International Directory of
COMPANY
HISTORIES

International Directory of

COMPANY HISTORIES

VOLUME 99

Editor

Jay P. Pederson

ST. JAMES PRESS
A part of Gale, Cengage Learning

Detroit • New York • San Francisco • New Haven, Conn • Waterville, Maine • London

International Directory of Company Histories, Volume 99

Jay P. Pederson, Editor

Project Editor: Miranda H. Ferrara

Editorial: Virgil Burton, Donna Craft, Louise Gagné, Peggy Geeseman, Julie Gough, Linda Hall, Sonya Hill, Keith Jones, Daniel King, Lynn Pearce, Holly Selden, Justine Ventimiglia

Production Technology Specialist: Mike Weaver

Imaging and Multimedia: John Watkins

Composition and Electronic Prepress: Gary Leach, Evi Seoud

Manufacturing: Rhonda Dover

Product Manager: Jenai Mynatt

For product information and technology assistance, contact us at **Gale Customer Support, 1-800-877-4253.**
For permission to use material from this text or product, submit all requests online at **www.cengage.com/permissions.**
Further permissions questions can be emailed to **permissionrequest@cengage.com**

Gale
27500 Drake Rd.
Farmington Hills, MI, 48331-3535

LIBRARY OF CONGRESS CATALOG NUMBER 89-190943
ISBN-13: 978-1-55862-633-1
ISBN-10: 1-55862-633-6

This title is also available as an e-book
ISBN-13: 978-1-55862-782-6   ISBN-10: 1-55862-782-0
Contact your Gale, a part of Cengage Learning sales representative for ordering information.

BRITISH LIBRARY CATALOGUING IN PUBLICATION DATA
International directory of company histories, Vol. 99
Jay P. Pederson
33.87409

Printed in the United States of America
1 2 3 4 5 6 7 13 12 11 10 09

Contents

Preface vii
Notes on Contributors ix
List of Abbreviations xi

AbitibiBowater Inc. 1
Advanced Micro Devices, Inc. 12
Ainsworth Lumber Co. Ltd. 18
Alfa Group 23
AMCON Distributing
    Company 270
American Commercial Lines Inc. . . .31
The Andrews Institute 35
Anhui Conch Cement Company
    Limited 39
Arena Leisure Plc 43
Baxters Food Group Ltd. 47
Bci 51
Bechtel Corporation 55
Beggars Group Ltd. 61
Bolt Technology Corporation 66
Bowlin Travel Centers, Inc. 71
Cains Beer Company PLC 76
Campagna-Turano Bakery, Inc. 81
Canada Bread Company,
    Limited 85
CF Industries Holdings, Inc. 89
CiCi Enterprises, L.P. 94
CNH Global N.V. 100
Coach, Inc. 113

Craig Hospital 121
Dana Holding Corporation 127
Drie Mollen Holding B.V. 135
Dylan's Candy Bar, LLC 139
Dynatronics Corporation 142
EnerSys Inc. 147
Euromarket Designs Inc. 152
Fastenal Company 158
Fisher Communications, Inc. 164
Five Guys Enterprises, LLC 169
France Telecom S.A. 173
FTD Group, Inc. 180
Green Dot Public Schools 186
GreenMan Technologies Inc. 190
Grupo Brescia 194
H. J. Heinz Company 198
Harps Food Stores, Inc. 206
Hemisphere GPS Inc. 210
IDT Corporation 214
IGA, Inc. .220
Ikonics Corporation 225
J. Lohr Winery Corporation 229
John Lewis Partnership plc 233
K.A. Rasmussen AS 241
Kooperativa Förbundet 245
Lehman Brothers Holdings Inc. . . .249
Linear Technology Corporation . . .254
Lionel L.L.C. 259

Luby's, Inc. 266
Lunardi's Super Market, Inc. 274
Mechel OAO 278
Meguiar's, Inc. 282
Mexichem, S.A.B. de C.V. 286
Mitsubishi UFJ Financial
    Group, Inc. 291
Noble Roman's, Inc. 297
North American Galvanizing &
    Coatings, Inc. 303
O'Reilly Media, Inc. 307
OJSC Novolipetsk Steel 311
Omega Protein Corporation 316
Organic To Go Food
    Corporation 319
Orgill, Inc. 323
Panattoni Development
    Company, Inc. 327
Parker-Hannifin Corporation 331
Perma-Fix Environmental
    Services, Inc. 338
Petro-Canada 342
Quinn Emanuel Urquhart
    Oliver & Hedges, LLP 350
Raisio PLC 354
The Real Good Food
    Company plc 358
Renfro Corporation 362
Retractable Technologies, Inc. 366
Riedel Tiroler Glashuette
    GmbH 370
Rostelecom Joint Stock Co. 374
Royal Brunei Airlines Sdn Bhd 378
Ryan Companies US, Inc. 382

Sanders\Wingo 386
Sara Lee Corporation 390
Savers, Inc. 399
Schering-Plough Corporation 404
Silverstar Holdings, Ltd. 415
Sine Qua Non 419
Southeast Frozen Foods
    Company, L.P. 423
The Structure Tone
    Organization 427
Sutherland Lumber
    Company, L.P. 431
TBA Global, LLC 435
TechTarget, Inc. 439
Tengasco, Inc. 444
Terremark Worldwide, Inc. 448
Toshiba Corporation 453
TVI Corporation 462
United Internet AG 466
Uzbekistan Airways National Air
    Company 470
Vanderbilt University Medical
    Center .474
Vita Food Products Inc. 4781
Woodbridge Holdings
    Corporation 482
Wyndham Worldwide
    Corporation 486
Yamaha Corporation 494
Zentiva N.V./Zentiva, a.s. 502
Zogby International, Inc. 507

Cumulative Index to Companies 511
Index to Industries 595
Geographic Index 661

Preface

The St. James Press series *The International Directory of Company Histories* (*IDCH*) is intended for reference use by students, business people, librarians, historians, economists, investors, job candidates, and others who seek to learn more about the historical development of the world's most important companies. To date, *IDCH* has covered more than 9,915 companies in 99 volumes.

INCLUSION CRITERIA

Most companies chosen for inclusion in *IDCH* have achieved a minimum of US$25 million in annual sales and are leading influences in their industries or geographical locations. Companies may be publicly held, private, or nonprofit. State-owned companies that are important in their industries and that may operate much like public or private companies also are included. Wholly owned subsidiaries and divisions are profiled if they meet the requirements for inclusion. Entries on companies that have had major changes since they were last profiled may be selected for updating.

The *IDCH* series highlights 25% private and nonprofit companies, and features updated entries on approximately 35 companies per volume.

ENTRY FORMAT

Each entry begins with the company's legal name; the address of its headquarters; its telephone, toll-free, and fax numbers; and its web site. A statement of public, private, state, or parent ownership follows. A company with a legal name in both English and the language of its headquarters country is listed by the English name, with the native-language name in parentheses.

The company's founding or earliest incorporation date, the number of employees, and the most recent available sales figures follow. Sales figures are given in local currencies with equivalents in U.S. dollars. For some private companies, sales figures are estimates and indicated by the abbreviation *est.* The entry lists the exchanges on which the company's stock is traded and its ticker symbol, as well as the company's NAICS codes.

Entries generally contain a *Company Perspectives* box which provides a short summary of the company's mission, goals, and ideals; a *Key Dates* box highlighting milestones in the company's history; lists of *Principal Subsidiaries, Principal Divisions, Principal Operating Units, Principal Competitors*; and articles for *Further Reading*.

American spelling is used throughout *IDCH*, and the word "billion" is used in its U.S. sense of one thousand million.

SOURCES

Entries have been compiled from publicly accessible sources both in print and on the Internet such as general and academic periodicals, books, and annual reports, as well as material supplied by the companies themselves.

CUMULATIVE INDEXES

IDCH contains three indexes: the **Cumulative Index to Companies**, which provides an alphabetical index to companies profiled in the *IDCH* series, the **Index to Industries**, which allows researchers to locate companies by their principal industry, and the **Geographic Index**, which lists companies alphabetically by the country of their headquarters. The indexes are cumulative and specific instructions for using them are found immediately preceding each index.

SPECIAL TO THIS VOLUME

This volume of *IDCH* contains the first entries for the countries of Brunei (Royal Brunei Airlines Sdn Bhd) and Uzbekistan (Uzbekistan Airways National Air Company).

SUGGESTIONS WELCOME

Comments and suggestions from users of *IDCH* on any aspect of the product as well as suggestions for companies to be included or updated are cordially invited. Please write:

The Editor
International Directory of Company Histories
St. James Press
Gale, Cengage Learning
27500 Drake Rd.
Farmington Hills, Michigan 48331-3535

St. James Press does not endorse any of the companies or products mentioned in this series. Companies appearing in the *International Directory of Company Histories* were selected without reference to their wishes and have in no way endorsed their entries.

Notes on Contributors

M. L. Cohen
Novelist, business writer, and researcher living in Paris.

Jeffrey L. Covell
Seattle-based writer.

Ed Dinger
Writer and editor based in Bronx, New York.

Paul R. Greenland
Illinois-based writer and researcher; author of two books and former senior editor of a national business magazine; contributor to *The Encyclopedia of Chicago History, The*

Encyclopedia of Religion, and the *Encyclopedia of American Industries.*

Robert Halasz
Former editor in chief of *World Progress* and *Funk & Wagnalls New Encyclopedia Yearbook*; author, *The U.S. Marines* (Millbrook Press, 1993).

Frederick C. Ingram
Writer based in South Carolina.

Kathleen Peippo
Minnesota-based writer.

Nelson Rhodes
Editor, writer, and consultant in the Chicago area.

Carrie Rothburd
Writer and editor specializing in corporate profiles, academic texts, and academic journal articles.

David E. Salamie
Part-owner of InfoWorks Development Group, a reference publication development and editorial services company.

Mary Tradii
Colorado-based writer.

Frank Uhle
Ann Arbor-based writer; movie projectionist, disc jockey, and staff member of *Psychotronic Video* magazine.

List of Abbreviations

¥ Japanese yen
£ United Kingdom pound
$ United States dollar

A

AB Aktiebolag (Finland, Sweden)
AB Oy Aktiebolag Osakeyhtiot (Finland)
A.E. Anonimos Eteria (Greece)
AED Emirati dirham
AG Aktiengesellschaft (Austria, Germany, Switzerland, Liechtenstein)
aG auf Gegenseitigkeit (Austria, Germany)
A.m.b.a. Andelsselskab med begraenset ansvar (Denmark)
A.O. Anonim Ortaklari/Ortakligi (Turkey)
ApS Amparteselskab (Denmark)
ARS Argentine peso
A.S. Anonim Sirketi (Turkey)
A/S Aksjeselskap (Norway)
A/S Aktieselskab (Denmark, Sweden)
Ay Avoinyhtio (Finland)
ATS Austrian shilling
AUD Australian dollar
ApS Amparteselskab (Denmark)
Ay Avoinyhtio (Finland)

B

B.A. Buttengewone Aansprakeiijkheid (Netherlands)
BEF Belgian franc

BHD Bahraini dinar
Bhd. Berhad (Malaysia, Brunei)
BND Brunei dollar
BRL Brazilian real
B.V. Besloten Vennootschap (Belgium, Netherlands)

C

C.A. Compania Anonima (Ecuador, Venezuela)
CAD Canadian dollar
C. de R.L. Compania de Responsabilidad Limitada (Spain)
CEO Chief Executive Officer
CFO Chief Financial Officer
CHF Swiss franc
Cia. Companhia (Brazil, Portugal)
Cia. Compania (Latin America [except Brazil], Spain)
Cia. Compagnia (Italy)
Cie. Compagnie (Belgium, France, Luxembourg, Netherlands)
CIO Chief Information Officer
CLP Chilean peso
CNY Chinese yuan
Co. Company
COO Chief Operating Officer
Coop. Cooperative
COP Colombian peso
Corp. Corporation
C. por A. Compania por Acciones (Dominican Republic)
CPT Cuideachta Phoibi Theoranta

(Republic of Ireland)
CRL Companhia a Responsabilidao Limitida (Portugal, Spain)
C.V. Commanditaire Vennootschap (Netherlands, Belgium)
CZK Czech koruna

D

D&B Dunn & Bradstreet
DEM German deutsche mark
Div. Division (United States)
DKK Danish krone
DZD Algerian dinar

E

EC Exempt Company (Arab countries)
Edms. Bpk. Eiendoms Beperk (South Africa)
EEK Estonian Kroon
eG eingetragene Genossenschaft (Germany)
EGMBH Eingetragene Genossenschaft mit beschraenkter Haftung (Austria, Germany)
EGP Egyptian pound
Ek For Ekonomisk Forening (Sweden)
EP Empresa Portuguesa (Portugal)
E.P.E. Etema Pemorismenis Evthynis (Greece)
ESOP Employee Stock Options and Ownership
ESP Spanish peseta

xi

Et(s). Etablissement(s) (Belgium, France, Luxembourg)

eV eingetragener Verein (Germany)

EUR euro

F

FIM Finnish markka

FRF French franc

G

G.I.E. Groupement d'Interet Economique (France)

gGmbH gemeinnutzige Gesellschaft mit beschraenkter Haftung (Austria, Germany, Switzerland)

G.I.E. Groupement d'Interet Economique (France)

GmbH Gesellschaft mit beschraenkter Haftung (Austria, Germany, Switzerland)

GRD Greek drachma

GWA Gewerbte Amt (Austria, Germany)

H

HB Handelsbolag (Sweden)

HF Hlutafelag (Iceland)

HKD Hong Kong dollar

HUF Hungarian forint

I

IDR Indonesian rupiah

IEP Irish pound

ILS new Israeli shekel

Inc. Incorporated (United States, Canada)

INR Indian rupee

IPO Initial Public Offering

I/S Interesentselskap (Norway)

I/S Interessentselskab (Denmark)

ISK Icelandic krona

ITL Italian lira

J

JMD Jamaican dollar

JOD Jordanian dinar

K

KB Kommanditbolag (Sweden)

KES Kenyan schilling

Kft Korlatolt Felelossegu Tarsasag (Hungary)

KG Kommanditgesellschaft (Austria, Germany, Switzerland)

KGaA Kommanditgesellschaft auf Aktien (Austria, Germany, Switzerland)

KK Kabushiki Kaisha (Japan)

KPW North Korean won

KRW South Korean won

K/S Kommanditselskab (Denmark)

K/S Kommandittselskap (Norway)

KWD Kuwaiti dinar

Ky Kommandiitiyhtio (Finland)

L

LBO Leveraged Buyout

Lda. Limitada (Spain)

L.L.C. Limited Liability Company (Arab countries, Egypt, Greece, United States)

L.L.P. Limited Liability Partnership (United States)

L.P. Limited Partnership (Canada, South Africa, United Kingdom, United States)

Ltd. Limited

Ltda. Limitada (Brazil, Portugal)

Ltee. Limitee (Canada, France)

LUF Luxembourg franc

M

mbH mit beschraenkter Haftung (Austria, Germany)

Mij. Maatschappij (Netherlands)

MUR Mauritian rupee

MXN Mexican peso

MYR Malaysian ringgit

N

N.A. National Association (United States)

NGN Nigerian naira

NLG Netherlands guilder

NOK Norwegian krone

N.V. Naamloze Vennootschap (Belgium, Netherlands)

NZD New Zealand dollar

O

OAO Otkrytoe Aktsionernoe Obshchestve (Russia)

OHG Offene Handelsgesellschaft (Austria, Germany, Switzerland)

OMR Omani rial

OOO Obschestvo s Ogranichennoi Otvetstvennostiu (Russia)

OOUR Osnova Organizacija Udruzenog Rada (Yugoslavia)

Oy Osakeyhtî (Finland)

P

P.C. Private Corp. (United States)

PEN Peruvian Nuevo Sol

PHP Philippine peso

PKR Pakistani rupee

P/L Part Lag (Norway)

PLC Public Limited Co. (United Kingdom, Ireland)

P.L.L.C. Professional Limited Liability Corporation (United States)

PLN Polish zloty

P.T. Perusahaan/Perseroan Terbatas (Indonesia)

PTE Portuguese escudo

Pte. Private (Singapore)

Pty. Proprietary (Australia, South Africa, United Kingdom)

Pvt. Private (India, Zimbabwe)

PVBA Personen Vennootschap met Beperkte Aansprakelijkheid (Belgium)

Q

QAR Qatar riyal

R

REIT Real Estate Investment Trust

RMB Chinese renminbi

Rt Reszvenytarsasag (Hungary)

RUB Russian ruble

S

S.A. Société Anonyme (Arab countries, Belgium, France, Jordan, Luxembourg, Switzerland)

S.A. Sociedad Anónima (Latin America [except Brazil], Spain, Mexico)

S.A. Sociedades Anônimas (Brazil, Portugal)

SAA Societe Anonyme Arabienne (Arab countries)

S.A.B. de C.V. Sociedad Anónima Bursátil de Capital Variable (Mexico)

S.A.C. Sociedad Anonima Comercial (Latin America [except Brazil])

S.A.C.I. Sociedad Anonima Comercial e Industrial (Latin America [except Brazil])

S.A.C.I.y.F. Sociedad Anonima Comercial e Industrial y Financiera (Latin America [except Brazil])

S.A. de C.V. Sociedad Anonima de Capital Variable (Mexico)

SAK Societe Anonyme Kuweitienne (Arab countries)

SAL Societe Anonyme Libanaise (Arab countries)

SAO Societe Anonyme Omanienne (Arab countries)

SAQ Societe Anonyme Qatarienne (Arab countries)

SAR Saudi riyal

S.A.R.L. Sociedade Anonima de Responsabilidade Limitada (Brazil, Portugal)

S.A.R.L. Société à Responsabilité Limitée (France, Belgium, Luxembourg)

S.A.S. Societá in Accomandita Semplice (Italy)

S.A.S. Societe Anonyme Syrienne (Arab countries)

S.C. Societe en Commandite (Belgium, France, Luxembourg)

S.C.A. Societe Cooperativa Agricole (France, Italy, Luxembourg)

S.C.I. Sociedad Cooperativa Ilimitada (Spain)

S.C.L. Sociedad Cooperativa Limitada (Spain)

S.C.R.L. Societe Cooperative a Responsabilite Limitee (Belgium)

Sdn. Bhd. Sendirian Berhad (Malaysia)

SEK Swedish krona

SGD Singapore dollar

S.L. Sociedad Limitada (Latin America [except Brazil], Portugal, Spain)

S/L Salgslag (Norway)

S.N.C. Société en Nom Collectif (France)

Soc. Sociedad (Latin America [except Brazil], Spain)

Soc. Sociedade (Brazil, Portugal)

Soc. Societa (Italy)

S.p.A. Società per Azioni (Italy)

Sp. z.o.o. Spólka z ograniczona odpowiedzialnoscia (Poland)

S.R.L. Sociedad de Responsabilidad Limitada (Spain, Mexico, Latin America [except Brazil])

S.R.L. Società a Responsabilità Limitata (Italy)

S.R.O. Spolecnost s Rucenim Omezenym (Czechoslovakia

S.S.K. Sherkate Sahami Khass (Iran)

Ste. Societe (France, Belgium, Luxembourg, Switzerland)

Ste. Cve. Societe Cooperative (Belgium)

S.V. Samemwerkende Vennootschap (Belgium)

S.Z.R.L. Societe Zairoise a Responsabilite Limitee (Zaire)

T

THB Thai baht

TND Tunisian dinar

TRL Turkish lira

TWD new Taiwan dollar

U

U.A. Uitgesloten Aansporakeiijkheid (Netherlands)

u.p.a. utan personligt ansvar (Sweden)

V

VAG Verein der Arbeitgeber (Austria, Germany)

VEB Venezuelan bolivar

VERTR Vertriebs (Austria, Germany)

VND Vietnamese dong

V.O.f. Vennootschap onder firma (Netherlands)

VVAG Versicherungsverein auf Gegenseitigkeit (Austria, Germany)

W–Z

WA Wettelika Aansprakalikhaed (Netherlands)

WLL With Limited Liability (Bahrain, Kuwait, Qatar, Saudi Arabia)

YK Yugen Kaisha (Japan)

ZAO Zakrytoe Aktsionernoe Obshchestve (Russia)

ZAR South African rand

ZMK Zambian kwacha

ZWD Zimbabwean dollar

AbitibiBowater Inc.

1155 Metcalfe Street, Suite 800
Montreal, Quebec H3B 5H2
Canada
Telephone: (514) 875-2160
Toll Free: (800) 361-2888
Fax: (514) 394-3444
Web site: http://www.abitibibowater.com

Public Company
Founded: 1912 as Abitibi Pulp & Paper Company
    Limited
Incorporated: 2007
Employees: 18,000
Sales: $3.88 billion (2007)
Stock Exchanges: New York Toronto
Ticker Symbol: ABH
NAICS: 322122 Newsprint Mills; 322121 Paper (Except
    Newsprint) Mills; 322110 Pulp Mills; 321113
    Sawmills; 113110 Timber Tract Operations

∎∎∎

Formed from the October 2007 merger of the Canadian
firm Abitibi-Consolidated Inc. and U.S.-based Bowater
Incorporated, AbitibiBowater Inc. is the world's largest
producer of newsprint. The company, headquartered in
Montreal and incorporated in Delaware, generates
around 41 percent of its revenues from newsprint, and
the capacity of its 16 newsprint facilities in North
America represents about 43 percent of the continent's
overall newsprint capacity. AbitibiBowater also runs
newsprint mills in England and South Korea, and it sells

about 45 percent of its newsprint production in more
than 80 countries outside North America. The company
is also a major producer of commercial printing papers
(35 percent of revenues), market pulp (16 percent), and
wood products (8 percent), and ranks as one of the
world's largest recyclers of newspapers and magazines. In
addition to the recycled fiber it generates, AbitibiBowater garners the wood it needs for its pulp, paper, and
wood products from the approximately 2.9 million acres
of timberlands it owns in Canada and the southeastern
United States and from the harvesting rights it holds on
roughly 49.5 million acres of Crown-owned land in
Canada.

EARLY HISTORY OF ABITIBI

The Abitibi-Consolidated side of AbitibiBowater was
itself the product of a May 1997 merger of Abitibi-Price
Inc. and Stone-Consolidated Corporation. Along with
much of the Canadian paper industry, Abitibi-Price
owed its existence to the bitter squabbling that
developed in the latter part of the 19th century between
U.S. manufacturers and consumers of newsprint. Ever
since the newspaper industry had converted from rag-
based paper to paper made from the pulp of trees in the
1870s, it had been troubled by recurring overcapacity
and disastrous price wars. These were usually followed
by attempts to moderate competition through mergers
and combinations. The most ambitious of these
consolidations was the 1898 creation of International
Paper Company from the assets of 17 U.S. paper
concerns. In the first decade of the 20th century
International Paper controlled nearly 75 percent of the
U.S. newsprint market, a situation that elicited charges

of monopoly and price gouging from the publishers of newspapers.

Newspaper publishers were able to publicize their accusations, sometimes coupling them with warnings about the need to protect freedom of the press from coercive economic forces. They eventually convinced the U.S. Congress to remove a longstanding tariff on imported paper products. The lifting of the tariff in 1913 prompted a rush to build plants in Canada, where abundant forests and water power made it a natural site for pulp and paper manufacturing. In the year 1911 alone, some 81 new forestry companies were created in Canada in anticipation of the lifting of the tariff. It was in the midst of this stampede that Abitibi Pulp & Paper Company Limited was established.

Abitibi's founder was an American named Frank H. Anson, born in 1859 in Niles, Michigan. Before coming to the paper business, Anson had worked as a railroad ticket agent, rubber prospector, exporter, and general superintendent of Ogilvie Flour Mills in Montreal. While at Ogilvie, Anson became interested in the mining wealth of Ontario's northern reaches, and in 1909 Anson hired two young men from McGill University to prospect for him in that remote part of Canada. The students found no minerals but did recommend that Anson start a paper mill along the Abitibi River, from whose swift current electrical and mechanical power could be generated to run such an operation.

With the abolition of the U.S. paper tariff drawing closer every day, Anson enlisted the financial backing of Shirley Ogilvie, son of the Ogilvie Flour Mills family. In 1912 he incorporated Abitibi Pulp & Paper Company Limited. In 1913 he built the company's first mill on the Abitibi River, some 300 miles north of Toronto at Iroquois Falls. In 1914 Abitibi Pulp & Paper changed its name and reincorporated as Abitibi Power & Paper Company Limited, because the firm also sold electric power from its hydroelectric facility. Anson's timing was very good: World War I soon drove up the price of newsprint to an all-time peak of $65 per ton, and the

new Canadian paper companies enjoyed unrestricted access to the immense U.S. markets.

ANTITRUST INVESTIGATIONS INTO NEWSPRINT ASSOCIATION, 1917

So successful were the paper companies on both sides of the border that another round of investigations of the industry was launched, and in 1917 the U.S. Department of Justice began antitrust prosecution of the members of an industrywide cooperative group called the News Print Manufacturers Association. The association's membership pleaded no contest, paid $11,000 in fines, and dissolved the organization. Still, the price of newsprint nearly doubled by 1920 to a new record of $112.60 per ton.

The newsprint industry's history of antitrust allegations and cyclical depressions seemed to be a result of three factors: the enormous cost of building new plant capacity; the relative inelasticity of demand for newsprint (sales do not tend to increase when the price drops); and the highly vocal and influential nature of the product's consumers, the newspaper community. Because competition often proved fatal, newsprint manufacturers tried to curb competition, resulting in well-publicized accusations by the newspapers of antitrust violations.

POST–WORLD WAR I EXPANSION

The postwar price peak encouraged a full decade of nonstop expansion in the Canadian paper industry, which nearly doubled its capacity by the year 1930. The consequence of this expansion was a long decline in the price of newsprint. By the end of the decade, it had fallen to about $62 per ton. There was also a growing overcapacity, which threw the industry into a premature depression of its own as early as 1928.

Abitibi Power & Paper had participated enthusiastically in the decade of expansion. It entered the fine-paper business with the purchase of a sulfite pulp mill at Smooth Rock Falls, Ontario; acquired substantial interests in Manitoba Paper Company and Sainte Anne Paper Company; and built its own mills. It became one of the industry's more important competitors.

Faced with the problems of increased capacity and falling prices, Abitibi and other paper manufacturers concluded that their best chance for collective survival was to amalgamate their holdings. Accordingly, in 1928 Abitibi engineered a quintuple merger, buying up the remainder of Manitoba Paper and Sainte Anne Paper and adding three others—Spanish River Pulp and Paper

---

KEY DATES

1912: Frank H. Anson incorporates Abitibi Pulp & Paper Company Limited.

1913: Abitibi opens its first mill in Ontario, Canada, at Iroquois Falls.

1914: Anson reincorporates his company as Abitibi Power & Paper Company Limited.

1928: Abitibi merges with several other Canadian pulp and paper companies.

1932: High debt and the Great Depression force Abitibi into receivership.

1938: London-based W.V. Bowater & Sons, Limited (later Bowater Paper Corporation Limited) expands into North America with the purchase of a massive pulp and newsprint mill in Corner Brook, Newfoundland.

1946: Abitibi emerges out of receivership and is formally independent once again.

1954: Bowater Paper makes its debut as a U.S. producer by building a newsprint mill in Calhoun, Tennessee.

1965: Abitibi is renamed Abitibi Paper Company Limited.

1974: Abitibi purchases a controlling stake in The Price Company Limited.

1978: Abitibi buys the remaining Price shares.

1979: Abitibi Paper Company changes its name to Abitibi-Price Inc.

1980: Olympia & York acquires control of Abitibi-Price.

1984: Bowater Paper demerges its North American newsprint and pulp operations into the independent, Darien, Connecticut-based Bowater Incorporated.

1992: After Olympia & York files for bankruptcy, Abitibi-Price comes under the control of a banking syndicate; Bowater moves its headquarters to Greenville, South Carolina.

1994: Syndicate divests itself of Abitibi-Price stock through a share offering.

1997: Abitibi-Price merges with Stone-Consolidated Corporation to become Abitibi-Consolidated Inc.

1998: Bowater scuttles Abitibi-Consolidated's hostile takeover bid of Avenor Inc. with a richer "white knight" offer.

2000: Abitibi-Consolidated acquires Donohue Inc. in a CAD 7.1 billion deal.

2007: Abitibi-Consolidated and Bowater merge to form AbitibiBowater Inc.

Mills, Fort William Power Company, and Murray Bay Paper Company. These, and a number of subsequent purchases by Abitibi, proved disastrous, but at the time it was hoped that by consolidating the industry could prevent price competition and increase production efficiency. That strategy might have succeeded in a thriving economy, but instead Abitibi was hit by the Great Depression of the 1930s and soon was in desperate straits.

DEPRESSION-ERA BANKRUPTCY

By 1932 sales had dropped to a fraction of their earlier levels, while the company's CAD 50 million debt was more than four times what it had been in 1927. This combination could not be sustained long, and on June 1, 1932, Abitibi defaulted on interest payments and was thrown into receivership. For the next 14 years Abitibi was directed by a court-appointed receiver, whose task it was to stabilize the company's finances, pay down the

outstanding debts, and return the company to its shareholders at some future date.

By 1933 the price of newsprint finally stabilized, allowing Abitibi to begin the long road back to solvency. The remainder of the 1930s was not a bad period for Abitibi, which managed to earn a fairly steady operating income to reduce its debt and maintain its physical assets. World War II revived the economy, and in 1940 Abitibi sales jumped immediately and remained between CAD 25 million and CAD 30 million for the duration of the war, providing the company with an excellent return and setting the stage for an end to receivership.

In 1943 the premier of Ontario appointed a committee for the purpose of designing a plan to take Abitibi out of receivership. After the committee's recommendations were accepted by all the creditors in 1946, the company was formally independent once again. Abitibi's 14-year receivership was the longest and most important in the history of Canadian industry, a trauma that would leave its mark in the form of a conservative corporate philosophy and deep skepticism about future expansion of capacity. Abitibi's experience during the Great Depression was an extreme example of the Canadian paper industry as a whole. When a remarkable postwar surge in demand for newsprint raised and prompted U.S. demands for increased capacity, the Canadian producers generally chose to increase production speed at existing plants rather than add new ones.

REBOUND AFTER WORLD WAR II

Abitibi CEO Douglas W. Ambridge strongly concurred with the prevalent conservatism, guiding Abitibi through two postwar decades of bountiful sales and profit increases while avoiding unnecessary capital expenditures. In this he was helped by the extraordinary expansion the company had undertaken in 1928, which provided Abitibi with a reserve of production capacity so great that corporate assets did not surpass those of 1928 until 30 years afterward. Abitibi thus merely made use of what plants it had to meet the rapidly growing demand of the 1950s, and Ambridge was able to keep debt low and earnings per share extremely high. After the years of receivership, the 1950s were a golden age.

1965 NAME CHANGE

In 1965 Abitibi Power & Paper Company Limited changed its name to Abitibi Paper Company Limited. Abitibi had been feeling the effects of the new U.S. presence as early as 1962, when, with the rest of the Canadian industry, it entered a decade of declining net income and diminished share of the critical U.S. market. To counteract this trend, Abitibi overcame its habitual reluctance to expand with the 1968 purchases of Cox Newsprint, Inc., and Cox Woodlands Company for $36.58 million. Cox, located in Augusta, Georgia, added 150,000 tons per year of newsprint capacity to Abitibi's Canadian holdings of 1.1 million tons and gave the company a presence in the booming southern U.S. industry.

1974 PURCHASE OF MAJORITY INTEREST IN THE PRICE COMPANY LIMITED

A new generation of leaders at Abitibi, headed by CEO Tom Bell and COO Harry Rosier, became increasingly aggressive in the search for additional capacity. Three exceptionally lean years were followed by an upsurge in fiscal 1974, when Abitibi sales soared from CAD 307 million to CAD 552 million. The company's capacity was strained, and Rosier suggested that it would be more economical for the company to buy existing mills than to build them from scratch. After a brief search for likely targets, Bell and Rosier gained control of 54 percent of the outstanding common shares of The Price Company Limited, another Canadian paper concern with 1974 sales of CAD 335 million.

Like Abitibi, Price was strongest in newsprint and kraft production, but it had no fine-paper and building-materials divisions. It recorded a significantly higher proportion of its sales outside North America than did Abitibi. Both companies had modest but profitable base-metal mining operations in Canada, and together they controlled rights to about 50,000 square miles of forest land, an area somewhat smaller than the state of Illinois. Price was a company much older than Abitibi, dating back to the early 19th century and the British navy's need for a new source of lumber for its masts. In 1810 William Price had been sent by a leading London lumber merchant to Canada to organize the new operation, and Price subsequently started the company bearing his name.

No sooner had Abitibi completed its 22-day, CAD 130.11 million conquest of The Price Company than the newsprint market collapsed, cutting the combined companies' 1975 net sales by two-thirds at a time when its debt had nearly doubled. Once again, Abitibi's poor timing led indirectly to a change in ownership. Caught in a cash squeeze, Abitibi tried to placate union demands with big pay hikes and thereby avoid a disastrous strike; instead the unions pushed their advantage and forced the strike anyway. The walkout was bitter and lasted for months, and by the time the economy rebounded in 1977 Abitibi was still trying to put its shaken house in order. In October 1978 Abitibi agreed to buy about 10 percent of Price's outstanding stock from Consolidated-Bathurst, a Canadian company that had bid against Abitibi for control of Price in 1974 and still held 10 percent of Price's stock. Later that month, Abitibi purchased Price's remaining shares. Abitibi paid about CAD 95 million for the 46 percent interest outstanding.

1980 TAKEOVER BY OLYMPIA & YORK

In December 1978 Consolidated-Bathurst bought 10 percent of Abitibi's stock and set off a prolonged bidding war for control of the company. When the dust settled 15 months later, Abitibi-Price Inc., which had changed its name in October 1979, was owned by Olympia & York, a Toronto-based real estate holding company run by the Reichmann family. Olympia & York, whose holdings were so vast that Abitibi-Price figured as a footnote in their annual reports, paid CAD

670 million for 92 percent of Abitibi-Price's stock. Olympia & York appeared to be the ideal silent partner for Abitibi-Price's management, offering great financial strength when needed but never meddling in the affairs of a business about which it knew little.

During the 1980s Abitibi-Price made a concerted effort to lessen its dependence on the brutally cyclical newsprint business. It sold plants, streamlined operations, and focused its efforts on markets where it felt it could be a leader. By the end of the decade the company's diversified group operated the largest network of paper distributors in Canada, the largest envelope manufacturer and largest school and office supplies maker, and one of the leading producers of building materials in the United States. The diversified group in 1990 accounted for approximately half of all corporate revenue, with the remainder generated by the paper group's two divisions of newsprint and printing papers. Newsprint remained the most profitable segment, however, and was the heart of Abitibi-Price's various holdings. After four straight years of bullish profits, the bottom dropped out once again in 1989, and in 1990 Abitibi-Price lost CAD 45 million.

DEEP NEWSPRINT MARKET DOWNTURN

In 1990 the newsprint industry entered its worst period since the Great Depression. From 1990 to 1995, Abitibi-Price lost hundreds of millions of dollars. In 1991 a global newspaper glut forced Abitibi-Price to close or sell mills and decentralize its operations to regain profitability. Ronald Oberlander became the company's new CEO. He adopted a new strategy to become the world's finest paper company rather than the world's largest. He also began shifting profit responsibilities away from corporate headquarters to the managers at the company's plants and mills.

In spite of falling pulp prices, Abitibi-Price managed to report an operating profit for the first six months of 1991. A CAD 20 million restructuring charge left the company with a net loss of CAD 11.2 million on revenue of CAD 1.46 billion for the first half of 1991. That was an improvement over the same period of 1990, when the company lost CAD 15 million on revenue of CAD 1.59 billion. The 1990 loss was affected by a one-time charge of CAD 42.6 million. Operating profits for the first half of 1990 were a strong CAD 45.5 million compared with CAD 2.6 million for the first half of 1991.

In June 1992 Abitibi-Price announced that it would sell its U.S. building products division for $100 million (CAD 120 million) to two separate buyers. Three of the

four units involved were sold to an investment group formed by New York-based investment banker Kohlberg & Co. and George T. Brophy. The fourth unit, a national supplier of interior wood products from facilities in Hiawatha, Kansas, and Lumberton, North Carolina, was sold to an investment group led by Alan J. Gitkin of Wayne, New Jersey. It would change its name to Flair Fold Corporation.

For 1992 Abitibi-Price reported a loss from continuing operations of CAD 200 million, compared with a loss of CAD 58 million for 1991. Overall, the company reported an after-tax loss of CAD 219 million for 1992 after discontinuing some of its noncore assets. That compared with an after-tax loss of CAD 76 million in 1991. Severe price erosion, caused by a continued oversupply of the company's paper products, was blamed for the poor results. Sales improved marginally to CAD 1.7 billion in spite of an almost 10 percent increase in tonnage sold. Included in the loss for 1992 was a charge of CAD 60 million relating to the permanent closure of the Thunder Bay newsprint mill. Ownership of a second mill in Thunder Bay was in the process of being transferred to its employees. The company was continuing to focus on its core business, the manufacture and marketing of groundwood papers. Other divisions included office products and converted products.

In 1992 Olympia & York, which held a controlling interest in Abitibi-Price, filed for protection from its creditors. It owned some 54.5 million shares of Abitibi-Price, an 82 percent stake. With Olympia & York's bankruptcy filing, the shares came under the control of a banking syndicate led by Hongkong and Shanghai Banking Corporation Limited, which appointed Salomon Brothers of New York and RBC Dominion Securities of Toronto to advise on their disposal. The syndicate eventually divested itself of its Abitibi-Price stock holdings through an early 1994 share offering. Afterward, Abitibi-Price shares were held widely, with two U.S. institutions holding about 20 percent of the stock between them.

In the spring of 1993 Abitibi-Price was targeted by the Energy and Paperworkers Union of Canada (CEP), which counted 4,000 Abitibi-Price employees among its 35,000 members in eastern Canada. Nationwide, CEP represented about 137,000 workers. Among the union demands were job security, significant wage hikes, cost-of-living indexing, and improved pensions. Abitibi-Price's labor force had been cut back from some 14,000 in 1990 to 8,600 at the end of 1992. Closing one of the Thunder Bay mills in 1992 eliminated 400 jobs.

For the first quarter of 1993, Abitibi-Price reported its first quarter-to-quarter improvement since 1988 when it cut losses from continuing operations by 24 percent. The company would not have a profitable quarter until 1995, when it reported annual net income of CAD 273 million on net sales of CAD 2.8 billion.

To cope better with the newsprint industry's cyclical downturns, Abitibi-Price developed what it called a "Cornerstone Strategy." Criteria were established for each mill that would enable it to turn a profit in even the most severe cyclical downturn. As part of its new cornerstone strategy, mills that did not meet those criteria were put up for sale. In early 1997 the company put up for sale its 75-year-old Fort Williams newsprint mill in Thunder Bay, Ontario, and associated timberlands.

1997 MERGER OF ABITIBI-PRICE AND STONE-CONSOLIDATED TO FORM ABITIBI-CONSOLIDATED

In May 1997 Abitibi-Price and Stone-Consolidated Corporation merged to become the world's largest newsprint and uncoated groundwood producer. The new company, called Abitibi-Consolidated Inc., was created by a tax-free amalgamation following an exchange of stock. The combined company had a market capitalization of CAD 4.1 billion, almost double the capitalization of CAD 2.2 billion of the industry's largest producer, MacMillan Bloedel Ltd. Shareholders of Abitibi-Price and Stone-Consolidated each received approximately one share of the new company for each share they held.

Chicago-based Stone Container Corporation had owned about half of Stone-Consolidated, an interest dating back to the latter firm's March 1989 purchase of Consolidated-Bathurst Inc. in a $2.2 billion deal. At the time, Consolidated-Bathurst Inc. was Canada's fifth largest pulp-and-paper company. In 1993 Stone Container sold 25 percent of Consolidated-Bathurst, renamed Stone-Consolidated Corporation, to the public. Stone Container's interest was reduced further, to around 47 percent, in 1995 when Stone-Consolidated merged with Rainy River Forest Products, Inc., a Toronto-based pulp and paper company. After the merger of Abitibi-Price and Stone-Consolidated, Stone Container owned about 25 percent of Abitibi-Consolidated. Before the end of 1997, Stone announced plans to sell its 48.8 million shares of Abitibi-Consolidated to raise cash needed to reduce its long-term debt of $4 billion; Stone, however, did not unload its Abitibi-Consolidated shares until 1999.

Abitibi-Price CEO Ronald Oberlander became the operating chairman of the new company, and Stone-Consolidated CEO James Doughan became Abitibi-Consolidated's new president and CEO. The two expected to achieve savings of CAD 100 million annually, later revised to CAD 200 million, just by eliminating duplications in the selling and administrative areas. At the time of the merger, Abitibi-Price was planning to sell its Fort Williams facility in Thunder Bay and was seeking to sell other noncore assets. Including those mills, Abitibi-Consolidated started operations with a total of 18 paper mills: 14 in Canada, three in the United States, and one in Great Britain, plus seven wholly owned or affiliated sawmills in Canada.

Analysts seemed to agree that the merger made sense, given the deeply cyclical nature of the North American newsprint industry. The emergence of stronger players through consolidations such as this one was seen as leading to more rational markets. Analysts expected shareholders to benefit as a result of the merger.

In terms of output, Abitibi-Consolidated had a total capacity of 2.8 millions tons for newsprint, exceeding current world leader Fletcher Challenge Ltd. of New Zealand's capacity of 1.8 million tons. For uncoated groundwood, Abitibi-Consolidated had a capacity of 1.5 million tons, more than leader UPM-Kymmene Corporation of Finland's capacity of 1.2 million tons. Overall, Abitibi-Consolidated ranked as the world's 11th largest pulp and paper producer in terms of tonnage and 17th internationally in sales. It had about a 15 percent share of the world's paper market. Abitibi-Consolidated's headquarters were placed in Montreal, where Stone-Consolidated had been headquartered, rather than in Toronto, where Abitibi-Price's main office had been located.

Although the merger was completed in May 1997, results for the new company were annualized for 1997. Abitibi-Consolidated reported a net loss of CAD 121 million after amalgamation and restructuring charges. Annualized net sales were CAD 4.16 billion. It reported an upbeat fourth quarter, however, posting net income before restructuring charges of CAD 57 million. For 1998, the company planned on keeping a tight lid on costs and capital spending to achieve profitability.

POST-MERGER DEVELOPMENTS

In the spring of 1998 Abitibi-Consolidated was unsuccessful in its hostile takeover attempt of one of its major competitors, the Montreal-based newsprint producer Avenor Inc. Its bid of CAD 2.8 billion was surpassed by a CAD 3.5 billion bid by U.S.-based Bowater Incorporated, Abitibi's later merger partner. Abitibi-Consolidated's bid was a sign that it was in an acquisition mode. Investor interest appeared to be increasing in the company, which saw the value of its stock rise by some CAD 500 million after it announced its bid for Avenor.

As part of its strategy to eliminate or sell off non-core assets, Abitibi-Consolidated announced in April 1998 that it had completed the sale of the U.S. and Mexican operations of its Office Products Division to United Stationers Inc. for approximately $110 million. The three business units that were sold were Azerty, which distributed computer supply consumables, peripherals, and accessories in the United States and Mexico; Positive ID, which distributed bar-code scanning products; and AP Support Services, which provided outsourcing services in direct marketing, telemarketing, and other areas. The three units had combined annual sales of about $350 million. Abitibi-Consolidated later sold the remainder of its Office Products Division, including its $150 million Axidata computer supplies distribution business. Also in 1998, the company acquired a newsprint mill in Snowflake, Arizona, from Stone Container for $266 million. The mill had the capacity to produce 287,000 metric tons of 70 percent recycled newsprint on an annual basis.

Seeking opportunities for further growth in its core newsprint area outside North America, Abitibi-Consolidated in 1999 entered into a three-way joint venture with Norway's Norske Skogindustrier ASA and South Korea's Hansol Paper Co. Ltd. The Singapore-based venture, called Pan Asia Paper Company Pte. Ltd., included Hansol's Korean and Chinese newsprint mills, as well as Norske Skog's interests in newsprint mills in Korea and Thailand. With these mills combining for an aggregate annual capacity of 1.425 million metric tons, Pan Asian Paper ranked as the largest newsprint and groundwood paper company in Asia outside of Japan. Abitibi-Consolidated spent $200 million for its one-third share in the venture.

Also in 1999, John Weaver was named chairman and CEO as both Oberlander and Doughan retired. Weaver had headed the company's newsprint operations. Seeking to lower its annual operating costs by an additional CAD 100 million as competition heated up with lower-cost competitors, Abitibi-Consolidated that year shut down its newsprint mill in Chandler, Arizona, as well as three paper machines at other mills, removing 450,000 metric tons of paper capacity from its system. The firm also reduced its workforce by about 10 percent, cutting 1,300 jobs, taking a pretax charge of CAD 110 million to implement the capacity and workforce cuts. The charge contributed to a full-year loss for 1999 of CAD 278 million.

2000 TAKEOVER OF DONOHUE

One of Abitibi-Consolidated's principal lower-cost competitors, and the third largest North American newsprint producer, was Donohue Inc. In April 2000 Abitibi-Consolidated acquired Donohue, also based in Montreal, for CAD 5.7 billion in cash and stock along with the assumption of CAD 1.4 billion in debt. The combined holdings of the two firms included about two dozen paper mills in North America as well as 19 wholly owned and five partially owned sawmills that made the enlarged Abitibi-Consolidated the continent's fifth largest lumber producer. Cost savings from synergies gained through the merger totaled nearly CAD 300 million by 2001, and the company also attempted to improve its efficiency by reducing its own newsprint capacity by a few hundred thousand metric tons.

After Hansol decided to end its involvement in the Pan Asia Paper joint venture, Abitibi-Consolidated and Norske Skog in August 2001 bought out Hansol's interest for $175 million each, increasing both firms' stakes to 50 percent. Around this time and into 2002, Abitibi-Consolidated felt the effects of an economic downturn that featured a sharp drop in advertising, which undercut both demand and prices for newsprint. Revenues for 2002 were down about 12 percent to CAD 5.12 billion, while the firm suffered a loss from continuing operations of CAD 47 million. Softness in the newsprint market continued into 2003, and the company suffered further blows from a rising Canadian dollar, lower paper and lumber prices, higher energy costs, and U.S. duties on its lumber exports. Abitibi-Consolidated was forced to slash its dividend as it reported a CAD 322 million loss from continuing operations.

Demand for newsprint in North America remained in a prolonged state of sluggishness. Print advertising failed to recover as Internet publishing and advertising continued their inexorable rise. At the same time, newspaper circulation was continuing a downward slide that began in the mid-1990s, and financially strained newspaper publishers were reducing the amount of newsprint they needed by shrinking the physical size of their pages, reducing the number of pages of news content, or both. Newsprint producers were therefore dealing with chronic overcapacity in North America, a situation compounded by the encroachment into the continent of low-cost producers from such areas as Latin America and the Asia-Pacific region. Abitibi-Consolidated responded with a string of further plant closings. The company's difficulties were compounded by the heavy debt load it had been saddled with since the Donohue acquisition. The result was two consecutive years of red ink—net losses of CAD 36 million and

CAD 350 million for 2004 and 2005, respectively—before the modest profit total of CAD 54 million for 2006. Abitibi-Consolidated attempted to shore up its financial position late in 2005 by selling its 50 percent stake in Pan Asia Paper to Norske Skog for $600 million. With this deal, Abitibi-Consolidated relinquished its claim as the world's largest newsprint maker to Norske Skog. In January 2007, however, the company moved to reclaim the top spot by agreeing to merge with Bowater as the two longtime rivals sought to bulk up to better compete in the intensely competitive environment.

HISTORY OF BOWATER

Bowater Incorporated evolved out of the paper wholesaling business founded by William Vansittart Bowater in London in 1881. This firm, which was later incorporated as W.V. Bowater & Sons, Limited, transitioned from paper wholesaling to paper manufacturing in the 1920s. Expansion into North America began in 1938 with the purchase of a massive pulp and newsprint mill at Corner Brook, Newfoundland's most important industrial undertaking with newsprint capacity of 200,000 tons per year and resources of 7,000 square miles of timberland.

After W.V. Bowater & Sons was reorganized under a holding company called Bowater Paper Corporation Limited in 1947, it made further inroads into the North American market, where demand for newsprint was rising relentlessly. The firm made its debut as a producer in the United States in 1954 with the construction of a paper mill in Calhoun, Tennessee, which had an initial annual capacity of 145,000 tons of newsprint. Already the largest producer of newsprint in the world, Bowater expanded further with the 1956 acquisition of Mersey Paper Company Limited of Liverpool, Nova Scotia, which added a further 140,000 tons of newsprint output. Around this same time, the capacity of the Calhoun plant was doubled. A desire for self-sufficiency in raw materials led to the opening of a new pulp mill at Catawba, South Carolina, in 1959.

Bowater Paper eventually diversified into a number of other areas and began reducing its newsprint operations in response to industry overcapacity. By 1982 the company had closed its last newsprint machine in the United Kingdom. This pullback culminated in 1984 when the North American newsprint and pulp operations were demerged from the rest of the firm as Bowater Incorporated, the stock of which was listed on the New York Stock Exchange. The U.K. firm was at this time renamed Bowater Industries plc but in 1995 was renamed Rexam PLC, ending a confusing period of

entirely separate Bowater companies on either side of the Atlantic.

Bowater Inc., which ranked as the largest newsprint producer in the United States, was initially headquartered in Darien, Connecticut, but moved its base to Greenville, South Carolina, in 1992. The company grew both organically and via acquisition over the years, with its most significant purchase coming in 1998. Bowater played "white knight" that year in besting rival Abitibi-Consolidated's CAD 2.8 billion hostile takeover bid for Avenor. Based in Montreal, Avenor was the former Canadian Pacific Forest Products Limited, which had been the forest products arm of the conglomerate Canadian Pacific Limited before being divested into a separate company in 1993. Bowater completed its CAD 3.5 billion purchase of Avenor in July 1998.

With the purchase of Avenor, Bowater gained additional newsprint mills in Dalhousie, New Brunswick; Gatineau, Quebec; Thunder Bay, Ontario; and Usk, Washington, thereby roughly doubling its annual newsprint capacity to 2.7 million metric tons and making it the second largest newsprint producer in the world (behind Abitibi-Consolidated). Avenor's assets also included two pulp mills in Canada and a lumber mill in Maniwaki, Quebec. Bowater expanded overseas as well in July 1998 by spending $223 million for Halla Pulp & Paper Co. Ltd., which operated a newsprint mill in Mokpo, South Korea, with annual capacity of around 250,000 metric tons. This low-cost mill, which started up in late 1996, produced newsprint using only recycled fiber.

Two other significant deals soon followed. In August 2000, in a $382.2 million deal, Bowater acquired a mill in Grenada, Mississippi, with annual capacity of 250,000 metric tons of newsprint. The following September, Bowater acquired Montreal-based Alliance Forest Products Inc. for $791 million, including assumed debt. Alliance's operations included two specialty paper mills in Quebec producing supercalendered paper used in magazines, ten Canadian sawmills, and a major newsprint mill in Coosa Pines, Alabama. The Coosa Pines facility was also a major supplier of fluff pulp, which was used by manufacturers of absorbent products such as diapers and feminine hygiene products.

Buffeted by the same set of challenges that Abitibi-Consolidated faced during this same period, Bowater posted net losses every year from 2002 to 2006. In addition to closing some newsprint mills and reducing its workforce, the company also worked to further reduce its exposure to the troubled newsprint sector by converting some of its newsprint machines to other uses. For example, the Catawba mill was converted to the production of lightweight coated paper in 2003, and one of the newsprint machines at the Calhoun mill was converted to specialty paper production in 2006. Coated and specialty papers commanded higher margins than newsprint and had greater growth potential. Ultimately, in January 2007, Bowater agreed to merge with rival Abitibi-Consolidated as the North American newsprint market continued to deteriorate.

2007 CREATION OF ABITIBIBOWATER INC.

The merger of Abitibi-Consolidated and Bowater, which was completed in October 2007, created the world's largest newsprint producer, AbitibiBowater Inc. The only regulatory condition placed on the merger was the divestment of Abitibi-Consolidated's newsprint mill in Snowflake, Arizona. After selling this mill to Catalyst Paper Corporation for $161 million in April 2008, AbitibiBowater ran 18 newsprint facilities in North America, England, and South Korea with an aggregate annual capacity of 5.4 million metric tons. Its share of the North American newsprint market stood at about 45 percent, and it was also the world's largest exporter of newsprint, generating 45 percent of its newsprint revenues outside North America. Although newsprint was its largest business, accounting for about 41 percent of overall revenues, the company was also a major supplier of commercial printing papers (35 percent), market pulp (16 percent), and wood products (8 percent). The head of Abitibi-Consolidated, John Weaver, was named executive chairman of AbitibiBowater, while Bowater's former leader, David Paterson, assumed the positions of president and CEO. In the spring of 2008, however, Weaver took the diminished role of nonexecutive chairman, leaving Paterson firmly in control. Although AbitibiBowater was incorporated in Delaware and reported its results in U.S. dollars, Montreal was selected as the firm's headquarters; Bowater's former base in Greenville, South Carolina, became AbitibiBowater's U.S. regional manufacturing and sales headquarters. The firm's stock was listed on both the New York and Toronto stock exchanges.

Among the main rationales for combining the two struggling companies were the synergies that could be realized and the opportunities for reducing production capacity that could be pursued. AbitibiBowater thus set a goal of attaining merger-related annual cost savings of $375 million by the end of 2009, and by early 2008 had also shut down six mills and one paper machine, all in Canada, cutting more than 1,600 jobs in the process. Another top priority was debt reduction, and the firm aimed to slash its debt by $1 billion by the end of 2010.

At the same time, AbitibiBowater was seeking to increase its exports of newsprint, given that the newsprint market was actually growing in other regions in sharp contrast to the situation in North America, and it also was investigating a further shift to the higher-value-added paper grades it was already making. A further challenge to the company's prospects arose in the form of the severe decline in the U.S. housing market that began during 2007 and undercut demand for lumber. In September 2008 AbitibiBowater announced the idling of four sawmills and resulting layoffs of 900 employees in response to the downturn.

Jonathan Martin
Updated, David Bianco; David E. Salamie

PRINCIPAL SUBSIDIARIES

Abitibi-Consolidated Alabama Corporation (U.S.A.); Abitibi-Consolidated Company of Canada; Abitibi-Consolidated Corp. (U.S.A.); Abitibi-Consolidated Inc.; Abitibi-Consolidated Canadian Office Products Holdings Inc.; Abitibi-Consolidated Hydro Inc.; Abitibi-Consolidated Nova Scotia Incorporated; Abitibi Consolidated Europe (Belgium); Abitibi-Consolidated Finance LP (U.S.A.); Abitibi Consolidated Sales Corp. (U.S.A.); Abitibi-Consolidated U.S. Funding Corp. (U.S.A.); ACH Calm Lake Inc.; ACH Fort Frances Inc.; ACH Iroquois Falls Inc.; ACH Island Falls Inc.; ACH Kenora Inc.; ACH Limited Partnership; ACH Norman Inc.; ACH Sturgeon Falls Inc.; ACH Twin Falls Inc.; Alabama River Newsprint Company (U.S.A.); Alliance Forest Products (2001) Inc.; The Apache Railway Company (U.S.A.); Augusta Newsprint Company (U.S.A.); Augusta Woodlands, LLC (U.S.A.); Bowater Alabama Inc. (U.S.A.); Bowater America Inc. (U.S.A.); Bowater Asia Pte Ltd. (Singapore); Bowater Canada Finance Corporation; Bowater Canada Inc.; Bowater Canada Treasury Corporation; Bowater Canadian Forest Products Inc.; Bowater Canadian Holdings Incorporated; Bowater Canadian Limited; Bowater Europe Limited (U.K.); Bowater Finance Company Inc. (U.S.A.); Bowater Incorporated (U.S.A.); Bowater-Korea Ltd.; Bowater LaHave Corporation; Bowater Maritimes Inc.; Bowater Mersey Paper Company Limited (51%); Bowater Mississippi LLC (U.S.A.); Bowater Nuway Inc. (U.S.A.); Bowater S. America Ltda. (Brazil); Bowater Shelburne Corporation; Bridgewater Paper Leasing Ltd. (U.K.); Bridgewater Paper Company Limited (U.K.); Calhoun Newsprint Company (U.S.A.; 51%); Cheshire Recycling Ltd. (U.K.); Donohue Corp. (U.S.A.); Donohue Malbaie Inc. (51%); Donohue Recycling Inc.; The International Bridge and Terminal Company; La Compagnie de Pulpe de Jonquiere; Lake Superior Forest

Products Inc. (U.S.A.); Manicouagin Power Company (60%); Marketing Donohue Inc.; Produits Forestiers La Tuque Inc. (83%); Produits Forestiers Saguenay Inc. (86%); Scramble Mining Ltd.; Star Lake Hydro Partnership (51%); St. Maurice River Drive Company Limited; Tenex Data Inc. (U.S.A.); Terra Nova Explorations Ltd.

PRINCIPAL DIVISIONS

Commercial Printing Papers; International Business; North American Newsprint; Wood Products.

PRINCIPAL COMPETITORS

Norske Skogindustrier ASA; International Paper Company; West Fraser Timber Co. Ltd.; NewPage Group Inc.; Catalyst Paper Corporation; Boise Inc.; Stora Enso Oyj; UPM-Kymmene Corporation; Domtar Corporation.

FURTHER READING

"Abitibi, 35,000 Workers Square Off for Pact Fight," *Toronto Star,* February 26, 1993, p. 7.

"AbitibiBowater Merger of Giants to Create 8th Largest Global Papermaker," *Pulp and Paper,* March 2007, p. 6.

Bary, Andrew, "Long Live Dead Trees," *Barron's,* April 2, 2007, pp. 24–25.

Chipello, Christopher J., "Abitibi Agrees to Purchase Donohue in $4 Billion Cash-and-Stock Accord," *Wall Street Journal,* February 14, 2000, p. A32.

———, "Bowater Agrees to Purchase Avenor for $1.76 Billion, Topping Abitibi's Bid," *Wall Street Journal,* March 10, 1998, p. A4.

Du Plessis, Jim, "Bowater to S.C.: 'Au Revoir,'" *Columbia (S.C.) State,* January 30, 2007, p. B7.

Evans, Richard, "The Tail Wagged This Dog Almost to Death," *International Management,* April 1988, pp. 57+.

Foot, Richard, "Bigger Is Better, Says Abitibi Chairman," *Calgary Herald,* January 31, 1998, p. E7.

Fowlie, Laura, "Abitibi-Price Pact May Bring Peace," *Financial Post,* May 26, 1993, p. 5.

Gibbens, Robert, "Abitibi-Consolidated Headquarters Will Be in Montreal," *Financial Post,* March 11, 1997, p. 8.

———, "Abitibi Shows a Profit As It Keeps a Tight Lid on Costs," *Financial Post,* February 12, 1998, p. 9.

———, "Stone Stays Cool Despite Rumors," *Financial Post,* April 12, 1997, p. 5.

———, "Stone to Sell Its Stake in Abitibi," *Financial Post,* October 28, 1997, p. 8.

———, "Two Struggling Newsprint Giants Merge," *Montreal Gazette,* January 30, 2007, p. B1.

Gibbon, Ann, and Tu Thahn Ha, "Abitibi Snaps Up Rival," *Globe and Mail,* February 12, 2000, p. B1.

Glowacki, Jeremy J., "Bowater Inc.: Refocuses, Restructures with New CEO," *Pulp and Paper,* October 1995, pp. 34+.

"Hard Choices Ahead for Abitibi-Consolidated," *Pulp and Paper,* March 2005, pp. 14–15.

Henriques, Diana, "No Paper Tiger: Bowater Has Become a Powerful Competitor," *Barron's,* September 8, 1986, p. 18.

Hill, Bert, and Michael Lewis, "Avenor Sold to Bowater for $3.5B: U.S. Bid Is 20% Higher Than One by Abitibi-Consolidated," *Ottawa Citizen,* March 10, 1998, p. B1.

Isaac, Debra, "How Bowater Broke Up," *Management Today,* August 1984, pp. 30+.

Kalawsky, Keith, "Paper Cuts," *Canadian Business,* November 12, 1999, pp. 85–86, 88–89.

Kennedy, Peter, "Abitibi Picture Brightens," *Financial Post,* April 20, 1993, p. 17.

Leger, Kathryn, "Abitibi Hunting Acquisitions," *Financial Post,* April 28, 1998, p. 3.

———, "Merger Creates Paper Giant," *Financial Post,* February 15, 1997, p. 1.

Lush, Patricia, "Merger to Create Paper-Making Giant," *Globe and Mail,* February 15, 1997, p. B1.

Marotte, Bertrand, "Abitibi Ends Bitter Board Battle," *Globe and Mail,* December 15, 2000, p. B1.

———, "Abitibi's Asian Assets Net $600-Million (U.S.)," *Globe and Mail,* September 8, 2005, p. B5.

Mathias, Philip, *Takeover: The 22 Days of Risk and Decision That Created the World's Largest Newsprint Empire, Abitibi-Price,* Toronto: Maclean-Hunter, 1976, 287 p.

McGovern, Sheila, "Abitibi Merger 'Doing Well,'" *Montreal Gazette,* November 5, 1997, p. C1.

McHugh, Michael, "Abitibi's Riding Out Pulp Slump," *Financial Post,* July 20, 1991, p. 20.

McKenna, Barrie, and Bertrand Marotte, "Abitibi, Bowater See Strength in Combining Paper Operations," *Globe and Mail,* January 30, 2007, p. B1.

"Merger Creates Paper Giant," *Northern Ontario Business,* March 1997, p. 3.

Mills, Patricia, "Abitibi-Price Selling Off Its Assets in Northwestern Ontario," *Northern Ontario Business,* March 1997, p. 22.

Moore, Lynn, "Deficit Deepens at Abitibi," *Montreal Gazette,* February 2, 2006, p. B2.

"Newsprint Mergers Continue with Bowater Set for Alliance Buy," *Pulp and Paper,* June 2001, p. 11.

Nulty, Peter, "Not Just Paper Profits," *Fortune,* April 11, 1988, pp. 118+.

Parker, Wendy, "New Direction at Abitibi-Price," *Northern Ontario Business,* September 1987, p. 35.

Reguly, Eric, "Abitibi Discards Big Dreams," *Financial Post,* June 13, 1991, p. 5.

Rosenberg, Jim, "Abitibi-Consolidated Promotes Newsprint Operations Chief to CEO," *Editor and Publisher,* January 30, 1999, p. 42.

Skelton, Chad, "Abitibi Dives into Asia," *Globe and Mail,* July 7, 1998, p. B1.

Swann, Charles, "Bowater: Going for Its Goals," *PIMA's Paper-maker,* June 1999, pp. 50–51, 54.

Werner, Ben, "Bowater Seeks Rebound from Debt, Red Ink," *Columbia (S.C.) State,* January 2, 2005, p. F1.

"White Knight Bowater Acquires Avenor for $2.5 Billion," *PIMA's Papermaker,* April 1998, pp. 10–11.

Yakabuski, Konrad, "Abitibi Successor Hints at Hard Choices," *Globe and Mail,* January 19, 1999, p. B11.

———, "A Bumpy Ride, an Early Exit," *Globe and Mail,* June 6, 2008, p. B1.

———, "Shrinking Giant," *Globe and Mail,* March 29, 2008, p. B6.

Advanced Micro Devices, Inc.

One AMD Place
Sunnyvale, California 94088
U.S.A.
Telephone: (408) 749-4000
Toll Free: (800) 538-8450
Fax: (408) 982-6164
Web site: http://www.amd.com

Public Company
Incorporated: 1969
Employees: 16,420
Sales: $6.01 billion (2007)
Stock Exchanges: New York
Ticker Symbol: AMD
NAICS: 334413 Semiconductor and Related Device
    Manufacturing

■ ■ ■

Advanced Micro Devices, Inc., (AMD) is one of the world leaders in the microprocessor industry, designing chips marketed in the computing and graphics markets. AMD sells single-core and multicore microprocessors for servers, workstations, laptops, and desktop personal computers. The company also sells embedded processors and other semiconductors for communications and networking applications as well as consumer electronics devices. AMD markets its products in North America, Europe, and Asia, deriving 40 percent of its annual revenue from sales to manufacturers based in China.

FINDING OPPORTUNITY: 1969–74

In 1968 Jerry Sanders (who had previously worked for Intel founder Robert Noyce) left his position as director of worldwide marketing at Fairchild Semiconductor. By May 1969 he and seven others officially launched Advanced Micro Devices, Inc. The company was incorporated with $100,000 with the purpose of building semiconductors for the electronics industry.

Although the company was initially headquartered in the living room of one of the cofounders, John Carey, it soon moved to two rooms in the back of a rug-cutting company in Santa Clara, California. By September of that year, AMD had raised the additional money it needed to begin manufacturing products and moved into its first permanent home, in Sunnyvale. In May 1970, AMD ended its first year with 53 employees and 18 products, but no sales.

The firm initially acted as an alternate source of chips, receiving products from other firms such as Fairchild and National Semiconductor and then redesigning them for greater speed and efficiency. Unlike other second-source companies, however, AMD was one of the first Silicon Valley firms to stress quality above all else, designing its chips to meet U.S. military specifications for semiconductors. At a time when the young computer industry was suffering from unreliable chips, this gave AMD an advantage. The firm began to cater to customers in the computer, telecommunications, and instrument industries who were growing quickly and who valued reliability highly enough to pay for it. AMD avoided producing chips for such inexpensive consumer

Over the course of AMD's three decades in business, silicon and software have become the steel and plastic of the worldwide digital economy. Technology companies have become global pacesetters, making technical advances at a prodigious rate—always driving the industry to deliver more and more, faster and faster. However, "technology for technology's sake" is not the way we do business at AMD. Our history is marked by a commitment to innovation that's truly useful for customers—putting the real needs of people ahead of technical one-upmanship. AMD founder Jerry Sanders has always maintained that "customers should come first, at every stage of a company's activities." Our current CEO, Hector de Jesus Ruiz, continues to carry the torch, saying, "Customer-centric innovation is the pre-eminent value at AMD. It is our reason for being and our strategy for success."

items as calculators and watches, determining that these were only short-term markets.

THE INFLUENCE OF JERRY SANDERS

Sanders, the driving force behind AMD, also began instituting price incentives, relying heavily on salesmanship to keep the company afloat. To do this, he kept the company decentralized, breaking it into several product profit centers. As a result, engineers and designers were more aware of the business implications of their work than were their counterparts.

A flamboyant leader who flaunted his love of materialism, Sanders used his personality to push his small company into the public eye, giving it a larger presence than its size merited. While attempting to motivate employees through the desire to be as rich as he was becoming, Sanders stressed respect for those low on the company's totem pole. He threw extravagant Christmas parties for everyone in the company and one year held a raffle, awarding $12,000 a year for 20 years to the winning employee, and showed up with a camera crew to record the prize delivery. These practices contrasted markedly with those of AMD's more conservative competitors, including Intel and National Semiconductor, and quickly gave the firm an aggressive reputation.

IPO IN 1972

In September 1972 the company went public, selling 525,000 shares at $15 a share, bringing in $7.87 million. In January of the following year, the company's first overseas manufacturing base, located in Penang, Malaysia, began volume production. By the end of AMD's fifth year, there were nearly 1,500 employees making over 200 different products, many of them proprietary, and bringing in nearly $26.5 million in annual sales. To commemorate its five-year anniversary in May 1974, AMD began what was to become a renowned tradition, holding a gala party, this one a street fair attended by employees and their families, in which televisions, ten-speed bicycles, and barbecue grills were given away.

DEFINING THE FUTURE: 1974–79

AMD's second five years gave the world a taste of the company's most enduring trait, tenaciousness. Despite a dogged recession in 1974–75, when sales briefly slipped, the company grew during this period to $168 million, representing an average annual compound growth rate of over 60 percent. Part of the success of the period was due to the implementation of a 44-hour work week for the company's staff. This was also a period of tremendous facilities expansion.

In 1975 the company received an infusion of cash ($30 million for 20 percent of its stock) from Siemens AG, a huge West German firm who wanted a foothold in the U.S. semiconductor market. In 1976 the company signed a cross-license agreement with Intel. Two years later the company formed a joint venture, called Advanced Micro Computers (AMC), with facilities in both Germany and the United States, to develop, produce, and market microcomputer products. The venture was dissolved a year later, in March 1979, and the company purchased the net assets of the domestic operations of AMC. Also in 1978, the company reached a major sales milestone of $100 million in annual revenue. In 1979 the company's shares were listed on the New York Stock Exchange for the first time under the ticker AMD; that same year, production began at AMD's newly constructed Austin, Texas, facility.

FINDING PREEMINENCE: 1980–83

The early 1980s were defined for AMD by two now famous corporate symbols. The first, called the "Age of Asparagus," represented the company's drive to increase the number of proprietary products offered to the marketplace. Like this lucrative crop, proprietary products take time to cultivate, but eventually bring

KEY DATES

1969: With $100,000 in start-up capital, Advanced Micro Devices (AMD) is founded.

1972: AMD completes its initial public offering of stock.

1985: AMD is included in the *Fortune* 500 list for the first time.

1994: AMD moves into its new headquarters facility.

2002: Hector de J. Ruiz is appointed chief executive officer, replacing founder Jerry Sanders.

2003: AMD becomes the first company to release a 64-bit processor for Windows-based personal computers.

2006: AMD acquires ATI Technologies in a $5.4 billion deal.

2007: Mubadala Development Co. acquires an 8.1 percent stake in AMD for $622 million.

excellent returns on the initial investment. The second symbol was a giant ocean wave. The "Catch the Wave" recruiting advertisements portrayed the company as an unstoppable force in the integrated circuit business, and unstoppable it was, at least for a time. AMD became a leader in research and development investment and by the end of fiscal 1981 the company had more than doubled its sales over 1979. Plants and facilities expanded with an emphasis on building in Texas. New production facilities were built in San Antonio, and more fabrication, or fab, space was added to the Austin plant as well. AMD had quickly become a major contender in the world semiconductor marketplace. In 1981 AMD's chips went into space aboard the space shuttle *Columbia*. The following year, AMD and Intel signed a technology exchange agreement centering on the iAPX86 family of microprocessors and peripherals. That same year, in a minor setback, a group of engineers left the company to found Cypress Semiconductor. In 1983 the company introduced INT.STD.1000, the highest quality standard in the industry, and incorporated AMD Singapore.

WEATHERING HARD TIMES: 1984–89

In 1984 the Austin facility added Building 2, and the company was listed in a new book titled *The 100 Best Companies to Work for in America*. The following year, AMD made the *Fortune* 500 list for the first time, and

Fabs 14 and 15 began operation in Austin. AMD celebrated its 15th year with one of the best sales years in company history. In the months following AMD's anniversary, employees received record-setting profit sharing checks and celebrated Christmas with musical groups Chicago in San Francisco and Joe King Carrasco and the Crowns in Texas.

By 1986, however, the tides of change had swept the industry. Japanese semiconductor makers came to dominate the memory markets (up until then a mainstay for AMD) and a fierce downturn had taken hold, limiting demand for chips in general. AMD, along with the rest of the semiconductor industry, began looking for new ways to compete in an increasingly difficult environment. In September 1986, Tony Holbrook was named president of the company; the following month, weakened by the long-running recession, AMD announced its first workforce restructure in over a decade. In April 1987, AMD initiated an arbitration action against Intel. Later that year, the company merged with Monolithic Memories, Inc., acquiring the latter's common stock in exchange for over 19 million shares of its own, a trade valued at $425 million. By 1989 AMD Chairman Jerry Sanders was talking about transformation: changing the entire company to compete in new markets, a process which began in October 1988, with the groundbreaking on the Submicron Development Center.

MAKING THE TRANSFORMATION: 1989–94

Finding new ways to compete led to the concept of AMD's "Spheres of Influence." For the transforming AMD, those spheres were microprocessors compatible with IBM computers, networking and communication chips, programmable logic devices, and high-performance memories. In addition, the company's long survival depended on developing submicron process technology that would fill its manufacturing needs into the next century.

By its 25th anniversary, AMD had put to work every ounce of tenaciousness it had to achieve those goals, growing to be either number one or number two worldwide in every market it served, including the Microsoft Windows–compatible business. AMD became a preeminent supplier of flash, networking, telecommunications, and programmable logic chips as well.

In May 1989, the company established the office of the chief executive, consisting of the top three company executives. In March 1991, AMD introduced new versions of the Am386 microprocessor family, breaking the Intel monopoly. A mere seven months later, the company had shipped its millionth Am386. That year, Siemens sold off its interest in AMD.

In February of the following year, the company's five-year arbitration with Intel ended, with AMD awarded full rights to make and sell the entire Am386 family of microprocessors. Early in 1993, the first members of the Am486 microprocessor family were introduced, and AMD and Fujitsu established a joint venture to produce flash memories, a new technology in which memory chips retained information even after the power was turned off. In July the Austin facility broke ground on Fab 25. In January 1994, computer reseller Compaq Computer Corporation and AMD formed a long-term alliance under which Am486 microprocessors would power Compaq computers. A month later, AMD employees began moving into One AMD Place in Sunnyvale, the company's new headquarters, and Digital Equipment Corporation became the foundry for Am486 microprocessors. In March 1994, a federal jury confirmed AMD's right to use Intel microcode in 287 math coprocessors, and the company celebrated its 25th anniversary with Rod Stewart in Sunnyvale and Bruce Hornsby in Austin.

FROM TRANSFORMATION TO TRANSCENDENCE: 1994–97

In January 1996, the company purchased Milpitas, California-based NexGen, Inc., a smaller semiconductor manufacturer founded in 1989. For fiscal 1998, the company posted net sales of $2.54 billion, a 7.9 percent increase, but also recorded a painful net loss on income of $104 million. In mid-1999, Hillsboro, Oregon-based Lattice Semiconductor Corp. purchased AMD's semiconductor manufacturing unit Vantis Corp. for $500 million in cash.

With Microsoft holding the software market in one fist, and Intel holding the microprocessor market in another, companies including National Semiconductor bowed out of the microprocessor manufacturing business in the late 1990s, refocusing their efforts instead on core competencies. Other companies, according to Kathleen Doler's August 1999 editorial in *Electronic Business,* "lost money six out of ... nine fiscal quarters." Indeed, AMD reported a 1999 second-quarter loss of $162 million. With "68 percent of its revenue derived from microprocessors and related products," Doler said, it seemed only prudent that AMD would diversify into other products in order to stay alive in the 21st century.

NEW LEADERSHIP IN 2002

The race between AMD and its archrival, Intel, defined AMD's progress during the first decade of the 21st

century. On AMD's side, the battle for market share would be led by a new face, as Sanders's more than 30-year reign of command came to an end, ushering in a new era of leadership at the Sunnyvale company. Hector de J. Ruiz was appointed chief executive officer in 2002 and chairman two years later. Born in Piedras Negras, Mexico, Ruiz earned bachelor's and master's degrees in electrical engineering from the University of Texas before earning his doctorate degree in electrical engineering from Rice University in 1973. He joined Texas Instruments after completing his education, the beginning of a career that would be largely spent at Motorola. Ruiz spent 22 years at Motorola, eventually becoming president of the company's semiconductor products division. He joined AMD as president and chief operating officer in 2000, quickly convincing Sanders that he had the skills and vision to lead AMD's fight against Intel.

AMD enjoyed the technological upper hand over Intel as Ruiz took the helm. The company developed a way for chips to handle data in both 32-bit and 64-bit allotments, which increased chip performance substantially. The Athlon 64 processor line debuted in 2003, causing considerable unease at Intel's headquarters. Intel followed AMD's lead, admitting in 2004 that it was working on a clone of the Athlon 64, and the company also followed AMD's lead in another important area. For years, AMD had maintained chip performance could be increased and energy consumption could be reduced by designing chips with more than one processing core. The company's Opteron chip featured two processing cores, a dual-core processor that caught Intel napping, enabling AMD to claim another technological victory over its rival. Intel, which had looked for performance increases by increasing clock speeds, embraced AMD's approach, revamped its microarchitecture, and, significantly, released its quad-core processor in November 2006, nearly a year before AMD released its first quad-core processor.

AMD FALTERS

After enjoying a technological advantage over Intel, AMD began to struggle, both financially and in keeping pace with Intel's product launches. AMD stumbled with the release of its quad-core processor, code-named Barcelona, and it experienced problems with profitability that were exacerbated by a massive acquisition it completed in 2006. AMD acquired Canadian graphics chip firm ATI Technologies, a $5.4 billion deal that helped contribute to a numbing $3.3 billion loss in 2007. The company received some relief in November 2007 when Abu Dhabi's Mubadala Development Co. paid $622 million for an 8.1 percent ownership stake, but the crux of its problems was its failure to execute in the market. Intel had cut costs, restructured its operations, and succeeded in beating AMD to market on several occasions with products that drew the applause of industry pundits. To keep pace with its larger rival, AMD needed to end a worrisome pattern of delayed and glitchy product launches and demonstrate the technological and marketing shrewdness that had underpinned its success for 40 years.

Scott Lewis
Updated, Daryl F. Mallett; Jeffrey L. Covell

PRINCIPAL SUBSIDIARIES

Advanced Micro Devices S.A.S. (France); AMD Corporation; ATI Technologies Systems Corp.; AMD (EMEA) Ltd.; AMD Far East Ltd.; AMD International Sales & Service, Ltd.; AMD Texas Properties, LLC; AMD Latin America Ltd.; AMD Saxony LLC; AMD US Finance Inc.; AMD (US) Holdings, Inc.; AMD Investments, Inc.; AMD FAB 36 LLC; Advanced Micro Devices Belgium N.V.; AMD South American Ltda. (Brazil); 1252986 Alberta Ulc (Canada); Advanced Micro Devices (China) Co. Ltd.; Advanced Micro Devices (Shanghai) Co. Ltd. (China); AMD Products (China) Co. Ltd.; Advanced Micro Devices GmbH (Germany); Advanced Micro Devices S.p.A. (Italy); AMD Japan Ltd.; Advanced Micro Devices Sdn. Bhd (Malaysia); AMD (Netherlands) B.V.; Advanced Micro Devices, AB (Sweden); Advanced Micro Devices (UK) Limited.

PRINCIPAL COMPETITORS

Intel Corporation; IBM Microelectronics; Freescale Semiconductor, Inc.

FURTHER READING

"Abu Dhabi Buys AMD Stake," *PC Magazine Online,* November 16, 2007.

"An Ailing AMD Faces Scrutiny," *eWeek,* December 6, 2007.

Brown, Ken, "Motorola Boosting R&D Through Joint Ventures," *Business Journal—Serving Phoenix & the Valley of the Sun,* July 24, 1998, p. 6.

Bruner, Richard, "AMD, Compaq Hit with Shareholder Suits," *Electronic News,* April 26, 1999, p. 10.

Calabro, Lori, "Closing Time," *CFO: The Magazine for Senior Financial Executives,* October 1994, p. 100.

Dillon, Nancy, "AMD Defies Intel's Monopoly Defense; Chip Maker's Loss Reflects Intel's Strength in Market, but K7 Chip Will Be Test of AMD's Competitive Position," *Computerworld,* July 5, 1999, p. 84.

Doler, Kathleen, "Jerry Sanders' Obsession," *Electronic Business,* August 1999, p. 4.

Dorsch, Jeff, "AMD to Use Leica Inspection/Review System," *Electronic News,* February 15, 1999, p. 26.

Fischer, Jack, "High-Tech Crime Wave Spreading Through Nation," *Knight-Ridder/Tribune Business News,* April 13, 1995, p. 4130273.

Fisher, Lawrence M., "Big Chip Maker Warns on Jobs and Earnings," *New York Times,* March 9, 1999, p. D1.

———, "Falling Chip Prices Bruise Manufacturers—and the Market," *International Herald Tribune,* April 16, 1999, p. 14.

Haber, Carol, "Posting a $32M 3Q Loss, AMD to Profit in 4Q ... If ... ," *Electronic News,* October 13, 1997, p. 92.

———, "Turmoil in the Desktop MPU Market: Intel Keeps Chugging As Rivals Bolt and Bleed," *Electronic News,* July 19, 1999, p. 1.

"Is AMD Doomed?" *eWeek,* November 19, 2007.

Morrison, Gale, "Sanders Under the Gun," *Electronic News,* April 13, 1998, p. 12.

Niccolai, James, "AMD Forecasts Large Loss; Chip Maker to Trim Workforce by 300," *Computerworld,* March 15, 1999, p. 27.

———, "AMD Posts Loss of $162M; President Resigns; Chip Battle Taking Toll on Intel Rival," *Computerworld,* July 19, 1999, p. 28.

Paul, Lauren Gibbons, "Eliminating the Procurement Middleman; AMD Taps a New Intranet-Based Solution to Buy Nonproduction Goods," *PC Week,* May 19, 1997, p. 135.

Quinlan, Tom, "Big Three of Microprocessors to Unveil New Designs," *Knight-Ridder/Tribune Business News,* October 7, 1998.

Reinhardt, Andy, and Ira Sager, "Can AMD Snap Its Losing Streak?" *Business Week,* December 8, 1997, p. 83.

Ristelhueber, Robert, "AMD Selling Vantis to Lattice," *Electronic News,* April 26, 1999, p. 1.

———, "The Long Goodbye," *Electronic News,* July 26, 1999, p. 8.

Rutledge, Tanya, "AMD Headquarters Sell for $95 Million," *Business Journal,* February 5, 1999, p. 1.

Schofield, Jack, "Crippling Battle Is on the Cards," *Guardian,* February 11, 1999, p. S2.

Slater, Michael, "Right Speed," *PC Magazine,* September 21, 1999, p. 100.

Takahashi, Dean, "Advanced Micro Devices Mulls Partnership," *Wall Street Journal,* July 29, 1999, p. B6.

———, "AMD Reports Record Loss for 2nd Period," *Wall Street Journal,* July 15, 1999, p. A3.

———, "More Bad News Puts Intel Rival Further Behind," *Wall Street Journal,* June 24, 1999, p. B1.

Takahashi, Dean, and Don Clark, "AMD's Search for No. 2 to Strong CEO Isn't Likely to Attract Many Outsiders," *Wall Street Journal,* July 16, 1999, p. B5.

Venezia, Carol, "Athlon vs. PIII at 600," *PC Magazine,* September 21, 1999, p. 41.

————, "Performance Tests: Athlon vs. PIII," *PC Magazine,* September 21, 1999, p. 44.

Willett, Hugh G., "Monopoly 101," *Electronic News,* May 24, 1999, p. 8.

Yates, Christopher, and Peter Coffee, "... and Why Intel Built the Chip Set," *PC Week,* June 21, 1999, p. 41.

Ainsworth®

Ainsworth Lumber Co. Ltd.

———————●———————

P.O. Box 49307
Suite 3194, Bentall 4
1055 Dunsmuir Street
Vancouver, British Columbia V7X 1L3
Canada
Telephone: (604) 661-3200
Toll Free: (877) 661-3200
Fax: (604) 661-3201
Web site: http://www.ainsworth.ca

Public Company
Founded: 1950
Employees: 1,700
Sales: CAD 544.2 million (2007)
Stock Exchanges: Toronto
Ticker Symbol: ANS
NAICS: 321219 Reconstituted Wood Products; 321999 All Other Miscellaneous Wood Product Manufacturing

■ ■ ■

Ainsworth Lumber Co. Ltd., a leading manufacturer of engineered wood products, has been ranked among the top five North American oriented strand board (OSB) makers in terms of capacity. In addition to OSB products, Ainsworth makes specialty overlaid plywood and veneer. Operating primarily in the structural wood panel sector, the company is sensitive to the ups and downs of the housing market. A significant industry downturn forced the Ainsworth family to give up control of the company in 2008 to bondholders. The Canadian company has scaled back both its homeland and U.S. operations.

BRITISH COLUMBIA BACKWOODS BEGINNING: 1950–92

Ainsworth Lumber Co. Ltd. traces its roots back to 1950. David Ainsworth and his wife, Susan, first set up a portable mill at 100 Mile House, British Columbia. Several years later they opened a sawmill at the south-central British Columbia location. In the 1980s, the lumber operation expanded into the production of veneer.

Along the away, Ainsworth Lumber had to contend with the inherent uncertainties of the Canadian forest industry. During the early 1980s, a downturn in the U.S. housing construction market forced the closure of competing mills in the area. At its 100 Mile House plant, Ainsworth cut positions and asked remaining employees to take pay cuts to allow the mill to keep running. The 100 Mile House plant and the company's Clinton, British Columbia, plant primarily produced two-by-four studs.

Toward the end of the decade, its Savona, British Columbia, stud mill was shut down in the wake of an export charge by the Canadian government on Canadian lumber sold to the United States. The action placed an added burden on producers of wall framing lumber, a low margin endeavor.

Then in 1990, Ainsworth Lumber came under scrutiny for layoffs at its Lillooet, British Columbia, mill. A job protection clause in place when Ainsworth

COMPANY PERSPECTIVES

Ainsworth is equipped with some of the most modern facilities in the industry. These state-of-the-art facilities are centrally located in contiguous timber supply areas, thereby ensuring that the right log goes to the right mill. Ainsworth's engineered wood products are marketed throughout the world and include oriented strand board (OSB), oriented strand lumber (OSL) and specialty overlaid panels.

took over the plant in 1987 was dropped when the company renewed its forest license agreement with the government, according to the *Vancouver Sun.* The company, for its part, said that mill was unprofitable and planned to add positions at its veneer mill.

Ainsworth produced sales of CAD 108 million for fiscal 1992. More than half of its sales came from lumber, but that was about to change.

NEW LEADERSHIP, NEW DIRECTION: 1993–95

Ainsworth Lumber went public in 1993. Under the leadership of the next generation, headed by Brian Ainsworth as CEO, the company moved to Vancouver and used the influx of funding to build a new plant for the production of OSB.

"First introduced by wood products manufacturers in the mid-1980s, OSB was dismissed by many as a second-rate alternative to plywood. OSB's crazy quilt appearance looked weird too," Gary Lamphier wrote in the *Vancouver Sun.*

Less expensive to produce than plywood, OSB offered similar structural performance, reason enough for forest-industry companies to get on board. Ainsworth would open its first OSB plant at 100 Mile House in 1994.

The newly public company, meanwhile, benefited from increased demand for lumber, veneer, and plywood during fiscal 1993. Revenue climbed to CAD 153 million. Profit rose CAD 1 a share over fiscal 1992, according to the *Globe and Mail.*

"U.S. countervailing duty refunds" helped out net earnings as the calendar year ran down. In a 14-month report, made as the company switched from an October to a December fiscal year end, Ainsworth Lumber said a lower Canadian dollar and a strong market also

contributed to improved performance. Yet operating figures were higher due to increases in labor costs, stumpage, and purchased logs, according to the *Vancouver Sun.*

As 1995 began, Ainsworth Lumber's British Columbia operations included the sawmill and OSB plant at 100 Mile House; the sawmill at Clinton; the sawmill and veneer plant at Lillooet; a specialty plywood plant at Savona; and a value-added plant at Abbotsford.

Ainsworth opened a second OSB plant in December. Located in Grande Prairie, Alberta, the facility was one of North America's largest, with annual capacity of 500 million square feet of product.

The company's plants also turned out products for the international market. Ainsworth Lumber claimed to be the first to introduce three-by-six-foot OSB panels (the standard size for the Japanese housing construction market), according to the *Globe and Mail.* Other markets outside North America included Taiwan, South Korea, Britain, Germany, Italy, and the Netherlands, although the Taiwanese market succumbed to tension with China. Ainsworth also was an early entrant in the nascent South African market.

The CAD 385-million-asset company was 60.5 percent owned by the Ainsworth family, via three holding companies. The three siblings in charge of the logging and solid wood processing operation included CEO and Chairman Brian Ainsworth; President and COO Allen Ainsworth; and CFO Catherine Ainsworth. During 1995, each received CAD 250,000 in compensation, an increase of 25 percent over the prior year. Net earnings for 1995 fell to CAD 14.6 million from CAD 24.2 million in 1994.

CLOSING OUT THE CENTURY

During the latter half of the 1990s, the popularity of OSB remained solid. The less-expensive alternative to plywood also provided a market for trees unsuitable for other lumber industry uses. The strength of the market triggered producer consolidation. Takeover speculation caused a spike in Ainsworth Lumber's share price around midyear 1999. The company had been climbing along with OSB demand and unprecedented pricing.

According to the *National Post,* an efficient mill could produce 1,000 square feet of OSB for CAD 150, while the going rate had climbed above CAD 500 per thousand square feet. However, with increased capacity within the industry, prices were expected to taper off.

Louisiana-Pacific Corp., based in Oregon, was the largest North American producer, holding a 21 percent market share. Ranked second, Weyerhaeuser Co., based

```
┌─────────────────────────────────────────┐
│                                           │
│             KEY DATES                     │
│              ──────■──────                │
│                                           │
│  1950:  David and Susan Ainsworth start   │
│         small Brit-ish Columbia wood      │
│         mill.                             │
│  1993:  Family operation goes public.     │
│  1999:  Company shifts primary focus to   │
│         oriented strand board market.     │
│  2001:  Grant Forest Products increases   │
│         stake in Ainsworth.               │
│  2004:  Oriented strand board price       │
│         recovery prompts expansion.       │
│  2006:  Bottom drops out of key U.S.      │
│         housing construction market.      │
│  2008:  Ainsworth family loses control    │
│         of company due to industry        │
│         downturn.                         │
│                                           │
└─────────────────────────────────────────┘
```

in Washington, had made a friendly bid for Vancouver-based MacMillan Bloedel Ltd. and its OSB business. Quebec's Groupe Forex Inc. factored into buyout plans on the table at both Louisiana-Pacific and Boise Cascade Corp. of Idaho. As for Ainsworth Lumber, the size of its debt and limited ownership mitigated chances of a takeover. In addition to the portion in the hands of the Ainsworth family, privately held Grant Forest Products controlled 20 percent of the Vancouver company.

In the summer of 1999, Ainsworth prepared to sell its plywood and lumber operations. Allen Ainsworth said in the *National Post:* "We want to be an engineered wood company." Ainsworth Lumber would concentrate on its fast-growing OSB business.

VOLATILE INDUSTRY: 2000–03

Ainsworth Lumber had to turn to outside financing, in the form of a CAD 52 million "bridge loan," in early 2001, to prevent a cash crisis, the *National Post* reported. The company had been channeling its cash into a joint venture project with Grant Forest Products. A drop in OSB prices precipitated the measure: more than 60 percent of Ainsworth's revenue came from OSB. The sale of a sawmill in Chasm, British Columbia, would bring in an additional CAD 22 million to the company's coffers.

Along with Grant Forest Products, Ainsworth had constructed a CAD 264 million OSB mill in High Level, Alberta, expected to be the largest OSB manufacturer in the world at full production. In December 2001, Grant Forest boosted its ownership of Ainsworth to about 32 percent through a Toronto Stock Exchange transaction.

Heavy investment by forest firms in plants to fabricate the board made of wood wafers, resin, and wax led to overcapacity. The condition worsened with an Asian economic crisis. The niche was set back on its heels. OSB prices and wood product manufacturers' profits tumbled.

By August 2003, however, the OSB segment of the forest product industry experienced resurgence. North American housing starts reached record levels. OSB prices shot up again, boosted by low inventories. Ainsworth, on the road to profitability, planned for an expansion at the Grande Prairie, Alberta, facility.

Ainsworth family members filled five of eight director chairs of Ainsworth Lumber. The company ranked as of one of the leading Canadian OSB producers, along with Slocan Forest Products Ltd. and Riverside Forest Products Ltd., also in British Columbia. According to the *National Post,* Ainsworth held about 5 percent of the North American OSB market.

The end of the housing construction season came with a predictable drop-off in sales. The threat of hurricanes on the southeast coast of the United States in 2003 had businesses and homeowners boarding up their structures against the storm, prolonging the period of strong sales for Canadian OSB producers. Of added benefit to Ainsworth, OSB, unlike other wood products from north of the border, was duty-free, according to the *Vancouver Sun.*

GOING FOR BROKE: 2004–07

Riding the OSB wave, Ainsworth's shares reached record levels in early 2004. Louisiana-Pacific, Weyerhaeuser, and fellow Canadian company Nexfor Inc. also were tied to the sector, but the smaller company's fate was more intimately bound to its ups and downs, according to the *National Post.* Nevertheless, Ainsworth deepened its commitment to OSB.

Seeking opportunities in new markets, the company acquired a plant in Barwick, Ontario, in April, and three in nearby Minnesota, in August. Ainsworth Lumber's OSB annual production capacity had swollen to 3.3 billion square feet. Its debt load also ballooned.

Profit and sales volume spiked with the additional plants. Banking on a continuation of the strong OSB market, Ainsworth planned an expansion of the Grande Prairie mill and new mills for interior British Columbia and upstate New York, according to the *Vancouver Sun.* However, Ainsworth Lumber was not alone in its drive to increase production, and prices were expected to fall again as capacity industrywide ramped up.

A significant downturn of U.S. housing starts led to slowdowns and layoffs at Ainsworth's Minnesota mills in the fall of 2006. Canadian housing starts had also fallen, but not as dramatically as in the United States. In the wake of declining business, the company posted negative earnings for the year.

In October 2007, Ainsworth was reducing production at Canadian plants as well. In addition to the depressed homebuilders' sector, the Canadian mills contended with an unfavorable monetary exchange rate.

To settle a complaint leveled in 2002, Ainsworth agreed during 2007 to pay $8.6 million to direct OSB purchasers. Nine forest product companies had been sued in U.S. District Court in Philadelphia for OSB price fixing. Ainsworth later added $1.3 million for indirect buyers. The company denied any wrongdoing, but settled to avoid costly litigation, according to *Canadian Business.*

Sales dropped to CAD 544.2 million in 2007, down from CAD 827.1 million in 2006. Net loss roughly doubled, rising from CAD 108 million in 2006 to CAD 216.5 million in 2007.

The critical U.S. market was mired in an oversupply of new and existing homes, a mortgage credit crisis, and weakened currency. U.S. housing starts experienced their steepest year-over-year decline since 1980, according to the company's annual report. OSB prices continued to fall. Ainsworth's jointly owned facility closed indefinitely and an expansion project was halted.

On the plus side, some raw material costs fell with the declining U.S. dollar. Ainsworth Lumber also introduced a promising engineered wood product. Overseas, the company led OSB sales in Japan and was preparing to enter the European Economic Area in 2008.

END OF AN ERA

In May 2008, Brian Ainsworth said the company was seeking strategic alternatives to strengthen its balance sheet and enhance its liquidity, *Canadian Business* reported. A bid in March to refinance debt had failed.

Year-end 2007 debt totaled CAD 977 million, and a semiannual interest payment of CAD 20 million was due June 30, according to the *Vancouver Sun.* Furthermore, liquidity had fallen below the threshold set in one loan covenant. In mid-May Ainsworth stock traded below CAD 3 per share.

A recapitalization plan, announced in June, ended the Ainsworth family's control of the company it founded. As negotiated with secured bondholders, debt was to be converted into equity in the company and new bonds issued. Old shares would be canceled. Existing shareholders as a group would receive 4 percent and bondholders would claim 96 percent of the new stock. Private equity funds HBK Master Fund L.P., Tricap Partners II L.P., and Barclays Bank PLC were the principal bondholders.

Sales continued to slide and losses climbed, as recapitalization headed toward completion. As for the company's future, one incoming director, Jonathan Mishkin, managing partner with Sanabe & Associates in New York, told *Canadian Business:* "What you can control is your cost of production and how much you produce. ... We plan to be really open minded about (what to do with Ainsworth)."

Kathleen Peippo

PRINCIPAL COMPETITORS

Louisiana-Pacific Corporation; Weyerhaeuser Company; Georgia-Pacific Corporation.

FURTHER READING

"Ainsworth Lumber Exploring Strategic Alternatives to Strengthen Balance Sheet," *Canadian Business Online,* May 1, 2008.

"Ainsworth to Lay Off 300 at 2 U.S. Plants," *European Intelligence Wire,* September 22, 2006.

"Ainsworth to Sell Solid Wood Assets," *National Post* (Ontario), September 4, 1999, p. D2.

Brissett, Jane, "Mills Cut Production," *Duluth News-Tribune,* October 25, 2007, p. B7.

Chow, Jason, "CEO Scorecard 2004: How They Performed, and How Much They Were Paid," *National Post* (Ontario), November 1, 2004, p. 88.

"Dismissed Ainsworth Executive Launches Suit," *Vancouver Sun,* January 30, 2003, p. C9.

"Forestry: Grant Increases Stake in Ainsworth Lumber to 32%," *National Post* (Ontario), December 12, 2001, p. FP9.

Garmoe, Patrick, "Ainsworth Family Steps Aside," *Duluth News-Tribune,* June 19, 2008, p. B5.

Greenwood, John, "Ainsworth Lumber Shares Ride Booming OSB Demand: Volatile Market," *National Post* (Ontario), February 17, 2004, p. FP6.

———, "Lumber Firms Cash In on Housing Boom," *National Post* (Ontario), September 9, 2003, p. FP7.

———, "Lumber Stocks Act Like Techs," *National Post* (Ontario), February 27, 2004, p. IN1F.

Hamilton, Gordon, "Bondholders Take Over Ainsworth," *Vancouver Sun,* June 18, 2008, p. D3.

———, "Briefly: Quarter Million for Ainsworth," *Vancouver Sun,* April 11, 1996, p. D6.

————, "Duty Refunds Fuel Ainsworth Net Earnings Rise," *Vancouver Sun,* February 24, 1995, p. D3.

————, "50-Year-Old Lumber Company Struggles with $88.2-Million Loss," *Vancouver Sun,* May 15, 2008, p. C4.

————, "Home Building Boom Fuels Run on Strandboard," *Vancouver Sun,* September 19, 2003, p. G1.

Hasselback, Drew, "Ainsworth Builds on Strength 'Wonder-wood,'" *National Post* (Ontario), July 21, 1999, p. 1D.

————, "Ainsworth Lumber Lands $52M Financing," *National Post* (Ontario), February 16, 2001, p. C5.

————, "Ainsworth Takes Aim at Hot OSB Market: US$457M Lumber Deal," *National Post* (Ontario), August 27, 2004, p. FP1FR.

Lamphier, Gary, "Price for Oriented Strandboard Goes Through the Roof," *Vancouver Sun,* August 6, 2003, p. D6.

Lush, Patricia, "Ainsworth Lumber Aims at Sales Hike," *Globe and Mail* (Toronto), May 8, 1996, p. B5.

"News Bulletins: Ainsworth Profit Up," *Globe and Mail* (Toronto), January 25, 1994, p. B2.

"Ontario Stud Mill Closes," *Vancouver Sun,* October 16, 1987, p. F6.

Parfitt, Ben, "Lillooet Report on Layoffs Hushed," *Vancouver Sun,* September 29, 1990, p. B12.

Penner, Derrick, "Ainsworth Lumber a Family Success: Sales Will Top $1 Billion This Year," *Vancouver Sun,* May 27, 2005, p. C1.

————, "Buoyed by $55-Million Profit, Panel Maker Ainsworth Looks to Expand," *Vancouver Sun,* May 11, 2005, p. D5.

Pynn, Larry, "Grizzly Habitat Logged After Cutting Permit Issued in Error," *Vancouver Sun,* October 2, 1996, p. B4.

Shackleton, Eric, "Norbord Settles U.S. Antitrust Case for US$30M, Avoids Trial Risks and Costs," *Canadian Business Online,* May 5, 2008.

Sirgurdson, Albert, "B.C. Workers Take Pay Cut to Save Jobs," *Globe and Mail* (Toronto), December 3, 1981, p. B1.

Vanderklippe, Nathan, "B.C.'s Pellet Bonanza?: The Answer for the Province's Beetle-Ravaged Forest May Be Wood Energy," *National Post,* January 23, 2007, p. FP3.

Alfa Group

---■---

31 B Shabolovka Street
Moscow, 115162
Russia
Telephone: (+7 495) 788-09-99
Fax: (+7 495) 785-08-88
Web site: http://www.alfagroup.org

Private Company
Incorporated: 1989
Total Assets: $32.2 billion (2007)
NAICS: 551112 Offices of Other Holding Companies

■ ■ ■

Alfa Group is one of Russia's largest conglomerates, with operations spanning a wide variety of industries, especially the oil and gas, banking, telecommunications, and retail industries. The company's major holdings include control of Alfa Bank, one of the largest privately held banks in Russia; TNK-BP, held in cooperation with British Petroleum, one of the leading oil and gas companies in Russia; controlling shares of number-two cellular telephone operator VimpelCom, as well as stakes in Megafon, another Russian mobile telephone provider; Ukraine's Kyivstar; Turkcell, in Turkey; and fixed line and Internet services provider Golden Telecom. Alfa Group's retail operations are conducted through the X5 Retail Group, which controls Pyaterochka, the largest grocery retailer in Russia, and Perekrestok, the country's leading supermarket chain.

Other holdings include CTC Media, one of the largest television broadcasters in Russia; Smirnov vodka;

and A1, a major capital investment firm. Alfa Group itself remains controlled by Mikhail Fridman, the company's founder and one of the wealthiest people in Russia, with a net worth valued at more than $21 billion. Friends, cofounders, and fellow billionaires German Khan and Alexei Kuzmichev also remain active in the company's operations. A number of Alfa Group's companies are listed on international stock exchanges, including Alfa Bank, VimpelCom, and Turkcell (New York Stock Exchange); CTC Media and Golden Telecom (NASDAQ); and X5 Retail (London Stock Exchange). Alfa Group's total assets were valued at $32.2 billion for the 2007 fiscal year.

PERESTROIKA-ERA COMMODITIES TRADER

Alfa Group was the brainchild of Mikhail Fridman and two schoolmates, German Khan and Alexei Kuzmichev. Born into a Jewish family in Lvov, Ukraine, in 1964, Fridman identified himself neither with Ukraine, nor with the anti-Semitic Soviet Empire, but instead as part of a larger European culture. This sense of identity was to play a role in Fridman's success in building Alfa Group, and in the company's survival during the Russian economic collapse of the late 1990s.

Fridman attended university at the Moscow Institute of Steel and Alloys, where he met Khan and Kuzmichev, graduating in 1986. Fridman's interest, however, turned to the business sector, which had just begun to develop under the perestroika era instituted by Mikhail Gorbachev. The Soviet government began allowing the creation of business cooperatives in the

COMPANY PERSPECTIVES

Alfa Group's Investment Philosophy: We rely on our investment philosophy to generate superior returns for our shareholders over the long term, to promote sound corporate governance and business practices, and to benefit our partners, counterparties, employees, the Russian consumer and society at large.

second half of the 1980s. This allowed Fridman and friends to form their first venture, a cooperative that specialized in window washing.

Fridman quickly proved an energetic entrepreneur, becoming involved in a wide variety of interests. By the late 1980s, Fridman had launched a courier service and become involved in real estate and rentals, and even a scheme for breeding mice for use in laboratory research. The import-export market was another area of interest for Fridman, and his operations in that sector included the import of cigarettes, perfume, computers, and photocopying machines, as well as the export of woolen shawls made in Siberia.

The launch of the partners' true path toward fortune came in 1988, when they founded Alfa-Eco, a commodities trading business. That company dealt in a broad range of commodities: sugar; tea; spirits, including control of the Smirnov vodka empire; and wine, later becoming Russia's top wine importer. Alfa-Eco also traded in oil, positioning itself among the earliest and largest players in what was soon to become one of the world's major oil and gas markets. Metals trading also became a significant part of Alfa-Eco's operations.

BANKING ON AN EMPIRE IN 1991

With the collapse of the Soviet Union, the Alfa-Eco partners found themselves in a strong position to take advantage of the new opportunities offered by the inauguration of a free market system in Russia. This period also saw the development of a new class of so-called oligarchs, a small group of politically connected individuals who built empires largely based on the privatization of Russia's natural resources. However, Fridman remained an outsider to this group. With few political connections, Fridman instead turned toward the financial sector. In 1991 the company founded its own bank, Alfa Bank. Although a full-service bank, Alfa's primary focus from the outset was on the corporate sector.

Alfa Bank grew strongly through the 1990s, providing a solid core to Alfa's expanding business interests. Nonetheless, Alfa still lacked the political influence necessary for success in the famously corrupt Russian economy of the 1990s. The company took a big step toward the political inside in 1992 when it recruited Pyotr Aven, the minister of foreign economic relations under the government led by Yegor Gaidar, to head Alfa Bank. Over the next several years, Fridman and Alfa continued to court Russia's political elite, eventually succeeding in developing close ties to the government under Boris Yeltsin.

In the meantime, Alfa's lack of political influence placed it on the losing end as the Russian government began handing out the former Soviet-run companies and industries to the country's oligarchs. Indeed, the period leading up to the country's economic crash was marked by the explosive growth of a number of wildly diversified conglomerates.

Alfa's inability to join in the feeding frenzy was to play a role in its survival: Unable to compete in the sell-off of the country's industries and resources, Alfa instead was required to optimize the operations it did own. In this way, the company maintained tight financial controls, avoiding the currency speculation and imprudent investments that proved the downfall of many of its competitors. Fridman's European leanings played a role in these financial policies, as he sought to emulate the corporate governance and financial responsibility more associated with the West.

Another consequence of Alfa's lack of influence in Moscow was the company's willingness to develop businesses from the ground up. Such was the case with Alfa's entry into the retail sector, with the creation of its own supermarket group, Perekrestok, in 1995. By founding a new company, rather than taking over one of Russia's notoriously inefficient retailers, Alfa quickly built Perekrestok into a leading supermarket and hypermarket group. By 1998 the company operated 20 supermarkets, and had acquired its own wholesale distribution facility. In 2002 Perekrestok, by then already among the leaders in Russia's supermarket sector, opened its first hypermarket as well. By the middle of the decade, the company was already the fifth largest hypermarket operator in Russia.

SURVIVING THE COLLAPSE IN 1998

While Fridman and partners built up Alfa Group during the 1990s, they also maintained their efforts to enter the political elite. Indeed, Fridman emerged as one of the most capable players in the seemingly lawless Russian

KEY DATES

1988: Mikhail Fridman, German Khan, and Alexei Kuzmichev found commodities trading company Alfa-Eco.

1991: Alfa-Eco founds its own bank, Alfa Bank.

1995: Alfa founds the Perekrestok supermarket group.

1997: Alfa Group gains control of the TNK oil group.

2001: Alfa enters telecommunications, acquiring stakes in Golden Telecom and VimpelCom.

2003: TNK merges with Russian and Ukrainian oil assets of British Petroleum (BP), forming TNK-BP.

2006: Perekrestok merges with rival Pyaterochka, forming the X5 Retail Group.

2008: Alfa Bank acquires 88 percent of Belarus's Mezhtorgbank.

economy of the mid-1990s. As Fridman told the *Financial Times:* "The rules of business are quite different to western standards. I don't want to lie and play this game. To say one can be completely clean and transparent is not realistic."

By 1996 Fridman himself counted among Russia's oligarchy, cementing his position by becoming one of the seven backers in the reelection of Yeltsin. In return, Fridman was rewarded with a prominent place at the table during the next round of often murky and usually suspect privatizations. In 1997 Alfa Group walked off with the prize: that of control of Tyumen Oil Co. (TNK), one of Russia's largest companies. In a shrewd move, Alfa recruited Simon Kukes, formerly with Amoco Corp., to take over the CEO spot at TNK. Kukes then launched a restructuring of the oil company, eliminating some 20 percent of jobs while achieving a 30 percent cut in operating costs.

Nevertheless, Alfa Bank remained at the group's core as Russia's banking system collapsed in 1998. As the country plunged into a deep economic crisis at the end of the 1990s, Alfa Bank, too, was hard hit, particularly by the devaluation of the ruble. While its rivals went bankrupt, however, Alfa Bank insisted on paying off its creditors and ensuring its customers' accounts. These efforts helped raise Alfa's profile, which attracted a new wave of clients. Through 1999 alone, the company added more than 6,000 new corporate clients. At the same time, Alfa took advantage of the

disarray in the Russian banking market, buying up the assets of its bankrupted rivals. At the beginning of the 2000s, Alfa Bank had emerged as Russia's largest private bank.

The rise of Vladimir Putin to political power also signaled a new era for Russia's economy. While most of the country's former oligarchs had been forced to flee Russia, Alfa Group now emerged as one of the country's leading conglomerates. This was in part because Fridman's reputation as a relative outsider to the Kremlin during the Yeltsin years enabled him to develop a strong lobbying arm within the Putin government. Alfa-Eco itself had emerged as a major force in the global commodities market particularly in the oil trading sector. This position was underscored in 2002 when the company negotiated a contract to purchase 20 million barrels of Iraqi crude oil. Meanwhile, TNK stepped up its position in the Russian oil market, gaining control of an 85 percent stake in rival oil company Onako in 2001. Two years later, Alfa led the merger of TNK with British Petroleum's (BP) oil assets in Russia and Ukraine, creating TNK-BP. In this way, Alfa became a major shareholder in Russia's third largest oil group.

TELECOMMUNICATIONS PLAYER IN THE 21ST CENTURY

Alfa Group spread its wings in the new century. The company opened a new trading subsidiary in the Netherlands. The company also acquired several insurance providers, including East European Insurance Agency and Ostra Kiev, which were then placed under a new company, Alfa Insurance, in 2001. The company also carried out a number of takeovers, including the buyout of the Smirnov vodka group in 2001. Unlike rival conglomerates, such as Interros and Millhouse, Alfa Group qualified itself as an investment-focused company. As Fridman told the Russian *St. Petersburg Times:* "We are neither bankers, nor oil men, nor telecommunications specialists—we are investors. We invest in projects and withdraw from them when we believe that it is the right time, place and price. We are sure that one day we will withdraw from our oil and banking assets and will possibly be investing in other assets."

Telecommunications became one of the group's most prominent investment targets in the first decade of the 2000s. The company's first step into that market came in 2001, when it paid $110 million to acquire nearly 44 percent of Golden Telecom, the leading Internet service provider in Russia. Just one month later, the company bought a major stake in the country's number two mobile telephone services provider, VimpelCom, paying nearly $250 million.

Alfa continued to pursue telecommunications investments into the second half of the decade, adding stakes in Ukraine's Kyivstar and Turkey's Turkcell, as well as control of the CTC broadcasting empire. By 2008 Alfa had increased its stake in VimpelCom, after that company merged with Golden Telecom. In the meantime, Alfa had also been building up its retail operations. The merger of Perekrestok with rival Pyaterochka in 2006 created Russia's leading retail group. The company was then renamed as X5 Retail Group. Alfa continued to seek new deals toward the decade's end. In August 2008 the company acquired 88 percent of Mezhtorgbank, in Belarus. The growth of the Alfa Group had also established its founders among Russia's, and the world's, richest. Alfa Group appeared certain to remain a major fixture in the Russian economy in the early decades of the new century.

M. L. Cohen

PRINCIPAL SUBSIDIARIES

A1 Group Limited BVI; ABH Financial Limited BVI; ABH Ukraine Limited (Cyprus; 100% owned and controlled by ABH Holdings Corp.); Alfa Capital Holdings (Cyprus) Limited; Alfa Finance Holdings S.A. (Luxemburg; 77.86%); Alfa Petroleum Holdings Limited; Altimo Holdings and Investments Limited BVI (73.69%); CJSC Alfa-Bank Ukraine (99.99%); CJSC Kyivstar GSM (Ukraine; 43.48%); Golden Telecom Inc. (U.S.A.; 29.26%); OJSC Alfa-Bank Russia; OJSC Vimpel-Communications (28.3%); Perekrestok Holdings Limited (Gibraltar); Turkcell Iletisim Hizmetleri Anonim Sirketi (Turkey; 13.22%); X5 Retail Group N.V. (Netherlands; 55.51%).

PRINCIPAL COMPETITORS

Interros Holding Co.; OBORONPROM United Industrial Corp.; Sistema Financial Corp.; Severstal Group; Savva Group Joint Stock Co.; Svyazinvest Joint Stock Co.; Evraz Holding Group Ltd.

FURTHER READING

"Alfa Group Considers Supermarket Merger," *International Herald Tribune,* April 7, 2006, p. 17.

"Alfa Group Grabs Stake in Cellular Operator," *St. Petersburg Times* (Russia), August 8, 2003.

"Alfa Group Officially Announces Purchase of Bank in Belarus," *Russia & CIS Business and Financial Newswire,* August 4, 2008.

"Alfa Group's Financial Business Valued at $10bln," *Russia & CIS Business and Financial Newswire,* December 4, 2007.

"Alfa Wins Tender to Run Sheremetyevo," *Moscow Times,* January 29, 2004.

Belton, Catherine, "Cast of Stakeholders Worth a Fortune," *Financial Times,* September 5, 2008, p. 19.

"The Big Get Bigger," *Business Week,* July 16, 2001, p. 22.

Fridman, Mikhail, Andrew Jack, and Arkady Ostrovsky, "Power Broker in Russia's Shifting Scene," *Financial Times,* August 29, 2003, p. 10.

Ostrovsky, Arkady, "Telecombative Oligarch Shares His Vision," *Financial Times,* July 7, 2005, p. 26.

"Russian Tycoon Moves into the Arms Industry," *International Herald Tribune,* December 6, 2006, p. 13.

"A Russian Tycoon Who's Doing Things Right," *Business Week,* June 14, 1999, p. 122B.

"Setting a Standard for Russian Business," *Business Week,* July 7, 2003, p. 54.

AMCON Distributing
Company

7405 Irvington Road
Omaha, Nebraska 68122
U.S.A.
Telephone: (402) 331-3727
Fax: (402) 331-4834
Web site: http://www.amcon.com

Public Company
Incorporated: 1986
Employees: 874
Sales: $853.6 million (2007)
Stock Exchanges: American
Ticker Symbol: DIT
NAICS: 424410 General Line Grocery Merchant
Wholesalers; 424940 Tobacco and Tobacco Product
Merchant Wholesalers

■ ■ ■

AMCON Distributing Company is an Omaha, Nebraska-based wholesale distributor of consumer products, serving the Great Plains and Rocky Mountain regions of the United States. One of the ten largest distributors in the country, AMCON serves about 5,000 retail customers, including convenience stores, drug stores, discount and general merchandise stores, gas stations, grocery stores, and supermarkets. Institutional customers include bars, restaurants, sporting venues, and other wholesalers. AMCON carried about 14,000 different products, primarily beverages, candy, cigarettes, groceries, health and beauty care products, paper products, and tobacco products. In addition to brand-

name products, AMCON markets private-label batteries, candy products, cigarettes and chewing tobacco, film, and water. Distribution centers are maintained in Quincy, Illinois; Springfield, Missouri; Omaha, Nebraska; Bismarck, North Dakota; and Rapid City, South Dakota. AMCON is also involved in the retail health food business through subsidiary Healthy Edge, Inc., which operates a pair of small health food store chains. Serving the Orlando, Florida, area with six stores is Chamberlin's Market, while seven stores in the Midwest carry the Akin's Natural Foods Market banner. The stores carry dairy products, delicatessen items, organic produce, as well as natural supplements and herbs. AMCON is a public company listed on the American Stock Exchange.

COMPANY FORMED: 1976

AMCON was established in Nebraska in 1976 by attorney William F. Wright as General Tobacco and Candy Company, growing out of a beer distributorship. One of his primary financial backers was Allen Petersen, whose grandfather, a Nebraska blacksmith, made a fortune through the invention of the Vise-Grip. Over the years, Petersen would invest in a number of Wright's projects. Wright earned a degree at the University of Nebraska before graduating from the Duke University School of Law. For several years he practiced law with a regional law firm, and then in 1968 founded his own law firm in Lincoln, Nebraska, involved in tax law, securities law, and mergers and acquisitions. Even after starting General Tobacco and Candy Company and serving as its chief executive, Wright continued to practice law until 1984. General Tobacco and Candy

COMPANY PERSPECTIVES

AMCON Distributing Company, together with its wholly-owned subsidiaries (collectively "AMCON"), is primarily engaged in the wholesale distribution of consumer products including cigarettes and tobacco products, candy and other confectionery, beverages, groceries, paper products and health and beauty care products. In addition, the Company operates thirteen retail health food stores in Florida and the Midwest.

launched an expansion program in 1981, mostly achieving growth through acquisitions, completing 19 deals over the next 15 years. The company was incorporated in Delaware in 1986 and took the AMCON Distributing Company name.

In February 1991 a new chief executive was installed, Kathleen M. Evans, who had been with the company or its subsidiaries since 1978. In 1985 she became vice-president of AMCON and was groomed for the top post. Under her guidance AMCON posted sales of $118.8 million in fiscal 1992. The company began looking to improve operating efficiency. Two small Omaha-area warehouses, for example, were replaced with a single distribution center that was larger, more modern, and better able to serve AMCON's growing business in eastern Nebraska and western Iowa. Additional refrigerated space permitted an increase in temperature-sensitive products, while extra warehouse space in general allowed AMCON to better participate in manufacturer promotions. Not only did AMCON merge smaller distribution facilities to create larger, more efficient operations, it began moving into contiguous markets through targeted acquisitions to take further advantage of those efficiencies. In late 1991, for example, Stillwater, Oklahoma-based Duckwall Wholesale Co., a tobacco and candy distributor, was acquired. AMCON also used acquisitions to add new product lines that could be offered throughout the AMCON system, such as health and beauty care products that were introduced in the early 1990s.

CABLE CAR BEVERAGE GAINS STAKE: 1993

AMCON returned to its roots as a beverage distributor in late 1992 when it arranged to acquire the distribution operation of Denver-based Cable Car Beverage Corporation, Sheya Brothers Specialty Beverages, Inc., which was a wholesaler of beer, malt beverage, and "New Age"

beverages. Cable Car received about a 15 percent stake in AMCON when the deal closed in June 1993. Two years later AMCON elected to sell the New Age beverage business to Vancol Industries, Inc., and in October 1996 sold the rest of the Sheya operation to Western Distributing Company. In the meantime, in June 1995, Cable Car distributed the AMCON stock to its shareholders, creating a large pool of shareholders for AMCON, whose stock was listed on NASDAQ. The distribution also created a nuisance for AMCON over the next decade, because the company had to contend with the expense of record keeping and issuing investment materials as required by law.

After posting sales in the $170 million range and earnings of about $1 million in fiscal 1994 and fiscal 1995, AMCON increased sales in fiscal 1996 to $176.1 million and net earnings to $1.3 million. The following year revenues approached $179 million and earnings reached $1.94 million. In early fiscal 1998, the company positioned itself for further growth to the balance sheet by acquiring Marcus Distributors Inc. of St. Louis, primarily a distributor of candy and cigarettes. In addition to St. Louis, AMCON gained entry into a number of new markets, including parts of eastern Missouri, Illinois, and Indiana.

The vast majority of AMCON sales came from cigarettes. In order to achieve some level of diversity, AMCON in November 1997 became involved in the distribution of health and natural foods and related products by acquiring Phoenix, Arizona-based Food For Health Company, Inc. (FFH), which supplied these items in southeastern and southwestern states from operations in Arizona, Florida, and Texas. FFH now became a wholly owned AMCON subsidiary. The addition of Marcus and FFH helped to push AMCON close to the $300 million mark ($294.3 million) in fiscal 1998 with net income of nearly $2.4 million.

NATURAL FOODS' ASSETS ACQUIRED: 1999

AMCON's aggressive growth push continued in fiscal 1999. In March of that year, FFH acquired a Winter Park, Florida, chain of six health and natural products retail stores, Chamberlin Natural Foods, Inc., which did business as Chamberlin's Market & Café. All units were located in the Orlando area. In September, before the fiscal year came to a close at the end of the month, FFH grew even larger, acquiring Health Food Associates, Inc., a Tulsa, Oklahoma-based operator of the Akin's Natural Food Market chain of six health and natural product retail stores. In addition to a pair of Tulsa stores, other Akin's units were located in Oklahoma City, Oklahoma; Lincoln, Nebraska; Springfield, Missouri; and Topeka,

KEY DATES

1976: Company is established as General Tobacco and Candy Company.
1986: Company incorporates as AMCON Distributing Company.
1991: Duckwall Wholesale Co. is acquired.
1997: Food For Health Company, Inc., is acquired.
1998: Marchus Distributors Inc. is acquired.
2002: Hawaiian Natural Water Co. Inc. is acquired.
2004: Trinity Spring Ltd. is acquired.
2006: Beverage assets are divested.

Kansas. AMCON managed its natural product stores collectively but opted to keep the Chamberlin and Akin's names, both of which were well established in their markets, both having been in business since 1935. Their partial contribution to the AMCON balance sheet helped to boost revenues to $385.5 million in fiscal 1999 and net income to $3.84 million. Due to its steady growth, AMCON was able to secure a listing on the American Stock Exchange at the start of 2000, providing greater visibility for AMCON stock.

The retail natural product business grew even larger in fiscal 2000 with the acquisition of Kissimmee, Florida-based T.I.N.K., Inc., operator of a single natural product food store under the Natural Way Foods banner. It was subsequently converted into a Chamberlin's Market & Café. A full-year contribution of Chamberlin and Akin's led to an increase in annual revenues for AMCON to $466.1 million and net income of $3.9 million in fiscal 2000.

While AMCON's management had high hopes for its natural products retail operations, the same could not be said for its wholesale health food and natural products business, which had to contend with stiff competition from national health food retail chains. By the end of fiscal 2001, AMCON sold the wholesale operation but kept the natural products retail stores. AMCON's traditional distribution business, primarily serving convenience stores, remained strong, and the company continued to build upon it in fiscal 2001, acquiring Quincy, Illinois-based Merchants Wholesale Inc. in February 2001 for about $50 million. Carrying much the same products as AMCON, Merchants Wholesale supplied customers in Arkansas, Illinois, Indiana, Iowa, Kansas, Missouri, Ohio, and Wisconsin. The addition of Merchants Wholesale increased AMCON's revenues to $582 million, but the cost of

integrating operations was high, resulting in a net loss of $3.34 million in fiscal 2001.

HAWAIIAN NATURAL WATER ACQUIRED: 2002

AMCON took steps to diversify in a new direction in fiscal 2002 by acquiring Hawaiian Natural Water Co. Inc., which produced premium bottled water for sale in the United States, the Middle East, and Asia. AMCON had been involved with the company for several years, distributing the water and also helping it build a new, state-of-the-industry bottling plant on the Big Island to help meet growing demand. It came online in fiscal 2003.

AMCON returned to profitability in fiscal 2002, netting nearly $2 million on sales of $847.1 million. A decrease in prices on Philip Morris and Brown & Williamson tobacco products adversely impacted AMCON the following year, leading to a drop in sales in fiscal 2003 to $772.1 million. Net income also fell to $1 million, due in large part to the cost of completing the Hawaiian Natural Water plant. During the year AMCON reorganized its beverage operation by forming a new subsidiary, The Beverage Group, Inc., established to distribute Hawaiian Natural Water and other premium products.

AMCON was also saddled with the ongoing cost of dealing with a multitude of small shareholders inherited from the Cable Car distribution of AMCON stock a decade earlier. Two-thirds of AMCON shareholders owned just 0.04 percent of the company. In 2004 AMCON took care of this problem by engineering a one-for-six reverse stock split in January 2004. One new share, worth six times as much as the old shares, would be exchanged for every six shares a person owned. If someone held fewer than six shares, and the vast majority did, the company would simply pay them in cash for the shares without charging a broker's commission, the cost of which had dissuaded most people from unloading AMCON stock in the past. As a result, small stockholders were able to liquidate their holdings without incurring a charge, and AMCON was able to achieve savings by eliminating the burden of communicating with a large number of small stakeholders.

In fiscal 2004 The Beverage Group acquired the assets of the Bahia Company, including the Bahia Aguas Frescas brand of exotic-flavored bottled drinks, catering to the Hispanic market. They were sold only in Southern California, but AMCON believed the drinks had national potential and began supplying them to their accounts. Later in fiscal 2004 The Beverage Group grew further with the acquisition of the assets of Trinity

Springs Ltd., an Idaho bottler of natural spring and mineral water, primarily serving the health food market. The beverage business proved extremely disappointing, however. The cost of product development, marketing, and building a distribution network drained cash from AMCON's coffers. Moreover, Trinity Beverage was embroiled in a costly legal dispute connected to the purchase.

ASSETS SHED: 2006

AMCON lost $4.2 million on sales of $821.8 million in fiscal 2004, and another $13 million in fiscal 2005 on sales of $845.9 million. Drastic changes were clearly in order, and in March 2006 Trinity Beverage was shut down and later in the year Hawaiian Natural Water was sold for $5.5 million, which included $3.8 million in cash and the assumption of $1.7 million in obligations. AMCON also saw a management shakeup. In October 2006 a new CEO, Christopher H. Atayan, was installed. A member of the company's board of directors, Atayan came with 25 years of Wall Street experience. He also had deep ties to the candy and tobacco distribution business: His family operated a wholesale business in Michigan and he began helping out at the age of eight.

Living in Westchester County, New York, Atayan worked off site and made occasional visits to turn around AMCON, cutting costs and returning the company to profitability. In fiscal 2007 sales totaled $853.6 million and the company netted $4 million. Having successfully righted the ship, Atayan replaced Wright as chairman of the board, completing a transition plan initiated earlier. Wright, who remained the largest shareholder, stayed on as a director and consultant to the company he founded.

Ed Dinger

PRINCIPAL SUBSIDIARIES

Healthy Edge, Inc.

PRINCIPAL COMPETITORS

Core-Mack Holding Company, Inc.; Eby-Brown Company, LLC; McLane Company, Inc.

FURTHER READING

"Cable Car Beverage Corp.: Company Plans to Distribute Amcon Shares to Its Holders," *Wall Street Journal,* June 26, 1995, p. B4.

"Cable Car Makes a Deal," *Beverage World,* December 1992, p. 12.

Jordon, Steve, "Amcon Distributing Co. Postpones Annual Shareholders Meeting," *Omaha World-Herald,* January 18, 2006.

———, "Amcon Is Able to Deliver," *Omaha World-Herald,* December 24, 2006.

———, "Omaha, Neb.-based Health-Food Distributor Amcon Assesses 'Alternatives,'" *Omaha World-Herald,* February 14, 2001.

Kawar, Mark, "Omaha, Neb.-based Amcon Distributing Thins Ownership with Reverse Stock Split," *Omaha World-Herald,* January 22, 2004.

Margulis, Ronald, "Warehouse Consolidation Gives Amcon Room to Grow," *U.S. Distribution Journal,* August 15, 1992, p. 29.

Rasmussen, Jim, "Amcon Distributing of Omaha, Neb., to Buy St. Louis Firm," *Omaha World-Herald,* September 16, 1997.

American Commercial
Lines Inc.

1701 East Market Street
Jefferson, Indiana 47130-4747
U.S.A.
Telephone: (812) 288-0100
Toll Free: (800) 457-6377
Fax: (812) 288-1664
Web site: http://www.aclines.com

Public Company
Incorporated: 1957 as American Commercial Barge Line
    Company
Employees: 3,000
Sales: $1.05 billion (2007)
Stock Exchanges: NASDAQ
Ticker Symbol: ACLI
NAICS: 483211 Inland Water Freight Transportation

■ ■ ■

A NASDAQ-listed public company, American Commercial Lines Inc. (ACL) is a leading U.S. diversified marine transportation and services company, primarily involved in barge transportation. Operating through the American Commercial Lines LLC subsidiary, the Jeffersonville, Indiana-based company maintains a fleet of more than 3,000 barges and about 120 towboats, plying some 15,000 miles of the Mississippi River System and connecting waterways as well as the Gulf Intracoastal Waterway. Often overlooked, barge transport is a highly economic way to ship goods: Each barge load is comparable to 15 railcar loads or 80 truckloads. The type of cargo ACL hauls includes chemicals, coal, construction materials, fertilizers, grain, petroleum products, and steel.

ACL is also involved in vessel manufacturing. The Jeffboat LLC subsidiary turns out dry cargo barges, tank barges, and special vessels, and also does repairs at its 68-acre facility fronting the Ohio River in Jeffersonville, serving the needs of third-party customers as well as ACL. Another subsidiary, ACL Transportation Services, owns and operates two facilities: a St. Louis rail-to-barge coal storage and transloading terminal, and a Memphis liquid storage and transfer terminal. In addition, the unit is responsible for nine other facilities serving the ACL transport network that provide repair, shifting, cleaning, and other services. Another subsidiary, ACL Professional Services Inc., provides naval architecture and marine engineering through the Elliott Bay Design Group unit, and environmental emergency response and remediating through Summit Contracting LLC.

MAJOR BARGE LINES MERGE: 1957

The foundation of ACL was the result of the 1957 merger between American Barge Line Company and the Commercial Transport Corporation. Serving as president of the combined concern, which took the name American Commercial Barge Line Company, was Jacob W. "Jake" Hershey, a giant in the barge transportation field and the man responsible for the birth of ACL and growing it into the world's largest commercial barge line.

Born in Harrisburg, Pennsylvania, a member of the famous Hershey chocolate family, Jake Hershey earned a

---

COMPANY PERSPECTIVES

Mission: Deliver premium transportation services and solutions to meet the evolving needs of our customers.

---

degree in applied economic sciences from Yale University in 1934. Upon graduation he went to work for Shell Oil Company in the oil-purchasing department. He left for Pan American Pipe Line Company in 1940 and spent two years serving as manager of oil purchases. Hershey moved to Texas in 1942 to take a job with a small Houston-based barge line called Commercial Petroleum and Transport Company, which used the waters of the Gulf Intracoastal Waterway to move petroleum products. Not only was Hershey responsible for growing his company, he influenced the national transportation and distribution field, helping to increase the influence of inland carriers by advocating a unified transportation policy that coordinated trucking and railroad industries with waterway carriers, often appearing before Congress and the Interstate Commerce Commission (ICC) to make his case. Moreover, during and after World War II he served his country as an appointed delegate to port conferences around the globe.

In 1955 Hershey engineered a buyout of the barge and motor carrier assets of Commercial Petroleum. With partners American Hawaiian Steamship of New York, Eastern Steamship Lines of Boston, and the New York investment bank of Lazard Freres & Co., he formed New York-based Commercial Transport Corporation, which paid $7.6 million for the assets, including Commercial Barge Lines of Detroit and Commercial Carriers, Inc., involved in the trucking of new automobiles. It was Commercial Transport Corporation that a year later agreed to merged with American Barge Line Company. The deal was completed in 1957, resulting in a company that boasted a combined fleet of 570 barges and 51 towboats, operating from the Great Lakes to the Gulf of Mexico. It also included Jeffersonville Boat and Machine Company, which possessed a solid foundation in shipbuilding.

In the 1800s Cincinnati native James Howard established works in Jeffersonville that became world famous for the stern-wheel paddle steamboats it turned out, such as the *Mississippi Queen* and *General Jackson.* The yards closed in 1931 due to the demise of steamboating, but seven years later Jefferson Boat was begun on part of the old Howard works and continued the tradition. It was soon taken over by the U.S. Navy dur-

ing World War II and was responsible for producing landing craft, tankers, and submarine chasers. Jefferson Boat continued to thrive during the postwar economic boom, with barges serving as its mainstay. Hershey renamed the company Jeffboat, Inc.

ISLAND CREEK FUEL AND TRANSPORTATION COMPANY ACQUIRED: 1963

Hershey soon became chairman of American Commercial Barge Line and continued to guide it into the 1960s. The company paid $6.5 million in 1963 for the Island Creek Fuel and Transportation Company, a subsidiary of West Virginia-based Island Creek Coal Company, which operated barges as part of a rail transport system to bring its coal to market. This addition helped the company to increase revenues to $42.4 million and net income to $5 million in 1963. Serving 5,000 miles of water routes in 18 states, it was by far the largest barge company in the United States.

Already the only barge company with a trucking component, American Commercial Barge Line sought to add to its trucking assets in 1963 by reaching an agreement to acquire Atlanta-based Terminal Transport Company, Inc., operator of routes between Chicago and Florida. The deal was not finalized until approval was granted by the ICC in 1965. Hershey also looked to diversify further in the transportation sector. A major hydraulic dredging company, Bauer Dredging Company of Port Lavaca, Texas, was acquired in that same year. As a result of this expansion revenues soared to about $120 million.

NAME CHANGE: 1968

American Commercial Barge Lines shortened its name to American Commercial Lines and in 1968 changed owners as well, merging with Texas Gas Transmission Co., a pipeline company that supplied fuel to utilities located in the Mississippi and Ohio River Valleys. The addition was part of a diversification strategy to offset seasonal fluctuations in the pipeline business. Hershey stayed on as ACL's chairman until 1978, when he retired after reaching age 65. He lived until 2000, having spent the final 20 years of his life actively involved with his wife in conservation projects before passing away at the age of 87.

Around the time Hershey retired, the barge sector began adding more capacity than needed because tax benefits encouraged investment, resulting in thousands of unneeded barges being built in the late 1970s and early 1980s. While the tax breaks were eventually

KEY DATES

1957: American Barge Line Company and Commercial Transport Corporation merge.
1968: Texas Gas Transmission Co. acquires company.
1978: Chairman Jacob Hershey retires.
1983: Company is sold to CSX Corporation.
1998: American Commercial Lines (ACL) is spun off and merges with Vectura Group assets.
2003: ACL files for Chapter 11 bankruptcy protection.
2005: Company emerges from bankruptcy, conducts initial public offering of stock.
2007: Elliott Bay Design Group is acquired.

rescinded, the need for the extra barges never materialized and to make matters worse, river transportation tailed off. As a result, work for shipbuilders including Jeffboat came to a sudden stop. At the peak of building in 1981, the company employed 2,200 people, who were completing 15 barges a week. Five years later that number was reduced to 225, and the yard was mostly used to make repairs and build offshore drilling rig components. It would have to wait until the 1990s, when the barges on the market began to surpass their useful life, and business picked up again.

In the midst of the downturn in river transportation, ACL was sold to CSX Corporation, a Richmond, Virginia-based railroad-holding company, as part of a 1983 acquisition of Texas Gas, which at the time was the subject of a hostile takeover bid by Coastal Corp. It was the first merger between a railroad and a barge line, and was part of an effort by CSX to provide intermodal services, essentially one-stop shipping for customers. Because ACL and CSX were competitors, ICC approval was needed. There were also fears that CSX would funnel all of its business to ACL and put other barge lines at an unfair disadvantage. It was not until the summer of 1984 that CSX was allowed to swallow ACL and three more years of legal wrangling followed before the matter was fully settled.

The Texas Gas and ACL acquisitions were also part of a diversification strategy that would see CSX purchase the Sea-Land service container shipping business as well as a chain of resort properties. As a result, CSX lost focus on its rail business and in the 1990s shed many of these noncore assets. ACL was retained for a while and expanded through further acquisitions. The addition of

a pair of small barge carriers—SCNO, operating mostly on the Missouri River, and Hines, a Kentucky bulk-liquid carrier—did not attract much attention. The reaction would be different, however, in 1992 when ACL arranged to acquire St. Louis-based Valley Line, among the top five of inland barge operators. ACL's main competitor, Ohio River Co., urged the ICC to reject the merger, claiming that ACL would now control one-sixth of the United States' dry-cargo barges. The ICC did not agree and the deal went through.

ACL REGAINS INDEPENDENCE: 1998

ACL regained its independence in 1998 when CSX decided to focus on its core rail business, selling the operation for $850 million to a new joint venture that took the American Commercial Lines name and simultaneously merged with the barge unit of New Orleans-based marine company Vectura Group Inc. Based in Jeffersonville, the new company was an industry behemoth, operating a fleet of 4,500 barges and 195 towboats. It was not the best of times for the barge business, however. Although rates had been low, barge companies were hoping that the North American Free Trade Agreement between the United States, Mexico, and Canada, would spur an increase in revenues. In recent years there had been a surge in the flow of products between the United States and Mexico, but the border infrastructure was not up to the task, resulting in stranded trains and trucks along the Texas-Mexico border. Barge companies such as ACL hoped that water transportation would now become an attractive alternative.

ACL continued to expand as the century came to an end, and also piled on debt. In 2000 the barge assets of ConAgra Inc., including Peavey Barge Lines and its St. Louis subsidiaries, Brown Water Towing and Superior Barge Lines, were acquired. It was not a particularly good time, however, for the barge industry, which was beset with high fuel prices, and ACL, saddled with debt, suffered more than most. In addition to a decrease in freight volumes and plummeting barge rates, ACL also had to contend with a ten-week labor strike at Jeffboat in 2002. Later in the year the company was sold for just $92 million to a New York insurance company, Danielson Holding Corp. Moreover, the bulk of that amount, $58.5 million, was debt forgiven by Danielson.

COMPANY FILES FOR BANKRUPTCY: 2003

With a debt load and other liabilities totaling $769 million at the end of 2002 and assets of $814 million, ACL and its dozen subsidiaries lurched into Chapter 11 bankruptcy protection in February 2003. Over the next two years ACL streamlined its organization and underwent changes in senior management under the leadership of interim CEO Richard Huber, a veteran of corporate turnaround efforts. The company finally emerged from bankruptcy in early 2005 with a $35 million revolving credit facility and $364 million of secured financing, as well as a new president and chief executive at the helm, Mark R. Holden, a transportation executive who oversaw a restructuring of Wabash National, a truck trailer manufacturer.

Holden brought in other former Wabash National executives to streamline operations to make the company more profitable. For example, barge trips were shortened by imposing charges on customers who failed to unload barges in a timely fashion. ACL was also able to charge higher rates. Further steps were taken to increase fleet usage, and plans were laid to add other types of transportation, part of a greater long-term plan to make ACL into a global transportation company. To fund these ambitions ACL conducted an initial public offering of stock in the fall of 2005.

ACL enjoyed a strong year in 2006, recording revenues of $942.6 million and net income of $92.3 million. The company looked to build on this success in 2007 by returning to a growth through acquisition strategy. In 2007 it acquired 20 towboats from the McKinney group of companies. Later in the year it acquired Elliott Bay Design Group, a Seattle-based naval architecture and marine engineering company that was added primarily to help Jeffboat in vessel design. While revenues grew to $1.1 billion in 2007, net earnings fell to $44.4 million, a disappointment that led to Holden stepping down in 2008 in favor of a new chief executive, Mike Ryan, a 27-year veteran of the transportation field. Whether he would be able to fulfill ACL's global aspirations remained to be seen.

Ed Dinger

PRINCIPAL SUBSIDIARIES

American Commercial Lines LLC; Jeffboat LLC; ACL Professional Services Inc.; ACL Transportation Services.

PRINCIPAL COMPETITORS

Ingram Industries Inc.; Kirby Corporation; Trinity Industries, Inc.

FURTHER READING

Bonney, Joseph, "CSX Barge Merger Under Attack," *American Shipper,* March 1992, p. 14.

Fabey, Michael, "ACL's Course Change," *Traffic World,* March 3, 2008, p. 1.

Hall, Henry Boyd, and Daniel Machalaba, "CSX's Purchase of a Barge Line Is Cleared by ICC," *Wall Street Journal,* July 25, 1984, p. 1.

Horne, George, "Barge Line Chairman Expects Doubling of Business in a Year," *New York Times,* May 14, 1965.

Lieber, Tammy, "Barge Company Floats Itself into Profitable Waters," *Indianapolis Business Journal,* June 5, 2006, p. 34.

Mathews, Anna Wilde, "CSX Corp. to Sell Its Barge Unit for $850 Million," *Wall Street Journal,* April 21, 1998, p. 1.

Norman, James R., "'We've Got a Clock on It,'" *Forbes,* June 25, 1990, p. 116.

"Tote That Barge," *Barron's National Business and Financial Weekly,* February 12, 1968, p. 9.

"Two Barge Lines Merge Services," *New York Times,* August 2, 1957.

"Winning Ways," *Barron's National Business and Financial Weekly,* September 7, 1964, p. 9.

The Andrews Institute

1040 Gulf Breeze Parkway
Gulf Breeze, Florida 32561
U.S.A.
Telephone: (850) 916-8700
Web site: http://www.theandrewsinstitute.com

Private Company
Incorporated: 2004
Employees: 120
NAICS: 621000 Ambulatory Health Care Services

■ ■ ■

Affiliated with Baptist Health Care of Pensacola, Florida, The Andrews Institute is the orthopedics and sports medicine complex headed by orthopedic surgeon Dr. James R. Andrews, acclaimed for his work on knee, shoulder, and elbow injuries suffered by some of the world's most famous athletes. The Andrews campus is located in Gulf Breeze, in northwest Florida, contiguous to the Gulf Breeze Hospital, and provides a full range of musculoskeletal and rehabilitation services geared toward both athletes and non-athletes (the Institute also offers physicals for executives), as well as research facilities. The multi-specialty Ambulatory Surgery Center occupies 26,000 square feet in the 85,000-square-foot Clinical Facility, and includes eight digital operating rooms. The center also houses the Diagnostic Imaging Center, featuring the most powerful magnetic resonance scanner (MRI) on the market; 38,000 square feet of medical office space for the Institute's more than 40 affiliated physicians; and 12,000 square feet dedicated to

the Outpatient Rehabilitation division, which offers individual programs for injury recovery and provides sports medicine services to area schools and community sports organizations.

Physical therapy and occupational therapy services are offered through partner Baptist First Rehab, which in addition to its space in the Clinical Facility treats outpatients in branch locations in Escambia and Santa Rosa counties in Florida. The 42,000-square-foot Athletic Performance and Research Pavilion houses a pair of divisions: the Athletic Performance Center and the Research and Education Institute. The former is a 10,000-square-foot athletic training facility that includes a sprint track, turf field, pitching mounds and a batter cage, performance pools, and an outdoor covered agility and court area. The 16,000 square feet of the Research and Education Institute is used for biomedical research related to athletic injuries and performance, and also provides classrooms and conference facilities for continuing medical education.

FOUNDER, 1967 MEDICAL SCHOOL GRADUATE

James Andrews was raised in Homer, Louisiana, where his father ran a laundry. His grandfather, a cotton farmer, was known for the homemade salves he provided to neighbors and insisted that the young man become a doctor when he grew up. "I never thought about doing anything else," Andrews told *Forbes*. Andrews also grew up with a passion for athletics. He was a high school quarterback who also played defense, but it was his skill

COMPANY PERSPECTIVES

Our mission is to provide the best medical care for the musculoskeletal system through orthopaedics and sports medicine, utilizing innovative clinical and surgical technologies, and to improve patient care through research and education, emphasizing prevention.

in track and field and a state championship in polevaulting that earned him a scholarship to Louisiana State University (LSU) to pursue a pre-med curriculum. At LSU he became the indoor and outdoor pole vaulting champion in the Southeastern Conference. He stayed at LSU to attend the School of Medicine, graduating in 1967. Andrews then began his orthopedic residency at Tulane Medical School.

Andrews was about two years into his residency when he went to Columbus, Georgia, to observe an operation by Dr. Jack Hughston, generally regarded as one of the fathers of sports medicine. Raised in Georgia, Hughston graduated from Auburn University and then earned his medical degree at LSU in 1943. After his internship in a New Orleans hospital, a stint in the U.S. Army Medical Corps during World War II, and a fellowship at Duke University School of Medicine, he returned to his hometown of Columbus and opened the Hughston Clinic in 1949. Three years later he was recruited by the Auburn University football team to become one of the first team physicians, a man who was ridiculed for patrolling football sidelines to observe injuries as they occurred. He was responsible for a number of groundbreaking techniques in sports medicine and was the inventor of the protective mouthpiece, which became mandatory for high school football players. After Hughston met Andrews, he invited the young man to join the clinic as a resident and then hired him on a full-time basis in 1973. Hughston became something of a father figure to Andrews, whose own father had died at the age of 43.

While at the Hughston clinic, Andrews began to make a name for himself in sports medicine, initially through baseball. Some minor-league baseball pitchers began showing up at the clinic with sore shoulders. "I didn't know what to do with them," Andrews explained to *Newsweek*. "We started watching films of the player and isolating instances of bad mechanics. One thing we determined was that it was bad business for boys to be throwing baseballs and footballs in the same season."

TOMMY JOHN SURGERY FIRST PERFORMED: 1974

Andrews was not the first physician to help repair pitching arms. In 1974 Dr. Frank Jobe performed the first surgery using a forearm or leg tendon to replace a damaged elbow ligament. The first patient was major-league pitcher Tommy John, and ever after the procedure became known as Tommy John surgery. Andrews became the master of the surgery, but an even greater contribution he made to sports medicine was his determination that surgery was not always the proper course. His film studies, later aided with computers, made him a pioneer in biomechanics, as he learned how athletic motions placed stress on various body parts. Should surgery be needed, Andrews laid out a plan for rehabilitation, providing a regimen to strengthen muscles needed in the rehabilitation process even before he cut.

Andrews's reputation was enhanced even further after performing rotator cuff surgery on a rookie pitcher named Roger Clemens in 1985. A year later Clemens became the American League's top pitcher, winning the Cy Young Award as well as Most Valuable Player while leading the Boston Red Sox to the World Series. As a result, Andrews was inundated with referrals from team physicians and sports agents. By this time Andrews was in his mid-40s and at the peak of his career, yet he was uncertain about his place at the Hughston Clinic. Hughston, who was in his late 60s, offered no insight to Andrews about succession plans, and so Andrews began to take seriously the interest hospitals around the country had expressed in setting up a practice for him.

About 150 miles away from Columbus in Birmingham, Alabama, South Highlands Hospital made a bid, and Andrews left Hughston along with orthopedist Dr. Lawrence Lemak to establish a clinic. Andrews's departure caused a rupture in the relationship between Andrews and Hughston. Matters would only grow colder after Auburn University took its orthopedic business to Andrews, ending a relationship of nearly four decades. Andrews made some attempts at reconciliation, inviting his mentor to visit his Alabama clinic, but Hughston would have none of it and they were never fully reconciled before Hughston's death in 2004.

HEALTHSOUTH ACQUIRES SOUTH HIGHLANDS: 1989

In 1989 HealthSouth bought South Highlands and HealthSouth's founder and chief executive, Richard Scrushy, invested an estimated $50 million to build an addition to the hospital to create the Alabama Sports Medicine & Orthopaedic Center, which only served to

KEY DATES

1973: Dr. James Andrews joins Hughston Clinic to practice sports medicine.

1986: Andrews founds Alabama Sports Medicine & Orthopaedic Center.

1989: HealthSouth becomes sponsor of Alabama Sports Medicine.

2003: Scandal at HealthSouth threatens Alabama Sports Medicine.

2004: Andrews agrees to open sports medicine institute in Gulf Breeze, Florida.

2007: Andrews Institute opens.

increase Andrews's profile and sports practice. Health-South also supported Andrews's nonprofit research and education foundation, the American Sports Medicine Institute. Thus, it was in Alabama that Andrews became a true superstar sports surgeon, developing a client list of superstar athletes in a variety of sports, including golfer Jack Nicklaus and even aerobics star Jane Fonda.

All went well for Andrews in Alabama until the early 2000s. Although there was no indication that he was unhappy with his situation with HealthSouth, Baptist Health Care of Pensacola made an overture to him in September 2002 through Chad Guilland, someone who had known Andrews since their days as high school football players. Guilland was also well aware of Andrews's passion for yachting, which Andrews pursued competitively, including a bid in the 2000 America's Cup. Guilland knew that the Gulf Breeze area of Pensacola would be appealing to Andrews, as well as the offer to open a facility in Andrews name that would include a full range of sports medicine services, from injury treatment to rehabilitation. The concept, while tempting, meant little to Andrews, who had made plans with HealthSouth to move to a new $300 million "digital" hospital, boasting wireless networking and bedside touch screens. Those plans would change a year later when unexpected circumstances intervened.

In March 2003 the Securities and Exchange Commission charged HealthSouth and Scrushy with accounting fraud to allow HealthSouth to meet earnings expectations. Scrushy resigned and the price of Health-South stock collapsed. With his patron desperately looking for new sources of capital to stave off bankruptcy, Andrews not only had to wonder about the viability of his move to a new hospital but also the funding and future of Alabama Sports Medicine, which received 27

percent of its annual budget from HealthSouth. Moreover, the hospital in which the Alabama Sports Medicine & Orthopaedic Center was housed was initially slated for liquidation to help HealthSouth pay off some debt. In June 2003 HealthSouth announced that the hospital would be retained, but Andrews's plans for a new facility were far from certain.

DEAL REACHED ON ANDREWS INSTITUTE: 2004

Talks with Baptist Health Care began in earnest, and in November 2004 the parties announced a joint venture that called for the construction of a state-of-the-art sports medicine clinic on six acres of land adjacent to Gulf Breeze Hospital to be headed by Dr. Andrews. The new 70,000-square-foot facility would include an ambulatory surgery center, diagnostic services, physicians' offices, an outpatient rehabilitation and athletic performance-enhancement facility, and a research center that included classrooms and conference space. The research operation would be part of Andrews's Birmingham-based American Sports Medicine Institute and would focus on golf injuries while the Birmingham component continued to mostly focus on baseball injuries. While the new facility was being constructed, Andrews began working with local physicians to start offering services at both the Baptist and Gulf Breeze hospitals.

Ground was broken on The Andrews Institute facility in May 2005, the same month that Andrews's practice left HealthSouth for St. Vincent's Hospital in Birmingham. While construction proceeded in Florida, Andrews endured a personal setback, suffering a heart attack in early 2006. He enjoyed a full recovery, however, and was soon seeing patients again. Andrews continued to work in Birmingham on a weekly basis as he disengaged from his practice there. In February 2007 he and his longtime partner, Larry Lemak, dissolved their sports medicine practice in what was described as an amicable split. Lemak planned to form a practice with his son David, an orthopedic surgeon at Alabama Sports Medicine, conducting business under the name Lemak Sports.

FIRST SURGERY AT NEW FACILITY: 2007

Andrews performed the first surgeries in The Andrews Institute for Orthopaedics & Sports Medicine in early March 2007. Construction on the entire two-building complex was soon completed, and the grand opening was celebrated in late April 2007. The Andrews Institute wasted little time in playing host to conferences and summits. Less than a week after the opening, an Injuries in Football Conference was held for athletic trainers, sports physicians, strength and conditioning coaches, orthopedic surgeons, and others. In mid-May 2007 The Andrews Institute hosted an aquatic therapy summit to discuss the advantages of aquatic therapy in rehabilitation from sports injuries.

More conferences and educational events followed in 2007 and 2008. The Andrews Institute also established a number of key relationships. In 2007 it began accepting Tricare health insurance, and a year later services became available to UnitedHealth Group members. In the fall of 2008 The Andrews Institute opened a 1,400-square-foot satellite rehabilitation center in a new healthcare facility, The Blake, located in Santa Rosa County, Florida. The Andrews Institute also forged a partnership with the University of West Florida, placing four of its doctors on the school's faculty to provide training to students studying athletic training and other healthcare disciplines. The arrangement was expected to be just the first in a number of educational alliances. Dr. Andrews, in the meantime, had reached retirement age. He expressed no interest in curtailing his activities, and remained one of the top surgeons in sports medicine. Unlike his mentor, however, he began taking steps to make sure there was a succession plan in place at The Andrews Institute, which was well positioned to remain a force in the field of sports medicine well after its illustrious founder contributed nothing more than his name.

Ed Dinger

PRINCIPAL SUBSIDIARIES

Andrews Institute Research and Education Institute.

PRINCIPAL COMPETITORS

Kerlin-Jobe Orthopaedic Clinic; Lemak Sports; The Sports Medicine Clinic.

FURTHER READING

Barra, Allen, "Arm and Leg Man," *Newsweek,* October 28, 1996, p. 56.

Brown, Ben, "Athletes in Pain Turn to Andrews," *USA Today,* April 30, 1991, p. 3C.

Burke, Monte, "Collateral Damage," *Forbes,* August 11, 2003, p. 94.

Carmichael, Fredie, "Orthopedic, Sports Medicine Facility Gets Its Official Start," *Pensacola News Journal,* May 11, 2005, p. 12C.

Kram, Mark, "The Jock Doc's Cutting Edge," *Philadelphia Daily News,* October 17, 2007, p. 82.

Nelson, Melissa, "Surgeon to the Stars," *Associated Press Archive,* October 26, 2007.

Proctor, Carlton, "Andrews Institute Not for Celebrities Only," *Pensacola News Journal,* December 22, 2006, p. 15.

Stewart, Michael, "Gulf Breeze Welcomes Pioneering Sports Surgeon," *Pensacola News Journal,* November 20, 2004, p. 1A.

Velasco, Anna, "Orthopedic Surgeons Remain in Limbo over Future Site of Clinic," *Birmingham News,* December 5, 2004, p. 1B.

———, "Sports Clinic Founders Pick Separate Paths," *Birmingham News,* October 3, 2007, p. 1D.

Williams, Chuck, "Top Surgeon Regrets Bitter Ending with Hughston," *Columbus (Ga.) Ledger-Enquirer,* February 2, 2008, p. A1.

Anhui Conch Cement Company Limited

---

209 Beijing E Rd.
Wuhu, 241000
China
Telephone: (+86 0553) 311 8688
Fax: (+86 0553) 311 4550
Web site: http://www.conch.cn

Public Company
Incorporated: 1997
Employees: 10,800
Sales: RMB 18.78 trillion ($2.74 billion) (2007)
Stock Exchanges: Hong Kong
Ticker Symbol: 00914
NAICS: 327310 Cement Manufacturing

■ ■ ■

Anhui Conch Cement Company Limited is the largest and most modern cement producer in the People's Republic of China. The company is also one of the fastest growing in the sector. In just ten years, the company's total production has expanded from three million metric tons to more than 90 million. Further expansion is expected to place the company among the world's largest by 2010. The company operates nearly 20 clinker plants, primarily in eastern and southern China, as well as 21 cement grinding mills. Most of Anhui Conch's cement output is produced using the more energy efficient Dry/Rotary process. The company also focuses on the higher-quality and specialty cement categories. Although Anhui Conch supplies some cement and clinker to the export market, China is the group's primary market. The Anhui province is its most important market, accounting for more than 60 percent of the group's sales. Anhui Conch is listed on both the Hong Kong and Shanghai Stock Exchanges. The company is led by Guo Wensan, chairman and CEO, who joined the company's predecessor in 1982. Anhui Conch's total revenues neared RMB 19 trillion (US$2.75 billion) in 2007.

MODERNIZING CHINA'S CEMENT INDUSTRY IN THE EIGHTIES

China claimed the position as the world's largest cement manufacturer by the middle of the 1980s. By the new millennium, the country's total output had doubled that of its four nearest competitors combined. This achievement was all the more remarkable considering the extremely backward state of the Chinese cement industry just 50 years earlier. Only a limited number of cement plants were in operation at the time of the Cultural Revolution. Among the oldest was the Lunan Cement Works in Tengzhou City, Shandong, founded in 1900. A number of other plants were created in the following decades, including a plant in Dalian in 1909, another in Tangshan in 1910, followed by a plant in Jinan Huanghai in 1920.

Much of the growth of the Chinese cement industry through the 1930s and into World War II was, in fact, attributed to the Japanese occupation of China. The Japanese instituted a vast infrastructure improvement program, particularly in the region around Manchuria.

KEY DATES

1980: Ningguo Cement Plant is established; production begins within two years.

1983: The Baimashan Cement Plant begins production.

1997: The Ningguo and Baimashan plants are merged into a new company, Anhui Conch, which lists its shares on the Hong Kong Stock Exchange.

2002: Anhui Conch adds its listing to the Shanghai Stock Exchange.

2008: Anhui Conch announces plans to build new clinker and cement grinding plants in Sichuan and other China provinces, adding nearly 50 million tons of clinker and cement capacity.

Nonetheless, the country's overall cement production remained exceedingly small in comparison to its size. At the declaration of the People's Republic of China in 1949, the country's total cement production represented just 660,000 metric tons. The need to rebuild and expand the country's existing infrastructure, however, made the growth of the cement industry a national priority.

Through the 1950s and 1960s, the Communist government launched the first expansion wave of the country's cement industry. Large numbers of the country's major cement production facilities were built during this time. These included a future Anhui Conch holding, the Donnguan Cement Plant, established in 1950.

The vast majority of early Chinese cement production was of lower-quality cement, used primarily in the construction of housing and other buildings in the country's rural provinces. Another hallmark of the country's cement industry was its tendency to locate its plants next to its major cities, rather than close to its raw materials supplies. Because of this, transportation costs helped boost the overall cost of cement. Meanwhile, the country's plants were largely of the outmoded wet production process type, which required significantly higher amounts of energy to produce.

By the late 1970s, China claimed the number four spot among the world's largest cement producers. In 1978, the country's total production stood at 65 million metric tons. In that year, however, the Chinese government instituted the first of a series of market reforms

designed to stimulate the country's economic expansion, particularly its lagging industrial infrastructure.

The cement industry's vital role in China's ambitions to become an industrial and economic power meant that the sector became particularly active in the early 1980s. The huge demand for construction materials, as the country transformed its urban and industrial environment, in turn stimulated the growth of the cement industry. The economic reforms had enabled and encouraged a massive increase in cement producers, and by the end of the decade, the country numbered more than 6,000 cement companies. The market was to remain highly fragmented, and many of the country's cement plants survived as small, locally based facilities using outmoded and inefficient production techniques. Nonetheless, by 1985, China had become the world's largest producer of cement.

PREDECESSOR FOUNDED IN 1982

The massive construction effort being undertaken in China's major cities demanded an increasing supply of cement. The development of large-scale construction projects also required higher-quality cements, and specialty cements. This in turn stimulated the growth of a new generation of more modern and efficient cement factories.

In Anhui province, this led to the construction of a cement factory in Ningguo. The Ningguo company was founded in 1980, and production was launched in 1982. Joining the company at this time was Guo Wensan. Guo had graduated from the Building Materials department at Shanghai Tongji University in 1978, and joined the Ningguo project at its outset just two years later. Then aged just 24, Guo became a major figure in the company's growth, becoming a deputy manager, then manager of its manufacturing division, before entering its administration. By the 1990s, Guo had become the general manager of the cement plant.

The Ningguo plant expanded rapidly to become one of the few cement manufacturers in China capable of producing more than one million tons of cement per year. By 1997, the plant had reached a total capacity of more than 1.4 million tons of clinker, with another 1.7 million tons of cement grinding capacity, making it not only one of the country's largest, but also one of its most modern.

By then, China's cement production had doubled the total combined production of the three next largest markets. However, the massive expansion of the country's cement sector had resulted in an oversupply of cement, especially lower-grade cement. The small size, antiquated facilities, and location far from their raw materials sources meant that the great majority of the many thousands of Chinese cement plants operated with little efficiency, and at high cost, both in production and environmental costs. Despite China's leadership in global cement production, none of its cement plants was capable of matching the annual output of the major Western cement companies, which had an average production capacity of 40 million tons.

LEADING THE REFORM OF THE CEMENT INDUSTRY

Recognizing the need to streamline and consolidate the country's cement industry, the Chinese government launched a reform effort in the late 1990s. The government's new policy called for the closure of vast numbers of smaller cement producers, and the consolidation of the industry into a smaller number of large-scale producers.

The Ningguo plant's status as one of the country's largest and most modern placed it in a prominent position to lead the reform of the cement sector. The company began preparations for its own expansion, adding a second cement factory to its operations, in Baimashan. That plant was also a modern facility, built in 1983, with a total capacity of 1.5 million tons of clinker and ground cement. Together, the company's total production now reached 2.2 million tons of clinker, and a grinding capacity of 2.5 million tons.

In 1997, the two plants were merged together to form Anhui Conch Cement Company, which then became the first in the Chinese cement industry to go public, listing its shares on the Hong Kong Exchange. Guo Wensan became the company's chairman and CEO and set into place a new expansion phase.

In 1998, the company completed several acquisitions, starting with a 75 percent stake in Hailuo Cement Product. This purchase was soon followed by a 68 percent stake in Tongling Hailuo Cement and a 99 percent share of Nanjing Hailuo Cement. By the end of the year, Anhui Conch had added stakes in another company, Anhui King Bridge Cement (40 percent). These acquisitions helped raise the company's total clinker production capacity to nearly four million tons.

The company's buying spree continued through 1999, as it boosted its total production capacity past 4.6 million tons. In that year, the group acquired Ningguo Cement, Nantong Cement Plant, and controlling stakes in Zhangjiagang Cement, Changfeng Cement, and Shanghai Hailuo Cement.

Meanwhile, the company also carried out a massive investment program, expanding the facilities of its existing plants as well as its new acquisitions. While boosting its clinker production, the company also carried out an extensive expansion of its grinding capacity. This effort included the creation of a joint venture with TCC Hong Kong Cement, called Anhui Zhujiaqiao Cement Co., which began construction of a 700,000-ton cement grinding mill in Wuhu. The company also acquired a 60 percent stake in Ningbo Hailuo Cement Co., which added another 700,000-ton powder grinding mill, as well as a pier on the Yangtze River capable of handling 1.2 million tons of cement product per year.

WORLD-CLASS IN THE 21ST CENTURY

Anhui Conch continued its drive to enter the ranks of the world's leading cement producers in the new century. While the company's acquisition efforts slowed, its investments in expanding its existing facilities took on greater steam. All of the company's plants benefited from this new expansion effort. As a result, capacity at a number of the group's facilities now passed the one million, and even two million ton marks. By the end of 2002, the company's production now topped 12.6 million tons. In that year, the company added its listing to the Shanghai Stock Exchange as well.

The company's push to add capacity was supported in part by the ongoing reforms being carried out by the Chinese government. Although these reforms, which called for the elimination of as much as half of the country's cement plants, came more slowly than originally projected, Anhui Conch nonetheless enjoyed the benefit of the steadily rising demand for its products. By then, too, the company had established the Anhui Conch brand as one of the best known in the Chinese cement industry, and one of the most valuable Chinese brand names overall.

By 2005, Anhui Conch's total production had passed 25 million tons, making the company not only the largest in China, but also twice the size of its next largest rival. The group's capacity still remained but a small minority, less than 3.5 percent, of the total Chinese market. At home in Anhui province, as well as in the broader East China market, however, the company had become a heavyweight, with a 25 percent market share.

Anhui Conch had set itself an objective of topping the 40-million-ton mark by 2010. This goal, however, quickly appeared too conservative. Indeed, in 2008, the company announced that its total production had reached 134 million tons, with sales of 113 million tons. Part of this enormous jump in capacity came through new acquisitions, including the purchase of local rival Anhui Chaodong Cement Co.

Into the later years of the first decade of the 2000s, more than 60 percent of Anhui Conch's sales came from its Anhui province home base. The company now set its sights on developing a broader geographical balance. In May 2008, the company announced that it had received approvals to expand into western China. The group's plans called for the addition of clinker and cement plants in the provinces of Sichuan, Guizhou, Shaanxi, and Gansu. Completion of the new plants was expected to raise the group's clinker production by nearly 25 million tons, with a jump of more than 20 million tons of cement grinding capacity as well. Anhui Conch had solidified its position among the world's major cement producers in the new century.

M. L. Cohen

PRINCIPAL SUBSIDIARIES

Anhui Changfeng Conch Cement Co., Ltd.; Anhui Chizhou Conch Cement Co., Ltd.; Anhui Conch Cement Product Co., Ltd.; Anhui Conch Machinery & Electric Co., Ltd.; Anhui Digang Conch Cement Co., Ltd.; Anhui Zongyang Conch Cement Co., Ltd.; Bengbu Conch Cement Co., Ltd.; Jianyang Conch Cement Co., Ltd.; Nanjing Conch Cement Co., Ltd.; Nantong Conch Cement Co., Ltd.; Ningbo Conch Cement Co.,; Ningguo Cement Plant 1985; Shanghai Conch Cement Co.,Ltd.; Shanghai Conch Cement Sales Co., Ltd.; Shanghai Mingzhu Conch Cement Co., Ltd.; Taizhou Conch Cement Co., Ltd.; Wenzhou Conch Cement Co., Ltd.; Zhangjiagang Conch Cement Co., Ltd.

PRINCIPAL COMPETITORS

Huzhou Nanxun Shengchuan Cement Company Ltd.; Liaoning Gongyuan Cement Company Ltd.; Liuzhou Yufeng Cement Group Company Ltd.; Huzhou Nanxun Shengchuan Cement Company Ltd.; Liaoning Gongyuan Cement Company Ltd.; Shanxi Antai International Enterprise Company Ltd.; Liuzhou Yufeng Cement Group Company Ltd.; Jiaoling Youkeng Cement Factory.

FURTHER READING

"Anhui Conch Builds Cement Production Lines in Xuzhou," *Alestron*, April 1, 2004.

"Anhui Conch Cement Is Most Competitive Company in China," *AsiaPulse News*, September 30, 2004.

"Anhui Conch Cement to Build Cement Production Base in Wuhu," *Alestron*, August 13, 2004.

"Anhui Conch Likely to Acquire Chaodong Cement," *Alestron*, May 12, 2006.

"China Conch Cement Kept No. 1 Cement Seller in 07," *Alestron*, February 29, 2008.

"China's Cement Industry to Raise Prices," *AsiaPulse News*, May 15, 2008, p. 20.

"Chinese Cement Firm Expands," *International Herald Tribune*, May 20, 2008, p. 20.

"Conch Cement Invests CNY 4.95bn in Expansion in West China," *Alestron*, May 15, 2008.

Spears, Lee, "Anhui Cement Less Than Concrete," *International Herald Tribune*, November 1, 2007.

———, "Big Projects Bolster Cement Firm," *International Herald Tribune*, November 1, 2007, p. 14.

Arena Leisure Plc

408 Strand
London, WC2R 0NE
United Kingdom
Telephone: (+44 020) 7632 2080
Fax: (+44 020) 7240 8032
Web site: http://www.arenaleisureplc.com

Public Company
Incorporated: 1997
Employees: 419
Sales: £57.92 million ($108 million) (2007)
Stock Exchanges: London
Ticker Symbol: ARE
NAICS: 722410 Drinking Places (Alcoholic Beverages);
    711212 Race Tracks

■ ■ ■

Arena Leisure Plc is the United Kingdom's leading operator of racecourses and related facilities. The London-based company operates seven of the country's approximately 50 racecourses, including Royal Windsor, Lingfield Park, Wolverhampton, Southwell, Folkestone, Worcester, and Doncaster. The Lingfield Park, Wolverhampton, and Southwell racecourses feature all-weather tracks, while the Wolverhampton facility is also the first floodlighted racecourse to operate in the United Kingdom. In this way Arena Leisure is able to extend its racing events to a 365-day-per-year schedule, including 35 evening events (known as "fixtures" in the United Kingdom). In addition to hosting races, Arena's racecourses feature restaurant and other catering and amenities, while a number of its parks include banquet and conference facilities, golf courses, and hotels. The company has also entered the bidding for a license to open a casino at its Wolverhampton facility, and hopes to launch casino operations as early as 2009. Arena Leisure has grown strongly since its founding, from just £6 million ($12 million) in revenues in the late 1990s to nearly £58 million ($108 million) in 2007. The company is led by CEO Mark Elliott and is listed on the London Stock Exchange.

FROM HOTELS TO RACECOURSES

Arena Leisure originated as part of the business empire built up by British businessman Trevor Hemmings, a former director at Scottish & Newcastle, through the 1980s and 1990s. Among Hemmings's business successes was his acquisition of the successful holiday camp group Pontins, which he then sold to Scottish & Newcastle for a large profit. The Pontins acquisition had also given Hemmings control of a small hotel on the Isle of Wight, Farringford, which had previously served as the home to the great British poet Alfred, Lord Tennyson. Hemmings himself came to control a major stake in the Farringford site through his own private company, TJH Group.

Hemmings's business interests turned toward the booming U.K. leisure sector during the 1990s. Hemmings sought to enter the British football (soccer) market, then undergoing a surge in activity because of the massive expansion of broadcasting revenues. Among Hemmings's acquisition targets at the time were the

Manchester City Football Club and the Bolton Wanderers.

At the same time, however, Hemmings had set his sights on developing a new company focused on another major British leisure sector, horse racing. Known as the cornerstone of the United Kingdom's highly liberalized gambling industry, horse racing had long played an important part in British leisure and entertainment. While horse racing had been introduced into Britain by the Romans, the first professional races were held in the early 18th century under the reign of Queen Anne. By the start of the following decade, many of the fixtures of the modern racing industry, including the breeding of thoroughbreds, had been established.

Hemmings's first investment in horse racing took place in the early 1990s, when TJH gained majority control of one of the United Kingdom's most prominent racecourses, Lingfield Park. Based on a 600-acre estate in Surrey and located near the borders of Kent and Sussex, Lingfield had been in operation since 1890, with the Prince of Wales and later King of England Edward VII overseeing the opening ceremonies.

Originally focused on horse jumping, Lingfield Park added a flat racing track in 1894.

The years following World War II were difficult ones at the Lingfield course, where flooding diminished its prestige in the racing world. The course came under control of betting group Ladbrokes during this period. Ladbrokes sold the site in 1982, and its new owners installed a flood-control system. By 1987 Lingfield Park also boasted its own 18-hole golf course. Into the 1990s, Lingfield Park also upgraded its racing track, installing one of the first all-weather tracks in the United Kingdom. In this way, the company was able to expand the number of events held at its course each year.

TAKEOVER LEADS TO ARENA LEISURE

TJH had acquired control of Lingfield Park in 1991. In that year, Farringford had been taken public, through the reverse takeover of a struggling soft-drinks company, Alpine Group. The completion of that deal gave Farringford a listing on the London Stock Exchange. By 1997, however, Hemmings's expanding interest in the leisure sector led to a new buyout with publicly listed Farringford acquiring Lingfield Park. This deal too proved to be a reverse takeover, as the Lingfield Park business emerged as the core operation of the company. With the completion of the takeover, the company changed its name to Arena Leisure Plc, maintaining its listing on the London Stock Exchange.

Arena, with sales of just £6 million into the late 1990s, now established a new goal for itself, to become the leading racecourse operator in the United Kingdom. Soon after completing the reverse takeover, the company announced its plans to spend some £30 million ($60 million) in building up what it expected to become a £500 million ($1 billion) company into the early 2000s.

While this goal ultimately proved too ambitious (into the last half of the first decade of the 2000s, the group's turnover remained at less than £60 million), Arena completed its first acquisition soon after. In 1998 the company agreed to pay £3.25 million to acquire the Folkestone racecourse in Kent. That site, opened in 1898, added 20 new racing days to Arena's schedule.

NEW MEDIA

Arena reached a new milestone in 1999 when it signed an agreement with RAM Racing to acquire its two racecourses, at Wolverhampton and Southwell. The Wolverhampton site, opened in 1887, was a particularly important addition in that it not only gave the company another all-weather track, but also the first U.K.

KEY DATES

1991: Trevor Hemmings' TJH Group acquires major stake in racecourse operator Lingfield Park (1991) Ltd. and hotel operator Farringford.

1997: Farringford acquires Lingfield Park through a reverse takeover, becoming the publicly listed Arena Leisure Plc.

1998: Arena acquires its second racecourse at Folkestone in Kent.

1999: Arena adds the Wolverhampton, Southwell, and Royal Windsor racecourses.

2001: Arena joins the At the Races television horse-racing joint venture.

2004: Arena acquires the lease to the Doncaster racecourse.

2007: The British government clears Arena's plans to construct a casino at its Wolverhampton site.

racecourse to feature floodlighting. Southwell too boasted an all-weather track, giving Arena control of the only three all-weather tracks operating in the United Kingdom at the time.

Soon after the RAM Racing acquisition, Arena scored new success. In August of that year, the company acquired the lease to operate the Worcester Racecourse, one of the United Kingdom's oldest, with racing dating back to 1718. While the city of Worcester remained the racecourse's owner, Arena gained a 99-year lease for its operations. The company then announced plans to invest some £10 million in the site, which included building a hotel and adding a new grandstand.

These acquisitions, which helped double Arena's share of the U.K. horse-racing market, encouraged the group to focus itself as a pure-play racecourse operator. In November 1999, therefore, the company sold the Farringford Hotel. Soon after, Arena completed another acquisition, paying £14 million to acquire the Royal Windsor racecourse. Founded in 1866 and located near Windsor Castle, the Royal Windsor track had also grown into one of the most famous racecourses in the world. As part of its financing of the Windsor purchase, Arena completed a secondary offering. In the course of that offering, TJH reduced its stake in Arena, which then became an independent company.

Arena's interests now turned to exploiting the new media opportunities available at the dawn of the 21st

century. The company recognized the growing importance of the online gambling market and in 2000 entered negotiations with Autotote Corporation to develop a cross-platform, global betting system. By 2001 the company had taken that operation fully in-house, forming Arena Online Services Ltd.

At the same time, Arena recognized the significant opportunities offered by the booming satellite television market. In 2001 the company formed a joint venture with satellite broadcast operator British Sky Broadcasting, also known as BskyB, and Channel 4 Television. The partnership agreed to create a new interactive television channel devoted to horse racing, called Go Racing. That company, subsequently renamed as At the Races, launched negotiations to acquire broadcast rights to all 49 of the United Kingdom's racecourses. To pay its share of that deal, worth £178 million, Arena completed a new equity offering for £85 million.

At the Races started off with a bang, leading to Arena Leisure AGM, a telebet service, in 2002. By the end of that year, the company had launched interactive betting service on the Sky Television platform, as well as on Channel 4 and on the NTL cable television service. The company also began broadcasting U.S. horse racing on Sky that year.

At the Races hit a snag when the Office of Fair Trade (OFT) declared that its deal with the British racecourses, which included all of the country's racecourses, gave Arena de facto monopoly on the market. As a result, the OFT declared the contract void and ordered At the Races to negotiate a new contract with the country's racecourse operators. Although At the Races was quickly relaunched, the suspension of its operations cost Arena some £49 million ($100 million).

LEADING RACECOURSE OPERATOR IN THE 21ST CENTURY

Although its troubles with At the Races proved a setback, Arena pushed forward with the development of its portfolio of racecourses. The company maintained a strong investment strategy, refurbishing and upgrading its existing facilities. The company also developed more ambitious plans, including the construction of hotels on several of its sites.

In 2003 Arena announced plans to team up with Gala to build a casino on its Wolverhampton site. In this way, Arena proposed to become the first "racino" operator in the United Kingdom's racing industry. The company's initial plans, which called for the casino to be operational as early as 2004, met with little success, as the government refused to give its permission. Nonetheless, Arena continued to develop its plans, and by 2006 had resubmitted the proposal, as well as a bid for one of 16 new casino licenses to be awarded by 2009.

Arena added a new racecourse to its portfolio in 2004 when it gained the lease to operate the Doncaster racecourse. Arena then announced plans to spend some £20 million upgrading the Doncaster operations, adding new facilities including a four-star hotel and conference center. By then, the company had committed some £20 million to the expansion of its Windsor operations, as well as carrying out an upgrade of the Lingfield Park racecourse.

Arena's racino hopes received a leg up in 2007 when the government passed the company's development plans for the Wolverhampton racecourse without objection. The company hoped to receive its license following the Parliament's review of the legislation governing the expansion of the country's casino sector in 2009. The addition of gambling, as well as the continued success of its media operations, gave Arena the hope that it might still achieve its original objective of breaking the £500 million mark in the new century.

M. L. Cohen

PRINCIPAL SUBSIDIARIES

Arena Leisure Catering Ltd.; Arena Leisure Racing Ltd.; Doncaster Racecourse Management Co. Ltd.; Folkestone Race Course Ltd.; Lingfield Park (1991) Ltd.; Southwell Racecourse Ltd.; Windsor Concessions Ltd.; Windsor Racecourse Co. Ltd.; Windsor Racing Ltd.; Wolverhampton Racecourse Ltd.; Worcester Racecourse Ltd.

PRINCIPAL COMPETITORS

Racecourse Holdings Trust Ltd.; Northern Racing PLC; Rabbah Bloodstock Ltd.; Gaming International Ltd.

FURTHER READING

"Arena Has Levy Support," *Investors Chronicle,* August 4, 2008.

"Arena Leisure Faces Hurdles," *Investors Chronicle,* March 7, 2008.

"Arena on Track As Increased Visitor Numbers Cover Development Costs," *Leisure Report,* June 2006, p. 7.

"Arena Wins Permission for Doncaster Racecourse Build," *Leisure Report,* April 2007, p. 12.

Blitz, Roger, "Arena Plans to Bid for Casino License," *Financial Times,* March 7, 2008, p. 25.

"First UK 'Racino' Awaits Approval in Wolverhampton," *International Gaming & Wagering Business,* November 2007, p. 10.

John, Peter, "Arena Reins in Its Losses After Channel Revamp," *Financial Times,* September 2, 2004, p. 22.

"Profits up As Arena Looks to Drive Growth," *Leisure Report,* October 2006, p. 6.

"Racing Is Riding High—And It's Not Only About the Ponies Anymore," *International Gaming & Wagering Business,* November 2007, p. 11.

Rivlin, Richard, "Hemmings Sets Sights on Bolton," *Daily Telegraph,* August 2, 1998.

Watkins, Mary, "Arena Leisure Settles into Its Stride," *Financial Times,* June 15, 2004, p. 26.

Baxters Food Group Ltd.

Northern Preserve Works
Fochabers, IV32 7LD
United Kingdom
Telephone: (+44 01343) 820393
Fax: (+44 01343) 820286
Web site: http://www.baxters.com

Private Company
Incorporated: 1868
Employees: 1,035
Sales: £100 million ($205.3 million) (2007 est.)
NAICS: 311421 Fruit and Vegetable Canning; 311412
     Frozen Specialty Food Manufacturing

■ ■ ■

Baxters Food Group Ltd. is one of the best-known and most respected of the United Kingdom's food companies. The company produces a wide range of premium soups, preserves, jams, pickles and peppers, condiments, and dressings, among other products. The company also produces frozen foods and other foods for the foodservice sector. Company brand names include the flagship Baxters line, Gamer's, Simply Delicious, PizzaExpress, Peppadew, and Mary Berry. Much of the produce used in the company's production comes from the surrounding region, including the company's own farms. Founded as a grocery store in Fochabers, Morayshire, in Scotland in the late 19th century, Baxters remains a family-run company, led by the founder's great-granddaughter, Audrey Baxter. Under her leadership, Baxters has launched expansion on an international level, exporting the group's products to other countries in Europe and to the North American market. In support of this effort, the company has added a number of foreign subsidiaries, including in Poland, the Netherlands, and Canada. Baxters remains headquartered in Fochabers and employs more than 1,000 people. In 2007 the company's sales topped £100 million ($205 million).

GROCERY STORE BEGINNINGS IN 1868

George Baxter originally worked as a gardener, one of 50, for the Duke of Richmond and Gordon. In 1868, however, he left that employ to open up his own grocery shop in nearby Fochabers, in the somewhat remote Moray region of Scotland. Encouraged by family members, Baxter borrowed £100 from his uncle to launch his business. Baxter was joined in the shop by his wife Margaret, who played an important role in Baxters' development as a food processing company.

The barter system remained an important part of the local economy at the time. This meant that the Baxters often took in locally grown fruits and vegetables in trade for goods sold in the store. The Moray region's coastal location made it a particularly fertile area of Scotland, noted not only for the quality of its product, but also for its beef. The region also boasted an abundance of game and seafood.

The steady supply of produce and meats led Margaret Baxter to set up a kitchen in the back of the shop. There, she began developing a range of jams, jellies, and other canned preserves for sale in the shop and

COMPANY PERSPECTIVES

∎

Since George Baxter opened his village grocery shop in 1868 his philosophy of Be Different, Be Better has prevailed upon all the activities of the Baxters Food Group. From humble beginnings of making jams and jellies in the back shop, today, we are one of the UK's premium food manufacturers, responsible for producing many of the country's finest products.

Those early principles, on which our business was founded, still drive our business success today. One of the biggest constants we have is the care and attention that goes into the making of our products and as a consequence our customers' delight in eating them.

elsewhere. Her recipes quickly proved popular with the local market. Before long, the shop had begun to supply its preserves to Gordon Castle, where they were introduced to the duke's guests from throughout Scotland and England. In this way, the Baxter name became known far beyond Fochabers.

The Baxter family's production remained on an artisanal level into the 20th century. Shortly before World War I, George and Margaret Baxter turned over the store to their son, William, who married the year the war began, 1914. His wife, Ethel, promptly took over Margaret's role in the shop's kitchen. The young couple decided to take the shop's preserves business to the next level. Soon after taking over the store, the Baxters purchased a parcel of land from the Duke of Gordon and set up the family's first dedicated factory.

NEW PRODUCTS DEVELOPED, INCLUDING SOUP

Ethel Baxter oversaw the company's food production, developing a wider range of preserves. She also began experimenting with new recipes and food products, especially the soups that were to establish the Baxters brand name throughout the United Kingdom. One of the most successful of Baxter's recipes was her Royal Game Soup, introduced in 1929, drawing both on the company's association with the Duke of Gordon and the Scottish traditional kitchen. By then, too, the company had pioneered the canning of beetroot (beets), which became a long-lived and popular product for the company. Other products developed by the company included Cock-a-Leekie Soup, Whole Roast Pheasant in

Burgundy Wine Jelly, Cream of Pheasant, and Game Consommé.

Ethel Baxter not only displayed a talent for developing tasty recipes, but also maintained the family's insistence on high-quality, premium products. Before long, William Baxter had traded in the family's shopkeeper role for that of traveling salesman. Over the next decades, Baxter traveled extensively throughout the United Kingdom, promoting his wife's products. In this way, Baxters had become a well-known brand in the United Kingdom through the 1920s and 1930s. Aiding the company's growth were orders from a number of the country's most prominent department stores, including London's Harrods and Fortram & Mason.

AMERICAN INSPIRATION AFTER WORLD WAR II

The Baxter family's business was nearly destroyed during World War II. With food supplies suddenly scarce, the company's production and sales dropped dramatically. Baxters limped along for the duration, supplying limited amounts of jams to the British Navy, Army, and Air Force Institutes. By the end of the war, the group's capital base had dropped down to just £4,000, and its number of employees to just 11. The company's sales had also dwindled, and into 1946 amounted to only £800 per week.

William and Ethel Baxter turned over the company to their son Gordon. Gordon Baxter became not only the company's managing director, but also helped lead the company's new product development, in addition to playing a major role in the group's postwar sales and marketing effort.

In 1952 Gordon Baxter met and married Ena Robertson, an artist and art teacher who had studied at the Gray's School of Art in Aberdeen. Like Margaret and Ethel Baxter before her, Ena Baxter played an important part behind the company's new rise to success. Ena Baxter took over the company's kitchen, becoming the creative force behind the company's product development. As Gordon Baxter told Julie Bain of *Scotland on Sunday:* "I'd still say the best thing I did in my life was marrying Ena. Without her, Baxters wouldn't be what it is today. She is a friend and a business partner."

Gordon Baxter's younger brother Ian also entered the family business. With his wife Margaret, Ian Baxter led the company into a new direction, farming, with the purchase of Scotsburn Farm in Lhanbryde. The farm grew into a major source of fresh produce for Baxters' expanding production. In addition to helping run the farm, Margaret Baxter also became an important part of Baxters' sales team.

KEY DATES

■

1868: George Baxter opens a grocery store in Fochabers, Scotland, where his wife Margaret begins canning jams and other preserves.
1914: Son William Baxter takes over as head of the company and, joined by wife Ethel, opens a factory and expands its operations into soups.
1946: Gordon Baxter takes over as managing director.
1970: Baxters Food Group becomes the first in the United Kingdom to package preserves in screw-top glass jars.
1992: Audrey Baxter becomes the company's managing director.
2003: Baxters acquires pickles and condiments producer CCL Foods.
2004: Baxters acquires first international operation, SoupExperts in Quebec, Canada.
2007: Baxters acquires CanGro Soup in Canada and establishes production base in Poland.

In the 1950s Gordon and Ena Baxter took the first of what was to become many trips to the United States. By 1959 the company had begun to export to North America, its sales backed by the efforts of both Baxters. Ena Baxter became particularly well known to Americans after appearing in the first of a number of televised cooking demonstrations. The couple functioned as unofficial Scottish ambassadors to the United States. At the same time, they came into contact with many of the United States' innovative retailing and marketing methods that were soon to transform food retailing in the United Kingdom and the rest of the world.

The Baxters correctly recognized that the U.S. supermarket, as yet unknown in the United Kingdom, represented the future of food retailing. Through the 1960s and 1970s, the company adapted its packaging, product development, and marketing efforts to the new retailing format as it became introduced in the United Kingdom. The company became one of the first in the United Kingdom to conduct consumer testing to develop a better understanding of its customers' preferences and expectations. This led the company, and Ena Baxter in particular, to adjust recipes in order to more closely match the taste of home-cooked food.

The opportunities provided by the larger supermarket shelves also encouraged the company to expand its product line. The company created its own lines of sauces and chutneys and developed new fruit-based jams, as well as added new beetroot varieties. The expanding product line also received new packaging. In 1970 the company became the first in the United Kingdom to begin packing its products in screw-top glass jars. During that decade the company also developed a new mini-jar format for its jams and jellies, after a suggestion from an executive with the Hilton Hotel group. The smaller, 1.5-ounce jar quickly became favored by hotel chains, including Hilton, and also found its way into the airline industry.

FOURTH GENERATION IN 1992

Baxters became especially known for its soups, and by the 1980s the company captured the lead in the U.K. premium soup category. The 1980s were also marked by a still-broader expansion of the group's product lines. During that decade, the company added ranges of luxury foods, such as Roasted Partridge in Sherry Wine Jelly, as well as exotic food dishes, such as Scampi Indienne and Scampi Thermidor. The group also became one of the first to recognize the coming demand for ready-made meals, for working families with less time to prepare foods at home, adding a line of microwavable dishes. Also during the period the group continued to build up its strong export operations, notably to the United States, Canada, Australia, and South Africa.

Baxters' success and strong brand name had long made it an attractive acquisition target for other food companies. Over the decades, the company claimed to have rejected more than 150 buyout offers. However, Baxters steadfastly clung to its family-owned format. Indeed, in the late 1980s, the company began preparing its transition to the next generation of the family.

Ian and Margaret Baxter retired from farming in the late 1980s, turning that operation over to Michael Baxter, then 25. Another Baxter, Andrew, joined the company in the late 1980s to head a new division producing frozen fish. Meanwhile, Gordon and Ena's daughter Audrey, then just 26, joined the company in 1988.

Audrey Baxter had initially been reluctant to join the family business, instead pursuing a career in London as a merchant banker. However by 1992, she had emerged as the family's candidate to lead the business, becoming managing director that year. While Gordon Baxter remained active in the group's day-to-day operations through the 1990s, Audrey Baxter led the group in a new phase of expansion into the next century. In 2000 Audrey Baxter became the company's president, finally taking over its chairman position in 2004.

INTERNATIONAL GROWTH IN
THE 21ST CENTURY

Into the late 1990s, Baxters announced its interest in pursuing a number of acquisitions to expand both its manufacturing operations and its range of brands and foods. In 2001, for example, the company acquired fellow Scottish company Ortega 2K Ltd., based in Clydebank. Ortega, which specialized in the production of pickles and sauces, had gone into receivership; Baxters' acquisition involved the purchase of the company's recipes, as well as its brand family, including Well Pickled, Well Preserved, and Well Soused. In 2003 Baxters expanded its brand range again, acquiring the contract to produce chilled ready meals for the Weight Watchers' brand.

The company also ventured into the retail arena in the early 2000s, opening the first of several stores in 2003. For this, the company targeted locations at Scottish tourist destinations, starting with the Ocean Terminal shopping center in Edinburgh. The success of that store, which also featured their own restaurants serving Baxters food products, encouraged the company to develop a new flagship store in Blackford, Perthshire, in 2006.

In the meantime, Baxters had completed a number of acquisitions. In 2003 the company acquired CCL Foods, a producer of condiments and pickles. That purchase also brought Baxters a range of new brand names, including PizzaExpress dressings, Simply Delicious, Peppadew, and Mary Berry.

With its export sales, including to the European continent, growing steadily, Baxters made a move to add an international production component as well. In 2004 the group entered Canada, buying Quebec-based SoupExperts. In 2007 the group added a production base in Poland as well, while announcing plans to add more production facilities in other markets, including Australia.

These moves came as part of the group's announced target of reaching £300 million ($600 million) in turnover in the new century. At the end of 2007, Baxters took another step closer to that goal, when it returned to Canada to acquire CanGro Soup and its Primo and Aylmer brands. The following year, Baxters opened its fifth retail store and restaurant in Selkirk,

Scotland. Family-owned Baxters appeared to have found the right recipe for growth into the 21st century.

M. L. Cohen

PRINCIPAL SUBSIDIARIES

SoupExperts Inc. (Canada).

PRINCIPAL COMPETITORS

Diageo PLC; Kraft Foods UK Ltd.; H.J. Heinz Company Ltd.; Edrington Group Ltd.; Premier Grocery Products Ltd.; Autobar Group Ltd.; Golden West Foods Ltd.

FURTHER READING

Bain, Julie, "Fine Food in the Family Way," *Scotland on Sunday*, July 30, 2000, p. B5.

"Baxters' Boss Cuts It with the Locals," *Selkirk Weekend Advertiser*, June 12, 2008.

"Baxters Bucks Market to Savour 14 Per Cent Rise in Sales," *Evening News*, January 25, 2008, p. 31.

"Baxters in European Push," *just-food.com*, October 15, 2007.

"Baxters Ready to Pounce Again Overseas," *just-food.com*, April 3, 2008.

"Baxters Set to Expand Operations Worldwide," *Aberdeen Press & Journal*, January 24, 2007.

"Baxters Soups Up Its Borders Presence," *Southern Reporter*, November 1, 2007.

"Baxters Takes Over Canadian Firm to Dish the Soup to US," *Aberdeen Press & Journal*, September 21, 2004.

"Canadian Deal Has Baxters Hungry for More Acquisitions," *Herald* (Glasgow), May 3, 2007, p. 30.

Clayton, Nick, "Baxters Looks to Grow Through Acquisitions," *Sunday Times*, November 13, 1994, p. 27.

"Death of Woman Who Was Driving Force with Baxters," *Aberdeen Press & Journal*, August 13, 2005.

Morais, Richard C., "Cock-a-Leekie," *Forbes*, September 7, 1987, p. 68.

"Mystery over Exit of Soutar from Baxters," *Scotsman*, September 5, 2006, p. 32.

Rogerson, Paul, "Baxters Expands Horizons with First-Ever Acquisition Overseas," *Herald* (Glasgow), September 21, 2004, p. 20.

————, "Master Chef Serves Up More Fine Fare at Baxters," *Herald* (Glasgow), March 15, 2005, p. 20.

————, "Success Tasting Sweeter at Baxters," *Herald* (Glasgow), January 27, 2006, p. 27.

Rutherford, Hamish, "Mass Exodus from Board Suggests Unrest at Baxters," *Scotsman*, January 19, 2007, p. 36.

Bci

———————————————— ■ ————————————————

Av. El Golf 125
Casilla 136-D
Los Condes, Santiago
Chile
Telephone: (56 2) 692-7000
Fax: (56 2) 698-8003
Web site: http://www.bci.cl

Public Company
Founded: 1937 as Banco de Crédito e Inversiones
Employees: 9,541
Total Assets: CLP 10.68 trillion ($20.19 billion) (2007)
Stock Exchanges: Bolsa de Comercio de Santiago
Ticker Symbol: CREDITO
NAICS: 522110 Commercial Banking; 522210 Credit
Card Issuing; 523120 Securities Brokerage; 524210
Insurance Agencies and Brokerages; 525910 Open-
End Investment Funds; 525990 Other Financial
Vehicles

■ ■ ■

Bci, formerly Banco de Crédito e Inversiones, is the
third largest non-governmental bank in Chile and the
largest one that is entirely Chilean-owned. Three generations of the Yarur family have presided over a team of
experienced managers since 1946, offering a model of
stability in hectic times that have included a revolution,
a counter revolution, and a financial crisis that shook
the nation's banking sector to its foundations. The
many mergers and acquisitions that have transformed
the nation's banking sector, and put many of the banks

in the hands of foreign investors, have left Bci
unscathed. Whether the "Lone Ranger" of Chilean
banking can survive in its present form remains an open
question.

THE FIRST FORTY YEARS: 1937–77

Juan Yarur Lolas, a Palestinian Arab, arrived in Chile in
1913 at the age of 18. After staying with his sister, he
and his younger brother moved to Bolivia, where a
cousin of theirs was living. They first became peddlers
and then opened a fabrics and clothing store. Yarur
became a textile manufacturer in Bolivia before returning to Chile in 1929 and opening a similar business.
This enterprise became the nation's largest cotton textile
plant and the first modern one in Chile.

Yarur was among a number of owners (some of
them also immigrants) of small and medium sized businesses who found it difficult to secure loans from
established banks, which were tied to established
economic groups. Banco de Crédito e Inversiones was
founded in 1937 by a group of Italian immigrants to
provide credit for small businesses. Yarur used his firm's
profits during World War II to acquire control of the
bank and become its president in 1946.

At first the bank did little except finance the
acquisition of machinery for the textile business. After
Yarur's death in 1954, he was succeeded by one of his
three sons, Jorge Yarur Banna. According to Jorge
Yarur's nephew and successor, the bank was on the
point of being liquidated by the shareholders at this
time. Under the new president, however, it soon opened
its first branch, in Valparaíso. Other branches were

COMPANY PERSPECTIVES

Our Mission: Bci defines itself as a Corporation of Financial Solutions that participates in all the business and financial operations that the General Banking Law allows, offering to the community products and services with quality processes of high efficiency, with a permanent technological innovation, prudent policies of risk administration and demanding ethical standards, which must be respected by all the people that play a role in our enterprises.

opened in Antofagasta, Iquique, and Curicó in the late 1950s.

According to Peter Winn's detailed and copiously footnoted account of the Yarur textile empire, Jorge Yarur converted Banco de Crédito e Inversiones "into a Yarur milch cow. ... The Banco de Crédito not only advanced the Yarurs and their companies large sums but also invested its funds directly in these ventures, purchasing large blocs of shares, which the depositors and shareholders of the bank financed but the Yarurs controlled. Jorge Yarur used every legal means—and some that were dubious—to maximize the bank's assets and channel them into the coffers of the Yarur textile companies, several of which were in need of continual capital infusions during the 1960s. In some years, more than three-quarters of Banco de Crédito's loans went to family members and enterprises, often at less than the normal bank rate and with no pressure for repayment."

By the mid-1960s Banco de Crédito y Inversiones was a much bigger, much more important institution. Jorge, and his brothers Amador and Carlos, held significant stock in the bank, and the three also owned Empresas Juan Yarur, which also had a stake in the bank. The biggest block of stock was owned by Yarur Manufacturas Chilenas de Algodón, which was controlled by the Yarur family and, perhaps, also by the U.S. firm W.R. Grace and Company. These shareholders, plus members of the influential and wealthy Larraín, Vial, and Prieto families, collectively owned more than half of the bank's shares.

The three Yarur Banna brothers formed a group that controlled 65 percent of Banco de Crédito e Inversiones in 1970. The group also held a two-thirds stake in another bank and all or most of two textile companies, an industrial chemicals firm, and two insurance companies. However, Salvador Allende was elected president of Chile that year, and he instituted a wide-ranging nationalization program that included the expropriation of the major companies in the textile industry. When Yarur opposed selling the bank to the state, it came under government control anyway.

Allende was ousted in 1973 by a military coup led by General Augusto Pinochet. Banco de Crédito e Inversiones was returned to its owners two years later. An agreement with the Bank of America provided it with technical support, including the help of assessors. By 1978 the Yarur Banna group had raised its share of the bank's stock to 78 percent. In all, the group had interests in about a dozen Chilean companies in 1978 with total assets bordering on $100 million.

GAINING ON ITS COMPETITORS: 1977–2000

In the late 1970s Chile's banks lent huge amounts to affiliated companies that were unable to continue making payments on the loans after a deep recession gripped the nation. The financial crisis became so severe that in 1983 five banks, including Banco de Chile, the largest, were placed under government control. Banco de Crédito e Inversiones was not among them, but, like others, took advantage of a provision allowing it to sell its bad debt portfolio to Banco Central de Chile and buy it back gradually.

During this period Banco de Crédito e Inversiones began offering more services to its clients, including securities trading through its own brokerage, founded in 1987, and mutual funds by means of another subsidiary. It established a "personal banking" department and had 89 branches by 1988. These included, in the far north, Iquique, where the economy benefited from a duty-free zone and profits from drugs filtering in from neighboring Peru and Bolivia, and, in the far south, an Antarctic branch where the sole staffer slept after closing hours when the weather was too bad to venture outside.

While addressing bank directors and managers, Yarur Banna was fatally stricken by a heart attack in 1991. Ironically, he died on the day he had made the last payment on the company's debt to the central bank. Yarur had earmarked all of Banco Crédito e Inversiones' profits to repayment of the debt, completing the task nine years ahead of schedule. He was succeeded as bank president by a nephew, Luis Enrique Yarur Rey. Under his leadership, Bci thrived, so much so that it was named the best bank in Chile in both 1998 and 1999 by the magazine *LatinFinance*.

By this time Banco de Crédito e Inversiones had became a full financial services institution. It established a financial assessment business in 1993 whose services

KEY DATES

1937: Banco de Crédito e Inversiones is founded.

1946: Juan Yarur Lolas becomes president of the bank.

1954: Juan Yarur's son Jorge Yarur Banna succeeds him on his death.

1960: Several branches have been opened as Banco de Crédito e Inversiones grows in stature.

1975: Following a few years of nationalization, the bank is returned to its owners.

1987: Banco de Crédito opens its own brokerage house; an insurance brokerage opens in 1998.

1988: The number of bank branches has reached 89.

1991: On Jorge Yarur's death, his nephew Luis Enrique Yarur Rey becomes bank president.

1999: Bci, for the second year in a row, is named best bank in Chile by *LatinFinance;* the bank opens its first foreign subsidiary, in Miami; the unit later becomes a branch office.

2001: Banco de Crédito e Inversiones is now Chile's third largest bank.

2002: Bci again is named best bank in Chile by the business magazine *LatinFinance.*

2006: A subsidiary is founded to manage various classes of funds, including the bank's 31 mutual funds.

2008: The number of Bci branches has reached 273.

included placement of company shares, bonds, and debentures and investment of funds in certain instruments in the national and world capital markets. The following year the bank founded a factoring subsidiary whose object was to purchase debt instruments from businesses needing short-term liquidity. An insurance brokerage was established in 1998.

Although it ranked only fifth in assets and deposits in 1998, Banco Crédito e Inversiones was well regarded by both bankers and analysts for its profitability, efficiency, fundamentals, and management. It had the highest return on equity of any Chilean bank that year and had a portfolio of loans praised for its quality. The bank accounted for more than half of all electronic payments made in Chile, testimony to the more than $70 million it had spent over the past five years on Internet and telephone banking systems. Bci's market share had increased 50 percent during that period.

Much of the gain came from the bank's emphasis on personal relations. Banco de Crédito e Inversiones' share of new checking accounts opened had reached 25 percent of the total, and the number of its branches had reached 107. In 1999 Bci opened its first foreign subsidiary, in Miami. Originally an agency, it became a branch office in 2001, which allowed it to take deposits from U.S. subsidiaries of foreign, mostly Chilean, companies as well as deposits from abroad.

STILL FAMILY CONTROLLED AND THRIVING IN THE EARLY 21ST CENTURY

Banco de Crédito e Inversiones was again voted Chile's bank of the year by *LatinFinance* in 2002. It had become the third largest Chilean bank the previous year, when its largest competitors grew by acquisition, leaving some of the customers of the swallowed banks dissatisfied and willing to look elsewhere. In spite of its growing share of new depositors, its proportion of past due loans to total loans had actually fallen. Yarur said Bci was able to lower prices to its clients because of its high proportion, 20 percent, of site deposits to total deposits.

Banco de Crédito continued to establish new subsidiaries in the early years of the 21st century. Founded in 2001, one of these was engaged in acquiring commercial loans by means of bonds issued and placed in the market. Another was founded in 2006 to manage various classes of funds, including the bank's own 31 mutual funds, investment funds, foreign capital investment funds, and housing funds.

By 2006 Banco de Crédito e Inversiones had shortened its name to Bci and had raised its market share to one-eighth of the total, mostly by its efforts alone, although in 2004 it purchased a much smaller institution, Banco Conosur (renamed Banco Nova), for $103 million. The number of its branches had grown to 221 and the number of current accounts to 299,125.

Bank assets deposited overseas had reached 7.5 percent of the total. Bci had, besides its Miami branch, offices in Lima, São Paulo, and Hong Kong. In addition it had an agreement with Banco Popular de España, which was active throughout Europe. Another office was being planned for Beijing. Bank officials were hoping that a greater part of its assets would be deposited abroad so that the enterprise would be less dependent on the fluctuations of the Chilean economy.

In 2008 Bci announced its intention to invest about $150 million during the year, of which two-thirds would be directed to adding 55 branches to the existing 273. The rest was earmarked for information systems intended to augment efficiency of operations and save about $45 million. The bank was also reported to be planning a unit for private banking, aimed at people of high net worth. Bci also indicated that it would soon introduce an investment bank, with the emphasis on engaging in mergers and acquisitions.

The private banking unit and the investment bank would have to compete for business with a number of Chilean institutions, including the two bigger Chilean banks and Canadian and Brazilian banks as well as the huge Wall Street investment houses and the British-based giant HSBC. Therefore, Bci was expected to act initially in alliance with an international affiliate. The executive of another bank speculated that the private banking model was aimed at people with salaries of $20,000 a month or more or assets of over $1 million. A business consultant estimated that there were 120,000 such persons in Chile.

In addition, Bci was engaged in a project called Bci 2010, a new system of information support that would allow its clients greater access to investment opportunities. Additionally, the plan called for centralizing the bank's operational units in the interests of cutting costs. This project was said to have been adopted at the recommendation of the McKinsey Corporation.

At the end of 2007 Empresas Juan Yarur S.A.C., the family holding company, held over 53 percent of Bci's shares. Two of Luis Yarur's nine children were bank employees, and some of his nephews were working in other enterprises of the group. Ignacio Yarur Arraste, Luis's 31-year-old eldest son, had been named assistant manager of finance. The quality and stability of Bci's management were considered above average. The bank was said to pay its employers better than other financial firms in Chile, and as a result turnover was lower than at other such firms.

Whether Bci could compete in the increasingly globalized banking market of the 21st century under its longstanding ownership structure was an open question. Interviewed for *AméricaEconomía,* Bci's director general, Lionel Olavarría, told Francisca Vega, "One imagines that in the future Bci will have a strong expansion plan and a much greater need for capital. [But today] the only possibility that I see are financial investors participating in limited form." Other sources said that Citibank had offered to buy Bci from the Yarur family before merging with Banco de Chile, but that the deal had not advanced because of a lack of agreement on price.

Robert Halasz

PRINCIPAL SUBSIDIARIES

Análisis y Servicios S.A.; Bci Administradora de Fondos Mutuos S.A.; Bci Administradora General de Fondos S.A.; Bci Asesoría Financiera S.A.; Bci Corredor de Bolsa S.A.; Bci Corredores de Seguros S.A.; Bci Factoring S.A.; Bci Securitizadora S.A.; Servicios de Normalización y Cobranza–Normaliza S.A.

PRINCIPAL DIVISIONS

Commercial and Branch Management; Comptroller's Division; Corporate Management, Planning and Financial Control; Corporate Personnel Performance Management; Corporate Risk Management; Finance and International Management; Innovation and Corporate Programs Management; Marketing Management; Retail Banking Management; Support Area Management.

FURTHER READING

Empresas en la historia, Santiago: Publicaciones Editorial Gestión, 1997, pp. 9–23.

Fidler, Stephen, and Leslie Crawford, "Chile Tries to Resolve Its Banking Problems," *Financial Times,* November 14, 1991, p. 32.

Freer, Jim, "Chilean Bank Gets OK to Take Resident Alien Deposits," *South Florida Business Journal,* November 9, 2001, p. 9.

Mark, Imogen, "Chilean Banks Recover and Diversify," *Euromoney,* March 1988, pp. 127–28, 131.

Moraga, Javiera, "Un Yarur que se las trae," *Capital,* June 30–July 13, 2006, pp. 40–41.

"Nimble and Feisty BCI," *LatinFinance,* November 2002, p. 33.

Vega, Francisca, "Llanero solitario," *AméricaEconomía,* May 5, 2008, pp. 39–40.

Wing, Lisa K., "Best Bank in Chile: Banco de Credito e Inversiones," *LatinFinance,* October 1999, p. 34.

Winn, Peter, *Weavers of Revolution,* New York: Oxford University Press, 1986, ch. 1, pp. 13–31.

Zegers V., and M. Angelica, "Banquero de sangre," *Capital,* August 25–September 7, 2006, pp. 30–32, 34.

Zeitlin, Maurice, and Richard Earl Ratcliff, *Landlords and Capitalists,* Princeton, N.J.: Princeton University Press, pp. 142–43.

Bechtel Corporation

---

50 Beale Street
San Francisco, California 94105-1895
U.S.A.
Telephone: (415) 768-1234
Fax: (415) 768-9038
Web site: http://www.bechtel.com

Private Company
Incorporated: 1925 as W. A. Bechtel Company
Employees: 42,500
Sales: $27 billion (2007 est.)
NAICS: 236210 Industrial Building Construction;
236116 New Multi-Family Housing Construction
(Except Operative Builders); 541330 Engineering
Services

■ ■ ■

Bechtel Corporation is one of the leading construction and engineering firms in the world, building everything from roads and bridges, to dams and pipelines, to power plants, and even entire cities. Through 40 offices located in more than 20 countries, Bechtel serves government and commercial customers, taking on some of the most daunting, high-profile construction projects in the world. As a private and predominantly family-controlled company, Bechtel has long been averse to publicity, an attitude that has sometimes been problematic in light of the firm's numerous links to prominent U.S. government officials.

EARLY HISTORY

In 1884 when he was 12 years old, Warren A. Bechtel moved with his family from a farm in Illinois to the frontier area of Peabody, Kansas. After graduating from high school, Bechtel ventured unsuccessfully into a music career. When "The Ladies Band" failed, Bechtel's father wired return fare to the stranded slide trombonist. The disappointed musician went back to work on the family farm. Some years later, poor farming conditions left Bechtel virtually without any possessions other than a team of 14 healthy mules. When the Chicago Rock Island and Peoria Railway Company pushed westward in 1889, Bechtel gathered up his mule team and worked his way across the continent grading railbed for frontier train lines.

Bechtel eventually sold his mule team, but he continued working for the rail industry in a variety of manual-labor positions. He managed to accumulate a small fortune and formed the W. A. Bechtel Company in 1898 with his three sons and his brother. The young company began many new ventures, including construction of the Northern California Highway and the Bowman Dam, which was at the time the second largest rock-fill dam in the world. By the time the company was incorporated in 1925, Bechtel was the largest construction firm in the western United States. When a six-company consortium received the $49 million contract for construction of the Hoover Dam, Warren Bechtel became president of the group. Work on the enormous dam lasted from 1931 to 1936. Warren Bechtel did not live to see the project completed, however; he died suddenly in 1933 at age 61.

Stephen Bechtel, one of the founder's three sons, took over the presidency in 1935. He had previously been a vice-president. The young executive directed the company to new financial and industrial heights, supervising completion of the Hoover Dam as well as work on the San Francisco–Oakland Bay Bridge, a hydrogeneration plant, and the Mene Grande Pipeline in Venezuela.

SHIPS AND TANKERS DURING WORLD WAR II

As the United States entered World War II, an already established partnership between Bechtel and John McCone, a steel salesman, grew to encompass a syndicate of companies participating in the construction of large shipyards. McCone and Stephen Bechtel had met at the University of California and had become business associates during work on the Hoover Dam. As an employee of Consolidated Steel, McCone secured the supply of necessary support structures for Bechtel. The business association proved so successful that after the dam was finished the former classmates formed a partnership. By 1940 McCone secured contracts for the partnership to build ships and tankers, and to modify aircraft for the war effort. Later the partnership developed the syndicate that built the Calship and Marinship yards in California, as well as a total of 500 ships. When McCone took a postwar position as undersecretary of defense, it was revealed that the directors of Calship earned 440 times their initial investment of $100,000, a profit of $44 million.

PIPELINE AND NUCLEAR POWER PLANTS HIGHLIGHT POSTWAR YEARS

Bechtel's operations continued to expand in the years following the war. The 1,100-mile Trans-Arabian

Pipeline, completed in 1947, is regarded as the first major structure of its kind. The South Korean Power Project effectively doubled that nation's energy output. In 1951 the pioneering company developed the first electricity-generating nuclear power plant, in Arco, Idaho. Later the company built a nuclear fuel reprocessing plant there. By the end of the 1950s Bechtel had construction and engineering projects on six continents and was ready to take advantage of the emerging market for nuclear power.

In 1960 Stephen Bechtel became chairman of the board, and Stephen, Jr., a Stanford Business School graduate and grandson of the founder, stepped into the CEO post. A 1978 estimate suggested that the two men controlled at least 40 percent of company stock. In the likely event of the younger Stephen one day inheriting his father's wealth, it was estimated that he could become the richest person in the United States. The other 60 percent of Bechtel stock was held by some 60 top executives who agreed to sell back their shares when they left the company or died.

With a new generation of leadership in place, the company sought to gain hegemony in the emerging nuclear power industry. In 1960 Bechtel completed the nation's first commercial nuclear station in Dresden, Illinois. Two years later the company built Canada's first nuclear power plant. Construction in foreign markets began to increase almost immediately thereafter. Although the nuclear power industry subsequently ran into difficulties such as cost overruns, questions about environmental safety, and stiff regulatory measures, Bechtel continued to promote nuclear energy as a necessary option to conventionally generated power.

Bechtel's construction projects in the 1960s and 1970s included the San Francisco Bay Area Rapid Transit system (BART), the subway transit system in-and-around Washington, D.C., a slurry pipe in Brazil, and an innovative tar sands project in Alberta, Canada.

In the 1970s two former Nixon cabinet members took executive posts at the company. Later both men, George Shultz and Caspar Weinberger, would leave Bechtel for positions in the Reagan administration. Bechtel has actively cultivated its ties to the federal government, and employs several former high officials, which has led to criticism of the company.

PLAN TO BUILD JUBAIL INDUSTRIAL CITY UNVEILED IN 1976

In 1976 Bechtel unveiled plans for its Jubail Project, the largest undertaking ever attempted by a construction company. The company spent more than 20 years build-

KEY DATES

1898: W. A. Bechtel Company is formed.

1925: The company ranks as the largest construction firm in the western United States by the time it is incorporated.

1936: Bechtel completes work on the Hoover Dam.

1947: Bechtel completes work on the 1,100-mile Trans-Arabian Pipeline.

1951: Bechtel develops the first electricity-generating nuclear power plant.

1960: The third generation of the Bechtel family, led by Stephen Bechtel, takes control of the company.

1976: Bechtel begins the more than $40 billion Jubail Project.

1995: Bechtel becomes the first U.S. company to be awarded a construction license by the Chinese government.

2003: Bechtel is chosen as the lead contractor in the reconstruction of Iraq.

2007: Revenues reach $27 billion, nearly triple the total generated five years earlier.

ing a futuristic industrial community on the site of an ancient fishing village on Saudi Arabia's Persian Gulf coast, at an estimated cost of more than $40 billion. The new city became the home of Saudi Arabia's integrated petrochemical industry. A 1973 meeting between Stephen Bechtel, Jr., and King Faisal was the catalyst for the project, which hauled off about 370 million cubic meters of sand and built a modern city complete with a five-million-gallon desalination plant, a national airport, a hospital and clinics, modular homes, mosques, a sex-segregated swimming marina, and a number of factories.

CONTROVERSY DURING SEVENTIES AND EIGHTIES

Due in part to a broad-based political effort to halt the use of nuclear power in the United States, in the 1970s and early 1980s Bechtel turned away from nuclear energy to less controversial markets. Nevertheless, problems in the nuclear power industry persisted. A 1978 lawsuit concerning malfunctions at the Palisades nuclear generator in Michigan cost Bechtel $14 million in settlement fees. In addition, a 1984 *Mother Jones* magazine article suggested that the company's use of irregular payments in attempting to secure nuclear power

contracts in South Korea may have violated the 1977 Foreign Corrupt Practices Act. The article also argued that certain Bechtel executives, who later became top U.S. government officials, may have known the payments warranted investigations by the Federal Bureau of Investigation and the U.S. Justice Department but said nothing. The company issued a point-by-point rebuttal of the article to its employees.

The company was the subject of negative publicity several times during the 1970s. A 1972 class-action suit alleging sex discrimination at Bechtel was settled out of court for $1.4 million. A bribery scheme involving construction of a New Jersey pipeline led to convictions for four Bechtel employees. Further unwanted publicity arose from the revelation that Bechtel had installed a 420-ton nuclear-reactor vessel backwards. Finally, in 1975 the Justice Department sued Bechtel for allegedly participating in an Arab boycott of Israel, a charge the company denied.

The decade was also a turning point for Bechtel's traditional business in construction and engineering. Prompted by increased government regulation and changing economic conditions, Bechtel embarked on a new program of financing and operational services. Soon after they began, the new divisions contributed 66 percent of total revenues. To defray increasing construction costs, Bechtel began securing financing for its customers, in some cases even putting up the company's own money. Bechtel's diversification program also included acquiring a 15 percent share of the Peabody Coal Company and a major interest in the prestigious Dillon, Read & Company investment firm. By 1982 over half of the company's business involved overseas markets.

During the Reagan presidency Bechtel's ties to the federal government increased considerably. Shultz left the presidency of Bechtel Corporation to become secretary of state after Alexander Haig, former chairman of United Technologies, left the post in 1982. Weinberger, previously the Bechtel general counsel, was secretary of defense for the first seven years of the Reagan administration. By 1984 Bechtel's connections in Washington also included Central Intelligence Agency (CIA) director William Casey, Middle East special envoy Philip Habib, and former CIA director Richard Helms, all of whom had worked for the company either as employees or as consultants in the past.

LACK OF BIG PROJECTS IN THE MID-EIGHTIES

By the mid-1980s, Stephen Bechtel, Jr., was chairman of the board. Alden P. Yates, who was Bechtel's president, led the firm into numerous projects previously regarded as too small for Bechtel. These included finishing jobs abandoned by the company's competitors and actively seeking contracts, even those as small as $2 million. Furthermore, remodification and modernization efforts at existing plants offset the lack of contracts for new construction. Finally, the company's operating services division kept skilled experts at work in their fields, mostly in ongoing maintenance of existing facilities.

Despite measures to locate new sources of income, Bechtel had to cut its workforce in 1984 to 35,000 (from 45,000 in 1982). The smaller projects that the company had been forced to take on were no replacement for the megaprojects of the past. The dearth of large projects stemmed from multiple developments. The U.S. nuclear power industry was virtually at a standstill in terms of new plants. In the Middle East, a traditional Bechtel area of strength, big construction projects were no longer the norm, thanks largely to significantly lower oil prices; in fact, the company suffered a severe blow when Saudi Arabia suddenly halted construction on a $1 billion refinery being built by Bechtel in Qasim. Bechtel and other U.S. engineering companies also faced increasing competition from European, South Korean, and Japanese construction firms. U.S. companies saw their share of the world's large construction projects fall from 50 percent in 1980 to 25 percent in 1988.

RESTRUCTURING IN THE 1980S

Bechtel's revenue fell from $14.13 billion in 1983 to $6.55 billion in 1986. New orders, meanwhile, dropped from $13.05 billion to $3.54 billion over the same period. One of the company's responses to this crisis was to reorganize into a more decentralized structure. In July 1986, its two main operating companies, Bechtel Power Corp. and Bechtel Inc., were restructured into five new units: Bechtel Western Power Corp., Bechtel Eastern Power Corp., Bechtel Civil Inc. (civil engineering projects), Bechtel Inc. (petroleum and mineral activities), and Bechtel National Inc. (advanced technical and research areas). At the same time, a separate Bechtel Inc. subsidiary was created, called Bechtel Ltd., which took over the company's British-based activities. These included one of the company's major projects of the later 1980s, the construction of the Channel Tunnel connecting England and France that began in 1986.

By early 1988 continuing difficulties forced the company to further slash its workforce to less than 18,000. That year Bechtel was once again the subject of negative news coverage after it was revealed that in 1984 and 1985 the company had been involved in an abortive effort to build a $1 billion pipeline from oil fields in

northern Iraq through Jordan to the Red Sea. Although the pipeline project had been scuttled when the Iraqi government began construction on an alternative pipeline, the special prosecutor investigating Attorney General Edwin Meese looked into an allegation that individuals acting on Bechtel's behalf tried to bribe Israeli officials into promising not to bomb the pipeline. Although no charges were ever filed against Bechtel in the case, this was another instance of unwelcome publicity for the company.

In 1989 Riley P. Bechtel, son of Stephen Bechtel, Jr., became president of Bechtel Group. That year also saw work begin on a major project in downtown Boston, the Boston Central Artery/Tunnel, which was the largest urban highway redevelopment effort in U.S. history. The project was a joint venture between Bechtel and Parsons Brinckerhoff.

REBOUND IN THE 1990S

Bechtel rebounded strongly during the 1990s under the direction of Riley Bechtel, who became chairman and CEO following Stephen Bechtel's retirement in 1991. After the Gulf War, Bechtel led the effort to restore the oil fields of Kuwait, putting out 650 oil-well fires and rebuilding the country's upstream oil and gas installations. Work on airports was significant in the 1990s as the company provided project management services for a $20 billion airport in Hong Kong and worked on the King Fahd International Airport in Saudi Arabia. From 1990 to 1993 Bechtel expanded a natural gas pipeline in the western United States owned by Pacific Gas Transmission Company. The end of the Cold War brought work to Bechtel in the form of the demilitarization of weapons for Russia. In 1993 the company began providing management, engineering, and support services for the $2.8 billion Athens Metro subway system.

Bechtel was also boosted in the 1990s by emerging markets in Asia, particularly China. In 1995 Bechtel became the first U.S. company to be granted a construction license by the Chinese government. The company had been active in the country since 1978 through a joint venture with the government-controlled China International Trust & Investment Corp. Among the venture's achievements was the building of a manufacturing complex for Motorola in Tianjin, China, which was due to open in 1999. Also in the mid-1990s, Bechtel helped to raise the funds for, and began supervision of, construction on a 430-kilometer toll road in China, the Greater Beijing Regional Expressway. In May 1998 the government of Ukraine selected a Bechtel-led consortium to stabilize a concrete shelter covering the damaged Unit 4 reactor of the Chernobyl nuclear power plant. Other consortium partners for the $760 million project were Electricité de France and the Battelle Memorial Institute.

From 1993 to 1996, annual revenues for Bechtel were no lower than $7.34 billion and no higher than $8.5 billion. After this steady performance, 1997 was perhaps a breakthrough year with revenues surging to $11.33 billion. New orders remained very strong as well, with $12.25 billion booked in 1997, following figures of $11.32 billion in 1996 and $12.47 billion in 1995.

Bechtel enjoyed a promising start to its second century of business, recording substantial financial growth in the wake of centennial celebrations in 1998. By 2000, revenues had increased to $15 billion thanks to projects such as the $600 million Trans-Thailand-Malaysia gas pipeline and a $300 million contract to build 30 Vehicle Certification Centers for iMotors.com. Further increases were expected after the company booked $23.3 billion of new contracts during the year, but the succeeding years saw Bechtel's annual volume decline. The company generated $13.4 billion in revenue in 2001 and $11.6 billion in 2002, slipping into a worrisome pattern of flagging sales. Help was the way, however, as the company soon reaped the rewards of its comprehensive capabilities and its close ties to influential figures in Washington, D.C.

BECHTEL BACK IN IRAQ

Several weeks before the United States invaded Iraq in March 2003, the U.S. Agency for International Development (AID) began planning for the repair of the infrastructure likely to be damaged during the bombing campaign in Iraq. AID solicited bids from a select group of the largest construction and engineering firms for the reconstruction of roads, airports, hospitals, power plants, and waste treatment systems. In April 2003, Bechtel emerged as the winning bidder, beating rivals such as Fluor Corporation, The Louis Berger Group, Inc., and Washington Group International. The contract, valued at $680 million over 18 months, but expected to be worth far more (some estimates at the time pegged the reconstruction cost at $100 billion), injected Bechtel with financial vitality, ushering in a period of staggering financial growth.

While Bechtel forces went to work on the herculean task of rebuilding Iraq, the company enjoyed bustling business across the globe. In 2006 Bechtel was named the primary contractor for the construction of as many as nine power-generating facilities for Texas-based TXU Corp. Also in 2006, the Federal Emergency Management Agency (FEMA) selected Bechtel to install more than 35,000 temporary housing units for Mississippi residents whose homes were destroyed by Hurricane Katrina. In 2007 the company was selected to spearhead the $1.8 billion expansion of Rio Tinto Aluminum's alumina refinery in Australia. The year also saw the company complete its first project, construction of an aluminum smelter, in Iceland. The massive projects coupled with the company's involvement in the reconstruction of Iraq sparked fantastic financial growth. Between 2002 and 2007, revenues skyrocketed from $11.6 billion to $27 billion.

As Bechtel prepared for the future, it could look ahead with confidence. The company ranked as the largest contractor in the country, possessing an impressive array of skills that ensured it would be sought after to complete the largest, most complex projects around the world. The enormous growth achieved during the first decade of the 21st century would be hard to match in the coming years, but Bechtel executives were confident their company would continue to shine.

Updated, David E. Salamie; Jeffrey L. Covell

PRINCIPAL SUBSIDIARIES

Bechtel Civil, Inc.; Bechtel Enterprises, Inc.; Bechtel Financing Services, Inc.; Bechtel National, Inc.; Bechtel Petroleum, Chemical & Industrial Co.; Bechtel Power Corporation; Bechtel Savannah River; Bechtel Construction Company, Inc.; The Fremont Group; Coldwell Banker Corporation.

PRINCIPAL DIVISIONS

Civil Infrastructure; Communications; Mining & Metals; Oil, Gas & Chemicals; Power; U.S. Government Services.

PRINCIPAL COMPETITORS

Fluor Corporation; AMEC Plc; Skanska AB.

FURTHER READING

"Bechtel Group Inc. Will Reorganize into Five Concerns," *Wall Street Journal*, May 28, 1996, p. 26.

The Bechtel Story: Seventy Years of Accomplishment in Engineering and Construction, San Francisco: Bechtel Group, Inc., 1968.

Building a Century: Bechtel, 1898–1998, San Francisco: Bechtel Group, Inc., 1997.

Crow, Robert Thomas, "The Business Economist at Work: The Bechtel Group," *Business Economics*, January 1994, p. 46.

Dwyer, Paula, et al., "Bechtel's Iraqi Pipe Dream Could Land It in Hot Water," *Business Week*, February 22, 1988, pp. 33–34.

Kahn, Joseph, "Bechtel Tests Waters for Big Jobs in China: Financing Arrangements for Projects May Be Model," *Wall Street Journal,* May 1, 1995, p. A10.

Labaton, Stephen, "Bechtel Faces Lack of Big Projects," *New York Times,* February 24, 1988, pp. D1, D4.

McCartney, Laton, *Friends in High Places: The Bechtel Story: The Most Secret Corporation and How It Engineered the World,* New York: Simon and Schuster, 1988.

Pitta, Julie, "Building a New World: Behind the Scenes with Bechtel," *World Trade,* August 2003, p. 16.

Shao, Maria, "A Bonanza for Bechtel? Well …," *Business Week,* May 6, 1991, p. 36.

Wherry, Rob, "Contacts for Contracts," *Forbes.* June 23, 2003, p. 62.

Zachary, G. Pascal, and Susan C. Faludi, "New Blueprint: Bechtel, Hurt by Slide in Heavy Construction, Re-Engineers Itself," *Wall Street Journal,* May 28, 1991, pp. A1, A16.

Beggars Group Ltd.

———◆———

17-19 Alma Road
London, SW18 1AA
United Kingdom
Telephone: (+44 208) 870 9912
Fax: (+44 208) 871 1766
Web site: http://www.beggars.com

Private Company
Incorporated: 1974 as Beggars Banquet Records
Employees: 90
Sales: £50 million (2008 est.)
NAICS: 512210 Record Production

■ ■ ■

Beggars Group Ltd. is one of England's leading independent record companies. The firm owns the 4AD label and half-stakes in XL Recordings, Rough Trade, and U.S.-based Matador. It also controls several smaller labels including Mantra, Wiiija, and Mo'Wax, and has a stake in music download service Playlouder. Over the years the company's imprints have achieved success with such artists as Gary Numan, The Smiths, The Prodigy, Throwing Muses, Radiohead, The Pixies, The Raconteurs, and The White Stripes. A sizable portion of Beggars Group revenues derive from sales of back catalog releases, but it also continues to seek new artists. The firm attributes its longevity to a focus on quality music rather than blockbuster hits. Beggars Group is owned by cofounder and Chairman Martin Mills.

BEGINNINGS

Beggars Group traces its roots to a record shop in London's Earls Court district that grew out of a disc jockey business cofounded by Oxford philosophy/politics/economics graduate Martin Mills. His firm, Giant Elf, became known as Beggars Banquet after merging with a competitor, and in 1974 Mills partnered with Nick Austin to found a retail store. It would offer both used discs and new releases, an unusual mix for the time.

The store was a success, and over the next several years the partners expanded to a half-dozen locations and began promoting concerts for major acts such as The Commodores and The Crusaders. At this time a new underground musical movement was starting to emerge that featured an aggressive, sometimes nihilistic attitude and a raw sound, exemplified by bands including The Sex Pistols and The Damned. Audiences rapidly embraced the music, and when ticket sales for mainstream artists plummeted the firm's concert unit changed its focus to booking the new "punk rock" bands.

The basement of one Beggars Banquet store soon became a rehearsal space for such groups, and its manager began to represent a band that practiced there called The Lurkers. When Mills and Austin took over this role they began seeking a record deal for the group, but found the major labels to be disinterested and decided to release a 45-rpm single on the Beggars Banquet imprint. At this time independent record companies were few and far between, but the firm worked out a distribution deal with Island and the

Lurkers single began to appear in shops around the country. With the enthusiastic support of influential disc jockey John Peel, it sold well and the newly established label began to seek other artists.

The first Beggars Banquet singles and albums sold well to consumers hungry for the new music, but early competitors such as Stiff and Chiswick were soon joined by a host of others and the market became saturated. The firm began to use cash flow from its record stores to support the discs, and the situation worsened when its distribution deal with Island fell through.

With things beginning to look bleak, the company was rescued by an act called Tubeway Army that had put out several poor-selling releases, which was fronted by one Gary Webb. The group was starting to prominently feature synthesizers rather than guitars, and with its lead singer (now calling himself Gary Numan) sporting an odd, robotic persona during television appearances, a single called "Are 'Friends' Electric?" zoomed up the British charts to the number one position in 1979 and stayed there for four weeks. An album was soon licensed to Warner Brothers for a £100,000 advance, which helped Beggars Banquet pay off debts and increase the activities of its record production unit.

4AD FOUNDED IN 1980

During the year store managers Ivo Watts-Russell and Peter Kent came to Mills and Austin with suggestions for bands to sign, and the partners suggested they found an offshoot label that the company would underwrite with a £2,000 investment. The first four single releases appeared in January 1980 on the Axis label, but when an existing firm of the same name complained, the label was changed to 4AD based on a phrase found on a concert flyer.

One 4AD group, Bauhaus, caught on with the public and was moved to the Beggars Banquet label

proper, but it would be the only such defection. Later signings with The Birthday Party, The Cocteau Twins, and Dead Can Dance would give 4AD a distinct "gothic" rock identity, and Beggars Banquet also signed its own roster of acts in this popular, if gloomy, musical genre.

In 1982 Nick Austin left the firm to focus on a New Age music label called Coda, which left Martin Mills as sole owner. A year later Peter Kent split from 4AD to found another new label called Situation 2, which was distributed by Pinnacle and Rough Trade and helped the firm reconnect with the vital independent-label charts via such popular acts as The Cult and The Associates. The latter group would subsequently shift to Warner Brothers in a deal that made Beggars Banquet again independent of major label distribution.

In 1987 the company formed a joint publishing venture with Andrew Heath called Momentum, signed a distribution deal with RCA in the United States, and created another new label called Citybeat with dance music record store owner Tim Palmer. The year also saw 4AD release the first independently distributed number one dance hit with a song called "Pump Up the Volume" by M.A.R.R.S.

XL RECORDINGS CREATED IN 1989

In 1989 Citybeat launched a new sub-label of its own called XL Recordings, which over time came to supplant its parent entirely. During this period the concept of an umbrella organization that would run the business functions of the labels, the Beggars Banquet Group, began to take shape. Several additional foreign offices were also established.

In 1990 4AD signed a commercially oriented band called The Charlatans, whose *Some Friendly* album soon reached number one. 4AD was also having success in the United States with such college radio/alternative rock bands as The Pixies and Throwing Muses. Two years later the label signed a deal with Warner Brothers to handle all of its U.S. distribution, having previously cut one-off deals for each release.

In 1991 major U.K. indie distributor and record label Rough Trade went bankrupt, leaving many small labels in financial peril. Beggars Banquet Group helped form a company called RTM to handle sales and distribution for such operators, and it also worked within the industry to redefine the independent record music charts. In 1993 the company signed a two-tier distribution agreement with Atlantic Records in the United States, with its smaller acts distributed by the Alternative Distribution Alliance (ADA).

In 1995 Beggars Banquet Group formed a new subsidiary in the United States and opened an office in New York, which was headed by U.K. press officer Lesley Bleakley. The firm's distribution deal with Atlantic was soon ended there and all distribution turned over to the ADA, with larger releases occasionally licensed to the majors. During the year the stake in XL owned by Tim Palmer was sold to Richard Russell, and a 4AD office was opened in Los Angeles, where Ivo Watts-Russell had moved. As he turned his attention to other projects like a series of books, Robin Hurley was named to run the label. In 1999 Hurley left and the L.A. office was closed, after which 4AD headquarters were moved back to London.

In 1997 XL artists The Prodigy had a number one album in 26 countries including the United States with *The Fat of the Land.* By that time Beggars Banquet Group had started or become affiliated with several other small labels including Mantra Recordings, Too Pure, Nation, Mo'Wax, and Wiiija.

In the late 1990s it became apparent that digital music recordings could easily be delivered over the Internet, and the firm began working on a strategy to take advantage of this opportunity. In 2000 Beggars Banquet Group partnered with U.K.-based Playlouder.com and

Avdeck to offer music online, and similar agreements were later reached with MP3.com and Apple's iTunes store. Popular acts at this time included Super Furry Animals, Badly Drawn Boy, and Cornershop, and the firm's music was finding strong sales in such markets as Australia and the Netherlands.

HALF OF MATADOR ACQUIRED IN 2002

In August 2002 Beggars Group (as the firm was now known) bought a 50 percent stake in New York-based Matador Records, a 13-year-old independent label that was home to a number of popular acts including Liz Phair, Yo La Tengo, and Pavement. Its New York offices would move into the larger Matador space nearby, with Matador founder Chris Lombardi and partner Gerard Coslov continuing to run that firm's operations. Both Matador and the Beggars Group labels were distributed by ADA, with smaller retailers serviced through Matador's own direct distribution unit. Beggars Group would represent Matador worldwide, although the latter firm would retain a U.K. office. Matador had been partly owned by Capitol Records for several years in the late 1990s, but had bought the stake back.

In 2003 Beggars Group signed online distribution deals with EMusic, Listen.com (owner of the Rhapsody service), and Musicmatch. Popular groups now included Basement Jaxx and Michigan rock duo The White Stripes, who had a number one album with *Elephant.* The firm's labels were also busy repackaging their back catalogs in new configurations that added previously unreleased or rare material. Sales for 2003 were a reported £35 million, up more than a third over the preceding year.

While CD sales were continuing to rise (in contrast with a decline for the major labels), the firm was seeing its biggest growth from music downloads and the licensing of material to outside projects including film soundtracks. In 2005 a deal was signed with Groove Mobile to offer downloads of songs to users' cellphones, and the firm was also working on deals to license its material to video jukebox operators and for use in cellphone ringtones. Sales fell to £15.6 million from £28.5 million the year before, although a profit of £2.2 million was recorded, the group's largest since 1997.

In 2006 Beggars Group launched a Japanese unit in association with Warner Music International. The firm had a total of nine international offices, with distribution in each territory handled via regional operators. Company Chairman Martin Mills was now also serving as chairman of Impala, a European trade association for independent record labels, and as vice-chair of the Association of Independent Music, which he had helped establish in 1999.

In early 2007 Beggars Group merged its public relations department for retail and online sales into a single unit, and doubled the number of web developers it employed to four. In the summer its U.S. arm released the third album of XL rapper Dizzee Rascal as a download only, which irritated retailers. The firm contended that Rascal was a relatively small name in the United States and the cost of producing and shipping CDs was not warranted by his sales there.

STAKE IN ROUGH TRADE PURCHASED IN JULY 2007

In July the firm bought 49 percent of Rough Trade Records from Sanctuary Records, which had owned it since 2001. Rough Trade's history dated to the late 1970s and its catalog included The Smiths and Babyshambles. The deal was worth £800,000, with Rough Trade's retail chain remaining under separate ownership. Founder Geoff Travis and his partner Jeannette Lee, who had relaunched the label in 2000, retained controlling interest.

In the fall of 2007 Beggars Group and other large independent labels signed a licensing deal with Slacker, Inc., a new Internet and wireless radio firm. The company also reshuffled some of its operations, bringing in Simon Halliday to run the Beggars Banquet, 4AD, and Too Pure labels and creating a separate XL public relations unit. At year's end cofounder Martin Mills was honored by the Queen of England and made a Member of the Order of the British Empire. He would join a long list of distinguished recipients that included The Beatles.

In early 2008 Beggars Group joined with several partners including Warner Music Entertainment to create the Lovelive Channel in the United Kingdom, which would broadcast advertiser-supported music performances. Some 300 concerts per year were expected to be filmed for the channel. The firm was also working with music download site AmieStreet, which offered music priced at whatever buyers were willing to pay, and ad-supported free download site Qtrax. Beggars Group now had three offices in London and seven worldwide.

In the spring the company announced it was shuttering the Too Pure and Beggars Banquet labels and shifting their artists to 4AD. The firm was now having hits with The Raconteurs (led by White Stripes frontman Jack White), Adele, Cat Power, Sigur Ros, Vampire Weekend, Radiohead, and Beck, several of which had left major labels. Half of the firm's sales came from the

back catalog, with such groups as The Pixies, The Prodigy, The Smiths, and others continuing to sell well year after year. The year 2008 was on track to be the firm's best ever, with sales expected to hit £50 million.

More than three decades after the first Beggars Banquet single was released, Beggars Group, Ltd., had become a major force in the music industry, both in England and abroad. It boasted a number of top artists and a strong-selling back catalog, and it continued to seek new acts for a portfolio of labels that included 4AD, XL, Matador, and Rough Trade. The company was growing in the face of an industry sales decline by seeking out new digital sales opportunities.

Frank Uhle

PRINCIPAL SUBSIDIARIES

Beggars USA; Beggars Canada; Beggars Germany; Beggars Italy; Beggars Japan; 4AD; XL Recordings (50%); Matador (50%); Rough Trade (49%); Playlouder (75%).

PRINCIPAL COMPETITORS

EMI Group plc; Sony Music Entertainment Inc.; Universal Music Group; Warner Music Group Corp.; The Gut Group; All Around the World; Warp Records; Ninja Tune Records; Wall of Sound Records; Sub Pop Ltd.; Touch & Go Records.

FURTHER READING

"Beggars: Blurring the Boundaries Between Marketing and Promotion," *Music Week,* February 10, 2007, p. 14.

"Beggars Can't Be Losers in Rough Trade Swoop," *Music Week,* August 4, 2007, p. 1.

Brandle, Lars, "The *Billboard* Q&A: Martin Mills & Geoff Travis," *Billboard,* January 12, 2008.

Cardew, Ben, "Beggars' Belief," *Music Week,* September 15, 2007, p. 10.

Cohen, Jonathan, and Chris Morris, "Beggars Purchases Half-Stake in Matador," *BPI Entertainment News Wire,* August 13, 2002.

Gettler, Leon, "Can't Stop the Music," *Age,* March 27, 2004, p. 5.

"Groove Mobile Signs Agreement with Beggars Group," *DMEurope,* August 17, 2005.

Harding, Cortney, "Beggars Group Shuffles Imprints," *Billboard.biz,* April 28, 2008.

Koranteng, Juliana, "Warners, Beggars Team on Gig Stream Service," *Billboard.biz,* February 11, 2008.

Martens, Todd, "Digital Dizzeeness; Beggars Anticipates Backlash for Rascal Decision," *Billboard,* June 9, 2007.

Paoletta, Michael, "Beggars Group Offers an Eclectic Feast of Dance Music," *Billboard,* April 14, 2001, p. 37.

"Plugging & PR: Beggars' Simple Strategy Earns Its Stripes," *Music Week,* July 30, 2005, p. 15.

"Profile: Simon Wheeler: Freedom of Expression," *New Media Age,* February 23, 2006, p. 17.

White, Dominic, "'Beggar' Who Does Just As He Chooses," *Daily Telegraph,* June 14, 2008, p. 37.

Williams, Paul, "Beggars Strikes Gold As UK Indie Group Makes Inroads in US Market," *Music Week,* August 23, 2008, p. 4.

Bolt Technology Corporation

4 Duke Place
Norwalk, Connecticut 06854-4632
U.S.A.
Telephone: (203) 853-0700
Fax: (203) 854-9601
Web site: http://www.bolt-technology.com

Public Company
Incorporated: 1962
Employees: 113
Sales: $61.6 million (2008)
Stock Exchanges: American
Ticker Symbol: BTJ
NAICS: 333132 Oil and Gas Field Machinery and
Equipment Manufacturing

■ ■ ■

Listed on the American Stock Exchange, Bolt Technology Corporation is a Norwalk, Connecticut-based oilfield services company specializing in geophysical equipment. The flagship product is the marine air gun, the foundation on which the company was built. Air guns are arranged in arrays and fired every eight seconds to send shockwaves to complete seismic exploration studies, mostly underwater as a way to locate oil and gas deposits but also conducted on land. The shockwaves are reflected by underlying rock layers, detected by instruments, and the signals converted into digital form for use with computer programs to create a representation of the subsurface. Geoscientists can then isolate likely pockets of oil and gas for exploratory drilling.

Because the air guns have to fire in unison, they must be well maintained, resulting in Bolt generating a large portion of its revenues from parts and repairs. The company also manufactures and sells marine air gun controllers and synchronizers, and other equipment associated with air gun use, including underwater cables, connectors, and hydrophones.

MARINE SEISMIC STUDIES: POST–WORLD WAR II ORIGINS

Marine seismic surveys, used to map underwater terrain in the search for oil and gas deposits, were first conducted in the 1950s. Initially, explosives such as dynamite were used to generate the sound waves needed in the process. The concussive effect of the charges, however, killed fish and harmed other marine life. The air gun was developed as an alternate signal source to eliminate the environmental damage caused by seismic studies. The man who invented the device was Stephen Chelminski, one of the cofounders of Bolt Technology.

Chelminski was born in New Jersey but was still quite young when his family moved to Wilton, Connecticut, in 1932. His father was a European-educated engineer with multifaceted abilities, licensed in electrical, chemical, and mining engineering in various states. While Chelminski inherited mechanical aptitude from his father, he was not certain what to do with his life after high school. Faced with the prospect of mandatory military service because of the Korean War, he volunteered for the draft and served a stint in the

CHELMINSKI LEAVES LAMONT TO START BUSINESS: 1960

In 1960 Beckmann left Lamont to establish his own company and asked Chelminski to join him. Instead, Chelminski decided to leave Lamont as well and start his own business. Beckmann formed Alpine Geophysical Associates, Inc., and it soon became apparent to Chelminski that, during the years he was at Lamont, Beckmann had been using Chelminski's work to set up a business to conduct survey work for the U.S. government, which wanted the entire East Coast of the United States surveyed for beach erosion, hence the need for sub-bottom exploration with a sound source and a machine able to take sand samples.

Chelminski set up shop in 1960 in his parents' barn in Norwalk, Connecticut, and brought in John Gilbert and Louis DeGeoffrey as his partners. Gilbert was a high school classmate who had earned a mechanical engineering degree from Pennsylvania State University and gone to work for Hamilton Standard in Hartford, Connecticut, but was not happy with life in a big company. DeGeoffrey was older, a friend of Chelminski's father and a man who enjoyed experimentation and invention. For the name of the company they chose Bolt Associates, the derivation of which was purely an inside joke, arrived at one evening when Chelminski and Gilbert were brainstorming in the living room of Chelminski's parents. They decided to name the company after Chelminski's older brother Paul, whose nickname was Bolt. The name was bestowed upon him because he dropped a bolt in the carburetor of a Volkswagen the youngest Chelminski was going to drive cross country to California. Stephen Chelminski had to spend an entire evening taking apart the engine to remove the bolt. Thus, Bolt Associates was born and Chelminski drew the company's first logo, which featured the earth forming the "O" of Bolt with a lightning bolt through it. In 1962 the company was incorporated and took its present-day name.

military. When he was discharged in 1954, Chelminski used the money he received from the government for his service to buy machine tools to make prototypes of his mechanical inventions, such as a controllable-thrust rocket motor. He also devoted time to another interest, trees, authoring a book called *The Tree Identification Book*. He then took advantage of the G.I. Bill of Rights to enroll at Columbia University's School of General Studies, taking pre-engineering courses.

At Columbia Chelminski was looking for a summer job when he met a researcher at Columbia University's Lamont Geological Observatory, Walter Beckmann, who was looking for some help in his work. In lieu of an interview, Beckmann asked Chelminski to show him some ideas on how to conduct deep-sea drilling. Impressed with the young man's sketches, and willingness to travel 60 miles through a blizzard to take a tour of his Lamont laboratory, Beckmann hired Chelminski. The summer job never came to an end, however. When fall arrived, Chelminski continued to work at Lamont and never would complete his degree.

Beckmann asked Chelminski to develop a sound source for seismic surveys, and he complied with a gas exploder machine, which mixed oxygen and propane to produce sound waves. Beckmann also asked him to develop a core-drilling machine, and Chelminski devised a way to take advantage of ocean bottom pressure to force core pipe into sediments to take samples. Chelminski took the prototype of the device for testing in the Atlantic Ocean for Lamont. Not only was the device damaged, Chelminski fell overboard and was fortunate that someone took notice and he was rescued after about 30 minutes in the water. The head of Lamont wanted Chelminski to continue the experiments, but he refused because he could not adequately repair the coring machine on the ship. From that point forward, his relationship with Lamont was strained and would grow more so in the years to come.

Starting out, Bolt Associates was a machine shop, relying on work Chelminski's father secured for the partners as a chemical engineer. They made parts for chemical plant equipment, and also landed work making drilling units for digging water wells. It was while working on water well drills that Chelminski began thinking about the work he had done at Lamont on the gas exploder. He began to tinker with the idea of making a device that could release air instead of exploding gases, and within a matter of weeks in the spring of 1961 he had designed and built a prototype for the first air gun.

Chelminski immediately applied for a patent, and Bolt trademarked the name PAR gun, standing for

KEY DATES

1960: Company is founded as Bolt Associated.
1962: Company is incorporated as Bolt Technology Corporation.
1964: Marine Air Gun is introduced to market.
1981: Company goes public.
1990: Company avoids bankruptcy.
1996: Stock is listed on American Stock Exchange.
1997: Custom Products is acquired.
2008: Custom Products is sold.

"pneumatic acoustical repeater." He demonstrated the device at the Lamont observatory, where it was suggested he should show the device to his old boss, Walter Beckmann. In June 1961 Beckmann received a demonstration and then rented one for use in a survey his company was conducting in Baychester, New York. The first time the air gun was used, in fact, was in a hole dug on dry land. Beckmann offered to license the technology from Chelminski but offered little money. When Chelminski turned him down, Beckmann (according to Chelminski in a 2008 phone interview) indicated Alpine would simply make the guns itself. When Chelminski suggested he might sue, Beckmann replied, "You don't have enough money." According to legal records in a later lawsuit filed by Bolt against Alpine, Alpine sold devices using Chelminski's method to Lamont.

AIR GUN INTRODUCED TO MARKET: 1964

In 1964 Bolt introduced to the market a refined version of the device that it now called the Marine Air Gun. Learning that Alpine was again interested in such a pneumatic sounder, Bolt supplied it with the latest model for testing, which Alpine kept for several days. Again negotiations proved fruitless, and once more Alpine began producing air guns, as did Lamont, using Bolt's trade secrets. The matter came to a head in 1965 when Bolt was negotiating to perform survey work in the English Channel, where a study was being conducted to determine the feasibility of a tunnel between England and France. Earlier studies, some of which had been done by Alpine, had not revealed enough detail. Fearing that Alpine might attempt to secure the Channel survey work using its bootleg version of the Marine Air Gun, Bolt went to court to stop Alpine. In the end, the court sided with Bolt and ordered Alpine not to divulge any of the features of

Bolt's pneumatic acoustical repeater until Bolt's patent was issued or denied. Chelminski would have to wait until 1976 before the patent was granted. The Society of Exploration Geophysicists did not wait as long, however. The previous year it had awarded Chelminski with the prestigious Kauffman Gold Medal.

Bolt was very much a small company in 1965 when it hired its sixth employee, Bernard Luskin, who became Bolt's longtime president and chairman. In the 1950s he was an engineer and Chelminski's colleague at Lamont, where he invented a precision depth recorder. He left Lamont on the same day as Chelminski to become a consultant and researcher for technology investors. When he learned of Bolt's air gun, Luskin immediately recognized that there was a ready market for the device with oil-and-gas-exploration companies. Once on board with Bolt, hired initially as general manager, he made a splash by taking out small ads in trade journals, challenging oil companies that still relied on explosives to a "shoot-out" with Bolt's air gun. Whoever produced the best survey results was the winner. Dynamite could not hope to match the timed arrays of the air gun, convincing Teledyne, Inc., a company involved in both electronics and geophysics, to sign up with Bolt. Using that contract as a calling card, Luskin was then able to land Mobil and other oil companies and quickly establish Bolt in the marine exploration market. Chelminski was becoming increasingly tied up with research and development and soon recommended that "Bernie" replace him as the company president. The board then approved Luskin as chief executive.

Bolt in the late 1970s extended its air gun technology for use onshore. The air gun released compressed air into a drilled hole, and underwater waves were emitted to reveal geological formations. With this additional revenue stream and revenues growing at an annual rate of nearly 40 percent, investors grew interested, and in 1981 Luskin took Bolt public, selling about one million shares of common stock to pay off debt, purchase additional machinery and equipment, and expand production of its new land seismic air guns. Revenues increased to $13.4 million in fiscal 1981 (which ended June 30) and jumped to more than $22.5 million in 1982, while net income grew from $2.4 million to $3.2 million during this period.

The early 1980s were not a good time for the oil and oil services industries, but until the end of 1982, Bolt defied the trend and continued to enjoy record growth. Finally, the drought began to affect Bolt, and it was still very much dependent on a single product. Sales fell to $16 million in fiscal 1984. During the previous decade Bolt had attempted to diversify through the development of new products, such as a pile driver Chelminski invented, but none of them fared well. In order to diversify the company, Luskin began scouting for acquisitions to take advantage of Bolt's strong cash position and lack of long-term debt. In 1984 Bolt acquired Tulsa, Oklahoma-based Zeligson Co., maker of heavy-duty specialty trucks used in geophysical exploration. Bolt's plan was to outfit the trucks with air guns and sell a complete seismic exploration truck package. Later in the year Bolt completed another purchase, adding Houston-based Criterion Exploration Inc., a geophysical data acquisition company that specialized in the transition space between land and sea. Also in 1984, Bolt picked up Kim Tech, an Englewood, Colorado, company that generated digital computer readouts from the information gathered by air guns.

Although Bolt widened its product offerings, in truth it did not diversify the business in a way that could shield it from the severe slump that visited the oil and gas industry in the late 1980s, when numerous well-established firms fell by the wayside. Bolt was at least strong enough to survive, although by 1990 it was in debt and unable to pay $6.7 million in debt principal. Luskin, now 65 years old, stepped down as president and chief executive officer, turning over day-to-day control to longtime CFO Raymond M. Soto. Luskin stayed on as chairman. Chelminski also reduced his commitment to a part-time basis, becoming director of special research and development projects in July 1990.

Soto was able to work with Bolt's bankers to avoid bankruptcy, and the company began to recover in the early 1990s. Sales reached $5.7 million in fiscal 1992 and the company turned a modest profit of $402,000. Revenues inched upward, reaching $8.7 million in fiscal 1996, when earnings also totaled $1.2 million. The company was doing well enough that in September 1996 Bolt gained a listing on the American Stock Exchange, after having been relegated to the over-the-counter market for several years.

CUSTOM PRODUCTS CORPORATION ACQUIRED: 1997

Bolt returned to growth mode in the second half of the 1990s. Not only did it come out with a new "long life" air gun that stimulated sales, it was again in the market for acquisitions and diversification. In November 1997 Bolt paid about $6 million in cash and stock for North Haven, Connecticut-based Custom Products Corporation, maker of miniature precision mechanical and pneumatic slip clutches, used in business machines, such as package labeling machines, laptop computers,

semiconductor manufacturing machines, medical equipment, and natural gas transmission meters.

With two business segments providing sales, Bolt saw revenues increase from $10.5 million in fiscal 1997 to more than $18 million in fiscal 1998. Net income also increased from $2.12 million to $5.13 million. Bolt completed another acquisition in April 1999, adding underwater electrical connectors and cables to the product mix through the purchase of Cypress, Texas-based A-G Geophysical Products Inc., a company that by itself posted annual sales of $10 million.

Bolt's revenues were very much dependent on the price of oil, which determined exploration and drilling activity. A downturn at the end of the 1990s resulted in revenues dropping from $19.6 million in fiscal 1999 to $14.8 million in fiscal 2000. Bolt introduced a new generation of the air gun, the Annular Port Air Gun, which featured a number of improvements and helped spur sales in fiscal 2001, when revenues increased to $15.5 million, but earnings were reduced to $396,000, a far cry from the $5.1 million the company netted in fiscal 1998. Sales continued to grow in fiscal 2002, but another dip in drilling activity led to plunging sales in fiscal 2003, when Bolt posted revenues of $10.8 million and a net loss of $161,000.

With the war in Iraq, oil prices soared, leading to boom times for the energy industry, and Bolt benefited accordingly. Sales jumped to $29.4 million in fiscal 2006, $46.9 million a year later, and $61.6 million in fiscal 2008, while net income during this period spiked to $14.6 million. Bolt took advantage of its good health in July 2007 to acquire Real Time Systems, a Fredericksburg, Texas-based developer of controllers and synchronizers for air guns. Several months later, in May 2008, Bolt decided to focus attention on its core oil services business and sold Custom Products for $5.25 million to a Wisconsin firm, A&S Manufacturing Co., Inc.

Ed Dinger

PRINCIPAL SUBSIDIARIES

A-G Geophysical Products, Inc.; Real Time Systems Inc.

PRINCIPAL COMPETITORS

CGGVeritas; ION Geophysical Corporation; OYO Geospace Corporation.

FURTHER READING

Brown, Paul R., "Will Bolt Make the Majors?" *Forbes*, March 14, 1983, p. 135.

Lee, Richard, "Norwalk's Bolt Technology Busy As a Thirsty World Seeks More Oil," *Stamford (Conn.) Advocate,* August 12, 2006.

Roberts, Jim, "Downturn in Oil Industry Pushed Bolt to the Brink," *Fairfield County Business Journal,* May 1, 1988, p. 1.

Soule, Alexander, "Chasing Talent That Chases Oil," *Fairfield County Business Journal,* February 4, 2008.

Bowlin Travel Centers, Inc.

---■---

150 Louisiana NE
Albuquerque, New Mexico 87108-2055
U.S.A.
Telephone: (505) 266-5985
Fax: (505) 266-7821
Web site: http://www.bowlintc.com

Public Company
Incorporated: 2000
Employees: 139
Sales: $28.65 million (2008)
Stock Exchanges: Over the Counter (OTC)
Ticker Symbol: BWTL
NAICS: 447110 Gasoline Stations with Convenience
Stores; 452990 All Other General Merchandise
Stores; 722110 Full-Service Restaurants; 722111
Limited-Service Restaurants

■ ■ ■

Bowlin Travel Centers, Inc., is one of the leading providers of roadside services to automotive travelers in the southwestern United States. The company offers gasoline, convenience foods, and a wide range of souvenirs to tourists, traveling sales representatives, and others along the rural yet well-traveled areas of Interstate 10 and Interstate 40. Bowlin Travel Centers sells known brands of gasoline (ExxonMobil, Mobil, and Shell) at three Arizona travel centers. At five travel centers, Dairy Queen Brazier restaurants provide casual meals as well as Dairy Queen's soft-serve ice-cream desserts. Although the company sells a variety of souvenirs, collectibles, and imported crafts, as trading posts the centers specialize in such Native American arts and crafts as handmade jewelry, pottery, baskets, Navajo rugs, and kachina dolls.

Bowlin Travel Centers operates nine travel centers in New Mexico and Arizona; they range in size from 6,000 to 11,000 square feet. In New Mexico, the Aleka Flats Trading Post and Butterfield Station Travel Center are located on Interstate 10 between Deming and Las Cruces, and the Continental Divide Trading Post is east of Lordsburg. The Old West Trading Post is on Highway 70, west of Las Cruces. On Interstate 40, the Bluewater Travel Center is located ten miles west of Grants, and the Flying C Ranch is 70 miles east of Albuquerque.

The three travel centers in Arizona include two at Picacho Peak, on Interstate 10 between Phoenix and Tucson, and another near Benson, 40 miles east of Tucson. The company advertises its travel centers and merchandise on billboards along the highways where the centers are located. While each travel center has a different atmosphere, the Benson store is the most unusual, luring visitors with advertisements of "The Thing," an unidentified attraction at the travel center museum. All of the travel centers promote nearby tourist sites, such as state and national parks, ghost towns, and museums.

NATIVE AMERICAN CRAFTS LEADS TO DEVELOPMENT OF TRADING POSTS

The development of Bowlin Travel Centers began in 1912, when Claude M. Bowlin began trading goods with Native Americans in New Mexico. Bowlin and his

COMPANY PERSPECTIVES

Bowlin Travel Centers shall continue to grow and serve our customers in our long standing tradition of honesty, integrity, and hospitality by providing high quality products and services at competitive prices, while providing financial stability and a reasonable return on equity for our stockholders, and compensation in excess of market along with a satisfying work environment for our employees.

wife, Willa, learned Native American languages and customs, and they appreciated the beauty of Native American arts and crafts. They began to trade in jewelry, pottery, baskets, blankets, and rugs handcrafted by Navajo and Zuni Indians at the pueblos in New Mexico. Initially, the Bowlins opened trading posts in the Gallup and Farmington areas. After owning and selling several such operations between 1919 and 1935, the Bowlins established a permanent location near Bluewater, on a wagon road that later became Route 66. The Old Crater Trading Post, which opened in 1935, took its name from an extinct volcano north of Bluewater.

After World War II, the Bowlins saw opportunity in the expansion of automotive travel and tourism of that era. They sought to expose visitors in New Mexico, known as the "Land of Enchantment," to Native American artisanship. Beginning in 1946, they built three additional trading posts, the Continental Divide Trading Post east of Lordsburg, the Akela Flats Travel Ranch east of Deming, and the Wagon Wheel, also located in southern New Mexico. The trading posts were located on Highway 70 or Highway 80, later renamed Interstate 10, where few travel services were available. In 1953 the Bowlins consolidated their holdings into a formal company, named Bowlin Incorporated. Expansion continued with three additional trading posts: Jack Rabbit Ranch; the Old West Trading Post, west of Las Cruces; and the Running Indian Trading Post at Alamogordo, on Highway 70, northeast of Las Cruces.

In 1972 Claude and Willa Bowlin's youngest son, Michael L. Bowlin, became president of the company as the ailing founder stepped down. Claude Bowlin passed away in 1974.

Bowlin continued to open new outlets, particularly along Interstate 40. In 1973 Bowlin closed the Bluewater operation when construction of Interstate 40 diverted traffic away from Route 66. The new Bluewater trading post opened on Interstate 40, west of Grants.

The company opened trading posts at Edgewood, east of Albuquerque, and Flying C Ranch, 70 miles east of Albuquerque and 40 miles west of Santa Rosa. In southern New Mexico, Bowlin opened a third trading post on Interstate 10, near several ghost towns and the Gila National Forest. Butterfield Station, 20 miles west of Deming, was named for the Butterfield Overland Mail, a stagecoach route that ran through southern New Mexico as it traveled from St. Louis, Missouri, to San Francisco, California, between 1857 and 1861.

Bowlin expanded into Arizona with the opening of Picacho Peak Plaza, 45 miles northwest of Tucson, on the much traveled stretch of Interstate 10 between Tucson and Phoenix. In 1985 the company opened a travel center near Benson, Arizona, east of Tucson, serving tourists traveling to Tombstone, site of the Earp brothers and Doc Holliday's infamous shootout against the Clantons at the O.K. Corral in 1881.

TRAVEL CENTERS DEVELOP WITH BRAND-NAME PRODUCTS

Over the years, the trading posts developed into full-service operations, selling food and gasoline to travelers. Bowlin offered convenience goods, such as prepackaged snacks and bottled and canned beverages, and brand-name gasoline, including CITGO, Conoco, Chevron, Texaco, and Diamond Shamrock. The Bowlins also became Dairy Queen and Dairy Queen Brazier franchisees. Dairy Queen offered soft-serve ice-cream desserts; the Dairy Queen Brazier restaurants, in addition to ice cream, provided customers with quick-service meals that included hamburgers, chicken, fish, and barbequed-meat sandwiches, side dishes, and soft drinks. The company added Dairy Queen restaurants at six travel centers between 1982 and 1986, including the Bluewater, Flying C Ranch, Butterfield, and Picacho Peak locations. At two locations, Bowlin added Stuckey's franchises, which offered souvenirs, gifts, and Stuckey's pecan candies. The Stuckey's franchises opened at Edgewood, New Mexico, in 1982 and in Benson, Arizona, in 1987. Also, Bowlin expanded its range of Native American crafts and added goods imported from Mexico.

During the 1980s, Bowlin expanded its business with outdoor advertising. Bowlin Outdoor Advertising emerged from the company's experience with advertising its travel centers on 300 billboards along highways. Billboards informed drivers of products and services available and the specific locations of the travel centers. The company soon acquired billboards in New Mexico, Arizona, Colorado, Oklahoma, and Texas. With an inventory of 1,700 outdoor advertising displays, the company leased billboards to hotels, motels, restaurants,

KEY DATES

1912: Claude and Willa Bowlin begin trading Native American goods in New Mexico.

1935: First longstanding trading post opens on wagon road near Bluewater, New Mexico.

1946: The Bowlins open several new trading posts in southern New Mexico.

1953: The company incorporates as Bowlin Inc.

1980s Bowlin enters the billboard leasing business.

1982: Dairy Queen and Stuckey's franchises expand trading post products and services.

1996: Company goes public as Bowlin Outdoor Advertising and Travel Centers, Inc.

2000: Bowlin Outdoor Advertising and Bowlin Travel Centers become separate businesses.

2005: A state-of-the-art travel center opens in Picacho Peak, Arizona.

tourist and entertainment businesses, and local consumer product manufacturers. By 1995 Bowlin Outdoor Advertising ranked among the largest 40 billboard leasing companies in the United States.

With the addition of new travel centers at Benson, Edgewood, and elsewhere, Bowlin operated 15 travel centers by 1996. These included two additional Stuckey's franchises and another Dairy Queen franchise. Revenues rose from $12 million in 1986 to $23.3 million in 1996. Travel centers accounted for $20.7 million in revenues, with 42 percent of sales originating from gasoline sales, 32 percent from merchandise, and 15 percent from food; outdoor advertising revenues, at $2.77 million, accounted for the balance, at 11 percent of revenues.

REINCORPORATION AND PUBLIC OFFERING OF STOCK

In 1996, in preparation for an initial public offering of stock, the company reincorporated as Bowlin Outdoor Advertising and Travel Centers, Inc. In December, Bowlin offered 1.1 million shares of stock at $8 per share. The company applied the $7.3 million net proceeds from the offering to pay long-term debt, to upgrade facilities, and for expansion, including new site development and outdoor advertising acquisitions. Facilities upgrades involved $5 million in renovations, including new lighting and furnishings, building and parking lot improvements, and new awnings, signage, and exterior facing. Travel center development included the opening

of the Rio Puerco Outpost on Interstate 40, located 17 miles east of Albuquerque.

Bowlin Travel Centers entered a new area of business when it began to offer CITGO gasoline wholesale to two smaller, independent gas stations in 1997. Over the next five years gasoline wholesaling contributed approximately $1 million to $2 million to revenues, averaging 5.5 percent of total revenues.

OUTDOOR ADVERTISING BUSINESS EXPANDS

Bowlin's primary focus involved expansion of the outdoor advertising business through the acquisition of several billboard leasing companies. In April 1997 the company acquired Pony Panels Outdoor Advertising for $4.2 million. The acquisition included 1,800 billboards in Oklahoma, west Texas, southern Colorado, Arizona, and New Mexico. Despite the name, most of the billboards were the largest size available, the "1448s," at 14 feet high and 48 feet wide. In late 1997 the company began an aggressive expansion strategy, pursuing opportunities in the lucrative markets of east and central Texas. Over the next 14 months Bowlin purchased eight companies for an aggregate $10.5 million. The acquisition of Sweezy Outdoor Advertising of Fort Hood included a manufacturing plant, providing Bowlin with the means to produce new billboards. Other acquired companies included Big-Tex Outdoor Advertising in Brownwood, Edgar Outdoor Advertising in Southlake, and GDM Outdoor Advertising of Tyler. Bowlin purchased another four companies by the end of 1999. The Texas acquisitions added more than 1,000 billboards to the company's inventory, for a total of 3,700 "faces."

Billboard leasing contributed to overall revenue increases, as earnings before interest, taxes, depreciation, and amortization for that segment of business increased 11.1 percent for the fiscal year that ended January 31, 2000, compared to a 4.7 percent increase for the company overall. That year Bowlin reported revenues of $34.62 million, a 14.3 percent increase over fiscal 1999.

Despite Bowlin's success in its two fields of operation, the combination of entirely different businesses, a media company and retail business, caused confusion in the public market. So, in June 2000, Bowlin announced that the company would separate the outdoor advertising and travel center operations. That year, Bowlin Outdoor Advertising and Travel Centers merged with Louisiana-based Lamar Advertising Company, and then followed with a spinoff of Bowlin Travel Centers. Michael Bowlin, who took the position of CEO at both companies, saw the changes as the best avenue to expand the billboard leasing business. The spinoff of Bowlin Travel Centers occurred through a stock exchange. Original shareholders of Bowlin Outdoor Advertising and Travel Centers received shares in both Lamar Advertising and Bowlin Travel Centers.

BOWLIN STREAMLINES TRAVEL CENTER OPERATIONS

With renewed focus on the travel centers, Bowlin streamlined operations with the closure of five of the centers. These included the Stuckey's travel centers at Benson, Arizona, and Edgewood, New Mexico. Bowlin sold both properties in the spring of 2001. The closures effectively ended Bowlin's affiliation with Stuckey's. The company also closed a freestanding Dairy Queen near Lordsburg. Bowlin's remaining operations consisted of 11 travel centers. Sales peaked at $26.77 million in 2001, and then decreased to $22.18 million in 2003. The company continued to be profitable, however, and sales incentives offset the decline in revenue.

To offset the decrease in travel center operations, Bowlin invested in real estate in New Mexico. The company purchased 12 acres of land near Alamogordo, and then divided them into 35 quarter-acre lots for residential construction. Infrastructure investment included paved roads; fencing; and sewer, water, and electrical connections. All lots were listed for sale, with the expectation that they would be sold during the next few years. By the end of 2005, Bowlin had sold three lots for manufactured houses.

NEW TRAVEL CENTERS ARE OPENED AND OTHERS CLOSE

Bowlin opened a state-of-the-art travel center in March 2005, the Picacho Peak Plaza, 45 miles northwest of Tucson, near its Picacho Peak Dairy Queen Travel Center. While the Picacho Peak Plaza unit did not offer Dairy Queen, with 10,000 square feet of retail space, the new travel center included a convenience store selling gourmet coffee and snacks. Nearby, a large-screen plasma television provided satellite news programming. In addition to southwestern arts and crafts, the souvenir and gifts section stocked imported goods from around the globe. Large items for sale, such as a 25-foot-tall totem pole, a life-sized statue of John Wayne on his horse, and life-sized stuffed animals, created a unique atmosphere in the store. Bowlin offered CITGO-brand gasoline at state-of-the-art super-pumpers, for 24-hour gasoline purchase with the use of a credit card.

Population growth fostered a rise in traffic between Phoenix and Tucson and seemed to merit the near duplication of services. The overlap, however, reduced revenues at the existing store. Merchandise sales at the existing store declined 34.8 percent, while higher gasoline prices contributed to an overall rise in revenues. Total sales increased 15.8 percent, from $24.09 million for the fiscal year ending January 31, 2006, to $27.9 million for fiscal 2007.

In 2007 Bowlin restructured its gasoline brand services, discontinuing its CITGO contract. Through an agreement with Arizona Fuel Distributors, LLC, Bowlin began selling Mobil brand gasoline at one of its Arizona outlets and Shell at the remaining two travel centers. Bowlin continued to offer ExxonMobil gasoline at New Mexico travel centers. The agreement with ExxonMobil for 2005 to 2010 included gasoline that Bowlin sold wholesale to three independent stations.

Operations at Bowlin continued to shrink in 2007, as the company closed the Rio Puerco Outpost and sold the property in May 2007. The company discontinued operations at the Alamogordo Running Indian Trading Post and the Edgewood Travel Center and listed both properties for sale in late 2007. All three units were relatively small, with Rio Puerco at 5,000 square feet, Alamogordo at 3,800 square feet, and Edgewood at 2,800 square feet. The changes left Bowlin with nine travel centers in operation, six in New Mexico and three in Arizona.

Mary Tradii

PRINCIPAL OPERATING UNITS

Akela Flats Trading Center; Benson Travel Center; Bluewater Travel Center; The Butterfield Station Travel Center; Continental Divide Trading Post; Flying C Ranch; Old West Trading Post; Picacho Peak Travel Center & Dairy Queen; Picacho Peak Plaza.

PRINCIPAL COMPETITORS

Giant Industries, Inc.; Love's Travel Stops & Country Stores, Inc.; Petro Corporation; Flying J Inc.

FURTHER READING

Baca, Aaron, "Albuquerque, N.M.-based Travel Center Company to Entertain Buyout Offer," *Albuquerque Journal*, October 9, 2003.

———, "Albuquerque, N.M.-based Travel Centers See Profits in Roadside Business," *Albuquerque Journal*, May 5, 2003.

———, "Shareholder Wants Remaining Stake in Albuquerque, N.M.-based Travel Center," *Albuquerque Journal*, March 9, 2002.

"Bowlin Increases Its Texas Presence with Acquisition," *Albuquerque Tribune,* March 9, 1999, p. B6.

"Bowlin Travel Centers, Inc.," *Plunkett's Retail Industry Almanac,* 2004.

Goodringer, Lisa, "Bowlin Travels Down IPO Road," *Business Journal—Serving Phoenix & the Valley of the Sun,* November 15, 1996, p. 6.

Mayfield, Dan, "Bowlin's Roadside Travel Centers on a 31-Year Winning Streak," *Albuquerque Tribune,* April 23, 2003, p. B5.

———, "The Trib 8," *Albuquerque Tribune,* September 25, 2000, p. 8.

Murphy, Michael G., "Billboard Company Expands," *Albuquerque Journal,* April 3, 1997, p. D4.

Robinson, Sherry, "Billboard Merger Returns Bowlin to Its Merchant Roots," *Albuquerque Tribune,* October 16, 2000, p. 9.

Rosales, Glen, "All Signs Point Up for Bowlin," *Albuquerque Journal,* March 22, 1999, p. 1.

Cains Beer Company PLC

The Robert Cain Brewery
Stanhope Street
Liverpool, L8 5XJ
United Kingdom
Telephone: (+44 0151) 709 8734
Fax: (+44 0151) 708 8395
Web site: http://www.cains.co.uk

Public Company
Incorporated: 1850 as Robert Cain & Company
Employees: 497
Sales: £47.4 million ($80.7 million) (2007)
Stock Exchanges: London
Ticker Symbol: CBC
NAICS: 312120 Breweries; 722410 Drinking Places
   (Alcoholic Beverages)

■ ■ ■

Cains Beer Company PLC is one of Liverpool, England's oldest and most popular breweries. Founded in 1850, the company has undergone a renaissance in the early 2000s, becoming one of the United Kingdom's fastest-growing regional breweries. Cains produces more than 120 million pints of beer each year. The company's labels include its flagship Robert Cain ale; Cains Finest Lager, which claims to be the first truly British lager; Organic Wheat Ale; and the award-winning Fine Raisin Beer. Cains distributes its beers through its own estate of 115 pubs, nearly all of which are located in the northwest region of England and Scotland. The company also sells its beer through the 450-pub Punch Taverns group, and has a number of national distribution contracts with supermarket groups, including Morrisons.

Cains Beer's revival is credited to brothers Ajmail and Sudarghara Dusanj, who acquired the company in 2002. Following the reverse takeover of Honeycombe Leisure in 2007, which also brought Cains to the London Stock Exchange, the company fell into financial difficulties. In 2008 the company was forced into receivership after its bank, Bank of Scotland, refused to support Cains' plans for future development. The Dusanj brothers have since been in negotiations to buy back the company. Despite these difficulties, Cains Beer Company has nonetheless shown strong revenue growth in the first decade of the 2000s, nearly doubling its sales to more than £47 million ($80 million) by the end of 2007.

IMMIGRANT SUCCESS STORY IN 1850

Robert Cain was born into poverty in County Cork, Ireland, in 1826. Cain's father had served in the British Army, and, after leaving the service, moved with his family to Liverpool. Robert Cain took to sea at a young age, serving on merchant ships linking Liverpool to the palm oil plantations on Africa's west coast. By the late 1840s, however, Cain had returned to Liverpool for good. Cain married in 1847 and by 1850 had settled on a new career as a brewer.

Cain opened his first brewery that year, setting up business in the Scotland Road/Vauxhall section of Liverpool. Cain's ales quickly proved popular in the local market. With sales rising strongly, Cain began acquiring his first pubs. Pub ownership was by then an important feature of the brewery market in England, which increasingly tended toward a tied pub system. Control of one's own pub estate provided brewers with a ready outlet for their beers. By the late 1850s, Cain controlled a number of pubs in Liverpool and the surrounding area.

The company's increasing beer sales led it to expand its capacity. In 1858 Cain moved to buy the former Hindey Brewery, a much larger brewery, located on Stanhope Street in Toxteth. Cain renamed the site as the Mersey Brewery. Through the second half of the 19th century, Cain continued to expand the site, buying up the surrounding tenement housing.

The acquisition of the Toxteth brewery had given Cain expanded quarters and a new range of brewery equipment. Additionally, the site provided another important feature for the future success of the company: its own underground spring. Control of its own water source, and the quality of the water itself, allowed the company to establish itself as a highly respected brewer. The company itself began to market its products as "Superior Ales and Stouts" and by the 1880s had grown into Liverpool's largest brewery. In addition to the expanded brewery, Cain also operated an estate of some 200 pubs, including many of the region's most iconic drinking establishments. The Cain family itself became one of the wealthiest in the region.

Cain, who had 11 children, brought two of his sons, William and Charles, into the business. In 1896 the company took on the new name of Robert Cain and Sons Ltd. Over the next few years, Cain transferred control of the company to his sons; Robert Cain died in 1907 at the age of 81.

BECOMING HIGSON'S IN 1923

William and Charles Cain continued to run the brewery business through the end of World War I and into the

difficult economic period of the early 1920s. In 1921, however, the company agreed to merge with Warrington-based brewer Peter Walker and Son. That company, which likewise had roots in the 19th century, had also completed the acquisition of a third brewery, Robert Blezard and Co. The purchase had added not only a brewery but also Blezard's estate of nearly 50 pubs. The newly enlarged company was then renamed as Peter Walker (Warrington) and Robert Cain & Sons Ltd. Shortly after, the company's brewing operations were transferred to its Warrington facility. Walker Cain, with a pub estate of 1,000 pubs, remained profitable, growing into one of the 50 largest companies in the United Kingdom by the beginning of the 1920s.

Having moved its own production to Warrington, Walker Cain put the historic Toxteth brewery on Stanhope Street up for sale. In 1923 that site was purchased by another local brewer, Daniel Higson Ltd., a company originally founded in 1827. Higson's then renamed the Toxteth brewery as the Freehold Brewery; nonetheless, the site became popularly known under the Higson's name over the next decades.

Higson's itself expanded in the 1930s. In 1937 the company completed a merger with another Liverpool-based brewer, Joseph Jones & Company, founded in 1869 in the Knotty Ash area. The merger also included the acquisition of the wine and spirits division of J. Sykes & Co., also based in Liverpool and founded in 1867. The new company was then renamed as Higson's Brewery Ltd.; it controlled a pub estate of nearly 200 licensed houses. The Freehold Brewery, with a total capacity of 5,000 barrels per week, remained the group's main production site.

Higsons (the company dropped the apostrophe in 1962) remained a modest, regionally focused brewery throughout most of the 20th century. The company profited during the surge of interest in Liverpool during the 1960s, particularly with the rise to fame of the Beatles and Liverpool's emergence as a major cultural center during this period.

During the 1960s, Higsons had acquired a new and important shareholder, Bass Plc, which gained more than a 12 percent stake in the Liverpool group. Although Higsons' traditional bitters and ales continued to enjoy the strong reputation originally established by Robert Cain, the company found itself racing to adapt to changes in the British beer-drinking market. The arrival of new beer types, especially the surging popularity of the lighter lagers brought in from continental Europe, had caused a downturn in traditional ale sales.

In response, Higsons, like many regional brewers, attempted to enter this beer category as well. After investing millions in new brewing equipment, however,

KEY DATES

1850: Irish immigrant Robert Cain founds a brewery in Liverpool.

1858: Cain acquires a larger brewery on Stanhope Street in Toxteth.

1896: Cain's sons join the business, which is renamed as Robert Cain & Sons.

1921: Robert Cain & Sons merges with Warrington-based brewer Peter Walker.

1923: Toxteth brewery is sold to Higson's.

1937: Higson's merges with Joseph Jones & Company and acquires the wine and spirits division of J. Sykes & Co.

1985: After a failed attempt to launch lager production, Higsons is sold to Boddingtons of Manchester.

1990: Boddingtons sells Higsons to Whitbread, which shuts down Toxteth brewery.

1991: The Danish Brewery Group, led by John Hughes, buys Toxteth brewery and relaunches production as Robert Cain & Co.

2002: The Dusanj brothers buy Robert Cain & Co. and launch a revitalization effort of the struggling brand.

2007: Cain acquires Honeycombe Leisure in a reverse takeover, gaining a listing on the London Stock Exchange.

2008: Cain is placed in receivership after suffering losses related to the Honeycombe takeover.

Higsons found itself still unable to capture the interest of the lager-drinking market, which maintained its preference for foreign brands. More successful for the company was its production of private-label beers for the supermarket sector. These operations grew to account for some 90 percent of the company's production. Nonetheless, the group continued to struggle against the trend toward foreign beers.

REBIRTH OF THE CAIN BRAND IN 1990

In the meantime, the collapse of Liverpool's shipping and shipbuilding industries and the overall economic malaise that lingered in the United Kingdom through much of the 1970s and into the 1980s added to Higsons' woes. By 1985 Higsons agreed to be sold to another northern England brewery group, Boddingtons, based in Manchester. In exchange, Bass gained a 12 percent stake in Boddingtons.

By the end of that year, Bass had agreed to sell its own Boddingtons stake to another major U.K. beer and spirits group, Whitbread, which already owned shares in Boddingtons. The purchase gave Whitbread control of 22 percent of the Boddingtons group, as well as the Higsons Brewery operation. The breakup of the tied pubs system, begun in the mid-1980s, then led Boddingtons to exit the brewery business to focus on its pub estate. As a result, Whitbread acquired full control of the Higsons brewery operations, minus its pubs, in 1990.

Whitbread promptly shifted production of Higsons ales to its own production facilities in Sheffield. The company then shut down the Freehold Brewery. Within weeks, however, the brewery found a rescuer, in the form of John Hughes, who had been successful in the frozen fish and food processing sectors, and later had established a business producing private-label soft drinks for the supermarket sector. Backed by The Danish Brewery Group, which became the Toxteth brewery's owners, Hughes renamed the company as Robert Cain & Co. Ltd., relaunching the Cain ale brand.

Over the next decade, Cain shifted the bulk of its production back to its own brands. By the early 2000s, own-label production accounted for the vast majority of the company's production. Yet Cain struggled against steady losses throughout most of this period. The company's sales declined, leaving its production capacity underused. In 2002 The Danish Brewery Group announced that it was putting the Cain brewery up for sale. Although the business was to be sold as a going concern, it appeared likely that the brewery itself would be shut down and production transferred to the new owner.

A NEW IMMIGRANT'S TALE FOR THE 21ST CENTURY

That announcement caught the attention of two brothers, Ajmail and Sudarghara Dusanj. Their father had emigrated from Punjab, India, to England in the early 1960s. From poverty, the elder Dusanj managed to build up savings to start his own business. In the early 1980s, he opened a fish-and-chips shop. Still in high school, the Dusanj brothers joined their father in the shop and helped the business grow strongly, opening a second shop soon after. After graduating from college, the brothers returned to the family business, helping to expand it to nine fish-and-chips shops, including several owned by the brothers themselves.

In the next decade, however, the Dusanj brothers began looking for new opportunities. In the mid-1990s, they sold their fish-and-chips shops to other family members and moved to the Midlands, where they acquired a struggling soft-drinks company. That business, which focused on bottling for the wholesale market, also included a cash-and-carry shop. The brothers succeeded in turning the business around, and by the early 2000s began looking for their next business venture.

By 2002 the Dusanj brothers had beaten out other bidders for the Cain brewery, and moved to Liverpool. The Dusanj brothers set out to revitalize the business, promising to maintain production at the historic Toxteth brewery. The brothers not only sought to expand production, but also to rejuvenate the Cain brand itself. For this, the company began focusing on improving the quality of its ales, as well as developing new beers.

Aiding the company in this effort was the rediscovery of the original spring beneath the property, which had been unused, and forgotten, for a number of decades. The company restored the spring as the group's water source, putting into place a new filter system. Control of its own water provided a significant cost savings for the company. At the same time, the spring water also enabled the company to improve the quality of its beers as well.

Despite long-term efforts to revitalize the U.K. ale market, notably through the Campaign for Real Ale, sales of lager continued to surpass sales of traditional British ales. At the same time, foreign lager brands, many of which were nonetheless brewed in the United Kingdom, also dominated the market. Even still the Dusanj brothers saw the opportunity for launching a truly British lager. In 2003 this led Cain to release its Premium British Lager, claiming it as the first lager to be developed and produced in the United Kingdom.

Cain had success with other recipes as well. The company introduced its Organic Wheat Beer in mid-2008. Cain also found success with its entry into the relatively young category of fruit-based beers, launching Fine Raisin Beer in 2003; in 2007 this beer won the first place award for fruit-based beer in the annual World Beer Awards, sponsored by the *Beers of the World* magazine.

EXPANSION LEADS TO FINANCIAL DIFFICULTIES

With the company's sales rising, the Dusanj brothers now sought to expand the company nationally for the first time. For this, the company began negotiating with the country's major supermarkets, and by 2008 had succeeded in winning a place on the shelves of the Morrisons supermarket chain.

As part of its expansion effort, Cain had also been taken public, gaining a listing on the London Stock Exchange in 2007. This was achieved through the reverse takeover of the larger Honeycombe Leisure, a pub operator with an estate of 100 pubs. The newly enlarged company, now Cains Beer Company Ltd., had more than doubled in size, topping £40 million by the end of the year.

The deal, which cost the company £37 million, also proved a heavy financial burden for the company. By early 2008 Cains had slipped into losses, which neared £3 million. Cains was equally hard hit by a ban on smoking that went into effect for the entire British brewery, pubs, and restaurant sector that year. By August of that year, the company's half-year losses had surged to £4.6 million.

As a result, the company was forced into receivership when Bank of Scotland refused to provide backing for the Dusanj brothers' business plan. Bank of Scotland then announced that it was putting the company up for sale. Among the bidders for the business was Marketing Management Services International, an investment group, which controlled a small brewery on the Isle of Arran and had announced plans to build up its own brewery portfolio.

The Dusanj brothers, who retained ownership of the Toxteth brewery facility itself, had not given up on Cains. In September 2008, the brothers returned to Bank of Scotland with an offer to buy back the company from its creditors. If successful, the Dusanj brothers expected to continue Cains tradition as Liverpool's most popular beer.

M. L. Cohen

PRINCIPAL COMPETITORS

Fuller Smith & Turner P.L.C.; Greene King Plc; Marston's Plc; Young & Co.'s Brewery P.L.C.; Compass Group PLC; Scottish & Newcastle plc; Luminar Group Holdings PLC; Punch Taverns plc; Mitchells and Butlers PLC; Enterprise Inns plc; Whitbread Group PLC; J D Wetherspoon plc.

FURTHER READING

"Brewery Is up for Sale," *Grocer,* April 27, 2002, p. 54.

"Brothers Toast Future of Pubs Group After Business Deal," *Birmingham Post* (U.K.), May 16, 2007, p. 23.

"Cains Beer Goes Flat As Losses Mount and Jobs Threatened," *Birmingham Post* (U.K.), August 8, 2008, p. 21.

"Cains Shuts 24 Pubs," *Liverpool Echo,* August 26, 2008, p. 1.

Gleeson, Bill, "Cains Aims to Become a National Household Name," *Liverpool Daily Post,* March 1, 2008, p. 12.

Hamilton, Douglas, "MMSI Blows Froth off Bid for Cains Beer," *Herald* (Glasgow), August 23, 2008, p. 23.

Hodgson, Neil, "Cains Launch First UK Pint in a Can," *Liverpool Echo,* January 11, 2008, p. 24.

"Honeycombe Reaps Sweet Harvest As Turnover Leaps," *Caterer & Hotelkeeper,* July 25, 2002, p. 10.

Houghton, Alistair, "Cains Makes Loss of £2.8m over 14 Months," *Liverpool Daily Post,* April 11, 2008, p. 15.

Jones, Adam, "FT Business School Case Study: Cains Beer," *Financial Times,* May 27, 2008.

Turnbull, Barry, "Cains' Output Highest Since 19th Century," *Liverpool Daily Post,* May 7, 2008, p. 1.

Turner, Alex, "Dusanj Brothers Move to Buy Back Cains," *Liverpool Daily Post,* September 3, 2008, p. 1.

Campagna-Turano Bakery, Inc.

—————————■—————————

6501 West Roosevelt Road
Berwyn, Illinois 60402-1100
U.S.A.
Telephone: (708) 788-9220
Toll Free: (800) 458-5662
Fax: (708) 788-3075
Web site: http://www.turanobakery.com

Private Company
Incorporated: 1966
Employees: 600
Sales: $100 million (2008 est.)
NAICS: 311812 Commercial Bakeries

■ ■ ■

Doing business as Turano Baking Company, Campagna-Turano Bakery, Inc., is a Berwyn, Illinois-based bakery wholesaler specializing in European-style artisan breads. The family-owned-and-operated company sells its products to Chicago-area grocery stores, including such major chains as Jewel Food Stores and Dominick's Finer Foods, as well as independent grocers. Grocery store products include Italian bread, French bread, Vienna bread, a wide variety of sandwich rolls, and plain and Italian bread crumbs. Turano also serves foodservice customers in major markets in Illinois, Wisconsin, and northwest Indiana, and provides custom manufacturing for several large national foodservice companies. Food-service products are available fully baked or partially baked (par-baked) and include Italian table breads, French breads, sandwich rolls, hamburger and hot dog buns, bagels, muffins, cannoli, chewy cookies, and biscotti. All told, Turano serves 35 of the top 100 national restaurant chains.

Turano maintains three production facilities in Illinois. The original plant, 100,000 square feet in size, is located in Berwyn and produces more than 120 bread items on four semiautomated lines. Specialty breads are also produced in small runs. Comparable in size is the Bolingbrook, Illinois, plant, which possesses the European-style equipment needed to automatically turn out fully baked or par-baked French bread and rolls. It includes a kneaded-dough baking facility, which makes frozen products for the company's national accounts, as well as for a joint venture with Sara Lee Bakery that also markets the frozen and par-baked products across the country. A 15,000-square-foot facility and pastry shop is maintained in Bloomingdale, Illinois, devoted to the baking of specialty bread items and cookies, cakes, and other sweet goods. Two new plants in Atlanta, Georgia, and Orlando, Florida, also turn out par-baked products. The company is run by the second generation of the Turano family, with a third generation beginning to assume top management positions.

TURANO FAMILY COMES TO THE UNITED STATES: 1922

Campagna-Turano Bakery, Inc., was created when brothers Carmen and Mariano Turano combined their bakeries. They hailed from Castrolibero, Calabria, Italy. Carmen, the eldest, came to the United States in 1922 and settled in Chicago. There he and his wife opened a small grocery store, in the back of which was

COMPANY PERSPECTIVES

The Turano Baking Company creates authentic, crusty breads from treasured family recipes, including one favorite dating back to 424 B.C.

a small bakery. When Mariano followed his brother to Chicago in 1955, he worked in construction digging ditches and also helped out at the store. The father of three sons, he had been a coffee salesman in Italy and wanted to start his own business, but was thwarted in that goal because he was not fluent in the English language. He returned home to Italy somewhat chastened, but soon concluded that his home country offered little hope for his young sons, and so he returned to Chicago and being a laborer.

On weekends Mariano began baking bread in the back of his brother's store, making use of the lessons taught to him by his mother. He used her recipes to bake authentic Calabresi-style breads, two-pound round loaves, which he then shared with friends and relatives who were also Italian born and missed the breads they had once enjoyed. Mariano's breads became so popular that people began asking him for loaves to take home. In this way he started a business and in 1958 he brought over his family. His sons helped him to bake 200 loaves of bread each weekend, which he then delivered to Italian households in a used Chevrolet, charging fewer than 50 cents for a two-pound loaf.

Mariano saved his money and in 1962 bought the Campagna Bakery on the northwest side of Chicago. In 1965 another brother, Eugenio Turano, became manager of the 1,000-square-foot bakery. With his used station wagon, Mariano made home deliveries several days a week and during the other days sold bread out of the shop, as well as authentic pizza, similar to a contemporary focaccia, essentially thick bread covered in tomato sauce and cheese.

FAMILY BAKERIES COMBINED: 1966

Carmen Turano, in the meantime, acquired a local bakery as well, renaming it the Turano Bakery. It offered products similar to Campagna's and served the same type of customers. In 1966 the brothers decided to join forces and merge their operations into a new bakery. Carmen was now nearing retirement age and agreed to the merger and to his younger brothers running the business, provided his children were involved. The result

was the Campagna-Turano Bakery built at 6441 West Roosevelt in Berwyn. In the beginning it was a retail bakery, 3,000 square feet in size, that made its mark with a popular four-pound loaf of bread. The first truck was purchased, replacing the station wagon for making deliveries.

The bakery expanded beyond Calabresi-style breads in 1967, adding French and Vienna breads, kaiser rolls, and Mamma Susi Pizzas. After building up a clientele, the bakery in the late 1960s and early 1970s expanded into wholesale, distributing its specialty hearth breads and rolls to Chicago-area supermarkets, delicatessens, and foodservice customers. Mamma Susi Pizzas, precooked and frozen in a pan, provided entrée to the supermarket trade. It was a product unique for the time and extremely popular. The supermarkets and other grocery stores had been Turano's competitors, but the company was interested in selling through the retail channels. The supermarkets also wanted to carry the pizzas, and soon an accommodation was reached so that Turano was not supplying stores while at the same time acting against the interests of their customers. Home deliveries were ceased, and now Turano trucks visited only grocery store customers, supplying them with bread and rolls as well as pizzas.

Turano also cracked the restaurant channel in an innovative way. After making their store deliveries, the Turano brothers often stopped for lunch at a restaurant and insisted on supplying their own bread, which they felt confident was far superior to what the restaurant had to offer. They would ask the chef to have the bread sliced, and invariably the chef would try it, and the brothers would invariably give him a loaf to take home. In some cases, other diners would see the bread on the table and ask for it as well. In this way, Turano began developing a roster of restaurant customers for the bakery.

PASTRY SHOP OPENS: 1974

As some of these restaurant and foodservice customers grew larger, Turano Bakery kept pace, expanding its Berwyn operation and delivering farther and farther away, northwest to Green Bay and Madison, Wisconsin, southwest to St. Louis, and southeast to Indianapolis. It was Eugenio Turano who developed the techniques for the mass baking of bread to meet the growing demand. The Turano family also became involved in the pastry business. In 1974 they opened a pastry shop in Bloomingdale, Illinois, which would evolve into the company's sweet goods operation that would produce and ship goods locally and nationally.

KEY DATES

1962: Mariano Turano acquires Chicago's Campagna Bakery.
1966: Campagna Bakery merges with Turano Bakery to form Campagna-Turano Bakery, Inc.
1974: Turano pastry shop opens in Bloomingdale, Illinois.
1989: Mariano Turano dies.
1994: New plant opens in Bolingbrook, Illinois.
1997: Joint venture is formed with Sara Lee Bakery.
2008: New plants open in Atlanta and Orlando.

Growing up, Mariano's sons—Renato, Umberto, and Giancarlo—had learned the business by helping out, from baking bread to more mundane chores such as cleaning up and making home deliveries. They had assumed leadership roles by the time their father died in 1989. Turano was generating about $25 million in annual revenues by this point and its name was well established in the Chicago market, so much so that it had emerged as the chief rival to Gonnella Baking Company, a 100-year-old Chicago bakery that was the market leader with approximately $32 million in annual sales. Moreover, Turano had managed to survive the onslaught of other Chicago Italian bakeries that had exploded onto the market in the early 1980s.

While both Turano and Gonnella offered similar lines of breads and rolls and delivered to grocery stores, specialty stores, and restaurants, Turano had a reputation for being more daring, while Gonnella was more conservative by nature. It was Turano, for example, that in the late 1980s began offering soft breadsticks, which became a signature item for the Olive Garden Italian restaurant chain, and Gonnella quickly followed suit. Turano also ventured beyond bread to begin offering imported pasta products under its own label. Gonnella could be an innovator as well, however. When it introduced a frozen garlic bread, Turano countered with its own frozen garlic bread in early 1990. The freezer case was perhaps the most competitive section of the supermarket, even more than the "knee-knocker" racks where specialty breads were displayed in front of supermarket delicatessens, or even the bread aisle, yet Turano raised the stakes again by introducing frozen cannoli.

In the late 1980s and early 1990s Turano expanded its foodservice operation, spurred in large part by the

national aspirations of some of its casual restaurants, pizza, and sandwich shop customers who began to see the advantage of serving quality warm breads and rolls to diners. To meet the need and ship its products greater distances, Turano looked to par-baked bread and rolls, which were about 90 percent baked, with the final minutes of baking completed onsite. The par-baked products proved so popular that by 1993 Turano had outgrown its Berwyn facility, which at the time was 65,000 square feet in size, and began making plans to open a second, more automated plant.

NEW PLANT OPENS: 1994

In 1994 Turano opened a 92,000-square-foot plant in Bolingbrook, Illinois. In order to mass produce fully baked and par-baked French baguettes, sub rolls, dinner rolls, and soft breadsticks, the company installed two state-of-the-art, high-speed production lines supplied by a French equipment maker. As a result the Berwyn plant could now focus all of its attention on fresh product for the Chicago-Milwaukee metropolitan markets. Turano anticipated that the two Bolingbrook lines would be able to accommodate demand through the end of the decade, but just six months after the plant opened in late 1994, a third line was installed. Only six more months would pass before the company added two more lines, and a sixth line would follow a few years later. Turano was now able to supply foodservice customers in 40 states.

In the 1990s Turano benefited from a trend that made hearth-baked products more mainstream, creating a need to install more lines in the Bolingbrook facility. Its capacity would be put to even greater use when Turano forged a joint venture with Sara Lee Bakery in 1997, a move that greatly enhanced Turano's foodservice distribution and market penetration across the United States. Under the terms of the arrangement, the Bolingbrook plant supplied Italian and French breads on a wholesale basis to Sara Lee, which in turn distributed them to foodservice customers and retail grocers under the Sara Lee brand as well as the Turano Old World Baker brand. For Sara Lee, the venture provided immediate entry into the flourishing specialty bread category, while Turano was able to tap into Sara Lee's extensive distribution capabilities.

In 1998 Turano launched its Pane di Campagna program, taking advantage of its experience serving foodservice customers across the country to further its retail and in-store bakery business. Turano offered retail and in-store bakery customers a turnkey merchandising solution. Not only would it provide fully baked or par-baked hearth breads, but Turano also supplied the packaging with the nutrition information along with the customer's brand. The Pane di Campagna brand was also made available to the stores, and should they prefer neither, the simple "country breads" banner was provided.

The last of the original Turano brothers, Eugenio, died in 1998. Renato Turano, a member of the second generation of the family, was now president; Anthony Turano was now an executive vice-president in charge of production and operations; and Giancarlo Turano was a vice-president overseeing sales and marketing. Soon after Eugenio Turano passed away, the third generation began to enter the ranks of the family company. After graduating from the Cornell University Hotel School in 1998, Joseph Turano worked for E. & J. Gallo Winery before joining Turano; within a few years he was named the company's operations manager. Another third-generation member, Giancarlo Turano II, also graduated from Cornell University, in 2001. He served as a consultant for HVS International before joining Turano. He too rose quickly through the ranks, becoming national sales manager.

Turano's president, Renato Turano, turned 65 in 2008, bringing closer the day that the third generation would take the helm of the company. He was also spending a large portion of his time getting involved in Italian national politics. In 2006 Italy reconfigured its legislature to allow representation of expatriate Italian citizens, and Turano ran for the Senate to represent more than 350,000 Italian citizens in North America. He won his election in April 2006 and became one of six senators and 12 deputies to represent expatriate Italians. He would now have less time to devote to Turano, spending part of each week in Rome to participate in Senate proceedings, and in addition paying visits to his immense legislative district.

NEW PLANT OPENINGS: 2008

The new century not only brought fresh blood but also new challenges. Popular low-carbohydrate diets hurt overall bread sales in the early years of the first decade of the 2000s, but rather than give ground and develop a less-tasty low-carb bread, Turano championed full-carb bread in 2003, spending $10 million on a "Bread for Life" marketing campaign in the Chicago area. The company did not see a decrease in sales. Rather, it actually benefited from another trend, the growing popularity of whole-grain and rustic artisan breads. In 2008 Turano opened new plants in Atlanta and Orlando, primarily to produce par-baked products. With sales around $100 million, Turano was well positioned to take an even more prominent role on the national stage and grow sales to a much higher level.

Ed Dinger

PRINCIPAL SUBSIDIARIES

Turano Baking Company; Turano Pastry Shops, Inc.

PRINCIPAL COMPETITORS

Gonnella Baking Co.; La Brea Holdings, Inc.; Ralcorp Frozen Bakery Products, Inc.

FURTHER READING

Chang, Rita, "Low-Carb Not Taking Bite Out of Turano," *Crain's Chicago Business,* July 12, 2004, p. 6.

Crown, Judith, "Breaking with Bread; Rival Italian Bakers Seek Dough in Pasta, Frozen Foods," *Crain's Chicago Business,* November 12, 1990, p. 19.

Malovany, Dan, "Artists at Work," *Snack Food & Wholesale Baker,* July 1998.

Pridmore, Jay, "The Breadwinner," *University of Chicago Magazine,* March–April 2008, p. 16.

Sullivan, JeanMarie, and Dan Malovany, "The Rustic Bread Revolution," *Bakery Production and Marketing,* April 24, 1995, p. 18.

Waters, Jennifer, "Sara Lee Bakery, Turano Will Make Dough Together," *Crain's Chicago Business,* February 24, 1997, p. 4.

Canada Bread Company, Limited

10 Four Seasons Place
Toronto, Ontario M9B 6H7
Canada
Telephone: (416) 926-2000
Fax: (416) 926-2018
Web site: http://investor.mapleleaf.ca/phoenix.
zhtml?c=189491&p=irol-irhome

Public Subsidiary of Maple Leaf Foods Inc.
Incorporated: 1911
Employees: 8,800
Sales: CAD 1.5 billion (2007)
Stock Exchanges: Toronto
Ticker Symbol: CBY
NAICS: 311812 Commercial Bakeries

■ ■ ■

Canada Bread Company, Limited is a Toronto-based manufacturer and distributor of flour-based bakery products. The company divides its business between two operating segments: Fresh Bakery Group and Frozen Bakery Group. Fresh Bakery products include sliced breads, artisan breads, and rolls, packaged under several brands, including Ben's, Dempster's, Healthy Way, McGavin's, Olafson's, and POM. In addition, the group offers tortillas, pitas, and other flatbreads; sweet goods, including cakes, cookies, doughnuts, pies, and tarts; as well as breakfast and snack products such as bagels, English muffins, waffles, and fruit breads. Also included in the group are fresh and frozen pasta and sauce sold under the Olivieri label. The group maintains 22 regional bakeries, serving all of Canada and the northeastern and northwestern United States.

Canada Bread's Frozen Bakery Group is one of North America's major providers of par-baked breads, products that are partially baked and then frozen, with the baking completed by the end user. Products include artisan and specialty breads, bagels, croissants, rolls, flatbreads, and frozen pie and tart shells. Serving the retail grocery, club store, and foodservice channels in Canada, the United States, and Asia, the group offers both private-label products and such brand labels as Bistolls dinner and sandwich rolls, California Goldminer sourdough breads, Dempster's Home Bakery breads, Grace Baking artisan breads, Maison Cousin crusty breads and rolls, and Tenderflake frozen pie shells. Production takes place in five Canadian bakery operations, and plants in three U.S. cities. The head office is also located in the United States, in Chicago. Although a public company listed on the Toronto Stock Exchange, Canada Bread is 89.8 percent owned by Maple Leaf Foods Inc.

Maple Leaf Bakery U.K. is part of the Frozen Bakery Group, and a leading specialty bakery in the United Kingdom producing bagels, croissants, Italian ciabatta, and other specialty bakery products in the U.K. and European markets. Maple Leaf Bakery U.K. operates seven facilities and employs approximately 1,200 people in the United Kingdom.

CANADA BREAD FORMED: 1911

Canada Bread was founded in August 1911 when several Canadian baking concerns were brought together, representing a combined capital of CAD 575,000 and an estimated net worth of CAD 5 million. Credited with the idea was C. R. Morden, a Niagara-area businessman, but it was a young Toronto financier, 29-year-old Cawthra Mulock, who made it a reality. Mulock was the son of one of Toronto's most prominent lawyers. His great-aunt left him an estate of about CAD 2.7 million when he was just 15, earning him the nickname "the boy millionaire." The money was parceled out to him in installments after he turned 21, allowing him to participate in a number of business ventures, including the building of Toronto's landmark Royal Alexandra Theatre and the Maple Leaf Milling Company. The latter was incorporated in 1904 and Mulock served as a vice-president, becoming responsible for executing the mergers that resulted in Canada Bread. He also owned a controlling stake in Canada Bread and served as its first president.

Canada Bread brought together the bakeries of George Weston, Mark Bredin, and Henry C. Tomlin of Toronto; Winnipeg's William J. Boyd; and Enoh James Stuart of Montreal. While little is known about Tomlin and Stuart, the other bakers were prominent figures of their times. George Weston, for example, was a baker's assistant who got his start maintaining a pair of bread routes. He built on this success to open a bread and cake bakery, Weston's Model Bakery, in Toronto in 1896. By the time he agreed to merge his bakery with the other Canada Bread founders, his Toronto operation was supplying more than 500 stores. Unlike some of the others, however, he had no interest in remaining involved with Canada Bread. In addition to selling his interest in Model Bakery for CAD 1 million, he agreed to stay out of the bread business, although he continued to bake cakes and cookies.

When his noncompete agreement was completed, he returned to the bread business by acquiring the H.C. Tomlin bakery located across the street from Canada Bread. It was presumably a venture of another Canada Bread founder, Henry Tomlin. After Weston's death in

1924, the business was taken over by his son Garfield Weston, who took the company public and nurtured it into George Weston Limited, one of Canada's largest food processors and distributors, and parent of Weston Foods Inc., involved in baked goods and other products.

Another of the Canada Bread founders was William Boyd, who at the age of 23 came to Winnipeg in 1885, establishing a confectionery business. Later he acquired Bateman Bread Company, which he would contribute (as Boyd Bakeries) to the holdings of Canada Bread, while concentrating on his confectionery business, Boyd Candy Company. The last of the Canada Bread founders was Mark Bredin. Born in Dublin, Ireland, Bredin immigrated to Canada as a 20-year-old in 1883, settling in Toronto, where he and his brother started a small bakery. In 1902 the business had grown so large that they opened a new state-of-the-industry plant, making the Bredin Bread Company one of Toronto's largest bakeries. It was Mark Bredin who succeeded Mulock as Canada Bread's president shortly after the company was formed. (Mulock would die young, just 36 when he became one of the victims of the Spanish influenza epidemic that swept the globe in 1918 and took as many as 100 million lives.)

NAME CHANGE: 1969

Bredin served as Canada Bread's president and general manager until his retirement in 1929. Although taken public, Canada Bread remained a majority owned company by Maple Leaf Milling. As such it became Canada's largest bread company. In October 1969 it changed its name to Corporate Foods Limited. The company did not limit itself to bread, however. It made investments in other areas as well, including the Gold-strike Mine in Nevada. In 1988 it acquired the Olivieri pasta business. By this stage sales topped the $100 million level.

A major U.K. food company, Hillsdown Holdings PLC, acquired Maple Leaf Mills and in 1990 acquired a controlling interest in Canada Packers Inc. The two units were brought together in 1991 as Maple Leaf Foods, which held a 66 percent stake in Corporate Foods. A year later Maple Leaf Foods made a bid to purchase 100 percent of Corporate Foods. Minority shareholders rejected the offer and Corporate Foods remained a public company, although it continued to be closely allied with Maple Leaf Foods. Later in 1992 Maple Leaf Foods sold McGavin Foods, the largest bakery company in Western Canada, to Corporate Foods, a move that strengthened Corporate Foods' national footprint.

Other acquisitions were to follow in the 1990s as Corporate Foods continued to expand. In the summer

1911: Canada Bread Company is formed.
1969: Name is changed to Corporate Foods Limited.
1988: Olivieri pasta brand is acquired.
1997: Canada Bread name is readopted.
2001: Multi-Marques Foods is acquired.
2002: Maple Leaf Foods' subsidiaries are acquired.
2007: Rising wheat prices hurt bakers worldwide.
2008: Aliments Martel Inc. is acquired.

of 1993 it acquired Dough Delight, a company with CAD 75 million in sales of frozen baked and unbaked pretzels, bagels, pizza dough, coffee cakes, Danish pastries, and croissants. About 30 percent of Dough Delight sales came from the United States. Corporate Foods' revenues also kept pace, topping CAD 200 million in 1992 and increasing to CAD 478.2 million in 1995. Net income also grew from CAD 15.5 million to CAD 21.9 million.

RETURN TO CANADA BREAD NAME: 1997

It was at this point that Corporate Foods elected to concentrate on its Canadian production operations and position the company as Canada's only national bakery company, although it planned to grow its export business as well, primarily in the United States. A major reason for this approach was consolidation in the grocery industry, with larger supermarket chains requiring vendors with a larger footprint to meet their needs. In keeping with the plan, management brought together its regional baking companies, reverting to the Canada Bread name in 1997, and uniting the bakeries under this common banner. It then built upon its fresh bakery business by acquiring Vancouver-based Venice Bakery, which brought with it CAD 36 million in sales of breads and rolls. Canada Bread also acquired Newfoundland's West Coast Bakery, and its Olivieri pasta and sauce brand was taken national through the acquisition of Bella Pasta, in Stoney Creek, Ontario. In keeping with maintaining company management in the country of operation, the company sold Chicago-based Brooklyn Bagels Boys, Inc., to Maple Leaf Foods in early 1997.

After posting sales of CAD 540.3 million and net earnings of CAD 25 million in 1996, Canada Bread continued to pursue its new strategy. At the start of 1997 the company began construction on a new CAD 26 million bakery in Calgary. Capable of producing fresh and frozen products for both the Canadian and U.S. markets, it opened later in the year. Canada Bread took its Dempster brand national in 1997, operating alongside the company's regional Canadian brands: Butternut in the east and McGavin's in the west. The Dempster's line was then expanded in 1998 with the national rollout of several new products: Dempster's Premium Bagels, Dempster's Hot & Crusty frozen retail bread and rolls, Dempster's Flatbreads of the World, and Dempster's Delicioso Italian bread.

The year was marred, however, by severe growing pains, as Canada Bread found it difficult to convert its regional bakery network into a streamlined national structure, struggling to consolidate management and administrative functions and ironing out problems in franchised delivery routes. One positive development in 1998 was the acquisition of Hamilton Baking Company, Limited, another bread and rolls baking operation. At the end of 1998 both Chairman Archibald C. McLean and CEO David H. Lees stepped down.

NEW MANAGEMENT TEAM: 1999

Canada Bread began 1999 with a fresh management team, headed by Chairman Richard A. Lan, and President and CEO Roger M. Dickhout, who was charged with leading a corporate turnaround. They led a resurgence in 1999, when Canada Bread sales grew from CAD 508.44 million in 1998 to CAD 567.25 million. Net income also increased from CAD 2.9 million to CAD 6.3 million. To help maintain its momentum, Canada Bread beefed up the senior and middle-level ranks of executives in 2000 and implemented a new evaluation and reward system to draw out optimum performance. Hundreds of underperforming products were eliminated, while new products, developed with the help of market research, were unveiled, including Dempster's Original White Bread with Fibre and the new WholeGrains bread products. Although sales slipped to CAD 553.7 million in 2000, Canada Bread increased earnings to CAD 17.24 million.

In 2001 Canada Bread became a fully national company by increasing its 25 percent interest in Multi-Marques Foods of Quebec to 100 percent. Canada Bread and Multi-Marques had a 30-year relationship, and now with the business in the fold, Canada Bread filled in a gap in its footprint, especially the fresh bread business in Quebec and Atlantic Canada. The company expanded its frozen bread business as well. Moreover, Canada Bread became involved in the sweet-goods business through the acquisition and added three new brands to its portfolio: Ben's, Bon Matin, and POM. The company also took advantage of the addition of

Multi-Marques to launch a "New Beginnings" improvement campaign that included plans to upgrade all of the company's manufacturing facilities in 2002.

In April 2002, Dickhout left Canada Bread having achieved his goal and set a new course for the company; Lan took over as CEO while relinquishing the chairmanship. Under Lan's watch the company grew further in 2002 through the acquisition of Olafson's Baking Company, Inc., a British Columbia baker of premium products, adding about CAD 30 million in annual sales. An even more important deal was completed later in the year when Canada Bread acquired Maple Leaf Food's U.S. bakery business and the U.K. Maple Leaf businesses for CAD 266 million. As a result, Canada Bread became the market leader in the U.S. par-baked category and the U.K. bagel category. With these additions and a full year's contribution from Multi-Marques, Canada Bread generated sales of CAD 1.03 billion in 2002 and net earnings of CAD 38.7 million.

HARVESTIME LIMITED BAKERY ACQUIRED: 2006

Canada Bread enjoyed steady growth in the middle years of the first decade of the 2000s, spurred by the introduction of new multigrain products in response to the popularity of low-carbohydrate diets. Maple Leaf Foods also increased its stake in the company to almost 90 percent.

In the United Kingdom, Canada Bread's Rotherham plant was twice doubled in size and became one of the country's largest specialty bakery operations. The unit grew even larger in 2006 with the acquisition of Walsall, England-based Harvestime Limited Bakery, a producer of par-baked products for the in-store bakery market; and Avance (U.K.) Ltd. and The French Croissant Company Ltd., maker of premium croissants. Canada Bread also became involved in the prepackaged sandwich business in 2006 through the acquisition of Toronto-based Royal Touch Foods.

Canada Bread, like all of the world's bakery concerns, had to contend with a spike in the price of wheat in 2007. Rather than pass all of the increases on to consumers, the company looked to lower production costs by upgrading manufacturing and distribution operations. Nevertheless, sales increased to CAD 1.51 billion and net income to CAD 84 million. The company's growth program continued in 2008 with the acquisition of Aliments Martel Inc., a Quebec maker of sandwiches, meals, and sweet goods with CAD 54 million in annual sales.

Ed Dinger

PRINCIPAL OPERATING UNITS

Fresh Bakery Group; Frozen Bakery Group.

PRINCIPAL COMPETITORS

George Weston Limited; Grupo Bimbo, S.A.B. de C.V.; Nature's Path Foods, Inc.

FURTHER READING

Avery, Simon, "Investors Build Appetite for New-Look Canada Bread," *Financial Post,* August 15, 1997, p. 17.

"Consolidation, Canadian-Style," *Snack Food & Wholesale Bakery,* February 2001, p. 8.

Dictionary of Canadian Biography, Vol. XV, Toronto: University of Toronto, 2005.

"Externally Focused," *Snack Food & Wholesale Bakery,* September 2001, p. 30.

Hopkins, J. Castell, *Canadian Annual Review of Public Affairs 1911,* Toronto: Annual Review Publishing Company.

"Mark Bredin," *New York Times,* October 20, 1935.

CF Industries Holdings, Inc.

———— ■ ————

4 Parkway North, Suite 400
Deerfield, Illinois 60015
U.S.A.
Telephone: (847) 405-2400
Fax: (847) 267-1004
Web site: http://www.cfindustries.com

Public Company
Incorporated: 1946 as Central Farmers Fertilizer Co.
Employees: 1,400
Sales: $2.76 billion (2007)
Stock Exchanges: New York
Ticker Symbol: CF
NAICS: 325311 Nitrogenous Fertilizer Manufacturing;
325312 Phosphatic Fertilizer Manufacturing

■ ■ ■

CF Industries Holdings, Inc., is one of the world's top fertilizer producers. The Illinois-based firm supplies North America with a quarter of its nitrogen and a fifth of its phosphate fertilizer, although its customers are largely located in the midwestern United States. CF operates nitrogen plants in southern Louisiana and Alberta, Canada (the latter through a joint venture); a phosphate mining and processing operation in Florida; and related distribution facilities. The company has boosted its exports through Swiss fertilizer trading company Keytrade AG, in which it bought a 50 percent stake in during 2007.

BEGINNINGS

CF Industries was founded in 1946 as a fertilizer brokerage operation called Central Farmers Fertilizer Co. (CFFC) by a group of regional agricultural cooperatives. Initially distributing fertilizer sourced from outside producers, the Chicago-based firm soon bought a minority stake in a nitrogen plant in Lawrence, Kansas. Nitrogen, applied as liquid ammonia or in solid granular forms such as urea, was generally made from natural gas. One of the three most-used fertilizers, it was essential for growing a variety of plants including corn and grains, which were among the top crops its cooperative owners produced. Other key fertilizers included potassium and phosphorus, which were largely mined from the earth as potash and phosphate, respectively.

In the 1950s CFFC attempted to develop a phosphate mine and processing plant in Idaho, but it was hampered by cost overruns and the cooperatives became unwilling to fund it any longer. The debacle led to a change of leadership, with Ken Lundberg appointed manager and E. V. Stevenson named board chair. The Idaho Phosphate Works project was subsequently shut down, and a financial reorganization implemented in which the value of CFFC ownership shares was written down by two-thirds.

In 1962 CFFC and three other farm cooperatives formed Central Nitrogen, Inc., to build a $20 million fertilizer plant in Terre Haute, Indiana. When operational in 1963, it would make 350 tons of ammonia per day. The firm also took stakes in National Potash Co., which owned a mine in New Mexico, and

COMPANY PERSPECTIVES

Corporate Vision: We will be recognized as a leading global marketer, producer and supplier of high-quality, low-cost fertilizer products and services, creating sustained value for shareholders, customers and employees.

St. Paul Ammonia Products, which operated a plant in Minnesota.

Seeking greater supplies of nitrogen fertilizer, in the mid-1960s CFFC announced plans to build a 1,000-ton-a-day ammonia plant in Donaldsonville, Louisiana, which would be completed in 1969. It was built by a company called First Nitrogen Corp., which would be co-owned by two member cooperatives before being acquired in full by the firm.

In early 1969 CFFC bought Central Phosphates, Inc., of Bartow, Florida, from International Minerals and Chemical Corp. The mine and processing facility, the largest of its kind, could produce 1.2 million tons of phosphate fertilizer per year. The move was considered a gamble because phosphate prices were then below the cost of production, but it soon paid off when they increased to a profitable level.

NAME CHANGE TO CF INDUSTRIES IN 1971

In 1970 CFFC bought a 49 percent stake in a Saskatchewan, Canada, potash plant owned by Noranda Mines, Ltd., which would run it. In 1971 CEO Ken Lundberg left the company and Donaldsonville Facility Manager R. R. "Barney" Baxter was named to head the firm. Soon afterward, its name was changed to CF Industries, Inc.

In 1972 CF started a multi-year, $65 million expansion program that would include a new 1,000-ton-a-day urea plant in Donaldsonville and a 250,000-ton-a-year phosphate plant in Plant City, Florida, as well as distribution warehouses, terminals, and a refrigerated storage tank. Owned by one Canadian and 17 U.S. cooperatives, CF was now the largest fertilizer producer in the United States.

Despite a sometimes difficult economic climate in the early 1970s, expansion was ongoing and in 1976 the firm joined with three Canadian cooperatives to build a nitrogen complex in Medicine Hat, Alberta, for $230.2 million. CF would take a 66 percent stake in the joint venture, which was operated under the name Canadian Fertilizers, Ltd. During the year the firm's headquarters were also moved to a new building in Long Grove, Illinois.

Other investments made by CF in the 1970s included ammonia storage facilities on rivers at St. Paul, Minnesota, and Kingston Mines, Illinois, and an inland site in eastern Illinois that was served by a pipeline. The company also bought a stake in barge transportation firm AgriTrans Corp., which would carry fertilizer north from Donaldsonville and grain south to the Gulf Coast.

In 1978 CF and Farmers Chemical Association were awarded $23.8 million by a judge to settle a lawsuit against oil company Transco, which they claimed had not honored a supply contract. A year later the firm sold its 49 percent stake in the Saskatchewan potash operation to Noranda Mines Ltd., after which it would continue to purchase potash from the Canadian firm.

By the start of the 1980s CF Industries had become the largest fertilizer supplier in the world, with over $1 billion in annual sales. It sold about ten million tons per year, 80 percent of which it produced. The company's cooperative owners distributed it to about one million farmers in 44 U.S. states and two Canadian provinces. The work was highly seasonal, with spring the critical time for distribution because farmers applied fertilizer at the start of the growing season.

In January 1985 40-year-old Executive Vice-President and COO Robert G. Liuzzi, who had joined the company as a lawyer ten years earlier, took over as president and CEO from R. R. Baxter. Two years later CF sold its Louisiana oil and gas properties to Kelly Oil Corp. for $5.5 million.

In 1991 CF proposed a land swap with officials in Florida, seeking a site where it planned a slightly radioactive gypsum waste storage area. The land the county was to receive would be used for a waterway linking a well field, and the proposal generated significant public comment. After several years of debate the exchange and gypsum deposit were approved, with CF agreeing to create a 1,900-acre wildlife preserve on the land. In 1992 the firm also offered to buy out homeowners in a Donaldsonville subdivision whose residents had complained their homes were devalued by proximity to CF facilities.

MORE DONALDSONVILLE IMPROVEMENTS COMPLETED IN 1993

In 1993 an $85 million upgrade was completed in Donaldsonville that included new urea and nitric acid

KEY DATES

1946: Central Farmers Fertilizer Co. is founded by agricultural cooperatives.

1960s: Company forms joint venture to build nitrogen facilities in Louisiana.

1969: Phosphate mine is acquired in Florida.

1971: Firm shortens name to CF Industries, Inc.

1970s: Company expands Louisiana, Florida production facilities.

1976: Joint venture in Alberta, Canada, is formed to build nitrogen plant.

1990s: Company completes new round of expansion in Louisiana and Florida.

2002: CF amends mission to emphasize financial stability over serving owners' needs.

2003: Forward Pricing Program is launched to reduce risks from gas price increases.

2005: Initial public offering on NYSE nets $622 million for cooperative owners.

2007: Company acquires stake in Swiss fertilizer trader Keytrade AG; wins Peruvian gas bid.

plants, and in 1994 the company doubled Florida phosphate production through the acquisition of a new mine five miles away, to which it relocated and expanded a processing facility. The firm's ownership consisted of 11 cooperatives which represented more than one million farmers and ranchers in 46 U.S. states and two Canadian provinces.

In April 1994 about two dozen members of the Oil, Chemical, and Atomic Workers' union in Rosemount, Minnesota, went on strike against CF. The Mississippi River terminal facility workers were the company's only remaining unionized employees out of 1,500. They had picketed over the firm's efforts to create an open shop, and in June 1995 an administrative law judge ordered that they be rehired because the company had not bargained in good faith.

In 1995 CF began another $305 million round of improvements and additions in Donaldsonville that would boost production of liquid and solid urea by more than 50 percent, and early the next year the firm's new phosphate mine was opened in Florida. CF had a 25-year permit to operate the facility, which was expected to cover the lifetime of the mine's ore, and it agreed to observe strict environmental standards that included returning the site to its original state when mining was over. The firm was praised by the state

Department of Environmental Protection, and CF subsequently created a national watershed award that was presented each year to one corporation and six communities.

In the summer of 1997 the company traded 7.2 million tons of developed and permitted phosphate it owned in Florida for 20 million unpermitted and undeveloped reserves near its existing mine. In December 1999 CF announced plans for a joint venture with Cargill Fertilizer and IMC Global to build a $40 million facility in Tampa to melt sulfur, which was needed for the production of phosphate fertilizer. The necessary permits were received two years later, and it was built. For 1999 the firm had sales of $1.1 billion on sales of 9.2 million tons of fertilizer.

In May 2000 an explosion at an ammonia processing facility in the firm's Donaldsonville, Louisiana, complex killed three workers and injured eight others. CF was later fined $150,000 for 14 safety and health violations related to the blast, which was traced to a defective storage vessel.

FORWARD PRICING PROGRAM CREATED IN 2003

Faced with growing competition from inexpensive imported Russian fertilizer, in 2002 CF joined with other industry leaders to lobby Washington for higher import duties. The company also changed its corporate priorities to emphasize strong financial performance rather than simply meeting the fertilizer needs of its members. In 2003 the firm instituted the Forward Pricing Program, in which buyers locked in prices for new fertilizer orders based on the price of natural gas, which enabled the company to buy a corresponding amount of gas at a fixed price on the futures market.

During the year CF idled its Donaldsonville nitrogen operation for a time to await lower rates, as natural gas prices quadrupled due to a cold winter in the north. Natural gas comprised nearly 80 percent of the cost of ammonia and urea production. The company also received a revolving line of credit worth $140 million from Harris Savings Bank and other lenders in 2003, and bought an ammonia terminal in North Dakota from bankrupt Farmland Industries for $200,000.

With gas prices remaining high, in August 2004, 23 of the Donaldsonville plant's 447 employees were laid off, the first to be let go since the 1980s. Despite the rise in gas prices, 2004 was the firm's first profitable year since the late 1990s, with net earnings of $68 million on sales of $1.65 billion. The company's bottom line was improving due to the successful Forward Pricing Program, as well as from increased sales outside the cooperatives. Sales to its cooperative owners had declined from 75 percent of output in 2002, to just 53 percent of the approximately 8.75 million tons it produced in 2004. With a spate of bankruptcies and plant closings rocking the industry, the firm was also finding more demand in the marketplace. CF now provided 22 percent of the nitrogen fertilizer and 14 percent of the phosphate fertilizer sold in the United States.

PUBLIC OFFERING IN 2005

In the spring of 2005 CF filed for an initial public offering (IPO) on the New York Stock Exchange. After completion in August the company became a subsidiary of CF Industries Holdings, Inc., and the $622 million proceeds were distributed to its eight cooperative owners, which included Land O'Lakes, Inc., CHS, Inc., Growmark, Inc., Southern States Cooperative, Intermountain Farmers Cooperative, MFA Inc., Tennessee Farmers Cooperative, and La Coop Federee. After the IPO, only CHS and Growmark would retain stakes in the company. Top stakeholder Land O'Lakes received just over half of the total.

During the summer CF also sold its stake in Florida-based CF Martin Sulphur to Martin Midstream Partners LP for $18.8 million, and boosted its revolving credit line to $250 million.

Although located just 40 miles from New Orleans, the firm's Donaldsonville facility suffered only minor damage in Hurricane Katrina, having been shut down and evacuated in advance of the storm that devastated the Gulf Coast. The price of natural gas doubled shortly after the disaster, however, and the company was forced to idle parts of the facility in the fall. For 2005, CF had sales of $1.9 billion and a net loss of $39 million, due to more than $125 million in one-time costs associated with the IPO and conversion from a cooperative ownership structure.

Rising gas prices had wreaked havoc with the fertilizer industry, which saw an $82 million trade surplus in 2004 fall to a $793 million trade deficit in 2005, and CEO Stephen Wilson joined other industry leaders to call for an increase in offshore drilling. At year's end President George W. Bush signed a law that would open new areas to exploration.

In May 2006 the firm reached an agreement to build a nitrogen fertilizer plant in Trinidad and Tobago through a joint venture with Terra Industries and ANSA McAL, but the deal fell through when a suitable site could not be found. In March 2007 CF moved its corporate headquarters to Deerfield, Illinois, slightly closer to downtown Chicago than Long Grove. The firm's sales were now going up as demand for nitrogen fertilizer grew due to the booming market for corn-based ethanol.

In the summer the company announced it was exploring building a $200 million uranium recovery operation at its Plant City, Florida, phosphate facility in conjunction with uranium trader Nukem, Inc. Reasonable amounts of uranium could be extracted from phosphate rock, and its price had gone up tenfold in three years.

KEYTRADE STAKE ACQUIRED IN 2007

In September the firm paid $25.9 million for 50 percent of Keytrade AG, an international trading company based in Zurich, Switzerland, that bought three million tons of fertilizer per year in 35 countries, and marketed it in 65. It would enable CF to better import nitrogen and sell phosphate overseas. Keytrade, which had sales of $685 million in 2006, would become the exclusive marketer of CF's exports.

In November the firm won a bid for a supply of natural gas in Peru, where it had plans to build plants that could produce 2,100 tons of ammonia and 3,300 tons of solid urea per day, at a cost of more than $1.2 billion. CF also began working with Uhde Corp. on plans to build a new gasification plant in Donaldsonville that could convert coal and petroleum coke into nitrogen fertilizer. Construction was expected to begin in 2009, with operations to start in 2012.

Fiscal 2007 was a record year for the company, with sales of $2.76 billion and net earnings of $372.7 million reported. Its nitrogen and phosphate plants operated at nearly full capacity as demand for fertilizer-consuming grain products remained high and prices rose as much as 40 percent. Although the firm's stock price rose to $150 in the summer, it dropped in the fall when prices for nitrogen fertilizer fell off.

After more than 60 years, CF Industries Holdings, Inc., had grown to become one of the leading fertilizer producers in North America. The firm's recent change in operating philosophy and switch to publicly owned status had helped bring it record sales and profits, although it continued to be vulnerable to shifting market prices and demand for the commodity items that it produced.

Frank Uhle

PRINCIPAL SUBSIDIARIES

CF Industries, Inc.; Canadian Fertilizers, Ltd. (Canada; 66%); Keytrade AG (Switzerland; 50%).

PRINCIPAL COMPETITORS

Agrium, Inc.; Koch Industries, Inc.; Terra Industries, Inc.; Potash Corporation of Saskatchewan, Inc.; BASF SE; Cargill, Inc.; Intrepid Potash, Inc.; J.R. Simplot Co.; LSB Industries, Inc.; The Mosaic Co.; Transammonia, Inc.

FURTHER READING

"CF Industries' Gas Prices Mitigated by Plant Slowdown, Hedging Program," *Gas Daily*, October 14, 2005, p. 6.

"CF Industries Plans $65 Million Expansion," *Wall Street Journal*, July 28, 1972, p. 23.

"CF Industries Sets Area Layoffs," *Associated Press Newswires*, August 27, 2003.

"CF Industries Wins Camisea Gas Supply Contract," *Business News Americas*, November 20, 2007.

Edgerton, Michael, "CF Industries Exec," *Chicago Tribune*, April 21, 1980, p. D9.

"EVS Memories—Chapter Five: FS/GROWMARK," http://www.familyinfo.us/home/node/349, June 14, 2007.

"Florida Phosphate Companies to Build Sulfur-Melting Plant," *Tampa Tribune*, December 12, 1999.

"Four Farmers' Groups Plan Fertilizer Plant in Indiana," *Wall Street Journal*, February 14, 1962, p. 2.

Graham, George, "CF Industries Among Top Fertilizer Distributors in U.S.," *Tampa Tribune*, May 17, 2003, p. 11.

Griggs, Ted, "CF Sets $305 Million Expansion Plan," *Saturday State Times*, October 7, 1995, p. 1E.

Harlin, Ted, "Fertilizer Maker Grows As Farmers Struggle to Meet Global Demand," *Investor's Business Daily*, April 23, 2008.

Hodges, Jill, "Judge Rules CF Industries Cannot Give Jobs Held by Strikers to Permanent Workers," *Star-Tribune Newspaper of the Twin Cities*, June 6, 1995, p. 1D.

Jackovics, Ted, "Rocking and Rolling," *Tampa Tribune*, February 6, 2006, p. 6.

———, "Uranium Extraction Facility Under Review for Phosphate Site," *Tampa Tribune*, July 31, 2007.

Keeton, Ann, "CF Industries Turns Fertilizer into Gold," *Dow Jones News Service*, March 17, 2008.

Newborn, Steve, "Company to Unveil New Hardee Mine," *Tampa Tribune*, March 18, 1996, p. 1.

"OSHA Fines Plant $149,850 in Blast, Deaths," *Baton Rouge Advocate*, November 23, 2000, p. 1B.

Pincus, Ted, "As Demand for Fertilizer Grows, So Does Corporation's Vibrancy," *Chicago Sun-Times*, February 27, 2007, p. 43.

"Pipe Line Liable for Users' Losses," *Chicago Tribune*, December 7, 1978.

Strawn, Catherine, "Long Grove Firm's IPO Raises $622.1 Million," *Chicago Daily Herald*, August 12, 2005, p. 1.

Tita, Bob, "CF Buys Trade Link to Global Market," *Crain's Chicago Business*, October 8, 2007, p. 22.

———, "Co-ops to Sell Off Fertilizer Firm," *Crain's Chicago Business*, June 13, 2005, p. 4.

CiCi Enterprises, L.P.

1080 West Bethel Road
Coppell, Texas 75019-4427
U.S.A.
Telephone: (972) 745-4200
Fax: (972) 745-4204
Web site: http://www.cicispizza.com

Private Company
Founded: 1985
Employees: 300
Sales: $6.5 million (2007 est.)
NAICS: 533110 Owners and Lessors of Other Non-
    Financial Assets; 722110 Full-Service Restaurants

▪ ▪ ▪

CiCi Enterprises, L.P. is the franchiser for more than 600 CiCi's all-you-can-eat pizza buffet restaurants in 29 states. CiCi's low-priced buffet provides between ten to 12 pizzas, from a range of 16 pizza flavorings. Classic options include basic pepperoni or Italian sausage and cheese. Signature pizzas include Spinach Alfredo, Macaroni and Cheese, Zesty Veggie, Mexican Style Olé, Buffalo Chicken, and Deep Dish. CiCi's will prepare individual pizzas to order, allowing customers to choose their favorite toppings. The buffet offers a ten-item salad bar and a selection of pasta with marinara or Alfredo sauce. Desserts include brownies, cinnamon rolls, and an apple dessert made with pizza dough. Some CiCi's outlets offer take-out pizza only.

PIZZA TAKE-OUT FINDS ITS IDENTITY IN ALL-YOU-CAN-EAT BUFFET

The CiCi's name came from the combination of the first letters of the company founders' last names, Croce and Cole. Joe Croce, then 26, and Mike Cole, then 38, founded CiCi's Pizza in Plano, Texas, in 1985, with an investment of $107,000. They each contributed $10,000, then borrowed the balance. Sweat equity involved remodeling the rented restaurant space, including installing the wainscoting and hanging wallpaper. The shop offered seating for only 32, as Croce wanted to put the emphasis on carryout business.

By offering pizza at the lowest price in Plano, CiCi's soon attracted a multitude of customers. Confident in their success, Croce and Cole opened a second location in Dallas County; with many national and local pizza shops near that location, however, the outlet failed to attract adequate business. Then Croce decided to offer an all-you-can-eat pizza buffet, with an array of six pizza offerings, at the low price of $1.99 per person. The business thrived, and CiCi's found its identity. Despite development of a take-out pizza operation, dining in the restaurant became central to CiCi's success. As the concept developed, CiCi's added to the buffet a pasta dish, a small salad bar, and desserts made with pizza dough.

The foundation of CiCi's success rested on three values, quality food served fresh and hot, a clean atmosphere, and excellent service. The quality of the pizza started with fresh ingredients, such as real mozzarella cheese, without added fillers. Pizza dough was

COMPANY PERSPECTIVES

CiCi's mission from the beginning has been to exceed each guest's expectation in food, service and cleanliness, all within our affordable price point.

made fresh on the premises. Having dry ingredients delivered once a week, rather than refrigerated pizza dough twice a week, proved less expensive, and the fresh dough improved product quality. CiCi's sought to exceed the public's expectations of service at a value-priced restaurant by being attentive to customer needs, such as accepting individual requests for pizza toppings. CiCi's responded to special requests by having raw pizza base ready for toppings; pizzas could be made quickly and served fresh and hot. The cleanliness of the restaurant, the low cost, and the service made CiCi's a favorite of families who wanted a quick meal.

CICI'S EXPANDS THROUGH FRANCHISING

With a winning formula in place, CiCi's began to offer franchises. The first franchise opened in Dallas in 1987. The company expanded slowly at first, but the low cost of opening a CiCi's franchise encouraged growth. With 3,500 to 4,000 square feet and seating for about 160 people, each unit averaged $325,000 in start-up costs, depending on local leasing rates. Annual sales averaged just under $1 million per unit, an amazing rate of return for such a low-priced food product. By 1990 CiCi's owned or franchised ten stores, but the rate of expansion increased afterward. Eleven stores opened in 1991 and another 20 stores opened in 1992. By the end of 1996, CiCi's operated 22 corporate-owned stores, and the company's 100 franchisees operated 141 stores in Texas, Georgia, Florida, and Louisiana.

To keep overhead low, Croce formed JMC Distribution, a food and paper products supplier, in 1991. JMC was not intended as a profit center but to facilitate profitability at the store level. By taking control of purchasing, JMC reduced food overhead from 33 percent to 28 percent of sales. Fresh products, such as lettuce, were purchased through local distributors, but paper and plastic products, cheese, flour, and other food supplies were provided by JMC. JMC operated a distribution center in Dallas, and as franchises opened in the southeastern United States, JMC opened a second distribution center in Atlanta in 1996.

Local and media marketing contributed to CiCi's success. Franchise fees paid for radio, television, and direct-mail advertisements, in which CiCi's highlighted its bargain price with the tagline, "Best pizza value anywhere." CiCi's encouraged local marketing by franchisees, which involved attracting sports teams, elementary schools, and church groups. CiCi's attracted repeat business as individuals from these groups returned with their families and friends.

The CiCi's concept evolved with the emphasis on family. The restaurants carried a plentiful supply of booster seats and high chairs, and televisions played Nickelodeon or the Cartoon Network. Video games and the low-price attracted groups of teenagers on weekend nights. CiCi's developed the store atmosphere, a maroon and green color scheme with potted plants. CiCi's expanded its pizza buffet, offering a variety of ten pizzas, some with unique flavorings, such as Alfredo or barbeque sauce. The variety included thick- and thin-crust pizza. Other products included pizza rolls and cheese bread. Desserts were made out of pizza dough and flavored with cinnamon and sugar or topped with hot chocolate sauce, vanilla custard, or apples.

The company expanded geographically with franchises in Alabama, Arkansas, Indiana, Kansas, Kentucky, Mississippi, Missouri, New Mexico, North and South Carolina, Ohio, Oklahoma, and Tennessee. By the end of 1997 systemwide sales surpassed $100 million, with 199 stores in operation. By 2000, with 345 stores open, systemwide sales reached $301 million. During this time CiCi's never closed a store, attributable to the company's diligence in accepting franchisees and to the comprehensive training and testing that preceded any store opening.

MARKET AND CONSUMER TASTES PROMPT CHANGES

By the end of the 1990s, the CiCi's concept began to grow stale and costs began to impinge upon profitability of a budget-priced concept. Although the company had raised the price of the buffet incrementally over the years, from $1.99 to $2.99, a 30 percent increase from $2.99 to $3.99 in 2000 began to affect customer traffic. Even though revenues in dollars compensated for the decline in business, CiCi's executives experienced it as a crisis. Customer count rebounded over the next two years, however, as new marketing strategies were implemented.

CiCi's recognized that its value-priced strategy was no longer sufficient to meet changing consumer tastes for quality and variety. The company began to offer fresh vegetable toppings for the pizza, added more fresh

KEY DATES

1985: First CiCi's Pizza restaurant opens in Plano, Texas.
1987: CiCi's begins franchising all-you-can-eat pizza buffet concept.
1991: Establishment of JMC Distribution reduces food costs.
1997: Systemwide sales reach $100 million.
2003: Management and investment partners purchase CiCi's.
2004: CiCi's opens 500th unit.
2007: CiCi's launches first national advertising campaign.

vegetables to the salad bar, and added a pasta bar to the buffet. The company expanded the pizza menu to 16 varieties and introduced a thicker-crust option. CiCi's improved the flavor of its pizza by increasing the amount of sauce and cheese put on each pizza and by replacing the pepperoni and oil with higher-quality brands. CiCi's introduced unique, limited-offer flavors, such as Philly Cheesesteak Pizza, with ingredients sourced from Philadelphia. The cheesesteak included mozzarella cheese, fresh green peppers and red onions, and cheesesteak sauce. Advertising emphasized the changes with the tagline, "Fresh taste at a great price." The new logo featured a tomato inside a circle representing a pizza.

CiCi's renewed its image with a new interior design. The company enlivened the store interior with a soft, light-green wall color, and earthy tile flooring replaced the dark, dour carpeting. CiCi's installed booths for adult comfort and picnic tables for children's play. A bright red awning attracted customer attention outside the restaurant. At new units, the changes resulted in higher average sales, from the $750,000 to $900,000 range to about $1.25 million. Remodeled units experienced sales increases, as well.

Unexpected changes afoot at CiCi's involved a management buyout. In February 2003 Croce relinquished his position as president and chief executive officer of CiCi's with the intention of selling his shares in the company. Cole had stepped down from management for other entrepreneurial pursuits. Now Croce wanted to devote his time to family, including two young children, and church activities. Levine Lechtman Capital Partners headed the buyout, purchasing a 28 percent ownership for $41.5 million. The company's

top 11 managers purchased most of the balance. When ownership and management changes were finalized in August, Craig Moore, vice-president of operations with ten years at CiCi's, took the position of president. Other owner-managers included Robert Kulick, president of JMC Restaurant Distribution, the company's food purchasing and distribution subsidiary; Forbes Anderson, chief financial officer for CiCi's and JMC; Joe Flannigan, vice-president of marketing; Robert Grossheusch, vice-president of training; and Robert Parent, vice-president of development.

GROWTH THROUGH MULTI-UNIT FRANCHISE CONTRACTS

Amid concept and ownership changes, CiCi's pursued plans to generate rapid growth. The simplicity and profitability of the CiCi's concept impressed many new franchisees. CiCi's attracted Pizza PALS, a high-profile franchise owned by veteran fast-food executives Allan Huston, former chief executive of Pizza Hut; Pat Williamson, former chief operating officer at Pizza Hut; and Larry Zwain, former chief executive at Boston Market, president at KFC International, and marketing chief at McDonald's. Pizza PALS took CiCi's into the Colorado market, with two stores opening in 2002 and a contract to open as many as 100 units in Colorado and Utah.

CiCi's developed other multi-unit contracts with franchise owners, rather than allocate one or two units per franchisee. Such contracts included a St. Louis market agreement with the Kolander Group that covered 25 stores to open over six years; development began with six stores opening in 2003. Mercury Ventures LLC signed franchise agreements to open stores in West Virginia, Maryland, and Ohio. Ohio markets included Columbus and Dayton, with 20 units planned, and Cincinnati, where 14 units were planned, beginning with three stores opening in 2004. Mercury Ventures' partner Marwin Management LLC oversaw operations. With the Equity Group of Dallas, Marwin Management acquired 15 franchises in the Houston market. CiCi's planned to expand to Michigan and Washington, D.C., as well.

In August 2004 CiCi's opened its 500th store, in Woodstock, Georgia. CiCi's commemorated the occasion with a pizza giveaway at Texas Stadium, home of the Dallas Cowboys football team. The company served 90 yards of pizza, the equivalent of 2,000 pizzas or 16,000 slices. About 3,500 people attended the event, which included carnival rides, games, a marching band, and other entertainment. For the July 2005 celebration of its 20th anniversary, the company hosted the "World's Largest Pizza Party" and offered a chance to win a trip to Naples, Italy, where pizza was first invented.

Multi-unit franchise development continued in 2005, when CiCi's signed 12 development contracts for 75 new stores. New CiCi's restaurants were planned for Chicago; Des Moines, Iowa; and Pittsburgh, Pennsylvania, as well as for new markets in such cities as Danville, Virginia; Macon, Georgia; Orlando, Florida; Palestine and Stephenville, Texas; and Youngstown, Ohio.

MARKETING STRATEGY CONTRIBUTES TO CICI'S NATIONAL RANKING

Franchise expansion gave CiCi's a larger budget for advertising, and in 2004 the company initiated a $15 million marketing campaign. Market research affirmed that the budget pizza approach no longer worked. Also, low prices generated low expectations of the product. The company was not marketing its service, recognized to be a high point given the low price. The new marketing strategy attempted to counter the negative expectations of the public.

Television commercials designed by Deutsch, Inc., of Los Angeles, satirized quick-service restaurants as rapid but inattentive. The advertisements emphasized the point by filming the stereotypical experience in black and white and the CiCi's experience in color. The former exemplified customer frustrations, such as staff talking on cellphones or going on break when a customer needed them. These were followed by color shots of CiCi's staff providing assistance at the buffet or taking soft-drink refills to the customer's table. The television commercials ran in 108 markets in 28 states, and radio and billboard advertising and in-store displays reinforced the service idea. The campaign succeeded in increasing same store sales, particularly as the emphasis on fast service conveyed the notion that the buffet was an option to drive-through windows. Television commercials produced by Anonymous Content of Culver City further emphasized CiCi's quality and service in 2005. One commercial showed a new clerk being too attentive and enthusiastic, requiring a manager to say, "You might want to tone that down a notch." The tagline followed, "Too good to be true."

Exponential growth through multi-unit franchising, along with extensive advertising, raised CiCi's ranking among fast-food pizza chains. In 2005 CiCi's ranked sixth behind Chuck E. Cheese, but rose to fifth place in 2006. Pizza Hut ranked at number one. With a 13 percent sales increase, from $490.3 million in 2005 to $540.9 million in 2006, CiCi's outranked Chuck E.

Cheese with $534 million in sales. On a sales per unit basis, Chuck E. Cheese ranked number one, with $1.05 million average sales, compared to CiCi's $915,200 and Papa John's, ranking third, $747,500 average sales. CiCi's growth stemmed from a 12 percent increase in number of stores, from 579 to 601 units in 2006, or 22 new units, although it was actually a slow year compared to 2005, when 62 units opened.

ECONOMIC OPERATIONS FOCUS SHIFTS TO MARKETING FOCUS

While CiCi's had always been operations driven, expansion encouraged the company to shift from a focus on operations to an emphasis on marketing. Nevertheless, the two concerns often tended to intermingle. For instance, in July 2006 CiCi's began to offer franchises with a take-out-only option. Revenues from carryout pizza ranged from 15 percent to 25 percent of sales at full-service units, with the higher percentage occurring only at high-volume stores. CiCi's, however, was unable to find real estate for buffet-style units, so the take-out option allowed franchisees to build infill between full-service restaurants. The take-out units offered one-stop, one-price pizzas available for $4.99 each, in direct competition with Little Caesars, known for its $5 pizza. CiCi's franchisees opened eight take-out stores in the first year.

The company prepared for franchise expansion with its first national media campaign in 2007, and it even aired commercials in markets where CiCi's had not opened. Advertising attracted traffic to the company's web site, at 5,000 hits per minute, causing the site to crash. A video on the web site introduced the public to CiCi's. President Craig Moore conducted a restaurant tour that appealed to potential customers, promising excellent service and a restaurant coming to their neighborhood soon. The tour caught the attention of hundreds of potential franchisees as well.

The company's marketing focus entailed a new approach to management training. The company's top executives went on the road to provide regional training to franchisees and store managers in 11 markets. To invigorate local marketing, CiCi's held four-hour multimedia presentations, titled "Guest First Fever," in movie theaters and hotel ballrooms throughout the Southeast. The company provided tools for marketing, such as shaker boards for outdoor advertising and a guide to in-store promotions and local marketing ideas. By providing a fun experience and giving formal and informal recognition attention to managers, CiCi's executives succeeded in educating and energizing store managers. Mystery shopping confirmed the success of the management "road shows." Coupled with a national media campaign, local marketing increased same store sales approximately $2,000 to $3,000 per week. CiCi's planned to expand the tour into another road show, titled "Wide Friggin' Open."

Economic imperatives fostered a commingling of attention to marketing and operations. CiCi's focus on operations enforced a habit of meeting rising costs through constant research into reducing overhead. Thus when the price of cheese quadrupled, JMC Distribution signed a nine-month contract to stabilize the cost. As inflation increased the cost of supplies, CiCi's slowly increased the price of the buffet, from $3.99 to $4.49, then $4.99 in September 2007. Markets with higher costs, such as rent, charged $5.49 or $5.99. CiCi's experienced increased competition from fast-serve restaurants, a proliferation of pizza places, form sandwich shops offering pizza-style sandwiches, and grocery stores offering take-and-bake pizzas. The company introduced competitive products, such as buffalo wings and tossed salads, and in certain markets CiCi's began to offer beer and wine.

For new franchises, CiCi's sought to reduce upfront building and utility costs by decreasing the size of new units, to 3,500 square feet from 4,200 square feet. Seating was similarly downsized from the 170-to-180 range to 140-to-160 seats, and CiCi's reduced the size of tables, as well. With concern for maintaining traffic volume, the company cut the size of the buffet by five feet, offering ten pizzas rather than 12. By presenting less food, CiCi's expected high food turnover to keep presentation and variety fresher. The company reorganized the kitchen operations to be more efficient to reduce the amount of space needed in the back of the house.

With new marketing strategies and operational efficiencies in place, CiCi's continued to expand into new markets in 2008. Franchises opened in Arizona, Illinois, Minnesota, Nevada, and South Dakota. Also, the company experienced substantial growth in new and existing markets in Florida, with 12 new units opened or planned for 2008. The company signed contracts for multi-unit franchise development in California, New Jersey, and New York. Overall, CiCi's expected to have 660 units in operation by the end of 2008 and 750 by the end of 2009.

Mary Tradii

PRINCIPAL SUBSIDIARIES

JMC Restaurant Distribution, L.P.

PRINCIPAL COMPETITORS

CEC Entertainment, Inc. (Chuck E. Cheese); Domino's Pizza Inc.; Little Caesar Enterprises; Papa John's International, Inc.; YUM! Brands, Inc. (Pizza Hut).

FURTHER READING

Abrams, Mike, "Pizza for Less; Careful Business Plan Has Paid Off for CiCi's, Home of the $2.99 Pizza, Pasta, Salad, and Dessert Bar," *Virginian-Pilot,* April 11, 1998, p. D1.

Berta, Dina, "CiCi's Pizza Executives Hit the Road to Bring Their Marketing Message to Franchisees and Managers," *Nation's Restaurant News,* September 17, 2007, p. 24.

Bertagnoli, Lisa, "Cheap Thrills: CiCi's Pizza Buffet's Challenge: To Keep Price Low and Service Levels High, All While Steadily Expanding," *Chain Leader,* October 2007, p. 82.

"Beyond Pizza," *Restaurants & Institutions,* May 15, 2008, p. 14.

Cebrynski, Gregg, "CiCi's Pizza Upgrades Products, Changes Logo and Store Image," *Nation's Restaurant News,* February 19, 2001, p. 22.

———, "Emerging CiCi's, Revitalized Little Caesars Intensify Competition in Pizza Segment with Expansion Pushes," *Nation's Restaurant News,* June 25, 2007, p. 102.

"CiCi's Franchise Expands in Texas with 15-Unit Buy," *Nation's Restaurant News,* July 12, 2004, p. 76.

"CiCi's Inks 12 Pacts for 74 Units in MW, SE, NE," *Nation's Restaurant News,* October 18, 2004, p. 104.

"CiCi's Inks 13 Deals for 64 New Units in 9 States," *Nation's Restaurant News,* January 10, 2005, p. 60.

"CiCi's Not-Frills Option," *Restaurants & Institutions,* July 1, 2006, p. 16.

"CiCi's Offers Low-Cost Pizza, Pasta, Salads," *Tampa Tribune,* July 11, 1998, p. 13.

"CiCi's Pizza," *Food Institute Report,* February 25, 2008, p. 6.

"CiCi's Pizza Inks Franchise Deal for Cincinnati Area," *Nation's Restaurant News,* April 5, 2004, p. 56.

Hein, Kenneth, "CiCi's Seeks Bigger Piece of Pie: Chain Builds Identity in Category Dominated by Pizza Hut, Domino's," *Brandweek,* May 30, 2005, p. 9.

Langheny, Marcia, "Hungry … with Children: CiCi's Pizza Is Fast, Cheap, and Full of Kids," *Atlanta Journal-Constitution,* March 27, 1999, p. E6.

Littman, Margaret, "In Living Color: CiCi's Pizza's New Campaign Shows Low Prices Doesn't Always Mean Bad Service," *Chain Leader,* September 2004, p. 26.

Ruggless, Ron, "CiCi's Pizza Expects Big Things from Smaller Units, Takeout-Only Variant," *Nation's Restaurant News,* October 29, 2007, p. 4.

———, "CiCi's Pizza Eyes Denver Market: Veteran Exec Trio Set for Colo. Debut," *Nation's Restaurant News,* May 6, 2002, p. 8.

———, "CiCi's Pizza Founder to Step Down; Mgmt. to Buy Chain," *Nation's Restaurant News,* February 17, 2003, p. 4.

———, "CiCi's Pizza Looks for Bigger Piece of American Pie in SE," *Nation's Restaurant News,* September 16, 1996, p. 3.

———, "CiCi's Pizza Scores 500th Store, Treats Fans to Yards of Pizza," *Nation's Restaurant News,* August 16, 2004, p. 100.

Shlacter, Barry, "A BIGGER Slice of the Pie—CiCi's Becomes Fastest-Growing Pizza Chain by Offering 'Good and Cheap' Fare," *Fort Worth Star-Telegram,* June 26, 2005, p. F1.

Silvan, Tricia Lynn, "CiCi's New Look," *San Antonio Business Journal,* April 20, 2001, p. 8.

Silver, Deborah, "A Piece of the Pie: As New Management Takes Command, CiCi's Pizza Mobilizes for Nationwide Expansion," *Chain Leader,* September 2003, p. 53.

Solman, Gregory, "Nothing 'Strange' About CiCi's Service," *Adweek Western Edition,* May 10, 2006.

Stroud, Jerri, "Dallas Pizza Chain Plans 25 Stores for St. Louis Area; First CiCi's Opens March 31 on Manchester in Rock Hill," *St. Louis Post-Dispatch,* March 5, 2003, p. C7.

CNH Global N.V.

World Trade Center
Amsterdam Airport
Tower B, 10th Floor
Schiphol Boulevard 217
Amsterdam, 1118 BH
Netherlands
Telephone: (+31 20) 446-0429
Fax: (+31 20) 446-0436
Web site: http://www.cnh.com
6900 Veterans Boulevard
Burr Ridge, Illinois 60527-5640
U.S.A.
Telephone: (630) 887-2229
Fax: (630) 887-2261

Public Company, 89 Percent Owned by Fiat S.p.A.
Incorporated: 1996
Employees: 28,100
Sales: $15.96 billion (2007)
Stock Exchanges: New York
Ticker Symbol: CNH
NAICS: 333111 Farm Machinery and Equipment
    Manufacturing; 333120 Construction Machinery
    Manufacturing; 333924 Industrial Truck, Tractor,
    Trailer, and Stacker Machinery Manufacturing;
    522220 Sales Financing; 532120 Truck, Utility
    Trailer, and RV (Recreational Vehicle) Rental and
    Leasing

CNH Global N.V. was the name adopted by the Dutch firm New Holland N.V. following its November 1999 acquisition of Case Corporation. CNH is the world's second largest maker of agricultural equipment, trailing Deere & Company, and third in construction equipment, following Caterpillar Inc. and Komatsu Ltd. The company's products are sold in 160 countries under a number of brands, including Case, Case IH, Kobelco, New Holland, and Steyr, through a network of more than 11,000 dealers and distributors. By region, 37 percent of sales are generated in North America, 33 percent in Western Europe, 12 percent in Latin America, and 18 percent elsewhere. Fiat S.p.A., the Italian automaker, holds a stake in CNH of approximately 89 percent. Although it is a Dutch firm by incorporation, CNH maintains its headquarters in Burr Ridge, Illinois, and its stock trades on the New York Stock Exchange.

19TH-CENTURY ORIGINS OF CASE

The history of Case is merged with the Industrial Revolution's impact on farming. Jerome Increase Case grew up threshing wheat by hand on his father's farmstead in the early 1800s. Wheat was cut with scythes, then beaten by hand to remove the grain. The blistering work meant that one person produced about half a dozen bushels a day, so farmers necessarily limited their acreage to prevent bottlenecks in production of their wheat. When Case was 16, he took his father to a demonstration of a crude, mechanized thresher patented around 1788 by Scotsman Andrew Meikle. His father was sufficiently impressed by the machine and applied for a franchise to sell them.

For five seasons, Jerome Case operated the machine for his father and his father's clients. During that time, Case became aware of the machine's flaws, as well as its indispensability to farming. In 1842 Jerome Case moved to Rochester, Wisconsin, then the growing heart of the wheat culture in the United States. He sold five thresher machines along the way, reserving one for himself.

Rochester was a village when Case arrived. That autumn, he did custom threshing and worked on his modifications of the machine. Case envisioned a machine that was both separator and thresher, constructed so that the straw would move to one end while grain fell underneath the machine. Such a machine had already been patented by inventors in Maine in 1837, but Case had not seen their invention. His machine differed in its operation. Case was helped by Stephen Thresher, a carpenter he met where he boarded in Rochester. The two were advised by Richard Ela, who made fanning mills and hailed from New Hampshire.

After a successful first demonstration of his new thresher-separator, Case decided to concentrate on manufacturing rather than custom threshering. When Rochester balked at his petition for water-power rights, Case moved to Racine, Wisconsin, in 1844, playing a

part in that town's explosive growth. Within three years, he had gone from renting a building to constructing his own factory. First named Jerome Increase Case Machinery Company, the name was changed to Racine Threshing Machine Works. By 1848, Case was producing 100 threshers a year and claimed he was meeting only half of the orders received. By 1854, water power was supplanted by a steam boiler and engine within the factory.

It was difficult to deliver such cumbersome equipment in the 1800s. There were no railroads in Wisconsin until the 1850s. Most roads were widened Indian trails, and rain could make them treacherous to wheels. Timely delivery of the heavy machines was not always possible, and timing remained as essential as rain to farmers. In addition, Case spent much time traveling to distant farms to collect back payments, credit being another necessity of his clients' business.

Many complementary farming products were appearing during the same period that the wheat belt of the Midwest and the Great Plains was burgeoning. While Case's business was growing, John Deere and Major Andrus were developing a steel plow in Illinois, and a reaper had been developed by Cyrus McCormick. Case purchased rights to the thresher and fanning mill invented before his, then added improvements. Acknowledging that his own strength was business and seeing the applications of machines, Case often acquired and improved upon the inventions of others. Case was established as a leading thresher manufacturer by the early 1850s.

Business was steady enough to allow Case to pursue civic interests; he was elected three times to the state Senate and served twice as Racine's mayor. The poor harvest and financial panic of 1857 did not prevent the company, then still specializing in threshers, from introducing new products. In 1862 Case began selling the "Sweepstakes," a thresher capable of producing 300 bushels of wheat a day. Pressures, including the Civil War, drove Case to create a co-partnership by 1863, established as J.I. Case & Co. The partnership included Case, Massena Erskine, and Stephen Bull until 1880.

The same year that Alexander Graham Bell won a bronze medal at the Philadelphia Centennial Exhibition, Case's new thresher, the 1869 Eclipse, also won a bronze and a commendation. The thresher took the gold medal at the World's Fair in Paris two years later. With the Homestead Act of 1862, farming burst into a new era, requiring equipment that could keep up. In 1878 Case produced its first steam traction engine, and by the following year had sold 109 of them. Sales

KEY DATES

1842: Jerome Increase Case builds his first thresher machine, and soon founds the Jerome Increase Case Machinery Company.

1863: Company is re-formed as a co-partnership, called J.I. Case & Co.

1878: Case produces its first steam traction engine.

1880: Partnership is incorporated as J.I. Case Threshing Machine Company.

1895: New Holland Machine Company is founded in New Holland, Pennsylvania.

1917: Ford Motor Company begins making the first mass-produced agricultural tractor.

1919: Fiat introduces its first mass-produced tractor to the market.

c. 1928: Case changes its name to J.I. Case Company.

1945: Case workers in Racine begin a 440-day strike.

1947: Sperry Corporation acquires New Holland, creating the subsidiary Sperry New Holland.

1957: Case relaunches its industrial equipment line and acquires American Tractor Corp.

1964: Kern County Land Company (KCL) gains majority control of Case.

1967: Tenneco Company acquires KCL and its stake in Case.

1970: Case becomes a wholly owned subsidiary of Tenneco; Fiat creates an earthmoving equipment subsidiary, Fiat Macchine Movimento Terra.

1974: Fiat Macchine creates joint venture with Allis Chalmers Corporation, Fiat-Allis.

1984: Fiat consolidates all of its agricultural machinery manufacturing under Fiatagri unit.

1985: Case acquires International Harvester's agricultural product line.

1986: Ford acquires Sperry New Holland and merges it with Ford Tractor Operations to form Ford New Holland, Inc.

1988: Fiat-Allis and Fiatagri are merged to form FiatGeotech S.p.A., which includes all of Fiat's agricultural and earthmoving equipment.

1991: Case posts a net loss of $1.1 billion; Fiat acquires an 80 percent interest in Ford New Holland, which is merged with FiatGeotech to form Netherlands-based N.H. Geotech N.V.

1993: N.H. Geotech changes its name to New Holland N.V.

1994: Tenneco takes Case Corporation public.

1996: Tenneco sells its remaining stake in Case, which gains its full independence.

1999: After acquiring Case, New Holland renames itself CNH Global N.V.

2000: Company endures first of four straight years in the red thanks principally to a difficult and lengthy integration process.

doubled in 1878, reaching the million-dollar mark by 1880. The partnership was incorporated as J.I. Case Threshing Machine Company in 1880. By 1890 Case was offering nine different horsepowers of steam traction engines, and continued improvements. Production peaked the same year the first gasoline tractor was introduced, 1911. Most steam engine products were eclipsed by the gasoline tractor by 1924. At that point, Case had built about one-third of the farm steam engines in the United States. It took time, though, for tractors to become standard farm equipment; as a power source on U.S. farms, draft animals outnumbered tractors until 1952.

Case died in 1891 at the age of 73. Leadership of the company was passed to one of his former partners,

Stephen Bull, who was assisted by his son Frank. Between 1893 and 1924, the company expanded to Europe, South America, and Australia. Competition between thresher manufacturers led to the dissolution of the Thresher Manufacturers Association in 1898 and increased rivalries. A depression between 1893 and 1897, a warehouse fire, and a Great Plains drought contributed to a decline in Case profits of nearly three-quarters between 1892 and 1896. Stockholder dissatisfaction led to new ownership, which resulted in Frank Bull as president. Bull became chairman of the board in 1916 and was succeeded in presidency by Warren J. Davis. The company name was changed to J.I. Case Company after further reorganization around 1928.

EARLY 20TH CENTURY: BECOMING A FULL-LINE MANUFACTURER

Case was advertising a full line of road machinery by 1912. The gasoline tractor became one of the company's most important products. Since 1902, many firms were fighting to produce the gasoline-powered successors to steam-powered engines. International Harvester began making them in 1905, and Ford in 1907. The design and manufacture of lighter, smaller versions of the engines made Case a major player in the gasoline tractor market by the 1920s. By the late 1920s, Case had become a full-line manufacturer, aided by its 1919 acquisition of Grand Detour, a tillage equipment company. Case also made expensive automobiles from 1912 to 1927: roadsters, coupes, and sedans in 14 different models over the years. Because of low profitability, the auto lines were phased out.

The depression in the U.S. economy in the wake of World War I greatly impacted the farm equipment industry. By 1929 only 18 of the 157 manufacturers of farm equipment operating 12 years earlier remained. Case's profits fell steadily, despite the addition of a combine to its line in 1923. The company was especially challenged by the dealer network of International Harvester. Case did not keep up with competitors' improvements while it was enjoying the sales of its steam traction engines and threshers. Between 1920 and 1922, annual gross sales plunged from $34 million to less than $16 million. In 1924 Case's new president, Leon R. Clausen, assumed the reins after leaving John Deere Company. He would remain president until 1948, and chairman of the board until 1958.

Clausen brought many ideas with him from Deere, including faith in aggressive marketing and the value of being a full-line manufacturer. He established three primary goals: improve tractor designs, establish a full line, and modernize the factories. The Model C tractor was introduced in 1929, and a tricycle tractor appeared in 1930. A line of "Motor Lift" implements arrived in 1935. Lines were expanded by acquisition as well as invention: Case purchased through the Emerson-Brantingham Company a line of farm equipment that included binders, mowers, reapers, and corn planters. The Rock Island Plow Company was acquired in 1937, adding drills, spreaders, and plows to the company's offerings.

Case also purchased a factory in Iowa to make small combines that year, sales of which had been growing steadily since they were introduced to the market. Case, Harvester, and Deere were responsible for three-quarters of the farm machinery sold in the United States by 1937. Although Case had, since 1912, offered an array

of road-building machinery, these products were not promoted under Clausen and it was not until the mid-1950s that Case became serious about marketing its construction equipment.

Clausen set to work on revamping the sales department and restructuring manufacturing. He is credited with building Case's dealer network. Although severe cutbacks were necessary to weather the Great Depression, Case managed to increase sales by 1936 on the strength of the company's tractor sales. In 1939 a new tractor line was introduced, as well as a small combine, hammer feed mills, and farm wagon gears.

With the start of World War II, Case's tractors were in even greater demand. More than 15,000 of its tractors went to the military between 1941 and 1945. New tractors were designed and manufactured with war needs in mind. Case also produced items such as shells, aircraft wings, and gun mounts for the war effort. Case devoted much more wartime engineering to federal production than did Deere or Caterpillar, which left it at a disadvantage at the war's end. Nonetheless, the postwar demand for farm machinery outpaced supply, and Case's lost wartime share soon seemed recoverable.

POSTWAR DIFFICULTIES FOR CASE

Regaining lost market share, however, was interrupted by a strike in 1945 that lasted 440 days. It was, at that time, the nation's longest strike. Clausen's animosity for unions—first noted when he was still with Deere—was mutual. Depleted by the strike and its aftermath, Clausen stepped down as president in 1948, staying on as chairman of the board. The strike hurt Case on every level: in its relationship with dealers, customers, and its union, and in its research and development, where it was lagging behind its competitors.

With the Marshall Plan and the lifted export restrictions, devastated Europe's need for working machinery became a fresh market for Case. In addition, U.S. farm machinery was in disrepair. There was a shortage of manpower on farms, because of deaths in the war, which increased the need for machinery. Sales growth on the West Coast led to a plant purchase in California in 1947. This purchase expanded Case's range into a new tobacco harvester. These factors helped Case post a profit through 1949, despite its costly strike.

Profits declined between 1950 and 1953, in part because of outdated products. Competitors introduced lighter models of tractors in the late 1930s, and these units became popular after the war. Case, on the other hand, had at the end of the war roughly the same heavy series it had at the beginning. Poor engineering hurt

Case during the early 1950s as well, as did a propensity to blame the dealer rather than the product. Items such as Case's hay baler, which had topped the market in 1941, lagged to less than 5 percent of baler sales in 1953 because Case failed to respond to a competitor's improvements.

All of these problems added up to a crisis in leadership at Case. According to Case's own published history, *J.I. Case: The First 150 Years,* Clausen consistently made decisions opposed to change. He opposed diesel engines for domestic sales; he believed farmers preferred "dependability" to changes such as a foot-operated clutch, a cab, and an oil filter—all of which a 1946 survey of farmers specified as desired. When Clausen left the presidency in 1948, Theodore Johnson took over. Johnson was 66 and had never worked outside of Case. The company continued to drift, with a lackluster response to competition and no notable innovations. Johnson was replaced in 1953 by John T. Brown.

Under Brown's direction, Case released a multitude of new or improved implements, including the 500 series tractor, which would become a popular line. The 500 had a six-cylinder, fuel-injected, diesel engine; power steering; and a push-button start. Two manure spreaders were unveiled in 1956. That same year, however, Case reported its second loss since 1953. For the first time, bankruptcy seemed a possibility. Diversification appeared to be the only remedy.

DIVERSIFYING CASE'S PRODUCT LINE

Case launched its industrial equipment line in 1957 as though it were new, but it had been making industrial units based on agricultural models for three decades. Street and highway builders, national forests and parks, and others had come to rely on industrial tractors adapted from farm use. Case applied itself to expanding this sector of its line, and turned to Caterpillar Company for marketing assistance. To revitalize its industrial line, Case acquired American Tractor Corporation (ATC) in 1957. ATC's volume around purchase time was $10 million, but the company was in debt because of recent rapid growth. Its assets included a vigorous president, Marc Bori Rojtman; a strong line of distributors and dealers; and a sturdy line of crawler tractors and backhoe loaders, the company's star product. Under Rojtman, Case's manufacturing capacity improved, new retailers were attracted, and the company moved confidently into the construction equipment business.

Rojtman's showman's personality led to dazzling regional shows to promote new product lines. Despite criticism, deliberate showmanship in marketing resulted in huge increases in orders. New product invention and marketing and overseas expansion proved financially taxing. However, sales rose 50 percent in 1957, reaching $124 million. Clausen, head of the board, strongly opposed Rojtman's presidency and his debt load, and resigned in 1958. An economic downturn in 1958 left the company in a precarious position. William Grede replaced Rojtman in 1960.

Case's debt load in 1959 was $236 million. It had become the country's fourth largest farm and construction equipment producer. Grede's first order of business was to reduce debt and consolidate manufacturing. A new offering of accessories such as batteries, oil, and hydraulic fluid proved successful. Between the new offering and special discounts, Case sales were still strong in 1960. A six-month strike occurred that same year. Unable to meet a $145 million bill due on short-term notes in 1962, the company negotiated a bank agreement that called for reorganization and deferment of most of the interest until 1967, so Case could focus on paying down principal. Reorganization included the ousting of Grede. He was succeeded by Merritt D. Hill, who had previously worked in Ford's Tractor and Implement Division.

Hill brought talent with him from Ford, including a chief product engineer. He completely restructured Case. Separate divisions were created for marketing, manufacturing, and engineering. Hill also ushered in a new era of labor-management relations, being the first of Case's presidents sympathetic to issues of labor and race. Money constraints impeded the development of new product lines, but Case managed to stay in the ring with competitors such as Ford and Deere, as the new head of its engineering department insisted. In 1964 Case introduced the 1200 Traction King, a 4-wheel drive, 120-horsepower giant that marked the company's entry into the large agricultural tractor market.

Case's operating loss had declined and its production levels were up. The company seemed on solid business ground by 1964, but was still not in a position to meet the terms of the 1962 agreement and have enough left over to fuel growth. Case shopped for a cash-rich partner to whom it could offer the use of its agreement's tax loss carry-forwards.

TAKEN OVER BY KCL (1964) AND THEN TENNECO (1967)

In May 1964 the Kern County Land Company (KCL) of California acquired majority stock in Case. KCL was founded in 1874 and began as a cattle-raising venture that branched into petroleum royalties after oil was discovered. It diversified into hard minerals, real estate, and businesses such as its Racine, Wisconsin-based parent company, Walker Manufacturing Company. KCL was cash-rich and agreed not to dictate Case's growth or internal decisions. These circumstances allowed Case to expand between 1964 and 1967, in accordance with a booming demand for existing products and the itch to produce new ones. Around 1965, the 450 crawler and the 1150 dozer debuted. A new series of backhoe loaders were introduced around this time also, among them Case's mainstay, the 580. By 1966, Case's income decline had been reversed. Hill became chairman of the board and Charles A. Anderson became president. Anderson had been with KCL and Walker.

Suddenly KCL, under threat of a hostile takeover by Armand Hammer, wooed a friendly buyer instead, and ended up being acquired by Tenneco Company of Houston. Gardiner Symonds, Tenneco's president, was familiar with KCL's natural resources but had no experience with manufacturing. Tenneco was a holding company. The deal closed in 1967. It was thought that Tenneco would quickly sell Case.

When investors began inquiring about Case's stock, Tenneco decided to run an analysis of the company and found it well-run but too low on liquid assets to grow. This shifted Tenneco's plan. Case would prosper from a shift to construction equipment, so Tenneco decided not to sell it. In 1968 Tenneco acquired Drott Manufacturing Company of Wausau, Wisconsin, and leased it to Case. Case had been buying loader buckets from Drott for years. That same year, Tenneco also bought Davis Manufacturing Company of Wichita, Kansas, a producer of crawler and rubber-tire mounted trenchers and cable-laying equipment. Tenneco allowed Case to expand by two product lines: log skidders for timber harvesting, through Beloit Woodlands of Wisconsin, and a "skid steer" loader, manufactured by the Uni-Loader Division of Universal Industries.

James Ketelsen succeeded Anderson as Case's president in 1967. Tenneco deferred to Case's manufacturing experience, but both agreed that the company's future was in construction equipment. The agricultural market had slowed, with replacements and larger machinery to accommodate fewer, larger farms, reflecting the bulk of sales. Case essentially exited the farm implement business by 1970. Yet, while Case dropped its combine business in 1972, an acquisition in 1985 returned harvesting equipment to Case's line.

After dropping so many of its lines, Case thought it could survive without being a full-line company. The farm economy was dire in the early 1970s, especially for smaller farmers. Case shifted its focus not away from agricultural implements altogether, but toward the large

tractor market. Tenneco "lent" Case $60 million from 1969 to mid-1970, giving the company enough fiscal strength to deal with healthy competitors such as Deere. Even Deere did not have access to such resources. By 1971, Case's entire construction equipment line had been replaced, and that year it unveiled more new machinery than any of its competitors. Tenneco's faith was repaid, as Case led all of Tenneco's companies in earnings gains the following year. Meantime, by 1970, Tenneco had purchased the remaining stock in Case, turning Case into a wholly owned subsidiary.

In 1972 Case bought David Brown, Ltd., a British agricultural equipment firm founded in 1860. Brown had a large distribution system in Britain, and Case concentrated its small tractor production in Brown. Thomas Guendel took over the company presidency in 1972 and commanded a chapter of unprecedented growth until he left Case seven years later. Sales quadrupled during that time and earnings improved more than 600 percent. The phenomenal growth was due largely to increased success in construction equipment and overseas markets.

The company reentered the military market during the 1970s. It was awarded a $55 million contract with the U.S. Army and U.S. Air Force in 1978. The economy was improving after the recession between 1974 and 1975, and Case was the country's third largest producer of construction equipment by 1975. By the late 1970s, 45 percent of Case's sales were overseas, while 80 percent of its production was domestic. France's Poclain Company, the largest manufacturer of hydraulic excavators in the world, was purchased by Case in 1977. Because Drott's excavators could not be sold in Europe due to trade restrictions, Poclain was a savvy purchase; it was a recognized worldwide market leader.

BLEAKEST TIMES YET

When Jerome K. Green replaced Guendel in 1979, Case passed the $2 billion mark in revenues. Case started the 1980s with 28,000 employees, but it did not anticipate the recession that would shatter the farming community. Shifting to the construction product line was no rescue, as that industry was equally hard hit. New general-purpose tractors had been introduced in 1983 and were languishing. Four more 94 series tractors were unveiled in 1984, but by that point, farms were in a real crisis. Case cut production to 55 percent of capacity and it still exceeded demand. Although overseas sales of construction equipment remained strong during the 1980s, Case's overseas sales did not balance the wounds of the recession in the United States: In 1983, Case lost

$68 million, and followed that with a deficit of $105 million in 1984.

Case acquired International Harvester's agricultural product line, production facilities, and distribution system in 1985. The history of Harvester was as long and as distinguished as Case's. (Harvester retained its trucking business, renaming it Navistar International Transportation Corp.) Case shut down its own factories for the start of 1985, reducing production to 45 percent of retail sales, and went on to close several Brown plants, and to retire the oldest and least efficient of Case's home plants. Trimming its agricultural product line to such things as tractors, tillage equipment, crop production, and combines, Case was prepared to compete head-on with John Deere, dominator of the farm equipment market.

Losses in 1986 were down to $1 million, despite the deepening farm recession. In addition, Case was among the top three farm equipment manufacturers in Germany, France, and the United Kingdom. Nevertheless, Tenneco was unhappy with Case's bad financial showing and unacceptably slow production in 1987. Green was replaced by James K. Ashford that same year. About 35 new agricultural products were introduced in 1987, while nine factories were closed or closing. Case was assisted by *Fortune*'s listing of its combines, planters, and backhoe loaders as among the best U.S. products in 1988. Ashford oversaw aggressive cutbacks and revamping, including the elimination of 300 jobs in Racine and an intended worldwide cut of 3,000 employees.

By 1989 Case had gone from a $142 million loss to a record profit of $228 million. The recovering farm economy and improved construction equipment sales were cause for celebration. Case's confidence was sufficient to announce a new headquarters complex, but the recovery was short-lived and sales began to weaken. Although John Deere was cutting back production, Ashford gambled that the recession was over and that Case would gain from a preparatory inventory.

This decision was disastrous. The market did not rebound. In the fourth quarter of 1990, Case's earnings were off by nearly $100 million and the year ended with a $42 million decline in operating profits. Part of this decline was due to a weakened dollar, which raised imported parts costs. Although Ashford was credited for Case's turnaround in 1989 and for replacing 80 percent of its divisions' managers and reviving a sluggish management, he resigned suddenly.

Losses continued in 1991 as Case scrambled to cut personnel by 5,000 and production schedules by as much as 23 percent. Sales were up, but discounts cut deeply into profits. Case ended 1991 with a $618 million operating loss.

Case had become a serious problem for Tenneco when Robert J. Carlson assumed the presidency in 1991. Carlson had spent nearly 30 years at Deere and inspired confidence at Case. The company announced extended factory shutdowns at all of its ten domestic plants and closure of some of its European facilities. Case had restructuring charges of $461 million in 1991. Added to Case's operating losses for that year, the loss was a staggering $1.1 billion. While Deere and Caterpillar had suffered from the extended recession as well, their trimmed production left them in better shape than Case. Tenneco executives, in fact, were so exasperated by the situation at Case that they offered to sell the subsidiary for $1 to anyone who was willing to assume the hefty $1 billion debt load; there were no takers.

Talk of further reducing the workforce by 4,000 employees started in 1992, when Edward J. Campbell assumed the presidency of Case. Campbell's approach to downsizing was different. He did not just slash, he reorganized and cut from the top, dismissing 21 of the company's 43 officers. Various European factories were closed or sold, including the Poclain plant at Carvin. An agreement was made with Sumitomo Heavy Industries of Japan to make midsized excavators for the North American market. Japan was an increasing presence in the agricultural and construction equipment industries.

These measures helped reduce losses for 1992, but revenues were also down. Operating losses were reduced by about 75 percent while agricultural equipment sales were down about 30 percent. The year closed with revenues of $3.8 billion and operating losses of $260 million, not including restructuring charges. From a high of 30,000 in 1990, Case's employees numbered 18,600 in 1992.

The farm economy appeared to have stabilized at the end of 1992, but construction equipment sales were sluggish. All manufacturers suffered from weak pricing, lower unit volume, the economic slump overseas, and cautious dealers. Caterpillar had a sales increase, but Deere and Case both reported losses. Although Case's performance improved, its progress was uneven, with profits in the second quarter of 1992 and losses in the third. Tenneco announced a $2 billion restructuring plan to revamp Case into three divisions: sales and marketing, manufacturing, and engineering. Jean-Pierre Rosso became president and chief executive of Case in 1993.

CASE'S RECOVERY AND SHORT-LIVED RETURN TO INDEPENDENCE

Case launched a three-year, $920 million restructuring program in March 1993. The program involved further plant closings and consolidations, revitalizing new product development with a renewed emphasis on customer input, abandoning money-losing product lines (such as smaller tractors and heavy construction equipment), and the gradual privatization of the 250 Case dealerships owned by the company. Sales of farm equipment were up by the summer of 1993, especially large tractor sales. Most farmers had not purchased new tractors or combines since the farming boom in the 1970s. Case announced that its 1993 combine production was sold out by June, but its Racine tractor plant was closed for 17 weeks following a $17 million loss in the first quarter of that year. The heavy equipment markets were proclaimed healthy by the end of 1993. The year ended well for Case: Operating income was $82 million in 1993, an improvement over its operating loss of $260 million the previous year, and revenues were $3.7 billion. Case was aided by a vast reduction in inventories, higher retail pricing, and increased demand for new products late in the year.

Case appeared to have recovered fully by 1994, as revenues increased to $4.3 billion while net income tripled to $165 million. The health of the company was also evident in Tenneco's successful sale of 56 percent of Case Corporation stock to the public during 1994, marking Case's first return to the public trading arena in nearly 30 years. During 1995 Tenneco further decreased its ownership of Case to 21 percent, then sold this remaining stake in March 1996, completing Case's return to independence.

Under Rosso's continued leadership, the revitalized Case adopted a more aggressive approach to developing new farm and construction equipment, earmarking $835 million in new product spending for 1996 through 1998, more than double the amount spent in the early 1990s. At the same time, Case pursued growth, particularly abroad, through acquisition and joint ventures. The company in 1995 had already entered the burgeoning market in China through the establishment of a joint venture with a leading Chinese construction equipment firm, Guangxi Liugong Machinery Co. Ltd., to make and market Case backhoe loaders. In 1996 and 1997 Case completed 11 acquisitions, nine of which were of agricultural equipment companies with the others being makers of construction equipment. Among the firms purchased in 1996 were Australia-based Austoft Holdings Limited, the world-leading maker of sugarcane harvesting equipment, with annual sales of $74 million; Steyr Landmaschinentechnik GmbH, an Austrian tractor manufacturer with annual sales of $176 million; and U.K. construction equipment maker Fermec Holdings Ltd., which had annual revenues of $154 million. In 1997 Case acquired Fortschritt Erntemaschinen GmbH, a German maker of

harvesting equipment, and the assets of two other German firms; the combined annual sales of the products acquired was about $110 million. The new and acquired products helped Case increase its revenues to a record $6 billion in 1997 while the company's cost-consciousness led to record net income that year of $403 million.

By 1998, however, economic difficulties in Asia and Russia, which reduced the grain exports of U.S. farmers, coupled with three straight years of record crops, drastically reduced crop prices (to 20-year lows) and in turn sharply depressed demand for farm equipment. Agricultural equipment makers, including Case, began once again laying off workers. In 1998 Case fired or laid off 2,100 workers; then, late that year, it said that it planned to lay off 1,300 more employees by the end of 1999. The latest downturn in the agricultural equipment market also led to pressure for consolidation within the industry as one way to cut production overcapacity and lessen competition, and in May 1999 Case agreed to be acquired by New Holland N.V.

THE ORIGINS OF NEW HOLLAND

New Holland's roots can be traced back to 1895, when handyman Abe Zimmerman made his first feed mill at his New Holland, Pennsylvania, repair shop. Zimmerman soon began making other agricultural products as well. He called his operation the New Holland Machine Company and incorporated it in 1903, the same year Henry Ford incorporated the automobile company he had started up in Detroit. Ford came out with the prototype for the world's first mass-produced agricultural tractor in 1907, and ten years later the tractor, known as the Fordson Model F, went into production. Decades later, these two fledgling operations would become linked.

Meanwhile, across the Atlantic, Italian automaker Fiat was developing a tractor of its own. That company's efforts resulted in the development of the 702, Fiat's first mass-produced tractor, which hit the market in 1919. In Belgium, another company, Claeys, was entering the picture. Founded in Zedelgem in 1906 by Leon Claeys, Claeys began manufacturing harvesting equipment in 1910. Back in the United States, Zimmerman's New Holland company was also thriving. It continued to do well until about 1930, when the Great Depression began to hit rural America hard. As farm income plummeted, so did New Holland's revenue.

SPERRY TAKES OVER IN 1947

After about a decade of struggle, New Holland was purchased by a group of four investors. The new owners

CNH Global N.V.

were able to turn the company around quickly by introducing a new product, the world's first successful automatic pickup, self-tying hay baler. The baler, invented by local thresherman Ed Nolt, was an instant hit among farmers. It almost singlehandedly put New Holland back on solid footing, and balers were a key company product line into the 21st century.

In 1947 New Holland Machine Company was acquired by electronics specialist Sperry Corporation, creating a subsidiary dubbed Sperry New Holland. In the years that followed, Sperry New Holland developed and manufactured a large number of agricultural machines. In particular, the company carved out a niche as a producer of high-quality harvesting equipment. Things were also developing quickly in the European agricultural equipment industry during this period. In 1952 Claeys unveiled the first European self-propelled combine harvester. By the early 1960s, Claeys was one of the biggest combine manufacturers in Europe. Sperry New Holland bought a major interest in Claeys in 1964. The same year, Sperry New Holland made a major breakthrough in hay harvesting technology with the introduction of the haybine mower-conditioner, model 460. This machine was capable of performing tasks that previously required two or three separate pieces of equipment. New Holland would go on to revolutionize harvesting equipment in 1974, with the introduction of the world's first twin rotor combine.

As the 1960s continued, Fiat became increasingly active in the manufacture of equipment for agriculture and construction. Late in the decade, that company created a Tractor and Earthmoving Machinery Division. Fiat's earthmoving segment was moved into its own subsidiary, Fiat Macchine Movimento Terra S.p.A., in 1970. Fiat continued to move further into heavy equipment through the 1970s. In 1974 Fiat Macchine Movimento Terra launched a joint venture with U.S. manufacturer Allis Chalmers Corporation, called Fiat-Allis. That year also marked the creation of the company's Fiat Trattori S.p.A. subsidiary. Fiat finally gained entry into the North American market in 1977, with the acquisition of Hesston, a Kansas-based manufacturer of hay and forage machinery. Fiat also purchased Agrifull, a small-sized tractor manufacturer, that year. In 1984 Fiat consolidated all of its agricultural machinery manufacturing under the umbrella of Fiatagri, the new name for Fiat Trattori.

THE EIGHTIES BELONG TO FORD

All the while, Ford was also becoming a global force in agricultural equipment. Its Ford Tractor division had been responsible for a number of industry breakthroughs, including the use of rubber pneumatic tires, power hydraulics, diesel engines, and the three-point hitch. Ford's inexpensive tractors had been largely responsible for the replacement of horses and mules by machines on U.S. farms over the first several decades of the 20th century. By 1985 Ford Tractor had 9,000 employees, about one-third of them located in North America, and 5,000 dealers worldwide, again about a third of them in the United States.

In 1986 Ford purchased Sperry New Holland and merged it with its Ford Tractor Operations to create a new company, Ford New Holland, Inc. By this time New Holland had grown to become one of the best performing companies in the farm equipment business, with 2,500 dealers and more than 9,000 employees of its own, working in 100 different countries. The merger was part of an overall consolidation taking place in the farm equipment industry at the time, occurring just one year after Case took over International Harvester. With combined annual sales of $2 billion, the new company made Ford the third largest farm equipment manufacturer in the world. Most of Ford Tractor's executives and managers were moved over to New Holland's Pennsylvania offices, which became Ford New Holland's corporate headquarters.

Within months of this merger, Ford New Holland added on the agricultural division of Versatile Farm and Equipment Co., an agricultural equipment manufacturer that had been founded in Canada in 1947. The combination of Ford's tractors, New Holland's harvesters, and Versatile's large four-wheel-drive machines created a company that produced a wide spectrum of agricultural equipment, and, best of all, there was almost no overlap in what the three entities manufactured and, therefore, little pruning to be done once they were united. One of the few major changes at New Holland was the gradual elimination of its company-store system. Between 1987 and 1989, New Holland's 53 company-owned outlets were sold or closed, in favor of a dealer development program that provided training and assistance for independent dealers.

Back in Europe, changes were also taking place at Fiat. In 1988 the activities of Fiat-Allis and Fiatagri were merged to form a new company, FiatGeotech S.p.A., which now encompassed Fiat's entire farm and earthmoving equipment sector. By the end of the 1980s, Fiat was Europe's leading manufacturer of tractors and hay and forage equipment. FiatGeotech's revenue for 1989 was $2.3 billion.

THE FIAT ERA

By 1990 Ford New Holland had 17,000 employees, revenue of $2.8 billion, and plants in the United States,

108

INTERNATIONAL DIRECTORY OF COMPANY HISTORIES, VOLUME 99

Canada, Belgium, England, and Brazil, plus joint ventures in India, Pakistan, Japan, Mexico, and Venezuela. In 1991 Fiat purchased an 80 percent interest in Ford New Holland. Ford New Holland was merged with FiatGeotech to create a huge new industrial equipment entity based in the Netherlands and dubbed N.H. Geotech N.V., although its North American operation kept the name Ford New Holland for the time being. The purchase surprised nobody in the industry, because Ford had been looking for a buyer for its tractor operation for the better part of a decade. The new international behemoth, headquartered in London, instantly became the world's largest producer of tractors and haying equipment, the second largest producer of combines, and one of the largest producers of diesel engines.

Between 1991 and 1993, the company undertook a number of measures designed to better integrate its many pieces into a coherent whole. Among the goals of this group of projects were a reduction in the time needed to bring new products to market and to focus manufacturing operations on core components. The company's supply chain was also streamlined. N.H. Geotech changed its name to New Holland N.V. in January 1993, although the company's North American operation stuck with the Ford New Holland name for two more years. The year 1993 also brought the introduction of the company's Genesis line of 140- to 210-horsepower tractors. The Genesis line proved so popular that it took only a little more than two years to sell 10,000 of them.

New Holland made the completion of its integration process official at its 1994 worldwide convention, at which the company unveiled its new corporate identity and logo. For that year, the company reported net income of $355 million on sales of $4.7 billion. Fiat eventually acquired the other 20 percent of New Holland previously owned by Ford, and in 1995, the 100th anniversary of the New Holland brand name, Ford New Holland was rechristened New Holland North America.

Operating as a wholly owned subsidiary of Fiat, New Holland N.V. brought in just more than $5 billion in sales in 1995. By this time, the company controlled 21 percent of the world market for agricultural tractors, 17 percent of the world market for combines, 42 percent of the market for forage harvesters, and significant shares of the world markets for just about every other category of agricultural or construction equipment one could name.

A PUBLIC OFFERING IN 1996

By 1996 New Holland was selling about 280 different products in 130 countries around the world. Globally, 5,600 dealers were selling the company's agricultural equipment and 250 were peddling its construction machinery. During the last quarter of that year, Fiat sold 31 percent of New Holland's stock, 46.5 million common shares, to the public at $21.50 per share, to raise capital to bolster its sagging core automobile business. On November 1, the first day New Holland stock was traded on the New York Stock Exchange, it was the most heavily traded stock on the market.

In addition to the stock offering, 1996 also brought a number of technological innovations and new product unveilings as well. New Holland's new E-Series backhoe loaders were chosen by *Construction Equipment* magazine as one of the construction industry's 100 most significant products. The company also introduced several new tractor lines, four Roll-Best round balers, and two large self-propelled forage harvesters. New Holland was also active in conducting research on futuristic, driverless machines. Working with the National Aeronautics and Space Administration (NASA) and Carnegie Mellon University as part of the NASA Robotics Engineering Consortium, New Holland created a prototype of a self-propelled windrower that cuts, conditions, and puts alfalfa into windrows without requiring a human operator. One further 1996 development at New Holland was the appointment of former U.S. Treasury secretary and vice-presidential candidate Lloyd Bentsen as its chairman of the board.

In July 1997 the 25,000th New Holland Twin Rotor combine rolled off the company's Grand Island, Nebraska, assembly line. As the year continued, the company announced the creation of a new Boomer line of light diesel tractors, including four brand-new models. Building on its longstanding philosophy of manufacturing products close to where they were sold, the company moved production of the light tractors from Japan to a new facility in Dublin, Georgia. The launch of the Boomer line reflected New Holland's commitment to the production of the kind of compact but powerful machines sought by customers for a variety of off-highway uses.

NEW HOLLAND + CASE = CNH GLOBAL

New Holland, like Case, was buffeted by the downturn in the worldwide agricultural equipment market in the late 1990s, and cut its workforce by 1,300 during the second half of 1998. The company in early 1999 announced that it would make further job cuts, then in May agreed to acquire Case. Completed in November 1999, the $4.6 billion acquisition involved the purchase by New Holland of all of Case's stock at $55 per share, after which New Holland renamed itself CNH Global

N.V. New Holland funded the transaction in part via a $1.4 billion advance to capital from Fiat. Thus, Fiat's initial 71.1 percent stake in CNH grew to 84.5 percent in June 2000 when this advance was converted into CNH common shares.

A symbol of globalization at the turn of the millennium, CNH was incorporated in the Netherlands; headquartered initially in Racine, Wisconsin (adopting Case's headquarters), later in Lake Forest, Illinois, and still later in Burr Ridge, Illinois; had its stock traded on the New York Stock Exchange; and was majority owned by an Italian automaker. Rosso, the Frenchman who had headed Case, was named cochairman and CEO, while the head of New Holland, Umberto Quadrino, an Italian, was the other cochairman.

As a condition of approval of the merger, the European Commission required CNH to divest itself of four business lines, including Fermec Holdings, which was sold to Terex Corporation in December 2000. CNH also began consolidating the operations of its predecessor companies, aiming to generate annual cost savings of around $600 million within four years. In early 2000 the company announced that it would close or sell ten of its 60 manufacturing plants around the world, cutting its 36,000-person workforce by 7,000. CNH also planned, within a few years, to reduce the number of chassis platforms used in its various products from 50 to about 35.

A DIFFICULT INTEGRATION

The post-merger integration was far from smooth, however. For 2000, its first full year of operation, CNH posted a loss of $269 million before restructuring and other merger-related charges. The red ink stemmed in part from economic woes, a continuing depression in commodity prices sending U.S. sales of large tractors and harvesting combines down. Another factor was CNH's failure to integrate the combined operations of New Holland and Case more quickly. As the integration dragged on, a significant portion of farmers and dealers, uncertain about which products CNH planned to continue to support, switched brands to Deere and other competitors. In the meantime, in November 2000, Rosso relinquished the CEO position but remained chairman. Promoted from president and COO to CEO was Paolo Monferino, who came to CNH through the New Holland side.

In 2001 CNH suffered a reduced loss before restructuring and merger-related charges of $170 million as the agricultural equipment market improved at the same time that the general downturn in the U.S. economy undercut demand for construction equipment.

Reflecting its financial struggles, the company slashed its dividend by 82 percent that year. As it continued to trim its workforce and close plants, and operate in the red, CNH by mid-2002 had reduced its annual operating costs by more than $450 million, putting it ahead of schedule on its cost-cutting plan. That year, the firm strengthened its balance sheet by cutting its net debt by $1.5 billion to roughly $4 billion through a financial restructuring. Fiat exchanged $1.3 billion in CNH debt for additional CNH shares, while the other $200 million was raised through a secondary stock offering. Fiat's stake in CNH consequently increased slightly to 85 percent.

Seeking new avenues for growth in global markets, CNH in 2002 launched an alliance with Kobelco Construction Machinery Co., Ltd., a subsidiary of Japanese steelmaker Kobe Steel, Ltd. The alliance centered on the worldwide development, production, and sale of crawler excavators, including mini-excavators. In conjunction with the formation of this venture, CNH acquired a 20 percent stake in Kobelco from Kobe Steel. Also in 2002, the company entered into a joint venture with a subsidiary of Shanghai Automotive Industry Corporation to make small farm tractors and engines in Shanghai, China.

In 2003 CNH effected another substantial cut in its debt load by issuing eight million shares of preferred stock to Fiat in exchange for the retirement of $2 billion in loans owed to Fiat. As agreed to by the two parties, these preferred shares automatically converted to CNH common shares in March 2006, boosting Fiat's stake to around 90 percent. CNH in 2003 also launched a new effort to further cut and contain costs, aiming to slash annual expenses by an additional $650 million by the end of 2006. More factories were closed and the workforce shrank even further, while $271 million in restructuring charges sent the firm into a net loss for 2003 of $157 million, the fourth straight loss-making year. From 2000 to 2003 CNH Global suffered cumulated net losses totaling nearly $1 billion.

A NEW ERA OF PROSPERITY

The company finally managed to turn a profit in 2004 (of $125 million) thanks to a stronger agricultural economy, the beginning of a major upsurge in construction spending worldwide, and successful new product introductions. Revenues jumped nearly 15 percent, to $11.55 billion. The following year, Monferino left CNH to head another Fiat unit. The career of Harold Boyanovsky, the new president and CEO, included stints at International Harvester and Case and then, within CNH, heading first its worldwide agricultural equipment business from 1999 to 2002 and then its construction equipment business.

In the fall of 2005 Boyanovsky announced the first major initiative of his tenure, a reorganization of the company around its four main brands: Case IH and New Holland in agricultural equipment and Case Construction and New Holland Construction in construction equipment. The new organization, which replaced the previous one that centered on regions of the world, was designed to better align CNH with its dealers and customers. It also provided the basis for a leaner and potentially quicker acting management team as the heads of the four brands began reporting directly to Boyanovsky. This reorganization, coupled with the preceding restructuring and integration efforts, seemed to have paid off by 2007 when, despite a sharp downturn in the North American construction market, CNH enjoyed a 91 percent net income surge, to $559 million, on record revenues of $15.96 billion, the latter a 23 percent increase over 2006. It appeared that the anticipated benefits of the New Holland–Case merger were at last being realized and that CNH was finally fulfilling its promise as a more formidable competitor to Deere, Caterpillar, and other rivals.

Robert R. Jacobson and Carol I. Keeley
Updated, David E. Salamie

PRINCIPAL SUBSIDIARIES

Case New Holland Inc. (U.S.A.); CNH America LLC (U.S.A.); CNH Australia Pty Limited; CNH Belgium N.V.; CNH Capital America LLC (U.S.A.); CNH Financial Services S.A.S. (France); CNH France S.A.; CNH Italia S.p.A. (Italy); CNH Latin America Ltda. (Brazil).

PRINCIPAL COMPETITORS

Deere & Company; Caterpillar Inc.; Komatsu Ltd.; AGCO Corporation.

FURTHER READING

Arndt, Michael, "A Merger's Bitter Harvest," *Business Week,* February 5, 2001, pp. 112, 114.

Bas, Ed, "Ford New Holland's Goal: The Blue Tractor Pulling a Red Harvester," *Ward's Auto World,* June 1987, p. 72.

Bowe, Christopher, "CNH Share Deal Set to Bolster Balance Sheet," *Financial Times,* March 28, 2002, p. 20.

Brezonick, Mike, "The Changing Face of CNH Global," *Diesel Progress North American Edition,* September 2000, pp. 16, 18, 20.

"CNH Global Names New Chief Executive," *Milwaukee Journal Sentinel,* November 10, 2000, p. 1D.

Content, Thomas, "CNH Global to Reorganize: Equipment Maker's New Strategy Will Emphasize Its Brands," *Milwaukee Journal Sentinel,* October 1, 2005, p. D1.

———, "CNH Plans to Eliminate $2 Billion Debt," *Milwaukee Journal Sentinel,* March 6, 2003, p. 1D.

Daykin, Tom, "CNH Global to Close Plants Outside U.S.," *Milwaukee Journal Sentinel,* June 27, 2003, p. 3D.

Deutsch, Claudia, "Former BMC Chairman Assumes Post at Case," *New York Times,* July 23, 1991, p. D4.

Eiben, Therese, "How the Industries Stack Up," *Fortune,* July 12, 1993, p. 102.

Emsden, Christopher, "Fiat Unit CNH Aims to Serve World's Small Farmers As Niche," *Wall Street Journal,* February 2, 2005, p. B2D.

Erb, David, and Eldon Brumbaugh, *Full Steam Ahead: J.I. Case Tractors and Equipment, 1842–1955,* St. Joseph, Mich.: American Society of Agricultural Engineers, 1993, 343 p.

Fisher, Lawrence, "Tenneco Names Head of Its J.I. Case Unit," *New York Times,* December 7, 1991, p. 39.

Fogarty, Bill, "Ford New Holland: Out of the Company Store Business," *Implement and Tractor,* July 1989, p. 15.

"Ford New Holland Here to Stay," *Construction Equipment,* March 1994, p. 14.

Gaines, Sallie L., "Here's a Case of Good Results," *Chicago Tribune,* May 30, 1999.

Gertzen, Jason, "CNH Global Makes Deal to Extend Overseas Reach," *Milwaukee Journal Sentinel,* March 30, 2001, p. 1D.

Gilpin, Kenneth, "Chief at Troubled J.I. Case Stepping Down," *New York Times,* September 16, 1992, p. D4.

Hawkins, Lee, Jr., "Farming Trends Prompt CNH Cutbacks," *Milwaukee Journal Sentinel,* July 19, 2000, p. 15D.

Haycraft, William R., *Yellow Steel: The Story of the Earthmoving Equipment Industry,* Urbana: University of Illinois Press, 2000, 465 p.

Hayes, Thomas, "Head of Tenneco Unit to Quit All His Posts," *New York Times,* March 16, 1991, p. 33.

———, "J.I. Case Plans to Cut Work Force by 4,000," *New York Times,* December 5, 1991, p. D4.

Holbrook, Stewart H., *Machines of Plenty: Chronicle of an Innovator in Construction and Agricultural Equipment,* New York: Macmillan, 1955, 269 p., reprinted, 1976.

Holmes, Michael, *J.I. Case: The First 150 Years,* Racine, Wis.: Case Corporation, 1992, 200 p.

"The Impact of Ford New Holland's Buyout," *Agri Marketing,* September 1990, p. 18.

Johnson, Robert, "Tenneco Restructuring Is Over, but Doubts Remain," *Wall Street Journal,* September 8, 1992, p. B4.

———, "Tenneco's Plans to Restructure Case Unit Include $843 Million After-Tax Charge," *Wall Street Journal,* March 23, 1993, p. A3.

Kelly, Kevin, "Case Digs Out from Way Under," *Business Week,* August 14, 1995, pp. 62–63.

Krebs, Michelle, "New Holland Called a 'Natural' for Ford," *Automotive News,* October 21, 1985, p. 53.

Mackintosh, James, "The Race to Drive Fiat Forward: The Italian Carmaker's Chief Executive Plans to Instill a New Sense of Urgency into Its CNH Division," *Financial Times,* July 25, 2006, p. 12.

Marsh, Peter, "Jean-Pierre Rosso Rolls Up His Sleeves at CNH," *Financial Times,* June 5, 2000, p. 23.

McKanic, Patricia Ann, "Tenneco's Ashford to Resign As Chief of Case Unit, Which He Turned Around," *Wall Street Journal,* March 18, 1991, p. B8.

McMurray, Scott, "Farm-Equipment Sales Are Running at Full Throttle," *Wall Street Journal,* June 15, 1993, p. B4.

Miller, James P., "Case Announces More Job Cuts As Demand Falls," *Wall Street Journal,* December 22, 1998, p. A3.

——, "CNH Global Pricing a Disappointment," *Chicago Tribune,* June 12, 2002, Business sec., p. 1.

Nesbitt, Scott, "Ford, Fiat Merger Brings Speculation," *Implement and Tractor,* September 1990, p. 1.

"New Holland Grows As Global Leader," *Lancaster (Pa.) Sunday News,* March 23, 1997, p. 32.

"New Holland Marks 100th Anniversary," *Implement and Tractor,* May/June 1995, p. 26.

Osenga, Mike, "Case Corporation," *Diesel Progress Engines and Drives,* June 1992, p. 102.

——, "A Look at New Holland's New Tractors," *Diesel Progress North American Edition,* July 1997, p. 10.

Raghavan, Anita, and Carl Quintanilla, "New Holland Agrees to Acquire Case for $4.2 Billion, Creating Rival to Deere," *Wall Street Journal,* May 17, 1999, p. A3.

Romell, Rick, "Racine Losing Its Case Tractor Plant," *Milwaukee Journal Sentinel,* July 19, 2000, p. 15A.

Rovito, Rich, "CNH Makes a New Case," *Business Journal of Milwaukee,* April 23, 2004.

——, "CNH Says Case, New Holland Tractors Will Harvest Profits," *Business Journal of Milwaukee,* June 28, 2002.

Savage, Mark, "Case Acquiring Global Influence," *Milwaukee Journal Sentinel,* October 12, 1997.

——, "Case to Lay Off 1,300 Workers," *Milwaukee Journal Sentinel,* December 22, 1998.

——, "Company Takes Best of All Worlds: Racine Farm Equipment Firm Has Global Look," *Milwaukee Journal Sentinel,* November 15, 1999.

——, "Deere Reaps Profits As CNH Stumbles," *Milwaukee Journal Sentinel,* August 16, 2000, p. 15D.

——, "Farm Equipment Slide Feeds Talk of Mergers," *Milwaukee Journal Sentinel,* May 16, 1999.

——, "Sale of Case Would Form Ag Giant," *Milwaukee Journal Sentinel,* May 18, 1999.

——, "Tenneco Cutting Link to Case: Move Will Leave Racine Firm Independent for the First Time Since 1964," *Milwaukee Journal Sentinel,* February 23, 1996.

Solomon, Caleb, "Tenneco Plans to Sell 35 Percent of Case Unit to Public, on Revival in Agriculture," *Wall Street Journal,* April 27, 1994, p. A2.

Stonehouse, Tom, and Eldon Brumbaugh, *J.I. Case Agricultural and Construction Equipment, 1956–1994,* St. Joseph, Mich.: American Society of Agricultural Engineers, [1996].

Sturani, Maria, "Fiat's Offering of New Holland Shares Expected to Swell Coffers by $1 Billion," *Wall Street Journal,* November 4, 1996, p. B11.

Tait, Nikki, "The Case for Working from a Platform," *Financial Times,* June 1, 1999, p. 27.

"Tenneco in Plan to Revamp Case," *New York Times,* January 23, 1992, p. D4.

Verespej, Michael A., "An Abrupt Turnaround," *Industry Week,* April 15, 1996, pp. 62–64, 66.

Wyatt, Edward A., "Case Reopened," *Barron's,* June 6, 1994, pp. 14–15.

Coach, Inc.

516 West 34th Street
New York, New York 10001-1394
U.S.A.
Telephone: (212) 594-1850
Fax: (212) 594-1682
Web site: http://www.coach.com

Public Company
Founded: 1941
Incorporated: 2000
Employees: 12,000
Sales: $3.18 billion (2008)
Stock Exchanges: New York
Ticker Symbol: COH
NAICS: 448320 Luggage and Leather Goods Stores; 448150 Clothing Accessories Stores; 454111 Electronic Shopping; 316992 Women's Handbag and Purse Manufacturing; 316993 Personal Leather Good (Except Women's Handbag and Purse) Manufacturing; 316999 All Other Leather Good Manufacturing

■ ■ ■

Coach, Inc., is a designer, marketer, and retailer of a prestige line of handbags, men's and women's accessories, and other fashion products. The company made its reputation selling sturdy leather purses in unchanging, traditional, classic styles, and it remains one of the best-known leather brands in the United States and has a growing reputation overseas while it has simultaneously earned a more fashion-forward reputation. Beyond its flagship handbags, the company offers Coach brand outerwear, belts, small leather goods, business cases, luggage, and jewelry. Although the firm began as a family-run workshop, all of these products are manufactured by independent contractors in Asia and Europe. Coach brand footwear, sunglasses, and watches are produced through agreements with licensing partners, while Coach fragrances are the result of a partnership with The Estée Lauder Companies Inc.

Nearly 80 percent of company sales are derived from direct-to-consumer channels. These include about 400 Coach stores in North America (of these, approximately 300 are retail stores and the remainder are factory outlets), direct-mail catalogs, and an online store. There are also around 150 Coach locations in fashion-trendsetting Japan. The company's indirect channels include the wholesaling of Coach brand products to approximately 900 department store locations in the United States and Canada, including Macy's, Bloomingdale's, Dillard's, Nordstrom, Lord and Taylor, Carson's, and Saks stores; and around 150 department store and freestanding retail locations in more than 20 international markets. Formed in 1941, Coach was family owned and operated until 1985, when Sara Lee Corporation purchased the firm. Coach remained a subsidiary of Sara Lee until 2001, when the firm regained its independence via a spinoff.

FAMILY-RUN BUSINESS BEGINNING IN 1941

Coach was founded in 1941 as a family-run workshop based in a loft on the edge of Manhattan's garment

Coach, Inc.

COMPANY PERSPECTIVES

Coach has grown from a family-run workshop in a Manhattan loft to a leading American marketer of fine accessories and gifts for women and men. Coach is one of the most recognized fine accessories brands in the U.S. and in targeted international markets. We offer premium lifestyle accessories to a loyal and growing customer base and provide consumers with fresh, relevant and innovative products that are extremely well made, at an attractive price. Coach's modern, fashionable handbags and accessories use a broad range of high quality leathers, fabrics and materials. In response to our customer's demands for both fashion and function, Coach offers updated styles and multiple product categories which address an increasing share of our customer's accessory wardrobe. Coach has created a sophisticated, modern and inviting environment to showcase our product assortment and reinforce a consistent brand position wherever the consumer may shop. We utilize a flexible, cost-effective global sourcing model, in which independent manufacturers supply our products, allowing us to bring our broad range of products to market rapidly and efficiently.

district. The company started with just six leather workers who made small leather goods, primarily wallets and billfolds, by hand. In 1946 Miles Cahn, a lifelong New Yorker, came to work for the company. By 1950 he was running the factory for its owners. The company's employees, members of Local 1 of the Pocketbook and Novelty Workers Union, continued to manufacture billfolds throughout the 1950s, producing small profits for the small concern.

By 1960 Cahn had taken notice of the distinctive properties of the leather used to make baseball gloves. With wear and abrasion, the leather in a glove became soft and supple. Following this model, Cahn devised a way of processing leather to make it strong, soft, flexible, and deep-toned in color, as it absorbed dye well. At his wife Lillian's suggestion, a number of women's handbags were designed to supplement the factory's low-margin wallet production. The purses, given the brand name Coach, were made of sturdy cowhide, in which the grain of the leather could still be seen, instead of the thin leather pasted over cardboard that was used for most women's handbags at the time. This innovation marked the company's entry into the field of classic, long-lasting, luxury women's handbags that Coach would come to define.

In 1961, after more than a decade of running the leather workshop, the Cahns borrowed money to buy out the factory's owners and take possession of Coach. Throughout the next decades, Coach produced solid handbags in an assortment of basic styles. For the most part, the company steered clear of fast-moving trends, opting instead for traditional, conservative elegance and quality. Gradually, high-priced Coach products developed a reputation and a certain cachet. In the late 1960s, as fashion changed radically, Coach deviated somewhat from its traditional product line, introducing additional models that were designed to complement trendier styles in clothing. In 1969 the company began to market items such as a structured bucket bag, which was produced for only one season, and a fringe "shimmy" bag.

By the early 1980s, the Coach plant occupied four floors of a building on West 34th Street. The company was manufacturing purses, briefcases, billfolds, and belts, using skilled laborers, many of whom had immigrated from Argentina. Paying their workers wages that were a dollar or more higher than rates in other factories, the Cahns enjoyed good labor relations with their employees, which allowed them to produce a steady flow of Coach products.

In the late 1970s and early 1980s, Coach took two steps to diversify its channels of distribution. Under a new vice-president for special products, the company began a mail-order business, and also began to open its own specialty stores, to sell Coach products outside a department store setting. Sales of Coach products grew steadily throughout this period, until demand began to outstrip supply. Department stores were selling all the Coach bags that the company could produce, and by the early 1980s it had become necessary to ration the products to various vendors. Despite the potential for vast expansion of their market share, the Cahns continued to run their business in the same way that they always had. They had little desire to move their factory out of its urban Manhattan setting to a place where rents and taxes might be lower, space more readily available, and wages cheaper. In addition, they did not want to change their methods of production so that goods could be made more quickly, at the expense of quality or workmanship. Instead, they continued to run their business on a personal level, maintaining first-name relationships with many of their workers, and inviting department store buyers from New York to tour their factory to observe the craftsmanship that went into each Coach bag.

KEY DATES

1941: Company is founded as a family-run workshop, making small leather goods in Manhattan.

1946: Miles Cahn joins the company.

1950: Cahn begins running the factory for its owners.

1960: Coach brand of sturdy cowhide purses is introduced and becomes the company's signature, luxury trademark.

1961: Cahn and his wife, Lillian, buy out the factory's owners.

Late 1970s/Early 1980s: Company begins a mail-order business and opens its first specialty stores.

1985: The Cahns sell Coach to Sara Lee Corporation for about $30 million; Sara Lee begins expanding Coach's product line and its channels of distribution.

1988: Company begins international push, opening boutiques in England and Japan.

1989: Sales reach $100 million, five times the level of 1985.

1992: Product line is expanded to include outerwear and luggage.

1997: Company enters into its first licensing agreement, a deal with Movado Group for a line of Coach watches.

1999: Company enters the e-commerce realm with the launch of coach.com.

2000: Sara Lee sells 17 percent of the newly named Coach, Inc., to the public.

2001: Sara Lee spins off remaining interest in Coach to Sara Lee shareholders; Coach Japan, Inc., is formed as a 50-50 joint venture with Sumitomo Corporation to facilitate expansion in Japan.

2004: Sales surpass $1 billion for the first time.

2005: Company acquires full control of Coach Japan.

2008: Company begins major push into China.

In 1983 the Cahns purchased a 300-acre dairy farm in Vermont as a weekend diversion from their business in New York. Although the property was intended to provide a vacation home and retirement destination, the Cahns began to raise goats and market goat cheese

under the brand name "Coach Farm" shortly after buying the farm. By 1985 they were commuting twice a week between Vermont and New York. In the summer of that year, after determining that none of their three children had any desire to take over the family leatherware business, the Cahns decided to sell Coach and retire to their goat farm.

EXPANDING UNDER SARA LEE STARTING IN 1985

In July 1985 the Cahns cemented an agreement with Sara Lee Corporation, which also sold foodstuffs and hosiery. In return for a sum reported to be around $30 million, the conglomerate took control of the company's factory, its six boutiques, and its flagship store on Madison Avenue in New York. Sara Lee promised that it would continue to operate Coach in the way in which it had always been run. At the time of the sale, the Cahns split $1 million of the proceeds with 200 longtime employees on the basis of their seniority. Taking over leadership of Coach as president was Lew Frankfort, who had joined the company in 1979 as vice-president of business development.

Under its new owners and new president, the company prepared for a rapid expansion. The basic strategy for this expansion was to add to the number of products that bore the Coach name and to increase the number of customers buying these goods. Accordingly, the company added several new styles of handbag in an updated classics line and also began a major expansion of its channels of distribution. In early 1986 new boutiques were opened in Macy's stores in New York and San Francisco and in two Bamberger's stores. Additional Coach outlets were under construction in stores in Denver and Seattle, and agreements had been reached to open similar boutiques within other major department stores later in the year. In addition, Coach opened its own stores in malls in New York, New Jersey, Texas, and California. By November, the company was operating 12 stores, along with nearly 50 boutiques within larger department stores. The company projected that the expansion would boost sales for 1986 to $25 million, a gain of 45 percent over the previous year.

A significant part of sales was expected to come from the newly introduced Coach Lightweights line of products, which featured lighter-weight leather and bags with new shapes. This line was intended to broaden the company's customer base by appealing to women who lived in the South and West, where warmer weather made lightweight handbags more desirable. The Lightweights line featured handbags in smaller sizes, for ease of access, and lighter spring colors, such as taupe, light brown, and navy. This line quickly came to constitute 15 percent of the company's overall sales.

To keep up with growing demand for Coach products, the company doubled its workforce, leased additional space for factory operations, and expanded the workweek to six days. Despite these measures, however, by the fall of 1987, Coach was again unable to meet all orders for its goods, and the company began to seek additional room for expansion. Also, to better control the circumstances under which its products were sold, Coach slashed the number of department stores retailing its goods by 50 percent. Despite continued strong demand, the company did not increase its prices to keep pace with a sharp rise in the cost of leather. By the end of 1987, Coach had nearly doubled its revenues.

In December 1987 Coach opened a new flagship store on Madison Avenue, in New York. The two-story store, with a marble and mahogany interior, featured an atrium and a gallery of leather art, as well as the full range of Coach products. The company expected to sell $5 million worth of handbags in the store's first year.

Coach solved its production problem by opening a plant near Miami, Florida, where its Lightweights collection was manufactured, in 1988. The plant's production supplied 22 freestanding stores and 300 different retailers, making Coach products available in more than 1,000 locations. Although the traditional line and the Lightweights products were emphasized, Coach further expanded its offerings to include more business items for men and women. Among the new products were briefcases, wallets, and diaries.

Coach's first nonleather product was introduced in 1988. Silk scarves, sold in four designs that related to leather goods, were planned to complement the other Coach products. Each of the 36-inch silk squares was manufactured in Italy and priced at $60. Although the company estimated that first-year sales of this line, which also grew to include men's ties and suspenders, would reach $2 million, the products were eventually discontinued after it was determined that their equestrian designs, featuring bridles and stirrups, made them look too much like products from a Coach competitor, Hermès.

AN INTERNATIONAL PUSH

Coach took its first steps overseas in 1988. The company had long noted that many of the customers in its New York store were foreign tourists, and Coach executives believed that this indicated that demand abroad justified international expansion. The company began by opening Coach boutiques in England and Japan, setting up one outlet in Harrods department store in London and five in Mitsukoshi stores in Tokyo and other Japanese locations. These stores carried a full line of Coach products and mimicked the look of Coach stores in the United States, with mahogany and brass fixtures and marble floors. The company planned to train foreign sales staff and hoped to take advantage of the low international value of the dollar to boost sales through lower prices.

As Coach continued its international push in 1989, opening a freestanding store on Sloane Street in London, company sales had quintupled to $100 million in a period of four years and the number of company stores had grown to 40. Coach established its first store in continental Europe, with a 500-square-foot outlet in Stuttgart, Germany. By 1990 the Coach push to enter international markets had created 19 in-store shops in Japanese Mitsukoshi department stores, with six more slated to open in 1991. Coach solidified its position in the Japanese market by renewing its agreement with Mitsukoshi Ltd., making it the exclusive distributor of Coach products in Japan. In addition, Coach joined with another company to open a boutique in a Singapore shopping area, and Coach opened a store in Taipei, Taiwan. With international sales making up 10 percent of the company's revenues, Coach saw the Pacific basin as a key area for further growth.

The company's Far East push was driven by the popularity of Coach goods with Asian tourists in New York, and also by the belief that the company's understated style, lacking in logos or obvious status symbols, was beginning to supplant the vogue for flashy designer goods. To support sales of its products in the Far East, Coach began an advertising campaign to stress the ways in which Coach expressed the American spirit.

Coach's expansion overseas was coupled with domestic expansion, and production again was increased. In addition to its new facility in Florida, the company moved its New York area operations from Manhattan to Carlstadt, New Jersey.

CONTINUING TO EXPAND THE PRODUCT LINE

Coach's success in expanding its brand awareness had caused other manufacturers to imitate the company's trademark styles and shapes in their own products. To prevent this infringement of the company's unique designs, Coach sued a number of other manufacturers to stop them from imitating Coach styles. In 1990 the company won a suit in federal court against several other companies, including Ann Taylor and Laura Leather Goods. The ruling awarded the company damages for trade dress infringement.

Coach sales continued to grow in the early 1990s. By May 1991, revenues had increased more than a fifth over the previous year, and annual sales had reached $150 million. The company continued to broaden its product line, while retaining the qualities identified with its prestigious brand name. Overall, Coach planned a dramatic shift in its identity in the 1990s. "We're going for positioning as Coach the brand, as opposed to Coach the leather company," the company's president told *Crain's New York Business.* "I can't see a limit to Coach's growth in the foreseeable future."

To bolster that growth, Coach hired a designer to lead a 16-person product development department to create new objects that could be marketed under the Coach name. In its women's line, the company sought to introduce products in more fashionable colors, without watering down the Coach reputation. In this way, the company hoped to overcome the built-in drawback to high quality and timeless styling, which was that customers rarely needed to replace a product. It launched a line of desk accessories, and an all-leather travel collection was introduced.

In addition, the company began to sell a line of goods for men that included suspenders and socks. This fast-moving category had grown to provide 40 percent of the company's sales. Coach capped off its growth in products for men by opening two Coach for Business stores, which were devoted specifically to products for men, on Madison Avenue in Manhattan and in Boston. With these stores, the company hoped to shift its image, repositioning itself as a full-range accessory maker, rather than merely a handbag manufacturer.

Coach announced that it would move more aggressively into the leather accessories market and also try to market its products to younger customers in 1991. To do so, the company hired a new, young advertising agency, which designed a campaign featuring descendants of famous Americans using Coach products, with the theme, "An American Legacy."

By early 1992 Coach had expanded its number of stores worldwide to 53 and had enhanced its line of men's and women's socks, to further exploit the appeal of the Coach brand name. Later that year, the company added gift items, including picture frames and belts. In the fall, Coach increased the scope of its handbag line, introducing the Sheridan collection, which featured textured, treated leather that would not burnish like other Coach items but was also more scratch resistant; and the Camden collection, which was styled with brass accents.

Coach stepped up its catalog sales effort in the fall of 1992, mailing ten million mail-order brochures to former customers and likely prospects. The company's

catalog operations, although small, were the most profitable of its branches. Coach turned to its mail-order operations to test-market its latest innovation in November 1992, when the company began to offer leather outerwear. Providing five styles for men and women, made of soft, waterproof leather, the outerwear was joined by fabric luggage, another departure from Coach tradition, as the company tried to push the boundaries of its identity even further.

NEW STYLES AND LICENSING ENDEAVORS

As Coach broadened its product offerings, it also broadened the variety of its handbags. Coach moved away from dark, staid colors to brightly hued bags, introducing the Manhattan collection in the spring of 1993. To keep up with demand for this wide variety of new products, Coach expanded its manufacturing activities to Puerto Rico. In late 1994 Coach opened a new flagship store in New York City, its first two-level unit and its largest store at that time. The following year Frankfort was named chairman and CEO of Coach. Around this time, Coach expanded its product line yet again with the launch of the Sonoma collection, which included handbags, backpacks, wallets, and belts featuring relaxed styling and suede and textured leathers. The firm also opened the first freestanding Coach store in Japan.

During the fiscal year ending in June 1996, Coach opened what it called its Pacific Rim flagship store in Waikiki, Hawaii, as a way to promote the brand to Asian tourists. In addition to continued international growth, the licensing of the prestigious Coach brand also came to the fore in the late 1990s. In 1997 the company entered into its first licensing agreement. It agreed to allow its name to be used on a line of watches to be developed by Movado Group. During fiscal 1998 a Coach leather phone case was introduced through a licensing deal with Motorola, Inc. The following year, a line of premium furniture bearing the Coach name was launched through a licensing deal with Baker Furniture Company.

Sales and profits at Coach suffered from 1997 to 1999 as a result of the combination of the economic difficulties in Asia and changes in consumer tastes, particularly a shift away from leather and toward mixed material and nonleather products. A revamp of the product line in 1999 aimed at reversing the sales slowdown, with an emphasis on attracting younger customers. The core handbag line began to feature more colorful cotton twill and other lightweight fabrics, and while the company maintained its classic leather offerings, a number of slow-moving colors were phased out.

Still more license agreements led to the introduction of Coach picture frames, eyewear, and footwear. Coach increasingly offered lower-priced accessory items whose affordability enabled younger consumers to buy a Coach product in its shops, stores, and catalogs. The company also began remodeling its major retail stores in late 1999, seeking to better showcase its new assortment of products. Another important development was the launch of coach.com in October 1999, which marked Coach's entrance into e-commerce.

On the manufacturing side, Coach looked to increase operating margins by turning increasingly to outsourcing and shifting from domestic production to production in lower cost markets. Whereas only about 25 percent of Coach products were produced by independent manufacturers in 1998, around 80 percent of the products were made by outsourcers just two years later. Coach was clearly making a rapid shift from manufacturer to designer and marketer while making sure that its manufacturing partners maintained the level of quality for which the brand was known.

A NEWLY INDEPENDENT COACH

While Frankfort was leading this revitalization effort, Sara Lee decided to spin off Coach as part of its own reorganization. As part of the much larger Sara Lee, Coach had seen its revenues increase from about $19 million in 1985 to $540.4 million in 1997, before declining to $507.8 million in 1999. By mid-2000 there were 106 Coach retail outlets in the United States and 63 outlet stores. Prior to the initial public offering (IPO), the improved financial condition of Coach was evident, as revenues for fiscal 2000 climbed 8.1 percent to $548.9 million and net income surged 130.9 percent, jumping from $16.7 million to $38.6 million. In early October 2000, Sara Lee sold off 17 percent of the newly named Coach, Inc., to the public. Through the IPO, 7.38 million shares of Coach stock were sold at $16 per share, raising $118 million on the New York Stock Exchange. Frankfort remained Coach's chairman and CEO. In April 2001 Sara Lee fully divested itself of its Coach holdings by spinning off the remaining interest to Sara Lee shareholders. Sara Lee netted $1.1 billion in the process. For the fiscal year ending in June 2001, Coach had very encouraging news in its first annual report: Net income had jumped 65.9 percent, to $64 million, and net sales had surged 12.2 percent, to $616.1 million.

In addition to accelerating the development of new products and new product categories, modernizing its store designs, and improving its margins through outsourcing, the newly independent Coach also sought to further expand its channels of distribution both at home and abroad in the early 21st century. After opening 15 new retail stores in the United States during fiscal 2001, Coach opened 20 more new stores in each of the following two years. Overseas, Coach continued to concentrate on the Japanese market, mainly because Japanese consumers spend a great deal more on a per-capita basis on handbags than U.S. consumers. Already boasting 76 outlets in Japan—62 department store boutiques and 14 retail stores—Coach sought to increase its presence in this important market by forming Coach Japan, Inc., a 50-50 joint venture with Japan's Sumitomo Corporation, in June 2001. Through Coach Japan, the company added a couple dozen more Coach locations in Japan over the next two years, including the first two flagship stores in that country, both located in Tokyo. By fiscal 2003, Coach Japan was responsible for more than 18 percent of overall revenues.

Another of the firm's growth strategies for the early 21st century was to promote the purchase of Coach products as gifts. It was clear that a substantial amount of the company's sales were gift purchases, but the company felt it could take greater advantage of this fact by developing new products tailored to gift giving and by improving advertising and promotion. One clear example of a product line perfectly suited to the gift-giving niche was jewelry, and in November 2001 Coach introduced its first jewelry collection in a joint effort with Carolee Designs, Inc. The silver jewelry line featured some items that combined silver and leather.

In April 2002 Coach shut down the last of its manufacturing facilities, a plant in Puerto Rico, thereby completing its shift from manufacturer to designer and marketer. From that point forward, Coach brand products were manufactured either via agreements with independent contractors or through its various deals with licensing partners.

GROWTH

Coach earned a reputation as one of the hottest growth companies of the early 21st century. Between fiscal 2001 and fiscal 2004, revenues more than doubled to $1.32 billion, while net income more than quadrupled, soaring from $64 million to $261.8 million. Thanks to its outsourcing initiative, other operational efficiencies, and improved terms with suppliers, Coach by 2004 enjoyed operating margins that were the highest of any publicly traded retailer in the United States. Wall Street had clearly hopped on the bandwagon as a March 29, 2004, *Business Week* article reported that the company's stock had leaped 900 percent since its 2000 IPO.

Frankfort of course received the lion's share of the credit for these accomplishments, but as a firm in the fashion business, Coach had also been propelled forward by what *Business Week* called a "design renaissance" led by Reed Krakoff. Serving as executive creative director since December 1996 and as president since September 1999, Krakoff led Coach's shift away from its traditional emphasis on classic leather products to a more eclectic, modern, and fashionable array of handbags and accessories made from a broader variety of fabrics and materials. To keep the brand fresh, Krakoff and his design team accelerated the pace of new product introductions. By fiscal 2004, more than 60 percent of Coach's net sales were from products introduced that year. Coach was particularly successful in designing new styles and types of bags and then selling women in the United States, Japan, and other markets on the need for such bags. For example, the company's designers created a six-inch by four-inch zippered bag dubbed a "wristlet" that featured a looped strap so that it could be either dangled from a wrist or clipped onto the inside of a larger bag. Introduced in the fall of 2001 and priced for as low as $38, the wristlet was a huge hit. During fiscal 2004 Coach sold more than a million of the items, generating revenue in excess of $40 million, about 3 percent of overall sales. In the United States, the new product drive was accompanied by the remodeling of Coach's stores and a revamped advertising effort.

Coach's accelerating profits enabled it to maintain an aggressive level of growth. In North America, 20 to 25 new Coach stores were being opened each year, bringing the store count on that continent to nearly 300 by the end of fiscal 2005. In Japan, which remained the firm's other main growth market, sales tripled between 2001 and 2005 as additional flagship stores and shops within department stores opened. During this period, Coach became the number two imported handbag and accessories brand in Japan, behind only Louis Vuitton. In July 2005 Coach set the stage for further growth in Japan by gaining full control of Coach Japan in a buyout of Sumitomo's share of the venture costing roughly $300 million.

Although handbags continued to make up the bulk (more than 60 percent) of sales, Coach sustained its efforts to experiment with other product lines. A line of Coach sunglasses was introduced in the fall of 2003 through a licensing deal with Marchon Eyewear, and the company in November 2006 launched a new jewelry line, mainly consisting of bangle bracelets. In March 2007 the first Coach fragrance debuted via a partnership with BeautyBank, a unit of The Estée Lauder Companies Inc. Coach also began augmenting its core handbag business by introducing major new lifestyle collections. In the fall of 2006, for example, the company introduced the up-market Legacy collection, which featured handbags costing about 48 percent more

on average than comparable Coach products. Among the collections debuting a year later was Ergo, a line of streamlined, lightweight bags that had minimal hardware.

At least through fiscal 2008, Coach appeared immune to the economic travails that had curtailed the growth and profits of many other retailers and had sent some into bankruptcy. Enjoying 32 consecutive quarters of increasing profits since going public in 2000, Coach set new records in 2008 for both sales, $3.18 billion, and net income, $783.1 million. The latter figure represented an 18 percent increase over the previous year.

Frankfort was ambitiously aiming to push Coach's sales to $5 billion by 2012, despite the possible impact of the economic downturn, via a slew of growth drivers. Already operating around 300 stores in the United States, Coach had identified more than 200 locations for additional outlets and planned to open about 40 per year. In addition, a specialty boutique for its Legacy collection debuted in New York City late in 2007. Overseas, Coach continued its Japanese expansion while also targeting China as its next big growth market. Hoping to duplicate its rapid ascension in Japan, the company in May 2008 announced plans to acquire the Coach retail businesses in Hong Kong, Macau, and mainland China from its distributor, the ImagineX group. These operations amounted to 24 Coach retail locations, including a flagship store in Hong Kong that opened in the spring of 2008. The acquisition was designed to enable Coach to gain greater control over its brand in China as it sought to open 50 new locations and generate sales of more than $250 million in that nation by 2013. Coach was also pushing into another emerging market, Russia, where it entered into a distributor agreement with Jamilco and opened its first store (in Moscow), both in 2008.

Elizabeth Rourke
Updated, David E. Salamie

PRINCIPAL SUBSIDIARIES

Coach Services, Inc.; Coach Leatherware International, Inc.; Coach Stores Puerto Rico, Inc.; Coach Japan Holdings, Inc.; Coach Japan Investments, Inc.; Coach Stores Canada Inc.; Coach International Holdings, Inc. (Cayman Islands); Coach Consulting (Shenzhen) Co. Limited (China); Coach Shanghai Limited (China); Coach International Limited (Hong Kong); Coach Manufacturing Limited (Hong Kong); Coach Hong Kong Limited; Coach Europe Services S.r.l. (Italy); Coach Japan, Inc.

PRINCIPAL COMPETITORS

LVMH Moët Hennessy Louis Vuitton SA; kate spade LLC; Dooney & Bourke Inc.; Gucci Group NV; Prada SpA Group; Kenneth Cole Productions, Inc.; Liz Claiborne, Inc.; Jones Apparel Group, Inc.; Hermès International; PreVu, Inc.; Polo Ralph Lauren Corporation; Etienne Aigner Group Inc.

FURTHER READING

Barker, Robert, "Coach May Carry Too Much Baggage," *Business Week,* September 11, 2000, p. 173.

Berman, Phyllis, "Goat Cheese, Anyone?" *Forbes,* September 18, 1989.

Berner, Robert, "Coach's Driver Picks Up the Pace," *Business Week,* March 29, 2004, pp. 98, 100.

Berry, Kate, "The Pocketbook Issues in the Future of Coach," *New York Times,* August 20, 2000, Sec. 3, p. 8.

Boorstin, Julia, "How Coach Got Hot," *Fortune,* October 28, 2002, pp. 131–32, 134.

Brady, Diane, "Coach's Split Personality: How the Retailer Manages to Keep Both Fashionistas and Outlet Shoppers Happy," *Business Week,* November 7, 2005, pp. 60, 62.

———, "Teaching an Old Bag Some New Tricks," *Business Week,* June 9, 2003, pp. 78, 80.

Byron, Ellen, "Case by Case: How Coach Won a Rich Purse by Inventing New Uses for Bags," *Wall Street Journal,* November 17, 2004, p. A1.

Fallon, James, "Coach Opens First Overseas Store in London," *Women's Wear Daily,* May 19, 1989.

Feitelberg, Rosemary, et al., "Sara Lee to Sell Non-Core Units," *Women's Wear Daily,* May 31, 2000, p. 2.

Gault, Ylonda, "Buyers Riding Coach; Leather Maker Growing," *Crain's New York Business,* May 6, 1991.

Gordon, Joanne, "Serial Tinkerer," *Forbes,* September 3, 2001, p. 86.

Grant, Lorrie, "Coach Bags Old Ideas: Classy Pursemaker Branches Out," *USA Today,* April 24, 2001, p. B3.

Karimzadeh, Marc, "Coach Inc. Expanding in Jewelry," *Women's Wear Daily,* June 26, 2001, p. 2.

Karr, Arnold J., "Coach Files for IPO in First Move to Part Company with Sara Lee," *Women's Wear Daily,* June 20, 2000, p. 2.

Lockwood, Lisa, "What Makes Coach a Winner? A Sharply Focused Game Plan," *HFN—The Weekly Newspaper for the Home Furnishing Network,* January 13, 2003, p. 20.

Much, Marilyn, "Japan's Handbag Hunger Feeds Designer's Growth," *Investor's Business Daily,* August 17, 2001.

Newman, Jill, "Coach Hits New Heights," *Women's Wear Daily,* January 8, 1988.

———, "Coach's International Approach," *Women's Wear Daily,* September 21, 1990.

O'Connell, Vanessa, "Coach Targets China—and Queens: Rather Than Hunker Down, CEO Opens Stores, Overhauls Fall Handbags, Adds Logo Pattern," *Wall Street Journal,* May 29, 2008, pp. B1, B2.

Rewick, C. J., "Trying New Accessories: Coach Builds on Handbag Success with Furniture, Towels, Other Items," *Crain's New York Business,* June 21, 1999, p. 25.

Ryan, Thomas J., "Coach IPO Heralds New Era," *Women's Wear Daily,* June 26, 2000, p. 10.

Ryan, Thomas J., and Brian Scott Lipton, "Coach Hopes to Raise $99 Million in IPO," *Daily News Record,* August 30, 2000, p. 13.

Strom, Stephanie, "A Women's Chain Beckons to Men," *New York Times,* July 24, 1991.

White, Erin, "How Stodgy Turned Stylish: Coach's Handbag Executives Used Marketing-by-Numbers to Create Hot Fashion Brand," *Wall Street Journal,* May 3, 2002, p. B1.

Young, Vicki M., "Bulking Up at Coach: Accessories Firm Eyes $5B in Sales by 2012," *Women's Wear Daily,* August 1, 2007, p. 1.

———, "Coach's Fourth-Quarter Net Leaps 32.9%," *Women's Wear Daily,* July 30, 2008, p. 5.

———, "Coach's Growth Drive: Adding Two New Lines, and Second Fragrance," *Women's Wear Daily,* April 25, 2007, p. 1.

———, "Coach's Pulling Power," *Women's Wear Daily,* August 3, 2005, p. 1.

———, "Riding the Wave: Coach Bullish on Bags As Net Leaps 120%," *Women's Wear Daily,* August 4, 2004, p. 1.

CRAIG HOSPITAL
Caring exclusively for patients with spinal cord and brain injuries.

Craig Hospital

——■——

3425 South Clarkson Street
Englewood, Colorado 80113-2811
U.S.A.
Telephone: (303) 789-8000
Fax: (303) 789-8219
Web site: http://www.craighospital.org

Nonprofit Company
Incorporated: 1910
Employees: 525
Operating Revenues: $34.4 million (2007)
NAICS: 622310 Specialty (Except Psychiatric and
    Substance Abuse) Hospitals

■ ■ ■

Craig Hospital is the only hospital in the United States to specialize in medical care for spinal cord injury and traumatic brain injury. A licensed acute care hospital, Craig provides complete treatment, from neurosurgery at the onset of injury to early rehabilitative therapy, long-term in-patient rehabilitation—which frequently exceeds 100 days—and outpatient care for lifelong well-being. Craig is also involved in leading-edge, clinical research. Craig's Center for Spinal Cord Injury Research is a worldwide pioneer in neuroscience research directed toward nervous system restoration. Collaboration between Craig and Karolinska Institutet in Sweden involves stem cell research in animals that shows promise for repairing spinal cord injuries.

Craig Hospital has consistently ranked among the top ten rehabilitation hospitals nationwide since 1990, when *U.S. News & World Report* began its annual surveys of hospital care. Since 1974 the National Institute on Disability Rehabilitation and Research has selected Craig as a Spinal Cord Injury Model Systems Center and, since 1998, as a Traumatic Brain Injury Model Systems Center. Over 23,000 spinal cord injury patients have been treated at Craig since 1956, more than at any other institution in the United States. Its specialized quality of care attracts patients from around the globe; about half of the patients at Craig come from outside of Colorado. Craig attracts many prominent people, such as actor Christopher Reeve, known for his role as Superman, who became paralyzed after a horseback-riding accident. Other high-profile patients include horse jockey Willie Shoemaker; Detroit Lions football player Mike Utley; and Roy Horn, of the Las Vegas entertainment duo Siegfried and Roy.

TENT COLONY FOR MEN WITH TUBERCULOSIS

Craig Hospital's origins can be traced back to a tuberculosis colony started by Frank Craig, who contracted tuberculosis in his early 20s and relocated to Colorado at the age of 30. The dry air and high altitude of Colorado were known to alleviate the symptoms of tuberculosis, a communicable and once deadly respiratory disease. Hence, Colorado attracted many people from the eastern United States who sought relief. When Craig set up a tent on vacant land near the west Denver neighborhood of Edgewater in 1907, indigent men with tuberculosis soon joined him. Despite his own ill health,

Craig provided shelter and care for anyone who asked. He provided food as well, beginning with donations of day-old bread and pastries from a local bakery.

When economic conditions declined and the number of sick, indigent men who required aid increased, the Denver Welfare Board asked Craig to accommodate them. Craig appealed to Denver citizens for help. Thus he obtained additional tents and donations of food. As the population of the tent colony increased, self-sufficiency became a hallmark of the "Colony of Brotherly Love," and everyone well enough to assist contributed to the daily operation of the place. In 1910 Craig formed a nonprofit corporation, the Brotherly Relief Colony, and became its official superintendent.

As the town of Edgewater grew, the neighbors complained to the landowner about the homeless men with the contagious disease. The landowner evicted Craig, but an article in the *Rocky Mountain News* prompted local citizens to act on the colony's behalf. In particular, Mrs. J. O. Cooper, wife of the sixth governor of Colorado, donated several pieces of property at West Colfax and Ingalls Street, only a few blocks away in Lakewood. The colony relocated to the site, which included a house for use as a sick ward. Sturdier tents were built, with wood floors, combination wood and canvas walls, and shingled roofs. Newspaper articles in the fall of 1910 inspired donations of food, clothing, cots, bedding, soap, cooking tools, stoves, and coal for cooking and heating through the winter.

Although Craig died in 1914, the Brotherly Relief Colony continued to expand. Beginning in 1916, three buildings were erected on the site, and by 1921 the colony consisted of 48 cottages. In memory of Craig,

the name of the site was renamed Craig Colony in 1919. That year, Mrs. Cooper died, but her heirs continued to generate philanthropic support for the institution.

NEW DIRECTION AS A HEALTHCARE PROVIDER

With the development of penicillin in 1928 and related refinement of antibiotics during World War II, the problem of tuberculosis diminished. Hence, the board of directors at Craig Colony deliberated the future of the institution. In 1947 the board conducted a study and determined that treatment of spinal cord injury (SCI) was an underserved, underdeveloped area of medicine. Antibiotics reduced infection, saving the lives of people with SCIs, who then required physical rehabilitation. Ironically, when antibiotics closed one area of medicine, it opened another. Craig provided care for polio patients during the late 1940s, but by 1955 the institution began to focus exclusively on rehabilitation from SCI and traumatic brain injury (TBI).

In 1957 Craig renovated existing buildings and completed construction on a 6,000-square-foot facility, the Craig Rehabilitation Center. That year, the board hired John Young, M.D., as medical director. Young established the innovative practices that made Craig a leader in SCI and TBI rehabilitation. To foster a relaxed atmosphere, staff wore casual clothing, rather than uniforms. Young developed the team structure for each patient's treatment. Single physician management, along with the same nurse, occupational therapist, physical therapist, speech pathologist, respiratory therapist, psychologist, and family counselor provided consistent care throughout an individual's rehabilitation process.

Despite the positive new direction taken at Craig, the costs of developing a complete treatment and rehabilitation center exceeded the institution's capacity. To rectify this situation, beginning in 1957, Craig initiated negotiations with a number of Denver area hospitals. An agreement, however, was not forthcoming. Meanwhile, Craig obtained a license as a rehabilitation hospital and changed its name to Craig Rehabilitation Hospital in 1966. Finally, Craig found compatibility with the Swedish Hospital in Englewood, Colorado. In 1968 the two hospitals signed a joint operating agreement, the first such agreement in the United States. With Robert R. Jackson, M.D., as medical director, Craig began a new chapter in its development as an SCI and TBI rehabilitation center.

KEY DATES

■

1907: "Tent Colony of Brotherly Love" provides refuge to homeless men with tuberculosis.

1916: Construction begins on three buildings as hospital develops.

1957: Dr. John Young initiates focus on spinal cord and traumatic brain injury rehabilitation.

1970: Neurosurgery unit adds medical services to rehabilitation program.

1975: Craig Rehabilitation Hospital becomes simply Craig Hospital.

1990: *U.S. News & World Report* lists Craig as a Top Ten Rehabilitation Hospital.

1996: Dr. Scott Falci performs the world's first spinal cord transplant in Stockholm, Sweden.

2003: Cell Center opens with a Class 10,000 Clean Room.

2007: Craig Hospital and staff celebrate 100th anniversary.

JOINT VENTURE FACILITATES CRAIG'S LEADERSHIP IN SCI/TBI REHABILITATION

The collaboration with Swedish Hospital provided Craig with ample space for expansion. In 1969 Craig began construction on a 63,000-square-foot, 80-bed facility on land leased from Swedish Hospital in Englewood. A tunnel between the two facilities provided reciprocal access to complementary facilities. In particular, Craig gained access to radiology, surgery, laboratory, and other medical services. Access to these facilities supported the establishment of a neurosurgical program by Robert Edgar, M.D., who joined Craig in 1970.

Craig expanded its rehabilitation program in 1973 when it purchased a nearby apartment building to provide transitional living quarters for rehabilitation patients and their families. The apartments facilitated the process of learning how to live self-sufficiently with a disability in a homelike setting, an innovative program at the time. Craig's leadership led the National Institute on Disability and Rehabilitation Research (NIDRR) to name Craig as a Spinal Cord Injury Model Systems Center in 1974.

Under the direction of a new president, Denny O'Malley, Craig further developed a local and national reputation for excellence in SCI and TBI treatment and care. In collaboration with Swedish Hospital, Craig opened a pioneering Neurotrauma Unit, an intensive

care and early rehabilitation therapy center at Swedish Hospital. Designed by Harry R. Hahn, M.D., the new facility allowed Craig to treat SCI and TBI from the onset of injury. Further development of medical services occurred in 1977, when Hahn created a separate Traumatic Brain Injury team, distinct from the SCI team. As Craig expanded its range of medical care, the organization had simplified its name to Craig Hospital in 1975.

Craig's prestige developed on the local level as the hospital played a role in expanding knowledge and services in Colorado and neighboring Wyoming. In 1980 Craig was instrumental in the formation of the Colorado Head Injury Foundation, later renamed the Brain Injury Association of Colorado. The organization compiled the first statewide study on brain injury in 1987. Craig opened SCI Outreach Clinics in Grand Junction, Colorado, and Casper, Wyoming, in 1980, then in Pueblo, Colorado, in 1987.

Craig Hospital sought to further improve its quality of care with the construction of a 62,000-square-foot expansion project in 1985. The new facility doubled the area available for patient treatment with a new outpatient clinic and more therapy rooms, while it maintained the same level of patient capacity. Other improvements included the addition of a large gymnasium, a media studio, and office space. The hospital established a Neuromuscular Laboratory; a Neuroscience Laboratory, which included electromyography/nerve conduction equipment; as well as a new Neurosurgery Laboratory. In 1989 Craig reorganized its SCI and TBI units, on separate floors, to accelerate advances in TBI treatment. Mark Cilo, M.D., played an integral role in cultivating Craig's expertise in TBI.

By the end of the 1980s, Craig's innovations and quality of care evolved into a national reputation. The medical community increasingly asked Craig physicians to contribute to publications and to present at conferences. The study and treatment of ventilator-dependent patients and high quadriplegia under "Pete" Peterson, M.D., led to the publication of *The Management of High Quadriplegia* and to the development of a national seminar in 1980. By the end of the decade, Craig staff provided an average of 75 presentations annually and contributed 20 to 25 articles or book chapters each year. National recognition culminated in being ranked among the Top Ten Rehabilitation Hospitals in the United States by *U.S. News & World Report* in 1990.

A national reputation increased Craig's opportunities for participation in clinical studies of leading-edge treatments. In 1991 Craig participated in a pre–Food and Drug Administration approval study of the Parastep Ambulation System, a neuromuscular electrical stimulation system intended to enable SCI patients to regain leg movement or mobility. Conversely, Craig maintained its reputation through research and publishing. The study and treatment of aging with SCI culminated in the 1993 publication *Aging with Spinal Cord Injury,* by Craig physician Robert Mentor, M.D.

EXPANSION FOSTERS FURTHER INNOVATIONS

Craig purchased the leased land from Swedish Hospital in 1994 and began a $9 million expansion. The project added space for 13 hospital beds, several new treatment areas, and research and office space, and it replaced the transitional patient-family rooms, thus improving the experience of self-sufficient living. A skybridge linked Swedish Hospital with the new building, and the aging tunnel link closed.

At this time, Craig developed a number of innovative programs that contributed to patient reentry into public and private life. These ranged from airline travel training to sexuality, intimacy, and fertility education. Craig began rehabilitation-equipment development with the formation of the Adaptive Equipment Company (AEC) in 1994. AEC provided patients with the medical equipment they needed after being discharged from the hospital, such as wheelchairs, other ambulatory aids, bathroom equipment, and hospital beds. The Adaptive Driving and Transportation Program provided patients with education and training in the use of specialized driving equipment and specialized motor vehicles.

A leader in therapeutic recreation, Craig developed the largest such department nationwide. With the help of the hospital's 175 volunteers, patients participated in individual projects, such as arts and crafts, ceramics, horticulture, and hand cycling, as well as group activities, such as bowling, scuba diving, sailing, hot-air ballooning, and attending movies and professional sports events. In addition to preparing patients for a normal life, the activities contributed to an uplifting psychological atmosphere.

CRAIG HOSPITAL LEADS 21ST-CENTURY RESEARCH

After three years of collaboration, and with a grant from the NIDRR, Karolinska Institutet of Stockholm, Sweden, and Craig Hospital jointly created the Craig Center for Spinal Cord Injury Research in 1996. Locally led by Scott Falci, M.D., the collaboration involved the use of fetal tissue to treat progressive post-traumatic cystic myelopathy, or syringomyelia, in which cysts erode normal spinal cord tissue. Adult nerve cells cannot repair themselves, and cysts sometimes fill the empty space at an injury site, thereby worsening the patient's condition. The new surgical technique involved the existing practice of draining the cyst, but added the new dimension of encouraging spinal cord tissue repair by transplanting embryonic spinal cord tissue from six- to eight-week-old aborted fetuses (used with the consent of the mothers). Because the embryonic cells were undeveloped, that is, had not determined their specific function, they held potential to adopt the role of connective tissue at the site of injury.

Karolinska scientists applied the method to restore movement in rats with injured spinal cords, laying the groundwork for a human transplant. In 1996 in Stockholm, Falci performed the first embryonic spinal cord transplant ever conducted on a human being. The surgery helped three paralyzed men to regain some sensation and motion. By 2002 Karolinska Institutet further developed the procedure with the use of stem cells. Research on rats showed that stem cells travel up and down the spinal cord and generate new nerve tissue connections.

Other research at Craig involved a 1996 trial of the intrathecal baclofen pump, which injected baclofen, a drug that reduces muscle spasms, directly into spinal cord fluid. In a 2001 NeoTherapeutics clinical study, Neotrofin was found to protect the nervous system and even showed nerve regeneration in the brain, spine, and peripheral nervous system. The Sygen Multicenter Acute Spinal Cord Injury Study showed improvement in sensation and related bowel and bladder function.

In 2003 Proneuron Biotechnologies and Craig Hospital received a $1 million grant from the BIRD Foundation, of Israel, to continue development of Proneuron's Activated Macrophage treatment for SCI. The Phase I trial took place in Israel, and two of the eight patients gained significant recovery of sensation or movement. Craig's new Cell Center with a Class 10,000 Clean Room became Proneuron's first trial site for the Phase II Activated Macrophage Clinical Trial. The Clean Room provided the correct atmosphere to isolate and supercharge white blood cells, or macrophage, taken from the patient. Injection at the SCI stimulates the immune response. While the spinal cord and brain have minimal immune capability, the supercharged macrophage was intended to compensate and thus speed the wound healing process by destroying bacteria that hinder healing. Hence, the treatment was intended for recently injured patients, within two weeks of injury.

Other innovations at Craig involved the construction of a new outpatient and family housing facility.

The 47-unit facility replaced the old apartments and the new units were wheelchair accessible, including roll-in showers. With two bedrooms and hide-a-beds, the apartments assisted in the transition process for patients and families, who stayed together in the apartments during the last ten days of a patient's stay.

Craig continued to be recognized as a national leader by the NIDRR, which provided grants for research. In July 2006 the NIDRR renewed Craig's designation as a Spinal Cord Injury Model Systems Center for 2006 to 2011. Along with the designation, Craig received $1.3 million of a $5.8 million grant to study SCI rehabilitation. The study, to be conducted by six rehabilitation centers and to be led by Craig, involved close examination of which programs among medical procedures, patient education, counseling, and therapeutic activities prove most effective.

In September 2006 the NIDRR gave Craig the designation of TBI Model Systems Center, a designation that originated in 1998. Craig was also named as the TBI National Statistical Data Center. In addition to being one of 16 model centers, Craig would gather and organize data from all model centers, which included the Mayo Clinic. A $3.1 million grant from NIDRR was to support brain injury research as well as administrative and technical support. The grant provided Craig with the opportunity to develop new research systems, as well as to meet the needs of data collection. Craig previously provided national leadership in this area with the Craig Hospital Assessment Reporting Technique and the Craig Hospital Inventory of Environmental Factors.

CRAIG HOSPITAL LOOKS TO THE FUTURE

In 2007, as Craig celebrated its 100th anniversary, the hospital prepared for the future. Craig planned for the advent of universal healthcare, which could impinge on Craig's insurance reimbursements. Craig executives were concerned that healthcare reforms might limit rehabilitation to 60 days, when most patients require 100 days. As such, the Craig Hospital Foundation began a high-profile fundraising effort, with the aim of raising $50 million over three years. For the first time in the hospital's history, Craig was willing to name wings or rooms after philanthropists and corporate contributors. The funds would compensate for the expected decline in income.

In June 2007 Craig's partnership with Karolinska Institutet continued with the study of the effectiveness of embryonic stem cells to treat SCIs. (Under the Bush administration, federal funding of embryonic stem cell research, a controversial and hotly debated topic among Americans, had been in place since 2001 but remained limited to a small number of existing stem cell lines.) The institute developed a line of stem cells and expected human trials to begin by 2012. Craig Medical Director Daniel Lammertse, M.D., expected Craig to seek funds, such as venture capital, to bring a stem cell laboratory to Englewood. Craig's annual PUSH fundraiser for stem cell research began in 2001 and had raised $4.1 million since its start.

Mary Tradii

PRINCIPAL SUBSIDIARIES

Adaptive Equipment Company.

PRINCIPAL COMPETITORS

Carolinas Rehabilitation; JFK Johnson Rehabilitation Institute; Mayo Clinic; Medical College of Virginia; Mt. Sinai Medical Center; Moss Rehabilitation; National Rehabilitation Hospital; The Ohio State University; Rehabilitation Institute of Michigan; Rehabilitation Institute of Chicago; Santa Clara University; Shepard Center; Spaulding Rehabilitation Hospital Network; University of Alabama at Birmingham; University of Pittsburgh; University of Texas; University of Washington–Seattle.

FURTHER READING

"Area Rehabilitation Center Offers Hope: 'Craig Has Taught Me That You Don't Have to Just Sit There and Be Disabled,' Patient Says," *Rocky Mountain News,* May 19, 1991, p. 6.

Davis, Joyzelle, "CEO Turned Craig into Top 10 Rehab Hospital," *Rocky Mountain News,* March 12, 2008, Business section, p. 1.

Duran, Marlys, "$9 Million Expansion Will Cut Patient Costs; Craig's New Services Also Will Help Disabled People Prepare for Life at Home," *Rocky Mountain News,* November 28, 1994, p. 23A.

Eicher, Diane, "Craig Enters Spinal Cord Pact," *Denver Post,* November 22, 1996, p. B4.

Fletcher, Amy, "Craig Hospital Awarded $3.1M to Fund Study," *Denver Business Journal,* September 29, 2006.

———, "Craig Hospital's $5.8M Grant Will Study Spinal Cord Injuries," *Denver Business Journal,* November 6, 2006.

Hubler, Eric, "Hospital an Island of Independence," *Denver Post,* May 2, 1999, p. I1.

Mook, Bob, "Campaign Trail," *Denver Business Journal,* June 1, 2007.

————, "Craig Seeks to Become Stem-Cell Center," *Denver Business Journal*, June 1, 2007.

"Nation's Doctors Rate Craig Hospital Among Top," *Rocky Mountain News*, April 26, 1990, p. 34.

"NeoTherapeutics Expands Neotrofin Trials to Additional Sites," *Pain & Central Nervous System Week*, September 22, 2001.

Noel, Tom, "Craig Left Legacy of Care, Compassion," *Rocky Mountain News*, March 24, 2007.

"Proneuron Biotechnologies and Craig Hospital Joint Experimental Program to Treat Spinal Cord Injury Receives US$1 Million Funding from the BIRD Foundation," *Business Wire*, June 24, 2002, p. 0092.

Romero, Tomas, "Our Turn to Lend a Hand," *Denver Post*, December 3, 1997, p. B7.

Scanlon, Bill, "Craig Front-Runner for Stem Cell Work— Englewood Hospital Could Be First in World to Transplant Them in Paralyzed Patients," *Rocky Mountain News*, April 29, 2002, p. 5A.

————, "Promise for the Paralyzed Groundbreaking Procedure at Craig Hospital Offers Hope to Those with Spinal Injuries," *Rocky Mountain News*, February 14, 2004, p. 21A.

Schrader, Ann, "Fetal Tissue Helps Ease Spine Condition; Transplant by Local Surgeon a World First," *Denver Post*, November 21, 1997, p. 1A.

Swafford, Bonnie Bauer, "A Practical Guide to Health Promotion After Spinal Cord Injury," *Physical Therapy*, November 1996, p. 1266.

Tabak, Herb, *Craig Hospital: A Century of Rebuilding Lives, 1907–2007*, Englewood: Craig Hospital, 2007.

Verrengia, Joseph B., "Fetal Cells Combat Paralysis/Denver Physicians Use Transplanted Spinal Tissue to Restore Some Motion in Three Men," *Rocky Mountain News*, November 21, 1997, p. 5A.

Wheeler, Sheba R., "Grateful Family Gives $1 Million to Craig," *Denver Post*, December 2, 2001, p. B1.

Wilmsen, Steven, "Craig Hospital Revamps Staff," *Denver Post*, July 7, 1989.

Dana Holding Corporation

4500 Dorr Street
P.O. Box 1000
Toledo, Ohio 43615-4040
U.S.A.
Telephone: (419) 535-4500
Toll Free: (800) 472-8810
Fax: (419) 535-4643
Web site: http://www.dana.com

Public Company
Founded: 1904 as C.W. Spicer
Incorporated: 1905 as Spicer Universal Joint Manufacturing Company
Employees: 35,000
Sales: $8.72 billion (2007)
Stock Exchanges: New York
Ticker Symbol: DAN
NAICS: 336330 Motor Vehicle Steering and Suspension Components (Except Spring) Manufacturing; 336350 Motor Vehicle Transmission and Power Train Parts Manufacturing

■ ■ ■

Dana Holding Corporation is a leading global manufacturer and supplier of axle, driveshaft, structural, sealing, thermal, and other products for automotive, commercial, and off-highway vehicles. Its automotive operations, which generate around 62 percent of sales, produce original-equipment auto parts for passenger cars and light trucks built by leading automakers. Around 20 percent of sales are attributable to parts made for medium- and heavy-duty trucks, buses, and other commercial vehicles. Dana secures its remaining 18 percent of revenues from the parts it makes for construction machinery, mining and forestry equipment, all-terrain vehicles, and other off-highway vehicles. The company enjoys a diversified customer base, with only Ford Motor Company, at 23 percent of sales, accounting for more than 10 percent of overall revenues. Serving customers in more than 125 countries with more than 100 major facilities in 26 nations, Dana is also diversified geographically with sales breaking down as North America, 55 percent; Europe, 26 percent; South America, 12 percent; and the Asia-Pacific region, 7 percent.

Founded in 1904 and developing concurrent to the automotive industry, Dana adapted to changes in that industry and remained a leader in its field. Like many other auto suppliers, however, the company (then known as Dana Corporation) ran into financial difficulties in the early 21st century under pressure from declining automotive production and rising raw-material and labor costs. The firm filed for Chapter 11 bankruptcy protection in March 2006, restructured its operations, and emerged from bankruptcy as Dana Holding Corporation in January 2008.

1904 FOUNDING BY CLARENCE W. SPICER

In 1902 company founder Clarence W. Spicer invented the Spicer universal joint and driveshaft to replace the loud, unreliable, and difficult to lubricate chain-and-sprocket devices then used in automobiles to transmit

COMPANY PERSPECTIVES

One of the industry's most experienced suppliers is also its newest. Welcome to our new beginning. As we enter this new chapter in Dana's history, we carry forward a rich heritage and expertise amassed during more than a century of operation. At the same time, Dana Holding Corporation is a new company benefiting from fundamental improvements achieved during our recent reorganization. We are energized by new leadership, we are committed to elevated standards for product and financial performance, and we are honored to build upon the successful relationships we maintain with thousands of customers in more than 125 countries. As we embark on this new beginning, we are united in our motivation to return Dana to its position as a premier, global leader in our markets.

engine power to the wheels. Spicer set up a company, initially called C.W. Spicer, in Plainfield, New Jersey, to begin making his universal joints for carmakers. The firm was well situated given that the U.S. automobile industry at that time was largely located in the Northeast. It shipped its first universal joints in September 1904 to the Corbin Motor Vehicle Company of New Britain, Connecticut.

Needing additional financing for expansion, Spicer incorporated the company in New Jersey in May 1905 as Spicer Universal Joint Manufacturing Company. The company was renamed Spicer Manufacturing Company in November 1909. Between 1904, when only 23,000 automobiles were built in the United States, and 1913, auto production increased 20-fold to almost half a million. During this period, Spicer's sales surpassed $10 million as the company's list of customers grew to more than 100 automakers, including American, Buick, Cadillac, Chevrolet, General Motors, Hudson, Olds, and Packard.

REVITALIZED AND EXPANDED UNDER CHARLES DANA

By 1914 Spicer Manufacturing was a company with great promise as a supplier of universal joints for a rapidly expanding industry, but it was struggling financially and needed better management. Both the financing and management acumen came on the scene in the form of the ambitious and well-connected Charles A. Dana, who was destined to guide the

company for half a century. Dana had graduated from Columbia University with both bachelor of arts and law degrees. After college, he practiced law for the State of New York, advancing to the position of assistant prosecutor in 1907. Dana went on to serve as a state legislator for six years.

Dana agreed to lend Spicer Manufacturing a desperately needed $15,000 and gradually became more deeply involved in the firm, providing financial, legal, and management advice. He became a director in 1914, owned nearly half the company a year later, and one year after that succeeded Clarence Spicer as company president. Spicer stayed onboard as vice-president and chief engineer. In 1915 all of Spicer Manufacturing's operations were moved to a new complex in South Plainfield, New Jersey, offering larger and more modern facilities. The company was reorganized and renamed Spicer Manufacturing Corporation in 1916. During World War I, the company continued to churn out universal joints, most of which ended up installed on military vehicles. War demand pushed sales over the $30 million mark for both 1918 and 1919.

During 1919 Spicer Manufacturing bolstered its production capability by acquiring Chadwick Engine Works of Pottstown, Pennsylvania, which at the time was producing 200,000 universal joints per month. More important for the company's long-term development, however, were two other acquisitions completed that same year: the buyouts of Reading, Pennsylvania-based Parish Pressed Steel Company, a producer of automotive frames, and Jamestown, New York-based Salisbury Axle Company, maker of automotive axles. A major postwar industry slump exacerbated by labor strikes and material shortages halted the acquisition spree and sent Spicer Manufacturing's sales down to just $5 million by 1921. The firm, and the industry, began recovering a year later, when Spicer's stock began trading on the New York Stock Exchange. Sales climbed back up to $17 million by 1929.

By the end of the 1920s, Detroit had clearly become the center of U.S. automotive production with that city's "Big Three" of General Motors, Ford, and Chrysler producing more than 80 percent of all new cars in the country. Thus, to be closer to its main customers, Spicer moved its corporate headquarters to Toledo, Ohio, in 1929 and then a year later moved its universal joint operations to Toledo from South Plainfield as well. Toledo, about 60 miles south of Detroit, was chosen instead of Detroit itself to enable Dana to continue living on the East Coast and commute to Spicer's new headquarters on a regular basis via an overnight train service. Also in 1929, Spicer Manufacturing further expanded its product line by purchasing Brown-

KEY DATES

1904: Clarence W. Spicer founds C.W. Spicer, in Plainfield, New Jersey, to begin making his Spicer universal joint for automakers.

1905: Firm is incorporated as Spicer Universal Joint Manufacturing Company.

1909: Company is renamed Spicer Manufacturing Company.

1916: Charles A. Dana becomes company president.

1919: Via acquisitions, Spicer Manufacturing expands into automotive frames and axles.

1922: Company stock begins trading on the New York Stock Exchange.

1929: Spicer Manufacturing shifts its headquarters to Toledo, Ohio; purchase of Brown-Lipe Gear Company propels the firm into production of automotive transmissions and clutches.

1946: Company is renamed Dana Corporation in honor of Charles Dana's long leadership tenure.

1974: Revenues pass the $1 billion mark.

1998: Dana spends $3.9 billion for Echlin Inc., a leading producer and distributor of aftermarket automotive parts.

2003: Company fends off a hostile takeover attempt from ArvinMeritor, Inc.

2004: Dana divests its aftermarket automotive components unit.

2006: Dana files for Chapter 11 bankruptcy protection.

2008: Company exits from bankruptcy under a new holding company, Dana Holding Corporation.

Lipe Gear Company of Syracuse, New York, a producer of automotive transmissions and clutches.

By 1932, at the height of the Great Depression, U.S. automobile production had fallen 75 percent, leading to a 90 percent plunge in Spicer's sales, to just $2 million. The company was forced to lay off employees and impose pay cuts on the remaining workforce. Sales rebounded somewhat by the late 1930s as the economy grew stronger and then reached new heights during World War II on the back of military orders. Although U.S. automakers had to suspend production of civilian cars and trucks for the duration of the war, much of

Spicer's factory output remained the same but was destined for installation on military vehicles. In addition to producing frames and other vehicle parts, the company also manufactured gun carriage mounts, field kitchens, housings for fighter planes, and other military supplies. Spicer's workforce grew to 10,000 by 1944, and sales swelled to $109 million the following year.

POSTWAR GROWTH AS DANA CORPORATION

As Spicer shifted back to civilian production after the war, the firm also decided that the time was right for a name change. The company had become known not only for Spicer brand products but also for products sporting such names as Parish, Salisbury, and Brown-Lipe. It therefore in July 1946 adopted the umbrella name Dana Corporation, which honored Charles Dana's more than 30 years of leadership. The Spicer brand continued to be used for the firm's universal joints and was later applied to such products as axles and transmissions.

Still headed by Charles Dana, Dana Corporation strengthened its product lineup in the postwar period by acquiring producers of clutches, power takeoffs, constant-velocity U-joints, and other automotive components. Dana positioned itself as a "growth company" within the automotive market, unlike many rivals who moved into new businesses and toward conglomerate status. New product development was another important growth avenue, and Dana in 1956 launched one of its most successful products ever, the Powr-Lok limited-slip differential. Vehicles equipped with the Powr-Lok offered better traction on slippery surfaces and better stability in turns. Through its growth initiatives, Dana achieved record revenues of $230 million by 1960.

By 1967 Dana ranked as one of the world's largest independent suppliers of automotive components and replacement parts with sales in excess of $500 million and an impressive customer list that included General Motors, Ford, International Harvester, Chrysler, and American Motors. Additional acquisitions had helped propel the company forward, including the 1963 purchase of Perfect Circle Corporation, a manufacturer of piston rings and related products, and the 1966 takeover of Victor Manufacturing and Gasket Company. As the U.S. automakers' dominance of the world car market began to erode, international expansion became increasingly important and was pursued in earnest. By 1966, $100 million of Dana's $453 million in sales was attributable to licensing agreements with 34 companies around the world, and the firm also held minority stakes in ten other foreign firms. In December 1966 Charles

Dana retired as chairman and CEO after 50 years at the helm. Jack Martin was his immediate successor.

THE MCPHERSON ERA

In 1968 Rene C. McPherson was appointed president of the company, and he was promoted to chairman and CEO in 1972. Described by *Fortune* magazine as a "maverick," McPherson was vital to the history of Dana Corporation because of his progressive policies regarding management and employee relations. He was also credited with turning a large, somewhat unwieldy, auto parts manufacturer into a "model of productivity." McPherson's first moves involved cutting 350 people from a staff of 500 at company headquarters and replacing the 17-inch stack of company operating manuals with a brief policy statement. McPherson decentralized the corporate bureaucracy by requiring managers to assume more responsibility in the decision-making process and encouraging personnel to participate in a Dana stock plan. At his insistence, managers met with employees instead of sending memos, time clocks were abolished, and managers helped personnel to establish their own production goals.

Another of McPherson's innovations was the establishment of "Dana University," an in-house training program for employees who wanted to move up through the ranks of the company. Moreover, Dana recruited "student teachers" to study excellence in manufacturing abroad and then return to their home plants to disseminate the human relations strategies, manufacturing techniques, and philosophies they had learned. The progressive policies of the company led one security analyst to note that McPherson brought "Japanese-style management to Dana before most people even knew what it was."

McPherson's business strategy was to make careful, small acquisitions while maintaining low costs and high productivity. As a result, Dana was considered one of the nation's best-run companies and maintained a sound financial record in the 1970s. During this time, McPherson shifted the company's focus away from its reliance on the original-equipment market and toward the light trucks market, which ultimately represented 35 percent of its sales during the decade.

Moreover, Dana became known for its ability to turn unprofitable companies around. For example, in 1974, Dana acquired Summit Engineering Corporation, a manufacturer of numerical controls for machinery. At the time, the company's sales were at $900,000; under Dana's direction, sales increased to $18 million by 1979.

Between 1963 and 1980, Dana Corporation purchased 24 companies outside its original-equipment

vehicle business, and company profits rose from $62 million in 1975 to $164 million by 1979. Revenues, which first hit $1 billion in 1974, soared to $2.76 billion by decade's end. By 1980 Dana had developed three distinct areas of business: original-equipment auto and truck parts, replacement parts, and industrial machine components.

SURVIVING AN ECONOMICALLY TURBULENT TIME

The changes implemented by McPherson were carried on by Gerald B. Mitchell when McPherson retired at the end of 1979. Having started as a Dana machine operator at the age of 16, Mitchell understood and appreciated the company's commitment to its workers' concerns. Economic recession during the early 1980s, however, made it increasingly difficult to honor McPherson's personnel policies; when light trucks declined in popularity during the early 1980s, prompting drastic declines in company earnings, Mitchell was forced to close five plants and lay off one-third of its employees in its American operations. Some United Auto Workers officials regarded the company's treatment of its employees as unfair. Nevertheless, the company strived to offer its unemployed workers preferential hiring at other plants and assisted with relocation expenses. Lists of laid-off employees were sent to other manufacturers in the area, and a two-week job counseling program was provided when Dana plants were shut down.

In 1983 Dana's original-equipment parts business had an unexpectedly profitable year, as earnings rose 119 percent to $112 million. Mitchell maintained, however, that Dana's best prospects for the future remained in the replacement market for its auto and truck parts. In 1984 Mitchell anticipated that the replacement parts business would make up 40 percent of the company's net earnings within five years, while the original-equipment business would account for only about 30 percent.

In 1984 Dana began manufacturing gears identical to those designed for a line of Clark Equipment Company truck transmissions. Through this tactic, Dana entered into direct competition with Clark's replacement sales, and Dana's success in this arena helped the company offset losses in other divisions. During this time, Dana also diversified into the financial service industry, acquiring the Cherokee Insurance Company, a small property and casualty insurance company. The venture proved unsuccessful, however, and Dana was forced to write off $6 million of its investment. While Dana considered its relationship with Cherokee Insurance over, many of Cherokee's clients were unsatisfied that the subsidiary had been unable to fulfill reinsurance obligations. Dana was subsequently sued for $1.7 million by St. Regis Corporation.

In 1985 Dana made its largest acquisition yet, the purchase of Warner Electric Brake & Clutch, which had annual sales of $200 million. Warner produced such products as industrial clutches and brakes, compressor clutches, and ball-bearing screws for production machinery, defense and aerospace equipment, and commercial and off-highway vehicles. Also in 1985 Southwood "Woody" Morcott, then a 20-year veteran of Dana, advanced to the firm's board of directors and was subsequently elected CEO and president, positions he would hold into the 1990s. Morcott began focusing on streamlining operations and cutting costs at Dana, investing $120 million in Project 90, a program for developing new technology, better facilities, and a new system of incentive payments which could be tied to higher productivity. The company hoped to reduce its costs to 90 percent of those of its major competitors.

In the late 1980s, however, global economic recession prompted increasing numbers of auto companies to manufacture parts in-house or to use less-expensive foreign-made parts. Dana's earnings declined during 1989, 1990, and 1991, and in 1992 Dana suffered a $382 million loss, despite a slight rebound in sales. Limiting its manufacture of passenger car components, Dana fortuitously expanded its production of engine parts for trucks. As that market segment, which constituted over 25 percent of Dana's business, rebounded in the early 1990s, the company was able to report net earnings of $80 million on 1993 sales of $5.46 billion.

As Dana's sales to Ford and Chrysler totaled 29 percent of its consolidated sales in 1993, Dana's future seemed inextricably linked to the fortunes of the automotive industry. Dana therefore focused on adapting its product lines in order to offset the effects of fluctuations in the industry. Management also persisted with its streamlining and cost-cutting measures and concentrated on penetration of international markets into the mid-1990s, with the goals of "Dana 2000" as incentive. According to the objectives stated in Dana's 1993 annual report, the company aimed to earn 50 percent of sales from distribution markets and 50 percent of total sales from outside the United States. Distribution sales amounted to 36.6 percent of sales and foreign sales contributed 17.8 percent as of 1993.

PHENOMENAL LATE-CENTURY GROWTH

A booming economy, a series of significant acquisitions, and the development of new products helped Dana

diversify, expand globally, and ultimately reap record sales of $13.2 billion by 1999. After purchasing the German gasket and sealing firm Reinz in 1993, Dana two years later built or purchased more than 30 facilities in nine countries, including axle and driveshaft operations in Brazil, Austria, Poland, Spain, India, and China. Back home, the company bought out Plumley Companies in 1995, gaining a maker of gaskets and fuel hoses based in Paris, Tennessee, that had 1994 sales of more than $100 million.

Early in 1997 Dana bought the piston ring and cylinder liner business of SPX Corporation for $223 million and also completed an even larger deal, the purchase of Clark-Hurth Corporation, that substantially bolstered the firm's position in off-highway vehicle components. Around 60 percent of Clark-Hurth's 1995 sales of $350 million were generated outside the United States. Clark-Hurth was combined with Dana's existing off-highway divisions to form the Off-Highway Components Group.

Continuing its deal-making, Dana in January 1998 engineered a swap of businesses with Eaton Corporation that bolstered a core Dana product line. Dana sold its clutch business to Eaton for $180 million, while simultaneously buying Eaton's heavy-duty truck and axle business for $287 million. The purchases of Clark-Hurth and the Eaton unit enabled Dana to begin producing entire chassis for heavy-duty vehicles. The divestment of the clutch business, meantime, was part of a larger effort to concentrate the firm more narrowly on a smaller set of core areas. During 1997 and 1998 Dana completed the divestiture of about a dozen operations with collective sales of about $1.2 billion.

In July 1998 Dana consummated what at the time was the largest acquisition ever in the automotive parts industry. The company paid around $3.9 billion for Echlin Inc. of Brandford, Connecticut. Echlin, with annual sales of $3.5 billion, was one of the leading producers and distributors of aftermarket automotive parts, including parts for brakes, engines, transmissions, steering systems, and suspensions. The company's 28,000 employees pushed Dana's workforce up to 80,000. To integrate the Echlin operations, Dana quickly announced a major overhaul that involved the closure of 15 factories and 30 warehouses and the elimination of 3,500 jobs. Most of the facilities shuttered were from the Echlin side as Dana sought to generate cost savings of $575 million. In December 1998 Dana paid $430 million to Federal-Mogul Corporation for the Glacier Vandervell bearings business and the AE Clevite aftermarket engine hard-parts business.

In early 1999 Joseph Magliochetti, a 32-year company veteran who had served as president since 1996, was named CEO as well, while Morcott remained chairman. Dana ended the 1990s with seven global operating units focusing on original-equipment automotive components, aftermarket automotive components, engine components, fluid system components, heavy truck components, off-highway components, and leasing services. Another unit, the Warner Electric industrial products business, was sold in early 2000.

RESTRUCTURING AND FENDING OFF HOSTILE TAKEOVER

The vehicle industry went into another deep cyclical downturn late in 1999, slicing into Dana's sales and profits and forcing the firm to restructure. From 2000 to early 2002 the firm announced overhauls encompassing a workforce reduction of more than 30,000, the closure of dozens of facilities, and the divestment of numerous businesses, including the leasing services unit. In addition, the engine and fluid system businesses were combined into a single unit, as were the heavy truck and off-highway operations. In the fall of 2001 Dana was forced to reduce its quarterly dividend to reserve cash, ending a 65-year streak of consecutively paying a dividend without any reductions. Restructuring charges of $317 million sent the company into a net loss of $298 million for 2001 on much reduced revenues of $10.27 billion.

After posting another loss of $182 million in 2002, Dana was the object of a hostile takeover bid of $2.2 billion from smaller rival ArvinMeritor, Inc., of Troy, Michigan, in mid-2003. Dana quickly rejected the offer, but ArvinMeritor kept its offer on the table. In September 2003, while the offer was still pending, Magliochetti died following a brief illness. Two months later, ArvinMeritor bumped its offer up to $2.67 billion but then walked away when Dana, operating under interim leadership, turned down the sweetened deal as well.

Shortly after the takeover drama ended, Dana announced its intention to focus exclusively on the original-equipment market by placing its aftermarket components unit up for sale, marking a strategy reversal from the brighter period in the late 1990s when Dana had boldly made its blockbuster Echlin acquisition. Carrying out this task eventually fell to Michael J. Burns, who was brought onboard as president and CEO in March 2004. Prior to joining Dana, Burns had spent his entire career at General Motors, where he had led a turnaround of that carmaker's European division. The aftermarket unit was sold to the private-equity firm Cypress Group for around $1 billion in November 2004. Also that year, Dana streamlined further by merging its engine and fluid systems unit into its main automotive components unit, the Automotive Systems Group (ASG). The company had slimmed down to two main units, the ASG and the Heavy Vehicle Technologies and Systems Group. Jettisoning the aftermarket unit trimmed Dana's workforce to just under 46,000 by the end of 2004, down from the more than 84,000 figure of five years earlier. It also represented a cut in revenues of nearly $2 billion, leaving Dana with sales for 2004 of just over $9 billion. The company eked out a profit of $82 million after taking $180 million in special charges.

INTO AND OUT OF BANKRUPTCY

During 2005 the state of the U.S. automotive industry deteriorated as Detroit's big automakers continued to lose market share to their overseas competitors. This left Dana highly vulnerable as General Motors and Ford accounted for around 35 percent of the company's revenues. At the same time that the costs of steel, other raw materials, energy, and labor were rising, the Detroit automakers had been pressing their suppliers for ever steeper price concessions, forcing some of them, including Delphi Corporation, to seek bankruptcy protection. Late in 2005, in an attempt to keep itself from meeting the same fate, Dana announced additional restructuring actions, including further plant closures and workforce reductions and the placement of its engine parts, fluids, and pumps businesses on the auction block. By early 2006, however, Dana began experiencing serious cash flow problems because of mounting debts. Unable to secure additional credit, the company was forced to file for Chapter 11 bankruptcy protection on March 3, 2006.

After securing $1.45 billion in debtor-in-possession financing that enabled it to continue operating as its bankruptcy case progressed, Dana pursued a series of restructuring initiatives. Most crucially, the company cut its annual operating expenses by $460 million by renegotiating unprofitable contracts with customers, closing several U.S. plants and shifting production to lower-wage countries, negotiating cuts in wages and benefits among its remaining workforce, and shifting responsibility for retiree health and welfare costs into trusts. In addition, by early 2008 Dana completed the divestment of its engine parts, fluids, and pumps businesses, which were sold in a series of transactions. Backed by $2 billion in exit financing and a much stronger balance sheet, the company emerged from bankruptcy on January 31, 2008, under a new holding company, Dana Holding Corporation. Burns stepped down from his position as CEO after successfully overseeing the bankruptcy and reorganization.

Burns's successor, Gary L. Convis, was a longtime Toyota Motor Corporation executive who had retired from that firm in 2007 after running its well regarded North American manufacturing operations for several years. Given the struggles of the U.S. automakers, and their nascent attempts to shift away larger vehicles at a time of surging gasoline prices, Convis planned to push Dana to expand its presence overseas, particularly in Asia but also in Europe and South America. He also wanted to take better advantage of the firm's strengths in components for commercial and off-highway vehicles to hedge against the vicissitudes of the light-vehicle market. Further restructuring was also on the agenda as Dana in August 2008 announced plans to cut 3,000 jobs from its 35,000-person workforce and also said that it was considering jettisoning noncore businesses to focus more narrowly on its core driveline products. The company was also in the process of selling its Toledo headquarters and shifting its global base to the suburb of Maumee, where it operated a technology center.

Updated, April Dougal Gasbarre; David E. Salamie

PRINCIPAL SUBSIDIARIES

Dana Automotive Aftermarket, Inc.; Dana Commercial Credit Corporation; Dana Corporation; Dana Credit Corporation; Dana Global Products, Inc.; Dana Lease Finance Corporation; Dana Technology Inc.; Echlin-Ponce, Inc.; Hose & Tubing Products, Inc.; Pasco Cogen Ltd.; Recap, Inc.; Redison, Inc.; Spicer Heavy Axle & Brake, Inc.; Victor Reinz Valve Seals, L.L.C.; Autometales, S.A. de C.V. (Mexico); Automotive Motion Technology Limited (U.K.); Axles India Limited; Chassis Systems Limited (U.K.); Dana (Deutschland) Grundstucksverwaltung GmbH (Germany); Dana (Wuxi) Technology Co. Ltd. (China); Dana Argentina S.A.; Dana Australia (Holdings) Pty. Ltd.; Dana Austria GmbH; Dana Automocion, S.A. (Spain); Dana Automotive Limited (U.K.); Dana Belgium BVBA; Dana Canada Corporation; Dana Canada Holding Company; Dana Canada Limited; Dana Capital Limited (U.K.); Dana Chassis Systems Limited (U.K.); Dana Comercializadora, S. de RL de CV (Mexico); Dana Commercial Credit (UK) Limited; Dana de Mexico Corporacion, S. de R.L. de C.V.; Dana do Brasil Ltda. (Brazil); Dana Ejes S.A. de C.V. (Mexico); Dana Equipamentos Ltda. (Brazil); Dana Europe Holdings B.V. (Netherlands); Dana Europe S.A. (Switzerland); Dana Finance (Ireland) Limited; Dana GmbH (Germany); Dana Heavy Axle Mexico S.A. de C.V.; Dana Holding GmbH (Germany); Dana Holdings Limited (U.K.); Dana Holdings Mexico S. de R.L. de C.V.; Dana Hungary kft; Dana India Private Limited; Dana Industrias Ltda. (Brazil); Dana Italia, SpA (Italy); Dana Japan, Ltd.; Dana Korea Co. Ltd.; Dana Limited (U.K.); Dana New Zealand Ltd.; Dana Queretaro, S. de R.L. de C.V. (Mexico); Dana SAS (France); Dana Spicer Limited (U. K.); Dana UK Automotive Limited; Dana UK Axle Limited; Dana UK Driveshaft Limited; Dana UK Holdings Limited; Dongfeng Dana Axle Co., Limited (China); Driveline Specialist Limited (U.K.); Ejes Tractivos, S.A. de C.V. (Mexico); Fujian Spicer Drivetrain System Co., Ltd. (China); Getrag Dana Holding GmbH (Germany); Hindustan Hardy Spicer Limited (India); Najico Spicer Co., Ltd. (Japan); Nippon Reinz Co. Ltd. (Japan); PT Spicer Axle Indonesia; PT. MCI Prima Gasket (Indonesia); Reinz-Dichtungs-GmbH (Germany); Shenyang Spicer Driveshaft Co. Ltd. (China); Spicer Axle Australia Pty Ltd; Spicer Ayra Cardan, S.A. (Spain); Spicer France S.A.R.L.; Spicer Gelenkwellenbau GmbH (Germany); Spicer India Limited; Spicer Nordiska Kardan AB (Sweden); Spicer Off-Highway Belgium N.V.; Spicer Philippines Manufacturing Co.; Stieber Formsprag Limited (U.K.); Tecnologia de Mocion Controlada S.A. de C.V. (Mexico); Thermal Products France SAS; Warner Electric do Brasil Ltda. (Brazil); Whiteley Rishworth Ltd (U.K.).

PRINCIPAL OPERATING UNITS

Automotive Systems Group; Heavy Vehicle Technologies and Systems Group.

PRINCIPAL COMPETITORS

American Axle & Manufacturing Holdings, Inc.; ZF Friedrichshafen AG; GKN plc; Magna International Inc.; Chrysler LLC; Ford Motor Company; Arvin-Meritor, Inc.; CARRARO S.p.A.; Klein Products, Inc.; Tower Automotive, LLC; Press Kogyo Co., Ltd.; Metalsa S. de R. L.; Modine Manufacturing Company; Martinrea International Inc.; ElringKlinger AG; Federal-Mogul Corporation; Freudenberg-NOK General Partnership; Behr GmbH & Co. KG; Delphi Corporation; Valeo; Denso Corporation.

FURTHER READING

Berman, Dennis K., "Cypress Is Set to Pay $1.1 Billion for Dana's Aftermarket Group," *Wall Street Journal*, July 9, 2004, p. B4.

Byrne, Harlan S., "Bigger and Better," *Barron's*, August 3, 1998, p. 18.

———, "Dana Corp.: After a Sluggish '91, Parts Supplier Readies a Kick into High," *Barron's*, September 30, 1991, pp. 41–42.

"Dana: As Light Trucks Stall, a Push into Financial Services," *Business Week*, July 21, 1980, pp. 98+.

"Dana: Repairing Its Profit Machine by Pushing Replacement Parts," *Business Week,* May 7, 1984, p. 63.

Flax, Steven, "How Dana Found Happiness in the Aftermarket," *Forbes,* March 29, 1982, pp. 110+.

Freeman, Sholnn, "ArvinMeritor Launches Bid for Dana," *Wall Street Journal,* July 9, 2003, p. A3.

Hussey, Allan F., "Beyond Autos," *Barron's,* June 27, 1983, pp. 50+.

Keenan, Tim, "Dana's Destiny: Morcott Shooting for 50% Sales Outside U.S.," *Ward's Auto World,* April 1996, pp. 53+.

Klayman, Ben, "Dana's in the Auto-Parts Driver's Seat," *Toledo Blade,* February 16, 1997, p. D1.

Kosdrosky, Terry, "Analysts Worry Dana Is Sputtering," *Wall Street Journal,* January 23, 2006, p. B3.

Mayersohn, Norman, "The Driver Behind Dana," *Chief Executive,* July 2001, pp. 18+.

McCarthy, Joseph L., "Engine of Growth," *Chief Executive,* May 1996, pp. 22+.

McCracken, Jeffrey, "Dana Follows Auto-Parts Peers into Chapter 11," *Wall Street Journal,* March 4, 2006, p. A1.

———, "Getting Back on the Road," *Wall Street Journal,* January 7, 2008, p. C1.

McKinnon, Julie M., "Dana Charts Course for Bumpy Roads: As Demand Plummets, Firm Weighs Where to Cut," *Toledo Blade,* March 4, 2001, p. D1.

———, "Dana Declares Bankruptcy," *Toledo Blade,* March 4, 2006, p. A1.

———, "Dana Fends Off Hostile Takeover Attempt," *Toledo Blade,* November 24, 2003, p. A1.

———, "Dana to Sell Wix, Other Parts Firms for $1.1 Billion in Cash," *Toledo Blade,* July 10, 2004, p. A1.

———, "Dana to Slash 11,200 Jobs, Close Facilities, Unload Subsidiary," *Toledo Blade,* October 18, 2001, p. A1.

———, "'You Must Continue Changing,' Burns Says: New CEO in Gear at Dana," *Toledo Blade,* June 27, 2004, p. D1.

McPherson, Rene C., *Dana: Toward the Year 2000,* New York: Newcomen Society in North America, 1973, 24 p.

Morrison, Ann M., "Dana Lays Off Its Stockholders," *Fortune,* October 6, 1980, p. 102.

Murphy, Tom, "Swap Meet: Dana, Eaton Trade Axles, Brakes for Clutches," *Ward's Auto World,* August 1997, p. 63.

Pakulski, Gary T., "Dana, Car-Parts Maker to Join," *Toledo Blade,* May 5, 1998, p. A1.

———, "Dana Files Its Map to Exit Bankruptcy," *Toledo Blade,* September 9, 2007, p. A1.

Simison, Robert L., "New Dana Illustrates Reshaping of Auto Parts Business," *Wall Street Journal,* September 2, 1997, p. B4.

Simison, Robert L., and Steven Lipin, "Dana to Acquire Echlin for $3.42 Billion," *Wall Street Journal,* May 5, 1998, p. A3.

Smith, David C., "Global Punch," *Ward's Auto World,* May 1997, pp. 34–36, 39.

Stoll, John D., "Dana Puts Convis at the Wheel," *Wall Street Journal,* April 17, 2008, p. B9.

The Story of the Dana Corporation, Toledo, Ohio: Dana Corporation, 2004, 160 p.

Teresko, John, "A Supplier on a Roll," *Industry Week,* March 2, 1998, pp. 48–50+.

Vellequette, Larry P., "Dana Lost Over $500M, Paid Ex-Leader $7.5M," *Toledo Blade,* March 18, 2008, p. A1.

———, "Dana to Cut 3,000 Jobs This Year," *Toledo Blade,* August 8, 2008, p. A1.

———, "Vanguard of a New Culture: Dana CEO, Veteran of Toyota, Hailed As Mentor," *Toledo Blade,* April 27, 2008, p. F1.

Ward, Sandra, "Back in the Fast Lane: Parts Maker Dana Gets a CEO and a Chance to Roar Ahead with a Revived Big-Truck Market," *Barron's,* February 9, 2004, pp. 34–35.

Drie Mollen Holding B.V.

Postbus 950
's Hertogenbosch, NL-5201 AZ
Netherlands
Telephone: (+31 073) 548 22 60
Fax: (+31 073) 548 22 61
Web site: http://www.driemollenholding.com

Private Company
Founded: 1818
Employees: 900
Sales: EUR 300 million ($450 million) (2007 est.)
NAICS: 311920 Coffee and Tea Manufacturing

■ ■ ■

Drie Mollen Holding B.V. is one of Europe's leading and fastest-growing specialist producers and distributors of coffee and tea. Drie Mollen (the name literally means "three moles") functions as a holding company overseeing the operations of a European-wide network of subsidiaries and sales offices. Based in the Netherlands, the company remains one of that country's leading coffee producers and distributors. The company targets especially the "out-of-home" market, including institutional, corporate, hospital, and governmental and related sales venues. Drie Mollen has also pursued an active internationalization strategy, buying major players in markets including Switzerland, Germany, France, the United Kingdom, and Spain. The company's subsidiaries include F. Cornelius Klipp in Germany; Gala Coffee and First Choice in the United Kingdom; Cafés Campanini in France; Merkur and Giger Café in Switzerland;

and Union Tostadura in Spain. Since 2007 the company has also served as the European distributor for California-based Javo, a specialist producer for the food-service industry. Drie Mollen was acquired by investment group CapVest Equity Partners in 2008. The company is led by CEO Kees Krikka. In 2007 Drie Mollen achieved revenues of more than EUR 300 million ($450 million).

COFFEE ROASTER IN 1818

Drie Mollen was founded as a small coffee-roaster shop in the Netherlands' 's Hertogenbosch in 1818. The shop took its name from its original location, a 16th-century building known as "In de Dry Swarte Mollen." The name possibly came from a plaque on the building's façade featuring three black moles. The shop's original owners, the Sweens family, had been active in coffee roasting and trade since at least the 1780s. The Sweens operated a number of other coffee shops and roasting facilities in the 's Hertogenbosch area.

Drie Mollen remained a relatively small business through the 19th century and the first half of the 20th century. In the years prior to World War II, Joseph Sweens married Mia Schute, daughter of another prominent local coffee roaster. The Sweens retained control of Drie Mollen throughout much of the 20th century. Mia Sweens-Schute survived her husband and became a director of the coffee company.

It was only in the years following World War II that Drie Mollen began to expand its operations beyond its local and regional base. This expansion took off especially in the 1980s when, under new ownership, the company developed into one of the Netherlands' leading coffee groups.

NETHERLANDS EXPANSION IN THE EIGHTIES

Acquisitions formed a major part of Drie Mollen's expansion effort. The company launched its new growth drive in 1981, buying a neighboring rival, Niemeyer, which operated a coffee-roasting and tea-production facility in Bolsward. The following year, the group boosted its 's Hertogenbosch-based operations again by buying Hamido. That company, in addition to its own coffee-roasting and tea-preparation operations, also added instant-coffee production capacity to Drie Mollen's business.

Through the 1980s, Drie Mollen vastly expanded its range of markets, becoming a major supplier to the restaurant and catering sector, while building a strong private-label business as well. The company also launched the production of coffee and teas for the airline sector, developing brands such as Mill House, for coffee, and Princess, for its tea. By the end of the decade, the company supplied its coffees and teas to a number of major airlines, such as KLM, Northwest, Aer Lingus, Qantas, and Cathay Pacific.

In the retail and supermarket sector, Drie Mollen launched its own brand, Gala coffee, which rose to the second place position behind Dutch leader Douwe Egberts. The company's private-label business, meanwhile, enabled it to build a strong export business through the decade. By the early 1990s, Drie Mollen had established coffee export sales to France and the United Kingdom, as well as in Poland, the Scandinavian markets, Greece, and elsewhere. At the same time, the company's Princess tea brand proved a popular export as well. That brand had, in fact, initially been developed for the international market, launched first in Finland, then rolled out to the Scandinavian market in general, before being introduced in the Netherlands.

In support of these operations, Drie Mollen continued to expand its industrial base. In 1985, for example, the company moved all of its coffee production, including its instant-coffee production, to the larger facilities in Bolsward. This site then became the company's main manufacturing center.

Drie Mollen continued to seek new acquisition candidates. The company added several more Dutch companies through the 1980s and the 1990s. These included Veka Coffee and Tea, based in Zoetermeer, in 1987; a stake in Otter Coffee & Tea, which operated in Nieuwegein and Gorredijk; Deventer's Knop en Co. in 1990; and Agem Coffee & Tea, located in Best, in 1994.

INTERNATIONAL MOVES IN THE NINETIES

In the meantime, Drie Mollen's success on the export market had led it to develop its own international component. The company took its first steps outside of Holland in 1987, when it acquired Dartford, England-based Calypsa, a producer of coffee and tea. Drie Mollen then renamed that company under the Gala brand name.

The collapse of the Soviet regime and the prospect of the emergence of a free market economy in the former Eastern bloc countries led Drie Mollen to make an initial entry into that market as well. In 1991 it acquired a stake in Poland's Prima SA, a coffee roaster and supplier based in Poznań. That company expanded strongly in the Polish market, becoming that country's leading coffee brand at the start of the 21st century.

The mid-1990s saw the launch of the next phase in Drie Mollen's international development. In 1996 the company added a new dimension to its European profile by entering the French, German, and Spanish markets. In France, one of the largest coffee markets in Europe, the company acquired Cafés Excella, a supplier to the private-label sector. The company went on to reinforce its French presence, acquiring Cafés Campanini, the French leader in the out-of-home market. Campanini was located in Clermont-Ferrand.

Drie Mollen found similar success in its drive into Germany in the same year when it acquired Gronau-based F. Cornelius Klipp. Klipp had been founded in Bremen in 1878. The acquisition gave Drie Mollen a strong position in the German private-label market, as well as operations in the out-of-home coffee segment, in addition to the foodservices and vending supplies channels. As in France, Drie Mollen soon reinforced its German operations, acquiring a 50 percent stake in Kaiser's Kaffee Geschaft, owned by the Tengelmann retail group, in 2000.

KEY DATES

1818: The Sweens family establishes a coffee-roasting plant and shop in a building known as "In de Dry Swarte Mollen" in 's Hertogenbosch, Netherlands, taking the name of Drie Mollen.

1981: Drie Mollen launches an expansion effort with the acquisition of Niemeyer in Bolsward.

1985: Drie Mollen transfers all production to its Bolsward facility.

1987: Company completes first international acquisition, of Dartford, England-based Calypsa, which changes its name to Gala Coffee & Tea.

1996: Drie Mollen enters France, Germany, and Spain through acquisitions.

2002: Gilde Buy Out Partners and AAC Capital Partners back management buyout of Drie Mollen.

2004: Drie Mollen acquires Merkur Kaffee AG of Switzerland.

2006: First Choice Coffee in the United Kingdom is acquired.

2008: CapVest acquires control of Drie Mollen from Gilde and AAC.

Drie Mollen also entered Spain in 1996, acquiring a share of Union Tostadora. Founded as a cooperative effort among Spain's coffee roasters in 1980, Union Tostadora had become the Spanish market's leading supplier to the private-label sector. Union Tostadora also claimed a top-five position in the out-of-home channel, through its El Templo brand.

FINANCIAL BACKERS IN 2002

Drie Mollen made a short-lived drive into the vending machine market, taking over Sweden's Olland AB in 1998. The purchase also brought Drie Mollen a strong vending-machine component in the Netherlands as well. The company's vending-machine business was boosted again in 2000, when it acquired Poland's Kawomat. The company sold its vending-machine operations in 2004, however.

Instead, Drie Mollen targeted further growth in the European coffee-roasting and distribution market. The company completed several new important acquisitions at the dawn of the 21st century. In 2000 the group

entered Switzerland, buying Rost AG, including its subsidiaries Cafag AG and Sima AG. The group's Swiss business grew again in 2002, when it bought Giger Café AG. That company was founded in Bern in 1904, and had grown into a leading supplier for the out-of-home category.

The out-of-home market became particularly important for Drie Mollen in the new century. Drie Mollen's ambitions to establish itself as a leading supplier to that sector achieved a boost in 2000, when the group acquired Smit & Dorlas, based in Mijdrecht, Netherlands, a leading out-of-home supplier with strong international operations. Other acquisitions completed in 2000 included Thermo-Centre, in the Netherlands, and Lyons, in the United Kingdom.

As it developed its European aspirations, Drie Mollen went in search of new financial backing. In 2002 the company underwent a management buyout, led by CEO Kees Krikka and backed by two Dutch investment firms, Gilde Buy Out Partners and AAC Capital Partners. The new owners then acquired Giger in Switzerland, as well as backed the acquisition of majority control of Union Tostadora in Spain.

TARGETING EUROPEAN LEADERSHIP IN THE 21ST CENTURY

The partnership with Gilde and AAC soon paid off, as Drie Mollen posted strong revenue gains through the middle of the decade. The company also shifted its focus more fully on building a leadership position in the European out-of-home sector, completing the sell-off of its vending-machine operations.

In its place, the company completed several more important acquisitions. In 2004, for example, the company acquired Merkur Kaffee AG, one of the oldest and largest coffee groups in Switzerland, with a strong business throughout Europe as well. This was followed by new expansion in the United Kingdom, where the group's Gala subsidiary had in the meantime grown into that market's leading coffee roaster. In 2006 the company acquired one of that market's top out-of-home suppliers, First Choice Coffee Ltd. of the United Kingdom.

Drie Mollen also sought to broaden its range of brand names in the second half of the decade. The company joined in the fair-trade movement, buying the rights to distribute the Max Havelaar brand to the out-of-home channel. Also that year, the company reached an agreement with California-based Javo, a specialist

Drie Mollen Holding B.V.

provider to the foodservice industry, to distribute its brand in Europe.

Drie Mollen then set its sights on further growth as it targeted the European leadership in its core markets. As part of that effort, the company announced its intention to continue seeking out new acquisitions, with a particular interest in acquiring smaller, family-owned businesses. The company's new foreign-growth objectives also led it to turn to a new financial partner. At the beginning of 2008 Gilde and AAC agreed to sell their stake in Drie Mollen to CapVest Equity Partners. Drie Mollen counted on CapVest's strong experience in the European food and beverage markets to support its own international ambitions for the new century.

M. L. Cohen

PRINCIPAL SUBSIDIARIES

Cafés Campanini SA (France); Drie Mollen Export B.V.; F. Cornelius Klipp (Germany); First Choice Coffee Ltd. (U.K.); Gala Coffee & Tea (U.K.); Giger Café (Switzerland); Merkur AG (Switzerland); Rost AG (Switzerland); Smit & Dorlas Koffiebranders; Union Tostadora (Spain).

PRINCIPAL COMPETITORS

Nestlé S.A.; Procter & Gamble Co.; Altria Group Inc.; Japan Tobacco Inc.; Kraft Foods Inc.; Astor Products Inc.; Cairns Foods Ltd.

FURTHER READING

Bell, Jonathan, "On Land, in Air, Around the World, You May Well Be Drinking Drie Mollen," *Tea & Coffee Trade Journal,* December 1991, p. 19.

Brennan, Joe, "CapVest Go Dutch and Are Smelling More Than Coffee," *Independent Ireland,* January 17, 2008.

"CapVest Grabs a Coffee Company," *European Venture Capital Journal,* February 2008, p. 18.

"Drie Mollen and Gilde Acquire Union Tostadora,'" *Expansion,* May 16, 2002.

"Drie Mollen Expands Activities in Germany and Poland," *Tea & Coffee Trade Journal,* March 1, 2000.

"Drie Mollen International," *Acquisitions Monthly,* February 2008, p. 55.

"Dutch Drie Mollen Enters Market," *Neue Zuercher Zeitung,* May 10, 2000, p. 14.

Joppen, Lucien, "Drie Mollen Heeft Europese Ambities," *Elsevier,* January 21, 2008.

Watson, Clare, "Drie Mollen to Distribute Javo Beverages Across Europe," *Drinks Review,* June 4, 2007.

Dylan's Candy Bar, LLC

315 East 62nd Street, 6th Floor
New York, New York 10065-7767
U.S.A.
Telephone: (646) 735-0078
Toll Free: (866) 9-DYLANS
Web site: http://www.dylanscandybar.com

Private Company
Incorporated: 2001
Employees: 200
Sales: $5.2 million (2008 est.)
NAICS: 445200 Specialty Food Stores

■ ■ ■

Dylan's Candy Bar, LLC, offers more than 5,000 types of candy—from classic American favorites to rare novelty and specialty treats from around the world—at its New York City flagship store and five other locations: inside Bloomingdale's at the Mall at Millenia and at the Florida Mall in Orlando, Florida; at the Houston Galleria Mall in Houston, Texas; at the Roosevelt Field Mall in Garden City, New York; and in East Hampton, New York. Each Dylan's store features nostalgia items, apparel, a bath and body department, a chocolate department, and candy art. With its streamlined, modern design and its cutting-edge retail concepts, the flagship store has earned several retail awards, including Fashion Group International's "Rising Star Award" for retail design and *Crain's* "40 under 40." The company has been showcased in *Vogue, Harper's Bazaar, Elle, Town*

and *Country,* the *New York Times,* and the *Wall Street Journal.*

CREATING AN EXPERIENCE WITH CANDY: 2001

On October 12, 2001, Dylan Lauren and Jeff Rubin opened Dylan's Candy Bar on Third Avenue and 60th Street in midtown Manhattan in a former Sam Goody music store. Lauren, daughter of Ralph Lauren and photographer Ricky Lauren, had studied art history and film at Duke University and was a lifelong aficionado of packaging design and of candy. After college, she toured Europe collecting indigenous treats and adding to her collection of unusual treats and packages. She next launched her own events firm, Dylan's Creative Events, which specialized in product launches and charity parties and frequently employed a candy theme for centerpieces, goody bags, and invitations.

Rubin's background included creating his own in-house candy concession, FAO Schweetz, at FAO Schwarz, which he sold to the world-famous toy store. When the two first met, Lauren reported in a 2001 *New York Times* article, she thought, "'Uh oh, this is the guy who's going to do the Willy Wonka store before I do.'" Instead they decided to partner on a store that featured "cotton candy flowers and gum ball trees and chocolate rivers."

Showcasing candy as a visual as well as a gastronomic treat, the store was a swirl of loud colors, dynamic graphics, and noise. (Ralph Lauren was, according to his daughter, put off by all the color at first.) The two-level, 10,000-square-foot store that Lauren

---

---

designed with Joanne Newbold and the architectural firm Allen & Killcoyne Associates had a giant lollipop tree, candy cane columns, translucent stairs embedded with gummi treats, benches that looked like peppermint swirls, tables that resembled licorice allsorts, and M & M mosaics. "Candy Land inspired the whole design of my store," Lauren explained in a July 2002 *New York Times* article.

Dylan's Candy Store was organized like a department store into boutiques. The 7,000-square-foot level one was arranged in departments by candy brands with ceiling-to-floor displays and a large party room, while 3,000-square-foot level two had bulk bins offering candy by the pound and an ice-cream parlor that rotated its 300 flavors. Songs such as "Sugar, Sugar" and "Honey Pie" were piped through the sound system. Packaging was more than a sideline; at Dylan's Candy Store it was everything. Aside from hot chocolate and banana splits, the business produced nothing. Instead, it presented and uniquely packaged its 5,000 different brands of candy and fun items.

It was an immediate success with all ages. "We've had more people over 50 in the store than kids," said Lauren in a 2001 *USA Today* article. "Park Avenue women come in, and the first thing they ask for is Gummi bears, not the most sophisticated chocolate. They love that it's very childhood, nostalgic." Rubin could boast that, "I've handled selling candy at FAO Schwarz in December. We are doing bigger numbers than that in October."

Paradoxically, the business could attribute part of its success to the destruction of the World Trade Center on September 11. "In a weird way," explained Lauren in a 2001 *New York Times* article, "the timing turned out to be a good thing. We were mobbed, and people kept coming up to me and saying 'I lost my mom' or 'I lost my brother, but thank you for making such a happy place to come and forget for a while about being sad.'"

The store was also something of a statement of independence, a stylistic coming of age for Lauren, who had chafed under the muted-toned sophistication of her father's lifestyle designs. "I guess it all started there," she reminisced in the *New York Times* in 2002, about her childhood pet rabbits, Chocolate and Vanilla, whom she secretly fed Oreos, noting that rabbits and candy still had a place in her decorating style. Rubin "wanted to think out of the chocolate box, to do for candy what Borders had done for books, and what Virgin had done for records. I wanted to make candy destinations."

For Lauren, who would "rather be known for what I'm doing than known for having a name," and for whom the "real bottom line" was finding something she wanted to be doing, the business was all about making people feel good. Willy Wonka, Disney, and her father, who bankrolled half of the venture, but who remained skeptical about its prospects at first, were her inspirations. "[He's] not a candy guy, but he understands Disneyland, how someone can take this concept and make a whole experience out of it. He knew that kids liked candy but when the store opened, he was amazed that all his friends had already been in buying Swedish fish," she explained in the *Sun Herald* in 2002.

EXPANDING DYLAN'S CONCEPT AND INCREASING STORE LOCATIONS: 2002–03

Lauren's dream included candy-centric lingerie, jewelry, handbags, and scented soaps, candles, and perfumes; T-shirts with messages such as "Bite Me"; and artworks made of or featuring images of candies. By 2002, the store, which was open until midnight on weekends, had become a hangout. It was also growing steadily. In the summer of 2003, three new Dylan's stores opened: in the Florida Mall in Orlando, Florida; in the Houston Galleria in Houston, Texas; and in the Roosevelt Field Mall on Long Island in New York. By 2005, business was up 16 percent over 2004 totals with estimated sales of $5 million, according to the *Professional Candy Buyer*. The business had plans to build ten large stores, each 10,000 square feet, and seven smaller stores and to invest in greater web development. It employed 40 people in its corporate offices and 200 in the four stores.

REFUSING TO MASS MARKET: 2004

In 2004, however, Lauren and Rubin went their separate ways with Lauren retaining ownership of the company. The split, which was purportedly amicable, was said to have occurred because Rubin wanted to take advantage of the various requests coming in to sell Dylan's Candy Bar products in other venues, including several big-box

KEY DATES

2001: Dylan Lauren and Jeff Rubin open Dylan's Candy Bar on Fifth Avenue in New York City.
2003: Three new Dylan's stores open.
2004: Lauren and Rubin dissolve their partnership, with Lauren retaining ownership of the company.
2005: The company adds a seasonal boutique at Bendel's in New York.
2007: The first Dylan's Mini Candy Bar opens in East Hampton, Long Island, New York.
2008: Dylan's Candy Bar in New York City expands from 10,000 to 15,000 square feet by adding a third floor; it becomes the world's largest candy store.

entities, such as Target, while Lauren preferred to take a more purist approach even if it meant smaller profits. British Selfridge's and Harrod's also approached Dylan's proposing distribution deals that Lauren turned down.

By 2006, the business was still not profitable. However, the absence of profit was, according to Lauren in the 2006 *Times* article, directly attributable to the company's growth: the four new locations added in 2003 and a seasonal boutique at Bendel's that opened in November 2005. Although some thought Lauren's position foolish, she explained in the 2006 *New York Times* article that "I always learned from my dad, 'Believe in your concept, and stick to your guts.' I knew we were going to make money. But I didn't need to make it in one year." Lauren reinvested all of Dylan's Candy Bar's proceeds as well as her salary in the business.

In fact, the near future saw more Dylan's Candy Bars open. During the summer of 2007, in the elite village of East Hampton on Long Island, a longstanding candy store became the first freestanding mini Dylan's Candy Bar. Lauren, referred to as the "candy girl" in the online newsletter *restaurantgirl*, was quoted as saying of this newest venture, that "'there will be more to boutique venues to come in the imminent future: Miami, Austin, resort towns and many more cities across America.'"

REMODELING THE FLAGSHIP STORE: 2008

In 2008, Dylan's flagship store on Third Avenue received a facelift and an expansion. Working with TSC Design Associates to remodel the interior and to add an additional floor, Lauren increased the size of the original Dylan's by 50 percent to 15,000 square feet. The renovated candy store had three floors, a larger party room, and a bar on the third floor that, in keeping with the company's overall concept, started serving candy-flavored martinis. Lauren described the bar in *Crain's New York Business*. "It's a fantastical theme, with peppermint stools, rather than a serious bar. We don't want people getting drunk."

"'Candy just makes people feel good. It makes you feel ageless,'" is how Lauren explained the success of her business in a 2005 *Philadelphia Inquirer* article. "'The store is a happy place. It's an extension of a childhood fantasy.'" Yet whether the hard economic times then troubling the nation would cause people to give up their sugar fix or whether, as before, the suffering would seek refuge and comfort at Dylan's, remained to be seen.

Carrie Rothburd

PRINCIPAL COMPETITORS

M & M Variety Stores (M & M World); FAO Schwarz Inc.; Godiva Chocolatier, Inc.; Harry & David Holdings, Inc.

FURTHER READING

"Candy Land," *Progressive Grocer*, December 1, 2003.

Epaminondas, George, "Sweet Little Rich Girl," *Sun Herald*, February 24, 2002, p. 8.

Finn, Robin, "Public Lives: Confections of an Enterprising Candy Lover," *New York Times*, November 30, 2001, p. 2.

"Gourmet Gossip: Dylan's Candy Bar Heads East to Hampton," *restaurantgirl*, July 13, 2007, http://www.restaurantgirl.com/gourmet_gossip/dylans_candy_bar_heads_to_east.html.

Green, Penelope, "Mirror, Mirror: Never Grow Up: A Toys 'R' Us Designer," *New York Times*, February 17, 2002, p. 9.

Heller, Karen, "The Sweet Life of Ralph Lauren's Daughter," *Philadelphia Inquirer*, November 13, 2005, p. M1.

Kinetz, Erika, "Candy-Colored Dreams," *New York Times*, January 1, 2006, p. 1.

Williams, Jeannie, "The Candy Is Dandy at This Store," *USA Today*, October 26, 2001, p. 4E.

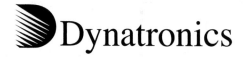

Dynatronics Corporation

7030 Park Centre Drive
Salt Lake City, Utah 84121-6618
U.S.A.
Telephone: (801) 568-7000
Toll Free: (800) 874-6251
Fax: (801) 568-7711
Web site: http://www.dynatronics.com

Public Company
Incorporated: 1983 as Dynatronics Research Corporation
Employees: 144
Sales: $32.59 million (2008)
Stock Exchanges: NASDAQ
Ticker Symbol: DYNT
NAICS: 334510 Electromedical and Electrotherapeutic Apparatus Manufacturing

■ ■ ■

Dynatronics Corporation is one of the leading designers and manufacturers of electrotherapy physical medicine devices in the United States. With its own research and development engineers, Dynatronics designs numerous patented technologies that relieve muscular pain and improve muscle function. Dynatronics' catalog offers more than 4,000 physical medicine and rehabilitation products. The company's sales network includes direct sales representation in 30 states, as well as a national and international network of dealers specializing in medical devices.

LEADING TECHNOLOGY FOR PAIN RELIEF

When Kelvyn Cullimore Sr. purchased Dynatronics Research Corporation in 1979, it was the only company in the United States to offer an advanced laser technology designed to relieve physical pain, particularly as associated with rheumatoid arthritis. The Dynatron low-power, laser device used a helium-neon laser at a low 632.8 nanometer wavelength that did not heat or cut tissue. When applied to muscle tissue, the one milliwatt beam of red light was intended to stimulate muscle relaxation and activate normal function.

Hoping to make something of this leading-edge technology, Cullimore relocated Dynatronics from Pittsburg, Kansas, to Salt Lake City, where the Cullimore family, along with investors, operated a wholesale bakery and a number of other companies. Cullimore applied to the Food and Drug Administration (FDA) for approval to commercialize the laser light therapy device. Until then, Dynatronics operated under the FDA's Pre-Market Approval (PMA). The designation prohibited general marketing but allowed the company to sell the product to physicians and physical therapists. Cullimore formed Dynatronics Marketing Corporation in 1980, to sell the laser product through dealers who specialized in medical devices. That year, Dynatronics introduced the Dynatron 820 low-power laser. The Dynatron 1120, launched in 1982, provided both laser therapy and electrical stimulation for muscle relaxation and pain relief.

Cullimore decided to take the company public to raise funds for the clinical trials on the Dynatron 1120, as necessary to meet FDA requirements. In 1983 he combined the engineering and marketing companies under Dynatronics Laser Corporation and took the company public in 1984. Despite some positive results, the FDA again refused to approve the device, and Cullimore decided to take Dynatronics into complementary areas of physical medicine.

ELECTROTHERAPY DEVICES PROVIDE FOUNDATION FOR GROWTH

In 1987 Dynatronics introduced its first proprietary electrotherapy machines, the Dynatron 100 and Dynatron 500. The Dynatron 100 featured microprocessor-based operation of interferential and premodulated electrical stimulus. Interferential electrotherapy worked by combining constant and variable sine waves into a beat frequency as the waves moved through body tissues. The premodulated electrotherapy generated a pulse frequency inside the machine, before the current entered the body. Both types of biostimulation aimed at reducing pain. The Dynatron 500, also referred to as the DynaStim, provided interferential, premodulated, and Russian electrical stimulus in one appliance, the first such device in the industry. The Russian current added a rehabilitative component, as it was designed to prevent or slow muscle atrophy by stimulating muscle contraction.

In 1988 Dynatronics introduced the Dynatron 2000, a diagnostic device for measuring and testing an array of nerve and muscle functions. Diagnostic testing included range of motion for neck and arms, grip strength for hands, and body balance equalizer, to test for "short leg" syndrome. The Dynatron 2000 included myotome testing for 300 nerve functions. The device assisted physical therapists with determining the degree of injury as well as provided monitoring through the rehabilitation process.

These groundbreaking technologies gave Dynatronics a reputation for technologically advanced physical

medicine products. Independent dealers sold the innovative products to physical therapists, chiropractors, podiatrists, family physicians, and athletic trainers. Revenue growth followed from Dynatronics' success, increasing from $2.45 million for the fiscal year ending June 30, 1987, to $7.34 million for fiscal 1989. That year *Inc.* magazine listed Dynatronics one of the fastest-growing small public companies in the United States.

MARKET LEADERSHIP SUSTAINED THROUGH INNOVATIVE TECHNOLOGY

With its position in the physical medicine market well-established, Dynatronics continued to develop new technology. In 1990 the company introduced two new diagnostic products. The Dynatron 330 Body Composition Analyzer determined the ratio between fat, lean tissue, and water. The Dynatron 350 Surface EMG (electromyography) tested nerve function by determining the electrical activity of the neuromuscular system. In addition to adding these capabilities to the Dynatron 5000, Dynatronics improved on the Dynatron 2000 with exercise recommendations and printed reports. New electrotherapy devices included the Dynatron 200 Microcurrent, which applied low-voltage electric stimulation.

Dynatronics introduced variations of existing products to meet different levels of financial resources. For instance, Dynatronics introduced the Dynatron 400, a midpriced device in a small, portable size; the model offered interferential and premodulated electrical current for pain relief but not the Russian stimulation current; the device treated up to four patients simultaneously. Dynatronics added new modalities to existing products. For instance, the Dynatron 100 Plus and Dynatron 500 Plus included the addition of microcurrent biostimulation to the Dynatron 100 and Dynatron 500 models. The Dynatron 100 Plus Target Sweep provided electrical current over a wide area to reduce pain and swelling.

With Kelvyn Cullimore Jr. as the president and chief executive officer, the company prepared for further growth, constructing a new headquarters in 1993. The 36,000-square-foot facility included space for research and development, as well as office space to accommodate expected growth.

Dynatronics restructured its product line to reflect the development of new technology. The "50 Series" title, introduced in 1994, featured new microprocessor technology which reduced the price of the electrotherapy devices while improving ease of use. The 50 Series products offered a display screen and menu

KEY DATES

1979: Kelvyn Cullimore Sr. acquires Dynatronics Research Corporation and its laser technology for muscular pain relief.

1984: Dynatronics becomes a public company in an attempt to raise funds for clinical research.

1987: Dynatronics launches first proprietary electrotherapy device.

1994: State-of-the-art ultrasound products are introduced to physical medicine market.

1996: Acquisitions expand product line to more than 900 orthopedic and physical rehabilitation products.

1998: Company enters aesthetic market with introduction of Synergie products.

2004: Dynatronics introduces light therapy products.

2007: Dynatronics pursues vertical integration with acquisition of six distributors.

choices for easy operation, and the computer technology enabled the company to design a compact, lightweight machine for portability. Computerization enabled the company to offer improved products at lower prices due to cost-savings from the smaller sized devices.

In conjunction with the 50 Series, Dynatronics began to offer ultrasound as an optional physical medicine modality. Although better known as a visual diagnostic tool, ultrasound delivered deep heat to release muscle tension and pain relief. Dynatronics' state-of-the-art technology provided three frequencies of ultrasound current, at one, two, or three megahertz, enabling the device to pinpoint injury at different depths within the muscle tissue. Under the 50 Series product line, Dynatronics offered existing products with the addition of ultrasound. For instance, the Dynatron 800 offered all of the features of the Dynatron 500 along with the ultrasound modality. Dynatronics received a patent for its Therapeutic Ultrasound in 1995.

The popularity of the 50 Series substantially increased the company's share of the physical medicine market, thus contributing to a significant rise in revenues over the next two years. Sales increased from $4.9 million in fiscal 1994 to $6.78 million for fiscal 1996. International expansion, including to Australia and South Africa, contributed to a 20 percent increase in sales. Dynatronics planned further international distribution and, in 1995, signed a distribution agree-

ment with a Japanese company. In December 1996, Dynatronics obtained approval to market the Dynatron 650 Electrotherapy and Dynatron 950 Combination Electrotherapy and Ultrasound devices in Japan. In preparation for distribution to European markets, Dynatronics implemented manufacturing and quality improvements to its 50 Series product line, launched as the 50 Series Plus line in 1997.

EXPANSION TO ORTHOPEDIC GOODS AND COMPLEMENTARY TECHNOLOGY

During the late 1990s, Dynatronics expanded its product offering through acquisition, new dealer agreements, and entry into the aesthetic product market. Dynatronics acquired Superior Orthopedics of Chattanooga, Tennessee, in 1996. A manufacturer and distributor of therapy tables and related products, such as cushions, pillows, straps, belts, and hot and cold packs, Superior Orthopedics complemented Dynatronics product offering to physical therapists, chiropractors, and athletic trainers. A $2.2 million company, the acquisition involved $1.7 million in cash, stock, and promissory notes.

Dynatronics expanded its therapy table and wood product-line and manufacturing capability through the acquisition of inventory and equipment and the lease of real and personal property from Charlton Floyd, the original owner of Midland Table Company of Columbia, South Carolina. Midland specialized in the design and manufacture of physical therapy treatment tables, parallel bars, and other rehabilitation therapy equipment. In purchasing Midland's assets, Dynatronics gained economies of scale in manufacturing, as well as extension of its rehabilitation product offering.

Dynatronics further expanded its product line through an exclusive distribution agreement with Life-Tech, Inc., producer of iontophoresis. The medical device delivered anti-inflammatory drugs and local anesthetics through the skin by electrical infusion, eliminating the use of needles. Dynatronics expected to increase sales of the iontophoresis through its existing distribution network, including its international dealers, although on a nonexclusive basis. By early 1997, when Dynatronics published its first catalog, acquisitions and product development expanded offerings to more than 900 products.

The company entered a new market when it launched the Synergie Lifestyle System of aesthetic products in 1998. The product line included the Synergie AMS, a vacuum massage tool, and Synergie MDA, the microdermabrasion device. The two-step process began with a massage to improve circulation, then exfoliation to remove the top layer of skin. The two-month treatment process resulted in clear, youthful looking skin. Dynatronics sold the Synergie product to spas and salons. Two national fitness and weight loss franchises purchased Synergie for use as private-label products. In 1999 Dynatronics gained FDA clearance to claim that the Synergie AMS vacuum massage temporarily reduced the appearance of cellulite.

To complement the microdermabrasion process, Dynatronics introduced a line of skin care products that assisted in maintaining the healthy look of the treated skin. Calisse brand products included cleanser, toner, moisturizer, hydrating serum, hydrating masque, and sunscreen.

CUTTING-EDGE PHYSICAL MEDICINE TECHNOLOGY

While most of Dynatronics' products were developed in-house, in 2000 the company became the exclusive licensee for a patented technology developed by Dr. Donald Rhodes. Dynatronics introduced the device as the Dynatron STS, for sympathetic therapy system. The device provided relief for neuromuscular pain usually associated with numbness due to problems in the sympathetic nervous system. The Dynatron STS was unique among the company's products in that the electrical current stimulated the nerves rather than the muscles. Pulse and beat frequencies stimulated the sympathetic nervous system through the peripheral nerves of the legs, feet, hands, and arms. The device attained immediate success, with 1,000 units in use within one year. In particular, Worker's Compensation Clinics found the technology to be an effective alternative to pain medication and an offset to recurring costs of pain management.

In 2002 and 2003, Dynatronics made unprecedented investments in product development, as the company returned to its roots in advanced light therapy products. Research culminated in the development of a "superluminous diode," introduced as Dynatron 880. An infrared probe provided 500 milliwatts of light energy, compared to one milliwatt in the original laser developed by Dynatronics Research during the 1970s. However, the market demanded laser technology, and the company found that a stronger light probe through laser light achieved the same results. Providing the market with such a product resulted in the Dynatron 890 laser probe, which received FDA approval in June 2004.

Dynatronics introduced the technology as the Solaris Series of light therapy products. The line provided

practitioners great flexibility, in that it allowed different kinds of probes, for different therapeutic applications, to be used with one central device. Dynatronics applied the technology for the aesthetic market with the Synergie LT, which adapted light wavelengths to improve skin health and appearance.

Solaris products significantly contributed to record sales at Dynatronics. In the fiscal year that ended June 30, 2004, sales increased 22 percent to $20.6 million. Net income reached a record high of $970,272.

At its annual dealer meeting in July 2005, Dynatronics introduced several new light therapy products, part of its new X-Series. These products included the Dynatron X3, a stand-alone light therapy device, and Dynatron DX2, a combination light therapy and spinal traction device, the first such device to be offered in the rehabilitation market. The Dynatron XP therapy pad allowed for the broad application of light therapy over the body or extremities. The XP was the first such product to allow treatment without requiring practitioner attention through the entire process. New probes for use with Solaris products included the D880 Plus high power light probe and the D405 infrared and blue light probe. Other new products included the Dynatron T3 and T4 motorized therapy tables and the iBox iontophoresis, a state-of-the-art drug delivery system.

COMPETITIVE ENVIRONMENT PROMPTS VERTICAL INTEGRATION

Operating at a loss in 2007 and facing projected growth in the medical rehabilitation industry, Dynatronics began to reevaluate its position in the market. Consolidation of dealers and manufacturers in the industry threatened to create a more competitive environment. The company developed a competitive strategy that centered on vertical integration of business operations and cost-saving operational improvements. Hence, Dynatronics pursued acquisitions that would broaden its product offering and distribution capabilities while improving economies of scale in its infrastructure.

In June and July 2007 Dynatronics purchased six of its major distributors for an aggregate $8.3 million, involving $3.3 million in cash and 4.6 million shares of stock. The primary acquisition involved Rajala Therapy Sales Associates, Dynatronics' largest product dealer. Rajala brought to Dynatronics a strong reputation in medical device marketing in southern California and a distribution facility in Pleasanton, California.

The other acquisitions involved several large medical device dealers: Therapy & Health Care Products, Inc., of Girard, Ohio; Responsive Providers, Inc., of

Houston, Texas; Cyman Therapy Products, Inc., of Detroit, Michigan; Theratech, Inc., of Minneapolis, Minnesota; and Al Rice and Associates, Inc., of Jeffersonville, Indiana. The six companies posted an aggregate $19 million in revenues in 2006, almost equal to Dynatronics' sales of $19.5 million; after selling overlapping inventory, however, the six acquired companies were expected to generate $15 million in revenues in fiscal 2008.

Dynatronics completed integration of the six companies in May 2008. Eight distribution centers were consolidated into three warehouse and distribution facilities, the company's original facilities in Salt Lake City and Chattanooga, plus the Pleasanton, California, operation. The move gave Dynatronics geographic scope while reducing aggregate labor and overhead expenses by $1.9 million per year.

Integration of the six dealers changed Dynatronics' marketing strategy as well. While maintaining its existing dealer network, the company began to emphasize direct sales representation as a means to growth. The acquisitions provided Dynatronics with a network of 26 sales representatives in 20 states. The company hired several more salespeople, including Jim Cavanaugh, one of the therapy device industry's top sales representatives, particularly in the lucrative southern California market. Dynatronics hired three direct sales representatives for the Oklahoma, Kansas, and Louisiana markets. By mid-May the company offered direct sales and distribution in 30 states.

Another aspect of the company's strategy focused on developing several new, state-of-the-art products that would ensure future growth. These included the Dynatron X5 Turbo, an improved version of soft-tissue oscillation therapy, a popular treatment in sports medicine. The DynaPro Spinal Health System combined spinal decompression with light therapy for the treatment of back pain associated with herniated discs, degenerative disc disease, sciatica, or pinched nerves.

Dynatronics launched a new line of aesthetic treatment equipment. The Synergie Elite included three products, a cellulite treatment, microdermabrasion, and bio-stimulation light therapy. The line featured new styling, smaller size, and it was easer to operate and use. The Synergie Elite Combination Unit was priced competitively, nearly 50 percent less than similar devices produced elsewhere.

In September 2008, Dynatronics began distribution of its new 2009–10 catalog, the company's largest catalog to date, with over 500 pages. Before vertical integration, the company sold 2,000 distinctive products. While the company continued to manufacture its core products, third-party distribution of numerous product lines came through the dealer acquisitions. Acquisitions expanded the Dynatronics product line to more than 4,000 items, all presented in the catalog.

Mary Tradii

PRINCIPAL COMPETITORS

Cynosure, Inc.; DJO Inc.; Encore Medical, L.P.; Hill Laboratories Company; Mettler Electronics Corp.; North American Medical Corporation.

FURTHER READING

"Back Pain Treatment," *Physical Therapy Products,* June 2007, p. 51.

Collins, Lois M., "Device Zaps Nerve Pain for Some—Dynatronics Product Offers Unique Therapy but Is Not a Panacea," *Deseret News,* February 8, 2002, p. C05.

"Dynatronics Becomes Leader—Cullimore Moves Device Firm Forward," *Deseret News,* June 13, 1999, p. M02.

"Dynatronics Breaks Ground for a New Research Facility," *Deseret News,* December 16, 1993, p. B7.

"Dynatronics Chief Announces 3 New Medical Products," *Deseret News,* January 2, 1990, p. D8.

"Dynatronics Corp.," *Health Industry Today,* July 1995, p. 12.

"Dynatronics Gets Clearance to Market New Laser Probe," *Deseret News,* June 15, 2004, p. E01.

"Dynatronics Laser Shipping New Device," *Deseret News,* June 16, 1992, p. D8.

"Dynatronics Named Master Distributor for IontoPlus Electrodes," *Medical Devices & Surgical Technology Week,* October 17, 2004, p. 100.

Rexroat, Brooks, "Dynatronics Acquisitions to Boost Growth," *Chattanooga Times/Free Press,* July 27, 2007.

"Solaris Maker Announces Record-Breaking Year-End Results," *Biotech Week,* September 22, 2004, p. 195.

Tierney, Jim, "Deal Making Dwindles," *Multichannel Merchant,* December 1, 2007.

"Traction and Therapy Table," *Physical Therapy Products,* May 2008, p. 34.

"Ultrasound Systems: Do You Offer Ultrasound Therapy in Your Practice," *Chiropractic Products,* July 2008, p. 28.

EnerSys Inc.

2366 Bernville Road
Reading, Pennsylvania 19605
U.S.A.
Telephone: (610) 208-1991
Toll Free: (800) 538-3627
Fax: (610) 372-8457
Web site: http://www.enersysinc.com

Public Company
Incorporated: 2000
Employees: 8,600
Sales: $2.03 billion (2008)
Stock Exchanges: New York
Ticker Symbol: ENS
NAICS: 335912 Primary Battery Manufacturing;
423610 Electrical Apparatus and Equipment, Wiring Supplies, and Related Equipment Merchant Wholesalers

∎ ∎ ∎

EnerSys Inc. is the world's largest industrial battery manufacturer. In addition to its headquarters in Reading, Pennsylvania, the company also has regional headquarters in Asia and Europe, as well as assembly and manufacturing operations in approximately 100 countries. EnerSys concentrates on two main market areas. The company's Motive Power division produces industrial forklift truck batteries, batteries for the rail transportation industry, mining and specialty equipment, chargers, and related systems. Operating in North America, South America, and Europe, the division serves

customers such as Toyota, Nissan, Carrefour, Opel, Lowe's, Yale, IKEA, and the United States Postal Service. EnerSys markets motive power batteries under brand names such as Hawker, EnerSys Ironclad, General Battery, FIAMM Motive Power, Uranio, and Oldham.

The company's Reserve Power division develops reserve power batteries for applications such as telecommunications, utilities, security, sports and leisure, aerospace and defense, and uninterruptible power supply. Operating globally, the division serves customers such as Motorola, Ericsson, Emerson, Verizon, Alcatel-Lucent, BT, and Nortel. EnerSys' line of reserve power batteries includes brands such as PowerSafe, DataSafe, Hawker, Genesis, Odyssey, Varta, and Cyclon.

ORIGINS: 2000–01

EnerSys Inc.'s roots date back to November 9, 2000, when Morgan Stanley Dean Witter Capital Partners acquired the Industrial Products Group of Japan's Yuasa Corp., which was given the new name, Yuasa Inc. The Industrial Products Group was comprised of Yuasa Corp.'s Motive Power and Stationary Power business units in both North America and South America.

Yuasa Corp.'s history can be traced to the early 1900s in Japan. After performing metal electrolysis research in 1913, Shichizaemon Yuasa started making batteries at Yuasa Iron Works in Sakai City, Osaka Prefecture. Yuasa Storage Battery Co. Ltd. was established in 1918. In 1954 it merged with Yuasa Dry Battery Co. Ltd., which had been formed in 1949, to create Yuasa Battery Co. Ltd. The company established a

U.S. operation named Yuasa Battery Inc. in 1963, and changed its name to Yuasa Corp. in 1992.

Yuasa Inc. was an established player within its industry niche at the time of the acquisition by Morgan Stanley, with a global workforce of about 3,000 people. Of these, some 2,500 worked in the United States, and 250 were based at the company's headquarters in Reading. The former Yuasa Corp. units that now made up Yuasa Inc. had generated revenues of $427.1 million for the fiscal year ending in September 2000.

John D. Craig, who had served as president and chief operating officer of Yuasa Corp.'s Industrial Products Group prior to the Morgan Stanley acquisition, was named chairman, president, and CEO of Yuasa Inc. following the deal.

Craig was joined by a team of other former Yuasa executives that included Charles K. McManus, who served as executive vice-president of the company's Stationary Power business, and John A. Shea, executive vice-president of the Motive Power business. In addition, Richard W. Zuidema was named executive vice-president of administration and international, while Michael T. Philion served as executive vice-president of finance and chief financial officer.

On January 1, 2001, Yuasa Inc. changed its name to EnerSys Inc., which was a more accurate representation of the company's focus on energy systems. A few months later, the company laid off 100 employees at its Sumter, South Carolina, plant, in the midst of a dispute with organized workers there. Some employees alleged that safety problems at the plant had caused occupational injuries, and that the layoffs were connected to their push for better working conditions. However, the company attributed the layoffs to a slowdown in business.

INTERNATIONAL EXPANSION: 2002–03

A major development unfolded on March 22, 2002, when EnerSys acquired the reserve power and motive power operations of London-based Invensys plc's Energy Storage Group (ESG). As part of a strategy to transform itself into a more than $1 billion enterprise, EnerSys had explored the potential acquisition of about 30 different battery manufacturers before settling on ESG.

EnerSys was able to take advantage of weak economic conditions and acquire ESG at a competitive price. The $505 million cash deal included a number of the group's subsidiaries, and transformed EnerSys into the largest industrial battery company in the world, with a global workforce of 7,500 people at offices in 27 different countries, including 22 manufacturing sites.

During the early 2000s Exide Corp. remained the leading manufacturer of batteries for the automotive and farm equipment markets. However, EnerSys owed the Exide brand name, which Yuasa had acquired in 1991, at the conclusion of an industrial battery joint venture the two companies had started during the 1980s. Around this time, EnerSys marketed its Exide Ironclad battery for electric forklifts. With a square tubular design, the battery offered up to 24 percent more power than competing products.

In an approach reminiscent of Japanese business strategy, EnerSys was able to take advantage of the close proximity of suppliers near its Cleveland, Ohio, plant and incorporate a "lean manufacturing" strategy. Quick, just-in-time deliveries and close relationships with key suppliers enabled the company to cut the production time for battery chargers from ten weeks to two weeks.

In early 2003, EnerSys grew via the acquisition of Japan's Hawker Battery. The deal led to the formation of a new business named EnerSys Japan. That year, the company's 6,500-member workforce helped it to generate earnings of $4.8 million on revenues of $969.1 million.

An interesting development occurred in the latter part of 2003, when EnerSys attempted to initiate negotiations with its bankrupt competitor, Exide Technologies Inc., about acquiring part of the company. At the time, the two firms were engaged in a legal battle over EnerSys' right to continue using the Exide brand name.

A letter filed with the U.S. Bankruptcy Court for the District of Delaware revealed that EnerSys had made a number of unsuccessful attempts to initiate discussions with the Blackstone Group, Exide's financial adviser. The letter, from EnerSys Chairman and CEO John Craig to Exide CEO Craig Mulhauser, indicated that EnerSys would be willing to pay more than the $950 million value that Blackstone had placed on Exide.

KEY DATES

2000: Morgan Stanley Dean Witter Capital Partners acquires the Industrial Products Group of Japan's Yuasa Corp., which is renamed Yuasa Inc.

2001: Yuasa Inc. changes its name to EnerSys Inc.

2002: EnerSys acquires the reserve power and motive power operations of London-based Invensys plc's Energy Storage Group and becomes the world's largest industrial battery company.

2004: The company begins trading on the New York Stock Exchange.

2008: EnerSys has an estimated 30 percent share of the industrial lead-acid battery market.

GOING PUBLIC: 2004–05

EnerSys had a busy year in 2004. In March, the company secured a $1 million contract to make submarine batteries for the U.S. Navy. That same month, it secured $580 million in credit, $270 million of which it used to pay a special dividend to Morgan Stanley Capital Partners. Two months later, Morgan Stanley announced plans to take EnerSys public, via an initial public offering (IPO) that it hoped would generate as much as $230 million.

A portion of the proceeds from the late July IPO, which actually generated about $156 million, were used to reduce the company's debt load, which by this time totaled around $511 million. Moving forward, EnerSys' stock started trading on the New York Stock Exchange under the symbol ENS.

Around the time of the IPO, a new Russian sales and service operation named ZAO EnerSys was formed. In August, the company announced the acquisition of Mandik Metal, a metal fabrication facility located in Hostimice, Czech Republic. A final development in 2004 was EnerSys Australia PTY Ltd.'s acquisition of Brisbane-based First National Battery (PTY) Ltd.

In early 2005, EnerSys announced a partnership with Aker Wade Power Technologies, in which the companies planned to offer a fast-charging battery system for heavy-duty electrical vehicles such as narrow aisle reach trucks and pallet jacks.

In April EnerSys earned $4.6 million in contracts to develop additional submarine batteries for the Naval Surface Warfare Center in Crane, Indiana. The deal strengthened the company's global defense business,

which included supplying batteries for ships, aircraft, and a variety of ground vehicles.

EnerSys expanded its presence within the global motive power industry two months later, when it acquired FIAMM S.p.A.'s motive power battery arm in a $32.71 million cash deal. EnerSys' growth continued in October, when it snapped up GAZ Gerate-und Akkumulatorwerk Zwickau GmbH, a specialty nickel-based battery maker serving the telecommunications, reserve power, and energy sectors, for about $3.6 million.

RISING MATERIAL COSTS: 2006–07

Developments continued at a blistering pace in 2006. EnerSys ushered in the year by responding to increasing prices of raw materials—such as copper, lead, and plastic—by hiking its product prices between 5 percent and 10 percent. In April, the company suffered a legal defeat when the U.S. Bankruptcy Court for the District of Delaware allowed Alpharetta, Georgia-based Exide to terminate the licensing agreements that had enabled EnerSys to use the Exide name on motive and network power batteries.

On the acquisition front, EnerSys strengthened its aerospace and defense business early in the year by obtaining a controlling interest in the lithium power source company Modular Energy Devices Inc. This was followed by a $2.2 million deal for Alliant Techsystems Inc.'s lithium primary battery operations in May. Three months later, EnerSys expanded into China when it acquired Chaozhou Xuntong Power Source Company Ltd. in a $5.3 million deal, gaining an additional lead acid battery plant. EnerSys ended 2006 with net income of $30.7 million, on sales of $1.28 billion.

Progress continued to unfold at EnerSys in 2007. In January, an $800,000 deal was made for Leclanche SA's lead-acid battery operations. This was followed by the formation of a strategic agreement to supply Hauppauge, New York-based Odyne Corp. with Genesis lead batteries for use in its fleet of plug-in vehicles.

A $17 million deal followed in May, when EnerSys snapped up the Targovishte, Bulgaria-based industrial battery firm Energia AD, which went on to assume some of its European production. This was followed by news that Metalmark Capital LLC and other institutional shareholders planned to sell six million shares of EnerSys stock to Jefferies & Co.

In late 2007 EnerSys continued to face skyrocketing lead costs. In the first half of its 2008 fiscal year alone (ending September 2007), lead prices increased 50 percent. In addition to raising the price of its products, the company's strategy for contending with this challenge included relocating production to countries including Mexico and China, where production costs were much lower. Production in these countries was expected to grow from about 30 percent to 50 percent in a few years.

Despite rising raw material costs, during the later years of the first decade of the 2000s EnerSys benefited from growth in developing countries such as China, which relied on the company's products to power forklifts in warehouses, and for the development of telecommunications systems. In addition, the military continued using the company's products in everything from submarines to tanks. By this time EnerSys had grown to serve approximately 10,000 customers in 100 countries.

EnerSys remained focused on the profitable lead battery market, even though it experimented with emerging nickel and lithium batteries, which were not likely to replace lead-acid batteries in the foreseeable future. The company capped off 2007 with net income of $45.2 million, on sales of $1.5 billion.

UNCERTAIN TIMES: 2008

In early 2008, EnerSys had an estimated 30 percent share of the industrial lead-acid battery market, ahead of competitor Exide, whose share was roughly 20 percent. By this time, 53 percent of the company's business came from Europe and 42 percent came from North America. About 5 percent of EnerSys' came from Asia, a market that held great potential as it moved toward the second decade of the 21st century.

In July 2008 EnerSys benefited from a $13 million submarine battery contract from the German shipbuilder HDW. Around the same time, a new industrial battery joint venture named EnerSys-Assad SARL was formed with Accumulateur Tunisie Assad SA (Assad), a manufacturer of automotive batteries in North Africa and Tunisia. In addition, the company earmarked $10 million to expand one of its factories in the United Kingdom, along with $40 million for the expansion of its Warrensburg, Missouri, plant.

In September 2008, EnerSys introduced its EcoSafe line of batteries, which were developed for use in emerging renewable energy generation storage applications, including solar and wind power.

EnerSys remained the world's largest industrial battery manufacturer and distributor in the fall of 2008. At that time, the world faced the greatest economic crisis since the Great Depression, created in large part by bad

mortgage-related investments. Corporations and consumers alike saw credit markets dry up and stock prices tumble. On October 10, 2008, the Dow Jones Industrial Average concluded the most devastating week in 112 years. Moving forward, the impact of the economic crisis on EnerSys remained to be seen.

Paul R. Greenland

PRINCIPAL SUBSIDIARIES

Acumuladores Industriales EnerSys SA (Spain); Chloride Industrial Batteries Ltd. (U.K.); EH Europe GmbH (Switzerland); Energia AD (Bulgaria; 97%); EnerSys (Chaozhou) Huada Batteries Company Ltd. (China); EnerSys Huada Batteries Company Ltd. (China); EnerSys (Jiangsu) Huada Batteries Company Ltd. (China; 91%); EnerSys A/S (Denmark); EnerSys AB (Sweden); EnerSys Advanced Systems Inc.; EnerSys AS (Norway); EnerSys Australia Pty Ltd.; EnerSys BV (Netherlands); EnerSys Canada Inc.; EnerSys Capital Inc.; EnerSys Cayman Euro L.P. (Cayman Islands); EnerSys Cayman Inc. (Cayman Islands); EnerSys Cayman L.P. (Cayman Islands); EnerSys CJSC (Russia); EnerSys de Mexico, S.A. de CV; EnerSys Delaware Inc.; EnerSys Delaware LLC I; EnerSys Delaware LLC II; EnerSys Energy Products Inc.; EnerSys Europe Oy (Finland); EnerSys European Holding Co.; EnerSys GmbH (Austria); EnerSys Holdings Sarl (Luxembourg); EnerSys Holdings UK Ltd.; EnerSys Hungária Kft. (Hungary); EnerSys Ltd. (U.K.); EnerSys Luxembourg Finance Sarl; EnerSys Mexico Management LLC; EnerSys Reserve Power Pte. Ltd. (Singapore); EnerSys S.r.l. (Italy); EnerSys SARL (France); EnerSys sp. z o.o. (Poland); EnerSys Specialty Products a.s. (Czech Republic); EnerSys SPRL (Belgium); EnerSys s.r.o. (Czech Republic); EnerSysAsia Ltd. (Hong Kong); ESECCO Inc.; Esfinco Inc.; Esrmco Inc.; GAZ GmbH (Germany); Hawker Batterien GmbH (Germany); Hawker GmbH (Germany); Hawker Power Systems Inc.; Hawker Powersource Inc.; Hawker Verteib GmbH (Germany); Modular Energy Devices Inc.; New Pacifico Realty Inc.; Oldham Italia S.R.L. (Italy); Powersafe Acumuladores Industrialis Lda. (Portugal); Powersonic S.A. de CV (Mexico); Shenzhen Huada Power Supply Mechanical & Electrical Co. Ltd. (China; 80%); YCI Inc. (Cayman Islands); Yecoltd S. de R.L. de CV (Mexico).

PRINCIPAL DIVISIONS

Motive Power; Reserve Power.

PRINCIPAL COMPETITORS

C&D Technologies Inc.; Exide Technologies; GS Yuasa Corp.

FURTHER READING

Harlin, Kevin, "EnerSys Inc. Reading, Pennsylvania Battery Maker Discovers New Ways to Keep the Lights On," *Investor's Business Daily,* July 29, 2008.

———, "EnerSys Inc. Reading, Pennsylvania; Lead-Acid Bat-tery Maker Holds Steady in Unglamorous Business," *Investor's Business Daily,* November 29, 2007.

Poole, Claire, "HIGHLIGHT: The Reading, Pa., Industrial Battery Maker Prices 12.5 Million Shares at $12.50 an Is-sue," *Daily Deal/The Deal,* August 2, 2004.

Euromarket Designs Inc.

725 Landwehr Road
Northbrook, Illinois 60062
U.S.A.
Telephone: (847) 272-2888
Toll Free: (800) 967-6696
Fax: (847) 272-5276
Web site: http://www.crateandbarrel.com

Private Company (Majority-Owned Subsidiary of Otto GmbH)
Incorporated: 1962
Employees: 6,000
Sales: $1.5 billion (2008 est.)
NAICS: 442110 Furniture Stores; 442299 All Other Home Furnishings Stores; 453220 Gift, Novelty, and Souvenir Shops; 454110 Electronic Shopping and Mail-Order Houses

■ ■ ■

Euromarket Designs Inc. is the corporate name of the famous Crate & Barrel contemporary home furnishings and housewares retail chain, and its two younger siblings, CB2 (geared toward Gen X and Gen Y shoppers) and the Land of Nod (a children's furniture and accessories retailer). Based in the Chicago suburb of Northbrook, Illinois, Crate & Barrel is considered a trendsetter in style and retail display and a significant amount of its store merchandise is exclusive to the company. In May 2008 cofounder Gordon Segal stepped down as chief executive to let Barbara Turf, who

had served as president of the growing retailer for 12 years, take charge of the company.

INNOVATIVE ROOTS: THE SIXTIES

Crate & Barrel was founded in 1962 by Gordon and Carole Segal. Gordon Segal had graduated from Northwestern University and was working as a real estate agent, while Carole was a schoolteacher. According to company lore, Gordon was inspired to open a store while doing the dishes at home one day. As he stood admiring a piece of imported German china in his hand, he mulled the fact that reasonably priced but classy houseware was not readily available to the Chicago consumer.

With the St. Lawrence Seaway newly opened, the Segals got the idea to have European goods shipped straight to Chicago, where they could be sold directly to the public. In this way, importers and wholesalers could be bypassed, allowing the fledgling merchants to keep prices in check. With their life savings of $12,000, plus $5,000 borrowed from Gordon's father, a successful Chicago restaurateur and caterer, the Segals went into business in spite of their complete lack of experience in either importing or retailing.

The first Crate & Barrel store was opened in a former elevator factory in Old Town, an area of Chicago in the process of gentrification. The store was put together in a mere two weeks. By opening day, Crate & Barrel consisted mainly of a big room, one employee, and a bunch of merchandise. Even the cash register had not yet arrived. With no tables or display cases, the

COMPANY PERSPECTIVES

■

At Crate & Barrel, our motto is "stay humble and stay nervous." We continually challenge ourselves to avoid getting too comfortable. Taking risks and anticipating trends helps us stay a step ahead in the marketplace— it's a tremendous outlet for the creativity of everyone here, and keeps us all on our toes. We like new ideas, and we keep evolving with the times, which makes it fun to come to work.

goods, mainly plates, glassware, and cookware, were stacked on overturned packing crates and barrels, hence the company name.

The Segals' inexperience showed in the earliest months of operation: in the first month, the store sold $8,000 worth of merchandise but began to fall afterward. The Segals realized they needed to broaden their product line to include more of everything as well as unique housewares for discerning shoppers.

In 1964 they took their first European buying trip to make direct contact with the independent crafts-people and manufacturers who would serve as the backbone of their merchandise for years to come.

Another key to the company's early survival was Gordon's ability to concoct unusual and advantageous leasing agreements with landlords. For example, in 1965, as the first Crate & Barrel was thriving in the Old Town location, the company found itself faced with the possibility of losing its lease. Segal was able to patch together a deal allowing Crate & Barrel to build a new store and rent it back from the landlord. Under the agreement, Crate & Barrel would then purchase the building in 15 years. This year, 1965, also marked Carole Segal's departure from the retailing operation to attend graduate business courses and study gourmet cooking.

In 1966 Gordon Segal and Lon Habkirk, a designer who remained affiliated with the company for two decades, traveled to Boston to study a store called Design Research. Design Research, the creation of architect Ben Thompson, dealt in imported housewares and furniture. Segal appreciated the store's clean, modern, Eurolook, heavily influenced by Thompson's unorthodox retail approach. Design Research, however, sold expensive and rare items and had trouble turning a profit in spite of a high dollar-per-square-foot sales ratio. Segal realized Crate & Barrel should focus on keeping prices low through volume buying. His goal was to keep prices 30 to 40 percent lower than competitors by importing goods directly from the manufacturer.

By 1968 Crate & Barrel had annual sales of around $500,000 and opened a second store at the Plaza del Lago shopping center in Wilmette, an upscale suburb of Chicago. As the company grew, Crate & Barrel began to face the problem of developing a reliable management team in an industry with traditionally low pay and high turnover. Segal's solution was to hire young college graduates into sales positions with the explicit goal of eventually moving them into management. He also aimed to create an inviting, stable environment to keep employees around, partly by expanding only to cities hospitable to workers, avoiding such rough-and-tumble markets as New York. This strategy paid off handsomely in employee loyalty. In 1970, for instance, a core of new staff members was brought on board; 15 years later, nearly two-thirds of the group held executive positions with the company.

EXPANSION AND GROWING RECOGNITION: 1970–88

Oak Brook, another affluent Chicago suburb, became home to Crate & Barrel's third store in 1971. By the middle of the 1970s, the chain was beginning to receive widespread attention for its unique marketing style and the quality of its wares. This attention was boosted by the 1975 opening of a new store at a highly visible location on Michigan Avenue in Chicago. Over the course of the next few years, Crate & Barrel began nationwide expansion, propelled by its sterling reputation among the growing class of young urban professionals, yuppies willing and able to spend money on their increasingly pricey homes.

Crate & Barrel's first non-Chicago markets were Boston and Dallas, with stores usually placed in upscale malls. Soon after, San Francisco and Washington, D.C., were added to the list. In 1981 Crate & Barrel tried its hand at retail furniture sales for the first time, converting one of the company's Boston stores into a furniture outlet. Used as a test location, Segal experimented with several different approaches and product lines without risking a heavy commitment to the furniture business. Ten years later, furniture sales were contributing about a fifth of the company's total revenue.

In 1983 Crate & Barrel raised $7 million to finance a new 136,000-square-foot complex in Northbrook, housing its corporate headquarters and a central warehouse. The chain had grown to 17 stores two years later and was generating about $50 million in sales with a workforce of 600 (twice as many during peak periods). By this time, Crate & Barrel stores were supplied by about 350 different manufacturers, many small

KEY DATES

1962: First Crate & Barrel store opens in Chicago, Illinois.
1967: Mail-order service commences.
1977: Crate & Barrel expands beyond Chicago with two stores in Boston.
1981: Crate & Barrel starts selling furniture in addition to housewares.
1989: Sales surpass the $100 million mark.
1990: The company opens flagship store on Michigan Avenue in Chicago.
1995: Crate & Barrel enters New York City market for the first time.
1996: Barbara Turf is named president of Crate & Barrel.
1998: Mail-order giant Otto GmbH buys a majority stake in the company.
1999: Crate & Barrel web site is launched and CB2, targeting younger customers, debuts in Chicago.
2000: The company purchases a half-interest in children's furniture retailer The Land of Nod.
2003: The company introduces online shopping through www.crateandbarrel.com.
2004: The second CB2 store opens in Chicago.
2006: Crate & Barrel sibling CB2 launches its own mail-order catalog.
2008: Barbara Turf takes the reins as chief executive with cofounder Gordon Segal remaining chairman.

independents, with 250 located overseas. Additionally, the company had launched a mail-order service, and was packing about 3,000 items a day.

In the mid'1980s Crate & Barrel found the tastes of its customers had become somewhat more expensive. This became especially apparent in its furniture operations which had consisted mainly of glass, chrome, and black leather in keeping with the clean, basic look of its tabletop merchandise. It soon became clear that its young, monied customers wanted more classic, comfortable furniture and were willing to pay for it. Turning from sleek to warmer wares soon seeped into the kitchen, where the demand for painted dinnerware and hand-decorated glassware began to increase.

Crate & Barrel's catalog also continued to thrive, although it was costly to run (50,000 orders a year

required to break even). Direct mail, however, had the helpful side effect of boosting in-store sales, with sales growing as much as 20 percent in a month immediately following a catalog release.

CONSERVATIVE GROWTH:
1989–97

Crate & Barrel doubled its sales over the next few years, passing the $100 million mark in 1989. By this time the chain had 27 stores, with Los Angeles and Houston added to Segal's carefully selected markets. The company's second furniture store was launched in 1989 on its home turf, as an extension of its Plaza del Lago store in Wilmette, Illinois. The Wilmette furniture store was an immediate hit, generating $1,000 in sales per square foot, especially robust for an industry in the midst of a lengthy slump. The success of the Wilmette furniture operation led to another planned furniture outlet in the Chicago area, this one an expansion of the chain's Oakbrook Center accessories location.

In 1990, with sales at about $150 million, Crate & Barrel opened a new flagship store on a ritzy stretch of Michigan Avenue in Chicago. The building was designed by John Buenz, whose firm (Solomon Cordwell Buenz & Associates) had been designing Crate & Barrel stores since 1976. The exterior of the four-story, 45,000-square-foot structure showed lots of glass and metal, reflecting the clean, modern feel of the standard Crate & Barrel interior. Two floors of the new outlet were to be devoted to furniture. This was a bold move, since furniture had not been sold successfully on this pricey stretch of Michigan Avenue—known as the Magnificent Mile—for many years, including failed attempts by such well-known retailers as John M. Smyth and Marshall Field's. The year also marked the closing of the oldest operating Crate & Barrel store, the 5,000-square-foot outlet opened in 1965 just down the street from the original Old Town store. This store was replaced by a new 10,000-square-foot location about a mile away, to be used primarily as an outlet for end-of-season and closeout merchandise.

Crate & Barrel had tapped into the Minneapolis and San Diego markets with new store locations and in 1991 the chain's total reached 34, with more than 1,000 employees nationwide. Merchandise sold at the various Crate & Barrel stores came from at least 25 different countries, although most of the furniture was manufactured in the United States. In 1992, the company entered the Florida market for the first time, opening stores in Palm Beach Gardens and Boca Raton, helping push sales to $170 million for the year.

By the mid-1990s Crate & Barrel had about 60 stores scattered across the United States, triple its size a decade earlier. The detail-oriented Segal, now in his mid-50s, continued to have his hands in every aspect of his creation. In the spring of 1995 Crate & Barrel entered the New York market by unveiling a store on expensive Madison Avenue in Manhattan. The Manhattan store, at about 55,000 square feet, was nearly twice the size of Chicago's Michigan Avenue flagship store and offered furniture and housewares. "We wanted to open a store that had some meaning," Segal told *Chief Executive.* "Most retailers are somewhat egomaniacal," Segal continued. "It's because you're competitive by nature—you're constantly trying to make a more important statement." Crate & Barrel followed up the Manhattan opening with two new stores in shopping malls in the Greater New York area.

Although 1995 had been a poor year for the retail industry overall, Crate & Barrel saw a 4 percent increase in sales. In early 1996 the traditionally conservative company began to step up its expansion efforts and announced plans to double its revenues in the next five years. Segal relinquished the role of president, giving the position to longtime employee Barbara Turf, in order to concentrate on accelerating growth. Segal particularly hoped to expand the furniture segment, which contributed about $70 million a year to store sales. Even though Crate & Barrel had been selling furniture since 1981, only eight stores offered furniture, with plans to open three additional furniture stores during 1996.

FUNDS FOR EXPANSION: LATE NINETIES

To fuel Crate & Barrel's growth, the company sold a majority interest to Otto Versand GmbH & Company (now Otto GmbH) in early 1998. Based in Hamburg, Germany, the privately held Otto was the largest mail-order company in the world, the parent of about 100 companies, all operating autonomously. Crate & Barrel needed outside assistance to remain competitive in the marketplace, which was increasingly filled with vendors similar to itself. The retailer planned to increase store openings from about four to six to about eight to ten new stores per year, and intended to continue opening larger-scale, flagship stores in major urban markets. Segal explained in the *Wall Street Journal,* "The whole marketplace is more dynamic and aggressive. ... You have just got to grow, and our only choices were to go public or find a strategic partner."

Segal had chosen not to go public, considering it far riskier than taking on a partner. Further, Segal did not want to be the largest chain but to be the best, and this was not usually a goal adopted by public companies. To reflect his new vision, Crate & Barrel was reinvented as Euromarket Designs, Inc., ready to take the home and housewares retail market by storm, with plans to increase its U.S. presence from 17 markets to 30, boost store numbers to 150 nationwide, and grow its catalog operations, which accounted for about 8 percent of sales at the time. The new partnership also benefited Otto, which picked up a popular company with robust revenues and major growth potential.

With a boost to its finances and a healthy economy, Euromarket Designs launched its five-year plan with gusto. In the summer of 1998 the company opened a new, 47,000-square-foot home furnishings store in Chicago. The store had many "firsts," including a fresh-flower market and a coffee shop. The home store featured furniture and accessories placed in homelike settings to provide customers with furnishing ideas and decorating possibilities. The new Crate & Barrel stores followed the chain's trend of moving outside of shopping malls; Segal believed convenience was the key to motivating busy shoppers, shoppers too busy to wander around malls. The company also finished construction of a national distribution center in Naperville, Illinois, where it planned to move its catalog operations. Mail-order sales had experienced significant growth, with sales leaping from 1997's $33 million to $40 million for 1998.

The end of the century heralded change for Euromarket, including plans to build a new 110,000-square-foot headquarters in Northbrook, and the launch of its web site (www.crateandbarrel.com). Crate & Barrel also announced a new retailing concept called CB2, offering basic housewares at lower prices than its increasingly upscale Crate & Barrel stores. CB2 stores, at about half the size of a standard Crate & Barrel, would enable the company to open more stores in more markets, such as college towns. While standard Crate & Barrel stores had a development period of about three to four years, CB2 stores would require less time and less money to launch. CB2 was also designed to lure customers seeking more affordable items, such as those offered when the company first opened its doors.

MIXING OLD AND NEW

The new millennium found Euromarket forging ahead with its multipronged expansion. Its online shopping site had become a phenomenal success, despite a few early hiccups including having to spell out "and" instead of using an ampersand (which did not translate). Interest had been immediate and sales had grown steadily, prompting the addition of a bridal registry and a wider range of products. It was hoped the combined sales of the web site and mail-order operations would account for 25 percent of Euromarket's overall revenues within two years.

Crate & Barrel's new 6,000-square-foot CB2 store concept had also become a reality, with the first store opening in Chicago. Targeting a younger, less wealthy demographic seemed like a prescient move, one followed by another segue into the children's furniture and accessories market. In December the company announced the purchase of a 50 percent interest in The Land of Nod, a catalog company specializing in high-end furniture and whimsical items for kids' rooms. At the end of 2000, Euromarket owned and operated 94 nationwide Crate & Barrel stores and one CB2 prototype.

In 2001 and 2002, Euromarket continued to eye new markets for upscale Crate & Barrel stores and added 3,000 square feet to its CB2 store. Buyers experimented with product lines and price levels, finding Crate & Barrel customers enjoyed dropping into the hipper store to browse knickknacks and accessories. Although CB2 struggled initially with its identity, the young sibling found its footing and began bringing in stronger sales. By the end of 2002 Euromarket brought in total revenues of a reported $850 million, marking Crate & Barrel's 40th year in retailing.

The company relaunched its CB2 concept in 2004, opening its second store. The new 9,000-square-foot location was in Chicago like its sibling, and offered colorful, offbeat products to Gen X and Gen Y shoppers who were trendy and cost-conscious, but willing to pay top dollar for stylish, artsy décor. As CB2 caught on in Chicago, additional Crate & Barrel stores continued to open across the country while the Land of Nod gained a foothold in the children's market. In 2005 came two significant milestones: Gordon Segal was inducted into the Retailing Hall of Fame and Euromarket surpassed the billion-dollar mark, hitting $1.1 billion in sales. In 2006 Euromarket continued to grow: Crate & Barrel opened additional locations in tony strip-malls and elsewhere, while CB2 opened in New York's SoHo and San Francisco's Union Square. In addition, CB2 launched a web site and debuted a 67-page mail-order catalog mailed to more than a million potential customers. Euromarket also announced the expansion of its primary warehouse in the Chicago suburbs, adding some 400,000 square feet to its size. Sales for 2007 were near $1.4 billion for the company's 160 nationwide locations, which included 151 Crate & Barrels, four CB2 stores, and five Land of Nod stores.

In May 2008 Segal stepped aside, leaving Barbara Turf, Crate & Barrel's president for a dozen years, to take the reins of the company. Segal remained chairman of the board, not yet ready to fully retire from his retail empire. Other developments for the year included the company's initial foray into international expansion with new Crate & Barrel and Land of Nod stores in Toronto (with a second Crate & Barrel slated to open in Calgary the next year), bringing Euromarket's total stores to just under 180. Although the economy suffered a significant slump in the second and third quarters of 2008, Euromarket's three specialty retailers were expected to survive the downturn.

Robert R. Jacobson
Updated, Mariko Fujinaka; Nelson Rhodes

PRINCIPAL OPERATING UNITS

Crate & Barrel; CB2; The Land of Nod.

PRINCIPAL COMPETITORS

Ashley Furniture Industries, Inc.; Bombay Brands LLC; Cost Plus, Inc.; Ethan Allen Interiors, Inc.; Inter IKEA Systems, B.V.; Pier 1 Imports, Inc.; Restoration Hardware, Inc.; Pottery Barn, Inc.; Target Corporation; Williams-Sonoma, Inc.

FURTHER READING

Baeb, Eddie, "Online Sales Clicking for Crate & Barrel," *Crain's Chicago Business,* March 20, 2000, p. 61.

Barnhart, Bill, and Sallie Gaines, "Fewer Fish in the Barrel?" *Chicago Tribune,* December 5, 1984, sec. 7, p. 1.

Berner, Robert, "Crate & Barrel Sells a Majority Stake to German Mail-Order Firm Versand," *Wall Street Journal,* February 13, 1998, p. B20.

Burton, Jonathan, "King of the House," *Chief Executive,* November 1, 1995, p. 20.

Carroll, Margaret, "Segals Create Barrel of Fun While Selling," *Chicago Tribune,* February 12, 1986, sec. 3, pp. 1–2.

Cavuto, Neil, "CEO Wire: Crate & Barrel Founder & CEO Interview," January 15, 2007.

Chandler, Susan, "Crate & Barrel Designs Smaller Store for Shoppers on Budgets," *Chicago Tribune,* September 18, 1999.

———, "Crate Gets Respect; A Customer at a Time," *Crain's Chicago Business,* November 26, 1990, p. 20.

———, "New Competition Rearranges the Furniture Business," *Seattle Times,* March 27, 1999, p. E4.

———, "Robust Retail: A League of Their Own," *Houston Chronicle,* December 29, 2002, p. 3.

Collins, Lisa, "Crate Expectations Fuel Furniture Push," *Crain's Chicago Business,* April 22, 1990, p. 1.

"Crate and Barrel Opens Its First International Store in Toronto," *CNW Group,* September 24, 2008.

Gapp, Paul, "Made to Order," *Chicago Tribune,* October 21, 1990, sec. 13, p. 14.

George, Melissa, "Uberdeal Has Crate over Otto's Barrel: A Look at Price Segal Will Pay for Euro-Giant's Cash," *Crain's Chicago Business,* February 16, 1998, p. 1.

"Gordon Segal of Crate & Barrel: Exit Interview," *Inc.,* May 2008, p. 26.

Greenberg, Herb, "Why Would You Want to Go Public?" *Fortune,* May 24, 1999, pp. 324+.

Gruber, William, "Crate & Barrel Plans for Florida and More," *Chicago Tribune,* July 22, 1991, sec. 4, p. 2.

Heher, Ashley M., "Crate & Barrel Cofounder Giving Up Day-to-Day Duties at Home Retailer," *Chicago Tribune,* January 30, 2008.

———, "Q&A: Ready to Ride Out the Storm," *Houston Chronicle,* June 9, 2008, p. 6.

Jones, Sandra, "Segal vs. Segal," *Crain's Chicago Business,* February 13, 2006, p. 3.

Kahn, Joseph P., "On Display," *Inc.,* November, 1985, pp. 110–22.

McNamara, Michael D., "Crate & Barrel Set to Launch Furniture Store in Chi. Area," *HFD,* April 10, 1989, p. 20.

Miller, Ellen, "Crate & Barrel Founder's Passion for Business Still Strong," *Indianapolis Star,* November 11, 2005.

Miller, Paul, "Following Otto's Lead," *Catalog Age,* March 15, 1999, p. 10.

Morrell, Lisa, "Crate Has Blueprint for Returning to Roots: Going After Low-Cost Housewares Set," *Crain's Chicago Business,* November 16, 1998, p. 4.

Nicksin, Carole, "CB2 Pins Down Its Identity with New Store," *HFN: The Weekly Newspaper for the Home Furnishing Network,* September 6, 2004, p. 4.

Palmeri, Christopher, "Stanley, This Is What I Want to Do," *Forbes,* January 20, 1992, pp. 90–92.

Podmolik, Mary Ellen, "Expansion for Crate & Barrel," *Chicago Sun-Times,* February 1, 1996, p. 39.

Schmitt, Anne, "Crate & Barrel Plans New Northbrook Headquarters," *Chicago Daily Herald,* November 24, 1998, p. 1.

Stankevich, Debby Garbato, "CB2 Balances Function with a Bit of Frivolity," *Retail Merchandiser,* May 2003, pp. 39+.

Strangenes, Sharon, "The Gambler," *Chicago Tribune,* August 26, 1990, sec. 15, p. 1.

Tisch, Carol, "Crate & Barrel Plans Home Store Rollout; Opens Prototype for Expanded Format in Chicago," *HFN,* June 15, 1998, p. 1.

Vincenti, Lisa, "Gordon Segal, Crate & Barrel: A Retailing Pioneer Who Not Only Survived but Thrived," *HFN,* November 27, 2000, p. 58S.

Fastenal Company

2001 Theurer Boulevard
Winona, Minnesota 55987-1500
U.S.A.
Telephone: (507) 454-5374
Fax: (507) 453-8049
Web site: http://www.fastenal.com

Public Company
Founded: 1967
Incorporated: 1968
Employees: 12,013
Sales: $1.81 billion (2007)
Stock Exchanges: NASDAQ
Ticker Symbol: FAST
NAICS: 444130 Hardware Stores; 423710 Hardware
   Merchant Wholesalers; 332722 Bolt, Nut, Screw,
   Rivet, and Washer Manufacturing

■ ■ ■

Fastenal Company is a major seller of industrial and
construction supplies at the wholesale and retail levels.
The firm sells nuts, bolts, screws, and other fasteners
and related supplies (the company's original product
line); power tools; cutting tools; hydraulics and
pneumatics products; material handling, storage, and
packaging products; janitorial supplies, chemicals, and
paints; electrical supplies; welding supplies; safety supplies; and metals, alloys, and materials. By late 2008,
after more than 40 years in business, it was selling
around 825,000 different products at its more than
2,160 company-operated stores, though each store car-

ried a much smaller inventory. Most of these stores were
located throughout the United States, Puerto Rico, and
Canada, but Fastenal had also opened some three dozen
stores in Mexico, Singapore, the Netherlands, and
China. The stores are stocked via 12 distribution
centers. Fastenal's core customers include general,
electrical, plumbing, sheet metal, and road contractors;
original-equipment manufacturers; and maintenance and
repair operations. Famous for the frugality of the
company founder, Fastenal is also distinguished by its
record of rapid, highly successful growth since going
public in 1987.

ROCKY BEGINNINGS

The idea for Fastenal was conceived by 11-year-old
Robert (Bob) A. Kierlin. When Kierlin assisted his
father at the family's auto supply shop in Winona, Minnesota, he noticed that customers typically drove from
store to store looking for fasteners that they needed for
particular jobs. If a hardware store did not have the
right nut or bolt, the owner would often send the
customer to the Kierlins' store, and vice-versa. In many
instances, Bob noted, the fastener simply could not be
found and the buyer would have to place a special order
and wait. "I wondered if you could put together a store
with all the parts," Kierlin recalled in the November 9,
1992, issue of *Forbes.*

The idea stuck with Kierlin. After graduating from
high school in 1957 he went on to major in mechanical
engineering at the University of Minnesota, where he
later earned his M.B.A. After college Kierlin accepted a
job with IBM in nearby Rochester. He worked as a

COMPANY PERSPECTIVES

Traditionally, Fastenal has fostered a management style that reflects its corporate philosophy: "Growth Through Customer Service." Our laboratory is currently A2LA accredited for mechanical/chemical testing and gauge calibration. Products are completely traceable and typically purchased to ANSI, ASTM, DIN, ISO, etc. standards. Quality products and quality service—that's what Fastenal is all about.

financial analyst for about ten years, but was itching to start his own business. According to Kierlin, the opportunity came when he missed an interview for an international position because of a late plane. Instead of getting the job, he ended up starting the company he had envisioned as a boy.

With some effort, he was able to persuade an IBM coworker, Jack Remick, to help him pursue his goal of selling nuts and bolts. Also joining Kierlin were former high school buddies Michael Gostomski, Dan McConnon, and Steve Slaggie. Slaggie, Kierlin, and McConnon had graduated from Winona Cotter High School in 1957, and Gostomski had followed in 1958. The five partners ponied up $30,000 and rented a 20-foot-wide storefront in Winona. The group's first dispute was over what to name the store. Someone suggested "Lightning Bolts," but two of the founders were so opposed to the name that they threatened to take their money and leave. The men finally settled on Fastenal, as in "Fasten All." Remick hand-painted the store sign, which one day would be framed and hung in the company's headquarters offices.

The founders' goal with Fastenal was to devise a means of making all kinds of nuts and bolts readily available to the general consumer. The group tinkered with various solutions, including an idea for a nuts and bolts vending machine. They finally settled on a retail strategy to stock a store with thousands of fasteners that would serve as a dependable one-stop shop. Most of the initial planning was done during the weekends and other times when the group could get time off from work. "It was almost like a hobby," Remick reminisced in the November 1994 *Corporate Report Minnesota.*

The first Fastenal shop opened its doors in 1967 on Winona's Lafayette Street. Despite sluggish sales, the group opened a second outlet in Rochester a few years later, thinking that the larger city might provide the customers that the Fastenal concept needed. It soon

became clear to the partners, however, that the venture was a flop. The partners were delivering nuts and bolts in a 1949 Cadillac and having to periodically chip in $1,000 from their savings just to keep the company afloat. "The ship almost went under," Slaggie recalled. "We'd look at the income statement and say, 'We lost how much money?' and then order a round of Budweisers. There was so much red ink."

FINDING THE RIGHT FORMULA AND EXPANDING IT

The group finally determined that their retail strategy was flawed. Rather than targeting the general consumer, they decided to focus on the commercial market. It turned out that price was much less of a factor than timeliness for that market segment, because contractors and companies often lost money searching or waiting for a particular part. Kierlin and his partners discovered that there was a great need for a service that could quickly provide the fastener or part that a buyer needed. The change turned out to be exactly what the stores needed to become profitable, and Kierlin left IBM in 1973 to run Fastenal full-time.

Kierlin continued to improve Fastenal's strategy during the 1970s and gradually began expanding with new stores. The concept became relatively simple: The partners would open outlets in small to medium-sized towns such as Winona and Rochester, where price competition tended to be lower than in large cities, which had special fasteners and parts more readily available. As a result, Fastenal was able to generate profits on the basis of reliability and quick service. The company also targeted towns that had healthy manufacturing and construction industries, seeking to become those customers' one-stop shop for fasteners and related parts. The stores stocked a large selection and promised prompt delivery of any item that was not on the shelf. Later, Fastenal even began manufacturing custom parts that could not be found on the market, at a manufacturing and distribution plant established in Winona.

Fastenal branched out during the early 1980s. Importantly, in 1981 Fastenal purchased the inventory and customer list of the fastener lines of Briese Steel in Rochester. That move spurred growth, first into La Crosse, Wisconsin, and then throughout the upper Midwest. By the early 1980s Fastenal was operating more than 30 company-owned stores. Although all of the original founders contributed to the venture's growth, Kierlin was always the driving force; in fact, the other founders, with the exception of Slaggie, went on to start their own small companies while remaining part-owners in Fastenal. Kierlin focused aggressively on

```
┌─────────────────────────────────────────────┐
│                                               │
│              KEY DATES                        │
│                    ■                          │
│  ─────────────────────────────────────        │
│  1967:  Robert A. Kierlin and partners open the first  │
│         Fastenal store in Winona, Minnesota.  │
│  1968:  Company is incorporated.              │
│  Early 1980s: Fastenal is operating more than 30  │
│         company-owned stores.                 │
│  1987:  To fund further growth, company is taken  │
│         public.                               │
│  1993:  Expansion beyond fasteners begins with the  │
│         launch of the FastTool line of power and  │
│         hand tools.                           │
│  2001:  Company opens its 1,000th store.      │
│  2002:  Customer Service Project is launched; Willard  │
│         Oberton succeeds Kierlin as CEO.      │
│  2004:  Revenues surpass $1 billion for the first time.  │
│                                               │
└─────────────────────────────────────────────┘
```

customer service and used his financial background to keep tight control on the company's finances.

Kierlin was a singular personality. His cluttered office in Winona housed a telescope that he used to birdwatch (Winona is perched along a scenic stretch of the Mississippi River about 100 miles south of Minneapolis). He rarely wore a tie to work and was known for his informal style, as well as a unique salary plan. Even when his company became a publicly traded, multimillion-dollar corporation, he paid himself only $120,000 annually, which was less than he paid several of his employees. In addition, unlike other chief executives who received low salaries, he paid himself no incentive bonus of any kind. Instead, he was content to watch his ownership interest in Fastenal grow along with the company. Also unusual was the fact that no employees had their own parking spaces and everyone, including Kierlin, received the same vacation benefits.

Beneath his casual exterior, Kierlin was an aggressive capitalist and ideologue with little patience for the methods of government or organized labor. He also held a fierce commitment to education. In a book that he self-published in the early 1990s, *The Unified Theory of Life*, Kierlin condemned the state of public education. "Increasingly," he wrote, "ownership of what goes on at the public schools resides not with the parents, nor even with local voters, but rather with state legislatures and state departments of education. ... 'Experts' impose their beliefs on what schools should teach and how the schools should teach them. The sense of omniscience leads the 'experts' to get into the minutiae of school

schedules, start-times, extra-curriculars and hot-lunch programs."

Kierlin backed his rhetoric financially. In 1987 he and the other Fastenal cofounders set up the Hiawatha Education Foundation to help Cotter, their alma mater, and other area Catholic schools. Within six years the foundation had contributed $25 million. Much of that was used to transform Cotter into a world-class, technology-rich institution that was ultimately attracting hundreds of boarding students from around the country and even the world. The Cotter campus was moved to the closed College of St. Teresa, where ceilings were lowered to house computer networking infrastructure. In addition, a $2 million sports complex was built that incorporated six indoor tennis courts. Because of the foundation's endowment, tuition to the school was a relatively low $1,225 by the mid-1990s, and each graduate was entitled to a college scholarship ranging from $500 to $7,000.

CONTINUING RAPID GROWTH

Kierlin continued to expand Fastenal at a rapid rate. By 1985 the chain had grown to a total of 35 company-owned stores. That number grew to 45 in 1986 and 58 in 1987. To generate cash for more expansion, Fastenal's founders took the company public in 1987. The stock jumped from $9 to $15 by year-end, making the Fastenal initial public offering (IPO) the most successful of the 627 conducted during the year of the October 1987 crash. Fastenal tapped the proceeds of the sale to add new outlets to its burgeoning chain. Seventeen shops were added in 1988, 28 in 1990, and 32 in 1991. By 1992 Fastenal was operating 200 stores throughout the industrial heartland of Pennsylvania, Ohio, Michigan, and Minnesota, but also as far away as Texas, New York, the Dakotas, and West Virginia.

Fastenal's gains were the result of Kierlin's profitable strategy and constant adaptation to markets. By the early 1990s each Fastenal store was offering 30,000 items. Four thousand of those were stocked, while the rest could be delivered within 24 hours from regional distribution facilities in Winona, Indianapolis, and Scranton (Pennsylvania). Store operators were trained to find the answer to any question posed to them by a customer, as service was the centerpiece of the Fastenal strategy, and any parts that Fastenal employees could not track down could be custom manufactured in the Winona plant. The stores were typically able to garner profit margins of between 50 percent and 80 percent, which was far above the industry average of about 37 percent. Costs were kept low by locating shops in low-rent districts and minimizing other overhead.

As Fastenal carried its successful strategy into small and medium-sized towns throughout the United States and into Canada, sales and profits surged. Even per-store sales continued to climb, despite economic recession in the early 1990s. Fastenal's revenues grew from $11.6 million in 1985 to $20.3 million and $41.2 million in 1987 and 1989, respectively, while net earnings climbed from $818,000 to $4.3 million. Between 1989 and 1992, sales doubled to $81.3 million as net income climbed to $8.83 million. In 1992 Fastenal opened a fourth distribution center in Dallas and agreed to purchase a fifth in Atlanta. It also entered its 29th state. Kierlin and the other cofounders, who still owned a combined 45 percent of the company, had become millionaires.

The reason for Fastenal's proliferating base of customers was readily apparent: Customers were willing to pay a premium for a dependable service that could save them a lot of money. About 50 percent of Fastenal's sales during the early 1990s came from manufacturing companies, while another 30 percent came from the construction industry. As an example, a contractor paying employees $30 per hour in wages and benefits could not afford to have a project held up by the lack of a special fastener for a piece of equipment, and he knew he could find it at Fastenal. In one instance, a Ford plant's assembly line was shut down by a breakdown that required a few dozen special bolts. Ford's regular supplier told the company it would have to wait until Monday, three days later. "Meanwhile, it's costing them something like $50,000 an hour to have this line not operating," Slaggie said in the March 11, 1992, *Successful Business.* "They called us and the part is an oddball, something we don't have in stock. We had them fax us the blueprint for the machine and we determined we could make it. … We had them finished Sunday afternoon."

Amazingly, Fastenal moved through the early 1990s with virtually no long-term debt, while expanding at a rampant pace. New stores were added from the East Coast to the West Coast, and the company opened up a sixth distribution center. The total number of Fastenal outlets grew to 256 in 1993 and 324 by the end of 1994. With solid gains in existing store sales, company revenues increased to $110 million in 1993 and $161 million in 1994. After posting record net earnings of $11.9 million in 1993, Fastenal's net income surged to $18.7 million in 1994.

Fastenal entered 1995 with 330 stores in 44 states, each of which offered 37,000 different items, and the company was planning to add 150 outlets to the chain within the next few years. Some of the stores were called FastTool, which debuted in 1993. Positioned next to Fastenal shops, FastTool carried the same concept to the tool market by offering about 3,000 different power and hand tools and safety products. The company also experimented in 1995 with a small Fastenal/FastTool combination store for small towns with 5,000 to 8,000 residents.

LATE-CENTURY EXPANSION OF PRODUCT LINE

The final years of the 20th century saw Fastenal expand both its product lines and the number of stores it operated. Product introductions during 1996 included the SharpCut line of metal cutting tools, the PowerFlow line of fluid transfer parts and accessories for hydraulic and pneumatic power, the EquipRite line of material handling and storage products, and the CleanChoice line of janitorial and paper products. Two more product lines were added the following year: the PowerPhase line of electrical supplies and the FastArc line of welding supplies. By this time, the company had nine distribution centers; it then opened two more in early 1998, in Winston-Salem, North Carolina, and Kansas City, Missouri. Expansions of the distribution centers in Scranton and Dallas were begun in 1998 and completed in 1999. Meanwhile, by year-end 1997, Fastenal was operating 644 stores, which were located in all 48 of the contiguous United States, as well as in Puerto Rico and Canada. Another 122 stores were opened in 1998, a year in which net sales reached $503.1 million, a 26.4 percent increase over the preceding year.

Another development in 1998 was the establishment of a subsidiary in Mexico, which employed a sales force dedicated to marketing within that country. Also that year came the distribution of the company's first all-inclusive catalog, an 824-page color-coded behemoth. The following year Fastenal began accepting orders via the company web site; as of mid-2001, however, only 1 percent of overall sales came in over the Internet. Sales and earnings growth slowed in 1998 and 1999 due in part to the aftereffects of the Asian financial crisis, which began in late 1997 and dampened demand for North American manufacturing exports. The opening of new stores was consequently slowed down, with only 43 stores opening in 1999 and 88 in 2000.

One area of increased growth was in so-called in-plant stores, which were supply depots set up and run by Fastenal within the plants of large customers. There were eight such locations at the beginning of 1999 and 21 at the end of that year. Another method that Fastenal employed to make up for the revenues that would have accrued from the previous faster pace of store openings was to place increased emphasis on sales of the newer product lines. Older Fastenal stores were seeing much of their growth coming from the sale of products outside the original fastener line. By 2000, 35.5 percent of overall sales were being generated by the newer, nonfastener product lines.

In 2000 Fastenal began operating a second manufacturing facility at its Fresno, California, distribution center. Sales for 2000 increased 22.4 percent over the previous year, reaching $745.7 million, while net earnings totaled $80.7 million, an increase of 23.3 percent. Toward the end of the year, the slowdown of the U.S. economy began affecting Fastenal's sales, a trend that continued into 2001. The U.S. manufacturing sector was hit particularly hard by the downturn, leading to substantial reductions in sales to some of Fastenal's industrial customers. The company still managed to post a revenue increase of more than 8 percent for 2001, but for the first time in a decade profits fell, declining 13.2 percent to $70.1 million. In spite of the economic climate, Fastenal maintained its growth agenda, opening another 128 stores. Among these were the firm's first outlets in Alaska and Hawaii—giving Fastenal locations in all 50 states—and the first ones in Mexico and Singapore. The first store in Hawaii was also the company's 1,000th overall. During the year, Fastenal additionally finished another expansion of its Scranton distribution center and added another satellite manufacturing facility at the Indianapolis distribution center.

CUSTOMER SERVICE PROJECT

In a key development from 2002, Fastenal launched what it called its Customer Service Project. The goal was to create a new store format that was better stocked and more customer friendly, and by doing so provide an incentive for the company's core customers to visit the stores more often. In addition to shifting a significant amount of inventory from warehouses to stores and expanding the range of products available in the stores, Fastenal also designed the new format to feature an increase in self-serve browsing areas, upgrades to store fixtures, and the first use of hanging merchandise signs. After testing out this new concept and finding that sales increased and inventory decreased, Fastenal started a multiyear process of converting all of its existing stores to the new format while all new stores were built using the new design. Another aspect of this project was to increasingly place new and relocated stores in higher traffic locations in major commercial and retail neighborhoods. Such locales promised to generate greater customer traffic than Fastenal's traditional sites within industrial parks.

In December 2002 Kierlin stepped down from the CEO slot to enable Willard Oberton to take over after serving as COO since March 1997 and as president since July 2001. Oberton had worked his way to the top from his 1980 start at Fastenal as a trainee. Kierlin left the CEO position owning about 9 percent of the company's stock, a holding then worth about $266 million. He remained chairman of the board.

The company stayed on the same path despite the management changeover. While continuing to roll out the Customer Service Project, Fastenal in 2003 also opened 151 new stores and began operating its first non-U.S. distribution center, located in Kitchener, Ontario. The firm that year enhanced its ability to source products directly from Asia, and thereby find alternative, and potentially lower-cost, supply sources by setting up a trading company in China called Fastenal Asia Shanghai Trading Co. (FASTCO). The company accelerated its pace of growth in 2004, opening a record 219 stores, including the first European unit, located in the Netherlands. Revenues surged past the $1 billion mark that year, jumping 24.5 percent to $1.24 billion. Profits were a record $131 million. Over the next two years, Fastenal opened 467 more stores, including its first one in China, bringing the total to more than 2,000. Profits reached $199 million by 2006, when revenues exceeded $1.8 billion.

In early 2007, as a slowing U.S. economy began curtailing sales to original-equipment manufacturing customers, Fastenal shifted strategy. Store openings were cut to just 161 that year. The money saved on start-up costs was reinvested in the existing stores in the form of the hiring of additional salespeople. The aim was to generate growth from both store openings and from increased sales at existing outlets via improved customer service. Early results were positive: record earnings and sales of $232.6 million and $2.06 billion, respectively, for 2007.

Going forward, Fastenal planned to increase its store count by between 7 percent and 10 percent each year. Its focus remained on North America, where it saw the potential for as many as 3,500 stores. Roughly 92 percent of its sales were generated in the United States, with most of the rest originating in Canada. Through late 2008, Fastenal had largely avoided any fallout from the economic travails that had beset the global economy. One reason for its good fortune was that it did not count among its core customer base two of the hardest hit sectors of the U.S. economy: home builders and the auto industry. Also noteworthy at the time of a debt-fueled economic crisis was the perpetuation of one of the ever-thrifty Kierlin's key strategies: Fastenal, after more than 40 years in business, continued to operate without the burden of any long-term debt.

Dave Mote
Updated, David E. Salamie

PRINCIPAL SUBSIDIARIES

Fastenal Canada Company; Fastenal Company Purchasing; Fastenal Company Leasing; Fastenal IP Company; Fastenal Mexico Services S. de R.L. de C.V.; Fastenal Mexico S. de R.L. de C.V.; Fastenal Singapore P.T.E. Ltd.; Fastenal Asia Pacific, Limited (China); FASTCO (Shanghai) Trading Co., Ltd. (China); Fastenal Europe, B.V. (Netherlands); Fastenal Air Fleet, LLC.

PRINCIPAL COMPETITORS

W.W. Grainger, Inc.; WinWholesale Inc.; Applied Industrial Technologies, Inc.; Lawson Products, Inc.; MSC Industrial Direct Co., Inc.; Park-Ohio Holdings Corp.; Anixter Pentacon Inc.; PennEngineering & Manufacturing Corp.; Production Tool Supply; WESCO International, Inc.; HD Supply, Inc.

FURTHER READING

Ballon, Marc, "The Cheapest CEO in America," *Inc.,* October 1997, pp. 52–54+.

Barrett, William P., "Bob Kierlin Versus the Shorts," *Forbes,* November 9, 1992, p. 204.

Bjorhus, Jennifer, "Fastenal CEO Steps Aside," *St. Paul Pioneer Press,* December 5, 2002, p. C3.

Burcum, Jill P., "Winona's Fastenal Bolts Past $100-Million Mark," *Corporate Report Minnesota,* November 1994, p. 22.

Buttweiler, Joe, "Fastenal Was Best IPO Performer," *Minneapolis-St. Paul CityBusiness,* February 8, 1988, p. 16.

Ciccantelli, Meg, "Corporate Capsule: Fastenal Co.," *Minneapolis-St. Paul CityBusiness,* November 26, 1993, p. 21.

Croghan, Lore, "The Wal-Mart of Nuts and Bolts," *Financial World,* July 18, 1995, p. 51.

DePass, Dee, "A New Nuts-and-Bolts Approach," *Minneapolis Star Tribune,* November 3, 2003, p. 10D.

Forster, Julie, "Nuts-and-Bolts Style Suits Fastenal's Kierlin," *Corporate Report Minnesota,* July 1999, p. 22.

Johnson, Gail, "On the Fastenal Track," *Electrical Wholesaling,* December 1999.

Kelly, Brad, "Fastenal Stays Up to Speed with Construction Industry," *Investor's Business Daily,* July 23, 2007.

Kickham, Victoria Fraza, "Still Room to Grow: Fastenal Stays Focused on Growth and Undeterred in Its Mission to Build a 3,500-Store Network Across North America," *Industrial Distribution,* June 2007, p. 42.

Lucy, Jim, "Fast-Growing Fastenal," *Electrical Wholesaling,* May 2008, p. 25.

Manthey, David J., "Fastenal Accelerates Growth," *Industrial Distribution,* November 2000, p. 16.

McLeod, Reggie, "Fastenal's Success Boon to Schools: Winona Firm's Founders Aid Private Education," *Successful Business,* August 29, 1989, p. 30.

Metzler, Melissa, "'Renaissance Man' Still Underpaid, Despite Raise," *Minneapolis-St. Paul CityBusiness,* July 7, 2000, p. S28.

Meyer, Harvey, "Cheap and Cheerful," *Journal of Business Strategy,* September/October 2001, pp. 14–17.

Morse, Dan, "Hardware Distributor Sticks to Nuts-and-Bolts Strategy," *Wall Street Journal,* July 3, 2001, p. B2.

Parker, Walter, "Fastenal Corp. Founders Remake a Tiny World-Class High School," *Knight-Ridder/Tribune Business News,* December 12, 1993.

Storm, Sheila, "Fastenal to Add New Stores," *Successful Business,* December 9, 1991, p. 1.

Swalboski, Gran, "Booming Fastenal Driven by Service," *Successful Business,* March 11, 1991, p. 22.

Teitelbaum, Richard, "Who Is Bob Kierlin—and Why Is He So Successful?" *Fortune,* December 8, 1997, pp. 245–46, 248.

Youngblood, Dick, "Fastenal Co. Doing Well by Sticking to Nuts and Bolts," *Minneapolis Star Tribune,* September 27, 1993.

———, "Fastenal Keeps on Growing, Making Life Tough for Short Sellers," *Minneapolis Star Tribune,* November 3, 1997, p. 1D.

Fisher Communications, Inc.

———————— ■ ————————

100 4th Avenue North, Suite 510
Seattle, Washington 98109
U.S.A.
Telephone: (206) 404-7000
Fax: (206) 404-6037
Web site: http://www.fsci.com

Public Company
Incorporated: 1910 as Fisher Flouring Mills Co.
Employees: 882
Sales: $160.42 million (2007)
Stock Exchanges: NASDAQ
Ticker Symbol: FSCI
NAICS: 515120 Television Broadcasting; 515112 Radio
　　Stations

■ ■ ■

Fisher Communications, Inc., operates 13 full-power and eight low-power television stations and eight radio stations in the Pacific Northwest. The firm also owns and manages a Seattle office building that houses its headquarters and several key broadcast properties, as well as tenants who use its telecommunications services. Most of Fisher's full-power TV stations are affiliated with CBS, with two linked to ABC and several others, including most of its low-power ones, broadcasting the Univision network. A sizable stake in the publicly traded firm is still owned by members of its founding family, who also occupy many of the seats on its board.

ROOTS

Fisher Communications traces its origins to 1910, when the O. W. Fisher family founded a flour mill in Seattle, Washington. Patriarch Oliver Williams Fisher was born in 1842 in Ohio, and as a young man worked in saw and flour mills. After fighting for the Union in the Civil War, he married and had five sons and a daughter. Fisher tried several lines of business, and had his first major success with a lumber company that he started in 1889 in Missouri. It was later expanded to other states including Louisiana, where the mill town of Fisher was founded in 1899.

As his sons grew up they entered the family businesses, as did daughter Lucy's husband. In 1905 Will P. Fisher moved to Seattle to found a flour brokerage called Fisher Trading Co., and the next year his brother Oliver David (O. D.) joined him there, seeking lumber to rebuild San Francisco following a devastating earthquake and fire. He also founded a mill with the Weyerhaeuser family, and began investing in other businesses including the Metropolitan Building Co. and First National Bank.

In 1910 O. D. Fisher founded Fisher Flouring Mills Co. to produce flour from the wheat of area farmers and transport it to market. The firm soon began construction of a milling facility on Seattle's new 350-acre, manmade Harbor Island that could grind 10,000 bushels of wheat per day, which opened for business the following April.

In 1917 the mill's capacity was more than doubled in an expansion that made it the largest flour mill in the western United States. The company had acquired

Fisher has a legacy of serving the community and setting the standard for innovation and journalistic excellence. Fisher envisions making life better in the communities served by connecting and empowering people through local news and information.

numerous warehouses in Seattle and more than two dozen grain elevators in Montana, as well as boats and a private rail line on the island to transport grain and flour.

When Oliver Williams Fisher died in 1922, O. D. Fisher was named president of all the family businesses. In addition to Fisher Flouring Mills, these now included Grandin-Coast Lumber, Louisiana Long Leaf Lumber, National Livestock and Mining Co., The Fisher-White-Henry Co., and Gallatin Valley Mining Co.

In 1923 O. D. Fisher helped found the General Insurance Company of America, serving as its chairman. It would later become known as Safeco, and over the years the Fisher family's stake became one of its most-prized assets, generating consistent dividend revenue.

KOMO GOES ON THE AIR IN 1927

In 1926 the firm expanded again when O. D. Fisher was approached by Birt Fisher (no relation) to help him build a new radio station in Seattle. O. D. happened to be a big fan of the then-new medium, and quickly recognized its advertising potential for the family businesses. At year's end the station went on the air from Harbor Island, operated by a new company unit called Fisher's Blend Station, Inc., which was named after the firm's flour. During its first year on the air, KOMO was moved to downtown Seattle, where it became affiliated with the NBC network. KOMO would go on to be the most popular station in Seattle for many years, with a powerful signal that could sometimes be picked up as far away as Hawaii.

In 1941 the firm bought radio station KJR from NBC, which switched frequencies with KOMO in 1944 and two years later was sold. In 1948 the Fisher lumber business was sold to the Weyerhaeuser Company and KOMO moved into new studios that included space for television broadcasting. Five years later, KOMO-TV was launched on Channel 4 as an NBC affiliate.

By this time Fisher Flouring Mills Co. had grown via numerous expansions to be the fifth largest mill in the United States, and was still the largest west of the Mississippi. In addition to domestic sales, the company's output was now being sold in the Far East and Central and South America.

When local rivals the Bullitt family wooed away NBC for their TV station KING in 1958, KOMO was forced to go with less-popular ABC, and lost a large chunk of market share. The firm was able to rebuild its ratings, however, and in 1962 launched another TV station in Portland, Oregon, called KATU. Initially an independent channel, it became an ABC affiliate two years later when it also boosted its signal.

In 1967 longtime company head O. D. Fisher died at the age of 91. He had continued to work into his late 80s, and also continued to serve on close to two dozen outside boards of directors. The firm remained in family control, with Fisher heirs running each of the firm's branches.

FORMATION OF FISHER COMPANIES, INC.: 1971

In 1971 a holding company called Fisher Companies, Inc., was created to oversee the family interests, which now included Fisher Flouring Mills, Fisher's Blend Stations, a candy company, a computer business, and a number of real estate properties. In 1976 the firm changed the name of Fisher's Blend to Fisher Broadcasting, Inc., and also expanded KOMO's studios.

Beginning in the late 1970s, real estate unit Fisher Properties, Inc., began a campaign of expansion by acquiring warehouses, offices, and unimproved land. In 1986 the firm opened a 195,000-square-foot office building called Fisher Business Center in a Seattle suburb, and began construction of Fisher Industrial Park in Kent, Washington. Revenues for the year hit $122 million. Three years later Fisher Broadcasting bought KZOK-FM from Adams Radio of Seattle.

In 1991 Donald Graham Jr. was named chairman and CEO of Fisher Companies and William Krippaehne was named president. Krippaehne added the CEO title two years later, becoming the first person outside the Fisher family to hold that job. Most of its directors continued to be descendants of the firm's founders.

In early 1994 Fisher bought radio stations KVI and KPLZ of Seattle from Golden West Broadcasters. KVI-AM of Tacoma, like KOMO, had been founded in 1926 and now aired conservative talk shows. In the fall the firm also acquired Sunbrook Communications, which owned 12 small stations in western Washington and Montana.

For 1995 Fisher Companies had revenues of $220 million and a profit of $22.7 million. In 1996 Fisher

KEY DATES

1910: Fisher Flouring Mills is founded in Seattle.
1926: KOMO radio station begins broadcasting.
1948: Firm sells lumber interests to Weyerhaeuser Co.
1953: KOMO-TV is launched.
1962: WATU-TV, Portland, goes on the air.
1971: Fisher Companies is organized as holding company for family interests.
1993: William Krippaehne, first non-Fisher to head company, is named CEO.
1994: Firm buys 14 additional radio stations.
1999: Construction of high-tech Fisher Plaza building begins.
2000: Company acquires 11 Retlaw TV stations for $215 million.
2001: Firm exits flour milling, food distribution businesses; name changes to Fisher Communications; stock lists on the NASDAQ.
2003: Firm completes sale of its real estate assets, keeping only Fisher Plaza.
2005: Company buys six Spanish-language TV stations for $20 million.

Mills formed a joint venture with Koch Agriculture called Blackfoot LLC to build a milling facility in Blackfoot, Idaho. Over the next three years the company would spend $33 million on the project, which it became sole owner of in 1999.

Even though the company was still controlled by the Fisher family, a few non-members owned stakes; in 1997 the firm issued its first annual report and registered with the U.S. Securities and Exchange Commission, as was required of companies with more than 500 shareholders. Its shares were available on the over-the-counter market, although trading activity was minimal.

In 1998 Fisher Broadcasting launched a Los Angeles-based production unit, Fisher Entertainment. It would produce and distribute programs for syndication, cable, and international markets. Most were in the so-called reality genre.

ELEVEN TELEVISION STATIONS ACQUIRED IN 1999

In June 1999 Fisher Broadcasting bought 11 television stations for $215 million from Retlaw Enterprises, Inc., which was owned by heirs of Walt Disney ("Retlaw" being "Walter" spelled backward). They included CBS network affiliates in Washington, Oregon, Idaho, and Fresno, California, as well as two Fox channels in Georgia. Eight of the 13 were either number one or two in their market in ratings or key demographics. With the company's 25 radio outlets, Fisher Broadcasting's reach was now extended to 5 percent of U.S. households. During the year the firm was also given a new unified brand identity, and Fisher Properties began construction of a 270,000-square-foot condominium project.

Fisher Companies was now building a new high-tech facility that would house its Seattle broadcast properties and its corporate offices, as well as space for rent to outside firms. Fisher Plaza was a new type of building designed for secure telecommunications operations, and the company would base a new unit there called Fisher Pathways to offer satellite and fiber-optic transmission services.

In 2000 Fisher Broadcasting sold the Fresno CBS television station it had acquired from Retlaw to the Ackerley Group for $60 million, and the following March the firm announced a deal to sell its flour milling operations to Pendleton Flour Mills for $31 million. Having invested $33 million in the Idaho operation alone, it took a sizable loss on the transaction, which also included Seattle, Portland, and California facilities. Soon afterward the company's related food distribution businesses were sold to Puratos Group of Belgium for $8 million.

FIRM BECOMES FISHER COMMUNICATIONS IN 2001

Focusing mainly on broadcasting, in March 2001 Fisher Companies changed its name to Fisher Communications, Inc., and moved its stock to the NASDAQ in a bid to gain greater visibility and value. In June the company pledged $3 million to renovate a former part of the 1962 Seattle World's Fair with parks and an entertainment facility, which would be known as Fisher Pavilion.

The dot-com bubble burst and slipping U.S. economy caused a big drop in advertising revenue, and during the summer the firm announced plans to cut operating costs by 10 percent. The September 11 terrorist attacks on the United States caused a further decline in earnings, and in October Fisher fell out of compliance with its lending agreements and announced plans to sell the bulk of its real estate assets. These included 1.3 million square feet of office and industrial space, as well as 201 boat slips, although the recently opened

Fisher Plaza would be kept off the block. For 2001 the firm lost $8.3 million, down from the previous year's profit of $14.5 million, and revenues fell $50 million to $162.5 million.

In early 2002 the company refinanced approximately $250 million in debt by using Fisher Plaza and its three million shares of Safeco as collateral. In April KOMO-AM signed a six-year agreement to broadcast Seattle Mariners baseball games, beating the bid of longtime Mariners station KIRO. The deal was reportedly worth over $10 million per year, the most paid to date for a Major League Baseball team's radio rights. Some Fisher shareholders criticized the company for the high price, and reports later surfaced that Fisher's attempt to raise ad rates to cover the cost had been unsuccessful. In July, the company suspended its shareholder dividend, and its already battered stock price dipped further. In an effort to cut costs, the firm had laid off 185 people over the preceding 12 months.

In August 2002 Fisher announced it would sell its two Georgia television stations, as well as revive a stalled effort to dispose of its commercial real estate properties. The money was needed to pay down debt and finish the $130 million Fisher Plaza, the second phase of which was still being completed. In November Goldman, Sachs was also retained to seek possible bidders for the firm.

By year's end Fisher had sold some of its real estate properties for more than $63 million, and early the next year the $40 million Georgia TV station deal was completed, although at a loss of $17 million to the company. Firms such as Clear Channel and Entercom were now bidding to buy Fisher Communications for a reported $430 million to $470 million.

In February 2003 the company backed off from a possible sale and announced plans to restructure operations and cut more costs. Challenges now included declining ratings at flagship TV station KOMO, and disappointing returns for KOMO-AM, which had switched to a more expensive 24-hour news format in a bid to unseat rival KIRO.

In the spring of 2003 Bill Gates's investment firm, which had bought a 5.3 percent stake in the company a year earlier, requested a position on its board, which still had nine Fisher family heirs among its 11 members. Soon afterward the firm added lucrative incentive packages for its top executives to stay with the company.

PORTLAND RADIO STATIONS SOLD IN 2003

In the spring Fisher announced it would sell two Portland radio stations, KWJJ-FM and KOTK-AM, to Entercom Communications for $44 million. In the fall the company's last two office properties were sold for $62 million, and its real estate unit was shuttered. These and other divestments helped decrease long-term debt by more than half, to $129 million.

With help from political advertisements, revenues for 2004 improved to $153.9 million, but a loss of nearly $12 million was booked. In January 2005 President and CEO William Krippaehne resigned under pressure from the company's board, and in October broadcast industry veteran Colleen Brown was named to replace him. The company's chairman was now Phelps K. Fisher.

In December the firm reached an agreement to purchase four Spanish-language television stations in Oregon and Idaho, and secured permits to build two others, for $20.3 million, from Equity Broadcasting. The most prominent were KPOU-TV and KPOU-LP of Portland, full-power stations which carried Univision, the top Spanish-language network in the United States. The others, and the permits, were for low-power community stations. During 2005 occupancy of Fisher Plaza also topped 90 percent for the first time.

In May 2006 the company reached an agreement to sell 18 of its small-market Washington and Montana stations to Cherry Creek Radio for $26.1 million. Six similar stations were also reserved for future sale. Shortly afterward the firm bought Seattle TV station KWOG for $16 million, making it a Univision outlet, and signed a local marketing agreement with WatchTV to manage four low-power Univision-affiliated TV stations in western Washington State. It also received the option to buy them at a later date. For 2006 the firm's sales grew to $154.7 million, and it reported a net profit of $16.8 million.

In 2007 Fisher bought Pegasus News, a Dallas, Texas, firm that offered a web-based news and advertising package, and sold one of its small-market radio stations for $3 million. For the year the firm had sales of $160.4 million and net earnings of $31.9 million. About two-thirds of revenues now came from television, with radio contributing about a quarter and the rest derived from Fisher Plaza. Though its earnings picture had improved, there were still rumors that the firm might sell Fisher Plaza or its radio stations.

In January 2008 the company bought two Bakersfield, California, TV stations, Fox affiliate KBFX and CBS affiliate KBKA, for $55 million. The deal was funded by the sale of 700,000 shares of Safeco stock. Soon afterward an agreement was reached for Safeco to be acquired by Liberty Mutual, and Fisher sold its remaining holdings for $153.4 million, after which it paid a special $3.50 per share dividend to investors. In

July the company announced that its six-year contract to broadcast Seattle Mariner baseball games would not be renewed after the current season ended.

Nearly a century after O. D. Fisher founded a flour mill in Seattle, Fisher Communications, Inc., had been transformed into one of the Pacific Northwest's leading television and radio broadcasters. The firm had returned to profitability after a period of transition in the early 2000s, although possible changes still lay ahead as it weighed the future of its radio and real estate properties.

Frank Uhle

PRINCIPAL SUBSIDIARIES

Fisher Broadcasting Co.; Fisher Mills Inc.; Fisher Properties Inc.; Fisher Media Services Co.; Fisher Radio Regional Group Inc.; Fisher Broadcasting - Seattle TV, L.L.C.; Fisher Broadcasting - Seattle Radio, L.L.C.; Fisher Broadcasting - Portland TV, L.L.C.; Fisher Broadcasting - Oregon TV, L.L.C.; Fisher Broadcasting - Washington TV, L.L.C.; Fisher Broadcasting - Idaho TV, L.L.C.; Fisher Broadcasting - S.E. Idaho TV, L.L.C.; Fisher Broadcasting - Bellevue TV, L.L.C.; Fisher Broadcasting - California TV, L.L.C.; Panlocal Media L.L.C.

PRINCIPAL COMPETITORS

Belo Corp.; CBS Broadcasting, Inc.; Tribune Company; Clear Channel Communications, Inc.; Entercom Communications Corporation; CBS Radio, Inc.; Cox Enterprises, Inc.; Journal Broadcast Group, Inc.; Meredith Corporation.

FURTHER READING

Corr, O. Casey, "Into the Spotlight," *Seattle Times,* June 5, 1994.

DeSilver, Drew, "Over-the-Counter Obscurity," *Seattle Times,* May 20, 2001, p. D1.

Dudley, Brier, "Gates' Fund Wants Role at Fisher," *Seattle Times,* March 8, 2003, p. C1.

"Fisher Announces Impending Layoffs," *Seattle Post-Intelligencer,* August 31, 2001, p. D1.

"Fisher Sells Small-Market Radio Stations to Cherry Creek Radio," *Entertainment Close-Up,* June 2, 2006.

Fryer, Alexander, "Flour, Broadcasting, Real Estate Fisher's Three Legs to Stand On," *Puget Sound Business Journal,* June 18, 1993, p. 33.

Goodman, Josh, "$20 Million Deal to Boost Fisher Role in Hispanic TV," *Seattle Times,* December 13, 2005, p. C1.

Kossen, Bill, and David Bowermaster, "Fisher Plays Hardball for M's," *Seattle Times,* April 25, 2002, p. C1.

Morgan, Richard, "Fisher Buys Retlaw: Disney Family Sells Affils for Tax Reasons," *Daily Variety,* November 20, 1998, p. 43.

"Oliver David Fisher Dies; Industrialist in Seattle, 91," *New York Times,* January 3, 1967, p. 35.

Ramsey, Bruce, "Fisher Companies Is Losing Some Privacy," *Seattle Post-Intelligencer,* May 28, 1996, p. B4.

———, "Fisher Seeks New Setup to Ensure Family's Control," *Seattle Post-Intelligencer,* March 31, 1999, p. C1.

Scott, Alwyn, "Fisher Communications CEO Quits Media Company at Board's Bid," *Seattle Times,* January 5, 2005.

———, "Fisher Pulls Out from Real-Estate Business," *Seattle Times,* November 8, 2001, p. C1.

———, "Fisher Selling Holdings," *Seattle Times,* August 15, 2002, p. E1.

———, "Seattle-Based Broadcast Empire Fisher Communications Facing Many Challenges," *Seattle Times,* February 23, 2003.

Scott, Alwyn, and Martin McOmber, "Debt Tangles Fisher's Future," *Seattle Times,* November 12, 2002, p. C1.

Steen, Herman, *The O.W. Fisher Heritage,* Seattle: F. McCaffrey, 1961.

Virgin, Bill, "By Going Public, Fisher Achieves Visibility, Faces Tough Questions," *Seattle Post-Intelligencer,* November 14, 2001, p. C1.

———, "Fisher Boosts Bottom Line with Sale of Safeco Stock," *Seattle Post-Intelligencer,* August 1, 2008, p. E1.

———, "Fisher to Sell Its Two Portland Radio Stations to Entercom," *Seattle Post-Intelligencer,* May 30, 2003, p. E6.

———, "In Leap at NASDAQ, Fisher Will Sell Mill," *Seattle Post-Intelligencer,* March 21, 2003, p. E1.

———, "Is Fisher Tuning Out Radio for TV?" *Seattle Post-Intelligencer,* May 1, 2008, p. E4.

———, "KOMO and KVI Are Turning 80," *Seattle Post-Intelligencer,* December 21, 2006, p. E2.

Wolcott, John, "Fisher: From a 'Mealy' Start to Media, Real Estate Glamour," *Puget Sound Business Journal,* June 24, 1991, p. 10.

Five Guys Enterprises, LLC

———■———

10440 Furnace Road, Suite 205
Lorton, Virginia 22079
U.S.A.
Telephone: (703) 339-9500
Toll Free: (866) 345-4897
Fax: (703) 339-9532
Web site: http://www.fiveguys.com

Private Company
Incorporated: 1986
Employees: 75
Sales: $200 million (2007 est.)
NAICS: 722211 Limited-Service Restaurants

■ ■ ■

Five Guys Enterprises, LLC, is the owner and franchiser of Five Guys Burgers and Fries, a chain of fast-food restaurants. The restaurants offer a limited menu of hamburgers, hot dogs, french fries, and soft drinks, but have garnered numerous awards from magazines and newspapers. During its first 17 years of existence, the company opened only five units, an era of its existence in sharp contrast to the succeeding years when the implementation of a franchising program sparked the rapid expansion of the concept. Five Guys Enterprises brokers multiunit agreements with franchisees, who pay $300,000 for an individual unit. From its home territory of northern Virginia, the chain has signed deals for the establishment of roughly 500 restaurants in 25 states and the District of Columbia.

ORIGINS

The decision to open the first Five Guys Burgers and Fries was made during a family meeting in the Murrell home in 1985. Jerry Murrell, who ran an estate- and tax-planning business with his wife, Janie, was ready to give his five sons the opportunity to determine their future. He asked his sons, Jim, Matt, Chad, Tyler, and Ben, whether they wanted to attend college or run their own business. The boys opted for the latter, embracing their father's suggestion of opening a takeout burger restaurant. "Nobody really knew how to cook," Matt Murrell recalled in an interview published in the November–December issue of *Power Magazine,* "but none of us was keen on college."

Jerry Murrell had cooked hamburgers while attending college in Michigan, which represented the sum total of the family's experience when they set out to open their first restaurant. Despite their lack of experience, the Murrells shined from the beginning, creating a concept whose simplicity was its greatest strength.

FIRST RESTAURANT OPENS IN ALEXANDRIA, VIRGINIA

The family business was started with the modest sum of $70,000, enough to lease 1,500 square feet on North Fayette Street in Alexandria, Virginia, and to pay for the equipment to outfit the store's kitchen. Although Jerry Murrell took the title of president of Five Guys Enterprises, responsibility for running the business was given to his wife, who managed the books, and to his oldest sons, Jim, Matt, and Chad. "I tried to make sure they kept it simple [and] didn't expand the menu," Jerry Murrell said in a November 2004 interview with *Chain Leader*. "[I made] sure they really got into the detail about the food."

Following their father's advice to keep the menu simple, the teenage boys offered basic items in generous portions, never impressing customers with selection, but winning their business with the quality of the food prepared. The menu consisted of four items: hamburgers, hot dogs, fries, and soft drinks. Only fresh, not frozen, meat was used to make the hamburgers, which were hand-formed and cooked to order. The hot dogs were 100 percent kosher. The fries were cooked in peanut oil. Soft drinks came in one size, 24 ounces, and refills were free. The only extravagances on the menu were the toppings for hamburgers. At no extra charge, customers could choose from more than a dozen toppings that included basic items such as onions and lettuce as well as jalapeno peppers, sautéed mushrooms, hot sauce, and barbecue sauce. While they waited for their food to be wrapped in foil and packaged in brown paper bags, customers could eat the free peanuts offered on the counter, contained, in typical Five Guys fashion, in a cardboard box.

The North Fayette Street shop opened in February 1986. There was no "grand opening" of the store, nor would there be for any of the restaurants to follow in its wake. The Murrells never advertised their restaurant either, but they never lacked for customers. Word spread about the unassuming hamburger and hot dog establishment and customers came in droves. At the end of its first year in business, the North Fayette Street location took in $600,000, enough to convince the Murrells they were doing something right, but the volume of business did not inspire the family to hatch bold expansion plans. Less than two decades later, Jerry Murrell, his wife, and his sons would be orchestrating an expansion campaign aimed at sweeping across the United States, but in the mid-1980s the family was content to keep their business small. Five Guys Enterprises, like its flagship North Fayette Street shop, kept things simple at first.

SLOW EXPANSION IN THE NINETIES

There were two contrasting chapters composing Five Guys Enterprises' history during the first 20 years of the company's development. For years, the company never ventured outside northern Virginia. Additional restaurants were opened methodically: two more restaurants were opened by 1994, one in Alexandria and another in Arlington. The company's fourth restaurant did not open until January 2001, a unit in Washington, D.C., that represented the Murrells' first foray outside Virginia and marked their 15th year in business. The family had never exhibited any desire to expand at a greater pace, and, in fact, had declared they would never do so. In a February 26, 1998, interview with the *Alexandria Gazette Packet*, Jerry Murrell said, "Lots of people have asked us to franchise," but he dismissed the idea, saying, "It just wouldn't be the same, and besides, this is my spirit thing." His thinking soon changed, ushering in the second chapter of Five Guys Enterprises' history and the vision of expanding the Five Guys concept throughout the country.

2002: THE MURRELLS DECIDE TO FRANCHISE

The turning point occurred in 2002, touching off a period of frenetic growth for a company that never showed an inkling of becoming a national player in the restaurant industry. Jerry Murrell set a new course for Five Guys Enterprises when he contacted Fransmart, an Alexandria-based consulting firm that helped restaurant operators franchise their concept. With Fransmart's help, Five Guys secured franchise status in December 2002 and began franchising Five Guys restaurants the following spring, signing its first deal in March 2003. From the start, the Murrells sold multiunit, regional franchising deals rather than single units for a specific location and it complemented its franchising deals with the expansion of corporately owned restaurants. The company's first deal was struck with a local restaurateur, Sean McCarthy, who agreed to open five restaurants in Washington, D.C. When the deal was announced, the Murrells revealed they intended to open between 15 and 20 company-owned units in addition to selling the franchise rights to another 60 to 75 units in the greater Washington, D.C., metropolitan area. Expansion, barely on display for nearly 20 years, was rushing forward.

RAPID EXPANSION

In June 2003, three months after the franchising campaign was launched, Five Guys Enterprises signed development deals with four parties who agreed to open

Survey began rating Five Guys in 2001, giving the company credentials that engendered lines of prospective franchisees willing to pay $300,000 for a Five Guys unit.

A NATIONAL COMPETITOR

Expansion of the Five Guys concept occurred at a torrid pace as the Murrells' bare-bones approach to competing in the fast-food business earned awards and accolades. Within three years, the concept ballooned from five units to 117 units by the end of 2006, nearly all operated by franchisees. The number increased to 220 units by the fall of 2007, when the first restaurant opened in New York City as part of a franchising deal that called for 30 Five Guys restaurants in Manhattan by 2015. Elsewhere, Five Guys restaurants were in operation in Alabama, Delaware, Florida, Georgia, Indiana, the Carolinas, Ohio, Wisconsin, and Pennsylvania, lending geographic diversity to a company that had taken nearly two decades to expand beyond its stronghold in northern Virginia.

After 20 years of business, little had changed on Five Guys' menu. Jerry Murrell's advice in 1986 to keep things simple had been followed even as the chain spread its presence throughout the United States. Hamburgers, hot dogs, fries, and soft drinks were the only items available, but the chain needed little else to power its rise as a national player. Although the company's franchising program did not target a specific demographic, it did require franchisees to agree to open multiple restaurants, a stipulation that fueled the expansion of the chain. Franchisees were advised to open their units in strip malls and shopping centers in trade areas populated by at least 25,000 people, which gave them a wealth of potential site locations.

Expansion showed no sign of slowing as Five Guys Enterprises prepared for the future. The chain had agreements in place for 500 restaurants to be in operation by 2008. Including units in operation and those slated to open, Five Guys Enterprises presided over a chain of restaurants that stretched from coast to coast in 25 states and the District of Columbia. Systemwide sales exploded as a result of the expansion, leaping from $9 million in 2003 to an estimated $200 million in 2007. In an interview published in the November 19, 2007, issue of *Nation's Restaurant News,* Jerry Murrell discussed the extent of the company's expansion efforts. "We don't have much territory left in the United States," he said. "We've sold almost everything, there's not much left, and we've reserved Phoenix, most of Chicago, and a big chunk of California for ourselves. So, we'll have to go into Canada, probably within the next six months." With international expansion on the horizon, Five Guys

KEY DATES

1986: The first Five Guys restaurant opens in Alexandria, Virginia.
2001: The first restaurant outside northern Virginia opens in Washington, D.C.
2002: The Murrell family decides to franchise the Five Guys concept.
2003: Franchising begins in March.
2006: By the end of the year, there are 117 Five Guys restaurants in operation.
2008: Expansion plans call for 500 restaurants to be in operation throughout the United States.

13 units in Virginia and 12 units in Maryland. By August 2003, when there were still only five Five Guys open for business, there were deals in place for the establishment of 80 additional units, all concentrated in the District of Columbia, Virginia, and Maryland. The first step out of the region was made in March 2004, when Five Guys Enterprises signed an 11-restaurant franchise agreement with Michael Ruffer, who purchased territory in southern Virginia and North Carolina, intending to open his first restaurant in North Carolina before March 2005.

By the fall of 2004, a year and a half after selling his first franchise, Jerry Murrell had signed development deals with 45 franchise groups promising to open 300 stores. Systemwide, Five Guys Enterprises was a $9 million business by the end of 2003. As the development deals came to fruition, systemwide sales were expected to reach $20 million by the end of 2004. The once sleepy Five Guys concept was beginning to become a notable player in the fast-food segment of the restaurant industry.

The rush to expand represented a dramatic change in Five Guys Enterprises' demeanor, but the Murrells were convinced their simple concept had the potential to become a franchise giant. Attention from the media supported their convictions. The restaurants had earned praise from food critics from the start, but in the years leading up to the launch of the franchising program, Five Guys Enterprises began to become a phenomenon. The company's hamburger was voted as the best hamburger by readers of *Washingtonian* in 1999, an honor it also received in the years 2001 through 2004. Readers of the Times Community Newspapers also selected Five Guys hamburgers as the "Best Burger" in 2000 and 2001. Perhaps most important, the Zagat

Enterprises pressed ahead, showing no lack of ambition as it neared its 25th anniversary.

Jeffrey L. Covell

PRINCIPAL COMPETITORS

McDonald's Corporation; Burger King Holdings, Inc.; Wendy's International, Inc.; YUM! Brands, Inc.

FURTHER READING

Elan, Elissa, "Fast-Grown Five Guys Chain Beefs Up, Eyes Meaty Growth," *Nation's Restaurant News,* November 19, 2007, p. 4.

"Five Guys Burgers Inks 4 Deals for 25 Units," *Nation's Restaurant News,* June 16, 2003, p. 88.

"Five Guys Burgers, Operator and Franchisor of an Eight-Unit Hamburger Chain, Signed 11-Restaurant Franchise Deal with Michael Ruffer," *Nation's Restaurant News,* March 4, 2004, p. 1.

Lyons, Lana, "Five Guys Draws Hamburger Lovers," *Alexandria Gazette Packet,* February 26, 1998, p. 45.

Norris, Maya, "Simple but Complicated: Five Guy's Bare-Bones Burger Menu Makes Its Way into the East," *Chain Leader,* November 2004, p. 20.

Rogow, Geoffrey, "Five Guys Burger Franchises Slated to Open in Region," *Roanoke Times,* August 5, 2003, p. A7.

Triplett, William, "Burger King," *Power Magazine,* November–December 2000.

france telecom

France Telecom S.A.

6 Pl. d'Alleray
Paris, F-75505 Cedex 15
France
Telephone: (+33 1 55) 78 60 56
Fax: (+33 1 44) 44 95 95
Web site: http://www.francetelecom.com

Public Company
Incorporated: 1878 as Société Générale du Telephones
Employees: 187,331
Sales: EUR 52.9 billion ($80 billion) (2007)
Stock Exchanges: Euronext Paris New York
Ticker Symbol: FTE
NAICS: 517110 Wired Telecommunications Carriers;
515210 Cable and Other Subscription Programming; 517212 Cellular and Other Wireless Telecommunications; 517910 Other Telecommunications

■ ■ ■

France Telecom S.A. is one of the world's largest telecommunications companies. The former French telephone monopoly has accomplished a breathtaking expansion at the dawn of the 21st century, establishing a global powerhouse reaching more than 170 million customers worldwide. France Telecom is the number three mobile telephone operator in Europe, with a customer base of 110 million. It is the leading European provider of ADSL-based broadband services, with nearly 12 million subscribers. A pioneer of VoIP (telephone over the Internet) and IPTV (television through the In-

ternet) technologies, France Telecom remains a European leader in both categories, with 4.8 million and 1.25 million subscribers, respectively. France Telecom is also leading the drive to convert customers to its "quad-play" model, combining Internet, telephony, television, and mobile telephone services. As such, most of France Telecom's operations have been rebranded under the Orange name; the company also operates under the Mobistar (Belgium), TP Group (Poland), and Amena and Ya.com (Spain) brands.

France, the United Kingdom, Spain, and Poland represent the company's main consumer markets, while its Enterprise division reaches 220 countries through a network of 166 offices. Other markets include Belgium, Switzerland, Luxembourg, Romania, Slovakia, Moldavia, Ivory Coast, Guinea-Bissau, Guinea, Equatorial Guinea, Cameroon, Botswana, Central African Republic, Niger, Mali, Senegal, Kenya, Madagascar, Mauritius, Egypt, Jordan, Mexico, Dominican Republic, Vietnam, and Vanuatu. The company is listed on the Euronext Paris Stock Exchange and the New York Stock Exchange (NYSE); the French government maintains a 55.5 percent stake in the company. Didier Lombard is France Telecom's CEO and chairman.

EARLY HISTORY

The history of French telecommunications is largely that of political intervention in scientific progress. As early as 1837, five years after Samuel Morse conceived his system of electromagnetic telegraphy, the Morse code, and when Carl von Steinheil had devised an electromagnetic machine through which messages were recorded by a needle, political control over telegraphic services was sought. The French king, Louis Philippe, perhaps saw this as a logical extension of the control of the press which Charles X had initiated as part of the July Ordinances of 1830. State monopoly of telegraphic services, for military and political reasons, was finally established in 1851.

Telegraphic communication was made practicable in the mid-19th century, after scientific experiments by André Ampère, Karl Friedrich Gauss, Wilhelm Eduard Weber, Michael Faraday, and Steinheil in Europe, and Morse in America, concerning the relationship between light waves and electromagnetic waves. The most celebrated technical advance in telegraphy was achieved by Émile Baudot, whose system of Rapid Telegraphy was patented in 1874. Other of Baudot's telegraphic inventions were contemporaneous with the development of the typewriter and by 1890 telegrams began to be transmitted in page form. The French Post Office gradually absorbed the telegraph service, one minister becoming responsible for both early in 1879.

From the last quarter of the 19th century the expansion of telephony in France was equally rapid. In 1880 the three private companies that the French government had licensed merged to form Société Générale du Telephones (SGT). The year 1883 saw the first telephone exchange installed in Rheims and 1887 the first international circuits connecting Paris to Brussels. SGT's telephone network was nationalized in September 1889, adopting the new name of Direction Générale des Télécommunications. The French government reserved the monopoly of telephonic developments and addressed itself to the problems of technical development with the assistance of scientists Ader and Berthon. In addition to the development of transmission equipment, work progressed on the refinement of switching equipment which automatically made the connections between the lines. In the United States, Al-

mon Strowger's automatic switchgear, patented in 1889, allowed subscriber connection without the interposition of a human operator. This new type of equipment became famous for its durability. The first automated exchange in France was installed in Nice in October 1913, the last being dismantled only in 1979.

Between 1890 and 1915 the number of telephones in France more than doubled every five years, from 15,432 to 357,515. However, the distribution of instruments in proportion to the population was modest. In 1911 there were 0.6 telephones per 100 people in France while in the United States there were 8.1, in Canada 3.7, in Denmark 3.5, in Sweden 3.4, and in Germany 1.6. One of the main reasons for this slow growth was the method of financing networks. The cities that wished to acquire a telephone system had to provide the administration with the initial finance. The administration later reimbursed the locality in proportion to the receipts from subscribers to the new network. Unequal distribution of telephone networks across the country, and lack of interregional connections, resulted from this approach.

Between the two world wars French government policy ensured that the telephone service was geared more closely to the needs of the commercial and industrial sectors, and that modern services were provided to all at the same price across the country. Originally there were many varieties of telephone sets available but a standard model was introduced in 1924. The setting of more, and better quality, lines was also begun, using underground cables. Long-distance connections, improved by the invention between 1904 and 1915 of the diode and the triode, the audion, and the hard valve lamps, were refined. Arteries of lines radiating from Paris to many regional telephone exchanges were constructed between 1924 and 1938. Finally, the replacement of manual by automatic exchanges was gradually achieved, using the rotary system.

Paris, its environs, and eventually the main provincial centers saw their exchanges automated from the 1930s. In the countryside, however, the problem of modernizing 25,000 exchanges, half of which supported fewer than five subscribers, had to be approached differently and a semiautomatic system resulted. Nevertheless, France still had one of the lowest ratios of telephones to people in 1938 with 3.79 percent whereas the United States had 15.27 percent, Sweden 12.47 percent, and the United Kingdom 6.74 percent. Most French telephones were used for business purposes and in the home the instrument barely penetrated below the upper middle classes. Most telephones were to be found in urban areas of northern France; elsewhere, only the

KEY DATES

1880: Three private companies holding telephone licenses merge to form Société Générale du Telephones (SGT).

1889: French government nationalizes telephone industry, and SGT becomes Direction Générale des Télécommunications (DGT).

1913: DGT inaugurates the first automatic telephone exchange in Nice.

1971: Intelsat II completes global satellite coverage.

1990: DGT becomes a limited liability company and changes name to France Télécom.

1997: France Telecom (the accents were removed from the name in 1993) completes a public offering, reducing the government's stake to 63 percent (later 55.5 percent).

2000: France Telecom pays $37 billion to acquire U.K.-based mobile telephone group Orange Plc.

2006: France Telecom launches rebranding of most of its operations as Orange.

2008: France Telecom fails in a bid to acquire Telia-Sonera AB.

exclusive resorts, such as Biarritz, Nice, and Cannes, were as well-equipped.

French telephonic, telegraphic, and radiocommunications services suffered greatly from World War II, the German occupation, and the fight for liberation. Out of 140 automatic exchanges, 39 were unusable as were 104 of the 228 manual exchanges. The cable network suffered similarly, with equipment and buildings destroyed or badly damaged. A quarter of the 105 main telegraph nodes were out of commission. Submarine lines connecting France with the United Kingdom, the United States, and Africa were destroyed, as was the huge Bordeaux-Croix d'Hins radio station.

POST-WORLD WAR II TECHNICAL ADVANCES

Of the several postwar economic plans, the telecommunications sector was not given priority and between 1947 and 1966 only 0.2 percent of the country's gross national product was spent on telecommunications. However, the creation of the Centre National d'Etudes des Télécommunications—CNET, now France Télécom's research and development organization—in 1944

was all-important in encouraging further experimentation. From the mid-1940s new technical advances were made as a result of this official collaboration with the French telecommunications and electronics industry. The first coaxial links connected Paris and Toulouse in 1947 and coaxial cable gradually replaced the old paired wire. Shortly after this date, NATO finance ensured the development of transatlantic coaxial connections.

Terrestrial telecommunications technology moved apace. The old rotary switching system was replaced by the crossbar system around 1960, the new equipment being sufficiently versatile to meet the needs of all types of telecommunication, from urban to international. In the mid-1960s digital switching experiments had begun in France and by 1970 fiber-optic cable began to be used to support signal transmission. This research was paralleled by work at CNET into the problems of electronic connection which resulted in the Aristote, Socrate, Périclès, and Platon systems of the 1960s and 1970s.

These programs of scientific experiment investigated the problems of electronic connection. With hindsight France Télécom of the pre-1970s appears to have had an under-equipped infrastructure, due to delayed technological development which represented around 2 percent of France's gross national product. However, at that time the system began to be modernized in a long-term strategy to digitalize it. During the same period interest in space-borne telecommunications was growing and in 1962 the United States launched the Telstar satellite. Franco-American experiments resulted in the capture and broadcast of the first television signals from the United States in July 1962.

The development of geostationary satellites, whose orbits keep them constantly above the same point on the earth's surface, led to the establishment of the Intelsat II fleet, which achieved full planetary coverage from 1971. France Télécom is the third largest user of these services. In 1977 Eutelsat, the European satellite organization, worked to achieve the ECS (European Communications Satellite) system. In 1979 France inaugurated a national system of space telecommunications via the Telecom I satellite, which serves the domestic market. The mission sought to establish links with French overseas territories, commercial satellite links, and videocommunications. ECS was eventually inaugurated in 1983. In 1991 France Télécom was the fifth largest shareholder in Inmarsat, the international maritime satellite, the culmination of over 60 years of development in intercontinental radio-electronic telephone traffic.

INCHING TOWARD THE MODERN ERA

By 1986 France Télécom had 25 million main lines that supported the connection of 96 percent of French homes, as well as the development of many innovative products and services, such as the Teletel videotex system. From 1983 Teletel began to replace paper telephone directories and its Minitel terminals were purchased by DGT in substantial quantities to create a largely captive market. In 1989 the Teletel system boasted a total of 85 million connection hours through five million terminals. The connection of Teletel to Transpac, the French national packet switching network, which handles data in the form of units or "packets" routed individually through the network, now meant that subscribers throughout the country could use other services, regardless of distance. National and international business connections combining voice and text distribution via the "Numeris" ISDN system became possible, although full utilization would wait until the mid-1990s.

Such successes could be attributable to a consistent and monopolistic government policy and efficient investment in telecommunications equipment and in the supplier companies, such as the E10 digital exchanges, a way of encoding information as a series of "on" or "off" signals, made by Alcatel. By the 1990s, France's 100 percent digital phone system was among the most modern in the world. Yet events in the telecommunications world would soon overtake the company, and its monopoly, and the burdens of bureaucracy soon left the company struggling to catch up to the rest of the worldwide industry, which was undergoing a process of deregulation and privatization that would transform the nature of the telecommunications business. Eyeing the success of other denationalized telephone providers, particularly the British system, renamed British Telecom, DGT adopted a new name, France Télécom, giving it at least the appearance of keeping up with modern industry trends.

Demands for full deregulation of the European telecommunications industry resulted from the Commission of the European Communities (CEC) Green Paper in 1987. In part, the inability of monopoly organizations to cope with rapid technological change, and also the need for the competition essential to support an economy driven more by information rather than production informed these moves. Once again, arguments about the provision of a universal telephone service prevailed over exclusive concentration on technological progress. However, various countries evolved different solutions to the problems of reorganization. Whereas in the United Kingdom British Telecom opted for full privatization, France Télécom resisted this and technological advance took place within a monopoly environment.

France Télécom nevertheless faced the loss of portions of its monopoly after 1993, under the terms of the European Community's Open Network Provision of 1989, which guaranteed to all value-added network (VAN) service providers equal access to its country's telecommunications infrastructure. The supply of terminal equipment such as telefax machines and telephone handsets, and VAN services such as home banking, would then become open to competition, although strictly licensed. Competition in the provision of computer data transfer was also to be allowed, provided that private firms did not undercut France Télécom.

NINETIES: STILL PLAYING CATCH-UP

The French legal act passed on July 2, 1990, on the organization of public posts and telecommunications services, transformed France Télécom (formerly Direction Générale des Télécommunications) into a public service carrier with corporate legal status. This legal reform substantially changed the contractual relations between France's national operator and its partners; from January 1, 1991, these relations became governed by the French concept of "private law." Thus France Télécom now gained budgetary, management, and organizational independence, like most of its European competitors. However, the company remained under the guardianship, and tight control, of the Ministry of Posts and Telecommunications. The company's monopoly status remained intact.

A frenzy of alliances and mergers would soon come to typify the French telecommunications industry in the late 1980s and 1990s, as it tried to achieve the international scale necessary to compete in new markets such as car telephones and radio telephone paging equipment. France Télécom and Matra, the recently privatized defense and electronics group, soon faced competition from France's largest private water distributor, Compagnie Générale des Eaux, which formed a partnership with Alcatel and Nokia of Finland to offer a second national car telephone network. Again, Alcatel, the telecommunications division of Compagnie Générale d'Electricité (CGE), absorbed ITT to form the world's second largest telecommunications venture after that of American Telephone and Telegraph. Matra, which in 1987 successfully bid with Ericsson of Sweden for control of CGCT, France's other major supplier of public switching equipment, later acquired a 15 percent stake in Société Anonyme de Télécommunications (SAT). Nevertheless, despite these incursions into its traditional market areas, France Télécom emerged as one of the world's top four public telecommunications carriers.

During the 1990s, France Télécom found itself rushing to catch up with many of the major developments in the telecommunications industry. In particular, the company was very late to the Internet table, a lateness blamed on the company's complacency with its Minitel "cash cow." The Minitel service, which had not seen any significant technological advancement since its introduction in 1983, quickly paled in comparison to the Internet, and particularly the rise of the World Wide Web. In May 1996, France Telecom finally introduced its own Internet provider service, dubbed Wanadoo. The company also joined the growing wave of mergers and partnerships sweeping the telecommunications industry, announcing its intention to form a partnership with Deutsche Telekom and Sprint Communications, called Global One. In 1997, the company joined another joint-venture partnership, Infostrada, formed by Olivetti Corporation and Bell Atlantic, which brought the company into Italy's recently deregulated telecommunications industry. During the 1990s, France Telecom began entering other international markets, including Argentina, Mexico, Indonesia, Senegal, and, in 1997, Vietnam. In recognition of its own growing international nature, the company removed the accents from the spelling of its name, becoming France Telecom in 1993.

In the meantime, France Telecom, at least its management, eyed with some envy the developments of the European telecommunications industry, as country after country denationalized their telephone carriers and ended their government monopolies, a process culminating in Deutsche Telekom's deregulation in 1996. An initial attempt to end French government control of the company and bring the company to the stock market was brutally rebuffed by France Telecom's own employees, 75 percent of whom participated in a strike protesting the move, which would end their civil servant status. The next attempt to denationalize the company waited until 1995, and again was quashed by an employee strike. Several months later, the French government passed a new law transforming the company into a *société anonyme,* an event that took place on January 1, 1997, creating a public company in name if not in fact. The date for the company's entry on the Paris Bourse, for a sale of shares worth from FRF 25 billion to 40 billion, the largest public offering ever in France, was set for June 1997.

FROM PUBLIC OFFERING TO EUROPEAN LEADER

The successful listing of France Telecom on both the Euronext Paris and NYSE marked the start of a new era for the company. While the French government maintained a majority stake in the company (63 percent, and then 55.5 percent into the end of the first decade of the 2000s), the company was now freed to pursue its ambitions to take a place on the global telecommunications stage. Led by Michel Bon, France Telecom now embarked on a new expansion drive, spending more than $50 billion in just three years.

France Telecom's ambitions got off to a shaky start, however. At home, the company faced increasing competition, as a number of new players, including Vivendi's Cegetel, entered the fixed-line market. France's mobile telephone unit, Itineris, grew only slowly, as the mobile telephone sector remained a niche market in the late 1990s. In the meantime, France Telecom had placed much of its international growth ambitions on the success of the Global One alliance. However, Sprint pulled out of the alliance after it was bought by MCI Worldcom in 1999. Soon after, France Telecom paid $1.8 billion to acquire a 17 percent stake in E-Plus Mobilfunk, the number three player in Germany's mobile telephone market, sparking a feud with partner Deutsche Telekom. In the meantime, Global One continued to lose money, nearly $800 million, on revenues of just $1.2 billion in 1998. By 2000, the alliance had been disbanded, as France Telecom bought out Deutsche Telekom's stake for $2.76 billion.

France Telecom soon found a new path for its global ambitions. In 2000, Germany's Mannesmann announced that it had agreed to acquire U.K. mobile phone icon Orange, founded in 1994 by Hans Snook. Before the ink was dry on that deal, however, Mannesmann itself was swallowed up by Vodafone AirTouch. To satisfy competition authorities, however, Orange was required to be sold before the Mannesmann takeover could proceed. France Telecom jumped at the opportunity, paying $37 billion for Orange. That deal initially took the form of something of a reverse takeover, as France Telecom merged its Itineris and other mobile operations into Orange. Snook and his management team were set to lead the newly enlarged Orange as it emerged as a major European mobile telephone player. Snook, however, decided to leave the company soon after.

Other France Telecom purchases during this period included $3.56 billion for a 28.5 percent stake in MobilCom, a Germany-based low-cost telephone provider. The company then snapped up Freeserve, a leading Internet access provider in the United Kingdom, at a cost of $2.5 billion. Then the company also beefed up its business services operations, largely grouped under the Global One franchise, with the $4 billion acquisition of the Netherlands' Equant. In the meantime, the company also launched construction of its 3G mobile telephone network, at a cost, including licensing fees, of more than $10 billion. By the end of 2001, the total bill for France Telecom's buying spree had topped $80 billion.

Yet, into the beginning of the 2000s, France Telecom also found itself struggling to carry a staggering $76 billion debt load. The company suddenly found itself vulnerable, as the telecommunications market crashed at the start of the first decade. From a high of $212 per share, France Telecom's share value now plunged, to just $8. The company was also forced to place its original plans to list Orange on the stock exchange, which would have raised much needed capital, on hold. In the end, France Telecom was forced to turn to the French government, which sponsored a $9 billion rescue package.

ORANGE QUAD PLAY FOR THE FUTURE

Bon was replaced by Thierry Breton, who had previously rescued Thomson Multimedia, in 2002. Breton set out a plan to lower the company's debt by some $30 billion, without selling off its prized assets, including Orange, Wanadoo, and Equant. Instead, the company increased its holdings in Orange and Wanadoo, both of which had launched their own public offerings. France Telecom paid nearly $7.7 billion for the outstanding 13.7 percent of Orange, and then $3 billion to acquire the 29.4 percent of Wanadoo that had previously been public. Two years later, the company completed a similar transaction for Equant, paying $736 million for the outstanding 45.8 percent in that company. Also in 2005, France Telecom struck out into new territory, buying Spain's number three mobile telephone operator, Amena, for $7.7 billion.

These moves came ahead of an ambitious new plan to rebrand much of France Telecom's non-fixed-line operations under the Orange name. The company began rolling out its new Orange-centric strategy in 2006, starting with its British, French, and Polish operations, before rolling out the Orange brand across its entire operations.

The move came as part of the evolving convergence of the telephone, Internet, television, and other media markets into the second half of the decade. In this France Telecom had been something of a pioneer, with the launch of its Livebox, an ADSL modem-router

outfitted not only for Internet access, but also to provide telephony services and reception of television broadcasts. The success of the Livebox, with more than six million in place by the later years of the first decade of the 2000s, had given France Telecom a leading share in the European "triple-play" market. By 2008, the company counted more than 4.8 million VoIP telephone users, and 1.25 IpTV subscribers.

In the meantime, Orange had grown into Europe's third largest mobile telephone provider, with a subscriber base of more than 110 million. Encouraged by the success of the Orange brand, France Telecom moved to convert still more of its empire to the brand family. By 2008, most of the company's non-fixed-line business had taken on the Orange name. This shift came as part of the company's new "quad-play" strategy, rolled out in May of that year, as the company launched a seamless integration of its mobile, Internet, and television offerings.

France Telecom continued to play catch-up to its chief rivals, Vodafone and Deutsche Telekom, however. The company hoped to correct this situation in June 2008, when it launched a bid to acquire Scandinavia's TeliaSonera AB. France Telecom's hopes were dashed, however, when TeliaSonera rejected the offer as too low. This did not prevent France Telecom from continuing to seek new markets. In October 2008, for example, the company announced its intention to launch the Orange brand in the Republic of Armenia, after winning a mobile operator's license there. In just a decade, France Telecom had grown from a national monopoly into one of the world's leading telecommunications companies.

Patrick Keeley
Updated, M. L. Cohen

PRINCIPAL SUBSIDIARIES

Amena SA (Spain); France Telecom North America (U. S.A.); Mobistar SA (Belgium); Orange S.A.; Orange UK Plc.; TP Group (Poland).

PRINCIPAL COMPETITORS

Nippon Telegraph and Telephone Corp.; Verizon Communications Inc.; Telefonica S.A.; AT&T Corporation; SK Group; Telecom Italia S.p.A.; Bouygues S.A.; ENDESA S.A.; Vodafone Group PLC.

FURTHER READING

Arvonny, M., "La Nouvelle Numérotation Téléphonique," *Le Monde*, October 28–29, 1985.

Bui, Doan, "Michel Bon Change de Telephone," *Le Nouvel Economiste,* May 23, 1997.

Carré, P. A., "France Télécom," *Revue France Télécom,* December 1990.

———, "Histoire des Télécommunications," *CNET/DGT,* 1989.

European High Technology and European Telecommunications Surveys, *Financial Times,* 1988–1990.

"France Telecom's $53 Billion Burden," *Business Week,* January 8, 2001, p. 22.

"France Telecom's Latest Effort to Buy TeliaSonera Collapses," *InformationWeek,* June 30, 2008.

"The Future's Quadplay," *Mobile Communications International,* April 1, 2007.

Garric, D., "Minitel," *Le Point,* April 15, 1985.

"Global One: One Big, Unhappy Family?" *Business Week,* July 26, 1999, p. 22.

Haquet, C., [On Telepoints], *Le Figaro,* September 14, 1983.

Holloway, Nigel, "Defensive Maneuvers," *Forbes,* November 29, 1999, p. 92.

Jacquin, Jean-Baptiste, "France Telecom: les Coulisses d'une Privatisation Géante," *L'Expansion,* March 20, 1997.

Montlack, Carol, "Untangling the Wires at France Telecom," *Business Week Online,* February 11, 2003.

Nora, Dominique, "France Telecom: Ca Passe ou Ca Casse," *Le Nouvel Observateur,* April 11, 1996.

———, "Telecom: La Bourse ou la Vie," *Le Nouvel Observateur,* May 25, 1995.

"Orange/France Telecom," *Economist,* June 3, 2000, p. 62.

"Orange Gets Armenia Mobile Licence," *Total Telecom Online,* October 8, 2008.

Rosenbush, Steve, "Can Anyone Answer Vodafone?" *Business Week Online,* July 28, 2005.

Schenker, Jennifer L., "France Telecom Goes to the Movies," *Business Week,* April 11, 2008.

Tussau, G., "Les Industries Electriques et Electroniques, Notes et Etudes Documentaires," *La Documentation Française,* 1980.

FTD Group, Inc.

3113 Woodcreek Drive
Downers Grove, Illinois 60515-5412
U.S.A.
Telephone: (630) 719-7800
Toll Free: (800) SEND FTD; (800) 736-3383
Fax: (630) 719-6170
Web site: http://www.ftd.com; http://www.interflora.co.uk

Wholly Owned Subsidiary of United Online, Inc.
Incorporated: 1910 as Florists' Telegraph Delivery
Employees: 984
Sales: $646.1 million (2008)
NAICS: 561422 Floral Wire Services; 453110 Florists

■ ■ ■

FTD Group, Inc., is one of the largest flowers-by-wire delivery companies worldwide, offering floral arrangements for every day and for every occasion. Supplementary products include greeting cards, wine, chocolate, gift baskets, stuffed animals, and holiday-specific gifts. FTD Group includes FTD, the wholesale flower business that sells floral products and gifts to affiliated retail florists, and FTD.com, which markets direct to customers through the company's web site and toll-free telephone number. FTD comprises approximately 20,000 independent retail florists in the United States and Canada, and more than 29,000 independent florists in 140 countries. Orders for FTD and FTD.com are processed on the company's online

computer network, and a local, affiliated florist packages and delivers the flowers.

The company's state-of-the-art Mercury Network is known as the "Floral Information Superhighway," because it processes more than 15 million orders and messages annually, not only for FTD but also for the major wire services used by florists. For FTD affiliates, the network determines the correct pay for local florists for their portion of a bouquet order and delivery, and it provides a variety of electronic business management tools. FTD affiliate services include national advertising, credit-card processing, and web site development. The Flower Exchange provides wholesale floral products and packaging, logistics and sales assistance, and easy online ordering. In business since 1910, FTD enjoys widespread name recognition, and the company's well-known Mercury Man logo is displayed at affiliated florist shops around the globe.

EARLY YEARS

FTD was organized on August 18, 1910, as Florists' Telegraph Delivery (FTD), by a group of 15 retail florists who agreed to exchange their out-of-town orders, signaling the orders to each other by telegraph. Even during its early years, FTD effected highly successful national advertising campaigns. In 1914 a Boston advertising executive coined the phrase "Say It with Flowers" for the company, a tagline that stuck with FTD for virtually the rest of the century. Also in 1914, FTD began using the Mercury Man logo, comprising the Greek god Mercury in a winged cap and winged sandals striding along with a bouquet of flowers held in his outstretched arm. The logo became prominent in FTD advertising and endured as one of the most recognizable logos in the United States.

FTD also began to use well-known personalities to advertise its services. In 1933 the company launched National Shut-In Day, a day to remember invalids, and hired to advertise the event actress Mary Pickford, gossip columnist and celebrity radio commentator Walter Winchell, and singer Kate Smith. Moreover, Winchell also added a routine to his radio show in which he presented "real orchids to real heroes." The orchids were provided by FTD, thus giving the florists' group prominent weekly exposure on a popular national broadcast.

GROWTH AFTER WORLD WAR II

FTD grew as a national retail member network, and after World War II it expanded abroad as well. On November 1, 1946, FTD established International Florists, Inc., to sell its flowers by wire all over the world. This allowed customers to send elaborate floral gifts across the ocean, and, in some cases, florists went to great lengths to keep up FTD's reputation for reliability. In one instance, a Spokane, Washington, businessman went on an around-the-world cruise, and his company ordered flowers sent to him at a dozen foreign ports of call. FTD handled the order with no problems, although it reported that its Kenyan member florist had to take a four-hour canoe trip downriver to make its delivery to the businessman's cruising steamer. The company was similarly proud of a British affiliate florist. Given the task of delivering a bouquet to a lighthouse keeper on a stormy day, the florist made four attempts by rowboat. Unable to land, the florist finally caught hold of a rope thrown out from the lighthouse and attached the box of flowers. The customer gratefully hauled it in.

Because of its growing international presence, Florists' Telegraph Delivery changed its name in 1965 to Florists' Transworld Delivery. The well-known initials stayed the same, and "Transworld" emphasized the company's expertise in delivering flowers across the globe. By 1969 FTD was processing more than 12 million orders annually. By 1974 the florists' cooperative had about 13,500 members. FTD's headquarters were in Southfield, Michigan, a suburb of Detroit, while its member retail florists were all across North America. Its international affiliates comprised approximately 40,000 florists in 130 countries, including countries behind the Iron Curtain.

With so many members to keep track of, FTD used computer tapes to handle records of its credits and debits, and such extensive computer files sometimes proved useful in unique applications. According to a 1974 article in *Nation's Business,* the Federal Bureau of Investigation (FBI) routinely paid visits to FTD's headquarters whenever a reputed mobster died. The FBI reportedly scanned FTD's records to keep tabs on who was sending flowers to the funeral. Because of the number of daily orders, and the importance of speed and accuracy to its business, FTD had to have the latest and best in computer equipment. From the computer tapes in use in 1974, the company finally launched its own computer network system in 1979, called the FTD Mercury Network. FTD delivered 6,500 computer consoles to member florists soon after adopting the system, allowing for faster and more reliable communication between retailers. In its first year of use, the FTD Mercury Network handled approximately 11,000 electronic orders every day.

BRAND DEVELOPMENT IN THE EIGHTIES AND NINETIES

A prominent national advertiser since its inception, FTD employed the Detroit ad agency of D'Arcy Masius Benton & Bowles in the 1980s. This agency focused on strengthening the identity of FTD as a brand by inventing memorable names for particular flower arrangements, including the FTD Pick-Me-Up Bouquet and the FTD Tickler Bouquet. In 1983 FTD began using former National Football League Hall of Fame star, sports announcer, and actor Merlin Olsen as a spokesperson in its television ads.

By 1990 FTD was spending between $20 million and $25 million annually on advertising. The company ran ads on television and radio, as well as in newspapers and magazines, continuing to use its longtime spokesperson Olsen. The advertising campaigns emphasized sending gift bouquets as a "kind, convenient, and above all, fun" activity, according to a

KEY DATES

1910: Fifteen florists form Florists' Telegraph Delivery (FTD), a cooperative association to provide rapid local delivery of flowers, regardless of where the order originated.

1914: FTD adopts the Mercury Man logo and the "Say It with Flowers" tagline.

1946: FTD forms International Florists, Inc., to provide wire service and floral delivery to international destinations.

1965: FTD changes its name to Florists' Transworld Delivery.

1979: The FTD Mercury Network is launched, providing state-of-the-art computer technology for processing 11,000 floral orders per day.

1994: As competition intensifies, FTD accepts merger proposal and becomes a for-profit company; FTD.com debuts.

2001: FTD Association breaks formal alliance with FTD, Inc.

2006: FlowerExchange.com is created to improve service to affiliated florists.

2008: United Online, Inc., acquires FTD for $754 million.

1990 *Advertising Age* report, which added that FTD strove to make available "the perfect bouquet for all occasions." Ads were targeted toward different audiences at different times of year, aiming at men for Valentine's Day, and women for Thanksgiving and Christmas, for example. Beginning in 1990 FTD tried to reach a younger audience, too, placing ads in such magazines as *Vogue, Rolling Stone,* and *Sports Illustrated.*

The company also launched promotions centered on new floral arrangements that featured the products of partner companies. For example, in 1991 FTD ran a cooperative venture with Gerber Products Co., the renowned baby food and baby products manufacturer. The FTD Bundle of Joy bouquet came attached to an assortment of Gerber products, including a baby bottle and a toy. In other joint ventures, FTD sponsored an international sweepstakes with credit-card company American Express in 1991 and conducted a similar contest with the Pontiac division of Detroit automaker General Motors.

The year 1993 saw the debut of the Chicken Soup Bouquet, a joint venture with Campbell's Soup Co. to combine a get-well floral bouquet with a Campbell's mug and a packet of instant chicken soup. Get-well bouquets made up approximately 14 percent of FTD member florists' business, and the new product was intended to boost that already large segment of the market. All the advertising for these various new products was overseen by the agency FTD had long been associated with, D'Arcy Masius Benton & Bowles.

COMPETITION INTENSIFIES IN THE NINETIES

Nevertheless, in spite of all the money FTD was spending on advertising, and the energy it was putting into creative marketing tie-ins with other companies, the company met with evidence of intensifying competition. Beginning in 1988, FTD experienced dropping market share and sales. From 1988 to 1994 FTD's share of floral orders fell from 80 percent to 58 percent, in part because of growing competition from less-expensive flower outlets. Supermarket sales ate into the retail florists' market, and competing floral telephone-order companies also stole some of FTD's traditional business.

One such competitor was 1-800-Flowers, a company that had been losing money in 1987 when it was bought by Jim McCann, a former social worker. By 1993 McCann had turned 1-800-Flowers around, and the company was reporting $100 million in annual sales. FTD launched its own toll-free number for use by the public in 1993: 1-800-Send-FTD. This move, however, not only managed to take orders away from FTD member retail florists but also lost an estimated $13 million in the process.

In the flower market as a whole, flower-by-wire sales dropped more than 13 percent from 1990 to 1994, and nonflorists accounted for almost half the flower sales in the United States. Consumers were also increasingly exposed to other flower venues, such as catalogs and online services. All this was bad news for FTD, made worse because FTD's advertising was clearly not getting its message across. The company conducted a focus group in 1992 in Atlanta, surveying 18- to 25-year-old women who had recently used a florist for their weddings. FTD's marketing department asked each of these women if the florist they had used was an FTD member. Not one of the women in the focus group either knew or cared. In response to this eye-opening news, FTD started a new advertising campaign. Instead of emphasizing a particular holiday or bouquet, the new ads sought to reinforce the image of FTD florists as high-quality and reliable vendors.

Another element in FTD's failure to compete involved its cooperative structure. With the company governed by a board and a series of committees, change took a lot of time to implement. For example, FTD explored instituting a toll-free number in the early 1990s, but by the time the idea was approved and implemented in 1993, 1-800-Flowers and several other companies already had thriving businesses and significant market share. FTD did launch its web site, FTD.com, in 1994, a year before 1-800-Flowers launched theirs.

COOPERATIVE BECOMES FOR-PROFIT BUSINESS THROUGH 1994 MERGER

The various marketing initiatives did not seem likely to turn the floral cooperative around, and in July 1994 FTD announced its interest in accepting a merger offer from a New York banking firm, Perry Capital Corp. Perry Capital was run by Richard Perry, formerly an executive with the investment firm Goldman Sachs & Co. Perry offered to buy FTD for $112 million, with the intention of converting it into a for-profit business.

Richard Perry brought in a marketing consultant, Jerry Siano, to help convince FTD members that the cooperative would do well to accept the merger. Siano had worked with N.W. Ayer, a New York advertising firm that had masterminded the "reach out and touch someone" campaign for AT&T. Perry used AT&T as a model for what he would like to do with FTD: emphasize the company's reliability and great service. The new company would "sell relationships, not just flowers," according to a September 26, 1994, report in *Advertising Age.*

FTD's board accepted Perry Capital's proposed merger, but only by a vote of ten to nine. While FTD members were mulling over the proposal, Roll International Corp., a privately held company that owned both commemorative platemaker Franklin Mint and the flower-delivery service Teleflora, offered $140 million for the company. Ultimately, however, FTD members opted for Perry Capital's deal. The new for-profit company, FTD Inc., organized in November 1994. At the same time, the company launched a nonprofit trade association, called FTD Association, as the educational arm of the organization.

One of the first things the new company did was to change its advertising agency, hiring Grey Advertising in 1995 to handle its account, worth an estimated $35 million. FTD also worked to improve its computer network. In 1996 FTD florists were relying on outdated monochrome computers that simply listed the different kinds of bouquets available. The company upgraded to a faster network that was able to transmit visual images of floral arrangements. The new computers were also capable of running CD-ROM versions of books important to florists and their customers, such as Emily Post's *Complete Guide to Weddings* and a dictionary of flowers and plants. Although the new system was expensive, it seemed to significantly enhance the service that individual FTD florists could offer their customers.

Competition continued to be fierce in the floral market. In 1997 two of FTD's rivals, Teleflora Inc. and Redbook Florists Service, announced that they would merge. Moreover, FTD experienced some challenges in the marketing department, as the company's vice-president for advertising left in 1997 and his duties were given to an outside consultant. Just two years after switching its advertising account from D'Arcy Masius Benton & Bowles to Grey Advertising, the company switched again, selecting W.B. Doner & Co. of South-field, Michigan. The company's advertising budget had gone up, from $12 million the year of its merger with Perry Capital to $35 million when Grey got the account, but ad spending fell to $16 million by 1996. The budget for new agency W.B. Doner was said to be in the broad range of between $20 million and $40 million.

In 1997 FTD consolidated its corporate headquarters, combining the operations of its Michigan offices with its Boston offices at a centrally located office in Downers Grove, Illinois, a suburb of Chicago. At this time, the company was handling approximately 12 million orders a year, down from around 22 million orders ten years earlier. Still billing itself as the leader in the flowers-by-wire business, FTD strove to counter the changing business conditions and increased competition that had hurt sales and market share in the past.

As a private company, FTD showed signs of trying to adapt to a more competitive floral market, witnessed by new advertising campaigns and a better computer network. With regard to technology, FTD announced an agreement in 1998 with Dell Computer Corp. to buy more than 20,000 Dell desktop computers, workstations, and servers. That year FTD also announced it was upping its ad spending, planning to spend $30 million on a new campaign, likely influenced by Richard Perry, focused on "selling relationships, not just flowers." The new 1998–99 campaign theme stressed that FTD was "The place to find quality."

FTD ADAPTS THROUGH OWNERSHIP CHANGES IN THE NEW MILLENNIUM

Perry Capital attempted several reorganizations to support growth and competitiveness at FTD. Believing that the online business would be more profitable on its own, in 1999 the company spun off FTD.com as an independent company, although Perry Capital's IOS Brands retained an 83.2 percent ownership. Under CEO Michael Soenen, FTD.com experienced rapid growth, with sales reaching $117.5 million in 2001. In 2002 FTD.com was able to acquire for cash Flowers Direct LLP.

In the meantime, other industry changes affected FTD in several ways. First, in 2001 the member organization, FTD Association, separated from FTD and formed a new organization. Teleflora, another major wire service, ceased using the Mercury Network, which had always been an open platform for floral order processing beyond the FTD affiliates. Competition from retail flower shops within grocery stores and big-box retailers continued, prompting FTD to reduce the price of a dozen roses from $50 to $29.99 plus $9.99 for delivery service. FTD did experience positive growth by offering gifts with a gardening or home decorating theme, as well as special occasion gifts, such as fine chocolates. General trends affecting the floral industry included some decline in regional economies and increases in the cost of Internet advertising.

By 2002 Richard Perry decided to fold FTD.com back into FTD to build the company into a billion-dollar business. First, FTD.com was merged back into IOS Brands, parent of FTD.com and FTD, Inc.; then IOS was renamed FTD, Inc. Perry prepared to take FTD public, but then, in October 2003, Leonard Green & Partners, L.P. announced that it would be purchasing FTD. Green completed the $420 million deal in February 2004 and renamed the company FTD Group. Green took the company public on the New York Stock Exchange a year later.

FTD Group intended to expand in the international market; European florists, however, operated through nonprofit cooperative organizations, much as FTD did before 1994, making it difficult to enter the market. Consequently, in July 2006 FTD acquired Interflora Holdings of England for $122 million. Interflora operated in a similar structure as FTD, with 1,800 florists in the United Kingdom and Ireland.

Meanwhile, FTD.com continued to be successful, but the Internet business grew at the expense of the network of local florists. To improve service to affiliated florists, in October 2006 the company revamped the FTD Flower Exchange, the service that provides FTD members with floral products. FTD expanded and improved its relationships with premium flower growers worldwide in order to provide better floral products at lower prices. Launching FlowerExchange.com, with daily "hot buys" and new pricing, FTD offered

discounts up to 40 percent below wholesale prices. FlowerExchange.com provided new options for same-day shipments and product selection. Online search capabilities included product photographs provided by the growers and new search criteria, such as color, flower, and origin. FTD expanded its sales team to provide improved customer service to local florists. The company established a logistics team to assist florists with product purchase decisions, that, in turn, would facilitate timely and appropriate freight solutions, thus improving florists' service to consumers. New quality-control initiatives sought to raise FTD's overall reputation by eliminating members who failed to meet service standards.

Ownership of FTD changed again in August 2008, when United Online, Inc., acquired the company. The $754 million transaction involved cash payment and share allocation to FTD stockholders. FTD provided a retail complement to United Online's Internet business services, which included Net Zero and Juno Internet e-mail services and Classmates Media.

A. Woodward
Updated, Mary Tradii

PRINCIPAL SUBSIDIARIES

Interflora Holdings Limited.

PRINCIPAL OPERATING UNITS

FTD; FTD.com; Mercury Network.

PRINCIPAL COMPETITORS

1-800-Flowers.com, Inc.; Provide Commerce, Inc.; Teleflora LLC.

FURTHER READING

"Campbell Joins FTD Bouquet," *Advertising Age*, January 11, 1993, p. 17.

Cortez, John P., "FTD Plans Blossom," *Advertising Age*, October 7, 1991, p. 65.

———, "Olsen Still in Blooms," *Advertising Age*, December 3, 1990, p. 51.

Fields-White, Mone, "An Imperfect Arrangement: FTD Expands on Web at Expense of Flower-Shop Biz," *Crain's Chicago Business*, April 9, 2007, p. 4.

"FTD Announces That It Will Merge with Perry Capital," *Wall Street Journal*, November 8, 1994, p. B4.

"FTD Is Back in Bloom: The Floral Outfit's Once Wilted Shares Have Come Back to Life, Thanks in Large Part to

Strong Growth in Its Gift Business and Improved Margins," *Business Week Online,* May 16, 2006.

"FTD Names Grey," *Wall Street Journal,* April 3, 1995, p. B12.

Hayes, Frank, "Electronic Commerce: No Place for Wallflowers," *Computerworld,* May 26, 1997, p. 117.

"How Kmart's Former CIO Had Bloomed Anew at FTD," *Chain Store Age Executive,* February 1996, p. 156.

Johnson, Stephen S., "Flower Power," *Forbes,* July 4, 1994, p. 144.

Johnsson, Julie, "People: 'Numbers Guy' Blooms at FTD into No. 2 Role," *Crain's Chicago Business,* October 21, 2002, p. 12.

———, "Tech Watch: Owner Takes Bloom of FTD.com Shareholders," *Crain's Chicago Business,* May 27, 2002, p. 6.

Louviere, Vernon, "Say It with Flowers, and the FBI Listens," *Nation's Business,* March 1974, p. 41.

Mahoney, Jerry, "Texas-Based Dell Computer Corp. Wins Two Big Orders," *Knight-Ridder/Tribune Business News,* November 3, 1998.

Manor, Robert, "Private Los Angeles Firm to Buy FTD Florists in $420 Million Deal," *Chicago Tribune,* October 7, 2003.

Moreira, Peter, "Green to Take FTD Public," *Daily Deal,* November 25, 2004.

Murphy, H. Lee, "Former Exec Returns to FTD for Shot at Top," *Crain's Chicago Business,* September 20, 2004, p. 22.

———, "In Debt, Will FTD Blossom or Sell? Report Says Retailer Is Sniffing for Buyers," *Crain's Chicago Business,* December 18, 2006, p. 11.

Petrecca, Laura, "FTD's Selection of Doner Surprises DiNoto Agency," *Advertising Age,* June 30, 1997, p. 2.

Rickard, Leah, "FTD Fights Back in $16M Image Ads," *Advertising Age,* September 27, 1993, p. 12.

———, "FTD Nurtures Plans for Healthy Growth," *Advertising Age,* September 26, 1994, p. 4.

Snavely, Brent, "Livonia Florists Group Splits from FTD," *Crain's Detroit Business,* June 25, 2001, p. 21.

Steinmetz, Greg, "FTD to Look at Bids to Make It Bloom Again," *Wall Street Journal,* November 2, 1994, p. B1.

Green Dot Public Schools

350 South Figueroa Street, Suite 213
Los Angeles, California 90091
U.S.A.
Telephone: (213) 621-0276
Fax: (213) 621-4419
Web site: http://www.greendot.org

Nonprofit Company
Incorporated: 1999
Employees: 250
Operating Revenues $30 million (2007 est.)
NAICS: 611110 Elementary and Secondary Schools

■ ■ ■

Green Dot Public Schools is a nonprofit organization that develops and operates charter schools primarily in the Los Angeles area. The organization has opened 18 charter schools in the Los Angeles Unified School District and one in New York City. Typically, Green Dot breaks large high schools into smaller campuses, starting with ninth grade and adding a class each year until the program develops into a full high school. Green Dot is supported by taxpayer dollars and through investments by supporters such as The Wasserman Foundation, The Bill and Melinda Gates Foundation, and The Broad Foundation. Green Dot is led by its founder, CEO Steve Barr.

BACKGROUND OF THE FOUNDER

Steve Barr formed Green Dot after he buried his brother and his mother, setting out to reform education in the Los Angeles area as a way to deal with the loss of his loved ones. The death of his brother, in particular, inspired Barr to risk his savings and launch Green Dot, a nonprofit organization whose underlying mission was to ensure that what happened to Michael Barr did not happen to others.

The Barr brothers experienced a less-than-idyllic childhood. Their father left home when Steve was two years old and Michael was an infant, which left their mother with the responsibility of caring for the two young boys. She struggled to make ends meet, and was forced to move frequently to find work, taking up temporary residence in places such as Fond du Lac, Wisconsin, and Ft. Leonard Wood, Missouri. When Steve Barr was five years old, he and his brother were put in foster care, where they remained for a year before being reunited with their mother. "My mom was a tough lady," Steve Barr said in a February 20, 2007 interview with the *Los Angeles Times*, "but always on the borderline of cracking up because it was just overwhelming. We had the basics, but for a few years there it was really tough. We were never incredibly hungry, but I was not unfamiliar with it."

After bouncing from one town to the next for years, the Barr family eventually landed in San Jose, California, where they resided in a one-bedroom apartment. It was the mid-1970s, and Steve Barr was about to enter high school, a juncture in his life when his mother made a decision that he credited with having a profound effect on his life. With her sons' high school education in mind, she moved the family near a highly regarded high school in neighboring Cupertino, finding

COMPANY PERSPECTIVES

Green Dot Public Schools is leading the charge to transform public education in Los Angeles and beyond so that all children receive the education they need to be successful in college, leadership, and life. Green Dot is achieving this mission in three ways. First, we create and operate high-achieving public schools where nearly all students graduate and go on to college. Second, we help parents throughout the city organize to strengthen their neighborhood schools. Finally, we push the Los Angeles Unified School District to move boldly to improve the city's public schools.

a place to rent just within the geographic boundaries that would make her sons eligible for enrollment.

At Cupertino High School, the Barr brothers found themselves surrounded by peers whose upbringing most assuredly had not included stints in foster care. Cupertino High was where well-paid Hewlett-Packard engineers sent their children, putting the Barr brothers in social circles that belied their modest means. Steve Barr thrived in the new environment, earning only average grades but excelling as a basketball player, which endeared him to his classmates. Michael Barr did not thrive at Cupertino. Overweight, not athletically gifted, and taunted for wearing ill-fitting glasses, Michael Barr struggled to gain acceptance. At the age of 16, he dropped out of high school. His brother Steve, meanwhile, began to come into his own, ready to show the world that he was much more than just a skilled basketball player.

After high school, Steve Barr enrolled in a local community college, later transferred to the University of California, Santa Barbara, and majored in political science. His first job after earning an undergraduate degree was working for the U.S. Olympic Torch Relay Committee for the 1984 Summer Olympic Games in Los Angeles. That stint led to Barr's full-time employment in the political arena, as he worked on the presidential campaigns of Gary Hart in 1984 and 1988, as wells as the campaigns of Bruce Babbitt and Michael Dukakis. In 1990, along with music executive Jeff Ayers, Barr cofounded Rock the Vote, a nonprofit organization that strove to involve young people in the political process. After Rock the Vote, Barr joined the effort to pass the Motor Voter Bill, which was signed into law by President Bill Clinton in 1994. Barr also

was involved in AmeriCorps, a federal program that fostered volunteerism in education, healthcare, and environmental cleanup. Barr oversaw AmeriCorps' after-school project in Los Angeles that concentrated on helping single mothers transition off welfare.

While Steve Barr compiled an impressive list of professional achievements, his brother led a decidedly different life. After dropping out of high school, Michael Barr struggled with drugs and ran afoul of the law, appearing before a judge who gave him the choice of time in jail or joining the U.S. Navy. Barr joined the Navy, but after he left the military his problems continued. A truck ran a red light and hit Barr while he was riding his motorcycle, which crushed his leg and led to dozens of surgeries to ease the pain. He eventually lost his leg. Barr later died, his life cut short after an accidental overdose of alcohol and painkillers.

The death of Steve Barr's brother was followed three years later by the death of his mother from lung cancer. "So there I was, at the age of 39, and I had just buried my family," Steve Barr said in a June 4, 2007 interview with the *Los Angeles Business Journal*. "I found myself wondering what happened to these people that I loved so much. At that point, I decided I wanted to do something different with my life. And the schools that had so failed my brother were a good place to start." In another interview published in the September 14, 2008 edition of the *New York Post*, Barr softened his assessment of Cupertino High School, but the inspiration to reform education remained: "I can't blame the high school totally," he said, "but I wanted to create a school where you didn't have to be an athlete to get attention, where you could find the dynamic of every kid."

BARR ESTABLISHES GREEN DOT

Barr, who was working as a news reporter on a nationally syndicated, Disney-produced television show titled *The Crusaders* when his mother died, launched his own crusade in 1999. He left the San Francisco Bay Area and moved to Venice, California, where he established Green Dot in a one-room office with $100,000 he had set aside for a down payment on a house. "For years," he said in his June 4, 2007 interview with the *Los Angeles Business Journal*, "the debate over schools basically fell into two camps: the Left was saying, 'Give the schools more money,' and the schools would show improvement; the Right was saying, 'Privatize the system and remove the unions.' I felt there just had to be a third way, one in which the money that was there could be spent more wisely and in which the unions could be given a buy-in."

KEY DATES

1999: Steve Barr forms Green Dot Public Schools and begins developing plans for his first charter school.

2000: Green Dot's first school, Ánimo Leadership High School, begins teaching ninth-grade students.

2002: Ánimo Inglewood becomes the second Green Dot school.

2003: A third school, Oscar De La Hoya Ánimo, is established.

2004: Two more schools, Ánimo South Los Angeles and Ánimo Venice, are opened.

2006: The Broad Foundation gives Green Dot a $10.5 million grant.

2007: The Bill and Melinda Gates Foundation invests $7.8 million in Green Dot.

2008: Green Dot opens a charter school in New York City.

THE BARR APPROACH TO EDUCATION

Through Green Dot, Barr was determined to establish charter schools in the Los Angeles Unified School District (LAUSD), the largest public school system in the United States. Charter schools are public institutions operated independently of a school district, but funded with tax revenue, which they receive provided they meet standards established by the state and their funders. Barr went to work in his Venice office on developing a plan for his first charter school. He studied the charter schools in operation in Los Angeles and he visited private schools, borrowing aspects from each of the examples to create the Green Dot approach to education.

When Barr set out to establish charter schools, LAUSD was graduating less than 50 percent of its students. He knew he could do better, and he developed a model based on six core principles, Green Dot's "Six Tenets of High Performing Schools": Small, Safe, Personalized Schools; High Expectations for All Students; Locally Managed Schools; Increased Parent Participation; Maximum Funding to the Classroom; and Keep Schools Open Longer.

Financially, Barr's efforts were aided greatly by donations and investments, none more important than the first infusion of cash he received to supplement his initial investment of $100,000. He became friends with

Reed Hastings, the founder of Netflix. Hastings, who was one of the primary financial supporters of the New Schools Venture Fund in Silicon Valley, gave Barr the money he needed to establish his first school. The first Green Dot school opened in August 2000 when 140 students and five teachers, using leased classrooms at the University of West Los Angeles School of Law, formed the nucleus of Ánimo Leadership High School. The school, limited to only the ninth grade during its first year, stood as the first test of Barr's approach to education. The majority of Ánimo Leadership's students would have attended the Centinela Valley Union High School District, where 20 percent of students passed the math portion of the state high school exit exam and 42 percent passed the English language arts portion. At the end of Ánimo Leadership's first year, 74 percent of the students passed the English language arts portion and 54 percent passed the math portion, giving Barr tangible evidence that the Green Dot approach to education could succeed.

THE FIRST FIVE SCHOOLS

Ánimo Leadership was the first of what Green Dot referred to as its "Founding Five Schools." A second charter school, Ánimo Inglewood, opened in 2002, followed by Oscar De La Hoya Ánimo in 2003 and Ánimo South Los Angeles and Ánimo Venice, both opened in 2004. By the time the first five schools had opened, the original 140 students at Ánimo Leadership had completed their senior year, with 96 percent earning their high school diploma, by far exceeding the average graduation rate within the LAUSD. Nearly two-thirds of the graduating class enrolled in a four-year university.

BENEFACTORS

The success of Green Dot accelerated its expansion after the first five schools were established. By 2006, there were ten high schools in operation, a year in which the schools graduated 78 percent of its students (the LAUSD graduated 46 percent of its students) and three out of every four graduates were accepted to four-year universities. The Broad Foundation, a venture philanthropic organization dedicated to improving achievement in urban public schools, gave Green Dot a $10.5 million grant during the year, which was earmarked for the establishment of 21 new, small high schools by 2010. In 2007, the Bill and Melinda Gates Foundation announced a $7.8 million investment in Green Dot, giving Barr the resources to open ten new high schools. With the money received from the two foundations, as well as contributions from The Wasserman Foundation, Barr set a goal of having one of every ten high school students in the LAUSD enrolled in a Green Dot School by 2010.

As Green Dot neared the completion of its first decade of existence, there were two major projects underway. In late 2007, Green Dot was given approval to take over management of Alain Locke Senior High School in Watts, one of the lowest-performing schools in the LAUSD. When the school opened in September 2008 under Green Dot's management it became the first time the organization had taken over an entire school instead of its usual practice of starting first with the freshman class. "The task Green Dot's taking on is monumental," the president of United Teachers Los Angeles—the district's teachers union—said in a September 18, 2008 interview with the *Los Angeles Times.* "The school district has shown for 20 years or more that they can't do this job."

GREEN DOT HEADS EAST

In scope and scale, the opening of Locke High School under Green Dot's management represented a significant leap forward; its other major project represented a major leap forward geographically. In 2008, Barr opened his first charter school outside the Los Angeles area, establishing a Green Dot presence in New York City. The president of the United Federation of Teachers, a teachers union based in the city, encouraged Barr to start a charter school in the south Bronx, where an inaugural class of 125 ninth graders set the foundation for what was expected to be a 500-student high school by 2011. "I think the partnership in New York is unique and I think it's going to be the future," Barr said in a September 14, 2008 interview with the *New York Post.*

In its first eight years of existence, Green Dot recorded impressive results in improving the graduation rate of high school students. In the years ahead, it was expected to carve out a presence in new markets while it continued to flesh out its presence in the LAUSD. Barr's continued involvement with Green Dot was not as certain, however, as rumors persisted that he might launch a political campaign and attempt to became mayor of Los Angeles. In a February 20, 2007 interview with the *Los Angeles Times,* he intimated as much, fueling speculation that he was hatching plans for a future beyond Green Dot. "My mission is systemic change," he said. "I don't want to be building charter school number 49."

Jeffrey L. Covell

PRINCIPAL COMPETITORS

Enterprise Charter Schools; Uncommon Schools; Bright Star Schools.

FURTHER READING

Blume, Howard, "Transformation of L.A. Unified's Locke High into a Charter School Is Green Dot's Biggest Test Yet," *Los Angeles Times,* September 18, 2008.

Fine, Howard, "Unsentimental Education," *Los Angeles Business Journal,* June 4, 2007, p. 21.

"Give Him an 'A' for Ambition," *Los Angeles Times,* February 20, 2007.

Gonen, Yoav, "Rock the Schools—Steve Barr Wants to Shake Up New York City Education," *New York Post,* September 14, 2008.

Murillo, Sandra, "Charter School Taking Shape in Inglewood," *Los Angeles Times,* July 16, 2002.

GreenMan Technologies Inc.

12498 Wyoming Avenue South
Savage, Minnesota 55378-1052
U.S.A.
Telephone: (781) 224-2411
Toll Free: (800) 526-0860
Fax: (781) 224-0114
Web site: http://www.greenman.biz

Public Company
Incorporated: 1992
Employees: 77
Sales: $20.2 million (2007)
Stock Exchanges: Over the Counter (OTC)
Ticker Symbol: GMTI
NAICS: 326199 All Other Plastics Product Manufacturing

■ ■ ■

Based in Savage, Minnesota, GreenMan Technologies Inc. collects, processes, and sells 12 million used scrap tires per year. In addition to operating processing facilities in Savage and Des Moines, Iowa, GreenMan Technologies produces playground safety tiles at a manufacturing site in Carlisle, Iowa, and operates a playground equipment warehouse in Macon, Missouri.

After collecting and processing old tires, GreenMan sells the after-products to local and regional tire outlets, parks and recreation departments, schools, state governments, and tire manufacturers for a wide range of applications. For example, its shredded tires are used in the construction of roadbeds, landfills, and septic fields.

Cement kilns, electric utilities, and paper mills also use the company's tire chips and whole tires as a secondary fuel source. Additionally, GreenMan Technologies sells crumb rubber for use in athletic surfaces, equestrian arenas, landscaping, playgrounds, public walkways, rubberized asphalt, and sport turf fields.

ORIGINS: 1992–94

GreenMan Technologies was established on September 16, 1992. The company was the brainchild of Jim Barker, a former Boston police officer who had worked as a salesman in the plastics industry for 25 years. After leaving New England in the mid-1980s, Barker moved to Dallas, Texas, and ultimately established his own company in Arkansas with assistance from Mitsubishi, for whom he had been selling plastic molding equipment.

In the January 12, 1996 issue of *Boston Business Journal,* Barker revealed some of the philosophy behind the establishment of GreenMan Technologies, commenting: "We're trying to contribute to a cleaner environment. I grew up in an age when cleaning up the environment was always left to the next generation. I started thinking, 'What can I do to help?' That's where GreenMan Technologies comes into play." Barker founded GreenMan Technologies along with former consultant Joseph Levangie, a Massachusetts Institute of Technology and Harvard Business School graduate who had experience helping numerous companies raise financing and engage in mergers and acquisitions.

A third partner was Barker's daughter, Cynthia, an investment banker who had worked for Levangie. Cynthia inspired her father to take action on his idea, and wrote the company's initial business plan. In the aforementioned *Boston Business Journal* article, Cynthia Barker explained: "My father understood the business. He had the concept for recycling tires and combining that with virgin plastics to make products. It was a great idea, but he just kept talking about it. Finally I just said, 'Let's stop talking about it and do it.'"

With Jim Barker serving as president, the founding partners collectively raised $250,000 to get their new enterprise off the ground. Initially focused on transforming old tires into consumer products, GreenMan's founders soon identified a shortage of reliable crumb rubber supply in the market. The company began producing crumb rubber from tires and combining it with plastics to develop products.

EARLY YEARS: 1995–98

With headquarters in Lynnfield, Massachusetts, and production operations in Malvern, Arkansas, the company saw events unfold at a rapid pace in the mid-1990s. In June 1995 GreenMan Technologies reincorporated in Delaware. That October the company made its initial public offering, generating $5.8 million.

As with many start-ups, profits were elusive at GreenMan Technologies during the company's formative years. The company ended its 1995 fiscal year with sales of $2.1 million and a $1.1 million loss. Nevertheless, with the introduction of new products in 1996, including playground furniture, recycling totes, and trash cans, better times seemed to be on the horizon.

In October 1995 GreenMan Technologies acquired DuraWear Corp., a manufacturer of polymer, ceramic, and alloy steel materials, in a cash-and-stock deal involving $400,000 and 75,000 shares. By this time the company had a workforce of 60 people at its plant in Malvern.

The following month, GreenMan Technologies ordered four cryogenic freezing systems from Queens,

New York-based Crumb Rubber Technology Inc. The systems were slated for inclusion within a 15,000-square-foot processing plant, which the company planned to build at a Jackson, Georgia-based tire-shredding facility operated by BFI Tire Recyclers of Georgia Inc.

With the new systems, GreenMan Technologies intended to shred tires into chips, freeze and granulate the rubber, and separate fiber and metal from the mix. Ultimately, the process produced crumb rubber that the company could combine with both virgin and recycled plastic to create material combinations of varying hardness. The challenge of getting the substances to adhere to one another was something GreenMan Technologies accomplished through extensive research.

In early 1996 GreenMan Technologies secured a $2 million deal to make recycled rubber display racks for Coca-Cola. That year, consolidated net sales increased to $4.34 million, with a net loss of $1.58 million.

Progress continued in early 1997 when GreenMan Technologies revealed plans to acquire the tire-recycling operations of Browning-Ferris Industries Inc. (BFI) in Savage, Minnesota, and Jackson, Georgia. The deal was completed in early July, with GreenMan shelling out $5.4 million for BFI Tire Recyclers of Minnesota Inc. and BFI Tire Recyclers of Georgia Inc., which subsequently became GreenMan Technologies of Minnesota Inc. and GreenMan Technologies of Georgia Inc., respectively.

Expansion continued during the latter part of the year when, in a $775,000 deal with Malvern, Pennsylvania-based MG Industries, the company acquired St. Francisville, Louisiana-based scrap tire processor Cryopolymers Inc. Following the deal, Cryopolymers was renamed GreenMan Technologies of Louisiana Inc.

GreenMan Technologies ushered in 1998 by shuttering its Malvern, Arkansas-based injection molding facility. A number of leadership changes occurred that year. CFO Levangie was named vice-chairman in March. Several months later, Robert H. Davis, who had served as vice-president of recycling for BFI, was named CEO, succeeding Maurice E. Needham, who stayed with GreenMan Technologies as chairman.

Growth continued in September when GreenMan Technologies struck a $4.1 million cash-and-stock deal with Republic Services Inc. for United Waste Service Inc.'s tire collection and processing assets, which were located in Batesburg, South Carolina, and Lawrenceville, Georgia. The deal meant an additional four million tires per year for GreenMan Technologies, as well as about $5 million per year in revenues.

KEY DATES

1992: GreenMan Technologies is established.
1995: Nearly $6 million is raised via an initial public offering.
1999: Company becomes solely focused on tire recycling following the sale of its DuraWear Corp. subsidiary; GreenMan Technologies achieves its first profitable quarter.
2004: *Waste Age* names GreenMan Technologies to its list of the industry's 100 leading firms.
2007: Company ceases to be a pure-play tire recycler upon acquisition of Welch Products Inc., a manufacturer of environmentally responsible products.

GreenMan Technologies' consolidated net sales skyrocketed 428 percent in the fiscal year ending May 1998, increasing to $11.01 million, thanks in large part to its acquisition of the BFI operations.

PURE-PLAY TIRE RECYCLER: 1999–2004

In early 1999 Frederickson Tire Recycling and Hiawatha Tire Recycling were acquired. A major change in focus occurred midway through the year when GreenMan Technologies became solely focused on tire recycling. This development unfolded when the company sold its DuraWear Corp. subsidiary to ETEC Technical Ceramics Corp. in June for $600,000.

President and CEO Davis remarked that DuraWear had contributed about $1.7 million in losses since GreenMan Technologies acquired the company. While GreenMan Technologies had proven that it was possible to produce products from combinations of crumb rubber and plastic, the company found it difficult to profitably manufacture these products, such as trash cans and picket fencing.

A major milestone was reached in June 1999 when GreenMan Technologies achieved its first profitable quarter in the company's history, earning $75,183 (1 cent per share). Unfortunately, the following month GreenMan Technologies' stock was pulled from the NASDAQ when the company did not meet the exchange's market activity standards. Following this, trading continued on the Boston Stock Exchange and the OTC Bulletin Board.

Midway through 2000 GreenMan Technologies consolidated its South Carolina operations with those in Georgia. Early the following year, the company's Technical Tire Recycling Inc. arm acquired Tennessee Tire Recyclers Inc., a provider of engineering services and scrap tire collection and disposal.

In early 2002 subsidiary GreenMan Technologies of Wisconsin Inc. bolstered the company's presence in the Midwest when it parted with $78,000 in cash and nearly $9,000 in stock to acquire the operations of scrap tire collector/processor An-Gun Inc.

Developments continued in March when Able Tire of Oklahoma LLC, a new scrap tire joint venture, was formed with Able Tire Co. LLC. The following month GreenMan Technologies furthered its midwestern expansion efforts by snapping up Utah Tire Recyclers Inc.'s Iowa operations in a deal worth $1.98 million, leading to the formation of GreenMan Technologies of Iowa Inc. More midwestern growth occurred in July, when GreenMan Technologies of Minnesota acquired R&J Recycling Co.'s tire collection assets.

It also was in July 2002 that Azusa, California-based scrap tire collector/processor Unlimited Tire Technologies Inc. was acquired, and a new subsidiary named GreenMan Technologies of California Inc. was established. A final development in 2002 occurred when GreenMan Technologies' common stock was listed on the American Stock Exchange under the symbol GRN.

Plans for a new high-volume tire-processing plant in LaVergne, Tennessee, with an initial annual capacity of four million tires, were announced in February 2003. GreenMan Technologies capped off the 2003 fiscal year with net sales of $29.68 million, up from $27.45 million in 2002, and a net loss of $2.89 million, compared to net income of $1.02 million in 2002.

GreenMan Technologies acquired American Tire Disposal Inc. in July 2004, expanding its presence in southern California. The following month, the company was named to *Waste Age*'s list of the waste industry's 100 leading firms, ranking number 50.

IMPROVEMENT FOCUS: 2005–06

As the company headed into 2005, it was collecting and processing about 30 million tires annually. Despite several years of operational expansion, however, GreenMan Technologies had recorded significant operating losses, especially in the southeastern United States. This quickly led to the development of a plan to turn things around.

In September 2005 an agreement was forged with Tennessee Tire Recyclers for the sale of GreenMan Technologies' operations in LaVergne. Three months later, the company's crumb rubber plant in Jackson,

Georgia, was closed down and eventually sold. Together, these two efforts were expected to generate monthly savings of approximately $500,000.

Several important developments occurred in 2006, beginning with the April appointment of Lyle E. Jensen as president and CEO. Prior to taking the head job, Jensen had served as a GreenMan Technologies board member, chairing the audit committee. It was around this same time that corporate headquarters were relocated from Massachusetts to Savage, which was closer to the company's more profitable midwestern operations.

On June 14, 2006, GreenMan Technologies' stock ceased trading on the American Stock Exchange after the company failed to meet minimum requirements related to stockholder equity. Subsequently, trading continued on the Pink Sheets under the new ticker symbol GMTI. At this time, the company continued to shed underperforming operations. GreenMan Technologies of California was divested in July, leaving facilities in Minnesota and Iowa that collectively processed 14 million tires annually.

RETURN TO MANUFACTURING: 2007–08

Better times seemed to be on the horizon as GreenMan Technologies headed into the last half of the first decade of the 2000s. In September 2007 the company announced its first annual profit in five years. Compared to a net loss of $3.71 million on net sales of $17.61 million in 2006, the company recorded net income of $313,000 on net sales of $20.18 million.

In October 2007 GreenMan Technologies ceased to be a pure-play tire recycler when it acquired Carlisle, Iowa-based Welch Products Inc. for eight million shares of stock. A manufacturer of environmentally responsible products, most of which were made from recycled materials, Welch was one of GreenMan's longtime crumb rubber customers. In addition to designing and installing playground equipment under the Playtribe brand name, Welch produced construction molds, highway guardrail rubber spacer blocks, playground safety tiles, and roadside antivegetation products.

By 2008 GreenMan Technologies' playground business was making meaningful progress. In September the company announced that Welch Products had received a playground surfacing contract from the LaTrobe School District of California, as well as a separate contract to install six playgrounds for California's Orland Unified School District. The two projects were worth more than $500,000. Around the same time, Welch Products also was awarded playground projects with five school districts in Minnesota, worth approximately $330,000.

After shedding unprofitable operations and getting back into the recycled products business, GreenMan Technologies approached the 21st century's second decade with renewed optimism. The company moved forward with an ample supply of used tires. While it processed some 12 million tires annually, roughly 300 million used tires became available in the United States each year.

Paul R. Greenland

PRINCIPAL SUBSIDIARIES

GreenMan Technologies of Georgia Inc.; GreenMan Technologies of Iowa Inc.; GreenMan Technologies of Minnesota Inc.; GreenMan Technologies of Tennessee Inc.; Technical Tire Recycling Inc.

PRINCIPAL COMPETITORS

Casella Waste Systems Inc.; North American Technologies Group Inc.; RB Rubber Products Inc.

FURTHER READING
"GreenMan Technologies Acquires Welch Products, Inc.; Acquisition Leverages GreenMan's Crumb Rubber Manufacturing Capabilities and Creates Vertically Integrated Products Subsidiary with Enhanced Growth Opportunity," *Market Wire,* October 2, 2007.

"GreenMan Technologies Completes Divestiture of Its DuraWear Subsidiary; Company Now a 'Pure Play' in Scrap-Tire Recycling," *Business Wire,* June 21, 1999.

McCormack, Ellie, "Tire Recycler Goes for the Green," *Boston Business Journal,* January 12, 1996.

"Molding a Business; Malvern Plant Owner Jim Barker Sees GreenMan Technologies Inc. Taking Some Clients' Reusable Plastic Throwaways and Transforming Them into Products That the Company Needs," *Arkansas Democrat-Gazette,* April 29, 1996.

Moore, Miles, "GreenMan Begins Cost-Cutting; Moves HQ; Troubled Recycler Relocates to Minnesota As It Implements Plan for Returning to Profitability," *Tire Business,* June 5, 2006.

———, "Learning from the School of Hard Knocks: Tough Path Pays Off for GreenMan," *Tire Business,* October 11, 1999.

Grupo Brescia

Calle Los Begonias 441
San Isidro
Lima,
Peru
Telephone: (51 1) 442-2030
Fax: (51 1) 442-3773

Private Company
Founded: 1889
Sales: $2.5 billion (2007 est.)
NAICS: 111310 Orange Groves; 111320 Citrus (Except Orange) Groves; 114111 Finfish Fishing; 212231 Lead Ore and Zinc Ore Mining; 212299 Other Metal Ore Mining; 311119 Other Animal Food Manufacturing; 325920 Explosives Manufacturing; 524113 Direct Life Insurance Carriers; 524114 Direct Health and Medical Insurance Carriers; 524126 Direct Property and Casualty Insurance Carriers; 524130 Reinsurance Carriers; 531110 Lessors of Nonresidential Buildings (Except Miniwarehouses); 621491 HMO Medical Centers; 721110 Hotels (Except Casino Hotels) and Motels

■ ■ ■

Grupo Brescia is the name given to the holdings of Pedro and Mario Brescia, brothers who own and administer what collectively forms the largest business conglomerate in Peru. They include the world's second largest tin mine, the nation's largest or second largest insurance company, and a large stake in its second largest bank, a hotel chain and an array of other kinds of real property, and a number of holdings in agriculture, fisheries, and chemicals. So vast and varied is the Brescia group, with a controlling interest in about 40 companies, that it operates through more than one holding company.

THE BRESCIAS' FIRST CENTURY: 1889–1989

Fortunato Brescia Tassano, an Italian immigrant, arrived in Peru in 1889 and became a farmer who provided grocers of Italian origin with dairy products, vegetables, and wheat for bread. He began buying land in the metropolitan area that included Lima, the capital, and its port, Callao, before the rapid growth of the urbanizing area in size and population. With a partner, Eugenio Raffo, he purchased a large suburban tract, Limatambo, in 1913, later buying out Raffo.

In 1940 the government expropriated Limatambo to construct the first commercial airport in Peru. Although a short-term loss, the measure enhanced the value of Brescia's other properties located between the airport and the main road from central Lima. Real estate became a principal focus of the family business group, which was taken over by his sons Pedro and Mario Brescia Cafferata after he died in 1952.

The Brescia brothers sold land for housing, industry, and shopping centers. Trained as agricultural engineers, they put much of their profits into farmland and by the 1960s were Peru's fifth largest landowners. They also became proprietors of four plants turning out fishmeal from anchovies, a product then in high demand as livestock feed. When the periodic El Niño

KEY DATES

1889: Fortunato Brescia, an Italian immigrant, arrives in Peru.

1913: Brescia purchases a large tract of land outside Lima.

1940: This tract is expropriated for an airport, which raises the value of other Brescia properties.

1952: Fortunato's two sons assume direction of the family fortune on his death.

1960: The Brescia brothers have become Peru's fifth largest landowners.

1971: The brothers enter the hotel and tourism sector.

1977: Now a conglomerate, Grupo Brescia includes insurance and mining companies.

1979: The group makes an ill-fated, decade-long venture into textiles and retail trade.

1995: The group, in a joint venture with a Spanish bank, acquires control of Peru's third largest bank.

2006: Grupo Brescia has formed the world's largest fishmeal company.

2008: The group's hotel chain is erecting the tallest building in Peru.

weather pattern disrupted the Pacific Ocean currents, drastically reducing the anchovy harvest, the boom ended, and the Brescias closed two of the plants.

Grupo Brescia's fishing companies were expropriated in 1973 by Peru's nationalist military government, which had seized power five years earlier. Some other industries were also nationalized, and large private holdings of land were broken up to be allotted to agricultural cooperatives or other uses. Half of the Brescia holdings in land were expropriated, much of it for housing that was never built, but the best properties were retained. Several years later, the urban land that had been seized was returned by means of a document signed by Vice Admiral Gerónimo Cafferata, a relative of the Brescia family who was minister of housing.

Although hostile to capitalism, the military government's policies provided opportunities for Grupo Brescia to enter new fields. Because the foreign stake in Peru's banks was reduced to a one-fifth share, Peruvian business groups, including the Brescia group, now vied for control of Banco del Crédito del Perú, the largest. Grupo Brescia raised its stake to at least 14 percent

before agreeing to be bought out by the larger Romero group in 1979. The Brescias then purchased 27 percent of the smaller Banco de Lima but were unable to win control because other shareholders feared the prospect of self dealing.

With regard to insurance the group was more successful, assuming majority control of Compañia de Seguros Rímac and Compañia Internacional de Seguros del Perú, which later merged and became Rímac Internacional Compañia de Seguros y Reaseguros S.A. Clínica Internacional S.A., proprietor of a medical center, became a subsidiary of Rímac in 1990.

The government also aided Grupo Brescia by forcing out New York-based W.R. Grace and Company, which had large holdings in agriculture and mining. In 1977 Brescia bought two-thirds of Grace's shares in Minsur Partnership Ltd. and 29 percent of its shares in Compañia Minera Atacocha S.A. Minsur held two mines, the largest of which yielded the only tin produced in Peru. The other one, closed in 1990, yielded concentrates of copper, lead, and silver. This enterprise, originally small, proved immensely lucrative as it expanded in the 1980s.

In 1979 Grupo Brescia purchased control of Fábrica de Tejidos La Unión Ltda. S.A., a large textile and clothing plant, from a British company long established in Peru. Two years later, the Brescias bought the retail chain Scala, consisting of 13 supermarkets, to strengthen La Unión's distribution chain. La Unión also had about two dozen subsidiaries. The textile industry was highly protected from foreign competition at the time but suffered from later free market reforms. La Unión also got into financial trouble by guaranteeing the debts of other companies in the Brescia group. It was losing $1 million a month when the Brescia group sold its 60 percent share to the company's executives in late 1989 for only $2.7 million.

Grupo Brescia also saw an opening when the military regime nationalized a number of hotel properties. The brothers founded Inversiones Nacionales de Turismo S.A. in 1971.

BANKING AND MINING: 1990–2000

In 1990 Grupo Brescia was a conglomerate with interests in finance, urban development, exporting, wholesaling, chemicals, minerals, and food production. In 1995 it achieved its goal of gaining a major stake in an important bank. Banco Continental, once a subsidiary of Chase Manhattan Bank, was in government hands when a 60 percent stake was sold to Holding Continental S.A., a joint venture of Grupo Brescia and the Spanish bank Banco Bilbao Viscaya (BBV), which later became Banco Bilbao Vizcaya Argentaria (BBVA). It paid $196.7 million in cash and assumed $60 million in debt in taking control of Peru's third largest bank. Although Pedro Brescia became the chairman of the board and Mario Brescia vice-chairman, management was in BBVA's hands. BBVA Banco Continental grew rapidly in the following years, advancing to second place in deposits in 1998, when it had more than 160 branches. It was also a leader in issuing credit cards.

Minsur (officially Minera del Sur S.A.) was Peru's only producer of tin, which it mined at an altitude of more than 14,000 feet in the province of Puno. The metal concentrate was smelted elsewhere, half in Bolivia, until 1995, when the company opened its own smelter. Grupo Brescia also had a stake in Atacocha and Compañia Minera Raura S.A., whose mines yielded lead, zinc, silver, and copper.

BRESCIA IN THE EARLY 21ST CENTURY

The Grupo Brescia of the early 21st century was divided into three subgroups: financial; industrial; and family holding companies. A complex web of cross ownerships connected the three. The main part of the financial subgroup was Brescia's half-share in the joint venture that owned 92 percent of BBVA Banco Continental in 2007. There was also a brokerage, a securities title company, a fund management company, and stakes in two pension funds. This part of Grupo Brescia was directed by nonfamily professional managers.

The industrial subgroup was also mostly administered by professional managers. It included Grupo Brescia's interests in mining, tourism, insurance, and chemicals, the latter represented by Explosivos S.A. (EXSA), a producer of nitrate and other explosives and also of welding supplies. These were typically public firms in which Brescia holding companies had a controlling, although not majority, stake. An exception was Minsur, which was wholly owned by Inversiones Breca S.A.

The family holdings group included investment holding companies and real estate development companies. The Brescia brothers' sister Rosa was, in 2004, a director of at least one of these companies, Inversiones Breca S.A. Her son Alex Fort Brescia and Mario's son Pedro Brescia Moreyra were directors of Banco Continental. Mario's two other sons were deputy directors of the bank.

By 2004 Fort was also managing director general of the Rímac insurance company. In that year Rímac purchased a majority share of rival Royal & Sun Alliance Seguros Fenix for $30 million. This gave Rímac a one-third share of the national insurance market. Earlier, it had acquired another insurance company, Wiese Atenia. Clínica Internacional, its subsidiary, was the largest company of its kind in Peru, with four medical centers in existence and a fifth planned for opening in 2010.

A VARIETY OF INTERESTS

Grupo Brescia was flush with cash, having sold its 24.3 percent stake in the Peruvian beer monopoly, Unión de Cervecerias Peruanas Backus y Johnston S.A.A., for more than $420 million in 2003. It chose to use some of this money to reenter the fisheries business, creating Tecnológica de Alimentos S.A. (TASA), which included the world's largest fishmeal plant. This company merged with Grupo Sindicato Pesquero del Perú S.A. (Sipesa) in 2006 to form the world's biggest fishmeal company. TASA in 2007 opened four refrigerated warehouses for the distribution of frozen seafood and two more by mid-2008. The company was accounting for 30 percent of Peru's production of fishmeal and fish oil and had a fishing fleet of more than 70 boats. Its sales were expected to reach $350 million during the year.

Agricola Hoja Redonda S.A. was growing citrus fruits and avocados, on land south of Lima that the Brescias had lost at the end of the 1960s but had repurchased from the peasants who won it in the redistribution program. The brothers were interested in recovering more land there, not to continue producing cotton, beans, or corn but, instead, grapes. A plant was being constructed to choose and process fruits for export. EXSA was also thinking of opening a plant to produce ammonia nitrate fertilizers there, at a cost of $300 million.

Intursa had grown into the proprietor of six Libertador hotels, all four- or five-star luxury establishments. In 2008 the company broke ground in the construction of the Westin Libertador Lima, a 30-story, 118-meter-high hotel that would be the tallest building in Peru. It was located on the same street as Grupo Brescia's headquarters, in the heart of the financial district of San Isidro, an affluent section of Lima. The hotel was expected to open in early 2010 at a cost of about $100 million. The Westin chain would operate the hotel but had no stake in it.

Intursa was also engaged in three other hotel projects that would require investment of more than $70 million. The first involved a total remodeling of the Libertador hotel in Cuzco, which would be renamed Libertador Luxury Collection, the trademark of luxury hotels owned by Starwood Hotels & Resorts Worldwide Inc., which also owned the Westin hotels. The second project, near Cuzco, would be a hotel called Libertador Urubamba Luxury Collection. A Paracas Libertador hotel would be built in Ica, in place of the former Paracas hotel. Three other hotels were also affiliated with the Hoteles Libertador Perú chain.

Grupo Brescia was also building a first-class office building in the San Isidro financial center at a cost of $23 million and was planning to build a second one nearby. Work had begun on a $20 million commercial center, Monterrico Plaza, that would include a hypermarket, a department store, a multiplex cinema, a gymnasium, a medical center, and retail stores on two levels. In addition to two existing Lima strip centers, three more were in development. Seven housing complexes were planned for Callao and northeastern Lima at a cost of more than $100 million.

In the mining field, Grupo Brescia was planning to open a gold mine in the far south of Peru and a tungsten mine near Minsur. A mine in Huancavelica would produce silver, zinc, lead, and copper.

FUTURE PLANS

The 87-year-old Pedro and 78-year-old Mario remained, in 2008, in total control of their empire. They had no plans to invest outside Peru until the unlikely event that the existing markets were saturated for their companies' products. Property development, mineral exploration, agroindustry, and petrochemicals were identified as the principal foci of their activities. Each Brescia company was expected to conduct its business independently and not to lean on another one. Presiding over all was Corporación AESA (formerly Administración de Empresas S.A.), the real estate arm of the group and also its "brain," which was responsible for decisions such as where new investments would be made. Its director general, Edgardo Arboccó, had been working for the Brescias for more than 40 years.

The Brescia brothers had no plans to retire. Both worked seven days a week and were present in the director boards of their companies. Pedro was spending every weekend in Chincha, south of Lima, to personally supervise Hoja Redonda's fruit growing, while Mario scoured every contract to see if even a comma was

missing. The candidates for the succession were Mario's three sons and their cousin Alex Fort. The former directed the mining, fishing, and hotel properties, respectively, while Fort was in charge of the Rímac insurance company.

Robert Halasz

PRINCIPAL HOLDING COMPANIES

Corporación AESA; Inversiones Breca S.A.; Inversiones San Borja S.A.; Urbanización Santa Marina S.A.

PRINCIPAL COMPETITORS

Banco del Crédito del Perú; El Pacifico–Peruana Suiza Compañia de Seguros y Reaseguros S.A.; Grupo Austral; PT Tambag Minah.

FURTHER READING

Chevarría León, Fernando, "Los Brescia se consolidan en pesca y apuntan al agro y la construcción," *El Comercio,* January 23, 2007.

———, "Los Monarcas," *AméricaEconomía,* May 25, 2008, pp. 28–30.

"Grupo Brescia alista varios proyectos immobiliarios y comerciales en el país," *El Comercio,* March 15, 2008.

"Hotel del grupo Brescia será edificio más alto de la capital," *El Comercio,* February 22, 2008.

Malpica Silva Santisteban, Carlos, *El poder económico en el Perú,* Lima: Ediciones La Escena Contemporánea, 1989, pp. 133–67.

"Minsur's Expansion Continues," *Mining Journal,* February 14, 1997, p. 3.

"Peru's Ailing Anchovy and Fishmeal Firms Are Nationalized by Military Government," *Wall Street Journal,* May 9, 1973, p. 5.

Qassim, Ali, "Fujimori's Open House," *Banker,* August 1995, pp. 56–57.

Shimizu, Tatsaya, *Family Business in Peru,* Chiba, Japan: Institute of Developing Economies, 2004 (www.apec.info/asia/jpapec5/007_shimizu.pdf).

Vásquez Huamán, Enrique, *Estrategias del poder,* Lima: Universidad del Pacífico, 2000, pp. 137–68.

H. J. Heinz Company

One PPG Place, Suite 1300
Pittsburgh, Pennsylvania 15222-5448
U.S.A.
Telephone: (412) 456-5700
Fax: (412) 456-6128
Web site: http://www.heinz.com

Public Company
Founded: 1869 as Heinz, Noble & Company
Incorporated: 1900
Employees: 32,500
Sales: $10.07 billion (2008)
Stock Exchanges: New York
Ticker Symbol: HNZ
NAICS: 311411 Frozen Fruit, Juice, and Vegetable Manufacturing; 311412 Frozen Specialty Food Manufacturing; 311421 Fruit and Vegetable Canning; 311422 Specialty Canning; 311941 Mayonnaise, Dressing, and Other Prepared Sauce Manufacturing; 311999 All Other Miscellaneous Food Manufacturing

■ ■ ■

Best known for its ketchup, H. J. Heinz Company manufactures thousands of food products in plants on five continents and markets these products in more than 200 countries and territories. The company's product line centers on ketchup, condiments and sauces, frozen food, soups, beans, pasta meals, and infant nutrition. It garners 70 percent of its revenues from 16 "power brands": Heinz (ketchup, beans; worldwide), ABC (soy sauce; Asia), Bagel Bites (frozen snacks; North America), Boston Market (frozen meals; North America), Chef Francisco (foodservice frozen soup; North America), Classico (pasta sauces; North America, Asia/Pacific), Delimex (frozen Mexican snacks; North America), Honig (soup, meals, pasta; Benelux), Lea & Perrins (sauces; worldwide), Ore-Ida (frozen potatoes; North America, Asia/Pacific), Plasmon (infant/nutrition products; Italy), Pudliszki (prepared meals, ketchup; Poland), Smart Ones (frozen entrees and desserts; North America), T.G.I. Friday's (frozen snacks and meals; North America), Wattie's (soups, sauces, baked beans; New Zealand), and Weight Watchers (canned goods, frozen meals and desserts; worldwide). Of the major U.S.-based food companies, H. J. Heinz is the most global, generating more than 60 percent of its sales outside the United States.

HENRY J. HEINZ AND THE FOUNDING OF HIS COMPANY

The origins of this vast food empire may be traced to Pennsylvania, where eight-year-old Henry John Heinz began selling produce from his family's plot to nearby neighbors. At ten he used a wheelbarrow, and, by the time he was 16, Heinz had several employees and was making three deliveries a week to Pittsburgh grocers. Born in 1844 to German immigrant parents, Heinz was the oldest of nine children. He grew up in Sharpsburg, Pennsylvania, near Pittsburgh, and, after graduating from Duff's Business College, he became the bookkeeper at his father's brickyard. At age 21, he became a partner. (Heinz retained an interest in bricks all his life; he personally supervised the buying and laying of brick

COMPANY PERSPECTIVES

The Heinz Vision: "To be the world's premier food company, offering nutritious, superior tasting foods to people everywhere."

As a global food company, Heinz is committed to enhancing the nutrition, health and wellness of people and their communities to make the world a better place to live. Heinz aims to manufacture safe, healthy, nutritious, high-quality food that satisfies appetites around the world. We define "premier" not necessarily in terms of size, but in terms of scope.

for his company's buildings, and his office desk was often piled with brick samples acquired on his travels.) In 1869 Heinz and L. C. Noble formed a partnership called Heinz, Noble & Company in Sharpsburg to sell bottled horseradish. Their product line soon expanded to include sauerkraut, vinegar, and pickles.

Following the panic of 1873 and subsequent economic chaos, the business failed in 1875, but Heinz quickly regrouped, and the following year started afresh with the determination to repay his creditors. With his brother John and cousin Frederick as partners and himself as manager, Heinz formed the partnership of F&J Heinz to manufacture condiments, pickles, and other prepared food. Ketchup was added to the product line in 1876. The business prospered, and Heinz made good on his obligations. In 1888 the partnership was reorganized as H. J. Heinz Company after Heinz gained financial control of the firm. Soon Heinz was known throughout the country as the "pickle king."

Small, energetic, and ambitious, Heinz was a cheerful man with courtly, old-fashioned manners. He exuded enthusiasm, whether for work, family, travel, religious activities, or good horses, and had a passion for involving others in his interests. According to his biographer, Robert C. Alberts, Heinz once installed an 800-pound, 14½-foot, 150-year-old live alligator in a glass tank atop one of his factory buildings so that his employees might enjoy the sight as much as he had in Florida.

In the late 1800s, the typical American diet was bland and monotonous, and the Heinz Company set out to spice it up with a multitude of products. The phrase "57 Varieties" was coined in 1892. Tomato soup and beans in tomato sauce were quickly added to the product line. Even as "57 Varieties" became a household slogan, the company had more than 60 products. At the

World's Columbian Exposition in Chicago in 1893, Heinz had the largest exhibit of any U.S. food company.

By 1900, the year the company was incorporated, H. J. Heinz Company occupied a major niche in U.S. business. It was first in the production of ketchup, pickles, mustard, and vinegar and fourth in the packing of olives. Overall the company made more than 200 products. Still, Heinz liked the lilt of his original slogan and in 1900 put it up in lights in New York City's first large electric sign, at Fifth Avenue and 23rd Street. A total of 1,200 lights illuminated a 40-foot-long green pickle and its advertising message.

Heinz's clever merchandising won him a reputation as an advertising genius, but he did not allow his ambitions to overshadow his religious convictions; during his lifetime, in deference to the Sabbath, Heinz's advertisements never ran on Sundays. Heinz Company factories were considered models in the industry, both in their facilities and their treatment of workers. The company received many awards, and Harry W. Sherman, grand secretary of the National Brotherhood of Electrical Workers of America, remarked after visiting a Heinz plant that it was "a utopia for working men."

In 1886 Henry Heinz went to England carrying a sample case, and came home with orders for seven products. By 1905, the company had opened its first factory in England. The following year, the Pure Food and Drug Act was vigorously opposed by most food manufacturers, but Heinz, who understood the importance of consumer confidence in the purity of processed foods, was all for it, and even sent his son to Washington, D.C., to campaign for its passage.

TRANSITION FROM FAMILY FIRM TO PUBLIC COMPANY

Henry Heinz died at age 75 in 1919. At that time, the company had a workforce of 6,500 employees and maintained 25 branch factories. Heinz was succeeded as president of the company by his son, Howard, who began his career with H. J. Heinz as advertising manager in 1905 and became sales manager in 1907. In 1931, at the height of the Great Depression, Howard Heinz saved the company by branching into two new areas: ready-to-eat soups and baby food. He remained president until his death in 1941. In 1939 *Fortune* estimated total sales for the still privately owned company at $105 million.

By the time Howard's son H. J. Heinz II (known as Jack) became president of the company at his father's death, he had worked in all the company's divisions, from the canning factories to the administrative offices. He chose to launch his career as a pickle-salter for $1 a

KEY DATES

1869: Henry J. Heinz and L. C. Noble form partnership, Heinz, Noble & Company, to sell bottled horseradish.

1875: Business fails following the panic of 1873.

1876: Business is reorganized in a new partnership, F&J Heinz; ketchup is added to the product line.

1888: Henry Heinz gains financial control of F&J Heinz and changes its name to H. J. Heinz Company.

1892: The slogan "57 Varieties" is first used.

1900: Company is incorporated.

1905: The first foreign factory is opened in England.

1919: Henry Heinz dies and is succeeded by his son, Howard.

1931: Company branches into ready-to-eat soups and baby food.

1946: Company goes public.

1963: StarKist Foods is acquired.

1965: Ore-Ida Foods, Inc., is acquired.

1978: Weight Watchers International is acquired.

1979: Anthony J. F. O'Reilly is named CEO.

1995: The North American pet food businesses of Quaker Oats Company are acquired, including such brands as Kibbles'n Bits, Gravy Train, and Ken-L Ration.

1997: Company initiates a major restructuring.

1998: William R. Johnson takes over as CEO.

1999: An even larger, multiyear restructuring is launched; the Weight Watchers diet class business is divested.

2002: Heinz spins off several sluggishly growing businesses, including its North American pet foods business and StarKist tuna.

2005: Company purchases the Lea & Perrins and HP sauce brands from Groupe Danone.

day in the Plymouth, Indiana, plant. Later he became part of the cleanup staff, then a salesperson for H. J. Heinz Company, Ltd., in England. In 1935, fresh out of Cambridge University, Jack Heinz was sent by his father to establish a plant in Australia. Heinz-Australia later became that country's biggest food processing plant.

From 1941, when Jack took over, to 1946, H. J. Heinz's sales nearly doubled. That year, Heinz made its first public stock offering and revealed that its net profit was more than $4 million. Foreign sales of baked beans and ketchup, particularly in England, contributed substantially to the company's success. During World War II, Jack Heinz was active in food relief and personally made four wartime trips to England to examine food problems there. The company insignia went to war, too; the 57th Squadron of the 446th Army Air Force chose for its emblem a winged pickle marked "57."

Jack Heinz's tenure was distinguished by expansion of the company, both internationally and at home. Subsidiaries were launched in the Netherlands, Venezuela, Japan, Italy, and Portugal. In 1960 and 1961, H. J. Heinz Company acquired the assets of Reymer & Bros., Inc., and Hachmeister, Inc. StarKist Foods was acquired in 1963 and Ore-Ida Foods, Inc., in 1965.

During the 25 years that H. J. Heinz II was chief executive, the food industry changed greatly. The era was marked by the rise of supermarket chains and the development of new distribution and marketing systems. In 1966 H. J. Heinz II stepped down as president and CEO, although he retained his position as chairperson until his death in February 1987.

THE O'REILLY REVOLUTION

In 1969 R. Burt Gookin, then CEO of Heinz, made Anthony (Tony) J. F. O'Reilly president of the company's profitable British subsidiary. O'Reilly, who was managing director of the Irish Sugar Company at the time, shook up the company by working 14-hour days and stressing a policy of winning through effort. O'Reilly was an uncommon executive; he was, among other things, a world-class rugby player. In 1973 O'Reilly was named president of the parent company, and in 1979 he became CEO. Shortly after the death of H. J. Heinz II, he was also made chairperson. From the beginning, O'Reilly stressed the importance of strong financial results. Some critics claimed that this emphasis created too stressful an atmosphere; in 1979, it was learned that managers of several subsidiaries had for years been misstating quarterly earnings to meet their target goals and impress top management.

Overall, O'Reilly's achievements were impressive, however. The timely acquisition of Hubinger Company in 1975 put Heinz in a position to cash in on the demand for high-fructose corn syrup when the price of sugar soared. In 1978 O'Reilly acquired Weight Watchers International, just ahead of the fitness craze that swept the nation.

At the same time that the company was branching out into new products, O'Reilly was cutting back on traditional businesses. By 1980, Heinz had increased volume, while cutting its number of plants from 14 to seven and reducing employment by 18 percent. O'Reilly also gave up the battle with Campbell Soup Company for the retail soup market. When generic products hit the supermarket shelves, Heinz countered not by producing for the generics industry but by "nickel and diming it," as he said. For example, Heinz switched to thinner glass bottles that cut the cost not only of packaging but also of transportation. When imports began to undersell StarKist tuna, StarKist decreased the size of the tuna can, just as Hershey had downsized its chocolate bar when cocoa prices soared. This ploy netted StarKist $7 million in savings. Other nickel-and-dime cost savings came from eliminating back labels from bottles, reclaiming heat, and reusing water.

O'Reilly's strategy in the 1980s was to pare costs to the bone and to use the savings to beef up marketing, primarily advertising, in an effort to increase market share. At the same time, Heinz pursued a cautious acquisition policy. By the mid-1980s, the company had spent $416 million to acquire more than 20 companies. Return on equity increased from 9 percent in 1972 to 23.3 percent in 1986.

O'Reilly's cost-cutting war included a threat to go to contract manufacturers rather than his own plants if the same products could be purchased elsewhere for less. Such tough talk elicited substantial concessions from labor unions in 1986. O'Reilly's hard-nosed, bottom-line strategies won Heinz recognition as one of the country's five best-managed companies in 1986. When H. J. Heinz died the following year, O'Reilly became the first nonfamily member to advance to Heinz's chair.

In 1988 Heinz bid $200 million for Bumble Bee Seafoods, the third largest tuna company in the country. The purchase would have given Heinz, whose StarKist brand ranked number one, more than 50 percent of the domestic tuna market. Accordingly, the U.S. Justice Department prevented the purchase on antitrust grounds. Also in 1988, Heinz reorganized StarKist Foods into StarKist Seafood and Heinz Pet Products to strengthen seafood operations for a push abroad. In pet foods, Heinz, already a leading canned cat food producer, strengthened its dog food position through the acquisition of several regional brands.

In overseas markets, Heinz began to expand into the Third World. It became the first foreign investor in Zimbabwe when it acquired a controlling interest in Olivine Industries, Inc., in 1982. Heinz also formed joint ventures in Korea and China, and in 1987 the company bought a controlling interest in Win-Chance Foods of Thailand. Win-Chance produced baby food

and milk products, and, of course, Heinz planned to add ketchup to the line.

LATE-CENTURY RESTRUCTURINGS AMID SLOWER GROWTH

O'Reilly's strategies succeeded in the 1980s. Heinz's sales doubled from $2.9 billion in 1980 to $6.1 billion in 1990, and net profits quadrupled to $504 million during the period. The CEO had hoped to increase Heinz's annual revenues to $10 billion by 1994, then retire at the close of his contract in 1995. Recession and competition from private-label products in the early 1990s, however, thwarted that plan and held the company's sales to $7 billion in 1993 and 1994. As Heinz's growth slowed from its double-digit pace of the previous decade, the company's stock declined as well—30 percent from 1992 to 1994—in spite of continuously rising dividends. As a result, O'Reilly postponed his retirement and embarked on a reorganization.

Divestments (most significantly, of the Hubinger subsidiary) in 1993 totaled $700 million. Internal cost-cutting measures included workforce and management staff reductions as well as achievement of manufacturing efficiencies. In the United States, O'Reilly cut brand advertising by 40 percent from 1990 levels and resorted to discounting to reverse 1991's market share losses to private labels. He shifted the company's domestic sales focus to the high-margin foodservice sector, acquiring J.L. Foods from Borden Inc. in 1994 for $500 million.

Domestic operations were little more than half of Heinz's operations in the 1990s. O'Reilly pinned his expectations for future growth on overseas markets, targeting baby food, in particular, for expansion. Heinz controlled 29 percent of the global infant food market in 1994 and completed the acquisition of Farley's baby food of Great Britain (from the Boots Company PLC) and Glaxo Holdings plc's baby food interests in India that year. Previously unchallenged in international baby food sales, Heinz faced a serious threat from the U.S. leader, Gerber, which was acquired by Swiss pharmaceutical giant Sandoz Ltd. and groomed for international expansion that year as well. Heinz also buttressed its interests in the Asia/Pacific region with the 1992 purchase of New Zealand's Wattie's Limited for $300 million. O'Reilly characterized the new addition as a "mini-Heinz" in a 1994 address to the New York Society of Securities Analysts. Heinz marked its 125th year in business with flat sales that O'Reilly himself characterized as disappointing.

The next two years, however, seemed to indicate that O'Reilly's restructuring efforts were paying off.

Sales surged ahead by more than $1 billion in each of those years, culminating in 1996 revenues of $9.11 billion. Further acquisitions played a role as well. In December 1994 Heinz paid $200 million to Kraft General Foods, Inc., for the All American Gourmet Company, maker of the Budget Gourmet line of frozen meals. Heinz nearly doubled the size of its pet food operation through the March 1995 purchase of the North American pet food businesses of the Quaker Oats Company for $725 million. Thereby added to the company's existing brands, which included 9-Lives and Amore, were Kibbles'n Bits, Cycle, Gravy Train, and Ken-L Ration, among others. In March 1996 Heinz acquired Boulder, Colorado-based Earth's Best, Inc., a maker of organic baby food. In June of that year William R. Johnson was named president and COO, positioning him as the likely successor of O'Reilly. Johnson, who had joined Heinz in 1982, was previously head of the tuna and pet food divisions, where he was noted for slashing costs and squeezing out profits from mature brands.

In March 1997 Heinz launched a major restructuring that involved the closure or sale of 25 plants and a workforce reduction of 2,500, as well as a plan to divest the foodservice operations of the Ore-Ida unit. The latter came to fruition in June 1997 with the sale of these operations to McCain Foods Limited of New Brunswick, Canada, for about $500 million (Heinz retained the Ore-Ida retail business). In connection with the restructuring, Heinz took pretax charges of $647.2 million in fiscal 1997, resulting in a reduction in net income to $301.9 million (compared with $659.3 million for 1996). Heinz also continued to make selective acquisitions, with one of the more important ones being the June 1997 purchase of John West Foods Limited from Unilever. John West was the leading brand of canned tuna and fish in the firm's home country, the United Kingdom. In May 1998 Johnson was named president and CEO of Heinz, with O'Reilly becoming nonexecutive chairman.

FURTHER RESTRUCTURING EFFORTS

Restructuring efforts continued into the early 21st century. In late 1998 the company took a $150 million charge to combine the operations of its Ore-Ida Foods and Weight Watchers Gourmet Foods units into a new unit called Heinz Frozen Food Company. Early the following year, Heinz announced its largest restructuring yet. In the first phase of a projected four-year program, the company planned to close 20 of its remaining 100 factories, reduce the workforce by an additional 4,000, and divest the diet class business of Weight Watchers. A key component of the program was the realigning of the company along global category lines, a major shift from the previous geographic arrangement. The six main categories, generating 80 percent of global revenues, were ketchup, tuna, frozen foods, infant foods, pet foods, and convenience meals. Heinz also planned to concentrate on the six countries that generated 80 percent of the company's revenues: the United States, the United Kingdom, Italy, Canada, Australia, and New Zealand. While the company hoped eventually to reap $200 million in annual savings from these efforts, it also planned to spend an additional $100 million during fiscal 2000 to increase its spending on marketing its flagship brands. Pretax restructuring charges for fiscal 1999 totaled $552.8 million.

In late 1999 Heinz completed the sale of the Weight Watchers diet class unit to Artal Luxembourg, S.A., a European venture capital firm, for about $735 million. Around this same time, with pressure for global consolidation among food companies growing, Heinz entered into merger talks with Bestfoods, maker of soups, sauces, bouillons, dressings, and other products. The talks collapsed, however, and Unilever soon stepped in to acquire Bestfoods. In the wake of this failed merger, Heinz continued its acquisitive ways. The company gained a foothold in the fast-growing natural and organic foods sector through the purchase of a 19.5 percent stake in Hain Food Group Inc. for $100 million. The Hain product line included Health Valley cereal and other products, Terra Chip snacks, and Westsoy soy beverages. Through the alliance with Heinz, Hain also acquired the Earth's Best line of organic baby foods. In May 2000 Hain acquired Celestial Seasonings, best known for its herbal teas, in a stock swap, leading Heinz to invest an additional $80 million in Hain to keep its stake at 19.5 percent. Other developments included the acquisition of the frozen foods business of U.K.-based United Biscuits PLC for $317 million. Sales for the unit in 1998 were $360 million, with the product line including frozen desserts, pizzas, potato products, and vegetarian/meat-free items.

In February 2000 Heinz announced that it had signed an agreement to acquire Milnot Holding Corporation, maker of the Beech-Nut brand of baby food, for $185 million. Beech-Nut was the number two baby food brand in the United States, with 13 percent of the market, while Heinz was number three with 11 percent. The commanding leader was Gerber, with 73 percent. Despite what Heinz officials called Gerber's virtual monopoly position, the Federal Trade Commission moved to block the deal in July 2000 under antitrust laws. Later in the year, a federal court refused the stop the acquisition, but in April 2001 Heinz abandoned its bid when an appeals court reversed the lower court's ruling.

During this same period, Heinz was stepping up its efforts to develop successful new products. In June 2000 Heinz began selling StarKist tuna in vacuum-sealed pouches, claiming that the tuna was fresher-tasting and firmer than the traditional canned variety. The company later in the year introduced a green version of its flagship Heinz ketchup. Identical to its traditional ketchup except for the addition of green food dyes, the product was aimed squarely at youngsters not only because of its color but also because it was packaged in what the company called an "EZ Squirt" bottle that released the ketchup in a thin stream, thus enabling kids to make designs on their hot dogs and hamburgers. With this debut, Heinz ketchup enjoyed its highest increase in sales in the brand's history. This product was the first of a series of colored Heinz ketchups.

The restructuring efforts launched under Johnson's leadership appeared to be paying off for Heinz. Although overall revenues remained flat (the $9.41 billion for 2000 was only marginally larger than the 1996 total of $9.11 billion), profits were growing. For fiscal 2000, a pretax restructuring charge of $392.7 million was more than offset by a pretax gain of $464.6 million on the sale of the Weight Watchers unit, resulting in overall net income for the year of $890.6 million.

In April 2001, the same month it had to abandon its Beech-Nut bid, Heinz was again thwarted when its offer to acquire the pickles business of Vlasic Foods International Inc. was topped by a higher offer from a buyout firm. Heinz did, however, manage to add a number of key brands in 2001 by completing three acquisitions for an aggregate total of $837.3 million. The purchase of Borden Food Corporation's pasta sauce, dry bouillon, and soup businesses brought the Classico pasta sauce and Wyler's bouillon and soup brands into the company fold. Heinz gained a major North American brand of frozen Mexican snacks via the acquisition of Delimex Holdings, Inc. The company also gained the rights to the T.G.I. Friday's and Poppers lines of frozen snacks and appetizers from Anchor Food Products. The latter two additions further bolstered Heinz's position in frozen foods, where it produced Ore-Ida potatoes, Boston Market meals, Bagel Bites snacks, and Smart Ones entrees and desserts. Heinz narrowed this frozen foods portfolio in another 2001 transaction that saw All American Gourmet Company and its Budget Gourmet line of frozen meals sold to Luigino's Inc.

CONCENTRATING ON CORE BRANDS

In a critical deal completed in December 2002, Heinz pared from its portfolio a group of sluggishly growing brands that had generated about 20 percent of its revenues, or $1.8 billion. Packaged in the spinoff were Heinz's North American pet foods business, including the 9-Lives and Kibbles'n Bits brands, StarKist tuna, Nature's Goodness baby food, College Inn broths, and the firm's U.S. private-label soup and gravy products. These assets were spun off into a separate company that then merged with Del Monte Foods Company. In the wake of this deal, Heinz began placing increased emphasis on 15 "power brands," which collectively represented more than 60 percent of the firm's total sales, and were centered around condiments, sauces, and frozen foods. Among these key brands were Heinz, Ore-Ida, Bagel Bites, Boston Market, Smart Ones, and Weight Watchers; Classico, Delimex, and T.G.I. Friday's; the New Zealand brand Wattie's and ABC, a leading sauce brand in Asia; and several European brands, including Honig, Plasmon, and Pudliszki. By devoting more of its resources to its top brands, Heinz hoped to spur revenue growth at a time when established brands were losing market share to private-label products.

The introduction of Heinz ketchup in an "Easy Squeeze" upside-down bottle offering instant pouring with "no mess" pushed the company's share of the U.S. ketchup market to a record 60 percent in fiscal 2004. Heinz's worldwide ketchup market share stood at an impressive 33 percent at this time. In August 2005 the company strengthened its array of sauce brands with the acquisition of HP Foods from France's Groupe Danone for roughly $877 million. In the deal, Heinz gained Lea & Perrins, the market-leading brand of Worcestershire sauce in the United States, Canada, and the United Kingdom, and HP, a leading brand of savory sauce in Canada and the United Kingdom.

In September 2005 Heinz unveiled a plan to unload another slate of noncore businesses, including its vegetable, frozen foods, and seafood businesses in Europe and its poultry arm in New Zealand. The annual sales of these operations totaled $1.4 billion. In the largest single divestment that subsequently occurred, Heinz in March 2006 sold its European seafood business to Lehman Brothers Merchant Banking for EUR 425 million. By fiscal 2008, when revenues surpassed the $10 billion mark for the first time, 96 percent of these sales stemmed from the firm's core product categories: ketchup, condiments, sauces, meals, snacks, and infant nutrition. This compared to the mark of approximately 70 percent that had prevailed prior to the 2002 spinoff of brands to Del Monte. Net income for 2008 totaled $844.9 million, an increase of 7.5 percent over the amount for 2007.

In 2006 Heinz became involved in a lengthy, well-publicized, and acrimonious proxy fight with activist investor Nelson Peltz, who had built up a stake in the company of around 5 percent. Peltz pushed for changes in the company's spending practices and an increase in marketing while also seeking to win five seats on Heinz's board. Eventually, Peltz and partner Michael Weinstein were added to the company board. The battle, perhaps, played a role in Heinz's stepped-up fiscal 2008 marketing efforts, which in part supported the aggressive introduction of more than 200 new products across the firm's core categories. Heinz was also working diligently to expand its existing product lines into such emerging markets as Russia and China, hoping to increase the portion of its sales originating in these locales from 13 percent to 20 percent by 2015. Selected acquisitions were also on the agenda. Heinz in October 2008 announced plans to acquire Golden Circle Limited for $225 million. Golden Circle was an iconic Australian brand of canned fruits, vegetables, and juices. Heinz's top executives were confident that the firm's product innovation, stable of top brands, and focus on productivity provided a platform for future growth despite the difficult economic climate that prevailed at this time.

April Dougal Gasbarre
Updated, David E. Salamie

PRINCIPAL SUBSIDIARIES

Heinz Italia S.p.A. (Italy); Heinz Wattie's Limited (New Zealand); H. J. Heinz B.V. (Netherlands); H. J. Heinz Company Australia Limited; H. J. Heinz Company of Canada Ltd.; H. J. Heinz Company, L.P.; H. J. Heinz Company Limited (U.K.); H. J. Heinz Frozen and Chilled Foods Limited (U.K.); H. J. Heinz Finance Company; Heinz Management L.L.C.; ProMark Brands; Heinz Investments Ltd. (Cyprus); H. J. Heinz Polska S.A. (Poland); Heinz Iberica S.A. (Spain): P.T. Heinz ABC Indonesia; Shanghai Guofu LongFong Co., Ltd. (China).

PRINCIPAL COMPETITORS

ConAgra Foods, Inc.; Nestlé S.A.; Kraft Foods Inc.; Campbell Soup Company; Del Monte Foods Company; Sara Lee Corporation.

FURTHER READING

Adamy, Janet, "Heinz Sets Overhaul Plans in Motion," *Wall Street Journal*, September 20, 2005, p. A6.

Alberts, Robert C., *The Good Provider: H. J. Heinz and His 57 Varieties,* Boston: Houghton Mifflin, 1973, 297 p.

Alexander, Keith L., and Stephen Baker, "The New Life of O'Reilly," *Business Week,* June 13, 1994, pp. 64–66.

Baker, Stephen, "The Odd Couple at Heinz," *Business Week,* November 4, 1996, p. 176.

Berner, Robert, "Ketchuping Up, or a Classic Condiment Returns As Top Dog," *Wall Street Journal,* November 5, 1999, p. A1.

Berner, Robert, and Kevin Helliker, "Heinz's Worry: 4,000 Products, Only One Star Winner," *Wall Street Journal,* September 17, 1999, p. B1.

Boyle, Matthew, "The Ketchup King Prospers," *Business Week,* September 8, 2008, p. 28.

Byrne, John A., "The CEO and the Board," *Business Week,* September 15, 1997, pp. 106+.

Campanella, Frank W., "Tomatoes, and More: H. J. Heinz, with $4 Billion in Yearly Sales, Lifts Profits in Stateside Business," *Barron's,* May 20, 1985, pp. 73+.

Creswell, Julie, "Bottled Up," *Fortune,* September 18, 2000, pp. 194+.

Dahm, Lori, "Innovator of the Year: H. J. Heinz Company," *Stagnito's New Products Magazine,* January 2007, pp. 52–54+.

Dienstag, Eleanor Foa, *In Good Company: 125 Years at the Heinz Table, 1869–1994,* New York: Warner, 1994, 352 p.

Eig, Jonathan, "Heinz's CEO Unveils Plans to Stimulate Growth," *Wall Street Journal,* June 16, 2000, p. B6.

Eig, Jonathan, and Robert Frank, "Heinz Spins Off Sluggish Units," *Wall Street Journal,* June 14, 2002, p. B4.

Fallon, Ivan, *The Luck of O'Reilly: A Biography of Tony O'Reilly,* New York: Warner, 1994, 406 p.

Gray, Steven, "Ketchup Fight: Peltz, Heinz CEO Go at It," *Wall Street Journal,* August 4, 2006, p. C1.

Hannon, Kerry, "The King of Ketchup," *Forbes,* March 21, 1988, pp. 58+.

"Heinz: Lucky or Good?" *Financial World,* February 15, 1981, p. 38.

Jargon, Julie, "Heinz Faces Challenges Keeping Flow," *Wall Street Journal,* August 8, 2007, p. C1.

Machan, Dyan, "Tony Who?" *Forbes,* June 15, 1998, pp. 98–102.

Mallory, Maria, "Heinz's New Recipe: Take a Dollop of Dollars," *Business Week,* September 30, 1991, pp. 86+.

Miles, Gregory L., "Heinz Ain't Broke, but It's Doing a Lot of Fixing," *Business Week,* December 11, 1989, pp. 84+.

Murray, Matt, "Heinz Unwraps Details of Restructuring," *Wall Street Journal,* March 17, 1997, p. A3.

———, "H. J. Heinz Chairman's Growth Prediction Comes True: Acquisitions and Volume Gains Boost Sales 12 Percent, but Weight Watchers Sags," *Wall Street Journal,* April 10, 1996, p. B4.

Murray, Matt, and Rekha Balu, "Corporate Icons Are a Hard Act to Follow, As Successors Discover: Heinz Chief Copes with Style and Expectations Born of a Very Different Era," *Wall Street Journal,* April 29, 1999, pp. A1+.

Saporito, Bill, "Heinz Pushes to Be the Low-Cost Producer," *Fortune,* June 24, 1985, pp. 44+.

Siklos, Richard, "I Want More of Everything," *Business Week,* December 20, 1999, pp. 158–62.

Symonds, William C., Andrew B. Wilson, and Marc Frons, "Tony O'Reilly of Heinz: His Day Has 57 Varieties," *Busi-*ness Week,* December 17, 1984, pp. 72+.

Troxell, Thomas N., Jr., "Spicy Results: Heinz Earnings Are Likely to Set Another All-Time Peak," *Barron's,* July 13, 1981, pp. 37+.

Willoughby, Jack, "Playing Ketchup," *Barron's,* June 28, 2004, pp. 23–25.

Harps Food Stores, Inc.

918 South Gutensohn Road
Springdale, Arkansas 72762-5165
U.S.A.
Telephone: (479) 751-7601
Fax: (479) 751-3625
Web site: http://www.harpsfood.com

Private Company
Founded: 1930 as Harps Cash Grocery
Employees: 3,000
Sales: $914.3 million (2007 est.)
NAICS: 445110 Supermarkets and Other Grocery (Except Convenience) Stores

■ ■ ■

Harps Food Stores, Inc., is a Springdale, Arkansas-based, employee-owned chain of supermarkets, operating under the Harps banner as well as Price Cutter and Food Warehouse. Stores range in size from 13,000 square feet to more than 60,000 square feet. Most of the more than 50 stores are located in Arkansas, but Harps is also represented in Missouri and Oklahoma. Focusing on small-town markets, Harps is one of the few retailers that has been able to survive, and prosper, in the shadow of Wal-Mart superstores, primarily by embracing a commitment to cleanliness, service, and quality, especially in the produce and meat departments. Harps, for example, refuses to add solution to its fresh beef, pork, and chicken, unlike Wal-Mart. Many of its stores offer delis and bakeries to produce fresh-baked goods, custom wedding cakes, Martha Harp fried chicken, en-

trées, and party trays. To help maintain a competitive edge, pharmacies are also included in many of the stores. A handful of Harps stores include gas pumps for further customer convenience. Majority-owned Associated Wholesale Grocers, based in Kansas City, supplies the stores with both brand-name and private-label merchandise. The company has been 100 percent employee-owned since 2001, when the company's employee stock ownership plan (ESOP) bought the remaining shares held by the Harp family. Each year employees receive about one-fifth of their pay in stock in addition to their hourly wages.

DEPRESSION-ERA ROOTS

The lineage of Harps Food Stores dates to 1930 when Harvard and Floy Harp opened a small grocery store called Harps Cash Grocery in Springdale, Arkansas, located on East Emma Avenue and Water Street. Harvard Harp was a native of the town, where his father had been a farmer, but his father died when Harp was just 13. Rather than pursue farming, the young man learned the ways of shopkeeping, in 1924 going to work for City Mercantile, a dry-goods store in Springdale. He left his hometown later in the decade, finding work in the citrus fields of California, where he saved $500. With that money he and his wife returned to Springdale to start their own grocery store.

Although small, and doing business during difficult economic times, Harps Cash Grocery prospered. In 1941 the business moved across the street to a bigger building, but soon outgrew that space as well. Harps Cash Grocery now moved to an even larger site and adopted a name more fitting to the enterprise: Publix Market. The Harps' eldest son, Don, joined his parents in 1953 after completing a stint in the U.S. Air Force. In that same year, the family replaced the Publix Market with the Food Palace, located at the intersection of U.S. highways 412 and 715. Just two years later, in 1955, the Harps relocated once again, this time across the street, opening Harps IGA Foodliner, one of the largest Arkansas supermarkets in its day. (It was affiliated with the Independent Grocers Alliance [IGA], a network of grocery stores that used their collective weight to gain a purchasing edge.) While at the time the Foodliner appeared to be something of a white elephant, given the small size of the Springdale market, in fact it laid the foundation for the Harps chain that was to follow.

SECOND STORE OPENS: 1964

In the early 1960s the younger brothers of Don Harp, Gerald and Reland, both graduates of the University of Arkansas, joined the family business on a full-time basis. They were already familiar with the operation, having worked in the store while growing up. The extra help would be needed in 1964 when the Harp family opened a second store, another IGA unit, located in the Plaza Shopping Center in North Springdale. In 1968 Harvard Harp died in an automobile accident and Don Harp took over as president of the emerging supermarket chain. His brothers would also play important roles, as did their mother, Floy, who remained actively involved, running the health and beauty departments until she retired in 1981. She lived another 13 years, dying in 1994 at the age of 86. Reland Harp in the meantime had died at an early age, passing away in 1986.

Although he never owned more than two stores at any one time, Harvard Harp had possessed an ambitious nature that greatly influenced his sons and the company he left behind. "He was always looking to expand," Gerald Harp told *Arkansas Business* in 1996. "So whenever the opportunity would come up, whenever we'd get a chance to grow, we'd take it." The Harp family expanded its operations to about two dozen stores by the end of the 1980s.

To help the company maintain its edge in a marketplace that now included another Arkansas-based retailer, Wal-Mart, Harps sought to leverage the commitment of its employees. In order to align their goals with the company's, in 1988 an ESOP was implemented. Another way the company tried to remain competitive was by adopting multiple formats. Aside from conventional supermarkets, the company pursued a warehouse store format under the Price Cutter banner; a handful of Harps Express convenience stores; and a limited assortment store, Cash/Mart, which opened in Rogers, Arkansas. Many of the Harps and Price Cutter supermarkets were also upgraded to include bakeries, which focused on scratch baking rather than thaw-and-sell, and did quite well, on average accounting for 3 percent of total store sales in the early 1990s. In addition, Harps owned Discount Distributors, a Springdale-based wholesaler that served as a purchasing distribution point for Harps stores, as well as outside customers, primarily convenience stores. Discount Distributors supplied Harps stores with general merchandise, cigarettes, and health and beauty care items. Food items were supplied by Kansas City-based Associated Wholesale Grocers (AWG), an independent supermarket cooperative.

GERALD HARP TAKES CHARGE: 1994

In 1994 Don Harp left the company to care for his ailing wife. He was replaced as president by his brother Gerald, initially a temporary move but one that became permanent a year later when Don Harp elected to formally retire and sell his interest back to the company. Gerald Harp took over a grocery chain with 24 units, employing 1,700 people and generating $176 million, making it the 16th largest privately held company in Arkansas.

Harps grew even larger. It filled in a gap in northwest Arkansas in February 1994 by acquiring three Phillips Foods Center stores, in Rogers, Bentonville, and Bella Vista, Arkansas. The Phillips stores had a similar history to Harps. The chain was launched in 1946 by Harlan Phillips who in that year opened the Phillips and Sons grocery store in Rogers and later added other units. The company was acquired by a Wal-Mart affiliate, Walton Enterprises, in 1981, and ten years later, following a management and employee buyout, it was purchased by Wal-Mart itself and became a subsidiary, Phillips Cos. In June 1995 Phillips Cos. sold ten Food-4-Less stores to Harps, all of which were converted to the Price Cutter format. As a result, by the summer of 1996, Harps was operating 38 stores, 31 in Arkansas and seven in Oklahoma. Annual sales also increased from $210 million to about $380 million.

KEY DATES

1930: Harvard and Floy Harp open Harps Cash Grocery.
1941: Store moves to larger building.
1964: Second store opens.
1968: Harvard Harp dies.
1988: Employee stock ownership plan is initiated.
1994: Gerald Harp replaces brother Don as president.
2001: Company becomes 100 percent employee-owned.

In the second half of the 1990s, Harps took time to assimilate the stores acquired from Phillips before adding further units. When it did, the chain ventured into Missouri and opened three other stores, bringing the total number of units to 42 as Harps entered the new century. Aside from adding stores, the company also looked to increase sales and margins by emphasizing nonfood items. The stores did particularly well with a DVD-rental program, especially in some of the rural areas where consumers had fewer video rental options. Harps also beefed up its general merchandise sections, adding a number of high-margin items. In addition to kitchen gadgets and office supplies, Harps looked to take advantage of seasonal opportunities, for example, devoting space to sell lawnmowers and outdoor furniture in the spring and holiday gift sets in the fall and winter.

EMPLOYEES BUY COMPANY: 2001

In 2000 Gerald Harp turned over the presidency to Roger Collins, who had been with Harps since 1986 when he joined the company as chief financial officer. A year after Collins took the helm, Harps became 100 percent employee owned when the ESOP bought out Gerald Harp with backing from a group of lenders led by Bank of America. Harp then retired and Collins became chief executive officer as well as chairman of the board. Soon after the employees gained control, an arrangement was also put into effect with AWG to form a new legal entity to serve as a wholesaler to Harps and other independent grocers. Harps would become the majority shareholder of the reconstituted AWG, while the original AWG assumed a minority position. By joining forces, Harps and AWG hoped to improve their ability to compete against Wal-Mart, which controlled about 60 percent of the Arkansas grocery market, compared to Harps' less than 6 percent.

Just as Harps' management had hoped, the employee commitment to the business helped the chain to hold its own against Wal-Mart and other competitors. In just two years the company was able to pay back the $20 million in debt taken on to buy out Gerald Harp. Moreover, the focus on quality and service was so successful that in 2003, for the first time in 11 years, no Wal-Mart Supercenter or Wal-Mart Neighborhood Market format opened in Harps' markets.

Harps continued to add new stores in the early 2000s, albeit at a measured pace. The 48th unit came as the result of an acquisition in 2005, when Harps bought the Town & Country Supermarket in Vilonia, Arkansas, a supermarket that opened in 1992. Later in the year Harps reached the 50-unit mark when it opened a new store in its hometown of Springdale. The following year Harps plied the acquisition route again, purchasing the last Dillon's grocery store in Arkansas, located in Prairie Grove. Unlike Dillon's and the other ill-fated supermarket chains that once dotted the Arkansas landscape, Harps continued to thrive despite the long shadow cast by Wal-Mart. In fact, the company had never been healthier, as evidenced by the value of its stock, which quadrupled in just a matter of years.

While employee commitment and a focus on quality and service was clearly a winning formula, Harps also took steps to be competitive in price. To help offset the purchasing power advantage of Wal-Mart, Harps hoped to gain an edge through technology. In the fall of 2006 the company unveiled a new computerized supply chain system that simplified its warehouse, inventory control, accounting, and general ledger operations. An auto replenishment system was added as well. The savings Harps enjoyed from the new system was then passed onto customers in the form of lower prices, thus helping the chain to maintain its competitive balance with Wal-Mart and other supermarket chains encroaching on its market.

NEW LOYALTY PROGRAM: 2007

Harps sought to better serve its customers in other ways as well. In 2007 it introduced a new loyalty program with S&H Greenpoints, an updated version of the old stamp books, which allowed customers to electronically accumulate points on their Harps discount card that could be redeemed for merchandise. Harps also rewarded loyal customers for buying certain items with discounts on gasoline provided by the new gas station format the company was rolling out. Because of the rising price of gasoline, it became a very popular program.

By 2008 Harps was doing an estimated $900 million in annual sales. By the end of the year another full-service supermarket was slated to open in the Pinnacle Hills shopping district of Rogers, Arkansas, including one of the new fuel stations. There was every reason to believe that more stores were to follow as Harps proved itself a strong competitor, so well entrenched in its market that it could prosper despite the challenge of giant Arkansas neighbor Wal-Mart.

Ed Dinger

PRINCIPAL SUBSIDIARIES

Associated Wholesale Grocers; Discount Distributors.

PRINCIPAL COMPETITORS

Affiliated Foods Southwest; The Kroger Co.; Wal-Mart Stores, Inc.

FURTHER READING

Bowden, Bill, "Harps ESOP Pays Off $20m in Debt," *Arkansas Business,* October 13, 2003, p. 13.

Brotherton, Velda, *Springdale: The Courage of Shiloh,* Charleston, S.C.: Arcadia Publishing, 2002, 160 p.

Elson, Joel, "Harps Plays Up High-Ticket Items to Sweeten Margins," *Supermarket News,* February 21, 2000, p. 73.

Greene, M. V., "Re-Tuning Harps," *Stores,* May 2008, p. 83.

Krumei, Doug, "Dressing Up a Sleeping Beauty," *Bakery Production and Marketing,* October 24, 1993, p. 36.

Kuykendall, Kristal L., "At 70, Harps Goes Head to Head with Competition," *Arkansas Democrat-Gazette,* January 30, 2000, p. BM 10.

Terry, Drew, "Harps Food Stores Celebrating 75 Years of Business," *Northwest Arkansas Times,* November 13, 2005.

Tobler, Christopher, "Harps Food's Presence Grows in Northwest," *Arkansas Business,* July 11, 1994, p. 27.

Treadway, Tyler, "From Modest Start, Harps Develops 38-Store Chain," *Arkansas Business,* July 8, 1996, p. 22.

Zwiebach, Elliot, "Harps Opting for Employee Ownership," *Supermarket News,* May 28, 2001, p. 4.

Hemisphere GPS Inc.

4110 9th Street Southeast
Calgary, Alberta T2G 3C4
Canada
Telephone: (403) 259-3311
Fax: (403) 259-8866
Web site: http://www.hemispheregps.com

Public Company
Incorporated: 1990 as Canadian Systems International Inc.
Employees: 252
Sales: CAD 58.09 million (2007)
Stock Exchanges: Toronto
Ticker Symbol: HEM
NAICS: 334220 Radio and Television Broadcasting and Wireless Communications Equipment Manufacturing; 334290 Other Communications Equipment Manufacturing

∎ ∎ ∎

Hemisphere GPS Inc. develops and manufactures advanced Global Positioning System (GPS) devices. The company is best known for its GPS products that aid in the guidance of agricultural vehicles, marketing devices that enable farmers to reduce human driving errors. The company also makes aerial guidance systems using GPS technology tailored for applications such as pest control, row crop spraying, and fighting forest fires. Through its precision products group, Hemisphere GPS develops GPS products for use in marine, mapping and surveying, and geographic information systems applications.

The company operates through facilities located in Australia, Canada, and the United States, marketing its products primarily in Europe and North America. Hemisphere GPS ranks as the world's largest supplier of aftermarket GPS products for the agricultural industry.

A COMMERCIAL MARKET FOR GPS

The market leadership enjoyed by Hemisphere GPS in the 21st century reflected its mastery of the technology underpinning NAVSTAR-GPS, the official name of the global navigation satellite system developed by the U.S. Department of Defense (DOD). The system did not become fully operational until 1995, but the commercial market for GPS products began taking shape a decade earlier. Initially a military research project, GPS was intended to be used exclusively by the federal government until Soviet jets shot down Korean Air Lines Flight 007 in 1983. The air disaster prompted President Ronald Reagan to issue a directive guaranteeing GPS microwave signals would be available for civilian use at no charge once the system became operational. The commercial sector needed no further inducement. Companies began developing GPS products for consumers shortly after the announcement. In 1990 Hemisphere GPS joined the pack, beginning its development into one of the world's premier GPS concerns.

Hemisphere GPS changed its corporate title on several occasions during its first 20 years in business. The company was incorporated in July 1990 as Canadian Systems International Inc., basing its opera-

COMPANY PERSPECTIVES

We believe that quality is about meeting and exceeding customer expectations. At Hemisphere GPS, we view quality as an integral part of business management. The quality of products and customer experiences depends on the quality of processes, which in turn is tied to the quality of management and continual improvement. Hemisphere GPS is fully committed to complying with product, industry, and customer requirements and to continually improving the effectiveness of the Quality Management System to ensure that all our customers are satisfied.

tions in Calgary, Alberta. From the start, the company was focused on developing Differential GPS (DGPS) products, designed to improve the positional accuracy of GPS devices. Although GPS represented a remarkable leap in technology, the system was not without faults. The system, which used microwave signals and a complex algorithm to determine geographic position, suffered from ionospheric errors, timing errors, and satellite orbit errors. The system also was intentionally flawed by order of the DOD. To maintain a strategic advantage, the DOD created two types of service, Precise Positioning Service (PPS), a service reserved for DOD personnel, and Standard Positioning Service (SPS), a less accurate service available to all users. The DOD artificially degraded the performance of SPS, adulterating it with what it called Selective Availability, thereby limiting its positioning accuracy to 100 meters with 95 percent confidence.

Canadian Systems International, through DGPS, sought to improve the accuracy of SPS by removing the effects of errors, both inherent and manmade errors. DGPS entailed using a reference GPS receiver at a point of known coordinates. The receiver calculated distance measurements to each of the GPS satellites, arriving at information that included any errors in the system. Next, the reference receiver, using its known coordinates, calculated what the true distance should have been, enabling it to determine the difference between the known and measured range, yielding an amount (the error range) that could be removed to correct for errors present in the system.

FIRST DGPS PRODUCT IN 1993

There were a variety of sources of differential corrections, including ground-based sources and space-based

sources. Initially, Canadian Systems used a network of radio beacons that constantly broadcasted DGPS corrections to receivers. In 1993, one year after the company changed its name to Communication Systems International Inc., it released its first DGPS product, MBX-1, a DGPS radio-beacon module that plugged into a GPS system to enhance its accuracy.

Communication Systems, which had licensed the beacon receiver technology in its first DGPS products, acquired the technology in 1996. The following year, the company completed its initial public offering (IPO) of stock, raising CAD 6 million in its debut on the Toronto Stock Exchange. After its IPO, the company was able to entertain the idea of adding to its capabilities and its product lines by acquiring other companies. Acquisitions played a defining role in the company's development from 1999 forward, guiding it into new markets and necessitating further alterations of its corporate title as its corporate profile changed.

ACQUISITION OF SATLOC IN 1999

Arguably the company's most important acquisition was its first major purchase, the April 1999 transaction that gave it ownership of Satloc, Inc. The acquisition established Communication Systems in the United States for the first time, giving it facilities in Satloc's hometown of Scottsdale, Arizona, and it provided entry into the company's single most important market, the agricultural market. Satloc, founded in 1992, made aerial- and ground-based precision guidance systems for agricultural applications. Using DGPS technology, Satloc's systems provided aerial swath guidance and precise guidance for tractors and sprayers used in farming applications.

DIVERSIFICATION INTO WIRELESS PRODUCTS IN 2000

Communication Systems' next acquisition prompted a name change to CSI Wireless Inc. In June 2000, the company added to its presence in the United States with the purchase of Wireless Link, a Silicon Valley, California-based company that made products associated with location-based wireless data communications applications. Wireless Link's products included wireless modems and asset-tracking products that could be integrated with GPS technology, giving the newly renamed CSI Wireless the ability to graft its technology onto products that competed in a variety of new markets.

CSI Wireless introduced a new product line in 2000, unveiling its Outback system, which became one

KEY DATES

1990: Hemisphere GPS is incorporated as Canadian Systems International Inc.

1993: The company introduces its first DGPS product, MBX-1.

1997: The company completes its initial public offering of stock.

1999: Satloc, Inc., is purchased, providing entry into the agricultural market and establishing its presence in the United States.

2000: After acquiring Wireless Link, the company changes its name to CSI Wireless Inc.

2005: CSI Wireless acquires RHS Inc., merges it with Satloc, and forms a division named Hemisphere GPS.

2006: CSI Wireless sells its wireless businesses.

2007: CSI Wireless changes its name to Hemisphere GPS Inc.

of the company's principal revenue generators. Developed by Satloc, the Outback S was a precision guidance system for agribusinesses that could be installed on virtually any tractor or sprayer in less than 15 minutes. The Outback S employed DGPS, enabling operators to save time and money when applying chemicals to their crops. Skipped rows and the overlapping of rows, which wasted time and money, were eliminated with the precise, automated control of an Outback S-equipped sprayer. For the marketing and distribution of Outback S and the later versions to follow, CSI Wireless turned to RHS, Inc., a Kansas-based company that became the exclusive source for purchasing what the American Society of Agricultural Engineers hailed as an outstanding innovation.

CSI Wireless entered the 21st century operating through two business units. The company's wireless business manufactured wireless products for mobile and fixed applications in commercial and consumer markets, scoring its greatest commercial success with its Asset-Link family of products that allowed companies to track the location of their vehicles. On the GPS side, CSI Wireless could point to several promising product lines despite a significant change in the DOD's policy regarding GPS. In mid-2000, the DOD reduced Selective Availability to zero, ending its practice of intentionally degrading the performance of GPS. The elimination of Selective Availability removed one of DGPS's main selling points, but the technology still offered greater ac-

curacy than conventional GPS by removing inherent errors. Consequently, CSI Wireless enjoyed rising sales from its agricultural products featuring DGPS and, beginning in 2002, from its Vector line of DGPS products developed for marine applications.

A NEW STRATEGY IN 2005

During CSI Wireless's second decade of business, management decided to focus the company's efforts in one area, a change in strategy that necessitated a complete reorganization of operations in Calgary and the United States. The profound changes began in 2005, when CSI Wireless acquired RHS's marketing and distribution assets associated with the Outback line. The acquisition led CSI Wireless's chief executive officer, Stephen Verhoeff, to combine RHS's assets with Satloc's operations, which created a new division named Hemisphere GPS. Hemisphere GPS became responsible for marketing CSI Wireless's Satloc and Outback products, as well as all the company's other GPS products. "Combined," Verhoeff said in a March 21, 2005, interview with *TelecomWeb News Digest*, "we become the industry leader in agricultural GPS products with strong research-and-development capabilities, marketing and sales strength, and distribution channel expertise. This is a rapidly growing market and we now hold the market leader position."

WIRELESS BUSINESSES SOLD IN 2006

CSI Wireless entered 2006 ranking as the world's largest supplier of aftermarket GPS products for the agricultural industry. The diversification into wireless products had proved useful, helping the company post record profits of $4.3 million in 2004, but the company determined its best chance for success was in its original line of business, GPS technology. "Our products are sold throughout the world and we have a very large percentage of the agricultural guidance and navigation markets," Verhoeff explained in a March 2006 interview with *GeoConnexion*. "Our challenge is in having our Hemisphere GPS brand become more widely known." Within months, Verhoeff sold the assets related to the company's wireless products business, executing CSI Wireless's transition into a purely GPS-focused company.

As CSI Wireless shed its wireless business, the company strengthened its GPS business. In 2006 the company purchased Texas-based Del Norte Technology, Inc., for roughly $1 million. Del Norte was combined with Satloc's aerial guidance unit to create the air products group, a unit of Hemisphere GPS that concentrated on developing GPS products for aerial guidance primarily for agricultural applications.

In the midst of CSI Wireless's transition into a purely GPS company, the company also underwent a change in leadership. In September 2006, Steven Koles was appointed president and chief executive officer. Formerly vice-president of AOL Canada Inc., Koles took the helm at the company's Calgary offices with the intention of completing the transition initiated by his predecessor.

CSI WIRELESS BECOMES HEMISPHERE GPS IN 2007

At the start of 2007, CSI Wireless announced the final step of its transformation into a GPS-only company, changing its name to Hemisphere GPS Inc. In a January 19, 2007, company press release, Koles explained the reasoning behind the third name change in the company's history. "We sold our wireless businesses last year," he said, "and this year as part of the refocusing on our GPS business, we are initiating a corporate re-branding strategy to leverage the leadership that our Hemisphere GPS brand enjoys in the market."

With a new name and a sharpened strategic focus, Hemisphere GPS held sway as the preeminent GPS company serving the agricultural industry. The company's agriculture products group, devoted to the ground-based use of GPS, was built around the successful Outback line of products, which included the Outback S3, the Outback S2, and the Outback eDriveTC models. According to the company's calculations, the use of an Outback guidance system on 3,000 acres of corn could save a farmer more than $19,000 a year by reducing human driving errors. Hemisphere GPS's air products group, which focused on the aerial applications of GPS in the agricultural industry, also enjoyed a dominant market position. Following the acquisition of Del Norte and its merger with Satloc, the operating unit controlled roughly 75 percent of the world's market for GPS aerial guidance for the agricultural industry. Hemisphere GPS's third operating unit, its precision products group, developed GPS devices for other applications, including marine, geographic information systems, and mapping and surveying.

BEELINE ACQUISITION

As Hemisphere GPS neared its 20th anniversary and prepared for the future, it added to its capabilities with one of the largest acquisitions in its history. In December 2007, the company paid $21 million in cash and stock for Beeline Technologies Pty. Ltd. Based in Brisbane, Australia, Beeline developed software for GPS precision guidance systems. The acquisition was intended to accelerate the evolution of Hemisphere GPS's guidance products from hydraulic-based steering to electronic vehicle control, the next technological leap the company intended to complete in the coming years.

Jeffrey L. Covell

PRINCIPAL SUBSIDIARIES

CSI Wireless Corporation; Hemisphere GPS LLC; CSI Wireless LLC; BEELINE Technologies, Inc.

PRINCIPAL OPERATING UNITS

Agriculture Products Group; Air Products Group; Precision Products Group.

PRINCIPAL COMPETITORS

Motorola, Inc.; NovAtel Inc.; Trimble Navigation Limited.

FURTHER READING

"CSI Wireless: Discussion with Stephen Verhoeff," *GeoConnexion,* March 2006, p. 38.

"CSI Wireless to Acquire RHS's Outback GPS Assets," *Wireless News,* April 10, 2005.

"CSI Wireless Transforms Completely to Hemisphere GPS," *GPS World,* June 2007, p. 18.

"CSI Wireless Unveils Revolutionary Product of Worldwide Mainstream Precision Agriculture," *Canadian Corporate News,* December 21, 2000.

"CSI's Hemisphere GPS Completes Del Norte Acquisition," *CNW Group,* January 19, 2006.

"Hemisphere GPS Completes Acquisition of Beeline," *CNW Group,* December 24, 2007.

IDT Corporation

520 Broad Street
Newark, New Jersey 07102
U.S.A.
Telephone: (973) 438-1000
Toll Free: (800) 225-5438
Fax: (973) 482-3971
Web site: http://www.idt.net

Public Company
Incorporated: 1990 as International Discount Telecommunications Corporation
Employees: 2,360
Sales: $2.01 billion (2007)
Stock Exchanges: New York
Ticker Symbol: IDT
NAICS: 513310 Wired Telecommunications Carriers; 513330 Telecommunications Resellers; 514191 On-Line Information Services

∎ ∎ ∎

IDT Corporation is a leading provider of telecommunications services. Its telecommunications activities include wholesale carrier services, prepaid calling cards, and consumer local, long distance, and wireless phone services. Under the brand name Net2Phone, the company provides voice over Internet protocol (VOIP) communications services. Telecommunications accounts for nearly 90 percent of the company's annual revenue. The balance is generated by diversified holdings such as IDT Energy, which sells electricity and natural gas in New York, and IDT Capital, which includes receivables

portfolio management collection, brochure distribution, and web sites that distribute content for mobile devices.

INTERNATIONAL TELEPHONE CALLBACK SERVICE: 1990–93

A native of New York City's borough of the Bronx, Howard Jonas graduated from Harvard University in 1978. During the next decade he built a small brochure distributing and publishing business into an enterprise with revenue exceeding $1 million a year, running it from a converted Bronx funeral home that he shared with his father's insurance brokerage. Shocked by the massive phone bills incurred by staffers who opened a company sales office in Israel, Jonas began thinking of ways to cut this cost of business. After a few months, and with the help of a computer engineer, he had, at an expense of $1,200, a working automatic-dialing device.

In 1990 Jonas entered the telecommunications industry with International Discount Telecommunications (IDT) Corporation, which introduced international call reorganization service. This service capitalized on the often prohibitive rates charged for long distance telephone calls in certain highly regulated international markets. Subscribers calling a designated number from a foreign carrier's standard international calling service contacted an IDT node in Hackensack, New Jersey, transmitting a dial tone and hanging up after the first ring. The node was equipped with custom designed call processors programmed to recognize such a call, routing it into the U.S. public switched telephone network and thereby enabling the client to place the call through the usually lower cost international calling service of the U.S. carrier chosen for this purpose.

COMPANY PERSPECTIVES

IDT's companies help people around the world communicate in new and better ways. We began by delivering reliable, low-cost long distance service to overseas customers. This strategy of seeking out opportunities and developing products and services to leverage them has led us to the creation of other successful telecommunications companies—and way beyond.

INTERNET AND OTHER SERVICES: 1993–98

IDT used the expertise derived from, and the calling volume generated by, its call reorigination business to enter the domestic long distance business in late 1993 by reselling the long distance services of other carriers to its domestic customers. As a value-added service for these customers, the company began offering Internet access in early 1994. IDT also introduced an international fax service, offering a new, brand name machine to any customer who would commit to sending $500 worth of such calls over the next two years and promising free e-mail and Internet access as well. Some 7,000 small businesses had signed up by midyear. The company also got a boost when the Federal Communications Commission denied AT&T Corp.'s 1992 petition to ban callback services.

In May 1994 IDT, in collaboration with the London-based Index on Censorship and other human rights groups, began publishing articles by political dissidents on the Internet. Its "Digital Freedom Network" web site offered a variety of material banned by various governments. The company's free access policy extended to pornography, which raised some eyebrows, since Jonas was an Orthodox Jew and father of six. While other Internet providers were shutting down access to some sites, radio host Barry Farber, as part of a $10 million per year ad campaign, was promoting IDT's $15.95 per month ($29.95 with images as well as text), no-time-limit service with the words, "I access *all* Internet services. I said *all* Internet services—get that naughty smirk off your face." By early 1996 IDT, seeking to survive the inevitable shakeout among the 1,350 or so U.S. Internet access providers, had 65,000 subscribers.

IDT had revenue of $3.17 million in fiscal 1994 (the year ended July 31, 1994), about half from domestic long distance service. The company lost $289,000 but had no long term debt. Revenue more than tripled in fiscal 1995, to $10.8 million, but rising expenses resulted in a loss of $2.15 million. Shortly after reincorporating as IDT Corporation, the company went public in February 1996, taking in $42.78 million by selling about 20 percent of its common stock at $10 a share. Jonas retained a 54 percent stake in the company. Revenue shot up fivefold in fiscal 1996, reaching $57.69 million, of which Internet, rather than telephone, service accounted for about 40 percent. IDT's costs rose even more rapidly, however, resulting in a net loss of $15.76 million for the fiscal year.

Under strain from its rapid expansion, IDT found itself flooded with mounting complaints from customers concerning technical problems, overbilling, and false or misleading advertising claims. At least some of the

For calls to the United States from such countries as Brazil, Italy, Spain, and the Soviet Union, the customer typically saved half the cost, sometimes more, by having these calls reoriginated in the United States. IDT billed its customers at rates high enough to cover its operational costs and make a profit. (Before long, however, the company began leasing its processors so that clients could avoid this markup.) Because touch tone phones were not readily available abroad, subscribers had to use handheld dialers to generate the dual tone multifrequency tones needed to enter access codes and telephone numbers into IDT's call processors. As part of the $250 per month service, IDT gave such callers a small electronic box with an automatic dialer and a device to coordinate conference calls. Each box could handle about 100 calls.

The company's first customer was NBC, which needed to be in frequent contact with a three-man team in Barcelona, Spain, preparing for the 1992 Summer Olympic Games. By the end of 1991 the company had 150 customers, some of them *Fortune* 500 firms, such as PepsiCo, Inc. Few, if any, were foreign enterprises, because they were fearful of angering their national telephone companies, most of them government-owned monopolies. France Telecom threatened legal action, for example, before reducing its own rates so much that Jonas pulled IDT out of the country.

In 1992 IDT relocated its headquarters in the windowless, two-story, cement block Hackensack building where it had placed the call receptors. Jonas sold 14 percent of IDT that year to an investor group for $1.4 million and bought new equipment, also hiring several Bell Laboratories engineers to improve the technology. By the spring of 1993 Jonas claimed that his company was taking in $400,000 a month in revenue from more than 1,000 customers in about 60 countries.

technical problems stemmed from IDT having become a national Internet provider without establishing a national infrastructure, instead contracting with more than 200 smaller service providers and thereby running the risk of incompatibility between carriers. In early 1997 IDT agreed to offer refunds to unhappy customers and to refrain from misleading and false statements in its advertising. (The company had, for example, neglected to inform Internet subscribers that they had to sign on for long distance telephone as well as Internet service to qualify for the $15.95 rate.)

IDT also agreed to pay $100,000 to settle claims that it was using unlicensed software. At this point the company had 150,000 Internet subscribers but was losing money on the service because of the growing cost of seeking new customers. It began de-emphasizing its Internet access service, and its revenue from this segment of its business peaked at $32.9 million in fiscal 1997.

IDT was offering Internet access to some 10,000 corporate clients in 80 countries in late 1995, when it announced that international computer users could soon use its links to make telephone calls to the United States or Great Britain over the Internet for the price of local calls.

In August 1996 the company introduced PC2Phone, which it called the first commercial telephone service to connect calls between personal computers and telephones over the Internet. There were about 350,000 customers for that service in late 1997, when IDT introduced Net2Phone Direct, which enabled users to make both international and domestic calls over the Internet using standard telephones. The company began marketing prepaid calling cards in January 1997.

IDT's revenues doubled in fiscal 1997, to $135.19 million, and its loss decreased to $3.84 million. Revenue soared to $335.38 million in fiscal 1998, during which the company lost $6.4 million. At the end of that fiscal year IDT was selling prepaid debit and rechargeable calling cards providing access to more than 230 countries and territories. The cards were being marketed to retail outlets throughout the United States through Union Telecard Alliance, LLC, a joint venture company in which IDT owned 51 percent of the equity. Customers were primarily members of ethnic communities in the United States who made calls to specific countries where IDT had favorable agreements. The cards also were being marketed to similar customers in Great Britain, France, and the Netherlands.

IDT sold another 4.6 million shares of stock to the public in January 1998 at $24.88 a share. It spun off Net2Phone as a separate business in August 1999, completing an initial public offering (IPO) of the stock that yielded $85.3 million in net proceeds to the parent company, which retained 56 percent of the shares. In March 2000 Net2Phone Inc. had a market value of $2.6 billion, about twice that of IDT itself. That month Liberty Media Group purchased almost 10 percent of IDT's common stock for about $130 million, or $34.50 a share.

IDT IN 1999

IDT earned its first profit in fiscal 1999, when it had net income of $2.92 million on revenue of $732.18 million, more than double the previous year's sum. Of this total, telecommunications accounted for 94 percent, Net2Phone, 4 percent, and Internet service, 2 percent. International sales accounted for 13 percent of revenue (compared with a high of 25 percent in fiscal 1997). The company had long-term debt of $112.97 million at the end of the fiscal year. Jonas held 32.2 percent of the stock in December 1999. IDT had offices in London, Paris, Mexico City, and Rotterdam, Netherlands. Its headquarters remained in Hackensack.

IDT was delivering its telecommunications service over a network of 70 switches in the United States and

Europe, and it owned and leased capacity on 16 undersea fiber optic cables. It was obtaining additional transmission capacity from other carriers. The company also was operating a domestic Internet dial up network consisting of multiple leased lines.

By acting as a "carrier's carrier," IDT was providing wholesale carrier service to about 125 domestic and international customers. Wholesale carrier sales represented 39.5 percent of the company's total consolidated revenues in fiscal 1999. Sales of prepaid calling cards, some 50 million in the fiscal year, generated even more money, amounting to 49.7 percent of total consolidated revenues. IDT's rechargeable cards, distributed primarily through in-flight magazines, allowed users to place calls from 43 countries through international toll free services.

IDT was also still offering international retail services to clients outside the United States, mainly through call reorigination. In 1999 it launched Debital-K, its first prepaid callback phone card. The company had more than 50,000 call reorganization customers in 170 countries during the fiscal year. Certain long distance services were being marketed directly to retail customers in the United States as a value added bundled service with dial-up Internet access for $15.95 a month plus a minimum of long distance billings of $40 a month. In 1999 IDT offered a plan with five-cent-a-minute calls for a $3.95 monthly fee that it believed made it the lowest cost long distance domestic provider in the United States.

IDT had three primary Internet access and online services: dial up access for individuals and businesses, direct connect dedicated Internet services for corporate customers, and Genie online entertainment and information services. A basic dial up Internet service was being offered for $19.95 a month and a premium service for $29.95 a month, both fully graphical accounts that included e-mail. An e-mail account only was available at $7.95 a month. Bundled customers who maintained monthly telephone billings of at least $150 a month could get basic Internet access for free. Internet customers also could receive e-mail by telephone, using text-to-speech technology. There were about 65,000 dial up retail customers and nearly 500 large and medium businesses using IDT Internet access.

IDT IN THE 21ST CENTURY

IDT's second decade of business, a period of profound change, showed the resilience of the Jonas-led organization and its founder's willingness to diversify into far-flung fields. For many of the company's competitors, these years represented a period of distress. The telecommunications industry's market value dropped by a staggering $1 trillion between 2000 and 2002 and seven of IDT's nine closest competitors filed for bankruptcy, contributing to $33 billion of debt left behind by bankrupt telecommunications firms in 2001. Jonas, in contrast, had $1 billion in cash, a sum obtained from the sale of Net2Phone stock to AT&T in 2000, and only $54 million of debt. He occupied an enviable position, surveying an industry strewn with heavily discounted assets he likened to "a battlefield full of smoldering tanks and downed airplanes," in an April 15, 2002, interview with *Forbes*. Jonas eyed his targets and pounced, using his vast financial resources to buy telecommunications assets and to diversify.

ACQUISITIONS AND DIVERSIFICATION

As Jonas executed his plan of attack, he relied on the aid of a trusted colleague. James A. Courter, an IDT director since 1996 and a former New Jersey congressman, was named chief executive officer in 2001. Jonas continued to serve as chairman. Together, the two executives pressed ahead, completing a number of deals that gave IDT assets for a pittance of their original cost. The company acquired its closest phone card competitor, PT-1, in February 2001 for $26.3 million. In 1998 PT-1 was trying to sell itself for roughly $420 million. The year also included the purchase of Winstar Communications, a bankrupt telecommunications company with a broadband wireless network that cost $5 billion to build. When Jonas acquired the company in December 2001 for $42.5 million, he hailed the purchase as representing "one of the greatest days in telecommunications history," according to the January 2, 2002, issue of the *Daily Deal*. Jonas also failed to complete some deals—a $5 billion bid for the long distance and local telephone operations of beleaguered WorldCom being the largest—but his successes added depth and breadth to IDT, particularly his deals outside the telecommunications industry.

IDT made several forays into new business areas during its second decade of business. Some of the diversifying moves remained part of the company at the end of the decade, while other ventures were divested. In 2003 IDT jumped into the entertainment business, acquiring computer graphics animator Mainframe Entertainment, the producer of the *Simpsons* television program, Film Roman Inc., and Anchor Bay Entertainment, a home video distributor. The purchases, along with investments in Vanguard Animations, Archie Comics Entertainment, and POW! Entertainment, composed IDT Entertainment, a business sold to Liberty Media Corporation in 2006. A more lasting business was launched in November 2004, when IDT entered the retail energy business. Through IDT Energy, the company sold natural gas and electricity to residential and business customers in New York.

Despite diversifying, IDT relied on its telecommunications business for the majority of its revenue. The company operated a business responsible for developing, incubating, and operating its newer assets, IDT Capital, which generated less than 5 percent of its total revenues. IDT Energy accounted for less than 10 percent of IDT's total revenues. The company also owned a brochure distribution business, Washington, D.C.-based radio station, WMET-AM, and a grocery distribution business, among other holdings, but it generated 86 percent of its revenue from IDT Telecom, its mainstay telecommunications business. Jonas focused his energies on the company's primary business in the wake of his diversification, courting a company that had once been part of his conglomeration of businesses.

NET2PHONE ACQUIRED IN 2006

In November 2005, Jonas announced he intended to regain control of Net2Phone. He wanted to gain control of the 58.9 percent of the VOIP company IDT did not already own. By March 2006, he gained control of 46.6 million shares of Net2Phone stock, paying $97.1 million for the company that had begun as a division of IDT.

IDT recorded uneven financial results as it acquired and shed businesses. Between 2003 and 2007, revenues fluctuated between $1.8 billion and $2.2 billion, falling to $2 billion in 2007. The period included consecutive annual losses as well. For four straight years, the company posted losses, including a substantial $178 million loss in 2006. In 2007 the worrisome pattern ended when IDT posted a $58 million profit, sparking hope that the years ahead would bring improved financial performance. Much of the company's future success depended on its mainstay telecommunications business, the business that served as IDT's foundation from the start and remained the primary engine driving its growth as it prepared for the future.

Robert Halasz
Updated, Jeffrey L. Covell

PRINCIPAL SUBSIDIARIES

225 Old NB Road Inc.; 226 Old NB Road, Corp.; Advanced Data Services, Inc.; Beltway Acquisition Corporation; CTM Brochure Display, Inc.; Dopchip Corp.; Entrix Telecom, Inc.; IDT America, Corp.; IDT Capital, Inc.; IDT Carmel Holdings, Inc.; IDT Carmel, Inc.; IDT Contact Services, Inc.; IDT Domestic Telecom, Inc.; IDT Energy, Inc.; IDT ESL. Inc.; IDT International, Corp.; IDT Internet Mobile Group, Inc.; IDT Investments Inc.; IDT Local Media, Inc.; IDT Nevada Holdings, Inc.; IDT Spectrum, Inc.; IDT Stored Value Services, Inc.; IDT Telecom, Inc.; IDT Venture Capital Corporation; IDT Venture Capital, Inc.; IDT Venture Holdings, Inc.; IDT Wireless, Inc.; Net2Phone, Inc.; Outside Counsel Solutions, Inc.; Powerlegal Support, Inc.; DirectTel Dutch Holdings B.V. (Netherlands); DYP C. V. (Netherlands); IDT Brazil Limitada; IDT Brazil Telecom Limitada; IDT Chile S. A.; IDT Corporation de Argentina S.A.; IDT Europe B.V. B.A. (Belgium); IDT France SARL (France); IDT Global Israel Ltd.; IDT Global Limited (U.K.); IDT Telecom Asia Pacific Limited; IDT Peru S.R.L.; IDT Puerto Rico & Co.; Phonecards Dominicana C por A (Dominican Republic); SPD Dutch Holdings B.V. (Netherlands); SPD Puerto Rico Corp.; TLL Dutch Holdings B.V. (Netherlands); TimeTel Dutch Holdings B.V. (Netherlands); Zedge Nordic NUF Limited (Norway).

PRINCIPAL COMPETITORS

AT&T Inc.; Verizon Communications Inc.; Movida Communications; Consolidated Edison, Inc.

FURTHER READING

Berreby, David, "Absolute Internet," *New York*, May 22, 1995, pp. 30, 35.

Cohen, David S., "Telecom Titan Takes Over Toons," *Variety*, August 9, 2004, p. A6.

Coughlin, Kevin, "Internet Firm Dials Up Refunds and Layoffs," *Newark Star-Ledger*, February 13, 1997, p. 43.

Crockett, Barton, "Start-Up Undercuts Foreign PTTs' Prices," *Network World*, June 24, 1991, p. 25.

Goetz, Thomas, "Down with IDT," *Village Voice*, May 21, 1996, pp. 24–25.

Hamerman, Joshua, "Sweetened Net2Phone Bid: Still Too Low?" *America's Intelligence Wire*, January 10, 2006.

Jonas, Howard, *On a Roll: From Hot Dog Buns to High-Tech Billions*, New York: Viking, 1998.

Lazaroff, Leon, "More Deals Ahead for IDT," *Daily Deal*, January 2, 2002.

Lee, Jeanne, "How IDT Hopes to Upend the Phone Biz," *Fortune*, November 9, 1998, p. 284.

Marshall, Jonathan, "New Long-Distance Service Uses the Net," *San Francisco Chronicle*, November 27, 1997, pp. E1, E5.

McKay, Martha, "Newark, N.J.-based Calling Card Seller Wants More of Internet Phone Firm," *Record*, December 9, 2004.

————, "Newark, N.J.-based Telecom Purchases Majority Stake in Animation Company," *Record,* May 16, 2003.

Meeks, Fleming, "David 1, Goliath 0," *Forbes,* June 20, 1994, p. 92.

————, "Dial H for Hustle," *Forbes,* May 24, 1993, pp. 62, 64.

Nolter, Chris, "IDT Picks Through Telecom Wreck," *Daily Deal,* September 21, 2002.

O'Shea, Dan, "IDT Finalizes Net2Phone Repurchase,"

Telephony, February 21, 2006.

Ramirez, Anthony, "Hot-Wiring Overseas Telephone Calls," *New York Times,* January 9, 1992, pp. D1, D6.

Schiesel, Seth, "IDT Says Liberty Media Will Buy Stake," *New York Times,* March 27, 2000, p. C8.

Weber, Thomas E., "Tiny IDT, an IPO, Bucks Trend Against Internet Porn," *Wall Street Journal,* March 22, 1996, p. B4.

Weinberg, Neil, "Malone Clone," *Forbes,* April 15, 2002, p. 82.

IGA, Inc.

8725 West Higgins Road
Chicago, Illinois 60631-2773
U.S.A.
Telephone: (773) 693-4520
Fax: (773) 693-4532
Web site: http://www.iga.com

Private Company
Incorporated: 1926 as Independent Grocers Alliance
Employees: 92,000
Sales: $21 billion (2007 est.)
NAICS: 424410 General Line Grocery Merchant Wholesalers

■ ■ ■

Maintaining its headquarters in Chicago, IGA, Inc., the former Independent Grocers Alliance, is the world's largest voluntary supermarket network, comprised of about 4,400 supermarkets located in 48 states of the United States and more than 40 countries, altogether generating more than $21 billion in annual sales. It is owned by about three dozen worldwide distribution companies. In addition to supplying IGA-member stores with major brand-label products, the company offers more than 2,300 IGA private-label products. IGA also provides independent grocers with a full range of other services. Store formats include IGA Express, ISA Super Saver, and IGA Foodliner, and owners can also add such options as banks, fast foods, fuel, and pharmacies. IGA offers an assessment program, using third-party experts to rate individual stores; hosts marketing events to help

stores increase traffic and customer loyalty; and through the IGA Trust Group Employee Benefits Programs helps both retailers and distributors to take advantage of their collective size to provide employees with healthcare and other benefits.

IGA FOUNDED: 1926

The man who conceived of IGA was J. (Joseph) Frank Grimes, an accountant who was a partner in the Chicago accounting firm of W.W. Thompson & Co., which mostly audited the books of wholesale grocers. During the 1920s grocery store chains were growing increasingly powerful and driving independent retailers, the customers of the wholesale grocers, out of business. Because of his work Grimes was well aware of the problem, and in order to combat the chains he thought of a way for independent grocers to band together to take advantage of the economies of scale enjoyed by the chains in terms of buying power and merchandising. In 1926 he developed his idea with colleagues at his accounting firm—William W. Thompson, Louis G. Groebe, H. V. Swenson, W. K. Hunter, and Gene Flack—and together they cofounded the Independent Grocers Alliance, which was quickly referred to by its initials. Grimes, Thompson, and Groebe split ownership between them.

Instead of attempting to service member stores themselves, the cofounders decided to work through established wholesalers, many of whom were already accounting clients. After they were able to arouse the interest of a Poughkeepsie, New York, wholesaler, W. T. Reynolds, all they needed were stores willing to join the network. A group of area retailers were brought together one night in the Poughkeepsie YMCA, and Grimes, named IGA's president, took the train from Chicago to meet with them and pitch the idea of joining the fledgling IGA. One of the retailers, George Sutcliff, expressed interest but wanted to see an actual IGA in operation. "My friend, there is no IGA store," Grimes told him. "IGA comes into existence in this room—tonight. If you would care to sign an application, you will be the first retail member in the country." Not only did Sutcliff sign, he was joined by 68 other grocers. The following evening Grimes made the same appeal in Sharon, Connecticut, and lined up another 25 members. These initial members decided to create a group identity and called themselves the Acorn Stores, in essence a seed that they hoped would one day grow into a large organization.

Grimes had national aspirations, and quickly looked to the South to expand IGA's footprint. A Memphis wholesaler, J.T. Fargarson Company, sponsored a group of Dixie stores, so that by the end of the first year the IGA network boasted more than 150 stores. Momentum quickly grew and a year later the IGA logo could be found on stores in 15 states, and the network did a business of $60 million. IGA helped members drive sales through merchandising programs. The first involved macaroni products, supported by window posters, point-of-sale signage, and direct-mail pieces. It was an overwhelming success, encouraged retailer participation, and led to the merchandising of other products.

FIRST PUBLICATION OF IGA GROCERGRAM: 1929

IGA was represented in 2,870 towns in 36 states by the end of 1928. To communicate with the growing number of retailers, at the start of 1929 IGA began publishing the IGA Grocergram, which espoused the evangelical zeal of Grimes for IGA while also informing members of new IGA programs and developed a sense of community by highlighting the successes of member stores and sharing ideas on how they could grow their businesses. Retailers began referring to one another in the pages of the Grocergram as Brother, another indication that IGA members felt they were on a mission, portraying the chains, such as A&P, as the Goliath to be conquered.

Not even the stock market crash of 1929 and the ensuing Great Depression could halt the national expansion of IGA. In 1930 the organization sponsored a six-times-a-week, national radio program, the IGA Home Town Hour, featuring mysteries set in small towns. In that same year, IGA signed legendary baseball star Babe Ruth as an endorser of IGA products. Later in the decade, popular cartoon character Popeye began endorsing IGA products, as did boxer Jack Dempsey and actor Jackie Cooper. IGA also promoted itself in a wide variety of national magazines, including the *Saturday Evening Post* and *McCall's*, with a combined subscription of 120 million. Early in 1932 IGA established a toehold in the lucrative California market, initially signing up retailers in San Francisco. Within three months, more than 600 California stores were displaying the IGA logo. In the mid-1930s IGA took on the chains in a different way, urging chain store managers to go independent and join IGA. Combined store sales reached $400 million during this period.

The 1930s also brought a change in ownership. The wholesalers that were a key element in IGA's success wanted a stake in the business, and in 1932 they received a half-interest and representation on the IGA board of directors. By mid-decade there would be 65 IGA wholesalers and 110 branches. The wholesalers paid IGA $4.74 a month per store for such services as layouts and merchandising advice. Stores, in the meantime, paid their wholesalers $3.50 per week for service and brokerage commissions to IGA, but enjoyed the benefits of lower prices, higher-margin private-label goods, and marketing clout.

At the start of the 1940s, IGA helped independents compete with chains by developing a prototype for a 2,000-square-foot store that could be built and equipped for about $4,500, including walk-in freezer, meat case, cash register, coffee mill, and scales. A model was built and taken across the country to local IGA conventions to drum up interest. Soon, everyone's attention would turn to foreign affairs, however, when the United States was drawn into World War II late in 1941. The next four years would be a time of shortages and rationing, making business difficult for IGA stores, which did their part in the war effort by encouraging customers to bring their own shopping bags to conserve paper, and also by marketing seeds for "Victory gardens" and setting up tables where war bonds were sold.

Even as the war was coming to a close in the summer of 1945, IGA resumed a growth strategy, which included larger store formats. The first IGA Foodliner opened in Wisconsin Rapids, Wisconsin, in July of that year. In the postwar era stores became increasingly

KEY DATES

1926: J. Frank Grimes founds Independent Grocers Alliance (IGA).
1930: Babe Ruth becomes IGA endorser.
1932: Wholesaler partners become co-owners.
1952: Frank Grimes retires, replaced by son Don.
1968: Don Grimes retires.
1978: Thomas Haggai is named chairman.
1986: Haggai takes over as CEO.
1995: IGA enters China market.
2006: U.S. and international operations split.
2008: IGA enters Russia.

larger, and left Main Street for outer locations, giving birth to the age of the highway supermarket. More than just groceries, IGA stores began to carry other merchandise, as competition with regional and national chains grew even stiffer. IGA also began competing outside of the United States, entering Canada in 1951.

FRANK GRIMES RETIRES: 1952

In 1952 Frank Grimes, now 70 years of age, resigned as IGA's president and turned over the reins to his 46-year-old son, Don R. Grimes. The younger Grimes had graduated from the University of Illinois and before joining IGA learned the grocery business working as a manager of an A&P store. He then worked his way up through the ranks at IGA, interrupted by a stint in the military during World War II. After the war, he played a key role in pushing a supermarket concept for IGA members. He took over an organization that was grossing $2.3 billion a year, and soon announced an ambitious goal of grossing more than $5 billion and 10,000 store members within ten years. A supermarket building boom actually swept the entire grocery industry, and IGA was challenged to keep up. In 1953 alone, 300 IGA stores were remodeled and $9 million was spent on 125 new IGA stores. Another important development came in 1954 when IGA entered the New York City market for the first time. To help retail members better grow their business, IGA headquarters offered member stores a new accounting service in 1957, and a year later added dairy and bakery departments to provide expertise to retailers in growing sales in these categories.

By the start of the 1960s the IGA network included 5,500 stores in 45 states. A new "package" available in two sizes was introduced at the four regional conventions in 1961. The pre-engineered and pre-designed stores were available in two sizes: 6,440 square feet, expected to generate about $21,000 a week in sales, and 8,880 square feet, slated to gross $30,000 a week. Within a matter of months, the formats were enlarged to meet the demands of member stores, to 7,755 square feet and 10,500 square feet. Some IGA stores would become even larger, such as a Foodliner that opened in Orland Park, Illinois. The store was 22,000 square feet in size and featured an in-store bakery, a novelty at the time.

Don Grimes did not reach his ambitious goal for IGA, which faced stiffer competition from chains than anticipated. When the organization celebrated its 40th anniversary in 1966 it was comprised of 4,300 stores in 46 states. A year later Grimes took a leave of absence, but he would never return. He was replaced as chief executive by Wilbur Pinney, who originally came to IGA to head the bakery department. In early 1968 Grimes officially retired and died four years later following a lengthy illness. Richard J. Jones, the head of an IGA-affiliated wholesaler, took over as president and tried to resume IGA's early pattern of strong growth and increased annual volume to the $10 billion level. In order to help member retailers develop new ideas, he urged affiliated wholesalers to open a corporate store where new concepts could be tried out for the good of the network. His efforts to refocus on the retail side of the organization began to pay dividends by the end of the 1960s, although the number of member stores continued to dwindle.

The early 1970s brought difficult economic times that hurt margins for IGA stores. In February 1973 a new president, William Olsen, replaced Jones, who remained involved in IGA as a part-owner of IGA stores in Urbana, Illinois. Olsen took over an organization that was in a state of flux. By the end of 1974 IGA was supplying about 3,400 stores in 45 states. Because the multi-unit operators were enjoying much higher volumes, Olsen encouraged members to seize opportunities to open additional stores and gain efficiencies. He applied the same principle to the home office in 1976 when operations were reorganized into two new divisions: procurement and member services. In that same year, IGA stores began installing scanning equipment to lower operational costs. While the number of member stores fell to 3,322 in 1976, IGA enjoyed a 10.7 percent increase to $4.7 billion in sales.

THOMAS HAGGAI NAMED CHAIRMAN: 1978

In 1978 Thomas S. Haggai was named chairman of IGA, and Olsen stayed on as president. Haggai was an ordained Baptist minister, a boy preacher who gave his first sermon at the age of 12. After completing his schooling he began speaking at business gatherings and later hosted a daily inspirational radio show. Frank Grimes, following his retirement, learned of Haggai and encouraged his son Don to book the minister as a speaker at one of the local IGA conventions. Around 1962 Haggai spoke for the first time before an IGA meeting and became a regular presence at IGA conventions for the next dozen years. In 1972 he became the first IGA board member without a background in the food industry. After Haggai became chairman, Olsen continued to maintain day-to-day control of the organization and grew sales to $7 billion by the start of the 1980s. By the middle of the decade the number of IGA-supplied stores fell to 3,200. With the IGA image in need of a upgrade, Haggai stepped in as CEO in 1986 and made growing the organization something of a divine mission. "If I didn't consider it as a ministry," he told the *Chicago Tribune,* in 1993, "I wouldn't work so hard."

Haggai's enthusiasm and devotion paid off. He visited hundreds of stores to entertain ideas and concerns of his constituents, and used his considerable political skills to push through changes that should have been made years earlier. Private labels were redesigned, new quality standards imposed, a partnership platform with national brand manufacturers formed, and new advertising campaigns launched. In 1987 IGA financed a very successful image-building campaign centered around the "Hometown Proud" theme, which would become the centerpiece of future campaigns as well. Five years later IGA boasted almost 4,000 affiliated supermarkets generating $16.2 billion in annual sales, making it the sixth largest supermarket chain in the United States.

Under Haggai IGA also began to extend its reach overseas. Japan and Australia were added in 1988, and in 1995 IGA expanded to St. Kitts in the Caribbean, and China, Singapore, and Malaysia in the Pacific Rim. IGA was the first U.S. grocer, in fact, to enter the Chinese and Singapore markets, where IGA partnered with established grocery chains that wanted to tap into the organization's expertise, including taking advantage of IGA University, a training program established by IGA and Coca-Cola Co. in 1992. Membership in IGA was also appealing overseas because IGA was able to provide operators with new technology and equipment as well as marketing help. In keeping with its expanded purview, IGA began referencing its initials as International Grocers Alliance.

IGA RESTRUCTURED: 2006

With supermarket chains growing ever larger through a consolidation trend, IGA had to contend with a greater degree of competition in the United States. By the start of the new century IGA had about 4,000 member stores in more than 40 countries, but by this point there were only about 1,100 units in the United States while overseas units had grown to nearly 3,000. IGA continued to take advantage of international opportunities, such as adding a third Chinese company to the IGA fold in 2005, bringing in 45 stores and $400 million in annual sales, and another 100 stores expected by 2008. Because of the growing international component, IGA was restructured in 2006, split between IGA USA and IGA Global, a Singapore corporation. Haggai took over as CEO of the latter while Mark Batenic, a veteran food industry executive with a long history working with independent grocery retailers and IGA, became the chairman, president, and CEO of IGA USA. Haggai also retained his title as nonexecutive chairman of IGA, Inc. While still retaining a strong presence in the United States, especially in small towns, it was apparent that the future of IGA lay beyond American shores. In 2008 IGA moved into another large market, Russia, teaming up with Megapolis Trading Company, the largest fast moving consumer goods (FMCG) distribution company in the country.

Ed Dinger

PRINCIPAL SUBSIDIARIES

IGA Global; IGA USA.

PRINCIPAL COMPETITORS

The Kroger Co.; Safeway Inc.; Wakefern Food Corporation.

FURTHER READING

"Cooperative Grocers," *Time,* October 19, 1936.

Gorman, John, "Grocers Thrive on Togetherness," *Chicago Tribune,* May 5, 1986, p. 3.

Haggai Thomas S., and Abby Ellin, "A Boy Preacher Grows Up," *New York Times,* March 3, 2002, p. 3.

"The Independents," *Time,* September 21, 1953.

Lewis, Leonard, "IGA, at 70, Is Still 'Hometown Proud,'" *Frozen Food Age,* June 1996, p. 1.

Matthews, Ryan, "Through the Looking Glass," *Progressive Grocer,* September 1996, p. 63.

Nowell, Paul, "IGA Chief Sets Standard for Small Grocery Stores," *Chicago Tribune,* January 10, 1993, p. 10.

Petreycik, Richard M., "IGA at 65: Hometown Is Where the Heart Is," *Progressive Grocer,* May 1991, p. 115.

Raphel, Murray, and Neil Raphel, "What the 'I' in IGA Stands For," *Progressive Grocer,* June 1996, p. 21.

Tanner, Richard, "60 Years with IGA," *Progressive Grocer,* June 1996, p. 25.

"Think Globally, Act Appropriately," *Progressive Grocer,* March 2001, p. 21.

Trotola, Jane Olszeski, "Extended Family," *Progressive Grocer,* April 1, 2005, p. 18.

Ikonics Corporation

4832 Grand Avenue
Duluth, Minnesota 55807
U.S.A.
Telephone: (218) 628-2217
Toll Free: (800) 328-4261
Fax: (218) 628-3245
Web site: http://www.ikonics.com

Public Company
Incorporated: 1952 as Chroma-Glo, Inc.
Employees: 75
Sales: $15.83 million (2007)
Stock Exchanges: NASDAQ
Ticker Symbol: IKNX
NAICS: 621512 Diagnostic Imaging Centers

■ ■ ■

Ikonics Corporation, an imaging-technology company, operates in two core manufacturing areas: photostencils for the screen printing industry and photoresists for abrasive etching. Both are slow growth, mature markets; sales are derived from both domestic and international markets. The company historically has driven growth through its commitment to research and development and ability to translate that knowledge into marketable products. Ikonics is applying the strategy in pursuit of a foothold in the industrial sector.

FIRST A LABEL MAKER: 1952–59

Ikonics Corporation is rooted in the advent of the chemical age. "The idea began in 1952, when the

Fitzgerald-Nelson Company incorporated to print plastic labels in rented quarters in Duluth's Northland Foods Building, on Lake Avenue," the *Duluthian* recounted.

Operating as Chroma-Glo, Inc., the company experimented with pigments, adhesives, and manufacturing processes. In addition to the challenges inherent to product development, the business faced supply limitations. Polyester film, a key component of its products, was produced in limited quantities, according to the *Duluth Herald*.

Chroma-Glo's pressure sensitive decals appeared on vehicles, lawnmowers, and pleasure boats. Intended for permanent use, the labels had to stand up under rigorous conditions. President Jim Fitzgerald tested the limits of the product further with the development of a decal for the fuselage of the Minnesota Air National Guard's F-94 Starfire jets.

"Our biggest worry was the sharp temperature changes which jets experience," Fitzgerald told the *Duluth Herald* in October 1954. "But the product is taking temperature, and 600-mile an hour speeds, with no trouble at all." By the end of the decade, the Duluth-based company reported net sales of $140,435.

KNOWLEDGE TRANSLATES TO GROWTH: 1960–79

Chroma-Glo climbed to $534,797 the next year, with net earnings of $16,604. The company entered a new phase in 1961, offering stock to the public for the first time. A move to automated screen printing equipment quickly followed.

COMPANY PERSPECTIVES

IKONICS has served as an international leader in the development of imaging technologies for over 50 years. IKONICS proudly introduces products and process solutions for a diverse array of imaging markets.

At the core of IKONICS' success is the ability to quickly adapt its fundamental, commercial and technological competencies to the needs of image-consumers everywhere.

Growth and innovation marked the 1960s. Demand for permanent labels rose as manufacturers began incorporating woodgrain and metallic designs into their consumer products. The company also embarked on a new area of business.

In 1964 Chroma-Glo developed and patented a photochemical imaging process and product. Stencil supply products were then manufactured and sold to other screen printers. Chroma-Glo relocated twice during the decade, to accommodate its expanding operation.

By the early 1970s Chroma-Glo materials were being used in the production of printed circuits for Japanese electronics manufacturers as well as for printing designs on English-made fine china.

Lewis C. Erickson, who joined the company in 1961, had led the charge, "bringing the theories and concepts of plastic label making to the present productive and profitable state of the art," according to a 1973 article in the *Duluthian*.

RISK AND REWARD: 1980–95

Another Erickson spearheaded a dramatic change in direction for the company in the early 1980s. Thomas L. Erickson, who succeeded his father Lewis as head of the company in 1976, persuaded the board to exit the mainstay printing business.

Chroma-Glo sold the printing operation, 70 percent of its business, and focused its resources on the photostencil business, manufacturing and marketing film, emulsions, and screen preparation products.

The sale of the screen printing business in 1982 allowed the company to retire long-term debt and gear up research and development (R&D). The company also took on a new name: Chromaline Corporation.

Erickson made the dramatic move in response to a combination of factors that threatened the company's future: an economic recession, the struggles of a key customer, and a 16-week labor strike.

Erickson stayed true to his vision for the company despite a challenging period of transition. In 1985 Chromaline sank $165,000 into research, while racking up $147,000 more in losses. In addition to R&D investment, the company committed itself to international sales.

Chromaline returned to the plus side in 1986, with $27,000 in earnings. In 1987 earnings surged more than tenfold, to $272,000.

The early 1990s afforded more opportunity and dangers. Chromaline brought its photochemical expertise to the abrasive etching industry but also faced another period of depressed earnings.

The increased R&D expenditures and marketing efforts paid off. Sales climbed from $4.9 million in 1993 to $6.5 million in 1994.

AT HOME AND ABROAD: 1996–99

Chromaline, which had begun selling its stock over-the-counter early in its history, was among a handful of locally owned, publicly traded companies in the Duluth area. "Small start-up companies that eventually go public 'just aren't part of the local economic culture,'" President and CEO Tom Erickson told the *Duluth News-Tribune*.

The area including the twin ports of Duluth, Minnesota, and Superior, Wisconsin, and extending into the surrounding lumber and mining regions, hosted many nonlocal, publicly traded companies. While the city's business climate in the 1990s suffered, its other qualities, including its natural beauty, low crime rate, and lack of congestion, garnered praise. "People we bring in from overseas, they're enchanted by Duluth," Erickson said.

The Duluth-based company had established an equity partnership in a European sales office and an Indian manufacturing plant. International sales accounted for 41 percent of revenue in 1997. Revenue for the year was $8.9 million with earnings of $638,000. According to the *Duluth News-Tribune*, the company was debt free, cash rich, and holding excess manufacturing capacity.

Philip Hourican succeeded Erickson as president and CEO about midyear 1998. The chemical industry executive, experienced in the international market, pledged to focus on growth.

```
┌─────────────────────────────────────────┐
│                                           │
│              KEY DATES                    │
│                  ■                        │
│ ─────────────────────────────────────    │
│  1952:  Label printing business begins    │
│         operation.                        │
│  1964:  Chroma-Glo introduces a photo-    │
│         chemical imaging process.         │
│  1982:  Company changes name to           │
│         Chromaline Corporation.           │
│  1992:  Chromaline applies photochemical  │
│         know-how to abrasive etching.     │
│  2000:  Company is listed on the NASDAQ.  │
│  2002:  The multiple product business     │
│         reorganizes as Ikonics            │
│         Corporation.                      │
│  2005:  Ikonics is named to *Fortune*     │
│         list of fastest-growing small     │
│         public companies.                 │
│  2007:  Company pushes forward with       │
│         products targeting industrial     │
│         markets.                          │
│                                           │
└─────────────────────────────────────────┘
```

During 1998 Chromaline had introduced two stencil-making products and two pieces of equipment into the market. Hourican wanted to escalate the rate. R&D spending was increased during his first full year in charge.

Besides spending more, Hourican wanted to get more out of his employees. Hourican told the *Duluth News-Tribune* in 1999, "We're trying to get everyone to be a bit more innovative, a bit more creative."

Chromaline's products were applied in processes including glass etching, textile design, artwork reproduction, and circuit board printing.

In addition to pushing for new products, Hourican expected the company to enter new markets and begin trading its stock on the NASDAQ instead of over the counter.

REACHING OUT: 2000–01

However, Hourican's tenure was short-lived. He resigned early in 2000. Longtime board member William Ulland succeeded him as president and CEO. His father, Oscar Ulland, preceded him on the board. While praising Hourican's leadership, Ulland set out to develop a new strategic plan for the company.

Meanwhile Chromaline moved closer to a listing on the NASDAQ, a market driven to record levels by the hot technology sector. The U.S. Securities and Exchange Commission filing and NASDAQ application, a yearlong process, cost the company about $60,000. According to Ulland the listing would "increase liquidity." Beginning in March 2000, Chromaline began trading

Competition kept sales flat during 2000, at $10.4 million. Legal costs and product expenses linked to a patent infringement lawsuit, losses related to the bankruptcy of its European distributor, and costs garnered in the redirection of the company depressed earnings to $0.20 per share, down from $0.62 in 1999.

Early in 2001, a longstanding patent dispute with Aicello Chemical Co. Ltd. of Japan and Aicello North America Ltd. was settled. Aicello first sued Chromaline over decorative sandblasting technology in 1996. Chromaline then countersued. The Minnesota-based company agreed to pay Aicello royalties for sales of its sandblasting product. Aicello, in turn, possibly would distribute Chromaline products in Japan and Europe.

The earnings slide continued in 2001. For the year, Chromaline reported losses of $0.16 a share. A recession in the electronics sector of the screen printing business drove down sales of higher margin film products in the United States. Moreover, the reintroduction of products withdrawn in 2000, due to the patent litigation, were returned slower than expected to market. Sales, though, rose slightly. Contributions of a screen-printing chemical manufacturer acquired in 2000 and of an alliance with Slee Corp. for the sale of glass and crystal helped out.

NEW IDENTITY: 2002–04

The company changed its name to Ikonics Corporation (IKNX) in December 2002. The move was geared to strengthen its brands by separating the corporate name from a product area. The company also wanted to clarify its identity with the investment community.

"Finding a good corporate name is a challenge in today's world," Ulland said in a *PR Newswire* release. "Ideally the name says something about your business, is 'dot-commable' and memorable. Ikonics stems from the Greek word *eikon* meaning image, which is appropriate since our core business is imaging and image transfer."

The company reconfigured into three divisions: Timeline Screen Printing Products, PhotoBrasive Systems, and SplitRock Technologies. The latter division, initially formed in 2001, was charged with commercializing new technologies for the marketplace.

Ikonics' Chromaline unit made strides in the fast-growing digital printing segment, during 2003, while the PhotoBrasive division pursued sales opportunities in Asia, Eastern and Central Europe, South America, and Australia. SplitRock Technologies, meanwhile, pursued a new metal etching technology.

The company's PhotoBrasive products for etching stone, glass, and other materials through sandblasting were not viable for metal. Consequently, Ikonics created a modified metal amenable to abrasive etching. Ikon-Metal's first application would be in the U.S. decorative sign market. The process competed against acid-resistant etching and cast-metal methods.

During 2004 Ikonics launched two new businesses using RapidMask technology acquired from DuPont in 2002. IKONSign Etch incorporated the IkonMetal technology, and IKONImage blended low-cost etching with RapidMask. Despite costs related to the new business units, Ikonics' profits rose 51 percent for the year.

ON A ROLL: 2005–08

Fortune magazine took note of Ikonics' efforts, in 2005, naming it one of the nation's 100 Fastest Growing Small Public Companies. During the year, the company prepared to tackle a new market segment with the establishment of Ikonics Industrial. Ikonics also acquired equity interest in Imaging Technology International, a developer, designer, and producer of industrial ink-jet systems.

Ikonics continued to work toward strengthening its product offerings during 2006, acquiring complementary screen printing products, deepening investment in the ink-jet business segment, and improving production processes for some of its newer lines.

Two technology initiatives for the industrial market took center stage during 2007. Ikonics strove to move into electronic wafer etching for large aerospace, electronic, and industrial materials companies, and into steel mold etching for plastics injection molding companies serving the automotive market.

In 2007 Ikonics marked its seventh consecutive year of record sales and third consecutive year of record earnings. Ikonics' sales were split 70 percent domestic and 30 percent international. Ikonics broke ground on a new $4.5 million warehouse and manufacturing facility in 2008 and looked to the future with optimism.

Kathleen Peippo

PRINCIPAL COMPETITORS

Minnesota Mining & Manufacturing Company; Eastman Kodak Company; Konica Minolta Corporation; Material Sciences Corporation; Agfa Gevaert.

FURTHER READING

"BIZbriefs," *Duluth News-Tribune,* February 9, 2001, p. 1E.

Brissett, Jane, "Board Names New Leader," *Duluth News-Tribune,* July 15, 1998, p. 1F.

———, "A New Image," *Corporate Report Minnesota,* April 1989, pp. 39–40.

"Chroma Glo Sells Labels and Ideas," *Duluthian,* May 1973.

Coleman, Herbert J., "Chromaline CEO Retiring," *Duluth News-Tribune,* May 1, 1998, p. 1F.

———, "Chromaline President, CEO Resigns," *Duluth News-Tribune,* February 9, 2000, p. 1E.

———, "Chromaline to Begin Trading on Nasdaq," *Duluth News-Tribune,* March 10, 2000, p. 4E.

———, "Nasdaq, New Products Top Chromaline Agenda," *Duluth News-Tribune,* April 15, 1999, p. 1F.

"Companies Reach Deal in Patent-Dispute Case," *Duluth News-Tribune,* January 25, 2001, p. 1C.

"Duluth-Based Ikonics Posts Significant Profit Increase," *Duluth News-Tribune,* February 22, 2008.

"Duluth Decal Firm Meets Challenge, Beats Elements," *Duluth Herald,* October 14, 1954.

"Duluth Firm Offers Public Stock Sale," *Duluth Herald,* June 16, 1961.

"Duluth, Minn.-based Imaging Technology Firm Sees 2003 Profits Jump 40%," *Knight-Ridder/Tribune Business News,* February 24, 2004.

"Duluth, Minn.-based Manufacturer Ikonics to Split Stock," *Knight-Ridder/Tribune Business News,* April 30, 2004.

"Ikonics Corp. Has Poor Quarter, Excellent Year," *Knight-Ridder/Tribune Business News,* February 17, 2005.

"Ikonics to Break Ground at Morgan Park Site," *Duluth News-Tribune,* May 1, 2008, p. B5.

Nelson, Wayne, "Chromaline in from the Cold," *Duluth News Tribune,* October 2, 1988.

Passi, Peter, "Duluth, Minn.-based Firm Patents New Metal-Etching Technology," *Knight-Ridder/Tribune Business News,* January 7, 2004.

Shipley, Jack D., "Slimmed-Down Chromaline Proves Less Is More," *Duluth News Tribune,* April 29, 1984.

Welbes, John, "Few Northland Firms Go Public," *Duluth News-Tribune,* January 1, 1996, p. 1B.

J. Lohr Winery Corporation

1000 Lenzen Avenue
San Jose, California 95126
U.S.A.
Telephone: (408) 288-5057
Fax: (408) 993-2276
Web site: http://www.jlohr.com

Private Company
Incorporated: 1974 as J. Lohr Vineyards & Wines
Employees: 150
Sales: $12.7 million (2007)
NAICS: 312130 Wineries; 111332 Grape Vineyards

■ ■ ■

J. Lohr Winery Corporation is an independent winemaker that produces red, white, sparkling, and nonalcoholic wines that are sold in 25 countries. The company owns three vineyards in the Arroyo Seco, Napa Valley, and Paso Robles regions of California. It maintains two tasting centers, one in downtown San Jose and the other next to its vineyard in Paso Robles. The company's wines are categorized according to their cost into three tiers, with the J. Lohr Cuvée Series ranking as the winery's most expensive brand. In descending order of price are the J. Lohr Vineyard Series and J. Lohr Estates brands, followed by two entry-level brands, Cypress Vineyards and Painter Bridge. J. Lohr Winery owns and manages more than 900 acres in the Arroyo Seco region in Monterey County. The company owns 2,000 acres in the Paso Robles region in San Luis Obispo County. In Napa Valley, where the company's

Carol's Vineyard is located, 33 acres are devoted to growing Cabernet Sauvignon, Sauvignon Blanc, and Petit Verdot grape varietals.

ORIGINS

For Jerome "Jerry" Lohr, memories of his youth inspired the formation of J. Lohr Winery. Lohr grew up on a wheat farm in South Dakota, but he did not immediately gravitate toward a career in agriculture. Instead, he chose a far different professional path, demonstrating an interest in civil engineering. After earning a degree from South Dakota State University in 1958, Lohr earned his master's degree in civil engineering from Stanford University and began pursuing a doctorate degree in his chosen field. He completed all his coursework for a Ph.D. by 1961, but ended his academic career before earning the degree. Lohr joined the U.S. Air Force in 1961 and rose to the rank of captain during a three-year stint that included serving as a research scientist at the National Aeronautics and Space Administration's Ames Research Center at Moffett Field, California.

Immediately after finishing his military service, Lohr decided to start his own business. In 1964, he founded what later became known as J. Lohr Properties, a land development and residential construction company. Lohr did well, quickly accumulating what he characterized as "a small fortune" in a June 13, 1994, interview with the *Business Journal.* He bought land and built homes, townhouses, and condominiums in the San Francisco Bay Area, eventually extending his activities throughout Santa Clara, Santa Cruz, and Monterey counties, a region known as California's Central Coast.

LOHR STARTS A SECOND CAREER

Lohr had no financial need to start another business, but he began planning for a second entrepreneurial venture before J. Lohr Properties celebrated its fifth anniversary. His years growing up on a farm in South Dakota, it appeared, had instilled a compelling need to follow in his family's footsteps. He did not return to the Midwest, however, choosing instead to perpetuate the Lohr tradition in agriculture near his thriving construction business. Lohr began surveying the Central Coast for the ideal conditions to grow grapes, intending to use some of the profits from J. Lohr Properties to start his own vineyard. For years, he searched for the perfect spot before settling on the Arroyo Seco region of Monterey County in 1971.

Lohr used $400,000 from his construction business to finance his entry into the winemaking business. He began planting grapes in 1972, spending the next year establishing 280 acres of vineyards in Arroyo Seco, the first of 900 acres in the region that would supply grapes for his winery. By 1974, he was ready to make his commercial debut. He formed his company, initially named J. Lohr Vineyards & Wines, and opened a tasting room in downtown San Jose. The year marked the release of the first J. Lohr wine, a Petite Sirah that heralded the construction magnate's arrival as a vintner.

A decade after starting his own construction business, Lohr began selling wine. Not only were his two professions dissimilar, they also were countercyclical, enabling Lohr to devote his time to each business when it needed it most. "I drop out of the building business during the fall and drive the Harvester in the vineyards," he explained in his June 13, 1994, interview with the *Business Journal.* When the construction business ramped up in the spring, he began building homes again while his grapes were growing.

WINE OFFERINGS EXPAND DURING THE SEVENTIES

Lohr's first years in business saw him establish his operations and demonstrate a flair for sales. New wines were released from J. Lohr Winery, beginning with a Cabernet Sauvignon, Sauvignon Blanc, Pinot Blanc, and Pinot Noir in 1975. The first vintage of the J. Lohr Chardonnay and Johannisberg Riesling followed in 1976, the year Lohr convinced local restaurateurs to offer his wines at their establishments. Lohr's efforts to promote his winery led to the rapid expansion of the business. By 1979, only five years after the first J. Lohr wine was produced, the brand had achieved national distribution.

Expansion would continue in the 1980s as the winery began to impress critics. Midway through the decade Lohr hired an employee who would play a central role in J. Lohr Winery's development for the decades to follow. Jeff Meier was hired to be part of the harvest staff in 1984, joining the winery after a brief stint working as a sales representative for a wine and spirits distributor. Raised in the San Francisco Bay Area, Meier was introduced to the winemaking business at an early age by accompanying his parents on frequent wine tasting trips to nearby Napa and Sonoma counties. The excursions left a lasting impression on Meier, prompting him to major in viticulture when he enrolled at the University of California, Davis. At J. Lohr Winery, Meier quickly distinguished himself, earning a promotion to bottling line supervisor only months after assisting in the harvest. In 1986, two years after joining the company, Meier was named assistant winemaker, a position he held until 1995, when he was put in charge of all winemaking operations and named vice-president.

NEW VINEYARDS ESTABLISHED IN EIGHTIES

As Meier's winemaking responsibilities increased, the scope of J. Lohr Winery's operations broadened as well. A nonalcoholic wine marketed under the name ARIEL was released in 1986, but the most significant development of the decade occurred on the vineyard front. In 1985, J. Lohr produced its first wine from Carol's Vineyard (named after Lohr's wife, Carol) in California's famed Napa Valley. In 1988, a third vineyard was established in Paso Robles, a winegrowing region located in San Luis Obispo County directly south of the company's vineyards in Arroyo Seco.

With three vineyards, a broad selection of wines, and an established brand name, J. Lohr Winery's stature swelled, becoming a bigger business than Lohr's construction company, J. Lohr Properties. The winery began to distribute its selection of wines internationally

<table>
<tr><td colspan="2">

KEY DATES

■
</td></tr>
<tr><td>**1972:**</td><td>Jerry Lohr begins planting grapes in the Arroyo Seco region of Monterey County, California.</td></tr>
<tr><td>**1974:**</td><td>J. Lohr Winery is founded and releases its first wine.</td></tr>
<tr><td>**1985:**</td><td>A second vineyard is established in Napa Valley.</td></tr>
<tr><td>**1986:**</td><td>J. Lohr Winery begins selling nonalcoholic wine under the brand name ARIEL.</td></tr>
<tr><td>**1988:**</td><td>A third vineyard is established in the Paso Robles region in San Luis Obispo County.</td></tr>
<tr><td>**1998:**</td><td>The J. Lohr Vineyard Series is released.</td></tr>
<tr><td>**2001:**</td><td>The J. Lohr Paso Robles Wine Center is opened.</td></tr>
<tr><td>**2002:**</td><td>The J. Lohr Cuvée Series is released.</td></tr>
<tr><td>**2004:**</td><td>J. Lohr Winery celebrates its 30th anniversary.</td></tr>
</table>

the same year it planted its first grapes in Paso Robles, which enabled it to sell more than 250,000 cases of wine annually by the beginning of the 1990s. As the business grew, Lohr put in place measures to foster loyalty within the winery's employee ranks. In 1994, Lohr created an employee stock ownership plan, enabling his workers to benefit from the growth of the business. Further, each employee was designated as a "co-owner," a title listed on every business card distributed to the winery's workers.

THE WINERY'S BRANDS TAKE SHAPE

From the winery's three vineyards, a distinct collection of brands was developed. The different labels composed J. Lohr Winery's portfolio of selections, constituting the breadth of its offerings in the 21st century. The first major brand to emerge was J. Lohr Estates with the release of J. Lohr Estates Riverstone Chardonnay in 1987. Produced from grapes planted in Paso Robles and Arroyo Seco, the J. Lohr Estates line was fleshed out in succeeding years to include Seven Oaks Cabernet Sauvignon, South Ridge Syrah, Bay Mist White Riesling, Wildflower Valdiguié, Los Osos Merlot, and Old Vines Zinfandel. Concurrent with the debut of the J. Lohr Estates line was the release of the winery's "entry-level" brand, Cypress Vineyards. Inaugurated with a Cabernet Sauvignon, the Cypress Vineyards line grew to include a Chardonnay, Merlot, Sauvignon Blanc, Shiraz, and

White Zinfandel. The Cypress Vineyards wines were produced by blending wines from the company's vineyards with grapes purchased from other California vineyards.

Roughly a decade after the J. Lohr Estates and Cypress Vineyards lines debuted, the winery entered the "luxury" segment of the wine market. In 1998, the J. Lohr Vineyard Series was released, a collection of wines intended to reflect and to capitalize upon the distinct characteristics of each of the winery's three vineyards. Limited in production, the J. Lohr Vineyard Series featured the Arroyo Vista Vineyard, a Chardonnay produced from the Arroyo Seco section of the winery's property in Monterey County. From the highest, best-drained slope in the winery's Paso Robles holdings, the J. Lohr Vineyard Series produced its Hilltop Cabernet. North of the town of St. Helena in Napa Valley, the gravelly loam soils produced two superior grape varieties showcased in the winery's Carol's Vineyard Sauvignon Blanc and Cabernet Sauvignon.

When J. Lohr Winery entered the 1990s, it sold more than 250,000 cases of wine for the first time in its history. By the end of the decade, sales eclipsed 500,000 cases of wine, reflecting the impressive progress achieved during the period. Expansion continued as the winery entered the 21st century, beginning with the grand opening of the J. Lohr Paso Robles Wine Center in 2001. Unlike the winery's first tasting room located in downtown San Jose, the Paso Robles facility was situated near the winery's vineyards, offering guests a sweeping view of the acreage that produced the wines to be sampled.

THE J. LOHR CUVÉE SERIES DEBUTS IN 2002

The most significant event of the new decade occurred one year after the J. Lohr Paso Robles Wine Center opened its doors. In 2002, the winery's third principal brand was released, the J. Lohr Cuvée Series. Developed as a more expensive brand than the J. Lohr Vineyard Series, the J. Lohr Cuvée Series was intended to represent the winery's masterstroke in winemaking, featuring three wines that only were produced during vintages that met strict criteria. The Cuvée PAU was a blend of at least 50 percent Cabernet Sauvignon combined with the grapes made up of Merlot, Cabernet Franc, Petite Verdot, and Malbec. The Cuvée St. E featured at least 50 percent Cabernet Franc blended with Merlot, Cabernet Sauvignon, and Petite Verdot. The Cuvée POM, at least 50 percent Merlot, also contained the grapes made up of Cabernet Franc, Cabernet Sauvignon, and Petite Verdot.

THIRTY YEARS AND BEYOND

As J. Lohr Winery prepared for the future, sales were increasing at an unprecedented pace. It took a decade for the winery to increase its annual sales volume from 250,000 to 500,000 cases, a plateau it reached in 1999. It took less than half the time for the winery to increase its volume by another 250,000 cases. J. Lohr Winery's sales surpassed 750,000 cases in 2003. The winery celebrated its 30th anniversary the following year, an occasion that also commemorated the impressive career of Jerry Lohr. Lohr had developed into an influential figure in the wine community during the period, serving in various capacities for a number of prestigious organizations. A onetime chairman of the Wine Institute, Lohr had led the Regional Winegrower's Council, helped found Wine Vision, an industry group devoted to promoting the wine industry, and served as a four-time president of the Monterey Vintners and Growers Association. In his capable hands, J. Lohr Winery could look forward to an enduring future as an independent wine producer of note.

Jeffrey L. Covell

PRINCIPAL COMPETITORS

Bronco Wine Company; The Wine Group, Inc.; Foster's Americas; Kendall-Jackson Wine Estates, Ltd.; Constellation Wines U.S., Inc.

FURTHER READING

Boyd, Gerald D., "Deep in the Heart of San Jose," *San Francisco Chronicle,* March 28, 2001, p. WB6.

Grover, Mary Beth, "The New Jugglers," *Forbes,* April 27, 1992, p. 182.

Lansford, Michael, "Lohr Accomplishes Much in Decade of Winemaking," *Houston Chronicle,* September 16, 1998, p. 7.

Sobers, Stefani, "J. Lohr Proves Winery Can Make a Go of It amid All the Pop and Fizz of Downtown," *Business Journal,* June 13, 1994, p. 24.

John Lewis Partnership plc

171 Victoria Street
London, SW1E 5NN
United Kingdom
Telephone: (+44-20) 7828-1000
Fax: (+44-20) 7592-5097
Web site: http://www.johnlewispartnership.co.uk

Partnership
Founded: 1864
Incorporated: 1929 as John Lewis Partnership Ltd.
Employees: 69,000
Sales: £6.05 billion ($12.04 billion) (2008)
NAICS: 452110 Department Stores; 445110 Supermarkets and Other Grocery (Except Convenience) Stores; 454111 Electronic Shopping; 454113 Mail-Order Houses

■ ■ ■

John Lewis Partnership plc is unique among large companies in Britain in that it is run for the benefit of its employees, as the majority of its profits are shared among them. Because of the independence this affords, it is perhaps less hungry for publicity than most companies of its size, and outsiders are often surprised to realize how large and successful it is. The company has two main arms. The original business was department stores, of which it has 27, nearly all of which operate under the John Lewis name. Around 40 percent of revenues are generated by the department store business. The other arm—the contributor of roughly 60 percent of sales—is supermarkets, of which it has 193, all trading as Waitrose. That these 220 outlets can generate total sales of more than £6 billion ($12 billion) is an indication of the size and efficiency of each unit. The group also includes the manufacturing firm Herbert Parkinson Limited, which supplies the stores with textiles, and Leckford Farm, supplier of flour, milk, apples, pears, apple juice, cider, mushrooms, free-range eggs, and free-range chicken. John Lewis is also involved in mail-order and e-commerce businesses; holds a 24 percent stake in Ocado, a grocery delivery business connected to Waitrose; and runs Greenbee, which through alliances with a variety of firms offers financial, travel, and leisure services. Among its limited activities outside the United Kingdom, John Lewis exports Waitrose-branded goods into some 20 countries and has entered into a licensing agreement with Dubai-based Spinneys Group Limited to open Waitrose outlets in the United Arab Emirates.

The business is essentially the creation of two men, John Lewis and his son John Spedan Lewis. The former created the first store and laid down its trading policy; the latter expanded it into a group of stores and gave the company its unique constitution. Since then the business has continued to thrive under nonfamily management, but a grandson of the first John Lewis, Peter Lewis, served as chairman from 1972 to 1993, and the ideas of John Spedan Lewis still permeate the whole enterprise.

COMPANY PERSPECTIVES

The John Lewis Partnership is a visionary and successful way of doing business, boldly putting the happiness of Partners at the centre of everything it does. It's the embodiment of an ideal, the outcome of nearly a century of endeavour to create a different sort of company, owned by Partners dedicated to serving customers with flair and fairness.

19TH-CENTURY ORIGINS: DEVELOPMENT OF THE FIRST JOHN LEWIS DEPARTMENT STORE

The company's first small shop opened in 1864, on part of the site that its main store occupied more than a century later in Oxford Street, London. This street was already well known for its shops, especially those supplying dresses and dress fabrics to the more prosperous classes. Other shops of this kind which were to become very successful included the well-established Debenham and Freebody (later Debenhams) and Marshall & Snelgrove.

John Lewis was 28 years old when he opened his first shop. He had come to London from Somerset eight years earlier, having served an apprenticeship in the drapery trade. In London he took a job with another Oxford Street drapery shop, Peter Robinson, and became its silk buyer.

The early days were hard and dreary, as John Lewis told his son, but the shop gradually became a success. At first his store specialized in dress fabrics, sewing threads, ribbons, and other trimmings, but then diversified into ready-made clothes, hats, and shoes. He did not advertise, but had a policy of displaying prices clearly, which was not common at that time. He offered a wide assortment, fair dealing, and retained low margins.

By 1875 Lewis was doing well enough to need more space, and he began to take over neighboring properties. With the extra space, he was able to stock more merchandise. From clothing, the store's range broadened to include furniture, carpets, china, and most household goods. During the 1870s Lewis's turnover almost tripled, and it continued growing throughout the 1880s.

By 1895 he was able to rebuild the whole store, which by then had a large corner site with fronts on Oxford Street and Holles Street. The new building occupied six floors, with impressive facades in Renaissance style, and the staff by this time numbered about 150.

In slightly more than 30 years Lewis had created a major department store in one of London's best shopping streets. Even more remarkably, he had done so entirely out of retained profits. In the early years he lived frugally and saved enough of the profits to finance each new step without the need to bring in partners or to turn the business into a joint stock company. The whole store belonged to him alone, and he ran it in a totally autocratic way.

Not until he was 48 did Lewis marry and start to raise a family. His wife was a teacher, 18 years younger than himself, and one of the first women to go to university. The couple had two sons, who received an excellent education and grew up with very different attitudes from those of their father. John Lewis had little education but had strongly individual views; he was an atheist and a liberal and once went to prison for defying a court order in a dispute with his landlord. He was considered a harsh employer, not prone to generosity. Both sons reacted against this hardness in different ways.

Lewis's sons both entered the business on leaving school and were given a quarter share in it upon reaching the age of 21. The younger son, Oswald, soon left the business to study law, provoking a long quarrel with his father, while Spedan became very interested in the business but increasingly critical of his father's methods.

The main issue of contention was staff wages. Spedan was shocked to find that the entire wage bill for 300 employees was a good deal less than the three partners were receiving in interest and profit. To him this was plainly unjust and probably bad for business too. He also discovered inefficiencies in the operation of the store; some departments were trading at a loss, and much of the upper floor space was being wasted. His father, however, angrily rejected all suggestions for change.

John Lewis was over 70 when his sons became partners but was still full of vigor. Satisfied with the profits the rebuilt store was making, he turned his attention to other things, becoming a member of the London County Council and investing some of his growing fortune in buying a second department store.

EARLY 20TH CENTURY: ADDING PETER JONES, CREATING THE PARTNERSHIP

The opportunity to do this arose in 1905, when one of his business rivals, Peter Jones, died. Jones had founded another successful store in Sloane Square. Some two

KEY DATES

■

1864: John Lewis opens a draper's shop in Oxford Street, London, and eventually develops it into a full-scale department store.

1905: Peter Jones department store in London is acquired.

1914: John Spedan Lewis, son of the founder, assumes control of Peter Jones and begins making radical changes.

1920: Spedan Lewis introduces a profit-sharing scheme at Peter Jones.

1925: Spedan Lewis introduces the slogan "Never Knowingly Undersold" as the pricing policy for Peter Jones.

1928: John Lewis dies; Spedan Lewis assumes full control of the Oxford Street store and of Peter Jones.

1929: Lewis transfers ownership of the company to a new firm called John Lewis Partnership Ltd., which holds the shares in trust for all employees, who in turn become full partners in the business and begin sharing in the profits.

1933: Company acquires its first provincial stores.

1937: Expansion into the food trade occurs with the acquisition of the Waitrose chain of ten grocery shops.

1940: John Lewis Partnership pays the Selfridge group £30,000 for 15 provincial department stores operating under various local names, which are retained.

1950s: Waitrose introduces self-service to its shops and begins converting the shops to the supermarket format.

1992: The 100th Waitrose supermarket opens.

1994: First Waitrose food & home store opens in London, marketing a full range of supermarket items along with a selection of household goods from John Lewis department stores.

2000: Founding of grocery delivery business Ocado, part-owned by the partnership; a £300 million, three-year makeover of the department store unit is launched, with local brands abandoned in favor of creating a nationwide John Lewis chain.

2004: Waitrose is expanded into the north of England via the purchase of 19 former Safeway stores.

2006: Waitrose gains its first Scottish locations.

---

miles away from John Lewis's store, it served a different clientele. The business, started in 1877, had grown rapidly and was by this time a limited company. Lewis bought Jones's controlling shareholding and became chairman, but seems not to have taken a close interest in the management of the business.

It proved to be an unrewarding investment. Without the flair of its founder, the store quickly went downhill. Sales dropped by a third, and for six years the company paid no dividends. Eventually, in 1914, Lewis decided to see what his son could do with it. He transferred his shares in the store to Spedan and made him chairman on the condition that he continue working at the Oxford Street store until 5 P.M. each day. Spedan jumped at the chance to try out his ideas, even though it meant giving up most of his evenings to the job.

Following a riding accident a few years earlier, Spedan had spent much time either in hospital or at home, using this time to work out his ideas in detail. At Peter Jones he immediately began to implement them. Pay and working conditions were improved, and sales incentives were introduced. In addition committees were set up to encourage new ideas, management functions were redefined, and new managers were hired. John Lewis became alarmed and demanded his shares back, but Spedan refused to relinquish them. As punishment, his father canceled Spedan's share in the partnership, banished him from Oxford Street, and reinstated Oswald there.

This at least enabled Spedan to give all his time to Peter Jones, and business there improved rapidly under his management. By 1919 the company was making a handsome profit, and John Lewis paid a visit of inspection. He said little to his son, relations between them still being cool, but afterward told his wife, "That place is a great credit to the boy—a very great credit."

Spedan took his reforms a stage further by introducing a profit-sharing scheme in 1920. Employees became known as partners and received weekly reports on sales and profits through a new house magazine, which also provided a forum for ideas and complaints. At the time, these practices were revolutionary and contrasted sharply with events at Oxford Street, where the employees went on strike for five weeks in 1920, earning the store much bad publicity. Over the next few years, however, there was a general slump in trade, which John Lewis withstood better than Peter Jones. This change in fortunes at last healed the rift between Spedan and his father, who advanced some much needed money to Peter Jones and restored Spedan's share in the Oxford Street business. Around this same time, in 1925 Spedan Lewis introduced the slogan "Never Knowingly Undersold" as the pricing policy for Peter Jones; this well-known motto was eventually adopted by the John Lewis Partnership.

By this time John Lewis was 88 and more or less content to let his sons manage the business. Oswald, however, did not agree with Spedan's radical views, and after two years Spedan persuaded him to give up his share in return for a cash settlement. Oswald was more interested in politics and soon afterward became a Conservative member of Parliament. From 1926, therefore, Spedan was effectively in control of both businesses and could begin to reorganize the Oxford Street store on the principles established at Peter Jones. All these were swiftly applied except that the transfer of profits had to be delayed until after John Lewis's death, which occurred in 1928. Spedan was left sole owner of the Oxford Street store as well as majority shareholder in Peter Jones. He immediately converted the former into a public company, John Lewis and Company Ltd. To raise capital for expansion he offered preferred shares to the public, but kept all the ordinary shares in his hands. Then he transferred these and his shares in Peter Jones to another company, John Lewis Partnership Ltd., which was to hold them in trust for the employees. The transfer was not a gift, but was made on very generous terms and was irrevocable. Spedan retained control of the trust for an experimental period.

From then on all employees were considered partners in the business. Spedan worked out an elaborate constitution for the partnership to ensure that all partners were represented in the decision-making process, while at the same time giving the board full powers to manage the business on their behalf. It was a unique structure for a business, devised by a very practical idealist. Having laid these foundations, Spedan and his colleagues turned their energies to building up the business. They proved to be a very able team. In the 1920s Spedan had begun to recruit men and women from the universities, the best of whom were given quick promotions to important jobs.

The capital raised by the public offer of 1928, and another in 1935, was used to enlarge and modernize the stores. John Lewis acquired two new buildings in seven years, one on the other side of Holles Street, followed by another part of the island site, which the John Lewis store now fills. At the same time Peter Jones was completely rebuilt in stages so that trading could continue. The new building was ultramodern in style, the first in Britain to make full use of curtain walling of steel and glass.

EXPANDING INTO THE PROVINCES, ACQUIRING WAITROSE

The company next began to broaden its base by acquiring some provincial stores: two in 1933 and two more the following year. All were in a rundown state but were gradually made profitable. With six stores in the group there was opportunity for more centralized buying, and a single warehouse was set up in London to service them all.

Most significantly for the future, although the move was not seen that way at the time, the company entered the food trade by buying a chain of ten grocery shops. The business traded as Waitrose, because its first partners were called Waite and Rose, and grew from a single shop in Acton in 1904 to ten in various parts of London by 1937. Like Sainsbury's, Waitrose was at the quality end of the grocery trade and was a well-run business, albeit a small one. As a result of this expansion, the turnover of the John Lewis Partnership grew from £1.25 million in 1928 to £3 million in 1939, and by then the company had some 6,000 partners. In 1940 the business again doubled in size by acquiring 15 more department stores and 4,000 more staff at one stroke.

Encouraged by its success in reviving the four provincial stores it already had, the John Lewis Partnership seized an opportunity to buy all the provincial stores in the Selfridge group. They had never been successful under Selfridge's ownership and were still losing money. Consequently, the John Lewis Partnership was able to buy control of these 15 stores, which had a combined turnover of £3.3 million, for a mere £30,000.

The stores had never traded under Selfridge's name, but had kept their various founders' names and continued to do so when they joined the John Lewis Partnership. Examples were Cole Brothers of Sheffield, Trewin Brothers of Watford, and Caleys of Windsor.

Their purchase, and the extensions to the Oxford Street store, were to prove a lifesaver over the next few years. By this time Britain was at war, and later in 1940 the main John Lewis building was almost completely destroyed by fire bombs. Four of the John Lewis Partnership's other stores were also destroyed. Had the business not been as widely scattered as it was, this would have been a calamity; as it was, it was just a bad setback. The loss of selling space was matched by shortages of staff and merchandise, which continued for some years after World War II. These shortages, and tight controls on building supplies, delayed further expansion of the John Lewis Partnership until the 1950s.

RAPID EXPANSION OF WAITROSE

Spedan was by then approaching retirement age, and management had largely passed into the hands of the people he had brought into the business. Unlike his father, who never formally retired, Spedan decided to do so at the age of 70, which he reached in 1955. Before retiring he signed over the last of his rights in the business to a corporate trustee. He also wrote two books about the John Lewis Partnership in the hope that its principles would be copied in other businesses. In fact, this did not happen. By 1955 the John Lewis Partnership had acquired the whole of its island site in Oxford Street and began to rebuild its store there. The work had to be done in stages and was not finished until 1960. The new building, still in use, gave the group a bigger selling area in central London than it had ever had before. The other war-damaged stores were also rebuilt at this time, and several more stores were acquired.

The biggest development in the business in the 1950s and 1960s, however, was the rapid expansion of the Waitrose chain. It had more shops than in 1937, but they were all small shops operated on the prewar pattern. In the United States self-service had largely superseded counter service in the 1940s, but retailers in Britain had been unable to experiment with this because of food rationing.

When rationing ended in the early 1950s, Waitrose was among the first British chains to try out self-service. It was also among the first to realize that self-service called for much larger shops. By 1959 it had built seven new-style supermarkets and owned 20 smaller shops. In the 1960s all the smaller shops were replaced by supermarkets. The total reached 50 in 1974 and 70 five years later. The John Lewis Partnership was quicker to embrace the new concept than many traditional food retailers and was rewarded with an increasing share of the retail food trade.

Waitrose became a far more important constituent of the John Lewis Partnership than it had been previously. Its contribution to group turnover jumped from under 15 percent in the early 1960s to over 40 percent by 1979. It developed its own trading style and own label products as well as its own distribution network and management hierarchy within the group.

CONTINUED EXPANSION THROUGH CENTURY'S END

Department stores, however, remained by far the more profitable part of the business, and investment in these continued. In the 1970s three new stores were started under the John Lewis name (in Edinburgh, Milton Keynes, and Brent Cross, London), and during the 1980s another seven were built or acquired from other owners. These new stores were much bigger than was the norm outside London. Some of the older stores were closed and others rebuilt or enlarged. As a result, the combined turnover of department stores rose almost as fast in the 1980s as that of the Waitrose food shops. Meanwhile, in 1988, the company expanded its manufacturing operations through the purchase of J.H. Birtwistle and Company, a textile supplier based in Lancashire. This brought to three the number of textile suppliers owned by the John Lewis Partnership, the company having decades earlier acquired two leading makers of household textiles, Herbert Parkinson, also based in Lancashire, and Stead McAlpin and Company, based in Cumbria.

By the end of the 1980s, almost 40,000 people shared the fruits of this business. Profits reached a peak in 1988 and 1989 of £131 million before taxes, of which £47 million was distributed among the employees.

During the recessionary period of the early 1990s, profits and the profit-sharing payout fell, totaling, for example, £93.2 million and £34.5 million, respectively, in 1993. By this time there were more than 100 Waitrose supermarkets and the partnership ran 22 department stores. The company expanded into the mail-order sector in 1993 with the purchase of Findlater Mackie Todd & Co., which sold wine through the mail and was the basis for Waitrose Wine Direct. Flowers Direct and Beer Direct were added later. Also in 1993 Stuart Hampson succeeded Peter Lewis to become the fourth chairman of the partnership. Hampson joined John Lewis in 1982, switching from a career as a high-ranking civil servant. During 1994, the first Waitrose food & home store opened in London's south end, marketing a full range of supermarket items along with a selection of household goods from John Lewis department stores.

Waitrose lost some ground during the early 1990s as its main rivals began opening on Sundays, in advance of a change in the law, and moved more rapidly to implement high-tech supply and distribution systems. It was not until 1995 that Waitrose began gaining additional revenues from opening its stores on Sundays and also completed the installation of electronic point-of-sale and ordering systems, which gave it better control over inventory and the ability to automatically reorder stock. The new initiatives had an almost immediate effect on sales, with Waitrose posting a 13 percent increase for the year ending in January 1996. This helped lift pretax profits to a record £150 million, an increase of 28 percent. The profit-sharing payout for that year amounted to £57 million, which translated into a bonus of 15 percent of salary.

From fiscal 1994 through fiscal 1998, the modernizing Waitrose chain saw its sales increase 50 percent and its profits triple. Although continuing to rely on word-of-mouth advertising over the huge television ad expenditures of its larger rivals Tesco, Sainsbury's, and Safeway, Waitrose did step up its print advertising budget during 1998 in a campaign aimed at encouraging its customers to spend more money. By 1999 the number of Waitrose outlets had been increased to more than 130. The John Lewis department store operation was also continuing its slow but steady expansion, with two stores opened in 1999 (in Bluewater, Kent, and in Glasgow) bringing the total to 25.

Also during 1999, a number of John Lewis partners began pushing for a breakup of the partnership through the sale or stock market flotation of the firm, a move that might have garnered each partner as much as £100,000. Hampson, however, strongly opposed the dissolution of the partnership and also noted that, according to the legal documents put together by John Spedan Lewis, the John Lewis trust could not be dissolved without a full Act of Parliament. He also argued that the increased investments that were being made in the group would pay off more handsomely for the partners in the long run than would a one-time payout generated by the sale or flotation of the partnership. In any event, at a meeting of representatives of John Lewis and Waitrose stores held in September 1999, little support for an end to the partnership was voiced, bringing at least a temporary end to talk of a sale.

Pressure for a breakup had arisen at least in part from a drop-off in sales during the first half of fiscal 2000. The group had a stronger second half, but pretax profits for the full year did fall 21 percent from the record level of the previous year. Profit-sharing bonuses totaled £78 million, compared to £98 million for fiscal 1999. During 2000 the company acquired 11 shops from Somerfield plc, which were then converted to Waitrose outlets. That year also saw the partnership

enter the burgeoning e-commerce sector with the launch of the John Lewis Now online shopping service and the purchase of a 40 percent interest in Last Mile Solutions, an Internet food retailer and delivery service later renamed Ocado. This was accompanied by the launch of Waitrose online shopping services for both home and workplaces, as well as the 2001 acquisition of the U.K. arm of Buy.com, an online retailer of electronic goods and computers. Buy.com was later merged into the firm's johnlewis.com online shopping site.

MAJOR OVERHAUL OF DEPARTMENT STORE ARM

Meanwhile, the profits of the John Lewis Partnership were continuing to decline in large measure because of heightened competition for the John Lewis department stores that was coming from discounters, who were forcing prices down. In late 2000 the company announced that it would begin a £300 million, three-year makeover of its 25-unit department store chain. In a perhaps belated modernizing of the operations, all of the stores not using the John Lewis name, with the exception of the flagship Peter Jones store (which was itself in the midst of an £80 million, three-year redesign), began doing so by the end of the restructuring/remodeling period. This created a unified, nationwide chain under the John Lewis name.

While sales surpassed the £4 billion mark for the first time for the year ending in January 2001, pretax profits fell once again, dropping 23 percent to £149.6 million. Profits were affected by the tough retailing environment, which was being hit by price deflation, as well as by the increased investments being made to restructure the department store operations and for the Internet initiatives. The profit-sharing payout for the 53,000 partners amounted to £58.1 million, equivalent to a 10 percent bonus, compared to the 15 percent of the preceding year.

After another down year, the John Lewis Partnership began an extended period of growing profits with the year ending in January 2003. During that year and the year that followed, the Waitrose chain was modestly expanded, with seven new stores opening. In August 2003 the partnership launched a £134 million plan to refurbish the 143 Waitrose supermarkets over a three-year period. The overhaul included new self-serve and cashier-operated checkouts, new refrigeration units, an expansion of the chain's home delivery business, and the devotion of more space to fresh foods.

In 2004 the group spent roughly £330 million to acquire and convert 19 former Safeway stores following that chain's acquisition by Wm Morrison Supermarkets

PLC. This purchase extended the Waitrose chain into the north of England for the first time. During the year ending in January 2005, four new Waitrose shops were also opened, bringing the chain total to 166. The following year a handful of additional Safeway stores were acquired and subsequently converted to the Waitrose banner, and then in the spring of 2006 the purchase of five supermarkets from Somerfield plc included what became Waitrose's first Scottish locations. By January 2007 the partnership was running 183 Waitrose outlets, and the chain over the previous three years had increased its store count by 40 and its selling space by 43 percent.

On the John Lewis department store side, the major remodeling program launched earlier in the decade began to bear fruit by the fiscal year ending in January 2007. That year, same-store sales were up more than 10 percent, sales per square foot increased nearly 10 percent, and operating profits surged 59 percent. These results were aided by a 64 percent increase in sales for the John Lewis online store, which garnered sales of £185.2 million and had begun operating in the black the previous year. As these improvements progressed, a major store expansion program was underway, starting with the May 2005 opening of a store in Manchester at Trafford Centre, the first new John Lewis outlet in four years.

AMBITIOUS EXPANSION PLANS
FOR NEW LEADER

In March 2007 Hampson retired as the partnership's chairman and was succeeded by Charlie Mayfield. The fifth and, at age 40, youngest chairman in the company's history, Mayfield was a former management consultant who had joined the John Lewis Partnership in 2000 and had served as managing director of the John Lewis department store arm since 2005. Soon after taking over the chairmanship, Mayfield outlined ambitious new growth targets, including a doubling of sales by 2017 to £12 billion, and plans for 20 more John Lewis stores and 50 more Waitroses during that period. A new John Lewis store opened in Cambridge late in 2007, followed by two more openings in 2008, in Liverpool and Leicester. A seemingly more confident group also began pursuing its first significant overseas venture. Already exporting Waitrose-branded goods into some 20 countries, the John Lewis Partnership late in 2007 entered into a licensing agreement with Dubai-based Spinneys Group Limited to open more than 20 Waitrose outlets in the United Arab Emirates by 2010.

In March 2008 the John Lewis Partnership paid out bonuses to its 69,000 partners for the previous fiscal year totaling £181 million, equivalent to 20 percent of salaries. The payout was based on the group's record results for the year, including an increase in sales of more than 6 percent and pretax profits of £379.8 million, an 18.7 percent jump over the preceding year. Later in 2008, however, the global credit crunch and resulting slump in the U.K. housing market began to hurt sales, particularly at the group's department stores, as consumers cut back on purchases of housewares and furniture. Pretax profits for the first six months of fiscal 2009 dropped nearly 27 percent, the first profit decline in six years. Despite this setback, Mayfield remained confident of the partnership's future and vowed to press on with the ambitious expansion, although he acknowledged the possibility that certain openings might be delayed if developers shelved plans for new shopping centers amid a deteriorating economic climate.

John Swan
Updated, David E. Salamie

PRINCIPAL SUBSIDIARIES

John Lewis plc; Findlater Mackie Todd & Co. Limited; Herbert Parkinson Limited; JLP Holdings BV (Netherlands); JLP Insurance Limited (Guernsey); JLP Victoria Limited; John Lewis Car Finance Limited; John Lewis Properties plc; John Lewis Transport Limited; Waitrose Limited.

PRINCIPAL COMPETITORS

Marks & Spencer Group p.l.c.; Tesco PLC; ASDA Group Limited; J Sainsbury plc; Wm Morrison Supermarkets PLC; Debenhams plc; House of Fraser PLC; NEXT plc; Arcadia Group.

FURTHER READING

Bidlake, Suzanne, "A Shopping Partner Is for Life," *Marketing*, June 27, 1991, p. 22.

Blackhurst, Chris, "Sir Stuart Hampson," *Management Today*, July 2005, p. 48.

Bradley, Keith, and Simon Taylor, *Business Performance in the Retail Sector: The Experience of the John Lewis Partnership*, Oxford: Clarendon Press, 1992, 194 p.

Brown, Malcolm, "Stuart Hampson," *Management Today*, August 1994, pp. 44, 46.

Brown-Humes, Christopher, "Goodwill Store," *Financial Times*, November 6, 1996, p. 19.

Day, Julia, "Waitrose Wises Up to Nineties Values," *Marketing Week*, June 4, 1998, pp. 21–22.

De Vita, Emma, "John Lewis: Partners on Board," *Management Today*, August 1, 2007, p. 44.

Finch, Julia, "John Lewis: Stores Group Hands £180m Bonus to Staff," *Guardian* (London), March 7, 2008, p. 34.

Hawkes, Steve, "Heady Times for John Lewis As Partnership Flexes Its Muscles," *Times* (London), March 17, 2008, p. 54.

———, "John Lewis Feels Chill of High Street As It Reports First Profit Decline in Six Years," *Times* (London), September 12, 2008, p. 61.

"The John Lewis Partnership," *Retail and Consumer Products,* September 1994, pp. 77+.

"John Lewis Profits Slump As Shoppers Demand Price Cuts," *Independent* (London), September 15, 2000, p. 18.

Kennedy, Carol, *The Merchant Princes: Family, Fortune, and Philanthropy,* London: Hutchinson, 2000, 309 p.

Lewis, John Spedan, *Fairer Shares,* London: Staples Press, 1954, 244 p.

———, *Partnership for All,* London: John Lewis Partnership, 1948, 532 p.

Macpherson, Hugh, ed., *John Spedan Lewis, 1885–1963, Remembered by Some of His Contemporaries in the Centenary Year of His Birth,* London: John Lewis Partnership, 1985.

Mesure, Susie, "Sir Stuart Hampson, Chairman of John Lewis: Urbane Retailer Who Is Never Knowingly Overstated," *Independent* (London), March 12, 2005.

Morrison, Dianne See, "Will a Bargain Boost John Lewis's Online Prospects?" *New Media Age,* March 22, 2001, p. 38.

Rigby, Elizabeth, "The Anointed Was Born for the Job," *Financial Times,* December 21, 2006, p. 19.

———, "John Lewis Bonuses at Five-Year High," *Financial Times,* March 11, 2005, p. 20.

———, "John Lewis Chairman to Depart Early," *Financial Times,* December 18, 2006, p. 23.

———, "Shopping Gets Tougher for Online Supermarkets," *Financial Times,* April 9, 2007, p. 19.

———, "Waitrose in First Move Overseas," *Financial Times,* December 31, 2007, p. 17.

Rigby, Elizabeth, and Maggie Urry, "JLP Feels the Pinch of Falling Sales," *Financial Times,* March 7, 2008, p. 22.

Rigby, Elizabeth, and Tom Braithwaite, "Crunch Knocks John Lewis," *Financial Times,* July 5, 2008, p. 1.

Rigby, Rhymer, "Never Knowingly Under-Generous," *Management Today,* October 1998, p. 126.

Ryle, Sarah, "But Is the Feeling Mutual?" *Observer* (London), April 11, 2004.

Spivey, Nigel, "The Dinosaur That Is Never Knowingly Undersold," *Financial Times,* March 22, 1997, p. 20.

"A Stake in the Store," *Economist,* June 11, 1994, p. 60.

Voyle, Susanna, "Long March to Re-energise Partnership: Luke Mayhew's Changes to Move John Lewis Out of the Doldrums Have Started to Pay Off," *Financial Times,* March 12, 2004, p. 25.

K.A. Rasmussen AS

Strandveien 165
Hamar, NO-2316
Norway
Telephone: (+47) 62 51 27 10
Fax: (+47) 62 53 26 44
Web site: http://www.ka-rasmussen.no

Private Company
Incorporated: 1872
Employees: 48
Sales: NOK 650 million ($124.3 million) (2007 est.)
NAICS: 332211 Cutlery and Flatware (Except Precious) Manufacturing; 339114 Dental Equipment and Supplies Manufacturing; 339912 Silverware and Plated Ware Manufacturing

■ ■ ■

K.A. Rasmussen AS is a leading Scandinavian-based producer of specialized semifinished and finished metals and metal products. Located in Hamar, Norway, Rasmussen produces a wide range of products, while focusing primarily on the precious metals and related alloys segments. The group's Semi-Manufactured Metals division is a leading producer of gold for the goldsmith and dental markets in the Scandinavian region, with products including gold sheets, granules, wires, solder, and anodes for gold-plating, as well as gold alloys for dental fillings and caps. This division also produces silver products, including sheets, wires, and other materials for the jewelry, silverware, and mint markets; and silver catalysts, solder, and flux powder. The

division's platinum production includes wire and sheets, crucibles and casting discs, and electrodes.

Other divisions include Catalysts, which supplies gold, silver, copper, and platinum-based catalysts and catalyst gauze. A major customer is Yara International, formerly part of Norsk Hydro. The Dental products division develops a full range of metals-based dental tools, equipment, and materials to the Scandinavian dentistry sector. The group's Consumer Goods division includes the luxury AB Gense brand of silverware, tableware, and related products, and the Eternum brand of cutlery and tableware. Rasmussen operates its own refinery division focused on processing gold, silver, and platinum for its own production. Since 2007, Rasmussen has also operated in the precious metals recovery market, through its acquisition of Swedish specialty recycling group ANA Adelmetaller. Rasmussen operates subsidiaries in Sweden, Finland, Denmark, Estonia, France, and Belgium. Founded in 1872, K.A. Rasmussen remains a private company. In 2007, the group's revenues were approximately NOK 650 million ($124 million).

GOLDSMITH IN 1872

K.A. Rasmussen was named after its founder, Knut Andreas Rasmussen, who opened a goldsmith's shop in Oslo in 1872. Rasmussen's first products consisted of decorative gold and silver pieces for bunads. These were highly ornate and largely festive costumes based on traditional clothing worn in Norway's provinces. By the late 19th century, the wearing of bunads by both men and women had become a popular part of the celebration of both national and religious holidays and festivals.

Among Rasmussen's popular designs was a series of roses and shells, first launched in 1880. These decorative pieces remained a part of the company's catalog into the 1930s. By then, however, the company had transformed itself from a small workshop into a prominent Norwegian industrial concern.

This process began toward the end of the 19th century, when Rasmussen added a new production site in Hamar, on the Mosje, the largest lake in Norway. That town had in fact been developed only since the 1850s, and had begun to grow into one of Norway's most modern towns. Rasmussen took advantage of the opportunities offered by the new city, and over the next decades the company steadily expanded its operation. Much of the group's transformation from artisan's workshop to industrial manufacturer came under Julius Rasmussen.

The company's metalworking expertise also developed strongly and by 1890 the company had won a silver medal at the Universal Exposition in Paris that year. In the years leading up to World War II, the company also extended its operations beyond decorative pieces. In 1927, for example, Rasmussen launched production of fishing lures, based on precious metals. While this product was not always the most profitable for the company, it remained in its catalog for nearly five decades, ceasing production only in 1975.

A more lucrative extension for the company came in 1932, when Rasmussen formed a partnership with Norwegian industrial giant Norsk Hydro. The two companies then worked together to develop a woven, platinum-based gauze for use as a catalyst in the production of nitric acid. Rasmussen and Norsk Hydro became close partners; even after Norsk Hydro spun off this division as Yara International, Rasmussen remained the company's exclusive provider of platinum gauze.

CREATING A PRECIOUS METALS CONGLOMERATE IN 1987

Following the war, Rasmussen regrouped its production operations at its Hamar facility. In 1950, the company completed the transition, and the Hamar site became its headquarters as well. The company quickly distinguished itself for the high quality of its products, helping to stimulate demand both in Norway and, increasingly, abroad. By the 1970s, Rasmussen had become determined to expand into the international markets.

For this, the company began acquiring companies outside of Norway, at first targeting the wider Scandinavian market. By the middle of the 1980s, the company had established operations in both Sweden and Finland, including the purchase of Sweden's MEMA-Märkström in 1987. This growth led the company to restructure itself into a holding company that year. The K.A. Rasmussen Group then became a prominent Scandinavian conglomerate focused on the precious metals sector.

Rasmussen joined forces with another Scandinavian company in the late 1980s, creating the joint venture Boliden KAR Adelmetaller in cooperation with Boliden Ore & Metals AB in 1988. The joint venture began refining and producing precious metals for the Swedish metals and mining giant, then in the process of launching a global expansion drive. As Boliden's attention turned more to its growth beyond the Scandinavian markets, the partners dissolved the joint venture in 1992. Rasmussen then took full control of Boliden KAR Adelmetaller, which was renamed as K.A. Rasmussen AB.

PRECIOUS METALS SPECIALIST IN THE 21ST CENTURY

Rasmussen completed several more acquisitions through the 1990s. These included Finland's Kultateolisuus OY in 1992, followed by a 33 percent stake in Juveel AS, based in Estonia, in 1993. Through the middle of the decade, Rasmussen sought to broaden its range of products, while keeping close to its core operations as a producer of specialist precious metals, including semifinished and finished products.

Rasmussen entered the silverware and tableware sector in 1995, with the acquisition of AB Gense. Founded in 1856 as Gustaf Eriksson NySilverfabriken in Eskilstuna, Sweden, Gense had become one of Europe's leading designers and producers of luxury silverware and tableware. Gense had also established an international presence, acquiring a number of silverware names, such as Denmark's Andersen & Burchart and silverware

KEY DATES

1872: Knut Andreas Rasmussen founds a goldsmith's shop in Oslo, producing decorative gold and silver pieces for bunads, a traditional Norwegian folk costume.

1880: Rasmussen adds a new series of designs featuring roses and shells, which become a popular part of the company's catalog into the 20th century.

1890: Under Julius Rasmussen, the company expands, adding a production facility in Hamar, and winning a silver medal at the Universal Exposition in Paris.

1927: Rasmussen launches the production of silver fishing lures.

1932: Rasmussen teams up with Norsk Hydro to develop its first platinum-based catalyst gauze for the production of nitric acid.

1950: Rasmussen consolidates its manufacturing and headquarters at its Hamar site.

1975: Rasmussen abandons production of fishing lures.

1987: Company acquires MEMA-Märkström and restructures as K.A. Rasmussen Group.

1988: Rasmussen forms a precious metals joint venture with Boliden called Boliden KAR Adelmetaller, in Sweden.

1992: Company acquires full control of the Boliden joint venture, which is then renamed as Rasmussen AB; the company acquires 33 percent of Juveel AS, in Estonia.

1995: Rasmussen adds a silverware component through the acquisition of AB Gense.

1996: Rasmussen expands its dental business with the purchase of John Sjödings AS in Sweden.

2005: Rasmussen opens a new research and development division, as well as a sales office in Washington, D.C.

2007: Company acquires precious metals recycling specialist ANA Adelmetaller, in Sweden.

specialist Carl M. Cohr. By the end of the 20th century, Gense had production centers in Sweden, Denmark, and Finland. The company had also acquired Belgian silver cutlery specialist Eternum, established in 1924, and its French subsidiary, Saint Médard, founded in 1898. In this way, Rasmussen's cutlery component became its most international, with sales throughout the world.

At the same time, the company had also boosted its dental products operations, through the acquisition of Sweden's John Sjödings AS. That company had been founded by John Sjödings, who had trained as a dental technician, in 1917 as Sjödings Dentalprodukter. The Stockholm-based company gained an international profile with the launch of the Hedström file, developed by Gustav Hedström in the 1940s. From there, Sjödings itself developed a number of its own innovative dental tools, including the S-file. In 1990, the company achieved new success with the launch of Sendoline, a nickel-titanium alloy that permitted mechanical rinsing. Rasmussen later sold the Sendoline operation, to dental equipment maker W&H, in 2005.

By then, Rasmussen itself had grown into a company posting revenues of nearly NOK 650 million (approximately $124 million) per year. In that year, Rasmussen inaugurated a new research and development department, both to develop new products and to provide solutions to technical questions and problems within the group's production divisions. In the meantime, the company boosted its international sales force, opening a sales office in Washington, D.C., that year.

Rasmussen had not abandoned external growth, however. The increasing scarcity of precious metals, and the soaring prices for metals in general in the middle of the first decade of the 2000s led the company to enter the growing new sector of precious metals recovery. For this, the company reached an agreement with Tricorona AB to acquire ANA Adelmetall in 2007. This company was the leading recycler of precious metals in the Swedish market. With roots in the late 19th century, K.A. Rasmussen looked forward to future expansion in the new century.

M. L. Cohen

PRINCIPAL SUBSIDIARIES

AB Gense (Sweden); AB John Sjöding (Sweden); AS Gense (Denmark); K.A. Rasmussen AS (Denmark); K.A. Rasmussen AS (Estonia); K.A. Rasmussen OY (Finland).

PRINCIPAL COMPETITORS

Gillette Co.; Kenwood Silver Company Inc.; Wella AG; Tramontina S.A.; Fiskars Oy Abp; Myrex International Company Ltd.; Lord Precision Industries; Tefal S.A.S.; Plata Lappas S.A.I.C. Y F.; WKI Holding Company Inc.

FURTHER READING

"Gense's Harlequin, Swedish-Designed Glass, to Bow in U.S.,"
*HFN: The Weekly Newspaper for the Home Furnishing
Network,* October 26, 1998, p. 66.

"Sweden's Tricorona AB Divests Precious Metals Recycling
Business to Norwegian Company KA Rasmussen AS,"
Nordic Business Report, November 30, 2007.

Kooperativa Förbundet

Box 15200
Stockholm, S-104 65
Sweden
Telephone: (+46 08) 743 25 00
Fax: (+46 08) 644 30 26
Web site: http://www.kf.se

Cooperative Company
Incorporated: 1900
Employees: 1,216
Sales: SEK 26.2 billion ($3.48 billion) (2007)
NAICS: 445110 Supermarkets and Other Grocery
(Except Convenience) Stores

■ ■ ■

Kooperativa Förbundet (The Swedish Cooperative Union, or KF) is the central body overseeing the operation of 51 consumer cooperative societies in Sweden, representing more than three million members. At the same time, KF is itself a retail holding company focused on the fast-moving consumer goods (FMCG) sector. KF's retail operations include Coop Sverige, one of the largest retail groups in Sweden, with approximately 700 stores. Coop Sverige's retail chains include Coop Forum, the largest hypermarket operator in the country, with 39 stores; Coop Konsum, the company's largest chain, with 167 largely urban stores; Coop Extra, a discount format, with 36 stores; the 98-store convenience format Coop Nära; and Coop Bygg, a do-it-yourself (DIY) and gardening format. In 2007, KF also acquired Daglivs, one of the largest supermarkets in Stockholm. Beyond

supermarkets, KF has a number of media-related operations, including publisher Norstedts Förlagsgrupp and the popular *Vi* magazine; academic bookstore operator Akademibokhandeln; and the Internet bookstore and media retailer Bokus. Other KF operations include banking (KF Sparkassa and MedMera Bank), as well as support operations including real estate, investment, and asset management. KF was formerly part of the Coop Norden joint venture, which has since been dismantled and replaced by a purchasing joint venture, Coop Trading, in 2008. KF remains a cooperative company, owned by its members. Lars Idermark serves as the group's CEO. In 2007, KF generated total revenues of SEK 26.2 billion ($3.48 billion).

CENTRAL COOPERATIVE BODY IN 1899

The cooperative movement swept across Europe in the first half of the 19th century, taking hold in nearly every commercial sector, from house-building to banking, and to groceries and consumer goods. In Sweden, government controls severely restricted commerce and trade in the country. This provided for little in the way of a competitive commercial environment, particularly in the country's rural areas. Consumers were dependent on local markets, held infrequently in the smaller villages. The rural villages also rarely supported more than one shop. The lack of modern transportation methods meant that travel to other villages, and their shops and markets, remained impractical, if not impossible.

As a result, a number of basic commodities and necessities, such as galoshes, had come under the control of monopolies and pricing cartels. Despite the growth of Sweden's urban population, as the country underwent a transformation from an agrarian society to an industrial economy, the lack of real competition in the marketplace meant that consumers, especially the growing ranks of the urban working class, continued to pay artificially high prices.

The first attempts to break this restrictive environment came in 1850, when a group of farmers put together a buying collective. The idea took hold, and over the next decade and a half, the Swedish government finally gave into the growing consumer pressure, passing the Freedom of Commerce Decree in 1864. The new economic freedom supported the rapid initial growth of Sweden's cooperative movement; by the mid-1870, the country already boasted more than 300 consumer cooperatives.

The new cooperatives remained for the most part small, local organizations. The cooperatives often lacked the necessary business and managerial expertise, leading to a large number of failures in the movement. Even into the years before World War I, the cooperative movement remained highly fragmented among many locally and independently operating smaller cooperatives, with an average of under 200 members each.

In the meantime, however, the cooperative movement had gained strong legal status, following the passage of legislation codifying their operation in 1895. The new regulations in turn stimulated the movement toward the creation of a central body overseeing the operations of the smaller cooperatives, which continued to operate independently of each other. In 1899, a group of 41 cooperatives joined together and founded Kooperativa Förbundet, or The Swedish Cooperative Union.

CHALLENGING THE CARTELS IN THE TWENTIES

KF, as the union was more popularly known, was initially founded to support its cooperative members with information and other advice on running their businesses. The union quickly expanded its influence, however, emerging as a major social force in Sweden. A first step in this direction came when KF launched a collective purchasing operation in 1904. By representing a larger volume, KF was able to negotiate lower wholesale prices for the small cooperatives. KF's wholesale wing grew into a major part of the union's operations through the 1920s.

KF added a number of other important components during this period as well. In 1908, the union founded KF Sparkassa, providing savings services for its members. In that year, also, the union joined with the Swedish Federation of Trade Unions to launch a jointly owned insurance company, Folksam General. That company offered fire insurance policies to the working class, which remained underserved by the country's insurance industry. By 1914, Folksam had expanded its insurance operations to include Folksam Life, offering mutual life insurance products.

These activities helped stimulate the movement of the country's still highly independent and fragmented cooperative sector toward a single centralized body. By 1910, KF counted 400 member cooperatives and nearly 75,000 members. By 1920, more than 1,000 cooperatives had joined KF, boosting its membership to 250,000. The individual societies remained characterized by their relatively small size. Nonetheless, into the 1950s, as KF's membership reached one million, the average size of its member cooperatives had already begun to grow, reaching an average of 1,500.

In the meantime, backed by a membership of a quarter of a million consumers, KF decided to attack the country's cartels and monopolies head on, by becoming a manufacturer. One of the more prominent monopolies in the country at the time controlled the sale of margarine, an important Swedish staple food. In 1909, KF bought its own factory and launched the own production of margarine, thereby breaking the monopoly on the sector. In this way, the union succeeded in reducing the price of margarine by nearly one-third.

Over the next 30 years, KF entered a number of other manufacturing sectors, including lightbulbs and galoshes. By the 1940s, the cooperative union had emerged as a major industrial force in Sweden in its own right. This industrial tradition continued into the 1960s, as the union targeted consumer sectors lacking a strong competitive environment. In 1964, for example,

KEY DATES

■

1850: The first farmers' cooperative is formed in Sweden.

1864: The passage of the Freedom of Commerce Decree stimulates the growth of the cooperative movement.

1899: Kooperativa Förbundet (KF) is created as a centralized body for the consumer cooperative movement.

1909: KF launches production of margarine, breaking up the monopoly in Sweden.

1941: KonsumStockholm becomes the first supermarket in Sweden.

1964: KF opens its first hypermarket.

1988: KF absorbs the OK Coop group.

1993: KF sells its manufacturing operations to focus on its retail holdings.

2001: KF joins Coop Norden grocery union with counterparts in Denmark and Norway.

2007: KF takes back control of its grocery operations following the breakup of Coop Norden and forms Coop Sverige.

the company added production of tampons, leading to strong price reductions for this product.

SUPERMARKET GROWTH IN THE POSTWAR ERA

KF's first entry into the supermarket and retail sector came as early as 1941, with the creation of Konsum, located in Stockholm, which became the country's first large-scale grocery store. By the end of that decade, KF had put into place a national distribution system. This in turn enabled the cooperative movement to develop a strong nationally operating retail and supermarket component.

The postwar period also represented a major period of change for the cooperative movement in general. By then, Sweden had completed its transformation into one of the world's most modern and industrial societies. The arrival of the automobile, and its new availability to the full range of the country's population, now made consumers more mobile than ever before. People were no longer confined to purchasing from their local shops or co-ops, because they were now able to easily drive the 20 or more kilometers to the next major supermarket.

KF and its members responded to this situation by developing their own chain of departments in the

1950s. By the end of the decade, the group had opened 100 department stores, covering the entire country. At the same time, KonsumStockholm had also expanded strongly, later becoming known as Coop Konsum. By the end of the century, there were nearly 170 Coop Konsum stores in Sweden, including its first hypermarket, opened in 1964.

During that decade as well, the Swedish cooperative movement carried out a first wave of consolidation among its membership, forming the first of a number of "mega-cooperatives," particularly in the country's more urban areas. This process was to continue through the 1990s, both through mergers within KF member cooperatives, as well as through mergers with other cooperative unions. In 1988, for example, KF took control of the OK Coop group. By the close of the century, while the number of individual cooperative members had swelled to more than 2.5 million, the numbers of independent cooperatives operating in Sweden had been shrinking. Into the 2000s, there remained just 75 local cooperatives, two-thirds of which were grouped under KF.

RETAIL FOCUS INTO THE 21ST CENTURY

KF increasingly focused on its fast-moving consumer goods retail operations. The Folksam insurance group, which had grown into one of Sweden's largest, had been split off from the company. The union also moved to exit the department store sector, shutting down these businesses at the beginning of the 1990s. At the same time, KF decided to refocus itself around its retail operations, and in 1993 sold the last of its manufacturing businesses.

Instead, KF developed a range of new retail formats through the 1990s and into the 2000s. These ranged from its Konsum supermarkets, to the Coop Extra discount format, as well as a convenience store format, Coop Nära, and a DIY and gardening specialist Coop Bygg. KF had also entered other retail areas, notably bookstores, including its Akademibokhandeln chain. By the late 1990s, KF had also developed an Internet-based bookstore and media retail outlet, Bokus, in a joint venture with Germany's Bertelsmann. KF subsequently bought out Bertelsmann's share in 2002.

KF had launched a number of other ventures as well. The company entered the publishing sector through its control of the Norstedts Förlagsgrupp; KF also acquired the popular *Vi* magazine, closely aligned with the cooperative movement. Another strong retail area for the company was women's clothing, led by the KappAhl chain of 240 stores in Sweden and elsewhere in Scandinavia. Less successful was the company's attempt to launch an Internet banking component, called Coop Bank, in a partnership with insurance group Skandia Liv and TeliaSonera, in 2000. KF pulled out of the venture, effectively ending it, in 2003.

KF also streamlined its retail operations during this period. The company had built up a chain of 26 Coop Power consumer electronics stores. In 2002, however, KF spun off this chain into a new joint venture company, led by Norway's Expert ASA, and including that country's consumer cooperative, Coop NKL. The new company, in which KF became a minority shareholder, was called Power AB. The company also exited the retail clothing sector, selling the KappAhl chain to Nordic Capital and Accent Equity Partners in 2004.

Another KF venture of the period lasted longer. In 2000, KF joined with its counterparts Forbrukersamvirket, in Norway and FDB in Denmark to combine their grocery operations into a single union, Coop Norden. The new company, which became operational in 2001, then claimed a 35 percent share of the total Scandinavian market, with sales of more than $7.5 billion. By 2007, however, the three Coop Norden members had agreed to go their separate ways, and KF resumed direct control of its Swedish supermarket empire. In Coop Norden's place, the three unions created a new joint purchasing venture, Coop Trading, in 2008. KF's own retail grocery operations in Sweden were now placed under a new umbrella group, Coop Sverige.

Total cooperative membership had continued to increase in the later years of the first decade of the 2000s, topping three million members by 2008. However, the cooperative movement itself had changed significantly since its origins in rural Sweden in the 19th century. Where members remained a controlling factor in the small, independently operating cooperatives at KF's origins, the cooperative union had long outgrown its initial democratic organization. From a cooperative union, KF had become one of Sweden's most powerful retail corporations.

M. L. Cohen

PRINCIPAL SUBSIDIARIES

AB Tidningen Vi; Akademibokhandelsgruppen AB; Bokus AB; Bopec Progress AB; Coop Norden AB; Coop Sverige AB; Daglivs AB; Fastighets AB; KF Cooperative Society; KF Fastigheter AB; KF Försäkrings AB; KF Invest AB; Kvarn AB; MedMera Bank AB; Norstedts Förlagsgrupp AB; PAN Vision Holding AB; Stockholms Dykeri AB.

PRINCIPAL COMPETITORS

ICA AB; Axel Johnson AB; Bergendahl and Son AB; Hemkoepskedjan AB; Konsum Nord AB; Konsum Vaermland; Konsum Norrbotten Ek-För; Konsumentföreningen Goeta Ek För; Konsumentföreningen Bohuslaen-Aelvsborg; Konsumentföreningen Gaevleborg; Hakon Invest AB.

FURTHER READING

Carnegy, Hugh, "Changes in Store at the Grocery," *Financial Times,* July 8, 1994, p. 14.
"Grocery Giant Formed from Coop Fusion," *Dagens Industri,* April 6, 2001, p. 17.
"Kooperativa Forbundet Buys Out Bertelsmann from Bokus," *M2 Best Books,* November 21, 2002.
"Kooperativa Forbundet to Divest KappAhl Chain to Nordic Capital and Accent Equity Partners," *Nordic Business Report,* October 28, 2004.
"Merger Plans for Cooperative Societies," *Dagens Naeringsliv,* October 8, 2000.
"Partners Row As Coop Bank Fails," *Retail Banker International,* September 17, 2003, p. 3.
"Swedish Competition Authorities Clear KF's Acquisition of Bokus," *Nordic Business Report,* January 29, 2003.

Lehman Brothers Holdings Inc.

---

745 Seventh Avenue
New York, New York 10019-6801
U.S.A.
Telephone: (212) 526-7000
Toll Free: (800) 666-2388
Fax: (212) 526-3738
Web site: http://www.lehman.com

Public Company
Founded: 1850 as H. Lehman & Bro.
Employees: 28,600
Total Assets: $691.06 billion (2007)
Stock Exchanges: Over the Counter (OTC)
Ticker Symbol: LEHMQ.PK
NAICS: 523120 Securities Brokerage; 523920 Portfolio
Management

■ ■ ■

Lehman Brothers Holdings Inc. is a venerable New York investment bank that was forced to file for liquidation in September 2008 after becoming a victim of the mortgage market crisis that began a year earlier. With offices in London as well as Tokyo, Lehman has evolved into a diversified, global financial services firm, heavily involved in investment banking, investment management, private equity, private banking, equity and fixed income sales, and research and trading. It has also been a major dealer in U.S. Treasury securities. Lehman caters to corporations, institutional clients, governments and municipalities, and high net worth individuals. Two weeks after filing for Chapter 11 bankruptcy protection,

Lehman sold its flagship North American capital markets division to Barclays PLC of the United Kingdom. Barclays also acquired the rights to use the Lehman Brothers name, leaving the future of the Lehman's brand far from certain.

MID-19TH-CENTURY ORIGINS

Lehman Brothers was founded in 1850 in Montgomery, Alabama, by immigrant brothers Henry, Emanuel, and Mayer Lehman. The eldest of the three, Henry, the son of a cattle merchant, had come to the United States in 1844 from the small Bavarian village of Rimpar. Just 23 years old, Henry Lehman settled in Montgomery, a town not much larger than Rimpar, for unknown reasons and initially earned his living as an itinerant merchant. A year later he had saved enough money to open a shop in town. He was soon joined by his 20-year-old brother Emanuel and together they grew the business, so that when another year passed they moved to a new location and hung a sign declaring "H. Lehman & Bro." The Lehman Brothers name was then adopted after the youngest brother, Mayer, made the transatlantic trip in 1850.

Although designated as grocers in the Montgomery City Directory, Lehman Brothers were really general merchants who increasingly focused on cotton, the king crop in town. Probably they accepted bales of cotton as cash from their planter customers and in time began buying cotton for trading. It was a natural step that they should become brokers, linking buyers and sellers. Soon, however, the company would have to do without Henry Lehman, who at the age of 33 succumbed to a yellow fever epidemic while on a business trip to New Orleans in 1855.

Emanuel and Mayer Lehman built upon what their elder brother began, enhancing the Lehman name with cotton planters and merchants across the country. By the late 1850s the center of the cotton trade had settled in New York City, the financial capital of the country. There transactions between growers and the mills of New England and Great Britain could be more effectively conducted. Hence, in 1858 Lehman Brothers opened a New York office and Emanuel Lehman made his home there. Mayer Lehman stayed in Montgomery, where he would reorganize the family business after the Civil War broke out and the brothers' New York office was cut off from the South. Loyal to the Southern cause, Mayer Lehman kept the business alive by forging an alliance with cotton merchant John Wesley Durr that resulted in the partnership Lehman, Durr & Co.

POST–CIVIL WAR
REORGANIZATION IN NEW YORK

At the end of the war in 1865 all of the Lehman stores, some 88,000 bales of cotton, were put to the torch lest federal troops confiscate them. Nevertheless, Lehman Brothers quickly reestablished itself in the cotton trade after hostilities ceased, with Emanuel reopening for business in New York while Mayer and Durr set up shop in Montgomery and Mayer's young brother-in-law, Benjamin Newgass, established a branch in New Orleans. With Durr and Newgass more than able to run the Southern operations, Mayer Lehman joined his older brother in New York City, which now became the base of operations for Lehman Brothers.

As before, the focus of Lehman Brothers was on cotton, and in the postwar years the firm helped establish the Cotton Exchange in 1870. The firm extended its interests to other commodities as well,

including coffee, grains, and sugar, and later became involved in the New York Petroleum Exchange after the discovery of oil in eastern Pennsylvania. In addition, Lehman Brothers began dealing in securities, using its growing capital and that of its clients and Southern associates to purchase stocks and bonds. To solidify its position, the firm acquired a seat on the New York Stock Exchange in 1887. Investment banking became another area of interest for Lehman Brothers during the Reconstruction Era. Soon after the Civil War, the firm became the Fiscal Agent of the State of Alabama and sold the state's bonds and serviced its debt. As the South began to rebuild and industrialize, Lehman Brothers was uniquely qualified among New York investment bankers to assess the viability of projects promoted in the South. In the final decades of the 1800s, the firm also became involved in some major land development deals, Southern railroads, and commercial banking.

Before turning over control of Lehman Brothers to a new generation, Emanuel and Mayer Lehman invested in the public utilities sector. Mayer Lehman died in 1897 at the age of 67, and while Emanuel lived another ten years he was no longer active in the firm by the start of the next century. Now leading Lehman Brothers was Emanuel's son, Philip, and other members of the second generation, including cousins Sigmund, Arthur, and Meyer H. They would later be joined by Herbert H. Lehman.

In the early years of the 1900s, the Montgomery and New Orleans branches were no longer playing an important role in Lehman Brothers and were phased out. The new generation of partners invested in many of the up-and-coming companies of the day, such as the Electric Vehicle Company, the Rubber Tire Wheel Company, the American Light and Traction Company, and the International Steam Pump Company, for which Lehman Brothers underwrote its first public stock offering in 1899. At the close of the century, the firm also became an early financial backer of a new breed of retailers, including Gimbel Brothers, F.W. Woolworth Company, R.H. Macy & Company, and Sears, Roebuck & Company.

INVESTMENT BANKS FOCUS:
WORLD WAR I ERA

The main business of Lehman Brothers by the end of World War I was investment banking, and the commodities business became increasingly less important. During the economic boom of the Roaring Twenties, the firm not only continued to focus on the retailing sector but also invested in new, high-growth areas, such as airlines and entertainment. Lehman Brothers arranged start-up financing for such film studios as 20th Century

Fox, Paramount, and RKO. In addition, in 1922 a municipal department and bond department were formed, and late in the decade the Investment Advisory Service was formed. During the final four years of the 1920s, the firm headed or co-managed about 60 public offerings of stock. During this period, Lehman Brothers helped form a number of investment companies, including The Lehman Corporation, created in 1929.

The stock market crash of 1929 that triggered the Great Depression of the 1930s forced Lehman Brothers to be innovative. Changes in law that created separation between commercial banking and investment banking forced the firm to sever longstanding ties with commercial banks. A scarcity of capital also led to Lehman Brothers pursuing new approaches to financing, such as the revolutionary concept of the "private placement" of stock, creating new sources of financing for blue-chip borrowers from insurance companies and other financial institutions. Lehman Brothers' reputation for providing funding for young industries continued as well during the 1930s. It helped fund the Radio Corporation of America, RCA, and was an early backer of television, underwriting the initial public offering (IPO) of the first television manufacturer, Dumont. An oil boom in the Southwest also led Lehman Brothers to back oil services companies including Haliburton and Kerr-McGee.

The Great Depression did not end until the United States' entry into World War II and military spending stoked the economy. Following a brief recession the year after the war ended in 1945, the economy embarked on another extended boom, and Lehman Brothers prospered as well, especially active in consumer industries, such as automaking and home appliances, as well as such consumer-oriented companies as Campbell Soup, General Foods, and Philip Morris. As the boom continued in the 1950s, Lehman Brothers was quick to become involved in the start of the electronics sector, backing Litton Industries and others, and the nascent computer sector, underwriting the IPO for Digital Equipment. With more cars on the highways and more highways to use, as well as a growing appetite among Americans for travel, the firm backed the IPO of Hertz Rent-a-Car in the 1950s, and in the following decade backed American Airlines, Continental Airlines, and TWA. In 1963 Lewis L. Glucksman was brought in to launch a commercial-paper operation, a lucrative business in selling promissory notes to provide short-term funding for corporations and other entities.

In the 1960s and 1970s Lehman Brothers looked increasingly overseas as many of the firm's clients expanded internationally. Hence, a Paris office opened in 1960, followed by a London office in 1972, and a Tokyo office in 1973. The early 1970s were also a time of extreme challenge and change in the upper ranks of management. In 1969 Robert Lehman, the last of the Lehman family to head the firm, died at the age of 77, and failed to leave a succession plan. Principal partner since 1925, Lehman was a skilled leader, described by the *New York Times* as "a prince in both personal lifestyle and Machiavellian management technique." He was especially adept at pitting one partner or clique against another to get his way. He was ill for the last four years of his life, yet left the matter of succession unsettled. To protect the partners' capital and limit liability, Lehman Brothers was incorporated in 1970.

LEHMAN BROTHERS AVERTS DISASTER: 1973

With a vacuum of leadership in the firm in the early 1970s, Glucksman attempted to take the commercial-paper department into government securities, but his timing proved faulty, because in the summer of 1973 interest rates soared at a time when Lehman Brothers held a large inventory of bonds. Not only did the firm have to pay high rates to finance the securities, buyers for the paper were scarce, leading to plummeting values, and an $8 million loss for Lehman Brothers in fiscal 1973 (which came to an end on September 30 of that year). In this time of uncertainty at the firm, Peter G. Peterson, a partner since only June 1973, was named chairman in what the *New York Times* characterized as a coup d'etat. Peterson, the former chairman and CEO of Bell & Howell Corporation, had served as the commerce secretary for the Nixon administration and had been ousted from his cabinet post, "presumably by his White House foes, H. R. Haldeman and John W. Ehrlichman," according to the *New York Times.*

Under Peterson, Lehman Brothers regained its feet. Lehman Holding Company, Inc., was formed to hold Lehman shares and a pair of European banks made a $7 million investment, replenishing the firm's coffers. In 1975 Lehman acquired the 60-year-old brokerage house of Abraham & Co., adding Abraham's proficiency in investment management and equity distribution. An even larger transaction was completed two years later with the merger with another well-known, old-line investment banking house, Kuhn Loeb & Company, founded in 1867. The resulting holding company entity, headed by Peterson, took the name Lehman Brothers Kuhn Loeb Inc., although overseas it would operate as Kuhn Loeb Lehman Brothers International. It immediately become one of the largest investment banks, boasting total capital of more than $78 million and trailing only three other firms: Salomon Brothers, Goldman Sachs, and First Boston.

While Peterson was successful in turning around Lehman, tension in the firm mounted between the investment bankers and Glucksman's traders, who were responsible for most of the profits. The matter came to a head in the early 1980s, and to keep peace Peterson named Glucksman as co-chief executive in May 1983. Just two months later, however, Glucksman informed Peterson that he wanted to run the firm by himself, and Peterson obliged, stepping aside but not before he arranged a financial settlement estimated at $15 million. The Lehman board was essentially presented with a fait accompli when it voted to accept Glucksman's ascension. Glucksman's tenure at the helm would be brief and tumultuous. He ruffled feathers by promoting friends, and more importantly began to change bonus allocations, heavily rewarding traders while slashing the payouts of the bankers, and altered share allocations in a similar manner. Some high-profile partners began to leave, and then Glucksman made the fatal error of allowing the board to meet without him. His grasp began to slip, and to make matters worse, a drop in the stock market crippled the firm, which now found itself in need of fresh capital. The board voted to put the firm up for sale and there was nothing Glucksman could do to prevent it. Thus, in May 1984, Lehman was sold to Shearson/American Express for $360 million and took the name Shearson Lehman Brothers Holdings Inc.

TAKEN PUBLIC: 1994

More changes were to follow in the ten years under American Express, which spun off Shearson in 1987. Lehman acquired a seat on the London Stock Exchange

in 1986 as well as a seat on the Tokyo Stock Exchange in 1988. In that same year, E.F. Hutton was acquired and the firm was renamed Shearson Lehman Hutton Holdings Inc. This entity was then split in two in 1990: Shearson brokerage operations and Lehman Brothers Investment banking. The former would be sold to Smith Barney in 1993, and the latter spun off in a $1.6 billion public stock offering in 1994 that made Lehman Brothers Holdings Inc. a New York Stock Exchange–listed company.

Lehman Brothers enjoyed a good run in the mid-1990s, when it became one of the major underwriters of IPOs of stock, and also did a thriving business in debt issue. The firm was overexposed, however, and in 1998 suffered severe trading losses that led to a plummeting stock price and rumors that it was on the verge of bankruptcy. Under the leadership of chief executive Richard S. Fuld Jr., Lehman Brothers quickly rebounded and resumed a growth strategy. In 1999 it acquired Delaware Savings Bank of Wilmington, renamed Lehman Brothers Bank, to serve as a platform for a national consumer banking business.

Even as the economy soured in 2001, the firm continued to perform well and unlike many of its rivals did not have to trim headcount. Later in the year, on September 11, 2001, Lehman Brothers was disrupted by the terrorist attacks of that day. Although the firm occupied three floors of one of the Twin Towers of the World Trade Center that collapsed, it lost but one employee. Its global headquarters located in Three World Financial Center, on the other hand, was severely damaged and could no longer house the firm's 6,500 employees. Lehman Brothers took up temporary quarters in Jersey City and returned to trading within the week, and over the next few months farmed out employees to more than 40 temporary locations. In March 2002, Lehman Brothers brought everyone together at a new headquarters in the Times Square area.

Lehman Brothers enjoyed some successes in its new home but would also experience some difficulties that would ultimately lead to its failure. It established a Wealth and Asset Management division, acquired Lincoln Capital Management's fixed income business, acquired Neuberger Berman to bolster its wealth and asset management business, and purchased The Crossroads Group to grow its private equity fund investment management business. Net revenues increased from $6.15 billion in fiscal 2002 to $19.26 billion in fiscal 2007, while net income increased from $975 million to near $4.2 billion. Despite this performance Lehman Brothers' image, and that of Wall Street in general, was tarnished in 2003 when it became one of ten firms to settle charges with federal and New York State regulators regarding the improper way analysts touted stocks to land underwriting opportunities for the investment banking divisions and other practices.

A far more serious problem would arise in the summer of 2007 when a crisis unfolded related to the subprime and prime mortgage markets in which Lehman Brothers was a major participant. Investors grew worried that the firm might be liable for significant losses and as a consequence began to bid down the price of Lehman Brothers' stock. For the next year the firm teetered on the edge of disaster but managed to keep its footing. The situation would grow more dire, however, as the firm not only had to contend with write-downs but its stock became the target of short sellers, further eroding confidence. When the mortgage industry was rocked by the government takeover of Fannie Mae and Freddie Mac in early September 2008, whatever hopes Lehman Brothers held out for a government bailout faded.

LIQUIDATION: 2008

Lehman Brothers filed for Chapter 11 bankruptcy protection on September 15, 2008, for purposes of liquidation. Many of the firm's assets in Europe, Asia, and the Middle East were acquired by Nomura Holdings of Japan, and the Neuberger Berman asset management unit was sold to Bain Capital and Hellman & Friedman. The United Kingdom's Barclays PLC acquired Lehman's North American capital markets division, including the firm's fixed income and equity sales, trading and research, prime services, investment banking, principal investing, and private investment management business. Although they would reopen under the Barclays Capital name, Barclays also acquired the rights to use the Lehman Brothers name. Given the brand value of the name, it was likely that Lehman Brothers would remain an operating company in some form. Whether it would ever regain a place of prominence in the financial world remained doubtful.

Ed Dinger

PRINCIPAL SUBSIDIARIES

Lehman Brothers Inc.

PRINCIPAL COMPETITORS

The Goldman Sachs Group, Inc.; Merrill Lynch & Co., Inc.; Morgan Stanley.

FURTHER READING

Auletta, Ken, "The Fall of Lehman Brothers: The Men, the Money, the Merger," *New York Times*, February 24, 1985.

———, *Greed and Glory on Wall Street: The Fall of the House of Lehman*, New York: Random House, Inc., 1986, 253 p.

Bender, Marylyn, "The White Knight at Lehman Brothers," *New York Times*, November 11, 1973.

A Centennial: Lehman Brothers, 1850–1950, New York: Lehman Brothers, 1950, 63 p.

de la Merced, Michael J., "Two Equity Firms Buy Lehman's Money Management Unit," *New York Times*, September 30, 2008.

Sloan, Allan, "Lessons from the House of Lehman," *Fortune*, July 7, 2008, p. 16.

Sloane, Leonard, "Lehman and Kuhn Loeb to Merge," *New York Times*, November 29, 1977.

Sorkin, Andrew Russ, "Lehman Files for Bankruptcy; Merrill Is Sold," *New York Times*, September 15, 2008.

Taylor, Alexander L., III, "Fire Sale; A Buyer for Lehman Brothers," *Time*, April 23, 1984, p. 68.

Linear Technology
Corporation

1630 McCarthy Boulevard
Milpitas, California 95035-7487
U.S.A.
Telephone: (408) 432-1900
Fax: (408) 434-0507
Web site: http://www.linear.com

Public Company
Incorporated: 1981
Employees: 4,173
Sales: $1.17 billion (2008)
Stock Exchanges: NASDAQ
Ticker Symbol: LLTC
NAICS: 334413 Semiconductor and Related Device
   Manufacturing

∎ ∎ ∎

Linear Technology Corporation develops, manufactures, and markets an array of high-performance linear integrated circuits. These circuits use analog waves to measure physical properties such as sound, pressure, weight, and light, and serve as the backbone for a wide range of products. The company's circuits are used in audio amplifiers, voltage regulators, power management products, and many other electronic devices, which in turn are used in computers, cellphones, satellites, cars and trucks, and other consumer products.

THE MAKING OF A CEO

Linear Technology is the progeny of engineer and semiconductor industry pioneer Robert Swanson, who founded the company in 1981. With three former coworkers, Swanson built the fledgling Linear into a $100 million company in the span of a decade, and established Linear as a technological leader in its niche. A self-proclaimed goof-off, Swanson nevertheless displayed his desire, early on, to succeed at what interested him. He lettered in football, baseball, and hockey at his western Massachusetts high school during the 1950s, for example, and spent his summers as a lifeguard. It was during high school that Swanson became intrigued with the burgeoning technology of semiconductors.

Swanson graduated from Northeastern University in 1960 with a degree in industrial engineering. Most colleges at the time were still teaching vacuum-tube technology, and semiconductors were in many ways considered to be experimental. Swanson started hunting for a job, walking into prospective employers' offices in Boston without a resume and asking for work. He turned down a $100-per-week offer from Polaroid to take a job with Transitron, then the nation's second largest chip manufacturer. It happened to be a great opportunity, as Transitron became a leader in military semiconductor applications. Swanson quickly became involved in a number of high-tech, high-profile projects, including the Polaris Missile program.

After three years at Transitron, Swanson yearned to move to California, where Silicon Valley was emerging as the center of the expanding semiconductor universe. After receiving a call from one of the soon-to-be famous founders of then-unknown Fairchild Semiconductor, he moved west. Swanson worked for chip pioneer Fairchild from 1963 to 1968 before joining National

Semiconductor Corporation. He spent ten years at National, helping it grow into one of the largest and most successful players in the chip business. However, as the company made the transition from a smaller, more entrepreneurial company to a big corporation, Swanson lost interest. "For 13 of 14 years at National, I was a gung-ho guy," Swanson later recalled in a May 13, 1991 *Business Journal-San Jose* article. When the company mushroomed in size, Swanson commented, "I kept looking at all the companies whose butts we'd been kicking. And then National started organizing itself like them. It was frustrating."

Swanson was eager to jump ship and start his own company. By the early 1980s the semiconductor industry was beginning to focus heavily on newer digital chips, which offered greater speed and power than traditional analog chips. Despite the new technology, Swanson believed that the demand for analog chips would continue to grow. Importantly, analog chips were better than digital chips at measuring real world properties including pressure and temperature, and digitals required support from analog chips in many applications. Swanson reasoned that as digital chips increased the potential applications for semiconductors, demand for analog chips would continue to grow despite the fact that they represented an increasingly smaller share of the overall semiconductor market.

THE START-UP: 1981–84

Swanson finally left National Semiconductor and in 1981 formed Linear Technology. His goal was to develop analog chips and to eventually profit from the growth of new applications created by digital chip

technology. He took three fellow executives from National with him and secured $5 million in venture capital funding. They subsequently hired away several of National's most talented minds. Swanson's former boss at National, Charlie Sporck, was furious his former coworkers were going to compete with his company. He tried to squelch the venture with lawsuits, claiming Linear had stolen technology developed at National. "We did choose to compete against them, and they accused us of misappropriating trade secrets, or stealing," Swanson told the *Business Journal-San Jose* (May 13, 1991). "But I'll tell you, for every guy we hired away from National, ten applied."

The tiny Linear Technology started out developing and supplying popular analog devices such as voltage regulators. It initially found its niche as a second-source supplier, providing chips to buyers whose main suppliers failed to fill an order. By filling that role, Linear was able to get its foot in the door and show the marketplace it could provide semiconductors that were less expensive, more reliable, and had more features than those provided by the competition. The second-source strategy was particularly effective during the chip boom in 1983 and 1984, when big suppliers reached capacity and equipment manufacturers had to turn to Linear to fulfill their analog semiconductor needs.

During the early 1980s Linear used the cash flow from its successful but relatively low-tech line of analog chips to fund research and development of more advanced linear devices. The company's goal was to become a leader in developing, making, and marketing advanced, high-profit analog chips that could be used in new applications made possible by digital technology. Such applications included miniature battery-powered devices, cellular phones and portable computers, for example, that required analog technology to regulate voltage or interpret analog sound waves. The challenge was to design analog chips that were simultaneously more powerful, more efficient, and smaller than those currently in use.

A SUCCESSFUL STRATEGY: 1985–89

Linear's legal battles with National Semiconductor turned out to be the greatest challenge of its early years. National filed a series of lawsuits as part of an effort to quash Linear and reduce its competitiveness. However, Swanson's bet on the analog chip market paid off big, allowing Linear to overcome huge legal bills that might have ruined most start-ups. Even when the overall semiconductor industry plummeted in 1985, Linear was able to double revenues in the wake of surging demand for its analog chips. Linear's success was due in part to

KEY DATES

1968: Robert Swanson joins National Semiconductor Corporation.
1981: Swanson creates Linear Technology with $5 million in funding.
1982: Linear opens its first wafer fabrication plant, near its offices in Milpitas.
1986: Linear Technology debuts on the NASDAQ.
1987: Linear partners with Texas Instruments to gain access to advanced chip processes.
1993: The company announces plans for a new fabrication plant in Washington State.
1995: Linear opens a manufacturing plant in Penang, Malaysia.
1999: Linear is reorganized into four business units with Clive Davies as president; Swanson gains the chairmanship.
2000: Linear is added to Standard & Poor's top 500 companies listing.
2003: Davies retires and David Bell succeeds him as president.
2005: Linear surpasses $1 billion in revenues.
2008: Linear is awarded its 440th patent with numerous others pending.

its growing reputation for quality products and good customer service.

As important as its service and quality focus, though, was the simple fact that Linear was the biggest of only a handful of U.S. companies targeting the analog market instead of chasing digital technology. Further, the analog chip industry differed from the digital sector in that the chips Linear produced were typically customized, and did not lend themselves to mass production. One important corollary of this attribute was that Linear was effectively excluded from the rash of Japanese competition that battered U.S. digital chip producers during the mid-1980s. Another advantage Linear enjoyed was a diversified customer base that reduced the risks larger digital chip manufactures faced in relying on a few major industries to buy their products.

A final boon for Linear was that it could rely on relatively old technology to produce its chips, while digital chip makers had to stay on the cutting edge to remain competitive. Swanson believed Linear would be able to post big profits once it had successfully developed more advanced analog chips, hence putting

every spare cent into research for the company's first several years. Everything changed in the middle of the decade as Linear hit several milestones. In May 1986 the company went public to raise capital for expansion and at the close of its fiscal year in June the company had earned its first net income of almost $1.2 million on sales of $20 million.

Over the next year Linear's sales shot up 60 percent to $35 million with income climbing to $3.3 million. Years of putting every spare cent back into research had finally paid off and Linear fought to keep up with demand. In June 1987 the company formed a partnership with Texas Instruments, gaining access to the firm's advanced chip processing technologies, low-cost assembly lines, and test facilities in Taiwan. In return, Texas Instruments was allowed to use several of Linear's proprietary chips for relatively negligible royalties. Expanded production capacity helped push Linear's sales to $51 million for 1988 and to $65 million the following year, generating nearly $16 million in annual profits.

EXTREME GROWTH: THE NINETIES

After wowing investors with big gains during the mid- and late 1980s, Linear went on to achieve even greater growth and profitability during the early 1990s—including expansion into Asia with an office and small plant in Singapore, a very prescient move. Company engineers and marketers attacked almost every niche of the semiconductor market, producing specialized, high-tech analog chips that were put to use in cars, trucks, cellphones, computer peripherals, satellites, medical instruments, and many other electronic products. "They're basically in anything that has a switch," said semiconductor industry analyst Carolyn Rogers in a 1992 *Business Journal-San Jose* article. Linear's sales increased to $119 million in 1992, while net income rose to $25 million. Investors made the company a Wall Street darling, pushing its stock price to record highs quarter after quarter, landing Linear as one of *Forbes* magazine's 200 best small public companies in the United States.

After several years of booming profits, Linear's war chest brimmed with $100 million in cash ready for investment. To take advantage of ongoing market growth, Swanson announced plans in 1993 to build a semiconductor wafer fabrication plant in Camas, Washington. Scheduled for phase-one completion in 1996, the plant was expected to consume up to $85 million in capital for up to a decade.

Linear sustained its rampant growth into the mid-1990s, increasing revenues to $150 million in 1993 and then to $201 million in 1994. Net income rose to $36.5 million and $56 million, respectively, proof positive of the value of Linear's premium chips. Their performance earned a reputation as one of the hottest prospects in Silicon Valley and Linear was considered one of the best-managed companies in the United States. For the first five years of the 1990s Linear was named to *Forbes* magazine's Best 200 Small Public Companies. It was also named *Business Week*'s 557th most valuable U.S. company in 1995. Semiconductor industry watcher *In-Stat* declared Linear "the best financially managed manufacturer in the semiconductor industry."

The company opened a manufacturing plant in Penang, Malaysia, for plastic packaging in 1995, which helped boost sales to $265 million, with an impressive $84.7 million in net income. As the semiconductor industry fell into a slump over the next three years, Linear continued its growth unabated. To keep up with demand, Linear had again gone to Asia: opening a design center in Singapore and assembly plant in Penang, Malaysia, in 1995 and 1996, respectively. At the same time, design centers popped up domestically as well, in Colorado, Massachusetts, and North Carolina. In 1997 Linear added 90,000 square feet to its Penang plant as sales had mushroomed to $484.8 million for fiscal 1998, despite a downturn in the overall semiconductor market.

As the decade came to a close, Linear underwent several major changes: not only did the firm reach $500 million in sales ($506.7 million), but Swanson and his fellow executives announced a major overhaul of the company. Among the changes were the appointment of Clive Davies, formerly chief operating officer, and a 17-year veteran of the company, as president. Swanson remained Linear's chief executive and added chairman of the board to his titles, but the bigger news was the company's restructuring with the stated goal of hitting $1 billion in sales within the next few years. To bring about such success, Linear's operations were divided into four major business units: power products (made up of converters, regulators, and other power-management devices); signal-conditioning products (amplifiers, filters, and other related products); mixed-signal (analog-to-digital and digital-to-analog items); and high-frequency products, which housed Linear's R&D department.

THE NEW MILLENNIUM: 2000–04

The new era opened with a bang for Linear as the company hit the big time, in financial terms, by landing a slot in the S&P 500. Being added to the market index meant Linear, the very profitable yet rarely touted company, had officially arrived in the semiconductor industry. As Swanson commented to *Electronic Buyers'*

News (May 15, 2000), about Linear's humble beginnings, "There were people questioning the wisdom of what we were trying to do. With the analog market now in excess of $22 billion, there are no doubters."

At that time the company's product line topped 5,000 items and another wafer manufacturing plant in Milpitas neared completion. Sales for fiscal 2000 reached just under $706 million, with net income leaping from the previous year's $194.3 million to $287.9 million. Linear continued exceeding expectations for 2001 as well, reaching sales of $972.6 million and net income of $427.4 million before the bottom fell out of the electronics industry. While Linear's reversal of fortune was not as extreme as others forced into bankruptcy, the company did close one of its wafer manufacturing plants and laid off nearly a fifth of its workforce for the first time in its two-decade history. The numbers were shocking nonetheless as sales nearly halved to $512.3 million. Despite the drop, Linear was still able to maintain net income of $197.6 million.

Davies saw Linear through the electronics slump and retired in June at the end of fiscal 2003. He was replaced by David Bell, who had served as vice-president and general manager of the Power Business unit, groomed for his post by Swanson who retained the duties of chief executive and chairman. Linear continued its steady climb in both sales and net income, reaching $606.6 million and $236.6 million, respectively, for 2003.

By 2004 Linear was back to its full steam ahead mentality, with production to match, especially overseas. International sales had increased over the last several years, amounting to a remarkable 71 percent or $569.7 million of Linear's 2004 revenues ($807.3 million), representing a healthy 33 percent climb from the previous year's annual figures. To stay ahead of its competitors, Linear spent $104.6 million on R&D, much of it in employee compensation, to keep its most talented workers. Unlike many billion-dollar companies, however, Linear spent a relatively paltry $6.2 million on advertising its products, since most of its customers were fully aware of what it had to offer and usually at a more attractive price than its competitors.

MILESTONES AND MORE: 2005 AND BEYOND

The mid-point of the first decade of the 2000s was significant for Linear on several levels: not only did the company reach its goal of hitting the billion-dollar mark in sales (just shy of $1.05 billion for the fiscal year), but a changing of the guard ushered in a new chief executive. Company founder and longtime head honcho

Swanson stepped aside for COO Lothar Maier to take the reins, with Swanson remaining chairman of the board. Further, to reflect the company's increasing international focus, Linear opened its first European design center in Munich, Germany, in early 2006. International sales amounted to $760.4 million or 70 percent of Linear's total revenues of $1.09 billion.

Although Linear's fortunes dipped a bit in 2007 as the economy weakened, the chip maker still managed revenues just short of $1.08 billion, and a healthy rebound for fiscal 2008 at $1.18 billion, a 9 percent increase from the previous year. Net income, though strong, had fallen to $387.6 million from 2007's $411.7 million due mostly to an accelerated stock repurchasing plan initiated during the last quarter of 2007. Sales to international distributors remained strong at 70 percent or $828.3 million, divided principally between Asia Pacific countries (39 percent), Europe (18 percent), and Japan (13 percent).

By 2008 Linear had been awarded 439 patents with dozens more pending, accounting for a good portion of its R&D budget. Over $197.1 million was spent on R&D for the year, up from 2007's $183.6 million. The company's products remained tied to three burgeoning consumer segments: communications (cellphones, modems, PBX, Internet/ethernet servers, voice-over), industrial applications (robotics, medical devices, security measures, factory automation), and computers (PCs, MP3s, LCDs, Bluetooth technology, toys, TVs). The remaining market share was comprised of military contracts (communications, satellites, radar, sonar, GPS, ordinance) and chips for the auto industry (dashboard, navigation, entertainment systems, safety systems, emission controls).

With Linear's fiscal year ending in June 2008, the company's figures came ahead of the disastrous upheaval of the financial markets and the economy in general in the fall. Despite belt-tightening by consumers worldwide, Linear's product lines remained fairly secure, though; the financial meltdown and volatile stock market were not expected to have a major impact on sales for fiscal 2009.

Dave Mote
Updated, Nelson Rhodes

PRINCIPAL SUBSIDIARIES

Linear Technology A.B. (Sweden); Linear Technology Foreign Sales Corporation; Linear Technology GmbH; Linear Technology Corporation Limited (Hong Kong); Linear Technology KK; Linear Technology Korea; Linear Technology PTE; Linear Technology S.A.R.L.; Linear Semiconductor Sdn Bhd; Linear Technology S.r.l. (Italy); Linear Technology (Taiwan) Corporation; Linear Technology (U.K.) Limited.

PRINCIPAL COMPETITORS

Advanced Analogic Technologies, Inc.; Fairchild Semiconductor International, Inc.; Intersil Corporation; Maxim Integrated Products, Inc.; Micril, Inc.; National Semiconductor Corporation; Semtech Corporation; Texas Instruments, Inc.

FURTHER READING

Cassell, Jonathan, "Linear: Straight to the S&P 500," *Electronic News,* April 3, 2000, p. 8.

Detar, James, "Linear Stayed in Black," *Investor's Business Daily,* September 12, 2003, p. A4.

Dunn, Darrell, "Analog Focus Paying Big Dividends for Linear," *Electronic Buyers' News (EBN),* May 15, 2000, p. 1.

Goldman, James S., "Bob Swanson: Hard-Driver Focuses on Low-Tech Chips," *Business Journal-San Jose,* May 13, 1991, p. 12.

———, "Linear Technology Profits in Manufacturing Analog Chips," *Business Journal-San Jose,* October 19, 1992, p. 5.

Jones, Stephen, "Linear Tech Projects New Growth in Analog Chip Market," *Business Journal-San Jose,* June 22, 1987, p. 9.

Plansky, Paul, "Reading Between the Headlines of Gloom & Doom," *Santa Clara County Business,* November 1986, p. 15.

Ristelhueber, Robert, "The Toughest CEO in Silicon Valley," *Electronic Business,* January 1998, pp. 40+.

Rose, Michael, "Linear Technology Eyes Camas Site for 350-Job Integrated Circuit Plant," *Business Journal-Portland,* July 26, 1993, pp. 1+.

Scouras, Ismini, "Linear Targets $1B Mark in Restructuring," *Electronic Buyers' News,* May 3, 1999, p. 5.

Smith, Tom, "Chipmakers' Circuits Are Humming," *Business Week Online,* January 20, 2004.

Smith, Tom W., and Amrit Tewary, "A Good Line for Linear Technology," *Business Week Online,* May 5, 2003.

Snyder, Bill, "The Amazing Margins of Linear," *PC Week,* July 10, 1995, p. A7.

Swanson, Bob, "Linear Labors to Lead Recovery," *EBN,* May 27, 2002, p. 1.

Wrubel, Robert, "Back to the Future," *Financial World,* April 19, 1988, p. 48.

Yanish, Donna Leigh, "Linear Tech Seeks at Least $11 Million in Offering," *Business Journal-San Jose,* April 21, 1986, p. 39.

Lionel L.L.C.

──────■──────

171 Madison Avenue, Suite 1100
New York, New York 10016-5110
U.S.A.
Telephone: (212) 488-5500
Fax: (212) 951-7162
Web site: http://www.lionel.com

Private Company
Founded: 1900 as Lionel Manufacturing Company
Incorporated: 1995
Employees: 100
Sales: $70 million (2007 est.)
NAICS: 339932 Game, Toy, and Children's Vehicle
   Manufacturing

■ ■ ■

Lionel L.L.C. is the leading manufacturer and marketer of model and toy trains in the United States and one of the largest in the world. With more than a century of experience, Lionel enjoys an established and respected name in the toy industry. Although the company suffered serious problems from the late 1950s through the 1960s, including bankruptcy proceedings, it recovered and regained some of the ground it lost by the 1990s. A trade-secrets dispute with a key U.S. rival sent Lionel back into bankruptcy in November 2004. While operating under bankruptcy protection, the firm managed to increase its sales by nearly 50 percent in part via a push into department and big-box stores. After reaching an agreement on the trade-secrets dispute, Lionel emerged from bankruptcy in May 2008 as a private company.

The company's largest shareholder, with a stake of more than 48 percent, is the private-equity firm Guggenheim Investment Management, LLC.

1900 FOUNDING

Joshua Lionel Cowen, born in New York City on August 25, 1877, did not set out to create the electric model train or to found one of the most successful 20th-century toy manufacturers in the United States. Cowen dropped out of Columbia University and began work as an assembler at an electric lamp factory. Cowen's natural skill with electric devices and his desire to innovate led him to conduct electrical experiments afterhours at work. About 1898 Cowen's tinkering led to his development of a fuse for igniting magnesium powder for photographers. The U.S. Navy heard about the invention and contacted Cowen to build fuses to be used for exploding mines. Cowen gained $12,000 from his subsequent contract with the Navy, which he used to open a small shop in New York City in 1900. The new enterprise, christened the Lionel Manufacturing Company, produced fuses, low-voltage motors, and electrical novelties. Cowen continued to experiment with electricity, and in 1900 he developed the first dry cell battery.

EARLY ELECTRIC TRAINS

In 1901 Cowen created a window display for his shop that would change the direction of his company. To showcase one of his small electrical motors, he placed one in a model railroad car and ran it on a track in his

COMPANY PERSPECTIVES

Our mission is to develop, manufacture, market and service the best electric toy trains and accessories in the world within a competitive environment. Lead the toy train industry with innovative engineering, flawless manufacturing and superior customer service. Employ the best people and inspire teamwork and strong communications in an atmosphere of teamwork, trust, openness and innovation. Expose children to the magic of Lionel trains and sprout interest in the toy train hobby. Work closely with our dealer network and share with them some of the decision making processes for future Lionel products. Keep the magic of the Lionel tradition living for another 100 years.

shop window. Cowen had hoped the train would grab the attention of passersby, and they would stay to buy his products. The train did indeed attract the attention of people, but what they wanted to buy was the train! Cowen was soon selling the trains to individual customers and other stores. Within two years, the Lionel Manufacturing Company was issuing catalogs for the trains. The first catalog, in 1903, featured 2 7/8-inch gauge trains and track. The gauge refers to the width between the rails of the track. In addition to locomotives, the catalog offered a steel derrick car and a gondola car. A particular train in this catalog, a steel reproduction of a Baltimore & Ohio Railroad locomotive powered by a wet cell battery, initiated a demand for small-scale reproductions of real trains. Designing and manufacturing reproductions for those interested in this new hobby would become a staple for Lionel.

Business grew rapidly. In 1905 Cowen hired Mario Caruso, a young engineer, to help with manufacturing. Soon a strict division of labor developed: Cowen handled the marketing of the trains, and Caruso ran the manufacturing plants. Caruso remained with the company until 1945. Production quickly outgrew the company's New York manufacturing plant, and in 1910 Lionel moved to a new factory in New Haven, Connecticut. In addition to an increase in the sheer number of trains produced, the selection expanded rapidly as well. The 1906 catalog offered a single locomotive, two electric trolley cars, two passenger cars, and seven freight cars, which included an oil tank, a coal car, a cattle car, a box car, a gondola, and a caboose. In contrast, the 1910 catalog offered several different locomotives, an increased number of freight and pas-

senger cars, and 11 trolley cars. The company had also introduced tin lithograph stations and small human figures to aid in the creation of realistic scenes.

Several important changes occurred in Lionel train design in the first decade of the century. First, the increasing number of homes wired for electricity meant that the trains no longer had to be powered by dry cell batteries. Cowen developed a transformer that reduced household current to a safe level for use with Lionel trains. Second, Lionel introduced in 1906 a three-rail track that measured 2 1/8 inch between rails. This gauge became so popular in the United States it was soon known as "standard gauge."

Gauge became an important marketing factor when Lionel competitor Ives Trains introduced the "O" gauge train in 1910. Smaller than the standard gauge train, the "O" gauge had only 1 1/4 inches between the rails. The gauge's popularity led Lionel into that market in 1915, when the company introduced nine sets of "O" gauge trains. At the time, Lionel offered 17 sets of trains in standard gauge.

RAPID GROWTH

The company, which changed its name in 1918 to the Lionel Corporation, continued to experience rapid growth through the 1920s. Increased production again forced the company to move to larger facilities in Irvinton, New Jersey. Lionel also increased its size and market share by acquiring its biggest competitor, Ives Trains, in 1928. Initially Lionel bought the company in partnership with the model train company American Flyer Trains, and both companies supplied some parts for Ives trains through 1929 and 1930. Lionel, however, bought out American Flyer's interest in Ives at the end of 1930. Lionel then closed the Ives plant in Bridgeport, Connecticut, and transferred the operations to its New Jersey facility.

The demand for reproductions of real trains grew through the 1920s. Throughout this time Lionel produced several sets of highly authentic trains as part of its numerous offerings of locomotives and train cars. During this "classic period" for Lionel, the company created model cars and engines with an astonishing attention to detail, including many models with brass and nickel trim. For example, the powerful 408E twin-motored engine featured six running lights, operating pantographs, and all brass detail. Lionel sets from this time, which included highly detailed passenger cars in addition to the locomotives, became valuable collectors' items, sought after by collectors and train enthusiasts into the 21st century.

KEY DATES
■

1900: Joshua Lionel Cowen founds Lionel Manufacturing Company in New York City to produce fuses, low-voltage motors, and electrical novelties.

1901: First toy trains are produced.

1915: Company begins producing "O" gauge trains.

1918: Company is renamed Lionel Corporation.

1934: Financial strains of the Great Depression force Lionel into receivership; introduction of a $1 Mickey Mouse and Minnie Mouse handcar helps spark a rebound.

1937: Company goes public.

1948: The Santa Fe Diesel, Lionel's all-time top-selling train engine, is introduced.

1953: Lionel ranks as the largest toy maker in the world.

1959: Founding family sells Lionel to a group of investors led by Roy Cohn.

1967: Lionel files for bankruptcy protection.

1969: As part of a reorganization under bankruptcy, General Mills, Inc., purchases the rights to the Lionel brand and the company's manufacturing equipment.

1970: Manufacturing operations are shifted to Mount Clemens, Michigan.

1985: Lionel becomes part of Kenner Parker Toys, Inc., which is spun off from General Mills.

1986: An investment group led by Richard P. Kughn acquires Lionel, incorporating it as Lionel Trains, Inc.

1994: TrainMaster control system is introduced.

1995: Wellspring Associates L.L.C. partners with Neil Young to purchase Lionel Trains, which is renamed Lionel L.L.C.

2004: Lionel is forced to file for bankruptcy protection after a jury imposes a $38.6 million judgment stemming from a trade-secret dispute with competitor M.T.H. Electric Trains.

2006: The jury verdict is overturned on appeal.

2008: After Lionel and M.T.H. reach an out-of-court settlement of their dispute, Lionel emerges from bankruptcy as a private company.

DEPRESSION PRODUCT LINES

The Great Depression forced a slight change in focus at Lionel. Sales dropped for the toy manufacturer early in the Depression, and Lionel lost money for the first time in 1931. Financial troubles forced the company into receivership in 1934, and the company was able to save itself by shifting production to lower-cost items. One new line in particular helped buoy company sales. In collaboration with The Walt Disney Company, Lionel created a Mickey Mouse and Minnie Mouse handcar in 1934. A single car that was wound by hand and was sold with a circle of track, the one-dollar toy enjoyed a vast popularity. Its success engendered a whole line of similar toys, including a Santa Claus handcar, introduced in 1935; Donald Duck and Peter Rabbit "chick mobiles," which came out the following year; and the Mickey Mouse Circus Train. Mickey, as the conductor of the tin locomotive, led the train filled with Disney passengers past a cardboard backdrop of a circus.

In its shift to lower-priced items, Lionel also placed increased emphasis on the smaller "O" gauge trains. Customers reacted favorably, and by 1939 Lionel had completely discontinued production of its standard gauge, three-rail trains. Despite the focus on lower costs, Lionel continued to introduce new models. The company's first steam-type "O" gauge locomotive debuted in 1930; within five years, Lionel made eight different "O" gauge steam engines. Streamlined passenger trains were introduced in the middle of the decade, as was the first steam whistle. Some demand for high-priced reproduction models remained, and Lionel filled it with its exact scale "O" gauge Hudson steam locomotive in 1937, which cost $75 at the time.

In 1938 Lionel introduced its first "OO" gauge train, a scale model of the Hudson engine with a tender and four freight cars. An immediate success in the "OO" gauge market, the Hudson model was the first of several that Lionel designed in the late 1930s. In 1942, however, Lionel stopped production of toy trains to join the war effort and never resumed its line of "OO" trains, even after the war ended.

Lionel's adjustments to the Depression market appeared successful. In 1937 the company employed 1,000 people and produced approximately 40,000 model train engines, 1.2 million railcars, and more than a million sets of track. That year Lionel offered stock to the public for the first time. With the entrance of the United States into World War II, Lionel suspended its model train production and began manufacturing navigation and communications equipment for the armed forces.

POSTWAR GROWTH

Toy train production resumed in 1945 under the direction of Lawrence Cowen, the son of Joshua Lionel Cowen. Having assumed the presidency that year, Lawrence remained at the head of the company until its sale in 1959. He oversaw the introduction of the company's all-time top-selling train engine, the Santa Fe Diesel, in 1948. Not only did Lionel begin producing diesel engines in 1948, it used plastic in its trains for the first time. The year of its 50th anniversary, 1950, Lionel unveiled Magne-Traction, a system designed to increase the pulling power of the locomotives. By inserting permanent magnets into the locomotive driving axles, a magnetic attraction was induced between the wheels and the steel track, enabling the locomotives to pull more cars and work better on steep grades.

Pent-up demand for consumer goods after the war led to some of Lionel's best years. By 1953 Lionel was the largest toy manufacturer in the world, with net sales of $32.9 million, and employed 2,000 people. Mismanagement and a shrinking market, however, reversed the company's fortunes. In the mid-1950s Lawrence Cowen attempted to diversify Lionel's products and holdings, perhaps in response to decreasing interest in model trains from the public. In 1957 the company began marketing "HO" gauge trains, licensed first from Rivarossi and later from Athearn, but the line did not sell and was dropped in 1967. Cohen also introduced a stereo camera and acquired Airex Corporation, a fishing reel manufacturer, but both ventures proved unprofitable. Labor disputes added to the company's misfortunes, disrupting production at the New Jersey plant with strikes. In 1958 Lionel lost $470,000 on sales of $14.5 million, the company's first yearly loss since the Depression.

The next year, 1959, Lawrence Cowen sold Lionel to a group of investors, sparking almost three decades of shifting ownership. Roy Cohn, Joshua Cowen's great-nephew and head of the investors—and infamous for his role as a key legal aide to the anticommunist demagogue Senator Joseph McCarthy—hoped to gain government missile contracts by acquiring electronics firms. Cohn placed John Maderis, a former major general, at the head of Lionel but replaced him in 1962 with Melvin Raney. Not only did government missile contracts fail to appear, but sales remained stagnant as well. Cohn sold Lionel at a significant loss in 1963 to financier Victor Muscat, who resold the company later the same year to a group led by A. M. Sonnabend of the Hotel Corporation of America. Sonnabend died the next year, and Robert Wolfe, a former toy company executive, was named president.

Wolfe took over a company that had suffered at the hands of its numerous leaders in the previous decade. Employees had been let go, and high-quality product lines had been discontinued to cut costs. Efforts to diversify the company's product line, including ventures into microscopes, science labs, and tape recorders, had served only to blur the company's focus. Wolfe was determined to return Lionel to its traditional niche as a high-quality toy train manufacturer. Nevertheless, even with the company's focus back on producing high-quality electric trains, Lionel continued to lose money. Its 1967 purchase of American Flyer Trains, its largest competitor, did nothing to stem the tide, and later that same year Lionel Corporation once again had to file for bankruptcy protection.

GENERAL MILLS/KENNER ERA, 1969–86

In 1969, as part of Lionel's bankruptcy reorganization, General Mills bought the rights to the Lionel name and all of the company's manufacturing equipment. What was left of the original Lionel Corporation emerged as a holding company for toy stores and hobby shops, and after a period of ups and downs this firm went bankrupt and was liquidated in 1993. At General Mills, in the meantime, the Lionel manufacturing equipment was moved from New Jersey to Mount Clemens, Michigan, in 1970 before production of Lionel trains was resumed. Fundimensions, a division of General Mills Fun Group, assumed responsibility for Lionel train production and revitalized the ailing brand.

In 1973 Fundimensions attempted to revive the Lionel "HO" gauge line, manufacturing the trains in Mount Clemens and Asia. However, the line once again failed to sell and was discontinued five years later. In 1979 Fundimensions reintroduced the American Flyer S Gauge trains as part of the Lionel line. In general, Lionel regained its health in the 1970s, enjoying increasing sales through the decade. In 1983, however, General Mills combined its toy manufacturing, including the production from Fundimensions, Kenner Toys, and Parker Brothers Games, and moved it all to Mexico. The new plant had a difficult time maintaining the quality of Lionel products and frequently missed delivery dates to retailers, injuring the reputation of the brand. When Kenner Parker Toys, Inc., spun off from General Mills in 1985, Lionel went with it as one of its divisions. That year Lionel moved its train production back to Mount Clemens.

LIONEL TRAINS, INC., ERA, 1986–95

In 1986 Richard P. Kughn, a Detroit real estate developer, formed a corporation with a group of investors to purchase Lionel. After paying an estimated $25 million, the group incorporated the enterprise as Lionel Trains, Inc. Kughn, who took over as the company's chairman, was an avid model train collector and, when he became interested in purchasing Lionel, already owned thousands of trains in a collection whose worth was estimated at nearly $1 million. Within two years of the purchase, Lionel's sales rose 150 percent, to $50 million a year, and market share reached 60 percent. Both the Collector and Traditional lines of trains showed record sales that year. Later, in 1990, the company's plant was moved to nearby Chesterfield, Michigan, where its headquarters were also situated.

Kughn, with his background as a model train collector, saw a market for reissues of classic Lionel trains. He initiated a new line in 1988, Lionel Classics, that directly reproduced the metal Lionel trains of the 1920s and 1930s. Kughn also encouraged innovation, particularly in the development of state-of-the-art technological features. RailScope, a locomotive with a miniature video camera in the nose, was introduced in 1988 to give railroading enthusiasts a chance to see the ride as an engineer would. The following year Rail-Sounds debuted in the Pennsylvania B6 Scale Switcher engine and the Reading T-1 Northern Locomotives. The microelectronic sound chip placed inside the engines held an exact sound recording from full-size trains. In 1994 Lionel incorporated a high-tech remote control device into a new series of trains. Through a joint venture with Lionel called Liontech, the rock musician Neil Young developed the TrainMaster to share his passion for model railroading with his son Ben, a victim of cerebral palsy. Easier to use than a traditional transformer, the handheld wireless controller used onboard electronic processors to move the train via electronic signal and incorporated digital sound to more closely reproduce such sounds as engines churning or cars uncoupling.

Completely new product lines also expanded Lionel's offerings during the late 1980s and early 1990s. Ready-to-run sets of trains with an "O27" gauge, slightly smaller than the "O" gauge, were first offered in the late 1980s. A new line of trains that were 1/24th the size of real trains was introduced in 1987. Roughly twice the size of the "O" gauge trains, the Lionel Large Scale was made of weather-resistant plastic to allow their use indoors or out. In collaboration with the Smithsonian Institution, Lionel created a collection of museum-quality "O" gauge engines. An exact replica of the 1938 New York Central Dreyfuss-Hudson locomotive, the first engine produced, was offered in a limited edition run of only 500.

BEGINNING OF LIONEL L.L.C. ERA

Young's interest in Lionel expanded in 1995 when he joined with former Paramount Communications, Inc., chairman Martin S. Davis to purchase Lionel from Kughn. The purchase was friendly, with Kughn remaining as chairman emeritus and retaining a minority share in the renamed Lionel L.L.C. Wellspring Associates L.L.C., an investment firm started by Davis, held Davis's majority share. As part of the deal, Lionel became the full owner of Liontech, the joint venture with Young.

In January 1996 the new owners brought Gary L. Moreau onboard as president and CEO. Moreau had been president and COO of tableware and giftware maker Oneida Ltd. That same year the company issued its first fully illustrated catalog in more than three decades. Lionel under Moreau continued its strategy of incorporating advanced technology into the company's traditional train sets to draw more enthusiasts into the Lionel fold. These efforts included ever-more sophisticated versions of the RailSounds system.

These trends continued after Moreau was succeeded by Richard N. Maddox in July 1999. Maddox had been the marketing vice-president at Bachmann Industries, Inc., one of Lionel's chief competitors. In his stint at the helm, Maddox placed an emphasis on leveraging the Lionel brand in myriad ways through licensing deals, from Lionel-themed Hallmark ornaments and computer games to Lionel train lunch boxes and clothing. He also stepped up new product development, pushing the company to deliver 24 new models of locomotives in 1999 and 2000, a faster pace than that of Lionel's golden era in the 1940s and 1950s. The company also launched a web site in 1999 and a year later celebrated its centennial by issuing its largest catalog ever, which was published in two volumes and contained nearly 200 pages of models, including new versions of several old engines and a centennial-themed train.

Facing increased competition from model-train makers relying on lower-cost manufacturing labor outside the United States, Lionel during this period increasingly shifted its production to contract manufacturers in South Korea and China. This trend culminated in August 2001 when Lionel closed its Michigan manufacturing plant. Also in 2001, Maddox retired and was replaced by Bill Bracy, a former Mattel, Inc., executive who also had a lengthy spell at General Mills' Fundimensions on his résumé.

DISPUTE WITH M.T.H. LEADING TO BANKRUPTCY

Lionel's relationship with Korea Brass Co., its Korean subcontractor, led to a lengthy trade-secrets dispute with the company's largest U.S. competitor and another trip to bankruptcy court. Mike's Train House, later known as M.T.H. Electric Trains, sued Lionel in 2000, accusing the company of selling trains built by Korea Brass that had been based on designs stolen from M.T.H.'s Korean subcontractor. In addition to the trains' actual physical look, the allegedly stolen designs also involved a computerized technology for synchronizing the sound, smoke, and speed of toy locomotives chugging around a track layout. M.T.H. had been founded by Mike Wolf, who had been a Lionel subcontractor in the late 1980s and early 1990s before developing his own model train lines after the Lionel work began to dry up.

In June 2004 a federal jury in Michigan issued a verdict siding with M.T.H. that ordered Lionel to pay M.T.H. a $38.6 million judgment. The amount was about 80 percent of Lionel's annual revenue at the time, and its size forced the company to file for Chapter 11 bankruptcy protection that November. Shortly before the filing, as part of a major management shakeup that saw Bracy's ouster, Jerry Calabrese was named CEO. Calabrese was a former president of Marvel Comics Group, part of Marvel Entertainment Inc. Ironically, given the legal travails, the 2004 holiday season featured what Calabrese claimed was the company's best-selling item in its history: the $249 Polar Express train set, a tie-in to that season's *Polar Express* holiday movie. The popularity of the set led to well-publicized shortages as Lionel ran out of stock and was unable to deliver additional sets to dealers until March 2005.

Lionel appealed the jury verdict. A loss at the appellate level had the potential to lead to a forced sale of the company to Wolf and M.T.H. However, in December 2006 a federal appeals court overturned the verdict and ordered a new trial, ruling that testimony had been erroneously admitted in the case and that the jury had unfairly assessed double damages. Rather than proceeding to a new trial, however, the two sides entered into settlement talks and reached a tentative deal in October 2007, the terms of which were not revealed. The settlement, coupled with the securing of exit financing, enabled Lionel L.L.C. to emerge from bankruptcy on May 1, 2008. The largest shareholder of the newly organized company was the private-equity firm Guggenheim Investment Management, LLC, which held a stake of 48.6 percent. The estate of Martin Davis, who had died in 1999, held a 28.6 percent stake, with other shareholders including Calabrese, who remained CEO, Kughn, and Young.

LOOKING FORWARD

Calabrese not only successfully shepherded Lionel through a resolution of the M.T.H. dispute and out of

bankruptcy, he also managed at the same time to place the business on a much firmer ground for future growth. He had assumed the company leadership at a time when Lionel was almost exclusively developing and selling trains for collectors willing to shell out a thousand dollars or more for a single locomotive. That this customer base was small, aging, and shrinking boded ill for Lionel's future. Calabrese aimed to attract new model-train enthusiasts with new starter sets aimed at kids, sporting much lower price tags ($129 to $300) and sold at department stores, high-end toy stores, and mass retailers, rather than the hobby shops to which the Lionel brand had long been confined.

Among the retailers that began carrying the new low-end Lionel train sets were F.A.O. Schwarz, Neiman Marcus, Fortunoff, and Macy's. The brand had not been showcased in these types of outlets in half a century. Lionel also began creating products specially tailored for particular retailers. In 2006, for example, Target offered a Lionel set carrying the theme "The Big Box of Trains You Wish Your Mother Had Not Given to Your Brother." Lionel also aggressively pursued potentially lucrative licensing deals to entice additional sales, including a 2007 release of a Harry Potter train set called the Hogwarts Express.

Between 2004 and 2007, sales of Lionel starter sets more than doubled to around 200,000, with a significant portion of the growth originating in department stores and big-box retailers. Total revenues during that period increased from around $48 million to $70 million. Building on this momentum, Calabrese was pursuing a larger vision for the Lionel brand, one that included parallels with Mattel's American Girl doll franchise, which enjoyed great popularity among girls. He hoped to establish a place at malls that might develop into an American Girl Place for boys. He also wanted to further broaden Lionel's customer base through film and television projects featuring the brand and had begun pursuing such projects with major studios and other partners.

Susan W. Brown
Updated, David E. Salamie

PRINCIPAL COMPETITORS

M.T.H. Electric Trains; Gebr. Märklin & Cie. GmbH; Bachmann Industries, Inc.; Athearn Trains; Kato USA, Inc.; Atlas Model Railroad Co., Inc.; Hornby Plc.

FURTHER READING

Barkholz, David, "Developing a New Train of Thought: Rocker Helps Lionel Make a Better Toy," *Crain's Detroit Business*, December 5, 1994, pp. 1+.

Bunkley, Nick, "Verdict Could Derail Model-Train Maker," *Detroit News,* June 8, 2004, p. 1C.

Carp, Roger, *The World's Greatest Toy Train Maker: Insiders Remember Lionel,* Waukesha, Wis.: Kalmbach Books, 1998, 112 p.

Craig, Charlotte W., "Rockers, Partners Will Take Control of Train Maker," *Detroit Free Press,* September 26, 1995, p. 1A.

Cross, Robert, "'Railroad Baron' Puts Lionel on Track," *Chicago Tribune,* December 18, 1986.

Donnelly, Francis X., "Lionel Ends Production in Macomb," *Detroit News,* February 2, 2001, p. 1B.

English, Susan, "Back on Track," *Spokane (Wash.) Spokesman-Review,* January 25, 2000, p. D1.

Fillon, Mike, "Lionel Trains," *Popular Mechanics,* April 2001, p. 90.

Fitzgerald, Patrick, "All Aboard: Lionel, MTH Settle Model-Trains Battle," *Wall Street Journal,* October 27–28, 2007, p. B3.

———, "Lionel Takes Steps to End Bankruptcy," *Wall Street Journal,* January 30, 2008, p. B3A.

———, "Toy Maker Lionel Emerges from Bankruptcy with Broader Plans," *Wall Street Journal,* May 5, 2008, p. B4.

Goldfarb, Zachary A., "Toy-Train Makers Engineer a Settlement of Patent Lawsuit," *Bergen County (N.J.) Record,* October 28, 2007, p. A9.

Green, Jeff, "The Toy-Train Company That Thinks It Can," *Business Week,* December 4, 2000, pp. 64–66, 69.

Grossmann, John, "Train Wreck," *Inc.,* February 2005, pp. 84–88, 90, 92.

Hoffman, Gary, "Domestic Production Helps Lionel; Model Train Maker Boosts Ads, Plans New Products," *Crain's Detroit Business,* December 15, 1986, p. 26.

Hollander, Ron, *All Aboard! The Story of Joshua Lionel Cowen and His Lionel Train Company,* New York: Workman Publishing, 1981, 253 p.

Ingersoll, Bruce, "Model-Train Industry Thinks It Can," *Wall Street Journal,* November 27, 2000, p. B16.

Jackson, Kathy, "Chugging Along: Lionel to Sell Board Game," *Crain's Detroit Business,* February 29, 1988, pp. 3+.

Jackson, Luther, "Lionel Trains Inc. Chugs Forward with a New Conductor," *Detroit Free Press,* December 21, 1987, p. 1C.

Johnson, Tom, "Engineering a Comeback: Jersey Native Is Turning Around Venerable Train Maker Lionel," *Newark (N.J.) Star-Ledger,* February 27, 2007, p. 43.

Jones, Tim, "Outsized Dispute over Nation's Toy Tracks," *Chicago Tribune,* July 24, 2007, p. 4.

Karush, Sarah, "Lionel Chugs Along Despite Woes," *Grand Rapids (Mich.) Press,* December 23, 2004, p. C1.

Lander, David, "Lionel: For Generations the Name Was As Closely Associated with Christmas As Santa Claus," *American Heritage,* November/December 2006, pp. 60+.

Line, Les, "Steam Meets Silicon in New Toy Trains," *New York Times,* November 26, 1998, pp. G1, G5.

"Lionel Brings in New CEO," *Macomb (Mich.) Daily,* October 8, 2004.

Lipin, Steven, "Toy Train Fanciers Team Up to Acquire, Modernize Lionel," *Wall Street Journal,* September 26, 1995, p. B9.

Marsh, Peter, "Baby Boomers Keep Model Train Industry on Track," *Financial Times,* May 30, 2005, p. 16.

McComas, Tom, and James Tuohy, *Lionel: A Collector's Guide and History,* 6 vols., Wilmette, Ill.: TM Productions, 1975–1981.

McCuan, Jess, "Lionel Is Hoping Web Site for Trains Will Click with Kids," *Wall Street Journal,* July 30, 1999, p. B5A.

Musial, Robert, "Back on Track: Lionel to Make Toy Trains in Michigan Again," *Detroit Free Press,* October 17, 1985, p. 1A.

Pereira, Joseph, and Ethan Smith, "A Christmas Derailed?" *Wall Street Journal,* November 17, 2004, p. B1.

Ponzol, Dan, *Lionel: A Century of Timeless Toy Trains,* New York: Freidman/Fairfax Publishers, 2000, 160 p.

"Rocker, Partner Buy Lionel," *Crain's Detroit Business,* October 2, 1995, p. 33.

Rozens, Aleksandrs, "Lionel's Next Stop: The Public Markets?" *Investment Dealers' Digest,* May 19, 2008.

Schleicher, Robert, *The Lionel Legend: An American Icon,* St. Paul, Minn.: Voyageur Press, 2008, 256 p.

Serwer, Andrew E., "An Odd Couple Aims to Put Lionel on the Fast Track," *Fortune,* October 30, 1995, p. 21.

Sprovieri, John, "Tradition Still Powers Lionel," *Assembly,* December 1998, pp. 34+.

Treece, James B., "The Little Train Company That Could: A Turnaround at Lionel," *Business Week,* December 26, 1988, pp. 70–71.

Weise, Elizabeth, "Hey, Hey, My My: Model Trains Will Never Die," *Austin (Tex.) American-Statesman,* July 19, 1997, p. C7.

Luby's, Inc.

———————■———————

13111 Northwest Freeway, Suite 600
Houston, Texas 77040-6392
U.S.A.
Telephone: (713) 329-6800
Toll Free: (800) 886-4600
Fax: (713) 329-6809
Web site: http://www.lubys.com

Public Company
Founded: 1947
Incorporated: 1959 as Cafeterias, Inc.
Employees: 7,500
Sales: $320.4 million (2007)
Stock Exchanges: New York
Ticker Symbol: LUB
NAICS: 722212 Cafeterias

■ ■ ■

Luby's, Inc., operates a chain of more than 120 cafeteria-style restaurants, mainly located in Texas. A handful of the eateries are located in the states of Arizona, Arkansas, Louisiana, and Oklahoma. Luby's cafeterias offer freshly prepared, home-style food at reasonable prices served in attractive settings. The cafeterias cater primarily to shoppers and to store and office personnel at lunchtime, and to families for the dinner meal, and all of them offer takeout service, which accounts for roughly 13 percent of revenues. Around 28 of the cafeterias serve breakfast on the weekends. Luby's outlets are located in shopping and business developments as well as in residential areas. Un-

like many restaurant chains, Luby's does not franchise its units, but it does compensate each unit manager with a generous portion of the profits from the unit the manager runs.

LUBY'S ORIGINS

Although Luby's was incorporated in 1959, the company's history dates back to 1909 when clothes merchant Harry Luby made a business trip from his home in Springfield, Missouri, to Chicago, Illinois. Luby was captivated by a new type of restaurant where patrons picked the food items they wanted from a counter and carried their own trays to dining tables.

Luby immediately saw that the Chicago restaurant was employing the then emerging concepts of mass production and assembly lines in the restaurant business. Two years later, Luby opened a similar operation in Springfield, Missouri. From a 12-foot counter he built himself, Luby dished out freshly prepared food at reasonable prices. One year later in 1912, Luby opened a second cafeteria in Springfield. From Missouri to Oklahoma to Texas, Luby opened one cafeteria after another over the next ten years. In stepping-stone fashion, Luby would sell outright or retain a partial interest in a unit before moving southward to establish his next eatery. In 1927 the 39-year-old Harry Luby had made enough money to retire in San Antonio, where he oversaw his investments in seven cafeterias in Texas and one in Kansas. Although ultimately his restaurants were operated under the Luby's Cafeteria name, Harry Luby had experimented with several other names, including New England Dairy Lunch, New England Cafeteria, and Luby's New England Cafeteria.

Amiable and generous, Harry Luby had operated his restaurants on some very simple concepts: good food at reasonable prices for the customers and a generous portion of profits for the managers. "Share the work, share the risks, share the profits" was a guiding principle for Luby. Thus, as an investor in eight cafeterias, Luby gave 40 percent of profits to the unit managers, an unusually large percentage at the time as well as in the years that followed.

A NEW GENERATION OF LEADERSHIP: THIRTIES THROUGH WORLD WAR II

Harry's son Robert (Bob) M. Luby grew up in the restaurant business, playing after school in cafeteria basements as a young child and working in cafeterias cleaning grease traps as a teenager. After graduating from college, Bob Luby and his cousin Earl Luby set their entrepreneurial sights on San Francisco, where they opened a cafeteria that failed to produce the Texas-sized profits his father's restaurants generated. Bob returned to Texas undeterred in his goal to establish and run a successful cafeteria. That goal was reached with a cafeteria in Dallas on Live Oak Street. Luby next enlisted his aunt, uncle, and brother-in-law George H. Wenglein to invest in, establish, and operate a cafeteria in El Paso, Texas.

While Bob Luby's cafeterias prospered during the 1930s, business was bleak for others. Homeless, hungry people often visited Luby's for sustenance. During the Great Depression, the cafeterias associated with Harry and Bob Luby served needy people from the food left over at closing time.

World War II and its wake profoundly altered the United States, sparking social changes and robust economic growth. Forced to sell his Dallas cafeteria when he enlisted in the Army Air Corps, Luby nonetheless continued to think about the food business, even while serving as an intelligence officer. The contacts he made while serving his country constituted the founda-

tion of a management team for the cafeteria chain to come.

POSTWAR EXPANSION

In 1946 Bob Luby hung up his military uniform and began plans with his cousin, Charles R. Johnston, to establish a cafeteria for the postwar era. In the decade following the war, household incomes would rise, families would move from cities to suburbs, and lifestyles calling for convenient products and services would reshape the fabric of American life. Amid such change, Americans also would seek the threads of the past.

In 1947 Luby and Johnston recognized the promise of these postwar stirrings and opened a cafeteria with capacity to seat 180 people. Located in downtown San Antonio, the restaurant was an immediate success thanks to returning servicemen in the area and to the postwar housing shortage, which had forced many people to live in downtown hotels. Nearby movie theaters provided brisk business in the evening. The cafeteria was managed by Norwood W. Jones, a fellow officer of Luby's while stationed at Santa Ana Army Air Base.

Luby and Johnston's next restaurant was located in the growing and affluent San Antonio suburb of Alamo Heights. Brother-in-law Wenglein was persuaded to co-manage the cafeteria with John Lee, a prewar Luby's associate. The Alamo Heights cafeteria served as a model for future Luby's units.

From the front seat of a sporty Studebaker serving as their office, the two entrepreneurs traveled the Lone Star state in search of new locations. Luby and Johnston were careful to open new cafeterias only when they had managers to operate the units according to the standards Harry Luby had pioneered.

By 1958, Luby and Johnston had opened 11 cafeterias, each of which had a different configuration of investors. In order to build and operate new Luby's cafeterias, the investors formed Cafeterias, Inc., on February 4, 1959. The preexisting cafeterias were not affected by the move, although those units provided the cash to help the investors finance the new corporation.

Cafeterias, Inc., launched its first cafeteria in March 1960 in a strip shopping center in Corpus Christi and two others followed within 60 days. Although in the black, the three units were not generating the profits normally associated with Luby's cafeterias. Downtown locations proved to be a problem, while an experiment to serve breakfast was a mild failure.

Luby's hit pay dirt with its fourth cafeteria located in a far north San Antonio suburb in a retail develop-

KEY DATES

1947: First Luby's cafeteria opens in San Antonio.
1959: Luby's, with 11 cafeterias, incorporates as Cafeterias, Inc.
1966: First non-Texas location opens in Las Cruces, New Mexico.
1973: Company goes public in the over-the-counter market.
1981: Cafeterias, Inc., is renamed Luby's Cafeterias Inc.
1982: Company stock begins trading on the New York Stock Exchange.
1996: Luby's records its 28th consecutive year of increased sales and earnings per share.
1999: Company is renamed Luby's, Inc.
2000: Declining sales and profits lead to suspension of dividend and near bankruptcy.
2001: Pappas brothers take over top management positions and begin turnaround bid.
2003: Company announces the pending closure of 50 restaurants, leaving the chain principally operating in Texas.
2004: Headquarters are shifted from San Antonio to Houston.
2007: A fresh expansion is launched with the opening of a new prototype Luby's in Cypress, Texas.

ated in the early 1960s, with its mission control headquarters in the area. In subsequent years, the oil industry and its attendant financiers would fuel the economy further. Meanwhile, the first Luby's located outside of Texas opened in Las Cruces, New Mexico, in 1966.

CONSOLIDATING OPERATIONS AND GOING PUBLIC

The corporation forged a link with the original Luby's cafeterias in 1969 when it agreed to manage those units for the next 15 years, bringing the number of corporate-managed units to 26, of which 17 were company-owned. Luby and Johnston passed their executive management reins to George Wenglein and Norwood Jones, respectively, in 1971. Luby, who remained chairman of the board, recalled the reason for stepping aside at age 61: "I had run the company with Charles since the beginning. ... Before we started selling stock to the public, I wanted to be darn sure the company could operate without me as president. So Charles and I stepped down earlier than we had to."

In January 1973 the company's stock was offered to the public in the over-the-counter market. The company continued to expand into new areas such as Dallas and to strengthen its internal operations, creating the new corporate position of area manager to oversee existing units and to launch new ones in a specific market.

The Yom Kippur War in October 1973 ushered in an era in which the Texas economy would be inexorably tied to Middle Eastern oil and the volatile political situation in that part of the world. The war created gasoline shortages in the United States but no shortages of customers at Luby's, which offered a reasonably priced, convenient suburban alternative for consumers whose pocketbooks were pinched by higher gas prices and whose auto travel was circumscribed by scarce fuel.

High oil prices soon began to work to Luby's advantage as energy exploration and development in Texas, Oklahoma, and Louisiana injected billions of dollars into the region's economy. With more cafeterias opening to meet the demand, Luby's created a formal training program to ensure that each new cafeteria would have adequate managerial staffers who were service-oriented to customers, sensitive to employees, and cost-conscious to the bottom line.

ESTABLISHING A SCHOOL OF MANAGEMENT

The Luby's Story, a history of the company published in 1988, explained that trainees were schooled in the

ment called North Star Mall. Bob Luby recalled, "Some people thought we had lost our minds because it was so far out that the city buses didn't serve the mall adequately. We actually had to subsidize the bus service to get our employees to work." However, the fast-growing affluent suburbs surrounding the mall would fill the fourth corporate Luby's restaurant with patrons and provide profits to build more cafeterias.

With Bob Luby as president and Charles Johnston as executive vice-president, Luby's entered the Houston market in 1965 with an upscale cafeteria that offered an expanded menu and more expensive food items. Operating under the Romano's Cafeteria name, the cafeteria quickly became a huge moneymaker. The modern structure with its rich decor served as a model for revamping efforts at existing Luby's and proved a market existed for cafeterias with a very modern style and design.

Luby's growth in the Houston market was propelled in part by the nation's space program, initi-

theory and practice of running a cafeteria. The boot-camp style training taught the recruits "the intricacies of butchering a side of beef, baking a lemon meringue pie, and mopping the floor," as well as how to clean the restaurant equipment and replenish the cafeteria serving line.

Trainees also learned to show respect to all Luby's employees. "In the kitchen, the young recruit is taught to show deference to his instructors—the fry cook, the baker, the butcher, and the salad maker. Clearly the young college graduate is the disciple and the veteran cook his master," the corporate history stated.

The deference and respect resulted in a stable workforce at the individual Luby's cafeterias. Luby's recorded one of the lowest turnovers of support staff in the restaurant industry. That low turnover translated into experienced and consistent service for the customers and minimal training costs for the individual units. After graduation, the prospective managers spent seven to ten years of additional training in individual cafeterias, moving from assistant manager to associate manager to manager, and from manager of a small unit to manager of larger and larger units.

Luby's cafeteria managers were given a high degree of autonomy. This enabled them to cater to customer tastes in their local markets with specialized menu offerings. The majority of the food ingredients were purchased locally by the individual cafeteria management team. This permitted managers to take advantage of price bargains in the local wholesale markets and to quickly respond to local product shortages.

A few items, such as fried haddock, were carried by every cafeteria in the Luby's network. Ingredients for these signature items were centrally sourced by the company. The management team of the individual cafeterias received their compensation based on the financial performance of each cafeteria. The management team consisted of a manager, an associate manager, and two to three assistant managers. Each team received 40 percent of the unit's operating profits. After the salaries of the assistant managers were deducted, the remainder in profits was divided in a 65/35 percent split between the manager and associate manager, respectively.

The opportunity for autonomy and for attractive financial compensation gave Luby's managers a strong incentive to operate profitably for the long-term. Approximately 85 percent of the company's unit managers remained with Luby's for ten years or more.

COMMENCEMENT OF PERIOD OF EXPANSION

The year 1980 saw corporate revenues surpass the $100 million mark, and the company adopted a new name, Luby's Cafeterias, Inc., in 1981. On February 22, 1982, Luby's entered the financial big league when its stock began trading on the New York Stock Exchange under the LUB symbol.

The 1980s represented a period of expansion outside Texas, which was suffering from slumping oil prices. Luby's Texas cafeterias weathered the economic downturn by avoiding waste and cutting labor costs. While others in the restaurant industry expended millions of dollars on advertising and borrowed heavily, Luby's relied on word-of-mouth recommendations to build its customer base and internally generated profits to build new cafeterias. The chain expanded into Oklahoma in 1980 and into Arizona, Arkansas, and Florida in 1988.

In a much publicized incident, random and bizarre violence hit a Luby's restaurant in Killeen, Texas, on October 16, 1991. A lone gunman entered the restaurant filled with patrons and employees, shot and killed 23 people, wounded 25 more, and then turned the gun on himself. When the killing ended, Luby's had acquired the unwanted distinction of being the site of the worst mass shooting in the history of the nation. The killer took his motive for the murders with him to the grave.

When word of the massacre reached company headquarters in San Antonio, Luby's chairman and several senior executives immediately flew to Killeen to provide aid and comfort to the victims' families, the survivors, and to the community. In fact, Luby's management was praised for its sensitive handling of the crisis surrounding the shooting. When the Killeen Luby's reopened on March 12, 1992, hundreds of people, including some of the survivors, came to the cafeteria to eat freshly prepared jalapeño corn bread, pan-grilled catfish, and Jefferson Davis pie.

NEW OPERATIONAL DIRECTIONS AMID CONTINUED STRONG GROWTH

The 1990s brought a more vibrant economy to the markets Luby's served and some new directions in its operations. In 1991 the company began developing a new marketing program using television and radio advertising to build repeat business and to position itself for youthful customers. "Luby's TV ads cut the mustard, go heavy on the wry" was the double-entendre headline over an article appearing in the December 5, 1994, issue of *Nation's Restaurant News.* The article noted Luby's ads used humor to convey the message that its restaurants catered to patrons of every age. Unlike the ads for other chains, Luby's did not merely feature glittery shots of the food and the cafeteria.

During fiscal 1994, Luby's conducted its first cooperative promotion, joining forces with Southwest Airlines, Sea World of Texas, and Karena Hotels of Texas to target families with children. Favorable results from the advertising and promotional campaigns led Luby's to earmark 2 percent of sales for marketing efforts in fiscal 1996.

At its January 1996 annual meeting, Luby's unveiled joint venture plans with Waterstreet Inc. for five to seven seafood restaurants over the next five years. Waterstreet's five restaurants in three cities served moderately priced, Gulf-of-Mexico-style seafood.

With a possible hint of a major new direction for the company as it moved toward the 21st century, Luby's Chairman Ralph "Pete" Erben told shareholders, "We will actively explore other potential concepts for diversification and enhancement of shareholder values." He said the company expected the joint venture to furnish Luby's with "restaurant concepts that provide growth and profitability into the future."

Luby's successful strategy was widely recognized by the press. "Why They're Lining Up at Luby's" was the headline for an article in the August 18, 1985, *New York Times* describing the company's recipe for success. *Kiplinger's Personal Finance Magazine* included Luby's in its list of "39 Stocks for Your Portfolio," which appeared in the August 1994 issue. An October 19, 1990, article in the *Wall Street Journal* examined how the company maintained its profitability during an economic recession. In addition, *Forbes* magazine named Luby's among the top 200 Best Small Companies for eight of the first ten years the publication conducted the survey.

Restaurant management publications also awarded Luby's top honors. *Restaurant Business* profiled Luby's in a May 1989 article titled "Slow and Steady Wins." In 1996, for the sixth time in seven annual surveys conducted nationally by *Restaurant and Institutions* magazine, consumers voted Luby's as their favorite in the cafeteria/buffet category.

With firm roots in the local communities it served, Luby's cafeterias were closely involved in local community events and philanthropic endeavors. When Hurricane Carla crashed into the Texas Gulf Coast in September 1961, the Corpus Christi Luby's served as an outpost for the National Guard and scores of emergency workers. Using gas-fired stoves, Luby's dispensed food and hot drinks to police, guardsmen, and neighbors.

"We didn't charge a thing, but we made a lot of friends," Cafeteria Manager Bill Lowe recalled. When the cafeteria reopened for normal business, Lowe remembered, "We were swamped with customers."

In addition to such ad hoc measures, unit managers were given a budget to spend on public service in their areas. The company's largest civic program was the Community Drug Education System. Initiated in 1987, the program received a Presidential Citation for educating students, parents, and teachers in 11 states about the dangers of substance abuse. By the end of fiscal 1996, Luby's had spent more than $1.3 million on the program.

LATE-CENTURY DOWNTURN

The final years of the 20th century saw Luby's falter. Although the results for fiscal 1997 showed another increase in sales, they also brought an end to a streak of 28 consecutive years of increased earnings per share, as net income fell from $39.2 million to $28.4 million. Luby's was finally being affected by the overall decline of the restaurant industry's cafeteria segment, which was now squeezed by the increasing popularity of both lower priced fast-food outlets and higher priced casual dining chains. Long known for its solid leadership, Luby's at the same time faced a sudden management crisis when, within the space of four days in March 1997, CEO and President John E. Curtis Jr. committed suicide, apparently triggered in part over concern about potential store closings, and the company's chairman, Ralph Erben, resigned unexpectedly. John B. Lahourcade, who had previously served as both CEO and chairman, was named interim chairman and David Daviss became acting CEO. The interim executive team announced in August 1997 that the company would close four stores and take a pretax charge of about $12 million in connection with the closures. Two months later, Barry J. C. Parker was hired as the company's new president and CEO. Parker was a former CEO of County Seat Stores, a nationwide clothing store chain. At the same time, Daviss replaced Lahourcade as chairman.

In 1998, the year that founder Bob Luby died, the new Luby's management team took steps aimed at sparking a turnaround. More than a dozen additional underperforming units were slated for closure with a $36.9 million charge taken in connection with asset impairments and store closings. Luby's began expanding its takeout service and opened its first unit with a drive-through window at a new restaurant in Tulsa, Oklahoma. These initiatives proved successful, leading to the rollout of food-to-go and drive-throughs at additional Luby's outlets. In January 1999 the company changed its name to Luby's, Inc., dropping the word "cafeteria." This move was in line with the company's new store prototype, which imparted a warmer, more casual dining feel by jettisoning the traditional stainless steel tray lines. The new units, which were smaller than usual at 9,600 square feet, also featured a hearth oven where a customer could pick out a steak to be cooked to order and ready by the time the customer reached the cash register. Luby's also introduced a "community restaurant" format in 1999, which was even smaller at about 7,000 square feet, and was specifically designed for markets that were previously considered not large enough to support a traditional Luby's. In a further retrenchment, Luby's sold its joint-venture interest in Water Street Seafood, having determined that the casual dining chain was not a good fit with the company's expertise in limited-service restaurateuring.

Despite price increases, both overall and same-store sales continued to decline through the fiscal year ending in August 2000. Net income that year totaled only $9.1 million, compared to $39.2 million just four years earlier. Another 15 stores were marked for closure during fiscal 2000, leading to a further charge of $14.5 million. With the company's stock price plummeting and a number of Luby's managers unhappy with a new compensation system Parker established that tied pay to specific sales targets, Parker resigned suddenly in October 2000. Daviss again assumed the positions of president and CEO on an interim basis. The company announced that it would suspend payment of its quarterly dividend for the first time in its history. It also reinstituted the old profit-sharing compensation plan for managers and launched new marketing campaigns.

The news grew bleaker by December 2000. Luby's reported a net loss of $2 million for the first quarter of fiscal 2001, a dissident group of shareholders began organizing a proxy fight for the annual meeting to be held in January 2001, and the company said it was nearing the end of its credit line, placing it on the verge of bankruptcy. Late that month, however, Christopher J. Pappas and Harris J. Pappas purchased about 6 percent of Luby's outstanding shares for about $6.6 million. The Pappas brothers were the principal owners of Pappas Restaurants Inc., which ran a number of successful casual dining chains, including Cajun, Mexican, and barbecue concepts.

PAPPAS BROTHERS-LED TURNAROUND

After Luby's survived the proxy battle in which the dissidents, angry over the depressed stock price as well as executive pay issues, aimed to gain three seats on the company board, the company gained some financial breathing room in March 2001 when the Pappas broth-

ers agreed to purchase as much as $10 million of the company's debt. At the same time, Chris Pappas was named president and CEO of Luby's while Harris Pappas became chief operating officer. The Pappases also gained seats on the board of directors. Robert T. Herres replaced Daviss as chairman of the company, although Daviss remained on the board. The Pappas brothers were determined to engineer a turnaround at Luby's, which they felt had failed to adapt to changing times, and they appeared eager to take a hands-on approach to doing so. According to the *Dallas Morning News,* Chris Pappas told a group of stock analysts, soon after taking over the reins, "Everything starts and stops at the store level. If it doesn't work at the store level, it won't work at the corporate level. ... We're great listeners to the market because we get out into the market. We're in the retail business."

In addition to boosting Luby's restaurant managers' pay, the Pappases' key early moves also included a renewed focus on serving dishes that had been freshly prepared onsite, reversing Parker's strategy of using ready-made food purchased from outside vendors. The Pappases also experimented with the menu, including the introduction of all-you-can-eat buffets at some locations, garnering mixed results. Most crucially, however, they had to stop the company from being swamped by its crushing debt load.

By this time it had become clear that Luby's had expanded much too rapidly in the 1990s, a growth spurt that had saddled the company with a total debt of $123 million by the time the Pappases had taken over the company management. Although the new leaders had managed to slightly reduce this total during their first year at the helm, Luby's ended up defaulting on $80 million in short-term debt in early 2003. After a deal to refinance this into long-term debt fell through, the Pappases staved off bankruptcy via a radical shrinking. In the spring of 2003 they announced that 50 Luby's outlets were to be closed over a two-year period. By closing and selling underperforming Luby's, capital was raised to reduce debt, while chainwide profits were improved through the concentration on top-performing units.

By the end of fiscal 2005, Luby's was on much firmer financial footing having reduced its total debt to just $13.5 million. The vast majority of its approximately 130 restaurants were now located in Texas as the company exited from the states of Mississippi, Tennessee, New Mexico, Florida, Missouri, and Kansas. Aided by new combo plates and the addition to the menu of more healthful items such as grilled and baked foods and entree salads, Luby's in fiscal 2005 enjoyed same-store sales growth of 6.3 percent while eking out a profit of $3.4 million on sales of $322.2 million, ending four straight years in the red. In December 2004, meantime, Luby's shifted its headquarters from San Antonio to Houston, the Pappas brothers' base of operations.

During fiscal 2006, Luby's eliminated its remaining long-term debt, while same-store sales increased again, by 4.6 percent, and net income shot up to $19.6 million. The Pappases' turnaround was further borne out by the reaction from Wall Street. After falling to nearly $1 a share in early 2003, Luby's stock rebounded to as high as $15.91 by March 2006. The Pappas brothers began planning for a new phase of growth.

NEW LUBY'S PROTOTYPE

In August 2007 Luby's opened its first new restaurant in seven years, a prototype of the next-generation Luby's that was located in the Houston suburb of Cypress. The new design was less "institutional" than a traditional Luby's and had more of the feel of a casual dining restaurant. The overall aim was to evoke the ambiance of the Texas Hill Country, while the specific design touches included an open kitchen, a granite serving line, a chilled salad display case, newly designed furniture and booths, exposed wood ceilings, oversized windows to let in a great deal of natural light, covered outdoor patio seating, and a dining counter inside for single diners. Early results at the prototype location were quite positive, including sales that were roughly 30 percent higher on average than a traditional Luby's.

Around the same time that the Cypress prototype opened, Luby's announced that it had secured $100 million in credit for an ambitious expansion plan calling for as many as 50 new units by 2013. The initial plan called for the building of four to six next-generation Luby's in 2008. By the middle of that year, however, the Pappases were forced to scale back their growth ambitions as the troubled economy and soaring gasoline prices forced many U.S. consumers to slash on their discretionary spending, including their dining-out outlays. Only two or three restaurants were now scheduled to be opened during 2008.

The Pappas brothers, in the meantime, faced a proxy battle of their own after the New York-based hedge fund Ramius Capital Group, L.L.C., built up a stake in Luby's of more than 7 percent and began agitating for a sale of the company, a sale-leaseback of the firm's cafeteria real estate, or some other move to enhance shareholder value. At Luby's annual meeting in January 2008, shareholders rejected Ramius's effort to replace four management-based incumbent board members with an alternative slate. With the company's

stock stuck in a range between $8 and $12 a share since mid-2006, however, Luby's did make one concession to disgruntled shareholders by setting in motion a plan to eventually allow shareholders to vote on all ten directors every year, ending the staggered election of board members.

Later that January, Ramius announced it had reduced its stake in Luby's to 4.5 percent, while the Pappas brothers upped their combined holding to more than 28 percent. As their restaurant expansion continued although more modestly because of the economic times, the Pappases had also turned the company in a new direction by launching a culinary contract service business. Luby's took over the food operations at a number of Texas hospitals, including two in Houston, St. Joseph Medical Center and Baylor College of Medicine. The company viewed its move into hospital food operations as a natural extension of its core business and a key way in which to further leverage the Luby's brand.

Lynn W. Adkins
Updated, David E. Salamie

PRINCIPAL SUBSIDIARIES

LUBCO, Inc.; Luby's Bevco, Inc.; Luby's Holdings, Inc.; Luby's Limited Partner, Inc.; Luby's Management, Inc.; Luby's Restaurants Limited Partnership.

PRINCIPAL COMPETITORS

Buffets Holdings, Inc.; Buffet Partners, L.P.; Piccadilly Restaurants, LLC; Pancho's Mexican Buffet, Inc.

FURTHER READING

Allen, Elizabeth, "Luby's Can't Dish Up $80 Million Loan Payment," *San Antonio Express-News,* January 30, 2003, p. 1A.

———, "Luby's to Shut More Cafeterias," *San Antonio Express-News,* April 1, 2003, p. 1A.

———, "S.A. Is Losing Luby's HQ," *San Antonio Express-News,* July 17, 2004, p. 1A.

Allen, Robin Lee, "Luby's Eyes Updated Image with Two New Campaigns," *Nation's Restaurant News,* June 6, 1994, p. 12.

Athavaley, Anjali, "Home Is Where the CEO Is: Luby's Will Move Its Headquarters to Houston, Bringing 80 Jobs," *Houston Chronicle,* July 17, 2004, Business sec., p. 1.

Bajaj, Vikas, "Pappas' Stake Infuses Luby's with Optimism," *Dallas Morning News,* December 28, 2000, p. 1D.

Barnhill, Steve, *The Luby's Story: Good Food from Good People,* San Antonio: Watercress Press, 1988, 107 p.

Barrett, William P., "The Best Little Hash House in Texas," *Forbes,* November 12, 1990, pp. 220–21.

Barrier, Michael, "First in Line at the Cafeteria," *Nation's Business,* February 1991, pp. 29–31.

Dawson, Carol, and Carol Johnston, *House of Plenty: The Rise, Fall, and Revival of Luby's Cafeterias,* Austin: University of Texas Press, 2006, 277 p.

Dorfman, John R., "Luby's Cafeterias' Steadiness Seems Suited to Withstand a Forced Diet for the Economy," *Wall Street Journal,* October 19, 1991, p. C2.

Fairbank, Katie, "Luby's to Close 50 Outlets," *Dallas Morning News,* April 1, 2003, p. 1D.

Hem, Brad, "Luby's Defeats Effort by Dissident Group," *Houston Chronicle,* January 16, 2008, Business sec., p. 1.

Hendricks, David, "Luby's Inc. Plans to Cede More Control," *San Antonio Express-News,* January 26, 2008, p. 1C.

———, "Management, Shareholder Battling for Control of Luby's Future," *San Antonio Express-News,* January 10, 2008, p. 1E.

Kaplan, David, "Cafeteria Chain Aims for Trendier Feel While Maintaining Its Signature Casual Convenience," *Houston Chronicle,* July 4, 2007, Business sec., p. 1.

———, "Taking the Cafeteria Up a Notch: Pappas Brothers Find Ways to Reinvigorate Luby's While Keeping the Comfort Food," *Houston Chronicle,* November 6, 2005, Business sec., p. 1.

Krajewski, Steve, "Luby's: Dining Humor," *Adweek,* August 22, 1994, p. 4.

Lee, Steven H., "Dishing Up Service: Pace-Setting Luby's Not Discouraged by Decline in Cafeterias," *Dallas Morning News,* December 22, 1996, p. 1H.

———, "Luby's Shareholders Angry, but Vote Re-elects Directors," *Dallas Morning News,* January 13, 2001, p. 2F.

———, "Luby's to Take Bottom-Up Approach: Menu Items and Prices May Need Tweaking, New CEO Pappas Says," *Dallas Morning News,* March 29, 2001, p. 3D.

———, "Luby's Will Suspend Dividend: Cafeteria Company Unveils Plan to Turn Eateries Around," *Dallas Morning News,* October 28, 2000, p. 1F.

———, "Nouvells Luby's: Cafeteria Chain Slims Down, Tries to Revive Profits with Scaled-Down Restaurants, New Features," *Dallas Morning News,* September 14, 1999, p. 1D.

———, "Plateful of Trouble: Conflicts over Leadership Loom at Luby's Meeting," *Dallas Morning News,* January 12, 2001, p. 1D.

McDowell, Bill, "The People's Choice," *Restaurants and Institutions,* February 1, 1996, pp. 43–65.

Monroe, Melissa S., "Luby's Completes Debt Refinancing Deal," *San Antonio Express-News,* June 9, 2004, p. 1E.

Reinhold, Robert, "Why They're Lining Up at Luby's," *New York Times,* August 18, 1985, p. F11.

Robinson-Jacobs, Karen, "Bracing for Boardroom Battle: Cafeteria Chain's White Knights Face Hedge Fund's Challenge," *Dallas Morning News,* January 15, 2008, p. 1D.

Rogers, Monica, "Buffet Gourmet," *Chain Leader,* April 2003, pp. 38–39+.

Ruggless, Ron, "Luby's Cafeterias Appoints New Chief," *Nation's Restaurant News,* September 29, 1997, pp. 3, 75.

———, "Luby's CEO Parker Quits After Warning About Lowered Profits, Unit Closures," *Nation's Restaurant News,* October 9, 2000, pp. 4, 145.

———, "Luby's Inc. Reverses Earnings Erosion, Cures Debt Default," *Nation's Restaurant News,* June 21, 2004, pp. 8, 59.

———, "Luby's Ongoing Slump Results in First Dividend Halt, Resignations," *Nation's Restaurant News,* November 6, 2000, p. 4.

———, "Luby's Seeks New Leaders," *Nation's Restaurant News,* March 31, 1997, p. 3.

———, "Luby's Sells Joint-Venture Interest in Water Street Seafood," *Nation's Restaurant News,* December 20, 1999, p. 11.

———, "Luby's Storms Texas Market with Wyatt's Buy," *Nation's Restaurant News,* July 29, 1996, p. 3.

———, "Luby's TV Ads Cut the Mustard, Go Heavy on the Wry," *Nation's Restaurant News,* December 5, 1994, p. 12.

———, "Pappas Brothers Take Two Top Luby's Posts," *Dallas Morning News,* March 10, 2001, p. 1F.

———, "Pappas Purchases a Piece of Luby's," *Nation's Restaurant News,* January 8, 2001, pp. 1, 62.

———, "Struggling Cafeteria Chains Draft Casual-Dining Vets in Recovery Bids," *Nation's Restaurant News,* May 28, 2001, pp. 4, 73.

Strauss, Gary, "Luby's Proxy Fight Illustrates Investors' Readiness to Act," *USA Today,* January 15, 2001, p. B1.

Tejada, Carlos, "Luby's CEO Takes Own Life, Police Say," *Wall Street Journal,* March 14, 1997, p. A4.

Waters, C. Dickinson, "Luby's Banking on Food-to-Go to Satisfy Wall Street Numbers Hunger," *Nation's Restaurant News,* June 26, 2000, p. 12.

Weil, Jonathan, "After Some Stale Years, Luby's May Have a Recipe for Success," *Wall Street Journal,* April 7, 1999, p. T2.

Weiss, Sebastian, "Luby's Sales Backslide Despite Major Upgrades, Ad Campaign," *San Antonio Business Journal,* February 25, 2000, p. 4.

Lunardi's Super Market, Inc.

---

432 North Canal Street, Unit 22
South San Francisco, California 94080
U.S.A.
Telephone: (650) 588-7507
Fax: (650) 588-0811
Web site: http://www.lunardis.com

Private Company
Incorporated: 1953
Employees: 400
Sales: $50 million (2007 est.)
NAICS: 445110 Supermarkets and Other Grocery (Except Convenience) Stores

■ ■ ■

Lunardi's Super Market, Inc., operates a regional chain of grocery stores in the San Francisco Bay Area, competing as an upscale grocer primarily in suburban markets. The company prides itself on the variety and the freshness of its produce, stocking more than 400 items it hand-selects daily at the produce market in South San Francisco. Its stores feature full-service departments, including meat, seafood, and hot deli. Lunardi's Super Market also boasts a comprehensive selection of wines and cheeses. A family-run operation, the company opened its first suburban supermarket in San Bruno in 1981, 28 years after its founding. Expansion after the San Bruno opening, which occurred at a pace of roughly one new store every five years, added locations in Los Gatos, San Jose, Walnut Creek, Danville, Belmont, and Burlingame. The company is led by Paul Lunardi, the son of founder Alfredo Lunardi.

ORIGINS

Around the time Alfredo Lunardi opened his first store, a relatively new breed of competitor in the grocery business was beginning to proliferate. Supermarkets, featuring self-service shelves and discounted prices, were becoming the rage and were soon to be the new standard for success in the grocery business. Lunardi's approach as a retailer bucked the industry trend, giving his grocery store distinctive qualities that endured for decades. Lunardi chose to compete on the quality of the items he sold, not on the price of the items, the basis of an operating philosophy he instilled in his son, Paul Lunardi. "I remember my father always saying, 'I can always explain my price, but I don't want to ever justify our quality,'" Paul Lunardi said in an April 2, 1999, interview with the *Business Journal.*

Born in Lucca, Italy, Alfredo Lunardi immigrated to the United States in 1950 when he was 20 years old. He settled in San Francisco and wasted little time before establishing himself in his new surroundings. By the age of 23, he was ready financially to start his own business. He used his savings to acquire a store in San Francisco's Sunset District, a 10,000-square-foot building located along Irving Street that operated under the name "Mother's Market." From the start, Lunardi concentrated on fresh produce, the financial mainstay of Lunardi's Super Market during its first half-century of business. The emphasis on produce demanded long hours from the young entrepreneur, requiring him to make daily visits to the South San Francisco terminal market to hand-select the best produce from the harvests of nearby farmers. He kept a rigorous schedule for years, shuttling from the produce stands to his store, a routine that left a lasting impression on his son Paul. "I remember as a kid my dad getting up at two in the morning to get to the produce market ... and then work until six at night [in the store]. He did that seven days a week."

EXPANSION BEGINS IN 1981

There were two distinct periods in Lunardi's Super Market's history. One era encompassed the years when Alfredo Lunardi tended his small downtown store, the nearly 30 years he spent managing the business before his sons, Paul and Ralph, joined the operation. The arrival of the second generation of the Lunardi family also coincided with the first major event in the company's history, touching off a second era of existence that would see Lunardi's Super Market develop into a retail chain.

By the beginning of the 1980s, rising rent prices in the Sunset District were forcing Alfredo Lunardi to consider closing his store and moving elsewhere. In 1981, when his two sons joined the business, he made his move, shuttering his downtown store and moving into a former Safeway store in San Bruno, California, 15 miles south of San Francisco. The store was twice the size of Lunardi's original location, giving him considerably more space to showcase the berries, peas, artichokes, asparagus, almonds, and other selections that had become his trademark. The store quickly became profitable, encouraging the three Lunardi's to expand a short time later.

LOS GATOS IN 1983

Lunardi's Super Market's upscale approach to the grocery business found ideal conditions in the upscale suburbs of San Francisco. The immediate success of the San Bruno store prompted the Lunardis to replicate the move in Los Gatos, an affluent community populated

primarily by people who worked for high-technology companies in Silicon Valley. Another former Safeway store provided entry into Los Gatos, a 27,000-square-foot store that the Lunardis spent $2 million to acquire and to remodel. "We are in a community where the average house sells for $300,000," Paul Lunardi said in a March 1986 interview with *Progressive Grocer,* referring to Los Gatos. "People who have that kind of money are not looking to save pennies on food shopping. We put out the best, and they are eager to buy."

Alfredo Lunardi's mantra of stressing quality over price paid dividends at the Los Gatos store. As a Safeway, the location generated $55,000 per week in volume. Once the Lunardis took over and stocked the store with more than 400 produce items, including hard-to-find fruits, vegetables, and fresh herbs, they increased the location's weekly volume by more than fivefold, generating $275,000 per week in sales. The store featured a full-service meat department, a full-service seafood department, and a full-service deli department, but the centerpiece of the store was the produce, which accounted for more than one-fifth of its weekly sales. The Los Gatos produce department generated more sales than the entire store generated under Safeway's management.

The Los Gatos store proved to be a resounding success, demonstrating that competing on price was not the only way to win market share in the fiercely competitive grocery business. Although Lunardi's Super Market competed against the massive, national chains operated by Kroger, Safeway, and Wal-Mart, the company's closest rivals in the upscale segment of the market were Menlo Park, California-based Draeger's Super Markets Inc. and San Jose, California-based Cosentinos Vegetable Haven Inc., companies that, like Lunardi's Super Market, emphasized quality over price. To compete against such foes, Lunardi's Super Market continued to hand-select its produce, dispatching Ralph Lunardi to South San Francisco to cull the best fruits and vegetables from the Golden Gate produce market. Although the Lunardis had opened two stores in two years, they dismissed speculation that an expansion campaign was underway. "When you're way ahead in the game," Paul Lunardi said in a March 1986 interview with *Progressive Grocer,* "you don't throw a long bomb." He soon changed his mind, however, ushering in a period of steady expansion that would see the company develop into a regional chain in the coming years.

EXPANSION INTO SAN JOSE IN 1988

Lunardi's Super Market's expansion efforts resumed five years after the San Bruno store opened. The company

KEY DATES

1953: Alfredo Lunardi opens a grocery store in San Francisco's Sunset District.
1981: After closing its store in the Sunset District, the company opens a store in San Bruno.
1983: A Lunardi's Super Market opens in Los Gatos.
1988: Lunardi's Super Market opens a store in San Jose.
1997: A store in Walnut Creek, the company's first store in the East Bay region, is opened.
2001: A sixth store in southeast San Jose is opened, becoming the anchor tenant of the Evergreen Village Square shopping center.
2006: Lunardi's Super Market acquires a store in Danville from Andronico's Market.
2007: The company closes its Evergreen Village Square store.

moved in on the home turf of Cosentinos Vegetable Haven, establishing a store in San Jose in 1988 during its 35th anniversary. Next, in 1992, the company opened a store in Belmont, halfway between San Jose and San Francisco in San Mateo County. A fifth store followed five years later, a 1997 grand opening in Walnut Creek, the first Lunardi's Super Market in the East Bay region.

By the end of the 1990s, Lunardi's Super Market had developed into a five-store regional chain with locations stretching from Los Gatos in the south to San Francisco in the north. Paul Lunardi had taken over leadership of the company by the end of the decade (his brother Ralph had passed away), but Alfredo Lunardi continued to make his daily rounds, visiting one or two stores every day to ensure the quality standards he established were being maintained. "He'll always find something he doesn't like," Paul Lunardi said, referring to his father in a May 7, 1999, interview with the *Business Journal.* "But the system works better than any of the efficiency reports we can generate," he added.

After nearly 50 years in business, Lunardi's Super Market continued to distinguish itself through its customer service and high-quality produce despite the increasing presence of upscale competitors in its markets. The company was the only grocery chain in the region that aged full sides of beef within its stores. Its seafood department stocked fish caught by hook-and-line rather than more inexpensive drag fishing methods.

The company boasted one of the broadest selections of cheese and wine available in northern California. As always, its produce department stood as the centerpiece of each store, offering unparalleled variety and freshness.

ENTERING THE NEW MILLENNIUM

To the thriving business it enjoyed at the end of the 1990s, the company planned to add a sixth store, a store whose grand opening was eagerly anticipated. A new shopping center was being built in southeast San Jose, the Evergreen Village Square, a 160,000-square-foot retail complex located in a rapidly developing area. Just north of the site where Cisco Systems Inc. planned to build a new campus that was expected to employ 20,000 workers, the shopping center was expected to benefit from the construction of nearly 3,000 new homes in the adjacent Evergreen Hills residential project. Lunardi's Super Market became the anchor tenant of the Evergreen Village Square when its 40,000-square-foot store opened in 2001.

A MOVE INTO DANVILLE IN 2006

Lunardi's Super Market's pattern of opening a new store every four or five years continued after the debut of the Evergreen Village Square store. One of the company's family-run competitors, Andronico's Market, an upscale, nine-store chain, decided to sell its store in Danville, a community south of Walnut Creek. "This decision was prompted by our need to satisfy debt obligations to our bank," Bill Andronico, the company's chief executive officer, said in a September 13, 2006, interview with the *San Francisco Chronicle.* "It was not an easy decision and it came only after two years of assessing all realistic alternatives and negotiating with landlords and a number of potential buyers."

Paul Lunardi seized the opportunity created by his rival's financial distress, acquiring the Danville store in 2006. The store was converted into a Lunardi's Super Market quickly, closing as an Andronico's on a Saturday and becoming the Lunardis' seventh retail location the following Tuesday. An expanded produce department was one of the major changes, as well as the addition of a 109-foot meat case, but the greatest difference between the two formats was the cooking school Andronico's had operated within the store. "We've never done that before, so this is all brand-new to us," a Lunardi's Super Market executive said in the September 13, 2006, edition of the *San Francisco Chronicle.* "But we do intend to kick it back up and run it."

STORE CLOSURE IN 2007

On the heels of the acquisition of the Danville store, Lunardi's Super Market suffered what arguably was the greatest setback in its history. In southeast San Jose, the promise of bustling business had failed to materialize, prompting the company to shut down its store in the Evergreen Village Square. Lunardi's Super Market's general counsel, in a September 6, 2007, interview with the *San Jose Mercury News,* explained the closure. "The center never really evolved into what we were anticipating," he said. "It's an expensive disappointment and unprecedented in their experience. Sometimes you have to make hard decisions."

The closure of the Evergreen Village Square store was a discouraging blow, but it was one blemish on an otherwise sterling record of performance. As Lunardi's Super Market celebrated its 55th anniversary and prepared for the future, the company could find ample reasons for optimism. Its measured pace of expansion, its entrenched market position, and its decades of experience lent an air of stability to a company well regarded in the San Francisco Bay Area. In the years ahead, as Lunardi's Super Market continued to adhere to the principles established by Alfredo Lunardi, the company was expected to remain a prominent player in the upscale segment of the grocery business.

Jeffrey L. Covell

PRINCIPAL COMPETITORS

Draeger's Super Markets Inc.; Cosentinos Vegetable Haven Inc.; Andronico's Market, Inc.; Whole Foods Market, Inc.

FURTHER READING

Molina, Joshua, "Evergreen Stunned: Lunardi's Market Closes in San Jose," *San Jose Mercury News,* September 6, 2007.

"Outstanding Progress in the Past 12 Months," *Progressive Grocer,* March 1986, p. 35.

Sarkar, Pia, "Andronico's Sells Danville Market," *San Francisco Chronicle,* September 13, 2006, p. C2.

Shappro, Dana, "Upscale Grocers Ride Demand for 'Yuppie' Food," *Business Journal,* October 20, 1986, p. 9.

Taylor, Dennis, "Fruits of Lunardi's Labors Grow with Hard Work, Business Savvy," *Business Journal,* May 7, 1999, p. 3.

———, "Lunardi's Planning Largest Store," *Business Journal,* April 2, 1999, p. 3.

Mechel OAO

Ul. Krasnoarmeyskaya 1
Moscow, 125993
Russia
Telephone: (+7 495) 221 88 88
Fax: (+7 495) 221 88 00
Web site: http://www.mechel.ru

Public Company
Incorporated: 2003
Employees: 85,032
Sales: $6.72 billion (2007)
Stock Exchanges: Moscow New York
Ticker Symbol: MTL
NAICS: 331111 Iron and Steel Mills

■ ■ ■

Mechel OAO is one of the leading integrated mining and steel companies in Russia. The company is Russia's leading producer of specialty steels and alloys, with a focus on long steel products. The company commands a 39 percent share of the total Russian specialty steel output, and ranks second in the long steel category. The company's steel operations include plants in Russia, Romania, and Lithuania. The Steel Division accounts for more than two-thirds of the group's total revenues, which topped $6.7 billion in 2007. Mechel's second division, Mining, is the fastest-growing segment. Mechel's mining interests include coal, nickel and non-ferrous metals, and iron ore, in Russia, Romania, and Lithuania. In 2006, the company produced 9.7 million tons of coking coal, 7.3 million tons of steam coal, 4.9 million

tons of iron ore concentrate, and 14,000 tons of nickel. The company ranks third in coking coal production in Russia, and holds a market share of 5.5 percent in the total Russian coal market. Mechel has grown rapidly from a minor Siberia-based coal trader to become a major force in the global steel market under the guidance of key shareholders Igor Syuzin and Vladimir Iorikh. The company is listed on the Moscow and New York stock exchanges.

WORLD WAR II STEEL PLANT

Mechel's history began in the years following the Soviet revolution, when the Stalinist government began developing plans to exploit the rich iron ore deposits in Bakal (later known as Chelyabinsk), in the Ural mountains. Although iron ore had been discovered in the Bakal field by the 18th century, it had been left untapped. The large-scale exploitation of the Ural region's rich mineral deposits became an important policy of the young Communist government. By the end of the 1920s, the country had already launched mining and steel production plants in Magnitogorsk, Kuznetsk, and Zoporozh'e. In 1930, the Communist government announced its intention to build two new metallurgical plants in the region at Tagil and Bakal.

Preparations for the Bakal/Chelyabinsk factory were drawn out over the next decade. In 1941, however, the government announced that it had completed the final specifications for the new facility. The outbreak of World War II just days after that announcement placed a new urgency on the factory's construction. Less than two years later, the Chelyabinsk factory was operational.

The name Mechel came from the contraction of the plant's original name, Metalurgicheckii Chelyabinskii.

Expansion of the site continued through the next decades in support of the Soviet government's industrialization and modernization policies through the 1980s. The operation developed into a highly integrated complex, capable of carrying out a broad range of metallurgical processes, from the production of coke and coke chemicals, to sintering, smelting, forging, and extrusion, as well as production of refractories and heat treatment systems. The Chelyabinsk plant's relative youth compared to the country's other steel plants meant that it soon became one of the most modern in the Soviet Union. Chelyabinsk's expertise grew to include in particular the production of specialty steels and long steel products.

Although an important component of the Soviet steel complex, the Chelyabinsk factory struggled in the early years following the Soviet Union's collapse. The institution of a free market system in Russia meant the company was now forced to compete against its larger counterparts, such as the Magnitogorsk steel plant. At the same time, the Chelyabinsk site's remote location meant that it was far from both the sources of its raw materials and fuel supply, but also from its principal markets.

COMBINING COAL AND STEEL ASSETS IN 2003

In the meantime, the new imperatives of the nascent Russian free market economy were also to have a profound impact on the country's coal industry. The legacy of the Soviet era had left the country with a highly inefficient, technologically backward coal industry. Few of the country's hundreds of coal mines even approached profitability, and the sector remained heavily dependent on government subsidies through much of the next decade.

The process of reforming and privatizing the sector began at the beginning of the 1990s, when Boris Yeltsin visited the heart of Russia's coal-production industry, the Kuzbass region. Following that visit, the companies there were granted a greater degree of autonomy in their operations, including the right to adopt new ownership structures. At this time, three new coal companies were created in the Kuznetsk Basin, also known as the Kuzbass region. These included Southern Kuznetsk Basin Company, or Yuzhny Kuzbass. The deregulation and privatization of the coal industry was then formally launched in 1993, as the Russian government announced its intention to sell off an initial 30 percent stake in the Kuzbass companies.

Among those acquiring stakes in Yuzhny Kuzbass were two ambitious partners, Igor Zyuzin and Vladimir Iorikh, who began amassing shares in the company from 1995. By 1996, the pair had acquired control of Yuzhny Kuzbass. Zyuzin and Iorikh, both in their 30s, had aspirations of joining Russia's booming oligarchy, a relatively small group of Kremlin insiders who amassed fortunes during the "wild west" years of the Yeltsin regime.

Through the end of the decade, Yuzhny Kuzbass began amassing a portfolio of mining interests. By 2000, the company had gained control of seven mining operations in the Mezhdurechensk region of southwestern Siberia. The mining interest also included the company's own coal processing plants.

However, Zyuzin's and Iorikh's ambitions of building a major industrial player in the Russian and even global market ran into a wall. The Russian government was approaching the end of its direct involvement in the country's coal industry. Over the decade, as the government phased out the subsidiaries that had kept the industry afloat, some 150 unprofitable coal companies had been shut down. From more than 900,000 mineworkers at the beginning of the 1990s, only 400,000 remained.

Yuzhny Kuzbass's ability to develop its own markets, especially the export market, remained highly limited, both by its remote location and by Russia's economic policies. Like the other coal producers, Yuzhny Kuzbass was forced to recognize the need to develop a close partnership with the steel industry. By 2000, the company had targeted Mechel as its proposed partner. The company offered to buy out the steel company's controlling shareholder, Glencore. Yet Zyuzin and Iorikh soon found themselves in a battle for control of Mechel, as rival steel group Evraz, which was also buying up mining interests, launched a bid to take over Mechel as well.

In the end, Yuzhny Kuzbass succeeded in pushing through the merger, resulting in the creation in 2001 of the new Mechel Group. At that time, the company

KEY DATES

1941: Construction begins on a steel factory, Metalurgicheckii Chelyabinskii (Mechel), which launches production two years later.

1993: Russian government launches privatization of Soviet-era coal mining industry, creating Yuzhny Kuzbass (Southern Kuznetsk Basin).

1996: Igor Zyuzin and Vladimir Iorikh gain control of the Yuzhny Kuzbass coal mining group.

2001: Yuzhny Kuzbass begins merger with Mechel, completed in 2003.

2004: Mechel becomes first Russian steel group to list its shares on the New York Stock Exchange.

2008: Vladimir Putin accuses Mechel of exporting its steel at a discount, causing the company's share value to plummet.

boasted a raw steel production of 4.2 million metric tons; 3.3 million metric tons of rolled steel products; and 2.6 million metric tons of coke. The company had by then also acquired the Southern Urals Nickel Plant, including a nickel processing plant and two nickel mines, adding an annual production of more than 13,500 metric tons of nickel.

INTERNATIONAL EXPANSION

Mechel now rolled out its expansion strategy. The company moved to develop both its commercial and export capacity with the acquisition of the Vyartsilya Metal Products Plant in 2002. The factory included a rolling mill producing more than 51,500 metric tons of finished product per year. The acquisition, located in Sortavala, Karelia, near the Finnish border, also provided Mechel with easier access to markets outside of Russia.

Closer to home, the company bought the Beloretsk Metallurgical Plant, located in the southern Urals. That plant added a rolling mill producing more than 500,000 metric tons annually, nearly half of which was wire rod. Also in 2002, Mechel acquired a limestone quarry and processing plant in Pugachev, near the Beloretsk plant.

The year 2002 also marked Mechel's first expansion outside of Russia. The company acquired COST, a steel mill in Targoviste, Romania, that year. This plant gave the group additional capacity of more than 725,000 metric tons of raw steel and steel products. The move

into Romania was soon followed by an extension into Croatia, with the purchase of the Zeljezara, a pipe producing plant. The softness of the pipe sector forced Mechel to shut down that operation in 2004.

By then, however, the company had completed a series of new acquisitions, including a stampings plant in Cheburkul, in the Urals. Mechel also added to its Romanian presence through the purchase of Idustria Sarmei, a steel mill in Campia Turzii, which added more than 450,000 metric tons to the group's production. The company then entered Lithuania, buying a small steel mill in Kaunas that year. In the meantime, Mechel added to its coal production as well, buying the Korshunov Mining Plant, in Siberia, and a coal washing facility in Kazakhstan. The group's operations there were quickly expanded in 2004, with the acquisition of a coal mine, the underground Gorbachev Mine. A further purchase was completed in 2004, as the company added Izhstal, a specialty steel producer with a total capacity of more than 700,000 metric tons.

FIRST RUSSIAN STEEL GROUP ON THE NYSE

These acquisitions had given Mechel the critical mass to enable it to achieve the next milestone in its history. In November 2004, Mechel became the first Russian metals group to launch an initial public offering on the New York Stock Exchange (NYSE). The offering of approximately 10 percent of the group's stock enabled it to raise $291 million. The listing also helped to confirm the aspirations of founding partners Zyuzin and Iorikh, as both men joined the ranks of Russia's billionaires. By the latter part of the decade, Mechel's market capitalization had soared past $15 billion. By then the company had become one of the largest steel groups in Russia, and the country's largest specialty steel producer.

Mechel continued to seek to enhance its vertically integrated profile. In 2006, for example, the company acquired Metals Recycling OOO, a scrap metal processor also located in Chelyabinsk. In this way, the company gained control of an annual scrap output of nearly 200,000 metric tons.

In 2008, the company signed an agreement to supply more than 400,000 metric tons of rail per year to Russian Railways. The contract represented half of Russian Railway's project rail needs as it carried out a massive modernization effort, including the addition of 20,000 kilometers of new railroad through 2030. Also that year, the company enhanced its international steel production capacity, with the acquisition of Ductil Steel for $221 million. The purchase marked the company's third steel plant in Romania.

Mechel continued to seek acquisition targets through 2008. In March of that year, the company announced it had reached an agreement to pay £749 million ($1.5 billion) to take over Oriel Resources. That company owned a chromite mine and nickel processing plant in Kazakhstan, as well as a smelter in Saint Petersburg. This acquisition was followed by a move into Western Europe, with the acquisition of German steel trading group HBL Holding GmbH in September of that year.

By then, however, Mechel faced a crisis that threatened its existence as an integrated steel and coal mining group. In August 2008, former Russian President Vladimir Putin, who continued to dominate Russian political life as its prime minister, publicly accused Mechel of selling its steel to the export markets at lower prices than in Russia. Putin followed up the accusation with more charges against Mechel, claiming that the company had been avoiding paying taxes, and making use of foreign subsidiaries to sell its Russian production.

The immediate result of Putin's accusations was a dramatic drop in Mechel's share price, slashing its value by more than half. The attack was viewed as a possible prelude to a breakup of Mechel. Members of the Russian government, including President Dmitry Medvedev, attempted to calm fears of a new round of Russian political intervention into its corporate sector.

Other observers questioned Putin's apparent unconcern about the possibility of destroying the already fragile confidence of the international investment community in the Russian market. Nonetheless, the move was seen as a possible prelude to Zyuzin's ouster from the company, in favor of an ally more closely aligned to Putin himself. Mechel's success in building one of Russia's largest integrated steel and mining companies had also succeeded in making it one of the country's most coveted in the new century.

M. L. Cohen

PRINCIPAL SUBSIDIARIES

Arshan OOO; Chelyabinsk Metallurgical Plant OAO; Magnitogorsk Metallurgical Plant OAO; Mechel Trading AG; Mechel Trading House OOO; South Ural Nickel Plant OAO; SUNP OAO; Yuzhny Kuzbass Coal Company.

PRINCIPAL COMPETITORS

Evraz Group S.A.; MMK; Severstal Group; OJSC Novolipetsk Steel; SKF (AB).

FURTHER READING

Gorst, Isobel, and Toby Shelley, "Oriel Resources Agrees to Takeover by Russia's Mechel," *Financial Times*, March 27, 2008, p. 22.

"Mechel Bashing, Business in Russia," *Economist* (U.S.), August 2, 2008.

"Mechel Completes Purchase of Scrap Processor," *American Metal Market*, May 2, 2006, p. 8.

"Mechel: Focusing on Growth," *Institutional Investor International Edition*, March 2005, p. 96.

"Mechel Looks to Bright Trading Future," *Trade Finance*, February 2008.

"Mechel OAO Announces Acquisition of HBL Holdings," *International Resource News*, September 25, 2008.

"Mechel OAO Commissions New Mining and Processing Plant," *International Resource News*, September 24, 2008.

"Mechel Steel Group Becomes First Russian Metals Firm to List on NYSE," *American Metal Market*, November 1, 2004, p. 5.

Mokrinskii, A. V., "The Company Mechel: Impressive Results from an Innovative Policy," *Metallurgist*, Vol. 47, Nos. 3–4, 2003.

Politi, James, "Wall St. Sceptical on Mechel US Listing," *Financial Times*, November 1, 2004, p. 28.

Robertson, Scott, "Mechel Completes $221m Ductil Buy," *American Metal Market*, April 9, 2008, p. 8.

———, "Mechel Investing $500m in Rail Mill," *American Metal Market*, February 27, 2008, p. 8.

Meguiar's, Inc.

17991 Mitchell South
Irvine, California 92614-6015
U.S.A.
Telephone: (949) 752-8000
Toll Free: (800) 347-5700
Fax: (949) 752-5784
Web site: http://www.meguiars.com

Private Company
Incorporated: 1901 as Mirror Bright Polish Company
Employees: 225
Sales: $100 million (2008 est.)
NAICS: 325612 Polish and Other Sanitation Good
Manufacturing

∎ ∎ ∎

Based in Irvine, California, Meguiar's, Inc., is a premier car care products company, long embraced by classic car collectors including talk show host Jay Leno as well as everyday car enthusiasts. Consumer products for exterior surfaces include car washes; paint cleaners; waxes; polishes; detailing clay; and wheel, tire, glass, trim and molding, and chrome and aluminum care products. Interior care products are available to care for leather, vinyl, rubber, and plastic, and also include cloth and carpet cleaners and odor elimination products. Consumer products are sold through auto parts chains such as Pep Boys and such mass retailers as Wal-Mart, Kmart, and Target. Meguiar's also offers a professional line of car care products, sold under the Mirror Glaze label, as well as car detailing accessories, including wash

mitts, detailing cloth, drying towels, chamois, and applicator pads. In addition, the company offers product lines for motorcycles, recreational vehicles, and boats.

Home care products include leather, metal, marble, glass, fiberglass, carpet, vinyl and rubber, and clear plastic cleaning solutions, as well as general cleaning solutions. Meguiar's also sells cleaners and degreasers for the garage, tool care products, and organizing products. The manufacture of Meguiar's 300 products is conducted at a 200,000-square-foot plant in Nashville, Tennessee. In addition to its California corporate headquarters, Meguiar's maintains its international headquarters in Hong Kong, as well as subsidiary offices in Toronto, Canada; Sydney, Australia; Tokyo, Japan; Dubai, United Arab Emirates; and Durban, South Africa. All told, Meguiar products are sold in about 100 countries. In September 2008 the Meguiar family agreed to sell the company to 3M Company.

BEGINNINGS IN INDIANA

Meguiar's Inc. was established in 1901 in Evansville, Indiana, as the Mirror Bright Polish Company by Frank Meguiar Jr., who developed a furniture polish in his garage that he sold under the Mirror Bright label. He had been a salesman for a furniture polish company, but the product he represented was poor in quality. Although he had no training in chemistry, he set to the task of developing a high-quality furniture polish. Relying mostly on trial and error, he developed a polish that made use of diminishing abrasives. In the beginning of the process the abrasives cut through dirt, but as they were worn down into smaller particles, they were able to

COMPANY PERSPECTIVES

What began a century ago as a simple furniture polish laboratory and plant in the garage of founder Frank Meguiar, Jr., now spans over 100 years of Meguiar family stewardship. Meguiar's, Inc., has become one of the world's leading surface care products companies, providing highly specialized products for almost every conceivable type of surface.

produce a smooth, shiny surface. Meguiar also developed a furniture cleaner that was used on wood that had previously been waxed, oiled, or polished, and was used before applying his Mirror Bright Furniture Polish. According to family lore, Meguiar used an egg-beater to mix up his polish one bottle at a time in his garage each night for sales the next day.

At the time Meguiar was establishing himself in the furniture polish business, the automobile industry was also taking shape. The early cars were very much horse-less carriages, relying on similar looking wooden bodies. Not surprisingly, Meguiar adopted his Mirror Bright polish for use on cars. When cars adopted metallic bodies, he followed the market and concocted a polish suitable for that surface while continuing to produce his furniture cleaner and polish. More importantly, he continued a commitment to producing the highest-quality product on the market that would ensure the company's ongoing success.

FAMILY MOVES TO PASADENA: 1913

In 1913 Frank Meguiar moved his family of 12 children to Pasadena, California, a major car center at the time. By 1915 it boasted the highest per capita rate of car ownership in the world. Here Meguiar continued to operate Mirror Bright Polish Company, which catered to the major coach builders such as Walter M. Murphy, who served the Hollywood elite and other high-end clients, building bodies for their Cord, Duesenberg, Minerva, Mercedes-Benz, and Packard automobiles. Meguiar's sons Maurice, Malcolm, and Kenneth joined him in running the business, although while growing up all of the children were expected to help out after school.

One son, Malcolm, was especially interested in the product development side of Mirror Bright. In 1923 at the age of eight he began working closely with his father

to formulate new polishes. Like his father he was self-taught, but years later when a team of chemists worked under him, Malcolm Meguiar often surprised his highly trained staff by displaying an inherent sense of what would work in a formulation. After his graduation from Pasadena City College and before he was entrusted by his father to develop products, Malcolm Meguiar was sent on the road as a salesman to learn the business while demonstrating Mirror Glaze products to new car dealers, body shops, and other potential customers.

FOUNDER DIES: 1950

Mirror Bright remained a home-based company until the late 1930s when demand grew large enough to warrant the opening of a combination storefront and plant on Colorado Boulevard in Pasadena. Unlike the furniture polish and cleaner, the company's car care products, marketed under the Mirror Glaze name, were no longer sold to the general public. Rather, they were marketed to automakers, car dealers, body shops, and detailers. In 1950 Frank Meguiar died and his sons Maurice, Malcolm, and Kenneth took charge as equal partners. The oldest was Maurice, who served as sales manager; Malcolm formulated the new products and was responsible for expanding offerings from 20 to about 230; and Kenneth, the youngest of the three, was responsible for operations.

Under the leadership of the second generation of the Meguiar family, Mirror Bright continued to grow, due in large part to excellent word of mouth. In the 1950s the company became more assertive in its marketing by sponsoring a car driven by Ray Crawford in the Indianapolis 500, the Meguiar Mirror Glaze Special. Mirror Bright received limited attention because Crawford failed to finish the 500 all three times he qualified, never finishing higher than 23rd. The former World War II fighter pilot fared better on other tracks around the world, however, and Mirror Bright and Meguiar's Inc. would continue to sponsor race cars, backing such drivers as Michael Andretti and Geoff Brabham as well as sponsoring races at Riverside International Raceway until the Riverside, California, road course was closed in 1989.

A third generation of the Mirror Bright Company became involved in the 1960s. Malcolm's son Barry joined his father, who was now heading the business, in 1964 after graduating, like his father, from Pasadena City College. Mirror Bright's annual sales had leveled off around $600,000, making it a difficult decision for the younger Meguiar, who had to question how much of a future there was with the company. He decided to take a chance and moved to Detroit, where Mirror Bright had recently lost its sales representative. Although

KEY DATES

1901: Frank Meguiar founds Mirror Bright Polish Company in Evansville, Indiana.
1913: Company moves to Pasadena, California.
1950: Three sons take control following Frank Meguiar's death.
1970: Company moves to Irvine, California.
1973: Consumer product line is introduced.
1980: Barry Meguiar is named president.
1995: After ten-year absence Barry Meguiar returns as chief executive.
2000: *Car Crazy* television program debuts on Speed Vision cable television channel.
2008: Company is sold to 3M Company.

very young for a rep, he had been working with Mirror Glaze products since his childhood summers. By high school he worked throughout the year in both manufacturing and order entry, and as a college student managed the accounting department. As a result he made an ideal advocate for Mirror Glaze products in Detroit and was well able to train much older field personnel.

Barry Meguiar was more than just a knowledgeable salesperson. He was a car enthusiast himself. After returning to California in the mid-1960s, he began attending and exhibiting at the increasingly popular car shows, including the Specialty Equipment Market Association (SEMA) show, which was to become one of the world's top automotive trade shows and a Las Vegas staple. Many of the winning show cars displayed a high-gloss look that came from Mirror Glaze products. Moreover, the custom painters who worked on show cars often provided their customers with a bottle of Meguiar's Mirror Glaze No. 7 Sealer & Reseal Glaze to help maintain the car's look. Such exposure created an awareness of Mirror Glaze products among enthusiasts, but the products were not supplied to retailers for sale to the general public, creating a groundswell for a consumer line of Mirror Bright products.

HEADQUARTERS MOVES TO IRVINE, CALIFORNIA: 1970

After the company moved to Irvine, California, in 1970 because of the Foothill Freeway project that forced Mirror Bright to vacate its longtime Pasadena home, Barry Meguiar spearheaded an effort to launch a consumer product line. Easy-to-use products were formulated for the general public and new packaging and a fresh brand, "Meguiar's," were developed. The consumer line was unveiled in 1973 and marked the beginning of a new era for the company, which was now renamed as Meguiar's Inc. The consumer products fared so well that in 1979 the company began offering them through mass retailers such as Wal-Mart and Kmart. It was also during the 1970s that Meguiar began traveling the globe establishing branch operations. In the early 1990s the company would make a push into the promising Asian market, first in Japan, leading to the establishment of the Hong Kong office that would become Meguiar's international headquarters.

Barry Meguiar replaced his father as president in 1980, although Malcolm Meguiar remained heavily involved in the business, serving as chairman until 1985. He also continued to supervise the laboratory until 1993. He remained chairman emeritus of the company, a title he held until his death in 1999 at the age of 84. Barry Meguiar served as president and chief executive officer of Meguiar's Inc. until 1985. In an effort to further grow the retail side of the business, the first nonfamily member, Lawrence Kerin, was installed as CEO. Meguiar's enjoyed success in this regard, but the Meguiar family was forever worried about jeopardizing its professional product sales and in particular its relationships with luxury automakers such as BMW, Lamborghini, and Mercedes-Benz. Kerin was replaced in 1992 by Meguiar's chief financial officer, Jack Swan, who served as president on an interim basis for a year before turning over the reins to Louis Basenese. In November 1995 Barry Meguiar, who had been chairman and provided advice to the company in the past decade while devoting a great deal of time to outside interests, returned to take day-to-day control of the family business.

With Barry Meguiar once again in direct control, Meguiar's Inc. in the late 1990s picked up the pace of its international expansion, especially in the Asian market where operations were established in Korea, the Philippines, and Thailand. The company also pursued further growth through the addition of new products. In 1999 Meguiar's introduced a major new product, Endurance. The result of two years of research and development, Endurance was a rubber and vinyl protectant for tires. Unlike less-expensive sprays, Endurance was a gel applied with a contoured washable foam applicator that greatly reduced waste. Moreover, Endurance, as its name suggested, was formulated to last longer than other tire treatments.

With the Internet becoming commonplace, Meguiar's took advantage of the web to establish a site that could provide a detailed maintenance program which customers could generate by completing an online questionnaire. Also to drive sales, the company began sponsoring awards in 1995, honoring people who had made a significant contribution to the collector car hobby. In 2000 Meguiar's pursued another way to promote its products, hosting a company-sponsored 30-minute program, *Car Crazy,* on the Speed Vision cable television channel. Soon a radio version of *Car Crazy* was added, as well as another radio show cosponsored with *Motor Trend* magazine. An Irvine production company, taking the name Car Crazy Productions, was acquired to handle the programming as well as take on audio and video projects for outside companies.

COMPANY SOLD: 2008

By the early 2000s, the fourth generation of the Meguiar family was involved in the business. Consumer products now accounted for 60 percent of Meguiar's sales. The family was circumspect about how well it was doing, but it was estimated that the company generated between $75 million and $100 million in sales. Barry Meguiar received frequent offers to buy the company, so much so that a form letter was developed to politely decline. In 2003, however, the company received "succession financing" from the private equity firm The Shansby Group. It was a difficult period in which to do business. With the economy faltering, the car wax market was hit especially hard, and it had already been on a downward trend because fewer car owners had the time or inclination to hand wax their cars. Fortunately, Meguiar's catered mostly to the car enthusiast market where its brand remained strong. To maintain its competitive position in the marketplace, the family decided in September 2008 to join forces with a major corporation, 3M Company, agreeing to sell the business

for an undisclosed amount. Barry Meguiar told the press, "Combining with 3M will greatly enhance our ability to serve and support Car Crazy people on a global basis." How much latitude the Meguiar family would retain in running the company Frank Meguiar established 107 years earlier remained to be seen.

Ed Dinger

PRINCIPAL SUBSIDIARIES

Car Crazy Productions; Meguiar's International.

PRINCIPAL COMPETITORS

The Clorox Company; Orica Limited; Turtle Wax, Inc.

FURTHER READING

Aguilera, Elizabeth, "Irvine, Calif.-based Car-Wax Maker Leads in Its Field," *Orange County Register,* September 1, 2001.

"'Car Crazy TV' Driving Sales As Vehicle for Meguiar's Inc.," *Los Angeles Business Journal,* May 10, 2004, p. 14.

Lee, Samantha, "Meguiar's Didn't Start with Cars, but Now Is Tied to Them," *Orange County Business Journal,* December 3, 2001.

Lyster, Michael, "Auto Wax Maker Meguiar's Selling to 3M," *Orange County Business Journal,* September 8, 2008.

Margolis, Dan, "Meguiar Back As Head of Family Business," *Los Angeles Times,* December 12, 1995.

Thapanachai, Somporn, "American Car-Care Product Maker Meguiar's Eyes 50 Percent Growth in Asia," *Bangkok Post,* October 3, 2003.

Yip, Jeff, "Calif. Firm Debuts Tire Protectant," *Tire Business,* January 18, 1999, p. 12.

Zintel, Ed, "After 100 Years the Passion Remains All in the Family for Meguiar's," *SEMA News,* November 2001.

Mexichem, S.A.B. de C.V.

Río San Javier 10
Tlalnepantla, Estado de México 54060
Mexico
Telephone: (52 55) 5366-4000
Fax: (52 55) 5397-8836
Web site: http://www.mexichem.com.mx

Public Company
Incorporated: 1953 as Cables Mexicanos, S.A.
Employees: 8,331
Sales: MXN 23.02 billion ($2.14 billion) (2007)
Stock Exchanges: Bolsa Mexicana de Valores
Ticker Symbol: MEXCHEM
NAICS: 325110 Petrochemical Manufacturing; 325120 Industrial Gas Manufacturing; 325181 Alkalines and Chlorine Manufacturing; 325211 Plastics Material and Resin Manufacturing; 326122 Plastics Pipe and Pipe Fitting Manufacturing; 326140 Polystyrene Foam Product Manufacturing; 551112 Offices of Other Holding Companies

■ ■ ■

Mexichem, S.A.B. de C.V., is the holding company for a Mexican group of chemical and petrochemical companies. Its plastic pipes, made from polyvinyl chloride (PVC), are widely used in construction, housing, drinking water, and urban sewage systems. Its PVC can also be found in a wide variety of products used in electronic and electrical applications, including computers, cellular phones, and power tools, in healthcare products, and also in the automotive market. In the construction market, besides pipes, Mexichem products are used in such materials as cement, paints, siding, roofing, floor and wall coverings, and fencing. Mexichem's hydrofluoric acid is chiefly used in the manufacture of refrigerating gases found in air conditioning but has other uses as well. An aggressive acquisition program has made the company a leader in chemicals and petrochemicals in Mexico, and it now exports products to more than 50 countries.

THE COMPLEX ASSEMBLAGE OF A CHEMICAL GIANT

Mexichem was created from the integration of a number of companies. One of these was Cables Mexicanos, S.A., founded in 1953 as a manufacturer of steel wires and cables. This company came to be controlled by Grupo Industrial Camesa, S.A. de C.V., which was founded in 1978 and entered the Bolsa Mexicana de Valores in the same year. In 1986 Camesa acquired Compañia Minera Las Cuevas, S.A. de C.V., a producer of fluorite, or fluorospar (calcium fluoride), founded in 1957.

Mexichem also derives from Industrial Química Pennwalt, S.A. de C.V. Founded in 1951 as Pennsalt de México, S.A. de C.V., a subsidiary of the Philadelphia-based Pennsylvania Salt Manufacturing Co. (later Pennwalt Corporation), the company originally focused mainly on the production of insecticides but later extended its range, becoming a leader in Mexico and Latin America in the production of caustic soda and chlorine. Pennwalt sold a majority stake in this company in a 1979 public offering.

In 1984 Química Pennwalt became one of three companies acquired by Antonio del Valle Ruíz, formerly the founder of Banco de Crédito y Servicio (Bancreser). Del Valle was at loose ends after a financial crisis had led the Mexican government to nationalize the country's banks in 1982. With the indemnization bonds he received from the government as compensation, he went shopping for other enterprises, acquiring a majority stake in Pennwalt quite by chance, simply because it was solvent and available, he later said.

Pennwalt acquired, in 1988, Cloro de Tehuantepec, S.A. de C.V., which enabled it to consolidate its leadership in Mexico in the production of chlorine and caustic soda, basic chemicals for the Mexican petrochemical industry. A joint undertaking of three companies and the national development bank, Cloro de Tehuantepec had opened a $72 million plant in 1971.

Del Valle returned to banking when Mexico's banks were reprivatized in 1992, as a principal shareholder of what became Grupo Financiero Bital, S.A. de C.V. After Camesa fell into deep financial trouble, its creditors, in 1994, named Bital as administrator of the company. In this way del Valle began the process of integrating disparate companies into a single holding under his proprietorship.

Química Pennwalt and Polímeros de México, S.A. de C.V., were members of an industrial group whose name became Mexichem in 1998. Majority control of Mexichem was held by Grupo Empresarial Privado Mexicano, S.A. de C.V., which had been founded the previous year and had a number of investors but was under del Valle's leadership. Elf Atochem, the chemical subsidiary of French oil company Elf Aquitaine S.A. (later Total S.A.), held 43.36 percent of the shares in Mexichem. Mexichem was merged into Camesa in 1999, with Camesa now holding the 50.4 percent stake in Mexichem that Grupo Empresarial Privado Mexicano had formerly held in this company. Mexichem became Camesa's division of plastics and chemicals.

FROM CAMESA TO MEXICHEM: 2002–05

By 2002 del Valle, who held one-fourth of Bital, had fallen out with his partners, Luis and Eduardo Berrondo. In return for his shares, he received a $300 million cash payment and, through Grupo Empresarial Kaluz, S.A. de C.V., the Berrondo's 70 percent stake in Camesa. Kaluz was a newly created holding company controlled by del Valle and his brother Adolfo, described in one publication as ranking 12th among wealthy Mexicans. In December 2003 Camesa purchased Total's stake in Mexichem. The remaining Mexichem shares were purchased by means of a tender offer on the Bolsa Mexicana.

In 2004 Camesa acquired Química Flúor, S.A. de C.V., a manufacturer of hydrofluoric acid and sulfuric acid founded in 1971 and devoted entirely to export. This company's operations were integrated with Compañia Minera las Cuevas, which had become the world's leading producer of fluorite. With the acquisition, Camesa became the largest vertically integrated producer of hydrofluoric acid in North America. To finance the purchase, Camesa issued convertible bonds with a nominal value of MXN 288 million (about $25 million) and an option that could be converted to a 12 percent shareholding.

Near the close of 2004, Camesa acquired Grupo Primex, S.A. de C.V., which, along with Polímeros de México, was the leader in Mexico and Latin America in the manufacture of PVC and PVC compounds, plasticizers, and plastic composites. Camesa was now the leading manufacturer in Mexico of products derived from the vinyl chlorine chemical chain.

Camesa, in June 2005, sold its steel and industrial division, consisting of six companies, to investors headed by Wire Rope Company of America, Inc., and WRCA, LLC, for about $130 million. Following this divestiture, Camesa, three months later, changed its name to Mexichem, S.A. de C.V., to more closely identify the enterprise with the sectors in which it was principally focused. The change of name was followed almost immediately by a public offering of stock in which the company obtained MXN 1.32 billion ($135 million) for 97.75 million shares of stock. Two years later, del Valle and related shareholders still held 70 percent of Mexichem.

A MULTINATIONAL PETROCHEMICAL PLAYER: 2005–07

With cash in hand, Mexichem quickly went shopping for more companies. Before the year was out, it had

Mexichem, S.A.B. de C.V.

KEY DATES

1978: Grupo Industrial Camesa, a precursor of Mexichem, is founded.
1984: Antonio del Valle Ruíz purchases a majority stake in Industrial Química Pennwalt.
1986: Camesa acquires Compañia Minera Las Cuevas, a producer of fluorite.
1988: Pennwalt acquires Cloro de Tehuantepec, a producer of chlorine and caustic soda.
1998: An industrial group that includes Pennwalt and Polímeros de México becomes Mexichem.
1999: Mexichem becomes Camesa's division of plastics and chemicals.
2004: Camesa is the world's largest producer of fluorite and a leading producer of hydrofluoric acid in North America; Camesa is also the Mexican leader in products derived from the vinyl chloride chain.
2005: Camesa changes its name to Mexichem and issues a public offering of stock.
2007: Mexichem acquires two big South American companies involved in making plastic pipes.
2008: Mexichem acquires 11 more companies by midyear.

acquired 69 percent of the capital stock of Dermet de México, S.A. de C.V. The purchase allowed Mexichem to gain access to the distribution channels for many chemical products and to market intelligence in its field, including both other producers and retail customers.

Mexichem entered the United States in early 2006, when it acquired Bayshore Vinyl Compounds, Inc., Bayshore Rigids LLC, and Riccia SA, LLC, of Manalapan, New Jersey. These enterprises were manufacturing PVC compounds for extrusion and molding, focusing on the construction sector. With this purchase, the Mexichem subsidiary Grupo Primex S.A. de C.V. became the principal producer of PVC, PVC compounds, and plasticizers in the Mexican market.

Also in 2006, in addition to creating a research and development center, Mexichem concluded two important projects in the fluor division: amplifying the flotation process in its San Luis Potosí salt mine and putting into production fluorite purifying in its hydrofluoric acid plant in Matamoros, Tamaulipas. This enabled the division to maintain its rank as the largest integrated producer of hydrofluoric acid in not only North America but the world.

The major news of 2007 was the acquisition, for $550 million, of Grupo Amanco, a Brazilian-based conglomerate that was the leader in Latin America in the production and sale of solutions for the conduction of fluids, consisting principally of plastic water transporting tubes. Amanco was the largest producer in Latin America of plastic tubing for the construction industry and had 18 production plants in 11 countries. Its businesses, which also included plastic compounds, agricultural solutions, and geosystems, had sales in 2006 that came to $811 million. Also in 2007, Mexichem acquired, for $250 million, Petroquímica Colombiana, S.A. (Petco), Colombia's largest producer of PVC resins, with 2006 sales of $375 million. To finance these two purchases, Mexichem borrowed $700 million from Citibank, N.A.

These transactions were well received by investors, and the Mexican business magazine *Expansión* named del Valle its entrepreneur of the year. The gains had indeed been spectacular. Mexichem's shares of stock were trading at a price almost five times as high at the end of 2007 as at the beginning. Its revenues grew 122 percent during the year.

MEXICHEM IN 2008

Mexichem's acquisition program continued into 2008 without a halt. Amanco's Brazilian subsidiary purchased 70 percent of Brazil-based DVG Industria e Comercio de Plásticos Limitada and took an option on the remaining stock. This company was a specialist in the production of PVC tubes for potable water and drainage, with three factories. Mexichem also acquired Dripsa, S.R.L., an Argentine company designing, selling, and installing irrigation equipment. This company was placed in a new unit, named Soluciones Agricolas, of a division that was renamed Transformed Products Chain.

By mid-2008 Mexichem had acquired nine more companies. Among these was Policyd, S.A. de C.V., a producer of PVC, and Plásticos Rex, S.A. de C.V. These companies were purchased from Grupo Cydsa, S.A. de C.V., in return for one of Mexichem's three chlorine soda plants. The other acquisitions consisted of a second one for agricultural solutions; another producer of fluorite; three more for the conduction of fluids; and two for a new unit called Geosystems.

Mexichem's operational units in 2008 consisted of three divisions, which it called chains. The chloro vinyl chain was based on the extraction of sodium chloride brine from underground salt domes at a site in the state of Veracruz. This brine served as the raw material for the manufacturing of chlorine soda, vinyl chloride, and polyvinyl chloride. Chlorine soda was being produced at two Mexican plants belonging to Mexichem Derivados,

S.A. de C.V. (consisting chiefly of the former Pennwalt and Cloro de Tehuantepec). Mexican Resinas Vinilicas, S.A. de C.V., had two Mexican plants producing PVC and other synthetic resins and special products. Petco was manufacturing the same products at an industrial complex in Cartagena, Colombia. Mexichem Colombia, S.A., located in Bogotá, was producing caustic soda, sodium hypochlorite, ferric chloride, ferric chloride solutions, and other specialized chemical products, bleaches, and liquids.

The fluorine chain depended on Mexichem's mine in the state of San Luis Potosí. It was the world's largest producer of fluorite, used in the manufacture of steel, cement production, and in the chemical and aluminum industries. This was available in metallurgic gravel for the steel, glass, and ceramic industries, and, in acid grade concentrate, the raw material for obtaining hydrofluoric acid, which was in turn the basis for the elaboration of fluorocarbons used in refrigeration, propellants, and thermoplastic polymers. The factory in Matamoros was producing both anhydrous and aqueous hydrofluoric acid. This facility was the second largest of its kind in the world and was exporting almost all of its production to the United States.

The transformed products chain included a compounds unit involving Mexichem in the production of additives for PVC to be utilized for specific applications. Two plants in Mexico were manufacturing plastic compounds, mostly from PVC, including cables, pipes, flexible and rigid film, shoes, Venetian blinds, window frames, castings, and medical instruments. The Bayshore plant, in Tennent, New Jersey, was producing high quality rigid and flexible PVC components. Another, in Cartagena, Colombia, was producing plastic compounds, including those derived from PVC and polyethylene. In addition, there were two Mexican factories producing styrene products. One was making polystyrene laminate for the food industry, thermoformed dishes and cups, and printed industrial containers. The other was producing expended polystyrene of different densities and presentation for several industries.

The other units in the transformed products chain consisted of acquisitions, namely Amanco's participation in making tubes, Dripsa's activities in equipment for irrigation, and two companies—one Brazilian, the other Peruvian—engaged in textiles: Bidim Industria e Comercio de Não-Teçidos Ltda. and Geotextiles del Perú S.A.

STRATEGIZING FOR THE FUTURE

Although Mexichem was producing the raw materials to make PVC and was manufacturing a large variety of products made from PVC, it did not have complete control of the production cycle because it lacked an intermediate process, the elaboration of monomer vinyl chloride for making PVC. Instead, Mexichem was selling the chlorine that its Mexichem Derivados subsidiary produced to Mexico's giant state-owned Petróleos Mexicanos (Pemex), which was combining the chemical with ethane and reselling the resulting monomer vinyl chloride to Mexichem's Grupo Primex and Polímeros to make PVC resins and compounds. This did not make economic sense to del Valle. However, the construction of a plant to manufacture the resin would cost between $400 million and $500 million and take three to four years to put in operation. The plant would also, company executives calculated, have to be placed in a country where the large amounts of electrical energy needed could be obtained at a price lower than that prevailing in Mexico.

Mexichem's most recent acquisitions were designed to secure necessary raw materials before they were subject to price increases from outside suppliers. This vertical expansion was being matched by horizontal expansion, such as the tubes it was constructing in South America and the variety of plastics compounds produced in its factories in Mexico, Colombia, and the United States. The feeling among investors was that Mexichem was on the right path because of the great need for spending on infrastructure in Latin America, including a severe shortage of housing in many of its countries.

Robert Halasz

PRINCIPAL SUBSIDIARIES

Amanco Tubosistemas Panamá S.A.; Construsistemas Amanco Panamá S.A.; Mexichem Amanco Holding, S.A. de C.V.; Mexichem CID, S.A. de C.V.; Mexichem Colombia, S.A.; Mexichem Compuestos, S.A. de C.V.; Mexichem Derivados, S.A. de C.V.; Mexichem Flúor, S.A. de C.V.; Mexichem Marcas, S.A. de C.V.; Mexichem Plastigama S.A.; Mexichem Resinas Colombia, S.A.; Mexichem Resinas Vinlicas, S.A. de C.V.; Mexichem Servicios Administrativos, S.A. de C.V.; Pavco Investment Inc.; Unión Minera del Sur, S.A. de C.V.

PRINCIPAL DIVISIONS

Chloro-Vinyl Chain; Fluor Chain; Transformed Products Chain.

PRINCIPAL COMPETITORS

Alpek, S.A. de C.V.; Comex, S.A. de C.V.; Petróleos Mexicanos Petroquímica.

FURTHER READING

Aguilar, Alberto, "Nombres, nombres y ... nombres," *Reforma,* January 25, 2002, p. 3.

Black, Thomas, "Mexichem Finds Boom Is a Catalyst," *International Herald Tribune,* October 18, 2007, p. 15.

Goyzueta, Verónica, and Andrés Piedragil, "Invisibles y Globales," *AméricaEconomía,* April 1, 2008, pp. 52–53.

Manley, C. Conrad, "Caustic Soda, Chlorine Output Hike Forecast," *Journal of Commerce,* May 2, 1975, p. 5.

"Mexican Mexichem Buys Latin American Pipe Producer Amanco for USD500 Million," *Noticias Financieras,* February 23, 2007.

Ortega, Adolfo, "Alta presión," *Expansión,* June 23, 2008, pp. 258–59.

———, "El empresario del año," *Expansión,* January 21, 2008 (cover story).

Román Pineda, Romina, "De banquero a Rey de los químicos," *El Universal,* April 10, 2006.

Vargas, Evangelina, "Vende Cydsa plantas a Mexichem," *El Norte,* April 23, 2008, p. 1.

Mitsubishi UFJ Financial Group, Inc.

———— ■ ————

2-7-1 Marunouchi
Chiyoda-ku
Tokyo, 100-8330
Japan
Telephone: (+81-3) 3240-8111
Fax: (+81-3) 3240-8203
Web site: http://www.mufg.jp

■ ■ ■

Public Company
Incorporated: 2001 as Mitsubishi Tokyo Financial Group,
    Inc.
Employees: 78,300
Total Assets: ¥194.07 trillion ($1.83 trillion) (2008)
Stock Exchanges: Tokyo Osaka Nagoya New York
Ticker Symbols: 8306 (Tokyo); MTU (New York)
NAICS: 551111 Offices of Bank Holding Companies;
    522110 Commercial Banking; 522210 Credit Card
    Issuing; 522220 Sales Financing; 522291 Consumer
    Lending; 523110 Investment Banking and Securi-
    ties Dealing; 523120 Securities Brokerage; 523920
    Portfolio Management; 523991 Trust, Fiduciary,
    and Custody Activities

In terms of assets, Mitsubishi UFJ Financial Group,
Inc., (MUFG) is the largest Japanese bank and one of
the ten largest in the world. Well diversified across the
spectrum of financial services, MUFG has five principal
operating companies: Bank of Tokyo-Mitsubishi UFJ,
Ltd., involved in commercial banking; Mitsubishi UFJ
Trust and Banking Corporation, involved in asset

management, pension management, and other trust
operations; securities specialist Mitsubishi UFJ Securities
Co., Ltd.; Mitsubishi UFJ NICOS Co., Ltd.,
concentrating on credit cards and consumer loans; and
the leasing/financing arm Mitsubishi UFJ Lease &
Finance Company Limited. Among Japanese banks,
MUFG operates the largest overseas network with offices and subsidiaries in 40 countries. Among its key
overseas assets is its majority stake in UnionBanCal
Corporation, parent of San Francisco-based Union Bank
of California, one of the 25 largest banks in the United
States. Mitsubishi UFJ Financial Group was formed in
October 2005 through the merger of Mitsubishi Tokyo
Financial Group, Inc., and UFJ Holdings, Inc., both of
which were themselves the creation of earlier mergers.

HISTORY OF MITSUBISHI BANK

In 1880 Yataro Iwasaki, the founder of the Mitsubishi
Shokai, the original Mitsubishi company and one of the
largest maritime shipping and warehousing enterprises
in Japan, established a money exchange office called the
Mitsubishi Exchange Office. Foreign-currency transactions were added to this business in 1890, and five years
later it was reorganized into a full-service banking
division. By 1917 the steadily growing Mitsubishi group
was forced to reorganize. Several divisions were spun off
into independent companies, including the bank, which
gained its independence in 1919 as the Mitsubishi
Bank, Limited, although it retained close ties to the
Mitsubishi *zaibatsu*, or conglomerate.

Immediately following Japan's defeat in World War
II, the U.S. occupation forces outlawed the *zaibatsu*,

COMPANY PERSPECTIVES

We have declared our message to the world as "Quality for You," with management's emphasis on quality. "Quality for You" means that by providing high-quality services, we aspire to help improve the quality of the lives of individual customers, and the quality of each corporate customer. The "You" expresses the basic stance of MUFG that we seek to contribute not only to the development of our individual customers but also communities and society. We believe that delivering superior quality services, reliability, and global coverage will result in more profound and enduring contributions to society.

broke them up into numerous smaller companies, and placed restrictions on their cooperating with one another. Mitsubishi Bank was reorganized as a city bank under the name Chiyoda Bank, Ltd., in 1948. The regulations were gradually relaxed over time until, in 1953, the bank readopted the name Mitsubishi.

Mitsubishi Bank quickly reestablished itself as a powerful trade coordinating entity and rebuilt its ties with the other Mitsubishi companies. As an institution increasingly involved in corporate finance, the bank during the 1960s followed its clients to both export and resource markets, opening offices in Los Angeles, Paris, and Seoul. It financed raw-material purchases, helped to build factories that turned out finished products, and participated in the distribution of those products worldwide. As such, Mitsubishi Bank became an integral contributor to Japan's export-led growth.

Still chartered as a city bank, Mitsubishi was prevented from engaging in certain foreign-exchange and long-term-financing activities. Individual banking, perhaps Japan's most stable business, was a low priority for Mitsubishi; the bank simply found greater opportunities in corporate business. Much of that opportunity grew from the influence the bank wielded inside the boardrooms of its clients.

During the 1970s, the bank established several more offices in Europe, the United States, and Asia. Mitsubishi also established an investment-banking operation and experimented in new areas of business, including leasing, asset management, and a number of other quasi-financial ventures. In 1984 Mitsubishi Bank purchased Bank of California, mainly because it held great promise for the bank's entry into trust banking

and securities. Two years later, in an effort to make Mitsubishi a universal, or full-service, international bank, the company was divided into five groups: international, merchant, corporate, national banking, and capital markets.

In the late 1980s, Japan's economy went through a period of extreme speculation as land prices and share prices soared beyond reason. When the "bubble" burst early in the 1990s, the banking industry in Japan was hit hard. Many banks had to take huge write-offs on unrecoverable loans. A very conservative operation, Mitsubishi was a known risk avoider, and, as a result, did not suffer much from the crisis. In fact, into the mid-1990s, Mitsubishi could boast of a lower than average ratio of nonperforming loans to total assets. The bank had wisely stayed away from speculative property loans and subsequently earned rewards for its prudence.

One such reward came in 1994 and involved Mitsubishi's takeover of Nippon Trust Bank Ltd., a bank founded in 1927. One of the many victims of the burst bubble, and also one of the largest, Nippon Trust's loan portfolio included as much as ¥500 billion in unrecoverable loans. Because Mitsubishi owned a 5 percent stake in Nippon, Japan's finance ministry pressured Mitsubishi to bail the company out. Thus Mitsubishi paid ¥200 billion ($2 billion) for 64 percent more of Nippon, bringing Mitsubishi's stake to 69 percent. Observers noted that Nippon Trust's bad loans exceeded its net asset value and therefore the acquisition could hardly be called a gain. However, the finance ministry rewarded Mitsubishi for taking on the Nippon burden by allowing the bank to begin managing pension funds ahead of the other city banks. Because all the city banks were anxious to move into various financial services and were frustrated at the slow pace of deregulation, this was a significant coup for Mitsubishi.

1996 CREATION OF BANK OF TOKYO-MITSUBISHI

In March 1995 Mitsubishi Bank and Bank of Tokyo, Ltd., announced that they intended to merge. Compared with Mitsubishi's strength in retail and corporate banking in the domestic market, Bank of Tokyo had a long history of involvement in overseas banking and finance since its founding in 1880 as the Yokohama Specie Bank, Ltd. (It took the Bank of Tokyo name in 1946.) The only bank in the country to employ more foreigners than Japanese, Bank of Tokyo developed into Japan's leading foreign exchange bank. This position led the bank to gain many foreign clients, as well as to successful operations in derivatives trading and overseas banking, notably its California-based Union

KEY DATES

■

1880: Mitsubishi Shokai, the original Mitsubishi company, establishes a money exchange office called the Mitsubishi Exchange Office; the Yokohama Specie Bank, Ltd., is established as a special foreign exchange bank.

1895: Mitsubishi Exchange Office is transformed into the banking division of the Mitsubishi group.

1919: Mitsubishi Bank, Limited gains its independence from the Mitsubishi *zaibatsu*.

1927: The Mitsubishi *zaibatsu* establishes Mitsubishi Trust Company, Limited; Nippon Trust Bank is founded.

1933: Three Osaka-based banks merge to form Sanwa Bank, Limited.

1941: Three Nagoya-based banks merge to form Tokai Bank, Limited.

1946: Yokohama Specie Bank is reorganized as Bank of Tokyo, Ltd.

1959: Toyo Trust Bank is founded.

1994: Mitsubishi takes control of Nippon Trust Bank Ltd.

1996: Mitsubishi Bank and Bank of Tokyo merge to form Bank of Tokyo-Mitsubishi, Ltd.

2001: Bank of Tokyo-Mitsubishi merges with Mitsubishi Trust under the newly formed holding company Mitsubishi Tokyo Financial Group, Inc. (MTFG); Nippon Trust is merged into Mitsubishi Trust; Sanwa Bank, Tokai Bank, and Toyo Trust & Banking Company, Limited are amalgamated under UFJ Holdings, Inc.

2002: Sanwa Bank and Tokai Bank merge to create UFJ Bank Limited.

2005: MTFG and UFJ merge to form Mitsubishi UFJ Financial Group, Inc.

2006: Bank of Tokyo-Mitsubishi and UFJ Bank merge to form Bank of Tokyo-Mitsubishi UFJ, Ltd.

Bank, which had been acquired in 1988. In fact, in terms of branches, Bank of Tokyo's success as an international operator was clear: it had just 37 domestic branches at the time of the merger, compared to 363 overseas. Furthermore, most of its loans were denominated in foreign currency.

The merger was consummated in April 1996, resulting in what was at its creation the world's largest bank, Bank of Tokyo-Mitsubishi, Ltd., with total assets of ¥72 trillion ($701.4 billion), 40 percent more than its nearest rival. Because of the complementary nature of the merged banks' holdings, there was remarkably little overlap in the new banking behemoth. Further, unlike in typical mergers in the United States, huge numbers of employee layoffs were not announced at the same time as the merger. Even one observer's estimate of the number of jobs to be shed (most likely through attrition and early retirements) was relatively small: 2,000. This was due both to how well the two operations meshed and to the more paternalistic nature of Japanese business.

Ironically, the one area in which significant overlap did exist was in California, where Mitsubishi's Bank of California and Bank of Tokyo's Union Bank were consolidated as the bank holding company UnionBanCal Corporation and its primary subsidiary Union Bank of California, N.A. At the time of the merger, UnionBanCal was the fourth largest bank in California with more than $25 billion in assets. Bank of Tokyo-Mitsubishi held an 81 percent stake in UnionBanCal, with the remaining stock publicly traded. In March 1999 Bank of Tokyo-Mitsubishi completed a secondary offering of 28.75 million shares of UnionBanCal stock, reducing its stake to 64 percent.

Back in Japan, the entire banking sector was in crisis as the post-bubble economy went into a prolonged period of stagnation. All the major banks were staggering under the weight of hefty exposures to loans that had gone sour. In the late 1990s the Japanese government stepped in to prop up the banks both through an ¥8 trillion ($80 billion) infusion of publicly backed loans and by enabling them to merge with each other to gain strength. For its part, Bank of Tokyo-Mitsubishi turned to other members of the Mitsubishi *keiretsu* to secure about ¥200 billion ($2 billion) in new capital. These capital infusions enabled the banks to begin writing off their bad loans. For the fiscal years ending in March 1998 and March 1999, Bank of Tokyo-Mitsubishi posted two straight net losses, as it wrote off some ¥2.3 trillion ($17 billion) in bad loans. The bank returned to the black a year later, despite a further ¥504.5 billion ($4.9 billion) bad-loan write-off, thanks to about ¥350 billion in gains on the sales of stockholdings.

MERGER-FILLED ROAD TO MITSUBISHI UFJ

As this financial crisis dragged on, the long-running deregulation of the Japanese financial system, known as the "Big Bang," moved to its completion in fiscal 2000. Through subsidiaries, banks were now able to own not only trust banks but also securities companies. The lifting of the regulatory barriers laid the ground for further mergers among Japanese financial institutions, leading eventually to the creation of a handful of major banking groups, all involved in a diversified array of financial services areas.

In April 2000 Bank of Tokyo-Mitsubishi announced plans to merge with Mitsubishi Trust and Banking Corporation. The latter had been formed in 1927 by the Mitsubishi *zaibatsu* as the Mitsubishi Trust Company, Limited and was one of the country's major trust banks. In April 2001 Bank of Tokyo-Mitsubishi, along with its Nippon Trust Bank subsidiary, merged with Mitsubishi Trust under the newly established holding company Mitsubishi Tokyo Financial Group, Inc. (MTFG), the stock of which was listed on the Tokyo, Osaka, New York, and London stock exchanges.

MTFG soon included three principal subsidiaries. Bank of Tokyo-Mitsubishi continued to concentrate on commercial banking. In October 2001 Nippon Trust Bank and Tokyo Trust Bank were merged into Mitsubishi Trust Bank, which was involved in pension management, asset management, real estate brokerage operations, and other trust operations. In September 2002 several of the group's securities and investment banking businesses were amalgamated as Mitsubishi Securities Co., Ltd. Mitsubishi Tokyo Financial was still burdened with a significant number of bad loans, but by 2004 it had substantially cut these back. Its portfolio of nonperforming loans was by that time down to around ¥1.4 trillion ($13 billion), representing only 3 percent of outstanding loans. MTFG thus had the strongest balance sheet of Japan's four major banking groups. The group also enjoyed a record profit of ¥822.83 billion ($7.9 billion) for the fiscal year ending in March 2004.

The weakest of the four Japanese banking behemoths was UFJ Holdings, Inc. Still saddled with ¥3.7 trillion ($36 billion) in nonperforming loans, about 8.5 percent of its outstanding loans, UFJ had posted a ¥403 billion ($3.6 billion) loss for the year ending in March 2004. The formation of UFJ had followed the same trajectory and occurred at the same time as that of MTFG. In April 2001 Sanwa Bank, Limited, Tokai Bank, Limited, and Toyo Trust & Banking Company, Limited were amalgamated under UFJ Holdings. Sanwa Bank had been established in 1933 from the merger of three Osaka-based banks—Konoike Bank, Yamaguchi Bank, and Sanjushi Bank. Similarly, three Nagoya-based banks, Aichi Bank, Ito Bank, and Nagoya Bank, consolidated in 1941 into Tokai Bank. Toyo Trust was founded in 1959. In January 2002

Sanwa and Tokai merged as UFJ Bank Limited, a subsidiary of UFJ Holdings. At the same time, Toyo Trust Bank was renamed UFJ Trust Bank Limited. The stock of UFJ Holdings was listed on the Tokyo, Osaka, and Nagoya exchanges.

2005 CREATION OF MITSUBISHI UFJ FINANCIAL GROUP

Despite UFJ's obvious weaknesses, MTFG agreed to a merger with UFJ in July 2004 in part because of the two group's complementary areas of strength. MTFG had traditionally done the bulk of its business with large Tokyo-based corporations, particularly those associated with the Mitsubishi industrial group. By contrast, the strength of UFJ resided in its consumer and small-business banking operations along with its solid presence in Nagoya, a key Japanese auto-making city. The merger of MTFG and UFJ thus created not only a much larger entity but also a banking group with a more diversified array of revenue sources.

The merger was completed on October 1, 2005, creating Mitsubishi UFJ Financial Group, Inc. (MUFG). At its creation, MUFG was the largest bank in the world in asset terms, with total assets of more than ¥190 trillion ($1.67 trillion), although its market capitalization of $130 billion was much smaller than that of Citigroup Inc.'s $230 billion. The stock of MUFG was listed on the Tokyo, Osaka, Nagoya, New York, and London exchanges, but the London listing was dropped the following year. Nobuo Kuroyanagi, the president and CEO of MTFG, was named to the same positions at MUFG, while UFJ Holdings' president and CEO, Ryosuke Tamakoshi, was named chairman of MUFG.

Of the predecessors' subsidiaries, UFJ Trust Bank was merged into Mitsubishi Trust Bank, which was renamed Mitsubishi UFJ Trust and Banking Corporation. In January 2006 Bank of Tokyo-Mitsubishi and UFJ Bank merged to form Bank of Tokyo-Mitsubishi UFJ, Ltd. In addition, the securities and investment banking unit Mitsubishi Securities Co. was merged with UFJ Tsubasa Securities Co., Ltd., to form Mitsubishi Securities Co., Ltd. In April 2007 two other key subsidiaries were created: Mitsubishi UFJ NICOS Co., Ltd., concentrating on credit cards and consumer loans, and the leasing/financing arm Mitsubishi UFJ Lease & Finance Company Limited.

In June 2006 MUFG paid off the remaining ¥835 billion ($7.1 billion) it owed to the Japanese government for loans that had been made during the post-bubble financial crisis. By doing so, the banking group had more freedom to pursue new and more aggressive business strategies, such as overseas expansions. During 2006, MUFG became the first Japanese bank to buy into a mainland Chinese bank when it invested $180 million for a 0.2 percent stake in Bank of China. It also invested $100 million into the nascent U.S. investment banking boutique Perella Weinberg Partners.

The major Japanese banks suffered much less than their U.S. and European counterparts during the initial months of the credit crisis that erupted in mid-2007. For the fiscal year ending in March 2008, MUFG suffered losses from exposure to subprime investments totaling around ¥120 billion ($1.15 billion), enabling it to still post a net profit of ¥636.6 billion ($6.1 billion). While the group was suffering from stagnant commercial lending in Japan, it was picking up additional business overseas funding acquisitions and infrastructure projects as U.S. and European banks reined in their credit activities.

In August and September 2008, as the Japanese domestic market remained sluggish and the U.S. financial sector drifted deeper into crisis, Mitsubishi UFJ Financial Group began to make larger, and riskier, bets in the United States. In August the group reached an agreement to acquire the 35 percent of UnionBanCal it did not already own for about $3.5 billion. This move if completed would make the San Francisco-based bank, at the time the 25th largest bank in the United States in asset terms, a wholly owned MUFG subsidiary and also provide a platform for possible additional takeovers of U.S. commercial banks. MUFG in September agreed to invest $9 billion in Morgan Stanley for which it would receive a stake in the U.S. investment bank of 21 percent and a seat on the company board. In the wake of the collapse of Lehman Brothers Holdings Inc., Morgan Stanley and the remaining independent U.S. investment banks needed capital infusions to shore up their battered balance sheets. MUFG pursued the deal seeking to partner with Morgan Stanley in such areas as corporate and investment banking, retail banking, and asset management. The deal highlighted the changing fortunes of two economies. Japanese banks, beset by bad debt a decade earlier, were now pursuing deals in a U.S. financial sector wracked by its own credit crisis.

David E. Salamie

PRINCIPAL SUBSIDIARIES

The Bank of Tokyo-Mitsubishi UFJ, Ltd.; The Senshu Bank, Ltd. (67.96%); Mitsubishi UFJ Trust and Banking Corporation; Mitsubishi UFJ Securities Co., Ltd.; kabu.com Securities Co., Ltd. (52.01%); Mitsubishi UFJ Wealth Management Securities, Ltd.; Mitsubishi

UFJ NICOS Co., Ltd.; Tokyo Credit Services, Ltd. (74%); Ryoshin DC Card Company, Ltd. (75.2%); Mitsubishi UFJ Lease & Finance Company Limited; NBL Co., Ltd. (89.74%); Tokyo Associates Finance Corp.; Mitsubishi UFJ Factors Limited; MU Frontier Servicer Co., Ltd. (94.44%); MU Hands-on Capital Co., Ltd. (50%); Defined Contribution Plan Consulting of Japan Co., Ltd. (77.49%); Kokusai Asset Management Co., Ltd. (53.08%); Mitsubishi UFJ Asset Management Co., Ltd.; MU Investments Co., Ltd.; Mitsubishi UFJ Real Estate Services Co., Ltd.; Mitsubishi UFJ Personal Financial Advisers Co., Ltd. (73.69%); Mitsubishi UFJ Research and Consulting Ltd. (69.45%); MU Business Engineering, Ltd.; UnionBanCal Corporation (U.S.A.; 65.4%); Mitsubishi UFJ Trust & Banking Corporation (U.S.A.); Mitsubishi UFJ Global Custody S.A. (Luxembourg); Mitsubishi UFJ Wealth Management Bank (Switzerland), Ltd.; Mitsubishi UFJ Securities International plc (U.K.); Mitsubishi UFJ Securities (USA), Inc.; Mitsubishi UFJ Trust International Limited (U.K.); Mitsubishi UFJ Securities (HK) Holdings, Limited (China); Mitsubishi UFJ Securities (Singapore), Limited (U.S.A.); BTMU Capital Corporation (U.S.A.); BTMU Leasing & Finance, Inc. (U.S.A.); PT U Finance Indonesia (95%); PT BTMU-BRI Finance (Indonesia; 55%); BTMU Lease (Deutschland) GmbH (Germany); Mitsubishi UFJ Baillie Gifford Asset Management Limited (U.K.; 51%); MU Trust Consulting (Shanghai) Co., Ltd. (China).

PRINCIPAL COMPETITORS

Mizuho Financial Group, Inc.; Sumitomo Mitsui Financial Group Inc.; HSBC Holdings plc; Citigroup Inc.

FURTHER READING

"The Big One," *Economist*, April 1, 1995, pp. 60–61.

Bremner, Brian, William Glasgall, and Kelley Holland, "Tokyo Mitsubishi Bank: Big, Yes. Bad, No," *Business Week*, April 10, 1995.

Dvorak, Phred, "Asahi Backs Out of 3-Way Bank Deal," *Asian Wall Street Journal*, June 16, 2000, p. 1.

———, "Japanese Bank Merger May Finish Industry's Major Consolidation," *Wall Street Journal*, March 15, 2000, p. A20.

———, "Sanwa Bank Is Facing a World of Giants," *Wall Street Journal*, October 29, 1999, p. A15.

Fackler, Martin, "Move Over, Citi, Mitsubishi UFJ Wants to Be a Global Player," *New York Times*, January 17, 2006, p. C4.

Fukase, Atsuko, "Japan Bank Could Gain More U.S. Assets," *Wall Street Journal*, August 14, 2008, p. C2.

Hayashi, Yuka, "Largest Japanese Banks Expand Overseas Business," *Wall Street Journal Asia,* May 23, 2006, p. 1.

———, "Mitsubishi UFJ Plans to Raise Its Global Profile," *Wall Street Journal Asia,* January 17, 2006, p. 1.

Hayashi, Yuka, Alison Tudor, and Matthew Karnitschnig, "MUFG Bid for UnionBanCal Shows Japan Banks' Revival," *Wall Street Journal,* August 13, 2008, pp. C1, C2.

Hayashi, Yuka, and Joanna Slater, "At Japan's Big Banks, Drive for Growth Sputters," *Wall Street Journal,* May 23, 2007, pp. C1, C2.

Hirsh, Michael, "Why Sanwa Leads the Pack," *Institutional Investor,* February 1994, pp. 155–58.

Holyoke, Larry, and William Glasgall, "The Japanese Bank That Knows How to Hustle," *Business Week,* May 30, 1994, p. 117.

Karmin, Craig, and Jason Singer, "Mitsubishi Tokyo Completes $2.32 Billion Sale," *Wall Street Journal,* March 4, 2003, p. C16.

"Mitsubeautiful," *Economist,* February 9, 1991, p. 86.

Mitsubishi Ginkoshi (History of Mitsubishi Bank), 2 vols., Tokyo: Mitsubishi Bank, 1980.

Nakamoto, Michiyo, "Consumer Finance Troubles Hit MUFG," *Financial Times,* November 22, 2007, p. 23.

Nakamoto, Michiyo, and Henny Sender, "MUFG to Take Control of UNBC," *Financial Times,* August 19, 2008, p. 23.

Nishio, Natsuo, "Japan Banks Unveil Integration Plan," *Asian Wall Street Journal,* October 5, 2000, p. 15.

———, "UFJ to Restructure Further, Push Up Sanwa, Tokai Merger," *Asian Wall Street Journal,* April 26, 2001, p. 7.

Rozens, Aleksandrs, "The Next Big Investment Bank? Mitsubishi UFJ, One of the World's Largest Commercial Banks, Plans Global Push into Investment Banking," *Investment Dealers' Digest,* October 29, 2007.

Sapsford, Jathon, and Robert Steiner, "Huge Japanese Merger Could Help Revitalize the Financial Sector," *Wall Street Journal,* March 29, 1995, pp. A1, A8.

Sender, Henny, "Bigger Is Better: Bank of Tokyo, Mitsubishi Create Banking Behemoth," *Far Eastern Economic Review,* April 6, 1995, p. 82.

Singer, Jason, "Mitsubishi Tokyo Loosens Up," *Asian Wall Street Journal,* December 8, 2003, p. M1.

Tudor, Alison, "Japanese Banks Roaring Up Wall Street," *Wall Street Journal,* September 23, 2008, pp. C1, C3.

Zaun, Todd, "Laggard Japanese Bank Decides It's Merger Time," *New York Times,* July 15, 2004, p. W1.

Noble Roman's, Inc.

One Virginia Avenue, Suite 800
Indianapolis, Indiana 46204-4269
U.S.A.
Telephone: (317) 634-3377
Toll Free: (800) 585-0669
Fax: (317) 636-3207
Web site: http://www.nobleromans.com

Public Company
Incorporated: 1972
Employees: 174
Sales: $11.6 million (2007)
Stock Exchanges: OTC
Ticker Symbol: NROM
NAICS: 722211 Limited-Service Restaurants; 533110 Lessors of Nonfinancial Intangible Assets (Except Copyrighted Works)

■ ■ ■

Noble Roman's, Inc., is the franchiser of the pizza chain Noble Roman's Pizza and sub purveyor Tuscano's Italian Style Subs. The company's franchise system includes more than 1,000 units in 45 states as well as Washington, D.C., Puerto Rico, Canada, Guam, and Italy. The vast majority of the units, in contrast to standard stand-alone restaurants, are located in so-called nontraditional locations, such as hospitals, military bases, universities, convenience stores, entertainment facilities, casinos, travel plazas, airports, hotels, and office complexes. More than 100 of the units are dual-branded traditional

stand-alone locations featuring both a Noble Roman's and a Tuscano's. Systemwide sales totaled about $120 million in 2007.

FOUNDING IN BLOOMINGTON, INDIANA

Noble Roman's was started in Bloomington, Indiana, by Stephen Huse and Gary Knackstedt. Huse had graduated from the business school at Indiana University in Bloomington before taking a sales job in 1965 with Ransburg Corporation. Eager to be on his own, Huse purchased an Arby's restaurant franchise in Bloomington and ran the operation for a few years. In 1969 he spearheaded the purchase of a struggling Bloomington pizza restaurant. During the early 1970s Huse and partner Knackstedt worked together to turn the restaurant around and then to expand in the Bloomington area with new Noble Roman's pizza outlets.

Huse and Knackstedt benefited during the early and mid-1970s from overall growth in the fast-food (particularly pizza) business. As the population of the college town swelled with increasing numbers of students, sales of Noble Roman's unique pizzas surged. To help them take advantage of growth opportunities, Huse and Knackstedt were joined by investor Paul Mobley in the early 1970s. Mobley helped to fund Noble Roman's expansion throughout the 1970s. He also became increasingly involved in the company's management. In 1977, in fact, Mobley became president of the company. By that time, Knackstedt had left the venture to pursue other interests. Huse, on the other

COMPANY PERSPECTIVES

∎

The story of Noble Roman's Pizza is the story of dedication to quality you can taste! Every ingredient we use, every mouthwatering product we bake, has been developed in such a way as to maximize the pleasure of your taste buds. Take our pizza crusts, for example. They're made from specially milled, high protein flour, flavorful cornmeal and lots of bakery yeast. Our fresh-packed, un-condensed sauce is made with secret spices, parmesan cheese and vine-ripened tomatoes straight from the fields of California. And our vegetables and mushrooms are always sliced and delivered fresh, never canned. It's a common way to cut corners and save a nickel, but our commitment to good taste means we never use soy fillers in our meats or cheeses. Our pizza cheese is 100% real Mozzarella and Muenster cheese blended together with a pinch of oregano. And our pepperoni, sausage, beef and bacon? Again, 100% real meat with no extenders or fillers. Seems like the way it ought to be done, right? We agree!

hand, would remain chairman and chief stockholder in the company until 1986.

Noble Roman's continued to grow during the late 1970s and early 1980s, expanding outside of Bloomington's borders in central Indiana and later throughout Indiana and into Ohio. During this period, the burgeoning restaurant chain rang up consistent, healthy profits. To garner more money for expansion, Mobley and Huse took the company public in 1982. They used proceeds from that stock offering to build new outlets and to branch out into other ventures. In addition, Noble Roman's management expanded the chain through franchising. Within a few years of the public offering the Noble Roman's chain had grown to include about 120 stores in Indiana and Ohio, 25 of which were company-owned stores.

FAILED GODFATHER'S DEAL

After posting hefty profit gains for more than a decade, Noble Roman's fortunes began to turn in 1985. The company netted income of $146,000 in 1984, after which profitability began deteriorating rapidly. Part of the problem stemmed from the chain's decision to intensify its expansion efforts in Ohio through the buyout of several ailing Godfather's Pizza outlets.

Godfather's called Noble Roman's executives in 1984 to see if they would be interested in buying their 21-store Dayton, Ohio, operations. Noble Roman's already had nine units in the area and was planning to open another five within the year. Executives initially rejected the offer, but finally agreed to purchase seven of the stores, which they planned to convert to Noble Roman's.

The deal was closed in March 1985, but problems immediately ensued. The management at Noble Roman's clashed with managers at the Godfather's stores. All seven of the store managers quit within a few months, and Mobley and fellow executives had trouble finding worthy replacements. To make matters worse, the deal had left Noble Roman's financially strapped and unable to invest funds necessary to revitalize the lagging Godfather's outlets. Rather than sell the new stores, Mobley decided to hire the best managers he could find at whatever price he would have to pay. Even that effort proved to be inadequate because the stores had already developed a bad reputation locally; little could be done to make amends.

Noble Roman's finally shuttered six of the seven stores, as well as three existing Noble Roman's in Dayton and another failing store in Decatur, Indiana. As a result of the failed Godfather's deal and other setbacks within the company, Noble Roman's net income plunged in 1985 to a deficit of $1.5 million. The company lost another $700,000 in the first quarter of 1986 and suffered another big deficit the next quarter when it wrote off losses related to the ten stores it closed in 1985. Noble Roman's eventually recorded a crushing $3.7 million loss for 1986. Management was left scrambling for a solution to the crisis.

While Mobley and fellow executives worked to repair the ailing company, Noble Roman's founder, Steve Huse, distanced himself from the company. In fact, Huse's influence on day-to-day operations had been declining since he and Mobley took the company public in December 1982. When the company negotiated the Godfather's deal, Huse increasingly began to turn his attention to other interests. He continued to own half of American Diversified Foods, Inc., which owned 11 Arby's Roast Beef franchises in Indiana and was connected to the first Arby's franchise he had started in 1967. Huse also dabbled in real estate and had owned a group of billiards/electronic game halls for a time (the halls were sold to Bally Manufacturing Corporation in 1983).

In 1985, the time when Noble Roman's first began to encounter serious problems, Huse opened a new restaurant in Bloomington called Mustard's. The venture, which represented a culmination of restaurant ideas that Huse had picked up during various travels, was ultimately a success. Shortly after opening that restaurant Huse purchased the well-known and respected St. Elmo Steak House in Indianapolis. Moreover, although Huse remained the largest single shareholder of Noble Roman's stock, he had been reducing his stake in the company since 1977. Finally, in 1986, Huse resigned from his position as chairman of the board. He later started the Huse Food Group, a holding company with various restaurant and real estate interests, and served for a few years as president and chief executive officer of the Indianapolis-based Consolidated Products, Inc., which owned the venerable Steak n Shake chain of eateries.

RECOVERY UNDER MOBLEY

Although Noble Roman's same-store sales improved during 1986, the company continued to struggle toward profitability. In an effort to buoy the company's sagging balance sheet, a group of company insiders led by Mobley purchased 12 stores from the company in 1987 for about $4.1 million. That left Noble Roman's with a chain of about 120 outlets, roughly 40 of which were owned by the company or by its executives. In addition, Mobley moved the company's headquarters from Bloomington to Indianapolis as part of an overall cost-cutting effort. He also reduced the headquarters staff from 30 to 23, closed some restaurants, and initiated several other measures that reduced the company's expenses by about $1.1 million annually. Mobley was aided in the effort by his 25-year-old son Scott, who joined the company in 1986.

During the late 1980s Noble Roman's went through a major reorganization. Managers became more responsible for their own budgets and improving efficiency in their operational area, and several stores changed ownership as part of an effort to boost cash flow and recover some of the $4.1 million that management invested in 1987. Importantly, Mobley made a decision to shift Noble Roman's focus away from the cut-throat, low-cost delivery segment and toward the upscale end of the pizza market. To that end, the restaurant introduced and began to emphasize its premium, high-profit products and to intensify its quality and service efforts. The menu was expanded to include pastas and other pizza-related products, and a late-night menu was introduced as well. Importantly, Noble Roman's also initiated a costly renovation program during the late 1980s designed to update the stores and give them a more upscale, progressive image.

As a result of the efforts of Mobley and his managers, Noble Roman's finances gradually recovered. The company's net loss of $500,000 in 1988 was reduced to a deficit of just $16,531 in 1990. Finally, in 1991 Noble Roman's returned to profitability with earnings of more than $200,000 on revenue of about $8.5 million. Throughout the period of recovery, however, some analysts remained skeptical of the company's strategy, citing several concerns. Even as late as 1989, for example, Noble Roman's was scrambling for cash to meet its burdensome liabilities, and observers noted that a variety of influences, such as a potential increase in the minimum wage, threatened to quash the company's gains. By the early 1990s, though, many skeptics were beginning to place more faith in Noble Roman's course of action. "I think they'll get this done," said stock analyst Ray Diggle in the *Indianapolis Business Journal* in January 1993. "Clearly, sales are doing exceptionally well. The company has done a good job of curtailing inventory costs. I think the company is poised for a period of solid growth."

After peaking at about 120 stores in the mid-1980s, the total number of Noble Roman's stores was reduced to around 75 by 1992. The reorganization and store reduction had allowed Noble Roman's to get back on track financially. In 1992, despite recessionary economic conditions, Noble Roman's increased its earnings to about $491,000 from sales of $9.1 million. In January 1993 the company bought back 27 of its restaurants from three companies that were franchising the outlets in Indiana. That left it with a total of 42 company-owned stores and 31 franchises. The purchase helped the chain to boost its sales to $24.2 million while profits grew to about $841,000. A drawback of the move was that it saddled Noble Roman's with a fat debt burden; long-term debt rocketed from $2.5 million to a lofty $8 million after the purchase. At the same time, Noble Roman's was still trying to pay off tax liabilities that had been accruing since the organization began experiencing problems in the mid-1980s.

Noble Roman's heavy debt and thin cash flow was reflected by its stock price, which had hovered around a low of $3 during much of the early 1990s. That situation began to change in 1994, though, when Noble Roman's performance continued to improve and Mobley began paring the company's liabilities. In 1994 Noble Roman's added a total of five new restaurants to its chain and announced plans to tag an additional 30 stores onto its portfolio by 1996.

The company also benefited from general industry trends. Indeed, although the pizza industry was growing, the big, low-cost delivery chains were not. Instead, smaller operators catering to the high-end segment were posting solid market share gains. Evidencing the validity of Noble Roman's upscale strategy, the chain reported record net income in 1994 of $1.5 million from revenues of $30.5 million.

Besides opening new stores in 1994 and 1995, Noble Roman's continued to buy outlets that were being operated as franchises. By mid-1995 Noble Roman's was operating 66 company-owned stores and 14 franchises in four states—Indiana, Ohio, Missouri, and Kentucky—a state of affairs that gave it ownership and control of more than 80 percent of the outlets in its chain. That increased ownership, combined with savvy management, allowed Noble Roman's to boost its sales and profits 63 percent and 87 percent, respectively, between 1991 and 1994. That achievement earned Noble Roman's a spot on *Business Week*'s 1995 list of "small, hot-growth" companies in 1995. (To be eligible for the list, a company had to have revenues between $10 million and $150 million and a market value of less than $1 million.)

FAILED PAPA GINO'S TAKEOVER

For its next phase of growth, Noble Roman's embarked on a strategy of acquiring and consolidating other regional pizza chains. In March 1996 the company signed a letter of intent to acquire Papa Gino's Holdings Corporation, Inc., for about $10 million in stock. Based in Dedham, Massachusetts, Papa Gino's owned and operated 180 pizza restaurants in seven northeastern states, and acquiring the chain would have turned Noble Roman's into a company with revenues of nearly $150 million and 265 restaurants. In June 1996, however, the deal fell apart for undisclosed reasons, although analysts speculated that Noble Roman's had been unable to secure the financing needed to complete the transaction.

Distracted by the takeover attempt, Noble Roman's top managers, by their own admission, failed to pay enough attention to the day-to-day operations of their chain, leading to an extended period of poor performance. At the same time, the firm took a second financial hit from the $768,000 it had spent on the failed acquisition of Papa Gino's, and the end result was a $3.9 million loss for 1996, plus the firm defaulted on the loan agreement with its primary lender, Provident Bank of Cincinnati.

In May 1997 Noble Roman's launched a major restructuring to pull itself out of this tailspin. It closed 19 of its restaurants and sold four others. The restructuring cost Noble Roman's $6.5 million, sending the firm into another loss totaling $5.5 million for 1997. Late in the year, Provident Bank agreed to a debt restructuring whereby it forgave more than $7 million in Noble Roman's debt while at the same time lending the firm an additional $2.6 million. Around this same time, Scott Mobley was named president of Noble Roman's, while his father, Paul Mobley, remained chairman.

SHIFT TO FRANCHISE MODEL AND NONTRADITIONAL LOCATIONS

As this restructuring was progressing, Noble Roman's in early 1997 began a shift to a franchise model centered on a concept originally called Noble Roman's Pizza Express. The Express concept, a stripped-down version of the traditional Noble Roman's full-service restaurant, was designed for so-called nontraditional locations. The company thus began selling and servicing Express franchises for placement in such locales as convenience stores, grocery stores, gas stations, hospitals, hotels, travel plazas, and airports, as well as alongside other fast-food restaurants, such as Subway and TCBY outlets. The units were relatively inexpensive to set up and operate and required only a small amount of space and minimal labor. Eventually, Noble Roman's turned its remaining company-owned full-service restaurants into franchises as well. By the end of 1999 more than 400 franchised Noble Roman's were in operation in nontraditional locations in around 30 states.

As this transition progressed, the company continued to operate in the red until 2000, when a profit of $531,000 was recorded, the first such gain since 1995. Revenues that year totaled just $5.6 million as Noble Roman's was now reliant on the royalties and fees it earned through its agreements with its franchisees. By the end of 2004 the Noble Roman's system included nearly 800 locations in 44 states. That year, the company spun off Noble Roman's sub sandwich line into a separate concept called Tuscano's Italian Style Subs and began offering franchises for this concept in nontraditional locations.

In 2005, in an attempt to accelerate its growth while continuing to expand its nontraditional franchises, Noble Roman's returned to the traditional, stand-alone restaurant model. It began selling development territories to area developers for the franchising of stand-alone, quick-service restaurants dual-branded under the Noble Roman's and Tuscano's names. By the end of 2007 the company had agreements in place with 20 area developers for more than 630 dual-branded franchise units, although only around 100 such units had actually opened. That year, Noble Roman's recorded net income of $2.5 million on revenue of $11.6 million. Systemwide sales for all the Noble Roman's and Tuscano's units totaled an estimated $120 million.

The dual-branded concept got off to a fairly rough start as several franchisees in various markets were forced to close their units and declare bankruptcy after garnering disappointing sales. In addition, a handful of area developers abandoned the venture, pulling the plug on more than 200 planned restaurants. In March 2008 Noble Roman's seized control of six dual-branded franchise restaurants in Indianapolis with plans to whip them into shape and then resell them to a new franchisee. By this time, the company had initiated a series of enhancements to its franchise standards, including adopting more rigorous criteria for selecting franchisees and implementing a more robust training process.

In June 2008 a group of ten current and former franchisees filed a lawsuit against Noble Roman's alleging that they had been sold a flawed concept and had not been given the support promised. Noble Roman's vigorously denied the allegations. The suit came at a difficult time for the company as restaurants across the United States were suffering from declining sales because of the poor economic climate and the pizza industry faced the further challenges of fierce competition and rising prices for wheat and cheese. Earlier in 2008 Noble Roman's announced it had retained the investment bank Roth Capital Partners to evaluate "various strategies to enhance shareholder value." This signaled the possibility that the company might be sold, but the tight credit markets and economic downturn lessened the chances for such an outcome.

Dave Mote
Updated, David E. Salamie

PRINCIPAL COMPETITORS

Pizza Hut, Inc.; Little Caesar Enterprises, Inc.; Domino's Pizza, Inc.; Papa John's International, Inc.; Sbarro, Inc.

FURTHER READING

Albert, Barb, "Investors Will Give Ailing Pizza Chain Money to Expand Its Express Division," *Indianapolis Star*, February 1, 2000, p. C1.

Allen, Robin Lee, "Noble Roman's Inc. to Acquire Papa Gino's in $10M Stock Transaction," *Nation's Restaurant News*, April 8, 1996, pp. 1+.

Andrews, Greg, "Noble Roman's Pays Up to Sever Ties with Vulture," *Indianapolis Business Journal*, September 12, 2005, p. 4A.

———, "Pizza Chain Fears 'Vulture,'" *Indianapolis Business Journal*, July 19, 2004, pp. 1, 44.

———, "Royal Payoff Awaits Longtime Noble Roman's CEO," *Indianapolis Business Journal*, January 29, 2007, p. 4.

Burton, Brian, "Improving the Recipe: A New Look at Noble Roman's, Inc.," *Indiana Business*, September 1986, p. 28.

Carlino, Bill, "Noble Roman's $1.7M Infusion Revives Expansion Plans," *Nation's Restaurant News*, January 20, 1997, pp. 7, 11.

———, "Noble Roman's, Papa Gino's Call Off Merger," *Nation's Restaurant News*, June 24, 1996, p. 3.

Culbertson, Katie, "Noble Roman's Looks for Bigger Piece of Pie," *Indianapolis Business Journal*, March 6, 2000, pp. 6, 50.

Dabney, Michael, "Noble Roman's Rebuilds Empire," *Indianapolis Business Journal*, August 20, 2007, pp. 3, 43.

Dobie, Maureen, "Noble Roman's Cashes in on Godfather's Turmoil," *Indianapolis Business Journal*, February 18, 1985, p. 5.

Eggert, David, "Concept Lands Pizzeria Profit," *Indianapolis Star*, July 20, 2000, p. C1.

Harton, Tom, "Following the Leader: Steak n Shake Parent Company Hires Two More Huse Group Execs," *Indianapolis Business Journal*, May 14, 1990, p. 9A.

Higgins, Will, "Bloomington-Based Noble Roman's Closes 10 Stores," *Indianapolis Business Journal*, July 7, 1986, p. 1.

Jeffrey, Don, "Huse Quits Noble Roman's," *Nation's Restaurant News*, September 15, 1986, p. 2.

Kukolla, Steve, "Noble Roman's Scores on *Business Week* List," *Indianapolis Business Journal*, May 22, 1995, p. 10A.

Murphy, Tom, "Seeking a Return to Glory: Once-Thriving Noble Roman's Cooks Up Ambitious Plan for 157 Pizza/ Sub Shops," *Indianapolis Business Journal*, August 7, 2006, pp. 1A, 41A.

Parent, Tawn, "Noble Roman's Digging Out of Deep Dish," *Indianapolis Business Journal*, January 25, 1993, p. 1A.

———, "Noble Roman's Would Reclaim 40 Franchises Through Stock Sale," *Indianapolis Business Journal*, July 6, 1992, p. 3.

Prewitt, Milford, "Noble Roman's to Fight Franchisees' Suit over Dual-Brand Rollouts," *Nation's Restaurant News,* July 21, 2008, p. 14.

Rettig, Ellen, "Noble Roman's Expands Express Concept," *Indianapolis Business Journal,* November 16, 1998, p. 6.

Rush, Jill, "Noble Roman's Still Losing Dough, but May Turn Corner This Year," *Indianapolis Business Journal,* July 3, 1989, p. 9A.

Schouten, Cory, "Chain Seizes 6 Stores: Struggling Noble Roman's Takes Over Franchisee's Units," *Indianapolis Business Journal,* March 24, 2008, pp. 3A, 42A.

———, "Noble Roman's Slapped with Suit: Former Franchisees Allege Fraud over Risks, Startup Costs," *Indianapolis Business Journal,* July 7, 2008, pp. 3A, 34A.

———, "Pie Fight at Noble Roman's: Failing Franchisees Say Chain Doesn't Deliver on Promises," *Indianapolis Business Journal,* December 24, 2007, pp. 1, 28.

Zuber, Amy, "Noble Roman's Slapped with Steep Fine for Child-Labor Violations," *Nation's Restaurant News,* July 20, 1998, p. 8.

North American Galvaniz-
ing & Coatings, Inc.

───■───

5214 South Yale Avenue, Suite 1000
Tulsa, Oklahoma 74135
U.S.A.
Telephone: (918) 488-9420
Fax: (918) 488-8172
Web site: http://www.nagalv.com

Public Company
Incorporated: 1955 as Kin-Ark Oil Company
Employees: 368
Sales: $88.4 million (2007)
Stock Exchanges: NASDAQ
Ticker Symbol: NGA
NAICS: 332812 Coating, Engraving, and Allied Services
    (Except Jewelry and Silverware) to Manufacturing

■ ■ ■

North American Galvanizing & Coatings, Inc., is the publicly traded holding company for North American Galvanizing Company (NAGC), a major provider of hot dip galvanizing coatings, offering corrosion protection for fabricated steel products used in the construction, commercial, and industrial markets. While more costly than paint, hot dip galvanizing is far more durable than paint, lasting 50 years rather than just ten, and is thus more cost-effective in the long term. The coating is the result of a metallurgical reaction between the underlying iron and molten zinc, and only after the product undergoes a thorough cleaning and degreasing, chemical pretreatment, and drying is it immersed in molten zinc, 835 degrees Fahrenheit. NAGC also offers the Infrashield Coating System, used in conjunction with hot dip galvanizing to permit specialty designed coatings to be added as well, providing further corrosion protection for steel products used in such applications as power plants, wastewater treatment plants, chemical processing facilities, and structural components with direct soil contact. NAGC is based in Tulsa, Oklahoma, where product engineering is conducted. Galvanizing and coatings take place in several plants strategically located throughout the United States, including Tulsa; Canton, Ohio; Denver, Colorado; Houston and Hurst, Texas; Kansas City and St. Louis, Missouri; Louisville, Kentucky; and Nashville, Tennessee.

COMPANY INCORPORATED IN 1955

NAGC was not originally involved in the hot dip galvanizing business. Rather, it was founded in Eldorado, Arkansas, as Kin-Ark Oil Company by Early Kinnard in 1955, when in January of that year the business was incorporated in Delaware, taken public, and gained a listing on the American Stock Exchange. The company held oil interests in Arkansas, Alabama, Colorado, Mississippi, and Texas. Kinnard sold control of the company in 1963 to Atlas Exploration Company, a Tulsa, Oklahoma, management group, and as a result Kin-Ark moved its headquarters to Tulsa.

Under new leadership, Kin-Ark began a diversification program in 1965, acquiring the 2,600-acre Caribou Ranch in Colorado, which the company planned to develop into a resort. A further step in the hospitality sector was taken three years later when Kin-Ark

---

COMPANY PERSPECTIVES

The mission of North American Galvanizing Company is based on sound fundamental principles. "To offer and deliver the most highly effective corrosion control products in the world." When it comes to protecting the life of your steel, our safe and environmentally friendly Hot Dip Galvanizing and Infrashield coating systems can offer proven solutions to your corrosion problems.

---

purchased the 350-room Camelot Hotel in Tulsa. It then built a 303-room Camelot Hotel in Little Rock, Arkansas, in 1973. Both properties were full-service convention hotels. Further diversification took place in 1968 with the acquisition of Lake River Corporation, a Chicago bulk storage liquid chemical company that leased tanks to customers, such as Union Carbide Corporation. It was also involved in chemical distribution, operating drum filling lines for specialty chemicals as well as bulk chemical bagging lines. In 1969 Kin-Ark became involved in the galvanizing field by acquiring Boyles Galvanizing Company. It was at this point that Kin-Ark changed its named to Kinark Corporation.

KINPAK FORMED: 1979

Kinark carried on as a mini-conglomerate through the 1970s, involved in a number of divergent fields. In 1979 it established Kinpak, Inc., to package chemicals and build upon the foundation of Lake River. The company decided in 1982 to exit the hotel business and put the Tulsa and Little Rock properties on the block. They were sold for $25 million, but after paying $8 million, the buyer defaulted on the note issued to Kinark, which repossessed the hotels in 1984. At that stage Kinark was more interested in pursuing the do-it-yourself home improvement market, in particular the packaging of swimming pool chemicals and lawn and garden chemicals, sold through the Kinpak subsidiary, as well as antifreeze and windshield washer fluid sold to the automotive market. The most profitable unit for Kinark at the time, however, was Boyles Galvanizing, which was the largest independent galvanizing company in the United States.

Through the remainder of the 1980s and into the 1990s, Kinark continued the attempt to change its business mix, primarily with frustrating results. In early 1989 the company had a deal to sell the Chicago Lake River terminals for $10 million, but it never came to

fruition. Late in the year Kinark again attempted to unload the money-losing Camelot hotels, which struggled to attract convention business, and once again the company had difficulty completing a transaction. A unidentified West Coast firm agreed to buy the properties for $12 million in 1990, but the deal was structured in a way that allowed the buyer to walk away from the deal by forfeiting a $50,000 deposit. A major Kinark shareholder, the New York partnership of Steel Partnership Ltd., was not pleased with this arrangement and made an offer to acquire Kinark to change the direction the company was taking. Another shareholder, Chicago-area Altair Corporation, was also highly critical of the Camelot sale.

Their skepticism was borne out later in 1990 when the buyer indeed terminated the sale agreement. The hotel properties were then put up for auction. The Tulsa property was purchased for $1.5 million, just $500,000 over the minimum bid, and the Little Rock hotel received no offers. To make matters worse the buyer for the Tulsa Camelot failed to show up for the closing, and the property was then awarded to the next highest bid, $1.35 million, submitted by a local group of Tulsa businessmen who already owned a pair of area hotels. That deal also fell apart, however, leading to the $1.25 million sale of the Tulsa Camelot to Illinois-based Lata Enterprises Ltd., which made a $300,000 down payment. When Lata defaulted on its note in 1992, Kinark elected to simply write off the balance of the note.

NORTH AMERICAN GALVANIZING COMPANY FORMED: 1996

Kinark was glad to be free of the hotel business and in 1993 began pursuing a plan to expand its galvanizing business, hiring an investment bank to help scout for possible acquisitions. Galvanizing had long been popular in Europe, but U.S. companies were beginning to realize the benefits of the process as well as the long-term cost savings. This change provided Kinark, which was already the United States' largest independent galvanizing company, with an opportunity to further its reach, which for many years had been limited to six plants, located in Denver, Louisville, Nashville, St. Louis, Houston, and Hurst, Texas (near Dallas). In keeping with this new strategy, the company began to divest noncore assets. In 1995 Kinpak was put up for sale. An agreement was forged in September of that year and completed in February 1996. Later in the year, Kinark was finally able to build on its galvanizing business by acquiring Rogers Galvanizing Company, another Tulsa-based company that operated five plants, four in Tulsa and a fifth in Kansas City, Missouri. Between Boyle and

Rogers, Kinark had the capacity to galvanize more than 200,000 tons of steel annually. Late in 1996 Kinark formed North American Galvanizing Company, which was then merged with Rogers before the end of the year, followed by Boyles in early 1997. NAGC then became the surviving entity.

About 20 percent of Kinark's revenues still came from its remaining bulk liquid chemical storage and warehousing operations. In 1997 these assets were combined to form North American Warehousing Company. Despite the name, it was very much a Chicago-area business, providing a turnkey service to companies in need of a presence in that large market. Kinark held onto the business until 2000, when North American Warehousing along with Lake River Corp. were sold to a management buyout group for $371,000 in cash. In the final three years of the 1990s, Kinark's revenues from chemical storage had dropped from $5.8 million to $5.2 million and warehousing revenues were cut in half, from $4.1 million to $2 million. Galvanizing had also fallen off, dipping to $37.8 million in 1999 after generating $39 million the previous year, but galvanizing held far more promise than chemical storage and warehousing, leading to the decision to sell North American Warehousing and Lake River and focusing exclusively on hot dip galvanizing, especially for use on the long poles needed for the wireless and communications and electric transmission markets. To better serve this niche, NAGC in 2000 began construction on a new Houston plant that would include a 62-foot galvanizing kettle designed to accommodate long poles. It became operational in the early months of 2001. The other Houston plant remained open as well, dedicated to the steel fabricating industry. When the economy began to struggle following the terrorist attacks against the United

States on September 11, 2001, the operation was closed by the end of the year.

Although NAGC suffered from a downturn in the economy, it was diversified in the types of industries it served as well as the regions it covered. The company was strong enough, in fact, to begin construction on a new $5 million St. Louis galvanizing and coating plant in 2002. When it opened later in the year it was the largest in the area, serving the growing commercial and industrial markets in the Midwest. In addition to galvanizing services, the plant offered Kinark's new Infrashield product, which allowed for the application of polymer coatings over galvanized material on the inside of tubular products ranging in size from 9 to 24 inches in diameter.

KINARK CHANGES NAME: 2003

By this time entirely devoted to galvanizing and coating products and services, Kinark in July 2003 adopted a name more suited to its business, as well as a move to build a brand, becoming North American Galvanizing & Coatings Inc. In the meantime, problems with the economy continued to hurt business, forcing NAGC to cut costs wherever possible. About 12 percent of the workforce, approximately 25 employees, were terminated. A plant in Houston that had been idle was closed, and the older St. Louis plant was expanded to make it more competitive. Also in 2003 the Nashville plant installed a centrifuge spinner line to attract new business galvanizing small products and threaded materials. Overall, 2003 was a difficult year for NAGC, which saw revenues fall to $33.2 million after posting sales of $38.2 million in 2002. A $1.1 million profit also turned into a $1 million net loss in 2003.

NAGC returned to profitability in 2004, netting $403,000 on revenues of $35.8 million, due to an upturn in the power distribution, communications, highway, and recreational markets. With business beginning to look up, NAGC acquired Canton, Ohio-based Gregory Industries through newly formed indirect subsidiary NAGalv-Ohio, Inc., adding a Canton facility that operated a pair of hot dip galvanizing lines and 16-foot and 52-foot kettles that could be used for a wide range of steel structures. Gregory also brought with it about $7 million in annual revenues.

An increase in zinc prices led to higher galvanizing prices through much of 2006, resulting in a surge in NAGC revenues for the year, but a significant portion of the $74 million in revenues the company recorded was due to increased demand, especially in the construction field. Net income increased to more than $4.5 million for the year. Fluctuating zinc prices again caused higher revenues in 2007, when NAGC improved by

19.4 percent to $88.4 million. Profits improved as well, leading to a doubling of net income to $9.2 million in 2007.

STOCK SPLITS: 2008

To better position itself for long-term growth, NAGC in 2008 opened a new Technical Center in Tulsa. Not only would it provide tech support to customers, it would also research and develop new products, and explore ways to improve product quality and plant operating efficiencies, as well as lower energy consumption, especially important given the high cost of energy. Management was confident about NAGC's future, as reflected by the decision in August 2008 to not only offer shareholders a four-for-three stock split as a dividend while making the stock available to a wider set of investors, but to also increase a stock buyback program.

Ed Dinger

PRINCIPAL SUBSIDIARIES

North American Galvanizing Company; NAGalv-Ohio, Inc.; Premier Coatings, Inc.; Reinforcing Services, Inc.; Rogers Galvanizing Company.

PRINCIPAL COMPETITORS

AZZ Incorporated; MNP Corporation; Steel Technologies Inc.

FURTHER READING

Carson, Jack, "Tulsa's Kinark Galvanizing Industry Niche," *Daily Oklahoman*, October 19, 1997, p. 16.

Fox, Sam, "Kinark Pressured on Offer," *Tulsa World*, May 16, 1990, p. 7B.

"Kinark Corp. Planning Sale of Tulsa's Camelot Hotel," *Daily Oklahoman*, August 31, 1982.

"Kinark Eyes Expansion," *Tulsa World*, August 7, 1993, p. B6.

"Kinark Sees Name Recognition in North American Galvanizing," *American Metal Market*, March 28, 2003, p. 5.

"Kinark to Focus on Core Business," *Tulsa World*, June 27, 2000, p. 8.

Schafer, Shaun, "Galvanizing Firms Cover Future of Kinark," *Tulsa World*, June 6, 1996, p. E1.

Stafford, Jim, "Focusing on Core Work Galvanizes Business," *Oklahoman*, November 5, 2006, p. 4.

Wiley, Elizabeth Camacho, "Tulsa, Okla.-based Kinark Corp.'s Change in Focus Fuels Big Gains," *Daily Oklahoman*, November 3, 2002.

O'REILLY®

O'Reilly Media, Inc.

■

1005 Gravenstein Highway North
Sebastopol, California 95472
U.S.A.
Telephone: (707) 827-7000
Toll Free: (800) 998-9938
Fax: (707) 829-0104
Web site: http://www.oreillymedia.com

Private Company
Incorporated: 1983 as O'Reilly & Associates, Inc.
Employees: 260
Sales: $50 million (2007 est.)
NAICS: 511130 Book Publishers; 511120 Periodical
 Publishers; 511140 Database and Directory
 Publishers

■ ■ ■

O'Reilly Media, Inc., is the second largest technical
book publisher in the United States. Targeting primarily
software developers, the company publishes more than
500 titles covering emerging technologies. O'Reilly
Media hosts numerous technical conferences as well,
including annual events such as Web 2.0, the O'Reilly
Tools of Change for Publishing Conference, and the
O'Reilly Emerging Technology Conference. The
company publishes a monthly magazine, *Make,* which
focuses on do-it-yourself technology projects. The
company is led by its founder, Tim O'Reilly.

THE FOUNDER

When he was growing up in San Francisco in the mid-
1960s, Tim O'Reilly met the man who had the greatest
influence on his life, his scoutmaster, George Simon. Simon was no ordinary leader within the Boy Scouts of
America. Born in Germany, Simon grew up in New
York City and eventually ended up in California, where
he made his living selling toilet paper. The occupation
told little about the eccentric and eclectic Simon, who
had spent years studying Zen Buddhism, semantics, and
yoga by the time the Explorer troop he led counted
Sean O'Reilly and his younger brother Tim as members.
Tim O'Reilly was only about ten years old when he met
Simon, but he was fascinated by his scoutmaster's attempts to build a language for consciousness. "When I
look back on what Simon wrote," O'Reilly said in an
October 2005 interview with *Wired,* "it's such cultish,
wacky stuff." A passage from O'Reilly's notes included
in the *Wired* interview offered a sense of the bizarre
theories developed by Simon. "In the end of Notebook
22," O'Reilly wrote, "George found that the UZ led on
to a C quadrant for HS4. He eventually came to feel
that the Z16 covered HS1-3, with a normal HS1 having
C and some D, and HS2 having C, D, B and HS3 having ABCD plus a sense of God."

 More comprehensible than Simon's mathematics-
based approach to expressing consciousness was the essence of his influence on O'Reilly. Through Simon's
teachings, O'Reilly embraced the philosophy that collective action would lead to the greater good, that the
larger the community in which thoughts could be
shared and exchanged, the greater the benefit to the
community. It was a way of thinking that would find

fertile ground in the global forum that the Internet represented, an opportunity O'Reilly would seize once the technology emerged.

In the years before the World Wide Web came into existence, O'Reilly made his living as a technical writer, a profession he came into by chance. He enrolled at Harvard College in the early 1970s and earned a degree in classics, graduating cum laude within three years. O'Reilly was the recipient of a National Endowment for the Arts grant to translate fables written by Greek philosophers and he wrote a biography of science-fiction writer Frank Herbert before his career took a defining turn in 1977.

O'REILLY BECOMES A TECHNICAL WRITER

O'Reilly was living in Boston with his wife, who was teaching a class in nonverbal communication. One of her students, a Hungarian engineer named Pater Brajer, was trying to get a job as a computer consultant and approached O'Reilly for help in writing his résumé. With O'Reilly's help, Brajer was offered a contract by Digital Equipment Corporation to write an equipment manual. Brajer asked O'Reilly to help him write the manual and O'Reilly, who reportedly had never seen a computer, took him up on the offer. Shortly after completing the project in 1978, O'Reilly and Brajer went into business together. "I actually feel like I did some of my best work as a technical writer in those early years because I didn't know anything," O'Reilly said in his interview with *Wired.* "I would just have to read stuff until I saw the patterns."

In 1983, O'Reilly started his own business, O'Reilly & Associates, the predecessor to O'Reilly Media, Inc. He converted an old barn in Newton, Massachusetts,

into an office, hired about a dozen employees, and began offering technical writing services on a contract basis. The business fared well, but began to do far better after a moment of inspiration during its fifth anniversary.

BOOK PUBLISHING BEGINNING IN THE LATE 1980S

In 1988, O'Reilly & Associates' work on a manual for the X-Windows System led toward an evolutional step. X-Windows, developed by the Massachusetts Institute of Technology (MIT) four years earlier, was the foundation used to construct graphical user interface environments. O'Reilly and his team had produced a two-volume guide to the programming libraries of X-Window and they were showing it to vendors for licensing. A conference on the systems, hosted by MIT, was about to take place. In the process of showing the two-volume guide to vendors, O'Reilly was besieged with requests for single copies, which spurred him to take action. "We went to a local copy shop that night and produced around 300 manuals," he explained in his interview with *Wired.* "Without any authorization, we set up a table in the lobby with a sign saying copies of an Xlib manual would be available at 4:30. By 4:00, there was this line of 150 people. They were literally throwing money at us, or sailing their credit cards over other people's heads. That was when we went, 'Publishing could be really big business.'"

O'Reilly decided to make the leap from contract work to book publishing, specifically the type of technical books that rarely found a place on bookstore shelves. He moved his company, which changed its name to O'Reilly Publishing, to Sebastopol, 50 miles north of San Francisco in California's apple-growing region, and began publishing books about programming languages and programming tools.

O'Reilly Publishing's titles sold well, developing a cultlike following within the burgeoning technology community. O'Reilly, more out of naïveté than from shrewdness, sold his books to bookstores at a trade discount of more than 40 percent, while his competitors sold their books at the textbook discount of 20 percent. Bookstore operators, who normally shied away from the type of technical titles offered by O'Reilly Publishing, were won over by heavily discounted wholesale prices and became more willing to take a chance on titles they otherwise would have ignored.

O'Reilly also paid heed to the powers of marketing as he moved into the commercial sector. He was aware he needed to attract customers with memorable cover designs for his books. He hired a designer, but balked at

KEY DATES

1983: Tim O'Reilly forms his own technical writing business, O'Reilly & Associates.

1988: O'Reilly's business, which becomes O'Reilly Publishing, begins publishing books.

1992: O'Reilly Publishing releases *The Whole Internet User's Guide and Catalog*, which sells more than one million copies.

1993: O'Reilly Publishing launches the Global Network Navigator, a portal regarded as the first genuine commercial web site on the Internet.

1997: The company hosts a conference on the scripting language Perl, marking its foray into the conference business.

2004: Safari Books Online is formed through a joint venture with Pearson Technology Group.

2007: The company adds audio files to its web site.

the bright colors and geometric patterns that were presented to him by the person he hired. One of his writers, who lived next door to a graphic designer named Edie Freedman, intervened, suggesting O'Reilly give Freedman a chance. Freedman, confronted with the names of programming utilities and languages such as AWK, sed, and Pascal—the subjects of O'Reilly's books—associated the strange titles with the names of strange animals. She turned to the Dover copyright-free archive and created book covers using woodcut drawings of animals such as the tarsier and Surinam toad, giving O'Reilly Publishing a distinctive look that stood out on bookstore shelves.

1992: *THE WHOLE INTERNET USER'S GUIDE AND CATALOG*

It was substance, not style, that turned O'Reilly Publishing into a phenomenon. The company's major breakthrough sprang from O'Reilly's foresight, from his ability to understand the enormous potential of the Internet at an early stage in its development. He saw an absence of documentation to guide users in cyberspace and quickly moved to fill the void. O'Reilly found a short, online document titled, "A Hitchhiker's Guide to the Internet," written by Ed Krol, and he commissioned Krol to turn his material into a book. Krol spent more than a year writing *The Whole Internet User's Guide and Catalog*, a book that recorded enormous commercial success immediately after being published in 1992.

Selected as one of the "Books of the Century" by the New York Public Library, *The Whole Internet User's Guide and Catalog* sold more than one million copies by the time its content became outdated in the mid-1990s.

O'Reilly Publishing's success in print form was followed quickly by a historic achievement in the form of web content. In 1993, the company launched the Global Network Navigator (GNN), an online version of *The Whole Internet User's Guide and Catalog*, which became the Web's first portal. GNN, the first commercial publication on the Internet, pioneered the advertiser-supported model of online publishing, featuring clickable advertisements that later became known as "banner ads." O'Reilly sold GNN to America Online in 1995 for $11 million.

As the launch of GNN demonstrated, O'Reilly Publishing was willing to venture beyond the traditional boundaries of a book publisher. "We see ourselves," O'Reilly said in a September 2007 interview with *Information Today*, "as technology activists and pundits who find technologies early in their life and make noise about them." It was an open-ended description that left the company free to explore new ways to "make noise" in the dot-com era. O'Reilly Publishing became O'Reilly Media because of the company's diversified approach to disseminating content, an approach that let O'Reilly capitalize on his talents as a technological visionary.

COMPANY BEGINS HOSTING CONFERENCES IN 1997

One of the ways O'Reilly evangelized leading-edge technology was through his company's conference business. In 1997, O'Reilly hosted a conference on Perl, the scripting language preferred for web development. Nearly 1,000 people attended the first event, encouraging O'Reilly to host numerous other events, including large conferences such as the Emerging Technology Conference, small gatherings of industry leaders in annual FOO (Friends of O'Reilly) camps, and the O'Reilly Tools of Change for Publishing Conference. The company hosted the first peer-to-peer technology conference in 2001 and the first Web 2.0 Conference in 2004. Web 2.0, a term coined by O'Reilly, referred to the idea of enhancing the interconnectivity and interactivity of Internet content, an idea whose essence harkened back to the teachings of George Simon.

SAFARI BOOKS ONLINE DEBUTS IN 2004

By the time O'Reilly Media hosted the first Web 2.0 Conference, it ranked as the second largest technology book publisher in the United States. Despite its forays into new ways to distribute information, the company continued to remain active as a traditional book publisher, selling more than 500 titles that helped it generate an estimated $50 million in revenue in 2004. That same year, the company formed a partnership with Pearson Technology Group, a division of Pearson Education, Inc., to establish Safari Books Online. The service enabled users to draw upon a database of more than 5,000 O'Reilly Media and Pearson Technology titles and articles, select passages or chapters they wanted, and digitally assemble their own books, which subsequently could be printed as hard copies. "If we establish this in just our segment of the market, computer science, it could easily be a $100 million business—bigger than our entire business is today," O'Reilly said in a September 2004 interview with *Business 2.0.*

Experimentation with new ways to deliver content to customers continued as O'Reilly celebrated his 30th year in the technical writing business. In late 2007 and early 2008, O'Reilly Media was letting users buy pieces of books to be read on their cellular telephones, enhancing the content with screen tips and video. The company formed a partnership with a specialist in synthetic voice technology to add audio files to the O'Reilly Media web site. Through a pilot program with the Open University in the United Kingdom, the company was producing interactive books that could be accessed with an offline viewer, enabling students and teachers to take notes or highlight passages and share them with each other. New ways of connecting to the community that O'Reilly Media catered to were being developed with each passing year. The extent to which Tim O'Reilly could use the power of computer science and the Internet to realize his central mission of sharing information on a broad scale was increasing as well, ensuring that in the years ahead O'Reilly Media would continue to redefine the business of distributing content.

Jeffrey L. Covell

PRINCIPAL SUBSIDIARIES

O'Reilly Network; Safari Books Online.

PRINCIPAL COMPETITORS

John Wiley & Sons, Inc.; SYS-CON Media, Inc.; Syngress Publishing Inc.

FURTHER READING

Hawkins, Donald T., "O'Reilly Media: Spreading the Knowledge of Innovation," *Information Today,* September 2007, p. 1.

Howe, Rob, "Ripping Up the Textbook Business," *Business 2.0,* September 2004, p. 66.

Levy, Steven, "The Trend Spotter," *Wired,* October 2005.

"NMA Interview: Secondary Schooling," *New Media Age,* November 30, 2006, p. 21.

"Safari Books Online," *Online,* January–February 2007, p. 8.

"What's the Big Idea?" *Revolution,* December 31, 2006, p. 48.

OJSC Novolipetsk Steel

Pl. Metallurgov 2
Lipetsk, 398040
Russia
Telephone: (+7 4742) 44 46 88
Fax: (+7 4742) 44 11 11
Web site: http://www.nlmksteel.com

Public Company
Incorporated: 1934
Employees: 44,358
Sales: $7.72 billion (2007)
Stock Exchanges: Moscow London
Ticker Symbol: NLMK
NAICS: 331111 Iron and Steel Mills; 325192 Cyclic Crude and Intermediate Manufacturing; 325311 Nitrogenous Fertilizer Manufacturing; 331221 Cold-Rolled Steel Shape Manufacturing

■ ■ ■

OJSC Novolipetsk Steel (NLMK) is one of Russia's top four integrated steel and mining concerns. Based in Lipetsk, a major iron ore mining region in Russia, NLMK's operations include iron ore, dolomite, and nickel mining; steel production; and steel product manufacturing. The company's main manufacturing facility in Lipetsk is one of the world's largest, covering an area of more than 27 square kilometers. The site's annual total steel production nears 9.5 million metric tons. Another NLMK business is VIZ-Stal, the second largest producer of electrical steel in Russia (after NLMK itself), giving NLMK control of 75 percent of

that market in Russia, and a 9 percent global share overall. NLMK owns Stoilensky GOK, one of the largest iron ore mining groups in Russia, which provides nearly all of NLMK's own iron ore materials needs. The company's mining holdings also include OJSC Dolomite and OJSC Stagdok, which produce dolomite and fluxing limestone, respectively.

NLMK has launched an internationalization strategy, buying steel and steel products producers Dan-Steel A/S in Denmark, and John Maneely Co. and Beta Steel Corp. in the United States. The company owns several steel trading companies in the Netherlands, Switzerland, Cyprus, the United Kingdom, and elsewhere. Listed on the Moscow Stock Exchange, NLMK is majority controlled by President and Chairman Vladimir Lisin. The company posted revenues of $7.72 billion in 2007.

SOVIET ORIGINS IN 1931

Industrialization became a major part of the young Soviet Union's objectives in the first half of the 20th century. Despite its great size and large population, the Soviet Union continued to lag behind the advances in technology and industrial infrastructure being made by its Western counterparts. The need to ensure the country's supply of steel occupied a central place in the government's planned expansion of the Soviet industrial complex.

With vast deposits of iron ore, coal, and other raw materials needed for the production of steel, the Soviet government launched a series of programs designed to upgrade and expand the country's existing steel

COMPANY PERSPECTIVES

Vision: We are committed to strengthening our leadership position in terms of profitability, product quality and technological advancement within the steel industry. Mission: Our mission is to be the preferred supplier of flat steel products to our core customer base and to be among the most profitable steel producers in the world, enjoying sustainable growth in revenues and profits.

factories. At the same time, the government planned to build a new series of steel foundries.

Lipetsk, located on the Voronezh River some 440 kilometers southwest of Moscow, had long been recognized as an important source of mineral wealth. The region in particular boasted large iron ore deposits. These were exploited for the first time in the early 18th century, when Czar Peter I (Peter the Great) established a foundry there to provide steel for weapons.

The Soviet government decided to build a modern, large-scale iron and steel foundry near the Lipetsk iron ore mines to take advantage of the region's rich iron ore deposits. Plans for the facility included two 930-cubic-meter blast furnaces, capable of producing up to 350,000 tons of iron per year. Construction of the site began in 1931, and the first blast furnace was completed in 1934. Production of pig iron was launched that year. By 1935, the Novolipetsk Iron and Steel Works had completed construction of the second blast furnace.

Novolipetsk ramped up its production through the end of the 1930s, doubling its output by the outbreak of World War II. The site also played a role in increasing the technological prowess of the Soviet metallurgy industry in general, carrying out successful testing of the use of steam in the blast-furnace process. This technique was later adopted throughout the Soviet steel industry.

DISMANTLED FOR THE DURATION

The plant's expansion was halted, however, with the German invasion of the Soviet Union in 1941. With the Nazi blitzkrieg moving rapidly into the Soviet Union, the Soviet government moved to dismantle the Novolipetsk facility and move its blast furnaces and other equipment to the Urals, another major Soviet metallurgy and iron ore mining center much farther from the front lines. When the Germans failed to capture Moscow, the

government ordered the return of the Novolipetsk blast furnaces to Lipetsk in 1942. This move again proved only temporary, and in 1944, all of the site's equipment, workers, and materials were transferred to Chelyabinsk, in the Urals.

Production nonetheless continued at the Lipetsk site, which saw its foundry and machine shop converted to the production of antitank obstacles, grenade casings, tools, machinery parts, and other items to support the Soviet war effort. By 1945, the workshop had been expanded to include a small electric arc furnace, as well as a plant for producing steel structural supports.

These operations came in part as a prelude to the reconstruction of the Lipetsk site as a major Soviet foundry. With the end of the war, the Gipromez, the state body responsible for the planning and construction of the country's metallurgy infrastructure, began drawing up plans for a new and still larger factory. The new plans called for the installation of two 1,000-cubic-meter blast furnaces, raising the site's total capacity to 600,000 tons per year. Construction began in 1947.

Great priority was given to construction of the site, and by 1950, Novolipetsk had restarted its production of pig iron. One year later, the site had already surpassed its prewar production levels. At the same time, the Gipromez plans included a major expansion to the site, to add the production of steel to its operations as well.

EXPANSION INTO THE SEVENTIES

In 1954, Novolipetsk added its first continuous casting equipment, beginning the site transformation to this technology. By 1957, the Novolipetsk facility included its first hot-rolled strip mill. One year later, the site added a new steelmaking facility, using electric arc technology as well. This permitted the launch of production of cold-rolled steel by 1960.

Expansion of the Novolipetsk plant continued through the 1960s, as the Lipetsk site became one of the largest in the Soviet Union. By the end of the decade, the site featured four blast furnaces, two hot rolling shops, an electric steelmaking factory, two sintering machines, and a sheet cold-rolling factory, among other operations.

Through the 1970s, the Novolipetsk site remained a central part of the Soviet Union's industrial growth. The site's operations continued to expand, and included a 3,200-cubic-meter blast furnace, the largest not only in the Soviet Union, but in all of Europe. The site had also added its first oxygen converters, allowing for the

KEY DATES

■

1934: The Novolipetsk Iron and Steel Plant, founded in 1931, launches pig iron production.

1947: Novolipetsk is relaunched following World War II.

1993: Russian government undertakes privatization of the country's steel industry, including Novolipetsk.

1998: Vladimir Lisin becomes chairman of Novolipetsk.

2002: Lisin gains full control of Novolipetsk.

2006: The company completes its first foreign acquisition, of DanSteel in Denmark.

2008: Novolipetsk acquires John Maneely Co. and Beta Steel in the United States.

continuous casting of curved billets. By 1980, Novolipetsk had begun manufacturing cold-rolled carbon steel as well.

By the mid-1980s, Novolipetsk had grown into the third largest steel producer in the Soviet Union. By then, the complex had completed its conversion to the continuous casting method. Increases made in production were significant, topping nine million metric tons by 1985.

VLADIMIR LISIN TAKES CONTROL IN THE NINETIES

These investments meant that Novolipetsk remained one of the most modern and efficient mills in the Soviet Union. This position allowed Novolipetsk to emerge from the collapse of the Soviet Union and the institution of a free market economy in relatively good shape. When the Russian government launched the privatization of the country's steel industry during the 1990s, Novolipetsk became an attractive target for both the Russian and foreign investment communities.

Among those gaining a share of Novolipetsk during the 1990s was Vladimir Lisin, then a member of the notorious TransWorld metal trading group. Lisin represented something of a proletariat rags-to-riches story. He was born in Moscow in 1956, and one of his first jobs was as an electrician in a coal mine in Siberia. Lisin attended the Siberian Metallurgical Institute, taking a job as a welder there during the mid-1970s. Lisin subsequently became a foreman at the Tulachermet

Metal Works, rising to the position of shop manager. Upon graduating in 1979, Lisin moved to Kazakhstan, where he became an engineer at the Karaganda Steel Plant.

Lisin once again moved quickly up the ranks, becoming deputy chief engineer of the site by 1981. It was then that Lisin developed a relationship with Oleg Soskovets, his superior at the Karaganda plant, and later to become minister of the metallurgical sector within the Soviet government. After Soskovets established his own private company, TSK-Steel, Lisin was named one of its directors. By the end of the 1990s, Lisin, who had by then earned a Ph.D. in engineering and a D.Sc. in economics, had become deputy director of the Karaganda site.

Soskovets's appointment as minister of metallurgy represented Lisin's own entry into the Moscow political and economic elite. Lisin returned to Moscow with Soskovets in 1991. By 1992, Lisin had joined TransWorld Group, described by *Forbes* magazine as a "tough group of traders ... [who] came to dominate Russia's aluminum and steel exports." Lisin quickly displayed a talent for negotiating the companies under his direction through the crisis years of the new Russian free market system. Lisin also took his place among the country's "oligarchs," a small group of businessmen close to Boris Yeltsin who gained control of many of the country's industrial sector during the 1990s.

By 1996, Lisin had become a member of the board at Novolipetsk, and through the end of the 1990s began quietly buying up shares in that company. The collapse of the Russian economy in 1998 enabled Lisin to increase his position within Novolipetsk, as he became chairman of the company that year. At the same time, Lisin's relatively low profile helped to spare him the fate of much of the Russian oligarchs, as the new government under Vladimir Putin came to power. Lisin successfully switched his loyalties to Putin, enabling him to retain control of his own growing empire.

By 2000, TransWorld had been broken up. Lisin's share of the breakup included majority control of Novolipetsk. Over the next year or two, Lisin battled with the company's other shareholders, including Vladimir Potanin, and by 2002, had managed to gain full control of the company.

EXPANSION IN THE 21ST CENTURY

Lisin had by then already launched Novolipetsk's expansion. The company bought metallurgical dolomite mining group OJSC Dolomite in 1997. In 1999, the company acquired OJSC Stagdok, adding its fluxing limestone mining and processing operations.

A major milestone in the company's drive toward becoming a fully integrated steel and mining concern came with its acquisition of a 97 percent stake in Stoilensky GOK in 2004. That purchase gave the company control over its own supply of iron ore.

At the same time, Novolipetsk continued to build up the other end of its operations, controlling its own logistics business, LLC, Independent Transport Company (or NTK). In 2004 the company also acquired a controlling stake in the Tuapse port on the Black Sea. In addition, the company began putting into place a move into energy production, gaining a license to build its own mining operations at the Zhernovskoie 1 coal deposit in the coal-rich Kuzbass region. That site became operational in 2008.

A crowning moment for Novolipetsk's growth into one of Russia's and the world's major integrated steel producers came in 2005, when Lisin successfully listed 6 percent of the company's shares on the London Stock Exchange. The listing not only helped raise new investor backing capital, it also gained Lisin a place among the world's super-rich. By 2008, Lisin had risen to 21st place, and second in Russia, on *Forbes* magazine's ranking of the world's wealthiest people.

INTERNATIONAL DRIVE TOWARD 2010

The listing also helped ensure the company's successful drive beyond Russia. The company's first move came in 2006, when it bought Denmark's DanSteel A/S, a specialist in rolled steel products. Later that year, Novolipetsk struck a deal with Duferco Group in Switzerland to form a $1.6 billion steel production and distribution joint venture. Novolipetsk agreed to pay $805 million for its 50 percent share of the joint venture, which then took over the operation of Duferco's 22 steel mills, including its Pennsylvania-based Duferco Farrel mill.

Having gained a foothold in the U.S. market, Novolipetsk next plotted its full scale entry into that market. The company found its target in August 2008, when it paid $3.5 billion to acquire New Jersey-based John Maneely Co. That acquisition gave the company control of ten steel mills in the United States, as well as one in Canada, with a total production capacity of three million tons. Just one month later, Novolipetsk returned to the United States, acquiring Beta Corp. for $400 million. Based in Portage, Indiana, Beta Steel added its production of steel pipes and tubes. In this way, Novolipetsk gained an outlet for its North American raw steel production.

Novolipetsk continued to expand back home as well. The company acquired Russia's second largest electrical steel manufacturer, VIZ Stal, in 2006. Combined with Novolipetsk's existing electrical steel production, the company now became Russia's dominant force in the sector, with a 75 percent share of the market, and a 9 percent share of the total global market. The company also boosted its coal assets, acquiring JSC Altai-koks, a coke producer, and the Prokopievskugol coal group. Other acquisitions included OJSC Maxi Group, an integrated steel products group, for $600 million in 2007, and several metal trading companies, including Switzerland's Novex Trading and Cyprus's Novexco in 2008. Under Vladimir Lisin's leadership, Novolipetsk had emerged as a major steel group not only in Russia but worldwide.

M. L. Cohen

PRINCIPAL SUBSIDIARIES

LLC Karamyshevskoye; LLC Larmet; LLC Lipetsk; LLC Novolipetskoye; LLC Steel; LLC Vimet; LLC VIZ-Stal; LLC Vtorchermet NLMK; LLC Vtormetsnab NLMK; NLMK International B.V.; Novolipetsky Metallurg (Ukraine); OJSC Altai-koks; OJSC Dolomite; OJSC Lipetsky Gipromez; OJSC Maxi-Group; OJSC North Oil and Gas Company (51%); OJSC Stoilensky GOK; OJSC Tuapsinsky Sea Commercial Port (TMTP).

PRINCIPAL COMPETITORS

Severstal Group; Evraz Group S.A.; Mechel Joint Stock Co.; Urals Mining and Metallurgical Co.; Magnitogorsk Iron and Steel Works Joint Stock Co. (MAGN).

FURTHER READING

Cook, Bradley, "European Steel Makers Strike Deal," *International Herald Tribune*, November 28, 2006, p. 15.

Forster, Harriet, "Russian Steel Plant Battles Shareholders," *American Metal Market*, March 25, 1997, p. 1.

Frantsenyuk, I. V., "The Novolipetsk Metallurgical Combine—60 Years," *Metallurgist*, October 1994, pp. 3–7.

Guzzo, Maria, "Size of NLMK-Maneely Deal Surprises Industry," *American Metal Market*, August 14, 2008, p. 1.

Kolpakov, S. V., "Forty Years of the Novolipetsk Metallurgical Plant," *Metallurgist*, November 1974, p. 16.

LaRue, Gloria T., "Novolipetsk Steel Plant Is Soviet Showpiece," *American Metal Market*, July 12, 1985, p. 1.

Lisin, Vladimir S., "Novolipetsk Iron & Steel Corporation," *WorldLink*, July–August 2000, p. 56.

Milner, Mark, and Charlotte Moore, "Russian Steel Firm Plans £6bn Float," *Guardian*, November 21, 2005, p. 23.

"Novolipetsk Buys Beta Steel for $400m to Expand US Presence," *Daily Telegraph*, September 5, 2008.

"Novolipetsk Iron & Steel Corporation," *WorldLink,* January–February 2001, p. 218.

Robertson, Scott, "NLMK $400m Beta Buy Aimed at Feeding JMC," *American Metal Market,* September 5, 2008, p. 1.

"Russians Who Caught a Cold," *Evening Standard,* September 29, 2008, p. 36.

"Vladimir Lisin Tames Russian Metal Sector," *Taipei Times,* December 19, 2005, p. 12.

Omega Protein
Corporation

———— ◼ ————

2105 City West Boulevard, Suite 500
Houston, Texas 77042-2838
U.S.A.
Telephone: (713) 623-0060
Toll Free: (800) 345-8805
Fax: (713) 940-6122
Web site: http://www.omegaproteininc.com

Public Company
Founded: 1878
Employees: 500
Sales: $157.1 million (2007)
Stock Exchanges: New York
Ticker Symbol: OME
NAICS: 311711 Seafood Canning; 311712 Fresh and
Frozen Seafood Processing

◼ ◼ ◼

Omega Protein Corporation is the largest manufacturer of specialty fish meals and fish oil for aquaculture, swine, other livestock feeds, and human consumption. Omega Protein catches more than 70 percent of the menhaden fished each year in the United States and is the leading manufacturer of marine protein and fish oil in North America. It is also one of the largest fish meal companies in the world with 40 fishing vessels and 35 spotter planes housed at the company's home ports and pressing plants in Abbeville and Cameron, Louisiana; Moss Point, Mississippi; and Reedville, Virginia. The company also has warehouses and storage facilities in Alabama, Illinois, Louisiana, Missouri, and Virginia.

THE FIRST HUNDRED YEARS

Omega Protein traces its roots back to 1878 when John A. Haynie and his younger brother, Thomas Haynie, opened a fish processing operation on Virginia's northern neck on the Haynie family's Reedville property. The Haynies processed menhaden fish, an ocean-swimming, foot-long, herring-like fish that feeds on algae and is rich in omega oils. Also known as pogy, porgy, bugmouth, fatback, alewife, shad, and shiner, menhaden is not often eaten because of its small size, its oiliness, and its many bones. The commercial domestic menhaden fishing industry began in the early 1800s when Europeans learned that the fish, which were abundant along the Gulf of Mexico and the Atlantic coast, were useful as fertilizer and for their extracted oil. The industry burgeoned after the Civil War when menhaden oil was used for lamps and fish meal was spread on fields as fertilizer.

In 1903, John A. Haynie Company became Haynie, Snow & Company, and, in 1913, it changed names again to Reedville Oil & Guano Company. Around 1978, Zapata Corporation, an oil and gas company founded by George H. W. Bush in 1953, acquired Reedville, which became a division of its parent company known as Zapata Haynie. Zapata Haynie focused on gaining Food and Drug Administration (FDA) approval of refined menhaden oil for human consumption throughout most of the 1980s and 1990s. Finally, in 1997, the FDA granted its approval of the oil that contains high levels of omega-3 fatty acids.

CONSOLIDATION AND GROWTH: THE EIGHTIES AND NINETIES

The 1980s and 1990s were decades of consolidation in the fish meal industry. In 1992, financier Malcolm Glazer acquired a stake in Zapata Corporation and Haynie's parent company purchased 60 percent of Venture Milling, a Delaware-based blender of animal protein products. Two years later, Zapata Haynie was renamed Zapata Protein. The name change reflected the division's expansion into the animal feed market. In 1997, Zapata Protein renamed itself again as Marine Genetics after it sold most of the assets of Venture Milling and acquired two of its four American rivals, Chesapeake Bay area-based American Protein and Louisiana-based Gulf Protein.

A year after Joseph von Rosenberg became president and CEO of Marine Genetics in 1997, Zapata Corporation spun off about 40 percent of the newly renamed Omega Protein in its initial public offering (IPO) in 1998. Rosenberg had been general counsel to Zapata Corporation for four years. Although August and September hurricanes severely limited the menhaden fishing season in 1998, Omega Protein reported record profits that year of $23.6 million, up from $10.4 million in 1997. The company, which launched its web site at www.buyomegaprotein.com, had five processing plants in the United States and made the Russell 3000 index of the largest companies in the U.S. stock market with 1998 revenues of $133.6 million, more than a 10 percent increase from the previous year's $117.6 million.

Despite this, Omega Protein's stock price plunged to 50 percent of its IPO price by the end of the year. The following year's severe drought, combined with a global glut in the fish meal and fish oil markets as well as record global production of soybeans in 1999 and 2000, depressed markets for Omega Protein's products. During late 1999 and early 2000, fish oil prices decreased 58 percent and fish meal prices 38 percent from levels a year earlier. As a result, in 1999, the company closed a plant in Louisiana and reduced its fishing fleet for the 2000 fishing season. The company, which experienced a net loss of $16.7 million for the year 2000, laid off 75 off-season employees.

CAPITALIZING ON HEALTH BENEFITS: 1999–2004

Fortunately the company had prepared to move forward in a new direction following the 1997 FDA approval of menhaden oil for use in foods. Hoping to capitalize on the health benefits of omega-3 fatty acids, which included improved brain and eye function; treatment for depression, arthritis, and other inflammatory diseases; and undoing some of the damage caused by the high-fat diet typical of Americans, Omega Protein partnered with Organic Food Products, Inc., one of the largest pasta sauce makers in the natural foods industry, in 1999. The two companies began to market a line of omega-3 fortified pasta sauces through natural foods and mass market retailers.

Fish oil was once again experiencing an upswing in popularity, aided by such organizations as the American Heart Association, which, in 2002, began recommending omega-3 oil for its coronary and vascular benefits. Omega Protein, one of only two menhaden processing operations remaining on the East Coast, saw its revenues rise to $117.9 million in 2003. In 2004, the company completed work on a $16.5 million refinery on the banks of the Chesapeake Bay. Up until then the company had focused on two products at its Virginia facility, fish meal and crude fish oil, for animal feeds and industrial and manufacturing uses. The new 100-metric-ton-per-day facility in Reedville, Virginia, roughly tripled Omega Protein's capacity to refine oil and allowed it to turn more attention to refining food-grade fish oil. The company also completed the Omega Protein Health and Science Center in Virginia in 2004, a laboratory for the research and development of omega-3 fortified foods.

The payback was immediate; in 2004, the company, which had three other processing plants in Mississippi and Louisiana, netted its first big contract with a Texas food processor that began adding Omega's fish oil to the tacos and tamales that it made for 38 school districts in its home state. "It's obvious to us the omega-3 story is something about to happen," Rosenberg commented in the *Richmond Times Dispatch.* "We hope [Texas] will be the first of many dominoes." The second domino proved to be a manufacturing and supply agreement that year with National Starch and Chemical Company, a leading producer of starch-based ingredients for the global food industry.

KEY DATES

1878: John A. and Thomas Haynie open a fish processing operation in Reedville, Virginia.

1903: John A. Haynie Company becomes Haynie, Snow & Company.

1913: The company changes its name to Reedville Oil & Guano Company.

1978: Zapata Corporation acquires Reedville, which becomes a division known as Zapata Haynie.

1992: Zapata Corporation purchases Venture Milling.

1994: Zapata Haynie becomes Zapata Protein.

1997: Zapata Protein becomes Marine Genetics after selling most of Venture Milling and acquiring competitors American Protein and Gulf Protein; the FDA approves menhaden oil for use in foods; von Rosenberg becomes chief executive officer of the company.

1998: Zapata Corporation spins off about 40 percent of the newly renamed Omega Protein in its initial public offering.

1999: The company partners with Organic Food Products, Inc., to make pasta sauces; the company dry-docks part of its fishing fleet for the 2000 fishing season.

2002: The American Heart Association begins recommending omega-3 oil for its health benefits.

2004: The company completes a new Chesapeake Bay refinery and the Omega Protein Health and Science Center laboratory.

2005: Omega Protein purchases a facility in Moss Point from the Shipley Company.

2006: Omega Protein acquires shares from Zapata Corporation, its majority shareholder.

PREPARING FOR THE FUTURE: 2005–08

Despite such optimistic forebodings, the year 2005 was a turbulent one for the company. The especially volatile hurricane season led to a net loss of $7.2 million on revenues of $109.9 million due to the closing of several facilities responsible for about 70 percent of the company's processing capacity. In addition, Greenpeace

activists staged a floating protest as part of their campaign to get state regulators to curtail the industrial harvest of menhaden from the Chesapeake Bay. The nonprofit, sport fishermen, and others argued that Omega Protein's factory fishing was depleting the bay's stock of menhaden and stressing the population of striped bass that fed on it.

Although the company agreed to limit its catch to its average catch of 2001 to 2005 indefinitely, it kept its eye on the future. In 2005, to reduce dependence on third-party warehousing, Omega Protein purchased a facility from the Shipley Company in Moss Point, Mississippi, into which it also moved its regional offices. In 2006, the company purchased Zapata Corporation's holdings in Omega Protein, and Joseph von Rosenberg replaced Glazer as president and chairman.

Revenues continued to rise as the use of omega-3 products expanded throughout the food and beverage markets. In 2007 the company reported revenues of $157.1 million. That year Omega Protein opened a new technical center, called the OmegaPure Technology and Innovation Center, in Houston, Texas, to further develop its OmegaPure food grade product line. The public's increased interest in omega-3 products offered new opportunities for Omega Protein to grow even as it invited competition due to the fish oil market's nascent supply structure.

Carrie Rothburd

PRINCIPAL COMPETITORS

American Seafoods Group LLC; Archer Daniels Midland Company; Cargill, Incorporated.

FURTHER READING

Antosh, Nelson, "Big Business for a Small Fish: Menhaden's Versatility Lands Net Profits for Omega Protein," *Houston Chronicle,* October 29, 1998, p. 1.

Colley, Jenna, "Omega Protein on the Menu for South Texas Schools," *Harvard Business Journal,* February 27, 2004, p. 2.

"'Frozen Fishing': A Proposal to Cap Harvests of a Single Fish in the Chesapeake Bay Is a Good Compromise—For Now," *Washington Post,* August 6, 2006, p. B6.

"Greenpeace Stages Floating Protest Outside Omega Plant," *Associated Press State & Local Wire,* July 24, 2005.

Latane, Lawrence, III, "Menhaden Plan Could Boost Virginia Fisheries: Omega Protein Will Supply Fish Oil for Texas School-Food Program," *Richmond Times Dispatch,* April 25, 2004, p. D1.

Organic To Go Food Corporation

3317 Third Avenue South
Seattle, Washington 98134
U.S.A.
Telephone: (206) 838-4670
Toll Free: (800) 304-4550
Fax: (425) 837-9622
Web site: http://www.organictogo.com

Public Company
Incorporated: 1994 as SP Holding Corporation
Employees: 251
Sales: $15.9 million (2007)
Stock Exchanges: Over the Counter (OTC)
Ticker Symbol: OTGO.OB
NAICS: 722110 Full-Service Restaurants; 424480 Fresh
  Fruit and Vegetable Merchant Wholesalers

■ ■ ■

Organic To Go Food Corporation is the first "fast casual" restaurant chain to be certified as organic by the U.S. Department of Agriculture (USDA). The company operates 33 retail locations in Seattle, Washington; Los Angeles and San Diego, California; and Washington, D.C. Organic To Go's wholesale business consists of branded "Grab-N-Go" locations at universities and airports, as well as 23 locations on the Microsoft Corporate Campus near Seattle. The company also provides delivery and catering service to corporate clientele, institutional customers, and consumers. Organic To Go's menu includes breakfast items, sandwiches, pizza, pasta, salads, soups, and snacks.

BACKGROUND OF THE FOUNDER

Jason Brown brought the speed and convenience of take-out foodservice to the organic foods industry, creating a first-of-its-kind dining concept that capitalized on one of the fastest-growing segments of the food industry. Organic To Go was not the first venture launched by Brown, a Pittsburgh, Pennsylvania, native who could be described as a serial entrepreneur. Earlier in his career Brown founded Cotton Comfort, a chain of retail stores he led for a dozen years. He also founded Columbia Sportswear Co. of New Zealand/Australia. In addition, Brown formed a distribution company to distribute salmon, soybeans, and other products. In the years leading up to Organic To Go's formation, Brown's other entrepreneurial achievements included founding Concept Developments, a company that developed AIDS-based pharmacies in New York, Florida, and Colorado. His last venture before founding Organic To Go was a company based in Carlsbad, California, named Custom Nutrition Services. Custom Nutrition provided consumers with personalized vitamin solutions. Brown sold the company to Bellevue, Washington-based Drugstore.com, an online retailer of health, beauty, and pharmacy products. The $5.3 million transaction, completed in June 2003, left Brown free to plot his next move, the founding of Organic To Go.

As Brown considered launching his own organic foods business, the sector was recording spirited growth, providing all the encouragement Brown needed. Beginning in the early 1990s, organic food began recording annual growth in the range of 20 percent, by far outpacing the growth of the food industry as a whole. Organic foods—those produced without the use of pesticides, artificial fertilizers, food additives, and ionizing radiation—had slipped into the mainstream. By 2003, organic products were available in 20,000 natural food stores and in 73 percent of conventional grocery stores, according to a study conducted by the USDA. Further, after more than a decade of lobbying efforts, certification by the USDA for the use of the organic label became federal law in October 2002, a piece of legislation that would enable Brown's future venture to become the first of its kind.

ORGANIC TO GO IS FORMED

Brown, along with colleagues from Custom Nutrition Services, developed a three-pronged attack on the robust organic food market. After hatching the idea of Organic To Go in early 2004, Brown and his associates developed a business model aimed at attracting white-collar office workers as well as students and employees of universities, Organic To Go's demographic. Organic To Go served its clientele through three channels: retail stores, wholesale accounts, and delivery and catering services. On the retail front, the company intended to open small cafés that would compete in the "fast casual" segment of the foodservice industry. The company's wholesale business, operated as branded "Grab-N-Go" locations, sold sandwiches and similar food items through independent coffee vendors and at universities, corporate campuses, and airports. Organic To Go's delivery and catering service provided meals and snacks to corporate clientele, universities, and institutional customers such as hospitals.

Organic To Go developed quickly, evolving from an idea on paper into a publicly traded company within three years. Far from a homespun start-up, the company gained its early strength from an impressive group of supporters, asserting itself as one of the premier organizations in the organic foods community from the start. Organic To Go's board of directors included some of the luminaries of the organic movement: Hass

Hassan, founder, president, and CEO of Alfalfa's Markets and founder of Fresh & Wild, the leading retailer of organic foods in the United Kingdom; Dave Smith, executive and consultant for Diamond Organics, Seeds of Change, and Organic Bouquet; Peter Meehan, CEO and cofounder of Newman's Own Organics; and Dr. Gunnar Weikert, founder and CEO of Inventages Venture Capital Investments, Inc., one of the world's largest venture capital funds focused on the life-sciences, nutrition, and wellness sector.

Incorporated as Organic Holding Company, Inc., in early 2004, Brown's company was prepared to serve customers by the end of the year. A commissary was established in Issaquah, just north of Seattle, late in the year that served as the hub of the company's operations, supplying each facet of its business: retail, wholesale, and catering. Organic To Go made its commercial debut at the start of 2005. In January, the company opened a retail café in Issaquah and its second outlet in downtown Seattle in the Columbia Tower.

January also marked the arrival of Organic To Go's culinary director, Greg Atkinson. A chef for more than 20 years when he joined Organic To Go, Atkinson was renowned for spearheading the revival of Seattle's Canlis restaurant, a once-prestigious steak house whose luster had faded considerably by the 1990s. Atkinson was appointed as executive chef of Canlis in 1996 and returned the restaurant to its former glory with "a new focus on seasonal influences and an orientation towards sustainably-raised, local products," as he explained on the Organic To Go web site. In 2001, Atkinson, while still serving as executive chef at Canlis, took on the duties of chef and food programs director at IslandWood, where he prepared organic food and designed educational programs about organic food for children. Next, he formed his own consulting company, Culinary Consulting, the company he ran when Brown offered him an executive position at Organic To Go.

COMPANY EXPANDS INTO LOS ANGELES IN 2005

Brown did not wait long to expand his company after opening his first two retail locations. In April 2005, he pushed south, entering the greater Los Angeles market with conviction. The purchase of certain assets owned by Briazz Inc., paved Organic To Go's entry into California. A Seattle-based sandwich café chain, Briazz filed for bankruptcy in June 2004, creating an ideal opportunity for Brown to purchase retail locations inexpensively. For $1.3 million, Brown gained six stores in the Greater Los Angeles area as well as three units in Seattle. By the end of the year, Organic To Go's

KEY DATES

2004: Jason Brown forms Organic To Go.

2005: The company opens its first retail location in Issaquah, Washington.

2006: Organic To Go becomes the first fast casual restaurant operator to be certified as organic by the U.S. Department of Agriculture (USDA).

2007: Organic To Go becomes a publicly traded company and expands into San Diego.

2008: Organic To Go acquires four retail locations in Washington, D.C.

first full year of operation, revenues reached $6.3 million.

USDA CERTIFICATION IN 2006

Organic To Go entered 2006 prepared to eclipse its expansion efforts in 2005. First, however, the company received a regulatory nod of approval that served as a powerful marketing tool. In February 2006, Quality Assurance International completed its inspection of Organic To Go to determine if the chain met the standards written into law four years earlier. The company passed the inspection, becoming the first fast casual chain in the country to be certified as organic by the USDA.

After devoting 2005 to establishing a retail presence, Organic To Go spent 2006 building its other two businesses, wholesale and catering. In October 2006, the company acquired Vinaigrettes LLC, a Los Angeles-based company that operated under the name Vinaigrettes Catering Company. Vinaigrettes, a $2.5 million-in-sales operation, had been in business for a decade supplying box lunches to corporate clientele and catering events hosted by the nearby film industry. Organic To Go also established its first Grab-N-Go location on the Microsoft Corporate Campus in 2006, the first of nearly two dozen locations that would be established in Redmond, Washington. The focus on expansion lifted revenues 61 percent by the end of 2006, when Organic To Go recorded $9.7 million in sales.

REVERSE MERGER IN 2007

Once Brown had laid the foundation for three streams of revenue, he moved to the next item on his agenda: taking Organic To Go public. He chose the most expedient route toward public ownership, brokering an unusual deal that saw an organic foods company merge with a former broadband wireless company, Speedcom Wireless Corp. Speedcom Wireless was formed in Florida in 1994, opened offices in Mexico, Canada, and China, but collapsed before its tenth year of business. All its assets were sold at the end of 2003, leaving its owner, SP Holding Corporation, existing as a public shell, a company whose only business activity was maintaining its status as a publicly traded concern. Brown used SP Holding to take Organic To Go public, executing a reverse merger, the same way Speedcom Wireless had gone public. The maneuver was completed in February 2007, when SP Holding acquired Organic To Go Holding, Inc., which became a subsidiary of SP Holding that was renamed Organic To Go, Inc. In May 2007, SP Holding changed its name to Organic To Go Food Corporation, the parent company of Organic To Go, Inc.

The reverse merger completed in 2007 was part of a busy year for Organic To Go. The company began the year by opening a retail café in Century City, California, the first of 11 cafés to open during the year. Increasingly, Brown turned to acquisitions to drive the expansion of Organic To Go, both on the retail and catering fronts. In March 2007, he purchased Jackrabbit, LLC, a Seattle-based catering operation that generated $1.8 million in annual revenue. In July 2007, the acquisition of an existing business led Organic To Go into the San Diego market for the first time. The company purchased Scott's Gourmet Sandwiches, a deal that gave it two retail locations and a catering service. Organic To Go's presence in San Diego was fleshed out several months later with the acquisition of Brother's Restaurant & Deli. Completed in October, the acquisition gave Organic To Go two catering facilities and two more retail locations in San Diego, making it a 25-store chain.

The flurry of acquisitions completed in 2007 spurred Organic To Go's physical and financial growth. The company's retail sales, invigorated by nearly doubling the size of the chain, increased 36 percent, reaching $7.1 million. Catering sales shot upward as well, nearly doubling to $6.6 million thanks largely to the acquisitions completed in Seattle and San Diego. The company's Grab-N-Go business doubled in size, generating $2.2 million in sales as the number of wholesale accounts eclipsed 100. The growth on all three fronts led to a 65 percent increase in sales, enabling Organic To Go to post $15.9 million in revenue at the end of 2007.

Brown pressed ahead with expansion as Organic To Go neared its fifth anniversary. In February 2008, when the company secured $10 million in private placement by Inventages Venture Capital Management, four new retail cafés opened their doors, two in Los Angeles, one in Seattle, and a fourth in San Diego. In the spring, a new dimension was added to the company's catering operations when Pizza Organica was launched in Seattle. The company began offering delivery service of pizza made with organic ingredients, a service that soon extended to Southern California. In May, Brown returned to acquisition mode, purchasing three retail locations and catering operations in Seattle. His next move set the tone for Organic To Go's future, giving industry observers a strong sense that expansion in the coming years would make the company a competitor on the national stage.

EAST COAST EXPANSION IN 2008

Within three years of opening his first retail location in Seattle, Brown had significantly extended his company's presence and honed his vision of making organic food conveniently available in three distinct ways. In Seattle, Los Angeles, and San Diego, he had impressed onlookers with a concerted development of retail, catering, and wholesale businesses, but no single move drew as much attention from pundits as the acquisition he completed in mid-2008, his eighth acquisition completed since 2005. In June, he engineered Organic To Go's giant geographic leap to the East Coast, acquiring a nine-year-old chain in Washington, D.C., named High Noon. The purchase, completed for an undisclosed price, gave Organic To Go four retail locations and a catering operation in the nation's capital. "This will serve as a tremendous launching pad for the Organic To Go brand on the East Coast," Brown said in a June 2, 2008, interview with the *Washington Business Journal*. The

years ahead were expected to see Brown take his concept to a higher level and extend the company's presence into major metropolitan markets across the country.

Jeffrey L. Covell

PRINCIPAL SUBSIDIARIES

Organic To Go, Inc.

PRINCIPAL COMPETITORS

Doctor's Associates Inc.; Fresh Choice LLC; Garden Fresh Restaurant Corp.

FURTHER READING

Allison, Melissa, "Quicker Than You Can Say IPO, Company Goes Public," *Seattle Times*, February 14, 2007, p. E1.

Elan, Elisa, "Having Words with Jason Brown: Founder, Organic To Go," *Nation's Restaurant News*, February 5, 2007, p. 50.

"Investors Cheer Realignment of Speedcom Board," *Sarasota Herald Tribune*, January 1, 2005, p. D1.

"Organic To Go Buys Four D.C.-Area Cafés," *Puget Sound Business Journal*, June 2, 2008.

"Organic To Go Buys High Noon," *Washington Business Journal*, June 2, 2008.

"Organic To Go Buys Three Seattle Restaurants," *Puget Sound Business Journal*, May 15, 2008.

"Organic To Go Goes Public," *Progressive Grocer*, February 14, 2007.

"Organic To Go Raises $4.7M, Goes Public," *Puget Sound Business Journal*, February 13, 2007.

Orgill, Inc.

3742 Tyndale Drive
Memphis, Tennessee 38125-8500
U.S.A.
Telephone: (901) 754-8850
Toll Free: (800) 347-2860
Fax: (901) 752-8989
Web site: http://www.orgill.com

Private Company
Incorporated: 1898 as Orgill Brothers & Co.
Employees: 1,710
Sales: $1.04 billion (2006)
NAICS: 423710 Hardware Merchant Wholesalers

■ ■ ■

With more than $1 billion in annual sales, Orgill, Inc., is the United States' largest independent hardware distributor, serving 48 states and more than 60 other countries from all corners of the world, including Africa, Asia, the Caribbean Basin, Central and South America, Europe, the Far East, and the Middle East. The family-owned company is based in Memphis, Tennessee, and maintains six distribution centers located in Memphis; Tifton, Georgia; Vandalia, Illinois; Inwood, West Virginia; Kilgore, Texas; and Hurricane, Utah. The international business, based in Jacksonville, Florida, is conducted through three export consolidation facilities in Jacksonville, Miami, and Los Angeles. In addition to its main customers, independent hardware stores and lumberyards, Orgill serves smaller format, non-big-box chains.

All told the company carries more than 70,000 products sourced from around the world, including hardware, lumber, building materials, paint and sundries, hand and power tools, plumbing, housewares, home furnishings, and camping and outdoor gear. It also offers a lock services program that provides retailers with everything they need to establish a locksmith service. Moreover, Orgill offers a number of retail services: a circular advertising program; assistance in product assortment planning; a floor care program; an equipment rental program; a catalog of clip strip, dump bin, and bucket displays of impulse sales items; a retail price sticker and bin label maintenance program; pricing assistance; and e-commerce solutions.

COMPANY FOUNDED: 1847

The roots of Orgill date back to April 1847 and the founding of the R.T. Lamb & Co. hardware store in Memphis. One of the principals of the business was William Orgill. Born in England, he had come to the United States to join his brother Joseph Orgill, who had immigrated in 1830 to establish a business importing hardware, tools, cutlery, and guns, primarily from manufacturers in Birmingham and Sheffield, England. William became a salesman for his brother and traveled throughout the Mid-Atlantic region, peddling his wares while waiting for an opportunity to strike out on his own. In 1846 he discovered a Petersburg, Virginia, hardware store that was liquidating its inventory, purchased it all, and relocated it to the boomtown of Memphis, Tennessee, which had emerged as one of the gateway cities to the West, where settlers arrived by steamboat and were outfitted for their journey. In addition to the goods of the Petersburg store, Orgill also brought a partner, the R. T. Lamb whose name graced the business. It was Lamb who ran the business. Orgill never actually lived in Memphis, although he paid regular visits. Other partners, in particular Henry Lownes, would succeed Lamb over the next few years, as demonstrated by a series of name changes that kept the local sign painter busy: Lownes & Co.; Holyoake, Lownes & Co.; and Lownes, Beekman & Co. It was not until 1854 that the Orgill name was included, the store now called Lownes, Orgill & Co. Upon Lownes's death, the enterprise took the name Orgill Brothers & Co., which it would keep for well over a century.

No matter what the name, the Memphis hardware venture prospered. It moved to a three-story building in 1850 at the corner of Front and Monroe streets in Memphis, the company's home for the next seven decades. A retail business operated out of Monroe side of the business, while the wholesale business was conducted on the Front Street side. In the rear of the building a shed was erected as an iron shop. With the construction of the railroads in the 1850s, Lownes, Orgill supplied the building operations in the area. The business also made its early mark in the sale of guns, and in 1856 published its first catalog, offering all manner of hardware and farm implements.

ORGILL BROTHERS
INCORPORATED: 1898

The Orgill Brothers name was taken after another Orgill brother, Edmund Orgill, moved his family to Memphis to become involved in the business. His sons Frederick, William, and Joseph would also join him, and in 1898 Orgill Brothers was incorporated. Edmund Orgill served as president, while Frederick became vice-president and Joseph was appointed secretary-treasurer. In 1905 Frederick replaced his father as president. Other changes also took place during the early 1900s. The business began carrying plumbing and electrical supplies, and in 1908 the retail business was spun off as DeSoto Hardware, leaving Orgill Brothers to concentrate on the wholesale distribution operation.

Orgill enjoyed steady expansion over the years. In 1922, having outgrown its space, the company relocated to new offices and warehouses in Memphis. A year later

it extended its reach by opening a branch in Jackson, Mississippi. In addition, the company looked to broaden its product mix by adding automotive parts in 1925. Although very much a family-owned-and-operated regional company, Orgill Brothers developed a reputation for being one of the more progressive distributors in its field. In 1952, for example, Orgill became one of the first wholesalers to install data processing equipment to keep track of inventory. In the mid-1950s it was in the vanguard of wholesalers to drop multistory warehouses for more efficient, larger footprint one-story distribution centers.

FIRST NON-FAMILY MEMBER
HEADS COMPANY: 1981

In the 1960s and 1970s Orgill continued to add volume and remained profitable, but it experienced an erosion in market share. The company attempted to rectify this condition through acquisition, sometimes absorbing less healthy rivals. In 1968 the fifth generation of the Orgill family took the helm when Joseph Orgill III became president. He ran the company for about a decade, at which point Orgill Brothers reached a turning point in its history. It was still very much a regional company, but to continue to prosper it would have to spread nationally. The Orgill family also decided that the time had come to bring in professional management to help run the company. Joseph Orgill III told *Do-It-Yourself Retailing,* "We didn't just want to depend on family members' interests or capabilities to run the company." In 1980 he became chairman of the board and William Fondren Jr. was brought in as general manager of the hardware division. A graduate of the Massachusetts Institute of Technology, he was a former IBM employee. A year later Fondren succeeded Joseph Orgill III as president and chief executive officer.

Not only did Fondren recruit a management team, he undertook market research to determine the perception of Orgill Brothers in the marketplace and help develop a plan for ongoing growth. Research conducted with retailers across the company's territories revealed three salient points. First, Orgill Brothers was regarded as a high-cost, high-priced distributor. Second, it was not the primary supplier for most of its customers. Rather, it was a second and sometimes third source. Finally, the research indicated that Orgill was losing market share to member-owner distributors. The report offered some rays of hope as well, however. Customers appreciated the company's wide variety of merchandise and valued the sales force, which many believed was a significant factor in the high prices.

Orgill took stock of itself to define a specific role in the marketplace. Serving as a secondary source providing

KEY DATES

1847: Company is founded as R.T. Lamb & Co.
1854: Business is renamed Lownes, Orgill & Co.
1898: Company incorporates as Orgill Brothers & Co.
1908: Retail hardware operation is spun off.
1952: Company installs data processing equipment.
1981: William Fondren Jr. becomes first non-Orgill family member to serve as president and CEO.
1985: Services are unbundled.
1998: Frederick Trading Co. is acquired.
2000: West Virginia distribution center opens.
2005: Hurricane, Utah, distribution center opens.
2006: Revenues exceed $1 billion for first time.

a minimum of service was not an appealing role for the company, which now tried to determine what was the suitable niche for Orgill in the contemporary scene. Further investigation revealed that a main reason for its high prices was the amount of services the company offered. While not every customer made use of these services, all paid the same price, resulting in a cost structure imbalance. The company decided to unbundle these services, so that customers paid for only what they wanted. In essence, customers could now select from a menu of services on an à la carte basis. Other than this rearrangement, all Orgill lacked to pursue its chosen role as a primary supplier was a store identification program. To fill this need, in 1983 the company became part of the Liberty Distributors' Trustworthy store franchise program.

MOVE INTO TEXAS MARKET: 1982

Service unbundling began in 1985, but already the company had expanded geographically through acquisitions. Memphis competitor Stratton-Warren Hardware Co. was acquired in 1980. The addition of Louisville Tin & Stove in 1981 brought markets to the north, as did the 1985 purchase of Ohio Valley, an Evansville, Indiana, distributor. Orgill also added a Dallas hub and moved into the Texas market in 1982 with the acquisition of Dallas-based Huey-Phillips Hardware.

The unbundled services were offered to customers at cost and included a space allocation program, in-store retail training, customized retail pricing, and in-store computer services. Moreover, salespeople were unbundled. If customers wanted to retain the service

provided by a salesperson, they had to pay a surcharge. The vast majority, about 97 percent as it turned out, opted to pay the surcharge. Orgill could now offer lower prices, provided the customer agreed to a prescribed amount of business each year. This arrangement was formalized in 1987 as the Value Plus program. In the warehouse, in the meantime, new materials-handling technology was installed, including a conveyor system added to the Memphis warehouse in 1984. The old mainframe computer card system was also scrapped for a contemporary data processing system. The efficiencies gained through these upgrades also helped to lower overhead and keep down prices, making Orgill at the very least competitive and in some cases the price leader.

Growth continued in the 1990s. Expanded service to Mississippi and Louisiana was achieved in 1990 through the inventory purchase of Feltus Brothers Hardware in Natchez, Mississippi. In late 1992 Orgill purchased some of the assets and inventory and hired some of the people of Odell Hardware's St. Petersburg, Florida, distribution center. Not only did the deal add to Orgill's Florida business but it also provided penetration into Latin America. A year later a similar transaction was completed with Columbia, South Carolina-based Palmetto Hardware's hardware deal division, a move that filled in gaps in South Carolina coverage and gave Orgill a presence in North Carolina and parts of Georgia. To better serve these markets, in 1995 Orgill broke ground on a $30 million, 334,000-square-foot distribution center, which opened in April 1996. The company also marked the occasion by announcing a name change: Orgill Brothers became Orgill, Inc. In 1998, Orgill gained a presence in the Mid-Atlantic region by acquiring Maryland-based Frederick Trading Co., which would also begin serving customers in the Northeast.

In the late 1990s Orgill once again demonstrated its progressive spirit by embracing the Internet and e-commerce ahead of the competition, becoming the first to offer a wide variety of products online as well as small-order fulfillment. The company already had in place a sophisticated warehouse operation that was capable of picking large and small orders. Moreover, Orgill was located in Memphis, the home of Federal Express, proximity that allowed it to ship any order within 24 hours. All the company really needed to add to its operation to become an e-commerce player was the acquisition of a facility close to its main Memphis warehouse that could take care of small-order fulfillment and serve as the hub for the new QuikShip program.

Orgill built on its momentum as it entered the new century to fulfill its goal of becoming a national company with international scope. In September 2000,

Orgill opened a new 543,000-square-foot distribution center in Martinsburg, West Virginia, the company's largest facility, which took over distribution to the northeastern United States from the much smaller Maryland distribution center that could now concentrate on the Mid-Atlantic region. Orgill opened a new 75,000-square-foot headquarters building in the Memphis area in 2002, and the following year completed a major expansion of the Tifton, Georgia, facility, which was the main export facility, distributing goods to the ports in Savannah, Jacksonville, and Miami for shipment to other countries. Sales topped $650 million in 2002, but Orgill was far from satisfied. In 2005 a new distribution center, the company's fifth, was opened in Hurricane, Utah. A 520,000-square-foot facility, it was strategically located to serve the western states. As a result, Orgill now covered all 48 of the contiguous states.

FONDREN NAMED CHAIRMAN: 2005

At the start of 2005 Joseph Orgill III turned over the chairmanship to Fondren, although he remained on the board of directors. Fondren was also replaced as president and CEO by Ron Beal, a 20-year veteran of the company. There was no indication that Orgill was satisfied with its position in the marketplace, as the company continued to grow. In 2006 it acquired Omaha-based Wright & Wilhelmy Co. to add to Orgill's business in Iowa, Kansas, Nebraska, North Dakota, and South Dakota. Also in fiscal 2006, Orgill cracked the $1 billion mark in annual sales for the first time in its history. To support further growth, Orgill in 2008 announced plans to expand its distribution network by opening a new Mid-America Supercenter, more than one million square feet in size, in Sikeston, Missouri, to replace the Vandalia, Illinois, and Memphis distribution centers. It was slated for completion in 2009. The company also planned to open a new distribution center in the Pacific Northwest, which would not only help Orgill better serve that corner of the country but also Alaska and Asia.

Ed Dinger

PRINCIPAL SUBSIDIARIES

Orgill Brothers & Co; Orgill International Logistics; Orgill Sales Inc.

PRINCIPAL COMPETITORS

Ace Hardware Corporation; Do It Best Corp.; True Value Company.

FURTHER READING

Cory, Jim, "Orgill Brothers: A Progressive Survivor at Age 144," *Chilton's Hardware Age*, April 1991, p. 95.

Jensen, Christopher A., "Orgill Brothers: Continuing a Tradition of Stability," *Do-It-Yourself Retailing*, March 1991, p. 116.

Magness, Perre, "Orgill's Roots Run Deep in Memphis," *Commercial Appeal*, July 17, 2003, p. CC2.

"Moving West: Orgill Inc.'s Construction of a Western DC Will Propel the Distributor onto the National Stage," *Do-It-Yourself Retailing*, December 2003, p. 35.

"Orgill Announces Plans for Major Expansion to Its Distribution Center in Tifton, Georgia," *Do-It-Yourself Retailing*, July 2002, p. 19.

"Orgill Announces Succession Plan for Executive Management of Company," *Do-It-Yourself Retailing*, October 2004, p. 12.

"Orgill Cuts the Ribbon on New West Virginia Distribution Center," *Do-It-Yourself Retailing*, September 2000, p. 25.

"Orgill Inc. Chairman Joe Orgill Discusses Changes Within the Industry," *Do-It-Yourself Retailing*, February 2001, p. 15.

Parrott, Mark, "One Retailer at a Time: Market-Focused Approach Serves As Foundation for Growth at Orgill Inc.," *Do-It-Yourself Retailing*, February 2005, p. 34.

Panattoni Development Company, Inc.

8775 Folsom Boulevard, Suite 200
Sacramento, California 95826
U.S.A.
Telephone: (916) 381-1561
Fax: (916) 381-7639
Web site: http://www.panattoni.com

Private Company
Incorporated: 1986
Employees: 160
Sales: $1.4 billion (2007 est.)
NAICS: 236210 Industrial Building Construction;
236220 Commercial and Institutional Building
Construction; 237210 Land Subdivision

■ ■ ■

Panattoni Development Company, Inc., develops, leases, owns, and manages industrial, office, and retail properties, ranking as one of the largest, privately owned developers in the United States. Through PDC Properties, Inc., Panattoni Construction, Inc., and Panattoni Law, the company provides comprehensive services to its clientele, offering development, property management, construction, financing, and asset management assistance. Panattoni Development's client list includes more than 500 companies, including Hewlett-Packard, Litton Systems, Dick's Sporting Goods, and Best Buy. Through main offices in the Netherlands, England, and Poland, the company offers its capabilities to European customers. Panattoni Development develops an average of 15 million square feet of space annually in North America and Europe.

ORIGINS

Carl D. Panattoni quietly and steadily built his company into one of the largest, privately owned real estate development companies in the United States, feeding the growth of his business with a constant stream of commercial and industrial projects. He founded Panattoni Development in 1986, starting from his base in the Sacramento area that served as a springboard for his march across the country. He moved into roughly 150 markets, taking on projects that ranged from as small as 2,500 square feet to upwards of one million square feet, refining skills within his expanding operation that gave him the confidence to make the bold leap overseas before his company celebrated its 20th anniversary.

One of the defining characteristics of Panattoni's approach as a developer was his penchant for collaborating with rivals. He favored forming joint ventures with other developers, a strategy that was on display only a few short years after Panattoni formed his company. In 1989, for instance, Panattoni Development forged an alliance with developer John Banchero, New York-based River Bank American, and Sacramento-based Crocker Development Co. to develop a $100 million industrial park in Sacramento County. The 220-acre project contained 3.5 million square feet of space, testifying to

COMPANY PERSPECTIVES

The goal of Panattoni Development Company is to strengthen our position as a leader within the commercial real estate development industry. This is accomplished with the dedication of each team member to perform beyond expectations within all aspects of project development. As a company, Panattoni emphasizes teamwork, local market knowledge, productivity and most importantly personal integrity. By applying these principles on each transaction, we achieve the ultimate goal of client satisfaction.

Panattoni Development's already considerable capabilities.

The project also reflected another signature trait of Panattoni's approach, his willingness to commit to speculation building. Many of Panattoni Development's projects were built before tenants agreed to occupy the space, projects undertaken in areas expected to experience vibrant growth. Such was the case with the warehouse project in Sacramento, which included a 330,000-square-foot warehouse that was the largest single building ever built locally on a speculation basis. "It's daring," an industrial broker commented in the March 5, 1990 edition of the *Business Journal Serving Greater Sacramento,* "but that's been Panattoni's history." Panattoni Development was confident it had selected what would become a prime real estate asset. "We've got a huge population base developing out there without any significant industrial-space support," a company spokesperson said in the January 1, 1990 edition of the *Business Journal.*

CROSS-COUNTRY EXPANSION

Panattoni Development did not remain confined to northern California for long. Before the end of the 1990s, the company had asserted itself fully as a developer of national scope, developing more than ten million square feet of industrial space annually during the latter half of the decade. During its first dozen years in business, Panattoni Development built $2 billion worth of commercial properties in more than 45 cities. In 1998, the company was working on a variety of projects that showed the extent of its geographic expansion. Panattoni Development was building a $5.5 million, 200,000-square-foot facility in Cartersville, Florida, for Anchor Glass Container Corp. It also was building a $16 million, 520,000-square-foot building in

Union County, South Carolina, for Disney Direct Marketing Services.

In 1998, Panattoni linked forces with another formidable developer, Ross Perot Jr., son of H. Ross Perot, the Texas billionaire who made a bid for the U.S. presidency twice in the 1990s. Ross Perot Jr. owned Hillwood Development Corp., a Dallas, Texas-based property development company that had developed 23,000 acres of land during the previous decade. Panattoni Development and Hillwood Development formed a joint venture to build industrial projects in northern Texas. Before the end of 1998, Panattoni-Hillwood Development Co. acquired its first land, an 89-acre tract in Lewisville, Texas, with the construction of three warehouses scheduled to begin at the start of 1999. "Soon we'll be able to show customers the type of quality, cost-effective buildings that this venture can produce," the head of the joint-venture company, Tal Hicks, said in a December 16, 1998 interview with *Knight-Ridder/Tribune Business News.*

PANATTONI DEVELOPMENT ENTERS THE PACIFIC NORTHWEST IN 1999

The partnership between Panattoni and Perot eventually developed nearly five million square feet of space in the Greater Dallas region before both parties amicably ended their alliance in November 2000. The dissolution of the joint venture had little impact on the growing business enjoyed by Panattoni Development, however. New territory was being explored during the period, including the company's first foray into the Pacific Northwest. In late 1999, Panattoni Development entered the Oregon market, purchasing the Fujitsu Computer Products of America headquarters site in Hillsboro, a property that contained 325,000 square feet of existing buildings on a 137-acre tract. The purchase led the company to open its first office in the region in early 2000, an office in Portland.

After completing its first full decade of business, Panattoni Development stood as a towering force. The company typically had $500 million worth of properties in its ownership and management portfolios at any given time. Annually, it developed close to 15 million square feet of space, building facilities for clients such as Procter & Gamble Co., Bristol-Myers Squibb, General Motors Corp., and Rite Aid Corp. The search for ideal land and properties had led the company into 25 states, giving it a presence in scores of markets, but Panattoni demonstrated a drive to expand further.

KEY DATES

1986: Carl D. Panattoni forms his own real estate development company.

1998: After 12 years in business, Panattoni Development builds $2 billion worth of commercial properties in 45 cities.

2000: A joint venture company formed with Hillwood Development Co. two years earlier is dissolved.

2001: Panattoni Development enters the Chicago market for the first time.

2005: The company begins establishing a presence in Europe.

2006: The first deal in Europe is completed, the construction of a warehouse in Poland.

2008: Panattoni begins developing Aviator Business Park, a $200 million project in Hazelwood, Missouri.

PANATTONI DEVELOPMENT ENTERS THE CHICAGO MARKET IN 2001

Panattoni and his senior executives continued to find promising prospects in new markets, such as the company's first step into Chicago in mid-2001. In July, Panattoni Development joined forces with Prudential Real Estate Investors to acquire four suburban Chicago business parks for $239 million. Under the terms of the agreement between the two parties, Panattoni Development purchased 278 acres of land, with options for an additional 250 acres, the largest land transaction in the history of the company. "It's our first time in Chicago, and the thing is, we're there instantly," a Panattoni Development senior partner said in a July 6, 2001 interview with the *Sacramento Bee.* "Usually you go into a new market and it takes a year or two to get started … we'll have two offices, and we're going to be building in August." With the land purchased in the deal, Panattoni Development possessed enough space to build 4.5 million square feet of commercial buildings.

As Panattoni Development neared its 20th anniversary, the company offered its customers comprehensive services that addressed all aspects of their needs. Through PDC Properties, Inc., the company offered property management services, helping clients ensure a stable and prosperous relationship with their tenants. Panattoni Construction, Inc., represented the heart of the organization, using 20 offices in the United States and Canada to provide design and build services for customers requiring the development of office, manufacturing, distribution, and retail space. Panattoni Law, the third arm of the organization, provided legal services related to property management and development.

A MOVE OVERSEAS IN 2005

On the eve of its 20th anniversary, Panattoni Development made the boldest move in its history. In early 2005, the company set it sights overseas, announcing a decision to enter the European market. The first deal was set to be completed in the United Kingdom, where Panattoni Development said it would fund the acquisition of a 9.6-acre site in Surrey by industrial developer Equity Estates. The company established an office in London that was intended to serve as a springboard into other European countries, but the development deal with Equity Estates was canceled by mid-2005. After Panattoni Development pulled out of the deal for undisclosed reasons, it put expansion in the United Kingdom on hold, opting instead to make a foray into Europe by establishing partnerships in Poland, France, and the Czech Republic.

Panattoni Development's official debut in the European property development market appeared to be set to occur in the Czech Republic, but, as in the United Kingdom, the deal never materialized. The company was narrowly beaten by a Dutch competitor to develop a 450,000-square-foot industrial warehouse near Prague for tire manufacturer Bridgestone Corporation. After failing to secure a foothold twice, the company succeeded in signing its first European deal in 2006, taking its first steps in Poland. Panattoni Development reached an agreement to build a 540,000-square-foot warehouse for a retail chain named H&M in Poznań, Poland. After its initial success in Poland, the company firmly established itself throughout Europe, taking on projects in France, Italy, the Czech Republic, and Spain that saw it develop more than three million square feet of warehouse space during the next two years.

With projects underway in North America and Europe, Panattoni Development's business grew. As it moved past its 20th anniversary, the company was developing 15 million square feet of space each year, fueling steady financial growth.

In 2007, the company completed numerous projects that contributed to its annual development total. In February, the company launched a 525,000-square-foot, speculative warehouse project in Memphis, Tennessee, on property at its Memphis Oaks complex, a 325-acre distribution park. At roughly the same time,

Panattoni Development announced its intention to buy and to develop a 105-acre property in Wawayanda, New York, where it intended to construct two warehouses totaling 770,000 square feet. Midway through the year, Panattoni Development received approval from the Tampa City Council on a zoning change that cleared the way for the construction of a 350,000-square-foot store for furniture retailer IKEA.

DEVELOPMENT OF AVIATOR BUSINESS PARK BEGINS IN 2008

Panattoni Development began 2008 by forming a partnership with ING Clarion Partners LLC. Together, the two companies purchased 61 acres of a 102-acre site in Anaheim, California, owned by Boeing Co. Plans called for the two partners to invest more than $350 million in the property to redevelop its existing 14 buildings into a mixed-use business park with office, industrial, and retail facilities. ING and Panattoni Development also began working together on an office and industrial park near Dallas in 2008, building three buildings with 280,000 square feet of space. The year also saw the beginning of a massive, speculative project in Hazelwood, Missouri. In June, Panattoni Development acquired a 155-acre site occupied by a shuttered assembly plant owned by Ford Motor Co. The project, expected to take five years to complete, involved demolishing an existing 3.5-million-square-foot building and developing new structures, beginning with a 100,000-square-foot warehouse. The warehouse was slated to be the first of 11 buildings to be constructed on a speculative basis for what was to become the $200 million Aviator Business Park.

For nearly a quarter-century, Panattoni Development maintained an impressive pace of expansion, reaching into new markets consistently without suffering the consequences of misguided growth. Each year of disciplined growth added to the company's strength, ensuring the years ahead would see the Panattoni Development name behind a bevy of industrial, office,

and retail development projects in North America and Europe.

Jeffrey L. Covell

PRINCIPAL SUBSIDIARIES

Panattoni Construction, Inc.; PDC Properties, Inc.; Panattoni Law.

PRINCIPAL COMPETITORS

Opus Corporation; Prologis; Industrial Developments International, Inc.

FURTHER READING

Brenneman, Kristina, "California Firm Stakes a Local Claim," *Business Journal-Portland,* February 23, 2001, p. 1.

Brown, Steve, "Perot Firm Buys Lewisville, Texas, Land for Industrial Project," *Knight-Ridder/Tribune Business News,* December 16, 1998.

Levensohn, Michael, "Developer to Construct Large Building in Wawayanda, N.Y., Area," *Times Herald-Record,* February 12, 2007.

Maki, Amos, "Developer Builds 525,000-Square-Foot Warehouse in Southeast Memphis, Tenn.," *Commercial Appeal,* February 16, 2007.

McCarthy, Mike, "Panattoni Builds Industrial Park," *Business Journal Serving Greater Sacramento,* January 1, 1990, p. 1.

———, "Panattoni on Warehouse Roll," *Business Journal Serving Greater Sacramento,* March 5, 1990, p. 2.

"Panattoni Crossed the Pond," *Property Week,* February 25, 2005, p. S6.

"Panattoni Picks Poland," *Estates Gazette,* April 8, 2006, p. 32.

Perez, Christine, "Panattoni-Hillwood Shakeout," *Dallas Business Journal,* December 1, 2000, p. 3.

Thomas, Daniel, "US Developer Readies European Campaign," *Property Week,* August 12, 2005, p. 10.

Trivedi-St. Clair, Riddhi, "Demolition Begins at Former Ford Plant in Hazelwood," *St. Louis Post-Dispatch,* August 7, 2008.

———, "Developer Closes on Purchase of Ford Plant," *St. Louis Post-Dispatch,* June 6, 2008.

"US Industrial Giant Arrives," *Estates Gazette,* February 26, 2005, p. 26.

Walter, Bob, "Sacramento, Calif.-based Developer Panattoni to Expand into Chicago," *Sacramento Bee,* July 6, 2001.

Parker-Hannifin
Corporation

———■———

6035 Parkland Boulevard
Cleveland, Ohio 44124-4141
U.S.A.
Telephone: (216) 896-3000
Fax: (216) 383-9414
Web site: http://www.parker.com

Public Company
Incorporated: 1918 as Parker Appliance Company
Employees: 60,000
Sales: $12.1 billion (2008)
Stock Exchanges: New York
Ticker Symbol: PH
NAICS: 332911 Industrial Valve Manufacturing

■ ■ ■

Motion control through the use of air, liquid, and gas is the principal concern of Parker-Hannifin Corporation, the industry's global leader. The company manufactures motion and control technologies for a wide range of applications within the aerospace, commercial, industrial, and mobile markets.

BEGINNINGS IN BRAKES

Parker-Hannifin started as an automobile brake company. Thought of at first as a rich man's domain, private transportation was within the reach of the middle class well before 1911, when Henry Ford sold 78,000 Tin Lizzies. By 1918, the first year of Parker Appliance Company's existence, there were more than one million cars a year coming out of factories in Detroit, Michigan; Cleveland, Ohio; and other centers.

Engineer-inventor Art Parker entered this profitable field modestly, with a pneumatic brake booster designed to make stopping easier for trucks and buses. This initial effort was doomed; the company's first promotional tour came to an abrupt end when an ice patch on a Pennsylvania hill sent Parker's only truck careening over a cliff. This catastrophe sank his bank balance but did not douse his dream of heading a motion control manufacturing business.

In 1924 he tried again, offering new flared-tube fitting components to expand his one-product line. Useful for many purposes, these attracted a wide variety of industrial manufacturers. The successful new start encouraged Parker to broaden his horizons. Noting opportunities in the fledgling aviation industry, he made lifelong customers of such pioneers as Donald Douglas of Douglas Aircraft Company and Robert Gross of Lockheed, who soon learned to rely on him as much for his knowledge of hydraulics as for dependable parts. Parker accepted their challenges willingly, helping them to design a hydraulic successor for the heavy gear-and-chain-driven parts then being used to move all airplane control surfaces. This cooperation was so valuable that neither Parker nor the flight industry suffered during the Great Depression. Instead, all parties flourished, aided by the growing military importance and commercial potential of their products.

Like the aviation section, the automotive division of the Parker Appliance Company grew during the Depression years. Although there was a drop of almost 500,000 in privately owned vehicles between 1930 and 1935, this decline did not affect Parker's profits. Travelers without their own cars simply used buses, which always needed parts for maintenance and repair.

By this time indispensable to two transport industries, the company achieved $2 million in sales in 1934. Other businesses were not so lucky: although almost four million cars rolled off assembly lines in 1935, many smaller factories had to close their doors. A victim of the Depression, the bankrupt Hupp Motor Car Corporation sold its Cleveland building to Parker.

WORLD WAR II ERA

By 1938 the company was ready to look for international markets for its aircraft components. Technologically advanced in both the automotive and the aviation fields, Germany seemed to be a good prospect. Parker and his wife, Helen, changed their minds after a three-month tour of German aircraft factories, because the activity they saw there convinced them that Adolf Hitler was arming for war.

Once back in Cleveland, Art Parker took immediate action. First, he licensed several patents for military aircraft parts that would broaden his previously patented product lines. His next step was to concentrate his energies on the aircraft market, shifting his focus from the automotive side of the business. Then, he placed an order for lathes, the largest that his manufacturer had ever filled.

Equipping his business for the demands of war took huge amounts of money. No longer able to channel capital from his recently abandoned commercial and industrial base, Parker insured himself against a cash-flow shortage by selling 10,000 shares of stock. During the final days of 1938, Art Parker saw his business become a public company.

By the time President Franklin Roosevelt declared war on Japan and its allies in December 1941, patents held by the Parker Appliance Company were setting standards for such components of military aircraft as hydraulic tube couplings, fuel system valves, and pumps. Two years later there were 5,000 employees, working three shifts seven days a week to produce these parts.

Though urgent at the time, this focus on purely military equipment to the exclusion of other business proved costly after the war. However, Art Parker, who died eight months before hostilities ended, was spared the sight of idle factory floors and the employment roll that had shrunk to 200 people as soon as the company's lone customer, the U.S. government, turned its attention back to peacetime pursuits. Although the prospect of bankruptcy now faced Helen Parker, she chose to keep the business running and to recruit new management.

With the help of the company's banker, Charles Sigmier, S. Blackwell Taylor was persuaded to assume the presidency of Parker and to bring his business associate, Robert Cornell, with him. The two men set to work immediately, selling surplus inventory and machinery before they did anything else.

Setting long-term goals to provide direction was their second task. The strategic operations plan they formulated, quickly dubbed the Corporate Creed, emphatically stated that the company was not for sale. It also stressed that management would begin to strive to reduce the percentage of government business, while still increasing sales to government customers, a wise precaution that would stand the company in good stead during the Korean War. Other proposals declared that growth would henceforth take place both internally, through research and development, and externally, through friendly acquisitions. Parker, however, had to be the dominant party in all acquisitions, which would be undertaken to expand the company's product lines and keep it on the cutting edge in the field of fluid power. Targets would be profitable family-owned businesses wherever possible, and each new subsidiary would enjoy considerable autonomy. Along with these decisions came the resolve to supply only top-quality products and service.

The postwar era also brought increasing interest in automation, much of which relied on fluid power to control motion through pneumatics and hydraulics. Making every effort to meet these needs by developing the range of their products, Parker also began to experiment with synthetic rubber to be used for more effective seals. The demand for these seals soon became so universal that the company became a leader in the worldwide standards that were benefiting original-equipment industries as well as many other engineering concerns. Another innovation was the decision to emphasize the production of replacement parts for those components whose constant motion caused them to wear out.

KEY DATES

■

1918: Engineer-inventor Art Parker establishes Parker Appliance Co.

1938: Parker becomes a public company.

1957: Hannifin Corp. is acquired and the company changes its name to Parker-Hannifin Corp.

1960: An international division is formed.

1968: President Robert Cornell is succeeded by Patrick S. Parker, son of founder Art Parker.

1980: Sales surpass $1 billion for the first time.

1984: Paul Schloemer succeeds Patrick Parker as president and CEO.

1989: Parker-Hannifin sells its three automotive aftermarket components divisions.

1999: President and CEO Duane E. Collins assumes the additional role of chairman, succeeding Patrick Parker, who is named chairman emeritus.

2000: Dana Corp.'s Gresen Hydraulic arm is acquired for $112 million; Youngstown, Ohio-based Commercial Intertech Corp. is acquired for $366 million; Donald E. Washkewicz is named president and chief operating officer.

2006: President and COO Nickolas W. Vande Steeg retires, and Washkewicz assumes the additional role of president.

ACQUISITION OF HANNIFIN, 1957

In 1957, a year that showed sales totaling $28.5 million, the Parker Appliance Company acquired the Hannifin Corporation of Des Plaines, Illinois. A manufacturer of hydraulic and air-power cylinders and of presses and other essential products used in liquid, gas, or air pressure systems, Hannifin was not a small company itself. Its $7.5 million price brought Parker two Illinois plants and one in Ohio, plus an employee roll of 600. It also brought a name change, for the Parker Appliance Company became the Parker-Hannifin Corporation. In line with company policy, the former Hannifin customers now became customers of the entire corporation. Also in line with company policy, the new acquisition was assured that there would be no competition for the original equipment manufactured by clients.

In 1960 Parker-Hannifin organized an international division to market its products worldwide. Situated in Amsterdam, it was followed in June 1962 by Parker-Hannifin NMF GmbH in Cologne, West Germany, a subsidiary gained by the purchase of Niehler Maschinenfabriek, a manufacturer of hydraulic components. These two new channels brought the company a stronger market for valves, pumps, hoses, air filters, and regulators, as well as for the industrial products of its other ten semi-autonomous subsidiaries.

Also burgeoning at this time was the aircraft division, which had entered the specialized field of cryogenics. Joining the product line of tube fittings, missiles, space vehicles, and systems for the control of wing flaps and landing gear was a ball valve handling liquid oxygen for the *Saturn* space booster. Other components for both commercial and military use included hydraulic torpedo parts and ground support equipment. Important for military action, these items played a significant strategic role when the United States entered the Vietnam War in 1965. Later this division would produce another important device, a special assembly for the main flight control of the Sikorsky Black Hawk helicopter. Consisting of only five pounds of bulletproof steel, it continued to function if damaged.

Keeping ahead of the competition in these ways had taken a great deal of prior planning. Mindful of the need for ultra-modern manufacturing plants, in 1961 the company had made a heavy investment in equipment to increase capacity and improve operating efficiency. This paid off handsomely the following year, with year-end sales of more than $61 million.

This modernizing, in addition to the strategic acquisition of profitable foreign companies that continued throughout the 1960s, added a line of refrigeration components and expanded the range of other Parker-Hannifin products now being made in Canada, Italy, France, and South Africa. Like domestic plants, overseas plants manufactured standardized components that were easily replaceable. The wisdom of this practice was reflected in 1967 sales, which totaled more than $152 million.

In 1968, President Robert Cornell was succeeded by the founder's son, Patrick S. Parker. Parker had spent three years running the seals division after gaining experience in various departments in Cleveland. Parker introduced training for machine operators to ensure skilled technical labor for affiliates and subsidiaries. Next came two 1973 courses for distributors and customers. Designed to explain the increasingly complex range of Parker-Hannifin products, the first course covered basic industrial hydraulic technology; the second, advanced circuit analysis.

GROWTH DURING THE SEVENTIES AND EIGHTIES

To reduce Parker-Hannifin's vulnerability to the cyclical swings of the capital goods field, the new CEO focused on the lucrative automotive aftermarket. Reasoning that wear on cars always makes replacement parts necessary, he set his sights on the Plews Manufacturing Company, a maker of quick-disconnect couplings, acquiring this concern in 1968. A 1971 newcomer was the Ideal Corporation, which manufactured hose clamps and turn indicators. Following shortly afterward were Roberk Company, which made windshield wipers and rearview mirrors, and in 1978, EIS Automotive Corporation, manufacturers of hydraulic replacement parts for drum- and disc-brake systems.

The automotive section was not the only business segment receiving company attention at this time. The aerospace division, although offering a profit potential of 14 percent—compared to 12 percent apiece from the other two units—was not growing fast enough. In 1978 Parker-Hannifin remedied this situation by broadening both its customer base and its product line. Parker-Hannifin acquired two new subsidiaries: Vansickle Industries, a maker of replacement wheels and brakes for lightweight private aircraft, and Bertea Corporation, providing electro-hydraulic flight controls for commercial airliners. Both companies had previously been leaders in their fields, with Bertea showing a 12-month backlog of orders, as well as a $19 million contract on primary flight-control actuators for new Boeing 767 airliners.

Internal efforts were also needed to pull the company successfully through business cycle troughs. A recession in 1971, causing profits to tumble, prompted a new strategic plan called cycle forecasting. The brainchild of Tommy McCuiston, vice-president of corporate planning, the forecasting plan was based on the premise that each industry followed its own cyclical rhythm for a period normally lasting three to four years. Six phases were apparent during this time span: growth, prosperity, warning, recession, depression, and recovery. Each phase demanded planning to provide for the next. During the growth phase, the company anticipated prosperity by expanding the workforce and speeding up its training programs. In line with its acquisition philosophy, it also looked for new manufacturing sources. The prosperity phase found Parker-Hannifin executives planning for the months of warning ahead. Expansion was curbed and superfluous companies were sold at this period of peak earning power. The kingpin of the strategy was strict inventory control, allowing for heavy manufacturing activity during depression periods, before growth phase demand made production expensive because of overtime wages.

Proof of the strategy's success came with the year-end sales figures for 1980, which surpassed $1 billion for the first time. Another benefit of the planning came to the fore in the research field, allowing the company to move actively into biomedical engineering. Here, long-used principles of hydraulics were applied to the development of life-enhancing equipment such as the implantable insulin dispenser for diabetics made by the aerospace division.

In 1984, Paul Schloemer succeeded Patrick Parker as CEO and president. Adding 14 acquisitions to Parker's previous 50, Schloemer guided the corporation into the untapped areas of industrial filters and pneumatics, with the addition of Schrader Bellows in 1984; and electromagnetic motion control, with the acquisition of Compumotor in 1986.

The 1980s brought other significant changes. A weaker dollar against the Japanese yen and the West German mark lost a considerable amount of value between 1984 and 1987. This brought down the price of U.S. technology and products to a level competitive with those of Japan and Europe, making it less expensive to produce components for foreign machinery in the United States than to import them for later assembly.

The automotive market scored heavily here. Quoted in a 1987 *Fortune* article, investment strategist John Connolly noted that, between 1986 and 1987, Honda had scaled down from one-half to one-quarter the number of parts it planned to import for cars assembled in the United States. This trend, along with joint product ventures including the Mazda/Ford Probe alliance, ensured a market for automotive components that helped Parker-Hannifin achieve more than $2 billion in sales in 1988, its 70th anniversary.

Other promising trends for growth came from the aerospace division. Several air disasters and near misses brought commercial airlines and air safety associations to the conclusion that tighter maintenance procedures and more frequent replacement of aircraft were necessary. This meant a greater need for complete hydraulic systems and parts for aircraft in frequent service.

In November 1989 Parker-Hannifin sold its three automotive aftermarket components divisions to an investor group headed by the president of the Parker automotive group. The company received about $80 million in exchange for its automotive parts business, and continued to manufacture original equipment for the automotive market. Parker-Hannifin also sold its small biomedical group in January 1990. The biomedical group had 1989 sales of about $4 million. These sectors were sold to allow Parker-Hannifin to concentrate on its core motion control markets, both industrial and aerospace.

FURTHER EXPANSION DURING THE NINETIES

Nevertheless, growth by acquisition continued into the 1990s under the leadership of CEO Duane E. Collins, driving sales above the $3 billion mark by 1995. The 1996 purchase of Swedish-based VOAC Hydraulics fortified the company's product line with hydraulic systems for mobile heavy equipment. The Abex/NWL division of Pneumo Abex, also acquired in 1996, supplied aerospace hydraulic actuation gears.

Parker-Hannifin bought New Jersey-based EWAL Manufacturing, a maker of fittings and valves, in 1997. That year, the company went on to establish its Mobile Hydraulics Division. After 60 years, Parker-Hannifin moved into a new 125,000-square-foot headquarters in August 1997. It donated the old headquarters building at 17325 Euclid Avenue to the Cleveland Clinic Foundation, an institution promoting medical research.

In 1998 Parker-Hannifin provided parts for a hydraulic platform that was used to move a 180-foot model of the *Titanic* for the hit movie of the same name. The company continued to acquire a wide range of other firms during the late 1990s, including Dynamic Valves Inc., regulator and valve maker Veriflo Corp., South Korea-based Jinyoung Electric Machinery Company Ltd., Fluid Power Industries' Fluid Power Systems division, and Avantech Corp. In all, Parker-Hannifin acquired approximately 50 companies during the 1990s.

Parker-Hannifin capped off the decade with a significant leadership change, as President and CEO Duane E. Collins took on the additional role of chairman in 1999, succeeding Patrick S. Parker, who was named chairman emeritus. Collins's long career with Parker-Hannifin had begun in 1961, when he joined the company as a sales engineer.

EXPANSION AND CHALLENGES IN THE 21ST CENTURY

Following the dawn of the new millennium, another important leadership change took place in March 2000, when Donald E. Washkewicz, a 27-year company veteran, was named president and chief operating officer. Acquisitions continued at a fast pace during this time, and included two of the largest deals in Parker-Hannifin's history.

In February 2000, Dana Corp.'s Gresen Hydraulic arm, which had about 1,000 employees, was acquired for $112 million in cash. This was followed by the April acquisition of Youngstown, Ohio-based Commercial Intertech Corp., which had some 4,000 employees, for $366 million. The two deals fleshed out the company's product offerings in the mobile hydraulics market. In July, another major deal unfolded when Parker-Hannifin acquired sealing products and technology firm Wynn's International Inc. for $497 million, creating the nation's third largest industrial seals maker.

During the early 2000s, Parker-Hannifin was tapped to provide NASA with more than 3,000 valve and seal assemblies for the International Space Station. While this was good news, slack demand in other areas prompted the company to begin selling peripheral business lines in 2001. Some 50 units were slated for closure over the following two years. Washkewicz called for the elimination of about 7,650 jobs and the closure of some 100 plants.

Following deals that included the $68 million acquisition of Italian hose, fittings, and rubber compounds maker ITR SpA in 2002, Parker-Hannifin saw its net income soar 50 percent in 2003, reaching $196.3 million on $6.4 billion in sales. The following year, the company added the nation's largest air-conditioning and refrigeration components maker, Sporlan Valve Co., to its lineup. Profits soared 76 percent on sales of $7.1 billion, reaching $349 million.

In 2005 Parker-Hannifin expanded in China via the formation of Parker Tejing Hydraulics Co. Ltd., a hydraulics components and systems joint venture the company established with Tianjin Tejing Hydraulics Co. Ltd. Other deals that year included the acquisition of India-based hydraulic hose products maker Markwel Hose Products PVT Ltd., as well as refrigeration and air conditioning components manufacturer Kenmore International.

Parker-Hannifin acquired approximately eight companies in 2006, including Resistoflex Aerospace and Saint-Ouen l'Aumone, France-based Acofab SAS and Adecem SARL. Late that year, the company received a $500 million contract to supply Airbus with fuel tank systems. Parker-Hannifin ended 2006 with the retirement of President and COO Nicklaus W. Vande Steeg. Following this development, Chairman and CEO Donald Washkewicz assumed the additional role of president.

Acquisition activity continued in 2007 as Parker-Hannifin snapped up Airtek, Rectus AG, Mitos Technologies Inc., and SSD Drives India. The following year, Vansco Electronics was acquired, followed by full ownership in Parker Seal de Mexico. The company finished the 2008 fiscal year with record sales of $12.1 billion and record earnings of $949.5 million.

International growth had helped Parker-Hannifin to offset the impact of regional economies. In the fall of 2008, however, the world faced the greatest economic crisis since the Great Depression, created in part by bad mortgage-related investments. Corporations and consumers alike saw credit markets dry up and stock prices tumble. On October 10, 2008, the Dow Jones Industrial Average concluded its most devastating week in 112 years. Moving forward, the impact of the economic crisis on Parker-Hannifin remained to be seen.

Gillian Wolf
Updated, Frederick C. Ingram; Paul R. Greenland

PRINCIPAL SUBSIDIARIES

Parker Baja Servicios S.A. de C.V. (Mexico); Parker Brownsville Servicios S.A. de C.V. (Mexico); Parker Filtration and Separation BV (Netherlands); Parker Filtration B.V. (Netherlands); Parker Hannifin (Australia) Pty. Ltd.; Parker Hannifin (Espana) S.A. (Spain); Parker Hannifin (Malaysia) Sdn Bhd; Parker Hannifin (N.Z.) Limited (New Zealand); Parker Hannifin (RAC) Ltd. (U.K.); Parker Hannifin (Thailand) Co. Ltd.; Parker Hannifin (UK) Ltd.; Parker Hannifin A/S (Norway); Parker Hannifin AB (Sweden); Parker Hannifin Argentina SAIC; Parker Hannifin B.V. (Netherlands); Parker Hannifin Bermuda L.P.; Parker Hannifin Canada; Parker Hannifin Cartera Industrial S.L. (Spain); Parker Hannifin Climate & Industrial Controls, Ltd. (South Korea); Parker Hannifin Connectors Ltd. (South Korea); Parker Hannifin Corp. Chile Limitada (Chile); Parker Hannifin Customer Support Inc.; Parker Hannifin Danmark A/S (Denmark); Parker Hannifin de Mexico S.A. de C.V.; Parker Hannifin de Venezuela, S.A.; Parker Hannifin Electronic Material (Shenzhen) Co. Ltd. (China); Parker Hannifin Europe SARL (Switzerland); Parker Hannifin Finance B.V. (Netherlands); Parker Hannifin Fluid Connectors (Qingdao) Co., Ltd. (China); Parker Hannifin Fluid Power Systems & Components (Shanghai) Co., Ltd. (China); Parker Hannifin Fluid Systems Namibia (Pty) Ltd.; Parker Hannifin France SAS; Parker Hannifin G.e. s.m.b.H (Austria); Parker Hannifin GB Ltd. (U.K.); Parker Hannifin Global Capital Management S.a.r.l. (Luxembourg); Parker Hannifin GmbH & Co. KG (Germany); Parker Hannifin Holding GmbH (Germany); Parker Hannifin Holding S. de R.L. de C.V. (Mexico); Parker Hannifin Hong Kong Limited; Parker Hannifin Industria e Comercio Ltda. (Brazil); Parker Hannifin Industrial s.r.o. (Czech Republic); Parker Hannifin Japan Ltd.; Parker Hannifin LLC (Russia); Parker Hannifin Ltd. (U.K.); Parker Hannifin Luxembourg S.a. r.l.; Parker Hannifin Motion & Control (Shanghai) Co. Ltd. (China); Parker Hannifin Oy (Finland); Parker Hannifin Portugal Lda.; Parker Hannifin S.p.A. (Italy); Parker Hannifin Singapore Private Ltd.; Parker Hannifin SNC (France); Parker Hannifin sp. z.o.o. (Poland); Parker Hannifin Taiwan Ltd.; Parker Hannifin Verwaltungs GmbH (Germany); Parker Hose BV (Netherlands); Parker Iklim Kontrol Sistemleri Sanayi Ve Ticaret AS. (Turkey); Parker Industrial S de RL de CV (Mexico); Parker Intangibles LLC; Parker International Capital Management Hungary Ltd.; Parker ITR Sr1 (Italy); Parker Korea Ltd. (South Korea); Parker Lucifer SA (Switzerland); Parker Mobile Control Division Asia Co. Ltd. (South Korea); Parker Pneumatic BV (Netherlands); Parker Polyflex BV (Netherlands); Parker Sales (Ireland) Limited; Parker Servicios de Mexico S.A. de C.V.; Parker Shelf LLC; Parker Sistemas de Automatizacion S.A. de C.V. (Mexico); Parker Tejing Hydraulics (Tianjin) Co. Ltd. (China); Parker-Hannifin (Africa) Pty. Ltd. (South Africa); Parker-Hannifin India Private Ltd.; Parker-Hannifin International Corp.; Parker-Hannifin N.V./S.A. (Belgium); Parker-Hannifin s.r.o. (Czech Republic); Parker-Markwel Industries Private Limited (India).

PRINCIPAL DIVISIONS

Aftermarket AC and Refrigeration Division; Air & Fuel Division; Aircraft Wheel & Brake Division; Chelsea Products Division; Chomerics Division; Climate Systems Division; Composite Sealing Systems Division; Control Systems Division; Cylinder Division; Cylinder Division - Europe; domnick hunter Industrial Division; domnick hunter Process Division; Electromechanical Division - Europe; Electromechanical Division - North America; Electronic Systems Division; Energy Products Division; Engineered Polymer Systems Division; Engineered Seals Division; Filtration & Separation Division - Balston Filter; Filtration & Separation Division - Finite Filter; Filtration Process Air and Gas Division; Fluid Control Division; Fluid Control Division - Europe; Gas Turbine Fuel Systems Division; Gear Pump Division; Hose Products Division; Hose Products Division - Europe; Hydraulic Accumulator Division; Hydraulic Cartridge Systems Division; Hydraulic Cartridge Systems Division - Europe; Hydraulic Filter Division - Europe; Hydraulic Pump & Motor Division; Hydraulic Pump Division; Hydraulic Systems Division; Hydraulic Systems Division - Europe; Hydraulic Valve Division; Industrial Hose Products Division; Instrumentation Products Division; Instrumentation Products Division - Europe; Integrated Sealing Systems Division; Mobile Climate Systems Division; Mobile Controls Division - Europe; Mobile Cylinder Division;

Nichols Airborne Division; Nichols Portland Division; O-Ring Division; O-Ring Division - Europe; Oildyne Division; Packing Division - Europe; Pan Am Division; Parflex Division; Partek Division; Pneumatics Division; Pneumatics Division - Europe; Pneutronics Division; Polyflex Division - Europe; Porter Instrument Division; Process Advanced Filtration Division; Pump and Motor Division - Europe; Quick Coupling Division; Quick Coupling Division - Europe; Racor Division - Europe; Refrigerating Specialties Division; Seal Aftermarket Products Division; Sporlan Division; Stratoflex Products Division; TechSeal Division; Tube Fittings Division; Tube Fittings Division Europe; Vane Pump Division.

PRINCIPAL OPERATING UNITS

Aerospace; Climate & Industrial Controls; Industrial.

FURTHER READING

Byrne, Harlan S., "High Stepper," *Barron's,* February 12, 1996, p. 18.

Heney, Paul J., "Parker Names New CEO, Acquires Dana's Gresen," *Hydraulics & Pneumatics,* March 2000.

Ozanian, Michael K., "17325 Euclid Avenue," *FW,* November 8, 1994, pp. 50–53.

Parker, Patrick, *Parker-Hannifin Corporation,* New York: Newcomen Society in North America, 1980.

"Parker President and COO Retires," *Diesel Progress North American Edition,* March 2007.

Wrubel, Robert, "Sum of the Parts," *Financial World,* February 23, 1988, pp. 24–25.

Zawacki, Michael, "Eyes Wide Open: Patrick S. Parker Led Parker Hannifin Corp. by Seeking and Encouraging Innovation," *Inside Business,* October 2004.

Perma-Fix Environmental Services, Inc.

———■———

8302 Dunwoody Place, Suite 250
Atlanta, Georgia 30350
U.S.A.
Telephone: (770) 587-9898
Toll Free: (800) 365-6066
Fax: (770) 587-9937
Web site: http://www.perma-fix.com

Public Company
Incorporated: 1990
Employees: 522
Sales: $54.1 million (2007)
Stock Exchanges: NASDAQ
Ticker Symbol: PESI
NAICS: 562111 Solid Waste Collection

■ ■ ■

Perma-Fix Environmental Services, Inc., is a waste management company that specializes in handling nuclear waste. The company's nuclear waste operations are comprised of four facilities that offer treatment, processing, and disposal services. Perma-Fix of Florida, Inc., based in Gainesville, Florida, operates under a hazardous waste permit and a radioactive materials license, serving nuclear utilities, commercial generators, pharmaceutical companies, and the U.S. Department of Energy (DOE). Kingston, Tennessee-based Diversified Scientific Services, Inc., another Perma-Fix subsidiary, specializes in storing, processing, and destroying certain types of mixed waste, operating as the only commercial facility of its kind in the United States licensed to destroy liquid organic mixed waste. A third subsidiary, East Tennessee Materials & Energy Corporation, operates a mixed waste facility in Oak Ridge, Tennessee, that ranks as Perma-Fix's largest waste facility. Perma-Fix Northwest, Inc., located in Richland, Washington, operates a low-level radioactive and mixed waste facility at the DOE's Hanford site. Perma-Fix also owns an engineering and regulatory consulting business, Schreiber, Yonley & Associates, located in Ellisville, Missouri.

ORIGINS

Incorporated in December 1990, Perma-Fix came under the control of Louis F. Centofanti two months later, marking the beginning of a leadership tenure that, except for one six-month period, would endure for years. No individual exerted greater influence over the development of Perma-Fix than Centofanti did, turning a small, Gainesville, Florida-based start-up into a company with operations spread across the United States.

Perma-Fix was not the first company led by Centofanti. After earning his doctorate degree in chemistry from the University of Michigan, he began a professional career that eventually led to his appointment as a regional administrator at the DOE. Centofanti took charge of the southeastern region of the country in 1978, beginning a three-year stint that ended when he decided to start his own company. He founded PPM, Inc., a hazardous waste management company that focused on treating oils contaminated by polychlorinated biphenyl. For four years he headed the company, building it into an asset that caught the attention of US-

COMPANY PERSPECTIVES

Looking ahead, legacy nuclear waste remains one of the nation's greatest environmental hazards, one that must be addressed by law, according to legislative and court mandates agreed to by the DOE. Moreover, we have begun treating higher level mixed waste—an opportunity that we believe may far exceed our current market for the treatment of low-level nuclear wastes. We are especially excited about the new opportunities at the Hanford Site and our goal is to demonstrate our ability to treat higher activity waste at this site in the near future. Overall, we believe we are uniquely positioned to capture a meaningful portion of the multibillion dollar market for nuclear waste treatment given our advanced technologies, proven track record in treating a multitude of waste streams, and the high regulatory barriers to entry.

PCI, Inc., a much larger hazardous waste company. In 1985, USPCI acquired PPM, a transaction that involved Centofanti becoming part of the senior management of the combined company. He served as USPCI's senior vice-president, taking over the management of the treatment, reclamation, and technical groups within the company. Centofanti remained at USPCI for six years until he became Perma-Fix's president and chief executive officer in February 1991.

STOCK OFFERING IN 1992

Centofanti's first major achievement at Perma-Fix was taking the company public. He guided the company through an initial public offering (IPO) of stock in 1992, securing the capital that would fuel expansion in the coming years. When Perma-Fix made its public debut, the company generated nearly $6 million in revenue, collecting the total from treating, storing, and disposing of hazardous and nonhazardous waste and by providing consulting and engineering services.

By 1996, impressive financial growth had been achieved, increasing revenues to more than $30 million. More than 80 percent of the company's annual volume of business came from handling the waste of government, industrial, and commercial customers at Perma-Fix-owned facilities. The company owned five facilities involved in treating, storing, and disposing of waste, operating the facilities as subsidiaries. In Tulsa, Oklahoma, the company controlled Perma-Fix Treat-

ment Services, Inc. In Dayton, Ohio, the company operated Perma-Fix of Dayton, Inc. The company's facility in Memphis, Tennessee, was operated through Perma-Fix of Memphis, Inc. The company operated two facilities in its home state of Florida, conducting operations through two subsidiaries, Perma-Fix of Ft. Lauderdale, Inc., and Perma-Fix of Florida, Inc. Perma-Fix of Florida was located near the company's main offices in Gainesville.

For the remaining 20 percent of its business volume, Perma-Fix relied on its consulting and engineering services. The company owned two subsidiaries engaged in such business, Schreiber, Yonley & Associates, based in Ellisville, Missouri, and Mintech, Inc., located in Tulsa, Oklahoma. Through these two subsidiaries, Perma-Fix offered industrial and government customers a broad range of services related to environmental issues, advising on environmental management programs, landfill design, regulatory permitting, and regulatory compliance and auditing.

PROFITS IN THE LATE NINETIES

Midway through the 1990s, Centofanti ceded some of his authority, but only for a relatively brief period. In September 1995, he handed the duties of CEO to Robert W. Foster Jr., an arrangement that, for undisclosed reasons, failed to pan out. In March 1996, Foster resigned, giving Centofanti the three most powerful positions: president, chief executive officer, and chairman of the board. Under his total control, the company ended the 1990s with $46.4 million in revenue. More important than the modest increase in sales volume during the second half of the 1990s was the company's marked improvement in profitability. After racking up five years of consecutive losses during the first half of the decade, Centofanti could point to a string of four years of profits, ending with the $1.5 million the company registered in net income in 1999.

Perma-Fix continued to generate more than four-fifths of its annual revenue from its offsite handling of hazardous and nonhazardous waste at the end of the 1990s. In scope, little had changed during the company's first decade of business, but internal expansion and acquisitions had made a significant change in the size of Perma-Fix. The company's waste management services business, its financial mainstay, was focused on two areas, industrial waste and nuclear mixed and low-level radioactive waste treatment. By the end of the 1990s, there were ten operating segments providing the company's waste management services, each representing a separate facility or location. In its hometown, the company operated its most distinguishable asset, one of only a few facilities in the country to

KEY DATES

1990: Perma-Fix is incorporated.
1992: Perma-Fix completes its initial public offering of stock.
1999: Sales climb to $46.4 million.
2006: Perma-Fix's main offices are moved from Gainesville to Atlanta.
2007: Perma-Fix begins selling its industrial waste segment and acquires a nuclear waste facility in Richland, Washington.

operate under both a hazardous waste permit and nuclear materials license. The treatment, storage, and disposal facility in Gainesville, operated through Perma-Fix of Florida, Inc., specialized in treating and processing waste liquid scintillation vials (LSVs), which were generated primarily by institutional research agencies and biotechnical companies. The company's Gainesville facility processed roughly 80 percent of the LSV waste in the United States.

Perma-Fix's operations in Florida also included several other facilities. Perma-Fix of Ft. Lauderdale, Inc., operated a plant that collected hazardous wastewaters, oily wastewaters, and used oil. In Orlando, Perma-Fix operated a hazardous and nonhazardous facility under the name Chemical Conservation Corporation, which the company acquired in mid-1999. The acquisition included Valdosta, Georgia-based Chemical Conservation of Georgia, Inc.; Chem-Met Services, Inc., a large bulk processing facility in Detroit, Michigan; and Chem-Met Government Services, a manager of large long-term federal and industrial onsite field service contracts.

Aside from facilities in Florida, Michigan, and Georgia, Perma-Fix maintained a presence in two other states. Perma-Fix Dayton, Inc., operated a treatment, storage, and disposal facility in Dayton, Ohio. The facility treated hazardous and nonhazardous wastewater by ultra filtration and metals precipitation that met the requirements of its Clean Water Act pretreatment permit. The facility also processed waste industrial oils and used motor oils through high-speed centrifuges that produced fuel used by industrial burners. Perma-Fix's most distant subsidiary was Perma-Fix of New Mexico, Inc., a company that offered onsite hazardous and nonhazardous waste treatment services from its main offices in Albuquerque, New Mexico.

A NEW STRATEGY IN THE 21ST CENTURY

During Perma-Fix's second decade of business, Centofanti and his management team restructured the company and sharpened its strategic focus. At the start of the decade, Perma-Fix's business was organized into three operating segments: industrial waste management services, nuclear waste management services, and consulting engineering services. Organized as such, the company generated $90.8 million in revenue in 2005, a total Perma-Fix would be hard-pressed to equal in the coming years. Centofanti, as part of his long-term plans for Perma-Fix, decided to shed what had been the company's original business. The tactical move meant a severe decline in the company's business volume, resulting in a leaner, more narrowly focused waste management company.

In 2007, Centofanti decided to remove one of the two principal pillars supporting Perma-Fix's operations. He announced a plan to divest the company's industrial business, a business segment that contributed 40 percent of Perma-Fix's revenues the previous year. "While the industrial segment may hold untapped potential," he said in a May 28, 2007 interview with *Waste News,* "we believe the nuclear segment represents the true long-term growth driver for our business," adding, "we see the Department of Energy increasing its allocation for the treatment of low-level mixed waste at nuclear weapons facilities across the country in the coming years." By cutting $35 million from the company's annual revenue total, Centofanti was taking a considerable step backward, but he also was discontinuing assets that had proven to be a drag on Perma-Fix's financial performance. The industrial segment posted a loss of $2 million in 2006 and nearly equaled that total during the first three months of 2007, when it lost $1.7 million.

The divestiture of the industrial segment was an ongoing process as Perma-Fix neared its 20th anniversary. In 2007, the company negotiated several deals to sell parts of its industrial assets, signing letters of intent to sell with several parties, but the agreements either expired or were terminated before being completed. In 2008, some progress was achieved, beginning with the sale of Perma-Fix Maryland, Inc., in January. In March, the company sold Perma-Fix Dayton, Inc., completing the deal as arrangements to sell Perma-Fix South Georgia, Inc., neared completion. As the process of selling the company's discontinued operations moved forward, the nuclear segment took center stage, becoming the most important part of Perma-Fix's business.

ACQUISITION OF NUVOTEC USA IN 2007

In 2006, the year Perma-Fix moved its headquarters from Gainesville to Atlanta, the company expanded its nuclear segment substantially. In October, the company signed a letter of intent to acquire Nuvotec USA, Inc., and its subsidiary, Pacific EcoSolutions, Inc. (PEcoS). PEcoS was a nuclear waste management company based in Richland, Washington, adjacent to the DOE's Hanford site, a decommissioned nuclear production complex. Perma-Fix paid $11.2 million to gain control of the PEcoS facility, which was permitted to treat, store, and process low-level radioactive and mixed waste. The deal was completed in June 2007, when Perma-Fix officially secured ownership of PEcoS and renamed it Perma-Fix Northwest. "This important milestone is beneficial to Perma-Fix on many levels," Centofanti explained in a June 14, 2007 Perma-Fix press release, "as it increases our treatment capacity, expands our West Coast presence, and secures PEcoS' radioactive and hazardous waste permits and licenses. This is an important step in the development of our strategy to become a focused nuclear services company."

The acquisition of the Hanford facility added a fourth element to Perma-Fix's nuclear segment. Aside from the relatively small percentage of revenue collected by the company's consulting engineering services business, Perma-Fix would rely on the PEcoS facility and three other subsidiaries to drive its growth during its third decade of business. Perma-Fix of Florida and Diversified Scientific Services were two of only a hand-ful of facilities in the United States to operate under both a hazardous waste permit and nuclear materials license. The company's other nuclear waste subsidiary, East Tennessee Materials & Energy Corporation, also operated under both a hazardous waste permit and nuclear materials license, ranking as the largest facility within the Perma-Fix fold. To these four nuclear waste subsidiaries and the engineering consulting service subsidiary, Centofanti looked for the impetus to carry his company forward in the coming years.

Jeffrey L. Covell

PRINCIPAL SUBSIDIARIES

Perma-Fix of Florida, Inc.; Diversified Scientific Services, Inc.; East Tennessee Materials and Energy Corporation; Perma-Fix of Northwest Richland, Inc.; Schreiber, Yonley & Associates.

PRINCIPAL COMPETITORS

American Ecology Corporation; Clean Harbors, Inc.; URS Corporation.

FURTHER READING

Johnson, Jim, "Perma-Fix Eyes Sale of Industrial Waste Segment," *Waste News,* May 28, 2007, p. 6.
"Perma-Fix Aims to Treat More Waste," *Tri-City Herald,* June 20, 2007.
"Perma-Fix to Acquire Radioactive Waste Management Company, Provides Access to DOE's Hanford Site," *Energy Resources,* October 24, 2006.
"Perma-Fix to Buy Radioactive Waste Treatment Facility," *America's Intelligence Wire,* October 24, 2006.

Petro-Canada

150 Sixth Avenue S.W.
Calgary, Alberta T2P 3E3
Canada
Telephone: (403) 296-8000
Fax: (403) 296-3030
Web site: http://www.petro-canada.ca

Public Company
Incorporated: 1975
Employees: 5,603
Sales: CAD 21.25 billion ($21.51 billion) (2007)
Stock Exchanges: Toronto New York
Ticker Symbols: PCA (Toronto); PCZ (New York)
NAICS: 211111 Crude Petroleum and Natural Gas Extraction; 211112 Natural Gas Liquids Extraction; 324110 Petroleum Refineries; 324191 Petroleum Lubricating Oil and Grease Manufacturing; 324199 All Other Petroleum and Coal Products Manufacturing; 325110 Petrochemical Manufacturing; 424710 Petroleum Bulk Stations and Terminals; 424720 Petroleum and Petroleum Products Merchant Wholesalers (Except Bulk Stations and Terminals); 447110 Gasoline Stations with Convenience Stores; 447190 Other Gasoline Stations; 454311 Heating Oil Dealers; 454312 Liquefied Petroleum Gas (Bottled Gas) Dealers; 454312 Other Fuel Dealers; 486110 Pipeline Transmission of Crude Oil; 486210 Pipeline Transportation of Natural Gas; 486910 Pipeline Transportation of Refined Petroleum Products

∎ ∎ ∎

Petro-Canada, commonly called Petrocan, is one of Canada's largest integrated oil and gas companies. On the upstream side, Petrocan produces on average more than 418,000 barrels of oil equivalent per day. In addition to exploring and producing natural gas, crude oil, and natural gas liquids in western Canada and the U.S. Rockies, the company has significant minority stakes in three major offshore oil projects in the North Atlantic off Canada's east coast: Terra Nova (which the firm also operates), Hibernia, and White Rose. Petro-Canada is also involved in several Albertan oil-sands projects involving the extraction or mining of heavy oil (or bitumen), which can be converted to crude oil or used for other purposes. International exploration and production activities are conducted in the North Sea, Libya, Syria, and Trinidad and Tobago.

Petrocan's downstream assets rank number two in Canada, behind Imperial Oil Limited. Its two refineries in Edmonton and Montreal have the capacity to process 255,000 barrels of crude oil per day, which accounts for roughly 13 percent of the total refinery capacity in Canada. These refineries produce a wide variety of petroleum products that are marketed at more than 1,300 Petro-Canada service stations across Canada and also distributed through 229 truck-stop facilities and via a bulk fuel sales channel. The company sells about 16 percent of the total petroleum products sold in Canada. Petrocan also holds a 51 percent stake in the ParaChem petrochemicals plant located adjacent to its Montreal refinery.

For much of its history, Petro-Canada's most distinguishing aspect was its operation as a Crown corporation substantially owned by the government of

COMPANY PERSPECTIVES

The Company believes its structure and scope strategically position Petro-Canada to deliver long-term shareholder value. With a base in Canada, Petro-Canada is situated in a stable, resource-rich and demand-driven market. An ever-increasing international presence and integration across businesses provide the Company access to more value-adding growth opportunities and an ability to better manage risk through having a diversified portfolio. As a mid-sized global company, even smaller sized investments can have a material impact. The Company remains committed to developing energy resources responsibly and providing growth opportunities for employees.

Canada. As such, the government owned any property held by the firm, and common shares in the company were held in the name of the Minister of Energy, Mines, and Resources. After 16 years under this ownership structure, the company's equity was transferred to the Minister of Privatization, who made an initial public offering of 15 percent of its equity in July 1991. Subsequent offerings reduced the government's holdings to about 70 percent of total equity by the fall of 1994. Then in September 1995 the government sold a further 50 percent of the company's common stock, reducing its stake to just 20 percent. The government sold the remainder of its shares in 2004.

CREATION AS CROWN CORPORATION IN 1975

Created by an act of parliament in 1975, Petro-Canada was a product of the oil crisis that shook the world in 1973 and 1974, driving oil prices up and creating havoc with the energy supply. When the Organization of Petroleum Exporting Countries (OPEC) substantially increased oil prices, Canada became aware of the vulnerability of its foreign oil supplies. The energy crisis focused the country's attention on the extent to which foreign countries dominated domestic oil production. Coincidental with the OPEC price increases, a sharp downward revision of Canada's oil reserves created substantial fears about whether supplies of domestic crude oil would be adequate for future needs. Petro-Canada was originally established as an effort to provide more Canadian control over the domestic oil industry, to ensure that the nation would receive its fair share of

remote and difficult-to-reach energy resources, and to provide the federal government with a listening post on the country's oil industry.

Maurice Strong, who earlier had helped establish Dome Petroleum Limited, served as Petro-Canada's first chairman. It was Wilbert Hopper, more than any other individual, however, who made Petro-Canada a success story. Ottawa-born Hopper, with degrees in geology and business administration, started in the oil business as a geologist for Imperial Oil Ltd. in the 1950s. In the early 1960s, he was senior economist for the Canadian National Energy Board, before joining the Cambridge, Massachusetts-based international consulting firm of Arthur D. Little, Inc. With a solid reputation in the oil industry, Hopper caught the attention of Canadian Prime Minister Pierre Elliott Trudeau, who sought Hopper's advice in forming a state-owned oil company. Thus began Petro-Canada. Hopper started his association with the company as a vice-president in 1976. Six months later, he was named president and chief executive officer. In 1979 he became chairman as well as CEO.

The initial holdings of Petrocan included properties previously owned by the government of Canada, which were conveyed to the company after its formation: a 12 percent interest in the Syncrude oil-sands mining project in northern Alberta; a 45 percent interest in Panarctic Oils; and a stake in the Polar Gas project, which was set up to operate a gas pipeline from the Arctic. With access to large amounts of money, Petro-Canada bought several Canadian-based oil companies that significantly increased its land holdings and oil and gas reserves and quickly made it a giant in the oil industry.

The company's first purchase, Atlantic Richfield Canada, was made in 1976 for CAD 342 million. Assets acquired from Atlantic Richfield included both producing and undeveloped oil and gas properties in western Canada, natural-gas-processing facilities, undeveloped oil and gas properties in the Arctic, and an additional interest in oil-sands leases. The cash flow from the producing assets funded exploration and development of new sources. Three years later, in 1979, Petro-Canada borrowed $1.25 billion from Canadian banks to finance the purchase of Pacific Petroleums Limited, which tripled the company's oil production and quintupled its gas production. Pacific Petroleums' assets also added coal leases in western Canada, oil properties outside of Canada, and distribution and sales facilities, including 400 retail outlets. In the meantime, the Syncrude consortium began mining-based production of the Athabasca oil sands in 1978.

Among Petro-Canada's mandates set forth by the federal government was that of special emphasis on exploration in remote frontier regions. In 1977 the

KEY DATES

1975: Petro-Canada (known as Petrocan) is created as a Crown corporation by an act of the Canadian parliament, inheriting the government's interests in the Syncrude and Panarctic Oils projects.

1976: Company increases its presence in western Canada via purchase of Atlantic Richfield Canada.

1979: Petrocan triples its oil production and quintuples its gas production through acquisition of Pacific Petroleums Limited.

1981: Acquisition of Petrofina Canada, Inc., provides Petro-Canada with a significant presence in Canadian refining and marketing.

1983: Petrocan buys the refining and marketing assets of BP Canada.

1985: Company purchases Gulf Canada Limited's refining, distribution, and marketing assets in Ontario and western Canada.

1991: Petro-Canada is partially privatized as the government sells about 19 percent of the company's shares in an initial public offering; major restructuring is launched.

1995: Canadian government sells 50 percent of the company's shares through an offering, reducing its stake to 20 percent.

1996: Amerada Hess Canada Limited is acquired, augmenting western Canadian upstream operations.

2002: Production begins at both the Terra Nova offshore field and the MacKay River oil-sands project; most of the international upstream oil and gas operations of Veba Oil & Gas GmbH are acquired.

2004: Canadian government sells its remaining 19 percent interest in Petrocan.

2005: Petro-Canada acquires majority control of the massive Fort Hills oil-sands mining project, which is still under development.

company made its first discoveries of oil and natural gas pools in the Brazeau River area, southwest of Edmonton, and in the late 1970s it participated in several oil discoveries in the Utikuma Lake area, northwest of Edmonton. Starting in 1979, Petrocan conducted an international exploration program that included activi-

ties in Colombia, Ecuador, Indonesia, Papua New Guinea, and offshore China.

Petro-Canada's development was controversial from the beginning. Members of the country's private oil industry charged that the state-owned corporation received preferential treatment and had a significant political and financial advantage over its private-sector competitors. Petro-Canada's easy access to government funding, which enabled it to expand through acquisition of competitors into one of the industry's top three players within barely a decade, was particularly irksome to the Canadian oil establishment. The counterargument was that Petro-Canada was required to undertake high-risk projects in the public interest, such as investment in frontier exploration, that could be done only with the infusion of government funds.

After briefly losing power in the late 1970s, the Liberal government forged ahead with its agenda, introducing federal legislation under the National Energy Program (NEP) that gave Petrocan 25 percent rights on all federal land, including potentially rich frontier acreage. Those rights were described by the Canadian Petroleum Association as retroactive confiscation of assets. The NEP also gave Petro-Canada more power over the nation's energy resources, including acquiescence to the company's continuing takeover of competitors.

1981 EXPANSION INTO REFINING AND MARKETING

One of Petro-Canada's few unquestionable successes was its major role in increasing domestic ownership of integrated oil companies from 26 percent of industry revenues in 1980 to 48.2 percent in 1985. The 1981 acquisition of Petrofina Canada, Inc., for $348 million represented not only the nationalization of a Belgian-owned oil company but also the expansion of Petro-Canada's activities from long-term frontier exploration and development projects (its original mandate) into refining and marketing. Petrofina's more than 1,100 service stations throughout Canada more than tripled the acquiring company's previous retail operations. Two years later, Petro-Canada bought the refining and marketing assets of BP Canada for CAD 425 million, adding another 1,640 service stations and 108 terminals and bulk plants.

Canada's private oil sector strongly protested these two major purchases, arguing that publicly funded competition in the oil industry had become a destructive practice. Hostility to the company was displayed in the press, and some oil men began to refer to Petro-Canada's 52-story red-granite-clad headquarters in downtown Calgary as "Red Square." The private sector also fumed over a federal government decision in mid-1982 awarding acreage in a Sable Island area off Nova Scotia to a group headed by Petro-Canada, protesting that Petro-Canada had not had to compete with other companies for the rights. Relations between the state-owned oil company and the private sector reached an all-time low in 1985 when Hopper announced at a public conference that his company was withdrawing membership from the Independent Petroleum Association of Canada.

By the mid-1980s Petro-Canada was an established major player on the Canadian oil industry scene, the existence and mandate of which was supported by a clear majority of Canadians. With the purchase of the Petrofina and BP interests, Petro-Canada became Canada's fifth largest company, with nearly 6,000 employees. It was the country's third largest gasoline marketer and the only nationwide station chain. The company continued with successful oil discoveries during the 1980s, most notably the Valhalla field in Alberta along with several in Saskatchewan, including the Cactus Lake field in 1980, the Salt Lake field in 1984, and the Hoosier South field in 1987. Petrocan also made its first major offshore discovery in 1984, the Terra Nova field off Newfoundland.

The Progressive Conservative Party swept into power in December 1984, determined to reduce the national government's role in business. "Reform is urgently needed," Prime Minister Brian Mulroney declared. "Crown corporations have become a state within a state," as reported in *Business Week* of September 24, 1984. Petro-Canada, the new government mandated, must be regarded less as an instrument of national policy and more as a commercial operation.

By the mid-1980s Petro-Canada seemed to be moving in this new direction, a change signaled by Chairman Hopper in the company's 1984 annual report. He wrote: "The corporation has now been given a new mandate by its shareholder [the Canadian government]—to operate in a commercial, private sector fashion with emphasis on profitability and the need to maximize return on the government of Canada's investment."

Soon after taking office, the Conservatives replaced Petrocan board members appointed by the previous Liberal government and canceled about $250 million in additional funding for 1985 that had been Liberal-approved. The government also told the company it had to finance its operation from revenues or market financing.

1985 GULF CANADA PURCHASE

In 1985 Petro-Canada made a deal that appeared to reflect its new mandate and to mark a turning point in the history of the company. Petro-Canada purchased Gulf Canada Limited's refining, distribution, and marketing assets in Ontario, western Canada, the Yukon Territory, and the Northwest Territories for CAD 896 million by using its own internally generated funds and short-term debt, not taxpayers' money. Among the assets acquired were a lubricants plant, an asphalt plant, and 1,800 additional retail outlets. The acquisition increased the size of Petrocan, giving the company at that time about $10 billion in assets and making it an even bigger force on the Canadian petroleum scene.

For the next three years, the federal government talked of privatization but allowed Petro-Canada to consolidate and rationalize its operation. In 1988, for example, Petro-Canada significantly increased its expenditures in natural gas development, reflecting the company's increased focus on the natural gas business, and also entered into a preliminary agreement providing for the potential development of an oil-sands mining project, the OSLO project, at Kearl Lake, Alberta, and for the Hibernia oilfield off Newfoundland's east coast.

By 1988 the private oil sector's hostility seemed to have dissipated. Peter Foster, a longstanding critic of Petro-Canada and the petroleum industry in general, speculated that private-sector oilmen had been mollified by the Crown corporation's investments in their high-risk joint exploration ventures. Hopper was elected president of the Canadian Petroleum Association and public support ran relatively high. One poll showed a 45 percent public approval of the company, with 35 percent of the public indifferent or ambivalent, and only 20 percent opposed outright to the company's existence. In order to maintain its improving public image, Petro-Canada sponsored an 18,000-kilometer cross-country relay of the Olympic torch dubbed "Share the Flame." The 80-day promotion in advance of the 1988 Calgary Winter Olympics drew 7,000 torch bearers and cost Petrocan CAD 5.5 million to stage. It was just one of many patriotic campaigns carried out during the late 1980s.

The future looked rosy indeed for the oil giant when it reported 1987 to be its most profitable year ever. However, when put in perspective, those "record earnings" were not much to crow about. Over the course of the 1980s, the company earned total profits of CAD 38 million. Its return on shareholders equity lagged comparable competitors by a wide margin. Whereas Imperial Oil Ltd. earned an average return on equity of 10.8 percent and Shell made 9.46 percent from 1980 to 1989, Petro-Canada made a mere 1.43 percent. CEO Hopper acknowledged this in a 1991 interview with *Maclean's,* noting that "compared with our competition, we are well aware of our lower performance." A high rate of debt service on the company's CAD 1 billion in long-term financing, in fact, led to a shift in the company's economic strategy from aggressively investing in remote areas toward enhancing the company's financial health and operating capability.

In 1989 Petrocan began a CAD 50 million internal reorganization that led to a staff reduction of over 1,000 positions. After several years of equivocation, the Progressive Conservative government appeared to be ready to move firmly toward privatizing the state oil company. Energy Minister Marcel Masse said the move would be carried out through a general sale to the public. Petro-Canada's continuing cash problems led the company to announce in December 1989 that it was looking for an infusion of money to help it develop the country's energy resources. In January 1990 Hopper gave testimony before a government panel studying Petrocan's future. He served notice that the oil company would not be able to carry out its commitment to costly frontier development without private capital.

1991 PRIVATIZATION

A new era began for Petro-Canada in February 1990, when Michael Wilson, Canada's Minister of Finance, indicated that Canada would begin the privatization of Petro-Canada. According to the announcement, in 1991 the government would offer to the public about 15 percent of the shares of the government-owned company, but individual ownership would be limited to 10 percent and foreign ownership to a cumulative 25 percent of the publicly held shares. Hopper welcomed the government's announcement. The generated equity capital, Hopper said, would help Petro-Canada participate in developing several oil projects, including the Hibernia oilfield.

In April 1990 the Canadian government went one step further, announcing that Petro-Canada would eventually be sold in its entirety to the public. After much talk and speculation, the Canadian government had decided to get out of this segment of the energy business.

After years of debate over whether or not Petro-Canada should be privatized, the decision to do so sparked new questions. Paramount among them was a dispute over who should receive the proceeds of the sale, the company or the government. Although the federal government, which was carrying a high debt of its own and had pumped billions into the enterprise over the years, certainly had a claim to the income, officials

turned the funds over to CEO Hopper with nary a peep. It would be used, he said, to finance continuing exploration of the frontier areas at Hibernia and Terra Nova. Petro-Canada expected its commitments there to cost CAD 3 billion between 1990 and 1996.

On February 1, 1991, the government-owned shares of Petro-Canada were transferred to the Minister of State for Privatization and Regulatory Affairs; and Petro-Canada was authorized to issue and sell its own shares. The company made its initial public offering (IPO) on July 3, 1991, selling 19.5 percent, or 42 million, of its shares on Canadian stock exchanges for CAD 13 each. The sale gave the federal government's remaining stake a market value of about half of its previously estimated worth and thereby effectively raised the nation's debt. To make matters worse, the IPO was poorly timed. Uncertainties related to the Persian Gulf War, as well as Petrocan's continuing poor performance combined to reduce its stock price to around CAD 9, where it remained through the end of 1992.

In 1991 CEO Hopper stepped up downsizing efforts that had already eliminated 1,000 employees from the corporate roster. By the fall of 1992, he had cut total debt by about CAD 1 billion to CAD 1.25 billion, slashed the employee roster from a high of 10,000 in 1985 to 8,200, and divested assets worth nearly CAD 850 million, including about 1,200 of the company's ubiquitous service stations. Although the company lost CAD 603 million in 1991, the changes began to reflect on the bottom line in 1992, when Petrocan recorded a CAD 5 million profit.

ACHIEVING CONSISTENT PROFITABILITY UNDER NEW LEADERSHIP

Ironically, the announcement of this return to profitability (albeit meager) brought with it the ouster of Hopper, the only leader Petro-Canada had ever known. Long criticized as a mere "civil servant" and "fat cat" who enjoyed taxpayer-funded perks such as an executive chef and jet, Hopper was nonetheless considered a "Teflon" man, able to deflect blame for his company's long-running problems. That reputation came to an end in January 1993, when he was removed without comment by Petrocan's board of directors. James Stanford, who had served as president of the company since April 1990 and was a 15-year veteran of the company, succeeded Hopper as CEO.

Stanford continued the rationalization program, reducing employment to 6,200 and maintaining a debt-to-equity ratio of around 28 percent (considered "reasonable" by petroleum industry standards) through the end of 1994. After declining throughout the early 1990s, revenues increased from CAD 4.6 billion in 1993 to CAD 4.73 billion in 1994. More importantly, the company achieved record earnings of CAD 262 million that year, nearly seven times its total take for the entire decade of the 1980s.

In Petrocan's 1994 annual report, Stanford complained that the government's controlling interest in the company was a significant factor in the undervaluing of its shares. The stock had fallen to a low of CAD 7.25 early in 1993 and rebounded to only about CAD 11.50 by the end of 1994. Around that time, the government committed itself to divesting its remaining 173 million shares "when market conditions permit."

In advance of a further stock offering, Petro-Canada in May 1995 launched another restructuring involving a further workforce reduction of 700. A key component of the overhaul was to merge three divisions into one with the aim of cutting annual expenses by CAD 40 million. In September 1995 the Canadian government sold 50 percent of Petrocan's shares through an extremely successful secondary offering. About 124 million shares were snapped up at CAD 14.62 per share, sending a net CAD 1.73 billion into the government's coffers. The sell-off reduced Ottawa's stake to just 20 percent.

In April 1996 Petro-Canada acquired Amerada Hess Canada Limited, the Canadian unit of Amerada Hess Corporation, for CAD 735 million. This takeover strengthened the company's position in western Canada and in particular boosted its natural gas production by 45 percent. That same year, Petrocan entered into an exchange of assets with Norsk Hydro ASA, trading portions of its stakes in the Hibernia and Terra Nova offshore Canada oilfields for small stakes in two oilfields in the North Sea off the Norwegian coast. Petrocan's stakes in Hibernia and Terra Nova were reduced to 20 percent and 29 percent, respectively.

Production began at the Hibernia field in November 1997, about 18 years after its discovery and following CAD 5.8 billion in preproduction spending. The field's reserves were estimated at this time to total 750 million barrels of oil, and by the end of 1999 production at Hibernia had reached 150,000 barrels per day. Development of the Terra Nova field, in the meantime, began in 1998. This field was estimated to contain around 370 million barrels of oil. Also in 1998, Petro-Canada entered into an agreement to combine into a joint venture its refinery and marketing assets with like assets in Michigan, New England, and eastern Canada overseen by Ultramar Diamond Shamrock Corporation. The deal fell through, however, after Canada's Competition Bureau raised serious concerns

about its potential to curtail competition at the wholesale and retail levels in eastern Canada.

In 1999 Petrocan completed the largest land acquisition program in its history, acquiring 2.7 million acres for exploration and development, including potential natural gas-producing acreage in the Northwest Territories' Mackenzie Delta and potential offshore oil-producing properties off both Newfoundland and Nova Scotia. Buoyed by higher crude oil prices and improved production from the Hibernia project, Petro-Canada posted profits of CAD 233 million for 1999, up 145 percent from the previous year. The company, in fact, had operated in the black ever since Stanford's 1993 promotion to the head post. Stanford ended his successful leadership reign in early 2000 when he retired. Taking over the helm was Ron A. Brenneman, a former executive at both Exxon Corporation and Petrocan rival Imperial Oil.

MULTIPRONGED GROWTH INITIATIVES

Among Brenneman's first action in 2000 was to carry out a previously announced divestment of Petro-Canada's western Canadian conventional oil business. As part of this sell-off, Petrocan traded certain oilfields in Alberta to Husky Oil Limited for increased stakes in two offshore east-coast oil projects, Terra Nova (up to 34 percent) and White Rose (27.5 percent). Petro-Canada's aim was to refocus its North American upstream oil activities on the higher growth areas of the offshore fields and the oil-sands projects, while continuing to produce natural gas in western Canada. The company delved further into oil sands by beginning construction of the wholly owned MacKay River project in northeastern Alberta, near Fort McMurray. Unlike Syncrude and other projects that mine oil-laden sand, MacKay River was a so-called in situ development involving the steam-driven extraction of bitumen from the onsite wells. Also in 2000, Petrocan sold its Norwegian offshore assets and restructured its downstream activities into the functional areas of refining and supply, sales and marketing, and lubricants.

As development of the MacKay River and other oil-sands projects progressed, Petro-Canada in 2001 launched a plan to augment its Edmonton refinery with equipment enabling it to process bitumen. In January 2002 production began at the Terra Nova offshore field, which by the end of 2003 was producing 134,000 barrels of oil per day. Construction also began that year on the CAD 2.3 billion White Rose project, which was slated to tap into an offshore field with as much as 250 million barrels of oil. On the oil-sands side, production began at MacKay River in November 2002, and nearly

11,000 barrels of oil were extracted there each day in 2003.

In May 2002 Petrocan nearly doubled its production and gained a new long-term growth platform by acquiring most of the international upstream oil and gas operations of Veba Oil & Gas GmbH in a CAD 2.23 billion deal. Included were North Sea fields mainly off the U.K. and Dutch shores, as well as fields in Syria and Libya. Thanks to the production start-ups and Veba acquisition, Petro-Canada's overall production of oil and gas in 2002 reached a record 382,400 barrels of oil equivalent per day, almost double the figure for 2001. Reserves at year-end 2002 totaled 1.29 billion barrels, a 57 percent increase from a year earlier.

In 2003 cost overruns led Petro-Canada to scale back its plans for further oil-sands projects, and the firm also announced plans to consolidate its eastern Canadian refining operations at its Montreal refinery. The company's Oakville, Ontario, refinery was partially shut down in 2004 and then shuttered a year later. This left Petrocan running two refineries, in Montreal and Edmonton. In 2004 the company further bolstered its international upstream operations with the purchase of a 29.9 percent stake in the Buzzard oilfield in the U.K. North Sea. During its first year of production in 2007, this field was producing as much as 200,000 barrels of oil per day. In another 2004 deal, Petrocan spent CAD 644 million for Prima Energy Corporation, which extended its natural gas production operations into the U.S. Rockies. At the time of the purchase, the acquired properties were producing 55 million cubic feet of gas per day; output had nearly doubled by the end of 2007.

FULL INDEPENDENCE AND FURTHER OIL-SANDS PROJECTS

Another milestone occurred in September 2004 when the Canadian government sold its remaining 19 percent interest in Petro-Canada through a public offering. Around 49 million Petrocan shares were sold at CAD 64.50 per share, generating gross proceeds for the government of roughly CAD 3.2 billion. Despite this divestment, the company remained subject to special restrictions outlined in the Petro-Canada Public Participation Act. The most important of these held that no individual or institution could own more than 20 percent of the company, which appeared to ensure its continued independence.

Reversing course on its pullback from the oil-sands sector, Petrocan in 2005 acquired majority control of the Fort Hills oil-sands mining project located near Fort McMurray. Production over the project's 40-year life span was projected to total 3.6 billion barrels of synthetic crude oil (after conversion from bitumen).

Bitumen production was expected to begin late in 2011, and the total cost of the project over its two proposed phases was estimated at CAD 26.2 billion, making it the largest single oil-sands project yet proposed. Soaring petroleum prices and rising worldwide demand for energy had made such ambitious oil-sands projects ever more viable. Petro-Canada in 2005 also announced plans for a second phase of the MacKay River in situ oil-sands project, and it began a multiyear project to convert the Edmonton refinery to exclusively refine oil-sands-based feedstock. In addition, production started at the White Rose offshore field. Profits for 2005 totaled a record CAD 1.79 billion on best-ever revenues of CAD 17.59 billion.

Although Petro-Canada was solidly profitable during this period, some analysts were critical of the firm's management, pointing to a decline in oil and gas production from a 2003 peak of 472,000 barrels per day to 345,000 barrels in 2006. Petrocan in 2006 was forced to shut down the Terra Nova platform for a six-month, CAD 225 million overhaul to fix flaws in its original design. The shutdown was a significant factor in the 2006 production decline. Production at Terra Nova returned to 100,000 barrels per day by the end of 2006, with Petro-Canada's share amounting to 34,000 barrels a day.

Oil-sands projects were expected to provide much of Petro-Canada's future growth opportunities, particularly Fort Hills, which was projected to produce 280,000 barrels of synthetic crude per day by 2014. In addition to the firm's expansion of the MacKay River project, Petrocan was involved in several other major growth endeavors: an expansion of the White Rose offshore project, the operation and further development of the Ebla natural gas project in Syria, and the development of oilfields in Libya in partnership with the state-controlled Libyan National Oil Company. In addition, Petro-Canada held a 22.7 percent stake in Hebron, another offshore project located off Newfoundland and Labrador. In August 2008 Chevron Corporation, the leader of the Hebron consortium, announced that the provincial government had approved the development, which was estimated to contain nearly 600 million barrels of recoverable heavy oil. Production was expected to commence between 2016 and 2018, with production projected to eventually top out at 150,000 barrels per day.

Ron Chepesiuk
Updated, April Dougal Gasbarre; David E. Salamie

PRINCIPAL SUBSIDIARIES

3908968 Canada Inc.; Petro-Canada U.K. Holdings Ltd.; Petro-Canada U.K. Limited.

PRINCIPAL COMPETITORS

Imperial Oil Limited; EnCana Corporation; Suncor Energy Inc.; Shell Canada Limited; ConocoPhillips; Canadian Natural Resources Limited; Talisman Energy Inc.; BP Canada Energy Company; Nexen Inc.; Husky Energy Inc.

FURTHER READING

Bliss, Michael, *Northern Enterprise: Five Centuries of Canadian Business,* Toronto: McClelland and Stewart, 1987, 640 p.

Brethour, Patrick, "Petrocan Antes Up for Major Oil Sands Project," *Globe and Mail,* March 2, 2005, p. B7.

———, "Petrocan Buying U.S. Rockies Foothold with Prima Acquisition," *Globe and Mail,* June 10, 2004, p. B1.

Carlisle, Tamsin, "Petro-Canada Has Resurgence," *Wall Street Journal,* March 14, 2003, p. B4.

Donville, Christopher, "Good Timing," *Globe and Mail,* May 18, 1991, p. B1.

Ebner, Dave, "Priming the Pump: Ron Brenneman's Challenge Is to Shake Off Petrocan's Government Origins to Become a Real Player," *Globe and Mail,* December 2, 2006, p. B4.

———, "'Stigma' Off Petrocan As Ottawa Gets Out," *Globe and Mail,* September 17, 2004, p. B1.

Fleming, James, "Petro-Canada Gets the Lead Out," *Globe and Mail,* January 28, 1994, p. 44.

Fossum, John Erik, *Oil, the State, and Federalism: The Rise and Demise of Petro-Canada As a Statist Impulse,* Toronto: University of Toronto Press, 1997, 368 p.

Foster, Peter, *The Blue-Eyed Sheiks: The Canadian Oil Establishment,* Don Mills, Ont.: Collins, 1979, 320 p.

———, "Hopper's Folly," *Globe and Mail,* July 19, 1991, p. 18.

———, *Self Serve: How Petro-Canada Pumped Canadians Dry,* Toronto: Macfarlane Walter & Ross, 1992, 323 p.

Jang, Brent, "Brenneman to Take Over Petrocan's Helm," *Globe and Mail,* December 18, 1999, p. B1.

———, "On the Firing Line Again," *Globe and Mail,* June 20, 1995, p. B14.

———, "Petro-Canada to Launch Major Oil Sands Project in Northern Alberta," *Globe and Mail,* December 20, 1999, p. B1.

———, "Petrocan Buys Amerada," *Globe and Mail,* April 4, 1996, p. B1.

———, "Petrocan Pumped Up to Go East," *Globe and Mail,* November 3, 1999, p. B13.

———, "Terra Nova Oil Project Launched," *Globe and Mail,* December 13, 1995, p. B1.

Jang, Brent, and Alan Freeman, "Petrocan Sale Gets Green Light," *Globe and Mail,* September 7, 1995, p. B1.

Kennedy, Peter, "Petrocan Buys Stake in North Sea Field," *Globe and Mail,* May 26, 2004, p. B1.

Lee, Hyun Young, "Petro-Canada Faces Challenge," *Wall Street Journal,* September 12, 2007, p. B5H.

McMurdy, Deirdre, "A Matter of Privacy," *Maclean's,* March 4, 1991, pp. 42–44.

Motherwell, Cathryn, "Petrocan Battles for Respect," *Globe and Mail,* 13 October 1992, p. B9.

"Mulroney Readies an Assault on 'Red Square,'" *Business Week,* September 24, 1984, p. 48.

Nguyen, Lily, "Petrocan to Buy Veba Assets for $3.2-Billion," *Globe and Mail,* January 30, 2002, p. B1.

Parkinson, David, "Petrocan Unveils Big Oil Projects," *Globe and Mail,* December 5, 2001, p. B1.

"Petro-Canada Emerging As a Model of State Oil Company Privatization," *Oil and Gas Journal,* December 25, 1995, pp. 21–26.

"Petro-Canada: How It Grew and Where It Likely Is Going," *Oil and Gas Journal,* December 9, 1985.

"Petro-Canada to Buy Veba's International Oil, Gas Assets," *Oil and Gas Journal,* February 11, 2002, p. 36.

Phillips, Ed, *Guts and Guile: True Tales from the Backrooms of the Pipeline Industry,* Vancouver, B.C.: Douglas & McIntyre, 1990, 222 p.

Scoffield, Heather, and Andrew Willis, "Ottawa Clearing Way for Petrocan Sale," *Globe and Mail,* April 12, 2004, p. B1.

Scott, Norval, "Petro-Canada Increases Investment in Oil Sands," *Globe and Mail,* December 14, 2007, p. B6.

———, "Petrocan's Libyan Dream: A Basin 'to Die For,'" *Globe and Mail,* December 15, 2007, p. B3.

Willoughby, Jack, "Petro-Canada Tries a New Drill," *Barron's,* November 28, 2005, p. 22.

quinn emanuel trial lawyers

los angeles | new york | san francisco | silicon valley | tokyo | london

Quinn Emanuel Urquhart Oliver & Hedges, LLP

865 South Figueroa Street, 10th Floor
Los Angeles, California 90017
U.S.A.
Telephone: (213) 443-3000
Fax: (213) 443-3100
Web site: http://www.quinnemanuel.com

Private Company
Incorporated: 1986
Employees: 900
Operating Revenues: $384.5 million (2007 est.)
NAICS: 541110 Offices of Lawyers

■ ■ ■

Quinn Emanuel Urquhart Oliver & Hedges, LLP is a law firm devoted exclusively to business litigation. Quinn Emanuel is involved in roughly 20 practice areas, including copyright litigation, antitrust litigation, and securities litigation, but the firm spends more than 50 percent of its time handling intellectual property lawsuits. Quinn Emanuel is known for its willingness and its success in arguing cases before a jury, having won more nine-figure verdicts than any other law firm in the United States. The firm has won 89.5 percent of the cases it has argued before a jury. Quinn Emanuel serves clients such as International Business Machines Corporation (IBM), Shell Oil Company, Northrop Grumman Corporation, and General Motors Corporation, as well as scores of other high-profile corporations. The firm maintains offices in Los Angeles, San Francisco, Silicon Valley, New York City, Tokyo, and London.

ORIGINS

One of the most profitable law firms in the United States sprang from the entrepreneurial efforts of Quinn Emanuel's cofounder, Managing Partner John Quinn. Quinn's success stood in sharp contrast to his first effort to establish his own firm, which foundered within months of its formation. "I thought my career had taken a detour for the worse," he recalled in an interview published in the June 2006 issue of the *American Lawyer,* referring to the failure of his first venture.

Quinn's career began with considerable promise, full of high expectations after a distinguished academic record. Quinn, who grew up in Bountiful, Utah, earned his undergraduate degree at Claremont Men's College (later renamed Claremont McKenna College) in 1973, leaving the institution as a magna cum laude graduate. Determined to practice law for a living, he was admitted to Harvard Law School, where he was elected to the most coveted post on campus, serving as editor of the *Harvard Review* between 1974 and 1976. A cum laude Harvard Law graduate, Quinn had his pick of law firms to join after completing his education. He was hired as an associate at one of the oldest, most prestigious firms in the country, Cravath, Swaine & Moore, a New York City-based firm where Quinn spent three years before a desire to return to the West Coast and strike out his own led to the first faltering steps in his career.

Quinn arrived in Los Angeles in 1979 ready to start his own law practice devoted to litigation. He and a colleague leased a small suite of offices and quickly discovered the difficulties of practicing law without the support of an established firm. Work was scarce, forcing the two partners to close up shop and find employment elsewhere. Quinn joined a midsized, New York City-based firm named Reboul, MacMurray, Hewitt, Maynard & Kristol, opened a one-room office in Los Angeles for his new employers, and began drumming up West Coast business for the firm any way he could. "I was shameless," he confided in his June 2006 interview with the *American Lawyer.*

QUINN EMANUEL ESTABLISHED IN 1986

By 1986, Quinn was ready to make a second attempt at establishing his own firm. Joining him in starting the practice were the three other founders of Quinn Emanuel: Eric Emanuel, whom Quinn had worked with at Cravath, Swaine in New York City; David Quinto, a 1982 graduate of Harvard Law School; and Phyllis Kupferstein, who earned her law degree at Loyola Marymount University. The firm was founded on January 1, 1986, touching off what Emanuel later remembered as "two years of misery," in a September 2008 interview with *Fast Company.*

Again, Quinn found it difficult to cultivate business. He and his partners scrounged for work, looking for clients by making cold calls to businesses in person and by telephone. The focus of Quinn Emanuel from the start was to operate as a litigation-only firm, and it found its first trickle of business by working for the human resources departments of large corporations, primarily taking on employment-termination cases. The firm charged low fees for its services, managing to eke out an existence while establishing a reputation. By the end of its second year, Quinn Emanuel had booked $3 million in revenue.

THE FIRM'S PRACTICE TAKES SHAPE

As the firm's business grew, it was able to progress beyond mundane employment matters to what would be its chief strengths: intellectual property and patent disputes. One of Quinn Emanuel's first major clients was Hughes Aircraft, which hired the firm in 1993 to handle an arbitration matter. Quinn Emanuel prevailed in the legal battle, paving the way for a stream of larger and larger clients. In 1996, the firm represented General Motors Corp. in a patent infringement suit against German automaker Volkswagen AG. The case resulted in a $1.1 billion settlement for Quinn Emanuel's client. In another notable case, the firm obtained dismissals of several class-action lawsuits filed in 1998 against senior officers of Northrop Grumman Corp. after its scuttled merger with Lockheed Martin Corp.

QUINN EMANUEL REAPS THE REWARDS OF SUCCESS

Quinn Emanuel's string of successes during the 1990s brought it out of obscurity, lifting it ever closer to Quinn's original vision of what he wanted the firm to become. In a June 2006 interview with the *American Lawyer,* Emanuel recalled an exchange with Quinn during the early years of the firm, saying, "He [Quinn] once said to me—when we were in a building with a view of the dumpster—he said, 'I want to be the go-to firm when someone needs the best.' That was when we were nothing; when we were shabby looking!" Success increased the firm's recognition in the corporate sector, which attracted additional clients and, significantly, enabled it to attract legal talent. At first, the firm had been unable to convince good students at second-tier schools in the Los Angeles area to interview, much less join the firm as associates, but as its reputation grew, Quinn Emanuel could pick and choose its next generation of litigators. The firm narrowed its sights, targeting only the best students from the best schools: Stanford, Yale, Columbia, Harvard, Chicago, and a small number of other prestigious institutions. The firm that once struggled to get law students to listen to its recruitment pitch turned into a highly selective employer, requiring Harvard graduates, for instance, to have at least an A−/B+ average to be considered as associates.

THE QUINN EMANUEL CULTURE

The new members of the Quinn Emanuel family joined an irreverent corporate culture when they arrived in Los Angeles. The firm's stylistic preferences stood in sharp

KEY DATES

1986: John Quinn and three other lawyers start their own law firm in Los Angeles.

1993: Quinn Emanuel prevails in an arbitration matter for one of its first large clients, Hughes Aircraft.

1996: Quinn Emanuel wins a $1.1 billion settlement for General Motors.

2001: The firm opens an office in New York City.

2003: Quinn Emanuel partners each generate $1 million in profits.

2007: Profits per partner climb to $3 million, a level reached by only three other law firms in the United States.

contrast with the décor and the attire characteristic of the nation's leading firms, a countercultural difference first seen by Quinn Emanuel recruits when A. William Urquhart, in charge of recruiting for the firm, appeared on university campuses wearing his trademark Hawaiian shirt, shorts, and sandals. Once new associates arrived at the firm's main offices, it was more of the same, a sea of lawyers, partners, and support personnel wearing T-shirts, jeans, and flip-flops. The wood-paneled walls and opulent trappings prevalent in the offices of the nation's leading firms were replaced by exposed ceilings, massive aquariums, and minimalistic décor at Quinn Emanuel.

Quinn Emanuel set itself apart from its rivals through style and through substance. The firm kept a narrow focus, eschewing the areas of corporate law practiced by its rivals. Quinn Emanuel concentrated exclusively on litigation, refusing to involve itself with corporate, tax, real estate, or structured finance cases. The firm relished an opportunity to try its cases before a jury, promoting itself as an expert in the courtroom. "They are what they claim to be," the general counsel for IBM said in the June 2006 issue of the *American Lawyer*. "They say they're trial lawyers, and they are. You can depend on the fact that these guys will have been in the courtroom multiple times." Quinn, of course, agreed, telling the *American Lawyer*, "It's the reason we're so successful. Corporate lawyers don't really understand what litigators do."

DECENTRALIZED STRUCTURE

The firm also stood out for the way it was organized, a loose, decentralized structure that befitted the attire

worn by its employees. Meetings were rarely held, and the plethora of committees that were part of other elite firms were absent at Quinn Emanuel. There was no executive committee, no management committee, no recruiting committee, no compensation committee, only a committee for determining contingency fees. "There is zero bureaucracy at this firm," a Quinn Emanuel partner told the *American Lawyer*. "Things get decided in a moment's notice."

By the end of the 1990s, Quinn Emanuel had grown to a 75-lawyer firm, having spent the decade making great strides toward distinguishing itself as a litigator of note. Within 15 years the firm had transformed from a four-lawyer practice that struggled to solicit business into a thriving firm nearly 20 times larger than it was at its inception. It bucked conventions in the legal field through its casual style, its willingness to try cases before a jury, and its practice of taking on cases on a contingency basis. "We like having skin in the game," Quinn said in his June 2006 interview with the *American Lawyer*. Much had been achieved, but in the years ahead, as Quinn Emanuel entered the 21st century, the firm's best years were to come.

2003–06: RAPID FINANCIAL GROWTH

During the first decade of the 21st century, Quinn Emanuel recorded impressive financial growth as the size of the firm increased exponentially. An office in New York City opened in 2001 after a client, Enron, asked Quinn Emanuel to identify experienced trial lawyers in the city. "We could not come up with a list of ten," Urquhart said in the June 2006 issue of the *American Lawyer*, prompting the firm to open its own three-lawyer office. Within five years, the New York City office had grown to 54 lawyers, with plans underway to move into offices that would accommodate 100 lawyers.

The firm's annual revenue eclipsed $100 million in 2002, a financial milestone upstaged the following year when Quinn Emanuel joined an elite group of law firms. For the first time, each of its partners generated $1 million in profits in 2003, lifting Quinn Emanuel to a level enjoyed by only the largest, most successful law firms in the country. The firm, after nearly 20 years in business, had secured a settlement or courtroom victory in 92.8 percent of its cases, a record of success that substantiated the firm's tagline, "Justice may be blind, but she sees it our way more than 90 percent of the time."

QUINN EMANUEL TURNS 20

Quinn Emanuel's 20th anniversary in 2006 was cause for justifiable celebration. For the third straight year, revenues increased more than 20 percent, reaching $193.5 million. The 244 lawyers under its employ represented a more than threefold increase from the size of the firm seven years earlier. Quinn Emanuel ranked as the most profitable law firm outside New York City, generating $1.9 million in profits per partner. The firm, it proudly proclaimed, had won more nine-figure verdicts—not settlements—than any other law firm in the United States.

As Quinn Emanuel looked to the future, it held sway as one of the most successful law firms in the country. Its capabilities in the courtroom distinguished it among its peers, enabling Quinn to realize his dream of leading a "go-to" firm. Quinn Emanuel's financial record reflected a firm that belonged among the upper-tier of the country's legal practices. In 2007, revenues swelled to $384.5 million and the firm's 109 partners took home on average just over $3 million, a nearly 25 percent increase from the previous year. There were only three other law firms in the country that had eclipsed the $3 million mark in profits per partner. With more than 440 lawyers working on its behalf, more than twice the total four years earlier, Quinn Emanuel promised to play a prominent role in business litigation for years to come.

Jeffrey L. Covell

PRINCIPAL COMPETITORS

Heller Ehrman LLP; Latham & Watkins LLP; O'Melveny & Myers LLP.

FURTHER READING

Beck, Susan, "The Mighty Quinn," *American Lawyer,* June 2006.

Bronstad, Amanda, "Aggressive Quinn Law Firm Joins Elite $1 Million Club," *Los Angeles Business Journal,* October 6, 2003, p. 10.

Fixtmer, Andy, "Growing Giant," *Los Angeles Business Journal,* May 2, 2005, p. 46.

Lacter, Mark, "Caffeinated, Aggressive & Brash," *Fast Company,* September 2008, p. 58.

York, Emily Bryson, "Still Waiting Out West," *Los Angeles Business Journal,* February 12, 2007, p. 7.

Raisio PLC

———— ■ ————

Box 101, Raisionkaari 55
Raisio, FIN-21201
Finland
Telephone: (+358 02) 443 21 11
Fax: (+358 02) 443 23 15
Web site: http://www.raisiogroup.com

Public Company
Incorporated: 1939 as Oy Vehnä Ab
Employees: 1,100
Sales: EUR 422 million ($619.6 million) (2007)
Stock Exchanges: OMX Nordic
Ticker Symbol: RAI
NAICS: 311225 Fats and Oils Refining and Blending; 311119 Other Animal Food Manufacturing; 311211 Flour Milling; 311213 Malt Manufacturing; 311423 Dried and Dehydrated Food Manufacturing

■ ■ ■

Raisio PLC is one of Finland's leading food and nutrition companies. The Raisio-based company operates through three main divisions, Food, Feed & Malt, and Ingredients. The Food division, which produces 45 percent of the group's total turnover, focuses primarily on the Finnish and Baltic Sea markets, including Sweden, Russia, Poland, and Ukraine, elsewhere. The company's food production focuses on plant-based products, and includes margarine, flour, pasta, potatoes, and flakes. The company's brand names include Elovena, Keiju, Herkku, and Sunnuntai (Finland);

Nordic, Dolina Skandi, and Voimix (Russia); and Pyszyny Duet and Masmix (Poland). The Feed & Malt division contributes 46 percent of Raisio's annual sales, with a focus on the Finnish and northwestern Russian markets. The company produces feeds for farm animals as well as fish farms, brewery malt, and oils and oil-based meals. Raisio's Ingredient's division, which added 9 percent to group sales in 2007, is perhaps best known for the international success of its patented cholesterol-lowering ingredient, Benecol, which is marketed in more than 30 countries. Raisio operates production facilities in nine countries, including the United States and Canada, as well as Russia, Ukraine, Latvia, Lithuania, and Estonia, and employs more than 1,100 people. Founded as a cooperative among Finnish wheat farmers in the 1950s, Raisio is listed on the OMX Nordic Exchange Helsinki. Matti Rihko serves as the company's CEO. Raisio's revenues reached EUR 422 million ($619.6 million) in 2007.

FARMERS' COOPERATIVE IN 1939

Raisio originated as a cooperative venture formed by a group of wheat farmers in Finland in 1939. The purpose of the cooperative was to build a mill to grind the farmers' produce into flour, which could then be sold at market. The upheavals of the outbreak of World War II delayed the construction of the mill; by 1942, however, the mill was in operation. The new company took the name of Oy Vehnä AB.

The strict rationing of foodstuffs during the war played to Vehnä's advantage, as the Finnish government took over responsibility for the distribution of the company's products. In this way, Vehnä's flour output had a guaranteed purchaser. Following the war, the continuing shortages of food and feed provided Vehnä with strong demand for its production. The food shortage also enabled the company to launch its first expansion, into the production of feed, using the mill's byproducts as primary ingredients. Vehnä's feed production was begun in 1948.

Vehnä's milling operations provided another production offshoot in 1950, when the company commenced production of brewery malts in 1950. That production was initially hampered by a lack of equipment and machinery, as the bulk of Finland's machinery production was being shipped to the Soviet Union as part of the country's war reparations. Nonetheless, Vehnä managed to piece together its first malting plant using leftover and spare parts.

GROWTH: 1950-80

Another important part of the future Raisio was founded in the postwar period. In 1950, a new company was established to build a vegetable oil milling factory in the town of Raisio. That company, Oy Kasviöljy-Växtolje Ab, then began to promote the cultivation of rapeseed, a new crop in Finland at the time, among the region's farmers, and soon after launched production of canola oil.

Kasviöljy-Växtolje initially had difficulty in convincing the area's margarine manufacturers to incorporate canola oil in their production. At the same time, a growing number of bakeries and retailers had expressed interest in developing their own margarine brands. In 1956, Kasviöljy-Växtolje with a group of retailer partners had formed a new production company, Margariini Oy. By then, Vehnä and Kasviöljy-Växtolje had already developed a strong partnership.

Through the 1960s and 1970s, the operations of the future Raisio continued to fall into place as the company established itself as a highly integrated company with operations extending from cultivation to consumer end products. The company founded a potato processing facility in 1961, located in Vihanti. By then,

the company had already begun the production of plant-based chemicals, such as varnish, wheat-based glues, and technical oils. These production activities were given a dedicated factory in 1961, founding the future Raisio Chemicals division.

The new division rapidly expanded its range of products. The inauguration of a fats chemistry unit enabled the company to produce distilled fatty acids, for example. These were used as ingredients in the production of detergents, soaps, candles, and other products, but also formed the basis for other fatty acids. In 1971, the chemicals division also established an alliance with the Finnish paper industry to develop vegetable-based paper coatings.

The next major milestone for the group came in 1976, when construction was completed on a new wheat starch factory. Over the next decade, this operation rose to become one of Finland's leading producers of starch and starch products. This leadership position was confirmed in 1984, when the company acquired Hämeen Peruna Oy, then the country's leading potato starch group. By then, also, the company had taken its first international steps, launching a starch processing factory in Sweden in 1981.

The longstanding partnership between Vehnä and Kasviöljy-Växtolje at last resulted in the merger of the two companies, forming Raisio Tehtaat Oy in 1987. The following year, the company went public, listing its shares on the Helsinki Stock Exchange. Nonetheless, voting rights in the group remained controlled by the founding farmer members of the original cooperative.

BENECOL DISCOVERY IN THE NINETIES

Through the 1990s, Raisio broadened its international scope, primarily through the Raisio Chemicals division. The company entered the North American market in 1995, establishing a subsidiary in the United States. By the beginning of the following year, the company had also entered Canada, buying the Canadian operations of the British-French company Roe Lee Chemical Group. Soon after, Raisio acquired a second Canadian company, Diachem Industries Ltd. The new operations were then merged with Raisio's U.S. business, forming Raisio Chemicals North America.

In other international extensions, the company added margarine production plants in Poland in 1995. The following year, the company added new margarine production capacity in Sweden by buying Carlshamn Mejeri AB.

Raisio had also been restructuring its operations in Finland, absorbing its margarine production subsidiary.

```
┌─────────────────────────────────────────┐
│                                           │
│              KEY DATES                    │
│                   ■                       │
│ ───────────────────────────────────────  │
│                                           │
│  1939:  A group of Finnish wheat farmers join │
│         together to found a flour mill, Oy Vehnä AB. │
│  1942:  Oy Vehnä AB launches flour production. │
│  1950:  Oy Vehnä AB begins producing brewers │
│         malts; Oy Kasviöljy-Växtolje Ab is founded to │
│         operate a vegetable oil factory in Raisio. │
│  1961:  The exspansion into wheat starch production │
│         leads to founding of Raisio Chemicals │
│         division. │
│  1987:  Oy Kasviöljy-Växtolje Ab and Oy Vehnä AB │
│         merge to form Raisio Tehtaat Oy. │
│  1988:  Raisio goes public on the Helsinki Stock │
│         Exchange. │
│  1995:  Raisio releases cholesterol-lowering ingredient │
│         and functional food brand, Benecol. │
│  2003:  Raisio refocuses as a Nutrition and Life Sci- │
│         ences company, selling Raisio Chemicals to │
│         Ciba Specialty Chemicals. │
│  2008:  Raisio reaches an agreement with British Bio- │
│         logicals to distribute Benecol to the Indian │
│         market. │
│                                           │
└─────────────────────────────────────────┘
```

This integration came as part of a new major milestone in Raisio's history. Scientists had long recognized the cholesterol-reducing effects of sterols, found in all plants. However, into the mid-1990s, efforts to isolate and incorporate sterols into foods for human consumption had been unsuccessful.

In 1995, however, Raisio's research and development team became the first to develop and patent a process for deriving a fat-soluble sterol from the stanols contained in pine trees. In this way, the company was able to produce concentrated amounts of sterols from pine waste pulp, a process said to require as much as 15 tons of pine trees to produce just one kilogram of the substance.

Raisio dubbed its new product as Benecol, and launched its first product to include the sterols, a margarine, in 1996. Success was immediate in Finland, where the traditional diet contributed to the development of high-cholesterol in the population. By 1997, the company had begun rolling out the Benecol-branded line of margarine and other products to the Swedish market as well.

Raisio's share price soared with the Benecol launch, which also established relatively tiny Raisio on the world food production scene. Rather than attempt to control

the production and distribution of Benecol on a global scale, Raisio went in search of a partner. In 1998, the company signed an international marketing agreement with McNeill Consumer Healthcare, giving the Johnson & Johnson subsidiary the exclusive right to market Benecol to the North American and European markets.

Raisio ramped up its Benecol production, as it began making its first foreign shipments. By the beginning of the 2000s, the company found itself overstocked as international demand for the breakthrough product fell far below initial expectations. The failure to develop the Benecol market hit the company hard financially, as it slipped into losses.

REFOCUSED FOR THE 21ST CENTURY

In 2000, Raisio renegotiated the distribution agreement with McNeill, gaining the right to supply sterol and stanol esters, both cholesterol-reducing agents, to third-parties, including such food industry giants as Unilever. Despite introducing direct competition for its own brand, Raisio hoped that the appearance of major players would help establish the validity of the functional food category, and consequently broaden sales of Benecol.

Raisio also launched a refocusing exercise. By 2003, the company had decided to redevelop itself as a specialist in Nutrition and Life Sciences. As a result, the company sold its Raisio Chemicals division to Ciba Specialty Chemicals in 2004. The sale, worth EUR 475 million, helped eliminate Raisio's debt.

Raisio now turned its attention to building its remaining business. In 2005, the company acquired Camelina Ltd., a Finnish company that specialized in the production of camelina seed. With an omega-3 fatty acid content of up to 40 percent, camelina seeds provided Raisio with a new extension for its functional foods operations.

The company also began targeting the extension of its Benecol product line into the Asian markets, many of which were just beginning to show an interest in the functional food category. This led the company to develop a partnership with India's British Biologicals, to distribute Benecol to the Indian market in 2008. The deal called for British Biologicals to sell Benecol both as an ingredient to food manufacturers as well as a powdered drink product for the consumer market.

Soon after, the company announced plans to extend the Benecol brand elsewhere in the Asian region. The company acknowledged its interest in entering the vast Chinese market in the near future. In the meantime,

Raisio turned to Thailand, where it opened an office in Bangkok in support of the launch of Benecol there. From a farmers' cooperative to an international functional foods group, Raisio looked forward to new growth as it neared the end of the decade.

M. L. Cohen

PRINCIPAL SUBSIDIARIES

Raisio Eesti AS (Estonia); Raisio Lietuva (Lithuania); Raisio Nutrition Ltd./Moscow (Russia); Raisio Polska Foods Sp.z o.o.; Raisio Staest US Inc.; Raisio Sverige AB; SIA Raisio Latvija; TOB Raisio Ukraina.

PRINCIPAL DIVISIONS

Food; Feed & Malt; Ingredients.

PRINCIPAL COMPETITORS

RGM International Private Ltd.; Cargill Inc.; Unilever N.V.; Archer Daniels Midland Co.; Wilmar International Ltd.; Sungai Budi Group; Orkla ASA; VION Food Group; Bunge Argentina S.A.; DANISH CROWN AmbA.

FURTHER READING

Anscombe, Nadya, "Seeing the Light," *ECN-European Chemical News,* July 21, 2003, p. 20.

"China Targeted As Raisio Plots Expansion," *just-food.com* February 21, 2008.

"Finland: Raisio Caution After 2007 Turnaround," *just-food. com,* February 13, 2008.

Haydon, Simon, "Benecol Owner Raisio Strikes India Deal," *just-food.com,* January 10, 2008.

Hume, Claudia, "Raisio Spreads Beyond Benecol," *Chemical Week,* March 8, 2000, p. 44.

Ipsen, Erik, "Finnish Firm Redefines Health Food," *International Herald Tribune,* January 9, 1997, p. 11.

"Raisio Acknowledges Problems with Benecol," *Nutraceuticals International,* March 2000.

"Raisio and Valio Collaboration Bears First Fruit with Cholesterol-Lowering Yogurt," *Nutraceuticals International,* May 2001.

"Raisio Considers Expansion of Its Paper Chemicals Business," *Chemical Market Reporter,* July 1, 2002, p. 4.

"Raisio Group's Financial Rise," *Nutraceuticals International,* September 2002.

"Raisio PLC Completes Outsourcing of Its Laboratory Operations," *TendersInfo,* September 2, 2008.

"Raisio to Close Russian Margarine Plant," *just-food.com,* June 28, 2007.

Wrong, Michela, "Rivals Get a Taste of Raisio's Market," *Financial Times,* February 25, 2000, p. 28.

The Real Good Food Company plc

International House
1 St. Katharine's Way
London, E1W 1XB
United Kingdom
Telephone: (+44 020) 7335 2500
Fax: (+44 020) 7335 2501
Web site: http://www.realgoodfoodplc.com

Public Company
Incorporated: 2003
Employees: 860
Sales: £231.1 million ($431.4 million) (2007)
Stock Exchanges: London AIM
Ticker Symbol: RGD
NAICS: 311812 Commercial Bakeries; 311311 Sugarcane Mills; 311330 Confectionery Manufacturing from Purchased Chocolate

■ ■ ■

The Real Good Food Company plc is a fast-growing supplier of sugar, bakery products, and ingredients to the U.K. retail grocery, wholesaler, and food processing industries. The company's largest component is its Sugar division, grouped around Napier Brown & Company, the third largest sugar processor and trader in the United Kingdom. This division produces a full range of packet, bagged, and bulk sugar, as well as dairy products and bakery mixes, and accounts for approximately 83 percent of the company's annual turnover of £231 million. The sugar division is also Real Good Food's most profitable, generating nearly two-thirds of its operating profit. The company's Bakery Ingredients division, which represents nearly 14 percent of sales, trades through the Renshaw and Sefcol brands, and produces marzipan, sugarpaste, caramel, chocolate flavored coatings, and other items for the retail, foodservice, and industrial markets. Real Good Food's smallest division is its Bakery division, which produces luxury cakes and pastries under the Hayden's Bakeries and Seriously Scrumptious brands. In 2007 Real Good Food sold its fourth division, a fish processing unit. Founded in 2003, Real Good Food is listed on the London Stock Exchange's AIM market. Cofounder Pieter Totté is company chairman, while Stephen Heslop is managing director.

FILLING A SHELL IN 2003

The U.K. retail supermarket industry by 2000 was marked by a heightened degree of competition. As a result, retailers placed increasing pressure on food producers to reduce their prices. Manufacturers unwilling or unable to meet the pricing demands of the major supermarket groups quickly found themselves shut out from their stores. However, many producers who attempted to retain their retailer clients by slashing their own margins paid the price of a drop in profits, and even a slip into losses.

The result of these pressures was that a growing number of smaller food manufacturers, some of which had been in operation since the 19th century and even beyond, were struggling to survive into the new century. Major food groups such as Nestlé and Unilever were able to make up for their lower margins through sheer

COMPANY PERSPECTIVES

The Real Good Food Company plc is a food group with three operating divisions supplying a wide range of ingredient and bakery products to grocery retailers, wholesalers and manufacturers. We aim to continue developing our assets by focusing on product excellence, customer service and innovation.

volume. The large-scale manufacturers were also able to adapt their production processes, adding modernized and automated machinery. Changes to their recipes, by incorporating lower cost ingredients, or even by replacing real ingredients with substitute products, was another way for the major producers to adjust to the ongoing demands for lower prices.

Smaller producers were unable to afford the same investments. While the market for higher-end, luxury products, generally shunned by the major mass food producers, continued to hold promise for smaller producers, the very nature of the market limited their ability to adjust their recipes. In the meantime, the surge in demand for raw food products from developing markets such as China and India, coupled with rising fuel costs, meant that the cost of the ingredients themselves had begun to rise sharply.

The situation of the U.K. food market stimulated the emergence of a number of new shell companies created with the specific intention of acquiring and regrouping the operations of smaller food companies into a larger holding company. The new type of shell company took advantage of the growing number of struggling and even failing firms, scooping them up for next to nothing, often for little more than the company's debt load.

Among the new players in the U.K. foods sector was a company called Real Good Food Company, created in 2003 by two food industry veterans, Pieter Totté and John Gibson. The initiative was led by the Dutch-born Totté, who had previously created another company, Finsbury Foods, from Megalomedia, itself a shell company formed by Lord Saatchi to acquire Internet companies in the late 1990s. Into the early 2000s, Totté had set himself up as a corporate financier, developing a number of investment vehicles. Gibson, meanwhile, had established his reputation as an interim CEO specializing in turning around struggling businesses. Gibson's previous career included stints at Grand Met, the Muller yogurt company, and Uniq.

Totté and Gibson started their new company by acquiring three small companies. The first, Hayden's Bakeries Limited, gave the company a large bakery facility. The second, Cake Co. UK Ltd., provided Real Good Food with a strong brand, Seriously Scrumptious, which produced "luxury" cakes for the supermarket sector. The third, a sandwich maker called Eurofoods Plc, attempted to cash in on the trend toward ready-made foods. That purchase added the Coolfresh line of sandwiches.

The acquisitions established Real Good Food as a company with more than £23 million in revenues, at a cost of just £2 million. Most of that cost, was in fact, the assumption of debt. In the case of Eurofoods, for example, Real Good Food paid just £3 for a company with revenues of more than £8.5 million per year. However, despite the strong revenue stream, Real Good Food had also acquired the three companies' losses. These amounted to approximately £1.2 million in the year before they were acquired. Much of those losses were produced at Devizes-based Hayden's, which had lost £1 million on sales of £10 million in 2002.

AIM LISTING ATTRACTS INVESTORS

Gibson led the effort to reinvigorate the group's businesses, which continued to operate under their own management for the most part, while Totté sought new acquisition candidates. Nonetheless, Real Good Food's ambitions were to build its existing operations as well. As Totté explained to *Grocer:* "We want to buy turnaround businesses and grow them. If we see a company that needs a different approach and it's in the real low cost arena with the right people, then we will see how we can improve it to get strong organic growth. You need to give these companies a blood transfusion."

Real Good Food itself sought a transfusion as it ramped up its future acquisition strategy. With three companies under its belt, and signs of progress already visible in their operations, Real Good Food went public. In September 2003, the company listed its shares on the London Stock Exchange's AIM (Alternative Investment Market) board. The offering initially valued the company at 105p per share. Three months later, the company completed a secondary offering, raising an additional £10 million, at 135p per share.

The new offering served to finance Real Good Food's latest acquisition of Five Star Fish Limited. The new operation established Real Good Food as a major supplier of processed fish products, including breaded, battered, and dusted cod, haddock, plaice, and pollock. The acquisition of Five Star Fish cost the company £16.6 million.

KEY DATES

2003: Pieter Totté and John Gibson found Real Good Food to acquire small companies and take Real Good Food public.
2004: Real Good Food acquires fish processor Five Star Fish.
2005: Real Good Food acquires Napier Brown & Company in a reverse takeover.
2007: Real Good Food sells Five Star Fish operations.

Real Good Food made good on its promise to invest in building its new businesses. The company beefed up management expertise and financial controls, adding new personnel. The company also invested in new machinery and production equipment, boosting quality. At the same time, the group's operations worked on developing new products, including private-label luxury cakes for supermarket firm Waitrose and other retailers, such as Marks and Spencer. Later, in 2005, the company consolidated its bakery operations at Hayden's Devizes factory, achieving strong cost savings.

These efforts paid off as both the Hayden's and Seriously Scrumptious businesses returned to profitability in 2004. The Hayden's operation had grown particularly strong, raising revenues by 50 percent to top £15 million that year. The company's total revenues topped £100 million in 2005.

Less successful for the company, however, was its Coolfresh sandwich division. After its major client, a chain of coffee shops, failed to roll out its own expansion, Coolfresh's losses continued to mount. Real Good Food attempted to breathe new life into the operations, launching a takeover attempt of a rival sandwich maker. When that offer failed, the company decided to shut down the Eurofoods and the Coolfresh brand, writing off a loss of £2 million.

SWEET REVERSE TAKEOVER IN 2005

The company's successes elsewhere encouraged Real Good Food to target a leap into the ranks of the U.K. food sector leaders at the middle of the first decade of the 2000s. In September 2005, the company spotted its next growth vehicle, launching the £67.74 million acquisition of Napier Brown & Company, the United Kingdom's third largest sugar trader.

While that company had originally been incorporated in 1982, its growth in the first decade of the 2000s mirrored Real Good Food. Napier Brown began seeking operations to help transform itself into a major sugar and related ingredients player. The company acquired Sefcol in 2000. That company had been founded in 1952, and produced sugar and nut products, such as sugarpaste, nut blends, caramel, and marzipan. Into the 2000s, Napier Brown's owners leveraged the company's operations in packaging and trading refined sugar and related products to launch an acquisition drive of its own. The company added its shares to the AIM board in 2003, raising £9 million. Napier Brown then went shopping, buying James Budgett Sugars, formerly part of Greencore, for £17.5 million, followed by Renshaw, a venerable Liverpool-based producer of marzipan, icing, baking chocolate, and other ingredients.

The Napier Brown acquisition in fact took the form of a reverse takeover, as the investment group behind the larger company gained the majority of Real Good Food's shares. The merger of the two companies helped transform Real Good Food, which reported revenues of more than £222 million at the end of 2006. Nonetheless, the acquisition, which boosted the company's debt load to £60 million, failed to excite the investor community, sending the group's share price sharply down. A month after the acquisition, Real Good Food's market value had dropped to £70 million, just two million more than it had paid for Napier Brown. Yet a major motivation for the merger had been Real Good Food's desire to gain a higher profile, and rating, enabling it to generate more funding for its future acquisition plans.

GROWTH TRACK TOWARD 2010

Totté and company remained confident in their ability to build the group, pointing to the growing diversity of its businesses as a buffer to market trends and individual sector cycles. Part of its confidence came from its willingness to invest in expanding the group's production capacity. The company spent some £400,000 in a new frying line for its Hayden's bakery factory. This brought the company's total investment in the facility up past £1 million over the previous three years.

These efforts began to pay off in 2007, as the company recorded new rises in both revenues and operating profits. The Napier Brown operations helped lead the company's return to fortune. However, the Five Star Fish business had also performed well. In June 2007, however, Real Good Food decided that fish processing would not become a core operation. The company decided to sell Five Star Fish, making a profit on the £35 million deal.

The sale refocused Real Good Food onto its three core divisions: Sugar, Bakery, and Ingredients. Despite the difficult trading conditions, the company continued to report trading increases, with its revenues passing £231 million in 2007. The company also remained profitable, with total operating profits of £9.6 million. At the same time, the company had stripped down its debt load, which stood at less than £26 million into 2008. Real Good Food appeared to have a recipe for success in the U.K. food production market.

M. L. Cohen

PRINCIPAL SUBSIDIARIES

Eurofoods plc; Garret Ingredients Ltd.; Gaywood Sugars Ltd.; Hayden's Bakeries Ltd.; J F Renshaw Ltd.; James Budgett Sugars Ltd.; Napier Brown & Company Ltd.; Napier Brown Foods Ltd.; Renshaw Scott Ltd.; Whitworths Sugars Ltd.

PRINCIPAL DIVISIONS

Bakery; Ingredients; Sugar.

PRINCIPAL COMPETITORS

Associated British Foods PLC; United Biscuits Holdings PLC; Wittington Investments Ltd.; RHM PLC; Northern Foods PLC; Geest Ltd; Greggs PLC; British Bakeries Ltd.; Warburtons Ltd.; Daniels Chilled Foods Ltd.; The Jacob's Bakery Ltd.; William Jackson and Son Ltd.

FURTHER READING

Cookson, Robert, "Warning Hurts Real Good Food," *Financial Times,* September 26, 2008, p. 26.

Davis, Glynn, "Time to Shell Out," *Grocer,* October 23, 2004, p. 38.

"Food Group Ready for a Bigger Slice," *Western Daily Press,* December 23, 2003.

Gleeson, Bill, "Firm's Sweet Taste of Success," *Daily Post,* July 12, 2007, p. 15.

Grande, Carlos, "Real Good Food Shares Hit by NBF Acquisition," *Financial Times,* May 25, 2006, p. 24.

"Keeping It Real," *Foodchain Home,* April–May 2006.

O'Connor, Brian, "Food for Thought," *Daily Mail,* October 9, 2005.

"Real Good Food Puts Sandwich Setbacks Behind It," *Western Daily Press,* September 9, 2005.

"Real Good Food Sees Operating Profit Fall," *just-food.com,* April 8, 2008.

"RGF Fights Its Way out from Sugar Mountain," *Western Daily Press,* January 17, 2007.

Warwick-Ching, Lucy, "Real Good Food Sells Frozen Fish Arm for £35m," *Financial Times,* June 12, 2007, p. 21.

Renfro Corporation

———————■———————

60 Linville Road
Mount Airy, North Carolina 27030
U.S.A.
Telephone: (336) 719-8000
Toll Free: (800) 334-9091
Fax: (336) 719-8215
Web site: http://www.renfro.com

Private Company
Incorporated: 1921 as Renfro Hosiery Mills Company
Employees: 5,500
Sales: $275.7 million (2007)
NAICS: 315119 Other Hosiery and Sock Mills

■ ■ ■

Renfro Corporation manufactures more than 3,000 different styles and colors of socks, including sports, casuals, and dress varieties, under its own brands—Fruit of the Loom, Starter, Fit First, and Hot Sox—and under license for other hosiery companies including Dr. Scholl's, John Deere, Wrangler, and Rider. The company sells socks across the country in such stores as Wal-Mart, Kmart, Target, J.C. Penney, Sears, Roebuck and Co., Montgomery Ward, and Foot Locker. The company has production facilities in South Carolina, Alabama, China, India, Pakistan, and Turkey and sales and distribution operations in the United States, Canada, Mexico, Europe, and Hong Kong.

RENFRO HOSIERY MILLS COMPANY'S BEGINNING: 1921

In 1921, Renfro Hosiery Mills Company began operations at Willow and Oak streets in Mount Airy, North Carolina. The 88,000-square-foot building in which the company set up its facilities was a former tobacco warehouse built in the 1890s that occupied a quarter of a city block. Renfro's 25 plant workers knitted socks there that were shipped to other plants for finishing and packaging.

CONSOLIDATION IN THE FACE OF DOMESTIC COMPETITION: LATE EIGHTIES TO MID-NINETIES

From the 1920s through the early 1980s, Renfro Hosiery grew by acquiring and absorbing other hosiery manufacturers, establishing itself as a premier domestic maker of socks for men, women, and children. Then, in the late 1980s, Renfro began to grow at a rapid pace, increasing both its production capability and its market share. The 1986 purchase of the former Virginia Maid Hosiery plant on Jefferson Street in downtown Pulaski, Virginia, was followed in 1989 with the opening of a second plant on Newbern Road on land leased from Pulaski County's Industrial Development Authority. Renfro also opened the Renfro Sock Shop in Pulaski's Maple Shade Shopping Center in 1990 and established a third facility in a former department store that it rented in Pulaski in 1993. In 1994, the company added 290 knitting machines and 200 jobs at its three Pulaski plants where it employed a total of 1,168 workers.

This growth, combined with Renfro's "zero defects" program, which encouraged employee participation in management decisions, coincided with a 78 percent increase between 1989 and 1999 in domestic sock production. By mid-decade, the domestic competition in socks was keen. "Pennies a dozen means whether we get an order or not," explained Renfro's Pulaski manager, James D. Reagan, in a 1996 *Roanoke Times & World News* article. "We have to come up with ways to produce [socks] for less money." Having produced between 300 million and 400 million socks in 1995, the company could boast that it was the second largest sock producer and the largest producer of ladies' and girls' socks in the world.

The solution to staying competitive, according to Reagan, was to consolidate operations. "The whole company is fixing itself to where we can knit, seam and finish the product in the same plant, which will lower our costs as far as transportation and handling, and give us a better product because we can control it," he told the *Roanoke Times & World News*. In 1996, Renfro moved its knitting and seaming facilities from the space it leased in a department store to the newly doubled 105,000-square-foot Newbern Road plant. This expansion was to lead to the addition of another 400 to 450 employees over several years, during which time the company's Jefferson Mills plant would install 315 new knitting machines costing $24,000 apiece and 27 new seaming machines costing $18,000 each. The plan was to bring on line 25 new knitting machines a month until all were installed.

ACQUISITIONS, REORGANIZATION, CHANGES IN PRODUCTION: LATE NINETIES

The company also grew through acquisitions during the second half of the 1990s. In 1995, it acquired Great American Knitting Mills, which operated Annedeen Hosiery Mills in Burlington, North Carolina. In 1996, the company purchased Fruit of the Loom's hosiery division with factories in North and South Carolina,

and Alabama for about $95 million. These two companies made plans to enter into a 20-year exclusive long-term licensing agreement that would allow Renfro to use the Fruit of the Loom name and trademark for its adult and children's athletic, casual, and dress socks. Also in 1996, the company purchased Pittsburg Knitting Mills, a small knitting company in South Pittsburg, Tennessee.

All told, Renfro's employee count reached slightly more than 4,000 with the addition of the 1,400 people working in Fruit of the Loom's hosiery operations in Alabama, North Carolina, and South Carolina. Approximately 1,500 of those worked at its headquarters, distribution center, and three factories in Mount Airy, while the rest worked at its three factories in Pulaski, Virginia, and a distribution center in Canada. It manufactured about 408 million socks a year.

Then, in 1997, Renfro began a period of reorganization. It gradually closed down operations at its 286-employee, four-story Willow Creek plant in Mount Airy, where its operations had started in 1921, and, a year later, its Jefferson Avenue plant in Pulaski and its Sock Shop. The equipment from these plants was moved to its other plants.

These closures in part reflected changes in domestic sock production. In 1998, socks, which then accounted for 70 percent of all domestic hosiery production, had increased by 177 million dozen pairs annually, while sheer hosiery had fallen. The top sock category was men's athletic socks with 33 percent of all production; women's athletic socks accounted for 11 percent. Consumer preference for casual dress was enforcing changes upon sock manufacturing.

Technology was shifting sock production from a labor-intensive to a capital-intensive industry. The newer, computer-controlled machines, knit yarn on huge spools into socks ever better and more efficiently. As a result, sock production remained domestic, although the industry's workforce began to globalize. Renfro relied on Hispanic immigrants in the United States to run its plants and sent partly finished socks to Mexico and Honduras for product finishing and packaging. There people worked for wages as much as 85 percent below U.S. levels.

However, in 1999, a tight labor market made it impossible for Renfro to hire enough people to justify running its larger Newbern plant, consisting of two 100,000-square-foot buildings designed to hold 1,200 workers. Renfro closed that plant and reopened the smaller one on Jefferson Avenue that it had closed just one year earlier.

KEY DATES

1921: Renfro Hosiery Mills Company is founded in Mount Airy, Virginia, with 25 employees at its Willow Creek plant.

1986: Renfro purchases Virginia Maid Hosiery's Jefferson Avenue plant in Pulaski, Virginia.

1989: Company adds another plant on Newbern Road in Pulaski, Virginia.

1990: Company opens the Renfro Sock Shop in Pulaski's Maple Shade Shopping Center.

1993: Company starts to rent department store space.

1995: Renfro acquires Great American Knitting Mills, which operates Annedeen Hosiery Mills in Burlington, North Carolina.

1996: Company acquires Fruit of the Loom's hosiery division; doubles the size of its plant on Newbern Road; purchases Pittsburg Knitting Mills in South Pittsburg, Tennessee.

1997: Company closes its Willow Creek plant.

1998: Company closes its Jefferson Avenue plant and its Sock Shop.

1999: Renfro shuts down its Newbern plant and reopens the plant on Jefferson Avenue.

2000: Renfro purchases Candor Hosiery Mills Inc., Hosiery Sales Inc. of New York, and Intersocks S.p.A.

2002: Renfro enters into a licensing agreement with SKECHERS.

2003: Company closes its plant on Jefferson Avenue.

2007: Sock production ends in Mount Airy; company purchases Hot Sox, which has licenses for Polo Ralph Lauren and Levi's.

OVERSEAS EXPANSION IN MANUFACTURING: 2000–04

Renfro, in effect, ran three businesses and had the market advantage of being a one-stop shopping place for its customers; it sold private-label socks, licensed brands, and a national consumer brand, Fruit of the Loom. In 2000, Renfro employed 3,800 people and had plants in Honduras, Mexico, and Pakistan where workers finished the socks it made in its five remaining domestic plants. It expanded operations to Europe for the first time in 2000 with the purchase of Intersocks S.p.A., which had its headquarters in Pieve d'Alpago, Italy, and

manufacturing, distribution, and sales offices throughout Europe. At the same time in 2000, Renfro also purchased Candor Hosiery Mills of Robbins, North Carolina, and Hosiery Sales Inc. of New York.

The sales of socks in the United States totaled only $5 billion a year in 2001. Renfro, which controlled a significant share of this market, expanded its reach further in 2002 by entering into an exclusive licensing agreement with SKECHERS hosiery, a global leader in lifestyle footwear in the United States. Renfro also expanded its manufacturing facilities in Pune, India, to bring its largest selling brand, Fruit of the Loom, overseas. It forged a joint venture and formed Renfro India Pvt. Ltd., increasing the number of knitting machines there from 82 to 300. Renfro India also became the manufacturing center for Renfro's U.S. markets and its product distribution center for Europe.

The next few years saw additional domestic plant closures for Renfro. In 2003, it eliminated 166 jobs in Pulaski when it moved its Jefferson Avenue plant's finishing department to Mexico. The company at this time had plants in South Carolina and Alabama and in Mexico, Honduras, India, and Pakistan. In the fall of 2003, it closed the plant entirely, shutting down its knitting and dyeing operations and eliminating another 315 jobs.

However, unlike some other hosiery manufacturers, Renfro opposed the 2004 Bush administration move to impose quotas on Chinese sock imports to quell the dramatic increase in the influx of Chinese socks into the U.S. market. In 2003, China had shipped 264 million pairs of socks to the United States, 48 times its total U.S. imports in 1999. By August 2004, that number had increased to more than half a billion, and the U.S. sock trade fell from 64 percent of the domestic market in 2001 to 31.4 percent for the year.

"If we're going to survive as a prominent player in this business, we have to be a global company," was the reason Warren Nichols, chief executive officer of Renfro, offered for his company's opposition to the quotas in a 2004 *Knight-Ridder* article. Renfro formed a partnership with Walt Knitting Co., a Chinese manufacturer of socks, in 2004.

CONTINUING PLANT CLOSURES: 2004–07

The company, which that year had sales of $274 million, had cut 1,631 jobs since 1997. Before 2004 was out, Renfro again cut 53 percent of the workforce at its Riverside plant in Mount Airy, firing about 280 people and bringing the total number of people laid off by the company in Mount Airy since 1997 to about 700. In 2007, it ended sock production in Mount Airy entirely, although Mount Airy remained the home of company headquarters, research and development, and distribution. The same week that it terminated production in Mount Airy, it bought Hot Sox Inc., thereby gaining access to the Polo Ralph Lauren and Levi's brands of socks as well as the Hot Sox brand.

Shortly afterward, the company agreed to be sold to members of its senior management and affiliates of a private equity firm, Kelso & Co. It also changed its position on import quotas; Renfro, a leader in moving production overseas, had steadfastly opposed trade safeguards against Chinese sock imports. It now joined other southern hosiery manufacturers in supporting safeguards against imports on Honduras in response to a 60 percent increase in sock imports from Honduras during the first six months of 2007. "This safeguard remedy … is necessary to level the playing field with companies shipping socks from Honduras to the U.S. market," explained Warren Nichols in a September 2007 *Winston-Salem Journal* article. Although the company had maintained in a March 2007 *Winston-Salem Journal*

article that it remained "a vibrant and growing company globally," Renfro clearly would face challenges from foreign manufacturers in years ahead.

Carrie Rothburd

PRINCIPAL COMPETITORS
Hanesbrands; MAST; Russell Corporation.

FURTHER READING
Craver, Richard, "Tariffs May Be Reset on Honduras Socks: 5,000 Triad Jobs at Stake in Import Fight," *Winston-Salem Journal,* September 25, 2007.

Dellinger, Paul, "Lots of Socks; Renfro Is the Nation's Second-Largest Sock Maker and Pulaski's No. 1 Employer," *Roanoke Times & World News,* February 25, 1996, p. 18.

Hopkins, Sheila M., "U.S. Ruling Means Chinese Sock Imports May Be Limited," *Knight-Ridder/Tribune Business News,* October 23, 2004, p. 1.

McCurry, John W., "Casual Trend Has Sock Mills Hopping," *Textile World,* October 1999, p. 26.

"102 Jobs to Be Cut: Plant Closing in Mount Airy," *Winston-Salem Journal,* March 15, 2007.

Wessel, David, "Socks Are Odd: Made in America," *Wall Street Journal,* May 3, 2001, A1.

Retractable Technologies, Inc.

---

511 Lobo Lane
Little Elm, Texas 75068
U.S.A.
Telephone: (972) 294-1010
Toll Free: (888) 806-2626
Fax: (972) 294-4400
Web site: http://www.vanishpoint.com

Public Company
Incorporated: 1994
Employees: 138
Sales: $26.29 million (2007)
Stock Exchanges: American
Ticker Symbol: RVP
NAICS: 339112 Surgical and Medical Instrument Manufacturing

■ ■ ■

Retractable Technologies, Inc., (RTI) sells safety syringes and other injection technologies that reduce the risk of accidental injuries in the healthcare industry. RTI's mainstay product line of VanishPoint safety syringes feature needles that automatically retract after injection, preventing accidental needle pricks that transmit blood-borne infections such as tuberculosis, hepatitis, and HIV. The company also makes a line of intravenous catheters and blood collection needles that feature similar technology. RTI's products are distributed nationally and internationally.

ORIGINS

As an engineering student at the University of Arizona, Thomas J. Shaw failed to make much of an impression. He was a mediocre student who rarely earned more than a "C" and who failed to secure his engineering credentials until his mid-30s, but after a slow and lackluster start to his professional career, Shaw began to shine. RTI became his crowning achievement. An inventor at heart, Shaw realized his greatest technological success with RTI's VanishPoint, but he also discovered that creative success did not confer success in the marketplace.

Shaw started his first company in 1984, a job-placement agency that occupied modest quarters in the corner of a bicycle shop in Little Elm, Texas, an hour north of Dallas. The business's profits gave him the money to earn his engineering credentials, which allowed him to establish his own engineering firm, Checkmate Engineering, four years later at the age of 37. Shaw's first customer was an amputee in a dispute with his insurance company. The man's prosthetic leg was cracked, and his insurer refused to replace it, insisting that the man had intentionally damaged the artificial limb. Shaw's customer argued that the crack resulted from a design flaw, a claim he hoped an independent engineering study would corroborate. Shaw analyzed the artificial limb, discovered an inherent weakness in its design, and his customer prevailed, receiving a new prosthetic limb paid for by his insurance company.

SHAW'S INSPIRATION

After his first success, Shaw relied on more conventional engineering business, assisting in the construction of civil projects in and around Little Elm. Checkmate Engineering subsisted on projects related to building roads and buildings, but the work was not enough to satisfy Shaw's desire to tinker and to invent. He was fascinated by medical devices, eager to develop new products that answered unaddressed needs. When a friend expressed concern that her grandmother was not taking her medication regularly, Shaw applied for a federal grant and developed an electronic pill machine that measured and dispensed medication, employing a monitoring system that telephoned caregivers if the proper medication was not taken. When Shaw learned of a doctor dying from AIDS because of an accidental needle prick while using a hypodermic syringe, he began laying the foundation for RTI.

In 1989, one year after founding Checkmate Engineering, Shaw was at home watching the nightly news. One segment featured the plight of a doctor who had been infected with HIV while caring for a patient diagnosed with the disease. The doctor, who had contracted AIDS, had become infected because he had accidentally pricked himself with the syringe's needle—not an isolated incident, Shaw learned, in the healthcare industry. The U.S. Centers for Disease Control and Prevention estimated that roughly 800,000 accidental needle-stick injuries were reported annually in hospitals, primarily by nurses and lab technicians who typically pricked themselves while capping the needle. Shaw studied the design of a hypodermic syringe and knew he could do better.

THE DEVELOPMENT OF VANISHPOINT

The idea of safety needles was not a novel concept in the late 1980s. They had been around for years, but nurses and other healthcare personnel had found them awkward to use. Further, the cost of a safety needle was an issue, with a safety needle sold by Becton Dickinson

and Company, the largest syringe maker in the country, priced at three times the total of a standard needle. Shaw believed he could make a lower cost, easier-to-use safety needle and he began experimenting with designs.

After spending a year working on preliminary design concepts, Shaw, as he had with his electronic medication project, received federal funding. The National Institute on Drug Abuse, part of the National Institutes of Health (NIH), awarded Shaw a $50,000 grant to continue his work on designs. By 1991, he had developed a prototype, a syringe with a needle that retracted into the syringe barrel after the medicine was dispensed. Shaw felt his work was done, unwilling to take the next step and form a company to manufacture his device. He hoped to license the device to a company already involved in making syringes and use the licensing fee to purchase a new piece of equipment for his fishing excursions. "I was willing to let it go for the price of a bass boat," he recalled in a March 1, 2005 interview with *FSB*. "I thought the design was worth maybe $50,000," he said.

To help bring his invention to market, Shaw turned to the biggest syringe maker in the United States, Franklin Lakes, New Jersey-based Becton Dickinson. The response took roughly a year, a note sent to Shaw that thanked him for his submission and informed him that Becton Dickinson, busy developing its own new safety syringe design, was not interested.

RTI INCORPORATED IN 1994

Rebuffed by Becton Dickinson, Shaw, somewhat reluctantly, decided to self-manufacture his safety syringes. He received additional funding through the NIH, a $600,000 grant to commercialize the production of his retractable syringe design and to produce 10,000 samples for clinical trials. He incorporated RTI in 1994 and shortly thereafter began testing the device at three major hospitals in Texas. The reaction to his retractable syringe was overwhelmingly positive, particularly from Presbyterian Hospital in Dallas, typified by the words of Dr. Lawrence Mills, chief of thoracic surgery at the institution. "I thought the biggest problem was the company wouldn't be able to make them fast enough to keep up with the demand," he said in the March 1, 2005 issue of *FSB*.

Shaw's elation quickly faded, however, when he was informed by administrators at Presbyterian Hospital that the institution could not purchase his retractable syringes because of contractual stipulations with a group purchasing organization (GPO), Premier Purchasing Partners. "I grew up in the desert, and I know a scorpion when I see one," Shaw said in his March 1, 2005 interview with *FSB*. "At that moment, I knew the

KEY DATES

1994: Thomas J. Shaw incorporates Retractable Technologies, Inc. (RTI).
1998: A year after commercial production of VanishPoint safety syringes begins, Shaw files an antitrust lawsuit to restore his free trade rights.
2001: RTI completes its initial public offering of stock.
2003: Premier, Novation, and Tyco International settle antitrust charges for $50 million.
2004: Becton Dickinson agrees to pay RTI $100 million to settle its lawsuit.
2007: RTI files another lawsuit against Becton Dickinson, accusing the company of patent infringement, antitrust practices, and false advertising.

healthcare system was rotten to the core."

Shaw's frustrations were just beginning. To build a manufacturing facility and to hire workers to begin volume production, he needed capital. He turned to Wall Street investors and received an encouraging amount of interest (investment bankers from Goldman Sachs made six separate visits to Little Elm) but one after another, the investors backed away from supporting Shaw. They knew what he was beginning to realize, that the hospital-supply market was virtually impenetrable. The largest hospital-supply manufacturers had supply agreements with the largest GPOs, who served as purchasing agents for many of the hospitals in the country, thereby controlling, under contract, the supplies purchased by hospitals. Shaw faced a formidable barrier, one that made the widespread distribution of his VanishPoint safety syringe a decidedly uphill battle.

LEGAL FIGHT ERUPTS IN 1998

Shaw tried to break through the barrier where he could. He approached hospitals in areas overlooked by the giants of the healthcare industry, focusing on markets GPOs deemed too small or too poor. Shaw sold VanishPoint syringes to federal prisons, to Native American reservations, and to the Mississippi Health Department, but the trickle of business did not lessen his frustration at what he perceived to be a cabal united against him. In 1998, he took action, filing a lawsuit in state court against three Texas hospitals and two syringe suppliers,

Tyco International and Becton Dickinson, accusing his adversaries of antitrust violations, specifically restraint of trade. The defendants were ready for a fight, Becton Dickinson in particular. The country's largest syringe manufacturer dispatched more than a dozen attorneys to Brazoria County, Texas, marshaling its forces to combat the tiny company in Little Elm.

Pretrial proceedings dragged on for years, offering little hope that Shaw would prevail in proving the defendants contracted among themselves and others to the detriment of RTI. The prospects for Shaw's legal battle brightened considerably when an attorney named Mark Lanier intervened on Shaw's behalf, agreeing to take the case on a contingency basis. Lanier's Houston-based firm agreed to invest the money and resources to bring the case to trial in exchange for one-third of the damages awarded. Ultimately, Lanier's firm would spend $6 million to argue its case, using a strategy that differed from Shaw's original lawsuit. In 2001, Lanier re-filed the case in federal court in Texarkana, Texas, a move that meant any damages would be tripled under federal antitrust law, and he dropped the three Texas hospitals from the lawsuit. RTI's legal fight became focused on the two large syringe makers, Tyco International and Becton Dickinson, and the GPOs that negotiated the contracts between syringe manufacturers and two-thirds of the nation's hospitals, Novation and Premier Purchasing Partners. RTI was seeking $600 million in damages.

SUCCESS OVERSEAS

While the tussle over the $6 billion syringe market continued in Texarkana, Shaw recorded some encouraging victories outside the legal arena. He succeeded in completing RTI's initial public offering (IPO) on the American Stock Exchange in 2001, raising $42 million primarily from doctors in Texas. He also made progress overseas, finding international markets far more penetrable than domestic markets. In June 2002, RTI signed a long-term agreement with Double Dove Co., Ltd., the largest syringe maker in China. The agreement called for Double Dove to dedicate 100,000 square feet of its manufacturing facility near Shanghai to the production of VanishPoint syringes, which was expected to reduce the average unit cost of RTI's needles to 8.5 cents. Less than a week after the partnership with Double Dove was forged, RTI signed marketing agreements with three of Europe's leading medical supply firms, paving the way for the distribution of VanishPoint syringes to healthcare facilities in Belgium, the Netherlands, Luxembourg, Denmark, and Sweden.

2003–04: LEGAL ISSUES RESOLVED

On the heels of RTI's international success, attention turned to its legal struggle, with its trial in Texarkana scheduled to begin in April 2003. The trial was postponed, however, "under a veil of secrecy," according to the May 2003 issue of *Hospital Materials Management*. The defendants, it was reported, had filed a motion to delay, which postponed the trial for nearly a year. Shortly after the judge's decision to reschedule the trial, three of the defendants reconsidered their legal strategy. In May 2003, Premier, Novation, and Tyco International decided to settle out of court, agreeing to pay a total of $50 million to RTI and to change their business practices. Their decision to bow out left RTI pitted against one foe, Becton Dickinson.

In February 2004, after six years of litigation, Shaw's battle against the industry giants came to a close. Hours before the trial was to begin, Becton Dickinson offered to settle charges it had illegally manipulated the market. The company offered to pay RTI $100 million, but, unlike its fellow defendants, it did not agree to change the manner in which it operated. Shaw, under pressure from shareholders who urged him to take the money, reluctantly agreed, concerned he would continue to face the same impenetrable barrier he had faced for the previous decade. "I never wanted the money, I just want to get into hospitals," he said in his March 1, 2005 interview with *FSB*.

MURKY FUTURE

Shaw's difficulties in shepherding VanishPoint into the mainstream persisted after his legal victory. Becton Dickinson made no promise to change its business practices and any changes made by Novation, Premier, and Tyco International were indiscernible to Shaw's eyes. RTI needed to control more than a fraction of the market to succeed financially, with losses of $3.8 million in 2006 and $6.9 million in 2007 indicative of the urgent need to wrest business away from its much larger rivals (Becton Dickinson generated $6.3 billion in revenue in 2007; RTI generated $26 million). Shaw continued to believe he was being unfairly blocked from market access by Becton Dickinson, prompting him to file another lawsuit against Becton Dickinson in 2007, accusing the company of patent infringement, antitrust practices, and false advertising. The cash settlement in 2004 was regarded as a "bittersweet victory," according to RTI's web site in late 2008. "Although it validated our position and provided an infusion of cash, our lifesaving products are still blocked from many hospitals." The passage on the web site concluded with four words that typified Shaw's experience since the formation of RTI—"So the struggle continues."

Jeffrey L. Covell

PRINCIPAL COMPETITORS

Becton, Dickinson, and Company; Covidien Ltd.; Terumo Corporation.

FURTHER READING

Becker, Cinda, "Federal Legislation Seals the Deal," *Modern Healthcare*, October 23, 2000, p. 40.

———, "Needling the Competition," *Modern Healthcare*, May 12, 2003, p. 10.

———, "'60 Minutes' Invades Safety Needle Seminar," *Modern Healthcare*, November 6, 2000, p. 94.

Colucci, Deana, "Accurate Assembly Leads to Safer Syringes," *Design News*, June 8, 1998, p. 111.

"GPO Antitrust Trial Delayed for a Year," *Hospital Materials Management*, May 2003, p. 2.

Gray, Patricia B., "Stick It to 'Em," *FSB*, March 1, 2005, p. 82.

"Groups, Suppliers, to Face Off in Court Following Lawsuit by Retractable Tech.," *Hospital Materials Management*, February 2003, p. 6.

"More Safety Needle Contracts Emerge Following New Law," *Hospital Materials Management*, January 2001, p. 7.

"Retractable Tech Signs Syringe Deal with China's Double Dove," *AsiaPulse News*, June 25, 2002, p. 499.

"Retractable Technologies Signs Agreements to Market VanishPoint Safety Needle Devices to the Benelux Countries, Denmark, and Sweden," *Canadian Corporate News*, June 28, 2002.

Smith, Heather, "Retractable v. Becton, Dickinson Et Al.," *Corporate Counsel*, August 2003.

Riedel Tiroler Glashuette GmbH

Weissachstrasse 28-34
Kufstein, A-6330
Austria
Telephone: (+43) 05372 648 96 0
Fax: (+43) 05372 632 25
Web site: http://www.riedelcrystal.co.at

Private Company
Incorporated: 1956
Employees: 1,900
Sales: EUR 300 million ($345 million) (2005 est.)
NAICS: 327215 Glass Product Manufacturing Made of Purchased Glass

■ ■ ■

Riedel Tiroler Glashuette GmbH is a world-renowned designer and producer of glassware. The Austrian company focuses on the production of glasses specially designed for drinking wine. Riedel's range includes the high-end, hand-blown Sommelier series, which includes more than 100 glass shapes, each developed for a specific variety of wine. The company also produces the best-selling O series, a stemless wine glass, and the mid-priced machine-blown Vinum line. Since 2004, Riedel has also controlled German rival Nachtmann, adding its crystal glass and tableware designs, as well as the discount-priced Spiegelau line. Riedel remains controlled by the founding Riedel family, and led by Georg Riedel and his son Maximilian Riedel. The company's sales are estimated at more than EUR 300 million ($345 million).

18TH-CENTURY ORIGINS

The history of the Riedel family's involvement in glass-making reaches back to early 18th-century Bohemia. The family started out as a glass merchant, as Johann Christoph Riedel, born in 1678, became a prosperous glass trader covering much of Europe. Riedel was murdered, however, in 1823, a crime that was said to have inspired the late 19th-century poem "The Cranes of Ibykus" by Friedrich Schiller.

Riedel's son, Johann Carl Riedel, who became a glasscutter and gilder by trade, became the first in the family to move into glass production. Born in 1701, Riedel went on to establish a glassmaking workshop in Antoniwald. Like much of the Bohemian glassmaking industry at the time, the workshop was established in the heart of the region's forests, close to the abundant source of fuel for the glassworks' furnace.

Riedel's nephew, Johann Leopold Riedel, proved himself an active entrepreneur. Born in 1826, Riedel went to work in the glassworks, then owned by his cousin, learning the craft and becoming a highly skilled glassmaker. A collapse in the glassware market, however, forced the glassworks to shut down. Johann Leopold stepped in to arrange a loan and reopen the glassworks. By 1756, Riedel had not only succeeded in paying off the loan, but he also had obtained authorization to operate as an independent business, paying rent to the local nobility.

The outbreak of the Seven Year War between Prussia and Austria in that year provided an opportunity for the glassworks. The war had destroyed many of the windows in the surrounding region. Riedel therefore

COMPANY PERSPECTIVES

Claus Riedel was the first person in the long history of the glass to design its shape according to the characters of the wine. He is thus the inventor of the functional wine glass.

converted much of his production to window panes. He also developed a system for replacing stained glass windows with ordinary clear glass.

This success enabled Riedel to build a new and larger glassworks in the Antoniwald forests, in Zenckner. Construction of the site was completed in 1775. Soon after, the fourth generation of Riedels, represented by Anton Leopold Riedel, joined the family trade. The younger Riedel, born in 1761, soon took over the business and by the end of the century had shifted its production from window panes to the production of more luxurious glass and crystal objects. The company's production grew to include a range of vases and glasses, as well as glass parts for chandeliers. Riedel also developed new production techniques, and built a new works.

Both of Anton Leopold Riedel's sons entered the family business. It was his son Franz Xavier Riedel who became the next in the line of famed Riedel glassmakers. Franz Xavier Riedel displayed a particular talent as a glass engraver, and became a well-known artist. Riedel also innovated, developing a technique for producing colored glass using uranium. At the same time, Riedel retained the family's gift for entrepreneurship. Capturing the spirit of the times, the company launched production of a wide range of beads, buttons, and other "notions" as the popular glass objects were known.

THE GLASS KING IN 1830

With no male heir of his own, Franz Xavier brought his nephew Josef Riedel into the business in 1830. Then just 14 years old, the younger Riedel proved himself not only as an avid apprentice, but also as an able businessman. In 1840, Riedel married his cousin, Anna Maria, settling questions of succession. When Franz Xavier Riedel died four years later, Josef Riedel became the head of what would soon be one of the region's most important glassworks.

By 1849, Riedel had already begun to expand the company, buying a rival glassworks that year. Riedel's success quickly earned him the nickname as the "Glass King of the Jizera Mountains." The death of his wife in

1855, however, marked a turning point for the company. Rather than remain in Antoniwald, Riedel decided to set up a new glassworks in Unter-Polaun, in the German-speaking Sudeten region. The choice of location was to have an important impact on the company's growth in the coming decades. In the meantime, Riedel continued to expand his operations, replacing the original Antoniwald works with a new and larger glassworks in Wilhelmshöhe in 1866.

The arrival of the railroad to Unter-Polaun in 1877 provided a major opportunity for Riedel. The company now began to import coal, which burned hotter and cost less than wood, and became the first to install modern gas furnaces. The company's production soared, focused on producing glass beads and unfinished glass blanks. The presence of the railroad facilitated shipments of the company's goods, further stimulating production growth. Rather than distribute its own products under its own name, the company established a network of traders. In this way, Riedel's production reached a worldwide market.

Josef Riedel the Elder brought his own sons into the family business, but youngest son Josef Riedel the Younger emerged as the leader of the next generation. Trained as a chemist and mechanical engineer, Riedel led the company into new directions, creating a range of more than 600 colors into the years of World War I. Glass beads became the company's most important product. Riedel's training as a mechanical engineer enabled him to develop machinery for drawing out glass tubes and rods, thereby permitting the mass production of glass beads. The invention represented a major breakthrough in the glassmaking industry.

SWITCHING TO STEMWARE

Walter Riedel became the next generation to take over the family business after his father's death in 1924. By then, the company, as well as the rest of the German-speaking Sudeten region, found itself part of the new Czech republic, created after the breakup of the Austria-Hapsburg Empire in the aftermath of World War I. The company nonetheless continued to grow, despite the turbulence of both the economic and political climate in the years leading up to World War II.

Through the 1930s, Riedel became a leading producer of bottles for the perfume industry, as well as gift items and chandeliers. Walter Riedel also continued to build on his father's production innovations, and introduced a number of new molding techniques. The German invasion and occupation of Czechoslovakia in 1938, however, placed the company under the control of the Nazi regime. Riedel's production was then converted to supporting the Nazi war effort.

```
┌─────────────────────────────────────────────┐
│                                               │
│              KEY DATES                        │
│                  ■                            │
│                                               │
│  1756:  Johann Leopold Riedel establishes an  │
│         independent glass workshop in the     │
│         Bohemian region, producing window     │
│         panes.                                │
│  1844:  Josef Riedel takes over the family    │
│         business, expanding it to become      │
│         one of the largest in the region.     │
│  1955:  Claus Riedel reestablishes the        │
│         family's glass-making business in     │
│         Austria and begins developing new     │
│         stemware designs.                     │
│  1973:  Riedel launches the Sommelier line    │
│         of wine glasses.                      │
│  1987:  Georg Riedel takes over as head of    │
│         the company and introduces the        │
│         lower-priced Vinnum line.             │
│  2004:  Riedel acquires F.X. Nachtmann in     │
│         Germany, including its Spiegelau      │
│         brand.                                │
│  2007:  Riedel launches the "O" line of       │
│         stemless wineglasses.                 │
│                                               │
└─────────────────────────────────────────────┘
```

The company at first began producing fiberglass. At the insistence of the Ministry of Aviation, the company formed a partnership with another company, led by Werner Schuller, who had developed a platinum-free method of producing fiberglass. Riedel's expertise in glass molding techniques also caught the attention of the ministry, which asked the company to deliver a 76-centimeter picture tube to be used as part of a new radar system. Despite the fact that at the time no one had succeeded in producing a picture tube larger than 38 centimeters, Riedel succeeded.

This success was to have dramatic consequences for Riedel following the war, as the Soviet Union took over control of Czechoslovakia. The Riedel family's operations were confiscated by the new government, and at first Walter Riedel was ordered to continue running the Riedel glassworks. When the Soviet Union discovered Riedel's picture tube, however, he was taken prisoner by the Soviets and was sent to Siberia. Riedel became a so-called forced contractor, initially with a five-year contract, and was put to work rebuilding the Soviet Union's glass factories. After the five-year period, however, the Stalinist government refused to allow him to return to Czechoslovakia. When Riedel complained to the Austrian embassy, he was arrested and sentenced to 25 years in jail. In the end, the intercession of German President Konrad Adenauer and the death of

Joseph Stalin permitted Riedel to be freed after just five years.

STARTING OVER IN THE FIFTIES

In the meantime, Riedel's son, Claus Riedel, had begun rebuilding the family's fortunes in Austria. The younger Riedel, born in 1925, had been conscripted into the German army and had engaged in fighting Italian partisans in the Tuscany region. At the end of the war, Claus Riedel was arrested by the Americans and placed in a prisoner of war camp. In 1946, while being transported back to Czechoslovakia, Riedel jumped the train. Riedel found himself in Austria, some 17 kilometers from the village where Daniel Swarovski operated his famed glassworks.

Swarovski had been an apprentice under Riedel's great-grandfather, and welcomed Riedel into his home, sending him to university, where he studied chemistry. Riedel worked a number of jobs over the next decade, and was joined by his father following his release. In 1955, however, Swarovski was offered the purchase of a failed stemware factory in Kufstein. While stemware did not fit in with Swarovski's own production, Daniel Swarovski agreed to back the Riedel family's purchase of the business.

The company, Tiroler Glashütte, specialized in mouth-blown stemware. Claus Riedel quickly developed a passion for the product, and soon emerged as one of the leading figures in stemware design. Indeed, over the next several years, Riedel transformed wineglass design from the traditionally innate styles to the sleeker and more delicate design now associated with the modern wineglass.

Riedel's background in chemistry and physics led him to investigate the properties of wine glasses and their influence on the taste of wine. By 1961, Riedel had developed the first wine glass specifically developed to enhance the wine drinking experience. Among Riedel's early designs was the enormous Burgundy Grand Cru, which was large enough to hold an entire bottle of wine. That design soon became a museum piece.

STEMWARE FOCUS IN THE EIGHTIES

Riedel continued his investigations into wineglass shapes. This led him to develop an entire range of wineglasses, each created to enhance a specific wine variety. The company at first found it difficult to convince a skeptical wine industry. By 1973, however, the group found the support of the Association of Italian Sommeliers. As a result, the company released the set of wine glasses. The line was given the name Sommelier.

Riedel was by then joined by his son Georg, who took up his father's ideas and helped to expand upon them over the next decades. The younger Riedel also proved himself a gifted and highly persuasive salesman; he would be credited with establishing the Riedel name and wineglass concept as a major presence in the global luxury wine market. Into the next century, Riedel expanded the Sommelier line to more than 100 different shapes.

Riedel also led the company's move into the North American market, where the wines from California were just beginning to achieve international recognition. An important milestone for the company came in the late 1980s when Georg Riedel was able to convince a somewhat skeptical Robert Mondavi of the company's claim that the shape of a wine glass could indeed enhance the flavor of the wine itself.

Georg Riedel took over as head of the company in 1987, and led the group into new commercial directions. The company, which had continued to produce a range of tableware and other glass items, refocused itself solely around its stemware. The group also decided to expand its range beyond its high-end, hand-blown Sommelier series. The company introduced a machine-blown line, Vinnum, which reproduced the shapes of the Sommelier series at a much lower cost. The company later introduced a second mid-priced, machine-blown series, Ouverture, which featured shorter stems. Into the 1990s, Riedel expanded its production to include the restaurant sector, producing the new Riedel Restaurant line. These wineglasses were specifically developed to withstand washing in a restaurant's dishwasher.

EXPANDING GROUP IN THE 21ST CENTURY

The 11th generation of Riedels joined the company in the late 1990s. Maximilian Josef Riedel emerged as a leader of this generation, joining the company in 1997. By 2004, the younger Riedel had taken over as head of the company's U.S. subsidiary. Riedel also joined the family's design legacy, developing the new "O" range of stemless wineglasses. The "O" designs proved immediately popular, and by the middle of the first decade of the 2000s had become the company's strongest seller, accounting for one-third of its total production.

Riedel expanded in 2004, buying German rival F.X. Nachtmann. The purchase not only gave the company a new strong luxury brand, it also added tableware back into the company's product mix. At the same time, the

acquisition gave the company control of Spiegelau, a glassmaker that had long been producing low-priced copies of Riedel's own designs. Riedel, however, recognized the opportunity presented by this production as well, enabling the company to extend its sales to the full range of price points. With roots in the 18th century, Riedel had become a thoroughly modern glassmaker in the 21st century.

M. L. Cohen

PRINCIPAL SUBSIDIARIES

F.X. Nachtmann AG; Riedel America Inc.

PRINCIPAL COMPETITORS

Corning Inc.; Magna Donnelly Corp.; D Swarovski and Co.; Andersen Corp.; Crystal Asfour; Arc International S.A.; Webasto Holdings Ltd.; Gerresheimer Glas AG; Lenox Inc.; Waterford Wedgwood PLC.

FURTHER READING
Atkin, Tim, "Glass with Class," *Guardian,* July 7, 1990, p. 19.

Bauer, Ann, "The Emperor Has Underwear … and Maybe a Pair of Socks," *Rake Magazine,* April 15, 2008.

Cooper, Bernie, "Crystal Gazing," *Bangkok Post,* October 29, 2004.

Fayard, Judy, "Toast of the Town," *Time International,* August 20, 2001, p. 84.

Huynh, Dai, "Glass Aficionado," *Houston Chronicle,* January 5, 2006, p. 25.

Mansson, Per-Hendrik, "The Riedel Dynasty," *Wine Spectator,* December 15, 1999, p. 101.

Prial, Frank J., "Claus Josef Riedel, Crystal Maker Who Suited Glass to Wine, Is Dead at 79," *New York Times,* March 24, 2004, p. A19.

Schubert, Siri, "Breaking Tradition," *Business 2.0.7.5,* June 2006, p. 46.

Teichgraeber, Tim, "As Riedel Wine Glasses Arrives at the Discount Chain, Georg Riedel Discusses Why They've Moved in That Direction," *Minneapolis Star Tribune,* September 5, 2007.

Webb, Carla, "Riedel Crystal Is in a Glass by Itself," *HFN: The Weekly Newspaper for the Home Furnishing Network,* August 16, 2004, p. 29.

———, "Riedel Sets Plans for Three Brands," *HFN: The Weekly Newspaper for the Home Furnishing Network,* November 22, 2004, p. 29.

Wylie, Ian, "Best in Glass," *Fast Company,* December 19, 2007.

Zisko, Allison, "Riedel Acquires Chief Competitor," *HFN: The Weekly Newspaper for the Home Furnishing Network,* November 22, 2004, p. 29.

Rostelecom Joint Stock Co.

1-aya Tverskaya-Yamskaya Ul. 14
Moscow, 125047
Russia
Telephone: (+7 495) 972 82 83
Fax: (+7 495) 972 82 22
Web site: http://www.rt.ru

Public Company
Incorporated: 1990 as AO Sovtelecom
Employees: 35,400
Sales: RUB 62.8 billion ($2.44 billion) (2007)
Stock Exchanges: Moscow New York (ADRs)
Ticker Symbols: RTKMG; ROS (New York)
NAICS: 517110 Wired Telecommunications Carriers

■ ■ ■

Rostelecom Joint Stock Co. is Russia's dominant provider of long-distance and international telephone services. Created following the breakup of the Soviet Union, Rostelecom has carried out a long series of infrastructure upgrades, giving it control of Russia's largest and most modern network. The company controls a fiber-optic network of more than 150,000 kilometers and offers voice, data, and Internet Protocol (IP) support for the fixed line domestic (inter-city) and international long-distance markets. In the last half of the first decade of the 2000s, Rostelecom has also begun providing advanced telecommunications services, such as videoconferencing, virtual private network (VPN), and intelligent network services (INS). On the international side, the company has international connection agree-

ments in place with more than 150 telecommunications services providers in 70 countries. Rostelecom also participates in 25 international cable systems. Despite the loss of its monopoly following Russia's telecommunications market deregulation, Rostelecom has retained a commanding 90 percent share of the market. Nonetheless, in expectation of a future decline in its domestic market share, the company has launched plans to expand into international markets starting in 2008. As part of this effort, the company expects to buy shares in providers in such markets as Ukraine, Azerbaijan, Uzbekistan, Kazakhstan, and Belarus. Rostelecom is listed on the Moscow Stock Exchange, with a secondary listing on the New York Stock Exchange. The Russian government remains Rostelecom's largest shareholder, with a 51 percent stake held through its Svyazinvest telecommunications holding company.

OUTMODED SOVIET-ERA TELECOMMUNICATIONS TECHNOLOGY

The first telephone exchange was introduced into Russia just one year after being introduced in Western Europe, and just five years after the invention of the telephone itself. By 1883, the country already counted some 1,000 telephones. Toward the end of the century, the country also introduced its first cross-country trunk line, permitting long-distance exchanges not only among the country's far-flung cities, as well as connections from Western Europe to Japan.

Despite this relatively early start, by the end of World War I and the start of the Soviet Revolution

Russia had already fallen far behind its European counterparts. Into the early 1920s, telephone penetration in Russia reached just one in 200 people in the country's urban centers, and telephones were far fewer to nonexistent in the country's rural regions. This compared with a penetration rate of one in 50 in the United Kingdom, and with one in ten in the United States.

The Soviet Era provided little hope that the country's telephone system would catch up to the rest of the world. Indeed, during the first decade of Soviet rule, the country's total number of telephones actually declined. The strict control of the Soviet government over the country's communications sector only intensified under Joseph Stalin and the subsequent Cold War period. The highly centralized, Moscow-dominated communications system left little autonomy, and investment, in the country's outlying regions. The Soviet requirement that the country's telecommunications technologies be self-produced also hampered the development of its fixed-line and long-distance networks.

In the 1960s, the government had recognized the need to ensure communications across the vast territory under its control: Russia alone crossed 11 time zones. In 1965, the government launched its own satellite communications system, the Molniya. While a success, the satellite system's technology quickly lagged behind the rapid advancements being made in the West and elsewhere.

The government's tight control over the population and its communications played a role in the U.S.S.R.'s inability to match the pace of its Western counterparts. While the government and military enjoyed access to telephones, the civilian sector remained heavily underserved. Long-distance access was particularly heavily restricted. All long-distance calls were completed through manual exchanges, enabling the government to maintain its strict surveillance.

Into the 1980s, the Russian system struggled to keep up with the increasing array of telecommunications technologies offered by the arrival of the computer age and digital communications systems. The country's own

technology quickly proved inadequate, particularly in the increasingly important area of data transmission. By the end of the decade, the country had been forced to turn to the West in order to modernize its increasingly outmoded telecommunications networks. The country began importing digital switching systems and other equipment. However, these were largely appropriated for military and government use, leaving the residential and newly developing commercial sector dependent on the country's notoriously unreliable telephone network.

CREATION OF A LONG-DISTANCE MONOPOLY IN 1993

By the end of the 1980s, telecommunications technology in the West had far exceeded the increasingly unstable Soviet Union. While digital technology became the norm in the West and other parts of the world, the Soviet Union's long-distance system remained 100 percent analog-based. In 1990, the soon-to-collapse Soviet government made an attempt at reforming its telecommunications sector, especially its anemic long-distance capacity. In that year, the government created AO Sovtelecom. The new company was given responsibility for the long-distance and international telecommunications systems across the Soviet Union.

The collapse of the Soviet Union itself, however, created the need for a new body to replace Sovtelecom. In 1991, the company was transformed into the International Joint-Stock Society Intertelecom. This company too proved only temporary, as the final shape of the new Russian Federation came into place.

In September 1993, the long-distance operator was renamed as Rostelecom Joint Stock Society. In 1994, the Russian government formally granted Rostelecom its license to operate the country's interurban and international telecommunications network. The license also centralized control of the country's primary and secondary trunk line networks, as well as the public data telecommunications network. In this way, Rostelecom gained the national monopoly for the country's long-distance services. Nonetheless, the creation of Rostelecom came as part of an effort by the Russian government to break up the country's former telecommunications monopoly. As a result, local and regional telephone services were spun off into a myriad of smaller operators.

In the meantime, the company had been making progress on upgrading the country's antiquated telecommunications systems. The company laid its first undersea digital fiber-optic line in 1993, reaching from Kingisepp in Russia to Denmark. The group also began construction of a digital radio-relay line linking Moscow

KEY DATES

1990: The Soviet Union creates Sovtelecom to oversee its long-distance telecommunications system.

1991: Sovtelecom becomes Intertelecom with the breakup of the Soviet Union.

1993: Intertelecom becomes Rostelecom, gaining the monopoly over long-distance telecommunications in the Russian Federation.

1996: Rostelecom becomes a subsidiary of state-owned telecommunications company Svyazinvest.

1998: Rostelecom places its ADRs on the New York Stock Exchange.

2004: Rostelecom quadruples capacity on its Moscow-Khabarovsk trunk line.

2008: Rostelecom announces plans to acquire stakes in long-distance providers in Ukraine, Belarus, Uzbekistan, and elsewhere.

with Khabarovsk in Siberia. In this way, Rostelecom participated in the completion of a global digital telecommunications ring linking four continents.

COMPLETING THE FIRST MODERNIZATION PHASE IN 2000

Through the 1990s, Rostelecom implemented its modernization strategy. The group launched construction of the Southern International Telecom System, including an undersea fiber-optic link. The new line linked Moscow with Odessa, Ukraine; Palermo, Italy; and Istanbul, Turkey. Another line, launched in 1995, placed a fiber-optic link between Russia and Japan and Korea.

By 1996, Rostelecom had commissioned its new Central Complex, giving it centralized control of its existing and future long-distance networks. These included the completion of the Moscow-Khabarovsk line, which became the longest digital radio relay in the world. By then, the government had recognized the failure of its attempt to abandon its telecommunications monopoly. This led to the creation of a state-owned holding company, Svyazinvest, which then took control of most of the country's telecommunications sector. In 1996, the government transferred its own 38 percent stake in Rostelecom to Svyazinvest. That company then became the de facto telecom monopoly in the country, mirroring the majority of Russia's European neighbors,

with control of some 96 percent of all telecommunications activities in the country.

Rostelecom remained a public company, however, with its shares listed on the Moscow exchange. In 1998, the company began wooing international investors, placing American Depositary Receipts (ADRs) on the New York Stock Exchange. This placement was later followed by ADRs on other major exchanges, including the Frankfurt and London exchanges. The listing also allowed Rostelecom to maintain its course through the end of the decade, despite the economic upheavals in Russia in the second half of the 1990s. Among other achievements, Rostelecom completed the trans-Russian fiber-optic line in 1999. The new line opened a direct link to the networks of Russia's neighbors, while also facilitating access through Russia. By 2000, the company had spent more than $500 million on its infrastructure investments.

Rostelecom had thus completed the first phase of its modernization effort. The company had installed a total digital capacity of 84,000 channels, half of which were already in operation. This expansion also meant that the company had nearly completed the automation of its long-distance network, with 98 percent of long-distance calls being completed automatically. This compared to nearly zero just ten years earlier. The addition of digital technologies also enabled the company to catch up to the rest of the world, with Internet and data transmission capacity up to 110 megabits per second.

INTERNATIONAL TARGETS FOR 2012

Rostelecom maintained an active expansion program into the 2000s. The company completed a fiber-optic line linking Samara, Saratov, and Volgograd, adding extensions of the line to Rostov-on-Don and Budennovsk, in 2001. By 2002, new lines also linked Lyuban and Issad, and Russia and Kazakhstan. In that year, the company also began incorporating new dense wavelength division multiplexing (DWDM) technologies. This effort was enhanced by a joint venture with Sweden's Telia to carry out the Baltic Cable System project. The move into new technologies also enabled the company to dismantle much of its remaining analog network starting in 2003.

On the consumer end, Rostelecom rolled out a number of initiatives, such as 800 numbers for corporations, and prepaid international calling cards for use with a variety of services, including Internet access, as well as domestic and international long-distance calls. By the end of 2004, Rostelecom had also completed an upgrade to its main Moscow-Khabarovsk trunk line, quadrupling its capacity.

The capacity increase came at an important time for the company, as the Russian government carried out a deregulation of the country's telecommunications sector, ending the de facto monopoly held by Svyazinvest, and by Rostelecom. The company now faced new competition for the long-distance sector as a number of new players, such as Golden Telecom, MTT, Synterra, and Transtelecom entered the market. By the later years of the first decade of the 2000s, while remaining the dominant long-distance provider in Russia, Rostelecom nonetheless saw its market share start to decline.

By 2008, the increasingly competitive market forced Rostelecom to respond. The company launched a price reduction initiative, dropping its daytime rates by 30 percent, and as much as 50 percent for large-scale clients. Rostelecom's continuing investments in modernizing and expanding its network had also helped reshape the company as a highly competitive player in the Russian market.

Nevertheless, Rostelecom began seeking new horizons into the next decade. In July 2008 the company announced the adoption of a new development strategy through 2012. This plan called for the company to move into international markets. For this, Rostelecom planned to target for acquisition many of its neighboring counterparts. Potential candidates included Farlep and Ukrtelekom in Ukraine, Beltelecom in Belarus, Uzbektelecom in Uzbekistan, and Kazakhstan's Kazhtelekom and Kaztranskom. The company also announced plans to construct new lines adding links among Russia and Turkmenistan, Azerbaijan, Georgia, and Turkey. Rostelecom had successfully transformed itself into one of the largest and most modern long-distance telecommunications group in the world.

M. L. Cohen

PRINCIPAL SUBSIDIARIES
MTT.

PRINCIPAL COMPETITORS
Moscow Long-Distance and International Telephone Joint Stock Co.; Uralsvyazinform Joint Stock Co.; Megaphone Joint Stock Co.; Golden Telecom Inc.; Sibirtelecom Joint Stock Co.; CentreTelecom Joint Stock Co.; Comstar-UTS Ltd.; VolgaTelecom Joint Stock Co.

FURTHER READING
"Rostelecom: An Ongoing Development Programme," *Euromoney,* January 2002, p. 87.

"Rostelecom CEO to Leave," *Total Telecom Online,* November 2, 2007.

"Rostelecom Eyes International Expansion," *Telegeography,* July 17, 2008.

"Rostelecom Faces Uncertain Future if State Excludes It from Svyazinvest Sell-Off," *Telegeography,* February 3, 2005.

"Rostelecom Introduces a New Interconnection and Pricing System for Fixed to Mobile Network Calls," *Tarifica Alert,* August 26, 2003.

"Rostelecom Links Kaliningrad with the Russian Digital Trunk Network," *Tarifica Alert,* March 2, 2004.

"Rostelecom: Rebounding and Growing," *Worldlink,* January–February 2000, p. 271.

"Russia Is Re-Creating a Telephone Monopoly," *New York Times,* November 16, 1996.

Royal Brunei Airlines Sdn Bhd

P.O. Box 737
Bandar Seri Begawan, BS 8671
Brunei
Telephone: (673) 221 2222
Fax: (673) 224 4737
Web site: http://www.bruneiair.com

State-Owned Company
Incorporated: 1974
Employees: 1,900
Sales: $200 million (1996 est.)
NAICS: 481111 Scheduled Passenger Air Transportation; 481112 Scheduled Freight Air Transportation; 481211 Nonscheduled Chartered Passenger Air Transportation; 488190 Other Support Activities for Air Transportation; 722310 Food Service Contractors

■ ■ ■

Royal Brunei Airlines Sdn Bhd (RBA) is the flag carrier of Brunei. Although Brunei is a small country and has been slow to develop itself as a tourist destination, the country's vast oil wealth and strategic location have enabled it to support an international airline with global reach. Its roles include connecting the country to distant trade centers and providing mobility and employment for the local population. Auxiliary activities including catering and aircraft maintenance help fortify the group's balance sheet.

RBA maintains a relatively young fleet of ten Boeing and Airbus airliners. About 1.5 million people fly the airline every year, some drawn by amenities such as gold-plated fixtures in the first-class sections. In keeping with Brunei's Muslim culture, the airline does not serve alcohol, and arranges charter flights for the annual *hajj* pilgrimage to Mecca.

AIRBORNE IN BORNEO

The island of Borneo has had commercial air service at least since the 1950s, when Shell Oil established a small operation there. Toward the end of the decade, British Overseas Airways Corporation (BOAC) helped set up Borneo Airways at Labuan, a group of islands that had once been a part of the Sultanate of Brunei.

Brunei, the tiny, oil-rich nation at the northern end of Borneo, eventually launched its own airline. Royal Brunei Airlines Sdn Bhd (RBA) was officially created on November 18, 1974, and commenced scheduled flights six months later. The initial route network included stops in Singapore, Malaysia, and Hong Kong. The next year Manila was added and in 1976, Bangkok.

RBA began with fewer than 100 employees. A pair of midsize Boeing 737s comprised the original fleet. Fewer than 50,000 passengers flew the airline in its first year, and it carried 500,000 kilograms of cargo.

Although launching an airline is an expensive proposition, from the beginning RBA had the backing of the Sultan of Brunei, who ranked for a time as the world's wealthiest man and was a licensed pilot himself. Its envisioned roles included carrying the flag to global trade centers and providing mobility and employment for the local population. It later became a key part of government efforts to diversify the economy beyond oil and natural gas production and was also a means of subsidized transportation to the *hajj*, the annual pilgrimage to Mecca (though it did assign many of these flights to a Saudi airline).

MATURING FAST

As typical with many start-ups from smaller countries, RBA was backed by technical assistance from an established European airline, in this case British Airways. By the end of its first decade, RBA was largely being run by Brunei nationals, although a few foreigners continued to occupy key technical positions and most all the pilot slots.

The company traditionally did not release financial results, but some hints slipped into the trade press. In 1990 the company's CEO reported it had been profitable every year but one. RBA's operating budget was then $60 million, and the carrier had about 250,000 passengers.

For RBA's first decade and a half, the carrier focused on service within Southeast Asia. The 1980 addition of a third Boeing 737 (this one configured to carry a flexible mix of freight and passengers) brought RBA to more of the Pacific's trading cities, beginning in 1981 with Kuala Lumpur. By the mid-1980s the airline was also flying to the north coast of Australia, first via Darwin in 1983, and to Jakarta, beginning in 1984.

By the late 1980s, RBA managers were preparing for the next ambitious stage in the airline's development. They signed into the Abacus distribution system and hired Cathay Pacific Airways Limited's consulting unit to train its cabin crew to a higher standard.

BEYOND REGIONAL

In the second half of the decade, RBA replaced its Boeing 737s with a more long-range plane. In 1986 the company acquired its first Boeing 757, which allowed it to reach Taipei. Two more Boeing 757s were delivered in the next couple of years and in 1988 RBA claimed a presence in Dubai, the Middle East destination that was fast becoming a hub for global commerce. The 757s replaced the 737s, which were all sold (at a profit) by July 1990.

With the target of serving more dense routes to distant global trade centers, RBA decided to purchase widebody aircraft. The airline chose the Boeing 767 in part to simplify training for pilots already qualified on the 757. The first Boeing 767, which had a capacity of 167 passengers when configured to RBA's commodious specifications, was delivered in the spring of 1990. This allowed it to begin flying to Europe for the first time, via Frankfurt. Service to London and Saudi Arabia (Jeddah) soon followed. The second 767 was an even larger version, configured to seat 203 passengers.

Within several years RBA was also flying to Bahrain, Zurich, and Cairo, its first stop in Africa. RBA added a couple more southern destinations in the mid-1990s, Bali and Brisbane. Even with its small fleet, the airline was still able to support a few charter missions. The airline added a route to London in December 1996, intending to build a hub there. RBA was flying to more than two dozen destinations in all.

While the airline was extending its reach, it was not seeking high-volume tourist traffic. An official explained to *Flight International*, RBA was unable to offset losses in highly competitive markets the way its larger international competitors could. Also, the country of Brunei itself did not yet have much to offer in the way of sightseeing or accommodations. Business and VFF (visiting friends and family) travelers made up the bulk of RBA's business.

INCREASINGLY SELF-SUFFICIENT

RBA had more than 1,000 employees in 1990. Nonnatives still held most of the flying and senior technical positions. The airline operated to British civil aviation standards and sent new flight crew hires to training in Scotland, while maintenance and engineering personnel went to the United Kingdom or New Zealand. There were 350 employees at the increasingly important maintenance unit.

Officials told *Flight International* in 1990 that the company's aircraft were as pampered as its first-class passengers. Royal Brunei performed much of its own

KEY DATES

1975: Royal Brunei Airlines (RBA) begins scheduled regional service with a pair of Boeing 737s.

1986: First of three long-range Boeing 757s connects RBA to long-haul destinations.

1990: Widebody Boeing 767s are added to the fleet; RBA's first European routes follow.

2003: European-made Airbus A310s and A320s join the fleet, replacing the Boeing 757s; BND 1 billion of aircraft are ordered for decade to come.

2008: RBA refocuses on core routes due to intense competition.

maintenance, and serious technical problems with the planes were almost unheard of. RBA was also slowly becoming more self-sufficient in training pilots. In 1997 the company even installed its own Boeing 757 and 767 flight simulator, a unique and expensive step for such a small carrier.

Both the maintenance and simulator facilities were made available to other airlines, in addition to a catering operation the company had taken over from Hong Kong's Dairy Farms group. This offered not only food but linen supply and cleaning services. It operated restaurants in the airport and at its own restaurants in the city.

CONFIGURING FOR A NEW MILLENNIUM

The carrier appeared relatively unaffected by the Asian financial crisis, although it did defer delivery of a few Airbus A319s (slated to replace its remaining two Fokker 100s, which had replaced the Fokker 50s in 1996). RBA also retreated from expensive ventures to Osaka and Beijing. China remained an important part of the company's plans. In October 2001 the airline began a twice-weekly service to Shanghai.

RBA traditionally divulged few financial details. However, over the years, various and sometimes contradictory reports emerged in the press. According to a survey in *Airline Business,* in 1997 RBA posted net revenues of $200.4 million as it carried 710,000 passengers. More than one official acknowledged that the airline was in financial trouble by 2001. Years of losses had consumed almost two-thirds of its equity.

The company had shuffled its management in 1998 and 1999, and the sultan rearranged the board again in

November 2001. A few months later he hired a former Cathay Pacific executive to lead a turnaround. The restructuring program included upgrading the 767 interiors and airport lounges and improving the frequent flyer program and online services. Although recovery efforts soon showed meaningful results, the SARS crisis in early 2003 had a profound but temporary effect on traffic at airlines throughout the region, from which RBA was not immune.

RBA continued to hold global aspirations. The government of Brunei began to enter into open skies agreements with other countries in 2001. Due to the small size of its tourist market, the country had had little to offer other nations as incentive in the bilateral agreements that nations traditionally used to trade access to each other's airports.

In harmony with evolving government policy, the airline was promoting Brunei as a vacation destination. It wooed travel agents from new stops along its slowly expanding network, such as those from Shanghai. There, it pitched its relative obscurity as a selling point to jaded Chinese tourists looking for more than discount shopping junkets to Hong Kong. At the same time, RBA continued to develop its home base as a hub for other vacation stops in the region. It had already been flying German tourists to Thailand, for example, for ten years.

EXPANSION AND RETRENCHMENT

In 2003, RBA announced an ambitious fleet renewal program in which more than BND 1 billion would be spent on new aircraft over the next ten years to keep up with demand. This would increase the number of planes in the fleet from 10 to 16. A small number of new Airbus A319 aircraft were delivered in 2003 and the first of two A320s followed in December 2004. These replaced the Boeing 757s on regional services.

RBA extended its operations down under through the addition of Auckland in October 2003 and Sydney a year later. In 2006 it added flights to Ho Chi Minh City (Saigon) to cater to Australia's sizable Vietnamese population.

In 2004 RBA flew 1.4 million passengers and hauled 37.5 million kilograms of freight. It connected 21 destinations spanning Australia to Europe. Codeshare arrangements with both small carriers and its much larger rivals Singapore Airlines Limited and Malaysian Airline System Berhad simplified connections for passengers beyond RBA's own network.

By 2008 the airline had grown to nearly 2,000 employees, including the latest in a succession of chief executives. RBA was operating a fleet of six Boeing 767s plus two each of the Airbus A319 and A320. There were plans to replace the 767s with new, larger, more fuel-efficient planes. In the meantime, RBA was navigating some business setbacks; in the spring of the year the carrier shut down its service to Sydney and Bali in the face of relentless competition and rising oil prices. It had also suspended its Shanghai route.

Frederick C. Ingram

PRINCIPAL SUBSIDIARIES

Royal Brunei Catering Sdn Bhd; Royal Brunei Trading; Malaut Abattoir Sdn Bhd; Abacus Distribution Systems (B) Sdn Bhd; RBA Golf Club Sdn Bhd; Brunei International Air Cargo Center (BIACC).

PRINCIPAL DIVISIONS

Engineering Department.

PRINCIPAL COMPETITORS

Malaysian Airline System Berhad; Singapore Airlines Limited; Cathay Pacific Airways Limited.

FURTHER READING

"Airline Business 100—Other Carriers," *Airline Business,* September 1, 1998, p. 38.

Anwar, M. K., "RBA's Fleet Expansion Meets Growing Demand," *Borneo Bulletin,* November 4, 2006.

Bailey, John, "Oil-Fired Ambition," *Flight International,* September 19, 1990, p. 50.

"Brunei: RBA CEO Peter Foster Steps Down," *Asia Africa Intelligence Wire,* August 9, 2005.

Fuller, Thomas, "Brunei Airline Takes Economy Under Its Wing," *International Herald Tribune,* August 3, 1998, p. 11.

Kj, Max, "Royal Brunei Is Forced to Delay A319s by New Management," *Flight International,* November 11, 1998, p. 11.

"Mysterious World Aims to Impress Chinese Tourists; Former Royal Playground Is Now Proving a Drawcard for Holiday-makers Tired of Low-End Shopping Tours," *Asia Africa Intelligence Wire,* from *South China Morning Post,* May 13, 2005.

Rina, Dk Suria, "Brunei: National Carrier Hit by SARS and Inefficiency," *Asia Africa Intelligence Wire,* from *Borneo Bulletin,* May 9, 2003.

"Tiny, Rich Brunei Is Opening Its Skies; Can It Become Another Singapore?" *Asian Aviation News,* February 7, 1997.

Tsang Shuk-wa, "Modern Carrier a Rising Star; The National Airline of the Oil-Rich State Is Spreading Its Wings to New Markets and More Services," *Asia Africa Intelligence Wire,* from *South China Morning Post,* May 13, 2005.

Vandyk, Anthony, "Building Up in Brunei," *Air Transport World,* June 1993, p. 205.

———, "Royal—Growing—Pains," *Air Transport World,* February 1990, pp. 52–54, 58.

Ryan Companies US, Inc.

---

50 South 10th Street, Suite 300
Minneapolis, Minnesota 55403-2012
U.S.A.
Telephone: (612) 492-4000
Fax: (612) 492-3000
Web site: http://www.ryancompanies.com

Private Company
Incorporated: 1938 as Ryan Lumber and Coal
Employees: 500
Sales: $800 million (2007 est.)
NAICS: 236220 Commercial and Institutional Building
   Construction

■■■

Ryan Companies US, Inc., is a family-owned-and-operated commercial real estate company based in Minneapolis, Minnesota, offering design-build, development, construction, and real estate management services. Customers in the office, industrial, retail, healthcare, and hospitality markets include 3M, AT&T, Byerly's, Citigroup, Cub Foods, First Bank System, Ford Motor Company, Honeywell, Sysco Corp., Target Stores, and US West. The company is also involved in multifamily and public sector projects. Ryan prides itself on maintaining long-term relationships with customers. For example, the company has been building Target stores since the mid-1960s. In order to better serve these customers, Ryan has opened branch offices around the country, including in Arizona, California, Florida, Illinois, and Iowa. The company is now led by the third

generation of the Ryan family, and other members are also well represented in the ranks. Family members are not automatically employed, however. First they must work elsewhere for three to five years, and are required to work in an area where they possess an expertise. They are also not allowed to work directly for a parent.

RYAN FAMILY ESTABLISHES DRAY LINE: 1909

The Ryan family became involved in the construction field more by accident than by design. Ryan Companies' founder James Henry Ryan had been involved in shipping, having founded Ryan Brothers Dray Line with his brother in 1909 in Hibbing, a small mining town in northern Minnesota. According to family lore, it was his love of Notre Dame University football that led to the career change. An alumnus of Notre Dame, Ryan made sure all of his children received a Notre Dame education, and also wanted them to develop a passion for the school's acclaimed football team. When the Fighting Irish of Notre Dame traveled to Minnesota in 1937 to play the University of Minnesota, Ryan and his wife paid a visit to a Firestone service station on their way to the game in order to see their son Francis ("Fran"), who was employed there. Because he was trying to nurture his career with Firestone Tire and Rubber Company, the younger Ryan was not sure he could take off work to attend the football game, a revelation that prompted his father to take action.

James Henry Ryan sold his share in the dray line to his brother, and looked for a different business to acquire in Hibbing. He found it in the Frederick

COMPANY PERSPECTIVES

For three generations Ryans have led the family business, and today we're staying true to the same principles the company was founded on—integrity, honesty, civic pride and a sincere regard for people.

Lumber Company, available for $18,000, and then told his son that he would complete the deal if the son agreed to return home to Hibbing to become his partner in the lumberyard. Fran agreed and in early 1938 Frederick Lumber was purchased and renamed Ryan Lumber and Coal. The Ryans knew little about the lumber business and even less about construction, but in order to compete in Hibbing where lumber was inexpensive, they were driven by necessity to become a contractor as well. While James Ryan managed the yard, Fran oversaw construction. The company's first project was a house built in Hibbing at a cost of $4,500.

SECOND SON JOINS COMPANY: 1939

Another of James Henry Ryan's four sons, Russell, joined the family business in 1939 after receiving a business administration degree from Notre Dame. James Henry Ryan soon retired, leaving sons Fran and Russell to run Ryan Lumber and Coal. Russell became the "numbers guy," while Fran drummed up business. They soon moved beyond home building, in 1940 completing their first commercial project, a Hibbing bowling alley. It was also Russell who oversaw the building business during the difficult years of World War II, taking on whatever projects that were available, such as ammunition boxes, milk houses, and grain boxes.

Following the war the Ryans became involved in their first "leaseback" project, building a store in 1946 that Ryan Lumber then leased to National Tea, which operated its stores under the name National Foods. Because the brothers could control all aspects of the project, they were attracted to the leaseback arrangement. Moreover, the National Tea project provided Ryan Lumber with a track record in supermarket construction, a thriving field in the economic and population boom taking place during the postwar years. Not only would the company build more than 60 National stores in five states, it would also construct stores for a number of other chains: Applebaum's, Kroger, Piggly Wiggly, Red Owl, Byerly's, Rainbow, and SuperValu, as well as food distribution

warehouses for the chains. In 1949 the Ryan brothers established Ryan Realty Company to own and manage these leaseback projects.

In the 1950s Ryan thrived on supermarket construction, which led in 1955 to the company's first project in Minneapolis, a new National Foods supermarket in the city. More projects were to follow in the Twin Cities, although not all were successful. One National Foods supermarket constructed in south Minneapolis during this period was not properly engineered and began to settle to such an extreme after opening that it could not be occupied. When all remedies failed, Ryan acquired a parcel of land across the street and simply built a new supermarket for National Foods. Ryan took a severe financial hit, but proved to National Foods and other clients that it was a company that stood behind its work, and so out of a bad situation emerged something positive.

FIRST TARGET STORE CONSTRUCTED: 1966

In a similar vein, in the late 1950s Ryan built a shopping center anchored by a supermarket in the Bloomington area, southwest of Minneapolis, which was just beginning to be developed. The market did not grow as quickly as anticipated, and Ryan was left with a costly white elephant. To make the best of this situation, Ryan negotiated its first deal with Target, demolished the site, and put up a Target store in its place in 1966.

Serving as the project manager for subsequent Target stores was 22-year-old Jim Ryan, Russell's son. By this time a number of changes had taken place in Ryan Lumber. In 1963 Ryan Lumber became Ryan Construction, and a year later Ryan Properties was formed to replace Ryan Realty. It was also in 1964 that a younger brother of Russell and Fran, Ed Ryan, joined the company and opened an office in Minneapolis. A year later Jim Ryan joined his uncle after graduating from Notre Dame. After working as a general laborer on the Bloomington Target, Jim took charge of construction while Ed assumed responsibility for development, finance, and management. (Another brother of Fran, Russell, and Ed was John R. Ryan, a Hibbing insurance broker who served on the board of directors of the Ryan Companies.) Jim Ryan's Notre Dame roommate, Tim Gray, also joined the company in 1969 and played a key role in modernizing accounting practices.

A year after Ryan built its first store for Target, it established a relationship with the Byerly's supermarket chain, building the first of what would become 24 midwestern stores in Golden Valley, Minnesota, in 1967. Two years later another long-term relationship with a supermarket chain was also established when Ryan built a store for SuperValu in Hibbing. Also in the 1960s Ryan constructed industrial facilities and office buildings in Minneapolis as well as nearby Wisconsin and North Dakota.

More personnel changes followed in the 1970s. Jim Ryan was named vice-president and the company's construction manager in 1973. His uncle Ed left the company in 1974 to move to Grand Rapids, Minnesota, and start his own company, Ryan Development, with his two sons. Eventually, Ryan Development would become involved in the Twin Cities market, but remained separate from Ryan Construction. Nevertheless, the cousin companies avoided competing with one another and often traded ideas. The 1970s also saw Ryan Construction take design in-house in 1976, forming an architectural team that set the stage for the company's transformation from contractor to a design-build firm. Ryan also became involved in speculative development. Its first speculative office project, the One Corporate Center in Edina, Minnesota, was completed in 1978.

JIM RYAN NAMED PRESIDENT: 1980

Jim Ryan assumed the presidency of the company in 1980, and under his guidance Ryan looked to grow its business in the Twin Cities as well as other midwest markets, especially in multitenant projects. To help spearhead this effort, he brought in a cousin, Pat Ryan,

who became vice-president of development. More important than his bloodlines was Pat Ryan's experience as a seasoned office-leasing specialist in Coldwell Banker's Twin Cities branch. He had also helped to lease One Corporate Center. Pat Ryan played a key role in Ryan's first downtown Minneapolis project, the largest the company had ever attempted: the 20-story, 330,000-square-foot International Centre Phase I office building, which broke ground in 1984. It was a risky project that paid off and led to the International Centre II project and a pair of office projects that were completed in 1987, the 505 Waterford Park building and Brookdale Corporate Center III. Together these developments provided the firm with national exposure and credibility that led in 1989 to winning the contract for the adjacent 34-story AT&T tower, beating out several well-known national developers.

In 1989 Jim and Pat Ryan along with Tim Gray became the active owner-managers of Ryan Construction, with Jim Ryan serving as chief executive, Pat Ryan as president, and Gray as chief financial officer. To keep pace with longtime customers, the company began opening branch offices in the 1990s. The first regional office was established in Cedar Rapids, Iowa, in 1991. It would soon be responsible for constructing 221 Towne Center, a 200,000-square-foot downtown office building in the city. Later in the 1990s the office would build a hotel and parking ramp in Bettendorf, Iowa, for Isle of Capri Casinos, Inc., as well as a new casino and hotel for the same client in Waterloo, Iowa.

RYAN COMPANIES US FORMED: 1992

In 1992 Ryan Construction was reorganized and took the name Ryan Companies US, Inc. With Target expanding across the country, Ryan opened an office in Phoenix, Arizona, in 1994 to meet the needs of the retail giant. Again to better serve Target, as well as Byerly's, Ryan opened a regional office in Chicago, Illinois, in 2000, and in the same year established a satellite office in Des Moines, Iowa. In Chicago, Ryan initially focused on shopping centers but soon expanded its purview to include the local industrial sector, constructing the Laraway Crossings Business Park in Joliet, Illinois, followed by a speculative industrial warehouse.

In the new century Ryan continued to grow as a nationally recognized developer. In 2001 the company completed the Phelps Dodge Tower, its first design-build downtown office tower in Phoenix. A year later Ryan made headlines in its hometown, completing a three-block redevelopment project in downtown Minneapolis, which included a new Target Corporate headquarters (along with the country's first two-story Target store), a

US Bancorp building, and the Retek on the Mall office building. In 2003 Ryan established a relationship with another developer, Ippidan, Inc., to build a pair of Gander Mountain outdoor stores. More than 30 store-building projects soon followed. Also in 2003 Ryan's Phoenix office constructed an office building for The Hartford Financial Services group in Santee, California. Two years later the Phoenix office established a satellite office in San Diego to pursue further contracts in the area. In addition, Ryan considered opening an office in either Texas or Florida, and in the end opted to add a branch in Tampa, Florida, in 2006, which became the center of the company's new Southeast Division.

In 2006 Russell Ryan died at the age of 89. His older brother Fran carried on, keeping the family heritage alive. The company he started with his father was enjoying a 15 percent annual growth rate, and fast approaching $1 billion in annual revenues as it continued to search for new opportunities. Ryan looked to become involved in the construction of ethanol plants through a company called Vision Fuels.

In 2007 the company broke ground on one of the most complex suburban land development projects in the Twin Cities, Twin Cities Army Ammunition Plant—Arden Hills, which when completed was to include 2,200 residential dwellings, 875,000 square feet of retail and mixed-use space, 575,000 square feet of industrial space, 1.2 million square feet of office space, as well 235 acres for wildlife corridors and park use. In June 2008 *Engineering News Record* published its annual rankings and Ryan was slotted 18th among the Top 100 Design-Build firms, an improvement over the number 22 ranking in 2006, and it was 54th on the Top 400 National Contractors list, a nine-place improvement over the previous year. Given the company's sterling reputation, ability to retain customers, and stable management, there was every reason to believe that Ryan Companies would rank even higher in the years to come.

Ed Dinger

PRINCIPAL SUBSIDIARIES

Ryan Properties.

PRINCIPAL COMPETITORS

Bovis Lend Lease; Duke Realty Corporation; Opus Corporation.

FURTHER READING

Derven, Ron, "Ryan Companies US, Inc.: Core Values Drive Company's Success," *Development*, Fall 2007.

Fiedler, Terry, "Building for the Future," *Minneapolis Star Tribune*, August 1, 2005, p. 1D.

Kukec, Anna Marie, "Ryan Companies US Inc. Celebrates 5th Anniversary, Move to Naperville," *Arlington Heights (Ill.) Daily Herald*, March 18, 2004, p. 1.

Murphy, H. Lee, "Developer Is Betting on Industrial Sector," *Crain's Chicago Business*, April 7, 2003, p. 11.

Patterson, Anne, "Ryan Companies Takes Challenges Others Refuse," *Ascent*, Spring 2000.

Peterson, Susan E., "'Developer of Year' Stresses Client Relationships," *Minneapolis Star Tribune*, April 21, 1986, p. 2M.

———, "Ryan Has Quietly Built an Enviable Reputation," *Minneapolis Star Tribune*, May 29, 1989, p. 1D.

SANDERS WINGO

Sanders\Wingo

———— ■ ————

2222 Rio Grande
Building C, 3rd Floor
Austin, Texas 78705
U.S.A.
Telephone: (512) 476-7949
Fax: (512) 476-7950
Web site: http://www.sanderswingo.com

Private Company
Incorporated: 1958 as Sanders Advertising
Employees: 90
Gross Billings: $89.6 million (2007)
NAICS: 541810 Advertising Agencies

■ ■ ■

Sanders\Wingo is a multicultural advertising and public relations firm offering such services as creative development for television, radio, print, and other media; interactive development, including web design, online marketing, and viral campaigns (information passed from person to person); media planning and placement; brand positioning; events and promotion; and consumer diaries to gauge the impact of marketing campaigns. Mostly targeting African Americans and Hispanic demographics, Sanders\Wingo works for many major corporations and other clients, including the American Heart Association, AT&T, Blockbuster, Chevrolet, Shell Oil, State Farm Insurance, and the U.S. Postal Service. Established in El Paso, Texas, Sanders\Wingo now maintains its headquarters in Austin, Texas. A satellite office is still operated in El Paso, as well as others in

Baltimore, Detroit, northern and southern California, and Las Vegas. With $89.6 million in billings, Sanders\Wingo ranks fifth on the *Black Enterprise* list of the top African American–owned advertising agencies. The agency is owned and headed by Robert V. Wingo, who took charge from founder David E. Sanders in 1992.

AGENCY ESTABLISHED: 1958

David Sanders was born in Parral, Mexico, in 1908, and raised in Mexico before coming to the United States. He became the merchandising director of the White House Department Stores in El Paso. He also developed a love for advertising. Like many he was especially influenced by legendary ad man Clyde Bedell and his seminal book, *How to Write Advertising That Sells,* first published in 1940 and reissued in 1952. In 1958, when Sanders was 50 years old and had two children in college, he decided to launch his own advertising agency, forming Sanders Advertising. It was very much a family affair, with his wife joining him in the business, as well as his daughter, Elizabeth Galvin, who earned a degree in journalism and advertising from Northwestern University in Chicago. She stayed in Chicago to start her career in advertising, but in time would return to El Paso to become a partner in her father's agency.

A seasoned merchandiser and bilingual with Mexican ties, Sanders was ideally qualified to provide advertising and marketing services to a border community such as El Paso. Thus, Sanders Advertising found a niche and attracted a number of regional and national accounts, primarily in the retail and apparel fields with an emphasis on mail order. Major clients included the Piggly Wiggly supermarket chain, for whom Sanders provided marketing services in the Southwest, including northern New Mexico where the agency was responsible for Navajo-language advertising. Another major client was BTK Industries, an El Paso-based maker of boys' jeans, slacks, and vests sold under the Billy the Kid and Mann Ranch labels, as well as Oscar de la Renta women's sportswear.

According to Galvin in a 2002 interview conducted for agency use, David Sanders eschewed advertising that was clever or edgy for its own sake. Rather, he emphasized research, so much so that he firmly believed admen should work in a store to get a firsthand understanding of what sells and why. Sanders developed advertising that grew out of that research of a client's brand or products. His greatest joy, his daughter maintained, was to nurture small clients. "He believed in helping a client, truly helping, not just sucking out their money." Moreover, he was known to be blunt, to tell clients what they needed to hear, not necessarily what they wanted to hear. He was also strict about maintaining a proper distance between the agency and its clients, forbidding people in the media department and elsewhere from accepting free lunches or other perquisites. Such an approach was also in keeping with his personality. He was "antisocial," according to his daughter, and although he wanted to grow the agency and take on new business, he was not willing to play the social and political games necessary to win many of those new contracts.

ROBERT WINGO JOINS AGENCY: 1983

Sanders Advertising was a 40-person shop by 1980 when David Sanders took on a pair of partners, Art Director Roy Morton and Account Executive Steve Perrault, resulting in a name change to Sanders, Perrault & Morton Advertising. In addition to apparel companies, the agency added an office retailer and some home furnishings retailers to its client roster. The agency struggled in the early 1980s, however, and David Sand-

ers looked to bring in a "rainmaker" to save the business. He found it in Robert V. Wingo, who joined the agency in 1983.

An African American, Wingo grew up with a keen interest in advertising, telling *AAA Newsletter* in 2006 that as a child he drove his grandmother "crazy endlessly singing the 'N-E-S-T-L-E-S … Nestlés makes the very best chocolate,' jingle. In school I gravitated toward marketing." After a stint in the army, Wingo enrolled at the University of Texas at El Paso and earned a degree in marketing/advertising in 1973. He applied for a sales position at BTK Industries, but because of his lack of experience was offered a customer service job instead. Confident in his abilities, Wingo told the recruiter, "I'll take this job, but I want to tell you right now I don't plan on making a career out of customer service."

True to his word, Wingo made sure his tenure in customer service lasted little more than a year. When the national sales manager at BTK needed an assistant, Wingo was determined to land the job, which involved the company's advertising program. His lobbying efforts paid off, but he was far from satisfied, instead devoting himself to learning all he could about BTK's marketing, and advertising in general. He was soon more versed in the field than his boss, whom he eventually replaced, and worked his way up to vice-president of advertising and sales. As such, he worked closely with BTK's ad agency, Sanders's shop, and particularly with David Sanders, who became something of a mentor to Wingo. At a young age, Wingo also had the opportunity to work with such luminaries in the apparel field as designers Bill Blass and Oscar de la Renta, as well as puppeteer Jim Henson.

In 1983, after they had worked together for a decade, Sanders offered Wingo the chance to be a partner in the agency. In that year, Perrault left and Galvin, who had become copy chief, also became a partner. The agency now took the name Sanders, Wingo, Galvin & Morton (SWG&M). Sanders remained the lead partner for another nine years, but Wingo took on an increasing amount of responsibility. Wingo had many of the qualities that Sanders lacked, including superior social skills, which Wingo put to good use bringing in new business. He was also more organized than Sanders, who, according to his daughter "planned, but he planned a quarter or two at a time." His protégé took a much different approach. "Every day Wingo would come in with his little pad of paper, his goals, and we'd all think, 'Oh no … ,' Galvin recalled in her company-conducted interview, adding, "They got along … to a point."

```
┌─────────────────────────────────────────────────┐
│                                                   │
│                 KEY DATES                         │
│                    ■                              │
│  ─────────────────────────────────────────────   │
│                                                   │
│  1958:  David Sanders founds Sanders Advertising  │
│         in El Paso, Texas.                        │
│  1980:  Name is changed to Sanders, Perrault &    │
│         Morton Advertising.                       │
│  1983:  Robert Wingo is named partner of what is  │
│         now Sanders, Wingo, Galvin & Morton.      │
│  1992:  Wingo takes charge following Sanders's    │
│         retirement.                               │
│  2000:  Austin, Texas, office opens.              │
│  2005:  Agency is renamed Sanders\Wingo.          │
│  2008:  Headquarters moves to Austin.             │
│                                                   │
└───────────────────────────────────────────────────┘
```

SANDERS RETIRES: 1992

Regardless of how dissimilar Sanders and Wingo were, they worked well together and grew the agency together. When Sanders retired in 1992 he entrusted the business he founded to the younger Wingo.

Free to run SWG&M as he desired, Wingo took the agency in new directions in the 1990s. It served a general market as well as African American and Asian markets. Located in El Paso, the agency was especially well positioned to also take advantage of the rising importance of Hispanic advertising. By the end of the decade, the Hispanic market was estimated at $275 billion and growing at an annual double-digit rate. To cater to the needs of this segment, SWG&M formed a dedicated Hispanic marketing arm, one that sought to correct the mistakes made by general advertisers. All too often, ad agencies had merely translated English ads into Spanish, not fully taking into account cultural differences, which resulted in ads that at best made no sense and at worse presented a conflicting message. The new Hispanic marketers were people who understood the culture and could craft advertisements that appealed to the target audience whether in Spanish or English or employing cross-language terms.

FIRST BRANCH OFFICE: 2000

To accommodate its regional work, SWG&M opened its first branch office in Austin, Texas, in 2000. The early part of the new century also saw the agency extend its reach to other parts of the country through its work for wireless telephone provider Sprint Alamosa PCS. According to *Black Enterprise,* Sprint spread into major markets outside of Texas, from Louisiana to Oregon, and "SWG&M was there every step of the way, billing in some 80 mid-level markets." The Sprint contract also

resulted in a major increase in revenues, so that in 2002 SWG&M made the *Black Enterprise* annual list of the top 20 African American-owned ad agencies, coming in at number ten. A year later, with $36 million in billings, SWG&M achieved the number 8 slot.

After helping clients in burnishing their own brands, SWG&M engaged in a rebranding effort for itself in 2005, changing its name to Sanders\Wingo as part of an effort to focus on "building bridges between visionary companies and the rapidly growing urban audience," which the agency believed was not just black or Hispanic but a melting pot of cultural influences, accented by particular tastes and preferences. "The urban audience is the new reality for growth-oriented companies," Wingo explained in a press statement. "And many of these companies are looking for expertise in building a brand that communicates authentically—speaking on the urban audience's own terms. Our collective experience in general market and African American brand marketing puts us in a unique position to benefit these companies." Some of the companies it was helping to tap the urban market included Blockbuster Entertainment, Shell Oil, and the U.S. Postal Service.

Sanders\Wingo increased billings to $71.7 million in 2006 and $89.6 million in 2007, according to *Black Enterprise,* which now listed it as the fifth largest African American–owned ad agency in the United States. Although Sanders\Wingo enjoyed a strong reputation for its work related to the Hispanic market, the El Paso agency was very much an African American agency, serving a market that was not just important because of its size, but also one that had the potential to be more easily tapped. According to the 2006 Multicultural Marketing study conducted by the consulting group Yankelovich, for example, 73 percent of African Americans said they enjoyed advertising, compared to just 34 percent for non-Hispanic whites.

NEW HEADQUARTERS IN
AUSTIN: 2008

Sanders\Wingo was poised to grow even larger when at the start of 2008 it won one of the most important contracts in the history of the agency, handling the $35 million African American marketing contract for General Motor Corporation's Chevrolet brand, wresting it away from Oakland, California-based Carol H. Williams Advertising. The contract also raised the agency's profile, which could very well lead to additional national contracts. To help produce the television, radio, print, and outdoor ads for Chevrolet, Sanders\Wingo hired about 20 employees for its El Paso and Austin offices.

The agency also concluded the time had come to shift its headquarters from El Paso to the larger and more important city of Austin, Texas. In August 2008 Sanders\Wingo moved into its new 13,000-square-foot Austin offices. The agency continued to maintain a major presence in El Paso, as well as satellite operations in Baltimore, Detroit, Las Vegas, and southern and northern California to better serve the needs of Chevrolet. Billings were expected to reach the $100 million mark by the end of the year, as Sanders\Wingo appeared poised to increase its national presence in the years to come.

Ed Dinger

PRINCIPAL COMPETITORS

Bromley Communications; GlobalHue; LatinWorks Marketing Inc.

FURTHER READING

"Advertising Firm Changes Its Name," *Austin Business Journal,* September 6, 2005.

"A Conversation with … Bob Wingo," *AAA Newsletter,* June 2006, p. 3.

Kolenc, Vic, "Sanders\Wingo to Target Car Ads to African-Americans," *El Paso Times,* January 30, 2008.

Ortega, Roy, "Boom Boosts Hispanic Ad Agencies," *El Paso Times,* June 24, 2000, p. 10B.

"Sanders\Wingo Marks a Year of Major Growth with Move to New Headquarters," *Target Market News,* August 26, 2008.

Sara Lee Corporation

3500 Lacey Road
Downers Grove, Illinois 60515-5424
U.S.A.
Telephone: (630) 598-6000
Toll Free: (800) 727-2533
Fax: (630) 598-8482
Web site: http://www.saralee.com

Public Company
Founded: 1939 as C.D. Kenny Company
Employees: 44,000
Sales: $13.21 billion (2008)
Stock Exchanges: New York Chicago London
Ticker Symbols: SLE (New York, Chicago); SRL (London)
NAICS: 311612 Meat Processed from Carcasses; 311615 Poultry Processing; 311812 Commercial Bakeries; 311813 Frozen Cakes, Pies, and Other Pastries Manufacturing; 311920 Coffee and Tea Manufacturing; 311991 Perishable Prepared Food Manufacturing; 325320 Pesticide and Other Agricultural Chemical Manufacturing; 325611 Soap and Other Detergent Manufacturing; 325612 Polish and Other Sanitation Good Manufacturing; 325620 Toilet Preparation Manufacturing

■ ■ ■

Sara Lee Corporation is a leading global manufacturer and marketer of brand-name consumer packaged goods concentrating principally on meats, bakery products, coffee and tea beverages, and household and body care products. The company is one of the largest producers of packaged meats in North America through such brands as Hillshire Farm, Jimmy Dean, and Ball Park. In bakery products, the firm produces fresh and frozen desserts, breads, buns, and other items in North America, including the famous Sara Lee cheesecake and Earthgrains bread. Sara Lee's bakery products business also extends to Western Europe and Australia and includes Bimbo, the leading fresh bread brand in Spain. Through such brands as Senseo, Douwe Egberts, Maison du Café, Marcilla, Merrild, and Pickwick, Sara Lee holds the top position in coffee and/or tea in several western European nations, is the leading coffee marketer in Brazil, and also maintains a presence in the Australian market. Household and body care products comprise Sara Lee's most global business, with the firm holding leading positions in four categories: shoe care, body care, air care, and insecticides. Brands include Kiwi shoe care products, Ambi Pur air care products, and Sanex body care products. Most Sara Lee products are considered staples, helping insulate the company from the effects of economic cycles. The company sells its products in roughly 200 countries, although 52 percent of sales originate in North America and a further 35 percent in Western Europe.

EARLY HISTORY: FROM C.D. KENNY TO CONSOLIDATED FOODS

Formally organized in 1939, what is now the Sara Lee Corporation spent the next three decades under the direction of founder Nathan Cummings. Although he retired from active management of the company in

---

COMPANY PERSPECTIVES

Mission: To simply delight you ... every day.

1968, Cummings remained the largest stockholder until his death in 1985, when Sara Lee bought back 1.8 million common shares from his estate.

Born in Canada in 1896, Cummings began his career in his father's shoe store. By 1917 he had built his own shoe manufacturing firm. Cummings's enterprise eventually expanded into a successful importer of general merchandise. This venture allowed him to purchase a small biscuit and candy company, which he later sold at a profit.

In 1939, at the age of 43, Cummings borrowed $5.2 million to buy C.D. Kenny Company, a small wholesale distributor of sugar, coffee, and tea established in 1870. The Baltimore-based company represented Cummings's first entry into U.S. markets, and he sought to increase the number of Kenny-label products.

Cummings broadened his geographic scope in 1942 with the purchase of Sprague, Warner & Company, a distributor of canned and packaged food nationwide. C.D. Kenny was relocated to Chicago and renamed Sprague Warner-Kenny Corporation. Under the established Richelieu label, sales came to $19 million that year, allowing Cummings to begin a significant expansion through acquisition, a strategy the company pursued consistently for much of its history.

After several smaller acquisitions, in 1945 Cummings acquired Reid, Murdoch and Company, the producer of the nationally recognized Monarch label. After this acquisition, C.D. Kenny Company changed its name to Consolidated Grocers Corporation, and in 1946 Consolidated made its first public stock offering, with a listing on the New York Stock Exchange. The Monarch purchase boosted sales to $123 million in 1946.

Smaller food companies struggled through a difficult period in the late 1950s and early 1960s as operational expenses and competition increased; continual development of new products and large promotional budgets were typically the only way to keep shelf space in supermarkets. Small companies, though, offered their already established brands to a large company such as Consolidated, saving the cost of internal development. By 1970, Cummings had supervised the purchase of more than 90 companies by

pursuing family-owned businesses who consented to mergers.

In 1951 Consolidated consisted of more than a dozen companies, and in 1953 sales passed $200 million. They did not remain that high for very long, however. Sales in 1954, the year Consolidated Grocers changed its name to Consolidated Foods Corporation, dropped to $133 million. Sales fell another $15 million the following year, when after-tax profits were only slightly greater than $1 million and earnings per common share fell almost 40 percent.

1956 ADDITION OF KITCHENS OF SARA LEE

Cummings met these losses with further diversification. The Kitchens of Sara Lee, a five-year-old maker of frozen baked goods with annual sales of $9 million, was acquired in 1956 for 164,890 shares—not Consolidated's biggest purchase to date, but eventually a significant one. The company had been founded by Charles Lubin, who had named it after his daughter, and the firm's best-selling product was Sara Lee cheesecake. A slightly larger purchase of 34 Piggly Wiggly supermarkets marked Consolidated's first venture into food retailing. An even larger purchase, of the Omaha Cold Store Company, demonstrated Consolidated's preference for distribution and marketing operations rather than direct-to-consumer sales.

Consolidated continued a rapid acquisition pace into the 1960s with Shasta beverages and the Eagle Supermarket chain in 1961. L.H. Parke Company, Michigan Fruit Canners, and Monarch Food Ltd. of Toronto together added $35 million in sales for 1962. The corporation first went international in 1960 by buying a controlling interest in a Venezuelan vinegar company; a second foreign investment came in 1962, with the purchase of Jonker Fris, a Dutch canner. Although growth was rapid, analysts considered Consolidated stock a risk because dividend increases depended on purchases.

During the 1960s recently acquired Booth Fisheries reported a 16 percent rise in sales volume for 1962, up to $56.6 million. By following the industry trend toward packaging seafood for the convenience market, Booth Fisheries fought off fish shortages and normally unstable prices, raising division earnings from $2.35 per share to $3.22.

In 1966 Consolidated agreed to a Federal Trade Commission (FTC) order to spin off its supermarket division within three years, principally its Piggly Wiggly and Eagle supermarket chains. This agreement came as a surprise to analysts, because the industry expected

KEY DATES

1939: Nathan Cummings buys C.D. Kenny Company, a small wholesale distributor of sugar, coffee, and tea based in Baltimore.

1942: Sprague, Warner & Company, distributor of canned and packaged food, is acquired; company relocates to Chicago and is renamed Sprague Warner-Kenny Corporation.

1945: Company changes name to Consolidated Grocers Corporation.

1946: Company goes public with a listing on the New York Stock Exchange.

1954: Company changes name to Consolidated Foods Corporation (CFC).

1956: The Kitchens of Sara Lee, maker of frozen baked goods, is acquired; CFC also acquires 34 Piggly Wiggly supermarkets.

1966: Under order from the Federal Trade Commission, CFC agrees to divest its supermarket division; the company acquires its first meat company, E. Kahn's Sons Company, and its first nonfood company, Oxford Chemical Corporation.

1968: CFC enters the apparel industry with the purchase of Gant shirts.

1971: Hillshire Farm is acquired.

1975: John H. Bryan becomes company CEO, beginning a long reign as head of the firm.

1978: CFC acquires Douwe Egberts, a Dutch coffee, tea, and tobacco producer.

1979: The hostile takeover of undergarment maker Hanes Corporation is completed.

1984: Jimmy Dean Meats is acquired.

1985: CFC changes its name to Sara Lee Corporation; the company acquires the foreign subsidiaries of Nicholas Kiwi Limited, an Australian maker of shoe care and other products, and also buys Coach leatherware.

1987: Dutch household goods conglomerate Akzo is acquired.

1991: Undergarment maker Playtex is acquired.

1998: Sara Lee sells its tobacco unit to Imperial Tobacco Group.

1999: Company acquires coffee brands Chock Full o' Nuts, Hills Bros., MJB, and Chase & Sanborn.

2000: Company acquires Courtaulds Textiles plc, leading seller of intimate apparel and underwear in the United Kingdom; partial interest in Coach is sold through a public offering; foodservice distributor PYA/Monarch is sold for $1.56 billion.

2001: Remaining stake in Coach is spun off to Sara Lee shareholders; Sara Lee purchases the second largest bakery in the United States, The Earthgrains Company.

2005: Sara Lee launches a massive overhaul including major divestments and newfound focus on its food, beverage, and household and body care businesses.

2006: Company sells its European branded apparel and European meats businesses; its branded apparel business in the Americas and Asia is spun off into the separate firm Hanesbrands Inc.

leniency from the FTC because of the high cost of small-scale food production and distribution. However, Consolidated Foods President William Howlett publicly welcomed the agreement, stating that Consolidated no longer wished to compete at the retail level with its other customers. Consolidated still kept its convenience retail outlets such as Lawson Milk, purchased in 1960.

As Cummings prepared for retirement, Consolidated searched for a larger share of European and American markets. New production facilities were planned for Shasta and Sara Lee in 1964, tripling the latter's output, and sales that year topped $600 million.

In 1966 Consolidated made two more important food purchases: E. Kahn's Sons Company (the firm's first meat company) and Idaho Frozen Foods.

BEGINNING OF NONFOOD ACQUISITIONS

Between 1966 and 1967, Consolidated made eight of its first nonfood acquisitions, including Oxford Chemical Corporation, a maker of cleaning products; Abbey Rents, a home furnishings company; Electrolux vacuum cleaners; and Fuller Brush Company. Consolidated also entered the apparel industry in 1968 when it purchased

Gant shirts and acquired several other clothing makers during this period. Within five years, nonfood businesses comprised 50 percent of the company's profits. William Howlett became Cummings's successor in 1968, but Cummings remained a director, and the largest shareholder, until his death. Howlett left two years later because of disagreements with the founding director. Despite the turbulence of the decade, sales tripled and after-tax earnings increased fivefold.

William A. Buzick Jr. became president in 1970, beginning a difficult decade for the corporation; by 1980, the selling price for a common share was almost 40 percent lower than 1970's purchase price. Although sales continued to rise, as a result of the diversification trend, Consolidated soon discovered the drawbacks of the strategy as well. Consolidated's profits rose only 4 percent from 1972 to 1973 (the year sales hit $2 billion) compared with an industry average of 17 percent. Sales continued to rise in 1974, but earnings dropped for the first time in 19 years as the nonfood businesses did poorly. Meantime, Hillshire Farm, maker of packaged meats, was acquired in 1971.

During Buzick's five-year reign, Consolidated sold many of its food distribution businesses and production facilities. Buzick also increased the company's commitment to nonfood products with the purchase of Max Klein, Inc., a Philadelphia-based clothing company and Erdal (later Intradal), a Dutch personal care products company.

Nonfood activity peaked in 1975 as durable goods provided almost two-thirds of corporate profits. The diversification was prompted in part by the company's belief that federal restraints on the food industry would continue. In addition, economic constraints made Consolidated's growth goals difficult to achieve as only a food company. Under President Richard Nixon's economic stabilization program of 1973, for instance, Sara Lee was allowed to increase prices on frozen baked goods only 6.35 percent; Consolidated had requested a 7.52 percent hike. Moving into nonfood businesses would make the corporation less dependent on federal decisions and less vulnerable to the antitrust suits that had impeded competitors.

MID-SEVENTIES START OF THE JOHN H. BRYAN ERA

Buzick left in 1975 and John H. Bryan became CEO; he was named chairman the following year. Bryan's family-owned business, Bryan Brothers Packing, was a 1968 Consolidated purchase. Bryan quickly sold more than 50 companies, most of which were smaller acquisitions made in the early 1970s. Fuller Brush and four furniture companies were singled out as problem units and divested. Earnings recovered the following year to $77.5 million, and Consolidated's operating margin returned to 7.6 percent.

Bryan continued to value nonfood sales, however. For the next ten years, nonfood products continued to make up more than 50 percent of corporate income but only 30 percent of total sales. Purchases during the 1980s continued the trend toward solidifying durable goods production.

Bryan's acquisition portfolio represented a more aggressive stance in all of its markets. Before the 1978 purchase of Douwe Egberts, a Dutch coffee, tea, and tobacco producer, only 11 percent of Consolidated's income came from abroad; by 1989 it made up nearly 30 percent. In 1979 Consolidated completed a hostile takeover of the Hanes Corporation, a family-owned undergarment manufacturer.

Despite difficulties—poor performance of some nonfood companies led to earnings losses in 1974 and 1975—Consolidated's performance excelled by the end of the 1970s. Between 1967 and 1973, sales doubled to $2 billion and total assets topped $1 billion. These figures allowed the company to set a goal of doubling sales volume by 1980; the actual amount achieved exceeded $5 billion.

Bryan's initial management goals were to keep the company diversified and decentralized, while keeping the corporate office responsible for financial control and strategic planning. Acquisition targets would be brands with leading market shares in new areas and "integrating acquisitions," large companies with established brands in Consolidated's markets. Chef Pierre pies, Superior Tea and Coffee Company, and Italian dry sausage product maker Gallo Salame, Inc., fell into the latter category, and were purchased in the late 1970s, building on Consolidated's pastry, coffee and tea, and meat market shares. Similarly, Jimmy Dean Meats was acquired in 1984.

EMERGING AS SARA LEE IN 1985

In 1985 Consolidated announced that it would change its name to Sara Lee Corporation. The name was chosen because it was the corporation's most prominent brand name, and as a corporate name would give the company higher visibility and make advertising efforts more cost-effective.

The first of two major foreign acquisitions came in 1985 when Nicholas Kiwi Limited's foreign subsidiaries were purchased for $330 million, in addition to 14 percent of its Australian domestic operations. Kiwi, seller of a variety of shoe care products, medicines, cleaners, and cosmetics, complemented Intradal, Sara Lee's Dutch subsidiary. Akzo, a Dutch conglomerate with annual sales of $720 million, was acquired in 1987 for approximately $600 million, the company's largest purchase ever. Another producer of household goods, Akzo was absorbed into Douwe Egberts and Kiwi. By mid-1987, just nine years since its first international venture, Sara Lee was among the largest U.S. multinationals, with foreign revenue reaching almost $2 billion, making up 24.1 percent of total sales, 26.8 percent of profits, and 40.5 percent of total corporate assets. Meantime, back home, Sara Lee acquired Coach Leatherware in 1985 and Hygrade Food Products, maker of Ball Park, Grillmaster, and Hygrade hot dogs, in 1989.

Although still very active in acquisitions, Bryan also drew praise for stressing internal product development. Return on total investment typically decreases in the wake of large purchases, but Bryan kept return on equity at more than 20 percent in nearly every year since 1985. This was especially unusual for a company whose growth was almost entirely through acquisition: 96 percent of Sara Lee's 141 entries into new businesses were through acquisition between 1950 and 1986.

Bryan was responsible for easing the uncertainty of the 1970s, shifting the company's focus to the marketing of consumer products only. He also improved manufacturing efficiency and product development. In 1986 sales dropped from $8.1 billion to $7.9 billion, yet income increased $17 million. Domestic consumer and institutional food divisions reported the largest sales drop, as Shasta, Idaho Frozen Foods, and Union Sugar were divested and Popsicle was restructured and eventually divested. Bryan also introduced lower-priced items to complement the corporation's premium Sara Lee and Hanes labels. Bryan hoped, with this tactic, to improve total sales volume as successfully as the meat division had done in the past. In 1989 the company began the divestiture of its foodservice operations, then its poorest performing division.

FURTHER ACQUISITIONS AND OVERSEAS GROWTH

During the early 1990s Sara Lee continued to grow through acquisition and increased its market presence abroad. During the first three years of the decade, it spent more than $1.7 billion in adding a variety of properties to the Sara Lee stable, including Playtex undergarments; Brylcreem men's hair-grooming products; Mark Cross leather goods; hosiery companies in France (Dim S.A.), Spain (Sans, S.A.), Italy (Filodoro), and the United Kingdom (Pretty Polly Limited);

the consumer food group of BP Nutrition; and Smith-Kline Beecham's European bath and body care business.

Perhaps most significant among these purchases was Playtex. Coupled with such existing holdings as Bali, the 1991 acquisition of Playtex gave Sara Lee a commanding presence in the intimate apparel market in the United States, with overall market share of more than 31 percent and market share in some niche areas surpassing 65 percent. Although some competitors expressed concerns about the monopolistic nature of the combination, they made little headway with the free marketers of the George H. W. Bush administration.

Ironically, Sara Lee's spending spree within another area, hosiery, quickly came back to haunt the company. A combination of several factors converged to lead to declining hosiery sales starting in late 1992. In the midst of a recession in Europe, the newly acquired hosiery units in France, Spain, and the United Kingdom experienced increasing competitive pressure. Sara Lee also erred in replacing the managers of the firms with U.S. personnel not as familiar with the local markets. Most important, both in Europe and the United States, the company failed to recognize quickly enough the trend toward more casual attire both at the office and for social events and, therefore, the resultant decreased demand for formal hosiery. Because hosiery comprised 25 percent of overall apparel sales, the decrease in hosiery sales presented a significant challenge. In response, Sara Lee quickly moved to decrease hosiery capacity by closing two U.S. plants as well as a plant in France. Sara Lee's apparel division also was realigned into a more flattened organizational structure.

Leading the way in these efforts was newly appointed President Cornelius Boonstra. A 20-year Sara Lee veteran with a strong background in operations, Boonstra provoked some disenchantment with his aggressive cost-cutting measures, which included reducing staff in the Chicago headquarters by 10 percent. Although praised by Wall Street for the cuts, several senior managers left Sara Lee soon after his appointment, and continuing friction with other executives led to his resignation in early 1994 after only six months in the job. No one was immediately appointed to succeed him.

In another irony, in June 1994 Sara Lee announced a major restructuring of its European personal products operations, which included cuts much more severe than those imposed by Boonstra. The company took a $732 million charge mainly to reduce capacity in its hosiery operations. Several more plants were closed and more than 8,000 jobs were cut.

Rebounding from the difficult restructuring year of 1994, Sara Lee enjoyed record sales of $17.71 billion (a

14 percent increase over 1994) and record operating income of $1.6 billion in fiscal 1995, with 12 Sara Lee brands racking up sales in excess of $250 million. For the year, 40 percent of Sara Lee's sales and 45 percent of its operating income were generated from its operations abroad.

MAJOR LATE-CENTURY RESTRUCTURING

After a relatively quiet couple of years on the acquisition front in fiscal 1995 and 1996, Sara Lee grew hungrier during the fiscal year ending in June 1997, spending nearly $700 million to gobble up several companies. The most prominent of these were Aoste, a French maker of processed meats; Lovable Italiana S.p.A., an Italian manufacturer of intimate apparel; and Brossard France S.A., a French producer of bakery products. Also during fiscal 1997, C. Steven McMillan was named president and chief operating officer of Sara Lee, with Bryan remaining chairman and CEO. McMillan, who had been executive vice-president, had joined the company in 1976.

In September 1997 Sara Lee embarked on a major restructuring designed to boost both profits, which had been growing just 6 percent a year since 1992, and the company's lagging stock price. As part of a program called "deverticalization," Sara Lee aimed to reduce its degree of vertical integration, shifting from a manufacturing and sales orientation to one focused foremost on marketing the firm's top brands. As many of its competitors had done, particularly those specializing in apparel and household products, Sara Lee began outsourcing more of its manufacturing; the company also sold more than 110 manufacturing and distribution facilities over the next two years. Nearly 10,000 employees, representing 7 percent of the workforce, were laid off. Sara Lee also exited from several noncore businesses. The Mark Cross leather goods operation was shut down, and Sara Lee sold its cut-tobacco unit, Douwe Egberts Van Nelle Tobacco, to Imperial Tobacco Group PLC for $1.08 billion in mid-1998. Proceeds from the divestments and the cost savings derived from the restructuring were earmarked for investment in the company's core brands and to buy back $3 billion in company stock.

In December 1998, while this restructuring was still being implemented, Sara Lee announced the recall of 35 million pounds of hot dogs and deli meats that were thought to have been contaminated with listeria, a life-threatening bacteria. The products were traced back to a plant in Zeeland, Michigan, run by the firm's Bil Mar Foods Inc. unit. The contaminated meat was eventually blamed for 15 deaths, six miscarriages, and more than 100 illnesses. By 2001 Sara Lee had settled several civil lawsuits for less than $5 million, and the company also pleaded guilty to a misdemeanor charge of selling tainted meat and agreed to pay the maximum fine of $200,000 and to spend $3 million on food-safety research. Sara Lee also spent $25 million to renovate the Bil Mar plant. The tainted-meat case hurt the company's profits, depressed its stock, and tarnished its credibility.

Meanwhile, Sara Lee completed several acquisitions in fiscal 1999 and 2000, with a particular emphasis on bolstering the firm's coffee operations. During the former year, Continental Coffee Products Company, a U.S. producer of roasted and ground coffee, was acquired from the Quaker Oats Company. Sara Lee spent $1 billion during fiscal 2000 to acquire: Chock Full o' Nuts Corporation, a U.S. coffee roaster and marketer; the North American coffee business of Nestlé S.A., including the Hills Bros., MJB, and Chase & Sanborn brands; Outer Banks Inc., maker of knit sports shirts; and Courtaulds Textiles plc, the number one producer of intimate apparel and underwear in the United Kingdom, under such brands as Gossard, Berlei, and Aristoc as well as private-label brands. At the end of fiscal 2000, McMillan moved up to president and CEO, while Bryan continued as chairman.

ANOTHER RESTRUCTURING AND MAJOR DIVESTMENTS

Despite the restructuring efforts of the late 1990s, Sara Lee continued to struggle. Profits had failed to grow at a faster pace, and annual sales growth for the five-year period from fiscal 1996 to fiscal 2000 was just 2.2 percent. The stock price, after jumping following the launch of the restructuring, was once again tumbling. In an attempt to reverse the company's fortunes, McMillan announced an even more ambitious restructuring in May 2000: Sara Lee would rein in its wide-ranging portfolio of businesses by focusing on three main areas: food and beverages, intimates and underwear, and household products; by reorganizing management to eliminate such duplicative efforts as running ten separate meat companies; and through a new round of divestments, including the leather goods company Coach, athletic apparel producer Champion, foodservice distributor PYA/Monarch, and the international fabrics manufacturing unit of Courtaulds. The restructuring efforts also would include the layoff of more than 13,000 employees, amounting to almost 10 percent of the workforce.

The divestment program proceeded in large part as outlined. In December 2000 PYA/Monarch was sold to Royal Ahold for $1.56 billion. In October 2000 Sara

Lee sold off 19.5 percent of the newly named Coach, Inc., to the public, raising $118 million. The following April Sara Lee fully divested itself of its Coach holdings by spinning off the remaining interest to Sara Lee shareholders, netting $1.1 billion in the process. The Courtaulds fabrics manufacturing unit was sold to Spanish fabric maker Dogi in April 2001. Although Sara Lee eventually decided to retain its Champion business in the United States, it did sell Champion Europe. A number of other smaller divestments were completed in 2001 and 2002 as well. Overall, the divestments equaled about 20 percent of company revenues.

Acquisitions were not a major feature of fiscal 2001, although Sara Lee did purchase Café Pilao Caboclo Ltda., the leading coffee company in Brazil, and Sol y Oro, the leading seller of women's underwear in Argentina. However, in August 2001 Sara Lee shifted back into a more serious growth mode by completing the largest acquisition in company history of The Earthgrains Company, purchased for $1.9 billion plus the assumption of $957 million in long-term debt. St. Louis-based Earthgrains was the nation's second largest bakery, with annual revenues of $2.6 billion, and it specialized in fresh packaged bread and refrigerated dough. The bakery operations of Earthgrains and Sara Lee were combined within the newly named Sara Lee Bakery Group. In October 2001 Bryan retired, ending his long stint as company chairman. McMillan added the chairman's post to his duties.

Also in 2001, the single-serve Senseo coffee-making system was launched in the Netherlands. The system was developed in concert with the Dutch electronics giant Royal Philips Electronics N.V., which produced the coffeemaker itself; Sara Lee was responsible for the one-cup coffee "pods" that the coffeemaker used to quickly brew a single cup of gourmet coffee. Senseo was later rolled out elsewhere in Europe and in the United States as well, although U.S. sales proved disappointing. Robust European sales nevertheless pushed Sara Lee's Senseo revenues over the $500 million mark by fiscal 2008.

MASSIVE OVERHAUL UNDER BARNES

Suffering from a prolonged bout of growth stagnation in part because only about half of the brands in its stable had higher-growth potential, Sara Lee brought a new top executive onboard to lead a turnaround drive. Brenda C. Barnes, named president and COO in July 2004, had earned accolades for her operational and branding skills during a long career at PepsiCo, Inc., where she had served as head of the PepsiCola North America division from 1996 to 1998. Barnes im-

mediately began placing a greater emphasis on Sara Lee's top brands, giving them additional marketing support, and also stepped up efforts to drive innovation and revitalize the firm's research and development. In June 2004 the company announced the elimination of 4,000 jobs from its clothing division coupled with the closure of five production plants.

In February 2005 Barnes was named Sara Lee CEO and took over the chairmanship as well later in the year upon McMillan's retirement. On assuming the CEO position, Barnes launched a massive overhaul of the firm's operations centering on the divestment of businesses that had been bringing in more than $8 billion in annual revenue, about 40 percent of the sales total. The operations to be disposed of included Sara Lee's apparel, European packaged meats, U.S. retail coffee, and direct selling businesses. The remaining operations were reorganized around customers, consumers, and geographies into six units concentrating on North American retail meats, North American bakery products, foodservice, international beverages, international bakery products, and household and body care products. As part of the overhaul, Sara Lee also moved into a new corporate headquarters in Downers Grove, Illinois, that also became the base for all of the firm's North American businesses and research and development operations.

The key divestments were carried out between December 2005 and September 2006. In the former month, Sara Lee off-loaded its direct selling business, which sold cosmetics, household products, and other consumer goods in several developing countries, to Tupperware Corporation for $557 million. Over the next several months, the company sold its U.S. retail coffee business (excluding Senseo) to Italy's Segafredo Zanetti Group, its European branded apparel unit to an affiliate of the private-investment firm Sun Capital Partners, Inc., and its European nuts and snacks business to PepsiCo's PepsiCo International unit. In August 2006 Sara Lee sold its European meats business to Smithfield Foods, Inc., in a transaction valued at $614 million. A month later the company wrapped up the divestitures by spinning off to its shareholders the branded apparel business in the Americas and Asia, which became a separate, publicly traded entity called Hanesbrands Inc. Sara Lee gained $2.4 billion in proceeds from the Hanesbrands spinoff plus an additional $1.3 billion from the other disposals.

Staking its future on developing innovative new products, Sara Lee committed a portion of these proceeds to the construction of a new 150,000-square-foot research and development facility at its Downers Grove headquarters. On its completion in 2009, the facility was expected to house 150 researchers charged with developing new products for the company's meats, bakery products, beverages, and foodservice units. By the fiscal year ending in June 2008, Sara Lee had already garnered some modest successes on the new product front, including Jimmy Dean breakfast skillets and breakfast bowls and new varieties of Sara Lee breads, and was also enjoying robust gains from its overseas coffee business.

Overall sales that year increased more than 10 percent to $13.21 billion, although a significant portion of the advance stemmed from the firm's ability to raise prices. The price increases were necessitated by the rising costs of such commodities as beef, pork, milk, and wheat, as well as by soaring energy costs. Sara Lee posted a net loss of $79 million for the year as it was forced to take an after-tax impairment charge of $851 million to write down the value of its 2001 Earthgrains acquisition, a deal widely seen in retrospect as one in which Sara Lee overpaid. On the bright side, revenues from the Sara Lee brand jumped 17 percent that year and for the first time surpassed the $1 billion mark. Going forward, Sara Lee Corporation was likely to continue its focus on new product development while simultaneously keeping an eye out for strategic acquisitions as it transitioned from restructuring to growth.

Updated, David E. Salamie

PRINCIPAL SUBSIDIARIES

Bryan Foods, Inc.; Earthgrains Baking Companies, Inc.; Gallo Salame, Inc.; Sara Lee—Kiwi Holdings, Inc.; Sara Lee Bakery Group, Inc.; Sara Lee Group (Australia) Pty. Ltd.; Sara Lee Coffee & Tea Belgium N.V./S.A.; Sara Lee Household and Body Care Belgium N.V.; Sara Lee Canada Holdings Limited; Fujian Sara Lee Consumer Products Co. Ltd. (China); Douwe Egberts Coffee Systems Limited (U.K.); Sara Lee Bakery UK Limited; Sara Lee Coffee & Tea UK Limited; Sara Lee UK Holdings Limited; Sara Lee Coffee & Tea France S.N.C.; Sara Lee France S.N.C.; Sara Lee Household and Body Care France S.N.C.; Sara Lee Coffee & Tea Germany GmbH; Sara Lee Deutschland GmbH (Germany); Sara Lee Foods Germany GmbH; Sara Lee Germany GmbH; Sara Lee Household & Body Care Deutschland (Germany); Sara Lee Hong Kong Ltd.; Godrej Sara Lee Ltd. (India); Sara Lee Household and Body Care India Pvt. Ltd.; P.T. Sara Lee Indonesia; Sara Lee Household and Body Care Italy S.p.A.; Sara Lee Malaysia Sdn. Bhd.; Sara Lee Household and Body Care de Mexico S. de R.L. de C.V.; Douwe Egberts Coffee Systems International B.V. (Netherlands); Sara Lee Foods Europe B.V. (Netherlands); Sara Lee International B.V.

(Netherlands); Sara Lee Group (N.Z.) Ltd. (New Zealand); Sara Lee Household & Body Care Norge AS (Norway); Sara Lee Household and Body Care Poland Sp.z.o.o.; Sara Lee Rus LLC (Russian Federation); Sara Lee Singapore Pte Ltd.; Sara Lee Slovakia, s.r.o. (Slovak Republic); Sara Lee (South Africa) Pty Ltd.; Sara Lee Bakery Iberia Corporativa, S.L. (Spain); Sara Lee Household and Body Care España, S.L. (Spain); Sara Lee Household & Body Care Sverige AB (Sweden); Sara Lee Household and Body Care Schweiz AG (Switzerland); Sara Lee (Thailand) Ltd.; Sara Lee Coffee & Tea (Thailand) Ltd.

PRINCIPAL OPERATING UNITS

North American Retail Meats; North American Retail Bakery; Foodservice; International Beverage; International Bakery; Household and Body Care.

PRINCIPAL COMPETITORS

Kraft Foods Inc.; Interstate Bakeries Corporation; Tyson Foods, Inc.; ConAgra Foods, Inc.; Pepperidge Farm, Inc.; Nestlé S.A.; Hormel Foods Corporation.

FURTHER READING

Adamy, Janet, "Sara Lee to Spin Off Apparel Arm," *Wall Street Journal,* February 11, 2005, p. A5.

"Added Polish: Consolidated Foods Plans Core Business Around Kiwi," *Barron's,* November 19, 1984, pp. 71+.

Balu, Rekha, and Ernest Beck, "Sara Lee Corp. Kicks Tobacco," *Wall Street Journal,* April 8, 1998, p. B1.

Bednarski, P. J., "For Sara Lee, the Land of Opportunity Is Hungary," *Chicago Sun-Times,* April 7, 1991, p. 51.

Berk, Christina Cheddar, "Barnes Is Back with Plan for Sara Lee," *Wall Street Journal,* November 10, 2004.

Byrne, Harlan S., "Sara Lee Corp.," *Barron's,* October 12, 1992, p. 51.

Cohen, Deborah L., "Sara Lee's Blunt-Spoken Chief," *Crain's Chicago Business,* February 28, 2000, p. 1.

———, "Sara Lee Welcomes Quiet After Storm," *Crain's Chicago Business,* October 25, 1999, p. 4.

Crown, Judith, "He Didn't Do Things Like Sara Lee: Cost-Cutting, Style Led to Boonstra's Quick Exit," *Crain's Chicago Business,* January 10, 1994, p. 3.

———, "John Bryan Hopes for Perfect Handoff," *Crain's Chicago Business,* September 22, 1997, p. 3.

———, "A Run in Sara Lee's Stockings Unit," *Crain's Chicago Business,* August 9, 1993, p. 1.

———, "Stale Goods? Sara Lee Seeks Recipe to Fire Up Sluggish Sales," *Crain's Chicago Business,* July 24, 1989, p. 1.

Cummings, Nathan, *Consolidated Foods: Blueprint for the Construction of a Diversified Company,* New York: Newcomen Society in North America, 1965, 24 p.

Curtis, Carol E., "Nothing Beats a Great Pair of L'Eggs," *Forbes,* September 29, 1980, p. 72.

"Designs on Europe's Knickers: Sara Lee," *Economist,* November 14, 1992, p. 86.

Eig, Jonathan, "Sara Lee Agrees to Acquire Earthgrains," *Wall Street Journal,* July 3, 2001, p. B5.

Feitelberg, Rosemary, "The New Sara Lee: Hosiery Giant Sends Message of Change," *Women's Wear Daily,* September 22, 1997, p. 1.

Feitelberg, Rosemary, et al., "Sara Lee to Sell Non-Core Units," *Women's Wear Daily,* May 31, 2000, p. 2.

Flores, Delia, and Steve Willey, "Consolidated Foods Triumphs in Offer for Kiwi," *Wall Street Journal,* November 1, 1984.

Forster, Julie, "Sara Lee: Changing the Recipe—Again," *Business Week,* September 10, 2001, pp. 125–26.

Gallagher, Patricia, "Sara Lee's Track Record Has a $732-Mil. Run in It," *Crain's Chicago Business,* June 13, 1994.

Gallun, Alby, "Mending Underwear Biz: Discounting Unravels Profits for Sara Lee," *Crain's Chicago Business,* November 12, 2001, p. 4.

———, "Sara Lee's Special Sweetener: Tax Breaks Key Ingredient in Profits," *Crain's Chicago Business,* March 18, 2002, p. 1.

———, "Wary Shopper: Investors Wonder If Sara Lee CEO Has a Plan," *Crain's Chicago Business,* May 21, 2001, p. 1.

Giges, Nancy, "ConFoods Gets Deeper into Distribution," *Advertising Age,* March 29, 1982, pp. 4+.

Gogoi, Pallavi, "Sara Lee: No Piece of Cake," *Business Week,* May 26, 2003, pp. 66, 68.

Gordon, Mitchell, "Baker's Dozen? That's Where Sara Lee Seems Headed with Yearly Profit Gains," *Barron's,* April 21, 1986, pp. 47+.

———, "Unbroken Stride: Consolidated Foods Appears Headed for Another Year of Record Net," *Barron's,* May 16, 1983, pp. 59+.

Gray, Steven, "How Sara Lee Spun White, Grain into Gold," *Wall Street Journal,* April 25, 2006, p. B1.

Griffin, Dick, "John Bryan Rewrites the Gospel According to Nate Cummings," *Fortune,* June 4, 1979, p. 100.

Heiman, Grover, "A Sprawling Company's Organization Man," *Nation's Business,* April 1983, pp. 48+.

James, Frank E., "Sara Lee to Buy Dutch Business, Sell Electrolux," *Wall Street Journal,* September 18, 1987.

Jargon, Julie, "A European Accent for Retooled Sara Lee," *Crain's Chicago Business,* August 22, 2005, p. 2.

———, "High Costs Put Sara Lee CEO in a Bind," *Wall Street Journal,* July 23, 2008, p. B1.

———, "Sara Lee Sees Benefits of Revamp As Sales Rise 12%," *Wall Street Journal,* August 8, 2008, p. B4.

Jargon, Julie, and Kate Ryan, "Welcome Brenda. Now Hurry Up," *Crain's Chicago Business,* February 14, 2005, p. 1.

"A Leaner Consolidated Foods Rediscovers Marketing," *Business Week,* August 29, 1983, pp. 58+.

Leonhardt, David, "Sara Lee: Playing with the Recipe," *Business Week,* April 27, 1998, pp. 114, 116.

Lloyd, Mary Ellen, "Sara Lee Prepares for Apparel Spinoff," *Wall Street Journal,* July 20, 2005.

McEntee, Helene, "John Bryan Leads a Leaner Sara Lee Corp.," *Chicago Sun-Times,* August 11, 1985.

McGill, Douglas C., "At Sara Lee, It's All in the Names," *New York Times,* June 19, 1989, p. D1.

McGough, Robert, "Icing on the Cake," *Financial World,* October 17, 1989, pp. 22–24.

Melcher, Richard A., "Sara Lee Isn't Exactly Cooking," *Business Week,* January 24, 1994.

Morgello, Clem, "John Bryan of Sara Lee Corp.: A Winning Global Strategy," *Institutional Investor,* May 1992, p. 17.

Our Corporate History, Chicago: Sara Lee Corporation, 1986.

Petterchak, Janice A., *To Share: The Heritage, Legend, and Legacy of Nathan Cummings,* Rochester, Ill.: Legacy Press, 2000, 165 p.

Rewick, C. J., "Sara Lee's New Recipe for a Post-Bryan Era," *Crain's Chicago Business,* October 26, 1998, p. 1.

Richardson, Karen, "Sara Lee's Coffee Sales Create Buzz," *Wall Street Journal,* April 24, 2008, p. C1.

Rutberg, Sidney, "Apparel Is the $3 Billion Frosting on Sara Lee's Cake," *Women's Wear Daily,* October 4, 1989, p. 23.

Schmeltzer, John, "New Menu at Sara Lee," *Chicago Tribune,* February 11, 2005, Business sec., p. 1.

———, "Tupperware Seals Deal for Sara Lee Unit," *Chicago Tribune,* August 11, 2005, Business sec., p. 1.

Sterrett, David, "Euro Coffee Perks Up Sara Lee," *Crain's Chicago Business,* December 10, 2007, p. 3.

"Stylish Acquisition: Fast-Stepping Hosiery Unit Sets the Pace at Consolidated Foods," *Barron's,* September 20, 1982, pp. 48+.

Therrien, Lois, "Sara Lee: No Fads, No Buyouts, Just Old-Fashioned Growth," *Business Week,* November 14, 1988, pp. 110+.

Waters, Jennifer, "After Euphoria, Can Sara Lee Be Like Nike?" *Crain's Chicago Business,* September 22, 1997, p. 3.

———, "Why Sara Lee Bagged Mark Cross," *Crain's Chicago Business,* September 8, 1997, p. 3.

Weber, Joseph, "No Cakewalk at Sara Lee," *Business Week,* June 12, 2000, p. 56.

Weiner, Steve, "How Do You Say L'Eggs in French?" *Forbes,* November 27, 1989, p. 73.

———, "On the Road to Eastern Europe," *Forbes,* December 10, 1990, p. 193.

Zweig, Phillip L., "Aris Doesn't Fit Sara Lee Like a Glove Anymore," *Business Week,* September 18, 1995.

savers

Savers, Inc.

———— ■ ————

11400 S.E. 6th Street
Bellevue, Washington 98004
U.S.A.
Telephone: (425) 462-1515
Fax: (425) 451-2250
Web site: http://www.savers.com

Private Company
Incorporated: 1971 as Thrift Village, Inc.
Employees: 10,000
Sales: $500 million (2006 est.)
NAICS: 452112 Discount Department Stores

■ ■ ■

Savers, Inc., is the largest for-profit chain of thrift stores in the United States and Canada, and the third largest thrift chain in the United States. The company operates more than 110 Value Village and Savers stores in 23 states and over 100 Village des Valeurs stores in ten Canadian provinces. Also, the company operates five Savers stores in Victoria province, Australia. All of the company's stores are full-line department stores. Merchandise includes clothing, shoes, and accessories for women, men, and children, as well as books, movies, toys, electronics, and sporting goods. Household goods include kitchenware, linens, furniture, and home decorating accents. While Savers' stores attract low-income shoppers and mothers of growing children, its primary customer earns $40,000 to $70,000 annually and enjoys the uniqueness of the thrift store shopping experience, akin to a treasure hunt for one-of-a-kind

items. Savers merchandise is obtained through partnerships with more than 120 charities, including many local chapters of Big Brothers Big Sisters. These nonprofit organizations collect donated goods and deliver them to a local Savers store for bulk sale. Savers pays over $117 million annually to charities for their collected goods; more than $1 billion has been paid since this unique business model was established in 1954.

The Savers business model accommodates other markets and also fulfills the company's environmental commitment to complete recycling of used goods. Of the collected items, Savers selects merchandise of sufficient quality for the retail sales floor. The remainder, about half of the goods, are shipped to developing countries where they are purchased by merchants for resale at local markets. Unsold merchandise is exported as well. Some remainders are sold to material wholesalers who then recycle the goods into thread, fabric, or cleaning rags; shoes are recycled into reusable rubber. Over 262 million pounds of used goods are exported or recycled annually, preventing reusable or recyclable goods from being sent to landfills.

SALVATION ARMY PROVIDES FOUNDATION FOR BUSINESS MODEL

TVI was started by William Ellison, whose father, Benjamin, managed a chain of thrift stores in Sacramento, California. Benjamin enticed his son to join the business by offering to bankroll a store in San Francisco. That was in 1954, when William, a graduate of the University of Washington, was selling advertising for a radio station in Seattle. However, it was almost inevitable that William would wind up in the thrift store business.

Benjamin and his brother, Orlo, joined the Salvation Army as career officers during the Depression and managed the charitable organization's secondhand clothing stores for more than two decades. Orlo's wife, Stella, was credited in family lore with coining the term "thrift store." Orlo left the Salvation Army in 1949 and opened his own thrift store. Benjamin left in 1951 and also went into business for himself. They were later joined by three younger brothers, and by the mid-1990s there were at least 100 members of the Ellison clan operating secondhand-clothing stores throughout the United States.

When William Ellison, then 24, opened The Thrift Shop in San Francisco's Mission District in 1954, he followed a successful business plan established by his father. He financed and managed the business, but the store was actually owned by a local charity. Six years later, Ellison had management contracts with several charities. He incorporated his business as the Salvage Management Corporation. Within a few years, however, Ellison decided to become the store owner as well as the manager. As he later explained, "Each time we got a store going well, the charity would terminate our contract because they figured they didn't need us anymore. When we lost six stores in one year, that's when we decided we needed to own our own stores."

NEW MODEL: FOR-PROFIT
COMPANY HELPING CHARITIES

In 1966 Ellison opened his first company-owned store in Renton, Washington, using the name Value Village. The next year, he opened a store in Redwood City, California, adopting the name Thrift Village. Within five years Ellison had stores in several more cities, including Los Angeles, Portland, and Seattle. In 1971 he incorporated the business as Thrift Village, Inc., and moved his company's headquarters to Renton.

By the mid-1970s, with the nation in recession, Thrift Village was operating nine stores. Yet only five were profitable. Thomas Ellison, William's son, later recalled a ski trip with his father in 1975 when they discussed "how to slice up" the company if it went under. "Contrary to what most people believe, the thrift business is not better in rough times," Thomas Ellison recalled. "In 1975, it was a matter of survival." Although Thrift Village, Inc., was turned down for loans by several banks, the company managed to hang on and began to grow again in the late 1970s. The company opened its first Canadian store in Vancouver in 1980.

By 1983, Thrift Village, Inc., was doing business in Canada as Value Village Stores and was operating 23 secondhand clothing outlets. However, as the for-profit company grew, its financial association with local charities came under scrutiny. When Orlo Ellison opened his first thrift store soon after World War II, he negotiated with veterans' organizations to supply secondhand merchandise. William Ellison had adopted the same practice. In a straightforward arrangement, Thrift Village, Inc., contracted with nonprofit organizations to provide used clothing and other items for specific stores. The company absorbed all the nonprofit organization's costs of soliciting and picking up the items, and then split the profits evenly at the end of the year. Thomas Ellison later defended the arrangement, explaining, "It would have been hard in the early days for nonprofits to function as a business. They didn't operate that way philosophically."

In 1979 a nonprofit organization that supplied a Thrift Village store in San Jose, California, suggested a more formal arrangement, with Thrift Village, Inc., contracting to buy used clothing directly from the nonprofit group. In the early 1980s the company began changing the way it treated nonprofit organizations. Ellison explained, "We also decided it was good to be totally at arm's length. We were spending too much time running [the nonprofit organization's] business and not enough time running ours." By the mid-1980s, Thrift Village, Inc., (which changed its name to TVI, Inc., when it became a Washington corporation in 1984) had signed all its nonprofit suppliers to bulk-purchase agreements.

In 1996 the company paid its suppliers per "OK" (an industry measurement of 2.7 cubic feet that approximated two grocery bags, or one box, of used goods). TVI paid nonprofit organizations $37 million for almost 7.5 million OKs in 1995, which amounted to more than 50,000 tons of secondhand clothing and merchandise. Jim McClurg, executive director of the Northwest Center for the Retarded in Seattle, which

KEY DATES

1954: Bill Ellison joins his father at the newly named Salvage Management Corporation.

1966: Ellison opens first independent Value Village stores.

1971: Salvage Management Corporation becomes a for-profit company, Thrift Village, Inc.

1974: Tom Ellison, representing the third generation of family involvement, joins the company.

1984: The company, now TVI, Inc., relocates main office to Bellevue, Washington.

1995: Five years of rapid expansion culminate in opening of TVI's 100th store.

2000: TVI, Inc., becomes Savers, Inc., in conjunction with sale of 50 percent of ownership to Berkshire Partners LLC.

2003: Former Pepsico executive Ken Alterman becomes CEO and initiates competitive improvements to Savers' operations.

2007: ReDesigners Campaign provides examples for teens to become their own fashion stylists with used clothing and accessories.

started supplying TVI in 1966, told the *Journal American* that "TVI is one of the lesser known companies in our community, but it has a greater impact on the success of nonprofits nationwide than any other I know of. I know it's a business, but the net result is that TVI finances social services across the United States and Canada." For example, the Northwest Center for the Retarded, which supplied eight Value Village stores in Washington, expected to receive $4 million from TVI in 1996, netting $1.5 million after expenses. In 1995, TVI estimated that it had paid more than $264 million to charitable organizations.

DEVELOPING THE THRIFT DEPARTMENT STORE CONCEPT

Thomas Ellison, who had gone to work for his father in 1974, became president of TVI in 1984, by which time he was 27 years old. Under the younger Ellison, the company nearly doubled the number of secondhand shops to 45 by 1990, expanding into Texas, Alaska, Arizona, Minnesota, Idaho, Utah, Hawaii, and three more Canadian provinces. TVI stores used the name Value Village in Canada and the Pacific Northwest, but adopted the name Savers to differentiate the company from secondhand stores using the "value" and/or "vil-

lage" name in other areas of the country. The Savers name was trademarked nationally.

In the late 1980s, TVI also introduced the concept of the "thrift department store," which proffered bright lights, wide aisles, neatly arranged displays, and clothing racks. In 1995, Thomas Ellison told the *Voice,* TVI's employee newsletter, "The goal was to take our stores mainstream. Back then, many people wouldn't admit to shopping in thrift stores. We wanted to create a store that would appeal to a broader segment of the population."

Forbes magazine, in 1993, noted, "TVI's outlets look more like Wal-Mart's than the dingy, cluttered Goodwills of years past." Likewise, in 1995, the *Toronto Star*'s fashion editor wrote, "Not every garment is a prize. You may find the perfect handknit sweater, but not necessarily in your size. And time and energy are required to rifle through the jam-packed racks. But that's half the fun."

One of the company's first "thrift department stores" was a Value Village in Redmond, Washington, which was an upscale suburb of Seattle and the home of Microsoft Corporation. TVI had started moving its stores out of low-income neighborhoods (where secondhand stores were traditionally located) into blue-collar communities in the early 1980s. Market research, however, showed that the stores were also attracting shoppers from more affluent neighborhoods looking for bargains. Indeed, the Redmond store, which opened in 1984, was TVI's best performing store for many years.

As the idea of the thrift department store caught on, Value Village and Savers stores became "anchor tenants" in retail strip malls. TVI, which had never before done any marketing, also began advertising its stores on television, starting in the Seattle market. Scott Blomquist, then a TVI vice-president, told the *Voice* in 1995, "We started seeing middle-income customers who were excited about our stores and had discovered them through hearsay or driving by. We wanted to speed up the process of 'hearsay' and get more of those people in." The company began by advertising sales, but soon introduced everyday advertising as well.

Under Thomas Ellison in the late 1980s, TVI also began selling overstocked or discontinued items, referred to as "Labels," from major department stores including Bon Marché, Nordstrom, Neiman Marcus, and Bloomingdale's. However, TVI eliminated its Labels department in 1996. "A lot of us at TVI liked to say we had new merchandise as well as used," Ellison said. "It made us feel good about ourselves. We had upscale people coming into our stores." Yet the new merchandise cut into the sales of used clothing, which ultimately hurt the bottom line. "We actually got good at marketing Labels," Ellison said. "But we agree to buy all the secondhand clothing the nonprofits can give us, and if it doesn't sell, we lose money."

The decision to eliminate Labels was not without risk. *Forbes* magazine had noted in 1993, "The new merchandise makes up only about 20 percent of TVI stores' sales, but it serves a more important marketing purpose by upgrading the entire store's image, bringing in customers that might otherwise never go into a secondhand store." Still, when TVI eliminated Labels in its Canadian stores in 1995, overall sales went up, which convinced TVI to eliminate new merchandise in all its stores.

TVI also abandoned two other efforts to expand beyond used clothing and household goods. In the early 1980s the company became a national distributor for Buck Stoves and Hunter Fans, and also opened secondhand furniture stores in Seattle and Spokane. Neither venture lasted long. "They were distractions," Ellison said in 1996. "My commitment now, as long as there is room for growth, is to stick with what we know."

The company doubled in size again between 1990 and 1995, opening its 100th store in Mount Vernon, Washington, and solidifying its place as the third largest thrift store chain in the United States, behind only the nonprofit groups Salvation Army and Goodwill. In 1995 the company formally adopted a business plan that called for 200 stores by the end of the century. Thomas Ellison predicted, "We will probably top out at 80 to 90 stores in Canada, but we could go as high as 600 in the United States, so we have lots of room for growth."

Market oversaturation hindered the rapid expansion Ellison sought, however, so he prepared the company to respond to heightened competition. As Goodwill Industries increasingly impinged on TVI's market, Ellison pursued outside investment. Although TVI had only 189 stores in operation in 2000, the sale of a 50 percent stake of TVI to Berkshire Partners, a private equity firm in Boston, provided $45 million in funds for further expansion. In 2003 the company, operating under the corporate name Savers, Inc., purchased Shop & Save, a chain of nine thrift stores in the Pacific Northwest.

NEW LEADERSHIP, CHANGES TO SAVERS' SYSTEM

After finding an investment partner, Ellison began looking for a new chief executive officer, who would bring a strong corporate mind-set to the company. In 2003 Savers hired former Pepsico executive Ken Alterman as chief executive officer, and Ellison took the role of "active

chairman." Under Alterman, Savers introduced a management training program to improve store operations. He streamlined pricing policies for quicker restocking, and also implemented inventory-tracking technology to better match turnover to demand. Alterman doubled the daily infusion of new merchandise from 2,500 items to 5,000 new items at each store. The company began to open larger stores that accommodated 100,000 items on the sales floor. Savers opened its largest store, 36,000 square feet, in the urban, Capital Hill neighborhood of Seattle.

In 2007, Savers capitalized on the interest that many teenagers had in the unique clothing often found in thrift stores by launching the ReDesigners Campaign. The company chose six teens as trendsetters and models for the creativity and individuality involved in developing a wardrobe from thrift store finds. The "ReDesigners" provided examples of how they changed vintage and used clothing styles by reconstructing the way pieces could be mixed and matched or by tailoring items to their personal taste through do-it-yourself sewing options. The six ReDesigners, each in a different Savers market, contributed to newsletters and blogs on the Savers web site and at the ReDesigners MySpace site, and they attended in-store events, such as grand openings.

With its operational improvements, Savers finally reached its 200-store goal in 2005 and began to expand rapidly. Between 2006 and 2008 Savers opened 34 stores. These included seven stores in Arizona, two in Texas (both in El Paso), and one store each in Washington, Idaho, Nevada, Colorado, Minnesota, Rhode Island, and Massachusetts. New markets included Wisconsin, with three stores, and New Mexico and Arkansas, with one store each. In Canada Savers opened eight stores in Ontario, and one each in Manitoba, British Columbia, New Brunswick, and Alberta. Alterman hoped to open another 100 stores over the next four years and to expand to Western Europe.

R. Dean Boyer
Updated, Mary Tradii

PRINCIPAL SUBSIDIARIES

Savers Australia Pty, Ltd.; Savers Recycling, Inc.; Value Village, Inc.; Village des Valeurs.

PRINCIPAL COMPETITORS

Goodwill Industries International, Inc.; The Salvation Army.

FURTHER READING

Boyer, Dean, "Secondhand Is First-Rate: Eastside-Based Chain Has 110 Stores, Still Growing," *Journal American*, January 21, 1996, p. D1.

"The Canadian Cousins," *Voice,* June 1995, p. 1.

"Cause Retailing: Thrift Chain Savers Looks to Drive Revenue by Better Emphasizing How Every Store Supports Non-Profits," *Retail Merchandiser,* October 2006, p. 18.

"The Early Years," *Voice,* February 1995, p. 1.

"The Early Years: The Extended Family," *Voice,* May 1995, p. 1.

"The Early Years: The Next Generation," *Voice,* April 1995, p. 1.

"The Early Years: TVI Arrives in Washington State," *Voice,* March 1995, p. 1.

Fox, Bruce, "The New Momentum in Used Merchandise," *Chain Store Age,* August 1995, pp. 23–32.

Gubernick, Lisa, "Secondhand Chic," *Forbes,* April 26, 1993, pp. 172–73.

Kearsely, Kelly, "Where the Used Shoe Fits: A Fife Distribution Center Thrives off the Used-Clothing Trade. Most of the Goods—Like Your Old College T-Shirt—Are Sold by the Pound for Export to Developing Countries," *News Tribune,* March 12, 2006, p. D1.

Kim, Nancy J. "Discount Chain Hopes for Bargain with Sale," *Puget Sound Business Journal,* June 23, 2000, p. 76.

Millares Bolt, Kristen, "Value Village Plans to Open up to 75 Stores in Coming Years," *Seattle-Post Intelligencer,* May 4, 2005.

Morra, Bernadette, "True Value: The Deals Are Real at the Value Village Thrift Store Chain," *Toronto Star,* October 26, 1995, p. C1.

Ouchi, Monica Soto, "Secondhand Stores Prove to Be First Rate," *Seattle Times,* March 30, 2005.

"Quarter of a Billion Paid to Charities," *Voice,* September 1995, p. 1.

"Savers Stores Bank on Thrifty Shoppers," *Leader-Telegram,* August 19, 2008.

"Savers/Value Village Thrift Stores Seek Style-Savvy Teens for Fashionable 'ReDesigner' Campaign; Six Trendsetting Teens Will Win Chance to Spotlight Their Unique Thrift-Style, Participate in Fashion-Filled Trip to Seattle, Star in a Back-to-School Photo Shoot, and More!" *Internet Wire,* June 12, 2007.

Trollinger, Amy, "Upscale Thrift Shops Come to Local Area," *Kansas City Business Journal,* September 5, 1997, p. 1.

Schering-Plough

Schering-Plough Corporation

———————————————■———————————————

2000 Galloping Hill Road
Kenilworth, New Jersey 07033-0530
U.S.A.
Telephone: (908) 298-4000
Fax: (908) 298-7653
Web site: http://www.schering-plough.com

Public Company
Incorporated: 1971
Employees: 55,000
Sales: $12.69 billion (2007)
Stock Exchanges: New York Boston Cincinnati Midwest
    Pacific Philadelphia
Ticker Symbol: SGP
NAICS: 325412 Pharmaceutical Preparation
    Manufacturing; 325414 Biological Product (Except
    Diagnostic) Manufacturing; 325620 Toilet Prepara-
    tion Manufacturing; 339113 Surgical Appliance and
    Supplies Manufacturing; 541710 Research and
    Development in the Physical, Engineering, and Life
    Sciences

■ ■ ■

Schering-Plough Corporation is a major U.S.-based manufacturer of pharmaceuticals. The company's leading prescription drug is Remicade, a treatment for rheumatoid arthritis, Crohn's disease, and other inflammatory disorders that generated $1.65 billion in 2007 sales; Schering-Plough markets Remicade via a licensing agreement with Johnson & Johnson subsidiary Centocor, Inc., and its marketing rights do not extend to the

United States and certain Asian countries. Among the firm's other top-selling prescription drugs are PEG-Intron, a treatment for hepatitis C (2007 sales of $911 million); Temodar, used to treat certain types of brain tumors ($861 million); and the allergy treatments Nasonex ($1.09 billion), Clarinex/Aerius ($799 million), and Claritin ($391 million); the company also sells an over-the-counter (OTC) version of Claritin ($462 million). In addition to its treatments in the areas of oncology, allergy/respiratory conditions, and immunology and infectious disease, Schering-Plough makes drugs to treat cardiovascular disease as well as disorders relating to the central nervous system and women's health. The company is also involved in a joint venture with Merck & Co., Inc., that develops and markets prescription cholesterol-management medications, namely, Vytorin and Zetia; revenues from this joint venture totaled $5.2 billion in 2007, although Schering-Plough's share of the proceeds is accounted as equity income rather than revenues.

Overall, prescription pharmaceuticals account for about 80 percent of company sales. Generating about 10 percent of sales are the company's animal health products, which include Nuflor, an antibiotic used to treat respiratory disease in cattle and other animals; and Bovilis, a line of vaccines to prevent infectious diseases in cattle. Another 10 percent of revenue comes from the sale of consumer products, including the aforementioned OTC version of Claritin, Afrin nasal sprays, Dr. Scholl's foot-care products, and Coppertone and Bain de Soleil sun-care products. Schering-Plough markets its products in more than 140 countries around the world aided by a network of subsidiaries that spans

55 countries outside the United States. Roughly 36 percent of revenues are generated at home, with Canada accounting for 4.5 percent; Europe, nearly 39 percent; Latin America, close to 11 percent; and the Asia-Pacific region, almost 10 percent.

HISTORY OF SCHERING CORPORATION

Schering-Plough Corporation was formed in 1971 through the merger of Schering Corporation and Plough, Inc., each with their own long and colorful histories. Schering began in the late 19th century as the U.S. subsidiary of Schering AG, a drug and chemical manufacturer founded in Berlin by Ernst Schering in 1864. In 1894 the company started to export diphtheria medication to the United States, and in 1928 Schering Corporation was incorporated in New York. Until the end of World War II, a sex hormone accounted for up to 75 percent of Schering's sales.

In 1935, on the eve of World War II, the U.S. government took over the assets of Schering Corporation because of its German ownership, thereby changing the course of the company's history. Frank Brown, a New Deal lawyer with no previous experience in the pharmaceutical business, was dealt a hand that would bind his future to Schering. Brown's legal career involved participating in government projects during the 1930s. He joined the Federal Deposit Insurance Corporation (FDIC), a creation of President Franklin D. Roosevelt's New Deal policies, and acted as legal counsel to Leo Crowley. Crowley was appointed the Alien Property Custodian, and Brown was given the job of managing Schering. He immediately filled vacated executive positions with associates from the FDIC. In 1943 Brown was formally appointed president of Schering, and under his direction the company soon proved a financial success.

Brown realized that research and development was the key to success in the pharmaceutical industry. To this end, Brown immediately began the development of a research department and, like many other pharmaceutical companies, conducted searches for those scientists and students on the verge of new discoveries or for noteworthy scientific contributions from medical colleges and universities across the country. Established in 1944, the Schering student competition fund found many worthy recipients over the years.

Because the postwar years marked a reduced demand for sex hormones, the newly expanded research department could not have found a better moment to discover a new antihistamine. Marketed as a proprietary drug (a drug directly advertised to consumers) under the name Trimeton and marketed also as an ethical drug (a drug advertised to healthcare professionals) under the name Chlor-Trimeton, the antihistamine marked a turning point in the history of Schering Corporation. By 1951, profits had quadrupled with sales reaching over $15 million.

That same year the U.S. attorney general put the company up for sale. A syndicate headed by Merrill Lynch outbid other prospective buyers, purchasing the company in 1952 and then proceeding to take it public that same year through the sale of $1.7 million of stock. The investors, however, asked Brown to remain on as company president. He accepted the offer and directed Schering to even greater profitability through the discovery of Meticorten and Meticortelone, two new corticosteroids that became the envy of the drug industry.

The discovery of synthetic cortisone dated back to 1949 when Merck & Co., an industry competitor, first made public its historic findings. Although the wonder drug's discovery rightfully belonged to Merck, the process for synthesizing the drug conflicted with several other patents for producing sex hormones. Schering was the owner of one of these patents, and through a "cross-licensing" agreement the company gained access to information about cortisone production.

Soon after production of cortisone began, Schering and its competitors raced to discover an improved line of the drug that would eliminate some of the side effects associated with the steroid. They all hoped to modify the cortisone molecule to find a more effective drug and, at the same time, eliminate hypertension, edema (water retention), and osteoporosis (a bone disease), all side effects connected with cortisone therapy. Using

KEY DATES

1864–Late 1800s: Ernst Schering founds Schering AG as a Berlin-based drug and chemical manufacturer and eventually forms a U.S. subsidiary to which his company begins exporting pharmaceuticals.

1908: Abe Plough begins his career of marketing consumer products by selling a concoction of linseed oil, carbolic acid, and camphor as an "antiseptic healing oil."

1918: Plough incorporates his business as Plough Chemical Co., later known as Plough, Inc.

1920: Plough acquires Chattanooga, Tennessee-based St. Joseph Company, maker of children's aspirin.

1928: Schering Corporation is incorporated in New York.

1935: The U.S. government takes over the assets of Schering Corporation because of its German ownership.

Mid-1940s: Schering establishes a research department and develops a new antihistamine marketed to consumers as Trimeton and as a prescription drug called Chlor-Trimeton.

1950s: Plough adds childproof caps to its children's aspirin products at a time when safety regulations are almost nonexistent.

1952: A syndicate headed by Merrill Lynch purchases Schering from the government and takes the company public.

1955: Schering introduces a new corticosteroid called Meticorten, soon followed by Meticortelone.

1965: Schering introduces Tinactin, an antifungal cream.

1966: Schering introduces Garamycin, an antibiotic used as a treatment for urinary tract infections and burn victims; it will soon become the company's leading product.

1967: Schering introduces the decongestant Afrin.

1971: Schering and Plough merge to form Schering-Plough Corporation, combining Schering's antibiotics, antihistamines, and other

pharmaceuticals with Plough's household consumer products such as Coppertone, Di-Gel, and Maybelline cosmetics.

1979: Scholl, Inc., maker of Dr. Scholl's foot-care products, is acquired.

1980: Patent for the company's top product, Garamycin, expires.

1982: Drive into biotechnology includes the acquisition of DNAX Research Institute, based in Palo Alto, California.

1986: Schering-Plough's Intron A interferon receives approval from the U.S. Food and Drug Administration (FDA); Key Pharmaceuticals, a maker of allergy, asthma, and cardiovascular drugs, is acquired.

1993: The company introduces Claritin, a nonsedating antihistamine, which quickly achieves blockbuster sales and becomes the firm's number one product.

1997: The animal health division of Mallinckrodt Inc. is acquired for $405 million.

2000: Company enters into a partnership with Merck & Co., Inc., to develop cholesterol-management medications; the company recalls 59 million asthma inhalers after finding that some of the devices contain little or none of the active ingredient.

2001: The FDA imposes a $500 million fine on Schering-Plough because of protracted manufacturing problems.

2002: FDA grants approval for the cholesterol-management drug Zetia, part of the Merck joint venture; Schering-Plough's main patent on Claritin expires.

2003: Fred Hassan is brought onboard to launch turnaround effort.

2007: Company acquires Organon BioSciences N.V. from Akzo Nobel N.V. for EUR 11 billion ($16.1 billion).

microorganisms to convert one chemical into another, Schering scientists discovered a drug in 1954 that fit the

desired guidelines. Clinical testing of the drug brought excellent results. When Schering was confronted with the prospect of full-scale production, however, the company realized it had no previous experience in manufacturing by fermentation, the process used to make the new drug. Schering first tried fermentation in a 150-gallon stainless steel container and later in a 1,000-gallon and finally a 22,000-gallon fermenter. This last container used $100,000 worth of cortisone and a few hundred gallons of microorganisms.

Having established a successful manufacturing technique, Schering released Meticorten in 1955 and Meticortelone soon afterward. Almost unbelievably, sales for the drugs jumped to over $20 million by the end of the year, $1 million more than total sales in 1954. By the end of 1955 sales for these drugs reached a new high of almost $46 million and by 1957 exceeded $80 million.

Other pharmaceutical companies manufacturing steroids immediately attempted to profit from Schering's success. Lederle, Upjohn, and Merck all developed similar drugs, and soon Schering found itself embroiled in lawsuits over patent and licensing rights. Merck's product arrived on the market only three months after Schering's, but because Schering had spent heavily on advertising it managed to retain a major share of the market. Furthermore, while Schering was forced to arrange licensing agreements with other companies, Brown demanded what other companies regarded as overpriced royalty payments. Although this initiated new litigation, it also allowed Schering profits to remain at an all-time high while agreements were worked out in time-consuming court processes.

In 1957 Schering acquired White Laboratories. During the mid-1960s the company completed a series of important introductions. In 1965 the company debuted Tinactin, an antifungal cream. The following year came the debut of Garamycin, an antibiotic used as a treatment for urinary tract infections and burn victims. This soon became the company's leading product. Schering introduced Afrin, a decongestant, in 1967.

HISTORY OF PLOUGH AND MERGER WITH SCHERING

Unrelated to Schering's historical development, a consumer product company in Memphis, Tennessee, won recognition for its own success story. Abe Plough, founder of Plough, Inc., began his career in marketing in 1908. He borrowed $125 from his father to create a concoction of linseed oil, carbolic acid, and camphor and sold the potion door-to-door from a horse-drawn buggy as a cure for "any ill of man or beast." Plough's inventory expanded to include a mysteriously named

C-2223. This relief for rheumatics became an immediate success; after four years Plough had sold 150,000 packages.

What Plough later claimed to be his shrewdest purchase occurred in 1915 when he paid $900 for the inventory of a bankrupt drug company. He netted a profit of $34,000 peddling the stock in the backwoods where there was still a large demand for oxidine chill tonic. In 1920 he bought the St. Joseph Company of Chattanooga, Tennessee, and began manufacturing children's aspirin. By the 1950s, Plough realized that a portion of the revenue for the popular aspirin was due to children taking overdoses of the product. To prevent this from reoccurring Plough ordered childproof caps added to the aspirin at a time when safety regulations were almost nonexistent. He went on to purchase 27 other companies during the course of his lifetime. In addition to being talented at making important acquisitions, he was also very adept at marketing: 25 percent of all income from sales was routinely spent on advertising. The success of radio advertising, in particular, convinced Plough to buy five AM and FM stations (which were later sold). Plough was best known in his own community for his philanthropic contributions. Upon his death in 1984 at age 92, flags throughout Memphis were lowered to half-staff.

Years before his death, however, the unlikely friendship between German-born Willibald Hermann Cozen, chief executive officer of Schering Corporation, and Plough was the antecedent to a company merger. At 17, after graduating from Kaiserin Augusta Gymnasium in Koblenz, Cozen began working for Schering AG, the German parent company. When the U.S. subsidiary of Schering AG was seized by the U.S. government in the 1930s and eventually sold to the public, Cozen became the CEO of the new independent company.

Although the 80-year-old Plough had initiated the merger because he was looking for a successor to run his firm, it was Cozen who actually designed the merger and, as a result, became the CEO of Schering-Plough; Plough served as chairman of the new company until 1976. The merger, which was completed in 1971, combined the comprehensive manufacturing of Schering's antibiotics, antihistamines, and other pharmaceuticals, and Plough's household consumer products with names as common as Coppertone, Di-Gel, and Maybelline cosmetics.

THE NEW SCHERING-PLOUGH

When the merger of the two companies was finally completed, combined sales reached $500 million in 1971. This marked the fastest sales growth for any merger in the industry. However, despite an earnings multiple of 46, Cozen, in his typically reserved style, spoke guardedly of continued expansion. The sales for Garamycin reached $90 million by 1972. This income accounted for almost half of both companies' growth for the period. The large profits, however, ironically concealed an "Achilles' heel." Garamycin's patent, scheduled to expire in 1980, signified the beginning of generic competition and the end of Schering-Plough's control over the manufacturing of this drug. The sound of competitors' footsteps could be heard following closely behind; Cozen's cautious remarks on continued expansion were well founded.

In 1974 reduced sales for Garamycin already affected company profit margins. In 1975 return on equity dropped from 31 to 27 percent and the company's stock dropped 10 percent from the previous year. Schering-Plough endured the ensuing decline in profits and increased funding for research and development. Several newly released drugs accounted for $100 million in sales in 1974. The following year Schering-Plough introduced Lotrimin AF, an antifungal product, and Vanceril, an antiasthma medicine, debuted in 1976. Similarly, Maybelline introduced a new line of makeup in 1974. The "Fresh and Lovely" cosmetic product line promised to catapult Maybelline into a competitive full-line makeup company.

These moves, however, were not remedies for the ailing profit margin. In 1979 Richard J. Bennet took over as CEO and continued the efforts to solve the Garamycin conundrum. Schering-Plough had historically been a conservative company with no major debt, maintaining an asset-to-liability ratio of 2.2 to 1 and a $350 million cash excess after seven acquisitions. Yet Schering-Plough continued to look like a "one-product" company because of its heavy reliance on Garamycin sales.

In 1979, 40 percent of all profits, or $220 million, was generated solely from Garamycin. Cozen's ineffective attempt to establish company profitability on the sales of a variety of drugs rather than a single product became Bennet's new challenge. Under his management the company released Netromycin, an antibiotic more potent that Garamycin but with fewer side effects. To ensure continued sales of Garamycin when the patent expiration date arrived, the company announced a discount plan to entice former customers into future contracts. Meanwhile, large sums of money continued to pour into the research facilities in the hope of discovering new drugs. Finally, to bolster consumer product sales, Schering-Plough purchased Scholl, Inc., the well-established maker of Dr. Scholl's foot-care products, for $30 million. Also acquired that year were the animal health business of Burns-Biotec and Kirby Pharmaceuticals Ltd. The company entered a new sector in 1980 with the acquisition of Wesley-Jensen Inc., maker of vision-care products and contact lenses.

Unfortunately, these maneuvers had only a limited effect on the company. Because doctors had already perfected methods for controlling Garamycin's side effects, they actually preferred to wait for generic and therefore less expensive versions of the drug rather than switch to Netromycin. Similarly, despite $75 million a year spent on research and development, no new discoveries were announced. Furthermore, while Scholl, Inc., had yearly revenues of $250 million and earnings of $12 million, its profits had barely kept pace with inflation since 1973.

FOCUSING STRONGLY ON HEALTHCARE

Next to all of these disappointments, however, one consumer product did exhibit strong signs of financial success. Maybelline, once known as a manufacturer of "me-too" or imitation products, matured into an aggressive full-line cosmetic company. Bennet claimed in 1980 that Maybelline held 34 percent of the mascara market and 24 percent of the eyeshadow market. Estimated sales for 1980 jumped to $150 million from $75 million in 1976. However, after Robert P. Luciano was appointed CEO in 1982, he refocused the company on healthcare, and Maybelline cosmetics and a household products group were eventually sold.

On May 28, 1980, the day the patent on Garamycin expired, Schering-Plough executives appeared unperturbed. In fact, the firm's stock on that day jumped from $39 to $45 a share. Not only was Netromycin on the market, but 80 percent of the hospitals who were previous customers of Garamycin had signed up for the deferred discount plan. More importantly, however, Schering-Plough had paid $12 million for a 14 percent equity stake in a Massachusetts-based genetic engineering company called Biogen Inc. This interest in Biogen was significant because it provided Schering-Plough with worldwide rights to the synthesis of human leukocyte interferons using recombinant DNA. The possibilities for using interferon, a chemical produced naturally in the body to fight viruses, were immense. It was hoped that the synthetic drug could be used to treat anything from cancer to the common cold. Moreover, gene-splicing promised to be highly cost-effective; this new method, on the cutting-edge of biotechnology, could produce the same amount of purer proteins in a week than old methods could in a year. Here was the long-awaited breakthrough.

By 1985, in an uncharacteristic move, Schering-Plough had made a more expensive investment in biotechnology than any of its competitors. Expenditures surpassed $100 million. In 1982 Schering-Plough, having reached an agreement to spend $31.5 million over ten years, formed a partnership with West Berlin politicians to establish a research institute on genetic engineering in Berlin. At the same time, plans were announced to build a fermentation and purification plant in Ireland to market the first commercial interferon. Schering-Plough also purchased another biotech firm in Palo Alto, California, called DNAX Research Institute.

Although Schering-Plough was the first to market a commercial interferon, patent problems with competitors gave Hoffmann-La Roche rights to market alpha interferons in the United States. On June 4, 1986, the U.S. Food and Drug Administration (FDA) approved Schering-Plough's Intron A and Hoffmann-La Roche's Rofeon-A for the U.S. market. Projected market sales for the interferon were $200 million in the United States and $150 million in Europe. By 1994, Intron A had sales of $426 million. With continued expansion in the United States and other international markets, Intron soon grew to be the market leader worldwide. The company continued its study in the field of biotechnology, spending about one-quarter of its research dollars in this area.

In the meantime, Schering-Plough completed additional acquisitions in the late 1980s. In 1986 Key Pharmaceuticals, Inc., a maker of allergy, asthma, and cardiovascular drugs, was acquired. Two years later, Schering-Plough acquired the Cooper Companies' U.S. contact lens solutions business as well as the rights to sell Aquaflex contact lenses in the United States and Japan. Then in 1989 the German animal health business of Byk Gulden was purchased.

THE CLARITIN DECADE

In the 1990s, Schering-Plough's largest and fastest-growing therapeutic category was in the area of asthma and allergy. Led by new product introductions, worldwide sales rose 24 percent in 1994 to approximately $1.46 billion. The most successful of these new drugs was Claritin (loratadine), a once-a-day, nonsedating antihistamine. Introduced in April 1993, Claritin was the third nonsedating antihistamine to reach the U.S. market. Despite its late arrival, in its first year on the market, Claritin had sales of nearly $200 million. It then captured the number one position in new prescriptions for plain antihistamines in less than a year and a half on the U.S. market, making it the largest single product for the company. Along with the November 1994 U.S. marketing clearance of Claritin-D,

a twice-daily formulation combining the decongestant pseudoephedrine, the company expected to capture a significant share of the antihistamine/decongestant market.

Also in the 1990s, fears of skin cancer and a depleting ozone layer turned sun care from a cosmetic segment to a healthcare one. With the introduction of Coppertone Kids and Shade UVAGuard, Schering-Plough proved to be a leader in the sun-care market. It heavily promoted Shade UVAGuard, the sunscreen positioned as a drug that protected against year-round UVA and UVB rays, both of which cause skin cancer. Schering was also one of the first companies to market sunless tanning and sport products. The year 1994 marked the 50th anniversary of the Coppertone brand, and, during that year, the company helped launch a national UV (ultraviolet) Index in a joint pilot program with the U.S. Environmental Protection Agency and the National Weather Service to help educate consumers about the importance of proper sun protection. With its broad product lines, Schering-Plough captured major shares in important segments of the entire sun-care market, and, in the fast-growing children's market, the company had a 60 percent share with its Coppertone Kids and Water Babies products.

An aging population, the popularity of self-medication, and active lifestyles were other trends that helped boost sales in Schering-Plough's foot-care division and build its position as North America's leading foot-care company. Schering-Plough's brands led in every segment of the market and, according to *Drug Topics* in 1995, Dr. Scholl's had a 72 percent share of the insole/insert category, an 86 percent share of the corn/callus/bunion category, and a 46 percent share of the odor/wetness/grooming category. The company, however, met increased competition from in-store and private-label brands during this time.

Continuing to concentrate more of its attention on pharmaceutical products, Schering-Plough sold its contact lens business to Bain Capital, Inc., in 1995 for $47.5 million. At the beginning of 1996, Richard J. Kogan succeeded Luciano as CEO. Luciano remained chairman until November 1998, when Kogan took on that position as well. Kogan had served as president and COO since 1986. Also in 1996, Schering-Plough acquired San Diego-based Canji, Inc., a gene therapy firm, for $54.5 million in stock. The following year the company substantially bolstered its animal health unit with the acquisition of the animal health division of Mallinckrodt Inc. for $405 million. Schering-Plough gained Mallinckrodt's lines of antiparasitic drugs and growth-enhancing products for cattle along with that firm's more extensive global distribution network. The newly enlarged animal health unit had annual revenues of about $650 million. In another extension of one of the company's nonpharmaceutical lines, Schering-Plough purchased from Pfizer Inc. the rights to sell Bain de Soleil sun-care products in the United States, Puerto Rico, and certain other markets.

On the pharmaceutical side, Schering-Plough in 1997 introduced Nasonex, a once-daily nasal spray for allergies that by 2000 achieved sales of $415 million. In 1998 the FDA approved a new drug regimen called Rebetron for the treatment of Hepatitis C. Rebetron was developed in partnership with ICN Pharmaceuticals, Inc., and was a combination of Schering-Plough's Intron A and ICN's Ribavirin. The company also purchased the marketing rights to several drugs in 1998, including Remicade, which had been developed by Centocor, Inc., for the treatment of Crohn's disease. During 1999, the FDA granted approval to Schering-Plough's Temodar for treating two serious types of malignant brain cancer.

FACING CLARITIN'S PATENT EXPIRATION

With the possible exception of Intron A, which through its various uses was generating $1.4 billion in annual revenues by 2000, none of these new products initially came close to approaching the blockbuster sales of the Claritin family of products. Worldwide sales of Claritin reached $3 billion in 2000, representing 36 percent of Schering-Plough's pharmaceutical revenues and nearly 31 percent of overall revenues. Part of the reason for the huge sales was the aggressive marketing campaign that had been mounted for the drug, a campaign that took full advantage of the loosening of FDA regulations relating to the advertising of prescription drugs. Claritin, in fact, was the most heavily advertised prescription drug in the United States in the late 1990s. Schering-Plough spent $322 million pitching Claritin to consumers in 1998 and 1999.

With Claritin generating so great a percentage of Schering-Plough's revenues and with the main patent on Claritin set to expire at the end of 2002, the company was faced with a near repeat of the situation it had faced in the late 1970s when the expiration of the patent on Garamycin was approaching. Schering-Plough took a multifaceted approach to the looming prospect of less expensive generic competition to its by far top-selling drug. In May 2000 the company entered into a partnership with Merck to develop two new drug combinations. One would combine Claritin with Merck's asthma drug Singulair in the hope of creating a highly effective asthma and allergy medication. Because Singulair's patent was slated to last until 2010, the

patent for the combined drug would extend to that year as well. Likewise, the two companies also began investigating a combination of Merck's cholesterol-reducing Zocor with ezetimibe (brand name Zetia), an experimental compound developed by Schering-Plough that interferes with the body's ability to absorb dietary cholesterol. Merck was facing the expiration of Zocor's patent in 2005, but ezetimibe's patent would not expire until 2015.

Schering-Plough also launched an intense lobbying campaign to get the U.S. Congress to extend Claritin's patent. The company argued that because the FDA approval process for Claritin had been so lengthy, lasting nearly six and a half years, the patent on the drug should be extended. These lobbying efforts failed. At the same time, Schering-Plough was attempting to get FDA approval for its next-generation allergy medication, desloratadine, which was to be marketed under the brand name Clarinex. This drug was closely related chemically to Claritin, and among scientists there was some debate about whether there was a marked difference between the two drugs. In any case, Schering-Plough was relying on getting Clarinex approved quickly enough so that it had adequate time to switch patients from Claritin to the new drug before the Claritin generics began flooding the market.

MANUFACTURING DIFFICULTIES AND OTHER TRAVAILS

Unfortunately, Schering-Plough was beset by difficulties at its drug manufacturing plants in New Jersey and Puerto Rico, and these troubles delayed the approval of Clarinex. In late 1999 and 2000, the company was forced to recall 59 million asthma inhalers after finding that some of the devices, which were potentially life-saving, contained little or none of the active ingredient. After the facilities failed further inspections, the FDA in February 2001 told the company that Clarinex would not be approved until the manufacturing problems were resolved. Following the uncovering of additional problems at the plants in June 2001, the company's president, Raul E. Cesan, who had been in charge of the manufacturing operations since 1994, was forced to resign. In a further blow, the consumer advocacy group Public Citizen in August 2001 called for a criminal investigation of the company, alleging that 17 deaths were associated with the use of faulty Schering-Plough asthma inhalers. Class-action lawsuits were soon filed related to the defective products and to allegations that the company had failed to alert shareholders to these problems (the company's stock fell substantially during this period).

The company also faced criticism for its marketing of Rebetron, in which the two-drug combination was sold for about $18,000 for the full year of treatment that was needed. Some patients wanted to take one of the drugs in combination with a drug produced by another company, but Schering-Plough refused to unbundle the drugs, contending that for safety reasons the drugs should only be taken together.

On the drug development front in 2001, Schering-Plough gained approval for just one new drug, PEG-Intron, a longer-lasting form of Intron A also used in the treatment of hepatitis C. Sales of PEG-Intron topped $1 billion in 2002 before falling the next two years because of the introduction of competitive new products. The drug's sales then began growing again as Schering-Plough introduced it into new markets around the world.

In the meantime, to solve its manufacturing problems, Schering-Plough spent $60 million on plant improvements and the hiring of 500 new employees, many of whom worked in quality control. Finally, in December 2001, the FDA granted approval to Clarinex but at the price of a fine of $500 million for the protracted manufacturing problems at Schering-Plough plants. The company paid the fine via two $250 million payments made in 2002 and 2003. The company immediately began selling the new drug, but it now had only one year to work at switching patients from Claritin to Clarinex.

Further complicating the situation was a petition to the FDA from WellPoint Health Networks Inc. of Thousand Oaks, California, which wanted Claritin and two other popular allergy medications, Allegra and Zyrtec, switched to OTC status, a move that would save money for WellPoint and other insurers while costing drugmakers and consumers with prescription drug coverage. After this petition won preliminary FDA approval in 2001, divisions of Johnson & Johnson and American Home Products Corporation filed registrations with the FDA for OTC versions of Claritin. This led Schering-Plough in February 2002 to file separate lawsuits against the two companies to block the OTC versions. At the same time, Schering-Plough was also involved in lawsuits with about 18 companies over generic versions of Claritin.

In the end, the lawsuits were little more than delaying tactics, and Schering-Plough soon reversed course and began making its own plans to sell an OTC version of Claritin. Late in 2002 the FDA approved the sale of Claritin as an over-the-counter drug. After garnering 2002 sales of $1.8 billion for prescription Claritin and nearly $600 million for Clarinex, Schering-Plough one year later brought in just $328 million for prescription Claritin sold outside the United States, $432 million for the OTC sales of Claritin in the United States, and $694 million for Clarinex worldwide, an overall revenue loss of nearly $1 billion.

As this hit to revenues was absorbed, Schering-Plough viewed its partnership with Merck as a potential key to future growth. In October 2002 the FDA gave the green light to the marketing of the cholesterol-management medication Zetia, which subsequently garnered worldwide sales of $471 million in 2003. In the United States alone, sales of this drug reached $1.2 billion by 2005 in part because many doctors began prescribing Zetia for their patients instead of increasing the dose of a statin. Schering-Plough and Merck then secured FDA clearance for a single-pill combination of Zetia and Merck's Zocor statin in July 2004, and the partners began marketing it as Vytorin. Sales of both Zetia and Vytorin were quite strong, totaling a combined $2.4 billion worldwide by 2005.

RESURGENCE UNDER HASSAN

Before the joint venture's sales began to take off, however, Schering-Plough was still contending with a host of difficulties, including a slumping stock price, that likely helped push chairman and CEO Kogan into retirement. Fred Hassan was brought onboard as Kogan's successor in April 2003 at a time when Schering-Plough's travails had left it vulnerable to a takeover. Hassan had earned a reputation as a turnaround artist as CEO of Pharmacia & Upjohn Inc., later Pharmacia Corporation. He jumped at the chance to lead a possible Schering-Plough renaissance when Pfizer Inc.'s then-pending takeover of Pharmacia promised to diminish his role at the combined company.

Hassan quickly launched plans to cut annual operating costs by $200 million and then in December 2003 announced job cuts totaling more than 3,000, or roughly 10 percent of the overall workforce. Special charges of nearly $600 million, some of which were related to the overhaul efforts, sent Schering-Plough into a net loss of $92 million for 2003. The charges included a $350 million increase in the firm's litigation reserves to cover anticipated legal expenses related to various government probes. Schering-Plough in the summer of 2004 pleaded guilty to a single federal charge of defrauding Medicaid and agreed to pay the U.S. government $345.5 million in fines and damages. Schering-Plough had used a kickback scheme to effectively cut the price at which it sold Claritin to certain private insurers and then billed Medicaid for the full price without the "discounts." The case, which had been brought by the U.S. Attorney in Philadelphia, involved actions that had occurred under the previous Schering-Plough regime.

The company suffered an even larger net loss of $947 million in 2004 thanks largely to a tax provision of $779 million taken to repatriate $9.4 billion in overseas earnings. These earnings were earmarked to fund R&D expenses, capital expenditures, and a dividend-reinvestment plan. Schering-Plough returned to profitability in 2005 aided by significant increases in sales of Remicade, Nasonex, and PEG-Intron along with the $268 million in equity income it booked from the Merck joint venture. Overall revenues increased 15 percent to $9.51 billion.

In August 2006 Schering-Plough reached an agreement to resolve what appeared to be the largest remaining legal issue that Hassan had inherited from prior management. In a case that had been brought by the U.S. Attorney in Boston and was similar to the one settled in 2004, Schering-Plough pled guilty to one count of criminal conspiracy and paid $435 million in fines and civil liabilities to settle charges of fraudulent drug marketing and pricing connected to a number of company drugs. Also in 2006, sales of Remicade passed the $1 billion mark, Nasonex revenues approached that same blockbuster level, and the company saw its income from the Zetia/Vytorin venture with Merck jump 50 percent to $403 million.

ORGANON ACQUISITION AND CONTROVERSY OVER VYTORIN

Already clearly on the upswing thanks to Hassan's turnaround efforts, Schering-Plough made a bold move to position itself for further growth by acquiring Organon BioSciences N.V. from Akzo Nobel N.V. in November 2007 for EUR 11 billion ($16.1 billion). The deal broadened Schering-Plough's range of human pharmaceutical offerings with the addition of Organon's strong line of women's health and fertility treatments, while also strengthening its position in animal health by gaining Organon's Intervet unit. Equally important was the addition to the company pipeline of several Organon compounds under development, particularly those falling into the area of central nervous system medicines. Chief among these was asenapine, a treatment for schizophrenia and bipolar disorder that Organon officials had viewed as a potential $1 billion blockbuster drug. It was in late-stage human testing at the time of the acquisition.

By 2007 the Schering-Plough-Merck joint venture was garnering more than $5 billion in worldwide sales from the sale of Zetia and Vytorin. The income booked from this venture was particularly important for Schering-Plough as it accounted for more than half of the firm's earnings. The company's stock thus went into a nosedive in early 2008 when a panel of cardiologists recommended that widespread use of Vytorin and Zetia should be curtailed after a study found they were no better at fighting heart disease than the far less expensive generic version of Zocor. Doctors and public officials began raising allegations that Schering-Plough and Merck had delayed release of the study's results to protect their sales of Vytorin and Zetia, and a Congressional committee launched a probe.

The companies denied the allegations and took exception to the panel's recommendation. Some researchers questioned the validity of the study's design and placed greater stock in a much larger study underway that was comparing how Vytorin stacked up against Zocor in preventing deaths and heart attacks in very high-risk patients. The results of this study were expected in 2012. In the meantime, in July 2008 the results of a different study raised additional questions about Vytorin's effectiveness while also showing a statistically significant increase in cancer in patients taking Vytorin. Sales of Vytorin and Zetia had already begun to fall because of the earlier study's findings and seemed likely to fall further following this additional bad news, although the FDA soon disputed the study's finding of a link between Vytorin and cancer.

Although the controversy over Vytorin appeared to have halted Schering-Plough's momentum and once again made the firm a possible takeover target, Hassan was undeterred. In the spring of 2008 he announced a plan to cut costs by $1.5 billion by 2012 that included a 10 percent, or 5,500 employee, workforce reduction, a cut in the number of manufacturing plants, a reduction of management layers, and a slimming down of the sales and marketing and R&D staffs. In a conference call with investors covered in the April 3, 2008, edition of the *Wall Street Journal,* Hassan said that with the cost-cutting plan launched, "We are taking control of our destiny." Brushing off calls to sell the company, Hassan contended that "we do believe we can power our way out of this difficulty."

Updated, Beth Watson Highman; David E. Salamie

PRINCIPAL SUBSIDIARIES

Diosynth RTP Inc.; Schering Corporation; Schering-Plough Animal Health Corporation; Schering-Plough del Caribe, Inc.; Schering-Plough HealthCare Products, Inc.; Schering-Plough Legislative Resources, L.L.C.; Schering-Plough Products LLC; Schering-Plough Canada, Inc.; Schering-Plough S.A. de C.V. (Mexico); Schering-Plough S.A. (Panama); Schering-Plough S.A.

(Argentina); Schering-Plough Produtos Farmacêuticos Ltda. (Brazil); Schering-Plough Compañia Limitada (Chile); Schering-Plough S.A. (Colombia); Schering-Plough del Ecuador, S.A.; Schering-Plough del Peru S.A.; Schering-Plough C.A. (Venezuela); AESCA Pharma GmbH (Austria); Schering-Plough N.V./S.A. (Belgium); Schering-Plough Labo N.V. (Belgium); Schering-Plough A/S (Denmark); Schering-Plough Oy (Finland); Schering-Plough S.A. (France); Essex Pharma GmbH (Germany); Schering-Plough S.A. (Greece); Schering-Plough (Ireland) Company; Schering-Plough S.p.A. (Italy); Intervet Holding B.V. (Netherlands); Organon BioSciences N.V. (Netherlands); Schering-Plough B.V. (Netherlands); Schering-Plough Farma Lda. (Portugal); Schering-Plough S.A. (Spain); Schering-Plough AB (Sweden); Essex Chemie A.G. (Switzerland); Schering-Plough Central East A.G. (Switzerland); Schering-Plough Ltd. (Switzerland); Schering-Plough Tibbi Urunler Ticaret, A.S. (Turkey); Schering-Plough Limited (U.K.); Schering Plough Israel A.G.; Schering-Plough (Proprietary) Limited (South Africa); Schering-Plough Pty. Limited (Australia); Schering-Plough (China), Ltd.; Shanghai Schering-Plough Pharmaceutical Company, Ltd. (China); Fulford (India) Limited; P.T. Schering-Plough Indonesia; Schering-Plough K.K. (Japan); Schering-Plough Sdn. Bhd. (Malaysia); Schering-Plough Corporation (Philippines); Schering-Plough (Singapore) Pte. Ltd.; Schering-Plough Korea (South Korea); Schering-Plough Limited (Taiwan); Schering-Plough Limited (Thailand).

PRINCIPAL OPERATING UNITS

Human Prescription Pharmaceuticals; Animal Health; Consumer Health Care; Schering-Plough Research Institute.

PRINCIPAL COMPETITORS

Pfizer Inc.; Novartis AG; Bristol-Myers Squibb Company; Sanofi-Aventis; GlaxoSmithKline plc; Bayer AG; Merck & Co., Inc.

FURTHER READING

Anand, Geeta, "Schering-Plough Hunts Deals," *Wall Street Journal,* October 24, 2005, p. B3.

Babcock, Charles R., "Patent Fight Tests Drug Firm's Clout: Claritin Maker Goes All Out in Congress," *Washington Post,* October 30, 1999, p. A1.

Bailey, Maureen, "Feeling No Pain?: Schering-Plough Suffers Loss of Market Share in Key Drug," *Barron's,* September 22, 1980, p. 11.

Baldo, Anthony, "Unlucky Luciano," *Financial World,* August 6, 1991, pp. 28+.

Barrett, Amy, "Schering's Dr. Feelbetter?" *Business Week,* June 23, 2003, pp. 55–56.

Breitstein, Joanna, "Being Fred Hassan," *Pharmaceutical Executive,* October 2007, pp. 73–74+.

Bronson, Gail, "Devour Thy Tail," *Forbes,* November 2, 1987, p. 85.

Carreyrou, John, "Turning Around a Drug Maker Takes Time," *Wall Street Journal,* August 2, 2006, pp. B1, B2.

Favole, Jared A., and Alicia Mundy, "FDA Disputes Vytorin Study's Results," *Wall Street Journal,* August 22, 2008, p. B7.

Fischl, Jennifer, "Schering-Plough: Just Say No," *Financial World,* April 15, 1997, pp. 24, 26.

Freudenheim, Milt, "U.S. Decision on New Drug Lifts Schering," *New York Times,* December 25, 2001, p. C1.

Gerena-Morales, Rafael, "Schering-Plough Can Sell Hepatitis C Drug Regimen," *Northern New Jersey Record,* June 5, 1998, p. A3.

Goetzl, David, "How to Follow a Blockbuster?" *Advertising Age,* November 19, 2001, pp. 4, 38.

Hall, Stephen S., "Prescription for Profit," *New York Times Magazine,* March 11, 2001, pp. 60+.

Harris, Gardiner, "Drug Makers Pair Up to Fight Key Patent Losses," *Wall Street Journal,* May 24, 2000, p. B1.

————, "Foul-Ups by Asthma-Drug Maker Draw FDA Fire," *Wall Street Journal,* January 28, 2000, p. B1.

————, "Guilty Plea Seen for Drug Maker," *New York Times,* July 16, 2004, p. A1.

————, "Schering Fines Could Total $500 Million," *Wall Street Journal,* December 24, 2001, p. A3.

————, "Wearing Off: Schering-Plough Faces a Future with Coffers Unfortified by Claritin," *Wall Street Journal,* March 22, 2002, p. A1.

Herper, Matthew, "Fix It, Fred," *Forbes,* February 11, 2008, pp. 88–90, 109.

Hunter, Kris, "Staff Cutbacks Begin at Schering-Plough," *Memphis Business Journal,* October 17, 1994, pp. 1+.

Jarvis, Lisa, "Manufacturing Problems Cast Pall on Schering-Plough Earnings," *Chemical Market Reporter,* July 9, 2001, p. 8.

————, "Schering-Plough Struggles to Land on Its Feet by 2005," *Chemical Market Reporter,* December 1, 2003, p. 12.

Johnson, Avery, "Schering Plans Cuts of $1.5 Billion by 2012," *Wall Street Journal,* April 3, 2008, p. B4.

Kogan, Richard J., "With Change Comes Opportunity," *Chemical Week,* April 26, 1995, p. 48.

Krause, Carey, "Schering-Plough Becomes Vulnerable to Takeover," *Chemical Market Reporter,* February 18, 2002, p. 10.

Landers, Peter, "Schering-Plough Says CEO Kogan to Retire by April," *Wall Street Journal,* November 14, 2002, p. A6.

Landers, Peter, Joann S. Lublin, and Vanessa Fuhrmans, "Bitter Pills for Schering-Plough's CEO," *Wall Street Journal,* October 29, 2002, p. B4.

Langreth, Robert, "Gene Therapy Is Dealt Setback by the FDA of Gene Drug," *Wall Street Journal,* October 11, 1999, p. B1.

———, "Pills and Poker," *Forbes,* March 15, 2004, pp. 82, 84.

———, "Schering-Plough Corp. to Acquire Mallinckrodt Animal-Health Unit," *Wall Street Journal,* May 20, 1997, p. B6.

Loftus, Peter, "Schering-Plough Posts Loss on Acquisition Charges," *Wall Street Journal,* February 13, 2008, p. A20.

Lueck, Sarah, "FDA Considers Unusual Bid to End Allergy Drugs' Prescription Status," *Wall Street Journal,* May 11, 2001, p. B1.

Marcial, Gene G., "Analysts See Schering-Plough on Rough Road As Drug Patent Lapses, Rival Product Gains," *Wall Street Journal,* June 2, 1980.

Martinez, Barbara, "Two Major Drug Firms Settle Suits," *Wall Street Journal,* August 2, 2004, p. B2.

Nayyar, Seema, "Coppertone Adapts to a Changing World," *Brandweek,* February 22, 1993, p. 28.

Novak, Viveca, "How One Firm Played the Patent Game," *Time,* November 22, 1999, p. 42.

Palmer, Jay, "Say Yes to Drugs? How Schering-Plough Aims to Survive Hillary Clinton," *Barron's,* October 4, 1993, p. 14.

Petersen, Melody, "At Schering, Optimism and Problems," *New York Times,* January 15, 2002, p. C1.

———, "Drug Maker to Pay $500 Million Fine for Factory Lapses," *New York Times,* May 18, 2002, p. A1.

———, "Factory Problems Unresolved, Schering-Plough President Is Out," *New York Times,* June 28, 2001, p. C4.

———, "Group Faults Drug Inhalers in Ten Deaths," *New York Times,* August 10, 2001, p. C1.

Power, Christopher, "Schering May Have a Cure for Anemic Profits," *Business Week,* September 15, 1986, pp. 118+.

Rubenstein, Sarah, and Avery Johnson, "Study Missteps Threaten Turnaround at Schering," *Wall Street Journal,* January 17, 2008, pp. B1, B2.

Rubenstein, Sarah, and Jeanne Whalen, "Schering-Plough Tries to Deal Its Way to Top," *Wall Street Journal,* March 13, 2007, p. B1.

"Schering, Plough Agree to Merger Put at $1.5 Billion," *Wall Street Journal,* June 24, 1970.

"Schering-Plough Banking on R&D," *Chemical Marketing Reporter,* July 11, 1994, pp. 7+.

Shaffer, Marjorie, "Schering-Plough: Against the Tide," *Financial World,* June 22, 1993, pp. 16+.

Silverman, Edward R., "Second N.J. Congressman Calls for Probe of Drug's Marketing," *Newark (N.J.) Star-Ledger,* April 27, 1999.

Simons, John, "Bitter Medicine," *Fortune,* October 14, 2002, pp. 169–70, 172, 174.

———, "Is It Too Late to Save Schering?" *Fortune,* September 15, 2003, pp. 145–46+.

Starr, Cynthia, "Schering's Claritin Promises Quick Onset, No Sedation," *Drug Topics,* June 7, 1993, pp. 22+.

"Step Up to Better Foot Care Sales," *Drug Topics,* March 20, 1995, pp. 68+.

"Touted Schering-Plough Feels the 'Clinton Effect,'" *Chemical Marketing Reporter,* February 22, 1993, pp. 8+.

Twitchell, Evelyn Ellison, "Nothing to Sneeze At: Schering-Plough Looks Like a Blue-Chip Bargain," *Barron's,* September 18, 2000, p. 52.

Verschoor, Curtis C., "Alleged Unethical Behaviors and Schering-Plough," *Strategic Finance,* July 2001, pp. 18, 20.

Waldholz, Michael, "Luciano to Quit Schering Post As Firm's CEO," *Wall Street Journal,* April 26, 1995, p. B7.

Weber, Joseph, "Is Kogan in a Corner?" *Business Week,* July 16, 2001, pp. 68–69.

Weintraub, Arlene, "Schering-Plough Climbs Out of Its Sickbed," *Business Week,* May 14, 2007, pp. 70–71.

Werdigier, Julia, "Schering Surprises Investors with Deal for Akzo Unit," *New York Times,* March 13, 2007, p. C7.

Westphal, Sylvia Pagan, Zachary M. Seward, and John Carreyrou, "Schering-Plough Settles Charges for $435 Million," *Wall Street Journal,* August 30, 2006, p. A2.

Wilke, John R., "Schering-Plough to Face Antitrust Charge: FTC to Allege Illegal Deal to Delay Generic Drugs from Reaching Market," *Wall Street Journal,* April 2, 2001, p. A3.

"Will Takeover Fever Strike Schering-Plough?" *Business Week,* October 23, 1989, p. 130.

Winslow, Ron, "Panel Deals Blow to Two Cholesterol Drugs," *Wall Street Journal,* March 31, 2008, p. B6.

Winslow, Ron, and Sarah Rubenstein, "Delays in Drug's Test Fuel Wider Data Debate," *Wall Street Journal,* March 24, 2008, pp. A1, A11.

———, "Study Deals Setback to Vytorin Cholesterol Drug," *Wall Street Journal,* January 15, 2008, p. A3.

Winslow, Ron, and Shirley S. Wang, "More Vytorin Bad News Hits Merck, Schering," *Wall Street Journal,* July 22, 2008, pp. B1, B2.

Silverstar Holdings, Ltd.

1900 Glades Road, Suite 435
Boca Raton, Florida 33431-7333
U.S.A.
Telephone: (561) 479-0040
Fax: (561) 479-0757
Web site: http://www.silverstarholdings.com

Public Company
Incorporated: 1995 as First South African Management
    Corporation
Employees: 102
Sales: $19.8 million (2007)
Stock Exchanges: NASDAQ
Ticker Symbol: SSTR
NAICS: 511210 Software Publishers

■ ■ ■

Silverstar Holdings, Ltd., is a Boca Raton, Florida-based public holding company listed on the NASDAQ. Portfolio companies include Empire Interactive PLC, Strategy First Inc., and Magnolia Broadband. A wholly owned subsidiary, Empire Interactive publishes interactive software for all game platforms, personal computers, and mobile and other digital platforms. Some of the company's top-selling titles include *Big Murtha Truckers, Hello Kitty, Starsky & Hutch,* and *Starship Troopers.* Maintaining its headquarters in the United Kingdom, Empire Interactive also has offices in France, Germany, Italy, Spain, and the United States. Another Silverstar subsidiary, Strategy First, is a Montreal, Canada-based developer and publisher of video games for personal

computers. Some of its award-winning titles include *Disciples, Jagged Alliance,* and *Space Empires.* Silverstar also owns a minority stake in Magnolia Broadband, a Bedminster, New Jersey-based developer of wireless technology focusing on smart antenna chipset solutions. Silverstar is headed by a pair of South Africa expatriates, Chairman Michael Levy and CEO Clive Kabatznik.

COMPANY INCORPORATES: 1995

Silverstar was established in September 1995 as First South African Management Corporation (First SA) by Levy and Kabatznik to invest in South African companies. According to South Africa's *Sunday Times Business Times,* in 1973 Kabatznik left South Africa and its apartheid system of racial segregation and discrimination "believing there was no hope of peace." He moved to the United States and in 1981 cofounded Learning Annex, Inc., serving as chief financial officer. In 1989 he cofounded Biltmore Capital Group, a holding company that controlled a stock brokerage, and in 1992 became president of a Miami, Florida, investment banking firm, Colonial Capital, Inc.

In 1995 Kabatznik teamed up with Levy, 11 years older and a cousin of his mother. With the situation in South Africa much improved, Kabatznik and Levy decided to use First SA as a vehicle to present Americans with investment opportunities in South Africa, focusing on the acquisition of middle market companies that had sales in the $5 million to $50 million range.

Initially working out of offices in Coconut Grove, Florida, First SA listed Bermuda as its headquarters. It conducted an initial public offering (IPO) of stock in

January 1996 and used the proceeds to complete three acquisitions: Starpak (Pty) Limited, a maker of plastic packaging machines; L.S. Pressings (Pty) Limited, a manufacturer of washers used in the fastener industry; and Europair Africa (Pty) Ltd., a company that manufactured and supplied air conditioning products. Europair also provided First SA with its principal South African offices. Levy was familiar with the plastic packaging machinery business, having served as chairman and chief executive officer of Chicago-based Arpac L.P.

First SA then used these three investments as a platform for further acquisitions in 1996. L.S. Pressings acquired Paper & Metal Industries, a maker of washers used by fastener manufacturers, while Europair acquired Universal Refrigeration, a refrigeration products supplier, followed later in the year by the purchase of First Strut (Pty) Ltd., which manufactured electrical trunking conduits. In June 1996 First SA also became involved in the food business, purchasing a meat-pie company, Pieman's Pantry, followed by the acquisitions of Astoria Bakery and Astoria Bakery Lesotho, which produced and distributed specialty baked breads and confectionery products. In addition, First SA gained entry into the plastic film and printed plastic bag business through the November acquisition of Alfapak (Pty) Ltd.

FIRST SA FOOD HOLDS STOCK OFFERING: 1997

First SA added to its food assets in 1997, picking up Seemanns Meat Products, a manufacturer and distributor of processed meat products, for $5.3 million, and paying another $9 million for Gull Foods, a value-added prepared foods manufacturer. In June 1997 First SA packaged its food assets into an entity called First SA Food, and sold off a 30 percent stake through an IPO of stock. A month later First SA Food grew larger through the $2.1 million acquisition of Fifers Bakery.

Meanwhile, in 1997 First SA added to its packaging holdings by acquiring Pakmatic Company (Pty), Ltd., which distributed automatic and process and packaging machinery, along with a company called Pacforce in a deal completed in October 1997. First SA also entered

the lifestyle market in 1997. In October of that year it paid $6.5 million for Republic Umbrella Manufacturers, producers of umbrellas and related outdoor products; $3.6 million for Galactex Outdoor, a distributor of such outdoor products as Weber grills; and $8.7 million for SA Leisure, a manufacturer of gardening, camping, outdoor furniture, and other products. These assets formed the basis for First SA Lifestyle Holdings, which grew even larger in March 1998 with the $1.23 million purchase of Tradewinds Parasol, South Africa's leading manufacturer of large canvas and wooden parasols.

LEISURE PLANET ACQUIRED: 1999

First SA veered away from manufacturing in 1999 with the acquisition of an 80 percent stake in LPI Limited, a global online travel service that did business as Leisure Planet. The business got its start in late 1991 in Cape Town, South Africa, as an electronic publisher of multimedia hotel information serving the travel industry, initially taking advantage of CD-ROM technology. The company's key asset was a hotel database. With the emergence of the Internet, Leisure Planet moved to the web, launching an Internet site in April 1996. As the Internet boom unfolded in the late 1990s, Leisureplanet, as it was now called, forged alliances with major search engines, including Lycos-Bertlesmann, Yahoo!, Infospace, and the French portal Nomade. Late in 1999 Leisureplanet was able to sell a $20 million interest (slightly less than 10 percent) to CNN News Group, a deal that included the news giant using its web sites to promote Leisureplanet and the codevelopment of a travel show to air on CNN International. At the same time as the CNN deal, a $20 million stake in the business was also sold to Warburg Dillon Read LLC and UBS Capital.

First SA was so enamored with the potential of Leisureplanet and the Internet that in May 1999 the company changed its name to Leisureplanet Holdings, Ltd. It would be a short-lived name, however. The company began casting off its other assets, now considered noncore, to focus on Leisureplanet and its stake in First SA Lifestyle Holdings, but less than a year later, in the early months of 2000, the Internet sector collapsed. In quick order, Leisureplanet was forced to cease operations by the end of August 2000.

SILVERSTAR NAME ADOPTED: 2000

Levy and Kabatznik shifted gears in 2000, dropping Leisureplanet and investing elsewhere. In April 2000 they gained a stake in Magnolia Broadband, investing $2.5 million in the start-up company, and invested a further

KEY DATES

1995: Company is founded as First South African Management Corporation to make investments in South Africa.
1996: Company goes public.
1999: Name is changed to Leisureplanet Holdings.
2000: Silverstar Holdings name is adopted.
2005: Strategy First is acquired.
2006: Empire Interactive is acquired.
2008: BigCityGame.com is launched.

$450,000 in October 2001. A more substantial deal was completed in November 2000 when they paid $3.5 million for Fantasy Sports, Inc., a seven-year-old company that operated subscription-based online fantasy games for college football, NASCAR, and other sports. A month later Leisureplanet Holdings changed its name to Silverstar Holdings, Ltd., essentially providing the company with a fresh start after having divested all of its South African assets and shutting down Leisureplanet.com and other unprofitable subsidiaries.

Silverstar sought to build upon its sports business in 2001. Early in the year it forged an alliance with Small World Media, Inc., another online fantasy sports games provider, which agreed to market Silverstar's NASCAR games to its two million members. Silverstar moved beyond fantasy games in September 2001 with the acquisition of Boca Raton, Florida-based Student Sports Inc., a major high school sports media and marketing company founded in 1989. The flagship product was *Student Sports Magazine,* a monthly magazine that covered high school sports, but the company also produced statistical high school sports record books, such as the *National High School Football Record Book,* local and regional television sports programming services, and recruiting content for such clients as CNNSI.com and TheSportingNews.com. Silverstar attempted to use Student Sports as the basis for a marketing service to large corporations looking to tap into this market, but like Leisure Planet, Student Sports did not pan out for Silverstar. In June 2003 the business was sold.

Silverstar was essentially a fantasy sports company until April 2005 when it acquired Strategy First out of Montreal bankruptcy court. The company had been founded in Montreal by some friends, video-game enthusiasts, who in 1990 were contracted to provide the art and graphics design for a role-playing game. The company continued to serve as a contract operator for

another two years before becoming a game developer, mostly for the personal computer (PC) platform, producing the *Solid Ice* title. More games followed but development costs proved too burdensome for Strategy First, because of salaries and other costs. Although the company attempted to rectify the problem in the early 2000s by publishing third-party titles to grow revenues, the shift in strategy came too late and the company lapsed into bankruptcy.

Changing tack again, Silverstar in April 2006 exited the fantasy sports business, selling Fantasy Sports to a Liberty Media Corporation unit for $4.4 million. In that same month, Silverstar beefed up Strategy First by acquiring the intellectual property assets of Santa Rosa, California-based Malfador Machinations. Established in 1995 Malfador was a space genre PC game developer and gained notice through the development of the award-winning *Space Empires* game series.

EMPIRE INTERACTIVE ACQUIRED: 2007

With the addition of the Malfador titles to Strategy First, Silverstar grew revenues from $353,000 in fiscal 2005 to $3.3 million in fiscal 2006. The company made a further commitment to video games in fiscal 2007 when it paid $16 million for a 90 percent stake in London, England-based Empire Interactive PLC. Empire was a game developer that focused on the major gaming platforms, including Microsoft's Xbox and Xbox 360, Sony's PlayStation and PlayStation 2, and Nintendo's Wii and DS. The company also adopted its games for play on PCs and mobile and other digital platforms.

Empire Interactive was formed in 1987 in the United Kingdom when Entertainment International (UK) Ltd. and Oxford Digital Enterprises merged their operations to become a software development contractor for original and licensed-based games. The company quickly made its mark developing games, such as *The Hunt for Red October* and the *Trivial Pursuit* board game, for Disney as well as for other licenses. Empire Interactive then became involved in the North American market with the development of the *Pipermania* game, which was also noteworthy because it was able to make the difficult transition to the arcade market. The company then sought to expand its purview by making its games available on all the major home console platforms. In order to achieve this goal, Empire Interactive in 2000 raised money via the London Stock Exchange's AIM (alternative investment market), and its shares remained listed on the AIM until the company was acquired by Silverstar. In addition to its frontline titles geared toward serious gamers, Empire Interactive introduced a value line in 2002. It was the combination of value and frontline games that attracted the attention of Silverstar.

With Empire Interactive in the fold, Silverstar grew revenues to $19.8 million in fiscal 2007. Silverstar deepened its commitment to video games in the summer of 2008. Strategy First launched BigCityGame.com, an e-commerce web distribution site catering to both younger and older gamers with dozens of casual games easier to play than many of the demanding and complex hardcore frontline games. At the same time, Silverstar looked to improve the performance of Empire Interactive, putting that company's internal development studio, Razorworks, on the block as part of a reorganization effort. Whether these changes would have the desired effect, or if Silverstar would remain committed to the gaming sector, were lingering questions as the company moved forward.

Ed Dinger

PRINCIPAL SUBSIDIARIES

Empire Interactive PLC; Strategy First Inc.

PRINCIPAL COMPETITORS

Activision Blizzard, Inc.; Midway Games Inc.; Take Two Interactive Software, Inc.

FURTHER READING

Arthur, Charles, "Two More Dot.com Firms Collapse As Capital Dries Up," *Independent* (London), August 4, 2000, p. 6.

"CNN Pays $20 Million for Stake in Service Booking Trips Online," *Wall Street Journal,* December 21, 1999, p. 1.

Efrat, Zilla, "Basket of Food Groups Offered to JSE," *Sunday Times Business Times* (South Africa), April 6, 1996.

"First South Africa Corp.: CEO Says Profit Triples and Revenue Quadruples," *Wall Street Journal,* November 12, 1996.

"Leisureplanet Holdings on Acquisition Trail," *Corporate Financing Week,* January 3, 2000, p. 3.

Moriarty, George, "Leisureplanet Taps Corporate, Euro VC," *Private Equity Week,* January 3, 2000, p. 8.

"Silverstar's Strategy First Launched BigCityGame.com," *Wireless News,* July 2, 2008.

Verkinderen, Frank, and Yochanan Altman, "Leisureplanet.com: Organization and HRM in the New Economy," *Human Resource Planning,* December 2002, p. 19.

Sine Qua Non

———■———

1750 North Ventura Avenue, #5
Ventura, California 93001
U.S.A.
Telephone: (805) 640-8901
Fax: (805) 640-8902

Private Company
Incorporated: 1994
Employees: 20
Sales: $12.6 million (2007 est.)
NAICS: 312130 Wineries

■ ■ ■

Sine Qua Non is one of the most critically acclaimed wineries in California. Owner and winemaker Manfred Krankl produces 3,500 cases of wine annually in a warehouse in Ventura, California. Before harvesting the first crop from his own vineyard in 2007, Krankl selected grapes grown by other vineyards, blending his selections into some of the most highly regarded wines in the world. He emphasizes red blends based on Syrah and Grenache grapes, but never makes the same wine twice. Each new bottling also is christened with a new name and a new label based on Krankl's artwork. The winery's selections retail for $300 per bottle, but do not appear on store shelves. Sine Qua Non wines are sold to customers who are on a mailing list, which is closed. Limited quantities of Sine Qua Non wines are available at restaurants.

ORIGINS

"It was all coincidental," Manfred Krankl said, referring to his career as a restaurateur and winemaker in a September 2008 interview with *Forbes Life*. "Nothing ever happened by design, other than I wanted to leave Austria." So resolute was his desire to leave his native country that Krankl did it twice, failing in his first attempt to stake out a new life, but succeeding beyond all expectations with his second attempt.

When he was 22 years old, Krankl bought a one-way plane ticket to Toronto. He was determined to find a job and make Toronto his new home. Difficulties in contending with the language barrier soon scuttled Krankl's hopes of starting a new life, however. Unable to land a job with only a smattering of English, he was forced to return to Austria, but his journey took far longer than a nine-hour flight home. Strapped for cash, Krankl was forced to travel by sea and booked passage on an ocean freighter that took him to Greece. He stopped on the island of Mykonos before completing the second leg of his journey and met a woman from California while hitchhiking. Less than a year after returning to Austria, Krankl purchased another one-way ticket out of Austria, using his memories of the woman on Mykonos as his compass. He arrived in California during the early 1980s ready to rekindle a love affair. He was virtually penniless, but determined to stay.

Unlike in Toronto, Krankl was able to find a job in Los Angeles. A fellow Austrian came to his aid, Norbert Wabnig, who owned The Cheese Store in Beverly Hills. Wabnig hired Krankl, whose duties were limited primarily to wrapping up cheese and sweeping the floor.

KEY DATES

1994: Manfred Krankl establishes Sine Qua Non and produces 100 cases of wine for sale.
1996: Krankl increases the winery's annual production volume to 2,000 cases.
2003: Krankl plants 22 acres of vineyards in Santa Barbara County, the first acreage under his control.
2008: Plans are underway to establish a new winery in Ventura County.

The job gave Krankl a chance to learn English and to acclimate to his new surroundings, a springboard he used to land a job at the Westwood Plaza, where he quickly rose to the position of general manager. Under his management, the hotel became the most profitable property within the chain, giving Krankl his first taste of professional success.

FOOD BEFORE WINE

By the late 1980s, Krankl had developed a network of friends and secured sufficient financial stability to begin entertaining bolder plans. He was offered the opportunity to become general manager and co-owner of a new restaurant opened by chefs Mark Peel and Nancy Silverton, a married couple who had earned distinction working in the kitchen of Wolfgang Puck's Spago restaurant. The restaurant, Campanile, opened in 1989 on La Brea Avenue, featuring a blend of Californian and Tuscan cuisine and wine programs developed by Krankl.

The restaurant became an immediate success, earning praise from food critics and recording surprising financial success with a sideline business. The restaurant baked its own bread, using an adjacent 2,000-square-foot space to supply its own needs and to sell the surplus on a retail basis. The owners put one employee behind the bakery's counter, but the unassuming business soon was besieged with orders. By 1991, La Brea Bakery was churning through 3,000 pounds of dough daily and in desperate need of additional space. The bakery was moved to a 12,000-square-foot facility near Culver City and began operating as a wholesale business, supplying bread to stores and restaurants. From there, the business only grew bigger. By the time Krankl took his equity out of the business in 2001, La Brea Bakery boasted 500 employees and enjoyed national exposure.

KRANKL'S HOBBY TURNS INTO SINE QUA NON

The success of Campanile and La Brea Bakery gave Krankl a comfortable living. He moved with his wife Elaine to an unincorporated part of West Ventura, where the couple lived on a rural plot near Lake Casitas, and turned one of his passions into a hobby. Krankl began making wine. The first to sample Krankl's skills as a vintner were his friends, who were overwhelmed by what they tasted. They encouraged him to try to sell his creations, and Krankl, tired of spending his days meeting with accountants and other appointments related to Campanile and La Brea Bakery, decided to give it a go. In 1994, the year Sine Qua Non was formed, he produced 100 cases. The supply sold out immediately, but far more encouraging than the eager demand displayed by Krankl's first customers was the reaction of one man, Robert M. Parker Jr.

A CRITICAL SUCCESS

In the wine world, Parker exerted tremendous influence as a critic, determining, to a large extent, the market value of a vintner's creation. He published the *Wine Advocate,* a direct-mail newsletter with subscribers in 37 countries, that expressed his opinions on wines. Parker used a point-based rating system that assayed wines on a scale from 50 to 100 points, with 100 points representing perfection. The Parker rating system changed the way some vintners made wine, a testament to the power of his opinion in the marketplace. Winemakers went to great lengths to earn high ratings from Parker, making what became known as "Parkerized" wines, wines that were specifically made to appeal to his perceived tastes.

Incredibly, Krankl caught the attention of the omnipotent Parker, gaining immediate legitimacy as a vintner of note. Somehow Parker received one of the bottles from Krankl's first 100 cases, judged it on its color, appearance, aroma, bouquet, flavor, and finish, and gave Krankl's inaugural effort a rating of 95, an unprecedented achievement for an unknown winemaker. Over the course of the next dozen years, Krankl racked up an astounding seven "Parker 100s," becoming in Parker's estimation, "One of the most creative and multidimensional winemakers on Planet Earth," as he was quoted in the September 2008 issue of *Forbes Life.* The seven perfect scores awarded within Krankl's first 12 years as a winemaker surpassed the achievements of some of the most heralded European vintners in the world, winemakers whose vintages had been rated for more than 60 years. During that time span, Chateau Lafite-Rothschild garnered four Parker 100s, Chateau Haut-Brion received three Parker 100s, and Chateau Latour netted three Parker 100s.

Krankl, from the gate, joined rarified company. Sine Qua Non became one of California's "cult wines," joining a coterie of wineries such as Screaming Eagle, Harlan Estate, and Dominus Estate whose wines were exceptionally difficult to obtain, extraordinarily expensive, and, typically, collected as investments rather than consumed. Krankl became the newest member of the wine industry's elite, but he was unlike his colleagues who based their operations in either Napa Valley or Sonoma Valley. Krankl established Sine Qua Non in what *Forbes Life* characterized as a "downtrodden suburb of Los Angeles," in Ventura, near "empty storefronts, chain-link-fence makers, lifting equipment leasers, and poker rooms." Sine Qua Non occupied an old, concrete warehouse, where one of the world's most promising winemakers worked next to a heap of corroding industrial equipment.

By 1996, Krankl had increased his annual production at the decidedly nondescript Sine Qua Non winery to 2,000 cases. Without his own vineyard, Krankl relied on the crops of other growers, selecting grapes grown by Alban Vineyards and Bien Nacido Vineyards for his first vintages. He established himself by emphasizing big-bodied Rhone-style blends, making wines based on Syrah and Grenache grape varieties, but the defining characteristic of his creations was diversity. Krankl never made the same wine twice. He used grapes assembled and blended from numerous sources—an approach that made his accumulation of Parker 100s all that more impressive—and he eschewed any sort of conventional branding with his ever-changing roster of selection. Each new bottling, in each vintage, bore a new name with a new label and design taken from Krankl's artwork. Sine Qua Non sold wines with names such as "Against the Wall," "Imposter McCoy," "Queen of Spades," and "The 17th Nail in My Cranium," each bearing its own distinct label.

DEMAND EXCEEDS SUPPLY

For many wine aficionados intrigued by the oddly named yet spectacular wines being produced in a Ventura warehouse there was little hope of ever tasting Krankl's work. He gradually increased his annual production to 3,500 cases, but he refused to expand production further, unwilling to diminish his control over the quality of his wines. Limited supply heightened already feverish demand, pushing the trading value of Sine Qua Non as high as $2,000 per bottle on the secondary market. Slots on the winery's mailing list were available briefly before the list was closed. The waiting list to get on the mailing list stretched for years. The last thing Krankl needed to be concerned about was finding customers for his wines.

Aside from waiting years to be put on Sine Qua Non's mailing list, Krankl's loyal followers could hope to purchase some of his wine at restaurants. Only a small supply was distributed to restaurants, however, and the limited supply was guarded closely by sommeliers, including one in New York who refused to offer Sine Qua Non if he felt the customer was unworthy— "too much money, too little soul," the sommelier explained in *Forbes Life*. One other opportunity to sample Krankl's work arose when he collaborated with a close friend, Alois Kracher Jr., an Austrian winemaker who also was hailed as a visionary. In 1998, Kracher and Krankl began making sweet dessert wines, selling a limited quantity of wines under the "Mr. K" label. The partnership continued until Kracher's death in late 2007, with the last Mr. K wines sold in 2008.

KRANKL PLANTS HIS FIRST VINEYARDS

As Sine Qua Non celebrated its tenth anniversary and prepared for its second decade of business, great changes were afoot. Krankl began laying the foundation for his own vineyards after years of relying on the crops of others. In 2003, he planted 22 acres of vineyards, dubbed the Eleven Confessions Vineyards, in the Santa Rita Hills of Santa Barbara County. The first harvest at Eleven Confessions occurred in 2007, by which time Krankl had announced plans to vacate the old warehouse in Ventura. He planned to build a new winery next to his home, a ranch property with 13 acres of vineyards. The combination of the two vineyards brought Krankl close to his goal of presiding over an estate-grown operation, an ideal arrangement for a perfectionist in the art of making wine and a major evolutional step for Sine Qua Non to take. The years ahead promised to see Krankl develop new award-winning wines and a growing legion of wine aficionados clamoring to get just one taste.

PRINCIPAL COMPETITORS

Harlan Estate; Colgin Cellars; Screaming Eagle Winery and Vineyards; Dominus Estate; Jericho Canyon Vineyards.

FURTHER READING

Asimov, Eric, "Alois Kracher, Austrian Winemaker and Advocate, Is Dead at 48," *New York Times*, December 10, 2007.

Kettman, Matt, "Sine Qua Non," *Ventana*, December 1, 2007.

Martin, Richard, "Campanile," *Nation's Restaurant News*, May 20, 1996, p. 20S.

Nalley, Richard, "The Krankl Cult," *Forbes Life,* September 2008, p. 126.

Stremfel, Michael, "Campanile's Bread Gets 'Hot,'" *Los Angeles Business Journal,* December 2, 1001, p. 25.

Southeast Frozen Foods
Company, L.P.

18770 N.E. 6th Avenue
Miami, Florida 33179
U.S.A.
Telephone: (305) 652-4622
Toll Free: (800) 662-4622
Fax: (305) 651-8329
Web site: http://www.seff.com

Private Company
Founded: 1958 as Poultry Inc.
Employees: 525
Sales: $550 million (2007 est.)
NAICS: 424410 General Line Grocery Merchant
   Wholesalers; 424420 Packaged Frozen Food
   Merchant Wholesalers; 424490 Other Grocery and
   Related Products Merchant Wholesalers

■ ■ ■

Southeast Frozen Foods Company, L.P. claims status as
the largest exclusive distributor of frozen foods in the
southeastern United States, serving 16 states. Through
five warehouse facilities, totaling 600,000 square feet,
Southeast Frozen Foods distributes products such as ice
cream, frozen foods, fruit, vegetables, breads, and
pastries. The company takes pride in its 99th percentile
order accuracy and fill rates and in its customer-friendly
ordering system. Southeast Frozen Foods entered the
wholesale dry food business in 2004, as Southeast
Wholesale Foods, to serve Florida, the Caribbean, and
South and Central America. Large supermarket chains
and distributors can also seek assistance with cold stor-

age and logistical services from one of the company's
business units, American Logistics Group of Southeast
Food Distribution.

FROZEN ASSETS: 1958–91

Southeast Frozen Foods Company dates back to a family
business established by Lawrence Udell in 1958 to
distribute frozen poultry in the Miami area. As Poultry
Inc., the company acquired other foodservice operations
and expanded its geographic area, according to the
company web site. Various businesses consolidated
under the Southeast Frozen Foods name in 1989. In addition to its core frozen poultry and dairy products, the
company distributed a full-line of brand-name items.

Southeast Frozen Foods made drastic job cuts during early 1991. Beginning with 189 employees in January 1991, only 89 remained by mid-March. Another 40
were expected to get their pink slips by the first of April,
the *Miami Herald* reported. The cutbacks came in the
wake of its parent company's bankruptcy filing.

Finevest Foods Inc., a holding company, based in
Greenwich, Connecticut, owned five companies with
total assets of $267.3 million. The financial woes of Fin-
evest's largest entity, Land-O-Sun Dairies based in
Johnson City, Tennessee, had spilled over to Southeast
Frozen Foods. Land-O-Sun Dairies had been hit by rising raw milk prices. The company purchased milk
rather than engaging in milk production, leaving it
vulnerable to fluctuating costs.

Meanwhile, Southeast Frozen Foods, the second
largest Finevest business, had been negotiating payment

COMPANY PERSPECTIVES

With nearly a half century of experience distributing frozen foods, Southeast Frozen Foods has established a reputation for reliability, efficiency and integrated customer service in the frozen and wholesale food business.

Southeast Food Distribution partners with customers and vendors to help them achieve growth and profitability objectives by being a leader in technology and providing best-in-class supply chain services, as well as retail support at a competitive price.

agreements with its vendors. On January 1, 1991, Finevest and its banking group agreed on a five-month debt repayment moratorium, Derek Reveron reported. "By early February, vendors were clamoring for payments 'like a run on a bank,'" Bob Goodale, vice-president of Finevest said in the *Miami Herald*.

Goodale, new to the company, came in the wake of an executive exodus. The president, chief financial officer, and two vice-presidents of Finevest had resigned. During the first nine months of fiscal 1990, the company had produced sales of $536.1 million with an operating loss of $3.4 million. Finevest's total liabilities were $212 million, according to Finevest legal counsel Brian C. Kelly. The Miami newspaper said the holding company owed a group of banks, led by Manufacturers Hanover and Barnett, $150.5 million.

Campbell Soup Co., Pillsbury Co., and other vendors filed a million-dollar lawsuit against Southeast Frozen Foods on February 4, 1991. Finevest filed for Chapter 11 bankruptcy protection on February 11, in U.S. District Court in Jacksonville.

TURNING THINGS AROUND: 1992–99

The Chapter 11 bankruptcy reorganization plan separated out Southeast Frozen Foods from Finevest and three dairy subsidiaries. Security holders were issued "limited voting Class B common stock convertible into 22.5% of Finevest common stock on a fully diluted basis," the *Wall Street Journal* reported in July 1992.

Philip J. Ablove, the turnaround specialist hired to direct the restructuring, stepped aside as president and CEO upon completion of the reorganization. Brian C.

Kelly, executive vice-president and general counsel, was named president. The Southeast Frozen Foods Inc. unit had been purchased in June 1991, by a partnership that included four former managers, according to the *Wall Street Journal*.

In 1994, the distributor was operating six warehouses and serving 18 southeastern states, *Supermarket News* reported. John Robinson was president of the company.

The next year, the company's Georgia-based operation settled with the U.S. Environmental Protection Agency over an administrative enforcement action, a *Business Wire* article reported. Southeast Frozen Foods Company, L.P. had allegedly violated the Emergency Planning and Community Right-to-Know Act: failing to submit Material Safety Data Sheets on time in 1987 and failing to submit completed Emergency and Hazardous Chemical Inventory forms to a state agency and local fire department from 1991 to 1993. The company paid a civil penalty; purchased and donated hazardous response equipment and paid for emergency response training for local fire departments; and contracted for an external analysis of its facilities and added ammonia detectors.

Difficulties aside, during the 1990s the company quadrupled in size. According to the company's web site, facilities were added in new locations in Florida, Georgia, Louisiana, Virginia, and South Carolina during the decade. Southeast Frozen Foods not only bought new warehouses, it built a "state-of-the-art fleet of refrigerated trucks," brought aboard "dedicated and experienced employees," and developed "cutting-edge technology for a uniquely customer-friendly order processing system."

STOCKING THE SHELVES: 2003–06

Southeast Frozen Foods leased a 300,000-square-foot warehouse in West Miami-Dade in the fall of 2003, preparing for a new subsidiary, Southeast Wholesale Foods, LLC. "It's the biggest industrial lease in at least three years," Benjamin Eisenberg, senior director at Cushman & Wakefield in Miami and a specialist in industrial properties, told the *Miami Daily Business Review*. "Most buildings of that size are owner occupied or build-to-suits." The food storage and delivery service for food wholesalers had been ranked 45th on *Florida Trend* magazine's list of the state's top 50 private companies, Terry Sheridan reported.

The frozen food business launched its dry groceries entity in February 2004. Southeast Wholesale Foods

KEY DATES

1958: Lawrence Udell begins distributing frozen poultry in Miami area.

1989: Food businesses are consolidated under Southeast Frozen Foods name.

1991: Bankruptcy results in divestment of frozen foods operation from holding company.

2004: Company expands into wholesale dry foods business.

2007: Company begins multimillion-dollar facility upgrade program.

would not only distribute to domestic customers, but act as an exporter.

Southeast Wholesale Foods picked up Presidente and Tropical Supermarket store groups as customers in March 2004. The south Florida stores wanted to switch to the Hy-Top brand distributed exclusively in its area by Southeast Wholesale Foods.

"Southeast led the re-setting and re-tagging of store shelves," *Today's Grocer* explained. "It took about one month to totally re-merchandise the stores now supplied by Southeast. Besides a full line of dry groceries, Hy-Top and its related labels can provide dairy items such as cheese (bagged, chunk and American singles), juices, butter and margarine. Frozen foods, such as ice cream, pizzas and vegetables and for the price conscious consumer, the better Valu trademark, your savings brand."

In addition to food items, Southeast Wholesale Foods could supply independent and chain supermarkets with items such as dry goods, health and beauty care products, and general merchandise.

In September 2004, Southeast Frozen Foods pitched in to help in the wake of a succession of hurricanes. The company provided its Florida retailers with refrigerated trucks and citizens with ice and drinking water. Potable water and ice was shipped to clients in the Caribbean and Cayman Islands. The company said it had developed an emergency plan prior to the onset of the hurricane season.

South Florida CEO reported that Southeast Frozen Foods had annual revenue of $525 million in 2005. Richard A. Bauer took over as president and CEO of the private company, in 2006, following the death of John Robinson. Bauer, who joined the company in 1993, had also served as controller.

UPDATING: 2007–08

Southeast Frozen Foods announced plans for the expansion of its Calhoun County, South Carolina, distribution center in September 2007. The $3.5 million project would add 1.2 million cubic feet of space, four more dock doors, and 3,500 additional pallet positions to the facility built in 1999. Thirty new jobs would be created.

"We certainly had a choice where we were going to expand our operations," Bauer said in an *Expansion Management* article. "We felt Calhoun County had a solid labor pool and logistical advantages. The expansion will help us increase our productivity and carry more products, which is so important to our business. In business you have to have partners to be successful, and we feel we have a true partner with the folks here in South Carolina." The company planned to invest in improvements and upgrades in its other facilities as well.

In 2008, Southeast Frozen Foods called itself "the largest exclusive distributor of frozen food products in the southeastern United States." Counted among its customers were large regional supermarkets and distributors. Its distribution network covered Florida, Georgia, North Carolina, South Carolina, Tennessee, Pennsylvania, Maryland, Delaware, West Virginia, Louisiana, and Virginia. Southeast Wholesale Foods, a subsidiary of Southeast Food Distribution, provided over 30,000 items and a marketing program to its retail customers in Florida and offshore. The food operations carried items supplied by more than 300 vendors. Another unit, American Logistics Group of Southeast Food Distribution, assisted the food industry in the southeastern United States with cold storage and logistical services. Among its customers were Dade County and Broward County schools.

Kathleen Peippo

PRINCIPAL SUBSIDIARIES

Southeast Food Distribution; Southeast Wholesale Foods; American Logistics Group.

PRINCIPAL COMPETITORS

Associated Grocers of Florida, Inc.; C&S Wholesale Grocers, Inc.; Nash-Finch Company.

FURTHER READING

"Corrections & Clarifications," *South Florida CEO,* September 2006, p. 6.

"Drawing Board," *Food Logistics,* October 2007.

"EPA Settles with Southeast Frozen Foods Company, LP of Cordele, Georgia, for Violations of the Emergency Planning and Community Right-to-Know Act," *Business Wire,* October 18, 1995.

Lunsford, Darcie, "Industrial Park Plans Spec Space," *South Florida Business Journal,* September 2, 2005.

"New Independent Supermarket Opens in Plantation," *Today's Grocer,* November 2004, p. 13.

Reveron, Derek, "Food Firm Slashes Workforce," *Miami Herald,* March 16, 1991.

Sheridan, Terry, "Food Distributor Signs Lease at Beacon Station," *Miami Daily Business Review,* September 30, 2003, p. A3.

"Southeast Frozen Appoints VP," *Supermarket News,* August 22, 1994, p. 46.

"Southeast Frozen Foods to Expand Distribution Center," *Food Logistics,* July 8, 2008.

"Southeast Frozen Foods to Expand Distribution Center in South Carolina," *Expansion Management,* September 21, 2007.

"Southeast Frozen Names Myers," *Supermarket News,* December 12, 1994, p. 33.

"Two Companies Pay for Unlicensed Software Use," *Miami Daily Business Review,* June 13, 2002, p. A7.

"Two Independent Groups Play Leading Role in Hy-Top Florida Debut," *Today's Grocer,* June 2004, p. 8.

Valeriano, Lourdes Lee, "Finevest Emerges from Capital 11 in Smaller Form," *Wall Street Journal* (Eastern Edition), July 15, 1992, p. A4.

The Structure Tone Organization

———■———

770 Broadway
New York, New York 10003-9522
U.S.A.
Telephone: (212) 779-0050
Fax: (212) 685-9267
Web site: http://www.structuretone.com

Private Company
Incorporated: 1971
Employees: 1,670
Sales: $3.16 billion (2006 est.)
NAICS: 236210 Industrial Building Construction; 236220 Commercial and Institutional Building Construction

■ ■ ■

The Structure Tone Organization is a privately owned group of six construction management companies. The flagship unit, Structure Tone Incorporated, is a New York City-based company providing construction management, project management, and general contracting services to a broad range of sectors: academia, broadcast and media, cultural and entertainment, financial and commercial, government, healthcare, hospitality, law, mission critical, nonprofit, parking facilities, residential, retail, and science and technology. Structure Tone is best known for its interior work. In addition to its Manhattan office, Structure Tone maintains branches in Lyndhurst and Princeton, New Jersey; Philadelphia, Pennsylvania; and Arlington, Virginia. Structure Tone International provides comparable services in England, France, Ireland, Italy, Spain, Hong Kong, and China. Another affiliate, ST Tech Services, Inc., is the organization's technology management division. Other affiliates include Constructors & Associates, a Texas construction management firm with offices in Austin, Dallas, Houston, and San Antonio; Pavarini Construction Company, Inc., a construction services firm with offices in Stamford, Connecticut, and Fort Lauderdale, Florida; and Pavarini McGovern LLC, a New York City-based provider of base building, core, and shell construction services in the greater New York metropolitan area. Structure Tone is owned by the Donaghy family and chief lieutenant of many years, John T. White.

COMPANY FOUNDED: 1971

Structure Tone was cofounded by its longtime CEO Patrick J. Donaghy in 1971. Born in Carrickmore, County Tyrone, Ireland, in 1941, he would come to the United States in 1959, and although he became a wealthy man he never forgot his roots. Over the years many people from Tyrone would find employment at Structure Tone, including students on break, a number of them athletes who filled the roster of the New York Tyrone Gaelic football team Donaghy supported. Before leaving his home country, Donaghy received an education at the Omagh Technical College, and put the skills he learned there to use in the United States, finding work as a carpenter. He was employed by Wicole Construction Company in New York City from 1960 until the time he left to start Structure Tone, with an Italian foreman, Lewis R. Marino.

According to company sources, Structure Tone's first project was work performed for Velcro USA. Another important job in the company's first year in operation was a $1.5 million contract with Simplicity Patterns at 200 Madison Avenue. Structure Tone also began working with its first *Fortune* 500 client, winning a contract for work at an IBM facility in Garden City, New York. According to Dublin, Ireland's *Sunday Business Post,* "It is believed that one of the company's first major jobs was the fit-out of several floors of the twin towers of the World Trade Center." Having gained acceptance in the marketplace, Structure Tone added other well-known clients, including financial institutions such as Citibank and Chemical Bank, and advertising agencies, including Cunningham & Walsh Advertising; Doyle, Dane & Bernback; and Grey Advertising.

JOHN T. WHITE JOINS COMPANY: 1977

It was in 1977 that John T. White, also Irish-born from County Sligo, joined Donaghy as executive vice-president and played a key role in the expansion of Structure Tone. In that same year, the firm entered the retail market, securing its first contract with Ohrbach's, a New York-based department store chain. More important to the company's success, however, were the management skills of Pat Donaghy. He was known as a tough businessman, and according to the *Sunday Business Post,* he was "personable when it comes to building new contacts in the construction game." As a result, Structure Tone entered the ranks of a select group of contractors that won the lion's share of interior work on Manhattan buildings. The city's skyline would be littered with buildings in which Structure Tone made a contribution.

Structure Tone expanded geographically in the 1980s, both home and abroad. An office was established in London in 1984, initially to do work for a U.S. client, Chemical Bank. A year later two offices in the United States opened as well: Boston and Washington, D.C. The Boston office started off strong. Early projects included a 250,000-square-foot interior fit-out at 260 Franklin Street, a 500,000-square-foot build-out at

20-21 Customer House, and another build-out, 750,000 square feet in size, at One International Place. Structure Tone's Lyndhurst, New Jersey, office was added in 1987 and made its debut on a project for MetLife Insurance Company project in Iselin, New Jersey. In that same year, Structure Tone also became involved in the mission critical market, taking on projects crucial to corporate operations, such as data centers and telecommunications switch rooms. With the rapid growth of information technology it was a field that would only grow in importance in the ensuing years.

CONSTRUCTORS & ASSOCIATES ACQUIRED: 1987

Structure Tone also grew via acquisition in 1987 and expanded well beyond the Northeast by bringing Dallas, Texas-based Constructors & Associates into the fold. The company was incorporated in Texas in 1977. It expanded beyond the Dallas area in 1986 when it opened an office in the state capital, Austin. Six years later the company would be charged with renovating the Texas State Capitol building. Constructors & Associates grew further under Structure Tone with the opening of an office in Houston in 1989.

By the 1990s Structure Tone was a prosperous company and Pat Donaghy was a wealthy man with personal interests to pursue. He remained very much involved in the business, but he had plenty of relatives to help shoulder the load, including some of his brothers and four sons. One of the personal projects close to his heart was the renovation of the Irish Arts Center in New York City in the late 1980s. He supplied labor from Structure Tone free of charge. Donaghy also became involved in the difficult and often violent conflict between loyalists and nationalists in Northern Ireland, spurred by the 1991 loyalist killing of a nephew. Donaghy became a major supporter and fund-raiser of the Sinn Fein nationalist political party. When he held fund-raisers for Sinn Fein in New York City, Structure Tone subcontractors could be counted on to attend and pay for the seats at the fund-raising tables. At one such event, according to *Sunday Business Times,* perhaps repeating an apocryphal tale, "One Italian-American was overheard saying, 'Who is Sinn Fein and has he arrived yet?'" As the newspaper summarized, "For many Italian-Americans, Donaghy was the only reason they handed over money to support a cause they knew little or nothing about." Donaghy was also among a group of Irish-American businessmen who successfully lobbied the Clinton administration in the early 1990s to provide Sinn Fein leader Gerry Adams, a close associate of Donaghy, with a U.S. visa, opening the way for a historic visit to the United States and lending legitimacy to Sinn Fein.

KEY DATES

1971: Company is founded by Patrick Donaghy and Lewis Marino.
1977: John T. White joins company.
1984: London office opens.
1987: Constructors & Associates is acquired.
1996: Pavarini Construction Co. is acquired.
1998: Structure Tone pleads guilty to bribery charges.
2000: Hong Kong office opens.
2001: Pavarini McGovern LLC is formed.
2005: Robert W. Mullen is named president.

COMPANY PLEADS GUILTY TO BRIBERY CHARGES: 1998

Aside from his connection with the controversial Sinn Fein party, Donaghy and Structure Tone experienced legal trouble in the 1990s. It was one of several construction companies ensnared in a five-year investigation, from 1992 to 1997, of the Manhattan District Attorney's office looking into bid rigging and kickback payments in the interior construction industry, which was controlled by a handful of companies, including Structure Tone. The company agreed in 1998 to plead guilty to bribe paying and accept a $10 million fine, but immediately after entering its plea in State Supreme Court in Manhattan, Structure Tone issued a public statement that maintained it was actually a victim of the bid-rigging scheme. It said it was forced to make payments, described as commissions, lest it risk losing work. Moreover, the company insisted that it only entered a guilty plea to get the matter behind it and get on with business. The District Attorney's office was far from pleased with the company's public relations move and its spokesman was quick to tell the press, "The fact that Structure Tone pleaded guilty to commercial bribery and has agreed to pay $10 million speaks for itself."

Shortly after the bribery case was settled, Pat Donaghy stepped down as Structure Tone's chairman, turning over the post to his son, James Donaghy. The interior construction firms that had been caught up in the scandal had good reason to fear that their reputations would be tarnished and they would lose business. Indeed, many New York City–area construction firms sensed an opportunity and launched interiors divisions to take away business from Structure Tone and the others. According to *Crain's New York Business* in 1999,

"at least 15 operations have sprung to life because of the investigation." In order to fend off this wave of new competition, Structure Tone "resorted to price-cutting for several months after the plea agreements," reported *Crain's*. "Competitors say they underbid other companies by 25%—until the fact that they were winning business strengthened their credibility enough so that they didn't have to lowball any more."

Even while Structure Tone was going through its legal difficulties, it continued to expand its operations in the second half of the 1990s. It entered the high education market, and in 1996 added another affiliate company, Pavarini Construction Co., which in that same year celebrated its centennial. Pavarini started out in Washington, D.C., in 1896, but relocated in 1945 to New York City, where it was involved in the construction of a number of prominent office buildings and department stores. It also did work at Princeton University; in Pittsburgh for U.S. Steel and Alcoa; and as far away as Oregon, where it constructed the Portland Building. In 1963 Pavarini opened an office in San Juan, Puerto Rico, and four years later added a Miami, Florida, office as well. To serve the southern New England market, Pavarini opened a Greenwich, Connecticut, office in 1979.

Having successfully overcome the stigma associated with its guilty plea, Structure Tone continued its steady growth pattern in the new century, both at home and abroad. In 2000, ST Tech Services, Inc., was added to the Structure Tone family of companies, providing technology management, communications network design, telecommunications management, and local area network and wide area network systems services and equipment. Also in 2000 Structure Tone opened an office in Hong Kong to serve its international clients in the Asia Pacific region. Additional offices in the area soon followed in Shenzhen, Guangzhou, and Souzhou, China. The company also registered to do business in Japan, Singapore, and Taiwan, making Structure Tone one of only a handful of foreign construction companies to be licensed to offer construction services in China and Japan.

In 2001 Structure Tone entered another new market, science and technology, and formed another affiliate construction company: Pavarini McGovern LLC, which complemented Structure Tone by providing base building, core, and shell construction services in the New York City area. In the Southwest, in the meantime, Constructors & Associates opened a San Antonio, Texas, office and began work on a project at the San Antonio Airport.

NEW CEO NAMED: 2005

In May 2005, Structure Tone brought in a new chief executive officer, Robert W. Mullen. He was a seasoned construction executive with 26 years of experience in the United States as well as overseas, primarily with Skanska USA Building. He took over a firm that in 2005 posted $2.59 billion in revenues, making it the 118th largest private company according to *Forbes* magazine. The company looked to generate even more revenues through real estate investments, in 2006 forming Structure Tone Equities to become co-investors with clients in real estate projects. Other changes were in store for the Texas affiliate. In late 2007 Constructors & Associates brought in real estate veteran Dan Busch to serve as president. One of his primary tasks would be to broaden the company's scope beyond corporate office interiors. With operations spread across the globe and participation in a broad range of industries, there was every reason to believe that Structure Tone was positioned to enjoy continued long-term success.

Ed Dinger

PRINCIPAL SUBSIDIARIES

Pavarini Construction Company, Inc.; Pavarini McGovern LLC; Structure Tone Incorporated; ST Tech Services, Inc.

PRINCIPAL COMPETITORS

Bovis Lend Lease; Skanska USA Building Inc.; The Turner Corporation.

FURTHER READING

Bagli, Charles V., "After Guilty Plea in Bribe Case, Company Calls the Payments Legal," *New York Times,* June 18, 1998.

———, "Guilty Pleas Are Expected in Office Construction Bid-Rigging," *New York Times,* June 16, 1998.

Carswell, Simon, and Paul T. Colgan, "Uncle Pat Pays the Piper," *Sunday Business Post* (Dublin), June 13, 2004.

Croghan, Lore, "After Scandal, New Firms Rush into Interiors," *Crain's New York Business,* May 10, 1999, p. 1.

Hethcock, Bill, "Busch Takes Helm of Constructors," *Dallas Business Journal,* December 3, 2007.

"Mullen Named Structure Tone CEO," *Constructioneer,* May 16, 2005, p. 51.

Smith, Geoffrey, "Firm Announces Formation of New Investment Arm," *Real Estate Weekly,* October 4, 2006, p. 34.

Sutherland Lumber Company, L.P.

———— ■ ————

4000 Main Street
Kansas City, Missouri 64111-2313
U.S.A.
Telephone: (816) 756-3000
Fax: (816) 756-3594
Web site: http://www.sutherlands.com

Private Company
Incorporated: 1917
Employees: 2,300
Sales: $1.18 billion (2006)
NAICS: 444190 Other Building Material Dealers

■ ■ ■

Sutherland Lumber Company, L.P. is a family-owned-and-operated chain of lumberyards, some small in size, and home improvement stores, many of which are warehouse operations more than 140,000 square feet in size. The Kansas City, Missouri-based business includes some 70 stores located in 13 states: Arizona, Arkansas, Colorado, Kansas, Louisiana, Mississippi, Missouri, New Mexico, Ohio, Oklahoma, Texas, Utah, and Wyoming. While Sutherland's focus is on lumber, it also offers building materials, doors and windows, flooring covering, hardware, electrical supplies, heating and ventilation supplies, plumbing supplies, paint, and lawn and garden products. Sutherland packages materials to build pre-designed houses, garages, sheds, pole buildings, decks, fences, backyard ponds, and swing and playground sets. The home centers also sell medicine cabinets and vanities, large appliances (washers, dryers, ranges, refrigera-

tors, and freezers), heaters, water heaters, and wood-burning and pellet stoves. In addition, the larger Sutherland outlets offer hunting supplies, including gloves and apparel, blinds, camouflage, gun cases and safes, scopes and binoculars, targets and traps, and other outdoor gear. Sutherland Lumber is owned by members of the Sutherland family, who are known for being circumspect about their business affairs.

COMPANY ESTABLISHED 1917

Sutherland Lumber began in 1917 when Robert Sutherland Jr. inherited some money from the life insurance policy of his father, Robert Sutherland Sr. According to his obituary in the *Kansas City Times,* the elder Sutherland was a 66-year-old "real estate man" of Canadian birth who moved to Kansas City in 1892. The wife of Robert Sutherland Jr. received a matching amount of money from her father, and in Durant, Oklahoma, the young couple opened a "house pattern yard," essentially a lumberyard that specialized in selling the materials needed to complete pre-designed home blueprints. Because of the United States' involvement in World War I and the devastated crops of Europe, which had been enveloped in the conflict since 1914, Oklahoma farmers were enjoying flush times, and the Sutherlands benefited from their prosperity. To take advantage, the family opened new yards in other Oklahoma towns, including Ada, Hugo, Idabel, Norman, and Shawnee.

It was near Ada in 1921 that a major oilfield was discovered, a turning point for both Oklahoma and Sutherland Lumber. The drilling operations needed lumber and other supplies and the Sutherlands' yard in

---

COMPANY PERSPECTIVES

Lumber is our business. ... Not a sideline!

Ada began expanding its product offerings to meet the needs of the oilmen. As oilfields cropped up around the state, Sutherland opened specialized oilfield yards. Through the rest of the 1920s Sutherland Lumber followed the oil boom, opening yards where discoveries were made and closing them as soon as the oilmen depleted what the earth had to offer. The number of companies that were large enough to possess the financial wherewithal to acquire leases and fund the drilling operations were limited to just a dozen or so in the Southwest, and Robert Sutherland proved adept at winning their business. As a result, Sutherland Lumber expanded beyond the Oklahoma oilfields, opening yards in boomtowns throughout Texas, Kansas, and New Mexico, 40 in all by the end of the 1920s.

GREAT DEPRESSION FORCES NEW STRATEGY

Reliance on the oilfields came to an end after the stock market crash of 1929 led to the Great Depression. Not only did oil prices plummet, decreasing the demand for new wells, producers switched from lumber rigs to steel ones, which could be reused and were less expensive in the long run. By the start of the 1930s the Sutherlands were at a crossroads and took stock of the lumber business. With oilfield sales no longer substantial, they decided to focus on farming communities, concluding that crops still had to be cultivated if people were to eat. Thus, Robert Sutherland and his wife invested what money they had left, moved to Des Moines, Iowa, and bought an existing business, Randall Lumber.

In Des Moines, as they were preparing to open, they recognized a new opportunity. At the stockyards, trucks brought hogs and cattle from the hinterlands and returned empty. Robert Sutherland realized that those trucks could very easily deliver lumber and other building materials to the farmers who had supplied the livestock. To attract this business, he developed an advertising piece that could be mailed to farmers, making a pitch about the returning stock trucks. Moreover, Sutherland offered low prices because the yard would be able to buy in larger quantities direct from manufacturers, cutting out jobbers, and passing on the savings to the farmers. It was also a cash-and-carry concept. Thus, Sutherland avoided the cost of delivery by making use

of the stock trucks and eliminated the problem of credit and the potential of uncollected accounts.

The main obstacle to Sutherland's plan was obtaining the mailing addresses of Iowa farmers. To help build the mailing list and run the yard, Robert Sutherland pulled his 19-year-old son, Herman, out of Princeton University (which he had transferred to after a year at a university in Kansas), and enlisted his help. The Des Moines venture had to be successful if the family were to survive these perilous times. In July 1932 Herman joined the Sutherland yard in Des Moines, working here during the spring, summer, and fall months, his first job unloading cement from boxcars. In the winter he was charged with obtaining the names and addresses of farmers, new targets for the yard's mailings. Because the post office did not permit employees to give out the information, Herman Sutherland traveled to all 80 of Iowa's counties and found a way to secure the information he wanted, sometimes paying retired mail carriers for it or bribing current carriers or their assistants at a penny a name if necessary.

KANSAS CITY YARD OPENS: 1936

Sutherland's cash-and-carry yard was also promoted in newspaper ads and on radio. It was well received by Iowa farmers but despised by competing yards around the state that had served customers for a long time and had enjoyed a tacit understanding with one another to maintain certain price levels. Sutherland upset that arrangement but there was nothing those yards could do until the Roosevelt administration and Congress enacted the National Industrial Recovery Act, which permitted the federal government to establish prices for goods, thus eliminating Sutherland's competitive edge. The law was challenged in the courts and eventually deemed unconstitutional, allowing Sutherland to resume its high-volume, low-price, cash-and-carry operation, which the family now took to Omaha, Nebraska, and downtown Oklahoma City, Oklahoma. In 1936 the Sutherlands opened a yard in Kansas City, which would become the headquarters for the parent company.

Robert Sutherland Jr. died of a heart attack in November 1941. Herman Sutherland and brothers Dwight, John, and Robert Q. took charge of the four stores that made up the family business, and two weeks later faced a major challenge when Japanese naval forces attacked the Pacific fleet of the U.S. Navy anchored at Pearl Harbor, Hawaii, an act that thrust the country into war. Materials of all sorts were now commandeered for military use, making it difficult to supply the Sutherland yards. One in East St. Louis was forced to close. Moreover, the company lost employees as men enlisted or were drafted into military service, including John and

KEY DATES

1917: Robert Sutherland Jr. and wife open first lumberyard.
1932: Cash-and-carry yard opens in Des Moines, Iowa.
1941: Robert Sutherland Jr. dies; four sons take over.
1992: Robert Q. Sutherland dies.
1994: New superstores open.
2006: Herman Sutherland dies.

Dwight Sutherland, who joined the Navy and Merchant Marines. Because of stomach ulcers, Herman Sutherland remained to lead the business, assisted by his brother Robert, who had been with the company since 1937. What kept the business afloat during this time was a contract to build shipping crates for the engines produced by the Pratt & Whitney Engine Co. plant in the Kansas City area. The military need for these engines made Sutherland Lumber a defense contractor and as a result provided it with the ability to secure raw materials.

POSTWAR GROWTH

After the war came to a close in 1945, Sutherland Lumber was quick to reopen the East St. Louis yard, and as the economy roared back to life following a brief recession, the company began opening more yards to take advantage of a building boom as returning veterans settled down to raise families in the new suburbs springing up across the country. Sutherland also repeated the success it enjoyed in Des Moines in other cities with stockyards, such as Sioux Falls and Ottumwa, Iowa, taking advantage of empty stock trucks to haul goods to farmers in those areas.

In the 1950s Sutherland Lumber became more vertically integrated. Timber was purchased in Colorado, where it was milled and planed. In South Dakota the company bought lumber from local mills and finished and dried the materials. The yards were also enlarged during this period to carry tools and hardware, followed by paint, electrical, and plumbing supplies. Sutherland Lumber took the concept further, adding finished building products. An aluminum door and window factory was opened in Marceline, Missouri, as well as a door frame and window plant in Goodman, Missouri, and a treating plant in Hatsfield, Arkansas, to turn out posts and poles. To handle the marketing needs of the

lumberyards, an advertising company, Cherokee Advertising, was launched. The Sutherland family also became involved in the wholesale business, establishing Cimarron Lumber and Supply, to supply the individual yards.

Sutherland Lumber consisted of 13 stores by the start of the 1960s. Because Herman Sutherland, his three brothers, and one sister were getting older, the family decided the time had come to split the operations among the five families. They also grew richer in the 1960s, according to *National Home Center News,* when their mother sold 1.8 million acres of Oklahoma and Arkansas southern yellow pine forests to Weyerhaeuser Co. The yards remained affiliated but each family was permitted to set their own policies. In this way they could learn from each other's mistakes and benefit from the others' successes. Sharing information with outsiders was frowned upon, however, as the Sutherlands earned a reputation for being secretive. Nevertheless, the number of units grew to 33 by the start of the 1970s. The company took advantage of a housing boom during the post–World War II era and opened new locations along the interstate highways that also emerged during this period.

Sutherland Lumber tripled in size over the next two decades, spurred by aggressive expansion in the South during the early 1980s. According to *Corporate Report Kansas City,* the company grossed about $350 million. In July 1981 Sutherland Lumber was reorganized, the five partnerships that had run the enterprise now splitting into 21 partnerships and private corporations, a move that likely eliminated some estate and capital gains taxes for the family. Some members of the Sutherland family tried to take the Sutherland brand into the warehouse sector, opening 80,000- to 100,000-square-foot units. The Indianapolis House Mart warehouse concept included salespeople on roller skates. While initially amusing, House Mart did not have staying power and eventually closed. An effort to become involved in the retail hardware market through the Crate Deals concept was also made, but it too did not connect with consumers and in time became a closeout store.

With divergent and overlapping family ownership of the stores, Sutherland Lumber was in reality a crazy-quilt operation. Although all relied on Cimarron Lumber for supplies and Cherokee Advertising for advertising, the stores ranged widely in size and manner of operation. While Herman Sutherland and his sons were more progressive than others in the family and embraced computerized inventory control systems, others did not. The yard in Corpus Christi, Texas, according to *National Home Center News* in a 1990 company profile, was "firmly entrenched in the 1960s, operating a barn-like lumberyard with no flourishes or customer amenities and cash boxes instead of computer terminals at the checkouts."

The Sutherland family received some notoriety in 1988 when Perry Sutherland, son of Dwight, joined forces with New York investor and corporate raider Asher Edelman to attempt a hostile takeover of a Kansas City-based building supplies chain, Payless Cashways Inc. To ward off the attempt, Payless went private. Sutherland and Edelman sold their stake, pocketing about $17 million in profits for their efforts. Payless took on excessive debt, eventually leading to its bankruptcy and liquidation. Also part of the investment group was Barry Rosenstein, an Edelman protégé. Two years later he and Perry Sutherland made an unsuccessful bid to acquire Justin Industries, a Texas manufacturing conglomerate.

Sutherland Lumber began the 1990s with 92 stores located in 18 states. The chain adjusted to the times, becoming more uniform under the leadership of a new generation of the Sutherland family. Robert Q. Sutherland retired in the late 1980s and died in 1992 at the age of 73. Dwight passed away at the age of 81 in 2003. The eldest brother, Herman, lived until late 2006, dying at the age of 93. During the 1990s Sutherland Lumber adopted the popular warehouse home improvement store model while closing some of the older, smaller lumberyards. By the early 2000s the Sutherland chain receded to about 60 units in 15 states, before beginning another expansion effort.

FAMILY SPAT ERUPTS: 2004

The Sutherland family continued to keep details of their business operation close to the vest, but some light was shed on the inner workings of the family and their concerns in 2004 when a family dispute led to litigation and filings. In that year, Dwight Sutherland's daughter Martha and son Dwight Jr. filed a lawsuit against one of the affiliated Sutherland Lumber companies—Kansas City-based Dardanelle Timber Co., which owned eight Sutherland Lumber stores—and their siblings, twins Perry and Todd Sutherland. Although part-owners of the business, Martha and Dwight Jr. were denied access to the books and records going back to 1990 that they requested following the 2003 death of their father. According to court filings, Martha Sutherland suspected that Perry and Todd were using the company for their own financial benefit. Even before the death of their father, there were tensions between the offspring, with Martha Sutherland refusing to sign a form that made

Perry Sutherland president of the family concern. According to court documents, he went around her by having a cousin replace her on the board and complete his appointment. She then sued in both Kansas City and in Delaware where Dardanelle was incorporated. The Kansas City case was settled in February 2006. No details of the deal were revealed.

The Delaware case continued, however, and in May 2006 a Delaware judge found that there was "a credible basis to believe that wrongdoing was afoot" and ordered the company to turn over financial documents to the fiscal year prior to Dwight Sr.'s death. The judge also chided Perry and Todd Sutherland for the perquisites they included in their employment agreements with Dardanelle. While the matter wound its way through the court system, Sutherland Lumber and its interconnecting ownership links continued on. How well it was faring remained uncertain, although estimates placed annual sales in the $1.2 billion range.

Ed Dinger

PRINCIPAL SUBSIDIARIES

Cherokee Advertising; Cimarron Lumber Supply.

PRINCIPAL COMPETITORS

84 Lumber Company; The Home Depot, Inc.; Lowe's Companies, Inc.

FURTHER READING

Cronkleton, Robert A., "Company to Enter New Arena," *Kansas City Star,* September 2, 2008, p. B1.

"Dwight D. Sutherland Sr. Dies at 81," *Kansas City Star,* October 27, 2005, p. B2.

Margolies, Dan, "Inside a Family Feud," *Kansas City Star,* June 7, 2006, p. C1.

———, "Sutherland Suit Reads a Little Like a CIA Dossier," *Kansas City Star,* November 22, 2005, p. D12.

Reddig, William M., Jr, "What's Next for the Secretive Sutherlands," *Corporate Report Kansas City,* September 1982, p. 33.

"Robert Q. Sutherland Dies at Age 73," *Kansas City Star,* January 23, 1992, p. B7.

Rudeman, Gary S., "Sutherland Lumber: The Old and the New Coexist," *National Home Center News,* September 3, 1990.

Smith, Joyce, "Sutherland Plans Opening for Waldo Warehouse Store," *Kansas City Star,* March 29, 1995, p. B3.

Tsai, Joyce, "Lumber Executive, KC Civic Leader Dies," *Kansas City Star,* December 29, 2006, p. B1.

TBA Global, LLC

21700 Oxnard Street, Suite 1430
Woodland Hills, California 91367
U.S.A.
Telephone: (818) 226-2800
Fax: (818) 226-2801
Web site: http://www.tbaglobal.com

Private Company
Incorporated: 1993 as Nashville Country Club, Inc.
Employees: 223
Sales: $110 million (2008 est.)
NAICS: 561920 Convention and Trade Show Organizers; 711320 Promoters of Performing Arts, Sports, and Similar Events Without Facilities

∎ ∎ ∎

TBA Global, LLC, is a communication and marketing services firm that produces entertainment programs, conferences, and other special events for major North American corporations including McDonald's, IBM, Wal-Mart, and Nike. In 2004 the firm was acquired by a group led by entertainment mogul Irving Azoff and industry executive Robert Geddes.

BEGINNINGS

The roots of TBA Global date to 1993, when former Hard Rock Café CEO Thomas J. "Jock" Weaver III founded a company to develop a chain of country music–themed concept restaurants called Nashville Country Club. Weaver had overseen the growth of the successful music-themed Hard Rock restaurant chain, and since its sale in 1988 had headed investment company Heritage Trust Co. He would receive assistance from restaurant industry executive Prab Nallamilli and Nashville investment firm Flood, Bumstead, McCready and Sayles.

In February 1994 Nashville Country Club sold 600,000 shares of stock on the NASDAQ for $5 each to help fund construction of the first restaurant. In May the firm announced it would also develop a chain of live music venues called The Road in partnership with Tribune Entertainment Co., which was planning spinoff radio and television programs.

On November 17 the first Nashville Country Club restaurant opened at 1811 Broadway on Nashville's famous Music Row, with numerous country music stars in attendance. It featured casual dining amid country-themed décor and displays of music memorabilia. As with the Hard Rock Café, a key part of the concept was sales of merchandise including T-shirts and other souvenirs at an in-house store.

In late 1995 the firm reached an agreement to buy the Village at Breckenridge Resort for $31 million. The 23-year-old, upscale Colorado ski country resort, which had two hotels and numerous condominiums, added eight more restaurants to the firm's portfolio and was expected to be the site of the next Nashville Country Club. In the spring of 1996 the company sold an additional $10 million in stock to fund the purchase, and in June the Village became affiliated with the prestigious Wyndham hotel chain. In the fall plans were also announced to expand the Nashville site to include a 110-room hotel, offices, and a parking garage.

MERGER WITH AVALON, NAME CHANGE TO TBA IN 1997

At the end of 1996 Nashville Country Club announced an agreement to merge with Avalon Entertainment Group, Inc., an eight-year-old marketing/corporate events planning firm that operated in part through a joint venture with Warner Custom Music Corp. The $7.2 million deal was consummated early the next year. In the spring of 1997 the firm also agreed to buy a majority stake in Avalon West Coast, which owned Eric Chandler Merchandising, Inc.; Eric Chandler, Ltd.; New Avalon, Inc.; TBA Media, Inc.; and the Irvine Meadows Amphitheater. In August 1997 the company raised another $9.1 million by selling 2.6 million shares of stock, and shortly afterward Nashville Country Club changed its name to TBA Entertainment Corporation, Inc.

While the initial inspiration for the company had been the surging popularity of country music (as exemplified by such young stars as Garth Brooks), the Nashville Country Club concept had failed to click with the public, and in November 1997 the first and only such restaurant to open was closed. With its focus now shifted to entertainment and marketing services, in May 1998 the company's West Coast amphitheater operation was sold to SFX Entertainment for $10 million, and in July Vail Resorts, Inc., bought the Village at Breckenridge for $34 million. TBA was named Vail's preferred entertainment provider in the deal.

During the year the firm continued to ramp up its entertainment/marketing side, in May paying $5 million to acquire Corporate Productions, Inc., of Chicago, which had revenues of $20 million and accounts with McDonald's, Harley-Davidson, and Motorola. In June TBA merged its artist management operations with Titley/Spalding & Associates, a 15-year-old agency that represented such top-selling country performers as Brooks & Dunn and Kathy Mattea, and in July a joint venture called TBA/Frank was created with Frank

Productions, Inc., an established Madison, Wisconsin, concert tour organizer.

In the latter half of 1998 the firm bought Image Entertainment Productions, a Tempe, Arizona-based producer of corporate events and festivals whose clients included Frito-Lay and Merrill Lynch, and added publicity firm Magnum Communications, whose clients included American Airlines and Novell. At year's end the flagship unit of the company's Corporate Communications and Entertainment division, Avalon Entertainment Group, was renamed TBA Entertainment, after which Warner/Avalon became Warner/TBA. A television unit, TBA TV, had also been established by this time, whose output included a television special starring Alabama.

For 1998 the firm's revenues more than quadrupled to $27.3 million, largely driven by its acquisitions, and it reported net income of $2.7 million. Recent successes of company units included securing corporate sponsors for lengthy tours by country stars LeAnn Rimes and Bryan White, and ex–Led Zeppelin frontmen Jimmy Page and Robert Plant, and producing eight dates for the Rolling Stones "Bridges to Babylon" tour.

In January 1999 TBA bought Indianapolis-based merchandising firm KGA, Inc., whose clients had included Nextel, the U.S. Open, and the Grammy Awards, for $5 million. It became part of the firm's Event Merchandising division, which also included Corporate Incentives and Eric Chandler Merchandising. During the month TBA sold the shuttered Nashville Country Club for $3.2 million to developers of an Embassy Suites hotel.

WEB SITE, RECORD LABEL ADDED IN 1999

In the spring of 1999 TBA launched a web site that offered concert tickets and merchandise, as well as information for investors, video clips, and other entertainment content. In June the company introduced a record label, whose debut release was a 43-track collection by Merle Haggard that was tied in to a pay-per-view TV special the firm's TV unit had produced. At year's end TBA bought Romeo Entertainment Group of Nebraska, a 45-year-old producer of fairs and other outdoor events, for $6.75 million, which was quickly followed by the purchase of Mike Atkins Management, a three-year-old firm whose clients included several top Christian music artists. Sales for 1999 topped $48 million, and a net profit of $2.1 million was recorded.

In April 2000 the company acquired outdoor event organizer EJD Concert Services, Inc., of Seattle. At this time TBA's combined units produced over 3,000 events

KEY DATES

1993: Former Hard Rock CEO Jock Weaver founds Nashville Country Club.

1994: Company completes its initial public offering on the NASDAQ; theme restaurant opens in Nashville.

1997: Restaurant is closed; firm merges with Avalon Entertainment and takes name TBA.

1998: Acquisitions ramp up as company expands entertainment, marketing units.

2004: Irving Azoff and Robert Geddes lead buyout of TBA for $6.15 million.

2008: Digital Entertainment unit TBA DEEP is founded.

or programs annually, including the Hard Rock Café Rockfest in Chicago and the 25-date Montreux Festival, both supported by Oldsmobile. In the fall the firm formed a London-based joint venture with Live Aid concert promoter Harvey Goldsmith called TBA Corporation Europe, of which it would own 51 percent. At year's end, the company's stock moved to the American Stock Exchange from the NASDAQ.

In January 2001 Avalon cofounder Greg Janese was named president of TBA, with Jock Weaver remaining chairman and CEO. During the month the firm acquired Moore Entertainment Corp., a Nashville-based concert promoter, and added agent Stewart Young, who brought a stable of acts that included Foreigner and The Scorpions. January also saw the production of a concert for the inauguration of George W. Bush that featured Destiny's Child and Jessica Simpson.

As the U.S. economy started to slide downward, the firm's management began to rethink corporate strategy. In April TBA's merchandising operations were sold and the concert and corporate events promotion business made its primary focus. In July the firm bought rock music talent agency Alliance Artists.

The concert tour business was seriously affected by the terrorist attacks against the United States on September 11, 2001, and in the months afterward TBA lost an estimated $15 million in canceled or unrealized bookings. It soon closed several underperforming units and took other cost-cutting measures, and for the year revenues fell to $60.4 million and a net loss of $6.9 million was recorded. The firm delayed filing its annual report because it was out of compliance with its primary

lender, although it was soon able to secure enough funds to make the payments.

The going continued to be hard in 2002 as sales fell to $49.1 million and a loss of $2.2 million was taken. In early 2003 the firm restructured $5.5 million in corporate debt and sold space it owned in Dallas for $589,000, as it combined several offices to cut costs. With the concert and events businesses continuing to remain stagnant, however, its stock price fell below a dollar.

AZOFF/GEDDES-LED BUYOUT TAKES FIRM PRIVATE IN 2004

In June 2004 talent manager/entrepreneur Irving Azoff, whose roster included The Eagles and Christina Aguilera, joined forces with entertainment industry executive Robert Geddes and JHW Greentree Capital to acquire TBA for $6.15 million. Geddes would take the title of CEO, while Azoff and JHW Greentree Managing Partner Mike Stone would be co-chairmen. After the sale, founder Jock Weaver exited the firm.

After taking the company private, TBA's new owners dissolved its talent management unit and components including Titley-Spalding and Alliance Artists became independent entities again. Concert promoter Steve Moore also left to resurrect Moore Entertainment.

The firm was subsequently renamed TBA Global Events, LLC, ("Events" was later dropped from the name) to reflect its new focus on producing corporate-sponsored events such as the Fruit of the Loom Countryfest, as well as private corporate concerts featuring big-name talent. The company had now pared down its offices to Nashville, New York, Los Angeles, Chicago, San Diego, Atlanta, and Salt Lake City.

In July 2005 TBA bought Production Group International (PGI), a struggling 15-year-old event production firm based in Washington, D.C. It operated in the United States, Canada, and Europe, with clients that included Exxon Mobil, Ford, and IBM. The deal was expected to boost TBA's annual revenues to approximately $175 million.

Major productions of this period included the Herbalife 25th Anniversary Extravaganza, which featured a performance by Elton John; the Sapphire conference sponsored by software firm SAP that included 16 theater setups; and the Bristol-Myers Squibb Tour of Hope national marketing campaign. Though the event business had been slow to recover from the downturn in the economy, TBA believed that corporations would increasingly look to special events as a valuable way to motivate both employees and customers in the increasingly cluttered advertising environment of the new millennium.

RESTRUCTURING IN THE FALL OF 2005

In September 2005 the company was restructured into four business units: strategic events/meeting planning services; destination management; consumer marketing; and fairs and festivals entertainment. In the fall of 2006 TBA signed a cooperative agreement with VOK DAMS Group of Germany, which had extensive operations in Europe and Asia. The two would produce events for each other in their respective territories.

In January 2007 TBA named former Citigate Broadstreet President Lee Rubenstein to the posts of president and chief operating officer, with Robert Geddes remaining CEO. In May a new unit called the Learning and Performance Solutions Group was launched to offer business training services, and in June TBA's new Branded Entertainment Group created McDonald's Live, a free ten-city concert tour with digital interactive elements. The firm had also produced the IBM PartnerWorld event in St. Louis, which was attended by 4,400, as well as corporate concerts by The Eagles, Brian Wilson of the Beach Boys, Jennifer Lopez, and ZZ Top.

In May 2008 the company announced the formation of TBA DEEP, which would focus on creating digital entertainment that would engage consumers and help strengthen brand identities. During the year TBA Global was named the fourth largest events planning company by *Special Events Magazine*. The firm now had 17 offices in North America and an affiliate office in London.

Following more than a decade of acquisitions and strategic shifts, TBA Global was coming together as an organizer of corporate events and concerts that helped develop brand identities and build customer and employee loyalty. Boasting many *Fortune* 500 clients, TBA had become one of the top players in its industry through the acquisition of a number of its key players.

Frank Uhle

PRINCIPAL DIVISIONS

Connective Strategy; B2B Events & Communication; Consumer Marketing; Learning & Performance; Destination Management; Branded Entertainment.

PRINCIPAL COMPETITORS

George P. Johnson Co.; Jack Morton Worldwide, Inc.; AMCI; Hartmann Studios; Imagination Group; VOK DAMS Group; CMS Communications; Blue Plate.

FURTHER READING

Bronikowski, Lynn, "Breckenridge Resort on Tap to Go a Little Bit Country," *Rocky Mountain News,* December 5, 1995, p. 46A.

"Corporate Event Specialist TBA Global Events Restructures," *Primedia Insight,* September 26, 2005.

Deckard, Lisa, "TBA Ventures into Europe with Goldsmith," *Amusement Business,* October 23, 2000, p. 1.

Emmons, Natasha, "TBA Corp. Expands Fair Presence with Acquisition of EJD," *Amusement Business,* April 24, 2000, p. 6.

Evans, Rob, "Nashville Country Club Agrees to Purchase Interest in Avalon," *Amusement Business,* June 30, 1997, p. 6.

Flaum, David, "Avalon Group's Sale Nearing," *Commercial Appeal,* December 20, 1996, p. B8.

———, "Nashville CC Revising Name," *Commercial Appeal,* July 1, 1997, p. B10.

"Former Hard Rock CEO Takes Nashville to the Country Club," *Billboard,* May 1, 1993, p. 26.

Hurley, Lisa, "Direct Connect," *Special Events Magazine,* July 1, 2007, p. 20.

Mahmud, Shahnaz, "TBA Global Deepens Its Entertainment Ties," *Adweek,* May 8, 2008.

Reynolds, Lisa, "TBA Entertain to Acquire Outdoor Fair Producer for $6.75 Million," *Dow Jones Business News,* November 29, 1999.

"TBA Global Events Buys PGI," *Meeting News,* July 29, 2005.

"Vail Resorts Agrees to Buy Village at Breckenridge," *Associated Press Newswires,* July 13, 1998.

Waddell, Ray, "TBA Forms Joint Venture with Frank Productions," *Amusement Business,* July 13, 1998, p. 9.

———, "TBA Goes Global with New Direction," *Billboard,* December 18, 2004, p. 21.

———, "TBA Quietly Turns into Powerhouse," *Billboard,* September 9, 2000, p. 12.

TechTarget, Inc.

117 Kendrick Street, Suite 800
Needham, Massachusetts 02494-2728
U.S.A.
Telephone: (781) 657-1000
Toll Free: (888) 274-4111
Fax: (781) 657-1100
Web site: http://www.techtarget.com

Public Company
Incorporated: 1999
Employees: 600
Sales: $94.7 million (2007)
Stock Exchanges: NASDAQ
Ticker Symbol: TTGT
NAICS: 511120 Software Publishers; 514191 On-Line
  Information Services; 541512 Computer Systems
  Design Services

■ ■ ■

TechTarget, Inc., holds a unique position in the field of Internet publication, as the company operates more than 50 web sites directed at information technology decision makers as well as the vendors that seek targeted market prospects. Each web site provides news and product analysis in computer specialties, such as storage, security, networking, data center management, enterprise applications, and web hosting. Web sites cover specific computer operating systems, such as Windows and Lotus, and computer systems, including IBM and Hewlett-Packard. By focusing on niche sectors of the information technology market, TechTarget creates a

targeted audience for paid sponsorships and advertising by product designers and manufacturers, such as IBM, Sun Microsystems, Oracle, Microsoft, and many others. Other TechTarget sites review basic products, such as desktop or laptop computers, printers, and smartphones. Examples of TechTarget print publications include *Storage* and *Information Security.* TechTarget has a registered subscriber base of more than 6.7 million prequalified information technology professionals, responsible for purchasing high-technology products.

TechTarget's success has earned the company many business and media awards. *Business to Business* magazine has named TechTarget to its "Media Power 50" list every year from 2001 to 2008. *Media Business* magazine has named cofounder Greg Strakosch to its "Top Innovators in Business Publishing" list from 2005 to 2008, and cofounder Don Hawk to the list in 2004. High standards for writing and editorial content have earned TechTarget more than 100 awards.

IT MARKETING AND PROFESSIONAL SUPPORT NICHE

TechTarget originated as a division of United Communications Group (UCG), publisher of numerous newsletters for professionals in several industries and government sectors. TechTarget cofounder Greg Strakosch joined UCG in 1992, when he and Kevin Beam sold Reliability Ratings, a disk drive review publication, to UCG. They stayed with UCG, and Strakosch moved on to form TechTarget in 1998.

That year Strakosch and Don Hawk designed a web site for information technology (IT) users and managers

---

COMPANY PERSPECTIVES

What TechTarget Does for IT Professionals and Executives: Tech Target provides IT professionals and executives with the information they need to perform their jobs—from developing strategy, to making cost-effective IT purchase decisions and managing their organizations' IT projects. What TechTarget Does for IT Marketers and Advertisers: TechTarget connects IT marketers with targeted, qualified communities of IT buyers, delivering measurable results that help IT companies generate leads, shorten sales cycles, and grow revenues.

---

based on Search 400, a newsletter created by Strakosch for IBM AS/400 computer systems. Search400.com provided the latest industry news and expert advice. Access to useful links was derived from more than 2,000 other web sites, supporting IT professionals in their search for specialized technical information, vendors, job listings, and other relevant content. The effective organization and prioritization of useful information quickly generated a user base of IT professionals. Moreover, while Strakosch intended the site to generate business for the newsletter and related conferences, high-technology product vendors inundated him with requests to purchase online advertising. Strakosch saw an opportunity to offer the newsletter subscriptions and online access for free and to earn revenues through the sale of advertising and sponsorships to vendors, serving this target audience of IT professionals. Hence, the company took the name TechTarget.

TechTarget used Hawk's first web site design as a template to develop multiple web sites for a wide variety of content areas. These included SearchDomino.com, which provided web support for users of Lotus Domino software. SearchNT.com served IT professionals using WindowsNT or Windows 2000, and SearchStorage.com provided technical information support to specialists in data storage architecture and management.

At the prompting of Strakosch, UCG spun off TechTarget as an independent company in September 1999. UCG provided $12 million in capital, and Strakosch raised an additional $22 million from private investors. With Strakosch as chief executive officer, and Hawk as president, TechTarget pursued acquisitions that provided the company with additional content. Through the February 2000 acquisition of vb-web-directory.com, TechTarget obtained a library of 22 web sites to adapt

to its own model, particularly the "user-centric interface" that made TechTarget sites easy to navigate. Vb-web-directory sites included searchSecurity.com, searchWebHosting.com, searchITServices.com, searchEnterpriseLinux.com, and whatis.com, a technical content web site. In some cases, TechTarget combined its sites with vb web sites, such as the merger of SearchDomino.com with Lotus411.com. The acquisition of DatabaseCentral.com provided TechTarget with a formidable array of database content. After integrating the search engine into the TechTarget network, the company relaunched the site as SearchDatabase.com.

By the end of 2000, TechTarget maintained 23 web sites and counted more than a million registered users. TechTarget published information on 100 newsletters, sent through 15 million monthly e-mails. Although TechTarget offered free access to the web sites, the company thrived on revenues from advertising sponsors, including such prominent vendors as IBM, Oracle, and Sun Microsystems. TechTarget's niche audience succeeded in generating qualified business leads for sponsors and advertisers. As such, the company garnered sponsorship fees from $50,000 to $300,000. Specialization of each web site also generated significant advertising revenues from banners, e-mail newsletters, keyword linkage, and event sponsorships. With more than 500 advertisers, TechTarget charged $100 to $250 CPM (cost per thousand page impressions), among the highest advertising rates for the Internet at that time.

ORIGINAL CONTENT, CONFERENCES, AND PRINT PUBLICATIONS

In March 2001, TechTarget obtained $30 million in capital funds, allowing the company to expand and improve its information products. In order to extend its services and generate business for its web sites, TechTarget began planning conferences for qualified IT professionals of large companies. The company planned five events for 2001: Storage Management, Windows Decisions, Security Decisions, Storage Decisions, and SearchSAP.com. The conferences filled a need for specialized information, and strong interest in these events prompted TechTarget to launch a division for conference development and management.

Another area of expansion involved the generation of original, long-form content, rather than simply gathering information from other sites. Hence, in March 2002 TechTarget introduced *Storage* magazine, a print publication with all original news gathering and analysis. TechTarget initiated the publication with a circulation of 50,000 copies. In July 2003 TechTarget acquired *Information Security* magazine, the top publication on

KEY DATES

1998: Niche web site for users of IBM AS/400 computer systems provides template for company development.

1999: United Communications Group spins off TechTarget with $12 million in seed capital.

2000: Company acquires vb-web-directory.com, which includes a library of 22 web sites.

2001: TechTarget launches conference planning division.

2002: The company's first print publication, *Storage,* is introduced.

2004: International expansion begins with agreements in China and Taiwan.

2007: IPO raises $100 million for expansion.

2008: Tech Target launches 50th web site.

IT security, with a circulation of 67,500. TechTarget redesigned the publication's format and relaunched *Information Security* in March 2004. In April 2005 TechTarget launched *CIO Decisions* magazine. Though unusually broad in its content focus, the publication was directed toward the underserved midsized business manager. A partnership with Windows Media Group led to development of the print publication *WinStorage*. However, the latter two publications were short-lived.

To improve target marketing for its sponsors, TechTarget produced webcasts that provided IT professionals with information on the latest products. Other avenues of improving and expanding the audience of IT professionals for its sponsors and advertisers involved renting e-mail opt-in subscription lists, in which the subscribers have given permission. TechTarget swapped lists with professional associations and provided online advertising for other conference planners to broaden the prospect base for advertisers.

Conversely, TechTarget sought to streamline its e-mail subscription base. In October 2003 the company announced its intention to convert its portfolio of e-mail newsletters to a controlled audience. By doing so, TechTarget would improve advertisers' return on investment, as a prequalified subscriber base would increase "click rates," the rate at which online viewers clicked on an advertisement. Although TechTarget expected the action to affect per-click advertising rates as well as to reduce e-mail circulation by 50 percent, the implementation of this direct-request model would generate more worthwhile prospects in each niche market.

A number of acquisitions deepened and expanded TechTarget's base of information. In late 2003, the company acquired LabMice.com, a Microsoft Windows specialty web site that complemented TechTarget's SearchWin2000.com. With $70 million in venture capital, TechTarget purchased the fast-growing Bitpipe. Bitpipe specialized in distributing peer-reviewed white papers that described real-life, problem-solving technology installations. The $40 million deal gave TechTarget a significant leap in competitiveness in its market. The acquisition of The ServerSide Communities, from Veritas Software Corporation, provided TechTarget with access to IT specialists in web server technology. TechTarget obtained the web sites TheServerSide.com and The ServerSide.net, and a conference, TheServerSide Java Symposium. The November 2005 acquisition of SecurityDocs.com expanded TechTarget's source of peer-reviewed white papers.

GLOBAL EXPANSION

International expansion at TechTarget involved providing content to foreign partners for translation into local languages. In 2004 TechTarget formed partnerships with ChinaByte in China, New Era International in Taiwan, and ITmedia in Japan. In South Korea, a partnership with Info Media Group involved security-related content as well as conference planning. In Europe expansion included partnerships with Internet media companies in Italy, Germany, Russia, and Bulgaria. The Spanish-language sites would serve IT professionals in Spain and in Spanish-speaking Latin American countries. In early 2006, Netremedia Pte. Ltd. of Singapore agreed to launch English-language web sites for IT professionals in Southeast Asia, including Indonesia, Brunei, Cambodia, Laos, Myanmar, Thailand, the Philippines, Vietnam, Malaysia, and Singapore. Netremedia planned to include versions of Bitpipe.com, SearchCIO.com, SearchStorage.com, SearchSecurity.com, and several Windows-related sites. Some global partners issued regional editions of *Information Security* and *Storage* magazines. Most international agreements involved a cooperative selling component, whereby the companies purchased advertising on one another's Internet sites.

Expansion to English-language markets overseas included a partnership with Reed Business Information UK. TechTarget began providing news, editorials, white papers, and advice to Reed's ComputerWeekly.com in the United Kingdom. Eventually, TechTarget formed a subsidiary in London to serve the European market. Web sites launched in the United Kingdom in March

2007 included SearchStorage.co.uk and SearchSecurity. co.uk, the first Internet sites to be developed by TechTarget outside of the United States. TechTarget launched three Internet sites in Australia, covering the security, storage, and networking niches. Through India Express Group, TechTarget reached into India's growing market for IT information services. Under the partnership agreement, India Express would handle local conference planning, launch a web site, and publish local editions of *Storage* and *Information Security* magazines. Operations began in early 2007.

ENTERING NEW MARKETS

Growing rapidly, TechTarget required capital to continue apace. Revenues increased more than 40 percent in both 2004 and 2005, with sales reaching $66.75 million in 2005. The company operated profitably, with net income of $8.89 million. Company executives considered the possibility of a sale, but they did not rule out a public offering of stock. In the meantime, TechTarget continued to develop new products and services.

In May 2006 TechTarget introduced a sales lead generation tool, TechTarget Magnifier. The technology identified prospects based on prior purchases, and it included the company's proprietary LeadPRISM technology, which prioritized leads based on demographics and history of specific web content access. Follow-up service provided to salespeople involved data on continuing web content interests that could be used for sending additional sales messages.

TechTarget moved into niche markets serving small- and medium-sized companies. The company acquired 20/20 Software, whose web site, 2020software.com, presented comparisons on a range of business software and provided trial versions of accounting, human resources, enterprise resource planning, and other software. TechTarget upgraded the content to cover project management, backup software, and unified threat management/integrated security. In November 2006 TechTarget launched web sites for the channel community of independent IT solutions professionals, such as resellers, systems integrators, and technology consultants. The five web sites included SearchITChannel.com and SearchSystemsChannel.com. The sites provided news, vendor programs, and other information relevant to these specialized areas.

Another new niche for TechTarget involved web development technology. The February 2007 acquisition of Ajaxiam, Inc., expanded TechTarget's range of IT resources into web development techniques using Asynchronous JavaScript and XML (hence Ajaxiam).

Ajaxiam operations included a prominent web site in the web development industry and an annual conference.

In April TechTarget acquired TechnologyGuide. com, which emphasized comparisons of mobile technology. Web sites included NotebookReview.com and Brighthand.com, the latter a smartphones review site.

By the end of 2006, TechTarget decided that the company was strong enough to stand on its own as a public company. Though revenues had slowed to an 18 percent increase in 2006, to $79 million, income rose nearly 50 percent, to $12.6 million. The initial public offering (IPO) of stock in May 2007 garnered net proceeds of $83.2 million. TechTarget applied the funds to pay debt and to acquire smaller companies that would increase the company's ability to capitalize on its existing infrastructure. For instance, the $58 million acquisition of KnowledgeStorm, an online product and service directory, brought a new base of advertisers to TechTarget, potentially adding more than $12 million in revenue annually.

TARGETING NEW IT NICHES AND EXPERT CONTENT

New web site development at TechTarget sought to serve the needs of diverse industries as well as specialization within areas of IT. New web sites launched in the fall of 2007 included SearchTelecom.com, for IT professionals in the wireless and telecommunications industries. Increased interest in virtual technology, a form of data storage, prompted TechTarget to complement its existing sites, including Search ServerVirtualization, with a site specifically for users of the VMware virtualization platform, SearchVMware.com. TechTarget employed virtual technology itself, when the company initiated virtual trade shows to provide vendors and buyers with real-time interactions via TechTarget web sites.

Other programs to improve advertisers' return on investment (ROI) included development of a client services department, which addressed concerns relating to verifying the value of online marketing. For the same purpose, TechTarget initiated an Online Marketing ROI Advisory Board, comprised of senior executives from several IT and marketing companies. Adobe Systems, Avaya, Microsoft, IBM, Hewlett-Packard, and OMD Worldwide were among many IT companies involved with the advisory board.

TechTarget supported interaction among IT professionals through the introduction of ITKnowledgeExchange.com, a forum for sharing information and experiences. The site provided unlimited space for user-created blogs, and MyWatchList tags facilitated easy navigation to topics of interest and tracked questions and answers. Operating in real time, the site allowed online collaboration of multiple users with TheAnswer-Wiki component. ITKnowledgeExchange followed from TechTarget's emphasis on expertise-based content, but allowed that expertise to flow from peer to peer.

TechTarget continued to develop new specialized web sites. TechTarget launched its 50th web site, SearchSMBStorage.com, in May 2008. The site addressed unique concerns of storage technology decisions for small- and medium-sized businesses (SMB). Other new web sites included DesktopReview.com and PrinterComparison.com, offshoots of TechnologyGuide. com. Two web sites, SearchFinancialSecurity.com and ConstructionSoftwareReview.com, reflected TechTarget's continuing effort to target the needs of specific industries and their IT product and service providers. In September 2008 TechTarget launched Search-DisasterRecovery.com. That site followed from market research showing an increased concern for data backup and recovery, with a significant number of IT professionals planning on budget increases in this area of data storage.

Mary Tradii

PRINCIPAL COMPETITORS

1105 Media, Inc.; CMP Media LLC; International Data Group, Inc.; Ziff-Davis Media Inc.

FURTHER READING

Callahan, Sean, "TechTarget Makes Trio of Big Moves; Flush with $70 Million in VC Funding, Company Buys Bitpipe, ServerSide; Plans New IT Magazine," *B to B*, December 13, 2004, p. 13.

———, "TechTarget Plans Entry into Japanese IT Market," *B to B*, April 4, 2005, p. 20.

Callahan, Sean, and Matthew Schwartz, "TechTarget to Pursue IPO in 2006; Three VPs Out As Technology Publisher Streamlines Its Management Structure," *B to B*, November 14, 2005, p. 3.

Clark, Philip B., "TechTarget Finds Conference Niche; Company Starts New Division to Focus on Narrowly Targeted Technology Sectors," *B to B*, February 11, 2002, p. 16.

"Company Spun off of UCG Is Reaping 'Extraordinary Results' from the Internet," *Newsletter on Newsletters*, January 31, 2000, p. 1.

Goodison, Donna, "Strong Web Presence Helps TechTarget Thrive," *Boston Herald*, November 3, 2005, p. 46.

"IT Media Company TechTarget Has Launched a Network of Five Web Sites," *Business Publisher*, November 1, 2006, p. 6.

"IT Search Central," *Info-Tech Advisor*, February 20, 2000.

Lehmann-Haupt, Rachel, "On Target," *Folio: The Magazine for Magazine Management*, August 1, 2004.

"9: TechTarget.com," *B to B*, April 30, 2001, p. 23.

Saucer, Patrick J. "Open Door Management," *Inc.*, June 2003.

Schwartz, Matthew, "No. 8 TechTarget, IT Media Company Boasts 50 Tech-Specific Sites, Continues to Focus on Narrow Vertical Segments," *B to B*, May 5, 2008, p. 32.

———, "TechTarget Acquires KnowledgeStorm for $58 Million," *B to B*, November 12, 2007, p. 4.

"Storage, New Mag to Debut," *Adweek Magazine's Technology Marketing*, November 2001, p. 8.

"TechTarget Acquires Software Site, Starts Marketing Blog & Enters UK Market," *Business Publisher*, June 1, 2006, p. 3.

"TechTarget and Windows Media Group Launch 'WinStorage' Magazine," *Business Publisher*, June 16, 2005, p. 4.

"TechTarget Enters Italian Market," *Business Publisher*, December 23, 2005, p. 3.

"TechTarget Gets $30M in Funding," *Boston Herald*, March 12, 2001, p. 25.

"TechTarget Has Opened a U.K. Subsidiary, TechTarget Ltd. (London), to Focus on the Company's International Clients," *Business Publisher*, October 17, 2006.

"TechTarget, Inc. Goes Public; Stock Climbs 'Sharply' in First Day of Trading," *Newsletter on Newsletters*, May 30, 2007, p. 1.

"TechTarget Joins Forces with Korean Event Producer," *Tradeshow Week*, May 16, 2005, p. T2.

"TechTarget Launches New Sites for Financial, Construction & U.K. Info Tech Markets," *Business Publishers*, April 1, 2008, p. 2.

"TechTarget Launches SearchTelecom.com," *Wireless News*, September 5, 2007.

"TechTarget Makes an Acquisition," *Adweek New England Edition*, November 3, 2005.

"TechTarget Partners to Launch Magazines and Websites for Southeast Asia Market," *Business Publisher*, February 1, 2006, p. 3.

"TechTarget—Print Newsletter Spin-Off Site Becomes Fastest Growing Ad-Based IT Media Site Online," *ContentBiz*, March 19, 2002.

"TechTarget Rolls with Search VMware.com," *Wireless News*, November 23, 2007.

"TechTarget to Stir IT Media Market," *Australasian Business Intelligence*, August 15, 2006.

Tengasco, Inc.

───■───

10215 Technology Drive, Suite 300
Knoxville, Tennessee 37932
U.S.A.
Telephone: (865) 675-1554
Fax: (865) 675-1621
Web site: http://www.tengasco.com

Public Company
Incorporated: 1916 as Gold Deposit Mining and Milling
    Co.
Employees: 27
Sales: $9.4 million (2007)
Stock Exchanges: American
Ticker Symbol: TGC
NAICS: 211111 Crude Petroleum and Natural Gas
    Extraction

■ ■ ■

Based in Knoxville, Tennessee, Tengasco, Inc., engages in the exploration for, and production and transportation of, oil and natural gas. The company's operations are located mainly in Kansas and Tennessee. As of late 2007, Tengasco had 1,134 Mcf (thousand cubic feet) of net proved gas reserves, and 2.28 million barrels of oil reserves. During the latter years of the first decade of the 2000s, Dolphin Offshore Partners held a 36 percent ownership interest in Tengasco.

AMBIGUOUS BEGINNINGS: 1916–90

Tengasco's roots officially date back to April 18, 1916, when the company was established in Utah as Gold

Deposit Mining and Milling Co. Although its early activities included mining, reducing, and smelting mineral ores, much of Tengasco's history prior to 1995, when the company first acquired oil and gas leases, is somewhat sketchy, with periods during which it did not engage in substantial operations.

Initially focused on about ten lode mining claims in Nevada's Battle Mountain Mining District, Gold Deposit Mining and Milling Co.'s mining operations were limited after the company's formation, according to a Form 10-SB filed with the U.S. Securities and Exchange Commission (SEC). The company's articles of incorporation, however, were amended numerous times over the years.

On November 10, 1972, Gold Deposit Mining and Milling ceased operations, according to the SEC documents. Control of the company changed in January 1983, and for the next eight years Gold Deposit Mining and Milling essentially was a shell company, existing solely for the purpose of acquiring assets of other businesses.

BRIEFLY IN BIOTECH: 1991–94

Following a reverse reorganization with Onasco Biotechnologies Inc. in December 1991, Gold Deposit Mining and Milling's name changed to Onasco Companies Inc., with a wholly owned subsidiary named Onasco Texas. The deal was intended to supply Robert C. Bohannon, Ph.D., a scientist who had trained at the Baylor College of Medicine, with $500,000 in funding.

Bohannon had developed vaccines for polio and an AIDS-like Type D retrovirus. In addition to developing

COMPANY PERSPECTIVES

Tengasco, Inc., focuses on acquisition, exploration and development of oil and natural gas in North America.

the vaccines, Onasco supplied laboratories at the U.S. Centers for Disease Control and Prevention and the U.S. Food and Drug Administration with diagnostic kits that detected the presence of the retrovirus.

Bohannon was Onasco Texas' principal stockholder, and filled the roles of president, CEO, vice-president, and director. When the deal failed to generate the $500,000 Bohannon had hoped for, the company fell on hard times. Research and development activities ceased in June 1994, at which time controlling interest was acquired by Duane S. Jenson and his son, Jeffrey D. Jenson. The Jensons acquired the 67 percent of stock that was not publicly held, and Bohannon resigned on June 13, after receiving a payment of $10,000. At this time, Jeffrey Jenson was named president, CEO, and secretary/treasurer.

COMPANY ENTERS OIL AND GAS INDUSTRY: 1995–97

Onasco changed its name to Tengasco, Inc., on April 28, 1995, after acquiring oil and gas leases, along with other assets, from Kentucky-based Industrial Resources Corp. (IRC). Specifically, IRC gained voting control of Tengasco in exchange for 60 percent of its assets. With headquarters in Knoxville, the company's stock began trading over the counter in June under the symbol TNGO. Ted Scallan served as Tengasco's president and CEO, and Jack Earnest as chairman.

By October 1995 Tengasco had forged an agreement with Williams Energy Services Co. to offer utilities and large industrial customers in middle and eastern Tennessee an alternative source of natural gas from the Gulf of Mexico. This development occurred in the wake of industry deregulation.

In early 1996 Tengasco announced plans to drill three natural gas wells on a 10,000-acre site in Tennessee's Appalachian region. The first to be drilled there in 13 years, the wells were completed in April, and another nine were planned by the year's end.

In mid-1996 Tengasco established a new wholly owned subsidiary named Tengasco Pipeline Corp. to transport natural gas to customers located in four counties. Construction of a new, 40-mile pipeline from

the company's Swan Creek field in Hancock County, to the city of Rogersville in Hawkins County, and ultimately to a major pipeline, was planned.

Midway through 1997, Tengasco announced that it had forged an agreement with the U.S. Department of Energy to provide power steam services at the East Tennessee Technology Park, which had previously produced uranium for both military and commercial purposes. After installing new turbines, Tengasco planned to convert the steam production facility to one that produced both electricity and steam.

EARLY GROWTH AND EXPANSION: 1998–2001

Tengasco expanded its operations west of the Mississippi River in February 1998, at which time the company acquired a number of oil and gas producing assets located near Hays, Kansas. In a deal with AFG Energy Inc., Tengasco spent $5.5 million to obtain 149 oil wells, 59 gas wells, 50 miles of pipeline, and a related gathering system that produced annual revenues of approximately $4 million.

One month after the AFG Energy deal, a major leadership change unfolded when Robert M. Carter, a former lumber and building supply company owner who had been with Tengasco since the company's formation, was elected president. By this time, Allen H. Sweeney was serving as Tengasco's chairman.

Around the same time, Tengasco celebrated the completion of a $10 million, 28-mile underground gas pipeline from its Swan Creek field to Rogersville, Tennessee, capping off an 18-month effort that involved laying pipeline through some of the roughest terrain in the state, including three mountain ranges.

Significant developments continued midway through 1998 when Tengasco announced what at the time was the most significant deal in its history: the $15 million cash and stock purchase of Oklahoma City, Oklahoma-based Twister Gas Services LLC and Twister Partners LLC. The transaction, which called for Twister to become a wholly owned Tengasco subsidiary, added 60 miles of natural gas pipeline, as well as 270 oil and natural gas wells, to Tengasco's lineup, which expanded to include a total of 490 oil and gas wells. In addition, the deal increased Tengasco's proved gas reserves to 80.7 billion cubic feet.

On July 7, 1998, the Tennessee Regulatory Authority granted a permit to Tengasco that allowed it to begin supplying natural gas to thousands of residential, municipal, and industrial customers via the company's new 28-mile pipeline. Service began the following day,

```
┌─────────────────────────────────────────┐
│                                           │
│              KEY DATES                    │
│                   ■                        │
│  ───────────────────────────────────      │
│                                           │
│  1916:  Company is established in Utah as Gold │
│         Deposit Mining and Milling Co.    │
│  1972:  Company ceases operations.        │
│  1983:  Organization operates as shell company, solely │
│         to acquire assets of other businesses. │
│  1991:  After a reverse reorganization with Onasco │
│         Biotechnologies Inc., name changes to │
│         Onasco Companies Inc.             │
│  1995:  Name is changed to Tengasco, Inc. │
│  1996:  Wholly owned subsidiary, Tengasco Pipeline │
│         Corp., is formed.                 │
│  1998:  Oklahoma-based Twister Gas Services LLC │
│         and Twister Partners LLC are acquired. │
│  1999:  Stock begins trading on the American Stock │
│         Exchange.                         │
│  2008:  Oil-producing properties in Rooks County, │
│         Kansas, are acquired from Black Diamond │
│         Oil Inc.                          │
│                                           │
└─────────────────────────────────────────┘
```

marking one of the most significant milestones in Tengasco's history.

In early 1999 Tengasco was being challenged by 20 local utility districts in Hawkins, Hancock, and Claiborne counties as it sought to bypass them and supply gas directly to industrial customers. The opposition came despite Tengasco having been granted approval by the Tennessee Regulatory Authority to transport the gas. In addition, the Tennessee Oil and Gas Association pledged its support to the company, arguing that the supply of lower-priced gas would have a positive impact on the state's economy.

Midway through 1999, Tengasco drilled its 16th successful natural well in the Swan Creek field, which some considered to be among the very largest natural gas fields in North America. In November, a reevaluation of the field by third-party engineers revealed that it had proved reserves of 611,000 barrels of oil and 30.7 billion cubic feet of natural gas. Compared to the previous year, these figures were increases of 100 percent and 54 percent, respectively.

In addition to energy-related developments, there also were several changes on the corporate front in 1999. In October, Terry W. Piesker was named president, succeeding Carter, who was named president of Tengasco Pipeline Co. At this time, Michael Ratliff remained CEO, and also was serving as chairman. The company capped off the year by announcing it would

begin trading on the American Stock Exchange on December 21, under the symbol TGC.

By the dawn of the new millennium, Tengasco had drilled 19 wells at Swan Creek. Both within and surrounding the field, the company had secured land leases for about 50,000 acres of land. Many of the wells contained oil, in addition to natural gas. The majority of the oil, however, was slated for production at a later time, given Tengasco's focus on natural gas.

In 2000 Tengasco planned to complete another 28-mile run of pipeline. The new run would supply gas to Eastman Chemical, which had signed a 20-year supply deal with Tengasco worth approximately $20 million. Tengasco ended the year with revenues of $5.24 million, up 74 percent from $3.02 million in 1999.

The completion of a $16 million, 60-mile intrastate pipeline system occurred in March 2001. The pipeline was expected to allow the company to generate about $25 million in annual gas and oil revenues. In April of that year, Tengasco secured a 20-year natural gas supply contract with BAE Systems Ordnance Systems Inc. to provide natural gas to the Kingsport, Tennessee-based Holston Army Ammunition Plant.

Midway through 2001, Tengasco drilled its 38th and 39th natural gas wells at Swan Creek. The company continued to have a remarkable success rate, and had yet to drill a "dry" well. In October Tengasco's board approved plans to buy back up to one million shares of the company's common stock. The following month, Tengasco obtained a $10 million line of credit from Bank One N.A.'s Energy Finance Division, which was expected to result in annual interest savings of about $600,000.

CHALLENGES AND LEADERSHIP CHANGES: 2002–05

In April 2002, only months after securing its credit line from Bank One, the bank notified Tengasco that, because the value of its oil and gas reserves had been reduced, the loan amount was being reduced to $3.1 million. Bank One demanded the remaining $6 million returned in 30 days. This ultimately led Tengasco to sue Bank One in federal court for $51 million in actual damages, and $100 million in punitive damages. Tengasco claimed Bank One was acting in bad faith, and that it had violated the credit agreement between the two companies.

In the midst of this difficult situation, significant leadership changes occurred. In July 2002 Benton Becker succeeded Ratliff (who remained CEO) as chairman, and Jeffrey Bailey was named president. In February 2003 health issues led Ratliff to relinquish the CEO title to COO Richard T. Williams. Although Ratliff remained on the company's board for a short while, he exited from the scene permanently in March, at which time he resigned from Tengasco's board.

Significant developments continued in 2004. In May, Tengasco settled its lawsuit against Bank One. After Tengasco agreed to pay the bank $3.66 million and drop the lawsuit, Bank One released its claims against the company. That October, Peter E. Salas was elected chairman. In addition, CEO Williams announced his intent to resign on December 31.

It also was in November 2004 that Tengasco announced that, on January 1, 2005, the duties performed by the CEO would be combined with the office of the president, and that the company would eliminate the CEO position altogether. This scenario was reversed in November 2005, when Tengasco eliminated the office of the president and named President Bailey as CEO.

During this period, things were beginning to look up for Tengasco's shareholders. After recording net losses of $3.45 million in 2003 and $1.99 million in 2004, the company saw its net income reach a record $1.09 million on revenues of $7.17 million in 2005.

FOCUS ON KANSAS OIL PRODUCTION: 2006–08

In 2006 Tengasco continued to break financial performance records, generating net income of $2.14 million on revenues of $9 million. That year, the company saw its oil production rise 36 percent, to more than 189,000 barrels. The increase was mainly in Kansas, where Tengasco was ramping up its exploration efforts.

New business activities were emerging in 2007, as Tengasco revealed plans to recover and market methane gas from landfills. After forging an agreement with Allied Waste in late 2006, a deal was struck to supply the gas to Eastman Chemical Co. Production was slated to begin later in the year at a location in Church Hill, Tennessee.

In September 2007 Tengasco announced a new oil drilling program in Kansas, in association with Hoactzin Partners LP, which was worth between $2.5 million and $4 million. At the year's end, an independent engineering report valued Tengasco's proved oil and gas reserves at $53.63 million. This was a substantial increase from $26.47 million a year before.

Developments continued in 2008. Midway through the year, Tengasco closed a $5.35 million deal with Black Diamond Oil Inc. for properties and assets in

Rooks County, Kansas, which produced approximately 80 barrels of oil per day. The purchase brought the company's daily oil production up to 680 barrels, and further strengthened its growth as an energy exploration and production firm.

Paul R. Greenland

PRINCIPAL SUBSIDIARIES

Manufactured Methane Corp.; Tengasco Pipeline Corp.; Tennessee Land and Mineral Corp.

PRINCIPAL COMPETITORS

Cabot Oil & Gas Corp.; Exxon Mobil Corp.; Miller Petroleum Inc.

FURTHER READING

"Form 10-SB," Washington, D.C.: U.S. Securities and Exchange Commission, August 7, 1997, available from http://www.secinfo.com.

Sabota, Danni, "Big Ideas, but Little Money; Biotech Wildcatter Stumbles on Wall Street," *Houston Business Journal,* March 29, 1993.

"Tengasco Agrees to Purchase Oklahoma City-based Twister Gas Services, LLC and Twister Partners, LLC.; Planned Acquisition Is Expected to Place Tengasco Among the Top 200 Ranked Publicly-Held Oil and Gas Companies in the United States," *PR Newswire,* June 9, 1998.

"Tengasco Announces Closing of Kansas Oil Purchase from Black Diamond Oil," *Internet Wire,* July 2, 2008.

"Tengasco Announces First Quarter 2004 Financial Results, Settlement of Litigation with Bank One, and Results of Recent Drilling in Swan Creek Field," *PR Newswire,* May 20, 2004.

"Tengasco Brings Deep Drilling to Appalachian Region; ET Natural Gas Reserves Could Be Boon to Area Industry," *Business Wire,* January 30, 1996.

"Tengasco Completes the First Three Gas Wells; Announces Pipeline Construction," *Business Wire,* April 30, 1996.

"Tengasco Completes 28-Mile Natural Gas Pipeline in Eastern Tennessee; Company Will Begin Serving Thousands of Industrial, Residential and Municipal Customers in April," *PR Newswire,* March 25, 1998.

"Tengasco Forms Wholly Owned Pipeline Subsidiary; Will Be Selling Natural Gas from Hancock County Field by End of Year," *Business Wire,* July 11, 1996.

"Tengasco Sparking Oil and Gas Boom in Tennessee, Says Industry Spokesman," *PR Newswire,* February 4, 2000.

"Tengasco to Begin Serving Natural Gas to Thousands of Industrial, Residential and Municipal Customers in East Tennessee Following Approval from the State of Tennessee Regulatory Authority," *PR Newswire,* July 8, 1998.

Terremark Worldwide, Inc.

———————■———————

One Biscayne Tower
2 South Biscayne Boulevard, Suite 2900
Miami, Florida 33131
U.S.A.
Telephone: (305) 856-3200
Toll Free: (800) 983-7060
Fax: (305) 856-8190
Web site: http://www.terremark.com

Public Company
Incorporated: 1980 as Terremark, Inc.
Employees: 759
Sales: $187.41 million (2008)
Stock Exchanges: NASDAQ
Ticker Symbol: TMRK
NAICS: 517110 Wired Telecommunications Carriers;
518210 Data Processing, Hosting, and Related
Services

■ ■ ■

Terremark Worldwide, Inc., builds and operates secure data hosting and networking facilities, and provides related services. Its sites in Florida, Virginia, California, Brazil, and Spain serve more than 1,000 clients including Microsoft, Google, Yahoo, the Library of Congress, and the U.S. Departments of State and Defense. The publicly traded firm is headed by founder Manuel "Manny" Medina.

BEGINNINGS

Terremark Worldwide was founded in Miami, Florida, by Manuel D. "Manny" Medina. Born in Cuba in 1952, Medina had immigrated to the United States with his family in 1965 and later earned an accounting degree from Florida Atlantic University. Upon graduation he started an accounting service with college roommate Julian Mesa, and also began helping Latin American investors purchase Florida real estate.

This sideline soon evolved into the firm's primary business, and in 1980 Medina established a company called Terremark, Inc., to develop and acquire properties. The seven-employee company's first major project was a 116-unit condominium complex in Ocala, and in 1981 its headquarters moved into the ten-story Terremark Building in Coral Gables.

On a visit to England in the early 1980s, Medina met financial consultant Timothy Elwes, whose firm made investments for wealthy Asian families. Elwes had been seeking a way to buy real estate in the United States, and he soon began funneling cash to Terremark, in which he became a partner. The firm subsequently opened an office in London, and Medina began to accompany Elwes on trips to meet Asian investors. At this time Julian Mesa parted ways with Terremark, and the firm shifted its focus to working exclusively with European and Asian clients and seeking larger development projects. By 1988 Terremark had developed some $350 million worth of properties. While it built some, it also bought and renovated others, including a 423-room Howard Johnson Hotel near Disney World and several office buildings.

Terremark Worldwide is a leading global provider of IT infrastructure services delivered on the industry's most robust and advanced operations platform. Leveraging purpose-built datacenters in the United States, Europe and Latin America and access to massive and diverse network connectivity from more than 160 global carriers, Terremark delivers government, enterprise and Web 2.0 customers a comprehensive suite of managed solutions including managed hosting, colocation, network and security services.

In 1990 the firm suffered a major blow when the 21-story Terremark Centre's primary tenant, General Development Corp., filed for bankruptcy and stopped paying rent amid charges of fraud. Medina soon became embroiled in a legal battle with lender Citibank, which eventually resulted in the loss of company assets valued at several hundred million dollars and the foreclosure of his home. Although he managed to retain the Terremark Tower and Terremark Centre, he decided to focus on working abroad and took assignments in Beijing and Kuwait, where he helped with rebuilding efforts following the Persian Gulf War.

In the mid-1990s Medina returned to Florida, and in 1997 formed a joint venture with Greenstreet Partners to fund $100 million in development projects there. In the spring of 1998 Terremark also merged with KB Commercial Real Estate Group, owned by Michael Katz and Bill Biondi. The firm would retain the name Terremark and Medina remained in place as chairman and CEO, with Katz serving as president and Biondi heading brokerage unit Terremark Realty. The two companies' combined assets were valued at upwards of $700 million.

FIRM CHANGES FOCUS TO TELECOMMUNICATIONS, GOES PUBLIC IN 2000

In 1998 Manny Medina was named a director of Fusion Telecommunications International of New York, where he became excited about the growing telecom industry. In November 1999 Terremark announced plans to merge with AmTec, Inc., an AMEX-listed communications services firm that was based in New York and primarily operated in China. AmTec had been increasing its Internet-related services and had formed a joint venture called IP.com with Fusion. The $30 million deal

was underwritten by longtime Terremark associate Chinese businessman Francis Lee, who would receive 35 percent of the stock. Manny Medina, who had already invested in both Fusion and AmTec, would hold a sizable stake as well.

The merger was initially intended to help Terremark install high-speed data, phone, and other telecommunications services in its buildings, a field which other real estate companies were rapidly entering as well. At this time the firm managed two million square feet of space in southern Florida, and had another five million square feet under development. The latter included a Ft. Lauderdale condominium tower and the 64-story Four Seasons Hotel and Tower in Miami, which it would manage for owner Millennium Partners of New York and which would be the tallest building in the state.

In March 2000 Terremark signed a deal to acquire Telecom Routing Exchange Developers, Inc., (known as T-Rex Developers), which built large, secure computer server centers around the United States that were rented to clients. In the spring the merger with AmTec was also finalized, after which the firm became known as Terremark Worldwide, Inc. It would continue to be headed by Chairman, CEO, and President Manny Medina. While based in Miami, it now had offices in other cities including New York and Washington, D.C. At the same time the firm closed a troubled chapter in its history by selling the Terremark Centre for $58.8 million, although it would continue to manage the building and house its headquarters there.

In April T-Rex Developers bought the 557-acre Blue Lake Technology Center in Boca Raton for $142 million, and the next month Terremark cut a deal to acquire Post Shell Technology Contractors, Inc., a 17-year-old construction firm based in Miami with $20 million in annual revenues. The firm was now planning to build a chain of what were dubbed telecom hotels under the T-Rex brand name, which would be rented to high-tech firms and would house fiber-optic networks, routers, and other equipment.

Terremark had also begun working with Miami area officials and the management of the Miami Heat basketball team, which owned land downtown, to build a network access point (NAP) that would serve as a major Internet link between the United States and Latin America. Its home would be the new $100 million Technology Center of the Americas (TECOTA) that was to be funded by outside investors, with Terremark holding a 1 percent ownership stake. The hurricane-proof, windowless, 750,000-square-foot concrete and steel structure's anchor tenant would be Global Crossing, Inc., which signed on before construction had begun. In the summer it was selected to house the fifth NAP in

KEY DATES

1980: Manuel Medina founds Terremark, Inc., to develop and acquire real estate projects.
1990: Following the loss of a key tenant, firm nearly goes bankrupt.
2000: Reverse merger with publicly traded AmTec creates Terremark Worldwide, Inc.; company's focus shifts to building secure IT facilities, Network Access Points.
2001: Technology Center of the Americas opens; Spanish, Brazilian deals are announced.
2007: Acquisition of Data Return LLC for $85 million boosts service offerings.
2008: First Phase of secure Virginia hosting facility opens.

the United States, which would be the first dedicated to linking North and South America.

During the year Terremark also bought Spectrum Telecommunications Corp. of Miami, which provided services in Argentina, Brazil, Chile, and Peru; launched a new subsidiary, ColoConnection, to offer fully furnished spaces in its planned T-Rex locations; established a unit called Asia Connect to market Internet services in China, and acquired IXS.net, a California-based Internet voice/fax service provider that served the Far East. In November, Terremark secured $109 million in financing to complete the already partially completed TECOTA.

HARD TIMES IN 2001

As the dot-com bubble began bursting and the telecommunications market started hitting the skids, in early 2001 the firm announced it was selling the T-Rex subsidiary it had bought less than a year before so it could concentrate on building the Miami NAP. It would also shed the Spectrum Telecommunications and Asia Connect units.

For the fiscal year ended March 31, the company reported sales of $40.1 million and a net loss of $103.9 million, which was due in large part to a write-down of $61.1 million for discontinued operations. The firm's auditor warned that it would not remain a "going concern" if it did not secure a significant source of funding in the near future.

In late June the Miami NAP became fully operational, and Terremark announced 34 contracts had

been signed for space there with such clients as AOL/Time Warner, Deutsche Telekom, Qwest, and Enron. The amount of space utilized was a small percentage of the total, however. The company was also continuing to divest its real estate portfolio, selling a condo project in Fort Lauderdale for $17.2 million. The firm now employed more than 230.

In August Terremark secured $48 million in funding from Ocean Bank to help it remain operational, which was personally guaranteed by CEO Medina. The firm was now facing millions of dollars worth of liens filed by contractors, and to cut costs it laid off a number of employees and closed a facility in California.

By the spring of 2002 Terremark had begun working on the NAPs for São Paolo, Brazil, and Madrid, Spain, but it was continuing to struggle, TECOTA client Global Crossing having recently filed for bankruptcy. The firm delayed filing its annual report until mid-July, when it revealed a loss of $57.4 million on revenues of $15.9 million. Of this, only $3.2 million had come from NAP operations. The TECOTA now hosted 75 clients, and the company was working to bring more from healthcare and other fields.

By the fall of 2002 Terremark had secured several new sources of funding, and had struck deals to convert $22.6 million that it owed to contractors into equity in the company. The firm's fortunes were also boosted by the closure of a rival Florida NAP operated by BellSouth.

In early 2003 the company's financial picture continued to stabilize, and in April its agreement with Ocean Bank was renegotiated to give the lender an equity stake. By the fall the Madrid and São Paolo NAPs were up and running, and the firm was also operating a facility in Santa Clara, California.

For fiscal 2004, ended in March, Terremark reported revenues of $18.2 million and a loss of $22.5 million. It was continuing to work on new financing deals, and, for the first time since its emergence as a public company, the firm's auditors did not warn it might not remain a "going concern."

TECOTA PURCHASED IN 2004

In July 2004 Terremark announced it would buy the TECOTA for $40 million plus assumption of $35 million in debt. After several delays, the deal was finalized in December. The payments on its loan were roughly equal to the $7.7 million it had been paying each year to rent the facility. In early 2005 the company also sold 60 million new shares of stock at 73 cents each to raise $40 million, and shortly afterward completed a one-for-ten reverse stock split.

Sales for the fiscal year ended in March increased to $48.1 million, although the company reported a loss of $9.9 million. Terremark was now receiving a sizable percent of revenues from U.S. government entities including the Departments of Defense and State, and had other important clients in the banking and healthcare industries. The firm was also winning new business after successfully remaining operational during a severe Florida hurricane season.

In August 2005 Terremark bought a small Dutch Internet services firm, Dedigate, and in 2006 launched a new unit, the Secure Information Services Group. The latter would offer vulnerability assessment, secure systems design, and incident preparation and response, among other services. The firm reported sales of $62.5 million and a net loss of $37 million for the year. Despite a blizzard of press releases touting new clients and other positive developments, the TECOTA facility remained less than 15 percent full.

In June 2006 Terremark hired an adviser to help it secure funding of up to $120 million to seek new customers and add infrastructure. It had announced plans to add an operation near Washington, D.C., and was seeking to expand in California.

In early 2007 the firm received $27.25 million from Credit Suisse to buy properties in Virginia and California, and in the spring sold another 11 million shares of stock for $8 each to raise $82.6 million. Soon afterward its stock was switched from the AMEX to the NASDAQ.

DATA RETURN ACQUIRED IN SPRING OF 2007

In May Terremark paid $85 million to buy Data Return LLC, an 11-year-old provider of data services with $55 million in annual revenues. The firm was now working to ramp up its service offerings, TECOTA space rental having yet to prove profitable. The company subsequently received $250 million in debt refinancing from Credit Suisse and Tennenbaum Capital Partners to help lower its interest payments. In November Terremark formed a new Interactive Entertainment Group to seek business in the online gaming and social networking fields, which not long afterward signed a deal to host Latin Interactive Network's gaming platform.

In 2008 the company began hosting a new interactive Library of Congress web site and a vast database of street-level images from major U.S. metropolitan areas run by Blue Dasher Technologies. For the fiscal year, Terremark reported revenues of $187.4 million and a net loss of $42.2 million. The firm now served close to 1,000 clients.

In the summer the first phase of the new NAP of the Capital Region opened in Culpeper, Virginia. The $250 million facility was surrounded by a ten-foot barbed wire fence and earthen berms designed to slow intruders. It also featured a 14-inch-thick solid concrete front wall and security checkpoints for visitors and vehicles to pass through. Its anchor tenant would be Computer Sciences Corporation, but the federal government was also expected to make heavy use of the complex, which was slated to be expanded fivefold.

During the year Terremark introduced a new service based on its Infinistructure computing platform called Enterprise Cloud. It would offer clients a dedicated pool of server and network resources that could be made operational in a short time for disaster recovery and similar uses.

Nearly three decades after Manny Medina founded it as a real estate development firm, Terremark Worldwide, Inc., had reconfigured itself as a secure data host and data recovery services provider. The firm was still seeking a path to profitability, but had passed a number of difficult hurdles and appeared to be closer to this goal than ever before.

Frank Uhle

PRINCIPAL SUBSIDIARIES

NAP of the Americas/West Inc.; Park West Telecommunications Investors, Inc.; TECOTA Services Corp.; Terremark Trademark Holdings, Inc.; TerreNAP Data Centers, Inc.; TerreNAP Services, Inc.; Optical Communications, Inc.; NAP of the Capital Region LLC; Terremark Federal Group, Inc.

PRINCIPAL COMPETITORS

AT&T, Inc.; International Business Machines Corp.; Level 3 Communications, Inc.; Rackspace Hosting, Inc.; SAVVIS, Inc.; Qwest Communications International, Inc.; SunGard Data Systems, Inc.; Switch & Data Facilities Company, Inc.; Verizon Business; Telefonica, S.A.

FURTHER READING

"Blue Dasher Chooses Terremark to Host Massive Image Database of N. America," *Optical Networks Daily*, May 1, 2008.

De Lollis, Barbara, "Miami Developer Seeks to Build Telecommunications Warehouses," *Miami Herald*, March 9, 2000.

———, "South Florida Real Estate Developers Merge Their Operations," *Miami Herald*, May 19, 1998.

———, "South Florida Realtor to Try Hand in Telecommunications Business," *Miami Herald*, November 10, 1999.

Garcia, Beatrice E., "Communications Company Terremark Warns Investors About Losses," *Miami Herald,* July 17, 2001.

———, "Miami-Based Telecommunications Firm Feels Good About Debt-for-Equity Deals," *Miami Herald,* December 7, 2002.

Hubbard, Richard, "Terremark NAP Could Put Miami on Map," *Dow Jones News Service,* September 20, 2000.

Johnson, Donnie, "Terremark Opens First Building in Culpeper," *Fredericksburg (Va.) Free Lance-Star,* June 26, 2008.

Lewis, Seth, "Once Near Brink, Terremark Perseveres," *Miami Herald,* April 17, 2006.

McQuay, Joseph, "Laying the Footings for a Towering Dream," *Florida Trend,* May 1, 1988, p. 23.

Owens, Paul, "T-Rex Developers, Manager of Ex-Blue Lake, to Be Sold," *Palm Beach Post,* January 20, 2001, p. 10B.

Rosenberg, Sharon Harvey, "Medina Faces Pressure of Funding Deadlines," *Miami Daily Business Review,* December 11, 2001.

Seemuth, Mike, "Billionaire Bets on Terremark's Future," *Broward Daily Business Review,* February 28, 2007, p. 3.

———, "Terremark CEO Sees Silver Lining in Hurricanes," *Broward Daily Business Review,* November 23, 2005, p. 3.

———, "Terremark Struggles, But Exec Boosts Holdings by 76%," *Broward Daily Business Review,* August 2, 2006, p. 3.

"Terremark Unveils 'Enterprise Cloud' Solution," *Wireless News,* June 10, 2008.

"Time Has Come for Miami-Based Internet Services Firm to Prove Itself," *Miami Herald,* January 27, 2002.

Villano, David, "Strategic Makeover," *Florida Trend,* August 1, 2001, p. 18.

Winter, Christine, "Series of Successful Deals Solidifies Miami Data Center Owner's Finances," *South Florida Sun-Sentinel,* May 1, 2003.

Zalewski, Peter, "Terremark Closes Deal to Buy Technology Center of Americas," *Palm Beach Daily Business Review,* January 5, 2005, p. 7.

TOSHIBA
Leading Innovation >>>

Toshiba Corporation

———————— ■ ————————

1-1-1 Shibaura
Minato-ku
Tokyo, 105-8001
Japan
Telephone: (+81-3) 3457-4511
Fax: (+81-3) 3456-1631
Web site: http://www.toshiba.co.jp

Public Company
Incorporated: 1939 as Tokyo Shibaura Electric Company, Ltd.
Employees: 198,000
Sales: ¥7.67 trillion ($76.68 billion) (2008)
Stock Exchanges: Tokyo Osaka Nagoya London
Ticker Symbols: 6502 (Tokyo); TOS (London)
NAICS: 237130 Power and Communication Line and Related Structures Construction; 333315 Photographic and Photocopying Equipment Manufacturing; 333415 Air-Conditioning and Warm Air Heating Equipment and Commercial and Industrial Refrigeration Equipment Manufacturing; 333611 Turbine and Turbine Generator Set Units Manufacturing; 333921 Elevator and Moving Stairway Manufacturing; 334111 Electronic Computer Manufacturing; 334112 Computer Storage Device Manufacturing; 334119 Other Computer Peripheral Equipment Manufacturing; 334210 Telephone Apparatus Manufacturing; 334220 Radio and Television Broadcasting and Wireless Communications Equipment Manufacturing; 334290 Other Communications Equipment Manufacturing; 334310 Audio and Video Equipment Manufacturing; 334411 Electron Tube Manufacturing; 334413 Semiconductor and Related Device Manufacturing; 334419 Other Electronic Component Manufacturing; 334510 Electromedical and Electrotherapeutic Apparatus Manufacturing; 334511 Search, Detection, Navigation, Guidance, Aeronautical, and Nautical System and Instrument Manufacturing; 334512 Automatic Environmental Control Manufacturing for Residential, Commercial, and Appliance Use; 334517 Irradiation Apparatus Manufacturing; 335110 Electric Lamp Bulb and Part Manufacturing; 335121 Residential Electric Lighting Fixture Manufacturing; 335122 Commercial, Industrial, and Institutional Electric Lighting Fixture Manufacturing; 335211 Electric Housewares and Household Fan Manufacturing; 335212 Household Vacuum Cleaner Manufacturing; 335221 Household Cooking Appliance Manufacturing; 335222 Household Refrigerator and Home Freezer Manufacturing; 335224 Household Laundry Equipment Manufacturing; 335228 Other Major Household Appliance Manufacturing; 335911 Storage Battery Manufacturing; 335912 Primary Battery Manufacturing; 336321 Vehicular Lighting Equipment Manufacturing; 336322 Other Motor Vehicle Electrical and Electronic Equipment Manufacturing

■ ■ ■

Toshiba Corporation is one of Japan's oldest and largest producers of consumer and industrial electric and electronic products. Toshiba is among the global leaders in notebook personal computers, mobile phones, flash-

COMPANY PERSPECTIVES

Toshiba delivers technology and products remarkable for their innovation and artistry—contributing to a safer, more comfortable, more productive life.

We bring together the spirit of innovation with our passion and conviction to shape the future and help protect the global environment—our shared heritage.

We foster close relationships, rooted in trust and respect, with our customers, business partners and communities around the world.

memory computer chips, LCDs, and nuclear power plants. A little more than half of the company's net sales are derived domestically, with about 16 percent from Asia (not including Japan), 15 percent from North America, and 13 percent from Europe. Toshiba is considered one of Japan's *sogo denki*, or general electric companies, a group that is typically said to also include Fujitsu Limited, Hitachi, Ltd., Mitsubishi Electric Corporation, and NEC Corporation. With a history that dates back to the 19th century and a product line that extends from semiconductors, batteries, and electro-medical devices to consumer electronics, home appliances, and elevators, Toshiba has played an active role in Japan's rise to the forefront of international business.

TWO-PRONGED ELECTRIC EQUIPMENT ROOTS

Toshiba was formed through the 1939 union of two manufacturers of electrical equipment, Shibaura Seisaku-sho (Shibaura Engineering Works) and Tokyo Electric Company, Ltd. The older of the two, Shibaura, traced its roots to Japan's first telegraph equipment shop, Tanaka Seizo-sho (Tanaka Engineering Works). Hisashige Tanaka, who has been called the "Edison of Japan," established the business in 1875. The business climate in which the company began, however, was far from the atmosphere in which it later operated. During the late 19th century, Japan lagged far behind Britain, France, Germany, and the United States in industrial development. Besieged with economic problems resulting from the overthrow of the Tokugawa government in 1869 and a tremendous influx of imported goods and machinery that threatened the nation's fledgling industries, Japan was vulnerable to colonization. Confronted with the task of strengthening its faltering

industries, the new government was quick to respond.

In October 1870 the Ministry of Industry (Kobusho) was formed and subsequently acted as a catalyst for the country's industrial development. In its attempt to integrate contemporary technologies into Japan, the government concentrated on hiring foreign engineers, technicians, and scientists to instruct domestic engineers in operating imported machinery; the government also sent its own engineers abroad with the intent of selecting machinery and manufacturing techniques for use in Japanese industries.

The integration of foreign technologies was first put into practice by Tanaka Seizo-sho. The company's 1,300-horsepower steam engine, copied from blueprints of an English counterpart, was successfully constructed in a plant in Kanebo, Japan. This venture convinced Japanese industrialists of their potential for technological advancement through the adoption of foreign technology and its adaptation to domestic skills and resources.

Tanaka Seizo-sho embraced this concept in the 1880s, determining that paying outright for technological knowledge was the most expedient means to upgrade its technological capabilities. This strategy helped the company expand into the manufacture of transformers, electric motors, and other heavy electric equipment in the 1890s.

Tanaka Seizo-sho made its own discoveries as well during this period, originating Japan's first hydroelectric generators in 1894. By 1902 the company's own technological capabilities had produced a 150-kilowatt three-phase-current dynamo for the Yokosuka Bay Arsenal, marking one of the initial transformations from foreign to Japanese-based technology, and the beginning of the company's rise to the forefront of international business. The company, which adopted the name Shibaura Seisaku-sho in 1904, developed Japan's first X-ray tubes in 1915.

While Shibaura and other Japanese corporations were growing in strength and increasing their capabilities, they were deeply debilitated by the advent of World War I. As the war began, Japanese manufacturers were cut off from Germany, England, and the United States, major suppliers of machines, industrial materials, and chemicals, forcing them to turn to one another for necessary materials and machinery to keep their fledgling industries alive. The hardships experienced during this period had long-term advantages, however, for they forced Japanese industry into self-sufficiency and paved the way for the country's industrial advancement.

Shibaura continued to grow in the interim between world wars and merged with Tokyo Electric Company,

KEY DATES

1875: Hisashige Tanaka establishes Japan's first telegraph equipment shop, Tanaka Seizo-sho.

1890: Hakunetsu-sha & Company is founded as Japan's first manufacturer of incandescent lamps.

1899: Hakunetsu-sha is renamed Tokyo Electric Company, Ltd.

1904: Tanaka Seizo-sho is renamed Shibaura Seisaku-sho.

1939: Tokyo Electric and Shibaura merge to form Tokyo Shibaura Electric Company, Ltd.

1949: Company's shares are first listed on the Tokyo and Osaka exchanges.

1954: Company produces Japan's first digital computers.

1978: Company is renamed Toshiba Corporation.

1985: Toshiba develops the first one-megabyte DRAM memory chip.

1986: Company begins producing laptop personal computers.

1987: The sale of submarine sound-deadening equipment to the then communist Soviet Union by a subsidiary half-owned by Toshiba leads to a U.S. Senate vote banning the import of Toshiba products for three years and the resignation of the company president and chairman.

1995: Toshiba, in partnership with Time Warner, develops the format for DVDs that becomes the industry standard.

1996: Company introduces its first DVD players and DVD drives for computers.

1998: Major restructuring is launched.

1999: Toshiba settles a U.S. class-action lawsuit over an allegedly faulty floppy disc drive in its laptops, agreeing to pay $1.1 billion.

2002: Exit from DRAM market and major restructuring sends the company into a record net loss.

2006: Toshiba acquires majority control of nuclear reactor group Westinghouse Electric Company.

Ltd., in 1939. Originally known as Hakunetsu-sha & Company before adopting the Tokyo Electric name in 1899, the firm was founded in 1890 by Dr. Ichisuke

Fujioka and Shoichi Miyoshi. Hakunetsu-sha had distinguished itself as Japan's first manufacturer of incandescent lamps. The newly merged company, named Tokyo Shibaura Electric Company, Ltd., soon became widely known as Toshiba (the company officially adopted the name Toshiba Corporation in 1978). The company's pre–World War II Japanese innovations included fluorescent lamps and radar.

FLOURISHING THEN FALTERING IN POSTWAR PERIOD

During the late 1940s, Japan rapidly passed from a period of self-isolation and self-reliance into a period of largely benevolent occupation and advocacy. With the assistance of the Japanese government and its citizens, the American Occupation Authority instituted social and economic reforms and poured resources into postwar financial markets. Japan's readmittance into the international trading community gave it access to overseas markets for manufactured goods and raw materials. The glut of raw materials available at the time enabled Japan to obtain necessary commodities in large quantities at favorable prices and, consequently, to regain its financial and industrial strength.

In this more favorable climate, Toshiba once again began to flourish. The company's shares were first listed on the Tokyo Stock and Osaka Securities Exchanges in 1949. Backed by the powerful trading house of the Mitsui Group, the company's financial status was well secured. Starting in the 1950s, Toshiba began a program to strengthen its competitiveness in both the domestic and international markets. The company produced Japan's first broadcasting equipment in 1952, launched Japan's first digital computers in 1954, and developed Japan's first microwave ovens in 1959.

It would be some time before modern business policies affected the company in any fundamental way. Toshiba executives were criticized for their rigid adherence to a feudal system of hierarchy and status. Top officials maintained lax working hours and were far removed from any operational business. An indisputable separation between a superior and his subordinates made the exchange of ideas virtually impossible. To reduce the burden of responsibility on any one executive, numerous signatures were needed to approve a document. Thus innovation was easily stymied in a chain of bureaucracy.

In the early 1960s, these internal problems were compounded by an economic recession. In one year Toshiba's pretax profits slid from $36 million to $13 million. To halt any further erosion, a radical change was in order. For only the second time in Toshiba's history the company sought an outsider to aid the ailing business. The company's board hired Toshiwo Doko to take charge of the company. Doko had won acclaim as the architect of the 1960 merger of Ishikawajima Heavy Industries and Harima Shipbuilding & Engineering Company, which formed the world's largest shipbuilder, IHI.

When he joined Toshiba as president in 1965, Doko retained his title as chairman of IHI. The combined status ranked Doko as Japan's leading industrialist. These two companies had shared interests prior to Doko's appointment at Toshiba; IHI owned over ten million shares in Toshiba and Toshiba controlled over four million shares in IHI. After Doko became president, Toshiba raised its stake in IHI as both companies shared executives on their boards and established trade agreements. This exchange, a *keiretsu* hallmark, strengthened Toshiba's financial standing.

Doko's other corrective measures included the reduction of Toshiba's dependence on borrowed capital. This was aided by the U.S.-based General Electric Company's agreement to purchase all of Toshiba's capital issue. General Electric's interest in Toshiba dated back to before World War II, but had declined in the intervening years. The infusion of capital enabled Toshiba to expand and modernize its operations.

The new company president also initiated a comprehensive campaign to export Toshiba products around the world. By establishing independent departments, the company could better facilitate the export of consumer and industrial goods. Major contracts were finalized with U.S. companies to export generators, transformers, and motors, as well as televisions and home appliances.

Other streamlining efforts took the form of expanding the sales force, hiring new management, and consolidating operations. By 1967 Toshiba controlled 63 subsidiaries and employed more than 100,000 people; the company ranked as the largest electronics manufacturer in Japan and the nation's fourth largest company. Yet in light of the dramatic expansion of such domestic competitors as Sony Corporation and Hitachi in the 1970s, Toshiba's performance was generally considered mediocre.

EMPHASIZING SEMICONDUCTORS, COMPUTERS, AND CONSUMER ELECTRONICS

In 1980 a new president, Shoichi Saba, brought renewed vigor to the company. Trained as an electrical engineer, Saba funneled vast resources into research and development, especially in the areas of semiconductors,

computers, and telecommunications. In October 1984 Toshiba formed an Information and Communications Systems Laboratory to develop and integrate office automation products. That same year, Toshiba was responsible for the world's first direct broadcast satellite. The company's R&D investment paid off handsomely in 1985, when Toshiba won the global race to develop the first one-megabyte DRAM memory chip. By 1987 the company was producing almost half of the world's one-megabyte chips.

Utilized in equipment from stereos to computers, semiconductors soon became an important part of Toshiba's portfolio. In 1986 alone, Toshiba's semiconductor facilities experienced a 55 percent increase thanks to contracts in France and West Germany, as well as burgeoning domestic demand. For the first time in its history, Toshiba surpassed its closest competitor, Hitachi, to become the second largest semiconductor manufacturer in the world, behind NEC Corporation.

Joint ventures and agreements with both Japanese and foreign corporations facilitated technology exchange. In 1986 Toshiba entered into a joint venture with Motorola, Inc., for its Japanese production of computer memories and microprocessors. The two companies became involved in the collective development of microcomputer and memory chips based on the exchange of technology, and also developed a manufacturing facility in Japan. Efforts of this type facilitated the development of voice recognition systems and digital private branch exchange systems (PBXs), which transmit telephone calls within private buildings. Through a 1986 agreement with AT&T Corporation, Toshiba began marketing these systems throughout Japan, as well as assisting that corporation with technological insight.

In the same year, Toshiba entered into an agreement with IBM-Japan to market their general-purpose computers domestically. Through this arrangement, Toshiba marketed its own communications equipment with IBM-Japan's computers, selling to governmental agencies, local governments, and other institutions to which IBM (as a foreign interest) had previously been blocked. An additional marketing contract with IBM introduced the first PC-compatible laptop computer, the T3100, to Japan, and met with great success. By 1991, Toshiba had garnered over one-fifth of the laptop market.

The area for which Toshiba became best known was its consumer products division, which grew at a rapid pace in the 1980s through acquisition and innovation. In April 1984 Toshiba reorganized the production, marketing, and research and development sections of its video and audio products, incorporating them into one centralized location. While sales of standard consumer products such as VCRs, compact disc players, televisions, and personal cassette recorders continued to grow, Toshiba was quick to capitalize on new markets as well. In 1986 the company entered the home video market, creating a wholly owned subsidiary and introducing 110 new video titles to the Japanese market. That same year, it inked an agreement to supply cable equipment to American Television and Communications Corporation.

Although Toshiba was best known in the United States for its computer-related and consumer products, it had a wide range of additional business ventures. Among Japanese corporations, Toshiba was a leader in the production of advanced medical electronic equipment. In 1986 the corporation initiated the supply of blood chemical analyzers, used to detect liver and kidney disease, to Allied Corporation, a leading U.S. chemical manufacturer. Other accomplishments suggested Toshiba's technological foresight in solving global and domestic problems. Toshiba began production of equipment for uranium fuel enrichment for use in nuclear power plants, marking an important step toward Japan's acquisition of a domestic nuclear fuel supply.

These many successes realized under Shoichi Saba were overshadowed by a 1987 scandal involving Toshiba Machine, a subsidiary half-owned by Toshiba. According to Washington sources, the subsidiary sold submarine sound-deadening equipment to the then communist Soviet Union. The equipment made detection more difficult and forced NATO to modernize its antisubmarine detection equipment. While Toshiba claimed that it was not able to control the subsidiary's daily operations, the sale broke a Western law concerning the sale of technologically advanced equipment to Communist countries. Two executives at the subsidiary under investigation were arrested and four top-ranking officials resigned. The Japanese government prohibited the subsidiary from exporting products to the Soviet Union for one year and repealed its right to sponsor visas for visiting personnel from Eastern-bloc countries. Amid growing protests in both Japan and the United States, Toshiba President Sugichiro Watari issued a public apology to the United States. Then, on July 1, 1987, both Watari and Chairman Shoichi Saba tendered their resignations from the Toshiba Corporation in the wake of a U.S. Senate vote to ban the import of Toshiba products for three years. Joichi Aoi, a former senior executive vice-president, assumed Toshiba's presidency.

Ironically, the anti-Japan mood roused by this episode may have revitalized morale at Toshiba. Perhaps to compensate for the loss of the U.S. market, Chairman Aoi led the company's energetic expansion into

global markets. In the latter years of the 1980s, Toshiba began offering its integrated circuit technology to the Chinese Electronics Import and Export Corporation to assist in development of television production. A 1991 joint venture with General Electric furthered this effort, with a special emphasis on large home appliances. The company also won a contract worth ¥12 billion to build a color television assembly plant in Russia, marking Moscow's first agreement of this nature with a Japanese company. Thus, in spite of losing up to ¥5 billion as a result of the U.S. embargo, the company's net income nearly doubled, from ¥61 billion in 1987 to ¥121 billion in 1990. Toshiba's fiscal triumphs were capped with the 1991 naming of Chairman Joichi Aoi as Asia's CEO of the Year.

REORGANIZATION AND STRATEGIC ALLIANCES

With the new decade came new economic imperatives, especially those created by a global recession and the rising value of the yen. While Toshiba's annual revenues remained essentially flat from 1990 to 1994, the electronics giant's profits declined more than 90 percent to ¥12 billion, their lowest level in well over a decade.

Toshiba Chairman Aoi and President Fumio Sato employed a variety of strategies in the hopes of reversing this downward course. A 1993 reorganization focused on fostering interaction between and flexibility among the company's hundreds of operations. In line with industry trends, the leaders worked to shorten product development cycles, lower production expenses, and more closely monitor consumer demands. They also moved to further diversify Toshiba's consumer product line, 50 percent of which was still in color televisions. The company worked to shift its emphasis to such high-potential products as cellular communications, multimedia, and mobile electronics. Amid all these changes, however, the company planned to continue its liberal use of strategic alliances for mutual benefit.

One of the company's key alliances in the early 1990s was with Time Warner Inc. In 1992 Toshiba spent $500 million for a 5.6 percent stake in Time Warner Entertainment, a subsidiary of Time Warner that owned cable television systems, Home Box Office, and Warner Bros. studios. The two companies began developing an industry standard for DVDs, or digital videodisks, CD-like disks capable of holding full-length films for play on television screens via players. By the mid-1990s, the Toshiba/Time Warner format became the industry standard, beating out a rival format developed by Sony and Philips. Toshiba then introduced its first DVD players and DVD drives for computers in 1996, becoming the first company to do so. In another alliance with a U.S. firm, Toshiba and IBM agreed to spend $1.2 billion to build a plant in the United States where 64-megabit DRAM memory chips would be made.

In June 1996 Taizo Nishimuro took over as president of Toshiba. With a background in marketing and multimedia Nishimuro became the first chief not to have an engineering background. The new president already faced the difficulty of contending with a Japanese economy in a prolonged state of stagnation, a situation soon compounded by the fallout from the Asian economic crisis, which erupted in mid-1997. The company's consumer electronics and semiconductor sectors, facing fierce international competition, were buffeted by sharp declines in prices and demand. As a result, for the fiscal year ending in March 1999, Toshiba suffered its first net loss in 23 years, a loss totaling ¥13.9 billion ($112.9 million).

SWEEPING RESTRUCTURING LAUNCHED IN 1998

In September 1998, even before these dismal results were released, Toshiba unveiled a multiyear restructuring plan that was radical by Japanese standards. About 6,500 jobs would be trimmed by March 2000 through attrition and hiring cutbacks. The most dramatic changes centered around a wide-ranging restructuring of operations. The company began placing some of its more peripheral businesses into joint ventures with other firms. In January 1999 its glassmaking subsidiary (a direct descendant of one of the company's founding lightbulb businesses) was merged with a subsidiary of Asahi Glass. Another of Toshiba's early business areas, electric motors, was the subject of another tie-up that same month, when the company and Mitsubishi Electric merged their large electric motor divisions into a joint venture called TMA Electric Corporation. In the area of nuclear fuel operations, Toshiba joined with General Electric Company and Hitachi to form Global Nuclear Fuel in January 2000. Another joint venture was formed with Carrier Corporation of the United States in the area of air conditioners. Toshiba also sold certain noncore units outright, such as its domestic automated teller machine business, which was bought by Oki Electric Industry Co., Ltd., in April 1999.

Another key move was the reorganization of the company's 15 rambling divisions into eight business groups (or "in-house companies"), each of which was given more independence and autonomy. The new structure was designed to speed decision making at what had been a fairly bureaucratic company, and for the same reason the size of the firm's board of directors was reduced from 34 to 12. The number of subsidiaries and affiliates was also drastically reduced from about 1,000 to 300. Aiming to place a greater emphasis on corporate profitability, Toshiba began to link executive pay more closely to performance. In another move to enhance profitability, the company adopted on a wide basis the Six Sigma quality approach made famous by General Electric and its longtime head, Jack Welch, leading to $1.3 billion in cost savings by 2000. Finally, at a company that had traditionally been engineer-focused, and where engineers essentially designed products for themselves, a new emphasis was placed on customer-driven new product development.

In the midst of implementing this sweeping reorganization, Toshiba suffered a potentially major setback when it decided to settle a class-action lawsuit that had been brought against the company in the United States over an allegedly faulty floppy disc drive used in more than five million Toshiba laptop computers. Although Toshiba denied that it was liable for the problem and said that there was no evidence that any data had been lost or corrupted because of the problem, Nishimuro decided to settle the suit, fearing that a jury trial could result in a judgment approaching $10 billion, potentially bankrupting the company. The company therefore agreed to a $1.1 billion settlement in October 1999 and was roundly criticized in some quarters for "caving in" too quickly.

The settlement led the company to post another loss for the year ending in March 2000, a net loss of ¥28 billion ($264.2 million). In June 2000 Nishimuro became chairman of Toshiba, while Tadashi Okamura took charge as president and CEO. Okamura, who also had a background in marketing, had been in charge of the sprawling Information and Industrial Systems and Services group, which included everything from telecommunications equipment and control systems to medical systems and elevators and escalators. Under Okamura's leadership, Toshiba continued to place non-core businesses into joint ventures, including rechargeable batteries, elevators, and satellites. The troubled and risky semiconductor sector was also targeted for alliances, including a tie-up with archrival Fujitsu. The company began placing increasing emphasis on information technology, targeting several areas within that sector as bases for future growth, including media cards, mobile applications, networked home appliances, digital broadcasting services, Internet services, and electronic devices for the automobile.

EXITING FROM DRAMS, LARGE WORKFORCE REDUCTION

Toshiba returned to profitability in the year ending in March 2001 only to then be battered when the global information technology industry went into freefall in the wake of the bursting of the U.S.-based Internet bubble. As demand for semiconductors plummeted, Toshiba took the decisive step of exiting from the highly volatile low-end DRAM market. In concert with this pullback, the company in August 2001 announced plans to cut nearly 19,000 employees from its payroll by March 2004, with 17,000 of this total concentrated in Japan. The cutbacks were carried out through a combination of attrition, spinoffs of units, and voluntary early retirement. The plan also involved the slashing of Toshiba's manufacturing operations in Japan by 30 percent, with some of the production shifting to lower-cost facilities in China. As part of its DRAM exit, Toshiba sold its DRAM plant in Virginia to Micron Technology, Inc. The tech downturn propelled sales 9 percent lower for the fiscal year ending in March 2002, to ¥5.39 trillion ($40.56 billion), and also sent the company into its first-ever operating loss. Restructuring charges totaling ¥208.9 billion ($1.57 billion) resulted in a record net loss of ¥254 billion ($1.91 billion).

As it exited from the DRAM market, Toshiba placed greater emphasis on the rapidly growing market for NAND flash-memory chips, a technology that had been invented at the company in the 1980s. These types of chips, which unlike DRAMs retained data when a device's power supply was shut off, were becoming an increasingly common storage medium for digital cameras, MP3 players, mobile phones, and USB drives. Toshiba attained a leading global position in this market in part by partnering with the U.S. firm SanDisk Corporation. Toshiba was also heavily involved in the fiercely competitive LCD panel market. The company elected to shore up its position in this burgeoning area by merging its LCD operations with those of Matsushita Electric Industrial Co., Ltd. This joint venture, 60 percent owned by Toshiba and created in April 2002, ranked among the top three producers of LCD panels in the world. Toshiba and Matsushita later merged their cathode-ray-tube businesses into another joint venture, and Toshiba and Mitsubishi Electric created a joint venture to amalgamate the parts of their businesses producing electrical and automation equipment for factories. Another important Toshiba alliance at this time was with Sony, for whom it was involved in the development of high-end microprocessors and mixed signal chips for the firm's PlayStation game consoles.

In notebook computers, where it had been the global leader throughout the 1990s, Toshiba by 2003 had not only been surpassed in market share by both Dell Inc. and Hewlett-Packard Company, it was also losing money. Under the guidance of Atsutoshi Nishida, Toshiba returned its notebook business to profitability in just one year by reducing its number of computer

configurations by half, shifting resources to the high-end Qosmio line, and slashing costs by turning to outside manufacturers in Taiwan and China for much of the production. Nishida was rewarded for this turnaround effort by being named Toshiba president and CEO in June 2005.

MAJOR INVESTMENTS IN ELECTRONICS AND NUCLEAR POWER

Among the billions of dollars the firm was investing during this period to develop new growth areas, Toshiba partnered with Sony and IBM to develop a multicore, cutting-edge microprocessor called Cell that was intended to compete with the segment's global leader, Intel Corporation. The Cell microprocessor's first commercial application was Sony's PlayStation 3 game console, which was introduced in late 2006. That same year, Toshiba introduced its first next-generation, high-definition DVD players and recorders using the format it had developed called HD DVD. This marked the beginning of a fierce battle between two competing, and incompatible, high-definition formats, HD DVD and Blu-ray, the latter of which had been developed by Toshiba's sometime partner Sony. Large investments were also made in Toshiba's increasingly important NAND flash-memory business, including the opening of a new production plant in Yokkaichi, Japan, in early 2005. This plant was constructed through a joint venture with SanDisk, and the two partners in 2006 agreed to invest about ¥600 billion ($5 billion) to build another flash-memory plant in Yokkaichi, where production began late in 2007. Together, Toshiba and SanDisk controlled about one-quarter of the global NAND flash-memory market.

Although better known for its electronic products, Toshiba still ran a number of industrial businesses that produced power plant equipment, elevators, and escalators. This area, later known as the firm's Infrastructure Systems group, was substantially bolstered in 2006 with the acquisition of a controlling 77 percent interest in nuclear reactor group Westinghouse Electric Company from British Nuclear Fuels plc for $5.4 billion. Westinghouse, based in Monroeville, Pennsylvania, was one of the world leaders in pressurized-water nuclear reactors, providing fuel, services, plant design, and equipment for this industry. Toshiba elected to delve further into nuclear power at a time when rising oil and gas prices and concerns about global warming appeared to signal a potential renaissance for a once-moribund industry. Much of the predicted growth was expected to occur in China, which had plans to build 20 new nuclear plants by 2020 to help fulfill the nation's exploding energy needs. In July 2007 Westinghouse signed contracts to build four nuclear plants in China, while Toshiba that same year was selected as the prime contractor for two boiling-water reactor plants in the United States. Also in 2007, Toshiba entered into an alliance with Kazatomprom, Kazakhstan's state-owned nuclear energy business, to purchase Kazakh uranium mining rights as part of its efforts to secure a stable uranium supply for its nuclear power businesses. Kazatomprom separately purchased a 10 percent stake in Westinghouse from Toshiba, cutting the Japanese firm's interest to 67 percent.

In December 2007 Toshiba entered into a major long-term alliance with Sharp Corporation. Toshiba agreed to supply Sharp with an array of customized computer chips for that company's high-end flat-screen television sets, while Sharp agreed to supply Toshiba with medium- and large-sized LCD panels in support of Toshiba's drive to capture a larger share of the fast-growing LCD TV market. Shortly after the announcement of this tie-up, the battle of the high-definition DVD formats came to a head, with Toshiba on the losing side. Toshiba and Sony had each lined up several major Hollywood studios to support their respective formats, but when Time Warner switched its allegiance from HD DVD to Blu-ray in January 2008 a number of major retailers that had been stocking both formats announced plans to discontinue their stocking of HD DVD players and movies. Toshiba quickly capitulated and pulled the plug on the business just two months later.

FURTHER FLASH-MEMORY INVESTMENTS

Undeterred by this setback, Toshiba pushed ahead with plans to boost its share of the rapidly expanding flash-memory market to 40 percent and overtake the sector leader Samsung. In February 2008 Toshiba announced that in partnership with SanDisk it planned to invest more than ¥1.7 trillion ($15.7 billion) to construct two more flash-memory plants in Japan, one each in Yokkaichi and Kitakami. Production at the plants was expected to commence by 2010. The company was also at the forefront of the development of flash-memory-based drives for personal computers, known as solid-state drives. These drives were expected to eventually supplant hard disk drives in computers in part because unlike conventional drives they contained no moving parts, making them faster, superior in shock resistance, and less demanding of energy.

For the fiscal year ending in March 2008 Toshiba pulled in record revenues of ¥7.67 trillion ($76.68 billion), a 7.8 percent increase over the previous year, while net income fell 7.3 percent to ¥127.41 billion ($1.27 billion). The decline in profits was partially attributable to declining prices for NAND flash memory and to costs associated with winding down the HD DVD business. Later in 2008 Toshiba began to feel the effects of the global economic crisis as demand for electronic products such as portable music players and digital cameras fell off, leading to a glut in the supply of computer chips, including flash memory, that pushed prices down further. During the first half of the fiscal year ending in March 2009, Toshiba's semiconductor business operated at a loss but its TV business had returned to profitability and it had enjoyed strong sales of personal computers in Europe and Japan. The potential for a prolonged global economic slowdown threatened to reverse this improved performance in consumer electronics. At the same time, SanDisk was suffering under the same pressures that Toshiba faced while also fending off a takeover bid from Samsung. In October 2008 Toshiba agreed to buy some of the manufacturing capacity of its flash-memory joint ventures with SanDisk in a deal valued at about $1 billion. Soon thereafter, Samsung dropped its takeover bid. Some analysts, however, speculated that a new Samsung offer was likely to materialize, leaving some doubt about the future of Toshiba's important partnership with SanDisk.

April Dougal Gasbarre
Updated, David E. Salamie

PRINCIPAL SUBSIDIARIES

Toshiba TEC Corporation (52.5%); Toshiba America Business Solutions, Inc. (U.S.A.); Toshiba Matsushita Display Technology Co., Ltd. (60%); AFPD Pte., Ltd. (Singapore); Toshiba Plant Systems & Services Corporation (61.6%); Toshiba Elevator and Building Systems Corporation (80%); Toshiba Solutions Corporation; Toshiba Medical Systems Corporation; Toshiba Nuclear Energy Holdings (US) Inc. (67%); Toshiba Nuclear Energy Holdings (UK) Ltd. (67%); Toshiba America Medical Systems, Inc. (U.S.A.); Toshiba Consumer Electronics Holding Corporation; Toshiba Capital Corporation; Toshiba America, Inc. (U.S.A.); Toshiba International Finance (UK) Plc; Toshiba Capital (Asia) Ltd. (Singapore); Taiwan Toshiba International Procurement Corporation.

PRINCIPAL OPERATING UNITS

Digital Products Group; Electronic Devices & Components Group; Infrastructure Systems Group.

PRINCIPAL COMPETITORS

Hitachi, Ltd.; Fujitsu Limited; NEC Corporation; Mitsubishi Electric Corporation; Samsung Electronics Co., Ltd.; Hewlett-Packard Company; Sony Corporation; International Business Machines Corporation; Panasonic Corporation; Dell Inc.; Sharp Corporation; SANYO Electric Co., Ltd.; Intel Corporation; LG Electronics, Inc.; Seiko Epson Corporation; Royal Philips Electronics N.V.; Acer Inc.; Pioneer Corporation; Siemens AG; Texas Instruments Incorporated; Infineon Technologies AG.

FURTHER READING

Abrahams, Paul, "Toshiba Soars As Deep Restructuring Bites," *Financial Times,* November 9, 1998, p. 25.

Abrams, Judith, "Toshiba Eyes New Media Frontier," *Dealerscope Merchandising,* July 1994, pp. 24–25.

Belson, Ken, "Japan Inc. Now Just a Memory, Toshiba Retools Its Image," *New York Times,* August 21, 2003, p. C1.

Bream, Rebecca, et al., "Nuclear Deal Set to Power Toshiba in China Market," *Financial Times,* January 24, 2006, p. 27.

Brull, Steven V., and Andy Reinhardt, "Toshiba's Digital Dreams," *Business Week,* October 13, 1997, pp. 76+.

Carlton, Jim, "Toshiba's U.S. Laptop Unit Fights to Regain Lost Turf," *Wall Street Journal,* February 8, 1999, p. B4.

Dvorak, Phred, "Toshiba's New CEO Is an Innovation: A Manager," *Wall Street Journal,* August 25, 2005, p. B3.

Einhorn, Bruce, "Rebooting Toshiba," *Business Week* (international ed.), May 31, 2004, p. 28.

Eisenstodt, Gale, "We Are Happy," *Forbes,* May 8, 1995, p. 44.

Fulford, Benjamin, "Gadget Colossus," *Forbes,* January 8, 2001, pp. 238–40.

Guth, Robert A., "Eroding Empires: Electronics Giants of Japan Undergo Wrenching Change," *Wall Street Journal,* June 20, 2002, p. A1.

———, "How Japan's Toshiba Got Its Focus Back," *Wall Street Journal,* December 28, 2000, pp. A6, A7.

———, "Toshiba Plans Strategic Shift to Fast Growth," *Wall Street Journal,* February 17, 2000, p. A12.

Holyoke, Larry, "How Toshiba's Laptops Retook the Heights," *Business Week,* January 16, 1995, p. 86.

Johnstone, Bob, "Industry: Quick As a Flash," *Far Eastern Economic Review,* January 7, 1993, p. 57.

Kane, Yukari Iwatani, "Toshiba Regroups After Losing DVD War," *Wall Street Journal,* February 20, 2008, p. B3.

Keenan, Faith, and Peter Landers, "Staggering Giants," *Far Eastern Economic Review,* April 1, 1999, pp. 10–13.

Kelly, Tim, "Calculated Risk: Atsutoshi Nishida Is Steering Toshiba in a Pronounced Direction by Buying the Westinghouse Nuclear Arm," *Forbes,* December 11, 2006, pp. 126–28.

Kunii, Irene M., "Toshiba Tries to Reboot," *Business Week,* July 24, 2000, p. 26.

———, "Under the Knife: The Global Tech Crunch Forces Chip Giants to Pare Down," *Business Week,* September 10, 2001, p. 62.

Landers, Peter, "Broken Up: Japan's Biggest Players Get Serious About Restructuring," *Far Eastern Economic Review,* February 11, 1999, p. 50.

———, "Japan's Toshiba Plans to Cut 20,000 Jobs by 2004," *Wall Street Journal,* August 28, 2001, p. A11.

Martin, Neil A., "Time for a Makeover," *Barron's,* December 8, 2003, pp. 20–22.

Meyer, Richard, "Asia's CEO of the Year: Joichi Aoi of Toshiba— 'We Just Stay with It,'" *Financial World,* October 15, 1991, pp. 50–54.

———, "Power Surge," *Financial World,* April 3, 1990, pp. 42–46.

Pasztor, Andy, and Peter Landers, "Toshiba Agrees to Settlement on Laptops," *Wall Street Journal,* November 1, 1999, p. A3.

Sato, Kazuo, ed., *Industry and Business in Japan,* New York: Croom Helm, 1980.

Schlender, Brenton R., "How Toshiba Makes Alliances Work," *Fortune,* October 4, 1993, pp. 116–20.

Shimamura, Kazuhiro, "Toshiba Plans Expansion to Boost Sales," *Wall Street Journal,* May 9, 2008, p. B7.

Tanzer, Andrew, "The Man Toshiba Hung Out to Dry," *Forbes,* September 7, 1987, pp. 96–98.

Uchida, Michio, "Toshiba Bounces Back," *Tokyo Business Today,* June 1989, pp. 14–19.

Woods, Ginny Parker, "Toshiba Looks to Long Term for Westinghouse," *Wall Street Journal,* February 8, 2006, p. B3B.

Yamaguchi, Yuzo, "Chip Glut Weighs on Toshiba, NEC," *Wall Street Journal,* October 30, 2008, p. B4.

Young, Lewis H., "Why Toshiba Likes the Component Business," *Electronic Business Buyer,* December 1994, pp. 52–56.

Zaun, Todd, "Toshiba Names New President with a Record of Turnarounds," *New York Times,* February 23, 2005, p. C6.

TVI Corporation

7100 Holladay Tyler Road
Glenn Dale, Maryland 20769
U.S.A.
Telephone: (301) 352-8800
Toll Free: (800) 598-9711
Fax: (301) 352-8818
Web site: http://www.tvicorp.com

Public Company
Incorporated: 1977
Employees: 205
Sales: $46.9 million (2007)
Stock Exchanges: NASDAQ
Ticker Symbol: TVIN
NAICS: 334511 Search, Detection, Navigation, Guidance, Aeronautical, and Nautical System and Instrument Manufacturing; 339999 All Other Miscellaneous Manufacturing

■ ■ ■

TVI Corporation makes emergency response and protection equipment used by the military, public health, and first-response agencies. TVI designs and manufactures rapid deployment shelters and tents that can decontaminate people exposed to biological or chemical agents. The company's line of mobile shelters are equipped with sinks, beds, heat, and lighting. The company also manufactures powered, air-purifying respirators and filter canisters for chemical, biological, radiological, and nuclear protection. TVI sells its products and systems worldwide, but primarily relies on domestic sales to state and local governments to sustain its operations.

ORIGINS

TVI experienced its fair share of struggles during its first 30 years in business, enduring bouts of financial distress and scandal that tested the resiliency of the small, publicly traded concern. The company was formed in 1977, basing its operations in Beltsville, Maryland, a small community in the Greater Washington, D.C., area. Initially, TVI made thermal targets for the U.S. military, using infrared material to produce fake, fold-up tanks. The tanks were used for target practice and to trick enemy gunners. During the first 15 years of its existence, the company developed a modestly sized business supplying thermal targets, gaining its greatest publicity when its fold-up tanks were used in the Persian Gulf War in the early 1990s. It soon became apparent, however, that the company's financial benefit from the uptick in business was as illusory as its decoy tanks. In March 1991, one month after the Persian Gulf War ended, TVI filed for bankruptcy.

SCANDAL IN THE NINETIES

At the time of the collapse, TVI was led by its chief executive officer and chairman, Brent Molovinsky. TVI remained in financial purgatory for five years, but insolvency was the least of its problems during the period. Molovinsky, according to his accusers, was engaged in criminal activity while TVI floundered financially.

> ## COMPANY PERSPECTIVES
>
> We continue to maintain a strong market position in our core businesses and are focused on achieving profitable growth. We firmly believe that TVI exhibits significant long-term growth potential.

The charges against Molovinsky were numerous. According to a U.S. Securities and Exchange Commission (SEC) investigation, Molovinsky was found to have misappropriated more than $1 million of investor proceeds between October 1992 and April 1995. The SEC charged that the TVI executive, who had exclusive control over the company's day-to-day operations and finances, fraudulently stimulated demand for TVI stock by making false and misleading statements concerning the company's revenues, earnings, and assets. He was accused of falsely stating that TVI had contracts to build tank gunnery ranges, of conducting illegal stock sales, and of falsely stating that TVI held patents for stealth material and thermal targets used in military applications. Molovinsky was ousted from his positions at TVI in an April 1995 shareholder takeover and, later, was barred by the SEC from acting as an officer or director of any public company.

TVI managed to survive the debacle, emerging from Chapter 11 protection in 1996 under the leadership of Allen Bender, who had replaced Molovinsky a year earlier. The company switched gears strategically and began using the material for its thermal targets (which was ultra-violet-stabilized, water-resistant, and durable) to make collapsible tents and display signs. The company subsisted off a trickle of revenue, limping along until it could point to the first genuinely positive development in a decade.

A CHANGE IN STRATEGY IN 1999

In 1999, TVI began exploring a new application for the technology underpinning its collapsible aluminum-and-vinyl tents and tanks. The company followed the suggestion of the lone executive left from the Molovinsky era, Chad Sample, and began looking for a way to make decontamination shelters, temporary facilities that could remove toxic agents from exposed people. TVI started work on the project, endeavoring to develop a family of products to assist in what were known as "Consequence Management" activities. As the company began developing a line of rapidly deployable decontamination shelters, the fear of chemical and biological attacks

ratcheted up to unprecedented heights, positioning TVI, for the first time, in what promised to be a lucrative market.

The terrorist attacks against the United States on September 11, 2001, turned the business of counterterrorism into a national priority of intense immediacy. The anthrax attacks that began the following week only aggravated widespread panic. A wave of biotechnology firms threw their efforts into developing ways to prevent and to detect biological and chemical agents, but TVI, before the attacks, had positioned itself in the less-crowded segment of what became known as the "homeland security" market, focusing its efforts on dealing with the aftermath of an attack.

When military, national, and local response teams launched recovery efforts at the Pentagon terrorist attack site, they were equipped with TVI's products. After struggling for decades to find firm footing, the company appeared to have found its niche, staking a presence in the homeland security market before the term was coined. The arrival of new business was greeted eagerly at the company's Beltsville headquarters, where Bender and his management team had watched TVI's stock value languish for years at less than $1 per share. In 2001, after more than two decades in business, its annual revenue volume amounted to only slightly more than $4 million. Yet TVI, which had operated in the shadows throughout its existence, was ready to record the first meaningful financial growth in its history.

RICHARD PRIDDY TAKES THE HELM IN 2002

As the company ramped up its efforts to flesh out its product line, a new leader was appointed to help capitalize on the anticipated surge in demand for decontamination systems. Bender was named chairman emeritus in early 2002, making room for Richard V. Priddy to become TVI's new chief executive officer. A graduate of the University of Iowa, where he earned a master's degree in business administration, Priddy brought with him extensive experience in manufacturing and government contracting. He had held management positions at ITT Industries, Rockwell Automation, and Allied Signal. "I am excited by the opportunity that has been given to me," he said in March 4, 2002, interview with *Market News Publishing*. "After only a week working with our customers and our employees, it is evident that TVI has developed a unique concept that is emerging as the cutting-edge technology for rapid deployment shelters."

Under Priddy's command, TVI began recording financial growth at a pace never experienced in the

KEY DATES

1977: TVI is founded in Beltsville, Maryland.
1991: TVI declares bankruptcy.
1995: Chairman Brent Molovinsky is removed from office amid accusations of embezzlement.
1999: TVI begins developing rapid deployment decontamination shelters.
2002: Richard V. Priddy is appointed chief executive officer and the company relocates to Glenn Dale, Maryland.
2005: TVI acquires SafetyTech International, a manufacturer of powered, air-purifying respirators.
2007: Priddy is fired and replaced by Harley A. Hughes.

company's history, courting customers with a "brochure [that] reads like an L.L. Bean catalogue from Armageddon," according to the March 13, 2003, issue of *America's Intelligence Wire.* By 2002, TVI had several systems for sale, including the Chem/Bio Infection Control System, which was an airtight tent equipped with filtration systems to remove toxic agents from exposed people. The company's Casualty Management Shelter featured a chemical-resistant exterior to protect injured people undergoing medical treatment. Its Temporary Morgue enabled the cold storage of cadavers. No system was more important than TVI's High Throughput Mass Decontamination Shelter, however. The decontamination shelter was equipped with roughly 50 shower nozzles threaded into its vinyl interior and three shower lanes to separate men, women, and the incapacitated after an attack. By attaching to a fire hose and using its own water pump, the shelter could sanitize 800 people an hour. Equally as impressive, the shelter could be transported in a pickup truck (it required as much storage space as a residential washing machine) and could be set up by four people in less than ten minutes.

RAPID FINANCIAL GROWTH

The High Throughput Mass Decontamination Shelter led TVI toward a banner year in 2002. In March, the company moved from a 17,000-square-foot basement to a 65,000-square-foot warehouse in Glenn Dale, Maryland, more than doubling its payroll to 90 workers to keep pace with demand for its flagship, $88,000 decontamination shelter. Sales shot upward during the

year, nearly tripling to $11.1 million, while profits swelled to $3 million, exponentially more than the $105,000 it posted in 2002. The increase in demand came primarily from state governments wishing to standardize decontamination technology throughout their jurisdictions. In 2002, Massachusetts became the first state to adopt TVI's technology statewide, and during the course of the ensuing year Delaware, Maine, Maryland, Rhode Island, and South Carolina followed suit. TVI, long ignored by the investment community, began to attract attention. The company's stock value increased 400 percent between early 2002 and early 2003, reaching $1.26 per share. "We were a garage-shop operation a year ago," Priddy noted in his March 13, 2003, interview with *America's Intelligence Wire.* "We're still a penny stock, but it's hard to argue with these numbers," he added, referring to TVI's financial totals for 2002.

More good news awaited TVI in 2003, a year that began with two TVI decontamination systems set up outside the U.S. House of Representatives' floor during President George W. Bush's State of the Union address. State governments continued to turn toward the company. In June, Washington became the first western state to standardize a decontamination system statewide, selecting TVI's systems to be used by the state's hospitals and first-responder agencies. TVI's successes with state governments encouraged Priddy to cultivate business overseas. In April, he formed a partnership with Professional Protection Systems, a U.K.-based decontamination system developer whose product was used after the 1995 sarin gas attack in Tokyo's subway. By the end of the year, there was much to celebrate, as revenues jumped 145 percent to $27 million. The following year, in 2004, the excitement in Glenn Dale continued when TVI's stock reached $6 per share and revenues leaped to $37.9 million, but from there the company slid backward, falling frustratingly short of expectations.

TVI FALTERS IN 2005

TVI's sales peaked in 2004, perhaps because the threat of biological or chemical attacks became less palpable, or perhaps because the emergency equipment market deflated as federal money was diverted to funding the war in Iraq. One certainty was that the declining financial health of TVI ignited problems in the executive offices in Glenn Dale, casting a pall over the company's 30th anniversary.

PRIDDY OUSTED IN 2007

In 2007, TVI posted a numbing loss of $29.6 million. The company's stock was trading at less than 50 cents per share. A boardroom battle erupted, leading to the dismissal of CEO Priddy and onetime hero, Executive Vice-President Charles Sample, for "questionable business transactions," as quoted in the June 18, 2006, edition of the *Baltimore Sun*. Bender, the chairman emeritus, emerged as the prominent figure voicing displeasure, taking exception with an overpayment of $1.7 million in supplies (TVI shareholders were informed in May 2008 that the SEC and the U.S. Justice Department were investigating the matter) and the acquisition of a party-tent rental company in 2005 that had proved a failure. Priddy was replaced by retired General Harley A. Hughes, a TVI director since 2003, who was named chief executive officer. Sample was replaced by Donald C. Yount Jr., a TVI director since 2005, who was named executive vice-president.

AN EMPHASIS ON PERSONAL PROTECTION EQUIPMENT

With Hughes at the helm, TVI focused on two acquisitions completed during the Priddy years that had proven worthwhile. The company added a new line of business in 2004 by acquiring CAPA Manufacturing, LLC, which became a TVI subsidiary named CAPA Manufacturing Corp. that sold a line of powered air-purifying respirators (PAPRs). In early 2005, TVI opened a new filter canister manufacturing facility in Glenn Dale, the first of its kind in the United States. At the facility, the company was capable of producing filter canisters for personnel responding to biological, chemical, or nuclear emergencies, gaining its first supply contract with the U.S. Army. In November 2005, the company greatly expanded its PAPR business by acquiring Frederick, Maryland-based SafetyTech International Inc. for $16.9 million. SafetyTech manufactured a wide range of PAPRs for chemical, biological, radiological, and nuclear protection, giving Hughes a new line of

business to exploit as he presided over TVI's turnaround efforts. Costs were being cut and new products were being developed, sparking hope that the company could regain the momentum it had built up earlier in the decade. "We can see the highway through the woods," Hughes said in a June 18, 2008, interview with the *Baltimore Sun*.

Jeffrey L. Covell

PRINCIPAL SUBSIDIARIES

CAPA Manufacturing Corp.; Safety Tech International, Inc.; Signature Special Events Services, Inc.

PRINCIPAL COMPETITORS

Zumro Manufacturing, Inc.; DHS Systems, LLC; Hughes Safety Showers Ltd.

FURTHER READING

Hancock, Jay, "Ready for Rumble at TVI Meeting," *Baltimore Sun,* June 18, 2008.

Lamb, Robyn, "Terrorism Threat Bolsters P.G. Co. Decontamination Firm," *Daily Record,* August 3, 2004.

"TVI Corp. New CEO," *Market News Publishing,* March 4, 2002.

"TVI Corp. Supports Terrorism Recovery Efforts at the Pentagon," *Market News Publishing,* October 2, 2001.

Waters, Ed, Jr., "TVI Corp Acquires Frederick, Md., Air Purifying Respirator Company," *Frederick News-Post,* November 15, 2005.

White, Bobby, "Possibility of Terrorist Attacks Good for One Business," *Daily Record,* June 11, 2003.

———, "TVI Corp. Capitalizes on Biological Warfare," *Daily Record,* June 27, 2003.

"A Worst-Case Enterprise," *America's Intelligence Wire,* March 13, 2003.

United Internet AG

Elgendorfer Strasse 57
Montabaur, D-56410
Germany
Telephone: (+49 02602) 96 1100
Fax: (+49 02602) 96 10 13
Web site: http://www.unitedinternet.de

Public Company
Incorporated: 1998 as 1&1 AG
Employees: 3,954
Sales: EUR 1.49 billion ($2.19 billion) (2007)
Stock Exchanges: Frankfurt
Ticker Symbol: UTDI
NAICS: 514191 On-Line Information Services; 541512
    Computer Systems Design Services

■ ■ ■

United Internet AG is one of Germany's, and Europe's, leading providers of Internet-related services. The Montabaur-based company operates through two primary business segments: Products and Online Marketing. The Products division is United Internet's largest, accounting for approximately 85 percent of the group's EUR 1.49 billion ($2.2 billion) in 2007. The Products division features such brands as GMX, the leading e-mail and messaging service in Germany; Web. de, the second largest web portal in Germany; Inter-NetX and Fasthosts, which provide web hosting products and services in Germany and the United Kingdom, respectively. A major part of the Products division is 1&1, which provides a range of Internet ac-

cess and web hosting services in Germany, Austria, the United Kingdom, France, and the United States. In 2008, 1&1 counted more than 3.2 million web hosting contracts, approximately half of which were outside of the Germany/Austria market. Through 1&1, United Internet has also emerged as Germany's second largest DSL-based Internet access provider, with nearly 2.7 million customers. The group's second division, Online Marketing, is grouped around its AdLINK Media advertising network; affiliate marketing specialist affilinet; and domain trader Sedo. United Internet was founded in 1988 by CEO Ralph Dommermuth. The company is listed on the Frankfurt stock exchange.

INTERNET WUNDERKIND IN 1988

United Internet AG was launched as a small computer shop in Montabaur, Germany, by Ralph Dommermuth in 1988. The then 24-year-old Dommermuth had initially apprenticed as a banker, but was quickly attracted by the opportunities offered by the nascent personal computer and online markets. Dommermuth set up a shop in a friend's office, and called his company 1&1 EDV Marketing GmbH.

From the start, Dommermuth recognized the future importance of marketing for the industry. The European software industry in the late 1980s and into the early 1990s was dominated by the big U.S. software companies, with nine of the top ten-selling software packages produced by U.S. companies. Most of the more than 30,000 European software companies in operation at the time, including 8,000 or so in Germany, remained too small to compete effectively against the marketing and distribution might of the larger U.S. companies. Dommermuth devised a means of providing pooled marketing, communication, data management, mailing, and distribution resources to these companies.

1&1's breakthrough came in 1992, when the company was hired by Deutsche Telekom to develop a marketing campaign for its struggling online service, then known as BTX. Dommermuth decided to make the campaign user-friendly, a novel approach at the time, renaming BTX as T-online, and drafting an easy-to-understand advertising campaign. The result was a surge in new subscribers, and by the middle of the 1990s, T-online had grown into the largest Internet services provider in Europe.

The company's involvement with T-online went beyond advertising, as 1&1 became responsible for developing the software that overhauled Deutsche Telekom's former portal, the tech-oriented Datex-J, into the popular and trendy T-online portal. The T-online launch also included one of the first Internet browsers, developed by 1&1, which played a significant factor in T-online's rapid success. 1&1's expertise grew to include

software development, content creation, marketing, and a range of services related to Internet access and operations. The success of T-online earned Dommermuth the reputation as a European Internet "wunderkind."

T-online remained 1&1's main customer through the mid-1990s. In 1996, however, T-online decided to bring its marketing and web portal operations in-house. Despite this blow to the company's operations, Dommermuth had already begun preparing 1&1 for life after its partnership with Deutsche Telekom. In the early 1990s, Dommermuth had recognized that the increasing complexity of the personal computer market would stimulate the demand for specialized technical support services. The company created its Customer Care Division, with just three employees.

The new division quickly landed a client, IBM, which hired the company to take over its help desk services for its OS2 operating software. As a result, 1&1's Customer Care Division expanded rapidly, growing to more than 60 employees in its first year. Through the mid-1990s, this division continued to focus on its work for IBM.

GOING PUBLIC IN 1998

Nonetheless, the loss of its T-online partnership forced Dommermuth to seek a new direction for the company. Rather than attempt to develop a relationship with a new Internet services provider (ISP), Dommermuth decided to enter that market directly. In 1996, the company launched its own ISP services. As Dommermuth explained to *Businessweek,* "With the rise of the Internet it had become relatively inexpensive to become a service provider ourselves."

At the same time, IBM had decided to bring its support services back in-house as well. Instead of folding the Customer Care Division, Dommermuth saw a means to build on its experience as part of the group's new drive to become a provider of Internet-related services. As a result, the division became a subsidiary, twenty4help Knowledge Service GmbH Europe. That company then began developing a new and broader client base by operating call center and helpline outsourcing services. By the end of the decade, twenty4help had already signed up more than 30 major clients.

In the meantime, Dommermuth's drive to transform 1&1 into an Internet services company led to the group's decision to go public in 1998. The company listed on the Frankfurt Stock Exchange that year, becoming one of the first of the web-oriented companies to do so. In this way, 1&1 found itself well positioned for the surge in investor interest in the sector.

KEY DATES

1988: Ralph Dommermuth founds 1&1 EDV Marketing GmbH to provide marketing services to young German software and online markets.

1992: 1&1 signs marketing contract with Deutsche Telekom, helping to create success of T-online.

1998: 1&1 goes public on the Frankfurt Stock Exchange and becomes 1&1 AG.

2000: The company reincorporates as United Internet and decides to refocus itself as an Internet services company.

2003: United Internet enters the United States, establishing a subsidiary there.

2008: United Internet enters the Spanish market, launching the 1&1 brand for that market.

The company's initial public offering had raised more than $60 million, which 1&1 now used to go on a shopping spree, buying a number of companies over the next two years. Among them was Schlund + Partner, an Internet marketing pioneer, which had become one of the first to develop a business around the hosting of web sites. The company then launched Puretec, a budget-priced web hosting package. Another important acquisition that year was of GMX, which provided e-mail accounts and messaging services. At the same time, 1&1 branched into online marketing, founding AdLINK, providing advertising booking services.

CHANGING DIRECTION IN 2000

The rising success of the company's Internet services operations led to a change in direction. In 2000, the company restructured itself into a holding company, changing its name to United Internet AG. The name change clearly signaled the company's decision to regroup around a core of Internet services, and as such, the company abandoned its non-core operations. This process was completed by 2007, with the sale of twenty4help to Teleperformance SA. 1&1, which formally acquired Schlund + Partner that year, now became United Internet's key Internet services subsidiary, renamed as 1&1 Internet.

United Internet now began a drive to develop itself on an international level. The company first targeted the United Kingdom, setting up a 1&1 subsidiary in Slough, England. The company also moved into the increasingly profitable domain name registration market, acquiring a stake in Afilia. In this way, the company gained control of the .info domain, the first major top level domain to be awarded by ICANN (the main domain name oversight body, Internet Corporation for Assigned Names and Numbers) in more than 15 years.

Success in England led to the launch of 1&1 subsidiaries in France and Ireland by the end of 2000. Into the middle of the first decade of the 2000s, the company added several new markets, including Belgium, Switzerland, Sweden, and elsewhere. The list expanded to include the United States, where the company set up a subsidiary in 2003. The U.S. operations, which went live in January 2004, had already signed up 200,000 subscribers by its official launch. The company's web hosting operations became one of the world's fastest-growing, and then the world's largest, with more than 3.2 million web hosting contracts under its control.

United Internet's relationship with T-online had remained a strong one into the early 2000s, despite the end of the original market contract. Into the beginning of the decade, the two companies appeared on the verge of deepening that relationship, with talks for T-online to acquire United Internet, and Dommermuth's elevation to head of T-online. In the end, however, the deal never materialized.

Instead, United Internet continued to go it alone, launching its own highly successful DSL-based Internet access service under the 1&1 brand in 2004. The new service grew quickly, and into the later years of the first decade of the 2000s had grown into Germany's second largest DSL provider, with more than 2.7 million customers.

WORLD LEADING INTERNET SERVICES GROUP IN THE 21ST CENTURY

United Internet's operations in Germany reached new heights in 2005 when the company agreed to acquire Web.de, the second largest web portal in the German market. The deal created a new subsidiary, United Internet Media, which now extended United Internet's reach to nearly half of the total German online market. The company also invested in the domain reseller market, acquiring InterNetX in Germany in 2005, and then Fasthosts in the United Kingdom in 2006.

United Internet also began to target a new advance in its DSL Internet operations. In late 2007, the company joined with Drisllisch AG to begin acquiring stakes in another major DSL provider in Germany, Freenet. By mid-2008, United Internet had joined the bidding war to acquire Freenet outright.

In the meantime, United Internet maintained its own organic growth, extending its operations into Switzerland and Belgium. In 2008, the company added Spain to its list, establishing a subsidiary there to roll out the range of 1&1 branded services. By then, United Internet's sales had grown to EUR 1.49 billion ($2.2 billion), with more than half coming from outside the German/Austrian market. Under Ralph Dommermuth, United Internet had successfully navigated the uncertain waters of the early Internet market, establishing itself as one of the world's leading Internet-related services groups.

M. L. Cohen

PRINCIPAL SUBSIDIARIES

1&1 Internet AG; 1&1 Internet Espana S.L.U.; 1&1 Internet Inc. (U.S.A.); 1&1 Internet Ltd. (U.K.); 1&1 Internet S.A.R.L. (France); 1&1 Internet Services (Philippines) Inc.; A1 Marketing Kommunikation und neue Medien GmbH; AdLINK Internet Media AB (Sweden); AdLINK Internet Media AG; AdLINK Internet Media N.V. (Belgium); Fasthosts Internet Ltd. (U.K.); GMX GmbH; GMX Internet Services Inc. (U.S.A.); InterNetX GmbH; MIP Multimedia Internet Park GmbH; United Internet Media AG; WEB.DE GmbH.

PRINCIPAL DIVISIONS

Products; Online Marketing.

PRINCIPAL COMPETITORS

T-online AG; Orange SA; Time Warner Inc.; Viacom Inc.; Centrica PLC; Groupe Cegetel; Terra Networks, S.A.

FURTHER READING

Boston, William, "United Internet-Europe's Hot Growth Companies," *Businessweek,* October 25, 2004.

O'Brien, Kevin J., "'Last Mile' Is Longest in German DSL Battle," *Forbes,* July 28, 2004.

Saunier, Fredric, "Unity in Europe," *Marketing Computers,* November 1992, p. 28.

"United Internet Acquires 80% of InternNetX," *RDSL Europe,* December 23, 2004.

"United Internet Buys Stake in Browser Game Provider E-Sport," *Telecompaper Europe,* December 27, 2006.

"United Internet Has Five Million Paying Customers," *Telecompaper Europe,* December 16, 2005.

"United Internet May Raise Freenet Bid if Debitel Buy Dropped," *Thomson Financial News,* April 27, 2008.

"United Internet Returns to Profit in 2002," *RDSL Europe,* March 21, 2003.

"United Internet Targets Break-Even by 2006 for 1+1," *RDSL Americas,* January 26, 2004.

"United Internet to Offer Mobile Phone Service," *Telecompaper Europe,* March 1, 2007.

"United Internet's Web Hosting Subsidiary to Rival Microsoft's E-mail Software," *Die Welt,* February 28, 2007.

Uzbekistan Airways National Air Company

41 A. Timur Street
Tashkent, 100061
Uzbekistan
Telephone: (998 71) 140 46 23
Web site: http://www.uzairways.com

State-Owned Company
Incorporated: 1992
Employees: 14,000
NAICS: 481111 Scheduled Passenger Air Transportation; 481112 Scheduled Freight Air Transportation; 481211 Nonscheduled Chartered Passenger Air Transportation; 488111 Air Traffic Control; 488119 Other Airport Operations

∎∎∎

Uzbekistan Airways National Air Company is the flag carrier of the Republic of Uzbekistan. It is also known as Uzbekistan Havo Yullary (hence the "HY" designation in its airline reservations code). Created a few months after Uzbekistan's September 1991 independence, the company inherited virtually all of the Soviet aviation assets in Uzbekistan, apart from aircraft production facilities. These included not just the airline, but operations at a dozen airports and an extensive maintenance unit. All of this was upgraded.

Thanks to its location, Uzbekistan has held a strategic position in global trade since the days of the ancient Silk Road. Aeroflot's Uzbek operation carried more than six million people in 1990, but after independence the airline's traffic settled to ap-

proximately two million passengers a year. Uzbekistan Airways operates an active fleet of more than 30 aircraft, more than half of them Western-made.

STRATEGIC LOCATION

Although carrying the flag of a relatively small country (2008 population: 27 million), Uzbekistan Airways has always manifested international ambitions. Perhaps this should not be surprising, given its location at the heart of the famed Silk Road.

The capital of Tashkent was a major hub for the Soviets before the end of the Soviet Union. Later, the government could count on a small, yet steady stream of hard currency from fees charged to foreign airlines for flying over its airspace, situated between East and West.

There were other commercial as well as cultural reasons for international carriers' interest in the region. Uzbekistan shares ethnic ties with the neighboring states of Azerbaijan, Kazakhstan, Kyrgyzstan, Turkmenistan, and Turkey. In addition to the airlines of these countries, Lufthansa AG began serving the area, catering to a small ethnic German population originally expelled from Russia by Joseph Stalin. Finally, Uzbekistan was home to a growing oil industry, although it at first had to rely on refineries in Russia to produce its aviation fuel.

INDEPENDENCE

After Uzbekistan became independent of the Soviet Union, it formed its own airline from the remnants of

COMPANY PERSPECTIVES

■

Uzbekistan Airways keeps a sound position on the international market and provides high quality competitive services. During the years of operation our company has been awarded the International fund for Aviation Safety Diploma and a Certificate from Airports International Association and "Euromarket-2000." We operate scheduled flights to more than forty cities of the world including America, Europe, Middle East, Southeast, Central Asia and the CIS. Uzbekistan Airways continues to establish long-term and reliable business contacts, to increase the number of countries where its aircraft flies to and to improve its services. It makes our company one of the world's dynamic airlines.

Aeroflot's local operation (one of 33 such units that had formed the monolithic Soviet carrier at its peak). Uzbekistan Airways National Air Company was officially signed into existence on January 28, 1992.

The company inherited virtually all of the Soviet aviation assets in Uzbekistan, apart from aircraft production facilities. This included not just the airline, but also airport operations, air traffic control, and an extensive maintenance unit. It also inherited a huge fleet, more than 100 planes, and an extensive network within the former Soviet Union. However, most of these flights were cut as the airline became independent, due to a lack of hard currency.

The group was profitable by the mid-1990s, when it had more than 11,000 employees. An official told *Aviation Week & Space Technology* that its international routes in particular helped it to earn a $7 million surplus in 1996. Even so, reports of government interest in possibly privatizing the airline later surfaced.

GROWING GLOBAL NETWORK

Reflecting the global scope of its ambition, the newly independent company was flying to London (Heathrow), Delhi, Karachi, Tel Aviv, Kuala Lumpur, and Beijing by the end of its first year. Frankfurt and Bangkok were added in 1993.

These routes were initially operated using Soviet airliners such as the Ilyushin Il-62M. The company received its first Western airliner, a leased Airbus A310, in June 1993. A second A310 joined the fleet in 1994 as

the route network expanded to Seoul, Athens, and Manchester. Uzbekistan Airways began operating Boeing 757 and 767 aircraft in 1996, placing these on long-haul international routes.

Eighty-five percent of the U.K. passengers were traveling on business—many of them continuing through to Delhi, India—a spokesperson told the *Times* (London), but ancient Uzbek cities such as Samarkand, Urghench, and Bukhara (all points on the airline's domestic network) were beginning to attract curious tourists. The airline was already operating a handful of charters from Japan.

By the mid-1990s the airline was flying to Athens and Amsterdam, the latter continuing on to New York. The company also soon established a hub at Sharjah in the United Arab Emirates, a fast-growing global trade center.

LOOKING WEST

In spite of a large and well-established maintenance unit of its own, the company turned to Lufthansa Technik for help when it received its first Airbus airliners. In 1997 Lufthansa agreed to help the airline develop the capacity for handling more of its own maintenance on its Airbus and Boeing aircraft.

In 1998 the maintenance department received European certification (JAR-145) to perform third-party work on Western-made airliners in 1998. The unit, previously known as Plant #243, became Uzbekistan Airways Technics a few years later.

The airline looked west for other advice as well. In a unique partnership, in the mid-1990s Uzbekistan Airways acquired a 40 percent stake in European Airways, a tiny U.K. carrier. This provided access to Western-style airline management expertise.

There were also partnerships closer to home. Uzbekistan Airways in late 1998 formed the "CIS Alliance" with Transaero, a small, privately owned Russian airline. The cooperation extended from coordinating routes to sharing maintenance tasks.

REBUILDING FLEET AND INFRASTRUCTURE

At the time of its independence, Uzbekistan's aviation infrastructure was inadequate for future growth. Some airports, including Tashkent, were too small and their runways too short to reliably accommodate large jets in the thin mountain air. The nation's outdated air traffic control equipment was soon upgraded, leapfrogging that of other former Soviet republics, but work on the

```
┌─────────────────────────────────────────────┐
│                                               │
│              KEY DATES                        │
│                   ◆                           │
│  ─────────────────────────────────────────   │
│  1992:  Newly independent Uzbekistan forms its own │
│         airline to take over local Aeroflot operation. │
│  1993:  Uzbekistan Airways begins to augment its │
│         fleet with Western-made aircraft.     │
│  1995:  The airline adds New York to expanding │
│         global route network.                 │
│  1998:  Uzbekistan's TAPO aircraft facility delivers │
│         the first Ilyushin Il-114 turboprop to the │
│         airline.                              │
│  2004:  An active fleet of more than 30 aircraft carries │
│         about two million passengers per year. │
│  2007:  Banking on expansion, the company places │
│         ambitious orders for new widebody aircraft. │
│                                               │
└─────────────────────────────────────────────┘
```

airports continued into the new millennium.

Only a fraction of the large fleet inherited from Aeroflot was put into commercial service by the new airline. It continued to fly locals on the smaller Antonov An-24 and Yakovlev Yak-40 aircraft as its new Airbuses plied the longer, international routes. Much of the Soviet-derived fleet was parked and scavenged for spare parts.

SOURCING AIRCRAFT AT HOME AND ABROAD

Uzbekistan had its own aircraft manufacturing plant, which dated to the Soviet era. In fact the country's president, Islam Karimov, had worked as a designer there. The factory, called the Tashkent Aircraft Production Organization, Named After Chkalov (TAPO), saw its orders disappear after the fall of the Soviet Union due to a lack of hard currency and a market preference for Western-made aircraft, which were perceived as safer and more efficient.

TAPO officials saw the Uzbek airline as a natural customer, but it took some time for the relationship to produce results. Finally, after eight years of development, in 1998 TAPO delivered to the carrier the first Ilyushin Il-114, a new, Soviet-designed twin-engine turboprop. Though assembled in Tashkent, most of the plane's components were imported from Russia, and the engines supplied by the Canadian unit of U.S. manufacturer Pratt & Whitney.

In July 1998 Uzbekistan Airways also added some Western-made regional jets (smaller airliners intended to replace turboprops on shorter hops), making it the first

in the Commonwealth of Independent States (CIS) to do so. The airline acquired three Avro RJ-85 Avroliners, each with a seating capacity of 85 people, from Aero International (Regional). These were placed into service on the regional routes most traveled by tourists.

A GROWING NETWORK

The network continued to expand as the airline added a third A310 in 1998 and a pair of Boeing 757s in 1999. Rome was among cities added in 2000, followed by Osaka the next year. Though passenger count fell from 1.8 million to about 1.6 million in 2001, Uzbekistan Airways enjoyed profits of $52 million, twice the previous year's figure.

Nevertheless, in the global aviation slowdown that followed the September 11, 2001 terrorist attacks on the United States, Uzbekistan Airways suspended some routes, such as its year-old service to New York (JFK) via Birmingham, England (this was relaunched in 2003). It temporarily shifted capacity from Europe to destinations within the CIS.

Additions to the growing international network tended to reflect fast-growing economies, such as Vietnam in 2003 (Ho Chi Minh City and Hanoi) and Shanghai in 2004. The airline also filled in the regional network with more stops in central Asia and the former Soviet Union. The airline began serving Cairo in 2007.

Uzbekistan Airways was still acquiring new aircraft to meet demand, and in 2004 it operated an active fleet of more than 30 planes, more than half of them modern, Western-made aircraft: five each of the Boeing 767 and 757, three Airbus A310s, and three RJ-85 regional jets. Traffic continued to hover at a little less than two million passengers a year.

AMBITIOUS PLANS

As in ancient days, Uzbekistan's central location continued to make it especially relevant to world trade. In August 2008 Korean Air's parent the Hanjin Group agreed to join the Uzbek airline in developing a new logistics center at Tashkent's Navoi International Airport. The partnership boosted Uzbekistan Airway's efforts to join the SkyTeam global alliance, of which Korean Air was a founding member, with the aim of associate status by 2009.

The airline was clearly banking on expansion. In May 2007 Uzbekistan Airlines ordered a pair of Boeing 787 Dreamliner aircraft, massive new long-haul planes (an extended version of the 767) capable of seating 290 passengers. The airline placed another important order for a half-dozen Airbus A320s in June 2007.

In August 2008, the company's director general, Valeriy Tyan, announced plans to acquire four more Boeing 767s within the next few years. These were substitutes for the two Boeing 787s, which were behind on their delivery schedule. The airline was also buying a half-dozen more Ilyushin Il-114s to replace its remaining Soviet-era Yakovlev Yak-40s to cater to international tourists on domestic routes.

Frederick C. Ingram

PRINCIPAL DIVISIONS

Uzaviatechsnab; Uzbekistan Airways Technics.

PRINCIPAL COMPETITORS

Lufthansa AG; Turkish Airlines Inc.; Aeroflot—Russian Airlines JSC; Air Astana JSC.

FURTHER READING

Anoshkin, Viktor, "Russia's Transaero, Uzbekistan Airways in Pact," *Reuters News,* December 19, 1997.

Blacklock, Mark, "Breaking Away," *Airline Business,* November 1993, pp. 36+.

Curphey, Marianne, "Uzbekis Re-Open the Silk Route," *Times* (London), December 2, 1993.

Guild, Sara, "Western Help Uzbek Style—Uzbekistan Airways/European Airlines," *Airline Business,* June 1, 1995, p. 18.

Jeziorski, Andrzej, "Lufthansa Signs Partnership with Uzbekistan," *Flight International,* March 26, 1997, p. 18.

Pain, Steve, "From Russia to NY Via Brum," *Birmingham Post* (U.K.), April 2, 2003, p. 20.

Proctor, Paul, "Uzbekistan Airways Rebuilds Its Central Asian Hub," *Aviation Week & Space Technology,* April 7, 1997, pp. 54+.

Sheppard, Ian, "AI(R) Achieves Breakthrough in Central Asia with RJ Avroliners," *Flight International,* July 16, 1998, p. 14.

———, "Central Asia's Rising Star," *Flight International,* August 27, 1997, p. 39.

"Under an Uzbek Sky," *Airfinance Journal,* October 2006, p. 48.

"Uzbek National Airline Head Rules Out 'Shock Therapy' in Privatization," *BBC Monitoring Central Asia,* January 6, 2001.

"Uzbekistan Airways Buys Two Boeing 787-8 Dreamliners," *UzReport.com,* May 31, 2007.

"Uzbekistan Airways Orders Six A320s," *UzReport.com,* June 28, 2007.

Winged Dynasties, movie, "Popular Science and Documentary Films Film Studio" Company, 2007.

Vanderbilt University Medical Center

1211 Medical Center Drive
Nashville, Tennessee 37232
U.S.A.
Telephone: (615) 322-5000
Fax: (615) 343-6388
Web site: http://www.mc.vanderbilt.edu

Private Affiliate of Vanderbilt University
Incorporated: 1874
Employees: 7,915
Operating Revenues: $2.04 billion (2007 est.)
NAICS: 611310 Colleges, Universities, and Professional
Schools

∎ ∎ ∎

Associated with Vanderbilt University in Nashville, Tennessee, Vanderbilt University Medical Center (VUMC) is a group of hospitals, clinics, outpatient centers, and schools of medicine and nursing. The VUMC includes the Vanderbilt University Hospital, offering more than 600 beds and the area's only Level 1 Trauma Center, Level 4 Neonatal Intensive Care Unit, and Level 3 Burn Unit; Monroe Carell Jr. Children's Hospital at Vanderbilt; Psychiatric Hospital at Vanderbilt; Vanderbilt Stallworth Rehabilitation Hospital, an 80-bed facility focusing on patients who have suffered stroke, head injuries, and other maladies requiring extensive rehabilitation; Vanderbilt Clinic, housing more than 100 ambulatory specialty practices; Vanderbilt-Ingram Cancer Center, Tennessee's only comprehensive cancer center; and the

Nashville Veterans Administration Medical Center, serving military veterans.

Education and research institutions associated with VUMC include the Vanderbilt University School of Medicine and Vanderbilt University School of Nursing; Ann and Roscoe R. Robinson Research Building and Preston Research Building, both dedicated to biomedical research; and the Annette and Irwin Eskind Biomedical Library, dedicated to medical care reference materials. VUMC boasts 50 fully endowed chairs and professorships. On the healthcare side, VUMC is regarded as one of the top hospitals in the United States, ranked 15th on *U.S. News and World Report*'s "America's Best Hospitals" in 2008. The publication also ranks the School of Medicine and School of Nursing within its top 20 listings.

19TH-CENTURY ORIGINS

VUMC was established in 1874 when the University of Nashville's School of Medicine was incorporated into Vanderbilt University. Even before Vanderbilt took shape, its founder, the Methodist Episcopal Church, was looking to include medical education. In 1858 the church established Shelby Medical College in Nashville to eventually provide medical education to a proposed "Central University." Due to the Civil War that broke out in 1861, Shelby closed its doors after just three years. It was not until 1872 that the Methodists revived their plans for Central University, and a year later shipping magnate Commodore Cornelius Vanderbilt provided a $1 million endowment to build the school. To honor its chief benefactor, Central University, which was chartered in 1872, changed its charter in 1873 to become Vanderbilt University. To replicate what it had previously in Shelby Medical College, the church added an existing school of medicine, established by the University of Nashville in 1851. Due to the merger, the 71 medical school graduates in 1875 were given the option of receiving diplomas from the University of Nashville or Vanderbilt. Most of them asked for diplomas from both.

Initially, as was customary for the time, the medical school was actually a private enterprise, owned and operated by the faculty, practicing physicians who received the tuition the students paid. The school was reorganized in 1895 and came under the auspices of the Vanderbilt University Board of Trust, and admission requirements were stiffened. Students had to at least have completed a high school education. In addition, laboratory work was added to the curriculum, which was now three six-month years in length. The number of months of instructions was increased to seven in 1898, and the number of years grew from three to four. Subsequently, requirements for admission were also stiffened: Applicants now had to have completed a full year of college work.

FLEXNER REPORT, 1910, CHANGES U.S. MEDICAL EDUCATION

Medical education in the United States changed dramatically following the 1910 release of the Flexner Report, issued by professional educator Abraham Flexner, who with funding from the Carnegie Foundation provided a critical assessment of American medical education. He argued for higher admission and graduation standards, and maintained that the country had too many shoddy schools turning out too many unqualified doctors. Almost overnight, about half the medical schools in the United States were either closed or merged. The changes Vanderbilt had already undertaken put it in good stead with the Flexner Report, which listed it as the best of Tennessee's medical schools. On the other hand, it lacked laboratory space and equipment and was in need of a full-time preclinical faculty. To address these and other issues, Vanderbilt supplied a

$4 million grant in 1919 and reorganized the Vanderbilt University School of Medicine.

Because it had originally been part of the University of Nashville, the medical school was a remote outpost in downtown Nashville, far from the Vanderbilt University campus. In 1920 a new dean of the School of Medicine, C. Canby Robinson, was appointed, and he lobbied for a reorganized school on the Vanderbilt campus. He succeeded in winning support for the idea, ground was broken in 1923, and two years later a new School of Medicine opened on campus as well as a building that housed the Vanderbilt University School of Nursing, which had been established in 1909 as part of Vanderbilt's liberal arts program. In addition to bricks and mortar, Dean Robinson worked to reshape the School of Medicine along the lines of what had been done in Baltimore, Maryland, at Johns Hopkins University, where a teaching institution was combined with an operating hospital, so that full-time teachers were intertwined with a clinical faculty. It was Dean Robinson who established the school's three original departments—medicine, surgery, and obstetrics and gynecology—as well as the initial laboratories in chemical, infectious disease, and physiological.

DEPRESSION ERA: NEW DEPARTMENTS ADDED

Dean Robinson resigned in 1928. Over the next dozen years more changes took place at VUMC. The Pediatrics department was added the same year as Robinson's departure. Radiology followed in 1936. The new medical center received its first addition in 1936, when a new corridor was erected to add more beds as well as space for the Gynecology, Obstetrics, and Pediatrics departments. During the 1930s VUMC also received one of its first major research grants, when in 1932 it was awarded $250,000 from the Rockefeller Foundation for clinical research. Vanderbilt garnered worldwide notice a year later for the research of Dr. Alfred Blalock on "blue baby syndrome," which led to cardiothoracic surgery for infants and was a stepping-stone for open heart surgery.

VUMC did its part during World War II, organizing a hospital unit that would be dispatched to Europe. Following the war, VUMC underwent a period of expansion. The department of Anesthesiology was established in 1945 shortly after the conflict came to an end. Work began on the Learned Laboratories in 1952, creating more space for graduate work, the final phases of the project completed in 1962. The first endowed chair of the medical school, the George W. Hale Professorship in Ophthalmology, was established in 1960. In that same year the Clinical Research Center was

KEY DATES

1874: Vanderbilt University assumes control of the University of Nashville's School of Medicine.
1895: School of Medicine is reorganized.
1925: New School of Medicine building opens.
1932: First major research grant is received from Carnegie Foundation.
1960: Clinical Research Center is established.
1971: Dr. Earl Sutherland wins Nobel Prize.
1985: Vanderbilt School of Nursing is integrated with Medical Center.
1992: Rehabilitation hospital opens.
1999: Alliance is forged with Meharry Medical College.
2003: New children's hospital opens.
2007: Vision 2020 is unveiled.

established using federal funds. A year later the Neonatology division was established, including a neonatal intensive care unit (NICU) that made its mark by becoming the first NICU in the United States to employ respiratory therapy for infants with damaged lungs.

Just as the Learned Laboratories added to VUMC's research space, the 1962 opening of a circular hospital wing, dubbed the Round Wing, increased patient care space. More additions to VUMC were to follow in the 1960s. The Joe and Howard Werthan Building opened in 1964, expanding Medical Center North while adding more laboratory space and a new library. Three years later, Medical Center South was renovated, and the Zerfoss Student Health Center opened.

VANDERBILT CHILDREN'S HOSPITAL OPENS: 1970

Vanderbilt Children's Hospital was established in 1970, leading to an emphasis on pediatric care at VUMC. The decade saw some other major advances for the organization as well. VUMC's research efforts were validated in 1971 when Vanderbilt's Dr. Earl Wilbur Sutherland Jr. won a Nobel Prize in Physiology or Medicine for his discoveries related to how hormones regulate body functions. A dormitory would be named in his honor at Vanderbilt as well as a prize for achievement in research awarded annually to a Vanderbilt faculty member, established in 1976, two years after Sutherland's death. The 1970s also brought the start of an extended building program that would last until the end of the

century. In 1977 the first building that resulted from this effort was Rudolph A. Light Hall, which greatly increased the number of classrooms and laboratories for the School of Medicine.

The start of the 1980s was marked by the opening of the twin-towered Vanderbilt University Hospital, which included space for the Vanderbilt Children's Hospital. In 1985 the Child and Adolescent Psychiatric Hospital was added, and in that same year, the Vanderbilt School of Nursing finally became part of VUMC. By the end of the decade the undergraduate nursing program was phased out and the school was exclusively a graduate program aimed at advanced level nurses. A bridge program, however, brought in students from non-nursing backgrounds and provided a course of work that led to enrollment in the graduate program. Other innovative programs offered by the School of Nursing included a Ph.D. in nursing science, introduced in 1993, and a partnership with Vanderbilt's School of Engineering to develop a program that led to dual degrees: an M.S.N. in nursing and a Ph.D. in biomedical engineering.

The Vanderbilt Clinic, a new outpatient center, was completed in 1988. A year later two more facilities opened: the Kim Dayani Human Performance Center and Medical Research Building I, later renamed the Ann and Roscoe Robinson Medical Research Building. The 1980s were also noteworthy because they produced VUMC's second Nobel laureate, Dr. Stanley Cohen, who shared the 1986 prize with longtime collaborator Dr. Rita Levi-Montalcini of Italy for the discovery of epidermal growth factors.

LATE CENTURY EXPANSION

The expansion of the VUMC footprint continued in the final decade of the 20th century. The Stallworth Rehabilitation Hospital, a joint enterprise with Health-South, was dedicated in 1992, adding a freestanding 80-bed hospital dedicated to rehabilitative medicine. It also included a therapeutic courtyard, treatment gyms, and a regulation-size gymnasium. A second medical research building was dedicated in 1993, later taking the name the Frances Williams Preston Building. The Annette and Irwin Eskind Biomedical Library opened in 1994.

The end of the century brought new challenges to VUMC as it did the entire medical profession in the United States. The rise of health maintenance organizations and pressure from both private insurers and the government had a significant impact on patient care. To cut costs, VUMC looked to improve efficiencies while not jeopardizing care. The Vanderbilt Medical Group was formed to reorganize faculty physicians, and satellite operations were established in various outside communities. VUMC researchers also had to contend with more competition for government grants, and responded by increasingly turning to private sources of research funds, including from entrepreneurs.

In order to expand its purview, VUMC continued to seek out partnerships. In 1999 it agreed to team up with Meharry Medical College, a well respected Nashville black academic health center, to share training and research. VUMC also took over the management of Meharry's Metro General Hospital. Four years later the relationship between the two institutions deepened with the establishment of the Vanderbilt-Meharry Development Center for AIDS Research, supported by a three-year, $750,000-a-year grant from the National Institutes of Health.

VUMC entered the new century facing financial concerns, due mostly to reduced payments from Medicare and TennCare, established by Tennessee in 1993 as an alternative to Medicaid, which had suffered extreme cuts. The financial situation became difficult enough that in early 2000 VUMC had to implement staff reductions to cut costs in an effort to close a budget shortfall. While it was an inauspicious beginning to the new century, VUMC over the next few years went on to enjoy one of its greatest growth spurts, with a much improved financial picture. The Medical Center's budget, which totaled $811 million in 1998, was projected to reach $1.4 billion by 2008. In fact, the budget reached the $2 billion level in 2007.

A wave of construction projects was undertaken in the early 2000s. Medical Research Building III was completed in 2002, followed by a new children's hospital, which opened in 2003. Other projects included the Vivarium, providing additional space for VUMC's fast-growing animal-based research program; the Vanderbilt-Ingram Cancer Center; the Bill Wilkerson Center, an addition to the south end of Medical Center East; and the Muskuloskeletal Institute, a 96,000-square-foot building. Moreover, another $210 million was earmarked in 2002 for the renovation and modernization of existing facilities. In 2004 plans were unveiled to build a third tower to the Vanderbilt University Hospital, a project that would be completed in phases over the next several years and with other work represented a total overhauling of the hospital. Rather than construct a new hospital from scratch at a projected cost of $1 billion, VUMC opted for a $300 million price tag for expansion and rebuilding.

In 2007 VUMC unveiled its "Vision 2020" strategy for growth over the next dozen years. Due to the new construction projects, available space on the VUMC campus became limited, leading VUMC to also adopt a "focused growth strategy" to take full advantage of all of its sites in the Nashville area. In 2007 VUMC launched plans to develop a second Medical Center campus at its 100 Oak Malls site. Clinics began to open there the following year, and a fifth medical research building also took shape. Additional research space was especially needed because of the strong growth in VUMC's efforts in that area in recent years. The Medical Center increased the amount of research dollars it received from $120 million in 1998 to $360 million in 2007. During the five years from 1999 to 2003, in fact, VUMC enjoyed a higher annual growth rate than any school in the country, including Duke University and the University of California at Los Angeles. Other building projects in the opening phase of Vision 2020 included an expansion of the Monroe Carell Jr. Children's Hospital, a new main hospital lobby, and renovation of the radiology unit.

Ed Dinger

PRINCIPAL SUBSIDIARIES

Monroe Carell Jr. Children's Hospital at Vanderbilt; Psychiatric Hospital at Vanderbilt; Vanderbilt Stallworth Rehabilitation Hospital; Vanderbilt University Hospital; Vanderbilt-Ingram Cancer Center.

PRINCIPAL COMPETITORS

Baptist Hospital; Chattanooga-Hamilton County Hospital Authority; HCA Inc.

FURTHER READING

Boerner, Craig, "Jacobson Outlines Bold Vision for VUMC," *Reporter* (Vanderbilt University Medical Center), March 8, 2007.

Campbell, Doug, "Growth Key to Future: Jacobson," *Reporter* (Vanderbilt University Medical Center), February 25, 2000.

Ferguson, Carrie, "Meharry Board Approves Plan to Join with VU," *Tennessean*, January 2, 1999, p. 7B.

Govern, Paul, "Growth Is Key to Success: Jacobson," *Reporter* (Vanderbilt University Medical Center), February 8, 2002.

Snyder, Bill, "Jacobson Outlines Vision 2020," *Reporter* (Vanderbilt University Medical Center), April 11, 2008.

———, "TennCare Cash Crunch Pushes Vanderbilt Hospital to Cut 51 Jobs," *Tennessean*, January 14, 2000, p. 1E.

———, "VUMC Has Plans for Big Expansion," *Tennessean*, February 22, 2000, p. 1B.

"Vanderbilt University Medical Center," *The Tennessee Encyclopedia of History and Culture,* http://www. tennesseeencyclopedia.net.

Wood, Wayne, "Vanderbilt Medical School Celebrates 125th Anniversary," *Reporter* (Vanderbilt University Medical Center), October 20, 2000.

Vita Food Products Inc.

2222 West Lake Street
Chicago, Illinois 60612
U.S.A.
Telephone: (312) 738-4500
Fax: (312) 738-3215
Web site: http://www.vitafoodproducts.com

Public Company
Incorporated: 1928
Employees: 178
Sales: $49.95 million (2007)
Stock Exchanges: Over the Counter (OTC)
Ticker Symbol: VFPI
NAICS: 311999 All Other Miscellaneous Food Manufacturing

■ ■ ■

Based in Chicago, Vita Food Products Inc. is a leading provider of seafood and specialty foods, with a separate division dedicated to each category. The company markets its offerings nationwide. Its customer base includes country clubs, cruise lines, food brokers, food-service companies, hotels, restaurants, and supermarkets.

Subsidiary Vita Specialty Foods makes and distributes products such as salad dressings, honey, marinades, steak sauces, and cooking sauces under such brand names as Virginia Brand, Oak Hill Farms, Scorned Woman, Jim Beam, and Budweiser.

Vita Food Products' seafood business markets pickled herring, nova salmon, and lox, as well as complementary products such as cocktail sauce, cream cheese with salmon, and horseradish, shrimp cocktail, and tartar sauces. The company's seafood products are marketed under the brand names Elf, Grand Isle, and Vita.

FORMATIVE YEARS: 1911–59

Although Vita Food Products was officially incorporated in 1928, its roots stretch back a few years earlier, when Victor H. Heller and his brother, R. George Heller, started the business in 1911. After Victor left his native Czechoslovakia for the United States in 1907, he and R. George established a delicatessen in the Yorkville area of Manhattan.

The brothers developed a niche as purveyors of pickled herring, a small, oily fish, which they first sold from barrels. After opening two additional locations and developing a reputation for their herring, the Hellers began packaging herring in cardboard containers and glass jars and selling the fish to other stores. Their success ultimately led them to give up the delicatessen and focus solely on selling packaged seafood.

In 1928 Victor Heller was named president of Vita Food Products. Midway through the 1930s, the company leased an eight-story building from Ideal Investing Inc. at 644-54 Greenwich Street in New York. Special alterations were made for Vita Food Products, including the installation of a large refrigeration plant.

In October 1944, Vita Food Products was one of seven smoked fish processing firms that received a collective 860 summons from New York Sheriff John J. McCloskey Jr. The companies were charged with violating the ceiling prices established by the Office of Price Administration (OPA). Specifically, they were alleged to have sold a variety of smoked fish, including chubs, salmon, sablefish, whitefish, lox, and kippered salmon, at an average of 25 percent over the OPA's ceiling price.

Besides Vita Food Products, the companies included Hellman's Smoked Fish Corp., Horowitz Brothers, Oxenberg Bros., Ten Eyck Smoked Fish Corp., Gem Smoked Fish Co., and Banner Smoked Fish Corp., all of which had been sued by the OPA in April 1943 for $4.07 million.

Of national importance, the case involved the largest number of prosecutions brought against a group of food wholesalers at one time in the Manhattan and Brooklyn Magistrates Courts. In December 1944, Vita Food Products was fined $200 for eight smoked fish sales that violated the OPA's price ceiling.

A number of noteworthy developments took place at Vita Food Products in the 1950s. In 1956 the company made a secondary stock offering of 69,480 common shares, which it priced at $8.38 each. The company rounded out the decade by elevating Victor Heller to the role of chairman in 1959. In addition, expansion was furthered by the acquisition of Mother's Food Products Inc.

EARLY GROWTH AND EXPANSION: 1960–68

In early 1961, plans were underway for the 73-acre Lake Street industrial district in Chicago, where Vita Food Products was one of several companies that had new facilities in the works. The area had ample access to transportation and was bordered by Lake and Leavitt streets, California Avenue, and the Chicago and North Western railway.

In July 1962, Vita Food Products broke ground on a 60,000-square-foot, one-story food processing plant in Chicago. Located at Lake Street and Oakley Avenue, the facility cost roughly $1 million and was a replacement for an existing processing plant at 659 West Lake Street.

Vita Food Products sales were roughly $20 million in 1963. That year, the company acquired Chicago

Smoked Fish Co., which had been founded in 1900, and launched what would become a very well-known advertising campaign featuring a character called the "Herring Maven," the latter being a Yiddish word for *expert*.

With an objective of introducing herring, which historically had been an ethnic food, to a broader audience, the Herring Maven commercials were designed by advertising agency Solow/Wexton Inc. With an initial budget of $50,000 for radio spots in the New York area, the commercials featured Allen Swift, "man of a thousand voices."

The Herring Maven campaign evolved further in 1965, when Vita Food Products ran an ad in the Sunday *New York Times Magazine* that included a free Herring Maven kit offer. Within two days, almost 780 people sent $1.10 to the company to receive the kit, which included a button that said "I'm a Herring Maven," along with a herring fork.

By 1966 Vita Food Products' sales had grown to approximately $40 million. On December 31, 1967, cofounder and Chairman Victor H. Heller died at the age of 81 in Phoenix, Arizona's Biltmore Hotel, where he was vacationing. R. George Heller remained active in the company's leadership as vice-chairman. Heading into the late 1960s, Aaron Gilman served as the president of Vita Food Products.

By 1967 Vita Food Products was receiving approximately 42 million pounds of fish at the Port of New York each year. That year, the company made plans to leave New York City for New Jersey or a nearby suburb. To prevent the loss of some 500 jobs, the city's Department of Marine and Aviation agreed to build a 200,000-square-foot facility on a roughly ten-acre site in the Bronx's Hunts Point Market, which the company agreed to lease for 20 years.

OWNERSHIP CHANGES: 1969–82

Vita Food Products was acquired by Brown & Williamson Tobacco Corp. in early 1969. The company was made a subsidiary of Brown & Williamson, which itself was owned by British-American Tobacco Co.

Within six years, Vita Food Products' Herring Maven radio commercials had become so popular that the Maven received fan mail at Vita Food Products' headquarters. In 1969 the company earmarked $500,000 for the spots, which had been successful at increasing sales. At this time the commercials ran on 14 New York radio stations, as well as 40 others throughout the United States.

In 1969 Vita Food Products' humorous commercials featured the Maven speaking to his son on a

KEY DATES

1911: After establishing a delicatessen in the Yorkville area of Manhattan, Victor H. Heller and his brother, R. George Heller, start selling pickled herring to stores.

1928: The Heller brothers incorporate Vita Food Products.

1963: The company launches its famous "Herring Maven" advertising campaign.

1967: Victor Heller dies at age 81.

1969: Brown & Williamson Tobacco Corp. acquires Vita Food Products.

1978: Vita Food Products is acquired by Dean Foods.

1982: Clark L. Feldman and Stephen D. Rubin acquire Vita Food Products.

1997: The company completes an initial public offering of its common stock, netting $4.1 million.

2000: The Virginia Honey Company Inc. is acquired.

2002: Halifax Group Inc. is acquired.

2007: The company announces it will voluntarily delist from the American Stock Exchange.

2008: After 25 years with Vita Food Products, Rubin retires but remains chairman emeritus.

wide range of topics, including poetry, sex, the theater, movies, and of course, herring. However, the advice suddenly stopped when Brown & Williamson decided to pull the Maven off the airwaves that year.

Despite the Herring Maven's exit, Vita Food Products continued to run radio advertisements. In 1971 four of its commercials landed the company in hot water. Actress Katharine Hepburn filed a $4 million lawsuit against Vita Food Products, as well as Brown & Williamson and advertising agency Solow/Wexton, for imitating her voice without permission.

In 1972 Vita Food Products combined five separate New York facilities—two in Brooklyn and three in Manhattan—into one. The operations were relocated to the 200,000-square-foot facility in the Bronx's Hunts Point Market, where Vita Food Products leased property from the city at an annual cost of $750,000.

In 1976 Vita Food Products relocated its headquarters from New York to an 18,000-square-foot leased location in Greenwich, Connecticut's Largo

Building. Headquarters operations had previously been situated within the Hunts Point Market facility. After announcing plans to cease all operations at Hunts Point by October, the company leased a 15,000-square-foot distribution center in Brooklyn's Greenpoint area.

At this time, Edwin F. Lewis was serving as president of Vita Food Products, which was generating annual sales of about $50 million. Beyond New York, the company had established operations in several other U.S. cities, including Billingham, Washington; Chicago; Dutch Harbor, Alabama; Newark, New Jersey; Philadelphia; and St. Louis, Missouri.

Brown & Williamson sold Vita Food Products to Dean Foods in 1978. However, another ownership change quickly followed when Clark L. Feldman and Stephen D. Rubin bought Vita Food Products in March 1982.

Under Brown & Williamson and Dean Foods, Vita Food Products had fallen from glory. Brown & Williamson had sold five of the company's plants, leaving only one facility. From a high of $67 million, sales continued to decline while Dean Foods owned the company, reaching approximately $10 million by the time Feldman and Rubin entered the picture.

BROADER FOCUS: 1983–2008

During the early 1980s, Vita Food Products generated roughly 65 percent of its sales in the eastern United States. In the North and Midwest, customers of Scandinavian descent contributed to strong sales in those regions, which collectively accounted for around 25 percent of the company's sales. The West Coast was Vita Food Products' smallest regional market, accounting for 10 percent of sales. At this time, the company competed against Noon Hour and Lasco, among others.

Feldman and Rubin quickly began infusing new life into Vita Food Products. This came in the form of many new product offerings, including cocktail, horseradish, and tartar sauces. In mid-1983 the owners introduced crab cocktail, seafood spread, and smoked whitefish.

In addition to new products, a more contemporary version of the Herring Maven was slated to return to the airwaves after 14 years of radio silence. Allen Swift was once again hired to provide the Maven's voice, with ads beginning in the New York market. By 1983 Vita Food Products sales had improved slightly, reaching approximately $12 million.

By the mid-1980s Vita Food Products claimed it was the largest herring and smoked fish processor in the United States. To maintain its position, the company had devoted roughly $350,000 annually to advertising efforts. In 1984 this figure increased to approximately $1 million.

During the early 1990s, Vita Food Products' workforce included approximately 100 employees. Several important developments occurred during the middle of the decade. In September 1996, the company was reincorporated in Nevada and merged with V-F Acquisition Inc.

Vita Food Products continued to unveil new offerings during the mid- to late 1990s, including a salmon burger in November 1996 and breaded, frozen Vita Salmon Nuggets in 1997. On January 23 of that year, the company completed an initial public offering of its common stock, netting $4.1 million. Strong salmon product sales and an expanding customer base helped Vita Food Products end the 1990s with revenues of $22.97 million in 1999, up from $22.30 million the previous year.

With Stephen Rubin still at the helm as president and CEO, and Clark Feldman serving as executive vice-president, Vita Food Products' sales continued to rise as the company entered the new millennium, reaching $25.13 million in 2000. In August of that year, the company acquired The Virginia Honey Company Inc., which had operations in Inwood, West Virginia, and Berryville, Virginia, in a deal with Terry W. Hess. The addition of Virginia Honey allowed Vita Food Products to beef up its product line with honey, salad dressings, jellies, jams, and sauces.

Another major deal unfolded in November 2002, when Atlanta, Georgia-based Halifax Group Inc. was acquired, adding a number of licensed items to Vita Food Products' lineup, including Jim Beam steak sauce, marinade, and barbeque sauce; Oak Hill Farms salad dressings and marinade; The Drambuie Gourmet Collection; and a line of food products marketed under the Scorned Woman brand name.

Vita Food Products' sales fell from $50.93 million in 2003 to $48.76 million in 2004, when the company recorded a consolidated net loss of $2.72 million. Sluggish sales to the retail trade, which represented virtually all of Vita Food Products' business, prompted the company to begin focusing on the institutional market, such as restaurants and hotels. The company hoped to generate as much as 25 percent of its business from the segment within two or three years.

In mid-2006, Vita Food Products began making four Budweiser-brand barbecue sauces under a licensing agreement with Anheuser-Busch. In August of that year, CFO and COO Clifford K. Bolen was named president and CEO. Rubin remained involved with the company as chairman.

Several important developments unfolded as Vita Food Products headed into the later years of the first decade of the 2000s. In May 2007, Rubin was named chairman emeritus, and David Lipson was appointed chairman. When the number of the company's shareholders dipped below 300, the company announced that it would voluntarily delist from the American Stock Exchange in late November.

After 25 years with Vita Food Products, Stephen Rubin announced his official retirement in January 2008, but retained his role as chairman emeritus. The company headed into 2009 under new leadership, but with nearly a century of experience in the food products industry.

Paul R. Greenland

PRINCIPAL SUBSIDIARIES

Halifax Group Inc.; The Virginia Honey Company Inc.; Vita Specialty Foods Inc.

PRINCIPAL DIVISIONS

Seafood; Specialty Foods.

PRINCIPAL COMPETITORS

Kraft Foods Inc.; R.A.B. Food Group LLC; Sioux Honey Association.

FURTHER READING

"Budweiser Brand Licensed to Area Firm for Barbecue Sauces," *Chicago Tribune,* May 9, 2006.

"Drive Stepped Up on Black Market; Sheriff's Office Discloses the Results of City Campaign Against Wholesalers," *New York Times,* December 20, 1944.

Murphy, H. Lee, "Vita Enters Food Service Biz, As Sales Fall and Costs Rise, Firm Seeks Growth from Colleges, Hotels," *Crain's Chicago Business,* July 18, 2005.

Robinson, Douglas, "Loss of 500 Jobs Averted by City; Vita Signs Lease in Bronx—Borden Going with 600," *New York Times,* November 9, 1967.

"Victor H. Heller Headed Vita Food; Fish Product Company's Co-founder Dies at 81," *New York Times,* January 1, 1968.

"Vita Looks to Herring Maven," *New York Times,* June 25, 1983.

Woodbridge Holdings
Corporation

2200 West Cypress Creek Road
Fort Lauderdale, Florida 33304-1825
U.S.A.
Telephone: (954) 940-4950
Fax: (954) 940-4960
Web site: http://www.woodbridgeholdings.com

Public Company
Incorporated: 1982 as Levitt Corporation
Employees: 125
Sales: $415.9 million (2007)
Stock Exchanges: New York
Ticker Symbol: WDG
NAICS: 551112 Offices of Other Holding Companies

■ ■ ■

Woodbridge Holdings Corporation is a New York Stock Exchange–listed investment company based in Fort Lauderdale, Florida, primarily dealing in real estate ventures. Through subsidiary Core Communities, LLC, the company is involved in master-planned community development in the southeastern United States. Its main projects are St. Lucie West and Tradition Florida, both in Florida, and Tradition Hilton Head, located in South Carolina. Another subsidiary, Cypress Creek Capital, is a real estate investment management company focusing on Florida commercial income-producing properties. Woodbridge also owns a 31 percent stake in Blugreen Corporation, which develops and acquires vacation ownership projects. In addition, Woodbridge is interested in diversifying beyond real estate, expressing a desire to acquire or invest in middle-market companies in other industries through its private equity affiliate, Snapper Creek Equity Management, LLC. Until May 2008, Woodbridge was known as Levitt Corporation.

FORMATION OF LEVITT
CORPORATION IN FLORIDA: 1982

While the predecessor to Woodbridge Holdings was incorporated in Florida as Levitt Corporation in 1982, the roots of the company reach further back and are inextricably bound to one of the legendary names in the homebuilding industry: Levitt and Sons, the company responsible for Levittown, the world's first mass-produced suburb. While Woodbridge prefers to focus on its connections to Levitt Corporation's owner, BankAtlantic, and trace its lineage through that branch, in truth the history of Woodbridge Holdings contains within it the dramatic arc of an iconic American company: the rise and fall of Levitt and Sons.

Like many histories of celebrated American companies, Levitt and Sons is an immigrant's tale. It began with a poor rabbi, Louis Levitt, who fled Russia and came to the United States in the 1800s. His German-born wife, Nellie, gave birth to a son named Abraham in 1880 in the Williamsburg section of Brooklyn, New York. Because the family was poor, Abraham had to leave school at the age of ten to help support the family through odd jobs. The young man was also an avid reader, however, and at the age of 20, despite a lack of formal education, he was able to pass the New York State Regents examination and enroll in the New York University Law School. After graduation

A diversified holding company with interests in master-planned community development, the vacation ownership industry, income producing real estate investment, and expanding to include investments in middle market operating companies.

he was admitted to the New York State Bar in 1903 and began practicing real estate law in New York City.

Abraham Levitt also married and began raising a family. He had two sons, William Jaird, the eldest, and Alfred Stuart Levitt, five years younger. In 1929 he took control of some unfinished house projects on land in Rockville Centre on Long Island and encouraged his sons to take advantage of the existing building crews to finish the homes. Hence, he formed a construction company his two sons called Levitt and Sons, Inc. While Abraham Levitt provided the legal underpinning and gravitas, William, just 22 at the time, served as president and became the driving force and public face of the firm. Less appreciated were the contributions of Alfred, vice-president of design, who was responsible for the house and community designs that were a key to the company's success.

Although Levitt and Sons would become synonymous with affordable housing, the company started out as a builder of upper-middle-class homes. The first Levitt house, in fact, was a six bedroom, two bathroom Tudor-style home that sold for $14,000, a far from modest price in 1929. All told, the company sold about 600 of these higher-end homes in the early 1930s, despite the Great Depression. More of these types of homes were to follow on Long Island and Westchester County in the 1930s.

GOVERNMENT CONTRACT, 1941, HELPS LEVITT REFINE BUILDING TECHNIQUES

Levitt and Sons began laying the groundwork for the mass production of homes in 1941 when it won a government contract to build 2,350 housing units in Norfolk, Virginia, needed to house defense workers as the U.S. economy geared up to support the military effort of World War II. As a result, the company learned some valuable lessons on how to streamline the house-building process. For example, the houses were slab-based, eliminating basements to dramatically speed up construction time.

William Levitt left the company to serve in the Navy Seabees during World War II. He became convinced that after the war there would be pent-up demand for low-cost housing and millions of veterans would be able to afford to buy houses through government loans made available to them for their service. Back home his father and brother were already acquiring land, about 1,000 acres used for growing potatoes, in Nassau County, enough land to accommodate a planned community of 6,000 low-cost homes that would take the name Levittown. Ground was broken in July 1947 and the development began to take shape. More land was acquired, 7,000 acres in all, and by the end of 1951 about 17,000 homes were built. At the height of construction, specialized teams completed 36 houses each day in the Long Island community.

More developments on Long Island, and in Pennsylvania and New Jersey, were to follow in the post–World War II building boom. The Levitt family also fell out during this time. The brothers went their separate ways in 1954 with Alfred engaged in other housing and apartment developments until his death in 1966. (Abraham Levitt had passed away four years earlier.) Left in charge of Levitt and Sons, William Levitt took the company public in 1960. The era of large tracts of land being available near large cities was over, however, forcing Levitt to shift gears. He took on smaller projects, and decentralized his authority to add developments in Chicago and Washington, D.C., as well as Puerto Rico and France.

ITT ACQUIRES LEVITT & SONS: 1967

In 1967 William Levitt sold Levitt and Sons to International Telephone & Telegraph Corporation (ITT) for a reported $92 million, leaving Levitt an extremely wealthy man. The bulk of his fortune was in the form of ITT stock, however, and rather than cash it in, in order to save on taxes, he used it as collateral for loans he took out to build subdivisions overseas. A ten-year non-compete agreement prevented him from developing projects in the United States. When the price of ITT stock plummeted in the early 1970s, losing 90 percent of its value, Levitt's stock was seized by Chase Manhattan Bank. He went into debt and attempted to revive his fortunes by building new housing projects in the United States after his non-compete agreement expired, but for the rest of his life William Levitt's finances were little more than a house of cards, as he moved money from project to project, no longer considered a good credit risk. Eventually he was forbidden from doing

KEY DATES

1929: Levitt and Sons, Inc., is founded.
1947: Company breaks ground on Levittown, New York, development.
1960: Company goes public.
1967: Levitt and Sons is sold to ITT and renamed Levitt Corporation.
1978: Starrett Corporation acquires Levitt.
1999: BankAtlantic Development Corp. acquires Levitt.
2003: Levitt is spun off as public company.
2007: Levitt files for Chapter 11 bankruptcy protection.
2008: Levitt is renamed Woodbridge Holdings Corporation.

business in his native state of New York. On the verge of bankruptcy, William Levitt died in 1984 from kidney failure at the age of 86.

After ITT acquired Levitt and Sons, the name was changed to Levitt Corporation, which was led by William Levitt's handpicked successor, Richard Wasserman. The company continued to build single-family homes, along with factory-built modular units, townhouses, and mobile homes, as well as becoming heavily involved in Florida land sales. Sales totaled $300 million in fiscal 1971, but the ITT subsidiary fell on hard times in 1972 due to a downturn in construction, which triggered the falling ITT stock prices that proved so devastating for William Levitt. ITT also had to contend with a federal antitrust lawsuit, and in 1974 it was ordered to divest some of its assets, which would include Levitt Corporation. For the next four years the company languished in receivership, its assets pared away until Starrett Corporation acquired what remained for $30 million in 1978.

Best known as the company that built the Empire State Building, Starrett was established in Chicago in 1922 as Starrett Brothers & Eken, a pioneer in skyscraper construction. The company went bankrupt during the Great Depression and was reorganized as Starrett Corporation in New Jersey in 1936. Following World War II, the company was heavily involved in the construction of large residential complexes in New York City for Metropolitan Life Insurance Company, including such notable developments as Manhattan's Stuyvesant Town and Peter Cooper Village.

HEADQUARTERS MOVED TO BOCA RATON: 1981

Under Starrett, Levitt moved its headquarters to Florida in 1979. Making its home in Boca Raton in 1981 it was incorporated in Florida a year later. A homebuilding slump in the early 1980s caused by a recession crippled Starrett, and it was Levitt that helped to keep the parent company afloat. In 1982 Levitt contributed two-thirds of Starrett's $44 million in revenues. In need of more funds, Starrett sold a 20 percent stake in Levitt in 1984 through a public offering of stock, resulting in an American Stock Exchange listing for Levitt. In that same year, Levitt began offering a new line of houses aimed at first-time buyers that proved very popular and spurred a turnaround. In 1987 Levitt generated more than $100 million in sales, and two years later Starrett was able to reacquire the 20 percent interest it had previously sold off.

Levitt remained a major contributor to Starrett in the 1990s when the subsidiary focused on building subdivisions along the southwestern and southeastern coasts of Florida and the San Juan, Puerto Rico, area, targeting for the most part an older demographic. The emphasis on Florida was perhaps a hasty move, given that the affluent Northeast where Levitt had made its mark continued to provide opportunities for such companies as Toll Brothers Inc. of Philadelphia. In Florida, on the other hand, Levitt was just one of many builders looking to develop "active adult communities" for the over-55 market. Nevertheless, the company remained profitable.

In 1997 Starrett sold Levitt to a New York investment firm. A year later the new owners put the business on the block again and in September 1999 Levitt was sold for $21 million to BankAtlantic Development Corp., the real estate unit of Fort Lauderdale, Florida-based BankAtlantic Bancorp Inc. BankAtlantic grew out of Atlantic Federal, established in 1952 as a single branch bank located in downtown Fort Lauderdale. The bank expanded over the years and was reorganized as BankAtlantic in 1987. Under the leadership of Chairman and Chief Executive Officer Alan B. Levan, BankAtlantic overcame the savings and loan crisis of the late 1980s and began to diversify in the 1990s, adding securities brokerage and commercial leasing subsidiaries. It also became involved in real estate development, forming BankAtlantic Development Corp., through which in 1997 it acquired Core Communities, LLC, developer of master-planned communities. BankAtlantic was well familiar with Levitt, having served as its banker for a number of years. BankAtlantic Development's president, John E. Abdo, had also been friends with Levitt's CEO, Elliott Wiener, since 1981.

Under new ownership, Levitt tripled sales in three years and also in 2002 acquired a 40 percent stake in Blue Green Corp., marketer of resort and golf communities. Investors, however, were not especially enthusiastic about BankAtlantic's ownership of Levitt Corporation, which put a damper on the price of BankAtlantic's stock. To address this concern and provide Levitt with the opportunity to raise capital for ongoing growth, BankAtlantic spun off Levitt in a tax-free transaction in 2003. The news brought an immediate 12 percent increase in the price of the stock of the parent company, which was seen as returning to its traditional roots.

With Levan serving as CEO even as he continued to run BankAtlantic, Levitt hoped to reestablish the Levitt and Sons subsidiary as a national builder. Unfortunately, when the housing boom in south Florida came to an end in 2006, the company faced mounting difficulties and began defaulting on its loans. To lower overhead, the company cut jobs, and then in September 2007, as it struggled to reorganize its growing debt due to a credit crunch, Levitt and Sons suspended building. Another Levan-controlled company, BFC Financial Corp., Levitt's controlling shareholder, attempted a fiscal rescue, but Levitt's collapsing stock price threatened to take BFC down with it, and BFC was forced to back away. Levitt then attempted to renegotiate loans with its five primary lenders, and when that too failed, the company had no choice but to file for Chapter 11 bankruptcy protection in November 2007.

WOODBRIDGE NAME TAKEN: 2008

On the same day as its filing, Levitt Corporation deconsolidated Levitt and Sons, removing the name from its books. Levan announced that the company would consider selling all or part of Levitt's assets, but court documents filed in June 2008 indicated that Levitt and Sons would not be reorganized. Rather it would be liquidated if the bankruptcy judge allowed. A month earlier Levitt asked its shareholders to change its name, to further divorce the company from the once-proud Levitt name. The request was approved and Levitt Corporation now became Woodbridge Holdings Corporation, a switch intended to reflect the change in direction the company was taking, which would include "acquisitions and investments both within and outside the real estate industry," Levan explained in a prepared statement.

Woodbridge settled claims from creditors of Levitt and Sons, agreeing to pay $12.5 million plus interest. As part of the effort to take the company in a new direction, Woodbridge engineered a one-for-five reverse split of its common stock in September 2008, a move that increased the share price to maintain a place on the New York Stock Exchange while making the stock a more viable investment for institutional and other investors. The decks cleared, Woodbridge looked to embark on the next leg of its journey.

Ed Dinger

PRINCIPAL SUBSIDIARIES

Core Communities, LLC; Cypress Creek Capital.

PRINCIPAL COMPETITORS

A.G. Spanos Companies; Caribe Homes, LLC; The St. Joe Company.

FURTHER READING

Braga, Michael, "Levitt Reports Giant Debt," *Sarasota Herald-Tribune,* November 13, 2007, p. D1.

Cordle, Ina Paiva, "BankAtlantic Agrees to Pay $21 Million for Levitt," *Miami Herald,* September 4, 1999, p. 1C.

Dunham, Kemba J., "Suburban Pioneer Looks to Remodel," *Wall Street Journal,* October 3, 2005, p. B8.

Freer, Jim, "BankAtlantic-Levitt Combo Could Spice Up the Balance Sheet," *South Florida Business Journal,* September 10, 1999, p. 14.

Gubernick, Lisa, "Too Long at the Party," *Forbes,* May 4, 1987, p. 40.

Molotsky, Irvin, "Levittown 30 Years Later," *New York Times,* October 2, 1977.

Owers, Paul, "Fort Lauderdale Builder Levitt and Sons to Liquidate," *South Florida Sun-Sentinel,* June 28, 2008.

Taylor, Angela, "25 Years Ago, Levittown Was a Joke, but Today It's Thriving," *New York Times,* April 18, 1972.

Thompson, Laura K., "Spinoff by BankAtlantic Signals Return to Roots," *American Banker,* April 4, 2003, p. 1.

Vanderhoof, Nadia, "Levitt Has New Name: Woodbridge," *Stuart News,* May 29, 2008, p. B6.

Wotapka, Dawn, and Kemba J. Dunham, "Levitt May Have a Last Chance in Offering," *Wall Street Journal,* September 5, 2007, p. B6.

www.WyndhamWorldwide.com

Wyndham Worldwide Corporation

7 Sylvan Way
Parsippany, New Jersey 07054-3805
U.S.A.
Telephone: (973) 753-6000
Fax: (973) 496-7658
Web site: http://www.wyndhamworldwide.com

Public Company
Founded: 1990
Employees: 33,200
Sales: $4.36 billion (2007)
Stock Exchanges: New York
Ticker Symbol: WYN
NAICS: 721110 Hotels (Except Casino Hotels) and Motels; 533110 Lessors of Nonfinancial Intangible Assets (Except Copyrighted Works); 531120 Lessors of Nonresidential Buildings (Except Miniwarehouses); 561599 All Other Travel Arrangement and Reservation Services

■ ■ ■

Wyndham Worldwide Corporation is one of the largest hospitality companies in the world. Through its Wyndham Hotel Group unit, the company franchises and provides hotel management services to owners of luxury, upscale, mid-market, and economy hotels. Its franchised lodging brands number 12: Wyndham, Ramada, Days Inn, Super 8, Wingate by Wyndham, Baymont Inn & Suites, Microtel Inns and Suites, Hawthorn Suites, Howard Johnson, Travelodge, Knights Inn, and AmeriHost Inn. The chains are linked through the

Wyndham Rewards frequent traveler program, which has approximately 6.8 million members. The Wyndham Hotel Group includes nearly 7,000 hotels containing around 581,000 rooms in 65 countries on six continents. Wyndham Worldwide is also involved in the time-share sector of the hospitality market through its vacation exchange and rentals business, Group RCI. This unit provides more than 3.6 million members access to more than 67,000 vacation properties in about 100 countries. A third unit, Wyndham Vacation Ownership, develops, markets, and sells time-share ownership interests through its network of around 145 vacation ownership resorts in the United States, Canada, Mexico, the Caribbean, and the South Pacific.

While the company's flagship Wyndham hotel chain was founded in 1981 by Dallas real estate developer Trammell Crow, Wyndham Worldwide more directly traces its origins to Hospitality Franchise Systems, Inc. (HFS), which was established by The Blackstone Group in 1990. HFS merged with CUC International, Inc., in December 1997, forming Cendant Corporation, which ranked as one of the world's largest franchisers in the fields of lodging, travel services, real estate, and car rental. In August 2006 Cendant spun off its hospitality group as Wyndham Worldwide Corporation.

FOUNDING OF HFS IN 1990

Hospitality Franchise Systems, Inc., was formed in 1990 by The Blackstone Group, a New York-based investment bank. Blackstone hired 50-year-old Henry Silverman, an attorney and investment banker with experience in the

COMPANY PERSPECTIVES

■

We provide directly to individual consumers our high quality products and services, including the various accommodations we market, such as hotels, vacation resorts, villas and cottages, and products we offer, such as vacation ownership interests. We also provide valuable products and services to our business customers, such as franchisees, hotel owners, affiliated resort developers and prospective developers. These products and services include marketing and central reservation systems, inventory networks and distribution channels, back office services and loyalty programs. We strive to provide value-added products and services that are intended to both enhance the travel experience of the individual consumer and drive revenue to our business customers. The depth and breadth of our businesses across different segments of the hospitality industry provide us with the opportunity to expand our relationships with our existing individual consumers and business customers in one or more segments of our business by offering them additional or alternative products and services from our other segments. Historically, we have pursued what we believe to be financially-attractive entrance points in the major global hospitality markets to strengthen our portfolio of products and services.

lodging industry, to run its merchant banking group. Blackstone formed HFS with the intent of purchasing ailing or undervalued franchise brands or the rights to those chain's brand names. It planned to generate profits by charging its member hotels up-front and annual franchise fees. Rather than own the hotels, it would simply provide marketing, reservation, and other value-added administrative services. In addition, it would target hotels that offered moderate- and low-priced rooms.

To the casual observer, Blackstone's entry into the lodging market may have seemed poorly timed. The U.S. hotel industry had just experienced its greatest period of expansion in history. By the early 1990s, in fact, there were more than three million hotel rooms in the nation, and about 30 percent of those had been built since the early 1980s. By the late 1980s, it was clear to hotel industry participants that the market was quickly fading. Indeed, after increasing at a rate of approximately 4 percent a year throughout the middle and late 1980s, the number of newly constructed hotel rooms plummeted. By the early 1990s, the growth rate had plunged to less than 1 percent, and most of the new rooms were built in the Las Vegas area.

The decline of the U.S. lodging industry was the result of several factors. First, the Tax Reform Act of 1986 gradually diminished the tax-favored status of commercial real estate developments, such as hotels, and decreased investment capital for new construction. Second, and more important, was a decline in demand. As the economy slowed in the late 1980s and early 1990s, both business and personal traveling declined. Many hoteliers that had expanded their chains during the 1980s with expectations of high demand and a preferred tax status suddenly found themselves burdened with half-empty, unprofitable properties that they could not sell.

By forming HFS, Blackstone hoped to exploit what it viewed as opportunities amidst the turmoil in the lodging industry. Fewer than one-third of all U.S. hotels going into the 1990s were affiliated with a national or regional chain. As a result, their operating costs were generally very high compared to members of national chains, which benefited from economies of scale. National chains could provide national advertising campaigns, centralized and automated reservation and billing departments, quality assurance programs, administrative support, and management training. Furthermore, HFS believed that the majority of the hotels that were affiliated with a chain could benefit from joining an even larger organization. Because so many hoteliers were strapped for cash by the early 1990s, HFS reasoned that it could sell large numbers of franchised rooms at low prices and profit, despite sluggish demand for hotel rooms.

FIRST ACQUISITIONS: HOWARD JOHNSON, RAMADA

In July 1990 HFS made its first acquisitions by purchasing the Howard Johnson franchise system and the rights to operate the domestic U.S. Ramada franchise system. HFS bought the troubled properties from Prime Motor Inns, Inc., for a scant $170 million. Prime Motor Inns was one of the fastest-growing hotel chains in the nation during the 1980s and had accrued an impressive list of holdings by the end of the decade. It had also racked up over $500 million in debt, however, causing it to seek refuge in bankruptcy court when the market finally soured. The profitability of its Ramada and Howard Johnson subsidiaries had deteriorated significantly by 1990; the Ramada chain was even losing money.

With its first purchase, HFS immediately became a major player in the U.S. lodging industry. The Ramada

KEY DATES

1990: Hospitality Franchise Systems, Inc., (HFS) is created by The Blackstone Group and immediately acquires the Howard Johnson franchise system and the U.S.-based Ramada franchise system.

1992: Company purchases Days Inn of America.

1993: HFS becomes the largest corporate hotel chain operator in the world with the purchase of the rights to Super 8 Motels, Inc.

1995: The Knights Inn chain is acquired; Hospitality Franchise Systems changes its name to HFS Incorporated.

1996: Company acquires the Travelodge hotel franchise system in North America, launches the Wingate Inn chain, and enters the time-share market via the purchase of Resort Condominiums International, Inc.

1997: HFS merges with CUC International, Inc., in a $14 billion deal, forming Cendant Corporation.

2000: Cendant acquires the AmeriHost Inn and AmeriHost Inn Suites brand names and franchising rights.

2001: Fairfield Resorts, Inc., marketer and manager of time-share properties, is acquired; Cendant also enters the vacation rentals business.

2002: Another time-share operator, Trendwest Resorts, Inc., is acquired.

2003: The TripRewards loyalty program is launched.

2004: Cendant gains full worldwide rights to the Ramada brand.

2005: The Wyndham hotel brand is acquired.

2006: Baymont Inn & Suites is acquired; Cendant spins off its hospitality businesses into the independent Wyndham Worldwide Corporation.

2008: TripRewards is succeeded by the Wyndham Rewards frequent guest program; the Microtel Inns & Suites and Hawthorn Suites hotel brands are acquired.

chain, which had been founded in Flagstaff, Arizona, in 1954, brought 472 hotels with more than 77,608 rooms under HFS's corporate umbrella. Howard Johnson, whose origins traced back to Savannah, Georgia, in 1954, added 417 properties with about 51,786 rooms.

HFS incurred about $91 million in debt during its first year of operation, but was able to recoup approximately $50 million in franchise fees for a net loss of about $1.9 million, not a bad outcome considering the company's start-up costs. HFS lost about $5 million in 1991 as it bolstered marketing efforts for its chains, began to establish a consolidated infrastructure that could also support future acquisitions, and pared its debt by about 15 percent.

In addition to trying to improve the efficiency of the hotels already in its chain, HFS sought to generate additional profits by adding independent hotels, other chain's hotels, and new construction to the Ramada and Howard Johnson chains. During 1990 and 1991, in fact, HFS added about 22,000 rooms to the two hotel chains. It profited immediately from the additions of these properties because hotel owners that joined the franchises paid HFS an up-front fee, typically around $20,000 to $30,000. In addition, the owners agreed to pay an annual franchise fee of 6 percent to 10 percent of gross receipts. The hotel owners benefited, of course, from access to a brand name and the reservation and marketing support proffered by HFS.

1992 PURCHASE OF DAYS INN

HFS's initial success prompted its second major acquisition. In January 1992 it purchased Days Inn of America, Inc., from the troubled Tollman-Hundley Lodging Corporation for $259 million. Days Inn had been started by Cecil B. Day on Tybee Island, Georgia, in 1970 and had grown into the third largest hotel brand in the world by 1992. It added about 1,220 hotels with about 133,127 rooms to HFS, thus almost doubling HFS's size. The Days Inn purchase proved to be a savvy buy for Silverman and his management team. Although HFS piled up a load of debt, it posted its first profit in 1992: net income leaped to more than $20 million from revenues of about $200 million. By the end of 1992, HFS's three chains included almost 2,500 hotels with about 300,000 rooms. After fewer than three years of operation, HFS had become one of the largest hotel franchisers in the world.

In addition to praise from many of its investors, Silverman and HFS also drew criticism following their rapid climb in 1992. The Days Inn acquisition represented the third time that a group associated with Silverman had purchased the chain in less than eight years, resulting in a profit of more than $100 million for him and his investors. The first purchase occurred in 1984 by an investment fund headed by Silverman and supported by felons-to-be Ivan Boesky, Michael Milken, and Victor Posner. They sold part of the chain to public investors at a 200 percent profit, bought it back in 1988 following the 1987 stock market crash, and then sold it a year later to Tollman-Hundley for a large profit. Now, Silverman was borrowing heavily, critics said, to buy the chain again.

Although Silverman's deals were all legal, his detractors argued that HFS was engaging in questionable strategies. For example, its practice of growing quickly by lowering franchise fees to attract independent hotels into the chain (instead of building new ones) suggested a possible lowering of chain standards to generate short-term royalties. In addition, critics derided HFS's financing strategy, claiming that it benefited certain top executives but reduced the long-term viability of the organization.

ACQUISITION OF SUPER 8 IN 1993

Despite criticism from a few analysts, HFS management and investors alike placed faith in the franchiser's growth strategy. The company's success throughout 1992 and into 1993 seemed to support their optimism. In April 1993, in fact, HFS edged out Holiday Inns as the largest corporate hotel chain operator in the world when it purchased the rights to hotels owned by Super 8 Motels, Inc. Established in 1974 in Aberdeen, South Dakota, Super 8 comprised 971 hotels totaling 59,532 rooms, for which HFS paid $125 million. Super 8 focused on serving government, senior, and family travelers, thus augmenting HFS's strength in the economy/limited service hotel niche. Because most of its franchises were located in the Midwest, HFS believed it offered significant potential for expansion into other regions of the United States.

The business strategy adopted by HFS in the early 1990s was to significantly expand each of its franchise systems while maintaining or improving their reputation and to offer high-quality, value-added services to each chain. By accomplishing these goals, HFS expected to continually increase revenues from franchise fees, thus generating capital for new acquisitions and forays into related businesses. An integral component of HFS's overall strategy was its state-of-the-art national reservation systems. Customers that called any of HFS's chains were channeled to one of four national clearinghouses, where an operator would process the hotel reservation and also link customer travel requests with related services, such as airlines and rental cars. HFS provided each of its franchisees with specialized reports tracking call patterns and reservation trends, thus allowing them to improve occupancy.

In addition to its reservation system, HFS boosted the value of its franchises through marketing programs.

Each of its companies had a separate marketing team to research and develop national and regional marketing initiatives, but the teams all benefitted from lower shared costs related to volume purchases of printed materials and media advertising. HFS developed a quality assurance program to complement its marketing efforts by ensuring that all franchise members adhered to brand-specific quality controls that created consistency for all hotels within each brand. HFS's training system educated each of its franchisees on how to get the most out of its reservation system and marketing programs.

One of the most important means of luring new hotels into its franchise system was its preferred vendor arrangements. Through volume buying, HFS allowed many of its franchise members to slash costs related to goods and services for everything from toilet paper to food. HFS also provided telephone support, via toll-free numbers, for each of its franchisees. In addition, it assisted existing hotels that were converting to a franchise with the design and construction services necessary to bring the unit up to its standards. The end result of HFS's various support services was that its hotel owners were typically able to improve occupancy and reduce operating costs, thus boosting profitability compared to most independent hoteliers.

In June 1993, shortly after acquiring Super 8, HFS added Park Inn International to its lineup. With 39 properties and 4,683 rooms in 13 states, Park Inn was a relatively small chain. HFS planned to market Super 8 and Park Inn chains separately and hoped to realize strong national growth for both brand names. Its expansion strategy resulted in an increase in the number of Super 8 franchisees of more than 12 percent during 1993, to more than 1,060. Meanwhile, HFS successfully enlarged its other chains as well. The Ramada chain, for example, swelled to 676 hotels with 107,000 rooms by the end of 1993, and Howard Johnson increased to 566 properties with 63,000 rooms. Days Inn grew similarly, expanding to 1,441 hotels with 145,000 rooms.

By the end of 1993, HFS had 3,783 hotels with 383,931 rooms in its systems. Although it had accrued a weighty $350 million in long-term debt, HFS managed to boost sales 27 percent in 1993, to $257 million, as net income climbed 34 percent to $21.5 million. Also during 1993, Silverman and comanagers took HFS truly public, selling all ownership shares held by The Blackstone Group on the stock market. It also increased the average occupancy rate of its hotels and was able to boost royalty fees for new members of its franchises.

HFS continued to grow each of its franchises early in 1994; by April it had about 4,000 hotels sending franchise fees to the home office. Furthermore, the company began branching out into new arenas. It formed several strategic alliances with transportation and foodservice companies in 1993 and 1994, such as Greyhound, Pizza Hut, and Carlson Hospitality Group, which owned several restaurants and hotels. The agreements provided services to franchise members, such as free in-room pizza delivery and reduced bus rates for HFS franchise guests.

As it entered the mid-1990s, HFS appeared well positioned to benefit from a projected increase in hotel room rates resulting from a dearth of new development in the early 1990s. Silverman continued on an acquisition spree, purchasing Century 21, Coldwell Banker, and ERA Real Estate. This expansion into the residential real estate brokerage sector prompted a name change. In September 1995 Hospitality Franchise Systems was renamed HFS Incorporated. Around this same time, HFS spent about $15 million for Knights Inn, an economy hotel franchise system consisting of around 115 hotels and 10,000 rooms in 19 states. Knights Inn had been founded in Columbus, Ohio, in 1974.

HFS's acquisition spree continued in 1996 with the January purchase of the Travelodge hotel franchise system in North America for $39.3 million. Originally known as the Motor Coach Court, Travelodge was a pioneer in economy lodging when it opened its first hotel in San Diego in 1939. By the time of its acquisition by HFS, the chain encompassed 450 hotels and 37,000 rooms. HFS also launched a new lodging brand in 1996, Wingate Inn, the first new-construction-only mid-market hotel chain to be introduced in a decade. Designed for business travelers, Wingate Inns were limited-service hotels featuring upscale amenities at mid-market prices. The first two Wingate Inns, which opened on successive days in August 1996, were located in Sevierville, Tennessee, and Alpharetta, Georgia.

HFS also expanded into the time-share market via the November 1996 purchase of Resort Condominiums International, Inc. (RCI), the largest time-share exchange organization in the world, for approximately $487 million. RCI, based in Indianapolis, Indiana, provided time-share vacation exchange opportunities for more than 2.2 million time-share owners from more than 150 nations and more than 3,100 resorts in 80 countries around the world.

In October 1996, meanwhile, HFS diversified further with the acquisition of the Avis, Inc., car rental business for $800 million. That same month, the company sold the Park Inn chain. Despite this divestment, HFS ended 1996 as the world's largest hotel franchiser, as measured by number of rooms and properties.

CREATION OF CENDANT VIA 1997 MERGER OF HFS AND CUC

During 1996, HFS began discussing the idea of a merger with CUC International, Inc. CUC offered individual consumers access to various services and discounts related to shopping, travel, insurance, automobiles, dining, vacationing, credit card enhancement packages, and various discount and coupon programs. The company provided its services primarily through memberships to clubs and programs. CUC had about 40 million members who paid $5 to $250 per year.

According to a 1997 *Journal of Business Strategy* article, the companies held beliefs that "merging will allow them to exploit their customer databases more fully, adding an estimated $250 million in annual incremental pretax earnings to their combined balance sheet over the next few years, and allow them to continue their swift growth, 25 percent to 30 percent, for longer than either could manage alone." Sure enough, in May 1997, HFS announced its plans to merge with CUC to create a $4.3 billion consumer services powerhouse. CUC was given marketing access to HFS's 80 million customer list, while HFS eyed CUC's Internet businesses as potentially lucrative distribution channels. The deal was completed in December 1997, and the two companies were folded into a new business entity called Cendant Corporation.

Silverman was named CEO of Cendant, which almost immediately was embroiled in a scandal. In April 1998 the company was forced to admit that its 1997 earnings were overstated by $100 million, prompting a precipitous decline in its stock price. Shareholders filed suit against Cendant for accounting fraud related to years of accounting inaccuracies at CUC. In December 1999 Cendant reached a $2.8 billion settlement with its shareholders, the largest recovery awarded in a securities class-action case at the time. In February 2000 Ernst & Young, which had been CUC's accountants at the time of the fraud, agreed to a $335 million settlement with Cendant shareholders.

Throughout the entire process of litigation, Silverman claimed that HFS knew nothing of CUC's fraudulent accounting practices before the merger. He pledged to restore shareholder confidence in Cendant, not only to boost the company's image, but that of his own. Having spent most of his career as a highly regarded and well-respected businessman in financial circles, Silverman spent most of 1999 and 2000 reestablishing Cendant as a leading consumer services firm. During 2000 the company began to resume acquisition activity, including the purchase of the AmeriHost Inn and AmeriHost Inn and Suites brand names and franchising rights. AmeriHost competed in the mid-market segment of the lodging market and had about 80 properties and 5,100 rooms at the time of the buyout.

In the spring of 2001, businesses began tightening their belts, cutting business travel and sending Cendant's hospitality business and the entire lodging industry into a downward spiral that accelerated in the aftermath of the September 11, 2001 terrorist attacks on the United States. Excluding the impact of acquisitions, revenues for Cendant's hospitality business were flat in 2002. Late that year a program was launched to improve the quality of the various Cendant hotel brands by purging from the system hotels deemed to be of substandard quality and franchisees who had defaulted on fee payments. The company also moved to improve the performance of its existing properties by providing them with additional support through increased marketing efforts.

VENTURING FURTHER INTO TIME-SHARES

In April 2001 Cendant ventured deeper into the time-share market by acquiring Fairfield Resorts, Inc., for about $760 million. Fairfield was one of the largest vacation ownership companies in the United States, with more than 324,000 time-share-owning households. The firm marketed and managed resort properties at 33 locations in 12 states and the Bahamas. The Fairfield deal was followed up 12 months later by the acquisition of another major time-share business, Trendwest Resorts, Inc., for $849 million. Trendwest had around 150,000 time-share owners and 48 properties. The two businesses meshed well together as the Fairfield properties were mainly located in the eastern United States, whereas Trendwest's resorts were principally in the western United States, Hawaii, Mexico, British Columbia, and the South Pacific. Between 2001 and 2004, Cendant also entered the vacation rentals business through a string of acquisitions.

Late in 2003 Cendant launched TripRewards, a frequent-traveler loyalty program that enabled customers to earn points from the full array of Cendant lodging brands, including its time-share operations. By the end of 2004, TripRewards had garnered more than three million members. At this same time, an overseas push was underway within Cendant's hospitality business. In December 2004 Cendant secured worldwide rights to the Ramada brand by purchasing the international rights to the Ramada brand from Marriott International, Inc. This brought within Cendant's orbit more than 200 additional franchised hotels with roughly 27,700 rooms located in 26 countries and territories. Cendant

was also making a concerted push into the Chinese market, targeting that nation's burgeoning middle class and anticipating surging demand for lodging during the 2008 Olympic Games in Beijing and the 2010 World Expo in Shanghai. In 2004 Cendant announced plans to add dozens of hotels in China at three lodging tiers: two- to three-star Super 8 hotels, three- to four-star Days Inn locations, and four- to five-star Howard Johnson hotels. The company also granted a master franchise to Moscow-based Hermitage Hospitality Ltd. for the opening of 45 Days Inns in Russia and 14 other countries of the former Soviet Union.

GAINING INDEPENDENCE AS WYNDHAM WORLDWIDE

The Cendant stable of hotels had always lacked an upscale brand. This hole was filled in October 2005 via the acquisition of the Wyndham hotel brand from Blackstone Group for $111 million. Wyndham, which had been founded in 1981 by Dallas real estate developer Trammell Crow, included 110 properties in the United States, Mexico, and the Caribbean. Most of the Wyndham hotels were franchised properties, but Cendant also gained management contracts for 29 of the hotels, marking the first time that the company would actual manage any of its hotels. By the end of 2005, Cendant's nine-brand hotel business included a total of approximately 6,350 properties and more than 532,000 rooms.

The Cendant hotel business was augmented further in April 2006 when the Baymont Inn & Suites brand and system of 115 franchised properties were acquired. Baymont, founded as Budgetel Inns in Oshkosh, Wisconsin, in 1974, strengthened Cendant's position in the limited-service, mid-market segment of the lodging sector. At this time, Cendant was in the process of splitting itself into smaller, focused, independent companies. In the breakup's last stage, Cendant spun three of its businesses off to its shareholders. The company's hospitality operations, including the lodging, time-share exchange, vacation rentals, and time-share ownership units, were spun off in August 2006 as Wyndham Worldwide Corporation. Steven A. Rudnitsky was named president and CEO of Wyndham Worldwide, having previously headed Cendant's hotel operations. After the spinoffs, Cendant was focused solely on the car rental business, and it renamed itself Avis Budget Group, Inc.

As was clear from the choice of company name, the Wyndham brand was intended to be the flagship around which Wyndham Worldwide would position itself, similar to the way other major hotel groups were centered around, for example, the Marriott and Hilton names. The Wyndham hotels themselves were at this time being revamped to attract the growing ranks of Generation X travelers. In 2007 the company began to extend its use of the Wyndham brand by rechristening the Wingate Inn chain as Wingate by Wyndham and with name changes of its time-share businesses, Fairfield Resort becoming Wyndham Vacation Resorts and Trendwest Resorts adopting the name WorldMark by Wyndham. In addition, the Wyndham ByRequest frequent guest program was integrated with TripRewards to create the newly named Wyndham Rewards program, which encompassed the firm's full range of lodging brands and debuted in May 2008.

In 2007, its full year as an independent firm, Wyndham Worldwide performed strongly, earning profits of $403 million on net revenues of $4.36 billion. The following July the company increased its hotel brand count to 12 by acquiring U.S. Franchise Systems, Inc., and its Microtel Inns & Suites and Hawthorn Suites brands from Global Hyatt Corporation for $131 million. This deal bolstered Wyndham's position in the economy segment with the addition of nearly 300 Microtel properties while also provided the company with its first foothold in the all-suites, extended-stay market in the form of Hawthorn and its more than 90 units.

At this time, Wyndham Worldwide was in an aggressive expansion mode, with more than 120 Wyndham or Wingate by Wyndham hotels in the development pipeline around the world. Several other company brands were also being expanded as the firm aimed to reach a goal of 700,000 rooms by 2010, with about 60 percent of the growth planned for outside North America. By October 2008, however, Wyndham began to feel the impact of the global economic crisis and announced some job cuts and restructuring charges. Most significantly, the company was forced to cut back on its time-share developments as it became increasingly difficult to find customers with sufficient credit quality. Wyndham also faced the possibility of curtailments in business and consumer travel spending from a potentially deep economic recession.

Dave Mote
Updated, Christina M. Stansell; David E. Salamie

PRINCIPAL SUBSIDIARIES

Wyndham Hotel Group, LLC; Group RCI, Inc.; Wyndham Vacation Ownership, Inc.; Wyndham Vacation Resorts, Inc.; Wyndham Consumer Finance, Inc.; Wyndham Resort Development Corporation.

PRINCIPAL OPERATING UNITS

Wyndham Hotels and Resorts; Wingate by Wyndham; Ramada; Baymont; Days Inn; Super 8; Howard Johnson; AmeriHost Inn; Travelodge; Knights Inn; Microtel Inns & Suites; Hawthorn Suites; Wyndham Rewards; RCI; The Registry Collection; Endless Vacation Rentals; Landal GreenParks; English Country Cottages; Novasol; Wyndham Vacation Resorts; WorldMark by Wyndham.

PRINCIPAL COMPETITORS

Marriott International, Inc.; Hilton Hotels Corporation; Starwood Hotels & Resorts Worldwide, Inc.; InterContinental Hotels Group PLC; Global Hyatt Corporation; Choice Hotels International, Inc.; Accor; Interval International, Inc.; Walt Disney Parks and Resorts.

FURTHER READING

Blitz, Roger, "Wyndham Shares Hit As It Cuts Jobs," *Financial Times,* October 7, 2008, p. 20.

Braue, Marilee Laboda, "N.J. Hotel Giant Always Has Room for More," *Bergen County (N.J.) Record,* January 7, 1993.

Brown, Steve, "Patriot-Wyndham Deal Valued at $1.1 Billion," *Dallas Morning News,* April 15, 1997, p. 4D.

Bryant, Adam, "Hospitality to Acquire Super 8 Motels," *New York Times,* February 17, 1993, p. D4.

"Buying Spree," *Hotels,* December 2005, pp. 22–24.

"Cendant Retools Hotel Division," *Hotel and Motel Management,* February 18, 2002, p. 36.

"Cendant to Buy Wyndham," *Hotels,* October 2005, p. 12.

Chittum, Ryan, "Cendant to Split into Four Companies," *Wall Street Journal,* October 24, 2005, p. A3.

———, "Wyndham International Gains Entry to New York," *Wall Street Journal,* August 25, 2004, p. B4.

Chittum, Ryan, and Alex Frangos, "Blackstone Group Will Purchase Wyndham Chain for $1.44 Billion," *Wall Street Journal,* June 15, 2005, p. A3.

DeMarrais, Kevin G., "No. 1 in Hospitality," *Bergen County (N.J.) Record,* July 7, 1993.

———, "Rooms with a Vision: Cendant Builds Hotel Brands," *Hackensack (N.J.) Record,* February 13, 2005, p. B1.

Der Hovanesian, Mara, "Cendant: Ready to Climb Again?" *Business Week,* March 12, 2001, p. 115.

Koss, Laura, "HFS Purchases Super 8," *Hotel and Motel Management,* March 8, 1993, pp. 1+.

Krauskopf, Lewis, "Cendant Acquires Upscale Brand: Will Pay $100M for Wyndham," *Hackensack (N.J.) Record,* September 15, 2005, p. B1.

Kyne, Phelim, "Cendant Looks to China's Drivers: More Days Inn Locations Will Cater to a Country with Big Traveling Public," *Wall Street Journal,* February 2, 2004, p. A16B.

Milligan, Michael, "Cendant Hotel Unit to Adopt Wyndham Name, Buy Baymont," *Travel Weekly,* March 20, 2006, p. 5.

Pacelle, Mitchell, and Neal Templin, "Buyout Magnates Watch Wyndham Stock Fall Despite Nascent Turnaround Effort," *Wall Street Journal,* November 3, 1999, p. C1.

Parker-Pope, Tara, "Wyndham Hotels Reaches for Upper Tier," *Wall Street Journal,* October 20, 1993, p. T3.

Pitock, Todd, "HFS and CUC: Perfect Together?" *Journal of Business Strategy,* July–August 1997, p. 36.

Preciphs, Joi, and Beth Jinks, "Wyndham Booked for $150 Million Hotel Purchase," *Newark (N.J.) Star-Ledger,* June 4, 2008, p. 58.

Prior, James T., "Hospitality Franchise Systems—A NJ Gem," *New Jersey Business,* April 1993, p. 22.

Strauss, Karyn, and Derek Gale, "New Name, New Game: Wyndham Worldwide," *Hotels,* September 2006, pp. 12–13.

Tsao, Amy, "Cendant: Ascendant Once Again?" *Business Week,* October 3, 2001.

Ward, Sandra, "Elephants and Memories," *Barron's,* November 24, 2003, pp. 22–23.

Watkins, Ed, "A Brand Transformed: A Revived Wyndham Targets Gen Xers," *Lodging Hospitality,* May 1, 2008, pp. 24–26, 28.

Wolff, Carlo, "Setting the Wyndham Tone," *Lodging Hospitality,* November 1995, pp. 24–26, 28.

"Wyndham Focuses on Next-Generation Marketing," *Hotels,* February 2008, p. 20.

Yee, Amy, "Cendant in Plan for China Hotels," *Financial Times,* April 22, 2004, p. 31.

Yamaha Corporation

10-1, Nakazawa-cho
Naka-ku
Hamamatsu, Shizuoka 430-8650
Japan
Telephone: (+83-53) 460-2800
Fax: (+83-53) 460-2802
Web site: http://www.global.yamaha.com

Public Company
Incorporated: 1897 as Nippon Gakki Co., Ltd.
Employees: 25,517
Sales: ¥548.75 billion ($5.48 billion) (2008)
Stock Exchanges: Tokyo
Ticker Symbol: 7951
NAICS: 339992 Musical Instrument Manufacturing; 334119 Other Computer Peripheral Equipment Manufacturing; 334310 Audio and Video Equipment Manufacturing; 334413 Semiconductor and Related Device Manufacturing; 611610 Fine Arts Schools

∎ ∎ ∎

Founded in 1887, Yamaha Corporation is the world's largest maker of musical instruments, including pianos and keyboards, wind instruments, string and percussion instruments, and digital musical instruments. Following World War II, the company diversified into other areas, becoming a major producer of audio products, semiconductors, and other electronics products. Yamaha also runs music schools in Japan and 40 other countries and operates a service that allows consumers in a number of countries to download ringtones to their mobile phones. Yamaha Motor Company, Ltd., the second largest Japanese motorcycle producer, is no longer an affiliate of Yamaha Corporation, although the latter does own a stake of roughly 15 percent in Yamaha Motor. Around three-fourths of Yamaha Corporation's net sales are derived from its musical instrument and audio products operations.

19TH-CENTURY ORIGINS

Yamaha founder Torakusu Yamaha's venture reflected late 19th-century Japan's enthusiasm for new technologies and the ability of its middle-class entrepreneurs to develop products based on them. Raised in what is now the Wakayama Prefecture, Yamaha received an unusual education for the time from his samurai father, a surveyor with broad interests in astronomy and mechanics and a remarkable library. The Meiji Restoration, a government-subsidized effort to hasten technological development in the late 19th century, put educated people such as Yamaha in a position to capitalize on the new growth.

At age 20 Yamaha studied watch repair in Nagasaki under a British engineer. He formed his own watchmaking company, but he was unable to stay in business because of a lack of money. He then took a job repairing medical equipment in Osaka after completing an apprenticeship at Japan's first school of Western medicine in Nagasaki.

As part of his job, Yamaha repaired surgical equipment in Hamamatsu, a small Pacific coastal fishing town. Because of the area's isolation, a township school

Since its establishment in 1887, Yamaha has been engaged in a broad spectrum of businesses, ranging from those with a focus on sound and music, such as musical instruments, AV equipment and semiconductors, to lifestyle-related products, metallic molds and components. Our operations in these businesses are expanding globally as we develop and propose truly satisfying products and services to people the world over. Going forward, we will continue to create "kando" (an inspired state of mind) and enrich culture together with people throughout the world, drawing on our expertise and rich vein of sensitivity in the realms of sound and music.

there asked him in 1887 to repair their prized U.S.-made Mason & Hamlin reed organ. Seeing the instrument's commercial potential in Japan, Yamaha produced his own functional version of the organ within a year and then set up a new business in Hamamatsu to manufacture organs for Japanese primary schools. In 1889 he established the Yamaha Organ Manufacturing Company, Japan's first maker of Western musical instruments. At the same time, the government granted Hamamatsu township status, which provided it with rail service and made it a regional commerce center.

Western musical traditions interested the Japanese government, which fostered and catered to growing enthusiasm for Western ideas. While Yamaha's technical education enabled him to manufacture a product, government investment in infrastructure made it possible for him to create a business. Yamaha Organ used modern mass-production methods, and by 1889 it employed 100 people and produced 250 organs annually.

During the 1890s the more inexpensive upright piano surpassed the reed organ in popularity in U.S. homes. Yamaha saw the potential of this market. In 1897 he renamed his company Nippon Gakki Co., Ltd., which literally means Japan musical instruments. He opened a new plant and headquarters in the Itaya-cho district of Hamamatsu.

In 1899 one of Yamaha's initial investors convinced other investors to pull out of Yamaha in favor of a competitor, a new organ maker that was near failure. Yamaha managed to borrow the money necessary to remain solvent and buy out his partners.

Japan's government not only supported industrialization through heavy manufacturing, but also encouraged upstart businesses to contact overseas markets directly. Expansion into pianos required more research, so the Japanese Ministry of Education sponsored a Yamaha tour of the United States in 1899. He was to study piano making and establish suppliers for the materials needed to produce pianos in Japan. In one year Nippon Gakki produced its first piano. Governmental and institutional orders were the first filled, including some for the Ministry of Education. In 1902, with U.S. materials and German technology, Nippon Gakki introduced its first grand piano. In 1903 the company produced 21 pianos.

Nippon Gakki demonstrated its new pianos in select international exhibitions. Between 1902 and 1920, the company received awards for its pianos and organs that had never before gone to a Japanese manufacturer, for example, a Grand Prix at the St. Louis World Exposition in 1904.

THE WORLD WARS

World War I curtailed sales by a German harmonica maker in Japan, so Nippon Gakki took the opportunity to broaden its product base and begin making and exporting harmonicas. Producing new products that required the same raw materials and manufacturing skills became a major operating principle for Nippon Gakki.

Yamaha died suddenly during the war. He had succeeded in introducing Western instruments and assembly techniques, but despite his assembly lines, piano making was still a craftsperson's industry at the time of his death. Vice-President Chiyomaru Amano assumed the presidency in 1917. His political contacts had helped the company expand. He saw the company through repeated labor strife for ten years before being replaced.

World War I produced tremendous growth in Japanese industry, and Nippon Gakki grew with it, supplying Asian markets cut off from traditional sources of supply. By 1920 it employed 1,000 workers and produced 10,000 organs and 1,200 pianos a year. The sales records set during the war continued afterward, despite recession. These gains were largely due to piano sales, which doubled to ¥2 million between 1919 and 1921.

The next five years nearly put the company in bankruptcy. Appreciation of the yen, which made Nippon Gakki products less competitive overseas, was part of the problem. In 1922 fire destroyed a new plant in Nakazawa and the main Itaya-cho plant in Hamamatsu. The next year the Great Kanto earthquake destroyed the

KEY DATES

1887: Company founder Torakusu Yamaha builds his first reed organ.

1889: Yamaha founds Yamaha Organ Manufacturing Company, Japan's first maker of Western musical instruments.

1897: Company's name is changed to Nippon Gakki Co., Ltd.

1900: Company produces its first upright piano.

1902: Production of grand pianos begins.

1930: Company opens an acoustics lab and research center.

1948: Japan's Education Ministry mandates musical education for Japanese children, expanding Yamaha's business.

1954: Yamaha Music Schools debut.

1955: An affiliated company, Yamaha Motor Company, Ltd., produces the first Yamaha motorcycle.

1958: First overseas subsidiary is established in Mexico.

1967: First concert grand piano is produced.

1971: Production of semiconductors begins.

1982: The first Disklavier pianos are produced.

1983: Company introduces the DX-7 digital synthesizer, a top seller.

1987: Company changes its name to Yamaha Corporation to celebrate the 100th anniversary of the firm.

1993: The Silent Piano series debuts.

2000: Yamaha posts a net loss of $384 million for the fiscal year ending in March; the newly installed president, Shuji Ito, initiates a restructuring program.

2004: Company establishes its first manufacturing presence in China.

2008: L. Bösendorfer Klavierfabrik GmbH, an Austrian maker of high-end pianos, is acquired.

of Sumitomo Wire Company, Kawakami made an unexpectedly nontraditional choice in accepting the position at the troubled company. Kawakami cut production costs and reorganized the company. Half of all debts were paid within 18 months of Kawakami taking over.

Between the world wars, Western imports still dominated the Japanese sales of Western instruments. Because Nippon Gakki's advantage was in price alone, Kawakami opened an acoustics lab and research center in 1930 to improve quality. He also hired advisers from C. Bechstein of Germany to improve the quality of the Yamaha piano.

The growth of the public school system of the 1930s expanded the market for Western instruments, and Nippon Gakki introduced lower priced accordions and guitars to capitalize on the expansion.

When World War II began, Nippon Gakki plants produced propellers for Zero fighter planes, fuel tanks, and wing parts. As with expansion during World War I, these items laid the groundwork for broader diversification in the postwar years. In the meantime, Nippon Gakki had to stop making musical instruments altogether in 1945.

POSTWAR EXPANSION AND DIVERSIFICATION

Only one Nippon Gakki factory survived the wartime U.S. bombing raids. Postwar financial assistance from the United States made possible the production of harmonicas and xylophones just two months after receipt of the funds. Within six months it produced organs, accordions, tube horns, and guitars. After the Allied powers approved civilian trade in 1947, Nippon Gakki began once again to export harmonicas.

Nippon Gakki already had experience with wooden aircraft parts dating back to 1920, but wartime activity exposed the company to new technologies. By 1947 Nippon Gakki could cast its own metal piano frames and produced its first pianos in three years. The company also produced its first audio component, a phonograph, in 1947.

Postwar growth was rapid. The Japanese government had fostered the growth of Western music in Japan since 1879, but Nippon Gakki received its biggest boost to date in 1948. That year the Education Ministry mandated musical education for Japanese children (it was only encouraged before the war) and greatly expanded business.

Kaichi Kawakami's son, Genichi Kawakami, became the company's fourth president in 1950. During

Tokyo office and again damaged company plants. Before the company recovered, labor unions went on strike after Amano refused to negotiate. Amano gave in to the union's demands 105 days later, after the company's reserves were depleted.

Board member Kaichi Kawakami, by request of the other directors, took the presidency in 1927. A director

his tenure the Japanese rebuilt their economy, and consumer buying power increased. Nippon Gakki became less reliant on institutional purchases. President for 27 years, Kawakami made more progress in popularizing Western music in Japan by beginning the Yamaha Music Schools in 1954 to train young musicians. With the help of the Ministry of Education, Nippon Gakki founded the nonprofit Yamaha Music Foundation in 1966 to sponsor festivals and concerts and run the music schools.

Kawakami's biggest accomplishments were in production, diversification, and the creation of foreign markets, all of which built the framework for the modern Yamaha Corporation. Kawakami toured the United States and Europe in 1953, a trip that inspired diversification into many areas unrelated to the music industry. Like Yamaha's tour of the United States in 1899, Kawakami's tour affected the company's product line and reputation for decades to come.

His return sparked research into new uses for materials because capital was scarce. The company researched uses for fiberglass reinforced plastics (FRP). In 1960 the company produced its first sailboat made of FRP. Later Yamaha expanded to produce yachts, patrol boats for Japan's Maritime Safety Agency, and oceangoing fishing vessels. Primarily serving the Asian market, the company eventually became Japan's largest FRP boat producer. FRP capability led to the introduction of other products, such as archery bows, skis, and bathtubs. Through metals research Nippon Gakki developed sophisticated alloys for electronics as well as less complex alloys for structural purposes. Nippon Gakki soon became a major producer of equipment for the household construction industry, such as boilers and central heating systems.

In its traditional line of pianos, Nippon Gakki expanded production, raised its quality standards, and cut production costs, already lower than the industry average, even further. Through a conveyer belt system and an innovative kiln drying technique that facilitated the rapid drying of wood used in pianos, Nippon Gakki decreased the amount of time required to produce a piano from two years to three months.

The first large-scale marketing drive toward the United States was not related to music at all. In 1954 the government returned the company's World War II–era metal-working factory, which had been among confiscated assets. Nippon Gakki produced its first motorcycle in 1955 and established the Yamaha Motor Company Ltd., of which it was partial owner. Later it produced smaller motorized vehicles such as snowmobiles, outboard engines, and golf carts. For the next 20 years, however, it was motorcycles for which the

West would recognize the Yamaha brand. Following Honda's lead, Yamaha introduced its first motorcycles in the United States in the early 1960s. Along with Suzuki, the three companies made smaller and lower-priced motorcycles and greatly expanded the U.S. market, which had been limited to large cycles for serious enthusiasts. Yamaha also marketed its motorcycles successfully in Asia.

Nippon Gakki began an ambitious drive into electronics in 1959, when it introduced the world's first all-transistor organ to replace electronic organs using vacuum tubes. Nippon Gakki's first electronic instrument represented the company's new competence in product development.

EXPORT PUSH

With its new variety of products Nippon Gakki began its first serious export push, establishing an overseas subsidiary in Mexico in 1958. In 1959 the company made a few pianos with a U.S. retailer's name on them, and in 1960 it created its own sales subsidiary in Los Angeles. Within a year Yamaha won a conspicuous contract to supply the Los Angeles Board of Education with 53 grand pianos. For the next seven years, the board annually purchased Yamaha pianos for schools in its jurisdiction. Because Nippon Gakki priced its pianos considerably lower than Western competition, this boost to its reputation for quality allowed it to bid with more success on U.S. institutional contracts.

Having worked well in Japan, Nippon Gakki sponsored overseas musical events and education beginning in 1964, when it opened the first Yamaha school in the United States. Like its Japanese counterpart, it was designed to teach music appreciation to students at an early age and create a long-term market. Financially independent of Yamaha, these nonprofit schools eventually operated throughout Europe and the United States and taught scores of students.

These educational efforts were just beginning to pay off in Japan. During the 1960s Nippon Gakki's domestic market grew tremendously. Annual piano output increased from 24,000 in 1960 to 100,000 in 1966, making the company the world's largest piano manufacturer.

In the mid-1960s Nippon Gakki began to produce wind instruments on a large scale. In 1968 Nippon Gakki started exporting trumpets, trombones, and xylophones. After five years in development, the company produced is first concert grand piano in 1967.

U.S. instrument makers did not welcome Yamaha's growth. In 1969 U.S. piano manufacturers sought a 30 percent tariff on imported pianos, but the U.S. Tariff Commission ruled in Yamaha's favor. Nonetheless, the hearings delayed for three years a tariff reduction that had already been scheduled and established a hostile precedent for Nippon Gakki expansion in North America. In 1973 Yamaha bought its first U.S. manufacturing facility, but a strike there further delayed Yamaha's U.S. drive.

ELECTRONICS DEVELOPMENTS

Just as transistors had once replaced tubes in electronics, integrated circuits (ICs) replaced transistors in the 1970s. Because no manufacturer would develop an IC for Nippon Gakki's relatively limited demand, the company built a plant in 1971 to make its own. By developing the technology early, Nippon Gakki established itself as a serious electronics firm, better able to serve the accelerating demand for electronic keyboards and audio components.

Large-scale integrated circuits (LSIs) allowed the company to digitalize its keyboards. Nippon Gakki built an LSI plant in 1976 so it could convert all of its electronic products from analog to digital formats. LSIs also made possible Yamaha's growth as an electronics supplier and the manufacture of advanced electronic systems such as industrial robots. Nippon Gakki developed electronic components more quickly than other types of components. In its traditional line of pianos and organs, by contrast, Nippon Gakki still depended on overseas suppliers for components in the 1970s. While Nippon Gakki's sales in 1979 remained steady, a favorable exchange rate boosted earnings to a record ¥15 billion. Nevertheless, the same exchange rate hurt motorcycle sales.

OVEREXTENSION IN THE EIGHTIES

The 1980s were a difficult decade for the company. While there were notable successes, Nippon Gakki was badly mismanaged in a case of imperial overreach. The company's first major blunder actually came from its affiliate, Yamaha Motor, which in 1981 unwisely tried to unseat Honda from its top position in motorcycles. Yamaha introduced new models and increased production. When Honda and other motorcycle manufacturers did the same, the industry faced overproduction. As a result Yamaha Motor posted two consecutive losses totaling $126.1 million. A relatively small motor manufacturer, Yamaha Motor was left with an inventory of one million motorcycles and debts that approached $1 billion. In addition, the price competition among Japanese motorcycle makers caused U.S.

manufacturer Harley-Davidson to request tariffs on imports, straining Yamaha's U.S. business, because it did not have any U.S. factories. Nippon Gakki remained profitable because it owned only 39.1 percent of Yamaha Motor (later reduced to 33 percent), but the debacle damaged the company's reputation and position at home.

On the positive side, synthesizers and LSIs brought the company success early in the decade. Electronics research paid off well with the 1983 introduction of the DX-7 digital synthesizer, which went on to become the best-selling synthesizer ever. The development of LSIs allowed Nippon Gakki to produce its first professional sound systems and to keep pace with the consumer audio industry during the early 1980s. In 1983 the company put its LSIs themselves on the market.

Also in the early 1980s, Nippon Gakki divided its research facilities to reflect its electronics emphasis. Research was then carried out by four sections: one on semiconductors and LSIs, a second for research applications to audiovisual equipment, a third on hall and theater acoustic design, and the fourth for product design.

While expanding its product line, Nippon Gakki also initiated a program to spread its manufacturing base overseas, adding to its network of marketing subsidiaries. Hiroshi Kawashima, former president of the U.S. subsidiary, spearheaded the U.S. drive. In 1980 Nippon Gakki opened an electronic keyboard plant in Georgia in the hope that basing this new venture in the United States would ease trade tension.

Further difficulties, however, were in store when Hiroshi, the third generation of Kawakamis, became the company's seventh president in 1983. His father, then chairman, reportedly distrusted Hiroshi and battles between the two helped lead the company astray. Hiroshi brought in outside consultants in end-runs around his father, but this only resulted in such unwise moves as building huge headquarters in London and Buena Park, California, which served simply as symbols of a global powerhouse that was not. The company also became notorious for moving ahead with ambitious projects after doing little, if any, market research. Before there was even the smallest market for it, for example, Nippon Gakki attempted to develop a multimedia computer in the early 1980s and, probably to the company's good fortune, failed. Another marketing miscalculation at the other end of the decade left Yamaha with 200,000 unsold wind instruments in 1990.

Such ventures might have been perceived as noble failures if it were not for the company's increasingly troubled finances. Throughout the 1980s, rising profitability became increasingly elusive. Hiroshi Kawakami's attempt at a reorganization from 1985 to 1987 had failed to turn the company around. Meanwhile, to celebrate the 100th anniversary of the firm, Kawakami changed the corporate name to Yamaha Corporation in 1987.

LATE-CENTURY RESTRUCTURING EFFORTS

Kawakami made another attempt to resurrect Yamaha but was thwarted by a demoralized and rebellious workforce. He reportedly had hoped to use early retirement as a means of reducing the company's number of employees, but the workers' labor union refused to go along with the plan and demanded that Kawakami be fired, and he was.

Taking over in 1992 was a 36-year Yamaha veteran with a marketing background, Seisuke Ueshima, who quickly moved to turn the company around. He demoted Kawakami cronies and brokered an agreement with the union that retained all nonmanagerial employees but led to the elimination of 30 percent of the administrative positions in Japan along with overseas employees (notably those in the London and Buena Park headquarters). Ueshima also downsized the non-core resorts and sporting goods operations, both of which were losing money.

For the longer term, Ueshima had to change the way new products were developed and marketed. Specifically, he wanted Yamaha employees to ask "Why are we building this product?," a question rarely raised during previous decades. In the face of the maturation of some markets, Ueshima decided to go after the high end of these markets where larger profits could be made. One example was the Disklavier series of pianos, originally introduced in 1982, with built-in computers for recording and playing back performances; individual Disklavier models could retail for more than $30,000.

Ueshima also pushed the company to develop innovative new products. In 1993 the Silent Piano series was introduced to great success. Costing $7,300 each, more than 17,000 were sold in Japan in their first 12 months on the market, 70 percent above the amount projected. These pianos could either be played as regular acoustic pianos or their sound could be muted and heard only by the pianist through headphones. In 1995 Yamaha introduced a similarly functional electronic trumpet mute and sold 13,000 of them in the first few months. Silent Drums followed in 1996, the Silent Violin in 1997, and the Silent Cello in 1998. Other successful musical introductions of this period included the VL1 and VP1 virtual acoustic synthesizers, which,

rather than storing libraries of sounds that could be replayed, stored computer models of the instruments themselves that were then able to reproduce a wider variety of sounds and in a more authentic fashion.

Other innovations during this time included the Yamaha FM sound chip used in many sound boards—an essential feature of multimedia computers—and a karaoke system that received music via phone lines connected to a central computer loaded with laser disks. Such successes returned Yamaha to healthy profitability: ¥6.4 billion in 1994 and ¥28.5 billion in 1995. In June 1997 Kazukiyo Ishimura took over as president of Yamaha, having headed the company's electronic parts unit, turning it into a ¥100 billion business. Yamaha went on to post solid results for the 1998 fiscal year: net income of ¥13.48 billion ($101.3 million) on revenues of ¥608.99 billion ($4.58 billion).

END-OF-CENTURY RED INK

The end of the 20th century saw Yamaha make another change at the top, as Shuji Ito was named president. By this time, the company had fallen into the red once again as a result of the stagnant Japanese economy, the appreciation in the yen, and a drop-off in results in the company's electronic parts unit. For the fiscal year ending in March 2000, Yamaha posted a net loss of ¥40.78 billion ($384.2 million) on sales of ¥527.9 billion ($4.97 billion). Part of this loss was attributable to restructuring costs, including the company's withdrawal from the manufacturing of storage heads (electronic components that write on and read from hard disks), the sale of a semiconductor plant, an early retirement program that cut the workforce by 11 percent, and additional restructuring efforts undertaken to turn around several underperforming businesses.

Seeking a quick return to profitability in the early 21st century, Ito aimed to further focus the company's efforts on the core musical instruments and audiovisual groups. Ito also sought to engender more cross-company cooperation by consolidating group management. Another new initiative was the Digital Media Business Strategy, which included a number of components, including an increased emphasis on equipment such as sound chips and digital content designed for mobile phones and other handheld devices; the formation of a new record company called Yamaha Music Communications Co., Ltd., with the eventual goal of offering online downloading of music content; and the development of network-enabled musical instruments and equipment.

In its biggest success to come out of this initiative, Yamaha posted huge gains from its sound chips that controlled mobile phone ringtones as these ringtones exploded in popularity. This one product line was the principal driving force behind the surge in the company's profits for fiscal 2004 to ¥43.54 billion ($412 million); the mobile-phone sound chips were responsible for about 60 percent of this total. Unfortunately, this boost proved temporary as market demand quickly shifted away from these chips toward ringtone software applications.

In its core musical instrument operations, Yamaha was contending at this time with a stagnant domestic market thanks in part to low birthrates, and consequently fewer potential young customers. In addition to continuing to launch new products, such as the Silent Guitar (2001) and Silent Viola and an electric violin (2002), the company strived to create new adult customers by developing products specifically designed for adult beginners and by launching a network of music schools for adults in Japan.

EARLY 21ST CENTURY: PUSH INTO CHINA, RESTRUCTURING MOVES, AND ACQUISITIONS

Yamaha also began making a concerted push into other Asian markets, including South Korea and China. The fast-growing Chinese market was particularly important, and in 2003 a newly established holding company began coordinating the firm's sales and marketing efforts there. Then in the fall of 2004 Yamaha began manufacturing pianos in China at a plant in Hangzhou. The establishment of a manufacturing base in China was part of an overall shift in production to lower cost countries. By 2007 Yamaha had consolidated its two piano manufacturing plants in Japan into a single base at Kakegawa, shut down a guitar plant in Taiwan, and ended production of musical instruments in the United States with the closure of a piano plant in Georgia and a facility in Michigan that had been producing wind instruments. The company's musical instrument manufacturing operations were now concentrated in Japan, Indonesia, and China. Late in 2006 Yamaha announced plans to boost musical instrument sales in the emerging markets of Brazil, Russia, India, and China. The previous year the company had begun opening up music schools in China.

In the latter stages of Ito's presidential stint, Yamaha began an effort to more forcefully concentrate on its core musical instrument business and unwind the ill-fated diversification efforts of its past. This effort continued under Ito's successor, Mitsuru Umemura, who took over as president in June 2007. That year, the company sold its electronic metal frames business to Dowa Metaltech Co., Ltd., and also sold four loss-making resort complexes. Yamaha hung onto two of its

resorts that were related to its music operations. Toward the same end of sharpening its focus on musical instruments, Yamaha in 2007 also sold off part of its remaining stake in Yamaha Motor, reducing its interest from 22.7 percent to 14.9 percent. After this sell-off, the company no longer had to account for Yamaha Motor's results by the equity method, which reduced the motorcycle maker's impact on Yamaha's earnings. In October 2008 Yamaha responded to the worldwide economic slowdown by announcing its intention to review a number of underperforming businesses for possible divestment, downsizing, or restructuring via alliances. The targets for review included the semiconductor, car interior, kitchen and bath unit, and magnesium parts operations.

Under Umemura, Yamaha also began seeking growth opportunities via acquisition. In January 2008 the company acquired L. Bösendorfer Klavierfabrik GmbH, a prestigious Austrian maker of high-end pianos established in 1828. Yamaha later in the year took over Paris-based Nexo S.A. Nexo specialized in loudspeakers for large venues, so this acquisition served to strengthen Yamaha's position in commercial audio equipment, an area being emphasized for its high growth potential owing to advances in digital and networking technology.

Ray Walsh
Updated, David E. Salamie

PRINCIPAL SUBSIDIARIES

Yamaha Music Hokkaido Co., Ltd.; Sakuraba Mokuzai Co., Ltd.; Yamaha Music Tohoku Co., Ltd.; Yamaha Music Kanto Co., Ltd.; Yamaha Music Tokyo Co., Ltd.; Yamaha Hall Co., Ltd.; Yamaha Music Trading Corporation; Yamaha Sound Technologies Inc.; Yamaha Electronics Marketing Corporation; Yamaha Music Entertainment Holdings, Inc.; Yamaha Music Communications Co., Ltd.; Yamaha A&R, Inc.; Yamaha Music Artist, Inc.; Yamaha Music Publishing, Inc.; Yamaha Music Nishi-Tokyo Co., Ltd.; Yamaha Music Media Corporation; Yamaha Music Yokohama Co., Ltd.; Yamanashi Kogei Co., Ltd.; Tsumagoi Co., Ltd.; D.S. Corporation; Katsuragi Co., Ltd.; YP Winds Corporation; Yamaha Hi-Tech Design Corporation; Yamaha Piano Service Co., Ltd.; Yamaha Music Craft Corporation; Yamaha Credit Corporation; Yamaha Music Lease Corporation; Yamaha Livingtec Corporation; Yamaha Living Products Corporation; Joywell Home Corporation; Yamaha Fine Technologies Co., Ltd.; YP Video Corporation; Yamaha Business Support Corporation; Yamaha Insurance Service Co., Ltd.; Yamaha Travel Service Co., Ltd.; YP Engineering Co., Ltd.; Nihon Jimu Center Co., Ltd.; Yamaha Music Tokai Co., Ltd.; Yamaha Music Osaka Co., Ltd.; Yamaha Music Setouchi Co., Ltd.; Yamaha Music Kyushu Co., Ltd.; Yamaha Kagoshima Semiconductor Inc.; Yamaha Corporation of America (U.S.A.); Yamaha Electronics Corporation, USA; Yamaha Commercial Audio Systems, Inc. (U.S.A.); Yamaha Music InterActive, Inc. (U.S.A.); Yamaha Artist Services, Inc. (U.S.A.); Yamaha Canada Music Ltd.; Yamaha de México, S.A. de C.V.; Yamaha Music Latin America, S.A. (Panama); Yamaha Musical do Brasil Ltda. (Brazil); Yamaha Music Europe GmbH (Germany); Steinberg Media Technologies GmbH (Germany); Kemble & Company Ltd. (U.K.); Kemble Music Ltd. (U.K.); Taiwan Yamaha Musical Instruments Manufacturing Co., Ltd.; Yamaha KHS Music Co., Ltd. (Taiwan); Yamaha Music & Electronics (China) Co., Ltd.; Yamaha Music Technical (Shanghai) Co., Ltd. (China); Yamaha Trading (Shanghai) Co., Ltd. (China); Yamaha Electronics (Suzhou) Co., Ltd. (China); Xiaoshan Yamaha Musical Instrument Co., Ltd. (China); Hangzhou Yamaha Musical Instruments Co., Ltd. (China); Tianjin Yamaha Electronic Musical Instruments, Inc. (China); Yamaha Music Korea Ltd. (South Korea); Yamaha Music (Asia) Pte Ltd. (Singapore); Yamaha Music (Malaysia) Sdn. Bhd.; Yamaha Electronics Manufacturing (M) Sdn Bhd (Malaysia); PT. Yamaha Indonesia; PT. Yamaha Music Manufacturing Indonesia; PT. Yamaha Musik Indonesia (Distributor); PT. Yamaha Music Manufacturing Asia (Indonesia); PT. Yamaha Musical Products Indonesia; PT. Yamaha Electronics Manufacturing Indonesia; Yamaha Music Gulf FZE (United Arab Emirates); Yamaha Music Australia Pty. Ltd.

PRINCIPAL OPERATING UNITS

Musical Instruments Business Group; Sound and IT Business Group; Productive Technology Business Group.

PRINCIPAL COMPETITORS

Kawai Musical Instruments Manufacturing Co., Ltd.; Roland Corporation; Steinway Musical Instruments, Inc.; Fender Musical Instruments Corporation; Gibson Guitar Corp.; C.F. Martin & Co., Inc.; Sony Corporation; Casio Computer Co., Ltd.; Panasonic Corporation.

FURTHER READING

Armstrong, Larry, "Sweet Music with Ominous Undertones for Yamaha," *Business Week,* November 15, 1993, pp. 119–20.

Henry, Lawrence, "Yamaha Stubs Its Imperial Toe," *Industry Week,* April 6, 1992, pp. 29–31.

Hirooka, Kazuo, "Yamaha Banks on Brand Name," *Nikkei Weekly,* November 13, 2006.

Komori, Keisuke, "Yamaha Returns to Musical Roots," *Nikkei Report,* July 9, 2002.

Lieberman, Richard K., "The Ivory Poachers: Steinway & Sons Was the Incomparable Maker of the Grand Piano—Until Yamaha Came Along," *Financial Times,* August 9, 1997, p. 1.

Morris, Kathleen, "Play It Again, Seisuke," *Financial World,* November 22, 1994, pp. 42–46.

"Perfect Pitch?" *Economist,* February 17, 1996, p. 60.

Sanchanta, Mariko, "Yamaha Aims to Boost Tempo in China," *Financial Times,* September 28, 2005, p. 26.

Schlender, Brenton R., "The Perils of Losing Focus," *Fortune,* May 17, 1993, p. 100.

Takahashi, Yoshio, "Yamaha to Retune Holdings: Instrument Maker Will Reduce Its Stake in Motorcycle Firm," *Wall Street Journal Asia,* May 22, 2007, p. 22.

Takeda, Jin, "Yamaha Refocuses on Musical Ops After Stepping Out of Kawakami's Shadow," *Nikkei Report,* May 21, 2008.

———, "Yamaha Seeks to Strengthen via Cross-Shareholdings," *Nikkei Report,* May 22, 2007.

Takeda, Jin, and Kaoru Sakuraba, "Yamaha Returning to Roots in Acquiring Storied Piano Maker," *Nikkei Report,* November 29, 2007.

Tanikawa, Miki, "Yamaha Is Mining Its Musical Strength," *New York Times,* August 5, 2001, p. BU5.

Yamaha: A Century of Excellence, 1887–1987, Hamamatsu, Japan: Yamaha Corporation, 1987.

"Yamaha Rebounds with Microchips," *Nikkei Weekly,* January 19, 2004.

"Yamaha's First Century," *Music Trades,* August 1987.

ZENTIVA

Zentiva N.V./Zentiva, a.s.

Fred Roeskestraat 123
Amsterdam, 1076 EE
Netherlands
Telephone: (+31 20) 6739753
Fax: (+31 20) 4708362

U kabelovny 130
Prague, 102 37 10
Czech Republic
Telephone: (+420 2) 67 241 111
Fax: (+420 2) 72 702 402
Web site: http://www.zentiva.cz

Public Company
Incorporated: 1993
Employees: 6,500
Sales: CZK 16.67 billion ($974 million) (2007)
Stock Exchanges: Prague London
Ticker Symbol: ZENTIVA
NAICS: 325412 Pharmaceutical Preparation Manufacturing; 424210 Drugs and Druggists' Sundries Merchant Wholesalers

■ ■ ■

Zentiva N.V. is one of the largest Central and Eastern European pharmaceuticals groups. The company, registered in the Netherlands but operating from the Czech Republic, is also a leading producer of generic drugs in the region, with a product portfolio of more than 400 products. The company's best-selling products include Ibalgin; Citalec, a citalopram-based antidepres-
sant; the anti-ulcer medication Helicid; Rispen, an antipsychotic based on risperidon; pain relievers, including Paralen, Tralgit, Veral, and Acylpirin; and the statin Simvacard. The company also produces vitamin supplements. Zentiva was formed through the 2003 merger of the Czech Republic's Leciva and Slovakia's Slovakafarm. The company has since acquired operations in Romania (Sicomed) and Turkey (Eczacibasi). Poland and Russia are also major markets for the company. Listed on the Prague Stock Exchange, Zentiva became the subject of a takeover from main shareholder Sanofi-Aventis in 2008. Sanofi-Aventis already holds nearly 25 percent of the company. Jiri Michal is company CEO and chairman. In 2007, Zentiva posted revenues of CZK 16.67 billion ($974 million).

FROM PHARMACY TO PHARMACEUTICALS IN THE LATE 19TH CENTURY

While Zentiva as a modern pharmaceutical company had its origins in the 19th century, the company's roots in fact reached back into medieval times. Records from the late 15th century already made mention of a pharmacy known as the U černého orla (the Black Eagle) in Lesser Prague. The pharmacy survived over the next centuries; Benjamin Fragner bought the shop in 1857, beginning nearly a century of Fragner family ownership.

The Black Eagle began to expand under son Karel Fragner, who, at the age of 25, took over after his father's death in 1886. The pharmacy's true growth came, however, with the third generation of the Fragner family. Jiri (or Jirfy) Fragner, born in 1900, took over the business after his father died in 1926. Fragner soon decided to launch the company into the preparation of pharmaceuticals on an industrial scale. By then, the newly independent Czechoslovakia had become an important focal point for European pharmaceutical research. Jiri Fragner soon emerged as a leading figure in the sector, and by the end of his life was known as the "father of the Czech pharmaceutical industry."

In 1928, Fragner acquired a site in Dolni Mecholupy, then on the outskirts of Prague, and launched construction of a new factory there. Construction of the facility, named after Fragner's grandfather, was completed in 1930. The company initially focused on the production of ointments, cough drops, and similar products. Over the next decade, however, the company began expanding its production to include a range of active substances as well. Fragner also expanded through the merger with fellow Prague pharmaceuticals group Interpharma, in 1931.

The German annexation of Czechoslovakia in 1939 had drastic consequences for the country's research community as well. Following the occupation, the Germans shut down the country's universities. The Fragner company stepped in to help preserve the country's research effort, and through the war years provided a workplace for many of the top Czech chemists, scientists, doctors, and students. Among them was Ivan Malek, who had begun work on the newly discovered antibiotics in the 1930s.

Cut off from the rest of Europe—where work on developing large-scale production of the penicillin molecule was well underway in England—by 1943 Malek and his team managed to extract a highly active substance similar to penicillin from rabbit droppings. Malek cautioned Fragner that in the event of the German defeat, the company's own antibiotic production would be rendered obsolete by the more advanced work done by the Allies. Nonetheless, Fragner authorized the continuation of Malek's work. Over the next year, the company succeeded in developing its own type of

penicillin. Throughout this period, the Fragner laboratory worked in secret to prevent the Germans from taking advantage of the new molecule, which was given the name Mykoin BF-510. By 1944, the new molecule had been successfully tested in clinical trials with critically ill patients.

GROWTH IN THE SOVIET ERA

Czechoslovakia came under Soviet dominance in the postwar period. By 1946, the new Communist government had begun to nationalize the country's pharmaceutical industry. As a result, the Fragner business was broken up, with the pharmacy separated from the pharmaceutical factory in Dolni Mecholupy. Despite the loss of ownership of his family's company, however, Jiri Fragner remained highly active in the industry. Following the nationalization of the pharmaceutical industry, Fragner became the first technical director of the newly created SPOFA (Spojené farmaceutické závody). The Dolni Mecholupy plant was then combined with three pharmaceutical factories in Modrany, Horatev, and Vyscocany, creating CS-12 National Enterprise.

SPOFA, and the rest of the pharmaceutical industry in Czechoslovakia, was initially considered as part of the country's chemicals industry, and therefore attached to the Ministry of Chemical Industry. In 1952, SPOFA moved a step closer to becoming the main pharmaceuticals operation in Czechoslovakia. In that year, the company took over direction of a Slovakian counterpart, Slovakofarma.

Slovakofarma had been created during the German occupation as Slovenské alkaloidy, in Bratislava in 1941. The company's initial production was limited to the production of morphine. Through the end of the war, however, the company expanded, taking over a number of factories, formerly used for the production of automobiles, in Hlohovec. Following the war, the group led the consolidation of the Slovak pharmaceutical sector, acquiring the Facet factory in Piest'any, among others. In 1950, the company took on the new name of Slovakofarma.

Two years after taking over Slovakofarma, SPOFA itself was transferred from the chemicals industry to the healthcare sector, and placed under the authority of the Supreme Drug Production Administration Office. At this time, SPOFA was expanded to stand for Sdružení podniků pro zdravotnickou výrobu, or Association of Healthcare Production Enterprises.

In this capacity, SPOFA oversaw both its own growth and the growth of the Czechoslovakian pharmaceuticals industry in general during the Cold

KEY DATES

∎

1857: Benjamin Fragner acquires the Black Eagle pharmacy in Prague.

1928: Grandson Jiri Fragner decides to open a factory and launch production of pharmacy and pharmaceutical products.

1944: Fragner becomes first in continental Europe to synthesize penicillin.

1946: The Czech government nationalizes the pharmaceutical industry, incorporating Fragner's operations into a state-run company, SPOFA.

1952: SPOFA adds Slovakofarma, becoming the central pharmaceuticals operation in Czechoslovakia.

1978: SPOFA completes a major expansion and modernization of its production capacity.

1990: SPOFA is broken up into Czech and Slovak components.

1993: The creation of Leciva replaces former SPOFA concern.

1998: Leciva is privatized through management buyout backed by Warburg Pincus.

2003: Leciva becomes Zentiva and acquires Slovakofarma.

2004: Zentiva goes public with an IPO on the Prague Stock Exchange.

2005: Zentiva acquires Sicomed in Romania.

2007: Zentiva acquires pharmaceuticals operations of Eczacibasi in Turkey.

2008: Sanofi-Aventis launches a takeover offer for Zentiva.

War era. By the late 1960s, demand for the group's products had risen steadily, leading the government to begin plans for a major expansion of SPOFA's production capacity. This expansion was carried out in the 1970s, as the Dolni Mecholupy site added a new, state-of-the-art factory and equipment. The extension elevated SPOFA to the status of a leading producer of pharmaceutical products in Central and Eastern Europe.

At the same time, the new facility enabled the company to achieve significant improvements in manufacturing processes and quality. In this way, SPOFA, unlike much of the Soviet-era industrial apparatus in the Eastern bloc nations, found itself reasonably prepared for the end of Soviet domination and the introduction of a new competitive free market economy in the 1990s.

PRIVATIZED IN 1998

The collapse of Communism and the breakup of Czechoslovakia itself had far-reaching consequences for SPOFA. Into the early 1990s, the company underwent a dismantling process, separated into its Czech and Slovak components. Both governments then began preparations for the privatization of their state-run industries. In Czechoslovakia, the CS-12 National Enterprise was split off from SPOFA in 1990, and subsequently placed under the authority of the Ministry of Industry.

In Slovakia, meanwhile, the new government prepared for the privatization of Slovakofarma, creating a new state-owned joint-stock company, Slovakofarma Hlohovec, in 1992. Two years later, the government launched the privatization of Slovakofarma. At this time, Slovakofarma found a new main shareholder, S.L. Pharma Holding, based in Austria.

By 1993, the remains of the former SPOFA operations had been regrouped under a new company, Leciva, which began preparing its own future privatization. As part of that process, the company instituted a new modernization program, raising its manufacturing plant to European and global standards. This effort was rewarded in 1993 with the receipt of the Best Manufacturing Practices Certificate from the World Health Organization, the first to be awarded in the Czech pharmaceutical industry. Leciva extended its modernization throughout its factories, which were all successfully certified by 1997.

Leading this effort was Jiri Michal, who had joined the company in 1974 as a chemist, and who had been named Leciva's first general director in 1993. Michal and his team set their sights on privatization, putting into place the structure for a management buyout. Instead of taking on debt, however, the company sought an investment partner to buy the company from the Czech government outright. In 1998, Michal found that partner in U.S.-based Warburg Pincus. Michal then turned to the Czech government and convinced them to sell the company, rather than put Leciva up for auction. The government agreed to the proposal on the faith of Warburg Pincus's financial backing and Michal's own highly regarded reputation.

BECOMING ZENTIVA IN THE 21ST CENTURY

Over the next several years, Leciva, already the largest pharmaceuticals concern in the Czech Republic, began restructuring its sales and marketing operations with an eye on a future expansion into international markets. By the early 2000s, the company recognized that this effort required that it achieve sufficient scale to make it possible to compete not only with major competitors in other Central and Eastern European markets, but also with increasing presence of major pharmaceutical giants from elsewhere in the world.

Leciva began acquisition talks with Slovak counterpart Slovakofarma. This led Leciva to restructure its own organization in preparation for the eventual merger. Part of this restructuring effort included a change of name, as the company adopted the more universal name Zentiva. By 2003, Zentiva had completed the acquisition of Slovakofarma. Zentiva's preparations meant that the integration of Slovakofarma went smoothly. Within weeks, the absorption of the Slovak operations had been completed, with the Zentiva name extended throughout the entire company.

With the successful completion of the Slovakofarma acquisition purchase, Zentiva now readied itself for further expansion. To this end, the company launched an initial public offering (IPO) in 2004. The IPO was highly successful, and notable as being the first IPO to be launched on the Prague Stock Exchange since the early 1990s. The share issue was accompanied by the placing of global depositary receipts on the London Stock Exchange. In this way, the company attracted investors both from within the Czech Republic and from abroad.

The IPO also provided Zentiva with the funding for an expansion effort, as the company established sales and distribution operations throughout much of Central and Eastern Europe. The company quickly established itself as a major presence in the growing generics market in much of the region, with a particularly strong presence in Poland, and operations reaching as far as Russia.

Zentiva now went in search of new acquisition opportunities to enable its expansion beyond the Czech and Slovak region. This search led the company to Romania, where it bought Bucharest-based Sicomed in 2005. Sicomed had originally been established in 1962 as a factory in Bucharest charged with supplying medicines and other pharmacy products to the city's pharmacies. The company initially operated under the name Bucharest Medicines Plant.

With the collapse of the Communist regime, the company took on a new name, Sicomed, in 1990. By 1998, Sicomed had begun its own privatization, listing its stock on the Bucharest Stock Exchange. The company's privatization was completed in 1999. Zentiva initially acquired 51 percent of Sicomed; by 2006, the group had raised its stake to nearly 75 percent. By the

end of that year, the company had completed its acquisition of Sicomed. The Romanian company was then integrated into Zentiva's own Romanian operations, forming a new subsidiary, Zentiva S.A. That company then became the leading generics supplier in Romania.

Zentiva's growth plans met new success in 2007 when the company reached an agreement with Turkey's Eczacibasi group to acquire its pharmaceuticals operations. Eczacibasi had been founded by a pharmacist in the early years of the Turkish Republic by Suleyman Ferit Bey, who had been granted the honorary title of "Eczacibasi" or "Master Pharmacist" in 1909. Bey acquired his own pharmacy in 1912, then began producing his own line of products, including creams, toothpaste, lotions, and even eau de cologne. Under his son, Nejat Eczacibasi (the family adopted the title as its surname in 1934), the company expanded strongly, creating its own pharmaceuticals laboratory in 1952. Eczacibasi went on to become a diversified conglomerate, with more that 40 companies under its control.

Zentiva paid EUR 460 million ($603 million) for the Eczacibasi operations. Following its integration into Zentiva, the Turkish operations were placed under the Eczacibasi-Zentiva name. The acquisition not only boosted Zentiva's annual revenues by more than EUR 200 million, it also solidified the company's status as one of the leading generics producers in Central and Eastern Europe.

TAKEOVER TARGET

In 2008, Zentiva itself became the target of a takeover offer. In 2006, French pharmaceuticals major Sanofi-Aventis became Zentiva's major stakeholder, paying $518 million for a nearly 25 percent stake. Initially, the French giant claimed that it was not interested in taking complete control of the Czech company. In August 2008, however, it launched a formal buyout offer for the rest of Zentiva's shares, in a deal that valued Zentiva at nearly $2.7 billion.

Zentiva quickly rejected the offer, with Michal telling shareholders in September 2008 (as reported by *Pharma Marketletter*) that the offer "fails to reflect the unique strategic position that we have built in the central and eastern European generics space over the last three years. It also fails to capture the significant improvement in operational and financial performance or the growth prospects which were reflected in our strong first-half 2008 results." Sanofi-Aventis's interest nonetheless underscored Zentiva's emergence as an important new force in the European generics market in the new century.

M. L. Cohen

PRINCIPAL SUBSIDIARIES

Eczacibaşi-Zentiva (Turkey); Zentiva A.S. (Czech Republic); Zentiva A.S. (Slovakia); Zentiva S.A (Romania).

PRINCIPAL COMPETITORS

Richter Gedeon AG; Ranbaxy Laboratories Ltd.; Dr Reddy's Laboratories Ltd.; Cipla Ltd.

FURTHER READING

Andress, Mark, "Zentiva Turns to Expansion," *Financial Times,* November 8, 2004, p. 20.

Breyerová, Petra, "Michal's Drug-Induced Visions," *Czech Business Weekly,* January 17, 2005.

Eisberg, Neil, "Dutch Headquartered Pharma Concern Zentiva, Which Operates in Central and Eastern Europe, Has Rejected an Unsolicited Takeover Bid by French Pharma Major Sanofi-Aventis," *Chemistry and Industry,* August 11, 2008, p. 15.

Evans, Julian, "Zentiva Livens Up Prague Exchange," *Euromoney,* August 2004, p. 21.

Krosnar, Katka, "Zentiva Acquires Turkey's Eczacibasi," *Financial Times,* March 6, 2007, p. 26.

Wells, Kathryn, "Zentiva's Prescription for Central European Growth," *Euromoney,* October 2006, p. 98.

"Zentiva Claims 40% of Czech Pharmaceuticals Market," *Czech Business News,* January 16, 2004.

"Zentiva Says $2B Sanofi Bid Undervalues Firm," *Pharma Marketletter,* September 15, 2008.

"Zentiva to Bring First Prague IPO for 14 Years via Merrill," *Euroweek,* June 4, 2004, p. 24.

Zogby International

Zogby International, Inc.

901 Broad Street
Utica, New York 13501
U.S.A.
Telephone: (312) 624-0200
Toll Free: (877) 462-7655
Fax: (315) 624-0210
Web site: http://www.zogby.com

Private Company
Incorporated: 1984
Employees: 166
Sales: $5 million (2007 est.)
NAICS: 541910 Marketing Research and Public
Opinion Polling

■ ■ ■

Zogby International, Inc., is an opinion polling and market research firm that polls, researches, and consults for the media, corporations, government organizations, and political groups. The company is best known for its polling during election cycles, but generates the bulk of its revenue by polling consumers and conducting focus groups for corporate clientele. Zogby International conducts opinion research in more than 70 countries through offices in New York, Washington, D.C., and Miami, and in Dubai, United Arab Emirates. The company is led by its founder, president, and chief executive officer, John Zogby.

ZOGBY'S BACKGROUND

John Zogby's success in assessing and articulating the opinions of others began by predicting his own failure.

For the Utica, New York, native, his impending doom inspired him to start a new chapter in his life and leave behind a career in academia. Zogby, who earned degrees in history from Le Moyne College and Syracuse University, was teaching history and political science at Utica College when he made his life-defining move. In 1981, at age 33, he decided to run for mayor of Utica as a Democrat and launched a campaign that enlisted the help of his students. "When I ran for mayor of Utica," Zogby recalled in a March 17, 2000 interview with *Investor's Business Daily,* "I had my students conduct a poll of the race." "There was good news and bad news," he continued. "The bad news was that I wasn't going to be elected mayor. The good news was that I knew before anyone else how much I was going to lose by."

Zogby's mayoral bid ended after the Democratic primary election, a loss that prompted him to reevaluate his life and make some changes. He left Utica College and joined the American Arab Anti-Discrimination Committee (ADC). Zogby, the son of Lebanese immigrants, spent three-and-a-half years working as a field representative for ADC (his brother, James Zogby, founded the Arab American Institute, a nonprofit, advocacy group, in 1985).

ZOGBY INTERNATIONAL
ESTABLISHED IN 1984

After his stint working for a grassroots, civil rights organization, Zogby decided to return to politics, but he did not return to teaching politics or running for an elected office. Instead, he started his own business, a political consultancy firm that bore his own name.

COMPANY PERSPECTIVES

Zogby International is constantly searching, testing and measuring hypotheses and principles on polling and public opinion research. Working with a panel of psychologists, sociologists, computer experts, linguists, political scientists, economists, and mathematicians, we explore every nuance in language and test new methods in public opinion research. It is this investment in time and money for research and development that makes us a leader in the public opinion field.

Zogby International was formed in 1984, with Zogby promoting himself as an activist and consultant. Of all the services he offered to clients, he preferred the task he had once assigned to his students at Utica College. "The thing I was doing best and liked the most were the occasional political polls," he said in his March 17, 2000 interview with *Investor's Business Daily.* "I've always been amazed at how one could get from a small sample an idea of how an election would turn."

Soon after establishing his company, Zogby began focusing exclusively on conducting polls. He spent the second half of the 1980s building his reputation in upstate New York, honing his skills, developing his methodology, and promoting his poll results from each election cycle. Every year ended with the formulation of new strategic plans, as Zogby and his small staff in Utica attempted to develop the most accurate way to ascertain and to predict voter behavior through probability and statistics.

ZOGBY GOES STATEWIDE IN 1991

Zogby operated as a regional pollster until 1991, the year he decided to elevate his business to the next level. Zogby set his sights on becoming the leading, independent pollster serving all of New York, a widening of Zogby International's scope that began with the company's first statewide poll in December 1991. Zogby set out to determine whether Democratic New York Governor Mario Cuomo should run for the presidency. The results of the survey, released in early 1992, showed that Cuomo would fail to carry his home state in a race against incumbent President George H. W. Bush. Numerous pundits focused on the presidential election credited Zogby International's findings with greatly influencing Cuomo's decision not to seek the presidency.

THE ZOGBY APPROACH

The first glimmer of Zogby's success in gauging the decisions made by voters drew attention to his polling methodology. Compared with the practices used by established pollsters such as The Gallup Organization and Opinion Research Corporation, there were differences in Zogby's methodology, although, as he conceded in a November 1, 2003 interview with *FSB,* there were not many. "Ninety-eight percent of what I do is what everybody else does," he said. To ensure his polling was as accurate as possible, Zogby polled only "likely" voters. Some pollsters, in contrast, polled all adults or all registered voters, which, Zogby believed, skewed the results because the findings included the opinions of people who did not intend to vote. He also weighted his polls, taking into account the party identification of the people his staff questioned. Zogby believed, for instance, that Republicans were less likely to answer telephone calls, which led him to give extra weighting to Republican responses. Despite his efforts to develop the most accurate way to determine what voters were thinking, Zogby realized there was a certain amount of guesswork and speculation in his findings. "Anyone who says there is not art in this is not facing reality," he said in his November 1, 2003 interview with *FSB.*

A few short years after launching his bid to become the leading pollster in the state of New York, Zogby was enjoying bustling business. In 1994, Zogby International signed a contract to conduct polling for the *New York Post* and the Fox affiliate in New York City, WNYW-TV. The year also saw Zogby gain national attention, as he again stood out for weighing in on the political chances of Mario Cuomo. Zogby was the first and only pollster to suggest Cuomo would lose his reelection bid for governor, which he did in the November 1994 election. Pundits and the press took note of Zogby's call, enabling the small company from Utica to expand its polling activities beyond New York and function as a national pollster in time for the 1996 presidential election. The state was set for Zogby's crowning achievement.

ZOGBY SHINES IN 1996

Zogby's debut in the national arena cemented his reputation as one of the country's most reliable pollsters. In the 1996 presidential race between Bill Clinton and Bob Dole, Zogby's prediction came within one-tenth of 1 percent of the actual result. When Zogby learned how close his call on the election had been, he realized his career as a pollster had reached a turning point. "My life was never going to be the same again," he said in his November 1, 2003 interview with *FSB.* Zogby's accuracy enabled his company to secure the high-profit-

KEY DATES

1984: John Zogby founds a political consultancy firm in Utica, New York.
1991: Zogby International begins conducting statewide political polls in New York.
1994: Zogby International is the only polling firm that correctly predicts an election loss for New York Governor Mario Cuomo.
1996: Zogby International's prediction in the presidential race comes within one-tenth of one percent of the actual result.
2000: Zogby International is one of only two national pollsters to predict Al Gore will win the popular vote.
2006: Zogby International's online polling correctly calls 17 of 18 U.S. Senate races.

margin corporate accounts that served as the lifeblood of Zogby International, accounting for roughly two-thirds of its annual sales. Major corporations such as Microsoft Corporation and Philip Morris hired Zogby International to poll consumers and to conduct focus groups, their confidence in the Utica firm bolstered by Zogby's pinpoint political prognostications. Not coincidentally, Reuters News Agency, the largest news agency in the world, hired Zogby International to conduct polls in 1996, beginning a relationship that would endure for years.

MISCUES

Making the correct call in the political arena enabled Zogby to win the business of corporations and advocacy groups, but when he incorrectly predicted elections, his reputation lost some of its luster. Such was the case in 1998 in the Senate race between incumbent Alfonse D'Amato and his challenger Charles Schumer, a mistake that led Zogby to alter his polling methodology. Zogby explained what happened in a March 17, 2000 interview with *Investor's Business Daily.* "I conducted a three-day running average poll," he said. "The last day of the poll Schumer was up five percent, but over the three days I had it as a tie. On the one hand, it was too close to call, but there was momentum for Schumer. On the other hand, I looked at history and saw where D'Amato had risen from the ashes so many times. So I said very qualifyingly that possibly D'Amato could win. This was treated as a prediction." In November 1998, D'Amato lost to Schumer by 11 percentage points,

delivering a stinging blow to Zogby's reputation. "It taught me to try to poll longer and later," he told *Investor's Business Daily.* "So instead of stopping Sunday at three P.M., we try to talk our clients into calling through Monday to try to catch any last-minute trends."

Zogby suffered a more profound setback as he led his company into the 21st century. After being one of only two national pollsters to predict that Al Gore would win the popular vote in the 2000 presidential election, he tripped up in the next election cycle. Zogby inaccurately called a number of strategically important congressional races in 2002, which exacerbated his company's declining billings from the corporate sector after the terrorist attacks against the United States on September 11, 2001. Strapped for cash, Zogby International began to suffer financially, its condition made more precarious when its bank demanded immediate payment of a loan. The company struggled for two years, operating without a line of credit while Zogby tried to recover from the downturn.

SUCCESSES OUTWEIGH FAILURES

Despite the slip-ups, Zogby had an impressive record as a pollster. Between 1984 and 2000, more than 95 percent of his election polls came within 1 percent of the results. Between 1996 and 2004, he was the most accurate pollster in the three presidential election cycles. Zogby also charted new ground in his industry, not only with new methodology such as weighting polls according to party identification, but also by conducting polls online. He began polling online in 1998, an effort that after years of research and development led to the formation of Zogby Interactive. Using a database of respondents that was reflective of the national population, Zogby Interactive made an impressive show in 2006, correctly predicting 17 of 18 U.S. Senate races and 84 percent of the 73 congressional and gubernatorial races.

ZOGBY OVERSEAS

Zogby's track record of success encouraged him to look beyond the United States, leading to Zogby International's expansion overseas. An office was established in Dubai, in the United Arab Emirates, to ascertain Arab attitudes toward the United States, particularly to poll Lebanese opinions regarding the United States. Zogby also interpreted the political landscape in foreign countries, correctly calling the Mexican presidential election of Vicente Fox in 2000 and Felipe Calderón in 2006, as well as the election of Ariel Sharon as prime minister of Israel in 2001.

Without question, Zogby was regarded as one of the most trusted pollsters in the political arena, delivering accurate snapshots of the mind-set of the electorate that, in turn, attracted corporate clientele. His non-political polling and research generated the majority of the revenue that fed Zogby International's growth, but his work during the election cycles determined his worth in the corporate sector. Accordingly, much was at stake for the financial health of Zogby International every two years, as Zogby was called upon by newspapers, radio stations, and television networks to interpret the mood of voters across the country. A series of serious blunders by Zogby augured disaster for Zogby International, but the company's influential leader rarely stumbled, making it highly likely that his company would play a prominent role in politics and in corporate boardrooms for years to come.

Jeffrey L. Covell

PRINCIPAL DIVISIONS

Zogby Interactive.

PRINCIPAL COMPETITORS

The Gallup Organization; Harris Interactive Inc.; YouGov; Angus Reid Strategies; Opinion Research Corporation.

FURTHER READING

Cleary, Peter, "Top Pollster John Zogby; Narrow Focus Keeps His Predictions on Target," *Investor's Business Daily,* March 17, 2000, p. A20.

Whitford, David, "The Battle for Poll Position: An Entrepreneur's Fate Depends on His Ability to Call the Next Election," *FSB,* November 1, 2003, p. 28.

Cumulative Index to Companies

Listings in this index are arranged in alphabetical order under the company name. Company names beginning with a letter or proper name such as Eli Lilly & Co. will be found under the first letter of the company name. Definite articles (The, Le, La) are ignored for alphabetical purposes as are forms of incorporation that precede the company name (AB, NV). Company names printed in **bold** *type have full, historical essays on the page numbers appearing in bold. Updates to entries that appeared in earlier volumes are signified by the notation* (**upd.**)*. This index is cumulative with volume numbers printed in bold type.*

A

A&E Television Networks, 32 3–7

A&P *see* The Great Atlantic & Pacific Tea Company, Inc.

A & W Brands, Inc., 25 3–5 *see also* Cadbury Schweppes PLC.

A-dec, Inc., 53 3–5

A-Mark Financial Corporation, 71 3–6

A.B. Chance Industries Co., Inc. *see* Hubbell Inc.

A.B.Dick Company, 28 6–8

A.B. Watley Group Inc., 45 3–5

A.C. Moore Arts & Crafts, Inc., 30 3–5

A.C. Nielsen Company, 13 3–5 *see also* ACNielsen Corp.

A. Duda & Sons, Inc., 88 1–4

A. F. Blakemore & Son Ltd., 90 1–4

A.G. Edwards, Inc., 8 3–5; 32 17–21 (upd.)

A.H. Belo Corporation, 10 3–5; 30 13–17 (upd.) *see also* Belo Corp.

A.L. Pharma Inc., 12 3–5 *see also* Alpharma Inc.

A.M. Castle & Co., 25 6–8

A. Moksel AG, 59 3–6

A. Nelson & Co. Ltd., 75 3–6

A. O. Smith Corporation, 11 3–6; 40 3–8 (upd.); 93 1–9 (upd.)

A.P. Møller - Maersk A/S, 57 3–6

A.S. Watson & Company Ltd., 84 1–4

A.S. Yakovlev Design Bureau, 15 3–6

A. Schulman, Inc., 8 6–8; 49 3–7 (upd.)

A.T. Cross Company, 17 3–5; 49 8–12 (upd.)

A.W. Faber-Castell Unternehmensverwaltung GmbH & Co., 51 3–6

AAF-McQuay Incorporated, 26 3–5

Aalborg Industries A/S, 90 5–8

AAON, Inc., 22 3–6

AAR Corp., 28 3–5

Aardman Animations Ltd., 61 3–5

Aarhus United A/S, 68 3–5

Aaron Brothers Holdings, Inc. *see* Michaels Stores, Inc.

Aaron Rents, Inc., 14 3–5; 35 3–6 (upd.)

AARP, 27 3–5

Aavid Thermal Technologies, Inc., 29 3–6

Abar Corporation *see* Ipsen International Inc.

Abaxis, Inc., 83 1–4

Abatix Corp., 57 7–9

ABB Ltd., II 1–4; 22 7–12 (upd.); 65 3–10 (upd.)

Abbey National plc, 10 6–8; 39 3–6 (upd.)

Abbott Laboratories, I 619–21; 11 7–9 (upd.); 40 9–13 (upd.); 93 10–18 (upd.)

ABC Appliance, Inc., 10 9–11

ABC Carpet & Home Co. Inc., 26 6–8

ABC Family Worldwide, Inc., 52 3–6

ABC, Inc. *see* Capital Cities/ABC Inc.

ABC Learning Centres Ltd., 93 19–22

ABC Rail Products Corporation, 18 3–5

ABC Stores *see* MNS, Ltd.

ABC Supply Co., Inc., 22 13–16

Abengoa S.A., 73 3–5

Abercrombie & Fitch Company, 15 7–9; 35 7–10 (upd.); 75 7–11 (upd.)

Abertis Infraestructuras, S.A., 65 11–13

ABF *see* Associated British Foods plc.

Abigail Adams National Bancorp, Inc., 23 3–5

Abiomed, Inc., 47 3–6

AbitibiBowater Inc., IV 245–47; 25 9–13 (upd.); 99 1–11 (upd.)

ABM Industries Incorporated, 25 14–16 (upd.)

ABN *see* Algemene Bank Nederland N.V.

ABN AMRO Holding, N.V., 50 3–7

Abrams Industries Inc., 23 6–8

Abraxas Petroleum Corporation, 89 1–5

Abril S.A., 95 1–4

Abt Associates Inc., 95 5–9

Abu Dhabi National Oil Company, IV 363–64; 45 6–9 (upd.)

Academic Press *see* Reed Elsevier plc.

Academy of Television Arts & Sciences, Inc., 55 3–5

Academy Sports & Outdoors, 27 6–8

Acadian Ambulance & Air Med Services, Inc., 39 7–10

Access Business Group *see* Alticor Inc.

ACCION International, 87 1–4

Acciona S.A., 81 1–4
Acclaim Entertainment Inc., 24 3–8
ACCO World Corporation, 7 3–5; 51 7–10 (upd.)
Accor S.A., 10 12–14; 27 9–12 (upd.); 69 3–8 (upd.)
Accredited Home Lenders Holding Co., 91 1–4
Accubuilt, Inc., 74 3–5
Accuray Incorporated, 95 10–13
AccuWeather, Inc., 73 6–8
ACE Cash Express, Inc., 33 3–6
Ace Hardware Corporation, 12 6–8; 35 11–14 (upd.)
Acer Incorporated, 16 3–6; 73 9–13 (upd.)
Acergy SA, 97 1–4
Aceros Fortuna S.A. de C.V. *see* Carpenter Technology Corp.
Aceto Corp., 38 3–5
AchieveGlobal Inc., 90 9–12
Acindar Industria Argentina de Aceros S.A., 87 5–8
Ackerley Communications, Inc., 9 3–5
Ackermans & van Haaren N.V., 97 5–8
ACLU *see* American Civil Liberties Union (ACLU).
Acme-Cleveland Corp., 13 6–8
Acme United Corporation, 70 3–6
ACNielsen Corporation, 38 6–9 (upd.)
Acorn Products, Inc., 55 6–9
Acosta Sales and Marketing Company,Inc., 77 1–4
ACS *see* Affiliated Computer Services, Inc.; Alaska Communications Systems Group, Inc.
Acsys, Inc., 44 3–5
Actelion Ltd., 83 5-8
Action Performance Companies, Inc., 27 13–15
Activision, Inc., 32 8–11; 89 6–11 (upd.)
Actuant Corporation, 94 1–8 (upd.)
Acuity Brands, Inc., 90 13–16
Acushnet Company, 64 3–5
Acuson Corporation, 10 15–17; 36 3–6 (upd.)
Acxiom Corporation, 35 15–18
Adam Opel AG, 7 6–8; 21 3–7 (upd.); 61 6–11 (upd.)
Adams Childrenswear Ltd., 95 14–19
The Adams Express Company, 86 1–5
Adams Golf, Inc., 37 3–5
Adams Media Corporation *see* F&W Publications, Inc.
Adani Enterprises Ltd., 97 9–12
Adaptec, Inc., 31 3–6
ADC Telecommunications, Inc., 10 18–21; 30 6–9 (upd.); 89 12–17 (upd.)
Adecco S.A., 36 7–11 (upd.)
Adelphia Communications Corporation, 17 6–8; 52 7–10 (upd.)
ADESA, Inc., 71 7–10
Adia S.A., 6 9–11 *see also* Adecco S.A.
adidas Group AG, 14 6–9; 33 7–11 (upd.); 75 12–17 (upd.)
Aditya Birla Group, 79 1–5

ADM *see* Archer Daniels Midland Co.
Administaff, Inc., 52 11–13
Administración Nacional de Combustibles, Alcohol y Pórtland, 93 23–27
Admiral Co. *see* Maytag Corp.
ADNOC *see* Abu Dhabi National Oil Co.
Adobe Systems Incorporated, 10 22–24; 33 12–16 (upd.)
Adolf Würth GmbH & Co. KG, 49 13–15
Adolfo Dominguez S.A., 72 3–5
Adolph Coors Company, I 236–38; 13 9–11 (upd.); 36 12–16 (upd.) *see also* Molson Coors Brewing Co.
Adolphe Lafont *see* Vivarte SA.
ADP *see* Automatic Data Processing, Inc.
ADT Security Services, Inc., 12 9–11; 44 6–9 (upd.)
Adtran Inc., 22 17–20
Advance Auto Parts, Inc., 57 10–12
Advance Publications Inc., IV 581–84; 19 3–7 (upd.); 96 1–7 (upd.)
Advanced Circuits Inc., 67 3–5
Advanced Fibre Communications, Inc., 63 3–5
Advanced Marketing Services, Inc., 34 3–6
Advanced Medical Optics, Inc., 79 6–9
Advanced Micro Devices, Inc., 6 215–17; 30 10–12 (upd.); 99 12–17 (upd.)
Advanced Neuromodulation Systems, Inc., 73 14–17
Advanced Technology Laboratories, Inc., 9 6–8
Advanced Web Technologies *see* Miner Group Int.
Advanstar Communications, Inc., 57 13–17
Advanta Corporation, 8 9–11; 38 10–14 (upd.)
Advantica Restaurant Group, Inc., 27 16–19 (upd.)
Adventist Health, 53 6–8
The Advertising Council, Inc., 76 3–6
The Advisory Board Company, 80 1–4 *see also* The Corporate Executive Board Co.
Advo, Inc., 6 12–14; 53 9–13 (upd.)
Advocat Inc., 46 3–5
AECOM Technology Corporation, 79 10–13
AEG A.G., I 409–11
Aegean Marine Petroleum Network Inc., 89 18–21
Aegek S.A., 64 6–8
Aegis Group plc, 6 15–16
AEGON N.V., III 177–79; 50 8–12 (upd.) *see also* Transamerica–An AEGON Company
AEI Music Network Inc., 35 19–21
AEON Co., Ltd., V 96–99; 68 6–10 (upd.)
AEP *see* American Electric Power Co.
AEP Industries, Inc., 36 17–19
Aer Lingus Group plc, 34 7–10; 89 22–27 (upd.)

Aero Mayflower Transit Company *see* Mayflower Group Inc.
Aeroflot - Russian Airlines JSC, 6 57–59; 29 7–10 (upd.); 89 28–34 (upd.)
AeroGrow International, Inc., 95 20–23
Aerojet-General Corp., 63 6–9
Aerolíneas Argentinas S.A., 33 17–19; 69 9–12 (upd.)
Aeronca Inc., 46 6–8
Aéroports de Paris, 33 20–22
Aéropostale, Inc., 89 35–38
Aeroquip Corporation, 16 7–9 *see also* Eaton Corp.
Aerosonic Corporation, 69 13–15
The Aérospatiale Group, 7 9–12; 21 8–11 (upd.) *see also* European Aeronautic Defence and Space Company EADS N.V.
AeroVironment, Inc., 97 13–16
The AES Corporation, 10 25–27; 13 12–15 (upd.); 53 14–18 (upd.)
Aetna, Inc., III 180–82; 21 12–16 (upd.); 63 10–16 (upd.)
Aetna Insulated Wire *see* The Marmon Group, Inc.
AFC Enterprises, Inc., 32 12–16 (upd.); 83 9-15 (upd.)
Affiliated Computer Services, Inc., 61 12–16
Affiliated Foods Inc., 53 19–21
Affiliated Managers Group, Inc., 79 14–17
Affiliated Publications, Inc., 7 13–16
Affinity Group Holding Inc., 56 3–6
AFLAC Incorporated, 10 28–30 (upd.); 38 15–19 (upd.)
African Rainbow Minerals Ltd., 97 17–20
Africare, 59 7–10
After Hours Formalwear Inc., 60 3–5
Aftermarket Technology Corp., 83 16-19
AG Barr plc, 64 9–12
Ag-Chem Equipment Company, Inc., 17 9–11 *see also* AGCO Corp.
Ag Services of America, Inc., 59 11–13
Aga Foodservice Group PLC, 73 18–20
AGCO Corp., 13 16–18; 67 6–10 (upd.)
Agence France-Presse, 34 11–14
Agere Systems Inc., 61 17–19
Agfa Gevaert Group N.V., 59 14–16
Aggregate Industries plc, 36 20–22
Aggreko Plc, 45 10–13
Agilent Technologies Inc., 38 20–23; 93 28–32 (upd.)
Agilysys Inc., 76 7–11 (upd.)
Agnico-Eagle Mines Limited, 71 11–14
Agora S.A. Group, 77 5–8
AGRANA *see* Südzucker AG.
Agri Beef Company, 81 5–9
Agrigenetics, Inc. *see* Mycogen Corp.
Agrium Inc., 73 21–23
AgustaWestland N.V., 75 18–20
Agway, Inc., 7 17–18; 21 17–19 (upd.) *see also* Cargill Inc.
AHL Services, Inc., 27 20–23

Ahlstrom Corporation, 53 22–25

Ahmanson *see* H.F. Ahmanson & Co.

AHMSA *see* Altos Hornos de México, S.A. de C.V.

Ahold *see* Koninklijke Ahold NV.

AHP *see* American Home Products Corp.

AICPA *see* The American Institute of Certified Public Accountants.

AIG *see* American International Group, Inc.

AIMCO *see* Apartment Investment and Management Co.

Ainsworth Lumber Co. Ltd., 99 18–22

Air & Water Technologies Corporation, 6 441–42 *see also* Aqua Alliance Inc.

Air Berlin GmbH & Co. Luftverkehrs KG, 71 15–17

Air Canada, 6 60–62; **23** 9–12 (upd.); **59** 17–22 (upd.)

Air China, 46 9–11

Air Express International Corporation, 13 19–20

Air France *see* Societe Air France.

Air-India Limited, 6 63–64; **27** 24–26 (upd.)

Air Jamaica Limited, 54 3–6

Air Liquide *see* L'Air Liquide SA.

Air Mauritius Ltd., 63 17–19

Air Methods Corporation, 53 26–29

Air Midwest, Inc. *see* Mesa Air Group, Inc.

Air New Zealand Limited, 14 10–12; **38** 24–27 (upd.)

Air Pacific Ltd., 70 7–9

Air Partner PLC, 93 33–36

Air Products and Chemicals, Inc., I 297–99; **10** 31–33 (upd.); **74** 6–9 (upd.)

Air Sahara Limited, 65 14–16

Air T, Inc., 86 6–9

Air Wisconsin Airlines Corporation, 55 10–12

Air Zimbabwe (Private) Limited, 91 5–8

AirAsia Berhad, 93 37–40

Airborne Freight Corporation, 6 345–47; **34** 15–18 (upd.) *see also* DHL Worldwide Network S.A./N.V.

Airborne Systems Group, 89 39–42

Airbus Industrie *see* G.I.E. Airbus Industrie.

Airgas, Inc., 54 7–10

Airguard Industries, Inc. *see* CLARCOR Inc.

Airlink Pty Ltd *see* Qantas Airways Ltd.

Airstream *see* Thor Industries, Inc.

AirTouch Communications, 11 10–12 *see also* Vodafone Group PLC.

Airtours Plc, 27 27–29, 90, 92

AirTran Holdings, Inc., 22 21–23

Aisin Seiki Co., Ltd., III 415–16; **48** 3–5 (upd.)

Aitchison & Colegrave *see* Bradford & Bingley PLC.

Aiwa Co., Ltd., 30 18–20

Ajegroup S.A., 92 1–4

Ajinomoto Co., Inc., II 463–64; **28** 9–11 (upd.)

AK Steel Holding Corporation, 19 8–9; **41** 3–6 (upd.)

Akamai Technologies, Inc., 71 18–21

Akbank TAS, 79 18–21

Akerys S.A., 90 17–20

AKG Acoustics GmbH, 62 3–6

Akin, Gump, Strauss, Hauer & Feld, L.L.P., 33 23–25

Akorn, Inc., 32 22–24

Akro-Mills Inc. *see* Myers Industries, Inc.

Aktiebolaget SKF, III 622–25; **38** 28–33 (upd.); **89** 401–09 (upd.)

Akzo Nobel N.V., 13 21–23; **41** 7–10 (upd.)

Al Habtoor Group L.L.C., 87 9–12

Al-Tawfeek Co. For Investment Funds Ltd. *see* Dallah Albaraka Group.

Alabama Farmers Cooperative, Inc., 63 20–22

Alabama National BanCorporation, 75 21–23

Alain Afflelou SA, 53 30–32

Alain Manoukian *see* Groupe Alain Manoukian.

Alamo Group Inc., 32 25–28

Alamo Rent A Car, 6 348–50; **24** 9–12 (upd.); **84** 5–11 (upd.)

ALARIS Medical Systems, Inc., 65 17–20

Alascom, Inc. *see* AT&T Corp.

Alaska Air Group, Inc., 6 65–67; **29** 11–14 (upd.)

Alaska Communications Systems Group, Inc., 89 43–46

Alaska Railroad Corporation, 60 6–9

Alba-Waldensian, Inc., 30 21–23 *see also* E.I. du Pont de Nemours and Co.

Albany International Corporation, 8 12–14; **51** 11–14 (upd.)

Albany Molecular Research, Inc., 77 9–12

Albemarle Corporation, 59 23–25

Alberici Corporation, 76 12–14

The Albert Fisher Group plc, 41 11–13

Albert Heijn NV *see* Koninklijke Ahold N.V. (Royal Ahold).

Albert's Organics, Inc. *see* United Natural Foods, Inc.

Alberta Energy Company Ltd., 16 10–12; **43** 3–6 (upd.)

Alberto-Culver Company, 8 15–17; **36** 23–27 (upd.); **91** 9–15 (upd.)

Albertson's, Inc., II 601–03; **7** 19–22 (upd.); **30** 24–28 (upd.); **65** 21–26 (upd.)

Alcan Aluminium Limited, IV 9–13; **31** 7–12 (upd.)

Alcatel S.A., 9 9–11; **36** 28–31 (upd.)

Alco Health Services Corporation, III 9–10 *see also* AmeriSource Health Corp.

Alco Standard Corporation, I 412–13

Alcoa Inc., 56 7–11 (upd.)

Alderwoods Group, Inc., 68 11–15 (upd.)

Aldi Einkauf GmbH & Co. OHG, 13 24–26; **86** 10–14 (upd.)

Aldila Inc., 46 12–14

Aldus Corporation, 10 34–36 *see also* Adobe Systems Inc.

Alès Groupe, 81 10–13

Alex Lee Inc., 18 6–9; **44** 10–14 (upd.)

Alexander & Alexander Services Inc., 10 37–39 *see also* Aon Corp.

Alexander & Baldwin, Inc., 10 40–42; **40** 14–19 (upd.)

Alexander's, Inc., 45 14–16

Alexandra plc, 88 5–8

Alfa Corporation, 60 10–12

Alfa Group, 99 23–26

Alfa-Laval AB, III 417–21; **64** 13–18 (upd.)

Alfa Romeo, 13 27–29; **36** 32–35 (upd.)

Alfa, S.A. de C.V., 19 10–12

Alfesca hf, 82 1–4

Alfred A. Knopf, Inc. *see* Random House, Inc.

Alfred Dunhill Limited *see* Vendôme Luxury Group plc.

Alfred Kärcher GmbH & Co KG, 94 9–14

Alfred Ritter GmbH & Co. KG, 58 3–7

Alga *see* BRIO AB.

Algemene Bank Nederland N.V., II 183–84

Algerian Saudi Leasing Holding Co. *see* Dallah Albaraka Group.

Algo Group Inc., 24 13–15

Alico, Inc., 63 23–25

Alienware Corporation, 81 14–17

Align Technology, Inc., 94 15–18

Alimentation Couche-Tard Inc., 77 13–16

Alitalia–Linee Aeree Italiane, S.p.A., 6 68–69; **29** 15–17 (upd.); **97** 21–27 (upd.)

Aljazeera Satellite Channel, 79 22–25

All American Communications Inc., 20 3–7

The All England Lawn Tennis & Croquet Club, 54 11–13

All Nippon Airways Co., Ltd., 6 70–71; **38** 34–37 (upd.); **91** 16–20 (upd.)

Alldays plc, 49 16–19

Allders plc, 37 6–8

Alleanza Assicurazioni S.p.A., 65 27–29

Alleghany Corporation, 10 43–45; **60** 13–16 (upd.)

Allegheny Energy, Inc., 38 38–41 (upd.)

Allegheny Ludlum Corporation, 8 18–20

Allegheny Power System, Inc., V 543–45 *see also* Allegheny Energy, Inc.

Allegheny Steel Distributors, Inc. *see* Reliance Steel & Aluminum Co.

Allegiance Life Insurance Company *see* Horace Mann Educators Corp.

Allegiant Travel Company, 97 28–31

Allegis Group, Inc., 95 24–27

Allen-Bradley Co. *see* Rockwell Automation.

Allen Canning Company, 76 15–17

Allen-Edmonds Shoe Corporation, 61 20–23

Allen Foods, Inc., 60 17–19

Allen Organ Company, 33 26–29

Allen Systems Group, Inc., 59 26–28
Allerderm *see* Virbac Corp.
Allergan, Inc., 10 46–49; 30 29–33
(upd.); 77 17–24 (upd.)
Allgemeine Elektricitäts-Gesellschaft *see*
AEG A.G.
Allgemeine Handelsgesellschaft der
Verbraucher AG *see* AVA AG.
Alliance and Leicester plc, 88 9–12
Alliance Assurance Company *see* Royal &
Sun Alliance Insurance Group plc.
Alliance Atlantis Communications Inc.,
39 11–14
Alliance Boots plc, 83 20-28 (upd.)
Alliance Capital Management Holding
L.P., 63 26–28
Alliance Entertainment Corp., 17 12–14
see also Source Interlink Companies,
Inc.
Alliance Resource Partners, L.P., 81
18–21
Alliance UniChem Plc *see* Alliance Boots
plc.
Alliant Techsystems Inc., 8 21–23; 30
34–37 (upd.); 77 25–31 (upd.)
Allianz AG, III 183–86; 15 10–14
(upd.); 57 18–24 (upd.)
Allied Corporation *see* AlliedSignal Inc.
The Allied Defense Group, Inc., 65
30–33
Allied Domecq PLC, 29 18–20
Allied Healthcare Products, Inc., 24
16–19
Allied Irish Banks, plc, 16 13–15; 43
7–10 (upd.); 94 19–24 (upd.)
Allied-Lyons plc, I 215–16 *see also*
Carlsberg A/S.
Allied Plywood Corporation *see* Ply Gem
Industries Inc.
Allied Products Corporation, 21 20–22
Allied-Signal Corp., I 414–16 *see also*
AlliedSignal, Inc.
Allied Signal Engines, 9 12–15
Allied Waste Industries, Inc., 50 13–16
Allied Worldwide, Inc., 49 20–23
AlliedSignal Inc., 22 29–32 (upd.) *see*
also Honeywell Inc.
Allison Gas Turbine Division, 9 16–19
Allmerica Financial Corporation, 63
29–31
Allou Health & Beauty Care, Inc., 28
12–14
Alloy, Inc., 55 13–15
The Allstate Corporation, 10 50–52; 27
30–33 (upd.)
ALLTEL Corporation, 6 299–301; 46
15–19 (upd.)
Alltrista Corporation, 30 38–41 *see also*
Jarden Corp.
Allwaste, Inc., 18 10–13
Alma Media Corporation, 98 1–4
Almacenes Exito S.A., 89 47–50
Almaden Vineyards *see* Canandaigua
Brands, Inc.
Almanij NV, 44 15–18 *see also*
Algemeene Maatschappij voor
Nijverheidskrediet.
Almay, Inc. *see* Revlon Inc.

Almost Family, Inc., 93 41–44
Aloha Airlines, Incorporated, 24 20–22
Alpargatas S.A.I.C., 87 13–17
Alpha Airports Group PLC, 77 32–35
Alpharma Inc., 35 22–26 (upd.)
Alpine Confections, Inc., 71 22–24
Alpine Electronics, Inc., 13 30–31
Alpine Lace Brands, Inc., 18 14–16 *see*
also Land O'Lakes, Inc.
Alps Electric Co., Ltd., II 5–6; 44
19–21 (upd.)
Alrosa Company Ltd., 62 7–11
Alsco *see* Steiner Corp.
Alside Inc., 94 25–29
Altadis S.A., 72 6–13 (upd.)
ALTANA AG, 87 18–22
AltaVista Company, 43 11–13
Altera Corporation, 18 17–20; 43
14–18 (upd.)
Alternative Living Services *see* Alterra
Healthcare Corp.
Alternative Tentacles Records, 66 3–6
Alternative Youth Services, Inc. *see*
Res-Care, Inc.
Alterra Healthcare Corporation, 42 3–5
Alticor Inc., 71 25–30 (upd.)
Altiris, Inc., 65 34–36
Altos Hornos de México, S.A. de C.V.,
42 6–8
Altran Technologies, 51 15–18
Altron Incorporated, 20 8–10
Aluar Aluminio Argentino S.A.I.C., 74
10–12
Alumalsa *see* Aluminoy y Aleaciones S.A.
Aluminum Company of America, IV
14–16; 20 11–14 (upd.) *see also* Alcoa
Inc.
Alvin Ailey Dance Foundation, Inc., 52
14–17
Alvis Plc, 47 7–9
ALZA Corporation, 10 53–55; 36
36–39 (upd.)
Amalgamated Bank, 60 20–22
AMAX Inc., IV 17–19 *see also* Cyprus
Amex.
Amazon.com, Inc., 25 17–19; 56 12–15
(upd.)
AMB Generali Holding AG, 51 19–23
AMB Property Corporation, 57 25–27
Ambac Financial Group, Inc., 65 37–39
Ambassadors International, Inc., 68
16–18 (upd.)
AmBev *see* Companhia de Bebidas das
Américas.
Amblin Entertainment, 21 23–27
AMC Entertainment Inc., 12 12–14; 35
27–29 (upd.)
AMCC *see* Applied Micro Circuits Corp.
AMCOL International Corporation, 59
29–33 (upd.)
AMCON Distributing Company, 99
27–30
Amcor Ltd., IV 248–50; 19 13–16
(upd.); 78 1–6 (upd.)
AMCORE Financial Inc., 44 22–26
AMD *see* Advanced Micro Devices, Inc.

Amdahl Corporation, III 109–11; 14
13–16 (upd.); 40 20–25 (upd.) *see also*
Fujitsu Ltd.
Amdocs Ltd., 47 10–12
Amec Spie S.A., 57 28–31
Amedysis, Inc., 53 33–36
Amer Group plc, 41 14–16
Amerada Hess Corporation, IV 365–67;
21 28–31 (upd.); 55 16–20 (upd.)
Amerchol Corporation *see* Union Carbide
Corp.
AMERCO, 6 351–52; 67 11–14 (upd.)
Ameren Corporation, 60 23–27 (upd.)
Ameri-Kart Corp. *see* Myers Industries,
Inc.
America Online, Inc., 10 56–58; 26
16–20 (upd.) *see also* CompuServe
Interactive Services, Inc.; AOL Time
Warner Inc.
America West Holdings Corporation, 6
72–74; 34 22–26 (upd.)
America's Car-Mart, Inc., 64 19–21
America's Favorite Chicken Company,
Inc., 7 26–28 *see also* AFC Enterprises,
Inc.
American & Efird, Inc., 82 5-9
American Airlines, I 89–91; 6 75–77
(upd.) *see also* AMR Corp.
American Apparel, Inc., 90 21–24
American Association of Retired Persons
see AARP.
American Axle & Manufacturing
Holdings, Inc., 67 15–17
American Banknote Corporation, 30
42–45
American Bar Association, 35 30–33
American Biltrite Inc., 16 16–18; 43
19–22 (upd.)
American Brands, Inc., V 395–97 *see*
also Fortune Brands, Inc.
American Builders & Contractors Supply
Co. *see* ABC Supply Co., Inc.
American Building Maintenance
Industries, Inc., 6 17–19 *see also* ABM
Industries Inc.
American Business Information, Inc., 18
21–25
American Business Interiors *see* American
Furniture Company, Inc.
American Business Products, Inc., 20
15–17
American Campus Communities, Inc.,
85 1–5
American Can Co. *see* Primerica Corp.
The American Cancer Society, 24 23–25
American Capital Strategies, Ltd., 91
21–24
American Cast Iron Pipe Company, 50
17–20
American Civil Liberties Union (ACLU),
60 28–31
American Classic Voyages Company, 27
34–37
American Coin Merchandising, Inc., 28
15–17; 74 13–16 (upd.)
American Colloid Co., 13 32–35 *see*
AMCOL International Corp.

American Commercial Lines Inc., 99 31–34

American Cotton Growers Association *see* Plains Cotton Cooperative Association.

American Crystal Sugar Company, 11 13–15; 32 29–33 (upd.)

American Cyanamid, I 300–02; 8 24–26 (upd.)

American Eagle Outfitters, Inc., 24 26–28; 55 21–24 (upd.)

American Ecology Corporation, 77 36–39

American Electric Power Company, V 546–49; 45 17–21 (upd.)

American Express Company, II 395–99; 10 59–64 (upd.); 38 42–48 (upd.)

American Family Corporation, III 187–89 *see also* AFLAC Inc.

American Financial Group Inc., III 190–92; 48 6–10 (upd.)

American Foods Group, 43 23–27

American Furniture Company, Inc., 21 32–34

American General Corporation, III 193–94; 10 65–67 (upd.); 46 20–23 (upd.)

American General Finance Corp., 11 16–17

American Girl, Inc., 69 16–19 (upd)

American Golf Corporation, 45 22–24

American Gramaphone LLC, 52 18–20

American Greetings Corporation, 7 23–25; 22 33–36 (upd.); 59 34–39 (upd.)

American Healthways, Inc., 65 40–42

American Home Mortgage Holdings, Inc., 46 24–26

American Home Products, I 622–24; 10 68–70 (upd.) *see also* Wyeth.

American Homestar Corporation, 18 26–29; 41 17–20 (upd.)

American Institute of Certified Public Accountants (AICPA), 44 27–30

American International Group, Inc., III 195–98; 15 15–19 (upd.); 47 13–19 (upd.)

American Italian Pasta Company, 27 38–40; 76 18–21 (upd.)

American Kennel Club, Inc., 74 17–19

American Lawyer Media Holdings, Inc., 32 34–37

American Library Association, 86 15–19

American Licorice Company, 86 20–23

American Locker Group Incorporated, 34 19–21

American Lung Association, 48 11–14

American Machine and Metals *see* AMETEK, Inc.

American Maize-Products Co., 14 17–20

American Management Association, 76 22–25

American Management Systems, Inc., 11 18–20

American Media, Inc., 27 41–44; 82 10–15 (upd.)

American Medical Association, 39 15–18

American Medical International, Inc., III 73–75

American Medical Response, Inc., 39 19–22

American Metals Corporation *see* Reliance Steel & Aluminum Co.

American Modern Insurance Group *see* The Midland Co.

American Motors Corp., I 135–37 *see also* DaimlerChrysler AG.

América Móvil, S.A. de C.V., 80 5–8

American MSI Corporation *see* Moldflow Corp.

American National Insurance Company, 8 27–29; 27 45–48 (upd.)

American Olean Tile Company *see* Armstrong Holdings, Inc.

American Oriental Bioengineering Inc., 93 45–48

American Pad & Paper Company, 20 18–21

American Pfauter *see* Gleason Corp.

American Pharmaceutical Partners, Inc., 69 20–22

American Pop Corn Company, 59 40–43

American Power Conversion Corporation, 24 29–31; 67 18–20 (upd.)

American Premier Underwriters, Inc., 10 71–74

American President Companies Ltd., 6 353–55 *see also* APL Ltd.

American Printing House for the Blind, 26 13–15

American Re Corporation, 10 75–77; 35 34–37 (upd.)

American Red Cross, 40 26–29

American Reprographics Company, 75 24–26

American Residential Mortgage Corporation, 8 30–31

American Restaurant Partners, L.P., 93 49–52

American Retirement Corporation, 42 9–12 *see also* Brookdale Senior Living.

American Rice, Inc., 33 30–33

American Rug Craftsmen *see* Mohawk Industries, Inc.

American Safety Razor Company, 20 22–24

American Savings Bank *see* Hawaiian Electric Industries, Inc.

American Science & Engineering, Inc., 81 22–25

American Seating Company, 78 7–11

American Skiing Company, 28 18–21

American Society for the Prevention of Cruelty to Animals (ASPCA), 68 19–22

The American Society of Composers, Authors and Publishers (ASCAP), 29 21–24

American Software Inc., 22 214; 25 20–22

American Standard Companies Inc., III 663–65; 30 46–50 (upd.)

American States Water Company, 46 27–30

American Steamship Company *see* GATX.

American Stores Company, II 604–06; 22 37–40 (upd.) *see also* Albertson's, Inc.

American Superconductor Corporation, 97 32–36

American Technical Ceramics Corp., 67 21–23

American Telephone and Telegraph Company *see* AT&T.

American Tobacco Co. *see* B.A.T. Industries PLC.; Fortune Brands, Inc.

American Tourister, Inc., 16 19–21 *see also* Samsonite Corp.

American Tower Corporation, 33 34–38

American Vanguard Corporation, 47 20–22

American Water Works Company, Inc., 6 443–45; 38 49–52 (upd.)

American Woodmark Corporation, 31 13–16

American Yearbook Company *see* Jostens, Inc.

AmeriCares Foundation, Inc., 87 23–28

Amerigon Incorporated, 97 37–40

AMERIGROUP Corporation, 69 23–26

Amerihost Properties, Inc., 30 51–53

AmeriSource Health Corporation, 37 9–11 (upd.)

AmerisourceBergen Corporation, 64 22–28 (upd.)

Ameristar Casinos, Inc., 33 39–42; 69 27–31 (upd.)

Ameritech Corporation, V 265–68; 18 30–34 (upd.) *see also* AT&T Corp.

Ameritrade Holding Corporation, 34 27–30

Ameriwood Industries International Corp., 17 15–17 *see also* Dorel Industries Inc.

Amerock Corporation, 53 37–40

Ameron International Corporation, 67 24–26

Amersham PLC, 50 21–25

Ames Department Stores, Inc., 9 20–22; 30 54–57 (upd.)

AMETEK, Inc., 9 23–25

N.V. Amev, III 199–202 *see also* Fortis, Inc.

Amey Plc, 47 23–25

AMF Bowling, Inc., 40 30–33

Amfac/JMB Hawaii L.L.C., I 417–18; 24 32–35 (upd.)

Amgen, Inc., 10 78–81; 30 58–61 (upd.); 89 51–57 (upd.)

AMI Metals, Inc. *see* Reliance Steel & Aluminum Co.

AMICAS, Inc., 69 32–34

Amkor Technology, Inc., 69 35–37

Ammirati Puris Lintas *see* Interpublic Group of Companies, Inc.

Amnesty International, 50 26–29

Amoco Corporation, IV 368–71; 14 21–25 (upd.) *see also* BP p.l.c.

Amoskeag Company, 8 32–33 *see also* Fieldcrest Cannon, Inc.

AMP, Inc., II 7–8; 14 26–28 (upd.)
Ampacet Corporation, 67 27–29
Ampco-Pittsburgh Corporation, 79 26–29
Ampex Corporation, 17 18–20
Amphenol Corporation, 40 34–37
AMR *see* American Medical Response, Inc.
AMR Corporation, 28 22–26 (upd.); 52 21–26 (upd.)
AMREP Corporation, 21 35–37
AMS *see* Advanced Marketing Services, Inc.
Amscan Holdings, Inc., 61 24–26
AmSouth Bancorporation, 12 15–17; 48 15–18 (upd.)
Amsted Industries Incorporated, 7 29–31
Amsterdam-Rotterdam Bank N.V., II 185–86
Amstrad plc, III 112–14; 48 19–23 (upd.)
AmSurg Corporation, 48 24–27
Amtech *see* American Building Maintenance Industries, Inc.; ABM Industries Inc.
Amtrak *see* The National Railroad Passenger Corp.
Amtran, Inc., 34 31–33
AMVESCAP PLC, 65 43–45
Amway Corporation, III 11–14; 13 36–39 (upd.); 30 62–66 (upd.) *see also* Alticor Inc.
Amy's Kitchen Inc., 76 26–28
Amylin Pharmaceuticals, Inc., 67 30–32
ANA *see* All Nippon Airways Co., Ltd.
Anacomp, Inc., 94 30–34
Anadarko Petroleum Corporation, 10 82–84; 52 27–30 (upd.)
Anadolu Efes Biracilik ve Malt Sanayii A.S., 95 28–31
Anaheim Angels Baseball Club, Inc., 53 41–44
Analex Corporation, 74 20–22
Analog Devices, Inc., 10 85–87
Analogic Corporation, 23 13–16
Analysts International Corporation, 36 40–42
Analytic Sciences Corporation, 10 88–90
Analytical Surveys, Inc., 33 43–45
Anam Group, 23 17–19
Anaren Microwave, Inc., 33 46–48
Anchor Bancorp, Inc., 10 91–93
Anchor Brewing Company, 47 26–28
Anchor Gaming, 24 36–39
Anchor Hocking Glassware, 13 40–42
Andersen, 10 94–95; 29 25–28 (upd.); 68 23–27 (upd.)
The Anderson-DuBose Company, 60 32–34
Anderson Trucking Service, Inc., 75 27–29
The Andersons, Inc., 31 17–21
Andis Company, Inc., 85 6–9
Andreas Stihl AG & Co. KG, 16 22–24; 59 44–47 (upd.)

Andrew Corporation, 10 96–98; 32 38–41 (upd.)
The Andrews Institute, 99 35–38
Andrews Kurth, LLP, 71 31–34
Andrews McMeel Universal, 40 38–41
Andritz AG, 51 24–26
Andronico's Market, 70 10–13
Andrx Corporation, 55 25–27
Angelica Corporation, 15 20–22; 43 28–31 (upd.)
AngioDynamics, Inc., 81 26–29
Angliss International Group *see* Vestey Group Ltd.
Anglo-Abrasives Ltd. *see* Carbo PLC.
Anglo American PLC, IV 20–23; 16 25–30 (upd.); 50 30–36 (upd.)
Anheuser-Busch Companies, Inc., I 217–19; 10 99–101 (upd.); 34 34–37 (upd.)
Anhui Conch Cement Company Limited, 99 39–42
Anixter International Inc., 88 13–16
Anker BV, 53 45–47
Annie's Homegrown, Inc., 59 48–50
AnnTaylor Stores Corporation, 13 43–45; 37 12–15 (upd.); 67 33–37 (upd.)
ANR Pipeline Co., 17 21–23
Anritsu Corporation, 68 28–30
The Anschutz Company, 12 18–20; 36 43–47 (upd.); 73 24–30 (upd.)
Ansell Ltd., 60 35–38 (upd.)
Ansoft Corporation, 63 32–34
Anteon Corporation, 57 32–34
Anthem Electronics, Inc., 13 46–47
Anthony & Sylvan Pools Corporation, 56 16–18
Anthracite Industries, Inc. *see* Asbury Carbons, Inc.
Anthropologie, Inc. *see* Urban Outfitters, Inc.
Antinori *see* Marchesi Antinori SRL.
The Antioch Company, 40 42–45
ANTK Tupolev *see* Aviacionny Nauchno-Tehnicheskii Komplex im. A.N. Tupoleva.
Antofagasta plc, 65 46–49
Antonov Design Bureau, 53 48–51
AOK-Bundesverband (Federation of the AOK), 78 12–16
AOL Time Warner Inc., 57 35–44 (upd.)
Aon Corporation, III 203–05; 45 25–28 (upd.)
AP *see* The Associated Press.
Apache Corporation, 10 102–04; 32 42–46 (upd.); 89 58–65 (upd.)
Apartment Investment and Management Company, 49 24–26
Apasco S.A. de C.V., 51 27–29
Apax Partners Worldwide LLP, 89 66–69
Apex Digital, Inc., 63 35–37
APH *see* American Printing House for the Blind.
APi Group, Inc., 64 29–32
APL Limited, 61 27–30 (upd.)
APLIX S.A. *see* Velcro Industries N.V.

Apogee Enterprises, Inc., 8 34–36
Apollo Group, Inc., 24 40–42
Applause Inc., 24 43–46 *see also* Russ Berrie and Co., Inc.
Apple & Eve L.L.C., 92 5–8
Apple Bank for Savings, 59 51–53
Apple Computer, Inc., III 115–16; 6 218–20 (upd.); 36 48–51 (upd.); 77 40–45 (upd.)
Apple Corps Ltd., 87 29–34
Applebee's International Inc., 14 29–31; 35 38–41 (upd.)
Appliance Recycling Centers of America, Inc., 42 13–16
Applica Incorporated, 43 32–36 (upd.)
Applied Bioscience International, Inc., 10 105–07
Applied Films Corporation, 48 28–31
Applied Materials, Inc., 10 108–09; 46 31–34 (upd.)
Applied Micro Circuits Corporation, 38 53–55
Applied Power Inc., 9 26–28; 32 47–51 (upd.) *see also* Actuant Corp.
Applied Signal Technology, Inc., 87 35–38
Applied Technology Solutions *see* RWD Technologies, Inc.
Aprilia SpA, 17 24–26
AptarGroup, Inc., 69 38–41
Aqua Alliance Inc., 32 52–54 (upd.)
aQuantive, Inc., 81 30–33
Aquarion Company, 84 12–16
Aquarius Platinum Ltd., 63 38–40
Aquent, 96 8–11
Aquila, Inc., 50 37–40 (upd.)
AR Accessories Group, Inc., 23 20–22
ARA *see* Consorcio ARA, S.A. de C.V.
ARA Services, II 607–08 *see also* Aramark.
Arab Potash Company, 85 10–13
Arabian Gulf Oil Company *see* National Oil Corp.
Aracruz Celulose S.A., 57 45–47
Aral AG, 62 12–15
ARAMARK Corporation, 13 48–50; 41 21–24 (upd.)
Arandell Corporation, 37 16–18
Arapuã *see* Lojas Arapuã S.A.
ARBED S.A., IV 24–27; 22 41–45 (upd.) *see also* Arcelor Gent.
Arbeitsgemeinschaft der öffentlich-rechtlichen Rundfunkanstalten der Bundesrepublick *see* ARD.
The Arbitron Company, 38 56–61
Arbor Drugs Inc., 12 21–23 *see also* CVS Corp.
Arby's Inc., 14 32–34
Arc International, 76 29–31
ARCA *see* Appliance Recycling Centers of America, Inc.
Arcadia Group plc, 28 27–30 (upd.)
Arcadis NV, 26 21–24
Arcelor Gent, 80 9–12
Arch Chemicals, Inc., 78 17–20
Arch Coal Inc., 98 5–8
Arch Mineral Corporation, 7 32–34

Arch Wireless, Inc., 39 23–26
Archer Daniels Midland Company, I 419–21; 11 21–23 (upd.); 32 55–59 (upd.); 75 30–35 (upd.)
Archie Comics Publications, Inc., 63 41–44
Archon Corporation, 74 23–26 (upd.)
Archstone-Smith Trust, 49 27–30
Archway Cookies, Inc., 29 29–31
ARCO *see* Atlantic Richfield Co.
ARCO Chemical Company, 10 110–11 *see also* Lyondell Chemical Co.
Arcor S.A.I.C., 66 7–9
Arctco, Inc., 16 31–34
Arctic Cat Inc., 40 46–50 (upd.); 96 12–19 (upd.)
Arctic Slope Regional Corporation, 38 62–65
ARD, 41 25–29
Arden Group, Inc., 29 32–35
Arena Leisure Plc, 99 43–46
Arena Resources, Inc., 97 41–44
AREVA NP, 90 25–30 (upd.)
Argentaria Caja Postal y Banco Hipotecario S.A. *see* Banco Bilbao Vizcaya Argentaria S.A.
Argon ST, Inc., 81 34–37
Argos S.A. *see* Cementos Argos S.A.
Argosy Gaming Company, 21 38–41 *see also* Penn National Gaming, Inc.
Argyll Group PLC, II 609–10 *see also* Safeway PLC.
Arianespace S.A., 89 70–73
Ariba, Inc., 57 48–51
Ariens Company, 48 32–34
ARINC Inc., 98 9–14
Aris Industries, Inc., 16 35–38
Aristocrat Leisure Limited, 54 14–16
Aristokraft Inc. *see* MasterBrand Cabinets, Inc.
The Aristotle Corporation, 62 16–18
AriZona Beverages *see* Ferolito, Vultaggio & Sons.
Arjo Wiggins Appleton p.l.c., 34 38–40
Ark Restaurants Corp., 20 25–27
Arkansas Best Corporation, 16 39–41; 94 35–40 (upd.)
Arkla, Inc., V 550–51
Arla Foods amba, 48 35–38
Armani *see* Giorgio Armani S.p.A.
Armco Inc., IV 28–30 *see also* AK Steel.
Armor All Products Corp., 16 42–44
Armor Holdings, Inc., 27 49–51
Armour *see* Tommy Armour Golf Co.
Armstrong Air Conditioning Inc. *see* Lennox International Inc.
Armstrong Holdings, Inc., III 422–24; 22 46–50 (upd.); 81 38–44 (upd.)
Army and Air Force Exchange Service, 39 27–29
Arnhold and S. Bleichroeder Advisers, LLC, 97 45–49
Arnold & Porter, 35 42–44
Arnold Clark Automobiles Ltd., 60 39–41
Arnoldo Mondadori Editore S.p.A., IV 585–88; 19 17–21 (upd.); 54 17–23 (upd.)

Arnott's Ltd., 66 10–12
Aro Corp. *see* Ingersoll-Rand Company Ltd.
Arotech Corporation, 93 53–56
ArQule, Inc., 68 31–34
ARRIS Group, Inc., 89 74–77
Arriva PLC, 69 42–44
Arrow Air Holdings Corporation, 55 28–30
Arrow Electronics, Inc., 10 112–14; 50 41–44 (upd.)
Arsenal Holdings PLC, 79 30–33
The Art Institute of Chicago, 29 36–38
Art Van Furniture, Inc., 28 31–33
Artesyn Technologies Inc., 46 35–38 (upd.)
ArthroCare Corporation, 73 31–33
Arthur Andersen & Company, Société Coopérative, 10 115–17 *see also* Andersen.
The Arthur C. Clarke Foundation, 92 9–12
Arthur D. Little, Inc., 35 45–48
Arthur J. Gallagher & Co., 73 34–36
Arthur Murray International, Inc., 32 60–62
Artisan Entertainment Inc., 32 63–66 (upd.)
Arts and Entertainment Network *see* A&E Television Networks.
Artsana SpA, 92 13–16
Arval *see* PHH Arval.
Arvin Industries, Inc., 8 37–40 *see also* ArvinMeritor, Inc.
ArvinMeritor, Inc., 54 24–28 (upd.)
A/S Air Baltic Corporation, 71 35–37
AS Estonian Air, 71 38–40
Asahi Breweries, Ltd., I 220–21; 20 28–30 (upd.); 52 31–34 (upd.)
Asahi Denka Kogyo KK, 64 33–35
Asahi Glass Company, Ltd., III 666–68; 48 39–42 (upd.)
Asahi Komag Co., Ltd. *see* Komag, Inc.
Asahi National Broadcasting Company, Ltd., 9 29–31
Asahi Shimbun, 9 29–30
Asanté Technologies, Inc., 20 31–33
ASARCO Incorporated, IV 31–34; 40 220–22, 411
Asatsu-DK Inc, 82 16–20
Asbury Automotive Group Inc., 60 42–44
Asbury Carbons, Inc., 68 35–37
ASC, Inc., 55 31–34
ASCAP *see* The American Society of Composers, Authors and Publishers.
Ascend Communications, Inc., 24 47–51 *see also* Lucent Technologies Inc.
Ascendia Brands, Inc., 97 50–53
Ascential Software Corporation, 59 54–57
Ascom AG, 9 32–34
ASDA Group Ltd., II 611–12; 28 34–36 (upd.); 64 36–38 (upd.)
ASEA AB *see* ABB Ltd.
ASG *see* Allen Systems Group, Inc.
Ash Grove Cement Company, 94 41–44

Ashanti Goldfields Company Limited, 43 37–40
Ashdown *see* Repco Corporation Ltd.
Ashland Inc., 19 22–25; 50 45–50 (upd.)
Ashland Oil, Inc., IV 372–74 *see also* Marathon.
Ashley Furniture Industries, Inc., 35 49–51
Ashtead Group plc, 34 41–43
Ashworth, Inc., 26 25–28
Asia Pacific Breweries Limited, 59 58–60
AsiaInfo Holdings, Inc., 43 41–44
Asiana Airlines, Inc., 46 39–42
ASIX Inc. *see* Manatron, Inc.
ASICS Corporation, 57 52–55
ASK Group, Inc., 9 35–37
Ask Jeeves, Inc., 65 50–52
ASML Holding N.V., 50 51–54
ASPCA *see* American Society for the Prevention of Cruelty to Animals (ASPCA).
Aspect Telecommunications Corporation, 22 51–53
Aspen Publishers *see* Wolters Kluwer NV.
Aspen Skiing Company, 15 23–26
Asplundh Tree Expert Co., 20 34–36; 59 61–65 (upd.)
Assicurazioni Generali SpA, III 206–09; 15 27–31 (upd.)
Assisted Living Concepts, Inc., 43 45–47
Associated British Foods plc, II 465–66; 13 51–53 (upd.); 41 30–33 (upd.)
Associated British Ports Holdings Plc, 45 29–32
Associated Estates Realty Corporation, 25 23–25
Associated Grocers, Incorporated, 9 38–40; 31 22–26 (upd.)
Associated International Insurance Co. *see* Gryphon Holdings, Inc.
Associated Milk Producers, Inc., 11 24–26; 48 43–46 (upd.)
Associated Natural Gas Corporation, 11 27–28
Associated Newspapers Holdings P.L.C. *see* Daily Mail and General Trust plc.
The Associated Press, 13 54–56; 31 27–30 (upd.); 73 37–41 (upd.)
Association des Centres Distributeurs E. Leclerc, 37 19–21
Association of Junior Leagues International Inc., 60 45–47
Assurances Générales de France, 63 45–48
Assured Guaranty Ltd., 93 57–60
AST Research, Inc., 9 41–43
Astec Industries, Inc., 79 34–37
Astellas Pharma Inc., 97 54–58 (upd.)
AstenJohnson Inc., 90 31–34
Aston Villa plc, 41 34–36
Astoria Financial Corporation, 44 31–34
Astra *see* PT Astra International Tbk.
AstraZeneca PLC, I 625–26; 20 37–40 (upd.); 50 55–60 (upd.)

Astronics Corporation, 35 52–54

Asur *see* Grupo Aeropuerto del Sureste, S.A. de C.V.

Asurion Corporation, 83 29-32

ASV, Inc., 34 44–47; 66 13–15 (upd.)

AT&T Bell Laboratories, Inc., 13 57–59 *see also* Lucent Technologies Inc.

AT&T Corporation, V 259–64; 29 39–45 (upd.); 61 68 38–45 (upd.)

AT&T Istel Ltd., 14 35–36

AT&T Wireless Services, Inc., 54 29–32 (upd.)

At Home Corporation, 43 48–51

ATA Holdings Corporation, 82 21–25

Atanor S.A., 62 19–22

Atari Corporation, 9 44–47; 23 23–26 (upd.); 66 16–20 (upd.)

ATC Healthcare Inc., 64 39–42

Atchison Casting Corporation, 39 30–32

ATE Investment *see* Atlantic Energy, Inc.

The Athlete's Foot Brands LLC, 84 17–20

The Athletics Investment Group, 62 23–26

ATI Technologies Inc., 79 38–41

Atkins Nutritionals, Inc., 58 8–10

Atkinson Candy Company, 87 39–42

Atlanta Bread Company International, Inc., 70 14–16

Atlanta Gas Light Company, 6 446–48; 23 27–30 (upd.)

Atlanta National League Baseball Club, Inc., 43 52–55

Atlantic & Pacific Tea Company (A&P) *see* The Great Atlantic & Pacific Tea Company, Inc.

Atlantic American Corporation, 44 35–37

Atlantic Coast Airlines Holdings, Inc., 55 35–37

Atlantic Coast Carton Company *see* Caraustar Industries, Inc.

Atlantic Energy, Inc., 6 449–50

The Atlantic Group, 23 31–33

Atlantic Premium Brands, Ltd., 57 56–58

Atlantic Richfield Company, IV 375–77; 31 31–34 (upd.)

Atlantic Southeast Airlines, Inc., 47 29–31

Atlantis Plastics, Inc., 85 14–17

Atlas Air, Inc., 39 33–35

Atlas Bolt & Screw Company *see* The Marmon Group, Inc.

Atlas Copco AB, III 425–27; 28 37–41 (upd.); 85 18–24 (upd.)

Atlas Tag & Label *see* BISSELL, Inc.

Atlas Van Lines, Inc., 14 37–39

Atmel Corporation, 17 32–34

ATMI, Inc., 93 61–64

Atmos Energy Corporation, 43 56–58

Atochem S.A., I 303–04, 676 *see also* Total-Fina-Elf.

Atos Origin S.A., 69 45–47

Atrix Laboratories, Inc. *see* QLT Inc.

Attachmate Corporation, 56 19–21

Attica Enterprises S.A., 64 43–45

Atwood Mobil Products, 53 52–55

Au Bon Pain Co., Inc., 18 35–38

AU Optronics Corporation, 67 38–40

Au Printemps S.A., V 9–11 *see also* Pinault-Printemps-Redoute S.A.

Aubert & Duval Holding *see* Eramet.

Auchan, 37 22–24

The Auchter Company, 78 21–24

Audible Inc., 79 42–45

Audio King Corporation, 24 52–54

Audiovox Corporation, 34 48–50; 90 35–39 (upd.)

August Schell Brewing Company Inc., 59 66–69

August Storck KG, 66 21–23

Ault Incorporated, 34 51–54

Auntie Anne's, Inc., 35 55–57

Aurea Concesiones de Infraestructuras SA *see* Abertis Infraestructuras, S.A.

Aurora Casket Company, Inc., 56 22–24

Aurora Foods Inc., 32 67–69

Austal Limited, 75 36–39

The Austin Company, 8 41–44; 72 14–18 (upd.)

Austin Nichols *see* Pernod Ricard S.A.

Austin Powder Company, 76 32–35

Australia and New Zealand Banking Group Limited, II 187–90; 52 35–40 (upd.)

Australian Wheat Board *see* AWB Ltd.

Austrian Airlines AG (Österreichische Luftverkehrs AG), 33 49–52

Authentic Fitness Corp., 20 41–43; 51 30–33 (upd.)

Auto Value Associates, Inc., 25 26–28

Autobacs Seven Company Ltd., 76 36–38

Autobytel Inc., 47 32–34

Autocam Corporation, 51 34–36

Autodesk, Inc., 10 118–20; 89 78–82 (upd.)

Autogrill SpA, 49 31–33

Autoliv, Inc., 65 53–55

Autologic Information International, Inc., 20 44–46

Automated Sciences Group, Inc. *see* CACI International Inc.

Automatic Data Processing, Inc., III 117–19; 9 48–51 (upd.); 47 35–39 (upd.)

Automobiles Citroën, 7 35–38

Automobili Lamborghini Holding S.p.A., 13 60–62; 34 55–58 (upd.); 91 25–30 (upd.)

AutoNation, Inc., 50 61–64

Autoridad del Canal de Panamá, 94 45–48

Autoroutes du Sud de la France SA, 55 38–40

Autotote Corporation, 20 47–49 *see also* Scientific Games Corp.

AutoTrader.com, L.L.C., 91 31–34

AutoZone, Inc., 9 52–54; 31 35–38 (upd.)

Auvil Fruit Company, Inc., 95 32–35

AVA AG (Allgemeine Handelsgesellschaft der Verbraucher AG), 33 53–56

Avado Brands, Inc., 31 39–42

Avalon Correctional Services, Inc., 75 40–43

AvalonBay Communities, Inc., 58 11–13

Avantium Technologies BV, 79 46–49

Avco Financial Services Inc., 13 63–65 *see also* Citigroup Inc.

Avecia Group PLC, 63 49–51

Aveda Corporation, 24 55–57

Avedis Zildjian Co., 38 66–68

Avendt Group, Inc. *see* Marmon Group, Inc.

Aventine Renewable Energy Holdings, Inc., 89 83–86

Avery Dennison Corporation, IV 251–54; 17 27–31 (upd.); 49 34–40 (upd.)

Aviacionny Nauchno-Tehnicheskii Komplek im. A.N. Tupoleva, 24 58–60

Aviacsa *see* Consorcio Aviacsa, S.A. de C.V.

Aviall, Inc., 73 42–45

Avianca Aerovías Nacionales de Colombia SA, 36 52–55

Aviation Sales Company, 41 37–39

Avid Technology Inc., 38 69–73

Avionics Specialties Inc. *see* Aerosonic Corp.

Avions Marcel Dassault-Breguet Aviation, I 44–46 *see also* Groupe Dassault Aviation SA.

Avis Group Holdings, Inc., 6 356–58; 22 54–57 (upd.); 75 44–49 (upd.)

Avista Corporation, 69 48–50 (upd.)

Aviva PLC, 50 65–68 (upd.)

Avnet Inc., 9 55–57

Avocent Corporation, 65 56–58

Avon Products, Inc., III 15–16; 19 26–29 (upd.); 46 43–46 (upd.)

Avondale Industries, Inc., 7 39–41; 41 40–43 (upd.)

AVTOVAZ Joint Stock Company, 65 59–62

AVX Corporation, 67 41–43

AWA *see* America West Holdings Corp.

AWB Ltd., 56 25–27

Awrey Bakeries, Inc., 56 28–30

AXA Colonia Konzern AG, III 210–12; 49 41–45 (upd.)

Axcan Pharma Inc., 85 25–28

Axcelis Technologies, Inc., 95 36–39

Axel Johnson Group, I 553–55

Axel Springer Verlag AG, IV 589–91; 20 50–53 (upd.)

Axsys Technologies, Inc., 93 65–68

Aydin Corp., 19 30–32

Aynsley China Ltd. *see* Belleek Pottery Ltd.

Azcon Corporation, 23 34–36

Azerbaijan Airlines, 77 46–49

Azienda Generale Italiana Petroli *see* ENI S.p.A.

Aztar Corporation, 13 66–68; 71 41–45 (upd.)

AZZ Incorporated, 93 69–72

B

B&D *see* Barker & Dobson.
B&G Foods, Inc., 40 51–54
B&J Music Ltd. *see* Kaman Music Corp.
B&Q plc *see* Kingfisher plc.
B.A.T. Industries PLC, 22 70–73 (upd.)
  see also Brown and Williamson Tobacco
  Corporation
B. Dalton Bookseller Inc., 25 29–31 *see
  also* Barnes & Noble, Inc.
B/E Aerospace, Inc., 30 72–74
B.F. Goodrich Co. *see* The BFGoodrich
  Co.
B.J. Alan Co., Inc., 67 44–46
The B. Manischewitz Company, LLC,
  31 43–46
B.R. Guest Inc., 87 43–46
B.W. Rogers Company, 94 49–52
BA *see* British Airways plc.
BAA plc, 10 121–23; 33 57–61 (upd.)
Baan Company, 25 32–34
Babbage's, Inc., 10 124–25 *see also*
  GameStop Corp.
The Babcock & Wilcox Company, 82
  26–30
Babcock International Group PLC, 69
  51–54
Babolat VS, S.A., 97 63–66
Baby Lock USA *see* Tacony Corp.
Baby Superstore, Inc., 15 32–34 *see also*
  Toys 'R Us, Inc.
Bacardi & Company Ltd., 18 39–42; 82
  31–36 (upd.)
Baccarat, 24 61–63
Bachman's Inc., 22 58–60
Bachoco *see* Industrias Bachoco, S.A. de
  C.V.
Back Bay Restaurant Group, Inc., 20
  54–56
Back Yard Burgers, Inc., 45 33–36
Backus y Johnston *see* Unión de
  Cervecerias Peruanas Backus y Johnston
  S.A.A.
Bad Boy Worldwide Entertainment
  Group, 58 14–17
Badger Meter, Inc., 22 61–65
Badger Paper Mills, Inc., 15 35–37
Badger State Ethanol, LLC, 83 33–37
BAE Systems Ship Repair, 73 46–48
Bahamas Air Holdings Ltd., 66 24–26
Bahlsen GmbH & Co. KG, 44 38–41
Baidu.com Inc., 95 40–43
Bailey Nurseries, Inc., 57 59–61
Bain & Company, 55 41–43
Baird & Warner Holding Company, 87
  47–50
Bairnco Corporation, 28 42–45
Bajaj Auto Limited, 39 36–38
Baker *see* Michael Baker Corp.
Baker and Botts, L.L.P., 28 46–49
Baker & Daniels LLP, 88 17–20
Baker & Hostetler LLP, 40 55–58
Baker & McKenzie, 10 126–28; 42
  17–20 (upd.)
Baker & Taylor Corporation, 16 45–47;
  43 59–62 (upd.)

Baker Hughes Incorporated, III 428–29;
  22 66–69 (upd.); 57 62–66 (upd.)
Bakkavör Group hf., 91 35–39
Balance Bar Company, 32 70–72
Balchem Corporation, 42 21–23
Baldor Electric Company, 21 42–44; 97
  63–67 (upd.)
Baldwin & Lyons, Inc., 51 37–39
Baldwin Piano & Organ Company, 18
  43–46 *see also* Gibson Guitar Corp.
Baldwin Technology Company, Inc., 25
  35–39
Balfour Beatty Construction Ltd., 36
  56–60 (upd.)
Ball Corporation, I 597–98; 10 129–31
  (upd.); 78 25–29 (upd.)
Ball Horticultural Company, 78 30–33
Ballantine Books *see* Random House, Inc.
Ballantyne of Omaha, Inc., 27 56–58
Ballard Medical Products, 21 45–48 *see
  also* Kimberly-Clark Corp.
Ballard Power Systems Inc., 73 49–52
Ballistic Recovery Systems, Inc., 87
  51–54
Bally Manufacturing Corporation, III
  430–32
Bally Total Fitness Corporation, 25
  40–42; 94 53–57 (upd.)
Balmac International, Inc., 94 58–61
Bâloise-Holding, 40 59–62
Baltek Corporation, 34 59–61
Baltika Brewery Joint Stock Company,
  65 63–66
Baltimore & Ohio Railroad *see* CSX
  Corp.
Baltimore Aircoil Company, Inc., 66
  27–29
Baltimore Gas and Electric Company, V
  552–54; 25 43–46 (upd.)
Baltimore Orioles L.P., 66 30–33
Baltimore Technologies Plc, 42 24–26
The Bama Companies, Inc., 80 13–16
Banamex *see* Grupo Financiero Banamex
  S.A.
Banana Republic Inc., 25 47–49 *see also*
  Gap, Inc.
Banc One Corporation, 10 132–34 *see
  also* JPMorgan Chase & Co.
Banca Commerciale Italiana SpA, II
  191–93
Banca Fideuram SpA, 63 52–54
Banca Intesa SpA, 65 67–70
Banca Monte dei Paschi di Siena SpA,
  65 71–73
Banca Nazionale del Lavoro SpA, 72
  19–21
Banca Serfin *see* Grupo Financiero Serfin,
  S.A.
Banco Bilbao Vizcaya Argentaria S.A., II
  194–96; 48 47–51 (upd.)
Banco Bradesco S.A., 13 69–71
Banco Central, II 197–98; 56 65 *see also*
  Banco Santander Central Hispano S.A.
Banco de Crédito del Perú, 9273–76
Banco de Crédito e Inversiones *see* Bci.
Banco Comercial Português, SA, 50
  69–72
Banco de Chile, 69 55–57

Banco de Comercio, S.A. *see* Grupo
  Financiero BBVA Bancomer S.A.
Banco do Brasil S.A., II 199–200
Banco Espírito Santo e Comercial de
  Lisboa, 15 38–40 *see also* Espírito
  Santo Financial Group S.A.
Banco Itaú S.A., 19 33–35
Banco Popular *see* Popular, Inc.
Banco Santander Central Hispano S.A.,
  36 61–64 (upd.)
Banco Serfin *see* Grupo Financiero Serfin,
  S.A.
Bancomer S.A. *see* Grupo Financiero
  BBVA Bancomer S.A.
Bandag, Inc., 19 36–38
Bandai Co., Ltd., 55 44–48
Banfi Products Corp., 36 65–67
Banfield, The Pet Hospital *see* Medical
  Management International, Inc.
Bang & Olufsen Holding A/S, 37
  25–28; 86 24–29 (upd.)
Bank Austria AG, 23 37–39
Bank Brussels Lambert, II 201–03
Bank Hapoalim B.M., II 204–06; 54
  33–37 (upd.)
Bank Leumi le-Israel B.M., 60 48–51
Bank of America Corporation, 46
  47–54 (upd.)
Bank of Boston Corporation, II 207–09
  see also FleetBoston Financial Corp.
Bank of China, 63 55–57
Bank of Cyprus Group, 91 40–43
Bank of East Asia Ltd., 63 58–60
Bank of Granite Corporation, 89 87–91
Bank of Hawaii Corporation, 73 53–56
Bank of Ireland, 50 73–76
Bank of Mississippi, Inc., 14 40–41
Bank of Montreal, II 210–12; 46 55–58
  (upd.)
Bank of New England Corporation, II
  213–15
Bank of New York Company, Inc., II
  216–19; 46 59–63 (upd.)
The Bank of Nova Scotia, II 220–23; 59
  70–76 (upd.)
The Bank of Scotland *see* The Governor
  and Company of the Bank of Scotland.
Bank of the Ozarks, Inc., 91 44–47
Bank of the Philippine Islands, 58
  18–20
Bank of Tokyo-Mitsubishi Ltd., II
  224–25; 15 41–43 (upd.) *see also*
  Mitsubishi UFJ Financial Group, Inc.
Bank One Corporation, 36 68–75
  (upd.) *see also* JPMorgan Chase & Co.
BankAmerica Corporation, II 226–28
  see also Bank of America.
Bankers Trust New York Corporation, II
  229–31
Banknorth Group, Inc., 55 49–53
Bankrate, Inc., 83 38–41
Banner Aerospace, Inc., 14 42–44; 37
  29–32 (upd.)
Banorte *see* Grupo Financiero Banorte,
  S.A. de C.V.
Banque Nationale de Paris S.A., II
  232–34 *see also* BNP Paribas Group.

Banta Corporation, 12 24–26; 32 73–77 (upd.); 79 50–56 (upd.)
Banyan Systems Inc., 25 50–52
Baptist Health Care Corporation, 82 37–40
Bar-S Foods Company, 76 39–41
Barbara's Bakery Inc., 88 21–24
Barclay Furniture Co. *see* LADD Furniture, Inc.
Barclays PLC, II 235–37; 20 57–60 (upd.); 64 46–50 (upd.)
BarclaysAmerican Mortgage Corporation, 11 29–30
Barco NV, 44 42–45
Barden Companies, Inc., 76 42–45
Bardwil Industries Inc., 98 15–18
Bare Escentuals, Inc., 91 48–52
Barilla G. e R. Fratelli S.p.A., 17 35–37; 50 77–80 (upd.)
Barings PLC, 14 45–47
Barlow Rand Ltd., I 422–24
Barmag AG, 39 39–42
Barnes & Noble, Inc., 10 135–37; 30 67–71 (upd.); 75 50–55 (upd.)
Barnes Group, Inc., 13 72–74; 69 58–62 (upd.)
Barnett Banks, Inc., 9 58–60 *see also* Bank of America Corp.
Barnett Inc., 28 50–52
Barney's, Inc., 28 53–55
Baron de Ley S.A., 74 27–29
Baron Philippe de Rothschild S.A., 39 43–46
Barr *see* AG Barr plc.
Barr Pharmaceuticals, Inc., 26 29–31; 68 46–49 (upd.)
Barratt Developments plc, I 556–57; 56 31–33 (upd.)
Barrett Business Services, Inc., 16 48–50
Barrett-Jackson Auction Company L.L.C., 88 25–28
Barrick Gold Corporation, 34 62–65
Barry Callebaut AG, 29 46–48; 71 46–49 (upd.)
Barry-Wehmiller Companies, Inc., 90 40–43
The Bartell Drug Company, 94 62–65
Barton Malow Company, 51 40–43
Barton Protective Services Inc., 53 56–58
The Baseball Club of Seattle, LP, 50 81–85
BASF Aktiengesellschaft, I 305–08; 18 47–51 (upd.); 50 86–92 (upd.)
Bashas' Inc., 33 62–64; 80 17–21 (upd.)
The Basketball Club of Seattle, LLC, 50 93–97
Bass PLC, I 222–24; 15 44–47 (upd.); 38 74–78 (upd.)
Bass Pro Shops, Inc., 42 27–30
Bassett Furniture Industries, Inc., 18 52–55; 95 44–50 (upd.)
BAT Industries plc, I 425–27 *see also* British American Tobacco PLC.
Bata Ltd., 62 27–30
Bates Worldwide, Inc., 14 48–51; 33 65–69 (upd.)

Bath Iron Works Corporation, 12 27–29; 36 76–79 (upd.)
Battelle Memorial Institute, Inc., 10 138–40
Batten Barton Durstine & Osborn *see* Omnicom Group Inc.
Battle Mountain Gold Company, 23 40–42 *see also* Newmont Mining Corp.
Bauer Publishing Group, 7 42–43
Bauerly Companies, 61 31–33
Baugur Group hf, 81 45–49
Baumax AG, 75 56–58
Bausch & Lomb Inc., 7 44–47; 25 53–57 (upd.); 96 20–26 (upd.)
Bavaria S.A., 90 44–47
Baxi Group Ltd., 96 27–30
Baxter International Inc., I 627–29; 10 141–43 (upd.)
Baxters Food Group Ltd., 99 47–50
The Bay *see* The Hudson's Bay Co.
Bay State Gas Company, 38 79–82
Bayard SA, 49 46–49
BayBanks, Inc., 12 30–32
Bayer A.G., I 309–11; 13 75–77 (upd.); 41 44–48 (upd.)
Bayerische Hypotheken- und Wechsel-Bank AG, II 238–40 *see also* HVB Group.
Bayerische Motoren Werke A.G., I 138–40; 11 31–33 (upd.); 38 83–87 (upd.)
Bayerische Vereinsbank A.G., II 241–43 *see also* HVB Group.
Bayernwerk AG, V 555–58; 23 43–47 (upd.) *see also* E.On AG.
Bayou Steel Corporation, 31 47–49
BB&T Corporation, 79 57–61
BB Holdings Limited, 77 50–53
BBA *see* Bush Boake Allen Inc.
BBA Aviation plc, 90 48–52
BBAG Osterreichische Brau-Beteiligungs-AG, 38 88–90
BBC *see* British Broadcasting Corp.
BBDO Worldwide *see* Omnicom Group Inc.
BBGI *see* Beasley Broadcast Group, Inc.
BBN Corp., 19 39–42
BBVA *see* Banco Bilbao Vizcaya Argentaria S.A.
BCE, Inc., V 269–71; 44 46–50 (upd.)
Bci, 99 51–54
BDO Seidman LLP, 96 31–34
BE&K, Inc., 73 57–59
BEA *see* Bank of East Asia Ltd.
BEA Systems, Inc., 36 80–83
Beacon Roofing Supply, Inc., 75 59–61
Bear Creek Corporation, 38 91–94
Bear Stearns Companies, Inc., II 400–01; 10 144–45 (upd.); 52 41–44 (upd.)
Bearings, Inc., 13 78–80
Beasley Broadcast Group, Inc., 51 44–46
Beate Uhse AG, 96 35–39
Beatrice Company, II 467–69 *see also* TLC Beatrice International Holdings, Inc.

BeautiControl Cosmetics, Inc., 21 49–52
Beazer Homes USA, Inc., 17 38–41
bebe stores, inc., 31 50–52
Bechtel Corporation, I 558–59; 24 64–67 (upd.); 99 55–60 (upd.)
Beckett Papers, 23 48–50
Beckman Coulter, Inc., 22 74–77
Beckman Instruments, Inc., 14 52–54
Becton, Dickinson & Company, I 630–31; 11 34–36 (upd.); 36 84–89 (upd.)
Bed Bath & Beyond Inc., 13 81–83; 41 49–52 (upd.)
Beech Aircraft Corporation, 8 49–52 *see also* Raytheon Aircraft Holdings Inc.
Beech-Nut Nutrition Corporation, 21 53–56; 51 47–51 (upd.)
Beer Nuts, Inc., 86 30–33
Beggars Group Ltd., 99 61–65
Behr GmbH & Co. KG, 72 22–25
Behring Diagnostics *see* Dade Behring Holdings Inc.
BEI Technologies, Inc., 65 74–76
Beiersdorf AG, 29 49–53
Bekaert S.A./N.V., 90 53–57
Bekins Company, 15 48–50
Bel *see* Fromageries Bel.
Bel Fuse, Inc., 53 59–62
Bel/Kaukauna USA, 76 46–48
Belco Oil & Gas Corp., 40 63–65
Belden CDT Inc., 19 43–45; 76 49–52 (upd.)
Belgacom, 6 302–04
Belk, Inc., V 12–13; 19 46–48 (upd.); 72 26–29 (upd.)
Bell and Howell Company, 9 61–64; 29 54–58 (upd.)
Bell Atlantic Corporation, V 272–74; 25 58–62 (upd.) *see also* Verizon Communications.
Bell Canada Enterprises Inc. *see* BCE, Inc.
Bell Canada International, Inc., 6 305–08
Bell Helicopter Textron Inc., 46 64–67
Bell Industries, Inc., 47 40–43
Bell Resources *see* TPG NV.
Bell Sports Corporation, 16 51–53; 44 51–54 (upd.)
Bellcore *see* Telcordia Technologies, Inc.
Belleek Pottery Ltd., 71 50–53
Belleville Shoe Manufacturing Company, 92 17–20
Bellisio Foods, Inc., 95 51–54
BellSouth Corporation, V 276–78; 29 59–62 (upd.) *see also* AT&T Corp.
Bellway Plc, 45 37–39
Belo Corporation, 98 19–25 (upd.)
Beloit Corporation, 14 55–57 *see also* Metso Corp.
Belron International Ltd., 76 53–56
Belvedere S.A., 93 77–81
Bemis Company, Inc., 8 53–55; 91 53–60 (upd.)
Ben & Jerry's Homemade, Inc., 10 146–48; 35 58–62 (upd.); 80 22–28 (upd.)
Ben Bridge Jeweler, Inc., 60 52–54

Ben E. Keith Company, 76 57–59
Benchmark Capital, 49 50–52
Benchmark Electronics, Inc., 40 66–69
Benckiser N.V. *see* Reckitt Benckiser plc.
Bendix Corporation, I 141–43
Beneficial Corporation, 8 56–58
Benesse Corporation, 76 60–62
Bénéteau SA, 55 54–56
Benetton Group S.p.A., 10 149–52; 67
    47–51 (upd.)
Benfield Greig Group plc, 53 63–65
Benguet Corporation, 58 21–24
Benihana, Inc., 18 56–59; 76 63–66
    (upd.)
Benjamin Moore and Co., 13 84–87; 38
    95–99 (upd.)
BenQ Corporation, 67 52–54
Benton Oil and Gas Company, 47
    44–46
Berean Christian Stores, 96 40–43
Beretta *see* Fabbrica D' Armi Pietro
    Beretta S.p.A.
Bergdorf Goodman Inc., 52 45–48
Bergen Brunswig Corporation, V
    14–16; 13 88–90 (upd.) *see also*
    AmerisourceBergen Corp.
Berger Bros Company, 62 31–33
Beringer Blass Wine Estates Ltd., 22
    78–81; 66 34–37 (upd.)
Berjaya Group Bhd., 67 55–57
Berkeley Farms, Inc., 46 68–70
Berkshire Hathaway Inc., III 213–15;
    18 60–63 (upd.); 42 31–36 (upd.);
    89 92–99 (upd.)
Berkshire Realty Holdings, L.P., 49
    53–55
Berlex Laboratories, Inc., 66 38–40
Berliner Stadtreinigungsbetriebe, 58
    25–28
Berliner Verkehrsbetriebe (BVG), 58
    29–31
Berlinwasser Holding AG, 90 58–62
Berlitz International, Inc., 13 91–93; 39
    47–50 (upd.)
Bernard C. Harris Publishing Company,
    Inc., 39 51–53
Bernard Chaus, Inc., 27 59–61
Bernard Hodes Group Inc., 86 34–37
Bernard Matthews Ltd., 89 100–04
The Bernick Companies, 75 62–65
Bernina Holding AG, 47 47–50
Bernstein-Rein, 92 21–24
The Berry Company *see* L. M. Berry and
    Company
Berry Petroleum Company, 47 51–53
Berry Plastics Group Inc., 21 57–59; 98
    26–30 (upd.)
Bertelsmann A.G., IV 592–94; 43 63–67
    (upd.); 91 61–68 (upd.)
Bertucci's Corporation, 16 54–56; 64
    51–54 (upd.)
Berwick Offray, LLC, 70 17–19
Besix Group S.A./NV, 94 66–69
Besnier SA, 19 49–51 *see also* Groupe
    Lactalis
Best Kosher Foods Corporation, 82
    41–44

Best Buy Co., Inc., 9 65–66; 23 51–53
    (upd.); 63 61–66 (upd.)
Bestfoods, 22 82–86 (upd.)
Bestseller A/S, 90 63–66
Bestway Transportation *see* TNT
    Freightways Corp.
BET Holdings, Inc., 18 64–66
Beth Abraham Family of Health
    Services, 94 70–74
Beth Israel Medical Center *see* Continuum
    Health Partners, Inc.
Bethlehem Steel Corporation, IV 35–37;
    7 48–51 (upd.); 27 62–66 (upd.)
Better Made Snack Foods, Inc., 90
    67–69
Bettys & Taylors of Harrogate Ltd., 72
    30–32
Betz Laboratories, Inc., I 312–13; 10
    153–55 (upd.)
Beverly Enterprises, Inc., III 76–77; 16
    57–59 (upd.)
Bewag AG, 39 54–57
BFC Construction Corporation, 25
    63–65
The BFGoodrich Company, V 231–33;
    19 52–55 (upd.) *see also* Goodrich
    Corp.
BFI *see* The British Film Institute;
    Browning-Ferris Industries, Inc.
BFP Holdings Corp. *see* Big Flower Press
    Holdings, Inc.
BG Products Inc., 96 44–47
BG&E *see* Baltimore Gas and Electric Co.
Bharti Tele-Ventures Limited, 75 66–68
BHC Communications, Inc., 26 32–34
BHP Billiton, 67 58–64 (upd.)
Bhs plc, 17 42–44
Bianchi International (d/b/a Gregory
    Mountain Products), 76 67–69
Bibliographisches Institut & F.A.
    Brockhaus AG, 74 30–34
BIC Corporation, 8 59–61; 23 54–57
    (upd.)
BICC PLC, III 433–34 *see also* Balfour
    Beatty plc.
Bicoastal Corporation, II 9–11
Biffa plc, 92 25–28
Big A Drug Stores Inc., 79 62–65
Big B, Inc., 17 45–47
Big Bear Stores Co., 13 94–96
Big Brothers Big Sisters of America, 85
    29–33
Big Dog Holdings, Inc., 45 40–42
Big 5 Sporting Goods Corporation, 55
    57–59
Big Flower Press Holdings, Inc., 21
    60–62 *see also* Vertis Communications.
The Big Food Group plc, 68 50–53
    (upd.)
Big Idea Productions, Inc., 49 56–59
Big Lots, Inc., 50 98–101
Big O Tires, Inc., 20 61–63
Big Rivers Electric Corporation, 11
    37–39
Big V Supermarkets, Inc., 25 66–68
Big Y Foods, Inc., 53 66–68
Bigard *see* Groupe Bigard S.A.
BigBen Interactive S.A., 72 33–35

Bilfinger & Berger AG, I 560–61; 55
    60–63 (upd.)
Bill & Melinda Gates Foundation, 41
    53–55
Bill Barrett Corporation, 71 54–56
Bill Blass Ltd., 32 78–80
Billabong International Ltd., 44 55–58
Billing Concepts, Inc., 26 35–38; 72
    36–39 (upd.)
Bimbo *see* Grupo Industrial Bimbo.
Bindley Western Industries, Inc., 9
    67–69 *see also* Cardinal Health, Inc.
The Bing Group, 60 55–58
Bingham Dana LLP, 43 68–71
Binks Sames Corporation, 21 63–66
Binney & Smith Inc., 25 69–72
Bio-Rad Laboratories, Inc., 93 82–86
Biogen Idec Inc., 14 58–60; 36 90–93
    (upd.); 71 57–59 (upd.)
Bioindustrias *see* Valores Industriales S.A.
Biokyowa *see* Kyowa Hakko Kogyo Co.,
    Ltd.
Biolase Technology, Inc., 87 55–58
bioMérieux S.A., 75 69–71
Biomet, Inc., 10 156–58; 93 87–94
    (upd.)
BioScrip Inc., 98 31–35
Biosite Incorporated, 73 60–62
Biovail Corporation, 47 54–56
BioWare Corporation, 81 50–53
Bird Corporation, 19 56–58
Birds Eye Foods, Inc., 69 66–72 (upd.)
Birkenstock Footprint Sandals, Inc., 12
    33–35; 42 37–40 (upd.)
Birmingham Steel Corporation, 13
    97–98; 40 70–73 (upd.) *see also* Nucor
    Corporation
Birse Group PLC, 77 54–58
Birthdays Ltd., 70 20–22
BISSELL, Inc., 9 70–72; 30 75–78
    (upd.)
The BISYS Group, Inc., 73 63–65
BIW *see* Bath Iron Works.
BJ Services Company, 25 73–75
BJ's Wholesale Club, Inc., 94 75–78
BKD LLP, 96 48–51
The Black & Decker Corporation, III
    435–37; 20 64–68 (upd.); 67 65–70
    (upd.)
Black & Veatch LLP, 22 87–90
Black Box Corporation, 20 69–71; 96
    52–56 (upd.)
Black Diamond Equipment, Ltd., 62
    34–37
Black Entertainment Television *see* BET
    Holdings, Inc.
Black Hills Corporation, 20 72–74
Blackbaud, Inc., 85 34–37
BlackBerry *see* Research in Motion Ltd.
Blackboard Inc., 89 105–10
Blackfoot Telecommunications Group,
    60 59–62
BlackRock, Inc., 79 66–69
Blacks Leisure Group plc, 39 58–60
Blackwater USA, 76 70–73
Blackwell Publishing (Holdings) Ltd.,
    78 34–37
Blair Corporation, 25 76–78; 31 53–55

Blessings Corp., 19 59–61
Blimpie International, Inc., 15 55–57; 49 60–64 (upd.)
Blish-Mize Co., 95 55–58
Blizzard Entertainment, 78 38–42
Block Communications, Inc., 81 54–58
Block Drug Company, Inc., 8 62–64; 27 67–70 (upd.) *see also* GlaxoSmithKline plc.
Blockbuster Inc., 9 73–75; 31 56–60 (upd.); 76 74–78 (upd.)
Blodgett Holdings, Inc., 61 34–37 (upd.)
Blokker Holding B.V., 84 21–24
Blonder Tongue Laboratories, Inc., 48 52–55
Bloomberg L.P., 21 67–71
Bloomingdale's Inc., 12 36–38
Blount International, Inc., 12 39–41; 48 56–60 (upd.)
BLP Group Companies *see* Boron, LePore & Associates, Inc.
Blue Bell Creameries L.P., 30 79–81
Blue Bird Corporation, 35 63–66
Blue Circle Industries PLC, III 669–71 *see also* Lafarge Cement UK.
Blue Coat Systems, Inc., 83 42–45
Blue Cross and Blue Shield Association, 10 159–61
Blue Diamond Growers, 28 56–58
Blue Heron Paper Company, 90 70–73
Blue Martini Software, Inc., 59 77–80
Blue Mountain Arts, Inc., 29 63–66
Blue Nile Inc., 61 38–40
Blue Rhino Corporation, 56 34–37
Blue Ridge Beverage Company Inc., 82 45–48
Blue Square Israel Ltd., 41 56–58
Bluefly, Inc., 60 63–65
Bluegreen Corporation, 80 29–32
BlueLinx Holdings Inc., 97 68–72
Blundstone Pty Ltd., 76 79–81
Blyth, Inc., 18 67–69; 74 35–38 (upd.)
BMC Industries, Inc., 17 48–51; 59 81–86 (upd.)
BMC Software, Inc., 55 64–67
BMG/Music *see* Bertelsmann AG.
BMHC *see* Building Materials Holding Corp.
BMI *see* Broadcast Music Inc.
BMW *see* Bayerische Motoren Werke.
BNA *see* Bureau of National Affairs, Inc.
BNE *see* Bank of New England Corp.
BNL *see* Banca Nazionale del Lavoro S.p.A.
BNP Paribas Group, 36 94–97 (upd.)
Boardwalk Pipeline Partners, LP, 87 59–62
Boart Longyear Company, 26 39–42
Boatmen's Bancshares Inc., 15 58–60 *see also* Bank of America Corp.
Bob Evans Farms, Inc., 9 76–79; 63 67–72 (upd.)
Bob's Red Mill Natural Foods, Inc., 63 73–75
Bobit Publishing Company, 55 68–70
Bobs Candies, Inc., 70 23–25

BOC Group plc, I 314–16; 25 79–82 (upd.); 78 43–49 (upd.)
Boca Resorts, Inc., 37 33–36
Boddie-Noell Enterprises, Inc., 68 54–56
Bodum Design Group AG, 47 57–59
Body Glove International LLC, 88 29–32
The Body Shop International plc, 11 40–42; 53 69–72 (upd.)
Bodycote International PLC, 63 76–78
Boehringer Ingelheim GmbH *see* C.H. Boehringer Sohn.
The Boeing Company, I 47–49; 10 162–65 (upd.); 32 81–87 (upd.)
Bogen Communications International, Inc., 62 38–41
Bohemia, Inc., 13 99–101
BÖHLER-UDDEHOLM AG, 73 66–69
Boiron S.A., 73 70–72
Boise Cascade Corporation, IV 255–56; 8 65–67 (upd.); 32 88–92 (upd.); 95 59–66 (upd.)
Boizel Chanoine Champagne S.A., 94 79–82
Boliden AB, 80 33–36
Bolt Technology Corporation, 99 66–70
Bojangles Restaurants Inc., 97 73–77
Bollinger Shipyards, Inc., 61 41–43
Bols Distilleries NV, 74 39–42
Bolsa Mexicana de Valores, S.A. de C.V., 80 37–40
Bolton Group B.V., 86 38–41
Bombardier Inc., 42 41–46 (upd.); 87 63–71 (upd.)
The Bombay Company, Inc., 10 166–68; 71 60–64 (upd.)
Bon Appetit Holding AG, 48 61–63
The Bon Marché, Inc., 23 58–60 *see also* Federated Department Stores Inc.
Bon Secours Health System, Inc., 24 68–71
The Bon-Ton Stores, Inc., 16 60–62; 50 106–10 (upd.)
Bond Corporation Holdings Limited, 10 169–71
Bonduelle SA, 51 52–54
Bongard *see* Aga Foodservice Group PLC.
Bongrain SA, 25 83–85
Bonhams 1793 Ltd., 72 40–42
Bonneville International Corporation, 29 67–70
Bonneville Power Administration, 50 102–05
Bonnier AB, 52 49–52
Book-of-the-Month Club, Inc., 13 105–07
Booker plc, 13 102–04; 31 61–64 (upd.)
Booker Cash & Carry Ltd., 68 57–61 (upd.)
Books-A-Million, Inc., 14 61–62; 41 59–62 (upd.); 96 57–61 (upd.)
Books Are Fun, Ltd. *see* The Reader's Digest Association, Inc.
Bookspan, 86 42–46
Boole & Babbage, Inc., 25 86–88 *see also* BMC Software, Inc.

Booth Creek Ski Holdings, Inc., 31 65–67
The Boots Company PLC, V 17–19; 24 72–76 (upd.) *see also* Alliance Boots plc.
Boots & Coots International Well Control, Inc., 79 70–73
Booz Allen & Hamilton Inc., 10 172–75
Boral Limited, III 672–74; 43 72–76 (upd.)
Borden, Inc., II 470–73; 22 91–96 (upd.)
Borders Group, Inc., 15 61–62; 43 77–79 (upd.)
Borealis AG, 94 83–86
Borg-Warner Automotive, Inc., 14 63–66; 32 93–97 (upd.)
Borg-Warner Corporation, III 438–41 *see also* Burns International.
BorgWarner Inc., 85 38–44 (upd.)
Borland International, Inc., 9 80–82
Boron, LePore & Associates, Inc., 45 43–45
Bosch *see* Robert Bosch GmbH.
Boscov's Department Store, Inc., 31 68–70
Bose Corporation, 13 108–10; 36 98–101 (upd.)
Boss Holdings, Inc., 97 78–81
Boston Acoustics, Inc., 22 97–99
The Boston Beer Company, Inc., 18 70–73; 50 111–15 (upd.)
Boston Celtics Limited Partnership, 14 67–69
Boston Chicken, Inc., 12 42–44 *see also* Boston Market Corp.
The Boston Consulting Group, 58 32–35
Boston Edison Company, 12 45–47
Boston Market Corporation, 48 64–67 (upd.)
Boston Pizza International Inc., 88 33–38
Boston Professional Hockey Association Inc., 39 61–63
Boston Properties, Inc., 22 100–02
Boston Scientific Corporation, 37 37–40; 77 58–63 (upd.)
The Boston Symphony Orchestra Inc., 93 95–99
Bou-Matic, 62 42–44
Bourbon *see* Groupe Bourbon S.A.
Bourbon Corporation, 82 49–52
Bouygues S.A., I 562–64; 24 77–80 (upd.); 97 82–87 (upd.)
Bovis *see* Peninsular and Oriental Steam Navigation Company (Bovis Division)
Bowater PLC, IV 257–59
Bowlin Travel Centers, Inc., 99 71–75
Bowne & Co., Inc., 23 61–64; 79 74–80 (upd.)
Bowthorpe plc, 33 70–72
The Boy Scouts of America, 34 66–69
Boyd Bros. Transportation Inc., 39 64–66
Boyd Coffee Company, 53 73–75
Boyd Gaming Corporation, 43 80–82

The Boyds Collection, Ltd., 29 71–73
Boyne USA Resorts, 71 65–68
Boys & Girls Clubs of America, 69 73–75
Bozell Worldwide Inc., 25 89–91
Bozzuto's, Inc., 13 111–12
BP p.l.c., 45 46–56 (upd.)
BPB plc, 83 46–49
Braathens ASA, 47 60–62
Brach's Confections, Inc., 15 63–65; 74 43–46 (upd.)
Bradford & Bingley PLC, 65 77–80
Bradlees Discount Department Store Company, 12 48–50
Bradley Air Services Ltd., 56 38–40
Brady Corporation, 78 50–55 (upd.)
Brake Bros plc, 45 57–59
Bramalea Ltd., 9 83–85
Brambles Industries Limited, 42 47–50
Brammer PLC, 77 64–67
The Branch Group, Inc., 72 43–45
BrandPartners Group, Inc., 58 36–38
Brannock Device Company, 48 68–70
Brascan Corporation, 67 71–73
Brasfield & Gorrie LLC, 87 72–75
Brasil Telecom Participaçoes S.A., 57 67–70
Brass Eagle Inc., 34 70–72
Brauerei Beck & Co., 9 86–87; 33 73–76 (upd.)
Braun GmbH, 51 55–58
Brazil Fast Food Corporation, 74 47–49
Brazos Sportswear, Inc., 23 65–67
Breeze-Eastern Corporation, 95 67–70
Bremer Financial Corp., 45 60–63
Brenntag AG, 8 68–69; 23 68–70 (upd.)
Brescia Group see Grupo Brescia.
Briazz, Inc., 53 76–79
The Brickman Group, Ltd., 87 76–79
Bricorama S.A., 68 62–64
Bridgeport Machines, Inc., 17 52–54
Bridgestone Corporation, V 234–35; 21 72–75 (upd.); 59 87–92 (upd.)
Bridgford Foods Corporation, 27 71–73
Briggs & Stratton Corporation, 8 70–73; 27 74–78 (upd.)
Brigham Exploration Company, 75 72–74
Brigham's Inc., 72 46–48
Bright Horizons Family Solutions, Inc., 31 71–73
Brightpoint, Inc., 18 74–77
Brillstein-Grey Entertainment, 80 41–45
The Brink's Company, 58 39–43 (upd.)
Brinker International, Inc., 10 176–78; 38 100–03 (upd.); 75 75–79 (upd.)
BRIO AB, 24 81–83
Brioche Pasquier S.A., 58 44–46
Brioni Roman Style S.p.A., 67 74–76
BRISA Auto-estradas de Portugal S.A., 64 55–58
Bristol Hotel Company, 23 71–73
Bristol-Myers Squibb Company, III 17–19; 9 88–91 (upd.); 37 41–45 (upd.)
Bristow Helicopters Ltd., 70 26–28
Britannia Soft Drinks Ltd. (Britvic), 71 69–71

Britannica.com see Encyclopaedia Britannica, Inc.
Brite Voice Systems, Inc., 20 75–78
British Aerospace plc, I 50–53; 24 84–90 (upd.)
British Airways plc, I 92–95; 14 70–74 (upd.); 43 83–88 (upd.)
British American Tobacco PLC, 50 116–19 (upd.)
British-Borneo Oil & Gas PLC, 34 73–75
British Broadcasting Corporation Ltd., 7 52–55; 21 76–79 (upd.); 89 111–14 (upd.)
British Coal Corporation, IV 38–40
British Columbia Telephone Company, 6 309–11
British Energy Plc, 49 65–68 see also British Nuclear Fuels PLC.
The British Film Institute, 80 46–50
British Gas plc, V 559–63 see also Centrica plc.
British Land Plc, 54 38–41
British Midland plc, 38 104–06
The British Museum, 71 72–74
British Nuclear Fuels PLC, 6 451–54
British Oxygen Co see BOC Group.
The British Petroleum Company plc, IV 378–80; 7 56–59 (upd.); 21 80–84 (upd.) see also BP p.l.c.
British Railways Board, V 421–24
British Sky Broadcasting Group plc, 20 79–81; 60 66–69 (upd.)
British Steel plc, IV 41–43; 19 62–65 (upd.)
British Sugar plc, 84 25–29
British Telecommunications plc, V 279–82; 15 66–70 (upd.) see also BT Group plc.
The British United Provident Association Limited, 79 81–84
British Vita plc, 9 92–93; 33 77–79 (upd.)
British World Airlines Ltd., 18 78–80
Britvic Soft Drinks Limited see Britannia Soft Drinks Ltd. (Britvic)
Broadcast Music Inc., 23 74–77; 90 74–79 (upd.)
Broadcom Corporation, 34 76–79; 90 80–85 (upd.)
The Broadmoor Hotel, 30 82–85
Broadwing Corporation, 70 29–32
Brobeck, Phleger & Harrison, LLP, 31 74–76
Brockhaus see Bibliographisches Institut & F.A. Brockhaus AG.
Brodart Company, 84 30–33
Broder Bros. Co., 38 107–09
Broderbund Software, Inc., 13 113–16; 29 74–78 (upd.)
Broken Hill Proprietary Company Ltd., IV 44–47; 22 103–08 (upd.) see also BHP Billiton.
Bronco Drilling Company, Inc., 89 118–21
Bronner Brothers Inc., 92 29–32
Bronner Display & Sign Advertising, Inc., 82 53–57

Brookdale Senior Living, 91 69–73
Brooke Group Ltd., 15 71–73 see also Vector Group Ltd.
Brookfield Properties Corporation, 89 122–25
Brooklyn Union Gas, 6 455–57 see also KeySpan Energy Co.
Brooks Brothers Inc., 22 109–12
Brooks Sports Inc., 32 98–101
Brookshire Grocery Company, 16 63–66; 74 50–53 (upd.)
Brookstone, Inc., 18 81–83
Brose Fahrzeugteile GmbH & Company KG, 84 34–38
Brother Industries, Ltd., 14 75–76
Brother's Brother Foundation, 93 100–04
Brothers Gourmet Coffees, Inc., 20 82–85 see also The Procter & Gamble Co.
Broughton Foods Co., 17 55–57 see also Suiza Foods Corp.
Brouwerijen Alken-Maes N.V., 86 47–51
Brown & Brown, Inc., 41 63–66
Brown & Haley, 23 78–80
Brown & Root, Inc., 13 117–19 see also Kellogg Brown & Root Inc.
Brown & Sharpe Manufacturing Co., 23 81–84
Brown and Williamson Tobacco Corporation, 14 77–79; 33 80–83 (upd.)
Brown Brothers Harriman & Co., 45 64–67
Brown-Forman Corporation, I 225–27; 10 179–82 (upd.); 38 110–14 (upd.)
Brown Group, Inc., V 351–53; 20 86–89 (upd.) see also Brown Shoe Company, Inc.
Brown Jordan International Inc., 74 54–57 (upd.)
Brown Printing Company, 26 43–45
Brown Shoe Company, Inc., 68 65–69 (upd.)
Browning-Ferris Industries, Inc., V 749–53; 20 90–93 (upd.)
Broyhill Furniture Industries, Inc., 10 183–85
Bruce Foods Corporation, 39 67–69
Bruegger's Corporation, 63 79–82
Bruno's Supermarkets, Inc., 7 60–62; 26 46–48 (upd.); 68 70–73 (upd.)
Brunschwig & Fils Inc., 96 62–65
Brunswick Corporation, III 442–44; 22 113–17 (upd.); 77 68–75 (upd.)
Brush Engineered Materials Inc., 67 77–79
Brush Wellman Inc., 14 80–82
Bruster's Real Ice Cream, Inc., 80 51–54
BSA see The Boy Scouts of America.
BSC see Birmingham Steel Corporation
BSH Bosch und Siemens Hausgeräte GmbH, 67 80–84
BSN Groupe S.A., II 474–75 see also Groupe Danone
BT Group plc, 49 69–74 (upd.)
BTG, Inc., 45 68–70

BTG Plc, 87 80–83
BTR plc, I 428–30
BTR Siebe plc, 27 79–81 *see also* Invensys PLC.
Buca, Inc., 38 115–17
Buck Consultants, Inc., 55 71–73
Buck Knives Inc., 48 71–74
Buckeye Partners, L.P., 70 33–36
Buckeye Technologies, Inc., 42 51–54
The Buckle, Inc., 18 84–86
Bucyrus International, Inc., 17 58–61
The Budd Company, 8 74–76 *see also* ThyssenKrupp AG.
Buderus AG, 37 46–49
Budgens Ltd., 59 93–96
Budget Group, Inc., 25 92–94 *see also* Cendant Corp.
Budget Rent a Car Corporation, 9 94–95
Budweiser Budvar, National Corporation, 59 97–100
Buena Vista Home Video *see* The Walt Disney Co.
Bufete Industrial, S.A. de C.V., 34 80–82
Buffalo Grill S.A., 94 87–90
Buffalo Wild Wings, Inc., 56 41–43
Buffets Holdings, Inc., 10 186–87; 32 102–04 (upd.); 93 105–09 (upd.)
Bugatti Automobiles S.A.S., 94 91–94
Bugle Boy Industries, Inc., 18 87–88
Buhrmann NV, 41 67–69
Buick Motor Co. *see* General Motors Corp.
Build-A-Bear Workshop Inc., 62 45–48
Building Materials Holding Corporation, 52 53–55
Bulgari S.p.A., 20 94–97
Bull *see* Compagnie des Machines Bull S.A.
Bull S.A., 43 89–91 (upd.)
Bulley & Andrews, LLC, 55 74–76
Bulova Corporation, 13 120–22; 41 70–73 (upd.)
Bumble Bee Seafoods L.L.C., 64 59–61
Bundy Corporation, 17 62–65
Bunge Ltd., 62 49–51
Bunzl plc, IV 260–62; 31 77–80 (upd.)
Burberry Group plc, 17 66–68; 41 74–76 (upd.); 92 33–37 (upd.)
Burda Holding GmbH. & Co., 23 85–89
Burdines, Inc., 60 70–73
The Bureau of National Affairs, Inc., 23 90–93
Bureau Veritas SA, 55 77–79
Burelle S.A., 23 94–96
Burger King Corporation, II 613–15; 17 69–72 (upd.); 56 44–48 (upd.)
Burgett, Inc., 97 88–91
Burke, Inc., 88 39–42
Burke Mills, Inc., 66 41–43
Burlington Coat Factory Warehouse Corporation, 10 188–89; 60 74–76 (upd.)
Burlington Industries, Inc., V 354–55; 17 73–76 (upd.)

Burlington Northern Santa Fe Corporation, V 425–28; 27 82–89 (upd.)
Burlington Resources Inc., 10 190–92 *see also* ConocoPhillips.
Burmah Castrol PLC, IV 381–84; 30 86–91 (upd.) *see also* BP p.l.c.
Burns International Security Services, 13 123–25 *see also* Securitas AB.
Burns International Services Corporation, 41 77–80 (upd.)
Burns, Philp & Company Ltd., 63 83–86
Burpee & Co. *see* W. Atlee Burpee & Co.
Burr-Brown Corporation, 19 66–68
Burroughs & Chapin Company, Inc., 86 52–55
Burt's Bees, Inc., 58 47–50
The Burton Corporation, V 20–22; 94 95–100 (upd.)
The Burton Group plc, *see also* Arcadia Group plc.
Burton Snowboards Inc., 22 118–20, 460
Busch Entertainment Corporation, 73 73–75
Bush Boake Allen Inc., 30 92–94 *see also* International Flavors & Fragrances Inc.
Bush Brothers & Company, 45 71–73
Bush Industries, Inc., 20 98–100
Business Men's Assurance Company of America, 14 83–85
Business Objects S.A., 25 95–97
Business Post Group plc, 46 71–73
Butler Manufacturing Company, 12 51–53; 62 52–56 (upd.)
Butterick Co., Inc., 23 97–99
Buttrey Food & Drug Stores Co., 18 89–91
buy.com, Inc., 46 74–77
Buzztime Entertainment, Inc. *see* NTN Buzztime, Inc.
BVR Systems (1998) Ltd., 93 110–13
BWAY Corporation, 24 91–93

C

C&A, 40 74–77 (upd.)
C&A Brenninkmeyer KG, V 23–24
C&G *see* Cheltenham & Gloucester PLC.
C&J Clark International Ltd., 52 56–59
C&K Market, Inc., 81 59–61
C & S Wholesale Grocers, Inc., 55 80–83
C-COR.net Corp., 38 118–21
C-Cube Microsystems, Inc., 37 50–54
C. Bechstein Pianofortefabrik AG, 96 66–71
C.F. Martin & Co., Inc., 42 55–58
The C.F. Sauer Company, 90 86–89
C. Hoare & Co., 77 76–79
C.H. Boehringer Sohn, 39 70–73
C.H. Guenther & Son, Inc., 84 39–42
C.H. Heist Corporation, 24 111–13
C.H. Robinson Worldwide, Inc., 11 43–44; 40 78–81 (upd.)
C.I. Traders Limited, 61 44–46
C. Itoh & Co., I 431–33 *see also* ITOCHU Corp.

C.R. Bard, Inc., 9 96–98; 65 81–85 (upd.)
C.R. Meyer and Sons Company, 74 58–60
C-Tech Industries Inc., 90 90–93
CAA *see* Creative Artists Agency LLC.
Cabela's Inc., 26 49–51; 68 74–77 (upd.)
Cable & Wireless HKT, 30 95–98 (upd.)
Cable and Wireless plc, V 283–86; 25 98–102 (upd.)
Cabletron Systems, Inc., 10 193–94
Cablevision Electronic Instruments, Inc., 32 105–07
Cablevision Systems Corporation, 7 63–65; 30 99–103 (upd.)
Cabot Corporation, 8 77–79; 29 79–82 (upd.); 91 74–80 (upd.)
Cache Incorporated, 30 104–06
CACI International Inc., 21 85–87; 72 49–53 (upd.)
Cactus Feeders, Inc., 91 81–84
Cactus S.A., 90 94–97
Cadbury Schweppes PLC, II 476–78; 49 75–79 (upd.)
Cadence Design Systems, Inc., 11 45–48; 48 75–79 (upd.)
Cadmus Communications Corporation, 23 100–03 *see also* Cenveo Inc.
CAE USA Inc., 48 80–82
Caere Corporation, 20 101–03
Caesars World, Inc., 6 199–202
Caffè Nero Group PLC, 63 87–89
Cagle's, Inc., 20 104–07
Cahners Business Information, 43 92–95
Cains Beer Company PLC, 99 76–80
Caisse des Dépôts et Consignations, 90 98–101
CAL *see* China Airlines.
Cal-Maine Foods, Inc., 69 76–78
CalAmp Corp., 87 84–87
Calavo Growers, Inc., 47 63–66
CalComp Inc., 13 126–29
Calcot Ltd., 33 84–87
Caldor Inc., 12 54–56
Calgon Carbon Corporation, 73 76–79
California Cedar Products Company, 58 51–53
California Pizza Kitchen Inc., 15 74–76; 74 61–63 (upd.)
California Sports, Inc., 56 49–52
California Steel Industries, Inc., 67 85–87
California Water Service Group, 79 85–88
Caliper Life Sciences, Inc., 70 37–40
Callanan Industries, Inc., 60 77–79
Callard and Bowser-Suchard Inc., 84 43–46
Callaway Golf Company, 15 77–79; 45 74–77 (upd.)
Callon Petroleum Company, 47 67–69
Calloway's Nursery, Inc., 51 59–61
CalMat Co., 19 69–72 *see also* Vulcan Materials Co.
Calpine Corporation, 36 102–04

Caltex Petroleum Corporation, 19 73–75 *see also* ChevronTexaco Corp.

Calvin Klein, Inc., 22 121–24; 55 84–88 (upd.)

Camaïeu S.A., 72 54–56

Camargo Corrêa S.A., 93 114–18

CamBar *see* Cameron & Barkley Co.

Cambrex Corporation, 16 67–69; 44 59–62 (upd.)

Cambridge SoundWorks, Inc., 48 83–86

Cambridge Technology Partners, Inc., 36 105–08

Camden Property Trust, 77 80–83

Cameco Corporation, 77 84–87

Camelot Music, Inc., 26 52–54

Cameron & Barkley Company, 28 59–61 *see also* Hagemeyer North America.

Campagna-Turano Bakery, Inc., 99 81–84

Campbell-Ewald Advertising, 86 56–60

Campbell-Mithun-Esty, Inc., 16 70–72 *see also* Interpublic Group of Companies, Inc.

Campbell Scientific, Inc., 51 62–65

Campbell Soup Company, II 479–81; 7 66–69 (upd.); 26 55–59 (upd.); 71 75–81 (upd.)

Campeau Corporation, V 25–28

The Campina Group, 78 61–64

Campo Electronics, Appliances & Computers, Inc., 16 73–75

Campofrío Alimentación S.A, 59 101–03

Canada Bread Company, Limited, 99 85–88

Canada Packers Inc., II 482–85

Canada Trust *see* CT Financial Services Inc.

Canadair, Inc., 16 76–78 *see also* Bombardier Inc.

The Canadian Broadcasting Corporation (CBC), 37 55–58

Canadian Imperial Bank of Commerce, II 244–46; 61 47–51 (upd.)

Canadian National Railway Company, 6 359–62; 71 82–88 (upd.)

Canadian Pacific Railway Limited, V 429–31; 45 78–83 (upd.); 95 71–80 (upd.)

Canadian Tire Corporation, Limited, 71 89–93 (upd.)

Canadian Utilities Limited, 13 130–32; 56 53–56 (upd.)

Canal Plus, 10 195–97; 34 83–86 (upd.)

Canandaigua Brands, Inc., 13 133–35; 34 87–91 (upd.) *see also* Constellation Brands, Inc.

Canary Wharf Group Plc, 30 107–09

Cancer Treatment Centers of America, Inc., 85 45–48

Candela Corporation, 48 87–89

Candie's, Inc., 31 81–84

Candle Corporation, 64 62–65

Candlewood Hotel Company, Inc., 41 81–83

Canfor Corporation, 42 59–61

Cannon Design, 63 90–92

Cannon Express, Inc., 53 80–82

Cannondale Corporation, 21 88–90

Cano Petroleum Inc., 97 92–95

Canon Inc., III 120–21; 18 92–95 (upd.); ; 79 89–95 (upd.)

Canstar Sports Inc., 16 79–81 *see also* NIKE, Inc.

Cantel Medical Corporation, 80 55–58

Canterbury Park Holding Corporation, 42 62–65

Cantine Giorgio Lungarotti S.R.L., 67 88–90

Cantor Fitzgerald, L.P., 92 38–42

CanWest Global Communications Corporation, 35 67–703

Cap Gemini Ernst & Young, 37 59–61

Cap Rock Energy Corporation, 46 78–81

Caparo Group Ltd., 90 102–06

Capcom Company Ltd., 83 50-53

Cape Cod Potato Chip Company, 90 107–10

Capel Incorporated, 45 84–86

Capezio/Ballet Makers Inc., 62 57–59

Capita Group PLC, 69 79–81

Capital Cities/ABC Inc., II 129–31

Capital Holding Corporation, III 216–19 *see also* Providian Financial Corp.

Capital One Financial Corporation, 52 60–63

Capital Radio plc, 35 71–73

Capital Senior Living Corporation, 75 80–82

Capitalia S.p.A., 65 86–89

Capitol Records, Inc., 90 111–16

CapStar Hotel Company, 21 91–93

Capstone Turbine Corporation, 75 83–85

Captain D's, LLC, 59 104–06

Captaris, Inc., 89 126–29

The Carphone Warehouse Group PLC, 83 54-57

Car Toys, Inc., 67 91–93

Caradon plc, 20 108–12 (upd.) *see also* Novar plc.

Carus Publishing Company, 93 128–32

Caraustar Industries, Inc., 19 76–78; 44 63–67 (upd.)

The Carbide/Graphite Group, Inc., 40 82–84

Carbo PLC, 67 94–96 (upd.)

Carbone Lorraine S.A., 33 88–90

Carborundum Company, 15 80–82 *see also* Carbo PLC.

Cardinal Health, Inc., 18 96–98; 50 120–23 (upd.)

Cardo AB, 53 83–85

Cardone Industries Inc., 92 43–47

Cardtronics, Inc., 93 119–23

Career Education Corporation, 45 87–89

CareerBuilder, Inc., 93 124–27

Caremark Rx, Inc., 10 198–200; 54 42–45 (upd.)

Carey International, Inc., 26 60–63

Cargill, Incorporated, II 616–18; 13 136–38 (upd.); 40 85–90 (upd.); 89 130–39 (upd.)

Cargolux Airlines International S.A., 49 80–82

Carhartt, Inc., 30 110–12; 77 88–92 (upd.)

Caribiner International, Inc., 24 94–97

Caribou Coffee Company, Inc., 28 62–65; 97 96–102 (upd.)

Caritas Internationalis, 72 57–59

Carl Allers Etablissement A/S, 72 60–62

Carl Kühne KG (GmbH & Co.), 94 101–05

Carl Zeiss AG, III 445–47; 34 92–97 (upd.); 91 85–92 (upd.)

Carl's Jr. *see* CKE Restaurants, Inc.

Carlisle Companies Inc., 8 80–82; 82 58-62 (upd.)

Carlsberg A/S, 9 99–101; 29 83–85 (upd.); 36–40 (upd.)

Carlson Companies, Inc., 6 363–66; 22 125–29 (upd.); 87 88–95 (upd.)

Carlson Restaurants Worldwide, 69 82–85

Carlson Wagonlit Travel, 55 89–92

Carlton and United Breweries Ltd., I 228–29 *see also* Foster's Group Limited

Carlton Communications plc, 15 83–85; 50 124–27 (upd.)

Carma Laboratories, Inc., 60 80–82

CarMax, Inc., 55 93–95

Carmichael Lynch Inc., 28 66–68

Carmike Cinemas, Inc., 14 86–88; 37 62–65 (upd.); 74 64–67 (upd.)

Carnation Company, II 486–89 *see also* Nestlé S.A.

Carnegie Corporation of New York, 35 74–77

Carnival Corporation, 6 367–68; 27 90–92 (upd.); 78 65–69 (upd.)

Carolina First Corporation, 31 85–87

Carolina Freight Corporation, 6 369–72

Carolina Power & Light Company, V 564–66; 23 104–07 (upd.) *see also* Progress Energy, Inc.

Carolina Telephone and Telegraph Company, 10 201–03

Carpenter Technology Corporation, 13 139–41; 95 81–86 (upd.)

CARQUEST Corporation, 29 86–89

Carr-Gottstein Foods Co., 17 77–80

Carrabba's Italian Grill *see* Outback Steakhouse, Inc.

CarrAmerica Realty Corporation, 56 57–59

Carrefour SA, 10 204–06; 27 93–96 (upd.); 64 66–69 (upd.)

The Carriage House Companies, Inc., 55 96–98

Carriage Services, Inc., 37 66–68

Carrier Access Corporation, 44 68–73

Carrier Corporation, 7 70–73; 69 86–91 (upd.)

Carrizo Oil & Gas, Inc., 97 103–06

Carroll's Foods, Inc., 46 82–85

Carrols Restaurant Group, Inc., 92 48–51

The Carsey-Werner Company, L.L.C., 37 69–72
Carson, Inc., 31 88–90
Carson Pirie Scott & Company, 15 86–88
CART *see* Championship Auto Racing Teams, Inc.
Carter Hawley Hale Stores, V 29–32
Carter Holt Harvey Ltd., 70 41–44
Carter Lumber Company, 45 90–92
Carter-Wallace, Inc., 8 83–86; 38 122–26 (upd.)
Cartier Monde, 29 90–92
Carvel Corporation, 35 78–81
Carver Bancorp, Inc., 94 106–10
Carver Boat Corporation LLC, 88 43–46
Carvin Corp., 89 140–43
Casa Bancária Almeida e Companhia *see* Banco Bradesco S.A.
Casa Cuervo, S.A. de C.V., 31 91–93
Casa Herradura *see* Grupo Industrial Herradura, S.A. de C.V.
Casa Saba *see* Grupo Casa Saba, S.A. de C.V.
Casas Bahia Comercial Ltda., 75 86–89
Cascade Corporation, 65 90–92
Cascade General, Inc., 65 93–95
Cascade Natural Gas Corporation, 9 102–04
Cascades Inc., 71 94–96
Casco Northern Bank, 14 89–91
Casey's General Stores, Inc., 19 79–81; 83 58-63 (upd.)
Cash America International, Inc., 20 113–15; 61 52–55 (upd.)
Cash Systems, Inc., 93 133–36
Casino Guichard-Perrachon S.A., 59 107–10 (upd.)
CASIO Computer Co., Ltd., III 448–49; 16 82–84 (upd.); 40 91–95 (upd.)
Castle & Cooke, Inc., II 490–92; 20 116–19 (upd.) *see also* Dole Food Company, Inc.
Castorama S.A. *see* Groupe Castorama-Dubois Investissements.
Castro Model Ltd., 86 61–64
Casual Corner Group, Inc., 43 96–98
Casual Male Retail Group, Inc., 52 64–66
Caswell-Massey Co. Ltd., 51 66–69
Catalina Lighting, Inc., 43 99–102 (upd.)
Catalina Marketing Corporation, 18 99–102
Catalytica Energy Systems, Inc., 44 74–77
Catellus Development Corporation, 24 98–101
Caterpillar Inc., III 450–53; 15 89–93 (upd.); 63 93–99 (upd.)
Cathay Pacific Airways Limited, 6 78–80; 34 98–102 (upd.)
Catherines Stores Corporation, 15 94–97
Catholic Charities USA, 76 82–84
Catholic Health Initiatives, 91 93–98

Catholic Order of Foresters, 24 102–05; 97 107–11 (upd.)
Cato Corporation, 14 92–94
Cattleman's, Inc., 20 120–22
Cattles plc, 58 54–56
Cavco Industries, Inc., 65 96–99
Cazenove Group plc, 72 63–65
CB&I *see* Chicago Bridge & Iron Company N.V.
CB Commercial Real Estate Services Group, Inc., 21 94–98
CB Richard Ellis Group, Inc., 70 45–50 (upd.)
CBI Industries, Inc., 7 74–77 *see also* Chicago Bridge & Iron Company N.V.
CBN *see* The Christian Broadcasting Network, Inc.
CBOT *see* Chicago Board of Trade.
CBP *see* Corporation for Public Broadcasting.
CBRL Group, Inc., 35 82–85 (upd.); 86 65–70 (upd.)
CBS Corporation, II 132–34; 6 157–60 (upd.); 28 69–73 (upd.) *see also* CBS Television Network.
CBS Television Network, 66 44–48 (upd.)
CBSI *see* Complete Business Solutions, Inc.
CCA *see* Corrections Corporation of America.
CCA Industries, Inc., 53 86–89
CCC Information Services Group Inc., 74 68–70
CCG *see* The Clark Construction Group, Inc.
CCH Inc., 14 95–97
CCM Inc. *see* The Hockey Co.
CDC *see* Control Data Corp.
CDC Corporation, 71 97–99
CDI Corporation, 6 139–41; 54 46–49 (upd.)
CDL *see* City Developments Ltd.
CDW Computer Centers, Inc., 16 85–87; 52 67–70 (upd.)
CEC Entertainment, Inc., 31 94–98 (upd.)
CECAB *see* Groupe CECAB S.C.A.
Cedar Fair Entertainment Company, 22 130–32; 98 41–45 (upd.)
CEDC *see* Central European Distribution Corp.
Celadon Group Inc., 30 113–16
Celanese Corp., I 317–19 *see also* Hoechst Celanese Corp.
Celanese Mexicana, S.A. de C.V., 54 50–52
Celebrate Express, Inc., 70 51–53
Celebrity, Inc., 22 133–35
Celera Genomics, 74 71–74
Celestial Seasonings, Inc., 16 88–91 *see also* The Hain Celestial Group, Inc.
Celestica Inc., 80 59–62
Celgene Corporation, 67 97–100
CellStar Corporation, 83 64-67
Cementos Argos S.A., 91 99–101
CEMEX S.A. de C.V., 20 123–26; 59 111–16 (upd.)

CEMIG *see* Companhia Energética De Minas Gerais S.A.
Cencosud S.A., 69 92–94
Cendant Corporation, 44 78–84 (upd.) *see also* Wyndham Worldwide Corp.
Centel Corporation, 6 312–15 *see also* EMBARQ Corp.
Centennial Communications Corporation, 39 74–76
Centerior Energy Corporation, V 567–68
Centerplate, Inc., 79 96–100
Centex Corporation, 8 87–89; 29 93–96 (upd.)
Centocor Inc., 14 98–100
Central and South West Corporation, V 569–70
Central European Distribution Corporation, 75 90–92
Central European Media Enterprises Ltd., 61 56–59
Central Florida Investments, Inc., 93 137–40
Central Garden & Pet Company, 23 108–10; 58 57–60 (upd.)
Central Hudson Gas And Electricity Corporation, 6 458–60
Central Independent Television, 7 78–80; 23 111–14 (upd.)
Central Japan Railway Company, 43 103–06
Central Maine Power, 6 461–64
Central National-Gottesman Inc., 95 87–90
Central Newspapers, Inc., 10 207–09 *see also* Gannett Company, Inc.
Central Parking Corporation, 18 103–05
Central Soya Company, Inc., 7 81–83
Central Sprinkler Corporation, 29 97–99
Central Vermont Public Service Corporation, 54 53–56
Centrica plc, 29 100–05 (upd.)
Centuri Corporation, 54 57–59
Century Aluminum Company, 52 71–74
Century Business Services, Inc., 52 75–78
Century Casinos, Inc., 53 90–93
Century Communications Corp., 10 210–12
Century Telephone Enterprises, Inc., 9 105–07; 54 60–63 (upd.)
Century Theatres, Inc., 31 99–101
Cenveo Inc., 71 100–04 (upd.)
CEPCO *see* Chugoku Electric Power Company Inc.
Cephalon, Inc., 45 93–96
Cepheid, 77 93–96
Ceradyne, Inc., 65 100–02
Cerner Corporation, 16 92–94; 94 111–16 (upd.)
CertainTeed Corporation, 35 86–89
Certegy, Inc., 63 100–03
Cerveceria Polar, I 230–31 *see also* Empresas Polar SA.
Ceské aerolinie, a.s., 66 49–51

Cesky Telecom, a.s., 64 70–73
Cessna Aircraft Company, 8 90–93; 27 97–101 (upd.)
Cetelem S.A., 21 99–102
CeWe Color Holding AG, 76 85–88
ČEZ a. s., 97 112–15
CF Industries Holdings, Inc., 99 89–93
CG&E see Cincinnati Gas & Electric Co.
CGM see Compagnie Générale Maritime.
Chadbourne & Parke, 36 109–12
Chadwick's of Boston, Ltd., 29 106–08
Chalk's Ocean Airways see Flying Boat, Inc.
The Chalone Wine Group, Ltd., 36 113–16
Champion Enterprises, Inc., 17 81–84
Champion Industries, Inc., 28 74–76
Champion International Corporation, IV 263–65; 20 127–30 (upd.) see also International Paper Co.
Championship Auto Racing Teams, Inc., 37 73–75
Chancellor Beacon Academies, Inc., 53 94–97
Chancellor Media Corporation, 24 106–10
Chanel SA, 12 57–59; 49 83–86 (upd.)
Channel Four Television Corporation, 93 141–44
Chantiers Jeanneau S.A., 96 78–81
Chaoda Modern Agriculture (Holdings) Ltd., 87 96–99
Chaparral Steel Co., 13 142–44
Charal S.A., 90 117–20
Chargeurs International, 6 373–75; 21 103–06 (upd.)
Charisma Brands LLC, 74 75–78
The Charles Machine Works, Inc., 64 74–76
Charles River Laboratories International, Inc., 42 66–69
The Charles Schwab Corporation, 8 94–96; 26 64–67 (upd.); 81 62–68 (upd.)
The Charles Stark Draper Laboratory, Inc., 35 90–92
Charles Vögele Holding AG, 82 63-66
Charlotte Russe Holding, Inc., 35 93–96; 90 121–25 (upd.)
The Charmer Sunbelt Group, 95 91–94
Charming Shoppes, Inc., 8 97–98; 38 127–29 (upd.)
Charoen Pokphand Group, 62 60–63
Chart House Enterprises, Inc., 17 85–88; 96 82–86 (upd.)
Chart Industries, Inc., 21 107–09
Charter Communications, Inc., 33 91–94
ChartHouse International Learning Corporation, 49 87–89
Chas. Levy Company LLC, 60 83–85
Chase General Corporation, 91 102–05
The Chase Manhattan Corporation, II 247–49; 13 145–48 (upd.) see also JPMorgan Chase & Co.
Chateau Communities, Inc., 37 76–79
Chattanooga Bakery, Inc., 86 75–78

Chattem, Inc., 17 89–92; 88 47–52 (upd.)
Chautauqua Airlines, Inc., 38 130–32
CHC Helicopter Corporation, 67 101–03
Checker Motors Corp., 89 144–48
Checkers Drive-In Restaurants, Inc., 16 95–98; 74 79–83 (upd.)
CheckFree Corporation, 81 69–72
Checkpoint Systems, Inc., 39 77–80
Chedraui see Grupo Comercial Chedraui S.A. de C.V.
The Cheesecake Factory Inc., 17 93–96
Chef Solutions, Inc., 89 149–52
Chello Zone Ltd., 93 145–48
Chelsea Milling Company, 29 109–11
Chelsea Piers Management Inc., 86 79–82
Chelsfield PLC, 67 104–06
Cheltenham & Gloucester PLC, 61 60–62
Chemcentral Corporation, 8 99–101
Chemed Corporation, 13 149–50
Chemfab Corporation, 35 97–101
Chemi-Trol Chemical Co., 16 99–101
Chemical Banking Corporation, II 250–52; 14 101–04 (upd.)
Chemical Waste Management, Inc., 9 108–10
Chemtura Corporation, 91 106–20 (upd.)
CHEP Pty. Ltd., 80 63–66
Cherokee Inc., 18 106–09
Cherry Lane Music Publishing Company, Inc., 62 64–67
Chesapeake Corporation, 8 102–04; 30 117–20 (upd.); 93 149–55 (upd.)
Chesapeake Utilities Corporation, 56 60–62
Cheshire Building Society, 74 84–87
Chesebrough-Pond's USA, Inc., 8 105–07
Cheung Kong (Holdings) Ltd., IV 693–95; 20 131–34 (upd.); 94 117–24 (upd.)
ChevronTexaco Corporation, IV 385–87;19 82–85 (upd.); 47 70–76 (upd.)
Cheyenne Software, Inc., 12 60–62
CHF Industries, Inc., 84 47–50
Chi-Chi's Inc., 13 151–53; 51 70–73 (upd.)
Chi Mei Optoelectronics Corporation, 75 93–95
Chiasso Inc., 53 98–100
Chiat/Day Inc. Advertising, 11 49–52 see also TBWA/Chiat/Day.
Chibu Electric Power Company, Incorporated, V 571–73
Chic by H.I.S, Inc., 20 135–37 see also VF Corp.
Chicago and North Western Holdings Corporation, 6 376–78 see also Union Pacific Corp.
Chicago Bears Football Club, Inc., 33 95–97
Chicago Blackhawk Hockey Team, Inc. see Wirtz Corp.

Chicago Board of Trade, 41 84–87
Chicago Bridge & Iron Company N.V., 82 67-73 (upd.)
Chicago Mercantile Exchange Holdings Inc., 75 96–99
Chicago National League Ball Club, Inc., 66 52–55
Chicago Pizza & Brewery, Inc., 44 85–88
Chicago Review Press Inc., 84 51–54
Chicago Tribune see Tribune Co.
Chick-fil-A Inc., 23 115–18; 90 126–31 (upd.)
Chicken of the Sea International, 24 114–16 (upd.)
Chico's FAS, Inc., 45 97–99
Children's Comprehensive Services, Inc., 42 70–72
Children's Hospitals and Clinics, Inc., 54 64–67
The Children's Place Retail Stores, Inc., 37 80–82; 86 83–87 (upd.)
ChildrenFirst, Inc., 59 117–20
Childtime Learning Centers, Inc., 34 103–06 see also Learning Care Group, Inc.
Chiles Offshore Corporation, 9 111–13
China Airlines, 34 107–10
China Automotive Systems Inc., 87 100–103
China Construction Bank Corp., 79 101–04
China Eastern Airlines Co. Ltd., 31 102–04
China Life Insurance Company Limited, 65 103–05
China Merchants International Holdings Co., Ltd., 52 79–82
China National Cereals, Oils and Foodstuffs Import and Export Corporation (COFCO), 76 89–91
China National Petroleum Corporation, 46 86–89
China Nepstar Chain Drugstore Ltd., 97 116–19
China Netcom Group Corporation (Hong Kong) Limited, 73 80–83
China Shenhua Energy Company Limited, 83 68-71
China Southern Airlines Company Ltd., 33 98–100
China Telecom, 50 128–32
Chinese Petroleum Corporation, IV 388–90; 31 105–08 (upd.)
Chipotle Mexican Grill, Inc., 67 107–10
CHIPS and Technologies, Inc., 9 114–17
Chiquita Brands International, Inc., 7 84–86; 21 110–13 (upd.); 83 72-79 (upd.)
Chiron Corporation, 10 213–14; 36 117–20 (upd.)
Chisholm-Mingo Group, Inc., 41 88–90
Chittenden & Eastman Company, 58 61–64
Chock Full o'Nuts Corp., 17 97–100
Chocoladefabriken Lindt & Sprüngli AG, 27 102–05

Choice Hotels International, Inc., 14 105–07; 83 80-83 (upd.)

ChoicePoint Inc., 65 106–08

Chorus Line Corporation, 30 121–23

Chr. Hansen Group A/S, 70 54–57

Chris-Craft Corporation, 9 118–19; 31 109–12 (upd.); 80 67–71 (upd.)

Christensen Boyles Corporation, 26 68–71

The Christian Broadcasting Network, Inc., 52 83–85

Christian Dalloz SA, 40 96–98

Christian Dior S.A., 19 86–88; 49 90–93 (upd.)

Christian Salvesen Plc, 45 100–03

The Christian Science Publishing Society, 55 99–102

Christie's International plc, 15 98–101; 39 81–85 (upd.)

Christofle SA, 40 99–102

Christopher & Banks Corporation, 42 73–75

Chromcraft Revington, Inc., 15 102–05

The Chronicle Publishing Company, Inc., 23 119–22

Chronimed Inc., 26 72–75

Chrysalis Group plc, 40 103–06

Chrysler Corporation, I 144–45; 11 53–55 (upd.) see also DaimlerChrysler AG

CHS Inc., 60 86–89

CH2M HILL Companies Ltd., 22 136–38; 96 72–77 (upd.)

Chubb Corporation, III 220–22; 14 108–10 (upd.); 37 83–87 (upd.)

Chubb, PLC, 50 133–36

Chubu Electric Power Company, Inc., V 571–73; 46 90–93 (upd.)

Chuck E. Cheese see CEC Entertainment, Inc.

Chugach Alaska Corporation, 60 90–93

Chugai Pharmaceutical Co., Ltd., 50 137–40

Chugoku Electric Power Company Inc., V 574–76; 53 101–04 (upd.)

Chunghwa Picture Tubes, Ltd., 75 100–02

Chupa Chups S.A., 38 133–35

Church & Dwight Co., Inc., 29 112–15; 68 78–82 (upd.)

Church's Chicken, 66 56–59

Churchill Downs Incorporated, 29 116–19

Cia Hering, 72 66–68

Cianbro Corporation, 14 111–13

Ciba-Geigy Ltd., I 632–34; 8 108–11 (upd.) see also Novartis AG.

CIBC see Canadian Imperial Bank of Commerce.

Ciber, Inc., 18 110–12

CiCi Enterprises, L.P., 99 94–99

CIENA Corporation, 54 68–71

Cifra, S.A. de C.V., 12 63–65 see also Wal-Mart de Mexico, S.A. de C.V.

CIGNA Corporation, III 223–27; 22 139–44 (upd.); 45 104–10 (upd.)

Cimarex Energy Co., 81 73–76

Cimentos de Portugal SGPS S.A. (Cimpor), 76 92–94

Ciments Français, 40 107–10

Cimpor see Cimentos de Portugal SGPS S.A.

Cinar Corporation, 40 111–14

Cincinnati Bell, Inc., 6 316–18

Cincinnati Financial Corporation, 16 102–04; 44 89–92 (upd.)

Cincinnati Gas & Electric Company, 6 465–68 see also Duke Energy Corp.

Cincinnati Lamb Inc., 72 69–71

Cincinnati Milacron Inc., 12 66–69 see also Milacron, Inc.

Cincom Systems Inc., 15 106–08

Cinemark Holdings, Inc., 95 95–99

Cinemas de la República, S.A. de C.V., 83 84-86

Cinemeccanica S.p.A., 78 70–73

Cineplex Odeon Corporation, 6 161–63; 23 123–26 (upd.)

Cinnabon, Inc., 23 127–29; 90 132–36 (upd.)

Cinram International, Inc., 43 107–10

Cintas Corporation, 21 114–16; 51 74–77 (upd.)

CIPSA see Compañia Industrial de Parras, S.A. de C.V. (CIPSA).

CIPSCO Inc., 6 469–72 see also Ameren Corp.

The Circle K Company, II 619–20; 20 138–40 (upd.)

Circon Corporation, 21 117–20

Circuit City Stores, 9 120–22; 29 120–24 (upd.); 65 109–14 (upd.)

Circus Circus Enterprises, Inc., 6 203–05

Cirque du Soleil Inc., 29 125–28; 98 46–51 (upd.)

Cirrus Design Corporation, 44 93–95

Cirrus Logic, Inc., 11 56–57; 48 90–93 (upd.)

Cisco-Linksys LLC, 86 88–91

Cisco Systems, Inc., 11 58–60; 34 111–15 (upd.); 77 97–103 (upd.)

Cisneros Group of Companies, 54 72–75

CIT Group Inc., 76 95–98

Citadel Communications Corporation, 35 102–05

CitFed Bancorp, Inc., 16 105–07 see also Fifth Third Bancorp.

CITGO Petroleum Corporation, IV 391–93; 31 113–17 (upd.)

Citi Trends, Inc., 80 72–75

Citibank see Citigroup Inc

CITIC Pacific Ltd., 18 113–15

Citicorp, II 253–55; 9 123–26 (upd.) see also Citigroup Inc.

Citicorp Diners Club, Inc., 90 137–40

Citigroup Inc., 30 124–28 (upd.); 59 121–27 (upd.)

Citizen Watch Co., Ltd., III 454–56; 21 121–24 (upd.); 81 77–82 (upd.)

Citizens Communications Company, 79 105–08 (upd.)

Citizens Financial Group, Inc., 42 76–80; 87 104–112 (upd.)

Citizens Utilities Company, 7 87–89 see also Citizens Communications Company

Citrix Systems, Inc., 44 96–99

Citroën see PSA Peugeot Citroen S.A.

City Brewing Company LLC, 73 84–87

City Developments Limited, 89 153–56

City Public Service, 6 473–75

CJ Banks see Christopher & Banks Corp.

CJ Corporation, 62 68–70

CJSC Transmash Holding, 93 446–49

CKE Restaurants, Inc., 19 89–93; 46 94–99 (upd.)

Claire's Stores, Inc., 17 101–03; 94 125–29 (upd.)

CLARCOR Inc., 17 104–07; 61 63–67 (upd.)

Clare Rose Inc., 68 83–85

Clarion Company Ltd., 64 77–79

The Clark Construction Group, Inc., 8 112–13

Clark Equipment Company, 8 114–16

Classic Vacation Group, Inc., 46 100–03

Clayton Homes Incorporated, 13 154–55; 54 76–79 (upd.)

Clayton Williams Energy, Inc., 87 113–116

Clean Harbors, Inc., 73 88–91

Clear Channel Communications, Inc., 23 130–32 see also Live Nation, Inc.

Clearly Canadian Beverage Corporation, 48 94–97

Clearwire, Inc., 69 95–97

Cleary, Gottlieb, Steen & Hamilton, 35 106–09

Cleco Corporation, 37 88–91

The Clemens Family Corporation, 93 156–59

Clement Pappas & Company, Inc., 92 52–55

Cleveland-Cliffs Inc., 13 156–58; 62 71–75 (upd.)

Cleveland Indians Baseball Company, Inc., 37 92–94

Click Wine Group, 68 86–88

Clif Bar Inc., 50 141–43

Clifford Chance LLP, 38 136–39

Clinton Cards plc, 39 86–88

Cloetta Fazer AB, 70 58–60

The Clorox Company, III 20–22; 22 145–48 (upd.); 81 83–90 (upd.)

Close Brothers Group plc, 39 89–92

The Clothestime, Inc., 20 141–44

Clougherty Packing Company, 72 72–74

Club Méditerranée S.A., 6 206–08; 21 125–28 (upd.); 91 121–27 (upd.)

ClubCorp, Inc., 33 101–04

CMC see Commercial Metals Co.

CME see Campbell-Mithun-Esty, Inc.; Central European Media Enterprises Ltd.; Chicago Mercantile Exchange Inc.

CMG Worldwide, Inc., 89 157–60

CMGI, Inc., 76 99–101

CMIH see China Merchants International Holdings Co., Ltd.

CML Group, Inc., 10 215–18

CMO see Chi Mei Optoelectronics Corp.

CMP Media Inc., 26 76–80

CMS Energy Corporation, V 577–79; 14 114–16 (upd.)

CN *see* Canadian National Railway Co.

CNA Financial Corporation, III 228–32; 38 140–46 (upd.)

CNET Networks, Inc., 47 77–80

CNG *see* Consolidated Natural Gas Co.

CNH Global N.V., 38 147–56 (upd.); 99 100–112 (upd.)

CNP *see* Compagnie Nationale à Portefeuille.

CNPC *see* China National Petroleum Corp.

CNS, Inc., 20 145–47 *see also* GlaxoSmithKline plc.

Co-operative Group (CWS) Ltd., 51 86–89

Coach, Inc., 10 219–21; 45 111–15 (upd.); 99 113–120 (upd.)

Coach USA, Inc., 24 117–19; 55 103–06 (upd.)

Coachmen Industries, Inc., 77 104–07

Coal India Ltd., IV 48–50; 44 100–03 (upd.)

Coastal Corporation, IV 394–95; 31 118–21 (upd.)

Coats plc, V 356–58; 44 104–07 (upd.)

COBE Cardiovascular, Inc., 61 68–72

COBE Laboratories, Inc., 13 159–61

Coberco *see* Friesland Coberco Dairy Foods Holding N.V.

Cobham plc, 30 129–32

Coborn's, Inc., 30 133–35

Cobra Electronics Corporation, 14 117–19

Cobra Golf Inc., 16 108–10

Coca-Cola Bottling Co. Consolidated, 10 222–24

The Coca-Cola Company, I 232–35; 10 225–28 (upd.); 32 111–16 (upd.); 67 111–17 (upd.)

Coca-Cola Enterprises, Inc., 13 162–64

Cochlear Ltd., 77 108–11

Cockerill Sambre Group, IV 51–53; 26 81–84 (upd.) *see also* Arcelor Gent.

Codelco *see* Corporacion Nacional del Cobre de Chile.

Coeur d'Alene Mines Corporation, 20 148–51

COFCO *see* China National Cereals, Oils and Foodstuffs Import and Export Corp.

The Coffee Beanery, Ltd., 95 100–05

Coffee Holding Co., Inc., 95 106–09

Coflexip S.A., 25 103–05 *see also* Technip.

Cogent Communications Group, Inc., 55 107–10

Cogentrix Energy, Inc., 10 229–31

Cognex Corporation, 76 102–06

Cognizant Technology Solutions Corporation, 59 128–30

Cognos Inc., 44 108–11

Coherent, Inc., 31 122–25

Cohu, Inc., 32 117–19

Coinmach Laundry Corporation, 20 152–54

Coinstar, Inc., 44 112–14

Colas S.A., 31 126–29

Cold Spring Granite Company, 16 111–14; 67 118–22 (upd.)

Cold Stone Creamery, 69 98–100

Coldwater Creek Inc., 21 129–31; 74 88–91 (upd.)

Coldwell Banker Co. *see* CB Richard Ellis Group, Inc.

Cole National Corporation, 13 165–67; 76 107–10 (upd.)

Cole's Quality Foods, Inc., 68 92–94

The Coleman Company, Inc., 9 127–29; 30 136–39 (upd.)

Coleman Natural Products, Inc., 68 89–91

Coles Express Inc., 15 109–11

Coles Group Limited, V 33–35; 20 155–58 (upd.); 85 49–56 (upd.)

Colfax Corporation, 58 65–67

Colgate-Palmolive Company, III 23–26; 14 120–23 (upd.); 35 110–15 (upd.); 71 105–10 (upd.)

Collectors Universe, Inc., 48 98–100

Colliers International Property Consultants Inc., 92 56–59

Collins & Aikman Corporation, 13 168–70; 41 91–95 (upd.)

Collins Industries, Inc., 33 105–07

Colonial Properties Trust, 65 115–17

Colonial Williamsburg Foundation, 53 105–07

Color Kinetics Incorporated, 85 57–60

Colorado Baseball Management, Inc., 72 75–78

Colorado MEDtech, Inc., 48 101–05

Colt Industries Inc., I 434–36

COLT Telecom Group plc, 41 96–99

Colt's Manufacturing Company, Inc., 12 70–72

Columbia Forest Products Inc., 78 74–77

The Columbia Gas System, Inc., V 580–82; 16 115–18 (upd.)

Columbia/HCA Healthcare Corporation, 15 112–14

Columbia House Company, 69 101–03

Columbia Sportswear Company, 19 94–96; 41 100–03 (upd.)

Columbia TriStar Motion Pictures Companies, II 135–37; 12 73–76 (upd.)

Columbus McKinnon Corporation, 37 95–98

Com Ed *see* Commonwealth Edison.

Comair Holdings Inc., 13 171–73; 34 116–20 (upd.)

Combe Inc., 72 79–82

Comcast Corporation, 7 90–92; 24 120–24 (upd.)

Comdial Corporation, 21 132–35

Comdisco, Inc., 9 130–32

Comerci *see* Controladora Comercial Mexicana, S.A. de C.V.

Comerica Incorporated, 40 115–17

COMFORCE Corporation, 40 118–20

Cominco Ltd., 37 99–102

Command Security Corporation, 57 71–73

Commerce Clearing House, Inc., 7 93–94 *see also* CCH Inc.

Commercial Credit Company, 8 117–19 *see also* Citigroup Inc.

Commercial Federal Corporation, 12 77–79; 62 76–80 (upd.)

Commercial Financial Services, Inc., 26 85–89

Commercial Metals Company, 15 115–17; 42 81–84 (upd.)

Commercial Union plc, III 233–35 *see also* Aviva PLC.

Commercial Vehicle Group, Inc., 81 91–94

Commerzbank A.G., II 256–58; 47 81–84 (upd.)

Commodore International, Ltd., 7 95–97

Commonwealth Edison, V 583–85

Commonwealth Energy System, 14 124–26

Commonwealth Telephone Enterprises, Inc., 25 106–08

CommScope, Inc., 77 112–15

Community Coffee Co. L.L.C., 53 108–10

Community Health Systems, Inc., 71 111–13

Community Newspaper Holdings, Inc., 91 128–31

Community Psychiatric Centers, 15 118–20

Compagnia Italiana dei Jolly Hotels S.p.A., 71 114–16

Compagnie de Saint-Gobain, III 675–78; 16 119–23 (upd.); 64 80–84 (upd.)

Compagnie des Alpes, 48 106–08

Compagnie des Cristalleries de Baccarat *see* Baccarat.

Compagnie des Machines Bull S.A., III 122–23 *see also* Bull S.A.; Groupe Bull.

Compagnie Financière de Paribas, II 259–60 *see also* BNP Paribas Group.

Compagnie Financière Richemont AG, 50 144–47

Compagnie Financière Sucres et Denrées S.A., 60 94–96

Compagnie Générale d'Électricité, II 12–13

Compagnie Générale des Établissements Michelin, V 236–39; 42 85–89 (upd.)

Compagnie Générale Maritime et Financière, 6 379–81

Compagnie Maritime Belge S.A., 95 110–13

Compagnie Nationale à Portefeuille, 84 55–58

Companhia Brasileira de Distribuiçao, 76 111–13

Companhia de Bebidas das Américas, 57 74–77

Companhia de Tecidos Norte de Minas - Coteminas, 77 116–19

Companhia Energética de Minas Gerais S.A., 65 118–20

Companhia Siderúrgica Nacional, 76 114–17

Companhia Suzano de Papel e Celulose S.A., 94 130–33

Companhia Vale do Rio Doce, IV 54–57; 43 111–14 (upd.)

Compania Cervecerias Unidas S.A., 70 61–63

Compañia de Minas BuenaventuraS.A.A., 92160–63

Compañia Española de Petróleos S.A. (Cepsa), IV 396–98; 56 63–66 (upd.)

Compañia Industrial de Parras, S.A. de C.V. (CIPSA), 84 59–62

Compaq Computer Corporation, III 124–25; 6 221–23 (upd.); 26 90–93 (upd.) *see also* Hewlett-Packard Co.

Compass Bancshares, Inc., 73 92–94

Compass Group PLC, 34 121–24

Compass Minerals International, Inc., 79 109–12

CompDent Corporation, 22 149–51

CompHealth Inc., 25 109–12

Complete Business Solutions, Inc., 31 130–33

Comprehensive Care Corporation, 15 121–23

Comptoirs Modernes S.A., 19 97–99 *see also* Carrefour SA.

CompuAdd Computer Corporation, 11 61–63

CompuCom Systems, Inc., 10 232–34

CompuDyne Corporation, 51 78–81

CompUSA, Inc., 10 235–36; 35 116–18 (upd.)

CompuServe Interactive Services, Inc., 10 237–39; 27 106–08 (upd.) *see also* AOL Time Warner Inc.

Computer Associates International, Inc., 6 224–26; 49 94–97 (upd.)

Computer Data Systems, Inc., 14 127–29

Computer Learning Centers, Inc., 26 94–96

Computer Sciences Corporation, 6 227–29

ComputerLand Corp., 13 174–76

Computervision Corporation, 10 240–42

Compuware Corporation, 10 243–45; 30 140–43 (upd.); 66 60–64 (upd.)

Comsat Corporation, 23 133–36 *see also* Lockheed Martin Corp.

Comshare Inc., 23 137–39

Comstock Resources, Inc., 47 85–87

Comtech Telecommunications Corp., 75 103–05

Comverse Technology, Inc., 15 124–26; 43 115–18 (upd.)

Con Ed *see* Consolidated Edison, Inc.

ConAgra Foods, Inc., II 493–95; 12 80–82 (upd.); 42 90–94 (upd.); 85 61–68 (upd.)

Conair Corporation, 17 108–10; 69 104–08 (upd.)

Conaprole *see* Cooperativa Nacional de Productores de Leche S.A. (Conaprole).

Concentra Inc., 71 117–19

Concepts Direct, Inc., 39 93–96

Concha y Toro *see* Viña Concha y Toro S.A.

Concord Camera Corporation, 41 104–07

Concord EFS, Inc., 52 86–88

Concord Fabrics, Inc., 16 124–26

Concurrent Computer Corporation, 75 106–08

Condé Nast Publications, Inc., 13 177–81; 59 131–34 (upd.)

Cone Mills LLC, 8 120–22; 67 123–27 (upd.)

Conexant Systems, Inc., 36 121–25

Confluence Holdings Corporation, 76 118–20

Congoleum Corporation, 18 116–19; 98 52–57 (upd.)

CONMED Corporation, 87 117–120

Conn-Selmer, Inc., 55 111–14

Conn's, Inc., 67 128–30

Connecticut Light and Power Co., 13 182–84

Connecticut Mutual Life Insurance Company, III 236–38

The Connell Company, 29 129–31

Conner Peripherals, Inc., 6 230–32

Connetics Corporation, 70 64–66

Connors Bros. Income Fund *see* George Weston Ltd.

ConocoPhillips, IV 399–402; 16 127–32 (upd.); 63 104–15 (upd.)

Conrad Industries, Inc., 58 68–70

Conseco Inc., 10 246–48; 33 108–12 (upd.)

Conso International Corporation, 29 132–34

CONSOL Energy Inc., 59 135–37

Consolidated Delivery & Logistics, Inc., 24 125–28 *see also* Velocity Express Corp.

Consolidated Edison, Inc., V 586–89; 45 116–20 (upd.)

Consolidated Freightways Corporation, V 432–34; 21 136–39 (upd.); 48 109–13 (upd.)

Consolidated Graphics, Inc., 70 67–69

Consolidated Natural Gas Company, V 590–91; 19 100–02 (upd.) *see also* Dominion Resources, Inc.

Consolidated Papers, Inc., 8 123–25; 36 126–30 (upd.)

Consolidated Products, Inc., 14 130–32

Consolidated Rail Corporation, V 435–37

Consorcio ARA, S.A. de C.V., 79 113–16

Consorcio Aviacsa, S.A. de C.V., 85 69–72

Consorcio G Grupo Dina, S.A. de C.V., 36 131–33

Constar International Inc., 64 85–88

Constellation Brands, Inc., 68 95–100 (upd.)

The Consumers Gas Company Ltd., 6 476–79; 43 154 *see also* Enbridge Inc.

Consumers Power Co., 14 133–36

Consumers Union, 26 97–99

Consumers Water Company, 14 137–39

The Container Store, 36 134–36

ContiGroup Companies, Inc., 43 119–22 (upd.)

Continental AG, V 240–43; 56 67–72 (upd.)

Continental Airlines, Inc., I 96–98; 21 140–43 (upd.); 52 89–94 (upd.)

Continental Bank Corporation, II 261–63 *see also* Bank of America.

Continental Cablevision, Inc., 7 98–100

Continental Can Co., Inc., 15 127–30

Continental Corporation, III 239–44

Continental General Tire Corp., 23 140–42

Continental Grain Company, 10 249–51; 13 185–87 (upd.) *see also* ContiGroup Companies, Inc.

Continental Group Co., I 599–600

Continental Medical Systems, Inc., 10 252–54

Continental Resources, Inc., 89 161–65

Continuum Health Partners, Inc., 60 97–99

Control Data Corporation, III 126–28 *see also* Seagate Technology, Inc.

Control Data Systems, Inc., 10 255–57

Controladora Comercial Mexicana, S.A. de C.V., 36 137–39

Controladora Mabe, S.A. de C.V., 82 74-77

Converse Inc., 9 133–36; 31 134–38 (upd.)

Conzzeta Holding, 80 76–79

Cooker Restaurant Corporation, 20 159–61; 51 82–85 (upd.)

Cookson Group plc, III 679–82; 44 115–20 (upd.)

CoolBrands International Inc., 35 119–22

CoolSavings, Inc., 77 120–24

Coop Schweiz Genossenschaftsverband, 48 114–16

Coopagri Bretagne, 88 53–56

Cooper Cameron Corporation, 20 162–66 (upd.); 58 71–75 (upd.)

The Cooper Companies, Inc., 39 97–100

Cooper Industries, Inc., II 14–17; 44 121–25 (upd.)

Cooper Tire & Rubber Company, 8 126–28; 23 143–46 (upd.)

Cooperativa Nacional de Productores de Leche S.A. (Conaprole),92 60–63

Coopers & Lybrand, 9 137–38 *see also* PricewaterhouseCoopers.

Coors Company *see* Adolph Coors Co.

Copa Holdings, S.A., 93 164–67

Copart Inc., 23 147–49

Copec *see* Empresas Copec S.A.

The Copley Press, Inc., 23 150–52

Coppel, S.A. de C.V., 82 78-81

The Copps Corporation, 32 120–22

Cora S.A./NV, 94 134–37

Corbis Corporation, 31 139–42

Corby Distilleries Limited, 14 140–42

The Corcoran Group, Inc., 58 76–78

Cordis Corporation, 19 103–05; 46 104–07 (upd.)

Cordon Bleu *see* Le Cordon Bleu S.A.

Corel Corporation, 15 131–33; 33 113–16 (upd.); 76 121–24 (upd.)

Corelio S.A./N.V., 96 87–90

CoreStates Financial Corp, 16 111–15 *see also* Wachovia Corp.

Corinthian Colleges, Inc., 39 101–04; 92 64–69 (upd.)

The Corky McMillin Companies, 98 58–62

Cornelsen Verlagsholding GmbH & Co., 90 141–46

Corning Inc., III 683–85; 44 126–30 (upd.); 90 147–53 (upd.)

Corporación Geo, S.A. de C.V., 81 95–98

Corporación Interamericana de Entretenimiento, S.A. de C.V., 83 87-90

Corporación Internacional de Aviación, S.A. de C.V. (Cintra), 20 167–69

Corporación José R. Lindley S.A., 92 70–73

Corporación Multi-Inversiones, 94 138–42

Corporacion Nacional del Cobre de Chile, 40 121–23

The Corporate Executive Board Company, 89 166–69

Corporate Express, Inc., 22 152–55; 47 88–92 (upd.)

Corporate Software Inc., 9 139–41

Corporation for Public Broadcasting, 14 143–45; 89 170–75 (upd.)

Correctional Services Corporation, 30 144–46

Corrections Corporation of America, 23 153–55

Correos y Telegrafos S.A., 80 80–83

Corrpro Companies, Inc., 20 170–73

CORT Business Services Corporation, 26 100–02

El Corte Inglés Group, 26 128–31 (upd.)

Cortefiel S.A., 64 89–91

Corticeira Amorim, Sociedade Gestora de Participaço es Sociais, S.A., 48 117–20

Corus Bankshares, Inc., 75 109–11

Corus Group plc, 49 98–105 (upd.)

Corvi *see* Grupo Corvi S.A. de C.V.

Cosi, Inc., 53 111–13

Cosmair Inc., 8 129–32 *see also* L'Oreal.

The Cosmetic Center, Inc., 22 156–58

Cosmo Oil Co., Ltd., IV 403–04; 53 114–16 (upd.)

Cosmolab Inc., 96 91–94

Cost Plus, Inc., 27 109–11

Cost-U-Less, Inc., 51 90–93

CoStar Group, Inc., 73 95–98

Costco Wholesale Corporation, 43 123–25 (upd.)

Coto Centro Integral de Comercializacion S.A., 66 65–67

Cott Corporation, 52 95–98

Cotter & Company, V 37–38 *see also* TruServ Corp.

Cotton Incorporated, 46 108–11

Coty, Inc., 36 140–42

Coudert Brothers, 30 147–50

Council on International Educational Exchange Inc., 81 99–102

Country Kitchen International, Inc., 76 125–27

Countrywide Credit Industries, Inc., 16 133–36

County Seat Stores Inc., 9 142–43

Courier Corporation, 41 108–12

Courtaulds plc, V 359–61; 17 116–19 (upd.) *see also* Akzo Nobel N.V.

Courts Plc, 45 121–24

Cousins Properties Incorporated, 65 121–23

Covance Inc., 30 151–53; 98 63–68 (upd.)

Covanta Energy Corporation, 64 92–95 (upd.)

Coventry Health Care, Inc., 59 138–40

Covidien Ltd., 91 132–35

Covington & Burling, 40 124–27

Cowen Group, Inc., 92 74–77

Cowles Media Company, 23 156–58 *see also* Primedia Inc.

Cox Enterprises, Inc., IV 595–97; 22 159–63 (upd.); 67 131–35 (upd.)

Cox Radio, Inc., 89 176–80

CP *see* Canadian Pacific Railway Ltd.

CPAC, Inc., 86 92–95

CPC International Inc., II 496–98 *see also* Bestfoods.

CPI Aerostructures, Inc., 75 112–14

CPI Corp., 38 157–60

CPL *see* Carolina Power & Light Co.

CPT *see* Chunghwa Picture Tubes, Ltd.

CR England, Inc., 63 116–18

CRA International, Inc., 93 168–71

CRA Limited, IV 58–61 *see also* Rio Tinto plc.

Cracker Barrel Old Country Store, Inc., 10 258–59 *see also* CBRL Group, Inc.

Craftmade International, Inc., 44 131–33

Craig Hospital, 99 121–126

craigslist, inc., 89 181–84

Crain Communications, Inc., 12 83–86; 35 123–27 (upd.)

Cram Company *see* The George F. Cram Company, Inc.

Cramer, Berkowitz & Co., 34 125–27

Crane & Co., Inc., 26 103–06; 30 42

Crane Co., 8 133–36; 30 154–58 (upd.)

Cranium, Inc., 69 109–11

Cranswick plc, 40 128–30

Crate and Barrel, 9 144–46 *see also* Euromarket Designs Inc.

Cravath, Swaine & Moore, 43 126–28

Crawford & Company, 87 121–126

Cray Inc., III 129–31; 16 137–40 (upd.); 75 115–21 (upd.)

Creative Artists Agency LLC, 38 161–64

Creative Technology Ltd., 57 78–81

Credence Systems Corporation, 90 154–57

Credit Acceptance Corporation, 18 120–22

Crédit Agricole Group, II 264–66; 84 63–68 (upd.)

Crédit Lyonnais, 9 147–49; 33 117–21 (upd.)

Crédit National S.A., 9 150–52

Crédit Suisse Group, II 267–69; 21 144–47 (upd.); 59 141–47 (upd.) *see also* Schweizerische Kreditanstalt.

Credito Italiano, II 270–72

Cree Inc., 53 117–20

Cremonini S.p.A., 57 82–84

Creo Inc., 48 121–24

Cresud S.A.C.I.F. y A., 63 119–21

Crete Carrier Corporation, 95 114–17

CRH plc, 64 96–99

Crispin Porter + Bogusky, 83 91-94

Cristalerias de Chile S.A., 67 136–38

Crit *see* Groupe Crit S.A.

Crocs, Inc., 80 84–87

Croda International Plc, 45 125–28

Crompton Corporation, 9 153–55; 36 143–50 (upd.) *see also* Chemtura Corp.

Croscill, Inc., 42 95–97

Crosman Corporation, 62 81–83

Cross Company *see* A.T. Cross Co.

CROSSMARK, 79 117–20

Crowley Maritime Corporation, 6 382–84; 28 77–80 (upd.)

Crowley, Milner & Company, 19 106–08

Crown Books Corporation, 21 148–50 *see also* Random House, Inc.

Crown Central Petroleum Corporation, 7 101–03

Crown, Cork & Seal Company, Inc., I 601–03; 13 188–90 (upd.); 32 123–27 (upd.) *see also* Crown Holdings, Inc.

Crown Crafts, Inc., 16 141–43

Crown Equipment Corporation, 15 134–36; 93 172–76 (upd.)

Crown Holdings, Inc., 83 95-102 (upd.)

Crown Media Holdings, Inc., 45 129–32

Crown Vantage Inc., 29 135–37

CRSS Inc., 6 142–44; 23 491

Cruise America Inc., 21 151–53

CryoLife, Inc., 46 112–14

Crystal Brands, Inc., 9 156–58

CS First Boston Inc., II 402–04

CSA *see* China Southern Airlines Company Ltd.

CSC *see* Computer Sciences Corp.

CSG Systems International, Inc., 75 122–24

CSK Auto Corporation, 38 165–67

CSM N.V., 65 124–27

CSR Limited, III 686–88; 28 81–84 (upd.); 85 73–80 (upd.)

CSS Industries, Inc., 35 128–31

CSX Corporation, V 438–40; 22 164–68 (upd.); 79 121–27 (upd.)

CT&T *see* Carolina Telephone and Telegraph Co.

CTB International Corporation, 43 129–31 (upd.)

CTG, Inc., 11 64–66
Ctrip.com International Ltd., 97
    120–24
CTS Corporation, 39 105–08
Cubic Corporation, 19 109–11; 98
    69–74 (upd.)
CUC International Inc., 16 144–46 *see
    also* Cendant Corp.
Cuisinart Corporation, 24 129–32
Cuisine Solutions Inc., 84 69–72
Culbro Corporation, 15 137–39 *see also*
    General Cigar Holdings, Inc.
CulinArt, Inc., 92 78–81
Cullen/Frost Bankers, Inc., 25 113–16
Culligan Water Technologies, Inc., 12
    87–88; 38 168–70 (upd.)
Culp, Inc., 29 138–40
Culver Franchising System, Inc., 58
    79–81
Cumberland Farms, Inc., 17 120–22; 84
    73–77 (upd.)
Cumberland Packing Corporation, 26
    107–09
Cummins Engine Co., Inc., I 146–48;
    12 89–92 (upd.); 40 131–35 (upd.)
Cumulus Media Inc., 37 103–05
CUNA Mutual Group, 62 84–87
Cunard Line Ltd., 23 159–62
CUNO Incorporated, 57 85–89
Current, Inc., 37 106–09
Curtice-Burns Foods, Inc., 7 104–06; 21
    154–57 (upd.) *see also* Birds Eye
    Foods, Inc.
Curtiss-Wright Corporation, 10 260–63;
    35 132–37 (upd.)
Curves International, Inc., 54 80–82
Cushman & Wakefield, Inc., 86 96–100
Custom Chrome, Inc., 16 147–49; 74
    92–95 (upd.)
Cutera, Inc., 84 78–81
Cutter & Buck Inc., 27 112–14
CVPS *see* Central Vermont Public Service
    Corp.
CVRD *see* Companhia Vale do Rio Doce
    Ltd.
CVS Corporation, 45 133–38 (upd.)
CWM *see* Chemical Waste Management,
    Inc.
Cybermedia, Inc., 25 117–19
Cyberonics, Inc., 79 128–31
Cybex International, Inc., 49 106–09
Cydsa *see* Grupo Cydsa, S.A. de C.V.
Cygne Designs, Inc., 25 120–23
Cygnus Business Media, Inc., 56 73–77
Cymer, Inc., 77 125–28
Cypress Semiconductor Corporation, 20
    174–76; 48 125–29 (upd.)
Cyprus Airways Public Limited, 81
    103–06
Cyprus Amax Minerals Company, 21
    158–61
Cyprus Minerals Company, 7 107–09
Cyrk Inc., 19 112–14
Cystic Fibrosis Foundation, 93 177–80
Cytec Industries Inc., 27 115–17
Cytyc Corporation, 69 112–14

Czarnikow-Rionda Company, Inc., 32
    128–30

D
D&B *see* Dun & Bradstreet Corp.
D&H Distributing Co., 95 118–21
D&K Wholesale Drug, Inc., 14 146–48
D-Link Corporation, 83 103-106
D. Carnegie & Co. AB, 98 79–83
D.F. Stauffer Biscuit Company, 82
    82–85
D.G. Yuengling & Son, Inc., 38 171–73
D.R. Horton, Inc., 58 82–84
Dachser GmbH & Co. KG, 88 57–61
D'Addario & Company, Inc. *see* J.
    D'Addario & Company, Inc.
Dade Behring Holdings Inc., 71 120–22
Daesang Corporation, 84 82–85
Daewoo Group, III 457–59; 18 123–27
    (upd.); 57 90–94 (upd.)
Daffy's Inc., 26 110–12
D'Agostino Supermarkets Inc., 19
    115–17
DAH *see* DeCrane Aircraft Holdings Inc.
Dai-Ichi Kangyo Bank Ltd., II 273–75
Dai Nippon *see also* listings under
    Dainippon.
Dai Nippon Printing Co., Ltd., IV
    598–600; 57 95–99 (upd.)
Daido Steel Co., Ltd., IV 62–63
The Daiei, Inc., V 39–40; 17 123–25
    (upd.); 41 113–16 (upd.)
Daihatsu Motor Company, Ltd., 7
    110–12; 21 162–64 (upd.)
Daiichikosho Company Ltd., 86
    101–04
Daikin Industries, Ltd., III 460–61
Daiko Advertising Inc., 79 132–35
Daily Mail and General Trust plc, 19
    118–20
The Daimaru, Inc., V 41–42; 42
    98–100 (upd.)
Daimler-Benz Aerospace AG, 16 150–52
Daimler-Benz AG, I 149–51; 15 140–44
    (upd.)
DaimlerChrysler AG, 34 128–37 (upd.);
    64 100–07 (upd.)
Dain Rauscher Corporation, 35 138–41
    (upd.)
Daio Paper Corporation, IV 266–67; 84
    86–89 (upd.)
Dairy Crest Group plc, 32 131–33
Dairy Farm International Holdings
    Ltd., 97 125–28
Dairy Farmers of America, Inc., 94
    143–46
Dairy Mart Convenience Stores, Inc., 7
    113–15; 25 124–27 (upd.) *see also*
    Alimentation Couche-Tard Inc.
Dairy Queen *see* International Dairy
    Queen, Inc.
Dairyland Healthcare Solutions, 73
    99–101
Daishowa Paper Manufacturing Co.,
    Ltd., IV 268–70; 57 100–03 (upd.)
Daisy Outdoor Products Inc., 58 85–88
Daisytek International Corporation, 18
    128–30

Daiwa Bank, Ltd., II 276–77; 39
    109–11 (upd.)
Daiwa Securities Company, Limited, II
    405–06
Daiwa Securities Group Inc., 55 115–18
    (upd.)
Daktronics, Inc., 32 134–37
Dal-Tile International Inc., 22 169–71
Dale Carnegie & Associates Inc., 28
    85–87; 78 78–82 (upd.)
Dalgety PLC, II 499–500 *see also* PIC
    International Group PLC
Dalhoff Larsen & Horneman A/S, 96
    95–99
Dalian Shide Group, 91 136–39
Dalkia Holding, 66 68–70
Dallah Albaraka Group, 72 83–86
Dallas Cowboys Football Club, Ltd., 33
    122–25
Dallas Semiconductor Corporation, 13
    191–93; 31 143–46 (upd.)
Dalli-Werke GmbH & Co. KG, 86
    105–10
Dallis Coffee, Inc., 86 111–14
Damark International, Inc., 18 131–34
    see also Provell Inc.
Damartex S.A., 98 84–87
Dames & Moore, Inc., 25 128–31 *see
    also* URS Corp.
Dan River Inc., 35 142–46; 86 115–20
    (upd.)
Dana Holding Corporation, I 152–53;
    10 264–66 (upd.); 99 127–134 (upd.)
Danaher Corporation, 7 116–17; 77
    129–33 (upd.)
Danaos Corporation, 91 140–43
Daniel Measurement and Control, Inc.,
    16 153–55; 74 96–99 (upd.)
Daniel Thwaites Plc, 95 122–25
Danisco A/S, 44 134–37
Dannon Co., Inc., 14 149–51
Danone Group *see* Groupe Danone.
Danske Bank Aktieselskab, 50 148–51
Danskin, Inc., 12 93–95; 62 88–92
    (upd.)
Danzas Group, V 441–43; 40 136–39
    (upd.)
D'Arcy Masius Benton & Bowles, Inc.,
    6 20–22; 32 138–43 (upd.)
Darden Restaurants, Inc., 16 156–58;
    44 138–42 (upd.)
Darigold, Inc., 9 159–61
Darling International Inc., 85 81–84
Dart Group PLC, 16 159–62; 77
    134–37 (upd.)
Darty S.A., 27 118–20
DASA *see* Daimler-Benz Aerospace AG.
Dassault-Breguet *see* Avions Marcel
    Dassault-Breguet Aviation.
Dassault Systèmes S.A., 25 132–34 *see
    also* Groupe Dassault Aviation SA.
Data Broadcasting Corporation, 31
    147–50
Data General Corporation, 8 137–40 *see
    also* EMC Corp.
Datapoint Corporation, 11 67–70
Datascope Corporation, 39 112–14

Datek Online Holdings Corp., 32
144–46
Dauphin Deposit Corporation, 14
152–54
Dave & Buster's, Inc., 33 126–29
The Davey Tree Expert Company, 11
71–73
The David and Lucile Packard
Foundation, 41 117–19
The David J. Joseph Company, 14
155–56; 76 128–30 (upd.)
David Jones Ltd., 60 100–02
David's Bridal, Inc., 33 130–32
Davide Campari-Milano S.p.A., 57
104–06
Davis Polk & Wardwell, 36 151–54
Davis Service Group PLC, 45 139–41
DaVita Inc., 73 102–05
DAW Technologies, Inc., 25 135–37
Dawn Food Products, Inc., 17 126–28
Dawson Holdings PLC, 43 132–34
Day & Zimmermann Inc., 9 162–64; 31
151–55 (upd.)
Day International, Inc., 84 90–93
Day Runner, Inc., 14 157–58; 41
120–23 (upd.)
Dayton Hudson Corporation, V 43–44;
18 135–37 (upd.) *see also* Target Corp.
DB *see* Deutsche Bundesbahn.
dba Luftfahrtgesellschaft mbH, 76
131–33
DC Comics Inc., 25 138–41; 98 88–94
(upd.)
DC Shoes, Inc., 60 103–05
DCN S.A., 75 125–27
DDB Worldwide Communications, 14
159–61 *see also* Omnicom Group Inc.
DDi Corp., 7 118–20; 97 129–32
(upd.)
De Beers Consolidated Mines Limited /
De Beers Centenary AG, IV 64–68; 7
121–26 (upd.); 28 88–94 (upd.)
De Dietrich & Cie., 31 156–59
De La Rue plc, 10 267–69; 34 138–43
(upd.); 46 251
Dean & DeLuca, Inc., 36 155–57
Dean Foods Company, 7 127–29; 21
165–68 (upd.); 73 106–15 (upd.)
Dean Witter, Discover & Co., 12 96–98
see also Morgan Stanley Dean Witter &
Co.
Dearborn Mid-West Conveyor
Company, 56 78–80
Death Row Records, 27 121–23 *see also*
Tha Row Records.
Deb Shops, Inc., 16 163–65; 76 134–37
(upd.)
Debeka Krankenversicherungsverein auf
Gegenseitigkeit, 72 87–90
Debenhams Plc, 28 95–97
Debevoise & Plimpton, 39 115–17
DEC *see* Digital Equipment Corp.
Deceuninck N.V., 84 94–97
Dechert, 43 135–38
Deckers Outdoor Corporation, 22
172–74; 98 95–98 (upd.)
Decora Industries, Inc., 31 160–62
Decorator Industries Inc., 68 101–04

DeCrane Aircraft Holdings Inc., 36
158–60
DeepTech International Inc., 21 169–71
Deere & Company, III 462–64; 21
172–76 (upd.); 42 101–06 (upd.)
Defiance, Inc., 22 175–78
Degussa-Hüls AG, IV 69–72; 32 147–53
(upd.)
DeKalb Genetics Corporation, 17
129–31 *see also* Monsanto Co.
Del Laboratories, Inc., 28 98–100
Del Monte Foods Company, 7 130–32;
23 163–66 (upd.)
Del Taco, Inc., 58 89–92
Del Webb Corporation, 14 162–64 *see
also* Pulte Homes, Inc.
Delachaux S.A., 76 138–40
Delaware North Companies Inc., 7
133–36; 96 100–05 (upd.)
Delco Electronics Corporation *see* GM
Hughes Electronics Corp.
Delhaize "Le Lion" S.A., 44 143–46
Deli Universal NV, 66 71–74
dELiA*s Inc., 29 141–44
Delicato Vineyards, Inc., 50 152–55
Dell Computer Corporation, 9 165–66;
31 163–66 (upd.); 63 122–26 (upd.)
Deloitte Touche Tohmatsu
International, 9 167–69; 29 145–48
(upd.)
De'Longhi S.p.A., 66 75–77
DeLorme Publishing Company, Inc., 53
121–23
Delphax Technologies Inc., 94 147–50
Delphi Automotive Systems
Corporation, 45 142–44
Delta and Pine Land Company, 33
133–37; 59 148–50
Delta Air Lines, Inc., I 99–100; 6
81–83 (upd.); 39 118–21 (upd.); 92
82–87 (upd.)
Delta Woodside Industries, Inc., 8
141–43; 30 159–61 (upd.)
Deltec, Inc., 56 81–83
Deltic Timber Corporation, 46 115–17
Deluxe Corporation, 7 137–39; 22
179–82 (upd.); 73 116–20 (upd.)
DEMCO, Inc., 60 106–09
DeMoulas / Market Basket Inc., 23
167–69
Den Norske Stats Oljeselskap AS, IV
405–07 *see also* Statoil ASA.
DenAmerica Corporation, 29 149–51
Denbury Resources, Inc., 67 139–41
Denby Group plc, 44 147–50
Dendrite International, Inc., 70 70–73
Denison International plc, 46 118–20
Denner AG, 88 62–65
Dennis Publishing Ltd., 62 93–95
Dennison Manufacturing Company *see*
Avery Dennison Corp.
DENSO Corporation, 46 121–26 (upd.)
Dentsply International Inc., 10 270–72
Dentsu Inc., I 9–11; 16 166–69 (upd.);
40 140–44 (upd.)
Denver Nuggets, 51 94–97
DEP Corporation, 20 177–80

Department 56, Inc., 14 165–67; 34
144–47 (upd.)
DEPFA BANK PLC, 69 115–17
Deposit Guaranty Corporation, 17
132–35
DePuy, Inc., 30 162–65; 37 110–13
(upd.)
Derco Holding Ltd., 98 99–102
Desarrolladora Homex, S.A. de C.V., 87
127–130
Desc, S.A. de C.V., 23 170–72
Deschutes Brewery, Inc., 57 107–09
Designer Holdings Ltd., 20 181–84
Desnoes and Geddes Limited, 79
136–39
Destec Energy, Inc., 12 99–101
Detroit Diesel Corporation, 10 273–75;
74 100–03 (upd.)
The Detroit Edison Company, V
592–95 *see also* DTE Energy Co.
The Detroit Lions, Inc., 55 119–21
The Detroit Pistons Basketball
Company, 41 124–27
Detroit Red Wings, 74 104–06
Detroit Tigers Baseball Club, Inc., 46
127–30
Deutsch, Inc., 42 107–10
Deutsche Babcock AG, III 465–66
Deutsche Bahn AG, 46 131–35 (upd.)
Deutsche Bank AG, II 278–80; 40
145–51 (upd.)
Deutsche Börse AG, 59 151–55
Deutsche BP Aktiengesellschaft, 7
140–43
Deutsche Bundepost Telekom, V
287–90 *see also* Deutsche Telekom AG
Deutsche Bundesbahn, V 444–47
Deutsche Fussball Bund e.V., 98 103–07
Deutsche Lufthansa AG, I 110–11; 26
113–16 (upd.); 68 105–09 (upd.)
Deutsche Post AG, 29 152–58
Deutsche Steinzeug Cremer & Breuer
Aktiengesellschaft, 91 144–48
Deutsche Telekom AG, 48 130–35
(upd.)
Deutscher Sparkassen- und Giroverband
(DSGV), 84 98–102
Deutz AG, 39 122–26
Deveaux S.A., 41 128–30
Developers Diversified Realty
Corporation, 69 118–20
DeVito/Verdi, 85 85–88
Devon Energy Corporation, 61 73–75
Devoteam S.A., 94 151–54
Devro plc, 55 122–24
DeVry Inc., 29 159–61; 82 86-90 (upd.)
Devtek Corporation *see* Héroux-Devtek
Inc.
Dewberry, 78 83–86
Dewey Ballantine LLP, 48 136–39
Dex Media, Inc., 65 128–30
Dexia NV/SA, 42 111–13; 88 66–69
(upd.)
The Dexter Corporation, I 320–22; 12
102–04 (upd.) *see also* Invitrogen
Corp.
DFS Group Ltd., 66 78–80
DH Technology, Inc., 18 138–40

DHB Industries Inc., 85 89–92
DHL Worldwide Network S.A./N.V., 6
  385–87; 24 133–36 (upd.); 69
  121–25 (upd.)
Di Giorgio Corp., 12 105–07
Diadora SpA, 86 121–24
Diageo plc, 24 137–41 (upd.); 79
  140–48 (upd.)
Diagnostic Products Corporation, 73
  121–24
Diagnostic Ventures Inc. *see* DVI, Inc.
Dial-A-Mattress Operating Corporation,
  46 136–39
The Dial Corporation, 8 144–46; 23
  173–75 (upd.)
Dialogic Corporation, 18 141–43
Diamond of California, 64 108–11
  (upd.)
Diamond Shamrock Corporation , IV
  408–11 *see also* Ultramar Diamond
  Shamrock Corp.
DiamondCluster International, Inc., 51
  98–101
Diana Shipping Inc., 95 126–29
Diavik Diamond Mines Inc., 85 93–96
Dibrell Brothers, Incorporated, 12
  108–10
dick clark productions, inc., 16 170–73
Dick Corporation, 64 112–14
Dick's Sporting Goods, Inc., 59 156–59
Dickten Masch Plastics LLC, 90 158–61
Dictaphone Healthcare Solutions, 78
  87–92
Diebold, Incorporated, 7 144–46; 22
  183–87 (upd.)
Diedrich Coffee, Inc., 40 152–54
Diehl Stiftung & Co. KG, 79 149–53
Dierbergs Markets Inc., 63 127–29
Diesel SpA, 40 155–57
D'Ieteren S.A./NV, 98 75–78
Dietrich & Cie *see* De Dietrich & Cie.
Dietz and Watson, Inc., 92 88–92
Digex, Inc., 46 140–43
Digi International Inc., 9 170–72
Digital Equipment Corporation, III
  132–35; 6 233–36 (upd.) *see also*
  Compaq Computer Corp.
Digital River, Inc., 50 156–59
Digitas Inc., 81 107–10
Dillard Paper Company, 11 74–76 *see
  also* International Paper Co.
Dillard's Inc., V 45–47; 16 174–77
  (upd.); 68 110–14 (upd.)
Dillingham Construction Corporation,
  44 151–54 (upd.)
Dillingham Corp., I 565–66
Dillon Companies Inc., 12 111–13
Dime Savings Bank of New York, F.S.B.,
  9 173–74 *see also* Washington Mutual,
  Inc.
Dimension Data Holdings PLC, 69
  126–28
DIMON Inc., 27 124–27
Dina *see* Consorcio G Grupo Dina, S.A.
  de C.V.
Diodes Incorporated, 81 111–14
Dionex Corporation, 46 144–46
Dior *see* Christian Dior S.A.

Dippin' Dots, Inc., 56 84–86
Direct Focus, Inc., 47 93–95
Direct Wines Ltd., 84 103–106
Directed Electronics, Inc., 87 131–135
Directorate General of
  Telecommunications, 7 147–49
DIRECTV, Inc., 38 174–77; 75 128–32
  (upd.)
Dirk Rossmann GmbH, 94 155–59
Discount Auto Parts, Inc., 18 144–46
Discount Drug Mart, Inc., 14 172–73
Discount Tire Company Inc., 84
  107–110
Discovery Communications, Inc., 42
  114–17
Discovery Partners International, Inc.,
  58 93–95
Discreet Logic Inc., 20 185–87 *see also*
  Autodesk, Inc.
Disney *see* The Walt Disney Co.
Distillers Co. plc, I 239–41 *see also*
  Diageo PLC.
Distribución y Servicio D&S S.A., 71
  123–26
Distrigaz S.A., 82 91-94
ditech.com, 93 181–84
The Dixie Group, Inc., 20 188–90; 80
  88–92 (upd.)
Dixon Industries, Inc., 26 117–19
Dixon Ticonderoga Company, 12
  114–16; 69 129–33 (upd.)
Dixons Group plc, V 48–50; 19 121–24
  (upd.); 49 110–13 (upd.)
Djarum PT, 62 96–98
DKB *see* Dai-Ichi Kangyo Bank Ltd.
DKNY *see* Donna Karan International
  Inc.
DLJ *see* Donaldson, Lufkin & Jenrette.
DMB&B *see* D'Arcy Masius Benton &
  Bowles.
DMGT *see* Daily Mail and General Trust.
DMI Furniture, Inc., 46 147–50
Do it Best Corporation, 30 166–70
Dobrogea Grup S.A., 82 95-98
Dobson Communications Corporation,
  63 130–32
Doctor's Associates Inc., 67 142–45
  (upd.)
The Doctors' Company, 55 125–28
Doctors Without Borders *see* Médecins
  Sans Frontières.
Documentum, Inc., 46 151–53
Dofasco Inc., IV 73–74; 24 142–44
  (upd.)
Dogan Sirketler Grubu Holding A.S.,
  83 107-110
Dogi International Fabrics S.A., 52
  99–102
Dolan Media Company, 94 160–63
Dolby Laboratories Inc., 20 191–93
Dolce & Gabbana SpA, 62 99–101
Dole Food Company, Inc., 9 175–76;
  31 167–70 (upd.); 68 115–19 (upd.)
Dollar Thrifty Automotive Group, Inc.,
  25 142–45
Dollar Tree Stores, Inc., 23 176–78; 62
  102–05 (upd.)

Dollywood Corporation *see* Herschend
  Family Entertainment Corp.
Doman Industries Limited, 59 160–62
Dominick & Dominick LLC, 92 93–96
Dominick's Finer Foods, Inc., 56 87–89
Dominion Homes, Inc., 19 125–27
Dominion Resources, Inc., V 596–99;
  54 83–87 (upd.)
Dominion Textile Inc., 12 117–19
Domino Printing Sciences PLC, 87
  136–139
Domino Sugar Corporation, 26 120–22
Domino's, Inc., 7 150–53; 21 177–81
  (upd.); 63 133–39 (upd.)
Domtar Corporation, IV 271–73; 89
  185–91 (upd.)
Don Massey Cadillac, Inc., 37 114–16
Donaldson Company, Inc., 16 178–81;
  49 114–18 (upd.)
Donaldson, Lufkin & Jenrette, Inc., 22
  188–91
Donatos Pizzeria Corporation, 58
  96–98
Donna Karan International Inc., 15
  145–47; 56 90–93 (upd.)
Donnelly Corporation, 12 120–22; 35
  147–50 (upd.)
Donnkenny, Inc., 17 136–38
Donruss Playoff L.P., 66 81–84
Dooney & Bourke Inc., 84 111–114
Dorel Industries Inc., 59 163–65
Dorian Drake International Inc., 96
  106–09
Dorling Kindersley Holdings plc, 20
  194–96 *see also* Pearson plc.
Dorsey & Whitney LLP, 47 96–99
Doskocil Companies, Inc., 12 123–25
  see also Foodbrands America, Inc.
Dot Foods, Inc., 69 134–37
Dot Hill Systems Corp., 93 185–88
Double-Cola Co.-USA, 70 74–76
DoubleClick Inc., 46 154–57
Doubletree Corporation, 21 182–85
Douglas & Lomason Company, 16
  182–85
Doux S.A., 80 93–96
Dover Corporation, III 467–69; 28
  101–05 (upd.); 90 162–67 (upd.)
Dover Downs Entertainment, Inc., 43
  139–41
Dover Publications Inc., 34 148–50
The Dow Chemical Company, I
  323–25; 8 147–50 (upd.); 50 160–64
  (upd.)
Dow Jones & Company, Inc., IV
  601–03; 19 128–31 (upd.); 47
  100–04 (upd.)
Dow Jones Telerate, Inc., 10 276–78 *see
  also* Reuters Group PLC.
DP World, 81 115–18
DPL Inc., 6 480–82; 96 110–15 (upd.)
DQE, 6 483–85; 38 40
Dr. August Oetker KG, 51 102–06
Dr Pepper/Seven Up, Inc., 9 177–78; 32
  154–57 (upd.)
Dr. Reddy's Laboratories Ltd., 59
  166–69

Drackett Professional Products, 12 126–28 *see also* S.C. Johnson & Son, Inc.

Draftfcb, 94 164–68

Dragados y Construcciones *see* Grupo Dragados SA.

Drägerwerk AG, 83 111-114

Drake Beam Morin, Inc., 44 155–57

Draper and Kramer Inc., 96 116–19

Draper Fisher Jurvetson, 91 149–52

Dräxlmaier Group, 90 168–72

Dreams Inc., 97 133–3

DreamWorks SKG, 43 142–46

The Drees Company, Inc., 41 131–33

Dresdner Bank A.G., II 281–83; 57 110–14 (upd.)

Dresdner Kleinwort Wasserstein, 60 110–13 (upd.)

The Dress Barn, Inc., 24 145–46

Dresser Industries, Inc., III 470–73; 55 129–31 (upd.)

Drew Industries Inc., 28 106–08

Drexel Burnham Lambert Incorporated, II 407–09 *see also* New Street Capital Inc.

Drexel Heritage Furnishings Inc., 12 129–31

Dreyer's Grand Ice Cream, Inc., 17 139–41 *see also* Nestlé S.A.

The Dreyfus Corporation, 70 77–80

DRI *see* Dominion Resources, Inc.

Drie Mollen Holding B.V., 99 135–138

Dril-Quip, Inc., 81 119–21

Drinker, Biddle and Reath L.L.P., 92 97–101

DriveTime Automotive Group Inc., 68 120–24 (upd.)

Drs. Foster & Smith, Inc., 62 106–08

DRS Technologies, Inc., 58 99–101

Drug Emporium, Inc., 12 132–34 *see also* Big A Drug Stores Inc.

Drypers Corporation, 18 147–49

DryShips Inc., 95 130–33

DS Smith Plc, 61 76–79

DSC Communications Corporation, 12 135–37 *see also* Alcatel S.A.

DSGV *see* Deutscher Sparkassen- und Giroverband (DSGV).

DSM N.V., I 326–27; 56 94–96 (upd.)

DSW Inc., 73 125–27

DTAG *see* Dollar Thrifty Automotive Group, Inc.

DTE Energy Company, 20 197–201 (upd.); 94 169–76 (upd.)

DTS, Inc., 80 97–101

Du Pareil au Même, 43 147–49

Du Pont *see* E.I. du Pont de Nemours & Co.

Dualstar Entertainment Group LLC, 76 141–43

Duane Reade Holding Corp., 21 186–88

Ducati Motor Holding SpA, 30 171–73; 86 125–29 (upd.)

Duck Head Apparel Company, Inc., 42 118–21

Ducks Unlimited, Inc., 87 140–143

Duckwall-ALCO Stores, Inc., 24 147–49

Ducommun Incorporated, 30 174–76

Duferco Group, 94 177–80

Duke Energy Corporation, V 600–02; 27 128–31 (upd.)

Duke Realty Corporation, 57 115–17

The Dun & Bradstreet Corporation, IV 604–05; 19 132–34 (upd.); 61 80–84 (upd.)

Dun & Bradstreet Software Services Inc., 11 77–79

Dunavant Enterprises, Inc., 54 88–90

Duncan Aviation, Inc., 94 181–84

Duncan Toys Company, 55 132–35

Dunham's Athleisure Corporation, 98 108–11

Dunn-Edwards Corporation, 56 97–99

Dunn Industries, Inc. *see* JE Dunn Construction Group, Inc.

Dunnes Stores Ltd., 58 102–04

Duplex Products, Inc., 17 142–44

Dupont *see* E.I. du Pont de Nemours & Co.

Duracell International Inc., 9 179–81; 71 127–31 (upd.)

Durametallic, 21 189–91 *see also* Duriron Company Inc.

Duriron Company Inc., 17 145–47 *see also* Flowserve Corp.

Dürkopp Adler AG, 65 131–34

Duron Inc., 72 91–93 *see also* The Sherwin-Williams Co.

Dürr AG, 44 158–61

Duty Free International, Inc., 11 80–82 *see also* World Duty Free Americas, Inc.

DVI, Inc., 51 107–09

Duvernay Oil Corp., 83 115-118

Dyax Corp., 89 192–95

Dyckerhoff AG, 35 151–54

Dycom Industries, Inc., 57 118–20

Dyersburg Corporation, 21 192–95

Dylan's Candy Bar, LLC, 99 139–141

Dylex Limited, 29 162–65

Dynatec Corporation, 87 144–147

Dynaction S.A., 67 146–48

Dynamic Materials Corporation, 81 122–25

Dynatech Corporation, 13 194–96

Dynatronics Corporation, 99 142–146

DynCorp, 45 145–47

Dynea, 68 125–27

Dyneff S.A., 98 112–15

Dynegy Inc., 49 119–22 (upd.)

Dyson Group PLC, 71 132–34

E

E. & J. Gallo Winery, I 242–44; 7 154–56 (upd.); 28 109–11 (upd.)

E! Entertainment Television Inc., 17 148–50

E-Systems, Inc., 9 182–85

E*Trade Financial Corporation, 20 206–08; 60 114–17 (upd.)

E-Z Serve Corporation, 17 169–71

E-Z-EM Inc., 89 196–99

E H Booth & Company Ltd., 90 173–76

E.I. du Pont de Nemours and Company, I 328–30; 8 151–54 (upd.); 26 123–27 (upd.); 73 128–33 (upd.)

E.On AG, 50 165–73 (upd.)

E.piphany, Inc., 49 123–25

E.W. Howell Co., Inc., 72 94–96 *see also* Obayashi Corporation

The E.W. Scripps Company, IV 606–09; 7 157–59 (upd.); 28 122–26 (upd.); 66 85–89 (upd.)

EADS N.V. *see* European Aeronautic Defence and Space Company EADS N.V.

EADS SOCATA, 54 91–94

Eagle Hardware & Garden, Inc., 16 186–89 *see also* Lowe's Companies, Inc.

Eagle-Picher Industries, Inc., 8 155–58; 23 179–83 (upd.) *see also* PerkinElmer Inc.

Eagle-Tribune Publishing Co., 91 153–57

Earl Scheib, Inc., 32 158–61

Earle M. Jorgensen Company, 82 99–102

The Earthgrains Company, 36 161–65

EarthLink, Inc., 36 166–68

East Japan Railway Company, V 448–50; 66 90–94 (upd.)

East Penn Manufacturing Co., Inc., 79 154–57

Easter Seals, Inc., 58 105–07

Eastern Airlines, I 101–03

The Eastern Company, 48 140–43

Eastern Enterprises, 6 486–88

EastGroup Properties, Inc., 67 149–51

Eastland Shoe Corporation, 82 103–106

Eastman Chemical Company, 14 174–75; 38 178–81 (upd.)

Eastman Kodak Company, III 474–77; 7 160–64 (upd.); 36 169–76 (upd.); 91 158–69 (upd.)

Easton Sports, Inc., 66 95–97

easyJet Airline Company Limited, 39 127–29; 52 330

Eateries, Inc., 33 138–40

Eaton Corporation, I 154–55; 10 279–80 (upd.); 67 152–56 (upd.)

Eaton Vance Corporation, 18 150–53

eBay Inc., 32 162–65; 67 157–61 (upd.)

Ebara Corporation, 83 119-122

EBSCO Industries, Inc., 17 151–53; 40 158–61 (upd.)

ECC Group plc, III 689–91 *see also* English China Clays plc.

ECC International Corp., 42 122–24

Ecco Sko A/S, 62 109–11

Echlin Inc., I 156–57; 11 83–85 (upd.) *see also* Dana Corp.

Echo Bay Mines Ltd., IV 75–77; 38 182–85 (upd.)

The Echo Design Group, Inc., 68 128–30

EchoStar Communications Corporation, 35 155–59

ECI Telecom Ltd., 18 154–56

Eckerd Corporation, 9 186–87 *see also* J.C. Penney Company, Inc.

Eckes AG, 56 100–03

Eclipse Aviation Corporation, 87 148–151

Ecolab Inc., I 331–33; **13** 197–200 (upd.); **34** 151–56 (upd.); **85** 97–105 (upd.)

eCollege.com, 85 106–09

Ecology and Environment, Inc., 39 130–33

The Economist Group Ltd., 67 162–65

Ecopetrol *see* Empresa Colombiana de Petróleos.

ECS S.A, 12 138–40

Ed S.A.S., 88 70–73

Edasa *see* Embotelladoras del Atlántico, S.A.

Eddie Bauer Holdings, Inc., 9 188–90; **36** 177–81 (upd.); **87** 152–159 (upd.)

Edeka Zentrale A.G., II 621–23; **47** 105–07 (upd.)

edel music AG, 44 162–65

Edelbrock Corporation, 37 117–19

Edelman, 62 112–15

EDF *see* Electricité de France.

EDGAR Online, Inc., 91 170–73

Edgars Consolidated Stores Ltd., 66 98–100

Edge Petroleum Corporation, 67 166–68

Edipresse S.A., 82 107–110

Edison Brothers Stores, Inc., 9 191–93

Edison International, 56 104–07 (upd.)

Edison Schools Inc., 37 120–23

Éditions Gallimard, 72 97–101

Editis S.A., 78 93–97

Editora Abril S.A *see* Abril S.A.

Editorial Television, S.A. de C.V., 57 121–23

EdK *see* Edeka Zentrale A.G.

Edmark Corporation, 14 176–78; **41** 134–37 (upd.)

EDO Corporation, 46 158–61

EDP Group *see* Electricidade de Portugal, S.A.

The Edrington Group Ltd., 88 74–78

EDS *see* Electronic Data Systems Corp.

Educate Inc., 86 130–35 (upd.)

Education Management Corporation, 35 160–63

Educational Broadcasting Corporation, 48 144–47

Educational Testing Service, 12 141–43; **62** 116–20 (upd.)

Edw. C. Levy Co., 42 125–27

Edward D. Jones & Company L.P., 30 177–79; **66** 101–04 (upd.)

Edward Hines Lumber Company, 68 131–33

Edward J. DeBartolo Corporation, 8 159–62

Edwards and Kelcey, 70 81–83

Edwards Brothers, Inc., 92 102–06

Edwards Theatres Circuit, Inc., 31 171–73

EFJ, Inc., 81 126–29

EG&G Incorporated, 8 163–65; **29** 166–69 (upd.)

Egan Companies, Inc., 94 185–88

EGAT *see* Electricity Generating Authority of Thailand (EGAT).

Egghead.com, Inc., 9 194–95; **31** 174–77 (upd.)

EGL, Inc., 59 170–73

Egmont Group, 93 189–93

EgyptAir, 6 84–86; **27** 132–35 (upd.)

Egyptian General Petroleum Corporation, IV 412–14; **51** 110–14 (upd.)

eHarmony.com Inc., 71 135–38

Eiffage, 27 136–38

8x8, Inc., 94 189–92

800-JR Cigar, Inc., 27 139–41

84 Lumber Company, 9 196–97; **39** 134–36 (upd.)

Eileen Fisher Inc., 61 85–87

Einstein/Noah Bagel Corporation, 29 170–73

eircom plc, 31 178–81 (upd.)

Eka Chemicals AB, 92 107–10

Ekco Group, Inc., 16 190–93

El Al Israel Airlines Ltd., 23 184–87

El Camino Resources International, Inc., 11 86–88

El Chico Restaurants, Inc., 19 135–38; **36** 162–63

El Corte Inglés, S.A., V 51–53; **26** 128–31 (upd.)

El Paso Corporation, 66 105–08 (upd.)

El Paso Electric Company, 21 196–98

El Paso Natural Gas Company, 12 144–46 *see also* El Paso Corp.

El Pollo Loco, Inc., 69 138–40

El Puerto de Liverpool, S.A.B. de C.V., 97 137–40

Elamex, S.A. de C.V., 51 115–17

Elan Corporation PLC, 63 140–43

Elano Corporation, 14 179–81

The Elder-Beerman Stores Corp., 10 281–83; **63** 144–48 (upd.)

Elders IXL Ltd., I 437–39

Electrabel N.V., 67 169–71

Electric Boat Corporation, 86 136–39

Electric Lightwave, Inc., 37 124–27

Electricidade de Portugal, S.A., 47 108–11

Electricité de France, V 603–05; **41** 138–41 (upd.)

Electricity Generating Authority of Thailand (EGAT), 56 108–10

Electro Rent Corporation, 58 108–10

Electrocomponents PLC, 50 174–77

Electrolux AB, 22 24–28 (upd.); **53** 124–29 (upd.)

Electrolux Group, III 478–81

Electromagnetic Sciences Inc., 21 199–201

Electronic Arts Inc., 10 284–86; **85** 110–15 (upd.)

Electronic Data Systems Corporation, III 136–38; **28** 112–16 (upd.) *see also* Perot Systems Corp.

Electronics Boutique Holdings Corporation, 72 102–05

Electronics for Imaging, Inc., 15 148–50; **43** 150–53 (upd.)

Elektra *see* Grupo Elektra, S.A. de C.V.

Elektra Entertainment Group, 64 115–18

Elektrowatt AG, 6 489–91 *see also* Siemens AG.

Element K Corporation, 94 193–96

Elementis plc, 40 162–68 (upd.)

Elephant Pharmacy, Inc., 83 123-126

Elf Aquitaine SA, 21 202–06 (upd.) *see also* Société Nationale Elf Aquitaine.

Eli Lilly and Company, I 645–47; **11** 89–91 (upd.); **47** 112–16 (upd.)

Elior SA, 49 126–28

Elite World S.A., 94 197–201

Elizabeth Arden, Inc., 8 166–68; **40** 169–72 (upd.)

Eljer Industries, Inc., 24 150–52

Elkay Manufacturing Company, 73 134–36

ElkCorp, 52 103–05

Ellen Tracy, Inc., 55 136–38

Ellerbe Becket, 41 142–45

Ellett Brothers, Inc., 17 154–56

Elma Electronic AG, 83 127-130

Elmer Candy Corporation, 88 79–82

Elmer's Restaurants, Inc., 42 128–30

Elpida Memory, Inc., 83 131-134

Elscint Ltd., 20 202–05

Elsevier NV, IV 610–11 *see also* Reed Elsevier.

Elsinore Corporation, 48 148–51

Elvis Presley Enterprises, Inc., 61 88–90

EMAP plc, 35 164–66

EMBARQ Corporation, 83 135-138

Embers America Restaurants, 30 180–82

Embotelladora Andina S.A., 71 139–41

Embraer *see* Empresa Brasileira de Aeronáutica S.A.

Embrex, Inc., 72 106–08

EMC Corporation, 12 147–49; **46** 162–66 (upd.)

EMCOR Group Inc., 60 118–21

EMCORE Corporation, 97 141–44

Emerson, 46 167–71 (upd.)

Emerson Electric Co., II 18–21

Emerson Radio Corp., 30 183–86

Emery Worldwide Airlines, Inc., 6 388–91; **25** 146–50 (upd.)

Emge Packing Co., Inc., 11 92–93

EMI Group plc, 22 192–95 (upd.); **81** 130–37 (upd.)

Emigrant Savings Bank, 59 174–76

The Emirates Group, 39 137–39; **81** 138–42 (upd.)

Emmis Communications Corporation, 47 117–21

Empi, Inc., 27 132–35

Empire Blue Cross and Blue Shield, III 245–46 *see also* WellChoice, Inc.

The Empire District Electric Company, 77 138–41

Empire Resorts, Inc., 72 109–12

Empire Resources, Inc., 81 143–46

Employee Solutions, Inc., 18 157–60

Empresa Brasileira de Aeronáutica S.A. (Embraer), 36 182–84

Empresa Colombiana de Petróleos, IV 415–18

Empresas Almacenes Paris S.A., 71 142–44
Empresas CMPC S.A., 70 84–87
Empresas Copec S.A., 69 141–44
Empresas ICA Sociedad Controladora, S.A. de C.V., 41 146–49
Empresas Polar SA, 55 139–41 (upd.)
Empresas Públicas de Medellín S.A.E.S.P., 91 174–77
Enbridge Inc., 43 154–58
ENCAD, Incorporated, 25 151–53 *see also* Eastman Kodak Co.
Encompass Services Corporation, 33 141–44
Encore Acquisition Company, 73 137–39
Encore Computer Corporation, 13 201–02; 74 107–10 (upd.)
Encore Wire Corporation, 81 147–50
Encyclopedia Britannica, Inc., 7 165–68; 39 140–44 (upd.)
Endemol Entertainment Holding NV, 46 172–74; 53 154
ENDESA S.A., V 606–08; 46 175–79 (upd.)
Endo Pharmaceuticals Holdings Inc., 71 145–47
Endurance Specialty Holdings Ltd., 85 116–19
Energen Corporation, 21 207–09; 97 145–49 (upd.)
Energis plc, 44 363; 47 122–25
Energizer Holdings, Inc., 32 171–74
Energy Brands Inc., 88 83–86
Energy Conversion Devices, Inc., 75 133–36
Enersis S.A., 73 140–43
EnerSys Inc., 99 147–151
Enesco Corporation, 11 94–96
Engelhard Corporation, IV 78–80; 21 210–14 (upd.); 72 113–18 (upd.)
Engineered Support Systems, Inc., 59 177–80
Engle Homes, Inc., 46 180–82
English China Clays Ltd., 15 151–54 (upd.); 40 173–77 (upd.)
Engraph, Inc., 12 150–51 *see also* Sonoco Products Co.
ENI S.p.A., 69 145–50 (upd.)
ENMAX Corporation, 83 139-142
Ennis, Inc., 21 215–17; 97 150–54 (upd.)
Enodis plc, 68 134–37
EnPro Industries, Inc., 93 194–98
Enquirer/Star Group, Inc., 10 287–88 *see also* American Media, Inc.
Enrich International, Inc., 33 145–48
Enron Corporation, V 609–10; 19 139–41; 46 183–86 (upd.)
ENSCO International Incorporated, 57 124–26
Enserch Corp., V 611–13 *see also* Texas Utilities.
Enskilda S.A. *see* Skandinaviska Enskilda Banken AB.
Enso-Gutzeit Oy, IV 274–77 *see also* Stora Enso Oyj.

Ente Nazionale Idrocarburi, IV 419–22 *see also* ENI S.p.A.
Ente Nazionale per l'Energia Elettrica, V 614–17
Entercom Communications Corporation, 58 111–12
Entergy Corporation, V 618–20; 45 148–51 (upd.)
Enterprise Inns plc, 59 181–83
Enterprise Oil plc, 11 97–99; 50 178–82 (upd.)
Enterprise Rent-A-Car Company, 6 392–93; 69 151–54 (upd.)
Entertainment Distribution Company, 89 200–03
Entravision Communications Corporation, 41 150–52
Entreprise Nationale Sonatrach, IV 423–25 *see also* Sonatrach.
Envirodyne Industries, Inc., 17 157–60
Environmental Industries, Inc., 31 182–85
Environmental Power Corporation, 68 138–40
Environmental Systems Research Institute Inc. (ESRI), 62 121–24
Enzo Biochem, Inc., 41 153–55
Eon Labs, Inc., 67 172–74
EPAM Systems Inc., 96 120–23
EPCOR Utilities Inc., 81 151–54
Epic Systems Corporation, 62 125–28
EPIQ Systems, Inc., 56 111–13
Equant N.V., 52 106–08
Equifax, Inc., 6 23–25; 28 117–21 (upd.); 90 177–83 (upd.)
Equistar Chemicals, LP, 71 148–50
Equitable Life Assurance Society of the United States, III 247–49
Equitable Resources, Inc., 6 492–94; 54 95–98 (upd.)
Equity Marketing, Inc., 26 136–38
Equity Office Properties Trust, 54 99–102
Equity Residential, 49 129–32
Equus Computer Systems, Inc., 49 133–35
Eram SA, 51 118–20
Eramet, 73 144–47
Ercros S.A., 80 102–05
ERGO Versicherungsgruppe AG, 44 166–69
Ergon, Inc., 95 134–37
Erickson Retirement Communities, 57 127–30
Ericsson *see* Telefonaktiebolaget LM Ericsson.
Eridania Béghin-Say S.A., 36 185–88
Erie Indemnity Company, 35 167–69
ERLY Industries Inc., 17 161–62
Ermenegildo Zegna SpA, 63 149–52
Ernie Ball, Inc., 56 114–16
Ernst & Young, 9 198–200; 29 174–77 (upd.)
Eroski *see* Grupo Eroski
Erste Bank der Osterreichischen Sparkassen AG, 69 155–57
ESCADA AG, 71 151–53
Escalade, Incorporated, 19 142–44

Eschelon Telecom, Inc., 72 119–22
ESCO Technologies Inc., 87 160–163
Eskimo Pie Corporation, 21 218–20
Espírito Santo Financial Group S.A., 79 158–63 (upd.)
ESPN, Inc., 56 117–22
Esporta plc, 35 170–72
Esprit de Corp., 8 169–72; 29 178–82 (upd.)
ESS Technology, Inc., 22 196–98
Essar Group Ltd., 79 164–67
Essef Corporation, 18 161–63 *see also* Pentair, Inc.
Esselte, 64 119–21
Esselte Leitz GmbH & Co. KG, 48 152–55
Esselte Pendaflex Corporation, 11 100–01
Essence Communications, Inc., 24 153–55
Essex Corporation, 85 120–23
Essilor International, 21 221–23
The Estée Lauder Companies Inc., 9 201–04; 30 187–91 (upd.); 92 199–207 (upd.)
Esterline Technologies Corp., 15 155–57
Estes Express Lines, Inc., 86 140–43
Etablissements Economiques du Casino Guichard, Perrachon et ie, S.C.A., 12 152–54 *see also* Casino Guichard-Perrachon S.A.
Etablissements Franz Colruyt N.V., 68 141–43
Établissements Jacquot and Cie S.A.S., 92 111–14
Etam Developpement SA, 44 170–72
ETBD *see* Europe Through the Back Door.
Eternal Word Television Network, Inc., 57 131–34
Ethan Allen Interiors, Inc., 12 155–57; 39 145–48 (upd.)
Ethicon, Inc., 23 188–90
Ethiopian Airlines, 81 155–58
Ethyl Corp., I 334–36; 10 289–91 (upd.)
Etienne Aigner AG, 52 109–12
Etihad Airways PJSC, 89 204–07
EToys, Inc., 37 128–30
ETS *see* Educational Testing Service.
Euralis *see* Groupe Euralis.
Eurazeo, 80 106–09
The Eureka Company, 12 158–60 *see also* White Consolidated Industries Inc.
Euro Disney S.C.A., 20 209–12; 58 113–16 (upd.)
Euro RSCG Worldwide S.A., 13 203–05
Eurocopter S.A., 80 110–13
Eurofins Scientific S.A., 70 88–90
Euromarket Designs Inc., 31 186–89 (upd.); 99 152–157 (upd.)
Euronet Worldwide, Inc., 83 143-146
Euronext N.V., 37 131–33; 89 208–11 (upd.)
Europe Through the Back Door Inc., 65 135–38

European Aeronautic Defence and Space Company EADS N.V., 52 113–16 (upd.)

European Investment Bank, 66 109–11

Eurotunnel Group, 13 206–08; 37 134–38 (upd.)

EVA Airways Corporation, 51 121–23

Evans & Sutherland Computer Corporation, 19 145–49; 78 98–103 (upd.)

Evans, Inc., 30 192–94

Everex Systems, Inc., 16 194–96

Evergreen Energy, Inc., 97 155–59

Evergreen International Aviation, Inc., 53 130–33

Evergreen Marine Corporation (Taiwan) Ltd., 13 209–11; 50 183–89 (upd.)

Everlast Worldwide Inc., 47 126–29

Evraz Group S.A., 97 160–63

EWTN *see* Eternal Word Television Network, Inc.

Exabyte Corporation, 12 161–63; 40 178–81 (upd.)

Exar Corp., 14 182–84

EXCEL Communications Inc., 18 164–67

Excel Technology, Inc., 65 139–42

Executive Jet, Inc., 36 189–91 *see also* NetJets Inc.

Executone Information Systems, Inc., 13 212–14; 15 195

Exel plc, 51 124–30 (upd.)

Exelon Corporation, 48 156–63 (upd.); 49 65

Exide Electronics Group, Inc., 20 213–15

Exito *see* Almacenes Exito S.A.

Expand SA, 48 164–66

Expedia, Inc., 58 117–21

Expeditors International of Washington Inc., 17 163–65; 78 104–08 (upd.)

Experian Information Solutions Inc., 45 152–55

Exponent, Inc., 95 138–41

Exportadora Bananera Noboa, S.A., 91 178–81

Express Scripts Inc., 17 166–68; 44 173–76 (upd.)

Extended Stay America, Inc., 41 156–58

Extendicare Health Services, Inc., 6 181–83

Extreme Pizza *see* OOC Inc.

EXX Inc., 65 143–45

Exxon Mobil Corporation, IV 426–30; 7 169–73 (upd.); 32 175–82 (upd.); 67 175–86 (upd.)

Eye Care Centers of America, Inc., 69 158–60

Ezaki Glico Company Ltd., 72 123–25

EZCORP Inc., 43 159–61

F

F&W Publications, Inc., 71 154–56

F.A.O. Schwarz *see* FAO Schwarz

The F. Dohmen Co., 77 142–45

F. Hoffmann-La Roche & Co. A.G., I 642–44; 50 190–93 (upd.)

F. Korbel & Bros. Inc., 68 144–46

F.W. Webb Company, 95 142–45

Fab Industries, Inc., 27 142–44

Fabbrica D' Armi Pietro Beretta S.p.A., 39 149–51

Faber-Castell *see* A.W. Faber-Castell Unternehmensverwaltung GmbH & Co.

Fabri-Centers of America Inc., 16 197–99 *see also* Jo-Ann Stores, Inc.

Facebook, Inc., 90 184–87

Facom S.A., 32 183–85

FactSet Research Systems Inc., 73 148–50

Faegre & Benson LLP, 97 164–67

FAG—Kugelfischer Georg Schäfer AG, 62 129–32

Fair Grounds Corporation, 44 177–80

Fair, Isaac and Company, 18 168–71

Fairchild Dornier GmbH, 9 205–08; 48 167–71 (upd.)

Fairclough Construction Group plc, I 567–68

Fairfax Financial Holdings Limited, 57 135–37

Fairfax Media Ltd., 94 202–08 (upd.)

Fairfield Communities, Inc., 36 192–95

Fairmont Hotels & Resorts Inc., 69 161–63

Faiveley S.A., 39 152–54

Falcon Products, Inc., 33 149–51

Falconbridge Limited, 49 136–39

Fallon Worldwide, 22 199–201; 71 157–61 (upd.)

Family Christian Stores, Inc., 51 131–34

Family Dollar Stores, Inc., 13 215–17; 62 133–36 (upd.)

Family Golf Centers, Inc., 29 183–85

Famous Brands Ltd., 86 144–47

Famous Dave's of America, Inc., 40 182–84

Fannie Mae, 45 156–59 (upd.)

Fannie May Confections Brands, Inc., 80 114–18

Fansteel Inc., 19 150–52

Fanuc Ltd., III 482–83; 17 172–74 (upd.); 75 137–40 (upd.)

FAO Schwarz, 46 187–90

Farah Incorporated, 24 156–58

Faribault Foods, Inc., 89 212–15

Farley Northwest Industries Inc., I 440–41

Farley's & Sathers Candy Company, Inc., 62 137–39

Farm Family Holdings, Inc., 39 155–58

Farm Journal Corporation, 42 131–34

Farmacias Ahumada S.A., 72 126–28

Farmer Bros. Co., 52 117–19

Farmer Jack Supermarkets, 78 109–13

Farmer Mac *see* Federal Agricultural Mortgage Corp.

Farmers Insurance Group of Companies, 25 154–56

Farmland Foods, Inc., 7 174–75

Farmland Industries, Inc., 48 172–75

FARO Technologies, Inc., 87 164–167

Farouk Systems, Inc., 78 114–17

Farrar, Straus and Giroux Inc., 15 158–60

Fastenal Company, 14 185–87; 42 135–38 (upd.); 99 158–163 (upd.)

FASTWEB S.p.A., 83 147-150

Fat Face Ltd., 68 147–49

Fatburger Corporation, 64 122–24

FATS, Inc. *see* Firearms Training Systems, Inc.

Faultless Starch/Bon Ami Company, 55 142–45

Faurecia S.A., 70 91–93

FAvS *see* First Aviation Services Inc.

Faygo Beverages Inc., 55 146–48

Fazoli's Management, Inc., 27 145–47; 76 144–47 (upd.)

Featherlite Inc., 28 127–29

Fedders Corporation, 18 172–75; 43 162–67 (upd.)

Federal Agricultural Mortgage Corporation, 75 141–43

Federal Deposit Insurance Corporation, 93 208–12

Federal Express Corporation, V 451–53 *see also* FedEx Corp.

Federal Home Loan Mortgage Corp. *see* Freddie Mac.

Federal-Mogul Corporation, I 158–60; 10 292–94 (upd.); 26 139–43 (upd.)

Federal National Mortgage Association, II 410–11 *see also* Fannie Mae.

Federal Paper Board Company, Inc., 8 173–75

Federal Prison Industries, Inc., 34 157–60

Federal Signal Corp., 10 295–97

Federated Department Stores Inc., 9 209–12; 31 190–94 (upd.) *see also* Macy's, Inc.

Fédération Internationale de Football Association, 27 148–51

Federation Nationale d'Achats des Cadres *see* FNAC.

Federico Paternina S.A., 69 164–66

FedEx Corporation, 18 176–79 (upd.); 42 139–44 (upd.)

Feed The Children, Inc., 68 150–52

FEI Company, 79 168–71

Feld Entertainment, Inc., 32 186–89 (upd.)

Feldmühle Nobel AG, III 692–95 *see also* Metallgesellschaft.

Fellowes Manufacturing Company, 28 130–32

Fenaco, 86 148–51

Fender Musical Instruments Company, 16 200–02; 43 168–72 (upd.)

Fenwick & West LLP, 34 161–63

Ferolito, Vultaggio & Sons, 27 152–55

Ferrara Fire Apparatus, Inc., 84 115–118

Ferrara Pan Candy Company, 90 188–91

Ferrari S.p.A., 13 218–20; 36 196–200 (upd.)

Ferrellgas Partners, L.P., 35 173–75

Ferrero SpA, 54 103–05

Ferretti Group SpA, 90 192–96

Ferro Corporation, 8 176–79; 56 123–28 (upd.)

Ferrovial *see* Grupo Ferrovial

F5 Networks, Inc., 72 129–31

FHP International Corporation, 6 184–86

Fiat SpA, I 161–63; 11 102–04 (upd.); 50 194–98 (upd.)

FiberMark, Inc., 37 139–42; 53 24

Fibreboard Corporation, 16 203–05 *see also* Owens Corning Corp.

Ficosa *see* Grupo Ficosa International.

Fidelity Investments Inc., II 412–13; 14 188–90 (upd.) *see also* FMR Corp.

Fidelity National Financial Inc., 54 106–08

Fidelity Southern Corporation, 85 124–27

Fieldale Farms Corporation, 23 191–93

Fieldcrest Cannon, Inc., 9 213–17; 31 195–200 (upd.)

Fielmann AG, 31 201–03

FIFA *see* Fédération Internationale de Football Association.

Fifth Third Bancorp, 13 221–23; 31 204–08 (upd.)

Le Figaro see Société du Figaro S.A.

Figgie International Inc., 7 176–78

Fiji Water LLC, 74 111–13

Fila Holding S.p.A., 20 216–18; 52 120–24 (upd.)

FileNet Corporation, 62 140–43

Fili Enterprises, Inc., 70 94–96

Filipacchi Medias S.A. *see* Hachette Filipacchi Medias S.A.

Film Roman, Inc., 58 122–24

Filtrona plc, 88 87–91

Fimalac S.A., 37 143–45

FINA, Inc., 7 179–81 *see also* Total Fina Elf S.A.

Finarte Casa d'Aste S.p.A., 93 213–16

Findel plc, 60 122–24

Findorff *see* J.H. Findorff and Son, Inc.

Fingerhut Companies, Inc., 9 218–20; 36 201–05 (upd.)

Finisar Corporation, 92 115–18

The Finish Line, Inc., 29 186–88; 68 153–56 (upd.)

FinishMaster, Inc., 24 159–61

Finlay Enterprises, Inc., 16 206–08; 76 148–51 (upd.)

Finmeccanica S.p.A., 84 119–123

Finnair Oy, 6 87–89; 25 157–60 (upd.); 61 91–95 (upd.)

Finning International Inc., 69 167–69

Fired Up, Inc., 82 111–14

Firearms Training Systems, Inc., 27 156–58

Fireman's Fund Insurance Company, III 250–52

Firmenich International S.A., 60 125–27

First Albany Companies Inc., 37 146–48

First Alert, Inc., 28 133–35

The First American Corporation, 52 125–27

First Aviation Services Inc., 49 140–42

First Bank System Inc., 12 164–66 *see also* U.S. Bancorp

First Brands Corporation, 8 180–82

First Cash Financial Services, Inc., 57 138–40

First Chicago Corporation, II 284–87 *see also* Bank One Corp.

First Choice Holidays PLC, 40 185–87

First Colony Coffee & Tea Company, 84 124–126

First Commerce Bancshares, Inc., 15 161–63 *see also* Wells Fargo & Co.

First Commerce Corporation, 11 105–07 *see also* JPMorgan Chase & Co.

First Data Corporation, 30 195–98 (upd.)

First Empire State Corporation, 11 108–10

First Executive Corporation, III 253–55

First Fidelity Bank, N.A., New Jersey, 9 221–23

First Financial Management Corporation, 11 111–13

First Hawaiian, Inc., 11 114–16

First Industrial Realty Trust, Inc., 65 146–48

First International Computer, Inc., 56 129–31

First Interstate Bancorp, II 288–90 *see also* Wells Fargo & Co.

The First Marblehead Corporation, 87 168–171

First Mississippi Corporation, 8 183–86 *see also* ChemFirst, Inc.

First Nationwide Bank, 14 191–93 *see also* Citigroup Inc.

First of America Bank Corporation, 8 187–89

First Pacific Company Limited, 18 180–82

First Security Corporation, 11 117–19 *see also* Wells Fargo & Co.

First Solar, Inc., 95 146–50

First Team Sports, Inc., 22 202–04

First Tennessee National Corporation, 11 120–21; 48 176–79 (upd.)

First Union Corporation, 10 298–300 *see also* Wachovia Corp.

First USA, Inc., 11 122–24

First Virginia Banks, Inc., 11 125–26 *see also* BB&T Corp.

The First Years Inc., 46 191–94

Firstar Corporation, 11 127–29; 33 152–55 (upd.)

FirstGroup plc, 89 216–19

Fiserv Inc., 11 130–32; 33 156–60 (upd.)

Fish & Neave, 54 109–12

Fisher Communications, Inc., 99 164–168

Fisher Companies, Inc., 15 164–66

Fisher Controls International, LLC, 13 224–26; 61 96–99 (upd.)

Fisher-Price Inc., 12 167–69; 32 190–94 (upd.)

Fisher Scientific International Inc., 24 162–66

Fisk Corporation, 72 132–34

Fiskars Corporation, 33 161–64

Fisons plc, 9 224–27; 23 194–97 (upd.)

5 & Diner Franchise Corporation, 72 135–37

Five Guys Enterprises, LLC, 99 169–172

FKI Plc, 57 141–44

Flagstar Companies, Inc., 10 301–03 *see also* Advantica Restaurant Group, Inc.

Flanders Corporation, 65 149–51

Flanigan's Enterprises, Inc., 60 128–30

Flatiron Construction Corporation, 92 119–22

Fleer Corporation, 15 167–69

FleetBoston Financial Corporation, 9 228–30; 36 206–14 (upd.)

Fleetwood Enterprises, Inc., III 484–85; 22 205–08 (upd.); 81 159–64 (upd.)

Fleming Companies, Inc., II 624–25; 17 178–81 (upd.)

Fletcher Challenge Ltd., IV 278–80; 19 153–57 (upd.)

Fleury Michon S.A., 39 159–61

Flexsteel Industries Inc., 15 170–72; 41 159–62 (upd.)

Flextronics International Ltd., 38 186–89

Flight Options, LLC, 75 144–46

FlightSafety International, Inc., 9 231–33; 29 189–92 (upd.)

Flint Ink Corporation, 13 227–29; 41 163–66 (upd.)

FLIR Systems, Inc., 69 170–73

Flo *see* Groupe Flo S.A.

Floc'h & Marchand, 80 119–21

Florida Crystals Inc., 35 176–78

Florida East Coast Industries, Inc., 59 184–86

Florida Gaming Corporation, 47 130–33

Florida Progress Corp., V 621–22; 23 198–200 (upd.) *see also* Progress Energy, Inc.

Florida Public Utilities Company, 69 174–76

Florida Rock Industries, Inc., 46 195–97 *see also* Patriot Transportation Holding, Inc.

Florida's Natural Growers, 45 160–62

Florists' Transworld Delivery, Inc., 28 136–38 *see also* FTD Group, Inc.

Florsheim Shoe Group Inc., 9 234–36; 31 209–12 (upd.)

Flotek Industries Inc., 93 217–20

Flour City International, Inc., 44 181–83

Flow International Corporation, 56 132–34

Flowers Industries, Inc., 12 170–71; 35 179–82 (upd.) *see also* Keebler Foods Co.

Flowserve Corporation, 33 165–68; 77 146–51 (upd.)

FLSmidth & Co. A/S, 72 138–40

Fluke Corporation, 15 173–75

Fluor Corporation, I 569–71; 8 190–93 (upd.); 34 164–69 (upd.)

FlyBE *see* Jersey European Airways (UK) Ltd.

Flying Boat, Inc. (Chalk's Ocean Airways), 56 135–37

Flying J Inc., 19 158–60

Flying Pigeon Bicycle Co. *see* Tianjin Flying Pigeon Bicycle Co., Ltd.

FMC Corp., I 442–44; **11** 133–35 (upd.); **89** 220–27 (upd.)

FMR Corp., 8 194–96; **32** 195–200 (upd.)

FNAC, 21 224–26

FNMA *see* Federal National Mortgage Association.

Foamex International Inc., 17 182–85

Focus Features, 78 118–22

Fokker *see* N.V. Koninklijke Nederlandse Vliegtuigenfabriek Fokker.

Foley & Lardner, 28 139–42

Follett Corporation, 12 172–74; **39** 162–65 (upd.)

Fonterra Co-Operative Group Ltd., 58 125–27

Food Circus Super Markets, Inc., 88 92–96

The Food Emporium, 64 125–27

Food For The Poor, Inc., 77 152–55

Food Lion LLC, II 626–27; **15** 176–78 (upd.); **66** 112–15 (upd.)

Foodarama Supermarkets, Inc., 28 143–45 *see also* Wakefern Food Corp.

FoodBrands America, Inc., 23 201–04 *see also* Doskocil Companies, Inc.; Tyson Foods, Inc.

Foodmaker, Inc., 14 194–96 *see also* Jack in the Box Inc.

Foot Locker, Inc., 68 157–62 (upd.)

Foot Petals L.L.C., 95 151–54

Foote, Cone & Belding Worldwide, I 12–15; **66** 116–20 (upd.)

Footstar, Incorporated, 24 167–69 *see also* Foot Locker, Inc.

Forbes Inc., 30 199–201; **82** 115–20 (upd.)

Force Protection Inc., 95 155–58

The Ford Foundation, 34 170–72

Ford Motor Company, I 164–68; **11** 136–40 (upd.); **36** 215–21 (upd.); **64** 128–34 (upd.)

Ford Motor Company, S.A. de C.V., 20 219–21

FORE Systems, Inc., 25 161–63 *see also* Telefonaktiebolaget LM Ericsson.

Foremost Farms USA Cooperative, 98 116–20

FöreningsSparbanken AB, 69 177–80

Forest City Enterprises, Inc., 16 209–11; **52** 128–31 (upd.)

Forest Laboratories, Inc., 11 141–43; **52** 132–36 (upd.)

Forest Oil Corporation, 19 161–63; **91** 182–87 (upd.)

Forever Living Products International Inc., 17 186–88

Forever 21, Inc., 84 127–129

FormFactor, Inc., 85 128–31

Formica Corporation, 13 230–32

Formosa Plastics Corporation, 14 197–99; **58** 128–31 (upd.)

Forrester Research, Inc., 54 113–15

Forstmann Little & Co., 38 190–92

Fort Howard Corporation, 8 197–99 *see also* Fort James Corp.

Fort James Corporation, 22 209–12 (upd.) *see also* Georgia-Pacific Corp.

Fortis, Inc., 15 179–82; **47** 134–37 (upd.); **50** 4–6

Fortum Corporation, 30 202–07 (upd.) *see also* Neste Oil Corp.

Fortune Brands, Inc., 29 193–97 (upd.); **68** 163–67 (upd.)

Fortunoff Fine Jewelry and Silverware Inc., 26 144–46

Forward Air Corporation, 75 147–49

Forward Industries, Inc., 86 152–55

The Forzani Group Ltd., 79 172–76

Fossil, Inc., 17 189–91

Foster Poultry Farms, 32 201–04

Foster Wheeler Corporation, 6 145–47; **23** 205–08 (upd.); **76** 152–56 (upd.)

Foster's Group Limited, 7 182–84; **21** 227–30 (upd.); **50** 199–203 (upd.)

FosterGrant, Inc., 60 131–34

Foundation Health Corporation, 12 175–77

Fountain Powerboats Industries, Inc., 28 146–48

Four Seasons Hotels Inc., 9 237–38; **29** 198–200 (upd.)

Four Winns Boats LLC, 96 124–27

4Kids Entertainment Inc., 59 187–89

Fourth Financial Corporation, 11 144–46

Fox Entertainment Group, Inc., 43 173–76

Fox Family Worldwide, Inc., 24 170–72 *see also* ABC Family Worldwide, Inc.

Fox, Inc. *see* Twentieth Century Fox Film Corp.

Fox's Pizza Den, Inc., 98 121–24

Foxboro Company, 13 233–35

FoxHollow Technologies, Inc., 85 132–35

FoxMeyer Health Corporation, 16 212–14 *see also* McKesson Corp.

Foxworth-Galbraith Lumber Company, 91 188–91

FPL Group, Inc., V 623–25; **49** 143–46 (upd.)

Framatome SA, 19 164–67 aee also Alcatel S.A.; AREVA.

France Telecom S.A., V 291–93; **21** 231–34 (upd.); **99** 173–179 (upd.)

Francotyp-Postalia Holding AG, 92 123–27

Frank J. Zamboni & Co., Inc., 34 173–76

Frank Russell Company, 46 198–200

Frank's Nursery & Crafts, Inc., 12 178–79

Franke Holding AG, 76 157–59

Frankel & Co., 39 166–69

Frankfurter Allgemeine Zeitung GmbH, 66 121–24

Franklin Covey Company, 11 147–49; **37** 149–52 (upd.)

Franklin Electric Company, Inc., 43 177–80

Franklin Electronic Publishers, Inc., 23 209–13

The Franklin Mint, 69 181–84

Franklin Resources, Inc., 9 239–40

Franz Inc., 80 122–25

Fraport AG Frankfurt Airport Services Worldwide, 90 197–202

Fraser & Neave Ltd., 54 116–18

Fred Alger Management, Inc., 97 168–72

Fred Meyer Stores, Inc., V 54–56; **20** 222–25 (upd.); **64** 135–39 (upd.)

Fred Usinger Inc., 54 119–21

The Fred W. Albrecht Grocery Co., 13 236–38

Fred Weber, Inc., 61 100–02

Fred's, Inc., 23 214–16; **62** 144–47 (upd.)

Freddie Mac, 54 122–25

Frederick Atkins Inc., 16 215–17

Frederick's of Hollywood Inc., 16 218–20; **59** 190–93 (upd.)

Freedom Communications, Inc., 36 222–25

Freeport-McMoRan Copper & Gold, Inc., IV 81–84; **7** 185–89 (upd.); **57** 145–50 (upd.)

Freescale Semiconductor, Inc., 83 151-154

Freeze.com LLC, 77 156–59

Freixenet S.A., 71 162–64

French Connection Group plc, 41 167–69

French Fragrances, Inc., 22 213–15 *see also* Elizabeth Arden, Inc.

Frequency Electronics, Inc., 61 103–05

Fresenius AG, 56 138–42

Fresh America Corporation, 20 226–28

Fresh Choice, Inc., 20 229–32

Fresh Enterprises, Inc., 66 125–27

Fresh Express Inc., 88 97–100

Fresh Foods, Inc., 29 201–03

FreshDirect, LLC, 84 130–133

Fretter, Inc., 10 304–06

Freudenberg & Co., 41 170–73

Fried, Frank, Harris, Shriver & Jacobson, 35 183–86

Fried. Krupp GmbH, IV 85–89 *see also* ThyssenKrupp AG.

Friedman, Billings, Ramsey Group, Inc., 53 134–37

Friedman's Inc., 29 204–06

Friedrich Grohe AG & Co. KG, 53 138–41

Friendly Ice Cream Corporation, 30 208–10; **72** 141–44 (upd.)

Friesland Coberco Dairy Foods Holding N.V., 59 194–96

Frigidaire Home Products, 22 216–18

Frisch's Restaurants, Inc., 35 187–89; **92** 128–32 (upd.)

Frito-Lay North America, 32 205–10; **73** 151–58 (upd.)

Fritz Companies, Inc., 12 180–82

Fromageries Bel, 23 217–19; 25 83–84

Frontier Airlines Holdings Inc., 22 219–21; 84 134–138 (upd.)

Frontier Corp., 16 221–23

Frontier Natural Products Co-Op, 82 121–24

Frontline Ltd., 45 163–65

Frost & Sullivan, Inc., 53 142–44

Frozen Food Express Industries, Inc., 20 233–35; 98 125–30 (upd.)

Frucor Beverages Group Ltd., 96 128–31

Fruehauf Corp., I 169–70

Fruit of the Loom, Inc., 8 200–02; 25 164–67 (upd.)

Fruth Pharmacy, Inc., 66 128–30

Fry's Electronics, Inc., 68 168–70

Frymaster Corporation, 27 159–62

FSI International, Inc., 17 192–94 *see also* FlightSafety International, Inc.

FTD Group, Inc., 99 180–185 (upd.)

FTI Consulting, Inc., 77 160–63

FTP Software, Inc., 20 236–38

Fubu, 29 207–09

Fuel Tech, Inc., 85 136–40

Fuel Systems Solutions, Inc., 97 173–77

FuelCell Energy, Inc., 75 150–53

Fugro N.V., 98 131–34

Fuji Bank, Ltd., II 291–93

Fuji Electric Co., Ltd., II 22–23; 48 180–82 (upd.)

Fuji Photo Film Co., Ltd., III 486–89; 18 183–87 (upd.); 79 177–84 (upd.)

Fuji Television Network Inc., 91 192–95

Fujisawa Pharmaceutical Company, Ltd., I 635–36; 58 132–34 (upd.) *see also* Astellas Pharma Inc.

Fujisawa-ICL Systems Inc., 11 150–51

Fujitsu Limited, III 139–41; 16 224–27 (upd.); 40 145–50 (upd.)

Fulbright & Jaworski L.L.P., 47 138–41

Fuller Smith & Turner P.L.C., 38 193–95

Funai Electric Company Ltd., 62 148–50

Funco, Inc., 20 239–41 *see also* GameStop Corp.

Fuqua Enterprises, Inc., 17 195–98

Fuqua Industries Inc., I 445–47

Furmanite Corporation, 92 133–36

Furniture Brands International, Inc., 39 170–75 (upd.)

Furon Company, 28 149–51 *see also* Compagnie de Saint-Gobain.

Furr's Restaurant Group, Inc., 53 145–48

Furr's Supermarkets, Inc., 28 152–54

Furukawa Electric Co., Ltd., III 490–92

Future Now, Inc., 12 183–85

Future Shop Ltd., 62 151–53

Fyffes Plc, 38 196–99

G

G&K Holding S.A., 95 159–62

G&K Services, Inc., 16 228–30

G A Pindar & Son Ltd., 88 101–04

G.D. Searle & Co., I 686–89; 12 186–89 (upd.); 34 177–82 (upd.)

G. Heileman Brewing Co., I 253–55 *see also* Stroh Brewery Co.

G.I.E. Airbus Industrie, I 41–43; 12 190–92 (upd.)

G.I. Joe's, Inc., 30 221–23 *see also* Joe's Sports & Outdoor.

G-III Apparel Group, Ltd., 22 222–24

G. Leblanc Corporation, 55 149–52

G.S. Blodgett Corporation, 15 183–85 *see also* Blodgett Holdings, Inc.

Gabelli Asset Management Inc., 30 211–14 *see also* Lynch Corp.

Gables Residential Trust, 49 147–49

Gadzooks, Inc., 18 188–90

GAF, I 337–40; 22 225–29 (upd.)

Gage Marketing Group, 26 147–49

Gaiam, Inc., 41 174–77

Gainsco, Inc., 22 230–32

Galardi Group, Inc., 72 145–47

Galaxy Investors, Inc., 97 178–81

Galaxy Nutritional Foods, Inc., 58 135–37

Gale International LLC, 93 221–24

Galenica AG, 84 139–142

Galeries Lafayette S.A., V 57–59; 23 220–23 (upd.)

Galey & Lord, Inc., 20 242–45; 66 131–34 (upd.)

Gallaher Group Plc, 49 150–54 (upd.)

Gallaher Limited, V 398–400; 19 168–71 (upd.)

Gallo Winery *see* E. & J. Gallo Winery.

The Gallup Organization, 37 153–56

Galoob Toys *see* Lewis Galoob Toys Inc.

Galp Energia SGPS S.A., 98 135–40

Galyan's Trading Company, Inc., 47 142–44

The Gambrinus Company, 40 188–90

Gambro AB, 49 155–57

The GAME Group plc, 80 126–29

GameStop Corp., 69 185–89 (upd.)

GAMI *see* Great American Management and Investment, Inc.

Gaming Partners InternationalCorporation, 92225–28

Gander Mountain Company, 20 246–48; 90 203–08 (upd.)

Gannett Company, Inc., IV 612–13; 7 190–92 (upd.); 30 215–17 (upd.); 66 135–38 (upd.)

Gano Excel Enterprise Sdn. Bhd., 89 228–31

Gantos, Inc., 17 199–201

Ganz, 98 141–44

GAP *see* Grupo Aeroportuario del Pacífico, S.A. de C.V.

The Gap, Inc., V 60–62; 18 191–94 (upd.); 55 153–57 (upd.)

Garan, Inc., 16 231–33; 64 140–43 (upd.)

The Garden Company Ltd., 82 125–28

Garden Fresh Restaurant Corporation, 31 213–15

Garden Ridge Corporation, 27 163–65

Gardenburger, Inc., 33 169–71; 76 160–63 (upd.)

Gardner Denver, Inc., 49 158–60

Garmin Ltd., 60 135–37

Garst Seed Company, Inc., 86 156–59

Gart Sports Company, 24 173–75 *see also* Sports Authority, Inc.

Gartner, Inc., 21 235–37; 94 209–13 (upd.)

Garuda Indonesia, 6 90–91; 58 138–41 (upd.)

Gas Natural SDG S.A., 69 190–93

GASS *see* Grupo Ángeles Servicios de Salud, S.A. de C.V.

Gasunie *see* N.V. Nederlandse Gasunie.

Gate Gourmet International AG, 70 97–100

GateHouse Media, Inc., 91 196–99

The Gates Corporation, 9 241–43

Gateway Corporation Ltd., II 628–30 *see also* Somerfield plc.

Gateway, Inc., 10 307–09; 27 166–69 (upd.); 63 153–58 (upd.)

The Gatorade Company, 82 129–32

Gatti's Pizza, Inc. *see* Mr. Gatti's, LP.

GATX, 6 394–96; 25 168–71 (upd.)

Gaumont S.A., 25 172–75; 91 200–05 (upd.)

Gaylord Container Corporation, 8 203–05

Gaylord Entertainment Company, 11 152–54; 36 226–29 (upd.)

Gaz de France, V 626–28; 40 191–95 (upd.)

Gazprom *see* OAO Gazprom.

GBC *see* General Binding Corp.

GC Companies, Inc., 25 176–78 *see also* AMC Entertainment Inc.

GE *see* General Electric Co.

GE Aircraft Engines, 9 244–46

GE Capital Aviation Services, 36 230–33

GEA AG, 27 170–74

GEAC Computer Corporation Ltd., 43 181–85

Geberit AG, 49 161–64

Gecina SA, 42 151–53

Gedney *see* M.A. Gedney Co.

Geerlings & Wade, Inc., 45 166–68

Geest Plc, 38 200–02 *see also* Bakkavör Group hf.

Gefco SA, 54 126–28

Geffen Records Inc., 26 150–52

GEHE AG, 27 175–78

Gehl Company, 19 172–74

GEICO Corporation, 10 310–12; 40 196–99 (upd.)

Geiger Bros., 60 138–41

Gelita AG, 74 114–18

GEMA (Gesellschaft für musikalische Aufführungs- und mechanische Vervielfältigungsrechte), 70 101–05

Gemini Sound Products Corporation, 58 142–44

Gemplus International S.A., 64 144–47

Gen-Probe Incorporated, 79 185–88

Gencor Ltd., IV 90–93; 22 233–37 (upd.) *see also* Gold Fields Ltd.

GenCorp Inc., 9 247–49

Genentech, Inc., I 637–38; 8 209–11 (upd.); 32 211–15 (upd.); 75 154–58 (upd.)

General Accident plc, III 256–57 *see also* Aviva PLC.

General Atomics, 57 151–54

General Bearing Corporation, 45 169–71

General Binding Corporation, 10 313–14; 73 159–62 (upd.)

General Cable Corporation, 40 200–03

The General Chemical Group Inc., 37 157–60

General Cigar Holdings, Inc., 66 139–42 (upd.)

General Cinema Corporation, I 245–46 *see also* GC Companies, Inc.

General DataComm Industries, Inc., 14 200–02

General Dynamics Corporation, I 57–60; 10 315–18 (upd.); 40 204–10 (upd.); 88 105–13 (upd.)

General Electric Company, II 27–31; 12 193–97 (upd.); 34 183–90 (upd.); 63 159–68 (upd.)

General Electric Company, PLC, II 24–26 *see also* Marconi plc.

General Employment Enterprises, Inc., 87 172–175

General Growth Properties, Inc., 57 155–57

General Host Corporation, 12 198–200

General Housewares Corporation, 16 234–36

General Instrument Corporation, 10 319–21 *see also* Motorola, Inc.

General Maritime Corporation, 59 197–99

General Mills, Inc., II 501–03; 10 322–24 (upd.); 36 234–39 (upd.); 85 141–49 (upd.)

General Motors Corporation, I 171–73; 10 325–27 (upd.); 36 240–44 (upd.); 64 148–53 (upd.)

General Nutrition Companies, Inc., 11 155–57; 29 210–14 (upd.) *see also* GNC Corp.

General Public Utilities Corporation, V 629–31 *see also* GPU, Inc.

General Re Corporation, III 258–59; 24 176–78 (upd.)

General Sekiyu K.K., IV 431–33 *see also* TonenGeneral Sekiyu K.K.

General Signal Corporation, 9 250–52 *see also* SPX Corp.

General Tire, Inc., 8 212–14

Generale Bank, II 294–95 *see also* Fortis, Inc.

Générale des Eaux Group, V 632–34 *see* Vivendi Universal S.A.

Generali *see* Assicurazioni Generali.

Genesco Inc., 17 202–06; 84 143–149 (upd.)

Genesee & Wyoming Inc., 27 179–81

Genesis Health Ventures, Inc., 18 195–97 *see also* NeighborCare,Inc.

Genesis Microchip Inc., 82 133–37

Genetics Institute, Inc., 8 215–18

Geneva Steel, 7 193–95

Genmar Holdings, Inc., 45 172–75

Genovese Drug Stores, Inc., 18 198–200

Genoyer *see* Groupe Genoyer.

GenRad, Inc., 24 179–83

Gentex Corporation, 26 153–57

Genting Bhd., 65 152–55

Gentiva Health Services, Inc., 79 189–92

Genuardi's Family Markets, Inc., 35 190–92

Genuine Parts Company, 9 253–55; 45 176–79 (upd.)

Genzyme Corporation, 13 239–42; 38 203–07 (upd.); 77 164–70 (upd.)

geobra Brandstätter GmbH & Co. KG, 48 183–86

Geodis S.A., 67 187–90

The Geon Company, 11 158–61

Georg Fischer AG Schaffhausen, 61 106–09

George A. Hormel and Company, II 504–06 *see also* Hormel Foods Corp.

The George F. Cram Company, Inc., 55 158–60

George P. Johnson Company, 60 142–44

George S. May International Company, 55 161–63

George W. Park Seed Company, Inc., 98 145–48

George Weston Ltd., II 631–32; 36 245–48 (upd.); 88 114–19 (upd.)

George Wimpey plc, 12 201–03; 51 135–38 (upd.)

Georgia Gulf Corporation, 9 256–58; 61 110–13 (upd.)

Georgia-Pacific Corporation, IV 281–83; 9 259–62 (upd.); 47 145–51 (upd.)

Geotek Communications Inc., 21 238–40

Gerald Stevens, Inc., 37 161–63

Gerber Products Company, 7 196–98; 21 241–44 (upd)

Gerber Scientific, Inc., 12 204–06; 84 150–154 (upd.)

Gerdau S.A., 59 200–03

Gerhard D. Wempe KG, 88 120–25

Gericom AG, 47 152–54

Gerling-Konzern Versicherungs-Beteiligungs-Aktiengesellschaft, 51 139–43

German American Bancorp, 41 178–80

Gerresheimer Glas AG, 43 186–89

Gerry Weber International AG, 63 169–72

Gesellschaft für musikalische Aufführungs-und mechanische Vervielfältigungsrechte *see* GEMA.

Getrag Corporate Group, 92 137–42

Getronics NV, 39 176–78

Getty Images, Inc., 31 216–18

Gevaert *see* Agfa Gevaert Group N.V.

Gévelot S.A., 96 132–35

Gevity HR, Inc., 63 173–77

GF Health Products, Inc., 82 138–41

GFI Informatique SA, 49 165–68

GfK Aktiengesellschaft, 49 169–72

GFS *see* Gordon Food Service Inc.

Ghirardelli Chocolate Company, 30 218–20

Gianni Versace SpA, 22 238–40

Giant Cement Holding, Inc., 23 224–26

Giant Eagle, Inc., 86 160–64

Giant Food LLC, II 633–35; 22 241–44 (upd.); 83 155–161 (upd.)

Giant Industries, Inc., 19 175–77; 61 114–18 (upd.)

Giant Manufacturing Company, Ltd., 85 150–54

GIB Group, V 63–66; 26 158–62 (upd.)

Gibbs and Dandy plc, 74 119–21

Gibraltar Steel Corporation, 37 164–67

Gibson, Dunn & Crutcher LLP, 36 249–52

Gibson Greetings, Inc., 12 207–10 *see also* American Greetings Corp.

Gibson Guitar Corp., 16 237–40

Giddings & Lewis, Inc., 10 328–30

GiFi S.A., 74 122–24

Gilbane, Inc., 34 191–93

Gildan Activewear, Inc., 81 165–68

Gildemeister AG, 79 193–97

Gilead Sciences, Inc., 54 129–31

Gillett Holdings, Inc., 7 199–201

The Gillette Company, III 27–30; 20 249–53 (upd.); 68 171–76 (upd.)

Gilman & Ciocia, Inc., 72 148–50

Ginnie Mae *see* Government National Mortgage Association.

Giorgio Armani S.p.A., 45 180–83

Girl Scouts of the USA, 35 193–96

Giesecke & Devrient GmbH, 83 162-166

The Gitano Group, Inc., 8 219–21

GIV *see* Granite Industries of Vermont, Inc.

Givaudan SA, 43 190–93

Given Imaging Ltd., 83 167-170

GKN plc, III 493–96; 38 208–13 (upd.); 89 232–41 (upd.)

Glaces Thiriet S.A., 76 164–66

Glacier Bancorp, Inc., 35 197–200

Glacier Water Services, Inc., 47 155–58

Glamis Gold, Ltd., 54 132–35

Glanbia plc, 59 204–07, 364

Glatfelter Wood Pulp Company *see* P.H. Glatfelter Company

Glaverbel Group, 80 130–33

Glaxo Holdings plc, I 639–41; 9 263–65 (upd.)

GlaxoSmithKline plc, 46 201–08 (upd.)

Glazer's Wholesale Drug Company, Inc., 82 142–45

Gleason Corporation, 24 184–87

Glen Dimplex, 78 123–27

Glico *see* Ezaki Glico Company Ltd.

The Glidden Company, 8 222–24

Global Berry Farms LLC, 62 154–56

Global Crossing Ltd., 32 216–19

Global Hyatt Corporation, 75 159–63 (upd.)

Global Imaging Systems, Inc., 73 163–65

Global Industries, Ltd., 37 168–72

Global Marine Inc., 9 266–67

Global Outdoors, Inc., 49 173–76

Global Payments Inc., 91 206–10
Global Power Equipment Group Inc., 52 137–39
GlobalSantaFe Corporation, 48 187–92 (upd.)
Globo Comunicação e Participações S.A., 80 134–38
Glock Ges.m.b.H., 42 154–56
Glon see Groupe Glon.
Glotel plc, 53 149–51
Glu Mobile Inc., 95 163–66
Gluek Brewing Company, 75 164–66
GM see General Motors Corp.
GM Hughes Electronics Corporation, II 32–36 see also Hughes Electronics Corp.
GMH Communities Trust, 87 176–178
GNC Corporation, 98 149–55 (upd.)
GNMA see Government National Mortgage Association.
The Go-Ahead Group Plc, 28 155–57
Go Sport see Groupe Go Sport S.A.
Go-Video, Inc. see Sensory Science Corp.
Godfather's Pizza Incorporated, 25 179–81
Godiva Chocolatier, Inc., 64 154–57
Goetze's Candy Company, Inc., 87 179–182
Gol Linhas Aéreas Inteligentes S.A., 73 166–68
Gold Fields Ltd., IV 94–97; 62 157–64 (upd.)
Gold Kist Inc., 17 207–09; 26 166–68 (upd.) see also Pilgrim's Pride Corp.
Gold'n Plump Poultry, 54 136–38
Gold's Gym International, Inc., 71 165–68
Goldcorp Inc., 87 183–186
Golden Belt Manufacturing Co., 16 241–43
Golden Books Family Entertainment, Inc., 28 158–61 see also Random House, Inc.
Golden Corral Corporation, 10 331–33; 66 143–46 (upd.)
Golden Enterprises, Inc., 26 163–65
Golden Krust Caribbean Bakery, Inc., 68 177–79
Golden State Foods Corporation, 32 220–22
Golden State Vintners, Inc., 33 172–74
Golden Telecom, Inc., 59 208–11
Golden West Financial Corporation, 47 159–61
The Goldman Sachs Group Inc., II 414–16; 20 254–57 (upd.); 51 144–48 (upd.)
Goldstar Co., Ltd., 12 211–13 see also LG Corp.
Golin/Harris International, Inc., 88 126–30
Golub Corporation, 26 169–71; 96 136–39 (upd.)
GOME Electrical Appliances Holding Ltd., 87 187–191
Gonnella Baking Company, 40 211–13
The Good Guys!, Inc., 10 334–35; 30 224–27 (upd.)

The Good Humor-Breyers Ice Cream Company, 14 203–05 see also Unilever PLC.
Goodby Silverstein & Partners, Inc., 75 167–69
Goodman Fielder Ltd., 52 140–43
Goodman Holding Company, 42 157–60
GoodMark Foods, Inc., 26 172–74
Goodrich Corporation, 46 209–13 (upd.)
GoodTimes Entertainment Ltd., 48 193–95
Goodwill Industries International, Inc., 16 244–46; 66 147–50 (upd.)
Goody Products, Inc., 12 214–16
Goody's Family Clothing, Inc., 20 265–67; 64 158–61 (upd.)
The Goodyear Tire & Rubber Company, V 244–48; 20 259–64 (upd.); 75 170–78 (upd.)
Google, Inc., 50 204–07
Gordmans, Inc., 74 125–27
Gordon Biersch Brewery Restaurant Group,Inc., 92229–32
Gordon Food Service Inc., 8 225–27; 39 179–82 (upd.)
The Gorman-Rupp Company, 18 201–03; 57 158–61 (upd.)
Gorton's, 13 243–44
Gosling Brothers Ltd., 82 146–49
Goss Holdings, Inc., 43 194–97
Gottschalks, Inc., 18 204–06; 91 211–15 (upd.)
Gould Electronics, Inc., 14 206–08
Gould Paper Corporation, 82 150–53
Goulds Pumps Inc., 24 188–91
The Governor and Company of the Bank of Scotland, 10 336–38
Goya Foods Inc., 22 245–47; 91 216–21 (upd.)
GP Strategies Corporation, 64 162–66 (upd.)
GPS Industries, Inc., 81 169–72
GPU see General Public Utilities Corp.
GPU, Inc., 27 182–85 (upd.)
Grace see W.R. Grace & Co.
GraceKennedy Ltd., 92 143–47
Graco Inc., 19 178–80; 67 191–95 (upd.)
Gradall Industries, Inc., 96 140–43
Graeter's Manufacturing Company, 86 165–68
Graham Corporation, 62 165–67
Graham Packaging Holdings Company, 87 192–196
Grampian Country Food Group, Ltd., 85 155–59
Grameen Bank, 31 219–22
Granada Group PLC, II 138–40; 24 192–95 (upd.)
Granaria Holdings B.V., 66 151–53
GranCare, Inc., 14 209–11
Grand Casinos, Inc., 20 268–70
Grand Hotel Krasnapolsky N.V., 23 227–29
Grand Metropolitan plc, I 247–49; 14 212–15 (upd.) see also Diageo plc.

Grand Piano & Furniture Company, 72 151–53
Grand Traverse Pie Company, 98 156–59
Grand Union Company, 7 202–04; 28 162–65 (upd.)
Grandoe Corporation, 98 160–63
Grands Vins Jean-Claude Boisset S.A., 98 164–67
GrandVision S.A., 43 198–200
Granite Broadcasting Corporation, 42 161–64
Granite City Food & Brewery Ltd., 94 214–17
Granite Construction Incorporated, 61 119–21
Granite Industries of Vermont, Inc., 73 169–72
Granite Rock Company, 26 175–78
Granite State Bankshares, Inc., 37 173–75
Grant Prideco, Inc., 57 162–64
Grant Thornton International, 57 165–67
Graphic Industries Inc., 25 182–84
Graphic Packaging Holding Company, 96 144–50 (upd.)
Gray Communications Systems, Inc., 24 196–200
Graybar Electric Company, Inc., 54 139–42
Great American Management and Investment, Inc., 8 228–31
The Great Atlantic & Pacific Tea Company, Inc., II 636–38; 16 247–50 (upd.); 55 164–69 (upd.)
Great Harvest Bread Company, 44 184–86
Great Lakes Bancorp, 8 232–33
Great Lakes Chemical Corp., I 341–42; 14 216–18 (upd.) see also Chemtura Corp.
Great Lakes Dredge & Dock Company, 69 194–97
Great Plains Energy Incorporated, 65 156–60 (upd.)
The Great Universal Stores plc, V 67–69; 19 181–84 (upd.) see also GUS plc.
Great-West Lifeco Inc., III 260–61 see also Power Corporation of Canada.
Great Western Financial Corporation, 10 339–41 see also Washington Mutual, Inc.
Great White Shark Enterprises, Inc., 89 242–45
Great Wolf Resorts, Inc., 91 222–26
Greatbatch Inc., 72 154–56
Grede Foundries, Inc., 38 214–17
Greek Organization of Football Prognostics S.A. (OPAP), 97 182–85
The Green Bay Packers, Inc., 32 223–26
Green Dot Public Schools, 99 186–189
Green Mountain Coffee, Inc., 31 227–30
Green Tree Financial Corporation, 11 162–63 see also Conseco, Inc.
The Greenalls Group PLC, 21 245–47

Greenberg Traurig, LLP, 65 161–63
The Greenbrier Companies, 19 185–87
Greencore Group plc, 98 168–71
Greene King plc, 31 223–26
Greene, Tweed & Company, 55 170–72
GreenMan Technologies Inc., 99 190–193
Greenpeace International, 74 128–30
GreenPoint Financial Corp., 28 166–68
Greenwood Mills, Inc., 14 219–21
Greg Manning Auctions, Inc., 60 145–46
Greggs PLC, 65 164–66
Greif Inc., 15 186–88; 66 154–56 (upd.)
Grévin & Compagnie SA, 56 143–45
Grey Global Group Inc., 6 26–28; 66 157–61 (upd.)
Grey Wolf, Inc., 43 201–03
Greyhound Lines, Inc., I 448–50; 32 227–31 (upd.)
Griffin Industries, Inc., 70 106–09
Griffin Land & Nurseries, Inc., 43 204–06
Griffon Corporation, 34 194–96
Grill Concepts, Inc., 74 131–33
Grinnell Corp., 13 245–47
Grist Mill Company, 15 189–91
Gristede's Foods Inc., 68 31 231–33; 180–83 (upd.)
Grohe *see* Friedrich Grohe AG & Co. KG.
Grolier Inc., 16 251–54; 43 207–11 (upd.)
Grolsch *see* Royal Grolsch NV.
Grossman's Inc., 13 248–50
Ground Round, Inc., 21 248–51
Group 4 Falck A/S, 42 165–68
Group Health Cooperative, 41 181–84
Group 1 Automotive, Inc., 52 144–46
Groupama S.A., 76 167–70
Groupe Air France, 6 92–94 *see also* Societe Air France.
Groupe Alain Manoukian, 55 173–75
Groupe André, 17 210–12 *see also* Vivarte SA.
Groupe Bolloré, 67 196–99
Groupe Bourbon S.A., 60 147–49
Groupe Bigard S.A., 96 151–54
Groupe Bull *see* Compagnie des Machines Bull.
Groupe Casino *see* Casino Guichard-Perrachon S.A.
Groupe Castorama-Dubois Investissements, 23 230–32 *see also* Kingfisher plc.
Groupe CECAB S.C.A., 88 131–34
Groupe Crit S.A., 74 134–36
Groupe Danone, 32 232–36 (upd.); 93 233–40 (upd.)
Groupe Dassault Aviation SA, 26 179–82 (upd.)
Groupe de la Cité, IV 614–16
Groupe DMC (Dollfus Mieg & Cie), 27 186–88
Groupe Euralis, 86 169–72
Groupe Flo S.A., 98 172–75
Groupe Fournier SA, 44 187–89
Groupe Genoyer, 96 155–58

Groupe Glon, 84 155–158
Groupe Go Sport S.A., 39 183–85
Groupe Guillin SA, 40 214–16
Groupe Herstal S.A., 58 145–48
Groupe Jean-Claude Darmon, 44 190–92
Groupe Lactalis, 78 128–32 (upd.)
Groupe Lapeyre S.A., 33 175–77
Groupe LDC *see* L.D.C. S.A.
Groupe Le Duff S.A., 84 159–162
Groupe Léa Nature, 88 135–38
Groupe Legris Industries, 23 233–35
Groupe Les Echos, 25 283–85
Groupe Limagrain, 74 137–40
Groupe Louis Dreyfus S.A., 60 150–53
Groupe Monnoyeur, 72 157–59
Groupe Open, 74 141–43
Groupe Partouche SA, 48 196–99
Groupe Pinault-Printemps-Redoute *see* Pinault-Printemps-Redoute S.A.
Groupe Promodès S.A., 19 326–28
Groupe Rougier SA, 21 438–40
Groupe SEB, 35 201–03
Groupe Sidel S.A., 21 252–55
Groupe Soufflet SA, 55 176–78
Groupe Vidéotron Ltée., 20 271–73
Groupe Yves Saint Laurent, 23 236–39 *see also* Gucci Group N.V.
Groupe Zannier S.A., 35 204–07
Grow Biz International, Inc., 18 207–10 *see also* Winmark Corp.
Grow Group Inc., 12 217–19
GROWMARK, Inc., 88 139–42
Groz-Beckert Group, 68 184–86
Grubb & Ellis Company, 21 256–58; 98 176–80 (upd.)
Gruma, S.A. de C.V., 31 234–36
Grumman Corp., I 61–63; 11 164–67 (upd.) *see aslo* Northrop Grumman Corp.
Grunau Company Inc., 90 209–12
Grundfos Group, 83 171-174
Grundig AG, 27 189–92
Gruntal & Co., L.L.C., 20 274–76
Grupo Aeroportuario del Centro Norte, S.A.B. de C.V., 97 186–89
Grupo Aeroportuario del Pacífico, S.A. de C.V., 85 160–63
Grupo Aeropuerto del Sureste, S.A. de C.V., 48 200–02
Grupo Ángeles Servicios de Salud, S.A. de C.V., 84 163–166
Grupo Bufete *see* Bufete Industrial, S.A. de C.V.
Grupo Brescia, 99 194–197
Grupo Carso, S.A. de C.V., 21 259–61
Grupo Casa Saba, S.A. de C.V., 39 186–89
Grupo Clarín S.A., 67 200–03
Grupo Comercial Chedraui S.A. de C.V., 86 173–76
Grupo Corvi S.A. de C.V., 86 177–80
Grupo Cydsa, S.A. de C.V., 39 190–93
Grupo Dina *see* Consorcio G Grupo Dina, S.A. de C.V.
Grupo Dragados SA, 55 179–82
Grupo Elektra, S.A. de C.V., 39 194–97
Grupo Eroski, 64 167–70

Grupo Ferrovial, S.A., 40 217–19
Grupo Ficosa International, 90 213–16
Grupo Financiero Banamex S.A., 54 143–46
Grupo Financiero Banorte, S.A. de C.V., 51 149–51
Grupo Financiero BBVA Bancomer S.A., 54 147–50
Grupo Financiero Galicia S.A., 63 178–81
Grupo Financiero Serfin, S.A., 19 188–90
Grupo Gigante, S.A. de C.V., 34 197–99
Grupo Herdez, S.A. de C.V., 35 208–10
Grupo IMSA, S.A. de C.V., 44 193–96
Grupo Industrial Bimbo, 19 191–93
Grupo Industrial Durango, S.A. de C.V., 37 176–78
Grupo Industrial Herradura, S.A. de C.V., 83 175-178
Grupo Industrial Lala, S.A. de C.V., 82 154–57
Grupo Industrial Saltillo, S.A. de C.V., 54 151–54
Grupo Leche Pascual S.A., 59 212–14
Grupo Lladró S.A., 52 147–49
Grupo Mexico, S.A. de C.V., 40 220–23
Grupo Modelo, S.A. de C.V., 29 218–20
Grupo Omnilife S.A. de C.V., 88 143–46
Grupo Planeta, 94 218–22
Grupo Portucel Soporcel, 60 154–56
Grupo Posadas, S.A. de C.V., 57 168–70
Grupo TACA, 38 218–20
Grupo Televisa, S.A., 18 211–14; 54 155–58 (upd.)
Grupo TMM, S.A. de C.V., 50 208–11
Grupo Transportación Ferroviaria Mexicana, S.A. de C.V., 47 162–64
Grupo Viz, S.A. de C.V., 84 167–170
Gruppo Coin S.p.A., 41 185–87
Gruppo Riva Fire SpA, 88 147–50
Gryphon Holdings, Inc., 21 262–64
GSC Enterprises, Inc., 86 181–84
GSD&M Advertising, 44 197–200
GSD&M's Idea City, 90 217–21
GSG&T, Inc. *see* Gulf States Utilities Co.
GSI Commerce, Inc., 67 204–06
GSU *see* Gulf States Utilities Co.
GT Bicycles, 26 183–85
GT Interactive Software, 31 237–41 *see also* Infogrames Entertainment S.A.
GTE Corporation, V 294–98; 15 192–97 (upd.) *see also* British Columbia Telephone Company; Verizon Communications.
GTSI Corp., 57 171–73
Guangzhou Pearl River Piano Group Ltd., 49 177–79
Guangzhou R&F Properties Co., Ltd., 95 167–69
Guardian Financial Services, 11 168–70; 64 171–74 (upd.)
Guardian Industries Corp., 87 197–204
Guardian Media Group plc, 53 152–55
Guardsmark, L.L.C., 77 171–74
Gucci Group N.V., 15 198–200; 50 212–16 (upd.)

Guenther *see* C.H. Guenther & Son, Inc.
Guerbet Group, 46 214–16
Guerlain, 23 240–42
Guess, Inc., 15 201–03; 68 187–91 (upd.)
Guest Supply, Inc., 18 215–17
Guida-Seibert Dairy Company, 84 171–174
Guidant Corporation, 58 149–51
Guilbert S.A., 42 169–71
Guilford Mills Inc., 8 234–36; 40 224–27 (upd.)
Guillemot Corporation, 41 188–91, 407, 409
Guillin *see* Groupe Guillin SA
Guinness/UDV, I 250–52; 43 212–16 (upd.) *see also* Diageo plc.
Guinot Paris S.A., 82 158–61
Guitar Center, Inc., 29 221–23; 68 192–95 (upd.)
Guittard Chocolate Company, 55 183–85
Gulf + Western Inc., I 451–53 *see also* Paramount Communications; Viacom Inc.
Gulf Air Company, 56 146–48
Gulf Agency Company Ltd., 78 133–36
Gulf Island Fabrication, Inc., 44 201–03
Gulf States Utilities Company, 6 495–97 *see also* Entergy Corp.
GulfMark Offshore, Inc., 49 180–82
Gulfstream Aerospace Corporation, 7 205–06; 28 169–72 (upd.)
Gund, Inc., 96 159–62
Gunite Corporation, 51 152–55
The Gunlocke Company, 23 243–45
Gunnebo AB, 53 156–58
GUS plc, 47 165–70 (upd.)
Guthy-Renker Corporation, 32 237–40
Guttenplan's Frozen Dough Inc., 88 151–54
Guy Degrenne SA, 44 204–07
Guyenne et Gascogne, 23 246–48
Gwathmey Siegel & Associates Architects LLC, 26 186–88
GWR Group plc, 39 198–200
Gymboree Corporation, 15 204–06; 69 198–201 (upd.)

H
H&R Block, Inc., 9 268–70; 29 224–28 (upd.); 82 162–69 (upd.)
H&M Hennes & Mauritz AB, 98 181–84 (upd.)
H.B. Fuller Company, 8 237–40; 32 254–58 (upd.); 75 179–84 (upd.)
H. Betti Industries Inc., 88 155–58
H.D. Vest, Inc., 46 217–19
H. E. Butt Grocery Company, 13 251–53; 32 259–62 (upd.); 85 164–70 (upd.)
H.F. Ahmanson & Company, II 181–82; 10 342–44 (upd.) *see also* Washington Mutual, Inc.
H. J. Heinz Company, II 507–09; 11 171–73 (upd.); 36 253–57 (upd.); 99 198–205 (upd.)

H.J. Russell & Company, 66 162–65
H. Lundbeck A/S, 44 208–11
H.M. Payson & Co., 69 202–04
H.O. Penn Machinery Company, Inc., 96 163–66
H-P *see* Hewlett-Packard Co.
The H.W. Wilson Company, 66 166–68
Ha-Lo Industries, Inc., 27 193–95
The Haartz Corporation, 94 223–26
Habersham Bancorp, 25 185–87
Habitat for Humanity International, 36 258–61
Hach Co., 18 218–21
Hachette Filipacchi Medias S.A., 21 265–67
Hachette S.A., IV 617–19 *see also* Matra-Hachette S.A.
Haci Omer Sabanci Holdings A.S., 55 186–89 *see also* Akbank TAS
Hackman Oyj Adp, 44 212–15
Hadco Corporation, 24 201–03
Haeger Industries Inc., 88 159–62
Haemonetics Corporation, 20 277–79
Haftpflichtverband der Deutschen Industrie Versicherung auf Gegenseitigkeit V.a.G. *see* HDI (Haftpflichtverband der Deutschen Industrie Versicherung auf Gegenseitigkeit V.a.G.).
Hagemeyer N.V., 39 201–04
Haggar Corporation, 19 194–96; 78 137–41 (upd.)
Haggen Inc., 38 221–23
Hagoromo Foods Corporation, 84 175–178
Hahn Automotive Warehouse, Inc., 24 204–06
Haier Group Corporation, 65 167–70
Haights Cross Communications, Inc., 84 179–182
The Hain Celestial Group, Inc., 27 196–98; 43 217–20 (upd.)
Hair Club For Men Ltd., 90 222–25
Hakuhodo, Inc., 6 29–31; 42 172–75 (upd.)
HAL Inc., 9 271–73 *see also* Hawaiian Airlines, Inc.
Hal Leonard Corporation, 96 167–71
Hale-Halsell Company, 60 157–60
Half Price Books, Records, Magazines Inc., 37 179–82
Hall, Kinion & Associates, Inc., 52 150–52
Halliburton Company, III 497–500; 25 188–92 (upd.); 55 190–95 (upd.)
Hallmark Cards, Inc., IV 620–21; 16 255–57 (upd.); 40 228–32 (upd.); 87 205–212 (upd.)
Hamilton Beach/Proctor-Silex Inc., 17 213–15
Hammacher Schlemmer & Company Inc., 21 268–70; 72 160–62 (upd.)
Hammerson plc, IV 696–98; 40 233–35 (upd.)
Hammond Manufacturing Company Limited, 83 179–182
Hamon & Cie (International) S.A., 97 190–94

Hamot Health Foundation, 91 227–32
Hampton Affiliates, Inc., 77 175–79
Hampton Industries, Inc., 20 280–82
Hampshire Group Ltd., 82 170–73
Hancock Fabrics, Inc., 18 222–24
Hancock Holding Company, 15 207–09
Handleman Company, 15 210–12; 86 185–89 (upd.)
Handspring Inc., 49 183–86
Handy & Harman, 23 249–52
Hanesbrands Inc., 98 185–88
Hang Seng Bank Ltd., 60 161–63
Hanger Orthopedic Group, Inc., 41 192–95
Hanjin Shipping Co., Ltd., 50 217–21
Hankyu Corporation, V 454–56; 23 253–56 (upd.)
Hankyu Department Stores, Inc., V 70–71; 62 168–71 (upd.)
Hanmi Financial Corporation, 66 169–71
Hanna Andersson Corp., 49 187–90
Hanna-Barbera Cartoons Inc., 23 257–59, 387
Hannaford Bros. Co., 12 220–22
Hanover Compressor Company, 59 215–17
Hanover Direct, Inc., 36 262–65
Hanover Foods Corporation, 35 211–14
Hansen Natural Corporation, 31 242–45; 76 171–74 (upd.)
Hansgrohe AG, 56 149–52
Hanson Building Materials America Inc., 60 164–66
Hanson PLC, III 501–03; 7 207–10 (upd.); 30 228–32 (upd.)
Hanwha Group, 62 172–75
Hapag-Lloyd AG, 6 397–99; 97 195–203 (upd.)
Happy Kids Inc., 30 233–35
Harbert Corporation, 14 222–23
Harbison-Walker Refractories Company, 24 207–09
Harbour Group Industries, Inc., 90 226–29
Harcourt Brace and Co., 12 223–26
Harcourt Brace Jovanovich, Inc., IV 622–24
Harcourt General, Inc., 20 283–87 (upd.)
Hard Rock Cafe International, Inc., 12 227–29; 32 241–45 (upd.)
Harding Lawson Associates Group, Inc., 16 258–60
Hardinge Inc., 25 193–95
HARIBO GmbH & Co. KG, 44 216–19
Harkins Amusement Enterprises, Inc., 94 227–31
Harland and Wolff Holdings plc, 19 197–200
Harland Clarke Holdings Corporation, 94 232–35 (upd.)
Harlem Globetrotters International, Inc., 61 122–24
Harlequin Enterprises Limited, 52 153–56
Harley-Davidson, Inc., 7 211–14; 25 196–200 (upd.)

Harleysville Group Inc., 37 183–86

Harman International Industries Inc., 15 213–15

Harmon Industries, Inc., 25 201–04 *see also* General Electric Co.

Harmonic Inc., 43 221–23

Harmony Gold Mining Company Limited, 63 182–85

Harnischfeger Industries, Inc., 8 241–44; 38 224–28 (upd.)

Harold's Stores, Inc., 22 248–50

Harper Group Inc., 17 216–19

HarperCollins Publishers, 15 216–18

Harpo Inc., 28 173–75; 66 172–75 (upd.)

Harps Food Stores, Inc., 99 206–209

Harrah's Entertainment, Inc., 16 261–63; 43 224–28 (upd.)

Harris Corporation, II 37–39; 20 288–92 (upd.); 78 142–48 (upd.)

Harris Interactive Inc., 41 196–99; 92 148–53 (upd.)

Harris Publishing *see* Bernard C. Harris Publishing Company, Inc.

The Harris Soup Company (Harry's Fresh Foods), 92 154–157

Harris Teeter Inc., 23 260–62; 72 163–66 (upd.)

Harrisons & Crosfield plc, III 696–700 *see also* Elementis plc.

Harrods Holdings, 47 171–74

Harry London Candies, Inc., 70 110–12

Harry N. Abrams, Inc., 58 152–55

Harry Winston Inc., 45 184–87

Harry's Farmers Market Inc., 23 263–66 *see also* Whole Foods Market, Inc.

Harry's Fresh Foods *see* The Harris Soup Company (Harry's Fresh Foods)

Harsco Corporation, 8 245–47 *see also* United Defense Industries, Inc.

Harte-Hanks Communications, Inc., 17 220–22; 63 186–89 (upd.)

Hartmann Inc., 96 172–76

Hartmarx Corporation, 8 248–50; 32 246–50 (upd.)

The Hartstone Group plc, 14 224–26

The Hartz Mountain Corporation, 12 230–32; 46 220–23 (upd.)

Harvey Norman Holdings Ltd., 56 153–55

Harveys Casino Resorts, 27 199–201 *see also* Harrah's Entertainment, Inc.

Harza Engineering Company, 14 227–28

Hasbro, Inc., III 504–06; 16 264–68 (upd.); 43 229–34 (upd.)

Haskel International, Inc., 59 218–20

Hastings Entertainment, Inc., 29 229–31

Hastings Manufacturing Company, 56 156–58

Hauser, Inc., 46 224–27

Havas, SA, 10 345–48; 33 178–82 (upd.) *see also* Vivendi Universal Publishing

Haverty Furniture Companies, Inc., 31 246–49

Hawaiian Airlines Inc., 22 251–53 (upd.) *see also* HAL Inc.

Hawaiian Electric Industries, Inc., 9 274–77

Hawaiian Holdings, Inc., 96 177–81 (upd.)

Hawk Corporation, 59 221–23

Hawker Siddeley Group Public Limited Company, III 507–10

Hawkeye Holdings LLC, 86 246–49

Hawkins Chemical, Inc., 16 269–72

Haworth Inc., 8 251–52; 39 205–08 (upd.)

Hay House, Inc., 93 241–45

Hayel Saeed Anam Group of Cos., 92 158–61

Hayes Corporation, 24 210–14

Hayes Lemmerz International, Inc., 27 202–04

Haynes International, Inc., 88 163–66

Haynes Publishing Group P.L.C., 71 169–71

Hays plc, 27 205–07; 78 149–53 (upd.)

Hazelden Foundation, 28 176–79

Hazlewood Foods plc, 32 251–53

HBO *see* Home Box Office Inc.

HCA—The Healthcare Company, 35 215–18 (upd.)

HCI Direct, Inc., 55 196–98

HDI (Haftpflichtverband der Deutschen Industrie Versicherung auf Gegenseitigkeit V.a.G.), 53 159–63

HDOS Enterprises, 72 167–69

HDR Inc., 48 203–05

Head N.V., 55 199–201

Headlam Group plc, 95 170–73

Headwaters Incorporated, 56 159–62

Headway Corporate Resources, Inc., 40 236–38

Health Care & Retirement Corporation, 22 254–56

Health Communications, Inc., 72 170–73

Health Management Associates, Inc., 56 163–65

Health O Meter Products Inc., 14 229–31

Health Risk Management, Inc., 24 215–17

Health Systems International, Inc., 11 174–76

HealthExtras, Inc., 75 185–87

HealthMarkets, Inc., 88 167–72 (upd.)

HealthSouth Corporation, 14 232–34; 33 183–86 (upd.)

Healthtex, Inc., 17 223–25 *see also* VF Corp.

The Hearst Corporation, IV 625–27; 19 201–04 (upd.); 46 228–32 (upd.)

Heartland Express, Inc., 18 225–27

The Heat Group, 53 164–66

Hechinger Company, 12 233–36

Hecla Mining Company, 20 293–96

Heekin Can Inc., 13 254–56 *see also* Ball Corp.

Heelys, Inc., 87 213–216

Heery International, Inc., 58 156–59

HEICO Corporation, 30 236–38

Heidelberger Druckmaschinen AG, 40 239–41

Heidelberger Zement AG, 31 250–53

Heidrick & Struggles International, Inc., 28 180–82

Heijmans N.V., 66 176–78

Heileman Brewing Co *see* G. Heileman Brewing Co.

Heilig-Meyers Company, 14 235–37; 40 242–46 (upd.)

Heineken N.V., I 256–58; 13 257–59 (upd.); 34 200–04 (upd.); 90 230–36 (upd.)

Heinrich Deichmann-Schuhe GmbH & Co. KG, 88 173–77

Heinz Co *see* H.J. Heinz Co.

Helen of Troy Corporation, 18 228–30

Helene Curtis Industries, Inc., 8 253–54; 28 183–85 (upd.) *see also* Unilever PLC.

Helix Energy Solutions Group, Inc., 81 173–77

Hella KGaA Hueck & Co., 66 179–83

Hellenic Petroleum SA, 64 175–77

Heller, Ehrman, White & McAuliffe, 41 200–02

Helly Hansen ASA, 25 205–07

Helmerich & Payne, Inc., 18 231–33

Helmsley Enterprises, Inc., 9 278–80; 39 209–12 (upd.)

Helzberg Diamonds, 40 247–49

Hemisphere GPS Inc., 99 210–213

Hemlo Gold Mines Inc., 9 281–82 *see also* Newmont Mining Corp.

Henderson Land Development Company Ltd., 70 113–15

Hendrick Motorsports, Inc., 89 250–53

Henkel KGaA, III 31–34; 34 205–10 (upd.); 95 174–83 (upd.)

Henkel Manco Inc., 22 257–59

The Henley Group, Inc., III 511–12

Hennes & Mauritz AB, 29 232–34 *see also* H&M Hennes & Mauritz AB

Henry Boot plc, 76 175–77

Henry Crown and Company, 91 233–36

Henry Dreyfuss Associates LLC, 88 178–82

Henry Ford Health System, 84 183–187

Henry Modell & Company Inc., 32 263–65

Henry Schein, Inc., 31 254–56; 70 116–19 (upd.)

Hensel Phelps Construction Company, 72 174–77

Hensley & Company, 64 178–80

HEPCO *see* Hokkaido Electric Power Company Inc.

Her Majesty's Stationery Office, 7 215–18

Heraeus Holding GmbH, IV 98–100; 54 159–63 (upd.)

Herald Media, Inc., 91 237–41

Herbalife Ltd., 17 226–29; 41 203–06 (upd.); 92 162–67 (upd.)

Hercules Inc., I 343–45; 22 260–63 (upd.); 66 184–88 (upd.)

Hercules Technology Growth Capital, Inc., 87 217–220

Herley Industries, Inc., 33 187–89

Herman Goelitz, Inc., 28 186–88 *see also* Jelly Belly Candy Co.

Herman Miller, Inc., 8 255–57; 77 180–86 (upd.)

Hermès International S.A., 14 238–40; 34 211–14 (upd.)

Héroux-Devtek Inc., 69 205–07

Herr Foods Inc., 84 188–191

Herradura *see* Grupo Industrial Herradura, S.A. de C.V.

Herschend Family Entertainment Corporation, 73 173–76

Hershey Foods Corporation, II 510–12; 15 219–22 (upd.); 51 156–60 (upd.)

Herstal *see* Groupe Herstal S.A.

Hertie Waren- und Kaufhaus GmbH, V 72–74

The Hertz Corporation, 9 283–85; 33 190–93 (upd.)

Heska Corporation, 39 213–16

Heublein Inc., I 259–61

Heuer *see* TAG Heuer International SA.

Hewitt Associates, Inc., 77 187–90

Hewlett-Packard Company, III 142–43; 6 237–39 (upd.); 28 189–92 (upd.); 50 222–30 (upd.)

Hexal AG, 69 208–10

Hexagon AB, 78 154–57

Hexcel Corporation, 28 193–95

hhgregg Inc., 98 189–92

HI *see* Houston Industries Inc.

Hibbett Sporting Goods, Inc., 26 189–91; 70 120–23 (upd.)

Hibernia Corporation, 37 187–90

Hickory Farms, Inc., 17 230–32

HickoryTech Corporation, 92 168–71

High Falls Brewing Company LLC, 74 144–47

High Tech Computer Corporation, 81 178–81

Highland Gold Mining Limited, 95 184–87

Highlights for Children, Inc., 95 188–91

Highmark Inc., 27 208–11

Highsmith Inc., 60 167–70

Highveld Steel and Vanadium Corporation Limited, 59 224–27

Hilmar Cheese Company, Inc., 98 193–96

Hilo Hattie *see* Pomare Ltd.

Hilb, Rogal & Hobbs Company, 77 191–94

Hildebrandt International, 29 235–38

Hill's Pet Nutrition, Inc., 27 212–14

Hillenbrand Industries, Inc., 10 349–51; 75 188–92 (upd.)

Hillerich & Bradsby Company, Inc., 51 161–64

The Hillhaven Corporation, 14 241–43 *see also* Vencor, Inc.

Hills Stores Company, 13 260–61

Hillsdown Holdings, PLC, II 513–14; 24 218–21 (upd.)

Hilti AG, 53 167–69

Hilton Group plc, III 91–93; 19 205–08 (upd.); 62 176–79 (upd.); 49 191–95 (upd.)

Hindustan Lever Limited, 79 198–201

Hines Horticulture, Inc., 49 196–98

Hino Motors, Ltd., 7 219–21; 21 271–74 (upd.)

HiPP GmbH & Co. Vertrieb KG, 88 183–88

Hiram Walker Resources Ltd., I 262–64

Hispanic Broadcasting Corporation, 35 219–22

HIT Entertainment PLC, 40 250–52

Hitachi, Ltd., I 454–55; 12 237–39 (upd.); 40 253–57 (upd.)

Hitachi Metals, Ltd., IV 101–02

Hitachi Zosen Corporation, III 513–14; 53 170–73 (upd.)

Hitchiner Manufacturing Co., Inc., 23 267–70

Hite Brewery Company Ltd., 97 204–07

HMI Industries, Inc., 17 233–35

HMV Group plc, 59 228–30

HNI Corporation, 74 148–52 (upd.)

Ho-Chunk Inc., 61 125–28

HOB Entertainment, Inc., 37 191–94

Hobby Lobby Stores Inc., 80 139–42

Hobie Cat Company, 94 236–39

Hochtief AG, 33 194–97; 88 189–94 (upd.)

The Hockey Company, 34 215–18; 70 124–26 (upd.)

Hodes *see* Bernard Hodes Group Inc.

Hodgson Mill, Inc., 88 195–98

Hoechst AG, I 346–48; 18 234–37 (upd.)

Hoechst Celanese Corporation, 13 262–65

Hoenig Group Inc., 41 207–09

Hoesch AG, IV 103–06

Hoffman Corporation, 78 158–12

Hoffmann-La Roche & Co *see* F. Hoffmann-La Roche & Co.

Hogan & Hartson L.L.P., 44 220–23

Hohner *see* Matth. Hohner AG.

HOK Group, Inc., 59 231–33

Hokkaido Electric Power Company Inc. (HEPCO), V 635–37; 58 160–63 (upd.)

Hokuriku Electric Power Company, V 638–40

Holberg Industries, Inc., 36 266–69

Holden Ltd., 62 180–83

Holderbank Financière Glaris Ltd., III 701–02 *see also* Holnam Inc

N.V. Holdingmaatschappij De Telegraaf, 23 271–73 *see also* Telegraaf Media Groep N.V.

Holiday Inns, Inc., III 94–95 *see also* Promus Companies, Inc.

Holiday Retirement Corp., 87 221–223

Holiday RV Superstores, Incorporated, 26 192–95

Holidaybreak plc, 96 182–86

Holland & Knight LLP, 60 171–74

Holland Burgerville USA, 44 224–26

The Holland Group, Inc., 82 174–77

Hollander Home Fashions Corp., 67 207–09

Holley Performance Products Inc., 52 157–60

Hollinger International Inc., 24 222–25; 62 184–88 (upd.)

Holly Corporation, 12 240–42

Hollywood Casino Corporation, 21 275–77

Hollywood Entertainment Corporation, 25 208–10

Hollywood Media Corporation, 58 164–68

Hollywood Park, Inc., 20 297–300

Holme Roberts & Owen LLP, 28 196–99

Holmen AB, 52 161–65 (upd.)

Holnam Inc., 8 258–60; 39 217–20 (upd.)

Holophane Corporation, 19 209–12

Holson Burnes Group, Inc., 14 244–45

Holt and Bugbee Company, 66 189–91

Holt's Cigar Holdings, Inc., 42 176–78

Holtzbrinck *see* Verlagsgruppe Georg von Holtzbrinck.

Homasote Company, 72 178–81

Home Box Office Inc., 7 222–24; 23 274–77 (upd.); 76 178–82 (upd.)

The Home Depot, Inc., V 75–76; 18 238–40 (upd.); 97 208–13 (upd.)

Home Hardware Stores Ltd., 62 189–91

Home Inns & Hotels Management Inc., 95 195–95

Home Insurance Company, III 262–64

Home Interiors & Gifts, Inc., 55 202–04

Home Products International, Inc., 55 205–07

Home Properties of New York, Inc., 42 179–81

Home Retail Group plc, 91 242–46

Home Shopping Network, Inc., V 77–78; 25 211–15 (upd.) *see also* HSN.

HomeBase, Inc., 33 198–201 (upd.)

Homestake Mining Company, 12 243–45; 38 229–32 (upd.)

Hometown Auto Retailers, Inc., 44 227–29

HomeVestors of America, Inc., 77 195–98

Homex *see* Desarrolladora Homex, S.A. de C.V.

Hon Hai Precision Industry Co., Ltd., 59 234–36

HON Industries Inc., 13 266–69 *see* HNI Corp.

Honda Motor Company Ltd., I 174–76; 10 352–54 (upd.); 29 239–42 (upd.); 96 187–93 (upd.)

Honeywell Inc., II 40–43; 12 246–49 (upd.); 50 231–35 (upd.)

Hong Kong and China Gas Company Ltd., 73 177–79

Hong Kong Dragon Airlines Ltd., 66 192–94

Hong Kong Telecommunications Ltd., 6 319–21 *see also* Cable & Wireless HKT.

Hongkong and Shanghai Banking Corporation Limited, II 296–99 *see also* HSBC Holdings plc.

Hongkong Electric Holdings Ltd., 6 498–500; 23 278–81 (upd.)

Hongkong Land Holdings Ltd., IV 699–701; 47 175–78 (upd.)

Honshu Paper Co., Ltd., IV 284–85 *see also* Oji Paper Co., Ltd.

Hoogovens *see* Koninklijke Nederlandsche Hoogovens en Staalfabricken NV.

Hooker Furniture Corporation, 80 143–46

Hooper Holmes, Inc., 22 264–67

Hooters of America, Inc., 18 241–43; 69 211–14 (upd.)

The Hoover Company, 12 250–52; 40 258–62 (upd.)

HOP, LLC, 80 147–50

Hops Restaurant Bar and Brewery, 46 233–36

Hopson Development Holdings Ltd., 87 224–227

Horace Mann Educators Corporation, 22 268–70; 90 237–40 (upd.)

Horizon Lines, Inc., 98 197–200

Horizon Organic Holding Corporation, 37 195–99

Hormel Foods Corporation, 18 244–47 (upd.); 54 164–69 (upd.)

Hornbach Holding AG, 98 201–07

Horsehead Industries, Inc., 51 165–67

Horseshoe Gaming Holding Corporation, 62 192–95

Horton Homes, Inc., 25 216–18

Horween Leather Company, 83 183-186

Hoshino Gakki Co. Ltd., 55 208–11

Hospira, Inc., 71 172–74

Hospital Central Services, Inc., 56 166–68

Hospital Corporation of America, III 78–80 *see also* HCA - The Healthcare Co.

Hospitality Franchise Systems, Inc., 11 177–79 *see also* Cendant Corp.

Hospitality Worldwide Services, Inc., 26 196–98

Hoss's Steak and Sea House Inc., 68 196–98

Host America Corporation, 79 202–06

Hot Dog on a Stick *see* HDOS Enterprises.

Hot Stuff Foods, 85 171–74

Hot Topic Inc., 33 202–04; 86 190–94 (upd.)

Hotel Properties Ltd., 71 175–77

Houchens Industries Inc., 51 168–70

Houghton Mifflin Company, 10 355–57; 36 270–74 (upd.)

House of Fabrics, Inc., 21 278–80 *see also* Jo-Ann Stores, Inc.

House of Fraser PLC, 45 188–91 *see also* Harrods Holdings.

House of Prince A/S, 80 151–54

Household International, Inc., II 417–20; 21 281–86 (upd.) *see also* HSBC Holdings plc.

Houston Industries Incorporated, V 641–44 *see also* Reliant Energy Inc.

Houston Wire & Cable Company, 97 214–17

Hovnanian Enterprises, Inc., 29 243–45; 89 254–59 (upd.)

Howard Hughes Medical Institute, 39 221–24

Howard Johnson International, Inc., 17 236–39; 72 182–86 (upd.)

Howmet Corporation, 12 253–55 *see also* Alcoa Inc.

HP *see* Hewlett-Packard Co.

HSBC Holdings plc, 12 256–58; 26 199–204 (upd.); 80 155–63 (upd.)

HSN, 64 181–85 (upd.)

Huawei Technologies Company Ltd., 87 228–231

Hub Group, Inc., 38 233–35

Hub International Limited, 89 260–64

Hubbard Broadcasting Inc., 24 226–28; 79 207–12 (upd.)

Hubbell Inc., 9 286–87; 31 257–59 (upd.); 76 183–86 (upd.)

The Hudson Bay Mining and Smelting Company, Limited, 12 259–61

Hudson Foods Inc., 13 270–72 *see also* Tyson Foods, Inc.

Hudson River Bancorp, Inc., 41 210–13

Hudson's Bay Company, V 79–81; 25 219–22 (upd.); 83 187-194 (upd.)

Huffy Corporation, 7 225–27; 30 239–42 (upd.)

Hughes Electronics Corporation, 25 223–25

Hughes Hubbard & Reed LLP, 44 230–32

Hughes Markets, Inc., 22 271–73 *see also* Kroger Co.

Hughes Supply, Inc., 14 246–47

Hugo Boss AG, 48 206–09

Huhtamäki Oyj, 64 186–88

HUK-Coburg, 58 169–73

Hulman & Company, 44 233–36

Hüls A.G., I 349–50 *see also* Degussa-Hüls AG.

Humana Inc., III 81–83; 24 229–32 (upd.)

The Humane Society of the United States, 54 170–73

Hummel International A/S, 68 199–201

Hummer Winblad Venture Partners, 97 218–21

Hungarian Telephone and Cable Corp., 75 193–95

Hungry Howie's Pizza and Subs, Inc., 25 226–28

Hunt Consolidated, Inc., 7 228–30; 27 215–18 (upd.)

Hunt Manufacturing Company, 12 262–64

Hunt-Wesson, Inc., 17 240–42 *see also* ConAgra Foods, Inc.

Hunter Fan Company, 13 273–75; 98 208–12 (upd.)

Hunting plc, 78 163–16

Huntingdon Life Sciences Group plc, 42 182–85

Huntington Bancshares Incorporated, 11 180–82; 87 232–238 (upd.)

Huntington Learning Centers, Inc., 55 212–14

Huntleigh Technology PLC, 77 199–202

Hunton & Williams, 35 223–26

Huntsman Corporation, 8 261–63; 98 213–17 (upd.)

Huron Consulting Group Inc., 87 239–243

Hurricane Hydrocarbons Ltd., 54 174–77

Husky Energy Inc., 47 179–82

Hutchinson Technology Incorporated, 18 248–51; 63 190–94 (upd.)

Hutchison Whampoa Limited, 18 252–55; 49 199–204 (upd.)

Huttig Building Products, Inc., 73 180–83

HVB Group, 59 237–44 (upd.)

Hvide Marine Incorporated, 22 274–76

Hy-Vee, Inc., 36 275–78

Hyatt Corporation, III 96–97; 16 273–75 (upd.) *see* Global Hyatt Corp.

Hyde Athletic Industries, Inc., 17 243–45 *see also* Saucony Inc.

Hyder plc, 34 219–21

Hydril Company, 46 237–39

Hydro-Quebéc, 6 501–03; 32 266–69 (upd.)

Hylsamex, S.A. de C.V., 39 225–27

Hypercom Corporation, 27 219–21

Hyperion Software Corporation, 22 277–79

Hyperion Solutions Corporation, 76 187–91

Hyster Company, 17 246–48

Hyundai Group, III 515–17; 7 231–34 (upd.); 56 169–73 (upd.)

I

I.C. Isaacs & Company, 31 260–62

I.M. Pei & Associates *see* Pei Cobb Freed & Partners Architects LLP.

IAC Group, 96 194–98

Iams Company, 26 205–07

IAWS Group plc, 49 205–08

Iberdrola, S.A., 49 209–12

Iberia Líneas Aéreas De España S.A., 6 95–97; 36 279–83 (upd.); 91 247–54 (upd.)

IBERIABANK Corporation, 37 200–02

IBJ *see* The Industrial Bank of Japan Ltd.

IBM *see* International Business Machines Corp.

IBP, Inc., II 515–17; 21 287–90 (upd.)

Ibstock Brick Ltd., 37 203–06 (upd.)

Ibstock plc, 14 248–50

IC Industries Inc., I 456–58 *see also* Whitman Corp.

ICA AB, II 639–40

ICEE-USA *see* J & J Snack Foods Corp.

Iceland Group plc, 33 205–07 *see also* The Big Food Group plc.

Icelandair, 52 166–69
Icelandic Group hf, 81 182–85
ICF International, Inc., 28 200–04; 94
   240–47 (upd.)
ICI *see* Imperial Chemical Industries plc.
ICL plc, 6 240–42
ICN Pharmaceuticals, Inc., 52 170–73
Icon Health & Fitness, Inc., 38 236–39
Idaho Power Company, 12 265–67
IDB Communications Group, Inc., 11
   183–85
IDB Holding Corporation Ltd., 97
   222–25
Idearc Inc., 90 241–44
Idemitsu Kosan Co., Ltd., IV 434–36;
   49 213–16 (upd.)
Identix Inc., 44 237–40
IDEO Inc., 65 171–73
IDEXX Laboratories, Inc., 23 282–84
IDG Books Worldwide, Inc., 27 222–24
   see also International Data Group, Inc.
IDG Communications, Inc *see*
   International Data Group, Inc.
IdraPrince, Inc., 76 192–94
IDT Corporation, 34 222–24; 99
   214–219 (upd.)
IDX Systems Corporation, 64 189–92
IEC Electronics Corp., 42 186–88
IFF *see* International Flavors & Fragrances
   Inc.
IG Group Holdings plc, 97 226–29
IGA, Inc., 99 220–224
Igloo Products Corp., 21 291–93
IGT *see* International Game Technology.
IHC Caland N.V., 71 178–80
IHI *see* Ishikawajima-Harima Heavy
   Industries Co., Ltd.
IHOP Corporation, 17 249–51; 58
   174–77 (upd.)
Ihr Platz GmbH + Company KG, 77
   203–06
IHS Inc., 78 167–70
IKEA Group, V 82–84; 26 208–11
   (upd.); 94 248–53 (upd.)
IKON Office Solutions, Inc., 50 236–39
Ikonics Corporation, 99 225–228
Il Fornaio (America) Corporation, 27
   225–28
ILFC *see* International Lease Finance
   Corp.
Ilitch Holdings Inc., 37 207–210; 86
   195–200 (upd.)
Illinois Bell Telephone Company, 14
   251–53
Illinois Central Corporation, 11 186–89
Illinois Power Company, 6 504–07 *see
   also* Ameren Corp.
Illinois Tool Works Inc., III 518–20; 22
   280–83 (upd.); 81 186–91 (upd.)
Illumina, Inc., 93 246–49
illycaffè SpA, 50 240–44
ILX Resorts Incorporated, 65 174–76
Image Entertainment, Inc., 94 254–57
Imagine Entertainment, 91 255–58
Imagine Foods, Inc., 50 245–47
Imasco Limited, V 401–02
Imation Corporation, 20 301–04 *see also*
   3M Co.

Imatra Steel Oy Ab, 55 215–17
IMAX Corporation, 28 205–08; 78
   171–76 (upd.)
IMC Fertilizer Group, Inc., 8 264–66
ImClone Systems Inc., 58 178–81
IMCO Recycling, Incorporated, 32
   270–73
Imerys S.A., 40 176, 263–66 (upd.)
Imetal S.A., IV 107–09
IMG, 78 177–80
IMI plc, 9 288–89; 29 364
Immucor, Inc., 81 192–96
Immunex Corporation, 14 254–56; 50
   248–53 (upd.)
Imo Industries Inc., 7 235–37; 27
   229–32 (upd.)
IMPATH Inc., 45 192–94
Imperial Chemical Industries plc, I
   351–53; 50 254–58 (upd.)
Imperial Holly Corporation, 12 268–70
   see also Imperial Sugar Co.
Imperial Industries, Inc., 81 197–200
Imperial Oil Limited, IV 437–39; 25
   229–33 (upd.); 95 196–203 (upd.)
Imperial Parking Corporation, 58
   182–84
Imperial Sugar Company, 32 274–78
   (upd.)
Imperial Tobacco Group PLC, 50
   259–63
IMS Health, Inc., 57 174–78
In Focus Systems, Inc., 22 287–90
In-N-Out Burgers Inc., 19 213–15; 74
   153–56 (upd.)
In-Sink-Erator, 66 195–98
InaCom Corporation, 13 276–78
Inamed Corporation, 79 213–16
Inchcape PLC, III 521–24; 16 276–80
   (upd.); 50 264–68 (upd.)
Inco Limited, IV 110–12; 45 195–99
   (upd.)
Incyte Genomics, Inc., 52 174–77
Indel, Inc., 78 181–84
Independent News & Media PLC, 61
   129–31
Indian Airlines Ltd., 46 240–42
Indian Oil Corporation Ltd., IV
   440–41; 48 210–13 (upd.)
Indiana Bell Telephone Company,
   Incorporated, 14 257–61
Indiana Energy, Inc., 27 233–36
Indianapolis Motor Speedway
   Corporation, 46 243–46
Indigo Books & Music Inc., 58 185–87
Indigo NV, 26 212–14 *see also*
   Hewlett-Packard Co.
Indosat *see* PT Indosat Tbk.
Indus International Inc., 70 127–30
Industria de Diseño Textil S.A.
   (Inditex), 64 193–95
Industrial Bank of Japan, Ltd., II
   300–01
Industrial Light & Magic *see* Lucasfilm
   Ltd.
Industrial Services of America, Inc., 46
   247–49
Industrias Bachoco, S.A. de C.V., 39
   228–31

Industrias Penoles, S.A. de C.V., 22
   284–86
Industrie Natuzzi S.p.A., 18 256–58
Industrie Zignago Santa Margherita
   S.p.A., 67 210–12
Infineon Technologies AG, 50 269–73
Infinity Broadcasting Corporation, 11
   190–92; 48 214–17 (upd.)
InFocus Corporation, 92 172–75
Infogrames Entertainment S.A., 35
   227–30
Informa Group plc, 58 188–91
Information Access Company, 17
   252–55
Information Builders, Inc., 22 291–93
Information Holdings Inc., 47 183–86
Information Resources, Inc., 10 358–60
Informix Corporation, 10 361–64; 30
   243–46 (upd.) *see also* International
   Business Machines Corp.
InfoSonics Corporation, 81 201–04
InfoSpace, Inc., 91 259–62
Infosys Technologies Ltd., 38 240–43
Ing. C. Olivetti & C., S.p.A., III
   144–46 *see also* Olivetti S.p.A
Ingalls Shipbuilding, Inc., 12 271–73
Ingenico—Compagnie Industrielle et
   Financière d'Ingénierie, 46 250–52
Ingersoll-Rand Company, III 525–27;
   15 223–26 (upd.); 55 218–22 (upd.)
Ingles Markets, Inc., 20 305–08
Ingram Industries, Inc., 11 193–95; 49
   217–20 (upd.)
Ingram Micro Inc., 52 178–81
INI *see* Instituto Nacional de Industria.
Initial Security, 64 196–98
Inktomi Corporation, 45 200–04
Inland Container Corporation, 8
   267–69 *see also* Temple-Inland Inc.
Inland Steel Industries, Inc., IV 113–16;
   19 216–20 (upd.)
Innovative Solutions & Support, Inc.,
   85 175–78
Innovo Group Inc., 83 195-199
INPEX Holdings Inc., 97 230–33
Input/Output, Inc., 73 184–87
Inserra Supermarkets, 25 234–36
Insight Enterprises, Inc., 18 259–61
Insilco Corporation, 16 281–83
Inso Corporation, 26 215–19
Instinet Corporation, 34 225–27
Insituform Technologies, Inc., 83
   200-203
Instituto Nacional de Industria, I
   459–61
Insurance Auto Auctions, Inc., 23
   285–87
Integra LifeSciences Holdings
   Corporation, 87 244–247
Integrated BioPharma, Inc., 83 204-207
Integrated Defense Technologies, Inc.,
   54 178–80
Integrity Inc., 44 241–43
Intel Corporation, II 44–46; 10 365–67
   (upd.); 36 284–88 (upd.); 75
   196–201 (upd.)
IntelliCorp, Inc., 45 205–07
Intelligent Electronics, Inc., 6 243–45

Inter Link Foods PLC, 61 132–34
Inter Parfums Inc., 35 235–38; 86 201–06 (upd.)
Inter-Regional Financial Group, Inc., 15 231–33 *see also* Dain Rauscher Corp.
Interbrand Corporation, 70 131–33
Interbrew S.A., 17 256–58; 50 274–79 (upd.)
Interceramic *see* Internacional de Ceramica, S.A. de C.V.
Interco Incorporated, III 528–31 *see also* Furniture Brands International, Inc.
IntercontinentalExchange, Inc., 95 204–07
Intercorp Excelle Foods Inc., 64 199–201
InterDigital Communications Corporation, 61 135–37
Interep National Radio Sales Inc., 35 231–34
Interface, Inc., 8 270–72; 29 246–49 (upd.); 76 195–99 (upd.)
Interfax News Agency, 86 207–10
Intergraph Corporation, 6 246–49; 24 233–36 (upd.)
The Interlake Corporation, 8 273–75
Intermec Technologies Corporation, 72 187–91
INTERMET Corporation, 32 279–82; 77 207–12 (upd.)
Intermix Media, Inc., 83 208–211
Intermountain Health Care, Inc., 27 237–40
Internacional de Ceramica, S.A. de C.V., 53 174–76
International Airline Support Group, Inc., 55 223–25
International Brotherhood of Teamsters, 37 211–14
International Business Machines Corporation, III 147–49; 6 250–53 (upd.); 30 247–51 (upd.); 63 195–201 (upd.)
International Controls Corporation, 10 368–70
International Creative Management, Inc., 43 235–37
International Dairy Queen, Inc., 10 371–74; 39 232–36 (upd.)
International Data Group, Inc., 7 238–40; 25 237–40 (upd.)
International Family Entertainment Inc., 13 279–81 *see also* ABC Family Worldwide, Inc.
International Flavors & Fragrances Inc., 9 290–92; 38 244–48 (upd.)
International Game Technology, 10 375–76; 41 214–16 (upd.)
International House of Pancakes *see* IHOP Corp.
International Lease Finance Corporation, 48 218–20
International Management Group, 18 262–65 *see also* IMG.
International Multifoods Corporation, 7 241–43; 25 241–44 (upd.) *see also* The J. M. Smucker Co.

International Olympic Committee, 44 244–47
International Paper Company, IV 286–88; 15 227–30 (upd.); 47 187–92 (upd.); 97 234–43 (upd.)
International Power PLC, 50 280–85 (upd.)
International Profit Associates, Inc., 87 248–251
International Rectifier Corporation, 31 263–66; 71 181–84 (upd.)
International Shipbreaking Ltd. L.L.C., 67 213–15
International Shipholding Corporation, Inc., 27 241–44
International Speedway Corporation, 19 221–23; 74 157–60 (upd.)
International Telephone & Telegraph Corporation, I 462–64; 11 196–99 (upd.)
International Total Services, Inc., 37 215–18
Interpool, Inc., 92 176–79
The Interpublic Group of Companies, Inc., I 16–18; 22 294–97 (upd.); 75 202–05 (upd.)
Interscope Music Group, 31 267–69
Intersil Corporation, 93 250–54
Interstate Bakeries Corporation, 12 274–76; 38 249–52 (upd.)
Interstate Hotels & Resorts Inc., 58 192–94
Intertek Group plc, 95 208–11
InterVideo, Inc., 85 179–82
Intevac, Inc., 92 180–83
Intimate Brands, Inc., 24 237–39
Intrado Inc., 63 202–04
Intrawest Corporation, 15 234–36; 84 192–196 (upd.)
Intres B.V., 82 178–81
Intuit Inc., 14 262–64; 33 208–11 (upd.); 73 188–92 (upd.)
Intuitive Surgical, Inc., 79 217–20
Invacare Corporation, 11 200–02; 47 193–98 (upd.)
Invensys PLC, 50 286–90 (upd.)
inVentiv Health, Inc., 81 205–08
The Inventure Group, Inc., 96 199–202 (upd.)
Inverness Medical Innovations, Inc., 63 205–07
Inversiones Nacional de Chocolates S.A., 88 199–202
Investcorp SA, 57 179–82
Investor AB, 63 208–11
Invitrogen Corporation, 52 182–84
Invivo Corporation, 52 185–87
Iogen Corporation, 81 209–13
Iomega Corporation, 21 294–97
IONA Technologies plc, 43 238–41
Ionatron, Inc., 85 183–86
Ionics, Incorporated, 52 188–90
Iowa Beef Processors *see* IBP, Inc.
Iowa Telecommunications Services, Inc., 85 187–90
Ipalco Enterprises, Inc., 6 508–09
IPC Magazines Limited, 7 244–47
Ipiranga S.A., 67 216–18

Ipsen International Inc., 72 192–95
Ipsos SA, 48 221–24
IranAir, 81 214–17
Irex Contracting Group, 90 245–48
Irish Distillers Group, 96 203–07
Irish Life & Permanent Plc, 59 245–47
Irkut Corporation, 68 202–04
iRobot Corporation, 83 212-215
Iron Mountain, Inc., 33 212–14
IRSA Inversiones y Representaciones S.A., 63 212–15
Irvin Feld & Kenneth Feld Productions, Inc., 15 237–39 *see also* Feld Entertainment, Inc.
Irwin Financial Corporation, 77 213–16
Irwin Toy Limited, 14 265–67
Isbank *see* Turkiye Is Bankasi A.S.
Iscor Limited, 57 183–86
Isetan Company Limited, V 85–87; 36 289–93 (upd.)
Ishikawajima-Harima Heavy Industries Company, Ltd., III 532–33; 86 211–15 (upd.)
The Island ECN, Inc., 48 225–29
Isle of Capri Casinos, Inc., 41 217–19
Ispat Inland Inc., 30 252–54; 40 267–72 (upd.)
Israel Aircraft Industries Ltd., 69 215–17
Israel Chemicals Ltd., 55 226–29
ISS A/S, 49 221–23
Istituto per la Ricostruzione Industriale S.p.A., I 465–67; 11 203–06 (upd.)
Isuzu Motors, Ltd., 9 293–95; 23 288–91 (upd.); 57 187–91 (upd.)
Itaú *see* Banco Itaú S.A.
ITC Holdings Corp., 75 206–08
Itel Corporation, 9 296–99
Items International Airwalk Inc., 17 259–61
ITM Entreprises SA, 36 294–97
Ito-Yokado Co., Ltd., V 88–89; 42 189–92 (upd.)
ITOCHU Corporation, 32 283–87 (upd.)
Itoh *see* C. Itoh & Co.
Itoham Foods Inc., II 518–19; 61 138–40 (upd.)
Itron, Inc., 64 202–05
ITT Educational Services, Inc., 33 215–17; 76 200–03 (upd.)
ITT Sheraton Corporation, III 98–101 *see also* Starwood Hotels & Resorts Worldwide, Inc.
ITW *see* Illinois Tool Works Inc.
i2 Technologies, Inc., 87 252–257
Ivar's, Inc., 86 216–19
IVAX Corporation, 11 207–09; 55 230–33 (upd.)
IVC Industries, Inc., 45 208–11
iVillage Inc., 46 253–56
Iwerks Entertainment, Inc., 34 228–30
IXC Communications, Inc., 29 250–52

J

J & J Snack Foods Corporation, 24 240–42
J&R Electronics Inc., 26 224–26

J. & W. Seligman & Co. Inc., 61
141–43

J.A. Jones, Inc., 16 284–86

J. Alexander's Corporation, 65 177–79

J.B. Hunt Transport Services Inc., 12
277–79

J. Baker, Inc., 31 270–73

J C Bamford Excavators Ltd., 83
216-222

J. C. Penney Company, Inc., V 90–92;
18 269–73 (upd.); 43 245–50 (upd.);
91 263–72 (upd.)

J. Crew Group, Inc., 12 280–82; 34
231–34 (upd.); 88 203–08

J.D. Edwards & Company, 14 268–70
see also Oracle Corp.

J.D. Power and Associates, 32 297–301

J. D'Addario & Company, Inc., 48
230–33

J.F. Shea Co., Inc., 55 234–36

J.H. Findorff and Son, Inc., 60 175–78

J.I. Case Company, 10 377–81 see also
CNH Global N.V.

J.J. Darboven GmbH & Co. KG, 96
208–12

J.J. Keller & Associates, Inc., 81
2180–21

The J. Jill Group, Inc., 35 239–41; 90
249–53 (upd.)

J.L. Hammett Company, 72 196–99

J Lauritzen A/S, 90 254–57

J. Lohr Winery Corporation, 99
229–232

The J. M. Smucker Company, 11
210–12; 87 258–265 (upd.)

J.M. Voith AG, 33 222–25

J.P. Morgan Chase & Co., II 329–32;
30 261–65 (upd.); 38 253–59 (upd.)

J.R. Simplot Company, 16 287–89; 60
179–82 (upd.)

J Sainsbury plc, II 657–59; 13 282–84
(upd.); 38 260–65 (upd.); 95 212–20
(upd.)

J. W. Pepper and Son Inc., 86 220–23

J. Walter Thompson Co. see JWT Group
Inc.

Jabil Circuit, Inc., 36 298–301; 88
209–14

Jack Henry and Associates, Inc., 17
262–65; 94 258–63 (upd.)

Jack in the Box Inc., 89 265–71 (upd.)

Jack Morton Worldwide, 88 215–18

Jack Schwartz Shoes, Inc., 18 266–68

Jackpot Enterprises Inc., 21 298–300

Jackson Hewitt, Inc., 48 234–36

Jackson National Life Insurance
Company, 8 276–77

Jacmar Companies, 87 266–269

Jaco Electronics, Inc., 30 255–57

Jacob Leinenkugel Brewing Company,
28 209–11

Jacobs Engineering Group Inc., 6
148–50; 26 220–23 (upd.)

Jacobs Suchard (AG), II 520–22 see also
Kraft Jacobs Suchard AG.

Jacobson Stores Inc., 21 301–03

Jacor Communications, Inc., 23 292–95

Jacques Whitford, 92 184–87

Jacquot see Établissements Jacquot and Cie
S.A.S.

Jacuzzi Brands Inc., 23 296–98; 76
204–07 (upd.)

JAFCO Co. Ltd., 79 221–24

Jaguar Cars, Ltd., 13 285–87

JAKKS Pacific, Inc., 52 191–94

JAL see Japan Airlines Company, Ltd.

Jalate Inc., 25 245–47

Jamba Juice Company, 47 199–202

James Avery Craftsman, Inc., 76 208–10

James Beattie plc, 43 242–44

James Hardie Industries N.V., 56
174–76

James Original Coney Island Inc., 84
197–200

James Purdey & Sons Limited, 87
270–275

James River Corporation of Virginia, IV
289–91 see also Fort James Corp.

Jani-King International, Inc., 85
191–94

Janssen Pharmaceutica N.V., 80 164–67

JanSport, Inc., 70 134–36

Janus Capital Group Inc., 57 192–94

Japan Airlines Company, Ltd., I
104–06; 32 288–92 (upd.)

Japan Broadcasting Corporation, 7
248–50

Japan Leasing Corporation, 8 278–80

Japan Pulp and Paper Company
Limited, IV 292–93

Japan Tobacco Inc., V 403–04; 46
257–60 (upd.)

Jarden Corporation, 93 255–61 (upd.)

Jardine Cycle & Carriage Ltd., 73
193–95

Jardine Matheson Holdings Limited, I
468–71; 20 309–14 (upd.); 93
262–71 (upd.)

Jarvis plc, 39 237–39

Jason Incorporated, 23 299–301

Jay Jacobs, Inc., 15 243–45

Jayco Inc., 13 288–90

Jays Foods, Inc., 90 258–61

Jazz Basketball Investors, Inc., 55
237–39

Jazzercise, Inc., 45 212–14

JB Oxford Holdings, Inc., 32 293–96

JCDecaux S.A., 76 211–13

JD Wetherspoon plc, 30 258–60

JDS Uniphase Corporation, 34 235–37

JE Dunn Construction Group, Inc., 85
195–98

The Jean Coutu Group (PJC) Inc., 46
261–65

Jean-Georges Enterprises L.L.C., 75
209–11

Jeanneau see Chantiers Jeanneau S.A.

Jefferies Group, Inc., 25 248–51

Jefferson-Pilot Corporation, 11 213–15;
29 253–56 (upd.)

Jefferson Properties, Inc. see JPI.

Jefferson Smurfit Group plc, IV 294–96;
19 224–27 (upd.); 49 224–29 (upd.)
see also Smurfit-Stone Container Corp.

Jel Sert Company, 90 262–65

Jeld-Wen, Inc., 45 215–17

Jelly Belly Candy Company, 76 214–16

Jenkens & Gilchrist, P.C., 65 180–82

Jennie-O Turkey Store, Inc., 76 217–19

Jennifer Convertibles, Inc., 31 274–76

Jenny Craig, Inc., 10 382–84; 29
257–60 (upd.); 92 188–93 (upd.)

Jenoptik AG, 33 218–21

Jeppesen Sanderson, Inc., 92 194–97

Jerónimo Martins SGPS S.A., 96
213–16

Jerry's Famous Deli Inc., 24 243–45

Jersey European Airways (UK) Ltd., 61
144–46

Jersey Mike's Franchise Systems, Inc.,
83 223-226

Jervis B. Webb Company, 24 246–49

Jet Airways (India) Private Limited, 65
183–85

JetBlue Airways Corporation, 44
248–50

Jetro Cash & Carry Enterprises Inc., 38
266–68

Jewett-Cameron Trading Company, Ltd.,
89 272–76

JFE Shoji Holdings Inc., 88 219–22

JG Industries, Inc., 15 240–42

Jillian's Entertainment Holdings, Inc.,
40 273–75

Jim Beam Brands Worldwide, Inc., 14
271–73; 58 194–96 (upd.)

The Jim Henson Company, 23 302–04

The Jim Pattison Group, 37 219–22

Jimmy Carter Work Project see Habitat
for Humanity International.

Jitney-Jungle Stores of America, Inc., 27
245–48

JJB Sports plc, 32 302–04

JLA Credit see Japan Leasing Corp.

JLG Industries, Inc., 52 195–97

JLL see Jones Lang LaSalle Inc.

JLM Couture, Inc., 64 206–08

JMB Realty Corporation, IV 702–03 see
also Amfac/JMB Hawaii L.L.C.

Jo-Ann Stores, Inc., 72 200–03 (upd.)

Joe's Sports & Outdoor, 98 218–22
(upd.)

Jockey International, Inc., 12 283–85;
34 238–42 (upd.); 77 217–23 (upd.)

The Joffrey Ballet of Chicago, 52
198–202

John B. Sanfilippo & Son, Inc., 14
274–76

John Brown plc, I 572–74

The John D. and Catherine T.
MacArthur Foundation, 34 243–46

John D. Brush Company Inc., 94
264–67

The John David Group plc, 90 266–69

John Deere see Deere & Co.

John Dewar & Sons, Ltd., 82 182–86

John Fairfax Holdings Limited, 7
251–54 see also Fairfax Media Ltd.

John Frieda Professional Hair Care Inc.,
70 137–39

John H. Harland Company, 17 266–69

John Hancock Financial Services, Inc.,
III 265–68; 42 193–98 (upd.)

John Laing plc, I 575–76; 51 171–73
(upd.) *see also* Laing O'Rourke PLC.
John Lewis Partnership plc, V 93–95;
42 199–203 (upd.); 99 233–240
(upd.)
John Menzies plc, 39 240–43
The John Nuveen Company, 21
304–065
John Paul Mitchell Systems, 24 250–52
John Q. Hammons Hotels, Inc., 24
253–55
John W. Danforth Company, 48
237–39
John Wiley & Sons, Inc., 17 270–72; 65
186–90 (upd.)
Johnny Rockets Group, Inc., 31
277–81; 76 220–24 (upd.)
Johns Manville Corporation, 64 209–14
(upd.)
Johnson *see* Axel Johnson Group.
Johnson & Higgins, 14 277–80 *see also*
Marsh & McLennan Companies, Inc.
Johnson & Johnson, III 35–37; 8
281–83 (upd.); 36 302–07 (upd.); 75
212–18 (upd.)
Johnson Controls, Inc., III 534–37; 26
227–32 (upd.); 59 248–54 (upd.)
Johnson Matthey PLC, IV 117–20; 16
290–94 (upd.); 49 230–35 (upd.)
Johnson Outdoors Inc., 84 201–205
(upd.)
Johnson Publishing Company, Inc., 28
212–14; 72 204–07 (upd.)
Johnson Wax *see* S.C. Johnson & Son,
Inc.
Johnson Worldwide Associates, Inc., 28
215–17 *see also* Johnson Outdoors Inc.
Johnsonville Sausage L.L.C., 63 216–19
Johnston Industries, Inc., 15 246–48
Johnston Press plc, 35 242–44
Johnstown America Industries, Inc., 23
305–07
Jolly Hotels *see* Compagnia Italiana dei
Jolly Hotels S.p.A.
Jones Apparel Group, Inc., 11 216–18;
39 244–47 (upd.)
Jones, Day, Reavis & Pogue, 33 226–29
Jones Intercable, Inc., 21 307–09
Jones Knowledge Group, Inc., 97
244–48
Jones Lang LaSalle Incorporated, 49
236–38
Jones Medical Industries, Inc., 24
256–58
Jones Soda Co., 69 218–21
Jongleurs Comedy Club *see* Regent Inns
plc.
Jordache Enterprises, Inc., 23 308–10
The Jordan Company LP, 70 140–42
Jordan Industries, Inc., 36 308–10
Jordan-Kitt Music Inc., 86 224–27
Jos. A. Bank Clothiers, Inc., 31 282–85
José de Mello SGPS S.A., 96 217–20
Joseph T. Ryerson & Son, Inc., 15
249–51 *see also* Ryerson Tull, Inc.
Jostens, Inc., 7 255–57; 25 252–55
(upd.); 73 196–200 (upd.)
Jotun A/S, 80 168–71

JOULÉ Inc., 58 197–200
Journal Communications, Inc., 86
228–32
Journal Register Company, 29 261–63
JPI, 49 239–41
JPMorgan Chase & Co., 91 273–84
(upd.)
JPS Textile Group, Inc., 28 218–20
JSC MMC Norilsk Nickel, 48 300–02
JSP Corporation, 74 161–64
j2 Global Communications, Inc., 75
219–21
The Judge Group, Inc., 51 174–76
Jugos del Valle, S.A. de C.V., 85
199–202
Juicy Couture, Inc., 80 172–74
Jujo Paper Co., Ltd., IV 297–98
Julius Baer Holding AG, 52 203–05
Julius Blüthner Pianofortefabric GmbH,
78 185–88
Julius Meinl International AG, 53
177–80
Jumbo S.A., 96 221–24
Jumeirah Group, 83 227–230
Jungheinrich AG, 96 225–30
Juniper Networks, Inc., 43 251–55
Juno Lighting, Inc., 30 266–68
Juno Online Services, Inc., 38 269–72
see also United Online, Inc.
Jupitermedia Corporation, 75 222–24
Jurys Doyle Hotel Group plc, 64
215–17
JUSCO Co., Ltd., V 96–99 *see also*
AEON Co., Ltd.
Just Bagels Manufacturing, Inc., 94
268–71
Just Born, Inc., 32 305–07
Just For Feet, Inc., 19 228–30
Justin Industries, Inc., 19 231–33 *see
also* Berkshire Hathaway Inc.
Juventus F.C. S.p.A, 53 181–83
JVC *see* Victor Company of Japan, Ltd.
JWP Inc., 9 300–02 *see also* EMCOR
Group Inc.
JWT Group Inc., I 19–21 *see also* WPP
Group plc.

K

K&B Inc., 12 286–88
K & G Men's Center, Inc., 21 310–12
K-Swiss Inc., 33 243–45; 89 277–81
(upd.)
K-tel International, Inc., 21 325–28
K.A. Rasmussen AS, 99 241–244
Kadant Inc., 96 231–34 (upd.)
Kaiser Aluminum Corporation, IV
121–23; 84 212–217 (upd.)
Kaiser Foundation Health Plan, Inc., 53
184–86
Kajima Corporation, I 577–78; 51
177–79 (upd.)
Kal Kan Foods, Inc., 22 298–300
Kaman Corporation, 12 289–92; 42
204–08 (upd.)
Kaman Music Corporation, 68 205–07
Kampgrounds of America, Inc., 33
230–33
Kamps AG, 44 251–54

Kana Software, Inc., 51 180–83
Kanebo, Ltd., 53 187–91
Kanematsu Corporation, IV 442–44; 24
259–62 (upd.)
Kansai Paint Company Ltd., 80 175–78
The Kansai Electric Power Company,
Inc., V 645–48; 62 196–200 (upd.)
Kansallis-Osake-Pankki, II 302–03
Kansas City Power & Light Company,
6 510–12 *see also* Great Plains Energy
Inc.
Kansas City Southern Industries, Inc., 6
400–02; 26 233–36 (upd.)
The Kansas City Southern Railway
Company, 92 198–202
Kao Corporation, III 38–39; 20 315–17
(upd.); 79 225–30 (upd.)
Kaplan, Inc., 42 209–12; 90 270–75
(upd.)
Kar Nut Products Company, 86 233–36
Karan Co. *see* Donna Karan Co.
Karl Kani Infinity, Inc., 49 242–45
Karlsberg Brauerei GmbH & Co KG,
41 220–23
Karmann *see* Wilhelm Karmann GmbH.
Karstadt Aktiengesellschaft, V 100–02;
19 234–37 (upd.)
Karstadt Quelle AG, 57 195–201 (upd.)
Karsten Manufacturing Corporation, 51
184–86
Kash n' Karry Food Stores, Inc., 20
318–20
Kashi Company, 89 282–85
Kasper A.S.L., Ltd., 40 276–79
kate spade LLC, 68 208–11
Katokichi Company Ltd., 82 187–90
Katy Industries Inc., I 472–74; 51
187–90 (upd.)
Katz Communications, Inc., 6 32–34 *see
also* Clear Channel Communications,
Inc.
Katz Media Group, Inc., 35 245–48
Kaufhof Warenhaus AG, V 103–05; 23
311–14 (upd.)
Kaufman and Broad Home
Corporation, 8 284–86 *see also* KB
Home.
Kaufring AG, 35 249–52
Kawai Musical Instruments
Manufacturing Co.,Ltd., 78 189–92
Kawasaki Heavy Industries, Ltd., III
538–40; 63 220–23 (upd.)
Kawasaki Kisen Kaisha, Ltd., V 457–60;
56 177–81 (upd.)
Kawasaki Steel Corporation, IV 124–25
Kay-Bee Toy Stores, 15 252–53 *see also*
KB Toys.
Kaydon Corporation, 18 274–76
KB Home, 45 218–22 (upd.)
KB Toys, Inc., 35 253–55 (upd.); 86
237–42 (upd.)
KC *see* Kenneth Cole Productions, Inc.
KCPL *see* Kansas City Power & Light Co.
KCSI *see* Kansas City Southern Industries,
Inc.
KCSR *see* The Kansas City Southern
Railway.
Keane, Inc., 56 182–86

Keebler Foods Company, 36 311–13
Keio Corporation, V 461–62; 96 235–39 (upd.)
The Keith Companies Inc., 54 181–84
Keithley Instruments Inc., 16 299–301
Kelda Group plc, 45 223–26
Kelley Blue Book Company, Inc., 84 218–221
Keller Group PLC, 95 221–24
Kelley Drye & Warren LLP, 40 280–83
Kellogg Brown & Root, Inc., 62 201–05 (upd.)
Kellogg Company, II 523–26; 13 291–94 (upd.); 50 291–96 (upd.)
Kellwood Company, 8 287–89; 85 203–08 (upd.)
Kelly-Moore Paint Company, Inc., 56 187–89
Kelly Services, Inc., 6 35–37; 26 237–40 (upd.)
The Kelly-Springfield Tire Company, 8 290–92
Kelsey-Hayes Group of Companies, 7 258–60; 27 249–52 (upd.)
Kemet Corp., 14 281–83
Kemira Oyj, 70 143–46
Kemper Corporation, III 269–71; 15 254–58 (upd.)
Ken's Foods, Inc., 88 223–26
Kendall International, Inc., 11 219–21
see also Tyco International Ltd.
Kendall-Jackson Winery, Ltd., 28 221–23
Kendle International Inc., 87 276–279
Kenetech Corporation, 11 222–24
Kenexa Corporation, 87 280–284
Kenmore Air Harbor Inc., 65 191–93
Kennametal, Inc., 13 295–97; 68 212–16 (upd.)
Kennecott Corporation, 7 261–64; 27 253–57 (upd.) see also Rio Tinto PLC.
Kennedy-Wilson, Inc., 60 183–85
Kenneth Cole Productions, Inc., 25 256–58
Kensey Nash Corporation, 71 185–87
Kensington Publishing Corporation, 84 222–225
Kent Electronics Corporation, 17 273–76
Kentucky Electric Steel, Inc., 31 286–88
Kentucky Fried Chicken see KFC Corp.
Kentucky Utilities Company, 6 513–15
Kenwood Corporation, 31 289–91
Kenya Airways Limited, 89 286–89
Keolis SA, 51 191–93
Kepco see Korea Electric Power Corporation; Kyushu Electric Power Company Inc.
Keppel Corporation Ltd., 73 201–03
Keramik Holding AG Laufen, 51 194–96
Kerasotes ShowPlace Theaters LLC, 80 179–83
Kerr Group Inc., 24 263–65
Kerr-McGee Corporation, IV 445–47; 22 301–04 (upd.); 68 217–21 (upd.)
Kerry Group plc, 27 258–60; 87 285–291 (upd.)

Kerry Properties Limited, 22 305–08
Kerzner International Limited, 69 222–24 (upd.)
Kesa Electricals plc, 91 285–90
Kesko Ltd (Kesko Oy), 8 293–94; 27 261–63 (upd.)
Ketchum Communications Inc., 6 38–40
Kettle Foods Inc., 48 240–42
Kewaunee Scientific Corporation, 25 259–62
Kewpie Kabushiki Kaisha, 57 202–05
Key Safety Systems, Inc., 63 224–26
Key Tronic Corporation, 14 284–86
KeyCorp, 8 295–97; 92272–81 (upd.)
Keyes Fibre Company, 9 303–05
Keys Fitness Products, LP, 83 231–234
KeySpan Energy Co., 27 264–66
Keystone International, Inc., 11 225–27
see also Tyco International Ltd.
KFC Corporation, 7 265–68; 21 313–17 (upd.); 89 290–96 (upd.)
Kforce Inc., 71 188–90
KGHM Polska Miedz S.A., 98 223–26
KHD Konzern, III 541–44
KI, 57 206–09
Kia Motors Corporation, 12 293–95; 29 264–67 (upd.); 56 173
Kiabi Europe, 66 199–201
Kidde plc, I 475–76; 44 255–59 (upd.)
Kiehl's Since 1851, Inc., 52 209–12
Kikkoman Corporation, 14 287–89; 47 203–06 (upd.)
Kimball International, Inc., 12 296–98; 48 243–47 (upd.)
Kimberly-Clark Corporation, III 40–41; 16 302–05 (upd.); 43 256–60 (upd.)
Kimberly-Clark de México, S.A. de C.V., 54 185–87
Kimco Realty Corporation, 11 228–30
Kinder Morgan, Inc., 45 227–30
KinderCare Learning Centers, Inc., 13 298–300
Kinetic Concepts, Inc., 20 321–23
King & Spalding, 23 315–18
The King Arthur Flour Company, 31 292–95
King Kullen Grocery Co., Inc., 15 259–61
King Nut Company, 74 165–67
King Pharmaceuticals, Inc., 54 188–90
King Ranch, Inc., 14 290–92; 60 186–89 (upd.)
King World Productions, Inc., 9 306–08; 30 269–72 (upd.)
Kingfisher plc, V 106–09; 24 266–71 (upd.); 83 235-242 (upd.)
Kingston Technology Corporation, 20 324–26
Kinki Nippon Railway Company Ltd., V 463–65
Kinko's Inc., 16 306–08; 43 261–64 (upd.)
Kinney Shoe Corp., 14 293–95
Kinray Inc., 85 209–12
Kinross Gold Corporation, 36 314–16
Kintera, Inc., 75 225–27

Kirby Corporation, 18 277–79; 66 202–04 (upd.)
Kirin Brewery Company, Limited, I 265–66; 21 318–21 (upd.); 63 227–31 (upd.)
Kirkland & Ellis LLP, 65 194–96
Kirlin's Inc., 98 227–30
Kirshenbaum Bond + Partners, Inc., 57 210–12
Kit Manufacturing Co., 18 280–82
Kitchell Corporation, 14 296–98
KitchenAid, 8 298–99
Kitty Hawk, Inc., 22 309–11
Kiva, 95 225–29
Kiwi International Airlines Inc., 20 327–29
KKR see Kohlberg Kravis Roberts & Co.
KLA-Tencor Corporation, 11 231–33; 45 231–34 (upd.)
Klabin S.A., 73 204–06
Klasky Csupo, Inc., 78 193–97
Klaus Steilmann GmbH & Co. KG, 53 192–95
Klein Tools, Inc., 95 230–34
Kleiner, Perkins, Caufield & Byers, 53 196–98
Kleinwort Benson Group PLC, II 421–23; 22 55 see also Dresdner Kleinwort Wasserstein.
Klement's Sausage Company, 61 147–49
KLM Royal Dutch Airlines see Koninklijke Luftvaart Maatschappij N.V.
Klöckner-Werke AG, IV 126–28; 58 201–05 (upd.)
Kluwer Publishers see Wolters Kluwer NV.
Kmart Corporation, V 110–12; 18 283–87 (upd.); 47 207–12 (upd.)
KN see Kühne & Nagel Group.
Knape & Vogt Manufacturing Company, 17 277–79
K'Nex Industries, Inc., 52 206–08
Knight-Ridder, Inc., IV 628–30; 15 262–66 (upd.); 67 219–23 (upd.)
Knight Trading Group, Inc., 70 147–49
Knight Transportation, Inc., 64 218–21
Knoll, Inc., 14 299–301; 80 184–88 (upd.)
Knorr-Bremse AG, 84 226–231
Knorr Co. see C.H. Knorr Co.
The Knot, Inc., 74 168–71
Knott's Berry Farm, 18 288–90
Knowledge Learning Corporation, 51 197–99; 54 191
Knowledge Universe, Inc., 54 191–94
KnowledgeWare Inc., 9 309–11; 31 296–98 (upd.)
KOA see Kampgrounds of America, Inc.
Koala Corporation, 44 260–62
Kobe Steel, Ltd., IV 129–31; 19 238–41 (upd.)
Kobrand Corporation, 82 191–94
Koç Holding A.S., I 478–80; 54 195–98 (upd.)
Koch Enterprises, Inc., 29 215–17
Koch Industries, Inc., IV 448–49; 20 330–32 (upd.); 77 224–30 (upd.)

Kodak *see* Eastman Kodak Co.

Kodansha Ltd., IV 631–33; 38 273–76 (upd.)

Koenig & Bauer AG, 64 222–26

Kohl's Corporation, 9 312–13; 30 273–75 (upd.); 77 231–35 (upd.)

Kohlberg Kravis Roberts & Co., 24 272–74; 56 190–94 (upd.)

Kohler Company, 7 269–71; 32 308–12 (upd.)

Kohn Pedersen Fox Associates P.C., 57 213–16

Kolbenschmidt Pierburg AG, 97 249–53

The Koll Company, 8 300–02

Kollmorgen Corporation, 18 291–94

Kolmar Laboratories Group, 96 240–43

Komag, Inc., 11 234–35

Komatsu Ltd., III 545–46; 16 309–11 (upd.); 52 213–17 (upd.)

Konami Corporation, 96 244–47

KONE Corporation, 27 267–70; 76 225–28 (upd.)

Konica Corporation, III 547–50; 30 276–81 (upd.)

König Brauerei GmbH & Co. KG, 35 256–58 (upd.)

Koninklijke Ahold N.V., II 641–42; 16 312–14 (upd.)

Koninklijke Grolsch BV *see* Royal Grolsch NV.

Koninklijke Houthandel G Wijma & Zonen BV, 96 248–51

Koninklijke KPN N.V. *see* Royal KPN N.V.

Koninklijke Luchtvaart Maatschappij N.V., I 107–09; 28 224–27 (upd.)

Koninklijke Nederlandsche Hoogovens en Staalfabrieken NV, IV 132–34

N.V. Koninklijke Nederlandse Vliegtuigenfabriek Fokker, I 54–56; 28 327–30 (upd.)

Koninklijke Nedlloyd N.V., 6 403–05; 26 241–44 (upd.)

Koninklijke Numico N.V. *see* Royal Numico N.V.

Koninklijke Philips Electronics N.V., 50 297–302 (upd.)

Koninklijke PTT Nederland NV, V 299–301 *see also* Royal KPN NV.

Koninklijke Vendex KBB N.V. (Royal Vendex KBB N.V.), 62 206–09 (upd.)

Koninklijke Wessanen nv, II 527–29; 54 199–204 (upd.)

Koo Koo Roo, Inc., 25 263–65

Kookmin Bank, 58 206–08

Kooperativa Förbundet, 99 245–248

Koor Industries Ltd., II 47–49; 25 266–68 (upd.); 68 222–25 (upd.)

Kopin Corporation, 80 189–92

Koppers Industries, Inc., I 354–56; 26 245–48 (upd.)

Korbel Champagne Cellars *see* F. Korbel & Bros. Inc.

Körber AG, 60 190–94

Korea Electric Power Corporation (Kepco), 56 195–98

Korean Air Lines Co. Ltd., 6 98–99; 27 271–73 (upd.)

Koret of California, Inc., 62 210–13

Korn/Ferry International, 34 247–49

Kos Pharmaceuticals, Inc., 63 232–35

Koss Corporation, 38 277–79

Kotobukiya Co., Ltd., V 113–14; 56 199–202 (upd.)

KPMG International, 10 385–87; 33 234–38 (upd.)

KPN *see* Koninklijke PTT Nederland N.V.

Kraft Foods Inc., II 530–34; 7 272–77 (upd.); 45 235–44 (upd.); 91 291–306 (upd.)

Kraft Jacobs Suchard AG, 26 249–52 (upd.)

KraftMaid Cabinetry, Inc., 72 208–10

Kraus-Anderson Companies, Inc., 36 317–20; 83 243-248 (upd.)

Krause Publications, Inc., 35 259–61

Krause's Furniture, Inc., 27 274–77

Kredietbank N.V., II 304–056

Kreditanstalt für Wiederaufbau, 29 268–72

Kreisler Manufacturing Corporation, 97 254–57

Krispy Kreme Doughnut Corporation, 21 322–24; 61 150–54 (upd.)

The Kroger Company, II 643–45; 15 267–70 (upd.); 65 197–202 (upd.)

Kroll Inc., 57 217–20

Kronos, Inc., 18 295–97; 19 468

Kruger Inc., 17 280–82

Krung Thai Bank Public Company Ltd., 69 225–27

Krupp AG *see* Fried. Krupp GmbH; ThyssenKrupp AG.

Kruse International, 88 227–30

The Krystal Company, 33 239–42

KSB AG, 62 214–18

KT&G Corporation, 62 219–21

K2 Inc., 16 295–98; 84 206–211 (upd.)

KU Energy Corporation, 11 236–38 *see also* LG&E Energy Corp.

Kubota Corporation, III 551–53

Kudelski Group SA, 44 263–66

Kuehne & Nagel International AG, V 466–69; 53 199–203 (upd.)

Kuhlman Corporation, 20 333–35

Kühne *see* Carl Kühne KG (GmbH & Co.).

Kühne & Nagel International AG, V 466–69

Kulicke and Soffa Industries, Inc., 33 246–48; 76 229–31 (upd.)

Kumagai Gumi Company, Ltd., I 579–80

Kumon Institute of Education Co., Ltd., 72 211–14

Kuoni Travel Holding Ltd., 40 284–86

Kurzweil Technologies, Inc., 51 200–04

The Kushner-Locke Company, 25 269–71

Kuwait Airways Corporation, 68 226–28

Kuwait Flour Mills & Bakeries Company, 84 232–234

Kuwait Petroleum Corporation, IV 450–52; 55 240–43 (upd.)

Kvaerner ASA, 36 321–23

Kwang Yang Motor Company Ltd., 80 193–96

Kwik-Fit Holdings plc, 54 205–07

Kwik Save Group plc, 11 239–41

Kymmene Corporation, IV 299–303 *see also* UPM-Kymmene Corp.

Kyocera Corporation, II 50–52; 21 329–32 (upd.); 79 231–36 (upd.)

Kyokuyo Company Ltd., 75 228–30

Kyowa Hakko Kogyo Co., Ltd., III 42–43; 48 248–50 (upd.)

Kyphon Inc., 87 292–295

Kyushu Electric Power Company Inc., V 649–51

L

L. and J.G. Stickley, Inc., 50 303–05

L-3 Communications Holdings, Inc., 48 251–53

L.A. Darling Company, 92 203–06

L.A. Gear, Inc., 8 303–06; 32 313–17 (upd.)

L.A. T Sportswear, Inc., 26 257–59

L.B. Foster Company, 33 255–58

L.D.C. SA, 61 155–57

L.L. Bean, Inc., 10 388–90; 38 280–83 (upd.); 91 307–13 (upd.)

The L.L. Knickerbocker Co., Inc., 25 272–75

L. Luria & Son, Inc., 19 242–44

L. M. Berry and Company, 80 197–200

L.S. Starrett Company, 13 301–03; 64 227–30 (upd.)

La Choy Food Products Inc., 25 276–78

La Madeleine French Bakery & Café, 33 249–51

La Poste, V 270–72; 47 213–16 (upd.)

The La Quinta Companies, 11 242–44; 42 213–16 (upd.)

La Reina Inc., 96 252–55

La Senza Corporation, 66 205–07

La-Z-Boy Incorporated, 14 302–04; 50 309–13 (upd.)

LAB *see* Lloyd Aéreo Boliviano S.A

LaBarge Inc., 41 224–26

Labatt Brewing Company Limited, I 267–68; 25 279–82 (upd.)

Labeyrie SAS, 80 201–04

LabOne, Inc., 48 254–57

Labor Ready, Inc., 29 273–75; 88 231–36 (upd.)

Laboratoires Arkopharma S.A., 75 231–34

Laboratoires de Biologie Végétale Yves Rocher, 35 262–65

Laboratory Corporation of America Holdings, 42 217–20 (upd.)

LaBranche & Co. Inc., 37 223–25

LaCie Group S.A., 76 232–34

Lacks Enterprises Inc., 61 158–60

Laclede Steel Company, 15 271–73

LaCrosse Footwear, Inc., 18 298–301; 61 161–65 (upd.)

Ladbroke Group PLC, II 141–42; 21 333–36 (upd.) *see also* Hilton Group plc.

LADD Furniture, Inc., 12 299–301 *see also* La-Z-Boy Inc.
Ladish Co., Inc., 30 282–84
Lafarge Cement UK, 54 208–11 (upd.)
Lafarge Coppée S.A., III 703–05
Lafarge Corporation, 28 228–31
Lafuma S.A., 39 248–50
Laidlaw International, Inc., 80 205–08
Laing O'Rourke PLC, 93 282–85 (upd.)
L'Air Liquide SA, I 357–59; 47 217–20 (upd.)
Lakeland Industries, Inc., 45 245–48
Lakes Entertainment, Inc., 51 205–07
Lakeside Foods, Inc., 89 297–301
Lala *see* Grupo Industrial Lala, S.A. de C.V.
Lam Research Corporation, 11 245–47; 31 299–302 (upd.)
Lam Son Sugar Joint Stock Corporation (Lasuco), 60 195–97
Lamar Advertising Company, 27 278–80; 70 150–53 (upd.)
The Lamaur Corporation, 41 227–29
Lamb Weston, Inc., 23 319–21
Lamborghini *see* Automobili Lamborghini S.p.A.
Lamonts Apparel, Inc., 15 274–76
The Lamson & Sessions Co., 13 304–06; 61 166–70 (upd.)
Lan Chile S.A., 31 303–06
Lancair International, Inc., 67 224–26
Lancaster Colony Corporation, 8 307–09; 61 171–74 (upd.)
Lance, Inc., 14 305–07; 41 230–33 (upd.)
Lancer Corporation, 21 337–39
Land O'Lakes, Inc., II 535–37; 21 340–43 (upd.); 81 222–27 (upd.)
Land Securities PLC, IV 704–06; 49 246–50 (upd.)
LandAmerica Financial Group, Inc., 85 213–16
Landauer, Inc., 51 208–10
Landec Corporation, 95 235–38
Landmark Communications, Inc., 12 302–05; 55 244–49 (upd.)
Landmark Theatre Corporation, 70 154–56
Landor Associates, 81 228–31
Landry's Restaurants, Inc., 15 277–79; 65 203–07 (upd.)
Lands' End, Inc., 9 314–16; 29 276–79 (upd.); 82 195–200 (upd.)
Landsbanki Islands hf, 81 232–35
Landstar System, Inc., 63 236–38
Lane Bryant, Inc., 64 231–33
The Lane Co., Inc., 12 306–08
Lanier Worldwide, Inc., 75 235–38
Lanoga Corporation, 62 222–24 *see also* Pro-Build Holdings Inc.
Lapeyre S.A. *see* Groupe Lapeyre S.A.
Larry Flynt Publishing Inc., 31 307–10
Larry H. Miller Group, 29 280–83
Las Vegas Sands, Inc., 50 306–08
Laserscope, 67 227–29
LaSiDo Inc., 58 209–11
Lason, Inc., 31 311–13
Lassonde Industries Inc., 68 229–31

Lasuco *see* Lam Son Sugar Joint Stock Corp.
Latham & Watkins, 33 252–54
Latrobe Brewing Company, 54 212–14
Lattice Semiconductor Corp., 16 315–17
Lauda Air Luftfahrt AG, 48 258–60
Laura Ashley Holdings plc, 13 307–09; 37 226–29 (upd.)
The Laurel Pub Company Limited, 59 255–57
Laurent-Perrier SA, 42 221–23
Laurus N.V., 65 208–11
Lavoro Bank AG *see* Banca Nazionale del Lavoro SpA.
Lawson Software, 38 284–88
Lawter International Inc., 14 308–10 *see also* Eastman Chemical Co.
Layne Christensen Company, 19 245–47
Lazard LLC, 38 289–92
Lazare Kaplan International Inc., 21 344–47
Lazio *see* Società Sportiva Lazio SpA.
Lazy Days RV Center, Inc., 69 228–30
LCA-Vision, Inc, 85 217–20
LCC International, Inc., 84 235–238
LCI International, Inc., 16 318–20 *see also* Qwest Communications International, Inc.
LDB Corporation, 53 204–06
LDC, 68 232–34
LDC S.A.*see* L.D.C. S.A.
LDDS-Metro Communications, Inc., 8 310–12 *see also* MCI WorldCom, Inc.
LDI Ltd., LLC, 76 235–37
Le Bon Marché *see* The Bon Marché.
Le Chateau Inc., 63 239–41
Le Cordon Bleu S.A., 67 230–32
Le Duff *see* Groupe Le Duff S.A.
Le Monde S.A., 33 308–10
Léa Nature *see* Groupe Léa Nature.
Leap Wireless International, Inc., 69 231–33
LeapFrog Enterprises, Inc., 54 215–18
Lear Corporation, 16 321–23; 71 191–95 (upd.)
Lear Siegler Inc., I 481–83
Learjet Inc., 8 313–16; 27 281–85 (upd.)
Learning Care Group, Inc., 76 238–41 (upd.)
The Learning Company Inc., 24 275–78
Learning Tree International Inc., 24 279–82
LeaRonal, Inc., 23 322–24 *see also* Rohm and Haas Co.
Leaseway Transportation Corp., 12 309–11
Leatherman Tool Group, Inc., 51 211–13
Lebhar-Friedman, Inc., 55 250–52
Leblanc Corporation *see* G. Leblanc Corp.
LeBoeuf, Lamb, Greene & MacRae, L.L.P., 29 284–86
LECG Corporation, 93 286–89
Leche Pascual *see* Grupo Leche Pascual S.A.

Lechmere Inc., 10 391–93
Lechters, Inc., 11 248–50; 39 251–54 (upd.)
Leclerc *see* Association des Centres Distributeurs E. Leclerc.
LeCroy Corporation, 41 234–37
Ledcor Industries Limited, 46 266–69
Ledesma Sociedad Anónima Agrícola Industrial, 62 225–27
Lee Apparel Company, Inc., 8 317–19
Lee Enterprises, Incorporated, 11 251–53; 64 234–37 (upd.)
Leeann Chin, Inc., 30 285–88
Lefrak Organization Inc., 26 260–62
Legal & General Group plc, III 272–73; 24 283–85 (upd.)
The Legal Aid Society, 48 261–64
Legal Sea Foods Inc., 96 256–60
Legent Corporation, 10 394–96 *see also* Computer Associates International, Inc.
Legg Mason, Inc., 33 259–62
Leggett & Platt, Inc., 11 254–56; 48 265–68 (upd.)
Lego A/S, 13 310–13; 40 287–91 (upd.)
Legrand SA, 21 348–50
Lehigh Portland Cement Company, 23 325–27
Lehman Brothers Holdings Inc., 99 249–253 (upd.)
Leica Camera AG, 35 266–69
Leica Microsystems Holdings GmbH, 35 270–73
Leidy's, Inc., 93 290–92
Leinenkugel Brewing Company *see* Jacob Leinenkugel Brewing Co.
Leiner Health Products Inc., 34 250–52
Lend Lease Corporation Limited, IV 707–09; 17 283–86 (upd.); 52 218–23 (upd.)
LendingTree, LLC, 93 293–96
Lennar Corporation, 11 257–59
Lennox International Inc., 8 320–22; 28 232–36 (upd.)
Lenovo Group Ltd., 80 209–12
Lenox, Inc., 12 312–13
LensCrafters Inc., 23 328–30; 76 242–45 (upd.)
L'Entreprise Jean Lefebvre, 23 331–33 *see also* Vinci.
Leo Burnett Company, Inc., I 22–24; 20 336–39 (upd.)
The Leona Group LLC, 84 239–242
Leoni AG, 98 231–36
Leprino Foods Company, 28 237–39
Leroux S.A.S., 65 212–14
Leroy Merlin SA, 54 219–21
Les Boutiques San Francisco, Inc., 62 228–30
Les Echos *see* Groupe Les Echos.
Les Schwab Tire Centers, 50 314–16
Lesaffre *see* Societe Industrielle Lesaffre.
Lesco Inc., 19 248–50
The Leslie Fay Company, Inc., 8 323–25; 39 255–58 (upd.)
Leslie's Poolmart, Inc., 18 302–04
Leucadia National Corporation, 11 260–62; 71 196–200 (upd.)
Leupold & Stevens, Inc., 52 224–26

Level 3 Communications, Inc., 67 233–35

Levenger Company, 63 242–45

Lever Brothers Company, 9 317–19 *see also* Unilever.

Levi, Ray & Shoup, Inc., 96 261–64

Levi Strauss & Co., V 362–65; 16 324–28 (upd.)

Levitz Furniture Inc., 15 280–82

Levy Restaurants L.P., 26 263–65

Lewis Drug Inc., 94 272–76

Lewis Galoob Toys Inc., 16 329–31

LEXIS-NEXIS Group, 33 263–67

Lexmark International, Inc., 18 305–07; 79 237–42 (upd.)

LG&E Energy Corporation, 6 516–18; 51 214–17 (upd.)

LG Corporation, 94 277–83 (upd.)

Li & Fung Limited, 59 258–61

Libbey Inc., 49 251–54

The Liberty Corporation, 22 312–14

Liberty Livewire Corporation, 42 224–27

Liberty Media Corporation, 50 317–19

Liberty Mutual Holding Company, 59 262–64

Liberty Orchards Co., Inc., 89 302–05

Liberty Property Trust, 57 221–23

Liberty Travel, Inc., 56 203–06

Libyan National Oil Corporation, IV 453–55 *see also* National Oil Corp.

Liebherr-International AG, 64 238–42

Life Care Centers of America Inc., 76 246–48

Life is good, Inc., 80 213–16

Life Technologies, Inc., 17 287–89

Life Time Fitness, Inc., 66 208–10

LifeCell Corporation, 77 236–39

Lifeline Systems, Inc., 32 374; 53 207–09

LifeLock, Inc., 91 314–17

LifePoint Hospitals, Inc., 69 234–36

Lifetime Brands, Inc., 27 286–89; 73 207–11 (upd.)

Lifetime Entertainment Services, 51 218–22

Lifetouch Inc., 86 243–47

Lifeway Foods, Inc., 65 215–17

LifeWise Health Plan of Oregon, Inc., 90 276–79

Ligand Pharmaceuticals Incorporated, 10 48; 47 221–23

LILCO *see* Long Island Lighting Co.

Lillian Vernon Corporation, 12 314–15; 35 274–77 (upd.); 92 207–12 (upd.)

Lilly & Co *see* Eli Lilly & Co.

Lilly Endowment Inc., 70 157–59

Limagrain *see* Groupe Limagrain.

The Limited, Inc., V 115–16; 20 340–43 (upd.)

LIN Broadcasting Corp., 9 320–22

Linamar Corporation, 18 308–10

Lincare Holdings Inc., 43 265–67

Lincoln Center for the Performing Arts, Inc., 69 237–41

Lincoln Electric Co., 13 314–16

Lincoln National Corporation, III 274–77; 25 286–90 (upd.)

Lincoln Property Company, 8 326–28; 54 222–26 (upd.)

Lincoln Snacks Company, 24 286–88

Lincoln Telephone & Telegraph Company, 14 311–13

Lindal Cedar Homes, Inc., 29 287–89

Linde AG, I 581–83; 67 236–39 (upd.)

Lindley *see* Corporación José R. Lindley S.A.

Lindsay Manufacturing Co., 20 344–46

Lindt & Sprüngli *see* Chocoladefabriken Lindt & Sprüngli AG.

Linear Technology Corporation, 16 332–34; 99 254–258 (upd.)

Linens 'n Things, Inc., 24 289–92; 75 239–43 (upd.)

Lintas: Worldwide, 14 314–16

The Lion Brewery, Inc., 86 248–52

Lion Corporation, III 44–45; 51 223–26 (upd.)

Lion Nathan Limited, 54 227–30

Lionel L.L.C., 16 335–38; 99 259–265 (upd.)

Lions Gate Entertainment Corporation, 35 278–81

Lipman Electronic Engineering Ltd., 81 236–39

Lipton *see* Thomas J. Lipton Co.

Liqui-Box Corporation, 16 339–41

Liquidnet, Inc., 79 243–46

LIRR *see* The Long Island Rail Road Co.

Litehouse Inc., 60 198–201

Lithia Motors, Inc., 41 238–40

Littelfuse, Inc., 26 266–69

Little Caesar Enterprises, Inc., 7 278–79; 24 293–96 (upd.) *see also* Ilitch Holdings Inc.

Little Switzerland, Inc., 60 202–04

Little Tikes Company, 13 317–19; 62 231–34 (upd.)

Littleton Coin Company Inc., 82 201–04

Littlewoods plc, V 117–19; 42 228–32 (upd.)

Litton Industries Inc., I 484–86; 11 263–65 (upd.) *see also* Avondale Industries; Northrop Grumman Corp.

LIVE Entertainment Inc., 20 347–49

Live Nation, Inc., 80 217–22 (upd.)

LivePerson, Inc., 91 318–21

Liz Claiborne, Inc., 8 329–31; 25 291–94 (upd.)

LKQ Corporation, 71 201–03

Lloyd Aéreo Boliviano S.A., 95 239–42

Lloyd's, III 278–81; 22 315–19 (upd.); 74 172–76 (upd.)

Lloyds TSB Group plc, II 306–09; 47 224–29 (upd.)

LM Ericsson *see* Telefonaktiebolaget LM Ericsson.

Loblaw Companies Limited, 43 268–72

Lockheed Martin Corporation, I 64–66; 11 266–69 (upd.); 15 283–86 (upd.); 89 306–11 (upd.)

Loctite Corporation, 8 332–34; 30 289–91 (upd.)

LodgeNet Entertainment Corporation, 28 240–42

Loehmann's Inc., 24 297–99

Loewe AG, 90 280–85

The Loewen Group, Inc., 16 342–44; 40 292–95 (upd.) *see also* Alderwoods Group Inc.

Loews Corporation, I 487–88; 12 316–18 (upd.); 36 324–28 (upd.); 93 297–304 (upd.)

Logan's Roadhouse, Inc., 29 290–92

Loganair Ltd., 68 235–37

Logica plc, 14 317–19; 37 230–33 (upd.)

Logicon Inc., 20 350–52 *see also* Northrop Grumman Corp.

Logitech International S.A., 28 243–45; 69 242–45 (upd.)

LoJack Corporation, 48 269–73

Lojas Americanas S.A., 77 240–43

Lojas Arapuã S.A., 22 320–22; 61 175–78 (upd.)

Loma Negra C.I.A.S.A., 95 243–46

London Drugs Ltd., 46 270–73

London Fog Industries, Inc., 29 293–96

London Regional Transport, 6 406–08

London Scottish Bank plc, 70 160–62

London Stock Exchange Limited, 34 253–56

Lone Star Steakhouse & Saloon, Inc., 51 227–29

Lonely Planet Publications Pty Ltd., 55 253–55

The Long & Foster Companies, Inc, 85 221–24

Long Island Bancorp, Inc., 16 345–47

Long Island Lighting Company, V 652–54

The Long Island Rail Road Company, 68 238–40

Long John Silver's, 13 320–22; 57 224–29 (upd.)

Long-Term Credit Bank of Japan, Ltd., II 310–11

The Longaberger Company, 12 319–21; 44 267–70 (upd.)

Longs Drug Stores Corporation, V 120; 25 295–97 (upd.); 83 249–253 (upd.)

Longview Fibre Company, 8 335–37; 37 234–37 (upd.)

Lonmin plc, 66 211–16 (upd.)

Lookers plc, 71 204–06

Loral Space & Communications Ltd., 8 338–40; 54 231–35 (upd.)

L'Oréal, III 46–49; 8 341–44 (upd.); 46 274–79 (upd.)

Los Angeles Lakers *see* California Sports, Inc.

Lost Arrow Inc., 22 323–25

LOT Polish Airlines (Polskie Linie Lotnicze S.A.), 33 268–71

LOT$OFF Corporation, 24 300–01

Lotte Confectionery Company Ltd., 76 249–51

Lotus Cars Ltd., 14 320–22

Lotus Development Corporation, 6 254–56; 25 298–302 (upd.)

LOUD Technologies, Inc., 95 247–50 (upd.)

Louis Dreyfus *see* Groupe Louis Dreyfus S.A.

Louis Vuitton, 10 397–99 *see also* LVMH Moët Hennessy Louis Vuitton SA.

The Louisiana Land and Exploration Company, 7 280–83

Louisiana-Pacific Corporation, IV 304–05; 31 314–17 (upd.)

Love's Travel Stops & Country Stores, Inc., 71 207–09

Lowe's Companies, Inc., V 122–23; 21 356–58 (upd.); 81 240–44 (upd.)

Löwenbräu AG, 80 223–27

Lowrance Electronics, Inc., 18 311–14

LPA Holding Corporation, 81 245–48

LSB Industries, Inc., 77 244–47

LSI *see* Lear Siegler Inc.

LSI Logic Corporation, 13 323–25; 64 243–47

LTU Group Holding GmbH, 37 238–41

The LTV Corporation, I 489–91; 24 302–06 (upd.)

The Lubrizol Corporation, I 360–62; 30 292–95 (upd.); 83 254-259 (upd.)

Luby's, Inc., 17 290–93; 42 233–38 (upd.); 99 266–273 (upd.)

Lucas Industries Plc, III 554–57

Lucasfilm Ltd., 12 322–24; 50 320–23 (upd.)

Lucent Technologies Inc., 34 257–60

Lucille Farms, Inc., 45 249–51

Lucky-Goldstar, II 53–54 *see also* LG Corp.

Lucky Stores Inc., 27 290–93

Ludendo S.A., 88 237–40

Lufkin Industries, Inc., 78 198–202

Lufthansa *see* Deutsche Lufthansa AG.

Luigino's, Inc., 64 248–50

Lukens Inc., 14 323–25 *see also* Bethlehem Steel Corp.

LUKOIL *see* OAO LUKOIL.

Luminar Plc, 40 296–98

Lunar Corporation, 29 297–99

Lunardi's Super Market, Inc., 99 274–277

Lund Food Holdings, Inc., 22 326–28

Lund International Holdings, Inc., 40 299–301

Lush Ltd., 93 305–08

Lutheran Brotherhood, 31 318–21

Luxottica SpA, 17 294–96; 52 227–30 (upd.)

LVMH Moët Hennessy Louis Vuitton SA, 33 272–77 (upd.) *see also* Christian Dior S.A.

Lycos *see* Terra Lycos, Inc.

Lydall, Inc., 64 251–54

Lyfra-S.A./NV, 88 241–43

Lyman-Richey Corporation, 96 265–68

Lynch Corporation, 43 273–76

Lynden Incorporated, 91 322–25

Lyondell Chemical Company, IV 456–57; 45 252–55 (upd.)

Lyonnaise des Eaux-Dumez, V 655–57 *see also* Suez Lyonnaise des Eaux.

M

M&F Worldwide Corp., 38 293–95

M-real Oyj, 56 252–55 (upd.)

M.A. Bruder & Sons, Inc., 56 207–09

M.A. Gedney Co., 51 230–32

M.A. Hanna Company, 8 345–47 *see also* PolyOne Corp.

M. DuMont Schauberg GmbH & Co. KG, 92 213–17

M.E.P.C. Ltd. *see* MEPC plc.

M.H. Meyerson & Co., Inc., 46 280–83

M. Shanken Communications, Inc., 50 324–27

Maatschappij tot Exploitatie van de Onderneming Krasnapolsky *see* Grand Hotel Krasnapolsky N.V.

Mabe *see* Controladora Mabe, S.A. de C.V.

Mabuchi Motor Co. Ltd., 68 241–43

Mac Frugal's Bargains - Closeouts Inc., 17 297–99 *see also* Big Lots, Inc.

Mac-Gray Corporation, 44 271–73

The Macallan Distillers Ltd., 63 246–48

MacAndrews & Forbes Holdings Inc., 28 246–49; 86 253–59 (upd.)

MacArthur Foundation *see* The John D. and Catherine T. MacArthur Foundation.

Mace Security International, Inc., 57 230–32

The Macerich Company, 57 233–35

MacGregor Golf Company, 68 244–46

Mack-Cali Realty Corporation, 42 239–41

Mack Trucks, Inc., I 177–79; 22 329–32 (upd.); 61 179–83 (upd.)

Mackay Envelope Corporation, 45 256–59

Mackays Stores Group Ltd., 92 218–21

Mackie Designs Inc., 33 278–81 *see also* LOUD Technologies, Inc.

Macklowe Properties, Inc., 95 251–54

Maclean Hunter Publishing Limited, IV 638–40; 26 270–74 (upd.) *see also* Rogers Communications Inc.

MacMillan Bloedel Limited, IV 306–09 *see also* Weyerhaeuser Co.

Macmillan, Inc., 7 284–86

The MacNeal-Schwendler Corporation, 25 303–05

MacNeil/Lehrer Productions, 87 296–299

Macquarie Bank Ltd., 69 246–49

Macromedia, Inc., 50 328–31

Macy's, Inc., 94 284–93 (upd.)

MADD *see* Mothers Against Drunk Driving.

Madden's on Gull Lake, 52 231–34

Madeco S.A., 71 210–12

Madeira Wine Company, S.A., 49 255–57

Madge Networks N.V., 26 275–77

Madison Dearborn Partners, LLC, 97 258–61

Madison Gas and Electric Company, 39 259–62

Madison-Kipp Corporation, 58 213–16

Madrange SA, 58 217–19

Mag Instrument, Inc., 67 240–42

Magellan Aerospace Corporation, 48 274–76

MaggieMoo's International, 89 312–16

Magma Copper Company, 7 287–90 *see also* BHP Billiton.

Magma Design Automation Inc., 78 203–27

Magma Power Company, 11 270–72

MagneTek, Inc., 15 287–89; 41 241–44 (upd.)

Magneti Marelli Holding SpA, 90 286–89

Magyar Telekom Rt, 78 208–11

MAI Systems Corporation, 11 273–76

Maid-Rite Corporation, 62 235–38

Maidenform, Inc., 20 352–55; 59 265–69 (upd.)

Mail Boxes Etc., 18 315–17; 41 245–48 (upd.) *see also* U.S. Office Products Co.

Mail-Well, Inc., 28 250–52 *see also* Cenveo Inc.

MAIN *see* Makhteshim-Agan Industries Ltd.

Maine & Maritimes Corporation, 56 210–13

Maine Central Railroad Company, 16 348–50

Maines Paper & Food Service Inc., 71 213–15

Maison Louis Jadot, 24 307–09

Majesco Entertainment Company, 85 225–29

The Major Automotive Companies, Inc., 45 260–62

Make-A-Wish Foundation of America, 97 262–65

Makhteshim-Agan Industries Ltd., 85 230–34

Makita Corporation, 22 333–35; 59 270–73 (upd.)

Malayan Banking Berhad, 72 215–18

Malaysian Airline System Berhad, 6 100–02; 29 300–03 (upd.); 97 266–71 (upd.)

Malcolm Pirnie, Inc., 42 242–44

Malden Mills Industries, Inc., 16 351–53 *see also* Polartec LLC.

Malév Plc, 24 310–12

Mallinckrodt Group Inc., 19 251–53

Malt-O-Meal Company, 22 336–38; 63 249–53 (upd.)

Mammoet Transport B.V., 26 278–80

Man Aktiengesellschaft, III 561–63

MAN Roland Druckmaschinen AG, 94 294–98

Management and Training Corporation, 28 253–56

Manatron, Inc., 86 260–63

Manchester United Football Club plc, 30 296–98

Mandalay Resort Group, 32 322–26 (upd.)

Mandom Corporation, 82 205–08

Manhattan Associates, Inc., 67 243–45
Manhattan Group, LLC, 80 228–31
Manheim, 88 244–48
Manila Electric Company (Meralco), 56 214–16
Manischewitz Company *see* B. Manischewitz Co.
Manitoba Telecom Services, Inc., 61 184–87
Manitou BF S.A., 27 294–96
The Manitowoc Company, Inc., 18 318–21; 59 274–79 (upd.)
Mannatech Inc., 33 282–85
Mannesmann AG, III 564–67; 14 326–29 (upd.); 38 296–301 (upd.) *see also* Vodafone Group PLC.
Mannheim Steamroller *see* American Gramophone LLC.
Manning Selvage & Lee (MS&L), 76 252–54
MannKind Corporation, 87 300–303
Manor Care, Inc., 6 187–90; 25 306–10 (upd.)
Manpower Inc., 9 326–27; 30 299–302 (upd.); 73 215–18 (upd.)
ManTech International Corporation, 97 272–75
Manufactured Home Communities, Inc., 22 339–41
Manufacturers Hanover Corporation, II 312–14 *see also* Chemical Bank.
Manulife Financial Corporation, 85 235–38
Manutan International S.A., 72 219–21
Manville Corporation, III 706–09; 7 291–95 (upd.) *see also* Johns Manville Corp.
MAPCO Inc., IV 458–59
MAPICS, Inc., 55 256–58
Maple Grove Farms of Vermont, 88 249–52
Maple Leaf Foods Inc., 41 249–53
Maple Leaf Sports & Entertainment Ltd., 61 188–90
Maples Industries, Inc., 83 260-263
Marble Slab Creamery, Inc., 87 304–307
March of Dimes, 31 322–25
Marchesi Antinori SRL, 42 245–48
Marchex, Inc., 72 222–24
marchFIRST, Inc., 34 261–64
Marco Business Products, Inc., 75 244–46
Marco's Franchising LLC, 86 264–67
Marcolin S.p.A., 61 191–94
Marconi plc, 33 286–90 (upd.)
Marcopolo S.A., 79 247–50
The Marcus Corporation, 21 359–63
Marelli *see* Magneti Marelli Holding SpA.
Marfin Popular Bank plc, 92 222–26
Margarete Steiff GmbH, 23 334–37
Marie Brizard et Roger International S.A.S., 22 342–44; 97 276–80 (upd.)
Marie Callender's Restaurant & Bakery, Inc., 28 257–59
Mariella Burani Fashion Group, 92 227–30

Marine Products Corporation, 75 247–49
MarineMax, Inc., 30 303–05
Marion Laboratories Inc., I 648–49
Marion Merrell Dow, Inc., 9 328–29 (upd.)
Marionnaud Parfumeries SA, 51 233–35
Marisa Christina, Inc., 15 290–92
Maritz Inc., 38 302–05
Mark IV Industries, Inc., 7 296–98; 28 260–64 (upd.)
Mark T. Wendell Tea Company, 94 299–302
The Mark Travel Corporation, 80 232–35
Märklin Holding GmbH, 70 163–66
Marks and Spencer p.l.c., V 124–26; 24 313–17 (upd.); 85 239–47 (upd.)
Marks Brothers Jewelers, Inc., 24 318–20 *see also* Whitehall Jewellers, Inc.
Marlin Business Services Corp., 89 317–19
The Marmon Group, Inc., IV 135–38; 16 354–57 (upd.); 70 167–72 (upd.)
Marquette Electronics, Inc., 13 326–28
Marriott International, Inc., III 102–03; 21 364–67 (upd.); 83 264-270 (upd.)
Mars, Incorporated, 7 299–301; 40 302–05 (upd.)
Mars Petcare US Inc., 96 269–72
Marsh & McLennan Companies, Inc., III 282–84; 45 263–67 (upd.)
Marsh Supermarkets, Inc., 17 300–02; 76 255–58 (upd.)
Marshall & Ilsley Corporation, 56 217–20
Marshall Amplification plc, 62 239–42
Marshall Field's, 63 254–63 *see also* Target Corp.
Marshalls Incorporated, 13 329–31
Martek Biosciences Corporation, 65 218–20
Martell and Company S.A., 82 213–16
Marten Transport, Ltd., 84 243–246
Martha Stewart Living Omnimedia, Inc., 24 321–23; 73 219–22 (upd.)
Martignetti Companies, 84 247–250
Martin-Baker Aircraft Company Limited, 61 195–97
Martin Guitar Company *see* C.F. Martin & Co., Inc.
Martin Industries, Inc., 44 274–77
Martin Marietta Corporation, I 67–69 *see also* Lockheed Martin Corp.
MartinLogan, Ltd., 85 248–51
Martini & Rossi SpA, 63 264–66
Martz Group, 56 221–23
Marubeni Corporation, I 492–95; 24 324–27 (upd.)
Maruha Group Inc., 75 250–53 (upd.)
Marui Company Ltd., V 127; 62 243–45 (upd.)
Maruzen Co., Limited, 18 322–24
Marvel Entertainment, Inc., 10 400–02; 78 212–19 (upd.)

Marvin Lumber & Cedar Company, 22 345–47
Mary Kay Inc., 9 330–32; 30 306–09 (upd.); 84 251–256 (upd.)
Maryland & Virginia Milk Producers Cooperative Association, Inc., 80 240–43
Maryville Data Systems Inc., 96 273–76
Marzotto S.p.A., 20 356–58; 67 246–49 (upd.)
The Maschhoffs, Inc., 82 217–20
Masco Corporation, III 568–71; 20 359–63 (upd.); 39 263–68 (upd.)
Maserati *see* Officine Alfieri Maserati S.p.A.
Mashantucket Pequot Gaming Enterprise Inc., 35 282–85
Masland Corporation, 17 303–05 *see also* Lear Corp.
Masonite International Corporation, 63 267–69
Massachusetts Mutual Life Insurance Company, III 285–87; 53 210–13 (upd.)
Massey Energy Company, 57 236–38
MasTec, Inc., 55 259–63 (upd.)
Master Lock Company, 45 268–71
MasterBrand Cabinets, Inc., 71 216–18
MasterCard Worldwide, 9 333–35; 96 277–81 (upd.)
MasterCraft Boat Company, Inc., 90 290–93
Matalan PLC, 49 258–60
Match.com, LP, 87 308–311
Material Sciences Corporation, 63 270–73
The MathWorks, Inc., 80 244–47
Matra-Hachette S.A., 15 293–97 (upd.) *see also* European Aeronautic Defence and Space Company EADS N.V.
Matria Healthcare, Inc., 17 306–09
Matrix Essentials Inc., 90 294–97
Matrix Service Company, 65 221–23
Matrixx Initiatives, Inc., 74 177–79
Matsushita Electric Industrial Co., Ltd., II 55–56; 64 255–58 (upd.)
Matsushita Electric Works, Ltd., III 710–11; 7 302–03 (upd.)
Matsuzakaya Company Ltd., V 129–31; 64 259–62 (upd.)
Matt Prentice Restaurant Group, 70 173–76
Mattel, Inc., 7 304–07; 25 311–15 (upd.); 61 198–203 (upd.)
Matth. Hohner AG, 53 214–17
Matthews International Corporation, 29 304–06; 77 248–52 (upd.)
Matussière et Forest SA, 58 220–22
Maui Land & Pineapple Company, Inc., 29 307–09
Maui Wowi, Inc., 85 252–55
Mauna Loa Macadamia Nut Corporation, 64 263–65
Maurices Inc., 95 255–58
Maus Frères SA, 48 277–79
Maverick Ranch Association, Inc., 88 253–56
Maverick Tube Corporation, 59 280–83

Max & Erma's Restaurants Inc., 19 258–60

Maxco Inc., 17 310–11

Maxicare Health Plans, Inc., III 84–86; 25 316–19 (upd.)

The Maxim Group, 25 320–22

Maxim Integrated Products, Inc., 16 358–60

MAXIMUS, Inc., 43 277–80

Maxtor Corporation, 10 403–05 *see also* Seagate Technology, Inc.

Maxus Energy Corporation, 7 308–10

Maxwell Communication Corporation plc, IV 641–43; 7 311–13 (upd.)

Maxwell Shoe Company, Inc., 30 310–12 *see also* Jones Apparel Group, Inc.

MAXXAM Inc., 8 348–50

Maxxim Medical Inc., 12 325–27

The May Department Stores Company, V 132–35; 19 261–64 (upd.); 46 284–88 (upd.)

May Gurney Integrated Services PLC, 95 259–62

May International *see* George S. May International Co.

Mayer, Brown, Rowe & Maw, 47 230–32

Mayfield Dairy Farms, Inc., 74 180–82

Mayflower Group Inc., 6 409–11

Mayo Foundation, 9 336–39; 34 265–69 (upd.)

Mayor's Jewelers, Inc., 41 254–57

Maytag Corporation, III 572–73; 22 348–51 (upd.); 82 221–25 (upd.)

Mazda Motor Corporation, 9 340–42; 23 338–41 (upd.); 63 274–79 (upd.)

Mazel Stores, Inc., 29 310–12

Mazzio's Corporation, 76 259–61

MBB *see* Messerschmitt-Bölkow-Blohm.

MBC Holding Company, 40 306–09

MBE *see* Mail Boxes Etc.

MBIA Inc., 73 223–26

MBK Industrie S.A., 94 303–06

MBNA Corporation, 12 328–30; 33 291–94 (upd.)

MC Sporting Goods *see* Michigan Sporting Goods Distributors Inc.

MCA Inc., II 143–45 *see also* Universal Studios.

McAfee Inc., 94 307–10

McAlister's Corporation, 66 217–19

McBride plc, 82 226–30

MCC *see* Morris Communications Corp.

McCain Foods Limited, 77 253–56

McCarthy Building Companies, Inc., 48 280–82

McCaw Cellular Communications, Inc., 6 322–24 *see also* AT&T Wireless Services, Inc.

McClain Industries, Inc., 51 236–38

The McClatchy Company, 23 342–44; 92 231–35 (upd.)

McCormick & Company, Incorporated, 7 314–16; 27 297–300 (upd.)

McCormick & Schmick's Seafood Restaurants, Inc., 71 219–21

McCoy Corporation, 58 223–25

McDATA Corporation, 75 254–56

McDermott International, Inc., III 558–60; 37 242–46 (upd.)

McDonald's Corporation, II 646–48; 7 317–19 (upd.); 26 281–85 (upd.); 63 280–86 (upd.)

McDonnell Douglas Corporation, I 70–72; 11 277–80 (upd.) *see also* Boeing Co.

McGrath RentCorp, 91 326–29

The McGraw-Hill Companies, Inc., IV 634–37; 18 325–30 (upd.); 51 239–44 (upd.)

MCI *see* Melamine Chemicals, Inc.

MCI WorldCom, Inc., V 302–04; 27 301–08 (upd.) *see also* Verizon Communications Inc.

McIlhenny Company, 20 364–67

McJunkin Corporation, 63 287–89

McKechnie plc, 34 270–72

McKee Foods Corporation, 7 320–21; 27 309–11 (upd.)

McKesson Corporation, I 496–98; 12 331–33 (upd.); 47 233–37 (upd.)

McKinsey & Company, Inc., 9 343–45

McLane Company, Inc., 13 332–34

McLeodUSA Incorporated, 32 327–30

McMenamins Pubs and Breweries, 65 224–26

McMoRan *see* Freeport-McMoRan Copper & Gold, Inc.

MCN Corporation, 6 519–22

McNaughton Apparel Group, Inc., 92 236–41 (upd.)

McPherson's Ltd., 66 220–22

McQuay International *see* AAF-McQuay Inc.

MCSi, Inc., 41 258–60

McWane Corporation, 55 264–66

MDC Partners Inc., 63 290–92

MDU Resources Group, Inc., 7 322–25; 42 249–53 (upd.)

The Mead Corporation, IV 310–13; 19 265–69 (upd.) *see also* MeadWestvaco Corp.

Mead Data Central, Inc., 10 406–08 *see also* LEXIS-NEXIS Group.

Mead Johnson & Company, 84 257–262

Meade Instruments Corporation, 41 261–64

Meadowcraft, Inc., 29 313–15

MeadWestvaco Corporation, 76 262–71 (upd.)

Measurement Specialties, Inc., 71 222–25

MEC *see* Mitsubishi Estate Company, Ltd.

Mecalux S.A., 74 183–85

Mechel OAO, 99 278–281

Mecklermedia Corporation, 24 328–30 *see also* Jupitermedia Corp.

Medarex, Inc., 85 256–59

Medco Containment Services Inc., 9 346–48 *see also* Merck & Co., Inc.

Médecins sans Frontières, 85 260–63

MEDecision, Inc., 95 263–67

Media Arts Group, Inc., 42 254–57

Media General, Inc., 7 326–28; 38 306–09 (upd.)

Mediacom Communications Corporation, 69 250–52

MediaNews Group, Inc., 70 177–80

Mediaset SpA, 50 332–34

Medical Information Technology Inc., 64 266–69

Medical Management International, Inc., 65 227–29

Medical Staffing Network Holdings, Inc., 89 320–23

Medicis Pharmaceutical Corporation, 59 284–86

Medifast, Inc., 97 281–85

MedImmune, Inc., 35 286–89

Mediolanum S.p.A., 65 230–32

Medis Technologies Ltd., 77 257–60

Meditrust, 11 281–83

Medline Industries, Inc., 61 204–06

Medtronic, Inc., 8 351–54; 30 313–17 (upd.); 67 250–55 (upd.)

Medusa Corporation, 24 331–33

Mega Bloks, Inc., 61 207–09

Megafoods Stores Inc., 13 335–37

Meggitt PLC, 34 273–76

Meguiar's, Inc., 99 282–285

Meidensha Corporation, 92 242–46

Meier & Frank Co., 23 345–47 *see also* Macy's, Inc.

Meijer Incorporated, 7 329–31; 27 312–15 (upd.)

Meiji Dairies Corporation, II 538–39; 82 231–34 (upd.)

Meiji Mutual Life Insurance Company, III 288–89

Meiji Seika Kaisha Ltd., II 540–41; 64 270–72 (upd.)

Mel Farr Automotive Group, 20 368–70

Melaleuca Inc., 31 326–28

Melamine Chemicals, Inc., 27 316–18 *see also* Mississippi Chemical Corp.

Melitta Unternehmensgruppe Bentz KG, 53 218–21

Mello Smello *see* The Miner Group International.

Mellon Financial Corporation, II 315–17; 44 278–82 (upd.)

Mellon-Stuart Co., I 584–85 *see also* Michael Baker Corp.

The Melting Pot Restaurants, Inc., 74 186–88

Melville Corporation, V 136–38 *see also* CVS Corp.

Melvin Simon and Associates, Inc., 8 355–57 *see also* Simon Property Group, Inc.

MEMC Electronic Materials, Inc., 81 249–52

Memorial Sloan-Kettering Cancer Center, 57 239–41

Memry Corporation, 72 225–27

The Men's Wearhouse, Inc., 17 312–15; 48 283–87 (upd.)

Menasha Corporation, 8 358–61; 59 287–92 (upd.)

Mendocino Brewing Company, Inc., 60 205–07

The Mentholatum Company Inc., 32 331–33

Mentor Corporation, 26 286–88

Mentor Graphics Corporation, 11 284–86

MEPC plc, IV 710–12

Mercantile Bankshares Corp., 11 287–88

Mercantile Stores Company, Inc., V 139; 19 270–73 (upd.) *see also* Dillard's Inc.

Mercer International Inc., 64 273–75

Mercian Corporation, 77 261–64

Merck & Co., Inc., I 650–52; 11 289–91 (upd.); 34 280–85 (upd.); 95 268–78 (upd.)

Mercury Air Group, Inc., 20 371–73

Mercury Communications, Ltd., 7 332–34 *see also* Cable and Wireless plc.

Mercury Drug Corporation, 70 181–83

Mercury General Corporation, 25 323–25

Mercury Interactive Corporation, 59 293–95

Mercury Marine Group, 68 247–51

Meredith Corporation, 11 292–94; 29 316–19 (upd.); 74 189–93 (upd.)

Merge Healthcare, 85 264–68

Meridian Bancorp, Inc., 11 295–97

Meridian Gold, Incorporated, 47 238–40

Merillat Industries, LLC, 13 338–39; 69 253–55 (upd.)

Merisant Worldwide, Inc., 70 184–86

Merisel, Inc., 12 334–36

Merit Medical Systems, Inc., 29 320–22

MeritCare Health System, 88 257–61

Meritage Corporation, 26 289–92

Merix Corporation, 36 329–31; 75 257–60 (upd.)

Merriam-Webster Inc., 70 187–91

Merrill Corporation, 18 331–34; 47 241–44 (upd.)

Merrill Lynch & Co., Inc., II 424–26; 13 340–43 (upd.); 40 310–15 (upd.)

Merry-Go-Round Enterprises, Inc., 8 362–64

The Mersey Docks and Harbour Company, 30 318–20

Mervyn's California, 10 409–10; 39 269–71 (upd.) *see also* Target Corp.

Merz Group, 81 253–56

Mesa Air Group, Inc., 11 298–300; 32 334–37 (upd.); 77 265–70 (upd.)

Mesaba Holdings, Inc., 28 265–67

Messerschmitt-Bölkow-Blohm GmbH., I 73–75 *see also* European Aeronautic Defence and Space Company EADS N.V.

Mestek, Inc., 10 411–13

Metal Box plc, I 604–06 *see also* Novar plc.

Metal Management, Inc., 92 247–50

Metaleurop S.A., 21 368–71

Metalico Inc., 97 286–89

Metallgesellschaft AG, IV 139–42; 16 361–66 (upd.)

Metalurgica Mexicana Penoles, S.A. *see* Industrias Penoles, S.A. de C.V.

Metatec International, Inc., 47 245–48

Metcash Trading Ltd., 58 226–28

Meteor Industries Inc., 33 295–97

Methanex Corporation, 40 316–19

Methode Electronics, Inc., 13 344–46

MetLife *see* Metropolitan Life Insurance Co.

Metris Companies Inc., 56 224–27

Metro AG, 50 335–39

Metro-Goldwyn-Mayer Inc., 25 326–30 (upd.); 84 263–270 (upd.)

Métro Inc., 77 271–75

Metro Information Services, Inc., 36 332–34

Metro International S.A., 93 309–12

Metrocall, Inc., 41 265–68

Metromedia Company, 7 335–37; 14 298–300 (upd.); 61 210–14 (upd.)

Métropole Télévision S.A., 76 272–74 (upd.)

Metropolitan Baseball Club Inc., 39 272–75

Metropolitan Financial Corporation, 13 347–49

Metropolitan Life Insurance Company, III 290–94; 52 235–41 (upd.)

The Metropolitan Museum of Art, 55 267–70

Metropolitan Opera Association, Inc., 40 320–23

Metropolitan Transportation Authority, 35 290–92

Metsä-Serla Oy, IV 314–16 *see also* M-real Oyj.

Metso Corporation, 30 321–25 (upd.); 85 269–77 (upd.)

Mettler-Toledo International Inc., 30 326–28

Mexican Restaurants, Inc., 41 269–71

Mexichem, S.A.B. de C.V., 99 286–290

Meyer International Holdings, Ltd., 87 312–315

MFS Communications Company, Inc., 11 301–03 *see also* MCI WorldCom, Inc.

MG&E *see* Madison Gas and Electric.

MGA Entertainment, Inc., 95 279–82

MGIC Investment Corp., 52 242–44

MGM MIRAGE, 17 316–19; 98 237–42 (upd.)

MGM/UA Communications Company, II 146–50 *see also* Metro-Goldwyn-Mayer Inc.

MGN *see* Mirror Group Newspapers Ltd.

Miami Herald Media Company, 92 251–55

Michael Anthony Jewelers, Inc., 24 334–36

Michael Baker Corporation, 14 333–35; 51 245–48 (upd.)

Michael C. Fina Co., Inc., 52 245–47

Michael Foods, Inc., 25 331–34

Michael Page International plc, 45 272–74

Michaels Stores, Inc., 17 320–22; 71 226–30 (upd.)

Michelin *see* Compagnie Générale des Établissements Michelin.

Michigan Bell Telephone Co., 14 336–38

Michigan National Corporation, 11 304–06 *see also* ABN AMRO Holding, N.V.

Michigan Sporting Goods Distributors, Inc., 72 228–30

Micrel, Incorporated, 77 276–79

Micro Warehouse, Inc., 16 371–73

MicroAge, Inc., 16 367–70

Microdot Inc., 8 365–68

Micron Technology, Inc., 11 307–09; 29 323–26 (upd.)

Micros Systems, Inc., 18 335–38

Microsemi Corporation, 94 311–14

Microsoft Corporation, 6 257–60; 27 319–23 (upd.); 63 293–97 (upd.)

MicroStrategy Incorporated, 87 316–320

Mid-America Apartment Communities, Inc., 85 278–81

Mid-America Dairymen, Inc., 7 338–40

Midas Inc., 10 414–15; 56 228–31 (upd.)

Middle East Airlines - Air Liban S.A.L., 79 251–54

The Middleby Corporation, 22 352–55

Middlesex Water Company, 45 275–78

The Middleton Doll Company, 53 222–25

Midland Bank plc, II 318–20; 17 323–26 (upd.) *see also* HSBC Holdings plc.

The Midland Company, 65 233–35

Midway Airlines Corporation, 33 301–03

Midway Games, Inc., 25 335–38

Midwest Air Group, Inc., 35 293–95; 85 282–86 (upd.)

Midwest Grain Products, Inc., 49 261–63

Midwest Resources Inc., 6 523–25

Miele & Cie. KG, 56 232–35

MiG *see* Russian Aircraft Corporation (MiG).

Migros-Genossenschafts-Bund, 68 252–55

MIH Limited, 31 329–32

Mikasa, Inc., 28 268–70

Mike-Sell's Inc., 15 298–300

Mikohn Gaming Corporation, 39 276–79

Milacron, Inc., 53 226–30 (upd.)

Milan AC S.p.A., 79 255–58

Milbank, Tweed, Hadley & McCloy, 27 324–27

Miles Laboratories, I 653–55 *see also* Bayer A.G.

Millea Holdings Inc., 64 276–81 (upd.)

Millennium & Copthorne Hotels plc, 71 231–33

Millennium Pharmaceuticals, Inc., 47 249–52

Miller Brewing Company, I 269–70; 12 337–39 (upd.) *see also* SABMiller plc.

Miller Industries, Inc., 26 293–95

Miller Publishing Group, LLC, 57 242–44

Milliken & Co., V 366–68; 17 327–30 (upd.); 82 235–39 (upd.)

Milliman USA, 66 223–26

Millipore Corporation, 25 339–43; 84 271–276 (upd.)

The Mills Corporation, 77 280–83

Milnot Company, 46 289–91

Milton Bradley Company, 21 372–75

Milton CAT, Inc., 86 268–71

Milwaukee Brewers Baseball Club, 37 247–49

Mine Safety Appliances Company, 31 333–35

Minebea Co., Ltd., 90 298–302

The Miner Group International, 22 356–58

Minerals & Metals Trading Corporation of India Ltd., IV 143–44

Minerals Technologies Inc., 11 310–12; 52 248–51 (upd.)

Minnesota Mining & Manufacturing Company, I 499–501; 8 369–71 (upd.); 26 296–99 (upd.) *see also* 3M Co.

Minnesota Power, Inc., 11 313–16; 34 286–91 (upd.)

Minntech Corporation, 22 359–61

Minolta Co., Ltd., III 574–76; 18 339–42 (upd.); 43 281–85 (upd.)

The Minute Maid Company, 28 271–74

Minuteman International Inc., 46 292–95

Minyard Food Stores, Inc., 33 304–07; 86 272–77 (upd.)

Miquel y Costas Miquel S.A., 68 256–58

Mirage Resorts, Incorporated, 6 209–12; 28 275–79 (upd.) *see also* MGM MIRAGE.

Miramax Film Corporation, 64 282–85

Mirant Corporation, 98 243–47

Miroglio SpA, 86 278–81

Mirror Group Newspapers plc, 7 341–43; 23 348–51 (upd.)

Misonix, Inc., 80 248–51

Mississippi Chemical Corporation, 39 280–83

Misys PLC, 45 279–81; 46 296–99

Mitchell Energy and Development Corporation, 7 344–46 *see also* Devon Energy Corp.

Mitchells & Butlers PLC, 59 296–99

Mitel Corporation, 18 343–46

MITRE Corporation, 26 300–02

MITROPA AG, 37 250–53

Mitsubishi Bank, Ltd., II 321–22 *see also* Bank of Tokyo-Mitsubishi Ltd.

Mitsubishi Chemical Corporation, I 363–64; 56 236–38 (upd.)

Mitsubishi Corporation, I 502–04; 12 340–43 (upd.)

Mitsubishi Electric Corporation, II 57–59; 44 283–87 (upd.)

Mitsubishi Estate Company, Limited, IV 713–14; 61 215–18 (upd.)

Mitsubishi Heavy Industries, Ltd., III 577–79; 7 347–50 (upd.); 40 324–28 (upd.)

Mitsubishi Materials Corporation, III 712–13

Mitsubishi Motors Corporation, 9 349–51; 23 352–55 (upd.); 57 245–49 (upd.)

Mitsubishi Oil Co., Ltd., IV 460–62 *see also* Nippon Mitsubishi Oil Corp.

Mitsubishi Rayon Co. Ltd., V 369–71

Mitsubishi Trust & Banking Corporation, II 323–24

Mitsubishi UFJ Financial Group, Inc., 99 291–296 (upd.)

Mitsui & Co., Ltd., I 505–08; 28 280–85 (upd.)

Mitsui Bank, Ltd., II 325–27 *see also* Sumitomo Mitsui Banking Corp.

Mitsui Marine and Fire Insurance Company, Limited, III 295–96

Mitsui Mining & Smelting Co., Ltd., IV 145–46

Mitsui Mining Company, Limited, IV 147–49

Mitsui Mutual Life Insurance Company, III 297–98; 39 284–86 (upd.)

Mitsui O.S.K. Lines Ltd., V 473–76; 96 282–87 (upd.)

Mitsui Petrochemical Industries, Ltd., 9 352–54

Mitsui Real Estate Development Co., Ltd., IV 715–16

Mitsui Trust & Banking Company, Ltd., II 328

Mitsukoshi Ltd., V 142–44; 56 239–42 (upd.)

Mity Enterprises, Inc., 38 310–12

MIVA, Inc., 83 271–275

Mizuho Financial Group Inc., 25 344–46; 58 229–36 (upd.)

MNS, Ltd., 65 236–38

Mo och Domsjö AB, IV 317–19 *see also* Holmen AB

Mobil Corporation, IV 463–65; 7 351–54 (upd.); 21 376–80 (upd.) *see also* Exxon Mobil Corp.

Mobile Mini, Inc., 58 237–39

Mobile Telecommunications Technologies Corp., 18 347–49

Mobile TeleSystems OJSC, 59 300–03

Mocon, Inc., 76 275–77

Modell's Sporting Goods *see* Henry Modell & Company Inc.

Modern Times Group AB, 36 335–38

Modern Woodmen of America, 66 227–29

Modine Manufacturing Company, 8 372–75; 56 243–47 (upd.)

MoDo *see* Mo och Domsjö AB.

Modtech Holdings, Inc., 77 284–87

Moen Incorporated, 12 344–45

Moët-Hennessy, I 271–72 *see also* LVMH Moët Hennessy Louis Vuitton SA.

Mohawk Industries, Inc., 19 274–76; 63 298–301 (upd.)

Mohegan Tribal Gaming Authority, 37 254–57

Moksel *see* A. Moksel AG.

MOL *see* Mitsui O.S.K. Lines, Ltd.

MOL Rt, 70 192–95

Moldflow Corporation, 73 227–30

Molex Incorporated, 11 317–19; 14 27; 54 236–41 (upd.)

Moliflor Loisirs, 80 252–55

Molinos Río de la Plata S.A., 61 219–21

Molins plc, 51 249–51

The Molson Companies Limited, I 273–75; 26 303–07 (upd.)

Molson Coors Brewing Company, 77 288–300 (upd.)

Monaco Coach Corporation, 31 336–38

Monadnock Paper Mills, Inc., 21 381–84

Monarch Casino & Resort, Inc., 65 239–41

The Monarch Cement Company, 72 231–33

Mondadori *see* Arnoldo Mondadori Editore S.p.A.

MoneyGram International, Inc., 94 315–18

Monfort, Inc., 13 350–52

Monnaie de Paris, 62 246–48

Monnoyeur Group *see* Groupe Monnoyeur.

Monoprix S.A., 86 282–85

Monro Muffler Brake, Inc., 24 337–40

Monrovia Nursery Company, 70 196–98

Monsanto Company, I 365–67; 9 355–57 (upd.); 29 327–31 (upd.); 77 301–07 (upd.)

Monsoon plc, 39 287–89

Monster Cable Products, Inc., 69 256–58

Monster Worldwide Inc., 74 194–97 (upd.)

Montana Coffee Traders, Inc., 60 208–10

The Montana Power Company, 11 320–22; 44 288–92 (upd.)

Montblanc International GmbH, 82 240–44

Montedison S.p.A., I 368–69; 24 341–44 (upd.)

Monterey Pasta Company, 58 240–43

Montgomery Ward & Co., Incorporated, V 145–48; 20 374–79 (upd.)

Montres Rolex S.A., 13 353–55; 34 292–95 (upd.)

Montupet S.A., 63 302–04

Moody's Corporation, 65 242–44

Moog Inc., 13 356–58

Moog Music, Inc., 75 261–64

Mooney Aerospace Group Ltd., 52 252–55

Moore Corporation Limited, IV 644–46 *see also* R.R. Donnelley & Sons Co.

Moore-Handley, Inc., 39 290–92

Moore Medical Corp., 17 331–33

Moran Towing Corporation, Inc., 15 301–03

The Morgan Crucible Company plc, 82 245–50
Morgan Grenfell Group PLC, II 427–29 see also Deutsche Bank AG.
The Morgan Group, Inc., 46 300–02
Morgan, Lewis & Bockius LLP, 29 332–34
Morgan Stanley Dean Witter & Company, II 430–32; 16 374–78 (upd.); 33 311–14 (upd.)
Morgans Hotel Group Company, 80 256–59
Morguard Corporation, 85 287–90
Morinaga & Co. Ltd., 61 222–25
Morinda Holdings, Inc., 82 251–54
Morningstar Inc., 68 259–62
Morris Communications Corporation, 36 339–42
Morris Travel Services L.L.C., 26 308–11
Morrison & Foerster LLP, 78 220–23
Morrison Knudsen Corporation, 7 355–58; 28 286–90 (upd.) see also The Washington Companies.
Morrison Restaurants Inc., 11 323–25
Morrow Equipment Co. L.L.C., 87 325–327
Morse Shoe Inc., 13 359–61
Morton International, Inc., 9 358–59 (upd.); 80 260–64 (upd.)
Morton Thiokol Inc., I 370–72 see also Thiokol Corp.
Morton's Restaurant Group, Inc., 30 329–31; 88 262–66 (upd.)
The Mosaic Company, 91 330–33
Mosinee Paper Corporation, 15 304–06 see also Wausau-Mosinee Paper Corp.
Moss Bros Group plc, 51 252–54
Mossimo, 27 328–30; 96 288–92 (upd.)
Mota-Engil, SGPS, S.A., 97 290–93
Motel 6, 13 362–64; 56 248–51 (upd.) see also Accor SA
Mothercare plc, 17 334–36; 78 224–27 (upd.)
Mothers Against Drunk Driving (MADD), 51 255–58
Mothers Work, Inc., 18 350–52
The Motley Fool, Inc., 40 329–31
Moto Photo, Inc., 45 282–84
Motor Cargo Industries, Inc., 35 296–99
Motorcar Parts & Accessories, Inc., 47 253–55
Motorola, Inc., II 60–62; 11 326–29 (upd.); 34 296–302 (upd.); 93 313–23 (upd.)
Motown Records Company L.P., 26 312–14
Mott's Inc., 57 250–53
Moulinex S.A., 22 362–65 see also Groupe SEB.
Mount see also Mt.
Mount Washington Hotel see MWH Preservation Limited Partnership.
Mountain States Mortgage Centers, Inc., 29 335–37
Mouvement des Caisses Desjardins, 48 288–91

Movado Group, Inc., 28 291–94
Movie Gallery, Inc., 31 339–41
Movie Star Inc., 17 337–39
Moy Park Ltd., 78 228–31
MPI see Michael Page International plc.
MPRG see Matt Prentice Restaurant Group.
MPS Group, Inc., 49 264–67
MPW Industrial Services Group, Inc., 53 231–33
Mr. Bricolage S.A., 37 258–60
Mr. Coffee, Inc., 15 307–09
Mr. Gasket Inc., 15 310–12
Mr. Gatti's, LP, 87 321–324
Mrs. Baird's Bakeries, 29 338–41
Mrs. Fields' Original Cookies, Inc., 27 331–35
Mrs. Grossman's Paper Company Inc., 84 277–280
MS&L see Manning Selvage & Lee.
MSC see Material Sciences Corp.
MSC Industrial Direct Co., Inc., 71 234–36
M6 see Métropole Télévision S.A..
Mt. see also Mount.
Mt. Olive Pickle Company, Inc., 44 293–95
MTA see Metropolitan Transportation Authority.
MTC see Management and Training Corp.
MTel see Mobile Telecommunications Technologies Corp.
MTG see Modern Times Group AB.
MTR Foods Ltd., 55 271–73
MTR Gaming Group, Inc., 75 265–67
MTS see Mobile TeleSystems.
MTS Inc., 37 261–64
Mueller Industries, Inc., 7 359–61; 52 256–60 (upd.)
Mulberry Group PLC, 71 237–39
Mullen Advertising Inc., 51 259–61
Multi-Color Corporation, 53 234–36
Multimedia Games, Inc., 41 272–76
Multimedia, Inc., 11 330–32
Munich Re (Münchener Rückversicherungs-Gesellschaft Aktiengesellschaft in München), III 299–301; 46 303–07 (upd.)
Murdock Madaus Schwabe, 26 315–19
Murphy Family Farms Inc., 22 366–68 see also Smithfield Foods, Inc.
Murphy Oil Corporation, 7 362–64; 32 338–41 (upd.); 95 283–89 (upd.)
Murphy's Pizza see Papa Murphy's International, Inc.
The Musco Family Olive Co., 91 334–37
Musco Lighting, 83 276–279
Musgrave Group Plc, 57 254–57
Music Corporation of America see MCA Inc.
Musicland Stores Corporation, 9 360–62; 38 313–17 (upd.)
Mutual Benefit Life Insurance Company, III 302–04
Mutual Life Insurance Company of New York, III 305–07

The Mutual of Omaha Companies, 98 248–52
Muzak, Inc., 18 353–56
MWA see Modern Woodmen of America.
MWH Preservation Limited Partnership, 65 245–48
MWI Veterinary Supply, Inc., 80 265–68
Mycogen Corporation, 21 385–87 see also Dow Chemical Co.
Myers Industries, Inc., 19 277–79; 96 293–97 (upd.)
Mylan Laboratories Inc., I 656–57; 20 380–82 (upd.); 59 304–08 (upd.)
MYOB Ltd., 86 286–90
Myriad Genetics, Inc., 95 290–95
Myriad Restaurant Group, Inc., 87 328–331
MySpace.com see Intermix Media, Inc.

N

N.F. Smith & Associates LP, 70 199–202
N M Rothschild & Sons Limited, 39 293–95
N.V. see under first word of company name
Naamloze Vennootschap tot Exploitatie van het Café Krasnapolsky see Grand Hotel Krasnapolsky N.V.
Nabisco Brands, Inc., II 542–44 see also RJR Nabisco.
Nabisco Foods Group, 7 365–68 (upd.) see also Kraft Foods Inc.
Nabors Industries Ltd., 9 363–65; 91 338–44 (upd.)
NACCO Industries, Inc., 7 369–71; 78 232–36 (upd.)
Nadro S.A. de C.V., 86 291–94
Naf Naf SA, 44 296–98
Nagasakiya Co., Ltd., V 149–51; 69 259–62 (upd.)
Nagase & Co., Ltd., 8 376–78; 61 226–30 (upd.)
NAI see Natural Alternatives International, Inc.; Network Associates, Inc.
Nalco Holding Company, I 373–75; 12 346–48 (upd.); 89 324–30 (upd.)
Nam Tai Electronics, Inc., 61 231–34
Nantucket Allserve, Inc., 22 369–71
Napster, Inc., 69 263–66
NAS see National Audubon Society.
NASCAR see National Association for Stock Car Auto Racing.
NASD, 54 242–46 (upd.)
The NASDAQ Stock Market, Inc., 92 256–60
Nash Finch Company, 8 379–81; 23 356–58 (upd.); 65 249–53 (upd.)
Nashua Corporation, 8 382–84
Naspers Ltd., 66 230–32
Nastech Pharmaceutical Company Inc., 79 259–62
Nathan's Famous, Inc., 29 342–44
National Amusements Inc., 28 295–97
National Aquarium in Baltimore, Inc., 74 198–200
National Association for Stock Car Auto Racing, 32 342–44

National Association of Securities
Dealers, Inc., 10 416–18 *see also*
NASD.
National Audubon Society, 26 320–23
National Auto Credit, Inc., 16 379–81
National Bank of Canada, 85 291–94
National Bank of Greece, 41 277–79
The National Bank of South Carolina,
76 278–80
National Beverage Corporation, 26
324–26; 88 267–71 (upd.)
National Broadcasting Company, Inc.,
II 151–53; 6 164–66 (upd.); 28
298–301 (upd.) *see also* General
Electric Co.
National Can Corp., I 607–08
National Car Rental System, Inc., 10
419–20 *see also* Republic Industries,
Inc.
National City Corporation, 15 313–16;
97 294–302 (upd.)
National Collegiate Athletic Association,
96 298–302
National Convenience Stores
Incorporated, 7 372–75
National Discount Brokers Group, Inc.,
28 302–04 *see also* Deutsche Bank
A.G.
National Distillers and Chemical
Corporation, I 376–78 *see also*
Quantum Chemical Corp.
National Educational Music Co. Ltd.,
47 256–58
National Enquirer see American Media,
Inc.
National Envelope Corporation, 32
345–47
National Equipment Services, Inc., 57
258–60
National Express Group PLC, 50
340–42
National Financial Partners Corp., 65
254–56
National Football League, 29 345–47 *see
also* NFL.
National Frozen Foods Corporation, 94
319–22
National Fuel Gas Company, 6 526–28;
95 296–300 (upd.)
National Geographic Society, 9 366–68;
30 332–35 (upd.); 79 263–69 (upd.)
National Grape Co-operative
Association, Inc., 20 383–85
National Grid USA, 51 262–66 (upd.)
National Gypsum Company, 10 421–24
National Health Laboratories
Incorporated, 11 333–35 *see also*
Laboratory Corporation of America
Holdings.
National Heritage Academies, Inc., 60
211–13
National Hockey League, 35 300–03
National Home Centers, Inc., 44
299–301
National Instruments Corporation, 22
372–74
National Intergroup, Inc., V 152–53 *see
also* FoxMeyer Health Corp.

National Iranian Oil Company, IV
466–68; 61 235–38 (upd.)
National Journal Group Inc., 67 256–58
National Media Corporation, 27
336–40
National Medical Enterprises, Inc., III
87–88 *see also* Tenet Healthcare Corp.
National Medical Health Card Systems,
Inc., 79 270–73
National Oil Corporation, 66 233–37
(upd.)
National Oilwell, Inc., 54 247–50
National Organization for Women, Inc.,
55 274–76
National Patent Development
Corporation, 13 365–68 *see also* GP
Strategies Corp.
National Picture & Frame Company, 24
345–47
National Power PLC, 12 349–51 *see also*
International Power PLC.
National Presto Industries, Inc., 16
382–85; 43 286–90 (upd.)
National Public Radio, 19 280–82; 47
259–62 (upd.)
National R.V. Holdings, Inc., 32
348–51
National Railroad Passenger
Corporation (Amtrak), 22 375–78;
66 238–42 (upd.)
National Record Mart, Inc., 29 348–50
National Research Corporation, 87
332–335
National Rifle Association of America,
37 265–68
National Sanitary Supply Co., 16
386–87
National Sea Products Ltd., 14 339–41
National Semiconductor Corporation, II
63–65; 6 261–63; 26 327–30 (upd.);
69 267–71 (upd.)
National Service Industries, Inc., 11
336–38; 54 251–55 (upd.)
National Standard Co., 13 369–71
National Starch and Chemical
Company, 49 268–70
National Steel Corporation, 12 352–54
see also FoxMeyer Health Corp.
National TechTeam, Inc., 41 280–83
National Thoroughbred Racing
Association, 58 244–47
National Transcommunications Ltd. *see*
NTL Inc.
National Weather Service, 91 345–49
National Westminster Bank PLC, II
333–35
National Wine & Spirits, Inc., 49
271–74
Nationale-Nederlanden N.V., III 308–11
Nationale Portefeuille Maatschappij
(NPM) *see* Compagnie Nationale à
Portefeuille.
NationsBank Corporation, 10 425–27
see also Bank of America Corporation
Natrol, Inc., 49 275–78
Natura Cosméticos S.A., 75 268–71
Natural Alternatives International, Inc.,
49 279–82

Natural Gas Clearinghouse *see* NGC
Corp.
Natural Ovens Bakery, Inc., 72 234–36
Natural Selection Foods, 54 256–58
Natural Wonders Inc., 14 342–44
Naturally Fresh, Inc., 88 272–75
The Nature Conservancy, 28 305–07
Nature's Path Foods, Inc., 87 336–340
Nature's Sunshine Products, Inc., 15
317–19
Natuzzi Group *see* Industrie Natuzzi
S.p.A.
NatWest Bank *see* National Westminster
Bank PLC.
Naumes, Inc., 81 257–60
Nautica Enterprises, Inc., 18 357–60;
44 302–06 (upd.)
Navarre Corporation, 24 348–51
Navigant International, Inc., 47 263–66;
93 324–27 (upd.)
The Navigators Group, Inc., 92 261–64
Navistar International Corporation, I
180–82; 10 428–30 (upd.) *see also*
International Harvester Co.
NAVTEQ Corporation, 69 272–75
Navy Exchange Service Command, 31
342–45
Navy Federal Credit Union, 33 315–17
NBC *see* National Broadcasting Company,
Inc.
NBD Bancorp, Inc., 11 339–41 *see also*
Bank One Corp.
NBGS International, Inc., 73 231–33
NBSC Corporation *see* National Bank of
South Carolina.
NBTY, Inc., 31 346–48
NCAA *see* National Collegiate Athletic
Assn.
NCH Corporation, 8 385–87
NCI Building Systems, Inc., 88 276–79
NCL Corporation, 79 274–77
NCNB Corporation, II 336–37 *see also*
Bank of America Corp.
NCO Group, Inc., 42 258–60
NCR Corporation, III 150–53; 6
264–68 (upd.); 30 336–41 (upd.); 90
303–12 (upd.)
NDB *see* National Discount Brokers
Group, Inc.
Nebraska Book Company, Inc., 65
257–59
Nebraska Furniture Mart, Inc., 94
323–26
Nebraska Public Power District, 29
351–54
NEBS *see* New England Business Services,
Inc.
NEC Corporation, II 66–68; 21 388–91
(upd.); 57 261–67 (upd.)
N.V. Nederlandse Gasunie, V 658–61
Nedlloyd Group *see* Koninklijke Nedlloyd
N.V.
Neenah Foundry Company, 68 263–66
Neff Corp., 32 352–53
NeighborCare, Inc., 67 259–63 (upd.)
The Neiman Marcus Group, Inc., 12
355–57; 49 283–87 (upd.)
Nektar Therapeutics, 91 350–53

Nelsons *see* A. Nelson & Co. Ltd.
Neogen Corporation, 94 327–30
Neopost S.A., 53 237–40
Neptune Orient Lines Limited, 47 267–70
NERCO, Inc., 7 376–79 *see also* Rio Tinto PLC.
NES *see* National Equipment Services, Inc.
Neste Oil Corporation, IV 469–71; 85 295–302 (upd.)
Nestlé S.A., II 545–49; 7 380–84 (upd.); 28 308–13 (upd.); 71 240–46 (upd.)
Nestlé Waters, 73 234–37
NetCom Systems AB, 26 331–33
NetCracker Technology Corporation, 98 253–56
Netezza Corporation, 69 276–78
Netflix, Inc., 58 248–51
NETGEAR, Inc., 81 261–64
NetIQ Corporation, 79 278–81
NetJets Inc., 96 303–07 (upd.)
Netscape Communications Corporation, 15 320–22; 35 304–07 (upd.)
Network Appliance, Inc., 58 252–54
Network Associates, Inc., 25 347–49
Network Equipment Technologies Inc., 92 265–68
Neuberger Berman Inc., 57 268–71
NeuStar, Inc., 81 265–68
Neutrogena Corporation, 17 340–44
Nevada Bell Telephone Company, 14 345–47 *see also* AT&T Corp.
Nevada Power Company, 11 342–44
Nevamar Company, 82 255–58
New Balance Athletic Shoe, Inc., 25 350–52; 68 267–70 (upd.)
New Belgium Brewing Company, Inc., 68 271–74
New Brunswick Scientific Co., Inc., 45 285–87
New Chapter Inc., 96 308–11
New Clicks Holdings Ltd., 86 295–98
New Dana Perfumes Company, 37 269–71
New England Business Service, Inc., 18 361–64; 78 237–42 (upd.)
New England Confectionery Co., 15 323–25
New England Electric System, V 662–64 *see also* National Grid USA.
New England Mutual Life Insurance Co., III 312–14 *see also* Metropolitan Life Insurance Co.
New Flyer Industries Inc., 78 243–46
New Holland N.V., 22 379–81 *see also* CNH Global N.V.
New Jersey Devils, 84 281–285
New Jersey Manufacturers Insurance Company, 96 312–16
New Jersey Resources Corporation, 54 259–61
New Line Cinema, Inc., 47 271–74
New Look Group plc, 35 308–10
New Orleans Saints LP, 58 255–57
The New Piper Aircraft, Inc., 44 307–10
New Plan Realty Trust, 11 345–47

New Seasons Market, 75 272–74
New Street Capital Inc., 8 388–90 (upd.) *see also* Drexel Burnham Lambert Inc.
New Times, Inc., 45 288–90
New Valley Corporation, 17 345–47
New World Development Company Limited, IV 717–19; 38 318–22 (upd.)
New World Pasta Company, 53 241–44
New World Restaurant Group, Inc., 44 311–14
New York City Health and Hospitals Corporation, 60 214–17
New York City Off-Track Betting Corporation, 51 267–70
New York Community Bancorp, Inc., 78 247–50
New York Daily News, 32 357–60
New York Eye and Ear Infirmary *see* Continuum Health Partners, Inc.
New York Health Care, Inc., 72 237–39
New York Life Insurance Company, III 315–17; 45 291–95 (upd.)
New York Philharmonic *see* Philharmonic-Symphony Society of New York, Inc.
New York Presbyterian Hospital *see* NewYork-Presbyterian Hospital.
New York Restaurant Group, Inc., 32 361–63
New York Shakespeare Festival Management, 92 328–32
New York State Electric and Gas Corporation, 6 534–36
New York Stock Exchange, Inc., 9 369–72; 39 296–300 (upd.)
The New York Times Company, IV 647–49; 19 283–85 (upd.); 61 239–43 (upd.)
Neways, Inc., 78 251–54
Newcor, Inc., 40 332–35
Newell Rubbermaid Inc., 9 373–76; 52 261–71 (upd.)
Newfield Exploration Company, 65 260–62
Newhall Land and Farming Company, 14 348–50
Newly Weds Foods, Inc., 74 201–03
Newman's Own, Inc., 37 272–75
Newmont Mining Corporation, 7 385–88; 94 331–37 (upd.)
Newpark Resources, Inc., 63 305–07
Newport Corporation, 71 247–49
Newport News Shipbuilding Inc., 13 372–75; 38 323–27 (upd.)
News America Publishing Inc., 12 358–60
News Corporation Limited, IV 650–53; 7 389–93 (upd.); 46 308–13 (upd.)
Newsquest plc, 32 354–56
NewYork-Presbyterian Hospital, 59 309–12
Nexans SA, 54 262–64
NEXCOM *see* Navy Exchange Service Command.
Nexen Inc., 79 282–85
Nexity S.A., 66 243–45

Nexstar Broadcasting Group, Inc., 73 238–41
Next Media Ltd., 61 244–47
Next plc, 29 355–57
Nextel Communications, Inc., 10 431–33; 27 341–45 (upd.)
Neyveli Lignite Corporation Ltd., 65 263–65
NFC plc, 6 412–14 *see also* Exel plc.
NFL *see* National Football League Inc.
NFL Films, 75 275–78
NFO Worldwide, Inc., 24 352–55
NGC Corporation, 18 365–67 *see also* Dynegy Inc.
NGK Insulators Ltd., 67 264–66
NH Hoteles S.A., 79 286–89
NHK Spring Co., Ltd., III 580–82
Niagara Corporation, 28 314–16
Niagara Mohawk Holdings Inc., V 665–67; 45 296–99 (upd.)
NICE Systems Ltd., 83 280–283
Nichii Co., Ltd., V 154–55
Nichimen Corporation, IV 150–52; 24 356–59 (upd.) *see also* Sojitz Corp.
Nichirei Corporation, 70 203–05
Nichiro Corporation, 86 299–302
Nichols plc, 44 315–18
Nichols Research Corporation, 18 368–70
Nicklaus Companies, 45 300–03
Nicole Miller, 98 257–60
Nicor Inc., 6 529–31; 86 303–07 (upd.)
Nidec Corporation, 59 313–16
Nielsen Business Media, Inc., 98 261–65
Nigerian National Petroleum Corporation, IV 472–74; 72 240–43 (upd.)
Nihon Keizai Shimbun, Inc., IV 654–56
NII *see* National Intergroup, Inc.
NIKE, Inc., V 372–74; 8 391–94 (upd.); 36 343–48 (upd.); 75 279–85 (upd.)
Nikken Global Inc., 32 364–67
The Nikko Securities Company Limited, II 433–35; 9 377–79 (upd.)
Nikon Corporation, III 583–85; 48 292–95 (upd.)
Niman Ranch, Inc., 67 267–69
Nimbus CD International, Inc., 20 386–90
Nine West Group Inc., 11 348–49; 39 301–03 (upd.)
99¢ Only Stores, 25 353–55
Nintendo Co., Ltd., III 586–88; 7 394–96 (upd.); 28 317–21 (upd.); 67 270–76 (upd.)
NIOC *see* National Iranian Oil Co.
Nippon Credit Bank, II 338–39
Nippon Electric Glass Co. Ltd., 95 301–05
Nippon Express Company, Ltd., V 477–80; 64 286–90 (upd.)
Nippon Life Insurance Company, III 318–20; 60 218–21 (upd.)
Nippon Light Metal Company, Ltd., IV 153–55
Nippon Meat Packers, Inc., II 550–51; 78 255–57 (upd.)

Nippon Mining Co., Ltd., IV 475–77
Nippon Oil Corporation, IV 478–79;
    63 308–13 (upd.)
Nippon Seiko K.K., III 589–90
Nippon Sheet Glass Company, Limited,
    III 714–16
Nippon Shinpan Co., Ltd., II 436–37;
    61 248–50 (upd.)
Nippon Soda Co., Ltd., 85 303–06
Nippon Steel Corporation, IV 156–58;
    17 348–51 (upd.); 96 317–23 (upd.)
Nippon Suisan Kaisha, Limited, II
    552–53; 92 269–72 (upd.)
Nippon Telegraph and Telephone
    Corporation, V 305–07; 51 271–75
    (upd.)
Nippon Yusen Kabushiki Kaisha (NYK),
    V 481–83; 72 244–48 (upd.)
Nippondenso Co., Ltd., III 591–94 *see
    also* DENSO Corp.
NIPSCO Industries, Inc., 6 532–33
Nissan Motor Company Ltd., I 183–84;
    11 350–52 (upd.); 34 303–07 (upd.);
    92 273–79 (upd.)
Nisshin Seifun Group Inc., II 554; 66
    246–48 (upd.)
Nisshin Steel Co., Ltd., IV 159–60
Nissho Iwai K.K., I 509–11
Nissin Food Products Company Ltd.,
    75 286–88
Nitches, Inc., 53 245–47
Nixdorf Computer AG, III 154–55 *see
    also* Wincor Nixdorf Holding GmbH.
NKK Corporation, IV 161–63; 28
    322–26 (upd.)
NL Industries, Inc., 10 434–36
Noah Education Holdings Ltd., 97
    303–06
Noah's New York Bagels *see*
    Einstein/Noah Bagel Corp.
Nobel Industries AB, 9 380–82 *see also*
    Akzo Nobel N.V.
Nobel Learning Communities, Inc., 37
    276–79; 76 281–85 (upd.)
Noble Affiliates, Inc., 11 353–55
Noble Roman's Inc., 14 351–53; 99
    297–302 (upd.)
Nobleza Piccardo SAICF, 64 291–93
Noboa *see also* Exportadora Bananera
    Noboa, S.A.
Nocibé SA, 54 265–68
NOF Corporation, 72 249–51
Nokia Corporation, II 69–71; 17
    352–54 (upd.); 38 328–31 (upd.); 77
    308–13 (upd.)
NOL Group *see* Neptune Orient Lines
    Ltd.
Noland Company, 35 311–14
Nolo.com, Inc., 49 288–91
Nomura Securities Company, Limited,
    II 438–41; 9 383–86 (upd.)
Noodle Kidoodle, 16 388–91
Noodles & Company, Inc., 55 277–79
Nooter Corporation, 61 251–53
Noranda Inc., IV 164–66; 7 397–99
    (upd.); 64 294–98 (upd.)
Norcal Waste Systems, Inc., 60 222–24
Norddeutsche Affinerie AG, 62 249–53

Nordea AB, 40 336–39
NordicTrack, 22 382–84 *see also* Icon
    Health & Fitness, Inc.
Nordisk Film A/S, 80 269–73
Nordson Corporation, 11 356–58; 48
    296–99 (upd.)
Nordstrom, Inc., V 156–58; 18 371–74
    (upd.); 67 277–81 (upd.)
Norelco Consumer Products Co., 26
    334–36
Norfolk Southern Corporation, V
    484–86; 29 358–61 (upd.); 75
    289–93 (upd.)
Norinchukin Bank, II 340–41
Norm Thompson Outfitters, Inc., 47
    275–77
Norrell Corporation, 25 356–59
Norsk Hydro ASA, 10 437–40; 35
    315–19 (upd.)
Norske Skogindustrier ASA, 63 314–16
Norstan, Inc., 16 392–94
Nortek, Inc., 34 308–12
Nortel Networks Corporation, 36
    349–54 (upd.)
North American Galvanizing &
    Coatings, Inc., 99 303–306
North Atlantic Trading Company Inc.,
    65 266–68
North Carolina National Bank
    Corporation *see* NCNB Corp.
The North Face, Inc., 18 375–77; 78
    258–61 (upd.)
North Fork Bancorporation, Inc., 46
    314–17
North Pacific Group, Inc., 61 254–57
North Star Steel Company, 18 378–81
The North West Company, Inc., 12
    361–63
North West Water Group plc, 11
    359–62 *see also* United Utilities PLC.
Northeast Utilities, V 668–69; 48
    303–06 (upd.)
Northern and Shell Network plc, 87
    341–344
Northern Foods plc, 10 441–43; 61
    258–62 (upd.)
Northern Rock plc, 33 318–21
Northern States Power Company, V
    670–72; 20 391–95 (upd.) *see also*
    Xcel Energy Inc.
Northern Telecom Limited, V 308–10
    see also Nortel Networks Corp.
Northern Trust Company, 9 387–89
Northland Cranberries, Inc., 38 332–34
Northrop Grumman Corporation, I
    76–77; 11 363–65 (upd.); 45 304–12
    (upd.)
Northwest Airlines Corporation, I
    112–14; 6 103–05 (upd.); 26 337–40
    (upd.); 74 204–08 (upd.)
Northwest Natural Gas Company, 45
    313–15
NorthWestern Corporation, 37 280–83
Northwestern Mutual Life Insurance
    Company, III 321–24; 45 316–21
    (upd.)
Norton Company, 8 395–97

Norton McNaughton, Inc., 27 346–49
    see also Jones Apparel Group, Inc.
Norwegian Cruise Lines *see* NCL
    Corporation
Norwich & Peterborough Building
    Society, 55 280–82
Norwood Promotional Products, Inc.,
    26 341–43
Nova Corporation of Alberta, V 673–75
NovaCare, Inc., 11 366–68
Novacor Chemicals Ltd., 12 364–66
Novar plc, 49 292–96 (upd.)
Novartis AG, 39 304–10 (upd.)
NovaStar Financial, Inc., 91 354–58
Novell, Inc., 6 269–71; 23 359–62
    (upd.)
Novellus Systems, Inc., 18 382–85
Noven Pharmaceuticals, Inc., 55 283–85
Novo Nordisk A/S, I 658–60; 61
    263–66 (upd.)
NOW *see* National Organization for
    Women, Inc.
NPC International, Inc., 40 340–42
The NPD Group, Inc., 68 275–77
NPM (Nationale Portefeuille
    Maatschappij) *see* Compagnie Nationale
    à Portefeuille.
NPR *see* National Public Radio, Inc.
NRG Energy, Inc., 79 290–93
NRT Incorporated, 61 267–69
NS *see* Norfolk Southern Corp.
NSF International, 72 252–55
NSK *see* Nippon Seiko K.K.
NSP *see* Northern States Power Co.
NSS Enterprises, Inc., 78 262–65
NTCL *see* Northern Telecom Ltd.
NTL Inc., 65 269–72
NTN Buzztime, Inc., 86 308–11
NTN Corporation, III 595–96; 47
    278–81 (upd.)
NTTPC *see* Nippon Telegraph and
    Telephone Public Corp.
NU *see* Northeast Utilities.
Nu-kote Holding, Inc., 18 386–89
Nu Skin Enterprises, Inc., 27 350–53;
    31 386–89; 76 286–90 (upd.)
Nucor Corporation, 7 400–02; 21
    392–95 (upd.); 79 294–300 (upd.)
Nufarm Ltd., 87 345–348
Nuplex Industries Ltd., 92 280–83
Nutraceutical International
    Corporation, 37 284–86
NutraSweet Company, 8 398–400
Nutreco Holding N.V., 56 256–59
Nutrexpa S.A., 92 284–87
NutriSystem, Inc., 71 250–53
Nutrition for Life International Inc., 22
    385–88
Nutrition 21 Inc., 97 307–11
Nuveen *see* John Nuveen Co.
NVIDIA Corporation, 54 269–73
NVR Inc., 8 401–03; 70 206–09 (upd.)
NWA, Inc. *see* Northwest Airlines Corp.
NYK *see* Nippon Yusen Kabushiki Kaisha
    (NYK).
NYMAGIC, Inc., 41 284–86
NYNEX Corporation, V 311–13 *see also*
    Verizon Communications.

NYRG *see* New York Restaurant Group, Inc.
NYSE *see* New York Stock Exchange.
NYSEG *see* New York State Electric and Gas Corp.

O

O&Y *see* Olympia & York Developments Ltd.
O.C. Tanner Co., 69 279–81
Oak Harbor Freight Lines, Inc., 53 248–51
Oak Industries Inc., 21 396–98 *see also* Corning Inc.
Oak Technology, Inc., 22 389–93 *see also* Zoran Corp.
Oakhurst Dairy, 60 225–28
Oakleaf Waste Management, LLC, 97 312–15
Oakley, Inc., 18 390–93; 49 297–302 (upd.)
Oaktree Capital Management, LLC, 71 254–56
Oakwood Homes Corporation, 13 155; 15 326–28
OAO AVTOVAZ *see* AVTOVAZ Joint Stock Co.
OAO Gazprom, 42 261–65
OAO LUKOIL, 40 343–46
OAO NK YUKOS, 47 282–85
OAO Severstal *see* Severstal Joint Stock Co.
OAO Siberian Oil Company (Sibneft), 49 303–06
OAO Tatneft, 45 322–26
Obayashi Corporation, 78 266–69 (upd.)
Oberto Sausage Company, Inc., 92 288–91
Obie Media Corporation, 56 260–62
Obrascon Huarte Lain S.A., 76 291–94
Observer AB, 55 286–89
Occidental Petroleum Corporation, IV 480–82; 25 360–63 (upd.); 71 257–61 (upd.)
Océ N.V., 24 360–63; 91 359–65 (upd.)
Ocean Beauty Seafoods, Inc., 74 209–11
Ocean Group plc, 6 415–17 *see also* Exel plc.
Ocean Spray Cranberries, Inc., 7 403–05; 25 364–67 (upd.); 83 284-290
Oceaneering International, Inc., 63 317–19
Ocesa *see* Corporación Interamericana de Entretenimiento, S.A. de C.V.
O'Charley's Inc., 19 286–88; 60 229–32 (upd.)
OCI *see* Orascom Construction Industries S.A.E.
OCLC Online Computer Library Center, Inc., 96 324–28
Octel Messaging, 14 354–56; 41 287–90 (upd.)
Ocular Sciences, Inc., 65 273–75
Odakyu Electric Railway Co., Ltd., V 487–89; 68 278–81 (upd.)
Odebrecht S.A., 73 242–44

Odetics Inc., 14 357–59
ODL, Inc., 55 290–92
Odwalla, Inc., 31 349–51
Odyssey Marine Exploration, Inc., 91 366–70
OEC Medical Systems, Inc., 27 354–56
OENEO S.A., 74 212–15 (upd.)
Office Depot, Inc., 8 404–05; 23 363–65 (upd.); 65 276–80 (upd.)
OfficeMax Inc., 15 329–31; 43 291–95 (upd.)
OfficeTiger, LLC, 75 294–96
Officine Alfieri Maserati S.p.A., 13 376–78
Offshore Logistics, Inc., 37 287–89
Obagi Medical Products, Inc., 95 310–13
Ogden Corporation, I 512–14; 6 151–53 *see also* Covanta Energy Corp.
Ogilvy Group Inc., I 25–27 *see also* WPP Group.
Oglebay Norton Company, 17 355–58
Oglethorpe Power Corporation, 6 537–38
Ohbayashi Corporation, I 586–87
The Ohio Art Company, 14 360–62; 59 317–20 (upd.)
Ohio Bell Telephone Company, 14 363–65; *see also* Ameritech Corp.
Ohio Casualty Corp., 11 369–70
Ohio Edison Company, V 676–78
Oil and Natural Gas Commission, IV 483–84; 90 313–17 (upd.)
Oil-Dri Corporation of America, 20 396–99; 89 331–36 (upd.)
Oil States International, Inc., 77 314–17
Oil Transporting Joint Stock Company Transneft, 92 450–54
The Oilgear Company, 74 216–18
Oji Paper Co., Ltd., IV 320–22; 57 272–75 (upd.)
OJSC Novolipetsk Steel, 99 311–315
OJSC Wimm-Bill-Dann Foods, 48 436–39
Oki Electric Industry Company, Limited, II 72–74; 15 125; 21 390
Oklahoma Gas and Electric Company, 6 539–40
Okuma Holdings Inc., 74 219–21
Okura & Co., Ltd., IV 167–68
Olan Mills, Inc., 62 254–56
Old America Stores, Inc., 17 359–61
Old Dominion Freight Line, Inc., 57 276–79
Old Kent Financial Corp., 11 371–72 *see also* Fifth Third Bancorp.
Old Mutual PLC, IV 535; 61 270–72
Old National Bancorp, 15 332–34; 98 266–70 (upd.)
Old Navy, Inc., 70 210–12
Old Orchard Brands, LLC, 73 245–47
Old Republic International Corporation, 11 373–75; 58 258–61 (upd.)
Old Spaghetti Factory International Inc., 24 364–66
Old Town Canoe Company, 74 222–24

Olga's Kitchen, Inc., 80 274–76
Olin Corporation, I 379–81; 13 379–81 (upd.); 78 270–74 (upd.)
Olivetti S.p.A., 34 316–20 (upd.)
Olsten Corporation, 6 41–43; 29 362–65 (upd.) *see also* Adecco S.A.
Olympia & York Developments Ltd., IV 720–21; 9 390–92 (upd.)
OM Group, Inc., 17 362–64; 78 275–78 (upd.)
OMA *see* Grupo Aeroportuario del Centro Norte, S.A.B. de C.V.
Omaha Steaks International Inc., 62 257–59
Omega Protein Corporation, 99 316–318
O'Melveny & Myers, 37 290–93
Omni Hotels Corp., 12 367–69
Omnicare, Inc., 13 49 307–10
Omnicell, Inc., 89 337–40
Omnicom Group Inc., I 28–32; 22 394–99 (upd.); 77 318–25 (upd.)
Omnilife *see* Grupo Omnilife S.A. de C.V.
OmniSource Corporation, 14 366–67
OMNOVA Solutions Inc., 59 324–26
Omrix Biopharmaceuticals, Inc., 95 314–17
Omron Corporation, 28 331–35 (upd.); 53 46
Omron Tateisi Electronics Company, II 75–77
OMV AG, IV 485–87; 98 271–74 (upd.)
On Assignment, Inc., 20 400–02
1-800-FLOWERS, Inc., 26 344–46
1-800-GOT-JUNK? LLC, 74 225–27
180s, L.L.C., 64 299–301
One Price Clothing Stores, Inc., 20 403–05
O'Neal Steel, Inc., 95 306–09
Oneida Ltd., 7 406–08; 31 352–55 (upd.); 88 280–85 (upd.)
ONEOK Inc., 7 409–12
Onet S.A., 92 292–95
Onex Corporation, 16 395–97; 65 281–85 (upd.)
Onion, Inc., 69 282–84
Onoda Cement Co., Ltd., III 717–19 *see also* Taiheiyo Cement Corp.
Ontario Hydro Services Company, 6 541–42; 32 368–71 (upd.)
Ontario Teachers' Pension Plan, 61 273–75
Onyx Acceptance Corporation, 59 327–29
Onyx Software Corporation, 53 252–55
OOC Inc., 97 316–19
OPAP S.A. *see* Greek Organization of Football Prognostics S.A. (OPAP)
Opel AG *see* Adam Opel AG.
Open *see* Groupe Open.
Open Text Corporation, 79 301–05
Openwave Systems Inc., 95 318–22
Operadora Mexicana de Aeropuertos *see* Grupo Aeroportuario del Centro Norte, S.A.B. de C.V.
Operation Smile, Inc., 75 297–99

Opinion Research Corporation, 46 318–22

The Oppenheimer Group, 76 295–98

Oppenheimer Wolff & Donnelly LLP, 71 262–64

Opsware Inc., 49 311–14

OPTEK Technology Inc., 98 275–78

Option Care Inc., 48 307–10

Optische Werke G. Rodenstock, 44 319–23

Opus Group, 34 321–23

Oracle Corporation, 6 272–74; 24 367–71 (upd.); 67 282–87 (upd.)

Orange Glo International, 53 256–59

Orange S.A., 84 286–289

Orascom Construction Industries S.A.E., 87 349–352

OraSure Technologies, Inc., 75 300–03

Orbital Sciences Corporation, 22 400–03

Orbitz, Inc., 61 276–78

Orbotech Ltd., 75 304–06

Orchard Supply Hardware Stores Corporation, 17 365–67

Ore-Ida Foods Inc., 13 382–83; 78 279–82 (upd.)

Oregon Chai, Inc., 49 315–17

Oregon Dental Service Health Plan, Inc., 51 276–78

Oregon Freeze Dry, Inc., 74 228–30

Oregon Metallurgical Corporation, 20 406–08

Oregon Steel Mills, Inc., 14 368–70

O'Reilly Automotive, Inc., 26 347–49; 78 283–87 (upd.)

O'Reilly Media, Inc., 99 307–310

Organic To Go Food Corporation, 99 319–322

Organic Valley (Coulee Region Organic Produce Pool), 53 260–62

Organización Soriana, S.A. de C.V., 35 320–22

Orgill, Inc., 99 323–326

ORI *see* Old Republic International Corp.

Orion Oyj, 72 256–59

Orion Pictures Corporation, 6 167–70 *see also* Metro-Goldwyn-Mayer Inc.

ORIX Corporation, II 442–43; 44 324–26 (upd.)

Orkla ASA, 18 394–98; 82 259–64 (upd.)

Orleans Homebuilders, Inc., 62 260–62

Ormat Technologies, Inc., 87 353–358

Ormet Corporation, 82 265–68

Orrick, Herrington and Sutcliffe LLP, 76 299–301

Orszagos Takarekpenztar es Kereskedelmi Bank Rt. (OTP Bank), 78 288–91

Orthodontic Centers of America, Inc., 35 323–26

Orthofix International NV, 72 260–62

The Orvis Company, Inc., 28 336–39

Oryx Energy Company, 7 413–15

Osaka Gas Company, Ltd., V 679–81; 60 233–36 (upd.)

Oscar Mayer Foods Corp., 12 370–72 *see also* Kraft Foods Inc.

Oshawa Group Limited, II 649–50

OshKosh B'Gosh, Inc., 9 393–95; 42 266–70 (upd.)

Oshkosh Corporation, 7 416–18; 98 279–84 (upd.)

Oshman's Sporting Goods, Inc., 17 368–70 *see also* Gart Sports Co.

OSI Restaurant Partners, Inc., 88 286–91 (upd.)

Osmonics, Inc., 18 399–401

Osram GmbH, 86 312–16

Österreichische Bundesbahnen GmbH, 6 418–20

Österreichische Elektrizitätswirtschafts-AG, 85 307–10

Österreichische Post- und Telegraphenverwaltung, V 314–17

O'Sullivan Industries Holdings, Inc., 34 313–15

Otari Inc., 89 341–44

Otis Elevator Company, Inc., 13 384–86; 39 311–15 (upd.)

Otis Spunkmeyer, Inc., 28 340–42

Otor S.A., 77 326–29

OTP Bank *see* Orszagos Takarekpenztar es Kereskedelmi Bank Rt.

OTR Express, Inc., 25 368–70

Ottakar's plc, 64 302–04

Ottaway Newspapers, Inc., 15 335–37

Otter Tail Power Company, 18 402–05

Otto Bremer Foundation *see* Bremer Financial Corp.

Otto Versand GmbH & Co., V 159–61; 15 338–40 (upd.); 34 324–28 (upd.)

Outback Steakhouse, Inc., 12 373–75; 34 329–32 (upd.) *see also* OSI Restaurant Partners, Inc.

Outboard Marine Corporation, III 597–600; 20 409–12 (upd.) *see also* Bombardier Inc.

Outdoor Research, Incorporated, 67 288–90

Outdoor Systems, Inc., 25 371–73 *see also* Infinity Broadcasting Corp.

Outlook Group Corporation, 37 294–96

Outokumpu Oyj, 38 335–37

Outrigger Enterprises, Inc., 67 291–93

Overhead Door Corporation, 70 213–16

Overhill Corporation, 51 279–81

Overnite Corporation, 14 371–73; 58 262–65 (upd.)

Overseas Shipholding Group, Inc., 11 376–77

Overstock.com, Inc., 75 307–09

Owens & Minor, Inc., 16 398–401; 68 282–85 (upd.)

Owens Corning, III 720–23; 20 413–17 (upd.); 98 285–91 (upd.)

Owens-Illinois, Inc., I 609–11; 26 350–53 (upd.); 85 311–18 (upd.)

Owosso Corporation, 29 366–68

Oxfam GB, 87 359–362

Oxford Health Plans, Inc., 16 402–04

Oxford Industries, Inc., 8 406–08; 84 290–296 (upd.)

P

P&C Foods Inc., 8 409–11

P & F Industries, Inc., 45 327–29

P&G *see* Procter & Gamble Co.

P.C. Richard & Son Corp., 23 372–74

P.F. Chang's China Bistro, Inc., 37 297–99; 86 317–21 (upd.)

P.H. Glatfelter Company, 8 412–14; 30 349–52 (upd.); 83 291–297 (upd.)

PACCAR Inc., I 185–86; 26 354–56 (upd.)

Pacer International, Inc., 54 274–76

Pacer Technology, 40 347–49

Pacific Basin Shipping Ltd., 86 322–26

Pacific Clay Products Inc., 88 292–95

Pacific Coast Building Products, Inc., 94 338–41

Pacific Coast Feather Company, 67 294–96

Pacific Coast Restaurants, Inc., 90 318–21

Pacific Dunlop Limited, 10 444–46 *see also* Ansell Ltd.

Pacific Enterprises, V 682–84 *see also* Sempra Energy.

Pacific Ethanol, Inc., 81 269–72

Pacific Gas and Electric Company, V 685–87 *see also* PG&E Corp.

Pacific Internet Limited, 87 363–366

Pacific Mutual Holding Company, 98 292–96

Pacific Sunwear of California, Inc., 28 343–45; 47 425

Pacific Telecom, Inc., 6 325–28

Pacific Telesis Group, V 318–20 *see also* SBC Communications.

PacifiCare Health Systems, Inc., 11 378–80

PacifiCorp, Inc., V 688–90; 26 357–60 (upd.)

Packaging Corporation of America, 12 376–78; 51 282–85 (upd.)

Packard Bell Electronics, Inc., 13 387–89

Packeteer, Inc., 81 273–76

Paddock Publications, Inc., 53 263–65

Paddy Power plc, 98 297–300

PagesJaunes Groupe SA, 79 306–09

Paging Network Inc., 11 381–83

Pagnossin S.p.A., 73 248–50

PaineWebber Group Inc., II 444–46; 22 404–07 (upd.) *see also* UBS AG.

Pakistan International Airlines Corporation, 46 323–26

Pakistan State Oil Company Ltd., 81 277–80

PAL *see* Philippine Airlines, Inc.

Palace Sports & Entertainment, Inc., 97 320–25

PALIC *see* Pan-American Life Insurance Co.

Pall Corporation, 9 396–98; 72 263–66 (upd.)

Palm Harbor Homes, Inc., 39 316–18

Palm, Inc., 36 355–57; 75 310–14 (upd.)

Palm Management Corporation, 71 265–68

Palmer & Cay, Inc., 69 285–87

Palmer Candy Company, 80 277–81

Palmer Co. *see* R. M. Palmer Co.

Paloma Industries Ltd., 71 269–71

Palomar Medical Technologies, Inc., 22 408–10

Pamida Holdings Corporation, 15 341–43

The Pampered Chef Ltd., 18 406–08; 78 292–96 (upd.)

Pamplin Corp. *see* R.B. Pamplin Corp.

Pan-American Life Insurance Company, 48 311–13

Pan American World Airways, Inc., I 115–16; 12 379–81 (upd.)

Panalpina World Transport (Holding) Ltd., 47 286–88

Panamerican Beverages, Inc., 47 289–91; 54 74

PanAmSat Corporation, 46 327–29

Panattoni Development Company, Inc., 99 327–330

Panavision Inc., 24 372–74

Pancho's Mexican Buffet, Inc., 46 330–32

Panda Restaurant Group, Inc., 35 327–29; 97 326–30 (upd.)

Panera Bread Company, 44 327–29

Panhandle Eastern Corporation, V 691–92 *see also* CMS Energy Corp.

Pantone Inc., 53 266–69

The Pantry, Inc., 36 358–60

Panzani, 84 297–300

Papa Gino's Holdings Corporation, Inc., 86 327–30

Papa John's International, Inc., 15 344–46; 71 272–76 (upd.)

Papa Murphy's International, Inc., 54 277–79

Papeteries de Lancey, 23 366–68

Papetti's Hygrade Egg Products, Inc., 39 319–21

Pappas Restaurants, Inc., 76 302–04

Par Pharmaceutical Companies, Inc., 65 286–88

The Paradies Shops, Inc., 88 296–99

Paradise Music & Entertainment, Inc., 42 271–74

Paradores de Turismo de Espana S.A., 73 251–53

Parametric Technology Corp., 16 405–07

Paramount Pictures Corporation, II 154–56; 94 342–47 (upd.)

Paramount Resources Ltd., 87 367–370

PAREXEL International Corporation, 84 301–304

Paribas *see* BNP Paribas Group.

Paris Corporation, 22 411–13

Parisian, Inc., 14 374–76 *see also* Belk, Inc.

Park Corp., 22 414–16

Park-Ohio Holdings Corp., 17 371–73; 85 319–23 (upd.)

Parker Drilling Company, 28 346–48

Parker-Hannifin Corporation, III 601–03; 24 375–78 (upd.); 99 331–337 (upd.)

Parlex Corporation, 61 279–81

Parmalat Finanziaria SpA, 50 343–46

Parque Arauco S.A., 72 267–69

Parras *see* Compañia Industrial de Parras, S.A. de C.V. (CIPSA).

Parsons Brinckerhoff, Inc., 34 333–36

The Parsons Corporation, 8 415–17; 56 263–67 (upd.)

PartnerRe Ltd., 83 298-301

Partouche SA *see* Groupe Partouche SA.

Party City Corporation, 54 280–82

Pathé SA, 29 369–71 *see also* Chargeurs International.

Pathmark Stores, Inc., 23 369–71

Patina Oil & Gas Corporation, 24 379–81

Patrick Industries, Inc., 30 342–45

Patriot Transportation Holding, Inc., 91 371–74

Patterson Dental Co., 19 289–91

Patterson-UTI Energy, Inc., 55 293–95

Patton Boggs LLP, 71 277–79

Paul Harris Stores, Inc., 18 409–12

Paul, Hastings, Janofsky & Walker LLP, 27 357–59

Paul Mueller Company, 65 289–91

Paul Reed Smith Guitar Company, 89 345–48

The Paul Revere Corporation, 12 382–83

Paul-Son Gaming Corporation, 66 249–51

Paul, Weiss, Rifkind, Wharton & Garrison, 47 292–94

Paulaner Brauerei GmbH & Co. KG, 35 330–33

Paxson Communications Corporation, 33 322–26

Pay 'N Pak Stores, Inc., 9 399–401

Paychex, Inc., 15 347–49; 46 333–36 (upd.)

Payless Cashways, Inc., 11 384–86; 44 330–33 (upd.)

Payless ShoeSource, Inc., 18 413–15; 69 288–92 (upd.)

PayPal Inc., 58 266–69

PBL *see* Publishing and Broadcasting Ltd.

PBS *see* Public Broadcasting Stations.

The PBSJ Corporation, 82 269–73

PC Connection, Inc., 37 300–04

PCA *see* Packaging Corporation of America.

PCA International, Inc., 62 263–65

PCC *see* Companhia Suzano de Papel e Celulose S.A.

PCC Natural Markets, 94 348–51

PCL Construction Group Inc., 50 347–49

PCM Uitgevers NV, 53 270–73

PCS *see* Potash Corp. of Saskatchewan Inc.

PDI, Inc., 52 272–75

PDL BioPharma, Inc., 90 322–25

PDO *see* Petroleum Development Oman.

PDQ Food Stores Inc., 79 310–13

PDS Gaming Corporation, 44 334–37

PDVSA *see* Petróleos de Venezuela S.A.

Peabody Energy Corporation, 10 447–49; 45 330–33 (upd.)

Peabody Holding Company, Inc., IV 169–72

Peace Arch Entertainment Group Inc., 51 286–88

The Peak Technologies Group, Inc., 14 377–80

Peapod, Inc., 30 346–48

Pearl Musical Instrument Company, 78 297–300

Pearle Vision, Inc., 13 390–92

Pearson plc, IV 657–59; 46 337–41 (upd.)

Peavey Electronics Corporation, 16 408–10; 94 352–56 (upd.)

Pechiney S.A., IV 173–75; 45 334–37 (upd.)

PECO Energy Company, 11 387–90 *see also* Exelon Corp.

Pediatric Services of America, Inc., 31 356–58

Pediatrix Medical Group, Inc., 61 282–85

Peebles Inc., 16 411–13; 43 296–99 (upd.)

Peek & Cloppenburg KG, 46 342–45

Peet's Coffee & Tea, Inc., 38 338–40

Peg Perego SpA, 88 300–03

Pegasus Solutions, Inc., 75 315–18

Pei Cobb Freed & Partners Architects LLP, 57 280–82

Pelican Products, Inc., 86 331–34

Pelikan Holding AG, 92 296–300

Pella Corporation, 12 384–86; 39 322–25 (upd.); 89 349–53 (upd.)

Pemco Aviation Group Inc., 54 283–86

Pemex *see* Petróleos Mexicanos.

Penaflor S.A., 66 252–54

Penauille Polyservices SA, 49 318–21

Pendleton Grain Growers Inc., 64 305–08

Pendleton Woolen Mills, Inc., 42 275–78

Penford Corporation, 55 296–99

Pengrowth Energy Trust, 95 323–26

The Peninsular and Oriental Steam Navigation Company, V 490–93; 38 341–46 (upd.)

Peninsular and Oriental Steam Navigation Company (Bovis Division), I 588–89 *see also* DP World.

Penn Engineering & Manufacturing Corp., 28 349–51

Penn National Gaming, Inc., 33 327–29

Penn Traffic Company, 13 393–95

Penn Virginia Corporation, 85 324–27

Penney's *see* J.C. Penney Company, Inc.

Pennington Seed Inc., 98 301–04

Pennon Group Plc, 45 338–41

Pennsylvania Blue Shield, III 325–27 *see also* Highmark Inc.

Pennsylvania Power & Light Company, V 693–94

Pennwalt Corporation, I 382–84

PennWell Corporation, 55 300–03

Pennzoil-Quaker State Company, IV 488–90; 20 418–22 (upd.); 50 350–55 (upd.)

Penske Corporation, V 494–95; 19 292–94 (upd.); 84 305–309 (upd.)

Pentair, Inc., 7 419–21; 26 361–64 (upd.); 81 281–87 (upd.)

Pentax Corporation, 78 301–05

Pentech International, Inc., 29 372–74

Pentland Group plc, 20 423–25

Penton Media, Inc., 27 360–62

Penzeys Spices, Inc., 79 314–16

People Express Airlines Inc., I 117–18

Peoples Energy Corporation, 6 543–44

PeopleSoft Inc., 14 381–83; 33 330–33 (upd.) *see also* Oracle Corp.

The Pep Boys—Manny, Moe & Jack, 11 391–93; 36 361–64 (upd.); 81 288–94 (upd.)

PEPCO *see* Potomac Electric Power Co.

Pepper *see* J. W. Pepper and Son Inc.

Pepper Hamilton LLP, 43 300–03

Pepperidge Farm, Incorporated, 81 295–300

The Pepsi Bottling Group, Inc., 40 350–53

PepsiAmericas, Inc., 67 297–300 (upd.)

PepsiCo, Inc., I 276–79; 10 450–54 (upd.); 38 347–54 (upd.); 93 333–44 (upd.)

Pequiven *see* Petroquímica de Venezuela S.A.

Perdigao SA, 52 276–79

Perdue Farms Inc., 7 422–24; 23 375–78 (upd.)

Perfetti Van Melle S.p.A., 72 270–73

Performance Food Group, 31 359–62; 96 329–34 (upd.)

Perini Corporation, 8 418–21; 82 274–79 (upd.)

PerkinElmer, Inc., 7 425–27; 78 306–10 (upd.)

Perkins Coie LLP, 56 268–70

Perkins Family Restaurants, L.P., 22 417–19

Perkins Foods Holdings Ltd., 87 371–374

Perma-Fix Environmental Services, Inc., 99 338–341

Pernod Ricard S.A., I 280–81; 21 399–401 (upd.); 72 274–77 (upd.)

Perot Systems Corporation, 29 375–78

Perrigo Company, 12 387–89; 59 330–34 (upd.)

Perry Ellis International, Inc., 41 291–94

Perry's Ice Cream Company Inc., 90 326–29

The Perseus Books Group, 91 375–78

Perstorp AB, I 385–87; 51 289–92 (upd.)

Pertamina, IV 491–93; 56 271–74 (upd.)

Perusahaan Otomobil Nasional Bhd., 62 266–68

Pescanova S.A., 81 301–04

Pet Incorporated, 7 428–31

Petco Animal Supplies, Inc., 29 379–81; 74 231–34 (upd.)

Pete's Brewing Company, 22 420–22

Peter Kiewit Sons' Inc., 8 422–24

Peter Piper, Inc., 70 217–19

Peterbilt Motors Company, 89 354–57

Petersen Publishing Company, 21 402–04

Peterson American Corporation, 55 304–06

Petit Bateau, 95 327–31

PetMed Express, Inc., 81 305–08

Petrie Stores Corporation, 8 425–27

Petro-Canada, IV 494–96; 99 342–349 (upd.)

Petrobrás *see* Petróleo Brasileiro S.A.

Petrobras Energia Participaciones S.A., 72 278–81

Petroecuador *see* Petróleos del Ecuador.

Petrofac Ltd., 95 332–35

PetroFina S.A., IV 497–500; 26 365–69 (upd.)

Petrogal *see* Petróleos de Portugal.

Petrohawk Energy Corporation, 79 317–20

Petróleo Brasileiro S.A., IV 501–03

Petróleos de Portugal S.A., IV 504–06

Petróleos de Venezuela S.A., IV 507–09; 74 235–39 (upd.)

Petróleos del Ecuador, IV 510–11

Petróleos Mexicanos, IV 512–14; 19 295–98 (upd.)

Petroleum Development Oman LLC, IV 515–16; 98 305–09 (upd.)

Petroleum Helicopters, Inc., 35 334–36

Petroliam Nasional Bhd (Petronas), 56 275–79 (upd.)

Petrolite Corporation, 15 350–52 *see also* Baker Hughes Inc.

Petromex *see* Petróleos de Mexico S.A.

Petron Corporation, 58 270–72

Petronas, IV 517–20 *see also* Petroliam Nasional Bhd.

Petrossian Inc., 54 287–89

PETsMART, Inc., 14 384–86; 41 295–98 (upd.)

Peugeot S.A., I 187–88 *see also* PSA Peugeot Citroen S.A.

The Pew Charitable Trusts, 35 337–40

Pez Candy, Inc., 38 355–57

The Pfaltzgraff Co. *see* Susquehanna Pfaltzgraff Co.

Pfizer Inc., I 661–63; 9 402–05 (upd.); 38 358–67 (upd.); 79 321–33 (upd.)

PFSweb, Inc., 73 254–56

PG&E Corporation, 26 370–73 (upd.)

PGA *see* The Professional Golfers' Association.

Phaidon Press Ltd., 98 310–14

Phantom Fireworks *see* B.J. Alan Co., Inc.

Phar-Mor Inc., 12 390–92

Pharmacia & Upjohn Inc., I 664–65; 25 374–78 (upd.) *see also* Pfizer Inc.

Pharmion Corporation, 91 379–82

Phat Fashions LLC, 49 322–24

Phelps Dodge Corporation, IV 176–79; 28 352–57 (upd.); 75 319–25 (upd.)

PHH Arval, V 496–97; 53 274–76 (upd.)

PHI, Inc., 80 282–86 (upd.)

Philadelphia Eagles, 37 305–08

Philadelphia Electric Company, V 695–97 *see also* Exelon Corp.

Philadelphia Gas Works Company, 92 301–05

Philadelphia Media Holdings LLC, 92 306–10

Philadelphia Suburban Corporation, 39 326–29

Philharmonic-Symphony Society of New York, Inc. (New York Philharmonic), 69 293–97

Philip Environmental Inc., 16 414–16

Philip Morris Companies Inc., V 405–07; 18 416–19 (upd.); 44 338–43 (upd.) *see also* Kraft Foods Inc.

Philip Services Corp., 73 257–60

Philipp Holzmann AG, 17 374–77

Philippine Airlines, Inc., 6 106–08; 23 379–82 (upd.)

Philips Electronics N.V., 13 400–03 (upd.) *see also* Koninklijke Philips Electronics N.V.

Philips Electronics North America Corp., 13 396–99

N.V. Philips Gloeilampenfabriken, II 78–80 *see also* Philips Electronics N.V.

Phillips, de Pury & Luxembourg, 49 325–27

Phillips Foods, Inc., 63 320–22; 90 330–33 (upd.)

Phillips International, Inc., 78 311–14

Phillips Petroleum Company, IV 521–23; 40 354–59 (upd.) *see also* ConocoPhillips.

Phillips-Van Heusen Corporation, 24 382–85

Phoenix AG, 68 286–89

Phoenix Footwear Group, Inc., 70 220–22

Phoenix Mecano AG, 61 286–88

The Phoenix Media/Communications Group, 91 383–87

Phones 4u Ltd., 85 328–31

Photo-Me International Plc, 83 302-306

PHP Healthcare Corporation, 22 423–25

PhyCor, Inc., 36 365–69

Physician Sales & Service, Inc., 14 387–89

Physio-Control International Corp., 18 420–23

Piaggio & C. S.p.A., 20 426–29

PianoDisc *see* Burgett, Inc.

PIC International Group PLC, 24 386–88 (upd.)

Picanol N.V., 96 335–38

Picard Surgeles, 76 305–07

Piccadilly Cafeterias, Inc., 19 299–302

Pick 'n Pay Stores Ltd., 82 280–83

PictureTel Corp., 10 455–57; 27 363–66 (upd.)

Piedmont Natural Gas Company, Inc., 27 367–69

Pier 1 Imports, Inc., 12 393–95; 34 337–41 (upd.); 95 336–43 (upd.)

Pierce Leahy Corporation, 24 389–92 *see also* Iron Mountain Inc.

Piercing Pagoda, Inc., 29 382–84

Pierre & Vacances SA, 48 314–16

Piggly Wiggly Southern, Inc., 13 404–06

Pilgrim's Pride Corporation, 7 432–33; 23 383–85 (upd.); 90 334–38 (upd.)

Pilkington Group Limited, II 724–27; 34 342–47 (upd.); 87 375–383 (upd.)

Pillowtex Corporation, 19 303–05; 41 299–302 (upd.)

Pillsbury Company, II 555–57; 13 407–09 (upd.); 62 269–73 (upd.)

Pillsbury Madison & Sutro LLP, 29 385–88

Pilot Air Freight Corp., 67 301–03

Pilot Corporation, 49 328–30

Pilot Pen Corporation of America, 82 284–87

Pinault-Printemps-Redoute S.A., 19 306–09 (upd.) *see also* PPR S.A.

Pindar *see* G A Pindar & Son Ltd.

Pinguely-Haulotte SA, 51 293–95

Pinkerton's Inc., 9 406–09 *see also* Securitas AB.

Pinnacle Airlines Corp., 73 261–63

Pinnacle West Capital Corporation, 6 545–47; 54 290–94 (upd.)

Pioneer Electronic Corporation, III 604–06; 28 358–61 (upd.) *see also* Agilysys Inc.

Pioneer Hi-Bred International, Inc., 9 410–12; 41 303–06 (upd.)

Pioneer International Limited, III 728–30

Pioneer Natural Resources Company, 59 335–39

Pioneer-Standard Electronics Inc., 19 310–14 *see also* Agilysys Inc.

Piper Jaffray Companies Inc., 22 426–30 *see also* U.S. Bancorp.

Pirelli & C. S.p.A., V 249–51; 15 353–56 (upd.); 75 326–31 (upd.)

Piscines Desjoyaux S.A., 84 310–313

Pitman Company, 58 273–75

Pitney Bowes, Inc., III 156–58, 159; 19 315–18 (upd.); 47 295–99 (upd.)

Pittsburgh Brewing Company, 76 308–11

Pittsburgh Plate Glass Co. *see* PPG Industries, Inc.

Pittsburgh Steelers Sports, Inc., 66 255–57

The Pittston Company, IV 180–82; 19 319–22 (upd.) *see also* The Brink's Co.

Pittway Corporation, 9 413–15; 33 334–37 (upd.)

Pixar Animation Studios, 34 348–51

Pixelworks, Inc., 69 298–300

Pizza Hut Inc., 7 434–35; 21 405–07 (upd.)

Pizza Inn, Inc., 46 346–49

PKF International, 78 315–18

Placer Dome Inc., 20 430–33; 61 289–93 (upd.)

Plain Dealer Publishing Company, 92 311–14

Plains Cotton Cooperative Association, 57 283–86

Planar Systems, Inc., 61 294–97

Planet Hollywood International, Inc., 18 424–26; 41 307–10 (upd.)

Planeta *see* Grupo Planeta.

Plantation Pipe Line Company, 68 290–92

Plante & Moran, LLP, 71 280–83

Platinum Entertainment, Inc., 35 341–44

PLATINUM Technology, Inc., 14 390–92 *see also* Computer Associates International, Inc.

Plato Learning, Inc., 44 344–47

Play by Play Toys & Novelties, Inc., 26 374–76

Playboy Enterprises, Inc., 18 427–30

PlayCore, Inc., 27 370–72

Players International, Inc., 22 431–33

Playmates Toys, 23 386–88

Playskool, Inc., 25 379–81 *see also* Hasbro, Inc.

Playtex Products, Inc., 15 357–60

Pleasant Company, 27 373–75 *see also* American Girl, Inc.

Pleasant Holidays LLC, 62 274–76

Plessey Company, PLC, II 81–82 *see also* Marconi plc.

Plexus Corporation, 35 345–47; 80 287–91 (upd.)

Pliant Corporation, 98 315–18

PLIVA d.d., 70 223–25

Plum Creek Timber Company, Inc., 43 304–06

Pluma, Inc., 27 376–78

Ply Gem Industries Inc., 12 396–98

The PMI Group, Inc., 49 331–33

PMP Ltd., 72 282–84

PMT Services, Inc., 24 393–95

The PNC Financial Services Group Inc., II 342–43; 13 410–12 (upd.); 46 350–53 (upd.)

PNM Resources Inc., 51 296–300 (upd.)

Pochet SA, 55 307–09

Pogo Producing Company, 39 330–32

Pohang Iron and Steel Company Ltd., IV 183–85 *see also* POSCO.

Polar Air Cargo Inc., 60 237–39

Polaris Industries Inc., 12 399–402; 35 348–53 (upd.); 77 330–37 (upd.)

Polartec LLC, 98 319–23 (upd.)

Polaroid Corporation, III 607–09; 7 436–39 (upd.); 28 362–66 (upd.); 93 345–53 (upd.)

Policy Management Systems Corporation, 11 394–95

Policy Studies, Inc., 62 277–80

Poliet S.A., 33 338–40

Polk Audio, Inc., 34 352–54

Polo/Ralph Lauren Corporation, 12 403–05; 62 281–85 (upd.)

Polski Koncern Naftowy ORLEN S.A., 77 338–41

PolyGram N.V., 23 389–92

PolyMedica Corporation, 77 342–45

PolyOne Corporation, 87 384–395 (upd.)

Pomare Ltd., 88 304–07

Pomeroy Computer Resources, Inc., 33 341–44

Ponderosa Steakhouse, 15 361–64

Poof-Slinky, Inc., 61 298–300

Poore Brothers, Inc., 44 348–50 *see also* The Inventure Group, Inc.

Pop Warner Little Scholars, Inc., 86 335–38

Pope & Talbot, Inc., 12 406–08; 61 301–05 (upd.)

Pope Cable and Wire B.V. *see* Belden CDT Inc.

Pope Resources LP, 74 240–43

Popular, Inc., 41 311–13

The Porcelain and Fine China Companies Ltd., 69 301–03

Porsche AG, 13 413–15; 31 363–66 (upd.)

The Port Authority of New York and New Jersey, 48 317–20

Port Imperial Ferry Corporation, 70 226–29

Portal Software, Inc., 47 300–03

Portillo's Restaurant Group, Inc., 71 284–86

Portland General Corporation, 6 548–51

Portland Trail Blazers, 50 356–60

Portmeirion Group plc, 88 308–11

Portucel *see* Grupo Portucel Soporcel.

Portugal Telecom SGPS S.A., 69 304–07

Posadas *see* Grupo Posadas, S.A. de C.V.

POSCO, 57 287–91 (upd.)

Post Office Group, V 498–501

Post Properties, Inc., 26 377–79

La Poste, V 470–72

Posterscope Worldwide, 70 230–32

Posti- Ja Telelaitos, 6 329–31

Potash Corporation of Saskatchewan Inc., 18 431–33

Potbelly Sandwich Works, Inc., 83 307–310

Potlatch Corporation, 8 428–30; 34 355–59 (upd.); 87 396–403 (upd.)

Potomac Electric Power Company, 6 552–54

Potter & Brumfield Inc., 11 396–98

Pou Chen Corporation, 81 309–12

Powell Duffryn plc, 31 367–70

Powell's Books, Inc., 40 360–63

Power Corporation of Canada, 36 370–74 (upd.); 85 332–39 (upd.)

Power-One, Inc., 79 334–37

PowerBar Inc., 44 351–53

Powergen PLC, 11 399–401; 50 361–64 (upd.)

Powerhouse Technologies, Inc., 27 379–81

POZEN Inc., 81 313–16

PP&L *see* Pennsylvania Power & Light Co.

PPB Group Berhad, 57 292–95

PPG Industries, Inc., III 731–33; 22 434–37 (upd.); 81 317–23 (upd.)

PPL Corporation, 41 314–17 (upd.)
PPR S.A., 74 244–48 (upd.)
PR Newswire, 35 354–56
PRS *see* Paul Reed Smith Guitar Co.
Prada Holding B.V., 45 342–45
Prairie Farms Dairy, Inc., 47 304–07
Pranda Jewelry plc, 70 233–35
Pratt & Whitney, 9 416–18
Praxair, Inc., 11 402–04; 48 321–24 (upd.)
Praxis Bookstore Group LLC, 90 339–42
Pre-Paid Legal Services, Inc., 20 434–37
Precision Castparts Corp., 15 365–67
Premark International, Inc., III 610–12 *see also* Illinois Tool Works Inc.
Premcor Inc., 37 309–11
Premier Industrial Corporation, 9 419–21
Premier Parks, Inc., 27 382–84 *see also* Six Flags, Inc.
Premium Standard Farms, Inc., 30 353–55
PremiumWear, Inc., 30 356–59
Preserver Group, Inc., 44 354–56
President Casinos, Inc., 22 438–40
Pressman Toy Corporation, 56 280–82
Presstek, Inc., 33 345–48
Preston Corporation, 6 421–23
Preussag AG, 17 378–82; 42 279–83 (upd.)
PreussenElektra Aktiengesellschaft, V 698–700 *see also* E.On AG.
PRG-Schultz International, Inc., 73 264–67
Price Communications Corporation, 42 284–86
The Price Company, V 162–64 *see also* Costco Wholesale Corp.
Price Pfister, Inc., 70 236–39
Price Waterhouse LLP, 9 422–24 *see also* PricewaterhouseCoopers
PriceCostco, Inc., 14 393–95 *see also* Costco Wholesale Corp.
Priceline.com Incorporated, 57 296–99
PriceSmart, Inc., 71 287–90
PricewaterhouseCoopers, 29 389–94 (upd.)
PRIDE Enterprises *see* Prison Rehabilitative Industries and Diversified Enterprises, Inc.
Pride International, Inc., 78 319–23
Primark Corp., 13 416–18 *see also* Thomson Corp.
Prime Hospitality Corporation, 52 280–83
Primedex Health Systems, Inc., 25 382–85
Primedia Inc., 22 441–43
Primerica Corporation, I 612–14
Prince Sports Group, Inc., 15 368–70
Princes Ltd., 76 312–14
Princess Cruise Lines, 22 444–46
The Princeton Review, Inc., 42 287–90
Principal Mutual Life Insurance Company, III 328–30
Printpack, Inc., 68 293–96

Printrak, A Motorola Company, 44 357–59
Printronix, Inc., 18 434–36
Prison Rehabilitative Industries and Diversified Enterprises, Inc. (PRIDE), 53 277–79
Pro-Build Holdings Inc., 95 344–48 (upd.)
The Procter & Gamble Company, III 50–53; 8 431–35 (upd.); 26 380–85 (upd.); 67 304–11 (upd.)
Prodigy Communications Corporation, 34 360–62
Proeza S.A. de C.V., 82 288–91
Professional Bull Riders Inc., 55 310–12
The Professional Golfers' Association of America, 41 318–21
Proffitt's, Inc., 19 323–25 *see also* Belk, Inc.
Programmer's Paradise, Inc., 81 324–27
Progress Energy, Inc., 74 249–52
Progress Software Corporation, 15 371–74
Progressive Corporation, 11 405–07; 29 395–98 (upd.)
Progressive Enterprises Ltd., 96 339–42
ProLogis, 57 300–02
Promus Companies, Inc., 9 425–27 *see also* Hilton Hotels Corp.
ProSiebenSat.1 Media AG, 54 295–98
Proskauer Rose LLP, 47 308–10
Protection One, Inc., 32 372–75
Provell Inc., 58 276–79 (upd.)
Providence Health System, 90 343–47
The Providence Journal Company, 28 367–69; 30 15
The Providence Service Corporation, 64 309–12
Provident Bankshares Corporation, 85 340–43
Provident Life and Accident Insurance Company of America, III 331–33 *see also* UnumProvident Corp.
Providian Financial Corporation, 52 284–90 (upd.)
Provigo Inc., II 651–53; 51 301–04 (upd.)
Provimi S.A., 80 292–95
Prudential Financial Inc., III 337–41; 30 360–64 (upd.); 82 292–98 (upd.)
Prudential plc, III 334–36; 48 325–29 (upd.)
PSA Peugeot Citroen S.A., 28 370–74 (upd.); 54 126
PSF *see* Premium Standard Farms, Inc.
PSI Resources, 6 555–57
Psion PLC, 45 346–49
Psychemedics Corporation, 89 358–61
Psychiatric Solutions, Inc., 68 297–300
PT Astra International Tbk, 56 283–86
PT Bank Buana Indonesia Tbk, 60 240–42
PT Indosat Tbk, 93 354–57
PTT Public Company Ltd., 56 287–90
Pubco Corporation, 17 383–85
Public Service Company of Colorado, 6 558–60

Public Service Company of New Hampshire, 21 408–12; 55 313–18 (upd.)
Public Service Company of New Mexico, 6 561–64 *see also* PNM Resources Inc.
Public Service Enterprise Group Inc., V 701–03; 44 360–63 (upd.)
Public Storage, Inc., 21 52 291–93
Publicis Groupe, 19 329–32; 77 346–50 (upd.)
Publishers Clearing House, 23 393–95; 64 313–16 (upd.)
Publishers Group, Inc., 35 357–59
Publishing and Broadcasting Limited, 54 299–302
Publix Super Markets Inc., 7 440–42; 31 371–74 (upd.)
Puck Lazaroff Inc. *see* The Wolfgang Puck Food Company, Inc.
Pueblo Xtra International, Inc., 47 311–13
Puerto Rico Electric Power Authority, 47 314–16
Puget Sound Energy Inc., 6 565–67; 50 365–68 (upd.)
Puig Beauty and Fashion Group S.L., 60 243–46
Pulaski Furniture Corporation, 33 349–52; 80 296–99 (upd.)
Pulitzer Inc., 15 375–77; 58 280–83 (upd.)
Pulsar Internacional S.A., 21 413–15
Pulte Homes, Inc., 8 436–38; 42 291–94 (upd.)
Puma AG Rudolf Dassler Sport, 35 360–63
Pumpkin Masters, Inc., 48 330–32
Punch International N.V., 66 258–60
Punch Taverns plc, 70 240–42
Puratos S.A./NV, 92 315–18
Pure World, Inc., 72 285–87
Purina Mills, Inc., 32 376–79
Puritan-Bennett Corporation, 13 419–21
Purolator Products Company, 21 416–18; 74 253–56 (upd.)
Putt-Putt Golf Courses of America, Inc., 23 396–98
PVC Container Corporation, 67 312–14
PW Eagle, Inc., 48 333–36
PWA Group, IV 323–25 *see also* Svenska Cellulosa.
Pyramid Breweries Inc., 33 353–55
Pyramid Companies, 54 303–05
PZ Cussons plc, 72 288–90

Q

Q.E.P. Co., Inc., 65 292–94
Qantas Airways Ltd., 6 109–13; 24 396–401 (upd.); 68 301–07 (upd.)
Qatar Airways Company Q.C.S.C., 87 404–407
Qatar National Bank SAQ, 87 408–411
Qatar Petroleum, IV 524–26; 98 324–28 (upd.)
Qatar Telecom QSA, 87 412–415

Qdoba Restaurant Corporation, 93 358–62

Qiagen N.V., 39 333–35

QLT Inc., 71 291–94

QRS Music Technologies, Inc., 95 349–53

QSC Audio Products, Inc., 56 291–93

Quad/Graphics, Inc., 19 333–36

Quaker Chemical Corp., 91 388–91

Quaker Fabric Corp., 19 337–39

Quaker Foods North America, II 558–60; 12 409–12 (upd.); 34 363–67 (upd.); 73 268–73 (upd.)

Quaker State Corporation, 7 443–45; 21 419–22 (upd.) see also Pennzoil-Quaker State Co.

QUALCOMM Incorporated, 20 438–41; 47 317–21 (upd.)

Quality Chekd Dairies, Inc., 48 337–39

Quality Dining, Inc., 18 437–40

Quality Food Centers, Inc., 17 386–88 see also Kroger Co.

Quality Systems, Inc., 81 328–31

Quanex Corporation, 13 422–24; 62 286–89 (upd.)

Quanta Computer Inc., 47 322–24

Quanta Services, Inc., 79 338–41

Quantum Chemical Corporation, 8 439–41

Quantum Corporation, 10 458–59; 62 290–93 (upd.)

Quark, Inc., 36 375–79

Québec Hydro-Electric Commission see Hydro-Quebéc.

Quebecor Inc., 12 412–14; 47 325–28 (upd.)

Quelle Group, V 165–67 see also Karstadt Quelle AG.

Quest Diagnostics Inc., 26 390–92

Questar Corporation, 6 568–70; 26 386–89 (upd.)

The Quick & Reilly Group, Inc., 20 442–44

Quick Restaurants S.A., 94 357–60

Quicken Loans, Inc., 93 363–67

Quidel Corporation, 80 300–03

The Quigley Corporation, 62 294–97

Quiksilver, Inc., 18 441–43; 79 342–47 (upd.)

QuikTrip Corporation, 36 380–83

Quill Corporation, 28 375–77

Quilmes Industrial (QUINSA) S.A., 67 315–17

Quinn Emanuel Urquhart Oliver & Hedges, LLP, 99 350–353

Quintiles Transnational Corporation, 21 423–25; 68 308–12 (upd.)

Quixote Corporation, 15 378–80

The Quizno's Corporation, 42 295–98

Quovadx Inc., 70 243–46

QVC Inc., 9 428–29; 58 284–87 (upd.)

Qwest Communications International, Inc., 37 312–17

R

R&B, Inc., 51 305–07

R.B. Pamplin Corp., 45 350–52

R.C. Bigelow, Inc., 49 334–36

R.C. Willey Home Furnishings, 72 291–93

R.G. Barry Corp., 17 389–91; 44 364–67 (upd.)

R. Griggs Group Limited, 23 399–402; 31 413–14

R.H. Macy & Co., Inc., V 168–70; 8 442–45 (upd.); 30 379–83 (upd.) see also Macy's, Inc.

R.J. Reynolds Tobacco Holdings, Inc., 30 384–87 (upd.)

R. M. Palmer Co., 89 362–64

R.P. Scherer Corporation, I 678–80 see also Cardinal Health, Inc.

R.R. Donnelley & Sons Company, IV 660–62; 38 368–71 (upd.)

Rabobank Group, 26 419; 33 356–58

RAC see Roy Anderson Corp.

Racal-Datacom Inc., 11 408–10

Racal Electronics PLC, II 83–84 see also Thales S.A.

Racing Champions Corporation, 37 318–20

Rack Room Shoes, Inc., 84 314–317

Radeberger Gruppe AG, 75 332–35

Radian Group Inc., 42 299–301 see also Onex Corp.

Radiation Therapy Services, Inc., 85 344–47

Radio Flyer Inc., 34 368–70

Radio One, Inc., 67 318–21

RadioShack Corporation, 36 384–88 (upd.)

Radius Inc., 16 417–19

RAE Systems Inc., 83 311–314

RAG AG, 35 364–67; 60 247–51 (upd.)

Rag Shops, Inc., 30 365–67

Ragdoll Productions Ltd., 51 308–11

Raiffeisen Zentralbank Österreich AG, 85 348–52

RailTex, Inc., 20 445–47

Railtrack Group PLC, 50 369–72

Rain Bird Corporation, 84 318–321

Rainforest Café, Inc., 25 386–88; 88 312–16 (upd.)

Rainier Brewing Company, 23 403–05

Raisio PLC, 99 354–357

Raleigh UK Ltd., 65 295–97

Raley's Inc., 14 396–98; 58 288–91 (upd.)

Rally's, 25 389–91; 68 313–16 (upd.)

Rallye SA, 54 306–09

Ralph Lauren see Polo/Ralph Lauren Corportion.

Ralphs Grocery Company, 35 368–70

Ralston Purina Company, II 561–63; 13 425–27 (upd.) see also Ralcorp Holdings, Inc.; Nestlé S.A.

Ramsay Youth Services, Inc., 41 322–24

Ramtron International Corporation, 89 365–68

Ranbaxy Laboratories Ltd., 70 247–49

Rand McNally & Company, 28 378–81; 53 122

Randall's Food Markets, Inc., 40 364–67 see also Safeway Inc.

Random House, Inc., 13 428–30; 31 375–80 (upd.)

Randon S.A. Implementos e Participações, 79 348–52

Randstad Holding n.v., 16 420–22; 43 307–10 (upd.)

Range Resources Corporation, 45 353–55

The Rank Group plc, II 157–59; 14 399–402 (upd.); 64 317–21 (upd.)

Ranks Hovis McDougall Limited, II 564–65; 28 382–85 (upd.)

RAO Unified Energy System of Russia, 45 356–60

Rapala-Normark Group, Ltd., 30 368–71

Rare Hospitality International Inc., 19 340–42

RAS see Riunione Adriatica di Sicurtà SpA.

Rascal House see Jerry's Famous Deli Inc.

Rasmussen Group see K.A. Rasmussen AS.

Rathbone Brothers plc, 70 250–53

RathGibson Inc., 90 348–51

ratiopharm Group, 84 322–326

Ratner Companies, 72 294–96

Raven Industries, Inc., 33 359–61

Ravensburger AG, 64 322–26

Raving Brands, Inc., 64 327–29

Rawlings Sporting Goods Co., Inc., 24 402–04

Raychem Corporation, 8 446–47

Raymond James Financial Inc., 69 308–10

Raymond Ltd., 77 351–54

Rayonier Inc., 24 405–07

Rayovac Corporation, 13 431–34; 39 336–40 (upd.)

Raytech Corporation, 61 306–09

Raytheon Aircraft Holdings Inc., 46 354–57

Raytheon Company, II 85–87; 11 411–14 (upd.); 38 372–77 (upd.)

Razorfish, Inc., 37 321–24

RCA Corporation, II 88–90

RCM Technologies, Inc., 34 371–74

RCN Corporation, 70 254–57

RCS MediaGroup S.p.A., 96 343–46

RDO Equipment Company, 33 362–65

RE/MAX International, Inc., 59 344–46

Read-Rite Corp., 10 463–64

The Reader's Digest Association, Inc., IV 663–64; 17 392–95 (upd.); 71 295–99 (upd.)

Reading International Inc., 70 258–60

The Real Good Food Company plc, 99 358–361

Real Madrid C.F., 73 274–76

Real Times, Inc., 66 261–65

Real Turismo, S.A. de C.V., 50 373–75

The Really Useful Group, 26 393–95

RealNetworks, Inc., 53 280–82

Reckitt Benckiser plc, II 566–67; 42 302–06 (upd.); 91 392–99 (upd.)

Reckson Associates Realty Corp., 47 329–31

Recording for the Blind & Dyslexic, 51 312–14

Recoton Corp., 15 381–83

Recovery Engineering, Inc., 25 392–94

Recreational Equipment, Inc., 18 444–47; 71 300–03 (upd.)

Recycled Paper Greetings, Inc., 21 426–28

Red Apple Group, Inc., 23 406–08

Red Bull GmbH, 60 252–54

Red McCombs Automotive Group, 91 400–03

Red Hat, Inc., 45 361–64

Red Robin Gourmet Burgers, Inc., 56 294–96

Red Roof Inns, Inc., 18 448–49 *see also* Accor S.A.

Red Spot Paint & Varnish Company, 55 319–22

Red Wing Pottery Sales, Inc., 52 294–96

Red Wing Shoe Company, Inc., 9 433–35; 30 372–75 (upd.); 83 315-321 (upd.)

Redback Networks, Inc., 92 319–22

Reddy Ice Holdings, Inc., 80 304–07

Redhook Ale Brewery, Inc., 31 381–84; 88 317–21 (upd.)

Redken Laboratories Inc., 84 327–330

Redland plc, III 734–36 *see also* Lafarge Cement UK.

Redlon & Johnson, Inc., 97 331–34

RedPeg Marketing, 73 277–79

RedPrairie Corporation, 74 257–60

Redrow Group plc, 31 385–87

Reebok International Ltd., V 375–77; 9 436–38 (upd.); 26 396–400 (upd.)

Reed & Barton Corporation, 67 322–24

Reed Elsevier plc, 31 388–94 (upd.)

Reed International PLC, IV 665–67; 17 396–99 (upd.)

Reeds Jewelers, Inc., 22 447–49

Regal-Beloit Corporation, 18 450–53; 97 335–42 (upd.)

Regal Entertainment Group, 59 340–43

The Regence Group, 74 261–63

Regency Centers Corporation, 71 304–07

Regent Communications, Inc., 87 416–420

Regent Inns plc, 95 354–57

Régie Nationale des Usines Renault, I 189–91 *see also* Renault S.A.

Regis Corporation, 18 454–56; 70 261–65 (upd.)

REI *see* Recreational Equipment, Inc.

Reichhold Chemicals, Inc., 10 465–67

Reiter Dairy, LLC, 94 361–64

Rejuvenation, Inc., 91 404–07

Reliance Electric Company, 9 439–42

Reliance Group Holdings, Inc., III 342–44

Reliance Industries Ltd., 81 332–36

Reliance Steel & Aluminum Company, 19 343–45; 70 266–70 (upd.)

Reliant Energy Inc., 44 368–73 (upd.)

Reliv International, Inc., 58 292–95

Remedy Corporation, 58 296–99

RemedyTemp, Inc., 20 448–50

Remington Arms Company, Inc., 12 415–17; 40 368–71 (upd.)

Remington Products Company, L.L.C., 42 307–10

Remington Rand *see* Unisys Corp.

Rémy Cointreau Group, 20 451–53; 80 308–12 (upd.)

Renaissance Learning Systems, Inc., 39 341–43

Renal Care Group, Inc., 72 297–99

Renault Argentina S.A., 67 325–27

Renault S.A., 26 401–04 (upd.); 74 264–68 (upd.)

Renfro Corporation, 99 362–365

Rengo Co., Ltd., IV 326

Renishaw plc, 46 358–60

RENK AG, 37 325–28

Renner Herrmann S.A., 79 353–56

Reno Air Inc., 23 409–11

Reno de Medici S.p.A., 41 325–27

Rent-A-Center, Inc., 45 365–67

Rent-Way, Inc., 33 366–68; 75 336–39 (upd.)

Rental Service Corporation, 28 386–88

Rentokil Initial Plc, 47 332–35

Rentrak Corporation, 35 371–74

Repco Corporation Ltd., 74 269–72

Repsol-YPF S.A., IV 527–29; 16 423–26 (upd.); 40 372–76 (upd.)

Republic Engineered Steels, Inc., 7 446–47; 26 405–08 (upd.)

Republic Industries, Inc., 26 409–11 *see also* AutoNation, Inc.

Republic New York Corporation, 11 415–19 *see also* HSBC Holdings plc.

Republic Services, Inc., 92 323–26

Res-Care, Inc., 29 399–402

Research in Motion Ltd., 54 310–14

Research Triangle Institute, 83 322-325

Réseau Ferré de France, 66 266–68

Reser's Fine Foods, Inc., 81 337–40

Resorts International, Inc., 12 418–20

Resource America, Inc., 42 311–14

Resources Connection, Inc., 81 341–44

Response Oncology, Inc., 27 385–87

Restaurant Associates Corporation, 66 269–72

Restaurants Unlimited, Inc., 13 435–37

Restoration Hardware, Inc., 30 376–78; 96 347–51 (upd.)

Retail Ventures, Inc., 82 299–03 (upd.)

Retractable Technologies, Inc., 99 366–369

Reuters Group PLC, IV 668–70; 22 450–53 (upd.); 63 323–27 (upd.)

Revco D.S., Inc., V 171–73 *see also* CVS Corp.

Revell-Monogram Inc., 16 427–29

Revere Electric Supply Company, 96 352–55

Revere Ware Corporation, 22 454–56

Revlon Inc., III 54–57; 17 400–04 (upd.); 64 330–35 (upd.)

Rewards Network Inc., 70 271–75 (upd.)

REX Stores Corp., 10 468–69

Rexam PLC, 32 380–85 (upd.); 85 353–61 (upd.)

Rexel, Inc., 15 384–87

Rexnord Corporation, 21 429–32; 76 315–19 (upd.)

The Reynolds and Reynolds Company, 50 376–79

Reynolds Metals Company, IV 186–88; 19 346–48 (upd.) *see also* Alcoa Inc.

RF Micro Devices, Inc., 43 311–13

RFC Franchising LLC, 68 317–19

RFF *see* Réseau Ferré de France.

RGI *see* Rockefeller Group International.

Rheinmetall AG, 9 443–46; 97 343–49 (upd.)

RHI AG, 53 283–86

Rhino Entertainment Company, 18 457–60; 70 276–80 (upd.)

RHM *see* Ranks Hovis McDougall.

Rhodes Inc., 23 412–14

Rhodia SA, 38 378–80

Rhône-Poulenc S.A., I 388–90; 10 470–72 (upd.)

Rica Foods, Inc., 41 328–30

Ricardo plc, 90 352–56

Rich Products Corporation, 7 448–49; 38 381–84 (upd.); 93 368–74 (upd.)

The Richards Group, Inc., 58 300–02

Richardson Electronics, Ltd., 17 405–07

Richardson Industries, Inc., 62 298–301

Richfood Holdings, Inc., 7 450–51; *see also* Supervalu Inc.

Richton International Corporation, 39 344–46

Richtree Inc., 63 328–30

Richwood Building Products, Inc. *see* Ply Gem Industries Inc.

Rickenbacker International Corp., 91 408–12

Ricoh Company, Ltd., III 159–61; 36 389–93 (upd.)

Ricola Ltd., 62 302–04

Riddell Sports Inc., 22 457–59; 23 449

Ride, Inc., 22 460–63

Ridley Corporation Ltd., 62 305–07

Riedel Tiroler Glashuette GmbH, 99 370–373

The Riese Organization, 38 385–88

Rieter Holding AG, 42 315–17

Riggs National Corporation, 13 438–40

Right Management Consultants, Inc., 42 318–21

Riklis Family Corp., 9 447–50

Rimage Corp., 89 369–72

Rinascente S.p.A., 71 308–10

Rinker Group Ltd., 65 298–301

Rio Tinto plc, 19 349–53 (upd.) 50 380–85 (upd.)

Ripley Entertainment, Inc., 74 273–76

Riser Foods, Inc., 9 451–54 *see also* Giant Eagle, Inc.

Ritchie Bros. Auctioneers Inc., 41 331–34

Rite Aid Corporation, V 174–76; 19 354–57 (upd.); 63 331–37 (upd.)

Ritter Sport *see* Alfred Ritter GmbH & Co. KG.

Ritter's Frozen Custard *see* RFC Franchising LLC.

Ritz Camera Centers, 34 375–77

The Ritz-Carlton Hotel Company, L.L.C., 9 455–57; 29 403–06 (upd.); 71 311–16 (upd.)

Ritz-Craft Corporation of Pennsylvania Inc., 94 365–68

Riunione Adriatica di Sicurtà SpA, III 345–48

Riva Fire *see* Gruppo Riva Fire SpA.

The Rival Company, 19 358–60

River Oaks Furniture, Inc., 43 314–16

River Ranch Fresh Foods LLC, 88 322–25

Riverwood International Corporation, 11 420–23; 48 340–44 (upd.) *see also* Graphic Packaging Holding Co.

Riviana Foods, 27 388–91

Riviera Holdings Corporation, 75 340–43

Riviera Tool Company, 89 373–76

RJR Nabisco Holdings Corp., V 408–10 *see also* R.J Reynolds Tobacco Holdings Inc., Nabisco Brands, Inc.; R.J. Reynolds Industries, Inc.

RM Auctions, Inc., 88 326–29

RMC Group p.l.c., III 737–40; 34 378–83 (upd.)

RMH Teleservices, Inc., 42 322–24

Roadhouse Grill, Inc., 22 464–66

Roadmaster Industries, Inc., 16 430–33

Roadway Express, Inc., V 502–03; 25 395–98 (upd.)

Roanoke Electric Steel Corporation, 45 368–70

Robbins & Myers Inc., 15 388–90

Roberds Inc., 19 361–63

Robert Bosch GmbH, I 392–93; 16 434–37 (upd.); 43 317–21 (upd.)

Robert Half International Inc., 18 461–63; 70 281–84 (upd.)

Robert Mondavi Corporation, 15 391–94; 50 386–90 (upd.)

Robert Talbott Inc., 88 330–33

Robert W. Baird & Co. Incorporated, 67 328–30

Robert Wood Johnson Foundation, 35 375–78

Robertet SA, 39 347–49

Roberts Pharmaceutical Corporation, 16 438–40

Robertson-Ceco Corporation, 19 364–66

Robins, Kaplan, Miller & Ciresi L.L.P., 89 377–81

Robinson Helicopter Company, 51 315–17

ROC *see* Royal Olympic Cruise Lines Inc.

Rocawear Apparel LLC, 77 355–58

Roche Biomedical Laboratories, Inc., 11 424–26 *see also* Laboratory Corporation of America Holdings.

Roche Bioscience, 14 403–06 (upd.)

Rochester Gas And Electric Corporation, 6 571–73

Rochester Telephone Corporation, 6 332–34

Röchling Gruppe, 94 369–74

Rock Bottom Restaurants, Inc., 25 399–401; 68 320–23 (upd.)

Rock-It Cargo USA, Inc., 86 339–42

Rock of Ages Corporation, 37 329–32

Rock-Tenn Company, 13 441–43; 59 347–51 (upd.)

The Rockefeller Foundation, 34 384–87

Rockefeller Group International Inc., 58 303–06

Rockford Corporation, 43 322–25

Rockford Products Corporation, 55 323–25

RockShox, Inc., 26 412–14

Rockwell Automation, 43 326–31 (upd.)

Rockwell International Corporation, I 78–80; 11 427–30 (upd.)

Rockwell Medical Technologies, Inc., 88 334–37

Rocky Mountain Chocolate Factory, Inc., 73 280–82

Rocky Shoes & Boots, Inc., 26 415–18

Rodale, Inc., 23 415–17; 47 336–39 (upd.)

Rodamco N.V., 26 419–21

Rodda Paint Company, 98 329–32

Rodriguez Group S.A., 90 357–60

ROFIN-SINAR Technologies Inc, 81 345–48

Rogers Communications Inc., 30 388–92 (upd.) *see also* Maclean Hunter Publishing Ltd.

Rogers Corporation, 61 310–13; 80 313–17 (upd.)

Rohde & Schwarz GmbH & Co. KG, 39 350–53

Röhm and Haas Company, I 391–93; 26 422–26 (upd.); 77 359–66 (upd.)

ROHN Industries, Inc., 22 467–69

Rohr Incorporated, 9 458–60 *see also* Goodrich Corp.

Roland Berger & Partner GmbH, 37 333–36

Roland Corporation, 38 389–91

Roland Murten A.G., 7 452–53

Rolex *see* Montres Rolex S.A.

Roll International Corporation, 37 337–39

Rollerblade, Inc., 15 395–98; 34 388–92 (upd.)

Rollins, Inc., 11 431–34

Rolls-Royce Allison, 29 407–09 (upd.)

Rolls-Royce Group PLC, 67 331–36 (upd.)

Rolls-Royce Motors Ltd., I 194–96

Rolls-Royce plc, I 81–83; 7 454–57 (upd.); 21 433–37 (upd.)

Rolta India Ltd., 90 361–64

Roly Poly Franchise Systems LLC, 83 326–328

Romacorp, Inc., 58 307–11

Roman Meal Company, 84 331–334

Ron Tonkin Chevrolet Company, 55 326–28

RONA, Inc., 73 283–86

Ronco Corporation, 15 399–401; 80 318–23 (upd.)

Ronson PLC, 49 337–39

Rooms To Go Inc., 28 389–92

Rooney Brothers Co., 25 402–04

Roosevelt Hospital *see* Continuum Health Partners, Inc.

Roots Canada Ltd., 42 325–27

Roper Industries, Inc., 15 402–04; 50 391–95 (upd.)

Ropes & Gray, 40 377–80

Rorer Group, I 666–68

Rosauers Supermarkets, Inc., 90 365–68

Rose Acre Farms, Inc., 60 255–57

Rose Art Industries, 58 312–14

Rose's Stores, Inc., 13 444–46

Roseburg Forest Products Company, 58 315–17

Rosemount Inc., 15 405–08 *see also* Emerson.

Rosenbluth International Inc., 14 407–09 *see also* American Express Co.

Rosetta Stone Inc., 93 375–79

Ross Stores, Inc., 17 408–10; 43 332–35 (upd.)

Rossignol Ski Company, Inc. *see* Skis Rossignol S.A.

Rossmann *see* Dirk Rossmann GmbH.

Rostelecom Joint Stock Co., 99 374–377

Rostvertol plc, 62 308–10

Rosy Blue N.V., 84 335–338

Rotary International, 31 395–97

Rothmans UK Holdings Limited, V 411–13; 19 367–70 (upd.)

Roto-Rooter, Inc., 15 409–11; 61 314–19 (upd.)

Rotork plc, 46 361–64

The Rottlund Company, Inc., 28 393–95

Rouge Steel Company, 8 448–50

Rougier *see* Groupe Rougier, SA.

Roularta Media Group NV, 48 345–47

Rounder Records Corporation, 79 357–61

Roundy's Inc., 14 410–12; 58 318–21 (upd.)

The Rouse Company, 15 412–15; 63 338–41 (upd.)

Roussel Uclaf, I 669–70; 8 451–53 (upd.)

Rover Group Ltd., 7 458–60; 21 441–44 (upd.)

Rowan Companies, Inc., 43 336–39

Rowntree Mackintosh PLC, II 568–70 *see also* Nestlé S.A.

The Rowohlt Verlag GmbH, 96 356–61

Roy Anderson Corporation, 75 344–46

Roy F. Weston, Inc., 33 369–72

Royal & Sun Alliance Insurance Group plc, 55 329–39 (upd.)

Royal Ahold N.V. *see* Koninklijke Ahold N.V.

Royal Appliance Manufacturing Company, 15 416–18

The Royal Bank of Canada, II 344–46; 21 445–48 (upd.); 81 349–55 (upd.)

The Royal Bank of Scotland Group plc, 12 421–23; 38 392–99 (upd.)

Royal Brunei Airlines Sdn Bhd, 99 378–381

Royal Canin S.A., 39 354–57

Royal Caribbean Cruises Ltd., 22 470–73; 74 277–81 (upd.)

Royal Crown Company, Inc., 23 418–20 *see also* Cott Corp.

Royal Doulton plc, 14 413–15; 38 400–04 (upd.)

Royal Dutch Petroleum Company, IV 530–32 *see also* Shell Transport and Trading Company p.l.c.

Royal Dutch/Shell Group, 49 340–44 (upd.)

Royal Grolsch NV, 54 315–18

Royal Group Technologies Limited, 73 287–89

Royal Insurance Holdings plc, III 349–51 *see also* Royal & Sun Alliance Insurance Group plc .

Royal KPN N.V., 30 393–95

Royal Nepal Airline Corporation, 41 335–38

Royal Numico N.V., 37 340–42

Royal Olympic Cruise Lines Inc., 52 297–99

Royal Packaging Industries Van Leer N.V., 30 396–98

Royal Ten Cate N.V., 68 324–26

Royal Vendex KBB N.V. *see* Koninklijke Vendex KBB N.V. (Royal Vendex KBB N.V.).

Royal Vopak NV, 41 339–41

RPC Group PLC, 81 356–59

RPC, Inc., 91 413–16

RPM International Inc., 8 454–57; 36 394–98 (upd.); 91 417–25 (upd.)

RSA Security Inc., 46 365–68

RSC *see* Rental Service Corp.

RSM McGladrey Business Services Inc., 98 333–36

RTI Biologics, Inc., 96 362–65

RTL Group SA, 44 374–78

RTM Restaurant Group, 58 322–24

RTZ Corporation PLC, IV 189–92 *see also* Rio Tinto plc.

Rubbermaid Incorporated, III 613–15; 20 454–57 (upd.) *see also* Newell Rubbermaid Inc.

Rubio's Restaurants, Inc., 35 379–81

Ruby Tuesday, Inc., 18 464–66; 71 317–20 (upd.)

Rudolph Technologies Inc., 94 375–78

The Rugby Group plc, 31 398–400

Ruger Corporation *see* Sturm, Ruger & Co., Inc.

Ruhrgas AG, V 704–06; 38 405–09 (upd.)

Ruhrkohle AG, IV 193–95 *see also* RAG AG.

Ruiz Food Products, Inc., 53 287–89

Rural Cellular Corporation, 43 340–42

Rural/Metro Corporation, 28 396–98

Rural Press Ltd., 74 282–85

Rush Communications, 33 373–75 *see also* Phat Fashions LLC.

Rush Enterprises, Inc., 64 336–38

Russ Berrie and Company, Inc., 12 424–26; 82 304–08 (upd.)

Russell Corporation, 8 458–59; 30 399–401 (upd.); 82 309–13 (upd.)

Russell Reynolds Associates Inc., 38 410–12

Russell Stover Candies Inc., 12 427–29; 91 426–32 (upd.)

Russian Aircraft Corporation (MiG), 86 343–46

Russian Railways Joint Stock Co., 93 380–83

Rust International Inc., 11 435–36

Rusty, Inc., 95 358–61

Ruth's Chris Steak House, 28 399–401; 88 338–42 (upd.)

RWD Technologies, Inc., 76 320–22

RWE Group, V 707–10; 50 396–400 (upd.)

Ryan Beck & Co., Inc., 66 273–75

Ryan Companies US, Inc., 99 382–385

Ryan's Restaurant Group, Inc., 15 419–21; 68 327–30 (upd.)

Ryanair Holdings plc, 35 382–85

Ryder System, Inc., V 504–06; 24 408–11 (upd.)

Ryerson Tull, Inc., 40 381–84 (upd.)

Ryko Corporation, 83 329-333

The Ryland Group, Inc., 8 460–61; 37 343–45 (upd.)

Ryoshoku Ltd., 72 300–02

RZB *see* Raiffeisen Zentralbank Österreich AG.

RZD *see* Russian Railways Joint Stock Co.

S

S&C Electric Company, 15 422–24

S&D Coffee, Inc., 84 339–341

S&K Famous Brands, Inc., 23 421–23

S&P *see* Standard & Poor's Corp.

S.A.C.I. Falabella, 69 311–13

S.A. Cockerill Sambre *see* Cockerill Sambre Group.

s.a. GB-Inno-BM *see* GIB Group.

S.C. Johnson & Son, Inc., III 58–59; 28 409–12 (upd.); 89 382–89 (upd.)

S-K-I Limited, 15 457–59

SAA (Pty) Ltd., 28 402–04

Saab Automobile AB, 32 386–89 (upd.); 83 334-339 (upd.)

Saab-Scania A.B., I 197–98; 11 437–39 (upd.)

Saarberg-Konzern, IV 196–99 *see also* RAG AG.

Saatchi & Saatchi plc, I 33–35; 33 328–31 (upd.)

SAB *see* South African Breweries Ltd.

Sabanci Holdings *see* Haci Omer Sabanci Holdings A.S.

Sabaté Diosos SA, 48 348–50 *see also* OENEO S.A.

Sabena S.A./N.V., 33 376–79

SABIC *see* Saudi Basic Industries Corp.

SABMiller plc, 59 352–58 (upd.)

Sabratek Corporation, 29 410–12

Sabre Holdings Corporation, 26 427–30; 74 286–90 (upd.)

Sadia S.A., 59 359–62

Safe Flight Instrument Corporation, 71 321–23

SAFECO Corporation, III 352–54

Safeguard Scientifics, Inc., 10 473–75

Safelite Glass Corp., 19 371–73

Safeskin Corporation, 18 467–70 *see also* Kimberly-Clark Corp.

Safety Components International, Inc., 63 342–44

Safety 1st, Inc., 24 412–15

Safety-Kleen Systems Inc., 8 462–65; 82 314–20 (upd.)

Safeway Inc., II 654–56; 24 416–19 (upd.); 85 362–69 (upd.)

Safeway PLC, 50 401–06 (upd.)

Saffery Champness, 80 324–27

Safilo SpA, 40 155–56; 54 319–21

Saga Communications, Inc., 27 392–94

The Sage Group, 43 343–46

SAGEM S.A., 37 346–48

Sagicor Life Inc., 98 337–40

Saia, Inc., 98 341–44

SAIC *see* Science Applications International Corp.

Sainsbury's *see* J Sainsbury PLC.

Saint-Gobain *see* Compagnie de Saint Gobain S.A.

St Ives plc, 34 393–95

St. James's Place Capital, plc, 71 324–26

The St. Joe Company, 31 422–25; 98 368–73 (upd.)

St. Joe Paper Company, 8 485–88

St. John Knits, Inc., 14 466–68

St. Jude Medical, Inc., 11 458–61; 43 347–52 (upd.); 97 350–58 (upd.)

St. Louis Music, Inc., 48 351–54

St. Luke's-Roosevelt Hospital Center *see* Continuum Health Partners, Inc.

St. Mary Land & Exploration Company, 63 345–47

St. Paul Bank for Cooperatives, 8 489–90

The St. Paul Travelers Companies, Inc., III 355–57; 22 492–95 (upd.); 79 362–69 (upd.)

Ste. Michelle Wine Estates Ltd., 96 408–11

Salem Communications Corporation, 97 359–63

salesforce.com, Inc., 79 370–73

Saks Inc., 24 420–23; 41 342–45 (upd.)

Salant Corporation, 12 430–32; 51 318–21 (upd.)

Salick Health Care, Inc., 53 290–92

Salix Pharmaceuticals, Ltd., 93 384–87

Sallie Mae *see* SLM Holding Corp.

Sally Beauty Company, Inc., 60 258–60

Salomon Inc., II 447–49; 13 447–50 (upd.) *see also* Citigroup Inc.

Salomon Worldwide, 20 458–60 *see also* adidas-Salomon AG.

Salt River Project, 19 374–76

Salton, Inc., 30 402–04; 88 343–48 (upd.)

The Salvation Army USA, 32 390–93

Salvatore Ferragamo Italia S.p.A., 62 311–13

Salzgitter AG, IV 200–01

Sam Ash Music Corporation, 30 405–07

Sam Levin Inc., 80 328–31

Sam's Club, 40 385–87

Sam's Wine & Spirits, 96 366–69

Samick Musical Instruments Co., Ltd., 56 297–300

Samsonite Corporation, 13 451–53; 43 353–57 (upd.)

Samsung Electronics Co., Ltd., 14 416–18; 41 346–49 (upd.)

Samsung Group, I 515–17

Samuel Cabot Inc., 53 293–95

Samuels Jewelers Incorporated, 30 408–10

San Diego Gas & Electric Company, V 711–14 *see also* Sempra Energy.

San Diego Padres Baseball Club L.P., 78 324–27

San Francisco Baseball Associates, L.P., 55 340–43

San Miguel Corporation, 15 428–30; 57 303–08 (upd.)

Sanborn Hermanos, S.A., 20 461–63

Sanborn Map Company Inc., 82 321–24

The Sanctuary Group PLC, 69 314–17

Sandals Resorts International, 65 302–05

Sanders Morris Harris Group Inc., 70 285–87

Sanders\Wingo, 99 386–389

Sanderson Farms, Inc., 15 425–27

Sandia National Laboratories, 49 345–48

Sandoz Ltd., I 671–73 *see also* Novartis AG.

Sandvik AB, IV 202–04; 32 394–98 (upd.); 77 367–73 (upd.)

Sanford L.P., 82 325–29

Sanitec Corporation, 51 322–24

Sankyo Company, Ltd., I 674–75; 56 301–04 (upd.)

Sanlam Ltd., 68 331–34

SANLUIS Corporación, S.A.B. de C.V., 95 362–65

The Sanofi-Synthélabo Group, I 676–77; 49 349–51 (upd.)

SanomaWSOY Corporation, 51 325–28

Sanpaolo IMI S.p.A., 50 407–11

Sanrio Company, Ltd., 38 413–15

Santa Barbara Restaurant Group, Inc., 37 349–52

The Santa Cruz Operation, Inc., 38 416–21

Santa Fe Gaming Corporation, 19 377–79 *see also* Archon Corp.

Santa Fe International Corporation, 38 422–24

Santa Fe Pacific Corporation, V 507–09 *see also* Burlington Northern Santa Fe Corp.

Santa Margherita S.p.A. *see* Industrie Zignago Santa Margherita S.p.A.

Santos Ltd., 81 360–63

Sanwa Bank, Ltd., II 347–48; 15 431–33 (upd.)

SANYO Electric Co., Ltd., II 91–92; 36 399–403 (upd.); 95 366–73 (upd.)

Sanyo-Kokusaku Pulp Co., Ltd., IV 327–28

Sao Paulo Alpargatas S.A., 75 347–49

SAP AG, 16 441–44; 43 358–63 (upd.)

Sapa AB, 84 342–345

Sappi Limited, 49 352–55

Sapporo Holdings Limited, I 282–83; 13 454–56 (upd.); 36 404–07 (upd.); 97 364–69 (upd.)

Saputo Inc., 59 363–65

Sara Lee Corporation, II 571–73; 15 434–37 (upd.); 54 322–27 (upd.); 99 390–398 (upd.)

Sarnoff Corporation, 57 309–12

Sarris Candies Inc., 86 347–50

The SAS Group, 34 396–99 (upd.)

SAS Institute Inc., 10 476–78; 78 328–32 (upd.)

Sasol Limited, IV 533–35; 47 340–44 (upd.)

Saturn Corporation, 7 461–64; 21 449–53 (upd.); 80 332–38 (upd.)

Satyam Computer Services Ltd., 85 370–73

Saucony Inc., 35 386–89; 86 351–56 (upd.)

Sauder Woodworking Co., 12 433–34; 35 390–93 (upd.)

Saudi Arabian Airlines, 6 114–16; 27 395–98 (upd.)

Saudi Arabian Oil Company, IV 536–39; 17 411–15 (upd.); 50 412–17 (upd.)

Saudi Basic Industries Corporation (SABIC), 58 325–28

Sauer-Danfoss Inc., 61 320–22

Saul Ewing LLP, 74 291–94

Saur S.A.S., 92 327–30

Savannah Foods & Industries, Inc., 7 465–67 *see also* Imperial Sugar Co.

Savers, Inc., 99 399–403 (upd.)

Sawtek Inc., 43 364–66 (upd.)

Sbarro, Inc., 16 445–47; 64 339–42 (upd.)

SBC Communications Inc., 32 399–403 (upd.)

SBC Warburg, 14 419–21 *see also* UBS AG.

Sberbank, 62 314–17

SBI *see* State Bank of India.

SBS Technologies, Inc., 25 405–07

SCA *see* Svenska Cellulosa AB.

SCANA Corporation, 6 574–76; 56 305–08 (upd.)

Scandinavian Airlines System, I 119–20 *see also* The SAS Group.

ScanSource, Inc., 29 413–15; 74 295–98 (upd.)

Scarborough Public Utilities Commission, 9 461–62

SCB Computer Technology, Inc., 29 416–18

SCEcorp, V 715–17 *see also* Edison International.

Schawk, Inc., 24 424–26

Scheels All Sports Inc., 63 348–50

Scheid Vineyards Inc., 66 276–78

Schell Brewing *see* August Schell Brewing Company Inc.

Schenck Business Solutions, 88 349–53

Schenker-Rhenus Ag, 6 424–26

Scherer *see* R.P. Scherer.

Scherer Brothers Lumber Company, 94 379–83

Schering A.G., I 681–82; 50 418–22 (upd.)

Schering-Plough Corporation, I 683–85; 14 422–25 (upd.); 49 356–62 (upd.); 99 404–414 (upd.)

Schibsted ASA, 31 401–05

Schieffelin & Somerset Co., 61 323–25

Schindler Holding AG, 29 419–22

Schlage Lock Company, 82 330–34

Schlotzsky's, Inc., 36 408–10

Schlumberger Limited, III 616–18; 17 416–19 (upd.); 59 366–71 (upd.)

Schmitt Music Company, 40 388–90

Schneider National, Inc., 36 411–13; 77 374–78 (upd.)

Schneider S.A., II 93–94; 18 471–74 (upd.)

Schneiderman's Furniture Inc., 28 405–08

Schnitzer Steel Industries, Inc., 19 380–82

Scholastic Corporation, 10 479–81; 29 423–27 (upd.)

Scholle Corporation, 96 370–73

School Specialty, Inc., 68 335–37

School-Tech, Inc., 62 318–20

Schott Brothers, Inc., 67 337–39

Schott Corporation, 53 296–98

Schottenstein Stores Corp., 14 426–28 *see also* Retail Ventures, Inc.

Schouw & Company A/S, 94 384–87

Schreiber Foods, Inc., 72 303–06

Schroders plc, 42 332–35

Schuff Steel Company, 26 431–34

Schultz Sav-O Stores, Inc., 21 454–56; 31 406–08 (upd.)

Schurz Communications, Inc., 98 345–49

The Schwan Food Company, 7 468–70; 26 435–38 (upd.); 83 340-346 (upd.)

Schwebel Baking Company, 72 307–09

Schweitzer-Mauduit International, Inc., 52 300–02

Schweizerische Post-, Telefon- und Telegrafen-Betriebe, V 321–24

Schweppes Ltd. *see* Cadbury Schweppes PLC.

Schwinn Cycle and Fitness L.P., 19 383–85 *see also* Huffy Corp.

SCI *see* Service Corporation International.

SCI Systems, Inc., 9 463–64

Science Applications International Corporation, 15 438–40

Scientific-Atlanta, Inc., 6 335–37; 45 371–75 (upd.)

Scientific Games Corporation, 64 343–46 (upd.)

Scientific Learning Corporation, 95 374–77

Scitex Corporation Ltd., 24 427–32

SCO *see* Santa Cruz Operation, Inc.

The SCO Group Inc., 78 333–37

Scope Products, Inc., 94 388–91

SCOR S.A., 20 464–66

The Score Board, Inc., 19 386–88

Scotiabank *see* The Bank of Nova Scotia.
Scotsman Industries, Inc., 20 467–69
Scott Fetzer Company, 12 435–37; 80 339–43 (upd.)
Scott Paper Company, IV 329–31; 31 409–12 (upd.)
Scottish & Newcastle plc, 15 441–44; 35 394–97 (upd.)
Scottish and Southern Energy plc, 13 457–59; 66 279–84 (upd.)
Scottish Media Group plc, 32 404–06; 41 350–52
Scottish Power plc, 49 363–66 (upd.)
Scottish Radio Holding plc, 41 350–52
ScottishPower plc, 19 389–91
Scottrade, Inc., 85 374–77
The Scotts Company, 22 474–76
Scotty's, Inc., 22 477–80
The Scoular Company, 77 379–82
Scovill Fasteners Inc., 24 433–36
SCP Pool Corporation, 39 358–60
Screen Actors Guild, 72 310–13
The Scripps Research Institute, 76 323–25
SDGE *see* San Diego Gas & Electric Co.
SDL PLC, 67 340–42
Sea Containers Ltd., 29 428–31
Seaboard Corporation, 36 414–16; 85 378–82 (upd.)
SeaChange International, Inc., 79 374–78
SEACOR Holdings Inc., 83 347-350
Seagate Technology, Inc., 8 466–68; 34 400–04 (upd.)
The Seagram Company Ltd., I 284–86; 25 408–12 (upd.)
Seagull Energy Corporation, 11 440–42
Sealaska Corporation, 60 261–64
Sealed Air Corporation, 14 429–31; 57 313–17 (upd.)
Sealed Power Corporation, I 199–200 *see also* SPX Corp.
Sealright Co., Inc., 17 420–23
Sealy Inc., 12 438–40
Seaman Furniture Company, Inc., 32 407–09
Sean John Clothing, Inc., 70 288–90
SeaRay Boats Inc., 96 374–77
Sears plc, V 177–79
Sears, Roebuck and Co., V 180–83; 18 475–79 (upd.); 56 309–14 (upd.)
Sears Roebuck de México, S.A. de C.V., 20 470–72
Seat Pagine Gialle S.p.A., 47 345–47
Seattle City Light, 50 423–26
Seattle FilmWorks, Inc., 20 473–75
Seattle First National Bank Inc., 8 469–71 *see also* Bank of America Corp.
Seattle Lighting Fixture Company, 92 331–34
Seattle Pacific Industries, Inc., 92 335–38
Seattle Seahawks, Inc., 92 339–43
Seattle Times Company, 15 445–47
Seaway Food Town, Inc., 15 448–50 *see also* Spartan Stores Inc.
SEB Group *see* Skandinaviska Enskilda Banken AB.

SEB S.A. *see* Groupe SEB.
Sebastiani Vineyards, Inc., 28 413–15
The Second City, Inc., 88 354–58
Second Harvest, 29 432–34
Securicor Plc, 45 376–79
Securitas AB, 42 336–39
Security Capital Corporation, 17 424–27
Security Pacific Corporation, II 349–50
SED International Holdings, Inc., 43 367–69
Seddon Group Ltd., 67 343–45
SEGA Corporation, 73 290–93
Sega of America, Inc., 10 482–85
Segway LLC, 48 355–57
SEI Investments Company, 96 378–82
Seibu Department Stores, Ltd., V 184–86; 42 340–43 (upd.)
Seibu Railway Company Ltd., V 510–11; 74 299–301 (upd.)
Seigle's Home and Building Centers, Inc., 41 353–55
Seiko Corporation, III 619–21; 17 428–31 (upd.); 72 314–18 (upd.)
Seino Transportation Company, Ltd., 6 427–29
Seita, 23 424–27 *see also* Altadis S.A.
Seitel, Inc., 47 348–50
The Seiyu, Ltd., V 187–89; 36 417–21 (upd.)
Sekisui Chemical Co., Ltd., III 741–43; 72 319–22 (upd.)
Select Comfort Corporation, 34 405–08
Select Medical Corporation, 65 306–08
Selecta AG, 97 370–73
Selectour SA, 53 299–301
Selee Corporation, 88 359–62
Selfridges Plc, 34 409–11
The Selmer Company, Inc., 19 392–94
SEMCO Energy, Inc., 44 379–82
Seminis, Inc., 29 435–37
Semitool, Inc., 18 480–82; 79 379–82 (upd.)
Sempra Energy, 25 413–16 (upd.)
Semtech Corporation, 32 410–13
Seneca Foods Corporation, 17 432–34; 60 265–68 (upd.)
Sennheiser Electronic GmbH & Co. KG, 66 285–89
Senomyx, Inc., 83 351-354
Sensient Technologies Corporation, 52 303–08 (upd.)
Sensormatic Electronics Corp., 11 443–45
Sensory Science Corporation, 37 353–56
La Senza Corporation, 66 205–07
Sephora Holdings S.A., 82 335–39
Sepracor Inc., 45 380–83
Sequa Corporation, 13 460–63; 54 328–32 (upd.)
Sequana Capital, 78 338–42 (upd.)
Serco Group plc, 47 351–53
Serologicals Corporation, 63 351–53
Serono S.A., 47 354–57
Serta, Inc., 28 416–18
Servco Pacific Inc., 96 383–86
Service America Corp., 7 471–73

Service Corporation International, 6 293–95; 51 329–33 (upd.)
Service Merchandise Company, Inc., V 190–92; 19 395–99 (upd.)
The ServiceMaster Company, 6 44–46; 23 428–31 (upd.); 68 338–42 (upd.)
Servpro Industries, Inc., 85 383–86
7-Eleven, Inc., 32 414–18 (upd.)
Sevenson Environmental Services, Inc., 42 344–46
Seventh Generation, Inc., 73 294–96
Severn Trent PLC, 12 441–43; 38 425–29 (upd.)
Severstal Joint Stock Company, 65 309–12
Seyfarth Shaw LLP, 93 388–91
SFI Group plc, 51 334–36
SFX Entertainment, Inc., 36 422–25
SGI, 29 438–41 (upd.)
Shakespeare Company, 22 481–84
Shaklee Corporation, 12 444–46; 39 361–64 (upd.)
Shanghai Baosteel Group Corporation, 71 327–30
Shanghai Petrochemical Co., Ltd., 18 483–85
Shangri-La Asia Ltd., 71 331–33
Shanks Group plc, 45 384–87
Shannon Aerospace Ltd., 36 426–28
Shared Medical Systems Corporation, 14 432–34 *see also* Siemens AG.
Sharp Corporation, II 95–96; 12 447–49 (upd.); 40 391–95 (upd.)
The Sharper Image Corporation, 10 486–88; 62 321–24 (upd.)
The Shaw Group, Inc., 50 427–30
Shaw Industries, Inc., 9 465–67; 40 396–99 (upd.)
Shaw's Supermarkets, Inc., 56 315–18
Shea Homes *see* J.F. Shea Co., Inc.
Sheaffer Pen Corporation, 82 340–43
Shearer's Foods, Inc., 72 323–25
Shearman & Sterling, 32 419–22
Shearson Lehman Brothers Holdings Inc., II 450–52; 9 468–70 (upd.) *see also* Lehman Brothers Holdings Inc.
Shedd Aquarium Society, 73 297–99
Sheetz, Inc., 85 387–90
Shelby Williams Industries, Inc., 14 435–37
Sheldahl Inc., 23 432–35
Shell Oil Company, IV 540–41; 14 438–40 (upd.); 41 356–60 (upd.) *see also* Royal Dutch/Shell Group.
Shell Transport and Trading Company p.l.c., IV 530–32 *see also* Royal Dutch Petroleum Company; Royal Dutch/Shell.
Sheller-Globe Corporation, I 201–02 *see also* Lear Corp.
Shells Seafood Restaurants, Inc., 43 370–72
Shenandoah Telecommunications Company, 89 390–93
Shenhua Group *see* China Shenhua Energy Company Limited
Shepherd Neame Limited, 30 414–16
Sheplers, Inc., 96 387–90

The Sheridan Group, Inc., 86 357–60

Shermag, Inc., 93 392–97

The Sherwin-Williams Company, III 744–46; 13 469–71 (upd.); 89 394–400 (upd.)

Sherwood Brands, Inc., 53 302–04

Shikoku Electric Power Company, Inc., V 718–20; 60 269–72 (upd.)

Shimano Inc., 64 347–49

Shionogi & Co., Ltd., III 60–61; 17 435–37 (upd.); 98 350–54 (upd.)

Shiseido Company, Limited, III 62–64; 22 485–88 (upd.); 81 364–70 (upd.)

Shochiku Company Ltd., 74 302–04

Shoe Carnival Inc., 14 441–43; 72 326–29 (upd.)

Shoe Pavilion, Inc., 84 346–349

Shoney's, Inc., 7 474–76; 23 436–39 (upd.)

ShopKo Stores Inc., 21 457–59; 58 329–32 (upd.)

Shoppers Drug Mart Corporation, 49 367–70

Shoppers Food Warehouse Corporation, 66 290–92

Shorewood Packaging Corporation, 28 419–21

Showa Shell Sekiyu K.K., IV 542–43; 59 372–75 (upd.)

ShowBiz Pizza Time, Inc., 13 472–74 *see also* CEC Entertainment, Inc.

Showboat, Inc., 19 400–02 *see also* Harrah's Entertainment, Inc.

Showtime Networks, Inc., 78 343–47

Shred-It Canada Corporation, 56 319–21

Shriners Hospitals for Children, 69 318–20

Shubert Organization Inc., 24 437–39

Shuffle Master Inc., 51 337–40

Shure Inc., 60 273–76

Shurgard Storage Centers, Inc., 52 309–11

Shutterfly, Inc., 98 355–58

SHV Holdings N.V., 55 344–47

The Siam Cement Public Company Limited, 56 322–25

Sideco Americana S.A., 67 346–48

Sidel *see* Groupe Sidel S.A.

Siderar S.A.I.C., 66 293–95

Sidley Austin Brown & Wood, 40 400–03

Sidney Frank Importing Co., Inc., 69 321–23

Siebe plc *see* BTR Siebe plc.

Siebel Systems, Inc., 38 430–34

Siebert Financial Corp., 32 423–25

Siegel & Gale, 64 350–52

Siemens AG, II 97–100; 14 444–47 (upd.); 57 318–23 (upd.)

The Sierra Club, 28 422–24

Sierra Health Services, Inc., 15 451–53

Sierra Nevada Brewing Company, 70 291–93

Sierra On-Line, Inc., 15 454–56; 41 361–64 (upd.)

Sierra Pacific Industries, 22 489–91; 90 369–73 (upd.)

SIFCO Industries, Inc., 41

SIG plc, 71 334–36

Sigma-Aldrich Corporation, I 690–91; 36 429–32 (upd.); 93 398–404 (upd.)

Signet Banking Corporation, 11 446–48 *see also* Wachovia Corp.

Signet Group PLC, 61 326–28

Sikorsky Aircraft Corporation, 24 440–43

Silhouette Brands, Inc., 55 348–50

Silicon Graphics Inc., 9 471–73 *see also* SGI.

Siliconware Precision Industries Ltd., 73 300–02

Siltronic AG, 90 374–77

Silver Lake Cookie Company Inc., 95 378–81

Silver Wheaton Corp., 95 382–85

SilverPlatter Information Inc., 23 440–43

Silverstar Holdings, Ltd., 99 415–418

Silverstein Properties, Inc., 47 358–60

Simco S.A., 37 357–59

Sime Darby Berhad, 14 448–50; 36 433–36 (upd.)

Simmons Company, 47 361–64

Simon & Schuster Inc., IV 671–72; 19 403–05 (upd.)

Simon Property Group Inc., 27 399–402; 84 350–355 (upd.)

Simon Transportation Services Inc., 27 403–06

Simplex Technologies Inc., 21 460–63

Simplicity Manufacturing, Inc., 64 353–56

Simpson Investment Company, 17 438–41

Simpson Thacher & Bartlett, 39 365–68

Simula, Inc., 41 368–70

SINA Corporation, 69 324–27

Sinclair Broadcast Group, Inc., 25 417–19

Sine Qua Non, 99 419–422

Singapore Airlines Limited, 6 117–18; 27 407–09 (upd.); 83 355-359 (upd.)

Singapore Press Holdings Limited, 85 391–95

Singer & Friedlander Group plc, 41 371–73

The Singer Company N.V., 30 417–20 (upd.)

The Singing Machine Company, Inc., 60 277–80

Sir Speedy, Inc., 16 448–50

Sirius Satellite Radio, Inc., 69 328–31

Sirti S.p.A., 76 326–28

Siskin Steel & Supply Company, 70 294–96

Sistema JSFC, 73 303–05

Six Flags, Inc., 17 442–44; 54 333–40 (upd.)

Sixt AG, 39 369–72

SJW Corporation, 70 297–99

SK Group, 88 363–67

Skadden, Arps, Slate, Meagher & Flom, 18 486–88

Skalli Group, 67 349–51

Skandia Insurance Company, Ltd., 50 431–34

Skandinaviska Enskilda Banken AB, II 351–53; 56 326–29 (upd.)

Skanska AB, 38 435–38

Skechers U.S.A. Inc., 31 413–15; 88 368–72 (upd.)

Skeeter Products Inc., 96 391–94

SKF *see* Aktiebolaget SKF.

Skidmore, Owings & Merrill LLP, 13 475–76; 69 332–35 (upd.)

SkillSoft Public Limited Company, 81 371–74

skinnyCorp, LLC, 97 374–77

Skipton Building Society, 80 344–47

Skis Rossignol S.A., 15 460–62; 43 373–76 (upd.)

Skoda Auto a.s., 39 373–75

Skyline Chili, Inc., 62 325–28

Skyline Corporation, 30 421–23

SkyMall, Inc., 26 439–41

SkyWest, Inc., 25 420–24

Skyy Spirits LLC, 78 348–51

SL Green Realty Corporation, 44 383–85

SL Industries, Inc., 77 383–86

Sleeman Breweries Ltd., 74 305–08

Sleepy's Inc., 32 426–28

SLI, Inc., 48 358–61

Slim-Fast Foods Company, 18 489–91; 66 296–98 (upd.)

Slinky, Inc. *see* Poof-Slinky, Inc.

SLM Holding Corp., 25 425–28 (upd.)

Slough Estates PLC, IV 722–25; 50 435–40 (upd.)

Small Planet Foods, Inc., 89 410–14

Smart & Final LLC, 16 451–53; 94 392–96 (upd.)

SMART Modular Technologies, Inc., 86 361–64

SmartForce PLC, 43 377–80

SMBC *see* Sumitomo Mitsui Banking Corp.

Smead Manufacturing Co., 17 445–48

SMG *see* Scottish Media Group.

SMH *see* Sanders Morris Harris Group Inc.; The Swatch Group SA.

Smith & Hawken, Ltd., 68 343–45

Smith & Nephew plc, 17 449–52; 41 374–78 (upd.)

Smith & Wesson Corp., 30 424–27; 73 306–11 (upd.)

Smith Barney Inc., 15 463–65 *see also* Citigroup Inc.

Smith Corona Corp., 13 477–80

Smith International, Inc., 15 466–68; 59 376–80 (upd.)

Smith-Midland Corporation, 56 330–32

Smith's Food & Drug Centers, Inc., 8 472–74; 57 324–27 (upd.)

Smithfield Foods, Inc., 7 477–78; 43 381–84 (upd.)

SmithKline Beckman Corporation, I 692–94 *see also* GlaxoSmithKline plc.

SmithKline Beecham plc, III 65–67; 32 429–34 (upd.) *see also* GlaxoSmithKline plc.

Smiths Industries PLC, 25 429–31

Smithsonian Institution, 27 410–13
Smithway Motor Xpress Corporation, 39 376–79
Smoby International SA, 56 333–35
Smorgon Steel Group Ltd., 62 329–32
Smucker's *see* The J.M. Smucker Co.
Smurfit-Stone Container Corporation, 26 442–46 (upd.) ; 83 360-368 (upd.)
Snap-On, Incorporated, 7 479–80; 27 414–16 (upd.)
Snapfish, 83 369-372
Snapple Beverage Corporation, 11 449–51
SNC-Lavalin Group Inc., 72 330–33
SNCF *see* Société Nationale des Chemins de Fer Français.
SNEA *see* Société Nationale Elf Aquitaine.
Snecma Group, 46 369–72
Snell & Wilmer L.L.P., 28 425–28
SNET *see* Southern New England Telecommunications Corp.
Snow Brand Milk Products Company, Ltd., II 574–75; 48 362–65 (upd.)
Soap Opera Magazine see American Media, Inc.
Sobeys Inc., 80 348–51
Socata *see* EADS SOCATA.
Società Finanziaria Telefonica per Azioni, V 325–27
Società Sportiva Lazio SpA, 44 386–88
Société Air France, 27 417–20 (upd.).
Société BIC S.A., 73 312–15
Société d'Exploitation AOM Air Liberté SA (AirLib), 53 305–07
Societe des Produits Marnier-Lapostolle S.A., 88 373–76
Société du Figaro S.A., 60 281–84
Société du Louvre, 27 421–23
Société Générale, II 354–56; 42 347–51 (upd.)
Société Industrielle Lesaffre, 84 356–359
Société Luxembourgeoise de Navigation Aérienne S.A., 64 357–59
Société Nationale des Chemins de Fer Français, V 512–15; 57 328–32 (upd.)
Société Nationale Elf Aquitaine, IV 544–47; 7 481–85 (upd.)
Société Norbert Dentressangle S.A., 67 352–54
Société Tunisienne de l'Air-Tunisair, 49 371–73
Society Corporation, 9 474–77
Sodexho SA, 29 442–44; 91 433–36 (upd.)
Sodiaal S.A., 19 50; 36 437–39 (upd.)
SODIMA, II 576–77 *see also* Sodiaal S.A.
Soft Sheen Products, Inc., 31 416–18
Softbank Corporation, 13 481–83; 38 439–44 (upd.); 77 387–95 (upd.)
Sojitz Corporation, 96 395–403 (upd.)
Sol Meliá S.A., 71 337–39
Sola International Inc., 71 340–42
Sole Technology Inc., 93 405–09
Solectron Corporation, 12 450–52; 48 366–70 (upd.)

Solo Serve Corporation, 28 429–31
Solutia Inc., 52 312–15
Solvay & Cie S.A., I 394–96; 21 464–67 (upd.)
Solvay S.A., 61 329–34 (upd.)
Somerfield plc, 47 365–69 (upd.)
Sommer-Allibert S.A., 19 406–09 *see also* Tarkett Sommer AG.
Sompo Japan Insurance, Inc., 98 359–63 (upd.)
Sonae SGPS, S.A., 97 378–81
Sonat, Inc., 6 577–78 *see also* El Paso Corp.
Sonatrach, 65 313–17 (upd.)
Sonera Corporation, 50 441–44 *see also* TeliaSonera AB.
Sonesta International Hotels Corporation, 44 389–91
Sonic Automotive, Inc., 77 396–99
Sonic Corp., 14 451–53; 37 360–63 (upd.)
Sonic Innovations Inc., 56 336–38
Sonic Solutions, Inc., 81 375–79
SonicWALL, Inc., 87 421–424
Sonoco Products Company, 8 475–77; 89 415–22 (upd.)
SonoSite, Inc., 56 339–41
Sony Corporation, II 101–03; 12 453–56 (upd.); 40 404–10 (upd.)
Sophus Berendsen A/S, 49 374–77
Sorbee International Ltd., 74 309–11
Soriana *see* Organización Soriana, S.A. de C.V.
Soros Fund Management LLC, 28 432–34
Sorrento, Inc., 19 51; 24 444–46
SOS Staffing Services, 25 432–35
Sotheby's Holdings, Inc., 11 452–54; 29 445–48 (upd.); 84 360–365 (upd.)
Soufflet SA *see* Groupe Soufflet SA.
Sound Advice, Inc., 41 379–82
Souper Salad, Inc., 98 364–67
The Source Enterprises, Inc., 65 318–21
Source Interlink Companies, Inc., 75 350–53
The South African Breweries Limited, I 287–89; 24 447–51 (upd.) *see also* SABMiller plc.
South Beach Beverage Company, Inc., 73 316–19
South Dakota Wheat Growers Association, 94 397–401
South Jersey Industries, Inc., 42 352–55
Southam Inc., 7 486–89 *see also* CanWest Global Communications Corp.
Southcorp Limited, 54 341–44
Southdown, Inc., 14 454–56 *see also* CEMEX S.A. de C.V.
Southeast Frozen Foods Company, L.P., 99 423–426
The Southern Company, V 721–23; 38 445–49 (upd.)
Southern Connecticut Gas Company, 84 366–370
Southern Electric PLC, 13 484–86 *see also* Scottish and Southern Energy plc.

Southern Financial Bancorp, Inc., 56 342–44
Southern Indiana Gas and Electric Company, 13 487–89 *see also* Vectren Corp.
Southern New England Telecommunications Corporation, 6 338–40
Southern Pacific Transportation Company, V 516–18 *see also* Union Pacific Corp.
Southern Peru Copper Corporation, 40 411–13
Southern Poverty Law Center, Inc., 74 312–15
Southern States Cooperative Incorporated, 36 440–42
Southern Union Company, 27 424–26
Southern Wine and Spirits of America, Inc., 84 371–375
The Southland Corporation, II 660–61; 7 490–92 (upd.) *see also* 7-Eleven, Inc.
Southtrust Corporation, 11 455–57 *see also* Wachovia Corp.
Southwest Airlines Co., 6 119–21; 24 452–55 (upd.); 71 343–47 (upd.)
Southwest Gas Corporation, 19 410–12
Southwest Water Company, 47 370–73
Southwestern Bell Corporation, V 328–30 *see also* SBC Communications Inc.
Southwestern Electric Power Co., 21 468–70
Southwestern Public Service Company, 6 579–81
Southwire Company, Inc., 8 478–80; 23 444–47 (upd.)
Souza Cruz S.A., 65 322–24
Sovran Self Storage, Inc., 66 299–301
SP Alpargatas *see* Sao Paulo Alpargatas S.A.
Spacehab, Inc., 37 364–66
Spacelabs Medical, Inc., 71 348–50
Spaghetti Warehouse, Inc., 25 436–38
Spago *see* The Wolfgang Puck Food Company, Inc.
Spangler Candy Company, 44 392–95
Spanish Broadcasting System, Inc., 41 383–86
Spansion Inc., 80 352–55
Spanx, Inc., 89 423–27
Spar Aerospace Limited, 32 435–37
SPAR Handels AG, 35 398–401
Spark Networks, Inc., 91 437–40
Spartan Motors Inc., 14 457–59
Spartan Stores Inc., 8 481–82; 66 302–05 (upd.)
Spartech Corporation, 19 413–15; 76 329–32 (upd.)
Sparton Corporation, 18 492–95
Spear & Jackson, Inc., 73 320–23
Spear, Leeds & Kellogg, 66 306–09
Spec's Music, Inc., 19 416–18 *see also* Camelot Music, Inc.
Special Olympics, Inc., 93 410–14
Specialist Computer Holdings Ltd., 80 356–59

Specialized Bicycle Components Inc., 50 445–48

Specialty Coatings Inc., 8 483–84

Specialty Equipment Companies, Inc., 25 439–42

Specialty Products & Insulation Co., 59 381–83

Spector Photo Group N.V., 82 344–47

Spectrum Control, Inc., 67 355–57

Spectrum Organic Products, Inc., 68 346–49

Spee-Dee Delivery Service, Inc., 93 415–18

SpeeDee Oil Change and Tune-Up, 25 443–47

Speedway Motorsports, Inc., 32 438–41

Speedy Hire plc, 84 376–379

Speidel Inc., 96 404–07

Speizman Industries, Inc., 44 396–98

Spelling Entertainment, 14 460–62; 35 402–04 (upd.)

Spencer Stuart and Associates, Inc., 14 463–65

Spherion Corporation, 52 316–18

Spie *see* Amec Spie S.A.

Spiegel, Inc., 10 489–91; 27 427–31 (upd.)

SPIEGEL-Verlag Rudolf Augstein GmbH & Co. KG, 44 399–402

Spin Master, Ltd., 61 335–38

Spinnaker Exploration Company, 72 334–36

Spirax-Sarco Engineering plc, 59 384–86

Spirit Airlines, Inc., 31 419–21

Sport Chalet, Inc., 16 454–56; 94 402–06 (upd.)

Sport Supply Group, Inc., 23 448–50

Sportmart, Inc., 15 469–71 *see also* Gart Sports Co.

Sports & Recreation, Inc., 17 453–55

The Sports Authority, Inc., 16 457–59; 43 385–88 (upd.)

The Sports Club Company, 25 448–51

The Sportsman's Guide, Inc., 36 443–46

Springs Global US, Inc., V 378–79; 19 419–22 (upd.); 90 378–83 (upd.)

Sprint Communications Company, L.P., 9 478–80 *see also* Sprint Corporation; US Sprint Communications.

Sprint Corporation, 46 373–76 (upd.)

SPS Technologies, Inc., 30 428–30

SPSS Inc., 64 360–63

SPX Corporation, 10 492–95; 47 374–79 (upd.)

Spyglass Entertainment Group, LLC, 91 441–44

Square D, 90 384–89

Squibb Corporation, I 695–97 *see also* Bristol-Myers Squibb Co.

SR Teleperformance S.A., 86 365–68

SRA International, Inc., 77 400–03

SRAM Corporation, 65 325–27

SRC Holdings Corporation, 67 358–60

SRI International, Inc., 57 333–36

SSA *see* Stevedoring Services of America Inc.

SSAB Svenskt Stål AB, 89 428–31

Ssangyong Cement Industrial Co., Ltd., III 747–50; 61 339–43 (upd.)

SSL International plc, 49 378–81

SSOE Inc., 76 333–35

St. *see under* Saint

STAAR Surgical Company, 57 337–39

The Stabler Companies Inc., 78 352–55

Stage Stores, Inc., 24 456–59; 82 348–52 (upd.)

Stagecoach Holdings plc, 30 431–33

Stanadyne Automotive Corporation, 37 367–70

StanCorp Financial Group, Inc., 56 345–48

Standard Candy Company Inc., 86 369–72

Standard Chartered plc, II 357–59; 48 371–74 (upd.)

Standard Commercial Corporation, 13 490–92; 62 333–37 (upd.)

Standard Federal Bank, 9 481–83

Standard Life Assurance Company, III 358–61

Standard Microsystems Corporation, 11 462–64

Standard Motor Products, Inc., 40 414–17

Standard Pacific Corporation, 52 319–22

The Standard Register Company, 15 472–74; 93 419–25 (upd.)

Standex International Corporation, 17 456–59; 44 403–06 (upd.)

Stanhome Inc., 15 475–78

Stanley Furniture Company, Inc., 34 412–14

Stanley Leisure plc, 66 310–12

The Stanley Works, III 626–29; 20 476–80 (upd.); 79 383–91 (upd.)

Staple Cotton Cooperative Association (Staplcotn), 86 373–77

Staples, Inc., 10 496–98; 55 351–56 (upd.)

Star Banc Corporation, 11 465–67 *see also* Firstar Corp.

Star of the West Milling Co., 95 386–89

Starbucks Corporation, 13 493–94; 34 415–19 (upd.); 77 404–10 (upd.)

Starcraft Corporation, 30 434–36; 66 313–16 (upd.)

StarHub Ltd., 77 411–14

Starkey Laboratories, Inc., 52 323–25

Starrett *see* L.S. Starrett Co.

Starrett Corporation, 21 471–74

StarTek, Inc., 79 392–95

Starter Corp., 12 457–458

Starwood Hotels & Resorts Worldwide, Inc., 54 345–48

Starz LLC, 91 445–50

The Stash Tea Company, 50 449–52

State Auto Financial Corporation, 77 415–19

State Bank of India, 63 354–57

State Farm Mutual Automobile Insurance Company, III 362–64; 51 341–45 (upd.)

State Financial Services Corporation, 51 346–48

State Street Corporation, 8 491–93; 57 340–44 (upd.)

Staten Island Bancorp, Inc., 39 380–82

Stater Bros. Holdings Inc., 64 364–67

Station Casinos, Inc., 25 452–54; 90 390–95 (upd.)

Statoil ASA, 61 344–48 (upd.)

The Staubach Company, 62 338–41

STC PLC, III 162–64 *see also* Nortel Networks Corp.

The Steak n Shake Company, 41 387–90; 96 412–17 (upd.)

Steamships Trading Company Ltd., 82 353–56

Stearns, Inc., 43 389–91

Steel Authority of India Ltd., IV 205–07; 66 317–21 (upd.)

Steel Dynamics, Inc., 52 326–28

Steel Technologies Inc., 63 358–60

Steelcase Inc., 7 493–95; 27 432–35 (upd.)

Stefanel SpA, 63 361–63

Steiff *see* Margarete Steiff GmbH.

Steilmann Group *see* Klaus Steilmann GmbH & Co. KG.

Stein Mart Inc., 19 423–25; 72 337–39 (upd.)

Steinberg Incorporated, II 662–65

Steiner Corporation (Alsco), 53 308–11

Steinway Musical Properties, Inc., 19 426–29

Stelco Inc., IV 208–10; 51 349–52 (upd.)

Stelmar Shipping Ltd., 52 329–31

Stemilt Growers Inc., 94 407–10

Stepan Company, 30 437–39

The Stephan Company, 60 285–88

Stephens Inc., 92 344–48

Stephens Media, LLC, 91 451–54

Steria SA, 49 382–85

Stericycle, Inc., 33 380–82; 74 316–18 (upd.)

Sterilite Corporation, 97 382–85

STERIS Corporation, 29 449–52

Sterling Chemicals, Inc., 16 460–63; 78 356–61 (upd.)

Sterling Drug Inc., I 698–700

Sterling Electronics Corp., 18 496–98

Sterling European Airlines A/S, 70 300–02

Sterling Software, Inc., 11 468–70 *see also* Computer Associates International, Inc.

STET *see* Società Finanziaria Telefonica per Azioni.

Steuben Glass *see* Corning Inc.

Steve & Barry's LLC, 88 377–80

Stevedoring Services of America Inc., 28 435–37

Steven Madden, Ltd., 37 371–73

Stew Leonard's, 56 349–51

Stewart & Stevenson Services Inc., 11 471–73

Stewart Enterprises, Inc., 20 481–83

Stewart Information Services Corporation, 78 362–65

Stewart's Beverages, 39 383–86
Stewart's Shops Corporation, 80 360–63
Stickley *see* L. and J.G. Stickley, Inc.
Stiefel Laboratories, Inc., 90 396–99
Stihl *see* Andreas Stihl AG & Co. KG.
Stillwater Mining Company, 47 380–82
Stimson Lumber Company Inc., 78 366–69
Stinnes AG, 8 494–97; 23 451–54 (upd.); 59 387–92 (upd.)
Stirling Group plc, 62 342–44
STMicroelectronics NV, 52 332–35
Stock Yards Packing Co., Inc., 37 374–76
Stoddard International plc, 72 340–43
Stoll-Moss Theatres Ltd., 34 420–22
Stollwerck AG, 53 312–15
Stolt-Nielsen S.A., 42 356–59; 54 349–50
Stolt Sea Farm Holdings PLC, 54 349–51
Stone & Webster, Inc., 13 495–98; 64 368–72 (upd.)
Stone Container Corporation, IV 332–34 *see also* Smurfit-Stone Container Corp.
Stone Manufacturing Company, 14 469–71; 43 392–96 (upd.)
Stonyfield Farm, Inc., 55 357–60
The Stop & Shop Supermarket Company, II 666–67; 24 460–62 (upd.); 68 350–53 (upd.)
Stora Enso Oyj, IV 335–37; 36 447–55 (upd.); 85 396–408 (upd.)
Storage Technology Corporation, 6 275–77
Storage USA, Inc., 21 475–77
Storehouse PLC, 16 464–66 *see also* Mothercare plc.
Stouffer Corp., 8 498–501 *see also* Nestlé S.A.
StrataCom, Inc., 16 467–69
Stratagene Corporation, 70 303–06
Stratasys, Inc., 67 361–63
Strattec Security Corporation, 73 324–27
Stratus Computer, Inc., 10 499–501
Straumann Holding AG, 79 396–99
Strauss Discount Auto, 56 352–54
Strauss-Elite Group, 68 354–57
Strayer Education, Inc., 53 316–19
Stride Rite Corporation, 8 502–04; 37 377–80 (upd.); 86 378–84 (upd.)
Strine Printing Company Inc., 88 381–84
Strix Ltd., 51 353–55
The Strober Organization, Inc., 82 357–60 *see also* Pro-Build Holdings Inc.
The Stroh Brewery Company, I 290–92; 18 499–502 (upd.)
Strombecker Corporation, 60 289–91
Stroock & Stroock & Lavan LLP, 40 418–21
Strouds, Inc., 33 383–86
The Structure Tone Organization, 99 427–430

Stryker Corporation, 11 474–76; 29 453–55 (upd.); 79 400–05 (upd.)
Stuart C. Irby Company, 58 333–35
Stuart Entertainment Inc., 16 470–72
Student Loan Marketing Association, II 453–55 *see also* SLM Holding Corp.
Stuller Settings, Inc., 35 405–07
Sturm, Ruger & Company, Inc., 19 430–32
Stussy, Inc., 55 361–63
Sub Pop Ltd., 97 386–89
Sub-Zero Freezer Co., Inc., 31 426–28
Suburban Propane Partners, L.P., 30 440–42
Subway, 32 442–44 *see also* Doctor's Associates Inc.
Successories, Inc., 30 443–45
Sucden *see* Compagnie Financière Sucres et Denrées.
Suchard Co. *see* Jacobs Suchard.
Sudbury Inc., 16 473–75
Südzucker AG, 27 436–39
Suez Lyonnaise des Eaux, 36 456–59 (upd.)
SUEZ-TRACTEBEL S.A., 97 390–94 (upd.)
Suiza Foods Corporation, 26 447–50 *see also* Dean Foods Co.
Sukhoi Design Bureau Aviation Scientific-Industrial Complex, 24 463–65
Sullivan & Cromwell, 26 451–53
Sulzer Ltd., III 630–33; 68 358–62 (upd.)
Sumitomo Bank, Limited, II 360–62; 26 454–57 (upd.)
Sumitomo Chemical Company Ltd., I 397–98; 98 374–78 (upd.)
Sumitomo Corporation, I 518–20; 11 477–80 (upd.)
Sumitomo Electric Industries, II 104–05
Sumitomo Heavy Industries, Ltd., III 634–35; 42 360–62 (upd.)
Sumitomo Life Insurance Company, III 365–66; 60 292–94 (upd.)
Sumitomo Metal Industries Ltd., IV 211–13; 82 361–66 (upd.)
Sumitomo Metal Mining Co., Ltd., IV 214–16
Sumitomo Mitsui Banking Corporation, 51 356–62 (upd.)
Sumitomo Realty & Development Co., Ltd., IV 726–27
Sumitomo Rubber Industries, Ltd., V 252–53
The Sumitomo Trust & Banking Company, Ltd., II 363–64; 53 320–22 (upd.)
The Summit Bancorporation, 14 472–74 *see also* FleetBoston Financial Corp.
Summit Family Restaurants Inc., 19 433–36
Sun Alliance Group PLC, III 369–74 *see also* Royal & Sun Alliance Insurance Group plc.
Sun Communities Inc., 46 377–79

Sun Company, Inc., IV 548–50 *see also* Sunoco, Inc.
Sun Country Airlines, I 30 446–49
Sun-Diamond Growers of California, 7 496–97 *see also* Diamond of California.
Sun Distributors L.P., 12 459–461
Sun Healthcare Group Inc., 25 455–58
Sun Hydraulics Corporation, 74 319–22
Sun International Hotels Limited, 26 462–65 *see also* Kerzner International Ltd.
Sun Life Financial Inc., 85 409–12
Sun-Maid Growers of California, 82 367–71
Sun Microsystems, Inc., 7 498–501; 30 450–54 (upd.); 91 455–62 (upd.)
Sun Pharmaceutical Industries Ltd., 57 345–47
Sun-Rype Products Ltd., 76 336–38
Sun Sportswear, Inc., 17 460–63
Sun Television & Appliances Inc., 10 502–03
Sun World International, LLC, 93 426–29
SunAmerica Inc., 11 481–83 *see also* American International Group, Inc.
Sunbeam-Oster Co., Inc., 9 484–86
Sunburst Hospitality Corporation, 26 458–61
Sunburst Shutters Corporation, 78 370–72
Suncor Energy Inc., 54 352–54
Suncorp-Metway Ltd., 91 463–66
Sundstrand Corporation, 7 502–04; 21 478–81 (upd.)
Sundt Corp., 24 466–69
SunGard Data Systems Inc., 11 484–85
Sunglass Hut International, Inc., 21 482–84; 74 323–26 (upd.)
Sunkist Growers, Inc., 26 466–69
Sunoco, Inc., 28 438–42 (upd.); 83 373-380 (upd.)
SunOpta Inc., 79 406–10
SunPower Corporation, 91 467–70
The Sunrider Corporation, 26 470–74
Sunrise Greetings, 88 385–88
Sunrise Medical Inc., 11 486–88
Sunrise Senior Living, Inc., 81 380–83
Sunsweet Growers *see* Diamond of California.
Suntech Power Holdings Company Ltd., 89 432–35
Sunterra Corporation, 75 354–56
Suntory Ltd., 65 328–31
SunTrust Banks Inc., 23 455–58
Super 8 Motels, Inc., 83 381-385
Super Food Services, Inc., 15 479–81
Supercuts Inc., 26 475–78
Superdrug Stores PLC, 95 390–93
Superior Energy Services, Inc., 65 332–34
Superior Essex Inc., 80 364–68
Superior Industries International, Inc., 8 505–07
Superior Uniform Group, Inc., 30 455–57

Supermarkets General Holdings
  Corporation, II 672–74 *see also*
  Pathmark Stores, Inc.
SUPERVALU INC., II 668–71; 18
  503–08 (upd.); 50 453–59 (upd.)
Suprema Specialties, Inc., 27 440–42
Supreme International Corporation, 27
  443–46
Suramericana de Inversiones S.A., 88
  389–92
OAO Surgutneftegaz, 48 375–78
Surrey Satellite Technology Limited, 83
  386-390
The Susan G. Komen Breast
  CancerFoundation, 78 373–76
Susquehanna Pfaltzgraff Company, 8
  508–10
Sutherland Lumber Company, L.P., 99
  431–434
Sutter Home Winery Inc., 16 476–78
Suzano *see* Companhia Suzano de Papel e
  Celulose S.A.
Suzuki Motor Corporation, 9 487–89;
  23 459–62 (upd.); 59 393–98 (upd.)
Sveaskog AB, 93 430–33
Svenska Cellulosa Aktiebolaget SCA, IV
  338–40; 28 443–46 (upd.); 85
  413–20 (upd.)
Svenska Handelsbanken AB, II 365–67;
  50 460–63 (upd.)
Sverdrup Corporation, 14 475–78 *see
  also* Jacobs Engineering Group Inc.
Sveriges Riksbank, 96 418–22
SWA *see* Southwest Airlines.
SWALEC *see* Scottish and Southern
  Energy plc.
Swales & Associates, Inc., 69 336–38
Swank, Inc., 17 464–66; 84 380–384
  (upd.)
Swarovski International Holding AG, 40
  422–25
The Swatch Group SA, 26 479–81
Swedish Match AB, 12 462–64; 39
  387–90 (upd.); 92 349–55 (upd.)
Swedish Telecom, V 331–33
SwedishAmerican Health System, 51
  363–66
Sweet Candy Company, 60 295–97
Sweetheart Cup Company, Inc., 36
  460–64
The Swett & Crawford Group Inc., 84
  385–389
SWH Corporation, 70 307–09
Swift & Company, 55 364–67
Swift Energy Company, 63 364–66
Swift Transportation Co., Inc., 42
  363–66
Swinerton Inc., 43 397–400
Swire Pacific Ltd., I 521–22; 16 479–81
  (upd.); 57 348–53 (upd.)
Swisher International Group Inc., 23
  463–65
Swiss Air Transport Company Ltd., I
  121–22
Swiss Army Brands, Inc. *see* Victorinox
  AG.
Swiss Bank Corporation, II 368–70 *see
  also* UBS AG.

The Swiss Colony, Inc., 97 395–98
Swiss Federal Railways (Schweizerische
  Bundesbahnen), V 519–22
Swiss International Air Lines Ltd., 48
  379–81
Swiss Reinsurance Company
  (Schweizerische
  Rückversicherungs-Gesellschaft), III
  375–78; 46 380–84 (upd.)
Swiss Valley Farms Company, 90
  400–03
Swisscom AG, 58 336–39
Swissport International Ltd., 70 310–12
Sybase, Inc., 10 504–06; 27 447–50
  (upd.)
Sybron International Corp., 14 479–81
Sycamore Networks, Inc., 45 388–91
Sykes Enterprises, Inc., 45 392–95
Sylvan, Inc., 22 496–99
Sylvan Learning Systems, Inc., 35
  408–11 *see also* Educate Inc.
Symantec Corporation, 10 507–09; 82
  372–77 (upd.)
Symbol Technologies, Inc., 15 482–84
  see also Motorola, Inc.
Symrise GmbH and Company KG, 89
  436–40
Syms Corporation, 29 456–58; 74
  327–30 (upd.)
Symyx Technologies, Inc., 77 420–23
Synaptics Incorporated, 95 394–98
Synchronoss Technologies, Inc., 95
  399–402
Syneron Medical Ltd., 91 471–74
Syngenta International AG, 83 391-394
Syniverse Holdings Inc., 97 399–402
SYNNEX Corporation, 73 328–30
Synopsys, Inc., 11 489–92; 69 339–43
  (upd.)
SynOptics Communications, Inc., 10
  510–12
Synovus Financial Corp., 12 465–67; 52
  336–40 (upd.)
Syntel, Inc., 92 356–60
Syntex Corporation, I 701–03
Synthes, Inc., 93 434–37
Sypris Solutions, Inc., 85 421–25
SyQuest Technology, Inc., 18 509–12
Syratech Corp., 14 482–84
SYSCO Corporation, II 675–76; 24
  470–72 (upd.); 75 357–60 (upd.)
System Software Associates, Inc., 10
  513–14
Systemax, Inc., 52 341–44
Systems & Computer Technology Corp.,
  19 437–39
Sytner Group plc, 45 396–98

T

T-Netix, Inc., 46 385–88
T-Online International AG, 61 349–51
T.J. Maxx *see* The TJX Companies, Inc.
T. Marzetti Company, 57 354–56
T. Rowe Price Associates, Inc., 11
  493–96; 34 423–27 (upd.)
TA Triumph-Adler AG, 48 382–85
TAB Products Co., 17 467–69

Tabacalera, S.A., V 414–16; 17 470–73
  (upd.) *see also* Altadis S.A.
TABCORP Holdings Limited, 44
  407–10
TACA *see* Grupo TACA.
Taco Bell Corporation, 7 505–07; 21
  485–88 (upd.); 74 331–34 (upd.)
Taco Cabana, Inc., 23 466–68; 72
  344–47 (upd.)
Taco John's International Inc., 15
  485–87; 63 367–70 (upd.)
Tacony Corporation, 70 313–15
TAG Heuer S.A., 25 459–61; 77 424–28
  (upd.)
Tag-It Pacific, Inc., 85 426–29
Taiheiyo Cement Corporation, 60
  298–301 (upd.)
Taittinger S.A., 43 401–05
Taiwan Semiconductor Manufacturing
  Company Ltd., 47 383–87
Taiwan Tobacco & Liquor Corporation,
  75 361–63
Taiyo Fishery Company, Limited, II
  578–79 *see also* Maruha Group Inc.
Taiyo Kobe Bank, Ltd., II 371–72
Takara Holdings Inc., 62 345–47
Takashimaya Company, Limited, V
  193–96; 47 388–92 (upd.)
Take-Two Interactive Software, Inc., 46
  389–91
Takeda Chemical Industries, Ltd., I
  704–06; 46 392–95 (upd.)
The Talbots, Inc., 11 497–99; 31
  429–32 (upd.); 88 393–98 (upd.)
Talisman Energy Inc., 9 490–93; 47
  393–98 (upd.)
Talk America Holdings, Inc., 70 316–19
Talley Industries, Inc., 16 482–85
TALX Corporation, 92 361–64
TAM Linhas Aéreas S.A., 68 363–65
Tambrands Inc., 8 511–13 *see also*
  Procter & Gamble Co.
Tamedia AG, 53 323–26
Tamfelt Oyj Abp, 62 348–50
Tamron Company Ltd., 82 378–81
TAMSA *see* Tubos de Acero de Mexico,
  S.A.
Tandem Computers, Inc., 6 278–80 *see
  also* Hewlett-Packard Co.
Tandy Corporation, II 106–08; 12
  468–70 (upd.) *see also* RadioShack
  Corp.
Tandycrafts, Inc., 31 433–37
Tanger Factory Outlet Centers, Inc., 49
  386–89
Tanimura & Antle Fresh Foods, Inc., 98
  379–83
Tanox, Inc., 77 429–32
TAP—Air Portugal Transportes Aéreos
  Portugueses S.A., 46 396–99 (upd.)
Tapemark Company Inc., 64 373–75
TAQA North Ltd., 95 403–06
Target Corporation, 10 515–17; 27
  451–54 (upd.); 61 352–56 (upd.)
Tarkett Sommer AG, 25 462–64
Targetti Sankey SpA, 86 385–88
Tarmac Limited, III 751–54; 28 447–51
  (upd.); 95 407–14 (upd.)

Taro Pharmaceutical Industries Ltd., 65 335–37

TAROM S.A., 64 376–78

Tarragon Realty Investors, Inc., 45 399–402

Tarrant Apparel Group, 62 351–53

Taser International, Inc., 62 354–57

Tasty Baking Company, 14 485–87; 35 412–16 (upd.)

Tata Iron & Steel Co. Ltd., IV 217–19; 44 411–15 (upd.)

Tata Tea Ltd., 76 339–41

Tate & Lyle PLC, II 580–83; 42 367–72 (upd.)

Tati SA, 25 465–67

Tatneft *see* OAO Tatneft.

Tattered Cover Book Store, 43 406–09

Tatung Co., 23 469–71

Taubman Centers, Inc., 75 364–66

TaurusHolding GmbH & Co. KG, 46 400–03

Taylor & Francis Group plc, 44 416–19

Taylor Corporation, 36 465–67

Taylor Devices, Inc., 97 403–06

Taylor Guitars, 48 386–89

Taylor Made Group Inc., 98 384–87

Taylor Nelson Sofres plc, 34 428–30

Taylor Publishing Company, 12 471–73; 36 468–71 (upd.)

Taylor Woodrow plc, I 590–91; 38 450–53 (upd.)

TaylorMade-adidas Golf, 23 472–74; 96 423–28 (upd.)

TB Wood's Corporation, 56 355–58

TBA Global, LLC, 99 435–438

TBS *see* Turner Broadcasting System, Inc.

TBWA/Chiat/Day, 6 47–49; 43 410–14 (upd.) *see also* Omnicom Group Inc.

TC Advertising *see* Treasure Chest Advertising, Inc.

TCBY Systems LLC, 17 474–76; 98 388–92 (upd.)

TCF Financial Corporation, 47 399–402

Tchibo GmbH, 82 382–85

TCI *see* Tele-Communications, Inc.

TCO *see* Taubman Centers, Inc.

TD Bank *see* The Toronto-Dominion Bank.

TDC A/S, 63 371–74

TDK Corporation, II 109–11; 17 477–79 (upd.); 49 390–94 (upd.)

TDL Group Ltd., 46 404–06

TDS *see* Telephone and Data Systems, Inc.

TEAC Corporation, 78 377–80

Teachers Insurance and Annuity Association-College Retirement Equities Fund, III 379–82; 45 403–07 (upd.)

Teamsters Union *see* International Brotherhood of Teamsters.

TearDrop Golf Company, 32 445–48

Tech Data Corporation, 10 518–19; 74 335–38 (upd.)

Tech-Sym Corporation, 18 513–15; 44 420–23 (upd.)

TechBooks Inc., 84 390–393

TECHNE Corporation, 52 345–48

Technical Olympic USA, Inc., 75 367–69

Technip, 78 381–84

Technitrol, Inc., 29 459–62

Technology Research Corporation, 94 411–14

Technology Solutions Company, 94 415–19

TechTarget, Inc., 99 439–443

Techtronic Industries Company Ltd., 73 331–34

Teck Corporation, 27 455–58

TECO Energy, Inc., 6 582–84

Tecumseh Products Company, 8 514–16; 71 351–55 (upd.)

Ted Baker plc, 86 389–92

Tee Vee Toons, Inc., 57 357–60

Teekay Shipping Corporation, 25 468–71; 82 386–91 (upd.)

Teijin Limited, V 380–82; 61 357–61 (upd.)

Tejon Ranch Company, 35 417–20

Tekelec, 83 395-399

Teknor Apex Company, 97 407–10

Tektronix, Inc., 8 517–21; 78 385–91 (upd.)

Telcordia Technologies, Inc., 59 399–401

Tele-Communications, Inc., II 160–62

Tele Norte Leste Participações S.A., 80 369–72

Telecom Argentina S.A., 63 375–77

Telecom Australia, 6 341–42 *see also* Telstra Corp. Ltd.

Telecom Corporation of New Zealand Limited, 54 355–58

Telecom Eireann, 7 508–10 *see also* eircom plc.

Telecom Italia Mobile S.p.A., 63 378–80

Telecom Italia S.p.A., 43 415–19

Teledyne Technologies Inc., I 523–25; 10 520–22 (upd.); 62 358–62 (upd.)

Telefonaktiebolaget LM Ericsson, V 334–36; 46 407–11 (upd.)

Telefónica de Argentina S.A., 61 362–64

Telefónica de España, S.A., V 337–40

Telefónica S.A., 46 412–17 (upd.)

Telefonos de Mexico S.A. de C.V., 14 488–90; 63 381–84 (upd.)

Telegraaf Media Groep N.V., 98 393–97 (upd.)

Telekom Malaysia Bhd, 76 342–44

Telekomunikacja Polska SA, 50 464–68

Telenor ASA, 69 344–46

Telephone and Data Systems, Inc., 9 494–96

TelePizza S.A., 33 387–89

Television de Mexico, S.A. *see* Grupo Televisa, S.A.

Television Española, S.A., 7 511–12

Télévision Française 1, 23 475–77

TeliaSonera AB, 57 361–65 (upd.)

Tellabs, Inc., 11 500–01; 40 426–29 (upd.)

Telsmith Inc., 96 429–33

Telstra Corporation Limited, 50 469–72

Telxon Corporation, 10 523–25

Tembec Inc., 66 322–24

Temple-Inland Inc., IV 341–43; 31 438–42 (upd.)

Tempur-Pedic Inc., 54 359–61

Ten Cate *see* Royal Ten Cate N.V.

Tenaris SA, 63 385–88

Tenet Healthcare Corporation, 55 368–71 (upd.)

TenFold Corporation, 35 421–23

Tengasco, Inc., 99 444–447

Tengelmann Group, 27 459–62

Tennant Company, 13 499–501; 33 390–93 (upd.); 95 415–20 (upd.)

Tenneco Inc., I 526–28; 10 526–28 (upd.)

Tennessee Valley Authority, 50 473–77

TenneT B.V., 78 392–95

TEP *see* Tucson Electric Power Co.

TEPPCO Partners, L.P., 73 335–37

Tequila Herradura *see* Grupo Industrial Herradura, S.A. de C.V.

Teradyne, Inc., 11 502–04; 98 398–403 (upd.)

Terex Corporation, 7 513–15; 40 430–34 (upd.); 91 475–82 (upd.)

The Terlato Wine Group, 48 390–92

Terra Industries, Inc., 13 502–04; 94 420–24 (upd.)

Terra Lycos, Inc., 43 420–25

Terremark Worldwide, Inc., 99 448–452

Terrena L'Union CANA CAVAL, 70 320–22

Terumo Corporation, 48 393–95

Tesco plc, II 677–78; 24 473–76 (upd.); 68 366–70 (upd.)

Tesoro Corporation, 7 516–19; 45 408–13 (upd.); 97 411–19 (upd.)

Tessenderlo Group, 76 345–48

The Testor Corporation, 51 367–70

Tetley USA Inc., 88 399–402

Teton Energy Corporation, 97 420–23

Tetra Pak International SA, 53 327–29

Tetra Tech, Inc., 29 463–65

Teva Pharmaceutical Industries Ltd., 22 500–03; 54 362–65 (upd.)

Texaco Inc., IV 551–53; 14 491–94 (upd.); 41 391–96 (upd.) *see also* ChevronTexaco Corp.

Texas Air Corporation, I 123–24

Texas Industries, Inc., 8 522–24

Texas Instruments Incorporated, II 112–15; 11 505–08 (upd.); 46 418–23 (upd.)

Texas Pacific Group Inc., 36 472–74

Texas Rangers Baseball, 51 371–74

Texas Roadhouse, Inc., 69 347–49

Texas Utilities Company, V 724–25; 25 472–74 (upd.)

Textron Inc., I 529–30; 34 431–34 (upd.); 88 403–07 (upd.)

Textron Lycoming Turbine Engine, 9 497–99

TFM *see* Grupo Transportación Ferroviaria Mexicana, S.A. de C.V.

TF1 *see* Télévision Française 1

Tha Row Records, 69 350–52 (upd.)

Thai Airways International Public Company Limited, 6 122–24; 27 463–66 (upd.)

Thai Union Frozen Products PCL, 75 370–72

Thales S.A., 42 373–76

Thames Water plc, 11 509–11; 90 404–08 (upd.)

Thane International, Inc., 84 394–397

Thanulux Public Company Limited, 86 393–96

Thermadyne Holding Corporation, 19 440–43

Thermo BioAnalysis Corp., 25 475–78

Thermo Electron Corporation, 7 520–22

Thermo Fibertek, Inc., 24 477–79 *see also* Kadant Inc.

Thermo Instrument Systems Inc., 11 512–14

Thermo King Corporation, 13 505–07 *see also* Ingersoll-Rand Company Ltd.

Thermos Company, 16 486–88

Things Remembered, Inc., 84 398–401

Thiokol Corporation, 9 500–02 (upd.); 22 504–07 (upd.)

Thistle Hotels PLC, 54 366–69

Thomas & Betts Corporation, 11 515–17; 54 370–74 (upd.)

Thomas & Howard Company, Inc., 90 409–12

Thomas Cook Travel Inc., 9 503–05; 33 394–96 (upd.)

Thomas Crosbie Holdings Limited, 81 384–87

Thomas H. Lee Co., 24 480–83

Thomas Industries Inc., 29 466–69

Thomas J. Lipton Company, 14 495–97

Thomas Nelson Inc., 14 498–99; 38 454–57 (upd.)

Thomas Publishing Company, 26 482–85

Thomaston Mills, Inc., 27 467–70

Thomasville Furniture Industries, Inc., 12 474–76; 74 339–42 (upd.)

Thomsen Greenhouses and Garden Center, Incorporated, 65 338–40

The Thomson Corporation, 8 525–28; 34 435–40 (upd.); 77 433–39 (upd.)

THOMSON multimedia S.A., II 116–17; 42 377–80 (upd.)

Thor Industries Inc., 39 391–94; 92 365–370 (upd.)

Thorn Apple Valley, Inc., 7 523–25; 22 508–11 (upd.)

Thorn EMI plc, I 531–32 *see also* EMI plc; Thorn plc.

Thorn plc, 24 484–87

Thorntons plc, 46 424–26

ThoughtWorks Inc., 90 413–16

Thousand Trails, Inc., 33 397–99

THQ, Inc., 39 395–97; 92 371–375 (upd.)

Threadless.com *see* skinnyCorp, LLC.

The 3DO Company, 43 426–30

365 Media Group plc, 89 441–44

3Com Corporation, 11 518–21; 34 441–45 (upd.) *see also* Palm, Inc.

3i Group PLC, 73 338–40

3M Company, 61 365–70 (upd.)

Thrifty PayLess, Inc., 12 477–79 *see also* Rite Aid Corp.

ThyssenKrupp AG, IV 221–23; 28 452–60 (upd.); 87 425–438 (upd.)

TI Group plc, 17 480–83

TIAA-CREF *see* Teachers Insurance and Annuity Association-College Retirement Equities Fund.

Tianjin Flying Pigeon Bicycle Co., Ltd., 95 421–24

Tibbett & Britten Group plc, 32 449–52

TIBCO Software Inc., 79 411–14

TIC Holdings Inc., 92 376–379

Ticketmaster, 13 508–10; 37 381–84 (upd.); 76 349–53 (upd.)

Tidewater Inc., 11 522–24; 37 385–88 (upd.)

Tiffany & Co., 14 500–03; 78 396–401 (upd.)

TIG Holdings, Inc., 26 486–88

Tiger Aspect Productions Ltd., 72 348–50

Tilcon-Connecticut Inc., 80 373–76

Tilia Inc., 62 363–65

Tilley Endurables, Inc., 67 364–66

Tillotson Corp., 15 488–90

TIM *see* Telecom Italia Mobile S.p.A.

Timber Lodge Steakhouse, Inc., 73 341–43

The Timberland Company, 13 511–14; 54 375–79 (upd.)

Timberline Software Corporation, 15 491–93

Time Out Group Ltd., 68 371–73

Time Warner Inc., IV 673–76; 7 526–30 (upd.) *see also* AOL Time Warner Inc.

The Times Mirror Company, IV 677–78; 17 484–86 (upd.) *see also* Tribune Co.

TIMET *see* Titanium Metals Corp.

Timex Corporation, 7 531–33; 25 479–82 (upd.)

The Timken Company, 8 529–31; 42 381–85 (upd.)

Tiscali SpA, 48 396–99

TISCO *see* Tata Iron & Steel Company Ltd.

Tishman Speyer Properties, L.P., 47 403–06

Tissue Technologies, Inc. *see* Palomar Medical Technologies, Inc.

Titan Cement Company S.A., 64 379–81

The Titan Corporation, 36 475–78

Titan International, Inc., 89 445–49

Titanium Metals Corporation, 21 489–92

TiVo Inc., 75 373–75

TJ International, Inc., 19 444–47

The TJX Companies, Inc., V 197–98; 19 448–50 (upd.); 57 366–69 (upd.)

TLC Beatrice International Holdings, Inc., 22 512–15

TMP Worldwide Inc., 30 458–60 *see also* Monster Worldwide Inc.

TNT Freightways Corporation, 14 504–06

TNT Limited, V 523–25

TNT Post Group N.V., 27 471–76 (upd.); 30 461–63 (upd.) *see also* TPG N.V.

Tobu Railway Company Ltd., 6 430–32; 98 404–08 (upd.)

Today's Man, Inc., 20 484–87

The Todd-AO Corporation, 33 400–04 *see also* Liberty Livewire Corp.

Todd Shipyards Corporation, 14 507–09

TODCO, 87 439–442

Todhunter International, Inc., 27 477–79

Tofutti Brands, Inc., 64 382–84

Tohan Corporation, 84 402–405

Toho Co., Ltd., 28 461–63

Tohuku Electric Power Company, Inc., V 726–28

The Tokai Bank, Limited, II 373–74; 15 494–96 (upd.)

Tokheim Corporation, 21 493–95

Tokio Marine and Fire Insurance Co., Ltd., III 383–86 *see also* Millea Holdings Inc.

Tokyo Electric Power Company, V 729–33; 74 343–48 (upd.)

Tokyo Gas Co., Ltd., V 734–36; 55 372–75 (upd.)

TOKYOPOP Inc., 79 415–18

Tokyu Corporation, V 526–28; 47 407–10 (upd.)

Tokyu Department Store Co., Ltd., V 199–202; 32 453–57 (upd.)

Toll Brothers Inc., 15 497–99; 70 323–26 (upd.)

Tollgrade Communications, Inc., 44 424–27

Tom Brown, Inc., 37 389–91

Tom Doherty Associates Inc., 25 483–86

Tom's Foods Inc., 66 325–27

Tom's of Maine, Inc., 45 414–16

Tombstone Pizza Corporation, 13 515–17 *see also* Kraft Foods Inc.

Tomen Corporation, IV 224–25; 24 488–91 (upd.)

Tomkins plc, 11 525–27; 44 428–31 (upd.)

Tommy Hilfiger Corporation, 20 488–90; 53 330–33 (upd.)

TomTom N.V., 81 388–91

Tomy Company Ltd., 65 341–44

Tone Brothers, Inc., 21 496–98; 74 349–52 (upd.)

Tonen Corporation, IV 554–56; 16 489–92 (upd.)

TonenGeneral Sekiyu K.K., 54 380–86 (upd.)

Tong Yang Cement Corporation, 62 366–68

Tonka Corporation, 25 487–89

Too, Inc., 61 371–73

Toolex International N.V., 26 489–91

Tootsie Roll Industries, Inc., 12 480–82; 82 392–96 (upd.)
The Topaz Group, Inc., 62 369–71
Topco Associates LLC, 60 302–04
Topcon Corporation, 84 406–409
Toppan Printing Co., Ltd., IV 679–81; 58 340–44 (upd.)
The Topps Company, Inc., 13 518–20; 34 446–49 (upd.); 83 400–406 (upd.)
Tops Appliance City, Inc., 17 487–89
Tops Markets LLC, 60 305–07
Toray Industries, Inc., V 383–86; 51 375–79 (upd.)
Torchmark Corporation, 9 506–08; 33 405–08 (upd.)
Toresco Enterprises, Inc., 84 410–413
The Toro Company, 7 534–36; 26 492–95 (upd.); 77 440–45 (upd.)
Toromont Industries, Ltd., 21 499–501
The Toronto-Dominion Bank, II 375–77; 49 395–99 (upd.)
Toronto Maple Leafs *see* Maple Leaf Sports & Entertainment Ltd.
Toronto Raptors *see* Maple Leaf Sports & Entertainment Ltd.
The Torrington Company, 13 521–24 *see also* Timken Co.
Torstar Corporation, 29 470–73 *see also* Harlequin Enterprises Ltd.
Tosco Corporation, 7 537–39 *see also* ConocoPhillips.
Toshiba Corporation, I 533–35; 12 483–86 (upd.); 40 435–40 (upd.); 99 453–461 (upd.)
Tosoh Corporation, 70 327–30
Total Compagnie Française des Pétroles S.A., IV 557–61 *see also* Total Fina Elf S.A.
Total Entertainment Restaurant Corporation, 46 427–29
Total Fina Elf S.A., 50 478–86 (upd.)
TOTAL S.A., 24 492–97 (upd.)
Total System Services, Inc., 18 516–18
Totem Resources Corporation, 9 509–11
TOTO LTD., III 755–56; 28 464–66 (upd.)
Tottenham Hotspur PLC, 81 392–95
Touchstone Films *see* The Walt Disney Co.
TouchTunes Music Corporation, 97 424–28
Toupargel-Agrigel S.A., 76 354–56
Touristik Union International GmbH. and Company K.G., II 163–65 *see also* Preussag AG.
TOUSA *see* Technical Olympic USA, Inc.
Touton S.A., 92 380–383
Tower Air, Inc., 28 467–69
Tower Automotive, Inc., 24 498–500
Towers Perrin, 32 458–60
Town & Country Corporation, 19 451–53
Town Sports International, Inc., 46 430–33
Townsends, Inc., 64 385–87
Toy Biz, Inc., 18 519–21 *see also* Marvel Entertainment, Inc.

Toymax International, Inc., 29 474–76
Toyo Sash Co., Ltd., III 757–58
Toyo Seikan Kaisha Ltd., I 615–16
Toyoda Automatic Loom Works, Ltd., III 636–39
Toyota Motor Corporation, I 203–05; 11 528–31 (upd.); 38 458–62 (upd.)
Toys 'R Us, Inc., V 203–06; 18 522–25 (upd.); 57 370–75 (upd.)
TPG N.V., 64 388–91 (upd.)
Tracor Inc., 17 490–92
Tractebel S.A., 20 491–93 *see also* Suez Lyonnaise des Eaux; SUEZ-TRACTEBEL S.A.
Tractor Supply Company, 57 376–78
Trader Classified Media N.V., 57 379–82
Trader Joe's Company, 13 525–27; 50 487–90 (upd.)
TradeStation Group, Inc., 83 407-410
Traffix, Inc., 61 374–76
Trailer Bridge, Inc., 41 397–99
Trammell Crow Company, 8 532–34; 57 383–87 (upd.)
Trane, 78 402–05
Trans-Lux Corporation, 51 380–83
Trans World Airlines, Inc., I 125–27; 12 487–90 (upd.); 35 424–29 (upd.)
Trans World Entertainment Corporation, 24 501–03; 68 374–77 (upd.)
Transaction Systems Architects, Inc., 29 477–79; 82 397–402 (upd.)
TransAlta Utilities Corporation, 6 585–87
Transamerica—An AEGON Company, I 536–38; 13 528–30 (upd.); 41 400–03 (upd.)
Transammonia Group, 95 425–28
Transatlantic Holdings, Inc., 11 532–33
TransBrasil S/A Linhas Aéreas, 31 443–45
TransCanada Corporation, V 737–38; 93 438–45 (upd.)
Transco Energy Company, V 739–40 *see also* The Williams Companies.
Transiciel SA, 48 400–02
Transitions Optical, Inc., 83 411–415
CJSC Transmash Holding, 93 446–49
Transmedia Network Inc., 20 494–97 *see also* Rewards Network Inc.
TransMontaigne Inc., 28 470–72
Oil Transporting Joint Stock Company Transneft, 92 450–54
Transnet Ltd., 6 433–35
Transocean Sedco Forex Inc., 45 417–19
Transport Corporation of America, Inc., 49 400–03
Transportes Aéreas Centro-Americanos *see* Grupo TACA.
Transportes Aereos Portugueses, S.A., 6 125–27 *see also* TAP—Air Portugal Transportes Aéreos Portugueses S.A.
TransPro, Inc., 71 356–59
The Tranzonic Companies, 15 500–02; 37 392–95 (upd.)
Travel Ports of America, Inc., 17 493–95

Travelers Corporation, III 387–90 *see also* Citigroup Inc.
Travelocity.com, Inc., 46 434–37
Travelzoo Inc., 79 419–22
Travis Boats & Motors, Inc., 37 396–98
Travis Perkins plc, 34 450–52
TRC Companies, Inc., 32 461–64
Treadco, Inc., 19 454–56
Treasure Chest Advertising Company, Inc., 32 465–67
Tredegar Corporation, 52 349–51
Tree of Life, Inc., 29 480–82
Tree Top, Inc., 76 357–59
TreeHouse Foods, Inc., 79 423–26
Trek Bicycle Corporation, 16 493–95; 78 406–10 (upd.)
Trelleborg AB, 93 455–64
Trend Micro Inc., 97 429–32
Trend-Lines, Inc., 22 516–18
Trendwest Resorts, Inc., 33 409–11 *see also* Jeld-Wen, Inc.
Trex Company, Inc., 71 360–62
Tri Valley Growers, 32 468–71
Triarc Companies, Inc., 8 535–37; 34 453–57 (upd.)
Tribune Company, IV 682–84; 22 519–23 (upd.); 63 389–95 (upd.)
Trico Marine Services, Inc., 89 450–53
Trico Products Corporation, 15 503–05
Tridel Enterprises Inc., 9 512–13
Trident Seafoods Corporation, 56 359–61
Trigen Energy Corporation, 42 386–89
Trilon Financial Corporation, II 456–57
TriMas Corp., 11 534–36
Trimble Navigation Limited, 40 441–43
Třinecké Železárny A.S., 92 384–87
Trinity Industries, Incorporated, 7 540–41
Trinity Mirror plc, 49 404–10 (upd.)
TRINOVA Corporation, III 640–42
TriPath Imaging, Inc., 77 446–49
Triple Five Group Ltd., 49 411–15
Triple P N.V., 26 496–99
Tripwire, Inc., 97 433–36
TriQuint Semiconductor, Inc., 63 396–99
Trisko Jewelry Sculptures, Ltd., 57 388–90
Triton Energy Corporation, 11 537–39
Triumph-Adler *see* TA Triumph-Adler AG.
Triumph Group, Inc., 31 446–48
Triumph Motorcycles Ltd., 53 334–37
Trizec Corporation Ltd., 10 529–32
The TriZetto Group, Inc., 83 416–419
TRM Copy Centers Corporation, 18 526–28
Tropicana Products, Inc., 28 473–77; 73 344–49 (upd.)
Troutman Sanders L.L.P., 79 427–30
True North Communications Inc., 23 478–80 *see also* Foote, Cone & Belding Worldwide.
True Religion Apparel, Inc., 79 431–34
True Temper Sports, Inc., 95 429–32
True Value Company, 74 353–57 (upd.)
Trump Organization, 23 481–84; 64 392–97 (upd.)

TRUMPF GmbH + Co. KG, 86 397–02

TruServ Corporation, 24 504–07 *see* True Value Co.

Trusthouse Forte PLC, III 104–06

TRW Automotive Holdings Corp., I 539–41; 11 540–42 (upd.); 14 510–13 (upd.); 75 376–82 (upd.)

TSA *see* Transaction Systems Architects, Inc.

Tsakos Energy Navigation Ltd., 91 483–86

TSB Group plc, 12 491–93

TSC *see* Tractor Supply Co.

Tsingtao Brewery Group, 49 416–20

TSMC *see* Taiwan Semiconductor Manufacturing Company Ltd.

TSYS *see* Total System Services, Inc.

TTL *see* Taiwan Tobacco & Liquor Corp.

TTX Company, 6 436–37; 66 328–30 (upd.)

Tubby's, Inc., 53 338–40

Tubos de Acero de Mexico, S.A. (TAMSA), 41 404–06

Tucows Inc., 78 411–14

Tucson Electric Power Company, 6 588–91

Tuesday Morning Corporation, 18 529–31; 70 331–33 (upd.)

TUF *see* Thai Union Frozen Products PCL.

TUI *see* Touristik Union International GmbH. and Company K.G.

TUI Group GmbH, 42 283; 44 432–35

Tulip Ltd., 89 454–57

Tullow Oil plc, 83 420–423

Tully's Coffee Corporation, 51 384–86

Tultex Corporation, 13 531–33

Tumaro's Gourmet Tortillas, 85 430–33

Tumbleweed, Inc., 33 412–14; 80 377–81 (upd.)

Tunisair *see* Société Tunisienne de l'Air-Tunisair.

Tupolev Aviation and Scientific Technical Complex, 24 58–60

Tupperware Brands Corporation, 28 478–81; 78 415–20 (upd.)

TurboChef Technologies, Inc., 83 424–427

Turkish Airlines Inc. (Türk Hava Yollari A.O.), 72 351–53

Turkiye Is Bankasi A.S., 61 377–80

Türkiye Petrolleri Anonim Ortaklığı, IV 562–64

Turner Broadcasting System, Inc., II 166–68; 6 171–73 (upd.); 66 331–34 (upd.)

Turner Construction Company, 66 335–38

The Turner Corporation, 8 538–40; 23 485–88 (upd.)

Turtle Wax, Inc., 15 506–09; 93 465–70 (upd.)

Tuscarora Inc., 29 483–85

The Tussauds Group, 55 376–78

Tutogen Medical, Inc., 68 378–80

Tuttle Publishing, 86 403–06

TV Azteca, S.A. de C.V., 39 398–401

TV Guide, Inc., 43 431–34 (upd.)

TVA *see* Tennessee Valley Authority.

TVE *see* Television Española, S.A.

TVI, Inc., 15 510–12; 99 462–465 *see also* Savers, Inc.

TW Services, Inc., II 679–80

TWA *see* Trans World Airlines.

TWC *see* The Weather Channel Cos.

Tweeter Home Entertainment Group, Inc., 30 464–66

Twentieth Century Fox Film Corporation, II 169–71; 25 490–94 (upd.)

24 Hour Fitness Worldwide, Inc., 71 363–65

24/7 Real Media, Inc., 49 421–24

Twin Disc, Inc., 21 502–04

Twinlab Corporation, 34 458–61

II-VI Incorporated, 69 353–55

Ty Inc., 33 415–17; 86 407–11 (upd.)

Tyco International Ltd., III 643–46; 28 482–87 (upd.); 63 400–06 (upd.)

Tyco Toys, Inc., 12 494–97 *see also* Mattel, Inc.

Tyler Corporation, 23 489–91

Tyndale House Publishers, Inc., 57 391–94

Tyson Foods, Inc., II 584–85; 14 514–16 (upd.); 50 491–95 (upd.)

U

U.S. *see also* US.

U.S. Aggregates, Inc., 42 390–92

U.S. Army Corps of Engineers, 91 491–95

U.S. Bancorp, 14 527–29; 36 489–95 (upd.)

U.S. Borax, Inc., 42 393–96

U.S. Can Corporation, 30 474–76

U.S. Cellular Corporation, 31 449–52 (upd.); 88 408–13 (upd.)

U.S. Delivery Systems, Inc., 22 531–33 *see also* Velocity Express Corp.

U.S. Foodservice, 26 503–06

U.S. Healthcare, Inc., 6 194–96

U.S. Home Corporation, 8 541–43; 78 421–26 (upd.)

U.S. News & World Report Inc., 30 477–80; 89 458–63 (upd.)

U.S. Office Products Company, 25 500–02

U.S. Physical Therapy, Inc., 65 345–48

U.S. Premium Beef LLC, 91 487–90

U.S. Robotics Corporation, 9 514–15; 66 339–41 (upd.)

U.S. Satellite Broadcasting Company, Inc., 20 505–07 *see also* DIRECTV, Inc.

U.S. Steel Corp *see* United States Steel Corp.

U.S. Timberlands Company, L.P., 42 397–400

U.S. Trust Corp., 17 496–98

U.S. Vision, Inc., 66 342–45

U S West, Inc., V 341–43; 25 495–99 (upd.)

UAL Corporation, 34 462–65 (upd.)

UAP *see* Union des Assurances de Paris.

UAW (International Union, United Automobile, Aerospace and Agricultural Implement Workers of America), 72 354–57

Ube Industries, Ltd., III 759–61; 38 463–67 (upd.)

Ubi Soft Entertainment S.A., 41 407–09

UBS AG, 52 352–59 (upd.)

UCB Pharma SA, 98 409–12

UFA TV & Film Produktion GmbH, 80 382–87

UGI Corporation, 12 498–500

Ugine S.A., 20 498–500

Ugly Duckling Corporation, 22 524–27 *see also* DriveTime Automotive Group Inc.

UICI, 33 418–21 *see also* HealthMarkets, Inc.

Ukrop's Super Market's, Inc., 39 402–04

UL *see* Underwriters Laboratories, Inc.

Ulster Television PLC, 71 366–68

Ulta Salon, Cosmetics & Fragrance, Inc., 92 471–73

Ultimate Electronics, Inc., 18 532–34; 69 356–59 (upd.)

Ultimate Leisure Group PLC, 75 383–85

Ultra Pac, Inc., 24 512–14

Ultra Petroleum Corporation, 71 369–71

Ultrak Inc., 24 508–11

Ultralife Batteries, Inc., 58 345–48

Ultramar Diamond Shamrock Corporation, IV 565–68; 31 453–57 (upd.)

ULVAC, Inc., 80 388–91

Umbro plc, 88 414–17

NV Umicore SA, 47 411–13

Umpqua Holdings Corporation, 87 443–446

Uncle Ben's Inc., 22 528–30

Uncle Ray's LLC, 90 417–19

Under Armour Performance Apparel, 61 381–83

Underberg AG, 92 388–393

Underwriters Laboratories, Inc., 30 467–70

UNG *see* United National Group, Ltd.

Uni-Marts, Inc., 17 499–502

Unibail SA, 40 444–46

Unibanco Holdings S.A., 73 350–53

Unica Corporation, 77 450–54

UNICEF *see* United Nations International Children's Emergency Fund (UNICEF).

Unicharm Corporation, 84 414–417

Unicom Corporation, 29 486–90 (upd.) *see also* Exelon Corp.

Uniden Corporation, 98 413–16

Unifi, Inc., 12 501–03; 62 372–76 (upd.)

Unified Grocers, Inc., 93 474–77

UniFirst Corporation, 21 505–07

Unigate PLC, II 586–87; 28 488–91 (upd.) *see also* Uniq Plc.

Unilever, II 588–91; 7 542–45 (upd.); 32 472–78 (upd.); 89 464–74 (upd.)

Unilog SA, 42 401–03
Union Bank of California, 16 496–98
see also UnionBanCal Corp.
Union Bank of Switzerland, II 378–79
see also UBS AG.
Union Camp Corporation, IV 344–46
Union Carbide Corporation, I 399–401;
9 516–20 (upd.); 74 358–63 (upd.)
Unión de Cervecerías Peruanas Backus y
Johnston S.A.A.,92 394–397
Union des Assurances de Paris, III
391–94
Union Electric Company, V 741–43 *see
also* Ameren Corp.
Unión Fenosa, S.A., 51 387–90
Union Financière de France Banque SA,
52 360–62
Union Pacific Corporation, V 529–32;
28 492–500 (upd.); 79 435–46 (upd.)
Union Planters Corporation, 54 387–90
Union Texas Petroleum Holdings, Inc.,
9 521–23
UnionBanCal Corporation, 50 496–99
(upd.)
Uniq plc, 83 428-433 (upd.)
Unique Casual Restaurants, Inc., 27
480–82
Unison HealthCare Corporation, 25
503–05
Unisys Corporation, III 165–67; 6
281–83 (upd.); 36 479–84 (upd.)
Unit Corporation, 63 407–09
United Airlines, I 128–30; 6 128–30
(upd.) *see also* UAL Corp.
United Auto Group, Inc., 26 500–02;
68 381–84 (upd.)
United Biscuits (Holdings) plc, II
592–94; 42 404–09 (upd.)
United Brands Company, II 595–97
United Business Media plc, 52 363–68
(upd.)
United Community Banks, Inc., 98
417–20
United Dairy Farmers, Inc., 74 364–66
United Defense Industries, Inc., 30
471–73; 66 346–49 (upd.)
United Dominion Industries Limited, 8
544–46; 16 499–502 (upd.)
United Dominion Realty Trust, Inc., 52
369–71
United Farm Workers of America, 88
418–22
United Foods, Inc., 21 508–11
United HealthCare Corporation, 9
524–26 *see also* Humana Inc.
The United Illuminating Company, 21
512–14
United Industrial Corporation, 37
399–402
United Industries Corporation, 68
385–87
United Internet AG, 99 466–469
United Jewish Communities, 33 422–25
United Merchants & Manufacturers,
Inc., 13 534–37
United Microelectronics Corporation,
98 421–24

United National Group, Ltd., 63
410–13
United Nations International Children's
Emergency Fund (UNICEF), 58
349–52
United Natural Foods, Inc., 32 479–82;
76 360–63 (upd.)
United Negro College Fund, Inc., 79
447–50
United News & Media plc, 28 501–05
(upd.) *see also* United Business Media
plc.
United Newspapers plc, IV 685–87 *see
also* United Business Media plc.
United Online, Inc., 71 372–77 (upd.)
United Overseas Bank Ltd., 56 362–64
United Pan-Europe Communications
NV, 47 414–17
United Paper Mills Ltd., IV 347–50 *see
also* UPM-Kymmene Corp.
United Parcel Service, Inc., V 533–35;
17 503–06 (upd.); 63 414–19; 94
425–30 (upd.)
United Press International, Inc., 25
506–09; 73 354–57 (upd.)
United Rentals, Inc., 34 466–69
United Retail Group Inc., 33 426–28
United Road Services, Inc., 69 360–62
United Service Organizations, 60
308–11
United States Cellular Corporation, 9
527–29 *see also* U.S. Cellular Corp.
United States Filter Corporation, 20
501–04 *see also* Siemens AG.
United States Health Care Systems, Inc.
see U.S. Healthcare, Inc.
United States Pipe and Foundry
Company, 62 377–80
United States Playing Card Company,
62 381–84
United States Postal Service, 14 517–20;
34 470–75 (upd.)
United States Shoe Corporation, V
207–08
United States Steel Corporation, 50
500–04 (upd.)
United States Surgical Corporation, 10
533–35; 34 476–80 (upd.)
United Stationers Inc., 14 521–23
United Talent Agency, Inc., 80 392–96
United Technologies Automotive Inc.,
15 513–15
United Technologies Corporation, I
84–86; 10 536–38 (upd.); 34 481–85
(upd.)
United Telecommunications, Inc., V
344–47 *see also* Sprint Corp.
United Utilities PLC, 52 372–75 (upd.)
United Video Satellite Group, 18
535–37 *see also* TV Guide, Inc.
United Water Resources, Inc., 40
447–50; 45 277
United Way of America, 36 485–88
Unitika Ltd., V 387–89; 53 341–44
(upd.)
Unitil Corporation, 37 403–06
Unitog Co., 19 457–60 *see also* Cintas
Corp.

Unitrin Inc., 16 503–05; 78 427–31
(upd.)
Univar Corporation, 9 530–32
Universal Compression, Inc., 59 402–04
Universal Corporation, V 417–18; 48
403–06 (upd.)
Universal Electronics Inc., 39 405–08
Universal Foods Corporation, 7 546–48
see also Sensient Technologies Corp.
Universal Forest Products, Inc., 10
539–40; 59 405–09 (upd.)
Universal Health Services, Inc., 6
191–93
Universal International, Inc., 25 510–11
Universal Manufacturing Company, 88
423–26
Universal Security Instruments, Inc., 96
434–37
Universal Stainless & Alloy Products,
Inc., 75 386–88
Universal Studios, Inc., 33 429–33
Universal Technical Institute, Inc., 81
396–99
The University of Chicago Press, 79
451–55
University of Phoenix *see* Apollo Group,
Inc.
Univision Communications Inc., 24
515–18; 83 434–439 (upd.)
UNM *see* United News & Media plc.
Uno Restaurant Holdings Corporation,
18 538–40; 70 334–37 (upd.)
Unocal Corporation, IV 569–71; 24
519–23 (upd.); 71 378–84 (upd.)
UNUM Corp., 13 538–40
UnumProvident Corporation, 52
376–83 (upd.)
Uny Co., Ltd., V 209–10; 49 425–28
(upd.)
UOB *see* United Overseas Bank Ltd.
UPC *see* United Pan-Europe
Communications NV.
UPI *see* United Press International.
Upjohn Company, I 707–09; 8 547–49
(upd.) *see also* Pharmacia & Upjohn
Inc.; Pfizer Inc.
UPM-Kymmene Corporation, 19
461–65; 50 505–11 (upd.)
UPS *see* United Parcel Service, Inc.
Uralita S.A., 96 438–41
Urban Outfitters, Inc., 14 524–26; 74
367–70 (upd.)
Urbi Desarrollos Urbanos, S.A. de C.V.,
81 400–03
Urbium PLC, 75 389–91
URS Corporation, 45 420–23; 80
397–400 (upd.)
URSI *see* United Road Services, Inc.
US *see also* U.S.
US Airways Group, Inc., I 131–32; 6
131–32 (upd.); 28 506–09 (upd.); 52
384–88 (upd.)
US 1 Industries, Inc., 89 475–78
USA Interactive, Inc., 47 418–22 (upd.)
USA Mobility Inc., 97 437–40 (upd.)
USA Truck, Inc., 42 410–13
USAA, 10 541–43; 62 385–88 (upd.)
USANA, Inc., 29 491–93

USCC *see* United States Cellular Corp.
USF&G Corporation, III 395–98 *see also* The St. Paul Companies.
USG Corporation, III 762–64; **26** 507–10 (upd.); **81** 404–10 (upd.)
Ushio Inc., 91 496–99
Usinas Siderúrgicas de Minas Gerais S.A., 77 454–57
Usinger's Famous Sausage *see* Fred Usinger Inc.
Usinor SA, IV 226–28; **42** 414–17 (upd.)
USO *see* United Service Organizations.
USPS *see* United States Postal Service.
USSC *see* United States Surgical Corp.
UST Inc., 9 533–35; **50** 512–17 (upd.)
USX Corporation, IV 572–74; **7** 549–52 (upd.) *see also* United States Steel Corp.
Utah Medical Products, Inc., 36 496–99
Utah Power and Light Company, 27 483–86 *see also* PacifiCorp.
Utilicorp United Inc., 6 592–94 *see also* Aquilla, Inc.
UTStarcom, Inc., 77 458–61
UTV *see* Ulster Television PLC.
Utz Quality Foods, Inc., 72 358–60
UUNET, 38 468–72
Uwajimaya, Inc., 60 312–14
Uzbekistan Airways National Air Company, 99 470–473

V

V&S Vin & Sprit AB, 91 504–11 (upd.)
VA TECH ELIN EBG GmbH, 49 429–31
Vail Resorts, Inc., 11 543–46; **43** 435–39 (upd.)
Vaillant GmbH, 44 436–39
Valassis Communications, Inc., 8 550–51; **37** 407–10 (upd.); **76** 364–67 (upd.)
Valeo, 23 492–94; **66** 350–53 (upd.)
Valero Energy Corporation, 7 553–55; **71** 385–90 (upd.)
Valhi, Inc., 19 466–68; **94** 431–35 (upd.)
Vallen Corporation, 45 424–26
Valley Media Inc., 35 430–33
Valley National Gases, Inc., 85 434–37
Valley Proteins, Inc., 91 500–03
ValleyCrest Companies, 81 411–14 (upd.)
Vallourec SA, 54 391–94
Valmet Oy, III 647–49 *see also* Metso Corp.
Valmont Industries, Inc., 19 469–72
Valora Holding AG, 98 425–28
Valorem S.A., 88 427–30
Valores Industriales S.A., 19 473–75
The Valspar Corporation, 8 552–54; **32** 483–86 (upd.); **77** 462–68 (upd.)
Value City Department Stores, Inc., 38 473–75 *see also* Retail Ventures, Inc.
Value Line, Inc., 16 506–08; **73** 358–61 (upd.)
Value Merchants Inc., 13 541–43
ValueClick, Inc., 49 432–34

ValueVision International, Inc., 22 534–36
Van Camp Seafood Company, Inc., 7 556–57 *see also* Chicken of the Sea International.
Van Hool S.A./NV, 96 442–45
Van Houtte Inc., 39 409–11
Van Lanschot NV, 79 456–59
Van Leer N.V. *see* Royal Packaging Industries Van Leer N.V.; Greif Inc.
Van's Aircraft, Inc., 65 349–51
Vance Publishing Corporation, 64 398–401
Vanderbilt University Medical Center, 99 474–477
The Vanguard Group, Inc., 14 530–32; **34** 486–89 (upd.)
Vanguard Health Systems Inc., 70 338–40
Vans, Inc., 16 509–11; **47** 423–26 (upd.)
Varco International, Inc., 42 418–20
Vari-Lite International, Inc., 35 434–36
Varian Associates Inc., 12 504–06
Varian, Inc., 48 407–11 (upd.)
Variety Wholesalers, Inc., 73 362–64
Variflex, Inc., 51 391–93
VARIG S.A. (Viação Aérea Rio-Grandense), 6 133–35; **29** 494–97 (upd.)
Varity Corporation, III 650–52 *see also* AGCO Corp.
Varlen Corporation, 16 512–14
Varsity Brands, Inc., 15 516–18; **94** 436–40 (upd.)
Varta AG, 23 495–99
VASCO Data Security International, Inc., 79 460–63
Vastar Resources, Inc., 24 524–26
Vattenfall AB, 57 395–98
Vauxhall Motors Limited, 73 365–69
VBA - Bloemenveiling Aalsmeer, 88 431–34
VCA Antech, Inc., 58 353–55
Veba A.G., I 542–43; **15** 519–21 (upd.) *see also* E.On AG.
Vebego International BV, 49 435–37
VECO International, Inc., 7 558–59 *see also* CH2M Hill Ltd.
Vector Aerospace Corporation, 97 441–44
Vector Group Ltd., 35 437–40 (upd.)
Vectren Corporation, 98 429–36 (upd.)
Vedior NV, 35 441–43
Veeco Instruments Inc., 32 487–90
Veidekke ASA, 98 437–40
Veit Companies, 43 440–42; **92** 398–402 (upd.)
Velcro Industries N.V., 19 476–78; **72** 361–64 (upd.)
Velocity Express Corporation, 49 438–41; **94** 441–46 (upd.)
Velux A/S, 86 412–15
Venator Group Inc., 35 444–49 (upd.) *see also* Foot Locker Inc.
Vencor, Inc., 16 515–17

Vendex International N.V., 13 544–46 *see also* Koninklijke Vendex KBB N.V. (Royal Vendex KBB N.V.).
Vendôme Luxury Group plc, 27 487–89
Venetian Casino Resort, LLC, 47 427–29
Ventana Medical Systems, Inc., 75 392–94
Ventura Foods LLC, 90 420–23
Venture Stores Inc., 12 507–09
VeraSun Energy Corporation, 87 447–450
Verbatim Corporation, 14 533–35; **74** 371–74 (upd.)
Vereinigte Elektrizitätswerke Westfalen AG, IV V 744–47
Veridian Corporation, 54 395–97
VeriFone, Inc., 18 541–44; **76** 368–71 (upd.)
Verint Systems Inc., 73 370–72
VeriSign, Inc., 47 430–34
Veritas Software Corporation, 45 427–31
Verity Inc., 68 388–91
Verizon Communications Inc., 43 443–49 (upd.); **78** 432–40 (upd.)
Verlagsgruppe Georg von Holtzbrinck GmbH, 35 450–53
Verlagsgruppe Weltbild GmbH, 98 441–46
Vermeer Manufacturing Company, 17 507–10
The Vermont Country Store, 93 478–82
Vermont Pure Holdings, Ltd., 51 394–96
The Vermont Teddy Bear Co., Inc., 36 500–02
Versace *see* Gianni Versace SpA.
Vertex Pharmaceuticals Incorporated, 83 440–443
Vertis Communications, 84 418–421
Vertrue Inc., 77 469–72
Vestas Wind Systems A/S, 73 373–75
Vestey Group Ltd., 95 433–37
Veuve Clicquot Ponsardin SCS, 98 447–51
VEW AG, 39 412–15
VF Corporation, V 390–92; **17** 511–14 (upd.); **54** 398–404 (upd.)
VHA Inc., 53 345–47
Viacom Inc., 7 560–62; **23** 500–03 (upd.); **67** 367–71 (upd.) *see also* Paramount Pictures Corp.
Viad Corp., 73 376–78
Viag AG, IV 229–32 *see also* E.On AG.
ViaSat, Inc., 54 405–08
Viasoft Inc., 27 490–93; **59** 27
VIASYS Healthcare, Inc., 52 389–91
Viasystems Group, Inc., 67 372–74
Viatech Continental Can Company, Inc., 25 512–15 (upd.)
Vicat S.A., 70 341–43
Vickers plc, 27 494–97
Vicon Industries, Inc., 44 440–42
VICORP Restaurants, Inc., 12 510–12; **48** 412–15 (upd.)

Victor Company of Japan, Limited, II 118–19; 26 511–13 (upd.); 83 444–449 (upd.)

Victoria Coach Station Ltd. see London Regional Transport.

Victoria Group, III 399–401; 44 443–46 (upd.)

Victorinox AG, 21 515–17; 74 375–78 (upd.)

Vicunha Têxtil S.A., 78 441–44

Victory Refrigeration, Inc., 82 403–06

Videojet Technologies, Inc., 90 424–27

Vidrala S.A., 67 375–77

Viel & Cie, 76 372–74

Vienna Sausage Manufacturing Co., 14 536–37

Viessmann Werke GmbH & Co., 37 411–14

Viewpoint International, Inc., 66 354–56

ViewSonic Corporation, 72 365–67

Viking Office Products, Inc., 10 544–46 see also Office Depot, Inc.

Viking Range Corporation, 66 357–59

Viking Yacht Company, 96 446–49

Village Roadshow Ltd., 58 356–59

Village Super Market, Inc., 7 563–64

Village Voice Media, Inc., 38 476–79

Villeroy & Boch AG, 37 415–18

Vilmorin Clause et Cie, 70 344–46

AO VimpelCom, 48 416–19

Vin & Spirit AB, 31 458–61 see also V&S Vin & Sprit AB.

Viña Concha y Toro S.A., 45 432–34

Vinci, 27 54; 43 450–52; 49 44

Vincor International Inc., 50 518–21

Vinson & Elkins L.L.P., 30 481–83

Vintage Petroleum, Inc., 42 421–23

Vinton Studios, 63 420–22

Vion Food Group NV, 85 438–41

Virbac Corporation, 74 379–81

Virco Manufacturing Corporation, 17 515–17

Virgin Group Ltd., 12 513–15; 32 491–96 (upd.); 89 479–86 (upd.)

Virginia Dare Extract Company, Inc., 94 447–50

Viridian Group plc, 64 402–04

Visa International, 9 536–38; 26 514–17 (upd.)

Viscofan S.A., 70 347–49

Vishay Intertechnology, Inc., 21 518–21; 80 401–06 (upd.)

Vision Service Plan Inc., 77 473–76

Viskase Companies, Inc., 55 379–81

Vista Bakery, Inc., 56 365–68

Vista Chemical Company, I 402–03

Vistana, Inc., 22 537–39

VistaPrint Limited, 87 451–454

VISX, Incorporated, 30 484–86

Vita Food Products Inc., 99 478–481

Vita Plus Corporation, 60 315–17

Vital Images, Inc., 85 442–45

Vitalink Pharmacy Services, Inc., 15 522–24

Vitamin Shoppe Industries, Inc., 60 318–20

Vitasoy International Holdings Ltd., 94 451–54

Vitesse Semiconductor Corporation, 32 497–500

Vitro Corp., 10 547–48

Vitro Corporativo S.A. de C.V., 34 490–92

Vivarte SA, 54 409–12 (upd.)

Vivartia S.A., 82 407–10

Vivendi Universal S.A., 46 438–41 (upd.)

Vivra, Inc., 18 545–47 see also Gambro AB.

Vlasic Foods International Inc., 25 516–19

VLSI Technology, Inc., 16 518–20

VMware, Inc., 90 428–31

VNU N.V., 27 498–501

Vocento, 94 455–58

Vodafone Group Plc, 11 547–48; 36 503–06 (upd.); 75 395–99 (upd.)

voestalpine AG, IV 233–35; 57 399–403 (upd.)

Voith Sulzer Papiermaschinen GmbH see J.M. Voith AG.

Volcan Compañia Minera S.A.A., 92 403–06

Volcom, Inc., 77 477–80

Volga-Dnepr Group, 82 411–14

Volkert and Associates, Inc., 98 452–55

Volkswagen Aktiengesellschaft, I 206–08; 11 549–51 (upd.); 32 501–05 (upd.)

Volt Information Sciences Inc., 26 518–21

Volunteers of America, Inc., 66 360–62

AB Volvo, I 209–11; 7 565–68 (upd.); 26 9–12 (upd.); 67 378–83 (upd.)

Von Maur Inc., 64 405–08

Vonage Holdings Corp., 81 415–18

The Vons Companies, Incorporated, 7 569–71; 28 510–13 (upd.)

Vontobel Holding AG, 96 450–53

Vornado Realty Trust, 20 508–10

Vorwerk & Co., 27 502–04

Vosper Thornycroft Holding plc, 41 410–12

Vossloh AG, 53 348–52

Votorantim Participaçoes S.A., 76 375–78

Vought Aircraft Industries, Inc., 49 442–45

VSM see Village Super Market, Inc.

VTech Holdings Ltd., 77 481–84

Vueling Airlines S.A., 97 445–48

Vulcan Materials Company, 7 572–75; 52 392–96 (upd.)

W

W + K see Wieden + Kennedy.

W.A. Whitney Company, 53 353–56

W. Atlee Burpee & Co., 27 505–08

W.B Doner & Co., 56 369–72

W.B. Mason Company, 98 456–59

W.C. Bradley Co., 69 363–65

W.H. Brady Co., 16 518–21 see also Brady Corp.

W. H. Braum, Inc., 80 407–10

W H Smith Group PLC, V 211–13

W Jordan (Cereals) Ltd., 74 382–84

W.L. Gore & Associates, Inc., 14 538–40; 60 321–24 (upd.)

W.P. Carey & Co. LLC, 49 446–48

W.R. Berkley Corporation, 15 525–27; 74 385–88 (upd.)

W.R. Grace & Company, I 547–50; 50 522–29 (upd.)

W.W. Grainger, Inc., V 214–15; 26 537–39 (upd.); 68 392–95 (upd.)

W.W. Norton & Company, Inc., 28 518–20

Waban Inc., 13 547–49 see also HomeBase, Inc.

Wabash National Corp., 13 550–52

Wabtec Corporation, 40 451–54

Wachovia Bank of Georgia, N.A., 16 521–23

Wachovia Bank of South Carolina, N.A., 16 524–26

Wachovia Corporation, 12 516–20; 46 442–49 (upd.)

Wachtell, Lipton, Rosen & Katz, 47 435–38

The Wackenhut Corporation, 14 541–43; 63 423–26 (upd.)

Wacker-Chemie GmbH, 35 454–58

Wacker Construction Equipment AG, 95 438–41

Wacoal Corp., 25 520–24

Waddell & Reed, Inc., 22 540–43

Waffle House Inc., 14 544–45; 60 325–27 (upd.)

Wagers Inc. (Idaho Candy Company), 86 416–19

Waggener Edstrom, 42 424–26

Wagon plc, 92 407–10

Wah Chang, 82 415–18

Wahl Clipper Corporation, 86 420–23

Wahoo's Fish Taco, 96 454–57

Wakefern Food Corporation, 33 434–37

Wal-Mart de Mexico, S.A. de C.V., 35 459–61 (upd.)

Wal-Mart Stores, Inc., V 216–17; 8 555–57 (upd.); 26 522–26 (upd.); 63 427–32 (upd.)

Walbridge Aldinger Co., 38 480–82

Walbro Corporation, 13 553–55

Waldbaum, Inc., 19 479–81

Waldenbooks, 17 522–24; 86 424–28 (upd.)

Walgreen Co., V 218–20; 20 511–13 (upd.); 65 352–56 (upd.)

Walker Manufacturing Company, 19 482–84

Walkers Shortbread Ltd., 79 464–67

Walkers Snack Foods Ltd., 70 350–52

Wall Drug Store, Inc., 40 455–57

Wall Street Deli, Inc., 33 438–41

Wallace Computer Services, Inc., 36 507–10

Walsworth Publishing Company, Inc., 78 445–48

The Walt Disney Company, II 172–74; 6 174–77 (upd.); 30 487–91 (upd.); 63 433–38 (upd.)

Walter Industries, Inc., III 765–67; 22 544–47 (upd.); 72 368–73 (upd.)

Walton Monroe Mills, Inc., 8 558–60 *see also* Avondale Industries.

WaMu *see* Washington Mutual, Inc.

Wanadoo S.A., 75 400–02

Wang Laboratories, Inc., III 168–70; 6 284–87 (upd.) *see also* Getronics NV.

Warburtons Ltd., 89 487–90

WARF *see* Wisconsin Alumni Research Foundation.

The Warnaco Group Inc., 12 521–23; 46 450–54 (upd.) *see also* Authentic Fitness Corp.

Warner Chilcott Limited, 85 446–49

Warner Communications Inc., II 175–77 *see also* AOL Time Warner Inc.

Warner-Lambert Co., I 710–12; 10 549–52 (upd.) *see also* Pfizer Inc.

Warner Music Group Corporation, 90 432–37 (upd.)

Warners' Stellian Inc., 67 384–87

Warrantech Corporation, 53 357–59

Warrell Corporation, 68 396–98

Warwick Valley Telephone Company, 55 382–84

Wascana Energy Inc., 13 556–58

The Washington Companies, 33 442–45

Washington Federal, Inc., 17 525–27

Washington Football, Inc., 35 462–65

Washington Gas Light Company, 19 485–88

Washington Mutual, Inc., 17 528–31; 93 483–89 (upd.)

Washington National Corporation, 12 524–26

Washington Natural Gas Company, 9 539–41 *see also* Puget Sound Energy Inc.

The Washington Post Company, IV 688–90; 20 515–18 (upd.)

Washington Scientific Industries, Inc., 17 532–34

Washington Water Power Company, 6 595–98 *see also* Avista Corp.

Wassall Plc, 18 548–50

Waste Connections, Inc., 46 455–57

Waste Holdings, Inc., 41 413–15

Waste Management, Inc., V 752–54

Water Pik Technologies, Inc., 34 498–501; 83 450–453 (upd.)

Waterford Wedgwood plc, 12 527–29; 34 493–97 (upd.)

Waterhouse Investor Services, Inc., 18 551–53

Waters Corporation, 43 453–57

Watkins-Johnson Company, 15 528–30

Watsco Inc., 52 397–400

Watson Pharmaceuticals Inc., 16 527–29; 56 373–76 (upd.)

Watson Wyatt Worldwide, 42 427–30

Wattie's Ltd., 7 576–78

Watts Industries, Inc., 19 489–91

Watts of Lydney Group Ltd., 71 391–93

Wausau-Mosinee Paper Corporation, 60 328–31 (upd.)

Waverly, Inc., 16 530–32

Wawa Inc., 17 535–37; 78 449–52 (upd.)

The Wawanesa Mutual Insurance Company, 68 399–401

Waxman Industries, Inc., 9 542–44

WAZ Media Group, 82 419–24

WB *see* Warner Communications Inc.

WD-40 Company, 18 554–57; 87 455–460 (upd.)

We-No-Nah Canoe, Inc., 98 460–63

The Weather Channel Companies, 52 401–04 *see also* Landmark Communications, Inc.

Weatherford International, Inc., 39 416–18

Weaver Popcorn Company, Inc., 89 491–93

Webasto Roof Systems Inc., 97 449–52

Webber Oil Company, 61 384–86

Weber et Broutin France, 66 363–65

Weber-Stephen Products Co., 40 458–60

WebEx Communications, Inc., 81 419–23

WebMD Corporation, 65 357–60

Weeres Industries Corporation, 52 405–07

Weetabix Limited, 61 387–89

Weg S.A., 78 453–56

Wegener NV, 53 360–62

Wegmans Food Markets, Inc., 9 545–46; 41 416–18 (upd.)

Weider Nutrition International, Inc., 29 498–501

Weight Watchers International Inc., 12 530–32; 33 446–49 (upd.); 73 379–83 (upd.)

Weil, Gotshal & Manges LLP, 55 385–87

Weiner's Stores, Inc., 33 450–53

Wieden + Kennedy, 75 403–05

Wienerberger AG, 70 361–63

Weingarten Realty Investors, 95 442–45

The Weir Group PLC, 85 450–53

Weirton Steel Corporation, IV 236–38; 26 527–30 (upd.)

Weis Markets, Inc., 15 531–33; 84 422–426 (upd.)

The Weitz Company, Inc., 42 431–34

Welbilt Corp., 19 492–94; *see also* Enodis plc.

Welcome Wagon International Inc., 82 425–28

Weleda AG, 78 457–61

The Welk Group, Inc., 78 462–66

Wella AG, III 68–70; 48 420–23 (upd.)

WellChoice, Inc., 67 388–91 (upd.)

Wellco Enterprises, Inc., 84 427–430

Wellcome Foundation Ltd., I 713–15 *see also* GlaxoSmithKline plc.

Wellman, Inc., 8 561–62; 52 408–11 (upd.)

WellPoint Health Networks Inc., 25 525–29

Wells Fargo & Company, II 380–84; 12 533–37 (upd.); 38 483–92 (upd.); 97 453–67

Wells-Gardner Electronics Corporation, 43 458–61

Wells Rich Greene BDDP, 6 50–52

Wells' Dairy, Inc., 36 511–13

Wendell *see* Mark T. Wendell Tea Co.

Wendy's International, Inc., 8 563–65; 23 504–07 (upd.); 47 439–44 (upd.)

Wenner Bread Products Inc., 80 411–15

Wenner Media, Inc., 32 506–09

Werner Enterprises, Inc., 26 531–33

Weru Aktiengesellschaft, 18 558–61

Wessanen *see* Koninklijke Wessanen nv.

West Bend Co., 14 546–48

West Coast Entertainment Corporation, 29 502–04

West Corporation, 42 435–37

West Fraser Timber Co. Ltd., 17 538–40; 91 512–18 (upd.)

West Group, 34 502–06 (upd.)

West Linn Paper Company, 91 519–22

West Marine, Inc., 17 541–43; 90 438–42 (upd.)

West One Bancorp, 11 552–55 *see also* U.S. Bancorp.

West Pharmaceutical Services, Inc., 42 438–41

West Point-Pepperell, Inc., 8 566–69 *see also* WestPoint Stevens Inc.; JPS Textile Group, Inc.

West Publishing Co., 7 579–81

Westaff Inc., 33 454–57

Westamerica Bancorporation, 17 544–47

Westar Energy, Inc., 57 404–07 (upd.)

WestCoast Hospitality Corporation, 59 410–13

Westcon Group, Inc., 67 392–94

Westdeutsche Landesbank Girozentrale, II 385–87; 46 458–61 (upd.)

Westell Technologies, Inc., 57 408–10

Western Atlas Inc., 12 538–40

Western Beef, Inc., 22 548–50

Western Company of North America, 15 534–36

Western Digital Corporation, 25 530–32; 92 411–15 (upd.)

Western Gas Resources, Inc., 45 435–37

Western Oil Sands Inc., 85 454–57

Western Publishing Group, Inc., 13 559–61 *see also* Thomson Corp.

Western Resources, Inc., 12 541–43

The WesterN SizzliN Corporation, 60 335–37

Western Union Financial Services, Inc., 54 413–16

Western Wireless Corporation, 36 514–16

Westfield Group, 69 366–69

Westin Hotels and Resorts Worldwide, 9 547–49; 29 505–08 (upd.)

Westinghouse Electric Corporation, II 120–22; 12 544–47 (upd.) *see also* CBS Radio Group.

WestJet Airlines Ltd., 38 493–95

Westmoreland Coal Company, 7 582–85

Weston Foods Inc. *see* George Weston Ltd.

Westpac Banking Corporation, II
388–90; 48 424–27 (upd.)

WestPoint Stevens Inc., 16 533–36 *see
also* JPS Textile Group, Inc.

Westport Resources Corporation, 63
439–41

Westvaco Corporation, IV 351–54; 19
495–99 (upd.) *see also* MeadWestvaco
Corp.

Westwood One, Inc., 23 508–11

The Wet Seal, Inc., 18 562–64; 70
353–57 (upd.)

Wetterau Incorporated, II 681–82 *see
also* Supervalu Inc.

Weyco Group, Incorporated, 32 510–13

Weyerhaeuser Company, IV 355–56; 9
550–52 (upd.); 28 514–17 (upd.); 83
454-461 (upd.)

WFS Financial Inc., 70 358–60

WFSC *see* World Fuel Services Corp.

WGBH Educational Foundation, 66
366–68

WH Smith PLC, 42 442–47 (upd.)

Wham-O, Inc., 61 390–93

Whatman plc, 46 462–65

Wheaton Industries, 8 570–73

Wheaton Science Products, 60 338–42
(upd.)

Wheelabrator Technologies, Inc., 6
599–600; 60 343–45 (upd.)

Wheeling-Pittsburgh Corporation, 7
586–88; 58 360–64 (upd.)

Wheels Inc., 96 458–61

Wherehouse Entertainment
Incorporated, 11 556–58

Whirlpool Corporation, III 653–55; 12
548–50 (upd.); 59 414–19 (upd.)

Whitbread PLC, I 293–94; 20 519–22
(upd.); 52 412–17 (upd.); 97 468–76
(upd.)

White & Case LLP, 35 466–69

White Castle Management Company,
12 551–53; 36 517–20 (upd.); 85
458–64 (upd.)

White Consolidated Industries Inc., 13
562–64 *see also* Electrolux.

The White House, Inc., 60 346–48

White Lily Foods Company, 88 435–38

White Mountains Insurance Group,
Ltd., 48 428–31

White Rose, Inc., 24 527–29

White Wave, 43 462–64

Whitehall Jewellers, Inc., 82 429–34
(upd.)

Whiting Petroleum Corporation, 81
424–27

Whiting-Turner Contracting Company,
95 446–49

Whitman Corporation, 10 553–55
(upd.) *see also* PepsiAmericas, Inc.

Whitman Education Group, Inc., 41
419–21

Whitney Holding Corporation, 21
522–24

Whittaker Corporation, I 544–46; 48
432–35 (upd.)

Whittard of Chelsea Plc, 61 394–97

Whole Foods Market, Inc., 20 523–27;
50 530–34 (upd.)

WHX Corporation, 98 464–67

Wickes Inc., V 221–23; 25 533–36
(upd.)

Widmer Brothers Brewing Company, 76
379–82

Wikimedia Foundation, Inc., 91 523–26

Wilbert, Inc., 56 377–80

Wilbur Chocolate Company, 66 369–71

Wilco Farm Stores, 93 490–93

Wild Oats Markets, Inc., 19 500–02; 41
422–25 (upd.)

Wildlife Conservation Society, 31
462–64

Wilh. Wilhelmsen ASA, 94 459–62

Wilhelm Karmann GmbH, 94 463–68

Wilkinson Hardware Stores Ltd., 80
416–18

Wilkinson Sword Ltd., 60 349–52

Willamette Industries, Inc., IV 357–59;
31 465–68 (upd.) *see also*
Weyerhaeuser Co.

Willamette Valley Vineyards, Inc., 85
465–69

Willbros Group, Inc., 56 381–83

William Grant & Sons Ltd., 60 353–55

William Hill Organization Limited, 49
449–52

William L. Bonnell Company, Inc., 66
372–74

William Lyon Homes, 59 420–22

William Morris Agency, Inc., 23 512–14

William Reed Publishing Ltd., 78
467–70

William Zinsser & Company, Inc., 58
365–67

Williams & Connolly LLP, 47 445–48

Williams Communications Group, Inc.,
34 507–10

The Williams Companies, Inc., IV
575–76; 31 469–72 (upd.)

Williams Scotsman, Inc., 65 361–64

Williams-Sonoma, Inc., 17 548–50; 44
447–50 (upd.)

Williamson-Dickie Manufacturing
Company, 14 549–50; 45 438–41
(upd.)

Willis Corroon Group plc, 25 537–39

Willkie Farr & Gallagher LLPLP, 95
450–53

Wilmington Trust Corporation, 25
540–43

Wilson Bowden Plc, 45 442–44

Wilson Sonsini Goodrich & Rosati, 34
511–13

Wilson Sporting Goods Company, 24
530–32; 84 431–436 (upd.)

Wilsons The Leather Experts Inc., 21
525–27; 58 368–71 (upd.)

Wilton Products, Inc., 97 477–80

Winbond Electronics Corporation, 74
389–91

Wincanton plc, 52 418–20

Winchell's Donut Houses Operating
Company, L.P., 60 356–59

WinCo Foods Inc., 60 360–63

Wincor Nixdorf Holding GmbH, 69
370–73 (upd.)

Wind River Systems, Inc., 37 419–22

Windmere Corporation, 16 537–39 *see
also* Applica Inc.

Windstream Corporation, 83 462-465

Windswept Environmental Group, Inc.,
62 389–92

The Wine Group, Inc., 39 419–21

Winegard Company, 56 384–87

Winmark Corporation, 74 392–95

Winn-Dixie Stores, Inc., II 683–84; 21
528–30 (upd.); 59 423–27 (upd.)

Winnebago Industries, Inc., 7 589–91;
27 509–12 (upd.); 96 462–67 (upd.)

WinsLoew Furniture, Inc., 21 531–33
see also Brown Jordan International Inc.

Winston & Strawn, 35 470–73

Winterthur Group, III 402–04; 68
402–05 (upd.)

Wipro Limited, 43 465–68

The Wiremold Company, 81 428–34

Wirtz Corporation, 72 374–76

Wisconsin Alumni Research
Foundation, 65 365–68

Wisconsin Bell, Inc., 14 551–53 *see also*
AT&T Corp.

Wisconsin Central Transportation
Corporation, 24 533–36

Wisconsin Dairies, 7 592–93

Wisconsin Energy Corporation, 6
601–03; 54 417–21 (upd.)

Wisconsin Public Service Corporation,
9 553–54 *see also* WPS Resources
Corp.

Wise Foods, Inc., 79 468–71

Witco Corporation, I 404–06; 16
540–43 (upd.) *see also* Chemtura Corp.

Witness Systems, Inc., 87 461–465

Wizards of the Coast Inc., 24 537–40

WLR Foods, Inc., 21 534–36

Wm. B. Reily & Company Inc., 58
372–74

Wm. Morrison Supermarkets PLC, 38
496–98

Wm. Wrigley Jr. Company, 7 594–97;
58 375–79 (upd.)

WMC, Limited, 43 469–72

WMF *see* Württembergische
Metallwarenfabrik AG (WMF).

WMS Industries, Inc., 15 537–39; 53
363–66 (upd.)

WMX Technologies Inc., 17 551–54

Wolfgang Puck Worldwide, Inc., 26
534–36; 70 364–67 (upd.)

Wolohan Lumber Co., 19 503–05 *see
also* Lanoga Corp.

Wolseley plc, 64 409–12

Wolters Kluwer NV, 14 554–56; 33
458–61 (upd.)

The Wolverhampton & Dudley
Breweries, PLC, 57 411–14

Wolverine Tube Inc., 23 515–17

Wolverine World Wide, Inc., 16
544–47; 59 428–33 (upd.)

Womble Carlyle Sandridge & Rice,
PLLC, 52 421–24

Wood Hall Trust plc, I 592–93

Wood-Mode, Inc., 23 518–20
Woodbridge Holdings Corporation, 99 482–485
Woodcraft Industries Inc., 61 398–400
Woodward Governor Company, 13 565–68; 49 453–57 (upd.)
Woolrich Inc., 62 393–96
The Woolwich plc, 30 492–95
Woolworth Corporation, V 224–27; 20 528–32 (upd.) *see also* Kingfisher plc; Venator Group Inc.
Woolworths Group plc, 83 466–473
WordPerfect Corporation, 10 556–59 *see also* Corel Corp.
Workflow Management, Inc., 65 369–72
Working Assets Funding Service, 43 473–76
Workman Publishing Company, Inc., 70 368–71
World Acceptance Corporation, 57 415–18
World Bank Group, 33 462–65
World Book, Inc., 12 554–56
World Color Press Inc., 12 557–59 *see also* Quebecor Inc.
World Duty Free Americas, Inc., 29 509–12 (upd.)
World Fuel Services Corporation, 47 449–51
World Publications, LLC, 65 373–75
World Vision International, Inc., 93 494–97
World Wide Technology, Inc., 94 469–72
World Wrestling Federation Entertainment, Inc., 32 514–17
World's Finest Chocolate Inc., 39 422–24
WorldCorp, Inc., 10 560–62
Worldwide Pants Inc., 97 481–84
Worldwide Restaurant Concepts, Inc., 47 452–55
Worms et Cie, 27 513–15 *see also* Sequana Capital.
Worthington Foods, Inc., 14 557–59 *see also* Kellogg Co.
Worthington Industries, Inc., 7 598–600; 21 537–40 (upd.)
WPL Holdings, 6 604–06
WPP Group plc, 6 53–54; 48 440–42 (upd.) *see also* Ogilvy Group Inc.
WPS Resources Corporation, 53 367–70 (upd.)
Wray & Nephew Group Ltd., 98 468–71
WRG *see* Wells Rich Greene BDDP.
Wright Express Corporation, 80 419–22
Wright Medical Group, Inc., 61 401–05
Writers Guild of America, West, Inc., 92 416–20
WS Atkins Plc, 45 445–47
WTD Industries, Inc., 20 533–36
Wunderman, 86 429–32
Württembergische Metallwarenfabrik AG (WMF), 60 364–69
WVT Communications *see* Warwick Valley Telephone Co.
Wyant Corporation, 30 496–98

Wyeth, 50 535–39 (upd.)
Wyle Electronics, 14 560–62 *see also* Arrow Electronics, Inc.
Wyman-Gordon Company, 14 563–65
Wyndham Worldwide Corporation, 99 486–493 (upd.)
Wynn's International, Inc., 33 466–70
Wyse Technology, Inc., 15 540–42

X

X-Rite, Inc., 48 443–46
Xantrex Technology Inc., 97 485–88
Xcel Energy Inc., 73 384–89 (upd.)
Xeikon NV, 26 540–42
Xerium Technologies, Inc., 94 473–76
Xerox Corporation, III 171–73; 6 288–90 (upd.); 26 543–47 (upd.); 69 374–80 (upd.)
Xilinx, Inc., 16 548–50; 82 435–39 (upd.)
XM Satellite Radio Holdings, Inc., 69 381–84
Xstrata PLC, 73 390–93
XTO Energy Inc., 52 425–27

Y

Yageo Corporation, 16 551–53; 98 472–75 (upd.)
Yahoo! Inc., 27 516–19; 70 372–75 (upd.)
Yamada Denki Co., Ltd., 85 470–73
Yamaha Corporation, III 656–59; 16 554–58 (upd.); 40 461–66 (upd.); 99 494–501 (upd.)
Yamaichi Securities Company, Limited, II 458–59
Yamato Transport Co. Ltd., V 536–38; 49 458–61 (upd.)
Yamazaki Baking Co., Ltd., 58 380–82
The Yankee Candle Company, Inc., 37 423–26; 38 192
YankeeNets LLC, 35 474–77
Yara International ASA, 94 477–81
Yarnell Ice Cream Company, Inc., 92 421–24
Yasuda Fire and Marine Insurance Company, Limited, III 405–07 *see also* Sompo Japan Insurance, Inc.
Yasuda Mutual Life Insurance Company, III 408–09; 39 425–28 (upd.)
The Yasuda Trust and Banking Company, Limited, II 391–92; 17 555–57 (upd.)
The Yates Companies, Inc., 62 397–99
Yell Group PLC, 79 472–75
Yellow Corporation, 14 566–68; 45 448–51 (upd.) *see also* YRC Worldwide Inc.
Yellow Freight System, Inc. of Deleware, V 539–41
Yeo Hiap Seng Malaysia Bhd., 75 406–09
YES! Entertainment Corporation, 26 548–50
YMCA of the USA, 31 473–76
YOCREAM International, Inc., 47 456–58

Yokado Co. Ltd *see* Ito-Yokado Co. Ltd.
The Yokohama Rubber Company, Limited, V 254–56; 19 506–09 (upd.); 91 527–33 (upd.)
The York Group, Inc., 50 540–43
York International Corp., 13 569–71; *see also* Johnson Controls, Inc.
York Research Corporation, 35 478–80
Yoshinoya D & C Company Ltd., 88 439–42
Youbet.com, Inc., 77 485–88
Young & Co.'s Brewery, P.L.C., 38 499–502
Young & Rubicam, Inc., I 36–38; 22 551–54 (upd.); 66 375–78 (upd.)
Young Broadcasting Inc., 40 467–69
Young Innovations, Inc., 44 451–53
Young's Bluecrest Seafood Holdings Ltd., 81 435–39
Young's Market Company, LLC, 32 518–20
Younkers, 76 19 510–12; 383–86 (upd.)
Youth Services International, Inc., 21 541–43; 30 146
YouTube, Inc., 90 443–46
YPF Sociedad Anónima, IV 577–78 *see also* Repsol-YPF S.A.
YRC Worldwide Inc., 90 447–55 (upd.)
The Yucaipa Cos., 17 558–62
YUKOS *see* OAO NK YUKOS.
Yule Catto & Company plc, 54 422–25
Yum! Brands Inc., 58 383–85
Yves Rocher *see* Laboratoires de Biologie Végétale Yves Rocher.
YWCA of the U.S.A., 45 452–54

Z

Zachry Group, Inc., 95 454–57
Zacky Farms LLC, 74 396–98
Zale Corporation, 16 559–61; 40 470–74 (upd.); 91 534–41 (upd.)
Zambia Industrial and Mining Corporation Ltd., IV 239–41
Zamboni *see* Frank J. Zamboni & Co., Inc.
Zanett, Inc., 92 425–28
Zany Brainy, Inc., 31 477–79
Zapata Corporation, 25 544–46
Zapf Creation AG, 95 458–61
Zappos.com, Inc., 73 394–96
Zara International, Inc., 83 474–477
Zatarain's, Inc., 64 413–15
ZCMI *see* Zion's Cooperative Mercantile Institution.
Zebra Technologies Corporation, 14 569–71; 53 371–74 (upd.)
Zed Group, 93 498–501
Zeneca Group PLC, 21 544–46 *see also* AstraZeneca PLC.
Zenith Data Systems, Inc., 10 563–65
Zenith Electronics Corporation, II 123–25; 13 572–75 (upd.); 34 514–19 (upd.); 89 494–502 (upd.)
Zentiva N.V./Zentiva, a.s., 99 502–506
ZERO Corporation, 17 563–65; 88 443–47 (upd.)
ZF Friedrichshafen AG, 48 447–51

Ziebart International Corporation, 30 499–501; 66 379–82 (upd.)
The Ziegler Companies, Inc., 24 541–45; 63 442–48 (upd.)
Ziff Davis Media Inc., 12 560–63; 36 521–26 (upd.); 73 397–403 (upd.)
Zila, Inc., 46 466–69
Zildjian *see* Avedis Zildjian Co.
ZiLOG, Inc., 15 543–45; 72 377–80 (upd.)
Zimmer Holdings, Inc., 45 455–57
Zindart Ltd., 60 370–72
Zingerman's Community of Businesses, 68 406–08
Zinifex Ltd., 85 474–77

Zinsser *see* William Zinsser & Company, Inc.
Zion's Cooperative Mercantile Institution, 33 471–74
Zions Bancorporation, 12 564–66; 53 375–78 (upd.)
Zipcar, Inc., 92 429–32
Zippo Manufacturing Company, 18 565–68; 71 394–99 (upd.)
Zodiac S.A., 36 527–30
Zogby International, Inc., 99 507–510
Zoltek Companies, Inc., 37 427–30
Zomba Records Ltd., 52 428–31
Zondervan Corporation, 24 546–49; 71 400–04 (upd.)

Zones, Inc., 67 395–97
Zoom Technologies, Inc., 18 569–71; 53 379–82 (upd.)
Zoran Corporation, 77 489–92
The Zubair Corporation L.L.C., 96 468–72
Zuffa L.L.C., 89 503–07
Zumiez, Inc., 77 493–96
Zumtobel AG, 50 544–48
Zurich Financial Services, III 410–12; 42 448–53 (upd.); 93 502–10 (upd.)
Zygo Corporation, 42 454–57
Zytec Corporation, 19 513–15 *see also* Artesyn Technologies Inc.

Index to Industries

Accounting

American Institute of Certified Public
    Accountants (AICPA), 44
Andersen, 29 (upd.); 68 (upd.)
Automatic Data Processing, Inc., III; 9
    (upd.); 47 (upd.)
BDO Seidman LLP, 96
BKD LLP, 96
CROSSMARK, 79
Deloitte Touche Tohmatsu International,
    9; 29 (upd.)
Ernst & Young, 9; 29 (upd.)
FTI Consulting, Inc., 77
Grant Thornton International, 57
Huron Consulting Group Inc., 87
KPMG International, 33 (upd.)
L.S. Starrett Co., 13
McLane Company, Inc., 13
NCO Group, Inc., 42
Paychex, Inc., 15; 46 (upd.)
PKF International 78
Plante & Moran, LLP, 71
PRG-Schultz International, Inc., 73
PricewaterhouseCoopers, 9; 29 (upd.)
Resources Connection, Inc., 81
Robert Wood Johnson Foundation, 35
RSM McGladrey Business Services Inc.,
    98
Saffery Champness, 80
Sanders\Wingo, 99
Schenck Business Solutions, 88
StarTek, Inc., 79
Travelzoo Inc., 79

Univision Communications Inc., 24; 83
    (upd.)

Advertising & Other Business Services

ABM Industries Incorporated, 25 (upd.)
Abt Associates Inc., 95
AchieveGlobal Inc., 90
Ackerley Communications, Inc., 9
ACNielsen Corporation, 13; 38 (upd.)
Acosta Sales and Marketing Company,
    Inc., 77
Acsys, Inc., 44
Adecco S.A., 36 (upd.)
Adia S.A., 6
Administaff, Inc., 52
The Advertising Council, Inc., 76
The Advisory Board Company, 80
Advo, Inc., 6; 53 (upd.)
Aegis Group plc, 6
Affiliated Computer Services, Inc., 61
AHL Services, Inc., 27
Allegis Group, Inc., 95
Alloy, Inc., 55
Amdocs Ltd., 47
American Building Maintenance
    Industries, Inc., 6
American Library Association, 86
The American Society of Composers,
    Authors and Publishers (ASCAP), 29
Amey Plc, 47
Analysts International Corporation, 36
aQuantive, Inc., 81
The Arbitron Company, 38
Ariba, Inc., 57
Armor Holdings, Inc., 27
Asatsu-DK Inc., 82
Ashtead Group plc, 34

The Associated Press, 13
Avalon Correctional Services, Inc., 75
Bain & Company, 55
Barrett Business Services, Inc., 16
Barton Protective Services Inc., 53
Bates Worldwide, Inc., 14; 33 (upd.)
Bearings, Inc., 13
Berlitz International, Inc., 13
Bernard Hodes Group Inc., 86
Bernstein-Rein, 92
Big Flower Press Holdings, Inc., 21
Billing Concepts, Inc., 26; 72 (upd.)
The BISYS Group, Inc., 73
Boron, LePore & Associates, Inc., 45
The Boston Consulting Group, 58
Bozell Worldwide Inc., 25
BrandPartners Group, Inc., 58
Bright Horizons Family Solutions, Inc., 31
Broadcast Music Inc., 23; 90 (upd.)
Buck Consultants, Inc., 55
Bureau Veritas SA, 55
Burke, Inc., 88
Burns International Services Corporation,
    13; 41 (upd.)
Cambridge Technology Partners, Inc., 36
Campbell-Ewald Advertising, 86
Campbell-Mithun-Esty, Inc., 16
Cannon Design, 63
Capita Group PLC, 69
Cardtronics, Inc., 93
Career Education Corporation, 45
Carmichael Lynch Inc., 28
Cash Systems, Inc., 93
Cazenove Group plc, 72
CCC Information Services Group Inc., 74
CDI Corporation, 6; 54 (upd.)
Central Parking Corporation, 18
Century Business Services, Inc., 52
Chancellor Beacon Academies, Inc., 53

ChartHouse International Learning Corporation, 49
Chiat/Day Inc. Advertising, 11
Chicago Board of Trade, 41
Chisholm-Mingo Group, Inc., 41
Christie's International plc, 15; 39 (upd.)
Cintas Corporation, 21
CMG Worldwide, Inc., 89
COMFORCE Corporation, 40
Command Security Corporation, 57
Computer Learning Centers, Inc., 26
Concentra Inc., 71
Corporate Express, Inc., 47 (upd.)
CoolSavings, Inc., 77
The Corporate Executive Board Company, 89
CORT Business Services Corporation, 26
Cox Enterprises, Inc., 22 (upd.)
CRA International, Inc., 93
craigslist, inc., 89
Creative Artists Agency LLC, 38
Crispin Porter + Bogusky, 83
CSG Systems International, Inc., 75
Cyrk Inc., 19
Daiko Advertising Inc., 79
Dale Carnegie & Associates Inc. 28; 78 (upd.)
D'Arcy Masius Benton & Bowles, Inc., 6; 32 (upd.)
Dawson Holdings PLC, 43
DDB Needham Worldwide, 14
Deluxe Corporation, 22 (upd.); 73 (upd.)
Dentsu Inc., I; 16 (upd.); 40 (upd.)
Deutsch, Inc., 42
Deutsche Post AG, 29
DeVito/Verdi, 85
Dewberry 78
DHL Worldwide Network S.A./N.V., 69 (upd.)
Digitas Inc., 81
DoubleClick Inc., 46
Draftfcb, 94
Drake Beam Morin, Inc., 44
The Dun & Bradstreet Corporation, 61 (upd.)
Earl Scheib, Inc., 32
eBay Inc., 67 (upd.)
EBSCO Industries, Inc., 17
Ecolab Inc., I; 13 (upd.); 34 (upd.); 85 (upd.)
Ecology and Environment, Inc., 39
Edelman, 62
Edison Schools Inc., 37
Educate Inc., 86 (upd.)
Education Management Corporation, 35
Electro Rent Corporation, 58
Employee Solutions, Inc., 18
Ennis, Inc., 21; 97 (upd.)
Equifax Inc., 6; 28 (upd.); 90 (upd.)
Equity Marketing, Inc., 26
ERLY Industries Inc., 17
Euro RSCG Worldwide S.A., 13
Expedia, Inc., 58
Fallon Worldwide, 22; 71 (upd.)
FileNet Corporation, 62
Finarte Casa d'Aste S.p.A., 93
Fiserv, Inc., 33 (upd.)
FlightSafety International, Inc., 29 (upd.)

Florists' Transworld Delivery, Inc., 28
Foote, Cone & Belding Worldwide, I; 66 (upd.)
Forrester Research, Inc., 54
Frankel & Co., 39
Franklin Covey Company, 37 (upd.)
Freeze.com LLC, 77
Frost & Sullivan, Inc., 53
FTI Consulting, Inc., 77
Gage Marketing Group, 26
The Gallup Organization, 37
Gartner, Inc., 21; 94 (upd.)
GEMA (Gesellschaft für musikalische Aufführungs- und mechanische Vervielfältigungsrechte), 70
General Employment Enterprises, Inc., 87
George P. Johnson Company, 60
George S. May International Company, 55
Gevity HR, Inc., 63
GfK Aktiengesellschaft, 49
Glotel plc, 53
Golin/Harris International, Inc., 88
Goodby Silverstein & Partners, Inc., 75
Grey Global Group Inc., 6; 66 (upd.)
Group 4 Falck A/S, 42
Groupe Crit S.A., 74
Groupe Jean-Claude Darmon, 44
GSD&M Advertising, 44
GSD&M's Idea City, 90
GSI Commerce, Inc., 67
Guardsmark, L.L.C., 77
Gwathmey Siegel & Associates Architects LLC, 26
Ha-Lo Industries, Inc., 27
Hakuhodo, Inc., 6; 42 (upd.)
Hall, Kinion & Associates, Inc., 52
Handleman Company, 15; 86 (upd.)
Harris Interactive Inc., 41; 92 (upd.)
Harte-Hanks, Inc., 63 (upd.)
Havas SA, 33 (upd.)
Hays plc, 27; 78 (upd.)
Headway Corporate Resources, Inc., 40
Heidrick & Struggles International, Inc., 28
Henry Dreyfuss Associates LLC, 88
Hewitt Associates, Inc., 77
Hildebrandt International, 29
Idearc Inc., 90
IKON Office Solutions, Inc., 50
IMS Health, Inc., 57
Interbrand Corporation, 70
Interep National Radio Sales Inc., 35
International Brotherhood of Teamsters, 37
International Management Group, 18
International Profit Associates, Inc., 87
International Total Services, Inc., 37
The Interpublic Group of Companies, Inc., I; 22 (upd.); 75 (upd.)
Intertek Group plc, 95
inVentiv Health, Inc., 81
Ipsos SA, 48
Iron Mountain, Inc., 33
ITT Educational Services, Inc., 39; 76 (upd.)
J.D. Power and Associates, 32
Jack Morton Worldwide, 88

Jackson Hewitt, Inc., 48
Jani-King International, Inc., 85
Japan Leasing Corporation, 8
JCDecaux S.A., 76
Jostens, Inc., 25 (upd.)
JOULÉ Inc., 58
JWT Group Inc., I
Katz Communications, Inc., 6
Katz Media Group, Inc., 35
Keane, Inc., 56
Kelly Services Inc., 6; 26 (upd.)
Ketchum Communications Inc., 6
Kforce Inc., 71
Kinko's Inc., 16; 43 (upd.)
Kirshenbaum Bond + Partners, Inc., 57
Kohn Pedersen Fox Associates P.C., 57
Korn/Ferry International, 34
Kroll Inc., 57
L. M. Berry and Company, 80
Labor Ready, Inc., 29; 88 (upd.)
Lamar Advertising Company, 27; 70 (upd.)
Landor Associates, 81
Le Cordon Bleu S.A., 67
Learning Care Group, Inc., 76 (upd.)
Learning Tree International Inc., 24
LECG Corporation, 93
Leo Burnett Company Inc., I; 20 (upd.)
The Leona Group LLC, 84
Lintas: Worldwide, 14
LivePerson, Inc., 91
Mail Boxes Etc., 18; 41 (upd.)
Manhattan Associates, Inc., 67
Manning Selvage & Lee (MS&L), 76
Manpower Inc., 30 (upd.); 73 (upd.)
Marchex, Inc., 72
marchFIRST, Inc., 34
Marco Business Products, Inc., 75
Maritz Inc., 38
Marlin Business Services Corp., 89
MAXIMUS, Inc., 43
MDC Partners Inc., 63
Mediaset SpA, 50
Milliman USA, 66
MIVA, Inc., 83
Monster Worldwide Inc., 74 (upd.)
Moody's Corporation, 65
MPS Group, Inc., 49
Mullen Advertising Inc., 51
Napster, Inc., 69
National Equipment Services, Inc., 57
National Media Corporation, 27
Navigant Consulting, Inc., 93
NAVTEQ Corporation, 69
Neopost S.A., 53
New England Business Services Inc., 18; 78 (upd.)
New Valley Corporation, 17
NFO Worldwide, Inc., 24
Nobel Learning Communities, Inc., 37; 76 (upd.)
Norrell Corporation, 25
Norwood Promotional Products, Inc., 26
The NPD Group, Inc., 68
O.C. Tanner Co., 69
Oakleaf Waste Management, LLC, 97
Obie Media Corporation, 56
Observer AB, 55

OfficeTiger, LLC, 75
The Ogilvy Group, Inc., I
Olsten Corporation, 6; 29 (upd.)
Omnicom Group, I; 22 (upd.); 77 (upd.)
On Assignment, Inc., 20
1-800-FLOWERS, Inc., 26
Opinion Research Corporation, 46
Oracle Corporation, 67 (upd.)
Orbitz, Inc., 61
Outdoor Systems, Inc., 25
Paris Corporation, 22
Paychex, Inc., 15; 46 (upd.)
PDI, Inc., 52
Pegasus Solutions, Inc., 75
Pei Cobb Freed & Partners Architects
    LLP, 57
Penauille Polyservices SA, 49
PFSweb, Inc., 73
Philip Services Corp., 73
Phillips, de Pury & Luxembourg, 49
Pierce Leahy Corporation, 24
Pinkerton's Inc., 9
Plante & Moran, LLP, 71
PMT Services, Inc., 24
Posterscope Worldwide, 70
Priceline.com Incorporated, 57
Publicis Groupe, 19; 77 (upd.)
Publishers Clearing House, 23; 64 (upd.)
Quintiles Transnational Corporation, 68
    (upd.)
Quovadx Inc., 70
Randstad Holding n.v., 16; 43 (upd.)
RedPeg Marketing, 73
RedPrairie Corporation, 74
RemedyTemp, Inc., 20
Rental Service Corporation, 28
Rentokil Initial Plc, 47
Research Triangle Institute, 83
Resources Connection, Inc., 81
Rewards Network Inc., 70 (upd.)
The Richards Group, Inc., 58
Right Management Consultants, Inc., 42
Ritchie Bros. Auctioneers Inc., 41
Robert Half International Inc., 18
Roland Berger & Partner GmbH, 37
Ronco Corporation, 15; 80 (upd.)
Russell Reynolds Associates Inc., 38
Saatchi & Saatchi, I; 42 (upd.)
Sanders\Wingo, 99
Schenck Business Solutions, 88
Securitas AB, 42
ServiceMaster Limited Partnership, 6
Servpro Industries, Inc., 85
Shared Medical Systems Corporation, 14
Sir Speedy, Inc., 16
Skidmore, Owings & Merrill LLP, 13; 69
    (upd.)
SmartForce PLC, 43
SOS Staffing Services, 25
Sotheby's Holdings, Inc., 11; 29 (upd.);
    84 (upd.)
Source Interlink Companies, Inc., 75
Spencer Stuart and Associates, Inc., 14
Spherion Corporation, 52
Steiner Corporation (Alsco), 53
Strayer Education, Inc., 53
Superior Uniform Group, Inc., 30
Sykes Enterprises, Inc., 45

Sylvan Learning Systems, Inc., 35
Synchronoss Technologies, Inc., 95
TA Triumph-Adler AG, 48
Taylor Nelson Sofres plc, 34
TBA Global, LLC, 99
TBWA/Chiat/Day, 6; 43 (upd.)
Thomas Cook Travel Inc., 33 (upd.)
Ticketmaster, 76 (upd.)
Ticketmaster Group, Inc., 13; 37 (upd.)
TMP Worldwide Inc., 30
TNT Post Group N.V., 30
Towers Perrin, 32
Trader Classified Media N.V., 57
Traffix, Inc., 61
Transmedia Network Inc., 20
Treasure Chest Advertising Company, Inc.,
    32
TRM Copy Centers Corporation, 18
True North Communications Inc., 23
24/7 Real Media, Inc., 49
Tyler Corporation, 23
U.S. Office Products Company, 25
Unica Corporation, 77
UniFirst Corporation, 21
United Business Media plc, 52 (upd.)
United News & Media plc, 28 (upd.)
Unitog Co., 19
Valassis Communications, Inc., 37 (upd.);
    76 (upd.)
ValleyCrest Companies, 81 (upd.)
ValueClick, Inc., 49
Vebego International BV, 49
Vedior NV, 35
Vertis Communications, 84
Vertrue Inc., 77
Viad Corp., 73
W.B Doner & Co., 56
The Wackenhut Corporation, 14; 63
    (upd.)
Waggener Edstrom, 42
Warrantech Corporation, 53
WebEx Communications, Inc., 81
Welcome Wagon International Inc., 82
Wells Rich Greene BDDP, 6
Westaff Inc., 33
Whitman Education Group, Inc., 41
Wieden + Kennedy, 75
William Morris Agency, Inc., 23
Williams Scotsman, Inc., 65
Workflow Management, Inc., 65
WPP Group plc, 6; 48 (upd.)
Wunderman, 86
Xerox Corporation, III; 6 (upd.); 26
    (upd.); 69 (upd.)
Young & Rubicam, Inc., I; 22 (upd.); 66
    (upd.)
Zogby International, Inc., 99

Aerospace

A.S. Yakovlev Design Bureau, 15
Aerojet-General Corp., 63
Aeronca Inc., 46
Aerosonic Corporation, 69
The Aerospatiale Group, 7; 21 (upd.)
AeroVironment, Inc., 97
AgustaWestland N.V., 75
Airborne Systems Group, 89
Alliant Techsystems Inc., 30 (upd.)

Antonov Design Bureau, 53
Arianespace S.A., 89
Aviacionny Nauchno-Tehnicheskii
    Komplex im. A.N. Tupoleva, 24
Aviall, Inc., 73
Avions Marcel Dassault-Breguet Aviation,
    I
B/E Aerospace, Inc., 30
Ballistic Recovery Systems, Inc., 87
Banner Aerospace, Inc., 14
BBA Aviation plc, 90
Beech Aircraft Corporation, 8
Bell Helicopter Textron Inc., 46
The Boeing Company, I; 10 (upd.); 32
    (upd.)
Bombardier Inc., 42 (upd.); 87 (upd.)
British Aerospace plc, I; 24 (upd.)
CAE USA Inc., 48
Canadair, Inc., 16
Cessna Aircraft Company, 8
Cirrus Design Corporation, 44
Cobham plc, 30
CPI Aerostructures, Inc., 75
Daimler-Benz Aerospace AG, 16
DeCrane Aircraft Holdings Inc., 36
Derco Holding Ltd., 98
Diehl Stiftung & Co. KG, 79
Ducommun Incorporated, 30
Duncan Aviation, Inc., 94
EADS SOCATA, 54
Eclipse Aviation Corporation, 87
EGL, Inc., 59
Empresa Brasileira de Aeronáutica S.A.
    (Embraer), 36
European Aeronautic Defence and Space
    Company EADS N.V., 52 (upd.)
Fairchild Aircraft, Inc., 9
Fairchild Dornier GmbH, 48 (upd.)
Finmeccanica S.p.A., 84
First Aviation Services Inc., 49
G.I.E. Airbus Industrie, I; 12 (upd.)
General Dynamics Corporation, I; 10
    (upd.); 40 (upd.); 88 (upd.)
GKN plc, III; 38 (upd.); 89 (upd.)
Goodrich Corporation, 46 (upd.)
Groupe Dassault Aviation SA, 26 (upd.)
Grumman Corporation, I; 11 (upd.)
Grupo Aeropuerto del Sureste, S.A. de
    C.V., 48
Gulfstream Aerospace Corporation, 7; 28
    (upd.)
HEICO Corporation, 30
International Lease Finance Corporation,
    48
Irkut Corporation, 68
Israel Aircraft Industries Ltd., 69
Kolbenschmidt Pierburg AG, 97
N.V. Koninklijke Nederlandse
    Vliegtuigenfabriek Fokker, I; 28 (upd.)
Kreisler Manufacturing Corporation, 97
Lancair International, Inc., 67
Learjet Inc., 8; 27 (upd.)
Lockheed Martin Corporation, I; 11
    (upd.); 15 (upd.); 89 (upd.)
Loral Space & Communications Ltd., 54
    (upd.)
Magellan Aerospace Corporation, 48
Martin Marietta Corporation, I

Martin-Baker Aircraft Company Limited, 61
McDonnell Douglas Corporation, I; 11 (upd.)
Meggitt PLC, 34
Messerschmitt-Bölkow-Blohm GmbH., I
Moog Inc., 13
Mooney Aerospace Group Ltd., 52
The New Piper Aircraft, Inc., 44
Northrop Grumman Corporation, I; 11 (upd.); 45 (upd.)
Orbital Sciences Corporation, 22
Pemco Aviation Group Inc., 54
Pratt & Whitney, 9
Raytheon Aircraft Holdings Inc., 46
Robinson Helicopter Company, 51
Rockwell International Corporation, I; 11 (upd.)
Rolls-Royce Allison, 29 (upd.)
Rolls-Royce plc, I; 7 (upd.); 21 (upd.)
Rostvertol plc, 62
Russian Aircraft Corporation (MiG), 86
Safe Flight Instrument Corporation, 71
Sequa Corp., 13
Shannon Aerospace Ltd., 36
Sikorsky Aircraft Corporation, 24
Smiths Industries PLC, 25
Snecma Group, 46
Société Air France, 27 (upd.)
Spacehab, Inc., 37
Spar Aerospace Limited, 32
Sukhoi Design Bureau Aviation Scientific-Industrial Complex, 24
Sundstrand Corporation, 7; 21 (upd.)
Surrey Satellite Technology Limited, 83
Swales & Associates, Inc., 69
Teledyne Technologies Inc., 62 (upd.)
Textron Lycoming Turbine Engine, 9
Thales S.A., 42
Thiokol Corporation, 9; 22 (upd.)
United Technologies Corporation, I; 10 (upd.)
Van's Aircraft, Inc., 65
Vector Aerospace Corporation, 97
Vought Aircraft Industries, Inc., 49
Whittaker Corporation, 48 (upd.)
Woodward Governor Company, 49 (upd.)
Zodiac S.A., 36

Airlines

Aer Lingus Group plc, 34; 89 (upd.)
Aeroflot - Russian Airlines JSC, 6; 29 (upd.); 89 (upd.)
Aerolíneas Argentinas S.A., 33; 69 (upd.)
Air Berlin GmbH & Co. Luftverkehrs KG, 71
Air Canada, 6; 23 (upd.); 59 (upd.)
Air China, 46
Air Jamaica Limited, 54
Air Mauritius Ltd., 63
Air New Zealand Limited, 14; 38 (upd.)
Air Pacific Ltd., 70
Air Partner PLC, 93
Air Sahara Limited, 65
Air Wisconsin Airlines Corporation, 55
Air Zimbabwe (Private) Limited, 91
Air-India Limited, 6; 27 (upd.)
AirAsia Berhad, 93

AirTran Holdings, Inc., 22
Alaska Air Group, Inc., 6; 29 (upd.)
Alitalia-Linee Aeree Italiana, S.p.A., 6; 29 (upd.); 97 (upd.)
All Nippon Airways Co., Ltd., 6; 38 (upd.); 91 (upd.)
Allegiant Travel Company, 97
Aloha Airlines, Incorporated, 24
America West Holdings Corporation, 6; 34 (upd.)
American Airlines, I; 6 (upd.)
AMR Corporation, 28 (upd.); 52 (upd.)
Amtran, Inc., 34
Arrow Air Holdings Corporation, 55
A/S Air Baltic Corporation, 71
AS Estonian Air, 71
Asiana Airlines, Inc., 46
ATA Holdings Corporation, 82
Atlantic Coast Airlines Holdings, Inc., 55
Atlantic Southeast Airlines, Inc., 47
Atlas Air, Inc., 39
Austrian Airlines AG (Österreichische Luftverkehrs AG), 33
Aviacionny Nauchno-Tehnicheskii Komplex im. A.N. Tupoleva, 24
Avianca Aerovías Nacionales de Colombia SA, 36
Azerbaijan Airlines, 77
Bahamas Air Holdings Ltd., 66
Banner Aerospace, Inc., 37 (upd.)
Braathens ASA, 47
Bradley Air Services Ltd., 56
Bristow Helicopters Ltd., 70
British Airways PLC, I; 14 (upd.); 43 (upd.)
British Midland plc, 38
British World Airlines Ltd., 18
Cargolux Airlines International S.A., 49
Cathay Pacific Airways Limited, 6; 34 (upd.)
Ceské aerolinie, a.s., 66
Chautauqua Airlines, Inc., 38
China Airlines, 34
China Eastern Airlines Co. Ltd., 31
China Southern Airlines Company Ltd., 33
Comair Holdings Inc., 13; 34 (upd.)
Consorcio Aviacsa, S.A. de C.V., 85
Continental Airlines, Inc., I; 21 (upd.); 52 (upd.)
Copa Holdings, S.A., 93
Corporación Internacional de Aviación, S.A. de C.V. (Cintra), 20
Cyprus Airways Public Limited, 81
dba Luftfahrtgesellschaft mbH, 76
Delta Air Lines, Inc., I; 6 (upd.); 39 (upd.); 92 (upd.)
Deutsche Lufthansa AG, I; 26 (upd.); 68 (upd.)
Eastern Airlines, I
easyJet Airline Company Limited, 39
EgyptAir, 6; 27 (upd.)
El Al Israel Airlines Ltd., 23
The Emirates Group, 39; 81 (upd.)
Ethiopian Airlines, 81
Etihad Airways PJSC, 89
Eurocopter S.A., 80
EVA Airways Corporation, 51

Finnair Oyj, 6; 25 (upd.); 61 (upd.)
Flight Options, LLC, 75
Flying Boat, Inc. (Chalk's Ocean Airways), 56
Frontier Airlines Holdings Inc., 22; 84 (upd.)
Garuda Indonesia, 6
Gol Linhas Aéreas Inteligentes S.A., 73
Groupe Air France, 6
Grupo Aeroportuario del Pacífico, S.A. de C.V., 85
Grupo TACA, 38
Gulf Air Company, 56
Hawaiian Holdings, Inc., 9; 22 (upd.); 96 (upd.)
Hong Kong Dragon Airlines Ltd., 66
Iberia Líneas Aéreas de España S.A., 6; 36 (upd.); 91 (upd.)
Icelandair, 52
Indian Airlines Ltd., 46
IranAir, 81
Japan Air Lines Company Ltd., I; 32 (upd.)
Jersey European Airways (UK) Ltd., 61
Jet Airways (India) Private Limited, 65
JetBlue Airways Corporation, 44
Kenmore Air Harbor Inc., 65
Kenya Airways Limited, 89
Kitty Hawk, Inc., 22
Kiwi International Airlines Inc., 20
Koninklijke Luchtvaart Maatschappij, N.V. (KLM Royal Dutch Airlines), I; 28 (upd.)
Korean Air Lines Co., Ltd., 6; 27 (upd.)
Kuwait Airways Corporation, 68
Lan Chile S.A., 31
Lauda Air Luftfahrt AG, 48
Lloyd Aéreo Boliviano S.A., 95
Loganair Ltd., 68
LOT Polish Airlines (Polskie Linie Lotnicze S.A.), 33
LTU Group Holding GmbH, 37
Malév Plc, 24
Malaysian Airlines System Berhad, 6; 29 (upd.); 97 (upd.)
Mesa Air Group, Inc., 11; 32 (upd.); 77 (upd.)
Mesaba Holdings, Inc., 28
Middle East Airlines - Air Liban S.A.L., 79
Midway Airlines Corporation, 33
Midwest Air Group, Inc., 35; 85 (upd.)
NetJets Inc., 96 (upd.)
Northwest Airlines Corporation, I; 6 (upd.); 26 (upd.); 74 (upd.)
Offshore Logistics, Inc., 37
Pakistan International Airlines Corporation, 46
Pan American World Airways, Inc., I; 12 (upd.)
Panalpina World Transport (Holding) Ltd., 47
People Express Airlines, Inc., I
Petroleum Helicopters, Inc., 35
PHI, Inc., 80 (upd.)
Philippine Airlines, Inc., 6; 23 (upd.)
Pinnacle Airlines Corp., 73
Preussag AG, 42 (upd.)

Qantas Airways Ltd., 6; 24 (upd.); 68 (upd.)
Qatar Airways Company Q.C.S.C., 87
Reno Air Inc., 23
Royal Brunei Airlines Sdn Bhd, 99
Royal Nepal Airline Corporation, 41
Ryanair Holdings plc, 35
SAA (Pty) Ltd., 28
Sabena S.A./N.V., 33
The SAS Group, 34 (upd.)
Saudi Arabian Airlines, 6; 27 (upd.)
Scandinavian Airlines System, I
Singapore Airlines Limited, 6; 27 (upd.); 83 (upd.)
SkyWest, Inc., 25
Société d'Exploitation AOM Air Liberté SA (AirLib), 53
Société Luxembourgeoise de Navigation Aérienne S.A., 64
Société Tunisienne de l'Air-Tunisair, 49
Southwest Airlines Co., 6; 24 (upd.); 71 (upd.)
Spirit Airlines, Inc., 31
Sterling European Airlines A/S, 70
Sun Country Airlines, 30
Swiss Air Transport Company, Ltd., I
Swiss International Air Lines Ltd., 48
TAM Linhas Aéreas S.A., 68
TAP—Air Portugal Transportes Aéreos Portugueses S.A., 46
TAROM S.A., 64
Texas Air Corporation, I
Thai Airways International Public Company Limited, 6; 27 (upd.)
Tower Air, Inc., 28
Trans World Airlines, Inc., I; 12 (upd.); 35 (upd.)
TransBrasil S/A Linhas Aéreas, 31
Transportes Aereos Portugueses, S.A., 6
Turkish Airlines Inc. (Türk Hava Yollari A.O.), 72
TV Guide, Inc., 43 (upd.)
UAL Corporation, 34 (upd.)
United Airlines, I; 6 (upd.)
US Airways Group, Inc., I; 6 (upd.); 28 (upd.); 52 (upd.)
VARIG S.A. (Viação Aérea Rio-Grandense), 6; 29 (upd.)
Virgin Group Ltd., 12; 32 (upd.); 89 (upd.)
Volga-Dnepr Group, 82
Vueling Airlines S.A., 97
WestJet Airlines Ltd., 38
Uzbekistan Airways National Air Company, 99

Automotive

AB Volvo, I; 7 (upd.); 26 (upd.); 67 (upd.)
Accubuilt, Inc., 74
Adam Opel AG, 7; 21 (upd.); 61 (upd.)
ADESA, Inc., 71
Advance Auto Parts, Inc., 57
Aftermarket Technology Corp., 83
Aisin Seiki Co., Ltd., 48 (upd.)
Alamo Rent A Car, Inc., 6; 24 (upd.); 84 (upd.)
Alfa Romeo, 13; 36 (upd.)

Alvis Plc, 47
America's Car-Mart, Inc., 64
American Motors Corporation, I
Amerigon Incorporated, 97
Applied Power Inc., 32 (upd.)
Arnold Clark Automobiles Ltd., 60
ArvinMeritor, Inc., 8; 54 (upd.)
Asbury Automotive Group Inc., 60
ASC, Inc., 55
Autobacs Seven Company Ltd., 76
Autocam Corporation, 51
Autoliv, Inc., 65
Automobiles Citroen, 7
Automobili Lamborghini Holding S.p.A., 13; 34 (upd.); 91 (upd.)
AutoNation, Inc., 50
AutoTrader.com, L.L.C., 91
AVTOVAZ Joint Stock Company, 65
Bajaj Auto Limited, 39
Bayerische Motoren Werke AG, I; 11 (upd.); 38 (upd.)
Belron International Ltd., 76
Bendix Corporation, I
Blue Bird Corporation, 35
Bombardier Inc., 42 (upd.)
BorgWarner Inc., 14; 32 (upd.); 85 (upd.)
The Budd Company, 8
Bugatti Automobiles S.A.S., 94
Canadian Tire Corporation, Limited, 71 (upd.)
CarMax, Inc., 55
CARQUEST Corporation, 29
Caterpillar Inc., 63 (upd.)
Checker Motors Corp., 89
China Automotive Systems Inc., 87
Chrysler Corporation, I; 11 (upd.)
Commercial Vehicle Group, Inc., 81
CNH Global N.V., 38 (upd.); 99 (upd.)
Consorcio G Grupo Dina, S.A. de C.V., 36
Crown Equipment Corporation, 15; 93 (upd.)
CSK Auto Corporation, 38
Cummins Engine Company, Inc., I; 12 (upd.); 40 (upd.)
Custom Chrome, Inc., 16
Daihatsu Motor Company, Ltd., 7; 21 (upd.)
Daimler-Benz A.G., I; 15 (upd.)
DaimlerChrysler AG, 34 (upd.); 64 (upd.)
Dana Holding Corporation, I; 10 (upd.); 99 (upd.)
Danaher Corporation, 77 (upd.)
Deere & Company, 42 (upd.)
Delphi Automotive Systems Corporation, 45
D'Ieteren S.A./NV, 98
Directed Electronics, Inc., 87
Discount Tire Company Inc., 84
Don Massey Cadillac, Inc., 37
Donaldson Company, Inc., 49 (upd.)
Douglas & Lomason Company, 16
Dräxlmaier Group, 90
DriveTime Automotive Group Inc., 68 (upd.)
Ducati Motor Holding SpA, 30; 86 (upd.)
Eaton Corporation, I; 10 (upd.); 67 (upd.)

Echlin Inc., I; 11 (upd.)
Edelbrock Corporation, 37
Faurecia S.A., 70
Federal-Mogul Corporation, I; 10 (upd.); 26 (upd.)
Ferrara Fire Apparatus, Inc., 84
Ferrari S.p.A., 13; 36 (upd.)
Fiat SpA, I; 11 (upd.); 50 (upd.)
FinishMaster, Inc., 24
Force Protection Inc., 95
Ford Motor Company, I; 11 (upd.); 36 (upd.); 64 (upd.)
Ford Motor Company, S.A. de C.V., 20
Fruehauf Corporation, I
General Motors Corporation, I; 10 (upd.); 36 (upd.); 64 (upd.)
Gentex Corporation, 26
Genuine Parts Company, 9; 45 (upd.)
GKN plc, III; 38 (upd.); 89 (upd.)
Group 1 Automotive, Inc., 52
Grupo Ficosa International, 90
Guardian Industries Corp., 87
Harley-Davidson Inc., 7; 25 (upd.)
Hastings Manufacturing Company, 56
Hayes Lemmerz International, Inc., 27
Hendrick Motorsports, Inc., 89
The Hertz Corporation, 33 (upd.)
Hino Motors, Ltd., 7; 21 (upd.)
Holden Ltd., 62
Holley Performance Products Inc., 52
Hometown Auto Retailers, Inc., 44
Honda Motor Company Limited (Honda Giken Kogyo Kabushiki Kaisha), I; 10 (upd.); 29 (upd.); 96 (upd.)
Hyundai Group, III; 7 (upd.); 56 (upd.)
Insurance Auto Auctions, Inc., 23
Isuzu Motors, Ltd., 9; 23 (upd.); 57 (upd.)
INTERMET Corporation, 77 (upd.)
Jardine Cycle & Carriage Ltd., 73
Kawasaki Heavy Industries, Ltd., 63 (upd.)
Kelsey-Hayes Group of Companies, 7; 27 (upd.)
Key Safety Systems, Inc., 63
Kia Motors Corporation, 12; 29 (upd.)
Kolbenschmidt Pierburg AG, 97
Kwik-Fit Holdings plc, 54
Lazy Days RV Center, Inc., 69
Lear Corporation, 71 (upd.)
Lear Seating Corporation, 16
Les Schwab Tire Centers, 50
Lithia Motors, Inc., 41
LKQ Corporation, 71
Lookers plc, 71
Lotus Cars Ltd., 14
Lund International Holdings, Inc., 40
Mack Trucks, Inc., I; 22 (upd.); 61 (upd.)
The Major Automotive Companies, Inc., 45
Marcopolo S.A., 79
Masland Corporation, 17
Mazda Motor Corporation, 9; 23 (upd.); 63 (upd.)
Mel Farr Automotive Group, 20
Metso Corporation, 30 (upd.)
Midas Inc., 10; 56 (upd.)

Mitsubishi Motors Corporation, 9; 23 (upd.); 57 (upd.)
Monaco Coach Corporation, 31
Monro Muffler Brake, Inc., 24
Montupet S.A., 63
National R.V. Holdings, Inc., 32
Navistar International Corporation, I; 10 (upd.)
New Flyer Industries Inc. 78
Nissan Motor Company Ltd., I; 11 (upd.); 34 (upd.); 92 (upd.)
O'Reilly Automotive, Inc., 26; 78 (upd.)
Officine Alfieri Maserati S.p.A., 13
Oshkosh Corporation, 7; 98 (upd.)
Paccar Inc., I
PACCAR Inc., 26 (upd.)
Park-Ohio Holdings Corp., 17; 85 (upd.)
Parker-Hannifin Corporation, III; 24 (upd.); 99 (upd.)
Pennzoil-Quaker State Company, IV; 20 (upd.); 50 (upd.)
Penske Corporation, V; 19 (upd.); 84 (upd.)
The Pep Boys—Manny, Moe & Jack, 11; 36 (upd.); 81 (upd.)
Perusahaan Otomobil Nasional Bhd., 62
Peterbilt Motors Company, 89
Peugeot S.A., I
Piaggio & C. S.p.A., 20
Pirelli & C. S.p.A., 75 (upd.)
Porsche AG, 13; 31 (upd.)
PSA Peugeot Citroen S.A., 28 (upd.)
R&B, Inc., 51
Randon S.A., 79
Red McCombs Automotive Group, 91
Regal-Beloit Corporation, 18; 97 (upd.)
Regie Nationale des Usines Renault, I
Renault Argentina S.A., 67
Renault S.A., 26 (upd.); 74 (upd.)
Repco Corporation Ltd., 74
Republic Industries, Inc., 26
The Reynolds and Reynolds Company, 50
Rheinmetall AG, 9; 97 (upd.)
Riviera Tool Company, 89
Robert Bosch GmbH., I; 16 (upd.); 43 (upd.)
RockShox, Inc., 26
Rockwell Automation, I; 11 (upd.); 43 (upd.)
Rolls-Royce plc, I; 21 (upd.)
Ron Tonkin Chevrolet Company, 55
Rover Group Ltd., 7; 21 (upd.)
Saab Automobile AB, I; 11 (upd.); 32 (upd.); 83 (upd.)
Safelite Glass Corp., 19
Safety Components International, Inc., 63
SANLUIS Corporación, S.A.B. de C.V., 95
Saturn Corporation, 7; 21 (upd.); 80 (upd.)
Sealed Power Corporation, I
Servco Pacific Inc., 96
Sheller-Globe Corporation, I
Sixt AG, 39
Skoda Auto a.s., 39
Sonic Automotive, Inc., 77
Spartan Motors Inc., 14
SpeeDee Oil Change and Tune-Up, 25

SPX Corporation, 10; 47 (upd.)
Standard Motor Products, Inc., 40
Strattec Security Corporation, 73
Superior Industries International, Inc., 8
Suzuki Motor Corporation, 9; 23 (upd.); 59 (upd.)
Sytner Group plc, 45
Titan International, Inc., 89
Toresco Enterprises, Inc., 84
Tower Automotive, Inc., 24
Toyota Motor Corporation, I; 11 (upd.); 38 (upd.)
CJSC Transmash Holding, 93
TransPro, Inc., 71
Triumph Motorcycles Ltd., 53
TRW Automotive Holdings Corp., 75 (upd.)
TRW Inc., 14 (upd.)
Ugly Duckling Corporation, 22
United Auto Group, Inc., 26; 68 (upd.)
United Technologies Automotive Inc., 15
Universal Technical Institute, Inc., 81
Valeo, 23; 66 (upd.)
Van Hool S.A./NV, 96
Vauxhall Motors Limited, 73
Volkswagen Aktiengesellschaft, I; 11 (upd.); 32 (upd.)
Wagon plc, 92
Walker Manufacturing Company, 19
Webasto Roof Systems Inc., 97
Wilhelm Karmann GmbH, 94
Winnebago Industries, Inc., 7; 27 (upd.); 96 (upd.)
Woodward Governor Company, 49 (upd.)
The Yokohama Rubber Company, Limited, V; 19 (upd.); 91 (upd.)
ZF Friedrichshafen AG, 48
Ziebart International Corporation, 30; 66 (upd.)

Beverages

A & W Brands, Inc., 25
Adolph Coors Company, I; 13 (upd.); 36 (upd.)
AG Barr plc, 64
Ajegroup S.A., 92
Allied Domecq PLC, 29
Allied-Lyons PLC, I
Anadolu Efes Biracilik ve Malt Sanayii A.S., 95
Anchor Brewing Company, 47
Anheuser-Busch Companies, Inc., I; 10 (upd.); 34 (upd.)
Apple & Eve L.L.C., 92
Asahi Breweries, Ltd., I; 20 (upd.); 52 (upd.)
Asia Pacific Breweries Limited, 59
August Schell Brewing Company Inc., 59
Bacardi & Company Ltd., 18; 82 (upd.)
Baltika Brewery Joint Stock Company, 65
Banfi Products Corp., 36
Baron de Ley S.A., 74
Baron Philippe de Rothschild S.A., 39
Bass PLC, I; 15 (upd.); 38 (upd.)
Bavaria S.A., 90
BBAG Osterreichische Brau-Beteiligungs-AG, 38
Belvedere S.A., 93

Beringer Blass Wine Estates Ltd., 22; 66 (upd.)
The Bernick Companies, 75
Blue Ridge Beverage Company Inc., 82
Boizel Chanoine Champagne S.A., 94
Bols Distilleries NV, 74
The Boston Beer Company, Inc., 18; 50 (upd.)
Brauerei Beck & Co., 9; 33 (upd.)
Britannia Soft Drinks Ltd. (Britvic), 71
Brown-Forman Corporation, I; 10 (upd.); 38 (upd.)
Brouwerijen Alken-Maes N.V., 86
Budweiser Budvar, National Corporation, 59
Cadbury Schweppes PLC, 49 (upd.)
Cains Beer Company PLC, 99
Canandaigua Brands, Inc., 13; 34 (upd.)
Cantine Giorgio Lungarotti S.R.L., 67
Caribou Coffee Company, Inc., 28; 97 (upd.)
Carlsberg A/S, 9; 29 (upd.); 98 (upd.)
Carlton and United Breweries Ltd., I
Casa Cuervo, S.A. de C.V., 31
Central European Distribution Corporation, 75
Cerveceria Polar, I
The Chalone Wine Group, Ltd., 36
The Charmer Sunbelt Group, 95
City Brewing Company LLC, 73
Clearly Canadian Beverage Corporation, 48
Clement Pappas & Company, Inc., 92
Click Wine Group, 68
Coca Cola Bottling Co. Consolidated, 10
The Coca-Cola Company, I; 10 (upd.); 32 (upd.); 67 (upd.)
Coffee Holding Co., Inc., 95
Companhia de Bebidas das Américas, 57
Compania Cervecerias Unidas S.A., 70
Constellation Brands, Inc., 68 (upd.)
Corby Distilleries Limited, 14
Cott Corporation, 52
D.G. Yuengling & Son, Inc., 38
Dallis Coffee, Inc., 86
Daniel Thwaites Plc, 95
Davide Campari-Milano S.p.A., 57
Dean Foods Company, 21 (upd.)
Delicato Vineyards, Inc., 50
Deschutes Brewery, Inc., 57
Desnoes and Geddes Limited, 79
Diageo plc, 79 (upd.)
Direct Wines Ltd., 84
Distillers Company PLC, I
Double-Cola Co.-USA, 70
Dr Pepper/Seven Up, Inc., 9; 32 (upd.)
Drie Mollen Holding B.V., 99
E. & J. Gallo Winery, I; 7 (upd.); 28 (upd.)
Eckes AG, 56
The Edrington Group Ltd., 88
Embotelladora Andina S.A., 71
Empresas Polar SA, 55 (upd.)
Energy Brands Inc., 88
F. Korbel & Bros. Inc., 68
Faygo Beverages Inc., 55
Federico Paternina S.A., 69
Ferolito, Vultaggio & Sons, 27

Fiji Water LLC, 74
Florida's Natural Growers, 45
Foster's Group Limited, 7; 21 (upd.); 50 (upd.)
Freixenet S.A., 71
Frucor Beverages Group Ltd., 96
Fuller Smith & Turner P.L.C., 38
G. Heileman Brewing Company Inc., I
The Gambrinus Company, 40
Gano Excel Enterprise Sdn. Bhd., 89
The Gatorade Company, 82
Geerlings & Wade, Inc., 45
General Cinema Corporation, I
Glazer's Wholesale Drug Company, Inc., 82
Gluek Brewing Company, 75
Golden State Vintners, Inc., 33
Gosling Brothers Ltd., 82
Grand Metropolitan PLC, I
Green Mountain Coffee, Inc., 31
The Greenalls Group PLC, 21
Greene King plc, 31
Grands Vins Jean-Claude Boisset S.A., 98
Groupe Danone, 32 (upd.); 93 (upd.)
Grupo Industrial Herradura, S.A. de C.V., 83
Grupo Modelo, S.A. de C.V., 29
Guinness/UDV, I; 43 (upd.)
The Hain Celestial Group, Inc., 43 (upd.)
Hansen Natural Corporation, 31; 76 (upd.)
Heineken N.V, I; 13 (upd.); 34 (upd.); 90 (upd.)
Heublein, Inc., I
High Falls Brewing Company LLC, 74
Hiram Walker Resources, Ltd., I
Hite Brewery Company Ltd., 97
illycaffè SpA, 50
Imagine Foods, Inc., 50
Interbrew S.A., 17; 50 (upd.)
Irish Distillers Group, 96
J.J. Darboven GmbH & Co. KG, 96
J. Lohr Winery Corporation, 99
Jacob Leinenkugel Brewing Company, 28
JD Wetherspoon plc, 30
Jim Beam Brands Worldwide, Inc., 58 (upd.)
John Dewar & Sons, Ltd., 82
Jones Soda Co., 69
Jugos del Valle, S.A. de C.V., 85
Karlsberg Brauerei GmbH & Co KG, 41
Kendall-Jackson Winery, Ltd., 28
Kikkoman Corporation, 14
Kirin Brewery Company, Limited, I; 21 (upd.); 63 (upd.)
Kobrand Corporation, 82
König Brauerei GmbH & Co. KG, 35 (upd.)
Labatt Brewing Company Limited, I; 25 (upd.)
Latrobe Brewing Company, 54
Laurent-Perrier SA, 42
The Lion Brewery, Inc., 86
Lion Nathan Limited, 54
Löwenbräu AG, 80
The Macallan Distillers Ltd., 63
Madeira Wine Company, S.A., 49
Maison Louis Jadot, 24

Marchesi Antinori SRL, 42
Marie Brizard et Roger International S.A.S., 22; 97 (upd.)
Mark T. Wendell Tea Company, 94
Martell and Company S.A., 82
Martignetti Companies, 84
Martini & Rossi SpA, 63
Maui Wowi, Inc., 85
MBC Holding Company, 40
Mendocino Brewing Company, Inc., 60
Mercian Corporation, 77
Miller Brewing Company, I; 12 (upd.)
The Minute Maid Company, 28
Mitchells & Butlers PLC, 59
Moët-Hennessy, I
Molson Coors Brewing Company, I; 26 (upd.); 77 (upd.)
Montana Coffee Traders, Inc., 60
Mott's Inc., 57
National Beverage Corporation, 26; 88 (upd.)
National Grape Cooperative Association, Inc., 20
National Wine & Spirits, Inc., 49
Nestlé Waters, 73
New Belgium Brewing Company, Inc., 68
Nichols plc, 44
Ocean Spray Cranberries, Inc., 7; 25 (upd.); 83 (upd.)
Odwalla, Inc., 31
OENEO S.A., 74 (upd.)
Old Orchard Brands, LLC, 73
Oregon Chai, Inc., 49
Panamerican Beverages, Inc., 47
Parmalat Finanziaria SpA, 50
Paulaner Brauerei GmbH & Co. KG, 35
Peet's Coffee & Tea, Inc., 38
Penaflor S.A., 66
The Pepsi Bottling Group, Inc., 40
PepsiAmericas, Inc., 67 (upd.)
PepsiCo, Inc., I; 10 (upd.); 38 (upd.); 93 (upd.)
Pernod Ricard S.A., I; 21 (upd.); 72 (upd.)
Pete's Brewing Company, 22
Philip Morris Companies Inc., 18 (upd.)
Pittsburgh Brewing Company, 76
Pyramid Breweries Inc., 33
Quilmes Industrial (QUINSA) S.A., 67
R.C. Bigelow, Inc., 49
Radeberger Gruppe AG, 75
Rainier Brewing Company, 23
Red Bull GmbH, 60
Redhook Ale Brewery, Inc., 31; 88 (upd.)
Rémy Cointreau Group, 20; 80 (upd.)
Robert Mondavi Corporation, 15; 50 (upd.)
Royal Crown Company, Inc., 23
Royal Grolsch NV, 54
S&D Coffee, Inc., 84
SABMiller plc, 59 (upd.)
Sam's Wine & Spirits, 96
San Miguel Corporation, 57 (upd.)
Sapporo Holdings Limited, I; 13 (upd.); 36 (upd.); 97 (upd.)
Scheid Vineyards Inc., 66
Schieffelin & Somerset Co., 61
Scottish & Newcastle plc, 15; 35 (upd.)

The Seagram Company Ltd., I; 25 (upd.)
Sebastiani Vineyards, Inc., 28
Shepherd Neame Limited, 30
Sidney Frank Importing Co., Inc., 69
Sierra Nevada Brewing Company, 70
Sine Qua Non, 99
Skalli Group, 67
Skyy Spirits LLC 78
Sleeman Breweries Ltd., 74
Snapple Beverage Corporation, 11
Societe des Produits Marnier-Lapostolle S.A., 88
The South African Breweries Limited, I; 24 (upd.)
South Beach Beverage Company, Inc., 73
Southcorp Limited, 54
Southern Wine and Spirits of America, Inc., 84
Starbucks Corporation, 13; 34 (upd.); 77 (upd.)
The Stash Tea Company, 50
Ste. Michelle Wine Estates Ltd., 96
Stewart's Beverages, 39
The Stroh Brewery Company, I; 18 (upd.)
Suntory Ltd., 65
Sutter Home Winery Inc., 16
Taittinger S.A., 43
Taiwan Tobacco & Liquor Corporation, 75
Takara Holdings Inc., 62
Tata Tea Ltd., 76
The Terlato Wine Group, 48
Tetley USA Inc., 88
Todhunter International, Inc., 27
Triarc Companies, Inc., 34 (upd.)
Tropicana Products, Inc., 73 (upd.)
Tsingtao Brewery Group, 49
Tully's Coffee Corporation, 51
Underberg AG, 92
Unilever, II; 7 (upd.); 32 (upd.); 89 (upd.)
Unión de Cervecerias Peruanas Backus y Johnston S.A.A., 92
V&S Vin & Sprit AB, 91 (upd.)
Van Houtte Inc., 39
Vermont Pure Holdings, Ltd., 51
Veuve Clicquot Ponsardin SCS, 98
Vin & Spirit AB, 31
Viña Concha y Toro S.A., 45
Vincor International Inc., 50
Whitbread PLC, I; 20 (upd.); 52 (upd.); 97 (upd.)
Widmer Brothers Brewing Company, 76
Willamette Valley Vineyards, Inc., 85
William Grant & Sons Ltd., 60
The Wine Group, Inc., 39
The Wolverhampton & Dudley Breweries, PLC, 57
Wray & Nephew Group Ltd., 98
Young & Co.'s Brewery, P.L.C., 38

Bio-Technology

Actelion Ltd., 83
Amersham PLC, 50
Amgen, Inc., 10; 30 (upd.)
ArQule, Inc., 68
Bio-Rad Laboratories, Inc., 93
Biogen Idec Inc., 71 (upd.)

Biogen Inc., 14; 36 (upd.)
bioMérieux S.A., 75
BTG Plc, 87
Caliper Life Sciences, Inc., 70
Cambrex Corporation, 44 (upd.)
Celera Genomics, 74
Centocor Inc., 14
Charles River Laboratories International, Inc., 42
Chiron Corporation, 10; 36 (upd.)
Covance Inc., 30; 98 (upd.)
CryoLife, Inc., 46
Cytyc Corporation, 69
Delta and Pine Land Company, 33
Dionex Corporation, 46
Dyax Corp., 89
Embrex, Inc., 72
Enzo Biochem, Inc., 41
Eurofins Scientific S.A., 70
Gen-Probe Incorporated, 79
Genentech, Inc., 32 (upd.)
Genzyme Corporation, 38 (upd.)
Gilead Sciences, Inc., 54
Howard Hughes Medical Institute, 39
Huntingdon Life Sciences Group plc, 42
IDEXX Laboratories, Inc., 23
ImClone Systems Inc., 58
Immunex Corporation, 14; 50 (upd.)
IMPATH Inc., 45
Incyte Genomics, Inc., 52
Inverness Medical Innovations, Inc., 63
Invitrogen Corporation, 52
The Judge Group, Inc., 51
Kendle International Inc., 87
Landec Corporation, 95
Life Technologies, Inc., 17
LifeCell Corporation, 77
Lonza Group Ltd., 73
Martek Biosciences Corporation, 65
Medarex, Inc., 85
Medtronic, Inc., 30 (upd.)
Millipore Corporation, 25; 84 (upd.)
Minntech Corporation, 22
Mycogen Corporation, 21
Nektar Therapeutics, 91
New Brunswick Scientific Co., Inc., 45
Omrix Biopharmaceuticals, Inc., 95
Pacific Ethanol, Inc., 81
Pharmion Corporation, 91
Qiagen N.V., 39
Quintiles Transnational Corporation, 21
Seminis, Inc., 29
Senomyx, Inc., 83
Serologicals Corporation, 63
Sigma-Aldrich Corporation, I; 36 (upd.); 93 (upd.)
Starkey Laboratories, Inc., 52
STERIS Corporation, 29
Stratagene Corporation, 70
Tanox, Inc., 77
TECHNE Corporation, 52
TriPath Imaging, Inc., 77
Waters Corporation, 43
Whatman plc, 46
Wisconsin Alumni Research Foundation, 65

Wyeth, 50 (upd.)

Chemicals

A. Schulman, Inc., 8
Aceto Corp., 38
Air Products and Chemicals, Inc., I; 10 (upd.); 74 (upd.)
Airgas, Inc., 54
Akzo Nobel N.V., 13; 41 (upd.)
Albemarle Corporation, 59
AlliedSignal Inc., 22 (upd.)
ALTANA AG, 87
American Cyanamid, I; 8 (upd.)
American Vanguard Corporation, 47
Arab Potash Company, 85
Arch Chemicals Inc. 78
ARCO Chemical Company, 10
Asahi Denka Kogyo KK, 64
Atanor S.A., 62
Atochem S.A., I
Avantium Technologies BV, 79
Avecia Group PLC, 63
Baker Hughes Incorporated, 22 (upd.); 57 (upd.)
Balchem Corporation, 42
BASF Aktiengesellschaft, I; 18 (upd.); 50 (upd.)
Bayer A.G., I; 13 (upd.); 41 (upd.)
Betz Laboratories, Inc., I; 10 (upd.)
The BFGoodrich Company, 19 (upd.)
BOC Group plc, I; 25 (upd.); 78 (upd.)
Brenntag AG, 8; 23 (upd.)
Burmah Castrol PLC, 30 (upd.)
Cabot Corporation, 8; 29 (upd.); 91 (upd.)
Calgon Carbon Corporation, 73
Caliper Life Sciences, Inc., 70
Cambrex Corporation, 16
Catalytica Energy Systems, Inc., 44
Celanese Corporation, I
Celanese Mexicana, S.A. de C.V., 54
CF Industries Holdings, Inc., 99
Chemcentral Corporation, 8
Chemi-Trol Chemical Co., 16
Chemtura Corporation, 91 (upd.)
Church & Dwight Co., Inc., 29
Ciba-Geigy Ltd., I; 8 (upd.)
The Clorox Company, III; 22 (upd.); 81 (upd.)
Croda International Plc, 45
Crompton Corporation, 9; 36 (upd.)
Cytec Industries Inc., 27
Degussa-Hüls AG, 32 (upd.)
DeKalb Genetics Corporation, 17
The Dexter Corporation, I; 12 (upd.)
Dionex Corporation, 46
The Dow Chemical Company, I; 8 (upd.); 50 (upd.)
DSM N.V., I; 56 (upd.)
Dynaction S.A., 67
E.I. du Pont de Nemours & Company, I; 8 (upd.); 26 (upd.)
Eastman Chemical Company, 14; 38 (upd.)
Ecolab Inc., I; 13 (upd.); 34 (upd.); 85 (upd.)
Eka Chemicals AB, 92
Elementis plc, 40 (upd.)

Engelhard Corporation, 72 (upd.)
English China Clays Ltd., 15 (upd.); 40 (upd.)
Enterprise Rent-A-Car Company, 69 (upd.)
Equistar Chemicals, LP, 71
Ercros S.A., 80
ERLY Industries Inc., 17
Ethyl Corporation, I; 10 (upd.)
Ferro Corporation, 8; 56 (upd.)
Firmenich International S.A., 60
First Mississippi Corporation, 8
FMC Corporation, 89 (upd.)
Formosa Plastics Corporation, 14; 58 (upd.)
Fort James Corporation, 22 (upd.)
G.A.F., I
The General Chemical Group Inc., 37
Georgia Gulf Corporation, 9; 61 (upd.)
Givaudan SA, 43
Great Lakes Chemical Corporation, I; 14 (upd.)
GROWMARK, Inc., 88
Guerbet Group, 46
H.B. Fuller Company, 32 (upd.); 75 (upd.)
Hauser, Inc., 46
Hawkins Chemical, Inc., 16
Henkel KGaA, III; 34 (upd.); 95 (upd.)
Hercules Inc., I; 22 (upd.); 66 (upd.)
Hoechst A.G., I; 18 (upd.)
Hoechst Celanese Corporation, 13
Huls A.G., I
Huntsman Corporation, 8; 98 (upd.)
IMC Fertilizer Group, Inc., 8
Imperial Chemical Industries PLC, I; 50 (upd.)
International Flavors & Fragrances Inc., 9; 38 (upd.)
Israel Chemicals Ltd., 55
Kemira Oyj, 70
Koppers Industries, Inc., I; 26 (upd.)
L'Air Liquide SA, I; 47 (upd.)
Lawter International Inc., 14
LeaRonal, Inc., 23
Loctite Corporation, 30 (upd.)
Lonza Group Ltd., 73
The Lubrizol Corporation, I; 30 (upd.); 83 (upd.)
Lyondell Chemical Company, 45 (upd.)
M.A. Hanna Company, 8
MacDermid Incorporated, 32
Makhteshim-Agan Industries Ltd., 85
Mallinckrodt Group Inc., 19
MBC Holding Company, 40
Melamine Chemicals, Inc., 27
Methanex Corporation, 40
Mexichem, S.A.B. de C.V., 99
Minerals Technologies Inc., 52 (upd.)
Mississippi Chemical Corporation, 39
Mitsubishi Chemical Corporation, I; 56 (upd.)
Mitsui Petrochemical Industries, Ltd., 9
Monsanto Company, I; 9 (upd.); 29 (upd.)
Montedison SpA, I
Morton International Inc., I; 9 (upd.); 80 (upd.)

The Mosaic Company, 91
Nagase & Company, Ltd., 8
Nalco Holding Company, I; 12 (upd.); 89 (upd.)
National Distillers and Chemical Corporation, I
National Sanitary Supply Co., 16
National Starch and Chemical Company, 49
NCH Corporation, 8
Nippon Soda Co., Ltd., 85
Nisshin Seifun Group Inc., 66 (upd.)
NL Industries, Inc., 10
Nobel Industries AB, 9
NOF Corporation, 72
Norsk Hydro ASA, 35 (upd.)
North American Galvanizing & Coatings, Inc., 99
Novacor Chemicals Ltd., 12
Nufarm Ltd., 87
NutraSweet Company, 8
Occidental Petroleum Corporation, 71 (upd.)
Olin Corporation, I; 13 (upd.); 78 (upd.)
OM Group, Inc., 17; 78 (upd.)
OMNOVA Solutions Inc., 59
Penford Corporation, 55
Pennwalt Corporation, I
Perstorp AB, I; 51 (upd.)
Petrolite Corporation, 15
Pfizer Inc., 79 (upd.)
Pioneer Hi-Bred International, Inc., 41 (upd.)
PolyOne Corporation, 87 (upd.)
Praxair, Inc., 11
Quaker Chemical Corp., 91
Quantum Chemical Corporation, 8
Reichhold Chemicals, Inc., 10
Renner Herrmann S.A., 79
Rhodia SA, 38
Rhône-Poulenc S.A., I; 10 (upd.)
Robertet SA, 39
Rohm and Haas Company, I; 26 (upd.); 77 (upd.)
Roussel Uclaf, I; 8 (upd.)
RPM International Inc., 8; 36 (upd.); 91 (upd.)
RWE AG, 50 (upd.)
S.C. Johnson & Son, Inc., III; 28 (upd.); 89 (upd.)
The Scotts Company, 22
SCP Pool Corporation, 39
Sequa Corp., 13
Shanghai Petrochemical Co., Ltd., 18
Sigma-Aldrich Corporation, I; 36 (upd.); 93 (upd.)
Solutia Inc., 52
Solvay S.A., I; 21 (upd.); 61 (upd.)
Stepan Company, 30
Sterling Chemicals, Inc., 16; 78 (upd.)
Sumitomo Chemical Company Ltd., I; 98 (upd.)
Takeda Chemical Industries, Ltd., 46 (upd.)
Teknor Apex Company, 97
Terra Industries, Inc., 13
Tessenderlo Group, 76
Teva Pharmaceutical Industries Ltd., 22

Tosoh Corporation, 70
Total Fina Elf S.A., 24 (upd.); 50 (upd.)
Transammonia Group, 95
Ube Industries, Ltd., 38 (upd.)
Union Carbide Corporation, I; 9 (upd.); 74 (upd.)
United Industries Corporation, 68
Univar Corporation, 9
The Valspar Corporation, 32 (upd.); 77 (upd.)
VeraSun Energy Corporation, 87
Vista Chemical Company, I
Witco Corporation, I; 16 (upd.)
Yule Catto & Company plc, 54
WD-40 Company, 87 (upd.)
Zeneca Group PLC, 21

Conglomerates

A.P. Møller - Maersk A/S, 57
Abengoa S.A., 73
Acciona S.A., 81
Accor SA, 10; 27 (upd.)
Ackermans & van Haaren N.V., 97
Adani Enterprises Ltd., 97
Aditya Birla Group, 79
Administración Nacional de Combustibles, Alcohol y Pórtland, 93
AEG A.G., I
Al Habtoor Group L.L.C., 87
Alcatel Alsthom Compagnie Générale d'Electricité, 9
Alco Standard Corporation, I
Alexander & Baldwin, Inc., 10, 40 (upd.)
Alfa, S.A. de C.V., 19
Alfa Group, 99
Alleghany Corporation, 60 (upd.)
Allied Domecq PLC, 29
Allied-Signal Inc., I
AMFAC Inc., I
The Anschutz Company, 73 (upd.)
The Anschutz Corporation, 36 (upd.)
Antofagasta plc, 65
Apax Partners Worldwide LLP, 89
APi Group, Inc., 64
Aramark Corporation, 13
ARAMARK Corporation, 41
Archer Daniels Midland Company, I; 11 (upd.); 75 (upd.)
Arkansas Best Corporation, 16
Associated British Ports Holdings Plc, 45
BAA plc, 33 (upd.)
Barlow Rand Ltd., I
Barratt Developments plc, 56 (upd.)
Bat Industries PLC, I
Baugur Group hf, 81
BB Holdings Limited, 77
Berjaya Group Bhd., 67
Berkshire Hathaway Inc., III; 18 (upd.); 42 (upd.); 89 (upd.)
Block Communications, Inc., 81
Bond Corporation Holdings Limited, 10
Brascan Corporation, 67
BTR PLC, I
Bunzl plc, 31 (upd.)
Burlington Northern Santa Fe Corporation, 27 (upd.)
Business Post Group plc, 46
C. Itoh & Company Ltd., I

C.I. Traders Limited, 61
Camargo Corrêa S.A., 93
Cargill, Incorporated, II; 13 (upd.); 40 (upd.); 89 (upd.)
CBI Industries, Inc., 7
Charoen Pokphand Group, 62
Chemed Corporation, 13
Chesebrough-Pond's USA, Inc., 8
China Merchants International Holdings Co., Ltd., 52
Cisneros Group of Companies, 54
CITIC Pacific Ltd., 18
CJ Corporation, 62
Colgate-Palmolive Company, 71 (upd.)
Colt Industries Inc., I
Compagnie Financiere Richemont AG, 50
The Connell Company, 29
Conzzeta Holding, 80
Cox Enterprises, Inc., 67 (upd.)
Cristalerias de Chile S.A., 67
CSR Limited, III; 28 (upd.); 85 (upd.)
Daewoo Group, 18 (upd.); 57 (upd.)
Dallah Albaraka Group, 72
De Dietrich & Cie., 31
Deere & Company, 21 (upd.)
Delaware North Companies Inc., 7; 96 (upd.)
Desc, S.A. de C.V., 23
The Dial Corp., 8
Dogan Sirketler Grubu Holding A.S., 83
Dr. August Oetker KG, 51
E.I. du Pont de Nemours and Company, 73 (upd.)
EBSCO Industries, Inc., 40 (upd.)
El Corte Inglés Group, 26 (upd.)
Elders IXL Ltd., I
Empresas Copec S.A., 69
Engelhard Corporation, 21 (upd.); 72 (upd.)
Essar Group Ltd., 79
Farley Northwest Industries, Inc., I
Fimalac S.A., 37
First Pacific Company Limited, 18
Fisher Companies, Inc., 15
Fletcher Challenge Ltd., 19 (upd.)
Florida East Coast Industries, Inc., 59
FMC Corporation, I; 11 (upd.)
Fortune Brands, Inc., 29 (upd.); 68 (upd.)
Fraser & Neave Ltd., 54
Fuqua Industries, Inc., I
General Electric Company, 34 (upd.); 63 (upd.)
Genting Bhd., 65
GIB Group, 26 (upd.)
Gillett Holdings, Inc., 7
The Gillette Company, 68 (upd.)
Granaria Holdings B.V., 66
Grand Metropolitan PLC, 14 (upd.)
Great American Management and Investment, Inc., 8
Greyhound Corporation, I
Groupe Bolloré, 67
Groupe Louis Dreyfus S.A., 60
Grupo Brescia, 99
Grupo Carso, S.A. de C.V., 21
Grupo Clarín S.A., 67
Grupo Industrial Bimbo, 19
Grupo Industrial Saltillo, S.A. de C.V., 54

Gulf & Western Inc., I
Haci Omer Sabanci Holdings A.S., 55
Hagemeyer N.V., 39
Hankyu Corporation, 23 (upd.)
Hanson PLC, III; 7 (upd.)
Hanwha Group, 62
Harbour Group Industries, Inc., 90
Hawk Corporation, 59
Henry Crown and Company, 91
Hitachi Zosen Corporation, 53 (upd.)
Hitachi, Ltd., I; 12 (upd.); 40 (upd.)
Ho-Chunk Inc., 61
Hutchison Whampoa Limited, 18; 49 (upd.)
Hyundai Group, III; 7 (upd.); 56 (upd.)
IC Industries, Inc., I
IDB Holding Corporation Ltd., 97
Ilitch Holdings Inc., 37; 86 (upd.)
Inchcape PLC, 16 (upd.); 50 (upd.)
Industria de Diseño Textil S.A. (Inditex), 64
Industrie Zignago Santa Margherita S.p.A., 67
Ingram Industries, Inc., 11; 49 (upd.)
Instituto Nacional de Industria, I
International Controls Corporation, 10
International Telephone & Telegraph Corporation, I; 11 (upd.)
Investor AB, 63
Ishikawajima-Harima Heavy Industries Company, Ltd., III; 86 (upd.)
Istituto per la Ricostruzione Industriale, I
ITOCHU Corporation, 32 (upd.)
J.R. Simplot Company, 60 (upd.)
Jardine Matheson Holdings Limited, I; 20 (upd.); 93 (upd.)
Jason Incorporated, 23
Jefferson Smurfit Group plc, 19 (upd.)
The Jim Pattison Group, 37
Jordan Industries, Inc., 36
José de Mello SGPS S.A., 96
Justin Industries, Inc., 19
Kanematsu Corporation, 24 (upd.)
Kao Corporation, 20 (upd.)
Katy Industries, Inc., I
Keppel Corporation Ltd., 73
Kesko Ltd. (Kesko Oy), 8; 27 (upd.)
Kidde plc, I; 44 (upd.)
King Ranch, Inc., 60 (upd.)
Knowledge Universe, Inc., 54
Koç Holding A.S., I; 54 (upd.)
Koch Industries, Inc., 77 (upd.)
Koninklijke Nedlloyd N.V., 26 (upd.)
Koor Industries Ltd., 25 (upd.); 68 (upd.)
Körber AG, 60
K2 Inc., 16; 84 (upd.)
The L.L. Knickerbocker Co., Inc., 25
Lancaster Colony Corporation, 8; 61 (upd.)
Larry H. Miller Group, 29
LDI Ltd., LLC, 76
Lear Siegler, Inc., I
Lefrak Organization Inc., 26
Leucadia National Corporation, 11; 71 (upd.)
Linde AG, 67 (upd.)
Litton Industries, Inc., I; 11 (upd.)

Loews Corporation, I; 12 (upd.); 36 (upd.); 93 (upd.)
Loral Corporation, 8
LTV Corporation, I; 24 (upd.)
LVMH Moët Hennessy Louis Vuitton SA, 33 (upd.)
The Marmon Group, Inc., 70 (upd.)
Marubeni Corporation, I; 24 (upd.)
MAXXAM Inc., 8
McKesson Corporation, I
McPherson's Ltd., 66
Melitta Unternehmensgruppe Bentz KG, 53
Menasha Corporation, 8
Metallgesellschaft AG, 16 (upd.)
Metromedia Company, 7; 61 (upd.)
Minnesota Mining & Manufacturing Company (3M), I; 8 (upd.); 26 (upd.)
Mitsubishi Corporation, I; 12 (upd.)
Mitsubishi Heavy Industries, Ltd., 40 (upd.)
Mitsui & Co., Ltd., I; 28 (upd.)
The Molson Companies Limited, I; 26 (upd.)
Montedison S.p.A., 24 (upd.)
NACCO Industries, Inc., 7; 78 (upd.)
Nagase & Co., Ltd., 61 (upd.)
National Service Industries, Inc., 11; 54 (upd.)
New Clicks Holdings Ltd., 86
New World Development Company Limited, 38 (upd.)
Nichimen Corporation, 24 (upd.)
Nichirei Corporation, 70
Nissho Iwai K.K., I
Norsk Hydro A.S., 10
Novar plc, 49 (upd.)
Ogden Corporation, I
Onex Corporation, 16; 65 (upd.)
Orkla ASA, 18; 82 (upd.)
Park-Ohio Holdings Corp., 17; 85 (upd.)
Pentair, Inc., 7; 26 (upd.); 81 (upd.)
Petrobras Energia Participaciones S.A., 72
Philip Morris Companies Inc., 44 (upd.)
Poliet S.A., 33
Powell Duffryn plc, 31
Power Corporation of Canada, 36 (upd.); 85 (upd.)
PPB Group Berhad, 57
Preussag AG, 17
The Procter & Gamble Company, III; 8 (upd.); 26 (upd.); 67 (upd.)
Proeza S.A. de C.V., 82
PT Astra International Tbk, 56
Pubco Corporation, 17
Pulsar Internacional S.A., 21
R.B. Pamplin Corp., 45
The Rank Organisation Plc, 14 (upd.)
Raymond Ltd., 77
Red Apple Group, Inc., 23
Roll International Corporation, 37
Rubbermaid Incorporated, 20 (upd.)
Samsung Group, I
San Miguel Corporation, 15
Sara Lee Corporation, II; 15 (upd.); 54 (upd.); 99 (upd.)
S.C. Johnson & Son, Inc., III; 28 (upd.); 89 (upd.)

Schindler Holding AG, 29
Scott Fetzer Company, 12; 80 (upd.)
Sea Containers Ltd., 29
Seaboard Corporation, 36; 85 (upd.)
Sealaska Corporation, 60
Sequa Corporation, 54 (upd.)
Sequana Capital, 78 (upd.)
ServiceMaster Inc., 23 (upd.)
SHV Holdings N.V., 55
Sideco Americana S.A., 67
Sime Darby Berhad, 14; 36 (upd.)
Sistema JSFC, 73
SK Group, 88
Société du Louvre, 27
Sojitz Corporation, 96 (upd.)
Sonae SGPS, S.A., 97
Standex International Corporation, 17; 44 (upd.)
Steamships Trading Company Ltd., 82
Stinnes AG, 23 (upd.)
Sudbury Inc., 16
Sumitomo Corporation, I; 11 (upd.)
Swire Pacific Limited, I; 16 (upd.); 57 (upd.)
Talley Industries, Inc., 16
Tandycrafts, Inc., 31
TaurusHolding GmbH & Co. KG, 46
Teijin Limited, 61 (upd.)
Teledyne, Inc., I; 10 (upd.)
Tenneco Inc., I; 10 (upd.)
Textron Inc., I; 34 (upd.); 88 (upd.)
Thomas H. Lee Co., 24
Thorn Emi PLC, I
Thorn plc, 24
TI Group plc, 17
Time Warner Inc., IV; 7 (upd.)
Tokyu Corporation, 47 (upd.)
Tomen Corporation, 24 (upd.)
Tomkins plc, 11; 44 (upd.)
Toshiba Corporation, I; 12 (upd.); 40 (upd.); 99 (upd.)
Tractebel S.A., 20
Transamerica–An AEGON Company, I; 13 (upd.); 41 (upd.)
The Tranzonic Cos., 15
Triarc Companies, Inc., 8
Triple Five Group Ltd., 49
TRW Inc., I; 11 (upd.)
Tyco International Ltd., 63 (upd.)
Unilever, II; 7 (upd.); 32 (upd.); 89 (upd.)
Unión Fenosa, S.A., 51
United Technologies Corporation, 34 (upd.)
Universal Studios, Inc., 33
Valhi, Inc., 19
Valorem S.A., 88
Valores Industriales S.A., 19
Veba A.G., I; 15 (upd.)
Vendôme Luxury Group plc, 27
Viacom Inc., 23 (upd.); 67 (upd.)
Virgin Group Ltd., 12; 32 (upd.); 89 (upd.)
Vivartia S.A., 82
Votorantim Participaçoes S.A., 76
W.R. Grace & Company, I; 50
Walter Industries, Inc., 72 (upd.)
The Washington Companies, 33

Watsco Inc., 52
Wheaton Industries, 8
Whitbread PLC, I; 20 (upd.); 52 (upd.);
    97 (upd.)
Whitman Corporation, 10 (upd.)
Whittaker Corporation, I
Wirtz Corporation, 72
WorldCorp, Inc., 10
Worms et Cie, 27
Yamaha Corporation, III; 16 (upd.); 40
    (upd.); 99 (upd.)

Construction

A. Johnson & Company H.B., I
ABC Supply Co., Inc., 22
Abertis Infraestructuras, S.A., 65
Abrams Industries Inc., 23
Acergy SA, 97
Aegek S.A., 64
Alberici Corporation, 76
Amec Spie S.A., 57
AMREP Corporation, 21
Anthony & Sylvan Pools Corporation, 56
Asplundh Tree Expert Co., 59 (upd.)
Astec Industries, Inc., 79
ASV, Inc., 34; 66 (upd.)
The Auchter Company, 78
The Austin Company, 8
Autoroutes du Sud de la France SA, 55
Balfour Beatty plc, 36 (upd.)
Baratt Developments PLC, I
Barton Malow Company, 51
Bauerly Companies, 61
BE&K, Inc., 73
Beazer Homes USA, Inc., 17
Bechtel Corporation, I; 24 (upd.); 99
    (upd.)
Bellway Plc, 45
BFC Construction Corporation, 25
Bilfinger & Berger AG, I; 55 (upd.)
Bird Corporation, 19
Birse Group PLC, 77
Black & Veatch LLP, 22
Boral Limited, 43 (upd.)
Bouygues S.A., I; 24 (upd.); 97 (upd.)
The Branch Group, Inc., 72
Brasfield & Gorrie LLC, 87
BRISA Auto-estradas de Portugal S.A., 64
Brown & Root, Inc., 13
Bufete Industrial, S.A. de C.V., 34
Building Materials Holding Corporation,
    52
Bulley & Andrews, LLC, 55
C.R. Meyer and Sons Company, 74
CalMat Co., 19
Cavco Industries, Inc., 65
Centex Corporation, 8; 29 (upd.)
Chugach Alaska Corporation, 60
Cianbro Corporation, 14
The Clark Construction Group, Inc., 8
Colas S.A., 31
Consorcio ARA, S.A. de C.V., 79
Corporación Geo, S.A. de C.V., 81
D.R. Horton, Inc., 58
Day & Zimmermann, Inc., 31 (upd.)
Desarrolladora Homex, S.A. de C.V., 87
Dick Corporation, 64

Dillingham Construction Corporation, I;
    44 (upd.)
Dominion Homes, Inc., 19
The Drees Company, Inc., 41
Dycom Industries, Inc., 57
E.W. Howell Co., Inc., 72
Edw. C. Levy Co., 42
Eiffage, 27
Ellerbe Becket, 41
EMCOR Group Inc., 60
Empresas ICA Sociedad Controladora,
    S.A. de C.V., 41
Encompass Services Corporation, 33
Engle Homes, Inc., 46
Environmental Industries, Inc., 31
Eurotunnel PLC, 13
Fairclough Construction Group PLC, I
Flatiron Construction Corporation, 92
Fleetwood Enterprises, Inc., III: 22 (upd.);
    81 (upd.)
Fluor Corporation, I; 8 (upd.); 34 (upd.)
Forest City Enterprises, Inc., 52 (upd.)
Fred Weber, Inc., 61
Furmanite Corporation, 92
George Wimpey plc, 12; 51 (upd.)
Gilbane, Inc., 34
Granite Construction Incorporated, 61
Granite Rock Company, 26
Great Lakes Dredge & Dock Company,
    69
Grupo Dragados SA, 55
Grupo Ferrovial, S.A., 40
H.J. Russell & Company, 66
Habitat for Humanity International, 36
Heery International, Inc., 58
Heijmans N.V., 66
Henry Boot plc, 76
Hensel Phelps Construction Company, 72
Hillsdown Holdings plc, 24 (upd.)
Hochtief AG, 33; 88 (upd.)
Hoffman Corporation 78
Horton Homes, Inc., 25
Hospitality Worldwide Services, Inc., 26
Hovnanian Enterprises, Inc., 29; 89 (upd.)
IHC Caland N.V., 71
Irex Contracting Group, 90
J.A. Jones, Inc., 16
J C Bamford Excavators Ltd., 83
J.F. Shea Co., Inc., 55
J.H. Findorff and Son, Inc., 60
Jarvis plc, 39
JE Dunn Construction Group, Inc., 85
JLG Industries, Inc., 52
John Brown PLC, I
John Laing plc, I; 51 (upd.)
John W. Danforth Company, 48
Kajima Corporation, I; 51 (upd.)
Kaufman and Broad Home Corporation,
    8
KB Home, 45 (upd.)
Kellogg Brown & Root, Inc., 62 (upd.)
Kitchell Corporation, 14
The Koll Company, 8
Komatsu Ltd., 16 (upd.)
Kraus-Anderson Companies, Inc., 36; 83
    (upd.)
Kumagai Gumi Company, Ltd., I
L'Entreprise Jean Lefebvre, 23

Laing O'Rourke PLC, 93 (upd.)
Ledcor Industries Limited, 46
Lennar Corporation, 11
Lincoln Property Company, 8
Lindal Cedar Homes, Inc., 29
Linde A.G., I
MasTec, Inc., 55
Matrix Service Company, 65
May Gurney Integrated Services PLC, 95
McCarthy Building Companies, Inc., 48
Mellon-Stuart Company, I
Michael Baker Corp., 14
Modtech Holdings, Inc., 77
Mota-Engil, SGPS, S.A., 97
Morrison Knudsen Corporation, 7; 28
    (upd.)
Morrow Equipment Co. L.L.C., 87
New Holland N.V., 22
Newpark Resources, Inc., 63
NVR Inc., 70 (upd.)
NVR L.P., 8
Obayashi Corporation 78
Obrascon Huarte Lain S.A., 76
Ohbayashi Corporation, I
Opus Group, 34
Orascom Construction Industries S.A.E.,
    87
Orleans Homebuilders, Inc., 62
Panattoni Development Company, Inc.,
    99
The Parsons Corporation, 56 (upd.)
PCL Construction Group Inc., 50
The Peninsular & Oriental Steam
    Navigation Company (Bovis Division),
    I
Perini Corporation, 8; 82 (upd.)
Peter Kiewit Sons' Inc., 8
Philipp Holzmann AG, 17
Post Properties, Inc., 26
Pulte Homes, Inc., 8; 42 (upd.)
Pyramid Companies, 54
Redrow Group plc, 31
Rinker Group Ltd., 65
RMC Group p.l.c., 34 (upd.)
Rooney Brothers Co., 25
The Rottlund Company, Inc., 28
Roy Anderson Corporation, 75
Ryan Companies US, Inc., 99
The Ryland Group, Inc., 8; 37 (upd.)
Sandvik AB, 32 (upd.)
Schuff Steel Company, 26
Seddon Group Ltd., 67
Shorewood Packaging Corporation, 28
Simon Property Group Inc., 27; 84 (upd.)
Skanska AB, 38
Skidmore, Owings & Merrill LLP, 69
    (upd.)
SNC-Lavalin Group Inc., 72
Speedy Hire plc, 84
Stabler Companies Inc. 78
Standard Pacific Corporation, 52
The Structure Tone Organization, 99
Stone & Webster, Inc., 64 (upd.)
Sundt Corp., 24
Swinerton Inc., 43
Tarmac Limited, III, 28 (upd.); 95 (upd.)
Taylor Woodrow plc, I; 38 (upd.)
Technical Olympic USA, Inc., 75

Terex Corporation, 7; 40 (upd.); 91 (upd.)
ThyssenKrupp AG, IV; 28 (upd.); 87 (upd.)
TIC Holdings Inc., 92
Toll Brothers Inc., 15; 70 (upd.)
Trammell Crow Company, 8
Tridel Enterprises Inc., 9
Turner Construction Company, 66
The Turner Corporation, 8; 23 (upd.)
U.S. Aggregates, Inc., 42
U.S. Home Corporation, 8; 78 (upd.)
Urbi Desarrollos Urbanos, S.A. de C.V., 81
VA TECH ELIN EBG GmbH, 49
Veidekke ASA, 98
Veit Companies, 43; 92 (upd.)
Wacker Construction Equipment AG, 95
Walbridge Aldinger Co., 38
Walter Industries, Inc., 22 (upd.)
The Weitz Company, Inc., 42
Whiting-Turner Contracting Company, 95
Willbros Group, Inc., 56
William Lyon Homes, 59
Wilson Bowden Plc, 45
Wood Hall Trust PLC, I
The Yates Companies, Inc., 62
Zachry Group, Inc., 95

Containers

Ball Corporation, I; 10 (upd.); 78 (upd.)
BWAY Corporation, 24
Chesapeake Corporation, 8; 30 (upd.); 93 (upd.)
Clarcor Inc., 17
Continental Can Co., Inc., 15
Continental Group Company, I
Crown Cork & Seal Company, Inc., I; 13 (upd.); 32 (upd.)
Crown Holdings, Inc., 83 (upd.)
Gaylord Container Corporation, 8
Golden Belt Manufacturing Co., 16
Graham Packaging Holdings Company, 87
Greif Inc., 15; 66 (upd.)
Grupo Industrial Durango, S.A. de C.V., 37
Hanjin Shipping Co., Ltd., 50
Inland Container Corporation, 8
Interpool, Inc., 92
Kerr Group Inc., 24
Keyes Fibre Company, 9
Libbey Inc., 49
Liqui-Box Corporation, 16
The Longaberger Company, 12
Longview Fibre Company, 8
The Mead Corporation, 19 (upd.)
Metal Box PLC, I
Molins plc, 51
National Can Corporation, I
Owens-Illinois, Inc., I; 26 (upd.); 85 (upd.)
Packaging Corporation of America, 51 (upd.)
Primerica Corporation, I
PVC Container Corporation, 67
Rexam PLC, 32 (upd.); 85 (upd.)
Reynolds Metals Company, 19 (upd.)

Royal Packaging Industries Van Leer N.V., 30
RPC Group PLC, 81
Sealright Co., Inc., 17
Shurgard Storage Centers, Inc., 52
Smurfit-Stone Container Corporation, 26 (upd.); 83 (upd.)
Sonoco Products Company, 8; 89 (upd.)
Thermos Company, 16
Toyo Seikan Kaisha, Ltd., I
U.S. Can Corporation, 30
Ultra Pac, Inc., 24
Viatech Continental Can Company, Inc., 25 (upd.)
Vidrala S.A., 67
Vitro Corporativo S.A. de C.V., 34

Drugs & Pharmaceuticals

A. Nelson & Co. Ltd., 75
A.L. Pharma Inc., 12
Abbott Laboratories, I; 11 (upd.); 40 (upd.); 93 (upd.)
Actelion Ltd., 83
Akorn, Inc., 32
Albany Molecular Research, Inc., 77
Allergan, Inc., 77 (upd.)
Alpharma Inc., 35 (upd.)
ALZA Corporation, 10; 36 (upd.)
American Home Products, I; 10 (upd.)
American Oriental Bioengineering Inc., 93
American Pharmaceutical Partners, Inc., 69
AmerisourceBergen Corporation, 64 (upd.)
Amersham PLC, 50
Amgen, Inc., 10; 89 (upd.)
Amylin Pharmaceuticals, Inc., 67
Andrx Corporation, 55
Astellas Pharma Inc., 97 (upd.)
AstraZeneca PLC, I; 20 (upd.); 50 (upd.)
Axcan Pharma Inc., 85
Barr Pharmaceuticals, Inc., 26; 68 (upd.)
Bayer A.G., I; 13 (upd.)
Berlex Laboratories, Inc., 66
Biovail Corporation, 47
Block Drug Company, Inc., 8
Boiron S.A., 73
Bristol-Myers Squibb Company, III; 9 (upd.); 37 (upd.)
BTG Plc, 87
C.H. Boehringer Sohn, 39
Caremark Rx, Inc., 10; 54 (upd.)
Carter-Wallace, Inc., 8; 38 (upd.)
Celgene Corporation, 67
Cephalon, Inc., 45
Chiron Corporation, 10
Chugai Pharmaceutical Co., Ltd., 50
Ciba-Geigy Ltd., I; 8 (upd.)
D&K Wholesale Drug, Inc., 14
Discovery Partners International, Inc., 58
Dr. Reddy's Laboratories Ltd., 59
Elan Corporation PLC, 63
Eli Lilly and Company, I; 11 (upd.); 47 (upd.)
Endo Pharmaceuticals Holdings Inc., 71
Eon Labs, Inc., 67
Express Scripts Inc., 44 (upd.)
F. Hoffmann-La Roche Ltd., I; 50 (upd.)

Fisons plc, 9; 23 (upd.)
Forest Laboratories, Inc., 52 (upd.)
FoxMeyer Health Corporation, 16
Fujisawa Pharmaceutical Company Ltd., I
G.D. Searle & Co., I; 12 (upd.); 34 (upd.)
Galenica AG, 84
GEHE AG, 27
Genentech, Inc., I; 8 (upd.); 75 (upd.)
Genetics Institute, Inc., 8
Genzyme Corporation, 13, 77 (upd.)
Glaxo Holdings PLC, I; 9 (upd.)
GlaxoSmithKline plc, 46 (upd.)
Groupe Fournier SA, 44
Groupe Léa Nature, 88
H. Lundbeck A/S, 44
Hauser, Inc., 46
Heska Corporation, 39
Hexal AG, 69
Hospira, Inc., 71
Huntingdon Life Sciences Group plc, 42
ICN Pharmaceuticals, Inc., 52
Immucor, Inc., 81
Integrated BioPharma, Inc., 83
IVAX Corporation, 55 (upd.)
Janssen Pharmaceutica N.V., 80
Johnson & Johnson, III; 8 (upd.)
Jones Medical Industries, Inc., 24
The Judge Group, Inc., 51
King Pharmaceuticals, Inc., 54
Kinray Inc., 85
Kos Pharmaceuticals, Inc., 63
Kyowa Hakko Kogyo Co., Ltd., 48 (upd.)
Laboratoires Arkopharma S.A., 75
Leiner Health Products Inc., 34
Ligand Pharmaceuticals Incorporated, 47
MannKind Corporation, 87
Marion Merrell Dow, Inc., I; 9 (upd.)
Matrixx Initiatives, Inc., 74
McKesson Corporation, 12; 47 (upd.)
Medicis Pharmaceutical Corporation, 59
MedImmune, Inc., 35
Merck & Co., Inc., I; 11 (upd.); 34 (upd.); 95 (upd.)
Merz Group, 81
Miles Laboratories, I
Millennium Pharmaceuticals, Inc., 47
Monsanto Company, 29 (upd.), 77 (upd.)
Moore Medical Corp., 17
Murdock Madaus Schwabe, 26
Mylan Laboratories Inc., I; 20 (upd.); 59 (upd.)
Myriad Genetics, Inc., 95
Nadro S.A. de C.V., 86
Nastech Pharmaceutical Company Inc., 79
National Patent Development Corporation, 13
Natrol, Inc., 49
Natural Alternatives International, Inc., 49
Nektar Therapeutics, 91
Novartis AG, 39 (upd.)
Noven Pharmaceuticals, Inc., 55
Novo Nordisk A/S, I; 61 (upd.)
Obagi Medical Products, Inc., 95
Omnicare, Inc., 49
Omrix Biopharmaceuticals, Inc., 95
Par Pharmaceutical Companies, Inc., 65
PDL BioPharma, Inc., 90

Perrigo Company, 59 (upd.)
Pfizer Inc., I; 9 (upd.); 38 (upd.); 79
    (upd.)
Pharmacia & Upjohn Inc., I; 25 (upd.)
Pharmion Corporation, 91
PLIVA d.d., 70
PolyMedica Corporation, 77
POZEN Inc., 81
QLT Inc., 71
The Quigley Corporation, 62
Quintiles Transnational Corporation, 21
R.P. Scherer, I
Ranbaxy Laboratories Ltd., 70
ratiopharm Group, 84
Reckitt Benckiser plc, II; 42 (upd.); 91
    (upd.)
Roberts Pharmaceutical Corporation, 16
Roche Bioscience, 14 (upd.)
Rorer Group, I
Roussel Uclaf, I; 8 (upd.)
Salix Pharmaceuticals, Ltd., 93
Sandoz Ltd., I
Sankyo Company, Ltd., I; 56 (upd.)
The Sanofi-Synthélabo Group, I; 49
    (upd.)
Schering AG, I; 50 (upd.)
Schering-Plough Corporation, I; 14
    (upd.); 49 (upd.); 99 (upd.)
Sepracor Inc., 45
Serono S.A., 47
Shionogi & Co., Ltd., III; 17 (upd.); 98
    (upd.)
Sigma-Aldrich Corporation, I; 36 (upd.);
    93 (upd.)
SmithKline Beecham plc, I; 32 (upd.)
Solvay S.A., 61 (upd.)
Squibb Corporation, I
Sterling Drug, Inc., I
Stiefel Laboratories, Inc., 90
Sun Pharmaceutical Industries Ltd., 57
The Sunrider Corporation, 26
Syntex Corporation, I
Takeda Chemical Industries, Ltd., I
Taro Pharmaceutical Industries Ltd., 65
Teva Pharmaceutical Industries Ltd., 22;
    54 (upd.)
UCB Pharma SA, 98
The Upjohn Company, I; 8 (upd.)
Vertex Pharmaceuticals Incorporated, 83
Virbac Corporation, 74
Vitalink Pharmacy Services, Inc., 15
Warner Chilcott Limited, 85
Warner-Lambert Co., I; 10 (upd.)
Watson Pharmaceuticals Inc., 16; 56
    (upd.)
The Wellcome Foundation Ltd., I
Zentiva N.V./Zentiva, a.s., 99
Zila, Inc., 46

Electrical & Electronics

ABB ASEA Brown Boveri Ltd., II; 22
    (upd.)
ABB Ltd., 65 (upd.)
Acer Incorporated, 16; 73 (upd.)
Acuson Corporation, 10; 36 (upd.)
ADC Telecommunications, Inc., 30 (upd.)
Adtran Inc., 22

Advanced Micro Devices, Inc., 6; 30
    (upd.); 99 (upd.)
Advanced Technology Laboratories, Inc., 9
Agere Systems Inc., 61
Agilent Technologies Inc., 38; 93 (upd.)
Agilysys Inc., 76 (upd.)
Aiwa Co., Ltd., 30
AKG Acoustics GmbH, 62
Akzo Nobel N.V., 13; 41 (upd.)
Alienware Corporation, 81
Alliant Techsystems Inc., 30 (upd.); 77
    (upd.)
AlliedSignal Inc., 22 (upd.)
Alpine Electronics, Inc., 13
Alps Electric Co., Ltd., II
Altera Corporation, 18; 43 (upd.)
Altron Incorporated, 20
Amdahl Corporation, 40 (upd.)
American Power Conversion Corporation,
    24; 67 (upd.)
American Superconductor Corporation,
    97
American Technical Ceramics Corp., 67
Amerigon Incorporated, 97
Amkor Technology, Inc., 69
AMP Incorporated, II; 14 (upd.)
Amphenol Corporation, 40
Amstrad plc, 48 (upd.)
Analog Devices, Inc., 10
Analogic Corporation, 23
Anam Group, 23
Anaren Microwave, Inc., 33
Andrew Corporation, 10; 32 (upd.)
Anixter International Inc., 88
Anritsu Corporation, 68
Apex Digital, Inc., 63
Apple Computer, Inc., 36 (upd.); 77
    (upd.)
Applied Power Inc., 32 (upd.)
Applied Signal Technology, Inc., 87
Argon ST, Inc., 81
Arotech Corporation, 93
ARRIS Group, Inc., 89
Arrow Electronics, Inc., 10; 50 (upd.)
Ascend Communications, Inc., 24
Astronics Corporation, 35
Atari Corporation, 9; 23 (upd.); 66 (upd.)
ATI Technologies Inc., 79
Atmel Corporation, 17
ATMI, Inc., 93
AU Optronics Corporation, 67
Audiovox Corporation, 34; 90 (upd.)
Ault Incorporated, 34
Autodesk, Inc., 10; 89 (upd.)
Avnet Inc., 9
AVX Corporation, 67
Axcelis Technologies, Inc., 95
Axsys Technologies, Inc., 93
Ballard Power Systems Inc., 73
Bang & Olufsen Holding A/S, 37; 86
    (upd.)
Barco NV, 44
Bell Microproducts Inc., 69
Benchmark Electronics, Inc., 40
Bicoastal Corporation, II
Black Box Corporation, 20; 96 (upd.)
Blonder Tongue Laboratories, Inc., 48
Blue Coat Systems, Inc., 83

BMC Industries, Inc., 59 (upd.)
Bogen Communications International,
    Inc., 62
Bose Corporation, 13; 36 (upd.)
Boston Acoustics, Inc., 22
Bowthorpe plc, 33
Braun GmbH, 51
Broadcom Corporation, 34; 90 (upd.)
Bull S.A., 43 (upd.)
Burr-Brown Corporation, 19
BVR Systems (1998) Ltd., 93
C-COR.net Corp., 38
Cabletron Systems, Inc., 10
Cadence Design Systems, Inc., 48 (upd.)
Cambridge SoundWorks, Inc., 48
Canon Inc., 18 (upd.); 79 (upd.)
Carbone Lorraine S.A., 33
Cardtronics, Inc., 93
Carl Zeiss AG, III; 34 (upd.); 91 (upd.)
Cash Systems, Inc., 93
CASIO Computer Co., Ltd., 16 (upd.);
    40 (upd.)
CDW Computer Centers, Inc., 52 (upd.)
Celestica Inc., 80
Checkpoint Systems, Inc., 39
Chi Mei Optoelectronics Corporation, 75
Chubb, PLC, 50
Chunghwa Picture Tubes, Ltd., 75
Cirrus Logic, Inc., 48 (upd.)
Cisco Systems, Inc., 34 (upd.); 77 (upd.)
Citizen Watch Co., Ltd., III; 21 (upd.);
    81 (upd.)
Clarion Company Ltd., 64
Cobham plc, 30
Cobra Electronics Corporation, 14
Coherent, Inc., 31
Cohu, Inc., 32
Color Kinetics Incorporated, 85
Compagnie Générale d'Électricité, II
Concurrent Computer Corporation, 75
Conexant Systems, Inc., 36
Cooper Industries, Inc., II
Cray Inc., 75 (upd.)
Cray Research, Inc., 16 (upd.)
Cree Inc., 53
CTS Corporation, 39
Cubic Corporation, 19; 98 (upd.)
Cypress Semiconductor Corporation, 20;
    48 (upd.)
D&H Distributing Co., 95
D-Link Corporation, 83
Dai Nippon Printing Co., Ltd., 57 (upd.)
Daiichikosho Company Ltd., 86
Daktronics, Inc., 32
Dallas Semiconductor Corporation, 13; 31
    (upd.)
DDi Corp., 97
De La Rue plc, 34 (upd.)
Dell Computer Corporation, 31 (upd.)
DH Technology, Inc., 18
Dictaphone Healthcare Solutions 78
Diehl Stiftung & Co. KG, 79
Digi International Inc., 9
Diodes Incorporated, 81
Directed Electronics, Inc., 87
Discreet Logic Inc., 20
Dixons Group plc, 19 (upd.)
Dolby Laboratories Inc., 20

Dot Hill Systems Corp., 93
DRS Technologies, Inc., 58
Dynatech Corporation, 13
E-Systems, Inc., 9
Electronics for Imaging, Inc., 15; 43
    (upd.)
Elma Electronic AG, 83
Elpida Memory, Inc., 83
EMCORE Corporation, 97
Emerson, II; 46 (upd.)
Emerson Radio Corp., 30
ENCAD, Incorporated, 25
Equant N.V., 52
Equus Computer Systems, Inc., 49
ESS Technology, Inc., 22
Essex Corporation, 85
Everex Systems, Inc., 16
Exabyte Corporation, 40 (upd.)
Exar Corp., 14
Exide Electronics Group, Inc., 20
Finisar Corporation, 92
First Solar, Inc., 95
Fisk Corporation, 72
Flextronics International Ltd., 38
Fluke Corporation, 15
FormFactor, Inc., 85
Foxboro Company, 13
Freescale Semiconductor, Inc., 83
Frequency Electronics, Inc., 61
FuelCell Energy, Inc., 75
Fuji Electric Co., Ltd., II; 48 (upd.)
Fuji Photo Film Co., Ltd., 79 (upd.)
Fujitsu Limited, 16 (upd.); 42 (upd.)
Funai Electric Company Ltd., 62
Gateway, Inc., 63 (upd.)
General Atomics, 57
General Dynamics Corporation, I; 10
    (upd.); 40 (upd.); 88 (upd.
General Electric Company, II; 12 (upd.)
General Electric Company, PLC, II
General Instrument Corporation, 10
General Signal Corporation, 9
Genesis Microchip Inc., 82
GenRad, Inc., 24
GM Hughes Electronics Corporation, II
Goldstar Co., Ltd., 12
Gould Electronics, Inc., 14
GPS Industries, Inc., 81
Grundig AG, 27
Guillemot Corporation, 41
Hadco Corporation, 24
Hamilton Beach/Proctor-Silex Inc., 17
Harman International Industries Inc., 15
Harris Corporation, II; 20 (upd.); 78
    (upd.)
Hayes Corporation, 24
Hemisphere GPS Inc., 99
Herley Industries, Inc., 33
Hewlett-Packard Company, 28 (upd.); 50
    (upd.)
Holophane Corporation, 19
Hon Hai Precision Industry Co., Ltd., 59
Honeywell Inc., II; 12 (upd.); 50 (upd.)
Hubbell Incorporated, 9; 31 (upd.)
Hughes Supply, Inc., 14
Hutchinson Technology Incorporated, 18;
    63 (upd.)
Hypercom Corporation, 27

IDEO Inc., 65
IEC Electronics Corp., 42
Illumina, Inc., 93
Imax Corporation, 28
In Focus Systems, Inc., 22
Indigo NV, 26
InFocus Corporation, 92
Ingram Micro Inc., 52
Innovative Solutions & Support, Inc., 85
Integrated Defense Technologies, Inc., 54
Intel Corporation, II; 10 (upd.); 75 (upd.)
Intermec Technologies Corporation, 72
International Business Machines
    Corporation, III; 6 (upd.); 30 (upd.);
    63 (upd.)
International Rectifier Corporation, 31; 71
    (upd.)
Intersil Corporation, 93
Ionatron, Inc., 85
Itel Corporation, 9
Jabil Circuit, Inc., 36; 88 (upd.)
Jaco Electronics, Inc., 30
JDS Uniphase Corporation, 34
Johnson Controls, Inc., 59 (upd.)
Juno Lighting, Inc., 30
Katy Industries, Inc., 51 (upd.)
Keithley Instruments Inc., 16
Kemet Corp., 14
Kent Electronics Corporation, 17
Kenwood Corporation, 31
Kesa Electricals plc, 91
Kimball International, Inc., 48 (upd.)
Kingston Technology Corporation, 20
KitchenAid, 8
KLA-Tencor Corporation, 45 (upd.)
KnowledgeWare Inc., 9
Kollmorgen Corporation, 18
Konami Corporation, 96
Konica Corporation, III; 30 (upd.)
Koninklijke Philips Electronics N.V., 50
    (upd.)
Koor Industries Ltd., II
Kopin Corporation, 80
Koss Corporation, 38
Kudelski Group SA, 44
Kulicke and Soffa Industries, Inc., 33; 76
    (upd.)
Kyocera Corporation, II; 79 (upd.)
LaBarge Inc., 41
The Lamson & Sessions Co., 61 (upd.)
Lattice Semiconductor Corp., 16
LeCroy Corporation, 41
Legrand SA, 21
Lenovo Group Ltd., 80
Leoni AG, 98
Lexmark International, Inc., 79 (upd.)
Linear Technology Corporation, 16; 99
    (upd.)
Littelfuse, Inc., 26
Loewe AG, 90
Loral Corporation, 9
LOUD Technologies, Inc., 95 (upd.)
Lowrance Electronics, Inc., 18
LSI Logic Corporation, 13; 64
Lucent Technologies Inc., 34
Lucky-Goldstar, II
Lunar Corporation, 29
Mackie Designs Inc., 33

MagneTek, Inc., 15; 41 (upd.)
Magneti Marelli Holding SpA, 90
Marconi plc, 33 (upd.)
Marquette Electronics, Inc., 13
Matsushita Electric Industrial Co., Ltd., II
Maxim Integrated Products, Inc., 16
McDATA Corporation, 75
Measurement Specialties, Inc., 71
Medis Technologies Ltd., 77
Merix Corporation, 36; 75 (upd.)
Methode Electronics, Inc., 13
Mitel Corporation, 18
MITRE Corporation, 26
Mitsubishi Electric Corporation, II; 44
    (upd.)
Molex Incorporated, 54 (upd.)
Monster Cable Products, Inc., 69
Motorola, Inc., II; 11 (upd.); 34 (upd.);
    93 (upd.)
N.F. Smith & Associates LP, 70
Nam Tai Electronics, Inc., 61
National Instruments Corporation, 22
National Presto Industries, Inc., 16; 43
    (upd.)
National Semiconductor Corporation, II;
    26 (upd.); 69 (upd.)
NEC Corporation, II; 21 (upd.); 57
    (upd.)
Network Equipment Technologies Inc., 92
Nexans SA, 54
Nintendo Co., Ltd., 28 (upd.)
Nokia Corporation, II; 17 (upd.); 38
    (upd.); 77 (upd.)
Nortel Networks Corporation, 36 (upd.)
Northrop Grumman Corporation, 45
    (upd.)
Oak Technology, Inc., 22
Océ N.V., 24; 91 (upd.)
Oki Electric Industry Company, Limited,
    II
Omnicell, Inc., 89
Omron Corporation, II; 28 (upd.)
OPTEK Technology Inc., 98
Orbotech Ltd., 75
Otari Inc., 89
Otter Tail Power Company, 18
Palm, Inc., 36; 75 (upd.)
Palomar Medical Technologies, Inc., 22
Parlex Corporation, 61
The Peak Technologies Group, Inc., 14
Peavey Electronics Corporation, 16
Philips Electronics N.V., II; 13 (upd.)
Philips Electronics North America Corp.,
    13
Pioneer Electronic Corporation, 28 (upd.)
Pioneer-Standard Electronics Inc., 19
Pitney Bowes Inc., 47 (upd.)
Pittway Corporation, 9
Pixelworks, Inc., 69
Planar Systems, Inc., 61
The Plessey Company, PLC, II
Plexus Corporation, 35; 80 (upd.)
Polk Audio, Inc., 34
Polaroid Corporation, III; 7 (upd.); 28
    (upd.); 93 (upd.)
Potter & Brumfield Inc., 11
Premier Industrial Corporation, 9
Protection One, Inc., 32

Quanta Computer Inc., 47; 79 (upd.)
Racal Electronics PLC, II
RadioShack Corporation, 36 (upd.)
Radius Inc., 16
RAE Systems Inc., 83
Ramtron International Corporation, 89
Raychem Corporation, 8
Rayovac Corporation, 13
Raytheon Company, II; 11 (upd.); 38 (upd.)
RCA Corporation, II
Read-Rite Corp., 10
Redback Networks, Inc., 92
Reliance Electric Company, 9
Research in Motion Ltd., 54
Rexel, Inc., 15
Richardson Electronics, Ltd., 17
Ricoh Company, Ltd., 36 (upd.)
Rimage Corp., 89
The Rival Company, 19
Rockford Corporation, 43
Rogers Corporation, 61
S&C Electric Company, 15
SAGEM S.A., 37
St. Louis Music, Inc., 48
Sam Ash Music Corporation, 30
Samsung Electronics Co., Ltd., 14; 41 (upd.)
SANYO Electric Co., Ltd., II; 36 (upd.); 95 (upd.)
Sarnoff Corporation, 57
ScanSource, Inc., 29; 74 (upd.)
Schneider S.A., II; 18 (upd.)
SCI Systems, Inc., 9
Scientific-Atlanta, Inc., 45 (upd.)
Scitex Corporation Ltd., 24
Seagate Technology, Inc., 34 (upd.)
SEGA Corporation, 73
Semitool, Inc., 79 (upd.)
Semtech Corporation, 32
Sennheiser Electronic GmbH & Co. KG, 66
Sensormatic Electronics Corp., 11
Sensory Science Corporation, 37
SGI, 29 (upd.)
Sharp Corporation, II; 12 (upd.); 40 (upd.)
Sheldahl Inc., 23
Shure Inc., 60
Siemens AG, II; 14 (upd.); 57 (upd.)
Silicon Graphics Incorporated, 9
Siltronic AG, 90
SL Industries, Inc., 77
SMART Modular Technologies, Inc., 86
Smiths Industries PLC, 25
Solectron Corporation, 12; 48 (upd.)
Sony Corporation, II; 12 (upd.); 40 (upd.)
Spansion Inc., 80
Spectrum Control, Inc., 67
SPX Corporation, 47 (upd.)
Square D, 90
Sterling Electronics Corp., 18
STMicroelectronics NV, 52
Strix Ltd., 51
Stuart C. Irby Company, 58
Sumitomo Electric Industries, Ltd., II

Sun Microsystems, Inc., 7; 30 (upd.); 91 (upd.)
Sunbeam-Oster Co., Inc., 9
SunPower Corporation, 91
Suntech Power Holdings Company Ltd., 89
Synaptics Incorporated, 95
Syneron Medical Ltd., 91
SYNNEX Corporation, 73
Synopsys, Inc., 69 (upd.)
Sypris Solutions, Inc., 85
SyQuest Technology, Inc., 18
Tandy Corporation, II; 12 (upd.)
Tatung Co., 23
TDK Corporation, II; 17 (upd.); 49 (upd.)
TEAC Corporation 78
Tech-Sym Corporation, 18
Technitrol, Inc., 29
Tektronix, Inc., 8
Teledyne Technologies Inc., 62 (upd.)
Telxon Corporation, 10
Teradyne, Inc., 11; 98 (upd.)
Texas Instruments Inc., II; 11 (upd.); 46 (upd.)
Thales S.A., 42
Thomas & Betts Corporation, 11; 54 (upd.)
THOMSON multimedia S.A., II; 42 (upd.)
THQ, Inc., 92 (upd.)
The Titan Corporation, 36
TomTom N.V., 81
Tops Appliance City, Inc., 17
Toromont Industries, Ltd., 21
Trans-Lux Corporation, 51
Trimble Navigation Limited, 40
TriQuint Semiconductor, Inc., 63
Tweeter Home Entertainment Group, Inc., 30
Ultimate Electronics, Inc., 69 (upd.)
Ultrak Inc., 24
Uniden Corporation, 98
United Microelectronics Corporation, 98
Universal Electronics Inc., 39
Universal Security Instruments, Inc., 96
Varian Associates Inc., 12
Veeco Instruments Inc., 32
VIASYS Healthcare, Inc., 52
Viasystems Group, Inc., 67
Vicon Industries, Inc., 44
Victor Company of Japan, Limited, II; 26 (upd.); 83 (upd.)
Vishay Intertechnology, Inc., 21; 80 (upd.)
Vitesse Semiconductor Corporation, 32
Vitro Corp., 10
VLSI Technology, Inc., 16
VTech Holdings Ltd., 77
Wells-Gardner Electronics Corporation, 43
Westinghouse Electric Corporation, II; 12 (upd.)
Winbond Electronics Corporation, 74
Wincor Nixdorf Holding GmbH, 69 (upd.)
Wyle Electronics, 14
Xantrex Technology Inc., 97

Xerox Corporation, III; 6 (upd.); 26 (upd.); 69 (upd.)
Yageo Corporation, 16; 98 (upd.)
York Research Corporation, 35
Zenith Data Systems, Inc., 10
Zenith Electronics Corporation, II; 13 (upd.); 34 (upd.); 89 (upd.)
Zoom Telephonics, Inc., 18
Zoran Corporation, 77
Zumtobel AG, 50
Zytec Corporation, 19

Engineering & Management Services

AAON, Inc., 22
Aavid Thermal Technologies, Inc., 29
Acergy SA, 97
AECOM Technology Corporation, 79
Alliant Techsystems Inc., 30 (upd.)
Altran Technologies, 51
Amey Plc, 47
American Science & Engineering, Inc., 81
Analytic Sciences Corporation, 10
Arcadis NV, 26
Arthur D. Little, Inc., 35
The Austin Company, 8; 72 (upd.)
Babcock International Group PLC, 69
Balfour Beatty plc, 36 (upd.)
BE&K, Inc., 73
Bechtel Corporation, I; 24 (upd.); 99 (upd.)
Birse Group PLC, 77
Brown & Root, Inc., 13
Bufete Industrial, S.A. de C.V., 34
C.H. Heist Corporation, 24
CDI Corporation, 6; 54 (upd.)
CH2M HILL Companies Ltd., 22; 96 (upd.)
The Charles Stark Draper Laboratory, Inc., 35
Coflexip S.A., 25
Corrections Corporation of America, 23
CRSS Inc., 6
Dames & Moore, Inc., 25
DAW Technologies, Inc., 25
Day & Zimmermann Inc., 9; 31 (upd.)
Donaldson Co. Inc., 16
Dycom Industries, Inc., 57
Edwards and Kelcey, 70
EG&G Incorporated, 8; 29 (upd.)
Eiffage, 27
Essef Corporation, 18
Exponent, Inc., 95
FKI Plc, 57
Fluor Corporation, 34 (upd.)
Forest City Enterprises, Inc., 52 (upd.)
Foster Wheeler Corporation, 6; 23 (upd.)
Foster Wheeler Ltd., 76 (upd.)
Framatome SA, 19
Fraport AG Frankfurt Airport Services Worldwide, 90
Fugro N.V., 98
Gale International Llc, 93
Georg Fischer AG Schaffhausen, 61
Gilbane, Inc., 34
Great Lakes Dredge & Dock Company, 69
Grupo Dragados SA, 55

Halliburton Company, 25 (upd.)
Harding Lawson Associates Group, Inc., 16
Harza Engineering Company, 14
HDR Inc., 48
HOK Group, Inc., 59
ICF Kaiser International, Inc., 28
IHC Caland N.V., 71
Jacobs Engineering Group Inc., 6; 26 (upd.)
Jacques Whitford, 92
The Judge Group, Inc., 51
JWP Inc., 9
The Keith Companies Inc., 54
Keller Group PLC, 95
Klöckner-Werke AG, 58 (upd.)
Kvaerner ASA, 36
Layne Christensen Company, 19
The MacNeal-Schwendler Corporation, 25
Malcolm Pirnie, Inc., 42
McDermott International, Inc., 37 (upd.)
McKinsey & Company, Inc., 9
Michael Baker Corporation, 51 (upd.)
Mota-Engil, SGPS, S.A., 97
Nooter Corporation, 61
Oceaneering International, Inc., 63
Odebrecht S.A., 73
Ogden Corporation, 6
Opus Group, 34
PAREXEL International Corporation, 84
Parsons Brinckerhoff, Inc., 34
The Parsons Corporation, 8; 56 (upd.)
The PBSJ Corporation, 82
Petrofac Ltd., 95
Quanta Services, Inc., 79
RCM Technologies, Inc., 34
Renishaw plc, 46
Ricardo plc, 90
Rosemount Inc., 15
Roy F. Weston, Inc., 33
Royal Vopak NV, 41
Rust International Inc., 11
Sandia National Laboratories, 49
Sandvik AB, 32 (upd.)
Sarnoff Corporation, 57
Science Applications International Corporation, 15
Serco Group plc, 47
Siegel & Gale, 64
Siemens AG, 57 (upd.)
SRI International, Inc., 57
SSOE Inc., 76
Stone & Webster, Inc., 13; 64 (upd.)
Sulzer Ltd., 68 (upd.)
Susquehanna Pfaltzgraff Company, 8
Sverdrup Corporation, 14
Tech-Sym Corporation, 44 (upd.)
Technip 78
Tetra Tech, Inc., 29
ThyssenKrupp AG, IV; 28 (upd.); 87 (upd.)
Towers Perrin, 32
Tracor Inc., 17
TRC Companies, Inc., 32
Underwriters Laboratories, Inc., 30
United Dominion Industries Limited, 8; 16 (upd.)
URS Corporation, 45; 80 (upd.)

U.S. Army Corps of Engineers, 91
VA TECH ELIN EBG GmbH, 49
VECO International, Inc., 7
Vinci, 43
Volkert and Associates, Inc., 98
The Weir Group PLC, 85
Willbros Group, Inc., 56
WS Atkins Plc, 45

Entertainment & Leisure
A&E Television Networks, 32
Aardman Animations Ltd., 61
ABC Family Worldwide, Inc., 52
Academy of Television Arts & Sciences, Inc., 55
Acclaim Entertainment Inc., 24
Activision, Inc., 32; 89 (upd.)
AEI Music Network Inc., 35
Affinity Group Holding Inc., 56
Airtours Plc, 27
Alaska Railroad Corporation, 60
All American Communications Inc., 20
The All England Lawn Tennis & Croquet Club, 54
Alliance Entertainment Corp., 17
Alternative Tentacles Records, 66
Alvin Ailey Dance Foundation, Inc., 52
Amblin Entertainment, 21
AMC Entertainment Inc., 12; 35 (upd.)
American Golf Corporation, 45
American Gramaphone LLC, 52
American Kennel Club, Inc., 74
American Skiing Company, 28
Ameristar Casinos, Inc., 33; 69 (upd.)
AMF Bowling, Inc., 40
Anaheim Angels Baseball Club, Inc., 53
Anchor Gaming, 24
AOL Time Warner Inc., 57 (upd.)
Applause Inc., 24
Apple Corps Ltd., 87
Aprilia SpA, 17
Arena Leisure Plc, 99
Argosy Gaming Company, 21
Aristocrat Leisure Limited, 54
Arsenal Holdings PLC, 79
The Art Institute of Chicago, 29
The Arthur C. Clarke Foundation, 92
Artisan Entertainment Inc., 32 (upd.)
Asahi National Broadcasting Company, Ltd., 9
Aspen Skiing Company, 15
Aston Villa plc, 41
The Athletics Investment Group, 62
Atlanta National League Baseball Club, Inc., 43
The Atlantic Group, 23
Autotote Corporation, 20
Aztar Corporation, 13
Bad Boy Worldwide Entertainment Group, 58
Baker & Taylor Corporation, 16; 43 (upd.)
Bally Total Fitness Holding Corp., 25
Baltimore Orioles L.P., 66
Barden Companies, Inc., 76
The Baseball Club of Seattle, LP, 50
The Basketball Club of Seattle, LLC, 50
Beggars Group Ltd., 99

Bertelsmann A.G., IV; 15 (upd.); 43 (upd.); 91 (upd.)
Bertucci's Inc., 16
Big Idea Productions, Inc., 49
BigBen Interactive S.A., 72
BioWare Corporation, 81
Blockbuster Inc., 9; 31 (upd.); 76 (upd.)
Boca Resorts, Inc., 37
Bonneville International Corporation, 29
Booth Creek Ski Holdings, Inc., 31
Boston Celtics Limited Partnership, 14
Boston Professional Hockey Association Inc., 39
The Boston Symphony Orchestra Inc., 93
The Boy Scouts of America, 34
Boyne USA Resorts, 71
Brillstein-Grey Entertainment, 80
British Broadcasting Corporation Ltd., 7; 21 (upd.); 89 (upd.)
The British Film Institute, 80
The British Museum, 71
British Sky Broadcasting Group plc, 20; 60 (upd.)
Brunswick Corporation, III; 22 (upd.); 77 (upd.)
Busch Entertainment Corporation, 73
Cablevision Systems Corporation, 7
California Sports, Inc., 56
Callaway Golf Company, 45 (upd.)
Canterbury Park Holding Corporation, 42
Capcom Company Ltd., 83
Capital Cities/ABC Inc., II
Capitol Records, Inc., 90
Carlson Companies, Inc., 6; 22 (upd.); 87 (upd.)
Carlson Wagonlit Travel, 55
Carmike Cinemas, Inc., 14; 37 (upd.); 74 (upd.)
Carnival Corporation, 6; 27 (upd.); 78 (upd.)
The Carsey-Werner Company, L.L.C., 37
CBS Inc., II; 6 (upd.)
Cedar Fair Entertainment Company, 22; 98 (upd.)
Central European Media Enterprises Ltd., 61
Central Independent Television, 7; 23 (upd.)
Century Casinos, Inc., 53
Century Theatres, Inc., 31
Championship Auto Racing Teams, Inc., 37
Channel Four Television Corporation, 93
Chello Zone Ltd., 93
Chelsea Piers Management Inc., 86
Chicago Bears Football Club, Inc., 33
Chicago National League Ball Club, Inc., 66
Chris-Craft Corporation, 9; 31 (upd.); 80 (upd.)
Chrysalis Group plc, 40
Churchill Downs Incorporated, 29
Cinar Corporation, 40
Cinemark Holdings, Inc., 95
Cinemas de la República, S.A. de C.V., 83
Cineplex Odeon Corporation, 6; 23 (upd.)
Cinram International, Inc., 43

Cirque du Soleil Inc., 29; 98 (upd.)
Classic Vacation Group, Inc., 46
Cleveland Indians Baseball Company, Inc., 37
Club Méditerranée S.A., 6; 21 (upd.); 91 (upd.)
ClubCorp, Inc., 33
CMG Worldwide, Inc., 89
Colonial Williamsburg Foundation, 53
Colorado Baseball Management, Inc., 72
Columbia Pictures Entertainment, Inc., II
Columbia TriStar Motion Pictures Companies, 12 (upd.)
Comcast Corporation, 7
Compagnie des Alpes, 48
Confluence Holdings Corporation, 76
Continental Cablevision, Inc., 7
Corporación Interamericana de Entretenimiento, S.A. de C.V., 83
Corporation for Public Broadcasting, 14; 89 (upd.)
Cox Enterprises, Inc., 22 (upd.)
Cranium, Inc., 69
Crown Media Holdings, Inc., 45
Cruise America Inc., 21
Cunard Line Ltd., 23
Dallas Cowboys Football Club, Ltd., 33
Dave & Buster's, Inc., 33
Death Row Records, 27
Denver Nuggets, 51
The Detroit Lions, Inc., 55
The Detroit Pistons Basketball Company, 41
Detroit Red Wings, 74
Detroit Tigers Baseball Club, Inc., 46
Deutsche Fussball Bund e.V., 98
dick clark productions, inc., 16
DIRECTV, Inc., 38; 75 (upd.)
Dover Downs Entertainment, Inc., 43
DreamWorks SKG, 43
Dualstar Entertainment Group LLC, 76
E! Entertainment Television Inc., 17
edel music AG, 44
Educational Broadcasting Corporation, 48
Edwards Theatres Circuit, Inc., 31
Egmont Group, 93
Electronic Arts Inc., 10; 85 (upd.)
Elektra Entertainment Group, 64
Elsinore Corporation, 48
Elvis Presley Enterprises, Inc., 61
Empire Resorts, Inc., 72
Endemol Entertainment Holding NV, 46
Entertainment Distribution Company, 89
Equity Marketing, Inc., 26
ESPN, Inc., 56
Esporta plc, 35
Euro Disney S.C.A., 20; 58 (upd.)
Europe Through the Back Door Inc., 65
Fair Grounds Corporation, 44
Family Golf Centers, Inc., 29
FAO Schwarz, 46
Fédération Internationale de Football Association, 27
Feld Entertainment, Inc., 32 (upd.)
Film Roman, Inc., 58
First Choice Holidays PLC, 40
First Team Sports, Inc., 22
Fisher-Price Inc., 32 (upd.)

Florida Gaming Corporation, 47
Focus Features 78
4Kids Entertainment Inc., 59
Fox Entertainment Group, Inc., 43
Fox Family Worldwide, Inc., 24
Fuji Television Network Inc., 91
The GAME Group plc, 80
GameStop Corp., 69 (upd.)
Gaumont SA, 25; 91 (upd.)
Gaylord Entertainment Company, 11; 36 (upd.)
GC Companies, Inc., 25
Geffen Records Inc., 26
Gibson Guitar Corp., 16
Girl Scouts of the USA, 35
Global Outdoors, Inc., 49
Glu Mobile Inc., 95
GoodTimes Entertainment Ltd., 48
Granada Group PLC, II; 24 (upd.)
Grand Casinos, Inc., 20
Great Wolf Resorts, Inc., 91
Greek Organization of Football Prognostics S.A. (OPAP), 97
The Green Bay Packers, Inc., 32
Grévin & Compagnie SA, 56
Groupe Partouche SA, 48
Grupo Televisa, S.A., 54 (upd.)
H. Betti Industries Inc., 88
Hallmark Cards, Inc., IV; 16 (upd.); 40 (upd.); 87 (upd.)
Hanna-Barbera Cartoons Inc., 23
Hard Rock Cafe International, Inc., 32 (upd.)
Harlem Globetrotters International, Inc., 61
Harpo Inc., 28; 66 (upd.)
Harrah's Entertainment, Inc., 16; 43 (upd.)
Harveys Casino Resorts, 27
Hasbro, Inc., 43 (upd.)
Hastings Entertainment, Inc., 29
The Hearst Corporation, 46 (upd.)
The Heat Group, 53
Hendrick Motorsports, Inc., 89
Herschend Family Entertainment Corporation, 73
Hilton Group plc, III; 19 (upd.); 49 (upd.)
HIT Entertainment PLC, 40
HOB Entertainment, Inc., 37
Holidaybreak plc, 96
Hollywood Casino Corporation, 21
Hollywood Entertainment Corporation, 25
Hollywood Media Corporation, 58
Hollywood Park, Inc., 20
Home Box Office Inc., 7; 23 (upd.); 76 (upd.)
Horseshoe Gaming Holding Corporation, 62
IG Group Holdings plc, 97
Imagine Entertainment, 91
IMAX Corporation 28; 78 (upd.)
IMG 78
Indianapolis Motor Speedway Corporation, 46
Infinity Broadcasting Corporation, 48 (upd.)

Infogrames Entertainment S.A., 35
Integrity Inc., 44
International Creative Management, Inc., 43
International Family Entertainment Inc., 13
International Game Technology, 41 (upd.)
International Olympic Committee, 44
International Speedway Corporation, 19; 74 (upd.)
Interscope Music Group, 31
Intrawest Corporation, 15; 84 (upd.)
Irvin Feld & Kenneth Feld Productions, Inc., 15
Isle of Capri Casinos, Inc., 41
iVillage Inc., 46
Iwerks Entertainment, Inc., 34
Jackpot Enterprises Inc., 21
Japan Broadcasting Corporation, 7
Jazz Basketball Investors, Inc., 55
Jazzercise, Inc., 45
Jillian's Entertainment Holdings, Inc., 40
The Jim Henson Company, 23
The Joffrey Ballet of Chicago, 52
Jurys Doyle Hotel Group plc, 64
Juventus F.C. S.p.A, 53
K'Nex Industries, Inc., 52
Kampgrounds of America, Inc. (KOA), 33
Kerasotes ShowPlace Theaters LLC, 80
Kerzner International Limited, 69 (upd.)
King World Productions, Inc., 9; 30 (upd.)
Klasky Csupo Inc. 78
Knott's Berry Farm, 18
Kuoni Travel Holding Ltd., 40
The Kushner-Locke Company, 25
Ladbroke Group PLC, II; 21 (upd.)
Lakes Entertainment, Inc., 51
Landmark Theatre Corporation, 70
Las Vegas Sands, Inc., 50
Lego A/S, 13; 40 (upd.)
Liberty Livewire Corporation, 42
Liberty Media Corporation, 50
Liberty Travel, Inc., 56
Life Time Fitness, Inc., 66
Lifetime Entertainment Services, 51
Lincoln Center for the Performing Arts, Inc., 69
Lionel L.L.C., 16; 99 (upd.)
Lions Gate Entertainment Corporation, 35
LIVE Entertainment Inc., 20
Live Nation, Inc., 80 (upd.)
LodgeNet Entertainment Corporation, 28
Lucasfilm Ltd., 12; 50 (upd.)
Luminar Plc, 40
Majesco Entertainment Company, 85
Manchester United Football Club plc, 30
Mandalay Resort Group, 32 (upd.)
Maple Leaf Sports & Entertainment Ltd., 61
The Marcus Corporation, 21
The Mark Travel Corporation, 80
Märklin Holding GmbH, 70
Martha Stewart Living Omnimedia, Inc., 73 (upd.)
Mashantucket Pequot Gaming Enterprise Inc., 35

MCA Inc., II
McMenamins Pubs and Breweries, 65
Media General, Inc., 7
Mediaset SpA, 50
Mega Bloks, Inc., 61
Metro-Goldwyn-Mayer Inc., 25 (upd.); 84 (upd.)
Metromedia Companies, 14
Métropole Télévision, 33
Métropole Télévision S.A., 76 (upd.)
Metropolitan Baseball Club Inc., 39
The Metropolitan Museum of Art, 55
Metropolitan Opera Association, Inc., 40
MGM Grand Inc., 17
MGM/UA Communications Company, II
Midway Games, Inc., 25
Mikohn Gaming Corporation, 39
Milan AC, S.p.A., 79
Milwaukee Brewers Baseball Club, 37
Miramax Film Corporation, 64
Mizuno Corporation, 25
Mohegan Tribal Gaming Authority, 37
Moliflor Loisirs, 80
Monarch Casino & Resort, Inc., 65
Motown Records Company L.P., 26
Movie Gallery, Inc., 31
Mr. Gatti's, LP, 87
MTR Gaming Group, Inc., 75
Multimedia Games, Inc., 41
Muzak, Inc., 18
National Amusements Inc., 28
National Aquarium in Baltimore, Inc., 74
National Association for Stock Car Auto Racing, 32
National Broadcasting Company, Inc., II; 6 (upd.)
National Collegiate Athletic Association, 96
National Football League, 29
National Hockey League, 35
National Public Radio, Inc., 19; 47 (upd.)
National Rifle Association of America, 37
National Thoroughbred Racing Association, 58
Navarre Corporation, 24
Navigant International, Inc., 47
NBGS International, Inc., 73
NCL Corporation, 79
New Jersey Devils, 84
New Line Cinema, Inc., 47
New Orleans Saints LP, 58
New York City Off-Track Betting Corporation, 51
New York Shakespeare Festival Management, 93
News Corporation Limited, 46 (upd.)
NFL Films, 75
Nicklaus Companies, 45
Nintendo Company, Ltd., 28 (upd.); 67 (upd.)
Nordisk Film A/S, 80
O'Charley's Inc., 19
Orion Pictures Corporation, 6
Outrigger Enterprises, Inc., 67
Palace Sports & Entertainment, Inc., 97
Paradise Music & Entertainment, Inc., 42
Paramount Pictures Corporation, II
Pathé SA, 29

Paul Reed Smith Guitar Company, 89
Paul-Son Gaming Corporation, 66
PDS Gaming Corporation, 44
Peace Arch Entertainment Group Inc., 51
Penn National Gaming, Inc., 33
Philadelphia Eagles, 37
Philharmonic-Symphony Society of New York, Inc. (New York Philharmonic), 69
Pierre & Vacances SA, 48
Pittsburgh Steelers Sports, Inc., 66
Pixar Animation Studios, 34
Platinum Entertainment, Inc., 35
Play by Play Toys & Novelties, Inc., 26
Players International, Inc., 22
Pleasant Holidays LLC, 62
PolyGram N.V., 23
Poof-Slinky, Inc., 61
Pop Warner Little Scholars, Inc., 86
Portland Trail Blazers, 50
Powerhouse Technologies, Inc., 27
Premier Parks, Inc., 27
President Casinos, Inc., 22
Preussag AG, 42 (upd.)
Princess Cruise Lines, 22
Professional Bull Riders Inc., 55
The Professional Golfers' Association of America, 41
Promus Companies, Inc., 9
ProSiebenSat.1 Media AG, 54
Publishing and Broadcasting Limited, 54
Putt-Putt Golf Courses of America, Inc., 23
Radio One, Inc., 67
Ragdoll Productions Ltd., 51
Rainforest Café, Inc., 25; 88 (upd.)
The Rank Group plc, II; 64 (upd.)
Rawlings Sporting Goods Co., Inc., 24
Real Madrid C.F., 73
The Really Useful Group, 26
Regal Entertainment Group, 59
Rentrak Corporation, 35
Rhino Entertainment Company, 18; 70 (upd.)
Ride, Inc., 22
Ripley Entertainment, Inc., 74
Riviera Holdings Corporation, 75
Rollerblade, Inc., 34 (upd.)
Roularta Media Group NV, 48
Rounder Records Corporation, 79
Royal Caribbean Cruises Ltd., 22; 74 (upd.)
Royal Olympic Cruise Lines Inc., 52
RTL Group SA, 44
Rush Communications, 33
Ryko Corporation, 83
S-K-I Limited, 15
Sabre Holdings Corporation, 74 (upd.)
Salomon Worldwide, 20
San Diego Padres Baseball Club LP 78
San Francisco Baseball Associates, L.P., 55
The Sanctuary Group PLC, 69
Santa Fe Gaming Corporation, 19
Schwinn Cycle and Fitness L.P., 19
Scientific Games Corporation, 64 (upd.)
Scottish Radio Holding plc, 41
Seattle FilmWorks, Inc., 20
Seattle Seahawks, Inc., 92

The Second City, Inc., 88
SEGA Corporation, 73
Sega of America, Inc., 10
Selectour SA, 53
SFX Entertainment, Inc., 36
Shedd Aquarium Society, 73
Shochiku Company Ltd., 74
Showboat, Inc., 19
Showtime Networks Inc. 78
Shubert Organization Inc., 24
Shuffle Master Inc., 51
Silverstar Holdings, Ltd., 99
The Singing Machine Company, Inc., 60
Sirius Satellite Radio, Inc., 69
Six Flags, Inc., 17; 54 (upd.)
Smithsonian Institution, 27
Società Sportiva Lazio SpA, 44
Sony Corporation, 40 (upd.)
Speedway Motorsports, Inc., 32
Spelling Entertainment Group, Inc., 14
Spin Master, Ltd., 61
The Sports Club Company, 25
Spyglass Entertainment Group, LLC, 91
Stanley Leisure plc, 66
Starz LLC, 91
Station Casinos, Inc., 25; 90 (upd.)
Stoll-Moss Theatres Ltd., 34
Stuart Entertainment Inc., 16
Sub Pop Ltd., 97
TABCORP Holdings Limited, 44
Take-Two Interactive Software, Inc., 46
TaylorMade-adidas Golf, 23; 96 (upd.)
Tee Vee Toons, Inc., 57
Tele-Communications, Inc., II
Television Española, S.A., 7
Texas Rangers Baseball, 51
Tha Row Records, 69 (upd.)
Thomas Cook Travel Inc., 9
The Thomson Corporation, 8
Thousand Trails, Inc., 33
THQ, Inc., 39
365 Media Group plc, 89
Ticketmaster Corp., 13
Tiger Aspect Productions Ltd., 72
The Todd-AO Corporation, 33
Toho Co., Ltd., 28
TOKYOPOP Inc., 79
Tomy Company Ltd., 65
The Topps Company, Inc., 13, 34 (upd.); 83 (upd.)
Tottenham Hotspur PLC, 81
Touristik Union International GmbH. and Company K.G., II
Town Sports International, Inc., 46
Toy Biz, Inc., 18
Trans World Entertainment Corporation, 24
Travelocity.com, Inc., 46
Tribune Company, 63 (upd.)
TUI Group GmbH, 44
Turner Broadcasting System, Inc., II; 6 (upd.); 66 (upd.)
The Tussauds Group, 55
Twentieth Century Fox Film Corporation, II; 25 (upd.)
24 Hour Fitness Worldwide, Inc., 71
Ubi Soft Entertainment S.A., 41
Ulster Television PLC, 71

Ultimate Leisure Group PLC, 75
United Pan-Europe Communications NV, 47
United States Playing Card Company, 62
United Talent Agency, Inc., 80
Universal Studios, Inc., 33
Univision Communications Inc., 24; 83 (upd.)
Urbium PLC, 75
USA Interactive, Inc., 47 (upd.)
Vail Resorts, Inc., 11; 43 (upd.)
Venetian Casino Resort, LLC, 47
Viacom Inc., 7; 23 (upd.)
Village Roadshow Ltd., 58
Vinton Studios, 63
Vivendi Universal S.A., 46 (upd.)
The Walt Disney Company, II; 6 (upd.); 30 (upd.); 63 (upd.)
Warner Communications Inc., II
Warner Music Group Corporation, 90 (upd.)
Washington Football, Inc., 35
The Welk Group Inc., 78
West Coast Entertainment Corporation, 29
WGBH Educational Foundation, 66
Wham-O, Inc., 61
Wherehouse Entertainment Incorporated, 11
Whitbread PLC, I; 20 (upd.); 52 (upd.); 97 (upd.)
Wildlife Conservation Society, 31
William Hill Organization Limited, 49
Wilson Sporting Goods Company, 24; 84 (upd.)
Wizards of the Coast Inc., 24
WMS Industries, Inc., 53 (upd.)
World Wrestling Federation Entertainment, Inc., 32
Worldwide Pants Inc., 97
Writers Guild of America, West, Inc., 92
XM Satellite Radio Holdings, Inc., 69
YankeeNets LLC, 35
YES! Entertainment Corporation, 26
YMCA of the USA, 31
Youbet.com, Inc., 77
Young Broadcasting Inc., 40
Zomba Records Ltd., 52
Zuffa L.L.C., 89

Financial Services: Banks

Abbey National plc, 10; 39 (upd.)
Abigail Adams National Bancorp, Inc., 23
ABN AMRO Holding, N.V., 50
Affiliated Managers Group, Inc., 79
Akbank TAS, 79
Alabama National BanCorporation, 75
Algemene Bank Nederland N.V., II
Alliance and Leicester plc, 88
Allianz AG, 57 (upd.)
Allied Irish Banks, plc, 16; 43 (upd.)
Almanij NV, 44
Amalgamated Bank, 60
AMCORE Financial Inc., 44
American Residential Mortgage Corporation, 8
AmSouth Bancorporation,12; 48 (upd.)
Amsterdam-Rotterdam Bank N.V., II

Anchor Bancorp, Inc., 10
Apple Bank for Savings, 59
Astoria Financial Corporation, 44
Australia and New Zealand Banking Group Limited, II; 52 (upd.)
Banca Commerciale Italiana SpA, II
Banca Fideuram SpA, 63
Banca Intesa SpA, 65
Banca Monte dei Paschi di Siena SpA, 65
Banca Nazionale del Lavoro SpA, 72
Banco Bilbao Vizcaya Argentaria S.A., II; 48 (upd.)
Banco Bradesco S.A., 13
Banco Central, II
Banco Comercial Português, SA, 50
Banco de Chile, 69
Banco de Crédito del Perú, 93
Banco do Brasil S.A., II
Banco Espírito Santo e Comercial de Lisboa S.A., 15
Banco Itaú S.A., 19
Banco Santander Central Hispano S.A., 36 (upd.)
Bank Austria AG, 23
Bank Brussels Lambert, II
Bank Hapoalim B.M., II; 54 (upd.)
Bank Leumi le-Israel B.M., 60
Bank of America Corporation, 46 (upd.)
Bank of Boston Corporation, II
Bank of China, 63
Bank of Cyprus Group, 91
Bank of East Asia Ltd., 63
Bank of Granite Corporation, 89
Bank of Hawaii Corporation, 73
Bank of Ireland, 50
Bank of Mississippi, Inc., 14
Bank of Montreal, II; 46 (upd.)
Bank of New England Corporation, II
The Bank of New York Company, Inc., II; 46 (upd.)
The Bank of Nova Scotia, II; 59 (upd.)
Bank of the Ozarks, Inc., 91
Bank of the Philippine Islands, 58
Bank of Tokyo-Mitsubishi Ltd., II; 15 (upd.)
Bank One Corporation, 10; 36 (upd.)
BankAmerica Corporation, II; 8 (upd.)
Bankers Trust New York Corporation, II
Banknorth Group, Inc., 55
Banque Nationale de Paris S.A., II
Barclays plc, II; 20 (upd.); 64 (upd.)
BarclaysAmerican Mortgage Corporation, 11
Barings PLC, 14
Barnett Banks, Inc., 9
BayBanks, Inc., 12
Bayerische Hypotheken- und Wechsel-Bank AG, II
Bayerische Vereinsbank A.G., II
BB&T Corporation, 79
Bci, 99
Beneficial Corporation, 8
BNP Paribas Group, 36 (upd.)
Boatmen's Bancshares Inc., 15
Bremer Financial Corp., 45
Brown Brothers Harriman & Co., 45
C. Hoare & Co., 77
Caisse des Dépôts et Consignations, 90

Canadian Imperial Bank of Commerce, II; 61 (upd.)
Capitalia S.p.A., 65
Carolina First Corporation, 31
Casco Northern Bank, 14
The Chase Manhattan Corporation, II; 13 (upd.)
Cheltenham & Gloucester PLC, 61
Chemical Banking Corporation, II; 14 (upd.)
China Construction Bank Corp., 79
Citicorp, II; 9 (upd.)
Citigroup Inc., 30 (upd.); 59 (upd.)
Citizens Financial Group, Inc., 42; 87 (upd.)
Close Brothers Group plc, 39
Commercial Credit Company, 8
Commercial Federal Corporation, 12; 62 (upd.)
Commerzbank A.G., II; 47 (upd.)
Compagnie Financiere de Paribas, II
Compass Bancshares, Inc., 73
Continental Bank Corporation, II
CoreStates Financial Corp, 17
Corus Bankshares, Inc., 75
Countrywide Credit Industries, Inc., 16
Crédit Agricole Group, II; 84 (upd.)
Crédit Lyonnais, 9; 33 (upd.)
Crédit National S.A., 9
Credit Suisse Group, II; 21 (upd.); 59 (upd.)
Credito Italiano, II
Cullen/Frost Bankers, Inc., 25
CUNA Mutual Group, 62
The Dai-Ichi Kangyo Bank Ltd., II
The Daiwa Bank, Ltd., II; 39 (upd.)
Danske Bank Aktieselskab, 50
Dauphin Deposit Corporation, 14
DEPFA BANK PLC, 69
Deposit Guaranty Corporation, 17
Deutsche Bank AG, II; 14 (upd.); 40 (upd.)
Deutscher Sparkassen- und Giroverband (DSGV), 84
Dexia NV/SA, 42; 88 (upd.)
Dime Savings Bank of New York, F.S.B., 9
Donaldson, Lufkin & Jenrette, Inc., 22
Dresdner Bank A.G., II; 57 (upd.)
Emigrant Savings Bank, 59
Erste Bank der Osterreichischen Sparkassen AG, 69
Espèrito Santo Financial Group S.A., 79 (upd.)
European Investment Bank, 66
Fidelity Southern Corporation, 85
Fifth Third Bancorp, 13; 31 (upd.)
First Bank System Inc., 12
First Chicago Corporation, II
First Commerce Bancshares, Inc., 15
First Commerce Corporation, 11
First Empire State Corporation, 11
First Fidelity Bank, N.A., New Jersey, 9
First Hawaiian, Inc., 11
First Interstate Bancorp, II
First Nationwide Bank, 14
First of America Bank Corporation, 8
First Security Corporation, 11

First Tennessee National Corporation, 11; 48 (upd.)
First Union Corporation, 10
First Virginia Banks, Inc., 11
Firstar Corporation, 11; 33 (upd.)
Fleet Financial Group, Inc., 9
FleetBoston Financial Corporation, 36 (upd.)
FöreningsSparbanken AB, 69
Fourth Financial Corporation, 11
The Fuji Bank, Ltd., II
Generale Bank, II
German American Bancorp, 41
Glacier Bancorp, Inc., 35
Golden West Financial Corporation, 47
The Governor and Company of the Bank of Scotland, 10
Grameen Bank, 31
Granite State Bankshares, Inc., 37
Great Lakes Bancorp, 8
Great Western Financial Corporation, 10
GreenPoint Financial Corp., 28
Grupo Financiero Banamex S.A., 54
Grupo Financiero Banorte, S.A. de C.V., 51
Grupo Financiero BBVA Bancomer S.A., 54
Grupo Financiero Galicia S.A., 63
Grupo Financiero Serfin, S.A., 19
H.F. Ahmanson & Company, II; 10 (upd.)
Habersham Bancorp, 25
Hancock Holding Company, 15
Hang Seng Bank Ltd., 60
Hanmi Financial Corporation, 66
Hibernia Corporation, 37
The Hongkong and Shanghai Banking Corporation Limited, II
HSBC Holdings plc, 12; 26 (upd.); 80 (upd.)
Hudson River Bancorp, Inc., 41
Huntington Bancshares Incorporated, 11; 87 (upd.)
HVB Group, 59 (upd.)
IBERIABANK Corporation, 37
The Industrial Bank of Japan, Ltd., II
Irish Life & Permanent Plc, 59
Irwin Financial Corporation, 77
J Sainsbury plc, II; 13 (upd.); 38 (upd.); 95 (upd.)
J.P. Morgan & Co. Incorporated, II; 30 (upd.)
J.P. Morgan Chase & Co., 38 (upd.)
Japan Leasing Corporation, 8
JPMorgan Chase & Co., 91 (upd.)
Julius Baer Holding AG, 52
Kansallis-Osake-Pankki, II
KeyCorp, 8; 93 (upd.)
Kookmin Bank, 58
Kredietbank N.V., II
Kreditanstalt für Wiederaufbau, 29
Krung Thai Bank Public Company Ltd., 69
Landsbanki Islands hf, 81
Lloyds Bank PLC, II
Lloyds TSB Group plc, 47 (upd.)
Long Island Bancorp, Inc., 16
Long-Term Credit Bank of Japan, Ltd., II

Macquarie Bank Ltd., 69
Malayan Banking Berhad, 72
Manufacturers Hanover Corporation, II
Manulife Financial Corporation, 85
Marfin Popular Bank plc, 92
Marshall & Ilsley Corporation, 56
MBNA Corporation, 12
Mediolanum S.p.A., 65
Mellon Bank Corporation, II
Mellon Financial Corporation, 44 (upd.)
Mercantile Bankshares Corp., 11
Meridian Bancorp, Inc., 11
Metropolitan Financial Corporation, 13
Michigan National Corporation, 11
Midland Bank PLC, II; 17 (upd.)
The Mitsubishi Bank, Ltd., II
The Mitsubishi Trust & Banking Corporation, II
Mitsubishi UFJ Financial Group, Inc., 99 (upd.)
The Mitsui Bank, Ltd., II
The Mitsui Trust & Banking Company, Ltd., II
Mizuho Financial Group Inc., 58 (upd.)
Mouvement des Caisses Desjardins, 48
N M Rothschild & Sons Limited, 39
National Bank of Greece, 41
National Bank of Canada, 85
The National Bank of South Carolina, 76
National City Corporation, 15; 97 (upd.)
National Westminster Bank PLC, II
NationsBank Corporation, 10
NBD Bancorp, Inc., 11
NCNB Corporation, II
New York Community Bancorp Inc. 78
Nippon Credit Bank, II
Nordea AB, 40
Norinchukin Bank, II
North Fork Bancorporation, Inc., 46
Northern Rock plc, 33
Northern Trust Company, 9
NVR L.P., 8
Old Kent Financial Corp., 11
Old National Bancorp, 15; 98 (upd.)
Orszagos Takarekpenztar es Kereskedelmi Bank Rt. (OTP Bank) 78
PNC Bank Corp., II; 13 (upd.)
The PNC Financial Services Group Inc., 46 (upd.)
Popular, Inc., 41
Provident Bankshares Corporation, 85
PT Bank Buana Indonesia Tbk, 60
Pulte Corporation, 8
Qatar National Bank SAQ, 87
Rabobank Group, 33
Raiffeisen Zentralbank Österreich AG, 85
Republic New York Corporation, 11
Riggs National Corporation, 13
Royal Bank of Canada, II; 21 (upd.); 81 (upd.)
The Royal Bank of Scotland Group plc, 12; 38 (upd.)
The Ryland Group, Inc., 8
St. Paul Bank for Cooperatives, 8
Sanpaolo IMI S.p.A., 50
The Sanwa Bank, Ltd., II; 15 (upd.)
SBC Warburg, 14
Sberbank, 62

Seattle First National Bank Inc., 8
Security Capital Corporation, 17
Security Pacific Corporation, II
Shawmut National Corporation, 13
Signet Banking Corporation, 11
Singer & Friedlander Group plc, 41
Skandinaviska Enskilda Banken AB, II; 56 (upd.)
Société Générale, II; 42 (upd.)
Society Corporation, 9
Southern Financial Bancorp, Inc., 56
Southtrust Corporation, 11
Standard Chartered plc, II; 48 (upd.)
Standard Federal Bank, 9
Star Banc Corporation, 11
State Bank of India, 63
State Financial Services Corporation, 51
State Street Corporation, 8; 57 (upd.)
Staten Island Bancorp, Inc., 39
The Sumitomo Bank, Limited, II; 26 (upd.)
Sumitomo Mitsui Banking Corporation, 51 (upd.)
The Sumitomo Trust & Banking Company, Ltd., II; 53 (upd.)
The Summit Bancorporation, 14
Suncorp-Metway Ltd., 91
SunTrust Banks Inc., 23
Svenska Handelsbanken AB, II; 50 (upd.)
Sveriges Riksbank, 96
Swiss Bank Corporation, II
Synovus Financial Corp., 12; 52 (upd.)
The Taiyo Kobe Bank, Ltd., II
TCF Financial Corporation, 47
The Tokai Bank, Limited, II; 15 (upd.)
The Toronto-Dominion Bank, II; 49 (upd.)
TSB Group plc, 12
Turkiye Is Bankasi A.S., 61
U.S. Bancorp, 14; 36 (upd.)
U.S. Trust Corp., 17
UBS AG, 52 (upd.)
Umpqua Holdings Corporation, 87
Unibanco Holdings S.A., 73
Union Bank of California, 16
Union Bank of Switzerland, II
Union Financière de France Banque SA, 52
Union Planters Corporation, 54
UnionBanCal Corporation, 50 (upd.)
United Community Banks, Inc., 98
United Overseas Bank Ltd., 56
USAA, 62 (upd.)
Van Lanschot NV, 79
Vontobel Holding AG, 96
Wachovia Bank of Georgia, N.A., 16
Wachovia Bank of South Carolina, N.A., 16
Washington Mutual, Inc., 17; 93 (upd.)
Wells Fargo & Company, II; 12 (upd.); 38 (upd.); 97 (upd.)
West One Bancorp, 11
Westamerica Bancorporation, 17
Westdeutsche Landesbank Girozentrale, II; 46 (upd.)
Westpac Banking Corporation, II; 48 (upd.)
Whitney Holding Corporation, 21

Wilmington Trust Corporation, 25
The Woolwich plc, 30
World Bank Group, 33
The Yasuda Trust and Banking Company, Ltd., II; 17 (upd.)
Zions Bancorporation, 12; 53 (upd.)

Financial Services: Excluding Banks

A.B. Watley Group Inc., 45
A.G. Edwards, Inc., 8; 32 (upd.)
ACCION International, 87
Accredited Home Lenders Holding Co., 91
ACE Cash Express, Inc., 33
Advanta Corporation, 8; 38 (upd.)
Ag Services of America, Inc., 59
Alliance Capital Management Holding L.P., 63
Allmerica Financial Corporation, 63
Ambac Financial Group, Inc., 65
America's Car-Mart, Inc., 64
American Capital Strategies, Ltd., 91
American Express Company, II; 10 (upd.); 38 (upd.)
American General Finance Corp., 11
American Home Mortgage Holdings, Inc., 46
Ameritrade Holding Corporation, 34
AMVESCAP PLC, 65
Apax Partners Worldwide LLP, 89
Arnhold and S. Bleichroeder Advisers, LLC, 97
Arthur Andersen & Company, Société Coopérative, 10
Avco Financial Services Inc., 13
Aviva PLC, 50 (upd.)
Bankrate, Inc., 83
Bear Stearns Companies, Inc., II; 10 (upd.); 52 (upd.)
Benchmark Capital, 49
Bill & Melinda Gates Foundation, 41
BlackRock, Inc., 79
Bolsa Mexicana de Valores, S.A. de C.V., 80
Bozzuto's, Inc., 13
Bradford & Bingley PLC, 65
Cantor Fitzgerald, L.P., 92
Capital One Financial Corporation, 52
Cardtronics, Inc., 93
Carnegie Corporation of New York, 35
Cash America International, Inc., 20; 61 (upd.)
Cash Systems, Inc., 93
Catholic Order of Foresters, 24; 97 (upd.)
Cattles plc, 58
Cendant Corporation, 44 (upd.)
Certegy, Inc., 63
Cetelem S.A., 21
The Charles Schwab Corporation, 8; 26 (upd.); 81 (upd.)
CheckFree Corporation, 81
Cheshire Building Society, 74
Chicago Mercantile Exchange Holdings Inc., 75
CIT Group Inc., 76
Citfed Bancorp, Inc., 16
Citicorp Diners Club, Inc., 90

Coinstar, Inc., 44
Comerica Incorporated, 40
Commercial Financial Services, Inc., 26
Compagnie Nationale à Portefeuille, 84
Concord EFS, Inc., 52
Coopers & Lybrand, 9
Cowen Group, Inc., 92
Cramer, Berkowitz & Co., 34
Credit Acceptance Corporation, 18
Cresud S.A.C.I.F. y A., 63
CS First Boston Inc., II
D. Carnegie & Co. AB, 98
Dain Rauscher Corporation, 35 (upd.)
Daiwa Securities Group Inc., II; 55 (upd.)
Datek Online Holdings Corp., 32
The David and Lucile Packard Foundation, 41
Dean Witter, Discover & Co., 12
Deutsche Börse AG, 59
ditech.com, 93
Dominick & Dominick LLC, 92
Dow Jones Telerate, Inc., 10
Draper Fisher Jurvetson, 91
Dresdner Kleinwort Wasserstein, 60 (upd.)
Drexel Burnham Lambert Incorporated, II
The Dreyfus Corporation, 70
DVI, Inc., 51
E*Trade Financial Corporation, 20; 60 (upd.)
Eaton Vance Corporation, 18
Edward D. Jones & Company L.P., 66 (upd.)
Edward Jones, 30
Eurazeo, 80
Euronet Worldwide, Inc., 83
Euronext N.V., 37; 89 (upd.)
Experian Information Solutions Inc., 45
Fair, Isaac and Company, 18
Fannie Mae, 45 (upd.)
Federal Agricultural Mortgage Corporation, 75
Federal Deposit Insurance Corporation, 93
Federal National Mortgage Association, II
Fidelity Investments Inc., II; 14 (upd.)
First Albany Companies Inc., 37
First Data Corporation, 30 (upd.)
The First Marblehead Corporation, 87
First USA, Inc., 11
FMR Corp., 8; 32 (upd.)
Forstmann Little & Co., 38
Fortis, Inc., 15
Frank Russell Company, 46
Franklin Resources, Inc., 9
Fred Alger Management, Inc., 97
Freddie Mac, 54
Friedman, Billings, Ramsey Group, Inc., 53
Gabelli Asset Management Inc., 30
Gilman & Ciocia, Inc., 72
Global Payments Inc., 91
The Goldman Sachs Group Inc., II; 20 (upd.); 51 (upd.)
Grede Foundries, Inc., 38
Green Tree Financial Corporation, 11
Gruntal & Co., L.L.C., 20
Grupo Financiero Galicia S.A., 63
H&R Block, Inc., 9; 29 (upd.); 82 (upd.)

H.D. Vest, Inc., 46
H.M. Payson & Co., 69
Hercules Technology Growth Capital, Inc., 87
Hoenig Group Inc., 41
Household International, Inc., II; 21 (upd.)
Hummer Winblad Venture Partners, 97
Huron Consulting Group Inc., 87
IDB Holding Corporation Ltd., 97
Ingenico—Compagnie Industrielle et Financière d'Ingénierie, 46
Instinet Corporation, 34
Inter-Regional Financial Group, Inc., 15
IntercontinentalExchange, Inc., 95
Investcorp SA, 57
The Island ECN, Inc., 48
Istituto per la Ricostruzione Industriale S.p.A., 11
J. & W. Seligman & Co. Inc., 61
JAFCO Co. Ltd., 79
Janus Capital Group Inc., 57
JB Oxford Holdings, Inc., 32
Jefferies Group, Inc., 25
John Hancock Financial Services, Inc., 42 (upd.)
The John Nuveen Company, 21
Jones Lang LaSalle Incorporated, 49
The Jordan Company LP, 70
Kansas City Southern Industries, Inc., 26 (upd.)
Kleiner, Perkins, Caufield & Byers, 53
Kleinwort Benson Group PLC, II
Knight Trading Group, Inc., 70
Kohlberg Kravis Roberts & Co., 24; 56 (upd.)
KPMG Worldwide, 10
La Poste, 47 (upd.)
LaBranche & Co. Inc., 37
Lazard LLC, 38
Legg Mason, Inc., 33
Lehman Brothers Holdings Inc. (updates Shearson Lehman), 99 (upd.)
LendingTree, LLC, 93
LifeLock, Inc., 91
Lilly Endowment Inc., 70
Liquidnet, Inc., 79
London Scottish Bank plc, 70
London Stock Exchange Limited, 34
M.H. Meyerson & Co., Inc., 46
MacAndrews & Forbes Holdings Inc., 28; 86 (upd.)
Madison Dearborn Partners, LLC, 97
MasterCard Worldwide, 9; 96 (upd.)
MBNA Corporation, 33 (upd.)
Merrill Lynch & Co., Inc., II; 13 (upd.); 40 (upd.)
Metris Companies Inc., 56
Morgan Grenfell Group PLC, II
Morgan Stanley Dean Witter & Company, II; 16 (upd.); 33 (upd.)
Mountain States Mortgage Centers, Inc., 29
NASD, 54 (upd.)
The NASDAQ Stock Market, Inc., 92
National Association of Securities Dealers, Inc., 10
National Auto Credit, Inc., 16

National Discount Brokers Group, Inc., 28
National Financial Partners Corp., 65
Navy Federal Credit Union, 33
Neuberger Berman Inc., 57
New Street Capital Inc., 8
New York Stock Exchange, Inc., 9; 39 (upd.)
The Nikko Securities Company Limited, II; 9 (upd.)
Nippon Shinpan Co., Ltd., II; 61 (upd.)
Nomura Securities Company, Limited, II; 9 (upd.)
Norwich & Peterborough Building Society, 55
NovaStar Financial, Inc., 91
Oaktree Capital Management, LLC, 71
Old Mutual PLC, 61
Ontario Teachers' Pension Plan, 61
Onyx Acceptance Corporation, 59
ORIX Corporation, II; 44 (upd.)
PaineWebber Group Inc., II; 22 (upd.)
PayPal Inc., 58
The Pew Charitable Trusts, 35
Piper Jaffray Companies Inc., 22
Pitney Bowes Inc., 47 (upd.)
Providian Financial Corporation, 52 (upd.)
Prudential Financial Inc., III; 30 (upd.); 82 (upd.)
The Quick & Reilly Group, Inc., 20
Quicken Loans, Inc., 93
Rathbone Brothers plc, 70
Raymond James Financial Inc., 69
Resource America, Inc., 42
Robert W. Baird & Co. Incorporated, 67
Ryan Beck & Co., Inc., 66
Safeguard Scientifics, Inc., 10
St. James's Place Capital, plc, 71
Salomon Inc., II; 13 (upd.)
Sanders Morris Harris Group Inc., 70
Sanlam Ltd., 68
SBC Warburg, 14
Schroders plc, 42
Scottrade, Inc., 85
SEI Investments Company, 96
Shearson Lehman Brothers Holdings Inc., II; 9 (upd.)
Siebert Financial Corp., 32
Skipton Building Society, 80
SLM Holding Corp., 25 (upd.)
Smith Barney Inc., 15
Soros Fund Management LLC, 28
Spear, Leeds & Kellogg, 66
State Street Boston Corporation, 8
Stephens Inc., 92
Student Loan Marketing Association, II
Sun Life Financial Inc., 85
T. Rowe Price Associates, Inc., 11; 34 (upd.)
Teachers Insurance and Annuity Association-College Retirement Equities Fund, 45 (upd.)
Texas Pacific Group Inc., 36
3i Group PLC, 73
Total System Services, Inc., 18
TradeStation Group, Inc., 83
Trilon Financial Corporation, II

United Jewish Communities, 33
The Vanguard Group, Inc., 14; 34 (upd.)
VeriFone Holdings, Inc., 18; 76 (upd.)
Viel & Cie, 76
Visa International, 9; 26 (upd.)
Wachovia Corporation, 12; 46 (upd.)
Waddell & Reed, Inc., 22
Washington Federal, Inc., 17
Waterhouse Investor Services, Inc., 18
Watson Wyatt Worldwide, 42
Western Union Financial Services, Inc., 54
WFS Financial Inc., 70
Working Assets Funding Service, 43
World Acceptance Corporation, 57
Yamaichi Securities Company, Limited, II
The Ziegler Companies, Inc., 24; 63 (upd.)
Zurich Financial Services, 42 (upd.); 93 (upd.)

Food Products

A. Duda & Sons, Inc., 88
A. Moksel AG, 59
Agri Beef Company, 81
Agway, Inc., 7
Ajinomoto Co., Inc., II; 28 (upd.)
Alabama Farmers Cooperative, Inc., 63
The Albert Fisher Group plc, 41
Alberto-Culver Company, 8; 36 (upd.); 91 (upd.)
Alfred Ritter GmbH & Co. KG, 58
Alfesca hf, 82
Allen Canning Company, 76
Alpine Confections, Inc., 71
Alpine Lace Brands, Inc., 18
American Crystal Sugar Company, 11; 32 (upd.)
American Foods Group, 43
American Italian Pasta Company, 27; 76 (upd.)
American Licorice Company, 86
American Maize-Products Co., 14
American Pop Corn Company, 59
American Rice, Inc., 33
Amfac/JMB Hawaii L.L.C., 24 (upd.)
Amy's Kitchen Inc., 76
Annie's Homegrown, Inc., 59
Archer-Daniels-Midland Company, 32 (upd.)
Archway Cookies, Inc., 29
Arcor S.A.I.C., 66
Arla Foods amba, 48
Arnott's Ltd., 66
Associated British Foods plc, II; 13 (upd.); 41 (upd.)
Associated Milk Producers, Inc., 11; 48 (upd.)
Atkinson Candy Company, 87
Atlantic Premium Brands, Ltd., 57
August Storck KG, 66
Aurora Foods Inc., 32
Auvil Fruit Company, Inc., 95
Awrey Bakeries, Inc., 56
B&G Foods, Inc., 40
The B. Manischewitz Company, LLC, 31
Bahlsen GmbH & Co. KG, 44
Bakkavör Group hf, 91
Balance Bar Company, 32

Baltek Corporation, 34
The Bama Companies, Inc., 80
Bar-S Foods Company, 76
Barbara's Bakery Inc., 88
Barilla G. e R. Fratelli S.p.A., 17; 50 (upd.)
Barry Callebaut AG, 71 (upd.)
Baxters Food Group Ltd., 99
Bear Creek Corporation, 38
Beatrice Company, II
Beech-Nut Nutrition Corporation, 21; 51 (upd.)
Beer Nuts, Inc., 86
Bel/Kaukauna USA, 76
Bellisio Foods, Inc., 95
Ben & Jerry's Homemade, Inc., 10; 35 (upd.); 80 (upd.)
Berkeley Farms, Inc., 46
Bernard Matthews Ltd., 89
Besnier SA, 19
Best Kosher Foods Corporation, 82
Bestfoods, 22 (upd.)
Better Made Snack Foods, Inc., 90
Bettys & Taylors of Harrogate Ltd., 72
Birds Eye Foods, Inc., 69 (upd.)
Blue Bell Creameries L.P., 30
Blue Diamond Growers, 28
Bob's Red Mill Natural Foods, Inc., 63
Bobs Candies, Inc., 70
Bolton Group B.V., 86
Bonduelle SA, 51
Bongrain SA, 25
Booker PLC, 13; 31 (upd.)
Borden, Inc., II; 22 (upd.)
Boyd Coffee Company, 53
Brach and Brock Confections, Inc., 15
Brake Bros plc, 45
Bridgford Foods Corporation, 27
Brigham's Inc., 72
Brioche Pasquier S.A., 58
British Sugar plc, 84
Brothers Gourmet Coffees, Inc., 20
Broughton Foods Co., 17
Brown & Haley, 23
Bruce Foods Corporation, 39
Bruegger's Corporation, 63
Bruster's Real Ice Cream, Inc., 80
BSN Groupe S.A., II
Bumble Bee Seafoods L.L.C., 64
Bunge Brasil S.A. 78
Bunge Ltd., 62
Bourbon Corporation, 82
Burns, Philp & Company Ltd., 63
Bush Boake Allen Inc., 30
Bush Brothers & Company, 45
The C.F. Sauer Company, 90
C.H. Robinson Worldwide, Inc., 40 (upd.)
C.H. Guenther & Son, Inc., 84
Cactus Feeders, Inc., 91
Cadbury Schweppes PLC, II; 49 (upd.)
Cagle's, Inc., 20
Cal-Maine Foods, Inc., 69
Calavo Growers, Inc., 47
Calcot Ltd., 33
Callard and Bowser-Suchard Inc., 84
Campagna-Turano Bakery, Inc., 99

Campbell Soup Company, II; 7 (upd.); 26 (upd.); 71 (upd.)
The Campina Group, 78
Campofrío Alimentación S.A, 59
Canada Bread Company, Limited, 99
Canada Packers Inc., II
Cape Cod Potato Chip Company, 90
Cargill, Incorporated, II; 13 (upd.); 40 (upd.); 89 (upd.)
Carnation Company, II
The Carriage House Companies, Inc., 55
Carroll's Foods, Inc., 46
Carvel Corporation, 35
Castle & Cooke, Inc., II; 20 (upd.)
Cattleman's, Inc., 20
Celestial Seasonings, Inc., 16
Cemoi S.A., 86
Central Soya Company, Inc., 7
Chaoda Modern Agriculture (Holdings) Ltd., 87
Charal S.A., 90
Chase General Corporation, 91
Chattanooga Bakery, Inc., 86
Chef Solutions, Inc., 89
Chelsea Milling Company, 29
Chicken of the Sea International, 24 (upd.)
China National Cereals, Oils and Foodstuffs Import and Export Corporation (COFCO), 76
Chiquita Brands International, Inc., 7; 21 (upd.); 83 (upd.)
Chock Full o'Nuts Corp., 17
Chocoladefabriken Lindt & Sprüngli AG, 27
Chr. Hansen Group A/S, 70
CHS Inc., 60
Chupa Chups S.A., 38
The Clemens Family Corporation, 93
Clif Bar Inc., 50
Cloetta Fazer AB, 70
The Clorox Company, III; 22 (upd.); 81 (upd.)
Clougherty Packing Company, 72
Coca-Cola Enterprises, Inc., 13
Coffee Holding Co., Inc., 95
Cold Stone Creamery, 69
Coleman Natural Products, Inc., 68
Community Coffee Co. L.L.C., 53
ConAgra Foods, Inc., II; 12 (upd.); 42 (upd.); 85 (upd.)
The Connell Company, 29
ContiGroup Companies, Inc., 43 (upd.)
Continental Grain Company, 10; 13 (upd.)
CoolBrands International Inc., 35
Coopagri Bretagne, 88
Cooperativa Nacional de Productores de Leche S.A. (Conaprole), 92
Corporación José R. Lindley S.A., 92
CPC International Inc., II
Cranswick plc, 40
CSM N.V., 65
Cuisine Solutions Inc., 84
Cumberland Packing Corporation, 26
Curtice-Burns Foods, Inc., 7; 21 (upd.)
Czarnikow-Rionda Company, Inc., 32
D.F. Stauffer Biscuit Company, 82

Daesang Corporation, 84
Dairy Crest Group plc, 32
Dalgery, PLC, II
Danisco A/S, 44
Dannon Co., Inc., 14
Darigold, Inc., 9
Dawn Food Products, Inc., 17
Dean Foods Company, 7; 21 (upd.); 73 (upd.)
DeKalb Genetics Corporation, 17
Del Monte Foods Company, 7; 23 (upd.)
Di Giorgio Corp., 12
Diageo plc, 24 (upd.)
Diamond of California, 64 (upd.)
Dietz and Watson, Inc., 92
Dippin' Dots, Inc., 56
Dobrogea Grup S.A., 82
Dole Food Company, Inc., 9; 31 (upd.); 68 (upd.)
Domino Sugar Corporation, 26
Doskocil Companies, Inc., 12
Dot Foods, Inc., 69
Doux S.A., 80
Dreyer's Grand Ice Cream, Inc., 17
The Earthgrains Company, 36
Elmer Candy Corporation, 88
Emge Packing Co., Inc., 11
Empresas Polar SA, 55 (upd.)
Eridania Béghin-Say S.A., 36
ERLY Industries Inc., 17
Eskimo Pie Corporation, 21
Établissements Jacquot and Cie S.A.S., 92
Exportadora Bananera Noboa, S.A., 91
Ezaki Glico Company Ltd., 72
Faribault Foods, Inc., 89
Farley's & Sathers Candy Company, Inc., 62
Farmland Foods, Inc., 7
Farmland Industries, Inc., 48
Ferrara Pan Candy Company, 90
Ferrero SpA, 54
Fieldale Farms Corporation, 23
First Colony Coffee & Tea Company, 84
Fleer Corporation, 15
Fleury Michon S.A., 39
Floc'h & Marchand, 80
Florida Crystals Inc., 35
Flowers Industries, Inc., 12; 35 (upd.)
Fonterra Co-Operative Group Ltd., 58
FoodBrands America, Inc., 23
Foremost Farms USA Cooperative, 98
Foster Poultry Farms, 32
Fred Usinger Inc., 54
Fresh America Corporation, 20
Fresh Express Inc., 88
Fresh Foods, Inc., 29
FreshDirect, LLC, 84
Friesland Coberco Dairy Foods Holding N.V., 59
Frito-Lay Company, 32
Frito-Lay North America, 73 (upd.)
Fromageries Bel, 23
Frontier Natural Products Co-Op, 82
Frozen Food Express Industries, Inc., 20; 98 (upd.)
Fyffes Plc, 38
Galaxy Nutritional Foods, Inc., 58
Gano Excel Enterprise Sdn. Bhd., 89

The Garden Company Ltd., 82
Gardenburger, Inc., 33; 76 (upd.)
Geest Plc, 38
General Mills, Inc., II; 10 (upd.); 36 (upd.); 85 (upd.)
George A. Hormel and Company, II
George Weston Ltd., II; 36 (upd.); 88 (upd.)
Gerber Products Company, 7; 21 (upd.)
Ghirardelli Chocolate Company, 30
Givaudan SA, 43
Glaces Thiriet S.A., 76
Glanbia plc, 59
Global Berry Farms LLC, 62
Godiva Chocolatier, Inc., 64
Goetze's Candy Company, Inc., 87
Gold Kist Inc., 17; 26 (upd.)
Gold'n Plump Poultry, 54
Golden Enterprises, Inc., 26
Gonnella Baking Company, 40
Good Humor-Breyers Ice Cream Company, 14
Goodman Fielder Ltd., 52
GoodMark Foods, Inc., 26
Gorton's, 13
Goya Foods Inc., 22; 91 (upd.)
Graeter's Manufacturing Company, 86
Grampian Country Food Group, Ltd., 85
Great Harvest Bread Company, 44
Greencore Group plc, 98
Grist Mill Company, 15
Groupe Bigard S.A., 96
Groupe CECAB S.C.A., 88
Groupe Danone, 32 (upd.); 93 (upd.)
Groupe Euralis, 86
Groupe Glon, 84
Groupe Lactalis, 78 (upd.)
Groupe Limagrain, 74
Groupe Soufflet SA, 55
Gruma, S.A. de C.V., 31
Grupo Comercial Chedraui S.A. de C.V., 86
Grupo Herdez, S.A. de C.V., 35
Grupo Industrial Lala, S.A. de C.V., 82
Grupo Leche Pascual S.A., 59
Grupo Viz, S.A. de C.V., 84
Guida-Seibert Dairy Company, 84
Guittard Chocolate Company, 55
Guttenplan's Frozen Dough Inc., 88
H.J. Heinz Company, II; 11 (upd.); 36 (upd.); 99 (upd.)
Hagoromo Foods Corporation, 84
The Hain Celestial Group, Inc., 27; 43 (upd.)
Hanover Foods Corporation, 35
HARIBO GmbH & Co. KG, 44
The Harris Soup Company (Harry's Fresh Foods), 92
Harry London Candies, Inc., 70
The Hartz Mountain Corporation, 12
Hayel Saeed Anam Group of Cos., 92
Hazlewood Foods plc, 32
Herman Goelitz, Inc., 28
Herr Foods Inc., 84
Hershey Foods Corporation, II; 15 (upd.); 51 (upd.)
Hill's Pet Nutrition, Inc., 27
Hillsdown Holdings plc, II; 24 (upd.)

Hilmar Cheese Company, Inc., 98
HiPP GmbH & Co. Vertrieb KG, 88
Hodgson Mill, Inc., 88
Horizon Organic Holding Corporation, 37
Hormel Foods Corporation, 18 (upd.); 54 (upd.)
Hot Stuff Foods, 85
Hudson Foods Inc., 13
Hulman & Company, 44
Hunt-Wesson, Inc., 17
Iams Company, 26
IAWS Group plc, 49
IBP, Inc., II; 21 (upd.)
Iceland Group plc, 33
Icelandic Group hf, 81
Imagine Foods, Inc., 50
Imperial Holly Corporation, 12
Imperial Sugar Company, 32 (upd.)
Industrias Bachoco, S.A. de C.V., 39
Intercorp Excelle Foods Inc., 64
International Multifoods Corporation, 7; 25 (upd.)
Interstate Bakeries Corporation, 12; 38 (upd.)
The Inventure Group, Inc., 96 (upd.)
Inversiones Nacional de Chocolates S.A., 88
Itoham Foods Inc., II; 61 (upd.)
J & J Snack Foods Corporation, 24
The J. M. Smucker Company, 11; 87 (upd.)
J.R. Simplot Company, 16
Jacobs Suchard A.G., II
Jays Foods, Inc., 90
Jel Sert Company, 90
Jelly Belly Candy Company, 76
Jennie-O Turkey Store, Inc., 76
Jim Beam Brands Co., 14
John B. Sanfilippo & Son, Inc., 14
John Lewis Partnership plc, V; 42 (upd.); 99 (upd.)
Johnsonville Sausage L.L.C., 63
Julius Meinl International AG, 53
Just Born, Inc., 32
Kal Kan Foods, Inc., 22
Kamps AG, 44
Kar Nut Products Company, 86
Kashi Company, 89
Katokichi Company Ltd., 82
Keebler Foods Company, 36
Kellogg Company, II; 13 (upd.); 50 (upd.)
Ken's Foods, Inc., 88
Kerry Group plc, 27; 87 (upd.)
Kettle Foods Inc., 48
Kewpie Kabushiki Kaisha, 57
Kikkoman Corporation, 14; 47 (upd.)
The King Arthur Flour Company, 31
King Nut Company, 74
King Ranch, Inc., 14
Klement's Sausage Company, 61
Koninklijke Wessanen nv, II; 54 (upd.)
Kraft Foods Inc., II; 7 (upd.); 45 (upd.); 91 (upd.)
Kraft Jacobs Suchard AG, 26 (upd.)
Krispy Kreme Doughnuts, Inc., 21; 61 (upd.)

Kuwait Flour Mills & Bakeries Company, 84
Kyokuyo Company Ltd., 75
L.D.C. SA, 61
La Choy Food Products Inc., 25
La Reina Inc., 96
Labeyrie SAS, 80
Lakeside Foods, Inc., 89
Lam Son Sugar Joint Stock Corporation (Lasuco), 60
Lamb Weston, Inc., 23
Lance, Inc., 14; 41 (upd.)
Land O'Lakes, Inc., II; 21 (upd.); 81 (upd.)
Lassonde Industries Inc., 68
LDC, 68
Ledesma Sociedad Anónima Agrícola Industrial, 62
Legal Sea Foods Inc., 96
Leidy's, Inc., 93
Leprino Foods Company, 28
Leroux S.A.S., 65
Lifeway Foods, Inc., 65
Liberty Orchards Co., Inc., 89
Lincoln Snacks Company, 24
Litehouse Inc., 60
Lotte Confectionery Company Ltd., 76
Lucille Farms, Inc., 45
Luigino's, Inc., 64
M.A. Gedney Co., 51
Madrange SA, 58
Malt-O-Meal Company, 22; 63 (upd.)
Maple Grove Farms of Vermont, 88
Maple Leaf Foods Inc., 41
Marble Slab Creamery, Inc., 87
Mars, Incorporated, 7; 40 (upd.)
Mars Petcare US Inc., 96
Maruha Group Inc., 75 (upd.)
Maryland & Virginia Milk Producers Cooperative Association, Inc., 80
The Maschhoffs, Inc., 82
Maui Land & Pineapple Company, Inc., 29
Mauna Loa Macadamia Nut Corporation, 64
Maverick Ranch Association, Inc., 88
McCain Foods Limited, 77
McCormick & Company, Incorporated, 7; 27 (upd.)
McIlhenny Company, 20
McKee Foods Corporation, 7; 27 (upd.)
Mead Johnson & Company, 84
Medifast, Inc., 97
Meiji Dairies Corporation, II; 82 (upd.)
Meiji Seika Kaisha, Ltd., II
Merisant Worldwide, Inc., 70
Michael Foods, Inc., 25
Mid-America Dairymen, Inc., 7
Midwest Grain Products, Inc., 49
Mike-Sell's Inc., 15
Milnot Company, 46
Molinos Río de la Plata S.A., 61
Monfort, Inc., 13
Morinda Holdings, Inc., 82
Morinaga & Co. Ltd., 61
Moy Park Ltd. 78
Mrs. Baird's Bakeries, 29
Mt. Olive Pickle Company, Inc., 44

MTR Foods Ltd., 55
Murphy Family Farms Inc., 22
The Musco Family Olive Co., 91
Nabisco Foods Group, II; 7 (upd.)
Nantucket Allserve, Inc., 22
Nathan's Famous, Inc., 29
National Presto Industries, Inc., 43 (upd.)
National Sea Products Ltd., 14
Natural Ovens Bakery, Inc., 72
Natural Selection Foods, 54
Naturally Fresh, Inc., 88
Nature's Path Foods, Inc., 87
Naumes, Inc., 81
Nestlé S.A., II; 7 (upd.); 28 (upd.); 71 (upd.)
New England Confectionery Co., 15
New World Pasta Company, 53
Newhall Land and Farming Company, 14
Newly Weds Foods, Inc., 74
Newman's Own, Inc., 37
Nichiro Corporation, 86
Niman Ranch, Inc., 67
Nippon Meat Packers, Inc., II; 78 (upd.)
Nippon Suisan Kaisha, Ltd., II; 92 (upd.)
Nisshin Seifun Group Inc., II; 66 (upd.)
Nissin Food Products Company Ltd., 75
Northern Foods plc, 10; 61 (upd.)
Northland Cranberries, Inc., 38
Nutraceutical International Corporation, 37
NutraSweet Company, 8
Nutreco Holding N.V., 56
Nutrexpa S.A., 92
NutriSystem, Inc., 71
Oakhurst Dairy, 60
Oberto Sausage Company, Inc., 92
Ocean Beauty Seafoods, Inc., 74
Ocean Spray Cranberries, Inc., 7; 25 (upd.); 83 (upd.)
OJSC Wimm-Bill-Dann Foods, 48
Olga's Kitchen, Inc., 80
Omaha Steaks International Inc., 62
Omega Protein Corporation, 99
Ore-Ida Foods Inc., 13; 78 (upd.)
Oregon Freeze Dry, Inc., 74
Organic To Go Food Corporation, 99
Organic Valley (Coulee Region Organic Produce Pool), 53
Orkla ASA, 18; 82 (upd.)
Oscar Mayer Foods Corp., 12
Otis Spunkmeyer, Inc., 28
Overhill Corporation, 51
Palmer Candy Company, 80
Panzani, 84
Papetti's Hygrade Egg Products, Inc., 39
Parmalat Finanziaria SpA, 50
Pendleton Grain Growers Inc., 64
Penford Corporation, 55
Penzeys Spices, Inc., 79
Pepperidge Farm, Incorporated, 81
PepsiCo, Inc., I; 10 (upd.); 38 (upd.); 93 (upd.)
Perdigao SA, 52
Perdue Farms Inc., 7; 23 (upd.)
Perfetti Van Melle S.p.A., 72
Performance Food Group, 96 (upd.)
Perkins Foods Holdings Ltd., 87
Perry's Ice Cream Company Inc., 90

Pescanova S.A., 81
Pet Incorporated, 7
Petrossian Inc., 54
Pez Candy, Inc., 38
Philip Morris Companies Inc., 18 (upd.)
Phillips Foods, Inc., 63
PIC International Group PLC, 24 (upd.)
Phillips Foods, Inc., 90 (upd.)
Pilgrim's Pride Corporation, 7; 23 (upd.); 90 (upd.)
The Pillsbury Company, II; 13 (upd.); 62 (upd.)
Pioneer Hi-Bred International, Inc., 9
Pizza Inn, Inc., 46
Poore Brothers, Inc., 44
PowerBar Inc., 44
Prairie Farms Dairy, Inc., 47
Premium Standard Farms, Inc., 30
Princes Ltd., 76
The Procter & Gamble Company, III; 8 (upd.); 26 (upd.); 67 (upd.)
Provimi S.A., 80
Punch Taverns plc, 70
Puratos S.A./NV, 92
Purina Mills, Inc., 32
Quaker Foods North America, 73 (upd.)
Quaker Oats Company, II; 12 (upd.); 34 (upd.)
Quality Chekd Dairies, Inc., 48
R. M. Palmer Co., 89
Raisio PLC, 99
Ralston Purina Company, II; 13 (upd.)
Ranks Hovis McDougall Limited, II; 28 (upd.)
The Real Good Food Company plc, 99
Reckitt Benckiser plc, II; 42 (upd.); 91 (upd.)
Reddy Ice Holdings, Inc., 80
Reser's Fine Foods, Inc., 81
Rica Foods, Inc., 41
Rich Products Corporation, 7; 38 (upd.); 93 (upd.)
Richtree Inc., 63
Ricola Ltd., 62
Ridley Corporation Ltd., 62
River Ranch Fresh Foods LLC, 88
Riviana Foods Inc., 27
Rocky Mountain Chocolate Factory, Inc., 73
Roland Murten A.G., 7
Roman Meal Company, 84
Rose Acre Farms, Inc., 60
Rowntree Mackintosh, II
Royal Numico N.V., 37
Ruiz Food Products, Inc., 53
Russell Stover Candies Inc., 12; 91 (upd.)
Sadia S.A., 59
Sanderson Farms, Inc., 15
Saputo Inc., 59
Sara Lee Corporation, II; 15 (upd.); 54 (upd.); 99 (upd.)
Sarris Candies Inc., 86
Savannah Foods & Industries, Inc., 7
Schlotzsky's, Inc., 36
Schreiber Foods, Inc., 72
The Schwan Food Company, 7; 26 (upd.); 83 (upd.)
Schwebel Baking Company, 72

Seaboard Corporation, 36; 85 (upd.)
See's Candies, Inc., 30
Seminis, Inc., 29
Seneca Foods Corporation, 60 (upd.)
Sensient Technologies Corporation, 52 (upd.)
Shearer's Foods, Inc., 72
Silhouette Brands, Inc., 55
Silver Lake Cookie Company Inc., 95
Skalli Group, 67
Slim-Fast Foods Company, 18; 66 (upd.)
Small Planet Foods, Inc., 89
Smithfield Foods, Inc., 7; 43 (upd.)
Snow Brand Milk Products Company, Ltd., II; 48 (upd.)
Société Industrielle Lesaffre, 84
Sodiaal S.A., 36 (upd.)
SODIMA, II
Sorbee International Ltd., 74
Sorrento, Inc., 24
Southeast Frozen Foods Company, L.P., 99
Spangler Candy Company, 44
Spectrum Organic Products, Inc., 68
Standard Candy Company Inc., 86
Star of the West Milling Co., 95
Starbucks Corporation, 13; 34 (upd.); 77 (upd.)
Stock Yards Packing Co., Inc., 37
Stollwerck AG, 53
Stolt Sea Farm Holdings PLC, 54
Stolt-Nielsen S.A., 42
Stonyfield Farm, Inc., 55
Stouffer Corp., 8
Strauss-Elite Group, 68
Südzucker AG, 27
Suiza Foods Corporation, 26
Sun-Diamond Growers of California, 7
Sun-Maid Growers of California, 82
Sun-Rype Products Ltd., 76
Sun World International, LLC, 93
Sunkist Growers, Inc., 26
SunOpta Inc., 79
Supervalu Inc., 18 (upd.); 50 (upd.)
Suprema Specialties, Inc., 27
Sweet Candy Company, 60
Swift & Company, 55
The Swiss Colony, Inc., 97
Swiss Valley Farms Company, 90
Sylvan, Inc., 22
Symrise GmbH and Company KG, 89
Syngenta International AG, 83
T. Marzetti Company, 57
Taiyo Fishery Company, Limited, II
Tanimura & Antle Fresh Foods, Inc., 98
Tasty Baking Company, 14; 35 (upd.)
Tate & Lyle PLC, II; 42 (upd.)
Taylor Made Group Inc., 98
TCBY Systems LLC, 17; 98 (upd.)
TDL Group Ltd., 46
Terrena L'Union CANA CAVAL, 70
Thai Union Frozen Products PCL, 75
Thomas J. Lipton Company, 14
Thorn Apple Valley, Inc., 7; 22 (upd.)
Thorntons plc, 46
TLC Beatrice International Holdings, Inc., 22
Tofutti Brands, Inc., 64

Tom's Foods Inc., 66
Tombstone Pizza Corporation, 13
Tone Brothers, Inc., 21; 74 (upd.)
Tootsie Roll Industries, Inc., 12; 82 (upd.)
Touton S.A., 92
Townsends, Inc., 64
Tree Top, Inc., 76
TreeHouse Foods, Inc., 79
Tri Valley Growers, 32
Trident Seafoods Corporation, 56
Tropicana Products, Inc., 28
Tulip Ltd., 89
Tumaro's Gourmet Tortillas, 85
Tyson Foods, Inc., II; 14 (upd.); 50 (upd.)
U.S. Foodservice, 26
U.S. Premium Beef LLC, 91
Uncle Ben's Inc., 22
Uncle Ray's LLC, 90
Unigate PLC, II; 28 (upd.)
Unilever, II; 7 (upd.); 32 (upd.); 89 (upd.)
Uniq plc, 83 (upd.)
United Biscuits (Holdings) plc, II; 42 (upd.)
United Brands Company, II
United Farm Workers of America, 88
United Foods, Inc., 21
Universal Foods Corporation, 7
Utz Quality Foods, Inc., 72
Van Camp Seafood Company, Inc., 7
Ventura Foods LLC, 90
Vestey Group Ltd., 95
Vienna Sausage Manufacturing Co., 14
Vilmorin Clause et Cie, 70
Vion Food Group NV, 85
Vista Bakery, Inc., 56
Vita Food Products Inc., 99
Vlasic Foods International Inc., 25
W Jordan (Cereals) Ltd., 74
Wagers Inc. (Idaho Candy Company), 86
Walkers Shortbread Ltd., 79
Walkers Snack Foods Ltd., 70
Warburtons Ltd., 89
Warrell Corporation, 68
Wattie's Ltd., 7
Weaver Popcorn Company, Inc., 89
Weetabix Limited, 61
Weis Markets, Inc., 84 (upd.)
Wells' Dairy, Inc., 36
Wenner Bread Products Inc., 80
White Lily Foods Company, 88
White Wave, 43
Wilbur Chocolate Company, 66
Wimm-Bill-Dann Foods, 48
Wisconsin Dairies, 7
Wise Foods, Inc., 79
WLR Foods, Inc., 21
Wm. B. Reily & Company Inc., 58
Wm. Wrigley Jr. Company, 7; 58 (upd.)
World's Finest Chocolate Inc., 39
Worthington Foods, Inc., 14
Yamazaki Baking Co., Ltd., 58
Yarnell Ice Cream Company, Inc., 92
Yeo Hiap Seng Malaysia Bhd., 75
YOCREAM International, Inc., 47
Young's Bluecrest Seafood Holdings Ltd., 81

Zacky Farms LLC, 74
Zatarain's, Inc., 64

Food Services & Retailers

A. F. Blakemore & Son Ltd., 90
Advantica Restaurant Group, Inc., 27 (upd.)
AFC Enterprises, Inc., 32 (upd.); 83 (upd.)
Affiliated Foods Inc., 53
Albertson's, Inc., II; 7 (upd.); 30 (upd.); 65 (upd.)
Aldi Einkauf GmbH & Co. OHG, 13; 86 (upd.)
Alex Lee Inc., 18; 44 (upd.)
Allen Foods, Inc., 60
Almacenes Exito S.A., 89
Alpha Airports Group PLC, 77
America's Favorite Chicken Company, Inc., 7
American Restaurant Partners, L.P., 93
American Stores Company, II
Andronico's Market, 70
Applebee's International, Inc., 14; 35 (upd.)
ARA Services, II
Arby's Inc., 14
Arden Group, Inc., 29
Arena Leisure Plc, 99
Argyll Group PLC, II
Ark Restaurants Corp., 20
Asahi Breweries, Ltd., 20 (upd.)
ASDA Group Ltd., II; 28 (upd.); 64 (upd.)
Associated Grocers, Incorporated, 9; 31 (upd.)
Association des Centres Distributeurs E. Leclerc, 37
Atlanta Bread Company International, Inc., 70
Au Bon Pain Co., Inc., 18
Auchan, 37
Auntie Anne's, Inc., 35
Autogrill SpA, 49
Avado Brands, Inc., 31
B.R. Guest Inc., 87
Back Bay Restaurant Group, Inc., 20
Back Yard Burgers, Inc., 45
Bashas' Inc., 33; 80 (upd.)
Bear Creek Corporation, 38
Ben E. Keith Company, 76
Benihana, Inc., 18; 76 (upd.)
Bertucci's Corporation, 64 (upd.)
Bettys & Taylors of Harrogate Ltd., 72
Big Bear Stores Co., 13
The Big Food Group plc, 68 (upd.)
Big V Supermarkets, Inc., 25
Big Y Foods, Inc., 53
Blimpie International, Inc., 15; 49 (upd.)
Bob Evans Farms, Inc., 9; 63 (upd.)
Bob's Red Mill Natural Foods, Inc., 63
Boddie-Noell Enterprises, Inc., 68
Bojangles Restaurants Inc., 97
Bon Appetit Holding AG, 48
Boston Market Corporation, 12; 48 (upd.)
Boston Pizza International Inc., 88
Brazil Fast Food Corporation, 74

Briazz, Inc., 53
Brinker International, Inc., 10; 38 (upd.); 75 (upd.)
Brookshire Grocery Company, 16; 74 (upd.)
Bruegger's Corporation, 63
Bruno's Supermarkets, Inc., 7; 26 (upd.); 68 (upd.)
Buca, Inc., 38
Budgens Ltd., 59
Buffalo Wild Wings, Inc., 56
Buffets Holdings, Inc., 10; 32 (upd.); 93 (upd.)
Burger King Corporation, II; 17 (upd.); 56 (upd.)
Busch Entertainment Corporation, 73
C&K Market, Inc., 81
C & S Wholesale Grocers, Inc., 55
C.H. Robinson, Inc., 11
Caffè Nero Group PLC, 63
Cains Beer Company PLC, 99
California Pizza Kitchen Inc., 15; 74 (upd.)
Captain D's, LLC, 59
Cargill, Incorporated, II; 13 (upd.); 40 (upd.); 89 (upd.)
Caribou Coffee Company, Inc., 28; 97 (upd.)
Carlson Companies, Inc., 6; 22 (upd.); 87 (upd.)
Carlson Restaurants Worldwide, 69
Carr-Gottstein Foods Co., 17
Carrols Restaurant Group, Inc., 92
Casey's General Stores, Inc., 19; 83 (upd.)
Casino Guichard-Perrachon S.A., 59 (upd.)
CBRL Group, Inc., 35 (upd.); 86 (upd.)
CEC Entertainment, Inc., 31 (upd.)
Centerplate, Inc., 79
Chart House Enterprises, Inc., 17
Checkers Drive-In Restaurants, Inc., 16; 74 (upd.)
The Cheesecake Factory Inc., 17
Chi-Chi's Inc., 13; 51 (upd.)
Chicago Pizza & Brewery, Inc., 44
Chick-fil-A Inc., 23; 90 (upd.)
Chipotle Mexican Grill, Inc., 67
Church's Chicken, 66
CiCi Enterprises, L.P., 99
Cinnabon Inc., 23; 90 (upd.)
The Circle K Corporation, II
CKE Restaurants, Inc., 19; 46 (upd.)
Coborn's, Inc., 30
The Coffee Beanery, Ltd., 95
Coffee Holding Co., Inc., 95
Cold Stone Creamery, 69
Coles Group Limited, V; 20 (upd.); 85 (upd.)
Compass Group PLC, 34
Comptoirs Modernes S.A., 19
Consolidated Products Inc., 14
Controladora Comercial Mexicana, S.A. de C.V., 36
Cooker Restaurant Corporation, 20; 51 (upd.)
The Copps Corporation, 32
Cosi, Inc., 53
Cost-U-Less, Inc., 51

Coto Centro Integral de Comercializacion S.A., 66
Country Kitchen International, Inc., 76
Cracker Barrel Old Country Store, Inc., 10
Cremonini S.p.A., 57
CulinArt, Inc., 92
Culver Franchising System, Inc., 58
D'Agostino Supermarkets Inc., 19
Dairy Mart Convenience Stores, Inc., 7; 25 (upd.)
Daniel Thwaites Plc, 95
Darden Restaurants, Inc., 16; 44 (upd.)
Dean & DeLuca, Inc., 36
Del Taco, Inc., 58
Delhaize "Le Lion" S.A., 44
DeMoulas / Market Basket Inc., 23
DenAmerica Corporation, 29
Denner AG, 88
Deschutes Brewery, Inc., 57
Diedrich Coffee, Inc., 40
Dierbergs Markets Inc., 63
Distribución y Servicio D&S S.A., 71
Doctor's Associates Inc., 67 (upd.)
Dominick's Finer Foods, Inc., 56
Domino's, Inc., 7; 21 (upd.); 63 (upd.)
Donatos Pizzeria Corporation, 58
E H Booth & Company Ltd., 90
Eateries, Inc., 33
Ed S.A.S., 88
Edeka Zentrale A.G., II; 47 (upd.)
Einstein/Noah Bagel Corporation, 29
El Chico Restaurants, Inc., 19
El Pollo Loco, Inc., 69
Elior SA, 49
Elmer's Restaurants, Inc., 42
Embers America Restaurants, 30
Etablissements Economiques du Casino Guichard, Perrachon et Cie, S.C.A., 12
Famous Brands Ltd., 86
Famous Dave's of America, Inc., 40
Farmer Jack Supermarkets 78
Fatburger Corporation, 64
Fazoli's Management, Inc., 27; 76 (upd.)
Fili Enterprises, Inc., 70
Fired Up, Inc., 82
5 & Diner Franchise Corporation, 72
Five Guys Enterprises, LLC, 99
Flagstar Companies, Inc., 10
Flanigan's Enterprises, Inc., 60
Fleming Companies, Inc., II
Food Circus Super Markets, Inc., 88
The Food Emporium, 64
Food Lion LLC, II; 15 (upd.); 66 (upd.)
Foodarama Supermarkets, Inc., 28
Foodmaker, Inc., 14
Fox's Pizza Den, Inc., 98
The Fred W. Albrecht Grocery Co., 13
Fresh Choice, Inc., 20
Fresh Enterprises, Inc., 66
Fresh Foods, Inc., 29
Friendly Ice Cream Corporation, 30; 72 (upd.)
Frisch's Restaurants, Inc., 35; 92 (upd.)
Fuller Smith & Turner P.L.C., 38
Furr's Restaurant Group, Inc., 53
Furr's Supermarkets, Inc., 28
Galardi Group, Inc., 72

Galaxy Investors, Inc., 97
Garden Fresh Restaurant Corporation, 31
Gate Gourmet International AG, 70
The Gateway Corporation Ltd., II
Genuardi's Family Markets, Inc., 35
George Weston Ltd., II; 36 (upd.); 88 (upd.)
Ghirardelli Chocolate Company, 30
Giant Eagle, Inc., 86
Giant Food LLC, II; 22 (upd.); 83 (upd.)
Godfather's Pizza Incorporated, 25
Golden Corral Corporation, 10; 66 (upd.)
Golden Krust Caribbean Bakery, Inc., 68
Golden State Foods Corporation, 32
The Golub Corporation, 26; 96 (upd.)
Gordon Biersch Brewery Restaurant Group, Inc., 93
Gordon Food Service Inc., 8; 39 (upd.)
Grand Traverse Pie Company, 98
The Grand Union Company, 7; 28 (upd.)
The Great Atlantic & Pacific Tea Company, Inc., II; 16 (upd.); 55 (upd.)
Greggs PLC, 65
Grill Concepts, Inc., 74
Gristede's Foods Inc., 31; 68 (upd.)
Ground Round, Inc., 21
Groupe Flo S.A., 98
Groupe Le Duff S.A., 84
Groupe Promodès S.A., 19
Grupo Corvi S.A. de C.V., 86
Guyenne et Gascogne, 23
H.E. Butt Grocery Company, 13; 32 (upd.); 85 (upd.)
Haggen Inc., 38
Hannaford Bros. Co., 12
Hard Rock Cafe International, Inc., 12
Harps Food Stores, Inc., 99
Harris Teeter Inc., 23; 72 (upd.)
Harry's Farmers Market Inc., 23
HDOS Enterprises, 72
Hickory Farms, Inc., 17
Holberg Industries, Inc., 36
Holland Burgerville USA, 44
Hooters of America, Inc., 18; 69 (upd.)
Hops Restaurant Bar and Brewery, 46
Hoss's Steak and Sea House Inc., 68
Host America Corporation, 79
Hotel Properties Ltd., 71
Houchens Industries Inc., 51
Hughes Markets, Inc., 22
Hungry Howie's Pizza and Subs, Inc., 25
Hy-Vee, Inc., 36
ICA AB, II
Iceland Group plc, 33
IGA, Inc., 99
IHOP Corporation, 17; 58 (upd.)
Il Fornaio (America) Corporation, 27
In-N-Out Burger, 19
In-N-Out Burgers Inc., 74 (upd.)
Ingles Markets, Inc., 20
Inserra Supermarkets, 25
Inter Link Foods PLC, 61
International Dairy Queen, Inc., 10; 39 (upd.)
ITM Entreprises SA, 36
Ito-Yokado Co., Ltd., 42 (upd.)
Ivar's, Inc., 86

J Sainsbury plc, II; 13 (upd.); 38 (upd.); 95 (upd.)
J. Alexander's Corporation, 65
Jack in the Box Inc., 89 (upd.)
Jacmar Companies, 87
Jamba Juice Company, 47
James Original Coney Island Inc., 84
JD Wetherspoon plc, 30
Jean-Georges Enterprises L.L.C., 75
Jerónimo Martins SGPS S.A., 96
Jerry's Famous Deli Inc., 24
Jersey Mike's Franchise Systems, Inc., 83
Jitney-Jungle Stores of America, Inc., 27
John Lewis Partnership plc, V; 42 (upd.); 99 (upd.)
Johnny Rockets Group, Inc., 31; 76 (upd.)
KFC Corporation, 7; 21 (upd.); 89 (upd.)
King Kullen Grocery Co., Inc., 15
Koninklijke Ahold N.V. (Royal Ahold), II; 16 (upd.)
Koo Koo Roo, Inc., 25
Kooperativa Förbundet, 99
The Kroger Co., II; 15 (upd.); 65 (upd.)
The Krystal Company, 33
Kwik Save Group plc, 11
La Madeleine French Bakery & Café, 33
Landry's Restaurants, Inc., 15; 65 (upd.)
The Laurel Pub Company Limited, 59
Laurus N.V., 65
LDB Corporation, 53
Leeann Chin, Inc., 30
Levy Restaurants L.P., 26
Little Caesar Enterprises, Inc., 7; 24 (upd.)
Loblaw Companies Limited, 43
Logan's Roadhouse, Inc., 29
Lone Star Steakhouse & Saloon, Inc., 51
Long John Silver's, 13; 57 (upd.)
Luby's, Inc., 17; 42 (upd.); 99 (upd.)
Lucky Stores, Inc., 27
Lund Food Holdings, Inc., 22
Lunardi's Super Market, Inc., 99
Madden's on Gull Lake, 52
MaggieMoo's International, 89
Maid-Rite Corporation, 62
Maines Paper & Food Service Inc., 71
Marble Slab Creamery, Inc., 87
Marco's Franchising LLC, 86
Marie Callender's Restaurant & Bakery, Inc., 28
Marsh Supermarkets, Inc., 17; 76 (upd.)
Matt Prentice Restaurant Group, 70
Maui Wowi, Inc., 85
Max & Erma's Restaurants Inc., 19
Mayfield Dairy Farms, Inc., 74
Mazzio's Corporation, 76
McAlister's Corporation, 66
McCormick & Schmick's Seafood Restaurants, Inc., 71
McDonald's Corporation, II; 7 (upd.); 26 (upd.); 63 (upd.)
Megafoods Stores Inc., 13
Meijer Incorporated, 7
The Melting Pot Restaurants, Inc., 74
Metcash Trading Ltd., 58
Métro Inc., 77
Metromedia Companies, 14

Mexican Restaurants, Inc., 41
The Middleby Corporation, 22
Minyard Food Stores, Inc., 33; 86 (upd.)
MITROPA AG, 37
Monterey Pasta Company, 58
Morrison Restaurants Inc., 11
Morton's Restaurant Group, Inc., 30; 88 (upd.)
Mr. Gatti's, LP, 87
Mrs. Fields' Original Cookies, Inc., 27
Musgrave Group Plc, 57
Myriad Restaurant Group, Inc., 87
Nash Finch Company, 8; 23 (upd.); 65 (upd.)
Nathan's Famous, Inc., 29
National Convenience Stores Incorporated, 7
New Seasons Market, 75
New World Restaurant Group, Inc., 44
New York Restaurant Group, Inc., 32
Noble Roman's, Inc., 14; 99 (upd.)
Noodles & Company, Inc., 55
NPC International, Inc., 40
O'Charley's Inc., 19; 60 (upd.)
Old Spaghetti Factory International Inc., 24
Organic To Go Food Corporation, 99
OOC Inc., 97
The Oshawa Group Limited, II
OSI Restaurant Partners, Inc., 88 (upd.)
Outback Steakhouse, Inc., 12; 34 (upd.)
P&C Foods Inc., 8
P.F. Chang's China Bistro, Inc., 37; 86 (upd.)
Pacific Coast Restaurants, Inc., 90
Palm Management Corporation, 71
Pancho's Mexican Buffet, Inc., 46
Panda Restaurant Group, Inc., 35; 97 (upd.)
Panera Bread Company, 44
Papa Gino's Holdings Corporation, Inc., 86
Papa John's International, Inc., 15; 71 (upd.)
Papa Murphy's International, Inc., 54
Pappas Restaurants, Inc., 76
Pathmark Stores, Inc., 23
Peapod, Inc., 30
Penn Traffic Company, 13
Performance Food Group Company, 31
Perkins Family Restaurants, L.P., 22
Peter Piper, Inc., 70
Petrossian Inc., 54
Phillips Foods, Inc., 63
Picard Surgeles, 76
Piccadilly Cafeterias, Inc., 19
Piggly Wiggly Southern, Inc., 13
Pizza Hut Inc., 7; 21 (upd.)
Planet Hollywood International, Inc., 18; 41 (upd.)
Players International, Inc., 22
Ponderosa Steakhouse, 15
Portillo's Restaurant Group, Inc., 71
Potbelly Sandwich Works, Inc., 83
Progressive Enterprises Ltd., 96
Provigo Inc., II; 51 (upd.)
Publix Super Markets Inc., 7; 31 (upd.)
Pueblo Xtra International, Inc., 47

Qdoba Restaurant Corporation, 93
Quality Dining, Inc., 18
Quality Food Centers, Inc., 17
The Quizno's Corporation, 42
Rainforest Café, Inc., 25; 88 (upd.)
Rally's, 25; 68 (upd.)
Ralphs Grocery Company, 35
Randall's Food Markets, Inc., 40
Rare Hospitality International Inc., 19
Raving Brands, Inc., 64
Red Robin Gourmet Burgers, Inc., 56
Regent Inns plc, 95
Restaurant Associates Corporation, 66
Restaurants Unlimited, Inc., 13
RFC Franchising LLC, 68
Richfood Holdings, Inc., 7
Richtree Inc., 63
The Riese Organization, 38
Riser Foods, Inc., 9
Roadhouse Grill, Inc., 22
Rock Bottom Restaurants, Inc., 25; 68
(upd.)
Roly Poly Franchise Systems LLC, 83
Romacorp, Inc., 58
Rosauers Supermarkets, Inc., 90
Roundy's Inc., 58 (upd.)
RTM Restaurant Group, 58
Rubio's Restaurants, Inc., 35
Ruby Tuesday, Inc., 18; 71 (upd.)
Ruth's Chris Steak House, 28; 88 (upd.)
Ryan's Restaurant Group, Inc., 15; 68
(upd.)
Safeway Inc., II; 24 (upd.); 50 (upd.); 85
(upd.)
Santa Barbara Restaurant Group, Inc., 37
Sapporo Holdings Limited, I; 13 (upd.);
36 (upd.); 97 (upd.)
Sbarro, Inc., 16; 64 (upd.)
Schlotzsky's, Inc., 36
Schultz Sav-O Stores, Inc., 21
The Schwan Food Company, 26 (upd.);
83 (upd.)
Seaway Food Town, Inc., 15
Second Harvest, 29
See's Candies, Inc., 30
Selecta AG, 97
Seneca Foods Corporation, 17
Service America Corp., 7
SFI Group plc, 51
Shaw's Supermarkets, Inc., 56
Shells Seafood Restaurants, Inc., 43
Shoney's, Inc., 7; 23 (upd.)
ShowBiz Pizza Time, Inc., 13
Skyline Chili, Inc., 62
Smart & Final, Inc., 16
Smith's Food & Drug Centers, Inc., 8; 57
(upd.)
Sobeys Inc., 80
Sodexho SA, 29; 91 (upd.)
Somerfield plc, 47 (upd.)
Sonic Corporation, 14; 37 (upd.)
Souper Salad, Inc., 98
Southeast Frozen Foods Company, L.P.,
99
The Southland Corporation, II; 7 (upd.)
Spaghetti Warehouse, Inc., 25
SPAR Handels AG, 35
Spartan Stores Inc., 8

Starbucks Corporation, 13; 34 (upd.); 77
(upd.)
Stater Bros. Holdings Inc., 64
The Steak n Shake Company, 41; 96
(upd.)
Steinberg Incorporated, II
Stew Leonard's, 56
The Stop & Shop Supermarket Company,
II; 68 (upd.)
Subway, 32
Super Food Services, Inc., 15
Supermarkets General Holdings
Corporation, II
Supervalu Inc., II; 18 (upd.); 50 (upd.)
SWH Corporation, 70
SYSCO Corporation, II; 24 (upd.); 75
(upd.)
Taco Bell Corporation, 7; 21 (upd.); 74
(upd.)
Taco Cabana, Inc., 23; 72 (upd.)
Taco John's International, Inc., 15; 63
(upd.)
TCBY Systems LLC, 17; 98 (upd.)
Tchibo GmbH, 82
TelePizza S.A., 33
Tesco PLC, II
Texas Roadhouse, Inc., 69
Thomas & Howard Company, Inc., 90
Timber Lodge Steakhouse, Inc., 73
Tops Markets LLC, 60
Total Entertainment Restaurant
Corporation, 46
Toupargel-Agrigel S.A., 76
Trader Joe's Company, 13; 50 (upd.)
Travel Ports of America, Inc., 17
Tree of Life, Inc., 29
Triarc Companies, Inc., 34 (upd.)
Tubby's, Inc., 53
Tully's Coffee Corporation, 51
Tumbleweed, Inc., 33; 80 (upd.)
TW Services, Inc., II
Ukrop's Super Market's, Inc., 39
Unified Grocers, Inc., 93
Unique Casual Restaurants, Inc., 27
United Dairy Farmers, Inc., 74
United Natural Foods, Inc., 32; 76 (upd.)
Uno Restaurant Holdings Corporation,
18; 70 (upd.)
Uwajimaya, Inc., 60
Vail Resorts, Inc., 43 (upd.)
Valora Holding AG, 98
VICORP Restaurants, Inc., 12; 48 (upd.)
Victory Refrigeration, Inc., 82
Village Super Market, Inc., 7
The Vons Companies, Incorporated, 7; 28
(upd.)
W. H. Braum, Inc., 80
Waffle House Inc., 14; 60 (upd.)
Wahoo's Fish Taco, 96
Wakefern Food Corporation, 33
Waldbaum, Inc., 19
Wall Street Deli, Inc., 33
Wawa Inc., 17; 78 (upd.)
Wegmans Food Markets, Inc., 9; 41
(upd.)
Weis Markets, Inc., 15
Wendy's International, Inc., 8; 23 (upd.);
47 (upd.)

The WesterN SizzliN Corporation, 60
Wetterau Incorporated, II
Whitbread PLC, I; 20 (upd.); 52 (upd.);
97 (upd.)
White Castle Management Company, 12;
36 (upd.); 85 (upd.)
White Rose, Inc., 24
Whittard of Chelsea Plc, 61
Whole Foods Market, Inc., 50 (upd.)
Wild Oats Markets, Inc., 19; 41 (upd.)
Winchell's Donut Houses Operating
Company, L.P., 60
WinCo Foods Inc., 60
Winn-Dixie Stores, Inc., II; 21 (upd.); 59
(upd.)
Wm. Morrison Supermarkets PLC, 38
Wolfgang Puck Worldwide, Inc., 26, 70
(upd.)
Worldwide Restaurant Concepts, Inc., 47
Yoshinoya D & C Company Ltd., 88
Young & Co.'s Brewery, P.L.C., 38
Yucaipa Cos., 17
Yum! Brands Inc., 58
Zingerman's Community of Businesses,
68

Health & Personal Care Products

Abaxis, Inc., 83
Abbott Laboratories, I; 11 (upd.); 40
(upd.); 93 (upd.)
Accuray Incorporated, 95
Advanced Medical Optics, Inc., 79
Advanced Neuromodulation Systems, Inc.,
73
Akorn, Inc., 32
ALARIS Medical Systems, Inc., 65
Alberto-Culver Company, 8; 36 (upd.); 91
(upd.)
Alco Health Services Corporation, III
Alès Groupe, 81
Allergan, Inc., 10; 30 (upd.); 77 (upd.)
American Oriental Bioengineering Inc., 93
American Safety Razor Company, 20
American Stores Company, 22 (upd.)
Amway Corporation, III; 13 (upd.)
AngioDynamics, Inc., 81
ArthroCare Corporation, 73
Artsana SpA, 92
Ascendia Brands, Inc., 97
Atkins Nutritionals, Inc., 58
Aveda Corporation, 24
Avon Products, Inc., III; 19 (upd.); 46
(upd.)
Bally Total Fitness Holding Corp., 25
Bare Escentuals, Inc., 91
Bausch & Lomb Inc., 7; 25 (upd.); 96
(upd.)
Baxter International Inc., I; 10 (upd.)
BeautiControl Cosmetics, Inc., 21
Becton, Dickinson & Company, I; 11
(upd.)
Beiersdorf AG, 29
Big B, Inc., 17
Bindley Western Industries, Inc., 9
Biolase Technology, Inc., 87
Biomet, Inc., 10; 93 (upd.)
BioScrip Inc., 98

Biosite Incorporated, 73
Block Drug Company, Inc., 8; 27 (upd.)
The Body Shop International plc, 53
    (upd.)
Boiron S.A., 73
Bolton Group B.V., 86
The Boots Company PLC, 24 (upd.)
Boston Scientific Corporation, 77 (upd.)
Bristol-Myers Squibb Company, III; 9
    (upd.)
Bronner Brothers Inc., 92
C.R. Bard Inc., 9
Candela Corporation, 48
Cantel Medical Corporation, 80
Cardinal Health, Inc., 18; 50 (upd.)
Carl Zeiss AG, III; 34 (upd.); 91 (upd.)
Carson, Inc., 31
Carter-Wallace, Inc., 8
Caswell-Massey Co. Ltd., 51
CCA Industries, Inc., 53
Chattem, Inc., 17; 88 (upd.)
Chesebrough-Pond's USA, Inc., 8
Chronimed Inc., 26
Church & Dwight Co., Inc., 68 (upd.)
Cintas Corporation, 51 (upd.)
The Clorox Company, III; 22 (upd.); 81
    (upd.)
CNS, Inc., 20
Colgate-Palmolive Company, III; 14
    (upd.); 35 (upd.)
Combe Inc., 72
Conair Corp., 17
CONMED Corporation, 87
Connetics Corporation, 70
Cordis Corp., 19
Cosmair, Inc., 8
Cosmolab Inc., 96
Coty, Inc., 36
Covidien Ltd., 91
Cybex International, Inc., 49
Cytyc Corporation, 69
Dade Behring Holdings Inc., 71
Dalli-Werke GmbH & Co. KG, 86
Datascope Corporation, 39
Del Laboratories, Inc., 28
Deltec, Inc., 56
Dentsply International Inc., 10
DEP Corporation, 20
DePuy, Inc., 30
DHB Industries Inc., 85
Diagnostic Products Corporation, 73
The Dial Corp., 23 (upd.)
Direct Focus, Inc., 47
Drackett Professional Products, 12
Drägerwerk AG, 83
Dynatronics Corporation, 99
E-Z-EM Inc., 89
Elizabeth Arden, Inc., 8; 40 (upd.)
Empi, Inc., 26
Enrich International, Inc., 33
The Estée Lauder Companies Inc., 9; 30
    (upd.); 93 (upd.)
Ethicon, Inc., 23
Farouk Systems Inc. 78
Forest Laboratories, Inc., 11
Forever Living Products International Inc.,
    17
FoxHollow Technologies, Inc., 85

French Fragrances, Inc., 22
G&K Holding S.A., 95
Gambro AB, 49
General Nutrition Companies, Inc., 11;
    29 (upd.)
Genzyme Corporation, 13; 77 (upd.)
GF Health Products, Inc., 82
The Gillette Company, III; 20 (upd.)
Given Imaging Ltd., 83
GNC Corporation, 98 (upd.)
Groupe Yves Saint Laurent, 23
Grupo Omnilife S.A. de C.V., 88
Guerlain, 23
Guest Supply, Inc., 18
Guidant Corporation, 58
Guinot Paris S.A., 82
Hanger Orthopedic Group, Inc., 41
Helen of Troy Corporation, 18
Helene Curtis Industries, Inc., 8; 28
    (upd.)
Henkel KGaA, III; 34 (upd.); 95 (upd.)
Henry Schein, Inc., 31; 70 (upd.)
Herbalife Ltd., 17; 41 (upd.); 92 (upd.)
Huntleigh Technology PLC, 77
Immucor, Inc., 81
Inamed Corporation, 79
Integra LifeSciences Holdings
    Corporation, 87
Integrated BioPharma, Inc., 83
Inter Parfums Inc., 35; 86 (upd.)
Intuitive Surgical, Inc., 79
Invacare Corporation, 11
IVAX Corporation, 11
IVC Industries, Inc., 45
The Jean Coutu Group (PJC) Inc., 46
John Paul Mitchell Systems, 24
Johnson & Johnson, III; 8 (upd.); 36
    (upd.); 75 (upd.)
Kanebo, Ltd., 53
Kao Corporation, III; 79 (upd.)
Kendall International, Inc., 11
Kensey Nash Corporation, 71
Keys Fitness Products, LP, 83
Kimberly-Clark Corporation, III; 16
    (upd.); 43 (upd.)
Kolmar Laboratories Group, 96
Kyowa Hakko Kogyo Co., Ltd., III
Kyphon Inc., 87
L'Oréal SA, III; 8 (upd.); 46 (upd.)
Laboratoires de Biologie Végétale Yves
    Rocher, 35
The Lamaur Corporation, 41
Lever Brothers Company, 9
Lion Corporation, III; 51 (upd.)
Lush Ltd., 93
Luxottica SpA, 17; 52 (upd.)
Mandom Corporation, 82
Mannatech Inc., 33
Mary Kay Inc., 9; 30 (upd.); 84 (upd.)
Matrix Essentials Inc., 90
Maxxim Medical Inc., 12
Medco Containment Services Inc., 9
MEDecision, Inc., 95
Medifast, Inc., 97
Medline Industries, Inc., 61
Medtronic, Inc., 8; 67 (upd.)
Melaleuca Inc., 31
The Mentholatum Company Inc., 32

Mentor Corporation, 26
Merck & Co., Inc., I; 11 (upd.); 34
    (upd.); 95 (upd.)
Merit Medical Systems, Inc., 29
Merz Group, 81
Natura Cosméticos S.A., 75
Nature's Sunshine Products, Inc., 15
NBTY, Inc., 31
NeighborCare, Inc., 67 (upd.)
Neutrogena Corporation, 17
New Dana Perfumes Company, 37
Neways Inc. 78
Nikken Global Inc., 32
NutriSystem, Inc., 71
Nutrition for Life International Inc., 22
Nutrition 21 Inc., 97
Ocular Sciences, Inc., 65
OEC Medical Systems, Inc., 27
Obagi Medical Products, Inc., 95
OraSure Technologies, Inc., 75
Orion Oyj, 72
Patterson Dental Co., 19
Perrigo Company, 12
Pfizer Inc., 79 (upd.)
Physician Sales & Service, Inc., 14
Playtex Products, Inc., 15
PolyMedica Corporation, 77
The Procter & Gamble Company, III; 8
    (upd.); 26 (upd.); 67 (upd.)
PZ Cussons plc, 72
Quidel Corporation, 80
Reckitt Benckiser plc, II; 42 (upd.); 91
    (upd.)
Redken Laboratories Inc., 84
Reliv International, Inc., 58
Retractable Technologies, Inc., 99
Revlon Inc., III; 17 (upd.)
Roche Biomedical Laboratories, Inc., 11
S.C. Johnson & Son, Inc., III; 28 (upd.);
    89 (upd.)
Safety 1st, Inc., 24
St. Jude Medical, Inc., 11; 43 (upd.); 97
    (upd.)
Schering-Plough Corporation, I; 14
    (upd.); 49 (upd.); 99 (upd.)
Sephora Holdings S.A., 82
Shaklee Corporation, 39 (upd.)
Shionogi & Co., Ltd., III; 17 (upd.); 98
    (upd.)
Shiseido Company, Limited, III; 22
    (upd.); 81 (upd.)
Slim-Fast Foods Company, 18; 66 (upd.)
Smith & Nephew plc, 17
SmithKline Beecham PLC, III
Soft Sheen Products, Inc., 31
Sola International Inc., 71
Spacelabs Medical, Inc., 71
STAAR Surgical Company, 57
Straumann Holding AG, 79
Stryker Corporation, 79 (upd.)
Sunrise Medical Inc., 11
Syneron Medical Ltd., 91
Synthes, Inc., 93
Tambrands Inc., 8
Terumo Corporation, 48
Thane International, Inc., 84
Tom's of Maine, Inc., 45
Transitions Optical, Inc., 83

The Tranzonic Companies, 37
Turtle Wax, Inc., 15; 93 (upd.)
Tutogen Medical, Inc., 68
Unicharm Corporation, 84
United States Surgical Corporation, 10;
    34 (upd.)
USANA, Inc., 29
Utah Medical Products, Inc., 36
Ventana Medical Systems, Inc., 75
VHA Inc., 53
VIASYS Healthcare, Inc., 52
Vion Food Group NV, 85
VISX, Incorporated, 30
Vitamin Shoppe Industries, Inc., 60
Water Pik Technologies, Inc., 34; 83
    (upd.)
Weider Nutrition International, Inc., 29
Weleda AG 78
Wella AG, III; 48 (upd.)
West Pharmaceutical Services, Inc., 42
Wright Medical Group, Inc., 61
Wyeth, 50 (upd.)
Zila, Inc., 46
Zimmer Holdings, Inc., 45

Health Care Services

Acadian Ambulance & Air Med Services,
    Inc., 39
Adventist Health, 53
Advocat Inc., 46
Almost Family, Inc., 93
Alterra Healthcare Corporation, 42
Amedysis, Inc., 53
The American Cancer Society, 24
American Healthways, Inc., 65
American Lung Association, 48
American Medical Association, 39
American Medical International, Inc., III
American Medical Response, Inc., 39
American Red Cross, 40
AMERIGROUP Corporation, 69
AmeriSource Health Corporation, 37
    (upd.)
AmSurg Corporation, 48
The Andrews Institute, 99
Applied Bioscience International, Inc., 10
Assisted Living Concepts, Inc., 43
ATC Healthcare Inc., 64
Baptist Health Care Corporation, 82
Beverly Enterprises, Inc., III; 16 (upd.)
Bon Secours Health System, Inc., 24
Brookdale Senior Living, 91
C.R. Bard, Inc., 65 (upd.)
Cancer Treatment Centers of America,
    Inc., 85
Capital Senior Living Corporation, 75
Caremark Rx, Inc., 10; 54 (upd.)
Catholic Health Initiatives, 91
Children's Comprehensive Services, Inc.,
    42
Children's Hospitals and Clinics, Inc., 54
Chronimed Inc., 26
COBE Laboratories, Inc., 13
Columbia/HCA Healthcare Corporation,
    15
Community Health Systems, Inc., 71
Community Psychiatric Centers, 15
CompDent Corporation, 22

CompHealth Inc., 25
Comprehensive Care Corporation, 15
Continental Medical Systems, Inc., 10
Continuum Health Partners, Inc., 60
Coventry Health Care, Inc., 59
Craig Hospital, 99
Cystic Fibrosis Foundation, 93
DaVita Inc., 73
Easter Seals, Inc., 58
Erickson Retirement Communities, 57
Express Scripts Incorporated, 17
Extendicare Health Services, Inc., 6
Eye Care Centers of America, Inc., 69
FHP International Corporation, 6
Fresenius AG, 56
Genesis Health Ventures, Inc., 18
Gentiva Health Services, Inc., 79
GranCare, Inc., 14
Group Health Cooperative, 41
Grupo Ángeles Servicios de Salud, S.A. de
    C.V., 84
Hamot Health Foundation, 91
Hazelden Foundation, 28
HCA - The Healthcare Company, 35
    (upd.)
Health Care & Retirement Corporation,
    22
Health Management Associates, Inc., 56
Health Risk Management, Inc., 24
Health Systems International, Inc., 11
HealthSouth Corporation, 14; 33 (upd.)
Henry Ford Health System, 84
Highmark Inc., 27
The Hillhaven Corporation, 14
Holiday Retirement Corp., 87
Hooper Holmes, Inc., 22
Hospital Central Services, Inc., 56
Hospital Corporation of America, III
Howard Hughes Medical Institute, 39
Humana Inc., III; 24 (upd.)
Intermountain Health Care, Inc., 27
Jenny Craig, Inc., 10; 29 (upd.); 92
    (upd.)
Kinetic Concepts, Inc. (KCI), 20
LabOne, Inc., 48
Laboratory Corporation of America
    Holdings, 42 (upd.)
LCA-Vision, Inc., 85
Life Care Centers of America Inc., 76
Lifeline Systems, Inc., 53
LifePoint Hospitals, Inc., 69
Lincare Holdings Inc., 43
Manor Care, Inc., 6; 25 (upd.)
March of Dimes, 31
Marshfield Clinic Inc., 82
Matria Healthcare, Inc., 17
Maxicare Health Plans, Inc., III; 25 (upd.)
Mayo Foundation, 9; 34 (upd.)
McBride plc, 82
Médecins sans Frontières, 85
Medical Management International, Inc.,
    65
Medical Staffing Network Holdings, Inc.,
    89
Memorial Sloan-Kettering Cancer Center,
    57
Merge Healthcare, 85
Merit Medical Systems, Inc., 29

MeritCare Health System, 88
Myriad Genetics, Inc., 95
National Health Laboratories
    Incorporated, 11
National Medical Enterprises, Inc., III
National Research Corporation, 87
New York City Health and Hospitals
    Corporation, 60
New York Health Care, Inc., 72
NewYork-Presbyterian Hospital, 59
NovaCare, Inc., 11
NSF International, 72
Operation Smile, Inc., 75
Option Care Inc., 48
Orthodontic Centers of America, Inc., 35
Oxford Health Plans, Inc., 16
PacifiCare Health Systems, Inc., 11
Palomar Medical Technologies, Inc., 22
Pediatric Services of America, Inc., 31
Pediatrix Medical Group, Inc., 61
PHP Healthcare Corporation, 22
PhyCor, Inc., 36
PolyMedica Corporation, 77
Primedex Health Systems, Inc., 25
Providence Health System, 90
The Providence Service Corporation, 64
Psychemedics Corporation, 89
Psychiatric Solutions, Inc., 68
Quest Diagnostics Inc., 26
Radiation Therapy Services, Inc., 85
Ramsay Youth Services, Inc., 41
Renal Care Group, Inc., 72
Res-Care, Inc., 29
Response Oncology, Inc., 27
Rural/Metro Corporation, 28
Sabratek Corporation, 29
St. Jude Medical, Inc., 11; 43 (upd.); 97
    (upd.)
Salick Health Care, Inc., 53
The Scripps Research Institute, 76
Select Medical Corporation, 65
Shriners Hospitals for Children, 69
Sierra Health Services, Inc., 15
Smith & Nephew plc, 41 (upd.)
Special Olympics, Inc., 93
The Sports Club Company, 25
SSL International plc, 49
Stericycle Inc., 33
Sun Healthcare Group Inc., 25
Sunrise Senior Living, Inc., 81
Susan G. Komen Breast Cancer
    Foundation 78
SwedishAmerican Health System, 51
Tenet Healthcare Corporation, 55 (upd.)
Twinlab Corporation, 34
U.S. Healthcare, Inc., 6
U.S. Physical Therapy, Inc., 65
Unison HealthCare Corporation, 25
United HealthCare Corporation, 9
United Nations International Children's
    Emergency Fund (UNICEF), 58
United Way of America, 36
Universal Health Services, Inc., 6
Vanderbilt University Medical Center, 99
Vanguard Health Systems Inc., 70
VCA Antech, Inc., 58
Vencor, Inc., 16
VISX, Incorporated, 30

Vivra, Inc., 18
Volunteers of America, Inc., 66
WellPoint Health Networks Inc., 25
World Vision International, Inc., 93
YWCA of the U.S.A., 45

Hotels

Accor S.A., 69 (upd.)
Amerihost Properties, Inc., 30
Ameristar Casinos, Inc., 69 (upd.)
Archon Corporation, 74 (upd.)
Arena Leisure Plc, 99
Aztar Corporation, 13; 71 (upd.)
Bass PLC, 38 (upd.)
Boca Resorts, Inc., 37
Boyd Gaming Corporation, 43
Boyne USA Resorts, 71
Bristol Hotel Company, 23
The Broadmoor Hotel, 30
Caesars World, Inc., 6
Candlewood Hotel Company, Inc., 41
Carlson Companies, Inc., 6; 22 (upd.); 87 (upd.)
Castle & Cooke, Inc., 20 (upd.)
Cedar Fair Entertainment Company, 22; 98 (upd.)
Cendant Corporation, 44 (upd.)
Choice Hotels International, Inc., 14; 83 (upd.)
Circus Circus Enterprises, Inc., 6
City Developments Limited, 89
Club Méditerranée S.A., 6; 21 (upd.); 91 (upd.)
Compagnia Italiana dei Jolly Hotels S.p.A., 71
Daniel Thwaites Plc, 95
Doubletree Corporation, 21
Extended Stay America, Inc., 41
Fairmont Hotels & Resorts Inc., 69
Fibreboard Corporation, 16
Four Seasons Hotels Inc., 9; 29 (upd.)
Fuller Smith & Turner P.L.C., 38
Gables Residential Trust, 49
Gaylord Entertainment Company, 11; 36 (upd.)
Global Hyatt Corporation, 75 (upd.)
Granada Group PLC, 24 (upd.)
Grand Casinos, Inc., 20
Grand Hotel Krasnapolsky N.V., 23
Great Wolf Resorts, Inc., 91
Grupo Posadas, S.A. de C.V., 57
Helmsley Enterprises, Inc., 9
Hilton Hotels Corporation, III; 19 (upd.); 49 (upd.); 62 (upd.)
Holiday Inns, Inc., III
Home Inns & Hotels Management Inc., 95
Hospitality Franchise Systems, Inc., 11
Hotel Properties Ltd., 71
Howard Johnson International, Inc., 17; 72 (upd.)
Hyatt Corporation, III; 16 (upd.)
ILX Resorts Incorporated, 65
Interstate Hotels & Resorts Inc., 58
ITT Sheraton Corporation, III
JD Wetherspoon plc, 30
John Q. Hammons Hotels, Inc., 24
Jumeirah Group, 83

Kerzner International Limited, 69 (upd.)
The La Quinta Companies, 11; 42 (upd.)
Ladbroke Group PLC, 21 (upd.)
Landry's Restaurants, Inc., 65 (upd.)
Las Vegas Sands, Inc., 50
Madden's on Gull Lake, 52
Mandalay Resort Group, 32 (upd.)
Manor Care, Inc., 25 (upd.)
The Marcus Corporation, 21
Marriott International, Inc., III; 21 (upd.); 83 (upd.)
McMenamins Pubs and Breweries, 65
MGM MIRAGE, 98 (upd.)
Millennium & Copthorne Hotels plc, 71
Mirage Resorts, Incorporated, 6; 28 (upd.)
Monarch Casino & Resort, Inc., 65
Morgans Hotel Group Company, 80
Motel 6, 13; 56 (upd.)
MTR Gaming Group, Inc., 75
MWH Preservation Limited Partnership, 65
NH Hoteles S.A., 79
Omni Hotels Corp., 12
Paradores de Turismo de Espana S.A., 73
Park Corp., 22
Players International, Inc., 22
Preussag AG, 42 (upd.)
Prime Hospitality Corporation, 52
Promus Companies, Inc., 9
Real Turismo, S.A. de C.V., 50
Red Roof Inns, Inc., 18
Regent Inns plc, 95
Resorts International, Inc., 12
The Ritz-Carlton Hotel Company, L.L.C., 9; 29 (upd.); 71 (upd.)
Riviera Holdings Corporation, 75
Sandals Resorts International, 65
Santa Fe Gaming Corporation, 19
The SAS Group, 34 (upd.)
SFI Group plc, 51
Shangri-La Asia Ltd., 71
Showboat, Inc., 19
Sol Meliá S.A., 71
Sonesta International Hotels Corporation, 44
Starwood Hotels & Resorts Worldwide, Inc., 54
Sun International Hotels Limited, 26
Sunburst Hospitality Corporation, 26
Super 8 Motels, Inc., 83
Thistle Hotels PLC, 54
Trusthouse Forte PLC, III
Vail Resorts, Inc., 43 (upd.)
WestCoast Hospitality Corporation, 59
Westin Hotels and Resorts Worldwide, 9; 29 (upd.)
Whitbread PLC, I; 20 (upd.); 52 (upd.); 97 (upd.)
Wyndham Worldwide Corporation (updates Cendant Corporation), 99 (upd.)
Young & Co.'s Brewery, P.L.C., 38

Information Technology

A.B. Watley Group Inc., 45
AccuWeather, Inc., 73
Acxiom Corporation, 35
Adaptec, Inc., 31

Adobe Systems Incorporated, 10; 33 (upd.)
Advanced Micro Devices, Inc., 6; 30 (upd.); 99 (upd.)
Agence France-Presse, 34
Agilent Technologies Inc., 38; 93 (upd.)
Akamai Technologies, Inc., 71
Aldus Corporation, 10
Allen Systems Group, Inc., 59
AltaVista Company, 43
Altiris, Inc., 65
Amdahl Corporation, III; 14 (upd.); 40 (upd.)
Amdocs Ltd., 47
America Online, Inc., 10; 26 (upd.)
American Business Information, Inc., 18
American Management Systems, Inc., 11
American Software Inc., 25
AMICAS, Inc., 69
Amstrad PLC, III
Analex Corporation, 74
Analytic Sciences Corporation, 10
Analytical Surveys, Inc., 33
Anker BV, 53
Ansoft Corporation, 63
Anteon Corporation, 57
AOL Time Warner Inc., 57 (upd.)
Apollo Group, Inc., 24
Apple Computer, Inc., III; 6 (upd.); 77 (upd.)
aQuantive, Inc., 81
The Arbitron Company, 38
Ariba, Inc., 57
Asanté Technologies, Inc., 20
Ascential Software Corporation, 59
AsiaInfo Holdings, Inc., 43
ASK Group, Inc., 9
Ask Jeeves, Inc., 65
ASML Holding N.V., 50
The Associated Press, 73 (upd.)
AST Research Inc., 9
At Home Corporation, 43
AT&T Bell Laboratories, Inc., 13
AT&T Corporation, 29 (upd.)
AT&T Istel Ltd., 14
Atos Origin S.A., 69
Attachmate Corporation, 56
Autodesk, Inc., 10; 89 (upd.)
Autologic Information International, Inc., 20
Automatic Data Processing, Inc., III; 9 (upd.); 47 (upd.)
Autotote Corporation, 20
Avantium Technologies BV, 79
Avid Technology Inc., 38
Avocent Corporation, 65
Aydin Corp., 19
Baan Company, 25
Baidu.com Inc., 95
Baltimore Technologies Plc, 42
Bankrate, Inc., 83
Banyan Systems Inc., 25
Battelle Memorial Institute, Inc., 10
BBN Corp., 19
BEA Systems, Inc., 36
Bell and Howell Company, 9; 29 (upd.)
Bell Industries, Inc., 47
Billing Concepts, Inc., 26; 72 (upd.)

Blackbaud, Inc., 85
Blackboard Inc., 89
Blizzard Entertainment 78
Bloomberg L.P., 21
Blue Martini Software, Inc., 59
BMC Software, Inc., 55
Boole & Babbage, Inc., 25
Booz Allen & Hamilton Inc., 10
Borland International, Inc., 9
Bowne & Co., Inc., 23
Brite Voice Systems, Inc., 20
Broderbund Software, 13; 29 (upd.)
BTG, Inc., 45
Bull S.A., 43 (upd.)
Business Objects S.A., 25
C-Cube Microsystems, Inc., 37
CACI International Inc., 21; 72 (upd.)
Cadence Design Systems, Inc., 11
Caere Corporation, 20
Cahners Business Information, 43
CalComp Inc., 13
Cambridge Technology Partners, Inc., 36
Candle Corporation, 64
Canon Inc., III
Cap Gemini Ernst & Young, 37
Captaris, Inc., 89
CareerBuilder, Inc., 93
Caribiner International, Inc., 24
Catalina Marketing Corporation, 18
CDC Corporation, 71
CDW Computer Centers, Inc., 16
Cerner Corporation, 16
CheckFree Corporation, 81
Cheyenne Software, Inc., 12
CHIPS and Technologies, Inc., 9
Ciber, Inc., 18
Cincom Systems Inc., 15
Cirrus Logic, Incorporated, 11
Cisco-Linksys LLC, 86
Cisco Systems, Inc., 11; 77 (upd.)
Citizen Watch Co., Ltd., III; 21 (upd.);
    81 (upd.)
Citrix Systems, Inc., 44
CMGI, Inc., 76
CNET Networks, Inc., 47
Cogent Communications Group, Inc., 55
Cognizant Technology Solutions
    Corporation, 59
Cognos Inc., 44
Commodore International Ltd., 7
Compagnie des Machines Bull S.A., III
Compaq Computer Corporation, III; 6
    (upd.); 26 (upd.)
Complete Business Solutions, Inc., 31
CompuAdd Computer Corporation, 11
CompuCom Systems, Inc., 10
CompUSA, Inc., 35 (upd.)
CompuServe Interactive Services, Inc., 10;
    27 (upd.)
Computer Associates International, Inc.,
    6; 49 (upd.)
Computer Data Systems, Inc., 14
Computer Sciences Corporation, 6
Computervision Corporation, 10
Compuware Corporation, 10; 30 (upd.);
    66 (upd.)
Comshare Inc., 23
Conner Peripherals, Inc., 6

Control Data Corporation, III
Control Data Systems, Inc., 10
Corbis Corporation, 31
Corel Corporation, 15; 33 (upd.); 76
    (upd.)
Corporate Software Inc., 9
CoStar Group, Inc., 73
craigslist, inc., 89
Cray Research, Inc., III
Credence Systems Corporation, 90
CSX Corporation, 79 (upd.)
CTG, Inc., 11
Ctrip.com International Ltd., 97
Cybermedia, Inc., 25
Dairyland Healthcare Solutions, 73
Dassault Systèmes S.A., 25
Data Broadcasting Corporation, 31
Data General Corporation, 8
Datapoint Corporation, 11
Dell Computer Corp., 9
Dendrite International, Inc., 70
Deutsche Börse AG, 59
Dialogic Corporation, 18
DiamondCluster International, Inc., 51
Digex, Inc., 46
Digital Equipment Corporation, III; 6
    (upd.)
Digital River, Inc., 50
Digitas Inc., 81
Dimension Data Holdings PLC, 69
ditech.com, 93
Documentum, Inc., 46
The Dun & Bradstreet Corporation, IV;
    19 (upd.)
Dun & Bradstreet Software Services Inc.,
    11
DynCorp, 45
E.piphany, Inc., 49
EarthLink, Inc., 36
eCollege.com, 85
ECS S.A, 12
EDGAR Online, Inc., 91
Edmark Corporation, 14; 41 (upd.)
Egghead Inc., 9
El Camino Resources International, Inc.,
    11
Electronic Arts Inc., 10; 85 (upd.)
Electronic Data Systems Corporation, III;
    28 (upd.)
Electronics for Imaging, Inc., 43 (upd.)
EMC Corporation, 12; 46 (upd.)
Encore Computer Corporation, 13; 74
    (upd.)
Environmental Systems Research Institute
    Inc. (ESRI), 62
EPAM Systems, Inc., 96
Epic Systems Corporation, 62
EPIQ Systems, Inc., 56
Evans and Sutherland Computer
    Company 19, 78 (upd.)
Exabyte Corporation, 12
Experian Information Solutions Inc., 45
Facebook, Inc., 90
FactSet Research Systems Inc., 73
FASTWEB S.p.A., 83
F5 Networks, Inc., 72
First Financial Management Corporation,
    11

Fiserv Inc., 11
FlightSafety International, Inc., 9
FORE Systems, Inc., 25
Franklin Electronic Publishers, Inc., 23
Franz Inc., 80
FTP Software, Inc., 20
Fujitsu Limited, III; 42 (upd.)
Fujitsu-ICL Systems Inc., 11
Future Now, Inc., 12
Gartner, Inc., 21; 94 (upd.)
Gateway, Inc., 10; 27 (upd.)
GEAC Computer Corporation Ltd., 43
Gericom AG, 47
Getronics NV, 39
GFI Informatique SA, 49
Global Imaging Systems, Inc., 73
Google, Inc., 50
Groupe Open, 74
GSI Commerce, Inc., 67
GT Interactive Software, 31
Guthy-Renker Corporation, 32
Handspring Inc., 49
Hewlett-Packard Company, III; 6 (upd.)
Hyperion Software Corporation, 22
Hyperion Solutions Corporation, 76
ICL plc, 6
Identix Inc., 44
IDX Systems Corporation, 64
IKON Office Solutions, Inc., 50
Imation Corporation, 20
Indus International Inc., 70
Infineon Technologies AG, 50
Information Access Company, 17
Information Builders, Inc., 22
Information Resources, Inc., 10
Informix Corporation, 10; 30 (upd.)
InfoSpace, Inc., 91
Infosys Technologies Ltd., 38
Ing. C. Olivetti & C., S.p.a., III
Inktomi Corporation, 45
Input/Output, Inc., 73
Inso Corporation, 26
Intel Corporation, 36 (upd.)
IntelliCorp, Inc., 45
Intelligent Electronics, Inc., 6
Interfax News Agency, 86
Intergraph Corporation, 6; 24 (upd.)
Intermix Media, Inc., 83
International Business Machines
    Corporation, III; 6 (upd.); 30 (upd.);
    63 (upd.)
InterVideo, Inc., 85
Intrado Inc., 63
Intuit Inc., 14; 33 (upd.); 73 (upd.)
Iomega Corporation, 21
IONA Technologies plc, 43
i2 Technologies, Inc., 87
J.D. Edwards & Company, 14
Jack Henry and Associates, Inc., 17
Janus Capital Group Inc., 57
Jones Knowledge Group, Inc., 97
The Judge Group, Inc., 51
Juniper Networks, Inc., 43
Juno Online Services, Inc., 38
Jupitermedia Corporation, 75
Kana Software, Inc., 51
Keane, Inc., 56
Kenexa Corporation, 87

Kintera, Inc., 75
KLA Instruments Corporation, 11
Knight Ridder, Inc., 67 (upd.)
KnowledgeWare Inc., 31 (upd.)
Komag, Inc., 11
Kronos, Inc., 18
Kurzweil Technologies, Inc., 51
LaCie Group S.A., 76
Lam Research Corporation, 11
Landauer, Inc., 51
Lason, Inc., 31
Lawson Software, 38
The Learning Company Inc., 24
Learning Tree International Inc., 24
Legent Corporation, 10
LendingTree, LLC, 93
Levi, Ray & Shoup, Inc., 96
LEXIS-NEXIS Group, 33
LifeLock, Inc., 91
Logica plc, 14; 37 (upd.)
Logicon Inc., 20
Logitech International S.A., 28; 69 (upd.)
LoJack Corporation, 48
Lotus Development Corporation, 6; 25 (upd.)
The MacNeal-Schwendler Corporation, 25
Macromedia, Inc., 50
Madge Networks N.V., 26
Magma Design Automation Inc. 78
MAI Systems Corporation, 11
Manatron, Inc., 86
ManTech International Corporation, 97
MAPICS, Inc., 55
Maryville Data Systems Inc., 96
Match.com, LP, 87
The MathWorks, Inc., 80
Maxtor Corporation, 10
Mead Data Central, Inc., 10
Mecklermedia Corporation, 24
MEDecision, Inc., 95
Medical Information Technology Inc., 64
Mentor Graphics Corporation, 11
Mercury Interactive Corporation, 59
Merge Healthcare, 85
Merisel, Inc., 12
Metatec International, Inc., 47
Metro Information Services, Inc., 36
Micro Warehouse, Inc., 16
Micron Technology, Inc., 11; 29 (upd.)
Micros Systems, Inc., 18
Microsoft Corporation, 6; 27 (upd.); 63 (upd.)
MicroStrategy Incorporated, 87
Misys plc, 45; 46
MITRE Corporation, 26
MIVA, Inc., 83
Moldflow Corporation, 73
Morningstar Inc., 68
The Motley Fool, Inc., 40
National Research Corporation, 87
National Semiconductor Corporation, 6
National TechTeam, Inc., 41
National Weather Service, 91
Navarre Corporation, 24
NAVTEQ Corporation, 69
NCR Corporation, III; 6 (upd.); 30 (upd.); 90 (upd.)
NetCracker Technology Corporation, 98

Netezza Corporation, 69
NetIQ Corporation, 79
Netscape Communications Corporation, 15; 35 (upd.)
Network Appliance, Inc., 58
Network Associates, Inc., 25
Nextel Communications, Inc., 10
NFO Worldwide, Inc., 24
NICE Systems Ltd., 83
Nichols Research Corporation, 18
Nimbus CD International, Inc., 20
Nixdorf Computer AG, III
Noah Education Holdings Ltd., 97
Novell, Inc., 6; 23 (upd.)
NVIDIA Corporation, 54
Océ N.V., 24; 91 (upd.)
OCLC Online Computer Library Center, Inc., 96
Odetics Inc., 14
Onyx Software Corporation, 53
Open Text Corporation, 79
Openwave Systems Inc., 95
Opsware Inc., 49
Oracle Corporation, 6; 24 (upd.); 67 (upd.)
Orbitz, Inc., 61
Packard Bell Electronics, Inc., 13
Packeteer, Inc., 81
Parametric Technology Corp., 16
PC Connection, Inc., 37
Pegasus Solutions, Inc., 75
PeopleSoft Inc., 14; 33 (upd.)
Perot Systems Corporation, 29
Phillips International Inc. 78
Pitney Bowes Inc., III
PLATINUM Technology, Inc., 14
Policy Management Systems Corporation, 11
Policy Studies, Inc., 62
Portal Software, Inc., 47
Primark Corp., 13
The Princeton Review, Inc., 42
Printrak, A Motorola Company, 44
Printronix, Inc., 18
Prodigy Communications Corporation, 34
Programmer's Paradise, Inc., 81
Progress Software Corporation, 15
Psion PLC, 45
Quality Systems, Inc., 81
Quantum Corporation, 10; 62 (upd.)
Quark, Inc., 36
Quicken Loans, Inc., 93
Racal-Datacom Inc., 11
Razorfish, Inc., 37
RCM Technologies, Inc., 34
RealNetworks, Inc., 53
Red Hat, Inc., 45
Remedy Corporation, 58
Renaissance Learning Systems, Inc., 39
Reuters Group PLC, 22 (upd.); 63 (upd.)
The Reynolds and Reynolds Company, 50
Ricoh Company, Ltd., III
Rocky Mountain Chocolate Factory, Inc., 73
Rolta India Ltd., 90
RSA Security Inc., 46
RWD Technologies, Inc., 76
SABRE Group Holdings, Inc., 26

The Sage Group, 43
salesforce.com, Inc., 79
The Santa Cruz Operation, Inc., 38
SAP AG, 16; 43 (upd.)
SAS Institute Inc., 10; 78 (upd.)
Satyam Computer Services Ltd., 85
SBS Technologies, Inc., 25
SCB Computer Technology, Inc., 29
Schawk, Inc., 24
Scientific Learning Corporation, 95
The SCO Group Inc., 78
SDL PLC, 67
Seagate Technology, Inc., 8
Siebel Systems, Inc., 38
Sierra On-Line, Inc., 15; 41 (upd.)
SilverPlatter Information Inc., 23
SINA Corporation, 69
SkillSoft Public Limited Company, 81
SmartForce PLC, 43
Softbank Corp., 13; 38 (upd.); 77 (upd.)
Sonic Solutions, Inc., 81
SonicWALL, Inc., 87
Spark Networks, Inc., 91
Specialist Computer Holdings Ltd., 80
SPSS Inc., 64
SRA International, Inc., 77
Standard Microsystems Corporation, 11
STC PLC, III
Steria SA, 49
Sterling Software, Inc., 11
Storage Technology Corporation, 6
Stratus Computer, Inc., 10
Sun Microsystems, Inc., 7; 30 (upd.); 91 (upd.)
SunGard Data Systems Inc., 11
Sybase, Inc., 10; 27 (upd.)
Sykes Enterprises, Inc., 45
Symantec Corporation, 10; 82 (upd.)
Symbol Technologies, Inc., 15
Synchronoss Technologies, Inc., 95
SYNNEX Corporation, 73
Synopsys, Inc., 11; 69 (upd.)
Syntel, Inc., 92
System Software Associates, Inc., 10
Systems & Computer Technology Corp., 19
T-Online International AG, 61
TALX Corporation, 92
Tandem Computers, Inc., 6
TechTarget, Inc., 99
TenFold Corporation, 35
Terra Lycos, Inc., 43
Terremark Worldwide, Inc., 99
The Thomson Corporation, 34 (upd.); 77 (upd.)
ThoughtWorks Inc., 90
3Com Corporation, 11; 34 (upd.)
The 3DO Company, 43
TIBCO Software Inc., 79
Timberline Software Corporation, 15
TomTom N.V., 81
TradeStation Group, Inc., 83
Traffix, Inc., 61
Transaction Systems Architects, Inc., 29; 82 (upd.)
Transiciel SA, 48
Trend Micro Inc., 97
Triple P N.V., 26

Tripwire, Inc., 97
The TriZetto Group, Inc., 83
Tucows Inc. 78
Ubi Soft Entertainment S.A., 41
Unica Corporation, 77
Unilog SA, 42
Unisys Corporation, III; 6 (upd.); 36
    (upd.)
United Business Media plc, 52 (upd.)
United Internet AG, 99
United Online, Inc., 71 (upd.)
United Press International, Inc., 73 (upd.)
UUNET, 38
VASCO Data Security International, Inc.,
    79
Verbatim Corporation, 14
Veridian Corporation, 54
VeriFone Holdings, Inc., 18; 76 (upd.)
Verint Systems Inc., 73
VeriSign, Inc., 47
Veritas Software Corporation, 45
Verity Inc., 68
Viasoft Inc., 27
Vital Images, Inc., 85
VMware, Inc., 90
Volt Information Sciences Inc., 26
Wanadoo S.A., 75
Wang Laboratories, Inc., III; 6 (upd.)
WebMD Corporation, 65
WebEx Communications, Inc., 81
West Group, 34 (upd.)
Westcon Group, Inc., 67
Western Digital Corporation, 25; 92
    (upd.)
Wikimedia Foundation, Inc., 91
Wind River Systems, Inc., 37
Wipro Limited, 43
Witness Systems, Inc., 87
Wolters Kluwer NV, 33 (upd.)
WordPerfect Corporation, 10
Wyse Technology, Inc., 15
Xerox Corporation, III; 6 (upd.); 26
    (upd.); 69 (upd.)
Xilinx, Inc., 16; 82 (upd.)
Yahoo! Inc., 27; 70 (upd.)
YouTube, Inc., 90
Zanett, Inc., 92
Zapata Corporation, 25
Ziff Davis Media Inc., 36 (upd.)
Zilog, Inc., 15

Insurance

AEGON N.V., III; 50 (upd.)
Aetna Inc., III; 21 (upd.); 63 (upd.)
AFLAC Incorporated, 10 (upd.); 38
    (upd.)
Alexander & Alexander Services Inc., 10
Alfa Corporation, 60
Alleanza Assicurazioni S.p.A., 65
Alleghany Corporation, 10
Allianz AG, III; 15 (upd.); 57 (upd.)
Allmerica Financial Corporation, 63
The Allstate Corporation, 10; 27 (upd.)
AMB Generali Holding AG, 51
American Family Corporation, III
American Financial Group Inc., III; 48
    (upd.)

American General Corporation, III; 10
    (upd.); 46 (upd.)
American International Group, Inc., III;
    15 (upd.); 47 (upd.)
American National Insurance Company, 8;
    27 (upd.)
American Premier Underwriters, Inc., 10
American Re Corporation, 10; 35 (upd.)
N.V. AMEV, III
AOK-Bundesverband (Federation of the
    AOK) 78
Aon Corporation, III; 45 (upd.)
Arthur J. Gallagher & Co., 73
Assicurazioni Generali SpA, III; 15 (upd.)
Assurances Générales de France, 63
Assured Guaranty Ltd., 93
Atlantic American Corporation, 44
Aviva PLC, 50 (upd.)
Axa, III
AXA Colonia Konzern AG, 27; 49 (upd.)
B.A.T. Industries PLC, 22 (upd.)
Baldwin & Lyons, Inc., 51
Bâloise-Holding, 40
Benfield Greig Group plc, 53
Berkshire Hathaway Inc., III; 18 (upd.);
    42 (upd.); 89 (upd.)
Blue Cross and Blue Shield Association,
    10
British United Provident Association
    Limited (BUPAL), 79
Brown & Brown, Inc., 41
Business Men's Assurance Company of
    America, 14
Capital Holding Corporation, III
Catholic Order of Foresters, 24; 97 (upd.)
China Life Insurance Company Limited,
    65
ChoicePoint Inc., 65
The Chubb Corporation, III; 14 (upd.);
    37 (upd.)
CIGNA Corporation, III; 22 (upd.); 45
    (upd.)
Cincinnati Financial Corporation, 16; 44
    (upd.)
CNA Financial Corporation, III; 38
    (upd.)
Commercial Union PLC, III
Connecticut Mutual Life Insurance
    Company, III
Conseco Inc., 10; 33 (upd.)
The Continental Corporation, III
Crawford & Company, 87
Debeka Krankenversicherungsverein auf
    Gegenseitigkeit, 72
The Doctors' Company, 55
Empire Blue Cross and Blue Shield, III
Enbridge Inc., 43
Endurance Specialty Holdings Ltd., 85
Engle Homes, Inc., 46
The Equitable Life Assurance Society of
    the United States Fireman's Fund
    Insurance Company, III
ERGO Versicherungsgruppe AG, 44
Erie Indemnity Company, 35
Fairfax Financial Holdings Limited, 57
Farm Family Holdings, Inc., 39
Farmers Insurance Group of Companies,
    25

Federal Deposit Insurance Corporation,
    93
Fidelity National Financial Inc., 54
The First American Corporation, 52
First Executive Corporation, III
Foundation Health Corporation, 12
Gainsco, Inc., 22
GEICO Corporation, 10; 40 (upd.)
General Accident PLC, III
General Re Corporation, III; 24 (upd.)
Gerling-Konzern Versicherungs-
    Beteiligungs-Aktiengesellschaft, 51
GraceKennedy Ltd., 92
Great-West Lifeco Inc., III
Groupama S.A., 76
Gryphon Holdings, Inc., 21
Guardian Financial Services, 64 (upd.)
Guardian Royal Exchange Plc, 11
Harleysville Group Inc., 37
HDI (Haftpflichtverband der Deutschen
    Industrie Versicherung auf
    Gegenseitigkeit V.a.G.), 53
HealthExtras, Inc., 75
HealthMarkets, Inc., 88 (upd.)
Hilb, Rogal & Hobbs Company, 77
The Home Insurance Company, III
Horace Mann Educators Corporation, 22;
    90 (upd.)
Household International, Inc., 21 (upd.)
Hub International Limited, 89
HUK-Coburg, 58
Irish Life & Permanent Plc, 59
Jackson National Life Insurance Company,
    8
Jefferson-Pilot Corporation, 11; 29 (upd.)
John Hancock Financial Services, Inc., III;
    42 (upd.)
Johnson & Higgins, 14
Kaiser Foundation Health Plan, Inc., 53
Kemper Corporation, III; 15 (upd.)
LandAmerica Financial Group, Inc., 85
Legal & General Group plc, III; 24 (upd.)
The Liberty Corporation, 22
Liberty Mutual Holding Company, 59
LifeWise Health Plan of Oregon, Inc., 90
Lincoln National Corporation, III; 25
    (upd.)
Lloyd's, 74 (upd.)
Lloyd's of London, III; 22 (upd.)
The Loewen Group Inc., 40 (upd.)
Lutheran Brotherhood, 31
Manulife Financial Corporation, 85
Marsh & McLennan Companies, Inc., III;
    45 (upd.)
Massachusetts Mutual Life Insurance
    Company, III; 53 (upd.)
MBIA Inc., 73
The Meiji Mutual Life Insurance
    Company, III
Mercury General Corporation, 25
Metropolitan Life Insurance Company,
    III; 52 (upd.)
MGIC Investment Corp., 52
The Midland Company, 65
Millea Holdings Inc., 64 (upd.)
Mitsui Marine and Fire Insurance
    Company, Limited, III

Mitsui Mutual Life Insurance Company, III; 39 (upd.)

Modern Woodmen of America, 66

Munich Re (Münchener Rückversicherungs-Gesellschaft Aktiengesellschaft in München), III; 46 (upd.)

The Mutual Benefit Life Insurance Company, III

The Mutual Life Insurance Company of New York, III

The Mutual of Omaha Companies, 98

National Medical Health Card Systems, Inc., 79

Nationale-Nederlanden N.V., III

The Navigators Group, Inc., 92

New England Mutual Life Insurance Company, III

New Jersey Manufacturers Insurance Company, 96

New York Life Insurance Company, III; 45 (upd.)

Nippon Life Insurance Company, III; 60 (upd.)

Northwestern Mutual Life Insurance Company, III; 45 (upd.)

NYMAGIC, Inc., 41

Ohio Casualty Corp., 11

Old Republic International Corporation, 11; 58 (upd.)

Oregon Dental Service Health Plan, Inc., 51

Pacific Mutual Holding Company, 98

Palmer & Cay, Inc., 69

Pan-American Life Insurance Company, 48

PartnerRe Ltd., 83

The Paul Revere Corporation, 12

Pennsylvania Blue Shield, III

The PMI Group, Inc., 49

Preserver Group, Inc., 44

Principal Mutual Life Insurance Company, III

The Progressive Corporation, 11; 29 (upd.)

Provident Life and Accident Insurance Company of America, III

Prudential Financial Inc., III; 30 (upd.); 82 (upd.)

Prudential plc, III; 48 (upd.)

Radian Group Inc., 42

The Regence Group, 74

Reliance Group Holdings, Inc., III

Riunione Adriatica di Sicurtà SpA, III

Royal & Sun Alliance Insurance Group plc, 55 (upd.)

Royal Insurance Holdings PLC, III

SAFECO Corporaton, III

Sagicor Life Inc., 98

The St. Paul Travelers Companies, Inc. III; 22 (upd.); 79 (upd.)

SCOR S.A., 20

Skandia Insurance Company, Ltd., 50

Sompo Japan Insurance, Inc., 98 (upd.)

StanCorp Financial Group, Inc., 56

The Standard Life Assurance Company, III

State Auto Financial Corporation, 77

State Farm Mutual Automobile Insurance Company, III; 51 (upd.)

State Financial Services Corporation, 51

Stewart Information Services Corporation 78

Sumitomo Life Insurance Company, III; 60 (upd.)

The Sumitomo Marine and Fire Insurance Company, Limited, III

Sun Alliance Group PLC, III

Sun Life Financial Inc., 85

SunAmerica Inc., 11

Suncorp-Metway Ltd., 91

Suramericana de Inversiones S.A., 88

Svenska Handelsbanken AB, 50 (upd.)

The Swett & Crawford Group Inc., 84

Swiss Reinsurance Company (Schweizerische Rückversicherungs-Gesellschaft), III; 46 (upd.)

Teachers Insurance and Annuity Association-College Retirement Equities Fund, III; 45 (upd.)

Texas Industries, Inc., 8

TIG Holdings, Inc., 26

The Tokio Marine and Fire Insurance Co., Ltd., III

Torchmark Corporation, 9; 33 (upd.)

Transatlantic Holdings, Inc., 11

The Travelers Corporation, III

UICI, 33

Union des Assurances de Pans, III

United National Group, Ltd., 63

Unitrin Inc., 16; 78 (upd.)

UNUM Corp., 13

UnumProvident Corporation, 52 (upd.)

USAA, 10

USF&G Corporation, III

Victoria Group, 44 (upd.)

VICTORIA Holding AG, III

Vision Service Plan Inc., 77

W.R. Berkley Corporation, 15; 74 (upd.)

Washington National Corporation, 12

The Wawanesa Mutual Insurance Company, 68

WellChoice, Inc., 67 (upd.)

Westfield Group, 69

White Mountains Insurance Group, Ltd., 48

Willis Corroon Group plc, 25

Winterthur Group, III; 68 (upd.)

The Yasuda Fire and Marine Insurance Company, Limited, III

The Yasuda Mutual Life Insurance Company, III; 39 (upd.)

Zurich Financial Services, 42 (upd.); 93 (upd.)

Zürich Versicherungs-Gesellschaft, III

Legal Services

Akin, Gump, Strauss, Hauer & Feld, L.L.P., 33

American Bar Association, 35

American Lawyer Media Holdings, Inc., 32

Amnesty International, 50

Andrews Kurth, LLP, 71

Arnold & Porter, 35

Baker & Daniels LLP, 88

Baker & Hostetler LLP, 40

Baker & McKenzie, 10; 42 (upd.)

Baker and Botts, L.L.P., 28

Bingham Dana LLP, 43

Brobeck, Phleger & Harrison, LLP, 31

Cadwalader, Wickersham & Taft, 32

Chadbourne & Parke, 36

Cleary, Gottlieb, Steen & Hamilton, 35

Clifford Chance LLP, 38

Coudert Brothers, 30

Covington & Burling, 40

CRA International, Inc., 93

Cravath, Swaine & Moore, 43

Davis Polk & Wardwell, 36

Debevoise & Plimpton, 39

Dechert, 43

Dewey Ballantine LLP, 48

Dorsey & Whitney LLP, 47

Drinker, Biddle and Reath L.L.P., 92

Faegre & Benson LLP, 97

Fenwick & West LLP, 34

Fish & Neave, 54

Foley & Lardner, 28

Fried, Frank, Harris, Shriver & Jacobson, 35

Fulbright & Jaworski L.L.P., 47

Gibson, Dunn & Crutcher LLP, 36

Greenberg Traurig, LLP, 65

Heller, Ehrman, White & McAuliffe, 41

Hildebrandt International, 29

Hogan & Hartson L.L.P., 44

Holland & Knight LLP, 60

Holme Roberts & Owen LLP, 28

Hughes Hubbard & Reed LLP, 44

Hunton & Williams, 35

Jenkens & Gilchrist, P.C., 65

Jones, Day, Reavis & Pogue, 33

Kelley Drye & Warren LLP, 40

King & Spalding, 23

Kirkland & Ellis LLP, 65

Latham & Watkins, 33

LeBoeuf, Lamb, Greene & MacRae, L.L.P., 29

LECG Corporation, 93

The Legal Aid Society, 48

Mayer, Brown, Rowe & Maw, 47

Milbank, Tweed, Hadley & McCloy, 27

Morgan, Lewis & Bockius LLP, 29

Morrison & Foerster LLP 78

O'Melveny & Myers, 37

Oppenheimer Wolff & Donnelly LLP, 71

Orrick, Herrington and Sutcliffe LLP, 76

Patton Boggs LLP, 71

Paul, Hastings, Janofsky & Walker LLP, 27

Paul, Weiss, Rifkind, Wharton & Garrison, 47

Pepper Hamilton LLP, 43

Perkins Coie LLP, 56

Pillsbury Madison & Sutro LLP, 29

Pre-Paid Legal Services, Inc., 20

Proskauer Rose LLP, 47

Quinn Emanuel Urquhart Oliver & Hedges, LLP, 99

Robins, Kaplan, Miller & Ciresi L.L.P., 89

Ropes & Gray, 40

Saul Ewing LLP, 74

Seyfarth Shaw LLP, 93
Shearman & Sterling, 32
Sidley Austin Brown & Wood, 40
Simpson Thacher & Bartlett, 39
Skadden, Arps, Slate, Meagher & Flom, 18
Snell & Wilmer L.L.P., 28
Southern Poverty Law Center, Inc., 74
Stroock & Stroock & Lavan LLP, 40
Sullivan & Cromwell, 26
Troutman Sanders L.L.P., 79
Vinson & Elkins L.L.P., 30
Wachtell, Lipton, Rosen & Katz, 47
Weil, Gotshal & Manges LLP, 55
White & Case LLP, 35
Williams & Connolly LLP, 47
Willkie Farr & Gallagher LLP, 95
Wilson Sonsini Goodrich & Rosati, 34
Winston & Strawn, 35
Womble Carlyle Sandridge & Rice, PLLC, 52

Manufacturing

A-dec, Inc., 53
A. Schulman, Inc., 49 (upd.)
A.B.Dick Company, 28
A.O. Smith Corporation, 11; 40 (upd.); 93 (upd.)
A.T. Cross Company, 17; 49 (upd.)
A.W. Faber-Castell Unternehmensverwaltung GmbH & Co., 51
AAF-McQuay Incorporated, 26
Aalborg Industries A/S, 90
AAON, Inc., 22
AAR Corp., 28
Aarhus United A/S, 68
ABB Ltd., 65 (upd.)
ABC Rail Products Corporation, 18
Abiomed, Inc., 47
ACCO World Corporation, 7; 51 (upd.)
Accubuilt, Inc., 74
Acindar Industria Argentina de Aceros S.A., 87
Acme United Corporation, 70
Acme-Cleveland Corp., 13
Acorn Products, Inc., 55
Acuity Brands, Inc., 90
Acushnet Company, 64
Acuson Corporation, 36 (upd.)
Adams Golf, Inc., 37
Adolf Würth GmbH & Co. KG, 49
Advanced Circuits Inc., 67
Advanced Neuromodulation Systems, Inc., 73
AEP Industries, Inc., 36
AeroGrow International, Inc., 95
Aftermarket Technology Corp., 83
Ag-Chem Equipment Company, Inc., 17
Aga Foodservice Group PLC, 73
AGCO Corporation, 13; 67 (upd.)
Agfa Gevaert Group N.V., 59
Agrium Inc., 73
Ahlstrom Corporation, 53
Ainsworth Lumber Co. Ltd., 99
Airgas, Inc., 54
Aisin Seiki Co., Ltd., III
AK Steel Holding Corporation, 41 (upd.)

AKG Acoustics GmbH, 62
Aktiebolaget Electrolux, 22 (upd.)
Aktiebolaget SKF, III; 38 (upd.); 89 (upd.)
Alamo Group Inc., 32
ALARIS Medical Systems, Inc., 65
Alberto-Culver Company, 8; 36 (upd.); 91 (upd.)
Aldila Inc., 46
Alfa Laval AB, III; 64 (upd.)
Allen Organ Company, 33
Allen-Edmonds Shoe Corporation, 61
Alliant Techsystems Inc., 8; 30 (upd.); 77 (upd.)
The Allied Defense Group, Inc., 65
Allied Healthcare Products, Inc., 24
Allied Products Corporation, 21
Allied Signal Engines, 9
AlliedSignal Inc., 22 (upd.)
Allison Gas Turbine Division, 9
Alltrista Corporation, 30
Alps Electric Co., Ltd., 44 (upd.)
Alticor Inc., 71 (upd.)
Aluar Aluminio Argentino S.A.I.C., 74
Alvis Plc, 47
Amer Group plc, 41
American Axle & Manufacturing Holdings, Inc., 67
American Biltrite Inc., 43 (upd.)
American Business Products, Inc., 20
American Cast Iron Pipe Company, 50
American Greetings Corporation, 59 (upd.)
American Homestar Corporation, 18; 41 (upd.)
American Locker Group Incorporated, 34
American Power Conversion Corporation, 67 (upd.)
American Seating Company 78
American Standard Companies Inc., 30 (upd.)
American Technical Ceramics Corp., 67
American Tourister, Inc., 16
American Woodmark Corporation, 31
Ameriwood Industries International Corp., 17
Amerock Corporation, 53
Ameron International Corporation, 67
AMETEK, Inc., 9
AMF Bowling, Inc., 40
Ampacet Corporation, 67
Ampco-Pittsburgh Corporation, 79
Ampex Corporation, 17
Amway Corporation, 30 (upd.)
Analogic Corporation, 23
Anchor Hocking Glassware, 13
Andersen Corporation, 10
The Andersons, Inc., 31
Andis Company, Inc., 85
Andreas Stihl AG & Co. KG, 16; 59 (upd.)
Andritz AG, 51
Ansell Ltd., 60 (upd.)
Anthem Electronics, Inc., 13
Apasco S.A. de C.V., 51
Apex Digital, Inc., 63
Applica Incorporated, 43 (upd.)
Applied Films Corporation, 48

Applied Materials, Inc., 10; 46 (upd.)
Applied Micro Circuits Corporation, 38
Applied Power Inc., 9; 32 (upd.)
AptarGroup, Inc., 69
ARBED S.A., 22 (upd.)
Arc International, 76
Arctco, Inc., 16
Arctic Cat Inc., 40 (upd.); 96 (upd.)
AREVA NP, 90 (upd.)
Ariens Company, 48
The Aristotle Corporation, 62
Armor All Products Corp., 16
Armstrong Holdings, Inc., III; 22 (upd.); 81 (upd.)
Arotech Corporation, 93
Artesyn Technologies Inc., 46 (upd.)
ArthroCare Corporation, 73
ArvinMeritor, Inc., 54 (upd.)
Asahi Glass Company, Ltd., 48 (upd.)
Ashley Furniture Industries, Inc., 35
ASICS Corporation, 57
ASML Holding N.V., 50
Astec Industries, Inc., 79
Astronics Corporation, 35
ASV, Inc., 34; 66 (upd.)
Atlantis Plastics, Inc., 85
Atlas Copco AB, III; 28 (upd.); 85 (upd.)
ATMI, Inc., 93
Atwood Mobil Products, 53
AU Optronics Corporation, 67
Aurora Casket Company, Inc., 56
Austal Limited, 75
Austin Powder Company, 76
Avedis Zildjian Co., 38
Avery Dennison Corporation, 17 (upd.); 49 (upd.)
Avocent Corporation, 65
Avondale Industries, 7; 41 (upd.)
AVX Corporation, 67
AZZ Incorporated, 93
B.J. Alan Co., Inc., 67
The Babcock & Wilcox Company, 82
Badger Meter, Inc., 22
BAE Systems Ship Repair, 73
Baker Hughes Incorporated, III
Babolat VS, S.A., 97
Baldor Electric Company, 21; 97 (upd.)
Baldwin Piano & Organ Company, 18
Baldwin Technology Company, Inc., 25
Balfour Beatty plc, 36 (upd.)
Ballantyne of Omaha, Inc., 27
Ballard Medical Products, 21
Ballard Power Systems Inc., 73
Bally Manufacturing Corporation, III
Baltek Corporation, 34
Baltimore Aircoil Company, Inc., 66
Bandai Co., Ltd., 55
Barmag AG, 39
Barnes Group Inc., 13; 69 (upd.)
Barry Callebaut AG, 29
Barry-Wehmiller Companies, Inc., 90
Bassett Furniture Industries, Inc., 18; 95 (upd.)
Bath Iron Works, 12; 36 (upd.)
Baxi Group Ltd., 96
Beckman Coulter, Inc., 22
Beckman Instruments, Inc., 14
Becton, Dickinson & Company, 36 (upd.)

Behr GmbH & Co. KG, 72
BEI Technologies, Inc., 65
Beiersdorf AG, 29
Bekaert S.A./N.V., 90
Bel Fuse, Inc., 53
Belden CDT Inc., 76 (upd.)
Belden Inc., 19
Bell Sports Corporation, 16; 44 (upd.)
Belleek Pottery Ltd., 71
Belleville Shoe Manufacturing Company,
    92
Beloit Corporation, 14
Bemis Company, Inc., 8; 91 (upd.)
Bénéteau SA, 55
Benjamin Moore & Co., 13; 38 (upd.)
BenQ Corporation, 67
Berger Bros Company, 62
Bernina Holding AG, 47
Berry Plastics Group Inc., 21; 98 (upd.)
Berwick Offray, LLC, 70
Bianchi International (d/b/a Gregory
    Mountain Products), 76
BIC Corporation, 8; 23 (upd.)
BICC PLC, III
Billabong International Ltd., 44
The Bing Group, 60
Binks Sames Corporation, 21
Binney & Smith Inc., 25
bioMérieux S.A., 75
Biomet, Inc., 10; 93 (upd.)
Biosite Incorporated, 73
BISSELL Inc., 9; 30 (upd.)
The Black & Decker Corporation, III; 20
    (upd.); 67 (upd.)
Black Diamond Equipment, Ltd., 62
Blodgett Holdings, Inc., 61 (upd.)
Blount International, Inc., 12; 48 (upd.)
Blue Nile Inc., 61
Blundstone Pty Ltd., 76
Blyth Industries, Inc., 18
Blyth, Inc., 74 (upd.)
BMC Industries, Inc., 17; 59 (upd.)
Bodum Design Group AG, 47
BÖHLER-UDDEHOLM AG, 73
Boise Cascade Holdings, L.L.C., IV; 8
    (upd.); 32 (upd.); 95 (upd.)
Bolt Technology Corporation, 99
Bombardier Inc., 42 (upd.); 87 (upd.)
Boral Limited, 43 (upd.)
Borden, Inc., 22 (upd.)
Borg-Warner Corporation, III
BorgWarner Inc., 14; 32 (upd.); 85 (upd.)
Boston Scientific Corporation, 37; 77
    (upd.)
Bou-Matic, 62
The Boyds Collection, Ltd., 29
BPB plc, 83
Brach's Confections, Inc., 74 (upd.)
Brady Corporation 78 (upd.)
Brammer PLC, 77
Brannock Device Company, 48
Brass Eagle Inc., 34
Breeze-Eastern Corporation, 95
Bridgeport Machines, Inc., 17
Briggs & Stratton Corporation, 8; 27
    (upd.)
BRIO AB, 24
British Vita plc, 33 (upd.)

Brose Fahrzeugteile GmbH & Company
    KG, 84
Brother Industries, Ltd., 14
Brown & Sharpe Manufacturing Co., 23
Brown Jordan International Inc., 74
    (upd.)
Brown-Forman Corporation, 38 (upd.)
Broyhill Furniture Industries, Inc., 10
Brunswick Corporation, III; 22 (upd.); 77
    (upd.)
BSH Bosch und Siemens Hausgeräte
    GmbH, 67
BTR Siebe plc, 27
Buck Knives Inc., 48
Buckeye Technologies, Inc., 42
Bucyrus International, Inc., 17
Bugle Boy Industries, Inc., 18
Building Materials Holding Corporation,
    52
Bulgari S.p.A., 20
Bulova Corporation, 13; 41 (upd.)
Bundy Corporation, 17
Burelle S.A., 23
Burgett, Inc., 97
Burton Snowboards Inc., 22
Bush Boake Allen Inc., 30
Bush Industries, Inc., 20
Butler Manufacturing Company, 12; 62
    (upd.)
C&J Clark International Ltd., 52
C. Bechstein Pianofortefabrik AG, 96
C.F. Martin & Co., Inc., 42
C.R. Bard, Inc., 65 (upd.)
C-Tech Industries Inc., 90
California Cedar Products Company, 58
California Steel Industries, Inc., 67
Callaway Golf Company, 15; 45 (upd.)
Campbell Scientific, Inc., 51
Cannondale Corporation, 21
Canon Inc., 79 (upd.)
Capstone Turbine Corporation, 75
Caradon plc, 20 (upd.)
The Carbide/Graphite Group, Inc., 40
Carbo PLC, 67 (upd.)
Carbone Lorraine S.A., 33
Cardo AB, 53
Cardone Industries Inc., 92
Carhartt, Inc., 77 (upd.)
Carl Zeiss AG, III; 34 (upd.); 91 (upd.)
Carma Laboratories, Inc., 60
Carpenter Technology Corporation, 13;
    95 (upd.)
Carrier Corporation, 7; 69 (upd.)
Carter Holt Harvey Ltd., 70
Carver Boat Corporation LLC, 88
Carvin Corp., 89
Cascade Corporation, 65
Cascade General, Inc., 65
CASIO Computer Co., Ltd., III; 40
    (upd.)
Catalina Lighting, Inc., 43 (upd.)
Caterpillar Inc., III; 15 (upd.); 63 (upd.)
Cavco Industries, Inc., 65
Cementos Argos S.A., 91
CEMEX S.A. de C.V., 59 (upd.)
Central Garden & Pet Company, 58
    (upd.)
Central Sprinkler Corporation, 29

Centuri Corporation, 54
Century Aluminum Company, 52
Cenveo Inc., 71 (upd.)
Cepheid, 77
Ceradyne, Inc., 65
Cessna Aircraft Company, 27 (upd.)
Champion Enterprises, Inc., 17
Chanel SA, 12; 49 (upd.)
Chantiers Jeanneau S.A., 96
Charisma Brands LLC, 74
The Charles Machine Works, Inc., 64
Chart Industries, Inc., 21; 96 (upd.)
Chicago Bridge & Iron Company N.V.,
    82 (upd.)
Chittenden & Eastman Company, 58
Chris-Craft Corporation, 9, 31 (upd.); 80
    (upd.)
Christian Dalloz SA, 40
Christofle SA, 40
Chromcraft Revington, Inc., 15
Cinemeccanica SpA 78
Ciments Français, 40
Cincinnati Lamb Inc., 72
Cincinnati Milacron Inc., 12
Cinram International, Inc., 43
Circon Corporation, 21
Cirrus Design Corporation, 44
Citizen Watch Co., Ltd., III; 21 (upd.);
    81 (upd.)
CLARCOR Inc., 17; 61 (upd.)
Clark Equipment Company, 8
Clayton Homes Incorporated, 13; 54
    (upd.)
The Clorox Company, III; 22 (upd.); 81
    (upd.)
CNH Global N.V., 38 (upd.); 99 (upd.)
Coach, Inc., 45 (upd.); 99 (upd.)
Coachmen Industries, Inc., 77
COBE Cardiovascular, Inc., 61
Cobra Golf Inc., 16
Cochlear Ltd., 77
Cockerill Sambre Group, 26 (upd.)
Cognex Corporation, 76
Cohu, Inc., 32
Colas S.A., 31
The Coleman Company, Inc., 30 (upd.)
Colfax Corporation, 58
Collins & Aikman Corporation, 41 (upd.)
Collins Industries, Inc., 33
Color Kinetics Incorporated, 85
Colorado MEDtech, Inc., 48
Colt's Manufacturing Company, Inc., 12
Columbia Sportswear Company, 19
Columbus McKinnon Corporation, 37
CommScope, Inc., 77
Compagnie de Saint-Gobain, 64 (upd.)
Compass Minerals International, Inc., 79
CompuDyne Corporation, 51
Conair Corporation, 69 (upd.)
Concord Camera Corporation, 41
Congoleum Corporation, 18; 98 (upd.)
Conn-Selmer, Inc., 55
Conrad Industries, Inc., 58
Conso International Corporation, 29
Consorcio G Grupo Dina, S.A. de C.V.,
    36
Constar International Inc., 64
Controladora Mabe, S.A. de C.V., 82

Converse Inc., 9
Cooper Cameron Corporation, 58 (upd.)
The Cooper Companies, Inc., 39
Cooper Industries, Inc., 44 (upd.)
Cordis Corporation, 46 (upd.)
Corning, Inc., III; 44 (upd.); 90 (upd.)
Corrpro Companies, Inc., 20
Corticeira Amorim, Sociedade Gestora de
    Participaço es Sociais, S.A., 48
CPAC, Inc., 86
Crane Co., 8; 30 (upd.)
Cranium, Inc., 69
Creative Technology Ltd., 57
Creo Inc., 48
CRH plc, 64
Crosman Corporation, 62
Crown Equipment Corporation, 15; 93
    (upd.)
CTB International Corporation, 43 (upd.)
Cubic Corporation, 19; 98 (upd.)
Cuisinart Corporation, 24
Culligan Water Technologies, Inc., 12; 38
    (upd.)
Cummins Engine Company, Inc., 40
    (upd.)
CUNO Incorporated, 57
Curtiss-Wright Corporation, 10; 35 (upd.)
Custom Chrome, Inc., 74 (upd.)
Cutera, Inc., 84
Cutter & Buck Inc., 27
Cyberonics, Inc., 79
Cybex International, Inc., 49
Cymer, Inc., 77
Dade Behring Holdings Inc., 71
Daewoo Group, III
Daikin Industries, Ltd., III
Daisy Outdoor Products Inc., 58
Dalhoff Larsen & Horneman A/S, 96
Dalian Shide Group, 91
Danaher Corporation, 7; 77 (upd.)
Daniel Industries, Inc., 16
Daniel Measurement and Control, Inc.,
    74 (upd.)
Danisco A/S, 44
Day Runner, Inc., 41 (upd.)
DC Shoes, Inc., 60
DCN S.A., 75
De'Longhi S.p.A., 66
Dearborn Mid-West Conveyor Company,
    56
Deceuninck N.V., 84
Deckers Outdoor Corporation, 22; 98
    (upd.)
Decora Industries, Inc., 31
Decorator Industries Inc., 68
DeCrane Aircraft Holdings Inc., 36
Deere & Company, III; 42 (upd.)
Defiance, Inc., 22
Delachaux S.A., 76
Dell Inc., 63 (upd.)
Deluxe Corporation, 73 (upd.)
DEMCO, Inc., 60
Denby Group plc, 44
Denison International plc, 46
DENSO Corporation, 46 (upd.)
Department 56, Inc., 14
DePuy Inc., 37 (upd.)
Detroit Diesel Corporation, 10; 74 (upd.)

Deutsche Babcock A.G., III
Deutsche Steinzeug Cremer & Breuer
    Aktiengesellschaft, 91
Deutz AG, 39
Devro plc, 55
DHB Industries Inc., 85
Dial-A-Mattress Operating Corporation,
    46
Diadora SpA, 86
Diebold, Incorporated, 7; 22 (upd.)
Diehl Stiftung & Co. KG, 79
Diesel SpA, 40
Dixon Industries, Inc., 26
Dixon Ticonderoga Company, 12; 69
    (upd.)
Djarum PT, 62
DMI Furniture, Inc., 46
Domino Printing Sciences PLC, 87
Donaldson Company, Inc., 49 (upd.)
Donnelly Corporation, 12; 35 (upd.)
Dorel Industries Inc., 59
Dot Hill Systems Corp., 93
Douglas & Lomason Company, 16
Dover Corporation, III; 28 (upd.); 90
    (upd.)
Dresser Industries, Inc., III
Drew Industries Inc., 28
Drexel Heritage Furnishings Inc., 12
Dril-Quip, Inc., 81
Drypers Corporation, 18
DTS, Inc., 80
Ducommun Incorporated, 30
Duncan Toys Company, 55
Dunn-Edwards Corporation, 56
Duracell International Inc., 9; 71 (upd.)
Durametallic, 21
Duriron Company Inc., 17
Dürkopp Adler AG, 65
Duron Inc., 72
Dürr AG, 44
Dynatronics Corporation, 99
Dynea, 68
Dyson Group PLC, 71
E-Z-EM Inc., 89
EADS SOCATA, 54
Eagle-Picher Industries, Inc., 8; 23 (upd.)
East Penn Manufacturing Co., Inc., 79
The Eastern Company, 48
Eastman Kodak Company, III; 7 (upd.);
    36 (upd.); 91 (upd.)
Easton Sports, Inc., 66
Eaton Corporation, I; 10 (upd.); 67
    (upd.)
Ebara Corporation, 83
ECC International Corp., 42
Ecolab Inc., I; 13 (upd.); 34 (upd.); 85
    (upd.)
Eddie Bauer Holdings, Inc., 9; 36 (upd.);
    87 (upd.)
EDO Corporation, 46
EG&G Incorporated, 29 (upd.)
Ekco Group, Inc., 16
Elamex, S.A. de C.V., 51
Elano Corporation, 14
Electric Boat Corporation, 86
Electrolux AB, III; 53 (upd.)
Eljer Industries, Inc., 24
Elkay Manufacturing Company, 73

Elscint Ltd., 20
Empire Resources, Inc., 81
Encompass Services Corporation, 33
Encore Computer Corporation, 13; 74
    (upd.)
Encore Wire Corporation, 81
Energizer Holdings, Inc., 32
Energy Conversion Devices, Inc., 75
EnerSys Inc., 99
Enesco Corporation, 11
Engineered Support Systems, Inc., 59
English China Clays Ltd., 40 (upd.)
Ennis, Inc., 21; 97 (upd.)
Enodis plc, 68
EnPro Industries, Inc., 93
Entertainment Distribution Company, 89
Ernie Ball, Inc., 56
Escalade, Incorporated, 19
ESCO Technologies Inc., 87
Esselte, 64
Esselte Leitz GmbH & Co. KG, 48
Essilor International, 21
Esterline Technologies Corp., 15
Ethan Allen Interiors, Inc., 12; 39 (upd.)
The Eureka Company, 12
Everlast Worldwide Inc., 47
Excel Technology, Inc., 65
EXX Inc., 65
Fabbrica D' Armi Pietro Beretta S.p.A., 39
Facom S.A., 32
FAG—Kugelfischer Georg Schäfer AG, 62
Faiveley S.A., 39
Falcon Products, Inc., 33
Fannie May Confections Brands, Inc., 80
Fanuc Ltd., III; 17 (upd.); 75 (upd.)
Farah Incorporated, 24
Farmer Bros. Co., 52
FARO Technologies, Inc., 87
Fastenal Company, 14; 42 (upd.); 99
    (upd.)
Faultless Starch/Bon Ami Company, 55
Featherlite Inc., 28
Fedders Corporation, 18; 43 (upd.)
Federal Prison Industries, Inc., 34
Federal Signal Corp., 10
FEI Company, 79
Fellowes Manufacturing Company, 28
Fender Musical Instruments Company, 16;
    43 (upd.)
Ferretti Group SpA, 90
Ferro Corporation, 56 (upd.)
Figgie International Inc., 7
Firearms Training Systems, Inc., 27
First Alert, Inc., 28
First Brands Corporation, 8
First International Computer, Inc., 56
First Solar, Inc., 95
The First Years Inc., 46
Fisher Controls International, LLC, 13;
    61 (upd.)
Fisher Scientific International Inc., 24
Fisher-Price Inc., 12; 32 (upd.)
Fiskars Corporation, 33
Fisons plc, 9
Flanders Corporation, 65
Fleetwood Enterprises, Inc., III; 22 (upd.);
    81 (upd.)
Flexsteel Industries Inc., 15; 41 (upd.)

Flextronics International Ltd., 38
Flint Ink Corporation, 41 (upd.)
FLIR Systems, Inc., 69
Florsheim Shoe Company, 9
Flour City International, Inc., 44
Flow International Corporation, 56
Flowserve Corporation, 33; 77 (upd.)
FLSmidth & Co. A/S, 72
Force Protection Inc., 95
Fort James Corporation, 22 (upd.)
Forward Industries, Inc., 86
FosterGrant, Inc., 60
Fountain Powerboats Industries, Inc., 28
Four Winns Boats LLC, 96
Foxboro Company, 13
Framatome SA, 19
Francotyp-Postalia Holding AG, 92
Frank J. Zamboni & Co., Inc., 34
Franke Holding AG, 76
Franklin Electric Company, Inc., 43
The Franklin Mint, 69
Freudenberg & Co., 41
Friedrich Grohe AG & Co. KG, 53
Frigidaire Home Products, 22
Frymaster Corporation, 27
FSI International, Inc., 17
Fuel Systems Solutions, Inc., 97
Fuel Tech, Inc., 85
Fuji Photo Film Co., Ltd., III; 18 (upd.);
    79 (upd.)
Fujisawa Pharmaceutical Company, Ltd.,
    58 (upd.)
Fuqua Enterprises, Inc., 17
Furniture Brands International, Inc., 39
    (upd.)
Furon Company, 28
The Furukawa Electric Co., Ltd., III
G. Leblanc Corporation, 55
G.S. Blodgett Corporation, 15
Gaming Partners International
    Corporation, 93
Ganz, 98
Gardner Denver, Inc., 49
The Gates Corporation, 9
GE Aircraft Engines, 9
GEA AG, 27
Geberit AG, 49
Gehl Company, 19
Gelita AG, 74
Gemini Sound Products Corporation, 58
Gemplus International S.A., 64
Gen-Probe Incorporated, 79
GenCorp Inc., 8; 9 (upd.)
General Atomics, 57
General Bearing Corporation, 45
General Binding Corporation, 73 (upd.)
General Cable Corporation, 40
General Dynamics Corporation, I; 10
    (upd.); 40 (upd.); 88 (upd.
General Housewares Corporation, 16
Genmar Holdings, Inc., 45
geobra Brandstätter GmbH & Co. KG,
    48
Georg Fischer AG Schaffhausen, 61
The George F. Cram Company, Inc., 55
George W. Park Seed Company, Inc., 98
Georgia Gulf Corporation, 61 (upd.)
Gerber Scientific, Inc., 12; 84 (upd.)

Gerresheimer Glas AG, 43
Getrag Corporate Group, 92
Gévelot S.A., 96
Giant Manufacturing Company, Ltd., 85
Giddings & Lewis, Inc., 10
Gildemeister AG, 79
The Gillette Company, 20 (upd.)
GKN plc, III; 38 (upd.); 89 (upd.)
Glaverbel Group, 80
Gleason Corporation, 24
Glen Dimplex 78
The Glidden Company, 8
Global Power Equipment Group Inc., 52
Glock Ges.m.b.H., 42
Goodman Holding Company, 42
Goodrich Corporation, 46 (upd.)
Goody Products, Inc., 12
The Gorman-Rupp Company, 18; 57
    (upd.)
Goss Holdings, Inc., 43
Goulds Pumps Inc., 24
Graco Inc., 19; 67 (upd.)
Gradall Industries, Inc., 96
Graham Corporation, 62
Granite Industries of Vermont, Inc., 73
Grant Prideco, Inc., 57
Greatbatch Inc., 72
Greene, Tweed & Company, 55
Greif Inc., 66 (upd.)
GreenMan Technologies Inc., 99
Griffin Industries, Inc., 70
Griffon Corporation, 34
Grinnell Corp., 13
Groupe André, 17
Groupe Genoyer, 96
Groupe Guillin SA, 40
Groupe Herstal S.A., 58
Groupe Legis Industries, 23
Groupe SEB, 35
Grow Group Inc., 12
Groz-Beckert Group, 68
Grunau Company Inc., 90
Grundfos Group, 83
Grupo Cydsa, S.A. de C.V., 39
Grupo IMSA, S.A. de C.V., 44
Grupo Industrial Saltillo, S.A. de C.V., 54
Grupo Lladró S.A., 52
Guangzhou Pearl River Piano Group Ltd.,
    49
Guardian Industries Corp., 87
Gulf Island Fabrication, Inc., 44
Gund, Inc., 96
Gunite Corporation, 51
The Gunlocke Company, 23
Guy Degrenne SA, 44
H.B. Fuller Company, 8; 32 (upd.); 75
    (upd.)
H.O. Penn Machinery Company, Inc., 96
Hach Co., 18
Hackman Oyj Adp, 44
Haeger Industries Inc., 88
Haemonetics Corporation, 20
Haier Group Corporation, 65
Halliburton Company, III
Hallmark Cards, Inc., IV; 16 (upd.); 40
    (upd.); 87 (upd.)
Hammond Manufacturing Company
    Limited, 83

Hamon & Cie (International) S.A., 97
Hansgrohe AG, 56
Hanson PLC, 30 (upd.)
Hardinge Inc., 25
Harland and Wolff Holdings plc, 19
Harmon Industries, Inc., 25
Harnischfeger Industries, Inc., 8; 38
    (upd.)
Harsco Corporation, 8
Hartmann Inc., 96
Hartmarx Corporation, 32 (upd.)
The Hartz Mountain Corporation, 46
    (upd.)
Hasbro, Inc., III; 16 (upd.)
Haskel International, Inc., 59
Hastings Manufacturing Company, 56
Hawker Siddeley Group Public Limited
    Company, III
Haworth Inc., 8; 39 (upd.)
Head N.V., 55
Headwaters Incorporated, 56
Health O Meter Products Inc., 14
Heekin Can Inc., 13
HEICO Corporation, 30
Heidelberger Druckmaschinen AG, 40
Hella KGaA Hueck & Co., 66
Hemisphere GPS Inc., 99
Henkel Manco Inc., 22
The Henley Group, Inc., III
Heraeus Holding GmbH, 54 (upd.)
Herman Miller, Inc., 8; 77 (upd.)
Hermès International S.A., 34 (upd.)
Héroux-Devtek Inc., 69
Hexagon AB 78
High Tech Computer Corporation, 81
Hillenbrand Industries, Inc., 10; 75 (upd.)
Hillerich & Bradsby Company, Inc., 51
Hillsdown Holdings plc, 24 (upd.)
Hilti AG, 53
Hindustan Lever Limited, 79
Hitachi Zosen Corporation, III
Hitchiner Manufacturing Co., Inc., 23
HMI Industries, Inc., 17
HNI Corporation, 74 (upd.)
The Hockey Company, 70
The Holland Group, Inc., 82
Hollander Home Fashions Corp., 67
Holnam Inc., 8
Holson Burnes Group, Inc., 14
Home Products International, Inc., 55
HON INDUSTRIES Inc., 13
Hooker Furniture Corporation, 80
The Hoover Company, 12; 40 (upd.)
Horween Leather Company, 83
Hoshino Gakki Co. Ltd., 55
Host America Corporation, 79
Hubbell Inc., 76 (upd.)
Huffy Corporation, 7; 30 (upd.)
Huhtamäki Oyj, 64
Hummel International A/S, 68
Hunt Manufacturing Company, 12
Hunter Fan Company, 13; 98 (upd.)
Huntleigh Technology PLC, 77
Hydril Company, 46
Hyster Company, 17
Hyundai Group, III; 7 (upd.); 56 (upd.)
IAC Group, 96
Icon Health & Fitness, Inc., 38

IDEO Inc., 65
IdraPrince, Inc., 76
Igloo Products Corp., 21
Ikonics Corporation, 99
Illinois Tool Works Inc., III; 22 (upd.); 81 (upd.)
Illumina, Inc., 93
Imatra Steel Oy Ab, 55
IMI plc, 9
Imo Industries Inc., 7; 27 (upd.)
In-Sink-Erator, 66
Inchcape PLC, III; 16 (upd.); 50 (upd.)
Indel Inc., 78
Industrie Natuzzi S.p.A., 18
Infineon Technologies AG, 50
Ingalls Shipbuilding, Inc., 12
Ingersoll-Rand Company Ltd., III; 15 (upd.); 55 (upd.)
Insilco Corporation, 16
Insituform Technologies, Inc., 83
Interco Incorporated, III
Interface, Inc., 8
The Interlake Corporation, 8
INTERMET Corporation, 77 (upd.)
Internacional de Ceramica, S.A. de C.V., 53
International Controls Corporation, 10
International Flavors & Fragrances Inc., 38 (upd.)
International Game Technology, 10
Intevac, Inc., 92
Intuitive Surgical, Inc., 79
Invacare Corporation, 47 (upd.)
Invensys PLC, 50 (upd.)
Invivo Corporation, 52
Ionatron, Inc., 85
Ionics, Incorporated, 52
Ipsen International Inc., 72
iRobot Corporation, 83
Irwin Toy Limited, 14
Ishikawajima-Harima Heavy Industries Co., Ltd., III; 86 (upd.)
Itron, Inc., 64
J C Bamford Excavators Ltd., 83
J. D'Addario & Company, Inc., 48
J.I. Case Company, 10
J.M. Voith AG, 33
Jabil Circuit, Inc., 36; 88 (upd.)
Jacuzzi Brands Inc., 76 (upd.)
Jacuzzi Inc., 23
JAKKS Pacific, Inc., 52
James Avery Craftsman, Inc., 76
James Hardie Industries N.V., 56
James Purdey & Sons Limited, 87
JanSport, Inc., 70
Japan Tobacco Inc., 46 (upd.)
Jarden Corporation, 93 (upd.)
Jayco Inc., 13
Jeld-Wen, Inc., 45
Jenoptik AG, 33
Jervis B. Webb Company, 24
JLG Industries, Inc., 52
John Frieda Professional Hair Care Inc., 70
Johns Manville Corporation, 64 (upd.)
Johnson Controls, Inc., III; 26 (upd.); 59 (upd.)
Johnson Matthey PLC, 49 (upd.)

Johnson Outdoors Inc., 28; 84 (upd.)
Johnstown America Industries, Inc., 23
Jones Apparel Group, Inc., 11
Jostens, Inc., 7; 25 (upd.); 73 (upd.)
Jotun A/S, 80
JSP Corporation, 74
Julius Blüthner Pianofortefabrik GmbH 78
Jungheinrich AG, 96
K'Nex Industries, Inc., 52
K.A. Rasmussen AS, 99
Kaman Corporation, 12; 42 (upd.)
Kaman Music Corporation, 68
Kansai Paint Company Ltd., 80
Karsten Manufacturing Corporation, 51
Kasper A.S.L., Ltd., 40
Katy Industries, Inc., 51 (upd.)
Kawai Musical Instruments Mfg Co. Ltd. 78
Kawasaki Heavy Industries, Ltd., III; 63 (upd.)
Kaydon Corporation, 18
KB Toys, Inc., 35 (upd.); 86 (upd.)
Kelly-Moore Paint Company, Inc., 56
Kenmore Air Harbor Inc., 65
Kennametal Inc., 68 (upd.)
Keramik Holding AG Laufen, 51
Kerr Group Inc., 24
Kewaunee Scientific Corporation, 25
Key Safety Systems, Inc., 63
Key Tronic Corporation, 14
Keystone International, Inc., 11
KGHM Polska Miedz S.A., 98
KHD Konzern, III
KI, 57
Kimball International, Inc., 12; 48 (upd.)
Kit Manufacturing Co., 18
Klein Tools, Inc., 95
Knape & Vogt Manufacturing Company, 17
Knoll Group Inc., 14; 80 (upd.)
Knorr-Bremse AG, 84
Koala Corporation, 44
Kobe Steel, Ltd., IV; 19 (upd.)
Koch Enterprises, Inc., 29
Koenig & Bauer AG, 64
Kohler Company, 7; 32 (upd.)
Komatsu Ltd., III; 16 (upd.); 52 (upd.)
KONE Corporation, 27; 76 (upd.)
Konica Corporation, III; 30 (upd.)
Kyocera Corporation, 79 (upd.)
KraftMaid Cabinetry, Inc., 72
Kreisler Manufacturing Corporation, 97
KSB AG, 62
Kubota Corporation, III; 26 (upd.)
Kuhlman Corporation, 20
Kwang Yang Motor Company Ltd., 80
Kyocera Corporation, 21 (upd.)
L-3 Communications Holdings, Inc., 48
L. and J.G. Stickley, Inc., 50
L.A. Darling Company, 92
L.B. Foster Company, 33
L.S. Starrett Company, 64 (upd.)
La-Z-Boy Incorporated, 14; 50 (upd.)
LaCie Group S.A., 76
Lacks Enterprises Inc., 61
LADD Furniture, Inc., 12
Ladish Co., Inc., 30

Lafarge Cement UK, 28; 54 (upd.)
Lafuma S.A., 39
Lakeland Industries, Inc., 45
Lam Research Corporation, 31 (upd.)
The Lamson & Sessions Co., 13; 61 (upd.)
Lancer Corporation, 21
The Lane Co., Inc., 12
Laserscope, 67
LaSiDo Inc., 58
LeapFrog Enterprises, Inc., 54
Lear Corporation, 71 (upd.)
Leatherman Tool Group, Inc., 51
Leggett & Platt, Inc., 11; 48 (upd.)
Leica Camera AG, 35
Leica Microsystems Holdings GmbH, 35
Lennox International Inc., 8; 28 (upd.)
Lenox, Inc., 12
Leupold & Stevens, Inc., 52
Lexmark International, Inc., 18; 79 (upd.)
Liebherr-International AG, 64
Lifetime Brands, Inc., 73 (upd.)
Linamar Corporation, 18
Lincoln Electric Co., 13
Lindal Cedar Homes, Inc., 29
Lindsay Manufacturing Co., 20
Lionel L.L.C., 16; 99 (upd.)
Lipman Electronic Engineering Ltd., 81
Little Tikes Company, 13; 62 (upd.)
Loctite Corporation, 8
Logitech International S.A., 28; 69 (upd.)
The Longaberger Company, 12; 44 (upd.)
LOUD Technologies, Inc., 95 (upd.)
Louis Vuitton, 10
LSB Industries, Inc., 77
Lucas Industries PLC, III
Lufkin Industries Inc. 78
Luxottica SpA, 17; 52 (upd.)
Lydall, Inc., 64
Lynch Corporation, 43
M&F Worldwide Corp., 38
M.A. Bruder & Sons, Inc., 56
Mabuchi Motor Co. Ltd., 68
MacAndrews & Forbes Holdings Inc., 28; 86 (upd.)
Mace Security International, Inc., 57
MacGregor Golf Company, 68
Mackay Envelope Corporation, 45
Madeco S.A., 71
Madison-Kipp Corporation, 58
Mag Instrument, Inc., 67
Maidenform, Inc., 59 (upd.)
Mail-Well, Inc., 28
Makita Corporation, 22; 59 (upd.)
MAN Aktiengesellschaft, III
Manhattan Group, LLC , 80
Manitou BF S.A., 27
The Manitowoc Company, Inc., 18; 59 (upd.)
Mannesmann AG, III; 14 (upd.)
Marcolin S.p.A., 61
Margarete Steiff GmbH, 23
Marine Products Corporation, 75
Marisa Christina, Inc., 15
Mark IV Industries, Inc., 7; 28 (upd.)
Märklin Holding GmbH, 70
The Marmon Group, 16 (upd.)
Marshall Amplification plc, 62

Martin-Baker Aircraft Company Limited, 61
Martin Industries, Inc., 44
MartinLogan, Ltd., 85
Marvin Lumber & Cedar Company, 22
Mary Kay Inc., 9; 30 (upd.); 84 (upd.)
Masco Corporation, III; 20 (upd.); 39 (upd.)
Masonite International Corporation, 63
Master Lock Company, 45
MasterBrand Cabinets, Inc., 71
MasterCraft Boat Company, Inc., 90
Material Sciences Corporation, 63
Matsushita Electric Industrial Co., Ltd., 64 (upd.)
Mattel, Inc., 7; 25 (upd.); 61 (upd.)
Matth. Hohner AG, 53
Matthews International Corporation, 29; 77 (upd.)
Maverick Tube Corporation, 59
Maxco Inc., 17
Maxwell Shoe Company, Inc., 30
Maytag Corporation, III; 22 (upd.); 82 (upd.)
McClain Industries, Inc., 51
McDermott International, Inc., III
McKechnie plc, 34
McWane Corporation, 55
Meade Instruments Corporation, 41
Meadowcraft, Inc., 29
Measurement Specialties, Inc., 71
Mecalux S.A., 74
Medtronic, Inc., 67 (upd.)
Meggitt PLC, 34
Meguiar's, Inc., 99
Meidensha Corporation, 92
Meiji Seika Kaisha Ltd., 64 (upd.)
MEMC Electronic Materials, Inc., 81
Memry Corporation, 72
Menasha Corporation, 59 (upd.)
Merck & Co., Inc., I; 11 (upd.); 34 (upd.); 95 (upd.)
Mercury Marine Group, 68
Merillat Industries Inc., 13
Merillat Industries, LLC, 69 (upd.)
Mestek Inc., 10
Metso Corporation, 30 (upd.); 85 (upd.)
Mettler-Toledo International Inc., 30
Meyer International Holdings, Ltd., 87
MGA Entertainment, 95
Michael Anthony Jewelers, Inc., 24
Micrel, Incorporated, 77
Microdot Inc., 8
The Middleton Doll Company, 53
Midwest Grain Products, Inc., 49
Miele & Cie. KG, 56
Mikasa, Inc., 28
Mikohn Gaming Corporation, 39
Milacron, Inc., 53 (upd.)
Miller Industries, Inc., 26
Millipore Corporation, 25; 84 (upd.)
Milton Bradley Company, 21
Mine Safety Appliances Company, 31
Minebea Co., Ltd., 90
Minolta Co., Ltd., III; 18 (upd.); 43 (upd.)
Minuteman International Inc., 46
Misonix, Inc., 80

Mitsubishi Heavy Industries, Ltd., III; 7 (upd.)
Mity Enterprises, Inc., 38
Mobile Mini, Inc., 58
Mocon, Inc., 76
Modine Manufacturing Company, 8; 56 (upd.)
Modtech Holdings, Inc., 77
Moen Incorporated, 12
Mohawk Industries, Inc., 19; 63 (upd.)
Molex Incorporated, 11
The Monarch Cement Company, 72
Monnaie de Paris, 62
Monster Cable Products, Inc., 69
Montblanc International GmbH, 82
Montres Rolex S.A., 13; 34 (upd.)
Montupet S.A., 63
Moog Music, Inc., 75
The Morgan Crucible Company plc, 82
Morrow Equipment Co. L.L.C., 87
Motorcar Parts & Accessories, Inc., 47
Moulinex S.A., 22
Movado Group, Inc., 28
Mr. Coffee, Inc., 15
Mr. Gasket Inc., 15
Mueller Industries, Inc., 7; 52 (upd.)
Multi-Color Corporation, 53
Musco Lighting, 83
Nashua Corporation, 8
National Envelope Corporation, 32
National Gypsum Company, 10
National Oilwell, Inc., 54
National Picture & Frame Company, 24
National Semiconductor Corporation, 69 (upd.)
National Standard Co., 13
National Starch and Chemical Company, 49
Natrol, Inc., 49
Natural Alternatives International, Inc., 49
NCI Building Systems, Inc., 88
NCR Corporation, III; 6 (upd.); 30 (upd.); 90 (upd.)
Neenah Foundry Company, 68
Neopost S.A., 53
NETGEAR, Inc., 81
New Balance Athletic Shoe, Inc., 25
New Holland N.V., 22
Newcor, Inc., 40
Newell Rubbermaid Inc., 9; 52 (upd.)
Newport Corporation, 71
Newport News Shipbuilding Inc., 13; 38 (upd.)
Nexans SA, 54
NGK Insulators Ltd., 67
NHK Spring Co., Ltd., III
Nidec Corporation, 59
NIKE, Inc., 36 (upd.)
Nikon Corporation, III; 48 (upd.)
Nintendo Company, Ltd., III; 7 (upd.); 67 (upd.)
Nippon Electric Glass Co. Ltd., 95
Nippon Seiko K.K., III
Nippondenso Co., Ltd., III
NKK Corporation, 28 (upd.)
NOF Corporation, 72
NordicTrack, 22
Nordson Corporation, 11; 48 (upd.)

Nortek, Inc., 34
Norton Company, 8
Norton McNaughton, Inc., 27
Novellus Systems, Inc., 18
NSS Enterprises Inc. 78
NTN Corporation, III; 47 (upd.)
Nu-kote Holding, Inc., 18
O'Sullivan Industries Holdings, Inc., 34
Oak Industries Inc., 21
Oakley, Inc., 49 (upd.)
Oakwood Homes Corporation, 15
ODL, Inc., 55
The Ohio Art Company, 14; 59 (upd.)
Oil-Dri Corporation of America, 20; 89 (upd.)
The Oilgear Company, 74
Okuma Holdings Inc., 74
Old Town Canoe Company, 74
180s, L.L.C., 64
Oneida Ltd., 7; 31 (upd.); 88 (upd.)
Optische Werke G. Rodenstock, 44
Orange Glo International, 53
Orbotech Ltd., 75
O'Reilly Media, Inc., 99
Orthofix International NV, 72
Osmonics, Inc., 18
Osram GmbH, 86
Overhead Door Corporation, 70
Otis Elevator Company, Inc., 13; 39 (upd.)
Otor S.A., 77
Outboard Marine Corporation, III; 20 (upd.)
Outdoor Research, Incorporated, 67
Owens Corning, 20 (upd.); 98 (upd.)
Owosso Corporation, 29
P & F Industries, Inc., 45
Pacer Technology, 40
Pacific Coast Feather Company, 67
Pacific Dunlop Limited, 10
Pagnossin S.p.A., 73
Pall Corporation, 9; 72 (upd.)
Palm Harbor Homes, Inc., 39
Paloma Industries Ltd., 71
Panavision Inc., 24
Park Corp., 22
Park-Ohio Holdings Corp., 17; 85 (upd.)
Parker-Hannifin Corporation, III; 24 (upd.); 99 (upd.)
Parlex Corporation, 61
Patrick Industries, Inc., 30
Paul Mueller Company, 65
Pearl Corporation 78
Pechiney SA, IV; 45 (upd.)
Peg Perego SpA, 88
Pelican Products, Inc., 86
Pelikan Holding AG, 92
Pella Corporation, 12; 39 (upd.); 89 (upd.)
Penn Engineering & Manufacturing Corp., 28
Pennington Seed Inc., 98
Pentair, Inc., 7; 26 (upd.); 81 (upd.)
Pentax Corporation 78
Pentech International, Inc., 29
PerkinElmer Inc. 7; 78 (upd.)
Peterson American Corporation, 55
Phillips-Van Heusen Corporation, 24

Phoenix AG, 68
Phoenix Mecano AG, 61
Photo-Me International Plc, 83
Physio-Control International Corp., 18
Picanol N.V., 96
Pilkington Group Limited, III; 34 (upd.); 87 (upd.)
Pilot Pen Corporation of America, 82
Pinguely-Haulotte SA, 51
Pioneer Electronic Corporation, III
Pirelli & C. S.p.A., 75 (upd.)
Piscines Desjoyaux S.A., 84
Pitney Bowes, Inc., 19
Pittway Corporation, 33 (upd.)
Planar Systems, Inc., 61
PlayCore, Inc., 27
Playmates Toys, 23
Playskool, Inc., 25
Pleasant Company, 27
Pliant Corporation, 98
Ply Gem Industries Inc., 12
Pochet SA, 55
Polaris Industries Inc., 12; 35 (upd.); 77 (upd.)
Polaroid Corporation, III; 7 (upd.); 28 (upd.); 93 (upd.)
The Porcelain and Fine China Companies Ltd., 69
Portmeirion Group plc, 88
Pou Chen Corporation, 81
PPG Industries, Inc., III; 22 (upd.); 81 (upd.)
Prada Holding B.V., 45
Pranda Jewelry plc, 70
Praxair, Inc., 48 (upd.)
Precision Castparts Corp., 15
Premark International, Inc., III
Pressman Toy Corporation, 56
Presstek, Inc., 33
Price Pfister, Inc., 70
Prince Sports Group, Inc., 15
Printpack, Inc., 68
Printronix, Inc., 18
Puig Beauty and Fashion Group S.L., 60
Pulaski Furniture Corporation, 33; 80 (upd.)
Pumpkin Masters, Inc., 48
Punch International N.V., 66
Pure World, Inc., 72
Puritan-Bennett Corporation, 13
Purolator Products Company, 21; 74 (upd.)
PVC Container Corporation, 67
PW Eagle, Inc., 48
Q.E.P. Co., Inc., 65
QRS Music Technologies, Inc., 95
QSC Audio Products, Inc., 56
Quixote Corporation, 15
R. Griggs Group Limited, 23
Racing Champions Corporation, 37
Radio Flyer Inc., 34
Rain Bird Corporation, 84
Raleigh UK Ltd., 65
Rapala-Normark Group, Ltd., 30
RathGibson Inc., 90
Raven Industries, Inc., 33
Raychem Corporation, 8
Rayovac Corporation, 39 (upd.)

Raytech Corporation, 61
Recovery Engineering, Inc., 25
Red Spot Paint & Varnish Company, 55
Red Wing Pottery Sales, Inc., 52
Red Wing Shoe Company, Inc., 9; 30 (upd.); 83 (upd.)
Reed & Barton Corporation, 67
Regal-Beloit Corporation, 18; 97 (upd.)
Reichhold Chemicals, Inc., 10
Remington Arms Company, Inc., 12; 40 (upd.)
Remington Products Company, L.L.C., 42
RENK AG, 37
Renner Herrmann S.A., 79
Revell-Monogram Inc., 16
Revere Ware Corporation, 22
Revlon Inc., 64 (upd.)
Rexam PLC, 32 (upd.); 85 (upd.)
Rexnord Corporation, 21; 76 (upd.)
RF Micro Devices, Inc., 43
Rheinmetall AG, 9; 97 (upd.)
RHI AG, 53
Richardson Industries, Inc., 62
Rickenbacker International Corp., 91
Riddell Sports Inc., 22
Riedel Tiroler Glashuette GmbH, 99
Rieter Holding AG, 42
River Oaks Furniture, Inc., 43
Riviera Tool Company, 89
RMC Group p.l.c., 34 (upd.)
Roadmaster Industries, Inc., 16
Robbins & Myers Inc., 15
Robertson-Ceco Corporation, 19
Rock-Tenn Company, 59 (upd.)
Rockford Products Corporation, 55
RockShox, Inc., 26
Rockwell Automation, I; 11 (upd.); 43 (upd.)
Rockwell Medical Technologies, Inc., 88
Rodda Paint Company, 98
Rodriguez Group S.A., 90
ROFIN-SINAR Technologies Inc., 81
Rogers Corporation, 61
Rohde & Schwarz GmbH & Co. KG, 39
Rohm and Haas Company, 77 (upd.)
ROHN Industries, Inc., 22
Rohr Incorporated, 9
Roland Corporation, 38
Rollerblade, Inc., 15; 34 (upd.)
Rolls-Royce Group PLC, 67 (upd.)
Ronson PLC, 49
Roper Industries, Inc., 15; 50 (upd.)
Rose Art Industries, 58
Roseburg Forest Products Company, 58
Rotork plc, 46
Royal Appliance Manufacturing Company, 15
Royal Canin S.A., 39
Royal Doulton plc, 14; 38 (upd.)
Royal Group Technologies Limited, 73
RPC Group PLC, 81
RPM International Inc., 8; 36 (upd.); 91 (upd.)
RTI Biologics, Inc., 96
Rubbermaid Incorporated, III
Russ Berrie and Company, Inc., 12; 82 (upd.)
Rusty, Inc., 95

S.C. Johnson & Son, Inc., III; 28 (upd.); 89 (upd.)
Sabaté Diosos SA, 48
Safe Flight Instrument Corporation, 71
Safeskin Corporation, 18
Safety Components International, Inc., 63
Safilo SpA, 54
St. Jude Medical, Inc., 11; 43 (upd.); 97 (upd.)
Salant Corporation, 12; 51 (upd.)
Salton, Inc., 30; 88 (upd.)
Samick Musical Instruments Co., Ltd., 56
Samsonite Corporation, 13; 43 (upd.)
Samuel Cabot Inc., 53
Sandvik AB, 32 (upd.); 77 (upd.)
Sanford L.P., 82
Sanitec Corporation, 51
SANLUIS Corporación, S.A.B. de C.V., 95
Sanrio Company, Ltd., 38
SANYO Electric Co., Ltd., II; 36 (upd.); 95 (upd.)
Sapa AB, 84
Sara Lee Corporation, II; 15 (upd.); 54 (upd.); 99 (upd.)
Sauder Woodworking Company, 12; 35 (upd.)
Sauer-Danfoss Inc., 61
Sawtek Inc., 43 (upd.)
Schindler Holding AG, 29
Schlage Lock Company, 82
Schlumberger Limited, III
School-Tech, Inc., 62
Schott Corporation, 53
Scotsman Industries, Inc., 20
Scott Fetzer Company, 12; 80 (upd.)
The Scotts Company, 22
Scovill Fasteners Inc., 24
Sea Ray Boats Inc., 96
SeaChange International, Inc., 79
Sealed Air Corporation, 14; 57 (upd.)
Sealy Inc., 12
Seattle Lighting Fixture Company, 92
Segway LLC, 48
Seiko Corporation, III; 17 (upd.); 72 (upd.)
Select Comfort Corporation, 34
Selee Corporation, 88
The Selmer Company, Inc., 19
Semitool, Inc., 18
Sequa Corp., 13
Serta, Inc., 28
Severstal Joint Stock Company, 65
Shakespeare Company, 22
Shanghai Baosteel Group Corporation, 71
The Shaw Group, Inc., 50
Sheaffer Pen Corporation, 82
Shelby Williams Industries, Inc., 14
Shermag, Inc., 93
The Sherwin-Williams Company, III; 13 (upd.); 89 (upd.)
Sherwood Brands, Inc., 53
Shimano Inc., 64
Shorewood Packaging Corporation, 28
Shuffle Master Inc., 51
Shurgard Storage Centers, Inc., 52
SIFCO Industries, Inc., 41
Siliconware Precision Industries Ltd., 73

Simmons Company, 47
Simplicity Manufacturing, Inc., 64
Simula, Inc., 41
The Singer Company N.V., 30 (upd.)
The Singing Machine Company, Inc., 60
Skeeter Products Inc., 96
Skis Rossignol S.A., 15; 43 (upd.)
Skyline Corporation, 30
SL Industries, Inc., 77
SLI, Inc., 48
Smead Manufacturing Co., 17
Smith & Wesson Corp., 30; 73 (upd.)
Smith Corona Corp., 13
Smith International, Inc., 15
Smith-Midland Corporation, 56
Smiths Industries PLC, 25
Smoby International SA, 56
Snap-On, Incorporated, 7; 27 (upd.)
Société BIC S.A., 73
Sola International Inc., 71
Sonic Innovations Inc., 56
Sonoco Products Company, 8; 89 (upd.)
SonoSite, Inc., 56
Spacelabs Medical, Inc., 71
Sparton Corporation, 18
Spear & Jackson, Inc., 73
Specialized Bicycle Components Inc., 50
Specialty Equipment Companies, Inc., 25
Specialty Products & Insulation Co., 59
Spectrum Control, Inc., 67
Speidel Inc., 96
Speizman Industries, Inc., 44
Spin Master, Ltd., 61
Spirax-Sarco Engineering plc, 59
SPS Technologies, Inc., 30
SPX Corporation, 47 (upd.)
SRAM Corporation, 65
SRC Holdings Corporation, 67
Stanadyne Automotive Corporation, 37
The Standard Register Company, 15; 93 (upd.)
Standex International Corporation, 17
Stanley Furniture Company, Inc., 34
The Stanley Works, III; 20 (upd.); 79 (upd.)
Starcraft Corporation, 66 (upd.)
Stearns, Inc., 43
Steel Authority of India Ltd., 66 (upd.)
Steel Dynamics, Inc., 52
Steel Technologies Inc., 63
Steelcase, Inc., 7; 27 (upd.)
Steinway Musical Properties, Inc., 19
Stelco Inc., 51 (upd.)
The Stephan Company, 60
Sterilite Corporation, 97
Stewart & Stevenson Services Inc., 11
STMicroelectronics NV, 52
Stratasys, Inc., 67
Strattec Security Corporation, 73
Straumann Holding AG, 79
Strombecker Corporation, 60
Stryker Corporation, 11; 29 (upd.); 79 (upd.)
Sturm, Ruger & Company, Inc., 19
Sub-Zero Freezer Co., Inc., 31
Sudbury Inc., 16
Sulzer Brothers Limited (Gebruder Sulzer Aktiengesellschaft), III

Sumitomo Heavy Industries, Ltd., III; 42 (upd.)
Sun Hydraulics Corporation, 74
Sunburst Shutter Corporation 78
Superior Essex Inc., 80
Susquehanna Pfaltzgraff Company, 8
Swank, Inc., 17; 84 (upd.)
Swarovski International Holding AG, 40
The Swatch Group SA, 26
Swedish Match AB, 12; 39 (upd.); 92 (upd.)
Sweetheart Cup Company, Inc., 36
Sybron International Corp., 14
Synthes, Inc., 93
Syratech Corp., 14
Systemax, Inc., 52
TAB Products Co., 17
Tacony Corporation, 70
TAG Heuer International SA, 25; 77 (upd.)
Tag-It Pacific, Inc., 85
Taiheiyo Cement Corporation, 60 (upd.)
Taiwan Semiconductor Manufacturing Company Ltd., 47
Tamron Company Ltd., 82
Targetti Sankey SpA, 86
Tarkett Sommer AG, 25
Taser International, Inc., 62
Taylor Devices, Inc., 97
Taylor Guitars, 48
TaylorMade-adidas Golf, 23; 96 (upd.)
TB Wood's Corporation, 56
TDK Corporation, 49 (upd.)
TearDrop Golf Company, 32
Techtronic Industries Company Ltd., 73
Tecumseh Products Company, 8; 71 (upd.)
Tektronix Inc., 8; 78 (upd.)
Telsmith Inc., 96
Tempur-Pedic Inc., 54
Tenaris SA, 63
Tennant Company, 13; 33 (upd.); 95 (upd.)
Terex Corporation, 7; 40 (upd.); 91 (upd.)
The Testor Corporation, 51
Tetra Pak International SA, 53
Thales S.A., 42
Thermadyne Holding Corporation, 19
Thermo BioAnalysis Corp., 25
Thermo Electron Corporation, 7
Thermo Fibertek, Inc., 24
Thermo Instrument Systems Inc., 11
Thermo King Corporation, 13
Thiokol Corporation, 22 (upd.)
Thomas & Betts Corp., 11; 54 (upd.)
Thomas Industries Inc., 29
Thomasville Furniture Industries, Inc., 12; 74 (upd.)
Thor Industries Inc., 39; 92 (upd.)
3M Company, 61 (upd.)
ThyssenKrupp AG, IV; 28 (upd.); 87 (upd.)
Tianjin Flying Pigeon Bicycle Co., Ltd., 95
Tilia Inc., 62
Timex Corporation, 7; 25 (upd.)
The Timken Company, 8; 42 (upd.)

Titan Cement Company S.A., 64
Titan International, Inc., 89
TiVo Inc., 75
TJ International, Inc., 19
Todd Shipyards Corporation, 14
Tokheim Corporation, 21
Tomy Company Ltd., 65
Tong Yang Cement Corporation, 62
Tonka Corporation, 25
Toolex International N.V., 26
The Topaz Group, Inc., 62
Topcon Corporation, 84
Topps Company, Inc., 13; 34 (upd.)
Toray Industries, Inc., 51 (upd.)
The Toro Company, 7; 26 (upd.); 77 (upd.)
The Torrington Company, 13
TOTO LTD., 28 (upd.)
TouchTunes Music Corporation, 97
Town & Country Corporation, 19
Toymax International, Inc., 29
Toyoda Automatic Loom Works, Ltd., III
Trane 78
CJSC Transmash Holding, 93
TransPro, Inc., 71
Tredegar Corporation, 52
Trek Bicycle Corporation, 16; 78 (upd.)
Trelleborg AB, 93
Trex Company, Inc., 71
Trico Products Corporation, 15
TriMas Corp., 11
Trinity Industries, Incorporated, 7
TRINOVA Corporation, III
TriPath Imaging, Inc., 77
TriQuint Semiconductor, Inc., 63
Trisko Jewelry Sculptures, Ltd., 57
Triumph Group, Inc., 31
True Temper Sports, Inc., 95
TRUMPF GmbH + Co. KG, 86
TRW Automotive Holdings Corp., 75 (upd.)
Tubos de Acero de Mexico, S.A. (TAMSA), 41
Tultex Corporation, 13
Tupperware Corporation, 28
TurboChef Technologies, Inc., 83
Turtle Wax, Inc., 15; 93 (upd.)
TVI Corporation, 99
Twin Disc, Inc., 21
II-VI Incorporated, 69
Ty Inc., 33; 86 (upd.)
Tyco International Ltd., III; 28 (upd.)
Tyco Toys, Inc., 12
U.S. Robotics Corporation, 9; 66 (upd.)
Ube Industries, Ltd., 38 (upd.)
Ultralife Batteries, Inc., 58
ULVAC, Inc., 80
United Defense Industries, Inc., 30; 66 (upd.)
United Dominion Industries Limited, 8; 16 (upd.)
United Industrial Corporation, 37
United States Filter Corporation, 20
United States Pipe and Foundry Company, 62
Unitika Ltd., 53 (upd.)
Unitog Co., 19
Universal Manufacturing Company, 88

Ushio Inc., 91
Usinas Siderúrgicas de Minas Gerais S.A., 77
Utah Medical Products, Inc., 36
UTStarcom, Inc., 77
VA TECH ELIN EBG GmbH, 49
Vaillant GmbH, 44
Valley National Gases, Inc., 85
Vallourec SA, 54
Valmet Corporation (Valmet Oy), III
Valmont Industries, Inc., 19
The Valspar Corporation, 8
Vari-Lite International, Inc., 35
Varian, Inc., 48 (upd.)
Variflex, Inc., 51
Varity Corporation, III
Varlen Corporation, 16
Varta AG, 23
Velcro Industries N.V., 19; 72 (upd.)
Velux A/S, 86
Ventana Medical Systems, Inc., 75
Verbatim Corporation, 74 (upd.)
Vermeer Manufacturing Company, 17
Vestas Wind Systems A/S, 73
Viasystems Group, Inc., 67
Vickers plc, 27
Victor Company of Japan, Limited, II; 26 (upd.); 83 (upd.)
Victorinox AG, 21; 74 (upd.)
Videojet Technologies, Inc., 90
Vidrala S.A., 67
Viessmann Werke GmbH & Co., 37
ViewSonic Corporation, 72
Viking Range Corporation, 66
Viking Yacht Company, 96
Villeroy & Boch AG, 37
Virco Manufacturing Corporation, 17
Viscofan S.A., 70
Viskase Companies, Inc., 55
Vita Plus Corporation, 60
Vitro Corporativo S.A. de C.V., 34
voestalpine AG, 57 (upd.)
Vorwerk & Co., 27
Vosper Thornycroft Holding plc, 41
Vossloh AG, 53
VTech Holdings Ltd., 77
W.A. Whitney Company, 53
W.C. Bradley Co., 69
W.H. Brady Co., 17
W.L. Gore & Associates, Inc., 14; 60 (upd.)
W.W. Grainger, Inc., 26 (upd.); 68 (upd.)
Wabash National Corp., 13
Wabtec Corporation, 40
Wacker Construction Equipment AG, 95
Wahl Clipper Corporation, 86
Walbro Corporation, 13
Walter Industries, Inc., 72 (upd.)
Washington Scientific Industries, Inc., 17
Wassall Plc, 18
Waterford Wedgwood plc, 12; 34 (upd.)
Water Pik Technologies, Inc., 34; 83 (upd.)
Waters Corporation, 43
Watts Industries, Inc., 19
Watts of Lydney Group Ltd., 71
WD-40 Company, 18
We-No-Nah Canoe, Inc., 98

Webasto Roof Systems Inc., 97
Weber-Stephen Products Co., 40
Weeres Industries Corporation, 52
Weg S.A. 78
The Weir Group PLC, 85
Welbilt Corp., 19
Wellman, Inc., 8; 52 (upd.)
Weru Aktiengesellschaft, 18
West Bend Co., 14
Westell Technologies, Inc., 57
Westerbeke Corporation, 60
Western Digital Corporation, 25; 92 (upd.)
Wheaton Science Products, 60 (upd.)
Wheeling-Pittsburgh Corporation, 58 (upd.)
Whirlpool Corporation, III; 12 (upd.); 59 (upd.)
White Consolidated Industries Inc., 13
Wilbert, Inc., 56
Wilkinson Sword Ltd., 60
William L. Bonnell Company, Inc., 66
William Zinsser & Company, Inc., 58
Williamson-Dickie Manufacturing Company, 45 (upd.)
Wilson Sporting Goods Company, 24; 84 (upd.)
Wilton Products, Inc., 97
Wincor Nixdorf Holding GmbH, 69 (upd.)
Windmere Corporation, 16
Winegard Company, 56
Winnebago Industries, Inc., 7; 27 (upd.); 96 (upd.)
WinsLoew Furniture, Inc., 21
The Wiremold Company, 81
WMS Industries, Inc., 15; 53 (upd.)
Wolverine Tube Inc., 23
Wood-Mode, Inc., 23
Woodcraft Industries Inc., 61
Woodward Governor Company, 13; 49 (upd.)
Wright Medical Group, Inc., 61
Württembergische Metallwarenfabrik AG (WMF), 60
Wyant Corporation, 30
Wyman-Gordon Company, 14
Wynn's International, Inc., 33
X-Rite, Inc., 48
Xerox Corporation, III; 6 (upd.); 26 (upd.); 69 (upd.)
Yamaha Corporation, III; 16 (upd.); 40 (upd.); 99 (upd.)
The Yokohama Rubber Company, Limited, V; 19 (upd.); 91 (upd.)
The York Group, Inc., 50
York International Corp., 13
Young Innovations, Inc., 44
Zapf Creation AG, 95
Zebra Technologies Corporation, 53 (upd.)
ZERO Corporation, 17; 88 (upd.)
ZiLOG, Inc., 72 (upd.)
Zindart Ltd., 60
Zippo Manufacturing Company, 18; 71 (upd.)
Zodiac S.A., 36

Zygo Corporation, 42

Materials

AK Steel Holding Corporation, 19
American Biltrite Inc., 16
American Colloid Co., 13
American Standard Inc., III
Ameriwood Industries International Corp., 17
Anhui Conch Cement Company Limited, 99
Apasco S.A. de C.V., 51
Apogee Enterprises, Inc., 8
Asahi Glass Company, Limited, III
Asbury Carbons, Inc., 68
Bairnco Corporation, 28
Bayou Steel Corporation, 31
Berry Plastics Group Inc., 21; 98 (upd.)
Blessings Corp., 19
Blue Circle Industries PLC, III
Bodycote International PLC, 63
Boral Limited, III
British Vita PLC, 9
Brush Engineered Materials Inc., 67
California Steel Industries, Inc., 67
Callanan Industries, Inc., 60
Cameron & Barkley Company, 28
Carborundum Company, 15
Carl Zeiss AG, III; 34 (upd.); 91 (upd.)
Carlisle Companies Inc., 8; 82 (upd.)
Carter Holt Harvey Ltd., 70
Cementos Argos S.A., 91
Cemex SA de CV, 20
Century Aluminum Company, 52
CertainTeed Corporation, 35
Chargeurs International, 6; 21 (upd.)
Chemfab Corporation, 35
Cimentos de Portugal SGPS S.A. (Cimpor), 76
Cold Spring Granite Company Inc., 16; 67 (upd.)
Columbia Forest Products Inc. 78
Compagnie de Saint-Gobain S.A., III; 16 (upd.)
Cookson Group plc, III; 44 (upd.)
Corning Inc., III; 44 (upd.); 90 (upd.)
CSR Limited, III; 28 (upd.); 85 (upd.)
Dal-Tile International Inc., 22
The David J. Joseph Company, 14; 76 (upd.)
The Dexter Corporation, 12 (upd.)
Dicken Masch Plastics LLC, 90
Dyckerhoff AG, 35
Dynamic Materials Corporation, 81
Dyson Group PLC, 71
ECC Group plc, III
Edw. C. Levy Co., 42
84 Lumber Company, 9; 39 (upd.)
ElkCorp, 52
Empire Resources, Inc., 81
English China Clays Ltd., 15 (upd.); 40 (upd.)
Envirodyne Industries, Inc., 17
Feldmuhle Nobel A.G., III
Fibreboard Corporation, 16
Filtrona plc, 88
Florida Rock Industries, Inc., 46
Foamex International Inc., 17

Formica Corporation, 13
GAF Corporation, 22 (upd.)
The Geon Company, 11
Giant Cement Holding, Inc., 23
Gibraltar Steel Corporation, 37
Granite Rock Company, 26
GreenMan Technologies Inc., 99
Groupe Sidel S.A., 21
Harbison-Walker Refractories Company, 24
Harrisons & Crosfield plc, III
Heidelberger Zement AG, 31
Hexcel Corporation, 28
Holderbank Financière Glaris Ltd., III
Holnam Inc., 39 (upd.)
Holt and Bugbee Company, 66
Homasote Company, 72
Howmet Corp., 12
Huttig Building Products, Inc., 73
Ibstock Brick Ltd., 14; 37 (upd.)
Imerys S.A., 40 (upd.)
Imperial Industries, Inc., 81
Internacional de Ceramica, S.A. de C.V., 53
International Shipbreaking Ltd. L.L.C., 67
Joseph T. Ryerson & Son, Inc., 15
Lafarge Coppée S.A., III
Lafarge Corporation, 28
Lehigh Portland Cement Company, 23
Loma Negra C.I.A.S.A., 95
Lyman-Richey Corporation, 96
Manville Corporation, III; 7 (upd.)
Material Sciences Corporation, 63
Matsushita Electric Works, Ltd., III; 7 (upd.)
McJunkin Corporation, 63
Medusa Corporation, 24
Mitsubishi Materials Corporation, III
Nevamar Company, 82
Nippon Sheet Glass Company, Limited, III
North Pacific Group, Inc., 61
Nuplex Industries Ltd., 92
OmniSource Corporation, 14
Onoda Cement Co., Ltd., III
Otor S.A., 77
Owens-Corning Fiberglass Corporation, III
Pacific Clay Products Inc., 88
Pilkington Group Limited, III; 34 (upd.); 87 (upd.)
Pioneer International Limited, III
PolyOne Corporation, 87 (upd.)
PPG Industries, Inc., III; 22 (upd.); 81 (upd.)
Redland plc, III
Rinker Group Ltd., 65
RMC Group p.l.c., III
Rock of Ages Corporation, 37
Rogers Corporation, 80 (upd.)
Royal Group Technologies Limited, 73
The Rugby Group plc, 31
Scholle Corporation, 96
Schuff Steel Company, 26
Sekisui Chemical Co., Ltd., III; 72 (upd.)
Severstal Joint Stock Company, 65
Shaw Industries, 9

The Sherwin-Williams Company, III; 13 (upd.); 89 (upd.)
The Siam Cement Public Company Limited, 56
SIG plc, 71
Simplex Technologies Inc., 21
Siskin Steel & Supply Company, 70
Solutia Inc., 52
Sommer-Allibert S.A., 19
Southdown, Inc., 14
Spartech Corporation, 19; 76 (upd.)
Ssangyong Cement Industrial Co., Ltd., III; 61 (upd.)
Steel Technologies Inc., 63
Sun Distributors L.P., 12
Symyx Technologies, Inc., 77
Tarmac Limited, III, 28 (upd.); 95 (upd.)
Tilcon-Connecticut Inc., 80
TOTO LTD., III; 28 (upd.)
Toyo Sash Co., Ltd., III
Tuscarora Inc., 29
U.S. Aggregates, Inc., 42
Ube Industries, Ltd., III
United States Steel Corporation, 50 (upd.)
USG Corporation, III; 26 (upd.); 81 (upd.)
Usinas Siderúrgicas de Minas Gerais S.A., 77
Vicat S.A., 70
voestalpine AG, 57 (upd.)
Vulcan Materials Company, 7; 52 (upd.)
Wacker-Chemie GmbH, 35
Walter Industries, Inc., III
Waxman Industries, Inc., 9
Weber et Broutin France, 66
Wienerberger AG, 70
Wolseley plc, 64
ZERO Corporation, 17; 88 (upd.)
Zoltek Companies, Inc., 37

Mining & Metals

A.M. Castle & Co., 25
Acindar Industria Argentina de Aceros S.A., 87
African Rainbow Minerals Ltd., 97
Aggregate Industries plc, 36
Agnico-Eagle Mines Limited, 71
Aktiebolaget SKF, III; 38 (upd.); 89 (upd.)
Alcan Aluminium Limited, IV; 31 (upd.)
Alcoa Inc., 56 (upd.)
Alleghany Corporation, 10
Allegheny Ludlum Corporation, 8
Alliance Resource Partners, L.P., 81
Alrosa Company Ltd., 62
Altos Hornos de México, S.A. de C.V., 42
Aluminum Company of America, IV; 20 (upd.)
AMAX Inc., IV
AMCOL International Corporation, 59 (upd.)
Amsted Industries Incorporated, 7
Anglo American Corporation of South Africa Limited, IV; 16 (upd.)
Anglo American PLC, 50 (upd.)
Aquarius Platinum Ltd., 63
ARBED S.A., IV, 22 (upd.)
Arcelor Gent, 80

Arch Coal Inc., 98
Arch Mineral Corporation, 7
Armco Inc., IV
ASARCO Incorporated, IV
Ashanti Goldfields Company Limited, 43
Atchison Casting Corporation, 39
Barrick Gold Corporation, 34
Battle Mountain Gold Company, 23
Benguet Corporation, 58
Bethlehem Steel Corporation, IV; 7 (upd.); 27 (upd.)
BHP Billiton, 67 (upd.)
Birmingham Steel Corporation, 13; 40 (upd.)
Boart Longyear Company, 26
Bodycote International PLC, 63
Boliden AB, 80
Boral Limited, 43 (upd.)
British Coal Corporation, IV
British Steel plc, IV; 19 (upd.)
Broken Hill Proprietary Company Ltd., IV, 22 (upd.)
Brush Engineered Materials Inc., 67
Brush Wellman Inc., 14
Buderus AG, 37
Cameco Corporation, 77
Caparo Group Ltd., 90
Carpenter Technology Corporation, 13; 95 (upd.)
Chaparral Steel Co., 13
China Shenhua Energy Company Limited, 83
Christensen Boyles Corporation, 26
Cleveland-Cliffs Inc., 13; 62 (upd.)
Coal India Ltd., IV; 44 (upd.)
Cockerill Sambre Group, IV; 26 (upd.)
Coeur d'Alene Mines Corporation, 20
Cold Spring Granite Company Inc., 16; 67 (upd.)
Cominco Ltd., 37
Commercial Metals Company, 15; 42 (upd.)
Companhia Siderúrgica Nacional, 76
Companhia Vale do Rio Doce, IV; 43 (upd.)
Compañia de Minas Buenaventura S.A.A., 93
CONSOL Energy Inc., 59
Corporacion Nacional del Cobre de Chile, 40
Corus Group plc, 49 (upd.)
CRA Limited, IV
Cyprus Amax Minerals Company, 21
Cyprus Minerals Company, 7
Daido Steel Co., Ltd., IV
De Beers Consolidated Mines Limited/De Beers Centenary AG, IV; 7 (upd.); 28 (upd.)
Degussa Group, IV
Diavik Diamond Mines Inc., 85
Dofasco Inc., IV; 24 (upd.)
Dynatec Corporation, 87
Earle M. Jorgensen Company, 82
Echo Bay Mines Ltd., IV; 38 (upd.)
Engelhard Corporation, IV
Eramet, 73
Evergreen Energy, Inc., 97
Evraz Group S.A., 97

Falconbridge Limited, 49
Fansteel Inc., 19
Fluor Corporation, 34 (upd.)
Freeport-McMoRan Copper & Gold, Inc.,
    IV; 7 (upd.); 57 (upd.)
Fried. Krupp GmbH, IV
Gencor Ltd., IV, 22 (upd.)
Geneva Steel, 7
Gerdau S.A., 59
Glamis Gold, Ltd., 54
Gold Fields Ltd., IV; 62 (upd.)
Goldcorp Inc., 87
Grupo Mexico, S.A. de C.V., 40
Gruppo Riva Fire SpA, 88
Handy & Harman, 23
Hanson Building Materials America Inc.,
    60
Hanson PLC, 30 (upd.)
Harmony Gold Mining Company
    Limited, 63
Haynes International, Inc., 88
Hecla Mining Company, 20
Hemlo Gold Mines Inc., 9
Heraeus Holding GmbH, IV
Highland Gold Mining Limited, 95
Highveld Steel and Vanadium
    Corporation Limited, 59
Hitachi Metals, Ltd., IV
Hoesch AG, IV
Homestake Mining Company, 12; 38
    (upd.)
Horsehead Industries, Inc., 51
The Hudson Bay Mining and Smelting
    Company, Limited, 12
Hylsamex, S.A. de C.V., 39
IMCO Recycling, Incorporated, 32
Imerys S.A., 40 (upd.)
Imetal S.A., IV
Inco Limited, IV; 45 (upd.)
Industrias Penoles, S.A. de C.V., 22
Inland Steel Industries, Inc., IV; 19 (upd.)
Intermet Corporation, 32
Iscor Limited, 57
Ispat Inland Inc., 30; 40 (upd.)
JFE Shoji Holdings Inc., 88
Johnson Matthey PLC, IV; 16 (upd.)
JSC MMC Norilsk Nickel, 48
K.A. Rasmussen AS, 99
Kaiser Aluminum Corporation, IV; 84
    (upd.)
Kawasaki Heavy Industries, Ltd., 63
    (upd.)
Kawasaki Steel Corporation, IV
Kennecott Corporation, 7; 27 (upd.)
Kentucky Electric Steel, Inc., 31
Kerr-McGee Corporation, 22 (upd.)
Kinross Gold Corporation, 36
Klockner-Werke AG, IV
Kobe Steel, Ltd., IV; 19 (upd.)
Koninklijke Nederlandsche Hoogovens en
    Staalfabrieken NV, IV
Laclede Steel Company, 15
Layne Christensen Company, 19
Lonmin plc, 66 (upd.)
Lonrho Plc, 21
The LTV Corporation, I; 24 (upd.)
Lukens Inc., 14
Magma Copper Company, 7

The Marmon Group, IV; 16 (upd.)
Massey Energy Company, 57
MAXXAM Inc., 8
Mechel OAO, 99
Meridian Gold, Incorporated, 47
Metaleurop S.A., 21
Metalico Inc., 97
Metallgesellschaft AG, IV
Minerals and Metals Trading Corporation
    of India Ltd., IV
Minerals Technologies Inc., 11; 52 (upd.)
Mitsui Mining & Smelting Co., Ltd., IV
Mitsui Mining Company, Limited, IV
Mueller Industries, Inc., 52 (upd.)
National Steel Corporation, 12
NERCO, Inc., 7
Newmont Mining Corporation, 7
Neyveli Lignite Corporation Ltd., 65
Niagara Corporation, 28
Nichimen Corporation, IV
Nippon Light Metal Company, Ltd., IV
Nippon Steel Corporation, IV; 17 (upd.);
    96 (upd.)
Nisshin Steel Co., Ltd., IV
NKK Corporation, IV; 28 (upd.)
Noranda Inc., IV; 7 (upd.); 64 (upd.)
Norddeutsche Affinerie AG, 62
North Star Steel Company, 18
Nucor Corporation, 7; 21 (upd.); 79
    (upd.)
Oglebay Norton Company, 17
OJSC Novolipetsk Steel, 99
Okura & Co., Ltd., IV
O'Neal Steel, Inc., 95
Oregon Metallurgical Corporation, 20
Oregon Steel Mills, Inc., 14
Ormet Corporation, 82
Outokumpu Oyj, 38
Park Corp., 22
Peabody Coal Company, 10
Peabody Energy Corporation, 45 (upd.)
Peabody Holding Company, Inc., IV
Pechiney SA, IV; 45 (upd.)
Peter Kiewit Sons' Inc., 8
Phelps Dodge Corporation, IV; 28 (upd.);
    75 (upd.)
The Pittston Company, IV; 19 (upd.)
Placer Dome Inc., 20; 61 (upd.)
Pohang Iron and Steel Company Ltd., IV
POSCO, 57 (upd.)
Potash Corporation of Saskatchewan Inc.,
    18
Quanex Corporation, 13; 62 (upd.)
RAG AG, 35; 60 (upd.)
Reliance Steel & Aluminum Co., 19
Republic Engineered Steels, Inc., 7; 26
    (upd.)
Reynolds Metals Company, IV
Rio Tinto PLC, 19 (upd.); 50 (upd.)
RMC Group p.l.c., 34 (upd.)
Roanoke Electric Steel Corporation, 45
Rouge Steel Company, 8
The RTZ Corporation PLC, IV
Ruhrkohle AG, IV
Ryerson Tull, Inc., 40 (upd.)
Saarberg-Konzern, IV
Salzgitter AG, IV
Sandvik AB, IV

Saudi Basic Industries Corporation
    (SABIC), 58
Schnitzer Steel Industries, Inc., 19
Severstal Joint Stock Company, 65
Shanghai Baosteel Group Corporation, 71
Siderar S.A.I.C., 66
Silver Wheaton Corp., 95
Smorgon Steel Group Ltd., 62
Southern Peru Copper Corporation, 40
Southwire Company, Inc., 8; 23 (upd.)
SSAB Svenskt Stål AB, 89
Steel Authority of India Ltd., IV
Stelco Inc., IV
Stillwater Mining Company, 47
Sumitomo Metal Industries Ltd., IV; 82
    (upd.)
Sumitomo Metal Mining Co., Ltd., IV
Tata Iron & Steel Co. Ltd., IV; 44 (upd.)
Teck Corporation, 27
Tenaris SA, 63
Texas Industries, Inc., 8
ThyssenKrupp AG, IV; 28 (upd.); 87
    (upd.)
The Timken Company, 8; 42 (upd.)
Titanium Metals Corporation, 21
Tomen Corporation, IV
Total Fina Elf S.A., 50 (upd.)
Třinecké Železárny A.S., 92
U.S. Borax, Inc., 42
Ugine S.A., 20
NV Umicore SA, 47
Universal Stainless & Alloy Products, Inc.,
    75
Uralita S.A., 96
Usinor SA, IV; 42 (upd.)
Usinor Sacilor, IV
VIAG Aktiengesellschaft, IV
Voest-Alpine Stahl AG, IV
Volcan Compañia Minera S.A.A., 92
Vulcan Materials Company, 52 (upd.)
Wah Chang, 82
Walter Industries, Inc., 22 (upd.)
Weirton Steel Corporation, IV; 26 (upd.)
Westmoreland Coal Company, 7
Wheeling-Pittsburgh Corp., 7
WHX Corporation, 98
WMC, Limited, 43
Worthington Industries, Inc., 7; 21 (upd.)
Xstrata PLC, 73
Zambia Industrial and Mining
    Corporation Ltd., IV
Zinifex Ltd., 85

Paper & Forestry

AbitibiBowater Inc., IV; 25 (upd.); 99
    (upd.)
Albany International Corporation, 51
    (upd.)
Amcor Ltd, IV; 19 (upd.); 78 (upd.)
American Greetings Corporation, 59
    (upd.)
American Pad & Paper Company, 20
Aracruz Celulose S.A., 57
Arjo Wiggins Appleton p.l.c., 34
Asplundh Tree Expert Co.,20; 59 (upd.)
Avery Dennison Corporation, IV
Badger Paper Mills, Inc., 15
Beckett Papers, 23

Bemis Company, Inc., 8; 91 (upd.)
Blue Heron Paper Company, 90
Bohemia, Inc., 13
Boise Cascade Holdings, L.L.C.,, IV; 8
   (upd.); 32 (upd.); 95 (upd.)
Bowater PLC, IV
Bunzl plc, IV
Canfor Corporation, 42
Caraustar Industries, Inc., 19; 44 (upd.)
Carter Lumber Company, 45
Cascades Inc., 71
Central National-Gottesman Inc., 95
Champion International Corporation, IV;
   20 (upd.)
Chesapeake Corporation, 8; 30 (upd.); 93
   (upd.)
Consolidated Papers, Inc., 8; 36 (upd.)
Crane & Co., Inc., 26
Crown Vantage Inc., 29
CSS Industries, Inc., 35
Daio Paper Corporation, IV; 84 (upd.)
Daishowa Paper Manufacturing Co., Ltd.,
   IV; 57 (upd.)
Deltic Timber Corporation, 46
Dillard Paper Company, 11
Doman Industries Limited, 59
Domtar Corporation, IV; 89 (upd.)
DS Smith Plc, 61
Empresas CMPC S.A., 70
Enso-Gutzeit Oy, IV
Esselte Pendaflex Corporation, 11
Federal Paper Board Company, Inc., 8
FiberMark, Inc., 37
Fletcher Challenge Ltd., IV
Fort Howard Corporation, 8
Fort James Corporation, 22 (upd.)
Georgia-Pacific Corporation, IV; 9 (upd.);
   47 (upd.)
Gould Paper Corporation, 82
Graphic Packaging Holding Company, 96
   (upd.)
Groupe Rougier SA, 21
Grupo Portucel Soporcel, 60
Guilbert S.A., 42
Hampton Affiliates, Inc., 77
Holmen AB, 52 (upd.)
Honshu Paper Co., Ltd., IV
International Paper Company, IV; 15
   (upd.); 47 (upd.); 97 (upd.)
James River Corporation of Virginia, IV
Japan Pulp and Paper Company Limited,
   IV
Jefferson Smurfit Group plc, IV; 49 (upd.)
Jujo Paper Co., Ltd., IV
Kadant Inc., 96 (upd.)
Kimberly-Clark Corporation, 16 (upd.);
   43 (upd.)
Kimberly-Clark de México, S.A. de C.V.,
   54
Klabin S.A., 73
Koninklijke Houthandel G Wijma &
   Zonen BV, 96
Kruger Inc., 17
Kymmene Corporation, IV
Longview Fibre Company, 8; 37 (upd.)
Louisiana-Pacific Corporation, IV; 31
   (upd.)
M-real Oyj, 56 (upd.)

MacMillan Bloedel Limited, IV
Matussière et Forest SA, 58
The Mead Corporation, IV; 19 (upd.)
MeadWestvaco Corporation, 76 (upd.)
Mercer International Inc., 64
Metsa-Serla Oy, IV
Metso Corporation, 30 (upd.); 85 (upd.)
Miquel y Costas Miquel S.A., 68
Mo och Domsjö AB, IV
Monadnock Paper Mills, Inc., 21
Mosinee Paper Corporation, 15
Nashua Corporation, 8
National Envelope Corporation, 32
NCH Corporation, 8
Norske Skogindustrier ASA, 63
Oji Paper Co., Ltd., IV
P.H. Glatfelter Company, 8; 30 (upd.); 83
   (upd.)
Packaging Corporation of America, 12
Papeteries de Lancey, 23
Plum Creek Timber Company, Inc., 43
Pope & Talbot, Inc., 12; 61 (upd.)
Pope Resources LP, 74
Potlatch Corporation, 8; 34 (upd.); 87
   (upd.)
PWA Group, IV
Rayonier Inc., 24
Rengo Co., Ltd., IV
Reno de Medici S.p.A., 41
Rexam PLC, 32 (upd.); 85 (upd.)
Riverwood International Corporation, 11;
   48 (upd.)
Rock-Tenn Company, 13; 59 (upd.)
Rogers Corporation, 61
The St. Joe Company, 8; 98 (upd.)
Sanyo-Kokusaku Pulp Co., Ltd., IV
Sappi Limited, 49
Schweitzer-Mauduit International, Inc., 52
Scott Paper Company, IV; 31 (upd.)
Sealed Air Corporation, 14
Sierra Pacific Industries, 22; 90 (upd.)
Simpson Investment Company, 17
Smurfit-Stone Container Corporation, 83
   (upd.)
Sonoco Products Company, 8; 89 (upd.)
Specialty Coatings Inc., 8
Stimson Lumber Company 78
Stone Container Corporation, IV
Stora Enso Oyj, IV; 36 (upd.); 85 (upd.)
Svenska Cellulosa Aktiebolaget SCA, IV;
   28 (upd.); 85 (upd.)
Sveaskog AB, 93
Tapemark Company Inc., 64
Tembec Inc., 66
Temple-Inland Inc., IV; 31 (upd.)
Thomsen Greenhouses and Garden
   Center, Incorporated, 65
TJ International, Inc., 19
U.S. Timberlands Company, L.P., 42
Union Camp Corporation, IV
United Paper Mills Ltd. (Yhtyneet
   Paperitehtaat Oy), IV
Universal Forest Products, Inc., 10; 59
   (upd.)
UPM-Kymmene Corporation, 19; 50
   (upd.)
Wausau-Mosinee Paper Corporation, 60
   (upd.)

West Fraser Timber Co. Ltd., 17; 91
   (upd.)
West Linn Paper Company, 91
Westvaco Corporation, IV; 19 (upd.)
Weyerhaeuser Company, IV; 9 (upd.); 28
   (upd.); 83 (upd.)
Wickes Inc., 25 (upd.)
Willamette Industries, Inc., IV; 31 (upd.)
WTD Industries, Inc., 20

Personal Services

AARP, 27
ABC Learning Centres Ltd., 93
ADT Security Services, Inc., 12; 44 (upd.)
Africare, 59
Alderwoods Group, Inc., 68 (upd.)
Ambassadors International, Inc., 68 (upd.)
American Civil Liberties Union (ACLU),
   60
American Management Association, 76
American Retirement Corporation, 42
American Society for the Prevention of
   Cruelty to Animals (ASPCA), 68
AmeriCares Foundation, Inc., 87
Aquent, 96
Arthur Murray International, Inc., 32
Association of Junior Leagues
   International Inc., 60
Benesse Corporation, 76
Berlitz International, Inc., 39 (upd.)
Big Brothers Big Sisters of America, 85
Blackwater USA, 76
Bonhams 1793 Ltd., 72
Boys & Girls Clubs of America, 69
The Brickman Group, Ltd., 87
The Brink's Company, 58 (upd.)
Brother's Brother Foundation, 93
CareerBuilder, Inc., 93
Caritas Internationalis, 72
Carriage Services, Inc., 37
Catholic Charities USA, 76
CDI Corporation, 6; 54 (upd.)
CeWe Color Holding AG, 76
ChildrenFirst, Inc., 59
Childtime Learning Centers, Inc., 34
Chubb, PLC, 50
Corinthian Colleges, Inc., 39; 92 (upd.)
Correctional Services Corporation, 30
Correos y Telegrafos S.A., 80
Council on International Educational
   Exchange Inc., 81
CUC International Inc., 16
Curves International, Inc., 54
Cystic Fibrosis Foundation, 93
Davis Service Group PLC, 45
DeVry Inc., 29; 82 (upd.)
Educational Testing Service, 12; 62 (upd.)
eHarmony.com Inc., 71
Feed The Children, Inc., 68
Food For The Poor, Inc., 77
The Ford Foundation, 34
Franklin Quest Co., 11
Gold's Gym International, Inc., 71
Goodwill Industries International, Inc.,
   16; 66 (upd.)
GP Strategies Corporation, 64 (upd.)
Green Dot Public Schools, 99
Greenpeace International, 74

Greg Manning Auctions, Inc., 60
Gunnebo AB, 53
Hair Club For Men Ltd., 90
Herbalife Ltd., 17; 41 (upd.); 92 (upd.)
The Humane Society of the United States, 54
Huntington Learning Centers, Inc., 55
Imperial Parking Corporation, 58
Initial Security, 64
Jazzercise, Inc., 45
The John D. and Catherine T. MacArthur Foundation, 34
Jones Knowledge Group, Inc., 97
Kaplan, Inc., 42; 90 (upd.)
KinderCare Learning Centers, Inc., 13
Kiva, 95
Knowledge Learning Corporation, 51
Kumon Institute of Education Co., Ltd., 72
Labor Ready, Inc., 29; 88 (upd.)
Learning Care Group, Inc., 76 (upd.)
Lifetouch Inc., 86
The Loewen Group Inc., 16; 40 (upd.)
LPA Holding Corporation, 81
Mace Security International, Inc., 57
Make-A-Wish Foundation of America, 97
Management and Training Corporation, 28
Manpower, Inc., 9
Martin Franchises, Inc., 80
Match.com, LP, 87
Michael Page International plc, 45
Mothers Against Drunk Driving (MADD), 51
National Heritage Academies, Inc., 60
National Organization for Women, Inc., 55
Noah Education Holdings Ltd., 97
Nobel Learning Communities, Inc., 37; 76 (upd.)
Oxfam GB, 87
Prison Rehabilitative Industries and Diversified Enterprises, Inc. (PRIDE), 53
Recording for the Blind & Dyslexic, 51
Regis Corporation, 18; 70 (upd.)
Robert Half International Inc., 70 (upd.)
The Rockefeller Foundation, 34
Rollins, Inc., 11
Rosenbluth International Inc., 14
Rosetta Stone Inc., 93
Rotary International, 31
The Salvation Army USA, 32
Scientific Learning Corporation, 95
Screen Actors Guild, 72
Service Corporation International, 6; 51 (upd.)
The ServiceMaster Company, 68 (upd.)
Shutterfly, Inc., 98
SOS Staffing Services, 25
Spark Networks, Inc., 91
Special Olympics, Inc., 93
SR Teleperformance S.A., 86
Stewart Enterprises, Inc., 20
Supercuts Inc., 26
24 Hour Fitness Worldwide, Inc., 71

UAW (International Union, United Automobile, Aerospace and Agricultural Implement Workers of America), 72
United Negro College Fund, Inc., 79
United Service Organizations, 60
Weight Watchers International Inc., 12; 33 (upd.); 73 (upd.)
The York Group, Inc., 50
Youth Services International, Inc., 21
YWCA of the U.S.A., 45
World Vision International, Inc., 93

Petroleum

Abraxas Petroleum Corporation, 89
Abu Dhabi National Oil Company, IV; 45 (upd.)
Adani Enterprises Ltd., 97
Aegean Marine Petroleum Network Inc., 89
Agway, Inc., 21 (upd.)
Alberta Energy Company Ltd., 16; 43 (upd.)
Amerada Hess Corporation, IV; 21 (upd.); 55 (upd.)
Amoco Corporation, IV; 14 (upd.)
Anadarko Petroleum Corporation, 10; 52 (upd.)
ANR Pipeline Co., 17
Anschutz Corp., 12
Apache Corporation, 10; 32 (upd.); 89 (upd.)
Aral AG, 62
Arctic Slope Regional Corporation, 38
Arena Resources, Inc., 97
Ashland Inc., 19; 50 (upd.)
Ashland Oil, Inc., IV
Atlantic Richfield Company, IV; 31 (upd.)
Aventine Renewable Energy Holdings, Inc., 89
Badger State Ethanol, LLC, 83
Baker Hughes Incorporated, 22 (upd.); 57 (upd.)
Belco Oil & Gas Corp., 40
Benton Oil and Gas Company, 47
Berry Petroleum Company, 47
BG Products Inc., 96
BHP Billiton, 67 (upd.)
Bill Barrett Corporation, 71
BJ Services Company, 25
Blue Rhino Corporation, 56
Boardwalk Pipeline Partners, LP, 87
Boots & Coots International Well Control, Inc., 79
BP p.l.c., 45 (upd.)
Brigham Exploration Company, 75
The British Petroleum Company plc, IV; 7 (upd.); 21 (upd.)
British-Borneo Oil & Gas PLC, 34
Broken Hill Proprietary Company Ltd., 22 (upd.)
Bronco Drilling Company, Inc., 89
Burlington Resources Inc., 10
Burmah Castrol PLC, IV; 30 (upd.)
Callon Petroleum Company, 47
Caltex Petroleum Corporation, 19
Cano Petroleum Inc., 97
Carrizo Oil & Gas, Inc., 97

ChevronTexaco Corporation, IV; 19 (upd.); 47 (upd.)
Chiles Offshore Corporation, 9
Cimarex Energy Co., 81
China National Petroleum Corporation, 46
Chinese Petroleum Corporation, IV; 31 (upd.)
CITGO Petroleum Corporation, IV; 31 (upd.)
Clayton Williams Energy, Inc., 87
The Coastal Corporation, IV; 31 (upd.)
Compañia Española de Petróleos S.A. (Cepsa), IV; 56 (upd.)
Comstock Resources, Inc., 47
Conoco Inc., IV; 16 (upd.)
ConocoPhillips, 63 (upd.)
CONSOL Energy Inc., 59
Continental Resources, Inc., 89
Cooper Cameron Corporation, 20 (upd.)
Cosmo Oil Co., Ltd., IV; 53 (upd.)
Crown Central Petroleum Corporation, 7
DeepTech International Inc., 21
Den Norse Stats Oljeselskap AS, IV
Denbury Resources, Inc., 67
Deutsche BP Aktiengesellschaft, 7
Devon Energy Corporation, 61
Diamond Shamrock, Inc., IV
Distrigaz S.A., 82
Dril-Quip, Inc., 81
Duvernay Oil Corp., 83
Dyneff S.A., 98
Dynegy Inc., 49 (upd.)
E.On AG, 50 (upd.)
Edge Petroleum Corporation, 67
Egyptian General Petroleum Corporation, IV; 51 (upd.)
El Paso Corporation, 66 (upd.)
Elf Aquitaine SA, 21 (upd.)
Empresa Colombiana de Petróleos, IV
Enbridge Inc., 43
Encore Acquisition Company, 73
Energen Corporation, 21; 97 (upd.)
ENI S.p.A., 69 (upd.)
Enron Corporation, 19
ENSCO International Incorporated, 57
Ente Nazionale Idrocarburi, IV
Enterprise Oil PLC, 11; 50 (upd.)
Entreprise Nationale Sonatrach, IV
Equitable Resources, Inc., 54 (upd.)
Ergon, Inc., 95
Exxon Mobil Corporation, IV; 7 (upd.); 32 (upd.); 67 (upd.)
Ferrellgas Partners, L.P., 35
FINA, Inc., 7
Flying J Inc., 19
Flotek Industries Inc., 93
Forest Oil Corporation, 19; 91 (upd.)
Galp Energia SGPS S.A., 98
OAO Gazprom, 42
General Sekiyu K.K., IV
Giant Industries, Inc., 19; 61 (upd.)
Global Industries, Ltd., 37
Global Marine Inc., 9
GlobalSantaFe Corporation, 48 (upd.)
Grey Wolf, Inc., 43
Halliburton Company, 25 (upd.); 55 (upd.)

Hanover Compressor Company, 59
Hawkeye Holdings LLC, 89
Helix Energy Solutions Group, Inc., 81
Hellenic Petroleum SA, 64
Helmerich & Payne, Inc., 18
Holly Corporation, 12
Hunt Consolidated, Inc., 7; 27 (upd.)
Hunting plc 78
Hurricane Hydrocarbons Ltd., 54
Husky Energy Inc., 47
Idemitsu Kosan Co., Ltd., 49 (upd.)
Idemitsu Kosan K.K., IV
Imperial Oil Limited, IV; 25 (upd.)
Indian Oil Corporation Ltd., IV; 48
    (upd.); 95 (upd.)
INPEX Holdings Inc., 97
Input/Output, Inc., 73
Iogen Corporation, 81
Ipiranga S.A., 67
Kanematsu Corporation, IV
Kerr-McGee Corporation, IV; 22 (upd.);
    68 (upd.)
Kinder Morgan, Inc., 45
King Ranch, Inc., 14
Koch Industries, Inc., IV; 20 (upd.), 77
    (upd.)
Koppers Industries, Inc., 26 (upd.)
Kuwait Petroleum Corporation, IV; 55
    (upd.)
Libyan National Oil Corporation, IV
The Louisiana Land and Exploration
    Company, 7
OAO LUKOIL, 40
Lyondell Petrochemical Company, IV
MAPCO Inc., IV
Maxus Energy Corporation, 7
McDermott International, Inc., 37 (upd.)
Meteor Industries Inc., 33
Mexichem, S.A.B. de C.V., 99
Mitchell Energy and Development
    Corporation, 7
Mitsubishi Oil Co., Ltd., IV
Mobil Corporation, IV; 7 (upd.); 21
    (upd.)
MOL Rt, 70
Murphy Oil Corporation, 7; 32 (upd.);
    95 (upd.)
Nabors Industries Ltd., 9; 91 (upd.)
National Fuel Gas Company, 6; 95 (upd.)
National Iranian Oil Company, IV; 61
    (upd.)
National Oil Corporation, 66 (upd.)
Neste Oil Corporation, IV; 85 (upd.)
Newfield Exploration Company, 65
Nexen Inc., 79
NGC Corporation, 18
Nigerian National Petroleum Corporation,
    IV; 72 (upd.)
Nippon Oil Corporation, IV; 63 (upd.)
OAO NK YUKOS, 47
Noble Affiliates, Inc., 11
Occidental Petroleum Corporation, IV; 25
    (upd.); 71 (upd.)
Odebrecht S.A., 73
Oil and Natural Gas Corporation Ltd.,
    IV; 90 (upd.)
Oil States International, Inc., 77
OMV AG, IV; 98 (upd.)

Oryx Energy Company, 7
Pacific Ethanol, Inc., 81
Pakistan State Oil Company Ltd., 81
Paramount Resources Ltd., 87
Parker Drilling Company, 28
Patina Oil & Gas Corporation, 24
Patterson-UTI Energy, Inc., 55
Pengrowth Energy Trust, 95
Penn Virginia Corporation, 85
Pennzoil-Quaker State Company, IV; 20
    (upd.); 50 (upd.)
Pertamina, IV; 56 (upd.)
Petro-Canada, IV; 99 (upd.)
Petrobras Energia Participaciones S.A., 72
Petrofac Ltd., 95
PetroFina S.A., IV; 26 (upd.)
Petrohawk Energy Corporation, 79
Petróleo Brasileiro S.A., IV
Petróleos de Portugal S.A., IV
Petróleos de Venezuela S.A., IV; 74 (upd.)
Petróleos del Ecuador, IV
Petróleos Mexicanos, IV; 19 (upd.)
Petroleum Development Oman LLC, IV;
    98 (upd.)
Petroliam Nasional Bhd (Petronas), IV; 56
    (upd.)
Petron Corporation, 58
Phillips Petroleum Company, IV; 40
    (upd.)
Pioneer Natural Resources Company, 59
Pogo Producing Company, 39
Polski Koncern Naftowy ORLEN S.A., 77
Premcor Inc., 37
Pride International Inc. 78
PTT Public Company Ltd., 56
Qatar Petroleum, IV; 98 (upd.)
Quaker State Corporation, 7; 21 (upd.)
Range Resources Corporation, 45
Reliance Industries Ltd., 81
Repsol-YPF S.A., IV; 16 (upd.); 40 (upd.)
Resource America, Inc., 42
Rowan Companies, Inc., 43
Royal Dutch/Shell Group, IV; 49 (upd.)
RPC, Inc., 91
RWE AG, 50 (upd.)
St. Mary Land & Exploration Company,
    63
Santa Fe International Corporation, 38
Santos Ltd., 81
Sasol Limited, IV; 47 (upd.)
Saudi Arabian Oil Company, IV; 17
    (upd.); 50 (upd.)
Schlumberger Limited, 17 (upd.); 59
    (upd.)
Seagull Energy Corporation, 11
Seitel, Inc., 47
Shanghai Petrochemical Co., Ltd., 18
Shell Oil Company, IV; 14 (upd.); 41
    (upd.)
Showa Shell Sekiyu K.K., IV; 59 (upd.)
OAO Siberian Oil Company (Sibneft), 49
Smith International, Inc., 59 (upd.)
Société Nationale Elf Aquitaine, IV; 7
    (upd.)
Sonatrach, 65 (upd.)
Spinnaker Exploration Company, 72
Statoil ASA, 61 (upd.)
Suburban Propane Partners, L.P., 30

SUEZ-TRACTEBEL S.A., 97 (upd.)
Sun Company, Inc., IV
Suncor Energy Inc., 54
Sunoco, Inc., 28 (upd.); 83 (upd.)
Superior Energy Services, Inc., 65
OAO Surgutneftegaz, 48
Swift Energy Company, 63
Talisman Energy Inc., 9; 47 (upd.)
TAQA North Ltd., 95
OAO Tatneft, 45
Tengasco, Inc., 99
TEPPCO Partners, L.P., 73
Tesoro Corporation, 7; 45 (upd.); 97
    (upd.)
Teton Energy Corporation, 97
Texaco Inc., IV; 14 (upd.); 41 (upd.)
Tidewater Inc., 37 (upd.)
TODCO, 87
Tom Brown, Inc., 37
Tonen Corporation, IV; 16 (upd.)
TonenGeneral Sekiyu K.K., 54 (upd.)
Tosco Corporation, 7
TOTAL S.A., IV; 24 (upd.)
Transammonia Group, 95
TransCanada Corporation, 93 (upd.)
TransMontaigne Inc., 28
Oil Transporting Joint Stock Company
    Transneft, 93
Transocean Sedco Forex Inc., 45
Travel Ports of America, Inc., 17
Triton Energy Corporation, 11
Tullow Oil plc, 83
Türkiye Petrolleri Anonim Ortakliği, IV
Ultra Petroleum Corporation, 71
Ultramar Diamond Shamrock
    Corporation, IV; 31 (upd.)
Union Texas Petroleum Holdings, Inc., 9
Unit Corporation, 63
Universal Compression, Inc., 59
Unocal Corporation, IV; 24 (upd.); 71
    (upd.)
USX Corporation, IV; 7 (upd.)
Valero Energy Corporation, 7; 71 (upd.)
Valley National Gases, Inc., 85
Varco International, Inc., 42
Vastar Resources, Inc., 24
VeraSun Energy Corporation, 87
Vintage Petroleum, Inc., 42
Wascana Energy Inc., 13
Weatherford International, Inc., 39
Webber Oil Company, 61
Western Atlas Inc., 12
Western Company of North America, 15
Western Gas Resources, Inc., 45
Western Oil Sands Inc., 85
Westport Resources Corporation, 63
Whiting Petroleum Corporation, 81
The Williams Companies, Inc., IV; 31
    (upd.)
World Fuel Services Corporation, 47
XTO Energy Inc., 52
YPF Sociedad Anonima, IV
The Zubair Corporation L.L.C., 96

Publishing & Printing

A.B.Dick Company, 28
A.H. Belo Corporation, 10; 30 (upd.)

AbitibiBowater Inc., IV; 25 (upd.); 99 (upd.)

Abril S.A., 95

AccuWeather, Inc., 73

Advance Publications Inc., IV; 19 (upd.); 96 (upd.)

Advanced Marketing Services, Inc., 34

Advanstar Communications, Inc., 57

Affiliated Publications, Inc., 7

Agence France-Presse, 34

Agora S.A. Group, 77

Aljazeera Satellite Channel, 79

Alma Media Corporation, 98

American Banknote Corporation, 30

American Girl, Inc., 69

American Greetings Corporation, 7, 22 (upd.)

American Media, Inc., 27; 82 (upd.)

American Printing House for the Blind, 26

American Reprographics Company, 75

Andrews McMeel Universal, 40

The Antioch Company, 40

AOL Time Warner Inc., 57 (upd.)

Arandell Corporation, 37

Archie Comics Publications, Inc., 63

Arnoldo Mondadori Editore S.p.A., IV; 19 (upd.); 54 (upd.)

The Associated Press, 31 (upd.); 73 (upd.)

The Atlantic Group, 23

Audible Inc., 79

Axel Springer Verlag AG, IV; 20 (upd.)

Banta Corporation, 12; 32 (upd.); 79 (upd.)

Bauer Publishing Group, 7

Bayard SA, 49

Berlitz International, Inc., 13

Bernard C. Harris Publishing Company, Inc., 39

Bertelsmann A.G., IV; 15 (upd.); 43 (upd.); 91 (upd.)

Bibliographisches Institut & F.A. Brockhaus AG, 74

Big Flower Press Holdings, Inc., 21

Blackwell Publishing Ltd. 78

Blue Mountain Arts, Inc., 29

Bobit Publishing Company, 55

Bonnier AB, 52

Book-of-the-Month Club, Inc., 13

Bowne & Co., Inc., 23; 79 (upd.)

Broderbund Software, 13; 29 (upd.)

Brown Printing Company, 26

Burda Holding GmbH. & Co., 23

The Bureau of National Affairs, Inc., 23

Butterick Co., Inc., 23

Cadmus Communications Corporation, 23

Cahners Business Information, 43

Carl Allers Etablissement A/S, 72

Carus Publishing Company, 93

CCH Inc., 14

Central Newspapers, Inc., 10

Champion Industries, Inc., 28

Cherry Lane Music Publishing Company, Inc., 62

Chicago Review Press Inc., 84

ChoicePoint Inc., 65

The Christian Science Publishing Society, 55

The Chronicle Publishing Company, Inc., 23

Chrysalis Group plc, 40

CMP Media Inc., 26

Commerce Clearing House, Inc., 7

Community Newspaper Holdings, Inc., 91

Concepts Direct, Inc., 39

Condé Nast Publications, Inc., 13; 59 (upd.)

Consolidated Graphics, Inc., 70

Consumers Union, 26

The Copley Press, Inc., 23

Corelio S.A./N.V., 96

Cornelsen Verlagsholding GmbH & Co., 90

Courier Corporation, 41

Cowles Media Company, 23

Cox Enterprises, Inc., IV; 22 (upd.)

Crain Communications, Inc., 12; 35 (upd.)

Current, Inc., 37

Cygnus Business Media, Inc., 56

Dai Nippon Printing Co., Ltd., IV; 57 (upd.)

Daily Mail and General Trust plc, 19

Dawson Holdings PLC, 43

Day Runner, Inc., 14

DC Comics Inc., 25; 98 (upd.)

De La Rue plc, 10; 34 (upd.)

DeLorme Publishing Company, Inc., 53

Deluxe Corporation, 7; 22 (upd.); 73 (upd.)

Dennis Publishing Ltd., 62

Dex Media, Inc., 65

Donruss Playoff L.P., 66

Dorling Kindersley Holdings plc, 20

Dover Publications Inc., 34

Dow Jones & Company, Inc., IV; 19 (upd.); 47 (upd.)

The Dun & Bradstreet Corporation, IV; 19 (upd.)

Duplex Products Inc., 17

The E.W. Scripps Company, IV; 7 (upd.); 28 (upd.); 66 (upd.)

Eagle-Tribune Publishing Co., 91

The Economist Group Ltd., 67

Edipresse S.A., 82

Éditions Gallimard, 72

Editis S.A. 78

Edmark Corporation, 14

Edwards Brothers, Inc., 92

Egmont Group, 93

Electronics for Imaging, Inc., 43 (upd.)

EMAP plc, 35

EMI Group plc, 22 (upd.); 81 (upd.)

Encyclopaedia Britannica, Inc., 7; 39 (upd.)

Engraph, Inc., 12

Enquirer/Star Group, Inc., 10

Entravision Communications Corporation, 41

Essence Communications, Inc., 24

F&W Publications, Inc., 71

Farm Journal Corporation, 42

Farrar, Straus and Giroux Inc., 15

Flint Ink Corporation, 13

Follett Corporation, 12; 39 (upd.)

Forbes Inc., 30; 82 (upd.)

Frankfurter Allgemeine Zeitung GmbH, 66

Franklin Electronic Publishers, Inc., 23

Freedom Communications, Inc., 36

G A Pindar & Son Ltd., 88

Gannett Company, Inc., IV; 7 (upd.); 30 (upd.); 66 (upd.)

GateHouse Media, Inc., 91

Geiger Bros., 60

Gibson Greetings, Inc., 12

Giesecke & Devrient GmbH, 83

Golden Books Family Entertainment, Inc., 28

Goss Holdings, Inc., 43

Graphic Industries Inc., 25

Gray Communications Systems, Inc., 24

Grolier Incorporated, 16; 43 (upd.)

Groupe de la Cite, IV

Groupe Les Echos, 25

Grupo Clarín S.A., 67

Grupo Televisa, S.A., 54 (upd.)

Guardian Media Group plc, 53

The H.W. Wilson Company, 66

Hachette, IV

Hachette Filipacchi Medias S.A., 21

Haights Cross Communications, Inc., 84

Hal Leonard Corporation, 96

Hallmark Cards, Inc., IV; 16 (upd.); 40 (upd.); 87 (upd.)

Harcourt Brace and Co., 12

Harcourt Brace Jovanovich, Inc., IV

Harcourt General, Inc., 20 (upd.)

Harlequin Enterprises Limited, 52

HarperCollins Publishers, 15

Harris Interactive Inc., 41; 92 (upd.)

Harry N. Abrams, Inc., 58

Harte-Hanks Communications, Inc., 17

Havas SA, 10; 33 (upd.)

Hay House, Inc., 93

Haynes Publishing Group P.L.C., 71

Hazelden Foundation, 28

Health Communications, Inc., 72

The Hearst Corporation, IV; 19 (upd.); 46 (upd.)

Her Majesty's Stationery Office, 7

Herald Media, Inc., 91

Highlights for Children, Inc., 95

N.V. Holdingmaatschappij De Telegraaf, 23

Hollinger International Inc., 24; 62 (upd.)

HOP, LLC, 80

Houghton Mifflin Company, 10; 36 (upd.)

IDG Books Worldwide, Inc., 27

IHS Inc. 78

Independent News & Media PLC, 61

Informa Group plc, 58

Information Holdings Inc., 47

International Data Group, Inc., 7; 25 (upd.)

IPC Magazines Limited, 7

J.J. Keller & Associates, Inc., 81

Jeppesen Sanderson, Inc., 92

John Fairfax Holdings Limited, 7

John H. Harland Company, 17
John Wiley & Sons, Inc., 17; 65 (upd.)
Johnson Publishing Company, Inc., 28;
72 (upd.)
Johnston Press plc, 35
Jostens, Inc., 25 (upd.); 73 (upd.)
Journal Communications, Inc., 86
Journal Register Company, 29
Jupitermedia Corporation, 75
Kaplan, Inc., 42
Kelley Blue Book Company, Inc., 84
Kensington Publishing Corporation, 84
Kinko's, Inc., 43 (upd.)
Knight Ridder, Inc., 67 (upd.)
Knight-Ridder, Inc., IV; 15 (upd.)
The Knot, Inc., 74
Kodansha Ltd., IV; 38 (upd.)
Krause Publications, Inc., 35
Landmark Communications, Inc., 12; 55
(upd.)
Larry Flynt Publishing Inc., 31
Le Monde S.A., 33
Lebhar-Friedman, Inc., 55
Lee Enterprises Inc., 11; 64 (upd.)
LEXIS-NEXIS Group, 33
Lonely Planet Publications Pty Ltd., 55
M. DuMont Schauberg GmbH & Co.
KG, 92
M. Shanken Communications, Inc., 50
Maclean Hunter Publishing Limited, IV;
26 (upd.)
Macmillan, Inc., 7
Martha Stewart Living Omnimedia, Inc.,
24; 73 (upd.)
Marvel Entertainment Inc., 10; 78 (upd.)
Matra-Hachette S.A., 15 (upd.)
Maxwell Communication Corporation plc,
IV; 7 (upd.)
The McClatchy Company, 23; 92 (upd.)
The McGraw-Hill Companies, Inc., IV;
18 (upd.); 51 (upd.)
Mecklermedia Corporation, 24
Media General, Inc., 38 (upd.)
MediaNews Group, Inc., 70
Menasha Corporation, 59 (upd.)
Meredith Corporation, 11; 29 (upd.); 74
(upd.)
Merriam-Webster Inc., 70
Merrill Corporation, 18; 47 (upd.)
Metro International S.A., 93
Miami Herald Media Company, 92
Miller Publishing Group, LLC, 57
The Miner Group International, 22
Mirror Group Newspapers plc, 7; 23
(upd.)
Moore Corporation Limited, IV
Morris Communications Corporation, 36
Mrs. Grossman's Paper Company Inc., 84
Multimedia, Inc., 11
MYOB Ltd., 86
Naspers Ltd., 66
National Audubon Society, 26
National Geographic Society, 9; 30 (upd.);
79 (upd.)
National Journal Group Inc., 67
New Chapter Inc., 96
New Times, Inc., 45
New York Daily News, 32

The New York Times Company, IV; 19
(upd.); 61 (upd.)
News America Publishing Inc., 12
News Corporation Limited, IV; 7 (upd.)
Newsquest plc, 32
Next Media Ltd., 61
Nielsen Business Media, Inc., 98
Nihon Keizai Shimbun, Inc., IV
Nolo.com, Inc., 49
Northern and Shell Network plc, 87
Oji Paper Co., Ltd., 57 (upd.)
Onion, Inc., 69
Ottaway Newspapers, Inc., 15
Outlook Group Corporation, 37
PagesJaunes Groupe SA, 79
Pantone Inc., 53
PCM Uitgevers NV, 53
Pearson plc, IV; 46 (upd.)
PennWell Corporation, 55
Penton Media, Inc., 27
The Perseus Books Group, 91
Petersen Publishing Company, 21
Phaidon Press Ltd., 98
Philadelphia Media Holdings LLC, 92
The Phoenix Media/Communications
Group, 91
Plain Dealer Publishing Company, 92
Plato Learning, Inc., 44
Playboy Enterprises, Inc., 18
Pleasant Company, 27
PMP Ltd., 72
PR Newswire, 35
Primedia Inc., 22
The Providence Journal Company, 28
Publishers Group, Inc., 35
Publishing and Broadcasting Limited, 54
Pulitzer Inc., 15; 58 (upd.)
Quad/Graphics, Inc., 19
Quebecor Inc., 12; 47 (upd.)
R.L. Polk & Co., 10
R.R. Donnelley & Sons Company, IV; 9
(upd.); 38 (upd.)
Rand McNally & Company, 28
Random House Inc., 13; 31 (upd.)
Ravensburger AG, 64
RCS MediaGroup S.p.A., 96
The Reader's Digest Association, Inc., IV;
17 (upd.); 71 (upd.)
Real Times, Inc., 66
Recycled Paper Greetings, Inc., 21
Reed Elsevier plc, IV; 17 (upd.); 31 (upd.)
Reuters Group PLC, IV; 22 (upd.); 63
(upd.)
Rodale, Inc., 23; 47 (upd.)
Rogers Communications Inc., 30 (upd.)
The Rowohlt Verlag GmbH, 96
Rural Press Ltd., 74
St Ives plc, 34
Salem Communications Corporation, 97
Sanborn Map Company Inc., 82
SanomaWSOY Corporation, 51
Schawk, Inc., 24
Schibsted ASA, 31
Scholastic Corporation, 10; 29 (upd.)
Schurz Communications, Inc., 98
Scott Fetzer Company, 12; 80 (upd.)
Scottish Media Group plc, 32
Seat Pagine Gialle S.p.A., 47

Seattle Times Company, 15
The Sheridan Group, Inc., 86
The Sierra Club, 28
Simon & Schuster Inc., IV; 19 (upd.)
Singapore Press Holdings Limited, 85
Sir Speedy, Inc., 16
Société du Figaro S.A., 60
Softbank Corp., 13
The Source Enterprises, Inc., 65
Southam Inc., 7
SPIEGEL-Verlag Rudolf Augstein GmbH
& Co. KG, 44
The Standard Register Company, 15; 93
(upd.)
Stephens Media, LLC, 91
Strine Printing Company Inc., 88
Sunrise Greetings, 88
Tamedia AG, 53
Taylor & Francis Group plc, 44
Taylor Corporation, 36
Taylor Publishing Company, 12; 36 (upd.)
TechBooks Inc., 84
TechTarget, Inc., 99
Telegraaf Media Groep N.V., 98 (upd.)
Thomas Crosbie Holdings Limited, 81
Thomas Nelson, Inc., 14; 38 (upd.)
Thomas Publishing Company, 26
The Thomson Corporation, 8; 34 (upd.);
77 (upd.)
Time Out Group Ltd., 68
The Times Mirror Company, IV; 17
(upd.)
Tohan Corporation, 84
TOKYOPOP Inc., 79
Tom Doherty Associates Inc., 25
Toppan Printing Co., Ltd., IV; 58 (upd.)
The Topps Company, Inc., 13; 34 (upd.);
83 (upd.)
Torstar Corporation, 29
Trader Classified Media N.V., 57
Tribune Company, IV, 22 (upd.); 63
(upd.)
Trinity Mirror plc, 49 (upd.)
Tuttle Publishing, 86
Tyndale House Publishers, Inc., 57
U.S. News & World Report Inc., 30; 89
(upd.)
United Business Media plc, 52 (upd.)
United News & Media plc, IV; 28 (upd.)
United Press International, Inc., 25; 73
(upd.)
The University of Chicago Press, 79
Valassis Communications, Inc., 8
Value Line, Inc., 16; 73 (upd.)
Vance Publishing Corporation, 64
Verlagsgruppe Georg von Holtzbrinck
GmbH, 35
Verlagsgruppe Weltbild GmbH, 98
Village Voice Media, Inc., 38
VistaPrint Limited, 87
VNU N.V., 27
Volt Information Sciences Inc., 26
W.W. Norton & Company, Inc., 28
Wallace Computer Services, Inc., 36
Walsworth Publishing Co. 78
The Washington Post Company, IV; 20
(upd.)

Waverly, Inc., 16
WAZ Media Group, 82
Wegener NV, 53
Wenner Media, Inc., 32
West Group, 7; 34 (upd.)
Western Publishing Group, Inc., 13
WH Smith PLC, V; 42 (upd.)
William Reed Publishing Ltd. 78
Wolters Kluwer NV, 14; 33 (upd.)
Workman Publishing Company, Inc., 70
World Book, Inc., 12
World Color Press Inc., 12
World Publications, LLC, 65
Xeikon NV, 26
Yell Group PLC, 79
Zebra Technologies Corporation, 14
Ziff Davis Media Inc., 12; 36 (upd.); 73 (upd.)
Zondervan Corporation, 24; 71 (upd.)

Real Estate

Akerys S.A., 90
Alexander's, Inc., 45
Alico, Inc., 63
AMB Property Corporation, 57
American Campus Communities, Inc., 85
Amfac/JMB Hawaii L.L.C., 24 (upd.)
Apartment Investment and Management Company, 49
Archstone-Smith Trust, 49
Associated Estates Realty Corporation, 25
AvalonBay Communities, Inc., 58
Baird & Warner Holding Company, 87
Berkshire Realty Holdings, L.P., 49
Bluegreen Corporation, 80
Boston Properties, Inc., 22
Bouygues S.A., I; 24 (upd.); 97 (upd.)
Bramalea Ltd., 9
British Land Plc, 54
Brookfield Properties Corporation, 89
Burroughs & Chapin Company, Inc., 86
Camden Property Trust, 77
Canary Wharf Group Plc, 30
CapStar Hotel Company, 21
CarrAmerica Realty Corporation, 56
Castle & Cooke, Inc., 20 (upd.)
Catellus Development Corporation, 24
CB Commercial Real Estate Services Group, Inc., 21
CB Richard Ellis Group, Inc., 70 (upd.)
Central Florida Investments, Inc., 93
Chateau Communities, Inc., 37
Chelsfield PLC, 67
Cheung Kong (Holdings) Limited, IV; 20 (upd.)
City Developments Limited, 89
Clayton Homes Incorporated, 54 (upd.)
Colliers International Property Consultants Inc., 92
Colonial Properties Trust, 65
The Corcoran Group, Inc., 58
The Corky McMillin Companies, 98
CoStar Group, Inc., 73
Cousins Properties Incorporated, 65
CSX Corporation 79 (upd.)
Cushman & Wakefield, Inc., 86
Del Webb Corporation, 14
Desarrolladora Homex, S.A. de C.V., 87

Developers Diversified Realty Corporation, 69
Draper and Kramer Inc., 96
Duke Realty Corporation, 57
Ducks Unlimited, Inc., 87
EastGroup Properties, Inc., 67
The Edward J. DeBartolo Corporation, 8
Enterprise Inns plc, 59
Equity Office Properties Trust, 54
Equity Residential, 49
Erickson Retirement Communities, 57
Fairfield Communities, Inc., 36
First Industrial Realty Trust, Inc., 65
Forest City Enterprises, Inc., 16; 52 (upd.)
Gale International Llc, 93
Gecina SA, 42
General Growth Properties, Inc., 57
GMH Communities Trust, 87
Great White Shark Enterprises, Inc., 89
Griffin Land & Nurseries, Inc., 43
Grubb & Ellis Company, 21; 98 (upd.)
Guangzhou R&F Properties Co., Ltd., 95
The Haminerson Property Investment and Development Corporation plc, IV
Hammerson plc, 40
Harbert Corporation, 14
Helmsley Enterprises, Inc., 39 (upd.)
Henderson Land Development Company Ltd., 70
Home Properties of New York, Inc., 42
HomeVestors of America, Inc., 77
Hongkong Land Holdings Limited, IV; 47 (upd.)
Holiday Retirement Corp., 87
Hopson Development Holdings Ltd., 87
Hovnanian Enterprises, Inc., 29; 89 (upd.)
Hyatt Corporation, 16 (upd.)
ILX Resorts Incorporated, 65
IRSA Inversiones y Representaciones S.A., 63
J.F. Shea Co., Inc., 55
Jardine Cycle & Carriage Ltd., 73
JMB Realty Corporation, IV
Jones Lang LaSalle Incorporated, 49
JPI, 49
Kaufman and Broad Home Corporation, 8
Kennedy-Wilson, Inc., 60
Kerry Properties Limited, 22
Kimco Realty Corporation, 11
The Koll Company, 8
Land Securities PLC, IV; 49 (upd.)
Lefrak Organization Inc., 26
Lend Lease Corporation Limited, IV; 17 (upd.); 52 (upd.)
Liberty Property Trust, 57
Lincoln Property Company, 8; 54 (upd.)
The Loewen Group Inc., 40 (upd.)
The Long & Foster Companies, Inc., 85
The Macerich Company, 57
Mack-Cali Realty Corporation, 42
Macklowe Properties, Inc., 95
Manufactured Home Communities, Inc., 22
Maui Land & Pineapple Company, Inc., 29
Maxco Inc., 17

Meditrust, 11
Melvin Simon and Associates, Inc., 8
MEPC plc, IV
Meritage Corporation, 26
Mid-America Apartment Communities, Inc., 85
The Middleton Doll Company, 53
The Mills Corporation, 77
Mitsubishi Estate Company, Limited, IV; 61 (upd.)
Mitsui Real Estate Development Co., Ltd., IV
Morguard Corporation, 85
The Nature Conservancy, 28
New Plan Realty Trust, 11
New World Development Company Ltd., IV
Newhall Land and Farming Company, 14
Nexity S.A., 66
NRT Incorporated, 61
Olympia & York Developments Ltd., IV; 9 (upd.)
Panattoni Development Company, Inc., 99
Park Corp., 22
Parque Arauco S.A., 72
Perini Corporation, 8
Pope Resources LP, 74
Post Properties, Inc., 26
Potlatch Corporation, 8; 34 (upd.); 87 (upd.)
ProLogis, 57
Public Storage, Inc., 52
Railtrack Group PLC, 50
RE/MAX International, Inc., 59
Reading International Inc., 70
Reckson Associates Realty Corp., 47
Regency Centers Corporation, 71
Rockefeller Group International Inc., 58
Rodamco N.V., 26
The Rouse Company, 15; 63 (upd.)
The St. Joe Company, 8; 98 (upd.)
Sapporo Holdings Limited, I; 13 (upd.); 36 (upd.); 97 (upd.)
Shubert Organization Inc., 24
The Sierra Club, 28
Silverstein Properties, Inc., 47
Simco S.A., 37
SL Green Realty Corporation, 44
Slough Estates PLC, IV; 50 (upd.)
Sovran Self Storage, Inc., 66
Starrett Corporation, 21
The Staubach Company, 62
Storage USA, Inc., 21
Sumitomo Realty & Development Co., Ltd., IV
Sun Communities Inc., 46
Sunterra Corporation, 75
Tanger Factory Outlet Centers, Inc., 49
Tarragon Realty Investors, Inc., 45
Taubman Centers, Inc., 75
Taylor Woodrow plc, 38 (upd.)
Technical Olympic USA, Inc., 75
Tejon Ranch Company, 35
Tishman Speyer Properties, L.P., 47
Tokyu Land Corporation, IV
Trammell Crow Company, 8; 57 (upd.)
Trendwest Resorts, Inc., 33

Tridel Enterprises Inc., 9
Trizec Corporation Ltd., 10
The Trump Organization, 23; 64 (upd.)
Unibail SA, 40
United Dominion Realty Trust, Inc., 52
Vistana, Inc., 22
Vornado Realty Trust, 20
W.P. Carey & Co. LLC, 49
Weingarten Realty Investors, 95
William Lyon Homes, 59
Woodbridge Holdings Corporation, 99

Retail & Wholesale

A-Mark Financial Corporation, 71
A.C. Moore Arts & Crafts, Inc., 30
A.S. Watson & Company Ltd., 84
A.T. Cross Company, 49 (upd.)
Aaron Rents, Inc., 14; 35 (upd.)
Abatix Corp., 57
ABC Appliance, Inc., 10
ABC Carpet & Home Co. Inc., 26
Abercrombie & Fitch Company, 15; 75 (upd.)
Academy Sports & Outdoors, 27
Ace Hardware Corporation, 12; 35 (upd.)
Action Performance Companies, Inc., 27
Adams Childrenswear Ltd., 95
ADESA, Inc., 71
Adolfo Dominguez S.A., 72
AEON Co., Ltd., 68 (upd.)
Aéropostale, Inc., 89
After Hours Formalwear Inc., 60
Alabama Farmers Cooperative, Inc., 63
Alain Afflelou SA, 53
Alba-Waldensian, Inc., 30
Alberto-Culver Company, 8; 36 (upd.); 91 (upd.)
Albertson's, Inc., 65 (upd.)
Alimentation Couche-Tard Inc., 77
Alldays plc, 49
Allders plc, 37
Alliance Boots plc (updates Boots Group PLC), 83 (upd.)
Allou Health & Beauty Care, Inc., 28
Almacenes Exito S.A., 89
Alpha Airports Group PLC, 77
Alrosa Company Ltd., 62
Alticor Inc., 71 (upd.)
Amazon.com, Inc., 25; 56 (upd.)
AMCON Distributing Company, 99
AMERCO, 67 (upd.)
American Coin Merchandising, Inc., 28; 74 (upd.)
American Eagle Outfitters, Inc., 24; 55 (upd.)
American Furniture Company, Inc., 21
American Girl, Inc., 69 (upd.)
American Stores Company, 22 (upd.)
AmeriSource Health Corporation, 37 (upd.)
Ames Department Stores, Inc., 9; 30 (upd.)
Amscan Holdings, Inc., 61
Amway Corporation, 13; 30 (upd.)
The Anderson-DuBose Company, 60
The Andersons, Inc., 31
AnnTaylor Stores Corporation, 13; 37 (upd.); 67 (upd.)

Appliance Recycling Centers of America, Inc., 42
Arbor Drugs Inc., 12
Arcadia Group plc, 28 (upd.)
Army and Air Force Exchange Service, 39
Art Van Furniture, Inc., 28
ASDA Group plc, 28 (upd.)
Ashworth, Inc., 26
Au Printemps S.A., V
Audio King Corporation, 24
Authentic Fitness Corporation, 20; 51 (upd.)
Auto Value Associates, Inc., 25
Autobytel Inc., 47
AutoNation, Inc., 50
AutoTrader.com, L.L.C., 91
AutoZone, Inc., 9; 31 (upd.)
AVA AG (Allgemeine Handelsgesellschaft der Verbraucher AG), 33
Aveda Corporation, 24
Aviall, Inc., 73
Aviation Sales Company, 41
AWB Ltd., 56
B. Dalton Bookseller Inc., 25
Babbage's, Inc., 10
Baby Superstore, Inc., 15
Baccarat, 24
Bachman's Inc., 22
Bailey Nurseries, Inc., 57
Ball Horticultural Company 78
Banana Republic Inc., 25
Bare Escentuals, Inc., 91
Barnes & Noble, Inc., 10; 30 (upd.); 75 (upd.)
Barnett Inc., 28
Barney's, Inc., 28
Barrett-Jackson Auction Company L.L.C., 88
Bass Pro Shops, Inc., 42
Baumax AG, 75
Beacon Roofing Supply, Inc., 75
Bear Creek Corporation, 38
Bearings, Inc., 13
Beate Uhse AG, 96
bebe stores, inc., 31
Bed Bath & Beyond Inc., 13; 41 (upd.)
Belk Stores Services, Inc., V; 19 (upd.)
Belk, Inc., 72 (upd.)
Ben Bridge Jeweler, Inc., 60
Benetton Group S.p.A., 10; 67 (upd.)
Berean Christian Stores, 96
Bergdorf Goodman Inc., 52
Bergen Brunswig Corporation, V; 13 (upd.)
Bernard Chaus, Inc., 27
Best Buy Co., Inc., 9; 23 (upd.); 63 (upd.)
Bestseller A/S, 90
Bhs plc, 17
Big A Drug Stores Inc., 79
Big Dog Holdings, Inc., 45
Big 5 Sporting Goods Corporation, 55
The Big Food Group plc, 68 (upd.)
Big Lots, Inc., 50
Big O Tires, Inc., 20
Birkenstock Footprint Sandals, Inc., 42 (upd.)
Birthdays Ltd., 70

Black Box Corporation, 20; 96 (upd.)
Blacks Leisure Group plc, 39
Blair Corporation, 25; 31 (upd.)
Blish-Mize Co., 95
Blokker Holding B.V., 84
Bloomingdale's Inc., 12
Blue Nile Inc., 61
Blue Square Israel Ltd., 41
Bluefly, Inc., 60
BlueLinx Holdings Inc., 97
Blyth Industries, Inc., 18
The Body Shop International PLC, 11
The Bombay Company, Inc., 10; 71 (upd.)
The Bon Marché, Inc., 23
The Bon-Ton Stores, Inc., 16; 50 (upd.)
Booker Cash & Carry Ltd., 68 (upd.)
Books-A-Million, Inc., 14; 41 (upd.); 96 (upd.)
Bookspan, 86
The Boots Company PLC, V; 24 (upd.)
Borders Group, Inc., 15; 43 (upd.)
Boscov's Department Store, Inc., 31
Boss Holdings, Inc., 97
Bowlin Travel Centers, Inc., 99
Bozzuto's, Inc., 13
Bradlees Discount Department Store Company, 12
Brambles Industries Limited, 42
Bricorama S.A., 68
Brioni Roman Style S.p.A., 67
Brodart Company, 84
Broder Bros. Co., 38
Bronner Display & Sign Advertising, Inc., 82
Brooks Brothers Inc., 22
Brookstone, Inc., 18
Brown Shoe Company, Inc., 68 (upd.)
Brunswick Corporation, 77 (upd.)
The Buckle, Inc., 18
Buhrmann NV, 41
Build-A-Bear Workshop Inc., 62
Building Materials Holding Corporation, 52
Burdines, Inc., 60
Burlington Coat Factory Warehouse Corporation, 10; 60 (upd.)
Burt's Bees, Inc., 58
The Burton Group plc, V
Buttrey Food & Drug Stores Co., 18
buy.com, Inc., 46
C&A, V; 40 (upd.)
C&J Clark International Ltd., 52
Cabela's Inc., 26; 68 (upd.)
Cablevision Electronic Instruments, Inc., 32
Cache Incorporated, 30
Cactus S.A., 90
Caldor Inc., 12
Calloway's Nursery, Inc., 51
Camaïeu S.A., 72
Camelot Music, Inc., 26
Campeau Corporation, V
Campo Electronics, Appliances & Computers, Inc., 16
Car Toys, Inc., 67
The Carphone Warehouse Group PLC, 83
Carrefour SA, 10; 27 (upd.); 64 (upd.)

Carson Pirie Scott & Company, 15
Carter Hawley Hale Stores, Inc., V
Carter Lumber Company, 45
Cartier Monde, 29
Casas Bahia Comercial Ltda., 75
Casey's General Stores, Inc., 19; 83 (upd.)
Castro Model Ltd., 86
Casual Corner Group, Inc., 43
Casual Male Retail Group, Inc., 52
Catherines Stores Corporation, 15
Cato Corporation, 14
CDW Computer Centers, Inc., 16
Celebrate Express, Inc., 70
Celebrity, Inc., 22
CellStar Corporation, 83
Cencosud S.A., 69
Central European Distribution
    Corporation, 75
Central Garden & Pet Company, 23
Cenveo Inc., 71 (upd.)
Chadwick's of Boston, Ltd., 29
Charlotte Russe Holding, Inc., 35; 90
    (upd.)
Charming Shoppes, Inc., 38
Chas. Levy Company LLC, 60
ChevronTexaco Corporation, 47 (upd.)
Chiasso Inc., 53
The Children's Place Retail Stores, Inc.,
    37; 86 (upd.)
China Nepstar Chain Drugstore Ltd., 97
Christian Dior S.A., 49 (upd.)
Christopher & Banks Corporation, 42
Cifra, S.A. de C.V., 12
The Circle K Company, 20 (upd.)
Circuit City Stores, Inc., 9; 29 (upd.); 65
    (upd.)
Clare Rose Inc., 68
Clinton Cards plc, 39
The Clothestime, Inc., 20
CML Group, Inc., 10
Co-operative Group (CWS) Ltd., 51
Coach, Inc., 45 (upd.); 99 (upd.)
Coborn's, Inc., 30
Coinmach Laundry Corporation, 20
Coldwater Creek Inc., 21; 74 (upd.)
Cole National Corporation, 13; 76 (upd.)
Cole's Quality Foods, Inc., 68
Coles Group Limited, V; 20 (upd.); 85
    (upd.)
Collectors Universe, Inc., 48
Columbia House Company, 69
Comdisco, Inc., 9
Compagnie Financière Sucres et Denrées
    S.A., 60
Companhia Brasileira de Distribuiçao, 76
CompUSA, Inc., 10
Computerland Corp., 13
Concepts Direct, Inc., 39
Conn's, Inc., 67
The Container Store, 36
Controladora Comercial Mexicana, S.A.
    de C.V., 36
CoolSavings, Inc., 77
Coop Schweiz Genossenschaftsverband, 48
Coppel, S.A. de C.V., 82
Corby Distilleries Limited, 14
Corporate Express, Inc., 22; 47 (upd.)
Cortefiel S.A., 64

The Cosmetic Center, Inc., 22
Cost Plus, Inc., 27
Costco Wholesale Corporation, V; 43
    (upd.)
Cotter & Company, V
County Seat Stores Inc., 9
Courts Plc, 45
CPI Corp., 38
Crate and Barrel, 9
Croscill, Inc., 42
CROSSMARK, 79
Crowley, Milner & Company, 19
Crown Books Corporation, 21
Cumberland Farms, Inc., 17; 84 (upd.)
CVS Corporation, 45 (upd.)
D&H Distributing Co., 95
Daffy's Inc., 26
The Daiei, Inc., V; 17 (upd.); 41 (upd.)
The Daimaru, Inc., V; 42 (upd.)
Dairy Farm International Holdings Ltd.,
    97
Dairy Mart Convenience Stores, Inc., 25
    (upd.)
Daisytek International Corporation, 18
Damark International, Inc., 18
Dart Group Corporation, 16
Darty S.A., 27
David Jones Ltd., 60
David's Bridal, Inc., 33
Dayton Hudson Corporation, V; 18
    (upd.)
Deb Shops, Inc., 16; 76 (upd.)
Debenhams Plc, 28
Deli Universal NV, 66
dELiA*s Inc., 29
Department 56, Inc., 34 (upd.)
Designer Holdings Ltd., 20
Deveaux S.A., 41
DFS Group Ltd., 66
Dick's Sporting Goods, Inc., 59
Diesel SpA, 40
Digital River, Inc., 50
Dillard Department Stores, Inc., V; 16
    (upd.)
Dillard's Inc., 68 (upd.)
Dillon Companies Inc., 12
Discount Auto Parts, Inc., 18
Discount Drug Mart, Inc., 14
Dixons Group plc, V; 19 (upd.); 49
    (upd.)
Do it Best Corporation, 30
Dollar Tree Stores, Inc., 23; 62 (upd.)
Donna Karan International Inc., 56 (upd.)
Dorian Drake International Inc., 96
Dreams Inc., 97
The Dress Barn, Inc., 24; 55 (upd.)
Drs. Foster & Smith, Inc., 62
Drug Emporium, Inc., 12
DSW Inc., 73
Du Pareil au Même, 43
Duane Reade Holding Corp., 21
Duckwall-ALCO Stores, Inc., 24
Dunham's Athleisure Corporation, 98
Dunnes Stores Ltd., 58
Duron Inc., 72
Duty Free International, Inc., 11
Dylan's Candy Bar, LLC, 99
Dylex Limited, 29

E-Z Serve Corporation, 17
Eagle Hardware & Garden, Inc., 16
Eastman Kodak Company, III; 7 (upd.);
    36 (upd.); 91 (upd.)
eBay Inc., 32
Eckerd Corporation, 9; 32 (upd.)
Eddie Bauer Holdings, Inc., 9; 36 (upd.);
    87 (upd.)
Edgars Consolidated Stores Ltd., 66
Edward Hines Lumber Company, 68
Egghead.com, Inc., 31 (upd.)
Eileen Fisher Inc., 61
El Corte Inglés Group, V
El Puerto de Liverpool, S.A.B. de C.V., 97
The Elder-Beerman Stores Corp., 10; 63
    (upd.)
Electrocomponents PLC, 50
Electronics Boutique Holdings
    Corporation, 72
Elephant Pharmacy, Inc., 83
Ellett Brothers, Inc., 17
EMI Group plc, 22 (upd.); 81 (upd.)
Empresas Almacenes Paris S.A., 71
Ermenegildo Zegna SpA, 63
ESCADA AG, 71
The Estée Lauder Companies Inc., 9; 30
    (upd.); 93 (upd.)
Etablissements Franz Colruyt N.V., 68
Ethan Allen Interiors, Inc., 39 (upd.)
EToys, Inc., 37
Euromarket Designs Inc., 31 (upd.); 99
    (upd.)
Evans, Inc., 30
Eye Care Centers of America, Inc., 69
EZCORP, 43
F.W. Webb Company, 95
The F. Dohmen Co., 77
Family Christian Stores, Inc., 51
Family Dollar Stores, Inc., 13; 62 (upd.)
Fannie May Confections Brands, Inc., 80
Farmacias Ahumada S.A., 72
Fastenal Company, 14; 42 (upd.); 99
    (upd.)
Faultless Starch/Bon Ami Company, 55
Fay's Inc., 17
Federated Department Stores, Inc., 9; 31
    (upd.)
Fenaco, 86
Fielmann AG, 31
Fila Holding S.p.A., 20; 52 (upd.)
Finarte Casa d'Aste S.p.A., 93
Findel plc, 60
Fingerhut Companies, Inc., 9; 36 (upd.)
The Finish Line, Inc., 29; 68 (upd.)
Finlay Enterprises, Inc., 16; 76 (upd.)
Finning International Inc., 69
First Cash Financial Services, Inc., 57
Fleming Companies, Inc., 17 (upd.)
Florsheim Shoe Group Inc., 9; 31 (upd.)
FNAC, 21
Follett Corporation, 12
Foot Locker, Inc., 68 (upd.)
Footstar, Incorporated, 24
Forever 21, Inc., 84
Fortunoff Fine Jewelry and Silverware
    Inc., 26
The Forzani Group Ltd., 79
Foxworth-Galbraith Lumber Company, 91

Frank's Nursery & Crafts, Inc., 12
Fred Meyer Stores, Inc., V; 20 (upd.); 64 (upd.)
Fred's, Inc., 23; 62 (upd.)
Frederick Atkins Inc., 16
Frederick's of Hollywood, Inc., 59 (upd.)
Freeze.com LLC, 77
Fretter, Inc., 10
Friedman's Inc., 29
Fruth Pharmacy, Inc., 66
Fry's Electronics, Inc., 68
FTD Group, Inc., 99 (upd.)
Funco, Inc., 20
Future Shop Ltd., 62
G&K Holding S.A., 95
G.I. Joe's, Inc., 30
Gadzooks, Inc., 18
Gaiam, Inc., 41
Galeries Lafayette S.A., V; 23 (upd.)
Galyan's Trading Company, Inc., 47
GameStop Corp., 69 (upd.)
Gander Mountain, Inc., 20; 90 (upd.)
Gantos, Inc., 17
The Gap, Inc., V; 18 (upd.); 55 (upd.)
Garden Ridge Corporation, 27
Garst Seed Company, Inc., 86
Gart Sports Company, 24
GEHE AG, 27
General Binding Corporation, 10
General Host Corporation, 12
Genesco Inc., 17; 84 (upd.)
Genovese Drug Stores, Inc., 18
Genuine Parts Company, 45 (upd.)
Gerald Stevens, Inc., 37
Gerhard D. Wempe KG, 88
Giant Food Inc., 22 (upd.)
GIB Group, V; 26 (upd.)
Gibbs and Dandy plc, 74
GiFi S.A., 74
Glacier Water Services, Inc., 47
Global Imaging Systems, Inc., 73
GOME Electrical Appliances Holding Ltd., 87
The Good Guys, Inc., 10; 30 (upd.)
Goodwill Industries International, Inc., 16
Goody's Family Clothing, Inc., 20; 64 (upd.)
Gordmans, Inc., 74
Gottschalks, Inc., 18; 91 (upd.)
Grand Piano & Furniture Company, 72
GrandVision S.A., 43
Graybar Electric Company, Inc., 54
The Great Universal Stores plc, V; 19 (upd.)
Griffin Land & Nurseries, Inc., 43
Grossman's Inc., 13
Groupe Alain Manoukian, 55
Groupe Castorama-Dubois Investissements, 23
Groupe DMC (Dollfus Mieg & Cie), 27
Groupe Go Sport S.A., 39
Groupe Lapeyre S.A., 33
Groupe Monnoyeur, 72
Groupe Zannier S.A., 35
Grow Biz International, Inc., 18
Grupo Casa Saba, S.A. de C.V., 39
Grupo Elektra, S.A. de C.V., 39
Grupo Eroski, 64

Grupo Gigante, S.A. de C.V., 34
Gruppo Coin S.p.A., 41
GSC Enterprises, Inc., 86
GT Bicycles, 26
GTSI Corp., 57
Gucci Group N.V., 15; 50 (upd.)
Guilbert S.A., 42
Guitar Center, Inc., 29; 68 (upd.)
GUS plc, 47 (upd.)
Gymboree Corporation, 69 (upd.)
H&M Hennes & Mauritz AB, 29; 98 (upd.)
Hahn Automotive Warehouse, Inc., 24
Hale-Halsell Company, 60
Half Price Books, Records, Magazines Inc., 37
Hallmark Cards, Inc., IV; 16 (upd.); 40 (upd.); 87 (upd.)
Hammacher Schlemmer & Company Inc., 21; 72 (upd.)
Hancock Fabrics, Inc., 18
Hankyu Department Stores, Inc., V; 62 (upd.)
Hanna Andersson Corp., 49
Hanover Compressor Company, 59
Hanover Direct, Inc., 36
Harold's Stores, Inc., 22
Harrods Holdings, 47
Harry Winston Inc., 45
Harvey Norman Holdings Ltd., 56
Hasbro, Inc., 43 (upd.)
Haverty Furniture Companies, Inc., 31
Headlam Group plc, 95
Hechinger Company, 12
Heilig-Meyers Company, 14; 40 (upd.)
Heinrich Deichmann-Schuhe GmbH & Co. KG, 88
Helzberg Diamonds, 40
H&M Hennes & Mauritz AB, 29; 98 (upd.)
Henry Modell & Company Inc., 32
Hensley & Company, 64
Hertie Waren- und Kaufhaus GmbH, V
hhgregg Inc., 98
Hibbett Sporting Goods, Inc., 26; 70 (upd.)
Highsmith Inc., 60
Hills Stores Company, 13
Hines Horticulture, Inc., 49
HMV Group plc, 59
Hobby Lobby Stores Inc., 80
The Hockey Company, 34
Holiday RV Superstores, Incorporated, 26
Holt's Cigar Holdings, Inc., 42
The Home Depot, Inc., V; 18 (upd.); 97 (upd.)
Home Hardware Stores Ltd., 62
Home Interiors & Gifts, Inc., 55
Home Retail Group plc, 91
Home Shopping Network, Inc., V; 25 (upd.)
HomeBase, Inc., 33 (upd.)
Hornbach Holding AG, 98
Hot Topic Inc., 33; 86 (upd.)
House of Fabrics, Inc., 21
House of Fraser PLC, 45
Houston Wire & Cable Company, 97
HSN, 64 (upd.)

Hudson's Bay Company, V; 25 (upd.); 83 (upd.)
Huttig Building Products, Inc., 73
Ihr Platz GmbH + Company KG, 77
IKEA International A/S, V; 26 (upd.)
InaCom Corporation, 13
Indigo Books & Music Inc., 58
Insight Enterprises, Inc., 18
Intermix Media, Inc., 83
International Airline Support Group, Inc., 55
Intimate Brands, Inc., 24
Intres B.V., 82
Isetan Company Limited, V; 36 (upd.)
Ito-Yokado Co., Ltd., V; 42 (upd.)
J&R Electronics Inc., 26
J. Baker, Inc., 31
The J. Jill Group Inc., 35; 90 (upd.)
J. C. Penney Company, Inc., V; 18 (upd.); 43 (upd.); 91 (upd.)
J.L. Hammett Company, 72
J. W. Pepper and Son Inc., 86
Jack Schwartz Shoes, Inc., 18
Jacobson Stores Inc., 21
Jalate Inc., 25
James Beattie plc, 43
Jay Jacobs, Inc., 15
Jennifer Convertibles, Inc., 31
Jetro Cash & Carry Enterprises Inc., 38
Jewett-Cameron Trading Company, Ltd., 89
JG Industries, Inc., 15
JJB Sports plc, 32
Jo-Ann Stores, Inc., 72 (upd.)
Joe's Sports & Outdoor, 98 (upd.)
John Lewis Partnership plc, V; 42 (upd.); 99 (upd.)
Jordan-Kitt Music Inc., 86
Jumbo S.A., 96
JUSCO Co., Ltd., V
Just For Feet, Inc., 19
K & B Inc., 12
K & G Men's Center, Inc., 21
K-tel International, Inc., 21
Karstadt Aktiengesellschaft, V; 19 (upd.)
Kash n' Karry Food Stores, Inc., 20
Kasper A.S.L., Ltd., 40
kate spade LLC, 68
Kaufhof Warenhaus AG, V; 23 (upd.)
Kaufring AG, 35
Kay-Bee Toy Stores, 15
Keys Fitness Products, LP, 83
Kiabi Europe, 66
Kiehl's Since 1851, Inc., 52
Kingfisher plc, V; 24 (upd.); 83 (upd.)
Kinney Shoe Corp., 14
Kirlin's Inc., 98
Kmart Corporation, V; 18 (upd.); 47 (upd.)
Knoll Group Inc., 14
Kohl's Corporation, 9; 30 (upd.); 77 (upd.)
Koninklijke Vendex KBB N.V. (Royal Vendex KBB N.V.), 62 (upd.)
Kotobukiya Co., Ltd., V; 56 (upd.)
Krause's Furniture, Inc., 27
Krispy Kreme Doughnuts, Inc., 21; 61 (upd.)

Kruse International, 88
L. and J.G. Stickley, Inc., 50
L. Luria & Son, Inc., 19
L.A. T Sportswear, Inc., 26
L.L. Bean, Inc., 10; 38 (upd.); 91 (upd.)
La Senza Corporation, 66
La-Z-Boy Incorporated, 14; 50 (upd.)
Lamonts Apparel, Inc., 15
Lands' End, Inc., 9; 29 (upd.); 82 (upd.)
Lane Bryant, Inc., 64
Lanier Worldwide, Inc., 75
Lanoga Corporation, 62
Laura Ashley Holdings plc, 37 (upd.)
Lazare Kaplan International Inc., 21
Le Chateau Inc., 63
Lechmere Inc., 10
Lechters, Inc., 11; 39 (upd.)
LensCrafters Inc., 23; 76 (upd.)
Leroy Merlin SA, 54
Les Boutiques San Francisco, Inc., 62
Lesco Inc., 19
Leslie's Poolmart, Inc., 18
Leupold & Stevens, Inc., 52
Levenger Company, 63
Levitz Furniture Inc., 15
Lewis Galoob Toys Inc., 16
Li & Fung Limited, 59
Liberty Orchards Co., Inc., 89
Life is Good, Inc., 80
Lifetime Brands, Inc., 27; 73 (upd.)
Lillian Vernon Corporation, 12; 35 (upd.); 92 (upd.)
The Limited, Inc., V; 20 (upd.)
Linens 'n Things, Inc., 24; 75 (upd.)
Little Switzerland, Inc., 60
Littleton Coin Company Inc., 82
Littlewoods plc, V; 42 (upd.)
LivePerson, Inc., 91
Liz Claiborne, Inc., 25 (upd.)
LKQ Corporation, 71
Loehmann's Inc., 24
Lojas Americanas S.A., 77
Lojas Arapuã S.A., 22; 61 (upd.)
London Drugs Ltd., 46
Longs Drug Stores Corporation, V; 25 (upd.); 83 (upd.)
Lookers plc, 71
Lost Arrow Inc., 22
LOT$OFF Corporation, 24
Love's Travel Stops & Country Stores, Inc., 71
Lowe's Companies, Inc., V; 21 (upd.); 81 (upd.)
Ludendo S.A., 88
Luxottica SpA, 17; 52 (upd.)
Lyfra-S.A./NV, 88
Mac Frugal's Bargains - Closeouts Inc., 17
Mac-Gray Corporation, 44
Mackays Stores Group Ltd., 92
Manheim, 88
Manutan International S.A., 72
Maples Industries, Inc., 83
MarineMax, Inc., 30
Marionnaud Parfumeries SA, 51
Marks and Spencer Group p.l.c., V; 24 (upd.); 85 (upd.)
Marks Brothers Jewelers, Inc., 24
Marlin Business Services Corp., 89

Marshall Field's, 63
Marshalls Incorporated, 13
Marui Company Ltd., V; 62 (upd.)
Maruzen Co., Limited, 18
Mary Kay Inc., 9; 30 (upd.); 84 (upd.)
Matalan PLC, 49
Matsuzakaya Company Ltd., V; 64 (upd.)
Maurices Inc., 95
Maus Frères SA, 48
The Maxim Group, 25
The May Department Stores Company, V; 19 (upd.); 46 (upd.)
Mayor's Jewelers, Inc., 41
Mazel Stores, Inc., 29
McCoy Corporation, 58
McGrath RentCorp, 91
McJunkin Corporation, 63
McKesson Corporation, 47 (upd.)
McLane Company, Inc., 13
McNaughton Apparel Group, Inc., 92 (upd.)
MCSi, Inc., 41
Media Arts Group, Inc., 42
Meier & Frank Co., 23
Meijer Incorporated, 27 (upd.)
Melville Corporation, V
The Men's Wearhouse, Inc., 17; 48 (upd.)
Menard, Inc., 34
Mercantile Stores Company, Inc., V; 19 (upd.)
Mercury Drug Corporation, 70
Merry-Go-Round Enterprises, Inc., 8
Mervyn's California, 10; 39 (upd.)
Metal Management, Inc., 92
Metro AG, 50
Michael C. Fina Co., Inc., 52
Michaels Stores, Inc., 17; 71 (upd.)
Michigan Sporting Goods Distributors, Inc., 72
Micro Warehouse, Inc., 16
MicroAge, Inc., 16
Migros-Genossenschafts-Bund, 68
Milton CAT, Inc., 86
Mitsukoshi Ltd., V; 56 (upd.)
MNS, Ltd., 65
Monoprix S.A., 86
Monrovia Nursery Company, 70
Monsoon plc, 39
Montgomery Ward & Co., Incorporated, V; 20 (upd.)
Moore-Handley, Inc., 39
Morrow Equipment Co. L.L.C., 87
Morse Shoe Inc., 13
Moss Bros Group plc, 51
Mothercare plc, 78 (upd.)
Mothers Work, Inc., 18
Moto Photo, Inc., 45
Mr. Bricolage S.A., 37
MSC Industrial Direct Co., Inc., 71
MTS Inc., 37
Mulberry Group PLC, 71
Musicland Stores Corporation, 9; 38 (upd.)
MWI Veterinary Supply, Inc., 80
Nagasakiya Co., Ltd., V; 69 (upd.)
Nash Finch Company, 65 (upd.)
National Educational Music Co. Ltd., 47
National Home Centers, Inc., 44

National Intergroup, Inc., V
National Record Mart, Inc., 29
National Wine & Spirits, Inc., 49
Natura Cosméticos S.A., 75
Natural Wonders Inc., 14
Navy Exchange Service Command, 31
Nebraska Book Company, Inc., 65
Neff Corp., 32
NeighborCare, Inc., 67 (upd.)
The Neiman Marcus Group, Inc., 12; 49 (upd.)
Netflix, Inc., 58
New Look Group plc, 35
Next plc, 29
Nichii Co., Ltd., V
NIKE, Inc., 36 (upd.)
Nine West Group Inc., 11
99;ct Only Stores, 25
Nocibé SA, 54
Noland Company, 35
Noodle Kidoodle, 16
Nordstrom, Inc., V; 18 (upd.); 67 (upd.)
Norelco Consumer Products Co., 26
Norm Thompson Outfitters, Inc., 47
North Pacific Group, Inc., 61
The North West Company, Inc., 12
Norton McNaughton, Inc., 27
Nu Skin Enterprises, Inc., 27; 76 (upd.)
Oakley, Inc., 49 (upd.)
Office Depot, Inc., 8; 23 (upd.); 65 (upd.)
OfficeMax, Inc., 15; 43 (upd.)
Olan Mills, Inc., 62
Old America Stores, Inc., 17
Old Navy, Inc., 70
One Price Clothing Stores, Inc., 20
O'Neal Steel, Inc., 95
The Oppenheimer Group, 76
Orchard Supply Hardware Stores Corporation, 17
Organización Soriana, S.A. de C.V., 35
Orgill, Inc., 99
The Orvis Company, Inc., 28
OshKosh B'Gosh, Inc., 42 (upd.)
Oshman's Sporting Goods, Inc., 17
Ottakar's plc, 64
Otto Versand (GmbH & Co.), V; 15 (upd.); 34 (upd.)
Overstock.com, Inc., 75
Owens & Minor, Inc., 16; 68 (upd.)
P.C. Richard & Son Corp., 23
Pamida Holdings Corporation, 15
The Pampered Chef, Ltd., 18; 78 (upd.)
The Pantry, Inc., 36
The Paradies Shops, Inc., 88
Parisian, Inc., 14
Party City Corporation, 54
Paul Harris Stores, Inc., 18
Pay 'N Pak Stores, Inc., 9
Payless Cashways, Inc., 11; 44 (upd.)
Payless ShoeSource, Inc., 18; 69 (upd.)
PCA International, Inc., 62
PDQ Food Stores, Inc., 79
Pearle Vision, Inc., 13
Peebles Inc., 16; 43 (upd.)
Peet's Coffee & Tea, Inc., 38
Penzeys Spices, Inc., 79

The Pep Boys—Manny, Moe & Jack, 11; 36 (upd.); 81 (upd.)
Petco Animal Supplies, Inc., 29; 74 (upd.)
Petit Bateau, 95
PetMed Express, Inc., 81
Petrie Stores Corporation, 8
PETsMART, Inc., 14; 41 (upd.)
PFSweb, Inc., 73
Phar-Mor Inc., 12
Phones 4u Ltd., 85
Photo-Me International Plc, 83
Pick 'n Pay Stores Ltd., 82
Pier 1 Imports, Inc., 12; 34 (upd.); 95 (upd.)
Piercing Pagoda, Inc., 29
Pilot Corporation, 49
Pinault-Printemps Redoute S.A., 19 (upd.)
Pitman Company, 58
Polartec LLC, 98 (upd.)
Pomeroy Computer Resources, Inc., 33
Powell's Books, Inc., 40
PPR S.A., 74 (upd.)
Praxis Bookstore Group LLC, 90
The Price Company, V
PriceCostco, Inc., 14
PriceSmart, Inc., 71
Pro-Build Holdings Inc., 95 (upd.)
Proffitt's, Inc., 19
Provell Inc., 58 (upd.)
Provigo Inc., 51 (upd.)
Publishers Clearing House, 64 (upd.)
Puig Beauty and Fashion Group S.L., 60
Purina Mills, Inc., 32
Quelle Group, V
QuikTrip Corporation, 36
Quiksilver, Inc., 79 (upd.)
Quill Corporation, 28
QVC Inc., 58 (upd.)
R.C. Willey Home Furnishings, 72
R.H. Macy & Co., Inc., V; 8 (upd.); 30 (upd.)
RadioShack Corporation, 36 (upd.)
Rag Shops, Inc., 30
Raley's Inc., 14; 58 (upd.)
Rallye SA, 54
Rapala-Normark Group, Ltd., 30
Ratner Companies, 72
RDO Equipment Company, 33
Reckitt Benckiser plc, II; 42 (upd.); 91 (upd.)
Recoton Corp., 15
Recreational Equipment, Inc., 18; 71 (upd.)
Red McCombs Automotive Group, 91
Red Wing Shoe Company, Inc., 9; 30 (upd.); 83 (upd.)
Redlon & Johnson, Inc., 97
Reeds Jewelers, Inc., 22
Rejuvenation, Inc., 91
Reliance Steel & Aluminum Company, 70 (upd.)
Rent-A-Center, Inc., 45
Rent-Way, Inc., 33; 75 (upd.)
Restoration Hardware, Inc., 30; 96 (upd.)
Retail Ventures, Inc., 82 (upd.)
Revco D.S., Inc., V
REX Stores Corp., 10
Rhodes Inc., 23

Richton International Corporation, 39
Riklis Family Corp., 9
Rinascente S.p.A., 71
Rite Aid Corporation, V; 19 (upd.); 63 (upd.)
Ritz Camera Centers, 34
RM Auctions, Inc., 88
Roberds Inc., 19
Rocky Shoes & Boots, Inc., 26
Rogers Communications Inc., 30 (upd.)
RONA, Inc., 73
Ronco Corporation, 15; 80 (upd.)
Rooms To Go Inc., 28
Roots Canada Ltd., 42
Rose's Stores, Inc., 13
Ross Stores, Inc., 17; 43 (upd.)
Rosy Blue N.V., 84
Roundy's Inc., 14
Rush Enterprises, Inc., 64
Ryoshoku Ltd., 72
S&K Famous Brands, Inc., 23
S.A.C.I. Falabella, 69
Saks Inc., 24; 41 (upd.)
Sally Beauty Company, Inc., 60
Sam Ash Music Corporation, 30
Sam Levin Inc., 80
Sam's Club, 40
Samuels Jewelers Incorporated, 30
Sanborn Hermanos, S.A., 20
SanomaWSOY Corporation, 51
Savers, Inc., 99 (upd.)
Scheels All Sports Inc., 63
Schmitt Music Company, 40
Schneiderman's Furniture Inc., 28
School Specialty, Inc., 68
Schottenstein Stores Corp., 14
Schultz Sav-O Stores, Inc., 31
The Score Board, Inc., 19
Scotty's, Inc., 22
The Scoular Company, 77
SCP Pool Corporation, 39
Seaman Furniture Company, Inc., 32
Sean John Clothing, Inc., 70
Sears plc, V
Sears Roebuck de México, S.A. de C.V., 20
Sears, Roebuck and Co., V; 18 (upd.); 56 (upd.)
SED International Holdings, Inc., 43
Seibu Department Stores, Ltd., V; 42 (upd.)
Seigle's Home and Building Centers, Inc., 41
The Seiyu, Ltd., V; 36 (upd.)
Selfridges Plc, 34
Service Merchandise Company, Inc., V; 19 (upd.)
7-Eleven, Inc., 32 (upd.)
Seventh Generation, Inc., 73
Shaklee Corporation, 12
The Sharper Image Corporation, 10; 62 (upd.)
Sheetz, Inc., 85
Sheplers, Inc., 96
The Sherwin-Williams Company, 89 (upd.)
Shoe Carnival Inc., 14; 72 (upd.)
ShopKo Stores Inc., 21; 58 (upd.)

Shoppers Drug Mart Corporation, 49
Shoppers Food Warehouse Corporation, 66
SIG plc, 71
Signet Group PLC, 61
skinnyCorp, LLC, 97
SkyMall, Inc., 26
Sleepy's Inc., 32
Smith & Hawken, Ltd., 68
Snapfish, 83
Solo Serve Corporation, 28
Sophus Berendsen A/S, 49
Sound Advice, Inc., 41
Source Interlink Companies, Inc., 75
Southern States Cooperative Incorporated, 36
Spartan Stores Inc., 66 (upd.)
Spec's Music, Inc., 19
Spector Photo Group N.V., 82
Spiegel, Inc., 10; 27 (upd.)
Sport Chalet, Inc., 16
Sport Supply Group, Inc., 23
Sportmart, Inc., 15
Sports & Recreation, Inc., 17
The Sports Authority, Inc., 16; 43 (upd.)
The Sportsman's Guide, Inc., 36
Stage Stores, Inc., 24; 82 (upd.)
Stanhome Inc., 15
Staple Cotton Cooperative Association (Staplcotn), 86
Staples, Inc., 10; 55 (upd.)
Starbucks Corporation, 13; 34 (upd.); 77 (upd.)
Starcraft Corporation, 30
Stefanel SpA, 63
Stein Mart Inc., 19; 72 (upd.)
Steve & Barry's LLC, 88
Stewart's Shops Corporation, 80
Stinnes AG, 8
The Stop & Shop Companies, Inc., 24 (upd.)
Storehouse PLC, 16
Strauss Discount Auto, 56
Stride Rite Corporation, 8
The Strober Organization, Inc., 82
Strouds, Inc., 33
Stuller Settings, Inc., 35
Successories, Inc., 30
Sun Television & Appliances Inc., 10
Sunglass Hut International, Inc., 21; 74 (upd.)
Superdrug Stores PLC, 95
Supreme International Corporation, 27
Sutherland Lumber Company, L.P., 99
Swarovski International Holding AG, 40
The Swiss Colony, Inc., 97
Syms Corporation, 29; 74 (upd.)
Systemax, Inc., 52
Takashimaya Company, Limited, V; 47 (upd.)
The Talbots, Inc., 11; 31 (upd.); 88 (upd.)
Target Corporation, 61 (upd.)
Target Stores, 10; 27 (upd.)
Tati SA, 25
Tattered Cover Book Store, 43
Tech Data Corporation, 10; 74 (upd.)
Tengelmann Group, 27

Tesco plc, 24 (upd.); 68 (upd.)
Things Remembered, Inc., 84
Thomsen Greenhouses and Garden
    Center, Incorporated, 65
Thrifty PayLess, Inc., 12
Tiffany & Co., 14; 78 (upd.)
The Timberland Company, 54 (upd.)
The TJX Companies, Inc., V; 19 (upd.);
    57 (upd.)
Today's Man, Inc., 20
Tokyu Department Store Co., Ltd., V; 32
    (upd.)
Too, Inc., 61
Topco Associates LLC, 60
Tops Appliance City, Inc., 17
Total Fina Elf S.A., 50 (upd.)
Toys 'R' Us, Inc., V; 18 (upd.); 57 (upd.)
Tractor Supply Company, 57
Trans World Entertainment Corporation,
    68 (upd.)
Travis Boats & Motors, Inc., 37
Travis Perkins plc, 34
Trend-Lines, Inc., 22
True Value Company, 74 (upd.)
TruServ Corporation, 24
Tuesday Morning Corporation, 18; 70
    (upd.)
Tupperware Corporation, 28; 78 (upd.)
TVI, Inc., 15
Tweeter Home Entertainment Group,
    Inc., 30
U.S. Vision, Inc., 66
Ulta Salon, Cosmetics & Fragrance, Inc.,
    93
Ultimate Electronics, Inc., 18; 69 (upd.)
Ultramar Diamond Shamrock
    Corporation, 31 (upd.)
Uni-Marts, Inc., 17
United Rentals, Inc., 34
The United States Shoe Corporation, V
United Stationers Inc., 14
Universal International, Inc., 25
Uny Co., Ltd., V; 49 (upd.)
Urban Outfitters, Inc., 14; 74 (upd.)
Uwajimaya, Inc., 60
Vallen Corporation, 45
Valley Media Inc., 35
Value City Department Stores, Inc., 38
Value Merchants Inc., 13
ValueVision International, Inc., 22
Vans, Inc., 47 (upd.)
Variety Wholesalers, Inc., 73
VBA - Bloemenveiling Aalsmeer, 88
Venator Group Inc., 35 (upd.)
Vendex International N.V., 13
Venture Stores Inc., 12
The Vermont Country Store, 93
The Vermont Teddy Bear Co., Inc., 36
VF Corporation, 54 (upd.)
Viewpoint International, Inc., 66
Viking Office Products, Inc., 10
Vivarte SA, 54 (upd.)
Volcom, Inc., 77
Von Maur Inc., 64
Vorwerk & Co., 27
W. Atlee Burpee & Co., 27
W.B. Mason Company, 98
W.W. Grainger, Inc., V

Waban Inc., 13
Wacoal Corp., 25
Wal-Mart de Mexico, S.A. de C.V., 35
    (upd.)
Wal-Mart Stores, Inc., V; 8 (upd.); 26
    (upd.); 63 (upd.)
Waldenbooks, 17; 86 (upd.)
Walgreen Co., V; 20 (upd.); 65 (upd.)
Wall Drug Store, Inc., 40
Warners' Stellian Inc., 67
Weiner's Stores, Inc., 33
West Marine, Inc., 17; 90 (upd.)
Western Beef, Inc., 22
The Wet Seal, Inc., 18; 70 (upd.)
Weyco Group, Incorporated, 32
WH Smith PLC, V; 42 (upd.)
The White House, Inc., 60
Whitehall Jewellers, Inc., 82 (upd.)
Whole Foods Market, Inc., 20
Wickes Inc., V; 25 (upd.)
Wilco Farm Stores, 93
Wilkinson Hardware Stores Ltd., 80
Williams Scotsman, Inc., 65
Williams-Sonoma, Inc., 17; 44 (upd.)
Wilsons The Leather Experts Inc., 21; 58
    (upd.)
Wilton Products, Inc., 97
Windstream Corporation, 83
Winmark Corporation, 74
Wolohan Lumber Co., 19
Wolverine World Wide, Inc., 59 (upd.)
Woolworth Corporation, V; 20 (upd.)
Woolworths Group plc, 83
World Duty Free Americas, Inc., 29
    (upd.)
Yamada Denki Co., Ltd., 85
The Yankee Candle Company, Inc., 37
Young's Market Company, LLC, 32
Younkers, 76 (upd.)
Younkers, Inc., 19
Zale Corporation, 16; 40 (upd.); 91
    (upd.)
Zany Brainy, Inc., 31
Zappos.com, Inc., 73
Zara International, Inc., 83
Ziebart International Corporation, 30
Zion's Cooperative Mercantile Institution,
    33
Zipcar, Inc., 92
Zones, Inc., 67
Zumiez, Inc., 77

Rubber & Tires
Aeroquip Corporation, 16
Bandag, Inc., 19
The BFGoodrich Company, V
Bridgestone Corporation, V; 21 (upd.); 59
    (upd.)
Canadian Tire Corporation, Limited, 71
    (upd.)
Carlisle Companies Incorporated, 8
Compagnie Générale des Établissements
    Michelin, V; 42 (upd.)
Continental AG, V; 56 (upd.)
Continental General Tire Corp., 23
Cooper Tire & Rubber Company, 8; 23
    (upd.)
Day International, Inc., 84

Elementis plc, 40 (upd.)
General Tire, Inc., 8
The Goodyear Tire & Rubber Company,
    V; 20 (upd.); 75 (upd.)
The Kelly-Springfield Tire Company, 8
Les Schwab Tire Centers, 50
Myers Industries, Inc., 19; 96 (upd.)
Pirelli S.p.A., V; 15 (upd.)
Safeskin Corporation, 18
Sumitomo Rubber Industries, Ltd., V
Trelleborg AB, 93
Tillotson Corp., 15
Treadco, Inc., 19
Ube Industries, Ltd., 38 (upd.)
The Yokohama Rubber Company,
    Limited, V; 19 (upd.); 91 (upd.)

Telecommunications
A.H. Belo Corporation, 30 (upd.)
Abertis Infraestructuras, S.A., 65
Abril S.A., 95
Acme-Cleveland Corp., 13
ADC Telecommunications, Inc., 10; 89
    (upd.)
Adelphia Communications Corporation,
    17; 52 (upd.)
Adtran Inc., 22
Advanced Fibre Communications, Inc., 63
AEI Music Network Inc., 35
AirTouch Communications, 11
Alaska Communications Systems Group,
    Inc., 89
Alcatel S.A., 36 (upd.)
Alliance Atlantis Communications Inc., 39
ALLTEL Corporation, 6; 46 (upd.)
América Móvil, S.A. de C.V., 80
American Tower Corporation, 33
Ameritech Corporation, V; 18 (upd.)
Amstrad plc, 48 (upd.)
AO VimpelCom, 48
AOL Time Warner Inc., 57 (upd.)
Arch Wireless, Inc., 39
ARD, 41
ARINC Inc., 98
ARRIS Group, Inc., 89
Ascom AG, 9
Aspect Telecommunications Corporation,
    22
Asurion Corporation, 83
AT&T Bell Laboratories, Inc., 13
AT&T Corporation, V; 29 (upd.); 68
    (upd.)
AT&T Wireless Services, Inc., 54 (upd.)
BCE Inc., V; 44 (upd.)
Beasley Broadcast Group, Inc., 51
Belgacom, 6
Bell Atlantic Corporation, V; 25 (upd.)
Bell Canada, 6
BellSouth Corporation, V; 29 (upd.)
Belo Corporation, 98 (upd.)
Bertelsmann A.G., IV; 15 (upd.); 43
    (upd.); 91 (upd.)
BET Holdings, Inc., 18
Bharti Tele-Ventures Limited, 75
BHC Communications, Inc., 26
Blackfoot Telecommunications Group, 60
Bonneville International Corporation, 29
Bouygues S.A., I; 24 (upd.); 97 (upd.)

Brasil Telecom Participaçoes S.A., 57
Brightpoint, Inc., 18
Brite Voice Systems, Inc., 20
British Broadcasting Corporation Ltd., 7;
  21 (upd.); 89 (upd.)
British Columbia Telephone Company, 6
British Telecommunications plc, V; 15
  (upd.)
Broadwing Corporation, 70
BT Group plc, 49 (upd.)
C-COR.net Corp., 38
Cable & Wireless HKT, 30 (upd.)
Cable and Wireless plc, V; 25 (upd.)
Cablevision Systems Corporation, 30
  (upd.)
CalAmp Corp., 87
The Canadian Broadcasting Corporation
  (CBC), 37
Canal Plus, 10; 34 (upd.)
CanWest Global Communications
  Corporation, 35
Capital Radio plc, 35
Carlton Communications PLC, 15; 50
  (upd.)
Carolina Telephone and Telegraph
  Company, 10
The Carphone Warehouse Group PLC, 83
Carrier Access Corporation, 44
CBS Corporation, 28 (upd.)
CBS Television Network, 66 (upd.)
Centel Corporation, 6
Centennial Communications Corporation,
  39
Central European Media Enterprises Ltd.,
  61
Century Communications Corp., 10
Century Telephone Enterprises, Inc., 9; 54
  (upd.)
Cesky Telecom, a.s., 64
Chancellor Media Corporation, 24
Channel Four Television Corporation, 93
Charter Communications, Inc., 33
Chello Zone Ltd., 93
China Netcom Group Corporation (Hong
  Kong) Limited, 73
China Telecom, 50
Chris-Craft Corporation, 9, 31 (upd.); 80
  (upd.)
The Christian Broadcasting Network, Inc.,
  52
Chrysalis Group plc, 40
Chugach Alaska Corporation, 60
CIENA Corporation, 54
Cincinnati Bell, Inc., 6
Citadel Communications Corporation, 35
Citizens Communications Company, 79
  (upd.)
Clear Channel Communications, Inc., 23
Clearwire, Inc., 69
Cogent Communications Group, Inc., 55
COLT Telecom Group plc, 41
Comcast Corporation, 24 (upd.)
Comdial Corporation, 21
Commonwealth Telephone Enterprises,
  Inc., 25
CommScope, Inc., 77
Comsat Corporation, 23
Comtech Telecommunications Corp., 75

Comverse Technology, Inc., 15; 43 (upd.)
Corning Inc., III; 44 (upd.); 90 (upd.)
Corporation for Public Broadcasting, 14;
  89 (upd.)
Cox Radio, Inc., 89
Craftmade International, Inc., 44
Cumulus Media Inc., 37
DDI Corporation, 7
Deutsche Telekom AG, V; 48 (upd.)
Dialogic Corporation, 18
Directorate General of
  Telecommunications, 7
DIRECTV, Inc., 38; 75 (upd.)
Discovery Communications, Inc., 42
Dobson Communications Corporation, 63
DSC Communications Corporation, 12
EchoStar Communications Corporation,
  35
ECI Telecom Ltd., 18
Egmont Group, 93
eircom plc, 31 (upd.)
Electric Lightwave, Inc., 37
Electromagnetic Sciences Inc., 21
EMBARQ Corporation, 83
Emmis Communications Corporation, 47
Empresas Públicas de Medellín S.A.E.S.P.,
  91
Energis plc, 47
Entercom Communications Corporation,
  58
Entravision Communications Corporation,
  41
Equant N.V., 52
Eschelon Telecom, Inc., 72
ESPN, Inc., 56
Eternal Word Television Network, Inc., 57
EXCEL Communications Inc., 18
Executone Information Systems, Inc., 13
Expand SA, 48
Facebook, Inc., 90
FASTWEB S.p.A., 83
Fisher Communications, Inc., 99
4Kids Entertainment Inc., 59
Fox Family Worldwide, Inc., 24
France Telecom S.A., V; 21 (upd.); 99
  (upd.)
Frontier Corp., 16
Fuji Television Network Inc., 91
Gannett Co., Inc., 30 (upd.)
Garmin Ltd., 60
General DataComm Industries, Inc., 14
Geotek Communications Inc., 21
Getty Images, Inc., 31
Global Crossing Ltd., 32
Globo Comunicação e Participações S.A.,
  80
Glu Mobile Inc., 95
Golden Telecom, Inc., 59
Granite Broadcasting Corporation, 42
Gray Communications Systems, Inc., 24
Groupe Vidéotron Ltée., 20
Grupo Televisa, S.A., 18; 54 (upd.)
GTE Corporation, V; 15 (upd.)
Guthy-Renker Corporation, 32
GWR Group plc, 39
Harmonic Inc., 43
Havas, SA, 10
HickoryTech Corporation, 92

Hispanic Broadcasting Corporation, 35
Hong Kong Telecommunications Ltd., 6
Huawei Technologies Company Ltd., 87
Hubbard Broadcasting Inc., 24; 79 (upd.)
Hughes Electronics Corporation, 25
Hungarian Telephone and Cable Corp.,
  75
IDB Communications Group, Inc., 11
IDT Corporation, 34; 99 (upd.)
Illinois Bell Telephone Company, 14
Indiana Bell Telephone Company,
  Incorporated, 14
PT Indosat Tbk, 93
Infineon Technologies AG, 50
Infinity Broadcasting Corporation, 11
InfoSonics Corporation, 81
InterDigital Communications
  Corporation, 61
Iowa Telecommunications Services, Inc.,
  85
IXC Communications, Inc., 29
Jacor Communications, Inc., 23
Jones Intercable, Inc., 21
j2 Global Communications, Inc., 75
Koninklijke PTT Nederland NV, V
Landmark Communications, Inc., 55
  (upd.)
LCC International, Inc., 84
LCI International, Inc., 16
LDDS-Metro Communications, Inc., 8
Leap Wireless International, Inc., 69
Level 3 Communications, Inc., 67
LIN Broadcasting Corp., 9
Lincoln Telephone & Telegraph Company,
  14
LodgeNet Entertainment Corporation, 28
Loral Space & Communications Ltd., 54
  (upd.)
MacNeil/Lehrer Productions, 87
Magyar Telekom Rt. 78
Manitoba Telecom Services, Inc., 61
Mannesmann AG, 38
MasTec, Inc., 19; 55 (upd.)
McCaw Cellular Communications, Inc., 6
MCI WorldCom, Inc., V; 27 (upd.)
McLeodUSA Incorporated, 32
Mediacom Communications Corporation,
  69
Mercury Communications, Ltd., 7
Metrocall, Inc., 41
Metromedia Companies, 14
Métropole Télévision, 33
Métropole Télévision S.A., 76 (upd.)
MFS Communications Company, Inc., 11
Michigan Bell Telephone Co., 14
MIH Limited, 31
MITRE Corporation, 26
Mobile Telecommunications Technologies
  Corp., 18
Mobile TeleSystems OJSC, 59
Modern Times Group AB, 36
The Montana Power Company, 44 (upd.)
Motorola, Inc., II; 11 (upd.); 34 (upd.);
  93 (upd.)
Multimedia, Inc., 11
National Broadcasting Company, Inc., 28
  (upd.)
National Grid USA, 51 (upd.)

National Weather Service, 91
NCR Corporation, III; 6 (upd.); 30
    (upd.); 90 (upd.)
NetCom Systems AB, 26
NeuStar, Inc., 81
Nevada Bell Telephone Company, 14
New Valley Corporation, 17
Nexans SA, 54
Nexstar Broadcasting Group, Inc., 73
Nextel Communications, Inc., 27 (upd.)
Nippon Telegraph and Telephone
    Corporation, V; 51 (upd.)
Nokia Corporation, 77 (upd.)
Norstan, Inc., 16
Nortel Networks Corporation, 36 (upd.)
Northern Telecom Limited, V
NTL Inc., 65
NTN Buzztime, Inc., 86
NYNEX Corporation, V
Octel Messaging, 14; 41 (upd.)
Ohio Bell Telephone Company, 14
Olivetti S.p.A., 34 (upd.)
Orange S.A., 84
Österreichische Post- und
    Telegraphenverwaltung, V
Pacific Internet Limited, 87
Pacific Telecom, Inc., 6
Pacific Telesis Group, V
Paging Network Inc., 11
PanAmSat Corporation, 46
Paxson Communications Corporation, 33
The Phoenix Media/Communications
    Group, 91
PictureTel Corp., 10; 27 (upd.)
Portugal Telecom SGPS S.A., 69
Posti- ja Telelaitos, 6
Price Communications Corporation, 42
ProSiebenSat.1 Media AG, 54
Publishing and Broadcasting Limited, 54
Qatar Telecom QSA, 87
QUALCOMM Incorporated, 20; 47
    (upd.)
QVC Network Inc., 9
Qwest Communications International,
    Inc., 37
RCN Corporation, 70
Regent Communications, Inc., 87
Research in Motion Ltd., 54
RMH Teleservices, Inc., 42
Rochester Telephone Corporation, 6
Rogers Communications Inc., 30 (upd.)
Rostelecom Joint Stock Co., 99
Royal KPN N.V., 30
Rural Cellular Corporation, 43
Saga Communications, Inc., 27
Salem Communications Corporation, 97
Sawtek Inc., 43 (upd.)
SBC Communications Inc., 32 (upd.)
Schweizerische Post-, Telefon- und
    Telegrafen-Betriebe, V
Scientific-Atlanta, Inc., 6; 45 (upd.)
Seat Pagine Gialle S.p.A., 47
Securicor Plc, 45
Shenandoah Telecommunications
    Company, 89
Sinclair Broadcast Group, Inc., 25
Sirius Satellite Radio, Inc., 69
Sirti S.p.A., 76

Società Finanziaria Telefonica per Azioni,
    V
Softbank Corporation, 77 (upd.)
Sonera Corporation, 50
Southern New England
    Telecommunications Corporation, 6
Southwestern Bell Corporation, V
Spanish Broadcasting System, Inc., 41
Spelling Entertainment, 35 (upd.)
Sprint Corporation, 9; 46 (upd.)
StarHub Ltd., 77
StrataCom, Inc., 16
Swedish Telecom, V
Swisscom AG, 58
Sycamore Networks, Inc., 45
Syniverse Holdings Inc., 97
SynOptics Communications, Inc., 10
T-Netix, Inc., 46
Talk America Holdings, Inc., 70
TDC A/S, 63
Tekelec, 83
Telcordia Technologies, Inc., 59
Tele Norte Leste Participações S.A., 80
Telecom Argentina S.A., 63
Telecom Australia, 6
Telecom Corporation of New Zealand
    Limited, 54
Telecom Eireann, 7
Telecom Italia Mobile S.p.A., 63
Telecom Italia S.p.A., 43
Telefonaktiebolaget LM Ericsson, V; 46
    (upd.)
Telefónica de Argentina S.A., 61
Telefónica S.A., V; 46 (upd.)
Telefonos de Mexico S.A. de C.V., 14; 63
    (upd.)
Telekom Malaysia Bhd, 76
Telekomunikacja Polska SA, 50
Telenor ASA, 69
Telephone and Data Systems, Inc., 9
Télévision Française 1, 23
TeliaSonera AB, 57 (upd.)
Tellabs, Inc., 11; 40 (upd.)
Telstra Corporation Limited, 50
Terremark Worldwide, Inc., 99
Thomas Crosbie Holdings Limited, 81
Tiscali SpA, 48
The Titan Corporation, 36
Tollgrade Communications, Inc., 44
TV Azteca, S.A. de C.V., 39
U.S. Satellite Broadcasting Company, Inc.,
    20
U S West, Inc., V; 25 (upd.)
U.S. Cellular Corporation, 9; 31 (upd.);
    88 (upd.)
UFA TV & Film Produktion GmbH, 80
United Pan-Europe Communications NV,
    47
United Telecommunications, Inc., V
United Video Satellite Group, 18
Univision Communications Inc., 24; 83
    (upd.)
USA Interactive, Inc., 47 (upd.)
USA Mobility Inc., 97 (upd.)
UTStarcom, Inc., 77
Verizon Communications Inc. 43 (upd.);
    78 (upd.)
ViaSat, Inc., 54

Vivendi Universal S.A., 46 (upd.)
Vodafone Group Plc, 11; 36 (upd.); 75
    (upd.)
Vonage Holdings Corp., 81
The Walt Disney Company, II; 6 (upd.);
    30 (upd.); 63 (upd.)
Wanadoo S.A., 75
Watkins-Johnson Company, 15
The Weather Channel Companies, 52
West Corporation, 42
Western Union Financial Services, Inc., 54
Western Wireless Corporation, 36
Westwood One, Inc., 23
Williams Communications Group, Inc.,
    34
The Williams Companies, Inc., 31 (upd.)
Wipro Limited, 43
Wisconsin Bell, Inc., 14
Working Assets Funding Service, 43
Worldwide Pants Inc., 97
XM Satellite Radio Holdings, Inc., 69
Young Broadcasting Inc., 40
Zed Group, 93
Zoom Technologies, Inc., 53 (upd.)

Textiles & Apparel

Abercrombie & Fitch Company, 35
    (upd.); 75 (upd.)
Adams Childrenswear Ltd., 95
adidas Group AG, 14; 33 (upd.); 75
    (upd.)
Adolfo Dominguez S.A., 72
Aéropostale, Inc., 89
Alba-Waldensian, Inc., 30
Albany International Corp., 8
Alexandra plc, 88
Algo Group Inc., 24
Alpargatas S.A.I.C., 87
American & Efird, Inc., 82
American Apparel, Inc., 90
American Safety Razor Company, 20
Amoskeag Company, 8
Angelica Corporation, 15; 43 (upd.)
AR Accessories Group, Inc., 23
Aris Industries, Inc., 16
ASICS Corporation, 57
AstenJohnson Inc., 90
The Athlete's Foot Brands LLC, 84
Authentic Fitness Corporation, 20; 51
    (upd.)
Babolat VS, S.A., 97
Banana Republic Inc., 25
Bardwil Industries Inc., 98
Bata Ltd., 62
Benetton Group S.p.A., 10; 67 (upd.)
Bill Blass Ltd., 32
Birkenstock Footprint Sandals, Inc., 12
Blair Corporation, 25
Body Glove International LLC, 88
Boss Holdings, Inc., 97
Brazos Sportswear, Inc., 23
Brioni Roman Style S.p.A., 67
Brooks Brothers Inc., 22
Brooks Sports Inc., 32
Brown Group, Inc., V; 20 (upd.)
Brunschwig & Fils Inc., 96
Bugle Boy Industries, Inc., 18

Burberry Group plc, 17; 41 (upd.); 92 (upd.)

Burke Mills, Inc., 66

Burlington Industries, Inc., V; 17 (upd.)

Calcot Ltd., 33

Calvin Klein, Inc., 22; 55 (upd.)

Candie's, Inc., 31

Canstar Sports Inc., 16

Capel Incorporated, 45

Capezio/Ballet Makers Inc., 62

Carhartt, Inc., 30, 77 (upd.)

Cato Corporation, 14

Chargeurs International, 6; 21 (upd.)

Charles Vögele Holding AG, 82

Charming Shoppes, Inc., 8

Cherokee Inc., 18

CHF Industries, Inc., 84

Chic by H.I.S, Inc., 20

Chico's FAS, Inc., 45

Chorus Line Corporation, 30

Christian Dior S.A., 19; 49 (upd.)

Christopher & Banks Corporation, 42

Cia Hering, 72

Cintas Corporation, 51 (upd.)

Citi Trends, Inc., 80

Claire's Stores, Inc., 17

Coach Leatherware, 10

Coats plc, V; 44 (upd.)

Collins & Aikman Corporation, 13

Columbia Sportswear Company, 19; 41 (upd.)

Companhia de Tecidos Norte de Minas - Coteminas, 77

Compañia Industrial de Parras, S.A. de C.V. (CIPSA), 84

Concord Fabrics, Inc., 16

Cone Mills LLC, 8; 67 (upd.)

Converse Inc., 31 (upd.)

Cotton Incorporated, 46

Courtaulds plc, V; 17 (upd.)

Crocs, Inc., 80

Croscill, Inc., 42

Crown Crafts, Inc., 16

Crystal Brands, Inc., 9

Culp, Inc., 29

Cygne Designs, Inc., 25

Damartex S.A., 98

Dan River Inc., 35; 86 (upd.)

Danskin, Inc., 12; 62 (upd.)

Deckers Outdoor Corporation, 22; 98 (upd.)

Delta and Pine Land Company, 59

Delta Woodside Industries, Inc., 8; 30 (upd.)

Designer Holdings Ltd., 20

The Dixie Group, Inc., 20; 80 (upd.)

Dogi International Fabrics S.A., 52

Dolce & Gabbana SpA, 62

Dominion Textile Inc., 12

Donna Karan International Inc., 15; 56 (upd.)

Donnkenny, Inc., 17

Dooney & Bourke Inc., 84

Duck Head Apparel Company, Inc., 42

Dunavant Enterprises, Inc., 54

Dyersburg Corporation, 21

Eastland Shoe Corporation, 82

Ecco Sko A/S, 62

The Echo Design Group, Inc., 68

Edison Brothers Stores, Inc., 9

Eileen Fisher Inc., 61

Ellen Tracy, Inc., 55

Ennis, Inc., 21; 97 (upd.)

Eram SA, 51

Ermenegildo Zegna SpA, 63

ESCADA AG, 71

Esprit de Corp., 8; 29 (upd.)

Etam Developpement SA, 44

Etienne Aigner AG, 52

Evans, Inc., 30

Fab Industries, Inc., 27

Fabri-Centers of America Inc., 16

Fat Face Ltd., 68

Fieldcrest Cannon, Inc., 9; 31 (upd.)

Fila Holding S.p.A., 20

Florsheim Shoe Group Inc., 31 (upd.)

Foot Petals L.L.C., 95

Fossil, Inc., 17

Frederick's of Hollywood Inc., 16

French Connection Group plc, 41

Fruit of the Loom, Inc., 8; 25 (upd.)

Fubu, 29

G&K Services, Inc., 16

G-III Apparel Group, Ltd., 22

Galey & Lord, Inc., 20; 66 (upd.)

Garan, Inc., 16; 64 (upd.)

Gerry Weber International AG, 63

Gianni Versace SpA, 22

Gildan Activewear, Inc., 81

Giorgio Armani S.p.A., 45

The Gitano Group, Inc. 8

Gottschalks, Inc., 18; 91 (upd.)

Grandoe Corporation, 98

Great White Shark Enterprises, Inc., 89

Greenwood Mills, Inc., 14

Groupe DMC (Dollfus Mieg & Cie), 27

Groupe Yves Saint Laurent, 23

Gucci Group N.V., 15; 50 (upd.)

Guess, Inc., 15; 68 (upd.)

Guilford Mills Inc., 8; 40 (upd.)

Gymboree Corporation, 15; 69 (upd.)

Haggar Corporation, 19; 78 (upd.)

Hampshire Group Ltd., 82

Hampton Industries, Inc., 20

Hanesbrands Inc., 98

Happy Kids Inc., 30

Hartmarx Corporation, 8

The Hartstone Group plc, 14

HCI Direct, Inc., 55

Healthtex, Inc., 17

Heelys, Inc., 87

Helly Hansen ASA, 25

Hermès S.A., 14

The Hockey Company, 34

Horween Leather Company, 83

Hugo Boss AG, 48

Hummel International A/S, 68

Hyde Athletic Industries, Inc., 17

I.C. Isaacs & Company, 31

Industria de Diseño Textil S.A., 64

Innovo Group Inc., 83

Interface, Inc., 8; 29 (upd.); 76 (upd.)

Irwin Toy Limited, 14

Items International Airwalk Inc., 17

J. Crew Group, Inc., 12; 34 (upd.); 88 (upd.)

JLM Couture, Inc., 64

Jockey International, Inc., 12; 34 (upd.); 77 (upd.)

The John David Group plc, 90

John Lewis Partnership plc, V; 42 (upd.); 99 (upd.)

Johnston Industries, Inc., 15

Jones Apparel Group, Inc., 39 (upd.)

Jordache Enterprises, Inc., 23

Jos. A. Bank Clothiers, Inc., 31

JPS Textile Group, Inc., 28

Juicy Couture, Inc., 80

K-Swiss, Inc., 33; 89 (upd.)

Karl Kani Infinity, Inc., 49

Kellwood Company, 8; 85 (upd.)

Kenneth Cole Productions, Inc., 25

Kinney Shoe Corp., 14

Klaus Steilmann GmbH & Co. KG, 53

Koret of California, Inc., 62

L.A. Gear, Inc., 8; 32 (upd.)

L.L. Bean, Inc., 10; 38 (upd.); 91 (upd.)

LaCrosse Footwear, Inc., 18; 61 (upd.)

Laura Ashley Holdings plc, 13

Lee Apparel Company, Inc., 8

The Leslie Fay Company, Inc., 8; 39 (upd.)

Levi Strauss & Co., V; 16 (upd.)

Liz Claiborne, Inc., 8

London Fog Industries, Inc., 29

Lost Arrow Inc., 22

Maidenform, Inc., 20; 59 (upd.)

Malden Mills Industries, Inc., 16

Maples Industries, Inc., 83

Mariella Burani Fashion Group, 92

Marzotto S.p.A., 20; 67 (upd.)

Maurices Inc., 95

Milliken & Co., V; 17 (upd.); 82 (upd.)

Miroglio SpA, 86

Mitsubishi Rayon Co., Ltd., V

Mossimo, Inc., 27; 96 (upd.)

Mothercare plc, 17; 78 (upd.)

Movie Star Inc., 17

Mulberry Group PLC, 71

Naf Naf SA, 44

Nautica Enterprises, Inc., 18; 44 (upd.)

New Balance Athletic Shoe, Inc., 25; 68 (upd.)

Nicole Miller, 98

NIKE, Inc., V; 8 (upd.); 75 (upd.)

Nine West Group, Inc., 39 (upd.)

Nitches, Inc., 53

The North Face Inc., 18; 78 (upd.)

Oakley, Inc., 18

Ormat Technologies, Inc., 87

OshKosh B'Gosh, Inc., 9; 42 (upd.)

Oxford Industries, Inc., 8; 84 (upd.)

Pacific Sunwear of California, Inc., 28

Peek & Cloppenburg KG, 46

Pendleton Woolen Mills, Inc., 42

Pentland Group plc, 20

Perry Ellis International, Inc., 41

Petit Bateau, 95

Phat Fashions LLC, 49

Phoenix Footwear Group, Inc., 70

Pillowtex Corporation, 19; 41 (upd.)

Plains Cotton Cooperative Association, 57

Pluma, Inc., 27

Polo/Ralph Lauren Corporation, 12; 62
(upd.)
Pomare Ltd., 88
Prada Holding B.V., 45
PremiumWear, Inc., 30
Puma AG Rudolf Dassler Sport, 35
Quaker Fabric Corp., 19
Quiksilver, Inc., 18; 79 (upd.)
R.G. Barry Corporation, 17; 44 (upd.)
Rack Room Shoes, Inc., 84
Raymond Ltd., 77
Recreational Equipment, Inc., 18
Red Wing Shoe Company, Inc., 9; 30
(upd.); 83 (upd.)
Reebok International Ltd., V; 9 (upd.); 26
(upd.)
Reliance Industries Ltd., 81
Renfro Corporation, 99
Rieter Holding AG, 42
Robert Talbott Inc., 88
Rocawear Apparel LLC, 77
Rollerblade, Inc., 15
Royal Ten Cate N.V., 68
Russell Corporation, 8; 30 (upd.); 82
(upd.)
Rusty, Inc., 95
St. John Knits, Inc., 14
Salant Corporation, 51 (upd.)
Salvatore Ferragamo Italia S.p.A., 62
Sao Paulo Alpargatas S.A., 75
Saucony Inc., 35; 86 (upd.)
Schott Brothers, Inc., 67
Seattle Pacific Industries, Inc., 92
Shaw Industries, Inc., 40 (upd.)
Shelby Williams Industries, Inc., 14
Shoe Pavilion, Inc., 84
Skechers U.S.A. Inc., 31; 88 (upd.)
skinnyCorp, LLC, 97
Sole Technology Inc., 93
Sophus Berendsen A/S, 49
Spanx, Inc., 89
Springs Global US, Inc., V; 19 (upd.); 90
(upd.)
Starter Corp., 12
Stefanel SpA, 63
Steiner Corporation (Alsco), 53
Steven Madden, Ltd., 37
Stirling Group plc, 62
Stoddard International plc, 72
Stone Manufacturing Company, 14; 43
(upd.)
Stride Rite Corporation, 8; 37 (upd.); 86
(upd.)
Stussy, Inc., 55
Sun Sportswear, Inc., 17
Superior Uniform Group, Inc., 30
Tag-It Pacific, Inc., 85
The Talbots, Inc., 11; 31 (upd.); 88
(upd.)
Tamfelt Oyj Abp, 62
Tarrant Apparel Group, 62
Ted Baker plc, 86
Teijin Limited, V
Thanulux Public Company Limited, 86
Thomaston Mills, Inc., 27
Tilley Endurables, Inc., 67
The Timberland Company, 13; 54 (upd.)

Tommy Hilfiger Corporation, 20; 53
(upd.)
Too, Inc., 61
Toray Industries, Inc., V
True Religion Apparel, Inc., 79
Tultex Corporation, 13
Under Armour Performance Apparel, 61
Unifi, Inc., 12; 62 (upd.)
United Merchants & Manufacturers, Inc.,
13
United Retail Group Inc., 33
Unitika Ltd., V
Umbro plc, 88
Vans, Inc., 16; 47 (upd.)
Varsity Spirit Corp., 15
VF Corporation, V; 17 (upd.); 54 (upd.)
Vicunha Têxtil S.A. 78
Volcom, Inc., 77
Walton Monroe Mills, Inc., 8
The Warnaco Group Inc., 12; 46 (upd.)
Wellco Enterprises, Inc., 84
Wellman, Inc., 8; 52 (upd.)
West Point-Pepperell, Inc., 8
WestPoint Stevens Inc., 16
Weyco Group, Incorporated, 32
Williamson-Dickie Manufacturing
Company, 14
Wolverine World Wide, Inc., 16; 59
(upd.)
Woolrich Inc., 62
Zara International, Inc., 83

Tobacco

Altadis S.A., 72 (upd.)
American Brands, Inc., V
B.A.T. Industries PLC, 22 (upd.)
British American Tobacco PLC, 50 (upd.)
Brooke Group Ltd., 15
Brown & Williamson Tobacco
Corporation, 14; 33 (upd.)
Culbro Corporation, 15
Dibrell Brothers, Incorporated, 12
DIMON Inc., 27
800-JR Cigar, Inc., 27
Gallaher Group Plc, V; 19 (upd.); 49
(upd.)
General Cigar Holdings, Inc., 66 (upd.)
Holt's Cigar Holdings, Inc., 42
House of Prince A/S, 80
Imasco Limited, V
Imperial Tobacco Group PLC, 50
Japan Tobacco Incorporated, V
KT&G Corporation, 62
Nobleza Piccardo SAICF, 64
North Atlantic Trading Company Inc., 65
Philip Morris Companies Inc., V; 18
(upd.)
R.J. Reynolds Tobacco Holdings, Inc., 30
(upd.)
RJR Nabisco Holdings Corp., V
Rothmans UK Holdings Limited, V; 19
(upd.)
Seita, 23
Souza Cruz S.A., 65
Standard Commercial Corporation, 13; 62
(upd.)
Swedish Match AB, 12; 39 (upd.); 92
(upd.)

Swisher International Group Inc., 23
Tabacalera, S.A., V; 17 (upd.)
Taiwan Tobacco & Liquor Corporation,
75
Universal Corporation, V; 48 (upd.)
UST Inc., 9; 50 (upd.)
Vector Group Ltd., 35 (upd.)

Transport Services

Abertis Infraestructuras, S.A., 65
The Adams Express Company, 86
Aegean Marine Petroleum Network Inc.,
89
Aéroports de Paris, 33
Air Express International Corporation, 13
Air Partner PLC, 93
Air T, Inc., 86
Airborne Freight Corporation, 6; 34
(upd.)
Alamo Rent A Car, Inc., 6; 24 (upd.); 84
(upd.)
Alaska Railroad Corporation, 60
Alexander & Baldwin, Inc., 10, 40 (upd.)
Allied Worldwide, Inc., 49
AMCOL International Corporation, 59
(upd.)
Amerco, 6
AMERCO, 67 (upd.)
American Classic Voyages Company, 27
American Commercial Lines Inc., 99
American President Companies Ltd., 6
Anderson Trucking Service, Inc., 75
Anschutz Corp., 12
APL Limited, 61 (upd.)
Aqua Alliance Inc., 32 (upd.)
Arriva PLC, 69
Atlas Van Lines, Inc., 14
Attica Enterprises S.A., 64
Avis Group Holdings, Inc., 75 (upd.)
Avis Rent A Car, Inc., 6; 22 (upd.)
BAA plc, 10
Bekins Company, 15
Berliner Verkehrsbetriebe (BVG), 58
Bollinger Shipyards, Inc., 61
Boyd Bros. Transportation Inc., 39
Brambles Industries Limited, 42
The Brink's Company, 58 (upd.)
British Railways Board, V
Broken Hill Proprietary Company Ltd.,
22 (upd.)
Buckeye Partners, L.P., 70
Budget Group, Inc., 25
Budget Rent a Car Corporation, 9
Burlington Northern Santa Fe
Corporation, V; 27 (upd.)
C.H. Robinson Worldwide, Inc., 40
(upd.)
Canadian National Railway Company, 71
(upd.)
Canadian National Railway System, 6
Canadian Pacific Railway Limited, V; 45
(upd.); 95 (upd.)
Cannon Express, Inc., 53
Carey International, Inc., 26
Carlson Companies, Inc., 6; 22 (upd.); 87
(upd.)
Carolina Freight Corporation, 6
Celadon Group Inc., 30

Central Japan Railway Company, 43
Chargeurs International, 6; 21 (upd.)
CHC Helicopter Corporation, 67
CHEP Pty. Ltd., 80
Chicago and North Western Holdings Corporation, 6
Christian Salvesen Plc, 45
Coach USA, Inc., 24; 55 (upd.)
Coles Express Inc., 15
Compagnie Générale Maritime et Financière, 6
Compagnie Maritime Belge S.A., 95
Consolidated Delivery & Logistics, Inc., 24
Consolidated Freightways Corporation, V; 21 (upd.); 48 (upd.)
Consolidated Rail Corporation, V
CR England, Inc., 63
Crete Carrier Corporation, 95
Crowley Maritime Corporation, 6; 28 (upd.)
CSX Corporation, V; 22 (upd.); 79 (upd.)
Ctrip.com International Ltd., 97
Dachser GmbH & Co. KG, 88
Danaos Corporation, 91
Danzas Group, V; 40 (upd.)
Dart Group PLC, 77
Deutsche Bahn AG, V; 46 (upd.)
DHL Worldwide Network S.A./N.V., 6; 24 (upd.); 69 (upd.)
Diana Shipping Inc., 95
Dollar Thrifty Automotive Group, Inc., 25
Dot Foods, Inc., 69
DP World, 81
DryShips Inc., 95
East Japan Railway Company, V; 66 (upd.)
EGL, Inc., 59
Emery Air Freight Corporation, 6
Emery Worldwide Airlines, Inc., 25 (upd.)
Enterprise Rent-A-Car Company, 6
Estes Express Lines, Inc., 86
Eurotunnel Group, 37 (upd.)
EVA Airways Corporation, 51
Evergreen International Aviation, Inc., 53
Evergreen Marine Corporation (Taiwan) Ltd., 13; 50 (upd.)
Executive Jet, Inc., 36
Exel plc, 51 (upd.)
Expeditors International of Washington Inc., 17; 78 (upd.)
Federal Express Corporation, V
FedEx Corporation, 18 (upd.); 42 (upd.)
FirstGroup plc, 89
Forward Air Corporation, 75
Fritz Companies, Inc., 12
Frontline Ltd., 45
Frozen Food Express Industries, Inc., 20; 98 (upd.)
Garuda Indonesia, 58 (upd.)
GATX Corporation, 6; 25 (upd.)
GE Capital Aviation Services, 36
Gefco SA, 54
General Maritime Corporation, 59
Genesee & Wyoming Inc., 27
Geodis S.A., 67
The Go-Ahead Group Plc, 28

The Greenbrier Companies, 19
Greyhound Lines, Inc., 32 (upd.)
Groupe Bourbon S.A., 60
Grupo Aeroportuario del Centro Norte, S.A.B. de C.V., 97
Grupo Aeroportuario del Pacífico, S.A. de C.V., 85
Grupo TMM, S.A. de C.V., 50
Grupo Transportación Ferroviaria Mexicana, S.A. de C.V., 47
Gulf Agency Company Ltd. 78
GulfMark Offshore, Inc., 49
Hanjin Shipping Co., Ltd., 50
Hankyu Corporation, V; 23 (upd.)
Hapag-Lloyd AG, 6; 97 (upd.)
Harland and Wolff Holdings plc, 19
Harper Group Inc., 17
Heartland Express, Inc., 18
The Hertz Corporation, 9
Holberg Industries, Inc., 36
Horizon Lines, Inc., 98
Hospitality Worldwide Services, Inc., 26
Hub Group, Inc., 38
Hvide Marine Incorporated, 22
Illinois Central Corporation, 11
International Shipholding Corporation, Inc., 27
J.B. Hunt Transport Services Inc., 12
J Lauritzen A/S, 90
John Menzies plc, 39
Kansas City Southern Industries, Inc., 6; 26 (upd.)
The Kansas City Southern Railway Company, 92
Kawasaki Kisen Kaisha, Ltd., V; 56 (upd.)
Keio Corporation, V; 96 (upd.)
Keolis SA, 51
Kinki Nippon Railway Company Ltd., V
Kirby Corporation, 18; 66 (upd.)
Knight Transportation, Inc., 64
Koninklijke Nedlloyd Groep N.V., 6
Kuehne & Nagel International AG, V; 53 (upd.)
La Poste, V; 47 (upd.)
Laidlaw International, Inc., 80
Landstar System, Inc., 63
Leaseway Transportation Corp., 12
Loma Negra C.I.A.S.A., 95
London Regional Transport, 6
The Long Island Rail Road Company, 68
Lynden Incorporated, 91
Maine Central Railroad Company, 16
Mammoet Transport B.V., 26
Marten Transport, Ltd., 84
Martz Group, 56
Mayflower Group Inc., 6
Mercury Air Group, Inc., 20
The Mersey Docks and Harbour Company, 30
Metropolitan Transportation Authority, 35
Miller Industries, Inc., 26
Mitsui O.S.K. Lines Ltd., V; 96 (upd.)
Moran Towing Corporation, Inc., 15
The Morgan Group, Inc., 46
Morris Travel Services L.L.C., 26
Motor Cargo Industries, Inc., 35
National Car Rental System, Inc., 10
National Express Group PLC, 50

National Railroad Passenger Corporation (Amtrak), 22; 66 (upd.)
Neptune Orient Lines Limited, 47
NFC plc, 6
Nippon Express Company, Ltd., V; 64 (upd.)
Nippon Yusen Kabushiki Kaisha (NYK), V; 72 (upd.)
Norfolk Southern Corporation, V; 29 (upd.); 75 (upd.)
Oak Harbor Freight Lines, Inc., 53
Ocean Group plc, 6
Odakyu Electric Railway Co., Ltd., V; 68 (upd.)
Odyssey Marine Exploration, Inc., 91
Oglebay Norton Company, 17
Old Dominion Freight Line, Inc., 57
OMI Corporation, 59
The Oppenheimer Group, 76
Oshkosh Corporation, 7; 98 (upd.)
Österreichische Bundesbahnen GmbH, 6
OTR Express, Inc., 25
Overnite Corporation, 14; 58 (upd.)
Overseas Shipholding Group, Inc., 11
Pacer International, Inc., 54
Pacific Basin Shipping Ltd., 86
Patriot Transportation Holding, Inc., 91
The Peninsular and Oriental Steam Navigation Company, V; 38 (upd.)
Penske Corporation, V; 19 (upd.); 84 (upd.)
PHH Arval, V; 53 (upd.)
Pilot Air Freight Corp., 67
Plantation Pipe Line Company, 68
Polar Air Cargo Inc., 60
The Port Authority of New York and New Jersey, 48
Port Imperial Ferry Corporation, 70
Post Office Group, V
Preston Corporation, 6
RailTex, Inc., 20
Railtrack Group PLC, 50
Réseau Ferré de France, 66
Roadway Express, Inc., V; 25 (upd.)
Rock-It Cargo USA, Inc., 86
Royal Olympic Cruise Lines Inc., 52
Royal Vopak NV, 41
Russian Railways Joint Stock Co., 93
Ryder System, Inc., V; 24 (upd.)
Saia, Inc., 98
Santa Fe Pacific Corporation, V
Schenker-Rhenus AG, 6
Schneider National, Inc., 36; 77 (upd.)
Seaboard Corporation, 36; 85 (upd.)
SEACOR Holdings Inc., 83
Securicor Plc, 45
Seibu Railway Company Ltd., V; 74 (upd.)
Seino Transportation Company, Ltd., 6
Simon Transportation Services Inc., 27
Smithway Motor Xpress Corporation, 39
Société Nationale des Chemins de Fer Français, V; 57 (upd.)
Société Norbert Dentressangle S.A., 67
Southern Pacific Transportation Company, V
Spee-Dee Delivery Service, Inc., 93
Stagecoach Holdings plc, 30

Stelmar Shipping Ltd., 52
Stevedoring Services of America Inc., 28
Stinnes AG, 8; 59 (upd.)
Stolt-Nielsen S.A., 42
Sunoco, Inc., 28 (upd.); 83 (upd.)
Swift Transportation Co., Inc., 42
The Swiss Federal Railways
    (Schweizerische Bundesbahnen), V
Swissport International Ltd., 70
Teekay Shipping Corporation, 25; 82
    (upd.)
Tibbett & Britten Group plc, 32
Tidewater Inc., 11; 37 (upd.)
TNT Freightways Corporation, 14
TNT Post Group N.V., V; 27 (upd.); 30
    (upd.)
Tobu Railway Company Ltd., 6; 98
    (upd.)
Tokyu Corporation, V
Totem Resources Corporation, 9
TPG N.V., 64 (upd.)
Trailer Bridge, Inc., 41
Transnet Ltd., 6
Transport Corporation of America, Inc.,
    49
Trico Marine Services, Inc., 89
Tsakos Energy Navigation Ltd., 91
TTX Company, 6; 66 (upd.)
U.S. Delivery Systems, Inc., 22
Union Pacific Corporation, V; 28 (upd.);
    79 (upd.)
United Parcel Service of America Inc., V;
    17 (upd.)
United Parcel Service, Inc., 63
United Road Services, Inc., 69
United States Postal Service, 14; 34 (upd.)
US 1 Industries, Inc., 89
USA Truck, Inc., 42
Velocity Express Corporation, 49
Werner Enterprises, Inc., 26
Wheels Inc., 96
Wincanton plc, 52
Wisconsin Central Transportation
    Corporation, 24
Wright Express Corporation, 80
Yamato Transport Co. Ltd., V; 49 (upd.)
Yellow Corporation, 14; 45 (upd.)
Yellow Freight System, Inc. of Delaware,
    V
YRC Worldwide Inc., 90 (upd.)

Utilities

AES Corporation, 10; 13 (upd.); 53
    (upd.)
Aggreko Plc, 45
Air & Water Technologies Corporation, 6
Alberta Energy Company Ltd., 16; 43
    (upd.)
Allegheny Energy, Inc., V; 38 (upd.)
Ameren Corporation, 60 (upd.)
American Electric Power Company, Inc.,
    V; 45 (upd.)
American States Water Company, 46
American Water Works Company, Inc., 6;
    38 (upd.)
Aquarion Company, 84
Aquila, Inc., 50 (upd.)
Arkla, Inc., V

Associated Natural Gas Corporation, 11
Atlanta Gas Light Company, 6; 23 (upd.)
Atlantic Energy, Inc., 6
Atmos Energy Corporation, 43
Avista Corporation, 69 (upd.)
Baltimore Gas and Electric Company, V;
    25 (upd.)
Bay State Gas Company, 38
Bayernwerk AG, V; 23 (upd.)
Berlinwasser Holding AG, 90
Bewag AG, 39
Big Rivers Electric Corporation, 11
Black Hills Corporation, 20
Bonneville Power Administration, 50
Boston Edison Company, 12
Bouygues S.A., I; 24 (upd.); 97 (upd.)
British Energy Plc, 49
British Gas plc, V
British Nuclear Fuels plc, 6
Brooklyn Union Gas, 6
California Water Service Group, 79
Calpine Corporation, 36
Canadian Utilities Limited, 13; 56 (upd.)
Cap Rock Energy Corporation, 46
Carolina Power & Light Company, V; 23
    (upd.)
Cascade Natural Gas Corporation, 9
Centerior Energy Corporation, V
Central and South West Corporation, V
Central Hudson Gas and Electricity
    Corporation, 6
Central Maine Power, 6
Central Vermont Public Service
    Corporation, 54
Centrica plc, 29 (upd.)
ČEZ a. s., 97
Chesapeake Utilities Corporation, 56
China Shenhua Energy Company
    Limited, 83
Chubu Electric Power Company, Inc., V;
    46 (upd.)
Chugoku Electric Power Company Inc.,
    V; 53 (upd.)
Cincinnati Gas & Electric Company, 6
CIPSCO Inc., 6
Citizens Utilities Company, 7
City Public Service, 6
Cleco Corporation, 37
CMS Energy Corporation, V, 14
The Coastal Corporation, 31 (upd.)
Cogentrix Energy, Inc., 10
The Coleman Company, Inc., 9
The Columbia Gas System, Inc., V; 16
    (upd.)
Commonwealth Edison Company, V
Commonwealth Energy System, 14
Companhia Energética de Minas Gerais
    S.A. CEMIG, 65
Compañia de Minas Buenaventura S.A.A.,
    93
Connecticut Light and Power Co., 13
Consolidated Edison, Inc., V; 45 (upd.)
Consolidated Natural Gas Company, V;
    19 (upd.)
Consumers Power Co., 14
Consumers Water Company, 14
Consumers' Gas Company Ltd., 6
Covanta Energy Corporation, 64 (upd.)

Dalkia Holding, 66
Destec Energy, Inc., 12
The Detroit Edison Company, V
Dominion Resources, Inc., V; 54 (upd.)
DPL Inc., 6; 96 (upd.)
DQE, Inc., 6
DTE Energy Company, 20 (upd.)
Duke Energy Corporation, V; 27 (upd.)
E.On AG, 50 (upd.)
Eastern Enterprises, 6
Edison International, 56 (upd.)
El Paso Electric Company, 21
El Paso Natural Gas Company, 12
Electrabel N.V., 67
Electricidade de Portugal, S.A., 47
Electricité de France, V; 41 (upd.)
Electricity Generating Authority of
    Thailand (EGAT), 56
Elektrowatt AG, 6
The Empire District Electric Company,
    77
Empresas Públicas de Medellín S.A.E.S.P.,
    91
Enbridge Inc., 43
ENDESA S.A., V; 46 (upd.)
Enersis S.A., 73
ENMAX Corporation, 83
Enron Corporation, V; 46 (upd.)
Enserch Corporation, V
Ente Nazionale per L'Energia Elettrica, V
Entergy Corporation, V; 45 (upd.)
Environmental Power Corporation, 68
EPCOR Utilities Inc., 81
Equitable Resources, Inc., 6; 54 (upd.)
Exelon Corporation, 48 (upd.)
Florida Progress Corporation, V; 23 (upd.)
Florida Public Utilities Company, 69
Fortis, Inc., 15; 47 (upd.)
Fortum Corporation, 30 (upd.)
FPL Group, Inc., V; 49 (upd.)
Gas Natural SDG S.A., 69
Gaz de France, V; 40 (upd.)
General Public Utilities Corporation, V
Générale des Eaux Group, V
GPU, Inc., 27 (upd.)
Great Plains Energy Incorporated, 65
    (upd.)
Gulf States Utilities Company, 6
Hawaiian Electric Industries, Inc., 9
Hokkaido Electric Power Company Inc.
    (HEPCO), V; 58 (upd.)
Hokuriku Electric Power Company, V
Hong Kong and China Gas Company
    Ltd., 73
Hongkong Electric Holdings Ltd., 6; 23
    (upd.)
Houston Industries Incorporated, V
Hyder plc, 34
Hydro-Québec, 6; 32 (upd.)
Iberdrola, S.A., 49
Idaho Power Company, 12
Illinois Bell Telephone Company, 14
Illinois Power Company, 6
Indiana Energy, Inc., 27
International Power PLC, 50 (upd.)
IPALCO Enterprises, Inc., 6
ITC Holdings Corp., 75

The Kansai Electric Power Company, Inc., V; 62 (upd.)
Kansas City Power & Light Company, 6
Kelda Group plc, 45
Kenetech Corporation, 11
Kentucky Utilities Company, 6
KeySpan Energy Co., 27
Korea Electric Power Corporation (Kepco), 56
KU Energy Corporation, 11
Kyushu Electric Power Company Inc., V
LG&E Energy Corporation, 6; 51 (upd.)
Long Island Lighting Company, V
Lyonnaise des Eaux-Dumez, V
Madison Gas and Electric Company, 39
Magma Power Company, 11
Maine & Maritimes Corporation, 56
Manila Electric Company (Meralco), 56
MCN Corporation, 6
MDU Resources Group, Inc., 7; 42 (upd.)
Middlesex Water Company, 45
Midwest Resources Inc., 6
Minnesota Power, Inc., 11; 34 (upd.)
Mirant Corporation, 98
The Montana Power Company, 11; 44 (upd.)
National Fuel Gas Company, 6; 95 (upd.)
National Grid USA, 51 (upd.)
National Power PLC, 12
Nebraska Public Power District, 29
N.V. Nederlandse Gasunie, V
Nevada Power Company, 11
New England Electric System, V
New Jersey Resources Corporation, 54
New York State Electric and Gas, 6
Neyveli Lignite Corporation Ltd., 65
Niagara Mohawk Holdings Inc., V; 45 (upd.)
Nicor Inc., 6; 86 (upd.)
NIPSCO Industries, Inc., 6
North West Water Group plc, 11
Northeast Utilities, V; 48 (upd.)
Northern States Power Company, V; 20 (upd.)
Northwest Natural Gas Company, 45
NorthWestern Corporation, 37
Nova Corporation of Alberta, V
NRG Energy, Inc., 79
Oglethorpe Power Corporation, 6
Ohio Edison Company, V
Oklahoma Gas and Electric Company, 6
ONEOK Inc., 7
Ontario Hydro Services Company, 6; 32 (upd.)
Osaka Gas Company, Ltd., V; 60 (upd.)
Österreichische Elektrizitätswirtschafts-AG, 85
Otter Tail Power Company, 18
Pacific Enterprises, V
Pacific Gas and Electric Company, V
PacifiCorp, V; 26 (upd.)
Panhandle Eastern Corporation, V
Paddy Power plc, 98
PECO Energy Company, 11
Pennon Group Plc, 45
Pennsylvania Power & Light Company, V
Peoples Energy Corporation, 6
PG&E Corporation, 26 (upd.)

Philadelphia Electric Company, V
Philadelphia Gas Works Company, 92
Philadelphia Suburban Corporation, 39
Piedmont Natural Gas Company, Inc., 27
Pinnacle West Capital Corporation, 6; 54 (upd.)
PNM Resources Inc., 51 (upd.)
Portland General Corporation, 6
Potomac Electric Power Company, 6
Power-One, Inc., 79
Powergen PLC, 11; 50 (upd.)
PPL Corporation, 41 (upd.)
PreussenElektra Aktiengesellschaft, V
Progress Energy, Inc., 74
PSI Resources, 6
Public Service Company of Colorado, 6
Public Service Company of New Hampshire, 21; 55 (upd.)
Public Service Company of New Mexico, 6
Public Service Enterprise Group Inc., V; 44 (upd.)
Puerto Rico Electric Power Authority, 47
Puget Sound Energy Inc., 6; 50 (upd.)
Questar Corporation, 6; 26 (upd.)
RAO Unified Energy System of Russia, 45
Reliant Energy Inc., 44 (upd.)
Revere Electric Supply Company, 96
Rochester Gas and Electric Corporation, 6
Ruhrgas AG, V; 38 (upd.)
RWE AG, V; 50 (upd.)
Salt River Project, 19
San Diego Gas & Electric Company, V
SCANA Corporation, 6; 56 (upd.)
Scarborough Public Utilities Commission, 9
SCEcorp, V
Scottish and Southern Energy plc, 66 (upd.)
Scottish Hydro-Electric PLC, 13
Scottish Power plc, 19; 49 (upd.)
Seattle City Light, 50
SEMCO Energy, Inc., 44
Sempra Energy, 25 (upd.)
Severn Trent PLC, 12; 38 (upd.)
Shikoku Electric Power Company, Inc., V; 60 (upd.)
SJW Corporation, 70
Sonat, Inc., 6
South Jersey Industries, Inc., 42
The Southern Company, V; 38 (upd.)
Southern Connecticut Gas Company, 84
Southern Electric PLC, 13
Southern Indiana Gas and Electric Company, 13
Southern Union Company, 27
Southwest Gas Corporation, 19
Southwest Water Company, 47
Southwestern Electric Power Co., 21
Southwestern Public Service Company, 6
Suez Lyonnaise des Eaux, 36 (upd.)
SUEZ-TRACTEBEL S.A., 97 (upd.)
TECO Energy, Inc., 6
Tennessee Valley Authority, 50
Tennet BV 78
Texas Utilities Company, V; 25 (upd.)
Thames Water plc, 11; 90 (upd.)
Tohoku Electric Power Company, Inc., V

The Tokyo Electric Power Company, 74 (upd.)
The Tokyo Electric Power Company, Incorporated, V
Tokyo Gas Co., Ltd., V; 55 (upd.)
TransAlta Utilities Corporation, 6
TransCanada PipeLines Limited, V
Transco Energy Company, V
Trigen Energy Corporation, 42
Tucson Electric Power Company, 6
UGI Corporation, 12
Unicom Corporation, 29 (upd.)
Union Electric Company, V
The United Illuminating Company, 21
United Utilities PLC, 52 (upd.)
United Water Resources, Inc., 40
Unitil Corporation, 37
Utah Power and Light Company, 27
UtiliCorp United Inc., 6
Vattenfall AB, 57
Vectren Corporation, 98 (upd.)
Vereinigte Elektrizitätswerke Westfalen AG, V
VEW AG, 39
Viridian Group plc, 64
Warwick Valley Telephone Company, 55
Washington Gas Light Company, 19
Washington Natural Gas Company, 9
Washington Water Power Company, 6
Westar Energy, Inc., 57 (upd.)
Western Resources, Inc., 12
Wheelabrator Technologies, Inc., 6
Wisconsin Energy Corporation, 6; 54 (upd.)
Wisconsin Public Service Corporation, 9
WPL Holdings, Inc., 6
WPS Resources Corporation, 53 (upd.)
Xcel Energy Inc., 73 (upd.)

Waste Services

Allied Waste Industries, Inc., 50
Allwaste, Inc., 18
American Ecology Corporation, 77
Appliance Recycling Centers of America, Inc., 42
Azcon Corporation, 23
Berliner Stadtreinigungsbetriebe, 58
Biffa plc, 92
Brambles Industries Limited, 42
Browning-Ferris Industries, Inc., V; 20 (upd.)
Chemical Waste Management, Inc., 9
Clean Harbors, Inc., 73
Copart Inc., 23
Darling International Inc., 85
E.On AG, 50 (upd.)
Ecolab Inc., I; 13 (upd.); 34 (upd.); 85 (upd.)
Ecology and Environment, Inc., 39
Empresas Públicas de Medellín S.A.E.S.P., 91
Fuel Tech, Inc., 85
Industrial Services of America, Inc., 46
Ionics, Incorporated, 52
ISS A/S, 49
Jani-King International, Inc., 85
Kelda Group plc, 45
MPW Industrial Services Group, Inc., 53

Newpark Resources, Inc., 63
Norcal Waste Systems, Inc., 60
Oakleaf Waste Management, LLC, 97
1-800-GOT-JUNK? LLC, 74
Onet S.A., 92
Pennon Group Plc, 45
Perma-Fix Environmental Services, Inc.,
   99
Philip Environmental Inc., 16
Philip Services Corp., 73
Republic Services, Inc., 92

Roto-Rooter, Inc., 15; 61 (upd.)
Safety-Kleen Systems Inc., 8; 82 (upd.)
Saur S.A.S., 92
Sevenson Environmental Services, Inc., 42
Severn Trent PLC, 38 (upd.)
Servpro Industries, Inc., 85
Shanks Group plc, 45
Shred-It Canada Corporation, 56
Stericycle, Inc., 33; 74 (upd.)
TRC Companies, Inc., 32
Valley Proteins, Inc., 91

Veit Companies, 43; 92 (upd.)
Waste Connections, Inc., 46
Waste Holdings, Inc., 41
Waste Management, Inc., V
Wheelabrator Technologies, Inc., 60
   (upd.)
Windswept Environmental Group, Inc.,
   62
WMX Technologies Inc., 17

Geographic Index

Algeria
Sonatrach, IV; 65 (upd.)

Argentina
Acindar Industria Argentina de Aceros
  S.A., 87
Aerolíneas Argentinas S.A., 33; 69 (upd.)
Alpargatas S.A.I.C., 87
Aluar Aluminio Argentino S.A.I.C., 74
Arcor S.A.I.C., 66
Atanor S.A., 62
Coto Centro Integral de Comercializacion
  S.A., 66
Cresud S.A.C.I.F. y A., 63
Grupo Clarín S.A., 67
Grupo Financiero Galicia S.A., 63
IRSA Inversiones y Representaciones S.A.,
  63
Ledesma Sociedad Anónima Agrícola
  Industrial, 62
Loma Negra C.I.A.S.A., 95
Molinos Río de la Plata S.A., 61
Nobleza Piccardo SAICF, 64
Penaflor S.A., 66
Petrobras Energia Participaciones S.A., 72
Quilmes Industrial (QUINSA) S.A., 67
Renault Argentina S.A., 67
Sideco Americana S.A., 67
Siderar S.A.I.C., 66
Telecom Argentina S.A., 63
Telefónica de Argentina S.A., 61
YPF Sociedad Anonima, IV

Australia
ABC Learning Centres Ltd., 93
Amcor Limited, IV; 19 (upd.), 78 (upd.)
Ansell Ltd., 60 (upd.)
Aquarius Platinum Ltd., 63
Aristocrat Leisure Limited, 54

Arnott's Ltd., 66
Austal Limited, 75
Australia and New Zealand Banking
  Group Limited, II; 52 (upd.)
AWB Ltd., 56
BHP Billiton, 67 (upd.)
Billabong International Ltd., 44
Blundstone Pty Ltd., 76
Bond Corporation Holdings Limited, 10
Boral Limited, III; 43 (upd.)
Brambles Industries Limited, 42
Broken Hill Proprietary Company Ltd.,
  IV; 22 (upd.)
Burns, Philp & Company Ltd., 63
Carlton and United Breweries Ltd., I
Coles Group Limited, V; 20 (upd.); 85
  (upd.)
Cochlear Ltd., 77
CRA Limited, IV; 85 (upd.)
CSR Limited, III; 28 (upd.)
David Jones Ltd., 60
Elders IXL Ltd., I
Fairfax Media Ltd., 94 (upd.)
Foster's Group Limited, 7; 21 (upd.); 50
  (upd.)
Goodman Fielder Ltd., 52
Harvey Norman Holdings Ltd., 56
Holden Ltd., 62
James Hardie Industries N.V., 56
John Fairfax Holdings Limited, 7
Lend Lease Corporation Limited, IV; 17
  (upd.); 52 (upd.)
Lion Nathan Limited, 54
Lonely Planet Publications Pty Ltd., 55
Macquarie Bank Ltd., 69
McPherson's Ltd., 66
Metcash Trading Ltd., 58
MYOB Ltd., 86

News Corporation Limited, IV; 7 (upd.);
  46 (upd.)
Nufarm Ltd., 87
Pacific Dunlop Limited, 10
Pioneer International Limited, III
PMP Ltd., 72
Publishing and Broadcasting Limited, 54
Qantas Airways Ltd., 6; 24 (upd.); 68
  (upd.)
Repco Corporation Ltd., 74
Ridley Corporation Ltd., 62
Rinker Group Ltd., 65
Rural Press Ltd., 74
Santos Ltd., 81
Smorgon Steel Group Ltd., 62
Southcorp Limited, 54
Suncorp-Metway Ltd., 91
TABCORP Holdings Limited, 44
Telecom Australia, 6
Telstra Corporation Limited, 50
Village Roadshow Ltd., 58
Westpac Banking Corporation, II; 48
  (upd.)
WMC, Limited, 43
Zinifex Ltd., 85

Austria
AKG Acoustics GmbH, 62
Andritz AG, 51
Austrian Airlines AG (Österreichische
  Luftverkehrs AG), 33
Bank Austria AG, 23
Baumax AG, 75
BBAG Österreichische
  Brau-Beteiligungs-AG, 38
BÖHLER-UDDEHOLM AG, 73
Borealis AG, 94
Erste Bank der Österreichischen
  Sparkassen AG, 69

Gericom AG, 47
Glock Ges.m.b.H., 42
Julius Meinl International AG, 53
Lauda Air Luftfahrt AG, 48
OMV AG, IV; 98 (upd.)
Österreichische Bundesbahnen GmbH, 6
Österreichische Elektrizitätswirtschafts-AG, 85
Österreichische Post- und Telegraphenverwaltung, V
Raiffeisen Zentralbank Österreich AG, 85
Red Bull GmbH, 60
RHI AG, 53
Riedel Tiroler Glashuette GmbH, 99
VA TECH ELIN EBG GmbH, 49
voestalpine AG, IV; 57 (upd.)
Wienerberger AG, 70
Zumtobel AG, 50

Azerbaijan
Azerbaijan Airlines, 77

Bahamas
Bahamas Air Holdings Ltd., 66
Kerzner International Limited, 69 (upd.)
Sun International Hotels Limited, 26
Teekay Shipping Corporation, 25; 82 (upd.)

Bahrain
Gulf Air Company, 56
Investcorp SA, 57

Bangladesh
Grameen Bank, 31

Barbados
Sagicor Life Inc., 98

Belgium
Ackermans & van Haaren N.V., 97
Agfa Gevaert Group N.V., 59
Almanij NV, 44
Arcelor Gent, 80
Bank Brussels Lambert, II
Barco NV, 44
Bekaert S.A./N.V., 90
Belgacom, 6
Besix Group S.A./NV, 94
Brouwerijen Alken-Maes N.V., 86
C&A, 40 (upd.)
Cockerill Sambre Group, IV; 26 (upd.)
Compagnie Maritime Belge S.A., 95
Compagnie Nationale à Portefeuille, 84
Cora S.A./NV, 94
Corelio S.A./N.V., 96
Deceuninck N.V., 84
Delhaize "Le Lion" S.A., 44
Dexia NV/SA, 88 (upd.)
DHL Worldwide Network S.A./N.V., 69 (upd.)
D'Ieteren S.A./NV, 98
Distrigaz S.A., 82
Electrabel N.V., 67
Etablissements Franz Colruyt N.V., 68
Generale Bank, II

GIB Group, V; 26 (upd.)
Glaverbel Group, 80
Groupe Herstal S.A., 58
Hamon & Cie (International) S.A., 97
Interbrew S.A., 17; 50 (upd.)
Janssen Pharmaceutica N.V., 80
Kredietbank N.V., II
Lyfra-S.A./NV, 88
PetroFina S.A., IV; 26 (upd.)
Picanol N.V., 96
Punch International N.V., 66
Puratos S.A./NV, 92
Quick Restaurants S.A., 94
Rosy Blue N.V., 84
Roularta Media Group NV, 48
Sabena S.A./N.V., 33
Solvay S.A., I; 21 (upd.); 61 (upd.)
Spector Photo Group N.V., 82
SUEZ-TRACTEBEL S.A., 97 (upd.)
Tessenderlo Group, 76
Tractebel S.A., 20
UCB Pharma SA, 98
NV Umicore SA, 47
Van Hool S.A./NV, 96
Xeikon NV, 26

Belize
BB Holdings Limited, 77

Bermuda
Assured Guaranty Ltd., 93
Bacardi & Company Ltd., 18; 82 (upd.)
Central European Media Enterprises Ltd., 61
Covidien Ltd., 91
Endurance Specialty Holdings Ltd., 85
Frontline Ltd., 45
Gosling Brothers Ltd., 82
Jardine Matheson Holdings Limited, I; 20 (upd.); 93 (upd.)
Nabors Industries Ltd., 91 (upd.)
PartnerRe Ltd., 83
Sea Containers Ltd., 29
Tyco International Ltd., III; 28 (upd.); 63 (upd.)
VistaPrint Limited, 87
Warner Chilcott Limited, 85
White Mountains Insurance Group, Ltd., 48

Bolivia
Lloyd Aéreo Boliviano S.A., 95

Brazil
Abril S.A., 95
Aracruz Celulose S.A., 57
Banco Bradesco S.A., 13
Banco Itaú S.A., 19
Brasil Telecom Participaçoes S.A., 57
Brazil Fast Food Corporation, 74
Bunge Brasil S.A. 78
Camargo Corrêa S.A., 93
Casas Bahia Comercial Ltda., 75
Cia Hering, 72
Companhia Brasileira de Distribuiçao, 76
Companhia de Bebidas das Américas, 57
Companhia de Tecidos Norte de Minas - Coteminas, 77

Companhia Energética de Minas Gerais S.A. CEMIG, 65
Companhia Siderúrgica Nacional, 76
Companhia Suzano de Papel e Celulose S.A., 94
Companhia Vale do Rio Doce, IV; 43 (upd.)
Empresa Brasileira de Aeronáutica S.A. (Embraer), 36
G&K Holding S.A., 95
Gerdau S.A., 59
Globo Comunicação e Participações S.A., 80
Gol Linhas Aéreas Inteligentes S.A., 73
Ipiranga S.A., 67
Klabin S.A., 73
Lojas Americanas S.A., 77
Lojas Arapua S.A., 22; 61 (upd.)
Marcopolo S.A. 79
Natura Cosméticos S.A., 75
Odebrecht S.A., 73
Perdigao SA, 52
Petróleo Brasileiro S.A., IV
Randon S.A. 79
Renner Herrmann S.A. 79
Sadia S.A., 59
Sao Paulo Alpargatas S.A., 75
Souza Cruz S.A., 65
TAM Linhas Aéreas S.A., 68
Tele Norte Leste Participações S.A., 80
TransBrasil S/A Linhas Aéreas, 31
Unibanco Holdings S.A., 73
Usinas Siderúrgicas de Minas Gerais S.A., 77
VARIG S.A. (Viação Aérea Rio-Grandense), 6; 29 (upd.)
Vicunha Têxtil S.A. 78
Votorantim Participaçoes S.A., 76
Weg S.A. 78

Brunei
Royal Brunei Airlines Sdn Bhd, 99

Canada
AbitibiBowater Inc., V; 25 (upd.); 99 (upd.)
Abitibi-Price Inc., IV
Agnico-Eagle Mines Limited, 71
Agrium Inc., 73
Ainsworth Lumber Co. Ltd., 99
Air Canada, 6; 23 (upd.); 59 (upd.)
Alberta Energy Company Ltd., 16; 43 (upd.)
Alcan Aluminium Limited, IV; 31 (upd.)
Alderwoods Group, Inc., 68 (upd.)
Algo Group Inc., 24
Alimentation Couche-Tard Inc., 77
Alliance Atlantis Communications Inc., 39
ATI Technologies Inc. 79
Axcan Pharma Inc., 85
Ballard Power Systems Inc., 73
Bank of Montreal, II; 46 (upd.)
The Bank of Nova Scotia, II; 59 (upd.)
Barrick Gold Corporation, 34
Bata Ltd., 62
BCE Inc., V; 44 (upd.)
Bell Canada, 6

BFC Construction Corporation, 25
BioWare Corporation, 81
Biovail Corporation, 47
Bombardier Inc., 42 (upd.); 87 (upd.)
Boston Pizza International Inc., 88
Bradley Air Services Ltd., 56
Bramalea Ltd., 9
Brascan Corporation, 67
British Columbia Telephone Company, 6
Brookfield Properties Corporation, 89
Cameco Corporation, 77
Campeau Corporation, V
Canada Bread Company, Limited, 99
Canada Packers Inc., II
Canadair, Inc., 16
The Canadian Broadcasting Corporation
    (CBC), 37
Canadian Imperial Bank of Commerce, II;
    61 (upd.)
Canadian National Railway Company, 6,
    71 (upd.)
Canadian Pacific Railway Limited, V; 45
    (upd.); 95 (upd.)
Canadian Tire Corporation, Limited, 71
    (upd.)
Canadian Utilities Limited, 13; 56 (upd.)
Canfor Corporation, 42
Canstar Sports Inc., 16
CanWest Global Communications
    Corporation, 35
Cascades Inc., 71
Celestica Inc., 80
CHC Helicopter Corporation, 67
Cinar Corporation, 40
Cineplex Odeon Corporation, 6; 23
    (upd.)
Cinram International, Inc., 43
Cirque du Soleil Inc., 29; 98 (upd.)
Clearly Canadian Beverage Corporation,
    48
Cognos Inc., 44
Cominco Ltd., 37
Consumers' Gas Company Ltd., 6
CoolBrands International Inc., 35
Corby Distilleries Limited, 14
Corel Corporation, 15; 33 (upd.); 76
    (upd.)
Cott Corporation, 52
Creo Inc., 48
Diavik Diamond Mines Inc., 85
Discreet Logic Inc., 20
Dofasco Inc., IV; 24 (upd.)
Doman Industries Limited, 59
Dominion Textile Inc., 12
Domtar Corporation, IV; 89 (upd.)
Dorel Industries Inc., 59
Duvernay Oil Corp., 83
Dynatec Corporation, 87
Dylex Limited, 29
Echo Bay Mines Ltd., IV; 38 (upd.)
Enbridge Inc., 43
ENMAX Corporation, 83
EPCOR Utilities Inc., 81
Extendicare Health Services, Inc., 6
Fairfax Financial Holdings Limited, 57
Fairmont Hotels & Resorts Inc., 69
Falconbridge Limited, 49
Finning International Inc., 69

Fortis, Inc., 15; 47 (upd.)
The Forzani Group Ltd. 79
Four Seasons Hotels Inc., 9; 29 (upd.)
Future Shop Ltd., 62
Ganz, 98
GEAC Computer Corporation Ltd., 43
George Weston Ltd., II; 36 (upd.); 88
    (upd.)
Gildan Activewear, Inc., 81
Goldcorp Inc., 87
GPS Industries, Inc., 81
Great-West Lifeco Inc., III
Groupe Vidéotron Ltée., 20
Hammond Manufacturing Company
    Limited, 83
Harlequin Enterprises Limited, 52
Hemisphere GPS Inc., 99
Hemlo Gold Mines Inc., 9
Héroux-Devtek Inc., 69
Hiram Walker Resources, Ltd., I
The Hockey Company, 34; 70
Hollinger International Inc., 62 (upd.)
Home Hardware Stores Ltd., 62
The Hudson Bay Mining and Smelting
    Company, Limited, 12
Hudson's Bay Company, V; 25 (upd.); 83
    (upd.)
Hurricane Hydrocarbons Ltd., 54
Husky Energy Inc., 47
Hydro-Québec, 6; 32 (upd.)
Imasco Limited, V
IMAX Corporation 28, 78 (upd.)
Imperial Oil Limited, IV; 25 (upd.); 95
    (upd.)
Imperial Parking Corporation, 58
Inco Limited, IV; 45 (upd.)
Indigo Books & Music Inc., 58
Intercorp Excelle Foods Inc., 64
Intrawest Corporation, 15; 84 (upd.)
Iogen Corporation, 81
Irwin Toy Limited, 14
Jacques Whitford, 92
The Jean Coutu Group (PJC) Inc., 46
The Jim Pattison Group, 37
Kinross Gold Corporation, 36
Kruger Inc., 17
La Senza Corporation, 66
Labatt Brewing Company Limited, I; 25
    (upd.)
LaSiDo Inc., 58
Lassonde Industries Inc., 68
Le Chateau Inc., 63
Ledcor Industries Limited, 46
Les Boutiques San Francisco, Inc., 62
Linamar Corporation, 18
Lions Gate Entertainment Corporation,
    35
Loblaw Companies Limited, 43
The Loewen Group, Inc., 16; 40 (upd.)
London Drugs Ltd., 46
Maclean Hunter Publishing Limited, IV;
    26 (upd.)
MacMillan Bloedel Limited, IV
Magellan Aerospace Corporation, 48
Manitoba Telecom Services, Inc., 61
Manulife Financial Corporation, 85
Maple Leaf Foods Inc., 41

Maple Leaf Sports & Entertainment Ltd.,
    61
Masonite International Corporation, 63
McCain Foods Limited, 77
MDC Partners Inc., 63
Mega Bloks, Inc., 61
Methanex Corporation, 40
Métro Inc., 77
Mitel Corporation, 18
The Molson Companies Limited, I; 26
    (upd.)
Moore Corporation Limited, IV
Morguard Corporation, 85
Mouvement des Caisses Desjardins, 48
National Bank of Canada, 85
National Sea Products Ltd., 14
Nature's Path Foods, Inc., 87
New Flyer Industries Inc. 78
Nexen Inc. 79
Noranda Inc., IV; 7 (upd.); 64 (upd.)
Nortel Networks Corporation, 36 (upd.)
The North West Company, Inc., 12
Northern Telecom Limited, V
Nova Corporation of Alberta, V
Novacor Chemicals Ltd., 12
Olympia & York Developments Ltd., IV;
    9 (upd.)
1-800-GOT-JUNK? LLC, 74
Onex Corporation, 16; 65 (upd.)
Ontario Hydro Services Company, 6; 32
    (upd.)
Ontario Teachers' Pension Plan, 61
Open Text Corporation 79
The Oppenheimer Group, 76
The Oshawa Group Limited, II
Paramount Resources Ltd., 87
PCL Construction Group Inc., 50
Peace Arch Entertainment Group Inc., 51
Pengrowth Energy Trust, 95
Petro-Canada, IV; 99 (upd.)
Philip Environmental Inc., 16
Placer Dome Inc., 20; 61 (upd.)
Potash Corporation of Saskatchewan Inc.,
    18
Power Corporation of Canada, 36 (upd.);
    85 (upd.)
Provigo Inc., II; 51 (upd.)
QLT Inc., 71
Quebecor Inc., 12; 47 (upd.)
Research in Motion Ltd., 54
Richtree Inc., 63
Ritchie Bros. Auctioneers Inc., 41
RM Auctions, Inc., 88
Rogers Communications Inc., 30 (upd.)
RONA, Inc., 73
Roots Canada Ltd., 42
Royal Bank of Canada, II; 21 (upd.), 81
    (upd.)
Royal Group Technologies Limited, 73
Saputo Inc., 59
Scarborough Public Utilities Commission,
    9
The Seagram Company Ltd., I; 25 (upd.)
Shermag, Inc., 93
Shoppers Drug Mart Corporation, 49
Shred-It Canada Corporation, 56
Silver Wheaton Corp., 95
Sleeman Breweries Ltd., 74

SNC-Lavalin Group Inc., 72
Sobeys Inc., 80
Southam Inc., 7
Spar Aerospace Limited, 32
Spin Master, Ltd., 61
Steinberg Incorporated, II
Stelco Inc., IV; 51 (upd.)
Sun Life Financial Inc., 85
Sun-Rype Products Ltd., 76
Suncor Energy Inc., 54
SunOpta Inc. 79
Talisman Energy Inc., 9; 47 (upd.)
TAQA North Ltd., 95
TDL Group Ltd., 46
Teck Corporation, 27
Tembec Inc., 66
The Thomson Corporation, 8; 34 (upd.);
    77 (upd.)
Tilley Endurables, Inc., 67
Toromont Industries, Ltd., 21
The Toronto-Dominion Bank, II; 49
    (upd.)
Torstar Corporation, 29
TransAlta Utilities Corporation, 6
TransCanada Corporation, V; 93 (upd.)
Tridel Enterprises Inc., 9
Trilon Financial Corporation, II
Triple Five Group Ltd., 49
Trizec Corporation Ltd., 10
Tucows Inc. 78
Van Houtte Inc., 39
Varity Corporation, III
Vector Aerospace Corporation, 97
Vincor International Inc., 50
Wascana Energy Inc., 13
The Wawanesa Mutual Insurance
    Company, 68
West Fraser Timber Co. Ltd., 17; 91
    (upd.)
Western Oil Sands Inc., 85
WestJet Airlines Ltd., 38
Xantrex Technology Inc., 97

Cayman Islands

Garmin Ltd., 60
Herbalife Ltd., 92 (upd.)
United National Group, Ltd., 63

Chile

Banco de Chile, 69
BCI, 99
Cencosud S.A., 69
Compania Cervecerias Unidas S.A., 70
Corporacion Nacional del Cobre de Chile,
    40
Cristalerias de Chile S.A., 67
Distribución y Servicio D&S S.A., 71
Embotelladora Andina S.A., 71
Empresas Almacenes Paris S.A., 71
Empresas CMPC S.A., 70
Empresas Copec S.A., 69
Enersis S.A., 73
Farmacias Ahumada S.A., 72
Lan Chile S.A., 31
Madeco S.A., 71
Parque Arauco S.A., 72
S.A.C.I. Falabella, 69

Viña Concha y Toro S.A., 45

China

Air China, 46
American Oriental Bioengineering Inc., 93
Anhui Conch Cement Company Limited,
    99
Asia Info Holdings, Inc., 43
Baidu.com Inc., 95
Bank of China, 63
China Automotive Systems Inc., 87
China Construction Bank Corp. 79
China Eastern Airlines Co. Ltd., 31
China Life Insurance Company Limited,
    65
China National Cereals, Oils and
    Foodstuffs Import and Export
    Corporation (COFCO), 76
China National Petroleum Corporation,
    46
China Nepstar Chain Drugstore Ltd., 97
China Netcom Group Corporation (Hong
    Kong) Limited, 73
China Shenhua Energy Company
    Limited, 83
China Southern Airlines Company Ltd.,
    33
China Telecom, 50
Chinese Petroleum Corporation, IV; 31
    (upd.)
Ctrip.com International Ltd., 97
Dalian Shide Group, 91
Egmont Group, 93
Guangzhou Pearl River Piano Group Ltd.,
    49
Haier Group Corporation, 65
Home Inns & Hotels Management Inc.,
    95
Huawei Technologies Company Ltd., 87
Li & Fung Limited, 59
Noah Education Holdings Ltd., 97
Shanghai Baosteel Group Corporation, 71
Shanghai Petrochemical Co., Ltd., 18
SINA Corporation, 69
Suntech Power Holdings Company Ltd.,
    89
Tianjin Flying Pigeon Bicycle Co., Ltd.,
    95
Tsingtao Brewery Group, 49
Zindart Ltd., 60

Colombia

Almacenes Exito S.A., 89
Avianca Aerovías Nacionales de Colombia
    SA, 36
Bavaria S.A., 90
Cementos Argos S.A., 91
Empresa Colombiana de Petróleos, IV
Empresas Públicas de Medellín S.A.E.S.P.,
    91
Inversiones Nacional de Chocolates S.A.,
    88
Suramericana de Inversiones S.A., 88

Valorem S.A., 88

Croatia

PLIVA d.d., 70

Cyprus

Bank of Cyprus Group, 91
Cyprus Airways Public Limited, 81
Marfin Popular Bank plc, 92

Czech Republic

Budweiser Budvar, National Corporation,
    59
Ceské aerolinie, a.s., 66
Cesky Telecom, a.s., 64
EZ a. s., 97
Skoda Auto a.s., 39
Tinecké Železárny A.S., 92
Zentiva N.V./Zentiva, a.s., 99

Denmark

A.P. Møller - Maersk A/S, 57
Aalborg Industries A/S, 90
Aarhus United A/S, 68
Arla Foods amba, 48
Bang & Olufsen Holding A/S, 37; 86
    (upd.)
Bestseller A/S, 90
Carl Allers Etablissement A/S, 72
Carlsberg A/S, 9; 29 (upd.); 98 (upd.)
Chr. Hansen Group A/S, 70
Dalhoff Larsen & Horneman A/S, 96
Danisco A/S, 44
Danske Bank Aktieselskab, 50
Ecco Sko A/S, 62
FLSmidth & Co. A/S, 72
Group 4 Falck A/S, 42
Grundfos Group, 83
H. Lundbeck A/S, 44
House of Prince A/S, 80
Hummel International A/S, 68
IKEA International A/S, V; 26 (upd.)
ISS A/S, 49
J Lauritzen A/S, 90
Lego A/S, 13; 40 (upd.)
Nordisk Film A/S, 80
Novo Nordisk A/S, I; 61 (upd.)
Schouw & Company A/S, 94
Sophus Berendsen A/S, 49
Sterling European Airlines A/S, 70
TDC A/S, 63
Velux A/S, 86
Vestas Wind Systems A/S, 73

Ecuador

Exportadora Bananera Noboa, S.A., 91
Petróleos del Ecuador, IV

Egypt

EgyptAir, 6; 27 (upd.)
Egyptian General Petroleum Corporation,
    IV; 51 (upd.)
Orascom Construction Industries S.A.E.,
    87

El Salvador

Grupo TACA, 38

Estonia
AS Estonian Air, 71

Ethiopia
Ethiopian Airlines, 81

Fiji
Air Pacific Ltd., 70

Finland
Ahlstrom Corporation, 53
Alma Media Corporation, 98
Amer Group plc, 41
Dynea, 68
Enso-Gutzeit Oy, IV
Finnair Oyj, 6; 25 (upd.); 61 (upd.)
Fiskars Corporation, 33
Fortum Corporation, 30 (upd.)
Hackman Oyj Adp, 44
Huhtamäki Oyj, 64
Imatra Steel Oy Ab, 55
Kansallis-Osake-Pankki, II
Kemira Oyj, 70
Kesko Ltd. (Kesko Oy), 8; 27 (upd.)
KONE Corporation, 27; 76 (upd.)
Kymmene Corporation, IV
M-real Oyj, 56 (upd.)
Metsa-Serla Oy, IV
Metso Corporation, 30 (upd.); 85 (upd.)
Neste Oil Corporation, IV; 85 (upd.)
Nokia Corporation, II; 17 (upd.); 38
   (upd.); 77 (upd.)
Orion Oyj, 72
Outokumpu Oyj, 38
Posti- ja Telelaitos, 6
Raisio PLC, 99
Sanitec Corporation, 51
SanomaWSOY Corporation, 51
Sonera Corporation, 50
Stora Enso Oyj, 36 (upd.); 85 (upd.)
Tamfelt Oyj Abp, 62
United Paper Mills Ltd. (Yhtyneet
   Paperitehtaat Oy), IV
UPM-Kymmene Corporation, 19; 50
   (upd.)
Valmet Corporation (Valmet Oy), III

France
Accor S.A., 10; 27 (upd.); 69 (upd.)
Aéroports de Paris, 33
The Aerospatiale Group, 7; 21 (upd.)
Agence France-Presse, 34
Akerys S.A., 90
Alain Afflelou SA, 53
Alcatel S.A., 9; 36 (upd.)
Alès Groupe, 81
Altran Technologies, 51
Amec Spie S.A., 57
Arc International, 76
AREVA NP, 90 (upd.)
Arianespace S.A., 89
Association des Centres Distributeurs E.
   Leclerc, 37
Assurances Générales de France, 63
Atochem S.A., I
Atos Origin S.A., 69
Au Printemps S.A., V

Auchan, 37
Automobiles Citroen, 7
Autoroutes du Sud de la France SA, 55
Avions Marcel Dassault-Breguet Aviation,
   I
Axa, III
Babolat VS, S.A., 97
Baccarat, 24
Banque Nationale de Paris S.A., II
Baron Philippe de Rothschild S.A., 39
Bayard SA, 49
Belvedere S.A., 93
Bénéteau SA, 55
Besnier SA, 19
BigBen Interactive S.A., 72
bioMérieux S.A., 75
BNP Paribas Group, 36 (upd.)
Boiron S.A., 73
Boizel Chanoine Champagne S.A., 94
Bonduelle SA, 51
Bongrain SA, 25
Bouygues S.A., I; 24 (upd.); 97 (upd.)
Bricorama S.A., 68
Brioche Pasquier S.A., 58
BSN Groupe S.A., II
Buffalo Grill S.A., 94
Bugatti Automobiles S.A.S., 94
Bull S.A., 43 (upd.)
Bureau Veritas SA, 55
Burelle S.A., 23
Business Objects S.A., 25
Camaïeu S.A., 72
Caisse des Dépôts et Consignations, 90
Canal Plus, 10; 34 (upd.)
Cap Gemini Ernst & Young, 37
Carbone Lorraine S.A., 33
Carrefour SA, 10; 27 (upd.); 64 (upd.)
Casino Guichard-Perrachon S.A., 59
   (upd.)
Cemoi S.A., 86
Cetelem S.A., 21
Chanel SA, 12; 49 (upd.)
Chantiers Jeanneau S.A., 96
Charal S.A., 90
Chargeurs International, 6; 21 (upd.)
Christian Dalloz SA, 40
Christian Dior S.A., 19; 49 (upd.)
Christofle SA, 40
Ciments Français, 40
Club Mediterranée S.A., 6; 21 (upd.); 91
   (upd.)
Coflexip S.A., 25
Colas S.A., 31
Compagnie de Saint-Gobain, III; 16
   (upd.); 64 (upd.)
Compagnie des Alpes, 48
Compagnie des Machines Bull S.A., III
Compagnie Financiere de Paribas, II
Compagnie Financière Sucres et Denrées
   S.A., 60
Compagnie Générale d'Électricité, II
Compagnie Générale des Établissements
   Michelin, V; 42 (upd.)
Compagnie Générale Maritime et
   Financière, 6
Comptoirs Modernes S.A., 19
Coopagri Bretagne, 88
Crédit Agricole Group, II; 84 (upd.)

Crédit Lyonnais, 9; 33 (upd.)
Crédit National S.A., 9
Dalkia Holding, 66
Damartex S.A., 98
Darty S.A., 27
Dassault Systèmes S.A., 25
DCN S.A., 75
De Dietrich & Cie., 31
Delachaux S.A., 76
Deveaux S.A., 41
Devoteam S.A., 94
Dexia Group, 42
Doux S.A., 80
Du Pareil au Même, 43
Dynaction S.A., 67
Dyneff S.A., 98
EADS SOCATA, 54
ECS S.A, 12
Ed S.A.S., 88
Éditions Gallimard, 72
Editis S.A. 78
Eiffage, 27
Electricité de France, V; 41 (upd.)
Elf Aquitaine SA, 21 (upd.)
Elior SA, 49
Eram SA, 51
Eramet, 73
Eridania Béghin-Say S.A., 36
Essilor International, 21
Etablissements Economiques du Casino
   Guichard, Perrachon et Cie, S.C.A., 12
Établissements Jacquot and Cie S.A.S., 92
Etam Developpement SA, 44
Eurazeo, 80
Euro Disney S.C.A., 20; 58 (upd.)
Euro RSCG Worldwide S.A., 13
Eurocopter S.A., 80
Eurofins Scientific S.A., 70
Euronext Paris S.A., 37
Expand SA, 48
Facom S.A., 32
Faiveley S.A., 39
Faurecia S.A., 70
Fimalac S.A., 37
Fleury Michon S.A., 39
Floc'h & Marchand, 80
FNAC, 21
Framatome SA, 19
France Telecom S.A., V; 21 (upd.); 99
   (upd.)
Fromageries Bel, 23
G.I.E. Airbus Industrie, I; 12 (upd.)
Galeries Lafayette S.A., V; 23 (upd.)
Gaumont S.A., 25; 91 (upd.)
Gaz de France, V; 40 (upd.)
Gecina SA, 42
Gefco SA, 54
Générale des Eaux Group, V
Geodis S.A., 67
Gévelot S.A., 96
GFI Informatique SA, 49
GiFi S.A., 74
Glaces Thiriet S.A., 76
Grands Vins Jean-Claude Boisset S.A., 98
GrandVision S.A., 43
Grévin & Compagnie SA, 56
Groupama S.A., 76
Groupe Air France, 6

Groupe Alain Manoukian, 55
Groupe André, 17
Groupe Bigard S.A., 96
Groupe Bolloré, 67
Groupe Bourbon S.A., 60
Groupe Castorama-Dubois
    Investissements, 23
Groupe CECAB S.C.A., 88
Groupe Crit S.A., 74
Groupe Danone, 32 (upd.); 93 (upd.)
Groupe Dassault Aviation SA, 26 (upd.)
Groupe de la Cite, IV
Groupe DMC (Dollfus Mieg & Cie), 27
Groupe Euralis, 86
Groupe Flo S.A., 98
Groupe Fournier SA, 44
Groupe Genoyer, 96
Groupe Glon, 84
Groupe Go Sport S.A., 39
Groupe Guillin SA, 40
Groupe Jean-Claude Darmon, 44
Groupe Lactalis 78 (upd.)
Groupe Lapeyre S.A., 33
Groupe Le Duff S.A., 84
Groupe Léa Nature, 88
Groupe Legris Industries, 23
Groupe Les Echos, 25
Groupe Limagrain, 74
Groupe Louis Dreyfus S.A., 60
Groupe Monnoyeur, 72
Groupe Monoprix S.A., 86
Groupe Open, 74
Groupe Partouche SA, 48
Groupe Promodès S.A., 19
Groupe Rougier SA, 21
Groupe SEB, 35
Groupe Sequana Capital 78 (upd.)
Groupe Sidel S.A., 21
Groupe Soufflet SA, 55
Groupe Yves Saint Laurent, 23
Groupe Zannier S.A., 35
Guerbet Group, 46
Guerlain, 23
Guilbert S.A., 42
Guillemot Corporation, 41
Guinot Paris S.A., 82
Guy Degrenne SA, 44
Guyenne et Gascogne, 23
Hachette, IV
Hachette Filipacchi Medias S.A., 21
Havas, SA, 10; 33 (upd.)
Hermès International S.A., 14; 34 (upd.)
Imerys S.A., 40 (upd.)
Imetal S.A., IV
Infogrames Entertainment S.A., 35
Ingenico—Compagnie Industrielle et
    Financière d'Ingénierie, 46
ITM Entreprises SA, 36
JCDecaux S.A., 76
Keolis SA, 51
Kiabi Europe, 66
L'Air Liquide SA, I; 47 (upd.)
L'Entreprise Jean Lefebvre, 23
L'Oréal SA, III; 8 (upd.); 46 (upd.)
L.D.C. SA, 61
La Poste, V; 47 (upd.)
Labeyrie SAS, 80
Laboratoires Arkopharma S.A., 75

Laboratoires de Biologie Végétale Yves
    Rocher, 35
LaCie Group S.A., 76
Lafarge Coppée S.A., III
Lafuma S.A., 39
Laurent-Perrier SA, 42
Lazard LLC, 38
LDC, 68
Le Cordon Bleu S.A., 67
Le Monde S.A., 33
Legrand SA, 21
Leroux S.A.S., 65
Leroy Merlin SA, 54
Ludendo S.A., 88
LVMH Möet Hennessy Louis Vuitton SA,
    I; 10; 33 (upd.)
Lyonnaise des Eaux-Dumez, V
Madrange SA, 58
Maison Louis Jadot, 24
Manitou BF S.A., 27
Manutan International S.A., 72
Marie Brizard & Roger International
    S.A.S., 22; 97 (upd.)
Marionnaud Parfumeries SA, 51
Martell and Company S.A., 82
Matra-Hachette S.A., 15 (upd.)
Matussière et Forest SA, 58
MBK Industrie S.A., 94
Metaleurop S.A., 21
Métropole Télévision, 33
Métropole Télévision S.A., 76 (upd.)
Moliflor Loisirs, 80
Monnaie de Paris, 62
Montupet S.A., 63
Moulinex S.A., 22
Mr. Bricolage S.A., 37
Naf Naf SA, 44
Neopost S.A., 53
Nestlé Waters, 73
Nexans SA, 54
Nexity S.A., 66
Nocibé SA, 54
OENEO S.A., 74 (upd.)
Onet S.A., 92
Otor S.A., 77
PagesJaunes Groupe SA 79
Panzani, 84
Papeteries de Lancey, 23
Pathé SA, 29
Pechiney SA, IV; 45 (upd.)
Penauille Polyservices SA, 49
Pernod Ricard S.A., I; 21 (upd.); 72
    (upd.)
Petit Bateau, 95
Peugeot S.A., I
Picard Surgeles, 76
Pierre & Vacances SA, 48
Pinault-Printemps Redoute S.A., 19 (upd.)
Pinguely-Haulotte SA, 51
Piscines Desjoyaux S.A., 84
Pochet SA, 55
Poliet S.A., 33
PPR S.A., 74 (upd.)
Provimi S.A., 80
PSA Peugeot Citroen S.A., 28 (upd.)
Publicis S.A., 19; 77 (upd.)
Rallye SA, 54
Regie Nationale des Usines Renault, I

Rémy Cointreau Group, 20, 80 (upd.)
Renault S.A., 26 (upd.); 74 (upd.)
Réseau Ferré de France, 66
Rhodia SA, 38
Rhône-Poulenc S.A., I; 10 (upd.)
Robertet SA, 39
Rodriguez Group S.A., 90
Roussel Uclaf, I; 8 (upd.)
Royal Canin S.A., 39
Sabaté Diosos SA, 48
SAGEM S.A., 37
Salomon Worldwide, 20
The Sanofi-Synthélabo Group, I; 49
    (upd.)
Saur S.A.S., 92
Schneider S.A., II; 18 (upd.)
SCOR S.A., 20
Seita, 23
Selectour SA, 53
Sephora Holdings S.A., 82
Simco S.A., 37
Skalli Group, 67
Skis Rossignol S.A., 15; 43 (upd.)
Smoby International SA, 56
Snecma Group, 46
Société Air France, 27 (upd.)
Société BIC S.A., 73
Société d'Exploitation AOM Air Liberté
    SA (AirLib), 53
Societe des Produits Marnier-Lapostolle
    S.A., 88
Société du Figaro S.A., 60
Société du Louvre, 27
Société Générale, II; 42 (upd.)
Société Industrielle Lesaffre, 84
Société Nationale des Chemins de Fer
    Français, V; 57 (upd.)
Société Nationale Elf Aquitaine, IV; 7
    (upd.)
Société Norbert Dentressangle S.A., 67
Sodexho SA, 29; 91 (upd.)
Sodiaal S.A., 36 (upd.)
SODIMA, II
Sommer-Allibert S.A., 19
SR Teleperformance S.A., 86
Steria SA, 49
Suez Lyonnaise des Eaux, 36 (upd.)
Taittinger S.A., 43
Tati SA, 25
Technip 78
Télévision Française 1, 23
Terrena L'Union CANA CAVAL, 70
Thales S.A., 42
THOMSON multimedia S.A., II; 42
    (upd.)
Total Fina Elf S.A., IV; 24 (upd.); 50
    (upd.)
Toupargel-Agrigel S.A., 76
Touton S.A., 92
Transiciel SA, 48
Ubi Soft Entertainment S.A., 41
Ugine S.A., 20
Unibail SA, 40
Unilog SA, 42
Union des Assurances de Pans, III
Union Financière de France Banque SA,
    52
Usinor SA, IV; 42 (upd.)

Valeo, 23; 66 (upd.)
Vallourec SA, 54
Veuve Clicquot Ponsardin SCS, 98
Vicat S.A., 70
Viel & Cie, 76
Vilmorin Clause et Cie, 70
Vinci, 43
Vivarte SA, 54 (upd.)
Vivendi Universal S.A., 46 (upd.)
Wanadoo S.A., 75
Weber et Broutin France, 66
Worms et Cie, 27
Zodiac S.A., 36

Germany

A. Moksel AG, 59
A.W. Faber-Castell
    Unternehmensverwaltung GmbH &
    Co., 51
Adam Opel AG, 7; 21 (upd.); 61 (upd.)
adidas Group AG, 14; 33 (upd.); 75
    (upd.)
Adolf Würth GmbH & Co. KG, 49
AEG A.G., I
Air Berlin GmbH & Co. Luftverkehrs
    KG, 71
Aldi Einkauf GmbH & Co. OHG 13; 86
    (upd.)
Alfred Kärcher GmbH & Co KG, 94
Alfred Ritter GmbH & Co. KG, 58
Allianz AG, III; 15 (upd.); 57 (upd.)
ALTANA AG, 87
AMB Generali Holding AG, 51
Andreas Stihl AG & Co. KG, 16; 59
    (upd.)
AOK-Bundesverband (Federation of the
    AOK) 78
Aral AG, 62
ARD, 41
August Storck KG, 66
AVA AG (Allgemeine Handelsgesellschaft
    der Verbraucher AG), 33
AXA Colonia Konzern AG, 27; 49 (upd.)
Axel Springer Verlag AG, IV; 20 (upd.)
Bahlsen GmbH & Co. KG, 44
Barmag AG, 39
BASF Aktiengesellschaft, I; 18 (upd.); 50
    (upd.)
Bauer Publishing Group, 7
Bayer A.G., I; 13 (upd.); 41 (upd.)
Bayerische Hypotheken- und
    Wechsel-Bank AG, II
Bayerische Motoren Werke AG, I; 11
    (upd.); 38 (upd.)
Bayerische Vereinsbank A.G., II
Bayernwerk AG, V; 23 (upd.)
Beate Uhse AG, 96
Behr GmbH & Co. KG, 72
Beiersdorf AG, 29
Berliner Stadtreinigungsbetriebe, 58
Berliner Verkehrsbetriebe (BVG), 58
Berlinwasser Holding AG, 90
Bertelsmann A.G., IV; 15 (upd.); 43
    (upd.); 91 (upd.)
Bewag AG, 39
Bibliographisches Institut & F.A.
    Brockhaus AG, 74
Bilfinger & Berger AG, I; 55 (upd.)

Brauerei Beck & Co., 9; 33 (upd.)
Braun GmbH, 51
Brenntag AG, 8; 23 (upd.)
Brose Fahrzeugteile GmbH & Company
    KG, 84
BSH Bosch und Siemens Hausgeräte
    GmbH, 67
Buderus AG, 37
Burda Holding GmbH. & Co., 23
C&A Brenninkmeyer KG, V
C. Bechstein Pianofortefabrik AG, 96
C.H. Boehringer Sohn, 39
Carl Kühne KG (GmbH & Co.), 94
Carl Zeiss AG, III; 34 (upd.); 91 (upd.)
CeWe Color Holding AG, 76
Commerzbank A.G., II; 47 (upd.)
Continental AG, V; 56 (upd.)
Cornelsen Verlagsholding GmbH & Co.,
    90
Dachser GmbH & Co. KG, 88
Daimler-Benz Aerospace AG, 16
DaimlerChrysler AG, I; 15 (upd.); 34
    (upd.); 64 (upd.)
Dalli-Werke GmbH & Co. KG, 86
dba Luftfahrtgesellschaft mbH, 76
Debeka Krankenversicherungsverein auf
    Gegenseitigkeit, 72
Degussa Group, IV
Degussa-Huls AG, 32 (upd.)
Deutsche Babcock A.G., III
Deutsche Bahn AG, 46 (upd.)
Deutsche Bank AG, II; 14 (upd.); 40
    (upd.)
Deutsche BP Aktiengesellschaft, 7
Deutsche Bundesbahn, V
Deutsche Bundespost TELEKOM, V
Deutsche Börse AG, 59
Deutsche Fussball Bund e.V., 98
Deutsche Lufthansa AG, I; 26 (upd.); 68
    (upd.)
Deutsche Post AG, 29
Deutsche Steinzeug Cremer & Breuer
    Aktiengesellschaft, 91
Deutsche Telekom AG, 48 (upd.)
Deutscher Sparkassen- und Giroverband
    (DSGV), 84
Deutz AG, 39
Diehl Stiftung & Co. KG 79
Dirk Rossmann GmbH, 94
Dr. August Oetker KG, 51
Drägerwerk AG, 83
Dräxlmaier Group, 90
Dresdner Bank A.G., II; 57 (upd.)
Dürkopp Adler AG, 65
Dürr AG, 44
Dyckerhoff AG, 35
E.On AG, 50 (upd.)
Eckes AG, 56
Edeka Zentrale A.G., II; 47 (upd.)
edel music AG, 44
ERGO Versicherungsgruppe AG, 44
ESCADA AG, 71
Esselte Leitz GmbH & Co. KG, 48
Etienne Aigner AG, 52
FAG—Kugelfischer Georg Schäfer AG, 62
Fairchild Dornier GmbH, 48 (upd.)
Feldmuhle Nobel A.G., III
Fielmann AG, 31

Francotyp-Postalia Holding AG, 92
Frankfurter Allgemeine Zeitung GmbH,
    66
Fraport AG Frankfurt Airport Services
    Worldwide, 90
Fresenius AG, 56
Freudenberg & Co., 41
Fried. Krupp GmbH, IV
Friedrich Grohe AG & Co. KG, 53
GEA AG, 27
GEHE AG, 27
Gelita AG, 74
GEMA (Gesellschaft für musikalische
    Aufführungs- und mechanische
    Vervielfältigungsrechte), 70
geobra Brandstätter GmbH & Co. KG,
    48
Gerhard D. Wempe KG, 88
Gerling-Konzern Versicherungs-
    Beteiligungs-Aktiengesellschaft, 51
Gerresheimer Glas AG, 43
Gerry Weber International AG, 63
Getrag Corporate Group, 92
GfK Aktiengesellschaft, 49
Giesecke & Devrient GmbH, 83
Gildemeister AG 79
Groz-Beckert Group, 68
Grundig AG, 27
Hansgrohe AG, 56
Hapag-Lloyd AG, 6; 97 (upd.)
HARIBO GmbH & Co. KG, 44
HDI (Haftpflichtverband der Deutschen
    Industrie Versicherung auf
    Gegenseitigkeit V.a.G.), 53
Heidelberger Druckmaschinen AG, 40
Heidelberger Zement AG, 31
Heinrich Deichmann-Schuhe GmbH &
    Co. KG, 88
Hella KGaA Hueck & Co., 66
Henkel KGaA, III; 34 (upd.); 95 (upd.)
Heraeus Holding GmbH, IV; 54 (upd.)
Hertie Waren- und Kaufhaus GmbH, V
Hexal AG, 69
HiPP GmbH & Co. Vertrieb KG, 88
Hochtief AG, 33; 88 (upd.)
Hoechst A.G., I; 18 (upd.)
Hoesch AG, IV
Hornbach Holding AG, 98
Hugo Boss AG, 48
HUK-Coburg, 58
Huls A.G., I
HVB Group, 59 (upd.)
Ihr Platz GmbH + Company KG, 77
Infineon Technologies AG, 50
J.J. Darboven GmbH & Co. KG, 96
J.M. Voith AG, 33
Jenoptik AG, 33
Julius Blüthner Pianofortefabrik GmbH
    78
Jungheinrich AG, 96
Kamps AG, 44
Karlsberg Brauerei GmbH & Co KG, 41
Karstadt Quelle AG, V; 19 (upd.); 57
    (upd.)
Kaufhof Warenhaus AG, V; 23 (upd.)
Kaufring AG, 35
KHD Konzern, III
Klaus Steilmann GmbH & Co. KG, 53

Klöckner-Werke AG, IV; 58 (upd.)
Knorr-Bremse AG, 84
Koenig & Bauer AG, 64
Kolbenschmidt Pierburg AG, 97
König Brauerei GmbH & Co. KG, 35 (upd.)
Körber AG, 60
Kreditanstalt für Wiederaufbau, 29
KSB AG, 62
Leica Camera AG, 35
Leica Microsystems Holdings GmbH, 35
Leoni AG, 98
Linde AG, I; 67 (upd.)
Loewe AG, 90
Löwenbräu AG, 80
LTU Group Holding GmbH, 37
M. DuMont Schauberg GmbH & Co. KG, 92
MAN Aktiengesellschaft, III
MAN Roland Druckmaschinen AG, 94
Mannesmann AG, III; 14 (upd.); 38 (upd.)
Margarete Steiff GmbH, 23
Märklin Holding GmbH, 70
Matth. Hohner AG, 53
Melitta Unternehmensgruppe Bentz KG, 53
Merz Group, 81
Messerschmitt-Bölkow-Blohm GmbH., I
Metallgesellschaft AG, IV; 16 (upd.)
Metro AG, 50
Miele & Cie. KG, 56
MITROPA AG, 37
Montblanc International GmbH, 82
Munich Re (Münchener Rückversicherungs-Gesellschaft Aktiengesellschaft in München), III; 46 (upd.)
Nixdorf Computer AG, III
Norddeutsche Affinerie AG, 62
Optische Werke G. Rodenstock, 44
Osram GmbH, 86
Otto Versand GmbH & Co., V; 15 (upd.); 34 (upd.)
Paulaner Brauerei GmbH & Co. KG, 35
Peek & Cloppenburg KG, 46
Philipp Holzmann AG, 17
Phoenix AG, 68
Porsche AG, 13; 31 (upd.)
Preussag AG, 17; 42 (upd.)
PreussenElektra Aktiengesellschaft, V
ProSiebenSat.1 Media AG, 54
Puma AG Rudolf Dassler Sport, 35
PWA Group, IV
Qiagen N.V., 39
Quelle Group, V
Radeberger Gruppe AG, 75
RAG AG, 35; 60 (upd.)
ratiopharm Group, 84
Ravensburger AG, 64
RENK AG, 37
Rheinmetall AG, 9; 97 (upd.)
Robert Bosch GmbH, I; 16 (upd.); 43 (upd.)
Röchling Gruppe, 94
Rohde & Schwarz GmbH & Co. KG, 39
Roland Berger & Partner GmbH, 37
The Rowohlt Verlag GmbH, 96

Ruhrgas AG, V; 38 (upd.)
Ruhrkohle AG, IV
RWE AG, V; 50 (upd.)
Saarberg-Konzern, IV
Salzgitter AG, IV
SAP AG, 16; 43 (upd.)
Schenker-Rhenus AG, 6
Schering AG, I; 50 (upd.)
Sennheiser Electronic GmbH & Co. KG, 66
Siemens AG, II; 14 (upd.); 57 (upd.)
Siltronic AG, 90
Sixt AG, 39
SPAR Handels AG, 35
SPIEGEL-Verlag Rudolf Augstein GmbH & Co. KG, 44
Stinnes AG, 8; 23 (upd.); 59 (upd.)
Stollwerck AG, 53
Südzucker AG, 27
Symrise GmbH and Company KG, 89
T-Online International AG, 61
TA Triumph-Adler AG, 48
Tarkett Sommer AG, 25
TaurusHolding GmbH & Co. KG, 46
Tchibo GmbH, 82
Tengelmann Group, 27
ThyssenKrupp AG, IV; 28 (upd.); 87 (upd.)
Touristik Union International GmbH. and Company K.G., II
TRUMPF GmbH + Co. KG, 86
TUI Group GmbH, 44
UFA TV & Film Produktion GmbH, 80
United Internet AG, 99
Vaillant GmbH, 44
Varta AG, 23
Veba A.G., I; 15 (upd.)
Vereinigte Elektrizitätswerke Westfalen AG, V
Verlagsgruppe Georg von Holtzbrinck GmbH, 35
Verlagsgruppe Weltbild GmbH, 98
VEW AG, 39
VIAG Aktiengesellschaft, IV
Victoria Group, III; 44 (upd.)
Viessmann Werke GmbH & Co., 37
Wilhelm Karmann GmbH, 94
Villeroy & Boch AG, 37
Volkswagen Aktiengesellschaft, I; 11 (upd.); 32 (upd.)
Vorwerk & Co., 27
Vossloh AG, 53
Wacker-Chemie GmbH, 35
Wacker Construction Equipment AG, 95
WAZ Media Group, 82
Wella AG, III; 48 (upd.)
Weru Aktiengesellschaft, 18
Westdeutsche Landesbank Girozentrale, II; 46 (upd.)
Wincor Nixdorf Holding GmbH, 69 (upd.)
Württembergische Metallwarenfabrik AG (WMF), 60
Zapf Creation AG, 95

ZF Friedrichshafen AG, 48

Ghana
Ashanti Goldfields Company Limited, 43

Greece
Aegean Marine Petroleum Network Inc., 89
Aegek S.A., 64
Attica Enterprises S.A., 64
Danaos Corporation, 91
Diana Shipping Inc., 95
DryShips Inc., 95
Greek Organization of Football Prognostics S.A. (OPAP), 97
Hellenic Petroleum SA, 64
Jumbo S.A., 96
National Bank of Greece, 41
Royal Olympic Cruise Lines Inc., 52
Stelmar Shipping Ltd., 52
Titan Cement Company S.A., 64
Tsakos Energy Navigation Ltd., 91
Vivartia S.A., 82

Guatemala
Corporación Multi-Inversiones, 94

Hong Kong
A.S. Watson & Company Ltd., 84
Bank of East Asia Ltd., 63
Cable & Wireless HKT, 30 (upd.)
Cathay Pacific Airways Limited, 6; 34 (upd.)
CDC Corporation, 71
Chaoda Modern Agriculture (Holdings) Ltd., 87
Cheung Kong (Holdings) Ltd., IV; 20 (upd.); 94 (upd.)
China Merchants International Holdings Co., Ltd., 52
CITIC Pacific Ltd., 18
Dairy Farm International Holdings Ltd., 97
First Pacific Company Limited, 18
The Garden Company Ltd., 82
GOME Electrical Appliances Holding Ltd., 87
Guangzhou R&F Properties Co., Ltd., 95
Hang Seng Bank Ltd., 60
Henderson Land Development Company Ltd., 70
Hong Kong and China Gas Company Ltd., 73
Hong Kong Dragon Airlines Ltd., 66
Hong Kong Telecommunications Ltd., 6
The Hongkong and Shanghai Banking Corporation Limited, II
Hongkong Electric Holdings Ltd., 6; 23 (upd.)
Hongkong Land Holdings Limited, IV; 47 (upd.)
Hopson Development Holdings Ltd., 87
Hutchison Whampoa Limited, 18; 49 (upd.)
Kerry Properties Limited, 22
Meyer International Holdings, Ltd., 87
Nam Tai Electronics, Inc., 61

New World Development Company
Limited, IV; 38 (upd.)
Next Media Ltd., 61
Pacific Basin Shipping Ltd., 86
Playmates Toys, 23
Shangri-La Asia Ltd., 71
The Singer Company N.V., 30 (upd.)
Swire Pacific Limited, I; 16 (upd.); 57
(upd.)
Techtronic Industries Company Ltd., 73
Tommy Hilfiger Corporation, 20; 53
(upd.)
Vitasoy International Holdings Ltd., 94
VTech Holdings Ltd., 77

Hungary
Magyar Telekom Rt. 78
Malév Plc, 24
MOL Rt, 70
Orszagos Takarekpenztar es Kereskedelmi
Bank Rt. (OTP Bank) 78

Iceland
Alfesca hf, 82
Bakkavör Group hf., 91
Baugur Group hf, 81
Icelandair, 52
Icelandic Group hf, 81
Landsbanki Islands hf, 81

India
Adani Enterprises Ltd., 97
Aditya Birla Group 79
Air Sahara Limited, 65
Air-India Limited, 6; 27 (upd.)
Bajaj Auto Limited, 39
Bharti Tele-Ventures Limited, 75
Coal India Limited, IV; 44 (upd.)
Dr. Reddy's Laboratories Ltd., 59
Essar Group Ltd. 79
Hindustan Lever Limited 79
Indian Airlines Ltd., 46
Indian Oil Corporation Ltd., IV; 48
(upd.)
Infosys Technologies Ltd., 38
Jet Airways (India) Private Limited, 65
Minerals and Metals Trading Corporation
of India Ltd., IV
MTR Foods Ltd., 55
Neyveli Lignite Corporation Ltd., 65
Oil and Natural Gas Corporation Ltd.,
IV; 90 (upd.)
Ranbaxy Laboratories Ltd., 70
Raymond Ltd., 77
Reliance Industries Ltd., 81
Rolta India Ltd., 90
Satyam Computer Services Ltd., 85
State Bank of India, 63
Steel Authority of India Ltd., IV; 66
(upd.)
Sun Pharmaceutical Industries Ltd., 57
Tata Iron & Steel Co. Ltd., IV; 44 (upd.)
Tata Tea Ltd., 76
Wipro Limited, 43

Indonesia
Djarum PT, 62
Garuda Indonesia, 6; 58 (upd.)

PERTAMINA, IV
Pertamina, 56 (upd.)
PT Astra International Tbk, 56
PT Bank Buana Indonesia Tbk, 60
PT Indosat Tbk, 93

Iran
IranAir, 81
National Iranian Oil Company, IV; 61
(upd.)

Ireland
Aer Lingus Group plc, 34; 89 (upd.)
Allied Irish Banks, plc, 16; 43 (upd.); 94
(upd.)
Baltimore Technologies Plc, 42
Bank of Ireland, 50
CRH plc, 64
DEPFA BANK PLC, 69
Dunnes Stores Ltd., 58
eircom plc, 31 (upd.)
Elan Corporation PLC, 63
Fyffes Plc, 38
Glanbia plc, 59
Glen Dimplex 78
Greencore Group plc, 98
Harland and Wolff Holdings plc, 19
IAWS Group plc, 49
Independent News & Media PLC, 61
IONA Technologies plc, 43
Irish Distillers Group, 96
Irish Life & Permanent Plc, 59
Jefferson Smurfit Group plc, IV; 19
(upd.); 49 (upd.)
Jurys Doyle Hotel Group plc, 64
Kerry Group plc, 27; 87 (upd.)
Musgrave Group Plc, 57
Paddy Power plc, 98
Ryanair Holdings plc, 35
Shannon Aerospace Ltd., 36
SkillSoft Public Limited Company, 81
Telecom Eireann, 7
Thomas Crosbie Holdings Limited, 81
Waterford Wedgwood plc, 34 (upd.)

Israel
Amdocs Ltd., 47
Bank Hapoalim B.M., II; 54 (upd.)
Bank Leumi le-Israel B.M., 60
Blue Square Israel Ltd., 41
BVR Systems (1998) Ltd., 93
Castro Model Ltd., 86
ECI Telecom Ltd., 18
El Al Israel Airlines Ltd., 23
Elscint Ltd., 20
Given Imaging Ltd., 83
IDB Holding Corporation Ltd., 97
Israel Aircraft Industries Ltd., 69
Israel Chemicals Ltd., 55
Koor Industries Ltd., II; 25 (upd.); 68
(upd.)
Lipman Electronic Engineering Ltd., 81
Makhteshim-Agan Industries Ltd., 85
NICE Systems Ltd., 83
Orbotech Ltd., 75
Scitex Corporation Ltd., 24
Strauss-Elite Group, 68

Syneron Medical Ltd., 91
Taro Pharmaceutical Industries Ltd., 65
Teva Pharmaceutical Industries Ltd., 22;
54 (upd.)

Italy
AgustaWestland N.V., 75
Alfa Romeo, 13; 36 (upd.)
Alitalia—Linee Aeree Italiana, S.p.A., 6;
29 (upd.); 97 (upd.)
Alleanza Assicurazioni S.p.A., 65
Aprilia SpA, 17
Arnoldo Mondadori Editore S.p.A., IV;
19 (upd.); 54 (upd.)
Artsana SpA, 92
Assicurazioni Generali SpA, III; 15 (upd.)
Autogrill SpA, 49
Automobili Lamborghini Holding S.p.A.,
13; 34 (upd.); 91 (upd.)
Banca Commerciale Italiana SpA, II
Banca Fideuram SpA, 63
Banca Intesa SpA, 65
Banca Monte dei Paschi di Siena SpA, 65
Banca Nazionale del Lavoro SpA, 72
Barilla G. e R. Fratelli S.p.A., 17; 50
(upd.)
Benetton Group S.p.A., 10; 67 (upd.)
Brioni Roman Style S.p.A., 67
Bulgari S.p.A., 20
Cantine Giorgio Lungarotti S.R.L., 67
Capitalia S.p.A., 65
Cinemeccanica SpA 78
Compagnia Italiana dei Jolly Hotels
S.p.A., 71
Credito Italiano, II
Cremonini S.p.A., 57
Davide Campari-Milano S.p.A., 57
De'Longhi S.p.A., 66
Diadora SpA, 86
Diesel SpA, 40
Dolce & Gabbana SpA, 62
Ducati Motor Holding SpA, 30; 86 (upd.)
ENI S.p.A., 69 (upd.)
Ente Nazionale Idrocarburi, IV
Ente Nazionale per L'Energia Elettrica, V
Ermenegildo Zegna SpA, 63
Fabbrica D' Armi Pietro Beretta S.p.A., 39
FASTWEB S.p.A., 83
Ferrari S.p.A., 13; 36 (upd.)
Ferrero SpA, 54
Ferretti Group SpA, 90
Fiat SpA, I; 11 (upd.); 50 (upd.)
Fila Holding S.p.A., 20; 52 (upd.)
Finarte Casa d'Aste S.p.A., 93
Finmeccanica S.p.A., 84
Gianni Versace SpA, 22
Giorgio Armani S.p.A., 45
Gruppo Coin S.p.A., 41
Gruppo Riva Fire SpA, 88
Guccio Gucci, S.p.A., 15
illycaffè SpA, 50
Industrie Natuzzi S.p.A., 18
Industrie Zignago Santa Margherita
S.p.A., 67
Ing. C. Olivetti & C., S.p.a., III
Istituto per la Ricostruzione Industriale
S.p.A., I; 11
Juventus F.C. S.p.A, 53

Luxottica SpA, 17; 52 (upd.)
Magneti Marelli Holding SpA, 90
Marchesi Antinori SRL, 42
Marcolin S.p.A., 61
Mariella Burani Fashion Group, 92
Martini & Rossi SpA, 63
Marzotto S.p.A., 20; 67 (upd.)
Mediaset SpA, 50
Mediolanum S.p.A., 65
Milan AC, S.p.A. 79
Miroglio SpA, 86
Montedison SpA, I; 24 (upd.)
Officine Alfieri Maserati S.p.A., 13
Olivetti S.p.A., 34 (upd.)
Pagnossin S.p.A., 73
Parmalat Finanziaria SpA, 50
Peg Perego SpA, 88
Perfetti Van Melle S.p.A., 72
Piaggio & C. S.p.A., 20
Pirelli & C. S.p.A., 75 (upd.)
Pirelli S.p.A., V; 15 (upd.)
RCS MediaGroup S.p.A., 96
Reno de Medici S.p.A., 41
Rinascente S.p.A., 71
Riunione Adriatica di Sicurtè SpA, III
Safilo SpA, 54
Salvatore Ferragamo Italia S.p.A., 62
Sanpaolo IMI S.p.A., 50
Seat Pagine Gialle S.p.A., 47
Sirti S.p.A., 76
Società Finanziaria Telefonica per Azioni,
   V
Società Sportiva Lazio SpA, 44
Stefanel SpA, 63
Targetti Sankey SpA, 86
Telecom Italia Mobile S.p.A., 63
Telecom Italia S.p.A., 43
Tiscali SpA, 48

Jamaica

Air Jamaica Limited, 54
Desnoes and Geddes Limited 79
GraceKennedy Ltd., 92
Wray & Nephew Group Ltd., 98

Japan

AEON Co., Ltd., 68 (upd.)
Aisin Seiki Co., Ltd., III; 48 (upd.)
Aiwa Co., Ltd., 30
Ajinomoto Co., Inc., II; 28 (upd.)
All Nippon Airways Co., Ltd., 6; 38
   (upd.); 91 (upd.)
Alpine Electronics, Inc., 13
Alps Electric Co., Ltd., II; 44 (upd.)
Anritsu Corporation, 68
Asahi Breweries, Ltd., I; 20 (upd.); 52
   (upd.)
Asahi Denka Kogyo KK, 64
Asahi Glass Company, Ltd., III; 48 (upd.)
Asahi National Broadcasting Company,
   Ltd., 9
Asatsu-DK Inc., 82
ASICS Corporation, 57
Astellas Pharma Inc., 97 (upd.)
Autobacs Seven Company Ltd., 76
Bandai Co., Ltd., 55
Bank of Tokyo-Mitsubishi Ltd., II; 15
   (upd.)

Benesse Corporation, 76
Bourbon Corporation, 82
Bridgestone Corporation, V; 21 (upd.); 59
   (upd.)
Brother Industries, Ltd., 14
C. Itoh & Company Ltd., I
Canon Inc., III; 18 (upd.); 79 (upd.)
Capcom Company Ltd., 83
CASIO Computer Co., Ltd., III; 16
   (upd.); 40 (upd.)
Central Japan Railway Company, 43
Chubu Electric Power Company, Inc., V;
   46 (upd.)
Chugai Pharmaceutical Co., Ltd., 50
Chugoku Electric Power Company Inc.,
   V; 53 (upd.)
Citizen Watch Co., Ltd., III; 21 (upd.);
   81 (upd.)
Clarion Company Ltd., 64
Cosmo Oil Co., Ltd., IV; 53 (upd.)
Dai Nippon Printing Co., Ltd., IV; 57
   (upd.)
The Dai-Ichi Kangyo Bank Ltd., II
Daido Steel Co., Ltd., IV
The Daiei, Inc., V; 17 (upd.); 41 (upd.)
Daihatsu Motor Company, Ltd., 7; 21
   (upd.)
Daiichikosho Company Ltd., 86
Daikin Industries, Ltd., III
Daiko Advertising Inc. 79
The Daimaru, Inc., V; 42 (upd.)
Daio Paper Corporation, IV, 84 (upd.)
Daishowa Paper Manufacturing Co., Ltd.,
   IV; 57 (upd.)
The Daiwa Bank, Ltd., II; 39 (upd.)
Daiwa Securities Group Inc., II; 55 (upd.)
DDI Corporation, 7
DENSO Corporation, 46 (upd.)
Dentsu Inc., I; 16 (upd.); 40 (upd.)
East Japan Railway Company, V; 66
   (upd.)
Ebara Corporation, 83
Elpida Memory, Inc., 83
Ezaki Glico Company Ltd., 72
Fanuc Ltd., III; 17 (upd.); 75 (upd.)
The Fuji Bank, Ltd., II
Fuji Electric Co., Ltd., II; 48 (upd.)
Fuji Photo Film Co., Ltd., III; 18 (upd.);
   79 (upd.)
Fuji Television Network Inc., 91
Fujisawa Pharmaceutical Company, Ltd.,
   I; 58 (upd.)
Fujitsu Limited, III; 16 (upd.); 42 (upd.)
Funai Electric Company Ltd., 62
The Furukawa Electric Co., Ltd., III
General Sekiyu K.K., IV
Hakuhodo, Inc., 6; 42 (upd.)
Hankyu Department Stores, Inc., V; 23
   (upd.); 62 (upd.)
Hagoromo Foods Corporation, 84
Hino Motors, Ltd., 7; 21 (upd.)
Hitachi, Ltd., I; 12 (upd.); 40 (upd.)
Hitachi Metals, Ltd., IV
Hitachi Zosen Corporation, III; 53 (upd.)
Hokkaido Electric Power Company Inc.
   (HEPCO), V; 58 (upd.)
Hokuriku Electric Power Company, V

Honda Motor Company Ltd., I; 10
   (upd.); 29 (upd.); 96 (upd.)
Honshu Paper Co., Ltd., IV
Hoshino Gakki Co. Ltd., 55
Idemitsu Kosan Co., Ltd., IV; 49 (upd.)
Isetan Company Limited, V; 36 (upd.)
Ishikawajima-Harima Heavy Industries
   Company, Ltd., III; 86 (upd.)
Isuzu Motors, Ltd., 9; 23 (upd.); 57
   (upd.)
Ito-Yokado Co., Ltd., V; 42 (upd.)
ITOCHU Corporation, 32
Itoham Foods Inc., II; 61 (upd.)
Japan Airlines Company, Ltd., I; 32
   (upd.)
JAFCO Co. Ltd. 79
Japan Broadcasting Corporation, 7
Japan Leasing Corporation, 8
Japan Pulp and Paper Company Limited,
   IV
Japan Tobacco Inc., V; 46 (upd.)
JFE Shoji Holdings Inc., 88
JSP Corporation, 74
Jujo Paper Co., Ltd., IV
JUSCO Co., Ltd., V
Kajima Corporation, I; 51 (upd.)
Kanebo, Ltd., 53
Kanematsu Corporation, IV; 24 (upd.)
The Kansai Electric Power Company, Inc.,
   V; 62 (upd.)
Kansai Paint Company Ltd., 80
Kao Corporation, III; 20 (upd.); 79
   (upd.)
Katokichi Company Ltd., 82
Kawai Musical Instruments Mfg Co. Ltd.
   78
Kawasaki Heavy Industries, Ltd., III; 63
   (upd.)
Kawasaki Kisen Kaisha, Ltd., V; 56 (upd.)
Kawasaki Steel Corporation, IV
Keio Corporation, V; 96 (upd.)
Kenwood Corporation, 31
Kewpie Kabushiki Kaisha, 57
Kikkoman Corporation, 14; 47 (upd.)
Kinki Nippon Railway Company Ltd., V
Kirin Brewery Company, Limited, I; 21
   (upd.); 63 (upd.)
Kobe Steel, Ltd., IV; 19 (upd.)
Kodansha Ltd., IV; 38 (upd.)
Komatsu Ltd., III; 16 (upd.); 52 (upd.)
Konami Corporation, 96
Konica Corporation, III; 30 (upd.)
Kotobukiya Co., Ltd., V; 56 (upd.)
Kubota Corporation, III; 26 (upd.)
Kumagai Gumi Company, Ltd., I
Kumon Institute of Education Co., Ltd.,
   72
Kyocera Corporation, II; 21 (upd.); 79
   (upd.)
Kyokuyo Company Ltd., 75
Kyowa Hakko Kogyo Co., Ltd., III; 48
   (upd.)
Kyushu Electric Power Company Inc., V
Lion Corporation, III; 51 (upd.)
Long-Term Credit Bank of Japan, Ltd., II
Mabuchi Motor Co. Ltd., 68

Makita Corporation, 22; 59 (upd.)
Mandom Corporation, 82
Marubeni Corporation, I; 24 (upd.)
Maruha Group Inc., 75 (upd.)
Marui Company Ltd., V; 62 (upd.)
Maruzen Co., Limited, 18
Matsushita Electric Industrial Co., Ltd., II; 64 (upd.)
Matsushita Electric Works, Ltd., III; 7 (upd.)
Matsuzakaya Company Ltd., V; 64 (upd.)
Mazda Motor Corporation, 9; 23 (upd.); 63 (upd.)
Meidensha Corporation, 92
Meiji Dairies Corporation, II; 82 (upd.)
The Meiji Mutual Life Insurance Company, III
Meiji Seika Kaisha Ltd., II; 64 (upd.)
Mercian Corporation, 77
Millea Holdings Inc., 64 (upd.)
Minebea Co., Ltd., 90
Minolta Co., Ltd., III; 18 (upd.); 43 (upd.)
The Mitsubishi Bank, Ltd., II
Mitsubishi Chemical Corporation, I; 56 (upd.)
Mitsubishi Corporation, I; 12 (upd.)
Mitsubishi Electric Corporation, II; 44 (upd.)
Mitsubishi Estate Company, Limited, IV; 61 (upd.)
Mitsubishi Heavy Industries, Ltd., III; 7 (upd.); 40 (upd.)
Mitsubishi Materials Corporation, III
Mitsubishi Motors Corporation, 9; 23 (upd.); 57 (upd.)
Mitsubishi Oil Co., Ltd., IV
Mitsubishi Rayon Co., Ltd., V
The Mitsubishi Trust & Banking Corporation, II
Mitsubishi UFJ Financial Group, Inc., 99 (upd.)
Mitsui & Co., Ltd., 28 (upd.)
The Mitsui Bank, Ltd., II
Mitsui Bussan K.K., I
Mitsui Marine and Fire Insurance Company, Limited, III
Mitsui Mining & Smelting Co., Ltd., IV
Mitsui Mining Company, Limited, IV
Mitsui Mutual Life Insurance Company, III; 39 (upd.)
Mitsui O.S.K. Lines, Ltd., V; 96 (upd.)
Mitsui Petrochemical Industries, Ltd., 9
Mitsui Real Estate Development Co., Ltd., IV
The Mitsui Trust & Banking Company, Ltd., II
Mitsukoshi Ltd., V; 56 (upd.)
Mizuho Financial Group Inc., 58 (upd.)
Mizuno Corporation, 25
Morinaga & Co. Ltd., 61
Nagasakiya Co., Ltd., V; 69 (upd.)
Nagase & Co., Ltd., 8; 61 (upd.)
NEC Corporation, II; 21 (upd.); 57 (upd.)
NGK Insulators Ltd., 67
NHK Spring Co., Ltd., III
Nichii Co., Ltd., V

Nichimen Corporation, IV; 24 (upd.)
Nichirei Corporation, 70
Nichiro Corporation, 86
Nidec Corporation, 59
Nihon Keizai Shimbun, Inc., IV
The Nikko Securities Company Limited, II; 9 (upd.)
Nikon Corporation, III; 48 (upd.)
Nintendo Co., Ltd., III; 7 (upd.); 28 (upd.); 67 (upd.)
Nippon Credit Bank, II
Nippon Electric Glass Co. Ltd., 95
Nippon Express Company, Ltd., V; 64 (upd.)
Nippon Life Insurance Company, III; 60 (upd.)
Nippon Light Metal Company, Ltd., IV
Nippon Meat Packers Inc., II, 78 (upd.)
Nippon Oil Corporation, IV; 63 (upd.)
Nippon Seiko K.K., III
Nippon Sheet Glass Company, Limited, III
Nippon Shinpan Co., Ltd., II; 61 (upd.)
Nippon Soda Co., Ltd., 85
Nippon Steel Corporation, IV; 17 (upd.); 96 (upd.)
Nippon Suisan Kaisha, Ltd., II; 92 (upd.)
Nippon Telegraph and Telephone Corporation, V; 51 (upd.)
Nippon Yusen Kabushiki Kaisha (NYK), V; 72 (upd.)
Nippondenso Co., Ltd., III
Nissan Motor Company Ltd., I; 11 (upd.); 34 (upd.); 92 (upd.)
Nisshin Seifun Group Inc., II; 66 (upd.)
Nisshin Steel Co., Ltd., IV
Nissho Iwai K.K., I
Nissin Food Products Company Ltd., 75
NKK Corporation, IV; 28 (upd.)
NOF Corporation, 72
Nomura Securities Company, Limited, II; 9 (upd.)
Norinchukin Bank, II
NTN Corporation, III; 47 (upd.)
Obayashi Corporation 78
Odakyu Electric Railway Co., Ltd., V; 68 (upd.)
Ohbayashi Corporation, I
Oji Paper Co., Ltd., IV; 57 (upd.)
Oki Electric Industry Company, Limited, II
Okuma Holdings Inc., 74
Okura & Co., Ltd., IV
Omron Corporation, II; 28 (upd.)
Onoda Cement Co., Ltd., III
ORIX Corporation, II; 44 (upd.)
Osaka Gas Company, Ltd., V; 60 (upd.)
Otari Inc., 89
Paloma Industries Ltd., 71
Pearl Corporation 78
Pentax Corporation 78
Pioneer Electronic Corporation, III; 28 (upd.)
Rengo Co., Ltd., IV
Ricoh Company, Ltd., III; 36 (upd.)
Roland Corporation, 38
Ryoshoku Ltd., 72
Sankyo Company, Ltd., I; 56 (upd.)

Sanrio Company, Ltd., 38
The Sanwa Bank, Ltd., II; 15 (upd.)
SANYO Electric Co., Ltd., II; 36 (upd.); 95 (upd.)
Sanyo-Kokusaku Pulp Co., Ltd., IV
Sapporo Holdings Limited, I; 13 (upd.); 36 (upd.); 97 (upd.)
SEGA Corporation, 73
Seibu Department Stores, Ltd., V; 42 (upd.)
Seibu Railway Company Ltd., V; 74 (upd.)
Seiko Corporation, III; 17 (upd.); 72 (upd.)
Seino Transportation Company, Ltd., 6
The Seiyu, Ltd., V; 36 (upd.)
Sekisui Chemical Co., Ltd., III; 72 (upd.)
Sharp Corporation, II; 12 (upd.); 40 (upd.)
Shikoku Electric Power Company, Inc., V; 60 (upd.)
Shimano Inc., 64
Shionogi & Co., Ltd., III; 17 (upd.); 98 (upd.)
Shiseido Company, Limited, III; 22 (upd.), 81 (upd.)
Shochiku Company Ltd., 74
Sompo Japan Insurance, Inc., 98 (upd.)
Showa Shell Sekiyu K.K., IV; 59 (upd.)
Snow Brand Milk Products Company, Ltd., II; 48 (upd.)
Softbank Corp., 13; 38 (upd.)
Sojitz Corporation, 96 (upd.)
Sony Corporation, II; 12 (upd.); 40 (upd.)
The Sumitomo Bank, Limited, II; 26 (upd.)
Sumitomo Chemical Company Ltd., I; 98 (upd.)
Sumitomo Corporation, I; 11 (upd.)
Sumitomo Electric Industries, Ltd., II
Sumitomo Heavy Industries, Ltd., III; 42 (upd.)
Sumitomo Life Insurance Company, III; 60 (upd.)
The Sumitomo Marine and Fire Insurance Company, Limited, III
Sumitomo Metal Industries Ltd., IV; 82 (upd.)
Sumitomo Metal Mining Co., Ltd., IV
Sumitomo Mitsui Banking Corporation, 51 (upd.)
Sumitomo Realty & Development Co., Ltd., IV
Sumitomo Rubber Industries, Ltd., V
The Sumitomo Trust & Banking Company, Ltd., II; 53 (upd.)
Suntory Ltd., 65
Suzuki Motor Corporation, 9; 23 (upd.); 59 (upd.)
Taiheiyo Cement Corporation, 60 (upd.)
Taiyo Fishery Company, Limited, II
The Taiyo Kobe Bank, Ltd., II
Takara Holdings Inc., 62
Takashimaya Company, Limited, V; 47 (upd.)
Takeda Chemical Industries, Ltd., I; 46 (upd.)

Tamron Company Ltd., 82
TDK Corporation, II; 17 (upd.); 49 (upd.)
TEAC Corporation 78
Teijin Limited, V; 61 (upd.)
Terumo Corporation, 48
Tobu Railway Company Ltd., 6; 98 (upd.)
Tohan Corporation, 84
Toho Co., Ltd., 28
Tohoku Electric Power Company, Inc., V
The Tokai Bank, Limited, II; 15 (upd.)
The Tokio Marine and Fire Insurance Co., Ltd., III
The Tokyo Electric Power Company, 74 (upd.)
The Tokyo Electric Power Company, Incorporated, V
Tokyo Gas Co., Ltd., V; 55 (upd.)
Tokyu Corporation, V; 47 (upd.)
Tokyu Department Store Co., Ltd., V; 32 (upd.)
Tokyu Land Corporation, IV
Tomen Corporation, IV; 24 (upd.)
Tomy Company Ltd., 65
TonenGeneral Sekiyu K.K., IV; 16 (upd.); 54 (upd.)
Topcon Corporation, 84
Toppan Printing Co., Ltd., IV; 58 (upd.)
Toray Industries, Inc., V; 51 (upd.)
Toshiba Corporation, I; 12 (upd.); 40 (upd.); 99 (upd.)
Tosoh Corporation, 70
TOTO LTD., III; 28 (upd.)
Toyo Sash Co., Ltd., III
Toyo Seikan Kaisha, Ltd., I
Toyoda Automatic Loom Works, Ltd., III
Toyota Motor Corporation, I; 11 (upd.); 38 (upd.)
Trend Micro Inc., 97
Ube Industries, Ltd., III; 38 (upd.)
ULVAC, Inc., 80
Unicharm Corporation, 84
Uniden Corporation, 98
Unitika Ltd., V; 53 (upd.)
Uny Co., Ltd., V; 49 (upd.)
Ushio Inc., 91
Victor Company of Japan, Limited, II; 26 (upd.); 83 (upd.)
Wacoal Corp., 25
Yamada Denki Co., Ltd., 85
Yamaha Corporation, III; 16 (upd.); 40 (upd.); 99 (upd.)
Yamaichi Securities Company, Limited, II
Yamato Transport Co. Ltd., V; 49 (upd.)
Yamazaki Baking Co., Ltd., 58
The Yasuda Fire and Marine Insurance Company, Limited, III
The Yasuda Mutual Life Insurance Company, III; 39 (upd.)
The Yasuda Trust and Banking Company, Ltd., II; 17 (upd.)
The Yokohama Rubber Company, Limited, V; 19 (upd.); 91 (upd.)

Yoshinoya D & C Company Ltd., 88

Jordan
Arab Potash Company, 85

Kenya
Kenya Airways Limited, 89

Kuwait
Kuwait Airways Corporation, 68
Kuwait Flour Mills & Bakeries Company, 84
Kuwait Petroleum Corporation, IV; 55 (upd.)

Latvia
A/S Air Baltic Corporation, 71

Lebanon
Middle East Airlines - Air Liban S.A.L. 79

Libya
National Oil Corporation, IV; 66 (upd.)

Liechtenstein
Hilti AG, 53

Luxembourg
ARBED S.A., IV; 22 (upd.)
Cactus S.A., 90
Cargolux Airlines International S.A., 49
Elite World S.A., 94
Esp[00ed]rito Santo Financial Group S.A. 79 (upd.)
Gemplus International S.A., 64
Metro International S.A., 93
RTL Group SA, 44
Société Luxembourgeoise de Navigation Aérienne S.A., 64
Tenaris SA, 63

Malaysia
AirAsia Berhad, 93
Berjaya Group Bhd., 67
Gano Excel Enterprise Sdn. Bhd., 89
Genting Bhd., 65
Malayan Banking Berhad, 72
Malaysian Airlines System Berhad, 6; 29 (upd.); 97 (upd.)
Perusahaan Otomobil Nasional Bhd., 62
Petroliam Nasional Bhd (Petronas), IV; 56 (upd.)
PPB Group Berhad, 57
Sime Darby Berhad, 14; 36 (upd.)
Telekom Malaysia Bhd, 76
Yeo Hiap Seng Malaysia Bhd., 75

Mauritius
Air Mauritius Ltd., 63

Mexico
Alfa, S.A. de C.V., 19
Altos Hornos de México, S.A. de C.V., 42
América Móvil, S.A. de C.V., 80
Apasco S.A. de C.V., 51

Bolsa Mexicana de Valores, S.A. de C.V., 80
Bufete Industrial, S.A. de C.V., 34
Casa Cuervo, S.A. de C.V., 31
Celanese Mexicana, S.A. de C.V., 54
CEMEX S.A. de C.V., 20; 59 (upd.)
Cifra, S.A. de C.V., 12
Cinemas de la República, S.A. de C.V., 83
Compañia Industrial de Parras, S.A. de C.V. (CIPSA), 84
Consorcio ARA, S.A. de C.V. 79
Consorcio Aviacsa, S.A. de C.V., 85
Consorcio G Grupo Dina, S.A. de C.V., 36
Controladora Comercial Mexicana, S.A. de C.V., 36
Controladora Mabe, S.A. de C.V., 82
Coppel, S.A. de C.V., 82
Corporación Geo, S.A. de C.V., 81
Corporación Interamericana de Entretenimiento, S.A. de C.V., 83
Corporación Internacional de Aviación, S.A. de C.V. (Cintra), 20
Desarrolladora Homex, S.A. de C.V., 87
Desc, S.A. de C.V., 23
Editorial Televisa, S.A. de C.V., 57
Empresas ICA Sociedad Controladora, S.A. de C.V., 41
El Puerto de Liverpool, S.A.B. de C.V., 97
Ford Motor Company, S.A. de C.V., 20
Gruma, S.A. de C.V., 31
Grupo Aeroportuario del Centro Norte, S.A.B. de C.V., 97
Grupo Aeroportuario del Pacífico, S.A. de C.V., 85
Grupo Aeropuerto del Sureste, S.A. de C.V., 48
Grupo Ángeles Servicios de Salud, S.A. de C.V., 84
Grupo Carso, S.A. de C.V., 21
Grupo Casa Saba, S.A. de C.V., 39
Grupo Comercial Chedraui S.A. de C.V., 86
Grupo Corvi S.A. de C.V., 86
Grupo Cydsa, S.A. de C.V., 39
Grupo Elektra, S.A. de C.V., 39
Grupo Financiero Banamex S.A., 54
Grupo Financiero Banorte, S.A. de C.V., 51
Grupo Financiero BBVA Bancomer S.A., 54
Grupo Financiero Serfin, S.A., 19
Grupo Gigante, S.A. de C.V., 34
Grupo Herdez, S.A. de C.V., 35
Grupo IMSA, S.A. de C.V., 44
Grupo Industrial Bimbo, 19
Grupo Industrial Durango, S.A. de C.V., 37
Grupo Industrial Herradura, S.A. de C.V., 83
Grupo Industrial Lala, S.A. de C.V., 82
Grupo Industrial Saltillo, S.A. de C.V., 54
Grupo Mexico, S.A. de C.V., 40
Grupo Modelo, S.A. de C.V., 29
Grupo Omnilife S.A. de C.V., 88
Grupo Posadas, S.A. de C.V., 57
Grupo Televisa, S.A., 18; 54 (upd.)
Grupo TMM, S.A. de C.V., 50

Grupo Transportación Ferroviaria
    Mexicana, S.A. de C.V., 47
Grupo Viz, S.A. de C.V., 84
Hylsamex, S.A. de C.V., 39
Industrias Bachoco, S.A. de C.V., 39
Industrias Penoles, S.A. de C.V., 22
Internacional de Ceramica, S.A. de C.V.,
    53
Jugos del Valle, S.A. de C.V., 85
Kimberly-Clark de México, S.A. de C.V.,
    54
Mexichem, S.A.B. de C.V., 99
Nadro S.A. de C.V., 86
Organización Soriana, S.A. de C.V., 35
Petróleos Mexicanos, IV; 19 (upd.)
Proeza S.A. de C.V., 82
Pulsar Internacional S.A., 21
Real Turismo, S.A. de C.V., 50
Sanborn Hermanos, S.A., 20
SANLUIS Corporación, S.A.B. de C.V.,
    95
Sears Roebuck de México, S.A. de C.V.,
    20
Telefonos de Mexico S.A. de C.V., 14; 63
    (upd.)
Tubos de Acero de Mexico, S.A.
    (TAMSA), 41
TV Azteca, S.A. de C.V., 39
Urbi Desarrollos Urbanos, S.A. de C.V.,
    81
Valores Industriales S.A., 19
Vitro Corporativo S.A. de C.V., 34
Wal-Mart de Mexico, S.A. de C.V., 35
    (upd.)

Nepal
Royal Nepal Airline Corporation, 41

Netherlands
ABN AMRO Holding, N.V., 50
AEGON N.V., III; 50 (upd.)
Akzo Nobel N.V., 13; 41 (upd.)
Algemene Bank Nederland N.V., II
Amsterdam-Rotterdam Bank N.V., II
Arcadis NV, 26
ASML Holding N.V., 50
Avantium Technologies BV 79
Baan Company, 25
Blokker Holding B.V., 84
Bols Distilleries NV, 74
Bolton Group B.V., 86
Buhrmann NV, 41
The Campina Group, The 78
Chicago Bridge & Iron Company N.V.,
    82 (upd.)
CNH Global N.V., 38 (upd.); 99 (upd.)
CSM N.V., 65
Deli Universal NV, 66
Drie Mollen Holding B.V., 99
DSM N.V., I; 56 (upd.)
Elsevier N.V., IV
Endemol Entertainment Holding NV, 46
Equant N.V., 52
Euronext N.V., 89 (upd.)
European Aeronautic Defence and Space
    Company EADS N.V., 52 (upd.)
Friesland Coberco Dairy Foods Holding
    N.V., 59

Fugro N.V., 98
Getronics NV, 39
Granaria Holdings B.V., 66
Grand Hotel Krasnapolsky N.V., 23
Greenpeace International, 74
Gucci Group N.V., 50
Hagemeyer N.V., 39
Head N.V., 55
Heijmans N.V., 66
Heineken N.V., I; 13 (upd.); 34 (upd.);
    90 (upd.)
IHC Caland N.V., 71
IKEA Group, 94 (upd.)
Indigo NV, 26
Intres B.V., 82
Ispat International N.V., 30
Koninklijke Ahold N.V. (Royal Ahold), II;
    16 (upd.)
Koninklijke Houthandel G Wijma &
    Zonen BV, 96
Koninklijke Luchtvaart Maatschappij,
    N.V. (KLM Royal Dutch Airlines), I;
    28 (upd.)
Koninklijke Nederlandsche Hoogovens en
    Staalfabrieken NV, IV
Koninklijke Nedlloyd N.V., 6; 26 (upd.)
Koninklijke Philips Electronics N.V., 50
    (upd.)
Koninklijke PTT Nederland NV, V
Koninklijke Vendex KBB N.V. (Royal
    Vendex KBB N.V.), 62 (upd.)
Koninklijke Wessanen nv, II; 54 (upd.)
KPMG International, 10; 33 (upd.)
Laurus N.V., 65
Mammoet Transport B.V., 26
MIH Limited, 31
N.V. AMEV, III
N.V. Holdingmaatschappij De Telegraaf,
    23
N.V. Koninklijke Nederlandse
    Vliegtuigenfabriek Fokker, I; 28 (upd.)
N.V. Nederlandse Gasunie, V
Nationale-Nederlanden N.V., III
New Holland N.V., 22
Nutreco Holding N.V., 56
Océ N.V., 24; 91 (upd.)
PCM Uitgevers NV, 53
Philips Electronics N.V., II; 13 (upd.)
PolyGram N.V., 23
Prada Holding B.V., 45
Qiagen N.V., 39
Rabobank Group, 33
Randstad Holding n.v., 16; 43 (upd.)
Rodamco N.V., 26
Royal Dutch/Shell Group, IV; 49 (upd.)
Royal Grolsch NV, 54
Royal KPN N.V., 30
Royal Numico N.V., 37
Royal Packaging Industries Van Leer N.V.,
    30
Royal Ten Cate N.V., 68
Royal Vopak NV, 41
SHV Holdings N.V., 55
Telegraaf Media Groep N.V., 98 (upd.)
Tennet BV 78
TNT Post Group N.V., V, 27 (upd.); 30
    (upd.)
Toolex International N.V., 26

TomTom N.V., 81
TPG N.V., 64 (upd.)
Trader Classified Media N.V., 57
Triple P N.V., 26
Unilever N.V., II; 7 (upd.); 32 (upd.)
United Pan-Europe Communications NV,
    47
Van Lanschot NV 79
VBA - Bloemenveiling Aalsmeer, 88
Vebego International BV, 49
Vedior NV, 35
Velcro Industries N.V., 19
Vendex International N.V., 13
Vion Food Group NV, 85
VNU N.V., 27
Wegener NV, 53
Wolters Kluwer NV, 14; 33 (upd.)
Zentiva N.V./Zentiva, a.s., 99

Netherlands Antilles
Orthofix International NV, 72
Velcro Industries N.V., 72

New Zealand
Air New Zealand Limited, 14; 38 (upd.)
Carter Holt Harvey Ltd., 70
Fletcher Challenge Ltd., IV; 19 (upd.)
Fonterra Co-Operative Group Ltd., 58
Frucor Beverages Group Ltd., 96
Nuplex Industries Ltd., 92
Progressive Enterprises Ltd., 96
Telecom Corporation of New Zealand
    Limited, 54
Wattie's Ltd., 7

Nigeria
Nigerian National Petroleum Corporation,
    IV; 72 (upd.)

Norway
Braathens ASA, 47
Den Norse Stats Oljeselskap AS, IV
Helly Hansen ASA, 25
Jotun A/S, 80
K.A. Rasmussen AS, 99
Kvaerner ASA, 36
Norsk Hydro ASA, 10; 35 (upd.)
Norske Skogindustrier ASA, 63
Orkla ASA, 18; 82 (upd.)
Schibsted ASA, 31
Statoil ASA, 61 (upd.)
Stolt Sea Farm Holdings PLC, 54
Telenor ASA, 69
Veidekke ASA, 98
Wilh. Wilhelmsen ASA, 94
Yara International ASA, 94

Oman
Petroleum Development Oman LLC, IV;
    98 (upd.)
The Zubair Corporation L.L.C., 96

Pakistan
Pakistan International Airlines
    Corporation, 46
Pakistan State Oil Company Ltd., 81

Panama
Autoridad del Canal de Panamá, 94
Copa Holdings, S.A., 93

Panamerican Beverages, Inc., 47
Willbros Group, Inc., 56

Papua New Guinea
Steamships Trading Company Ltd., 82

Peru
Ajegroup S.A., 92
Banco de Crédito del Perú, 93
Compañia de Minas Buenaventura S.A.A.,
    93
Corporación José R. Lindley S.A., 92
Grupo Brescia, 99
Southern Peru Copper Corporation, 40
Unión de Cervecerias Peruanas Backus y
    Johnston S.A.A., 92
Volcan Compañia Minera S.A.A., 92

Philippines
Bank of the Philippine Islands, 58
Benguet Corporation, 58
Manila Electric Company (Meralco), 56
Mercury Drug Corporation, 70
Petron Corporation, 58
Philippine Airlines, Inc., 6; 23 (upd.)
San Miguel Corporation, 15; 57 (upd.)

Poland
Agora S.A. Group, 77
LOT Polish Airlines (Polskie Linie
    Lotnicze S.A.), 33
KGHM Polska Miedz S.A., 98
Polski Koncern Naftowy ORLEN S.A., 77
Telekomunikacja Polska SA, 50

Portugal
Banco Comercial Português, SA, 50
Banco Espírito Santo e Comercial de
    Lisboa S.A., 15
BRISA Auto-estradas de Portugal S.A., 64
Cimentos de Portugal SGPS S.A.
    (Cimpor), 76
Corticeira Amorim, Sociedade Gestora de
    Participaço es Sociais, S.A., 48
Electricidade de Portugal, S.A., 47
Galp Energia SGPS S.A., 98
Grupo Portucel Soporcel, 60
Jerónimo Martins SGPS S.A., 96
José de Mello SGPS S.A., 96
Madeira Wine Company, S.A., 49
Mota-Engil, SGPS, S.A., 97
Petróleos de Portugal S.A., IV
Portugal Telecom SGPS S.A., 69
Sonae SGPS, S.A., 97
TAP—Air Portugal Transportes Aéreos
    Portugueses S.A., 46
Transportes Aereos Portugueses, S.A., 6

Puerto Rico
Puerto Rico Electric Power Authority, 47

Qatar
Aljazeera Satellite Channel 79
Qatar Airways Company Q.C.S.C., 87
Qatar General Petroleum Corporation, IV
Qatar National Bank SAQ, 87
Qatar Petroleum, 98

Qatar Telecom QSA, 87

Republic of Yemen
Hayel Saeed Anam Group of Cos., 92

Romania
Dobrogea Grup S.A., 82
TAROM S.A., 64

Russia
A.S. Yakovlev Design Bureau, 15
Aeroflot - Russian Airlines JSC, 6; 29
    (upd.); 89 (upd.)
Alfa Group, 99
Alrosa Company Ltd., 62
AO VimpelCom, 48
Aviacionny Nauchno-Tehnicheskii
    Komplex im. A.N. Tupoleva, 24
AVTOVAZ Joint Stock Company, 65
Baltika Brewery Joint Stock Company, 65
Evraz Group S.A., 97
Golden Telecom, Inc., 59
Interfax News Agency, 86
Irkut Corporation, 68
JSC MMC Norilsk Nickel, 48
Mechel OAO, 99
Mobile TeleSystems OJSC, 59
OAO Gazprom, 42
OAO LUKOIL, 40
OAO NK YUKOS, 47
OAO Siberian Oil Company (Sibneft), 49
OAO Surgutneftegaz, 48
OAO Tatneft, 45
OJSC Novolipetsk Steel, 99
OJSC Wimm-Bill-Dann Foods, 48
RAO Unified Energy System of Russia, 45
Rostelecom Joint Stock Co., 99
Rostvertol plc, 62
Russian Aircraft Corporation (MiG), 86
Russian Railways Joint Stock Co., 93
Sberbank, 62
Severstal Joint Stock Company, 65
Sistema JSFC, 73
Sukhoi Design Bureau Aviation
    Scientific-Industrial Complex, 24
CJSC Transmash Holding, 93
Oil Transporting Joint Stock Company
    Transneft, 93
Volga-Dnepr Group, 82

Saudi Arabia
Dallah Albaraka Group, 72
Saudi Arabian Airlines, 6; 27 (upd.)
Saudi Arabian Oil Company, IV; 17
    (upd.); 50 (upd.)
Saudi Basic Industries Corporation
    (SABIC), 58

Scotland
Arnold Clark Automobiles Ltd., 60
Distillers Company PLC, I
General Accident PLC, III
The Governor and Company of the Bank
    of Scotland, 10
The Royal Bank of Scotland Group plc,
    12
Scottish & Newcastle plc, 15

Scottish Hydro-Electric PLC, 13
Scottish Media Group plc, 32
ScottishPower plc, 19
Stagecoach Holdings plc, 30
The Standard Life Assurance Company,
    III

Singapore
Asia Pacific Breweries Limited, 59
City Developments Limited, 89
Creative Technology Ltd., 57
Flextronics International Ltd., 38
Fraser & Neave Ltd., 54
Hotel Properties Ltd., 71
Jardine Cycle & Carriage Ltd., 73
Keppel Corporation Ltd., 73
Neptune Orient Lines Limited, 47
Pacific Internet Limited, 87
Singapore Airlines Limited, 6; 27 (upd.);
    83 (upd.)
Singapore Press Holdings Limited, 85
StarHub Ltd., 77
United Overseas Bank Ltd., 56

South Africa
African Rainbow Minerals Ltd., 97
Anglo American Corporation of South
    Africa Limited, IV; 16 (upd.)
Barlow Rand Ltd., I
De Beers Consolidated Mines Limited/De
    Beers Centenary AG, IV; 7 (upd.); 28
    (upd.)
Dimension Data Holdings PLC, 69
Edgars Consolidated Stores Ltd., 66
Famous Brands Ltd., 86
Gencor Ltd., IV; 22 (upd.)
Gold Fields Ltd., IV; 62 (upd.)
Harmony Gold Mining Company
    Limited, 63
Highveld Steel and Vanadium
    Corporation Limited, 59
Iscor Limited, 57
Naspers Ltd., 66
New Clicks Holdings Ltd., 86
Pick 'n Pay Stores Ltd., 82
SAA (Pty) Ltd., 28
Sanlam Ltd., 68
Sappi Limited, 49
Sasol Limited, IV; 47 (upd.)
The South African Breweries Limited, I;
    24 (upd.)
Transnet Ltd., 6

South Korea
Anam Group, 23
Asiana Airlines, Inc., 46
CJ Corporation, 62
Daesang Corporation, 84
Daewoo Group, III; 18 (upd.); 57 (upd.)
Electronics Co., Ltd., 14
Goldstar Co., Ltd., 12
Hanjin Shipping Co., Ltd., 50
Hanwha Group, 62
Hite Brewery Company Ltd., 97
Hyundai Group, III; 7 (upd.); 56 (upd.)
Kia Motors Corporation, 12; 29 (upd.)
Kookmin Bank, 58

Korea Electric Power Corporation
(Kepco), 56
Korean Air Lines Co., Ltd., 6; 27 (upd.)
KT&G Corporation, 62
LG Corporation, 94 (upd.)
Lotte Confectionery Company Ltd., 76
Lucky-Goldstar, II
Pohang Iron and Steel Company Ltd., IV
POSCO, 57 (upd.)
Samick Musical Instruments Co., Ltd., 56
Samsung Electronics Co., Ltd., I; 41
(upd.)
SK Group, 88
Ssangyong Cement Industrial Co., Ltd.,
III; 61 (upd.)
Tong Yang Cement Corporation, 62

Spain

Abengoa S.A., 73
Abertis Infraestructuras, S.A., 65
Acciona S.A., 81
Adolfo Dominguez S.A., 72
Altadis S.A., 72 (upd.)
Banco Bilbao Vizcaya Argentaria S.A., II;
48 (upd.)
Banco Central, II
Banco do Brasil S.A., II
Banco Santander Central Hispano S.A.,
36 (upd.)
Baron de Ley S.A., 74
Campofrío Alimentación S.A, 59
Chupa Chups S.A., 38
Compania Española de Petróleos S.A.
(Cepsa), IV; 56 (upd.)
Cortefiel S.A., 64
Correos y Telegrafos S.A., 80
Dogi International Fabrics S.A., 52
El Corte Inglés Group, V; 26 (upd.)
ENDESA S.A., V; 46 (upd.)
Ercros S.A., 80
Federico Paternina S.A., 69
Freixenet S.A., 71
Gas Natural SDG S.A., 69
Grupo Dragados SA, 55
Grupo Eroski, 64
Grupo Ferrovial, S.A., 40
Grupo Ficosa International, 90
Grupo Leche Pascual S.A., 59
Grupo Lladró S.A., 52
Grupo Planeta, 94
Iberdrola, S.A., 49
Iberia Líneas Aéreas de España S.A., 6; 36
(upd.); 91 (upd.)
Industria de Diseño Textil S.A., 64
Instituto Nacional de Industria, I
Mecalux S.A., 74
Miquel y Costas Miquel S.A., 68
NH Hoteles S.A. 79
Nutrexpa S.A., 92
Obrascon Huarte Lain S.A., 76
Paradores de Turismo de Espana S.A., 73
Pescanova S.A., 81
Puig Beauty and Fashion Group S.L., 60
Real Madrid C.F., 73
Repsol-YPF S.A., IV; 16 (upd.); 40 (upd.)
Sol Meliá S.A., 71
Tabacalera, S.A., V; 17 (upd.)
Telefónica S.A., V; 46 (upd.)

TelePizza S.A., 33
Television Española, S.A., 7
Terra Lycos, Inc., 43
Unión Fenosa, S.A., 51
Uralita S.A., 96
Vidrala S.A., 67
Viscofan S.A., 70
Vocento, 94
Vueling Airlines S.A., 97
Zara International, Inc., 83
Zed Group, 93

Sweden

A. Johnson & Company H.B., I
AB Volvo, I; 7 (upd.); 26 (upd.); 67
(upd.)
Aktiebolaget Electrolux, 22 (upd.)
Aktiebolaget SKF, III; 38 (upd.); 89
(upd.)
Alfa Laval AB, III; 64 (upd.)
Astra AB, I; 20 (upd.)
Atlas Copco AB, III; 28 (upd.); 85 (upd.)
Autoliv, Inc., 65
Boliden AB, 80
Bonnier AB, 52
BRIO AB, 24
Cardo AB, 53
Cloetta Fazer AB, 70
D. Carnegie & Co. AB, 98
Electrolux AB, III; 53 (upd.)
Eka Chemicals AB, 92
FöreningsSparbanken AB, 69
Gambro AB, 49
Gunnebo AB, 53
H&M Hennes & Mauritz AB, 98 (upd.)
Hennes & Mauritz AB, 29
Hexagon AB 78
Holmen AB, 52 (upd.)
ICA AB, II
Investor AB, 63
Kooperativa Förbundet, 99
Mo och Domsjö AB, IV
Modern Times Group AB, 36
NetCom Systems AB, 26
Nobel Industries AB, 9
Nordea AB, 40
Observer AB, 55
Perstorp AB, I; 51 (upd.)
Saab Automobile AB, I; 11 (upd.); 32
(upd.); 83 (upd.)
Sandvik AB, IV; 32 (upd.); 77 (upd.)
Sapa AB, 84
The SAS Group, 34 (upd.)
Scandinavian Airlines System, I
Securitas AB, 42
Skandia Insurance Company, Ltd., 50
Skandinaviska Enskilda Banken AB, II; 56
(upd.)
Skanska AB, 38
SSAB Svenskt Stål AB, 89
Stora Kopparbergs Bergslags AB, IV
Sveaskog AB, 93
Svenska Cellulosa Aktiebolaget SCA, IV;
28 (upd.); 85 (upd.)
Svenska Handelsbanken AB, II; 50 (upd.)
Sveriges Riksbank, 96
Swedish Match AB, 12; 39 (upd.); 92
(upd.)

Swedish Telecom, V
Telefonaktiebolaget LM Ericsson, V; 46
(upd.)
TeliaSonera AB, 57 (upd.)
Trelleborg AB, 93
Vattenfall AB, 57
V&S Vin & Sprit AB, 91 (upd.)
Vin & Spirit AB, 31

Switzerland

ABB ASEA Brown Boveri Ltd., II; 22
(upd.)
ABB Ltd., 65 (upd.)
Actelion Ltd., 83
Adecco S.A., 36 (upd.)
Adia S.A., 6
Arthur Andersen & Company, Société
Coopérative, 10
Ascom AG, 9
Bâloise-Holding, 40
Barry Callebaut AG, 29; 71 (upd.)
Bernina Holding AG, 47
Bodum Design Group AG, 47
Bon Appetit Holding AG, 48
Charles Vögele Holding AG, 82
Chocoladefabriken Lindt & Sprüngli AG,
27
Ciba-Geigy Ltd., I; 8 (upd.)
Compagnie Financiere Richemont AG, 50
Conzzeta Holding, 80
Coop Schweiz Genossenschaftsverband, 48
Credit Suisse Group, II; 21 (upd.); 59
(upd.)
Danzas Group, V; 40 (upd.)
De Beers Consolidated Mines Limited/De
Beers Centenary AG, IV; 7 (upd.); 28
(upd.)
Denner AG, 88
Duferco Group, 94
Edipresse S.A., 82
Elektrowatt AG, 6
Elma Electronic AG, 83
F. Hoffmann-La Roche Ltd., I; 50 (upd.)
Fédération Internationale de Football
Association, 27
Fenaco, 86
Firmenich International S.A., 60
Franke Holding AG, 76
Galenica AG, 84
Gate Gourmet International AG, 70
Geberit AG, 49
Georg Fischer AG Schaffhausen, 61
Givaudan SA, 43
Holderbank Financière Glaris Ltd., III
International Olympic Committee, 44
Jacobs Suchard A.G., II
Julius Baer Holding AG, 52
Keramik Holding AG Laufen, 51
Kraft Jacobs Suchard AG, 26 (upd.)
Kudelski Group SA, 44
Kuehne & Nagel International AG, V; 53
(upd.)
Kuoni Travel Holding Ltd., 40
Liebherr-International AG, 64
Logitech International S.A., 28; 69 (upd.)
Lonza Group Ltd., 73
Maus Frères SA, 48
Médecins sans Frontières, 85

Mettler-Toledo International Inc., 30
Migros-Genossenschafts-Bund, 68
Montres Rolex S.A., 13; 34 (upd.)
Nestlé S.A., II; 7 (upd.); 28 (upd.); 71 (upd.)
Novartis AG, 39 (upd.)
Panalpina World Transport (Holding) Ltd., 47
Pelikan Holding AG, 92
Phoenix Mecano AG, 61
Ricola Ltd., 62
Rieter Holding AG, 42
Roland Murten A.G., 7
Sandoz Ltd., I
Schindler Holding AG, 29
Schweizerische Post-, Telefon- und Telegrafen-Betriebe, V
Selecta AG, 97
Serono S.A., 47
STMicroelectronics NV, 52
Straumann Holding AG 79
Sulzer Ltd., III; 68 (upd.)
Swarovski International Holding AG, 40
The Swatch Group SA, 26
Swedish Match S.A., 12
Swiss Air Transport Company, Ltd., I
Swiss Bank Corporation, II
The Swiss Federal Railways (Schweizerische Bundesbahnen), V
Swiss International Air Lines Ltd., 48
Swiss Reinsurance Company (Schweizerische Rückversicherungs-Gesellschaft), III; 46 (upd.)
Swisscom AG, 58
Swissport International Ltd., 70
Syngenta International AG, 83
Synthes, Inc., 93
TAG Heuer International SA, 25; 77 (upd.)
Tamedia AG, 53
Tetra Pak International SA, 53
UBS AG, 52 (upd.)
Underberg AG, 92
Union Bank of Switzerland, II
Valora Holding AG, 98
Victorinox AG, 21; 74 (upd.)
Vontobel Holding AG, 96
Weleda AG 78
Winterthur Group, III; 68 (upd.)
Xstrata PLC, 73
Zurich Financial Services, 42 (upd.); 93 (upd.)
Zürich Versicherungs-Gesellschaft, III

Taiwan
Acer Incorporated, 16; 73 (upd.)
AU Optronics Corporation, 67
BenQ Corporation, 67
Chi Mei Optoelectronics Corporation, 75
China Airlines, 34
Chunghwa Picture Tubes, Ltd., 75
D-Link Corporation, 83
Directorate General of Telecommunications, 7
EVA Airways Corporation, 51
Evergreen Marine Corporation (Taiwan) Ltd., 13; 50 (upd.)

First International Computer, Inc., 56
Formosa Plastics Corporation, 14; 58 (upd.)
Giant Manufacturing Company, Ltd., 85
High Tech Computer Corporation, 81
Hon Hai Precision Industry Co., Ltd., 59
Kwang Yang Motor Company Ltd., 80
Pou Chen Corporation, 81
Quanta Computer Inc., 47
Siliconware Precision Industries Ltd., 73
Taiwan Semiconductor Manufacturing Company Ltd., 47
Taiwan Tobacco & Liquor Corporation, 75
Tatung Co., 23
United Microelectronics Corporation, 98
Winbond Electronics Corporation, 74
Yageo Corporation, 16; 98 (upd.)

Thailand
Charoen Pokphand Group, 62
Electricity Generating Authority of Thailand (EGAT), 56
Krung Thai Bank Public Company Ltd., 69
Pranda Jewelry plc, 70
PTT Public Company Ltd., 56
The Siam Cement Public Company Limited, 56
Thai Airways International Public Company Limited, 6; 27 (upd.)
Thai Union Frozen Products PCL, 75
Thanulux Public Company Limited, 86
The Topaz Group, Inc., 62

Tunisia
Société Tunisienne de l'Air-Tunisair, 49

Turkey
Akbank TAS 79
Anadolu Efes Biracilik ve Malt Sanayii A.S., 95
Dogan Sirketler Grubu Holding A.S., 83
Haci Omer Sabanci Holdings A.S., 55
Koç Holding A.S., I; 54 (upd.)
Turkish Airlines Inc. (Türk Hava Yollari A.O.), 72
Turkiye Is Bankasi A.S., 61
Türkiye Petrolleri Anonim Ortakli&gcaron;i, IV

Ukraine
Antonov Design Bureau, 53

United Arab Emirates
Abu Dhabi National Oil Company, IV; 45 (upd.)
Al Habtoor Group L.L.C., 87
DP World, 81
The Emirates Group, 39; 81 (upd.)
Etihad Airways PJSC, 89
Gulf Agency Company Ltd. 78
Jumeirah Group, 83

United Kingdom
A. F. Blakemore & Son Ltd., 90
A. Nelson & Co. Ltd., 75

Aardman Animations Ltd., 61
Abbey National plc, 10; 39 (upd.)
Acergy SA, 97
Adams Childrenswear Ltd., 95
Aegis Group plc, 6
AG Barr plc, 64
Aga Foodservice Group PLC, 73
Aggregate Industries plc, 36
Aggreko Plc, 45
AgustaWestland N.V., 75
Air Partner PLC, 93
Airtours Plc, 27
The Albert Fisher Group plc, 41
Alexandra plc, 88
The All England Lawn Tennis & Croquet Club, 54
Alldays plc, 49
Allders plc, 37
Alliance and Leicester plc, 88
Alliance Boots plc, 83 (upd.)
Allied Domecq PLC, 29
Allied-Lyons PLC, I
Alpha Airports Group PLC, 77
Alvis Plc, 47
Amersham PLC, 50
Amey Plc, 47
Amnesty International, 50
Amstrad plc, III; 48 (upd.)
AMVESCAP PLC, 65
Anglo American PLC, 50 (upd.)
Anker BV, 53
Antofagasta plc, 65
Apax Partners Worldwide LLP, 89
Apple Corps Ltd., 87
Arcadia Group plc, 28 (upd.)
Arena Leisure Plc, 99
Argyll Group PLC, II
Arjo Wiggins Appleton p.l.c., 34
Arriva PLC, 69
Arsenal Holdings PLC 79
ASDA Group Ltd., II; 28 (upd.); 64 (upd.)
Ashtead Group plc, 34
Associated British Foods plc, II; 13 (upd.); 41 (upd.)
Associated British Ports Holdings Plc, 45
Aston Villa plc, 41
AstraZeneca PLC, 50 (upd.)
AT&T Istel Ltd., 14
Avecia Group PLC, 63
Aviva PLC, 50 (upd.)
BAA plc, 10; 33 (upd.)
Babcock International Group PLC, 69
Balfour Beatty plc, 36 (upd.)
Barclays plc, II; 20 (upd.); 64 (upd.)
Barings PLC, 14
Barratt Developments plc, I; 56 (upd.)
Bass PLC, I; 15 (upd.); 38 (upd.)
Bat Industries PLC, I; 20 (upd.)
Baxi Group Ltd., 96
Baxters Food Group Ltd., 99
BBA Aviation plc, 90
Beggars Group Ltd., 99
Belleek Pottery Ltd., 71
Bellway Plc, 45
Belron International Ltd., 76
Benfield Greig Group plc, 53
Bernard Matthews Ltd., 89

Bettys & Taylors of Harrogate Ltd., 72
Bhs plc, 17
BICC PLC, III
Biffa plc, 92
The Big Food Group plc, 68 (upd.)
Birse Group PLC, 77
Birthdays Ltd., 70
Blacks Leisure Group plc, 39
Blackwell Publishing Ltd. 78
Blue Circle Industries PLC, III
BOC Group plc, I; 25 (upd.); 78 (upd.)
The Body Shop International plc, 11; 53
    (upd.)
Bodycote International PLC, 63
Bonhams 1793 Ltd., 72
Booker Cash & Carry Ltd., 13; 31 (upd.);
    68 (upd.)
The Boots Company PLC, V; 24 (upd.)
Bowater PLC, IV
Bowthorpe plc, 33
BP p.l.c., 45 (upd.)
BPB plc, 83
Bradford & Bingley PLC, 65
Brake Bros plc, 45
Brammer PLC, 77
Bristow Helicopters Ltd., 70
Britannia Soft Drinks Ltd. (Britvic), 71
British Aerospace plc, I; 24 (upd.)
British Airways PLC, I; 14 (upd.); 43
    (upd.)
British American Tobacco PLC, 50 (upd.)
British Broadcasting Corporation Ltd., 7;
    21 (upd.); 89 (upd.)
British Coal Corporation, IV
British Energy Plc, 49
The British Film Institute, 80
British Gas plc, V
British Land Plc, 54
British Midland plc, 38
The British Museum, 71
British Nuclear Fuels plc, 6
The British Petroleum Company plc, IV;
    7 (upd.); 21 (upd.)
British Railways Board, V
British Sky Broadcasting Group plc, 20;
    60 (upd.)
British Steel plc, IV; 19 (upd.)
British Sugar plc, 84
British Telecommunications plc, V; 15
    (upd.)
British United Provident Association
    Limited (BUPA) 79
British Vita plc, 9; 33 (upd.)
British World Airlines Ltd., 18
British-Borneo Oil & Gas PLC, 34
BT Group plc, 49 (upd.)
BTG Plc, 87
BTR PLC, I
BTR Siebe plc, 27
Budgens Ltd., 59
Bunzl plc, IV; 31 (upd.)
Burberry Group plc, 17; 41 (upd.); 92
    (upd.)
Burmah Castrol PLC, IV; 30 (upd.)
The Burton Group plc, V
Business Post Group plc, 46
C&J Clark International Ltd., 52
C. Hoare & Co., 77

C.I. Traders Limited, 61
Cable and Wireless plc, V; 25 (upd.)
Cadbury Schweppes PLC, II; 49 (upd.)
Caffè Nero Group PLC, 63
Cains Beer Company PLC, 99
Canary Wharf Group Plc, 30
Caparo Group Ltd., 90
Capita Group PLC, 69
Capital Radio plc, 35
Caradon plc, 20 (upd.)
Carbo PLC, 67 (upd.)
Carlton Communications PLC, 15; 50
    (upd.)
The Carphone Warehouse Group PLC, 83
Cartier Monde, 29
Cattles plc, 58
Cazenove Group plc, 72
Central Independent Television, 7; 23
    (upd.)
Centrica plc, 29 (upd.)
Channel Four Television Corporation, 93
Chello Zone Ltd., 93
Chelsfield PLC, 67
Cheltenham & Gloucester PLC, 61
Cheshire Building Society, 74
Christian Salvesen Plc, 45
Christie's International plc, 15; 39 (upd.)
Chrysalis Group plc, 40
Chubb, PLC, 50
Clifford Chance LLP, 38
Clinton Cards plc, 39
Close Brothers Group plc, 39
Co-operative Group (CWS) Ltd., 51
Coats plc, V; 44 (upd.)
Cobham plc, 30
COLT Telecom Group plc, 41
Commercial Union PLC, III
Compass Group PLC, 34
Cookson Group plc, III; 44 (upd.)
Corus Group plc, 49 (upd.)
Courtaulds plc, V; 17 (upd.)
Courts Plc, 45
Cranswick plc, 40
Croda International Plc, 45
Daily Mail and General Trust plc, 19
Dairy Crest Group plc, 32
Dalgety, PLC, II
Daniel Thwaites Plc, 95
Dart Group PLC, 77
Davis Service Group PLC, 45
Dawson Holdings PLC, 43
De La Rue plc, 10; 34 (upd.)
Debenhams Plc, 28
Denby Group plc, 44
Denison International plc, 46
Dennis Publishing Ltd., 62
Devro plc, 55
Diageo plc, 24 (upd.); 79 (upd.)
Direct Wines Ltd., 84
Dixons Group plc, V; 19 (upd.); 49
    (upd.)
Domino Printing Sciences PLC, 87
Dorling Kindersley Holdings plc, 20
Dresdner Kleinwort Wasserstein, 60 (upd.)
DS Smith Plc, 61
Dyson Group PLC, 71
E H Booth & Company Ltd., 90
easyJet Airline Company Limited, 39

ECC Group plc, III
The Economist Group Ltd., 67
The Edrington Group Ltd., 88
Electrocomponents PLC, 50
Elementis plc, 40 (upd.)
EMAP plc, 35
EMI Group plc, 22 (upd.); 81 (upd.)
Energis plc, 47
English China Clays Ltd., 15 (upd.); 40
    (upd.)
Enodis plc, 68
Enterprise Inns plc, 59
Enterprise Oil PLC, 11; 50 (upd.)
Esporta plc, 35
Eurotunnel Group, 13; 37 (upd.)
Exel plc, 51 (upd.)
Fairclough Construction Group PLC, I
Fat Face Ltd., 68
Filtrona plc, 88
Findel plc, 60
First Choice Holidays PLC, 40
FirstGroup plc, 89
Fisons plc, 9; 23 (upd.)
FKI Plc, 57
French Connection Group plc, 41
Fuller Smith & Turner P.L.C., 38
G A Pindar & Son Ltd., 88
Gallaher Group Plc, 49 (upd.)
Gallaher Limited, V; 19 (upd.)
The GAME Group plc, 80
The Gateway Corporation Ltd., II
Geest Plc, 38
General Electric Company PLC, II
George Wimpey PLC, 12; 51 (upd.)
Gibbs and Dandy plc, 74
GKN plc, III; 38 (upd.); 89 (upd.)
GlaxoSmithKline plc, I; 9 (upd.); 46
    (upd.)
Glotel plc, 53
The Go-Ahead Group Plc, 28
Grampian Country Food Group, Ltd., 85
Granada Group PLC, II; 24 (upd.)
Grand Metropolitan PLC, I; 14 (upd.)
The Great Universal Stores plc, V; 19
    (upd.)
The Greenalls Group PLC, 21
Greene King plc, 31
Greggs PLC, 65
Guardian Financial Services, 64 (upd.)
Guardian Media Group plc, 53
Guardian Royal Exchange Plc, 11
Guinness/UDV, I; 43 (upd.)
GUS plc, 47 (upd.)
GWR Group plc, 39
Hammerson plc, 40
The Hammerson Property Investment and
    Development Corporation plc, IV
Hanson PLC, III; 7 (upd.); 30 (upd.)
Harrisons & Crosfield plc, III
Harrods Holdings, 47
The Hartstone Group plc, 14
Hawker Siddeley Group Public Limited
    Company, III
Haynes Publishing Group P.L.C., 71
Hays Plc, 27; 78 (upd.)
Hazlewood Foods plc, 32
Headlam Group plc, 95
Henry Boot plc, 76

Her Majesty's Stationery Office, 7
Highland Gold Mining Limited, 95
Hillsdown Holdings plc, II; 24 (upd.)
Hilton Group plc, 49 (upd.)
HIT Entertainment PLC, 40
HMV Group plc, 59
Holidaybreak plc, 96
Home Retail Group plc, 91
House of Fraser PLC, 45
HSBC Holdings plc, 12; 26 (upd.); 80 (upd.)
Hunting plc 78
Huntingdon Life Sciences Group plc, 42
Huntleigh Technology PLC, 77
IAC Group, 96
Ibstock Brick Ltd., 14; 37 (upd.)
ICL plc, 6
IG Group Holdings plc, 97
IMI plc, 9
Imperial Chemical Industries PLC, I; 50 (upd.)
Imperial Tobacco Group PLC, 50
Inchcape PLC, III; 16 (upd.); 50 (upd.)
Informa Group plc, 58
Inter Link Foods PLC, 61
International Power PLC, 50 (upd.)
Intertek Group plc, 95
Invensys PLC, 50 (upd.)
IPC Magazines Limited, 7
J C Bamford Excavators Ltd., 83
J Sainsbury plc, II; 13 (upd.); 38 (upd.); 95 (upd.)
James Beattie plc, 43
James Purdey & Sons Limited, 87
Jarvis plc, 39
JD Wetherspoon plc, 30
Jersey European Airways (UK) Ltd., 61
JJB Sports plc, 32
John Brown PLC, I
The John David Group plc, 90
John Dewar & Sons, Ltd., 82
John Laing plc, I; 51 (upd.)
John Lewis Partnership plc, V; 42 (upd.); 99 (upd.)
John Menzies plc, 39
Johnson Matthey PLC, IV; 16 (upd.); 49 (upd.)
Johnston Press plc, 35
Kelda Group plc, 45
Keller Group PLC, 95
Kennecott Corporation, 7; 27 (upd.)
Kesa Electricals plc, 91
Kidde plc, 44 (upd.)
Kingfisher plc, V; 24 (upd.); 83 (upd.)
Kleinwort Benson Group PLC, II
Kvaerner ASA, 36
Kwik-Fit Holdings plc, 54
Ladbroke Group PLC, II; 21 (upd.)
Lafarge Cement UK, 54 (upd.)
Land Securities PLC, IV; 49 (upd.)
Laing O'Rourke PLC, 93 (upd.)
Laura Ashley Holdings plc, 13; 37 (upd.)
The Laurel Pub Company Limited, 59
Legal & General Group plc, III; 24 (upd.)
Littlewoods plc, V; 42 (upd.)
Lloyd's, III; 22 (upd.); 74 (upd.)
Lloyds TSB Group plc, II; 47 (upd.)
Loganair Ltd., 68

Logica plc, 14; 37 (upd.)
London Regional Transport, 6
London Scottish Bank plc, 70
London Stock Exchange Limited, 34
Lonmin plc, 66 (upd.)
Lonrho Plc, 21
Lookers plc, 71
Lotus Cars Ltd., 14
Lucas Industries PLC, III
Luminar Plc, 40
Lush Ltd., 93
The Macallan Distillers Ltd., 63
Mackays Stores Group Ltd., 92
Madge Networks N.V., 26
Manchester United Football Club plc, 30
Marconi plc, 33 (upd.)
Marks and Spencer Group p.l.c., V; 24 (upd.); 85 (upd.)
Marshall Amplification plc, 62
Martin-Baker Aircraft Company Limited, 61
Matalan PLC, 49
Maxwell Communication Corporation plc, IV; 7 (upd.)
May Gurney Integrated Services PLC, 95
McBride plc, 82
McKechnie plc, 34
Meggitt PLC, 34
MEPC plc, IV
Mercury Communications, Ltd., 7
The Mersey Docks and Harbour Company, 30
Metal Box PLC, I
Michael Page International plc, 45
Midland Bank PLC, II; 17 (upd.)
Millennium & Copthorne Hotels plc, 71
Mirror Group Newspapers plc, 7; 23 (upd.)
Misys plc, 45; 46
Mitchells & Butlers PLC, 59
Molins plc, 51
Monsoon plc, 39
The Morgan Crucible Company plc, 82
Morgan Grenfell Group PLC, II
Moss Bros Group plc, 51
Mothercare plc, 17; 78 (upd.)
Moy Park Ltd. 78
Mulberry Group PLC, 71
N M Rothschild & Sons Limited, 39
National Express Group PLC, 50
National Power PLC, 12
National Westminster Bank PLC, II
New Look Group plc, 35
Newsquest plc, 32
Next plc, 29
NFC plc, 6
Nichols plc, 44
North West Water Group plc, 11
Northern and Shell Network plc, 87
Northern Foods plc, 10; 61 (upd.)
Northern Rock plc, 33
Norwich & Peterborough Building Society, 55
Novar plc, 49 (upd.)
NTL Inc., 65
Ocean Group plc, 6
Old Mutual PLC, 61
Orange S.A., 84

Ottakar's plc, 64
Oxfam GB, 87
Pearson plc, IV; 46 (upd.)
The Peninsular & Oriental Steam Navigation Company (Bovis Division), I
The Peninsular and Oriental Steam Navigation Company, V; 38 (upd.)
Pennon Group Plc, 45
Pentland Group plc, 20
Perkins Foods Holdings Ltd., 87
Petrofac Ltd., 95
Phaidon Press Ltd., 98
Phones 4u Ltd., 85
Photo-Me International Plc, 83
PIC International Group PLC, 24 (upd.)
Pilkington Group Limited, III; 34 (upd.); 87 (upd.)
PKF International 78
The Plessey Company, PLC, II
The Porcelain and Fine China Companies Ltd., 69
Portmeirion Group plc, 88
Post Office Group, V
Posterscope Worldwide, 70
Powell Duffryn plc, 31
Powergen PLC, 11; 50 (upd.)
Princes Ltd., 76
Prudential plc, 48 (upd.)
Psion PLC, 45
Punch Taverns plc, 70
PZ Cussons plc, 72
R. Griggs Group Limited, 23
Racal Electronics PLC, II
Ragdoll Productions Ltd., 51
Railtrack Group PLC, 50
Raleigh UK Ltd., 65
The Rank Group plc, II; 14 (upd.); 64 (upd.)
Ranks Hovis McDougall Limited, II; 28 (upd.)
Rathbone Brothers plc, 70
The Real Good Food Company plc, 99
The Really Useful Group, 26
Reckitt Benckiser plc, II; 42 (upd.); 91 (upd.)
Redland plc, III
Redrow Group plc, 31
Reed Elsevier plc, IV; 17 (upd.); 31 (upd.)
Regent Inns plc, 95
Renishaw plc, 46
Rentokil Initial Plc, 47
Reuters Group PLC, IV; 22 (upd.); 63 (upd.)
Rexam PLC, 32 (upd.); 85 (upd.)
Ricardo plc, 90
Rio Tinto PLC, 19 (upd.); 50 (upd.)
RMC Group p.l.c., III; 34 (upd.)
Rolls-Royce Group PLC, 67 (upd.)
Rolls-Royce plc, I; 7 (upd.); 21 (upd.)
Ronson PLC, 49
Rothmans UK Holdings Limited, V; 19 (upd.)
Rotork plc, 46
Rover Group Ltd., 7; 21 (upd.)
Rowntree Mackintosh, II
Royal & Sun Alliance Insurance Group plc, 55 (upd.)

The Royal Bank of Scotland Group plc,
  38 (upd.)
Royal Doulton plc, 14; 38 (upd.)
Royal Dutch Petroleum Company/ The
  Shell Transport and Trading Company
  p.l.c., IV
Royal Insurance Holdings PLC, III
RPC Group PLC, 81
The RTZ Corporation PLC, IV
The Rugby Group plc, 31
Saatchi & Saatchi PLC, I
SABMiller plc, 59 (upd.)
Safeway PLC, 50 (upd.)
Saffery Champness, 80
The Sage Group, 43
St. James's Place Capital, plc, 71
The Sanctuary Group PLC, 69
SBC Warburg, 14
Schroders plc, 42
Scottish & Newcastle plc, 35 (upd.)
Scottish and Southern Energy plc, 66
  (upd.)
Scottish Power plc, 49 (upd.)
Scottish Radio Holding plc, 41
SDL PLC, 67
Sea Containers Ltd., 29
Sears plc, V
Securicor Plc, 45
Seddon Group Ltd., 67
Selfridges Plc, 34
Serco Group plc, 47
Severn Trent PLC, 12; 38 (upd.)
SFI Group plc, 51
Shanks Group plc, 45
Shepherd Neame Limited, 30
SIG plc, 71
Signet Group PLC, 61
Singer & Friedlander Group plc, 41
Skipton Building Society, 80
Slough Estates PLC, IV; 50 (upd.)
Smith & Nephew plc, 17;41 (upd.)
SmithKline Beecham plc, III; 32 (upd.)
Smiths Industries PLC, 25
Somerfield plc, 47 (upd.)
Southern Electric PLC, 13
Specialist Computer Holdings Ltd., 80
Speedy Hire plc, 84
Spirax-Sarco Engineering plc, 59
SSL International plc, 49
St Ives plc, 34
Standard Chartered plc, II; 48 (upd.)
Stanley Leisure plc, 66
STC PLC, III
Stirling Group plc, 62
Stoddard International plc, 72
Stoll-Moss Theatres Ltd., 34
Stolt-Nielsen S.A., 42
Storehouse PLC, 16
Strix Ltd., 51
Superdrug Stores PLC, 95
Surrey Satellite Technology Limited, 83
Sun Alliance Group PLC, III
Sytner Group plc, 45
Tarmac Limited, III; 28 (upd.); 95 (upd.)
Tate & Lyle PLC, II; 42 (upd.)
Taylor & Francis Group plc, 44
Taylor Nelson Sofres plc, 34
Taylor Woodrow plc, I; 38 (upd.)

Ted Baker plc, 86
Tesco plc, II; 24 (upd.); 68 (upd.)
Thames Water plc, 11; 90 (upd.)
Thistle Hotels PLC, 54
Thorn Emi PLC, I
Thorn plc, 24
Thorntons plc, 46
3i Group PLC, 73
365 Media Group plc, 89
TI Group plc, 17
Tibbett & Britten Group plc, 32
Tiger Aspect Productions Ltd., 72
Time Out Group Ltd., 68
Tomkins plc, 11; 44 (upd.)
Tottenham Hotspur PLC, 81
Travis Perkins plc, 34
Trinity Mirror plc, 49 (upd.)
Triumph Motorcycles Ltd., 53
Trusthouse Forte PLC, III
TSB Group plc, 12
Tulip Ltd., 89
Tullow Oil plc, 83
The Tussauds Group, 55
Ulster Television PLC, 71
Ultimate Leisure Group PLC, 75
Ultramar PLC, IV
Umbro plc, 88
Unigate PLC, II; 28 (upd.)
Unilever, II; 7 (upd.); 32 (upd.); 89
  (upd.)
Uniq plc, 83 (upd.)
United Biscuits (Holdings) plc, II; 42
  (upd.)
United Business Media plc, 52 (upd.)
United News & Media plc, IV; 28 (upd.)
United Utilities PLC, 52 (upd.)
Urbium PLC, 75
Vauxhall Motors Limited, 73
Vendôme Luxury Group plc, 27
Vestey Group Ltd., 95
Vickers plc, 27
Virgin Group Ltd., 12; 32 (upd.); 89
  (upd.)
Viridian Group plc, 64
Vodafone Group Plc, 11; 36 (upd.); 75
  (upd.)
Vosper Thornycroft Holding plc, 41
W Jordan (Cereals) Ltd., 74
Wagon plc, 92
Walkers Shortbread Ltd. 79
Walkers Snack Foods Ltd., 70
Warburtons Ltd., 89
Wassall Plc, 18
Waterford Wedgwood Holdings PLC, 12
Watson Wyatt Worldwide, 42
Watts of Lydney Group Ltd., 71
Weetabix Limited, 61
The Weir Group PLC, 85
The Wellcome Foundation Ltd., I
WH Smith PLC, V, 42 (upd.)
Whatman plc, 46
Whitbread PLC, I; 20 (upd.); 52 (upd.);
  97 (upd.)
Whittard of Chelsea Plc, 61
Wilkinson Hardware Stores Ltd., 80
Wilkinson Sword Ltd., 60
William Grant & Sons Ltd., 60
William Hill Organization Limited, 49

William Reed Publishing Ltd. 78
Willis Corroon Group plc, 25
Wilson Bowden Plc, 45
Wincanton plc, 52
Wm. Morrison Supermarkets PLC, 38
Wolseley plc, 64
The Wolverhampton & Dudley Breweries,
  PLC, 57
Wood Hall Trust PLC, I
The Woolwich plc, 30
Woolworths Group plc, 83
WPP Group plc, 6; 48 (upd.)
WS Atkins Plc, 45
Xstrata PLC, 73
Yell Group PLC 79
Young & Co.'s Brewery, P.L.C., 38
Young's Bluecrest Seafood Holdings Ltd.,
  81
Yule Catto & Company plc, 54
Zeneca Group PLC, 21
Zomba Records Ltd., 52

United States

A & E Television Networks, 32
A & W Brands, Inc., 25
A-dec, Inc., 53
A-Mark Financial Corporation, 71
A. Schulman, Inc., 8; 49 (upd.)
A.B. Watley Group Inc., 45
A.B.Dick Company, 28
A.C. Moore Arts & Crafts, Inc., 30
A. Duda & Sons, Inc., 88
A.G. Edwards, Inc., 8; 32
A.H. Belo Corporation, 10; 30 (upd.)
A.L. Pharma Inc., 12
A.M. Castle & Co., 25
A.O. Smith Corporation, 11; 40 (upd.);
  93 (upd.)
A.T. Cross Company, 17; 49 (upd.)
AAF-McQuay Incorporated, 26
AAON, Inc., 22
AAR Corp., 28
Aaron Rents, Inc., 14; 35 (upd.)
AARP, 27
Aavid Thermal Technologies, Inc., 29
Abatix Corp., 57
Abaxis, Inc., 83
Abbott Laboratories, I; 11 (upd.); 40
  (upd.); 93 (upd.)
ABC Appliance, Inc., 10
ABC Carpet & Home Co. Inc., 26
ABC Family Worldwide, Inc., 52
ABC Rail Products Corporation, 18
ABC Supply Co., Inc., 22
Abercrombie & Fitch Company, 15; 35
  (upd.); 75 (upd.)
Abigail Adams National Bancorp, Inc., 23
Abiomed, Inc., 47
ABM Industries Incorporated, 25 (upd.)
Abrams Industries Inc., 23
Abraxas Petroleum Corporation, 89
Abt Associates Inc., 95
Academy of Television Arts & Sciences,
  Inc., 55
Academy Sports & Outdoors, 27
Acadian Ambulance & Air Med Services,
  Inc., 39
ACCION International, 87

Acclaim Entertainment Inc., 24
ACCO World Corporation, 7; 51 (upd.)
Accredited Home Lenders Holding Co., 91
Accubuilt, Inc., 74
Accuray Incorporated, 95
AccuWeather, Inc., 73
ACE Cash Express, Inc., 33
Ace Hardware Corporation, 12; 35 (upd.)
Aceto Corp., 38
AchieveGlobal Inc., 90
Ackerley Communications, Inc., 9
Acme United Corporation, 70
Acme-Cleveland Corp., 13
ACNielsen Corporation, 13; 38 (upd.)
Acorn Products, Inc., 55
Acosta Sales and Marketing Company, Inc., 77
Acsys, Inc., 44
Action Performance Companies, Inc., 27
Activision, Inc., 32; 89 (upd.)
Actuant Corporation, 94 (upd.)
Acuity Brands, Inc., 90
Acushnet Company, 64
Acuson Corporation, 10; 36 (upd.)
Acxiom Corporation, 35
The Adams Express Company, 86
Adams Golf, Inc., 37
Adaptec, Inc., 31
ADC Telecommunications, Inc., 10; 30 (upd.); 89 (upd.)
Adelphia Communications Corporation, 17; 52 (upd.)
ADESA, Inc., 71
Administaff, Inc., 52
Adobe Systems Inc., 10; 33 (upd.)
Adolph Coors Company, I; 13 (upd.); 36 (upd.)
ADT Security Services, Inc., 12; 44 (upd.)
Adtran Inc., 22
Advance Auto Parts, Inc., 57
Advance Publications Inc., IV; 19 (upd.); 96 (upd.)
Advanced Circuits Inc., 67
Advanced Fibre Communications, Inc., 63
Advanced Marketing Services, Inc., 34
Advanced Medical Optics, Inc. 79
Advanced Micro Devices, Inc., 6; 30 (upd.); 99 (upd.)
Advanced Neuromodulation Systems, Inc., 73
Advanced Technology Laboratories, Inc., 9
Advanstar Communications, Inc., 57
Advanta Corporation, 8; 38 (upd.)
Advantica Restaurant Group, Inc., 27 (upd.)
Adventist Health, 53
The Advertising Council, Inc., 76
The Advisory Board Company, 80
Advo, Inc., 6; 53 (upd.)
Advocat Inc., 46
AECOM Technology Corporation 79
AEI Music Network Inc., 35
AEP Industries, Inc., 36
AeroGrow International, Inc., 95
Aerojet-General Corp., 63
Aeronca Inc., 46
Aéropostale, Inc., 89

Aeroquip Corporation, 16
Aerosonic Corporation, 69
AeroVironment, Inc., 97
The AES Corporation, 10; 13 (upd.); 53 (upd.)
Aetna Inc., III; 21 (upd.); 63 (upd.)
AFC Enterprises, Inc., 32; 83 (upd.)
Affiliated Computer Services, Inc., 61
Affiliated Foods Inc., 53
Affiliated Managers Group, Inc. 79
Affiliated Publications, Inc., 7
Affinity Group Holding Inc., 56
AFLAC Incorporated, 10 (upd.); 38 (upd.)
Africare, 59
After Hours Formalwear Inc., 60
Aftermarket Technology Corp., 83
Ag Services of America, Inc., 59
Ag-Chem Equipment Company, Inc., 17
AGCO Corporation, 13; 67 (upd.)
Agere Systems Inc., 61
Agilent Technologies Inc., 38; 93 (upd.)
Agilysys Inc., 76 (upd.)
Agri Beef Company, 81
Agway, Inc., 7; 21 (upd.)
AHL Services, Inc., 27
Air & Water Technologies Corporation, 6
Air Express International Corporation, 13
Air Methods Corporation, 53
Air Products and Chemicals, Inc., I; 10 (upd.); 74 (upd.)
Air T, Inc., 86
Air Wisconsin Airlines Corporation, 55
Airborne Freight Corporation, 6; 34 (upd.)
Airborne Systems Group, 89
Airgas, Inc., 54
AirTouch Communications, 11
AirTran Holdings, Inc., 22
AK Steel Holding Corporation, 19; 41 (upd.)
Akamai Technologies, Inc., 71
Akin, Gump, Strauss, Hauer & Feld, L.L.P., 33
Akorn, Inc., 32
Alabama Farmers Cooperative, Inc., 63
Alabama National BanCorporation, 75
Alamo Group Inc., 32
Alamo Rent A Car, 6; 24 (upd.); 84 (upd.)
ALARIS Medical Systems, Inc., 65
Alaska Air Group, Inc., 6; 29 (upd.)
Alaska Communications Systems Group, Inc., 89
Alaska Railroad Corporation, 60
Alba-Waldensian, Inc., 30
Albany International Corporation, 8; 51 (upd.)
Albany Molecular Research, Inc., 77
Albemarle Corporation, 59
Alberici Corporation, 76
Alberto-Culver Company, 8; 36 (upd.); 91 (upd.)
Albertson's, Inc., II; 7 (upd.); 30 (upd.); 65 (upd.)
Alco Health Services Corporation, III
Alco Standard Corporation, I
Alcoa Inc., 56 (upd.)

Aldila Inc., 46
Aldus Corporation, 10
Alex Lee Inc., 18; 44 (upd.)
Alexander & Alexander Services Inc., 10
Alexander & Baldwin, Inc., 10; 40 (upd.)
Alexander's, Inc., 45
Alfa Corporation, 60
Alico, Inc., 63
Alienware Corporation, 81
Align Technology, Inc., 94
All American Communications Inc., 20
Alleghany Corporation, 10; 60 (upd.)
Allegheny Energy, Inc., 38 (upd.)
Allegheny Ludlum Corporation, 8
Allegheny Power System, Inc., V
Allegiant Travel Company, 97
Allegis Group, Inc., 95
Allen Canning Company, 76
Allen Foods, Inc., 60
Allen Organ Company, 33
Allen Systems Group, Inc., 59
Allen-Edmonds Shoe Corporation, 61
Allergan, Inc., 10; 30 (upd.); 77 (upd.)
Alliance Capital Management Holding L.P., 63
Alliance Entertainment Corp., 17
Alliance Resource Partners, L.P., 81
Alliant Techsystems Inc., 8; 30 (upd.); 77 (upd.)
The Allied Defense Group, Inc., 65
Allied Healthcare Products, Inc., 24
Allied Products Corporation, 21
Allied Signal Engines, 9
Allied Waste Industries, Inc., 50
Allied Worldwide, Inc., 49
AlliedSignal Inc., I; 22 (upd.)
Allison Gas Turbine Division, 9
Allmerica Financial Corporation, 63
Allou Health & Beauty Care, Inc., 28
Alloy, Inc., 55
The Allstate Corporation, 10; 27 (upd.)
ALLTEL Corporation, 6; 46 (upd.)
Alltrista Corporation, 30
Allwaste, Inc., 18
Almost Family, Inc., 93
Aloha Airlines, Incorporated, 24
Alpharma Inc., 35 (upd.)
Alpine Confections, Inc., 71
Alpine Lace Brands, Inc., 18
Alside Inc., 94
AltaVista Company, 43
Altera Corporation, 18; 43 (upd.)
Alternative Tentacles Records, 66
Alterra Healthcare Corporation, 42
Alticor Inc., 71 (upd.)
Altiris, Inc., 65
Altron Incorporated, 20
Aluminum Company of America, IV; 20 (upd.)
Alvin Ailey Dance Foundation, Inc., 52
ALZA Corporation, 10; 36 (upd.)
Amalgamated Bank, 60
AMAX Inc., IV
Amazon.com, Inc., 25; 56 (upd.)
AMB Property Corporation, 57
Ambac Financial Group, Inc., 65
Ambassadors International, Inc., 68 (upd.)
Amblin Entertainment, 21

AMC Entertainment Inc., 12; 35 (upd.)
AMCOL International Corporation, 59 (upd.)
AMCON Distributing Company, 99
AMCORE Financial Inc., 44
Amdahl Corporation, III; 14 (upd.); 40 (upd.)
Amdocs Ltd., 47
Amedysis, Inc., 53
Amerada Hess Corporation, IV; 21 (upd.); 55 (upd.)
Amerco, 6
AMERCO, 67 (upd.)
Ameren Corporation, 60 (upd.)
America Online, Inc., 10; 26 (upd.)
America West Holdings Corporation, 6; 34 (upd.)
America's Car-Mart, Inc., 64
America's Favorite Chicken Company, Inc., 7
AmeriCares Foundation, Inc., 87
American & Efird, Inc., 82
American Airlines, I; 6 (upd.)
American Apparel, Inc., 90
American Axle & Manufacturing Holdings, Inc., 67
American Banknote Corporation, 30
American Bar Association, 35
American Biltrite Inc., 16; 43 (upd.)
American Brands, Inc., V
American Building Maintenance Industries, Inc., 6
American Business Information, Inc., 18
American Business Products, Inc., 20
American Campus Communities, Inc., 85
The American Cancer Society, 24
American Capital Strategies, Ltd., 91
American Cast Iron Pipe Company, 50
American Civil Liberties Union (ACLU), 60
American Classic Voyages Company, 27
American Coin Merchandising, Inc., 28; 74 (upd.)
American Colloid Co., 13
American Commercial Lines Inc., 99
American Crystal Sugar Company, 9; 32 (upd.)
American Cyanamid, I; 8 (upd.)
American Eagle Outfitters, Inc., 24; 55 (upd.)
American Ecology Corporation, 77
American Electric Power Company, Inc., V; 45 (upd.)
American Express Company, II; 10 (upd.); 38 (upd.)
American Family Corporation, III
American Financial Group Inc., III; 48 (upd.)
American Foods Group, 43
American Furniture Company, Inc., 21
American General Corporation, III; 10 (upd.); 46 (upd.)
American General Finance Corp., 11
American Girl, Inc., 69 (upd.)
American Golf Corporation, 45
American Gramaphone LLC, 52
American Greetings Corporation, 7; 22 (upd.); 59 (upd.)

American Healthways, Inc., 65
American Home Mortgage Holdings, Inc., 46
American Home Products, I; 10 (upd.)
American Homestar Corporation, 18; 41 (upd.)
American Institute of Certified Public Accountants (AICPA), 44
American International Group, Inc., III; 15 (upd.); 47 (upd.)
American Italian Pasta Company, 27; 76 (upd.)
American Kennel Club, Inc., 74
American Lawyer Media Holdings, Inc., 32
American Library Association, 86
American Licorice Company, 86
American Locker Group Incorporated, 34
American Lung Association, 48
American Maize-Products Co., 14
American Management Association, 76
American Management Systems, Inc., 11
American Media, Inc., 27; 82 (upd.)
American Medical Association, 39
American Medical International, Inc., III
American Medical Response, Inc., 39
American Motors Corporation, I
American National Insurance Company, 8; 27 (upd.)
American Pad & Paper Company, 20
American Pharmaceutical Partners, Inc., 69
American Pop Corn Company, 59
American Power Conversion Corporation, 24; 67 (upd.)
American Premier Underwriters, Inc., 10
American President Companies Ltd., 6
American Printing House for the Blind, 26
American Re Corporation, 10; 35 (upd.)
American Red Cross, 40
American Reprographics Company, 75
American Residential Mortgage Corporation, 8
American Restaurant Partners, L.P., 93
American Retirement Corporation, 42
American Rice, Inc., 33
American Safety Razor Company, 20
American Science & Engineering, Inc., 81
American Seating Company 78
American Skiing Company, 28
American Society for the Prevention of Cruelty to Animals (ASPCA), 68
The American Society of Composers, Authors and Publishers (ASCAP), 29
American Software Inc., 25
American Standard Companies Inc., III; 30 (upd.)
American States Water Company, 46
American Stores Company, II; 22 (upd.)
American Superconductor Corporation, 97
American Technical Ceramics Corp., 67
American Tourister, Inc., 16
American Tower Corporation, 33
American Vanguard Corporation, 47
American Water Works Company, Inc., 6; 38 (upd.)

American Woodmark Corporation, 31
Amerigon Incorporated, 97
AMERIGROUP Corporation, 69
Amerihost Properties, Inc., 30
AmeriSource Health Corporation, 37 (upd.)
AmerisourceBergen Corporation, 64 (upd.)
Ameristar Casinos, Inc., 33; 69 (upd.)
Ameritech Corporation, V; 18 (upd.)
Ameritrade Holding Corporation, 34
Ameriwood Industries International Corp., 17
Amerock Corporation, 53
Ameron International Corporation, 67
Ames Department Stores, Inc., 9; 30 (upd.)
AMETEK, Inc., 9
AMF Bowling, Inc., 40
Amfac/JMB Hawaii L.L.C., I; 24 (upd.)
Amgen, Inc., 10; 30 (upd.); 89 (upd.)
AMICAS, Inc., 69
Amkor Technology, Inc., 69
Amoco Corporation, IV; 14 (upd.)
Amoskeag Company, 8
AMP Incorporated, II; 14 (upd.)
Ampacet Corporation, 67
Ampco-Pittsburgh Corporation 79
Ampex Corporation, 17
Amphenol Corporation, 40
AMR Corporation, 28 (upd.); 52 (upd.)
AMREP Corporation, 21
Amscan Holdings, Inc., 61
AmSouth Bancorporation, 12; 48 (upd.)
Amsted Industries Incorporated, 7
AmSurg Corporation, 48
Amtran, Inc., 34
Amway Corporation, III; 13 (upd.); 30 (upd.)
Amy's Kitchen Inc., 76
Amylin Pharmaceuticals, Inc., 67
Anacomp, Inc., 94
Anadarko Petroleum Corporation, 10; 52 (upd.)
Anaheim Angels Baseball Club, Inc., 53
Analex Corporation, 74
Analog Devices, Inc., 10
Analogic Corporation, 23
Analysts International Corporation, 36
Analytic Sciences Corporation, 10
Analytical Surveys, Inc., 33
Anaren Microwave, Inc., 33
Anchor Bancorp, Inc., 10
Anchor Brewing Company, 47
Anchor Gaming, 24
Anchor Hocking Glassware, 13
Andersen, 10; 29 (upd.); 68 (upd.)
Anderson Trucking Service, Inc., 75
The Anderson-DuBose Company, 60
The Andersons, Inc., 31
Andis Company, Inc., 85
Andrew Corporation, 10; 32 (upd.)
The Andrews Institute, 99
Andrews Kurth, LLP, 71
Andrews McMeel Universal, 40
Andronico's Market, 70
Andrx Corporation, 55
Angelica Corporation, 15; 43 (upd.)

AngioDynamics, Inc., 81
Anheuser-Busch Companies, Inc., I; 10
  (upd.); 34 (upd.)
Anixter International Inc., 88
Annie's Homegrown, Inc., 59
AnnTaylor Stores Corporation, 13; 37
  (upd.); 67 (upd.)
ANR Pipeline Co., 17
The Anschutz Company, 12; 36 (upd.);
  73 (upd.)
Ansoft Corporation, 63
Anteon Corporation, 57
Anthem Electronics, Inc., 13
Anthony & Sylvan Pools Corporation, 56
The Antioch Company, 40
AOL Time Warner Inc., 57 (upd.)
Aon Corporation, III; 45 (upd.)
Apache Corporation, 10; 32 (upd.); 89
  (upd.)
Apartment Investment and Management
  Company, 49
Apex Digital, Inc., 63
APi Group, Inc., 64
APL Limited, 61 (upd.)
Apogee Enterprises, Inc., 8
Apollo Group, Inc., 24
Applause Inc., 24
Apple & Eve L.L.C., 92
Apple Bank for Savings, 59
Apple Computer, Inc., III; 6 (upd.); 36
  (upd.); 77 (upd.)
Applebee's International Inc., 14; 35
  (upd.)
Appliance Recycling Centers of America,
  Inc., 42
Applica Incorporated, 43 (upd.)
Applied Bioscience International, Inc., 10
Applied Films Corporation, 48
Applied Materials, Inc., 10; 46 (upd.)
Applied Micro Circuits Corporation, 38
Applied Power, Inc., 9; 32 (upd.)
Applied Signal Technology, Inc., 87
AptarGroup, Inc., 69
Aqua Alliance Inc., 32 (upd.)
aQuantive, Inc., 81
Aquarion Company, 84
Aquent, 96
Aquila, Inc., 50 (upd.)
AR Accessories Group, Inc., 23
ARA Services, II
ARAMARK Corporation, 13; 41 (upd.)
Arandell Corporation, 37
The Arbitron Company, 38
Arbor Drugs Inc., 12
Arby's Inc., 14
Arch Chemicals Inc. 78
Arch Coal Inc., 98
Arch Mineral Corporation, 7
Arch Wireless, Inc., 39
Archer Daniels Midland Company, I; 11
  (upd.); 32 (upd.); 75 (upd.)
Archie Comics Publications, Inc., 63
Archon Corporation, 74 (upd.)
Archstone-Smith Trust, 49
Archway Cookies, Inc., 29
ARCO Chemical Company, 10
Arctco, Inc., 16
Arctic Cat Inc., 40 (upd.); 96 (upd.)

Arctic Slope Regional Corporation, 38
Arden Group, Inc., 29
Arena Resources, Inc., 97
Argon ST, Inc., 81
Argosy Gaming Company, 21
Ariba, Inc., 57
Ariens Company, 48
ARINC Inc., 98
Aris Industries, Inc., 16
The Aristotle Corporation, 62
Ark Restaurants Corp., 20
Arkansas Best Corporation, 16; 94 (upd.)
Arkla, Inc., V
Armco Inc., IV
Armor All Products Corp., 16
Armor Holdings, Inc., 27
Armstrong Holdings, Inc., III; 22 (upd.);
  81 (upd.)
Army and Air Force Exchange Service, 39
Arnhold and S. Bleichroeder Advisers,
  LLC, 97
Arnold & Porter, 35
Arotech Corporation, 93
ArQule, Inc., 68
ARRIS Group, Inc., 89
Arrow Air Holdings Corporation, 55
Arrow Electronics, Inc., 10; 50 (upd.)
The Art Institute of Chicago, 29
Art Van Furniture, Inc., 28
Artesyn Technologies Inc., 46 (upd.)
ArthroCare Corporation, 73
The Arthur C. Clarke Foundation, 92
Arthur D. Little, Inc., 35
Arthur J. Gallagher & Co., 73
Arthur Murray International, Inc., 32
Artisan Entertainment Inc., 32 (upd.)
ArvinMeritor, Inc., 8; 54 (upd.)
Asanté Technologies, Inc., 20
ASARCO Incorporated, IV
Asbury Automotive Group Inc., 60
Asbury Carbons, Inc., 68
ASC, Inc., 55
Ascend Communications, Inc., 24
Ascendia Brands, Inc., 97
Ascential Software Corporation, 59
Ash Grove Cement Company, 94
Ashland Inc., 19; 50 (upd.)
Ashland Oil, Inc., IV
Ashley Furniture Industries, Inc., 35
Ashworth, Inc., 26
ASK Group, Inc., 9
Ask Jeeves, Inc., 65
Aspect Telecommunications Corporation,
  22
Aspen Skiing Company, 15
Asplundh Tree Expert Co., 20; 59 (upd.)
Assisted Living Concepts, Inc., 43
Associated Estates Realty Corporation, 25
Associated Grocers, Incorporated, 9; 31
  (upd.)
Associated Milk Producers, Inc., 11; 48
  (upd.)
Associated Natural Gas Corporation, 11
The Associated Press, 13; 31 (upd.); 73
  (upd.)
Association of Junior Leagues
  International Inc., 60
AST Research Inc., 9

Astec Industries, Inc. 79
AstenJohnson Inc., 90
Astoria Financial Corporation, 44
Astronics Corporation, 35
Asurion Corporation, 83
ASV, Inc., 34; 66 (upd.)
At Home Corporation, 43
AT&T Bell Laboratories, Inc., 13
AT&T Corporation, V; 29 (upd.); 68
  (upd.)
AT&T Wireless Services, Inc., 54 (upd.)
ATA Holdings Corporation, 82
Atari Corporation, 9; 23 (upd.); 66 (upd.)
ATC Healthcare Inc., 64
Atchison Casting Corporation, 39
The Athlete's Foot Brands LLC, 84
The Athletics Investment Group, 62
Atkins Nutritionals, Inc., 58
Atkinson Candy Company, 87
Atlanta Bread Company International,
  Inc., 70
Atlanta Gas Light Company, 6; 23 (upd.)
Atlanta National League Baseball Club,
  Inc., 43
Atlantic American Corporation, 44
Atlantic Coast Airlines Holdings, Inc., 55
Atlantic Energy, Inc., 6
The Atlantic Group, 23
Atlantic Premium Brands, Ltd., 57
Atlantic Richfield Company, IV; 31 (upd.)
Atlantic Southeast Airlines, Inc., 47
Atlantis Plastics, Inc., 85
Atlas Air, Inc., 39
Atlas Van Lines, Inc., 14
Atmel Corporation, 17
ATMI, Inc., 93
Atmos Energy Corporation, 43
Attachmate Corporation, 56
Atwood Mobil Products, 53
Au Bon Pain Co., Inc., 18
The Auchter Company, The 78
Audible Inc. 79
Audio King Corporation, 24
Audiovox Corporation, 34; 90 (upd.)
August Schell Brewing Company Inc., 59
Ault Incorporated, 34
Auntie Anne's, Inc., 35
Aurora Casket Company, Inc., 56
Aurora Foods Inc., 32
The Austin Company, 8; 72 (upd.)
Austin Powder Company, 76
Authentic Fitness Corporation, 20; 51
  (upd.)
Auto Value Associates, Inc., 25
Autobytel Inc., 47
Autocam Corporation, 51
Autodesk, Inc., 10; 89 (upd.)
Autologic Information International, Inc.,
  20
Automatic Data Processing, Inc., III; 9
  (upd.); 47 (upd.)
AutoNation, Inc., 50
Autotote Corporation, 20
AutoTrader.com, L.L.C., 91
AutoZone, Inc., 9; 31 (upd.)
Auvil Fruit Company, Inc., 95
Avado Brands, Inc., 31
Avalon Correctional Services, Inc., 75

AvalonBay Communities, Inc., 58
Avco Financial Services Inc., 13
Aveda Corporation, 24
Avedis Zildjian Co., 38
Aventine Renewable Energy Holdings,
    Inc., 89
Avery Dennison Corporation, IV; 17
    (upd.); 49 (upd.)
Aviall, Inc., 73
Aviation Sales Company, 41
Avid Technology Inc., 38
Avis Group Holdings, Inc., 75 (upd.)
Avis Rent A Car, Inc., 6; 22 (upd.)
Avista Corporation, 69 (upd.)
Avnet Inc., 9
Avocent Corporation, 65
Avon Products, Inc., III; 19 (upd.); 46
    (upd.)
Avondale Industries, 7; 41 (upd.)
AVX Corporation, 67
Awrey Bakeries, Inc., 56
Axcelis Technologies, Inc., 95
Axsys Technologies, Inc., 93
Aydin Corp., 19
Azcon Corporation, 23
Aztar Corporation, 13; 71 (upd.)
AZZ Incorporated, 93
B&G Foods, Inc., 40
B. Dalton Bookseller Inc., 25
The B. Manischewitz Company, LLC, 31
B/E Aerospace, Inc., 30
B.J. Alan Co., Inc., 67
B.R. Guest Inc., 87
B.W. Rogers Company, 94
Babbage's, Inc., 10
The Babcock & Wilcox Company, 82
Baby Superstore, Inc., 15
Bachman's Inc., 22
Back Bay Restaurant Group, Inc., 20
Back Yard Burgers, Inc., 45
Bad Boy Worldwide Entertainment
    Group, 58
Badger Meter, Inc., 22
Badger Paper Mills, Inc., 15
Badger State Ethanol, LLC, 83
BAE Systems Ship Repair, 73
Bailey Nurseries, Inc., 57
Bain & Company, 55
Baird & Warner Holding Company, 87
Bairnco Corporation, 28
Baker & Daniels LLP, 88
Baker & Hostetler LLP, 40
Baker & McKenzie, 10; 42 (upd.)
Baker & Taylor Corporation, 16; 43
    (upd.)
Baker and Botts, L.L.P., 28
Baker Hughes Incorporated, III; 22
    (upd.); 57 (upd.)
Balance Bar Company, 32
Balchem Corporation, 42
Baldor Electric Company, 21; 97 (upd.)
Baldwin & Lyons, 51
Baldwin Piano & Organ Company, 18
Baldwin Technology Company, Inc., 25
Ball Corporation, I; 10; 78 (upd.)
Ball Horticultural Company 78
Ballantyne of Omaha, Inc., 27
Ballard Medical Products, 21

Ballistic Recovery Systems, Inc., 87
Bally Manufacturing Corporation, III
Bally Total Fitness Corporation, 25; 94
    (upd.)
Balmac International, Inc., 94
Baltek Corporation, 34
Baltimore Aircoil Company, Inc., 66
Baltimore Gas and Electric Company, V;
    25 (upd.)
Baltimore Orioles L.P., 66
The Bama Companies, Inc., 80
Banana Republic Inc., 25
Bandag, Inc., 19
Banfi Products Corp., 36
Bank of America Corporation, 46 (upd.)
Bank of Boston Corporation, II
Bank of Granite Corporation, 89
Bank of Hawaii Corporation, 73
Bank of Mississippi, Inc., 14
Bank of New England Corporation, II
The Bank of New York Company, Inc., II;
    46 (upd.)
Bank of the Ozarks, Inc., 91
Bank One Corporation, 10; 36 (upd.)
BankAmerica Corporation, II; 8 (upd.)
Bankers Trust New York Corporation, II
Banknorth Group, Inc., 55
Bankrate, Inc., 83
Banner Aerospace, Inc., 14; 37 (upd.)
Banta Corporation, 12; 32 (upd.); 79
    (upd.)
Banyan Systems Inc., 25
Baptist Health Care Corporation, 82
Bar-S Foods Company, 76
BarclaysAmerican Mortgage Corporation,
    11
Barbara's Bakery Inc., 88
Barden Companies, Inc., 76
Bardwil Industries Inc., 98
Bare Escentuals, Inc., 91
Barnes & Noble, Inc., 10; 30 (upd.); 75
    (upd.)
Barnes Group Inc., 13; 69 (upd.)
Barnett Banks, Inc., 9
Barnett Inc., 28
Barney's, Inc., 28
Barr Pharmaceuticals, Inc., 26; 68 (upd.)
Barrett Business Services, Inc., 16
Barrett-Jackson Auction Company L.L.C.,
    88
Barry-Wehmiller Companies, Inc., 90
The Bartell Drug Company, 94
Barton Malow Company, 51
Barton Protective Services Inc., 53
The Baseball Club of Seattle, LP, 50
Bashas' Inc., 33; 80 (upd.)
The Basketball Club of Seattle, LLC, 50
Bass Pro Shops, Inc., 42
Bassett Furniture Industries, Inc., 18; 95
    (upd.)
Bates Worldwide, Inc., 14; 33 (upd.)
Bath Iron Works, 12; 36 (upd.)
Battelle Memorial Institute, Inc., 10
Battle Mountain Gold Company, 23
Bauerly Companies, 61
Bausch & Lomb Inc., 7; 25 (upd.); 96
    (upd.)
Baxter International Inc., I; 10 (upd.)

Bay State Gas Company, 38
BayBanks, Inc., 12
Bayou Steel Corporation, 31
BB&T Corporation 79
BBN Corp., 19
BDO Seidman LLP, 96
BE&K, Inc., 73
BEA Systems, Inc., 36
Beacon Roofing Supply, Inc., 75
Bear Creek Corporation, 38
Bear Stearns Companies, Inc., II; 10
    (upd.); 52 (upd.)
Bearings, Inc., 13
Beasley Broadcast Group, Inc., 51
Beatrice Company, II
BeautiControl Cosmetics, Inc., 21
Beazer Homes USA, Inc., 17
bebe stores, inc., 31
Bechtel Corporation, I; 24 (upd.); 99
    (upd.)
Beckett Papers, 23
Beckman Coulter, Inc., 22
Beckman Instruments, Inc., 14
Becton, Dickinson & Company, I; 11
    (upd.); 36 (upd.)
Bed Bath & Beyond Inc., 13; 41 (upd.)
Beech Aircraft Corporation, 8
Beech-Nut Nutrition Corporation, 21; 51
    (upd.)
Beer Nuts, Inc., 86
BEI Technologies, Inc., 65
Bekins Company, 15
Bel Fuse, Inc., 53
Bel/Kaukauna USA, 76
Belco Oil & Gas Corp., 40
Belden CDT Inc., 76 (upd.)
Belden Inc., 19
Belk Stores Services, Inc., V; 19 (upd.)
Belk, Inc., 72 (upd.)
Bell and Howell Company, 9; 29 (upd.)
Bell Atlantic Corporation, V; 25 (upd.)
Bell Helicopter Textron Inc., 46
Bell Industries, Inc., 47
Bell Microproducts Inc., 69
Bell Sports Corporation, 16; 44 (upd.)
Belleville Shoe Manufacturing Company,
    92
Bellisio Foods, Inc., 95
BellSouth Corporation, V; 29 (upd.)
Belo Corporation, 98 (upd.)
Beloit Corporation, 14
Bemis Company, Inc., 8; 91 (upd.)
Ben & Jerry's Homemade, Inc., 10; 35
    (upd.); 80 (upd.)
Ben Bridge Jeweler, Inc., 60
Ben E. Keith Company, 76
Benchmark Capital, 49
Benchmark Electronics, Inc., 40
Bendix Corporation, I
Beneficial Corporation, 8
Benihana, Inc., 18; 76 (upd.)
Benjamin Moore & Co., 13; 38 (upd.)
Benton Oil and Gas Company, 47
Berean Christian Stores, 96
Bergdorf Goodman Inc., 52
Bergen Brunswig Corporation, V; 13
    (upd.)
Berger Bros Company, 62

Beringer Blass Wine Estates Ltd., 66 (upd.)
Beringer Wine Estates Holdings, Inc., 22
Berkeley Farms, Inc., 46
Berkshire Hathaway Inc., III; 18 (upd.); 42 (upd.); 89 (upd.)
Berkshire Realty Holdings, L.P., 49
Berlex Laboratories, Inc., 66
Berlitz International, Inc., 13; 39 (upd.)
Bernard C. Harris Publishing Company, Inc., 39
Bernard Chaus, Inc., 27
Bernard Hodes Group Inc., 86
The Bernick Companies, 75
Bernstein-Rein, 92
Berry Plastics Group Inc., 21; 98 (upd.)
Berry Plastics Corporation, 21
Bertucci's Corporation, 16; 64 (upd.)
Berwick Offray, LLC, 70
Best Buy Co., Inc., 9; 23 (upd.); 63 (upd.)
Best Kosher Foods Corporation, 82
Bestfoods, 22 (upd.)
BET Holdings, Inc., 18
Beth Abraham Family of Health Services, 94
Bethlehem Steel Corporation, IV; 7 (upd.); 27 (upd.)
Better Made Snack Foods, Inc., 90
Betz Laboratories, Inc., I; 10 (upd.)
Beverly Enterprises, Inc., III; 16 (upd.)
The BFGoodrich Company, V; 19 (upd.)
BG Products Inc., 96
BHC Communications, Inc., 26
Bianchi International (d/b/a Gregory Mountain Products), 76
BIC Corporation, 8; 23 (upd.)
Bicoastal Corporation, II
Big A Drug Stores Inc. 79
Big B, Inc., 17
Big Bear Stores Co., 13
Big Brothers Big Sisters of America, 85
Big Dog Holdings, Inc., 45
Big 5 Sporting Goods Corporation, 55
Big Flower Press Holdings, Inc., 21
Big Idea Productions, Inc., 49
Big Lots, Inc., 50
Big O Tires, Inc., 20
Big Rivers Electric Corporation, 11
Big V Supermarkets, Inc., 25
Big Y Foods, Inc., 53
Bill & Melinda Gates Foundation, 41
Bill Barrett Corporation, 71
Bill Blass Ltd., 32
Billing Concepts Corp., 26
Billing Concepts, Inc., 72 (upd.)
Bindley Western Industries, Inc., 9
The Bing Group, 60
Bingham Dana LLP, 43
Binks Sames Corporation, 21
Binney & Smith Inc., 25
Bio-Rad Laboratories, Inc., 93
Biogen Idec Inc., 71 (upd.)
Biogen Inc., 14; 36 (upd.)
Biolase Technology, Inc., 87
Biomet, Inc., 10; 93 (upd.
BioScrip Inc., 98
Biosite Incorporated, 73

Bird Corporation, 19
Birds Eye Foods, Inc., 69 (upd.)
Birkenstock Footprint Sandals, Inc., 12; 42 (upd.)
Birmingham Steel Corporation, 13; 40 (upd.)
BISSELL Inc., 9; 30 (upd.)
The BISYS Group, Inc., 73
BJ Services Company, 25
BJ's Wholesale Club, Inc., 94
BKD LLP, 96
The Black & Decker Corporation, III; 20 (upd.); 67 (upd.)
Black & Veatch LLP, 22
Black Box Corporation, 20; 96 (upd.)
Black Diamond Equipment, Ltd., 62
Black Hills Corporation, 20
Blackbaud, Inc., 85
Blackboard Inc., 89
Blackfoot Telecommunications Group, 60
BlackRock, Inc. 79
Blackwater USA, 76
Blair Corporation, 25; 31
Blessings Corp., 19
Blimpie International, Inc., 15; 49 (upd.)
Blish-Mize Co., 95
Blizzard Entertainment 78
Block Communications, Inc., 81
Block Drug Company, Inc., 8; 27 (upd.)
Blockbuster Inc., 9; 31 (upd.); 76 (upd.)
Blodgett Holdings, Inc., 61 (upd.)
Blonder Tongue Laboratories, Inc., 48
Bloomberg L.P., 21
Bloomingdale's Inc., 12
Blount International, Inc., 12; 48 (upd.)
Blue Bell Creameries L.P., 30
Blue Bird Corporation, 35
Blue Coat Systems, Inc., 83
Blue Cross and Blue Shield Association, 10
Blue Diamond Growers, 28
Blue Heron Paper Company, 90
Blue Martini Software, Inc., 59
Blue Mountain Arts, Inc., 29
Blue Nile Inc., 61
Blue Rhino Corporation, 56
Blue Ridge Beverage Company Inc., 82
Bluefly, Inc., 60
Bluegreen Corporation, 80
BlueLinx Holdings Inc., 97
Blyth, Inc., 18; 74 (upd.)
BMC Industries, Inc., 17; 59 (upd.)
BMC Software, Inc., 55
Boardwalk Pipeline Partners, LP, 87
Boart Longyear Company, 26
Boatmen's Bancshares Inc., 15
Bob Evans Farms, Inc., 9; 63 (upd.)
Bob's Red Mill Natural Foods, Inc., 63
Bobit Publishing Company, 55
Bobs Candies, Inc., 70
Boca Resorts, Inc., 37
Boddie-Noell Enterprises, Inc., 68
Body Glove International LLC, 88
The Boeing Company, I; 10 (upd.); 32 (upd.)
Bogen Communications International, Inc., 62
Bohemia, Inc., 13

Boise Cascade Holdings, L.L.C., IV; 8 (upd.); 32 (upd.); 95 (upd.)
Bojangles Restaurants Inc., 97
Bollinger Shipyards, Inc., 61
Bolt Technology Corporation, 99
The Bombay Company, Inc., 10; 71 (upd.)
The Bon Marché, Inc., 23
Bon Secours Health System, Inc., 24
The Bon-Ton Stores, Inc., 16; 50 (upd.)
Bonneville International Corporation, 29
Bonneville Power Administration, 50
Book-of-the-Month Club, Inc., 13
Books-A-Million, Inc., 14; 41 (upd.); 96 (upd.)
Bookspan, 86
Boole & Babbage, Inc., 25
Booth Creek Ski Holdings, Inc., 31
Boots & Coots International Well Control, Inc. 79
Booz Allen & Hamilton Inc., 10
Borden, Inc., II; 22 (upd.)
Borders Group, Inc., 15; 43 (upd.)
Borg-Warner Corporation, III
BorgWarner Inc., 14; 32 (upd.); 85 (upd.)
Borland International, Inc., 9
Boron, LePore & Associates, Inc., 45
Boscov's Department Store, Inc., 31
Bose Corporation, 13; 36 (upd.)
Boss Holdings, Inc., 97
Boston Acoustics, Inc., 22
The Boston Beer Company, Inc., 18; 50 (upd.)
Boston Celtics Limited Partnership, 14
The Boston Consulting Group, 58
Boston Edison Company, 12
Boston Market Corporation, 12; 48 (upd.)
Boston Professional Hockey Association Inc., 39
Boston Properties, Inc., 22
Boston Scientific Corporation, 37; 77 (upd.)
The Boston Symphony Orchestra Inc., 93
Bou-Matic, 62
Bowlin Travel Centers, Inc., 99
Bowne & Co., Inc., 23; 79 (upd.)
The Boy Scouts of America, 34
Boyd Bros. Transportation Inc., 39
Boyd Coffee Company, 53
Boyd Gaming Corporation, 43
The Boyds Collection, Ltd., 29
Boyne USA Resorts, 71
Boys & Girls Clubs of America, 69
Bozell Worldwide Inc., 25
Bozzuto's, Inc., 13
Brach and Brock Confections, Inc., 15
Brach's Confections, Inc., 74 (upd.)
Bradlees Discount Department Store Company, 12
Brady Corporation 78 (upd.)
The Branch Group, Inc., 72
BrandPartners Group, Inc., 58
Brannock Device Company, 48
Brasfield & Gorrie LLC, 87
Brass Eagle Inc., 34
Brazos Sportswear, Inc., 23
Breeze-Eastern Corporation, 95

Bremer Financial Corp., 45
Briazz, Inc., 53
The Brickman Group, Ltd., 87
Bridgeport Machines, Inc., 17
Bridgford Foods Corporation, 27
Briggs & Stratton Corporation, 8; 27 (upd.)
Brigham Exploration Company, 75
Brigham's, Inc., 72
Bright Horizons Family Solutions, Inc., 31
Brightpoint, Inc., 18
Brillstein-Grey Entertainment, 80
The Brink's Company, 58 (upd.)
Brinker International, Inc., 10; 38 (upd.); 75 (upd.)
Bristol Hotel Company, 23
Bristol-Myers Squibb Company, III; 9 (upd.); 37 (upd.)
Brite Voice Systems, Inc., 20
Broadcast Music Inc., 23; 90 (upd.)
Broadcom Corporation, 34; 90 (upd.)
The Broadmoor Hotel, 30
Broadwing Corporation, 70
Brobeck, Phleger & Harrison, LLP, 31
Brodart Company, 84
Broder Bros. Co., 38
Broderbund Software, Inc., 13; 29 (upd.)
Bronco Drilling Company, Inc., 89
Bronner Brothers Inc., 92
Bronner Display & Sign Advertising, Inc., 82
Brookdale Senior Living, 91
Brooke Group Ltd., 15
Brooklyn Union Gas, 6
Brooks Brothers Inc., 22
Brooks Sports Inc., 32
Brookshire Grocery Company, 16; 74 (upd.)
Brookstone, Inc., 18
Brother's Brother Foundation, 93
Brothers Gourmet Coffees, Inc., 20
Broughton Foods Co., 17
Brown & Brown, Inc., 41
Brown & Haley, 23
Brown & Root, Inc., 13
Brown & Sharpe Manufacturing Co., 23
Brown & Williamson Tobacco Corporation, 14; 33 (upd.)
Brown Brothers Harriman & Co., 45
Brown Jordan International Inc., 74 (upd.)
Brown Printing Company, 26
Brown Shoe Company, Inc., V; 20 (upd.); 68 (upd.)
Brown-Forman Corporation, I; 10 (upd.); 38 (upd.)
Browning-Ferris Industries, Inc., V; 20 (upd.)
Broyhill Furniture Industries, Inc., 10
Bruce Foods Corporation, 39
Bruegger's Corporation, 63
Bruno's Supermarkets, Inc., 7; 26 (upd.); 68 (upd.)
Brunschwig & Fils Inc., 96
Brunswick Corporation, III; 22 (upd.); 77 (upd.)
Brush Engineered Materials Inc., 67
Brush Wellman Inc., 14

Bruster's Real Ice Cream, Inc., 80
BTG, Inc., 45
Buca, Inc., 38
Buck Consultants, Inc., 55
Buck Knives Inc., 48
Buckeye Partners, L.P., 70
Buckeye Technologies, Inc., 42
The Buckle, Inc., 18
Bucyrus International, Inc., 17
The Budd Company, 8
Budget Group, Inc., 25
Budget Rent a Car Corporation, 9
Buffalo Wild Wings, Inc., 56
Buffets Holdings, Inc., 10; 32 (upd.); 93 (upd.)
Bugle Boy Industries, Inc., 18
Build-A-Bear Workshop Inc., 62
Building Materials Holding Corporation, 52
Bulley & Andrews, LLC, 55
Bulova Corporation, 13; 41 (upd.)
Bumble Bee Seafoods L.L.C., 64
Bundy Corporation, 17
Bunge Ltd., 62
Burdines, Inc., 60
The Bureau of National Affairs, Inc., 23
Burger King Corporation, II; 17 (upd.); 56 (upd.)
Burgett, Inc., 97
Burke, Inc., 88
Burke Mills, Inc., 66
Burlington Coat Factory Warehouse Corporation, 10; 60 (upd.)
Burlington Industries, Inc., V; 17 (upd.)
Burlington Northern Santa Fe Corporation, V; 27 (upd.)
Burlington Resources Inc., 10
Burns International Services Corporation, 13; 41 (upd.)
Burr-Brown Corporation, 19
Burroughs & Chapin Company, Inc., 86
Burt's Bees, Inc., 58
The Burton Corporation, 22; 94 (upd.)
Busch Entertainment Corporation, 73
Bush Boake Allen Inc., 30
Bush Brothers & Company, 45
Bush Industries, Inc., 20
Business Men's Assurance Company of America, 14
Butler Manufacturing Company, 12; 62 (upd.)
Butterick Co., Inc., 23
Buttrey Food & Drug Stores Co., 18
buy.com, Inc., 46
BWAY Corporation, 24
C&K Market, Inc., 81
C & S Wholesale Grocers, Inc., 55
C-COR.net Corp., 38
C-Cube Microsystems, Inc., 37
C.F. Martin & Co., Inc., 42
The C.F. Sauer Company, 90
C.H. Guenther & Son, Inc., 84
C.H. Heist Corporation, 24
C.H. Robinson Worldwide, Inc., 11; 40 (upd.)
C.R. Bard, Inc., 9; 65 (upd.)
C.R. Meyer and Sons Company, 74
C-Tech Industries Inc., 90

Cabela's Inc., 26; 68 (upd.)
Cabletron Systems, Inc., 10
Cablevision Electronic Instruments, Inc., 32
Cablevision Systems Corporation, 7; 30 (upd.)
Cabot Corporation, 8; 29 (upd.); 91 (upd.)
Cache Incorporated, 30
CACI International Inc., 21; 72 (upd.)
Cactus Feeders, Inc., 91
Cadence Design Systems, Inc., 11; 48 (upd.)
Cadmus Communications Corporation, 23
Cadwalader, Wickersham & Taft, 32
CAE USA Inc., 48
Caere Corporation, 20
Caesars World, Inc., 6
Cagle's, Inc., 20
Cahners Business Information, 43
Cal-Maine Foods, Inc., 69
CalAmp Corp., 87
Calavo Growers, Inc., 47
CalComp Inc., 13
Calcot Ltd., 33
Caldor Inc., 12
Calgon Carbon Corporation, 73
California Cedar Products Company, 58
California Pizza Kitchen Inc., 15; 74 (upd.)
California Sports, Inc., 56
California Steel Industries, Inc., 67
California Water Service Group 79
Caliper Life Sciences, Inc., 70
Callanan Industries, Inc., 60
Callard and Bowser-Suchard Inc., 84
Callaway Golf Company, 15; 45 (upd.)
Callon Petroleum Company, 47
Calloway's Nursery, Inc., 51
CalMat Co., 19
Calpine Corporation, 36
Caltex Petroleum Corporation, 19
Calvin Klein, Inc., 22; 55 (upd.)
Cambrex Corporation, 16; 44 (upd.)
Cambridge SoundWorks, Inc., 48
Cambridge Technology Partners, Inc., 36
Camden Property Trust, 77
Camelot Music, Inc., 26
Cameron & Barkley Company, 28
Campagna-Turano Bakery, Inc., 99
Campbell-Ewald Advertising, 86
Campbell-Mithun-Esty, Inc., 16
Campbell Scientific, Inc., 51
Campbell Soup Company, II; 7 (upd.); 26 (upd.); 71 (upd.)
Campo Electronics, Appliances & Computers, Inc., 16
Canandaigua Brands, Inc., 13; 34 (upd.)
Cancer Treatment Centers of America, Inc., 85
Candela Corporation, 48
Candie's, Inc., 31
Candle Corporation, 64
Candlewood Hotel Company, Inc., 41
Cannon Design, 63
Cannon Express, Inc., 53
Cannondale Corporation, 21

Cano Petroleum Inc., 97
Cantel Medical Corporation, 80
Canterbury Park Holding Corporation, 42
Cantor Fitzgerald, L.P., 92
Cap Rock Energy Corporation, 46
Cape Cod Potato Chip Company, 90
Capel Incorporated, 45
Capezio/Ballet Makers Inc., 62
Capital Cities/ABC Inc., II
Capital Holding Corporation, III
Capital One Financial Corporation, 52
Capitol Records, Inc., 90
Capital Senior Living Corporation, 75
CapStar Hotel Company, 21
Capstone Turbine Corporation, 75
Captain D's, LLC, 59
Captaris, Inc., 89
Car Toys, Inc., 67
Caraustar Industries, Inc., 19; 44 (upd.)
The Carbide/Graphite Group, Inc., 40
Carborundum Company, 15
Cardinal Health, Inc., 18; 50 (upd.)
Cardone Industries Inc., 92
Cardtronics, Inc., 93
Career Education Corporation, 45
CareerBuilder, Inc., 93
Caremark Rx, Inc., 10; 54 (upd.)
Carey International, Inc., 26
Cargill, Incorporated, II; 13 (upd.); 40
   (upd.); 89 (upd.)
Carhartt, Inc., 30; 77 (upd.)
Caribiner International, Inc., 24
Caribou Coffee Company, Inc., 28; 97
   (upd.)
Carlisle Companies Inc., 8; 82 (upd.)
Carlson Companies, Inc., 6; 22 (upd.); 87
   (upd.)
Carlson Restaurants Worldwide, 69
Carlson Wagonlit Travel, 55
Carma Laboratories, Inc., 60
CarMax, Inc., 55
Carmichael Lynch Inc., 28
Carmike Cinemas, Inc., 14; 37 (upd.); 74
   (upd.)
Carnation Company, II
Carnegie Corporation of New York, 35
Carnival Corporation, 6; 27 (upd.); 78
   (upd.)
Carolina First Corporation, 31
Carolina Freight Corporation, 6
Carolina Power & Light Company, V; 23
   (upd.)
Carolina Telephone and Telegraph
   Company, 10
Carpenter Technology Corporation, 13;
   95 (upd.)
CARQUEST Corporation, 29
Carr-Gottstein Foods Co., 17
CarrAmerica Realty Corporation, 56
The Carriage House Companies, Inc., 55
Carriage Services, Inc., 37
Carrier Access Corporation, 44
Carrier Corporation, 7; 69 (upd.)
Carrizo Oil & Gas, Inc., 97
Carroll's Foods, Inc., 46
Carrols Restaurant Group, Inc., 92
The Carsey-Werner Company, L.L.C., 37
Carson Pirie Scott & Company, 15

Carson, Inc., 31
Carter Hawley Hale Stores, Inc., V
Carter Lumber Company, 45
Carter-Wallace, Inc., 8; 38 (upd.)
Carus Publishing Company, 93
Carvel Corporation, 35
Carver Bancorp, Inc., 94
Carver Boat Corporation LLC, 88
Carvin Corp., 89
Cascade Corporation, 65
Cascade General, Inc., 65
Cascade Natural Gas Corporation, 9
Casco Northern Bank, 14
Casey's General Stores, Inc., 19; 83 (upd.)
Cash America International, Inc., 20; 61
   (upd.)
Cash Systems, Inc., 93
Castle & Cooke, Inc., II; 20 (upd.)
Casual Corner Group, Inc., 43
Casual Male Retail Group, Inc., 52
Caswell-Massey Co. Ltd., 51
Catalina Lighting, Inc., 43 (upd.)
Catalina Marketing Corporation, 18
Catalytica Energy Systems, Inc., 44
Catellus Development Corporation, 24
Caterpillar Inc., III; 15 (upd.); 63 (upd.)
Catherines Stores Corporation, 15
Catholic Charities USA, 76
Catholic Health Initiatives, 91
Catholic Order of Foresters, 24; 97 (upd.)
Cato Corporation, 14
Cattleman's, Inc., 20
Cavco Industries, Inc., 65
CB Commercial Real Estate Services
   Group, Inc., 21
CB Richard Ellis Group, Inc., 70 (upd.)
CBI Industries, Inc., 7
CBRL Group, Inc., 35 (upd.); 86 (upd.)
CBS Corporation, II; 6 (upd.); 28 (upd.)
CBS Television Network, 66 (upd.)
CCA Industries, Inc., 53
CCC Information Services Group Inc., 74
CCH Inc., 14
CDI Corporation, 6; 54 (upd.)
CDW Computer Centers, Inc., 16; 52
   (upd.)
CEC Entertainment, Inc., 31 (upd.)
Cedar Fair Entertainment Company, 22;
   98 (upd.)
Celadon Group Inc., 30
Celanese Corporation, I
Celebrate Express, Inc., 70
Celebrity, Inc., 22
Celera Genomics, 74
Celestial Seasonings, Inc., 16
Celgene Corporation, 67
CellStar Corporation, 83
Cendant Corporation, 44 (upd.)
Centel Corporation, 6
Centennial Communications Corporation,
   39
Centerior Energy Corporation, V
Centerplate, Inc. 79
Centex Corporation, 8; 29 (upd.)
Centocor Inc., 14
Central and South West Corporation, V
Central European Distribution
   Corporation, 75

Central Florida Investments, Inc., 93
Central Garden & Pet Company, 23; 58
   (upd.)
Central Hudson Gas and Electricity
   Corporation, 6
Central Maine Power, 6
Central National-Gottesman Inc., 95
Central Newspapers, Inc., 10
Central Parking Corporation, 18
Central Soya Company, Inc., 7
Central Sprinkler Corporation, 29
Central Vermont Public Service
   Corporation, 54
Centuri Corporation, 54
Century Aluminum Company, 52
Century Business Services, Inc., 52
Century Casinos, Inc., 53
Century Communications Corp., 10
Century Telephone Enterprises, Inc., 9; 54
   (upd.)
Century Theatres, Inc., 31
Cenveo Inc., 71 (upd.)
Cephalon, Inc., 45
Cepheid, 77
Ceradyne, Inc., 65
Cerner Corporation, 16; 94 (upd.)
CertainTeed Corporation, 35
Certegy, Inc., 63
Cessna Aircraft Company, 8; 27 (upd.)
CF Industries Holdings, Inc., 99
Chadbourne & Parke, 36
Chadwick's of Boston, Ltd., 29
The Chalone Wine Group, Ltd., 36
Champion Enterprises, Inc., 17
Champion Industries, Inc., 28
Champion International Corporation, IV;
   20 (upd.)
Championship Auto Racing Teams, Inc.,
   37
Chancellor Beacon Academies, Inc., 53
Chancellor Media Corporation, 24
Chaparral Steel Co., 13
Charisma Brands LLC, 74
The Charles Machine Works, Inc., 64
Charles River Laboratories International,
   Inc., 42
The Charles Schwab Corporation, 8; 26
   (upd.); 81 (upd.)
The Charles Stark Draper Laboratory,
   Inc., 35
Charlotte Russe Holding, Inc., 35; 90
   (upd.)
The Charmer Sunbelt Group, 95
Charming Shoppes, Inc., 8; 38
Chart House Enterprises, Inc., 17
Chart Industries, Inc., 21; 96 (upd.)
Charter Communications, Inc., 33
ChartHouse International Learning
   Corporation, 49
Chas. Levy Company LLC, 60
Chase General Corporation, 91
The Chase Manhattan Corporation, II; 13
   (upd.)
Chateau Communities, Inc., 37
Chattanooga Bakery, Inc., 86
Chattem, Inc., 17; 88 (upd.)
Chautauqua Airlines, Inc., 38
Checker Motors Corp., 89

Checkers Drive-In Restaurants, Inc., 16; 74 (upd.)

CheckFree Corporation, 81

Checkpoint Systems, Inc., 39

The Cheesecake Factory Inc., 17

Chef Solutions, Inc., 89

Chelsea Milling Company, 29

Chelsea Piers Management Inc., 86

Chemcentral Corporation, 8

Chemed Corporation, 13

Chemfab Corporation, 35

Chemi-Trol Chemical Co., 16

Chemical Banking Corporation, II; 14 (upd.)

Chemical Waste Management, Inc., 9

Chemtura Corporation, 91 (upd.)

CHEP Pty. Ltd., 80

Cherokee Inc., 18

Cherry Lane Music Publishing Company, Inc., 62

Chesapeake Corporation, 8; 30 (upd.); 93 (upd.)

Chesapeake Utilities Corporation, 56

Chesebrough-Pond's USA, Inc., 8

ChevronTexaco Corporation, IV; 19 (upd.); 47 (upd.)

Cheyenne Software, Inc., 12

CHF Industries, Inc., 84

Chi-Chi's Inc., 13; 51 (upd.)

Chiasso Inc., 53

Chiat/Day Inc. Advertising, 11

Chic by H.I.S, Inc., 20

Chicago and North Western Holdings Corporation, 6

Chicago Bears Football Club, Inc., 33

Chicago Board of Trade, 41

Chicago Mercantile Exchange Holdings Inc., 75

Chicago National League Ball Club, Inc., 66

Chicago Review Press Inc., 84

Chick-fil-A Inc., 23; 90 (upd.)

Chicken of the Sea International, 24 (upd.)

Chico's FAS, Inc., 45

Children's Comprehensive Services, Inc., 42

Children's Hospitals and Clinics, Inc., 54

The Children's Place Retail Stores, Inc., 37; 86 (upd.)

ChildrenFirst, Inc., 59

Childtime Learning Centers, Inc., 34

Chiles Offshore Corporation, 9

Chipotle Mexican Grill, Inc., 67

CHIPS and Technologies, Inc., 9

Chiquita Brands International, Inc., 7; 21 (upd.); 83 (upd.)

Chiron Corporation, 10; 36 (upd.)

Chisholm-Mingo Group, Inc., 41

Chittenden & Eastman Company, 58

Chock Full o' Nuts Corp., 17

Choice Hotels International Inc., 14; 83 (upd.)

ChoicePoint Inc., 65

Chorus Line Corporation, 30

Chris-Craft Corporation, 9; 31 (upd.); 80 (upd.)

Christensen Boyles Corporation, 26

The Christian Broadcasting Network, Inc., 52

The Christian Science Publishing Society, 55

Christopher & Banks Corporation, 42

Chromcraft Revington, Inc., 15

The Chronicle Publishing Company, Inc., 23

Chronimed Inc., 26

Chrysler Corporation, I; 11 (upd.)

CHS Inc., 60

CH2M HILL Companies Ltd., 22; 96 (upd.)

The Chubb Corporation, III; 14 (upd.); 37 (upd.)

Chugach Alaska Corporation, 60

Church & Dwight Co., Inc., 29; 68 (upd.)

Church's Chicken, 66

Churchill Downs Incorporated, 29

Cianbro Corporation, 14

Ciber, Inc., 18

CiCi Enterprises, L.P., 99

CIENA Corporation, 54

CIGNA Corporation, III; 22 (upd.); 45 (upd.)

Cimarex Energy Co., 81

Cincinnati Bell, Inc., 6

Cincinnati Financial Corporation, 16; 44 (upd.)

Cincinnati Gas & Electric Company, 6

Cincinnati Lamb Inc., 72

Cincinnati Milacron Inc., 12

Cincom Systems Inc., 15

Cinemark Holdings, Inc., 95

Cinnabon, Inc., 23; 90 (upd.)

Cintas Corporation, 21; 51 (upd.)

CIPSCO Inc., 6

The Circle K Company, II; 20 (upd.)

Circon Corporation, 21

Circuit City Stores, Inc., 9; 29 (upd.); 65 (upd.)

Circus Circus Enterprises, Inc., 6

Cirrus Design Corporation, 44

Cirrus Logic, Inc., 11; 48 (upd.)

Cisco-Linksys LLC, 86

Cisco Systems, Inc., 11; 34 (upd.); 77 (upd.)

CIT Group Inc., 76

Citadel Communications Corporation, 35

Citfed Bancorp, Inc., 16

CITGO Petroleum Corporation, IV; 31 (upd.)

Citi Trends, Inc., 80

Citicorp Diners Club, Inc., 90

Citigroup Inc., II; 9 (upd.); 30 (upd.); 59 (upd.)

Citizens Communications Company 7; 79 (upd.)

Citizens Financial Group, Inc., 42; 87 (upd.)

Citrix Systems, Inc., 44

City Brewing Company LLC, 73

City Public Service, 6

CKE Restaurants, Inc., 19; 46 (upd.)

Claire's Stores, Inc., 17; 94 (upd.)

CLARCOR Inc., 17; 61 (upd.)

Clare Rose Inc., 68

The Clark Construction Group, Inc., 8

Clark Equipment Company, 8

Classic Vacation Group, Inc., 46

Clayton Homes Incorporated, 13; 54 (upd.)

Clayton Williams Energy, Inc., 87

Clean Harbors, Inc., 73

Clear Channel Communications, Inc., 23

Clearwire, Inc., 69

Cleary, Gottlieb, Steen & Hamilton, 35

Cleco Corporation, 37

The Clemens Family Corporation, 93

Clement Pappas & Company, Inc., 92

Cleveland Indians Baseball Company, Inc., 37

Cleveland-Cliffs Inc., 13; 62 (upd.)

Click Wine Group, 68

Clif Bar Inc., 50

The Clorox Company, III; 22 (upd.); 81 (upd.)

The Clothestime, Inc., 20

Clougherty Packing Company, 72

ClubCorp, Inc., 33

CMG Worldwide, Inc., 89

CMGI, Inc., 76

CML Group, Inc., 10

CMP Media Inc., 26

CMS Energy Corporation, V, 14

CNA Financial Corporation, III; 38 (upd.)

CNET Networks, Inc., 47

CNH Global N.V., 99 (upd.)

CNS, Inc., 20

Coach, Inc., 10; 45 (upd.); 99 (upd.)

Coach USA, Inc., 24; 55 (upd.)

Coachmen Industries, Inc., 77

The Coastal Corporation, IV, 31 (upd.)

COBE Cardiovascular, Inc., 61

COBE Laboratories, Inc., 13

Coborn's, Inc., 30

Cobra Electronics Corporation, 14

Cobra Golf Inc., 16

Coca Cola Bottling Co. Consolidated, 10

The Coca-Cola Company, I; 10 (upd.); 32 (upd.); 67 (upd.)

Coca-Cola Enterprises, Inc., 13

Coeur d'Alene Mines Corporation, 20

The Coffee Beanery, Ltd., 95

Coffee Holding Co., Inc., 95

Cogent Communications Group, Inc., 55

Cogentrix Energy, Inc., 10

Cognex Corporation, 76

Cognizant Technology Solutions Corporation, 59

Coherent, Inc., 31

Cohu, Inc., 32

Coinmach Laundry Corporation, 20

Coinstar, Inc., 44

Cold Spring Granite Company, 16

Cold Spring Granite Company Inc., 67 (upd.)

Cold Stone Creamery, 69

Coldwater Creek Inc., 21; 74 (upd.)

Cole National Corporation, 13; 76 (upd.)

Cole's Quality Foods, Inc., 68

The Coleman Company, Inc., 9; 30 (upd.)

Coleman Natural Products, Inc., 68

Coles Express Inc., 15
Colfax Corporation, 58
Colgate-Palmolive Company, III; 14 (upd.); 35 (upd.); 71 (upd.)
Collectors Universe, Inc., 48
Colliers International Property Consultants Inc., 92
Collins & Aikman Corporation, 13; 41 (upd.)
Collins Industries, Inc., 33
Colonial Properties Trust, 65
Colonial Williamsburg Foundation, 53
Color Kinetics Incorporated, 85
Colorado Baseball Management, Inc., 72
Colorado MEDtech, Inc., 48
Colt Industries Inc., I
Colt's Manufacturing Company, Inc., 12
Columbia Forest Products Inc., 78
The Columbia Gas System, Inc., V; 16 (upd.)
Columbia House Company, 69
Columbia Sportswear Company, 19; 41 (upd.)
Columbia TriStar Motion Pictures Companies, II; 12 (upd.)
Columbia/HCA Healthcare Corporation, 15
Columbus McKinnon Corporation, 37
Comair Holdings Inc., 13; 34 (upd.)
Combe Inc., 72
Comcast Corporation, 7; 24 (upd.)
Comdial Corporation, 21
Comdisco, Inc., 9
Comerica Incorporated, 40
COMFORCE Corporation, 40
Command Security Corporation, 57
Commerce Clearing House, Inc., 7
Commercial Credit Company, 8
Commercial Federal Corporation, 12; 62 (upd.)
Commercial Financial Services, Inc., 26
Commercial Metals Company, 15; 42 (upd.)
Commercial Vehicle Group, Inc., 81
Commodore International Ltd., 7
Commonwealth Edison Company, V
Commonwealth Energy System, 14
Commonwealth Telephone Enterprises, Inc., 25
CommScope, Inc., 77
Community Coffee Co. L.L.C., 53
Community Health Systems, Inc., 71
Community Newspaper Holdings, Inc., 91
Community Psychiatric Centers, 15
Compaq Computer Corporation, III; 6 (upd.); 26 (upd.)
Compass Bancshares, Inc., 73
Compass Minerals International, Inc. 79
CompDent Corporation, 22
CompHealth Inc., 25
Complete Business Solutions, Inc., 31
Comprehensive Care Corporation, 15
CompuAdd Computer Corporation, 11
CompuCom Systems, Inc., 10
CompuDyne Corporation, 51
CompUSA, Inc., 10; 35 (upd.)

CompuServe Interactive Services, Inc., 10; 27 (upd.)
Computer Associates International, Inc., 6; 49 (upd.)
Computer Data Systems, Inc., 14
Computer Learning Centers, Inc., 26
Computer Sciences Corporation, 6
Computerland Corp., 13
Computervision Corporation, 10
Compuware Corporation, 10; 30 (upd.); 66 (upd.)
Comsat Corporation, 23
Comshare Inc., 23
Comstock Resources, Inc., 47
Comtech Telecommunications Corp., 75
Comverse Technology, Inc., 15; 43 (upd.)
ConAgra Foods, Inc., II; 12 (upd.); 42 (upd.); 85 (upd.)
Conair Corporation, 17; 69 (upd.)
Concentra Inc., 71
Concepts Direct, Inc., 39
Concord Camera Corporation, 41
Concord EFS, Inc., 52
Concord Fabrics, Inc., 16
Concurrent Computer Corporation, 75
Condé Nast Publications, Inc., 13; 59 (upd.)
Cone Mills LLC, 8; 67 (upd.)
Conexant Systems, Inc., 36
Confluence Holdings Corporation, 76
Congoleum Corporation, 18; 98 (upd.)
CONMED Corporation, 87
Conn's, Inc., 67
Conn-Selmer, Inc., 55
Connecticut Light and Power Co., 13
Connecticut Mutual Life Insurance Company, III
The Connell Company, 29
Conner Peripherals, Inc., 6
Connetics Corporation, 70
ConocoPhillips, IV; 16 (upd.); 63 (upd.)
Conrad Industries, Inc., 58
Conseco, Inc., 10; 33 (upd.)
Conso International Corporation, 29
CONSOL Energy Inc., 59
Consolidated Delivery & Logistics, Inc., 24
Consolidated Edison, Inc., V; 45 (upd.)
Consolidated Freightways Corporation, V; 21 (upd.); 48 (upd.)
Consolidated Graphics, Inc., 70
Consolidated Natural Gas Company, V; 19 (upd.)
Consolidated Papers, Inc., 8; 36 (upd.)
Consolidated Products Inc., 14
Consolidated Rail Corporation, V
Constar International Inc., 64
Constellation Brands, Inc., 68 (upd.)
Consumers Power Co., 14
Consumers Union, 26
Consumers Water Company, 14
The Container Store, 36
ContiGroup Companies, Inc., 43 (upd.)
Continental Airlines, Inc., I; 21 (upd.); 52 (upd.)
Continental Bank Corporation, II
Continental Cablevision, Inc., 7
Continental Can Co., Inc., 15

The Continental Corporation, III
Continental General Tire Corp., 23
Continental Grain Company, 10; 13 (upd.)
Continental Group Company, I
Continental Medical Systems, Inc., 10
Continental Resources, Inc., 89
Continuum Health Partners, Inc., 60
Control Data Corporation, III
Control Data Systems, Inc., 10
Converse Inc., 9; 31 (upd.)
Cooker Restaurant Corporation, 20; 51 (upd.)
CoolSavings, Inc., 77
Cooper Cameron Corporation, 20 (upd.); 58 (upd.)
The Cooper Companies, Inc., 39
Cooper Industries, Inc., II; 44 (upd.)
Cooper Tire & Rubber Company, 8; 23 (upd.)
Coopers & Lybrand, 9
Copart Inc., 23
The Copley Press, Inc., 23
The Copps Corporation, 32
Corbis Corporation, 31
The Corcoran Group, Inc., 58
Cordis Corporation, 19; 46 (upd.)
CoreStates Financial Corp, 17
Corinthian Colleges, Inc., 39; 92 (upd.)
The Corky McMillin Companies, 98
Corning Inc., III; 44 (upd.); 90 (upd.)
The Corporate Executive Board Company, 89
Corporate Express, Inc., 22; 47 (upd.)
Corporate Software Inc., 9
Corporation for Public Broadcasting, 14; 89 (upd.)
Correctional Services Corporation, 30
Corrections Corporation of America, 23
Corrpro Companies, Inc., 20
CORT Business Services Corporation, 26
Corus Bankshares, Inc., 75
Cosi, Inc., 53
Cosmair, Inc., 8
The Cosmetic Center, Inc., 22
Cosmolab Inc., 96
Cost Plus, Inc., 27
Cost-U-Less, Inc., 51
CoStar Group, Inc., 73
Costco Wholesale Corporation, V; 43 (upd.)
Cotter & Company, V
Cotton Incorporated, 46
Coty, Inc., 36
Coudert Brothers, 30
Council on International Educational Exchange Inc., 81
Country Kitchen International, Inc., 76
Countrywide Credit Industries, Inc., 16
County Seat Stores Inc., 9
Courier Corporation, 41
Cousins Properties Incorporated, 65
Covance Inc., 30; 98 (upd.)
Covanta Energy Corporation, 64 (upd.)
Coventry Health Care, Inc., 59
Covington & Burling, 40
Cowen Group, Inc., 92
Cowles Media Company, 23

Cox Enterprises, Inc., IV; 22 (upd.); 67 (upd.)
Cox Radio, Inc., 89
CPAC, Inc., 86
CPC International Inc., II
CPI Aerostructures, Inc., 75
CPI Corp., 38
CR England, Inc., 63
CRA International, Inc., 93
Cracker Barrel Old Country Store, Inc., 10
Craftmade International, Inc., 44
Craig Hospital, 99
craigslist, inc., 89
Crain Communications, Inc., 12; 35 (upd.)
Cramer, Berkowitz & Co., 34
Crane & Co., Inc., 26
Crane Co., 8; 30 (upd.)
Cranium, Inc., 69
Crate and Barrel, 9
Cravath, Swaine & Moore, 43
Crawford & Company, 87
Cray Inc., 75 (upd.)
Cray Research, Inc., III; 16 (upd.)
Creative Artists Agency LLC, 38
Credence Systems Corporation, 90
Credit Acceptance Corporation, 18
Cree Inc., 53
Crete Carrier Corporation, 95
Crispin Porter + Bogusky, 83
Crocs, Inc., 80
Crompton Corporation, 9; 36 (upd.)
Croscill, Inc., 42
Crosman Corporation, 62
CROSSMARK 79
Crowley Maritime Corporation, 6; 28 (upd.)
Crowley, Milner & Company, 19
Crown Books Corporation, 21
Crown Central Petroleum Corporation, 7
Crown Crafts, Inc., 16
Crown Equipment Corporation, 15; 93 (upd.)
Crown Holdings, Inc., 83 (upd.)
Crown Media Holdings, Inc., 45
Crown Vantage Inc., 29
Crown, Cork & Seal Company, Inc., I; 13; 32 (upd.)
CRSS Inc., 6
Cruise America Inc., 21
CryoLife, Inc., 46
Crystal Brands, Inc., 9
CS First Boston Inc., II
CSG Systems International, Inc., 75
CSK Auto Corporation, 38
CSS Industries, Inc., 35
CSX Corporation, V; 22 (upd.); 79 (upd.)
CTB International Corporation, 43 (upd.)
CTG, Inc., 11
CTS Corporation, 39
Cubic Corporation, 19; 98 (upd.)
CUC International Inc., 16
Cuisinart Corporation, 24
Cuisine Solutions Inc., 84
Culbro Corporation, 15
CulinArt, Inc., 92
Cullen/Frost Bankers, Inc., 25

Culligan Water Technologies, Inc., 12; 38 (upd.)
Culp, Inc., 29
Culver Franchising System, Inc., 58
Cumberland Farms, Inc., 17; 84 (upd.)
Cumberland Packing Corporation, 26
Cummins Engine Company, Inc., I; 12 (upd.); 40 (upd.)
Cumulus Media Inc., 37
CUNA Mutual Group, 62
Cunard Line Ltd., 23
CUNO Incorporated, 57
Current, Inc., 37
Curtice-Burns Foods, Inc., 7; 21 (upd.)
Curtiss-Wright Corporation, 10; 35 (upd.)
Curves International, Inc., 54
Cushman & Wakefield, Inc., 86
Custom Chrome, Inc., 16; 74 (upd.)
Cutera, Inc., 84
Cutter & Buck Inc., 27
CVS Corporation, 45 (upd.)
Cybermedia, Inc., 25
Cyberonics, Inc. 79
Cybex International, Inc., 49
Cygne Designs, Inc., 25
Cygnus Business Media, Inc., 56
Cymer, Inc., 77
Cypress Semiconductor Corporation, 20; 48 (upd.)
Cyprus Amax Minerals Company, 21
Cyprus Minerals Company, 7
Cyrk Inc., 19
Cystic Fibrosis Foundation, 93
Cytec Industries Inc., 27
Cytyc Corporation, 69
Czarnikow-Rionda Company, Inc., 32
D&H Distributing Co., 95
D&K Wholesale Drug, Inc., 14
D'Agostino Supermarkets Inc., 19
D'Arcy Masius Benton & Bowles, Inc., VI; 32 (upd.)
D.F. Stauffer Biscuit Company, 82
D.G. Yuengling & Son, Inc., 38
D.R. Horton, Inc., 58
Dade Behring Holdings Inc., 71
Daffy's Inc., 26
Dain Rauscher Corporation, 35 (upd.)
Dairy Farmers of America, Inc., 94
Dairy Mart Convenience Stores, Inc., 7; 25 (upd.)
Dairyland Healthcare Solutions, 73
Daisy Outdoor Products Inc., 58
Daisytek International Corporation, 18
Daktronics, Inc., 32
Dal-Tile International Inc., 22
Dale Carnegie & Associates Inc. 28; 78 (upd.)
Dallas Cowboys Football Club, Ltd., 33
Dallas Semiconductor Corporation, 13; 31 (upd.)
Dallis Coffee, Inc., 86
Damark International, Inc., 18
Dames & Moore, Inc., 25
Dan River Inc., 35; 86 (upd.)
Dana Holding Corporation, I; 10 (upd.); 99 (upd.)
Danaher Corporation, 7; 77 (upd.)
Daniel Industries, Inc., 16

Daniel Measurement and Control, Inc., 74 (upd.)
Dannon Co., Inc., 14
Danskin, Inc., 12; 62 (upd.)
Darden Restaurants, Inc., 16; 44 (upd.)
Darigold, Inc., 9
Darling International Inc., 85
Dart Group Corporation, 16
Data Broadcasting Corporation, 31
Data General Corporation, 8
Datapoint Corporation, 11
Datascope Corporation, 39
Datek Online Holdings Corp., 32
Dauphin Deposit Corporation, 14
Dave & Buster's, Inc., 33
The Davey Tree Expert Company, 11
The David and Lucile Packard Foundation, 41
The David J. Joseph Company, 14; 76 (upd.)
David's Bridal, Inc., 33
Davis Polk & Wardwell, 36
DaVita Inc., 73
DAW Technologies, Inc., 25
Dawn Food Products, Inc., 17
Day & Zimmermann Inc., 9; 31 (upd.)
Day International, Inc., 84
Day Runner, Inc., 14; 41 (upd.)
Dayton Hudson Corporation, V; 18 (upd.)
DC Comics Inc., 25; 98 (upd.)
DC Shoes, Inc., 60
DDB Needham Worldwide, 14
DDi Corp., 97
Dean & DeLuca, Inc., 36
Dean Foods Company, 7; 21 (upd.); 73 (upd.)
Dean Witter, Discover & Co., 12
Dearborn Mid-West Conveyor Company, 56
Death Row Records, 27
Deb Shops, Inc., 16; 76 (upd.)
Debevoise & Plimpton, 39
Dechert, 43
Deckers Outdoor Corporation, 22; 98 (upd.)
Decora Industries, Inc., 31
Decorator Industries Inc., 68
DeCrane Aircraft Holdings Inc., 36
DeepTech International Inc., 21
Deere & Company, III; 21 (upd.); 42 (upd.)
Defiance, Inc., 22
DeKalb Genetics Corporation, 17
Del Laboratories, Inc., 28
Del Monte Foods Company, 7; 23 (upd.)
Del Taco, Inc., 58
Del Webb Corporation, 14
Delaware North Companies Inc., 7; 96 (upd.)
dELiA*s Inc., 29
Delicato Vineyards, Inc., 50
Dell Inc., 9; 31 (upd.); 63 (upd.)
Deloitte Touche Tohmatsu International, 9; 29 (upd.)
DeLorme Publishing Company, Inc., 53
Delphax Technologies Inc., 94

Delphi Automotive Systems Corporation, 45
Delta Air Lines, Inc., I; 6 (upd.); 39 (upd.); 92 (upd.)
Delta and Pine Land Company, 33; 59
Delta Woodside Industries, Inc., 8; 30 (upd.)
Deltec, Inc., 56
Deltic Timber Corporation, 46
Deluxe Corporation, 7; 22 (upd.); 73 (upd.)
DEMCO, Inc., 60
DeMoulas / Market Basket Inc., 23
DenAmerica Corporation, 29
Denbury Resources, Inc., 67
Dendrite International, Inc., 70
Denison International plc, 46
Dentsply International Inc., 10
Denver Nuggets, 51
DEP Corporation, 20
Department 56, Inc., 14; 34 (upd.)
Deposit Guaranty Corporation, 17
DePuy Inc., 30; 37 (upd.)
Derco Holding Ltd., 98
Deschutes Brewery, Inc., 57
Designer Holdings Ltd., 20
Destec Energy, Inc., 12
Detroit Diesel Corporation, 10; 74 (upd.)
The Detroit Edison Company, V
The Detroit Lions, Inc., 55
The Detroit Pistons Basketball Company, 41
Detroit Red Wings, 74
Detroit Tigers Baseball Club, Inc., 46
Deutsch, Inc., 42
Developers Diversified Realty Corporation, 69
DeVito/Verdi, 85
Devon Energy Corporation, 61
DeVry Inc., 29; 82 (upd.)
Dewberry 78
Dewey Ballantine LLP, 48
Dex Media, Inc., 65
The Dexter Corporation, I; 12 (upd.)
DFS Group Ltd., 66
DH Technology, Inc., 18
DHB Industries Inc., 85
DHL Worldwide Express, 6; 24 (upd.)
Di Giorgio Corp., 12
Diagnostic Products Corporation, 73
The Dial Corp., 8; 23 (upd.)
Dial-A-Mattress Operating Corporation, 46
Dialogic Corporation, 18
Diamond of California, 64 (upd.)
Diamond Shamrock, Inc., IV
DiamondCluster International, Inc., 51
Dibrell Brothers, Incorporated, 12
dick clark productions, inc., 16
Dick Corporation, 64
Dick's Sporting Goods, Inc., 59
Dickten Masch Plastics LLC, 90
Dictaphone Healthcare Solutions 78
Diebold, Incorporated, 7; 22 (upd.)
Diedrich Coffee, Inc., 40
Dierbergs Markets Inc., 63
Dietz and Watson, Inc., 92
Digex, Inc., 46

Digi International Inc., 9
Digital Equipment Corporation, III; 6 (upd.)
Digital River, Inc., 50
Digitas Inc., 81
Dillard Paper Company, 11
Dillard's Inc., V; 16 (upd.); 68 (upd.)
Dillingham Construction Corporation, I; 44 (upd.)
Dillon Companies Inc., 12
Dime Savings Bank of New York, F.S.B., 9
DIMON Inc., 27
Diodes Incorporated, 81
Dionex Corporation, 46
Dippin' Dots, Inc., 56
Direct Focus, Inc., 47
Directed Electronics, Inc., 87
DIRECTV, Inc., 38; 75 (upd.)
Discount Auto Parts, Inc., 18
Discount Drug Mart, Inc., 14
Discount Tire Company Inc., 84
Discovery Communications, Inc., 42
Discovery Partners International, Inc., 58
ditech.com, 93
The Dixie Group, Inc., 20; 80 (upd.)
Dixon Industries, Inc., 26
Dixon Ticonderoga Company, 12; 69 (upd.)
DMI Furniture, Inc., 46
Do it Best Corporation, 30
Dobson Communications Corporation, 63
Doctor's Associates Inc., 67 (upd.)
The Doctors' Company, 55
Documentum, Inc., 46
Dolan Media Company, 94
Dolby Laboratories Inc., 20
Dole Food Company, Inc., 9; 31 (upd.); 68 (upd.)
Dollar Thrifty Automotive Group, Inc., 25
Dollar Tree Stores, Inc., 23; 62 (upd.)
Dominick & Dominick LLC, 92
Dominick's Finer Foods, Inc., 56
Dominion Homes, Inc., 19
Dominion Resources, Inc., V; 54 (upd.)
Domino Sugar Corporation, 26
Domino's Pizza, Inc., 7; 21 (upd.)
Domino's, Inc., 63 (upd.)
Don Massey Cadillac, Inc., 37
Donaldson Company, Inc., 16; 49 (upd.)
Donaldson, Lufkin & Jenrette, Inc., 22
Donatos Pizzeria Corporation, 58
Donna Karan International Inc., 15; 56 (upd.)
Donnelly Corporation, 12; 35 (upd.)
Donnkenny, Inc., 17
Donruss Playoff L.P., 66
Dooney & Bourke Inc., 84
Dorian Drake International Inc., 96
Dorsey & Whitney LLP, 47
Doskocil Companies, Inc., 12
Dot Foods, Inc., 69
Dot Hill Systems Corp., 93
Double-Cola Co.-USA, 70
DoubleClick Inc., 46
Doubletree Corporation, 21
Douglas & Lomason Company, 16

Dover Corporation, III; 28 (upd.); 90 (upd.)
Dover Downs Entertainment, Inc., 43
Dover Publications Inc., 34
The Dow Chemical Company, I; 8 (upd.); 50 (upd.)
Dow Jones & Company, Inc., IV; 19 (upd.); 47 (upd.)
Dow Jones Telerate, Inc., 10
DPL Inc., 6; 96 (upd.)
DQE, Inc., 6
Dr Pepper/Seven Up, Inc., 9; 32 (upd.)
Drackett Professional Products, 12
Draftfcb, 94
Drake Beam Morin, Inc., 44
Draper and Kramer Inc., 96
Draper Fisher Jurvetson, 91
Dreams Inc., 97
DreamWorks SKG, 43
The Drees Company, Inc., 41
The Dress Barn, Inc., 24; 55 (upd.)
Dresser Industries, Inc., III
Drew Industries, Inc., 28
Drexel Burnham Lambert Incorporated, II
Drexel Heritage Furnishings Inc., 12
Dreyer's Grand Ice Cream, Inc., 17
The Dreyfus Corporation, 70
Dril-Quip, Inc., 81
Drinker, Biddle and Reath L.L.P., 92
DriveTime Automotive Group Inc., 68 (upd.)
DRS Technologies, Inc., 58
Drs. Foster & Smith, Inc., 62
Drug Emporium, Inc., 12
Drypers Corporation, 18
DSC Communications Corporation, 12
DSW Inc., 73
DTE Energy Company, 20 (upd.); 94 (upd.)
DTS, Inc., 80
Dualstar Entertainment Group LLC, 76
Duane Reade Holding Corp., 21
Duck Head Apparel Company, Inc., 42
Ducks Unlimited, Inc., 87
Duckwall-ALCO Stores, Inc., 24
Ducommun Incorporated, 30
Duke Energy Corporation, V; 27 (upd.)
Duke Realty Corporation, 57
The Dun & Bradstreet Corporation, IV; 19 (upd.); 61 (upd.)
Dun & Bradstreet Software Services Inc., 11
Dunavant Enterprises, Inc., 54
Duncan Aviation, Inc., 94
Duncan Toys Company, 55
Dunham's Athleisure Corporation, 98
Dunn-Edwards Corporation, 56
Dunn Inc., 72
Duplex Products Inc., 17
Duracell International Inc., 9; 71 (upd.)
Durametallic, 21
Duriron Company Inc., 17
Duron Inc., 72
Duty Free International, Inc., 11
DVI, Inc., 51
Dyax Corp., 89
Dycom Industries, Inc., 57
Dyersburg Corporation, 21
Dylan's Candy Bar, LLC, 99

Dynamic Materials Corporation, 81
Dynatech Corporation, 13
Dynatronics Corporation, 99
DynCorp, 45
Dynegy Inc., 49 (upd.)
E! Entertainment Television Inc., 17
E*Trade Financial Corporation, 20; 60 (upd.)
E. & J. Gallo Winery, I; 7 (upd.); 28 (upd.)
E.I. du Pont de Nemours and Company, I; 8 (upd.); 26 (upd.); 73 (upd.)
E.piphany, Inc., 49
E-Systems, Inc., 9
E.W. Howell Co., Inc., 72
The E.W. Scripps Company, IV; 7 (upd.); 28 (upd.); 66 (upd.)
E-Z Serve Corporation, 17
E-Z-EM Inc., 89
Eagle Hardware & Garden, Inc., 16
Eagle-Picher Industries, Inc., 8; 23 (upd.)
Eagle-Tribune Publishing Co., 91
Earl Scheib, Inc., 32
Earle M. Jorgensen Company, 82
The Earthgrains Company, 36
EarthLink, Inc., 36
East Penn Manufacturing Co., Inc. 79
Easter Seals, Inc., 58
Eastern Airlines, I
The Eastern Company, 48
Eastern Enterprises, 6
EastGroup Properties, Inc., 67
Eastland Shoe Corporation, 82
Eastman Chemical Company, 14; 38 (upd.)
Eastman Kodak Company, III; 7 (upd.); 36 (upd.); 91 (upd.)
Easton Sports, Inc., 66
Eateries, Inc., 33
Eaton Corporation, I; 10 (upd.); 67 (upd.)
Eaton Vance Corporation, 18
eBay Inc., 32; 67 (upd.)
EBSCO Industries, Inc., 17; 40 (upd.)
ECC International Corp., 42
Echlin Inc., I; 11 (upd.)
The Echo Design Group, Inc., 68
EchoStar Communications Corporation, 35
Eckerd Corporation, 9; 32 (upd.)
Eclipse Aviation Corporation, 87
Ecolab Inc., I; 13 (upd.); 34 (upd.); 85 (upd.)
eCollege.com, 85
Ecology and Environment, Inc., 39
Eddie Bauer, Inc., 9; 36 (upd.); 87 (upd.)
Edelbrock Corporation, 37
Edelman, 62
EDGAR Online, Inc., 91
Edge Petroleum Corporation, 67
Edison Brothers Stores, Inc., 9
Edison International, 56 (upd.)
Edison Schools Inc., 37
Edmark Corporation, 14; 41 (upd.)
EDO Corporation, 46
Educate Inc. 86 (upd.)
Education Management Corporation, 35
Educational Broadcasting Corporation, 48

Educational Testing Service, 12; 62 (upd.)
Edw. C. Levy Co., 42
Edward D. Jones & Company L.P., 30; 66 (upd.)
Edward Hines Lumber Company, 68
The Edward J. DeBartolo Corporation, 8
Edwards and Kelcey, 70
Edwards Brothers, Inc., 92
Edwards Theatres Circuit, Inc., 31
EFJ, Inc., 81
EG&G Incorporated, 8; 29 (upd.)
Egan Companies, Inc., 94
Egghead.com, Inc., 9; 31 (upd.)
EGL, Inc., 59
eHarmony.com Inc., 71
8x8, Inc., 94
84 Lumber Company, 9; 39 (upd.)
800-JR Cigar, Inc., 27
Eileen Fisher Inc., 61
Einstein/Noah Bagel Corporation, 29
Ekco Group, Inc., 16
El Camino Resources International, Inc., 11
El Chico Restaurants, Inc., 19
El Paso Corporation, 66 (upd.)
El Paso Electric Company, 21
El Paso Natural Gas Company, 12
El Pollo Loco, Inc., 69
Elamex, S.A. de C.V., 51
Elano Corporation, 14
The Elder-Beerman Stores Corp., 10; 63 (upd.)
Electric Boat Corporation, 86
Electric Lightwave, Inc., 37
Electro Rent Corporation, 58
Electromagnetic Sciences Inc., 21
Electronic Arts Inc., 10; 85 (upd.)
Electronic Data Systems Corporation, III; 28 (upd.)
Electronics Boutique Holdings Corporation, 72
Electronics for Imaging, Inc., 15; 43 (upd.)
Elektra Entertainment Group, 64
Element K Corporation, 94
Elephant Pharmacy, Inc., 83
Eli Lilly and Company, I; 11 (upd.); 47 (upd.)
Elizabeth Arden, Inc., 8; 40 (upd.)
Eljer Industries, Inc., 24
Elkay Manufacturing Company, 73
ElkCorp, 52
Ellen Tracy, Inc., 55
Ellerbe Becket, 41
Ellett Brothers, Inc., 17
Elmer Candy Corporation, 88
Elmer's Restaurants, Inc., 42
Elsinore Corporation, 48
Elvis Presley Enterprises, Inc., 61
EMBARQ Corporation, 83
Embers America Restaurants, 30
Embrex, Inc., 72
EMC Corporation, 12; 46 (upd.)
EMCOR Group Inc., 60
EMCORE Corporation, 97
Emerson, II; 46 (upd.)
Emerson Radio Corp., 30

Emery Worldwide Airlines, Inc., 6; 25 (upd.)
Emge Packing Co., Inc., 11
Emigrant Savings Bank, 59
Emmis Communications Corporation, 47
Empi, Inc., 26
Empire Blue Cross and Blue Shield, III
The Empire District Electric Company, 77
Empire Resorts, Inc., 72
Empire Resources, Inc., 81
Employee Solutions, Inc., 18
ENCAD, Incorporated, 25
Encompass Services Corporation, 33
Encore Acquisition Company, 73
Encore Computer Corporation, 13; 74 (upd.)
Encore Wire Corporation, 81
Encyclopaedia Britannica, Inc., 7; 39 (upd.)
Endo Pharmaceuticals Holdings Inc., 71
Energen Corporation, 21; 97 (upd.)
Energizer Holdings, Inc., 32
Energy Brands Inc., 88
Energy Conversion Devices, Inc., 75
Enesco Corporation, 11
EnerSys Inc., 99
Engelhard Corporation, IV; 21 (upd.); 72 (upd.)
Engineered Support Systems, Inc., 59
Engle Homes, Inc., 46
Engraph, Inc., 12
Ennis, Inc., 21; 97 (upd.)
EnPro Industries, Inc., 93
Enquirer/Star Group, Inc., 10
Enrich International, Inc., 33
Enron Corporation, V, 19; 46 (upd.)
ENSCO International Incorporated, 57
Enserch Corporation, V
Entercom Communications Corporation, 58
Entergy Corporation, V; 45 (upd.)
Enterprise Rent-A-Car Company, 6; 69 (upd.)
Entertainment Distribution Company, 89
Entravision Communications Corporation, 41
Envirodyne Industries, Inc., 17
Environmental Industries, Inc., 31
Environmental Power Corporation, 68
Environmental Systems Research Institute Inc. (ESRI), 62
Enzo Biochem, Inc., 41
Eon Labs, Inc., 67
EPAM Systems Inc., 96
Epic Systems Corporation, 62
EPIQ Systems, Inc., 56
Equifax Inc., 6; 28 (upd.); 90 (upd.)
Equistar Chemicals, LP, 71
Equitable Life Assurance Society of the United States, III
Equitable Resources, Inc., 6; 54 (upd.)
Equity Marketing, Inc., 26
Equity Office Properties Trust, 54
Equity Residential, 49
Equus Computer Systems, Inc., 49
Ergon, Inc., 95
Erickson Retirement Communities, 57

GEOGRAPHIC INDEX

Erie Indemnity Company, 35
ERLY Industries Inc., 17
Ernie Ball, Inc., 56
Ernst & Young, 9; 29 (upd.)
Escalade, Incorporated, 19
Eschelon Telecom, Inc., 72
ESCO Technologies Inc., 87
Eskimo Pie Corporation, 21
ESPN, Inc., 56
Esprit de Corp., 8; 29 (upd.)
ESS Technology, Inc., 22
Essef Corporation, 18
Esselte, 64
Esselte Pendaflex Corporation, 11
Essence Communications, Inc., 24
Essex Corporation, 85
The Estée Lauder Companies Inc., 9; 30
    (upd.); 93 (upd.)
Esterline Technologies Corp., 15
Estes Express Lines, 86
Eternal Word Television Network, Inc., 57
Ethan Allen Interiors, Inc., 12; 39 (upd.)
Ethicon, Inc., 23
Ethyl Corporation, I; 10 (upd.)
EToys, Inc., 37
The Eureka Company, 12
Euromarket Designs Inc., 31 (upd.); 99
    (upd.)
Euronet Worldwide, Inc., 83
Europe Through the Back Door Inc., 65
Evans and Sutherland Computer
    Company 19; 78 (upd.)
Evans, Inc., 30
Everex Systems, Inc., 16
Evergreen International Aviation, Inc., 53
Evergreen Energy, Inc., 97
Everlast Worldwide Inc., 47
Exabyte Corporation, 12; 40 (upd.)
Exar Corp., 14
EXCEL Communications Inc., 18
Excel Technology, Inc., 65
Executive Jet, Inc., 36
Executone Information Systems, Inc., 13
Exelon Corporation, 48 (upd.)
Exide Electronics Group, Inc., 20
Expedia, Inc., 58
Expeditors International of Washington
    Inc., 17; 78 (upd.)
Experian Information Solutions Inc., 45
Exponent, Inc., 95
Express Scripts Inc., 17; 44 (upd.)
Extended Stay America, Inc., 41
EXX Inc., 65
Exxon Corporation, IV; 7 (upd.); 32
    (upd.)
Exxon Mobil Corporation, 67 (upd.)
Eye Care Centers of America, Inc., 69
EZCORP Inc., 43
F&W Publications, Inc., 71
The F. Dohmen Co., 77
F. Korbel & Bros. Inc., 68
F.W. Webb Company, 95
Fab Industries, Inc., 27
Fabri-Centers of America Inc., 16
Facebook, Inc., 90
FactSet Research Systems Inc., 73
Faegre & Benson LLP, 97
Fair Grounds Corporation, 44

Fair, Isaac and Company, 18
Fairchild Aircraft, Inc., 9
Fairfield Communities, Inc., 36
Falcon Products, Inc., 33
Fallon McElligott Inc., 22
Fallon Worldwide, 71 (upd.)
Family Christian Stores, Inc., 51
Family Dollar Stores, Inc., 13; 62 (upd.)
Family Golf Centers, Inc., 29
Famous Dave's of America, Inc., 40
Fannie Mae, 45 (upd.)
Fannie May Confections Brands, Inc., 80
Fansteel Inc., 19
FAO Schwarz, 46
Farah Incorporated, 24
Faribault Foods, Inc., 89
Farley Northwest Industries, Inc., I
Farley's & Sathers Candy Company, Inc.,
    62
Farm Family Holdings, Inc., 39
Farm Journal Corporation, 42
Farmer Bros. Co., 52
Farmer Jack Supermarkets 78
Farmers Insurance Group of Companies,
    25
Farmland Foods, Inc., 7
Farmland Industries, Inc., 48
FARO Technologies, Inc., 87
Farouk Systems Inc. 78
Farrar, Straus and Giroux Inc., 15
Fastenal Company, 14; 42 (upd.); 99
    (upd.)
Fatburger Corporation, 64
Faultless Starch/Bon Ami Company, 55
Fay's Inc., 17
Faygo Beverages Inc., 55
Fazoli's Management, Inc., 76 (upd.)
Fazoli's Systems, Inc., 27
Featherlite Inc., 28
Fedders Corporation, 18; 43 (upd.)
Federal Agricultural Mortgage
    Corporation, 75
Federal Deposit Insurance Corporation,
    93
Federal Express Corporation, V
Federal National Mortgage Association, II
Federal Paper Board Company, Inc., 8
Federal Prison Industries, Inc., 34
Federal Signal Corp., 10
Federal-Mogul Corporation, I; 10 (upd.);
    26 (upd.)
Federated Department Stores Inc., 9; 31
    (upd.)
FedEx Corporation, 18 (upd.); 42 (upd.)
Feed The Children, Inc., 68
FEI Company 79
Feld Entertainment, Inc., 32 (upd.)
Fellowes Manufacturing Company, 28
Fender Musical Instruments Company, 16;
    43 (upd.)
Fenwick & West LLP, 34
Ferolito, Vultaggio & Sons, 27
Ferrara Fire Apparatus, Inc., 84
Ferrara Pan Candy Company, 90
Ferrellgas Partners, L.P., 35
Ferro Corporation, 8; 56 (upd.)
F5 Networks, Inc., 72
FHP International Corporation, 6

FiberMark, Inc., 37
Fibreboard Corporation, 16
Fidelity Investments Inc., II; 14 (upd.)
Fidelity National Financial Inc., 54
Fidelity Southern Corporation, 85
Fieldale Farms Corporation, 23
Fieldcrest Cannon, Inc., 9; 31 (upd.)
Fifth Third Bancorp, 13; 31 (upd.)
Figgie International Inc., 7
Fiji Water LLC, 74
FileNet Corporation, 62
Fili Enterprises, Inc., 70
Film Roman, Inc., 58
FINA, Inc., 7
Fingerhut Companies, Inc., 9; 36 (upd.)
Finisar Corporation, 92
The Finish Line, Inc., 29; 68 (upd.)
FinishMaster, Inc., 24
Finlay Enterprises, Inc., 16; 76 (upd.)
Firearms Training Systems, Inc., 27
Fired Up, Inc., 82
Fireman's Fund Insurance Company, III
First Albany Companies Inc., 37
First Alert, Inc., 28
The First American Corporation, The 52
First Aviation Services Inc., 49
First Bank System Inc., 12
First Brands Corporation, 8
First Cash Financial Services, Inc., 57
First Chicago Corporation, II
First Colony Coffee & Tea Company, 84
First Commerce Bancshares, Inc., 15
First Commerce Corporation, 11
First Data Corporation, 30 (upd.)
First Empire State Corporation, 11
First Executive Corporation, III
First Fidelity Bank, N.A., New Jersey, 9
First Financial Management Corporation,
    11
First Hawaiian, Inc., 11
First Industrial Realty Trust, Inc., 65
First Interstate Bancorp, II
The First Marblehead Corporation, 87
First Mississippi Corporation, 8
First Nationwide Bank, 14
First of America Bank Corporation, 8
First Security Corporation, 11
First Solar, Inc., 95
First Team Sports, Inc., 22
First Tennessee National Corporation, 11;
    48 (upd.)
First Union Corporation, 10
First USA, Inc., 11
First Virginia Banks, Inc., 11
The First Years Inc., 46
Firstar Corporation, 11; 33 (upd.)
Fiserv Inc., 11; 33 (upd.)
Fish & Neave, 54
Fisher Communications, Inc., 99
Fisher Companies, Inc., 15
Fisher Controls International, LLC, 13;
    61 (upd.)
Fisher Scientific International Inc., 24
Fisher-Price Inc., 12; 32 (upd.)
Fisk Corporation, 72
5 & Diner Franchise Corporation, 72
Five Guys Enterprises, LLC, 99
Flagstar Companies, Inc., 10

Flanders Corporation, 65
Flanigan's Enterprises, Inc., 60
Flatiron Construction Corporation, 92
Fleer Corporation, 15
FleetBoston Financial Corporation, 9; 36 (upd.)
Fleetwood Enterprises, Inc., III; 22 (upd.); 81 (upd.)
Fleming Companies, Inc., II; 17 (upd.)
Flexsteel Industries Inc., 15; 41 (upd.)
Flight Options, LLC, 75
FlightSafety International, Inc., 9; 29 (upd.)
Flint Ink Corporation, 13; 41 (upd.)
FLIR Systems, Inc., 69
Florida Crystals Inc., 35
Florida East Coast Industries, Inc., 59
Florida Gaming Corporation, 47
Florida Progress Corporation, V; 23 (upd.)
Florida Public Utilities Company, 69
Florida Rock Industries, Inc., 46
Florida's Natural Growers, 45
Florists' Transworld Delivery, Inc., 28
Florsheim Shoe Group Inc., 9; 31 (upd.)
Flotek Industries Inc., 93
Flour City International, Inc., 44
Flow International Corporation, 56
Flowers Industries, Inc., 12; 35 (upd.)
Flowserve Corporation, 33; 77 (upd.)
Fluke Corporation, 15
Fluor Corporation, I; 8 (upd.); 34 (upd.)
Flying Boat, Inc. (Chalk's Ocean Airways), 56
Flying J Inc., 19
FMC Corporation, I; 11 (upd.); 89 (upd.)
FMR Corp., 8; 32 (upd.)
Foamex International Inc., 17
Focus Features 78
Foley & Lardner, 28
Follett Corporation, 12; 39 (upd.)
Food Circus Super Markets, Inc., 88
The Food Emporium, 64
Food For The Poor, Inc., 77
Food Lion LLC, II; 15 (upd.); 66 (upd.)
Foodarama Supermarkets, Inc., 28
FoodBrands America, Inc., 23
Foodmaker, Inc., 14
Foot Locker, Inc., 68 (upd.)
Foot Petals L.L.C., 95
Foote, Cone & Belding Worldwide, I; 66 (upd.)
Footstar, Incorporated, 24
Forbes Inc., 30; 82 (upd.)
Force Protection Inc., 95
The Ford Foundation, 34
Ford Motor Company, I; 11 (upd.); 36 (upd.); 64 (upd.)
FORE Systems, Inc., 25
Foremost Farms USA Cooperative, 98
Forest City Enterprises, Inc., 16; 52 (upd.)
Forest Laboratories, Inc., 11; 52 (upd.)
Forest Oil Corporation, 19; 91 (upd.)
Forever Living Products International Inc., 17
Forever 21, Inc., 84
FormFactor, Inc., 85
Formica Corporation, 13

Forrester Research, Inc., 54
Forstmann Little & Co., 38
Fort Howard Corporation, 8
Fort James Corporation, 22 (upd.)
Fortune Brands, Inc., 29 (upd.); 68 (upd.)
Fortunoff Fine Jewelry and Silverware Inc., 26
Forward Air Corporation, 75
Forward Industries, Inc., 86
Fossil, Inc., 17
Foster Poultry Farms, 32
Foster Wheeler Corporation, 6; 23 (upd.)
Foster Wheeler Ltd., 76 (upd.)
FosterGrant, Inc., 60
Foundation Health Corporation, 12
Fountain Powerboats Industries, Inc., 28
Four Winns Boats LLC, 96
4Kids Entertainment Inc., 59
Fourth Financial Corporation, 11
Fox Entertainment Group, Inc., 43
Fox Family Worldwide, Inc., 24
Fox's Pizza Den, Inc., 98
Foxboro Company, 13
FoxHollow Technologies, Inc., 85
FoxMeyer Health Corporation, 16
Foxworth-Galbraith Lumber Company, 91
FPL Group, Inc., V; 49 (upd.)
Frank J. Zamboni & Co., Inc., 34
Frank Russell Company, 46
Frank's Nursery & Crafts, Inc., 12
Frankel & Co., 39
Franklin Covey Company, 11; 37 (upd.)
Franklin Electric Company, Inc., 43
Franklin Electronic Publishers, Inc., 23
The Franklin Mint, 69
Franklin Resources, Inc., 9
Franz Inc., 80
Fred Alger Management, Inc., 97
Fred Meyer Stores, Inc., V; 20 (upd.); 64 (upd.)
Fred Usinger Inc., 54
The Fred W. Albrecht Grocery Co., 13
Fred Weber, Inc., 61
Fred's, Inc., 23; 62 (upd.)
Freddie Mac, 54
Frederick Atkins Inc., 16
Frederick's of Hollywood, Inc., 16; 59 (upd.)
Freedom Communications, Inc., 36
Freeport-McMoRan Copper & Gold, Inc., IV; 7 (upd.); 57 (upd.)
Freescale Semiconductor, Inc., 83
Freeze.com LLC, 77
French Fragrances, Inc., 22
Frequency Electronics, Inc., 61
Fresh America Corporation, 20
Fresh Choice, Inc., 20
Fresh Enterprises, Inc., 66
Fresh Express Inc., 88
Fresh Foods, Inc., 29
FreshDirect, LLC, 84
Fretter, Inc., 10
Fried, Frank, Harris, Shriver & Jacobson, 35
Friedman's Inc., 29
Friedman, Billings, Ramsey Group, Inc., 53

Friendly Ice Cream Corporation, 30; 72 (upd.)
Frigidaire Home Products, 22
Frisch's Restaurants, Inc., 35; 92 (upd.)
Frito-Lay North America, 32; 73 (upd.)
Fritz Companies, Inc., 12
Frontier Airlines Holdings Inc., 22; 84 (upd.)
Frontier Corp., 16
Frontier Natural Products Co-Op, 82
Frost & Sullivan, Inc., 53
Frozen Food Express Industries, Inc., 20; 98 (upd.)
Fruehauf Corporation, I
Fruit of the Loom, Inc., 8; 25 (upd.)
Fruth Pharmacy, Inc., 66
Fry's Electronics, Inc., 68
Frymaster Corporation, 27
FSI International, Inc., 17
FTD Group, Inc., 99 (upd.)
FTI Consulting, Inc., 77
FTP Software, Inc., 20
Fubu, 29
Fuel Systems Solutions, Inc., 97
Fuel Tech, Inc., 85
FuelCell Energy, Inc., 75
Fujitsu-ICL Systems Inc., 11
Fulbright & Jaworski L.L.P., 47
Funco, 20
Fuqua Enterprises, Inc., 17
Fuqua Industries, Inc., I
Furmanite Corporation, 92
Furniture Brands International, Inc., 39 (upd.)
Furon Company, 28
Furr's Restaurant Group, Inc., 53
Furr's Supermarkets, Inc., 28
Future Now, Inc., 12
G&K Services, Inc., 16
G-III Apparel Group, Ltd., 22
G. Heileman Brewing Company Inc., I
G. Leblanc Corporation, 55
G.A.F., I
G.D. Searle & Company, I; 12 (upd.); 34 (upd.)
G.I. Joe's, Inc., 30
G.S. Blodgett Corporation, 15
Gabelli Asset Management Inc., 30
Gables Residential Trust, 49
Gadzooks, Inc., 18
GAF Corporation, 22 (upd.)
Gage Marketing Group, 26
Gaiam, Inc., 41
Gainsco, Inc., 22
Galardi Group, Inc., 72
Galaxy Investors, Inc., 97
Galaxy Nutritional Foods, Inc., 58
Gale International Llc, 93
Galey & Lord, Inc., 20; 66 (upd.)
The Gallup Organization, 37
Galyan's Trading Company, Inc., 47
The Gambrinus Company, 40
GameStop Corp., 69 (upd.)
Gaming Partners International Corporation, 93
Gander Mountain Company, 20; 90 (upd.)

GEOGRAPHIC INDEX

Gannett Company, Inc., IV; 7 (upd.); 30
(upd.); 66 (upd.)
Gantos, Inc., 17
The Gap, Inc., V; 18 (upd.); 55 (upd.)
Garan, Inc., 16; 64 (upd.)
Garden Fresh Restaurant Corporation, 31
Garden Ridge Corporation, 27
Gardenburger, Inc., 33; 76 (upd.)
Gardner Denver, Inc., 49
Gart Sports Company, 24
Gartner, Inc., 21; 94 (upd.)
Garst Seed Company, Inc., 86
GateHouse Media, Inc., 91
The Gates Corporation, 9
Gateway, Inc., 10; 27 (upd.); 63 (upd.)
The Gatorade Company, 82
GATX Corporation, 6; 25 (upd.)
Gaylord Container Corporation, 8
Gaylord Entertainment Company, 11; 36
(upd.)
GC Companies, Inc., 25
GE Aircraft Engines, 9
GE Capital Aviation Services, 36
Geerlings & Wade, Inc., 45
Geffen Records Inc., 26
Gehl Company, 19
GEICO Corporation, 10; 40 (upd.)
Geiger Bros., 60
Gemini Sound Products Corporation, 58
Gen-Probe Incorporated 79
GenCorp Inc., 8; 9
Genentech, Inc., I; 8 (upd.); 32 (upd.);
75 (upd.)
General Atomics, 57
General Bearing Corporation, 45
General Binding Corporation, 10; 73
(upd.)
General Cable Corporation, 40
The General Chemical Group Inc., 37
General Cigar Holdings, Inc., 66 (upd.)
General Cinema Corporation, I
General DataComm Industries, Inc., 14
General Dynamics Corporation, I; 10
(upd.); 40 (upd.); 88 (upd.)
General Electric Company, II; 12 (upd.);
34 (upd.); 63 (upd.)
General Employment Enterprises, Inc., 87
General Growth Properties, Inc., 57
General Host Corporation, 12
General Housewares Corporation, 16
General Instrument Corporation, 10
General Maritime Corporation, 59
General Mills, Inc., II; 10 (upd.); 36
(upd.); 85 (upd.)
General Motors Corporation, I; 10 (upd.);
36 (upd.); 64 (upd.)
General Nutrition Companies, Inc., 11;
29 (upd.)
General Public Utilities Corporation, V
General Re Corporation, III; 24 (upd.)
General Signal Corporation, 9
General Tire, Inc., 8
Genesco Inc., 17; 84 (upd.)
Genesee & Wyoming Inc., 27
Genesis Health Ventures, Inc., 18
Genesis Microchip Inc., 82
Genetics Institute, Inc., 8
Geneva Steel, 7

Genmar Holdings, Inc., 45
Genovese Drug Stores, Inc., 18
GenRad, Inc., 24
Gentex Corporation, 26
Gentiva Health Services, Inc. 79
Genuardi's Family Markets, Inc., 35
Genuine Parts Company, 9; 45 (upd.)
Genzyme Corporation, 13; 38 (upd.); 77
(upd.)
The Geon Company, 11
George A. Hormel and Company, II
The George F. Cram Company, Inc., 55
George P. Johnson Company, 60
George S. May International Company,
55
George W. Park Seed Company, Inc., 98
Georgia Gulf Corporation, 9; 61 (upd.)
Georgia-Pacific Corporation, IV; 9 (upd.);
47 (upd.)
Geotek Communications Inc., 21
Gerald Stevens, Inc., 37
Gerber Products Company, 7; 21 (upd.)
Gerber Scientific, Inc., 12; 84 (upd.)
German American Bancorp, 41
Getty Images, Inc., 31
Gevity HR, Inc., 63
GF Health Products, Inc., 82
Ghirardelli Chocolate Company, 30
Giant Cement Holding, Inc., 23
Giant Eagle, Inc., 86
Giant Food LLC, II; 22 (upd.); 83 (upd.)
Giant Industries, Inc., 19; 61 (upd.)
Gibraltar Steel Corporation, 37
Gibson Greetings, Inc., 12
Gibson Guitar Corp., 16
Gibson, Dunn & Crutcher LLP, 36
Giddings & Lewis, Inc., 10
Gilbane, Inc., 34
Gilead Sciences, Inc., 54
Gillett Holdings, Inc., 7
The Gillette Company, III; 20 (upd.); 68
(upd.)
Gilman & Ciocia, Inc., 72
Girl Scouts of the USA, 35
The Gitano Group, Inc., 8
Glacier Bancorp, Inc., 35
Glacier Water Services, Inc., 47
Glamis Gold, Ltd., 54
Glazer's Wholesale Drug Company, Inc.,
82
Gleason Corporation, 24
The Glidden Company, 8
Global Berry Farms LLC, 62
Global Crossing Ltd., 32
Global Hyatt Corporation, 75 (upd.)
Global Imaging Systems, Inc., 73
Global Industries, Ltd., 37
Global Marine Inc., 9
Global Outdoors, Inc., 49
Global Payments Inc., 91
Global Power Equipment Group Inc., 52
GlobalSantaFe Corporation, 48 (upd.)
Glu Mobile Inc., 95
Gluek Brewing Company, 75
GM Hughes Electronics Corporation, II
GMH Communities Trust, 87
GNC Corporation, 98 (upd.)
Godfather's Pizza Incorporated, 25

Godiva Chocolatier, Inc., 64
Goetze's Candy Company, Inc., 87
Gold Kist Inc., 17; 26 (upd.)
Gold'n Plump Poultry, 54
Gold's Gym International, Inc., 71
Golden Belt Manufacturing Co., 16
Golden Books Family Entertainment, Inc.,
28
Golden Corral Corporation, 10; 66 (upd.)
Golden Enterprises, Inc., 26
Golden Krust Caribbean Bakery, Inc., 68
Golden State Foods Corporation, 32
Golden State Vintners, Inc., 33
Golden West Financial Corporation, 47
The Goldman Sachs Group Inc., II; 20
(upd.); 51 (upd.)
Golin/Harris International, Inc., 88
Golub Corporation, 26; 96 (upd.)
Gonnella Baking Company, 40
The Good Guys, Inc., 10; 30 (upd.)
Good Humor-Breyers Ice Cream
Company, 14
Goodby Silverstein & Partners, Inc., 75
Goodman Holding Company, 42
GoodMark Foods, Inc., 26
Goodrich Corporation, 46 (upd.)
GoodTimes Entertainment Ltd., 48
Goodwill Industries International, Inc.,
16; 66 (upd.)
Goody Products, Inc., 12
Goody's Family Clothing, Inc., 20; 64
(upd.)
The Goodyear Tire & Rubber Company,
V; 20 (upd.); 75 (upd.)
Google, Inc., 50
Gordmans, Inc., 74
Gordon Biersch Brewery Restaurant
Group, Inc., 93
Gordon Food Service Inc., 8; 39 (upd.)
The Gorman-Rupp Company, 18; 57
(upd.)
Gorton's, 13
Goss Holdings, Inc., 43
Gottschalks, Inc., 18; 91 (upd.)
Gould Electronics, Inc., 14
Gould Paper Corporation, 82
Goulds Pumps Inc., 24
Goya Foods Inc., 22; 91 (upd.)
GP Strategies Corporation, 64 (upd.)
GPU, Inc., 27 (upd.)
Graco Inc., 19; 67 (upd.)
Gradall Industries, Inc., 96
Graeter's Manufacturing Company, 86
Graham Corporation, 62
Graham Packaging Holdings Company,
87
GranCare, Inc., 14
Grand Casinos, Inc., 20
Grand Piano & Furniture Company, 72
Grand Traverse Pie Company, 98
The Grand Union Company, 7; 28 (upd.)
Grandoe Corporation, 98
Granite Broadcasting Corporation, 42
Granite City Food & Brewery Ltd., 94
Granite Construction Incorporated, 61
Granite Industries of Vermont, Inc., 73
Granite Rock Company, 26
Granite State Bankshares, Inc., 37

Grant Prideco, Inc., 57
Grant Thornton International, 57
Graphic Industries Inc., 25
Graphic Packaging Holding Company, 96
 (upd.)
Gray Communications Systems, Inc., 24
Graybar Electric Company, Inc., 54
Great American Management and
 Investment, Inc., 8
The Great Atlantic & Pacific Tea
 Company, Inc., II; 16 (upd.); 55 (upd.)
Great Harvest Bread Company, 44
Great Lakes Bancorp, 8
Great Lakes Chemical Corporation, I; 14
 (upd.)
Great Lakes Dredge & Dock Company,
 69
Great Plains Energy Incorporated, 65
 (upd.)
Great Western Financial Corporation, 10
Great White Shark Enterprises, Inc., 89
Great Wolf Resorts, Inc., 91
Greatbatch Inc., 72
Grede Foundries, Inc., 38
The Green Bay Packers, Inc., 32
Green Dot Public Schools, 99
Green Mountain Coffee, Inc., 31
Green Tree Financial Corporation, 11
Greenberg Traurig, LLP, 65
The Greenbrier Companies, 19
GreenMan Technologies Inc., 99
Greene, Tweed & Company, 55
GreenPoint Financial Corp., 28
Greenwood Mills, Inc., 14
Greg Manning Auctions, Inc., 60
Greif Inc., 15; 66 (upd.)
Grey Advertising, Inc., 6
Grey Global Group Inc., 66 (upd.)
Grey Wolf, Inc., 43
Greyhound Lines, Inc., I; 32 (upd.)
Griffin Industries, Inc., 70
Griffin Land & Nurseries, Inc., 43
Griffon Corporation, 34
Grill Concepts, Inc., 74
Grinnell Corp., 13
Grist Mill Company, 15
Gristede's Foods Inc., 31; 68 (upd.)
Grolier Incorporated, 16; 43 (upd.)
Grossman's Inc., 13
Ground Round, Inc., 21
Group 1 Automotive, Inc., 52
Group Health Cooperative, 41
Grow Biz International, Inc., 18
Grow Group Inc., 12
GROWMARK, Inc., 88
Grubb & Ellis Company, 21; 98 (upd.)
Grumman Corporation, I; 11 (upd.)
Grunau Company Inc., 90
Gruntal & Co., L.L.C., 20
Gryphon Holdings, Inc., 21
GSC Enterprises, Inc., 86
GSD&M Advertising, 44
GSD&M's Idea City, 90
GSI Commerce, Inc., 67
GT Bicycles, 26
GT Interactive Software, 31
GTE Corporation, V; 15 (upd.)
GTSI Corp., 57

Guangzhou Pearl River Piano Group Ltd.,
 49
Guardian Industries Corp., 87
Guccio Gucci, S.p.A., 15
Guess, Inc., 15; 68 (upd.)
Guest Supply, Inc., 18
Guida-Seibert Dairy Company, 84
Guidant Corporation, 58
Guilford Mills Inc., 8; 40 (upd.)
Guitar Center, Inc., 29; 68 (upd.)
Guittard Chocolate Company, 55
Gulf & Western Inc., I
Gulf Island Fabrication, Inc., 44
Gulf States Utilities Company, 6
GulfMark Offshore, Inc., 49
Gulfstream Aerospace Corporation, 7; 28
 (upd.)
Gund, Inc., 96
Gunite Corporation, 51
The Gunlocke Company, 23
Guardsmark, L.L.C., 77
Guthy-Renker Corporation, 32
Guttenplan's Frozen Dough Inc., 88
Gwathmey Siegel & Associates Architects
 LLC, 26
Gymboree Corporation, 15; 69 (upd.)
H&R Block, Inc., 9; 29 (upd.); 82 (upd.)
H.B. Fuller Company, 8; 32 (upd.); 75
 (upd.)
H. Betti Industries Inc., 88
H.D. Vest, Inc., 46
H.E. Butt Grocery Company, 13; 32
 (upd.); 85 (upd.)
H.F. Ahmanson & Company, II; 10
 (upd.)
H.J. Heinz Company, II; 11 (upd.); 36
 (upd.); 99 (upd.)
H.J. Russell & Company, 66
H.M. Payson & Co., 69
H.O. Penn Machinery Company, Inc., 96
The H.W. Wilson Company, 66
Ha-Lo Industries, Inc., 27
The Haartz Corporation, 94
Habersham Bancorp, 25
Habitat for Humanity International, 36
Hach Co., 18
Hadco Corporation, 24
Haeger Industries Inc., 88
Haemonetics Corporation, 20
Haggar Corporation, 19; 78 (upd.)
Haggen Inc., 38
Hahn Automotive Warehouse, Inc., 24
Haights Cross Communications, Inc., 84
The Hain Celestial Group, Inc., 27; 43
 (upd.)
Hair Club For Men Ltd., 90
HAL Inc., 9
Hal Leonard Corporation, 96
Hale-Halsell Company, 60
Half Price Books, Records, Magazines
 Inc., 37
Hall, Kinion & Associates, Inc., 52
Halliburton Company, III; 25 (upd.); 55
 (upd.)
Hallmark Cards, Inc., IV; 16 (upd.); 40
 (upd.); 87 (upd.)
Hamilton Beach/Proctor-Silex Inc., 17

Hammacher Schlemmer & Company Inc.,
 21; 72 (upd.)
Hamot Health Foundation, 91
Hampshire Group Ltd., 82
Hampton Affiliates, Inc., 77
Hampton Industries, Inc., 20
Hancock Fabrics, Inc., 18
Hancock Holding Company, 15
Handleman Company, 15; 86 (upd.)
Handspring Inc., 49
Handy & Harman, 23
Hanesbrands Inc., 98
Hanger Orthopedic Group, Inc., 41
Hanmi Financial Corporation, 66
Hanna Andersson Corp., 49
Hanna-Barbera Cartoons Inc., 23
Hannaford Bros. Co., 12
Hanover Compressor Company, 59
Hanover Direct, Inc., 36
Hanover Foods Corporation, 35
Hansen Natural Corporation, 31; 76
 (upd.)
Hanson Building Materials America Inc.,
 60
Happy Kids Inc., 30
Harbert Corporation, 14
Harbison-Walker Refractories Company,
 24
Harbour Group Industries, Inc., 90
Harcourt Brace and Co., 12
Harcourt Brace Jovanovich, Inc., IV
Harcourt General, Inc., 20 (upd.)
Hard Rock Cafe International, Inc., 12;
 32 (upd.)
Harding Lawson Associates Group, Inc.,
 16
Hardinge Inc., 25
Harkins Amusement, 94
Harland Clarke Holdings Corporation, 94
 (upd.)
Harlem Globetrotters International, Inc.,
 61
Harley-Davidson Inc., 7; 25 (upd.)
Harleysville Group Inc., 37
Harman International Industries Inc., 15
Harmon Industries, Inc., 25
Harmonic Inc., 43
Harnischfeger Industries, Inc., 8; 38
 (upd.)
Harold's Stores, Inc., 22
Harper Group Inc., 17
HarperCollins Publishers, 15
Harpo Inc., 28; 66 (upd.)
Harps Food Stores, Inc., 99
Harrah's Entertainment, Inc., 16; 43
 (upd.)
Harris Corporation, II; 20 (upd.); 78
 (upd.)
Harris Interactive Inc., 41; 92 (upd.)
The Harris Soup Company (Harry's Fresh
 Foods), 92
Harris Teeter Inc., 23; 72 (upd.)
Harry London Candies, Inc., 70
Harry N. Abrams, Inc., 58
Harry Winston Inc., 45
Harry's Farmers Market Inc., 23
Harsco Corporation, 8
Harte-Hanks, Inc., 17; 63 (upd.)

Hartmann Inc., 96
Hartmarx Corporation, 8; 32 (upd.)
The Hartz Mountain Corporation, 12; 46 (upd.)
Harveys Casino Resorts, 27
Harza Engineering Company, 14
Hasbro, Inc., III; 16 (upd.); 43 (upd.)
Haskel International, Inc., 59
Hastings Entertainment, Inc., 29
Hastings Manufacturing Company, 56
Hauser, Inc., 46
Haverty Furniture Companies, Inc., 31
Hawaiian Electric Industries, Inc., 9
Hawaiian Holdings, Inc., 22 (upd.); 96 (upd.)
Hawk Corporation, 59
Hawkeye Holdings LLC, 89
Hawkins Chemical, Inc., 16
Haworth Inc., 8; 39 (upd.)
Hay House, Inc., 93
Hayes Corporation, 24
Hayes Lemmerz International, Inc., 27
Haynes International, Inc., 88
Hazelden Foundation, 28
HCA - The Healthcare Company, 35 (upd.)
HCI Direct, Inc., 55
HDOS Enterprises, 72
HDR Inc., 48
Headwaters Incorporated, 56
Headway Corporate Resources, Inc., 40
Health Care & Retirement Corporation, 22
Health Communications, Inc., 72
Health Management Associates, Inc., 56
Health O Meter Products Inc., 14
Health Risk Management, Inc., 24
Health Systems International, Inc., 11
HealthExtras, Inc., 75
HealthMarkets, Inc., 88 (upd.)
HealthSouth Corporation, 14; 33 (upd.)
Healthtex, Inc., 17
The Hearst Corporation, IV; 19 (upd.); 46 (upd.)
Heartland Express, Inc., 18
The Heat Group, 53
Hechinger Company, 12
Hecla Mining Company, 20
Heekin Can Inc., 13
Heelys, Inc., 87
Heery International, Inc., 58
HEICO Corporation, 30
Heidrick & Struggles International, Inc., 28
Heilig-Meyers Company, 14; 40 (upd.)
Helen of Troy Corporation, 18
Helene Curtis Industries, Inc., 8; 28 (upd.)
Helix Energy Solutions Group, Inc., 81
Heller, Ehrman, White & McAuliffe, 41
Helmerich & Payne, Inc., 18
Helmsley Enterprises, Inc., 9; 39 (upd.)
Helzberg Diamonds, 40
Hendrick Motorsports, Inc., 89
Henkel Manco Inc., 22
The Henley Group, Inc., III
Henry Crown and Company, 91
Henry Dreyfuss Associates LLC, 88

Henry Ford Health System, 84
Henry Modell & Company Inc., 32
Henry Schein, Inc., 31; 70 (upd.)
Hensel Phelps Construction Company, 72
Hensley & Company, 64
Herald Media, Inc., 91
Herbalife International, Inc., 17; 41 (upd.)
Hercules Inc., I; 22 (upd.); 66 (upd.)
Hercules Technology Growth Capital, Inc., 87
Herley Industries, Inc., 33
Herman Goelitz, Inc., 28
Herman Miller, Inc., 8; 77 (upd.)
Herr Foods Inc., 84
Herschend Family Entertainment Corporation, 73
Hershey Foods Corporation, II; 15 (upd.); 51 (upd.)
The Hertz Corporation, 9; 33 (upd.)
Heska Corporation, 39
Heublein, Inc., I
Hewitt Associates, Inc., 77
Hewlett-Packard Company, III; 6 (upd.); 28 (upd.); 50 (upd.)
Hexcel Corporation, 28
hhgregg Inc., 98
Hibbett Sporting Goods, Inc., 26; 70 (upd.)
Hibernia Corporation, 37
Hickory Farms, Inc., 17
HickoryTech Corporation, 92
High Falls Brewing Company LLC, 74
Highlights for Children, Inc., 95
Highmark Inc., 27
Highsmith Inc., 60
Hilb, Rogal & Hobbs Company, 77
Hildebrandt International, 29
Hill's Pet Nutrition, Inc., 27
Hillenbrand Industries, Inc., 10; 75 (upd.)
Hillerich & Bradsby Company, Inc., 51
The Hillhaven Corporation, 14
Hills Stores Company, 13
Hilmar Cheese Company, Inc., 98
Hilton Hotels Corporation, III; 19 (upd.); 62 (upd.)
Hines Horticulture, Inc., 49
Hispanic Broadcasting Corporation, 35
Hitchiner Manufacturing Co., Inc., 23
HMI Industries, Inc., 17
HNI Corporation, 74 (upd.)
Ho-Chunk Inc., 61
HOB Entertainment, Inc., 37
Hobby Lobby Stores Inc., 80
Hobie Cat Company, 94
Hodgson Mill, Inc., 88
Hoechst Celanese Corporation, 13
Hoenig Group Inc., 41
Hoffman Corporation 78
Hogan & Hartson L.L.P., 44
HOK Group, Inc., 59
Holberg Industries, Inc., 36
Holiday Inns, Inc., III
Holiday Retirement Corp., 87
Holiday RV Superstores, Incorporated, 26
Holland & Knight LLP, 60
Holland Burgerville USA, 44
The Holland Group, Inc., 82

Hollander Home Fashions Corp., 67
Holley Performance Products Inc., 52
Hollinger International Inc., 24
Holly Corporation, 12
Hollywood Casino Corporation, 21
Hollywood Entertainment Corporation, 25
Hollywood Media Corporation, 58
Hollywood Park, Inc., 20
Holme Roberts & Owen LLP, 28
Holnam Inc., 8; 39 (upd.)
Holophane Corporation, 19
Holson Burnes Group, Inc., 14
Holt and Bugbee Company, 66
Holt's Cigar Holdings, Inc., 42
Homasote Company, 72
Home Box Office Inc., 7; 23 (upd.); 76 (upd.)
The Home Depot, Inc., V; 18 (upd.); 97 (upd.)
The Home Insurance Company, III
Home Interiors & Gifts, Inc., 55
Home Products International, Inc., 55
Home Properties of New York, Inc., 42
Home Shopping Network, Inc., V; 25 (upd.)
HomeBase, Inc., 33 (upd.)
Homestake Mining Company, 12; 38 (upd.)
Hometown Auto Retailers, Inc., 44
HomeVestors of America, Inc., 77
HON INDUSTRIES Inc., 13
Honda Motor Company Limited, I; 10 (upd.); 29 (upd.)
Honeywell Inc., II; 12 (upd.); 50 (upd.)
Hooker Furniture Corporation, 80
Hooper Holmes, Inc., 22
Hooters of America, Inc., 18; 69 (upd.)
The Hoover Company, 12; 40 (upd.)
HOP, LLC, 80
Hops Restaurant Bar and Brewery, 46
Horace Mann Educators Corporation, 22; 90 (upd.)
Horizon Lines, Inc., 98
Horizon Organic Holding Corporation, 37
Hormel Foods Corporation, 18 (upd.); 54 (upd.)
Horsehead Industries, Inc., 51
Horseshoe Gaming Holding Corporation, 62
Horton Homes, Inc., 25
Horween Leather Company, 83
Hospira, Inc., 71
Hospital Central Services, Inc., 56
Hospital Corporation of America, III
Hospitality Franchise Systems, Inc., 11
Hospitality Worldwide Services, Inc., 26
Hoss's Steak and Sea House Inc., 68
Host America Corporation 79
Hot Stuff Foods, 85
Hot Topic, Inc., 33; 86 (upd.)
Houchens Industries Inc., 51
Houghton Mifflin Company, 10; 36 (upd.)
House of Fabrics, Inc., 21
Household International, Inc., II; 21 (upd.)

Houston Industries Incorporated, V
Houston Wire & Cable Company, 97
Hovnanian Enterprises, Inc., 29; 89 (upd.)
Howard Hughes Medical Institute, 39
Howard Johnson International, Inc., 17;
    72 (upd.)
Howmet Corp., 12
HSN, 64 (upd.)
Hub Group, Inc., 38
Hub International Limited, 89
Hubbard Broadcasting Inc., 24; 79 (upd.)
Hubbell Inc., 9; 31 (upd.); 76 (upd.)
Hudson Foods Inc., 13
Hudson River Bancorp, Inc., 41
Huffy Corporation, 7; 30 (upd.)
Hughes Electronics Corporation, 25
Hughes Hubbard & Reed LLP, 44
Hughes Markets, Inc., 22
Hughes Supply, Inc., 14
Hulman & Company, 44
Humana Inc., III; 24 (upd.)
The Humane Society of the United States,
    54
Hummer Winblad Venture Partners, 97
Hungarian Telephone and Cable Corp.,
    75
Hungry Howie's Pizza and Subs, Inc., 25
Hunt Consolidated, Inc., 27 (upd.)
Hunt Manufacturing Company, 12
Hunt Oil Company, 7
Hunt-Wesson, Inc., 17
Hunter Fan Company, 13; 98 (upd.)
Huntington Bancshares Incorporated, 11;
    87 (upd.)
Huntington Learning Centers, Inc., 55
Hunton & Williams, 35
Huntsman Corporation, 8; 98 (upd.)
Huron Consulting Group Inc., 87
Hutchinson Technology Incorporated, 18;
    63 (upd.)
Huttig Building Products, Inc., 73
Hvide Marine Incorporated, 22
Hy-Vee, Inc., 36
Hyatt Corporation, III; 16 (upd.)
Hyde Athletic Industries, Inc., 17
Hydril Company, 46
Hypercom Corporation, 27
Hyperion Software Corporation, 22
Hyperion Solutions Corporation, 76
Hyster Company, 17
I.C. Isaacs & Company, 31
Iams Company, 26
IBERIABANK Corporation, 37
IBP, Inc., II; 21 (upd.)
IC Industries, Inc., I
ICF International, Inc., 28; 94 (upd.)
ICN Pharmaceuticals, Inc., 52
Icon Health & Fitness, Inc., 38
Idaho Power Company, 12
IDB Communications Group, Inc., 11
Idearc Inc., 90
Identix Inc., 44
IDEO Inc., 65
IDEXX Laboratories, Inc., 23
IDG Books Worldwide, Inc., 27
IdraPrince, Inc., 76
IDT Corporation, 34; 99 (upd.)
IDX Systems Corporation, 64

IEC Electronics Corp., 42
IGA, Inc., 99
Igloo Products Corp., 21
IHOP Corporation, 17; 58 (upd.)
IHS Inc. 78
IKON Office Solutions, Inc., 50
Il Fornaio (America) Corporation, 27
Ilitch Holdings Inc., 37; 86 (upd.)
Illinois Bell Telephone Company, 14
Illinois Central Corporation, 11
Illinois Power Company, 6
Illinois Tool Works Inc., III; 22 (upd.); 81
    (upd.)
Illumina, Inc., 93
Ikonics Corporation, 99
ILX Resorts Incorporated, 65
Image Entertainment, Inc., 94
Imagine Entertainment, 91
Imagine Foods, Inc., 50
Imation Corporation, 20
IMC Fertilizer Group, Inc., 8
ImClone Systems Inc., 58
IMCO Recycling, Incorporated, 32
IMG 78
Immucor, Inc., 81
Immunex Corporation, 14; 50 (upd.)
Imo Industries Inc., 7; 27 (upd.)
IMPATH Inc., 45
Imperial Holly Corporation, 12
Imperial Industries, Inc., 81
Imperial Sugar Company, 32 (upd.)
IMS Health, Inc., 57
In Focus Systems, Inc., 22
In-N-Out Burgers Inc., 19; 74 (upd.)
In-Sink-Erator, 66
InaCom Corporation, 13
Inamed Corporation 79
Incyte Genomics, Inc., 52
Indel Inc. 78
Indiana Bell Telephone Company,
    Incorporated, 14
Indiana Energy, Inc., 27
Indianapolis Motor Speedway
    Corporation, 46
Indus International Inc., 70
Industrial Services of America, Inc., 46
Infinity Broadcasting Corporation, 11; 48
    (upd.)
InFocus Corporation, 92
Information Access Company, 17
Information Builders, Inc., 22
Information Holdings Inc., 47
Information Resources, Inc., 10
Informix Corporation, 10; 30 (upd.)
InfoSonics Corporation, 81
InfoSpace, Inc., 91
Ingalls Shipbuilding, Inc., 12
Ingersoll-Rand Company Ltd., III; 15
    (upd.); 55 (upd.)
Ingles Markets, Inc., 20
Ingram Industries, Inc., 11; 49 (upd.)
Ingram Micro Inc., 52
Initial Security, 64
Inktomi Corporation, 45
Inland Container Corporation, 8
Inland Steel Industries, Inc., IV; 19 (upd.)
Innovative Solutions & Support, Inc., 85
Innovo Group Inc., 83

Input/Output, Inc., 73
Inserra Supermarkets, 25
Insight Enterprises, Inc., 18
Insilco Corporation, 16
Insituform Technologies, Inc., 83
Inso Corporation, 26
Instinet Corporation, 34
Insurance Auto Auctions, Inc., 23
Integra LifeSciences Holdings
    Corporation, 87
Integrated BioPharma, Inc., 83
Integrated Defense Technologies, Inc., 54
Integrity Inc., 44
Intel Corporation, II; 10 (upd.); 36
    (upd.); 75 (upd.)
IntelliCorp, Inc., 45
Intelligent Electronics, Inc., 6
Inter Parfums Inc., 35; 86 (upd.)
Inter-Regional Financial Group, Inc., 15
Interbrand Corporation, 70
Interco Incorporated, III
IntercontinentalExchange, Inc., 95
InterDigital Communications
    Corporation, 61
Interep National Radio Sales Inc., 35
Interface, Inc., 8; 29 (upd.); 76 (upd.)
Intergraph Corporation, 6; 24 (upd.)
The Interlake Corporation, 8
Intermec Technologies Corporation, 72
INTERMET Corporation, 32, 77 (upd.)
Intermix Media, Inc., 83
Intermountain Health Care, Inc., 27
International Airline Support Group, Inc.,
    55
International Brotherhood of Teamsters,
    37
International Business Machines Corpora-
    tion, III; 6 (upd.); 30 (upd.); 63 (upd.)
International Controls Corporation, 10
International Creative Management, Inc.,
    43
International Dairy Queen, Inc., 10; 39
    (upd.)
International Data Group, Inc., 7; 25
    (upd.)
International Family Entertainment Inc.,
    13
International Flavors & Fragrances Inc., 9;
    38 (upd.)
International Game Technology, 10; 41
    (upd.)
International Lease Finance Corporation,
    48
International Management Group, 18
International Multifoods Corporation, 7;
    25 (upd.)
International Paper Company, IV; 15
    (upd.); 47 (upd.); 97 (upd.)
International Profit Associates, Inc., 87
International Rectifier Corporation, 31; 71
    (upd.)
International Shipbreaking Ltd. L.L.C., 67
International Shipholding Corporation,
    Inc., 27
International Speedway Corporation, 19;
    74 (upd.)
International Telephone & Telegraph
    Corporation, I; 11 (upd.)

International Total Services, Inc., 37
Interpool, Inc., 92
The Interpublic Group of Companies, Inc., I; 22 (upd.); 75 (upd.)
Interscope Music Group, 31
Intersil Corporation, 93
Interstate Bakeries Corporation, 12; 38 (upd.)
Interstate Hotels & Resorts Inc., 58
InterVideo, Inc., 85
Intevac, Inc., 92
Intimate Brands, Inc., 24
Intrado Inc., 63
Intuit Inc., 14; 33 (upd.); 73 (upd.)
Intuitive Surgical, Inc. 79
Invacare Corporation, 11; 47 (upd.)
inVentiv Health, Inc., 81
The Inventure Group, Inc., 96 (upd.)
Inverness Medical Innovations, Inc., 63
Invitrogen Corporation, 52
Invivo Corporation, 52
Iomega Corporation, 21
Ionatron, Inc., 85
Ionics, Incorporated, 52
Iowa Telecommunications Services, Inc., 85
IPALCO Enterprises, Inc., 6
Ipsen International Inc., 72
Irex Contracting Group, 90
iRobot Corporation, 83
Iron Mountain, Inc., 33
Irvin Feld & Kenneth Feld Productions, Inc., 15
Irwin Financial Corporation, 77
The Island ECN, Inc., 48
Isle of Capri Casinos, Inc., 41
Ispat Inland Inc., 40 (upd.)
ITC Holdings Corp., 75
Itel Corporation, 9
Items International Airwalk Inc., 17
Itron, Inc., 64
ITT Educational Services, Inc., 33; 76 (upd.)
ITT Sheraton Corporation, III
i2 Technologies, Inc., 87
Ivar's, Inc., 86
IVAX Corporation, 11; 55 (upd.)
IVC Industries, Inc., 45
iVillage Inc., 46
Iwerks Entertainment, Inc., 34
IXC Communications, Inc., 29
J & J Snack Foods Corporation, 24
J&R Electronics Inc., 26
J. & W. Seligman & Co. Inc., 61
J. Alexander's Corporation, 65
J. Baker, Inc., 31
J. Crew Group. Inc., 12; 34 (upd.); 88 (upd.)
J. C. Penney Company, Inc., V; 18 (upd.); 43 (upd.); 91 (upd.)
J. D'Addario & Company, Inc., 48
The J. Jill Group, Inc., 35; 90 (upd.)
J.A. Jones, Inc., 16
J.B. Hunt Transport Services Inc., 12
J.D. Edwards & Company, 14
J.D. Power and Associates, 32
J.F. Shea Co., Inc., 55
J.H. Findorff and Son, Inc., 60

J.I. Case Company, 10
J.J. Keller & Associates, Inc., 81
J.L. Hammett Company, 72
J. Lohr Winery Corporation, 99
The J. M. Smucker Company, 11; 87 (upd.)
J.P. Morgan Chase & Co., II; 30 (upd.); 38 (upd.)
J.R. Simplot Company, 16; 60 (upd.)
J. W. Pepper and Son Inc., 86
Jabil Circuit, Inc., 36; 88 (upd.)
Jack Henry and Associates, Inc., 17; 94 (upd.)
Jack in the Box Inc., 89 (upd.)
Jack Morton Worldwide, 88
Jack Schwartz Shoes, Inc., 18
Jackpot Enterprises Inc., 21
Jackson Hewitt, Inc., 48
Jackson National Life Insurance Company, 8
Jacmar Companies, 87
Jaco Electronics, Inc., 30
Jacob Leinenkugel Brewing Company, 28
Jacobs Engineering Group Inc., 6; 26 (upd.)
Jacobson Stores Inc., 21
Jacor Communications, Inc., 23
Jacuzzi Brands Inc., 76 (upd.)
Jacuzzi Inc., 23
JAKKS Pacific, Inc., 52
Jalate Inc., 25
Jamba Juice Company, 47
James Avery Craftsman, Inc., 76
James Original Coney Island Inc., 84
James River Corporation of Virginia, IV
Jani-King International, Inc., 85
JanSport, Inc., 70
Janus Capital Group Inc., 57
Jarden Corporation, 93 (upd.)
Jason Incorporated, 23
Jay Jacobs, Inc., 15
Jayco Inc., 13
Jays Foods, Inc., 90
Jazz Basketball Investors, Inc., 55
Jazzercise, Inc., 45
JB Oxford Holdings, Inc., 32
JDS Uniphase Corporation, 34
JE Dunn Construction Group, Inc., 85
Jean-Georges Enterprises L.L.C., 75
Jefferies Group, Inc., 25
Jefferson-Pilot Corporation, 11; 29 (upd.)
Jel Sert Company, 90
Jeld-Wen, Inc., 45
Jelly Belly Candy Company, 76
Jenkens & Gilchrist, P.C., 65
Jennie-O Turkey Store, Inc., 76
Jennifer Convertibles, Inc., 31
Jenny Craig, Inc., 10; 29 (upd.); 92 (upd.)
Jeppesen Sanderson, Inc., 92
Jerry's Famous Deli Inc., 24
Jersey Mike's Franchise Systems, Inc., 83
Jervis B. Webb Company, 24
JetBlue Airways Corporation, 44
Jetro Cash & Carry Enterprises Inc., 38
Jewett-Cameron Trading Company, Ltd., 89
JG Industries, Inc., 15

Jillian's Entertainment Holdings, Inc., 40
Jim Beam Brands Worldwide, Inc., 14; 58 (upd.)
The Jim Henson Company, 23
Jitney-Jungle Stores of America, Inc., 27
JLG Industries, Inc., 52
JLM Couture, Inc., 64
JMB Realty Corporation, IV
Jo-Ann Stores, Inc., 72 (upd.)
Jockey International, Inc., 12; 34 (upd.); 77 (upd.)
Joe's Sports & Outdoor, 98 (upd.)
The Joffrey Ballet of Chicago, The 52
John B. Sanfilippo & Son, Inc., 14
The John D. and Catherine T. MacArthur Foundation, 34
John D. Brush Company Inc., 94
John Frieda Professional Hair Care Inc., 70
John H. Harland Company, 17
John Hancock Financial Services, Inc., III; 42 (upd.)
The John Nuveen Company, 21
John Paul Mitchell Systems, 24
John Q. Hammons Hotels, Inc., 24
John W. Danforth Company, 48
John Wiley & Sons, Inc., 17; 65 (upd.)
Johnny Rockets Group, Inc., 31; 76 (upd.)
Johns Manville Corporation, 64 (upd.)
Johnson & Higgins, 14
Johnson & Johnson, III; 8 (upd.); 36 (upd.); 75 (upd.)
Johnson Controls, Inc., III; 26 (upd.); 59 (upd.)
Johnson Outdoors Inc., 28; 84 (upd.)
Johnson Publishing Company, Inc., 28; 72 (upd.)
Johnsonville Sausage L.L.C., 63
Johnston Industries, Inc., 15
Johnstown America Industries, Inc., 23
Jones Apparel Group, Inc., 11; 39 (upd.)
Jones, Day, Reavis & Pogue, 33
Jones Intercable, Inc., 21
Jones Knowledge Group, Inc., 97
Jones Lang LaSalle Incorporated, 49
Jones Medical Industries, Inc., 24
Jones Soda Co., 69
Jordache Enterprises, Inc., 23
The Jordan Company LP, 70
Jordan Industries, Inc., 36
Jordan-Kitt Music Inc., 86
Jos. A. Bank Clothiers, Inc., 31
Joseph T. Ryerson & Son, Inc., 15
Jostens, Inc., 7; 25 (upd.); 73 (upd.)
JOULÉ Inc., 58
Journal Communications, Inc., 86
Journal Register Company, 29
JPI, 49
JPMorgan Chase & Co., 91 (upd.)
JPS Textile Group, Inc., 28
j2 Global Communications, Inc., 75
Juicy Couture, Inc., 80
The Judge Group, Inc., 51
Juniper Networks, Inc., 43
Juno Lighting, Inc., 30
Juno Online Services, Inc., 38
Jupitermedia Corporation, 75

Just Bagels Manufacturing, Inc., 94
Just Born, Inc., 32
Just For Feet, Inc., 19
Justin Industries, Inc., 19
JWP Inc., 9
JWT Group Inc., I
K & B Inc., 12
K & G Men's Center, Inc., 21
K'Nex Industries, Inc., 52
K-Swiss, Inc., 33; 89 (upd.)
K-tel International, Inc., 21
Kadant Inc., 96 (upd.)
Kaiser Aluminum Corporation, IV; 84
    (upd.)
Kaiser Foundation Health Plan, Inc., 53
Kal Kan Foods, Inc., 22
Kaman Corporation, 12; 42 (upd.)
Kaman Music Corporation, 68
Kampgrounds of America, Inc. 33
Kana Software, Inc., 51
Kansas City Power & Light Company, 6
Kansas City Southern Industries, Inc., 6;
    26 (upd.)
The Kansas City Southern Railway
    Company, 92
Kaplan, Inc., 42; 90 (upd.)
Kar Nut Products Company, 86
Karl Kani Infinity, Inc., 49
Karsten Manufacturing Corporation, 51
Kash n' Karry Food Stores, Inc., 20
Kashi Company, 89
Kasper A.S.L., Ltd., 40
kate spade LLC, 68
Katy Industries, Inc., I; 51 (upd.)
Katz Communications, Inc., 6
Katz Media Group, Inc., 35
Kaufman and Broad Home Corporation,
    8
Kaydon Corporation, 18
KB Home, 45 (upd.)
KB Toys, 15; 35 (upd.); 86 (upd.)
Keane, Inc., 56
Keebler Foods Company, 36
The Keith Companies Inc., 54
Keithley Instruments Inc., 16
Kelley Blue Book Company, Inc., 84
Kelley Drye & Warren LLP, 40
Kellogg Brown & Root, Inc., 62 (upd.)
Kellogg Company, II; 13 (upd.); 50
    (upd.)
Kellwood Company, 8; 85 (upd.)
Kelly Services Inc., 6; 26 (upd.)
Kelly-Moore Paint Company, Inc., 56
The Kelly-Springfield Tire Company, 8
Kelsey-Hayes Group of Companies, 7; 27
    (upd.)
Kemet Corp., 14
Kemper Corporation, III; 15 (upd.)
Ken's Foods, Inc., 88
Kendall International, Inc., 11
Kendall-Jackson Winery, Ltd., 28
Kendle International Inc., 87
Kenetech Corporation, 11
Kenexa Corporation, 87
Kenmore Air Harbor Inc., 65
Kennametal Inc., 68 (upd.)
Kennedy-Wilson, Inc., 60
Kenneth Cole Productions, Inc., 25

Kensey Nash Corporation, 71
Kensington Publishing Corporation, 84
Kent Electronics Corporation, 17
Kentucky Electric Steel, Inc., 31
Kentucky Utilities Company, 6
Kerasotes ShowPlace Theaters LLC, 80
Kerr Group Inc., 24
Kerr-McGee Corporation, IV; 22 (upd.);
    68 (upd.)
Ketchum Communications Inc., 6
Kettle Foods Inc., 48
Kewaunee Scientific Corporation, 25
Key Safety Systems, Inc., 63
Key Tronic Corporation, 14
KeyCorp, 8; 93 (upd.)
Keyes Fibre Company, 9
Keys Fitness Products, LP, 83
KeySpan Energy Co., 27
Keystone International, Inc., 11
KFC Corporation, 7; 21 (upd.); 89 (upd.)
Kforce Inc., 71
KI, 57
Kidde, Inc., I
Kiehl's Since 1851, Inc., 52
Kolmar Laboratories Group, 96
Lewis Drug Inc., 94
Lifetouch Inc., 86
LifeWise Health Plan of Oregon, Inc., 90
Kikkoman Corporation, 47 (upd.)
Kimball International, Inc., 12; 48 (upd.)
Kimberly-Clark Corporation, III; 16
    (upd.); 43 (upd.)
Kimco Realty Corporation, 11
Kinder Morgan, Inc., 45
KinderCare Learning Centers, Inc., 13
Kinetic Concepts, Inc. (KCI), 20
King & Spalding, 23
The King Arthur Flour Company, 31
King Kullen Grocery Co., Inc., 15
King Nut Company, 74
King Pharmaceuticals, Inc., 54
King Ranch, Inc., 14; 60 (upd.)
King World Productions, Inc., 9; 30
    (upd.)
Kingston Technology Corporation, 20
Kinko's, Inc., 16; 43 (upd.)
Kinney Shoe Corp., 14
Kinray Inc., 85
Kintera, Inc., 75
Kirby Corporation, 18; 66 (upd.)
Kirkland & Ellis LLP, 65
Kirlin's Inc., 98
Kirshenbaum Bond + Partners, Inc., 57
Kit Manufacturing Co., 18
Kitchell Corporation, 14
KitchenAid, 8
Kitty Hawk, Inc., 22
Kiva, 95
Kiwi International Airlines Inc., 20
KLA-Tencor Corporation, 11; 45 (upd.)
Klasky Csupo Inc. 78
Klein Tools, Inc., 95
Kleiner, Perkins, Caufield & Byers, 53
Klement's Sausage Company, 61
Kmart Corporation, V; 18 (upd.); 47
    (upd.)
Knape & Vogt Manufacturing Company,
    17

Knight Ridder, Inc., 67 (upd.)
Knight Trading Group, Inc., 70
Knight Transportation, Inc., 64
Knight-Ridder, Inc., IV; 15 (upd.)
Knoll, Inc., 14; 80 (upd.)
The Knot, Inc., 74
Knott's Berry Farm, 18
Knowledge Learning Corporation, 51
Knowledge Universe, Inc., 54
KnowledgeWare Inc., 9; 31 (upd.)
Koala Corporation, 44
Kobrand Corporation, 82
Koch Enterprises, Inc., 29
Koch Industries, Inc., IV; 20 (upd.); 77
    (upd.)
Kohl's Corporation, 9; 30 (upd.); 77
    (upd.)
Kohlberg Kravis Roberts & Co., 24; 56
    (upd.)
Kohler Company, 7; 32 (upd.)
Kohn Pedersen Fox Associates P.C., 57
The Koll Company, 8
Kollmorgen Corporation, 18
Komag, Inc., 11
Koo Koo Roo, Inc., 25
Kopin Corporation, 80
Koppers Industries, Inc., I; 26 (upd.)
Koret of California, Inc., 62
Korn/Ferry International, 34
Kos Pharmaceuticals, Inc., 63
Koss Corporation, 38
Kraft Foods Inc., II; 7 (upd.); 45 (upd.);
    91 (upd.)
KraftMaid Cabinetry, Inc., 72
Kraus-Anderson Companies, Inc., 36; 83
    (upd.)
Krause Publications, Inc., 35
Krause's Furniture, Inc., 27
Kreisler Manufacturing Corporation, 97
Krispy Kreme Doughnuts, Inc., 21; 61
    (upd.)
The Kroger Company, II; 15 (upd.); 65
    (upd.)
Kroll Inc., 57
Kronos, Inc., 18
Kruse International, 88
The Krystal Company, 33
K2 Inc., 16; 84 (upd.)
KU Energy Corporation, 11
Kuhlman Corporation, 20
Kulicke and Soffa Industries, Inc., 33; 76
    (upd.)
Kurzweil Technologies, Inc., 51
The Kushner-Locke Company, 25
Kyphon, 87
L-3 Communications Holdings, Inc., 48
L. and J.G. Stickley, Inc., 50
L. Luria & Son, Inc., 19
L.A. Darling Company, 92
L.A. Gear, Inc., 8; 32 (upd.)
L.A. T Sportswear, Inc., 26
L.B. Foster Company, 33
L.L. Bean, Inc., 10; 38 (upd.); 91 (upd.)
The L.L. Knickerbocker Co., Inc., 25
L. M. Berry and Company, 80
L.S. Starrett Company, 13; 64 (upd.)
La Choy Food Products Inc., 25
La Madeleine French Bakery & Café, 33

The La Quinta Companies, 11; 42 (upd.)
La Reina Inc., 96
La-Z-Boy Incorporated, 14; 50 (upd.)
LaBarge Inc., 41
LabOne, Inc., 48
Labor Ready, Inc., 29; 88 (upd.)
Laboratory Corporation of America
    Holdings, 42 (upd.)
LaBranche & Co. Inc., 37
Lacks Enterprises Inc., 61
Laclede Steel Company, 15
LaCrosse Footwear, Inc., 18; 61 (upd.)
LADD Furniture, Inc., 12
Ladish Co., Inc., 30
Lafarge Corporation, 28
Laidlaw International, Inc., 80
Lakeland Industries, Inc., 45
Lakes Entertainment, Inc., 51
Lakeside Foods, Inc., 89
Lam Research Corporation, 11; 31 (upd.)
Lamar Advertising Company, 27; 70
    (upd.)
The Lamaur Corporation, 41
Lamb Weston, Inc., 23
Lamonts Apparel, Inc., 15
The Lamson & Sessions Co., 13; 61
    (upd.)
Lancair International, Inc., 67
Lancaster Colony Corporation, 8; 61
    (upd.)
Lance, Inc., 14; 41 (upd.)
Lancer Corporation, 21
Land O'Lakes, Inc., II; 21 (upd.); 81
    (upd.)
LandAmerica Financial Group, Inc., 85
Landauer, Inc., 51
Landec Corporation, 95
Landmark Communications, Inc., 12; 55
    (upd.)
Landmark Theatre Corporation, 70
Landor Associates, 81
Landry's Restaurants, Inc., 65 (upd.)
Landry's Seafood Restaurants, Inc., 15
Lands' End, Inc., 9; 29 (upd.); 82 (upd.)
Landstar System, Inc., 63
Lane Bryant, Inc., 64
The Lane Co., Inc., 12
Lanier Worldwide, Inc., 75
Lanoga Corporation, 62
Larry Flynt Publishing Inc., 31
Larry H. Miller Group, 29
Las Vegas Sands, Inc., 50
Laserscope, 67
Lason, Inc., 31
Latham & Watkins, 33
Latrobe Brewing Company, 54
Lattice Semiconductor Corp., 16
Lawson Software, 38
Lawter International Inc., 14
Layne Christensen Company, 19
Lazare Kaplan International Inc., 21
Lazy Days RV Center, Inc., 69
LCA-Vision, Inc., 85
LCC International, Inc., 84
LCI International, Inc., 16
LDB Corporation, 53
LDDS-Metro Communications, Inc., 8
LDI Ltd., LLC, 76

Leap Wireless International, Inc., 69
LeapFrog Enterprises, Inc., 54
Lear Corporation, 71 (upd.)
Lear Seating Corporation, 16
Lear Siegler, Inc., I
Learjet Inc., 8; 27 (upd.)
Learning Care Group, Inc., 76 (upd.)
The Learning Company Inc., 24
Learning Tree International Inc., 24
LeaRonal, Inc., 23
Leaseway Transportation Corp., 12
Leatherman Tool Group, Inc., 51
Lebhar-Friedman, Inc., 55
LeBoeuf, Lamb, Greene & MacRae,
    L.L.P., 29
LECG Corporation, 93
Lechmere Inc., 10
Lechters, Inc., 11; 39 (upd.)
LeCroy Corporation, 41
Lee Apparel Company, Inc., 8
Lee Enterprises Inc., 11; 64 (upd.)
Leeann Chin, Inc., 30
Lefrak Organization Inc., 26
The Legal Aid Society, 48
Legal Sea Foods Inc., 96
Legent Corporation, 10
Legg Mason, Inc., 33
Leggett & Platt, Inc., 11; 48 (upd.)
Lehigh Portland Cement Company, 23
Lehman Brothers Holdings Inc., 99 (upd.)
Leidy's, Inc., 93
Leiner Health Products Inc., 34
LendingTree, LLC, 93
Lennar Corporation, 11
Lennox International Inc., 8; 28 (upd.)
Lenovo Group Ltd., 80
Lenox, Inc., 12
LensCrafters Inc., 23; 76 (upd.)
Leo Burnett Company Inc., I; 20 (upd.)
The Leona Group LLC, 84
Leprino Foods Company, 28
Les Schwab Tire Centers, 50
Lesco Inc., 19
The Leslie Fay Companies, Inc., 8; 39
    (upd.)
Leslie's Poolmart, Inc., 18
Leucadia National Corporation, 11; 71
    (upd.)
Leupold & Stevens, Inc., 52
Level 3 Communications, Inc., 67
Levenger Company, 63
Lever Brothers Company, 9
Levi, Ray & Shoup, Inc., 96
Levi Strauss & Co., V; 16 (upd.)
Levitz Furniture Inc., 15
Levy Restaurants L.P., 26
Lewis Galoob Toys Inc., 16
LEXIS-NEXIS Group, 33
Lexmark International, Inc., 18; 79 (upd.)
LG&E Energy Corporation, 6; 51 (upd.)
Libbey Inc., 49
The Liberty Corporation, 22
Liberty Livewire Corporation, 42
Liberty Media Corporation, 50
Liberty Mutual Holding Company, 59
Liberty Orchards Co., Inc., 89
Liberty Property Trust, 57
Liberty Travel, Inc., 56

Life Care Centers of America Inc., 76
Life is Good, Inc., 80
Life Technologies, Inc., 17
Life Time Fitness, Inc., 66
LifeCell Corporation, 77
Lifeline Systems, Inc., 53
LifeLock, Inc., 91
LifePoint Hospitals, Inc., 69
Lifetime Brands, Inc., 73 (upd.)
Lifetime Entertainment Services, 51
Lifetime Hoan Corporation, 27
Lifeway Foods, Inc., 65
Ligand Pharmaceuticals Incorporated, 47
Lillian Vernon Corporation, 12; 35
    (upd.); 92 (upd.)
Lilly Endowment Inc., 70
The Limited, Inc., V; 20 (upd.)
LIN Broadcasting Corp., 9
Lincare Holdings Inc., 43
Lincoln Center for the Performing Arts,
    Inc., 69
Lincoln Electric Co., 13
Lincoln National Corporation, III; 25
    (upd.)
Lincoln Property Company, 8; 54 (upd.)
Lincoln Snacks Company, 24
Lincoln Telephone & Telegraph Company,
    14
Lindal Cedar Homes, Inc., 29
Lindsay Manufacturing Co., 20
Linear Technology Corporation, 16; 99
    (upd.)
Linens 'n Things, Inc., 24; 75 (upd.)
Lintas: Worldwide, 14
The Lion Brewery, Inc., 86
Lionel L.L.C., 16; 99 (upd.)
Liqui-Box Corporation, 16
Liquidnet, Inc., 79
Litehouse Inc., 60
Lithia Motors, Inc., 41
Littelfuse, Inc., 26
Little Caesar Enterprises, Inc., 7; 24
    (upd.)
Little Tikes Company, 13; 62 (upd.)
Littleton Coin Company Inc., 82
Litton Industries, Inc., I; 11 (upd.)
LIVE Entertainment Inc., 20
Live Nation, Inc., 80 (upd.)
LivePerson, Inc., 91
Liz Claiborne, Inc., 8; 25 (upd.)
LKQ Corporation, 71
Lockheed Martin Corporation, I; 11
    (upd.); 15 (upd.); 89 (upd.)
Loctite Corporation, 8; 30 (upd.)
LodgeNet Entertainment Corporation, 28
Loehmann's Inc., 24
Loews Corporation, I; 12 (upd.); 36
    (upd.); 93 (upd.)
Logan's Roadhouse, Inc., 29
Logicon, 20
LoJack Corporation, 48
London Fog Industries, Inc., 29
Lone Star Steakhouse & Saloon, Inc., 51
The Long & Foster Companies, Inc., 85
Long Island Bancorp, Inc., 16
Long Island Lighting Company, V
The Long Island Rail Road Company, 68
Long John Silver's, 13; 57 (upd.)

The Longaberger Company, 12; 44 (upd.)
Longs Drug Stores Corporation, V; 25 (upd.); 83 (upd.)
Longview Fibre Company, 8; 37 (upd.)
Loral Space & Communications Ltd., 8; 9; 54 (upd.)
Lost Arrow Inc., 22
LOT$OFF Corporation, 24
Lotus Development Corporation, 6; 25 (upd.)
LOUD Technologies, Inc., 95 (upd.)
The Louisiana Land and Exploration Company, 7
Louisiana-Pacific Corporation, IV; 31 (upd.)
Love's Travel Stops & Country Stores, Inc., 71
Lowe's Companies, Inc., V; 21 (upd.); 81 (upd.)
Lowrance Electronics, Inc., 18
LPA Holding Corporation, 81
LSB Industries, Inc., 77
LSI Logic Corporation, 13; 64
The LTV Corporation, I; 24 (upd.)
The Lubrizol Corporation, I; 30 (upd.); 83 (upd.)
Luby's, Inc., 17; 42 (upd.); 99 (upd.)
Lucasfilm Ltd., 12; 50 (upd.)
Lucent Technologies Inc., 34
Lucille Farms, Inc., 45
Lucky Stores, Inc., 27
Lufkin Industries Inc. 78
Luigino's, Inc., 64
Lukens Inc., 14
Lunar Corporation, 29
Lunardi's Super Market, Inc., 99
Lund Food Holdings, Inc., 22
Lund International Holdings, Inc., 40
Lutheran Brotherhood, 31
Lydall, Inc., 64
Lyman-Richey Corporation, 96
Lynch Corporation, 43
Lynden Incorporated, 91
Lyondell Chemical Company, IV; 45 (upd.)
M&F Worldwide Corp., 38
M. Shanken Communications, Inc., 50
M.A. Bruder & Sons, Inc., 56
M.A. Gedney Co., 51
M.A. Hanna Company, 8
M.H. Meyerson & Co., Inc., 46
Mac Frugal's Bargains - Closeouts Inc., 17
Mac-Gray Corporation, 44
MacAndrews & Forbes Holdings Inc., 28; 86 (upd.)
MacDermid Incorporated, 32
Mace Security International, Inc., 57
The Macerich Company, 57
MacGregor Golf Company, 68
Mack Trucks, Inc., I; 22 (upd.); 61 (upd.)
Mack-Cali Realty Corporation, 42
Mackay Envelope Corporation, 45
Mackie Designs Inc., 33
Macklowe Properties, Inc., 95
Macmillan, Inc., 7
MacNeil/Lehrer Productions, 87
The MacNeal-Schwendler Corporation, 25
Macromedia, Inc., 50

Macy's, Inc., 94 (upd.)
Madden's on Gull Lake, 52
Madison Dearborn Partners, LLC, 97
Madison Gas and Electric Company, 39
Madison-Kipp Corporation, 58
Mag Instrument, Inc., 67
MaggieMoo's International, 89
Magma Copper Company, 7
Magma Design Automation Inc. 78
Magma Power Company, 11
MagneTek, Inc., 15; 41 (upd.)
MAI Systems Corporation, 11
Maid-Rite Corporation, 62
Maidenform, Inc., 20; 59 (upd.)
Mail Boxes Etc., 18; 41 (upd.)
Mail-Well, Inc., 28
Make-A-Wish Foundation of America, 97
Maine & Maritimes Corporation, 56
Maine Central Railroad Company, 16
Maines Paper & Food Service Inc., 71
Majesco Entertainment Company, 85
The Major Automotive Companies, Inc., 45
Malcolm Pirnie, Inc., 42
Malden Mills Industries, Inc., 16
Mallinckrodt Group Inc., 19
Malt-O-Meal Company, 22; 63 (upd.)
Management and Training Corporation, 28
Manatron, Inc., 86
Mandalay Resort Group, 32 (upd.)
Manhattan Associates, Inc., 67
Manhattan Group, LLC, 80
Manheim, 88
The Manitowoc Company, Inc., 18; 59 (upd.)
Mannatech Inc., 33
Manning Selvage & Lee (MS&L), 76
MannKind Corporation, 87
Manor Care, Inc., 6; 25 (upd.)
Manpower Inc., 9; 30 (upd.); 73 (upd.)
ManTech International Corporation, 97
Manufactured Home Communities, Inc., 22
Manufacturers Hanover Corporation, II
Manville Corporation, III; 7 (upd.)
MAPCO Inc., IV
MAPICS, Inc., 55
Maple Grove Farms of Vermont, 88
Maples Industries, Inc., 83
Marble Slab Creamery, Inc., 87
March of Dimes, 31
Marchex, Inc., 72
marchFIRST, Inc., 34
Marco Business Products, Inc., 75
Marco's Franchising LLC, 86
The Marcus Corporation, 21
Marie Callender's Restaurant & Bakery, Inc., 28
Marine Products Corporation, 75
MarineMax, Inc., 30
Marion Laboratories, Inc., I
Marisa Christina, Inc., 15
Maritz Inc., 38
Mark IV Industries, Inc., 7; 28 (upd.)
Mark T. Wendell Tea Company, 94
The Mark Travel Corporation, 80
Marks Brothers Jewelers, Inc., 24

Marlin Business Services Corp., 89
The Marmon Group, Inc., IV; 16 (upd.); 70 (upd.)
Marquette Electronics, Inc., 13
Marriott International, Inc., III; 21 (upd.); 83 (upd.)
Mars, Incorporated, 7; 40 (upd.)
Mars Petcare US Inc., 96
Marsh & McLennan Companies, Inc., III; 45 (upd.)
Marsh Supermarkets, Inc., 17; 76 (upd.)
Marshall & Ilsley Corporation, 56
Marshall Field's, 63
Marshalls Incorporated, 13
Marshfield Clinic Inc., 82
Martek Biosciences Corporation, 65
Marten Transport, Ltd., 84
Martha Stewart Living Omnimedia, Inc., 24; 73 (upd.)
Martignetti Companies, 84
Martin Franchises, Inc., 80
Martin Industries, Inc., 44
Martin Marietta Corporation, I
MartinLogan, Ltd., 85
Martz Group, 56
Marvel Entertainment Inc., 10; 78 (upd.)
Marvin Lumber & Cedar Company, 22
Mary Kay Inc., 9; 30 (upd.); 84 (upd.)
Maryland & Virginia Milk Producers Cooperative Association, Inc., 80
Maryville Data Systems Inc., 96
The Maschhoffs, Inc., 82
Masco Corporation, III; 20 (upd.); 39 (upd.)
Mashantucket Pequot Gaming Enterprise Inc., 35
Masland Corporation, 17
Massachusetts Mutual Life Insurance Company, III; 53 (upd.)
Massey Energy Company, 57
MasTec, Inc., 19; 55 (upd.)
Master Lock Company, 45
MasterBrand Cabinets, Inc., 71
MasterCard Worldwide, 9; 96 (upd.)
MasterCraft Boat Company, Inc., 90
Match.com, LP, 87
Material Sciences Corporation, 63
The MathWorks, Inc., 80
Matria Healthcare, Inc., 17
Matrix Essentials Inc., 90
Matrix Service Company, 65
Matrixx Initiatives, Inc., 74
Matt Prentice Restaurant Group, 70
Mattel, Inc., 7; 25 (upd.); 61 (upd.)
Matthews International Corporation, 29; 77 (upd.)
Maui Land & Pineapple Company, Inc., 29
Maui Wowi, Inc., 85
Mauna Loa Macadamia Nut Corporation, 64
Maurices Inc., 95
Maverick Ranch Association, Inc., 88
Maverick Tube Corporation, 59
Max & Erma's Restaurants Inc., 19
Maxco Inc., 17
Maxicare Health Plans, Inc., III; 25 (upd.)
The Maxim Group, 25

Maxim Integrated Products, Inc., 16
MAXIMUS, Inc., 43
Maxtor Corporation, 10
Maxus Energy Corporation, 7
Maxwell Shoe Company, Inc., 30
MAXXAM Inc., 8
Maxxim Medical Inc., 12
The May Department Stores Company, V;
    19 (upd.); 46 (upd.)
Mayer, Brown, Rowe & Maw, 47
Mayfield Dairy Farms, Inc., 74
Mayflower Group Inc., 6
Mayo Foundation, 9; 34 (upd.)
Mayor's Jewelers, Inc., 41
Maytag Corporation, III; 22 (upd.); 82
    (upd.)
Mazel Stores, Inc., 29
Mazzio's Corporation, 76
MBC Holding Company, 40
MBIA Inc., 73
MBNA Corporation, 12; 33 (upd.)
MCA Inc., II
McAfee Inc., 94
McAlister's Corporation, 66
McCarthy Building Companies, Inc., 48
McCaw Cellular Communications, Inc., 6
McClain Industries, Inc., 51
The McClatchy Company, 33; 92 (upd.)
McCormick & Company, Incorporated, 7;
    27 (upd.)
McCormick & Schmick's Seafood
    Restaurants, Inc., 71
McCoy Corporation, 58
McDATA Corporation, 75
McDermott International, Inc., III; 37
    (upd.)
McDonald's Corporation, II; 7 (upd.); 26
    (upd.); 63 (upd.)
McDonnell Douglas Corporation, I; 11
    (upd.)
McGrath RentCorp, 91
The McGraw-Hill Companies, Inc., IV;
    18 (upd.); 51 (upd.)
MCI WorldCom, Inc., V; 27 (upd.)
McIlhenny Company, 20
McJunkin Corporation, 63
McKee Foods Corporation, 7; 27 (upd.)
McKesson Corporation, I; 12; 47 (upd.)
McKinsey & Company, Inc., 9
McLane Company, Inc., 13
McLeodUSA Incorporated, 32
McMenamins Pubs and Breweries, 65
McNaughton Apparel Group, Inc., 92
    (upd.)
MCN Corporation, 6
MCSi, Inc., 41
McWane Corporation, 55
MDU Resources Group, Inc., 7; 42 (upd.)
The Mead Corporation, IV; 19 (upd.)
Mead Data Central, Inc., 10
Mead Johnson & Company, 84
Meade Instruments Corporation, 41
Meadowcraft, Inc., 29
MeadWestvaco Corporation, 76 (upd.)
Measurement Specialties, Inc., 71
Mecklermedia Corporation, 24
Medarex, Inc., 85
Medco Containment Services Inc., 9

MEDecision, Inc., 95
Media Arts Group, Inc., 42
Media General, Inc., 7; 38 (upd.)
Mediacom Communications Corporation,
    69
MediaNews Group, Inc., 70
Medical Information Technology Inc., 64
Medical Management International, Inc.,
    65
Medical Staffing Network Holdings, Inc.,
    89
Medicis Pharmaceutical Corporation, 59
Medifast, Inc., 97
MedImmune, Inc., 35
Medis Technologies Ltd., 77
Meditrust, 11
Medline Industries, Inc., 61
Medtronic, Inc., 8; 30 (upd.); 67 (upd.)
Medusa Corporation, 24
Megafoods Stores Inc., 13
Meguiar's, Inc., 99
Meier & Frank Co., 23
Meijer Incorporated, 7; 27 (upd.)
Mel Farr Automotive Group, 20
Melaleuca Inc., 31
Melamine Chemicals, Inc., 27
Mellon Bank Corporation, II
Mellon Financial Corporation, 44 (upd.)
Mellon-Stuart Company, I
The Melting Pot Restaurants, Inc., 74
Melville Corporation, V
Melvin Simon and Associates, Inc., 8
MEMC Electronic Materials, Inc., 81
Memorial Sloan-Kettering Cancer Center,
    57
Memry Corporation, 72
The Men's Wearhouse, Inc., 17; 48 (upd.)
Menard, Inc., 34
Menasha Corporation, 8; 59 (upd.)
Mendocino Brewing Company, Inc., 60
The Mentholatum Company Inc., 32
Mentor Corporation, 26
Mentor Graphics Corporation, 11
Mercantile Bankshares Corp., 11
Mercantile Stores Company, Inc., V; 19
    (upd.)
Mercer International Inc., 64
Merck & Co., Inc., I; 11 (upd.); 34
    (upd.); 95 (upd.)
Mercury Air Group, Inc., 20
Mercury General Corporation, 25
Mercury Interactive Corporation, 59
Mercury Marine Group, 68
Meredith Corporation, 11; 29 (upd.); 74
    (upd.)
Merge Healthcare, 85
Meridian Bancorp, Inc., 11
Meridian Gold, Incorporated, 47
Merillat Industries Inc., 13
Merillat Industries, LLC, 69 (upd.)
Merisant Worldwide, Inc., 70
Merisel, Inc., 12
Merit Medical Systems, Inc., 29
MeritCare Health System, 88
Meritage Corporation, 26
Merix Corporation, 36; 75 (upd.)
Merrell Dow, Inc., I; 9 (upd.)
Merriam-Webster Inc., 70

Merrill Corporation, 18; 47 (upd.)
Merrill Lynch & Co., Inc., II; 13 (upd.);
    40 (upd.)
Merry-Go-Round Enterprises, Inc., 8
Mervyn's California, 10; 39 (upd.)
Mesa Air Group, Inc., 11; 32 (upd.); 77
    (upd.)
Mesaba Holdings, Inc., 28
Mestek Inc., 10
Metal Management, Inc., 92
Metalico Inc., 97
Metatec International, Inc., 47
Meteor Industries Inc., 33
Methode Electronics, Inc., 13
Metris Companies Inc., 56
Metro Information Services, Inc., 36
Metro-Goldwyn-Mayer Inc., 25 (upd.); 84
    (upd.)
Metrocall, Inc., 41
Metromedia Company, 7; 14; 61 (upd.)
Metropolitan Baseball Club Inc., 39
Metropolitan Financial Corporation, 13
Metropolitan Life Insurance Company,
    III; 52 (upd.)
The Metropolitan Museum of Art, 55
Metropolitan Opera Association, Inc., 40
Metropolitan Transportation Authority, 35
Mexican Restaurants, Inc., 41
MFS Communications Company, Inc., 11
MGA Entertainment, Inc., 95
MGIC Investment Corp., 52
MGM MIRAGE, 17; 98 (upd.)
MGM/UA Communications Company, II
Miami Herald Media Company, 92
Michael Anthony Jewelers, Inc., 24
Michael Baker Corporation, 14; 51 (upd.)
Michael C. Fina Co., Inc., 52
Michael Foods, Inc., 25
Michaels Stores, Inc., 17; 71 (upd.)
Michigan Bell Telephone Co., 14
Michigan National Corporation, 11
Michigan Sporting Goods Distributors,
    Inc., 72
Micrel, Incorporated, 77
Micro Warehouse, Inc., 16
MicroAge, Inc., 16
Microdot Inc., 8
Micron Technology, Inc., 11; 29 (upd.)
Micros Systems, Inc., 18
Microsemi Corporation, 94
Microsoft Corporation, 6; 27 (upd.); 63
    (upd.)
MicroStrategy Incorporated, 87
Mid-America Apartment Communities,
    Inc., 85
Mid-America Dairymen, Inc., 7
Midas Inc., 10; 56 (upd.)
The Middleby Corporation, 22
Middlesex Water Company, 45
The Middleton Doll Company, 53
The Midland Company, 65
Midway Airlines Corporation, 33
Midway Games, Inc., 25
Midwest Air Group, Inc., 35; 85 (upd.)
Midwest Grain Products, Inc., 49
Midwest Resources Inc., 6
Mikasa, Inc., 28
Mike-Sell's Inc., 15

Mikohn Gaming Corporation, 39
Milacron, Inc., 53 (upd.)
Milbank, Tweed, Hadley & McCloy, 27
Miles Laboratories, I
Millennium Pharmaceuticals, Inc., 47
Miller Brewing Company, I; 12 (upd.)
Miller Industries, Inc., 26
Miller Publishing Group, LLC, 57
Milliken & Co., V; 17 (upd.); 82 (upd.)
Milliman USA, 66
Millipore Corporation, 25; 84 (upd.)
The Mills Corporation, 77
Milnot Company, 46
Milton Bradley Company, 21
Milton CAT, Inc., 86
Milwaukee Brewers Baseball Club, 37
Mine Safety Appliances Company, 31
The Miner Group International, 22
Minerals Technologies Inc., 11; 52 (upd.)
Minnesota Mining & Manufacturing
    Company (3M), I; 8 (upd.); 26 (upd.)
Minnesota Power, Inc., 11; 34 (upd.)
Minntech Corporation, 22
The Minute Maid Company, 28
Minuteman International Inc., 46
Minyard Food Stores, Inc., 33; 86 (upd.)
Mirage Resorts, Incorporated, 6; 28 (upd.)
Miramax Film Corporation, 64
Mirant Corporation, 98
Misonix, Inc., 80
Mississippi Chemical Corporation, 39
Mitchell Energy and Development
    Corporation, 7
MITRE Corporation, 26
Mity Enterprises, Inc., 38
MIVA, Inc., 83
MNS, Ltd., 65
Mobil Corporation, IV; 7 (upd.); 21
    (upd.)
Mobile Mini, Inc., 58
Mobile Telecommunications Technologies
    Corp., 18
Mocon, Inc., 76
Modern Woodmen of America, 66
Modine Manufacturing Company, 8; 56
    (upd.)
Modtech Holdings, Inc., 77
Moen Incorporated, 12
Mohawk Industries, Inc., 19; 63 (upd.)
Mohegan Tribal Gaming Authority, 37
Moldflow Corporation, 73
Molex Incorporated, 11; 54 (upd.)
Molson Coors Brewing Company, 77
    (upd.)
Monaco Coach Corporation, 31
Monadnock Paper Mills, Inc., 21
Monarch Casino & Resort, Inc., 65
The Monarch Cement Company, 72
MoneyGram International, Inc., 94
Monfort, Inc., 13
Monro Muffler Brake, Inc., 24
Monrovia Nursery Company, 70
The Mosaic Company, 91
Monsanto Company, I; 9 (upd.); 29
    (upd.); 77 (upd.)
Monster Cable Products, Inc., 69
Monster Worldwide Inc., 74 (upd.)
Montana Coffee Traders, Inc., 60

The Montana Power Company, 11; 44
    (upd.)
Monterey Pasta Company, 58
Montgomery Ward & Co., Incorporated,
    V; 20 (upd.)
Moody's Corporation, 65
Moog Inc., 13
Moog Music, Inc., 75
Mooney Aerospace Group Ltd., 52
Moore Medical Corp., 17
Moore-Handley, Inc., 39
Moran Towing Corporation, Inc., 15
The Morgan Group, Inc., 46
Morgan, Lewis & Bockius LLP, 29
Morgan Stanley Dean Witter &
    Company, II; 16 (upd.); 33 (upd.)
Morgans Hotel Group Company, 80
Morinda Holdings, Inc., 82
Morningstar Inc., 68
Morris Communications Corporation, 36
Morris Travel Services L.L.C., 26
Morrison & Foerster LLP 78
Morrison Knudsen Corporation, 7; 28
    (upd.)
Morrison Restaurants Inc., 11
Morrow Equipment Co. L.L.C., 87
Morse Shoe Inc., 13
Morton International Inc., I; 9 (upd.); 80
    (upd.)
Morton Thiokol, Inc., I
Morton's Restaurant Group, Inc., 30; 88
    (upd.)
Mosinee Paper Corporation, 15
Mossimo, 27; 96 (upd.)
Motel 6, 13; 56 (upd.)
Mothers Against Drunk Driving
    (MADD), 51
Mothers Work, Inc., 18
The Motley Fool, Inc., 40
Moto Photo, Inc., 45
Motor Cargo Industries, Inc., 35
Motorcar Parts & Accessories, Inc., 47
Motorola, Inc., II; 11 (upd.); 34 (upd.);
    93 (upd.)
Motown Records Company L.P., 26
Mott's Inc., 57
Mountain States Mortgage Centers, Inc.,
    29
Movado Group, Inc., 28
Movie Gallery, Inc., 31
Movie Star Inc., 17
MPS Group, Inc., 49
MPW Industrial Services Group, Inc., 53
Mr. Coffee, Inc., 15
Mr. Gasket Inc., 15
Mr. Gatti's, LP, 87
Mrs. Baird's Bakeries, 29
Mrs. Fields' Original Cookies, Inc., 27
Mrs. Grossman's Paper Company Inc., 84
MSC Industrial Direct Co., Inc., 71
Mt. Olive Pickle Company, Inc., 44
MTR Gaming Group, Inc., 75
MTS Inc., 37
Mueller Industries, Inc., 7; 52 (upd.)
Mullen Advertising Inc., 51
Multi-Color Corporation, 53
Multimedia Games, Inc., 41
Multimedia, Inc., 11

Murdock Madaus Schwabe, 26
Murphy Family Farms Inc., 22
Murphy Oil Corporation, 7; 32 (upd.);
    95 (upd.)
The Musco Family Olive Co., 91
Musco Lighting, 83
Musicland Stores Corporation, 9; 38
    (upd.)
The Mutual Benefit Life Insurance
    Company, III
The Mutual Life Insurance Company of
    New York, III
The Mutual of Omaha Companies, 98
Muzak, Inc., 18
MWH Preservation Limited Partnership,
    65
MWI Veterinary Supply, Inc., 80
Mycogen Corporation, 21
Myers Industries, Inc., 19; 96 (upd.
Mylan Laboratories Inc., I; 20 (upd.); 59
    (upd.)
Myriad Restaurant Group, Inc., 87
Myriad Genetics, Inc., 95
N.F. Smith & Associates LP, 70
Nabisco Foods Group, II; 7 (upd.)
Nabors Industries, Inc., 9
NACCO Industries Inc., 7; 78 (upd.)
Nalco Holding Company, I; 12 (upd.); 89
    (upd.)
Nantucket Allserve, Inc., 22
Napster, Inc., 69
NASD, 54 (upd.)
The NASDAQ Stock Market, Inc., 92
Nash Finch Company, 8; 23 (upd.); 65
    (upd.)
Nashua Corporation, 8
Nastech Pharmaceutical Company Inc. 79
Nathan's Famous, Inc., 29
National Amusements Inc., 28
National Aquarium in Baltimore, Inc., 74
National Association for Stock Car Auto
    Racing, 32
National Association of Securities Dealers,
    Inc., 10
National Audubon Society, 26
National Auto Credit, Inc., 16
The National Bank of South Carolina, 76
National Beverage Corporation, 26; 88
    (upd.)
National Broadcasting Company, Inc., II;
    6 (upd.); 28 (upd.)
National Can Corporation, I
National Car Rental System, Inc., 10
National City Corporation, 15; 97 (upd.)
National Collegiate Athletic Association,
    96
National Convenience Stores
    Incorporated, 7
National Discount Brokers Group, Inc.,
    28
National Distillers and Chemical
    Corporation, I
National Educational Music Co. Ltd., 47
National Envelope Corporation, 32
National Equipment Services, Inc., 57
National Financial Partners Corp., 65
National Football League, 29
National Frozen Foods Corporation, 94

National Fuel Gas Company, 6; 95 (upd.)
National Geographic Society, 9; 30 (upd.); 79 (upd.)
National Grape Cooperative Association, Inc., 20
National Grid USA, 51 (upd.)
National Gypsum Company, 10
National Health Laboratories Incorporated, 11
National Heritage Academies, Inc., 60
National Hockey League, 35
National Home Centers, Inc., 44
National Instruments Corporation, 22
National Intergroup, Inc., V
National Journal Group Inc., 67
National Media Corporation, 27
National Medical Enterprises, Inc., III
National Medical Health Card Systems, Inc. 79
National Oilwell, Inc., 54
National Organization for Women, Inc., 55
National Patent Development Corporation, 13
National Picture & Frame Company, 24
National Presto Industries, Inc., 16; 43 (upd.)
National Public Radio, Inc., 19; 47 (upd.)
National R.V. Holdings, Inc., 32
National Railroad Passenger Corporation (Amtrak), 22; 66 (upd.)
National Record Mart, Inc., 29
National Research Corporation, 87
National Rifle Association of America, 37
National Sanitary Supply Co., 16
National Semiconductor Corporation, II; VI, 26 (upd.); 69 (upd.)
National Service Industries, Inc., 11; 54 (upd.)
National Standard Co., 13
National Starch and Chemical Company, 49
National Steel Corporation, 12
National TechTeam, Inc., 41
National Thoroughbred Racing Association, 58
National Weather Service, 91
National Wine & Spirits, Inc., 49
NationsBank Corporation, 10
Natrol, Inc., 49
Natural Alternatives International, Inc., 49
Natural Ovens Bakery, Inc., 72
Natural Selection Foods, 54
Natural Wonders Inc., 14
Naturally Fresh, Inc., 88
The Nature Conservancy, 28
Nature's Sunshine Products, Inc., 15
Naumes, Inc., 81
Nautica Enterprises, Inc., 18; 44 (upd.)
Navarre Corporation, 24
Navigant Consulting, Inc., 93
Navigant International, Inc., 47
The Navigators Group, Inc., 92
Navistar International Corporation, I; 10 (upd.)
NAVTEQ Corporation, 69
Navy Exchange Service Command, 31
Navy Federal Credit Union, 33

NBD Bancorp, Inc., 11
NBGS International, Inc., 73
NBTY, Inc., 31
NCH Corporation, 8
NCI Building Systems, Inc., 88
NCL Corporation 79
NCNB Corporation, II
NCO Group, Inc., 42
NCR Corporation, III; 6 (upd.); 30 (upd.); 90 (upd.)
Nebraska Book Company, Inc., 65
Nebraska Furniture Mart, Inc., 94
Nebraska Public Power District, 29
Neenah Foundry Company, 68
Neff Corp., 32
NeighborCare, Inc., 67 (upd.)
The Neiman Marcus Group, Inc., 12; 49 (upd.)
Nektar Therapeutics, 91
Neogen Corporation, 94
NERCO, Inc., 7
NetCracker Technology Corporation, 98
Netezza Corporation, 69
Netflix, Inc., 58
NETGEAR, Inc., 81
NetIQ Corporation 79
NetJets Inc., 96 (upd.)
Netscape Communications Corporation, 15; 35 (upd.)
Network Appliance, Inc., 58
Network Associates, Inc., 25
Network Equipment Technologies Inc., 92
Neuberger Berman Inc., 57
NeuStar, Inc., 81
Neutrogena Corporation, 17
Nevada Bell Telephone Company, 14
Nevada Power Company, 11
Nevamar Company, 82
New Balance Athletic Shoe, Inc., 25; 68 (upd.)
New Belgium Brewing Company, Inc., 68
New Brunswick Scientific Co., Inc., 45
New Chapter Inc., 96
New Dana Perfumes Company, 37
New England Business Service Inc., 18; 78 (upd.)
New England Confectionery Co., 15
New England Electric System, V
New England Mutual Life Insurance Company, III
New Jersey Devils, 84
New Jersey Manufacturers Insurance Company, 96
New Jersey Resources Corporation, 54
New Line Cinema, Inc., 47
New Orleans Saints LP, 58
The New Piper Aircraft, Inc., 44
New Plan Realty Trust, 11
New Seasons Market, 75
New Street Capital Inc., 8
New Times, Inc., 45
New Valley Corporation, 17
New World Pasta Company, 53
New World Restaurant Group, Inc., 44
New York City Health and Hospitals Corporation, 60
New York City Off-Track Betting Corporation, 51

New York Community Bancorp Inc. 78
New York Daily News, 32
New York Health Care, Inc., 72
New York Life Insurance Company, III; 45 (upd.)
New York Restaurant Group, Inc., 32
New York Shakespeare Festival Management, 93
New York State Electric and Gas, 6
New York Stock Exchange, Inc., 9; 39 (upd.)
The New York Times Company, IV; 19 (upd.); 61 (upd.)
Neways Inc. 78
Newcor, Inc., 40
Newell Rubbermaid Inc., 9; 52 (upd.)
Newfield Exploration Company, 65
Newhall Land and Farming Company, 14
Newly Weds Foods, Inc., 74
Newman's Own, Inc., 37
Newmont Mining Corporation, 7; 94 (upd.)
Newpark Resources, Inc., 63
Newport Corporation, 71
Newport News Shipbuilding Inc., 13; 38 (upd.)
News America Publishing Inc., 12
NewYork-Presbyterian Hospital, 59
Nexstar Broadcasting Group, Inc., 73
Nextel Communications, Inc., 10; 27 (upd.)
NFL Films, 75
NFO Worldwide, Inc., 24
NGC Corporation, 18
Niagara Corporation, 28
Niagara Mohawk Holdings Inc., V; 45 (upd.)
Nichols Research Corporation, 18
Nicklaus Companies, 45
Nicole Miller, 98
Nicor Inc., 6; 86 (upd.)
Nielsen Business Media, Inc., 98
NIKE, Inc., V; 8 (upd.); 36 (upd.); 75 (upd.)
Nikken Global Inc., 32
Niman Ranch, Inc., 67
Nimbus CD International, Inc., 20
Nine West Group, Inc., 11; 39 (upd.)
99¢ Only Stores, 25
NIPSCO Industries, Inc., 6
Nitches, Inc., 53
NL Industries, Inc., 10
Nobel Learning Communities, Inc., 37; 76 (upd.)
Noble Affiliates, Inc., 11
Noble Roman's Inc., 14; 99 (upd.)
Noland Company, 35
Nolo.com, Inc., 49
Noodle Kidoodle, 16
Noodles & Company, Inc., 55
Nooter Corporation, 61
Norcal Waste Systems, Inc., 60
NordicTrack, 22
Nordson Corporation, 11; 48 (upd.)
Nordstrom, Inc., V; 18 (upd.); 67 (upd.)
Norelco Consumer Products Co., 26
Norfolk Southern Corporation, V; 29 (upd.); 75 (upd.)

Norm Thompson Outfitters, Inc., 47
Norrell Corporation, 25
Norstan, Inc., 16
Nortek, Inc., 34
North American Galvanizing & Coatings, Inc., 99
North Atlantic Trading Company Inc., 65
The North Face, Inc., 18; 78 (upd.)
North Fork Bancorporation, Inc., 46
North Pacific Group, Inc., 61
North Star Steel Company, 18
Northeast Utilities, V; 48 (upd.)
Northern States Power Company, V; 20 (upd.)
Northern Trust Company, 9
Northland Cranberries, Inc., 38
Northrop Grumman Corporation, I; 11 (upd.); 45 (upd.)
Northwest Airlines Corporation, I; 6 (upd.); 26 (upd.); 74 (upd.)
Northwest Natural Gas Company, 45
NorthWestern Corporation, 37
Northwestern Mutual Life Insurance Company, III; 45 (upd.)
Norton Company, 8
Norton McNaughton, Inc., 27
Norwood Promotional Products, Inc., 26
NovaCare, Inc., 11
NovaStar Financial, Inc., 91
Novell, Inc., 6; 23 (upd.)
Novellus Systems, Inc., 18
Noven Pharmaceuticals, Inc., 55
NPC International, Inc., 40
The NPD Group, Inc., 68
NRG Energy, Inc. 79
NRT Incorporated, 61
NSF International, 72
NSS Enterprises Inc. 78
NTN Buzztime, Inc., 86
Nu Skin Enterprises, Inc., 27; 76 (upd.)
Nu-kote Holding, Inc., 18
Nucor Corporation, 7; 21 (upd.); 79 (upd.)
Nutraceutical International Corporation, 37
NutraSweet Company, 8
Nutrition 21 Inc., 97
NutriSystem, Inc., 71
Nutrition for Life International Inc., 22
NVIDIA Corporation, 54
NVR Inc., 8; 70 (upd.)
NYMAGIC, Inc., 41
NYNEX Corporation, V
O.C. Tanner Co., 69
Oak Harbor Freight Lines, Inc., 53
Oak Industries Inc., 21
Oak Technology, Inc., 22
Oakhurst Dairy, 60
Oakleaf Waste Management, LLC, 97
Oakley, Inc., 18; 49 (upd.)
Oaktree Capital Management, LLC, 71
Oakwood Homes Corporation, 15
Obagi Medical Products, Inc., 95
Oberto Sausage Company, Inc., 92
Obie Media Corporation, 56
Occidental Petroleum Corporation, IV; 25 (upd.); 71 (upd.)
Ocean Beauty Seafoods, Inc., 74

Ocean Spray Cranberries, Inc., 7; 25 (upd.); 83 (upd.)
Oceaneering International, Inc., 63
O'Charley's Inc., 19; 60 (upd.)
OCLC Online Computer Library Center, Inc., 96
Octel Messaging, 14; 41 (upd.)
Ocular Sciences, Inc., 65
Odetics Inc., 14
ODL, Inc., 55
Odwalla, Inc., 31
Odyssey Marine Exploration, Inc., 91
OEC Medical Systems, Inc., 27
Office Depot, Inc., 8; 23 (upd.); 65 (upd.)
OfficeMax, Inc., 15; 43 (upd.)
OfficeTiger, LLC, 75
Offshore Logistics, Inc., 37
Ogden Corporation, I; 6
The Ogilvy Group, Inc., I
Oglebay Norton Company, 17
Oglethorpe Power Corporation, 6
The Ohio Art Company, 14; 59 (upd.)
Ohio Bell Telephone Company, 14
Ohio Casualty Corp., 11
Ohio Edison Company, V
Oil-Dri Corporation of America, 20; 89 (upd.)
Oil States International, Inc., 77
The Oilgear Company, 74
Oklahoma Gas and Electric Company, 6
Olan Mills, Inc., 62
Old America Stores, Inc., 17
Old Dominion Freight Line, Inc., 57
Old Kent Financial Corp., 11
Old National Bancorp, 15; 98 (upd.)
Old Navy, Inc., 70
Old Orchard Brands, LLC, 73
Old Republic International Corporation, 11; 58 (upd.)
Old Spaghetti Factory International Inc., 24
Old Town Canoe Company, 74
Olga's Kitchen, Inc., 80
Olin Corporation, I; 13 (upd.); 78 (upd.)
Olsten Corporation, 6; 29 (upd.)
OM Group Inc. 17; 78 (upd.)
Omaha Steaks International Inc., 62
Omega Protein Corporation, 99
O'Melveny & Myers, 37
OMI Corporation, 59
Omni Hotels Corp., 12
Omnicare, Inc., 49
Omnicell, Inc., 89
Omnicom Group, Inc., I; 22 (upd.); 77 (upd.)
OmniSource Corporation, 14
OMNOVA Solutions Inc., 59
Omrix Biopharmaceuticals, Inc., 95
On Assignment, Inc., 20
180s, L.L.C., 64
One Price Clothing Stores, Inc., 20
1-800-FLOWERS, Inc., 26
O'Neal Steel, Inc., 95
Oneida Ltd., 7; 31 (upd.); 88 (upd.)
ONEOK Inc., 7
Onion, Inc., 69
Onyx Acceptance Corporation, 59

Onyx Software Corporation, 53
OOC Inc., 97
Openwave Systems Inc., 95
Operation Smile, Inc., 75
Opinion Research Corporation, 46
Oppenheimer Wolff & Donnelly LLP, 71
Opsware Inc., 49
OPTEK Technology Inc., 98
Option Care Inc., 48
Opus Group, 34
Oracle Corporation, 6; 24 (upd.); 67 (upd.)
Orange Glo International, 53
OraSure Technologies, Inc., 75
Orbital Sciences Corporation, 22
Orbitz, Inc., 61
Orchard Supply Hardware Stores Corporation, 17
Ore-Ida Foods Inc., 13; 78 (upd.)
Oregon Chai, Inc., 49
Oregon Dental Service Health Plan, Inc., 51
Oregon Freeze Dry, Inc., 74
Oregon Metallurgical Corporation, 20
Oregon Steel Mills, Inc., 14
O'Reilly Automotive, Inc., 26; 78 (upd.)
O'Reilly Media, Inc., 99
Organic To Go Food Corporation, 99
Organic Valley (Coulee Region Organic Produce Pool), 53
Orgill, Inc., 99
Orion Pictures Corporation, 6
Orleans Homebuilders, Inc., 62
Ormat Technologies, Inc., 87
Ormet Corporation, 82
Orrick, Herrington and Sutcliffe LLP, 76
Orthodontic Centers of America, Inc., 35
The Orvis Company, Inc., 28
Oryx Energy Company, 7
Oscar Mayer Foods Corp., 12
OshKosh B'Gosh, Inc., 9; 42 (upd.)
Oshkosh Corporation, 7; 98 (upd.)
Oshman's Sporting Goods, Inc., 17
OSI Restaurant Partners, Inc., 88 (upd.)
Osmonics, Inc., 18
O'Sullivan Industries Holdings, Inc., 34
Otis Elevator Company, Inc., 13; 39 (upd.)
Otis Spunkmeyer, Inc., 28
OTR Express, Inc., 25
Ottaway Newspapers, Inc., 15
Otter Tail Power Company, 18
Outback Steakhouse, Inc., 12; 34 (upd.)
Outboard Marine Corporation, III; 20 (upd.)
Outdoor Research, Incorporated, 67
Outdoor Systems, Inc., 25
Outlook Group Corporation, 37
Outrigger Enterprises, Inc., 67
Overhead Door Corporation, 70
Overhill Corporation, 51
Overnite Corporation, 14; 58 (upd.)
Overseas Shipholding Group, Inc., 11
Overstock.com, Inc., 75
Owens & Minor, Inc., 16; 68 (upd.)
Owens Corning, III; 20 (upd.); 98 (upd.)
Owens-Illinois, Inc., I; 26 (upd.); 85 (upd.)

Owosso Corporation, 29
Oxford Health Plans, Inc., 16
Oxford Industries, Inc., 8; 84 (upd.)
P&C Foods Inc., 8
P & F Industries, Inc., 45
P.C. Richard & Son Corp., 23
P.F. Chang's China Bistro, Inc., 37; 86 (upd.)
P.H. Glatfelter Company, 8; 30 (upd.); 83 (upd.)
Paccar Inc., I; 26 (upd.)
Pacer International, Inc., 54
Pacer Technology, 40
Pacific Clay Products Inc., 88
Pacific Coast Building Products, Inc., 94
Pacific Coast Feather Company, 67
Pacific Coast Restaurants, Inc., 90
Pacific Ethanol, Inc., 81
Pacific Enterprises, V
Pacific Gas and Electric Company, V
Pacific Mutual Holding Company, 98
Pacific Sunwear of California, Inc., 28
Pacific Telecom, Inc., 6
Pacific Telesis Group, V
PacifiCare Health Systems, Inc., 11
PacifiCorp, V; 26 (upd.)
Packaging Corporation of America, 12; 51 (upd.)
Packard Bell Electronics, Inc., 13
Packeteer, Inc., 81
Paddock Publications, Inc., 53
Paging Network Inc., 11
PaineWebber Group Inc., II; 22 (upd.)
Palace Sports & Entertainment, Inc., 97
Pall Corporation, 9; 72 (upd.)
Palm Harbor Homes, Inc., 39
Palm Management Corporation, 71
Palm, Inc., 36; 75 (upd.)
Palmer & Cay, Inc., 69
Palmer Candy Company, 80
Palomar Medical Technologies, Inc., 22
Pamida Holdings Corporation, 15
The Pampered Chef, Ltd., 18; 78 (upd.)
Pan American World Airways, Inc., I; 12 (upd.)
Pan-American Life Insurance Company, 48
Panamerican Beverages, Inc., 47
PanAmSat Corporation, 46
Panattoni Development Company, Inc., 99
Panavision Inc., 24
Pancho's Mexican Buffet, Inc., 46
Panda Restaurant Group, Inc., 35; 97 (upd.)
Panera Bread Company, 44
Panhandle Eastern Corporation, V
Pantone Inc., 53
The Pantry, Inc., 36
Papa Gino's Holdings Corporation, Inc., 86
Papa John's International, Inc., 15; 71 (upd.)
Papa Murphy's International, Inc., 54
Papetti's Hygrade Egg Products, Inc., 39
Pappas Restaurants, Inc., 76
Par Pharmaceutical Companies, Inc., 65
The Paradies Shops, Inc., 88

Paradise Music & Entertainment, Inc., 42
Parametric Technology Corp., 16
Paramount Pictures Corporation, II; 94 (upd.)
PAREXEL International Corporation, 84
Paris Corporation, 22
Parisian, Inc., 14
Park Corp., 22
Park-Ohio Industries Inc., 17; 85 (upd.)
Parker Drilling Company, 28
Parker-Hannifin Corporation, III; 24 (upd.); 99 (upd.)
Parlex Corporation, 61
Parsons Brinckerhoff, Inc., 34
The Parsons Corporation, 8; 56 (upd.)
Party City Corporation, 54
Pathmark Stores, Inc., 23
Patina Oil & Gas Corporation, 24
Patrick Industries, Inc., 30
Patriot Transportation Holding, Inc., 91
Patterson Dental Co., 19
Patterson-UTI Energy, Inc., 55
Patton Boggs LLP, 71
Paul Harris Stores, Inc., 18
Paul, Hastings, Janofsky & Walker LLP, 27
Paul Mueller Company, 65
Paul Reed Smith Guitar Company, 89
The Paul Revere Corporation, 12
Paul, Weiss, Rifkind, Wharton & Garrison, 47
Paul-Son Gaming Corporation, 66
Paxson Communications Corporation, 33
Pay 'N Pak Stores, Inc., 9
Paychex, Inc., 15; 46 (upd.)
Payless Cashways, Inc., 11; 44 (upd.)
Payless ShoeSource, Inc., 18; 69 (upd.)
PayPal Inc., 58
The PBSJ Corporation, 82
PC Connection, Inc., 37
PCA International, Inc., 62
PCC Natural Markets, 94
PDI, Inc., 52
PDL BioPharma, Inc., 90
PDQ Food Stores, Inc. 79
PDS Gaming Corporation, 44
Peabody Coal Company, 10
Peabody Energy Corporation, 45 (upd.)
Peabody Holding Company, Inc., IV
The Peak Technologies Group, Inc., 14
Peapod, Inc., 30
Pearle Vision, Inc., 13
Peavey Electronics Corporation, 16; 94 (upd.)
PECO Energy Company, 11
Pediatric Services of America, Inc., 31
Pediatrix Medical Group, Inc., 61
Peebles Inc., 16; 43 (upd.)
Peet's Coffee & Tea, Inc., 38
Pegasus Solutions, Inc., 75
Pei Cobb Freed & Partners Architects LLP, 57
Pelican Products, Inc., 86
Pella Corporation, 12; 39 (upd.); 89 (upd.)
Pemco Aviation Group Inc., 54
Pendleton Grain Growers Inc., 64
Pendleton Woolen Mills, Inc., 42

Penford Corporation, 55
Penn Engineering & Manufacturing Corp., 28
Penn National Gaming, Inc., 33
Penn Traffic Company, 13
Penn Virginia Corporation, 85
Pennington Seed Inc., 98
Pennsylvania Blue Shield, III
Pennsylvania Power & Light Company, V
Pennwalt Corporation, I
PennWell Corporation, 55
Pennzoil-Quaker State Company, IV; 20 (upd.); 50 (upd.)
Penske Corporation, V; 19 (upd.); 84 (upd.)
Pentair, Inc., 7; 26 (upd.); 81 (upd.)
Pentech International, Inc., 29
Penton Media, Inc., 27
Penzeys Spices, Inc. 79
People Express Airlines, Inc., I
Peoples Energy Corporation, 6
PeopleSoft Inc., 14; 33 (upd.)
The Pep Boys—Manny, Moe & Jack, 11; 36 (upd.); 81 (upd.)
Pepper Hamilton LLP, 43
Pepperidge Farm, Incorporated, 81
The Pepsi Bottling Group, Inc., 40
PepsiAmericas, Inc., 67 (upd.)
PepsiCo, Inc., I; 10 (upd.); 38 (upd.); 93 (upd.)
Perma-Fix Environmental Services, Inc., 99
Perdue Farms Inc., 7; 23 (upd.)
Performance Food Group, 31; 96 (upd.)
Perini Corporation, 8; 82 (upd.)
PerkinElmer Inc. 7; 78 (upd.)
Perkins Coie LLP, 56
Perkins Family Restaurants, L.P., 22
Perot Systems Corporation, 29
Perrigo Company, 12; 59 (upd.)
Perry Ellis International, Inc., 41
Perry's Ice Cream Company Inc., 90
The Perseus Books Group, 91
Pet Incorporated, 7
Petco Animal Supplies, Inc., 29; 74 (upd.)
Pete's Brewing Company, 22
Peter Kiewit Sons' Inc., 8
Peter Piper, Inc., 70
Peterbilt Motors Company, 89
Petersen Publishing Company, 21
Peterson American Corporation, 55
PetMed Express, Inc., 81
Petrie Stores Corporation, 8
Petrohawk Energy Corporation 79
Petroleum Helicopters, Inc., 35
Petrolite Corporation, 15
Petrossian Inc., 54
PETsMART, Inc., 14; 41 (upd.)
The Pew Charitable Trusts, 35
Pez Candy, Inc., 38
Pfizer Inc., I; 9 (upd.); 38 (upd.); 79 (upd.)
PFSweb, Inc., 73
PG&E Corporation, 26 (upd.)
Phar-Mor Inc., 12
Pharmacia & Upjohn Inc., I; 25 (upd.)
Pharmion Corporation, 91
Phat Fashions LLC, 49

Phelps Dodge Corporation, IV; 28 (upd.); 75 (upd.)
PHH Arval, V; 53 (upd.)
PHI, Inc., 80 (upd.)
Philadelphia Eagles, 37
Philadelphia Electric Company, V
Philadelphia Gas Works Company, 92
Philadelphia Media Holdings LLC, 92
Philadelphia Suburban Corporation, 39
Philharmonic-Symphony Society of New York, Inc. (New York Philharmonic), 69
Philip Morris Companies Inc., V; 18 (upd.); 44 (upd.)
Philip Services Corp., 73
Philips Electronics North America Corp., 13
Phillips, de Pury & Luxembourg, 49
Phillips Foods, Inc., 63; 90 (upd.)
Phillips International Inc. 78
Phillips Petroleum Company, IV; 40 (upd.)
Phillips-Van Heusen Corporation, 24
Phoenix Footwear Group, Inc., 70
The Phoenix Media/Communications Group, 91
PHP Healthcare Corporation, 22
PhyCor, Inc., 36
Physician Sales & Service, Inc., 14
Physio-Control International Corp., 18
Piccadilly Cafeterias, Inc., 19
PictureTel Corp., 10; 27 (upd.)
Piedmont Natural Gas Company, Inc., 27
Pier 1 Imports, Inc., 12; 34 (upd.); 95 (upd.)
Pierce Leahy Corporation, 24
Piercing Pagoda, Inc., 29
Piggly Wiggly Southern, Inc., 13
Pilgrim's Pride Corporation, 7; 23 (upd.); 90 (upd.
Pillowtex Corporation, 19; 41 (upd.)
The Pillsbury Company, II; 13 (upd.); 62 (upd.)
Pillsbury Madison & Sutro LLP, 29
Pilot Air Freight Corp., 67
Pilot Corporation, 49
Pilot Pen Corporation of America, 82
Pinkerton's Inc., 9
Pinnacle Airlines Corp., 73
Pinnacle West Capital Corporation, 6; 54 (upd.)
Pioneer Hi-Bred International, Inc., 9; 41 (upd.)
Pioneer Natural Resources Company, 59
Pioneer-Standard Electronics Inc., 19
Piper Jaffray Companies Inc., 22
Pitman Company, 58
Pitney Bowes Inc., III; 19; 47 (upd.)
Pittsburgh Brewing Company, 76
Pittsburgh Steelers Sports, Inc., 66
The Pittston Company, IV; 19 (upd.)
Pittway Corporation, 9; 33 (upd.)
Pixar Animation Studios, 34
Pixelworks, Inc., 69
Pizza Hut Inc., 7; 21 (upd.)
Pizza Inn, Inc., 46
Plain Dealer Publishing Company, 92
Plains Cotton Cooperative Association, 57

Planar Systems, Inc., 61
Planet Hollywood International, Inc., 18; 41 (upd.)
Plantation Pipe Line Company, 68
Plante & Moran, LLP, 71
Platinum Entertainment, Inc., 35
PLATINUM Technology, Inc., 14
Plato Learning, Inc., 44
Play by Play Toys & Novelties, Inc., 26
Playboy Enterprises, Inc., 18
PlayCore, Inc., 27
Players International, Inc., 22
Playskool, Inc., 25
Playtex Products, Inc., 15
Pleasant Company, 27
Pleasant Holidays LLC, 62
Plexus Corporation, 35; 80 (upd.)
Pliant Corporation, 98
Plum Creek Timber Company, Inc., 43
Pluma, Inc., 27
Ply Gem Industries Inc., 12
The PMI Group, Inc., 49
PMT Services, Inc., 24
The PNC Financial Services Group Inc., II; 13 (upd.); 46 (upd.)
PNM Resources Inc., 51 (upd.)
Pogo Producing Company, 39
Polar Air Cargo Inc., 60
Polaris Industries Inc., 12; 35 (upd.); 77 (upd.)
Polaroid Corporation, III; 7 (upd.); 28 (upd.); 93 (upd.)
Polartec LLC, 98 (upd.)
Policy Management Systems Corporation, 11
Policy Studies, Inc., 62
Polk Audio, Inc., 34
Polo/Ralph Lauren Corporation, 12; 62 (upd.)
PolyGram N.V., 23
PolyMedica Corporation, 77
PolyOne Corporation, 87 (upd.)
Pomare Ltd., 88
Pomeroy Computer Resources, Inc., 33
Ponderosa Steakhouse, 15
Poof-Slinky, Inc., 61
Poore Brothers, Inc., 44
Pop Warner Little Scholars, Inc., 86
Pope & Talbot, Inc., 12; 61 (upd.)
Pope Resources LP, 74
Popular, Inc., 41
The Port Authority of New York and New Jersey, 48
Port Imperial Ferry Corporation, 70
Portal Software, Inc., 47
Portillo's Restaurant Group, Inc., 71
Portland General Corporation, 6
Portland Trail Blazers, 50
Post Properties, Inc., 26
Potbelly Sandwich Works, Inc., 83
Potlatch Corporation, 8; 34 (upd.); 87 (upd.)
Potomac Electric Power Company, 6
Potter & Brumfield Inc., 11
Powell's Books, Inc., 40
Power-One, Inc. 79
PowerBar Inc., 44
Powerhouse Technologies, Inc., 27

POZEN Inc., 81
PPG Industries, Inc., III; 22 (upd.); 81 (upd.)
PPL Corporation, 41 (upd.)
PR Newswire, 35
Prairie Farms Dairy, Inc., 47
Pratt & Whitney, 9
Praxair, Inc., 11; 48 (upd.)
Praxis Bookstore Group LLC, 90
Pre-Paid Legal Services, Inc., 20
Precision Castparts Corp., 15
Premark International, Inc., III
Premcor Inc., 37
Premier Industrial Corporation, 9
Premier Parks, Inc., 27
Premium Standard Farms, Inc., 30
PremiumWear, Inc., 30
Preserver Group, Inc., 44
President Casinos, Inc., 22
Pressman Toy Corporation, 56
Presstek, Inc., 33
Preston Corporation, 6
PRG-Schultz International, Inc., 73
Price Communications Corporation, 42
The Price Company, V
Price Pfister, Inc., 70
PriceCostco, Inc., 14
Priceline.com Incorporated, 57
PriceSmart, Inc., 71
PricewaterhouseCoopers, 9; 29 (upd.)
Pride International Inc. 78
Primark Corp., 13
Prime Hospitality Corporation, 52
Primedex Health Systems, Inc., 25
Primedia Inc., 22
Primerica Corporation, I
Prince Sports Group, Inc., 15
Princess Cruise Lines, 22
The Princeton Review, Inc., 42
Principal Mutual Life Insurance Company, III
Printpack, Inc., 68
Printrak, A Motorola Company, 44
Printronix, Inc., 18
Prison Rehabilitative Industries and Diversified Enterprises, Inc. (PRIDE), 53
Pro-Build Holdings Inc., 95 (upd.)
The Procter & Gamble Company, III; 8 (upd.); 26 (upd.); 67 (upd.)
Prodigy Communications Corporation, 34
Professional Bull Riders Inc., 55
The Professional Golfers' Association of America, 41
Proffitt's, Inc., 19
Programmer's Paradise, Inc., 81
Progress Energy, Inc., 74
Progress Software Corporation, 15
The Progressive Corporation, 11; 29 (upd.)
ProLogis, 57
Promus Companies, Inc., 9
Proskauer Rose LLP, 47
Protection One, Inc., 32
Provell Inc., 58 (upd.)
Providence Health System, 90
The Providence Journal Company, 28
The Providence Service Corporation, 64

Provident Bankshares Corporation, 85
Provident Life and Accident Insurance
  Company of America, III
Providian Financial Corporation, 52
  (upd.)
Prudential Financial Inc., III; 30 (upd.);
  82 (upd.)
PSI Resources, 6
Psychemedics Corporation, 89
Psychiatric Solutions, Inc., 68
Pubco Corporation, 17
Public Service Company of Colorado, 6
Public Service Company of New
  Hampshire, 21; 55 (upd.)
Public Service Company of New Mexico,
  6
Public Service Enterprise Group Inc., V;
  44 (upd.)
Public Storage, Inc., 52
Publishers Clearing House, 23; 64 (upd.)
Publishers Group, Inc., 35
Publix Supermarkets Inc., 7; 31 (upd.)
Pueblo Xtra International, Inc., 47
Puget Sound Energy Inc., 6; 50 (upd.)
Pulaski Furniture Corporation, 33; 80
  (upd.)
Pulitzer Inc., 15; 58 (upd.)
Pulte Corporation, 8
Pulte Homes, Inc., 42 (upd.)
Pumpkin Masters, Inc., 48
Pure World, Inc., 72
Purina Mills, Inc., 32
Puritan-Bennett Corporation, 13
Purolator Products Company, 21; 74
  (upd.)
Putt-Putt Golf Courses of America, Inc.,
  23
PVC Container Corporation, 67
PW Eagle, Inc., 48
Pyramid Breweries Inc., 33
Pyramid Companies, 54
Q.E.P. Co., Inc., 65
Qdoba Restaurant Corporation, 93
QRS Music Technologies, Inc., 95
QSC Audio Products, Inc., 56
Quad/Graphics, Inc., 19
Quaker Chemical Corp., 91
Quaker Fabric Corp., 19
Quaker Foods North America, 73 (upd.)
The Quaker Oats Company, II; 12 (upd.);
  34 (upd.)
Quaker State Corporation, 7; 21 (upd.)
QUALCOMM Incorporated, 20; 47
  (upd.)
Quality Chekd Dairies, Inc., 48
Quality Dining, Inc., 18
Quality Food Centers, Inc., 17
Quality Systems, Inc., 81
Quanex Corporation, 13; 62 (upd.)
Quanta Services, Inc. 79
Quantum Chemical Corporation, 8
Quantum Corporation, 10; 62 (upd.)
Quark, Inc., 36
Quest Diagnostics Inc., 26
Questar Corporation, 6; 26 (upd.)
The Quick & Reilly Group, Inc., 20
Quicken Loans, Inc., 93
Quidel Corporation, 80

The Quigley Corporation, 62
Quiksilver, Inc., 18; 79 (upd.)
QuikTrip Corporation, 36
Quill Corporation, 28
Quinn Emanuel Urquhart Oliver &
  Hedges, LLP, 99
Quintiles Transnational Corporation, 21;
  68 (upd.)
Quixote Corporation, 15
The Quizno's Corporation, 42
Quovadx Inc., 70
QVC Inc., 9; 58 (upd.)
Qwest Communications International,
  Inc., 37
R&B, Inc., 51
R.B. Pamplin Corp., 45
R.C. Bigelow, Inc., 49
R.C. Willey Home Furnishings, 72
R.G. Barry Corporation, 17; 44 (upd.)
R.H. Macy & Co., Inc., V; 8 (upd.); 30
  (upd.)
R.J. Reynolds Tobacco Holdings, Inc., 30
  (upd.)
R.L. Polk & Co., 10
R. M. Palmer Co., 89
R.P. Scherer, I
R.R. Donnelley & Sons Company, IV; 9
  (upd.); 38 (upd.)
Racal-Datacom Inc., 11
Racing Champions Corporation, 37
Rack Room Shoes, Inc., 84
Radian Group Inc., 42
Radiation Therapy Services, Inc., 85
Radio Flyer Inc., 34
Radio One, Inc., 67
RadioShack Corporation, 36 (upd.)
Radius Inc., 16
RAE Systems Inc., 83
Rag Shops, Inc., 30
RailTex, Inc., 20
Rain Bird Corporation, 84
Rainforest Café, Inc., 25; 88 (upd.)
Rainier Brewing Company, 23
Raley's Inc., 14; 58 (upd.)
Rally's, 25; 68 (upd.)
Ralphs Grocery Company, 35
Ralston Purina Company, II; 13 (upd.)
Ramsay Youth Services, Inc., 41
Ramtron International Corporation, 89
Rand McNally & Company, 28
Randall's Food Markets, Inc., 40
Random House, Inc., 13; 31 (upd.)
Range Resources Corporation, 45
Rapala-Normark Group, Ltd., 30
Rare Hospitality International Inc., 19
RathGibson Inc., 90
Ratner Companies, 72
Raven Industries, Inc., 33
Raving Brands, Inc., 64
Rawlings Sporting Goods Co., Inc., 24
Raychem Corporation, 8
Raymond James Financial Inc., 69
Rayonier Inc., 24
Rayovac Corporation, 13; 39 (upd.)
Raytech Corporation, 61
Raytheon Aircraft Holdings Inc., 46
Raytheon Company, II; 11 (upd.); 38
  (upd.)

Razorfish, Inc., 37
RCA Corporation, II
RCM Technologies, Inc., 34
RCN Corporation, 70
RDO Equipment Company, 33
RE/MAX International, Inc., 59
Read-Rite Corp., 10
The Reader's Digest Association, Inc., IV;
  17 (upd.); 71 (upd.)
Reading International Inc., 70
Real Times, Inc., 66
RealNetworks, Inc., 53
Reckson Associates Realty Corp., 47
Recording for the Blind & Dyslexic, 51
Recoton Corp., 15
Recovery Engineering, Inc., 25
Recreational Equipment, Inc., 18; 71
  (upd.)
Recycled Paper Greetings, Inc., 21
Red Apple Group, Inc., 23
Red Hat, Inc., 45
Red McCombs Automotive Group, 91
Red Robin Gourmet Burgers, Inc., 56
Red Roof Inns, Inc., 18
Red Spot Paint & Varnish Company, 55
Red Wing Pottery Sales, Inc., 52
Red Wing Shoe Company, Inc., 9; 30
  (upd.); 83 (upd.)
Redback Networks, Inc., 92
Reddy Ice Holdings, Inc., 80
Redhook Ale Brewery, Inc., 31; 88 (upd.)
Redken Laboratories Inc., 84
Redlon & Johnson, Inc., 97
RedPeg Marketing, 73
Reebok International Ltd., V; 9 (upd.); 26
  (upd.)
Reed & Barton Corporation, 67
Reeds Jewelers, Inc., 22
Regal Entertainment Group, 59
Regal-Beloit Corporation, 18; 97 (upd.)
The Regence Group, 74
Regency Centers Corporation, 71
Regent Communications, Inc., 87
Regis Corporation, 18; 70 (upd.)
Reichhold Chemicals, Inc., 10
Reiter Dairy, LLC, 94
Rejuvenation, Inc., 91
Reliance Electric Company, 9
Reliance Group Holdings, Inc., III
Reliance Steel & Aluminum Company,
  19; 70 (upd.)
Reliant Energy Inc., 44 (upd.)
Reliv International, Inc., 58
Remedy Corporation, 58
RemedyTemp, Inc., 20
Remington Arms Company, Inc., 12; 40
  (upd.)
Remington Products Company, L.L.C., 42
Renaissance Learning Systems, Inc., 39
Renal Care Group, Inc., 72
Renfro Corporation, 99
Reno Air Inc., 23
Rent-A-Center, Inc., 45
Rent-Way, Inc., 33; 75 (upd.)
Rental Service Corporation, 28
Rentrak Corporation, 35
Republic Engineered Steels, Inc., 7; 26
  (upd.)

Republic Industries, Inc., 26
Republic New York Corporation, 11
Republic Services, Inc., 92
Res-Care, Inc., 29
Research Triangle Institute, 83
Reser's Fine Foods, Inc., 81
Resorts International, Inc., 12
Resource America, Inc., 42
Resources Connection, Inc., 81
Response Oncology, Inc., 27
Restaurant Associates Corporation, 66
Restaurants Unlimited, Inc., 13
Restoration Hardware, Inc., 30; 96 (upd.)
Retail Ventures, Inc., 82 (upd.)
Retractable Technologies, Inc., 99
Revco D.S., Inc., V
Revell-Monogram Inc., 16
Revere Electric Supply Company, 96
Revere Ware Corporation, 22
Revlon Inc., III; 17 (upd.); 64 (upd.)
Rewards Network Inc., 70 (upd.)
REX Stores Corp., 10
Rexel, Inc., 15
Rexnord Corporation, 21; 76 (upd.)
The Reynolds and Reynolds Company, 50
Reynolds Metals Company, IV; 19 (upd.)
RF Micro Devices, Inc., 43
RFC Franchising LLC, 68
Rhino Entertainment Company, 18; 70
  (upd.)
Rhodes Inc., 23
Rica Foods, Inc., 41
Rich Products Corporation, 7; 38 (upd.);
  93 (upd.)
The Richards Group, Inc., 58
Richardson Electronics, Ltd., 17
Richardson Industries, Inc., 62
Richfood Holdings, Inc., 7
Richton International Corporation, 39
Rickenbacker International Corp., 91
Riddell Sports Inc., 22
Ride, Inc., 22
The Riese Organization, 38
Riggs National Corporation, 13
Right Management Consultants, Inc., 42
Riklis Family Corp., 9
Rimage Corp., 89
Ripley Entertainment, Inc., 74
Riser Foods, Inc., 9
Rite Aid Corporation, V; 19 (upd.); 63
  (upd.)
Ritz Camera Centers, 34
The Ritz-Carlton Hotel Company, L.L.C.,
  9; 29 (upd.); 71 (upd.)
Ritz-Craft Corporation of Pennsylvania
  Inc., 94
The Rival Company, 19
River Oaks Furniture, Inc., 43
River Ranch Fresh Foods LLC, 88
Riverwood International Corporation, 11;
  48 (upd.)
Riviana Foods Inc., 27
Riviera Holdings Corporation, 75
Riviera Tool Company, 89
RJR Nabisco Holdings Corp., V
RMH Teleservices, Inc., 42
Roadhouse Grill, Inc., 22
Roadmaster Industries, Inc., 16

Roadway Express, Inc., V; 25 (upd.)
Roanoke Electric Steel Corporation, 45
Robbins & Myers Inc., 15
Robins, Kaplan, Miller & Ciresi L.L.P., 89
Roberds Inc., 19
Robert Half International Inc., 18; 70
  (upd.)
Robert Mondavi Corporation, 15; 50
  (upd.)
Robert Talbott Inc., 88
Robert W. Baird & Co. Incorporated, 67
Robert Wood Johnson Foundation, 35
Roberts Pharmaceutical Corporation, 16
Robertson-Ceco Corporation, 19
Robinson Helicopter Company, 51
Rocawear Apparel LLC, 77
Roche Bioscience, 11; 14 (upd.)
Rochester Gas and Electric Corporation, 6
Rochester Telephone Corporation, 6
Rock Bottom Restaurants, Inc., 25; 68
  (upd.)
Rock-It Cargo USA, Inc., 86
Rock of Ages Corporation, 37
Rock-Tenn Company, 13; 59 (upd.)
The Rockefeller Foundation, 34
Rockefeller Group International Inc., 58
Rockford Corporation, 43
Rockford Products Corporation, 55
RockShox, Inc., 26
Rockwell Automation, 43 (upd.)
Rockwell International Corporation, I; 11
  (upd.)
Rockwell Medical Technologies, Inc., 88
Rocky Mountain Chocolate Factory, Inc.,
  73
Rocky Shoes & Boots, Inc., 26
Rodale, Inc., 23; 47 (upd.)
Rodda Paint Company, 98
ROFIN-SINAR Technologies Inc., 81
Rogers Corporation, 61; 80 (upd.)
Rohm and Haas Company, I; 26 (upd.);
  77 (upd.)
ROHN Industries, Inc., 22
Rohr Incorporated, 9
Roll International Corporation, 37
Rollerblade, Inc., 15; 34 (upd.)
Rollins, Inc., 11
Rolls-Royce Allison, 29 (upd.)
Roly Poly Franchise Systems LLC, 83
Romacorp, Inc., 58
Roman Meal Company, 84
Ron Tonkin Chevrolet Company, 55
Ronco Corporation, 15; 80 (upd.)
Rooms To Go Inc., 28
Rooney Brothers Co., 25
Roper Industries, Inc., 15; 50 (upd.)
Ropes & Gray, 40
Rorer Group, I
Rosauers Supermarkets, Inc., 90
Rose Acre Farms, Inc., 60
Rose Art Industries, 58
Rose's Stores, Inc., 13
Roseburg Forest Products Company, 58
Rosemount Inc., 15
Rosenbluth International Inc., 14
Rosetta Stone Inc., 93
Ross Stores, Inc., 17; 43 (upd.)
Rotary International, 31

Roto-Rooter, Inc., 15; 61 (upd.)
The Rottlund Company, Inc., 28
Rouge Steel Company, 8
Rounder Records Corporation 79
Roundy's Inc., 14; 58 (upd.)
The Rouse Company, 15; 63 (upd.)
Rowan Companies, Inc., 43
Roy Anderson Corporation, 75
Roy F. Weston, Inc., 33
Royal Appliance Manufacturing Company,
  15
Royal Caribbean Cruises Ltd., 22; 74
  (upd.)
Royal Crown Company, Inc., 23
RPC, Inc., 91
RPM International Inc., 8; 36 (upd.); 91
  (upd.)
RSA Security Inc., 46
RSM McGladrey Business Services Inc.,
  98
RTI Biologics, Inc., 96
RTM Restaurant Group, 58
Rubbermaid Incorporated, III; 20 (upd.)
Rubio's Restaurants, Inc., 35
Ruby Tuesday, Inc., 18; 71 (upd.)
Rudolph Technologies Inc., 94
Ruiz Food Products, Inc., 53
Rural Cellular Corporation, 43
Rural/Metro Corporation, 28
Rush Communications, 33
Rush Enterprises, Inc., 64
Russ Berrie and Company, Inc., 12; 82
  (upd.)
Russell Corporation, 8; 30 (upd.); 82
  (upd.)
Russell Reynolds Associates Inc., 38
Russell Stover Candies Inc., 12; 91 (upd.)
Rust International Inc., 11
Rusty, Inc., 95
Ruth's Chris Steak House, 28; 88 (upd.)
RWD Technologies, Inc., 76
Ryan Beck & Co., Inc., 66
Ryan Companies US, Inc., 99
Ryan's Restaurant Group, Inc., 15; 68
  (upd.)
Ryder System, Inc., V; 24 (upd.)
Ryerson Tull, Inc., 40 (upd.)
Ryko Corporation, 83
The Ryland Group, Inc., 8; 37 (upd.)
S&C Electric Company, 15
S&D Coffee, Inc., 84
S&K Famous Brands, Inc., 23
S-K-I Limited, 15
S.C. Johnson & Son, Inc., III; 28 (upd.);
  89 (upd.)
Saatchi & Saatchi, 42 (upd.)
Sabratek Corporation, 29
SABRE Group Holdings, Inc., 26
Sabre Holdings Corporation, 74 (upd.)
Safe Flight Instrument Corporation, 71
SAFECO Corporaton, III
Safeguard Scientifics, Inc., 10
Safelite Glass Corp., 19
Safeskin Corporation, 18
Safety Components International, Inc., 63
Safety 1st, Inc., 24
Safety-Kleen Systems Inc., 8; 82 (upd.)
Safeway Inc., II; 24 (upd.); 85 (upd.)

Saga Communications, Inc., 27
Saia, Inc., 98
The St. Joe Company, 31; 98 (upd.)
St. Joe Paper Company, 8
St. John Knits, Inc., 14
St. Jude Medical, Inc., 11; 43 (upd.); 97 (upd.)
St. Louis Music, Inc., 48
St. Mary Land & Exploration Company, 63
St. Paul Bank for Cooperatives, 8
The St. Paul Travelers Companies, Inc. III; 22 (upd.); 79 (upd.)
Ste. Michelle Wine Estates Ltd., 96
Saks Inc., 24; 41 (upd.)
Salant Corporation, 12; 51 (upd.)
Salem Communications Corporation, 97
salesforce.com, Inc. 79
Salick Health Care, Inc., 53
Salix Pharmaceuticals, Ltd., 93
Sally Beauty Company, Inc., 60
Salomon Inc., II; 13 (upd.)
Salt River Project, 19
Salton, Inc., 30; 88 (upd.)
The Salvation Army USA, 32
Sam Ash Music Corporation, 30
Sam Levin Inc., 80
Sam's Club, 40
Sam's Wine & Spirits, 96
Samsonite Corporation, 13; 43 (upd.)
Samuel Cabot Inc., 53
Samuels Jewelers Incorporated, 30
San Diego Gas & Electric Company, V
San Diego Padres Baseball Club LP 78
Sanborn Map Company Inc., 82
Sandals Resorts International, 65
Sanders Morris Harris Group Inc., 70
Sanders\Wingo, 99
Sanderson Farms, Inc., 15
Sandia National Laboratories, 49
Sanford L.P., 82
Santa Barbara Restaurant Group, Inc., 37
The Santa Cruz Operation, Inc., 38
Santa Fe Gaming Corporation, 19
Santa Fe International Corporation, 38
Santa Fe Pacific Corporation, V
Sara Lee Corporation, II; 15 (upd.); 54 (upd.); 99 (upd.)
Sarnoff Corporation, 57
Sarris Candies Inc., 86
SAS Institute Inc., 10; 78 (upd.)
Saturn Corporation, 7; 21 (upd.); 80 (upd.)
Saucony Inc., 35; 86 (upd.)
Sauder Woodworking Company, 12; 35 (upd.)
Sauer-Danfoss Inc., 61
Saul Ewing LLP, 74
Savannah Foods & Industries, Inc., 7
Savers, Inc., 99 (upd.)
Sawtek Inc., 43 (upd.)
Sbarro, Inc., 16; 64 (upd.)
SBC Communications Inc., 32 (upd.)
SBS Technologies, Inc., 25
SCANA Corporation, 6; 56 (upd.)
ScanSource, Inc., 29; 74 (upd.)
SCB Computer Technology, Inc., 29
SCEcorp, V

Schawk, Inc., 24
Scheels All Sports Inc., 63
Scheid Vineyards Inc., 66
Scherer Brothers Lumber Company, 94
Schering-Plough Corporation, I; 14 (upd.); 49 (upd.); 99 (upd.)
Schieffelin & Somerset Co., 61
Schlage Lock Company, 82
Schlotzsky's, Inc., 36
Schlumberger Limited, III; 17 (upd.); 59 (upd.)
Schmitt Music Company, 40
Schenck Business Solutions, 88
Schneider National, Inc., 36; 77 (upd.)
Schneiderman's Furniture Inc., 28
Schnitzer Steel Industries, Inc., 19
Scholastic Corporation, 10; 29 (upd.)
Scholle Corporation, 96
School Specialty, Inc., 68
School-Tech, Inc., 62
Schott Brothers, Inc., 67
Schott Corporation, 53
Schottenstein Stores Corp., 14
Schreiber Foods, Inc., 72
Schuff Steel Company, 26
Schultz Sav-O Stores, Inc., 21; 31 (upd.)
Schurz Communications, Inc., 98
The Schwan Food Company, 83 (upd.)
Schwan's Sales Enterprises, Inc., 7; 26 (upd.)
Schwebel Baking Company, 72
Schweitzer-Mauduit International, Inc., 52
Schwinn Cycle and Fitness L.P., 19
SCI Systems, Inc., 9
Science Applications International Corporation, 15
Scientific-Atlanta, Inc., 6; 45 (upd.)
Scientific Games Corporation, 64 (upd.)
Scientific Learning Corporation, 95
The SCO Group Inc. 78
Scope Products, Inc., 94
The Score Board, Inc., 19
Scotsman Industries, Inc., 20
Scott Fetzer Company, 12; 80 (upd.)
Scott Paper Company, IV; 31 (upd.)
The Scotts Company, 22
Scottrade, Inc., 85
Scotty's, Inc., 22
The Scoular Company, 77
Scovill Fasteners Inc., 24
SCP Pool Corporation, 39
Screen Actors Guild, 72
The Scripps Research Institute, 76
Sea Ray Boats Inc., 96
Seaboard Corporation, 36; 85 (upd.)
SeaChange International, Inc. 79
SEACOR Holdings Inc., 83
Seagate Technology, Inc., 8; 34 (upd.)
Seagull Energy Corporation, 11
Sealaska Corporation, 60
Sealed Air Corporation, 14; 57 (upd.)
Sealed Power Corporation, I
Sealright Co., Inc., 17
Sealy Inc., 12
Seaman Furniture Company, Inc., 32
Sean John Clothing, Inc., 70
Sears, Roebuck and Co., V; 18 (upd.); 56 (upd.)

Seattle City Light, 50
Seattle FilmWorks, Inc., 20
Seattle First National Bank Inc., 8
Seattle Lighting Fixture Company, 92
Seattle Pacific Industries, Inc., 92
Seattle Seahawks, Inc., 92
Seattle Times Company, 15
Seaway Food Town, Inc., 15
Sebastiani Vineyards, Inc., 28
The Second City, Inc., 88
Second Harvest, 29
Security Capital Corporation, 17
Security Pacific Corporation, II
SED International Holdings, Inc., 43
See's Candies, Inc., 30
Sega of America, Inc., 10
Segway LLC, 48
SEI Investments Company, 96
Seigle's Home and Building Centers, Inc., 41
Seitel, Inc., 47
Select Comfort Corporation, 34
Select Medical Corporation, 65
Selee Corporation, 88
The Selmer Company, Inc., 19
SEMCO Energy, Inc., 44
Seminis, Inc., 29
Semitool, Inc., 18; 79 (upd.)
Sempra Energy, 25 (upd.)
Semtech Corporation, 32
Seneca Foods Corporation, 17; 60 (upd.)
Senomyx, Inc., 83
Sensient Technologies Corporation, 52 (upd.)
Sensormatic Electronics Corp., 11
Sensory Science Corporation, 37
Sepracor Inc., 45
Sequa Corporation, 13; 54 (upd.)
Serologicals Corporation, 63
Serta, Inc., 28
Servco Pacific Inc., 96
Service America Corp., 7
Service Corporation International, 6; 51 (upd.)
Service Merchandise Company, Inc., V; 19 (upd.)
The ServiceMaster Company, 6; 23 (upd.); 68 (upd.)
Servpro Industries, Inc., 85
7-11, Inc., 32 (upd.)
Sevenson Environmental Services, Inc., 42
Seventh Generation, Inc., 73
Seyfarth Shaw LLP, 93
SFX Entertainment, Inc., 36
SGI, 29 (upd.)
Shakespeare Company, 22
Shaklee Corporation, 12; 39 (upd.)
Shared Medical Systems Corporation, 14
The Sharper Image Corporation, 10; 62 (upd.)
The Shaw Group, Inc., 50
Shaw Industries, Inc., 9; 40 (upd.)
Shaw's Supermarkets, Inc., 56
Shawmut National Corporation, 13
Sheaffer Pen Corporation, 82
Shearer's Foods, Inc., 72
Shearman & Sterling, 32

Shearson Lehman Brothers Holdings Inc., II; 9 (upd.)
Shedd Aquarium Society, 73
Sheetz, Inc., 85
Shelby Williams Industries, Inc., 14
Sheldahl Inc., 23
Shell Oil Company, IV; 14 (upd.); 41 (upd.)
Sheller-Globe Corporation, I
Shells Seafood Restaurants, Inc., 43
Shenandoah Telecommunications Company, 89
Sheplers, Inc., 96
The Sheridan Group, Inc., 86
The Sherwin-Williams Company, III; 13 (upd.); 89 (upd.)
Sherwood Brands, Inc., 53
Shoe Carnival Inc., 14; 72 (upd.)
Shoe Pavilion, Inc., 84
Shoney's, Inc., 7; 23 (upd.)
ShopKo Stores Inc., 21; 58 (upd.)
Shoppers Food Warehouse Corporation, 66
Shorewood Packaging Corporation, 28
ShowBiz Pizza Time, Inc., 13
Showboat, Inc., 19
Showtime Networks Inc. 78
Shriners Hospitals for Children, 69
Shubert Organization Inc., 24
Shuffle Master Inc., 51
Shure Inc., 60
Shurgard Storage Centers, Inc., 52
Shutterfly, Inc., 98
Sidley Austin Brown & Wood, 40
Sidney Frank Importing Co., Inc., 69
Siebel Systems, Inc., 38
Siebert Financial Corp., 32
Siegel & Gale, 64
The Sierra Club, 28
Sierra Health Services, Inc., 15
Sierra Nevada Brewing Company, 70
Sierra On-Line, Inc., 15; 41 (upd.)
Sierra Pacific Industries, 22; 90 (upd.)
SIFCO Industries, Inc., 41
Sigma-Aldrich Corporation, I; 36 (upd.); 93 (upd.)
Signet Banking Corporation, 11
Sikorsky Aircraft Corporation, 24
Silhouette Brands, Inc., 55
Silicon Graphics Incorporated, 9
Silver Lake Cookie Company Inc., 95
SilverPlatter Information Inc., 23
Silverstar Holdings, Ltd., 99
Silverstein Properties, Inc., 47
Simmons Company, 47
Simon & Schuster Inc., IV; 19 (upd.)
Simon Property Group Inc., 27; 84 (upd.)
Simon Transportation Services Inc., 27
Simplex Technologies Inc., 21
Simplicity Manufacturing, Inc., 64
Simpson Investment Company, 17
Simpson Thacher & Bartlett, 39
Simula, Inc., 41
Sinclair Broadcast Group, Inc., 25
Sine Qua Non, 99
The Singing Machine Company, Inc., 60
Sir Speedy, Inc., 16
Sirius Satellite Radio, Inc., 69

Siskin Steel & Supply Company, 70
Six Flags, Inc., 17; 54 (upd.)
SJW Corporation, 70
Skadden, Arps, Slate, Meagher & Flom, 18
Skechers U.S.A. Inc., 31; 88 (upd.)
Skeeter Products Inc., 96
Skidmore, Owings & Merrill LLP, 13; 69 (upd.)
skinnyCorp, LLC, 97
Skyline Chili, Inc., 62
Skyline Corporation, 30
SkyMall, Inc., 26
SkyWest, Inc., 25
Skyy Spirits LLC 78
SL Green Realty Corporation, 44
SL Industries, Inc., 77
Sleepy's Inc., 32
SLI, Inc., 48
Slim-Fast Foods Company, 18; 66 (upd.)
SLM Holding Corp., 25 (upd.)
Small Planet Foods, Inc., 89
Smart & Final LLC, 16; 94 (upd.)
SMART Modular Technologies, Inc., 86
SmartForce PLC, 43
Smead Manufacturing Co., 17
Smith & Hawken, Ltd., 68
Smith & Wesson Corp., 30; 73 (upd.)
Smith Barney Inc., 15
Smith Corona Corp., 13
Smith International, Inc., 15; 59 (upd.)
Smith's Food & Drug Centers, Inc., 8; 57 (upd.)
Smith-Midland Corporation, 56
Smithfield Foods, Inc., 7; 43 (upd.)
SmithKline Beckman Corporation, I
Smithsonian Institution, 27
Smithway Motor Xpress Corporation, 39
Smurfit-Stone Container Corporation, 26 (upd.); 83 (upd.)
Snap-On, Incorporated, 7; 27 (upd.)
Snapfish, 83
Snapple Beverage Corporation, 11
Snell & Wilmer L.L.P., 28
Society Corporation, 9
Soft Sheen Products, Inc., 31
Softbank Corporation, 77 (upd.)
Sola International Inc., 71
Sole Technology Inc., 93
Solectron Corporation, 12; 48 (upd.)
Solo Serve Corporation, 28
Solutia Inc., 52
Sonat, Inc., 6
Sonesta International Hotels Corporation, 44
Sonic Automotive, Inc., 77
Sonic Corp., 14; 37 (upd.)
Sonic Innovations Inc., 56
Sonic Solutions, Inc., 81
SonicWALL, Inc., 87
Sonoco Products Company, 8; 89 (upd.)
SonoSite, Inc., 56
Sorbee International Ltd., 74
Soros Fund Management LLC, 28
Sorrento, Inc., 24
SOS Staffing Services, 25
Sotheby's Holdings, Inc., 11; 29 (upd.); 84 (upd.)

Sound Advice, Inc., 41
Souper Salad, Inc., 98
The Source Enterprises, Inc., 65
Source Interlink Companies, Inc., 75
South Beach Beverage Company, Inc., 73
South Dakota Wheat Growers Association, 94
South Jersey Industries, Inc., 42
Southdown, Inc., 14
Southeast Frozen Foods Company, L.P., 99
The Southern Company, V; 38 (upd.)
Southern Connecticut Gas Company, 84
Southern Financial Bancorp, Inc., 56
Southern Indiana Gas and Electric Company, 13
Southern New England Telecommunications Corporation, 6
Southern Pacific Transportation Company, V
Southern Poverty Law Center, Inc., 74
Southern States Cooperative Incorporated, 36
Southern Union Company, 27
Southern Wine and Spirits of America, Inc., 84
The Southland Corporation, II; 7 (upd.)
Southtrust Corporation, 11
Southwest Airlines Co., 6; 24 (upd.); 71 (upd.)
Southwest Gas Corporation, 19
Southwest Water Company, 47
Southwestern Bell Corporation, V
Southwestern Electric Power Co., 21
Southwestern Public Service Company, 6
Southwire Company, Inc., 8; 23 (upd.)
Sovran Self Storage, Inc., 66
Spacehab, Inc., 37
Spacelabs Medical, Inc., 71
Spaghetti Warehouse, Inc., 25
Spangler Candy Company, 44
Spanish Broadcasting System, Inc., 41
Spansion Inc., 80
Spanx, Inc., 89
Spark Networks, Inc., 91
Spartan Motors Inc., 14
Spartan Stores Inc., 8; 66 (upd.)
Spartech Corporation, 19; 76 (upd.)
Sparton Corporation, 18
Spear & Jackson, Inc., 73
Spear, Leeds & Kellogg, 66
Spec's Music, Inc., 19
Special Olympics, Inc., 93
Specialized Bicycle Components Inc., 50
Specialty Coatings Inc., 8
Specialty Equipment Companies, Inc., 25
Specialty Products & Insulation Co., 59
Spectrum Control, Inc., 67
Spectrum Organic Products, Inc., 68
Spee-Dee Delivery Service, Inc., 93
SpeeDee Oil Change and Tune-Up, 25
Speedway Motorsports, Inc., 32
Speidel Inc., 96
Speizman Industries, Inc., 44
Spelling Entertainment, 14; 35 (upd.)
Spencer Stuart and Associates, Inc., 14
Spherion Corporation, 52
Spiegel, Inc., 10; 27 (upd.)

Spinnaker Exploration Company, 72
Spirit Airlines, Inc., 31
Sport Chalet, Inc., 16; 94 (upd.)
Sport Supply Group, Inc., 23
Sportmart, Inc., 15
Sports & Recreation, Inc., 17
The Sports Authority, Inc., 16; 43 (upd.)
The Sports Club Company, 25
The Sportsman's Guide, Inc., 36
Springs Global US, Inc., V; 19 (upd.); 90 (upd.)
Sprint Corporation, 9; 46 (upd.)
SPS Technologies, Inc., 30
SPSS Inc., 64
SPX Corporation, 10; 47 (upd.)
Spyglass Entertainment Group, LLC, 91
Square D, 90
Squibb Corporation, I
SRA International, Inc., 77
SRAM Corporation, 65
SRC Holdings Corporation, 67
SRI International, Inc., 57
SSOE Inc., 76
STAAR Surgical Company, 57
Stabler Companies Inc. 78
Stage Stores, Inc., 24; 82 (upd.)
Stanadyne Automotive Corporation, 37
StanCorp Financial Group, Inc., 56
Standard Candy Company Inc., 86
Standard Commercial Corporation, 13; 62 (upd.)
Standard Federal Bank, 9
Standard Microsystems Corporation, 11
Standard Motor Products, Inc., 40
Standard Pacific Corporation, 52
The Standard Register Company, 15, 93 (upd.)
Standex International Corporation, 17; 44 (upd.)
Stanhome Inc., 15
Stanley Furniture Company, Inc., 34
The Stanley Works, III; 20 (upd.); 79 (upd.)
Staple Cotton Cooperative Association (Staplcotn), 86
Staples, Inc., 10; 55 (upd.)
Star Banc Corporation, 11
Star of the West Milling Co., 95
Starbucks Corporation, 13; 34 (upd.); 77 (upd.)
Starcraft Corporation, 30; 66 (upd.)
Starkey Laboratories, Inc., 52
Starrett Corporation, 21
StarTek, Inc. 79
Starter Corp., 12
Starwood Hotels & Resorts Worldwide, Inc., 54
Starz LLC, 91
The Stash Tea Company, 50
State Auto Financial Corporation, 77
State Farm Mutual Automobile Insurance Company, III; 51 (upd.)
State Financial Services Corporation, 51
State Street Corporation, 8; 57 (upd.)
Staten Island Bancorp, Inc., 39
Stater Bros. Holdings Inc., 64
Station Casinos, Inc., 25; 90 (upd.)
The Staubach Company, 62

The Steak n Shake Company, 41; 96 (upd.)
Stearns, Inc., 43
Steel Dynamics, Inc., 52
Steel Technologies Inc., 63
Steelcase, Inc., 7; 27 (upd.)
Stein Mart Inc., 19; 72 (upd.)
Steiner Corporation (Alsco), 53
Steinway Musical Properties, Inc., 19
Stemilt Growers Inc., 94
Stepan Company, 30
The Stephan Company, 60
Stephens Media, LLC, 91
Stephens Inc., 92
Stericycle, Inc., 33; 74 (upd.)
Sterilite Corporation, 97
STERIS Corporation, 29
Sterling Chemicals Inc., 16; 78 (upd.)
Sterling Drug, Inc., I
Sterling Electronics Corp., 18
Sterling Software, Inc., 11
Steve & Barry's LLC, 88
Stevedoring Services of America Inc., 28
Steven Madden, Ltd., 37
Stew Leonard's, 56
Stewart & Stevenson Services Inc., 11
Stewart Enterprises, Inc., 20
Stewart Information Services Corporation 78
Stewart's Beverages, 39
Stewart's Shops Corporation, 80
Stiefel Laboratories, Inc., 90
Stillwater Mining Company, 47
Stimson Lumber Company 78
Stock Yards Packing Co., Inc., 37
Stone & Webster, Inc., 13; 64 (upd.)
Stone Container Corporation, IV
Stone Manufacturing Company, 14; 43 (upd.)
Stonyfield Farm, Inc., 55
The Stop & Shop Supermarket Company, II; 24 (upd.); 68 (upd.)
Storage Technology Corporation, 6
Storage USA, Inc., 21
Stouffer Corp., 8
StrataCom, Inc., 16
Stratagene Corporation, 70
Stratasys, Inc., 67
Strattec Security Corporation, 73
Stratus Computer, Inc., 10
Strauss Discount Auto, 56
Strayer Education, Inc., 53
The Stride Rite Corporation, 8; 37 (upd.); 86 (upd.)
Strine Printing Company Inc., 88
The Strober Organization, Inc., 82
The Stroh Brewery Company, I; 18 (upd.)
Strombecker Corporation, 60
Stroock & Stroock & Lavan LLP, 40
Strouds, Inc., 33
The Structure Tone Organization, 99
Stryker Corporation, 11; 29 (upd.); 79 (upd.)
Stuart C. Irby Company, 58
Stuart Entertainment Inc., 16
Student Loan Marketing Association, II
Stuller Settings, Inc., 35
Sturm, Ruger & Company, Inc., 19

Stussy, Inc., 55
Sub Pop Ltd., 97
Sub-Zero Freezer Co., Inc., 31
Suburban Propane Partners, L.P., 30
Subway, 32
Successories, Inc., 30
Sudbury Inc., 16
Suiza Foods Corporation, 26
Sullivan & Cromwell, 26
The Summit Bancorporation, 14
Summit Family Restaurants, Inc. 19
Sun Communities Inc., 46
Sun Company, Inc., IV
Sun Country Airlines, 30
Sun-Diamond Growers of California, 7
Sun Distributors L.P., 12
Sun Healthcare Group Inc., 25
Sun Hydraulics Corporation, 74
Sun-Maid Growers of California, 82
Sun Microsystems, Inc., 7; 30 (upd.); 91 (upd.)
Sun Sportswear, Inc., 17
Sun Television & Appliances Inc., 10
Sun World International, LLC, 93
SunAmerica Inc., 11
Sunbeam-Oster Co., Inc., 9
Sunburst Hospitality Corporation, 26
Sunburst Shutter Corporation 78
Sundstrand Corporation, 7; 21 (upd.)
Sundt Corp., 24
SunGard Data Systems Inc., 11
Sunglass Hut International, Inc., 21; 74 (upd.)
Sunkist Growers, Inc., 26
Sunoco, Inc., 28 (upd.); 83 (upd.)
SunPower Corporation, 91
The Sunrider Corporation, 26
Sunrise Greetings, 88
Sunrise Medical Inc., 11
Sunrise Senior Living, Inc., 81
Sunterra Corporation, 75
SunTrust Banks Inc., 23
Super 8 Motels, Inc., 83
Super Food Services, Inc., 15
Supercuts Inc., 26
Superior Essex Inc., 80
Superior Energy Services, Inc., 65
Superior Industries International, Inc., 8
Superior Uniform Group, Inc., 30
Supermarkets General Holdings Corporation, II
SUPERVALU Inc., II; 18 (upd.); 50 (upd.)
Suprema Specialties, Inc., 27
Supreme International Corporation, 27
Susan G. Komen Breast Cancer Foundation 78
Susquehanna Pfaltzgraff Company, 8
Sutherland Lumber Company, L.P., 99
Sutter Home Winery Inc., 16
Sverdrup Corporation, 14
Swales & Associates, Inc., 69
Swank, Inc., 17; 84 (upd.)
SwedishAmerican Health System, 51
Sweet Candy Company, 60
Sweetheart Cup Company, Inc., 36
The Swett & Crawford Group Inc., 84
SWH Corporation, 70

Swift & Company, 55
Swift Energy Company, 63
Swift Transportation Co., Inc., 42
Swinerton Inc., 43
Swisher International Group Inc., 23
The Swiss Colony, Inc., 97
Swiss Valley Farms Company, 90
Sybase, Inc., 10; 27 (upd.)
Sybron International Corp., 14
Sycamore Networks, Inc., 45
Sykes Enterprises, Inc., 45
Sylvan Learning Systems, Inc., 35
Sylvan, Inc., 22
Symantec Corporation, 10; 82 (upd.)
Symbol Technologies, Inc., 15
Syms Corporation, 29; 74 (upd.)
Symyx Technologies, Inc., 77
Synaptics Incorporated, 95
Synchronoss Technologies, Inc., 95
Syniverse Holdings Inc., 97
SYNNEX Corporation, 73
Synopsys, Inc., 11; 69 (upd.)
SynOptics Communications, Inc., 10
Synovus Financial Corp., 12; 52 (upd.)
Syntel, Inc., 92
Syntex Corporation, I
Sypris Solutions, Inc., 85
SyQuest Technology, Inc., 18
Syratech Corp., 14
SYSCO Corporation, II; 24 (upd.); 75
    (upd.)
System Software Associates, Inc., 10
Systemax, Inc., 52
Systems & Computer Technology Corp.,
    19
T-Netix, Inc., 46
T. Marzetti Company, 57
T. Rowe Price Associates, Inc., 11; 34
    (upd.)
TAB Products Co., 17
Taco Bell Corporation, 7; 21 (upd.); 74
    (upd.)
Taco Cabana, Inc., 23; 72 (upd.)
Taco John's International, Inc., 15; 63
    (upd.)
Tacony Corporation, 70
Tag-It Pacific, Inc., 85
Take-Two Interactive Software, Inc., 46
The Talbots, Inc., 11; 31 (upd.); 88
    (upd.)
Talk America Holdings, Inc., 70
Talley Industries, Inc., 16
TALX Corporation, 92
Tambrands Inc., 8
Tandem Computers, Inc., 6
Tandy Corporation, II; 12 (upd.)
Tandycrafts, Inc., 31
Tanger Factory Outlet Centers, Inc., 49
Tanimura & Antle Fresh Foods, Inc., 98
Tanox, Inc., 77
Tapemark Company Inc., 64
Target Corporation, 10; 27 (upd.); 61
    (upd.)
Tarragon Realty Investors, Inc., 45
Tarrant Apparel Group, 62
Taser International, Inc., 62
Tasty Baking Company, 14; 35 (upd.)
Tattered Cover Book Store, 43

Taubman Centers, Inc., 75
Taylor Corporation, 36
Taylor Devices, Inc., 97
Taylor Guitars, 48
Taylor Made Group Inc., 98
TaylorMade-adidas Golf, 23; 96 (upd.)
Taylor Publishing Company, 12; 36 (upd.)
TB Wood's Corporation, 56
TBA Global, LLC, 99
TBWA/Chiat/Day, 6; 43 (upd.)
TCBY Systems LLC, 17; 98 (upd.)
TCF Financial Corporation, 47
Teachers Insurance and Annuity
    Association-College Retirement Equities
    Fund, III; 45 (upd.)
TearDrop Golf Company, 32
Tech Data Corporation, 10; 74 (upd.)
Tech-Sym Corporation, 18; 44 (upd.)
TechBooks Inc., 84
TECHNE Corporation, 52
Technical Olympic USA, Inc., 75
Technitrol, Inc., 29
Technology Research Corporation, 94
Technology Solutions Company, 94
TechTarget, Inc., 99
TECO Energy, Inc., 6
Tecumseh Products Company, 8; 71
    (upd.)
Tee Vee Toons, Inc., 57
Tejon Ranch Company, 35
Tekelec, 83
Teknor Apex Company, 97
Tektronix Inc., 8; 78 (upd.)
Telcordia Technologies, Inc., 59
Tele-Communications, Inc., II
Teledyne Technologies Inc., I; 10 (upd.);
    62 (upd.)
Telephone and Data Systems, Inc., 9
Tellabs, Inc., 11; 40 (upd.)
Telsmith Inc., 96
Telxon Corporation, 10
Temple-Inland Inc., IV; 31 (upd.)
Tempur-Pedic Inc., 54
Tenet Healthcare Corporation, 55 (upd.)
TenFold Corporation, 35
Tengasco, Inc., 99
Tennant Company, 13; 33 (upd.); 95
    (upd.)
Tenneco Inc., I; 10 (upd.)
Tennessee Valley Authority, 50
TEPPCO Partners, L.P., 73
Teradyne, Inc., 11; 98 (upd.)
Terex Corporation, 7; 40 (upd.); 91
    (upd.)
The Terlato Wine Group, 48
Terra Industries, Inc., 13; 94 (upd.)
Terremark Worldwide, Inc., 99
Tesoro Corporation, 7; 45 (upd.); 97
    (upd.)
The Testor Corporation, 51
Tetley USA Inc., 88
Teton Energy Corporation, 97
Tetra Tech, Inc., 29
Texaco Inc., IV; 14 (upd.); 41 (upd.)
Texas Air Corporation, I
Texas Industries, Inc., 8
Texas Instruments Inc., II; 11 (upd.); 46
    (upd.)

Texas Pacific Group Inc., 36
Texas Rangers Baseball, 51
Texas Roadhouse, Inc., 69
Texas Utilities Company, V; 25 (upd.)
Textron Inc., I; 34 (upd.); 88 (upd.)
Textron Lycoming Turbine Engine, 9
Tha Row Records, 69 (upd.)
Thane International, Inc., 84
Thermadyne Holding Corporation, 19
Thermo BioAnalysis Corp., 25
Thermo Electron Corporation, 7
Thermo Fibertek, Inc., 24
Thermo Instrument Systems Inc., 11
Thermo King Corporation, 13
Thermos Company, 16
Things Remembered, Inc., 84
Thiokol Corporation, 9; 22 (upd.)
Thomas & Betts Corporation, 11; 54
    (upd.)
Thomas & Howard Company, Inc., 90
Thomas Cook Travel Inc., 9; 33 (upd.)
Thomas H. Lee Co., 24
Thomas Industries Inc., 29
Thomas J. Lipton Company, 14
Thomas Nelson, Inc., 14; 38 (upd.)
Thomas Publishing Company, 26
Thomaston Mills, Inc., 27
Thomasville Furniture Industries, Inc., 12;
    74 (upd.)
Thomsen Greenhouses and Garden
    Center, Incorporated, 65
Thor Industries Inc., 39; 92 (upd.)
Thorn Apple Valley, Inc., 7; 22 (upd.)
ThoughtWorks Inc., 90
Thousand Trails, Inc., 33
THQ, Inc., 39; 92 (upd.)
3Com Corporation, 11; 34 (upd.)
The 3DO Company, 43
3M Company, 61 (upd.)
Thrifty PayLess, Inc., 12
TIBCO Software Inc. 79
TIC Holdings Inc., 92
Ticketmaster, 76 (upd.)
Ticketmaster Group, Inc., 13; 37 (upd.)
Tidewater Inc., 11; 37 (upd.)
Tiffany & Co., 14; 78 (upd.)
TIG Holdings, Inc., 26
Tilia Inc., 62
Tillotson Corp., 15
Timber Lodge Steakhouse, Inc., 73
The Timberland Company, 13; 54 (upd.)
Timberline Software Corporation, 15
Time Warner Inc., IV; 7 (upd.)
The Times Mirror Company, IV; 17
    (upd.)
Timex Corporation, 7; 25 (upd.)
The Timken Company, 8; 42 (upd.)
Tishman Speyer Properties, L.P., 47
The Titan Corporation, 36
Titan International, Inc., 89
Titanium Metals Corporation, 21
TiVo Inc., 75
TJ International, Inc., 19
The TJX Companies, Inc., V; 19 (upd.);
    57 (upd.)
TLC Beatrice International Holdings, Inc.,
    22
TMP Worldwide Inc., 30

TNT Freightways Corporation, 14
Today's Man, Inc., 20
TODCO, 87
Todd Shipyards Corporation, 14
The Todd-AO Corporation, 33
Todhunter International, Inc., 27
Tofutti Brands, Inc., 64
Tokheim Corporation, 21
TOKYOPOP Inc. 79
Toll Brothers Inc., 15; 70 (upd.)
Tollgrade Communications, Inc., 44
Tom Brown, Inc., 37
Tom Doherty Associates Inc., 25
Tom's Foods Inc., 66
Tom's of Maine, Inc., 45
Tombstone Pizza Corporation, 13
Tone Brothers, Inc., 21; 74 (upd.)
Tonka Corporation, 25
Too, Inc., 61
Tootsie Roll Industries, Inc., 12; 82 (upd.)
Topco Associates LLC, 60
The Topps Company, Inc., 13; 34 (upd.);
    83 (upd.)
Tops Appliance City, Inc., 17
Tops Markets LLC, 60
Torchmark Corporation, 9; 33 (upd.)
Toresco Enterprises, Inc., 84
The Toro Company, 7; 26 (upd.); 77
    (upd.)
The Torrington Company, 13
Tosco Corporation, 7
Total Entertainment Restaurant
    Corporation, 46
Total System Services, Inc., 18
Totem Resources Corporation, 9
TouchTunes Music Corporation, 97
Tower Air, Inc., 28
Tower Automotive, Inc., 24
Towers Perrin, 32
Town & Country Corporation, 19
Town Sports International, Inc., 46
Townsends, Inc., 64
Toy Biz, Inc., 18
Toymax International, Inc., 29
Toys 'R Us, Inc., V; 18 (upd.); 57 (upd.)
Tracor Inc., 17
Tractor Supply Company, 57
Trader Joe's Company, 13; 50 (upd.)
TradeStation Group, Inc., 83
Traffix, Inc., 61
Trailer Bridge, Inc., 41
Trammell Crow Company, 8; 57 (upd.)
Trane 78
Trans World Airlines, Inc., I; 12 (upd.);
    35 (upd.)
Trans World Entertainment Corporation,
    24; 68 (upd.)
Trans-Lux Corporation, 51
Transaction Systems Architects, Inc., 29;
    82 (upd.)
Transamerica–An AEGON Company, I;
    13 (upd.); 41 (upd.)
Transammonia Group, 95
Transatlantic Holdings, Inc., 11
Transco Energy Company, V
Transitions Optical, Inc., 83
Transmedia Network Inc., 20
TransMontaigne Inc., 28

Transocean Sedco Forex Inc., 45
Transport Corporation of America, Inc.,
    49
TransPro, Inc., 71
The Tranzonic Companies, 37
Travel Ports of America, Inc., 17
The Travelers Corporation, III
Travelocity.com, Inc., 46
Travelzoo Inc. 79
Travis Boats & Motors, Inc., 37
TRC Companies, Inc., 32
Treadco, Inc., 19
Treasure Chest Advertising Company, Inc.,
    32
Tredegar Corporation, 52
Tree of Life, Inc., 29
Tree Top, Inc., 76
TreeHouse Foods, Inc. 79
Trek Bicycle Corporation, 16; 78 (upd.)
Trend-Lines, Inc., 22
Trendwest Resorts, Inc., 33
Trex Company, Inc., 71
Tri Valley Growers, 32
Triarc Companies, Inc., 8; 34 (upd.)
Tribune Company, IV; 22 (upd.); 63
    (upd.)
Trico Products Corporation, 15
Trico Marine Services, Inc., 89
Tilcon-Connecticut Inc., 80
Trident Seafoods Corporation, 56
Trigen Energy Corporation, 42
TriMas Corp., 11
Trimble Navigation Limited, 40
Trinity Industries, Incorporated, 7
TRINOVA Corporation, III
TriPath Imaging, Inc., 77
Triple Five Group Ltd., 49
TriQuint Semiconductor, Inc., 63
Tripwire, Inc., 97
Trisko Jewelry Sculptures, Ltd., 57
Triton Energy Corporation, 11
Triumph Group, Inc., 31
The TriZetto Group, Inc., 83
TRM Copy Centers Corporation, 18
Tropicana Products, Inc., 28; 73 (upd.)
Troutman Sanders L.L.P. 79
True North Communications Inc., 23
True Religion Apparel, Inc. 79
True Temper Sports, Inc., 95
True Value Company, 74 (upd.)
The Trump Organization, 23; 64 (upd.)
TruServ Corporation, 24
TRW Automotive Holdings Corp., 75
    (upd.)
TRW Inc., I; 11 (upd.); 14 (upd.)
TTX Company, 6; 66 (upd.)
Tubby's, Inc., 53
Tucson Electric Power Company, 6
Tuesday Morning Corporation, 18; 70
    (upd.)
Tully's Coffee Corporation, 51
Tultex Corporation, 13
Tumaro's Gourmet Tortillas, 85
Tumbleweed, Inc., 33; 80 (upd.)
Tupperware Corporation, 28; 78 (upd.)
TurboChef Technologies, Inc., 83
Turner Broadcasting System, Inc., II; 6
    (upd.); 66 (upd.)

Turner Construction Company, 66
The Turner Corporation, 8; 23 (upd.)
Turtle Wax, Inc., 15; 93 (upd.)
Tuscarora Inc., 29
Tutogen Medical, Inc., 68
Tuttle Publishing, 86
TV Guide, Inc., 43 (upd.)
TVI, Inc., 15
TVI Corporation, 99
TW Services, Inc., II
Tweeter Home Entertainment Group,
    Inc., 30
Twentieth Century Fox Film Corporation,
    II; 25 (upd.)
24 Hour Fitness Worldwide, Inc., 71
24/7 Real Media, Inc., 49
Twin Disc, Inc., 21
Twinlab Corporation, 34
II-VI Incorporated, 69
Ty Inc., 33; 86 (upd.)
Tyco Toys, Inc., 12
Tyler Corporation, 23
Tyndale House Publishers, Inc., 57
Tyson Foods, Inc., II; 14 (upd.); 50
    (upd.)
U S West, Inc., V; 25 (upd.)
U.S. Aggregates, Inc., 42
U.S. Army Corps of Engineers, 91
U.S. Bancorp, 14; 36 (upd.)
U.S. Borax, Inc., 42
U.S. Can Corporation, 30
U.S. Cellular Corporation, 31 (upd.); 88
    (upd.)
U.S. Delivery Systems, Inc., 22
U.S. Foodservice, 26
U.S. Healthcare, Inc., 6
U.S. Home Corporation, 8; 78 (upd.)
U.S. News & World Report Inc., 30; 89
    (upd.)
U.S. Office Products Company, 25
U.S. Physical Therapy, Inc., 65
U.S. Premium Beef LLC, 91
U.S. Robotics Corporation, 9; 66 (upd.)
U.S. Satellite Broadcasting Company, Inc.,
    20
U.S. Timberlands Company, L.P., 42
U.S. Trust Corp., 17
U.S. Vision, Inc., 66
UAL Corporation, 34 (upd.)
UAW (International Union, United
    Automobile, Aerospace and Agricultural
    Implement Workers of America), 72
UGI Corporation, 12
Ugly Duckling Corporation, 22
UICI, 33
Ukrop's Super Market's, Inc., 39
Ulta Salon, Cosmetics & Fragrance, Inc.,
    93
Ultimate Electronics, Inc., 18; 69 (upd.)
Ultra Pac, Inc., 24
Ultra Petroleum Corporation, 71
Ultrak Inc., 24
Ultralife Batteries, Inc., 58
Ultramar Diamond Shamrock
    Corporation, 31 (upd.)
Umpqua Holdings Corporation, 87
Uncle Ben's Inc., 22
Uncle Ray's LLC, 90

Under Armour Performance Apparel, 61
Underwriters Laboratories, Inc., 30
Uni-Marts, Inc., 17
Unica Corporation, 77
Unicom Corporation, 29 (upd.)
Unifi, Inc., 12; 62 (upd.)
Unified Grocers, Inc., 93
UniFirst Corporation, 21
Union Bank of California, 16
Union Camp Corporation, IV
Union Carbide Corporation, I; 9 (upd.);
    74 (upd.)
Union Electric Company, V
Union Pacific Corporation, V; 28 (upd.);
    79 (upd.)
Union Planters Corporation, 54
Union Texas Petroleum Holdings, Inc., 9
UnionBanCal Corporation, 50 (upd.)
Unique Casual Restaurants, Inc., 27
Unison HealthCare Corporation, 25
Unisys Corporation, III; 6 (upd.); 36
    (upd.)
Unit Corporation, 63
United Airlines, I; 6 (upd.)
United Auto Group, Inc., 26; 68 (upd.)
United Brands Company, II
United Community Banks, Inc., 98
United Dairy Farmers, Inc., 74
United Defense Industries, Inc., 30; 66
    (upd.)
United Dominion Industries Limited, 8;
    16 (upd.)
United Dominion Realty Trust, Inc., 52
United Farm Workers of America, 88
United Foods, Inc., 21
United HealthCare Corporation, 9
The United Illuminating Company, 21
United Industrial Corporation, 37
United Industries Corporation, 68
United Jewish Communities, 33
United Merchants & Manufacturers, Inc.,
    13
United National Group, Ltd., 63
United Nations International Children's
    Emergency Fund (UNICEF), 58
United Natural Foods, Inc., 32; 76 (upd.)
United Negro College Fund, Inc. 79
United Online, Inc., 71 (upd.)
United Parcel Service of America Inc., V;
    17 (upd.)
United Parcel Service, Inc., 63; 94 (upd.)
United Press International, Inc., 25; 73
    (upd.)
United Rentals, Inc., 34
United Retail Group Inc., 33
United Road Services, Inc., 69
United Service Organizations, 60
United States Cellular Corporation, 9
United States Filter Corporation, 20
United States Pipe and Foundry
    Company, 62
United States Playing Card Company, 62
United States Postal Service, 14; 34 (upd.)
The United States Shoe Corporation, V
United States Steel Corporation, 50 (upd.)
United States Surgical Corporation, 10;
    34 (upd.)
United Stationers Inc., 14

United Talent Agency, Inc., 80
United Technologies Automotive Inc., 15
United Technologies Corporation, I; 10
    (upd.); 34 (upd.)
United Telecommunications, Inc., V
United Video Satellite Group, 18
United Water Resources, Inc., 40
United Way of America, 36
Unitil Corporation, 37
Unitog Co., 19
Unitrin Inc., 16; V
Univar Corporation, 9
Universal Compression, Inc., 59
Universal Corporation, V; 48 (upd.)
Universal Electronics Inc., 39
Universal Foods Corporation, 7
Universal Forest Products, Inc., 10; 59
    (upd.)
Universal Health Services, Inc., 6
Universal International, Inc., 25
Universal Manufacturing Company, 88
Universal Security Instruments, Inc., 96
Universal Stainless & Alloy Products, Inc.,
    75
Universal Studios, Inc., 33
Universal Technical Institute, Inc., 81
The University of Chicago Press 79
Univision Communications Inc., 24; 83
    (upd.)
Uno Restaurant Corporation, 18
Uno Restaurant Holdings Corporation, 70
    (upd.)
Unocal Corporation, IV; 24 (upd.); 71
    (upd.)
UnumProvident Corporation, 13; 52
    (upd.)
The Upjohn Company, I; 8 (upd.)
Urban Outfitters, Inc., 14; 74 (upd.)
URS Corporation, 45; 80 (upd.)
US Airways Group, Inc., I; 6 (upd.); 28
    (upd.); 52 (upd.)
US 1 Industries, Inc., 89
USA Interactive, Inc., 47 (upd.)
USA Mobility Inc., 97 (upd.)
USA Truck, Inc., 42
USAA, 10; 62 (upd.)
USANA, Inc., 29
USF&G Corporation, III
USG Corporation, III; 26 (upd.); 81
    (upd.)
UST Inc., 9; 50 (upd.)
USX Corporation, IV; 7 (upd.)
Utah Medical Products, Inc., 36
Utah Power and Light Company, 27
UtiliCorp United Inc., 6
UTStarcom, Inc., 77
Utz Quality Foods, Inc., 72
UUNET, 38
Uwajimaya, Inc., 60
Vail Resorts, Inc., 11; 43 (upd.)
Valassis Communications, Inc., 8; 37
    (upd.); 76 (upd.)
Valero Energy Corporation, 7; 71 (upd.)
Valhi, Inc., 19; 94 (upd.)
Vallen Corporation, 45
Valley Media Inc., 35
Valley National Gases, Inc., 85
Valley Proteins, Inc., 91

ValleyCrest Companies, 81 (upd.)
Valmont Industries, Inc., 19
The Valspar Corporation, 8; 32 (upd.); 77
    (upd.)
Value City Department Stores, Inc., 38
Value Line, Inc., 16; 73 (upd.)
Value Merchants Inc., 13
ValueClick, Inc., 49
ValueVision International, Inc., 22
Van Camp Seafood Company, Inc., 7
Van's Aircraft, Inc., 65
Vance Publishing Corporation, 64
Vanderbilt University Medical Center, 99
The Vanguard Group, Inc., 14; 34 (upd.)
Vanguard Health Systems Inc., 70
Vans, Inc., 16; 47 (upd.)
Varco International, Inc., 42
Vari-Lite International, Inc., 35
Varian, Inc., 12; 48 (upd.)
Variety Wholesalers, Inc., 73
Variflex, Inc., 51
Varlen Corporation, 16
Varsity Spirit Corp., 15
VASCO Data Security International, Inc.
    79
Vastar Resources, Inc., 24
VCA Antech, Inc., 58
VECO International, Inc., 7
Vector Group Ltd., 35 (upd.)
Vectren Corporation, 98 (upd.)
Veeco Instruments Inc., 32
Veit Companies, 43; 92 (upd.)
Velocity Express Corporation, 49; 94
    (upd.)
Venator Group Inc., 35 (upd.)
Vencor, Inc., 16
Venetian Casino Resort, LLC, 47
Ventana Medical Systems, Inc., 75
Ventura Foods LLC, 90
Venture Stores Inc., 12
VeraSun Energy Corporation, 87
Verbatim Corporation, 14; 74 (upd.)
Veridian Corporation, 54
VeriFone Holdings, Inc., 18; 76 (upd.)
Verint Systems Inc., 73
VeriSign, Inc., 47
Veritas Software Corporation, 45
Verity Inc., 68
Verizon Communications, 43 (upd.); 78
    (upd.)
Vermeer Manufacturing Company, 17
The Vermont Country Store, 93
Vermont Pure Holdings, Ltd., 51
The Vermont Teddy Bear Co., Inc., 36
Vertex Pharmaceuticals Incorporated, 83
Vertis Communications, 84
Vertrue Inc., 77
VF Corporation, V; 17 (upd.); 54 (upd.)
VHA Inc., 53
Viacom Inc., 7; 23 (upd.); 67 (upd.)
Viad Corp., 73
ViaSat, Inc., 54
Viasoft Inc., 27
VIASYS Healthcare, Inc., 52
Viasystems Group, Inc., 67
Viatech Continental Can Company, Inc.,
    25 (upd.)
Vicon Industries, Inc., 44

VICORP Restaurants, Inc., 12; 48 (upd.)
Victory Refrigeration, Inc., 82
Videojet Technologies, Inc., 90
Vienna Sausage Manufacturing Co., 14
Viewpoint International, Inc., 66
ViewSonic Corporation, 72
Viking Office Products, Inc., 10
Viking Range Corporation, 66
Viking Yacht Company, 96
Village Super Market, Inc., 7
Village Voice Media, Inc., 38
Vinson & Elkins L.L.P., 30
Vintage Petroleum, Inc., 42
Vinton Studios, 63
Virbac Corporation, 74
Virco Manufacturing Corporation, 17
Virginia Dare Extract Company, Inc., 94
Visa International, 9; 26 (upd.)
Vishay Intertechnology, Inc., 21; 80 (upd.)
Vision Service Plan Inc., 77
Viskase Companies, Inc., 55
Vista Bakery, Inc., 56
Vista Chemical Company, I
Vistana, Inc., 22
VISX, Incorporated, 30
Vita Food Products Inc., 99
Vita Plus Corporation, 60
Vital Images, Inc., 85
Vitalink Pharmacy Services, Inc., 15
Vitamin Shoppe Industries, Inc., 60
Vitesse Semiconductor Corporation, 32
Vitro Corp., 10
Vivra, Inc., 18
Vlasic Foods International Inc., 25
VLSI Technology, Inc., 16
VMware, Inc., 90
Volcom, Inc., 77
Volkert and Associates, Inc., 98
Volt Information Sciences Inc., 26
Volunteers of America, Inc., 66
Von Maur Inc., 64
Vonage Holdings Corp., 81
The Vons Companies, Incorporated, 7; 28 (upd.)
Vornado Realty Trust, 20
Vought Aircraft Industries, Inc., 49
Vulcan Materials Company, 7; 52 (upd.)
W. Atlee Burpee & Co., 27
W.A. Whitney Company, 53
W.B Doner & Co., 56
W.B. Mason Company, 98
W.C. Bradley Co., 69
W. H. Braum, Inc., 80
W.H. Brady Co., 17
W.L. Gore & Associates, Inc., 14; 60 (upd.)
W.P. Carey & Co. LLC, 49
W.R. Berkley Corporation, 15; 74 (upd.)
W.R. Grace & Company, I; 50 (upd.)
W.W. Grainger, Inc., V; 26 (upd.); 68 (upd.)
W.W. Norton & Company, Inc., 28
Waban Inc., 13
Wabash National Corp., 13
Wabtec Corporation, 40
Wachovia Bank of Georgia, N.A., 16

Wachovia Bank of South Carolina, N.A., 16
Wachovia Corporation, 12; 46 (upd.)
Wachtell, Lipton, Rosen & Katz, 47
The Wackenhut Corporation, 14; 63 (upd.)
Waddell & Reed, Inc., 22
Waffle House Inc., 14; 60 (upd.)
Wagers Inc. (Idaho Candy Company), 86
Waggener Edstrom, 42
Wah Chang, 82
Wahl Clipper Corporation, 86
Wahoo's Fish Taco, 96
Wakefern Food Corporation, 33
Wal-Mart Stores, Inc., V; 8 (upd.); 26 (upd.); 63 (upd.)
Walbridge Aldinger Co., 38
Walbro Corporation, 13
Waldbaum, Inc., 19
Waldenbooks, 17; 86 (upd.)
Walgreen Co., V; 20 (upd.); 65 (upd.)
Walker Manufacturing Company, 19
Wall Drug Store, Inc., 40
Wall Street Deli, Inc., 33
Wallace Computer Services, Inc., 36
Walsworth Publishing Co. 78
The Walt Disney Company, II; 6 (upd.); 30 (upd.); 63 (upd.)
Walter Industries, Inc., II; 22 (upd.); 72 (upd.)
Walton Monroe Mills, Inc., 8
Wang Laboratories, Inc., III; 6 (upd.)
The Warnaco Group Inc., 12; 46 (upd.)
Warner Communications Inc., II
Warner Music Group Corporation, 90 (upd.)
Warner-Lambert Co., I; 10 (upd.)
Warners' Stellian Inc., 67
Warrantech Corporation, 53
Warrell Corporation, 68
Warwick Valley Telephone Company, 55
The Washington Companies, 33
Washington Federal, Inc., 17
Washington Football, Inc., 35
Washington Gas Light Company, 19
Washington Mutual, Inc., 17; 93 (upd.)
Washington National Corporation, 12
Washington Natural Gas Company, 9
The Washington Post Company, IV; 20 (upd.)
Washington Scientific Industries, Inc., 17
Washington Water Power Company, 6
Waste Connections, Inc., 46
Waste Holdings, Inc., 41
Waste Management, Inc., V
Water Pik Technologies, Inc., 34; 83 (upd.)
Waterhouse Investor Services, Inc., 18
Waters Corporation, 43
Watkins-Johnson Company, 15
Watsco Inc., 52
Watson Pharmaceuticals Inc., 16; 56 (upd.)
Watson Wyatt Worldwide, 42
Watts Industries, Inc., 19
Wausau-Mosinee Paper Corporation, 60 (upd.)
Waverly, Inc., 16

Wawa Inc., 17; 78 (upd.)
Waxman Industries, Inc., 9
WD-40 Company, 18; 87 (upd.)
We-No-Nah Canoe, Inc., 98
The Weather Channel Companies, The 52
Weatherford International, Inc., 39
Weaver Popcorn Company, Inc., 89
Webasto Roof Systems Inc., 97
Webber Oil Company, 61
Weber-Stephen Products Co., 40
WebEx Communications, Inc., 81
WebMD Corporation, 65
Weeres Industries Corporation, 52
Wegmans Food Markets, Inc., 9; 41 (upd.)
Weider Nutrition International, Inc., 29
Weight Watchers International Inc., 12; 33 (upd.); 73 (upd.)
Weil, Gotshal & Manges LLP, 55
Weiner's Stores, Inc., 33
Weingarten Realty Investors, 95
Weirton Steel Corporation, IV; 26 (upd.)
Weis Markets, Inc., 15; 84 (upd.)
The Weitz Company, Inc., 42
Welbilt Corp., 19
Welcome Wagon International Inc., 82
The Welk Group Inc. 78
WellChoice, Inc., 67 (upd.)
Wellco Enterprises, Inc., 84
Wellman, Inc., 8; 52 (upd.)
WellPoint Health Networks Inc., 25
Wells Fargo & Company, II; 12 (upd.); 38 (upd.); 97 (upd.)
Wells Rich Greene BDDP, 6
Wells' Dairy, Inc., 36
Wells-Gardner Electronics Corporation, 43
Wendy's International, Inc., 8; 23 (upd.); 47 (upd.)
Wenner Bread Products Inc., 80
Wenner Media, Inc., 32
Werner Enterprises, Inc., 26
West Bend Co., 14
West Coast Entertainment Corporation, 29
West Corporation, 42
West Group, 34 (upd.)
West Linn Paper Company, 91
West Marine, Inc., 17; 90 (upd.)
West One Bancorp, 11
West Pharmaceutical Services, Inc., 42
West Point-Pepperell, Inc., 8
West Publishing Co., 7
Westaff Inc., 33
Westamerica Bancorporation, 17
Westar Energy, Inc., 57 (upd.)
WestCoast Hospitality Corporation, 59
Westcon Group, Inc., 67
Westell Technologies, Inc., 57
Westerbeke Corporation, 60
Western Atlas Inc., 12
Western Beef, Inc., 22
Western Company of North America, 15
Western Digital Corporation, 25; 92 (upd.)
Western Gas Resources, Inc., 45
Western Publishing Group, Inc., 13
Western Resources, Inc., 12

The WesterN SizzliN Corporation, 60
Western Union Financial Services, Inc., 54
Western Wireless Corporation, 36
Westfield Group, 69
Westin Hotels and Resorts Worldwide, 9; 29 (upd.)
Westinghouse Electric Corporation, II; 12 (upd.)
Westmoreland Coal Company, 7
WestPoint Stevens Inc., 16
Westport Resources Corporation, 63
Westvaco Corporation, IV; 19 (upd.)
Westwood One, Inc., 23
The Wet Seal, Inc., 18; 70 (upd.)
Wetterau Incorporated, II
Weyco Group, Incorporated, 32
Weyerhaeuser Company, IV; 9 (upd.); 28 (upd.); 83 (upd.)
WFS Financial Inc., 70
WGBH Educational Foundation, 66
Wham-O, Inc., 61
Wheaton Industries, 8
Wheaton Science Products, 60 (upd.)
Wheelabrator Technologies, Inc., 6; 60 (upd.)
Wheeling-Pittsburgh Corporation, 7; 58 (upd.)
Wheels Inc., 96
Wherehouse Entertainment Incorporated, 11
Whirlpool Corporation, III; 12 (upd.); 59 (upd.)
White & Case LLP, 35
White Castle Management Company, 12; 36 (upd.); 85 (upd.)
White Consolidated Industries Inc., 13
The White House, Inc., 60
White Lily Foods Company, 88
White Rose, Inc., 24
Whitehall Jewellers, Inc., 82 (upd.)
Whiting Petroleum Corporation, 81
Whiting-Turner Contracting Company, 95
Whitman Corporation, 10 (upd.)
Whitman Education Group, Inc., 41
Whitney Holding Corporation, 21
Whittaker Corporation, I; 48 (upd.)
Whole Foods Market, Inc., 20; 50 (upd.)
WHX Corporation, 98
Wickes Inc., V; 25 (upd.)
Widmer Brothers Brewing Company, 76
Wieden + Kennedy, 75
Wilbert, Inc., 56
Wilbur Chocolate Company, 66
Wilco Farm Stores, 93
Wild Oats Markets, Inc., 19; 41 (upd.)
Wildlife Conservation Society, 31
Wikimedia Foundation, Inc., 91
Willamette Industries, Inc., IV; 31 (upd.)
Willamette Valley Vineyards, Inc., 85
William L. Bonnell Company, Inc., 66
William Lyon Homes, 59
William Morris Agency, Inc., 23
William Zinsser & Company, Inc., 58
Williams & Connolly LLP, 47
Williams Communications Group, Inc., 34
The Williams Companies, Inc., IV; 31 (upd.)

Williams Scotsman, Inc., 65
Williams-Sonoma, Inc., 17; 44 (upd.)
Williamson-Dickie Manufacturing Company, 14; 45 (upd.)
Willkie Farr & Gallagher LLP, 95
Wilmington Trust Corporation, 25
Wilson Sonsini Goodrich & Rosati, 34
Wilson Sporting Goods Company, 24; 84 (upd.)
Wilsons The Leather Experts Inc., 21; 58 (upd.)
Wilton Products, Inc., 97
Winchell's Donut Houses Operating Company, L.P., 60
WinCo Foods Inc., 60
Wind River Systems, Inc., 37
Windmere Corporation, 16
Windstream Corporation, 83
Windswept Environmental Group, Inc., 62
The Wine Group, Inc., 39
Winegard Company, 56
Winmark Corporation, 74
Winn-Dixie Stores, Inc., II; 21 (upd.); 59 (upd.)
Winnebago Industries, Inc., 7; 27 (upd.); 96 (upd.)
WinsLoew Furniture, Inc., 21
Winston & Strawn, 35
The Wiremold Company, 81
Wirtz Corporation, 72
Wisconsin Alumni Research Foundation, 65
Wisconsin Bell, Inc., 14
Wisconsin Central Transportation Corporation, 24
Wisconsin Dairies, 7
Wisconsin Energy Corporation, 6; 54 (upd.)
Wisconsin Public Service Corporation, 9
Wise Foods, Inc. 79
Witco Corporation, I; 16 (upd.)
Witness Systems, Inc., 87
Wizards of the Coast Inc., 24
WLR Foods, Inc., 21
Wm. B. Reily & Company Inc., 58
Wm. Wrigley Jr. Company, 7; 58 (upd.)
WMS Industries, Inc., 15; 53 (upd.)
WMX Technologies Inc., 17
Wolfgang Puck Worldwide, Inc., 26, 70 (upd.)
Wolohan Lumber Co., 19
Wolverine Tube Inc., 23
Wolverine World Wide, Inc., 16; 59 (upd.)
Womble Carlyle Sandridge & Rice, PLLC, 52
Wood-Mode, Inc., 23
Woodbridge Holdings Corporation, 99
Woodcraft Industries Inc., 61
Woodward Governor Company, 13; 49 (upd.)
Woolrich Inc., 62
Woolworth Corporation, V; 20 (upd.)
WordPerfect Corporation, 10
Workflow Management, Inc., 65
Working Assets Funding Service, 43
Workman Publishing Company, Inc., 70

World Acceptance Corporation, 57
World Bank Group, 33
World Book, Inc., 12
World Color Press Inc., 12
World Duty Free Americas, Inc., 29 (upd.)
World Fuel Services Corporation, 47
World Publications, LLC, 65
World Vision International, Inc., 93
World Wide Technology, Inc., 94
World Wrestling Federation Entertainment, Inc., 32
World's Finest Chocolate Inc., 39
WorldCorp, Inc., 10
Worldwide Restaurant Concepts, Inc., 47
Worldwide Pants Inc., 97
Worthington Foods, Inc., 14
Worthington Industries, Inc., 7; 21 (upd.)
WPL Holdings, Inc., 6
WPS Resources Corporation, 53 (upd.)
Writers Guild of America, West, Inc., 92
Wright Express Corporation, 80
Wright Medical Group, Inc., 61
WTD Industries, Inc., 20
Wunderman, 86
Wyant Corporation, 30
Wyeth, 50 (upd.)
Wyle Electronics, 14
Wyman-Gordon Company, 14
Wyndham Worldwide Corporation, 99 (upd.)
Wynn's International, Inc., 33
Wyse Technology, Inc., 15
X-Rite, Inc., 48
Xcel Energy Inc., 73 (upd.)
Xerium Technologies, Inc., 94
Xerox Corporation, III; 6 (upd.); 26 (upd.); 69 (upd.)
Xilinx, Inc., 16; 82 (upd.)
XM Satellite Radio Holdings, Inc., 69
XTO Energy Inc., 52
Yahoo! Inc., 27; 70 (upd.)
Yarnell Ice Cream Company, Inc., 92
The Yankee Candle Company, Inc., 37
YankeeNets LLC, 35
The Yates Companies, Inc., 62
Yellow Corporation, 14; 45 (upd.)
Yellow Freight System, Inc. of Delaware, V
YES! Entertainment Corporation, 26
YMCA of the USA, 31
YOCREAM International, Inc., 47
The York Group, Inc., 50
York International Corp., 13
York Research Corporation, 35
Youbet.com, Inc., 77
YouTube, Inc., 90
Young & Rubicam, Inc., I; 22 (upd.); 66 (upd.)
Young Broadcasting Inc., 40
Young Innovations, Inc., 44
Young's Market Company, LLC, 32
Younkers, 76 (upd.)
Younkers, Inc., 19
Youth Services International, Inc., 21
YRC Worldwide Inc., 90 (upd.)
Yucaipa Cos., 17
Yum! Brands Inc., 58

YWCA of the United States, 45
Zachry Group, Inc., 95
Zacky Farms LLC, 74
Zale Corporation, 16; 40 (upd.); 91 (upd.)
Zanett, Inc., 92
Zany Brainy, Inc., 31
Zapata Corporation, 25
Zappos.com, Inc., 73
Zatarain's, Inc., 64
Zebra Technologies Corporation, 14; 53 (upd.)
Zenith Data Systems, Inc., 10
Zenith Electronics Corporation, II; 13 (upd.); 34 (upd.); 89 (upd.)
ZERO Corporation, 17; 88 (upd.)
Ziebart International Corporation, 30; 66 (upd.)
The Ziegler Companies, Inc., 24; 63 (upd.)
Ziff Davis Media Inc., 12; 36 (upd.); 73 (upd.)
Zila, Inc., 46
ZiLOG, Inc., 15; 72 (upd.)
Zimmer Holdings, Inc., 45
Zingerman's Community of Businesses, 68
Zion's Cooperative Mercantile Institution, 33

Zions Bancorporation, 12; 53 (upd.)
Zipcar, Inc., 92
Zippo Manufacturing Company, 18; 71 (upd.)
Zogby International, Inc., 99
Zoltek Companies, Inc., 37
Zondervan Corporation, 24; 71 (upd.)
Zones, Inc., 67
Zoom Technologies, Inc., 18; 53 (upd.)
Zoran Corporation, 77
Zuffa L.L.C., 89
Zumiez, Inc., 77
Zygo Corporation, 42
Zytec Corporation, 19

Uruguay
Administración Nacional de Combustibles, Alcohol y Pórtland, 93
Cooperativa Nacional de Productores de Leche S.A. (Conaprole), 92

Uzbekistan
Uzbekistan Airways National Air Company, 99

Vatican City
Caritas Internationalis, 72

Venezuela
Cerveceria Polar, I

Cisneros Group of Companies, 54
Empresas Polar SA, 55 (upd.)
Petróleos de Venezuela S.A., IV; 74 (upd.)

Vietnam
Lam Son Sugar Joint Stock Corporation (Lasuco), 60

Virgin Islands
Little Switzerland, Inc., 60

Wales
Hyder plc, 34
Iceland Group plc, 33
Kwik Save Group plc, 11

Zambia
Zambia Industrial and Mining Corporation Ltd., IV

Zimbabwe
Air Zimbabwe (Private) Limited, 91

DATE DUE

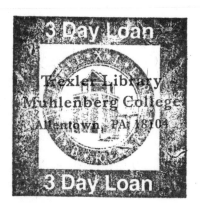

DEMCO